EXPLORATION & DISCOVERY

Robert E. Peary en route to the North Pole.

EXPLORATION & DISCOVERY

As Reported By
The New York Times

Edited by
Suri Fleischer
and
Arleen Keylin

NYT

ARNO PRESS
New York • 1976

Distributed by Crown Publishers, Inc., One Park Avenue, New York, New York 10016

A Note to the Reader

Original copies of **The New York Times** were not available to the publisher. This volume, therefore, was created from 35mm microfilm.

Library of Congress Cataloging in Publication Data

Main entry under title:

Exploration and discovery.

1. Discoveries (in geography) I. Fleischer, Suri.
II. Keylin, Arleen. III. New York times.
G99.E88 910 76-23398
ISBN 0-405-09187-7

Editorial Assistant: Sandra Jones

Manufactured in the United States of America

2 3 4 5 6 7 8 9 10

CONTENTS

1930-1939

1940-1949

1950-1959

1960-1969

1970-1976

EXPLORATION & DISCOVERY

Dr. Fridtjof Nansen, discoverer of the North Pole.

"All the News That's Fit to Print."

The New York Times.

THE WEATHER.
Fair, slightly warmer Thursday; Friday, fair, warmer; moderate winds, becoming south.
For full weather report see Page 21.

VOL. XLV....NO. 13,881. NEW-YORK, SUNDAY, FEBRUARY 16, 1896.—FOUR PARTS—THIRTY-TWO PAGES.—COPYRIGHTED, 1896, BY THE NEW-YORK TIMES PUBLISHING CO. PRICE FIVE CENTS.

LONDON AND SALISBURY

The Indiscretions of Utterance That Balfour Has to Defend.

CHAMBERLAIN'S SUCCESSFUL LABOR

Views of Greater Dividends and Less Responsibility in Chartered Company Circles.

CZAR AND SULTAN ARM-IN-ARM IN SOFIA

Austria's Emperor and French President to Meet at Mentone—Bourgeois Ministry—Ruin of The Daily News.

By Commercial Cable from Our Own Correspondent.

LONDON, Feb. 15.—A week of the Parliament has not done much to illumine the perplexed British mind or to tranquilize the British nerves. Undoubtedly its chief effect has been to rub into public consciousness new doubts and reservations about Lord Salisbury's fitness for his place. Every debate which has arisen has automatically swung round like the needle in a compass to point out some new foolishness or wanton contradiction in his speeches, and Balfour had to get up so many times to defend or explain away his uncle's indiscretions and banalities of utterance that, latterly, when he rose the whole House tittered and even the nephew's loyalty could not prevent his showing that he saw the joke, and, privately, was rather tempted to laugh himself.

The perception of this curious situation may be the sole source of the rumor which I have heard hinted at from several and different quarters of the House of Commons last night, namely, that Lord Salisbury's health is very queer, and his disappearance from the public scene will not be long postponed. It must be several years ago that I reported information coming to me from a perfect source to the effect that Salisbury had been warned by physicians that he was definitely in the grip of Bright's disease; but that is a malady which often gives to its victims a very long rope, and nothing now recalls it to mind except the general feeling among politicians that, except on the theory that he is going to pieces, his recent performances are unaccountable.

Nobody, however, suggests that there is anything the matter with Chamberlain. His triumphs at Westminster have been quite of a piece with the popular success which he won before the session began. It is true that a close observer may discover that the bulk of the Tory members sit sourly silent when he is cheered, and eye him with moody dislike, but they do not dare to do more, and he flaunts his orchid boutonnière and his smart, glib, cocksure deportment in their sulky faces with evident enjoyment. According to his story, he has figuratively mopped the earth with Cecil Rhodes. He grew almost pathetic in his picture of that once great man's reduced dimensions. One would think that he returned to South Africa like a prodigal son, whose father slammed the door in his face, destitute, dejected, friendless, to begin life all over again in remote exile. Mr. Chamberlain's cold, sparkling eyes almost managed a tear for this melancholy spectacle, and the listening House uttered sympathetic hear-hears which might have been taken for groans. But if you talk in Chartered Company circles it is to find an extraordinarily different view prevailing as to the position of Rhodes and his partners. They got rid of the costly responsibility of police and other administration without any curtailment of benefits, and they began to see in the whole transaction merely a promise of larger dividends than ever; being gentlemen who are not engaged in expanding the empire for their health, they are able to contemplate this prospect with a smile.

It is not likely that much new light will be thrown on the present or future state of the Venezuelan controversy by the debate which is expected to begin Monday. Sir William Vernon-Harcourt has made a specialty of the subject the last two months, and prepared for a comprehensive and powerful attack on the Government, but the Queen's speech rather takes the wind out of his sails. No disposition has been disclosed among the private Tories to say disagreeable things on the topic, and the official Tories profess such a complete anxiety to settle everything to America's liking that it seems somewhat bootless to bombard the long-since abandoned fortifications where Salisbury intrenched himself on the Schomburgk line. There is no reason whatever to suspect that these official professions of a desire to arrange the matter amicably conceal any ulterior design, and, that being the case, it seems as if the thing might with profit be taken out of newspaper discussion, for a week or so at least, and left to the two Foreign Offices where it belongs.

Somehow it had not been easy at any time during the week wholly to credit the finality of Sexton's refusal to become the head of his party. Healy's letter to-day, in which he goes to the length of offering to retire from public life if Sexton will say that it will promote harmony and enable him to accept the post, removes the last chance of the Dillon and O'Brien clique to misrepresent the situation from at least that point of view. If Sexton still persists in holding back, it will be interesting to wait and see how long it is before he gets the post of President of the Irish National Bank. No secret is made of the fact that if Dillon forces his own election to the Chairmanship on Tuesday the party will at once break up.

Western Europe, and even America, may ponder with profit on the fact that the only visible result of the slaughter of many thousands of Armenians has been that the Czar and the Sultan are now warm allies. It is interesting, too, to note that they find their first opportunity to appear together arm-in-arm in Sofia, where Stambouloff's butchery and Ferdinand's base violation of the oath sworn to his bride and her parents have made it possible for the Czar to be friendly with the Bulgarians, and for the Sultan to bestir himself to secure his vassal's recognition by the Courts of Europe. It was as if little Prince Boris had received a double baptism of blood; once in the murder pit of Sassoun and once in the gutter in front of the Sofia Club. Not even in Paris do men pretend that this spectacle is not repulsive. Nobody is to object to the recognition of Ferdinand, however.

More importance attaches to the impending interview at Mentone between the Emperor of Austria and President Faure than is generally imagined. It will not be surprising, indeed, if this meeting will not come, in after years, to be regarded as a historical event. Berthelot was somewhat sniffed at when he left his laboratory to take charge of the foreign affairs of the republic, but men laugh no longer. He has already done great things toward lifting France out of the ruinous Chauvinistic morass in which she has floundered, and this sign of possible understanding with Austria promises even more notable results, but very likely these soon will be exhibiting themselves.

This present French Cabinet has as many lives as the proverbial cat. On Thursday morning the whole press of Paris agreed in the prediction that the Ministry would be dead by nightfall, but when evening came, lo and behold! Bourgeois was not only still Premier, but had a rousing vote of confidence by the Chamber of Deputies to show to his enemies. That these continued triumphs of the Ministry, which has really only a small minority of true friends in the Chamber, have something queer underlying them is, of course, perfectly well known, but there are many widely varying explanations of what this something is. There seems to be a portion of truth in each of a dozen of these different solutions of the problem. The Ministry now possesses such a huge collection of compromising facts relating to any number of separate scandals that it is believed to hold a threat of disclosure over fully 300 Deputies, which is more than half the Chamber. It is said, on apparently good authority, that not less than 250 are involved in some phase of the South of France Railway and Telephone contract scandals alone, and these are only two out of a large assorted collection. Thus it happens that even when the present Minister of Public Instruction is confronted by extremely embarrassing proof of his own bad behavior in the railway matter the Cabinet is able to force the Chamber to ignore the thing and to embark instead on a combat with the Senate. These two bodies have not before been in open conflict since the Constitution of the republic was adopted, and no precedents exist to help guesswork as to how the dead-lock will terminate. Under ordinary circumstances such a struggle might easily precipitate a grave Constitutional crisis, but nobody seems to fear that it may happen in this case, for the simple, though unpleasant, reason that the Ministry is believed to have enough secrets of personal corruption up its sleeve to bring the Senate to its knees if a real emergency arises.

Hungary's spirited determination to make her millennial celebration memorable in the history of the world, regardless of expense, has already produced one very painful side result. Among the numerous magnificent plans was one to found a Museum of Fine Arts at Buda-Pesth which should make the whole rest of the world green with envy, and the sum of $1,500,000 was voted for a start. Of this $200,000 was intrusted to Director Pulszky, who is the eldest son of one of Hungary's most cherished patriots of Kossuth's time, to travel through Europe and buy old masters' art with. Subsequently much more money was sent to him, but soon it was discovered that he was buying only absurd, pitiful rubbish at wild prices, and not even paying for that, but running the Government in debt. Then came the disclosure that he had embezzled practically the whole huge sum and allowed it to be taken from him by a pack of adventurers of both sexes. His conduct was so idiotic that friends of his father had him certified as insane and ran him into a lunatic asylum, but a parliamentary hubbub was raised by the Clericals in revenge for the civil marriage legislation, with the result that Pulszky is decided to be sane and must be tried and punished. A more unwelcome overture to a year's national celebration may hardly be imagined.

Scarcely subordinate in interest to the direct issue of the Chartered Company has been the extraordinary capture of the virtuous old Daily News by the Rhodes-Barnato combination. The change began sharply on Monday, when the new editor, E. T. Cook, took charge, and the amazement has been growing day by day through the week. It is supposed that there must also have been some change in proprietorship, or, perhaps, a change in proprietorial investments, to explain the thing, but of this nothing is known. The Liberals are aghast at the suggestion that their time-honored official organ has sold them out, and are only less disgusted to see that W. T. Stead, who was Cook's first chief on the old Pall Mall Gazette, has now a free hand all over The Daily News's columns to boom Rhodes, Mme. Noviskoff, telepathy, ghosts, and all the rest of his either venal or asinine obsessions. Whatever the explanation may be, and however soon a change again may be made, it is clear enough that The Daily News is irretrievably ruined. One week has sufficed to destroy the work of fifty years. Naturally, this is advantageous for The Daily Chronicle, which has been climbing up over its decrepit rival ever since Massingham and Norman received their head in its control, and now it steps into the position of the chief Liberal paper of England quite by acclamation.

Although it is evident that America is fully abreast, if not ahead, of Europe in expanding and developing Röntgen's discovery, some quaint incidents of the process here may not be duplicated on the other side. For instance, the Vienna Museum for some time has possessed as its chief treasure an Egyptian mummy, which is swathed to resemble a human being, but the inscription on which suggested it to be an ibis instead. The thing was too rare and precious to run the risk of unwinding its bandages to solve this problem, but the shadow photograph now plainly reveals the skeleton of a large bird. Prof. Bergmann of Berlin utilized the discovery the other day for a surgical operation, but at the same time made a speech to the students in the university class, warning them of the possible dangers involved in this new and weird multiplication of facilities for diagnosis. He foresees that, now that the position of metal substances inside the human form may be traced with ease, everybody who has been carrying bullets, needles, and shot for years without harm to himself will be possessed with the passion to have them located and dug out, and against this he protests fervently. He says he made his special reputation in surgery in the Russo-Turkish war by never extracting a bullet if it was not absolutely necessary, more than anything else, and even in time of peace, where antiseptic aids are at their best, he earnestly deprecates all but strictly essential operations of this nature.

The Prussian general staff is enthusiastic over Count Zeppelin's steerable balloon, which can rise 1,200 yards, travel eleven miles an hour, carry two tons, stay up fully a week, and ascend and descend without throwing ballast or losing gas. It utilizes aluminium in the motor and steering gear, but the principal novelty is a secret preparation, or sizing, making silk entirely gastight. The cost of one will be $75,000, but its value in time of war as a look-out over a vast range, either by sea or land, will be incalculable.

The evening papers Thursday picked up bushels of extra pennies on the subject of the north pole, but otherwise, in the opinion of scientists here, nothing has been changed. It is not believed by them that news from Nansen could possibly come by the way that this report is said to have traveled, but laymen remember that scientists have often been beaten by facts before, and so keep an open mind.

When I reported the rumor reaching me that Dunraven already had an apology on the way to America, it seems that my informant had information that such a course had been insisted on by the Prince of Wales at Sandringham, and took it for granted that Dunraven had not delayed to act on it; but he appears to have held out over two or three ocean mails before he finally acted. This characteristic behavior prepares everybody here for the disclosure that the communication itself is inadequate and grudging in tone, and if this be the case, after the elaborate and persistent courtesy of the New-York Yacht Club, you may be sure that no one here whose opinion you value will resent his being dealt with as he deserves.

S. J. Solomon's election as Associate by the Royal Academy is popular among painters, and at another time would have called forth many congratulations, but it happens to be rather overshadowed by the choice of Edwin A. Abbey, which excites a wider and more vigorous outburst of enthusiasm. Despite his magnificent Boston Library creations, he is still regarded primarily as a black-and-white man, and illustrators hail his election as a long-belated recognition of this art. It is noteworthy, too, perhaps, that at such a time an American, the vast bulk of whose work has been done for America, should be chosen over many Englishmen, without a hint in any quarter of the slightest jealousy on national grounds.

It is understood now that plans to pass over Sir John Everett Millais have all come to naught, and that he will be elevated to the Presidency Thursday without opposition or any pledge to regard himself as a warming pan for somebody else. H. F.

GASOLINE IN SLEEPING CAR EXPLODED

Two Women and a Man Injured—Three Cars Damaged.

PITTSBURG, Feb. 15.—Gasoline exploded this morning in the Pullman sleeping car Wyndham, in the Pennsylvania Railroad yards, Eighteenth Street, near Union Station. Mrs. Laura Foss, who lives on Twenty-first Street, Pittsburg, and Miss Sadie Conroy of Allegheny, car cleaners, and the car porter, James Richards, colored, whose home is in Cincinnati, were injured. Their injuries consist of cuts and bruises about their heads, hands, and faces.

The women were cleaning the carpets and plush trimmings of the Wyndham, using gasoline for the purpose. Suddenly there was a terrific explosion that hurled the occupants of the sleeper aside with great force, rendering them unconscious. The sides of the car bulged out and the roof was lifted. Every window and door was blown from its fastenings, and, in fact, the car above the trucks is a complete wreck.

The sleeping cars Zita and New-England, standing on either side of the Wyndham, were also badly damaged, not a window remaining in place. The damage will amount to several thousand dollars. The manner in which the gasoline became ignited has not yet been explained, nor has it been learned how seriously the victims of the explosion were injured.

A Young Singer Seriously Ill.

NEWARK, N. J., Feb. 15.—Mrs. Irene Wheeler of Washington, a young singer who recently appeared in the burlesque, "Thrilby," in this city, is hovering between life and death at the German Hospital. She is suffering with typhoid fever, and the doctors say her condition is critical. Miss Wheeler is the daughter of an attache of the First Auditor's office, at the Treasury Department, at Washington.

Kept His Confessional Secrets.

MONTREAL, Feb. 15.—The Rev. M. Gill, curé of the Church of Notre Dame of Granby, Quebec, has been committed to prison by a magistrate for contempt of court in refusing to disclose the secrets heard in the confessional.

OTRANTO RUNS AGROUND

The Steamship Stranded Near Fire Island Light Friday Night—Wrecking Tugs Cannot Reach It

PATCHOGUE, L. I., Feb. 15.—After being delayed and driven far out of her course by heavy storms the steamer Otranto of the Wilson Line, from Shields, England, to New-York, with a general cargo, lies hard aground on one of the most dangerous sand bars on the Long Island coast. She lies two miles west of Fire Island Lighthouse, on the east side of Fire Island Bar, which is a part of the treacherous shoals that swallowed up the schooner Kennebec and part of her crew last Winter, the memory of which is fresh in the minds of people here.

The Otranto lies headed northeast, although her course was west. She probably swung around as she struck. The big steamship has settled hard in the sand, and experienced surfmen say she will surely break up, as she lies in such a position that the very strong tide which runs here will carry out the sands from her stem and stern and will leave her keel on a ridge.

The sea came up strong this evening, with the wind in the southwest. The Merritt wrecking steamer that came up early this morning from the work of unloading the steamer Lamington, opposite Patchogue, has stood by the Otranto all day, but cannot get to her, or get a boat to her, on account of the breaking seas and dangerous shoals.

The life-saving crew went aboard this morning and offered to take the crew of thirty-five men off, but they remained aboard. The life-savers put a line aboard this afternoon, and will rig the breeches buoy to be prepared for any emergency.

The steamer's agents, Sanderson Brothers, 22 State Street, New-York, sent the Chapman Wrecking Company's tug down this morning, but they found the Merritt steamer already on the ground.

The steamer struck at 11:30 o'clock last night, still under good headway. The night was clear and starlight, and the wind was off shore. When Capt. Charles Weeks of the Fire Island life-saving crew put out to the vessel this morning, Capt. Richard Hubby would make no statement as to how he came ashore under such favorable conditions, and with Fire Island's lights streaming over the waters, not two miles away.

It is supposed that the Captain was misled by the depth of water, as his lead might mark sixteen fathoms a short distance from where his vessel struck. Still his chart should have apprised him of the position of the shoals. As he was east of the bell buoy, which marks the outer edge of the shoals, he could not hear the bell.

When the steamer struck last night her lights could be plainly seen from Babylon, yet, while the people thus early learned of the wreck, boats did not put off from there until to-day. The I. J. Merritt appeared to be getting ready to float a line to the steamer to-night.

The steamer has a full head of steam on, and if the line is made fast will use her screws to help the Merritt get her off.

The life savers think the attempt will prove futile, even if the Merritt succeeds in getting the line aboard. They think the ship will stay where she is. Owing to the bulky nature of the cargo, which consists of iron and steel, it will be very difficult for the lighters of the wrecking company to unload her.

Tugs Sent to Otranto's Relief.

Sanderson & Son, the agents in this city for the steamer Otranto, have received no particulars as yet of the grounding of the vessel. The agents are anxiously awaiting word from the Otranto's Captain, and until he is heard from the company has declined the services of the wrecking companies. However, the wrecking tug W. E. Chapman has gone to the scene of the accident, and will stand by in case help is required. The large ocean tugs L. Luckenbach and Ocean King have been sent to the assistance of the Otranto.

Mr. Sanderson says he believes the vessel is all right, and will come off the beach without assistance.

The Otranto is a British freight steamer, and is commanded by Capt. Hubby. She carries no passengers, and has a crew of about thirty men.

She left Shields, England, Jan. 23, with a general cargo, consigned to Sanderson & Son. The cargo consists principally of iron, steel, and wood pulp.

The Otranto is 305 feet long, 36 feet beam, 27 feet deep, and of 2,379 tons. She was built in Hull, England, in 1877, and is owned by T. Wilson, Sons & Co., Hull, England.

El Dorado Still Aground.

The Morgan Line steamship El Dorado, which grounded south of Liberty Island Thursday evening during a dense fog, is still fast in the mud. An attempt was made last night to float the vessel. At that time her keel forward and aft was free, but was hard aground amidships.

The vessel's cargo is being discharged and the Chapman Wrecking Company will make an effort at high tide to-day to get her afloat. She has lost two blades of her propeller, but is otherwise uninjured.

OIL CLOTH WORKS IN CAMDEN BURNED

Farr & Bailey's Loss $100,000—A Hose Carriage Driver Hurt.

CAMDEN, N. J., Feb. 15.—Farr & Bailey's oil cloth works in this city were destroyed by fire this evening, causing a loss of $100,000 on buildings, machinery, and stock. There is some insurance, but how much could not be learned this evening. The cause of the blaze is said to have been a spark caused by electricity in the printing room.

The works consisted of three large buildings. The wind was strong and carried the sparks a considerable distance. Some of them set fire to a storehouse filled with chemicals. The roof of this building was blazing when the firemen reached it. They managed to quench the flames before the fire worked to the interior of the building. Other sparks set fire to a house at Ninth and Chestnut Streets, and it was badly damaged.

While returning from the fire, Wilson Broomly, driver of a hose carriage, was severely injured by the axle of the hose carriage breaking. When the side of the carriage dropped to the ground, Broomly was thrown to the street. He was cut and bruised.

Made Director of Public Safety.

PHILADELPHIA, Feb. 15.—Mayor Warwick this afternoon appointed Frank M. Riter to be Director of Public Safety, to succeed Abraham M. Beitler, whose appointment by Gov. Hastings as a Judge of Common Pleas Court was announced to-day. The salary is $10,000 per annum. Mr. Riter is a well-known attorney, and for four years was an Assistant City Solicitor of Philadelphia. He has been a member of the Pennsylvania House of Representatives from this city since 1889.

Conference on New-York Bills.

There was a conference yesterday afternoon at Police Headquarters between Senators Pavey and Laimbeer, Frank Moss of the Parkhurst Society, and Commissioners Roosevelt and Parker.

The conference was held behind closed doors in President Roosevelt's private office.

After the conference was over Commissioner Roosevelt said bills before the Legislature affecting the police had been talked over.

Gen. Harrison Preparing to Marry.

INDIANAPOLIS, Feb. 15.—Gen. Harrison has begun to prepare for his marriage to Mrs. Dimmick. His sister, Mrs. Bettie Eaton, of North Bend, Ohio, has arrived here to assist him in putting his house in order for the reception of the bride. The date of the wedding has not been announced, but it is believed it will not be later than April 10.

HARMONY STILL AFAR OFF

The Governor's Dinner Failed of Its Chief Object.

PLATT'S FRIGID GREETING TO STRONG

An Incident of the Evening Which Pained Dr. Depew and Other Conciliationists More than They Care to Tell.

ALBANY, Feb. 15.—The "harmony," which was supposed to develop at Gov. Morton's dinner, was scattered like a mist before a wind by an incident just at the close of the evening, as the guests had arisen from the table. It was the meeting of Mr. Platt and Mayor Strong. That meeting was so cold, and so lacking in all evidence of harmonious feeling, that it almost created a scene.

It was more than cold. Mayor Strong was willing to make up, but Mr. Platt gave him the "icy hand."

The incident has been pretty widely discussed to-day, by those who were interested in the "harmony" part of the entertainment.

The Mayor and Mr. Platt did not greet each other during the informal hand-shaking that followed the arrival of the guests in the drawing room of the Executive Mansion. They were literally the observed of all, for one of the great things necessary to bringing together all the elements in New-York City politics is a reconciliation between these two. During the dinner Mayor Strong and Mr. Platt sat at a considerable distance apart. Afterward, when the cigars were still passing the guests arose from the table and formed little groups, as they found congenial society. Mayor Strong and Mr. Platt chose opposite ends of the dining room.

Finally it occurred to Col. Cole, the Governor's private secretary, who appreciates the humor of any situation, that these two gentlemen ought to know each other, and he brought Mayor Strong to Mr. Platt and presented him.

Mayor Strong had an olive branch of modest proportions in his left hand, and as he approached the chieftain he extended his right hand and remarked that he had "no personal feeling in the political relations" which he had maintained.

Speaker Fish, Chairman Hackett, William Barnes, Jr., Assemblyman O'Grady, and two or three others were watching with eager interest. The situation at once became so awkward that Mr. Fish could not endure the sight, and stepped into an adjoining room. It looked as if Mr. Platt was about to refuse to clasp hands. But Mr. Platt is nothing if not a gentleman, and, moreover, he is not likely to create a "scene," unless there is absolute necessity for it. He hesitated a moment, gave the Mayor a dignified, not to say freezing, look, and then extended his hand reluctantly. He made a remark which no one remembers accurately. A half-dozen attempts have been made to quote it, but no two guests have the same version. All must have been somewhat "rattled." Whatever may have been the precise wording of it, it conveyed to Mayor Strong the information that the Tioga chieftain considered that there was a personal matter between them which is as yet unadjusted.

Commonplace remarks were exchanged for the space of half a minute, and the two passed on. Mr. Platt's behavior has been characterized as one of "Harrison civility."

This incident was the one which has oftenest been spoken of to-day. Dr. Depew is said to have been more nearly "rattled" than any one present had ever before seen him. He forgot to tell a story for several minutes.

The occurrence is talked of chiefly as an indication of the likelihood of all factions in New-York City coming together, and with this as the closing incident of the harmony feast, opinion is general that the breach is no nearer healed now than it was before the feast.

Mr. Platt and Chairman Hackett left for New-York at 1:35 o'clock, Mr. Platt having had luncheon with the Governor just before going to the train. Mayor Strong and those who had remained over night departed on an earlier train.

Mr Platt said before his departure: "I have seen some proposed amendments to the Raines bill, but I cannot divulge them, because that is a matter for the committee. The bill, in my opinion, is now a perfect measure, and I think it will meet the approval of the majority of the members of the Legislature."

MR. PLATT IS SILENT.

Nothing to Say Regarding His Meeting with Mayor Strong.

Mr. Platt, Chairman Hackett, and Republican Leader O'Grady reached this city from Albany at 6 o'clock last night. Mr. Lauterbach and others who were at the so-called "harmony" feast were in the city earlier in the day. Some of them gave a few details of what took place at the dinner. One related a conversation that he said took place between Mr. Platt and Gen. Horace Porter, whose prominence in the Union League Club did not spare him from one of Mr. Platt's sarcastic cuts. The two were discussing the Greater New-York bill, and the likelihood that it would become a law. Mr. Platt, of course, is in favor of the bill.

"The Union League Club," said Gen. Porter, "has decided to oppose the bill."

"Yes; so I heard," replied Mr. Platt: "I'm glad of it."

"I said," repeated Gen. Porter, thinking Mr. Platt had misunderstood him, "I said 'oppose' it."

"Yes," replied Mr. Platt. "I'm glad."

"Why?" asked Gen. Porter, turning and facing the Tioga man.

"Because," said Mr. Platt, "if the Union League is against it, it's sure to pass."

Mr. Platt was not disposed to discuss last night the incident of his meeting with Mayor Strong.

MAYOR STRONG LOST HIS VOICE.

Mayor Wurster Says He Could Not Respond to "Mr. Platt's Health."

Mayor Wurster of Brooklyn was one of the guests at the harmony dinner given by Gov. Morton at Albany Friday night. He arrived home yesterday evening, and, in speaking of the dinner, said:

"It was one of the most enjoyable dinners I ever attended, but there was no singing. Mrs. Morton is a delightful conversationalist, and a charming woman."

Mayor Wurster was asked if Mr. Platt had converted him to his belief upon the subject of consolidation.

"I devoted myself almost entirely to Mrs. Morton, and there was very little said about consolidation. By the way, some one proposed the health of ex-Senator Platt, and called on Mayor Strong to second the toast, but he said he had lost his voice."

Mayor Wurster said he regarded Mr. Platt as the leader of the State, and then said: "Mr. Platt takes counsel of the other leaders, and whatever they decide upon is the will of Mr. Platt, and he is held responsible for it. No man in either the Republican or Democratic Party is a dictator. He must consult with other leaders. No man knows it all."

He denied that he had changed his views upon the question of consolidation since he had seen Mr. Platt.

MANIAC'S DASH FOR LIBERTY

Edward Rodgers Knocked Down a Keeper and Jumped Into the Water at Bellevue Hospital.

An exciting chase after an insane man took place in the Bellevue Hospital grounds yesterday afternoon. The patient was Edward Rodgers, who escaped from the insane pavilion, after knocking down one of the keepers, and jumped overboard. He was pulled out of the water with some difficulty.

Rodgers is a clerk, forty-five years old, and lives at 422 Hudson Street. It is said that he became insane a few days ago, and yesterday afternoon his brother, Michael Rodgers, and three friends decided to take him to Bellevue Hospital. He insisted on walking all the way. At Twenty-third Street and Fourth Avenue he became unmanageable and refused to go any further. His brother called upon a policeman, who assisted them in bringing Rodgers to Bellevue. He was taken into the insane pavilion, where the policeman left him and went into the reception room.

As Rodgers was brought in, several patients were being transferred from the rear door of the pavilion. Rodgers, watching his chance, made a dash for liberty. Thomas Butler, one of the keepers, was passing near the door, when the insane man sprung up, struck Butler, knocking him down.

He dashed out of the door and ran across the lawn to the sea wall. His brother Michael, who was still present, raised an alarm, which was heard by the policeman, O'Connell, who ran after the insane man.

Warden O'Rourke, Deputy Warden Rickard, and Policeman Morrell, who was on duty at the Morgue, joined him. Rodgers jumped over several benches, and, reaching the sea wall, jumped overboard into eighteen feet of water. He swam around close to the wall and threw aside a rope which was thrown to him. Several attempts were made to rescue him, but he evaded his rescuers. At the end of about ten minutes he showed signs of exhaustion, and a life ladder was formed in order to pull him out.

Harold Logan reached down over the wall and was held by Warden O'Rourke and some others. He managed to get hold of Rodgers's coat while he was sinking for the second time and pulled him out.

When he was brought to the ground Michael Rodgers struck his brother in the face. The men there wanted to have Michael arrested, but this was not done. The insane man, addressing the crowd, said: "My name is Edward Rodgers. I live at 422 Hudson Street. They are trying to put me away. I have money and they want it." He was taken back to the insane pavilion and put under restraint.

Butler was unconscious from Rodgers's blow. He has a gash on the head, and was removed to the hospital.

ENTERTAINED THE PRESIDENT

A Brilliant Dinner Party Given by Secretary and Mrs. Hoke Smith, with Novel Electrical Effects.

WASHINGTON, Feb. 15.—The Secretary of the Interior and Mrs. Hoke Smith entertained the President and Mrs. Cleveland at dinner to-night, and treated their guests to a novel surprise in the way of floral and electrical effects. Their dining room was canopied with asparagus vines, which twinkled with numerous electric lights, all radiating from an electric star in the centre of the ceiling. The garlands of green hung down over the mirrors and buffets, and each strand was fastened off with a light. The table had an oblong lake down the centre, in which floated tiny goldfish around a centrepiece of pineapple ferns. Pink lilies were here and there in the lake, and it was bordered with maidenhair ferns, veiling a ring of electric lights. The entire effect was exquisitely soft and pretty, and caused great comment and pleasure.

Besides the President and Mrs. Cleveland, there were present Secretary and Mrs. Olney, Secretary and Mrs. Carlisle, Secretary and Miss Herbert, Secretary and Mrs. Lamont, Secretary and Miss Morton, Postmaster General and Mrs. Wilson, Representative Turner, and Mrs. Gordon of Georgia. A mandolin orchestra played softly throughout the dinner, which was composed entirely of Southern dishes and dainties, served on old family plate and china.

Miss Batcheller gave an informal tea this afternoon for old friends to meet Mrs. Cyrus Field Judson of New-York, formerly Miss Alice Condit-Smith of this city.

Prof. and Mrs. Alexander Graham Bell gave a reception to-night which was largely attended by the official and resident circles of society.

The Chilean Minister and Mrs. Gana entertained at dinner to-night, to meet the Vice President.

The Brazilian Minister and Mrs. Mendonça to-night entertained at dinner Gen. and Mrs. Miles, Admiral and Mrs. Ramsay, Gen. and Mrs. Henderson, Gen. and Mrs. Rochester, Gen. and Mrs. Willcox, Gen. and Mrs. Sternberg, Mr. and Mrs. Pollock, Mrs. Audenreid, and Mr. Langley.

THREE KILLED IN A MINE SHAFT

Skip in Which They Were Ascending Overturned—One Fatally Hurt.

REPUBLIC, Mich., Feb. 15.—Eleven men were riding from the bottom of No. 1 shaft of the Republic Mine in a skip this morning just before 7 o'clock. In some way unknown, the skip overturned, precipitating the men to the bottom of the shaft.

James Dridge, H. Pegeleber, Andrew Bailed and William McGrath were killed, and Andrew Petersen was so badly injured that he cannot live. Eric Martin's leg was broken and only one of the others escaped injury.

The shaft is an inclined one and very deep, so that the men were raised and lowered in the skip, it being too far to climb the ladders. The skip began turning soon after starting from the bottom of the shaft, and all the men had been thrown out before a height of sixty feet had been reached.

All the men killed, excepting McGrath, were married and leave families. Petersen, who cannot live, is also married. All were old hands at the mine.

A New Financial Scheme.

WASHINGTON, Feb. 15.—Mr. Fowler of New-Jersey offered in the House to-day a bill to take the Government out of the banking business, refund the National debt, and to improve the banking system. The bill provides for a Board of Finance to consist of the Controller of the Currency and four Ministers of Finance, to be appointed by the President, which would have supervision of all National banks in accordance with existing rules or rules which hereafter may be established.

Mr. Lauterbach Makes No Comment.

Edward Lauterbach said yesterday afternoon that he had no comment to make on the action of the Union League Club in passing a resolution against the consolidation of New-York and Brooklyn. Mr. Lauterbach's tone clearly indicated that he thought the action of the Union League men would make very little difference in the final result.

Mr. Lauterbach was asked if there was much harmony at Gov. Morton's dinner Friday night.

"Lots of it," he replied, "but we didn't talk any politics."

Small Conscience Contribution.

WASHINGTON, Feb. 15.—A sixteen-dollar conscience contribution from an unknown party in Millintown, Penn., was received at the Treasury to-day.

NANSEN'S ARCTIC TRAVEL

Siberian Report of His Discovery Confirmed or Reiterated.

ADVICE OF CONSUL AT ARCHANGEL

Details of Previous Rumors that the Norwegian Had Been Successful—Opinion of Charles P. Daly.

LONDON, Feb. 15.—A dispatch from the British Consul at Archangel has been received at the Foreign Office, in which the report that Dr. Nansen, the arctic explorer, has discovered the north pole, and is now on his return from his successful voyage is confirmed.

The correspondent of The St. James's Gazette at St. Petersburg telegraphs that the report of Dr. Nansen's having discovered the north pole is confirmed.

The first dispatch announcing Dr. Nansen's supposed discovery was received from Kouchtenareff, the explorer's agent and dog supplier, stationed near the mouth of the Lena River. Kouchtenareff may have received his first report through the interchange of visits between the people of the Lena River district, and the inhabitants of New Siberia, where it is thought that Nansen was awaiting.

Various items of news purporting to come from Nansen have been published from time to time since his start from Christi-

Dr. Fridtjof Nansen.

ania June 24, 1893. Le Figaro of Paris circulated a rumor in April last that the explorer had found the north pole, and that it was situated in a chain of mountains.

Again, in September of last year, it was reported in dispatches to London from Angmagsalik, a trading station on the east coast of Greenland, that the Fram had been sighted in July, stuck in an ice drift.

A report was published last December that Mrs. Nansen had received a letter by carrier pigeon from her husband, saying that the expedition was prospering. This story was generally disbelieved, as no carrier pigeons were taken by the party.

The last authentic news received personally from Dr. Nansen was in August, 1895, when he reported that he was about to sail into the Kara Sea, and that the Fram had behaved splendidly.

Fridtjof Nansen is a Norwegian, about thirty-five years old, and well known as a scientist. He studied at the University of Christiania, and in 1882 made a sealing trip to Denmark Straits, on the east coast of Denmark. Later he was appointed Curator of the Museum at Bergen, which position he held until 1888, when he made a second trip to Greenland.

He had already become a believer in the possibility of discovering the north pole, and it was probably on this expedition that he conceived the idea of an attempt to reach the pole in a specially constructed vessel.

The construction of the Fram and his plans have already been described in THE NEW-YORK TIMES. With him on the expedition were Otto Sverdrup, master of the ship, who was Nansen's companion in his journey across Greenland; Sigurd Scott Hansen, Lieutenant in the Norwegian Navy and leader of the meteorological, astronomical, magnetic, and geodetic observations; Henrik Blessing, physician of the expedition and botanist; Claudius Theodor Jacobsen, mate of the Fram, formerly sealer and shipmaster in the Arctic Sea around Spitzbergen and Novaya Zembla; Peter Hendriksen, harpooner, formerly sealer and shipmaster in the Arctic Sea; Hjalmar Johannesen, Lieutenant in Norwegian army, (on the Fram he is fireman and general utility man;) Ivar Mogstad, carpenter, &c., also acts as steward; Bernhard Nordahl, electrical assistant and fireman; Anton Amundsen and Lars Pettersen, engineers; Adolf Juell, steward and sailor, formerly shipmaster; Bernt Bentsen, sailor.

The following list of attempts to reach the North Pole, with their results, may be of interest in connection with Dr. Nansen's reported success:

1827—Capt. Parry reached latitude 82.45.
1827—Capt. Ross, (with the Victory,) lost in the ice, reached latitude 81.27.
1845—Sir John Franklin, (with the Erebus and Terror,) lost in the ice.
1853—Dr. Kane, (Advance,) reached latitude 80.35.
1871—Capt. Peterman, (Hansa,) 81.05.
1871—Capt. Hall, (Polaris,) 82.16.
1876—Capt. Nares, (Alert and Discovery,) 83.10.
1879—Lieut. De Long, (Jeannette,) lost, 72.15.
1881—Lieut. Greely, (Proteus,) 83.20.
1891—Lieut. Peary, (Kite,) 83.24.
1892—Bjorling and Kalshmins, (Ripple,) lost in 76.49.
1893—Lieut. Peary, (Falcon,) 82.34.

DOUBTS AS TO NANSEN'S SUCCESS.

Washington Scientific Men Give Reasons for Being Incredulous.

WASHINGTON, Feb. 15.—In scientific circles in Washington the interest in the report of Dr. Nansen's alleged achievement would be much greater if the news came in a more authentic shape and with more definite particulars.

The fact that the two points from which confirmatory dispatches are alleged to have been received—Irkutsk, in Eastern Siberia, and Archangel, in European Russia—are more than 3,500 miles apart, in the opinion of Lieut. William H. Schuetz of the navy, who is thoroughly familiar with the Siberian coast, casts grave doubts upon the authenticity of the reports. That is to say, the possibility of Dr. Nansen having accomplished his mission by reaching the north pole and planting there the Norwegian flag, in the dramatic way stated in the Irkutsk dispatch, is absolutely questioned. But a reservation is made in favor of the theory that the hardy Norwegian explorer may have escaped alive, and that some intelligence to that effect may have been conveyed by natives in the mysterious way in which rumors travel among savages, and may possibly have reached

"All the News That's Fit to Print"

The New York Times

LATE CITY EDITION

Weather: Fair, very cold today and tonight. Chance of snow tomorrow. Temp. range: today 24-14; Sunday 33-26. Full U.S. report on Page 30.

VOL. LIII...NO. 16,925. NEW YORK, SATURDAY, APRIL 2, 1904.—14 Pages with Review of Books and Art. ONE CENT. In Greater New York, Jersey City and Newark. | Elsewhere, TWO CENTS.

QUESTION HAWLEY ON COTTON DEALS

Says that He, Sully, and Ray Were "Interested.'

WON'T ADMIT JOINT ACCOUNTS

Memoranda of Deals in Evidence—Array of Eminent Counsel in Court.

The examination of Edwin Hawley and Frank H. Ray as witnesses in the bankruptcy proceedings against Daniel J. Sully & Co. was begun yesterday before Thomas Alexander, United States Commissioner, sitting as a Special Examiner in the United States District Court. The courtroom was filled with an interested crowd, consisting mainly of creditors, newspaper reporters, and clerks for the principals in the proceedings.

There was also an imposing array of counsel for various creditors, and the courtroom was well filled when Mr. Alexander took the bench. Among the eminent lawyers present were Elihu Root, acting for the receivers; Henry W. Taft and David H. Miller, who occupied seats next to him. John R. Dos Passos appeared for Mr. Sully. Bootnoy & Baldwin represented the creditors' committee. A member of the law firm of Guggenheimer, Untermyer & Marshall represented Lehman Brothers, large creditors of the defunct firm. W. M. Evans was in attendance on behalf of Fereira, Wilson & Co., and Turner, Rolston & Horace appeared for S. M. Weld & Co. Messrs. Hawley and Ray were represented by Julien T. Davies of Davies, Stone & Auerbach.

Of the creditors' committee were present Reinhard Siedenburg, J. Temple Gwathmey, and G. H. Chapman. R. H. McDougall, President of the Cotton Exchange, occupied a prominent seat, and among other prominent cotton merchants present were George Bailey, George Brennecke, and J. Mandelbaum.

Daniel J. Sully came in late and took a seat by his counsel. He was immaculately dressed in a black English walking coat, a white silk waistcoat, and a tie of the latest design. He wore four large rings. His cuff buttons were jeweled, and in his tie was a large four-leaf clover stickpin with a diamond dewdrop. His white waistcoat set off a heavy gold watch chain. His manner was one of assurance. He did not stop to shake hands or greet the men who were taking steps to recover their money from his alleged partners.

Edwin Hawley, who took the witness stand first, was equally self-possessed, and only once or twice did he show any irritation.

The proceedings were opened by Mr. Root, who stated the circumstances to the examiner. He had hardly finished when Julien T. Davies obtained the privilege of speaking, and said that his clients had been served with subpoenas duces tecum only late on Thursday afternoon, but that, as they had nothing to conceal, and as the interests of so many persons were concerned, he had advised them not to test the legality of the examination, which was doubtful, but to appear ready for the proceedings.

Mr. Davies also asked the privilege to act as counsel for his clients in court, but Mr. Root objected on the ground that this was an ex parte proceeding, in which only the petitioners had any standing in court. The Commissioner so ruled, thereby excluding the right of Mr. Davies or any other lawyer to interfere in any way with the examination. Nevertheless, Mr. Davies tried to enter an objection a few minutes after that, but after a little talk with Mr. Root gave way.

Answering Mr. Root's questions, Mr. Hawley said that he was a President and Director of several railroads, and also a member of the firm of Hawley & Davis. He said he had known Daniel J. Sully for a year and a half, and that his relations with him were those of a customer to his broker. He had also lent $600,000 to Mr. Sully in September, 1903. The loan was secured by stocks and bonds. This loan he had since closed out.

All his transactions with the Sully firm, he said, were conducted with but little writing. He gave his orders. Sully and his clerks did not enter their results on his ledger, but various memoranda were kept of the transactions.

These memoranda were produced in court, and they showed that there were eight distinct accounts between Mr. Hawley and the Sully firm. In all of these Sully and Ray were interested with Hawley, except in transaction "No. 3," when there were five participants. In the other transactions each of them had a one-third interest, except in Transaction "No. 5," in which Sully had a half interest, while Ray and Hawley had a quarter interest each.

These transactions ranged from Dec. 3, 1903, the date of the first transaction, to March 18, 1904, when the last account was closed. The transactions were not for nearly so large amounts as has been commonly supposed. The following table shows the size of the transactions and the profits of the men interested, as far as they appeared from yesterday's testimony.

No.	Bales.	Profit of— Sully.	Ray.	Hawley.
1	30,100	$45,220	....	$45,220
2	10,000	15,200	$15,200	15,200
3	35,100	65,205	65,205	65,205
4	1,500	10,000	10,000	10,000
5	19,100	20,310	10,140	10,140
6	84,100	50,000	50,000	50,000
7	10,000	4,006	4,006	4,006
8	60,700		(loss not stated.)	
	240,600	$210,901	$155,511	$200,731

In addition to these transactions there was another in which five men, whose names did not become known yesterday, were interested. This account was for 30,000 bales of May cotton, and was open on March 17, the day before the suspension of the Sully firm. Some of the profits as set forth were only approximated by Mr. Hawley, who did not have his check book along, and was therefore unable to give exact figures.

"No. 8" is the one over which there is the dispute as to Mr. Hawley's liability, as it was not closed until the day of the suspension. It is understood to have resulted in a loss of over $200,000.

With the exception of the first transaction all of these were marked on the statements "joint three account." Mr. Root tried to make Mr. Hawley explain what "joint three account" meant.

"I don't know," replied Mr. Hawley, "why D. J. Sully should have marked any account 'joint three account.'"

"Can't you give us some light on this?"

"No," said Mr. Hawley, and he declined to admit that the accounts were joint accounts, although he said that he, Sully, and Ray were all interested in the transactions.

Mr. Root asked Mr. Hawley if he had ever made a division with Mr. Sully.

"I never did to my knowledge, but I divided with Mr. Ray and other parties," was the answer.

"Then," asked Mr. Root, "Mr. Sully retained his share before he sent you a check?"

"I don't know," said Mr. Hawley. "The assumption was that he did."

There were also put in evidence a number of letters written on the day of the failure. In one of these Mr. Hawley speaks of inclosing a check of $82,420. This check has since been paid.

The rest of the session was taken up with identification of the handwritings of the various memoranda and letters. At 2 o'clock an adjournment was taken until next Thursday at 11 A. M.

INDEX TO DEPARTMENTS.

CLARK WON'T NAME LOBBY.

Senator Declines to Tell Who Is Pushing Repeal of Land Laws.

Special to The New York Times.

WASHINGTON, April 1.—Senator Clark of Wyoming declined to-day to name the men whom he stated before the Senate yesterday were employed as a lobby at Washington to bring about a repeal of the land and homestead laws. Senator Clark says, however, that he will privately give the names to any Senator who wants them.

The charges are likely to produce further debate and perhaps lead to an investigation. Mr. Clark's charge was not veiled, but was open and direct. He said:

"I say with a full knowledge and with responsibility for my words that never in the history of public land legislation has there been such a determined and such an insistent lobby as has been behind this proposition for the last three years to repeal the land laws of the United States.

"It is no secret that they have a bureau established here in this city for that purpose. It is no secret that they maintain a weekly organ of publication devoted to this, and to this alone. It is no secret that one of the greatest of these holders boasted in a public speech at a banquet within the last two months that his company alone had contributed $25,000 to this propaganda."

Mr. Patterson thought the name of the man engaged in lobbying ought to be made known to the Senate, "that he would be known from one end of the country to the other."

SAN FRANCISCO, April 1.—John H. Fimple, Assistant Commissioner in the United States General Land Office, testified in the Hyde-Diamond land fraud case to-day. He is a witness for the prosecution, but was called, under protest, by the attorneys for the defense. He stated that about fifty-three forest reservations, comprising 2,000,000 acres, had been created under the act of March 30, 1888.

He added that probably 1,000 selectors of these lands had appeared by attorneys.

TWO WOMEN KILLED BY TRAIN.

One Sacrificed Her Life by Turning Back to Save the Other.

Side by side in the Jersey City Morgue lie the bodies of Mrs. Minnie Langerfeld, thirty years old, of 31 Wales Avenue, and Mrs. Josephine Steingraver, thirty-two years old, of 37 Wales Avenue. They were killed on the Pennsylvania Railroad near James Avenue shortly after noon yesterday by an express train on its way to Philadelphia.

Mrs. Mary Woolraven, who saw the accident from her window, says Mrs. Steingraver had crossed the track, and, Mrs. Langerfeld following, stopped on the track of the west-bound passenger train. A freight train hid the approaching train from the two women. Mrs. Langerfeld appeared paralyzed with fear, and Mrs. Steingraver turning back either to assist her or because she was confused, was hurled to one side. Mrs. Langerfeld shot upward and forward and dropped sixty feet in front of the train and her body was dragged forty feet by the wheels of the locomotive.

Mrs. Steingraver leaves three children and Mrs. Langerfeld two. Frederick Steingraver, husband of one of the women, who works in New York, was notified by telephone of his wife's death immediately after the accident, but denounced his informant as an "April fool joker," and paid no attention to the matter until the police sent him a telegram informing him of the tragedy.

GOT REVELATION NOT TO WED.

Woman Wouldn't Remarry Former Husband Because He Was Not Saved.

Special to The New York Times.

ST. LOUIS, April 1.—Mrs. Nora Hardman to-day forsook her fiancé just before the time set for the wedding and explained to the minister and assembled guests: "I cannot marry the man I love until I know that he is saved."

R. J. Caldwell and Mrs. Hardman were formerly man and wife, but last Fall she became interested in the "holiness" movement and the resulting differences of opinion resulted in Mr. Caldwell obtaining a divorce. The woman resumed the name of a former husband. Recently a reconciliation was effected and a second marriage arranged.

On the way for the license the bride-elect prayed twenty minutes on the steps of the City Hall for a revelation as to the Divine opinion of the match. Her decision, she says, was due to the asked-for revelation.

SUICIDE LEAPS FROM TWENTY-FIRST STORY

S. J. Haydon Seeks Death from Dizzy Height of Skyscraper.

A PROMINENT RAILROAD MAN

Jump Is Taken from an Unoccupied Office in the New "Forty-two Broadway" Building.

Sidney Johnston Haydon, a well-known railroad man, who for the last year and a half lived in the Holley, an apartment hotel at 36 Washington Square West, committed suicide yesterday afternoon by jumping from the twenty-first story of the new "Forty-two Broadway" Building. The police say that the man's choice of a means of ending life was one of the most remarkable in the annals of the city. Those persons who were acquainted with Haydon say that he had always appeared to be perfectly sane. It is believed that he feared being in financial straits.

Haydon is supposed to have entered the building about 3 o'clock, which was half an hour before he made his leap. The building is new, and few of the offices are occupied. Those unrented are left unlocked during the day for inspection by prospective tenants. The room to which Haydon made his way in order to end his life is in the south wing on the New Street side. From the sill the distance to the ground is 320 feet. It being an unoccupied office, the windows were closed. Haydon placed his umbrella in a corner, raised a sash as far as it would go to admit of the passage of his huge form, and stepped out on the three-foot sill. Then he closed the window behind him and leaped.

The body struck feet first directly in front of a saloon in the rear of the building. The impact, according to scores of persons in the neighborhood, made a noise like the report of a large calibre pistol. Two boys, Frank McLaughlin and Joseph Allimento, were the only persons, so far as is known, who saw the body of the man as it came tumbling down from the dizzy height. So fast did it descend that the boys did not at first realize that it was a man. When it struck the ground the boys darted up the street to where Policeman Esmond Gray of the Old Slip Station was, and managed to make him understand that something awful had happened.

"The man shot himself," faltered McLaughlin, and Allimento stammered a similar explanation of the affair.

The policeman investigated their story and then sent for an ambulance from the Hudson Street Hospital, though it was evident that the man was dead.

The news of Haydon's jump spread like wildfire through the neighborhood, and although it was after most of the brokers, bankers, and other business men had gone home, a tremendous crowd soon gathered. The body was removed to the Old Slip Station. In the pockets were found $44.40, several letters, and a cardcase with engraved cards bearing Haydon's name. It also was ascertained from papers in the pockets that the man lived at the Holley, and Mr. Knott, the manager of the house, was summoned by telephone. He positively identified the body as that of his tenant.

So far as Mr. Knott knew, Haydon was a man of leisure, and, although everybody in the Holley knew him, he had never seen fit to tell any one of his affairs. The manager himself, he said, did not know the address of any of his relatives.

Mr. Knott said that Haydon was not married and that he always appeared to have plenty of money. A clerk at the hotel said later that the dead man was a Southerner and it was remarked that he bore the name of the famous Confederate commander Albert Sidney Johnston. One of the women guests said that Mr. Haydon had been worried very much lately by the fact that he was becoming deaf. He remarked yesterday morning, she added, that unless he improved everybody would soon be screaming at him.

The building known as "The Forty-two Broadway" was visited yesterday by about 5,000 persons, a majority of them being prospective tenants, and twelve of the elevators were kept busy all day. No one could be found who remembered seeing a man 6 feet 4 inches in height, weighing 240 pounds, well dressed, of rather distinguished appearance, enter the building. One of the employes in the Edison Building, however, said that he knew Haydon and that he believed him to have been a speculator.

Coroner Brown late last night made public one of the letters found on Haydon by the police. It was from Erastus Young, the General Auditor of the Union Pacific Railroad. The letter was dated San Francisco, March 5, and read:

Your letter of the 27th, addressed to me at Omaha and forwarded to me here, just received. I am very glad to have it, and will certainly keep you in mind for anything in your line that may come under my notice. I fear I cannot offer much encouragement for a position in our service, as there are usually more men qualified for promotion than we can find places for. I will, however, take great pleasure in aiding you in any way in my power. I trust that if you desire to re-engage in railroad work you will not have to wait long before finding a suitable opening.

Another letter was from a woman, whose name Coroner Brown would not make public, in which the writer told Haydon she was sure that everything would end well, and that she was certain that Mr. Young was sincere in his desire to aid him.

An envelope, from which a letter had been removed, also was found. It bore the name of Eugene Talcott of 108-110 Franklin Street, this city. There is no Eugene Talcott in the New York directory, but there is an A. W. Talcott, who has an office at that Franklin Street address. His home is in Rye, N. Y.

LOUISVILLE, April 1.—Sidney Johnston Haydon, who committed suicide in New York by jumping from the top floor of a skyscraper, was prominent as a railroad man and related to many prominent Kentuckians. During his residence in Louisville some years ago he was one of the chief clerks in the Auditor's office of the Louisville and Nashville Railroad. After leaving Louisville he became Auditor of the Choctaw, Oklahoma and Gulf Road. Later he opened an office as expert accountant in New York.

He was a bachelor. His mother, Mrs. Anna G. Haydon of Louisville, is the only surviving member of his immediate family.

Damage by Ice to Erie Canal.

ALBANY, April 1.—According to the latest estimates made by employes in the Department of Public Works, the cost of repairing the damage to the Erie Canal caused by the floods and the breaking of the ice gorges in the Mohawk Valley may considerably exceed $100,000.

NAVAL OFFICER A SUICIDE.

Lieut. Commander Warburton Kills Himself on the Maine.

Special to The New York Times.

PENSACOLA, Fla., April 1.—Lieut. Commander Edgar Townsend Warburton, Chief Engineer of the battleship Maine, now at Pensacola, sent a bullet through his brain to-day, death resulting almost instantly. His fellow-officers are at a loss to understand his reasons for the act, as he has been in good spirits since the arrival of the ship at Pensacola.

The executive officer was the first to discover the suicide. He was passing the door of the cabin of the Chief Engineer, when he was startled by the report of a revolver and heard a bullet whiz by his ear. The bullet, after having passed through the brain of the Chief Engineer, passed through the screen door of the cabin and struck the rail near where the executive officer was standing.

It was apparent from the position that the Commander occupied when he was first found that he had shot himself deliberately. The pistol was clasped firmly in the right hand, and the ball had penetrated just above the right temple, passing out just over the left ear. His fellow-officers claim that it was an accident, but the circumstances do not admit of a doubt as to suicidal intent.

All the ships of the squadron have been ordered in mourning, and the remains will be shipped to-morrow to his widow in Philadelphia.

Special to The New York Times.

PHILADELPHIA, April 1.—Lieut. Commander Warburton is survived by a widow, a brother, and two sisters, all of whom live in this city. At his home, 4412 Chestnut Street, to-night his widow was prostrated with grief. She could ascribe no use for her husband's deed. His brother said that a letter was received from the Commander on March 28 in which he wrote as though in the best of health and spirits.

He was appointed from Pennsylvania cadet engineer at the Naval Academy Oct. 1, 1872, and was commissioned assistant engineer July 1, 1878, and passed assistant engineer July 1, 1887. He was on the Huron when that vessel was wrecked off Nag's Head, N. C. Nov. 24, 1877.

From November, 1886, to September, 1887, he was Secretary of the Examining Board of Naval Engineers in this city. After service on the Pacific Coast and three years of inspection duty at Cramps' Shipyards in this city he was promoted chief engineer May, 1897, and served on the New Orleans during the Spanish-American war, taking part in the bombardments of the fortifications at the entrance of the harbor and also on the blockade of San Juan, Porto Rico. He was commissioned Lieut. Commander March 3, 1899. He was transferred from the Indiana to the Maine a few months ago.

KILLED BY BIRTHDAY ROSE.

Thorn Scratches Aged Woman's Finger, Causing Blood Poisoning.

BLOOMFIELD, N. J., April 1.—Mrs. Francis Dannbacher of Maolis Avenue, Bloomfield, died this afternoon from blood poisoning. A few days ago she celebrated the seventy-first anniversary of her birth, and among the presents received was a handsome bouquet of roses. While exhibiting them to her friends the aged woman accidentally scratched one of her fingers with a thorn.

Mrs. Dannbacher paid no attention to the wound at the time, but the next day her arm and hand began to swell to such proportions that the family physician was called in. He pronounced her ailment blood poisoning. Yesterday a New York specialist was called in consultation with other physicians, but the septic condition was too extensive to be mastered.

HILL PLOT YARN DENIED.

Story That Tammany Would Not Be Allowed to Name Its Delegates.

Special to The New York Times.

ALBANY, April 1.—A story was started here to-day that David B. Hill, now that he is certain of controlling the State Convention which will meet in Albany on April 18, intends to secure a united delegation for Parker to go to the St. Louis Convention by denying to Tammany the privilege of naming the delegates from the Congressional districts included within the City of New York. The delegates to the Democratic National Convention have in this State customarily been ratified by the State Convention.

The story has it that Mr. Hill, in order to avoid the possibility of division in the New York delegation on the candidacy of Judge Parker, would see to it that the selections of delegates made by Tammany were rejected, and men selected in their stead who could absolutely be relied upon to vote for Judge Parker.

An authoritative denial was to-night obtained from Mr. Hill's headquarters that Mr. Hill has any such intention as imputed to him.

TWO SOLID PARKER COUNTIES.

Herkimer and Albany Both Declare for the Judge's Nomination.

ALBANY, N. Y., April 1.—The Democrats of the Second Albany District to-day elected delegates to the State Convention and instructed them for Judge Parker. All of the Albany delegation, now complete, have been thus instructed.

Democratic caucuses were held to-day throughout Herkimer County, and were carried, without exception, for Judge Parker, who got 51 votes to 6 for Hearst.

The Second District Democratic Assembly Convention, held at Wilson this afternoon, also elected delegates to the State Convention and indorsed Judge Parker for President.

SUE TWENTY-SIX RAILROADS.

Chicago Coal Men Allege Illegal Combination in Restraint of Trade.

Special to The New York Times.

CHICAGO, April 1.—Eight specific charges alleging violations of the Sherman anti-trust law are brought against the twenty-six leading railroads running into Chicago in a bill prepared for the Chicago Coal Shippers' Association, to be filed in the United States Circuit Court. The action is an attempt by the coal men to put the Chicago Car Service Association out of business on the ground that it is an illegal combination of railroads. The bill is a petition for injunction against each of the railroads.

The charges are summed up in the last clause, wherein it is alleged that the purpose and object of the association and the direct and necessary effect of its operations is artificially to restrain trade and the maintenance of unreasonable and arbitrary regulations for the conduct of the business of the defendant railroad companies in defiance of the law.

The railroads will be given their first hearing a week from Friday.

EXPLORERS FOUND GREAT ANTARCTIC PLATEAU

Interior of South Victoria Rises to Height of 9,000 Feet.

SCOTT'S BOLD TRIP WESTWARD

Party from the Ship Discovery Tried to Cut Canal Through Ice—Relief Ships Used Dynamite.

LYTTELTON, New Zealand, April 1.—The British antarctic steamer Discovery and the relief steamers Morning and Terra-nova arrived here to-day.

The relief ships, which left Hobart Dec. 5, reached the Discovery Feb. 14, and found all the members of the expedition in excellent health and spirits. There was great excitement among the crews of all the ships when they sighted each other, and the rescuers found that all was well on board the long-absent Discovery.

Scientific work was continued by the explorers throughout the Winter of 1903. They established the fact that the interior of Victorialand continues at a height of 9,000 feet, and is evidently a vast continental plateau. A new route to the west was found and a depot was established 2,000 feet up the glacier.

CHRISTCHURCH, New Zealand, April 1.—Capt. R. F. Scott, R. N., of the Discovery says that the Winter of 1903 passed pleasantly and that the members of the expedition enjoyed much greater comfort than in 1902. Sledging operations began in September under severe conditions, owing to extremely low temperatures, which frequently fell to 60 degrees below zero.

In November one party reached a point 160 geographical miles southeast of the ship. There was no trace of land, and evidence was obtained showing that this was a vast floating ice plain.

Capt. Scott with another party made two excursions westward in October over a glacier. They gained the summit Oct. 11 and crossed the magnetic meridian Oct. 20 in longitude 155½ east. Proceeding still westward the party reached a point 270 miles from the ship in latitude 78, south longitude 146¼ east. The interior of South Victoria is evidently a vast continental plateau stretching continuously upward for 9,000 feet. The glacier valley affords magnificent scenery and gives a natural geological section of the mountains.

In the middle of December the party attempted to cut a canal through the ice, which was from 7 to 8 feet thick, but the effort was futile owing to constant refreezing. The open water was then seventeen miles from the ship.

The relief ships arrived simultaneously Jan. 5. The ice began to break at the end of January, assisted by systematic dynamiting. On Feb. 12 a general break-up brought the relief ships to Hut Point, and on Feb. 14 two heavy charges of dynamite placed the Discovery in open water.

In the succeeding days the heavy gales drove the vessels apart and the Discovery was driven ashore, where she remained for eight hours in a critical position before she freed herself.

"On Feb. 19," said Capt. Scott, "we got seventy-five tons of coal from the relief ships. Before a fresh gale drove us north we kept close along the coast line and parted company with the other ships at Cape Washington, with a clear sea to the north. We entered Wood Bay and Robertson Bay, but in attempting to pass around Cape North we met with heavy pack ice.

"We found that we had not sufficient coal to enter Smith Inlet and skirted the pack to the east and north, and proceeded west along Parallel 66½ latitude, and on March 2 found that Balleny and Russel Islands were identical. We passed through the group and continued west to longitude 156, when want of coal obliged us to turn north. The coast line reported in this direction we found to be a mistake, as no such land exists.

"We arrived at Auckland Island March 15 with only ten tons of coal in our bunkers. The Terra Nova and the Morning rejoined us March 20, after experiencing terrible weather. The shortage of coal alone compelled our early return."

FAST TRAIN'S NARROW ESCAPE.

Ontario and Western Engine Leaves Track, but Cars Don't.

Special to The New York Times.

MIDDLETOWN, N. Y., April 1.—Fast express train No. 6, on the Ontario and Western Railroad, had a narrow escape from disaster this morning about four miles from this city. The train of five coaches was on one of the fastest stretches of the road and was going sixty miles an hour, when the engine left the rails.

Engineer E. P. Dewitt threw back the throttle and stuck to his post. The heavy coaches stayed on the rails, and, although the engine ran over the ties for thirty rods before being stopped, it stayed upright. No one was injured.

WOMAN'S MYSTERIOUS DEATH.

Her Body Found Bearing the Marks of Several Stiletto Wounds.

WESTON, Mass., April 1.—The authorities of Middlesex County are investigating the death of Miss Mabel Page, aged forty, whose body was found by her father in her room at home here yesterday. The case was thought to be one of suicide at first glance, but the location of one or more of the wounds on the body raised a doubt that they could have been self-inflicted.

Miss Page was alone at her home for several hours yesterday, and it was during this interval that her death occurred. No weapon has been found, but the police are of the opinion that the wounds were inflicted with a stiletto. In this connection it is recalled that some time ago a tramp, apparently an Italian, called at the Page house, asking for food and his request was refused.

INSTRUCTED FOR ROOSEVELT.

New York and Louisiana Republicans Want His Nomination.

WATERTOWN, N. Y., April 1.—At nearly all the Republican caucuses held in the towns of Jefferson County to-day resolutions were adopted calling for the nomination of President Roosevelt.

NEW ORLEANS, La., April 1.—The Republican Convention of the Sixth Congressional District has indorsed the Roosevelt Administration and elected delegates to the National Convention instructed to vote for Roosevelt.

DECLINES $1,800,000 BEQUEST.

Denver Doctor Turns Inherited Fortune Over to His Sister.

Special to The New York Times.

DENVER, April 1.—Dr. William A. Harroun of the city has telegraphed his sister, Mrs. J. M. Lewis of Portland, Me., that he will not accept the $1,800,000 estate just bequeathed him by his uncle, J. A. Harroun, and that it shall all go to her and her family. Dr. Harroun says:

"I have refused to accept a penny of $1,800,000 and have turned it over to my sister because I am able to make my own living. Every penny that I have made and every penny that I ever have I shall make."

The inheritance came to Dr. Harroun as the heir of James A. Harroun, who died a few weeks ago in Kilkenny, Ireland. He was the last of Dr. Harroun's father's brothers and, according to an agreement between the elder Harrouns that whatever either should leave at death should go to the oldest son of the other or to whomsoever he should designate, the property, consisting of lands and cash, was willed to the Denver doctor.

LANDSLIDE AT DEVIL'S HOLE.

Comes with an Explosion and Revives Up-State Volcano Tradition.

Special to The New York Times.

ROCHESTER, April 1.—Inhabitants in the vicinity of Devil's Hole, near Dansville, Livingston County, are terrified over a big landslide occasioned by some subterranean phenomena as yet unexplained.

The landslide occurred this morning at 3 o'clock, a muffled explosion being heard at the same time and apparently coming from the bowels of the earth. In 1796 a large stream of water burst from the east hill with a sound like thunder, hurling rocks weighing hundreds of pounds high in the air, and causing a rent in the mountains, known as Devil's Hole. Since then there has been a tradition that Devil's Hole is located over the mouth of a volcano.

TELEPHONE GIRL MADE DEAF.

Jury Awards Her $15,000 Damages Against Chicago Company.

Special to The New York Times.

CHICAGO, April 1.—For deafness in her left ear, caused by an electric shock from a telephone receiver, Miss Mary Schultz, 2,614 Wallace Street, secured to-day a verdict of $15,000 against the Chicago Telephone Company.

The accident occurred April 23, 1899, at the switchboard station of the telephone company at 151 Twenty-second Street, where Miss Schultz, then seventeen years old, was employed as an operator. While she had the receiving apparatus around her head and ear a bolt of electricity was transmitted through the wires and she received such a shock that she was thrown violently to the floor.

HAVANA EXPRESS ABLAZE.

Stops Amid Flames from Woodpile—Cars Burned, Passengers Escape.

SANTIAGO, Cuba, April 1.—The Havana express, on the Cuba Railroad, due at Santiago at 10 o'clock last night, ran into the flames from one of the company's woodpiles which was burning alongside the track at a curve east of Las Tunas. The engineer being unable to stop, attempted to speed through, but the heat had caused the rails to spread, and the train, which was crowded with passengers, was derailed in the midst of the fire.

All on board the train escaped by the sides of the cars, which were not immediately exposed to the flames. Among the passengers was Terazzine, the Italian opera singer.

A sleeper, two coaches, and an observation car were burned. The mail, baggage, and express consignments were saved.

WOMAN HELD UP AT HOME.

Facing Two Revolvers, She Hands Over Money and Rings.

POMPTON LAKES, N. J., April 1.—Mrs. Harry Burgess was confronted by an armed thief in her home here yesterday afternoon, and, under threats of instant death, was compelled to give up $29 and several valuable rings. The man appeared at the Burgess home at about 4 o'clock, and, finding Mrs. Burgess alone with her little children, pointed two revolvers at her head and ordered her not to make an outcry.

After satisfying himself that he had everything of value that could be easily carried away the thief again threatened to kill his victim if she made an outcry before he had a chance to escape. Mrs. Burgess collapsed after the man fled, and when her husband returned from work in the evening he found her prostrated.

Mrs. Burgess gave a good description of the burglar. The Borough Marshal was notified and a posse started out in search of the thief, but failed to get him.

STRIKES HIT NEW ORLEANS.

Series of Tie-Ups Promise to Spoil Banner Building Year.

Special to The New York Times.

NEW ORLEANS, April 1.—To-day witnessed the first of what it is feared will be a series of tie-ups of building construction in this city. Three strikes went into effect to-day in the building trades—the painters, the tinners, and building laborers. All stopped work this morning because their demands had been refused.

On April 7 strikes of the carpenters, lathers, and hod carriers will come on, for no settlement of their demands is in sight.

This year would have been a record-breaking building season in New Orleans. Already $6,000,000 worth of contracts had been let.

MRS. McKINLEY'S FRANK.

Good Only for Mail Sent by Her—Mrs. Garfield's Wider Privilege.

WASHINGTON, April 1.—Acting Postmaster General Wynne has issued an order calling the attention of Postmasters to the terms of the statutes now in force extending the franking privilege to Mrs. Lucretia R. Garfield and Mrs. Ida S. McKinley, widows of late Presidents.

There is a striking difference in the two acts. The one of Dec. 20, 1881, under which Mrs. Garfield has enjoyed the franking privilege, allows free carriage in the mails of all mail matter sent to her and sent out by her under her autograph signature, while the act of Jan. 22, 1902, under which Mrs. McKinley has had the franking privilege, limits the privilege to mail sent by her.

ANOTHER NIGHT DASH AT PORT ARTHUR

Togo Seeks to Ascertain Effect of Last "Bottling" Expedition.

ALEXIEFF VISITS WARSHIPS

He Presents Gold Swords of Honor to the Captains of the Cruisers Bayan, Novik and Askold.

LONDON, April 1.—A dispatch to the Central News from Tokio says Vice Admiral Togo made another attack on Port Arthur during the night of March 30 and 31.

The dispatch adds that it is understood the attack was for the purpose of taking soundings and ascertaining the effects of the last attempt to bottle up the Russian fleet. No details of the attack are obtainable.

ST. PETERSBURG, April 1.—The Associated Press is officially informed that up to the present the Government has received no news to confirm the statement sent by a new agency from Tokio that the Japanese made another attack on Port Arthur during the night of March 30 and 31.

Viceroy Alexieff is at Port Arthur on a tour of inspection. He arrived there yesterday and his stay will be brief. With Admiral Makaroff and Gen. Stoessel, respectively commanders of the Russian naval and military forces at Port Arthur, and Gen. Smirnoff, he visited the battleships Petropavlovsk, Retvisan, and Czarevitch, the protected cruiser Pallada, and other ships in the harbor, and later conferred gold swords of honor, with St. George's ribbons inscribed "For Gallantry," upon the Captains of the cruisers Bayan, Novik, and Askold.

According to information received here it is believed the Japanese are preparing to repeat their attempts on Port Arthur. There is a growing conviction in naval and military circles that Vice Admiral Togo's desperate endeavors to bottle up or cripple the squadron there are for the purpose of definitely immobilizing it while the Japanese effect a landing at Niu-Chwang or some other point.

Vice Admiral Makaroff's capture of a Japanese steamer near an island between the extremity of the Liao-Tung Peninsula and the Shan-Tung Peninsula proves that he is watching the entrance of the Gulf of Pe-Chi-Li. It is not believed the Japanese will attempt to debark on the shores of the Liao-Tung Gulf while Makaroff's fleet is uncrippled.

The Emperor has ordered the Koriets, Variag, Sungaruchtchi, and Yenisei stricken from the navy list.

BRITAIN "OUT IN THE COLD."

Continent's Sympathy for Russia as a Russian Paper Pictures It.

LONDON TIMES—NEW YORK TIMES Special Cablegram.
Copyright, 1904, THE NEW YORK TIMES.

ST. PETERSBURG, April 1.—The Novoe Vremya, referring to the visits of the Kaiser and President Loubet to Italy, declares that the connecting link between the Triple and Dual Alliances is the sincere sympathy with Russia cherished by the States composing the two alliances.

The article asserts that in recent professions of international friendship there has been no mention of England, in spite of the fact that England has thrust her friendship upon Italy, France, Germany, and Russia.

England's manysidedness, it is argued, and the sympathy she has displayed with Japan, is causing other nations to hold aloof from her. The paper warns its readers not to be led aside by the recent change in the tone of the English press in reference to the war. It goes on to say:

"It is simply a display of great political tact, in forgetfulness of which the English press went to the greatest extremes, to the danger of England herself."

The Brigheviya Viedomosti suggests that England is disappointed with the proceedings of her ally, and that she is inclined to estimate the strength of Russia more favorably than hitherto.

The Sviet joins the Novoe Vremya in urging that China be informed that merely external neutrality is insufficient, and that any breach of neutrality, whether formal or informal, will be regarded in effect as a breach for which China will be held responsible.

MAY BUY SHIPS IN GERMANY.

Japanese Officers Inspect the Vulcan Yards at Stettin.

LONDON TIMES—NEW YORK TIMES Special Cablegram.
Copyright, 1904, THE NEW YORK TIMES.

BERLIN, April 1.—A number of Japanese officers under the guidance of a Japanese Naval Attaché at Berlin were conducted over the Vulcan Shipbuilding Yard at Stettin yesterday.

It is anticipated that Japan may place in Germany orders for the construction of some of the new vessels which are to be built at once in order to maintain the strength of the Japanese Navy.

SINKING OF JAPANESE SHIP.

Russian Version Says Maps and Torpedoes Were Found on Junk.

ST. PETERSBURG, April 1.—A semi-official dispatch from Port Arthur bearing to-day's date says:

"Our entire squadron left the harbor March 28, making for the Miaotao Islands. At 11 o'clock the cruiser Novik signaled a steamer towing a Chinese junk. She would not stop until the torpedo boat Vrimaniny fired two shots. It was the Japanese steamer Hanien Maru, on board which were found ten Japanese and eleven Chinamen, various papers, telegrams, and maps, and two Whitehead torpedoes. The crew was taken on board our ships, after which the vessel was taken in tow and subsequently sunk.

"The Novik and accompanying torpedo

Robert F. Scott in the first photograph taken on his South Pole expedition.

Captain Roald Amundsen, navigator of the Northwest Passage.

"All the News That's Fit to Print."

The New York Times.

THE WEATHER.
Fair, slightly warmer Thursday; Friday, fair, warmer; moderate winds, becoming south.
For full weather report see Page 12.

VOL. LV...NO. 17,484. **** NEW YORK, THURSDAY, DECEMBER 7, 1905.—SIXTEEN PAGES. ONE CENT In Greater New York, Jersey City and Newark. Elsewhere, TWO CENTS.

ATTACK BEGUN IN HOUSE ON THE CANAL ACCOUNT

Members on Both Sides Object to Miscellaneous Expenditures.

TALK OF $10,000 PRESS AGENT

Mr. Williams Will Move to Scale Down Emergency Appropriation—Debate Will Continue To-day.

Special to The New York Times.

WASHINGTON, Dec. 6.—Full evidence that members of the House are dissatisfied with the expenditure of $10,000,000 on preparatory work for the Panama Canal and that they mean to have closer supervision over future appropriations was given in the House to-day. The bill to appropriate $16,500,000 for the work of the Isthmian Commission was up for general debate, and four and a half hours were spent in sharp discussion of the general subject. The debate will be resumed to-morrow.

Objection centred upon the statement of the expenditures and estimate of needed appropriations made by Auditor Benson of the commission. It is made up largely of items of "miscellaneous" material purchases and other "miscellaneous" needs. The word miscellaneous was a challenge to half the men in the House. They fired questions at Col. Hepburn, who was in charge of the bill, with machine-gun-like rapidity.

Forty times he was obliged to say that he didn't know; that a fuller statement was desirable; that it would be found in the report of the Secretary of War; that it would be had later; that anything would be done, except furnishing an immediate answer to the questions. Representative Mann, Col. Hepburn's associate on the committee, who is supposed to be the best-informed Representative on the canal, tried to go to Hepburn's assistance and was promptly mixed up in the tangle.

Col. Hepburn was stirred out of his easy assumption of indifference to vigorous and animated retort, once when Mr. Fitzgerald of New York got after him on the subject of the commission's so-called "press agent." Fitzgerald had heard that such a person was employed by the commission at a salary of $10,000 a year, and he wanted to know. He insisted so hard that Col. Hepburn finally accused him of endeavoring to make political capital out of his objection. Fitzgerald retorted hotly that it was not so, and that when he tried to make political capital the other side would know it.

John Sharp Williams came to the defense of his adherent by saying that he was surprised to have Col. Hepburn take a question of that sort in such manner.

"Are not Republicans as interested in the proper appropriation and expenditure of money as Democrats?" he asked.

The Republicans were as hard on the auditor's statement as the Democrats. It was Mr. Olmsted of Pennsylvania, a member of the Judiciary Committee, who said "the whole country is demanding, and properly, that the Government shall see that there is the fullest publicity exacted with regard to the affairs of large corporations. But not a corporation or business firm in the United States would stand for a minute such a statement as this on which we are asked to appropriate sixteen and a half millions of dollars."

Mr. Hepburn admitted that it might have been better if the estimates had been more in detail, but saw no good reason why the appropriation should not be made. He read items in the estimates for river and harbor improvements to show that they were not in detail and not in form to give information on their face to be understood except by the engineers. It would be impertinence on his part, he maintained, to set up his judgment against the expert officials, who had been selected because of their fitness for this work.

This statement furnished the text for a lively speech by Bourke Cockran of New York, who demanded to know, if members of the House were to blindly follow estimates, what were they here for? If that was the case, he did not want to occupy his position on the House floor.

He asked Mr. Hepburn what the President meant when he said in his message: "I earnestly recommend to the Congress the need of economy and to this end a rigid scrutiny of appropriations."

"If the power of appropriation is superfluous and impertinent," continued Mr. Cockran, "it is all a mockery. But I ask this House to declare now that this function is not impertinence, but pertains to the oath which we took no longer ago than Monday, which includes that the Treasury shall be guarded by us and not in a perfunctory manner."

Mr. Hepburn retorted that he had not denied the right of scrutiny of any member of the House with regard to appropriations.

Mr. Williams, the Democratic leader, gave notice of certain amendments he should offer to the bill when it comes up to-morrow. He expressly declared, however, that the canal is a non-partisan question.

The principal one would be to strike out the sum of $16,500,000 and insert an amount he should endeavor to ascertain as the amount actually necessary to carry on the work until Jan. 1.

Asserting that there were at least $40,000,000 belonging to the United States now on deposit without interest in National banks, he said he would object to the issuance of bonds on which 2 per cent. interest should be paid to secure money to build the canal. Failing in striking out the entire bonding provision he should move to strike out the provision reimbursing the Treasury the amount appropriated in the bill from the proceeds of the bond sale. He maintained that the position he took was not against National banks.

Gen. Grosvenor of Ohio led off to-day with a move that is certain to have the approval of the Chicago beef packers. He introduced a reprint of the bill passed four years ago taxing oleomargarine colored like butter at the rate of 10 cents a pound, with a single change in the text. This change was to scratch out the word "ten" and insert the word "two." If passed the bill would reduce the tax on oleo to the same rate now paid on the uncolored product.

But for the fact that Grosvenor is a member of Ways and Means and that he was opposed to the original Oleomargarine bill the matter would have attracted little attention. Two years ago the Ways and Means Committee was all ready to report such a bill, which had been prepared by Mr. Boutell of Illinois.

The bill was in the hands of Representative Dalzell of Pennsylvania to report when the fact got into the newspapers. The commotion was so great that the attempt was abandoned.

INDEX TO DEPARTMENTS.

McCALL SAYS HE'LL STICK.

New York Life's President Declares He Has No Intention of Resigning.

Reports that President John A. McCall of the New York Life would soon follow the example set by George W. Perkins, in determining to leave that company at an early date, crystalized yesterday in a story to the effect that Mr. McCall would certainly resign before the next annual meeting in April, and might place his resignation in the hands of the Trustees before their meeting next Wednesday. Mr. McCall himself said last night that he had no intention of resigning.

"I believe that the policy holders are for me," he declared. "Nobody has asked me to resign, and I don't expect to be asked to resign, nor do I expect to resign. The resignation of Mr. Perkins was suggested by Mr. Morgan, to whom the question of Mr. Perkins holding his dual position was referred when Mr. Perkins entered the firm of J. P. Morgan & Co. It is solely at Mr. Morgan's suggestion that Mr. Perkins is retiring from the New York Life."

President McCall complained that the newspapers had treated his testimony before the Armstrong committee unfairly.

One report about the New York Life yesterday was that, should John A. McCall resign, the Presidency would be offered to John Claflin. Still another was that the office had been offered to Mr. Claflin and he had refused it on the ground that his business interests made it impossible for him to accept. Mr. Claflin would not discuss the matter.

THREAT FROM ISLE OF PINES.

Americans There Talk of Possibility of Bloodshed.

HAVANA, Dec. 6.—Edward C. Ryan, chosen by the Americans on the Isle of Pines as a Territorial Delegate to Congress, will leave Havana for Washington Dec. 9.

Mr. Ryan said to-day that he would present to the House of Representatives his credentials from the "Isle of Pines Legislative Assembly." He expected that these credentials would be referred to a committee, before which would then come the question as to whether the island was American territory. He said that if the House should seat him and the Senate meanwhile ratified the treaty conceding the island to Cuba the contention would then be raised that the island could not be constitutionally disposed of except by the act of both houses. If the House did not seat him the matter would be taken to the United States Supreme Court in another form.

Mr. Ryan has a statement signed by the leaders of the movement, in which they assert that in the pending treaty both the Government of the United States and that of Cuba recognize the island as American territory. The statement contends that Cuba temporarily has the right of police jurisdiction and to no other function.

After referring to alleged injustices of the Cuban Government, the statement complains that while Panama's declaration of independence was immediately recognized by the United States, "we of your own race have prayed four years for justice without effect. If the time comes when the shedding of blood shall be necessary for obtaining these people's rights, much responsibility will rest upon the United States Government."

Special to The New York Times.

WASHINGTON, Dec. 6.—When "Delegate" Ryan from the Isle of Pines attempts to get his credentials before Congress he will run up against a stone wall. There is simply no chance at all for the least success of that endeavor. The Administration is committed thoroughly by Secretary Root's recent letter and Ryan's attempt will be met by the whole force of the Administration machinery, which controls the House absolutely on such a matter.

MRS. F. M. THAW REMARRIES.

Wedded to J. Dodridge Peet at the Euclid Hall.

Mrs. Freda Marsh Thaw, who recently divorced her husband, was married last night to J. Dodridge Peet, a wealthy New Yorker who has lived much abroad. The ceremony was performed in Mrs. Thaw's apartment in the Euclid Hall, Broadway and Eighty-sixth Street. The greatest efforts were made to prevent details of the wedding from reaching reporters who, having heard of it in advance, went to the house to make inquiries.

The order excluding reporters worked out rather awkwardly for several persons, who were not what the Superintendent of the house thought they were. The musicians and a special chef who was to cook the wedding supper had trouble in getting into the hotel. The latter was at the point of walking away and leaving the hotel help to cook the supper when he was recognized and admitted at a side door.

The wedding was on the second floor. A woman who wanted to see a friend on that floor, and who it was suspected might be a woman reporter, was obliged to sit in the reception room on the first floor for an hour and a half before she was allowed to see her friend.

The explanation was that all the servants had been tipped to do battle against any reporters who might try to get in. Even the postman, it was said, had trouble in delivering a registered letter.

Cards sent to the wedding party were refused, and when, as the guests emerged after the ceremony, a reporter drew a piece of paper from his pocket and began to make notes, the lights illuminating the front of the house went out. They went out afterward whenever guests appeared to go to their carriages.

The newly married couple departed at 10:30 o'clock. A woman in pink followed them to the door, danced for them on the steps, and showered confetti on them.

The ceremony was performed by the Rev. Dr. Butler of this city, an Episcopalian minister. The bridesmaid was Mrs. David Coykendall, a sister of the bride. A brother of Mr. Peet was best man.

J. Dodridge Peet is about 32 years old. His residence recently has been the Republican Club, and he is a member of several other well-known clubs.

Mrs. Thaw was Freda L. Marsh. She and her husband lived at 1 West Seventy-second Street, until their domestic troubles resulted in divorce. Edward Thaw, from whom Mrs. Thaw was divorced, is a half-brother of Harry Kendall Thaw, husband of Florence Evelyn Nesbit, and of the Countess of Yarmouth. He is a stepson of the present Mrs. William Thaw of Pittsburg.

Three days had been spent in decorating the rooms in which the wedding took place last night.

PEABODY'S NAME TABLED BY MUTUAL TRUSTEES

But a Committee Is to Report To-morrow on Presidency.

ROGERS-BAKER PARTY GAINS

Not Likely, However, to Force Action Which Would Show Its Ascendency—By-Laws Amended.

The expected test of strength between the two elements in the Board of Trustees of the Mutual Life came yesterday, when the faction headed by H. H. Rogers and George F. Baker, which has been reported as seeking to control a reorganization before the investigating committee completes its work, brought forward the name of Charles A. Peabody for the President of the company. The nomination was tabled by a majority vote, which was subsequently made unanimous, and a committee of five was appointed to report at another meeting to be held to-morrow.

On this committee are two of the members of the Mutual's present Finance Committee, which is understood to be in sympathy with Mr. Baker and Mr. Rogers, with James N. Jarvie of Arbuckle & Co., Stuyvesant Fish and William H. Truesdale of the Mutual's Investigating Committee. The majority of this nominating committee is thus supposed to be favorable to the Rogers-Baker party in the board. After yesterday's experience, however, in which Mr. Peabody's nomination was tabled, the Trustees who oppose having the control of the Mutual tied up to any particular financial interest believe that it will not be possible to-morrow to put through a candidate who is subject to this criticism.

For all that, the result is contrary to one contention of the Mutual's investigating committee, that no permanent organization should be undertaken until the investigation is finished.

It was learned that yesterday's session was a strenuous one. Mr. Peabody's name came up soon after 12:30, when the meeting began, and an animated discussion followed in which many members of the board took part. What militated against the programme of the investigating committee was Acting President Cromwell's announced intention to retire at the earliest possible moment. This he made known as soon as the Rogers-Baker faction had brought forward Mr. Peabody as its candidate. Mr. Peabody is the law partner of Fisher Baker, George F. Baker's brother, and is Mr. Baker's personal counsel.

After the nominating committee had been appointed and Mr. Peabody's name disposed of, the Board took up the proposed amendments to the by-laws of the company which had been held up since the investigating committee made its first report on Nov. 16. This resulted in a victory for the investigating committee, the by-laws being all passed as recommended. The most important was a modification of Section 25 of the present by-laws of the company. This section as proposed for amendment was as follows; the words in fullface indicate the additions made by the investigating committee:

No commission or compensation, direct or indirect, for procuring or facilitating loans from the company, **or sales to or purchases from the company** shall be received by any trustee or by any of its officers or any other persons in its employment; **no trustee or officer shall act as a member of a committee or vote at a meeting of the board upon the approval of any purchase from the company or any sale to the company in which he has an interest, direct or indirect, of any kind whatsoever.**

When this section was originally proposed it met with considerable opposition, and attempts were made to eliminate the committee's addition of "sales to or purchases from the company" and to substitute for the word "interest" the word "ownership." It was argued that if Directors were prohibited from voting on propositions in which they had an interest it would be practically impossible to obtain a quota of committeemen who would give to the company the service required by a large financial institution. H. H. Rogers had urged this very strongly, and had personally made several motions in previous meetings of the board to postpone consideration of it indefinitely. There was further discussion of the section yesterday, but it became apparent that the majority of the Trustees favored the adoption of the by-law, and so the vote was unanimous.

Other amendments of the by-laws adopted yesterday placed specifically under the charge of the general solicitor of the company all "legislative business," provided that contracts for printing shall be on a competitive basis and that the committee on expenditures shall not approve the payment of any moneys except upon vouchers disclosing fully the nature of the payment, the person paid, the services rendered, and the property furnished. A committee was also appointed yesterday to take up the work of transferring the agencies of the company from a commission to a salary basis.

When yesterday's meeting was over temporary President Cromwell, who was the only one of the Trustees who would talk for publication, came out strongly for harmony.

"We are in perfect accord," he said, "and are not disposed to hurry in the disposition of any business. Our meeting to-day was devoted to the consideration of changes in the by-laws. That there is absolute harmony among the Trustees of the company is evident in the fact that every motion was carried unanimously."

The fifty agents of the Mutual Life, who held a meeting yesterday, issued a statement in which they said that in their previous resolution favoring the promotion of Supt. of Agencies Dexter they did not mean to insist upon the retirement of General Manager Robert H. McCurdy.

THREE YEARS FOR REPEATER.

Illegal Voting Must Stop, Said Court, in Sentencing O'Brien.

James O'Brien, an ex-convict, found guilty of illegal voting, was sentenced to three years and two months in Sing Sing by Justice Rogers in the Supreme Court yesterday. Although having no right to vote at all on account of his criminal record, O'Brien managed to vote twice on election day, once under his own name and the second time under the name of William Gallagher.

"There is too much illegal voting done in this city," said Justice Rogers in pronouncing the sentence. "It must stop."

The sentence is said to be the severest ever inflicted in this city for this offense.

STATEMENT BY W. E. COREY.

Domestic Differences Irreconcilable, Says Steel Trust's Head.

William E. Corey, President of the United States Steel Corporation, made this statement yesterday afternoon at his office, 71 Broadway, about his domestic troubles:

"The subject matter of recent publications, personal to myself and some others, is of such a painful character that I have hesitated to say anything in regard to it and have perhaps been unjust to myself and to the press in declining to admit the whole truth when questioned. However, in view of what has been published I have decided to make a statement which covers the situation. I do this more to cover the good name of others than my own.

"Mrs. Corey and I have had disagreements. Our differences are irreconcilable. I have been informed and believe she is residing in Nevada. She may have contemplated a divorce, and if she applies for one I shall not oppose it if it is legally obtained and does not involve moral turpitude. Whether she does or not, I am in duty bound to provide for her a comfortable support and shall do so.

"I have been for a long time acquainted with a lady whose name has been prominently connected with mine, but there has never been any conduct between us of which either of us need be ashamed. Any suggestion to the contrary would be a great injustice."

FLAMES SWEEP STEAMBOAT.

Joy Liner Badly Damaged—Transport McClellan Saved.

Fire starting from some unknown cause in the stern of the Joy Line steamer Rosalie, in Winter quarters at the Morse Iron Works, Fifty-seventh Street, South Brooklyn, shortly after one o'clock this morning, swept the vessel to her bow.

Capt. Stephen Merritt who, with a crew of five men, was keeping the ship, was unable to do anything to check the progress of the flames and two of the crew were driven overboard, but were rescued.

The others fled across the decks of the United States transport McClellan, also out of commission and moored alongside.

Three alarms were turned in, bringing the fireboats Seth Low and David A. Boody. Soon after 2 o'clock the Rosalie listed heavily and threatened to turn turtle. The plates of the McClellan were then red hot in places, but the action of her crew in playing the ship's hose on threatened parts is believed to have saved the vessel from serious damage.

About twenty vessels are in Winter quarters at the iron works. The City of Key West and several others nearest the blazing wreck were towed into the stream. The Rosalie was laid up three days ago. Her fires were drawn, and there was no cargo aboard. No theory satisfactorily accounts for the fire. The Rosalie is an old wooden side-wheeler and had lately been plying between this city and Boston. The damage is placed at $50,000.

DRIVER SAVES WOMEN.

Turns Railway Emergency Team Into Pole—One Horse Sacrificed.

The promptness of Charles Reynolds, the driver of a Metropolitan Street Railway emergency wagon, in sacrificing his team rather than endanger the lives of two women, who in a hansom were on their way to the Waldorf-Astoria late yesterday afternoon, averted what might have been a fatal accident.

Reynolds's team was dashing down Sixth Avenue in response to an emergency call, when at Thirtieth Street the cab pulled directly in his path. There was but a moment in which to act, but that was sufficient for Reynolds, who swerved his team around into a sign pole that stood on the edge of the sidewalk, narrowly missing the cab and its screaming occupants.

Both of Renold's horses fell, and one of them was so badly hurt that he will have to be shot. The other was more fortunate, although seriously injured. The occupants of the cab escaped uninjured and drove on without giving their names.

PLEAS FOR MRS. ROGERS.

Petitions Sent to Gov. Bell—Her Attorneys to Act.

RUTLAND, Vt., Dec. 6.—Attorneys for Mrs. Mary Rogers, whose execution is fixed for Friday next, have not given up hope of obtaining another reprieve from Gov. Charles J. Bell, who is now on his way home from Chicago. Preparations were made by one of Mrs. Rogers's attorneys to intercept the Governor and present to him the papers prepared.

Special to The New York Times.

CINCINNATI, Dec. 6.—Miss Jessie M. Partlon is speeding across the country with 27,648 signatures to a petition to Gov. Bell protesting against the execution of Mrs. Mary Rogers. The signatures have all been gathered in three days, and, as thousands more are expected, they will be shipped by express on an early train to-morrow morning.

Special to The New York Times.

OWINGSVILLE, Ky., Dec. 6.—Within the last few days a large number of petitions, signed by several thousand Kentuckians, have been forwarded to Gov. Bell, pleading that executive clemency be extended Mrs. Rogers.

GIRLS IN A STORE FIRE PANIC.

Flames Wrecked the Storeroom of a Fifth Avenue Millinery Shop.

A fire in the room once used as the kitchen of the old St. Marc's Hotel, with entrances on Thirty-eighth and Thirty-ninth Streets and on Fifth Avenue, but now the storeroom of Wilson's millinery store, caused a lot of excitement last evening.

The fifty girls working in the millinery store were getting ready to go home when smoke was seen coming from the storeroom. Some girls with their hats and coats, others without them, all made for the Thirty-eighth Street entrance.

There are several firms in the building, and hundreds of girls are employed there. When the smoke got into the hallways there was one grand rush to reach the street on the Fifth Avenue side. On the way down one girl fainted and another became hysterical, but all got out safely. A sick child in one of the shops was carried out by its mother. They were taken home in a cab.

The fire was confined to the storeroom. The loss was $2,000.

Federal Judge Arrested Here.

William O. Beery, a Federal Court Judge, of Santa Fe, New Mexico, was arrested yesterday by Detective Sergts. Munday and Fogarty at the Hotel Roland, in West Fifty-ninth Street, on a telegraphic order from the Chief of Police of Santa Fe, on a charge of having passed a bad check for $100. Magistrate Walsh in the Tombs Police Court paroled him for a hearing on Friday. The Judge said he got in a poker game in Santa Fe and lost $1,700. He had payment on the check stopped, believing he had lost enough in the game.

AMUNDSON NAVIGATES NORTHWEST PASSAGE

Norwegian Reaches Alaska by Sailing Arctic Channels.

THIRTY MONTHS ON THE TRIP

Explorer Finds True Magnetic Pole on King William Island—Telegraphs to Nansen.

SEATTLE, Wash., Dec. 6.—Capt. Roand Amundson of Norway, who has made his way through a northwest passage from the Atlantic to the Western Arctic Ocean, is at Fort Egbert, Alaska, near Eagle City. Trouble with the land wires from Valdes to Eagle City to-day made it impossible to get his story of the details of his expedition. Amundson sent the following message to Dr. Nansen, the explorer, at Christiania:

"Fort Egbert, Eagle City, Alaska, Dec. 5.—To Nansen, Christiania, Norway:

"Gjoa is wintering at King Point, 69 degrees 45 minutes west. All well.

"Left there Aug. 13, at which time the harbor was free from ice. On Aug. 26 sighted the first vessel, the schooner Charles Hansen of San Francisco, Capt. McKenna, twenty-five kilometers south of Nelson Head, Baring Land. Passed two whalers east of Cape Bathurst, and saw two whalers, the Alexander and Brawhead of San Francisco, Capts. Tilton and Cook, anchored at Cooper Island.

"Passed the schooner Bananza of San Francisco, grounded off King Point.

"Fleet of American whalers overtaken here by rapid progress of Winter. Twelve wintering here, five at Herschel Island, six to the east, and one wrecked on the shore. Out of the twelve only three intended wintering.

"Land surveyed in the Spring of 1905 to 72 degrees and 10 minutes north. Magnetic observation, King William Land, finished June 1.

"Left Herschel Oct. 24 with dog sled and arrived here to-day. Will be at Fort Yukon in six days, where mail will reach me.

"Wire $500 as soon as possible.

"How is the political situation?"

Capt. Amundson left Norway at midnight on June 1, 1903, and his first stop was at God Haven, Greenland, for dogs. The first base station was King William Island, in the Summer of this year. There Amundson set up his self-registering instruments.

He also found the true magnetic pole on King William Island and, it is believed, found the monument erected by Sir John Franklin's expedition.

The original intention of Amundson was to reach Herschel Island, in Mackenzie Bay, north of the Yukon Territory, in the Summer of 1906, and establish his base there, opening communication with Fort McPherson of the Hudson Bay Company, on the Mackenzie River. Later his plans were altered, and he brought the Gjoa from Herschel to King Point to winter. King Point, in Mackenzie Bay, is on the mainland, fifty miles southeast of Herschel Island.

Capt. Amundson left Herschel Island on Oct. 24, and arrived overland at Fort Egbert, near Eagle City, Alaska, on Dec. 5.

The search for the northwest passage began in the latter part of the sixteenth century, but it was not until 1819 that William E. Parry opened to the westward the series of magnificent waterways that led to the Arctic Ocean. Repeated attempts to follow in the track that he had pursued resulted in failure, including that of Sir John Franklin in 1845, whose expedition was lost and whose fate was unknown until 1859.

Franklin's absence caused many search expeditions, which added largely to the knowledge of the American Arctic, but the northwest passage was not accomplished.

READING ALSO STOPS PASSES.

Baer Abolishes Free Transportation—One Result in Politics.

Special to The New York Times.

PHILADELPHIA, Dec. 6.—"The Reading and the Central Railroad of New Jersey," said George F. Baer, President of the two roads, to-day, "will abolish every form of free transportation after the end of the present year. Every other railroad with which I am connected will do the same thing if I have my way."

Mr. Baer is also a Director of the Lehigh Valley Railroad and is closely identified with the management of several of the larger Eastern railroads.

"I intend," Mr. Baer went on, "that the order shall be carried out to the very letter. Ever since I have been connected with railroads I have opposed the giving of passes to members of courts, legislators, Mayors, members of City Councils, and the thousand and one others who felt they were entitled to be hauled around over railroads free of charge. The courtesy has been abused ever since it has been in vogue, and now is the time to stop it. The Pennsylvania Railroad Company was the proper road to start the reform, and I am glad to have the opportunity to follow."

An officer of the Pennsylvania Road said to-day: "You would be surprised to know that it would take a train of ten coaches every day, including Sundays, to handle the passengers holding free transportation on our line East of Pittsburg and Erie. We have known for a long time that passes have been traded, sold, loaned and passed around promiscuously, and there was nothing left for us to do but 'wipe the slate clean.' On some of the suburban trains there are forty and fifty political passes used five and six days a week."

The drastic measures of the Pennsylvania and the Reading Railroad managements will have a telling effect on many political clubs of the city. They have been held together largely by the knowledge that the club leaders would take the members on junkets to conventions and provide the more faithful with passes for themselves and the members of their families.

TO ANNEX SANTO DOMINGO.

Heyburn Offers a Bill to Take in Haiti with It.

WASHINGTON, Dec. 6.—Senator Heyburn to-day introduced a resolution providing for the annexation of San Domingo and Haiti to the United States.

RUSSIAN ARMY STARVING.

Soldiers Pillage Harbin—Linevitch in a Difficult Position.

PARIS, Thursday, Dec. 7.—The St. Petersburg correspondent of the Matin says that letters received from Manchuria describe a terrible situation among the soldiers there.

The men are practically starving and refuse to listen to their officers.

Harbin has been pillaged.

The position of Gen. Linevitch is an extremely difficult one.

DENY VANDERBILT'S REQUEST.

Commissioners Decide That Lake Success Road Shall Remain Public.

William K. Vanderbilt, Jr., is not to obtain exclusive possession of little Success Lake, in Nassau County.

The Lake Success Road, which runs near the Vanderbilt house at Deepdale, belongs to the public.

The commission has decided against closing the road for Mr. Vanderbilt.

WICKES FOUND GUILTY.

Author of "Lewis Jarvis" Letters to be Sentenced Next Wednesday.

A verdict of "guilty as charged" was returned yesterday afternoon after less than an hour's deliberation by the jury trying Lawyer Thomas Parmelee Wickes, author of the "Lewis Jarvis" letters, for attempted blackmail.

According to an agreement between District Attorney Jerome and counsel for the defendant, Justice Rogers remanded Wickes to the Tombs until next Wednesday, when sentence will be imposed, unless his counsel has succeeded in obtaining a stay by that time.

Wickes heard the verdict without moving a muscle. His young wife, who was sitting by his side, looked very pale, but did not stir.

REJECTS $100,000 AND WEDS.

Miss Bagnell of Pittsburg Married Despite Guardian's Protest.

Special to The New York Times.

YOUNGSTOWN, Ohio, Dec. 6.—Miss Louisa Bagnell, 18 years old, of Pittsburg, rejected a fortune here to-day when she was married to William Meider, also of Pitsburg. Both came here this morning and got a marriage license at the Probate Court.

As they were leaving the Court House, they were arrested on instructions from William Bagnall, a Pittsburg steel man, who is the girl's guardian. The two spent the afternoon in the police station, and to-night Mr. Bagnell arrived.

He offered the girl $100,000 cash if she would leave Meider and return home, but she refused it and went with Meider to the home of the Rev. Mr. Frasier, where they were wedded. They left for Pittsburg to-night.

MAURICE GRAU VERY ILL.

News Reaches This City in a Dispatch from Paris to a Friend.

Maurice Grau, the impresario and former manager of the Metropolitan Opera Company, according to a private cable dispatch received in this city yesterday, is seriously ill at his home, in Paris.

When Mr. Grau gave up his management of opera two years ago, to be succeeded by Heinrich Conrieu, he was completely broken in health, and went abroad to recuperate.

He has never returned. After a year of complete rest, for the greater part of the time in the south of France, his health was greatly improved. Then, with his wife and daughter, he took up his residence in Paris.

Nearly two months ago his health began to fail again, and since the last of October he has been steadily losing ground. His trouble is an affection of the heart.

ARMOUR COUP IN WHEAT.

4,000,000 Bushels Bought, Turning Prices Upward on Chicago Board.

Special to The New York Times.

CHICAGO, Dec. 6.—The Armour interests put wheat where they wanted today, buying fully 4,000,000 bushels on the Board of Trade. Early in the session President A. I. Valentine bought the December in person, but sold May through brokers, and caused the report that deliveries on December contracts late in the afternoon would approximate 2,000,000 bushels.

In the scare which followed prices were carried down about 1 cent a bushel, but a brisk export demand created an undertone of strength, which resulted in a rally of 1⅝ cents for December, and 1⅛ cents for May to the highest figure of the day. The market bounded upward, while scared shorts poured in their orders. For ten days the Armour house has been steadily bulling the wheat market. While buying the futures here the firm sold cash wheat to Eastern millers, and it is believed that the house will ship nearly 1,000,000 bushels to Buffalo before Dec. 10.

MR. ROOT WILL GO TO BRAZIL.

Pan-American Congress to Meet at Rio Janeiro on July 21.

WASHINGTON, Dec. 6.—The third international congress of American Republics will meet in Rio Janeiro July 21, 1906. This decision was reached at a meeting of the Executive Council of the bureau to-day, presided over by Secretary Root.

Mr. Root reiterated his purpose of attending the congress as the head of the American delegation, the other members of which have not yet been chosen. It is probable that the American delegation will be conveyed to Rio on a fine naval squadron.

The Mexican Ambassador was particularly active in bringing about to-day's conclusion. The meeting was harmonious and several felicitous speeches were exchanged, the references of the President in his message to the general subject of improved relations between the countries of this hemisphere being especially commended.

WOMAN'S LONE FIGHT ENDED.

Police Use Ammonia Fumes in Storming Railroad Car Fort.

GIRARD, Kan., Dec. 6.—Mrs. Ina Berry, who since last Friday had held the town officers at bay in a railroad car, was removed to-day shortly before noon after she had been partially overcome by the fumes of ammonia.

GEN. SAKHAROFF SLAIN BY A WOMAN

Ex-War Minister Had Been Having Peasants Whipped.

INFANTRY AT MOSCOW REBEL

Troops in the Capital on the Verge of Revolt — Outbreaks in Poland and Finland.

LONDON, Thursday, Dec. 7.—The St. Petersburg correspondent of The Daily Telegraph in a dispatch dated Dec. 5, sent by way of Eydtkuhnen, says:

"Lieut. Gen. Sakharoff, ex-Minister of War, was assassinated to-day.

"The Government had deputed Gen. Sakharoff to visit the Province of Saratoff for the purpose of quelling the agrarian riots there.

"A woman belonging to the so-called 'flying columns' of the revolutionary movement called at the house of the Governor of Saratoff at noon to-day and asked to see Gen. Sakharoff.

"She fired three revolver shots at the General, killing him on the spot."

"The tidings reached St. Petersburg to-night. Count Witte charged Lieut. Gen. Rudiger, Minister of War, with the task of breaking the news to Mme. Sakharoff.

"The event has created a profound impression in St. Petersburg, owing to fears that the revolutionists here will follow the example thus set.

"The spectre of a military dictatorship, which has been looming on the horizon, is slowly gaining consistency and sharpness of outline.

"I am personally convinced that Count Witte's faith in the good sense and political tact of the Russian thinking classes, which recently was as firm as a rock, is gradually weakening, and with it his hopes for the carrying out of the liberties promised in the Emperor's manifesto.

"There are signs of a collapse of the post and telegraph strike. Two-thirds of the telegraph operators are daily offering to resume work, but they are prevented from so doing because the wires have been cut or the stations fail to answer signals.

"Father Gapon has gone to Paris under very mysterious conditions, which I am not at liberty to unfold."

ST. PETERSBURG, Tuesday, Dec. 5.—The non-official papers print harrowing details of Gen. Sakharoff's whipping of peasants whom he was sent to pacify.

The military situation has become so critical as a result of the mutinies at Kieff, Veronezh, Viborg, Poland, and St. Petersburg that the dreams of a dictatorship may be regarded as at an end.

I am informed on excellent authority that a revolt is bound to break out in the garrison of St. Petersburg. The greatest discontent prevails, especially among the gunners and sappers. The officers are resigning in large numbers.

The unrest here is not so much due to the food and clothing, because the garrison here is particularly favored in these respects, but to political reasons, chiefly on account of the manifesto. No official pronouncement has yet been made regarding its application to the army, and hence individual commanders interpret it according to their own private views, most of them declaring that the manifesto does not concern the army, which is of course absurd.

Details of the Kieff mutiny show that the outbreak began with a sapper battalion when it was ordered to take the place of postal and telegraph employes. The mutineers assaulted their commander and marched out of their barracks fully armed and preceded by a band and a red flag. They were joined by infantry and Cossacks and a large number of workmen.

The procession was ambushed and nearly 100 were killed or wounded, mostly civilians.

ST. PETERSBURG, Dec. 5, via Eydtkuhnen, Dec. 6.—Private accounts from Kieff say that the mutinous troops there were shot down in a narrow lane by Cossacks, the mutineers being caught between two fires. The mutiny, however, is said not to be quelled.

It is reported here to-day that symptoms of mutiny have appeared in the Seventh Finnish Regiment at Viborg. It is also reported that outbreaks have occurred in various regiments in Poland.

At the review of the Smonovsky Regiment at Tsarskoe-Selo yesterday the Emperor addressed the troops, commenting on their tried loyalty. At the subsequent regimental banquet given by the officers his Majesty thanked the regiment for its exemplary services and expressed the hope that it would always show itself as firmly united as it was at present.

Advices from Voronezh, dated Dec. 5, say that the soldiers of a disciplinary battalion are parading the town in gangs and intimidating the populace. One contingent, it is added, is touring the surrounding villages and estates and levying blackmail.

LONDON, Thursday, Dec. 7.—A dispatch to a news agency from St. Petersburg, dated Dec. 5, says that twenty-two men were killed and forty were wounded at Kieff after a regular battle.

A dispatch of the same date from [illegible]

Amundsen's ship the *Gjoa*, which made the historic voyage.

Captain Amundsen

Roald Amundsen (at left) and the crew that traveled the Northwest Passage with him.

The marker that Amundsen left to designate the magnetic North Pole. The *Gjoa* was Amundsen's ship.

The New York Times.

THE NEW YORK TIMES, SUNDAY, JANUARY 7, 1906.

Another Attempt to Solve Aerial Navigation Problem

Flying Machine Invented by the Wright Brothers Sails Through the Air Without Aid of Balloon or Gas Bag--Working On It in Secret for Years.

A FLYING machine, or aeroplane, constructed by two young brothers, Orville and Wilbur Wright, has been propelled by its own power and without any aid of balloon or gas bag, for a distance of twenty-four miles in thirty-eight minutes, or at the rate of very nearly thirty-eight miles an hour.

These young inventors are the sons of a minister, now residing at Dayton, Ohio. They have been experimenting in strict secrecy for several years, but their final success is to be made public in connection with the exhibition of the Aero Club, to be held in conjunction with the Automobile Show at the Sixty-ninth Regiment Armory, Jan. 13 to 20. A model and photographs of the machines in flight will be there on view.

Not more than a dozen persons have been in the secret. Among these is A. I. Root, the apiculturist of Medina, Ohio, from whose statements the following details are mainly derived. The chief facts have been indorsed by members of the Aero Club.

+ + +

The Wright brothers first turned their attention to the subject of aeroplanes when, as boys, they made an apparatus on which they could slide down hill in the air a few inches from the ground. They made a number of these gliding machines, and experimented with them during their Summer vacations until they found that they could to a considerable extent control their movements while in the air, and turn them from side to side, as well as slightly up or down. They then began the study of the flight of birds and insects, and read up the history of the numberless attempts that have been made to solve the problem of aerial navigation. The Wrights now possess one of the largest collections of books on this subject in the world.

Thus the boys developed into scientific explorers. They were familiar with what others had done or were trying to do, and they laid their own plans so carefully that there has been no waste of effort, but a progressive accumulation of experiences on which to build up both theory and practice. At the same time they have maintained a discreet and consistent silence.

They experimented with their gliding machines for several Summers. They used to glide down hill against the wind, so that the wind helped them to carry the machine up again. When they were satisfied both that the wings were constructed as nearly perfect as possible, and that they were able to control the machine within broad limits, they bought a gasoline engine, attached a propeller to the apparatus, and obtained some slight success in flying through the air at the end of the Summer of 1903.

+ + +

They resumed their secret experiments in the Summer of 1904, and conducted their investigations in a large level field of eighty-seven acres of pasture near Dayton, Ohio. The location allowed them a straight run of about half a mile, and a circular course of a little less than a full mile. In their first trials with gasoline propulsion they kept near the marshy ground, but this precaution proved unnecessary, because in none of their experiments did any accidents happen that occasioned more than a scratch either to the machine or the brothers.

At first the aeroplane, when driven by the engine, persisted in going up and down with a wave-like motion, but when, after a large number of trials, fifty pounds of cast iron were placed on the "nose" of the machine, or at the head of the forward steering gear, this fault was remedied. Other defects were likewise overcome with patience and ingenuity.

Toward the end of the Summer of 1904 the brothers were able to fly one at a time in their machine for a few seconds, and to attain a height of fifty or sixty feet above the ground. On these short flights, and going against the wind on the straight course, they attained a velocity of from thirty to forty miles an hour, with the ba[illegible] increased to seventy pounds. They did not at that time try going with the wind, but they experimented turning corners, until on Sept. 20, 1904, the aeroplane went round the circular track of about one mile and came back to its starting point without touching the ground once. This achievement was witnessed by Mr. Root and a few others, and proper notes were made of the

OR[illegible]LE WRIGHT IN HIS GLIDING MACHINE.

facts connected with the event. In the next few weeks they succeeded in making as many as four complete circles without alighting, and on one night the machines remained in the air for five minutes and twenty seconds.

The last flight of the season, made on Dec. 1, could have been prolonged but that the operator's hand became cramped on the rudder. In the season of 1904 altogether a hundred flights were made, and certain facts as to the behavior of the aeroplane had been positively ascertained. In rounding corners it was found that it was necessary to ascend to at least twenty or thirty feet, so that the tip of the inner wing (the wings being forty feet long) would always clear the ground. The machine turns corners in the same manner as a bird, by raising the outer wing. In the earlier trials the machine was always run against the wind, so that the operator would be longer in the air, and have more opportunity to make experiments, and also because the inventors did not at first wish to go very far from the shed in which the machine was housed. After they found that they could turn around, they felt it advisable to start with the wind, and in this way, for short distances, they attained a speed of one mile a minute.

+ + +

Last Summer the experiments were continued, and late in the Fall the machine, with one of the brothers on board, went round and round the circular track for a distance of twenty-four miles in thirty-eight consecutive minutes, or at the rate of nearly thirty-eight miles an hour. On the half-mile straight portion of the course the speed was greater. This flight was accomplished at a height of from seventy-five to one hundred feet above the ground, but no attempt was made to drive the engines at the fullest speed nor to mount any higher. The gasoline gave out at the twenty-fourth mile, but seeing that forty pounds of ballast were carried, it would have been easily possible to carry enough fuel for a full hour's flight or even longer. But the Wright brothers have not sought for spectacular success, such as flying from city to city, but are determined to go along step by step and test everything that they do.

The Wright aeroplane consists of two wings or planes, forty feet long, about four feet broad, and arranged above each other on a slight wooden framework, with the planes about five feet apart. The sails are of white canvas, and the framework, strengthened by diagonal wire braces, is painted white. The "planes" or wings are not strictly speaking planes, but each is slightly concave. The front edges of the wings are stiffened by means of light wooden rods, but at the rear the canvas is free to bend. The whole construction is built on the same principle as the wing of an albatross, except that it is rectangular in shape. In the middle of the machine, a rudder, controlling the up and down movement, projects about six feet in front, and a turning rudder is attached in a similar manner at the rear. The front rudder is a small independent plane, which can be raised or lowered by the hand of the operator. The rear rudder consists of two vertical planes made to rotate on a pivot.

+ + +

The operator reclines across the middle of the lower wing and the gasoline engines are beside him. The engines are of aluminium, and of about the power required to drive a two-passenger automobile. Each of the two engines has four cylinders, which drive a shaft stretching out at the rear. On each shaft is a two-bladed propeller working on either side of the back rudder. When preparing for a trip through the air the machinery is started and gets up speed gradually, and at the right moment an ingenious tripping device releases the mooring, and the aeroplane quickly soars aloft from the short metal track on which it reposes when not in use. The aeroplane can be started as quickly as an automobile. When the power is shut off while flying, the apparatus glides quietly to the ground and slides along its runners for perhaps six yards. There is no difficulty in alighting on a fairly smooth field, and it is found better to come down while traveling at a good rate, say, thirty miles an hour, rather than to drop down straight on stopping the engine. Speed can be reduced by raising the forward rudder, so that the air acts as a brake.

New York Assembly's Youthful Speaker---His Task and Opportunity

TO leap at a single bound from the rank and file of the Assembly to the Speakership is a tremendous achievement, viewed from any standpoint, and he who is able to perform such a feat becomes at once an object of great interest. And when that result has been brought about through the intervention of all the power that a National and a State Administration can wield, the talk and comment are not confined to people who live and have their being in the highways and byways of politics. James Wolcott Wadsworth, Jr., elected Wednesday to preside over the 129th regular session of the New York Assembly, is, therefore, perhaps more in the limelight just now than any legislator in either the State or Nation. It is true with reference to the country at large in view of the fact that he was snatched from comparative obscurity by President Roosevelt and Secretary of State Root. And anything these two men do these days comes in for general observation.

It is not inaccurate to state that the election of Wadsworth of Livingston has stunned scores upon scores of legislative war horses. His sudden accession has forced a rearrangement on many chess boards. State committeemen who carry whole counties in their pockets are figuring how they can "get a line" on the new Speaker. They are trying to recall if they or any members of their families ever did a favor for a Wadsworth; if any of their ancestors fought with Gen. Wadsworth in his last battle at The Wilderness; if anybody to whom they are related or with whom they have close political relations has ever done a favor for Congressman Wadsworth, Chairman of Agriculture. They think if, perchance, there should be an affirmative to any or all of these propositions it will help them in what they want or don't want at Albany this session.

The conditions surrounding the election of Wadsworth have no precedent since the inception of the Republican Party. It is true that others have been elected Speaker at the beginning of their second term, and even some at the beginning of their first term, but in none of these instances were the incumbents placed in their high position because a powerful National Administration wished it. There have been six Speakers in the past sixty years who had as brief a legislative experience to their credit when elected as Wadsworth: Horatio Seymour of Oneida, elected in 1845; Henry Jarvis Raymond, Seventh New York, elected in 1851; George G. Hoskins, Wyoming, elected in 1865; George B. Sloan, First Oswego, elected in 1877; George H. Sharpe, First Ulster, elected in 1880; Alfred C. Chapin, Eleventh Kings, elected in 1883. There were six who did not have even one term to their credit when elected: Alonzo B. Cornell, Eleventh New York, elected in 1873; Thomas G. Alvord, Second Onondaga, elected in 1858; Robert H. Pruyn, Third Albany, elected in 1854; Henry Smith, Second Albany, elected in 1872; Jeremiah McGuire, Chemung, elected in 1875; William Hitchman, Twenty-first New York, elected in 1868.

Of these some rose to higher honors. Cornell and Seymour became Governor, Raymond and Hoskins and Alvord became Lieutenant Governor, Chapin became Controller of the State and Mayor of Brooklyn, Sloan became a State Senator and was for years the leader of Oswego.

The career of Cornell alone affords the only elements of similarity to that of Wadsworth. Like Cornell, Wadsworth was born to wealth. But perhaps there the similarity ceases, for Cornell had already been long a power in the party and had been honored with a nomination for Lieutenant Governor. Though elected from New York County, Cornell, like Wadsworth, had his forebears in the region of the State known as "Western New York." As Congressman Wadsworth has high hopes for his son and has the money and power to help put him into places of great power, honor, and trust, no less did Ezra Cornell have the power and wealth to advance his son. As Cornell University is a monument to the Cornells, no less are the beautiful estates at Geneseo a monument to the Wadsworths. Alonzo B. Cornell headed the Republican State Committee for years and became Governor and went into the history of the Stalwart-Half Breed titanic struggle as "The Lizard On the Hill," conferred by Roscoe Conkling. Some of the Republican ancients are wondering if conditions will ever come about whereby young Wadsworth will become the important man that Cornell became.

Certainly, in view of the important legislation that the people of the State are demanding this session, young Wadsworth is already in an important place. Already he is the centre of a vortex. Insurance, railroad, traction, banking, agricultural, good roads, water company, real estate, lumbering, and other interests have been pounding him and his advisers during the week. They want safe men on the committees; they want guarantees that "it's all right"; they want assurances that they won't be held up; they want to know that the new Speaker recognizes their potency. And not less are they fearful of the Roosevelt-Higgins "new deal."

Those who can tell almost at a glance at the committees which are "safe" and which are not, what interests will be served, and whether the people have a show on earth with this committee or that, are anxiously awaiting Wadsworth's appointments. That will be the barometer of the new Speaker's intentions.

Behind Wadsworth stand two leaders—Aldridge of Monroe and O'Brien of Clinton. They played the practical end of the Wadsworth canvass to a large extent. Roosevelt, Root, and Higgins furnished the munitions, and Aldridge and O'Brien saw to it that they were distributed or promised. Superintendent of Public Works Franchot beamed o'er all and on the night of the Republican caucus took personal charge of the caucus nominee's room. Outside the Assembly, Wadsworth's cabinet will be Aldridge, O'Brien, Higgins, and Franchot, with Health Officer Alvah H. Doty and Frank Sullivan Smith as provisional advisers. Some of the wise ones concede that Wadsworth can't go far wrong with these people to advise and direct. Other wise ones don't believe the new Regency can long endure. It is built of some sentiment and considerable patronage. Odell's organization was built wholly of patronage, and, for the time, is shattered.

James Wolcott Wadsworth, Jr., is one of the very few recently in New York State politics who may be said to have been born with a golden spoon in his mouth. There have been Speakers of wealth, Lieutenant Governors of wealth, Governors of wealth, and United States Senators of wealth, but in nearly every instance these officials had started with a shoestring. Flower was such a one. Depew is wealthy, but he made his money by his own efforts. Platt has a few dollars, but he worked for them. On the other hand, Roosevelt and Higgins, like Wadsworth, were born to moderate wealth. Of the three heads of the State Government—Higgins, Bruce, and Wadsworth—Lieut. Gov. Bruce alone has risen to his office through sheer ability and political perspicacity. He had no money to purchase advancement for himself, and nobody stood behind him to pave the way with dollars. These conditions have led many to make the observation that Roosevelt and Root and Higgins apparently believe in handing out honors in New York State as they are handed in the countries of the Guelphs, the Hapsburgs, the Hohenzollerns, the Bernadottes. Some of the mean men at Albany say the Roosevelt-Root-Higgins programme is to recognize only the crown prince in the landed families of the State.

The successor of the late Speaker Samuel Frederick Nixon of Chautauqua is probably as young at the time of taking office as Speaker as any of the long line of predecessors. He told nothing more than the truth when he said he could not hope to equal Nixon as a presiding officer. That candid statement helped him.

"Young Wadsworth," as he will be called for some weeks to come, despite his election to the Speakership, was born on Aug. 12, 1877. He belongs to the family that is best known in the Genesee Valley, which stretches from the Pennsylvania line on the south to Lake Ontario on the north. One can walk for miles in this valley without putting foot on other than Wadsworth land. Part of it afforded a battle-ground for Gen. Sullivan and his Indian foes in the first Washington Administration.

The home of the new Speaker is at Groveland, about three miles from Geneseo, where for years the Wadsworths have held fox hunts every Autumn. President Roosevelt has ridden to the hounds here. The Groveland farm is a model. Plenty of money for equipment and plenty of money for keeping the buildings in first-class condition make it so. Cattle and sheep are raised here. Farming as Speaker Wadsworth is able to pursue it becomes almost a joy forever.

It can be said that social Albany is pleased beyond expression by the election of Speaker Wadsworth. Social Albany is powerful in its way. The Higgins administration is popular with social Albany, because the Governor has the means to entertain. For the same reason, the Morton Administration was popular. The Black Administration achieved only nominal social success. Black was not rich. Gov. Odell was so busy with politics that the social side received just ordinary consideration. The Roosevelt Administration was just what social Albany wanted. Roosevelt pleased the old Dutch patroons—the Ten Broecks, the Ten Eycks, the Van Santvoords, the Van Rensselaers, and the Van Wormers.

Social Albany is also hugging itself in view of the social standing of Mrs. Wadsworth's family—the Hays. With the son of Congressman Wadsworth and the daughter of the late Secretary Hay to join with the Higgins household at the Executive Mansion in entertaining this Winter, social Albany is quite beside itself. It is expected the new Speaker will take a residence for the session where the social side and the political end of his administration may have room for play or development.

Alexander E. Orr, the New York Life's New President

WHEN Alexander Ector Orr was elected to the Presidency of the New York Life Insurance Company last week he received fitting laurels for a half century of prominence and activity in the financial centre of the hemisphere. It is doubtful, however, if Mr. Orr will be best known in history as the head of this great corporation or as the Chairman of the Board of Rapid Transit Commissioners, which built the subway. Either position alone would entitle him to eminence; the two show the position the man has made for himself in the regard and confidence of his fellows.

Kindly, courteous, fair, but at all times watchful and careful for the great interests in his charge, few who know Mr. Orr and his activities would take him for a man nearing the three-quarter century mark in the march of time. He carries himself with altogether too much firmness of step and alertness of manner to impress one as a man seventy-five years of age, and yet he will reach that mark on March 2 of this year, less than two months away. Fifty-five years of that life have been spent in this city, in its activities and in its upbuilding.

During that time Mr. Orr saw the great growth of the city as a grain centre, and to him more than to any other single man the city owed its prominence as a grain port. He, too, saw the decadence of New York's shipping, and saw the falling away of the great industry he did so much to upbuild before railroad discriminations took grain shipments to Boston, to Baltimore, to Newport News, and to New Orleans.

He has seen the passing of the Broadway stages to the horse cars, of the horse cars to the cable roads; has watched the development of the steam elevated roads, the trolleys, the electric elevated service, and finally the Subway, which he did so much to make an established fact. He was able to study the transit problem from its real beginning, to study the growth of New York through its greatest years, and now, at the time when most men are willing to lay aside business pursuits and rest, he is called to the head of one of the leading financial institutions of the world, and does not drop a single one of his other many activities to take on the new burden, which would be far too much for many a younger man.

Mr. Orr is a native of Ireland, having been born in Strabane, County Tyrone, in 1831. His parentage was Scottish, his ancestors having left their own country and settled in Ireland the century before. Young Orr was destined for a seafaring life by his parents, and, therefore, they entered him in the service of the East India Company's college at Addiscombe, England, but he had barely passed his entrance examination when he met with a serious accident that checked his career and compelled him to study under a tutor.

Afterward he was sent on a sea voyage and made a trip to this country, landing at Wilmington, N. C. He stayed several months here, and then returned to Ireland, but with the determination to make America his home of the future. The next year after his return, in 1851, he came to this country and settled permanently in New York, entering the shipping trade. Shortly after he made a connection with the establishment of David Dows & Co., and about that time married Miss Juliet B. Dows, daughter of Ami Dows, the original head of the house. He was admitted to partnership in the firm in 1861, and for years has been its head, as he is to-day, as well as being the executor of the estate of David Dows, which is exceedingly wealthy.

For a quarter of a century, under the management of Dows and Orr, this house was one of the leading commission houses of the country, the business being in flour, grain, and provisions, chiefly home products. To the firm largely was due the maintenance of a leading place as a grain market for the port of New York, and the largest grain elevator in the world, at the time, was erected for the Dows stores, at Pacific Street, Brooklyn, in the early eighties. The buildings and machinery cost $1,000,000, and the capacity was [illegible]0,000 bushels of wheat. Since the death of David Dows, in 1885, the business of the firm has been discontinued and is in process of liquidation, but its many investments have kept the firm intact, and there is no need nor prospect of winding up its affairs further than they now are wound up.

ALEXANDER ECTOR ORR

Mr. Orr joined the Produce Exchange in 1859, and has been President more times than he can remember. He was the Chairman of the committee which constructed the present fine home of the Exchange, and he also was the author of the gratuity system of the organization. He has taken a leading part in the work of the Chamber of Commerce, and has served as its President. As Chairman of the Rapid Transit Commission, since its creation in 1897, he has guided and watched the progress of the work from the beginning with an eye to the interests of the public, and has been found ready at all times to take forceful action when needed either to curb the interests in control of the construction and operation of the subway lines, or to force the advancement of new routes and projects. Progressive when progress is needed, he is conservative when care and conservatism are required.

In politics Mr. Orr always has been active and independent. He was associated with John Bigelow, Daniel Magone, and John D. Van Buren in the Canal Commission appointed by Governor Tilden in 1875, and which worked eight months in exposing the Canal Ring frauds, which led to placing the State canals under the State Superintendent of Public Works. He was an intimate friend of Tilden's, and was a Tilden Presidential Elector in 1876. In 1881 he supported Seth Low for Mayor of Brooklyn, Mr. Orr at that time living, as he has for years, on Brooklyn Heights. In all of Mayor Low's campaigns Mr. Orr supported him, but last year was with Mayor McClellan for re-election. He was a Civil Service Commissioner under Mayor Chapin, and during his entire career has been identified with charitable, benevolent, and financial institutions to such a number that space does not permit of their enumeration.

Mr. Orr has been twice married. His first wife died in 1872. His second marriage was in 187[illegible] to Miss Margaret S. Luquer.

From the zest with which President Orr has entered upon his new duties with the New York Life, it is apparent to all his friends that he finds his greatest enjoyment in business activity. He has no thought of retirement, and frowns at the mere suggestion that his new duties may occupy him so that he may have to lay down the Chairmanship of the Rapid Transit Board.

Largest Buyer of Diamonds

SOME few years ago there was a general impression among dealers in precious stones that the value of the diamond, in view of the constant and increasing supply and the indestructibility of the article, must necessarily decrease. So far from this being the case, the value of diamonds within the last ten years has increased enormously, and this accretion in value bids fair to continue.

The reason for this abnormal state of trade is declared by experts to be due to the demands of a comparatively new and apparently an inexhaustible market in the United States.

According to the returns of the Appraiser of New York, over £6,640,000 worth of diamonds and other precious stones entered the port in 1904—an increase of £2,200,000 over the imports of the preceding year. Last year £2,056,000 of uncut stones were entered, as against barely £100,000 worth in 1904.

"America is undoubtedly far and away our best market," said the London representative of a firm which deals with a large part of the diamond output. "The great majority of the best stones mined in South Africa are sent to the States, not less, in fact, than five-eighths of the total value. Several Amsterdam firms have recently established diamond cutting works in New York."—London Mail.

Sure He Would Get It

IT is a fact, made well known by the press, that President Roosevelt uses a phrase of greeting of which he is very fond. He is often "de-lighted" to see one and says so with great heartiness.

Last Winter a man from the West, who had met the President many years before, came to Washington for the purpose of laying a certain request before the Chief Executive. As he sat in an ante room, awaiting his turn to see the President, the latter had occasion to enter the room for a word with his Secretary. Mr. Loeb made the usual presentation; whereupon the President grasped the visitor's hand, said he was "de-lighted," and returned to his own office. In a short time the President re-appeared and, glancing at the Westerner again, evidently recognized him as one he had seen before, for he again shook hands, repeating the favorite phrase of greeting.

This happened a third time, for the President was extremely busy that day, and much pre-occupied.

"I regret that you have to wait so long," said the Secretary, after a while.

"Oh, I don't mind in the least," was the cheerful response of the man from the West, "I'm going to wait till I can see the President. When a man is delighted to see me three times, I think he will give me what I want."

No man has more money than brains who has brains enough to hang on to it.

The greatest follies are often committed by the smallest fools.

When two young people embark on the sea of matrimony one of them is pretty sure to rock the boat.

The Wright Brothers experimenting with gliders at Kitty Hawk in 1902.

Wilbur Wright flying at Pau, France.

"All the News That's Fit to Print."

The New York Times.

THE WEATHER.
Fair, slightly warmer Thursday; Friday, fair, warmer; moderate winds, becoming south.
For full weather report see Page 9.

VOL. LVI...NO. 17,815. *** NEW YORK, SATURDAY, NOVEMBER 3, 1906.—EIGHTEEN PAGES and Section Devoted to Review of Books. ONE CENT In Greater New York, Jersey City, and Newark. | Elsewhere, TWO CENTS.

HUGHES TALKS TO 30,000 IN BROOKLYN AND QUEENS

Up to You, He Says, to Deal a Death Blow to Hearstism.

ELEVEN CROWDED MEETINGS

The Candidate, in Fine Fettle, Ridicules His Opponent with Snappy Epigrams—A Strenuous Night.

Charles E. Hughes talked to more than 30,000 people in Queens and Brooklyn last night, covering in all eleven meetings from the time he arrived in Weehawken from his trip through the State.

Mr. Hughes had not a moment's rest after his arrival. He had just time to bolt a dinner after he arrived in New York, and at 7:30 he and State Chairman Woodruff entered their automobile, in waiting at Republican headquarters, and were whirled away on one of the most remarkable tours of the campaign.

In both boroughs Mr. Hughes was received with tremendous acclaim. Notwithstanding his arduous work through the State, those who saw him last night marveled that he had kept his voice and the buoyant spirits that marked his entrance into the campaign. Last night he had both.

His impromptu style of speaking caught the audience in each place at once.

Some Striking Epigrams.

Mr. Hughes ran to epigrams last night and kept up this crisp style of oratory throughout his trip. While expressing his confidence in the result, based as he said, on what he had seen and heard through the State, he warned his hearers against overconfidence and said that he wanted his opponent and his methods to get a blow from which he would not recover. Here are some of the things he said:

"We don't want sensations. We want things done. There are things that you can't put into a headline."

"We've got too good a country to spoil, and the Government of this Empire State shall not be spoiled."

"We should be more anxious to be just than to be famous—more anxious to be fair than to get office. Let us stand by our principles even if we fall in supporting them."

"We want corporation evils, whether they originate with the railroads or the newspapers, corrected."

"What we want is more business, not less business. We want the man with money in bank to add to it, and the man who is out of debt to keep out of it."

"I have no political debts to pay, no axes to grind, and no grudges to satisfy."

These and dozens of other terse things were greeted with great applause. In Brooklyn Mr. Hughes gave some attention to the Brooklyn Traction Company abuses, and said that if he was elected he would do what was possible for a Governor to do to see that they were corrected.

The first stop was at the Civic Club in Long Island City, where Mr. Hughes held an informal reception. In introducing him the President of the club said that the workers in the First District wanted to shake his hand.

"I am glad to meet the workers," he said. "I have been in all the counties of the State but seven, and the reliable information I have gathered there tells me that things up the State are all right. But we don't want to take chances. We want to deal a death blow to the tactics of our opponents, and we'll do it if you see that the votes are brought out. We have got the election all right, I am sure of that, now it's up to you men of Queens to do your share."

"And you bet we'll do it," came back the answer.

Mr. Hughes, Mr. Woodruff, and the rest of the party, escorted by Police Capt. Hayes and a squad and led by a brass band, then marched over to Frenz's Casino, a block away, where 2,000 persons were packed into the hall, although it was not yet 8 o'clock, and where Mr. Hughes got an ovation. His first utterance, "Queens is all right," brought down the house. Mr. Hughes said:

Queens Is All Right.

"Fellow-Citizens: I tell you Queens is all right. [Applause.]

"I am very glad to come to Queens, and I am sorry that I have such a short time. But we have got a great many meetings to-night, and a great deal to do before next Tuesday, and I want to tell you a few things in a very plain and direct manner.

"We have got great prosperity in this country, and we want to keep it. [Applause.]

"We have got business enterprises constantly expanding, and we want them to increase. We have got opportunities for men to get employment, and we want more of them and not less. [Applause.]

"It is a great deal better that work should seek the workingman rather than that the workingman should look for work. [Applause.]

"Now, it is the easiest thing in the world to destroy that prosperity. Talk about the diffusion of prosperity—I believe in it, but you have got to have the prosperity first before you can diffuse it.

"Talk about the distribution of wealth—I believe in it, and in doing everything that we can, to be fair and just, but before you can have a distribution of wealth you have got to have wealth to distribute.

Good Order the Prime Requisite.

"Now, everything depends on good order. Everything depends upon doing things in a straightforward and decent way. If anybody comes around trying to stir up one class against another and making people believe that business in this country is organized robbery he aims a blow at all business, and if that sort of thing lasts it will throw labor out of employment, and it will paralyze our business prosperity.

"Now, I do not say that as standing in the way of a single reform. On the contrary, I am for everything that can be done to get rid of abuses in our corporate life, and get rid of abuses in connection with politics.

"We want clean business and we want clean politics. We want men to run for office who are disinterested. We want men to understand that it is a great deal more important to have the administration of this Government conducted in a proper way than it is to sell some newspapers. [Great applause.]

"We want people to understand that it is more important in government that a

Continued on Page 2.

BROOKLYN TRAINS CRASH.

Seven Persons Hurt, Two Severely, in Collision on Fulton Street Line.

In a rear-end collision between two elevated trains on the Fulton Street line at 6 o'clock last night a dozen or more persons were injured, two of them severely, while the crowds beneath the Rockaway Avenue station transferring to the several surface lines converging there were showered with broken glass.

At the time of the accident a five-car train, bound for the Brooklyn Bridge, in charge of Conductor John Enhoff, was standing at the station, while passengers were leaving and entering it. Before the downtown track of the line passes by the Rockaway Avenue station there is a sharp hill, which the trains are accustomed to climb at a high velocity. Up this another five-car train, controlled by Motorman Edward Colbert, rushed.

Apparently Colbert did not see the train at the station in time to check his own train, for the moving string of cars bumped into the stationary train with force sufficient to break every window in both. The platform of the rear train crushed into the one on the car in front, crumpling it into splintered sections and carrying away the gates of the two cars. The motorman's box on the rear train was torn off, while one of the forward cars of the stationary train was derailed.

Some one sent in a call for an ambulance, which arrived from St. Mary's Hospital. The ambulance surgeon found in the struck car Henry Bulew, of Avenue S and Seventy-second Street, Flatbush, a man of 78, who had been sitting near the rear. He had been thrown across the car, receiving in the fall a fractured ankle and several cuts on the head.

In the forward car of the rear train a young man, Albert Monga, living near the junction of Rockaway Avenue and Avenue G, Canarsie, was lying on the floor unconscious. He had been thrown against a seat and partially through a window. His arms and back were bruised and cut. Both men were later taken to their homes, while others who had received small cuts and bruises saw the claim agents and left.

It was several hours before the tracks were ready for the use of trains, as the derailed car prevented both up and down traffic.

UTES MAY GIVE IN.

Holding Conference with Army Officers, Who Offer Liberal Terms.

SHERIDAN, Wyoming, Nov. 2.—A messenger who arrived at Arvada late this afternoon reported that Col. Rodgers and Major Grierson were in conference with the Ute Indians, who, nearly 400 strong and with 1,100 ponies, are still camped on Little Powder River, in Montana, thirty-five miles northeast of Moorehead. The indications were that the Indians would give in.

It is said that the military offered to take the Utes home, issue rations during the Winter, and promised to take up the question of allowing them another abiding place by next Spring.

Further details of the raiding of a Government supply train bound for the camps of the Tenth and Sixth Cavalry from Arvada, characterizes it as a clever piece of work, evidently planned by some of the older heads of the Ute tribe. According to Driver James Forgen, no Indians were in sight until about a hundred mounted redskins dashed out of a defile in the hills and surrounded him. They made little noise outside of a few sharp yells in the nature of commands, and while several Indians kept Forgen under their rifles, the balance rifled his wagon train of 3,000 pounds of flour, and the band then disappeared into the hills.

As the result of the raiding of the supply train the troopers are in need, and the operations looking to a chase of the Utes are practically at a standstill until supplies can be had. More supply trains will be sent out from Arvada at once. Troops from Fort Keogh with supplies are now at Ashland, en route to the camp of the Tenth near Moorehead.

A correspondent in the field denies positively reports that there has been a clash between the Cheyennes and the soldiers.

EXTENT OF THE CANAL JOB.

Estimates of Excavation to be Done and Structural Material Required.

WASHINGTON, Nov. 2.—Some idea of the vastness of the Panama Canal project is conveyed in a circular issued by the commission to-day for the information of prospective bidders for constructing the canal. The summary shows that the estimated excavation and structural material in these sections are approximately as follows:

Colon section, 9,445,000 cubic yards; Mindi, 11,000,000 yards; Gatun locks, excavation, 3,660,000 yards; concrete, 1,302,080 yards; steel gates, 29,230,000 pounds; Gatun dam, earth filled, 21,200,000 yards; Gatun regulating works, excavation, 1,580,000 yards; concrete, 189,000 yards; sluices, 5,000,000 pounds; lake section, excavation, 24,000,000 yards; Culebra, excavation, 39,000,000 yards; Pedro Miguel, excavation, 6,835,000 yards; Pedro Miguel lock, excavation, 1,170,000 yards; embankment, 1,100,000 yards; back fill, 390,000 yards; concrete, 513,612 yards; cast iron, 732,000 pounds; steel gates, 19,500,000 pounds; Lake Sosa section, excavation, 1,680,000 yards; Sosa locks, excavation, 1,430,000 yards; back fill, 950,000 yards; concrete, 902,800 yards; cut stone, 600,000 yards; brick, 14,000 yards; cast iron, 1,281,000 pounds; steel gates, 37,180,000 pounds; La Boca Dam, 6,300,000 yards; Corozal-Sosa Dam, 5,397,000 yards; Panama Bay, excavation, 8,528,000 yards.

INDEX TO DEPARTMENTS.

RARE BURNS ORIGINALS BOUGHT BY J. P. MORGAN

Financier May Have Got the Best of the Bard's Poems.

APPRAISED HERE AT $50,000

English and Scotch Have Been Protesting at the Purchases of the Rare Manuscripts.

It became known yesterday that in the last week J. Pierpont Morgan has received from Europe two scrapbooks, each filled with manuscript. At the Appraiser's Stores Mr. Morgan's agent put their value at $25,000 each, and on the two Mr Morgan paid $10,000 duty.

Efforts apparently have been made to keep the arrival of the scrapbooks a secret, perhaps for the reason that the knowledge of their arrival in this country would arouse in the United Kingdom, and especially in Scotland, a vigorous protest. Hints of such a protest have been seen in the British newspapers at intervals for years.

For the manuscripts, pasted into the two scrapbooks, are the originals of the best poems of Robert Burns, the Ayrshire bard, and of many of that fervid rhymester's impassioned letters to his ladies and his creditors.

The British Museum, the Kensington Museum, and the various institutions in Edinburgh and Glasgow where historical and literary relics are stored, have never boasted a very extensive collection of original manuscripts by the author of "Tam o' Shanter," "Auld Lang Syne," and such world-famous poems.

Manuscripts Were Scattered.

It is known that the reason for this is that Burns had a habit of writing verses on the moment, handing them to the person who inspired the poems, or, where they related to impersonal subjects, to friends who sympathized or to creditors whom the poet sought to humor. Thus were many of the manuscripts of Burns scattered, figuratively speaking, to the winds.

In the last ten years it has been rumored in Scotland from time to time that the agents of a rich American were scouring the kingdom in efforts to collect all the manuscripts of Burns that could possibly be purchased. Many of these were found in humble places; many, on the other hand, in the private archives of noble families to whom they had been given by the poet in his flowery days in Edinburgh.

The name of the rich American who employed these agents was never made public in Great Britain, but that some knew the source of search is certain from the fact that Queen Victoria, King Edward, and others interested in national relics interested themselves to the extent of urging that the manuscripts be allowed to remain in the country where they were written.

The British press at intervals also protested against the removal to America of literary remains which, it was said at the time, included not only many Burns originals, but manuscripts from the pen of Sir Walter Scott, Byron, and other famous writers.

Whether the manuscripts contained in Mr. Morgan's scrapbooks are those purchased by the rich American in the United Kingdom in the last ten years cannot definitely be ascertained at this time. But the fact that they are Burns manuscripts, and that Mr. Morgan has placed upon them such a high assessment, seems to indicate that they are of a value that cannot easily be figured in a mercantile way.

Mr. Morgan's Agents Busy.

According to information received in support of the belief that originals of the best of "Bobby" Burns have arrived in this country, Mr. Morgan's agents have been busy for the last fifteen years collecting Burns manuscripts in Great Britain, and it is said that those agents have spent about $200,000 in their search.

The manuscripts obtained by Mr. Morgan's agents have been purchased, many of them, at figures which were far beyond what even the National and literary pride of Great Britain could offer in order to keep them in the country. From time to time, as the purchase of an original was made public, the storm of patriotic protest, especially in Scotland, rose high in the British newspapers. It was urged repeatedly that some wealthy collector or lore-loving philanthropist should save them, but in the end the American went over the highest British offers.

The scrapbooks full of manuscript arrived here this week. They were turned over to Appraiser Fowler by the Customs officials. Mr. Morgan was notified, and his agent, on going to the Appraisers' Stores, said that the scrapbooks were worth $25,000 each. The duty of 20 per cent., amounting to $10,000, was promptly paid, and the books removed to Mr. Morgan's residence.

The scrapbooks are large volumes of the usual letter-file size and about five inches thick. They contain, a person who had seen them said last night, poems and letters signed by Robert Burns. The titles of these poems were not noticed, or, if noticed, they did not make an impression for the reason that the person who saw them was not particularly an admirer of the poet.

Collectors, however, have an idea that perhaps these scrapbooks contain originals of "The Jolly Beggars," "The Cottar's Saturday Night," "Bonnie Mary o' Argyll," and the wonderful letters to the idealized Clarinda and to Miss Chalmers.

Scotch May Protest.

Anything pertaining to the wild, romantic rhymer of the tavern and the furrow has a value to the Scots that nothing material can measure. Should it happen, as seems likely, that the scrapbooks imported by Mr. Morgan contain originals of Burns's best works, Scotch indignation is expected to materialize.

The arrival of these manuscripts in this country is taken incidentally as a sign that Mr. Morgan has given up his fight against the Dingley tariff on art works. The Dingley tariff decrees that all works of art intended for public exhibition in this country shall enter free, but that works of art intended for private collections shall pay 20 per cent. of their assessed value.

It is generally believed that Mr. Morgan has numerous valuable collections of literary and artistic value in Europe, and that, while his fight was on against the Dingley tariff, he preferred to let them stay in Europe with his agents there. The Burns collection, which has been accumulated in fifteen years and on which Mr. Morgan has just paid $10,000 duty, is believed to be the first of a series of art "sensations" which he intends to bring to the United States.

NEW ILLINOIS CENTRAL TALE.

Chicago Hears of a Meeting Called to Replace Fish with Harahan.

Special to The New York Times.

CHICAGO, Ill., Nov. 2.—According to a report widely circulated here yesterday a special meeting of the Directors of the Illinois Central Railway will be held in New York next week. The report went on to say that at this meeting J. T. Harahan, now Vice President in charge of operation, will be elected President by the Harriman interests to succeed Stuyvesant Fish.

Mr. Harahan himself and John C. Welling, another Vice President of the road, are the only Directors in Chicago. Mr. Welling is ill and could not be seen. Mr. Harahan said that if he had been chosen for election as President he had not been informed of it, and that he had received no notice of a special meeting.

"I have been expecting a meeting to be called at almost any time," he added, "but if one has been decided upon I do not know it. The next regular Directors' meeting will take place on Nov. 21."

Attorney Ralph Shaw, who with William Nelson Cromwell of New York represented the Harriman interests at the Illinois Central's annual meeting, said he had not heard of a call for a special meeting, but would not be surprised if one were issued. He declined to say more.

E. H. Harriman said last night through his secretary at his home in Tuxedo that he didn't know whether a special meeting of the Directors with any such programme before it had been called or not. The secretary explained that Mr. Harriman had not been to business for several days.

NEGRO SOLDIERS RIOT AGAIN.

Man Killed and Two Men Wounded Near El Paso.

Special to The New York Times.

EL PASO, Texas, Nov. 2.—Negro soldiers at Fort Bliss, five miles from here, went on a rampage to-night and started a general fight in a saloon outside the reservation. One man was killed and two were seriously wounded. Other troops from the fort have been dispatched to arrest the rioters and further trouble is feared before morning.

The negroes belong to the Twenty-fifth Infantry, members of which, while stationed at Fort Brown, made a raid on Brownsville, Texas, shot into homes and business houses, and killed one white man and wounded another. The affair aroused so much indignation that the War Department at Washington ordered the negro troops transferred from Fort Brown to Fort Bliss.

The man killed in to-night's affray was Private Matthews. Private Lewis and Alexander Johnson, a saloonkeeper, were wounded. It is said Johnson cannot live.

Advices concerning the origin of the trouble are conflicting, but a card game is said to have prompted the affair.

DUNDEE HONORS REID.

He Speaks of the Billions of Reasons for Anglo-American Peace.

DUNDEE, Nov. 2.—The freedom of the City of Dundee was to-day conferred on Whitelaw Reid, the American Ambassador.

In the course of his speech thanking the municipality, the Ambassador, referring to the relations between the United States and Great Britain, said the statesmen of either country had no higher task than to preserve them. When it was remembered that nearly one-third of the entire trade of New York and nearly half the whole trade of the United States were with the British Empire all would recognize that there were billions of reasons for maintaining and perpetuating the present cordial relations.

Mr. Reid delivered an address to-night on "How the United States Faced Its Educational Problems." After reviewing what this problem meant to a new and vast country developing at the outset with painful slowness and later with startling rapidity under a self-governing people, he called attention to the fact that now the total enrollment in schools, colleges, and universities in the United States was 18,187,000, of which number 16,127,000 persons were in public institutions supported by taxation. Thus nearly one-fourth of the total population was at school in a nation of 80,000,000. From primary school to university, Mr. Reid said, American education aimed first of all to give every human being within the country his chance, and make America more than ever the home of opportunity.

POLICEMAN BADLY BEATEN.

Thrashed by Three Men in Stopping a Saloon Row—May Die.

Three men, who had been drinking, wrecked the saloon of James J. Collins at 140th Street and Seventh Avenue last night and nearly killed Policeman John Hanley of the West 125th Street Police Station, who went to the assistance of the bartender.

Liquor had been refused to the men. When Hanley entered to quell the disturbance they made one of them tripped him up, another jumped on him, and the third grabbed his nightstick and began to beat him on the head.

A woman who was passing aroused the neighborhood, and the police reserves from the West 125th Street Station rescued Hanley. He was picked up bleeding and unconscious. His face was a mass of bruises, his skull was fractured and he is in the J. Hood Wright Hospital in a critical condition.

Only one of the men was captured. He described himself as Gustave Thompson of 220 East 113th Street, a furniture mover. He was locked up.

HORSE IN EIGHT-FOOT HOLE.

Ran Away with Four Occupants of Surrey and Falls in Areaway.

A horse belonging to Herman Senner of 74 West 114th Street ran away from 153d Street and St. Nicholas Avenue to 121st Street and Manhattan Avenue last night, and there fell into an areaway eight feet deep. The shafts parted from the surrey, in which were seated Senner, Abraham Lopan, and his daughter Bella, and another friend, just before the horse went over the curb and into the inclosure. The occupants of the vehicle were badly shaken up and slightly cut.

A tackle was rigged up and the horse was treated by a veterinary. Two windows were broken in the house at the southwest corner of Manhattan Avenue and 121st Street, where the horse ended its long and exciting run.

CURB ODDS NOW 4 TO 1 IN FAVOR OF HUGHES

Hearst Men Alarmed by Roosevelt and Croker Utterances.

SOME SMALL BETS AT 5 TO 1

Odds in Wall Street Climbed Steadily Throughout the Day, Starting at $3\frac{1}{2}$ to 1.

If the betting market is a fair political barometer, the President's denunciation of Hearst through the speech of the Secretary of State, coupled with ex-Boss Croker's cabled condemnation of Tammany's policy and his attack on the Democratic candidate, have knocked the last pegs from under the Hearst boom. The holders of Hearst money in the financial district were fairly panic-stricken at the opening of business yesterday, and the odds climbed steadily from $2\frac{1}{2}$ to 1 to 5 to 1 in the late afternoon.

Even with the higher odds the brokers with Hughes money to place found it hard to find takers for large sums. The betting was the heaviest since the campaign began, but the sum total, estimated at over $100,000, was made up chiefly of bets in which the Hearst end was less than four figures.

At $3\frac{1}{2}$ to 1 a number of bets were placed. Two of $3,500 each were made by M. Joseph at these odds, with W. W. Bagley. An offer of $17,500 on Hughes, made by Batcheller, Adee & Rawlins, cleaned out about all the Hearst money in sight, and the odds went up another ½ point, to 4 to 1, at which Wasserman Brothers' representative put $1,600 against $400 put up by Rothschild & Cammerer.

Vail Brothers reported a bet of $20,000 on Hughes at 4 to 1, and W. W. Bagley put out $4,000 at the same odds with Leo Levy. About this time Wolf Brothers announced that they had $40,000 to bet against $10,000 on Hughes. They got no takers. Those who had Hughes money to bet in amounts of less than $1,000 had great difficulty in unearthing Hearst commissioners willing to take 4 to 1. A number of small bets were reported at 5 to 1.

W. S. Dugan, who announced that he had $10,000 to put on Hearst against $50,000, was reported to have put half of this sum late in the afternoon with A. J. Smith at 4 to 1.

Betting on Hughes's plurality took the form of even money that the Republican candidate would win by 100,000. A representative of Henry Clews & Co. announced that his firm had $5,000 to bet on this proposition, but no taker was found. Allen, McGraw & Co., however, succeeded in putting $8,500 at even money on this bet, of which $3,000 was covered by Phildrick & Hall. W. A. Scott took $1,000 of the same money.

Stakeholders and bettors at the Broadway hotels were inclined to laugh last night at the stories that came up from Wall Street to the effect that 4 and 5 to 1 on Hughes were the current odds for the election.

Most of the 3 to 1 bets recorded yesterday were at the Metropole, where "Eddie" Hines took charge of about $3,000 of Hughes money put against $1,000 furnished by Hearst supporters. Richard Bernard took the long end of the bet, and part of the $1,000 belonged to Franz Ebert.

At the Jamaica race track yesterday Maxey Blumenthal, one of the largest operators among the bookmakers on the New York race tracks, announced before the racing began that he stood ready to accept all wagers that might be offered on the election of Hearst. Blumenthal made the offer of 5 to 2 on Hughes as his first challenge to the backers of Hearst, and, receiving no offers, raised the odds to 3 to 1, at which odds, he said through his commissioners, he had $250,000 to wager.

Blumenthal's offer drew no response from the backers of Hearst, and he said after the races were over that he had not succeeded in placing any of the great sum he offered. The only effect was to make a quick change in the odds and cause those of the bookmakers and bettors who had backed Hearst earlier to attempt to hedge their bets. Joe Vendig, who in past years was agent for Richard Croker in the placing of heavy election bets, was said to have been betting on Hearst at 3 to 1, but in the last few days Vendig has refused many offers at the current odds.

JOHNSON MAY BE RE-ELECTED

Democratic Governor Still in Favor in Republican Minnesota.

Special to The New York Times.

ST. PAUL, Minn., Nov. 2.—The campaign in Minnesota has been strenuous. Gov. John A. Johnson, a Democrat, who was elected two years ago because of a spontaneous sentiment in opposition to stories sprung by his opponents that his mother was a washerwoman and his father an inmate of the poor farm, is holding good this year. Roosevelt polled 156,000 plurality in this State, but the indications are that Johnson will be re-elected. A ten-thousand-dollar wager on Johnson, at 2 to 1, had no taker.

Aside from the Gubernatorial contest, interest centres in the Second Congressional District, where James T. McCleary, Republican, is struggling for re-election. McCleary is standing on the stand-pat tariff platform. The opinion prevails that he will be defeated by Republican voters.

SHOT BROTHER, THEN FLED.

Child, After Accidental Killing, Ran Away and Has Not Returned.

BRIDGEPORT, Conn., Nov. 2.—Michael Santa, the eleven-year-old boy who accidentally shot and killed his five-year-old brother, John, yesterday in their home in a secluded part of the town of Fairfield, has not been found, and it is the general opinion that the lad is too frightened to return.

In the absence of their father and mother, the boys took down a rifle and it exploded, the ball going completely through John's head. When he died Michael rode away on a bicycle, and five other children of the Santas, all under 12 years of age, walked four miles through the country in a vain attempt to find their parents, who returned later in the day to find their boy dead and the home deserted.

TO RAISE WAGES 10 PER CENT.

Pennsylvania Road Will Pay Out $1,000,000 More Each Month.

Special to The New York Times.

PHILADELPHIA, Nov. 2.—The wages of all employes of the Pennsylvania system, numbering nearly 200,000 on all lines East and West of Pittsburg, are to be increased on Jan. 1. This, as far as the Pennsylvania system is concerned, will forestall the concerted action of organized labor to demand a raise in wages.

The management is considering a proposition to grant an increase of 10 per cent. to all employes whose salary per month is less than $500. The monthly pay roll of the system averages about $10,000,000 and an increase would mean the additional payment of $1,000,000.

BENCH CANDIDATE DIES.

Appendicitis Kills William Hughes—R. A. Miles in His Place.

Assistant Corporation Counsel William Hughes, one of the Democratic candidates for Justice of the Supreme Court, in the Second District, died late yesterday afternoon in St. Peter's Hospital, Brooklyn. He had been ill for a month and last week he entered the hospital to be operated on for appendicitis.

Rowland A. Miles of Northport, Suffolk County, was named in place of Mr. Hughes. As it is too late to have it printed on the ballot, the name of Mr. Miles will be pasted over that of Mr. Hughes, as provided by law, by those who wish to vote for the Northport man.

ICE-HOLDING CO. TO PAY UP

Dividend on a 7 Per Cent. Basis After the Ice Famine.

The first returns on the stock of the American Ice Securities Company was declared yesterday in the shape of a quarterly dividend of 1¾ per cent., thus placing the stock on a 7 per cent. basis. This dividend was made possible by the recent declaration of back dividends on the preferred stock of the American Ice Company, amounting to 9 per cent., and aggregating $1,275,831, on the $14,175,900 of this stock held by the American Ice Securities Company.

The dividend on the preferred stock of the subsidiary company is not to be paid into the securities company's treasury until Dec. 15.

STRIKE NEAR IN ST. PAUL.

Switchmen on Ten Roads Entering City Fail to Get 8-Hour Day.

Special to The New York Times.

ST. PAUL, Minn., Nov. 2.—The switchmen of the ten railroads entering St. Paul will probably go on a strike within a few days. The men demand 10 cents per hour additional in wages and the eight-hour day.

The roads have consented to the increase in pay, but have held to the ten-hour day. This proposition the men refuse. A general strike is imminent.

FIRE TRUCK KILLS A MAN.

An Engine Going to the Same Fire Breaks Man's Legs.

One man was killed and another had both legs broken last night by fire apparatus going to a fire at 35 City Hall Place. The fire was a small one.

The dead man is supposed to be John Doyle, 36 years old, a sailor on the steamship Majestic. He slipped from behind a car in front of Hook and Ladder Truck 10 at Centre Street, near City Hall Park, and was instantly killed. Driver John Zeigler was held on a technical charge of homicide.

Engine No. 31, going to the same fire, ran down Thomas Daly, 50 years old, of 180 Park Row. The heavy engine passed over Daly's legs and they were broken. He was taken to the Hudson Street Hospital.

CASTRO STILL VERY ILL.

Uncertainty Regarding the Future Is Paralyzing Business.

FORT DE FRANCE, Martinique, Nov. 2.—Passengers arriving here from Venezuela by the steamer Canada bring the information that President Castro, whose health has not improved, was moved on Oct. 25 from the coast to Caracas and on Oct. 27 from Caracas to Sabana Grande, near the capital. With the exception of those ministering to him no one is permitted to come near the President.

Business in Venezuela is in a condition of paralysis because of the general uneasiness regarding the future.

Señor Velutini, the Second Vice President of Venezuela, is expected here shortly.

NIGHT TRIP IN A BALLOON.

Stevens Went Up from Pittsfield and Landed at South Sandisfield.

PITTSFIELD, Mass., Nov. 2.—Leo Stevens, the balloonist, made an ascent from this city this afternoon in the balloon Eagle, which has a capacity of 18,000 feet of gas. A strong northeasterly wind was blowing when Mr. Stevens went up at 4 o'clock. He reached a height of about 2,000 feet, and then disappeared in a southerly direction.

Late to-night the officials of the Aero Club received a telephone message from Mr. Stevens saying that he had landed at South Sandisfield, near the Connecticut line, about 9 o'clock. In the darkness he lost his bearings completely and had no idea of his whereabouts when he succeeded in making a safe landing.

HAS HIS SQUAD KILL HIM.

German Sergeant Adopts a New Means of Committing Suicide.

TREVES, Nov. 2.—While several squads of the Twenty-ninth Regiment of Infantry were exercising in a field to-day undergoing instruction, with blank cartridges, in how to use their rifles on the firing line, a Sergeant of one squad fell dead, with four bullets through his breast.

He had himself loaded the rifles of the squad with ball cartridges and had directed the recruits to aim at his breast and pull the triggers. As the men fired he exclaimed: "His Majesty! Hurrah!"

The cause of the Sergeant's suicide has not been ascertained.

MR. ROOT SEES HIS BROTHER.

Visits with Him at Hamilton College—Coming Here To-day.

UTICA, N. Y., Nov. 2.—Secretary of State Root, who spoke at the Republican mass meeting in this city last night, went to Clinton to-day to visit his brother, Prof. Oren Root of Hamilton College.

He will leave for New York at noon Saturday.

PEARY HAS GONE FARTHEST NORTH

Brings Us the Honor Held by an Italian.

203 MILES FROM THE POLE

The Duke of the Abruzzi Missed It by 237 Miles.

EXPLORER COMING HOME

Message Sent Here from Labrador Tells How He Got to 87°6' North Latitude Last Spring.

Commander Robert E. Peary has gained for the United States the record of "farthest North." Although he failed to reach the north pole, as he hoped, in his vessel, the Roosevelt, he got up to 87 degrees and 6 minutes, north latitude, beating by 32 minutes the record of the Duke of the Abruzzi, 86 degrees and 34 minutes.

The Duke of the Abruzzi got within 237 statute miles of the pole. Commander Peary got within about 203 miles of the arctic explorers' goal.

The news of Commander Peary's achievement came here last night in the shape of this cablegram to Herbert L. Bridgman, Secretary of the Peary Arctic Club, which financed the expedition:

Peary's Message Home.

Hopedale, Labrador, via Twillingate, Newfoundland, Nov. 2.

Herbert L. Bridgman: Roosevelt wintered north coast Grant Land, somewhat north Alert Winter quarters. Went north with sledges February, via Heckla and Columbia. Delayed by open water between 84 and 85 degrees. Beyond 85 six days. Gale disrupted ice, destroyed caches, cut off communication with supporting bodies and drifted due east.

Reached 87 degrees 6 minutes, north latitude, over ice, drifting steadily eastward. Returning, ate eight dogs. Drifted eastward, delayed by open water, reached north coast Greenland in straitened conditions. Killed musk oxen and returned along Greenland coast to ship. Two supporting parties driven on north coast Greenland, one rescued by me in starving condition.

After one week recuperation on Roosevelt sledged west, completing north coast Grant Land and reaching other land, near one hundredth meridian.

Homeward voyage incessant battle with ice, storms, and headwinds. Roosevelt magnificent ice fighter and sea boat. No deaths or illness in expedition.

PEARY.

Mr. Bridgman's Comment.

After furnishing the contents of Commander Peary's message to the reporters, Mr. Bridgman said that the receipt of any news from the explorer at this time was quite a surprise to him. Mr. Bridgman had supposed that it had become too late in the season for Commander Peary to send news of his venture. Mr. Bridgman added that the message spoke for itself, and that since he did not know anything more of the results of Commander Peary's effort to reach the pole than was in the message, he could hardly comment on the dispatch.

There was little doubt, however, Mr. Bridgman said, that Commander Peary was coming home. This seems to be borne out by the routing of the dispatch. Hopedale, or Hoffenthal, is a Moravian mission station on the east coast of Labrador. Twillingate is a port on the east coast of Newfoundland. Mr. Bridgman said the message was probably mailed by Commander Peary from Hopedale to the most accessible cable point.

What the Duke of the Abruzzi Did.

The Duke of the Abruzzi's expedition, which started in 1900, suffered many hardships, and were compelled to eat their sledge dogs. An engineer from Norway and two Italians perished.

The Duke's ship was the Stella Polare. She remained fast in the ice for eleven months, and the pressure opened up a hole in her side a foot and a half across. Her machinery was also damaged. The party had planned to reach the pole if possible by means of sleds, and to make only a limited use of the vessel. It went therefore provided with twenty sleds, each weighing 48½ pounds, and carrying eight aluminum boxes packed with stores and a canoe.

Dr. Fridtjof Nansen held the record before this. When he returned from the arctic regions in August, 1896, he reported that he had left his vessel, the Fram, in 84 degrees north latitude and traversed the Polar Sea to a point 86 degrees 14 minutes north.

Started July 16, 1905.

Commander Peary's steamship, the Roosevelt, left New York on her long journey in search of the north pole on July 16 of last year. The Roosevelt was built in Maine and came down to New York, where she was refitted before starting. The vessel, for which funds were furnished by the Peary Arctic Club of New York, was designed by Naval Architect William E. Winant particularly for arctic exploration. She cost about $100,000. The Roosevelt had a crew of twenty men under Capt. Bartlett.

Commander Peary did not go with the ship from New York, but joined her later at Sydney, C. B., where she took on coal and additional supplies. The Roosevelt left Sydney on July 26. She was next reported at Domino Run, Labrador, on July 29. From that point she crossed to Greenland. The next heard from the vessel was from Etah, North Greenland. She passed Cape York on Aug. 7. The expedition's auxiliary steamer Erik had visited various settlements in Greenland meanwhile and had obtained natives and dogs for the explorer, and turned them over to the Roosevelt on Aug. 12.

At Etah the Roosevelt overhauled her machinery, took on board her last supply of coal from the Erik, and thence [illegible]

Commander Robert E. Peary, the first man to get within 203 miles of the North Pole.

The Bettmann Archive

Dr. Frederick A. Cook claimed to be the first man to reach the North Pole.

"All the News That's Fit to Print."

The New York Times.

THE WEATHER.
Fair, continued cool to-day and Friday; north to variable winds.

VOL. LVIII...NO. 18,849. * * * NEW YORK, THURSDAY, SEPTEMBER 2, 1909.—SIXTEEN PAGES ONE CENT In Greater New York, Jersey City, and Newark { Elsewhere, TWO CENTS.

SHOOTS HER DOCTOR AND THEN HERSELF

Mrs. William Condon of Dunton, L. I., Calls Physician to Her Home and Begins Firing.

DYING, SHE IS REPENTANT

He Was Shot in the Leg and Will Live, but Refuses to Talk—Due to "Nervousness," Woman's Explanation.

Dr. S. N. C. Hicks of 28 Hardenbrook Avenue, Jamaica, L. I., while visiting at the home of William Condon, a plumber, residing on Dakota Avenue, near Wyoming Avenue, Dunton, L. I., yesterday afternoon, was shot by Mrs. Condon. Afterward Mrs. Condon turned the revolver upon herself inflicting a probably mortal wound over the heart. She is believed to be dying in St. Mary's Hospital. Dr. Hicks is painfully wounded, the shot having entered his left leg near the knee.

Dr. Hicks resolutely refused to make a charge against Mrs. Condon, and she appeared solicitous regarding his condition while in the ambulance on the way to the hospital.

The shooting took place in the Condon home about 2 o'clock in the absence of the husband, who was in Williamsburg upon a plumbing job. When the husband returned, in response to a message sent to him by telephone, he declined to make any statement whatever.

The Condons have lived at the address given for about six years. Mrs. Condon is 36 years old. They have two children, Lillie, 13, and Walter, 11 years. According to neighbors Dr. Hicks had been a very frequent visitor at the Condon home. Some neighbors asserted yesterday that he spent three or four hours every day at the house, although none appeared to know of any illness in the home. Yesterday a telephone message was sent to Dr. Hicks's house, asking him to call at the Condon home.

At 1:30 o'clock Mrs. Condon went to the home of her next-door neighbor, Mrs. Hannah Meisel. She had on her hat and was apparently attired for the street.

"Mrs. Meisel," she said, "I am going out for a while, and wish you would have an eye upon Lillie and Walter while I am gone."

The neighbor promised and the children were left by their mother playing in the Meisel back yard. Whether or not Mrs. Condon went further than the front gate is not known to the neighbors. Dr. Hicks appeared upon the scene some little time after or about 2 o'clock.

After Dr. Hicks had been in the house about ten or fifteen minutes there were some shots, and Lillie and Walter, who were the first to hear them, began crying. They called out to Mrs. Meisel, who aroused other neighbors. None seemed to dare to enter the house. Singularly enough, the shooting did not seem to wholly surprise the neighbors, many of whom had noticed Dr. Hicks's automobile standing in front of the Condon house frequently and for long periods.

Mrs. Meisel finally screwed up her courage sufficiently to enter the house just as Dr. Hicks staggered through the front door.

"'I'm shot! I'm shot!'" said the physician in an agonized voice, his face pale and drawn with pain.

Dr. Hicks saw Emile Texter, a Dakota Avenue neighbor of the Condons, in his doorway, and called out to him again that he was shot.

"Send for the ambulance. Send for the police," said Dr. Hicks, who was unable to walk, but hobbled along mainly upon his right leg, the bullet having entered his left leg above the knee.

Texter telephoned to St. Mary's Hospital of Jamaica for an ambulance and notified the police of the Richmond Hill Precinct. Capt. John Barnes hastened to the house. As the ambulance was out when the message was received it did not arrive for nearly an hour.

Meanwhile Texter telephoned, at Dr. Hicks's request, for Dr. George K. Meyned of Clinton Avenue, Jamaica, Chief Surgeon of the Long Island Railroad, and Dr. Meyned hurried to the Condon house and attended both the injured persons. The ambulance arrived and took Mrs. Condon to the hospital, while Dr. Meyned conveyed Dr. Hicks to the institution in his own carriage.

"Oh, doctor, I didn't mean to shot either Dr. Hicks or myself," said Mrs. Condon.

She made no explanation as to how she chanced to have a revolver in her hands if she intended to do no harm with it, and Dr. Meynen did not ask her, nor would he permit any one to enter the private rooms in which Mrs. Condon and Dr. Hicks were lying.

"Mrs. Condon was hysterical when the shooting occurred, and I do not believe she meant to shoot me," was all the comment Dr. Hicks vouchsafed.

Mrs. Condon is under arrest in the hospital upon a charge of attempted suicide, as Dr. Hicks would make no charge against her.

When Capt. Barnes examined the revolver, with which the shooting was done, he found three chambers had been discharged, although only two shots have been accounted for. None of the neighbors knew of Mrs. Condon ever having practiced with a revolver before yesterday's shooting, although her husband told one that she sometimes handled a revolver.

Last night Dr. Meynen said that he could not tell whether Mrs. Condon would die from her wound, which was in the left breast, above the heart. The bullet was too far in the body to admit of its removal. Coroner Ambler went to St. Mary's Hospital last evening and took Mrs. Condon's ante-mortem statement.

In it she denied all intention of shooting Dr. Hicks or herself. She said her husband always kept a revolver under his pillow. She telephoned to Dr. Hicks before noon, she said, as she felt a nervous turn coming on, and just as he was entering the house she felt she simply must get that revolver and shoot something. She said she had no idea how many shots she fired.

DANGER IN ROOSEVELT BAG.

Ex-President's Trophies Found to Carry Eggs of Dreaded Tse-tse Fly.

Special to The New York Times.

WASHINGTON, Sept. 1.—The possibility of sleeping sickness developing from germs brought recently from Africa in the Roosevelt trophies is causing a mild alarm in Washington. Officials of the institution began unpacking the specimens yesterday, and to-day, in skins of a specie of hair that is frequently infested with tse-tse fly eggs, several egg deposits in perfect condition were discovered.

It happened that these skins were not packed in brine, but merely dried in the sun, and that fact accounts for the preservation of the eggs. The tse-tse fly is said to carry sleeping sickness much as the ordinary mosquito of certain breed carries malaria. The officers of the institution started at first to destroy the eggs by sterilization, but scientific curiosity prevailed, and it is not unlikely that the eggs will be hatched out for purposes of experimentation.

The point the scientists wish to discover is whether the sleeping sickness is merely a hereditary or contagious disease carried by the flies, or a sickness resulting from the flies' own venom.

The scientists of the Smithsonian Institution are now satisfying their curiosity as to what the first consignment of boxes containing trophies of Col. Roosevelt's African hunt have within their sides.

Upon opening the casks containing the skins they were found to be in good shape, and Major Mearns, in charge of the Smithsonian forces with Col. Roosevelt, has been notified of the fact. The work of stuffing the skins will not be undertaken for some time, and it will probably be two years before the work is completed. The scientists of the institution have expressed themselves as having never seen a more interesting and well preserved collection of mammals and birds.

MARS IN ECLIPSE.

Fine Sight for Amateur Astronomers—Planet Coming Nearer.

New Yorkers who looked out of their eastern windows at about 8:30 o'clock last night saw the big, full moon, glistening and brilliant as a gigantic reflector, surge suddenly out of a bank of clouds over Long Island.

Clinging close to its lower eastern rim was the planet Mars, looking a little paler, smaller, and less brilliant than it has been during the last few days. Side by side, the big and the small planet soared up together through the blue-black nocturnal ether. Little Mars, indeed, seemed to be following up the large moon with very much the same persistence that a small, angry kingbird, whose nest has been robbed, chases a big blundering bird of prey.

As planet and moon mounted the heavens, they also kept getting nearer and nearer together. Finally, at eight minutes to 9 o'clock, Mars gradually slid behind the moon, and the moon slipped in front of Mars. The planet disappeared for almost exactly an hour. At seven minutes and fifty-three seconds before 10 o'clock, it suddenly shot out from behind the moon's western side, about half way up the circumference. The two continued to climb side by side, but gradually diverged.

MET ALLIGATOR ON HIGHWAY.

It Was Pointing Toward Sagamore Hill When Notts Gave Combat.

Bound for Sagamore Hill to await the return of his friend, Bwana Tumbo, a romantic young alligator, met a cruel fate on the highway outside Jamaica yesterday. It was discovered and beaten to death by Richard Notts, a baker, of Lefferts Avenue, Hoffman Park.

Mounted on his bicycle Notts encountered the monster face to face and there followed a combat which would have made St. George and the dragon turn pale. Putting on speed, says Baker Notts, he charged down upon the monster which opened its mouth as if about to swallow bicycle and rider.

His machine shied, and quickly dismounting and seizing his trusty bicycle pump Notts advanced to the fray shoving the pump down the alligator's throat. Then having it hors de combat, he cracked it over the snout with a club, hitched it on the back of his wheel, and rode back to town.

By the tape line the alligator measured just four and a half feet, and the oldest inhabitant stood by and wiped the tears from his eyes as it breathed its last.

VENEZUELA PAYS INDEMNITY.

Settles with American Corporation for Claim of $475,000 After Many Years.

CARACAS, Sept. 1.—W. W. Russell, American Minister, has received a check for $30,375, to be paid to the New York and Venezuela Company, and also the signed protocol by which the Venezuelan Government binds itself to pay $415,625 more in seven yearly installments. These $475,000 are the first of several large sums which Venezuela must pay in atonement for the confiscation and destruction of American property rights in Venezuela by the late Castro Government. The whole amount will be more than a million dollars, as a large monetary indemnity will probably be paid also to the Orinoco Corporation.

To attain the above satisfactory outcome of the negotiations Mr. Russell had been working for months on the transaction, and the State Department had paid thousands of dollars in cable tolls. The New York and Venezuela Company releases all of its rights in Venezuela in view of the indemnity to be paid.

The Orinoco Corporation is trying to effect a settlement similar to that just successfully carried through by Mr. Russell in behalf of the New York and Venezuela Company. They are willing to give up all their rights in Venezuela if they are given a large enough indemnity. It is understood that Venezuela is willing to pay $400,000 to the Orinoco Corporation, but no agreement is near because there is some hitch either in the State Department or with the Directors of the Corporation. If settlement is not made by Sept. 13 the case will go to The Hague and be arbitrated together with that of the Orinoco Shipping Company.

Balloon Ascends 12,000 Feet.

DAYTON, Ohio, Sept. 1.—The new balloon, The Delight, in its initial voyage yesterday reached a height of 12,000 feet. It landed fourteen miles beyond Delaware, Ohio.

BALLOONIST FALLS ON TELEPHONE WIRES

Clinging to Parachute and Dragged Over Roofs, Drew Is Saved by Policemen.

WIND-SWEPT FROM JERSEY

Bluecoats Get Him Down from Fifty Feet in Midair with Aid of a Rope—Crowds See Rescue.

George B. Drew, a young aeronaut, who has been making balloon ascensions from a Park, near Edgewater, N. J., and then coming down with a parachute, narrowly escaped serious injury and possible death late yesterday afternoon.

After being swept across the river by the wind, his parachute caught on a line of telephone wires running from the roof of an apartment house on Morningside Heights, and he hung, helpless and exhausted, in midair more than fifty feet above the pavement. The quick action of three policemen from the West 125th Street police station saved the young man from serious trouble, and brought him out of the difficulty none the worse for the experience except for slightly bruised knees and elbows.

Women and children and home-going business men in the neighborhood of Riverside Drive and 122d Street just before dark last evening were thrown into a frenzy of excitement by the sight of Drew hanging from the slender bar of a small parachute, who shot down out of the sky and was swept by the wind across the roofs of several apartment houses, in the direction of the East River. While they stood shouting on the sidewalks, the young aeronaut bumped back and forth between the chimneys, and then disappeared back of the Lincoln Court Apartments, at 136 Claremont Avenue, between 122d and 123d Streets. The crowd rushed around the corner, expecting to find the young man dashed to pieces on the ground. They found him dangling from the parachute, which was caught on the wires running from the roof, six or eight feet from the wall, between the fourth and fifth stories.

Policemen Wegge had run up in the meantime, attracted by the commotion. He shouted to Drew to hold on, and quickly cutting down a clothesline in a neighboring vacant lot rushed up to the roof of the apartment house. Before entering the building he blew his whistle for assistance, and Policemen Hamilton and Ruth were soon on the scene. They saw the situation at a glance, and the former ran to a telephone and called out Fire Truck 23. Before it arrived, however, Wegge had reached the roof and succeeded in throwing the rope to Drew. The wires were sagging heavily by this time, and it was clear that the parachute would not hold much longer. The side of the apartment by which the young man was caught is a blank wall, and the onlookers realized that the rescuers would still have some trouble in getting him out of his predicament. Hamilton and Ruth ran upstairs to the apartment of George W. French, on the fourth floor of the building, and shouted to Wegge to swing the young man to the window just around the corner. Drew tied the rope around his waist and swung off. Wegge's hold was good, but the young man struck heavily against the side of the building, and, before the policeman could get him around the corner of the roof so that his fellow policemen could reach him, his knees and elbows were badly bruised. Then he was dragged to safety.

Dr. Brothers had arrived from the J. Hood Wright Hospital in an ambulance and he dressed young Drew's wounds in the French apartments. The young man was clad only in a bathing suit, and the doctor took him to the West 130th Street ferry after he had rested a bit. Drew then returned to Palisades Park. then returned to New Jersey.

DESTROYER MAKES 33.7 KNOTS

The Flusser Establishes New Speed Record for United States Warships.

ROCKLAND, Me., Sept. 1.—A record three knots faster than that of any ship in the United States Navy was scored today by the Bath-built torpedo boat destroyer Flusser in a standardization trial, the first of her official acceptance trials on the Rockland mile course. Her fastest mile was made at the rate of 33.7 knots an hour, while another was at the rate of 33.4 knots. The average of her five top speed runs was 32.7 knots. The contract speed requirement is 28 knots.

The British destroyer Swift has a record of nearly 36 knots, but she was designed for that speed, and is a 1,800 ton ship, while the Flusser has a displacement of only 700 tons.

A fog set in so thick that the officers could not see the marks, but this did not interfere with the trial. A shaft horse power of 14,400 was developed. Capt. Charles W. Dingley of Bath was the navigating officer and Charles P. Weatherbee was superintending engineer.

The Flusser is equipped with Parsons turbines. She will be ready for delivery on Sept. 28.

BLIND BRIDE WON BY MUSIC.

Blind Pianist Attracted Her at a Concert—Married Yesterday.

Among the applicants for marriage licenses who appeared at the License Bureau in Brooklyn yesterday was a blind musician who had won a blind bride by his piano playing. He was Clement Coffin, 44 years old, of 83 Putnam Avenue, Brooklyn, and his bride-to-be, Miss Antoinette Barton, 29 years old, of 48 Ralph Avenue, that borough.

Miss Barton heard Mr. Coffin play at a concert some time ago and the two became acquainted. After that the blind pianist visited the young woman frequently and entertained her with his piano playing. Although neither could see the other they spent many hours happily together at the piano, and their newly found friendship soon ripened to love.

The pair left the License Bureau to get married, and said they would make their home at 243 Albany Avenue.

LUSITANIA MAKING A RECORD.

Two Hours Ahead of Mauretania's Best—May Be in To-night.

By Marconi Wireless to THE TIMES.

S. S. LUSITANIA, Sept. 1, (via Halifax.)—At 10 o'clock to-night, New York time, the Lusitania is 480 miles from Sandy Hook. For more than eighty-seven hours she has averaged slightly above 26 knots an hour, and at this time she is more than two hours ahead of the Mauretania's best record at the same stage of voyage.

With good luc kthe Lusitania will reach Sandy Hook by 5 o'clock to-morrow afternoon, and will dock between 7 and 8, landing her passengers on Thursday evening for the first time in the history of the westward voyages of the two big Cunarders, and establishing a new record of about four days twelve hours for the transatlantic trip.

The Lusitania's day's runs have been, so far, 632 miles to Monday noon, 656 miles to noon on Tuesday, 651 miles to noon to-day.

LEFT $15,000 ON A TRAIN.

Brooklyn Woman Wouldn't Trust Banks with It—Offers $1,000 Reward.

A poorly dressed, elderly woman, evidently greatly troubled, entered the law offices of Page, Crawford & Tuska at 32 Liberty Street yesterday afternoon.

"I want you to help me find $15,000 which I have lost. It represents my savings for years as well as some money I recently inherited," she told Benjamin Tuska, the only member of the firm in the office at the time.

"I am a trained nurse and live in Brooklyn. I have always earned a good salary and have put by most of it. I was in the habit of depositing it in a trust company. Then I inherited some money. I deposited that in a trust company, too.

"But the panic shook my faith in trust companies, and recently I have been keeping the money in my house. It was done up in a sealed package, exactly as when I took it from the trust company.

"A friend told me of a safe mortgage in which to invest the money, and a week ago I put the sealed package of money in a black handbag and, leaving my home in Brooklyn, came over to Manhattan in the Subway. I placed the bag beside me on the seat and, in quitting the train, left the bag behind.

"I discovered my loss as soon as I had left the Subway station and ran back, only to find that the train was gone. Since then I have visited the offices of the railway company every day in hopes that the package would be returned. But it hasn't been."

WANTS NO COLLEGE CLIQUES.

Harvard's New Head Would Have His Student Body Democratic.

Special to The New York Times.

CAMBRIDGE, Mass., Sept. 1.—President A. Lawrence Lowell, Harvard's newly elected head, will have many new ideas to offer for the betterment of the university's standing in the educational world, which he will outline in his inaugural address Oct. 6. He will read his address from a large outdoor platform before the college offices.

He believes the academic degree of to-day is held too lightly and in many cases is too easily obtained. He wishes the Harvard degree to be one well earned and to be regarded as a standard. He does not wish to see Harvard the home of the athlete with no student ties, or a resort for the idle rich.

He believes that men go to college to study. He also aims to discourage the forming of cliques, though he believes that the freshman class should have dormitories of its own. In general, however, he thinks that the students would become more democratic if they were not divided off into cliques.

THE EATONS TOGETHER AGAIN.

Rear Admiral's Wife and Daughters Go to House Where Boy Died.

Special to The New York Times.

SCITUATE, Mass., Sept. 1.—Mrs. Joseph G. Eaton, wife of Rear Admiral Eaton, retired, and her two daughters, June and Dorothy, returned to the home in Assinippi last night from the Sandhills and were received by Admiral Eaton. Admiral Eaton had nothing to say, on the ground that "too much about their family differences had already been said." Mrs. Eaton and her two daughters had nothing to say, either.

The Eatons went to the Beach in July. They occupied the Isis cottage, which had been hired to Sept. 1. Two weeks ago the Eatons' adopted child, Joseph Giles Eaton, Jr., died suddenly, and the mother demanded an autopsy. The stomach was sent to the Harvard Medical School for analysis, it being feared that the child had died of poison.

LOEB STOPS BAND CONCERTS.

Ocean Liners' Musicians Suspected of Smuggling by Trombone Route.

By a new order Collector Loeb has done away with an old custom in which the people of Hoboken have taken considerable pleasure and pride. It is the habit of the bands of the various ocean liners landing in Hoboken to go ashore and give concerts in the various gardens and other resorts in Hoboken. All this has been stopped.

Six customs men held up the band of the Scandinavian-American Liner Oscar II on Tuesday night. Supt. Lassen of the company declares he will appeal to the Collector to have the new order rescinded.

Mr. Loeb's action, it is understood, was taken only after he had become convinced that some of the bandmen were smuggling goods into the country, carrying them ashore in their instruments.

TRIED TO SAVE DOG; IS DYING.

Bride's Skull Fractured While Seeking to Keep Pet Terrier from Under a Car.

Mrs. Mae Peterson, the six months' bride of Ernest T. Peterson, President of the National Cipher Code Corporation of 91 Wall Street, is critically ill in St. Joseph's Hospital, Far Rockaway, and it was not expected last night that she would live until morning. The woman has a fractured skull. She received her injury yesterday morning while trying to save her pet Boston terrier Mugglns from being run over by a car.

Mrs. Peterson had the dog on the Boulevard, Rockaway Beach, early yesterday morning, and the animal ran toward a swiftly approaching trolley car. Mrs. Peterson ran after him to pull him off the tracks, and the car hit her.

Mrs. Peterson and her husband have been residents of the Tent City at Rockaway Beach, this Summer. Their home is at 794 Washington Avenue, Brooklyn.

COOK REPORTS HE HAS FOUND THE NORTH POLE

Reached It April 21, 1908, After Prolonged Fight with Famine and Frost.

MADE DASH OF 600 MILES

Started with Ten Eskimos and 103 Dogs with Sledges.

NO LAND AT THE POLE

But New Territory Discovered Far North on the Way.

STARTED TWO YEARS AGO

Chose Winter, When Ice Pack Was Welded, for Final Effort.

SENDS NEWS TO WIFE HERE

Expedition Fitted Out by John R. Bradley, Who Went as Far as Labrador.

PARIS, Sept. 2.—The Paris edition of The New York Herald publishes this morning a signed statement from Dr. Frederick A. Cook, which is dated "Hans Egede, Lerwick, Wednesday," on his experiences in the arctic regions.

"After a prolonged fight with famine and frost," says Dr. Cook, "we have at last succeeded in reaching the north pole. A new highway, with an interesting strip of animated nature, has been explored, and big game haunts located, which will delight sportsmen and extend the Eskimo horizon.

"Land has been discovered on which rest the earth's northernmost rocks. A triangle of 30,000 square miles has been cut out of the terrestrial unknown.

"The expedition was the outcome of a Summer cruise in the arctic seas on the schooner Bradley, which arrived at the limits of navigation in Smith Sound late in August, 1907. Here conditions were found to launch a venture to the pole. J. R. Bradley liberally supplied from his vessel suitable provisions for local use.

All Elements Favorable.

"My own equipment for emergencies served well for every purpose of arctic travel. Many Eskimos had gathered on the Greenland shores at Annatok for the Winter bear hunt. Immense quantities of meat had been collected, and about the camp were plenty of strong dogs. The combination was lucky, for there was good material for equipment. All that was required was conveniently arranged for at a point only 700 miles from the boreal centre.

Ready to Try New Route.

A house and workshop were built of packing boxes by willing hands, and this northernmost tribe of 250 people set themselves to the problem of devising a suitable outfit. Before the end of the long Winter night we were ready for the enterprise and plans had matured to force a new route over Grinnell Land northward along its west coast out onto the polar sea.

"The campaign opened with a few scouting parties being sent over the American shores to explore the way and seek the game haunts. Their mission was only partly successful because of the storms.

Main Expedition Starts.

"At sunrise of 1908 (Feb. 19) the main expedition embarked on its voyage to the pole. It consisted of eleven men and 103 dogs drawing eleven heavily laden sledges. The expedition left the Greenland shore and pushed westward over the troubled ice of Smith Sound. The gloom of the long night was relieved only by a few hours of daylight. The chill of the Winter was felt at its worst.

"As we crossed the heights of Ellesmere Sound to the Pacific slope the temperature sank to minus 83 Centigrade. Several dogs were frozen, and the men suffered severely, but we soon found the game trails, along which the way was easy.

"We forced through Nansen Sound to Land's End. In this march we secured 101 musk oxen, seven bears, and 335 hares. We pushed out into the polar sea from the southern point of Herbert Island on March 18. Six Eskimos returned from here.

Six Eskimos Return.

"With four men and forty-six dogs moving supplies for eighty days, the crossing of the circumpolar pack was begun. Three days later two other Eskimos, forming the last supporting party, returned and the trials had now been reduced by the survival of the fittest. The two best men and twenty-six dogs were picked for the final effort.

"There, before us in an unknown line of 460 miles, lay our goal. The first days provided long marches, and we made encouraging progress. A big lead, which separated the land from the ice of the central pack, was crossed with little delay.

"The low temperature was persistent and the winds made life a torture. But cooped up in our snow houses, eating dried beef tallow and drinking hot tea, there were some animal comforts occasionally to be gained.

New Land Discovered.

"For several days after the sight of known land was lost, the overcast sky prevented an accurate determination of our positions. On March 30 the horizon was partly cleared and new land was discovered. Our observations gave our position as latitude 84.47, longitude 86.36.

"There was urgent need of rapid advance. Our main mission did not permit a détour for the purpose of exploring the coast.

"Here were seen the last signs of solid earth, beyond there was nothing stable to be seen.

"We advanced steadily over the monotony of moving sea ice, and now found ourselves beyond the range of all life—neither footprints of bears nor the blowholes of seals were detected. Even the microscopic creatures of the deep were no longer under us.

Frost Almost Unendurable.

"The maddening influence of the shifting desert of frost became almost unendurable in the daily routine. The surface of the pack offered less and less trouble and the weather improved, but there still remained the life-sapping wind, which drove despair to its lowest recess.

"The extreme cold compelled physical action. Thus day after day our weary legs spread over big distances. Incidents and positions were recorded, but adventure was promptly forgotten in the next day's efforts.

Sunburns and Frost Bites.

"The night of April 7 was made notable by the swinging of the sun at midnight over the northern ice. Sunburns and frost bites now were recorded on the same day, but the double day's glitter infused quite an incentive into one's life of shivers.

"Our observation on April 8 placed the camp in latitude 86.36, longitude 94.2. In spite of what seemed long marches we advanced but little over a hundred miles. Much of our work was lost in circuitous twists, around troublesome pressure lines and high, irregular fields. A very old ice drift, too, was driving eastward with sufficient force to give some anxiety.

"Although still equal to about 50 miles daily, the extended marches and the long hours for traveling with which fortune favored us earlier, were no longer possible. We were now about 200 miles from the pole and sledge loads were reduced. One dog after another went into the stomachs of the hungry survivors until the teams were considerably diminished in number, but there seemed to remain a sufficient balance for man and brute to push along into the heart of the mystery to which we had set ourselves."

"On April 21 we had reached 89 degrees 59 minutes 46 seconds. The pole was in sight. We covered the remaining fourteen seconds and made a few final observations. I told Etukishook and Ahwelsh (the accompanying Eskimos) that we had reached the great nail.'

Every Direction South.

Everywhere we turned was south. With a single step we could pass from one side of the earth to the other: from midday to midnight. At last the flag floated to the breezes at the pole. It was April 21, 1908. The temperature was minus 38 Centigrade, barometer 29.83, latitude 90; as for the longitude, it was nothing, as it was but a word.

"Although crazy with joy, our spirits began to undergo a feeling of weariness. Next day, after taking all our observations, a sentiment of intense solitude penetrated us while we looked at the horizon. Was it possible that this desolate region, without a patch of earth, had aroused the ambition of so many men for so many centuries.

There was no ground, only an immensity of dazzling white snow, no living being, no point to break the frightful monotony.

"On April 23 we started on our return."

TELLS OF LAND FAR NORTH.

Dr. Cook Wires News of Discovery to the Brussels Observatory.

Special Cable to THE NEW YORK TIMES.

BRUSSELS, Sept. 1.—The Brussels Observatory received the following message this afternoon, dated Lerwick, Shetland Islands:

"Lecointe, Observatory, Brussels:

"Reached north pole April 21, 1908. Discovered land far north. Return to Copenhagen by steamer Hans Eged.

(Signed) "FREDERICK COOK."

This telegram caused a deep sensation at the Observatory. Director Lecointe was absent.

I was unable to get further information with regard to the tremendous achievement of the American explorer. All I could learn was that the statement was perfectly correct and authentic.

COPENHAGEN, Sept. 1.—A message announcing that the north pole had been reached on April 21, 1908, by Dr. Frederick A. Cook, the American explorer, was received at the Colonial Office here to-day from an official on board the Danish Government steamer Hans Egede.

Reaches Shetland Islands.

The steamer on which Dr. Cook is returning from the arctic regions passed Lerwick in the Shetland Islands today, and it was from there the message was sent. It read as follows:

"We have on board the American traveler, Dr. Cook, who reached the north pole April 21, 1908. Dr. Cook arrived at Upernavik in May of 1908 from Cape York. The Eskimos of Cape York confirm Dr. Cook's story of his journey."

Due at Copenhagen Saturday.

It is understood that the Danish Consul at Lerwick, where the Hans Egede remained for two hours, was officially notified of Dr. Cook's success in his attempt to reach the pole, but that he was bound to secrecy concerning the extent and nature of the explorer's discoveries.

Director Ryberg, head of the Greenland Administration Bureau, said to-night that he did not expect to receive any further details of Dr. Cook's achievement before the arrival of the Hans Egede at this port, which probably would be Saturday afternoon. The vessel will make no stops on the voyage from Lerwick to Copenhagen.

American Legation Advised.

Director Ryberg proceeded to the American Legation and informed the Minister, Dr. Maurice F. Egan, that Dr. Cook had reached the north pole. The announcement caused the greatest enthusiasm throughout the city, and many Americans called at the legation to congratulate the Minister. Among these was Alexander Kolla of New York, a warm personal friend of Dr. Cook, who said that he had believed the explorer had perished long ago. The legation was overcrowded with visitors to-night.

Great Reception Planned.

The noted explorer, Commander Hovgaard, leader of various north pole expeditions, was convinced that the message that Dr. Cook had reached the pole was true, but remarked that it was strange that no mention was made in the cable as to whether or not there is land at the pole. It is the intention of the people of Copenhagen, on Dr. Cook's arrival there, to give him a most enthusiastic reception.

The Eskimos at Cape York, mentioned in the dispatch, are said to be connected with the expedition of the Danish explorer Knud Rasmussen, who is now at Cape York.

It is believed here that Dr. Cook was accompanied on his dash to the pole only by a few Eskimos.

DOUBT CAST IN LONDON.

Reports There That Only the Magnetic Pole Was Found.

Special Cable to THE NEW YORK TIMES.

LONDON, Sept. 1.—A telegram from Lerwick, Shetland Islands, where Dr. Cook's ship touched, says that Cook reached the north magnetic pole. The Daily Mail points out that if this is correct and that the magnetic pole is the north pole meant in the Copenhagen telegrams the exploit is not so remarkable, as the magnetic north pole is a long distance south of the north pole, and was attained by Ross so far back as 1831.

No definite [illegible] are obtainable

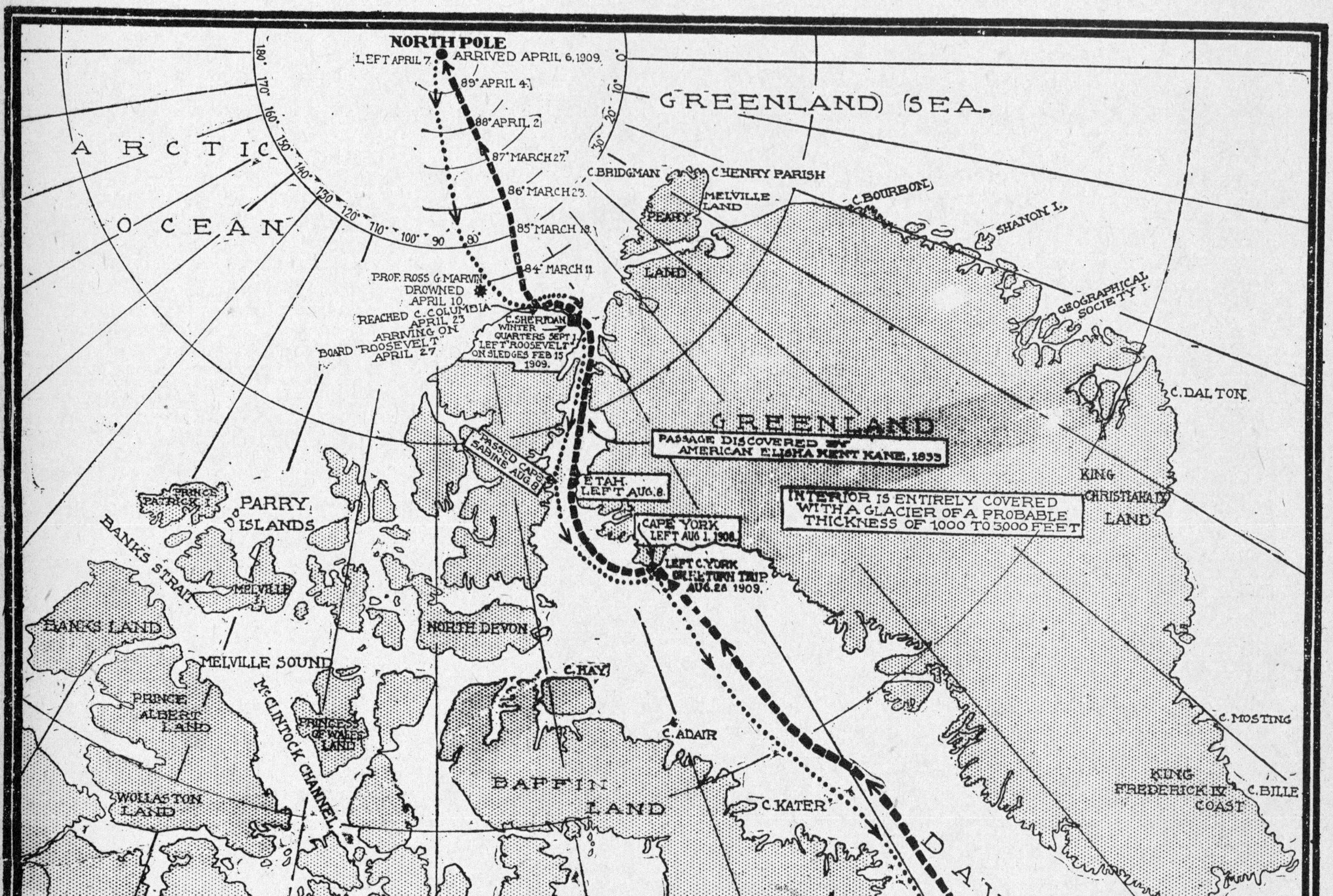

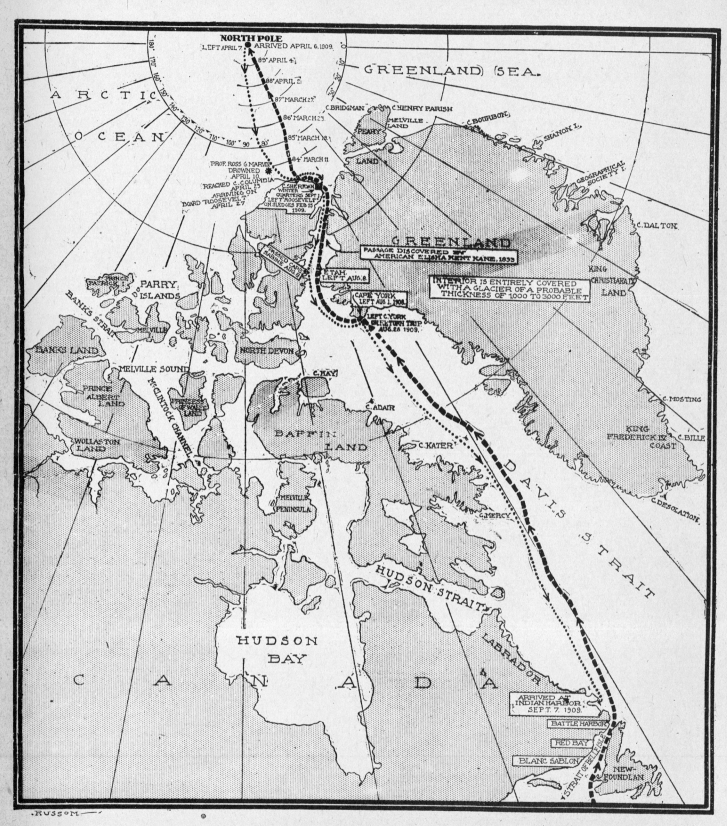

Map showing in detail Peary's progress to the Pole.

"All the News That's Fit to Print"

The New York Times

LATE CITY EDITION

Weather: Fair, very cold today and tonight. Chance of snow tomorrow. Temp. range: today 24-14; Sunday 33-26. Full U.S. report on Page 30.

VOL. LVIII...NO. 18,854. * * * NEW YORK, TUESDAY, SEPTEMBER 7, 1909.—EIGHTEEN PAGES. ONE CENT In Greater New York, Jersey City, and Newark | Elsewhere, TWO CENTS.

GAYNOR, UNPLEDGED, CONSENTS TO RUN

Writes Business Men He Will Accept Support of Any Party, but Make No Promises.

SAYS TAMMANY IS FOR HIM

Assured by Leaders of the Nomination, He Declares—Is for War on Machine Control and "City Spoliation."

Supreme Court Justice William J. Gaynor of Brooklyn has announced his willingness to become a candidate for Mayor in a letter written to a committee of influential Brooklyn citizens who urged him soon after his return from Europe to enter the fight. The long-awaited declaration of his position was made public last night together with the names of the committee of citizens and their letter to the Brooklyn jurist.

Justice Gaynor reviews the entire Mayoralty situation, assails "mere political control," which has resulted in "spoliation of the city treasury." He declares, however, that he has reason to believe that he will receive the Democratic nomination and Republican support, as well as that of the Independence League.

An interesting part of the letter is that in which Justice Gaynor refers to the printed statements that he would not receive the indorsement of the Republican organization unless he made some definite pledge of his position. While declaring that he does not believe that the majority of the organization demand any such condition of him, he emphatically states that he will pledge himself to no organization.

"I shall not take a nomination from any organization to which is annexed any pledge, promise or condition whatsoever other than to be Mayor in fact, and do my duty if elected," says he.

In referring to his expectation of welcoming all voters to his standard, Justice Gaynor says: "When an organization or party vouches for one and nominates him and wants him elected I have always understood that it welcomes help from any and all quarters to elect him."

Promises from Tammany.

He goes on to make the significant declaration that he has received assurance from influential Democrats that the Tammany City Convention will give him an "unconditional nomination" and that "no one can prevent the election of delegates who will nominate me." He states that he is aware that there is opposition to him in the organization, but that he does not believe "an undivided delegation can be brought into the convention opposed to my nomination."

"As to the Independence League," he continues, "inasmuch as it has always stood for the uplifting of city government, I think I may justly expect its support."

Justice Gaynor concludes with a solemn pledge to discharge his trust with fidelity and honesty, ending with the words, "No party or party machine can drag us down if we stand fast together; on the contrary, we may lift city politics up in all parties, and make the spoliation of the city's treasury, through mere machine political control, a thing impossible in the future."

Here is Justice Gaynor's answer:

Justice Gaynor's Letter.

Sept. 4, 1909.

"Messrs. Abraham Abraham, James McMahon, Archibald R. Watson, Judson G. Wall, Michael H. Drummond, James Creelman, Charles M. Higgins M. M. Belding, Jr., and Frank J. Price.

Dear Sirs—Your letter added to my very great anxiety, already caused by similar letters and requests and public discussion, but has finally helped to enable me to see my way through it. I put myself in your hands, and consent to be a candidate for nomination for Mayor. No doubt you have observed that several bodies of citizens have nominated me already. I specially note your statement, 'We do not care who, or what party convention, joins in nominating and voting for you if you will give us your consent to run,' etc. It requires me to say something of recent occurrences in order that there may be no misunderstanding, and I trust I may say it without a bit of unkindness to any one.

The Republican City Committee has met since your letter was written and apparently give out a statement that the Republican City Convention will not nominate any one who will not pledge himself in advance not to accept a nomination from the Democratic City Convention also. Although published in all of the newspapers, and in no way questioned, I have doubted whether it was in fact authorized. I know that many Republicans will not acquiesce in it. As is well enough known, I have long been of those who look upon such extreme partisanship in city or local elections as most unfortunate. Its main result is to play everything year after year into the hands of party machines.

In years gone by I have worked shoulder to shoulder with Republicans and Democrats alike and together in efforts to prevent official wrongdoing and lift the city Government up and make it intelligent and decent. I so worked successfully with those who prevented the fraudulent purchase of the water company, and other even worse things, still in general remembrance, and with those who moved upon and destroyed John Y. McKane and his corrupt control, results and benefits from which were accepted by leaders and the machines of both parties in turn through series of years.

We never paused then to inquire of one another's politics, or to put any ban or bar on one another because of politics, and we shall not do the like now. Must I now in order to run for Mayor first get up and unjustly offend men who so worked with us then, and thousands of others who gave us their good-will and sympathy in such work, by saying that I shall not suffer the city convention of their party to also nominate me? If I should do so I could not expect their votes.

The great bulk of the voters here who are Democrats in National politics are in favor of intelligent and good local government the same as the corresponding bulk of Republican voters are. How much better it would be for the city if they should work together instead of proscribing and ostracizing each other.

Base Men in the Minority.

Base men are in the minority in all parties and everywhere. There are 75,000 or more voters in this great city who now never allow National politics to influence their votes in city elections. What,

Continued on Page 7.

HARRIMAN SUFFERS RELAPSE.

Diagnosed as Acute Indigestion—His Physician Says, 'We Hope for the Best.'

Special to The New York Times.

TURNER'S, N. Y., Sept. 6.—That E. H. Harriman has had a relapse was admitted this afternoon by Dr. W. M. Gordon Lyle, his physician, at the Harriman home here. Acute indigestion is Dr. Lyle's diagnosis of his patient's trouble.

The attack came on yesterday after Mr. Harriman had appeared to be doing nicely for several days. A telephone message was sent from the Harriman home in the early hours of this morning to Miss Taylor, Superintendent of St. Luke's Hospital nurses' registry, at 214 West 106th Street, Manhattan, asking her to send her best nurse here with all speed. The nurse arrived within three hours.

According to Dr. Lyle, Mr. Harriman is resting easily to-night. He said that it was he who sent for the nurse. There is a report that there are four other nurses here, but this could not be confirmed. Certain it is that Mr. Harriman's state of health is such that both day and night nurses are required.

When Dr. Lyle was seen this afternoon he was much perturbed over the presence here again of newspaper men. It was pointed out to him, however, that they were withdrawn on the understanding that the press was to be apprised of any change in Mr. Harriman's condition through his office at 120 Broadway. He was told that nothing could be learned from that source to-day.

"It is true," said Dr. Lyle, "that Mr. Harriman has had a relapse. Yesterday he had a sharp attack of indigestion, but he is better to-day, and is now resting comfortably. We hope for the best."

Mr. Harriman's entire family is at Tower Hill, while Judge Robert S. Lovett, general counsel to most of the important Harriman interests, was summoned to Arden and arrived last night. It is said that two of the physicians who were called into consultation with Dr. George W. Crile, the Cleveland surgeon, shortly after Mr. Harriman's return from Europe, are again at Arden. They are Dr. Walter B. James of 17 West Fifty-fourth Street and Dr. George E. Brewer of 61 West Forty-eighth Street.

Dr. Lyle gave out this bulletin at 4 P. M.: "Mr. Harriman had an attack of acute indigestion at 11 P. M. last night, having partaken of a dinner a little heartier than his strength would allow. His condition is improved to-day, although there are still slight indications of a bad stomach."

At Dr. Brewer's home last night it was said that the doctor was at Cedar Camp in the Adirondacks, so far as any of his household here knew. He may have gone to Arden from there, however. There was no response to the telephone when a TIMES reporter tried to reach Dr. James's house over the wire.

DYNAMITE HOUSE AND PLANT.

Official Who Had Discharged Men Kicks Explosive to the Ground.

Special to The New York Times.

TYRONE, Penn., Sept. 6.—The handsome residence of Thomas Calderwood, an official of the American Lime and Stone Company, and all of the buildings of the company at the quarry near here, were completely wrecked and one unidentified fire engineer was killed by explosions of dynamite early to-day.

Calderwood some time ago discharged some foreign employes of his company, and it was the general belief here that the explosions were acts of revenge.

Mr. Calderwood arose at 5 o'clock and smelled something burning. Upon investigation he found a large bundle of dynamite securely bound with wire on his kitchen window. He immediately tore the window open, and kicked it to the ground, and shouted for his wife and daughter to run for their lives. They had barely reached the street before the explosion occurred. Every window in the house was smashed to atoms. The doors and walls were badly damaged. Windows for blocks were broken.

At the quarries a ton of dynamite had been stored. The whole amount was exploded, completely destroying the buildings about the works, and blowing a large steel car 100 feet from the tracks.

The home of Harry Houck, near the quarries, was completely destroyed. The scales used for weighing cars were wrecked, and windows were broken in the houses within a radius of five miles.

HUGHES'S DEPUTIES AT RACES

Make No Secret of Their Mission, but Find No Betting at Sheepshead Bay.

Four investigators of race-track conditions from Albany visited the Sheepshead Bay race course yesterday, as the representatives of Gov. Hughes, after presenting themselves, with credentials which were accepted, to Sheriff Hobley of Kings County

The investigators made no secret of their mission, but made no claim to official standing of any kind, except to say that they came to observe what was going on and ascertain the conditions concerning betting at the race track for a report to the Governor.

The visitors watched the proceedings of the holiday crowd through the afternoon, and agreed that they saw nothing fitting the description of race-track betting published in an afternoon newspaper early last week, which report caused Gov. Hughes to request reports from the New York police officials and the officials of Kings County on the matter of race-track bookmaking.

MISS STEWART A PRINCESS.

Emperor Francis Joseph Confers the Rank in Her Own Right.

VIENNA, Sept. 6.—Emperor Francis Joseph has conferred upon Miss Anita Stewart, whose marriage to Prince Miguel of Braganza will take place Sept. 15, the rank of Princess in her own right.

Miss Anita Stewart is the daughter of Mrs. James Henry Smith by her first husband, William Rhinelander Stewart, whom she divorced in South Dakota to marry Mr. Smith. When Mr. Smith died in Kobe, Japan, he left his stepdaughter an income of $40,000 a year, to which her mother will add another $40,000 a year on her marriage to Prince Miguel next month in London.

In order to get the consent of his father, Dom Miguel, the Prince had to renounce all claim to the throne of Portugal in favor of his younger brother, Prince Francis Joseph.

LONDON APPLAUDS PEARY'S EXPLOIT

Instant Acceptance of His Report a Contrast to Skepticism Toward Dr. Cook.

HAD AWAITED HIS VERDICT

Admiral Nares Thinks It Peculiar That the Announcements Should Come So Close Together.

Special Cable to THE NEW YORK TIMES.

LONDON, Sept. 6.—The news that Commander Robert E. Peary had reached the north pole was made known throughout London by late editions of the evening papers, which displayed the brief announcement under headlines which suggested none of the reservations with which the reports of the discovery by Dr. Cook have been received.

In marked contrast with the skepticism with which Dr. Cook's reports were printed is the immediate and whole-hearted acceptance of Peary's dispatch. Nothing could show this better than a comparison of headlines upon the two announcements.

A Difference in Headlines.

"North pole reached by Peary. Official news that the American flag was hoisted April 6, 1909." That is the way in which Commander Peary's dispatch is presented to its readers by a London paper which headed Dr. Cook's report as follows: "The north pole reported discovered. American explorer's statement."

With the general public a similar readiness to accept Commander Peary's statement is strikingly apparent and bears out the saying frequently heard here recently to the effect that had it been Commander Peary instead of Dr. Cook who had come forward with a bare announcement of the discovery of the pole not a single voice would have been raised in question. It is a testimony to Commander Peary's high reputation as a man and an explorer that the world accepts his word without a shadow of hesitation.

Had Awaited Peary's Testimony

Mr. Peary's announcement is hailed with peculiar satisfaction, because, throughout the controversy that has been raging in the last few days, it has been stated again and again that Mr. Peary's testimony would settle the question definitely. "Peary will know the truth," it was said. Thus, Peary is the witness for whom the whole world is waiting. There was a consensus of opinion among the people with whom I talked to-night that if Commander Peary contests the claims put forward by Dr. Cook, the latter will find it an extremely difficult task to establish his pretensions to be the discoverer of the pole, even should the "proofs" which he is now withholding prove to be as good as he says they are.

Cook Expects Confirmation.

Dr. Cook, on being informed in Copenhagen to-night of the news from Mr. Peary, said:

"I hope it is true, for Peary's reports will confirm all my claims."

An arctic explorer to whom to-night I showed Mr. Peary's message to THE NEW YORK TIMES, saying, "I have the pole," made the comment that Mr. Peary, by implication, denied any other claim to the honor of discovering the pole, and that, consequently, it was to be inferred that the confirmation which Dr. Cook expects from Mr. Peary is hardly likely to be forthcoming.

Peculiar Coincidence, Says Nares.

Sir George Nares, who led the arctic expedition of 1875-6, when interviewed to-night with regard to Commander Peary's message announcing the discovery, said:

"It is difficult to avoid the conclusion that Commander Peary's Eskimos at Etah must have known that Dr. Cook had crossed Smith's Sound and passed Etah last Winter to reach Ellesmere Land. Dr. Cook, then," continued the Admiral, "gets down from his Eskimo headquarters at Annotook to Upernavik by a Greenland route never before traversed, passing all the sea glaciers in Baffin Bay just in time to catch a Danish Government vessel which leaves Upernavik early in the year before the whaling vessels are due.

"My first impression was that Dr. Cook had got hold of Commander Peary's Eskimos in some way or other and ought to have communicated either with Commander Peary or with the Eskimos at Etah.

"The question now arises how it comes about that Cook and Peary announce at practically the same time the discovery of the north pole. Is it not a peculiar fact that this coincidence takes place, in view of the possibility of news having reached Etah of the success of one or the other of the men?"

Capt. Scott of the exploring ship Discovery stated to-night that Commander Peary's message put it beyond doubt that the Stars and Stripes was the first flag to fly at the north pole.

The Proper Witness Arrives.

"Just at the very moment when men were saying that only the evidence of an independent witness who had himself visited the north pole could estab-

Continued on Page 2.

In order not to miss The New York Times of to-morrow, in which will be printed exclusively Lieut. Peary's own story of his discovery of the North Pole, order a copy from your newsdealer early to-day.

COOK GLAD PEARY REACHED THE POLE

Unmoved When, Wreathed with Flowers at Banquet, He Hears the News.

HOPE NOW FOR OTHERS

Believes More Expeditions Will Reach the Pole Within the Next Ten Years.

COPENHAGEN, Sept. 6.—Copenhagen was electrified to-night by the report of Commander Peary's announcement that he had reached the north pole. Dr. Cook was immensely interested and said:

"That is good news. I hope Peary did get to the pole. His observations and reports on that region will confirm mine."

Asked if there was any probability of Peary's having found the tube containing his records, Dr. Cook replied:

"I hope so, but that is doubtful on account of the drift. Commander Peary would have reached the pole this year, probably, while I was there last year. His route was several hundred miles east of mine. We are rivals, of course, but the pole is good enough for two.

"The fact of two men having reached the pole along different paths," continued the explorer, "should furnish large additions to scientific knowledge. Probably other parties will reach it in the next ten years, since every explorer is helped by the experience of his predecessors, just as Sverdrup's observations and reports were of immeasurable help to me.

"I can say nothing more concerning Commander Peary's success without knowing further details, than that I am glad of it."

While Dr. Cook was conversing casually this morning with some friends, a possibility of the dénouement which electrified the world to-day was laughingly suggested. Dr. Cook remarked:

"It is quite possible that Peary will turn up now. He is about due to get back if he carries out his plans."

Those who have had the best opportunities to become acquainted with Dr. Cook here believe that he is not likely to enter into a controversy with Commander Peary.

It is doubtful if history furnishes a more dramatic episode than the breaking of the news to Dr. Cook that Peary had realized the goal of his life's ambition and repeated struggles. Dr. Cook was seated at a dinner, surrounded by explorers and correspondents, in the gilded ballroom of the Tivoli Casino. Around his neck was hung a garland of pink roses, according to the Scandinavian method of honoring heroes, which the explorer wore blushingly and with visible embarrassment. Several speeches, acclaiming him, had been given and repeated toasts to him drunk with clamorous cheers.

Amid this scene a whisper went around that Peary had planted the Stars and Stripes at the pole. Cook was perfectly cool and unmoved. He made a striking speech, in which he paid high tribute to the work of Sverdrup, who sat near, to whose discoveries he largely owed his success; to John R. Bradley, who had financed the expedition; to "the intelligence, endurance, and faithfulness" of the Eskimos who had assisted in the preparations, and those who had accompanied him. The whole story of the expedition, he said, has not come out, and will not come out for some time, nor will it come out in installments, but only when it is completed.

Dr. Cook did not permit the whispers which came to his ear of Peary's success to move him in the least, but when he had finished he was surrounded by correspondents who looked for some sign of emotion, but the explorer said smilingly: "I am glad."

Nothing but arctic exploration has been thought of here for the last few days. The people at first refused to believe that such a report as that telling of Peary's success had been received. They thought it must be a canard or a practical joke. The Danish news agency, which received the telegram from London, feared that it had been imposed upon and cabled to London for confirmation before it would circulate the report.

Minister Egan characterized it as one of the most dramatic events of history. The rumor spread that Peary was returning by way of Denmark, and this made an immense sensation. Some questioned the authority of the Peary telegram on the ground that it was improbable that a scientific man would use such dramatic language.

After the dinner to-night Dr. Cook stood about talking with Sverdrup and the other guests in a most unconcerned manner. Later, with the roses still decorating his shoulders, his hosts led him through the Casino grounds to an automobile. A crowd of several hundred, half of the number being women, surrounded and followed him, cheering, but the people were not able to get near enough to shake hands, because of a cordon of police.

PEARY DISCOVERS THE NORTH POLE AFTER EIGHT TRIALS IN 23 YEARS

Notifies The New York Times That He Reached It on April 6, 1909.

HE WIRES FROM LABRADOR

Returning on the Roosevelt, Which He Reports to Bridgman Is Safe.

IS NEARING NEWFOUNDLAND

Expects to Reach Chateau Bay To-day, When He Will Send Full Particulars.

McMILLAN SENDS WORD

Explorer's Companion Telegraphs Sister: "We Have the Pole on Board."

SEVEN VAIN EXPEDITIONS

Many Years Consumed in Learning the Feasible Route—Picked Men Were His Assistants.

Commander Robert E. Peary, U. S. N., has discovered the north pole. Following the report of Dr F. A. Cook that he had reached the top of the world comes the certain announcement from Mr. Peary, the hero of eight polar expeditions, covering a period of twenty-three years, that at last his ambition has been realized, and from all over the world comes full acknowledgment of Peary's feat and congratulations on his success.

The first announcement of Peary's exploit was received in the following message to THE NEW YORK TIMES:

> Indian Harbor, Labrador, via Cape Ray, N. F., Sept. 6.
> THE NEW YORK TIMES, New York:
> I have the pole, April sixth. Expect arrive Chateau Bay, September seventh. Secure control wire for me there and arrange expedite transmission big story. PEARY.

Following the receipt of Commander Peary's message to THE NEW YORK TIMES several other messages were received in this city from the explorer to the same effect.

Soon afterward The Associated Press received the following:

> INDIAN HARBOR, Via Cape Ray, N. F., Sept. 6.—To Associated Press, New York.
> Stars and Stripes nailed to the pole. PEARY.

To Herbert L. Bridgman, Secretary of the Peary Arctic Club, he telegraphed as follows:

> Herbert L. Bridgman, Brooklyn, N. Y.:
> Pole reached. Roosevelt safe. PEARY.

This message was received at the New York Yacht Club in West Forty-fourth Street:

> INDIAN HARBOR, Via Cape Ray, N. F., Sept. 6.—George A. Carmack, Secretary New York Yacht Club:
> Steam yacht Roosevelt, flying club burgee, has enabled me to add north pole to club's other trophies. (Signed) PEARY.

Cipher Shows Authenticity.

The telegram to Mr. Bridgman was sent in cipher. The cipher used was a private one and indicated clearly that the dispatch was undoubtedly from Commander Peary.

Commander Peary also sent a message to his wife at South Harpswell, Me., where she has been spending the Summer.

"Have made good at last," said the explorer to his wife. "I have the old pole. Am well. Love. Will wire again from Chateau."

The message was signed simply "Bert," an abbreviation of Robert, Commander Peary's first name. Mrs. Peary sent a wife's characteristic reply, with love and a blessing and a request for him to "hurry home."

By a strange coincidence, Mrs. Frederick A. Cook, too, was in South Harpswell, Me., when she received the first news from her husband.

Peary's Companion Reports.

Two messages were received in this country also from Donald B. McMillan, who accompanied Peary. Mr. McMillan was an instructor in mathematics and physical training at the academy in Worcester, Mass., until the close of school last year, when he obtained a leave of absence of two years to go on the Peary expedition.

In addition to his message to Dr. D. L. Abercrombie, Principal of the academy, Mr. McMillan sent the following to Mrs. W. C. Fogg, his sister, who is Postmistress at Freeport, Me.:

> Indian Harbor, Sept. 6, 1909.
> Mrs. W. C. Fogg, Freeport, Me.:
> Arrived safe. Pole on board. Best year of my life. BEN.

Follows Cook's Report Quickly.

These messages, flashed from the coast of Labrador to New York and thence to the four corners of the globe while Dr. Frederick A. Cook is being acclaimed by the crowned heads of Europe and the world at large as the discoverer of the north pole, added a remarkable chapter to the story of an achievement that has held the civilized world up to the highest pitch of interest since Sept. 1, when Dr. Cook's claim to having reached the "top of the world" was first telegraphed from the Shetland Islands.

The two explorers, Dr. Frederick A. Cook and Commander Robert E. Peary, both Americans, had been in the arctic seeking the goal of centuries, the impossible north pole, whose attainment has at times seemed beyond the reach of man. Both were determined and courageous, and both had started expressing the belief that their efforts would be crowned with success.

Peary the Better Known.

Peary was well known to both scientists and the general public as a persistent striver for the honor of reaching the "farthest north." Dr. Cook, on the other hand, had held the public attention to a lesser degree. He made his departure quietly and his purpose was hardly known except to those keenly interested in polar research.

Then suddenly, and with no word of warning, a steamer touched at Lerwick, in the Shetland Islands, and Dr. Cook's claim to having succeeded where expedition after expedition of the hardiest explorers of the world had failed was made known. Dr. Cook's announcement was that he had reached the pole on April 21, 1908.

Three days later Dr. Cook arrived at Copenhagen and received a welcome such as no explorer had ever received before.

Peary Announces Success.

Five days after the receipt of the Lerwick message, almost to the hour, came the sensational statement from Indian Harbor, Labrador, that Commander Peary also had been successful on his third expedition to the common goal, the date being April 6, 1909.

He filed his brief messages and continued on his way to the south, leaving the world to marvel at a dramatic situation such as has seldom been recorded—the double achievement of a purpose that for almost ten centuries had baffled the endeavor of man and taken many an explorer to his death in the frozen north.

It is almost certain that Commander Peary did not know of Dr. Cook's announcement when he sent his message from Indian Harbor.

Under ordinary circumstances Commander Peary's announcement would have evoked world-wide interest, but the existing conditions conspired to add many times to the importance of his communication.

According to Dr. Cook's account of his expedition, he buried the American flag at the pole in a metal tube; Peary's words would indicate that the Stars and Stripes were raised by him and left standing.

How the News Came.

The message from Commander Peary to THE NEW YORK TIMES was received in New York at 12:39 yesterday through the Postal Telegraph Company. It was handed in at Indian Harbor, Labrador, and was sent from there by wireless telegraph to Cape Ray, Newfoundland, and from Cape Ray to Port aux Basques by the Newfoundland Government land lines; thence to Canso, Nova Scotia, by cable, and to New York from there over the lines of the Commercial Cable Company.

WASHINGTON CREDITS PEARY.

Believes Cook, Too, but Has Said That He Must Produce Records.

Special to The New York Times.

WASHINGTON, Sept. 6.—There was instant acceptance among the geographers in Washington of the assertion in Commander Peary's laconic cable message that he had discovered the north pole. And there was just as ready rejoicing for Peary is popular with the scientific men in the National capitol, and they are ready to take his word at its face value without examination or delay.

In the manner of their acceptance this announcement of a second discovery of the point that has baffled discoverers for so many years there is a sharp contrast to the attitude of the same men toward the announcement from Dr. Cook. Most of them, indeed, accept Cook's assertion, and announce their belief that the Brooklyn man actually did reach the north pole in April, 1908. [illegible]

PEARY REPORTS TO THE TIMES

ANNOUNCES HIS DISCOVERY OF THE POLE AND WILL SEND A FULL AND EXCLUSIVE ACCOUNT TO-DAY.

Indian Harbor, Labrador, via Cape Ray, N. F., Sept. 6.

The New York Times, New York:

I have the pole, April sixth. Expect arrive Chateau Bay September seventh. Secure control wire for me there and arrange expedite transmission big story.

PEARY.

PEARY'S MESSAGE TO HIS WIFE.

SOUTH HARPSWELL, Me., Sept. 6.—Commander Robert E. Peary announced his success in discovering the North Pole to his wife, who is summering at Eagle Island here, as follows:

INDIAN HARBOR, via Cape Ray, Sept. 6, 1909.

Mrs. R. E. Peary, South Harpswell, Me.:

Have made good at last. I have the old Pole. Am well. Love. Will wire again from Chateau.

(Signed) BERT.

In replying Mrs. Peary sent the following dispatch:

SOUTH HARPSWELL, Me., Sept. 6, 1909.

To Commander R. E. Peary, Steamer Roosevelt, Chateau Bay:

All well. Best love. God bless you. Hurry home.

(Signed) JO.

CONFIRMED BY FELLOW-VOYAGER.

INDIAN HARBOR, Labrador, Sept. 6, 1909.

Dr. D. W. Abercrombie, Worcester Academy, Worcester, Mass.:

Top of the earth reached at last. Greetings to Faculty and boys.

(Signed) D. B. McMILLAN.

DR. COOK CABLES THE TIMES.

To the Editor of The New York Times:

COPENHAGEN, Sept. 6.

Glad Peary did it. Two records are better than one, and the work over a more easterly route has added value.

COOK.

"All the News That's Fit to Print."

The New York Times.

THE WEATHER.
Fair, slightly warmer Thursday; Friday, fair, warmer; moderate winds, becoming south.
For full weather report see Page 22.

VOL. LVIII...NO. 18,856. * * * NEW YORK, THURSDAY, SEPTEMBER 9, 1909.—TWENTY PAGES. ONE CENT In Greater New York, Jersey City, and Newark | Elsewhere, Two Cents.

COOK NOT NEAR POLE, SAYS PEARY; PROOFS STILL HELD BACK BY COOK

Two Eskimos Cited by Cook Told Peary He Never Went Far from Land.

SAYS "I HAVE COOK NAILED"

Cables His Wife Not to Worry About the Doctor's Claim to the Pole.

COOK TO ASK FOR AN INQUIRY

Says He Will Submit His Observations to Competent Scientists.

DOUBT OF HIS STORY GROWS

Cook's Supporters Here and Throughout Europe Greatly Worried by His Failure to Refute Peary.

This message from Commander Peary to The New York Times was received at 4:57 o'clock yesterday morning:

INDIAN HARBOR, via Cape Ray, N. F., Sept. 8.—Cook's story should not be taken too seriously. The Eskimos who accompanied him say that he went no distance north. He did not get out of sight of land. Other men of the tribe corroborate their statements. Kindly give this to all home and foreign news associations for the same wide distribution as Cook's story. PEARY.

Commander Peary also sent this message to Mrs. Peary at Portland, Me., yesterday, telling her not to worry about Dr. Cook's assertions:

"Indian Harbor, Labrador,
"Via Cape Ray, N. F., Sept. 8.
"Good morning. Delayed by gale. Don't let Cook story worry you. Have him nailed.
"BERT."

COOK DEMANDS A TRIBUNAL.

Still Declares He Has Proofs—Withholds Them, Despite Urging.

COPENHAGEN, Sept. 8.—This is Dr. Cook's reply to Commander Peary:

"I have been to the north pole. As I said last night when I heard of Commander Peary's success, if he says he has been to the north pole, I believe him.

"I am willing to place facts, figures, and worked-out observations before a joint tribunal of the scientific bodies of the world. In due course I shall be prepared to make public an announcement that will effectually dispel any doubt, if there can be such, of the fact that I reached the pole. But, knowing that I am right and that right must prevail, I will submit at the proper time my full story to the court of last resort—the people of the world.

Won't Enter Into a Controversy.

"I will not enter into any controversy over the subject with Commander Peary, further than to say that if he says I have taken his Eskimos my reply is that Eskimos are nomads. They are owned by nobody and are not the private property of either Commander Peary or myself. The Eskimos engaged by me were paid ten times what they agreed to accompany me for.

"As to the story that Commander Peary says I took provisions stored by him, my reply is that Peary took my provisions, obtaining them from the custodian on the plea that I had been so long absent that he was going to organize relief stations for me in case I should be alive. For this I have documentary proof."

Concern in Copenhagen.

Coming so quickly upon other dramatic incidents of the week, Commander Peary's dispatch denying that Dr. Cook had achieved the triumph for which he has been fêted and honored in Copenhagen beyond the lot of any other private person, has been read here with feelings of amazement and concern.

But Dr. Cook himself seems in no wise disturbed. He was perfectly cool and apparently unmoved when confronted to-light with telegrams from the United States saying that Commander Peary had denounced him as an imposter. His demeanor has not changed in the slightest from the day he landed at Copenhagen.

Dr. Cook's friends had urged him to their utmost to make any statement possible for the public, but he had said repeatedly that all he had to say for the present was that he possessed proofs that he had visited the north pole on April 21, 1908. Those proofs were convincing and would in due time be given to the world.

Doesn't Fear Public Clamor.

When it was suggested to him that his chances of proving his case might be ruined unless he made a satisfactory statement immediately, he smiled—his usual quiet smile, and asked how could a man be ruined by popular clamor calling him an imposter when he had proofs in his case which could and would be published, as he had oftimes repeated, when they were in proper form to be given out.

Dr. Cook told Capt. Sverdrup and another friend the day after he landed here that he hoped there would be no unpleasantness over supplies with the Peary party; that he had found some of Peary's men in possession of one of his depots and had turned them out unceremoniously.

It is settled that Cook will send a ship back to bring to America the two Eskimos who accompanied him on the last stage of his journey to the pole, as well as some of the party who were sent back when the start of the last stage began. Capt. Sverdrup may command the expedition. It is Dr. Cook's desire that he shall do so, and they conferred for some hours to-day regarding the details of the expedition.

Dr. Cook's purpose in bringing his Eskimo comrades to America is to have them relate their stories of the trip to the pole. He proposes to have them examined by any men familiar with the arctic and the Eskimo, including the members of Commander Peary's party, if they wish. Dr. Cook's apparent confidence is the greatest factor working in his support in Copenhagen. Those who have had the opportunity to talk with him are only of one mind, that he is an absolutely sincere, simple man, or deserves a pedestal in history as one of the greatest of actors.

PROOFS TO-DAY, SAYS COOK.

But Grave Doubt Is Felt That He Can Supply Them.

By PHILIP GIBBS.

Special Cable to THE NEW YORK TIMES.
Dispatch to The London Daily Chronicle.

COPENHAGEN, Sept. 8.—The most profound sensation was produced and great excitement prevailed to-day in Copenhagen after Dr. Cook's lecture last night. People who would have staked their lives upon his honesty were now full of the most terrible doubts. The lecture was a fiasco of the first magnitude and seemed so obviously a story of the imagination, wildly improbable and unsupported by a shred of scientific facts, that those many explorers who were present in this city of explorers and who stood by Cook now felt shattered in their belief. Some of them went to Cook early this morning and told him that unless he produced the strongest evidence of his claim within twenty-four hours they would denounce him as an impostor. To this he said:

"I will produce my proofs within twenty-four hours."

Immediately after that declaration Peary's telegrams were published in Copenhagen. The effect was immediately seen in the Danish newspapers. They had upheld Dr. Cook, and had denounced me personally for my daily criticism of Cook's story. Now they come out with articles headed "Is Cook an Impostor?" and Danish journalists came to interview the English journalist who had been alone in his disbelief. That was the only amusing thing in a day which had been too exciting and too strenuous. I had many things to do. I had first of all to see Cook himself and ask him what he had to say about Peary's words. He said:

"I shall say very little about what Peary says. It does not matter to me. Wait a little while and you will see."

I must now say that this man Frederick Cook is the most remarkable, most amazing man I have ever met. He calls me his enemy, but I have no personal animosity against him, and I will say honestly that I am filled with a sense of profound admiration for him. If he is an impostor he is also a very brave man—a man with such iron nerve, such miraculous self-control, and such magnificent courage in playing his game, that he will count for ever among the greatest impostors of the world. That and not the discovery of the north pole shall be his claim to immortality.

Here was this man doubted by all who had acclaimed him a hero, with his story strongly discounted by Peary, pursued by circumstantial evidence, and threatened within twenty-four hours by the almost certain possibility of final exposure, and yet he faced the world, defied criticism, and smiled and smiled again.

I was in the same room with him for two hours to-day, a drawing room into which came a stream of distinguished people, full of suspicion about him. But, ceremoniously polite, he stood among them haking hands and bowing and smiling. He was haggard, and there were deep lines upon his face, but his hand was perfectly steady as he took a cup of tea and still he smiled.

Now what is Cook's answer to the challenge of Peary; to that ultimatum given by the explorers and scientists of Denmark? His answer is:

"I will produce my observations and records and instruments before the university to-morrow. They shall see everything, and I shall prove the truth of my story to the world."

To these words I say Cook cannot prove his story to-morrow or the day after. Cook has no proof in Copenhagen to give the university, and if the committee which is to make the examination says, "We are satisfied," then I say beforehand they will be satisfied without proof, without any trustworthy evidence whatever, as Prof. Stromgren was satisfied without proof or evidence, because I had evidence to-day still further proving that Cook cannot produce proof to-morrow. I had that evidence from one of the most distinguished men of science in Europe, whose word cannot be doubted, and who still believes, or tries to believe, in Cook, and I had that evidence from Frederick Cook himself. I will give briefly the gist of two remarkable interviews, first with Dr. de Querlain Chief of the Swiss-German expedition and joint Director of the Swiss Central Meteorological Institute. This interview was before three witnesses and the special correspondent of a London journal, Comte de Lesdain, and myself. The following questions were asked and answered:

"Do you know Cook well?"

"I was four weeks with him. Upon his return, coming back with him in the Hans Egede, we had long conversations."

"Did he show you any of his observations?"

"No; but he said he would show them to me. I pointed out to him the importance of putting forward proofs to satisfy public opinion, and it was for that reason I suggested he should show me his observations, as, of course, I have had long training experience in these matters."

"And did he?"

"No. I regret to say that when I asked him again he said he would prefer not to do so."

No Observations on Hans Egede.

"Are you sure he had any observations on board?"

"I could not be sure. He had a box on board in which he said he had papers. Most of his books went by boat—Whitney's boat—from Greenland to America."

"Would it be possible for him to make imaginary observations?"

"I do not say it would be impossible, but it would be very difficult."

"Did he have proper instruments with him?"

"He had a sextant and chronometers."

"Was this sextant an ordinary one?"

"He told me it was a better sextant than the ordinary one used in the navy."

"Has he brought his instruments to Copenhagen?"

"No, he sent them to America."

"But is it not necessary to test these instruments before the value of the observations can be proved?"

"Strictly speaking, that is so."

After this interview, in which every answer was drawn painfully and reluctantly from a man desiring to shield his friend but compelled by conscience to tell the truth. Dr. de Querlain signed a document in which he made this remarkable statement. The following are his exact words:

"I recognize that Cook, with whom I passed several weeks on board the Hans Egede, has given me the impression of a man who understands quite well how to take observations. Moreover, Knud Rasmussen, who passed some time with Cook after the return of the latter from the pole, has received favorable evidence of Cook's story from Eskimos who knew two men who accompanied Cook and believes Cook has been to the pole.

Didn't Tell of Meeting Rasmussen.

The later part of his statement is startling. Cook never referred to his meeting with Rasmussen upon his homeward journey. Rasmussen's letter to his wife suggests a direct contradiction of Cook upon a material point, and from the lips of Mrs. Rasmussen and Mr. Freuken, an explorer in whose hands I first saw this letter, I heard the words that Mr. Rasmussen does not believe in Cook's claim. They have repeated that to others.

This, however, is not part of my main evidence. The essential point in the above interview is Cook's refusal to show Querlain his observations after his promise to do so, and Querlain's statement that Cook's instruments and most of his books have been sent to America by way of Greenland. I now come to Cook himself. This morning I put the following questions to him in the presence of Comte de Lesdain.

"Have you any original observations in Copenhagen?"

"At first Cook refused to answer this question. He then said:

"I have in Copenhagen results of my observations only, but my instruments and the working out of my observations have been packed with great care and are on their way to America."

"Why have you not shown your observations and instruments to any Danish or other scientist?"

"I have not done so because I prom-

Continued on Page 3.

Latest Shipping News.

Arrived—Steamer Pennsylvania, Hamburg, Aug. 28.

COMMANDER PEARY'S PRELIMINARY ACCOUNT OF HIS SUCCESSFUL VOYAGE TO THE NORTH POLE

He Sends to The Times by Wireless a Summary, to be Followed by His Full Report—Record of His Swift Progress to the Utmost North.

FROM CAPE COLUMBIA UP IN 37 DAYS, BACK IN 16 DAYS

Prof. Ross G. Marvin, of Cornell, Drowned on April 10, Forty-five Miles North of Cape Columbia, While Leading the Supporting Party.

BATTLE HARBOR, Labrador, Via Wireless Cape Ray, N. F., Sept. 8.—As it may be impossible to get my full story through in time for to-morrow's TIMES, partly as a prelude which may stimulate interest and partly to forestall possible leaks, I am sending you a brief summary of my voyage to the North Pole, which is to be printed exactly as written.

SUMMARY OF NORTH POLAR EXPEDITION OF THE PEARY ARCTIC CLUB.

The steamer Roosevelt left New York on July 6, 1908; left Sydney on July 17; arrived at Cape York, Greenland, August 1; left Etah, Greenland, August 8; arrived Cape Sheridan, at Grantland, September 1; wintered at Cape Sheridan.

The sledge expedition left the Roosevelt February 15, 1909, and started for the North. Arrived at Cape Columbia March 1; passed British record March 2; delayed by open water March 2 and 3; held up by open water March 4 to 11; crossed the 84th parallel March 11; encountered open lead March 15; crossed 85th parallel March 1[illegible]; crossed 86th parallel March 23d; encountered open lead March 23d; passed Norwegian record March 23d; passed Italian record March 24th; encountered open lead March 26th; crossed 87th parallel March 27th; passed American record March 28; encountered open lead March 28; held up by open water March 29; crossed 88th parallel April 2; crossed 89th parallel April 4; North Pole April 6.

All returning left North Pole April 7, reached Cape Columbia April 23, arriving on board Roosevelt April 27.

The Roosevelt left Cape Sheridan July 18; passed Cape Sabine August 8; left Cape York August 26; arrived at Indian Harbor with all members of expedition returning in good health except Prof. Ross G. Marvin, unfortunately drowned April 10, when forty-five miles north of Cape Columbia, returning from 86° North Latitude in command of the supporting party.

ROBERT E. PEARY.

MAP SHOWING PEARY'S ROUTE TO THE POLE.

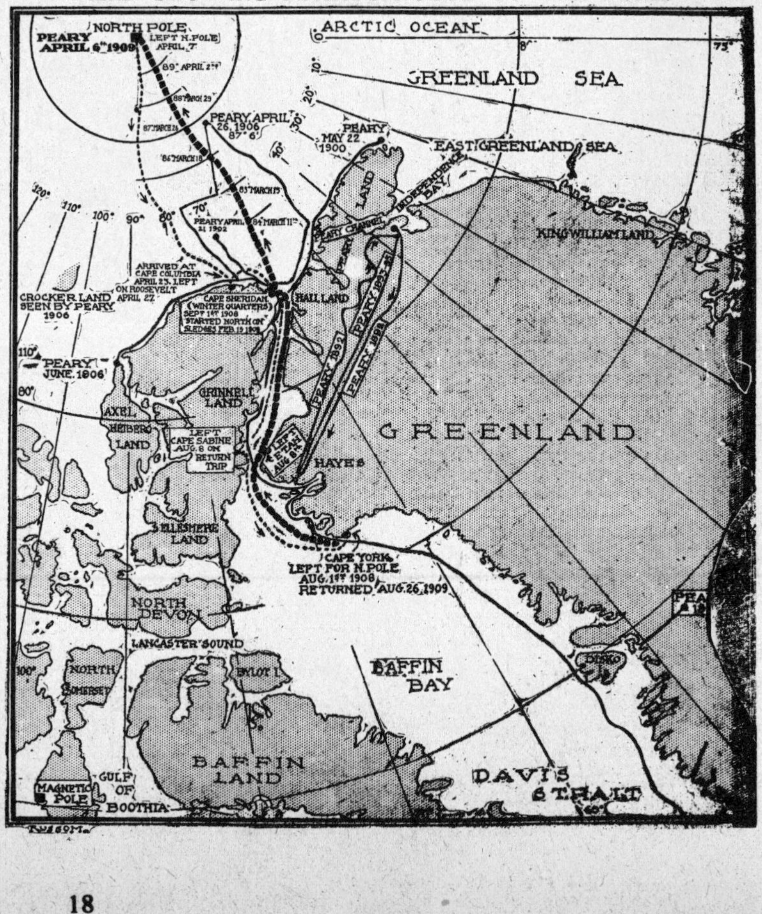

Dr. Cook in the Polar regions.

The Bettmann Archive

Robert E. Peary aboard his ship, the *Roosevelt*.

"All the News That's Fit to Print."

The New York Times.

THE WEATHER.
Fair, slightly warmer Thursday; Friday, fair, warmer; moderate winds, becoming south.
For full weather report see Page 22.

VOL. LVIII...NO. 18,857. * * * NEW YORK, FRIDAY, SEPTEMBER 10, 1909.—TWENTY PAGES. ONE CENT In Greater New York, Jersey City, and Newark { Elsewhere, TWO CENTS.

HARRIMAN DEAD; NEWS DELAYED

Financier's End Came at 1:30 o'Clock, with His Family About His Bedside.

SISTER LETS SECRET OUT

The Official Announcement Had Set the Hour of Death Some Two Hours Later.

HIS AILMENT UNREVEALED

Cancer or Tuberculosis of the Bowels Each Said to be the Cause.

GREAT RAILROAD ORGANIZER

Universal Tributes to His Genius and Indomitable Courage—The Financial World Not Taken Unaware.

Special to The New York Times.

TURNER, N. Y., Sept. 9.—Edward H. Harriman died at Arden House this afternoon at 1:30 o'clock. The news of his death was withheld for two hours, when official announcement was made that the financier had passed away at 3:35 o'clock.

All the members of Mr. Harriman's family were around his bedside when the end came. Dr. William Gordon Lyle, the family physician, was the only medical man present. The cause of death has not been made public yet, but there seems little doubt that it was cancer in the abdominal region, although another theory heard here is that the ailment was tuberculosis of the bowels.

It is impossible to get into communication with Arden House to-night, either by road or by telephone. Guards armed with heavy sticks block all the approaches to the house on the hill; the telephone operator refuses to answer calls.

Mrs. Cornelia Simons, sister of the dead financier and wife of Charles D. Simons, is authority for the statement that her brother passed away at about 1:30 o'clock. Reporters found her at her home at the foot of Tower Hill immediately after her return from the death bed. With her was her husband, who, however, was not present when Mr. Harriman died. When the reporters approached her as she was about to enter her home she said:

"Of course, you have heard the sad news. I was with him when he died."

Died at 1:30 Sister Says.

A reporter offered his condolences, remarking that many people considered Mr. Harriman the greatest man in America.

"Yes, he was the prince of them all," said Mrs. Simons.

"What time did Mr. Harriman die?" asked a reporter.

"About 1:30," she replied without hesitation.

"What was the cause of death?"

Mrs. Simons held up her hand deprecatingly.

"Don't ask me that," she said. "I cannot talk to you. You will have to see Dr. Lyle about that."

Mr. Simons explained that he had been in New York all day, and arrived back at Arden station on the 5:25 o'clock train with Judge Robert S. Lovett, Mr. Harriman's general counsel.

"What time did Mr. Harriman die?" a reporter asked him.

"Why, he died at 3:35 o'clock," was the answer.

"Then Mrs. Simons was mistaken when she said he died at 1:30?" he was asked.

Mr. Simons appeared confused.

"I wasn't there, you see," he said. "I got here after he died."

"What was the cause of death?"

"I have my suspicions. I don't care to say. You had better ask Dr. Lyle."

Family at His Bedside.

At the request of the reporters, Mrs. Simons named those who were present at the bedside when the end came. They were Mrs. Harriman, Orlando H. Harriman, brother; Mrs. Cornelia Simons, sister; Walter Averell Harriman, eldest surviving son; Mr. and Mrs. Robert Livingston Gerry, the latter of whom is a daughter of Mr. Harriman; Miss Mary Harriman and Miss Carol Harriman, daughters; Roland Harriman, the youngest son; Dr. W. G. Lyle, and two nurses.

That the end came suddenly and unexpectedly is asserted by all at the house with whom the reporters talked. That it was not a surprise, however, was admitted by Mr. Simons, who when asked the question replied: "No, we have realized his condition."

The first intimation of the end reached the watching newspaper men here just before 4 o'clock this afternoon. It came from the office of a morning newspaper, and said: "The Union Pacific office announces Harriman's death at 3:35."

A few moments earlier the Rev. J. Holmes McGuinness, rector of St. John's Episcopal Church at Arden and Mr. Harriman's chaplain, had driven past Turner Station in an automobile on his way to Arden House. The machine was speeding at something like fifty miles an hour. It was learned later that he had been summoney from the Harriman home by telephone at 1:10 o'clock, but was out then. Consequently he was not present when Mr. Harriman died.

No Operation Performed.

On receiving the message from New York, Arden House was communicated with by telephone. After a good deal of hesitation and delay the operator there said: "The news is correct; Mr. Harriman died at 3:35."

"Was an operation performed?"

At this question Mrs. Simons, who had overheard the interview with her husband came forward.

"No, there has been no operation," she said. Then both retired into the house.

At 9:30 o'clock yesterday morning Judge Lovett had stopped at the press room at Turner Station on his way to New York just long enough to hand in this bulletin, signed by Dr. Lyle:

"Mr. Harriman's condition remains unchanged."

All the morning persistent rumors of Mr. Harriman's death were in circulation here, as well as in New York. Finally, at 1:45 P. M., Arden House was again communicated with by telephone and told that the report was so strong that only a direct statement from Dr. Lyle could set the matter at rest.

After a little delay the answer came back: "Dr. Lyle authorizes me to say that Mr. Harriman is not dead. You cannot emphasize this too strongly, he says."

Was Conscious to the Last.

From excellent authority it is learned that Mr. Harriman was conscious almost to the last. In fact, in the earlier part of the morning his condition was such that Judge Lovett did not hesitate to go to New York. The fact that only one physician was in the house at the end shows that death came suddenly.

It was about noon that a change for the worse in the financier's condition became apparent. Oxygen and all known methods were used to prolong his life, but to no avail. He sank rapidly and died an hour and a half after the change was noticed.

Wedding Party Just After Death.

Within four hours of the death of Mr. Harriman a wedding party left Arden House. For some days it has been known that the wedding of Mary Spalding, a parlor maid, who has been in the employ of Mr. Harriman for some time, had been arranged for this afternoon to George Murphy, head machinist on the Harriman estate. With their master in so serious a condition, the bride went to Mrs. Harriman this morning and suggested a postponement of the nuptials. Mrs. Harriman, evidently not knowing how ill her husband was, would not hear of any delay, and the marriage was set for 4:30 o'clock this afternoon at St. Mary's, the pretty little Roman Catholic church, at the foot of Tower Hill.

Just before 4 o'clock this afternoon the wedding party, numbering some forty people, all employes at Arden House, left the sorrowful Harriman home and proceeded in a wagonette down the hill to the church. Thirty-eight of them knew the sad news, but it had been kept from the bride and bridegroom. They were married by the Rev. Father H. F. MacAran without knowing of the death of their employer, and departed for New York at 6:15 o'clock on a train which was stopped specially for them at Arden. The bridegroom had received as a wedding gift from Mr. Harriman a check for $500.

Deep Regret in Arden.

Charles T. Ford, who is superintendent of the Harriman estate here and whom the dead financier honored with his personal friendship, was greatly overcome by his employer's death. With tears streaming down his cheeks he said to the reporters:

"I suppose you know that Mr. Harriman passed away. He had been sinking rapidly since noon. Dr. Lyle told me he was conscious almost to the last. There was no operation. Dr. Lyle has just told me he has nothing further to say at this time, except that Mr. Harriman sank very rapidly, and passed away at 3:35."

Mr. Ford said that about noon, when the change for the worse set in, he stopped the men at work on the grounds of Arden House, of whom there were some 300 or 400. They were not, however, sent down the hill until just before 4 o'clock. This was in order not to rouse suspicion among the villagers. Most of the men are employed on the mountain railway, which is nearing completion.

Harriman Thought He Improved.

That Mr. Harriman sincerely believed he was improving when he sent the note to the newspapers requesting the withdrawal of their representatives last week is borne out by the fact that there were no physicians at the Harriman home in the latter part of last week. Dr. Lyle left Arden House on Wednesday, intending to stay in New York for a few days. When Mr. Harriman had the first relapse on Sunday, Dr. Lyle was immediately summoned by telephone, and arrived on Sunday evening. Since then he had been in constant attendance on his patient up to the end.

On Monday Dr. Walter B. James of New York was summoned here. He did not leave until last night.

Saw Harriman, Clerk Said.

Among the callers at Arden House this morning was T. B. Price of Mr. Harriman's office in New York. He arrived on the 10:40 train, bringing with him papers for Mr. Harriman's perusal, he said. He went to the house, and returned to the station at 1:45 o'clock, to catch the train back to New York.

Mr. Price must have left Arden house only about an hour before his chief died, yet he was emphatic in saying he had seen Mr. Harriman. Asked concerning the latter's condition, he said it was "fairly encouraging."

An attempt was made by the reporters to get to Arden house shortly before 6 o'clock to-night. Within 200 yards of it they were met by a band of guards, who said their instructions were to allow no one to pass and to take no communications to the house.

While the reporters were parleying with the guards an automobile came from the house. In it was the Rev. Dr. McGuinness. Within two minutes Mrs. Simmons, weeping, followed in a runabout driven by a Harriman coachman. Then from the opposite direction came an automobile containing Judge Lovett and two other men who had just arrived from New York. Judge Lovett later sent out word that he had nothing to say.

"End of a Worn-Out Man."

"The real cause of Mr. Harriman's death will probably never be known," said Robert L. Gerry, son-in-law of the dead financier, to-night, "that is, unless an autopsy is performed, which at present seems improbable."

Charles A. Peabody, Orlando H. Harriman, and the latter's nephew, before leaving Arden for New York to-night, refused to discuss the nature of the disease of which Mr. Harriman died.

It was learned to-night that the funeral will take place at Arden on Sunday at 3:30 o'clock and will be private. The burial will be in the little cemetery attached to St. John's Episcopal Church at Arden. It is here that Mr. Harriman's eldest son, Edward H. Harriman, Jr., was buried some twenty years ago, about a year after the Harrimans came here to live.

A member of the Harriman family, when asked to-night as to the cause of death, replied: "It was simply the end of a worn-out man."

The news of Mr. Harriman's death caused some consternation among the villagers here and at Central Valley and Highland Mills, many of whom are dependent for their livelihood on the Harriman estate. Everywhere groups of them are to be seen earnestly talking over the future. One and all are deeply affected, and vie with each other in telling of some kind action which emanated from the "House on the Hill."

TRIBUTES TO HARRIMAN.

Men of Prominence Make Estimates of His Worth.

Bankers, railway Presidents, railroad managers, Wall Street men, old friends, the men who financed Mr. Harriman's properties, those who had been counted his strong rivals in the railroad world and finance, and his associates and coworkers generally, all united yesterday in paying their tribute of praise to Mr. Harriman's genius as a wonderful organizer and executive whose place it would be impossible to fill, as he had filled it so uniquely.

James J. Hill, who has been E. H. Harriman's keenest rival since the latter first became a real factor in the railroad world, was much moved at the news of Mr. Harriman's death. He was loath to comment on Mr. Harriman's work in the railroad world or to discuss the question of a successor. "Poor fellow," he said, "this has been a long time coming. He has suffered a lot. It would seem that he was beyond human aid. Perhaps he is better off. I believe he is happy now. It is too bad that he could not have been spared to carry on his work. Perhaps if he had lived longer he would have settled down more."

Mr. Hill said he anticipated no financial disturbance as a result of Mr. Harriman's death. The affairs of his roads were in fine shape, he said.

Burned Candle at Both Ends, Hill Says.

"We all die, but the world goes on somehow," said Mr. Hill, "yet Mr. Harriman's place will be a hard one to fill. He did the work of many men, but he burned the candle at both ends."

Mr. Hill, although the so-called Hill-Harriman fights for supremacy in the Northwest have waged almost continuously for many years, always maintained pleasant personal relations with his rival, as he indicated yesterday.

"I have done a great deal of business with Mr. Harriman," said Mr. Hill. "Some of it was pretty strenuous, but we have always remained good friends. I had a high regard for his personality and was his warm admirer."

Jacob H. Schiff, when asked to comment on Mr. Harriman's career, said that his relations with Mr. Harriman had been so long standing and personal and the sense of loss in his death so keen that at the moment he felt it impossible to give expression to his thoughts.

James Stillman, Chairman of the Board of Directors of the National City Bank, said: "Mr. Harriman's death grieves me so keenly, in the loss that it brings of a close friend, that I hesitate to trust myself to speak at any length of his career or his genius. I have long regarded him as one of the most remarkable geniuses that ever developed in business life. He has been an upbuilder and has left a permanent impression on the map and in the development of the country. The world has known few minds that had such a grasp of large relations and problems, and at the same time such a firm grip upon details and such ability for successful execution."

President Brown's Tribute.

W. C. Brown, President of the New York Central and a co-Director of Mr. Harriman, said of him: "The death of Mr Harriman removed one of the greatest figures of the generation in the business and financial world. The Union and Southern Pacific Railroads, both transformed by his materful hand from financial and physical wrecks to the magnificent properties they are to-day, will perhaps be the most enduring monument to his marvelous executive ability and constructive genius. In all he did his first thought was to do that which would contribute most to the growth and development of the country.

"The world knows of his greatness in

Continued on Page 6.

NEWSPAPERS ENJOINED.

In view of the fact that The New York World and The New York Sun published yesterday Commander Peary's preliminary report, taken from The London Times and cabled to New York, in violation of The New York Times's copyright, Federal Judge Hand issued last night an order restraining those two newspapers from infringing the copyright on Commander Peary's report in this morning's issue of The New York Times. The order is returnable before Judge Hand in the Federal Building at noon to-day.

INJUNCTION IN CHICAGO.

Judge Grosscup in Chicago last night granted at the instance of The Chicago Tribune an order restraining The Record-Herald, The Inter-Ocean, The Examiner and the American of that city from publishing the copyrighted Peary article or any part of it.

INJUNCTION IN TORONTO.

A similar order was granted in Toronto to the Toronto Globe against the Toronto Mail and Empire.

PEARY'S STORY OF HIS MARCH OVER THE ICE FROM CAPE COLUMBIA TOWARD THE NORTH POLE

His Narrative, So Far As Received, Takes Him to a Point Above the "Farthest North" of Nansen and the Duke of the Abruzzi.

SWIFT DASH DESPITE ROUGH ICE, LAKES, AND MISHAPS

Borup Thrown Into the Water—McMillan Frostbitten, is Sent Back—"Beware of the Leads" is Peary's Last Warning to Marvin—Story Teems with Praise for Others.

BATTLE HARBOR, Labrador, (via Marconi Wireless, Cape Ray, N. F.,) Sept. 9.—The steamer Roosevelt, bearing the North Polar expedition of the Peary Arctic Club, parted company with the Erik and steamed out of Etah Ford late in the afternoon of Aug. 18, 1908, setting the usual course for Cape Sabine. The weather was dirty, with fresh southerly winds. We had on board 22 Eskimo men, 17 women, and 10 children, 226 dogs, and some 40-odd walrus.

We encountered the ice a short distance from the mouth of the harbor, but it was not closely packed and was negotiated by the Roosevelt without serious difficulty. As we neared Cape Sabine the weather cleared somewhat, and we passed close by Three Voort Island and Cape Sabine, easily making out with the naked eye the house at Hayes Harbor occupied by me in the Winter of 1901-2.

From Cape Sabine north there was so much water that we thought of setting the lug sail before the southerly wind; but a little later appearance of ice to the northward stopped this. There was clean open water to Cape Albert, and from there scattered ice to a point about abreast of Victoria Head, thick weather and dense ice bringing us some ten or fifteen miles away.

From here we drifted south somewhat, and then got a slant to the northward out of the current. We worked a little further north, and stopped again for some hours. Then we again worked westward and northward till we reached a series of lakes, coming to a stop a few miles south of the Windward's Winter quarters at Cape Durville. From here, after some delay, we slowly worked a way northeastward through fog and broken ice of medium thickness through one night and the forenoon of the next day, only emerging into open water and clear weather off Cape Fraser.

From this point we had a clear run through the middle of Robeson Channel, uninterrupted by either ice or fog, to Lady Franklin Bay. Here we encountered both ice and fog, and while working along in search of a practicable opening were forced across to the Greenland coast at Thank God Harbor.

The fog lifted there, and enabled us to make out our whereabouts; and we steamed north through a series of leads past Cape Lupton, and thence southward toward Cape Union. A few miles off that cape we were stopped by impracticable ice, and we drifted back south to Cape Union, where we stopped again.

TWICE FORCED AGROUND.

We lay for some time in a lake of water, and then, to prevent being drifted south again, took refuge under the north shore of Lincoln Bay, in nearly the identical place where we had our unpleasant experiences three years before. Here we remained for several days during a period of constant and at times violent northeasterly winds.

Twice we were forced aground by the heavy ice; we had our port quarter rail broken and a hole stove in the bulwarks; and twice we pushed out in an attempt to get north, but we were forced back each time to our precarious shelter.

Fnally, on Sept. 2, we squeezed around Cape Union and made fast in a shallow niche in the ice; but after some hours we made another short run to Black Cape, and hung on to a grounded bit of ice. At last, a little after midnight of Sept. 5, we passed through extremely heavy running ice into a stream of open water, rounded Cape Rawson, and passed Cape Sheridan.

Within a quarter of an hour of the same time we arrived three years before—7 A. M., Sept. 5—we reached the open water extending beyond Cape Sheridan. We steamed up to the end of it, and it appeared practicable at first to reach Porter Bay, near Cape Joseph Henley, which I had for my Winter quarters. But the outlook being unsatisfactory, I went back and put the Roosevelt into the only opening in the floe, being barred close to the mouth of the Sheridan River, a little north of our position three years prior.

The season was further advanced than in 1905; there was more snow on the ground, and the new ice inside the floe bergs was much thicker. The work of discharging the ship was commenced at once and rushed to completion. The supplies and equipment we sledged across ice and sea and deposited on shore. A house and workshop were built of board, covered with sails and fitted with stoves, and the ship was snug for Winter in shoal water, where she touched bottom at low tide. This settlement on the stormy shores of the Arctic Ocean was christened Hubbardville.

Hunting parties were sent out Sept. 10, and a bear was brought in on the 12th and some deer a day or two later.

MOVING THE SUPPLIES.

On Sept. 15 the full work of transporting supplies to Cape Columbia was inaugurated. Marvin, with Dr. Goodsall and Borup and the Eskimos, took sixteen sledge loads of supplies to Cape Belknap, and on the 27th the same party started with loads to Porter Bay. The work of hunting and transporting supplies was prosecuted continuously by the members of the party and the Eskimos until Nov. 5, when the supplies for the Spring sledge trip had been removed from Winter quarters and deposited at various places from Cape Colan to Cape Columbia.

In the latter part of September the movement of the ice subjected the ship to a pressure which listed her to port some 8 or 10 degrees, and she did not recover till the following Spring. On Oct. 1 I went on a hunt with two Eskimos across the field and Parr Bay and the peninsula, made the circuit of Clemants Markham Inlet, and returned to the ship in seven days with fifteen musk oxen, a bear, and a deer. Later, in October, I repeated the trip, obtaining five musk oxen and hunting parties secured some forty deer.

Prof. McMillan went to Columbia in November and obtained a month of tidal observations, returning in December. In the December moon Borup moved the Hecla depot to Cape Colan; Bartlett made a hunting trip overland to Lake Hazen, and Hansen went to Clemants Markham Inlet. In the January moon Marven crossed Robeson Channel and went to Cape Bryant for tidal and meteorological observations; Bartlett crossed the channel and made the circuit of Newman Bay, and explored the peninsula. After he returned Goodsell went to Markham Inlet and Borup toward Lake Hazen, in the interior, on hunting trips.

In the February moon Bartlett went to Cape Hecla, Goodsell moved some more supplies from Hecla to Cape Colan, and Borup went to Markham Inlet on a hunting trip. On Feb. 15 Bartlett left the Roosevelt with his division for Cape Columbia and Parr Bay. Goodsell, Borup, McMillan, and Hansen followed on successive days with their provisions. Marven returned from Bryants on Feb. 17 and left for Cape Columbia Feb. 21. I brought up the rear Feb. 22.

The total of all divisions leaving the Roosevelt were 7 members of the party, 59 Eskimos, 140 dogs, and 23 sledges. By Feb. 27 such of the Cape Colan depot as was needed had been brought up to Cape Columbia, the dogs were rested and the rationed and harnessed, and the sledges and other gear overhauled.

HEWING THROUGH ICE.

Four months of northerly winds during the Fall and Winter instead of southerly ones, as during the previous season, led me to expect less open water than before, but a great deal of rough ice and I was prepared to hew a road through the jagged ice for the first hundred miles or so and then cross the big lead.

On the last day of February Bartlett, with his pioneer division, accomplished this, and his division got away due north over the ice on March 1. The remainder of the party got away on Bartlett's trail, and I followed an hour later.

The party now comprised 7 members of the expedition, 17 Eskimos, 133 dogs, and 19 sledges. One Eskimo and seven dogs had gone to pieces.

A strong easterly wind, drifting snow, and temperature in the minus marked our departure from the camp at Cape Columbia, which I had christened Crane City. Rough ice in the first march damaged several sledges and smashed two beyond repair, the teams going back to Columbia for other sledges in reserve there.

We camped ten miles from Crane City. The easterly wind and low temperature continued. In the second march we pased the British record made by Markham in May 1876—82.20—and were stopped by open water, which had been formed by the wind after Bartlett passed. In this march we negotiated the lead and reached Bartlett's third camp. Borup had gone back from here, but missed his way, owing to the faulting of the trail by the movement of the ice.

Marvin came back also for more fuel and alcohol. The wind continued forming open water all about us. At the end of the fourth march we came upon Bartlett, who had been stopped by a wide lake of open water. We remained here from March 4 to March 11.

At noon of March 5 the sun, red and shaped like a football by excessed reflection, just raised itself above the horizon for a few minutes, and then disappeared again. It was the first time I had seen it since Oct. 1.

I now began to feel a good deal of anxiety because there were no signs of Marvin and Borup, who should have been there for two days. Besides, they had the alcohol and oil, which were indispensable for us. We concluded that they had either lost the trail or were imprisoned on an island by open water, probably the latter.

ACROSS 84TH PARALLEL.

Fortunately, on March 11 the lead was practicable, and leaving a note for Marvin and Borup to push

A typical shelter, built of packed snow, used for overnight stops.

A raft chopped out of ice, used as a ferry.

"All the News That's Fit to Print."

The New York Times.

THE WEATHER
Fair today; showers tomorrow; variable winds, becoming light southwest.
For full weather report see Page 17.

VOL. LVIII...NO. 18,858. NEW YORK, SATURDAY, SEPTEMBER 11, 1909.—TWENTY PAGES. ONE CENT In Greater New York, Jersey City, and Newark { Elsewhere, TWO CENTS.

EMPLOYES TO BEAR HARRIMAN'S BODY

Simplicity the Keynote of the Funeral at Little Church at Arden.

ESTATE FOR A STATE PARK?

Some Expectation That Provision to This End Is Made in His Will, to be Read Next Week.

Special to The New York Times.

TURNER'S, N. Y., Sept. 10.—Simplicity will be the keynote of the funeral services over E. H. Harriman, to be held here on Sunday. It was announced to-night that the services will be conducted by Bishop Doane of Albany and Archdeacon Nelson of the Cathedral of St. John the Divine, New York City. They will be assisted by the Rev. D. J. Holmes McGuinnis, rector of St. John's Church at Arden and spiritual adviser of the Harriman family. In speaking of the funeral arrangements to-night Dr. McGuinnis said: "There will be family services at 10 o'clock on Sunday morning at Arden House. Communion will be celebrated at St. John's Church at 11 o'clock, followed by a memorial service at which I will make the address.

"The funeral service will be in St. John's Church at 3 o'clock in the afternoon. The choir of Grace Church in New York will furnish the music. This service will be strictly private, and only the members of the family or close personal friends of Mr. Harriman and some employes of the estate will attend. Bishop Doane and Archdeacon Nelson, who will officiate, are very close personal friends of the family, and have been for many years."

Preparations for the funeral are being pushed forward. Sixty men worked in the rain to-day on the new road now nearing completion, leading down the 1,300 feet from Arden House to the village of Arden. This road is so constructed that the grade is scarcely perceptible. Mr. Harriman took great interest in the work on it, and it is said that one of the last wishes he expressed was that, in the event of his death, he should be carried to the grave by this route.

Another interesting announcement here to-night is that at 3 o'clock on Sunday afternoon, the time set for the funeral, every wheel then in motion on the 64,000 miles of railroads controlled by the Harriman interests will be stopped for five minutes.

Six men have been at work all day digging the grave in which Mr. Harriman will lie. It is in the village churchyard about a hundred yards from St. John's Church, and only about ten yards from the main road, from which it can readily be seen by passersby. The formation of the ground is quartz, and the grave has to be blasted out of the rock.

In the church to-day villagers are busily engaged in draping the pews in mourning. There is seating accommodation for 150 persons. The Harriman pew is the first row on the north side of the aisle. The active pall bearers are to be Charles T. Ford, Superintendent of the Arden estate; William Viner, manager of the Harriman farms; William Robbins, manager of the stock farms; R. W. Mandigo, master carpenter; E. P. Schultz, master mason; W. A. McClellan, manager of the Arden farm dairy; J. Barlow Ford and George W. Bush, both of whom hold responsible positions on the estate.

So far the death certificate has not been filed with E. L. Fitch, Town Clerk of Highland Mills, the township in which Arden House is situated. According to Supt. Ford, this will be done to-morrow. As to the cause of death, Judge Robert S. Lovett, who went to New York to-night on the 6 o'clock train from Arden, when shown the statement of Prof. Struempell of Vienna to the effect that he had diagnosed Mr. Harriman's ailment as cancer, said:

"I cannot say anything about that. Dr. Lyle has been the chief medical adviser, and is complying with the wishes of the family in maintaining an attitude of silence."

Asked for the reason of the great secrecy which distinguished Mr. Harriman's illness, Judge Lovett replied:

"Mr. Harriman's life was so interwoven with Wall Street and the financial world at large that any change in his condition would have affected the market, and we thought it advisable, in order to run no danger of misrepresentation, to say nothing about his condition. Any statement one way or the other would have been misunderstood."

Judge Lovett would not discuss the will left by Mr. Harriman or give any idea of the value of the estate, saying it would all come out in good time.

Among those who have wired messages of sympathy are Ogden Mills, Ogden Armour, Chauncey M. Depew, William Rockefeller, Whitelaw Reid, Jacob H. Schiff, Mrs. Elsie French Vanderbilt, Mrs. Cornelius Vanderbilt, August Belmont, Robert Goelet, Benjamin B. Odell, Frank A. Munsey, Mayor Tideman of Savannah, and the Lieutenant Governor of California.

Supt. Ford said to-night that all work on the estate would be resumed on Monday. Plans had been made by the dead financier which would take another five years to complete. His death will not interfere with these arrangements.

Mrs. Cornelia Simons, sister of Mr. Harriman, said to-night that she might have been mistaken when she fixed 1:30 P. M. as the hour of her brother's death yesterday. She explained that she would naturally be much upset at the time the reporters saw her yesterday afternoon, and that really she did not know the exact time the end came. Now, however, she believed it to be 3:35 o'clock, the time given out in the official bulletin announcing the financier's death.

Mrs. Simons also corrected her statement of yesterday, that she was present at Mr. Harriman's death. She now says she was not present. In view of Dr. W. G. Lyle's statement issued in New York this morning positively denying the holding back of the death news for two hours, it may be said that Mrs. Simons not only fixed the time of death at 1:30 once yesterday, but reiterated it thrice.

Another person who is willing to go on record as asserting that Mr. Harriman died at 3:35 and not at 1:30 o'clock yesterday is the Rev. Dr. McGuinniss, who, however, was not present when the end came. He also said that up to the day before yesterday the whole Harriman family believed that the financier was going to get better.

In an appreciation of Mr. Harriman Dr. McGuinniss said that the keynote of the personal side of the dead man was his simplicity and approachableness.

"Any workman on the estate could get to him instantly," said the rector. "He

Continued on Page 4.

PEARY DENOUNCES COOK.

Says "He Has Sold the Public a Gold Brick"—Will Produce Proofs.

To the Editor of The New York Times:

BATTLE HARBOR, Labrador, (via Marconi Wireless, Capt Ray, N. F.,) Sept. 10.—The Roosevelt will remain here three or four days coaling and overhauling ship. I expect to arrive at Sydney about Sept. 15.

Do not trouble about Cook's story or attempt to explain any discrepancies in his statements. The affair will settle itself.

He has not been at the pole on April 21st, 1908, or at any other time. He has simply handed the public a gold brick.

These statements are made advisedly, and I have proof of them. When he makes a full statement of his journey over his signature to some geographical society or other reputable body, if that statement contains the claim that he has reached the pole, I shall be in a position to furnish material that may prove distinctly interesting reading for the public.

ROBERT E. PEARY.

GROSSCUP AGAIN ENJOINS.

Says The Times's Copyright Is Good—Will Punish Contempt Severely.

Special to The New York Times.

CHICAGO, Sept. 11.—At 12:45 Judge Grosscup issued a second injunction against the Chicago Examiner based on The New York Times copyright of the Peary articles. He explained that in his judgment the grounds for the previous injunction based on the copyright of the pamphlet were sufficient.

Judge Grosscup paid little attention to Judge Hand's decision, and riddled Beck's argument.

He concluded by saying that if contempt were proved he would visit upon the defendants penalties which they would not soon forget.

He emphasized the point that paraphrase was piracy.

Judge Grosscup refused to consider motion based on Hand's decision by The Examiner attorneys.

YES, THE WIRELESS WAS BUSY

Commander Peary Was Sending More to The New York Times.

By The Associated Press.

ST. JOHN'S, N. F., Sept. 10.—The Roosevelt was at Battle Harbor late today, and the wireless station at that point was still working overtime on Peary's detailed account of his Far Northern journey.

It is understood that Peary's long stay at that point was not so much for the purpose of coaling, but was decided upon as a stopping place where the Commander could send the account of his trip to a syndicate of newspapers, of which THE NEW YORK TIMES is the head.

MADE $2,250 ON $285.

How a Lucky Buyer of a "Call" on Union Pacific Fared Yesterday.

When the stock market was soaring yesterday stories were many of those who had profited by their belief that E. H. Harriman's death had been sufficiently discounted to prevent anything like a real break in the market. None of the stories of those who had bought the market in London or who had put in overnight orders to buy at the opening could quite touch the experience of a customer of Arthur Lewin of the Consolidated Exchange, who went into the New Street put and call crowd on Thursday afternoon and snapped up a call on 1,000 shares of Union Pacific, good yesterday or to-day, at 198½. This man for $285 purchased a call on 1,000 shares at that figure. The call was put out by a customer of Ball & Whicher, who was long of the stock, and indorsed by that firm. If the buyer had covered at 207¼ his profit at the high price of the day would have been $7,250 on his investment of $285. Like most regulars in Wall Street, however, he was not willing to risk his profits, and began to cover at 200⅝, selling one-half of his call between that price and 206 at an average of 203. At this average his profit was $2,250, with 500 shares still left on which to realize to-day.

The fact that a call on 1,000 shares of Union Pacific at 198½, 4 points above Thursday's closing price, was being offered after, seemed attractive to many speculators, and there were at least four men yesterday who said they had tried to take up the offer, but were too late. Lewin's lucky customer himself had tried to get a call on 5,000 shares on the same terms, but Ball & Whicher's customer had only 1,000 shares to offer. He was long of the stock, and his loss represents only his prospective profits.

The New York Times to-morrow (Sunday) will contain the full story of Commander Peary's successful expedition to discover the north pole.

Owing to the tremendous difficulties of transmitting this thrilling narrative from the ice-bound shores of Labrador by wireless telegraphy, The New York Times has been able to print his story only in daily installments. A problem of this magnitude has never before confronted a newspaper, and The New York Times has used every known means to give its readers the first authentic news of this great achievement.

The New York Times will assemble this great story to-morrow in a continuous narrative, and no one interested in the culmination of centuries of heroic endeavor can afford to be without it.

BOOK COPYRIGHT AND PEARY REPORT

Lower Court Dissolves The Times Writ of Injunction on a Technicality.

DECIDED ON THE CONTRACT

Judge Remarking on "Unreasonable" Construction Which Leaves No Protection Against Appropriation of News.

Judge Learned Hand, sitting in the United States District Court, yesterday afternoon, dissolved the injunction he had issued on Thursday night restraining The New York Sun and The New York World from reprinting from The London Times Commander Peary's copyrighted dispatches to THE NEW YORK TIMES describing his discovery of the north pole. The failure of this attempt to protect Commander Peary's interest in the financial proceeds of his achievement was due to a technicality in the contract made by THE NEW YORK TIMES with Commander Peary on July 6, 1908.

Upon this contract with Commander Peary the issue turned yesterday afternoon, after Judge Hand had declared in the morning that if THE TIMES were shown to be technically within its rights he would grant the injunction to prevent the reprinting of the Peary dispatches unless the newspapers it was sought to enjoin wanted to agree that there should be no further infringements.

Times's Contract With Peary.

The contract itself was produced and read as follows:

July 6, 1908.

NEW YORK TIMES, New York City.

Gentlemen: I herewith ackowledge the receipt of the sum of four thousand dollars ($4,000) from THE NEW YORK TIMES on behalf of itself and associates. It is understood that in making this advance THE TIMES does not assume any responsibility for or any connection with the expedition on which I am about to embark and which has for its purpose the finding of the north pole. The money is advanced to me as a loan to be repaid to THE NEW YORK TIMES and its associates out of the proceeds of the news and literary rights resulting from this expedition, it being understood that if for any reason the expedition is abandoned before the Fall of 1908 the money is to be reunded to THE TIMES. If the expedition is successful and the pole is discovered, I promise to use every means in my power to reach civilization and wire to THE TIMES the full story of the discovery over my own signature. THE TIMES is to have the sole rights to the news of the discovery, and is to have the exclusive right of its publication in all parts of the world.

My understanding is that THE TIMES on its part agrees to syndicate the news both in Europe and America, and to give to me the entire amount it receives after deducting costs of cable tolls, &c. THE TIMES and its associates will pay me what they consider a reasonable amount for the use of the material in their own publications. From the sum thus raised the $4,000 is to be repaid, and I am free to sell the magazine and book rights to my best advantage.

It is understood, however, that should the news reports by any possibility not realize the sum of $4,000, any deficit will be reimbursed to THE TIMES from the magazine and book rights.

Should the expedition not be successful in finding the pole, but should simply result in explorations in the Far North, THE TIMES is to be repaid $4,000 out of the news, magazine, and book rights of the expedition, so far as they may go toward the liquidation of that claim.

Yours very truly,
R. E. PEARY.

It may be stated that the sum realized for the Peary dispatches has been greatly in excess of the amount advanced to Commander Peary.

Judge Hand's Decision.

Judge Hand's decision makes clear the ground on which he decided to dissolve the injunction. Here it is:

At the time when the injunction was granted the complainants had attempted to acquire a copyright by the publication of a pamphlet with notice of copyright, and had mailed the requisite copies to the Librarian of Congress. Had the complainants received from Lieut. Peary the right to publish the story of this discovery in pamphlet form the copyright would have been perfected by these acts. The contract gave to them, however, only the right to a news publication of the story, which I understand to mean that they meant to publish it in what fairly came within the description of being a newspaper. If so, the antecedent publication of a pamphlet was not the publication which the statute requires, for that must be a publication by the proprietor. Assuming that Lieut. Peary could, in fact, split up his rights, as to which I decide nothing, he had not given to the complainant any magazine or book rights which I can conceive to include pamphlets. This publication must follow their title, and until they published in a newspaper I cannot think they published as required by the statute. I should be disposed to stretch the reading of the contract, in so far as in justice I might, to protect the complainant, but I cannot construe this pamphlet as in any sense a newspaper without a clear perversion of the parties' meaning.

The Sun to Reprint No More.

When the case had been closed James M. Beck, as attorney for The Sun, stated in court that his client would not reprint from London any more of the Peary dispatches to THE TIMES.

"I am glad you have come to that decision," said Judge Hand.

The afternoon's argument was entirely devoted to a discussion of the construction of the Peary contract. Mr. Beck

Continued on Page 2.

THE GOAL OF CENTURIES ACHIEVED BY PEARY; THRILLING CONCLUSION OF THE EXPLORER'S NARRATIVE OF HIS CONQUEST OF THE NORTH POLE

How, With Five Companions, One a Washington Negro and the Others Eskimos He Planted American Flags at the Top of the World, Over a Fathomless Sea.

SOUNDING OF 9,000 FEET AT THE POLE FINDS NO BOTTOM

One Eskimo Went to the Pole to Win the Hand of a Girl—Great Speed Explained by Fact That in the Unexplored Regions Ice Was Level and So Easy That Dogs Could Gallop—Photographs Taken at Pole—No Mention of Any Land—Only 33 Below Zero, Sometimes Only 12.

BATTLE HARBOR, Labrador, (via Marconi Wireless, Cape Ray, N. F.,) Sept. 10.—With the disappearance of Bartlett I turned to the problem before me. This was that for which I had worked for thirty-two years; for which I had lived the simple life; for which I had conserved all my energy on the upward trip; for which I had trained myself as for a race, crushing down every worry about success.

For success now, in spite of my years, I felt in trim—fit for the demands of the coming days and eager to be on the trail. As for my party, my equipment, and my supplies, I was in shape beyond my most sanguine dreams of earliest years. My party might be regarded as an ideal which had now come to realization—as loyal and responsive to my will as the fingers of my right hand.

Four of them carried the technique of dogs, sledges, ice, and cold as their heritage. Two of them, Hansen and Ootam, were my companions to the furthest point three years before. Two others, Egingwah and Sigloo, were in Clark's division, which had such a narrow escape at that time, and now were willing to go anywhere with my immediate party and willing to risk themselves again in any supporting party.

The fifth was a young man who had never served before in any expedition, but who was, if possible, even more willing and eager than the others for the princely gifts—a boat, a rifle, a shotgun, ammunition, knives, &c.—which I had promised to each of them who reached the pole with me; for he knew that these riches would enable him to wrest from a stubborn father the girl whose image filled his hot young heart.

All had blind confidence so long as I was with them, and gave no thought for the morrow, sure that whatever happened I should somehow get them back to land. But I dealt with the party equally. I recognized that all its impetus centred in me, and that whatever pace I set it would make good. If any one was played out, I would stop for a short time.

HE PLANS FIVE MARCHES.

I had no fault to find with the conditions. My dogs were the very best, the pick of 122 with which I left Columbia. Almost all were powerful males, hard as nails, in good flesh, but without a superfluous ounce, without a suspicion of fat anywhere; and, what was better yet, they were all in good spirits.

My sledges, now that the repairs were completed, were in good condition. My supplies were ample for forty days, and, with the reserve represented by the dogs themselves, could be made to last fifty.

Pacing back and forth in the lee of the pressure ridge where our igloos were built, while my men got their loads ready for the next marches, I settled on my programme. I decided that I should strain every nerve to make five marches of fifteen miles each, crowding these marches in such a way as to bring us to the end of the fifth long enough before noon to permit the immediate taking of an observation for latitude.

Weather and leads permitting, I believed I could do this. If my proposed distances were cut down by any chance, I had two means in reserve for making up the deficit:

First—To make the last march a forced one, stopping to make tea and rest the dogs, but not to sleep.

Second—At the end of the fifth march to make a forced march with a light sledge, a double team of dogs and one or two of the party, leaving the rest in camp.

Underlying all these calculations was a recognition of the ever-present neighborhood of open leads and impassable water and the knowledge that a twenty-four hours' gale would knock all my plans into a cocked hat, and even put us in imminent peril.

NOTCHES IN HIS BELT.

At a little after midnight of April 1, after a few hours of sound sleep, I hit the trail, leaving the others to break up camp and follow. As I climbed the pressure ridge back of our igloos I set another hole in my belt, the third since I started. Every man and dog of us was lean and fat-bellied as a board and as hard.

It was a fine morning. The wind of the last two days had subsided, and the going was the best and most equable of any I had had yet. The floes were large and old, hard and clear, and were surrounded by pressure ridges, some of which were almost stupendous. The biggest of them, however, were easily negotiated, either through some crevice or up some huge brink.

I set a good pace for about ten hours. Twenty-five miles took me well beyond the 88th parallel. While I was building my igloos a long lead formed by the east and southeast of us at a distance of a few miles.

A few hours' sleep and we were on the trail again. As the going was now practically horizontal, we were unhampered and could travel as long as we pleased and sleep as little as we wish. The weather was fine and the going like that of the previous day, except at the beginning, when pickaxes were required. This and a brief stop at another lead cut down our distance. But we had made twenty miles in ten hours and were half way to the 89th parallel.

The ice was grinding audibly in every direction, but no motion was visible. Evidently it was settling back into equilibrium, and probably sagging due northward with its release from the wind pressure.

Again there was a few hours' stop, and we hit the trail before midnight. The weather and going were even better. The surface, except as interrupted by infrequent ridges, was as level as the glacial fringe from Hecla to Columbia, and harder.

A DANGEROUS DASH.

We marched something over ten hours, the dogs being often on the trot, and made 20 miles. Near the end of the march we rushed across a lead 100 yards wide, which buckled under our sledges and finally broke as the last sledge left it.

We stopped in sight of the 89th parallel, in a temperature of 40 degrees below. Again a scant sleep, and we were on our way once more and across the 89th parallel.

This march duplicated the previous one as to weather and going. The last few hours it was on young ice, and occasionally the dogs were galloping.

We made 25 miles or more, the air, the sky, and the bitter wind burning the face till it crackled. It was like the great interior ice cap of Greenland. Even the natives complained of the bitter air. It was as keen as frozen steel.

A little longer sleep than the previous ones had to be taken here, as we were all in need of it. Then on again.

Up to this time, with each successive march, our fear of an impossible lead had increased. At every inequality of the ice I found myself hurrying breathlessly forward, fearing that it marked a lead, and when I arrived at the summit would catch my breath with relief—only to find myself hurrying on in the same way at the next one.

But on this march, by some strange shift of feeling, this fear fell from me completely. The weather was thick, but it gave me no uneasiness.

Before I turned in I took an observation which indicated our position as 89.25. A dense, lifeless pall hung overhead. The horizon was black and the ice beneath was a ghastly, chalky white with no relief—a striking contrast to the glimmering, sunlit fields of it over which we had been traveling for the previous four days.

The going was even better and there was scarcely any snow on the hard, granular, last Summer's surface of the old floes, dotted with the sapphire ice of the previous Summer's lakes.

A rise in temperature to 15 below reduced the friction of the sledges and gave the dogs the appearance of having caught the spirits of the party. The more sprightly ones, as they went along with tightly curled tails, frequently tossed their heads, with short, sharp barks and yelps.

In 12 hours we made 40 miles. There was no sign of a lead in the march.

THE POLE AT LAST!

I had now made my five marches, and was in time for a hasty noon observation through a temporary break in the clouds, which indicated our position as 89.57. I quote an entry from my journal some hours later:

"The pole at last! The prize of three centuries, my dream and goal for twenty years, mine at last! I cannot bring myself to realize it.

"It all seems so simple and commonplace. As Bartlett said when turning back, when speaking of his being in these exclusive regions, which no mortal has ever penetrated before:

"'It is just like every day!'"

Of course, I had many sensations that made sleep impossible for hours, despite my utter fatigue—

The *Roosevelt*, frozen in coastal ice, was the winter base for Peary's party.

Peary with the dogs that powered the sledges.

Mat Henson, the faithful companion who accompanied Commander Peary on his Arctic expeditions.

"All the News That's Fit to Print."

The New York Times.

THE WEATHER.
Fair, slightly warmer Thursday; Friday, fair, warmer; moderate winds, becoming south.
For full weather report see Page 23.

VOL. LIX...NO. 18,960. * * * NEW YORK, WEDNESDAY, DECEMBER 22, 1909.—TWENTY PAGES. ONE CENT In Greater New York, Jersey City, and Newark. | Elsewhere, TWO CENTS.

COOK'S CLAIM TO DISCOVERY OF THE NORTH POLE REJECTED; OUTRAGED DENMARK CALLS HIM A DELIBERATE SWINDLER; HAVING NO ORIGINAL OBSERVATIONS, HE USED LOOSE'S 'FAKES'

UNIVERSITY FINDS THAT COOK'S PAPERS CONTAIN NO PROOF THAT HE REACHED THE NORTH POLE.

DOCUMENTS SUBMITTED BY DR. COOK.

First, a typewritten report prepared by Dr. Cook's secretary, Walter Lounsdale, and covering sixty-one pages of foolscap.

Second, a typewritten copy made by Mr. Lounsdale from Dr. Cook's notebooks. This occupies sixteen pages of foolscap, and includes a description of the expedition during the period from March 18, 1908, to June 13, 1908, during which, according to the statement, Dr. Cook journeyed fom Svartevog to the North Pole and returned to a point on the polar ice not specifically indicated, but west of the Axel Heiberg land.

FINDINGS REPORTED BY THE EXAMINING COMMISSION.

First, the report of the expedition sent to the University by Dr. Cook is the same as that printed in The New York Herald during the months of September and October last.

Second, the copy of Cook's notebooks does not contain any original astronomical observations whatsoever, but only results.

Third, the documents presented are inexcusably lacking in information which would prove that the astronomical observations therein referred to were really made; and also contain no details regarding the practical work of the expedition and the sledge journey which would enable the Committee to determine their reliability.

The Committee therefore is of the opinion that the material transmitted for examination contains no proof that Dr. Cook reached the Pole.

VERDICT OF COPENHAGEN UNIVERSITY CONSISTORY.

The documents handed the University for examination do not contain observations and information which can be regarded as proof that Dr. Cook reached the North Pole on his recent expedition.

PEARY'S WARNINGS AGAINST COOK.

The New York Times, New York:

Indian Harbor, Labrador, via Marconi Wireless to Cape Ray, N. F., Sept. 8, 1909.—Cook's story should not be taken too seriously. The Eskimos who accompanied him say that he went no distance north. He did not get out of sight of land. Other men of the tribe corroborate their statements Kindly give this to all home and foreign news associations for the same wide distribution as Cook's story.

PEARY.

To the Editor of The New York Times.

Battle Harbor, Labrador, via Marconi Wireless to Cape Ray, N. F., Sept. 10, 1909.—Do not trouble about Cook's story, or attempt to explain any discrepancies in his statements. The affair will settle itself. He has not been at the Pole on April 21st, 1908, or at any other time. He has simply handed the public a gold brick.

These statements are made advisedly, and I have proof of them.

ROBERT E. PEARY.

PEARY'S FIRST MESSAGE TO THE TIMES

The New York Times, New York:

Indian Harbor, Labrador, via Cape Ray, N. F., Sept. 6.—I have the Pole, April sixth. Expect arrive Chateau Bay September seventh. Secure control wire for me there and arrange expedite transmission big story.

PEARY.

PEARY SENDS CONGRATULATIONS TO THE TIMES

Washington, Dec. 21, 1909.

To the Editor of The New York Times.

Congratulations to The New York Times for its steady, insistent, victorious stand for the truth.

PEARY.

Only Two Typewritten Documents Submitted to Copenhagen University, and These Found to Contain No Proof at All.

TALE OF PLOT TOLD AGAIN

Lounsdale Tried to Convince the Danes That Original Records Were Being Brought Over by Mrs. Cook.

INSANITY THEORY IS DROPPED

"Shameless," Says Stroemgren, "Scandal," Says Rasmussen, "A Swindler," Says Holm, of the Examining Board.

ABSURD TALE ABOUT DOGS

Rasmussen Flouts Cook's Assertion That After Feeding His Dogs Pemmican He Used Them as Foot Warmers.

SOME LOOSE FIGURES USED

Then Cook Evidently Became Scared and Fled—Wrote to Lounsdale from Marseilles—His Whereabouts Are Not Known.

Special Cable to THE NEW YORK TIMES.

COPENHAGEN, Dec. 21.—A formal decision was rendered by the University of Copenhagen to-day, which disposed once and forever of Dr. Frederick A. Cook's claim that he discovered the north pole. I am able to add that there is accumulated circumstantial and other evidence sufficient to brand him as a deliberate swindler.

The consistory of the university did not consider itself called upon to do more than pronounce upon the evidence submitted for its opinion. This evidence consisted wholly of typewritten matter, part of which was alleged to have been copied from Cook's original notebooks. On it the commission and the consistory decided simply that there was no proof that Cook had reached the pole.

Hallucination Theory Abandoned.

Various members of the commission whom I have seen, however, do not hesitate to speak out their minds about Cook. The most flattering opinion expressed of him is that he was an incredibly stupid bungler. The theory which at one time obtained among some of those who doubted Cook's claims, that he was suffering from a hallucination, is no longer held by a single member of the commission which examined the so-called proofs.

The news that Cook had not sent his original diaries to the university created a tremendous sensation in Copenhagen. Readers of THE NEW YORK TIMES were already aware that these famous records had played much the same role as the fictitious Crawford will in Mme. Humbert's safe. The omission by Cook of original astronomical calculations upon which were based the alleged records of travel, similarly related in advance in THE NEW YORK TIMES dispatches, was in itself sufficient to put Cook out of court for serious consideration, but the cock and bull story offered here by Walter Lounsdale, Cook's secretary, in explanation of his failure to send the original diaries [illegible]

ROUT ZELAYA'S ARMY, BATTLE AGAIN TO-DAY

Forces of Gen. Estrada Successful in Engagement at Rama Lasting Several Hours.

FIGHT NOW FOR SURRENDER

Revolutionists Under Gen. Estrada Confident of Complete Victory in Next Attack—Joy in Central America.

BLUEFIELDS, Nicaragua, Dec. 21.—The revolutionists under command of Gen. Estrada have completely routed the Zelayan forces near Rama. Estrada has captured Recreo, Vasquez's strongest position, and has been victorious all along the line, which stretches for a distance of eight miles.

Yesterday the forward movement began, detachments being sent out under Gen. Luis Mena, Fornos Diaz, Alfredo Diaz, Chamorro, and Matuty. It was Gen. Mena's task to outflank Gonzales, who directed the defense of the main body of the Government troops. These in large numbers were well intrenched, but Estrada's followers were armed with the latest equipment and machine guns were brought into play to clear the trenches.

The casualties on the Government side were high, the greatest execution being done at Recreo, which the revolutionists finally took by assault.

Among those in the revolutionary ranks was Capt. Godfrey Fowler, formerly of the Thirty-third Infantry, U. S. A., who was in command of the artillery in the firing line.

WASHINGTON, Dec. 21.—Fighting will be resumed in Nicaragua to-morrow, according to advices received here to-day, and the Estrada army will bend all efforts to compel the unconditional surrender of the Government forces.

There is some doubt as to the exact extent of Estrada's success. From revolutionary sources the word is sent that the victory over the Zelayan troops is "complete." The State Department has received word from Thomas H. Moffat, United States Consul at Bluefields, that Estrada had "partially routed and defeated the forces of Zelaya." It is agreed, however, that the moral effect of such initial success on the part of the revolutionists can hardly be exaggerated.

The first announcement of the success of the Estrada arms came in a cablegram to Dr. Castrillo, the representative here of the Provisional Government. It was signed "Diaz." Diaz is Secretary of State of the Provisional Government. The cablegram said:

> Complete victory is ours. Zelaya's troops are in retreat.

Later this evening the State Department gave out the following message from Consul Moffat, which had been sent by wireless telegraph from Colon:

> Estrada forces at Tatumbla and Recreo, near Rama, commanded by Gen. Mena at the former place and Gens. Chamorro, Mattuti, and Fornos Diaz at the latter place, partially routed and defeated the forces of Zelaya after desperate fighting of several hours. The Zelayan forces were commanded by Gen. Gonzales.
>
> A great many were killed, the number being unknown. One hundred were wounded, and 150 prisoners were taken by the revolutionists.
>
> The Zelayan troops at Recreo have occupied what has been considered a strong position. Estrada is confident of defeating the enemy, when he renews the attack to-morrow, and of forcing their surrender.

The clash between the two armies was not unexpected here. For days on end they have been lying practically idle in their trenches around Rama, skirmishes only marring the peace that brooded over that district. Estrada played a waiting game in the hope that the Zelayan commanders would take the initiative and attempt the capture of his position, which was reported to be very strong. Furthermore, with the waning of President Zelaya's star he expected a large number of accessions from the Zelayan army.

When Zelaya abdicated and practically dictated the election of Dr. Madriz as his successor, Estrada, according to his diplomatic friends here, determined to strike. Accordingly he moved his army forward early to-day and took the field actively against his enemy. Dr. Castrillo and his friends look forward confidently to the receipt to-morrow of word of a complete victory and the beginning of the march of the victorious army on the capital.

None of the officials of the State Department to-night would discuss the reported victory of Estrada. It is known, however, that the news was not unwelcome. Had the Zelayan army defeated Estrada, this Government would have been in a somewhat embarrassing position, having espoused openly the cause of the Provisional Government.

In Central American diplomatic circles the word brought joy, and there was a general celebration to-night. The diplomats join in the prediction that this first victory is the "beginning of the end" of Zelayaism, and that the next step will be to force the retirement of President Madriz on the ground that he is a tool of Zelaya, and not the real choice of the country. The State Department has not yet received news of the election of Madriz to the Presidency.

The consulate at Bluefields, in a telegram dated last Sunday, reports that the people in that locality recognized the fact that the election of any President by the present National Assembly would undoubtedly mean the continuance of Zelaya's domination. The same dispatch stated that in the event of Estrada's election as Provisional President he will guarantee free elections.

Nicaragua has defaulted in making the second payment of $50,000 toward the liquidation of the celebrated Emery claim against that country. This sum fell due last Saturday, but the State Department has received neither the money nor any communication from any authoritative source in regard to it.

As at present there is no responsible Government in Nicaragua, the State Department will take no immediate steps in the matter. Should it be found advisable, however, the United States would have little difficulty in taking possession

Continued on Page 7.

STEEL TRUST GIVES $1,000,000

Finance Committee Appropriates That Sum for Christmas Present to Workers

A million-dollar Christmas present was voted by the Finance Committee of the United States Steel Corporation yesterday to its employes, making the biggest package by far that the Wall Street St. Nick will handle this year. It will be distributed among the employes of the Steel Trust in all parts of the country. It is the annual bonus for efficiency. The gift will not be in cash, but in the corporation's common or preferred stock, according to the choice of the beneficiaries. The men who have been picked out to receive the annual reward of merit were offered an option by the vote of the Finance Committee yesterday to take common stock to the amount of their award at the rate of $80 a share or preferred at $124 a share. The closing prices of these issues yesterday were 91⅝ for the common and 124⅝ for the preferred. The practice of distributing stock as a bonus was inaugurated in 1906, when about 21,000 shares of common stock were included in the year's distribution.

In his report for that year President Corey explained that the stock would not be delivered "until the expiration of three years, and compliance had been made with various condition named for the protection of the companies." It is supposed that the same conditions attach to this year's allotment. This Christmas distribution is, of course, quite separate from the privileges annually given to employes to subscribe to the stock of the company on a deferred payment plan.

Wall Street employes generally are looking for a cheerful Christmas this year after two successive seasons of slim Christmas stockings following the panic. The custom of paying employes a substantial cash bonus at Christmas or New Year's is more general among banking institutions and brokerage houses than it is uptown, and at this season the working forces of the financial district are on tip-toe to learn what the Christmas envelope is to contain. The bonuses extend from the smallest office boy to the bank President in most institutions, and in good years often amount to substantial sums. This year of rising prices has been a profitable one for the brokers, and the office forces of the Street are looking for a return to ante-panic standards.

Most houses enjoin their employes to secrecy as to the amount they receive, but the custom of the large houses is to pay a percentage of the year's salary, which ranges from 5 to 20 per cent.

In several of the larger National banks a round sum is paid, which goes upward in keeping with the importance of the position.

In recent years there has been a tendency to do away with the Christmas present and substitute awards in the shape of salary increases in recognition of efficient service. This method was adopted by the First National Bank last season.

INVESTIGATE 'PHONE SALE.

Ohio Attorney General Thinks Morgan Deal May Mean a Trust.

Special to The New York Times.

COLUMBUS, Ohio, Dec. 21.—Action against what is alleged to have been a merger of the independent and trust telephone lines of Ohio by the recent purchase of the Cuyahoga Telephone Company by the firm of J. P. Morgan & Co. is seen in the announcement made this evening by Attorney General U. G. Denman of Ohio.

Mr. Denman stated that he has struck a lead which will in all probability bring him to the fact that the purchase of the company was not one "for speculation only," as pronounced by the Morgan Company, but that it was an illegal merger.

He would not say what his lead is. However, he did say that if action is brought to annul the sale it would be under the telephone statutes of Ohio, and not under the Valentine anti-trust law. The deal, he said, was of too broad a scope to be included under the anti-trust statutes.

It is known that soon after the sale was forecasted in the newspapers, Attorney General Denman was visited in his offices here by stockholders of the Cuyahoga Company. They are the men who did not want the company sold and fought against the transaction from beginning to end.

Since Mr. Denman is a Toledo man and used to be a corporation lawyer there, it is surmised that his information comes from Toledo capitalists.

This afternoon the Attorney General said he felt free to say that the suit would probably be brought, and that it would be in the courts here, and not at Toledo.

HARDEN IN McCARREN'S SEAT.

Wins the Senatorship in the Seventh District by 3,305 Plurality.

In the special election ordered by Gov. Hughes to fill the vacancy in the Seventh Senate District in Brooklyn caused by the death of Senator McCarren, Thomas C. Harden, the Democratic nominee, was chosen last night.

There were four candidates, Harden, (Dem.,) John McCrate, (Rep.,) a young lawyer; John J. Clancy, (Ind. League,) and Albert Pauly, (Socialist.) The total number of votes cast was 12,500, of which Harden received 6,386; McCrate, 3,081; Clancy, 2,039; Pauly, 96.

The election passed off without incident, and required no police interference. Supt. Leary, with several of his deputies, made a tour of certain lodging houses in the Thirteenth, Fourteenth, and Fifteenth Assembly Districts looking for floaters. It was said that he came across sixty-five and obtained warrants for their arrest. None of the alleged floaters presented himself at the polls, however, so no arrests were made.

The voting was light. The total enrolled voting strength of the Seventh District is 19,500.

Washington Town Goes Wet.

WALLA WALLA, Wash., Dec. 21.—After an exciting campaign Walla Walla yesterday voted wet by a majority of 622.

Latest Shipping News.

SS St. Paul, incoming from Southampton, was reported by Marconi wireless 1,143 miles east of Sandy Hook at 8:30 P. M. yesterday. Due, if not delayed, Friday afternoon.

SS Oscar II., Copenhagen, Dec. 9.

INDICT 27; ARREST 20 IN SMUGGLING CASE

Importers and Pier Employes Accused After Discovery of Big Frauds Here.

LEADER OF THE GANG DEAD

Innocent Voyagers' Names Used to Get Finery Through—Government's Loss $1,000,000 a Year.

A wholesale round-up of the importers of gowns, laces, silks, and millinery, together with other persons involved in the smuggling frauds uncovered on the piers of the American Line and Red Star Line last Spring, was begun yesterday by United States Attorney Henry A. Wise. An indictment naming twenty-seven individual defendants was brought out before Judge Holt, in the United States Circuit Court, and bench warrants issued for the persons therein named. Deputy United States Marshals, under the direction of Marshal Henkel, started immediately to serve the warrants, and before the close of the day sixteen defendants had been brought in to give bail before United States Commissioner Shields.

Meantime in both Chicago and Boston, the Federal authorities were busy. Two arrests were made in each city, thus accounting for twenty of the twenty-seven defendants named in the indictment. To-day the Deputy Marshals will round up the rest of the New Yorkers who are involved, some of whom are already under bail on other charges of smuggling. Following are those arrested here yesterday:

Who the Prisoners Are.

PHILIP A. PHILLIPSEN, a city or merchants' weigher, who made his headquarters on the American Line pier and is accused of being the American head of the system of underground expressage, whereby smuggled goods were taken away from the pier without examination by customs officials. Phillipsen gave $5,000 bail.

ROBERT SCHWARTZ, baggage master of the American Line pier, who was arrested last March and is accused of being Phillipsen's right hand man in sorting out the trunks belonging to those who stood in with the smuggling scheme. He was released on $5,000 bail.

THOMAS MURPHY, a subordinate of Schwartz's, accused of complicity in the handling of the trunks, and released as a material witness for the Government.

MARGARET DONELSON, and MARY KENNEY of 15 East Forty-sixth Street, released on $1,500 bail.

ALFRED J. O'DONOVAN of 381 Fifth Avenue, released on $1,500 bail.

ELLEN McNAMARA, alias Ellen O'Donovan, and MARGARET J. SMITH of 37 West Thirty-sixth Street, released on $1,500 bail each.

ANNA E. CONLIN, 55 West Thirty-eighth Street, released on $1,500 bail.

JOHN McMARAUGH of K. L. Carey & Co. of 71 West Thirty-fifth Street, released on $1,500 bail.

THERESA MAHONEY of 69 West Forty-eighth Street, released on $1,500 bail.

CAROLINE WINDMULLER, alias Mme. Thurn, of 426 Fifth Avenue, released on $5,000 bail.

AUGUSTA WICKSTROM of 205 West Forty-eighth Street, released on $2,500 bail.

TERESA F. HANNON and THOMAS F. J. HANNON of 26 West Forty-seventh Street, already under $3,000 bail.

ALICE McEVOY of 41 West Forty-fifth Street, released on $1,500 bail.

All of these defendants, with the exception of Phillipsen, Schwartz, and Murphy, were importers, who are accused of availing themselves of the advantages of the system which Phillipsen is said to have represented. In addition, counsel for Mary A. Moore and Isabel Holland of Boston appeared yesterday and gave bail in the sum of $8,000 for their appearance here on Jan. 3, when all of the defendants named in the indictment will be up for arraignment.

The Charge Against Them.

The indictment itself was not made public yesterday, but the bail bonds contained a summary of the legal charges against the defendants. According to these bonds the Government charges that the defendants "knowingly, unlawfully, and willfully conspired to defraud the United States by bringing in and causing to be brought in on and by divers vessels of the American and Red Star Lines, to the piers and docks of said lines, in the Port of New York, and then and there clandestinely removing and causing to be clandestinely removed from said docks and piers and entered into domestic commerce of the United States without making any entry or declaration thereof, or presenting any invoice to the United States Collector for the Port of New York and without at any time paying or causing to be paid any customs duties on certain goods, wares, and merchandise." Then follows a description of the general classes of merchandise smuggled in, namely, "model gowns, women's dresses, silks, laces, and dressmaking materials and general merchandise."

The story behind these arrests goes back to the time, last March, when a seizure was made on the American Line pier of five trunks containing silks, laces, and other articles of large value, representing a total of approximately $52,000. The arrest of Schwartz, head baggage man at the pier, followed, and then the Government, through Mr. Wise, took up an investigation of the whole subject of the frauds involving the smuggling of millinery and dressmaking materials into this country, which eventually unraveled a remarkable story of an underground express route that had cost the Government a million dollars or more a year in duties.

More Indictments to Come.

Collector Loeb readily gave his assistance to the task, which Mr. Wise placed in the hands of Assistant United States Attorney Goldthwaite Dorr, and the result was the complete exposure of the system under which the Government has been defrauded. The facts relating to these swindles and others which are yet to be made the subject of arrests were in process of presentation before the Federal Grand Jury, which sat from last June until the first of October, and the investigation was wound up before the October Grand Jury, which just went out of office.

Various indictments were handed down and placed under the seal of the court until a convenient time should be reached for making a general round-up of the persons accused, and it is expected that in addition to the twenty-seven persons named in the present indictment several other individuals or firms, among them one of the most prominent millinery firms in the city, will eventually be brought in with the rest.

The system had at its head, according to discoveries which the Government made, a man named Frank Faucett, who is now dead. He was once in the Customs Service here and was dismissed for some misconduct or other, whereupon he took up his residence in Paris and got up what is considered the cleverest scheme ever devised for general smuggling of anything that might be brought into this country in trunks accompanying passengers on the high-class steamship lines.

In order not to miss the many notable features in next Sunday's Times it is important to place orders with news dealers to-day.

SNEAD SUICIDE NOTE MAY BE GENUINE

Handwriting Expert Said to Have Found That the Bathtub Victim Wrote It.

PROSECUTION WON'T HALT

Authorities Said to Have New Evidence of a Murder Plot—Indictments Expected To-day.

It was learned on good authority yesterday that William J. Kinsley, the handwriting expert, declares that Mrs. Ocey W. M. Snead, whose body was found in a bathtub in East Orange, N. J., on Nov. 29, after she had been dead twenty-four hours, did write the suicide note, and all the other suicide notes and letters since found.

Prosecutor Mott of Essex County would neither admit nor deny it. Mr. Kinsley did not deny it, saying that any statement would have to come from Mr. Mott. The report is borne out by collateral statements from both Mr. Mott and Mr. Kinsley.

Some days ago when asked what he would do in the event that the handwriting expert found the suicide note to be genuine, Mr. Mott said he would not submit the note to any other expert, but on the other hand, if Mr. Kinsley found the note a forgery he would employ a second expert. Last night when both he and Mr. Kinsley admitted that the latter had reached a decisive finding in the case of the notes, Mr. Mott said no more experts would be employed. Mr. Kinsley advised Mr. Mott to employ other experts, but the prosecutor said he was satisfied.

How the girl came to write so many notes is not explained. It is suggested that she may have had suicide mania, as her mother, Mrs. Caroline B. Martin, says she had, but it was learned also last night that Mr. Mott within the last two or three days has discovered among the papers of Mrs. Martin and Mrs. Snead, one of the aunts, much new evidence tending to show that there was a conspiracy against the life of the dead girl, despite the report on the suicide notes.

So strong is this new evidence, according to the statement of an important witness, that the testimony of Mr. Kinsley, whatever its character might have been, would not have halted the prosecution. The exact nature and source of this new light which has broken on the Prosecutor could not be learned.

Through the activity of his own and the East Orange detectives, assisted by the police of this city, Mr. Mott has come into possession of a large quantity of the three prisoners' papers. Their character was not made known to the Essex County Grand Jury yesterday with any degree of completeness, it is believed. They are said to contain five new "suicide notes," found among the papers belonging to Mrs. Mary Snead, at 466 West Twenty-second Street, making in all, according to the Prosecutor, about thirty-five or forty suicide notes and letters.

When the Grand Jury adjourned last night, after having given much of the afternoon to investigating the causes of Mrs. Snead's death, there was little doubt in the minds of those about the Court House that indictments against all three women would be reported, probably this afternoon.

Prosecutor Mott announced at the close of the Grand Jury session that the inquiry had been completed.

"Did you exhaust the list of your witnesses summoned here to testify before the Grand Jury?" he was asked.

"I did not," he said.

One of the witnesses said that of his own knowledge of the case he had no doubt of the finding of indictments. Mr. Mott admitted that he had asked the Grand Jury to make its report in this case at the earliest possible moment. It is believed to be his purpose to have extradition papers for Mrs. Martin and Mrs. Snead when they appear in the Tombs Court on Friday morning.

Among those testifying before the Grand Jury were Chief of Police Bell, Detective Sergeant O'Neil of East Orange, Mr. Kinsley, and Charles Kirk and William Howard, two boys of East Orange, who have identified Mrs. Martin as one of the women they saw leave the East Orange house in which Mrs. Snead died. The Howard boy picked up her veil, according to the detectives.

Dr. William H. Hicks, who is analyzing the stomach of the woman to ascertain if it contained poison, was at the court house, but not ready with his report.

Special to The New York Times.

ST. CATHERINES, Ontario, Dec. 21.—The police here have so far received no communication from the police of New York or New Jersey concerning the arrest of Fletcher Snead. They are keeping him under surveillance, however, and wait only the word to take him into custody.

He rented a lock box at the Post Office to-day and gave orders to have all his mail kept there until he called for it. Heretofore it has been sent to his hotel.

STEALS A PURSE FROM BABY.

But Mother, Out Shopping, Catches the Boy Who Did It.

Mrs. Anna Silverstein of 16 West 113th Street, who left her pocketbook in a baby carriage in which was her baby outside of a shop at 1,350 Fifth Avenue yesterday afternoon, saw two boys grab the pocketbook and run. She chased and caught one of the boys, on whom she found $7. Her purse had contained $16.50, she said.

Reuben Greenblatt, who is 11 years old and lives at 7 East 115th Street, said another boy had given him the money. Reuben was arrested and paroled in the custody of his parents.

HIGH WIND SPREADS BIG FIRE IN NEWBURG

Night Blaze Started in Marvel's Shipyards and Rapidly Worked Over to the Factory District.

NEARBY TOWNS SEND AID

Fire Apparently Beyond Control and Nearly All of the Residents of the City Out to View It.

Special to The New York Times.

NEWBURG, N. Y., Dec. 22, (Wednesday.)—The biggest fire which has occurred along the Hudson River shores in years started in the Marvel shipyards here at 1:30 o'clock this morning and half an hour later had spread to several factory buildings and dwellings adjoining. Requests for assistance were sent to all the nearby twons, for the fire was entirely uncontrollable. At present it is impossible to tell where it will end.

Poughkeepsie, Fiskill Landing Matteawan, and several other towns are among those which have promised help in the way of fire apparatus and men. A stiff northwest wind is blowing, driving the flames over the territory south of the shipyards.

How the fire started is not known. Once it started, however, it gained headway with remarkable speed and was beyond the control of the local Fire Department almost before men or apparatus reached the yards.

A steamer of the Citizens' Line was tied to the pier at the shipyards undergoing repairs, but was floated away into the river before the fire had spread to its decks. Other shipping, much of it in course of construction by the company, has been destroyed or is in a position where there is no hope that it may be saved.

Among the work at present on hand by the shipyards are a steel ferryboat intended for use in Manhattan by the New York Central Railroad, and another similar vessel destined for service between this place and New York. Both of these will be destroyed.

The Marvel Shipyards is one of the biggest industries in Newburg and employs many men. Thomas F. Marvel, the founder of the company, is its President, and ex-Gov. Odell is the Vice President and Treasurer.

Crowds line the streets at the edge of the burning territory, everybody in Newburg having been aroused by the blaze, and across the river the shore for miles is lined with interested spectators. The fire is a spectacular one, the flames mounting skyward to a great height.

Every available man has been pressed into service as a fireman, but their efforts have had no noticeable effect on the spread of the flames, which threaten to extend the burned area unless help arrives from other towns in the way of more fire apparatus.

WOMAN CAPTURES A BURGLAR.

Mrs. Kenny Got Dowd by the Neck and Kept Him Until Police Came.

Mrs. Patrick Kenny, widow of Assessment Commissioner of Jersey City, returning home early yesterday morning from a visit to her daughter, Mrs. Thomas Lally, caught John Dowd of 278 Twelfth Street breaking into her home at 183 [illegible]

Dowd is frail and Mrs. Kenny is big and strong. She took Dowd by the neck and marched him into her parlor and kept him under subjection until a policeman arrived.

In the First Criminal Court Judge Farmer held Dowd for the Grand Jury.

The Bettmann Archive

Dr. Cook retraces his steps on a map as he lectures before the King of Denmark and 1500 people at the Royal Geographical Society of Denmark. Cook enjoyed great honors and acclaim before his claims were rejected on grounds of insufficient evidence.

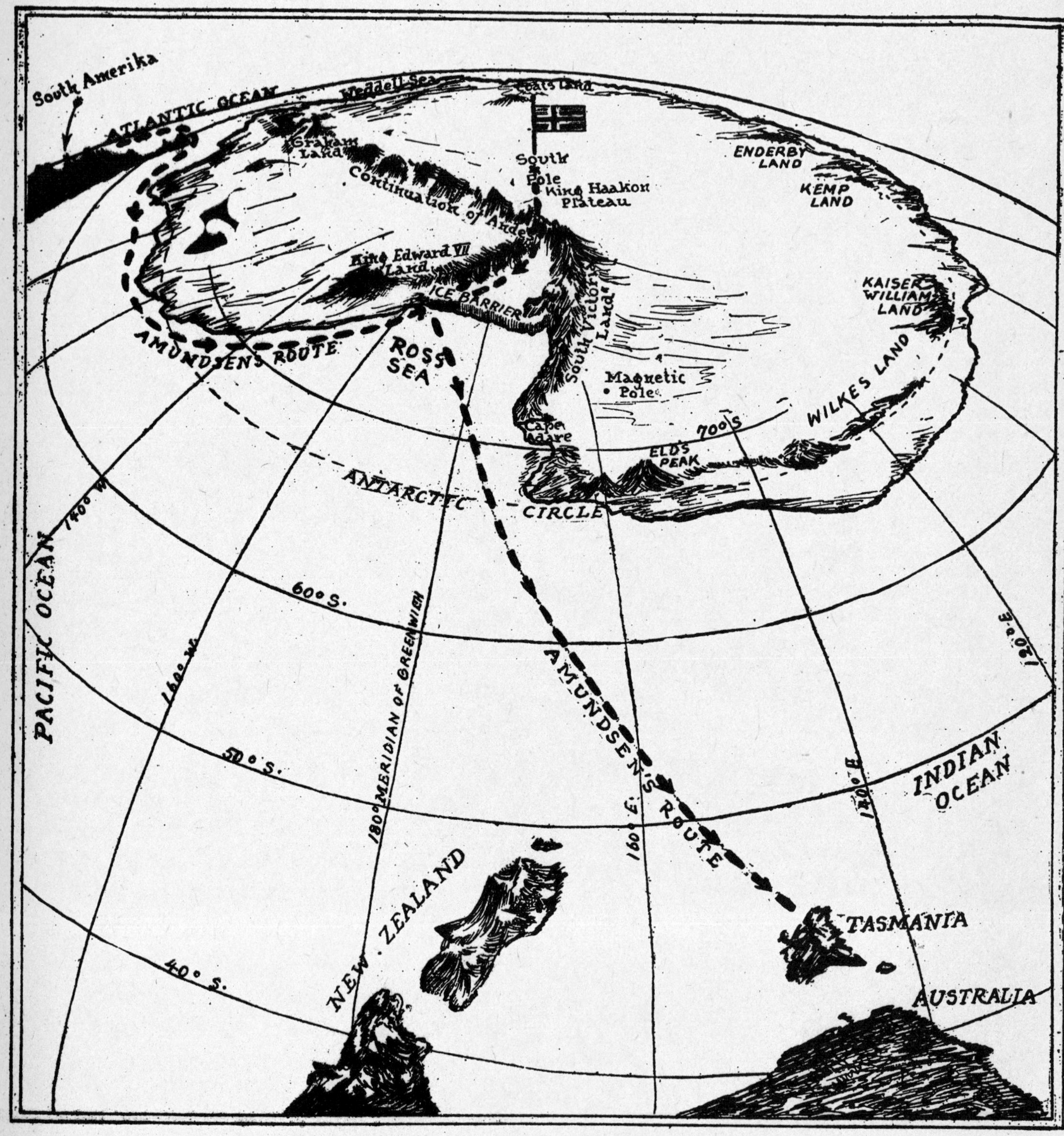

Amundsen's route to the South Pole.

"All the News That's Fit to Print."

The New York Times.

THE WEATHER.
Fair, slightly warmer Thursday; Friday, fair, warmer; moderate winds, becoming south.
For full weather report see Page 23.

VOL. LXI...NO. 19,767. NEW YORK, FRIDAY, MARCH 8, 1912.—TWENTY-TWO PAGES. ONE CENT

MRS. W. W. JACOBS IS SENT TO PRISON

Wife of Novelist Sentenced to Month's Hard Labor for Smashing Windows in London.

"DUTY TO HER CHILDREN"

Her Defense and Husband's Plea Fail —More Suffragette Window-Breaking Yesterday.

By Marconi Transatlantic Wireless Telegraph to The New York Times.

LONDON, Friday, March 8.—Undeterred by the hard labor sentences passed by the Magistrates on suffragists earlier in the week, a number of women early yesterday morning waited in the West End for the taking down of the shutters in front of the shops, and as soon as the glass was exposed smashed the expensive windows of some big establishments. Among the windows destroyed were some of the largest in London. Half a dozen of the "militants" were arrested, and doubtless heavy sentences await them.

The latest prominent convict-recruit to the ranks of the militant suffragettes is Mrs. Eleanor Jacobs, wife of W. W. Jacobs, the novelist, who was sentenced to a month's imprisonment at hard labor by Magistrate Fordham at the West London Police Court yesterday for breaking four windows in the Earl's Court Road Post Office on Wednesday afternoon. When asked by the Magistrate what she had to say, she replied:

"I have done this because I think it is my duty as the mother of five children."

"Was it your duty as the mother of children to smash property?" asked the Magistrate.

"Yes, that is the only way we can protest against the action, or rather the inaction of the Government in refusing us justice," responded Mrs. Jacobs.

The Magistrate remarked that her statement was absurd and started to remand her for eight days to have a doctor report on her state of mind.

The defendant smilingly replied:

"My mind is quite sound. I have done my duty to my children for twelve years. I think my daughters, when they grow up, should have equal rights and responsibilities and duties with my sons."

Later in the afternoon Mr. Jacobs appeared before the Magistrate and pleaded for his wife, saying that she had taken this attitude because she conceived it her duty to her children that she should support the movement. He asked the Magistrate to consider that for a long time persons like his wife had been under the influence of two leaders of the movement, Mr. and Mrs. Pethick Lawrence.

He said he could not speak too highly of her as a wife and mother, and hoped the court would extend leniency to her and not inflict on her the hardships which very properly, no doubt, had been inflicted on many of these misguided women. His wife, he said, could not stand hardship, and if called upon to endure it her health would be permanently affected; she did not realize what she was doing.

He wished to say that if the Government had not played with the question, his wife and those other unhappy women would not have been brought into their present position.

The Magistrate, while expressing sympathy with the novelist, said there was no reason why he should deal more leniently with Mrs. Jacobs than with a vagabond who broke a window for a night's lodging, and passed sentence of one month's imprisonment at hard labor.

LONDON, Friday, March 8.—The extent to which the window-smashing raids of the suffragettes has aroused public feeling against them was evidenced by the large force of foot and mounted police necessary to protect them from a great mob, carrying an effigy of Miss Christabel Pankhurst, which gathered outside Oscar Hammerstein's London Opera House, where the militant section of the suffragists held a meeting last night. The speeches at the meeting were tame and there was a noticeable absence of all incitement to violence.

One woman speaker said that, if any woman desired to judge the panic the latest actions of the suffragettes had caused, let her go to the nearest store and try to borrow a hammer.

A large band of medical students created disorderly scenes outside the Opera House.

The excitement into which London has been thrown by the activity of the suffragettes is indicated by the instructions last night that ladies will not be admitted to Buckingham Palace for the Court tonight unless they present their invitation cards, and also by the announcement that both Houses of Parliament will be closed to the public to-day.

The public was practically asked yesterday to help the police catch the window smashers. The Commissioner of Police issued a circular calling attention to the fact that under the common law anybody is empowered to restrain persons attempting to do such damage and to hold them until a policeman arrives, and, similarly, persons detected after the damage is done.

WOULD SMASH IN PHILADELPHIA

Militant Suffragist Threatens Violence Like That in London.

Special to The New York Times.

PHILADELPHIA, March 7.—Miss Lida Stokes Adams, prominent in the National Women's Suffrage Association, declares that unless the women of Pennsylvania get the ballot the suffragette riots of London may be repeated in this city.

Miss Adams is a militant suffragist. She believes that the women of this country are seeking the ballot in too mild a manner and that if they would use a little muscle instead of voice for argument the cause would advance in a more rapid manner.

FOUR DEAD IN TRAIN WRECK.

Thirty Also Hurt in Wabash Crash—Six Coaches Off the Track.

Special to The New York Times.

LAFAYETTE, Ind., March 7.—The Continental Limited No. 1 of the Wabash Railroad, which left Lafayette an hour and a half late, was wrecked at Redwood Curve, a mile and a half west of West Lebanon, Ind., thirty-five miles from here, at 5 o'clock this afternoon, and as the accident tore down all wires, communication with the scene of the wreck was difficult.

Four persons were killed and thirty injured.

The dead are Mrs. U. G. Good, who boarded the train at Fort Wayne, Ind., en route to St. Louis, and died almost instantly, her back being broken; Mrs. Grant, en route from Adrian, Mich., to Kansas City; a Pullman porter, name unknown, and an unknown youth about 18 years old.

The seriously injured are Mrs. Paul Triesce, Danville, internally hurt; May Hudson, Sidney, Ill., cut and bruised; Fred Henschen, St. Louis, traveling auditor Wabash Railroad, hurt about head. Among those less seriously hurt are William P. Howell, Indianapolis; W. C. Thoms, Toledo; Sherman Sayres, Lafayette, Ind.; A. R. Kitsero, Peru, Ind.; Charles Rhodenburg, Dallas, Texas; E. F. Jennings, Buffalo, N. Y.; E. C. Kohl, Crawfordsville, Ind.; L. H. Robinson, Camden, N. J., and F. Barker, Elmira, N. Y.

The entire train of six coaches left the track, but the engine remained on the rails. A wreck train with physicians on board hurried to the scene.

A broken rail is believed to have caused the wreck. The coaches are piled in confusion on the side of a thirty-foot embankment. The tracks are all blocked, and other trains are detouring.

LONE WINDOW SMASHER HERE

Staten Island Girl Takes a Cue from the London Suffragettes.

Miss Annie Glisman, 22 years old, whose home is between Prince's Bay and Pleasant Plains, S. I., has been deeply interested in reading of the exploits of the London suffragettes, and last night she started out on a lone window-smashing crusade.

Miss Glisman first made her way to the home of Alderman Charles Cole, in Prince's Bay, and, after announcing her presence by breaking a window with a stone, rang the doorbell. The Alderman opened the door, and to him the young woman announced that she was a suffragette and had come to demand her rights. She did not explain what she deemed her rights, but declared that if the Alderman did not do something she would stone the house.

Mr. Cole tried to calm her and cautioned her against violence. Then he called his wife to the door to talk to the young woman while he went to the telephone to notify the police. While he was at the telephone the young woman went away, but she was soon heard from in the neighborhood. Stopping in front of several houses, she hurled stones through the windows.

Detectives responded to the call of Alderman Cole, but Miss Glisman eluded them for some time. Finally she was taken to the station, and from there was sent to the City Farm Colony in New Springville, where she will be examined as to her sanity.

OLD MAN-O'-WAR IN CHAIRS.

Daedalus, Sea-Fighter of a Century Ago, Done Into Furniture.

Timbers from the man-o-war Daedalus, which was an aristocrat of the British Navy a century ago when fighting ships were wearing oak armor belts, have been lying for the past month in the wood yard of F. Eckenroth & Son, 921 East Fifth Street.

They were brought over from England several weeks ago in the Mesaba, of the Atlantic Transportation Company's line to be worked up into household furniture for a residence which is being built at 46 East Seventeenth Street for Stephen C. Clark, a real estate dealer at 149 Broadway.

The timbers were square sawed stanchions of oak fourteen and sixteen inches in thickness, which had acted as supports to the main deck of the man-o'-war. It took several weeks to get them ready for the saw by drawing out the spikes and bolts with which every piece was found to be loaded.

The timbers, cut up, were taken yesterday to Sherwin & Co., wood workers, at 287 East 137th Street, where they will be finished into chairs, tables and trimmings for the dining room and library of Mr. Clark's house.

Mr. Clark said last night that seasoned oak had been ordered from England and that it was purely accidental that the wood purchased had been part of a dismantled warship.

JUMPS INTO NIAGARA RAPIDS.

Man on Freight Train Seeks Death in the Whirlpool.

Special to The New York Times.

BUFFALO, N. Y., March 7.—An unidentified man jumped from a Michigan Central freight train to death in the Niagara whirlpool rapids late this evening. The train was on its way from Canada, and it is believed by the Niagara Falls police that the suicide boarded the train at the Canadian end of the bridge.

When the train was about half way across the cantilever bridge and directly over the whirlpool one of the crew saw a man climb to the top of a car, jump over the low rail a few feet away, and disappear.

NEW OIL CAPITAL $30,000,000.

Standard Company of Indiana Arranging for Increase of Stock.

WHITING, Ind., March 7.—The stockholders of the Standard Oil Company of Indiana to-day voted to increase the capital stock of the Indiana corporation from $1,000,000 to $30,000,000.

After the increase has been referred to the Indiana State authorities and a certificate issued by the Secretary of State the Directors of the Standard Oil Company of Indiana will direct the distribution of the stock of the company in accordance with the reorganization plan approved by the United States Court.

HONORS FOR MRS. ROOSEVELT

Costa Rica Government Put Special Train at Her Disposal.

SAN JOSE, Costa Rica, March 7.—Mrs. Theodore Roosevelt and her daughter, Miss Ethel, arrived at Port Limon this morning.

The visit of the wife and daughter of the ex-President of the United States was a surprise to the Government, which took steps immediately to place a special train at their disposal to bring them to San Jose. Preparations are being made by a women's Reception Committee to entertain the visitors.

TREATIES, SHORN, PASS SENATE, 76 TO 3

Clause Invading Senate's Rights Is Eliminated and Other Restrictions Are Added.

ROOSEVELTIAN VOTES DECIDE

Four Such Senators Defeat Taft's Arbitration Aims—Existing Treaties Suffice, Say Opponents.

Special to The New York Times.

WASHINGTON, March 7.—The Senate brought the debate on the general arbitration treaties with Great Britain and France to an end to-day by unanimous consent, and then proceeded to take from the treaties nearly everything that marked their least advance on the fifteen treaties drafted in 1908 and 1909, when Senator Root was Secretary of State. The single point of advance left in the treaties provides for a Joint High Commission of Inquiry to investigate disputes and their arbitrability, but gives the commission no powers of award. As amended, the treaties were ratified by a vote of 76 to 3.

The turn of affairs adverse to the textual integrity of the treaties came as a surprise to the leaders of the Senate and the supporters of the Administration. It had been known that the ratification of the treaties by the Senate could be obtained only by means of some device like the Lodge resolution of ratification, which, while leaving the treaties unamended internally, so construed them as to deprive the Joint High Commission of its final powers of sending disputes to arbitration and reserved the Senate's full powers of advice and consent. But it had been hoped that the appearance of victory would be saved to the Administration by retaining unimpaired, the language in which the treaties were submitted to the Senate.

The defeat of Mr. Taft's plans resulted from the defection of four Roosevelt Senators, who, with two other Republicans, joined the almost solid Democratic vote in insisting upon the elimination bodily from the treaties of the third clause of Article III., which made the decisions of the High Commission final as to the arbitrability of differences.

Col. Roosevelt has sharply assailed the treaties in editorials and speeches. In general, it can be said that the amendments seeking to weaken the treaties had the support of the Democrats, Roosevelt Republicans, and a few unclassified Republicans. But by a strange coincidence the only Senator who voted throughout for every proposal to weaken the treaties was William Lorimer of Illinois, who is Mr. Roosevelt's bitterest enemy in the Senate. At the last it was he who, with Mr. Reed of Missouri, and Mr. Martine of New Jersey—two radical Democrats—voted against ratification.

Bone of Contention Removed.

The test vote came as soon as debate ended. It was on the original amendment reported last Summer from the Committee on Foreign Relations eliminating Clause 3 of Article III., which has always been the bone of contention. The clause was stricken out by a vote of 42 to 40.

The vote for the amendment was made up of thirty-six Democrats and six Republicans. The vote against the amendment was made up of thirty-seven Republicans and three Democrats. The Republicans who voted to strike out the important clause were Mr. Borah of Idaho, Mr. Bourne of Oregon, Mr. Bristow of Kansas, and Mr. Dixon of Montana—all Roosevelt sympathizers—and Mr. Lorimer of Illinois and Mr. Smith of Michigan. The Democrats who voted for the retention of the clause were Mr. Rayner of Maryland, Mr. Thornton of Alabama, and John Sharp Williams of Mississippi.

Then Mr. Culberson of Texas offered an amendment to the body of the treaties exempting from its terms all questions of vital interest, independence, honor, or the interests of third parties. That amendment failed by a vote of 37 to 45, though subsequently the object of the amendment was accomplished in an amendment to the resolution of ratification. Mr. Bacon then unsuccessfully offered to the body of the treaties the amendment, subsequently adopted as part of the resolution of ratification, exempting from the operation of the treaty all questions of immigration, State bonds, Territorial integrity, the Monroe Doctrine, and all issues of American policy. As an amendment to the body of the treaty this motion was lost by a tie vote, 41 to 41.

The second change actually made in the text of the treaties was contained in an amendment offered by Mr. Chamberlain, a Democrat from Oregon. He excepted from the operation of the treaties all questions concerning the admission of aliens to the schools of the several States or their admission into the United States. This amendment, which, of course, has no bearing upon the present treaties, but looks merely to the possible negotiation of similar treaties with Japan and China, was adopted by a vote of 40 to 38.

The question of final ratification then came up, and Mr. Lodge, after explaining that the elimination of Clause 3 of Article III. made his carefully worded resolution of ratification unnecessary, withdrew it and offered instead a simple resolution declaring the treaty with Great Britain ratified. To that Mr. Bacon of Georgia offered his former amendment, and by the change in half a dozen votes it was adopted, 46 to 36. The amended resolution was then adopted, a two-thirds vote being necessary. All votes affecting the British treaty were then voted to apply to the French convention.

Treaties' Purpose Destroyed.

The language of the Bacon amendment shows how completely the significance of the new treaties has been destroyed. It reads:

> Resolved further, That the Senate advises and consents to the ratification of the said treaty with the understanding, to be made a part of such ratification, that the treaty does not authorize the submission to arbitration of any question which affects the admission of aliens into the United States, or the admission of aliens to the educational institutions of the several States, or the territorial integrity of the several States or of the United States, or concerning the question of the alleged indebtedness or moneyed obligation of any State of the United States, or any question which depends upon or involves the maintenance of the traditional attitude of the United States concerning American questions, commonly described as the Monroe Doctrine, or other purely Governmental policy.

The debate was significant from the fact that all the opponents of the pending treaties, declared their belief that the treaties already in force as negotiated by Mr. Root as Secretary of State were superior in phraseology and definiteness. Mr. Root himself made a striking address in behalf of the treaties, though, like Mr. Lodge, who also supported them, he favored the Lodge resolution of ratification on striking out the plenary powers of the Joint High Commission.

TRIES TO KILL GIRLS, BLOWS HIMSELF UP

Coachman George Mead Terribly Beats Young Women with Steel Molding, Then Ends His Life.

USED A STICK OF DYNAMITE

Fancied Injury by the Girls' Father, the Rev. Frank Hartfield, Cause of Tragedy Near Brewsters, N. Y.

Special to The New York Times.

BREWSTERS, N. Y., March 7.—In their home, Stonehenge Cottage, in Sodom, twelve miles from here, the Misses Ruby and Amy Hartfield, daughters of the Rev. Frank Hartfield, rector of the Episcopal Church here, and granddaughters of Mrs. Seth B. Howes, widow of a wealthy showman and owner of a large estate known as the Castle, about a mile and a half from this village, are recovering from the attack made on them yesterday by George Mead, their grandmother's coachman and the caretaker of her house, in her absence.

All that remains of Mead was taken to-day from the morgue to the little cottage near the Howes estate, to which he brought his bride less than six months ago. Mead, facing capture at the hands of employes of H. H. Vreeland, former head of the Metropolitan Street Railway Company, blew himself to pieces with a stick of dynamite. His young wife is prostrated.

Miss Ruby Hartfield is 20 years old, and her sister is 18. Mead was 32 years old, having entered the employ of Mr. Howes 16 years ago.

Apparently, Mead intended to kill both the girls and perhaps himself at the same time, to avenge a fancied wrong at the hands of their father. Mead is known to have believed it was by the rector's advice that Mrs. Howes, on leaving for the Winter, four months ago, refused to allow him the use of her automobiles, that he might learn to be a chauffeur, and also reduced his coachman's wages of $45 a month to $30 a month for acting as caretaker. No later than Tuesday Mead threatened to "get square" with the rector.

The attack on the girls was made at about 5 o'clock, when they reached The Castle, after a twelve-mile drive from home, bringing keys to the place, in response to a telephone message from Mead that the wind had blown loose a shutter and he must enter the house to repair this. The girls drove into the stable, from an upper window of which they had seen Mead peering as they ascended the driveway. The man was down the stairs almost before the girls were in the stable, and he bolted the door behind them.

Struck Girls Down.

Both girls were alarmed at his action, but alighted from their pony carriage. Ruby stepped toward Mead to hand him the keys, and he sprang at her, bringing up a steel moulding which he had held behind him, and striking her on the head. As the girl sank, he caught her and struck her again and again.

As Mead dragged Ruby into a washroom, Amy stood, too frightened to scream. Then she rushed toward Mead, crying:

"If you are going to kill her, kill me, too."

Mead dropped the elder sister and sprang at Amy. He struck her once on the head, and the girl fell to her knees. Evidently believing that he had stunned her, Mead jumped back to the other girl. Amy, however, staggered to the stable door, pushed it outward a few inches, and screamed.

Her cries were heard by Dennis Hogan, gardener on the Vreeland estate, who hurried to the stable. Amy faltered an explanation. On the floor of the washroom he found Ruby, her face covered with blood. Mead was not to be seen, but a door into the carriage house showed how he had escaped.

Hogan raised the girl, and carrying her started toward the Vreeland place with Amy clinging to his arm. They had nearly reached the road when they were prostrated by an explosion.

The report reached the ears of A. B. Yates in the Vreeland stable, and he hurried to the scene. With Hogan he got the girls to a safe place, and telephoned to Dr. F. Robert Ritchey, who came with Constable Arthur Brown and Deputy Sheriff H. S. Brown.

The officers found the front of the building almost blown to pieces. Every window was shattered and the south wall bulged outward. Within, the flooring was blown into splinters, but the pony and the cart stood unharmed in the wreckage. The post to which the pony had been tethered was torn from the floor. The two-inch oak partition, which separated the washroom from the main stable, was blown out.

Man Blown to Pieces.

In a corner of the washroom lay Mead's head, neck, part of his left shoulder, and his left arm. His body had been blown to pieces, and his legs and right arm were found in different corners of the room. Most of the damage was confined to the washroom. In the stable two horses, besides the pony, were unhurt, and both of Mrs. Howes's automobiles were not damaged.

On a shelf in the washroom the officers found two sticks of dynamite. One end of the shelf on which they rested was blown away, but the sticks had not exploded. It was with one like these, it is believed, that Mead killed himself. He had the dynamite there to blow up stumps on the place.

Mead's body was taken to the morgue here and afterward claimed by his young wife. Coroner Smith said he would hold an inquest as soon as the Misses Hartfield were well enough to appear before him as witnesses.

Seven stitches were taken in Amy's scalp and thirteen in patching up wounds on the head of Ruby. The girls are still confined to their bed.

PREDICT STOCKING FAMINE.

White Costumes Will Be Incomplete Unless the Retailers Hurry Up.

The increased demand for white dress fabrics for summer is regarded in the New York hosiery market as an infallible indication that white hosiery will be popular.

Many of the stocking mills are preparing to meet the expected demand, which it is believed will exceed that of last year. It is predicted that the failure of retail buyers to appreciate this will cause a shortage in the supply before the season is very far advanced. At the present time buyers are ordering sparingly, and it is said that the rush of orders later on will overwhelm the mills.

AMUNDSEN REACHES THE SOUTH POLE; STAYS FOUR DAYS, DEC. 14 TO 17, 1911; PARTY ALL WELL, HE TELLS THE TIMES

Norwegian Explorer Sends Word of His Success From Tasmania.

NO NEWS FROM CAPT. SCOTT

London Waits Anxiously for Word That He, Too, Has Attained the Goal.

AMUNDSEN'S FULL STORY

Will Be Published Exclusively in The New York Times, Probably To-morrow.

SHACKLETON GIVES PRAISE.

Believes Norwegian Was Aided by Good Weather and His Special Equipment.

EXPLORERS MAY HAVE MET

Possible That Their Parties Came Together on the Routes Converging Toward the Goal.

AMUNDSEN ANNOUNCES HIS DISCOVERY

Special Cable to The New York Times.

Christiania, Norway, March 7.

I have received the following message:

HOBART, Tasmania, Thursday, March 7, 1912—Pole attained, fourteenth—seventeenth December, 1911. All well. ROALD AMUNDSEN.

(Signed) LEON AMUNDSEN.

WARNING.

For the protection of Capt. Amundsen, who has risked his life in the attainment of the south pole, and whose chief material reward must be the proceeds of the sale of his narrative, The New York Times, which has purchased the rights thereto for the United States, to be duly protected by copyright, gives notice that it will prosecute any infringement whatsoever of such copyright.

(Photograph, American Press Association.)

Roald Amundsen

He Discovered the Northwest Passage, and To-day His Triumphant Attainment of the South Pole Is Announced.

SHACKLETON ON THE FEAT.

Famous Antarctic Explorer Analyzes the Performance of Amundsen.

By SIR ERNEST SHACKLETON.

Specially Contributed to The New York Times and London Chronicle.

Special Cable to THE NEW YORK TIMES.

LONDON, March 7.—Analyzing the somewhat brief cable to hand, announcing Capt. Amundsen's attainment of the south pole, one, from previous experience, would assume that the journey was done with extreme rapidity and under very favorable conditions as regards the weather.

Capt. Amundsen has attained the geographical south pole, the long-sought-for spot, and that finishes record breaking as far as the ends of the earth are concerned.

Assuming that the latitude of Amundsen's Winter quarters was 74° 44', that is only 676 geographical miles from the south pole. This place was named Bay of Whales by me on my expedition, and was formerly known as Balloon Bight. If Amundsen did fifteen miles a day and reached the south pole on Dec. 14, he would have started south about the beginning of November, but it is much more likely that he did not travel at that rate, especially for the first hundred or two odd miles, so we may assume that he started for the pole about the beginning of October.

There is no indication in the cable whether Amundsen followed the route of my expedition in reaching the mountains that guard the approach to the pole. It may be possible that he found a new route and an easier one up to the plateau which lies about 9,000 to 11,000 feet above sea level. He may have had good weather.

Took Three Days to be Sure.

The words of the cablegram, "Pole attained, Dec. 14 to 17," evidently mean that on reaching the geographical pole, so that no uncertainty should exist as to his exact position, he waited three days, taking noon observations so as accurately to determine his position.

The advantage of taking three days of continuous observations at the pole are as follows:

Assuming that an explorer took a noon observation of the altitude of the sun and found that he was at the pole, a degree of uncertainty would still exist because of the slow movement of the sun, which completes the circle with hardly any perceptible rise or fall. If an observation is taken for the second day at the same spot, and the difference of declination of the sun in its north or south path corresponds with his observation of the day before, and it does this for the third day, he may safely assume that his position is accurate.

A flying snapshot is not as reliable as a continuous series of observations. If he were using a theodolite, undoubtedly the most accurate instrument, there is no doubt that he could ascertain the position of the pole to one mile.

If Capt. Amundsen left the pole on Dec. 17 he would very likely, with a fair wind behind him, return to Winter quarters in about forty-five days. We left our "furthest south," which was, roughly speaking, 100 miles north of the pole, on Jan. 9, and reached our Winter quarters on Feb. 28. They were 650 geographical miles from the pole, approximately the same length of journey that Amundsen would have covered from the pole to his Winter quarters, as they were ninety miles further south than ours.

We then assume that Capt. Amundsen reached Bay of Whales at the end of January. He would take two or three days loading up and getting under way with the Fram. He would then presumably go north and work to the westward of Cape Adare, and then get into the westerly winds and make Hobart, Tasmania. The Fram, being a slow vessel, doing about five knots, it would take quite a month, unless there were strong winds behind her, to reach Hobart.

Did Scott Reach the Pole?

The question naturally arises in one's mind, did Capt. Scott reach the pole before Dec. 14?

If so, the honor flies with the British flag, but the same endurance, the same skill, and the same meed of endeavor must be granted to Capt. Amundsen as the Norwegian people would grant to Capt.

"All the News That's Fit to Print."

The New York Times.

THE WEATHER.
Fair, slightly warmer Thursday; Friday, fair, warmer; moderate winds, becoming south.
For full weather report see Page 22.

VOL. LXI...NO. 19,768. * * * * NEW YORK, SATURDAY, MARCH 9, 1912.—TWENTY-FOUR PAGES. ONE CENT In Greater New York, Jersey City, and Newark. { Elsewhere, TWO CENTS.

TAFT SHOWS PERIL IN ROOSEVELT POLICY

Recall of Decisions Would Sow Seeds of Confusion and Tyranny, He Says.

CHEERED BY TOLEDO THRONG

Judiciary Would Be Deprived of Independence, He Asserts, and Life and Property Endangered.

Special to The New York Times.

TOLEDO, Ohio, March 8.—After a day spent for the most part on the rear platform of his private car President Taft concluded his brief "campaign" through Eastern and Northern Ohio here to-night with a speech in the Coliseum.

On the way north from Pittsburgh to Toledo the President made more than a dozen speeches from the car platform. Although rain or snow was falling the Ohioans turned out in good numbers.

President Taft spoke on prosperity and peace, the tariff and business, farming, and conservation. None of his talks was long.

The President was in good humor and the crowds were apparently in good humor, too. At Canton somebody raised a laugh that brought an answering smile to the President's face by yelling after Mr. Taft was through speaking:

"Don't let the lion tamer get you."

The President reached Toledo late this afternoon, driving from the station to the Commercial Club over muddy streets, between sidewalks filled with people.

President Taft's appearance at the Coliseum was attended by prolonged cheering and waving of myriads of small flags held up by the seat holders. Crowds of people were turned away because of the lack of seats. His topic was "The Judiciary and Progress." He made no direct reference to Col. Theodore Roosevelt, nor to the latter's speech at Columbus, but referred freely to some of the policies that were enunciated by the former President before the Ohio Constitutional Convention.

Taft on Recall of Judges.

Utterly without merit or utility, and reactionary instead of progressive; crude, revolutionary, fitful, and unstable were the terms in which the President referred to the recall method of reversing judicial constructions of the Constitution.

"I have examined this proposed method of reversing judicial decisions on Constitutional questions with care," President Taft said. "I do not hesitate to say that it lays the axe at the foot of the tree of well-ordered freedom and subjects the guaranties of life, liberty, and property without remedy to the fitful impulse of a temporary majority of an electorate."

The President began with a reference to the development of representative government in the United States. The best government, he said, and that which was most certain to provide for and protect the [illegible] of every class, was that government in which every class had a voice.

"Government by unanimous vote of the electorate," he said, "is impossible, and therefore the majority of the electorate must rule. We find that government by the people, is, therefore, under our present system, government by a majority of one-fourth of those whose rights and happiness are to be affected by the course and conduct of the Government. This is the nearest to a government by the whole people we have ever had. Women's suffrage will change this, and it is doubtless coming as soon as the electorate can be certain that most women desire it, and will assume its burden and responsibility.

Constitution a Protection.

"It was long ago recognized that direct action of a temporary majority of the existing electorate must be limited by fundamental law; that is by a Constitution intended to protect the individual and the minority of the electorate and the non-voting majority of the people against the unjust or the arbitrary action of the majority of the electorate."

President Taft quoted at length from Daniel Webster's speeches on the necessity of maintaining checks and balances in a Constitution to secure the guaranty of individual rights and well-ordered liberty, and then led up to his discussion of the judiciary.

"It is a complete misunderstanding of our form of government," the President said, "or any kind of government that exalts justice and righteousness, to assume that Judges are bound to follow the will of a majority of an electorate in respect of the issue for their decision."

The judiciary, he said, was not representative in the sense that the Executive and the legislators were, whether Judges be appointed or elected, because they must enforce the law as they found it.

"In many cases before the Judges that temporary majority is a real party to the controversy to be decided," the President continued. "It may be seeking to deprive an individual or a minority of a right secured by the fundamental law. In such a case if the Judges were mere representatives or agents of the majority to carry out its will they would lose their judicial character entirely and the so-called administration of justice would be a farce."

At this point the President repeated his former declarations that the judicial system was not as perfect as it might be made, and called attention to his speeches and messages to Congress urging reform in procedure. He spoke of delays and the costs of litigation.

Judges and Popular Opinion.

"But these humdrum defects and their tedious remedies," he declared, "are not of the spectacular character to call for political discussion or to attract effort from politicians in the passage of remedial legislation. The formidable attack upon our judiciary now is that the Judges do not respond sufficiently to popular opinion. It is said that courts are interposing their obstructive power to the enforcement of legislation looking to the relief of the oppressed by declaring laws unconstitutional and by so-called judicial legislation in interpreting into statutes words not intended by the Legislature."

Such charges, if reduced to specific instances, the President thought, could be shown to be unfounded for the most part, but for the purposes of his discussion he might admit that courts had erred in that regard, had unduly broadened Constitutional restrictions to invalidate useful statutes, or had given to statutes a wrong construction.

"Indeed, I do not hesitate to say that I do not concur in the reasoning of certain courts of last resort as to the Constitutional validity of certain social reform statutes, and I am very anxious that the remedies proposed in those statutes should be given effective operation."

Independence of the Judiciary.

The President then took up the proposed remedies: First the recall of Judges and later the recall of judicial decisions. Than the recall of Judges, he declared, there could not be a system better adapted to deprive the judiciary of "that independence without which the liberty and other rights of the individual cannot be maintained against the Government and the majority.

"But it is said we may have corrupt Judges. How are we going to get rid of them? They can be impeached under our present system. But that is said to be too [illegible]. Well, amend the procedure [illegible]. Create a tribunal for [illegible] of Judges for cause. Give them

Continued on Page 10.

AMUNDSEN SILENT ASHORE

Has Told Nothing at Hobart About His Trip, Even to His Friend the Consul.

From THE TIMES Correspondent at Hobart, Tasmania.

HOBART, Tasmania, Saturday Afternoon, March 9.—Capt. Amundsen has absolutely refused to disclose any information here. He showed your correspondent to-day a cable despatch from THE NEW YORK TIMES congratulating him on the result of his expedition, and says that he is forwarding further information to THE NEW YORK TIMES.

Amundsen's ship, the Fram, is still anchored in the stream, and no one is allowed aboard her.

Last night Capt. Amundsen cabled to The London Daily Chronicle and to THE NEW YORK TIMES. To-day he lunched with Henry D. Baker, the American Consul, but notwithstanding that press men seeking information were close around him he was as hard as adamant to their inquiries. Even Consul Baker could get nothing from him about his expedition and its results.

J. B. McNAMARA VERY ILL.

His Brother Also in Serious Condition in San Quentin Prison.

Special to The New York Times.

LOS ANGELES, Cal., March 8.—J. B. McNamara is dying in the State Penitentiary at San Quentin and his brother, J. J. McNamara, former Secretary-Treasurer of the International Association of Bridge and Structural Iron Workers, is seriously ill in the same institution, is the word brought from the prison to-day by Malcolm McLaren, the Burns detective who worked on the case against the dynamiters.

J. B. McNamara was sentenced to life imprisonment upon his plea of guilty of dynamiting the Los Angeles Times Building. His brother is serving a ten-year sentence. J. B. McNamara is suffering with tuberculosis and the dust in the jute mill where he is employed is aggravating the disease, according to McLaren.

DEVANEY OFF TO NEW DORP.

Capt. O'Connor, in His Place, Expected to Stop Burglaries in Bath Beach.

Police Commissioner Waldo transferred Capt. Michael Devaney yesterday from the Bath Beach Station to the station at New Dorp, S. I., and replaced him by Capt. John O'Connor from New Dorp. Devaney lives at 365 Union Street, Brooklyn, within about twenty minutes journey of his former command.

The transfer was made following an inspection of the district by Chief Inspector Max Schmittberger on Thursday night. Among other things the Inspector found that Sergt. John McAuliffe and Patrolman James Robinson were loitering in the B. R. T.'s station at Ulmer Park instead of patroling, and these men were suspended yesterday pending a hearing of charges against them.

The inspection was brought about by the South Side Board of Trade. Robberies have been frequent in the Bath Beach precinct, and residents have complained that the few policemen in the streets failed absolutely to perform such ordinary duties as seeing to the observance of city ordinances. A committee from the Board of Trade called on Commissioner Waldo on Thursday and on their statements the Commissioner sent Inspector Schmittberger to make an investigation.

WIFE SENTENCES HUSBAND.

Philadelphia Judge Allows Woman to Act in His Stead.

Special to The New York Times.

PHILADELPHIA, March 8.—Magistrate Morris to-day solved the problem of family difficulties to the satisfaction of three women who had caused the arrest of their husbands when he made the wives, judge, jury and court and had them pass sentance upon the husbands. In two cases the women relented but in the third the wife decided that about three months in the House of Correction would be a mighty good thing for her husband.

Mrs. Patrick Mackin of 1812 Lambert Street was the strong willed woman who sentenced her husband to three months. She said they had been married seventeen years and in that time she had supported the family and had been forced to give money to her husband to purchase liquor. To-day, the woman said, was the first time she really was boss of the household and she meant to "see how it felt to give orders."

Mrs. Marie Gegenhimer of 1826 Judson Street told a harrowing tale of her seven years of married life. When the time came for passing sentence, however, she decided that it might be just as well to give her husband one more chance and she took him home.

HALT PITNEY'S CONFIRMATION

Senate Approves Judge, Then Defers Action on Culberson Objecting.

WASHINGTON, March 8.—The Senate to-day confirmed President Taft's nomination of Mahlon Pitney, Chancellor of the State of New Jersey, to succeed the late Associate Justice Harlan on the Supreme Court bench, and then set aside its action for further consideration because of opposition to Chancellor Pitney which developed in executive session.

The nomination was quickly confirmed in the routine way. Suddenly Senator Bacon asked its status. Vice President Sherman announced that the nomination had been confirmed. Senator Bacon then suggested that the confirmation should be held up until Senator Culberson was present. Senator Culberson, who has been inquiring into the decisions made by the Chancellor, came into the chamber a moment afterward and joined in the debate.

Senator Culberson called attention to Chancellor Pitney's decision in what is known as the Glass Bottle Blowers' case, and a lively discussion followed. In that case Chancellor Pitney, speaking for the majority of the court, sustained an injunction restraining the bottle blowers from coercing or persuading other workmen to break contracts with employers or from interfering in any way with persons willing to work, or from picketing strikers or enforcing boycotts at places where employes had struck.

The nomination may come up again tomorrow.

PLOT TO ROB RICH WIDOW IS CHARGED

Mrs. Harriet Wells Smith Causes the Arrest of a Niece and a Grandnephew.

COURT IS HELD IN HER ROOM

She Is an Aged Paralytic and the Disappearance of an Indorsed Check Made Her Suspicious.

Because Mrs. Harriet Wells Smith, 75 years old and a helpless paralytic, could not appear before him Magistrate McQuade adjourned the afternoon session of the West Side Court yesterday and went to Mrs. Smith's boarding house, 156 West Seventy-eighth Street, to investigate the charge made by her lawyer that an attempt had been made to swindle the aged woman out of the income of $500,000 left to her by her husband, S. Newton Smith, a banker and at one time a member of the firm of E. D. Morgan & Co., who died in December, 1907. The Magistrate made the trip in an ambulance which chanced to be standing outside the court.

After a hearing held in Mrs. Smith's room Magistrate McQuade issued warrants for Mrs. Smith's niece and ward, Mrs. Antoinette W. Brown, wife of a well-to-do cotton broker of Chicago, and Mrs. Brown's son, Newton Davis. Both were arrested later and locked up in the West Sixty-eighth Street Station.

Mrs. Smith, who, despite her age and the fact that her right side is completely paralyzed, is in full possession of her faculties, told Magistrate McQuade that she had sent for her lawyer, George Malraison of 41 Park Row, after her suspicions had been aroused that her niece was trying to swindle her.

The aged woman told the Magistrate that on last Tuesday she had received a check for $119.82 from the United States Trust Company, trustee of Mr. Smith's estate, and that Mrs. Brown, who was present, had opened the letter containing this check and had said to her:

"Indorse this check for me, will you, please?"

Mrs. Smith said that she refused to do this and suggested to Mrs. Brown:

"I think it is time that I got some of my own money now."

Mrs. Brown then informed her, she said, that she owed $1,400 to Miss Mary Clark, her nurse, on a note once given by Mrs. Smith to Miss Clark. Mrs. Smith said she told her niece that she thought this note had been taken up, but finally was persuaded by Mrs. Brown that something was still due on it, and therefore she indorsed the check and gave it to Mrs. Brown. Mrs. Brown and her son, who had accompanied her, left immediately, Mrs. Brown saying as she went out:

"Here, you see, I'll put the check on the mantelpiece."

Blank Paper in Place of Check.

Mrs. Smith said that as soon as Miss Clark arrived she spoke to her about the note, and was told by the nurse that it had been paid already. At Mrs. Smith's direction, so she told the Magistrate, Miss Clark then went to the mantelpiece and found there only a blank piece of paper the size and shape of a check. Mrs. Smith declared that the occurrence had convinced her that an attempt was being made to swindle her, and she thereupon sent word to Mr. Malraison, who straightway visited the West Side Court.

Assistant District Attorney Deacon Murphy began an investigation of the case, and said later that he had learned that Mrs. Brown practically had complete control over Mrs. Smith until quite recently, when the elder woman refused to do her bidding. At Mrs. Brown's direction, he said, Mrs. Smith had moved from the Hotel Savoy, where she and her husband had made their home, to the Great Northern Hotel in Fifty-seventh Street, then to the Holly Apartments, 55 West 116th Street, and finally to the boarding house in Seventy-eighth Street.

He said that when the time came he would be able to show that the transaction on which warrants were issued for Mrs. Brown and her son was not the only one in which Mrs. Smith had been victimized. She said that in the case of the $119.82 check he had learned that Mrs. Brown had deposited it to her own account in the Lincoln Trust Company.

Mr. Malraison called attention to a fact which he suggested would be of extreme importance in the event of a trial. He said that several years ago some of the heirs to Mr. Smith's estate had tried to break his will and that as a result the United States Trust Company was appointed trustee by the Surrogate. He said that Mrs. Brown at once started suit to have the estate transferred so that Mrs. Smith might have control of it.

Mrs. Smith has been under the treatment of Dr. E. Le Roy Satterlee of 6 West Fifty-sixth Street for more than ten years. The physician said last night that he had been suspicious regarding the handling of the estate. Mrs. E. L. Hatch, who keeps the boarding house where Mrs. Smith lives, contributed to the investigation the statement that Mrs. Brown never called on her aunt when Dr. Satterlee was present.

Calls Her Arrest a Conspiracy.

Mrs. Brown's maiden name was Antoinette Wells Steele. She was married to a man named Davis and later divorced him, according to Mr. Murphy, the divorce being granted in Texas in 1906. Two months ago she was married to Wilson T. Brown. When arrested she said she was forty-five years old and lived at 111 West Seventy-sixth Street. Her son, who gave his age as twenty-two, gave the same address.

Henry B. Wesselman of the law firm of Wesselman & Kraus of 55 Liberty Street visited Mrs. Brown and Davis in their cells in the West Sixty-eighth Street Station last night and afterward said that Mrs. Brown declared that her arrest was due to a conspiracy on the part of certain lawyers whom she had blocked in an attempt to extort an excessive fee from Mrs. Smith.

Mr. Wesselman said that Mrs. Brown spoke of a suit instituted in the Surrogates' Court against Mrs. Smith for $2,500, and that after the case had been disposed of the lawyers sent in a bill for $3,500, which she persuaded Mrs. Smith not to pay. He also said that two weeks ago Mrs. Brown visited him and laid the fact before him, later retaining him to look after the widow's interests in respect to this bill. He said that Mrs. Smith appeared when he saw her to be perfectly satisfied with the manner in which Mrs. Brown was looking after her estate, and spoke of her as "my protector."

Mr. Wesselman also said that there was no misappropriation in connection with the check, as it had been given to his client to pay the nurse with. He denied that Mr. Smith's estate was worth $500,000, saying that it was $100,000, and that Mrs. Smith had only a life interest in the estate, of which Newton Davis will inherit $20,000 at her death.

"Mrs. Smith is simply weak-minded. There has been no disagreement between the two women. Mrs. Brown lived with Mrs. Smith up to a few weeks ago," he said.

Mrs. Brown is a large woman, weighing perhaps 180 pounds. She is quite deaf and has to use an ear trumpet.

Shortly after 8 o'clock last night a carriage drove up to Mrs. Smith's home. Two young men went into the house, and a few minutes later Mrs. Smith was carried out on a chair and put into the carriage. Two trunks were put on the carriage, which was then driven away. Mrs. Hatch declared afterward she did not know where Mrs. Smith had been taken to.

From her cell Mrs. Brown sent a message to the nurse attending Mrs. Smith, asking the nurse to take care of her younger son, Britton.

FORSAKE EXPLORER IN ARCTIC WILDS

Indian Guides Tell of Deserting Harry V. Radford in the Barren Lands.

FEARS FOR HIS SAFETY

No Word Yet from Supply Ship Sent to Aid Him in His Trip Around the Top of the Continent.

Harry V. Radford, arctic explorer, Fellow of the American Geographical Society, and member of the Arctic Club, who left this city on Feb. 12, 1909, to engage in four years of exploration and hunting in Northern Canada, is reported to have been forsaken by his guides in the heart of the Barren Lands between Chesterfield Inlet on the northern end of Hudson Bay and Great Bear Lake, about 500 miles inland. He is believed to have been left without provisions, and much fear is expressed for his welfare.

A letter telling of Radford's plight reached the Arctic Club yesterday. The letter is dated Fort Smith, Northwest Territories, Canada, Jan. 15, 1912, and is written by A. J. Bell, Canadian agent stationed at Fort Smith.

"I beg to inform you," wrote Mr. Bell, "that word has reached me from Fort Resolution, Great Bear Lake, stating that the two Indians hired by Mr. Radford during last Summer to accompany him for one year into the Barren Lands, had visited Fort Resolution last month and stated that they had left Mr. Radford last Fall owing to disagreement, and that he did not know they were leaving, as they left at night. Kindly take steps to inform those interested in Mr. Radford of this fact."

Mr Radford made his first trip into Northern Canada about five years ago. He went to study the wood bison, an almost extinct animal, and he succeeded in shooting a beast of this species which weighed more than a ton. Its skeleton is now in the National Museum at Washington, and is the finest of its kind on exhibition. Mr. Radford has written a book on his search for the wood bison, and is a recognized authority on the subject.

Around the Continent's Top.

When he last left New York he announced his intention of proceeding from Great Slave Lake, the northern end of Hudson Bay, then working around the fringe of land to Coronation Bay and Mackenzie Bay, ultimately crossing Alaska to Dawson. He left Edmonton, Alberta, on Oct. 4, 1910, proceeding by way of Fort Vermillion and Fort Smith. He wrote a letter to his friends in the United States on Dec. 26, 1910, from Fort Smith, and in this letter he spoke of his disappointment because of the Canadian Government's refusal to send a supply ship up Hudson Bay to Chesterfield Inlet, which should meet him after he had crossed the Barren Lands. He said that he had then traveled 1,100 miles from Edmonton, and that he had traveled 17,000 miles since leaving New York City.

Mr. Radford next corresponded with the Arctic Club of New York, and this club agreed to send the explorer provisions. More than $500 worth of provisions were bought by Anthony Fiala, Secretary of the club, and shipped from Montreal by a Mr. Grahame of the Hudson Bay Company. They were to be sent to Fort Churchill on the western coast of Hudson Bay, and if Mr. Radford were not found there they were to be sent on to Chesterfield Inlet, about 350 miles further north. The provisions left Montreal on July 5, 1911. Mr. Fiala received a letter from Mr. Grahame on Feb. 19, 1912, in which Mr. Grahame stated that he had not yet learned whether the boatload of provisions had reached Fort Churchill. Nothing had been heard, he said, of either Radford or the ship which was carrying the provisions.

Mr. Fiala also showed a TIMES reporter a letter from Mr. Radford received on Aug. 28, 1911, and postmarked Fort Resolution, which is 600 miles north of Edmonton. It had been written July 9, 1911. In this letter the explorer spoke of having another white man with him, T. George Street of Ottawa, Canada. He said that they would start out for Hudson Bay immediately, and that they expected to reach Chesterfield Inlet by September. He spoke of having been deserted by four other white men whom he had hired to help him in making the rough trip, and said that the trip would no doubt be lonely, especially since there were no Indians between Artillery Lake, which is a haunt for the Yellow Knife Indians, and Baker Lake, where there is a trible of Eskimo.

Depending on Chance.

"Two Indians will accompany us in another canoe," he wrote. "We can stow away 473 pounds of food supplies in addition to the bedding, arms, ammunition, clothing, medicines, and scientific equipment that must be carried. Street and I are depending upon procuring game and fish along the way."

Mr. Radford further said that he and his partner expected to be out of supplies by the time they reached Hudson Bay and that if they did not find the supplies which had been asked for from the Arctic Club at Chesterfield Inlet they would start for Fort Churchill, trusting to find game along the way. Friends of the explorer are anxious to learn whether Mr. Street really made the dangerous trip with Mr. Radford. The two Indians, of which the explorer spoke in his letter, are presumed to be those who deserted him in the wilderness. The supply ship has now been on its way for eight months and it is considered strange that no word has come from Mr. Radford or the crew of the supply ship in all that time. If the explorer reached Chesterfield Inlet or Fort Churchill by last September he should have been heard from by this time, his friends say. Mr. Grahame in his letter to Mr. Fiala said that he would inform the Arctic Club as soon as he had definite news. In the meantime Mr. Fiala will try and get into touch with Mr. Bell in Fort Smith.

Mr. Radford is known to have a fine zoological and ethnological harvest, which is to be sent to the United States Biological Survey for determination. When the explorer was last heard from he said that the collection included 67 mammals, 22 birds, 47 insects, 150 plants, 10 geological specimens, 40 ethnological specimens, and 400 tereoscopic photographs. Aside from the collection Mr. Radford announced that he had prepared two maps covering his explorations east and west of the Slave River and that he had discovered a large river fully 600 miles long, and many lakes, one of them 100 miles long, which he named after Lady Grey, wife of the ex-Governor General of Canada, who had befriended him.

CAPT. AMUNDSEN'S FULL STORY OF HIS DASH TO THE SOUTH POLE WITH FOUR OF HIS MEN AND 18 DOGS

Crosses Ice Barrier and Reaches the Goal In Fifty-five Days.

AT POLE DEC. 14, 3 P. M.

On a Vast Plateau, the Norwegian Flag Is Unfurled in a Light Breeze.

ONLY 9.4 BELOW ZERO THEN

Though on Previous Days the Thermometer Had Dropped as Far as 76 Below.

HAD TO KILL 34 DOGS

At 10,600 Feet Altitude, a Blizzard Keeps the Little Party in Camp Four Days.

NEW MOUNTAINS ARE SEEN

Range Runs South from King Edward Land—Discoverer's Route Over New Course.

AMUNDSEN KNOWS NOTHING OF SCOTT

The following message from Capt. Amundsen is in reply to a cable from The New York Times informing him that dispatches from New Zealand credited him with the statement that Capt. Scott had reached the South Pole, and asking whether these reports were true or not. It will be noted that Amundsen replies in the third person:

Special Cable to The New York Times.

HOBART, Tasmania, March 8.

Amundsen knows nothing about Scott.

FROM HENRY D. BAKER, UNITED STATES CONSUL:

Special Cable to The New York Times.

HOBART, Tasmania, March 8.—Amundsen denies knowledge of Scott's expedition, refuses to disclose anything regarding himself, and has isolated his ship's crew. He is reticent, according to his contracts with newspapers. BAKER.

ROALD AMUNDSEN.
Picture of the South Pole Discoverer Taken Just Before He Left Norway.

WARNING.

For the protection of Capt. Amundsen, who has risked his life in the attainment of the south pole, and whose chief material reward must be the proceeds of the sale of his narrative, The New York Times, which has purchased the rights thereto for the United States, to be duly protected by copyright, gives notice that it will prosecute any infringement whatsoever of such copyright.

SPECIAL NOTICE.

The narrative below was published by The New York Times Company yesterday as a book, duly entered for copyright and publicly exposed for sale. Its reproduction in this newspaper is of course duly authorized. Its reproduction elsewhere, in any form, except by permission from The New York Times Company, is forbidden.

United States Judge Holt issued last night a temporary injunction restraining such newspapers in New York as had not agreed to respect The Times copyright, from publishing or otherwise disposing of Amundsen's narrative.

CAPT. AMUNDSEN'S OWN NARRATIVE

Of His Attainment of the South Pole, Dec. 14-17, 1911.

By ROALD AMUNDSEN.

Special Cable to THE NEW YORK TIMES.

HOBART, Tasmania, March 8, 11:20 A. M.—On the 10th of February, 1911, we commenced to work our way toward the south, from that day to the 11th of April establishing three depots, which in all contained a quantity of provisions of about 3,000 kilos. One thousand six hundred kilos, including 1,100 kilos of seal meat, were cached in 80 degrees, 700 kilos in 81 degrees, and 800 kilos in 82 degrees South Latitude.

As no landmarks were to be seen, these depots were marked with flags, seven kilometers on each side in the easterly and westerly directions.

The ground and the state of the Barrier were of the best, and specially well adapted to driving with dogs. On Feb. 15, we had thus traveled about 100 kilometers. The weight of the sledges was 300 kilos, and the number of dogs was six for each sledge. The surface of the Barrier was smooth and fine with no sastrugi. [Snow furrows thrown up by the wind.] The crevices were very local and were found dangerous in only two places. For the rest—long, smooth undulations.

The weather was excellent—calm or a light breeze. The lowest temperature on these depot trips was minus 45 Celsius or centigrade. (49 degrees below zero, Fahrenheit.) On the 4th of March, on our return from the first trip beginning on the 15th of February, we found out that the Fram had already left us. With pride and delight we heard that her smart captain had succeeded in sailing her furthest south and there hoisting the colors of his country—a glorious moment for him and his comrades—the furthest north and the furthest south—good old Fram! The highest south latitude attained was 78 degrees 41 minutes.

Winter on the Ice Barrier.

Before the arrival of Winter we had 6,000 kilos of seal meat in the depots, enough for ourselves and 110 dogs. Eight dog houses, a combination of tents and snow huts, were built.

Having cared for the dogs, the turn came to use our solid little hut. It was almost entirely covered with snow by the middle of April. First we had to get light and air. The Lux lamp, which had a power of 200 standard candles, gave us a brilliant light and kept the temperature up to 20 degrees Celsius (68 degrees Fahrenheit) throughout the Winter, and our excellent ventilation system gave us all the air we wanted.

In direct communication with the hut and dug-out on the barrier were workshops, packing-rooms, cellars for provisions, coal, wood, and oil, a plain bath, a steam bath, and observatories. Thus we had everything within doors if the weather should be too cold and stormy.

The sun left us on the 22d of April and did not return until four months later. The Winter was spent in changing our whole outfit, which on the depot trips was found to be too clumsy and solid for the smooth surface of the barrier. Besides this, as much scien-

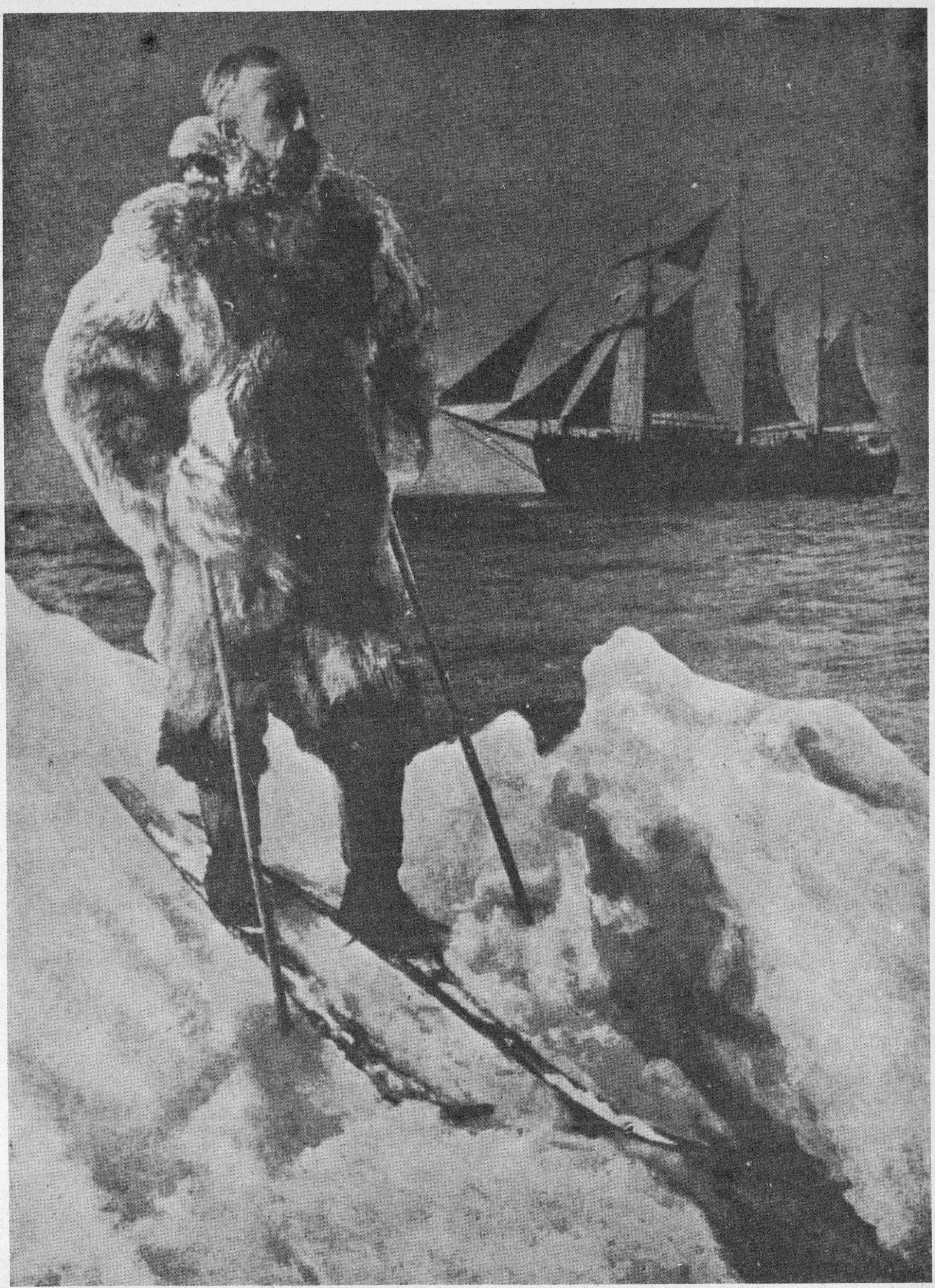

Captain Roald Amundsen on skis with his ship, the *Fram*, in the background.

Captain Amundsen taking a sighting to confirm for posterity that he reached the South Pole.

"All the News That's Fit to Print."

The New York Times.

THE WEATHER.

Fair, slightly warmer Thursday; Friday, fair, warmer; moderate winds, becoming south.

For full weather report see Page [illegible].

VOL. LXI...NO. 19,770. * * NEW YORK, MONDAY, MARCH 11, 1912.—TWENTY-TWO PAGES. ONE CENT In Greater New York, Jersey City, and Newark. { Elsewhere, TWO CENTS.

AMUNDSEN DESCRIBES HIS POLAR DASH; FOUND THE POLE'S ALTITUDE 10,500 FEET; FORCED TO KILL AND EAT HIS DOGS

COAL STRIKE NOW NEAR WORLD WIDE

Prussian Miners Follow the Lead of English Workers and Quit.

SUPPLY FAST DECREASING

A Real Coal Famine Feared—More Than 1,000,000 Men Out—Silesians Gain Demands.

HOPE TO AVERT STRIKE HERE

Committees Representing the Operators and the Workers to Confer in This City Wednesday.

With more than 1,000,000 coal miners on strike in England the Prussian workers also decided yesterday to quit work.

In France there is much unrest. A shortage in supply is already feared, and the action of the English and German workers is likely to influence the French miners.

In this country preparations are being made to face a great walkout of anthracite workers, who threaten to quit on April 1. Coal owners are guarding their stockades in the Pennsylvania fields by barbed wire. The men's demands have thus far been refused, and strenuous efforts are being made to accumulate sufficient reserves to meet the situation.

GERMANS VOTE TO STRIKE.

150,000 Miners Agree to Quit Work to Force Higher Wages.

ESSEN, Rhenish Prussia, March 10.—A strike throughout the Ruhr region was overwhelmingly voted to-day at a meeting of the delegates representing the three coal miners' organizations. The Christian Unionists, who were not represented at the meeting, have issued a protest against the strike, but it is said that they will approve the demand for increased wages, and it would not be surprising to see them eventually join the movement. The strike will become effective to-morrow.

Eighty different meetings were held in the various mining districts to-day, and not less than 150,000 miners attended. Much enthusiasm was manifested and the men enthusiastically favored a fight to a finish with the employers. All the meetings were orderly. The official notification of the proposed strike appeals to the miners to be law abiding and "strictly avoid liquor."

A strong police guard is on hand throughout the district, and troops will be summoned if necessary.

ZWICKAU, Saxony, March 10.—Fifteen hundred miners met to-day and decided to present an ultimatum to the mine owners on Tuesday respecting a demand for an increase of wages, which has already been refused by the owners.

WALDENBURG, Silesia, March 10.—The Lower Silesian mine owners, in compliance with the demand of all the organizers in the district, have decided to increase wages to the 1908 scale, the highest ever paid. The increase becomes effective on April 1.

The demand of the men was for a 15 per cent. increase in their wages, and the employers' action meets the demand part way, with the result that the men will probably continue at work.

COAL SCARCE IN ENGLAND.

More Conferences Planned, but Strike's End Is Not Yet in Sight.

LONDON, March 10.—As the coal strike in England continues the fear increases that, unless it is settled soon, there will be a general coal famine. Already precautionary measures have been taken by the railways and the big industrial concerns. They are practicing the severest economy, and may be forced to reduce their operations in order to make their supply of fuel last until the strike is at an end.

The representatives of the miners have agreed to meet Premier Asquith again and they are expected to decide whether or not they will have a joint conference with the mine owners. The Premier is hopeful of the outcome, but by many his views of the situation are regarded as too optimistic.

The effect of the strike is keenly felt in France, the west coast of which is dependent a great deal upon England for its supply of coal. It is also reported from France that the coal miners here are threatening to go out.

TO ANSWER MINERS' DEMAND.

Conference Between Miners and Employes to be Held Wednesday.

None of the anthracite operators was willing yesterday to predict the result of the joint conference between the committee of ten of the operators, which will meet to-day to prepare a detailed reply to the rejected demands of the anthracite miners, and the Conference Committee of the mine workers, which will be held on Wednesday. The details of the reply will not be made public until it is first submitted to the representatives of the mine workers at this conference.

The demand for domestic anthracite in Brooklyn was greater last week than in Manhattan and the Bronx. The head of one of the largest coal firms in Brooklyn said that in every case the good customer who can be relied on for payment would be taken care of. He will get enough to last him through the Spring, in any case. The coal might cost him more than in ordinary years. Many Brooklyn homes are already stocked with coal at the highest seasonal price, $6.50 a ton, with a premium added. The average tide water price of anthracite remained the same last week, it was stated. The average tide water price for domestic anthracite is $4.95 for egg coal, used in household heating furnaces; the same price for stove and from $5.20 to $6 for chestnut.

It was said yesterday that briquettes are now being used in a number of hotels and apartment houses as a substitute for steam coal. Despite the talk of the scarcity of small steam sizes it was stated on good authority yesterday that there was [illegible] a month's supply on hand.

CHURCH TEST OF PUBLICITY.

Forward Movement Makes Its Appeal Through Paid Advertisements.

The sporting pages of all New York newspapers this morning are carrying display advertisements of the Men and Religion Forward Movement which will be organized in this city in April. Three illuminated signs on Broadway are also a part of the modern publicity campaign in behalf of the up-to-date religious revival that has proved successful in seventy-five cities on this continent. The advertising is in charge of the Publicity Commission of the Christian Conservation Congress.

The Congress meets here April 19-24, and will conduct the Men and Religion Forward Movement during its session. The movement is non-sectarian. It is intended to be of benefit to the Catholic, Protestant, and Hebrew Churches. The converts which it makes are turned into the fold of local churches. The National organization behind the movement goes out of existence after the congress in April.

The Publicity Commission is made up of newspaper men from all parts of America. Secretary William T. Ellis said: "These new methods of advertising merely illustrate what we think the organized forces of religion will have to come to in presenting their claims to all men everywhere. We recognize that the only way to reach literally all the people is through the daily press. Whatever savors of propaganda or of the people's affairs, so to speak, should be set forth in direct appeal by paid display advertisements."

CITY DRIVERS' STRIKE TALK.

Dissatisfaction Reported Among Street Cleaners—Edwards Doesn't Know of It.

There was talk last night of the different meeting halls of the local unions of the International Brotherhood of Teamsters that dissatisfaction in the ranks of the Street Cleaning Department drivers might lead to another strike. It was said that the dissatisfaction was due chiefly over the night work, which caused the recent unsuccessful strike and put practically all of the old drivers out of their jobs.

It was said that when the new drivers were taken on Commissioner Edwards had taken back 400 of the old drivers to teach the new ones, and that when Mayor Gaynor heard about this he ordered the discharge of the 400 ex-strikers. This was denied last night by Commissioner Edwards, who said that only 150 drivers had been discharged and that the Civil Service Commission, and not the Mayor, had ordered the discharges, the reason being that the men had not been certified by the commission. Commissioner Edwards said that, as far as he knew, there was no trouble now among his men.

William H. Ashton, the strike leader who has led so many losing fights in recent years, said, however, that he had heard that the men were dissatisfied and said that a strike might be one of the happenings of the near future.

RICH, BUT PREFERS JAIL.

Lives There Voluntarily for Seclusion and to Escape Relatives.

Special to The New York Times.

CHICAGO, March 10.—Louis Kruse, a retired farmer of Dupage County, who is said to be worth more than $60,000, is to spend the rest of his days in the county jail at Wheaton, because he is weary of the monotony of freedom. He was not arrested.

Cynical and suspicious of friends and relatives, Kruse decided that jail was the safest place and ideal for quiet and seclusion. So Kruse went to jail. He pays Sheriff Kuhn $1 a day for permitting him to be a prisoner.

This fact was disclosed by an investigation conducted by Judge Landis of the United States District Court, into charges that Sheriff Kuhn was showing special favors to "Dutch" Heitler, a West Side character, serving thirty days for violation of the White Slave act.

Kuhn testified that Kruse was shown a few favors because he paid for his keep, and was merely a voluntary prisoner.

GOETHALS GUEST OF KAISER.

"Why Didn't You Make the Locks Wider?" Asked the Emperor.

BERLIN, March 10.—Lieut. Col. George W. Goethals, Chief Engineer of the Panama Canal, was the guest of the Emperor to-day at luncheon. The Empress, Princess Victoria Luise, Admiral von Tirpitz, Minister of Marine, and Herr von Breitenbach, Minister of Public Works, were also present.

Col. Goethals in an interview later praised the Emperor, not as a war lord but as a pleasant host. In the discussion of the Panama Canal he found that the Emperor was surprisingly conversant with every detail of the work.

"I was personally introduced to your steam shovels on the Northeast Sea Canal," the Emperor explained. He praised the Panama construction, added Col. Goethals, but asked: "Why didn't you make the locks as wide as those of the Kaiser Wilhelm Canal?"

The Colonel replied that they were wide enough for the largest existing warships, and the Emperor said:

"Yes, now. When we built the Kaiser Wilhelm locks they sufficed for that period, but we have had to expend much money on them since."

AVIATOR NEAR DEATH.

Berry Has Trouble With Parachute in Repeating Airship Jump.

ST. LOUIS, March 10.—Albert Berry again leaped from a flying aeroplane in a parachute to-day. The performance was the second of its kind in the history of aviation, Berry having been the first to attempt the feat when he leaped from a machine ten days ago as it was speeding over Jefferson Barracks.

He narrowly escaped death to-day, when the parachute became tangled under him. He succeeded in righting in before reaching earth.

FALL KILLS GIRL AVIATOR.

Suzanne Bernard Meets Death in Final Test for License.

ETAMPES, France, March 10.—A woman aviator, Suzanne Bernard, was killed to-day while undergoing examination for a pilot's license. She was only 19 years of age and had successfully made most of the tests.

Contrary to the advice of the examining officials, she attempted a sharp turn to the right. The machine was caught by an eddy and capsized. It fell 200 feet and the woman was crushed beneath the motor.

BOMB WRECKS BAKE SHOP.

Police Search for Man Who Dropped It Down Chimney of Newark House.

A bomb dropped by an unknown person down the chimney of a one-story bake shop in the rear of 35 Adams Street, Newark, late last night wrecked the brick oven in the shop and seriously injured the proprietor, Thomas Mistretta. His son Vito and Salvatore Macoluso, helper, escaped injury.

Vigorous efforts are being made by the police to find the person who dropped the bomb. Mistretta has been running a non-union shop and has had trouble with the Bakers' Union.

NANSEN CALLS IT MATCHLESS TRIP

No Luck, No Chance, but Well-Laid Plans Were What Won for Amundsen.

ITS RESULTS INVALUABLE

Glacial Conditions at the South Pole Can Now Be Understood.

THE NEW MOUNTAINS SEEN

Probably Extend Beyond the Pole Toward South America—Praise for the Fram's Crew.

BY FRIDTJOF NANSEN.

Specially Contributed to The New York Times and The London Chronicle.

Special Cable to THE NEW YORK TIMES.

CHRISTIANIA, March 10.—It was in 1910 that Capt. Amundsen was starting on his great expedition to the north pole in the Fram, but there was scanty interest shown in him and his undertaking, and still scantier were his funds.

Ever since his first expedition with the Gjoa, however, he had had to sail heavily burdened with debt, for which he was personally responsible, and now, as then, he put out to sea one Summer night in the silence.

It was in the Autumn that there came a message from him that in order to raise the necessary funds for his north pole expedition he was bound for the south pole.

At first the people were amazed, hardly knowing what to think or what to say. Such a thing was unheard of—to go to the south pole on his way to the north. Some thought it grand, but others, and these were the many, considered the venture doubtful. There were many who exclaimed that it was wrong, and that it was unfair. There were even some who would have had him stopped, but the echoes of the controversy reached him not. He had set his course, as he had determined, and without looking back.

The matter was soon forgotten, and people reverted to their own affairs.

It was foggy day after day, week after week—a charitable fog of mediocrities in which all that is high and great is shrouded, when all at once, and unexpectedly, a sunny Spring day dispels the fog.

A new message comes. Men stop and look up, and there, high above them shines a deed—a man. It is irresistible. It goes like a whirl of rapture through the minds of all. Flags fly aloft and flutter in the bright air. Men look into new and unknown tracts, and for a moment are forgetful of themselves.

Yes, we have looked in upon a new land and have read the story of Amundsen's matchless journey from beginning to end like a new and wonderful tale. So grand—it could not be more magnificent. It is unique as a deed, as a voyage of discovery, and in its results, and is told so simply as if it were an Easter pleasure trip on the mountains.

And yet what does it not convey of sage, well-laid plans and splendid execution, of determined courage, endurance, and manly power! Must not even those who know him not glow and rejoice over this man of iron will, who goes on his own way quietly and, as is his wont, without looking to right or left?

New Light on Age-Old Problems.

And what has he now discovered? New light is thrown upon large questions. Portions of the veil that rests on antarctic problems are raised. Amundsen has taken a great stride toward solving the last great geographical enigma. Not only is there light cast upon the antarctic of the present day, but it reaches also over the ice caps of the ice periods of remote ages.

It is as yet too early to attempt to measure the extent of the new discoveries that he has made, but much light already gleams through what he told us of his sledge journey over the antarctic ice cap.

In 1902 Capt. Scott made the important discovery that South Victoria Land continued from 78 degrees south latitude due south, with a high chain of mountains, or rather, a mountainous coast line, far beyond his most southerly point, 82 degrees 17 minutes, and he further found that the glacier surface he was traveling on, along the foot of these high mountains, did not rise noticeably to the southward, for which reason he concluded that it probably must be ice, more or less floating on the sea.

Shackleton continued, in 1908, the discovery of this mountainous coast further southward, past 84 degrees south latitude, and he penetrated on his bold journey by way of Beardmore Glacier on to King Edward VII. plateau, 8,000 feet to 10,000 feet high inside these mountains, and reached on it 88 degrees 73 minutes south.

Amundsen, now for the present, has completed these researches and has reached the pole itself.

From a purely meteorological point of view, Amundsen seems to have made the discovery that the amount of precipitation was comparatively small in the parts he was in. This will perhaps provide the key to enable us to understand the remarkable glacial conditions that have been found, and explain why the entire land, with its mountains and valleys, is not buried deep under a continuous ice cap similar to the ice cap of Greenland.

An important discovery is probable in the connection between South Victoria Land and Capt. Scott's King Edward VII. Land.

The New Mountain Range.

Perhaps even more remarkable is the vast chain of Queen Maud Mountains, which appears to be a continuation of the Queen Alexandra range, and with peaks of 12,000 feet and 15,000 feet in height stretches southeastward into the unknown, probably to the other side of the pole in the direction of Weddell Sea, south of South America.

This is an important step in the advance toward an understanding of the geography of these hitherto unknown regions, and also a new link in our knowledge of the mountain chains of the world.

Through Amundsen's observations we also achieve a final comprehension of the nature of Ross Barrier. It is obviously an enormous glacial mass, floating more or less on the sea in the great bay between South Victoria Land and King Edward VII. Land. This floating mass of ice is formed and fed by the glaciers which force their way down through the valleys and passes in the great mountain range which stretches southward from South Victoria Land, and similar glaciers may quite possibly originate from the south of Amundsen's newly found continuation of King Edward VII. Land.

It was on such an ice slope, or glacier, which comes down from the higher plateau, that he made his remarkable ascent with his dogs in four days to a height of over 7,000 feet. Another glacier of this kind is Beardmore Glacier, where Shackleton made his dangerous ascent. These glaciers obviously originate from the inner ice cap, which, at a height of from 8,000 feet to 10,000 feet, stretches over the land west and south of the high mountains. Part of this ice cap is King Edward VII.'s plateau, which Shackleton reached, and King Haakon's plateau, which surrounds the pole itself.

The Smooth Surface at the Pole.

On account of the unusually low temperature in this region and the resulting small precipitation, this ice cap is not able to grow so great that it can bury the mountains in this case. In the inner parts of Greenland these glacial masses correspond to what in the Alps are called firn, from which the glaciers originate and descend into the valleys.

Amundsen's descriptions of what he calls the Devil's Glacier and the Devil's Ballroom are very remarkable, the ice surface being there so hard that they could not even use skis. As he himself gives minus 5 degrees Centigrade as the maximum temperature during the whole journey at midsummer and after, and as the temperature in these inner regions must be much lower than this, the ice cannot, so far as one can judge, be formed by melting. It must rather be a phenomenon of crystallization of a similar kind to that which occurred on the snow fields and on drifting ice near the north pole, where the snow in Winter, in the severe frost and wind, was covered with a sharp and hard ice crust composed of great ice crystals. By the force of the wind, such a surface is kept smooth and hard.

As the temperature on the glacial plateau traveled over by Amundsen and Shackleton is so low and precipitation is so small, it is probable that the glaciers originating from it have very little movement.

Amundsen's many height measurements and observations during his journey across these glaciers and the inner plateau, combined with Shackleton's earlier observations, will be of the greatest importance in enabling us to understand conditions in this remarkable land, which is so perfectly different from all other lands on earth. They will help us to a clearer understanding of what conditions have been during the former great ice ages.

Lieut. Prestrud's Discoveries.

In addition to all this and a great deal more discovered by Amundsen, Lieut. Prestrud also explored King Edward VII. Land, the Bay of Whales, and the ice barrier in the surrounding neighborhood. We can also expect that this will give information of great geographical and geological importance.

All who are acquainted with Amundsen's previous scientific work will know that his observations of every description are as reliable as the careful use of the instruments at his command can make them. The heights are measured both with the aid of a hypsometer (by determining the boiling point of pure water) and by an aneroide.

And his determination of his position at the pole itself. Is it not like him for the four of his party to take on Dec. 16 an observation every hour for twenty-four hours with the sextant and artificial horizon, in addition to the series of observations on the previous day, and then explore the surrounding neighborhood?

There is not much room left for doubt that the expedition, from first to last, has been carried out on Amundsen's own plans and calculations, and without a single mishap.

No Luck, No Chance.

Let no one in this instance speak of luck and chance. He has had the good fortune that accompanies the strong. Even such a difficult thing as to lay

Continued on Page 2.

Marched 6 Hours a Day, Slept 6 Hours; Always Hungry, But Never Without Food.

HOPES SCOTT GOT THERE

And Thinks He Probably Did, but No Trace of His Expedition Was Found.

ALWAYS CALM AT THE POLE

Norwegian Explorer Believes No Storms Sweep the Earth's Southernmost Point.

THREE DOGS DESERTED

And Plundered Food Depots—Only Eleven Made the Trip Back.

BIRD OF NEW SPECIES SEEN

Beards of the Party Clipped with a Machine, and One Tooth Extracted.

SPECIAL NOTICE.

The following supplementary narrative by Capt. Amundsen has been copyrighted by The New York Times Company, and its reproduction in the United States without the express permission of The New York Times is forbidden.

Capt. Amundsen himself states that he wishes this narrative to be published only in the newspapers which, by purchasing his first narrative, have helped to reimburse him. It is pathetically pointed out by Nansen, elsewhere in this morning's Times, that Amundsen set out on his expedition burdened with debt; and it is understood that he mortgaged all he possessed to secure the necessary equipment. It is therefore the purpose of The New York Times to prevent as far as possible the loss to Capt. Amundsen of the just reward of his achievement.

Special Cable to THE NEW YORK TIMES.

HOBART, Sunday, March 10.—Capt. Roald Amundsen received me to-day, and not only materially added to the information already cabled by him respecting his journey to and from the south pole, but also discussed the question of whether it is likely that he was preceded by his English rival, Capt. Scott. He said:

"I saw no traces whatever showing that Capt. Scott had been at the pole, but it is possible that he had been there and had left some unsubstantial memorial which had afterward been destroyed by the storms.

"The chances, however, are heavily against this theory, for during the three days that I was there the weather was calm and still, and I think that is the prevalent condition. There was nothing but the vast level plains of snow, and hence there was no possibility of erecting a permanent cairn of stones.

"The season was very favorable, and therefore it is exceedingly likely that Capt. Scott did reach the pole later, if not sooner, than myself. I most sincerely hope he did arrive there, for he well deserves success.

How the Dash Was Made.

"On my sledging journey to the pole a new plan was tried. At first the expedition daily traveled fifteen miles in five hours, then spent two hours eating and in feeding the dogs, and then we attempted to spend the other seventeen hours in sleep. This period of rest was found to be too long both for the men and dogs, and a new plan was tried. This was to march fifteen miles in about six hours, spend two hours eating and attending to the dogs, sleep six hours, and then breakfast and march again. This accounts for the remarkable speed of over twenty miles a day attained on the return journey.

Had Difficulty in Breathing.

"The greatest difficulties of the expedition were caused by the heights encountered. During the latter part of the journey to the pole we spent nearly six weeks at great elevations, which sometimes reached 16,750 feet. [This may be an error in cabling, as Capt. Amundsen, in an earlier report, mentioned 10,750 feet as the greatest reached.] The pole itself is at an elevation of 10,500 feet. When we were working hard, great difficulty was experienced in breathing at these heights, and we panted and struggled for breath.

"With regard to food, we had full rations all the way, but in that climate full rations are a very different thing to having as much as a man can eat. There seems little limit to one's eating powers when doing a hard sledging journey. However, on the return journey we had not merely full rations, but as much as we could eat from the depots after passing 86 degrees.

Eating Dog Meat No Hardship.

"The first dogs were eaten on the journey to the pole in 85½ degrees, when twenty-four were killed. In spite of the fact that they had not always been able to obtain full meals, the dogs were fat and proved most delicious eating. It is anything but a real hardship to eat dog flesh.

"Two skua gulls were seen at 84½ degrees. A small cairn had previously been erected as a mark to guide us on our return, and just when he had left this the gulls came flying past and alighted on the cairn.

Three Dogs Deserted.

"Three of the best dogs deserted the party at 83 degrees. We had killed a female dog at 82½ degrees, and the dogs went back, searching for her. This caused us great anxiety, for it was feared that the dogs would pillage the depots on which the party depended. When we returned to 83 degrees, after being at the pole, we saw fresh dog tracks around the large snow cairn used as a depot there. Curiously enough, the pemmican in the depot was untouched.

"Traces of the dogs were followed to 82½ degrees, where the female dog had been killed. They had found the body, which was placed on the top of a heap of snow as a food reserve for the party, and, having eaten it, the dogs had gone to the depot at 82 degrees, where a large number of cases were piled up. They had got at one of the cases of pemmican and had not only eaten that, but had also eaten the leather straps and other indigestible articles. They had also eaten two dogs which we had killed and left for food at this depot.

"Eleven dogs survived the whole journey and safely reached the Fram.

Christmas Dinner Near the Pole.

"I and my four companions on the pole party kept the Christmas festival in the high mountains, not a great distance from the pole. The feast consisted of an extra allowance of biscuits cooked in a [illegible] abundance of the Norwegian Christmas, but we enjoyed it heartily.

"On the return journey we had not a single day's rest. We did not even rest on Christmas Day, but passed on, day after day, through all weathers. There was little that was adventurous about the trip, but it was very hard work.

"I attribute my success to my splendid comrades and to the magnificent work of the dogs, and next to them to our skis.

"The splendid condition of the dogs on landing in the antarctic was due mainly to the precautions taken on the Fram. In order to keep the dogs in good health while crossing the tropics a special double-deck planking had been fixed above the deck of the Fram with a space several inches deep left for the circulation of fresh air. This device was constructed before leaving Norway, and in the hot weather sails stretched above kept the dogs always in the shade. As a result, little trouble was experienced with the dogs, which landed fit for work.

Kept Fat on Polar Dash.

"Of real hardships in the way of food on the pole journey there were none. Rather the reverse, for when my companions reached the ship they were almost fat, and could not eat as much as when they started. The dogs, too, were fat, and that they had lived well during the last part of the journey was shown by the fact that they would hardly touch the seal meat which was lying in large quantities about the base of the camp.

"Washing was a luxury never indulged in on the journey, nor was there any shaving, but as the beard has to be kept short to prevent ice accumulating from one's breath, a beard-cutting machine which we had taken along proved invaluable.

"Another article taken was a tooth extractor, and this also proved valuable, for one man had a tooth which became so bad that it was absolutely essential that it should be pulled out, and this could hardly have been done without a proper instrument.

"The party which explored King Edward VII. Land reports seeing a bird of a new species. They are certain of that, as they got close to it and saw it distinctly.

Protecting His Narrative.

"I am gratified to learn that the steps taken to prevent the results of the expedition prematurely leaking out proved successful, and that The New York Times was the first to publish the news in America.

"The method adopted here was simple. Nobody was allowed on board the ship, and no member of the expedition other than myself was allowed to go ashore. All necessary business and other business for the crew was transacted by myself.

"I arrived Thursday and sent you a brief cablegram announcing my success, and on Friday dispatched a long account of my journey to the pole and the discoveries we had made.

"From all over the world telegrams had been pouring into Hobart, chiefly from newspapers in England and America, begging for messages from me. I had arranged that The London Chronicle, The New York Times, and their associates should have the story exclusively, and that promise I have been glad to fulfill.

Will Now Seek the Arctic.

"I have been most gratified to-day to receive hearty congratulations from King George.

"Before sailing to Buenos Aires I have arranged to go on a month's lecturing tour in Australia. From Buenos Aires I intend to make my way to the arctic via Bering Strait, thus carrying out my original programme."

More than 100 telegrams of congratulation were received at Hobart yesterday by Capt. Amundsen, fifty being delivered [illegible]

"All the News That's Fit to Print."

The New York Times

THE WEATHER.
Rain, somewhat warmer Tuesday; Wednesday clearing; moderate to brisk southerly winds.
For full weather report see Page 23.

VOL. LXI...NO. 19,792. * * * NEW YORK, TUESDAY, APRIL 2, 1912.— TWENTY-FOUR PAGES. ONE CENT In Greater New York, Jersey City, and Newark. | Elsewhere, TWO CENTS.

CAPT. SCOTT'S THRILLING STORY OF HIS TRIP; MANY PERILS, HAIRBREADTH ESCAPES; FIVE OF PARTY PROBABLY REACHED POLE

Leader of Expedition Saved as by a Miracle—Party, Adrift on Ice, Rescued by Ropes.

THE PONIES GAVE TROUBLE

And Some of the Dogs Died in a Few Hours from a Mysterious New Disease.

EXPLORERS' HUT BLOWN AWAY

Men, Half Buried Under Snow, Without Food for Forty-eight Hours.

MOTOR SLEDGES ABANDONED

But They Had Proved the Value in Antarctic Travel of This Means of Transportation.

MOVING PICTURES TAKEN

And a Telephone Line Fifteen Miles Long Constructed—Storms Delayed Progress.

FIVE MEN GOING TO POLE

Ready to Advance on Jan. 3 on the Goal 150 Miles Away—London Thinks They Have Won.

CAPT. ROBERT F. SCOTT.

[Title under which the narrative is copyrighted in the United States, Great Britain, and Canada.]

CAPT. SCOTT'S STORY

Trying Experiences—Miraculous Escapes—Daring Winter Operations—Valuable Scientific Work—First Antarctic Telephone Installed—Motor Sledges Did Good Work—Cinematograph Records Taken—Expedition Steadily Approaching Pole When Last Heard From.

Special Cable to THE NEW YORK TIMES.

AKAROA, New Zealand, Tuesday, April 2.—Lieut. Pennell, Commander of the Terra Nova of the British Antarctic Expedition of 1910, which arrived here yesterday, brought with him a long and intensely interesting account of the work and experiences of the expedition up to Jan. 3 last, written expressly for The New York Times by Capt. Robert F. Scott, the leader of the expedition.

Capt. Scott's story is as follows:

By CAPT. ROBERT F. SCOTT.

McMURDO SOUND, Oct. 30, 1911.—Shortly after the departure of the depot-laying party from Cape Evans on Jan. 25, 1911, the sea ice broke at South Cape and severed communication with the station. The depot party consisting of twelve men, eight ponies, and two dog teams occupied till Jan. 30 in establishing a base camp at the barrier seven miles east, southeast, of Hut Point. Owing to the heavy weights to be transported the main part of the supplies were left at this camp. The party proceeded with single loads east, southeast, twenty-seven miles to a spot named Corner Camp, before turning south to avoid the crevasses of White Island. The snow surface proved very soft, making terribly hard work for the ponies. A three days' heavy blizzard at Corner Camp was a further severe trial to the animals, which were not in good condition.

On Feb. 8 we proceeded south, marching by night and resting by day. The weather was exceptionally bad, but the surface improved. The three weakest ponies were sent back, but these unfortunately were caught in another bad blizzard and two succumbed. With the remaining ponies and the dogs we reached latitude 79½ degrees on the 16th, when I decided, owing to the condition of the weather and the animals to make a depot here and return. We left more than a ton of stores at this point, which we named One Ton Camp, and which should be a great help to us this season. We then returned to our base camp with dog teams.

Perched on a Crevasse Bridge.

Whilst cutting a corner of White Island in a bad light the whole of one dog team fell into a crevasse. Meares, myself, and the sledge were miraculously held up on part of a bridge across the crevasse, along which we had been traveling, and most of the dogs hung by their harness. With great difficulty and after three hours' work we extricated the animals. One, which was badly injured by falling sixty feet, afterward died.

At Base Camp I found every single pony well, and visiting Hut Point I received news of the Terra Nova and Fram. On Feb. 24, with men on skis, and a single pony, I started to take more stores to Corner Camp. On the outward journey we passed returning ponies going well. Returning from Corner Camp, I was held up by a blizzard on the 27th, but reached Base Camp on the 28th. I found the storm had been phenomenal at this place, raging for three days and causing enormous accumulations of snow. Shifts of wind had baffled all efforts to shelter the ponies with snow walls, and the animals had suffered very badly, so I decided to retire to Hut Point without delay.

Wilson and Meares, driving dog teams, reached Hut Point in safety. Oates, Grain and I remained to try and save one pony which had been badly hit by the blizzard, whilst Bowers, Cherry, Gerrard, and Crean with the four best ponies set out to follow the dogs. Nearing Hut Point they found badly working cracks in the sea ice, and hastily turned and marched four miles south.

Adrift on Floating Ice.

There at 2 A. M. on March 1 the tired condition of the ponies obliged the party to camp. At 4:30 Bowers, awakened by a noise, found the ice broken all around the camp and moving with the heavy swell. One pony had disappeared from the picketing line and was not seen again. Hastily packing their sledges, the party decided to try and work

DESERTER GOT $1,500 FOR KILLING WOMAN

THAW INQUIRY HALTED BY SUPREME COURT WRIT

Justice Prohibits Taking of More Testimony at Present.

A SURPRISE TO PROSECUTION

Mr. Hartridge Insists He Is Thaw's Counsel—Prisoner's Mother Urges Olcott to Remain in Case.

John B. Gleason, a member of the Clifford W. Hartridge division of counsel for Harry Kendall Thaw, appeared yesterday morning before Supreme Court Justice Blanchard and obtained a writ of prohibition restraining District Attorney Jerome and the July Grand Jury from taking further evidence as to the murder of Stanford White or issuing further subpoenas in connection with the case.

The writ was made returnable to-day, when Acting District Attorney Smyth, upon whom it was served, will appear before Justice Blanchard and ask for an adjournment of the matter for a week on the ground that Assistant District Attorney Garvan, who has had charge of the Thaw case, is now out of the city.

The issuance of the order granting the application for the writ was not the only development yesterday in the Thaw case. Mrs. William Thaw, with her daughter, Mrs. George L. Carnegie, and Mrs. Carnegie's husband, ran over from Roslyn, L. I., and held a conference with Lewis L. Delafield, Mrs. Thaw's personal counsel, and ex-Judge William M. K. Olcott. Josiah Thaw, Harry Thaw's brother, was also present at this conference.

It is understood that Mrs. Thaw repeated her request that ex-Judge Olcott continue as counsel for her son, and that the lawyer took the matter under advisement. A statement may be issued by his firm to-day. The attitude taken by ex-Gov. Black, senior member of the firm, probably will decide the matter.

Mr. Hartridge Stands Firm.

In the meantime Mr. Hartridge, standing pat on the proposition that Harry Thaw, being free, white, and 21, is entitled to select his own counsel and reject counsel whose views he believes are antagonistic to his own, insists that he is in charge of Thaw's case, and he alone. Mr. Gleason, he says, is working with him. That he considers that he is in charge of the defense he made clear yesterday in a letter addressed by him to the District Attorney's office.

In his application for the writ of prohibition Mr. Gleason, as counsel for Thaw, makes the following affidavit:

In June, 1908, a Grand Jury in the County of New York, in the Court of General Sessions, inquired into the facts of a crime alleged to have been committed in New York County, involving the shooting of Stanford White, and the Grand Jury presented to the court an indictment against Harry K. Thaw, charging him with murder in the first degree for the killing of Stanford White, to which indictment the defendant has pleaded not guilty, and is now in the City Prison awaiting his trial. For the purpose of preparing the case for trial subpoenas are made by the District Attorney and addressed to witnesses, requiring them to appear and testify before the Grand Jury in an investigation before it.

These subpoenas are not made for the purpose of procuring any new indictment for the killing of Stanford White, but for the purpose of procuring evidence to be used against the defendant at the trial. The witnesses are required by the District Attorney to be sworn before the Grand Jury and the depositions are taken. The newspapers keep track of the witnesses thus produced and undertake to state the facts to which they have testified. The taking of these depositions against the defendant has been chiefly intrusted to Assistant District Attorney Garvan, and from time to time interviews purporting to have come from him have appeared in the public press, in which the intent to take the depositions before the Grand Jury for use against Harry K. Thaw at his trial has been plainly stated.

Has Forty-three Depositions.

The affidavit quotes an alleged interview with Mr. Garvan which was published in an afternoon paper, in which Mr. Garvan is quoted as saying: "I have already taken the depositions of forty-three witnesses for use at the trial of Harry K. Thaw." It continues:

Deponent personally knows of at least two subpoenas which have been issued and served for attendance before the Grand Jury on July 17 in this proceeding. Deponent has only been retained recently in this case and by reason of the fact that the hearing is set down to continue upon July 17 has not the time to procure the personal affidavit of the various reporters and persons who have informed him of the statement by Assistant District Attorney Garvan admitting that the depositions are taken solely for the purpose of preparing for the trial of the defendant, but deponent alleges that he knows the fact to be that this is the sole purpose for the taking of these depositions, and that the circumstances in this case are so open and notorious, and so well understood, that there is no room for any claim or allegation that these depositions are being taken for use against any one except the defendant, Harry K. Thaw.

The order issued by Justice Blanchard reads:

On the reading and filing of the affidavit of John B. Gleason, the attorney for the relator, Harry K. Thaw, above named, and the court being satisfied of this authority, it is

Ordered, That a writ of prohibition issue, directed to the Court of General Sessions and William Travers Jerome and the July Grand Jury in the Court of General Sessions, commanding them to desist and refrain from any further proceedings in the matter of the investigation by said Grand Jury of the question of the killing of Stanford White and of the

Continued on Page 2.

INDEX TO DEPARTMENTS.

COAL FILLS DINING SALOON.

The Olympic Taking No Chances of Running Short at This Port.

By Marconi Transatlantic Wireless Telegraph to The New York Times.

LONDON, April 1.—To guard against a possible shortage of fuel on her arrival at New York, the White Star liner Olympic, which sails on Wednesday, has been coaled to her utmost capacity. The third-class dining saloon has been completely filled with coal, accommodation for the passengers being provided in another part of the vessel.

Justice Bargrave Deane in the Admiralty Court to-day gave judgment in a test action brought by two members of the crew of the Olympic against the owners for a month's wages in lieu of the three days' wages that were offered after the Olympic's collision with the cruiser Hawke.

The case turned on the legal definition of a wreck. The court held that the Olympic was a wreck within the meaning of the Merchant Shipping act, and that consequently the crew were entitled to only three days' wages.

Judgment was accordingly entered for the defendants.

MARY GARDEN OPERA HOUSE.

Prima Donna to Direct It—Americans Backing Paris Scheme.

By Marconi Transatlantic Wireless Telegraph to The New York Times.

PARIS, April 1.—With reference to the report previously sent to THE NEW YORK TIMES that a section of the actionnaires of the Opéra Comique are about to take over another theatre and turn it into an opera house run on business lines, it is now rumored that an American syndicate which is backing Mary Garden is likely to join the French enterprise with a view to renting the Vaudeville Theatre in the Boulevard des Italiens and making it a luxurious lyric house in which a modern, and especially a French, répertoire will be given.

It is further said that the house will be called the Mary Garden Opera House, and that the American prima donna will have the artistic direction of it besides interpreting star rôles.

SENATE'S NEW CHESTERFIELD

Ashurst of Arizona Arrives with His Courtly Manners.

Special to The New York Times.

WASHINGTON, April 1.—Of the four new Senators from Arizona and New Mexico who have presented themselves at the Capitol, one made a deep impression to-day, though they will not take the oath until to-morrow. That one is Henry F. Ashurst of Arizona, and it was his manners that did it. Though Mr. Ashurst is a Democrat from the Far West, he was welcomed by the old guard as a new Chesterfield.

On the arm of a member of the House, Mr. Ashurst began his progress toward the Senate Chamber shortly before convening. He was attired faultlessly in a becoming frock coat and striped pants—yes, they were pants—with only a broad black sombrero in honor of the West. His escort was tastefully attired in blue, with a combrero of the tan Rough Rider variety.

As no announcement of the approaching statesmen had gone ahead of them, there was only a single doorkeeper to receive them, but the statesmen made the most of them. Five feet this side of the door they stopped, doffed their hats to the doorkeeper, and bowed profoundly. Then they advanced and introduced themselves with warm handclasps that until to-day had been considered distinctly Southern. After that they entered the Chamber.

Mr. Martine of New Jersey is the sociable member of the Senate, and he took Mr. Ashurst in tow, presenting him to everybody he could find. Then the Senators saw the fine shadings in Mr. Ashurst's manner. To the older members he bowed till his frock coat was at right angles to his trousers; to the venerable Senator Cullom he bowed even lower than that. But to the young Senators his greeting was more virile; no bowing, just a giant's grasp and a long look into the eyes, man fashion.

His softest manner he reserved for Mr. Martine alone, and he and the friendly Senator from New Jersey made the circuit of the Chamber, hand in hand.

Mr. Ashurst, his colleague, Mark Smith, and the two Senators-elect from New Mexico, A. B. Fall and T. B. Catron, both Republicans, will take the oath to-morrow. They will draw lots for their assignments to the Senatorial classes. Two of them will draw terms of six years, one of four years, and one of two years.

POISON AFTER APRIL JOKE.

Girl, Believing She Is Jilted, Swallows Tablets of Mercury.

Special to The New York Times.

ST. LOUIS, Mo., April 1.—Ida Kaiser, 19 years old, living in Vonversen Avenue, ran to meet the mail carrier this morning. She broke the seal of the letter she received, and the opening sentence read "I have married another."

She went to her room and swallowed a dozen mercury tablets. Physicians removed her to the Jewish Hospitl, where it is doubtful if she will live. Frank Davidson, to whom she was to have been married in two weeks, hurried to the hospital and is at her beside begging forgiveness. He sent the letter as an April Fool joke. Miss Kaiser's parents are from Washington County, Ala.

MUMPS DON'T HALT WEDDING.

Miss Lola Gaskill Takes Max Kirsh, Swollen Face and All.

Special to The New York Times.

PLEASANTVILLE, N. J., April 1.—Even the fact that the bridegroom had the mumps did not stop the wedding last night in the Wesley Methodist Church of Miss Lola Gaskill and Max Kirsh. The bride thought it would be unlucky to postpone the ceremony, so it went on according to programme, except for the absence of half a dozen men who allowed their fear of the disease to keep them away.

The Rev. Dr. Wells, the officiating clergyman, warned the guests in advance of the infectious nature of the bridegroom's affliction.

PRIEST IS ELECTED MAYOR.

Gets a Majority of One Hundred in Lapeer, Mich.

DETROIT, April 1.—The first seventeen counties heard from in to-day's "wet" and "dry" election contests, embracing twenty-five counties, showed a gain of two counties for the "drys" in "wet" territory, and a "wet" majority in four "dry" counties.

The Rev. E. W. Dunnigan, a Catholic priest, was elected Mayor of Lapeer by a majority of 100.

GAGGED AND BOUND BY THIEVES, HE SAYS

Brooklyn Merchant Found Dazed in a Deep Cut of the Long Island Railroad.

THROWN THERE AT NIGHT

Robbed at Noon, Thieves Who Felled Him Kept Him a Prisoner in Cellars Until After Dark.

Robert H. Cooper, a wholesale produce merchant, with offices at the foot of Forty-seventh Street, at the Bush Stores, South Brooklyn, was found gagged, blindfolded, and bound at the bottom of the Long Island Railroad cut at Fifth Avenue and Sixty-seventh Street last night. His groans attracted the attention of persons who chanced to be passing by. He was bruised and dazed.

When assisted to the Fourth Avenue Police Station, Cooper told a most remarkable story of having been robbed of $1,200 in cash and $300 in checks by two men, who attacked him at noon yesterday at Forty-fourth Street and Second Avenue, Brooklyn, and who after felling him had carried him around Brooklyn, bound, gagged, and blindfolded, sometimes in a cart and sometimes in and out of cellars, for the next eight hours.

According to the story he told in the Police Station, Cooper, who lives with his wife and one child at 566 Decatur Street, Brooklyn, received a telephone message from a customer yesterday at noon. The customer, who lived nearby and whose name the police will not make public, told Mr. Cooper over the 'phone that he was anxious to meet him and to pay a certain debt. Putting $1,200 in cash and $300 in checks in his breast pocket and meaning to deposit both this and the customer's money in the Flatbush Avenue Branch of the Corn Exchange Bank, Cooper set out to meet the customer.

Attacked at Noon.

"It was just noon time and the streets were crowded," he told the police. "But, as I was walking through Second Avenue at Forty-fourth Street, two ratherly poorly dressed young men, each about 25 years old, came up to me and struck me heavily on the breast with some metal instrument, and I fell to the sidewalk.

"I don't know what happened then, but when I came to I found that I was bound and gagged. The bandage over my eyes was sufficiently thin so that I could detect the quality of the light around me. Judging from this and from the damp smell and feeling of the atmosphere, I judged I was in a cellar. I seemed to be half sitting, half lying on a box.

"I could hear the two men talking near me. They seemed to be discussing how badly I was hurt. I lay still, so as not to excite them. But gradually I began to feel faint and became unconscious again. Finally I felt myself lifted out of the cellar and carried, one man being at my head and the other at my feet, to an open wagon. I wasn't shrouded or screened in any way, so far as I know.

"The wagon seemed to travel quite a distance. I don't know exactly how far, because I was very weak and kept relapsing into unconsciousness, then partly recovering.

"Finally I was lifted out of the cart. The two men lifted me up high, as though over a fence. Then they let me go. I seemed to be falling a long, an endlessly long distance, before again becoming unconscious."

The place where Cooper's fall apparently took place was the 40-foot excavation of the Long Island Railroad at Sixty-seventh Street and Fifth Avenue. While Dennis Mahoney of 366 Sixty-ninth Street was passing through Fifth Avenue at this point last night he heard groans issuing from the excavation.

Clambering down to the tracks he found Cooper with his hands tied behind him and cloths bound around his mouth and eyes. He seemed stunned and bruised as a result of his fall, but to be otherwise uninjured. His hat was gone and his clothes disheveled.

Bruised by His Fall.

Mahoney ran up to the street and called several other men. Cooper was carried to the street by them and given restoratives. He was then assisted to the Fourth Avenue Police Station, and Dr. Carter was summoned with an ambulance from the Norwegian Hospital. Dr. Carter found that Mr. Cooper was suffering from bruises apparently resulting from his fall down the embankment. He seemed to be otherwise uninjured. Neither the police nor the doctor believe he had been drinking.

One of the puzzling features of the case is that Cooper's gold watch and chain were found in his waistcoat, as well as $60 in cash and several checks in his hip hip pocket. A diamond ring also was left upon his finger by the thieves.

Cooper refused to go to the hospital. While he was recovering from his experience and describing his assailants to the detectives in the police station, his brother, the Rev. Hedley Cooper of Greenwood Lake, L. I., was summoned and came to the station.

Detective Lieut. Fay and ten other detectives set out on Mr. Cooper's suggestion to try to find the produce merchant's assailants. Their search up to a late hour was fruitless.

Cooper can give no clue to the cellar to which, he says, he was carried. The place on Second Avenue where he says he was assaulted, is about two miles from the railroad cut where he was found.

PARK AVENUE BARRIER DOWN.

First Vehicles in 40 Years Cross It at Fifty-first Street.

For the first time in more than forty years it was possible yesterday for both foot passengers and vehicles to cross Park Avenue at Fifty-first Street, as a result of the completion of improvements by the New York Central.

For twoscore of years the tunnel through Park Avenue prevented vehicles from crossing between Forty-second and Fifty-fifth Streets, although bridges were built over the tracks for pedestrians at Fifty-fourth, Fifty-second, Fiftieth, Forty-eighth, and Forty-sixth Streets. Now the street has been built over the tracks from Fiftieth to Fifty-fourth Street. At Fifty-first Street the wall was taken down and a roof erected over the tracks.

HELD BY MEXICAN BANDITS.

American, in a Smuggled Letter, Tells of His Comrades' Plight.

LACROSSE, Wis., April 1.—Harry Conklin of Lacrosse, in a letter smuggled through the revolutionary lines from Lluvia De Oro, Chihuahua, Mexico, to his mother in this city, says that he and a party of Americans are held captive there by about 300 Mexican bandits and that their lives are in danger. The letter is dated March 19.

Lluvia De Oro is a small settlement of American miners.

CONTINUATION OF SCOTT'S STORY

The second part of Capt. Scott's thrilling account of his journey toward the South Pole and his explorations and scientific discoveries in the Antarctic region will be published in to-morrow's NEW YORK TIMES.

BERLIN BACKS DOWN ON KAISER'S DENIAL

Only Meant to Say He Did Not Advise Goethals to Fortify the Canal Against Japan.

ASTONISHED AT THE COLONEL

Press Gibe at "Garrulous Foreigners"—Observers Think Denial Was Intended to Soothe the Japanese.

By Marconi Transatlantic Wireless Telegraph to The New York Times.

BERLIN, April 1.—Col. George W. Goethals's action in giving the lie to the official "denial" of the German Government with reference to his conversation with the Kaiser on the subject of fortifying the Panama Canal has caused a profound sensation in Berlin.

American cablegrams having reported that Col. Goethals sticks to his guns, the Foreign Office to-night deemed it wise to issue a statement which considerably qualifies, if it does not wholly withdraw, the flat-footed "denial" published on Saturday.

The Foreign Office now declares that the Kaiser never meant to say that he had not discussed the fortification question. His Majesty meant merely to deny that he advised America to fortify against Japan or England or any other power which might eventually attempt to seize a coaling station in the region of the Isthmus. The Kaiser, in fact, carefuly avoided the discussion of anything so concrete and confined his remarks strictly to general observations.

The Foreign Office adds that the version of Col. Goethals's remarks which reached Germany was doubtless distorted and that the official contradiction was leveled at a palpable garbled reproduction.

The newspapers have not yet been favored with this post-mortem effort of the Foreign Office to close what they describe as "a most painful incident." Meantime the papers are full of articles abusing the "garrulous foreigners" who gain access to the Kaiser's presence. They declare the Kaiser's experience with Col. Goethals ought finally to teach him that it is unsafe to open the doors of the German Court to Americans, Frenchmen, and others, who unburden themselves to the first reporters who run across them.

The press universally assume that Saturday's denial was issued for the purpose of assuaging Japan. The Kaiser rubbed the Japanese the wrong way under identical circumstances five or six years ago, when he discussed the "yellow peril" with a talkative member of the American House of Representatives. The Japanese Ambassador in Berlin protested, and thereupon an official "denial" was issued, stating that the Kaiser had discussed yellow fever, not the "yellow peril," and Japan was appeased.

LEFT $2,500 TO HER PARROT.

"Rattlesnake Pete" to be the Guardian of Rich Spinster's Bird.

Special to The New York Times.

ROCHESTER, N. Y., April 1.—Clara Ide, a wealthy spinster, whose estate in the town of Riga, near Rochester, is a show place of the county, willed 160 acres and $30,000 to found a model farm for the benefit of persons who may wish to study agriculture in a practical way. The will, admitted to probate to-day directs the organization of a corporation with a Board of Managers, to include the Master of the Riga Grange, the Supervisor of the town, and the Chairman of the County Board of Supervisors.

Miss Ide left the income of $2,500 to a person, to be selected by the executors, who will care for her parrot, "Capt. Flint." "Rattlesnake Pete" Gruber, who cured the bird of a distemper, will be appointed guardian of the bird. He says "Capt. Flint" will live fifty years more, barring sickness or accident.

Miss Ide's will directs that her saddle horse Pollux be cared for by the model farm corporation, and that he be buried alongside Castor, another favorite horse already dead, and she orders that the ground shall never be plowed in the part of the farm known as the horse cemetery.

WEDS FOR THIRD TIME.

Mrs. Staunton Elliott Now the Wife of Daniel A. MacRae.

Mrs. W. Staunton Elliott, daughter of William H. Henriques, a stock broker of 84 Riverside Drive, became the wife of Daniel A. MacRae, a salesman for the Paul Lacriox Automobile Company about eight months ago, it was learned yesterday. They were married in Europe.

Mrs. MacRae obtained a divorce from her first husband, Douglas J. Neame, of London, in 1892. He refused to recognize the American decree and sued for divorce in London, naming Frank Ellison as corespondent. Ellison, who was often seen in company of Mrs. Neame, was a witness in her divorce suit. Later he attacked Mrs. Neame's father, for which he served a prison term.

Her second husband was W. Staunton Elliott, a Boston commissioned merchant. They were married in 1890 and divorced a year and a half ago.

Latest Shipping News.

ARRIVED—SS Prins Willem V., (Royal Dutch Mail,) Trinidad, March 13.

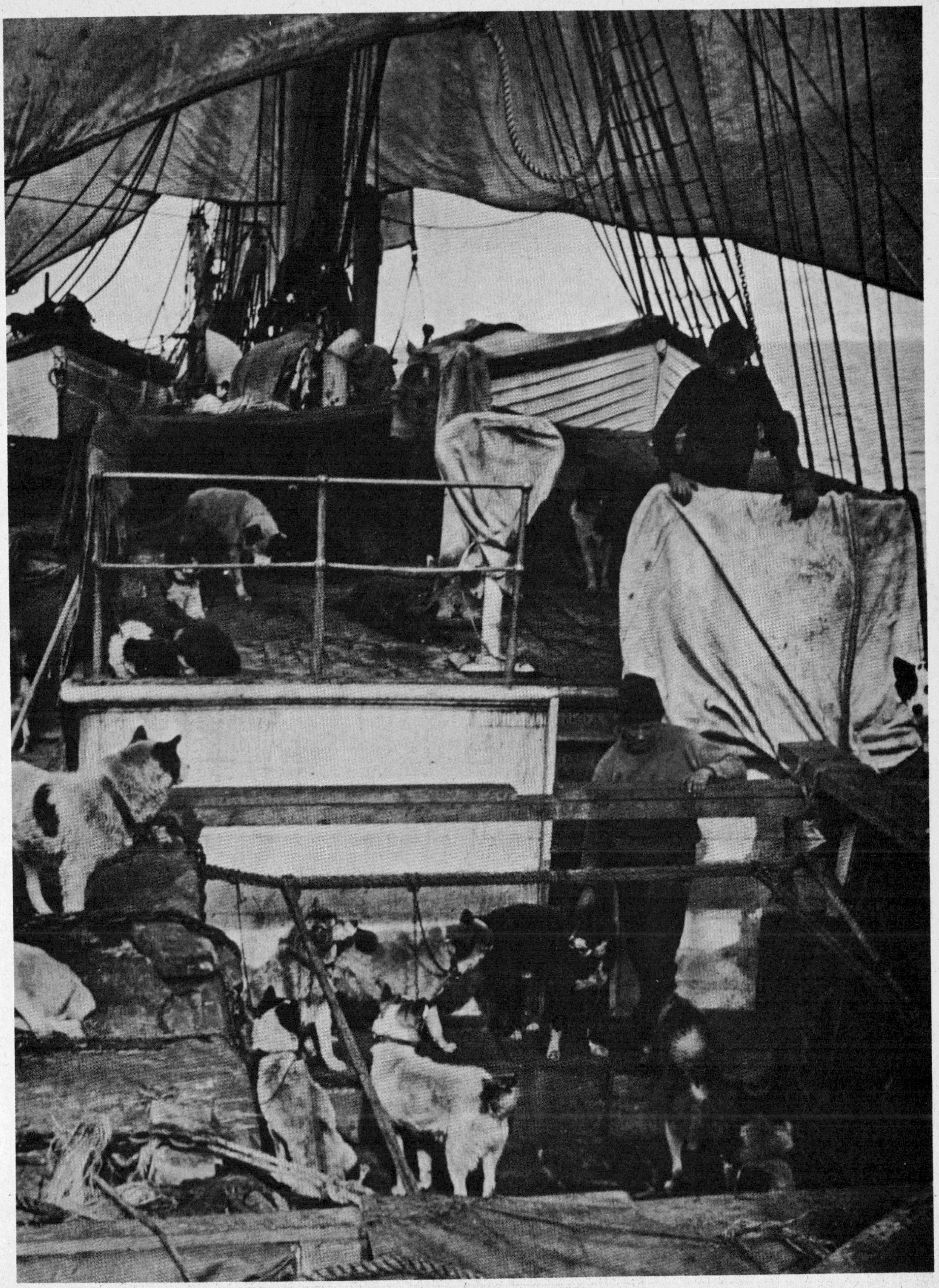

On board the *Terra Nova*, Captain Scott's ship.

Unloading the motor sledge which later fell through the ice and sank.

Scott believed that ponies would be hardier and more useful to his expedition than dogs. He was tragically proven wrong. Here he is shown leading one of the ponies to shore at Cape Evans, Antarctica.

Some of the members of Scott's last expedition, Captain Scott is fifth from right.

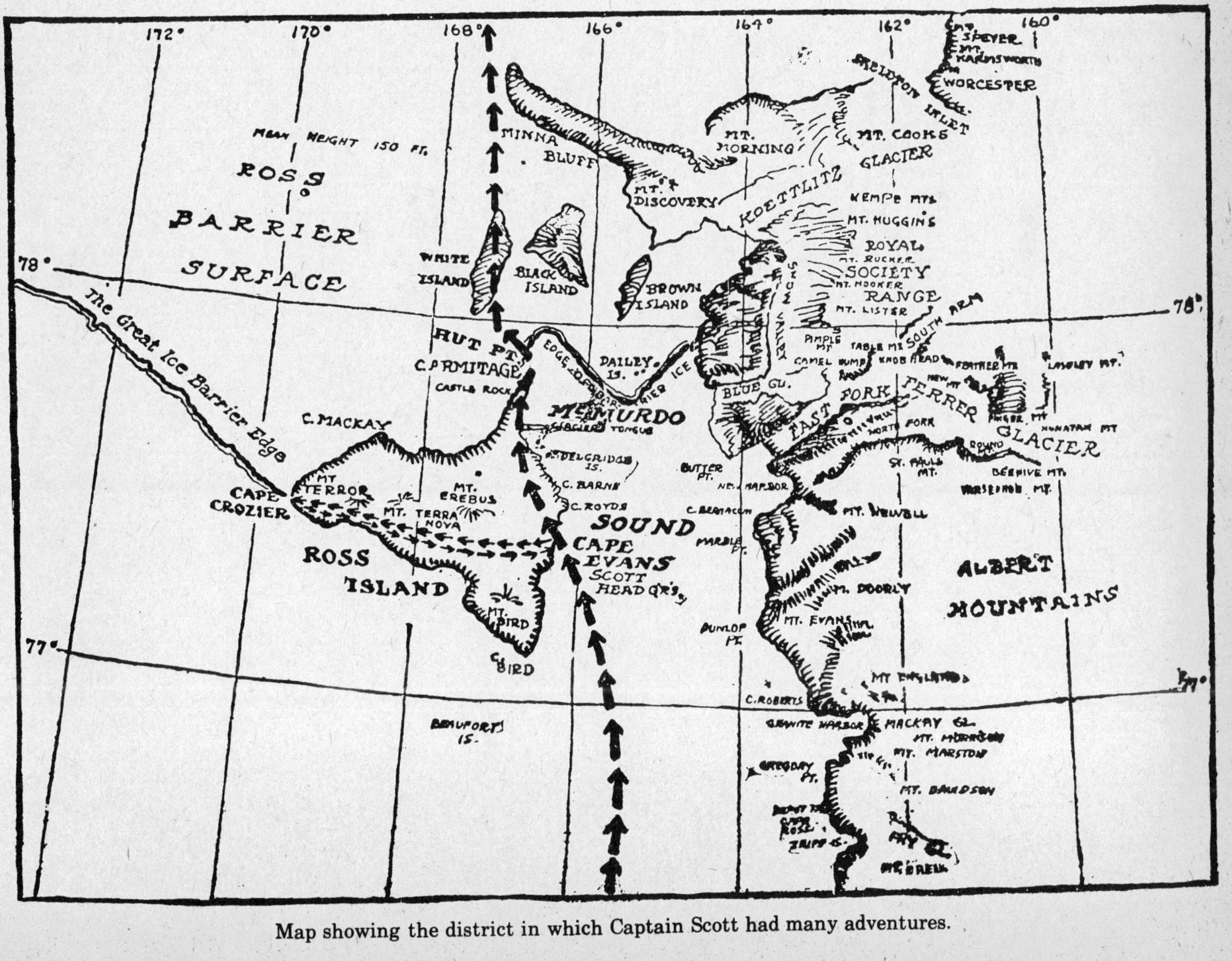

Map showing the district in which Captain Scott had many adventures.

"All the News That's Fit to Print."

The New York Times.

THE WEATHER.
Fair, slightly warmer Thursday; Friday, fair, warmer; moderate winds, becoming south.
For full weather report see Page 22.

VOL. LXI...NO. 19,793. * * * NEW YORK, WEDNESDAY, APRIL 3, 1912.—TWENTY-TWO PAGES. ONE CENT In Greater New York, Jersey City, and Newark. { Elsewhere, TWO CENTS.

FINDING SECOND CITY AT POMPEII

Results of New Excavations Indicate Discoveries More Remarkable Than Any Before.

TREASURES IN A WINESHOP

Over 800 Objects, All of Artistic Beauty, Include Exquisite Cups and Lamps.

FINE FRESCOES LAID BARE

One of Enormous Size—Women's Appeal for Votes for Aldermanic Candidate Written on a Wall.

By Marconi Transatlantic Wireless Telegraph to The New York Times.

LONDON, Wednesday, April 3.—Additional particulars regarding the new excavations at Pompeii are given in the Daily Mail, which says that about eight houses in the Street of Abundance, leading toward the Amphitheatre, have now been brought to light. The account goes on:

"The first house to the left is lofty and forms the angle of the newly excavated street with a narrower street still buried. The house has a wide door, above which is a fresco some six feet long, in which is depicted a rejoicing crowd playing around a throne on which is a seated divinity. Many of the figures are playing citharas, and a woman stretches out her arms, inviting them to contribute gifts, while two other female figures hold baskets in which to receive the gifts. Wreaths of flowers and foliage form a border to the whole.

"On the wall above, separated from one another by large red squares, are figures larger than life of Jupiter, Mercury, and Apollo, while a fourth figure is not yet identified. The features of Jupiter are rude, with a cruel expression. The coloring of the fresco is very vivid, and the proportions of the figures are just.

"Above juts out a roof four or five feet wide, [illegible] not only protected the paintings, but also people walking below on the footway of the street. One portion of the projection, which is still intact, is a balcony about eighteen feet long, again protruding for some three feet, with a parapet two feet high and fifteen inches wide. The parapet is in fragments, which have all been found. In the still existing corner of the parapet is a piece of clay gutter.

Scribbled Election.

"The wall of the house toward the side street is covered with red stucco, on which are scribbled notices of elections.

"Then, going on beyond the intersection with the outside street, comes a second house more than thirty feet high, with a balcony running along its two sides. Part has fallen, but the rest is connected with the balcony of a third house. Below in the side street is a foundation like all those found in Pompeii, and on the side of the house mentioned is an enormous fresco divided into upper and lower portions. In the upper part are figured twelve gods, Jupiter being in the centre, with a small inscription below. On the lower part is a procession of four priests performing a sacrifice before an altar.

"Opposite a fountain in the street is a small altar about three feet high, belonging evidently to the public shrine represented by the fresco described. In this little altar there is cut a channel for the blood of the sacrifice to run off into the street.

Women in Politics.

"The walls of the third house are plastered with white stucco covered with inscriptions in favor of a Duumvir. They are supposed to have been written by two women, whose names are written aslant beneath in angular characters between Runic and Latin. The inscription composed by these women runs:

Aselinas non sine Smvrine pro C Pollio Fusco rogant.

"Probably this means roughly, 'Aselinas and Smyrine say, Vote for Fuscus as your Alderman.'

"Some adversary or wag has crossed out the word 'Smyrine' by a thin line and substituted a name scarcely decipherable.

"Beyond the wall comes the door of a wine shop or bar similar to all those found in Pompeii, but so well preserved that it seems to have been only quite recently buried. There is the usual table or counter, its surface of glazed white tiles, in round apertures of which are inserted very large terracotta wine jars. In a corner of the shop lie a number of amphorae of various dimensions leaning against the wall.

"On the counter is a small square box made of bone, in which were found gold and silver coins, while others in copper lay open on the counter. All about the place lie a quantity of objects, among which are two rude clay amphorae in the shape of cocks, the

Continued on Page 3.

ENGINEERS FOR A STRIKE.

Brotherhood Members Said to Favor Stand of Their Officials.

The officials of the Brotherhood of Locomotive Engineers announced yesterday that the ballots so far received from the engineers on Eastern railroads indicated that the general sentiment among the men was in favor of a strike unless the demands of the brotherhood were acceded to. The men on the ballots were asked to declare whether they were willing to support those instructed to carry out a strike if one was deemed necessary. In this connection the ballots said:

"Your representatives having exhausted every effort to obtain a peaceful settlement and failed are firmly of the opinion that the managers representing the aforesaid lines are seeking to take an unfair advantage of our well-known conservatism and attempting to force the organization to accept a settlement that would bring the engineers a much smaller rate of pay than they honestly earn, and would also destroy our prestige and cast dishonor upon the organization to an extent that would practically prevent any future committee from obtaining results. With such a condition it would only be a short time before the rules and working conditions that have taken years of hard work to build up would be destroyed and engineers would be in the same condition as they were before the organization was founded.

"The prestige of the organization is at stake. Are you willing to support those intrusted with the carrying out of the plan of concerted action to the extent of a strike if in their judgment it is deemed necessary?"

MAN OF MYSTERY MURDERED.

Italian Who May Be of Noble Birth Shot by Unknown Assassin.

A young Italian who, in the seven months he had been in this country, was an object of no little mystery to the people of the Italian colony on the lower east side reeled into a drug store on Eleventh Street near First Avenue a little after 10 o'clock last night, spitting blood and bleeding profusely from a wound over the heart.

He had time just before he died to whisper to those who bent over him that he had been shot as he was walking along Eleventh Street, but that was all he said, and the detectives who went to work on the case found themselves without clue as to motive or the identity of the man or woman who did the shooting.

The dead man was known as Frank Cardinale, and he lived at 514 East Sixteenth Street. To the people of that neighborhood he was an object of absorbing interest, for he was of fine bearing, always well dressed, and yet he did no work of any sort. It was common knowledge that he received money regularly from Italy, so that he was what is known as a "remittance man." Some of his neighbors believe that he was of noble blood.

Shortly after the police had started work on the case a small boy marched into the Fifth Street Station carrying a revolver with one chamber discharged. He said that he had found it on Tenth Street, near Avenue A.

CHICAGO DEMOCRATIC.

Only 10 of 36 Aldermen Elected Are Republicans.

Special to The New York Times.

CHICAGO, April 2.—In the city election to-day the Democrats elected 26 Aldermen and the Republicans 10. The voters also approved three of the five bond issues asked for by Mayor Carter H. Harrison's administration, one of which is for $5,000,000 for new outer harbor improvements.

There was a bitter factional fight between the adherents of Mayor Harrison and Roger Sullivan, Democratic National Committeeman from Illinois. The Sullivan followers lost, eighteen of the victorious Democrats being aligned with the Harrison wing. But with all these victories the Sullivan Democrats, combining with Republicans in the Twenty-sixth Ward, dealt the Harrison forces a serious blow by defeating the re-election of Alderman Peter Reinberg, Chairman of the Commission on Local Transportation.

FORMER WAIF NOW MAYOR.

Henry L. Jost Elected by the Democrats of Kansas City.

KANSAS CITY, Mo., April 2.—Henry L. Jost, 31 years old, Democrat, was elected Mayor of Kansas City to-day over Mayor Darius A. Brown, Republican, by a majority estimated at 3,500 votes. With Mr. Jost the entire Democratic ticket, outside of a few Aldermen, was elected. The Council stands eighteen Democrats and six Republicans.

Mayor Brown, who formerly was President of the League of American Municipalities, ran on a platform that favored municipal ownership of gas and electric light plants.

Mr. Jost is an Assistant Prosecuting Attorney. He was a waif in New York and was sent West for adoption when a small boy.

HARTFORD IS REPUBLICAN.

Col. Cheney Elected—Council a Tie—Aldermanic Board Democratic.

Special to The New York Times.

HARTFORD, Conn., April 2.—Col. Louis R. Cheney, Republican, was elected Mayor of Hartford to-day over State Senator Thomas J. Spellacy, Democrat, by 658 majority. The total vote cast was 13,500, and Cheney's majority is the largest of any Mayoralty candidate in the last eight years. The Democrats have had the Mayor since 1910.

The Republicans were successful in carrying all the other important offices.

In the Board of Councilmen there is a tie, while the Democrats still retain a majority in the Board of Aldermen, owing to the number of members holding over.

HUNGARIANS ATTACK KING.

Violent Scenes in Parliament—Heir to Throne Also Denounced.

LONDON, Wednesday, April 3.—The Hungarian crisis has not abated in violence and the prospect of a settlement appears remote, according to a Vienna dispatch to The Daily Mail.

At a sitting of the Hungarian Parliament yesterday brutal attacks were made upon the Emperor-King and the Crown Prince.

The session was disorderly throughout and the President was powerless to check the unbridled speech.

MILWAUKEE REJECTS RULE BY SOCIALISTS

Dr. Gerhard Bading, Fusion Candidate for Mayor, Defeats Seidel by 12,972 Majority.

ALSO CAPTURE CITY COUNCIL

Socialists Will Have Only One-Third the Members—Americanism the Chief Campaign Issue.

Special to The New York Times.

MILWAUKEE, Wis., April 2.—Milwaukee is no longer a Socialist city. After a campaign in which the issue was the Stars and Stripes as against the red flag of Socialism the voters of Milwaukee, by a vote never before equalled in this city, demanded that the Socialistic banner be hauled down from the City Hall flagstaff, where it has fluttered metaphorically for the last two years, and a fusion ticket, headed by one Republican and two Democrats with practically a non-partisan City Council, has been elected to take over the reins of Government.

The majority of Dr. Gerhard Bading, the non-partisan candidate for Mayor, against Mayor Emil Seidel is 12,972, his vote being 43,172 to Seidel's 30,200. The total vote of 73,372 is 14,000 more votes than were cast in the election of two years ago, when the Socialists took control of the municipality.

The returns as to the City Council are as yet indefinite, but the Council is certainly anti-Socialistic. The Socialists will have no more than eleven of the thirty-seven Aldermen, four Socialists holding over. J. P. Carney, non-partisan candidate for City Treasurer, against whom the Socialists waged their hottest fight, ran ahead of his ticket nearly 20,000.

Dr. Bading, the Mayor-elect, said:

"Once more Milwaukee stands in the eyes of the world redeemed, an American city, believing in the American Constitution and the American Government.

"We have thrown off the disgrace under which we have suffered for the last two years and have made it apparent to the world that Milwaukee people are loyal Americans and not Socialists or Anarchists."

Mayor Seidel said: "We are coming back stronger than ever next Fall. We are going to recover our voices first. Then we are going back into the struggle and fight as we never fought before."

To-day's result shows that two years ago the Socialists were elected by a revolt of the old party members against the regular machines, and not because the people of Milwaukee believed in Socialism as the best form of government. The difficulty in Milwaukee has been that the Socialists lacked the administrative ability to accomplish the reforms they sought at a minimum expense.

Americanism was made the chief issue of the campaign. The Fusionists declared that it was the American flag against the Socialist red flag. One newspaper went so far as to portray this issue in colors on its first page to-day, and though the Socialists answered with the phrase, "Patriotism is the last refuge of a scoundrel," the flag issue won and is responsible for the tremendous anti-Socialist majority.

The demonstration of Saturday night, when the Socialists tried to break up a Fusion meeting by walking out of the hall when the American flag was unfurled, precipitated this issue, which was caught up until the supply of flags in Milwaukee was insufficient to meet the demand of the Fusionists, who nailed flags to their houses, wore them in hats and on their coat lapels.

The Socialists declare that they are not through in Milwaukee, and that their defeat is the only logical effort of capitalism to forget the National parties and combine to meet the advance of the proletariat. They say they will continue to march onward until they carry the city even in the face of the enactment of the majority election law, which will be the next development in Wisconsin politics.

In the coming session of the State Legislature, to be held the last of this month, a bill will be introduced and undoubtedly passed to allow Wisconsin cities to eliminate the Republican and Democratic Parties, and hold municipal campaigns on local issues, without regard to National party designations. An attempt to pass such a law at the regular session of the Legislature failed through the efforts of the Milwaukee Socialists, who by trading votes with farmer members obtained the passage of measures they wished and the defeat of those they opposed.

The day of Socialism in Milwaukee, however, has gone, and the home rulers will be able to pass the law for majority non-partisan elections. Milwaukee's course will be followed throughout the State.

WISCONSIN FOR LA FOLLETTE.

Returns Indicate Full Delegation for Him—Wilson Defeats Clark.

Special to The New York Times.

MILWAUKEE, Wis., April 2.—Incomplete returns from the Wisconsin Presidential preference primaries indicate that Senator La Follette will have practically a complete delegation from this State to the Republican National Convention, and that Gov. Woodrow Wilson of New Jersey will have just as strong a following among the Democrats. Both President Taft and Speaker Champ Clark were snowed under.

Taft managers concede the State to La Follette, with probably 22 out of the State's 26 delegates.

The figures from the State in general indicate a total vote of about 120,000 for La Follette and 50,000 for Taft. A review of the State shows that the La Follette men have carried the four delegates at large, and the First, Second, Third, Fourth, Sixth, Seventh, Eighth, and Eleventh Districts. This much is certain, and the other three also are probably La Follette's.

Clark's manager, ex-Congressman Weiss, admits that Clark has probably lost every delegate to Wilson.

Col. Roosevelt's name did not figure to any extent in the primary, as his supporters did not have his name printed on the ballot.

MONTANA ELECTIONS.

Helena Elects Democratic Mayor—Butte Socialists Lose Ground.

HELENA, Mont., April 2.—Municipal elections were held throughout Montana yesterday.

In Helena Ex-Mayor R. R. Purcell, Democrat, now ill in an eastern hospital was elected over Republican and Socialist opposition. Republican aldermen were returned from six out of seven wards.

Socialists carried only one of the eight wards in Butte where there is a hold over Socialist mayor.

Missoula in its first election since the adoption of the commission form of government re-elected but one of the original three commissioners and the element in favor of an open Sunday gained control.

SPRING BOOK NUMBER

Next Sunday The New York Times will issue its Spring Book Number, which will be filled with special articles by well-known writers, and many other features, including an annotated list of 500 books for Spring reading.

NEAR TO FISTICUFFS IN STEEL COMMITTEE

Gardner, Senator Lodge's Son-in-Law, Twice Aims Blows at Chairman Stanley.

INSISTS THAT HE'S A LIAR

Row Starts Over Publicity Given to Secrets of the Committee Hearings.

Special to The New York Times.

WASHINGTON, April 2.—Representative Augustus P. Gardner of Massachusetts, the son-in-law of Senator Lodge, made two sincere and well-meant attempts to punch the face of Representative Augustus O. Stanley of Kentucky, Chairman of the Steel Trust investigating committee, at an executive session of the committee to-day.

Mr. Gardner is an upstanding sort of person with plenty of sinews. It is the regret of his life that two large Republican Congressmen named Young and Sterling intercepted him and prevented him from denting Stanley's crown. While he was about it he called Stanley a liar and prefaced the word with profane adjectives. At a late hour to-night Stanley was still glad that Young and Sterling were there at the time.

The fracas, or rather the two fracases, of to-day were the outcome of a long series of incidents which have created great ill-feeling in the committee. Mr. Stanley has excited the derision of several of his colleagues, especially Gardner and McGillicuddy of Maine, who have done all the real directing of the work while Stanley has sought diversion in divers ways.

To-day, when the executive session of the committee began, Gardner pulled out a newspaper clipping reporting what had taken place in the executive session of last Saturday.

"This whole story," said Gardner, "is false so far as I am concerned, and I am sick and tired of the leaks that are coming out of this committee."

He then proceeded to intimate in the most unmistakable manner that Stanley was responsible for the leaks and also that the stories Stanley gave out to his favorite newspapers were not true.

"If you mean," Stanley broke in, "that I have been giving these stories out, you are saying what is an untruth."

"I'll show you who is telling an untruth!" Gardner shouted. "This thing has gone far enough."

With that he made a jump for the Chairman, but Young and Sterling got hold of him and forced him back into his seat. Meantime, Representative Bartlett of Georgia, who weighs about ninety pounds, was holding Stanley, but it was a work of supererogation. So far as anybody could see the Chairman was not belligerent. Martin Littleton sat by and chuckled unrestrainedly, and in a few minutes the orderly course of the committee was resumed.

But Gardner was still ruffled, and as the proceedings went on he kept interjecting remarks not calculated to please the Chairman. Most of them related to the way in which the Chairman had handled or mishandled the investigation. The trouble was chiefly over the question whether the investigation should be continued further and J. Pierpont Morgan and other witnesses should be summoned—Gardner was in favor of that—or whether, as Stanley preferred, it should wind up its proceedings immediately so that a good campaign document could be turned in as a report.

Gardner's comments kept getting more and more personal, and quite a number of them related to Stanley's convivial disposition and his willingness to let the other members of the committee work while he slept.

Finally, Stanley, goaded beyond endurance, interrupted him with a contradiction.

"You're a liar!" cried Gardner, "and I'll break your head this time in spite of all the butters-in on this committee!"

And he very nearly did it. Young and Sterling were promptly on the spot, but before they could catch his arm he had made a glancing blow along Stanley's jaw. Young caught him in time to prevent it from taking full effect and Stanley dodged, but before Sterling could get the left arm Gardner had made a swing with it at Stanley, who again ducked. This time Sterling caught him again just in time to prevent him from catching Stanley on the nose. Gardner, swearing mad and still struggling vainly to get at Stanley, was finally forced back into his seat and quieted.

There were no casualties.

CHICAGO ALL-NIGHT THEATRE

Provides Moving Pictures for Prowlers from Midnight Until 6 A. M.

Special to The New York Times.

CHICAGO, Ill., April 2.—The weary sufferer from insomnia and the prowling night hawk, together with the man who has stayed out so late that he is afraid finally to go home and face his wife—all have been provided for at last. The Lyric Theatre, a moving picture house in State Street, in the heart of the retail shopping district of Chicago, has been converted into a day and night house.

The result of the experiment for the first 24 hours is declared to have been satisfactory.

"We have established the only all-night and all-day theatre in the world," said Aaron J. Jonas, President of the syndicate operating the theatre, to-night; "and we are going to give the experiment a six months' trial, whether we make a penny by it or not."

To operate the theatre, which combines vaudeville with motion pictures, three shifts of employes will be required, while 96,000 feet of film will be operated during each 24 hours. From midnight until 6 A. M. nothing but pictures will be shown.

RARE MINERALS, STRANGE FORMS OF LIFE, AND PICTURESQUE NATURAL MARVELS FOUND BY SCOTT'S ANTARCTIC EXPLORERS

Coal and Marble, with Only a Trace of Gold, and Many Well Preserved Fossils.

A STREAM UNDERGROUND

Twenty-five Miles Long, Winding Through Crystalline Caves, and Alive with Seals.

STRANGE, WINGLESS INSECTS

Of Two Varieties, Found in Thousands, Clustered, Half Frozen, Under Pebbles.

NEW ROUTE TO THE PLATEAU

Crater of the Late Glacial Age Found, and Basalt Flows 80 Feet Thick.

EXPLORED NOT ONLY ON LAND

But Sounded the Seas for New Forms of Life, and Sent Up Balloons to Test the Air.

HEROIC WORK SAVED EVANS

Officer Suffering from Scurvy Carried to Coast, Now Convalescent—Exhaustive Marine Biological Observations.

Special Cable to THE NEW YORK TIMES.

AKAROA, New Zealand, April 2.—Acting on behalf of Capt. Scott, Commander Pennell to-day gave me short accounts of the journeys of the first two parties which were detached from the southern party as it advanced toward the pole.

Day and Hooper, who left the southern party on Nov. 4, arrived safely at Cape Evans on Jan. 21.

Atkinson, Wright, Cherry, Garrard, and Keohane, who left the southern party at Upper Glacier Depot on Dec. 21, reached Cape Evans on Jan. 28. On their way down the Beardmore Glacier they spent Christmas Day visiting a moraine near Cloudmaker Mountain and collected some geological specimens.

A depot party left Cape Evans on Dec. 26 and placed special rations at One Ton Depot for the returning parties.

While returning opportunity was taken by Day to repair the motor sledge, which was left on the barrier near Safety Cape last Spring, the necessary parts having been brought out on the outward journey. The sledge is now in working order. It is intended, if possible, to bring this motor sledge back to the ship next year.

Returning Party's Perils.

The last supporting party had an exciting time. The report states that during the forenoon of Jan. 4 the party, consisting of Lieut. Evans, Lashley, and Crean, marched three miles south with Scott's advanced party. Then, bidding their leader and his comrades farewell, they turned northward at latitude 87 degrees 35 minutes and commenced their homeward march. The southern party were then traveling rapidly, yet easily, and the members appeared to be exceptionally fit.

The last returning party retraced their steps, feeling confident that Scott would reach the south pole. They covered eighteen miles a day until Jan. 9, when a blizzard of moderate severity blew from the south, lasting three days and severely hampering the party. Accordingly, to insure full rations for the early part of the homeward march, they shaped their course direct for the depot near Mount Darwin. This necessitated crossing Shackleton's ice falls at the head of Beardmore

BOMB EXPLODES AT UNION MEETING

Found in Hall, It Mortally Injures Man Appointed to Carry It Out.

HAYWOOD STIRS PASSAIC MEN

Denounces Peaceful Methods and Promises a General Walk-Out—8,000 Now Idle.

RED BANK, N. J., April 2.—Just as Chairman Marato was about to call to order a meeting of the Garment Workers' Union in Columbus Hall to-night he saw an object on the floor that had the appearance of a bomb. He pointed it out to Andrew Shkulsky, a member, and told him to take it out to the street.

Shkulsky picked it up and carried it out. A moment later an explosion was heard. The garment workers ran out and found Shkulsky prostrate. His left hand had been torn off by the explosion, his right hand was mangled, and his right arm broken. In spite of his injuries he got to his feet and staggered to his home, where he fell unconscious in the doorway. His condition is serious. He was taken to the Long Branch Hospital.

When the police arrived the hall was deserted. Detective Minugh says that on Friday last a boy told the police that he had seen what he thought were several bombs in the closet in Columbus Hall. When the police expressed doubt the boy went off and came back with what looked like a bomb and which he said he had taken from the closet in the meeting room. Chief Wymbs put the bomb in a safe place and told the lad to go and get the others, as he had said there were two more in the closet. The boy went back, but when he reached the hall he found it closed for the night.

When there was a strike at Fisner's factory about two years ago a number of Polaks were brought from New York to take the places of the strikers, who were Italians. After the strike some of the Polaks remained in the employ of the firm. When the strike occurred Shkulsky, Minugh said, came from New York with other Polaks, and besides getting work in the factory, opened a boarding house for the Polak workers. At the present time, the detective said, there are fifteen or twenty Polaks and about 400 Italians employed in the factory.

The detective said it struck him as rather peculiar that a Polak should have been asked to remove the suspicious object when there were so many Italians in the hall.

HAYWOOD AT PASSAIC.

Takes Command of Strikers, Denouncing Peaceable Methods.

William D. Haywood, who directed the strikes at Lawrence and Lowell, Mass., recently, visited Passaic, N. J., yesterday. He made two addresses to the striking mill operatives there and boasted that before he was through he would "put Passaic on the map and show the world what the capitalists of Passaic really are."

After several weeks the strike situation in Passaic and the neighboring towns is not such as to encourage the strikers greatly. Three mills out of several dozen are shut down. These are the New Jersey Worsted Spinning Company, at Garfield, and two plants of the Forstmann & Hoffmann Company at Clifton and Garfield. Other mills are somewhat crippled by lack of hands, but there remain many that are running on full time. Only about 4,000 operatives are on strike, but their failure to work has thrown about an equal number out of employment, so that all told about 8,000 persons, men and women, are idle.

Haywood's arrival was marked by enthusiasm among many of the strikers who have wearied of the peaceable methods ordered by Boris Reinstein, who first began enrolling the workers in the Industrial Workers of the World. Haywood immediately denounced Reinstein as an impostor who had illegally used the name of the Industrial Workers of the World and promised his hearers that he would drive him from the field.

Reinstein has contented himself with enrolling about 4,000 weavers. Haywood proposes enrolling workers of all branches and nationalities. Most of his hearers last night were Italians.

Haywood promised a general strike which would cripple the whole mill business. He urged his hearers to combine as the strikers at Lawrence and Lowell did, and promised them that if they did so they could defeat the police, the militia, and the capitalists.

What influence the arrival of Haywood may have had to do with it is not known, but it was remarked that few of the employes returned yesterday to three of the mills which offered the increases in wages demanded by the strikers, though continuing to hold out against recognition of shop committees. It had been expected that many of the strikers would seize this offering, and there was considerable amazement on the part of the mill owners when the strikers failed to avail themselves of the opportunity to return to work.

DIES OF JOY OVER ELECTION.

Peter Schofield Thought His Son Had Been Chosen Alderman.

Special to The New York Times.

CHICAGO, Ill., April 2.—Joy over a false report that his son William had been elected Alderman in the Twenty-first Ward, caused the death of Peter Schofield this evening.

Schofield had been working in his son's interest at the polls all day and was exhausted when he returned to his home. Another son, James, informed him of the progress of the counting of the votes, and finally announced that William had received enough votes to assure his election.

The father sank back in his chair with a sigh, and died almost immediately.

Later reports from the polls showed that William Schofield's Republican opponent, J. F. Burns, was elected by a majority of 119 votes.

CROKER GOING BACK.

Comes Up from Florida and Sails for Ireland To-morrow.

Richard Croker, the former Tammany chieftain, sails for Ireland to-morow on the White Star liner Adriatic, accompanied by his friend Edward Cahill.

Mr. Croker returned from Florida at the end of last week and has been spending his time since his arrival in New York visiting his old friends at the National Democratic Club. They will give him a farewell dinner to-night.

COSTLY 10-MINUTE STORM.

Philadelphia Property Suffers—Two Women Hurt in Wrecked Car.

Special to The New York Times.

PHILADELPHIA, Penn., April 2.—A storm of ten minutes' duration at 7:05 to-night did property damage to the extent of thousands of dollars in the business section along the waterfront and in Camden. Countless trees were blown down, an office building was unroofed, night hawk cabs were overturned, and the windows of several of the larger hotels were smashed, showering the guests with glass.

Only two persons were reported seriously injured, Miss Anna Cleary of Camden and Mrs. Anna Behrend of Philadelphia. They were in a Camden trolley car when a tin roof, which had been carried several hundred feet, struck the car and wrecked it. The women were buried in the débris.

The wind reached a velocity of forty miles an hour, and subsided as quickly as it arose. The storm came out of the northwest and apparently followed the course of the Delaware River to the southeast. The residential districts of Philadelphia were only slightly affected.

GEMS AT $5 A QUART.

Those That Studded Mrs. Anthony's Heels So Valued by Husband.

Special to The New York Times.

MUNCIE, Ind., April 2.—A desire to outdo Alice Roosevelt Longworth in popularity is given by Charles H. Anthony of Muncie as the reason for the lavish display of jewelry by his wife, Harriet B. Anthony, who recently attracted widespread attention by appearing at a Washington ball wearing slippers with the heels studded with diamonds.

"You can buy that kind of gems at about $5 a quart," said Mr. Anthony to-day, in listing his property for taxation with the Township Assessor, Clem V. Powell; but the other jewelry displayed by Mrs. Anthony in the East will run up into the thousands in value, according to the Assessor's schedule.

NELLIE BLY TO GO TO JAIL.

Judge Hough Signs an Order Committing Her for Contempt of Court.

An order committing Mrs. Elizabeth S. Seaman, (Nellie Bly,) owner of the Iron Clad Manufacturing Company, to jail for contempt of court and failure to pay a fine of $600 imposed therefor was signed yesterday afternoon by Judge Hough in the United States District Court. Because of the lateness of the hour it was not given to a Marshal to serve, but it will be handed over to the Marshal this morning.

Charles A. Riegelman, Edwin T. Rice, and John M. Carver, attorneys for some of the Iron Clad Company's creditors, obtained a certificate from the Clerk of the United States District Court in Brooklyn on Monday that Mrs. Seaman had not paid her fine, and they presented this to Judge Hough yesterday.

The contempt in which Mrs. Seaman was held grew out of failure properly to answer questions put to her regarding the relations between the Iron Clad Company, now in bankruptcy, and the $2,000,000 American Steel Barrel Company.

SAYS BOY ALIENATED WIFE.

Pennsylvania Merchant Causes Arrest of Student, 17 Years Old.

Special to The New York Times.

PHILADELPHIA, Penn., April 2.—William P. Becker, a student of the Northeast Manual Training School, was arrested to-night on a charge of alienating the affections of Mrs. B. H. Caldwell, wife of a wealthy business man of Fernwood, Delaware County.

Caldwell accuses the boy of trying to induce Mrs. Caldwell to put poison in the coffee which she gave her husband. This charge is embodied in the complaint upon which the warrant is based.

Becker was arrested at his home, 2126 East Chelten Avenue, Germantown. He stoutly declared his innocence when the charges were read to him, and declared that he would have an entirely different version of the affair when he was given a chance to tell his side of the story. He alleged that the arrest is due to insane jealousy upon the part of Caldwell.

Becker is 17 and Mrs. Caldwell is about twice his age.

SIGN OF TAFT'S CONFIDENCE.

Approves Naval Fleet's Plans Extending Beyond His Present Term.

Special to The New York Times.

WASHINGTON, April 2.—President Taft is credited with having a firm and settled conviction that he is to be re-elected. Evidence of this was the general topic of comment in the Navy Department to-day when the memorandum for the operations of the Atlantic fleet was discussed.

Plans for the work of the fleet are seldom made out for a longer period than three or four months at a time. The Summer programme is usually made out in the Spring and covers the Spring manoeuvres, the Summer cruise, and closes with the orders for the Fall docking. The memorandum for the coming Summer's work was completed on Saturday, and after a careful examination by the President received his approval. It has the force of a military order and is obeyed as such.

Beginning with April 15 the fleet is to be sent to home yards for docking, which will occupy the time until May 1. Then the successive operations of the fleet are set forth, covering the time from May 1, 1912, until May 5, 1913, two months after the expiration of the present term of the President.

Robert F. Scott on skis at the South pole.

Scott wearing the wallet in which his journals were preserved.

Oates, Bowers, Scott, Wilson and Evans stand at the South Pole, exhausted from their ordeal and sorely disappointed to discover that Amundsen's party preceded theirs to the Pole by one month.

"All the News That's Fit to Print."

The New York Times.

THE WEATHER.
Showers Monday. Tuesday generally fair; moderate southwest and west winds.
For full weather report see Page 17.

VOL. LXI...NO. 19,910. * * * * NEW YORK, MONDAY, JULY 29, 1912. EIGHTEEN PAGES. ONE CENT. In Greater New York, Jersey City, and Newark. Elsewhere, TWO CENTS.

TELLS HOW POLICE CLEARED STREET FOR MURDERERS

The Times Finds a Witness of Rosenthal's Killing Who Was Hustled About and Clubbed.

HAD DINED IN METROPOLE

Stood Talking in Front of Hotel Just Before the Crime and Was Ordered Away.

POLICE FOLLOWED TO CORNER

Ordered Again to Move On, He Crossed the Street Just as Murder Car Drew Up.

THREE FIRED AT GAMBLER

One of These, a Bald Man, Felt Victim's Pulse, Then Jumped on Moving Auto.

DESCRIPTION FITS ROSE

Bystander Who Tried to Halt the Gray Car Was Roughly Handled by Assassins' Lookout.

THE TIMES found yesterday a witness of the shooting of Herman Rosenthal on the sidewalk in front of the Hotel Metropole on the morning of July 16, whose story tends to support the assertions frequently made since the murder that the plan by which it was carried out included the clearing of the immediate vicinity by policemen and conspirators of bystanders who might have been in the way of the murderers. His story further tends to corroborate the oft-repeated assertion of District Attorney Whitman that pursuit of the murderers after the crime was the "merest pretext."

In making his statement the witness for personal reasons, which he set forth, refused to disclose his name for publication. He has lived in New York for four years, and up to the time of the murder was employed by a concern in the vicinity of Times Square. Two days after the murder he left the city for a vacation, which was spent at his home in another State. He returned to New York several days ago, after having obtained employment in another city, for which he starts to-day. The fact that he was about to leave town for a place where he could not be harassed on account of what he had witnessed, played no small part in his willingness to tell what he saw. Here is his story:

Sat Near Rosenthal in Metropole.

On the night of the Rosenthal murder he attended a performance at the Globe Theatre with a young woman friend and another couple whose acquaintance he had made through his companion. The four left the Globe Theatre at 11:45 o'clock and strolled leisurely down Broadway to Twenty-eighth Street and back. They reached Forty-third Street at 1 o'clock and went into the café of the Metropole, where they sat at a table in the rear of the place and on the east side.

Soon after the party was seated two men at an adjoining table began a conversation which centred on the disclosures made and threatened by Rosenthal of graft in the Police Department. Suddenly one of the men exclaimed, "There is Rosenthal now," and he pointed to a man seated about three tables to the front of the one at which the witness's party sat.

Near Rosenthal another man was sitting, but apparently he was a stranger to the gambler. At any rate, no words passed between them. Rosenthal was drinking from a tall glass when observed by the witness.

With his friends, the witness stated, he tarried in the café of the Metropole until about 1:40 o'clock, when they decided to separate, each couple returning home.

Police Kept His Party Moving.

"As we stepped from the door of the café," the witness declared, "we stopped for just a minute to say good-bye. As we drew up about three or four feet to the side of the door a policeman came up and ordered us to move along. We shifted our position a little bit, and were still exchanging remarks when a second policeman approached us and told us to keep moving.

"We then walked slowly west to the northeast corner of Broadway and Forty-third Street and halted just about in front of the entrance to the bar of the Hotel Cadillac. The second policeman who had ordered us to move on came up to where we were standing and again ordered us to move.

"Then we crossed to the south side of Forty-third Street and returned in a leisurely way to a point just opposite the Metropole. We were standing under one of the balconies of the Cohan Theatre Building and about to bid each other good-night when a big gray touring car with four men on the rear seat and only the chauffeur in the front rolled up just in front of us, having come from Sixth Avenue.

"Two of the men on the rear seat jumped out of the machine, walked back toward Sixth Avenue about thirty-five or forty feet, and crossed over to the north side of the street. As these two returned toward the entrance of the Metropole Café, the other two men on the rear seat stepped out on to the sidewalk almost where we were standing, and as the chauffeur turned the car around walked

Continued On Page 2.

NUPTIAL LAW UNCHANGED.

Report of Repeal by Pope Was Due to a Misunderstanding.

ROME, July 28.—The report that the Pope has repealed the decree, "Ne Temere," is unfounded, nor is it likely ever to be revoked, as it embodies provisions which have governed church procedure for two centuries.

It is probable that the misunderstanding with respect to the repeal of the decree arose through the suspension of the provision relating to mixed marriages in Germany and Hungary.

The other provisions of the "Ne Temere," however, are in full force in those two countries, while in the United States and England all the provisions of the decree without exception are still in force. Thus a marriage betwen Catholic and Protestant without the sanction of the parish priest is null. It is declared that possibly the United States and England may later obtain a change in that provision.

YACHT BURNS IN THE HUDSON

Tarrytown Harbor Master Suspects an Enemy Set It Afire.

Special to The New York Times.

TARRYTOWN, N. Y., July 28.—The yacht Rambler, owned by Dr. T. V. Roe of this town, was destroyed by fire early this morning under suspicious circumstances. Dr. Roe, who yesterday stocked the boat with provisions preparatory to a cruise up the St. Lawrence, says it was the work of an enemy, or some one, who, knowing that the lockers were full, went aboard the boat to rob it, and dropped a match among the oil rags. The blaze was discovered at 3 o'clock in the morning, but the boat was then doomed.

The fire burned for an hour, when the waves from the Albany night boat sank the hull after the flames had eaten their way to the water's edge. Dr. Roe was made Harbor Master a short time ago, and since then he has had trouble. For a month he has had a man sleep on his boat. Last night, through a misunderstanding, no one wos on board.

$75,000,000 IN KANSAS WHEAT

Abundant Crops and Good Prices Promise Prosperity in Middle West.

Special to The New York Times.

KANSAS CITY, Mo., July 28.—With the biggest wheat crop on record, a favorable season thus far for a heavy corn crop, unusually large hay crops already put up, a favorable outlook for cotton, abundant yield of most fruits, and remunerative prices for all commodities, a big season is ahead for the railroads, the merchants, the bankers, and all branches of industry in the Middle West.

Wheat worth $2,500,000, in 2,500 cars, was marketed in Kansas City last week. The live stock receipts were valued at about the same sum. A multitude of minor commodities added several hundred thousand dollars more to the money paid for Western products. They give some indication of the commercial activity that has started with the beginning of the big crop movement.

The Kansas wheat crop alone is worth about $75,000,000.

MacARTHUR'S TRIUMVIRATE.

Pastor Calls on Carnegie, Rockefeller, and Morgan to Save the World.

Special to The New York Times.

BOSTON, Mass., July 28.—The Rev. Dr. Robert S. MacArthur, in his sermon in Tremont Temple to-day, said he had prayed that men like Carnegie, Rockefeller, and J. Pierpont Morgan would give their best brains to God for missionary work in China, Japan, India, and Continental Europe. Dr. MacArthur declared that if these three men would get their hearts and wealth together they would evangelize the world in twenty-five years.

"Business men should not only give one day in seven to rest and recreation, but they should contribute one-seventh of their wealth for missionary work both home and foreign," said the preacher.

"The men who wrote the Bible," he continued, "were greater scientists than we have in America to-day. They tell us how bad traits are of great physical injury to men. Only a few years ago Dr. Oliver Wendell Holmes said that soon we should have an instrument that would record the characteristics of men, and I am not prepared to say that the learned gentleman was wrong.

"It was only a short while ago when a professor of the Smithsonian Institution at Washington saw two Italians exhibiting much anger toward each other. He got one of them to speak into a vessel from which he prepared a mixture and later gave it to a cat, and the cat died."

MAY GET ONE BATTLESHIP.

Democrats Alarmed by Growth of Sulzer Movement in House.

Special to The New York Times.

WASHINGTON, July 28.—The conflict within Democratic ranks over the naval increase programme, precipitated by the decision of the House Democratic caucus against any battleships at this time, has become so serious that party leaders have arranged a postponement of the contest in the House in the hope that the big and little navy factions may be brought together without injury or stultification to the party.

Originally it was the plan to call up the conference report on the Naval Appropriation bill in the House on Tuesday. This is only a partial report in which the conferees agreed on everything but the disputed naval programme. The Senate has adopted the partial report.

Representative Sulzer's petition urging Democrats to join with the Republican minority in voting for a motion to concur in the Senate two battleship amendment is being circulated, and the leaders are hoping the factions may compromise on one battleship. In an effort to line up the forces that way, Chairman Padgett of the House Naval Committee has announced that he will not call up the naval conference report before Thursday, instead of Tuesday, and if a compromise cannot be reached by that day, there may be no action before next week.

The battleship advocates feel confident they will force through at least one battleship, possibly two.

Latest Shipping News.

ARRIVED—SS Athenai, from Patras, July 12.

DILLON WON'T RUN FOR OHIO GOVERNOR

Republican Nominee Withdraws Because the Party Is So Badly Divided.

ROOSEVELT STATE TICKET

Colonel Overrules His Advisers, Who Wanted to Indorse the Judge—Committee to Name Successor.

Special to The New York Times.

COLUMBUS, Ohio, July 28.—Judge Edmond B. Dillon, nominated as the Republican candidate for Governor of Ohio at the State Convention last month, announced to-day his withdrawal from the ticket, his reason being the determination of the Roosevelt people to put up a third ticket in the State.

Judge Dillon's announcement came in a telegram from Mackinac Island, where he is spending the Summer. The telegram said:

> My written declination, placed in the hands of Chairman Burton, was not read to the convention, and I accepted the nomination in the full presumption and belief that my acceptance would mean a united party and a single ticket in Ohio.
>
> All endeavor in that behalf has failed despite the kind offices of my friends in each following of the party.
>
> The measure of justice due me, even though a mere individual, requires my resignation as nominee for Governor, and the same will be presented to the State Central Committee at its next meeting, Wednesday.

The committee, a Taft body by a slight margin, is empowered to fill the vacancy. That it do so, is not mandatory. It may decide to reconvene the delegates in another State Convention.

The nomination of Judge Dillon was made against his own wish. When the delegates were gathered for the State Convention he steadfastly refused to allow his named to be used in connection with the Governorship, wanting only the nomination for Judge of the Supreme Court. Two ballots had been taken in a vain endeavor to choose between Arthur L. Garford, Lawrence K. Langdon, Bernard H. Kroger, and D. F. Anderson. Roosevelt delegates steadfastly clung to Garford. Taft men sought to concentrate on Langdon, but were unable to do so. They needed the eighty-seven votes which were cast regularly for Kroger by his Cincinnati friends and other votes.

Warren G. Harding started the stampede to Judge Dillon when, appearing dramatically on the platform after the second ballot, he proposed that the Judge should be nominated by acclamation. The Dillon boom once started never abated, and the candidate who had been considered only as a remote possibility at the opening of the convention was nominated on the fifth ballot.

Judge Dillon thought when he was nominated that his selection marked the end of the new party movement in this State, and in a brief speech to the convention accepting the nomination, he said: "I will give to the party and the people of the State the best that is in me."

The Judge's decision now not to run is due solely to the fact that Col. Roosevelt has delivered to his Ohio supporters instructions to arrange for putting a new party ticket in the field. Arthur L. Garford would be the logical candidate for Governor on the third ticket.

When Nat C. Wright, the Cleveland editor, returned from Oyster Bay after a talk with Col. Roosevelt last week the intimation was made clear that the proposed Bull Moose nominee for President could not be persuaded to give up his contention that there should be a State ticket in Ohio, just as in other States. Mr. Wright told Col. Roosevelt that the plan favored by his supporters in Ohio was to indorse Judge Dillon and the rest of the Republican State ticket and put their names in the Roosevelt column on the ballot under the Roosevelt candidates for Presidential Electors. But the Colonel would not assent to this.

Col. Roosevelt's attitude was made known to Judge Dillon late last week, and he had a talk with State Chairman Walter F. Brown in Toledo on his way to Mackinac. Mr. Brown led the Roosevelt movement prior to the May primaries, but since the Chicago Convention has made no public statement which in the slightest would indicate that he intended to join the third party or to resign his membership on the State or National Republican Committee, which might be expected if he changed his affiliations.

It was learned here to-day that Arthur I. Vorys, former Republican National Committeeman for Ohio, would be named as a member of the Advisory Committee of the Republican National Committee. The Advisory Committee will be the real controlling force in the party organization.

GOV. FORBES HAD RELAPSE.

Condition Was Serious for a Time, but He Is Now Recovering.

WOOD'S HOLE, Mass., July 28.—W. Cameron Forbes, Governor General of the Philippines, is ill on Nashawena Island, but his condition is not regarded as critical. The Governor has suffered a recurrence of a trouble which affected him in the Philippines, and at one time within a week was considered seriously ill. Since then, however, he has improved considerably. Dr. F. S. Watson of Boston is with Gov. Forbes on the island continuously.

Edward Forbes, a brother of the Governor, who is staying at Falmouth for the Summer, said to-day that his brother is getting along very well. Mr. Forbes said that the Governor's original complaint had been complicated somewhat by another trouble which attending physicians had not been able definitely to diagnose. The Governor's condition, his brother said, is that of a man who has been seriously run down, but who is recuperating and whose condition need cause no alarm.

ROBBED AS COTTAGE BURNS.

Kenneth Murchison at Narragansett Loses $7,000 in Jewels.

Special to The New York Times.

NARRAGANSETT PIER, July 28.—Mr. and Mrs. Kenneth M. Murchison of New York, who had a cottage at Kentara Green partly burned Saturday, were robbed of jewels valued at $7,000 to $8,000. Included in the list of jewels stolen are several diamond rings owned by Mrs. Murchison, and prized as family heirlooms.

During the fire Mrs. Murchison tried to aid the other cottagers, and burglars took advantage of the opportunity.

CAR SMASHES AUTO; TWO MORTALLY HURT

Anton Homan and His Son Have Their Skulls Fractured in Wreck at Woodhaven, L. I.

SEVEN PERSONS HURLED OUT

Driver Trying to Pass Ahead of the Trolley When Another He Could Not See Struck Machine.

Persons in Jamaica Avenue, Woodhaven, Queens, near the corner of Manor Avenue, about 7 o'clock last night, saw a big automobile, in which were three men, a woman, and five children, suddenly dart out behind a wagon and a trolley car, which blocked its progress on its own side of the road, and dodge across the tracks as if to swing around the outside of the trolley car. Another trolley car, evidently unseen by the motorists, was bearing rapidly down on them, and as their motor car emerged from behind the trolley which they sought to pass, this other car struck them, head on.

The automobile was sent flying across the road and overturned. All the occupants except one man and a boy were thrown from the car. These two were pinned beneath the wreckage. Passengers from the two trolley cars ran to the automobile and assisted all the injured persons to the office of Dr. A. L. Voltz, on the corner. There, as the physician attended them, their names were learned. The worst injured were found to be:

HOMAN, ANTON, 628 Glenmore Avenue, Brooklyn, fractured skull.
HOMAN, Mrs. ANTON, both ankles sprained.
HOMAN, AUGUST, 19 years old, brother of Anton, badly cut and bruised.
HOMAN, FRANCIS, 3 years old, fractured skull.

The others in the party were August Becker of 106 Reid Avenue, Brooklyn, an uncle of Mrs. Homan, three other children of the Homans, Florence, 9 years old; Elizabeth, 5, and Margaret, 2, and Charles Emmerich of 291 Gates Avenue, a cousin of the Homan children, 15 years old. All of these persons were bruised and shaken, but they were not hurt otherwise, and Dr. Voltz took them all to their homes in his own automobile. Mr. Becker owned the car in which the party had been riding, and it was wrecked.

An ambulance was called from St. Mary's Hospital in Jamaica for Mr. Homan and his son, and they were taken there, where it was said that both probably would die. There was some hope held out for the father, but it was said that Francis Homan had almost no chance of recovery.

On the way from the hospital in response to the call the ambulance, a motor car, was making nearly forty miles an hour, when John McCracken of 15 Vine Street, Richmond Hill, stepped in front of it as it passed through Richmond Hill. He was flung to the side of the road and Dr. Halstead, who had started with Dr. Agan from the hospital, dropped off and found that McCracken was badly bruised and cut, but that no bones were broken. He assisted the man to a hotel near by and stayed with him there until the ambulance returned for them after having carried Mr. Homan and his son to the hospital.

No one on the trolley car with which the Homan automobile collided was injured, though the vestibule of the car was smashed in about Motorman Patrick Reilly, and he was covered with broken glass. He escaped without a cut.

LOST DIAMOND IN AUTO FALL.

Mrs. Walter's Touring Car Skids Into Broadway Hole.

Receiving word that one of her big sight-seeing cars had been disabled down in Lower Manhattan last night about 9 o'clock, Mrs. W. Walter of 105 East Fifteenth Street, who manages the Knickerbocker Sightseeing Company, started down Broadway from Times Square in a touring car to investigate. Her machine was driven by Edward Regan of 242 East Forty-ninth Street.

Reaching Thirty-seventh Street, the chauffeur attempted to steer the automobile to the left around a large excavation about six feet deep, which is blocked off there by the Consolidated Telegraph and Electrical Subway Company. As the automobile turned across the car tracks the left front wheel began to slide along the rail. The front of the machine skidded over the pavement, made wet and slippery by the light rain, directly into the excavation. The machine was saved from overturning by the network of pipes and cables extending north and south across the excavation.

Thrown suddenly forward in the machine by the plunge, Mrs. Walter tried to grasp one of the arms supporting the top of the automobile. A blow broke a diamond ring with three large settings, and one of the stones was lost.

The automobile was pulled out of the excavation after a rope was run from its rear axle to a Broadway car. Immediately after the machine was taken away several men with lanterns entered the excavation in search of the lost diamond, valued by Mrs. Walter at $500.

AUTOS CRASH IN FIFTH AV.

Mrs. D. E. Duclos Thrown to the Pavement—Two Others a Little Hurt.

In a collision between two automobiles in Fifth Avenue in front of St. Patrick's Cathedral last night, one woman was injured and two others were badly shaken up. Mrs. David E. Duclos was thrown from one car, and her left ankle was sprained. She refused medical aid, and was taken to her home in the machine. Two other women who were riding in the car with Mrs. Duclos were a little hurt, but refused to allow Policeman Miller of the East Fifty-first Street Station to call an ambulance, and did not give their names.

Mr. Duclos was driving his car south

Continued On Page 3.

CAPT. EJNAR MIKKELSEN'S OWN STORY OF TWO YEARS OF ARCTIC TORTURE

Disease, Hunger, and Cold Fought for Lives of Danish Explorer and His Comrade.

WENT DAYS WITHOUT FOOD

Forced to Eat Their Dogs and Struggle Alone Down the Bleak Greenland Coast.

SCURVY PROSTRATED LEADER

And Iversen Dragged Him a Hundred Miles by Sledge to Winter Station.

FOUND LOOKING LIKE BEASTS

Long Hair Made Them Resemble Musk Oxen and Rescuers Started to Shoot Them.

ERICHSEN RECORDS FOUND

Diaries Once Left Behind to Save Their Lives, but They Returned and Brought Them Home.

CAPT. EJNAR MIKKELSEN

Saved from the Arctic After He Had Long Been Given Up as Dead.

THE TIMES herewith presents the personal narrative of Capt. Ejnar Mikkelsen of his two years of hardship and suffering in the wastes of Northern Greenland, during the latter part of which he had been given up as dead. The story was cabled exclusively to this paper last night from Copenhagen by the explorer's brother, Thorvald Mikkelsen, to whom he had sent it on his arrival at Aalesund, Norway, where, after their rescue, Capt. Ejnar Mikkelsen and his companion, Iversen, the engineer, first came into touch with the outside world. At the same time came from the rescuers pitiable accounts of the condition in which the explorers were found after two years' exile—more like wild animals than human beings, nearly naked, rushing out of their hut, guns in hand, prepared to fight off the beasts they believed had interrupted their solitude.

Mikkelsen and Iversen set out in March, 1910, northward from Shannon Island across Northern Greenland to find the depot and records of Mylius Erichsen, the explorer, who with two companions had perished there the year before. As told in yesterday's TIMES, Knud Rasmussen, failing to find any trace of them last year, reported them dead, and it was only when Norwegian fishermen, coming by chance upon their refuge on Bass Rock, brought them to Aalesund on Saturday, that the world learned differently. They have succeeded in their quest, and have brought back the data that Erichsen gave his life to obtain.

BY CAPT. EJNAR MIKKELSEN.

Special Cable to THE NEW YORK TIMES.

COPENHAGEN, July 28.—Having taken leave of our comrades at Shannon Island on April 19, we [Capt. Mikkelsen's engineer Iverson was his only companion] proceeded northward over the inland ice with provisions sufficient for a 100 days' journey.

We were much hindered from the outset by the tempestuous weather. The surface was very hilly and full of abysses, and as a consequence we and the dogs fell very often through snowbraes.

We reached an altitude of 3,600 feet and passed several high mountains between Queen Louise's Land and Piede Gerlache, mapping the border of the land from there and southward to Denmark Fiord.

On May 12 we stepped down from the inland ice to a lake, connected with the bottom of Denmark Fiord. We shot two musk oxen soon afterward in this neighborhood.

We sledged along the north coast of the fiord and found the first cairn of Erichsen at 80.25 north latitude. Erichsen left this place on Sept. 12, 1907, in good order, starting on his return journey along the coast. He had had good hunting, and carried sixteen days' provisions. All were well, and they had seven dogs.

Found Erichsen's Records.

In his Summer camp was found a second cairn, containing information of the results of this journey. Peary Channel did not run through and Navy Cliff was connected with Heilprint Land. He had left his Summer camp on the 25th. He had only a small supply of provisions and took all with him.

We started on our return journey on May 25 from Cape Rigsdagen. The snow was very soft, and the going was slow. We searched all through the land, and found no trace of Erichsen.

At this point I became very ill of scurvy.

We found a depot on Northeast Bend. The depot contained very little food, and nothing besides that. A depot on Andrups Land was untouched.

We reached Molemuk Mountain on June 21, and had to lie low until the snow was melted from the ice. I found very little hunting in this neighborhood, but shot a few seagulls.

I recovered soon afterward from the scurvy and could work again.

At the beginning of July we proceeded southward on the ice without snow, but were much delayed by the water and crevasses.

We lost our instruments and other things when a sledge fell into the water. The provisions were damaged by salt water, and again we had to lie low on Havgaads Island until the beginning of August, the outdrifting inland ice being impassable.

The depot here was quite destroyed by water, but it had not been touched.

We got no game, and were very hungry, having been on short allowances since the beginning of July.

Driven Southward by Hunger.

Hunger forced us southward in August. We had only seven pounds of provisions and two dogs.

Deep water spots and rivers on outdrifted inland ice delayed us very much. Finally we had to turn a sledge into a ferryboat which could carry the load of dogs and one man. The dogs were quite broken down, and had to be carried on the sledges.

We shot twelve ptarmigans and a hare-kid on the north coast of Lambert's Land. From there we walked on to the next depot. We had to eat both the dogs.

My comrade was very ill, and both of us were very much exhausted.

We moved along slowly with the sledge. There was much water on the ice and we came upon broad crevasses.

We reached the depot a long time after we had eaten the last of the dog meat. The depot gave us a good supply, but we had to lie down for seven days to recover our strength. We suffered from poisoning from having eaten the dog liver.

We could not do any hunting here, so we started south again on Sept. 2. The sledging was much better as new ice is always very uneven and difficult to pass.

We found the north depot partly damaged when we reached there.

On Sept. 10 open water to the south compelled us to leave the sledge behind, also our tent and other things. At the Bear Rocks we walked on the land, carrying our diaries and provisions, consisting of three pounds of pemmican.

Marooned on Rock in Fiord.

A storm broke the new ice in Skaergaards Fiord. Here we shot four ptarmigans.

We had to wait a day on a rock before the new ice was strong enough to carry us, but severe storms broke it again when we were out on it. So we had to seek refuge again on a rock in the middle of the fiord.

The storms were incessant and we waited two days and ate our last provisions. We had no water or fuel.

Finally we had to go, and left the diaries in a cairn. We reached land after ten hours of hard labor.

We walked along the coast to Cape Marie Valdemar. There we found two cans with meat extract, and rested a few hours.

From there we proceeded, very much broken by hunger and cold. We tried to rest behind a stone the following night, but it was blowing too much for sleep. Because of the wind becoming stronger and the intense cold, we were forced to leave this refuge, where we found two small cans of soup between stones.

From there we went straight across country and reached Denmark Harbor at noon on Sept. 19.

We tried to go back from here for our diaries in October, but had to give up the attempt after a day's striving.

Uninterrupted storms delayed our journey southward to Winter Harbor. We started finally on Nov. 3, and reached the harbor on the 5th, after forty hours of continuous walking.

We spent the Winter there, and sledged southward to the depot on the southeastern point of Shannon Island. We shot bears, and I was cured of the last remnant of the scurvy.

We wanted to go to Bass Rock Island, but the conditions were too difficult, open water and deep snow on the inland ice preventing.

Dug Diaries Out of Snow.

We decided first to return for the diaries, and sledged to Skaergaard's Fiord to get them. Bears had destroyed the depot and spread the contents about. We dug the snow away with our hands and found nearly everything.

We returned to Shannon Island on June 6. In the middle of July we drifted on the shore and we remained until Aug. 30, but there was still no water in view.

We tried to go southward with the boat, but had to leave it, as we could not get it out from Winter Harbor.

We had plenty of hunting of musk-

Scott's grave, marked by a tall cairn and a cross, erected by the rescue party.

The *Terra Nova* being towed into a London dock in 1913.

"All the News That's Fit to Print."

The New York Times.

THE WEATHER.

Fair, slightly warmer Thursday; Friday, fair, warmer; moderate winds, becoming south.

For full weather report see Page 22.

VOL. LXII...NO. 20,107. NEW YORK, TUESDAY, FEBRUARY 11, 1913.—TWENTY-FOUR PAGES. ONE CENT In Greater New York, Jersey City, and Newark. { Elsewhere, TWO CENTS.

SCOTT FINDS SOUTH POLE; THEN PERISHES WITH FOUR MEN IN ANTARCTIC BLIZZARD; BODIES FOUND AFTER EIGHT MONTHS

ARMED TRUCE IN MEXICO CITY; MADERO RETURNS

Called Upon by Diaz for His Resignation, the President Cries, "I Will Die First!"

REBEL LEADER INSISTENT

Says He Held Off to Prevent Slaughter, but the Federals Have Not Done the Same.

BATTLE PREDICTED TO-DAY

Both Sides Have Been Strengthening Their Positions and Seeking Reinforcements.

FOREIGNERS NOT MOLESTED

Executions Take Place at the Palace—Son of Reyes Kills Himself.

NORTHERN GENERALS WAITING

Washington Hurries Warships to Convenient Ports to Watch Events in Republic.

General Diaz to The Times.

By Cable to the Editor of The New York Times.

MEXICO CITY, Feb. 10.—The revolt is in progress and in a few hours will have to be decided. All the chances are in our favor. I will protect all your citizens and properties.

FELIX DIAZ.

Special Cable to The New York Times.

MEXICO CITY, Feb. 10.—The city at 10 o'clock to-night was quiet.

The Federals and Revolutionists still held their positions. The Government was taking ammunition to the palace under a heavy guard.

Gen. Diaz says he delayed battle in order to avoid slaughter of non-combatants, but as the Government has not refrained from hostile movements he has about lost patience.

Fighting, it is expected, will begin at daybreak.

Special Cable to The New York Times.

MEXICO CITY, Feb. 10.—An armed truce prevailed between the Federals and the revolutionists all day.

Gen. Diaz still held the arsenal and had practical control of all the heavy artillery. He is equipped with rifles and machine guns and has an unlimited supply of ammunition. According to reports, he is arming and drilling several hundred men in the arsenal.

A conference was held this morning between Gen. Diaz, two of his suporters, and Cabinet Ministers at a café in the centre of the city. What occurred at the conference was not made public, but after it was over a red flag was raised on the arsenal, and war without quarter was declared.

Several cannon were taken from the arsenal last night to the suburbs. They were placed where they would command the Chapultepec Castle. Officers in the castle say they will raze it if necessary to save it.

The movements of President Madero are kept secret. It is reported that he went to Cuernavaca last night and returned to the city at dawn this morning. Gen. Felipe Angeles, commander of Cuernavaca, it is said, is at Contreras, twelve miles south of the capital, with about a thousand Madero troops.

Gen. Angeles, it is said, has some heavy artillery.

The populace is maintaining neutrality.

A small riot in the Colonia del Carmen early this morning was stopped by mounted police.

The number of dead has not been reported, as it is impossible to pass the lines.

Genoveve de la O and Felipe Neri, rebel leaders from the State of Mexico, occupy a position within ten miles of the capital at Tlalpam and Xicpimilco, awaiting the orders of Gen. Diaz to enter the capital. Tlalpam is five miles beyond the Country Club. Foreigners are leaving that place.

Messengers were sent to Gen. Diaz this morning, protesting loyalty to him and asking permission to enter and join his forces. He sent an officer with instructions to take the positions and walt further orders.

Higinio Aguilar and Gaudencio de la

Continued on Page 8.

EDISON 66 YEARS OLD TO-DAY

Wife Will Make Him Quit Work Long Enough to Dine with Friends.

Special to The New York Times.

WEST ORANGE, N. J., Feb. 10.—Thomas A. Edison, who will be 66 years old to-morrow, will pass the day just as he does the other 364 in the year, with the exception of an occasional Sunday, when he yields to the insistence of Mrs. Edison and goes to church. He will work in the laboratory and offices, but has promised to "knock off" in the evening to be the guest at a family dinner party which Mrs. Edison is arranging.

The employes of the works will observe the day by wearing buttons or pins bearing the numerals "66." The workers at the Edison plant are grateful because since Edison took charge of the commercial branches in December many of the pay envelopes of the humbler employes have been fattened.

The production of the kinetophone, the further perfection of the storage battery, and the development of the disk phonograph record are among the achievements of the inventor during the past year. For his storage battery Edison received the Rathenau medal, donated by Emile Rathenau of Berlin.

"I feel like twenty-five," said Edison this afternoon. "I'm sure I'm going to keep right at it, too, for a good many years more."

POPE DECORATES EDITORS.

Medals to Cardinal for Those Who Compiled Catholic Encyclopedia.

Cardinal Farley received from Pope Pius X. yesterday the "Pro Ecclesia et Pontifice," an important decoration, to be bestowed upon the Board of Editors of the Catholic Encyclopedia. The order was instituted by Pope Leo XIII., July 17, 1888, and the decoration was made a permanent distinction only in October, 1898. It is to reward those, who, in a general way, deserve well of the Pope. The medal is made of gold, silver, and bronze. It is cross shaped, made rectangular in form by fleurs de lis, fixed in the angles of the cross. In the centre of the cross is a small medal with an image of its founder, Pope Leo XIII. The ribbon is purple, with delicate lines of white and yellow on each border. The decoration is worn on the right side of the chest.

The Board of Editors of the Catholic Encyclopedia consists of Charles G. Herbman, Ph. D., L. L. D., Professor of Latin Language and Literature at the College of the City of New York; Edward A. Pace, Ph. D., D. D., Professor of Philosophy at the Catholic University in Washington; Conde B. Pallen, Ph. D., L. L. D., of New Rochelle; Mgr. Thomas J. Shahan, D. D., rector of the Catholic University, Washington, and the Rev. J. J. Wynnee, S. J.

Dr. Pallen has just returned from Rome, where he presented the Pope with a set of the Vatican edition of the encyclopedia.

LEFT CHANGE FOR $50 BILL.

Clerks Wonder if Their Customer Was Absent-Minded or Crazy.

All day yesterday the clerks at the Broadway and Thirtieth Street store of Hackett Carhart & Co. expected to see a wild-eyed man run in and demand if any one had seen on Saturday a perfectly good $50 bill. No such person turned up, and last night as the employes put out the lights they wondered if there really could be any one in this city who cared so little for money.

On Saturday afternoon a customer asked to be shown some neckties. He seemed perfectly rational and betrayed no more than the proper amount of interest in the adornment of his person. He selected ties worth $4.50 and handed the salesman a $50 bill. This was sent on its way to the cashier for change and the ties were wrapped up. The man took his parcel, put it in his pocket, and quit the store. When the salesman received the change he had gone. The man ran out into Broadway, but the customer had disappeared.

The salesman reported the incident and the cashier decided at once that the note must be a counterfeit. But examination proved that it was genuine.

SOON TO WED, DISAPPEARS.

Rockfellow's Friends Unable to Account for His Sudden Departure.

Special to The New York Times.

PLAINFIELD, N. J., Feb. 10.—Rowland C. Rockfellow, son of the late Mayor George W. Rockfellow, disappeared from his home on Saturday, leaving two notes for his mother, who was prostrated by his absence. His wedding to Miss Rae Warnock, daughter of Mr. and Mrs. W. W. Warnock, was set for Tuesday night, Feb. 18, and one of the letters addressed to his mother said:

"I wil not be responsible for any debts unless contracted by myself." The wedding invitations had been issued when the young man disappeared.

Mrs. Rockfellow said to-day that she could not account for her son's action. She exhibited the other note he had left, which read:

> Dear Mother: I have been a good boy. I am not dishonest, but I can't help going away. Don't blame me.

W. R. Causbrook, district manager of the Public Service Corporation's local office, where Rockfellow was employed as cashier, said this afternoon that his accounts were correct. His fiancée, Miss Warnock, said she had not had any quarrel with Rockfellow. The first intimation she had had of his absence, she asserted, was on Saturday night when he failed to appear at a dinner party given to them.

WILSON WON'T SEE CASTRO.

Declines Request of ex-President of Venezuela for an Interview.

TRENTON, N. J., Feb. 10.—Representatives of ex-President Castro of Venezuela came to Trenton to-day to obtain an interview for the General with President-elect Wilson. Castro wished to see the Governor, but Mr. Wilson declined to receive him on the ground that he would not mix in any affairs of the Taft Administration before his inauguration as President.

Castro has been building hopes on the possibility of friendly action by Mr. Wilson. He has said that if Mr. Wilson was President instead of Mr. Taft he would have no trouble in obtaining admission to this country. When Mr. Wilson visited Ellis Island some time ago the ex-President expressed much regret that he had been unable to see him. One of Mr. Wilson's companions on that trip, Mrs. J. Borden Harriman, did ask Commissioner Williams to let the Governor's party talk with Castro, but Mr. Williams refused the request curtly. Mr. Wilson seemingly did not know of Mrs. Harriman's request at the time it was made.

SCOTT'S LAST MESSAGE TO THE WORLD.

Not Faulty Organization, but Misfortune, Caused the Disaster Which He Foresaw—Asks Aid for Families of the Dead.

MESSAGE TO THE PUBLIC.

The causes of this disaster are not due to faulty organization, but to misfortune in all the risks which had to be undertaken. One, the loss of pony transport in March 1911, obliged me to start later than I had intended, and obliged the limits of stuff transported to be narrowed. The weather throughout the outward journey, and especially the long gale in 83 degrees south, stopped us. The soft snow in the lower reaches of the glacier again reduced the pace.

We fought these untoward events with will and conquered, but it ate into our provisions reserve. Every detail of our food supplies, clothing and depots made on the interior ice-sheet and on that long stretch of 700 miles to the pole and back worked out to perfection. The advance party would have returned to the glacier in fine form and with a surplus of food but for the astonishing failure of the man whom we had least expected to fail. Seaman Edgar Evans was thought to be the strongest man of the party, and Beardmore glacier is not difficult in fine weather. But on our return we did not get a single completely fine day. This, with a sick companion, enormously increased our anxieties. I have said elsewhere that we got into frightfully rough ice, and Edgar Evans received a concussion of the brain. He died a natural death, but left us a shaken party, with the season unduly advanced.

But all the facts above enumerated were as nothing to the surprise which awaited us at the Barrier. I maintain that our arrangements for returning were quite adequate, and that no one in the world would have done better in the weather which we encountered at this time of the year. On the summit, in latitude 85 degrees to 86 degrees, we had minus twenty to minus thirty. On the Barrier, in latitude 82 degrees, 10,000 feet lower, we had minus thirty in the day and minus forty-seven at night pretty regularly, with a continuous headwind during our day marches.

These circumstances came on very suddenly, and our wreck is certainly due to this sudden advent of severe weather, which does not seem to have any satisfactory cause.

I do not think human beings ever came through such a month as we have come through, and we should have got through in spite of the weather but for the sickening of a second companion, Capt. Oates, and a shortage of fuel in our depots, for which I cannot account, and, finally, but for the storm which has fallen on us within eleven miles of the depot at which we hoped to secure the final supplies. Surely misfortune could scarcely have exceeded this last blow!

We arrived within eleven miles of our old One Ton camp with fuel for one hot meal and food for two days. For four days we have been unable to leave the tent, the gale blowing about us. We are weak.

Writing is difficult, but for my own sake I do not regret this journey, which has shown that Englishmen can endure hardships, help one another, and meet death with as great a fortitude as ever in the past. We took risks. We knew we took them. Things have come out against us, and therefore we have no cause for complaint, but bow to the will of Providence, determined still to do our best to the last.

But if we have been willing to give our lives to this enterprise, which is for the honor of our country, I appeal to our countrymen to see that those who depend on us are properly cared for. Had we lived, I should have had a tale to tell of the hardihood, endurance, and courage of my companions, which would have stirred the heart of every Englishman.

These rough notes and our dead bodies must tell the tale, but surely, surely, a great, rich country like ours will see that those who are dependent on us are properly provided for.

March 25, 1912. (Signed) R. SCOTT.

INDICT WALSH, NEWELL AND FOYE

True Bills Found Against Police Captain and Lawyer on Bribery Charge.

WHITMAN AFTER HOCHSTIM

Ready Now to Indict One of the Heads of Syndicate Running Disorderly Hotels.

WALDO HUNTING DOWN GRAFT

Big Police Official Reported Called for Examination To-day—Costigan Aids Curran Inquiry.

The Extraordinary Grand Jury returned indictments yesterday against Police Capt. Thomas W. Walsh, Patrolman Charles E. Foye, and Edward J. Newell, the lawyer. Walsh and Newell were charged with bribery and against the lawyer there was a second indictment charging him also with misdemeanor. The first bill found against Newell a fortnight ago was dismissed and the new ones returned. Foye was charged with perjury because of his sworn testimony before the Curran Committee that Chairman Curran had tried to persuade him not to press a charge against a saloonkeeper whom he had arrested.

The witnesses against Walsh and Newell were Thomas I. Dorian and Nathan J. Michaels, the managers of the Hotel Avenel; George A. Sipp, and Patrolman Eugene Fox. All of them were willing witnesses except Michaels. Sipp's story, covering five years of paying graft to Capt. Walsh for protection, was corroborated by Dorian before the Curran Committee, and then Dorian fled the city. District Attorney Whitman made a long and fruitless effort to find him. It was learned that he was receiving his weekly pay from the hotel syndicate that employed him, and a search began for evidence to show that these payments were really made to keep Dorian away.

Mr. Whitman threatened to proceed against the syndicate and to indict Dorian. Then Dorian returned and told a story to Mr. Whitman that not only confirmed the confession made by Fox, but gave information that showed that the disorderly hotel syndicate had paid graft to the police for many years in the many districts in which they owned hotels. It was discovered that there were several of these hotels in various sections of the city. Yesterday Mr. Whitman said that he was ready to submit enough evidence before the Grand Jury to indict at least one of the leading spirit of the syndicate.

Whitman After Hochstim.

The man that Mr. Whitman is after is Max Hochstim, who, with Philip Blau, Jacob Spielberg, and a man named Fromberg, composed the Baltic Hotel Company that owns the Hotel Avenel and other hotels of the same character. Mr. Whitman learned yesterday that Mrs. Hochstim owns thirty-nine shares of the Baltic Hotel Company, and that Hochstim owns one share. The sixty other shares are scattered. Some of the information against the syndicate was gathered yesterday in the course of the investigation in connection with police graft bearing upon the cases directly aimed against Walsh and Newell.

The moment the indictment against Newell was returned Justice Goff issued a bench warrant for his arrest. It was served by Detective Flood of Mr. Whitman's office, who found Newell in his office at 42 Broadway. He was brought before Justice Goff and his bail on the bribery charge was fixed at $2,000, while the $1,000 on which he was held on the misdemeanor charge was continued. A surety company furnished the bail, and Newell went about his business. Foye is away on a vacation. He will be taken into custody this morning as soon as he returns and bail will be set. If he fails to furnish it he will be locked up. No action was taken against Capt. Walsh because of his illness. As soon as he is physically able to go abroad he will be arraigned and released on bail.

W. M. K. Olcott, Newell's lawyer, had a talk with Mr. Whitman between the time of Newell's indictment and his arraignment in court. Before Mr. Whitman went home last night it was said that there were prospects that Newell would tell all he knew of his connection with Sipp and Capt. Walsh.

It was explained that if he told all he knew it would be to the effect that a well known lawyer handed him $1,000 to give to Sipp in return for Sipp's promise to remain out of this State until after Jan. 1, 1914; that he held out $300 to pay himself for the services he had rendered Sipp while the latter was a prisoner at Atlantic City on the charge made against him by the police and that the money came originally from Capt. Walsh. But if Newell's story goes beyond this transaction it might reach a point where the system of the police to get legal services from certain influential sources, directly or indirectly, would be uncovered.

Newell Proved Obdurate.

When Newell was indicted, first for a misdemeanor, under Section 2,441 of the

Continued on Page 9.

Death Wipes Out Brave Party on Return Trip to Winter Quarters

LEAVES MESSAGE TO PUBLIC

Disaster Not Due to Faulty Organization, but to Misfortune, His Last Word.

THREE BODIES IN ONE TENT

There Scott, Wilson, and Bowers Succumbed to Starvation and Exhaustion.

OATES BRAVED DEATH ALONE

Knowing His Fate, He Marched Out Into the Blizzard—"Brave Soul," Wrote Scott.

EVANS KILLED BY A FALL

Storm Wrecked Last Hope of Saving Themselves When Only 11 Miles from a Food Depot.

REACHED POLE JAN. 18, 1912

Found Amundsen's Records There—Perished March 29, 1912, and Bodies Were Found in the Following November.

By Lieut. E. R. G. R. EVANS, R.N.
Second in Command of the Scott Expedition.

Special Cable to The New York Times.

CHRISTCHURCH, New Zealand, Feb. 10.—Capt. Robert F. Scott's antarctic ship, the Terra Nova, on Jan. 18, this year, arrived at Cape Evans, the base on McMurdo Sound, where it was to meet the explorers on their return from the expedition in search of the south pole and bring them back, if they were ready. It was learned from the shore party found at this base that Capt. Scott and the four men with him had reached the pole on Jan. 18, 1912, but all had perished on the return journey, about the end of March. Their bodies were not found until a searching party discovered them on Nov. 12, nearly eight months after the disaster.

Capt. Scott, Dr. Edward A. Wilson, chief of the scientific staff, and Lieut. H. R. Bowers had made their way back to within 155 miles of Cape Evans, when they were caught in a blizzard and were overcome about March 29. They were then within eleven miles of One Ton Depot, where they would have found shelter and supplies.

Previously Petty Officer Edgar Evans and Capt. L. E. G. Oates of the Inniskillen Dragoons, who had been in charge of the ponies and dogs, had succumbed. Evans was the first to give way, dying from concussion of the brain due to a fall on Feb. 17. Oates died from exposure on March 17.

Found Amundsen's Records.

The records of Capt. Scott were recovered by a relief expedition. They showed that he and his party had reached the south pole on Jan. 18, 1912. There they found the tent and records left by Capt. Roald Amundsen when he quit the pole on Dec. 17, 1911.

Six other men of the Scott expedition who had been through a perilous experience were found to be safe and well. They composed Lieut. V. L. A. Campbell's expedition, which had been sent to make geological investigations to the east of Cape Evans. The Terra Nova had been unable to take the men off the year before on account of ice, and they were left to spend another Winter in the antarctic. In this party were Dr. Levick, Priestly, Abott, Browning, and Dickerson.

Relief Party Had to Return.

Before the Terra Nova sailed for New Zealand last March Surgeon Atkinson, who had been left in charge of the western party until Capt. Scott's return, dispatched Garrard and Demetri with two dog teams to assist the southern party, whose return to Hut Point was expected about March 10, 1912. Atkinson would have accompanied this party, but was kept back in medical charge of Lieut. Evans, the second in command, who, it will be remembered, nearly died from scurvy.

This relief party reached One Ton Depot on March 3, but was compelled to return on March 10, owing primarily to the dog food running short, also to persistent bad weather and the poor condition of the dogs after the strain of a hard season's work. The dog teams returned to Hut Point on March 16, the poor animals being mostly frostbitten and incapable of furthe work.

Garrard collapsed through an overstrained heart. His companion was also sick. It was impossible to communicate with Cape Evans, the ship having sailed on March 4, and the open sea lying between Atkinson and Keohane.

The only two men left sledged out to Corner Camp to render any help that might be wanted by the southern party. They fought their way out to Corner Camp against the unusually severe weather, and, realizing that they could be of no assistance, they were forced to return to Hut Point after depoting one week's provisions.

In April, when communication with Cape Evans was established, a gallant attempt to relieve Lieut. Campbell was made by Atkinson, Wright, Williamson, and Keohane. This party reached Butter Point, when they were stopped by open water. Their return was exciting and nearly ended in disaster, owing to the sea ice breaking up.

Search Party's Journey.

The search party left Cape Evans after the Winter on Oct. 30 last. The party, which was organized by Surgeon Atkinson, consisted of two divisions, Atkinson taking the dog teams with Garrard and Demetri, and Mr. Wright being in charge of a party including Nelson, Gran, Lashley, Crean, Williamson, Keohane, and Hooper, with seven Indian mules. They were provisioned for three months, as they expected an extended search.

One Ton camp was found in order, and all provisioned.

Proceeding along the old southern route, Wright's party sighted Capt. Scott's tent on Nov. 12. Within it were found the bodies of Capt. Scott, Dr. Wilson, and Lieut. Bowers. They had saved their records, hard pressed as they were.

From these papers the following information was gleaned:

The first death was that of Seaman Edgar Evans, petty officer

Capt. Robert Falcon Scott.

The continuation of the authentic narrative of Capt. Scott's expedition will appear exclusively in The New York Times to-morrow.

Sir Ernest Shackleton

"All the News That's Fit to Print"

The New York Times

LATE CITY EDITION

Weather: Fair, very cold today and tonight. Chance of snow tomorrow. Temp. range: today 24-14; Sunday 33-26. Full U.S. report on Page 30.

VOL. LXIII...NO. 20,429. • • • NEW YORK, TUESDAY, DECEMBER 30, 1913.—EIGHTEEN PAGES. ONE CENT In Greater New York, Jersey City and Newark. | Elsewhere TWO CENTS.

SHACKLETON PLANS RECORD POLAR TRIP

Expedition Across Antarctic Continent and Pole the Most Difficult Ever Attempted.

AEROPLANE TO BE USED

One with Clipped Wings to Help Drive Sledge—Sir Ernest Sends Message to Americans.

By Marconi Transatlantic Wireless Telegraph to The New York Times.

LONDON, Dec. 29.—The news that Sir Ernest Shackleton is about to lead another expedition to the antarctic has awakened the greatest interest here.

The main object of the expedition will be to cross the south polar continent from Weddell Sea to Ross Sea, a distance roughly of 1,700 miles, making the south pole a "halfway house" on the great journey, of which at least half will be over an entirely new route.

It will be the biggest polar journey ever attempted, and if successful will open up in the Weddell quadrant a vast unexplored region which is still a blank on the map.

Sir Ernest Shackleton in an interview to-day gave to a NEW YORK TIMES correspondent this message to the American people:

"My hopes are bright. I do not believe hope is the courage of despair. I know the men who are going with me. I feel we can face anything, and I do hope that as much interest and sympathy will be shown by the great American people this time as I personally experienced before.

"I recall with pleasure the great kindness and hospitality shown to me when I was in America, and I hope to go again. Science knows no country. The scientific results of this expedition are sure to be as much appreciated in America as in my home country.

"We hope to carry our country's flag across the south polar continent. If we succeed, I feel sure the generous spirit of the American people will appreciate it."

Sir Ernest's Plans.

In describing the plans and scope of the expedition, Sir Ernest said:

"The main object of the expedition will be the crossing of the polar continent. The unknown fields in the world which are still unconquered are rapidly narrowing down, but there still remains this great work. Of recent years the interest of geographers and the public has been concentrated on the approach to the pole from Ross Sea.

"Except Dr. Bruce's discovery of Coats Land in 1904 and the results of the Filchner expedition of last year, we know scarcely more of the Weddell quadrant than we did in Weddell's day. There is a vast unexplored region on the big white space on the map.

"The crossing of the south polar continent will be the biggest polar journey ever attempted, a longer journey than to the pole and back, and infinitely more difficult, because we shall always be advancing over new ground, with no depots to draw upon.

"The minimum distance from sea to sea is roughly 1,700 statute miles, and more than half the distance will be positively a new route. With good fortune it is probable that the whole journey will cover new ground—that is to say, after reaching the pole from Weddell Sea we may strike out a route to Ross Sea which will be neither that which I followed on my previous journey and which Capt. Scott took, nor the other and shorter one adopted by Capt. Amundsen.

The Geographical Problem.

"From a geographical point of view the complete continental nature of the antarctic can be absolutely solved by such a journey. No one now knows whether the great plateau dips gradually from the pole toward Weddell Sea; no one knows whether the great Victoria chain of mountains, which has been traced to the pole, extends across the continent and links up with the Andes. The solution of this problem is naturally of intense interest to geographers all over the world, and the discovery of the great mountain range which we assume to be there will be one of the biggest geographical triumphs possible."

Sir Ernest Shackleton expects that the geological collections which he purposes to make will be of the greatest scientific value. He will also take continuous magnetic observations with the object of determining the general dip of the magnetic needle. He intends to set up a magnetic observatory at the Winter quarters on Weddell Sea and to take observations throughout the Winter. Continuous meteorological observations will be another important branch of the work.

Ships to Have Oil Fuel.

The expedition will have two ships, both driven by oil fuel, giving a radius for operations four times greater than coal. The larger vessel will leave Buenos Aires early next October for the antarctic, reaching, if possible, 78 degrees, where a good landing place was discovered by the German expedition.

If the ice conditions permit, the expedition will reach the base at the beginning of November. A shore party

Continued on Page 2.

THE TASMAN FILLING.

Passengers Will Be Taken Off by Dutch or Australian Ship.

Special Cable to THE NEW YORK TIMES.

LONDON, Tuesday, Dec. 30.—A telegram to The Times from Sydney says:

"Authentic news about the Tasman is still very scanty. There are fourteen feet of water in the hold.

"The Captain expects to float the ship off, but the harbormaster at Thursday Island considers this doubtful.

"There is no anxiety concerning the passengers, who will be taken off either by the Dutch steamer Houtman or the Australian steamer Aldenham."

MELBOURNE, Dec. 29.—A wireless message received at noon to-day from the Dutch steamer Tasman, ashore in the Gulf of Papua, reported fifteen feet of water in the hold and gaining rapidly.

At that hour the steamers which had been dispatched to the assistance of the Tasman had not arrived.

It is considered possible that the Tasman will be a total wreck.

In addition to Mme. Lillian Nordica, Alva Adams, ex-Governor of Colorado, and Thomas G. Stallsmith of California, previously mentioned in the dispatches as passengers, Major Sydney A. Cloman, a member of the Panama-Pacific Exposition Commission and ex-Military Attaché of the United States at London, is on board the stranded vessel.

AMSTERDAM, Dec. 29.—The Tasman usually carries about sixty cabin passengers and a crew of 120, mostly natives, according to the owners of the vessel.

Late advices from the wreck say that the Tasman has water in her first and second holds and the double bottom is badly damaged.

The vessel is in a serious condition, as the weather is stormy.

George W. Young, husband of Mme. Nordica, received the following cablegram from her yesterday:

"Steamship Tasman, Thursday Island, Dec. 28. Just struck reef Torres Strait. No danger so far. Will keep you posted. Lillian."

NEW TUBERCULOSIS TOXIN.

Its Isolation Tends to Prove Consumption Vaccines Useless.

By Marconi Transatlantic Wireless Telegraph to The New York Times.

PARIS, Dec. 29.—A striking communication, giving the results of the researches of M. Marino, a young scientist, at the Pasteur Institute, was made this afternoon before the Academy of Medicine by Dr. Pierre Roux.

According to Marino, all anti-tuberculosis serums employed at the present time and hitherto are quite useless for their purpose. Marino discovered that the toxic products secreted by tuberculosis bacilli were less effectively neutralized by anti-tuberculosis serums than by the normal serums of the blood. All anti-tuberculosis serums, he says, act similarly, that is to say, less efficaciously than common blood serums. The result, it is explained, is that tuberculosis toxins, which are probably tubercolins, do not form any counter-poison in animals. The existing anti-tuberculosis vaccines are in the same case. Serums and vaccines are, therefore, inefficacious.

PAYS $20,000 GAME FINE.

Penalty Heaviest Ever Imposed Under Law Protecting Wild Life.

August Silz, President of the Franco-American Poultry Company, one of the largest distributors of poultry and game in the country, paid a fine of $20,000 yesterday to the New York Conservation Commission in the office of John A. Fleming, President of the commission, at Albany. This is said to be the largest fine ever paid in this country for a violation of the game laws. The commission, which has power to compromise such cases, accepted $20,000, although if the company had been convicted of every offense charged the fine would have amounted to more than $200,000.

Silz was charged with more than a thousand violations of the law regulating the importation of wild ducks from other States. Evidence that the law was being violated was obtained originally by the United States Bureau of Biological Survey. The case against Silz was prepared by the American Game Protective and Propagation Association.

A representative of the association was sent to the farm of Mr. Silz at Goshen, where it was represented that the ducks sold by his company were grown. The detective of the association gained access to the books of the company and was able to show that several thousand of the ducks shipped to New York, instead of being reared on the farm, had been caught alive in large numbers from flocks of wild ducks and had been taken to the Silz farm in Goshen, N. Y., where they were immediately killed and put on the market.

'NO HONESTY IN CONGRESS.'

Whitacre of Ohio, After Playing Role of Diogenes, Won't Go Back.

CANTON, Ohio, Dec. 29.—In announcing to-night that he would not be a candidate for re-election, Congressman J. J. Whitacre of the Eighteenth Ohio District declared that "no man who wants to be intellectually honest has any business in Congress."

"All I've done since I've been down in Washington," said Whitacre, "has been to sit around and try to look wise, and that's what any man has to do who isn't willing to barter his convictions for political expediency.

"I thought there might be a chance for an honest, wide-awake, frank, and open business man in Congress, but I was quickly disillusioned."

Whitacre is serving his second term as a Representative, having been elected as a Democrat. He was the first "Wilson" Congressman from Ohio.

BODY IN A TRUNK LEFT ON SIDEWALK

May Be John Kremen, a Driver, Who Was Found Bound, His Neck Broken.

GET CART THAT BROUGHT IT

Police Now Seek Man Who Put Trunk at Tenement Door and Asked Boys to Watch It.

A brand new trunk which two men with a pushcart had left on the sidewalk just at the entrance to the tenement at 47 Pitt Street shortly after 11 o'clock yesterday morning stood there for an hour, jutting into the unending stream of hurrying passers-by and attracting only a passing curiosity, until a woman of imagination, who had been watching it from a doorway across the street, took it upon herself to go down to the Broome Street corner and tell Patrolman Storjohan about it.

A few moments later, in the centre of a jostling crowd that had assembled in a twinkling, the policeman struck off the lock of the trunk with a hatchet he had borrowed from a store across the street and inside, beneath a rough, straw-stuffed ticking, he found the body of a young man. The woman's curiosity had started the police on the task of solving a new murder mystery.

The body of the dead man was still warm and limp. Death had come from a broken neck only a little while before, quite possibly after he had been placed inside the trunk, perhaps by the very force of the jar with which the trunk was dumped from the pushcart to the sidewalk.

A two-yard length of wash line encircled the ankles and the neck as if to hold the huddled body in position.

Within half an hour after the trunk had been opened Second Deputy Police Commissioner Dougherty was standing over it in the court yard of the Clinton Street Station, a dozen of the best detectives in the city were starting off on their various assignments, and every bit of available strength in the department was being strained to solve this murder riddle before the last hour of 1913, so that the detective branch of the force could wind up the present administration in a blaze of glory.

Detective's Theory Correct.

"This man," said Dougherty, after he had carefully examined every atom of physical evidence before him, "was a Slav, probably a Pole. He was accustomed to work with horses, most likely as a driver, and the chances are that the murder was committed inside a stable."

This bit of induction, rather like that of a certain famous detective of fiction, Mr. Dougherty went on to explain to his men. Inside the cuff of the dead man's trousers he had found a little accumulation of stable dust, the index finger of the dead man's right hand was calloused as from continuous holding of reins, and the five-foot skimpy mattress which served to cover the body in the trunk was of the sort much used on the seat of heavy trucks.

Four hours after Mr. Dougherty had decided on this much the murdered man was identified as John Kremen, a young Ruthenian from Southeastern Poland, and those who knew him said that he had usually worked as a stableman. This information came just before 6 o'clock, and by that time the police knew also what manner of men had brought the trunk to Pitt Street, where and when they had obtained the pushcart, and where the trunk had been manufactured.

They did not know where or how the murder was committed or by whom. They did not know who were the men who carried the trunk to Pitt Street. It was in search of this information that detectives were raking every Polish corner of New York last night while Dougherty directed their work from the Waldorf-Astoria, whither he had gone to attend a dinner given in honor of his retiring chief. In direct charge at the Clinton Street Station was Inspector Faurot.

The Man in Charge.

No one was found yesterday who seemed to know from which direction came the pushcart in which the trunk was brought to Pitt Street. Out of the ceaseless caravan of such carts it was halted at the curb there about 11:10 o'clock in the morning, and the first the neighborhood remembers was the sight of a tall, rather conspicuously well-dressed man in a long gray overcoat, who walked along the sidewalk and signaled to the pushcart trundler to approach the curb.

He of the pushcart was a shabby, swarthy little man who seemed in a hurry to do what he was told. He let the trunk land with a bang on the sidewalk and then, under the direction of the man in the gray overcoat, carried it to the wall just at the side of the entrance to the tenement. He tipped his hat then, clutched at the 50-cent piece that was tossed him and shuffled off. The unconcerned director of these proceedings was left standing beside the trunk, and he stood there long enough to let the ash grow long on his cigar.

Then he signalled to two boys standing near by, 14-year-old Morris Feinstein, in charge of the candy stand at 50 Pitt Street, and his friend, Sammie Mable, who lives in the tenement outside which the trunk was standing. The tall stranger told them they could earn ten cents if they would keep their eyes on that trunk for a few moments, and they assented with alacrity. Whereupon the stranger turned on his heel and sauntered off into the crowd. They did not see him again.

An hour passed and he had not returned. Then the possibilities of the unexplained trunk became too much for the curiosity of Mrs. Esther Leznick of 149 Broome Street, who had watched the episode from the doorway across Pitt Street. When an hour had passed and the trunk still remained unopened and unexplained she went to the police.

The News Spreads.

Patrolman Storjohan had hardly lifted the ticking from the top of the trunk and seen the body huddled up beneath it than the word sped along the streets, shouted in a dozen different tongues from fire escape to fire escape, from pushcart to pushcart, from curb to curb, and within a few moments the crowd in Pitt Street was enormous. Leaving Patrolman Kelly in charge, Storjohan went to summon a patrol wagon. The excited, curious crowd was too much for the lone guard. Kelly was fairly bowled off his feet as the crowd of men and women pushed forward to get a glimpse of the trunk, to stroke the trunk, to touch the trunk. So many grimy hands were laid upon it in the next two minutes that there were a thousand jumbled stories left upon it to bewilder the finger-print experts who attempted vainly to read the cover later in the day.

At the station the coarse ticking was lifted out. Beneath it was an old silk waist, and wrapped around the dead man's head was a petticoat of cheap striped cotton. The man in the trunk

Continued on Page 3.

SCHMIDT JURY NOT AGREED; LOCKED UP

Eleven Hours After Retiring They Stood 9 to 3 for Conviction.

The jury, which has been engaged for three weeks in the trial of Hans Schmidt, the priest, for the murder of Anna Aumuller, retired to deliberate at 1:26 o'clock yesterday afternoon. At 12:47 o'clock this morning they had failed to agree on a verdict, and were ordered locked up by Judge Foster of General Sessions until 9:30 o'clock this morning.

At 11:40 o'clock last night, when the jury first reported its failure to agree, the foreman, Lawrence Ottinger, shook his head and said:

"Your Honor, I fear it is a hopeless case."

When the jury returned again to the court room at 12:20 A. M. Juror No. 6 was missing, and was found by an attendant in the corridor. The foreman again said that the jury had been unable to agree, and also that they found the jury room uncomfortably cold.

Judge Foster told the jurors that if they had any reasonable doubt to give the verdict to the defendant. He requested that they should return and discuss the matter a while longer.

The foreman said that some of the jurors had refused to discuss the case. The court then said it was the duty of all the jurors to discuss the questions over which they disagreed. After that he gave the order for locking them up.

Schmidt, who was brought into the courtroom with his counsel on both occasions when the jury returned, was visibly relieved at each announcement of a disagreement.

It was reported in the courtroom that the jurors stood 9 to 3 for conviction of murder in the first degree. The only alternative verdict is not guilty on the ground of insanity.

Ridicules the Alienists.

The summing-up of Assistant District Attorney James A. Delehanty was full of ridicule and invective.

"This prisoner," he said, "is a liar, a thief, a perjurer, a counterfeiter, a seducer, an abortionist, and a murderer, and, cringing like a rat, he pretends to be insane, in order to escape the punishment he deserves."

Spreading out the ancestral chart prepared by the defense to show that many of Schmidt's family had been insane, Mr. Delehanty said:

"The tree had sixty-two members, or limbs, on it, and this alienist, Dr. Jelliffe, tried to show that because one member of the family was insane the others must be also. He did not tell you how he arrived at the conclusion that they were insane, but I can tell you. It was by the children's method, 'eeny, meeny, miney, mo, catch a nigger by the toe; if he hollers, let him go, eeny, meeny, miney, mo.' Dr. Jelliffe simply tagged the one he wished to tag. As for Dr. White, another of the defense's alienists, he simply went to the Tombs, and as soon as he caught sight of Schmidt's whiskers decided that he was insane.

"Drs. Jelliffe and White are writing a book, and I guess if they should be successful in this case Schmidt's picture will occupy a prominent place in the next volume, with a Laura Jean Libby title, 'Insanity at a Glance; or, Saved by His Whiskers.'"

Mr. Delehanty said that the latest feature of Schmidt's shamming was his pretense that he was being persecuted. The Assistant District Attorney strongly intimated that the prisoner had been coached. The theory that he had committed the murder by divine command was suggested to Schmidt by the alienists, Mr. Delehanty said. He called attention to the many discrepancies in the language used by Schmidt in conversation with different alienists, the discrepancies showing, he said, that Schmidt's memory failed him temporarily and that he found it difficult to play the complicated part that had been cut out for him as a supposed sufferer from dementia praecox.

"This Schmidt was no more a priest than a tramp in the gutter is," said Mr. Delehanty. "He obtained his place in the order through forgery and fraud. He went into the priesthood simply because the priesthood furnished him with a cloak for his crimes. He got no sign from St. Elizabeth. This was only one of his fakes. He received no divine commands."

The prosecutor said in closing that Schmidt's pretense of insanity was made possible by the man's own superior education and intelligence, working in co-operation with a "medical mind."

Judge Foster's charge to the jury was brief, and the counsel for the prosecution were better satisfied with the tenor of it than were Schmidt's lawyers. Judge Foster said that if the prisoner, at the time of committing the crime, knew the nature and quality of his act he must be held responsible. If the defendant knew that the act was wrong and that the law forbade it, the plea of insanity is no defense. Judge Foster said. He said that if the jury had any doubt as to Schmidt's sanity it was their duty to give him the benefit of the doubt. He added, however, that the jury should use common sense in arriving at a verdict. The only verdicts admissible under Judge Foster's charge were guilty of murder in the first degree or not guilty because insane.

Last Plea For Priest.

The morning session began with the plea for Schmidt by ex-Judge W. M. K. Olcott.

"The act was plainly that of an insane man," he said. "That the family was predisposed to insanity and that they held life lightly is proved by the fact that of the sixty-two known members of the family ten had been insane or suicides.

"We have before us a half educated, half ignorant, poor German philosopher, a man cursed with hereditary insanity and hereditary abnormal tendencies. He is charged with the murder of the only person in the world except his mother and sister that he loved. Could such an act be committed by a sane man? The deeper you look into the evidence in this case the more surely you will find that the only possible motive for the killing of the unfortunate woman was an insane, morbid love, which was a result of a disease of the mind beginning soon after he was admitted to the priesthood in 1906—or rather, beginning at that time to show its symptoms."

SEE 'POISON NEEDLE' IN GIRL'S ILLNESS

Miss Marion Brindle Falls Into Stupor After Walking Home from Her Work.

Accompanied by his wife and a physician, George R. Nielson hurried late last night from his home at 352 West Twenty-third Street to Police Headquarters with the story that his sister-in-law, Marion Brindle, had been jabbed in the arm with some instrument which had been so poisoned that she became first drowsy, then half-stupified, then unconscious, and so remained for more than two hours. The girl seemed to have no idea when this poison—if poison it was—had been injected.

Miss Brindle, who is 18 years old, makes her home with her sister, Mrs. Nielson, and works as a stenographer in the Japanese house of H. Ohashi & Co. of 395 Broadway. She left there yesterday afternoon after 5:30 o'clock and made her way up Broadway and across Twenty-third Street.

She was helping Mrs. Nielson set the supper table when she stood still as if she was dizzy and her astonished sister saw the plates slip from the girl's limp hands. Then the girl swayed a little as if she were going to faint. Next she dropped to the floor and was soon in a complete stupor.

Dr. Walter Benney whose office is at the West Twenty-third Street address, was out at the time and a call was sent to Dr. Louis H. Schneider of 349 West Twenty-second Street. Dr. Schneider was considerably puzzled by the girl's illness and finally, baring her left arm, he found in the flesh above the elbow two fine small scratches as though the needle of some instrument had been thrust through the skin there.

According to the story which Dr. Benney and Mr. Nielson told Lieut. Fogarty at headquarters, Dr. Schneider was of the opinion that this was a real poison needle case—a real case of some subtle poison having been injected.

When finally the girl was revived she was questioned closely, but she seemed utterly bewildered by what they told her, and said she had no recollection of any sudden hurt in her arm that might place the time when this injection was made.

Her brother-in-law told the Lieutenant that a month ago Miss Brindle had been annoyed by a man who had tried to scrape an acquaintance with her, and had made unsuccessful efforts to learn where she lived and what her telephone number was. The Lieutenant was sufficiently impressed with the story to arrange for the girl to be brought to Headquarters this morning to look through the pictures of the Rogues' Gallery to see if by chance this annoyer of a month ago was any one of a familiar few recognized by the police as engaged in the traffic in women.

Mr. Nielson was further directed to submit his evidence to Detective Griffin of the West Seventeenth Street Station, and at 1 o'clock this morning the detective was at work on the case.

CAPTURE AUTO BANDITS.

Police Pursue Two Highwaymen Who Flee in a Taxicab.

At 1 o'clock this morning two men entered the restaurant of Herman Wertz of 2,146 Broadway and, threatening Wertz with a revolver, demanded money. Wertz broke away from the thieves and ran to the street. The robbers jumped into a taxicab outside the store and ordered the chauffeur to drive up Broadway.

Three policemen ran up and commandeered another taxicab. They chased the men in the taxicab from Seventy-fifth Street to Seventy-ninth Street, where with drawn revolvers they commanded the driver of the thieves' cab to stop. He did so, and the highwaymen were arrested. The taxicab driver was not held. On the floor of the cab a revolver was found.

The men arrested say they are George Kenneth, a chauffeur, of 503 Amsterdam Avenue, and John Warren, address refused, a salesman. They are charged with robbery.

SAYS GERAGHTY IS ELIGIBLE

Mayor of Woburn Carries Disputed Election to Supreme Court.

WOBURN, Mass., Dec. 29.—The election to the Board of Aldermen of John E. Geraghty, son-in-law of Amos Tuck French of New York, and the subsequent ruling that he was ineligible to serve because he has lived here less than a year, have caused such complications that the Supreme Court was called upon to-day to act in the matter. A petition for a writ of mandamus to compel eight members of the Board of Aldermen to show cause why they should not sign a certificate of election prepared by the City Clerk was filed to-day by City Solicitor Maloney at the request of Mayor Henchey.

The Aldermen declined to sign the certificate because it declared Geraghty to have been elected despite his alleged ineligibility.

The City Solicitor contends that Geraghty was legally elected, and that the question of his eligibility is a matter for subsequent consideration. The failure of the Aldermen to sign the certificate, in the opinion of the Solicitor, makes the Mayor and members-elect of the city government ineligible to take office.

THINKS THE KARLUK DOOMED

New Bedford Sailor Writes of Arctic Ship's Danger on Oct. 13.

NEW BEDFORD, Dec. 29.—The fear that the Karluk, one of the vessels of the Stefansson arctic expedition, was doomed, was expressed by Stephen Cottle in a letter written Oct. 13 and just received here. Cottle was on board the steamer Belvedere, which was held fast in the ice ten miles off Demarkation Point, Alaska.

"Dr. Anderson," he wrote, "is stuck about seventy-five miles west of us with the two small vessels of the Stefansson expedition; the Karluk was last seen about ten miles off shore off Flaxman Island four days ahead of us. We can get no further news from them, and I am very much afraid it is the last of the Karluk. We are in hopes that the crew has been able to make a place of safety to the west of us."

WALDO RESIGNS; WILL GO WEDNESDAY

Police Department Headless When Mayor Mitchel's Administration Begins.

PROTEST FROM MAYOR KLINE

Commissioner Rescinds Order Transferring Heads of Bureaus and His Personal Staff.

Police Commissioner Rhinelander Waldo yesterday sent his resignation to Mayor Kline, to take effect at any time, but in any event not later than midnight to-morrow. The resignation followed the Commissioner's compliance with a request of Mayor Kline to rescind the order he made Saturday transferring heads of bureaus and members of his personal staff from Headquarters to precinct duty. The resignation, said Mr. Waldo, had no connection with the receipt of the message from the Mayor asking that the transferred men be restored to their old positions. This is the letter of resignation sent by Mr. Waldo to the Mayor:

Dec. 29, 1913.

Hon. Ardolph Kline, Mayor, City of New York.

Sir: I have the honor to tender my resignation as Police Commissioner, to take effect at your convenience, but not later than 12 o'clock, midnight, Dec. 31, 1913.

Very respectfully,

RHINELANDER WALDO, Commissioner.

The resignations of the four Deputy Police Commissioners had previously been placed in the hands of Commissioner Waldo. He said the deputies will all be out of the department before his own resignation takes effect. This will leave the department without a civilian head until Mitchel becomes Mayor and appoints Waldo's successor, a situation that has not occurred in the Police Department before, so far as any one could recall last night. After the receipt of Mr. Waldo's resignation the Mayor had the Commissioner called up on the telephone and protested against his leaving the department without a head before the new administration had an opportunity to make an appointment. This Mayor Kline will be unable to do, for his powers as Mayor will cease at the same time the Commissioner's resignation becomes effective.

Schmittberger in Charge.

"I suppose the Chief Inspector will be in charge," suggested Mr. Waldo. According to this programme Chief Inspector Max F. Schmittberger will be in command of the entire department until the new Commissioner takes charge.

Commissioner Waldo denied that his motive in the transfer of bureau heads was to embarrass the new administration. On the contrary, it was to leave the new Commissioner free to select his own men, those not so close to the present administration, he said, and chiefly was designed to relieve him of responsibility for the old men and their work under the supervision of his successor.

The order of transfer was to have gone into effect yesterday. A verbal order from Waldo held the men at their old assignments. Commissioner Waldo said:

"I transferred the men to prevent any question arising as to responsibility for them and their work during the next administration. They were all men close to me or under my immediate supervision, and should the occasion arise for any fault-finding regarding these men and their work, say within the next six months, for example, I did not want any shifting of responsibility and permit opportunity for any one to say they were all Waldo's men. The Mayor's desire to have these men kept in their old positions relieves me of all responsibility when I leave the department. That was all I wanted.

"In complying with the Mayor's request, I do it all the more willingly because there was nothing against the men in the order of transfer, and were I to continue as head of the department I should retain them in their present positions. Many of the men are my personal friends and have done splendid work. As I intimated, my only desire in making the transfer was to leave the new Commissioner unhampered and relieve myself of responsibility under the new administration.

"I have been the Police Commissioner," added Waldo. "No one has interfered with me. Only on one occasion was I requested to transfer a Sergeant at the suggestion of the late Mayor Gaynor. I believe I am leaving the department in good shape. It has been a big responsibility. I am glad to be relieved of it. The prospect of getting out makes me feel ten years younger."

A verbal request from Mayor Kline to restore the men was received at Police Headquarters, but the letter sent by the Mayor giving his reasons had not been received by Commissioner Waldo last night. Mayor Kline wants the men put back, on the ground that the senior clerks who were designated to perform their work were not familiar with the duties, and the absence of so many experienced men would tend to seriously handicap the business of the department.

It was unofficially stated on good authority last night that Mayor Kline had taken this action at the suggestion of Mayor-elect Mitchel. Mr. Mitchel, it was said, considered the transfer of the men on the eve of the beginning of his administration as suggestive of a desire to handicap the new head of the Police Department.

No Commissioner in Sight.

Yesterday morning Mr. Mitchel thought he had solved the Police Commissionership problem by offering the job to W. Cameron Forbes, former Governor General of the Philippines, but last night Mr. Forbes, who is in Boston, sent word that he would not take the office, and Mr. Mitchel began his quest all over again. As the situation now stands, Arthur Wood, a former Deputy Commissioner, is likely to be selected.

Mr. Mitchel has offered the Police Commissionership to at least four persons, but all declined. When he first offered the appointment to Mr. Forbes the latter sent word that he did not want it, but said he would take it under advisement. When the other refusals came along Mr. Mitchel again turned to Mr. Forbes, with the result that he got a decided refusal.

Henry Bruere, one of Mr. Mitchel's closest advisers and his selection for City Chamberlain, was then sent to Boston to plead with Mr. Forbes. At the same time Mr. Mitchel appealed to District Attorney Whitman to help him out of his difficulty. The Mayor-elect and the District Attorney had luncheon at the Whitehall Club down town, and they discussed the police situation yesterday.

Mr. Whitman, it was said, has virtually supplanted Samuel S. Koenig, President of the Republican County Committee, as the official spokesman of the Republican organization. Mr. Whitman and Mr. Koenig did not get along very well over the matter of ap-

Continued on Page 2.

ENDS PARIS-CAIRO FLIGHT.

Vedrines Brings 3,500-Mile Journey to Successful Conclusion.

By Marconi Transatlantic Wireless Telegraph to The New York Times.

CAIRO, Dec. 29.—Jules Vedrines, the French airman, reached Heliopolis, a suburb of Cairo, to-day. He thus completed the great air journey of about 3,500 miles from Paris across Europe and Asia Minor to Africa, which he began five weeks ago.

Vedrines will stay a fortnight at Cairo. He then intends to fly to Jerusalem, Beirut, Aleppo, Bagdad, Bombay, Calcutta, Singapore, and Australia, to cross the Pacific Ocean by steamer, and to fly over America, thus making a tour of the world.

PARIS, Dec. 30.—Jules Vedrines tells in a long dispatch of his memorable journey. Not once during the trip did his engine miss fire, and not a wire of the aeroplane was out of place when he landed.

Vedrines announces his intention to be the first aviator to fly to Australia. He will cross the intervening sea by way of the nearest island to the Australian Continent, a distance of little more than 200 miles.

The only difficult stretch of his Paris-to-Cairo journey was over the Taurus Mountains, compared to which the Pyrenees Mountains were "the merest trifle." He took on 240 litres of gasoline and forty litres of oil and flew over the plateaux at a height of nearly 16,000 feet. For two hours he was tossed about like a chip above the desolate peaks, where, should he have suffered a breakdown, help would have been impossible. He almost looped the loop, but not of his own volition, when he alighted on the seashore. Never had he experienced such a terrible sensation.

MEXICO SEIZES THE TIMES.

Copies Confiscated, Say News Agencies in the Capital.

Special Cable to THE NEW YORK TIMES.

MEXICO CITY, Dec. 29.—It is understood that the Government is confiscating copies of THE NEW YORK TIMES sent to agencies here for distribution, the paper being practically unobtainable except by individual subscribers.

The reason for this action is not ascertainable. It is denied by minor Government officials, although the news agencies confirm it.

MORGAN GIFT FOR POLICE.

$1,000 for Pension Fund as Tribute to Bluecoats' Service.

J. Pierpont Morgan yesterday sent a check for $1,000 to Police Commissioner Waldo to be applied to the Police Pension Fund.

The check was sent in recognition of the work done by the police at the funeral of Mr. Morgan's father, the late J. Pierpont Morgan.

MRS. MACKAY GONE AWAY.

Sublets House She Leased and Will Not Return to Town This Winter.

Mrs. Clarence H. Mackay, it came out yesterday, has sub-leased the St. John Smith residence at 129 East Seventieth Street, which she leased recently, to Robert C. Hill, President of a coal company, for immediate occupancy.

Mrs. Mackay leased the house for the season, and occupied it about the middle of November, but the condition of her health has now caused her to take a long rest away from town. Having disposed of the leasehold, she will probably not return to New York before next Winter.

MONTEREY IN A FIERCE GALE

Two of Ward Liner's Crew Injured on Her Trip to Havana.

Special Cable to THE NEW YORK TIMES.

HAVANA, Dec. 29.—The Ward liner Monterey arrived this morning a day late. Owing to a severe storm, lasting twenty-four hours, the steamer was compelled to lay to twelve hours.

Carmen Izquidero, a Cuban passenger, suffered a stroke of paralysis from fright. Two seamen were injured, one seriously. Capt. Smith says the storm was the worst in ten years. The waves sometimes went over the funnels, and some lifeboats were smashed, and some staterooms wrecked.

MAY AVERT FRISCO STRIKE.

Road's Receivers Offer Some Concessions to the Telegraphers.

ST. LOUIS, Dec. 29.—There will be no strike of telegraphers on the St. Louis & San Francisco Railroad, according to indications to-night. The Strike Committee of the Order of Railway Telegraphers will meet the receivers of the railroad again to-morrow in an attempt to reach an agreement.

The railroad company has agreed to a wage increase, but not to the 15 per cent. increase asked by the men. It also has agreed to pay overtime, but not double overtime as demanded.

LESS NOISE NEW YEAR'S EVE

Mayor Kline Puts His Ban on Horns and Bells.

The public ear will be spared the noise of the tin horn this New Year's Eve, if the authority of Mayor Kline is great enough to smite down the tradition. Commissioner Waldo is asked in a communication from the City Hall to suppress the tooting of the horn, which is briefly described by the Mayor as "noise."

Celebrators on Manhattan Island will be expected to adapt their tastes on New Year's Eve to the singing of carols in Madison Square Park and the chimes of old Trinity on lower Broadway. It is especially in the vicinity of these two places that Mayor Kline has asked the Police Commissioner to take strong measures to put down tin horns and other noise makers. But in all parts of the city tooting and bell ringing will be officially in bad taste.

Latest Ship News.

ARRIVED—SS Uranium, SS Finland, SS City of Montgomery.

BY WIRELESS—SS Cymric, from New York for Liverpool, reported 186 miles W. of Fastnet at 9 P. M. last night, and is due at Queenstown to-day.

ANGLO-GERMAN GENERAL ENTENTE

Covers Several Problems, Washington Admits—Doubts Anti-American Trade Compact.

BUT THE STORY PERSISTS

Sponsors Claim First-Hand Foreign Information—Say Events Will Vindicate Them.

DENIED BY BOTH NATIONS

Report Ascribed in London to Exposition Agent — Exhibit at Fair "Insurance Against Trouble."

Special to The New York Times.

WASHINGTON, Dec. 29.—It is difficult to arrive at a definite conclusion from what was said here to-day as to the application of the present British-German understanding to prospective efforts of American financial and commercial interests to extend their activities in South America. In authoritative quarters of the State Department, the report that an agreement existed between the two European nations to checkmate American enterprise was discountenanced, but, in the face of this, persons claiming to have inside information from abroad declared that there was ample evidence that the reputed agreement was in full force and would become apparent in due course.

State Department officials said frankly that they had known for some time that Great Britain and Germany were arranging their differences over several questions of importance, but none of these, it was declared, touched the United States—or the Western Hemisphere, for that matter—except as regarded the Panama-Pacific Exposition. These negotiations were a matter of common knowledge among nations, it was said, and constituted no reason to believe that the entente between the two Governments contemplated a general alliance to checkmate American trade.

The understanding between Germany and Great Britain that neither should participate in the Panama-Pacific Exposition without notifying the other of that intention was acknowledged to be in force, but officials gave the impression that they regarded it as entirely apart from the general understanding between the two European nations, and not a part of a compact to display an unfriendly attitude toward the United States.

Predict Early Developments.

Balancing these assertions are the emphatic assertions of the other persons to whom allusion has been made. While these persons say they are not willing to produce evidence at this time, they are emphatic in declaring that within a comparatively brief period it will become obvious that Great Britain and Germany are working in co-operation to prevent United States trade from gaining headway in the rich South American field, where the two European nations have had the lead for a long time.

The Government's information as to the reason for the agreement of Great Britain and Germany not to take part in the San Francisco fair was made known to-day. Each country, it was said, had arrived separately at the decision that official participation was neither desirable nor essential, the common reason being that such expositions were becoming too frequent, were of little value to foreign nations participating, and were too expensive. Germany, it was said, had arrived at this conclusion after the Imperial Industrial Commission had reported that it found no great desire among industrial interests to take part in the exposition.

It was while Great Britain and Germany were negotiating for an adjustment of their differences concerning the Bagdad Railway and German and British affairs in East Africa that the matter of the San Francisco fair was brought into prominence. Prior to that time both Governments had declined the invitation of the United States to take part in the exposition.

It was represented in the conference that if either Government should reconsider its decision to give no encouragement to the fair it should notify the other, a further cause for irritation between them might be prevented, and out of this suggestion grew an agreement that neither would accept the American invitation without previously notifying the other that it intended to do so.

Germany's Attitude Puzzling.

Out of knowledge of this condition apparently has grown, in part at least, the understanding that the British-German entente has a wider application to American affairs. But it is asserted by persons who claim first-hand knowledge of what has taken place that their information is based on fact and not on inference or deduction.

The story told would be accepted here with less questioning if it did not seek to place Germany in a position of being unfriendly to the United States. In recent years the German Government has shown a spirit of decided cordiality in its dealings with this country. This has been notably so in the case of the Mexican trouble.

The German attitude toward the efforts of President Wilson had been a source of satisfaction, particularly as the position of the British Government was regarded as unfriendly. In these circumstances many close observers find it hard to believe that whatever may be the German arrangement with Great Britain regarding South America, Germany did not enter into it with the intention of displaying opposition to American enterprise.

At the same time the United States Government has increasing evidence that Germany intends to drive hard bargains with this country in all matters affecting trade. Its latest manifestation is the refusal of the request of the United States to remove the discriminating duty imposed on certain grades of American steel and rubber shoes. Germany bases its refusal on the ground that some of the provisions of the Underwood tariff act discriminate against German products, and the hint is conveyed that if these provisions are changed the Berlin Government will rescind its own discriminations.

LONDON SCOUTS THE REPORT.

Intimates That Compact Story Came from Exposition Agent.

Special Cable to THE NEW YORK TIMES.

LONDON, Tuesday, Dec. 30.—The newspapers give prominence to New York and Washington dispatches

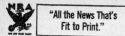

"All the News That's Fit to Print."

The New York Times.

LATE CITY EDITION
WEATHER—Fair today; tomorrow warmer and possibly rain.
Temperature Yesterday—Max., [illegible]; min., [illegible].
Detailed Weather Report, Page [illegible].

VOL. LXIII...NO. 20,470. NEW YORK, MONDAY, FEBRUARY 9, 1914.—SIXTEEN PAGES. ONE CENT In Greater New York, Jersey City and Newark. | Elsewhere TWO CENTS.

$50,000 BARRIE GIFT EQUIPS SHACKLETON

Anonymous Donor Who Made Antarctic Expedition Possible Is the Playwright.

HIS REGARD FOR SCOTT

Who Left Him a Last Blurred Message—His Mother's Influence Seen, Too—Mr. Frohman's Explanation.

The reason Sir Ernest Shackleton has been able to announce that he has finally collected the necessary funds for his antarctic expedition is that Sir J. M. Barrie, the playwright, has come forward with the remaining sum desired.

The Barrie contribution, without which the expedition would not have been possible, was made, so it was learned yesterday, with the single stipulation that it should be kept private. Even now the Barrie donation to the Shackleton fund is not known in London.

The sum with which Barrie rounded out the fund deemed necessary for this latest south polar exploration is $50,000. The entire equipment needed can now be furnished, according to the estimate of Sir Ernest Shackleton. The expedition will start from Buenos Aires in October, the object being to cross the south polar continent from the Weddell Sea to the Ross Sea, a distance of 1,700 land miles. More than half this distance will be over an entirely new route. Financially supported better than any other previous polar expedition, the Shackleton party will set out equipped with an aeroplane, motor sledges, 120 trained dogs and a complete supply of all the latest scientific apparatus. This will be Sir Ernest Shackleton's first polar expedition since, as Lieut. Shackleton, he led the famous dash which was checked and turned back 111 miles from the South pole. He had previously served in Scott's unsuccessful attempt to reach the pole.

Why Barrie Is Interested.

Charles Frohman, who has produced all of Sir J. M. Barrie's plays in England and America and is one of his closest friends, explained last night the probable reasons for Barrie's great interest in the Shackleton polar expedition.

"Knowing Mr. Barrie's extreme sensitiveness to any publicity concerning his gifts," said Mr. Frohman, "I won't either confirm or deny the fact that it was he who completed the sum necessary for the Shackleton expedition. But if you say it is so, I can easily explain the donation to you. Naturally, everybody will be interested to know the connection between one of the gentlest, shyest and most retiring of men with a huge, daring expedition into a land already so tragic for Englishmen. But, once you know J. M. Barrie, the explanation is simple.

"Two influences make Sir Ernest Shackleton's coming polar expedition an event of the most absorbing interest for J. M. Barrie. One influence is typical of Barrie sentiment, and the other is typical of Barrie heredity. One of the closest friends of the late Capt. Scott, among the living men of England, was J. M. Barrie. Peter Scott, only son of the dead explorer, is Mr. Barrie's godson, and gets his name from the playwright's 'Peter Pan.' Capt. Scott was Sir Ernest Shackleton's chief, and Mr. Barrie regards the Shackleton expedition as a fulfillment of an ambition that Capt. Scott gave his life for. Barrie now possesses one of the last messages found beside Capt. Scott's body in the tent that finally became his grave. It is a wonderfully heroic farewell message. I have seen it. It was written in lead pencil, and toward the end the words are very faint, going off finally into the obscurity of undecipherable scratches. Then it suddenly ends with the abruptness of a thing written by a dying hand.

"In the message Capt. Scott confides his son, Peter, to Barrie's care. I particularly remember one sentence in it: 'Give the boy a chance in life if the State won't do it. He ought to have good stuff in him.' Capt. Scott, Lieut. Shackleton, as he then was, and J. M. Barrie, all inveterate pipe smokers, were, as Barrie and Shackleton still are, wonderfully kindred souls; the link between them being a boundless curiosity in the unknown; Barrie experiencing in his writings the love of adventure that Shackleton and Scott experienced in their explorations.

His Mother's Influence.

"But heredity, too, enters largely into the explanation of Mr. Barrie's interest in the Shackleton expedition. J. M. Barrie is, above all else, his mother's son. He has told me that, as a lad, his mother's favorite reading was the biographies of explorers; only he says that his mother, to whom he invariably refers simply by her maiden name, Margaret Ogilvy, always said she hoped that every famous explorer would have the sense to stay at home, after finally getting there, although she would beam with admiration as each explorer disappointed her and went forth again.

"Now, this is the way a great admiration for explorers, felt all her life by Barrie's mother, worked out as an interesting bit of heredity in Barrie himself. As a lad it first fired him with an eagerness to venture forth into unknown lands very far to the south of his own native Kirriemuir in Scotland; so that he was one of the first of the very few of his generation who risked seeking a livelihood in London with barely a shilling in his pocket. After years of struggle and privation he succeeded as a writer, first of books and then of plays, largely concerned with the unknown world. In 'Peter Pan' he coined a name for it, the 'Never-Never Land'—the unmapped tract of country where all is thrilling adventure.

"When Capt. Scott failed to return from the 'Never-Never Land' no man felt it more keenly than Barrie. He had heard Capt. Scott tell by the hour of his adventures in each of the earlier expeditions, and, just as the biographies of famous explorers, read to him in his youth by his mother, affected Barrie's early life, close association with living explorers, like Shackleton and Scott, has left its traces in the present period of Barrie's life. You can see a most interesting example of this in his latest play, 'The Legend of Leonora,' where the character, 'Capt. Rattway,' described as an explorer but newly returned from a perilous expedition, is none other than Barrie's friend, Capt. Scott. The beauty of Capt. Rattway as a character in a play is the beauty that Capt. Robert Scott had in J. M. Barrie's eyes as a character in life. And as for Leonora and her love of explorers, of course, that again is heredity; for 'The Legend of Leonora' is the legend of Barrie's own mother.

"So you can see why nobody in England will be more solicitous for the safety and heartening of Sir Ernest

Continued on Page 2.

GLYNN SEES WILSON TO-DAY

Will Discuss with President Reorganization of New York Democracy.

WASHINGTON, Feb. 8.—Gov. Glynn of New York, accompanied by William F. McCombs, Democratic National Chairman, arrived here late to-night, and will have a conference to-morrow with President Wilson. Questions affecting the reorganization of the Empire State Democracy are to be discussed.

With members of Congress and a United States Senator to be elected there next Fall, President Wilson has been giving much attention in his recent talks with Chairman McCombs to the New York State situation. It is known that the national Administration is anxious to build up in New York State a new organization, and that it will look for assistance from Mayor Mitchel and Gov. Glynn. Neither Gov. Glynn nor Mr. McCombs would discuss politics to-night. Just how far the reorganization would affect Charles F. Murphy and the Tammany organization may be made clear after the conference.

Gov. Glynn said that, besides his visit to the White House, he came to Washington to appear before the Rivers and Harbors Committee in the interest of a deeper Hudson, and in connection with the Niagara water power question.

TO LECTURE LIKE BRYAN.

Secretary Wilson Booked for Chautauqua with Yodlers and Jugglers.

Special to The New York Times.

WASHINGTON, Feb. 8.—Undeterred by the criticism of Secretary Bryan last Summer, William B. Wilson, Secretary of Labor, is going on the lecture platform. His Chautauqua manager will be Dr. Paul W. Pearson of Swarthmore College in Pennsylvania, who arranged the Bryan tour.

Secretary Wilson is to talk for the Democratic cause in Pennsylvania from the same platform as Gifford Pinchot, Progressive candidate for the nomination for United States Senator in the Keystone State. An admission fee will be charged.

Dr. Pearson announces "the other talent" to appear on these Chautauqua platforms. This talent includes a band, motion pictures, both educational and comedy; Tyrolean yodlers, violinist, Tuskegee singers, a "Prince of Jugglers," a male quartet, an "operatic company," and other attractions. The Pennsylvania Chautauqua is the organization which utilized Secretary Bryan's services last Summer.

Dr. Pearson says: "Making a partisan speech on a non-partisan platform is no new thing in the Chautauqua. This method means that the people pay for their own political campaigns instead of letting the corporations and big business pay for them. Chautauquas put campaigning on a democratic basis."

These are the places in Pennsylvania where Secretary Wilson and Mr. Pinchot are to speak and the dates: Hazleton, April 18; South Bethlehem, April 20; West Chester, April 21; Carlisle, April 22; Lancaster, April 25; Coatesville, April 27, and Chester, April 28.

RUNAWAY INJURES FOUR.

Driver Thrown Out and Auto Party Bruised.

A team of horses drawing a heavy coach dashed through 125th Street, from Fifth to Eighth Avenue, early last night when the sidewalks were crowded and the street full of autos and wagons. At every crossing groups of pedestrians narrowly escaped being run down, but in spite of repeated efforts to stop the runaways, the frightened animals galloped on as far as Eighth Avenue, where Patrolman Bolk succeeded in stopping them.

The driver, John Heany, 37 years old, of 331 East 122d Street, was thrown from his seat when the team bolted, and was picked up unconscious. He was removed to the Harlem Hospital in an ambulance by Dr. Allen, who said that he was suffering from a fracture of the skull and possible internal injuries. In front of Hurtig & Seamon's Music Hall, between Seventh and Eighth Avenues, the runaways swerved, and the coach collided with an automobile in which were seated Harry Seamon, Joseph Hurtig, and Phil Wolf. All three occupants of the machine were thrown out, and the body of the touring car was badly damaged. Seamon and his companions escaped with a few bruises. The team of horses and the coach are owned by George B. Prior of 3,160 Broadway.

THIEF CHASE IN CHURCH.

Choir Boys Join in Pursuit of Man Who Interrupts Mass.

Priests were about to celebrate the mass at the morning service yesterday in St. Xavier's Church in West Fiftieth Street when persons in the congregation saw a white-haired man in ragged clothing edge over in his pew until he was directly behind a woman who was praying. The old man's hand stole over the back of the pew in front of him and came back with a large leather handbag.

When the thief had moved out to the aisle one or two arose to follow him. The old man started to run down the aisle to the door of the church. Cries of "Stop thief" aroused those who were at prayer and had not seen the incident. Several choir boys in cassocks and surplices, preparing to take part in the service, caught an idea of what was going on and ran down the aisle to join several others who were pursuing the thief. The priests looked from the chancel in astonishment at the uproar in the church.

The old man ran fast and had arrived at Sixth Avenue and Sixteenth Street before George Peyronnin, who was at the head of the pursuers, caught him.

The prisoner said that he was James Morton, 72 years old, of 153 Bowery, and that he had stolen the bag because he was starving. The police said that he was an old offender. Magistrate House heard the prisoner's story in the Men's Night Court and held him in $1,000 bail for Special Sessions.

RATHBURN CLINTON HELD.

New York Man Under Observation in Washington Hospital.

Special to The New York Times.

WASHINGTON, Feb. 8.—Rathburn Clinton, 29 years old, a resident of New York City, was arrested here to-day and sent to the Washington Asylum Hospital for observation as to his mental condition. The complaint was made by his brother, Capt. Thomas Clinton of the United States Marine Corps.

Capt. Clinton told the police that his brother recently threatened to kill him. A warrant was issued, but when Rathburn Clinton was found his condition was so pitiable that he was sent to the hospital for treatment. The police said he was suffering from drug poisoning.

JAPAN ONE REASON FOR LARGER NAVY

Vreeland Frank to House Committee—"Our Exclusion of Asiatics Challenged."

OTHER POLICIES TO DEFEND

Advocate of 48 Battleships Names Monroe Doctrine and Open Door —European Potentialities.

Special to The New York Times.

WASHINGTON, Feb. 8.—The House Naval Committee has made public testimony of Rear Admiral Charles E. Vreeland, a member of the General Board of the Navy, ranking next to Admiral Dewey, before that committee which contains significant references to Japan and American naval strategy in the Pacific. Some of Admiral Vreeland's remarks about Japan, Germany, and the international contest for sea power have been retained in the printed text of his testimony, but all those statements which he thought necessary to be kept confidential have been blue-penciled in his revision of the stenographers' record of what he said.

Admiral Vreeland recommended the construction of four dreadnoughts as part of this year's naval increase programme, and said the General Board urged the creation of a fleet of forty-eight battleships by 1920.

The report of the General Board to Secretary Daniels on naval increase this year stated the board's position in these words:

The General Board does not believe the nation stands ready to abandon or modify any of its well-established national policies, and repeats its position that the naval policy of the country should be to possess a fleet powerful enough to prevent or answer any challenge to these policies. The absolute strength necessary to accomplish this is a question that depends upon the national policies of prospective challengers and the force they can bring against us, and hence is relative and varies with their naval policies and building programmes.

Policies We Must Protect.

This statement was utilized by the "little navy" members of the Naval Committee for a grilling interrogation of Admiral Vreeland.

"Does that state your views?" inquired Representative Witherspoon of Mississippi.

"Yes, Sir," replied Admiral Vreeland. "That is straight."

"What are the national policies we should be able to resist or prevent any challenge of?"

"There is one for which we need a very large navy—the Monroe Doctrine," answered Admiral Vreeland.

"What are the others?" inquired Representative Witherspoon.

"Have we abandoned the open door in China?" flashed back Admiral Vreeland.

"No," said Mr. Witherspoon. "I am trying to get at the policies. You say we should have a fleet powerful enough to prevent or answer any challenge."

"Excluding the Asiatics," replied Admiral Vreeland, naming another policy.

"From California?" inquired Mr. Witherspoon.

"From our country," said the Admiral. "They are three big propositions that require force to maintain."

"Is that all?" asked Mr. Witherspoon.

"They occur to me as the most important," said the Admiral.

"Do you know of any reasonable apprehension that anybody is about to challenge the Monroe Doctrine, or the open door policy, or the exclusion of the Asiatics?"

"The exclusion of the Asiatics has been challenged," responded Admiral Vreeland.

"That is one reason why your belief is that we should increase the navy in order to prevent or answer any challenge to our policies?"

"Yes, Sir," said the Admiral.

"Have you any reasonable apprehension that the other policies will be challenged by any nation and that we should increase our navy for the purpose of preventing or answering that challenge—any one except the one?" insisted Mr. Witherspoon.

"The Monroe Doctrine," was Admiral Vreeland's answer.

Vreeland Differentiates Japan.

"What percentage of the navy of England could be spared," asked Mr. Williams of Illinois, "under ordinary conditions and complication in Europe, to be sent to America to attack us?"

"I do not think she could spare any—not without an understanding with the other powers," replied Admiral Vreeland. "I should say that is also true of Germany at the present time. I should say it is true of France, also."

"Is it true of Japan?" asked Mr. Williams.

"No, Sir," was Admiral Vreeland's reply.

"Would Japan be free under present conditions to send practically her whole navy across the Pacific to our west coast?"

"I don't think," said the Admiral, "she would have occasion to do that. She could inflict damage nearer home."

"I infer," said Mr. Williams, "from your answers that our need for a larger navy and extensive naval construction is in the Pacific rather than the Atlantic."

"At present," replied Admiral Vreeland. "You cannot tell what the case will be a year hence; no one can tell."

"I understood you to say the European powers could hardly spare a sufficient number of their navy to come this far from their base to attack us."

"At the present time," answered the Admiral. "No one can predict what alliances and ententes may exist a year hence. So long as our navy is comparatively weak, we should go ahead."

JAPAN SITUATION BRIGHTER.

House's Handling of Immigration Bill a Revelation to Tokio.

WASHINGTON, Feb. 8.—Notable improvement in the relations between the United States and Japan is believed to have resulted from the events in the House of Representatives last week connected with the passage of the Burnett Immigration bill. Reports from Tokio are that a profound impression was caused in the Japanese capital, not only by the refusal of the House to include in the bill the proposed prohibition against the entry of Japanese into the United States, but even more by the non-partisan appeal of Representative Mann.

The demonstration of the fact that in dealing with such large matters of international importance Americans stand ready to ignore mere party considerations, and that there is no reasonable ground for expecting a different viewpoint on international affairs to result from a change in the political cast of the Administration is said to have been something of a revelation.

The Japanese statesmen are declared to have been much pleased, moreover, by the House's reception of the appeal for fair treatment of aliens and for abstention from legislative interference with the Executive Department in its efforts to arrive at a settlement of the open issues between the two countries. Officials here are encouraged in the hope that the proceedings in the House have gone far to insure an early and satisfactory adjustment of all issues between the two Governments. So far as known, the only actual step that has been taken is the proposal that a new treaty be made declaring the right of Japanese to hold land in America on even terms with other foreigners.

Feminism and Woman Suffrage.

Prof. Sedgwick's recent article stirred up more comment probably than any other article ever printed on the subject. It especially aroused the ire of the champions of suffrage, and they hasten to reply.

Dr. Simon Flexner of the Rockefeller Institute,
Dr. Franklin P. Mall of Johns Hopkins,
Dr. William H. Howell of the same university,
Dr. Frederick Peterson, and
Prof. James Harvey Robinson, both of Columbia, join in the debate.

IN NEXT SUNDAY'S TIMES.

TRAIN'S WAY TO ROUT TICKET SPECULATORS

Whitman's Assistant Proposes a Central Ticket Office Run by Managers.

Assistant District Attorney Arthur Train will submit to Lee Shubert to-day a plan to do away with theatre ticket speculation in New York that will put an end even to ticket agencies in the hotels. The scheme already has been submitted to other leading theatrical managers, and although it is drastic in its provisions, Mr. Train believes that every one of them will work in harmony with his suggeston.

As worked out by Mr. Train, the plan calls for the establishment in Times Square of a central ticket office operated and controlled by the theatre managers themselves, where tickets for all of the amusement places will be offered for sale. To meet the expenses of such an establishment Mr. Train proposes to increase the price of tickets from $2 to $2.25.

This extra 25 cents on each ticket will, Mr. Train believes, pay all of the expenses of the central agency and also for the employment of a staff of special detectives to spot persons buying for speculators and so keep tickets from falling into the hands of persons who would resell them.

Mr. Train's idea is to have on sale at the central office only the first eight or ten rows of orchestra seats, and to keep the central office open only until 7 o'clock at night. After that hour all unsold tickets are to be returned to the box offices and put on sale there at the regular two-dollar rate.

In order to do away with the hotel agencies Mr. Train propses to amend the excise law making it a misdemeanor to sell a ticket to any place of amusement in any pice where liquor is sold.

If the theatre managers fail to adopt the plan suggested by Mr. Train, or fail to suggest another which meets with his approval, he will immediately suggest the passage of laws which will take the matter out of the hands of the managers altogether.

"When the matter of theatre ticket speculation was first brought to the attention of my office," said Mr. Train last night, "I was surprised to find how much damage the speculation in the tickets had done to the theatres and how widespread was the resentment of the public at the treatment it was receiving. As a matter of fact, the ticket agencies are kept alive by the large number of visitors to the city, who, having only a short time to stay and see the shows, are willing to pay almost any price to get good seats. New Yorkers object to paying the high prices asked for tickets and have been driven away from the theatres.

"While at the outset the managers may have encouraged the sale of tickets to speculators, I am convinced now of their sincerity when they say they will do everything in their power to help break up the practice. The health of the theatre business depends upon doing away with ticket speculation.

"My plan is for the establishment of a perfect agency where a large force of clerks will give prompt and courteous treatment to the public, and where a person knows he can get good seats—if not for to-night, then for to-morrow night, or for some other night. It may be necessary for the business to be strictly cash at first, but that will be up to the managers themselves. Later, if they wish to extend credit to persons they know, just as the agencies do now, that is entirely their own business.

"The public, while it objects to paying exorbitant prices for seats, has been educated up to a small advance at least, and the 25 cents extra which I suggest placing on all good seats sold at the central office would not be objectionable to any one. At the same time, with all of the theatres represented, it would bring in a large income which would make possible the employment of clerks of the highest class.

"I will also attempt to obtain legislation which will make it a crime for the manager of a theatre to sell or assist in the selling of tickets at a price higher than the one he has stamped on them. While any law which would attempt to prevent the buyer of a ticket from reselling it at a higher price probably would be unconstitutional, we will try to reach that evil in other ways. At all events, we will make it possible for the public to get what it wants at a fair price, and when that is done there will be no one to deal with the agencies.

"I have gone over the plan carefully many times, and I do not see any better way to do it. The report that Mr. Klaw said that Klaw & Erlanger did not believe in entering into any agreement with other managers is not true. I found Mr. Klaw most anxious to help me in every way. I have an appointment with Mr. Shubert on Monday, and will go into the plan with him, just as I have with the others. I am sure he will help, too."

"Last September," said Sargent Aborn of the Century Opera Company last night, "practically every agency and ticket speculator called upon us and tried to arrange for 'blocks of tickets' for each week's opera. The most important factor in their proposition was that they wished to return any unsold tickets to the box office each night as the curtain was rising.

"We said at the time we would not lend ourselves to such business methods in disposing of tickets to the public.

"We very soon got rid of the street speculator by having him arrested and fined. Some five or six speculators were so handled during the early part of our season, and that ended the nuisance. We are heartily in accord with any movement which will end forever the ticket-speculating nuisance and free the amusement public from the methods now employed to extort exorbitant prices for tickets for the opera."

VADERLAND BADLY DAMAGED

Red Star Liner Injured at Antwerp Docks—Return Trip Delayed.

ANTWERP, Feb. 8.—The Red Star Line steamer Vaderland was badly damaged while docking here to-day on her arrival from New York.

Her return trip, set for later in the week, has been canceled.

PASTOR SAID 'DAMN' TO DANCE OBJECTOR

Now Greenpoint's Reformed Episcopal Church Is to Lose the Rev. Charles Quinn.

Because he desired the young people of his congregation to dance as often as they wished, while a senior warden considered a dance in the church building an outrage on the fitness of things, the Rev. Charles Quinn, pastor of the Reformed Episcopal Church of the Redemption in Greenpoint, handed in his resignation last night. It is to take effect on March 1.

The announcement created a stormy scene during the evening service, during which William MacEwan, the first warden, shouted that the pastor was "a liar," and two young girls arose to remark that "after Mr. Quinn goes away the congregation will consist only of Mr. MacEwan and the four members of his family."

It was clear from the behavior of the congregation that its sympathies were with the pastor. The Rev. Mr. Quinn is a young man. He was ordained less than two years ago. Mr. MacEwan is one of the oldest residents of Greenpoint. He has served as church warden during the incumbency of half a dozen pastors.

The trouble started, according to a version on which the Rev. Mr. Quinn and Senior Warden MacEwan partially agree, at a meeting of an organization of church workers known as the Helping Hand Society. The members of this society went to the church for a meeting a few weeks ago only to find that the fires had not been lighted and that the rooms were very chilly. Some one suggested that the members dance for a few minutes in order to warm up for the society's session.

A telephone message to the young clergyman obtained his permission, and a few numbers were danced to music from the church organ. As the fourth waltz was in progress the Senior Warden burst in upon them, hot with indignation.

He announced that "this dancing business will not do," and when told that the pastor had given his permission for the dance, the Senior Warden said the pastor would not do any more than the dancing would. He ordered all present to leave the church, and said he would report the minister to Bishop Robert L. Rudolph next day.

Events of the next day led to friction and bad feeling that has driven asunder all thought of fellowship and reconciliation between the minister and the Senior Warden. The Rev. Mr. Quinn told the young people they could have another dance that night if they so desired. Senior Warden MacEwan said there never would be another dance, whereupon the clergyman, as he admitted last night, dropped a remark that "there were many things a damn sight worse than dancing at which the young people might become engaged if driven away from the church for their amusements."

The profane phrase in the clergyman's remarks was repeated to Bishop Rudolph that very day. There was an investigation, and in accordance with the Bishop's recommendation, the Rev. Mr. Quinn gave out his announcement that he was ready to seek a new congregation.

"No publicity in this, no publicity in this," said Mr. MacEwan when reporters sought for details from the Rev. Mr. Quinn last night.

"But if there has been publicity you are to blame," the clergyman retorted to the Senior Warden.

"Any one who says that is a liar," said Mr. MacEwan, and he added, "You don't dare tell it all anyhow."

But the Rev. Mr. Quinn insisted that he did dare to tell it all, and asked Mr. MacEwan to listen while he did so. He then narrated the story, including the phrase containing the word "damn" that had so stirred up Mr. MacEwan. He insisted that most of the trouble was due to the fact that Mr. MacEwan belonged to a generation that had passed and could not, even in a slight degree, interpret the desires of the young folks of the present day. He said that the three clergymen who had preceded him had remained only for very brief periods.

Miss Harriet Gieger, President of the Helping Hand Society, and Miss Florence MacMillan, its Secretary, announced that they would see to it that all of the young folks remained away from church until "Mr. MacEwan could be brought to his senses."

MEMPHIS BANK CLOSES.

Speculations of the Mercantile's President Blamed for It.

Special to The New York Times.

MEMPHIS, Tenn., Feb. 8.—The Directors of the Mercantile Bank formally declared the bank insolvent to-day and adopted a resolution ordering its doors closed. They also directed Gen. L. E. Wright and Caruthers Ewing, attorneys, to take such steps as are necessary to protect the remaining assets of the bank. The resolutions asserted that default by the President of the bank, Hunter Raine, made that action necessary.

The last report of the bank, on Jan. 6, put its capital at $200,000 and the surplus $100,000. The Directors said to-night that they could not give a detailed statement of the affairs of the bank because the books were under a time lock and could not be reached. Mr. Raine, who is said to have lost a large sum in speculation, turned over to the bank all of his personal estate, valued at some $400,000. It is believed the bank will pay its depositors in full. Mr. Raine's losses were said to have occurred almost entirely within the last forty to fifty days.

The name of Hunter Raine was familiar in these parts a dozen years ago when it was borne by a well known racehorse, named for the Memphis banker.

Latest Shipping News.

BY MARCONI WIRELESS SS. Oceanic (White Star Line), Southampton to New York, was 1,541 miles east of Sandy Hook at 7:20 P. M. yesterday, Feb. 8th, forenoon.

ACCUSE HUSBAND IN NEWARK MURDER

Manning Now Held as an Accessory of "Veiled Slayer" Who Shot His Wife.

HIS SISTER ALSO HELD

As a Material Witness—Evidence Obtained in Note Left By Suicide.

Chief of Police Long of Newark announced shortly after midnight last night that a charge of murder would be placed against Charles I. Manning, proprietor of a garage at Verona, N. J., for the death of his wife, Harriet Manning, of 219 Warren Street, Newark. Mrs. Manning was shot and killed on Friday night by Miss Hazel Herdman of Cedar Grove, N. J., who confessed just before she died on Saturday at the Mountainside Hospital in Montclair, N. J., of poison by bichloride of mercury, taken with suicidal intent, that she had murdered Mrs. Manning and had done so to free Manning to marry her. Manning and Miss Herdman had a child 18 months old, who is now in the care of relatives at Montclair.

At midnight the detectives brought two women into Newark Police Headquarters. After they had been questioned for an hour, Captain of Detectives Tuite announced that one of the women was Mrs. Sadie E. Garrabrant, a sister of Manning, who would be held as a material witness. Before his arrest Manning had lived with her at her home in Bloomfield Avenue, Verona. The second woman was released.

After questioning Manning's sister Capt. Tuite said:

"We have established to our satisfaction that Manning knew that Miss Herdman had committed the crime at least as early as the time that she was arrested on Friday night. There is also reason to believe that he knew in advance that the deed was committed."

Capt. Tuite was asked if Mrs. Garrabrant had admitted that words of her brother showed that he knew about the crime. Capt. Tuite, however, would not say whether the accusation against Manning was supported by his sister's testimony.

Miss Herdman in her dying statement attempted to exonerate Manning, but Chief Long said last night that evidence had been obtained tending to show that he was an accessory before and after the fact. One thing which the police in their investigation yesterday were seeking to show, was that Manning took Miss Herdman in his automobile to Newark before the murder was committed.

Last Monday Mrs. Manning received a check for $2,600, her share in the estate of her father, Reuben Cobb, a farmer. She had other property besides that. She died intestate, and under the New Jersey law Manning became her sole heir, as they had no children.

Shortly after the murder on Friday night the police of Newark called up Manning's garage at Verona and found him in. Later they took him to Police Headquarters in Newark and questioned him, but later released him.

Manning made no efforts to escape. On Saturday morning he drove with Miss Herdman to Newark and viewed the body of his wife in Mullin's morgue. After Miss Herdman had taken poison he carried her in his machine from Bloomfield to the hospital in Montclair, and later drove with the girl's mother and sister to the hospital, where he was taken into custody by Chief Long.

Physicians at the hospital in Montclair, who read the note the dying girl left for Manning, said that there was nothing in it which implicated Manning in any way with the crime or showed that he had any knowledge of it. Chief Long refused to say what the note contained, holding that it was a dying declaration and contained valuable information for the police. Chief Long refused last night to tell what the evidence was which led to the decision to charge Manning with murder.

Chief of Police Long of Newark questioned Manning yesterday afternoon in the presence of Mrs. Harriet Cobb and Mrs. William Reilly, mother and sister of the murdered woman. Chief Long later sent for a stenographer to take a statement. Chief Long, however, refused last night to say whether his investigation had thrown any light on the murder.

The body of Miss Herdman is at Kunz's Morgue in Orange. The funeral arrangements have not been completed, but it was said last night that the services would be conducted by the Rev. John R. Pratt, pastor of the Congregational Church at Verona, who was asked for on Saturday by Miss Herdman, but was unable to reach the hospital before her death.

$150,000 FOR A PICTURE.

American Buys Painting by El Greco at a Record Price.

Special Cable to THE NEW YORK TIMES.

PARIS, Feb. 8.—THE NEW YORK TIMES correspondent learns that Messrs. Knoedler have just sold to an American collector a very fine whole length life-size portrait by El Greco of a Spanish gentleman in armor. The price paid was $150,000. This is believed to be by far the highest price yet paid for a painting by this master, of whose work there are very few good examples outside of public collections, and these chiefly in Spain.

The portrait just sold was, it is understood, formerly in an English collection.

Roland F. Knoedler of Messrs. Knoedler & Co., 556 Fifth Avenue, said at the Hotel Savoy last night that his firm had not yet been formally notified of the sale of the portrait. Charles L. Knoedler, another brother, of 169 West Fifty-seventh Street, who retired from the firm two years ago, said he did not consider $150,000 an extravagant price for one of El Greco's works. "The works of this artist," he said, "are mostly to be found in the galleries of collectors in Madrid and other parts of Spain. Collectors here are just beginning to go after his paintings."

UNIONS ACCUSE A JUDGE.

Want Wilson to Put Dayton of West Virginia Under Investigation.

WHEELING, West Va., Feb. 8.—President Wilson will be asked to bring about an investigation of the official conduct of Circuit Judge Alston G. Dayton, of the Northern District of West Virginia. This was decided upon at a union labor mass meeting held here to-day under the auspices of the Ohio Valley Trades Council. A petition, signed by 5,000 men, will be taken to Washington this week.

The United Mine Workers of America started the fight on Judge Dayton charging him with having shown favoritism in cases growing out of the strike at Colliers, West Virginia.

MAYOR MITCHEL BETTER.

To be at His Office To-day—Will Cut Down Dinners.

Mayor Mitchel, who was confined to his home at 258 Riverside Drive on Saturday by a severe headache and a slight cold, was feeling much better yesterday. He said last night that he would be at his office this morning ready for work.

"It was only a headache," said the Mayor, "and I don't know that I can blame dinners and other social engagements for my slight illness, but I've got to cut down my social engagements in order to get more rest."

The Mayor missed two dinners on Saturday night where he was scheduled to make addresses.

FLIES 1,000 MILES STRAIGHT

German Aviator Stays Up 16 Hours 20 Minutes, Breaking All Records.

By Marconi Transatlantic Wireless Telegraph to The New York Times.

LONDON, Monday, Feb. 9.—A further demonstration of the fact that a transatlantic aeroplane flight is no longer to be regarded as an impossible achievement, says The Daily Mail, was given on Saturday by the German airman Ingold, who covered a distance of more than 1,000 miles in 16 hours and 20 minutes, breaking the endurance record, during which time he flew from Mülhausen, in Alsace, and ended his flight near Munich.

Ingold used a Pfeil biplane, fitted with a 100-horse power Mercedes engine, and carried 126 gallons of gasoline and 12 gallons of oil.

The previous record of 14 hours and 7 minutes was made by Bruno Langer at Johannisthal on Feb. 3.

HERE'S A HELLO WEDDING.

Preacher Stands Outside and Yells to Couple in Smallpox House.

Special to The New York Times.

SAVANNAH, Ga., Feb. 8.—A. D. Jernigan, a Valdosta jeweler, yesterday married Miss Bertha Stevens, whom he is nursing through a case of smallpox. When Jernigan went to visit the girl he found that she and other members of her family were suffering from smallpox, and that the house was under quarantine. He got through the quarantine lines and announced that he would nurse his sweetheart back to health, and that they would be married at once. Then another difficulty arose, for he could not induce any clergyman to come to the house.

The Rev. A. C. Pyle, a Baptist preacher, finally settled the difficulty by yelling the ceremony at them from the safety of the front yard, having first assured himself that all the windows and doors were closed.

GOETHALS TO JUDGE BURKE.

Charges of Graft to be Passed Upon by Canal Chairman.

PANAMA, Feb. 8.—The report of the investigation into the alleged irregularities in the Commissary Department, of which John Burke is manager, is now in the hands of Col. George W. Goethals, Chairman of the Panama Canal Commission, who will decide to-morrow what action, if any, is to be taken.

Allegations have been made that Mr. Burke has accepted illegal commissions from contractors for supplies, and his European dealings have been the subject of a special investigation. It is understood that the case has been left in the hands of Col. Goethals, to deal with in an administrative capacity.

LOSES POWER OF SPEECH.

Woman Suffers Nervous Breakdown on the Way to Atlantic City.

Special to The New York Times.

ATLANTIC CITY, N. J., Feb. 8.—Mrs. Lillie Oberhofer of 640 Sixtieth Street, Brooklyn, who arrived here to-night suffering from a nervous breakdown, lost the power of speech before the train arrived in this city.

She managed by signs to let the ticket agent at the Reading Station know that she wanted to talk to a policeman, and after walking away with one she recovered somewhat. In a newspaper she pointed out letters, and the policeman by spelling them out learned her name and that she had been out of a hospital two days. She was put in charge of the police matron, who took her to the Atlantic City Hospital.

HATS MIXED, DANCERS FIGHT

Lack of Hat Hooks Leads to Shooting at Mrs. Rosseny's Party.

When Mrs. Josephine Rosseny gave a dance on Saturday night in her flat at 353 East Twenty-third Street, there were not enough hat hooks for the fifteen couples who took part, and several hats were laid on the floor against the wall. As soon as the music struck up the couples danced along the hall and the hats were kicked into an inextricable mass.

The guests began to depart early yesterday morning and a quarrel at once began. One man became infuriated and fired four shots from his revolver. One guest was shot twice in the breast, and while he was being taken to Bellevue Hospital, the others went home hatless. A revolver was found in the gutter outside, but no arrests were made. The man wounded was James Saverano of 382 Keap Street, Brooklyn, a son-in-law of the hostess.

MARSHALL PREVENTS PANIC.

Helps Smother Shouts of "Fire!" in Crowded Hall—Bryan There Also.

Special to The New York Times.

WASHINGTON, Feb. 8.—The lives of more than 2,000 persons who had gathered to hear Secretary Bryan, Vice President Marshall, and others speak at the Interdenominational Bible Conference were endangered at Poliqué's Theatre this afternoon when fire started in the dressing rooms below the stage. The curtain was rung down and the people quietly passed out, thinking the meeting was over. Rats gnawing on matches caused the blaze.

Quiet on the stage was maintained by Vice President Marshall and others, who prevented cries of "Fire!" from being shouted. Among those on the stage were the Rev. G. Campbell Morgan, pastor of Westminster Chapel, London, and prominent church dignitaries from practically every State in the Union.

VILLA TELLS WILSON HE'LL PUNISH BANDIT

Bryan Carries Reassuring Messages from Rebel Leader to the White House.

ALL DEAD IN TRAIN WRECK

Only Charred Bones Found in Tunnel—Villa to Guard Spaniards in Torreon Attack.

WASHINGTON, Feb. 8.—After an hour's conference with President Wilson at the White House to-night, Secretary Bryan announced that assurances had been received from Gen. Francisco Villa of his intention to protect Spanish subjects when he attacked Torreon.

Word was also received from the Constitutionalist General of his intention to assist in every way possible in fixing the responsibility for the tragedy in Cumbre Tunnel, on the Mexico Northwestern Railroad, in which several Americans were suffocated. Gen. Villa has complied with the request of the State Department that a guard of soldiers accompany the party, composed of Americans, who hope to recover the bodies of the dead Americans. Secretary Bryan said he had ordered American Consul Edwards at Juarez to send a special messenger with the party to report on the facts of the affair.

Constitutionalists here say Maximo Castillo, who is charged with responsibility for the tunnel accident, is an irresponsible bandit with a small following, recognizing neither Huerta nor Carranza. He was the trusted bodyguard of Madero when the latter took the field against Diaz, and members of the Constitutionalist agency here say his present outlawry is the result of insanity. They say he will be summarily dealt with by Villa if captured.

All those aboard the ill-fated train appear to have perished. They include at least nine Americans and thirty Mexicans, according to a dispatch from American Consul Letcher at Chihuahua to the State Department to-night. The dispatch, which was dated to-day, gave information brought there by persons who had just arrived from Madera, the nearest point to the tunnel. It said the Americans known to have been aboard the train and whose bodies were being sought by a relief party included:

M. J. Gilmartin, Superintendent of the Mexican Northwestern Railroad at Chihuahua.
C. H. Marders, express agent.
Henry Schofield, Superintendent, Juarez.
K. L. Hatfield, business man, El Paso.
Thomas M. Kelly, conductor.
J. I. Morris, road master.
L. E. Williams, employe Madera Lumber Company.
J. Webster, conductor in charge of train.
Edward J. McCutcheon, engineer.

About thirty other persons, including some Americans, were aboard.

From American Consul Edwards at Juarez came the information that Vice Consul Zoeller had left with a special relief train for Cumbre tunnel, with about thirty Americans and a guard of fifty Constitutionalist soldiers. They took many coffins with them, as they had little hope of finding alive any of the passengers or crew of the train.

Mr. Edwards added that it had been positively established in the latest telegrams received from near the scene of the disaster that the train was not held up or in any way disturbed by the bandits before it entered the tunnel, and that it was also known that the bandits had departed about two hours before the train entered the south end of the tunnel. Seven stock cars had been set on fire at the north end, which ignited the timbers in the tunnel, and it is the supposition of those near the scene that the passenger train ran into and collided with the burning cars. The Consul said opinion was divided as to whether or not the bandits intended to destroy lives.

Secretary Bryan was busy at the State Department all day answering messages of inquiry concerning the Americans and telegraphing instructions to the nearest Consuls. The advices were shown to President Wilson. There is confidence at the State Department that the Constitutionalists will do everything possible to punish the offenders.

The announcement that Gen. Villa would protect Spanish subjects in his invasion of Torreon brought relief to officials here, who had been swamped with petitions and representations on behalf of the threatened Spaniards.

Urgent representations had been made to Villa by Consul Edwards at the instance of the American Government. Secretary Bryan said to-night that earlier dispatches to the effect that Villa had intended to execute all Spaniards were not confirmed. It is understood that Villa's warning was directed chiefly against Spaniards who were actively assisting Huerta. The State Department, however, regards its latest assurances as satisfactory and feels that all Spaniards will be safe. It is regarded as possible, however, that the Spanish Legation at Mexico City will advise Spaniards at Torreon to refrain from acting in any way as combatants in the revolution.

Word was received here to-day that Charles Myers Dobson, an American, formerly a newspaper man, was imprisoned in Torreon, and Secretary Bryan promptly dispatched a request for information to the American Consul there.

FIND NO BODIES IN TUNNEL.

Rescuers' Search for Castillo Victims Vain—May Be Buried by Debris.

Special to The New York Times.

CUMBRE TUNNEL, Chihuahua, Feb. 8.—Rescue workers in oxygen helmets have been at work since Saturday trying to reach the burning passenger train which was run into the tunnel by Maximo Castillo and his bandits. No more bodies have been located, and it is now believed by the officials of the Mexico Northwestern Railroad that all the passengers were suffocated and buried under the slime of the mountain tunnel.

The special train which left Juarez Saturday night arrived here at 1:55 this afternoon, and the entire crew and fire fighters on board went to work on the north portal, where the gas and fumes were worst. Lining the cars were seventy-five coffins, awaiting bodies that were not recovered. Mexicans sent to scour the mountains in the forlorn hope that Castillo might have kidnapped the passengers in the hills failed to find any trace of them.

At the Pearson Syndicate offices, which have been established at the tunnel mouth, the officials said they did not believe there was one chance in a hundred for the men in the tunnel to be alive. Rescuers working from the south end of the bore have penetrated only a third of the distance, but succeeded in discovering the locomotive of the passenger train. The pilot was broken, and the whole machine showed that the train had gone into the tunnel under full steam. This tends to verify the belief

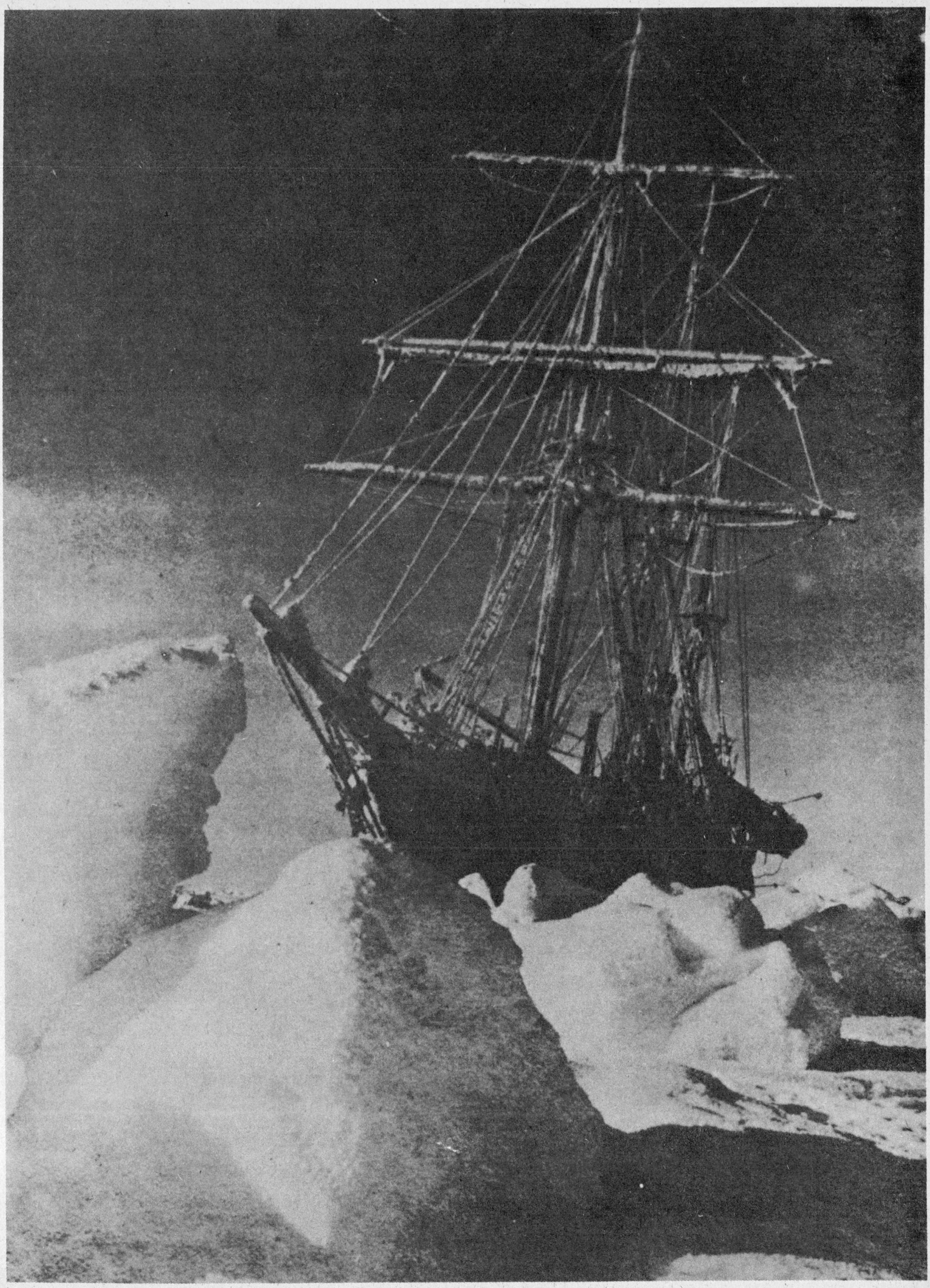

Shackleton's ship, the *Endurance*, locked in the ice of the Weddell Sea.

As the *Endurance* drifted slowly toward the interior of the ice pack imprisoning it, Shackleton and his 26 men had to abandon ship and camp on the ice floes. Here Shackleton is shown at a camp on the ice.

Trapped in the ice, the hull of the *Endurance* was inexorably crushed.

"All the News That's Fit to Print."

The New York Times.

THE WEATHER.
Fair, slightly warmer Thursday; Friday, fair, warmer; moderate winds, becoming south.
For full weather report see Page 22.

VOL. LXV...NO. 21,245. ... NEW YORK, SATURDAY, MARCH 25, 1916.—TWENTY PAGES. ONE CENT In Greater New York, Jersey City and Newark. | Elsewhere, TWO CENTS.

SHACKLETON SHIP HELPLESS IN ICE DRIFTS 500 MILES

Breaking from Moorings, Relief Vessel Wanders for Months in the Antarctic.

LEFT 10 MAROONED ASHORE

With No Anchors and Little Fuel, Vessel Makes for New Zealand.

HAS NO WORD OF EXPLORER

Was to Pick Him Up If He Succeeds in Crossing the South Polar Continent.

MELBOURNE, Saturday, March 25.—The auxiliary ship Aurora of the Shackleton antarctic expedition has been damaged and is proceeding to New Zealand for repairs, according to a wireless dispatch from the vessel received by the Navy Department here yesterday.

A. A. Jensen, Minister of the Navy, has received the following message from the Aurora:

"Hull severely strained. Ship released from ice March 14, latitude 64.30 south, longitude 161 east. Drift 500 miles.

"Case, commissariat officer; Richards, physicist; Hayward, Secretary, and Jack, biologist, ashore.

"Wireless appeals for relief ship sent during Winter. No acknowledgment.

"Ship proceeding to port Chalmers, New Zealand, with jury rudder. No anchors and short of fuel. Expect to arrive early in April.

"STENHOUSE."

J. R. Stenhouse is chief officer of the Aurora.

It is evident from the Aurora's wireless dispatch that the fate of Lieutenant Sir Ernest Shackleton and the rest of the party which is attempting to cross the antarctic region is yet unknown. Probably nothing will be heard from them until next November, when the ice breaks.

It is explained here that the wireless relief calls sent during the Winter by the Aurora probably were not answered because of the Australian Government's abandonment of Macquarie Island as a wireless station.

Concern Felt in London.

Special Cable to THE NEW YORK TIMES.

LONDON, Saturday, March 25.—A dispatch reached London yesterday saying that Shackleton's relief ship, the Aurora, had broken adrift from her Ross Sea base, leaving Lieutenant Mackintosh and nine men stranded ashore. The news aroused considerable apprehension here, as it places two parties of the expedition in grave peril. The Aurora left Hobart, Tasmania, at the end of 1914 for Ross Sea, on the New Zealand side of the antarctic, with picked men to go forward and establish depots to meet Lieut. Shackleton and his six companions who are crossing the antarctic continent from the South American side.

No news has come from the Endurance of Lieutenant Shackleton's definite start from Weddell Sea on his 1,700-mile journey, but there is every reason to suppose that it was made. There is now no vessel available to receive Shackleton on his arrival at Ross Sea and there is no apparent hope of relief reaching his party and the Mackintosh party before next Winter, when Ross Sea again becomes navigable. Much depends upon the amount of stores landed from the Aurora before she broke adrift, and how long they last the marooned men.

The news of the disaster comes from the Aurora's own wireless. The Aurora is now somewhere in the southern Pacific. The wireless message received here from her was picked up yesterday by a New Zealand station, but it would seem that the vessel had tried to communicate with land for several months. The message says that the Aurora, on her arrival at Cape Crozier on Jan. 9, 1915, finding conditions too bad to permit landing, sailed eastward along the Barrier and up the Sound, where the landing was made on Ross Sea coast. A safe harbor could not be found, so the Aurora moored off Cape Evans. From the end of January to the middle of March various expeditions ashore were made for the purpose of landing stores, arranging the depot testing motors, and doing scientific work.

Broke Away in Blizzard.

On May 6 during a violent blizzard the Aurora broke away from her Winter moorings. There were then ten men ashore, including Lieutenant Mackintosh, who was in charge of the expeditions on the Australian side of the antarctic continent, and four members of the scientific staff. The Aurora, with the remainder of the crew, then became locked in pack ice and drifted helplessly in this condition over ten months, sustaining heavy damage, traveling south and eastward about 1,200 miles.

On July 21, 1915, the ice pressure severely strained the hull and carried the rudder away. The vessel was then about ninety miles south of Coulmain Island. The Aurora finally got away from the ice on March 14 last. She was then in latitude 64.30 south, longitude 161 east.

The wireless appeals for a relief ship which the Aurora sent during the Winter were never received.

With a jury rudder and short of coal the Aurora is now making for New Zealand, where she expects to arrive early in April.

Mackintosh's party now ashore includes H. E. Wild, a brother of Frank Wild; Ernest Joyce, J. Cope, A. Stevens, A. Spencer Smith, and Victor Hayward.

Lady Shackleton Hopeful.

Lady Shackleton when seen last evening said that she had not heard from Sir Ernest, although she had heard that the Aurora had gone adrift. She was optimistic in the absence of fuller and more definite details, and added: "They may have got back to Buneos Aires. There is just a hope." No news of the breaking away of the Aurora had been received up to 5:30 o'clock last evening at the home of Dr. Shackleton, Sir Ernest's father.

Commander Evans, who took command of the Scott expedition after the

Continued on Page 5.

$2,650,000,000 Subscribed To Fourth German War Loan

BERLIN, (by Wireless to Sayville,) March 24.—Dr. Karl Helfferich, Secretary of the Imperial Treasury, told the Reichstag today that the fourth German war loan had been a brilliant success, the subscriptions having reached more than 10,600,000,000 marks, ($2,650,000,000,) not including subscriptions abroad and at the front.

It was pointed out that the German war loans have now reached a total of 36,300,000,000 marks ($9,075,000,000,) while the British loans have only totaled 19,000,000,000 marks, and those of France 11,944,000,000 marks.

As forecast in recent Berlin advices, the total in subscriptions for the fourth German war loan, incomplete as yet according to Dr. Helfferich's statement, is less than for the third loan, but in excess of that for the second loan. Final figures on the third loan showed total subscriptions of 12,160,000,000 marks, while the subscriptions for the second loan were 8,026,072,000 marks.

GAYNOR WARDED OFF A PUBLICITY BOOMER

His Letters to W. F. Clark Make a Merry Session for the Thompson Committee.

WILLCOX LAUDS CONTRACTS

Never Heard of Subway Offer Ellison Described—McAneny to Testify.

The Thompson legislative committee heard several witnesses in the Municipal Building yesterday, including Theodore P. Shonts, President of the Interborough Rapid Transit Company; William R. Willcox, former Chairman of the Public Service Commission, and William B. Ellison, former Corporation Counsel. The most important developments of the day were:

The production of several letters that passed between the late Mayor William J. Gaynor and W. F. Clark, a publicity promoter, in 1912, when Mr. Gaynor was an aspirant for the Democratic Presidential nomination. These letters were found by the committee's expert accountant in the letter files stored in the basement of City Hall.

Ex-Corporation Counsel Ellison told of an offer made to him by a Mr. Alexander and a Mr. Pollock, who, he understood, represented the Standard Oil Company, to furnish $500,000,000 to build all the subways needed by the city. Mr. Ellison took the men to see Mayor Gaynor, and the Mayor treated the matter as a joke, suggesting that the money be loaned to the Interborough, and that the Interborough undertake the work. The Public Service Commissioners also took little stock in the proposal.

McAneny Demands to be Called.

George McAneny, who was Borough President of Manhattan during the subway negotiations, followed Controller Prendergast and Mr. Willcox in writing to Senator Thompson, Chairman of the investigating committee, demanding an opportunity to go on the witness stand and tell all he knew about the negotiations. Senator Thompson said Mr. McAneny, Mr. Prendergast, and Mr. Willcox would receive the opportunity they sought "in due course of time." Mr. Willcox went on the stand and told of the dealings he had with President Shonts when the subway contracts were under discussion.

Mr. Shonts was again called and recounted in detail the conferences he had with Mayor Gaynor. Several letters that passed between Mr. Shonts and members of the firm of J. P. Morgan & Co. were read into the record.

The disclosure of the Gaynor-Clark letters furnished the most interesting feature of the day, and caused much laughter among the large audience when they were read. Frank Moss, counsel to the committee, put them in evidence in an attempt to show that Mayor Gaynor was on a friendly footing with President Shonts at the time.

In reply to a direct question Mr. Shonts denied that he had ever contributed money to the Gaynor pre-nomination campaign fund. He said he had never heard that the Interborough had contributed anything.

Mr. Moss prefaced the introduction of the letters by asking Mr. Shonts if he remembered Mr. Clark. Mr. Shonts replied that he had no recollection of him, whereupon Mr. Moss read this letter, written on stationery of "The Cosmographic Editorials and Correspondence for the American Press":

March 4, 1912.

My Dear Mr. Mayor:

No one holding a city position should be mixed up in national politics. They are bound to do something to hurt your Presidential prospects. The Gerard incident illustrates their lack of tact, to use no harder term. This is a big game, and it can't be successfully played by small men. You should instruct Adamson, Watson, and the other gentlemen who have been collecting funds, to quit. Hearst has a report of every move they have made. They mean well, no doubt, but they are only making it more difficult for your real friends to do the work in the South and West that will be necessary to give you the proper standing in the national convention. Sincerely yours,

W. F. CLARK.

Thought Clark Credulous.

The next letter was a reply from Mayor Gaynor as follows:

March 5, 1912.

Dear Mr. Clark: I think you are entirely mistaken in saying that Mr. Adamson, Mr. Watson, or anyone around me is collecting money. I cannot credit it. As for the "Gerard incident," I trust that you do not believe that I sat down to lunch with him and asked him for money. I never sat down with him in my life, nor have I any intimacy with him whatever. I fear you are rather credulous in this instance. If necessary I shall issue a statement that no one is authorized to collect any money in my behalf. Very truly yours,

W. J. GAYNOR, Mayor.

W. F. Clark, Esq., 1 Broadway, New York City.

Mr. Clark more than two months later wrote the following:

W. F. Clark,
New York, 1 Broadway, May 14, 1912.

My Dear Mr. Mayor:

A brisk newspaper campaign would, I'm sure, hasten along the subway negotiations. I did this work before, and I am sure if you would say the word to Mr. Shonts for me, another campaign would be inaugurated. The only way to get the New York public to understand anything is to keep hammering away in the newspapers

Continued on Page 5.

WAITE CONFESSES PROCURING POISON FOR FATHER-IN-LAW

Tells District Attorney He "Aided Peck in Suicide," and Expects to Die for It.

TO BE INDICTED ON MONDAY

Admits Tale Is Unbelievable and Offers $1,000 to Maid to Say Victim Wanted to Die.

NOW PRISONER IN BELLEVUE

Mother Breaks Down Upon Arrival Here—Wife Turns Against Him—Plaza Companion Found.

Dr. Arthur Warren Waite confessed yesterday afternoon to District Attorney Swann that he had bought arsenic three days before the death of his father-in-law, John E. Peck, millionaire drug manufacturer of Grand Rapids, Mich., on March 12 last, in Dr. Waite's apartment at the Colosseum, 435 Riverside Drive. Mr. Peck requested him to get the poison, Dr. Waite said, so that he could commit suicide.

The young dentist swore that he had not murdered his father-in-law, but admitted that he had no corroboration for his story, and told the District Attorney that he expected to go to the electric chair. Mr. Swann does not believe the story, and will proceed with the Grand Jury investigation, which he expects to result on Monday in an indictment against Dr. Waite for murder in the first degree. Desire for Mr. Peck's money will be the motive alleged.

Dr. Waite made his confession only after he had been confronted with his own signature signed on a druggist's receipt for the arsenic which he purchased on March 9. Before he had seen this evidence he had denied any knowledge of Mr. Peck's death, swore that he had purchased no poison of any kind, and called all suspicion of him "absurd." When Mr. Swann showed him the receipt, repeated the name of a Dr. Muller to whom he went for advice about buying arsenic, offered to produce the druggist who sold the poison, and laid other convicting details before the young man, he smiled and said, "Well, I guess I might as well tell the truth." His confession then followed.

Tries to Bribe Servant.

Although Dr. Waite admitted that he had no evidence to support his story, he attempted late yesterday afternoon, after making his confession, to prepare a defense for himself by bribing Dora Hillier, the negro servant, formerly employed in his apartment, to testify that she knew of Mr. Peck's desire to commit suicide, according to District Attorney Swann. Mr. Swann said that Dr. Waite had given Raymond C. Schindler, the private detective employed by the dead man's son, a check for $1,000 made to the order of the servant. Mr. Schindler reported the Doctor's bribe to the District Attorney.

The District Attorney charges no culpability against either Dr. Muller or the druggist, both of whom acted in good faith. Dr. Waite told them that he wanted arsenic to kill a cat and they believed him. They have given valuable assistance to the District Attorney.

Still weak from the powerful drugs which he took on Wednesday, Dr. Waite was removed from his apartment last night to the prison ward in Bellevue Hospital. One reason for his removal was fear that he might attempt suicide by jumping from a second story window near his bed. The prisoner denied that he had sought to destroy himself with the drugs he took on Wednesday, but he said yesterday that he wished they had killed him. Those who have watched and interviewed him in the last two days are convinced that his real motive in taking the drugs was suicide.

Mother Ill of Grief.

Mr. and Mrs. Warren W. Waite, the parents of the prisoner, arrived from Grand Rapids late yesterday afternoon. They obtained afternoon newspapers on the train before reaching New York, and learned thus for the first time of their son's confession. Mrs. Waite was overcome by the news, and by the time the train arrived in the city she was so nearly prostrated that it was impossible for her to go to see her son. Frank A. Waite, a brother of Dr. Waite, who is chief of the division of information at the Public Library and who lives at 3,210 Hull Avenue, the Bronx, met his parents and, observing the condition of his mother, hurried with them to his home, where Mrs. Waite was placed under the care of a physician. The elder Mr. Waite and his son then went to Bellevue Hospital.

Mr. Waite, senior, who is a commission merchant, is a tall, robust man who, though gray headed from years, shows strong character in his heavy, deeply lined face. When he was at the hospital he presented the picture of a strong man bewildered and almost crushed by an overwhelming disaster. He was almost speechless with amazement at what his son had done, and deeply moved with concern for his "boy."

He and Frank Waite waited for half an hour after applying to see Dr. Waite, and then the authorities at the hospital told them that they could not see the prisoner, as the District Attorney had given orders that no one was to be admitted to him without written permission.

"But I want to see him only to cheer him," pleaded the father.

The authorities regretted, though, that they must obey orders.

Mr. Waite then expressed concern over his son's health, and asked anxiously if "the boy" was in a dangerous condition. He was assured that Dr. Waite would recover, and he seemed greatly relieved.

When asked about his son's case Mr. Waite, speaking as one entirely uncomprehending, said:

Must Believe in Son.

"I know nothing except what I have read in the newspapers, and I simply can.

Continued on Page 4.

Channel Liner Sussex Mined or Torpedoed; All on Board, Including Americans, Saved

Special Cable to THE NEW YORK TIMES.

LONDON, March 24.—The steamship Sussex, one of the London, Brighton & South Coast Railway Company's cross-Channel fleet, came to grief off Dieppe today while on the Folkestone-Dieppe service, but it is understood that all the passengers and the crew were saved. She was outward bound from Dieppe under the French flag. It is understood that the Sussex was torpedoed.

News of the disaster was at once communicated by wireless to the French coast and every available vessel in Dieppe harbor was dispatched to her assistance. A message received late tonight said the vessel had been towed into a French port.

According to officials at the railway company's offices there were 386 passengers aboard the Sussex, which also carried a French crew of about fifty men.

The Sussex at the time of the attack was about three hours out from Folkestone. There were thirty American passengers aboard. The great majority of the passengers—some 70 per cent., it is estimated—were women and children, comprising chiefly returning Belgian refugees.

By The Associated Press.

LONDON, March 24.—Reports reached London this afternoon that the Sussex, a channel boat playing between Folkestone and Dieppe, had been torpedoed and there was grave fear that many lives had been lost, for the vessel carried a large number of passengers.

Several of the dispatches were conflicting and confusing, and alarm continued until the Brighton Railroad, which operates the boat, issued this statement late tonight:

"The Sussex, sailing under a French flag in the Folkestone-Dieppe service, met with a mishap somewhere off Dieppe on her passage today. There were 386 passengers aboard and a crew of about fifty, but it is impossible at present to give further particulars, nor is the passenger list available. At 8:30 o'clock this evening the vessel was still afloat in charge of a tug. It is assumed, therefore, that all the passengers were saved."

Fear of mines and torpedoes has caused special precautions to be taken by Channel boats during the last few days. Owing to their light draught, it has been generally believed that they were safe from torpedoes.

These boats make the trip from Folkestone to Dieppe in four hours and ten minutes, but for the last fortnight they have been sailing with the tide in order to increase their speed. The Folkestone-Dieppe route is one of two routes still open to travelers going to Paris and points beyond, and is mainly used by neutrals.

At both the American Embassy and the Consulate General there were rumors that the Sussex had been torpedoed, but neither had received any details.

There were thirty Americans aboard the Sussex, which left Folkestone yesterday shortly after noon in clear weather. The vessel proceeded without incident until 4:20 P. M., when she was struck amidships as she was approaching the coast of France. A terrific crash followed and several hands in the engine room were badly injured. Wireless messages brought help from both sides of the channel and all the passengers were rescued.

Lloyd's received a report tonight that the steamer Englishman of the Dominion Line had been sunk. It is stated that thus far sixty-eight survivors have been accounted for.

The British steamship Fulmar, 1,270 tons, also has been sunk. Eighteen of her crew were rescued.

Still another Danish steamship has been sunk—the Christianssund, 1,017 tons. Her entire crew of twenty-two was saved.

The Norwegian steamer Blaaklakken was torpedoed in the North Sea a week ago while on a voyage from England to Norway, according to a Copenhagen dispatch to the Exchange Telegraph Company. Four survivors were picked up half unconscious off the Doggerbank by the Norwegian steamer Activ and were landed at Copenhagen today. The other members of the crew are believed to have perished.

HAUCOURT TRENCHES TAKEN BY GERMANS

French Salient Is Narrowed by Heavy Pressure of the Foe West of the Meuse.

HILL 304 UNDER HOT FIRE

Germans Pour Shells from Three Sides on Eminence Which Is Key to the French Position.

LONDON, March 24.—By continued pressure in the hotly contested region near Malancourt, west of the Meuse, the German troops have won two more trenches west of Haillmont, according to the official bulletin of the German headquarters staff.

Paris does not mention any such loss, but the evening bulletin of the French War Office tells of the intense artillery fire which is being directed against the woods of Malancourt and Avocourt, just to the westward.

Closely connected with the operations in this region is the activity in the Eastern Argonne, only a few miles to the west. Here French guns were showering shells on German lines of communication today, and here, too, there was a brisk encounter at Vauquois, where the Kaiser's troops rushed in after a French mine explosion and occupied a first-line trench, but were later driven out.

A Berlin dispatch gives a clear picture of the situation west of the Meuse and of the crucial importance attached on the German side, at least, to Hill 304, the highest eminence in the Malancourt-Bettincourt region. The dispatch says:

"The capture of Avocourt Forest and Hill 287, northeast thereof, still further menaces the French salient on a line running along the southern slope of Dead Man's Hill northward to Bethincourt and thence southwestwardly.

"The new German position in Avocourt Forest not only enables them to direct a more effective flanking fire against the French to the east, but also makes it more difficult for the French to oppose the German advance to the south of Dead Man's Hill.

Hill Under Flanking Fire.

"The strongest French position commands Hill 304, but this already lies under flanking artillery fire on three sides, as does the whole line of their rear communications as far as Esnes.

"Hill 304, however, despite its exposure to flanking fire, is difficult to take. Its steep slopes are wooded more or less heavily, with the exception of a few hundred yards on the northwest. Its capture by the Germans, judging by a close study of military maps, would make untenable the whole French position north of a line drawn from Dead Man's Hill and passing south of Hill 304 to Avocourt.

"The summit of Hill 304 is four miles from Fort de Bois Bourrus, and five miles from Fort de Marre. It is nearly 100 meters in altitude above Verdun."

The statement by German Army Headquarters is as follows:

The violence of the artillery duels increased considerably at times in the Champagne, on the Somme-py-Souain high road and in the Argonne, and in the Meuse district as far as the Moselle.

Following up our successes of Wednesday, we occupied another couple of trenches west of Haucourt. On this occasion the number of prisoners increased to 32 officers and 879 men.

The afternoon bulletin of the French War Office says:

In the Argonne district our batteries last night cannonaded with energy the enemy positions in the wood of Malancourt. Near Hill No. 285 we caused the explosion of a mine and occupied the resulting crater.

To the west of the River Meuse the night passed quietly.

To the east of the river there was intermittent bombarding in the vicinity of Douaumont and Damloup.

In the Woevre district there have been some outbursts of artillery fire in the sectors of Moulainville and Eparges, both sides taking part.

There has been no other development of importance on the rest of the front.

The night bulletin of the French War Office reads:

In the Argonne, following the explosion of one of our mines at Vau-

Continued on Page 3.

ROOSEVELT RETURNS; SILENT ON POLITICS

Says Wilson's Mexican Policy Has Resulted as He Predicted It Would.

BAILED HIS OWN STATEROOM

And Discovered a Queer Cave-Dwelling Bird, Which Humboldt Found Before Him, in 1799.

After a stormy voyage during which the seas were so high at one time that he had to bail the water out of his stateroom with a bucket at 2 o'clock in the morning, Colonel Theodore Roosevelt got back to New York last night on the steamship Matura from his trip to the West Indies.

Although political leaders are agreed that he tossed his hat into the ring again by a statement issued at Port of Spain recently, the Colonel said that he must refuse to talk politics "for the present." He took another jab at the Wilson Administration because of the situation which has developed in Mexico, and then turned the conversation to the discussion of zoology. The fact is that the Colonel believes he has discovered a new species of bird which, however, Alexander von Humbolt seems to have discovered before him, about 1799.

Colonel Roosevelt never enjoyed better health in his life than he did last night as he stood in the smoking room of the Matura and discussed Mexico and his trip with the newspaper men who had met him at quarantine. He looked in every way fit for the strenuous political campaign that leaders believe is ahead of him, despite his refusal to discuss that possibility. His only reference to his Port of Spain statement was that he had meant every word he said and just what he said.

The return of the Colonel was arranged carefully so that there would be no attempt at a public demonstration. The only person who went down the bay in the revenue cutter to meet him, aside from the newspapermen, was his secretary, John W. McGrath, and representatives of the Collector's office. There was no one at the pier in South Brooklyn, not even George W. Perkins, Chairman of the Executive Committee of the Progressive Party, who returned yesterday from Stuart, Fla. All this was by the Colonel's request, made in a wireless sent on Thursday.

Volley of Questions Aimed at Colonel.

The moment the newspaper correspondents found the Colonel there was a volley of questions about politics and the developments in Mexico. They elicited this statement, which he dictated:

"I am not prepared to make any statement on politics at present, or on the international situation, beyond referring you to what I said in the book I published six weeks ago called 'Fear God and Take Your Own Part.' If you will turn to the chapter on Mexico you will see that everything I then said, and have for the last three years been saying, applies exactly to the present situation, and that all I said in prophecy has been made good by the event.

"And I call your special attention to what I said as to furnishing arms and munitions to one set of bandits in order to help them against another set of bandits instead of helping Uncle Sam against all of them. And I also call your attention to what I therein said as to the effect of adhering to the policy of refusal to prepare and of being too proud to fight. What I said in that volume needs no elaboration now, and exactly applies.

"I have greatly enjoyed my trip through the West Indies, and I am more impressed than ever with those islands and with Demerara as tourist resorts and with their industrial future. I wish to express my deep appreciation of the courtesy and hospitality with which the officials and the private citizens in the French, English, and Danish islands received me.

"I was immensely struck by the enthusiastic loyalty with which the people of the French and English islands had come forward to the aid of the mother country in this war. The islands have sent to the front or have in training to send to the front between 20,000 and

Continued on Page 5.

RING CLOSING IN ON VILLA AT EL OSO; PERSHING'S TROOPS USING RAILWAY; BANDIT TURNED BACK FROM PASSES

Obregon Declares Villa Will Soon Be Taken; Is Rushing More Mexican Troops to Front

Special Cable to THE NEW YORK TIMES.

QUERETARO, Mexico, March 24.—General Obregon, Minister of War, announced today that the bandit Villa was located three days ago in the town of Namiquipa, in the mountains of Western Chihuahua, where he was attacked by the Constitutionalist forces under direct command of General Benjamin Garza. This battle has been raging for the last three days and many reinforcements have been sent to the scene.

General Obregon expresses faith in the ultimate victory of the Constitutionalists, as they have enough troops already upon the ground, or rapidly arriving, to surround the Villistas.

Full details are anxiously awaited by Government officials, who are hoping for the speedy capture of Villa, which will do away with the danger of friction which could be caused by the presence of American troops upon Mexican soil. Officials say that while things are at present satisfactory, yet every day that foreign troops are in Mexico adds to the danger of a clash, which may be forced by the enemies of the Government, who are spending money lavishly to force intervention.

MEXICO CITY, March 24.—Villa is surrounded and cannot possibly escape, according to a message received tonight by the Minister of War from General Luis Gutierrez. The message adds that General Gutierrez's troops are spread out fan-shape in front of Namiquipa and that the General has divided his forces into four commands under General Benjamin Garza, General F. Cabasos, Colonel Hernandez, and Colonel Cano, for the purpose of hemming in Villa and his followers from the four points of the compass.

American Troops on Eve of Battle

SAN ANTONIO, Texas, March 24.—General Pershing's report to General Funston that two columns of his expeditionary forces were in the vicinity of Namiquipa, a town 120 miles southeast of Casas Grandes, and repeated reports from Mexican sources that Villa, with a comparatively small force, had been forced to a stand at El Oso, near there, has caused officers here to expect news at any time of a battle. General Funston thinks it probable a fight already may have occurred.

Consul Beltran of the Mexican Government said he received a message late today from Consul Garcia, at El Paso, saying confirmation had been received of the report that Villa had been defeated yesterday in the Santa Gertrudes Canon by the American and Mexican forces and that he had fled to El Oso, five miles from Namiquipa, where he was surrounded.

The Consul added that one of the American officers with the expeditionary forces had reported to General Pershing that they would attack Villa today.

DECIDES AGAINST CALLING MILITIA

Cabinet Studies Mexican Situation and Concludes More Troops Are Not Needed.

RESENTS ALARMIST STORIES

Lansing Blames Interventionists and Is Expected to Make a Formal Statement Today.

Special to The New York Times.

WASHINGTON, March 24.—President Wilson and his Cabinet canvassed the Mexican situation at their session today, considering especially the question whether there was need for calling out the National Guard for duty on the border. It was decided that there was no necessity for using the Guard at this time, as it was felt that to call volunteers or send the National Guard to the border might be misconstrued by Mexicans and prove an embarrassment to the Carranza Government. General Funston has not asked for additional troops since the Fifth Cavalry and the Twenty-fourth Infantry were ordered to join him.

What were regarded as evidences of activity of powerful influences to force intervention in Mexico through the spreading of alarmist reports were discussed at today's Cabinet meeting, and resulted in the preparation of a formal statement on the subject by Secretary Lansing, which will probably be made public tomorrow.

The Secretary of State said frankly today:

"I believe a large part of these stories originate in the minds of interested persons who desire intervention."

He added that they could have no other purpose than to inflame the minds of the Mexican people.

Administration officials in general believe that a definite effort is being made to bring about war between the United States and Mexico. One Cabinet member expressed the opinion, following today's meeting, that the attempts to force intervention were backed by interests owning property in Northern Mexico. Well defined steps were being taken, he said, to stir up public opinion in Mexico and the United States to the point where a clash between the two nations would be inevitable.

Several warnings against spreading alarmist reports have already been issued by Administration officials, and it was stated tonight that President Wilson, deeply resentful over the situation, was determined that the agitation should be brought to an end. Legal steps to stop the spreading of false news are under consideration, it is said, but officials have not decided yet what can be done.

In private conversation officials condemned the spreading of unfounded reports at "this critical juncture," when the Government was endeavoring to enter into a working arrangement by means of a protocol to further the sole purpose of the expedition into Mexico—the capture of Villa and the dispersal, if not the capture and punishment, of his band of outlaws.

Officials showed particular irritation today over the persistent report from the border that General Herrera, a Carranza chieftain, had revolted.

One dispatch said that General Bell, commanding the infantry brigade at El Paso, had sent a dispatch to Funston "confirming" the report of Herrera's alleged revolt. The War and State De-

Continued on Page 3.

INVASION TALK AROUSES STONE

Senator Says American Interests Are Trying to Bring On War with Mexico.

ALSO SEES POLITICS IN IT

Lewis Describes as Traitors Those Americans Who Would Aid Villa.

Special to The New York Times.

WASHINGTON, March 24.—Senator Stone of Missouri, Chairman of the Committee on Foreign Relations, today charged that interests in and out of Mexico were trying through false reports to force the United States to extend the expedition in search of Villa into a general invasion of Mexico. Turning angrily on the Republicans, Mr. Stone added that some of them were seeking political advantage by forcing a debate on Mexican questions. He had just come from the State and War Departments, he said, and any one could see that the situation in Mexico was critical and should not be further ruffled by public discussion.

The debate in the Senate was unusually bitter and personal. Mr. Stone used sharp language in characterizing the Republican course in the Senate, even denouncing particular Senators for attempting to force debate that would further emphasize the acute situation below the Rio Grande. But the debate, he deprecated, was really occasioned by a resolution introduced by the Democratic whip, Mr. Lewis of Illinois, describing as traitors any Americans selling or furnishing supplies to Villa. The debate was continued mostly by Mr. Stone, and it was brought to an end by Mr. Oliver of Pennsylvania, a Republican.

Mr. Lewis's resolution follows:

Whereas, It is known to the authorities of the United States that funds and supplies are being furnished to the force and following of Villa in Mexico from foreign countries and from sources in the United States of America; and,

Whereas, Such supplies and sustenance are being delivered for the purpose of being used against the soldiers of the United States:

Therefore, be it resolved, by the Senate of the United States, That those who are furnishing such supplies and sustenance to the forces of Villa for the purpose of opposing the United States are the enemies of the United States, and those in the United States who are furnishing supplies and sustenance to the said Villa and his forces, either of money or provisions, arms, and ammunition, are within the provisions of the laws of the United States defining treason as giving aid and comfort to the enemies of the United States;

Be it resolved, further, That those in the United States who are giving such support, affording supplies, ammunition, and aid to the Villa forces against the soldiers of the United States are guilty of indirect treason within the meaning of the law against the sovereignty of the United States and its authority.

Mr. Borah of Idaho, a Republican, who has indorsed President Wilson's course in ordering the pursuit of Villa, then had read a telegram from D. A. Richardson of Douglas, Ariz., addressed to Senator Fall of New Mexico, who was absent. Several other Senators from the Southwest had received identical telegrams, and Mr. Ashurst of Arizona said afterward that he knew Mr. Richard-

Continued on Page 3.

END OF PURSUIT IN SIGHT

El Paso Expects Outlaw Will Be Captured in Two Days.

AVIATORS SCAN MOUNTAINS

Pershing Springs Surprise by the Rapid Distribution of His Columns.

REPORTS NEAR NAMIQUIPA

More Soldiers Are Arriving at the Border, with Autos—New Radio Station.

Rumor of Three Americans Murdered Near Boundary

DOUGLAS, Ariz., March 24.—Three Americans, two women and one man, were killed near Gibson's Line Ranch, on the Mexico-New Mexico boundary line, eight miles west of Columbus, N. M., between 4 and 5 o'clock Wednesday afternoon, presumably by Mexicans, according to a story brought here by a party of five Douglas residents, who said they arrived on the scene shortly after the bodies had been removed by soldiers.

Samuel Collins, automobile dealer; Mr. and Mrs. Russel, T. W. Childers, Miss Lottie Milinowski, and Edward Freeman, who made up an automobile party, told of the alleged killing. The names of the persons said to have been killed were not learned. They said that at Hermanas a railroad section foreman told them he had seen through binoculars a mounted band of 100 or more men cross the border near the ranch and ride to a water hole a mile and a half north. After watering their horses they rode back across the line. He added that within a short time troopers of the Twelfth Cavalry had gone to the ranch house and moved about in an excited manner. The automobilists proceeded to the ranch, and they were guarded at the house all night by seven troopers, who had arrived in response to an alarm given when the bodies had been found.

The soldiers, according to the motorists, said the bodies had been found in an automobile near the ranch, but they did not know what disposition had been made of them.

Special to The New York Times.

EL PASO, Texas, March 24.—A ring of United States troops is tightening around Francisco Villa and the remnants of his bandit band. It is expected here tonight that he will be captured within the next two days and that the American troops will be marching out of Mexico within another week.

That was the information an American brought here from Casas Grandes today. Unknown to people on the border, General Pershing's troops have penetrated into the heart of the Guerrero district using trains on the Mexico North Western, and troops have been distributed throughout the entire district south of Casas Grandes and on both sides of the Sierra Madre.

The American who came out today reported that General Pershing has been using the Mexico North Western Railroad south of Casas Grandes to Madera for more than a week. Trains have been sent regularly between Casas Grandes and Cumbre Tunnel, and troops and supplies have been taken over the mountain on a switchback railroad which has been built since the Cumbre Tunnel was fired by Maximo Castillo and blocked with falling rock and débris of burning trains.

Advancing East and South.

The troops have been sent as far south as Temosachic and even to Matachic in their efforts to hem in Villa, and have been working east and southeast toward Namiquipa, Santa Ana, and the other settlements on the eastern slope of the Sierra Madre.

Co-operating with General Pershing's column has been Colonel George A. Dodd, with his field artillery and cavalry. He went down the Galeana road through Galeana City, El Valle, Las Cruces, and to Namiquipa, where he is believed to be co-operating with the Carranza forces.

Villa is reported to be in El Oso Cañon, where he made his stand and escaped from the Carranza troops three months ago, before he appeared at Santa Ysabel and ordered Pablo Lopez to commit the Santa Ysabel massacre. El Oso is five miles southeast of Namiquipa, on the trail toward Santa Clara, where General Pablo Bertani last night reported he had met and defeated Villa and his men with a loss of men and horses.

The news that the fugitive has turned sharply to the southeast of Namiquipa and apparently abandoned his plan to go west over the Sierra Madre at Babricora trail into the Babricora country tends to verify the American's report that General Pershing's cavalry column is in the Madera-Babricora country and that Villa did not dare risk a flight over the mountains in that direction, but chose the southeastern course, following

"All the News That's Fit to Print."

The New York Times.

THE WEATHER.
Fair, slightly warmer Thursday; Friday, fair, warmer; moderate winds, becoming south.
For full weather report see Page 22.

VOL. LXXI....No. 23,411. NEW YORK, TUESDAY, FEBRUARY 28, 1922. TWO CENTS In Greater New York | [illegible]

NEW TRANSIT BILLS GIVE HYLAN'S POWER TO THE STATE BOARD

Would Let Three Commissioners Serve on Control Body Instead of His Appointees.

PLAN HAS MILLER'S BACKING

Intended to Block Obstruction by the City in Test of Consolidated System.

EFFECTIVE FOR ONE YEAR

Mayor Could Then Name Appointees as Already Provided—Other Traction Law Changes Sought.

Special to The New York Times.

ALBANY, Feb. 27.—George McAneny, Chairman of the Transit Commission, had a conference with Governor Miller this afternoon, at which they discussed amendments to the Public Service Commission act.

A bill embodying the amendments was introduced at the session tonight by Senator William T. Simpson of Kings County and Assemblyman George N. Jesse of New York.

One of these amendments takes from the Mayor the right, conferred in the present plan for consolidating the New York traction lines, of naming three members of the proposed Board of Control of seven, and permits the three members of the commission, if they so elect, to act as members of the board. This is the most drastic of the amendments and the one that will draw the most opposition from city officials.

Under the consolidation plan made public on Sept. 29 the board was to consist of three members named by three operating companies and three by the Mayor, the six men to name a Chairman. If they could not agree, the Chairman was to be named by the commission. This right is not disturbed by the amendment, but the law, as proposed, would vest the three members of the commission with the right to serve on the board, remaining Transit Commissioners with the power to name a Chairman. This would give the commission four votes in the board.

Could Serve First Year.

The amendment limits the term of Commissioners on the board to one year. The Mayor then would have the power of naming three men to fill their places. Under the plan the five-cent fare must continue for a year. The purpose of placing the Commissioners in absolute power was to assure a fair test of the plan, it was said, as it was feared that representatives of the city would not act in accord with the other members.

It was explained at the office of the commission that the Commissioners might find it possible to serve on the board through appointment by one of the operating companies. But such a turn to the situation is not expected, and the purpose of the amendment is to place in the hands of the commission full control.

Chairman McAneny said in a statement that if the amendments were adopted the name of the control body should be the Board of Transit Control, and that it should have authority to issue bonds and other evidences of indebtedness; to hold stock and securities of subsidiary operating corporations; to supervise and control the management and operation of the railroads included in the plan, and all other authority necessary to make these powers effective.

The amendments provide that if title to the railroads is to be vested in the city the title shall first pass to an intervening corporation, which would be the board of control.

Control of Companies.

A further provision directs the commission to file with the Secretary of State a certificate of incorporation, granting the right to operate future extensions to the rapid transit systems. A further right conferred by the amendment reads:

"The Board of Transit Control may provide in the certificates of incorporation of such companies that the right to elect Directors thereof shall be vested in others than the stockholders in accordance with the conditions and stipulations contained in the contract and contracts or modifications of contracts executed under or in pursuance of the plan of readjustment.

"Every such corporation shall have power, in addition to the powers conferred by the general and stock corporation laws, to exercise all of the powers of the railroad companies whose properties have been, as in this act authorized, vested in the city and leased to such subsidiary operating companies, and all of the powers conferred by the railroad law, being Chapter 49 of the consolidated laws, and by Chapter 4 of the laws of 1921, as amended."

The next important amendment deals with the fare problem. The general provisions of the act of last year are amended so as to provide that the right, in any contingency, "to change, or authorize a change, in the rate of fare hitherto fixed either by contract, franchise or otherwise, shall apply only to such companies or such individual roads as may be included in the commission's plan of readjustment."

It was explained that this amendment eliminates all hope of present or future increase of fare for any roads not included in the plan. In other words, any company which refuses to join the proposed consolidation will not benefit by any possible increase allowed roads which have joined. The latter can be

Continued on Page Four.

Wilson Says Democrats' Time To Serve the Country Is Near

FORT WAYNE, Ind., Feb. 27.—Confidence that the "time is at hand when the Democrats will have an opportunity to serve the country," was expressed by former President Wilson in a letter to Claude G. Bowers, in response to a message sent to him on behalf of the Indiana Democratic Editorial Association by Mr. Bowers.

Mr. Wilson's letter read in part:

"It is very delightful to be associated with such a fighting and forward looking force as the Democrats of Indiana. I wish I had the opportunity to assure them of my confidence that the time is just at hand when the party will have an opportunity to serve the country in more ample measure, and with more lasting benefit than ever before."

BITTER ENDERS START ATTACK ON TREATIES

Johnson Leads in Denouncing Agreements—Calls Yap "Dismal Prologue."

ALL REPORTED TO SENATE

Glass Indicates That Wilson Is Taking No Part in the Controversy.

Special to The New York Times.

WASHINGTON, Feb. 27.—Lively attacks by "irreconcilables" upon the Yap treaty, the Four Power Pacific treaty, the "secrecy" of the arms conference and the alleged plans of the majority leaders to "jam through" the seven treaties and agreements resulting from that international gathering, were conspicuous features of today's Senate session.

The outburst coincided with the formal report from the Foreign Relations Committee of the seven treaties and agreements, but it centred mainly about the Yap treaty, which was the subject before the Senate.

In the course of a violent assault upon the agreement made with Japan relative to Yap and other mandated islands of the Pacific, Senator Johnson of California bluntly styled the treaty a "dismal prologue" of what is to come—"the initial bluff and first surrender."

Senators Reed of Missouri and Robinson of Arkansas joined him in the onslaught.

The majority leaders had originally planned to prolong the session until the Yap treaty was disposed of, but after hours of debate it was finally agreed this evening to postpone the final vote until 2 P. M. on Thursday.

Wilson Not Interfering.

One encouraging event of the day's session to the friends of the conference treaties was a statement by Senator Glass of Virginia, which was taken to mean that ex-President Wilson had not taken any part in the controversy and would not do so.

Senator Glass, who is one of Mr. Wilson's closest friends, told the senate late today that he has seen Mr. Wilson but once, and then only for a moment, in the last three months and that not a word passed between them regarding the treaties resulting from the arms conference.

The Virginia Senator, when recognized by the chair, said:

"Being a newspaper publisher myself, I very rarely take notice of the mistakes which commonly, and inevitably, are made with respect to public matters, because I readily understand how easy it is to make mistakes in the rush and hurry of a daily paper's routine; but there appeared yesterday in The Washington Herald a statement to this effect:

"'Senators Glass and Robinson, Democrats, are considering the advisability of attempting to organize Democratic opposition and hold the twenty-nine in line. Glass has recently had a talk with Woodrow Wilson and is said to have brought back word that the former President remained firm in his decision not to fight the treaty openly. Wilson opposed it, however, Glass was reported by Democrats to have told them.'

"That is the purest invention that ever appeared in a public print. I

Continued on Page Three.

MONDELL PROPOSES TO DELAY BONUS TILL FUNDS APPEAR

House Leader After Seeing Harding Favors Waiting for Clearer Skies.

COUNTS ON BRITISH BONDS

Admits President Is Against No-Revenue Bill — Longworth Says He Would Veto It.

MACNIDER USING PRESSURE

Sees Fordney and Will Confer With Harding Today—Insists Bill Must Be Passed.

Special to The New York Times.

WASHINGTON, Feb. 27.—In spite of assertions that President Harding would veto any soldier bonus bill that did not carry a revenue raising provision, the Republican members of the Ways and Means Committee went ahead today with preparations to report the bill in such form.

Representative Longworth expressed the opinion that formal action would be taken at the meeting tomorrow of the majority members to consider the subcommittee's report. He said he believed that if Congress passed the bonus bill without a revenue provision it would be vetoed.

Later, after a visit to the White House, he asserted that the President still felt that bonus legislation should include a sales tax or be postponed.

Apparently formal action by Congress on the whole proposition is to be delayed. The plans of the Republican leaders seem to be to wait until Senator Smoot and Representative Burton are confirmed by the Senate as members of the Debt Funding Commission and then to have the commission proceed with all dispatch to endeavor to obtain the British bonds, which are expected to result from the funding operations, so that they can be used to pay the bonus.

Chairman Fordney and Representative Mondell, the Republican House leader, conferred with President Harding this morning. Later Mr. Mondell said:

"The President would certainly not be pleased by the passage of a bill which made no specific provision for revenue. Everyone realizes, he thinks, that is the thing that should not be done.

"The country in the main has been for the bonus. Let us analyze the situation. The country in the main for the last two years has been for the bonus, either enthusiastically or indifferently. There has been very little active opposition to it. A number of members took a decided opposition to the bonus two years ago, but they were not sustained or supported by their constituents.

Says Country Favors a Bonus.

"In the meantime, local bonus bills were approved. Every man who wanted to be popular was peddling the bonus whether he was selling oil stock or running for corner, and either directly or inferentially a great majority of the members are pledged to adjust compensation. Not only men who talked openly, but those who have been carefully guarded in their statements said that the sentiment of their districts was for the bonus.

"Some people, who are finding it difficult to raise the money, are writing letters to me and marking them confidential and private. There are some, but not so many who are publicly announcing their opposition. Many are keeping an anchor to windward. Congress was elected by a people, a majority of whom expected a bonus bill and this Congress has been made to feel so obligated and is disposed to pass a bonus bill.

"The situation of meeting the payments is a trying one, as most of the plans proposed for raising the money have not met with general approval. We are still hoping for some little gap between expenditures and income. If the general conditions of the country improve we have every reason to believe, in the not distant future, the income will increase under operation of present revenue laws. In the near future we can secure funds through the sale of foreign securities. Taking that into consider-

Continued on Page Fourteen.

German Armament Secrets Sold to Japan; Seven Germans Tried for High Treason

BERLIN, Feb. 27.—German military and naval secrets of much importance have come into the hands of Japanese Government agents, according to information which has reached authoritative circles in Berlin. Among these are processes for the manufacture of star shells, the formula for a contact fuse which the Germans used advantageously for range finding when time-exploding fuses were unsatisfactory, and "certain submarine plans and naval secrets which have been betrayed, to the detriment of the German Empire."

For the theft of these submarine plans and other secrets, which took place several months ago in Kiel, at least seven Germans have been tried for high treason secretly before the Leipsic court, and four of them received sentences of from seven months to one and a half years' imprisonment. Four of the convicted men were former German officers; the others were employes of a well-known German manufacturing firm which filled huge war orders.

The trials, which were held last December, gave no indication that the Japanese Government was concerned, but reports in the hands of responsible diplomatic officials in Berlin say: "The defendants attempted with some success to dispose of their information to the Japanese Embassy in Berlin." It was added that "for the good of the German Empire it was necessary that the trials should be secret."

Complaint is heard in German industrial quarters that with the secrets already in the hands of the Japanese, through the seizure of many German patents during the war, the Germans are greatly handicapped commercially. Warning to the Japanese that they must have "care for German rights" has been issued from what is described as "an important high industrial circle."

MORSE, WITH 3 SONS, 8 OTHERS, INDICTED

Accused of a Conspiracy to Defraud the United States and Fleet Corporation.

THIRTY "OVERT ACTS" CITED

Morse Says Daugherty Has Bias Against Him, but Lasker Says Case Is Ship Board's Alone.

Special to The New York Times.

WASHINGTON, Feb. 27.—The Grand Jury for the District of Columbia returned indictments today against Charles W. Morse, his three sons and eight others, charging conspiracy to defraud the United States and the United States Shipping Board Emergency Fleet Corporation in connection with war contracts made by a number of so-called Morse companies.

The indictments follow investigations begun last Summer by the Shipping Board which resulted last December in Morse's arrest on a conspiracy charge and release under $30,000 bail.

Two true bills, each containing two counts, were filed with Chief Justice McCoy of the Supreme Court of the District of Columbia. One of the indictments charges that the twelve defendants conspired to defraud the United States in violation of Section 37 of the Criminal Code, while the other bill charges conspiracy to defraud the Emergency Fleet Corporation in violation of Section 35 of the code.

List of Men Indicted.

Along with Morse, all the indicted men were connected with shipbuilding companies in which Morse was interested—the Groton Iron Works of Groton, Conn.; the Virginia Shipbuilding Corporation of Alexandria, Va., and the United States Transport Company, Inc. They include the financier-shipbuilder's sons, Erwin A., Benjamin W. and Harry F. Morse, who, with their father, were Directors of the three shipping companies; George M. Burditt of New York, an attorney for the three corporations; former Judge W. W. Scott of Washington, who was attorney for the Virginia yards; Nehemiah H. Campbell of New York, Director of the Groton Iron Works and Assistant Treasurer of the United States Transport Company; Rupert M. Much, President of the United States Transport Company and Assistant Treasurer of the Virginia Shipbuilding Company; Richard O. White of New York, Assistant Treasurer of the Groton Iron Works and later President of the United States Transport Company; Colin H. Livingston of Washington, national head of the American Boy Scouts, who was President of the Virginia Shipbuilding Corporation; Leonard D. Christie of Washington, Treasurer of the Virginia Shipbuilding Corporation, and Philip Reinhardt of Baltimore, former auditor of the Emergency Fleet Corporation.

The contracts between the Emergency Fleet Corporation on the one side and the Groton Iron Works and the Virginia Shipbuilding Corporation on the other are said to involve $40,000,000. No estimate is made in the indictment of the full amount which the defendants are charged with having misappropriated, and Fletcher Dobyns, assistant to the Attorney General, who has handled the case from the start, declined after the indictments were returned to set any figure.

William G. McAdoo Mentioned.

One feature of the indictments is mention of the names of William G. McAdoo, former Secretary of the Treasury, and Stuart C. Gibboney of Barber & Gibboney, 165 Broadway, New York, who are alleged to have conveyed statements to Shipping Board officials concerning the excellent financial condition of the Virginia Shipbuilding Corporation. Although it states that Messrs. McAdoo and Gibboney acted as lawyers for the corporation, the indictment does not charge them with having knowledge of the alleged falsity of their representations to the Emergency Fleet Corporation.

Before he left for New York this afternoon, Charles W. Morse gave out a statement declaring that his indictment was "terribly unjust," and that it was due to the personal animosity of Attorney General Harry M. Daugherty. Morse stated that Daugherty acted as one of his attorneys in securing his release "in a dying condition" from the Atlanta Federal Penitentiary, and that the Attorney General harbored resentment against him on account of a disagreement over fees.

Attorney General Daugherty took no notice of the Morse statement, and no comment was made upon it by officials of the Department of Justice. A. D. Lasker, Chairman of the Shipping Board, declared, however, that the Attorney General had no part in the case against Morse, which, he said, was

Continued on Page Twelve.

RECEIVER FOR FOUR MORE BROKER FIRMS

Prosecutor to Start Magistrate's Inquiry Into Cotton Trading on Thursday

DIER APPLICATION IS DENIED

Court Allows Examination of Books—Grand Jury Gets More "Bucketing" Evidence.

Three more brokerage firms, Mosher & Wallace of 33 Broadway, Gamble & Yates of 82 Broad Street and Shewry & Falkland of 198 Broadway were thrown into involuntary bankruptcy yesterday, and one firm, C. W. Starbuck & Co., of 20 Broad Street, made an assignment for the benefit of its creditors. This increased the number of brokerage firms which have failed in the last five business days to fourteen.

District Attorney Joab H. Banton announced that he would start a John Doe inquiry into trading in cotton before Chief Magistrate William McAdoo at the Criminal Courts Building on Thursday. The inquiry will start with an investigation of the American Cotton Exchange and some of its members, and will be public, in accordance with the request of officials of the Exchange.

Judge Learned Hand of the United States District Court denied the application of Elmore D. Dier for an injunction to restrain the District Attorney from examining the books of E. D. Dier & Co., now in bankruptcy, in connection with complaints against the firm which have been received at the District Attorney's office. There were said to be two complaints against Dier & Co., and Mr. Banton said he would direct an examination of the firm's books at once.

Printers Sign Petition.

The petition against Mosher & Wallace, who were said to be members of the New York Curb Market Association, was signed by Charles D. Gilbert of the Gilbert-O'Farrell Printing Company, who presented a claim of $911. Judge Hand appointed Louis B. Wehle of 111 Broadway receiver, under bond of $30,000.

The petition declared that the firm, which is composed of William J. Mosher and Forrest W. Wallace, has liabilities of $175,000. The quick assets were estimated at $150,000, and there were said to be in addition "frozen" assets of considerable value. The failure was said to have been precipitated by the failure of other brokerage firms and "general unrest and lack of confidence." Saul S. Myers, attorney for the creditors, said that no charges of "bucketing" had been made against the firm.

Claims aggregating $5,450 were filed against Gamble & Yates by the three petitioning creditors, Stephen U. Hopkins, Marie E. Dow and Charles Witson. The firm is composed of Henry P. Gamble and George Stiles. Ben A. Matthews of 2 Rector Street was appointed receiver. The liabilities were estimated at $70,000, and the assets at $20,000. Olcott, Bonynge, McManus & Ernst are attorneys for the petitioning creditors. Gamble & Yates maintained an uptown branch at 587 Fifth Avenue, and were said to have many women customers.

The petitioner against the firm of Shewry & Falkman, composed of Charles W. Shewry and Donald Falkman, was the Peerless Quality Company with a claim of $516. The liabilities were estimated at $60,000 and the assets at $26,000. Henry B. Singer was appointed receiver. Saul S. Myers is attorney for the creditors.

The assignment of C. W. Starbuck & Co. for the benefit of its creditors was to Nelson M. Cooper of 247 West 104th Street. The partners in the firm are Calvin W. Starbuck and Frederick W. Wright and Edward Stetson of 140 Nassau Street is attorney for the assignee. The estimate of assets and liabilities was not disclosed in the assignment.

Wants Receiver Restrained.

Judge Hand signed an order directing Earl B. Barnes, receiver for Thomas H. Cowley & Co., which went into bankruptcy on Saturday, to show cause why he should not be restrained from disposing of certain securities that have come into his possession as receiver. The order was granted on petition of Henry L. Erney, who claimed ownership of 3,000 shares of Mexican Railway preferred and 200 shares each of Interborough Rapid Transit and Santa Cecilia Sugar.

District Attorney Banton's decision to conduct a John Doe inquiry into methods of trading in cotton was the result of a visit of officials and attorneys of the American Cotton Exchange, against which two complaints have been filed, in addition to complaints against several members. In the delegation that called on Mr. Banton were A. [illegible] Graham, President of the American Cotton Ex-

Continued on Page Five.

LINDSAY, INDICTED AS ARCH CROOK, CAUGHT NEAR PHILADELPHIA

Promoter Denounced by Women as $1,000,000 Swindler Jailed at Ardmore.

BROUGHT HERE EARLY TODAY

Prisoner Says He Has Been Lied About and Will Straighten Things Out.

MONEY IN HIS WIFE'S NAME

N. J. Fitzsimmons, Who Mobilized the Victims, Thinks Losses Can Be Recovered.

Special to The New York Times.

PHILADELPHIA, Feb. 27.—In a room he had occupied since Thursday at the fashionable Green Hill Farms apartment, Overbrook, Alfred E. Lindsay, for whom a nation-wide search was begun by the New York authorities on the charge of fleecing prominent New York women of upward of $1,000,000, was arrested tonight about 8 o'clock. He was traced to the apartment house where he was in hiding with his wife, through evidence obtained by a Pennsylvania Railroad detective, who turned up checks for trunks of Lindsay at his various stops since he disappeared, and turned over the information to the authorities.

Lindsay and his wife were registered at the Green Hill Farms as "A. R. Brooks and wife." None of the guests, many prominent socially, knew of their presence, as they took all their meals in their room. They were there when Detective Roddy of New York and Captain James I. Donaghy of the Ardmore police came to the hotel tonight in search of them. A head waiter was sent to knock on the door of their room and ask for the dishes.

"I'm in bed and the dishes were taken out a half hour ago," said a man's voice from inside.

The head waiter persisted, but the man repeated his refusal to let him in. The New York detective and Captain Donaghy then took a hand.

"You'll have to open the door," they said, "you're Lindsay and we want you."

"You're mistaken, men," he said as he opened the door. "I'm not Lindsay."

The police insisted that he was. Then he said: "Well, I might as well come along with you. A lot of people have been lying about me, and I guess I might as well see the thing out. I thought I had some friends, but they've all jumped out on me and left me alone. I'll straighten it out all right."

Lindsay was taken out of a side door of the hotel quietly and hustled to the Ardmore Police Station in an automobile. Since Lindsay left New York with his wife it was said they had stopped at the Robert Treat Hotel, Newark, N. J., where Lindsay registered in his right name, and from there to the Shoreham, in Washington. They left Washington last Thursday afternoon for Philadelphia and went to the Bellevue-Stratford. They then went to the Green Hill Farms Apartments on the western edge of the city. Lindsay tonight waived extradition and left for New York at midnight.

Arrives in New York.

Lindsay arrived at Pennsylvania Station at 2:30 o'clock this morning, in the custody of Detective Sergeant William Roddy of the New York police force. He rode in the rear sleeper of the train from Philadelphia and was not handcuffed to the policeman.

Assistant District Attorney Richard J. Murphy and Detective Sergeant Daley were awaiting the prisoner on his arrival. Mr. Murphy ordered the detectives to take Lindsay to the District Attorney's office downtown immediately, so that he could be questioned without loss of time regarding the charges of women that he swindled them out of enormous sums of money.

Mr. Murphy expressed surprise that Detective Roddy had not brought back Lindsay's wife, who accompanied him on his flight to Philadelphia. He asked where she was, and Roddy replied that he had left her in the apartment house in Overbrook, where Lindsay was arrested. Murphy said he would telegraph to Philadelphia to have Mrs. Lindsay put under surveillance.

Lindsay was calmly smoking a cigar when reporters at the Pennsylvania Station asked if he had any comment to make on the charges against him. "I have nothing to say," was his reply. Detective Roddy said his prisoner made

Continued on Page Seven.

Ex-Kaiser Is Hard Up, He Says, Refusing a Donation

Copyright, 1922, by Chicago Tribune Co.

BERLIN, Feb. 27.—"I am hard up and confining myself to the necessities of life."

The Association of War Veteran Cripples received the foregoing in a letter from former Kaiser Wilhelm in reply to the cripples' request for the Kaiser to send a donation. Instead of a donation the Kaiser sent a photograph of himself in the uniform of a Field Marshal, which action did not cause any particular joy to the cripples.

In explaining his failure to inclose a check, the Kaiser declared that living in Holland was terribly expensive, as he received his income from Germany, and he only got 1 guilder for 30 paper marks. Therefore, he had discharged most of his servants and restricted his table and he had no money left for charity.

HARDING TO PROPOSE SHIP SUBSIDY TODAY

Will Address Congress on Plan to Extend Aid of About $50,000,000 a Year.

$30,000,000 TO BE DIRECT

Raised by Diverting 10% of Customs Duties—Other Steps to Support Merchant Marine.

Special to The New York Times.

WASHINGTON, Feb. 27.—President Harding will appear in person before Congress tomorrow with a message outlining the Administration's recommendations for legislation extending Government aid to American shipping.

His message will embody the essential features of a report that has been made by United States Shipping Board experts who have spent the Winter studying the problem. This report was completed early this month and has been carefully gone over by the President, who has had a number of conferences on the subjects with Chairman Lasker of the Shipping Board.

From unquestioned sources it has been learned that the President will urge:

1. The direct appropriation from the Treasury of 10 per cent. of the customs duties, which, under the present estimated returns, will yield $30,000,000 for 1923.

2. The creation of a $125,000,000 ship construction loan fund, the Shipping Board being empowered to loan as much as two-thirds of the total cost of building a ship of approved type at a rate of interest of 2 per cent.

3. Relief from corporation taxes to the extent of 5 per cent. to firms consigning their imports and exports to American vessels.

4. The appropriation of all the revenues, derived from port and lighter charges, to a fund, from which retainers to the extent of $3,000,000 will be paid officers and men, enrolled in the United States Naval Reserve, which is to be created.

5. The allowance of a higher depreciation charge to shipowners than now is permitted by the Treasury Department in making out income taxes and other exemptions to steamship companies in taxation.

6. The broadening of the Shipping Board's powers in making sales, so that the board will be permitted to sell steamers at the world's market prices, without taking into account the replacement value or the original cost of production.

The indirect aids, which President Harding will recommend, will include:

1. The enforcement of Section 21 of the Merchant Marine act of 1920, by virtue of which the Shipping Board will restrict the granting of preferential rates on exports to those commodities to be shipped overseas in American vessels.

2. The enforcement of Section 28, by which the coastwise laws will be extended to the Philippines.

3. The passage of legislation requiring 50 per cent. of immigrants from maritime countries and all of the immigrants from non-maritime countries to embark on ships of American registry.

4. Granting specific permission to railroads to own ships operating in all foreign trades.

5. The assurance that the army and navy transport services will be discontinued when private interests establish adequate sailings.

It is estimated that subsidizing the merchant marine will result in a cost of about $50,000,000 a year upon the Treasury.

Legislation providing for the direct and indirect subsidies has been prepared un-

Continued on Page Three.

LONDON BEGINS FETE ON EVE OF WEDDING OF PRINCESS MARY

Sightseers and Holiday Makers Watch for a Glimpse of Bridal Couple.

CHEERED AS THEY APPEAR

Princess Limits Decorations' Cost, but Triumphal Arches Are Erected.

RECEIVES WANAMAKER GIFT

Ambassador and Mrs. Harvey to Be Only Americans Officially Present in Abbey.

Copyright, 1922, by The New York Times Company. Special Cable to THE NEW YORK TIMES.

LONDON, Feb. 27.—London gave itself up today, in preparation for Princess Mary's wedding tomorrow, to sightseeing and holiday making. All day long before Buckingham Palace crowds waited for a chance to see the bride and thronged around her when she drove out.

Along the route of the procession, and especially near Westminster Abbey, the crowd was so thick that omnibuses, motor cars and other wheeled traffic moved only with the greatest difficulty. People of all classes and all ages were out to see the preparations, and they came in numbers that surprised the police and put business out of gear.

It was a spontaneous demonstration, and the evident loyalty on the part of such an enormous proportion of the population which it expressed is likely to give pause to those people who, it is understood, have been considering the possibility of making trouble in the West End of London tomorrow. Various reports have been current regarding a projected demonstration of the unemployed, but whatever grounds there may or may not be for them, it is certain that the authorities are well prepared to deal with any attempt to cause disorder.

Lascelles Eludes Crowd.

The centre of interest today was naturally Buckingham Palace. For a week past little groups of people have been continually gathered outside the gates, hoping to see the King, Queen or Princess drive out. Today the crowd had swelled to considerable size. Some had come prepared for long vigils with stools, flasks and sandwiches, apparently expecting to be able to sit there all night. They were keenly interested in the smallest happenings within the palace court.

Lord Lascelles came to pay his regular morning visit to his betrothed, but he was too old a campaigner to be caught. He passed safely through the spectators' lines, having hired an ordinary taxicab and made his own big automobile follow immediately in its wake. The crowd saw the taxicab and turned from it in disdain. It surged toward the motorcar ready to cheer, but found it empty, and turned back just in time to see the tall figure of Lord Lascelles disappearing into the palace.

That disappointment was partly atoned for by the stream of visitors who came to the palace, and after a few words with the policemen at the gate were admitted. Many of them were coming to make presentations of gifts, for even today Princess Mary was obliged to give up several hours to a reception of deputations. Much interest was shown in a couple of working girls who had come unannounced and were permitted to cross the courtyard to leave their person present at the palace door.

Soon after noon a real thrill came. A big automobile was seen to leave the inner court of the palace and make for the main gate. Could it possibly be true that the Princess was really coming out? It was asked. With one impulse the crowd left its position and surged forward. The police ran hastily and tried to form a cordon on each side of the gate. The crowd paid no attention to them and pushed forward. It had caught sight of the Princess. She was there with Lord Lascelles and a lady in waiting. The very thing the crowd had been waiting for all those weary hours was happening and what were police to them; they just shoved the police to one side and dashed at the motorcar.

The car came to a standstill and for a moment or two the Princess was surrounded by a cheering, shouting throng. She leaned forward smiling and bowing, blushing as well, while Lord Lascelles, who seemed to be much amused, kept raising his hat. In a minute or so the police had forced their way around the car, and, holding on to it while they shoved back the people, they cleared a way for it to proceed to St. James's Palace.

When the Princess came back half an hour later the police were better prepared and the approach to Buckingham Palace was kept clear.

In the afternoon the last of the pre-wedding receptions was held. It was of a special character, being intended largely for farmers and other tenants of the King's and the bridegroom's estates. A number of the tenantry from the Harwood estate in Yorkshire, who have known Lord Lascelles from boyhood, were invited and were presented to the Princess, who is to live among them.

Whitehall, and Westminster Abbey were other places which drew the densest crowds. Along Whitehall the Government offices were hanging out their flags and placing scarlet, blue and gold cloths on their window sills. New flags had been placed on the cenotaph and stands were being rushed up in front of many of the shops.

More formal decorations had been confined to Parliament Square on which the houses of Parliament and Westminster Abbey are situated. Princess Mary had let it be known that she [illegible] with a great amount of [illegible]

Americans to Help Excavate Carthage; Body of Hannibal to Be Sought First

Copyright, 1922, by The New York Times Company. Special Cable to THE NEW YORK TIMES.

PARIS, Feb. 27.—A number of Americans and Frenchmen interested in archaeology have formed a project to undertake extensive excavation and restoration work on the site of the ancient City of Carthage.

The leader of the movement, Francis Byron Kuhn, who has already approached the French authorities, has obtained their sanction, and has also succeeded in interesting several French archaeologists and American residents of Paris, who are attracted by the artistic and historic importance of the scheme. The father of the plan is really the French savant P. Renaud, who for many years lived among the ruins of Carthage and gave all he possessed to his dream of restoring the wonderful Phoenician capital. He died there without seeing the fruits of his life's work, which are now to be gathered by others.

A preliminary expedition, starting out in the middle of March to examine the ground, will take photographic films. It will include, besides Mr. Kuhn, Miss J. Osborn, daughter of Professor Henry F. Osborn, the American explorer and geologist; Fred Singer, commercial attaché of the American Embassy in Paris, and Mrs. Singer; the Marquis d'Estailleur de Chanteraine, a young French writer, who recently returned from a diplomatic mission to Syria; Lieut. Col. Simmons and J. McLeod. The archaeologists in charge will be Father Delattre and Dr. Carton, who have spent most of their lives in Carthage.

It is planned subsequently to organize a lecture in the United States to show the films taken with a view to raising funds to carry out the excavation and restoration work. According to French law, archaeological finds become the property of the French Government, but the authorities have promised a percentage of all that is found in Carthage in order to enable donations to be made to American universities and museums.

The gain to the world from the historic point of view will be great if the plan is successfully carried out. The first work to be undertaken this Spring will be to search for the burial place of Hannibal, who lies buried in his armor among the public tombs.

Few sites are of fuller romantic interest than the ancient African port. It was there that St. Louis of France died. One cannot hear the name of Carthage without thinking of Dido, Hasdrubal and Hamilcar. It was there also that St. Cyprien, St. Maurice and St. Perpetua were martyred in the early Christian days, while the story of St. Augustine is closely linked with the city, from which venturesome trading ships sailed forth to the four corners of the earth.

Four Killed, Many Wounded, in Mexico City As Police Battle With Striking Chauffeurs

MEXICO CITY, Feb. 27 (Associated Press).—Four persons were killed and many wounded this afternoon when the police fired on a crowd of striking chauffeurs who were holding a demonstration in front of the City Hall. Two of those killed were chauffeurs and two policemen.

The chauffeurs called a strike this morning owing to a disagreement over the issuance of licenses and held numerous parades. They assembled in front of the National Palace shortly after noon, at the moment when Miguel Alessio Robles was being sworn in as Secretary of Commerce and Industries.

The police at first fired over the heads of the chauffeurs, but when the chauffeurs charged they fired point blank at the advancing men, two of whom were killed outright, while a score of others were wounded. The chauffeurs then retreated behind statues in the plaza, maintaining their fire, which resulted in the death of two policemen.

During their rush on the police the chauffeurs captured several swords and took them to the National Palace and delivered them to the Presidential Guard with great ceremony.

Desultory firing continued for more than an hour. It eventually was silenced when President Obregon, from the National Palace, sent out officers ordering a cessation of the sniping.

Virtually every electric light in the Zocalo was shot out during the fighting and business houses adjacent to the scene closed down. The Zocalo was crowded with people incidental to the swearing in of Señor Robles, and it is considered remarkable that only four persons were killed during the hour's hostilities.

The chauffeurs continued their demonstrations during the afternoon.

"All the News That's Fit to Print."

The New York Times.

THE WEATHER.
Fair, slightly warmer Thursday; Friday, fair, warmer; moderate winds, becoming south.
For full weather report see Page 22.

VOL. LXXI....No. 23,517. NEW YORK, WEDNESDAY, JUNE 14, 1922. TWO CENTS In Greater New York | THREE CENTS Within 200 Miles | FOUR CENTS Elsewhere

GOLD COINS MINTED BY CROESUS FOUND IN RUINS OF SARDIS

Greatest Archaeological Discovery in Ten Years Is Made by American Scientists.

METROPOLITAN MAY GET 15

Half the Priceless Treasures, Dating Back to 546 B. C., Sought for Museum Here.

DUG FROM AN ANCIENT TOMB

Believed Hidden There by a Rich Man When King Cyrus Was Warring on Lydia.

Thirty gold coins belonging to the first series of gold coins ever minted have been unearthed by American archaeologists who are working on the buried ruins of Sardis, the ancient Lydian capital in Asia Minor. Fifteen of them may come to the Metropolitan Museum of Art.

They are of the coinage of Croesus, the last King of Lydia and the first great international banker, whose name has been a symbol for wealth for nearly 2,500 years.

The coins were minted some time between 561 B. C., when Croesus ascended the throne of Lydia, and 546, when he was captured by Cyrus, the Persian king. Some of the thirty "staters," as they are called, are as bright as new-minted pieces of United States gold money. They are lighter in hue, as they are of pure gold.

Before this find, which is considered one of the greatest archaeological discoveries in many years, there were only five "staters" known to be in existence. Four of these were so rubbed and worn that the lion's head and bull's head were nearly effaced. One was in good condition. These five are in the British Museum.

News of this discovery was brought to the United States by Dr. T. Leslie Shear, an archaeologist of Columbia University, one of the members of the expedition who were present at the discovery. Other members of the party were Mrs. T. Leslie Shear, an authority on ancient painting and decorative work; W. R. Berry, E. R. Holden, an architect; Edward Stoever, engineer of the party; Cyrus McCormick of Chicago and his son, Gordon McCormick, an architect. The work is under the direction of Professor Howard Crosby Butler of Princeton, who arrived at Sardis after the discovery was made.

Many other interesting relics of the Lydian, Greek and Roman periods of the ancient capital were discovered.

Hidden During Siege by Cyrus.

The thirty pieces of gold, which was probably an enormous fortune in the days of the first gold currency, are thought to have been hidden by some wealthy Lydian in 546 while Sardis was besieged by Cyrus. They were found in a tomb.

Some of the coins were a little rubbed, indicating that they had been in circulation a few years. The fresh-minted condition of some of them makes it almost a certainty that they were fashioned late in the reign of Croesus.

The wealth of the Lydian Kings has been celebrated at length by Herodotus. The source of the gold is supposed to have been the River Pactolus, which flows through the kingdom. King Midas washed "the golden touch" from himself into this river and impregnated the sands with the noble metal before he had shaken off the curse of automatic transmutation. Some historians have discredited the theory that the Pactolus region was rich in gold and have argued that the undoubted wealth of the kingdom was due to its foreign trade. It is believed by the explorers of the site of Sardis that the riches of the kingdom were due to mineral wealth and to its geographical positions, which made it the greatest trading centre of the time.

The Lydian kings were forced to become the great international exchange bankers of the time, because their kingdom lay across the old Royal Road of trade from Persia, Babylon and all the Orient to the Greek cities, and probably to Egypt and other Mediterranean cities.

Croesus not only coined gold but adjusted his system of coinage to a convenient exchange basis with the silver and copper coins of the Greeks in the west and the Babylonians and other Orientals on the east. His father and predecessor, Alyattes, had made coins of electrum, an alloy of gold and silver, but the final step to put the kingdom on a gold basis was taken by Croesus.

During the fourteen-day siege of Sardis, ending in its capture by the Persians under Cyrus, some wealthy Lydian merchant or banker probably concealed his wealth in the little clay pot nine inches high in which it was found among the scattered fragments of a tomb.

Buried by Earthquakes.

Sardis, which many American and European archaeologists have pronounced to be the most promising site for archaeological research in the world, is for the most part deeply buried. Its famous acropolis of ancient times was a clay mountain, which has been shaken to pieces by earthquakes and washed down over a large part of the ancient city, preserving it, much as Pompeii was preserved. Such of the splendid architecture of Sardis as was not thus sealed up has been gnawed down to the foundations through the later centuries by degenerate inhabitants of Sardis who used the temples and monuments as stone quarries to supply materials

Continued on Page Three.

'Dead Beats' Becoming Fewer, Retail Credit Experts Say

CLEVELAND, June 13.—"Dead beats" are rapidly disappearing, according to members of the Retail Credit Men's National Association in annual convention here.

"The female of the dead beat species used to be more deadly than the male," Mrs. Verne Zimmerman, a credit manager, said. "The increasing number of women in business, education in the value of prompt payment and a credit rating are eliminating the thoughtless woman buyer."

"Neither men nor women buy luxuries as they did during the war and in the after-the-war flurry," George A. Law of Memphis, Tenn., former President of the association, said. "It is a combination of education and co-operation that is eliminating the bill-jumper."

$1,000,000 INCOMES DROP FROM 65 TO 33

1920 List Shows Number of Incomes of $1,000 to $2,000 Increased by 500,000.

1,927,184 RISE IN RETURNS

Net Incomes Reported Advance $3,876,137,735 Over 1919, but Taxes Fall $194,576,418.

WASHINGTON, June 13.—The preliminary statistics on personal incomes in 1920, made public tonight, show that only 33 persons reported incomes of $1,000,000 or more, as compared with 65 in 1919 and 67 in 1918. The falling off in large incomes reported, due to heavy investments in tax exempt bonds and declining profits, was further emphasized by the statement that the 33 net incomes of over $1,000,000 in 1920 totaled but $77,078,139. The comparative totals of net incomes of $1,000,000 or more for 1919 and 1918 were $152,650,245 and $137,486,892, respectively.

The high-water mark in net incomes of $1,000,000 or more reported came in 1916, when there were 206, aggregating $464,263,644. In 1917 the number had dropped to 141 with a total of $306,835,914.

The preliminary report does not supply the details as to the classification of incomes of $1,000,000 or more. Information of this kind will be presented in the final report to be rendered later.

While the number of those in the larger classes of income dropped heavily, the number of returns for smaller incomes rose sharply, increasing with each lower classification. Returns for incomes between $1,000 and $2,000 increased by more than 500,000 over 1919.

In commenting on the 1920 income conditions, Commissioner Blair said in his report:

"The number of personal returns filed as of the calendar year ended Dec. 31, 1920, was 7,250,944. The total amount of net income reported by these returns was $23,735,629,183 and the tax (normal tax and surtax), amounted to $1,075,053,686. As compared with 1919, the above figures show a growth of 1,927,184 in the number of returns filed and an increase in the total net income reported amounting to $3,876,137,735, but a decrease of $194,576,418 in the total tax. The average net income per return for 1920 was $3,269.40, the average amount of tax $148.08, and the average tax rate 4.53 per cent."

An interesting table in the report shows the growth of taxable income covering several years. The figures for 1920 and 1919 are here given:

NUMBER OF RETURNS.

Income Classes.	1920.	1919.
$1,000 to $2,000	2,671,950	1,924,872
2,000 to 3,000	2,569,316	1,569,741
3,000 to 5,000	1,337,116	1,180,488
5,000 to 10,000	455,442	438,851
10,000 to 25,000	171,830	162,485
25,000 to 50,000	38,548	37,477
50,000 to 100,000	13,002	13,320
100,000 to 150,000	2,191	2,983
150,000 to 200,000	1,003	1,864
200,000 to 500,000	239	425
500,000 to 1,000,000	122	180
1,000,000 and over	33	65
Total	7,250,944	5,332,760

The distribution by States and Territories is taken up in the report. New York State shows the largest total, the returns numbering 1,047,694, the net income $4,030,622,696, the amount of tax $284,607,280 and the percentage of the total tax 26.65.

Income reported by the various States for 1920 was as follows:

Alabama	$156,894,922
Alaska	19,480,775
Arizona	87,290,486
Arkansas	119,980,716
California	1,329,006,394
Colorado	219,277,154
Connecticut	451,727,792
Delaware	56,482,321
District of Columbia	206,386,174

Continued on Page Two.

RALPH WARD DEFIES GRAND JURY; FACES JAIL FOR CONTEMPT

Brother Refuses to Tell Conversations He Had With Confessed Slayer of Peters.

WILL BE RECALLED TODAY

Prosecutor to Ask Court to Compel Witnesses to Answer Questions About Blackmail.

4 OTHERS GIVE TESTIMONY

George Ward, the Father, Located in Pennsylvania—Two Called to Tell of Race Track Deals.

Ralph D. Ward, brother of Walter S. Ward, refused to tell the Grand Jury at White Plains yesterday what his brother and his father, George S. Ward, had told him about the shooting of Clarence Peters. His refusal caused the Grand Jury to adjourn until 10 o'clock this morning and sent Frederick E. Weeks, District Attorney of Westchester County, hurrying into a conference with Justice Morschauser, who has charge of the Grand Jury.

Ralph Ward will be recalled today. He faces jail if he persists in his refusal to answer questions. Mr. Weeks will get an order compelling the witness to testify, and then will ask again what the father and brother told him. If Ralph still refuses to answer, Justice Morschauser undoubtedly will commit him to the Westchester County jail for contempt of court.

If Ralph Ward can be made to talk, the prosecuting authorities hope to learn at last the real reason why his brother shot Peters and the real basis for the alleged blackmailing plot that led to the shooting. He is one of the two persons who should know the facts. The other is his father, George S. Ward, who slipped out of New York State and who cannot now be reached by a subpoena.

Father in Williamsport, Pa.

The father was discovered yesterday in Williamsport, Pa., where is a litigant in a civil suit in the United States District Court. He refused to say when or whether he would return to New York, or to answer any questions regarding the Ward death mystery.

Ralph Ward followed the example of Walter S. Ward's wife in refusing to answer important questions before the Grand Jury. If he follows the wife's example under the ruling of the Court, however, he will answer every question today. Under Justice Morschauser's ruling that she must tell everything that was not privileged as a confidential wife, she gave up her attempt to protect her husband and answered the questions. Ralph Ward as a brother has no privilege whatsoever.

The first witness heard after the Grand Jury convened at 10 o'clock yesterday morning was George W. Sutton of New Rochelle. Mr. Sutton is a neighbor and political ally of Ward. He lives at 60 Decatur Road, Sutton Manor, across the street from Ward, and is Commissioner of Assessment and Taxation. He was in the Grand Jury room only fifteen minutes.

Mr. Sutton testified, presumably, to what happened in the Ward house on the night of May 15. His testimony was favorable to Ward if it conformed to what he had previously told reporters. According to his newspaper statements, Sutton went to a moving picture show early on the evening of May 15, and did not reach the Ward house until after 10 o'clock. He remained until about 1 o'clock, playing poker. Ward was not present while he was in the house, nor did he see or hear anything out of the ordinary, Sutton told reporters.

Swiss Governess Is Called.

Miss Irme Ziegler, a Swiss governess, was the second witness. She was said to have been questioned about conversations she overheard at the breakfast table in the Ward home on May 16 and later.

Before going to the stand, Miss Ziegler told a reporter she was in Canada when she learned that the Wards needed a governess for their two children. She was employed about three days before the shooting and remained until June 1. According to her statement, Miss Ziegler once heard Ward say, "I couldn't do anything else." This was after the story of the shooting became known.

Miss Ziegler could not recall the wording of other remarks made by Ward to Mrs. Ward, but thought their general tenor supported his version of the shooting. She knew nothing of what time Ward came home on the morning of May 16, nor of his condition.

Miss Ziegler is now employed at the home of Martin Taylor, a New York lawyer, in Nissequogue, L. I.

Following Miss Ziegler's testimony,

Continued on Page Fourteen.

Mlle. Lenglen May Not Face Mrs. Mallory; Health Poor; American Champion Skeptical

LONDON, June 13 (Associated Press).—The English lawn tennis world is perturbed over the report from Paris that Suzanne Lenglen, for two years the holder of the women's grass court championship, has developed heart trouble and her family is insisting that she withdraw from the coming championship tournament at Wimbledon. There has been much enthusiasm over a possible meeting at Wimbledon between the French girl and Mrs. Molla Bjurstedt Mallory, the American woman singles champion, who since coming to England has rounded into form and now is playing at the top of her game.

Mrs. Mallory has been keenly anticipating another meeting with Mlle. Lenglen, and today, when she learned the news from Paris, she said:

"I am extremely disappointed over Mlle. Lenglen's failure to defend her title. I am skeptical regarding her recent statement saying how much she wants to play me again. I don't think she is ready to face me again across the tennis net."

Mrs. Mallory is said to have come to Europe especially with the hope of having another match with the French star, and only after Mlle. Lenglen had definitely declared she would play through all the championship rounds. Much sympathy has been extended to Mrs. Mallory in her present disappointment over again facing Mlle. Lenglen.

In the Kent tennis championship at Beckingham Mrs. Mallory has had two comfortable wins in the early rounds. Her first strong opponent will be Mrs. Peacock, former champion of India, in the fourth round of the singles. Mrs. Peacock recently defeated Miss Elizabeth Ryan of California and Miss McKane and Mrs. Beamish, two sterling British players.

$92,000 in Stock Certificates Stolen; Missing Messenger Sought at Coney Island

The theft yesterday of stock certificates worth $92,000 from Clark, Childs & Co., brokers, at 165 Broadway, became known last night.

A messenger left the firm's offices with the certificates and has not been seen since. Detectives are scouring the city for the missing man, and ferries and railroad stations were under strict watch all night.

This latest echo from the epidemic of bond robberies which occurred in Wall Street two years ago is being held as secret as possible by the police and by members of the firm itself. It was said by the Lieutenant on the desk of the Old Slip Police Station, in whose precinct the firm has its offices, that no report of the robbery had been made there. Charles A. Morse, a partner in the firm, who lives at the Great Northern Hotel, declined to discuss the robbery, saying that he "had heard nothing" of it.

The firm of Clark, Childs & Co. is a member of the New York Stock Exchange, has branches at the Hotel Belmont and the Murray Hill. They were formerly located at 135 Broadway, but moved to their present address about a year ago.

In the Fall of 1919 the firm lost heavily through dishonest messengers. On one occasion a man named Parnell, who had been with the company just one day, was entrusted with two Crucible Steel stock certificates worth $45,000. He started with them for Harriman & Co. and was never seen again. The certificates were recovered by private detectives after they had been put up as collateral against a loan for $25,000 with the National Savings and Trust Company of Washington, D. C.

About the same time representatives of the New York District Attorney's office found that Clark, Childs & Co. had been robbed of 100 shares of Baldwin Locomotive stock worth $14,300. This stock was likewise recovered.

It was learned that a private detective agency of international reputation had been called in to further the efforts of Police Headquarters in the case. Detectives from this agency made a hurried trip to Coney Island on a tip that the missing messenger had been last seen there.

CHARGES RACE SLUR AT NAVAL ACADEMY

Sutherland Calls Attention of Senate to Indignity Against a Jewish Midshipman.

SLIGHTED IN CLASS VOLUME

Name Omitted From Index and Page Bearing Sketch Is Unnumbered and Perforated.

Special to The New York Times.

WASHINGTON, June 13.—Senator Sutherland of West Virginia this afternoon called the attention of the Senate to an alleged indignity committed by the graduating class at the United States Naval Academy at Annapolis against Leonard Kaplan, one of the graduates. Kaplan, Senator Sutherland said, was of Jewish extraction, and he attributed the indignity of which he complained to racial and religious prejudice.

The slight put upon Kaplan, according to Mr. Sutherland's explanation to the Senate, was in perforation of the inner margin of the last page of the book of the graduating class, known as "The Lucky Bag," this page containing a photograph and a short sketch of Kaplan, the apparent object of the perforation being to suggest that the page could be torn out without defacing the volume, a very handsome and expensive publication, printed on fine paper and with sketches and photographs excellently reproduced. The photographs of all the members of the graduating class are contained in the book, each with a short biographical sketch containing ironical comment on the chief characteristics of the graduate.

Kaplan's name is omitted from the index to the biographies. There are two sketches to the page. On the page with Kaplan's photograph and biography, which is termed "an autobiography" in the book, is a crudely drawn picture of a fictitious member of the graduating class designated as "Porky," of whom it is said that he was "born in the Township of Zion, County of Cork, State of Ignorance, Sunday, the 17th day of March, 1900."

To Ascertain the Facts.

Senator Sutherland called attention to the incident by having one of the Senate clerks read an editorial article from The Washington News, headed "The Cruelty of Youth," which told the story of the perforated page of "The Lucky Bag." There was a short debate devoted in part to discussing whether the authorities of the Naval Academy were in any way responsible for the publication of "The Luck Bag." Nobody was able to shed any light on that subject, but Senator Sutherland said he intended to ascertain the facts. Senator King of Utah suggested that the case should be brought forward again in the Senate when the Naval Appropriation bill was under consideration.

When the article from The Washington News had been read, Senator Sutherland said:

"I cannot too strongly criticise the circumstances which have been set forth in the article which has just been read at the Secretary's desk. It relates to a boy from my State by the name of Leonard Kaplan, who is of Jewish extraction. Throughout the four years of his career at Annapolis, young Kaplan has maintained a very high standing; in fact, I understand he was very near the head of his class which has just been graduated; but because of his nationality, he has been subjected to a refinement of cruelty such as has been set forth in this article. It appears that his biography was printed on a page by itself, which was unnumbered, and perforated along the line of the binder in such a way that it could be torn from the yearbook of the academy for the current year, 1922, so that those who wished to do so could tear off the page containing this boy's biography without defacing the book."

When Senator Pomerene of Ohio asked whether "The Lucky Bag" was published by the authorities of the Naval Academy or the graduating class, Senator Sutherland said that it was printed by the midshipmen, but he declared that "a course of training that will permit such a condition of affairs to exist in one of our governmental schools, indeed, in any school in this country, discriminating against a man who has maintained such high standing, and subjecting him to such treatement as has been indicated, is utterly un-American and cannot be too scathingly condemned."

Thinks Authorities Responsible.

Senator McCumber of North Dakota said he believed the authorities of the Naval Academy were responsible for the book. He could not conceive, he said, of any system which would permit such

Continued on Page Two.

UNTERMYER THREAT FORCES CURB TO QUIT

Governors, Facing Grand Jury Inquiry, Withdraw Steel Merger Stock From List.

CANCEL ALL TRANSACTIONS

Lawyer Says Stock Exchange Should Ask Kuhn, Loeb & Co. to Dissolve Syndicate.

On the eve of the beginning of a Grand Jury investigation this morning into the circumstances surrounding the listing of the stock of the North American Steel Company on the curb market, the Board of Governors of the New York Curb Market Exchange held a special meeting late yesterday afternoon and took belated action on the ultimatum of Samuel Untermyer demanding that they cease transactions in the stock on a "when, as and if issued" basis.

The Board of Governors, under threat of felony and misdemeanor indictments, making those concerned liable to imprisonment for two years or a fine of $5,000 or both, cancelled and annulled all past dealings in the stock involving approximately 70,000 shares valued at $3,500,000, and struck it from the list, withdrawing all further dealings until after the corporation shall have been organized and a complete statement of all details shall have been made by the company and approved by the Listing Committee of the Exchange.

The announcement caused Mr. Untermyer to ask when the Stock Exchange would ask Kuhn, Loeb & Co., bankers for the merger, to dissolve the syndicate formed to market the stock, intimating that early action might save the Stock Exchange from trouble.

The action was taken following a conference between District Attorney Joab Banton and Mr. Untermyer.

Fifty Subpoenas Issued.

Directly the conference concluded fifty subpoenaes were issued returnable at 11 A. M. today before the Grand Jury. Process servers were sent out and, according to reports, had served some of the subpoenaes when hurried consultations were called by the committees of the Curb Exchange and messengers were sent for members of the Board of Governors. A majority of the board responded and a meeting was held.

W. A. Lockwood of Rumsey & Morgan, counsel to the Curb Association, it is understood, explained the situation to the Curb members. The Governors then reversed their stand of Monday when they informed Mr. Untermyer that they would continue to permit trading in the stock of the three-company steel merger on a "when, as and if issued" basis.

The following announcement, signed by A. B. Sturges, Secretary of the curb association, was made public:

"At a special meeting of the Board of Governors held June 13, 1922, the following resolution was unanimously adopted:

"Resolved, that the privilege to deal in the securities of the North American Steel Company that was granted by the Listing Committee on June 2, is hereby withdrawn. No further dealing in the stock 'when issued' or otherwise will be permitted until after the corporation has been duly organized or until the amount in terms of its capitalization and all other details have been settled and a complete statement thereof has been filed with and approved by the Listing Committee.

"All past dealings in the stock will be canceled and annulled except where, after the due organization of the corporation and the issuance of its stock, the transactions heretofore made are confirmed and approved in writing by the parties thereto."

Will Not Press Charge.

On learning of the action of the Board of Governors Mr. Untermyer said:

"What a pity these Stock Exchange men will never take disinterested, well meant advice except under pressure or until it is too late. Just see what a lot of unnecessary trouble they have caused me in bringing them to time.

"The instincts of common honesty should have prompted them to realise that any law student, by reading the penal code, could have told them that in authorising gamblings on their Exchange in a blind pool in this phantom stock they were doing an unethical and unlawful act.

"Now, with the permission of Judge Giegerich and the Grand Jury, and with the assent of the District Attorney, I shall refrain from further pressing the charge if all past dealings are canceled and annulled, the stock stricken from the list and future dealings prohibited, unless, when my back is turned an attempt is made to revive the game. In that event there will be some one here

Continued on Page Six.

GEORGE W. ALDRIDGE DIES AS HE GOLFS AT WESTCHESTER CLUB

Collector of Port, 65, and Seemingly Hale, Stricken With Apoplexy.

SINKS WITHOUT A WORD

Charles D. Hilles and George Sweeny Near Rochester Leader as Death Comes.

ENDS PICTURESQUE CAREER

Last Survivor of Big Three, Including Platt and Hendricks—Body to Be Taken Home Today.

George W. Aldridge, Collector of the Port of New York and long one of the big Republican figures of the State, dropped dead yesterday on the golf course at the Westchester-Biltmore Country Club near Rye.

Mr. Aldridge was 63 years old. In December, 1920, he had been near death with pneumonia in his Rochester home, but his recovery appeared to have been complete. He was apparently in rugged health and his spirits were excellent, when, in the act of driving, his grip on his club suddenly relaxed and he reeled and fell to the turf.

George Sweeny, President of the Hotel Commodore, was at Mr. Aldridge's side. He knelt a moment over the motionless figure, then called to Dr. Ira Hill of New York, who was playing a foursome at another part of the course. Dr. Hill said death had been instantaneous. Dr. Elmer L. Pennock, Health Officer of Harrison, who was summoned, pronounced death due to apoplexy and issued the death certificate. The body then was removed to W. H. Graham's undertaking rooms at Rye. It will be taken today to Rochester for burial. George W. Aldridge Jr., a son, who was notified by telephone, drove to Rye to make the arrangements.

Mr. Aldridge had motored to the country club in the afternoon with Charles D. Hilles, Republican National Committeeman from New York; Ralph A. Day, Prohibition Commissioner for New York State, and Mr. Sweeny, to participate in a hotel men's golf tournament.

Hilles Notifies Family.

It was just at 4:30 o'clock, while the contest was in full swing, that near-by players saw Mr. Aldridge totter and sink to the ground without a word. Mr. Hilles and others soon surrounded him. It was Mr. Hilles who summoned his son and who sent word to his widow in Rochester. Before the National Committeeman had left the clubhouse he had received a telegraphed reply from Rochester that James L. Hotchkiss, one of his closest friends, was starting for Rye to take the body home. Mr. Hilles promptly notified the National Republican Club here, and State Chairman George Glynn and others hurried to the Westchester club.

The death of Mr. Aldridge, familiarly known to a host as "Uncle George," removes the last of that triumvirate that once ruled the State—that one-time invincible Big Three whose other members were Thomas C. Platt and Francis K. Hendricks, both of whom preceded him to the grave.

As a member of Governor Whitman's "Kitchen Cabinet" he wielded a later influence, and in the political generation that succeeded Platt, Hendricks and Odell he became and remained one of that "Big Four" of Republican State politics, the other members of which were William L. Ward of Westchester, who was another of his associates who was at the club at the time of his death, Fred Greiner, veteran of Erie County, and Wadsworth of Western New York.

That his passing will be a shock and a source of genuine grief to many could be doubted by no one who recalled the warmth of the reception which accompanied his induction into the office he held at the time of his death. He was selected for the post traditionally belonging to an up-Stater at a conference here in March, 1921, among the two United States Senators from New York, James W. Wadsworth Jr. and William M. Calder, Mr. Hilles and Mr. Glynn. At the Republican National Convention in Chicago in 1920 he had voted consistently and persistently for Senator Warren G. Harding, from first to last.

Made Title to Office Clear.

The only other delegate from this State to vote for Mr. Harding on the first ballot was James L. Hotchkiss, Chairman of the Monroe County Republican Committee, Aldridge's chief political lieutenant. The two stuck to Harding throughout, although reviled by other members of the delegation whose votes were pretty evenly divided.

The credit for swinging the vote of the New York delegation practically

Continued on Page Five.

World-Wide War on War to Be Waged on Two July Days

Special to The New York Times.

WASHINGTON, June 13.—To further its object of "no more war," the National Council for Reduction of Armaments, at a meeting today, decided to spend $250,000 in the coming year. This is more than eight times the amount spent by it in the last year. It was announced by the council this evening that in the last two weeks it had received $10,000 in contributions. Some donations were $1,000.

The council plans to participate in a world wide demonstration against war on July 29 and 30. It will keep the wires hot on those days with messages to Members of Congress and others, backing up the results of the Washington Conference on Limitation of Armaments. Throughout the country hundreds of placards bearing the legend, "No More War," will be displayed. A chain of offices will be established to help get the $250,000.

LADD FOR ISSUING NEW BONUS MONEY

McCumber's North Dakota Colleague Proposes $2,500,000,000 Output of Legal Tender.

TO RETIRE IT BY BANK TAX

If This Proves Insufficient, Foreign Debt Interest Would Be Used.

Special to The New York Times.

WASHINGTON, June 13.—The newest of soldiers' bonus proposals came into the Senate this afternoon when Senator Ladd of North Dakota introduced an amendment to the McCumber bill providing for the issuance of legal tender Treasury notes to the extent of $2,500,000,000 in order that the bonus may be paid in cash.

The notes, according to the Ladd plan, would be retired in twenty-five years and would be paid by levying an excess profits tax on banks, trust companies, banking partnerships and other banking institutions. In the event that this tax fails to provide the money required to meet the notes, it is provided that the interest on the foreign debt would be used and if there was still a deficit the money would be taken out of the Treasury.

This is the first of the amendments which are to be offered to the bonus legislation now on the calendar. The Ladd amendment was considered significant in view of the fact that Senator McCumber, his colleague from North Dakota, is the author of the bill reported from the Finance Committee, a bill which Senator Ladd characterized as "not much more than a bread pill for the soldiers." Using another form of expression, he said that the soldiers asked for meat and in the McCumber bill received a stone.

The introduction of the Ladd amendment at this time caused considerable comment in Capitol circles, particularly as the North Dakota primary is less than three weeks away and Senator McCumber is seeking a renomination. His principal opponent is Lynn Frazier, the former Non-Partisan League Governor of the State. The Congressional Directory lists Ladd as a Non-Partisan Republican who was nominated by the Republicans and endorsed by the Frazier-Townley organization. Senator McCumber's ardent advocacy of bonus legislation is being urged in North Dakota as one of the principal reasons why he should be renominated.

Ladd Outlines His Proposal.

The financing of the Ladd plan is described by its author in this fashion:

"First, by taxing all banks, banking institutions, trust companies and banking partnerships that are incorporated for or in excess of $100,000 to the extent of 50 per cent. of their profits, after making an allowance of 12 per cent. for profits and deducting all other amounts paid in taxes. If the revenue derived from this source should prove insufficient to retire any annual instalment, he provides.

"Second, that the interest paid to the United States Government upon the refunded foreign debt shall be used in paying such annual instalment. Should these two sources prove insufficient to provide for any annual instalment, he proposes,

"Third, to make an appropriation out of any moneys in the Treasury not otherwise appropriated.

"The amendment also carries the provision that after twelve months from the passage of the act any holder of $100 or more of the currency issued under the act may convert the same into 3 per cent. gold bonds, non-tax-exempt; provided, however, that not

Continued on Page Two.

Man Jumps to Death Under Subway Train; Card Read: 'Herbert Thompson, Author'

Just before 1 o'clock this morning a well-dressed middle-aged man who had been pacing restlessly up and down the subway Interborough platform at Times Square, leaped in front of a northbound express train. A man near by lunged for him as he poised himself for a fraction of a second at the platform's edge, but he was too late. He landed under the wheels before Motorman Meehan could check the train and was crushed to death.

There were many persons in the station and the screams and shouts of those who saw the leap brought a crowd which several policemen, who ran from the street level, had difficulty in shoving back. Interboro employes found that the body was firmly wedged under the wheels and were forced to jack up a truck of the forward car before they could extricate the body.

Dr. Hauser had come from New York Hospital by the time the body had been extricated. He pronounced the man dead.

The body was taken to the West Forty-seventh Street Police Station, where it was found that all effects which might lead to identification had been removed except a card which read: "Herbert Thompson, Dramatic Author, 1,367 Broadway."

A policeman was unable to learn at that address, a building occupied by the Regal Shoe Company, whether the man had an office there or not; nor was it certain the card was that of the suicide himself.

He was about 5 feet 6 inches tall, and weighed about 140 pounds. He was well dressed and in a pocket was a considerable sum of money.

HARDING WILL CALL AN EXTRA SESSION IF SHIP BILL FAILS

Virtual Threat in Letter to Campbell Given Out as Revision Is Completed.

GOES TO THE HOUSE TODAY

Democrats Open Attack, Comparing Its Value to That of Muscle Shoals Bill.

MEASURES MAY BE LINKED

That Would Help Ship Bill in Both Houses, Leaders Say—Harding Not Opposing Ford Plan.

Special to The New York Times.

WASHINGTON, June 13.—President Harding has indicated in a letter to Chairman Campbell of the House Rules Committee that he would call Congress in special session if it failed to pass the ship subsidy bill at this session. The President's views were made public today by Representative Campbell on the eve of the introduction of the subsidy bill in the House in the face of marked opposition among Republican leaders and members in general.

The President's letter read as follows:

WHITE HOUSE, May 26, 1922.

My dear Congressman Campbell:

I understand that in a very short time the Merchant Marine bill is to be favorably reported to the House. I am writing to express the hope that your Committee on Rules will report whatever provision is necessary for its early and final consideration.

I cannot convey to you how very earnest I feel the necessity of passing this act. So much is involved and such difficult and discouraging situation will follow if Congress fails to sanction the Merchant Marine bill that I feel I should feel myself obligated to call Congress immediately in extraordinary session to especially consider it if it went over through any neglect or delay beyond the present term.

I should be more than glad to cooperate in any way that I can in impressing the House with the urgent necessity of the favorable consideration of this bill. I am writing an expression of my earnestness to you at this time because I understand it is within the province of the Rules Committee to report a provision under which there may be secured early, and I hope, favorable consideration.

Very truly yours,
WARREN G. HARDING.

The publication of this letter was followed up by a statement at the White House that constant pressure could be expected from the Administration to bring about the enactment of the ship subsidy bill. According to reports the President was made to feel that no greater disappointment could come to him than failure of Congress to push the measure through. One Administration spokesman remarked today that it was queer that members of Congress still came to the President, asking him if he wanted the measure passed.

Tied Up With Muscle Shoals.

After the President's letter came out a discussion as to the legislative program was precipitated in the House. Representative Garrett, acting Democratic leader, questioned Representative Mondell concerning published reports that the President was opposed to the Government accepting Ford's offer to Muscle Shoals. Mr. Mondell denied that the President had expressed opposition to the Muscle Shoals proposal in his conference yesterday, admitting, however, that the matter was discussed among other matters.

There was quick action in the House as the consequence of the attacks upon the Republican plans for legislation. The subcommittee of the Merchant Marine and Fisheries Committee, which had been revising the subsidy bill, completed the final draft for introduction tomorrow, and Representative Edmonds issued a statement explaining features of the bill and the changes made from the Shipping Board draft.

In the opinion of Republican leaders who have been telling the President that nothing could be accomplished unless the Senate also acted upon the ship subsidy bill, the determination of the President to call an extra session, if necessary to pass the measure will force the Senate to pass upon the measure before adjourning. House leaders said, however, that the Administration could not hope to pass the subsidy bill in the House unless assurance was given that a special rule was to be granted for the passage of the Muscle Shoals bill.

All the developments today went to show that the President was going to test his strength with Congress on the Ship Subsidy bill. The leaders are opposed to taking up the subsidy before election. The action of the President in admonishing the leaders that they must act on the measure at this session or be summoned in special session to do so is interpreted to mean that the President is willing to assume leadership and responsibility for disposing of the subsidy measure before November.

If the Ship Subsidy bill and the Muscle Shoals proposal are tied up together as part of the final legislative program, the House leaders say that there will be no great difficulty in forcing through the subsidy bill. Such a combination would also make the passage of the subsidy bill by the Senate less difficult.

Both Matters Up in House.

Both the subsidy question and the Muscle Shoals proposition came up in the House today as the result of Democratic prodding. Representative Garrett asked about the legislative program and whether it would include the Muscle Shoals bill. Representative Mondell declined to give any information as to the status of the Muscle Shoals bill, but did deny that the President

"All the News That's Fit to Print."

The New York Times.

THE WEATHER
Cloudy, warmer today; Thursday fair, fresh south to west winds.
Temperature yesterday—Max., 49; min., 42.
For weather report see next to last page.

VOL. LXXII....No. 23,650. NEW YORK, WEDNESDAY, OCTOBER 25, 1922. TWO CENTS In Greater New York | THREE CENTS Within 200 Miles | FOUR CENTS Elsewhere

LAW CABINET READY TO TAKE HOLD TODAY; THE CAMPAIGN OPENS

New Ministers Include Curzon, Baldwin, Derby and the Duke of Devonshire.

DIE-HARDS ARE LEFT OUT

Government Weak in Commons, Its Strong Men in Lords, Critics Say.

FIRST PARTY APPEALS OUT

Fear of Labor Vote and Desire to Avoid Further Cleavage Are Emphasized.

Special Cable to THE NEW YORK TIMES.

LONDON, Oct. 24.—Andrew Bonar Law announced tonight the principal members of his Cabinet. They will go tomorrow morning to Buckingham Palace, where they will receive from the King the seals of office and will thereby be formally installed. The retiring Ministers will visit the King a few minutes before to relinquish office.

The new Government will be made up as follows:

Premier and First Lord of the Treasury—ANDREW BONAR LAW.

Lord President of the Council—Marquis of SALISBURY.

Lord High Chancellor—Viscount CAVE.

Chancellor of the Exchequer—STANLEY BALDWIN.

Secretary for Home Affairs—WILLIAM C. BRIDGEMAN.

Secretary for Foreign Affairs—Marquis CURZON.

Secretary for the Colonies—The Duke of DEVONSHIRE.

Secretary for India—Viscount PEEL.

Secretary for War—The Earl of DERBY.

First Lord of the Admiralty—Lieut. Col. L. C. M. S. AMERY.

President of the Board of Trade—Sir PHILIP LLOYD-GREAME.

Minister of Health—Sir ARTHUR GRIFFITH-BOSCAWEN.

Minister of Agriculture—Sir ROBERT A. SANDERS.

Secretary for Scotland—Viscount NOVAR.

Attorney General—DOUGLAS McG. HOGG.

Lord Advocate—The Hon. W. A. WATSON.

President of the Board of Education—EDWARD F. L. WOOD.

Die-Hards Fare Badly.

The appointments announced tonight have been largely anticipated, but it is pointed out that perhaps the most interesting part of them is their omissions. The Die-Hards have come out poorly, Lord Salisbury their leader, being the only one included in the present list. As Lord President of the Council he has a post of dignity, but without any department duties; there is, however, plenty of opportunity to reward his followers in minor posts.

Lord Cave, the new Lord Chancellor, has been Lord of Appeal for the last two or three years. During a large part of the war he held the difficult position of Home Secretary and did not escape some of the criticism which was showered on the Government by perfervid patriots for his administration of the law concerning spies and aliens.

Stanley Baldwin's promotion to the Chancellorship of the Exchequer was foreseen and came in for a high compliment this afternoon from Reginald McKenna as representative of big banking interests. He was President of the Board of Trade in the last Ministry and stood out for his fight in the Cabinet for rigorous application of the Safeguarding of Industries act.

William Clive Bridgeman, the new Home Secretary, was in charge of the Mines Department in the Board of Trade under the Coalition. He has been in Commons for years and held several minor Government posts.

Marquis Curzon, as expected, remains at the Foreign Office and continues his leadership of the House of Lords, while the Duke of Devonshire can claim his successful Governor Generalship of Canada as qualification for his appointment to the Colonial Secretaryship.

Lord Peel, as expected, remains at the India Office, and Lord Derby will be no stranger at the War Office. During the war he had much to do with the army, first as originator of the scheme of voluntary recruiting known as the Derby scheme, and afterward as Secretary of State.

Lieut. Col. L. C. Amery becomes First Lord of the Admiralty, being promoted from the Secretaryship of that department to be its head, and the nomination of Sir Philip Lloyd-Greame to be President of the Board of Trade is also in the nature of a promotion. Under the coalition he held a hybrid post as Director of Overseas Trade, partly under the Foreign Office and partly under the Board of Trade.

Sir A. Griffith Boscawen succeeds Sir Alfred Mond at the Ministry of Health, rather to the general surprise, as it had been assumed he would remain at his old post as Minister of Agriculture, but that now has been given to Sir Robert Sanders, who was Under Secretary of War under the late Government.

Viscount Novar, new Secretary for Scotland, was well known in political life as Ronald Munro Ferguson till his elevation to the peerage in 1920, and served as Governor General of Australia during the war.

The two legal appointments announced, that of Douglas McGarrel Hogg to be Attorney General, and William Watson to be Lord Advocate for Scotland, are considered to illustrate the difficulties

Continued on Page Three.

New York Woman Leads White House Pickets

Special to The New York Times.

WASHINGTON, Oct. 24.—Under the captaincy of Mrs. Marguerite Tucker of New York, picketing of the White House gate as a protest over the failure of President Harding to release the remaining sixty-nine men in Federal prisons convicted of wartime offenses was resumed today.

Banners appropriate to the crusade were carried by several women. Most of them bore legends addressed directly to President Harding.

BIG MOVE BY ALLIES TO SAVE GERMANY

Britain Yields to French View and Reparation Board Is Going to Berlin.

WIRTH PLANS STEP APART

Will Invite Foreign Experts, including Americans, to Advise on Financial Crisis.

Special Cable to THE NEW YORK TIMES.

PARIS, Oct. 24.—After three days' discussion of M. Barthou's counterproposals to Sir John Bradbury's plan for a two-year moratorium for Germany, the Reparation Commission today decided to go to Berlin on Sunday to discuss with the German Government in a friendly spirit the means whereby in the commission's opinion Germany might be helped to balance her budget and stabilize the mark.

The Commission's decision is in many ways a compromise between the British and French points of view. Whereas Bradbury recommended the permanent transference of the Commission to Berlin, with the object of working together with the German Government on plans for payment of reparations, M. Barthou demanded that a Guarantees Committee be sent there with powers of control and dictation.

It appears that the present visit of the commission is to conform with the Bradbury suggestion in that it will be a of a friendly nature. The commission seeks only to give advice to the German Government and not to dictate terms. At the same time they will endeavor to secure the consent of the German Government to some measure of control such as suggested in M. Barthou's scheme.

It is recognized by the French Government that the terms of the Treaty of Versailles and the communications made by the German delegates during the Peace Conference in the nature, duties and status of the Reparation Commission do not permit such a degree of control of German finance as M. Barthou proposed. The consent of the German Government must, therefore, be obtained to any such measures, and this is what will be sought.

The rapid downward plunge of the German mark has had important influence on the decision of the commission. Bradbury is of the opinion that unless the mark is pegged at fifteen hundred to the dollar Germany will in two months fall into a state of financial chaos similar to that of Austria—and instead of having to discuss what can be obtained from Germany in payments the Reparation Commission may have to discuss what measures of relief must be given.

The French, too, have come to realize the urgency of the situation. M. Barthou, who is in close touch with Poincaré, is understood to be prepared to acquiesce with the Bradbury proposal that a two-year moratorium be granted in fact, if not in name. It is probable that in order to cover these two years a system of payments by bonds which was adopted for the last four months of this year will be again resorted to and further extended.

It will also be insisted on by the French that payments in kind under the Stinnes-Lubersac agreement be fully adoyted.

On the proposel of Henri Cheron, Minister of Agriculture, the French Council of Ministers this morning decided to include in the progra mof payments in kind to be demanded from Germany sufficient chemical fertilizer "for the needs of French agriculture." According to Cheron Germany produces a million and a half tons of this product annually.

France, on the other hand, produces

Continued on Page Nine.

TABLET OF 2100 B. C. MAKES ADAM VICTIM OF JEALOUS GODS

His Expulsion From Eden Due to Fear of His Rivaling Them in Wisdom.

LONG ANTEDATES GENESIS

Babylonian Version Refers to Forbidden Food, but Omits Eve and the Serpent.

STORY GIVEN IN DIALOGUE

Dr. Chiera of University of Pennsylvania Translates Account Found in Nippur Library.

Special to The New York Times.

PHILADELPHIA, Oct. 24.—Dr. Edward Chiera, Assistant Professor of Assyriology of the University of Pennsylvania, has deciphered a Babylonian clay tablet of about 2100 B. C. which contained an account of the fall of man paralleling the account in Genesis in many particulars.

The account is in the form of a dialogue between a man and a god. It resembles the biblical story in references to a forbidden food, to the disobedience of man, to man's unlawful attainment of knowledge, to his being driven into the desert and compelled to labor. His adoption of clothing as a result of knowledge is also indicated.

The god—which Babylonian god is not indicated—drives man away in self-defense rather than as a punishment. Man is accused of aspiring to a place with the gods, a theme which has been treated in other Babylonian literature.

A Babylonian Prometheus.

The moral consideration is unimportant in the Babylonian legend, man's position being like that of Prometheus, who was a criminal in the eyes of a god, but worthy of commendation from the point of view of man.

There is no allusion in the dialogue just deciphered to the serpent or the tempter; but, according to Dr. Chiera, the serpent was an honest friend and counselor of man, as the Babylonians looked at it. Other Babylonian texts tell of a god who befriended and advised man. Such a counselor of man has been metamorphosed into the serpent in later versions of the Fall, or of the break between man and the gods, according to the theory of Dr. Chiera.

"The date of this tablet is about 2100 or 2300 B. C.," said Dr. Chiera. "The writing of the Hebrew account took place, according to the best authorities, at some later date than 1000 B. C."

The flood story in Genesis has been shown to be closely paralleled in the Babylonian epic, but this parallel is established with the help of records in the library of Assur-ban-i-pal, who lived long after Genesis had been written, and it has been contended by some scholars that the Babylonians took their story from the Hebrews. According to Dr. Chiera, parts of the epic have been found in writings far anterior to Genesis, apparently establishing the priority of the Babylonian account.

Tablet Is from the Nippur Library.

The tablet is in the Sumerian language and formerly belonged to the library of the temple at Nippur, from which excavations for the University of Pennsylvania Museum have recovered several thousand tablets. The Sumerian is believed to be the earliest language of the country, and with the Egyptian to to be the earliest written language, its progress from picture-writing to the use of an alphabet having been clearly traced.

Since the deciphering of this tablet, Dr. Chiera has discovered other fragments, apparently belonging to the same legend or cycle of legends, in which there are references to the invention of writing and to the beginning of civilization. These, however, have not been fully translated. Twelve or thirteen other tablets have been found with similar characteristics and words showing them to be of mythological character. They are believed to develop further the early Babylonian mythology, and Dr. Chiera has started work on them.

According to the Assyriologist, the ancient Babylonian story was apparently taken over by the Hebrews and adjusted to fit their monotheistic system.

Continued on Page Two.

Big Shield Makes Start Today to Bore Vehicular Tunnel Under the Hudson

One of the big shields to be used in driving the vehicular tunnel under the Hudson River will begin to move forward this morning from the foot of Canal Street under a hydraulic pressure of 6,000 tons, and the actual work of tunneling will then be under way. The shield is 29 feet 6 inches in diameter. Within a few weeks six of them will be at work.

If the schedule prepared by the engineers is adhered to, the shields will advance about two and a half feet a day through rock and fifteen feet a day through silt. The shield will move on a downward grade of about 3½ per cent. for a distance of something like 1,200 feet and then it will proceed westward on a level line under the river. It is expected that the shield moving from the Jersey City waterline will meet with the westward-bound shield 700 feet from the Manhattan shore, for the reason that for this distance practically all of the obstructive rock will be encountered. The entire length of the tunnel will be 9,250 feet, of which 3,400 feet will be under the river.

The cost of preparing for the actual work of construction has amounted to nearly $2,000,000. Chief Engineer Clifford M. Holland of the Tunnel Commission said yesterday that he expected the work to progress according to schedule, and that if it does vehicles will be running through the tunnel within thirty-six months.

LINKS CITY BUS DEAL WITH TAMMANY MAN

Driver Tells of Buying Car From Farley After Promise He Would Be "Put to Work."

$600 PROFIT ON THE SALE

Witnesses at Transit Hearing Explain Methods Used to Obtain Grants.

A profit of $600 on the sale of a bus by Thomas M. Farley, Tammany leader of the Fourteenth Assembly District, to Harry Fautwasser, and its possible connection with the granting of a permit to Fautwasser, was the subject of investigation at the hearing yesterday before the Transit Commission.

Fautwasser, who is now driving the bus on the Seventy-ninth Street line, said Farley promised to see he was "put to work" before he made the purchase. John G. Succa, a bus driver, testified that Farley had bought and sold the bus for him and had paid him all the purchase money, part of which, he said, he had paid back to a man who lent him the money to buy the bus in the first place. Succa admitted, however, that he neither gave nor took receipts in these transactions, which were entirely in cash, although at the time he had a bank account.

Mr. Farley, who formerly was an Alderman and is now Deputy County Clerk, testified the preceding day that he purchased the bus for Joseph Succa, brother of John G. Succa, at Bridgeport, Conn., but Joseph Succa denied this.

John Succa testified that Mr. Farley bought the bus for him for $1,500 in April. He said the receipt for the bus was made out to "Thomas M. Farley," and that the bus was stored in a garage until Sept. 12 last, when it was sold to Fautwasser. Succa said Fautwasser paid $1,500 in cash and agreed to pay $1,000 in notes, and that $1,000 of the cash was paid in the office of Assemblyman F. L. Hackenburg, Mr. Farley's attorney.

Made a Profit of $600.

"Mr. Hackenburg didn't represent you, did he?" asked former Justice Clarence J. Shearn, special counsel of the commission.

"No, he represents the district," Succa replied.

Succa said that Fautwasser paid the remaining $500 in cash to Farley and that it was decided later to accept $600 in cash in place of the $1,000 in notes, making the purchase price of the bus $2,100, or $600 more than had been paid for it. Succa said that Farley turned the money over to him as soon as he received it. Succa said he gave Farley no receipt for the money and did not put any of the money in a bank, although he had a bank account at the time. He added that immediately after he received the first two payments, aggregating $1,500, he went to Bridgeport and gave the money to a man from whom he borrowed $1,500 to buy the bus in the first place.

"There is no paper in existence that shows either that you paid this man you talk about in Bridgeport, or that Farley paid you?" Judge Shearn asked.

"Not that I know of," said Succa.

Fautwasser corroborated the witness concerning the payments to Farley and said the latter had promised to use his influence in getting him a bus permit, and that this had influenced him in buying the bus.

"Didn't you say that you asked Mr. Farley to lend you a helping hand to get you on one of the bus lines, and that you bought the bus after he said he would help you get on the line?" Judge Shearn asked.

"He simply said that if I bought the bus he would see that I went to work," replied Fautwasser.

Politics and Permits.

Politics entered largely into the day's testimony, and in one case where a permit was granted the preliminary influence appeared to have been Republican rather than Democratic.

Leonard V. Antonelli, a bus operator, testified that he was informed his only chance of getting a permit was through Grover A. Whalen, Commissioner of Plant and Structures, that he did not know Mr. Whalen, and so went to State Senator William Duggan, a Republican. He said Senator Duggan introduced him to Collector of Internal Revenue Frank K. Bowers, a Republican district leader, then in the office of the President of the Board of Aldermen, and that Mr. Bowers introduced a Mr. Riegelmann in Mr. Whalen's office, whom he described as a friend of Mr. Bowers and a brother of the Borough President of Brooklyn.

Antonelli said Mr. Riegelmann gave him a letter to Frederick Rochter, superintendent of bus operation, and that the latter put him on the Flatbush Avenue line. Antonelli said he was laid off because he did not vote at the last city election, but received a permit again when he obtained his final naturalization papers. He said he had since joined the Highbridge Democratic Club in the Bronx, but denied that any one had suggested it.

Joseph J. Tino, another member of

Continued on Page Eight.

WILSON IN WARTIME AS LANE SAW HIM

Acted Alone on Big Questions, Letters and Notes of Ex-Secretary Show.

CABINET MEETINGS BARREN

Book, Now Issued, Also Contains Letter Noting Wilson's Lack of Sympathy With Preparedness.

BOSTON, Oct. 24 (Associated Press).—A series of letters, dealing with the American war Cabinet and giving an intimate picture of Woodrow Wilson as he appeared while presiding over the secret meetings of his official family, written by the late Franklin K. Lane, Secretary of the Interior from 1913 to 1920, have been collected and edited by his widow, Anne Wintermute Lane, and published by the Houghton Mifflin Company. [Some of the letters, including one commenting on Mr. Wilson's lack of sympathy with a preparedness campaign, were printed in THE NEW YORK TIMES last May.]

The correspondence shows, among other things, how the President sometimes lost patience with the tremendous problems confronting him and how at other times discouragement crowded him to such a degree that he was prompted to turn bitterly upon his advisers when they failed to agree with him. It is told that when great questions were pressing for decision, he encouraged his Cabinet to talk of trivialities while he went along on his own course.

In addition to his voluminous correspondence Mr. Lane made many notes on incidents in his daily life. Among these were copious comments on the Cabinet meetings. In one of these notes, dated March 1, 1918, he said:

"Yesterday, at the Cabinet meeting, we had the first real talk on the war in weeks, yes, in months. Burleson brought up the matter of Russia—would we support Japan in taking Siberia, or even Vladivostok? Should we join Japan actively—in force?

"The President said 'No,' for the very practical reason that we had no ships. We had difficulty in providing for our men in France and for our Allies. (The President never uses this word, saying that we are not Allies)."

In a note dated March 12, 1918, Secretary Lane wrote:

"Nothing talked of at Cabinet that would interest a nation, a family or a child. No talk of war. No talk of Russia or Japan. Talk by McAdoo about some bills in Congress, by the President about giving the veterans of the Spanish war leave, with pay, to attend their annual encampment. And he treated this seriously, as if it were a matter of first importance * * *"

"Yesterday we had a Cabinet meeting," he wrote under date of Oct. 23, 1918. "All were present. The President was manifestly disturbed. For some weeks we have spent our time at Cabinet meetings largely in telling stories. Even at the meeting of a week ago, the day on which the President sent his reply to Germany—his second note of the Paris series—we were given no view of the note, which was already in Lansing's hands and was emitted at 4 o'clock. Germany came back with an acceptance of the President's terms—a superficial acceptance at least—hence the appeal to the Cabinet yesterday.

"This was his opening: 'I do not know what to do. I must ask your advice. I may have made a mistake in not properly safeguarding what I said before. What do you think should be done?'

"This general query was followed by a long silence, which I broke by saying that Germany would do anything he said. 'What should I say?' he asked.

"That we would not treat until Germany was across the Rhine.

"This he thought impossible."

Mr. Lane became discouraged at times. On Jan. 19, 1920, he wrote:

"The whole world is skew-jee, awry, distorted and altogether perverse. The President is broken in body and obstinate in spirit. Clemenceau is beaten for an office he did not want. Einstein has declared the law of gravitation outgrown and decadent. Drink, consoling friend of a perturbed world, is shut off, and all goes merry as a dance in hell."

BRITISH LAW FORCES AMERICAN LINE SHIP TO CARRY BRANDY

Clearance Papers Refused the President Adams Until Steerage Rule Is Followed.

TAKES ABOARD FIVE QUARTS

Capt. Pendlebury Had Removed All Spirits—'Jolly Good Law,' Says Official.

APPEAL DRY SHIP RULING

Five Companies Take Action, With Seven to Move Today—Hope for Early Decision.

The President Adams of the United States Line, operated for the United States Government, had five quarts of brandy aboard when she arrived yesterday at Pier 3, Hoboken, from London, by way of Queenstown. The British law compels the steamers to carry a gallon of brandy for every 100 steerage passengers for use if needed in illness, and clearance papers were refused by the British Board of Trade until the required amount of "medical comforts" were on board for the 115 steerage passengers. The law is an old one and has always been rigidly enforced.

Captain Jonas Pendlebury of the President Adams said yesterday that he had received orders from the Shipping Board to bring his vessel into the United States "dry" and he thereupon unloaded all alcoholic liquid refreshments.

When he went to the British Board of Trade to obtain his clearance papers, all went well until a member of the board remarked:

"Well, Cap'n, I suppose you've got enough brandy aboard, eh, what?"

Captain Pendlebury then told him of his orders and the unloading of the liquor.

"Well, I'm sorry, Captain," said the British official: "but unless you have a gallon of brandy for every hundred steerage passengers aboard I can't give you your clearance papers. This is British law, and, if I do say it myself, it is jolly good law, too."

Five Lines File Appeals.

Five of the twelve foreign and domestic steamship companies who are contesting the dry-ship ruling of Attorney General Daugherty filed appeals yesterday to the United States Supreme Court from the decree of Judge Learned Hand dismissing their bills in equity and upholding the position of the Government. Other companies will file appeals this morning. The formal decrees were entered yesterday by Judge Hand.

The steamship companies will also seek from Justice Brandeis of the Supreme Court a supersedeas stay, holding up enforcement of the new dry ruling until the Supreme Court acts on the appeal from Judge Hand's decision. A special messenger from the law firm of Lord, Day & Lord, 25 Broadway, counsel for the Cunard and Anchor Lines, left last night for Washington with the appeal papers. The decree in this case was the first one signed yesterday by Judge Hand. Papers in the other cases will be sent to Washington by special messenger immediately.

Lucius H. Beers of the law firm of Lord, Day & Lord, and ex-Judge Van Vechten Veeder of counsel for half a dozen of the steamship companies, said last night that the supersedeas stay probably would be asked for within the next few days.

Hope for Early Hearing.

Counsel for the steamship companies, Mr. Beers said, will also make a motion for a preference, so as to get the case on the calendar of the United States Supreme Court for early hearing. In the ordinary course of events, it was said, it might be months before the case would be disposed of. Both Mr. Beers and Judge Veeder were inclined to think that the court would consent to an early disposition of the test cases and Mr. Beers said that there was a possibility of a decision before the end of the year.

The following companies were able yesterday afternoon to perfect their records and file them with the proper appeal bonds: The Cunard Line, the Anchor Line, the French Line, the International Mercantile Marine and the International Navigation Company, Ltd. The others, excepting those which procured from Judge Hand Monday, permission to submit a single question regarding American vessels, are expected to complete their appeal records today.

Cletus Keating, of counsel for the

Continued on Page Six.

Hylan Names Committee To Visit Berwind Mines

Pursuant to a resolution recently adopted by the Board of Estimate, Mayor Hylan last night appointed a committee of five to visit the Pennsylvania mines of the Berwind-White Coal Company to investigate mining and living conditions in connection with the coal supplied to the Interboro Rapid Transit Company. The committee is made up of David Hirshfield, Commissioner of Accounts; Amos T. Smith, engineer, connected with the Board of Estimate; Mrs. Louis R. Welzmiller, Deputy Commissioner of Public Markets; John Lohman, Assistant Corporation Counsel, and Thomas Moran of the Bureau of Investigations of the Finance Department.

J. J. ASTOR ACQUIRES LONDON TIMES SHARE

Brother of Viscount Astor Is Associated With John Walter in New Control.

FOLLOWS FATHER'S CAREER

Northcliffe's Shares Bring £1,390,000—Times and Mail Now Opposed in Politics.

Special Cable to THE NEW YORK TIMES.

LONDON, Oct. 24.—Major the Hon. John Jacob Astor is associated with John Walter in the repurchase of The London Times. A Times announcement says: "It is announced that the shares in The Times Publishing Company owned by the late Lord Northcliffe, as well as those owned by Sir John Ellerman, have been acquired by John Walter and that Major the Hon. John Jacob Astor is associated with Walter in their acquisition. It is the intention and object of Mr. Walter and Major Astor to maintain the highest traditions of The Times and to insure its continuance as a national institution, conducted solely in the best interests of the nation and empire."

It is said that the price paid for Lord Northcliffe's shares was £1,390,000.

Lord Rothermere's disposal of his interest in The Times newspaper is a fulfillment of general expectations. As soon as it was realized how heavy would be the death duties which Lord Northcliffe's estate would have to pay, it was foreseen that it would be necessary for his brother and heir to get rid of some of the newspaper properties. Of these it was very much easier for them to sell The Times than any of the others, as it never fitted in well with the rest of the Northcliffe press. Indeed, for months there had been rumors that it was on the market, and that its financial position was so precarious that Lord Northcliffe might be forced to let it go.

John Walter, who now in association with Major the Hon. John Jacob Astor has taken over the shares of Lord Rothermere and Sir John Ellerman, is a direct descendant of the John Walter who founded the newspaper in 1775. During the Northcliffe régime he retained a large interest in it, but he is understood to have had little to do with its active management.

Major Astor has not heretofore had anything to do with the London press, but his father, the first Lord Astor, owned from 1892 to 1917 The Pall Mall Gazette as well as The Pall Mall Budget and Pall Mall Magazine. He also bought The Observer from Lord Northcliffe in 1911, and this has been inherited by his eldest son, the present Viscount Astor.

Times and Mail Now Opposed.

That a change was coming in the ownership of The Times had been evident for several weeks, as there was a steadily growing divergence between the policy it advocated and that pursued by The Daily Mail and other publications from Carmelite House. Thus, in its comments on the Near Eastern crisis, when The Daily Mail was denouncing the warmongers The Times was markedly restrained in its editorials and took the line traditional in Printing House Square of supporting the Government of the day as far as it consistently could on a matter so gravely affecting the welfare of the nation.

In the same way there has been a clear distinction between the attitude of The Times and The Daily Mail toward the new Government. For example, The Times this morning declared that the smoothness with which the election of Bonar Law as Conservative leader had gone off was of good augury for the character and policy of the new administration and the sort of thing which the country would welcome, but The Daily Mail, in an editorial headed "Vague Promises Will Not Do," almost openly declared war on the new Premier. It sneered at him because it

Continued on Page Four.

HEARD HALL SLAYER CALLED BY HIS NAME, SWEARS MRS. GIBSON

Saw Pistol Flashes, but Darkness Prevented Identification of 2 Men and 2 Women.

EVIDENCE VALUE DISPUTED

Somerset and Middlesex Authorities in Conflict—Special Prosecutor Mott to Decide.

HEAR MAN STOLE LETTERS

Officials Running Down Clue That Church Member Then Turned Them Over to Woman.

Wilbur A. Mott, Special Deputy Attorney General of the State of New Jersey, appointed to take charge of the Hall-Mills murder investigation, established his headquarters yesterday in Somerville, county seat of Somerset County, and began active work in his efforts to solve the mystery which has baffled the county authorities for more than five weeks. Mr. Mott arrived in Somerville with James F. Mason, a Newark detective, whom he has chosen as his chief investigator, and they conferred for several hours yesterday morning and afternoon with Prosecutors Azariah M. Beekman of Somerset, Joseph E. Stricker of Middlesex and Detective George Totten of Somerset, who have been directing the investigation.

Another incident of the day was the disclosure by an official who said that he saw the affidavit of the details of the story said to have been told to the authorities by Mrs. Jane Gibson that she had seen two men and two women under the apple tree on the Phillips farm, that she had heard the shots and heard one of the women cry out to one of the men, mentioning him by name. The understanding is that because Mrs. Gibson could not identify any of the persons involved, the value of her information as legal evidence has become a subject of dispute.

Arrest Rumors Revived.

Mr. Mott concentrated his energies upon familiarizing himself with the details of the complex case, going back to the beginning and sifting out the information collected by the authorities since the discovery of the bodies on the Phillips farm outside New Brunswick on Sept. 16. Mr. Mott may require several days to study the mass of statements of witnesses and the information gathered in running down various clues. When he is ready to proceed on his own account another examination of members of the Hall and Mills families, together with further questioning of all the other known witnesses in the case, may be expected.

The arrival of the new chief prosecutor in Somerset County was accompanied by new rumors of impending arrests. Beekman has not asked for indictments or ordered arrests on information which other officials considered adequate. It was this difference of opinion among the officials which was responsible for the conflicting statements, for and against the possibility of the indictment of a woman and two men, which were issued by the authorities last week. It will be up to Mr. Mott to decide which officials were right—those who favored immediate action or those who feared the evidence was not strong enough.

New Witness Known as "Pig Woman."

The evidence turned over to Mr. Mott yesterday included an affidavit said to have been made by Mrs. Gibson, who is a widow about 50 years old, living with her 21-year-old son on a 60-acre farm near the Phillips farm. Mrs. Gibson is known in New Brunswick as "the pig woman," because she raises and sells pigs. She is a vigorous woman, with dark brown hair and a dark skin, who speaks English and German and appears to be much better educated than the average woman in her circumstances. Her home is in an old barn, converted into a dwelling, about 100 yards off Hamilton Avenue, which runs from the centre of New Brunswick, curves out in a semicircle based on Easton Avenue, and runs into De Russy's Lane, not far from the scene of the murder. The Gibson house is about a mile from the crab-apple tree under which the two bodies were found.

Barking Dog Gave Alarm.

Mrs. Gibson owns forty-eight pigs, five dogs, five mules and some chickens, and has a good crop of corn growing on her farm. She would never have figured in the events of the murder night—Thursday, Sept. 14—except that somebody had been stealing her corn and chickens.

According to the story which Mrs. Gibson is said to have embodied in affidavit form, she was sitting in her home a little before 9 o'clock on the night of Sept. 14, when one of her dogs, inside the house, began to bark and scratch at the door. She went to the door and saw a shadowy figure of a man leaving her corn patch and making his way toward the Phillips farm.

Thinking that the man was the thief who had been stealing corn and chickens, Mrs. Gibson mounted one of her mules and set off along Hamilton Avenue toward the Phillips place in an attempt to cut him off. Reaching De Russy's Lane, which runs into Easton Avenue near the Parker Home for the Aged, she branched off into the fields and began a zig-zag course that brought her up a little lane close to the abandoned Phillips farm house.

Standing close to the little crabapple tree, just off this lane and not far from the farm house, according to Mrs. Gibson's story to the authorities, were two men and two women. The time is supposed to have been "a little before 10 o'clock." She is reported to have said their figures were "silhouetted." It was a very dark night, with no moon, and

---

President Refuses to Oust Sawyer At Demand of the American Legion

Special to The New York Times.

WASHINGTON, Oct. 24.—The demand of the American Legion at its recent convention in New Orleans for the removal of Brig. Gen. Charles E. Sawyer, President Harding's physician, from the Chairmanship of the Federal Board of Hospitalization was met at the White House today with a flat statement that General Sawyer would not be removed or called upon to resign.

What was said was informal and oral, but it was known to have the sanction of President Harding. The President, it was clearly indicated, assumed full responsibility for the shortcomings attributed to General Sawyer. If there had been any failure of the Hospitalization Board, it was explained, General Sawyer was not at fault. The fault was the President's, and he was willing to let that be known.

According to the White House spokesman, the criticism of the Hospitalization Board and General Sawyer had its inception in the location of Government hospitals for disabled and sick war veterans in Wisconsin, Minnesota and Michigan. The President noted, when the board's selections of sites were laid before him, that another hospital was recommended for Chicago. His reports told him there were other Government hospital accommodations at Chicago, it was explained, and that all the beds in them were not occupied. He made inquiries, and concluded that there ought to be a hospital in Michigan, for several reasons.

Mr. Harding decided that the Camp Custer site in Michigan afforded a convenient place, as it could get the benefit for consultation purposes of physicians and surgeons of the Battle Creek Sanitarium, would be centrally located for Michigan men who had served in the war, and, as the State had furnished her full quota to the army during the great conflict, she was entitled to have a Government hospital of her own for the treatment of war veterans.

There was no politics in the selection of the Michigan site, it was stated at the White House. The President, it was declared, did not consult with the Michigan Senators and Representatives. He came to the conclusion that Michigan had better claims to have a hospital than Chicago, and therefore asked the Federal Hospitalization Board to reconsider its recommendation.

These and other similar occurrences, the White House spokesman said, had led to the criticism of General [illegible] and the board, but Mr. Harding wanted it understood that he, and not General Sawyer, was responsible.

No change in the personnel of the Hospitalization Board was contemplated, the White House spokesman said, with emphasis.

I. W. W. TRIED TO POISON SOLDIERS, SAYS WITNESS

Former Haywood Aid Testifies They Tampered With Food in Packing Plants in War.

SACRAMENTO, Cal., Oct. 24.—W. E. Townsend, who said he formerly was the "right-hand man" of William D. Haywood, head of the Industrial Workers of the World, testified at the trial of ten members of that organization here today that he and other members of the I. W. W. conspired to send poisoned canned goods to the American soldiers in France during the World War.

Townsend, who was a surprise witness for the State against the ten who are charged with violation of the State Criminal Syndicalism law, testified that in one of the big packing houses in Chicago 300 or 400 Industrial Workers were at work during the war and that part of their task was to test canned goods before shipment. Instead of condemning the cans, he said, the Industrial Workers would let them pass.

"We wanted to cripple the packers and also we were opposed to the war," Townsend testified. "We used to say, 'Let them poison Uncle Sam's damned gunners.'"

Further, to ruin food contained in the cans, Townsend said, the workers drove in the nails on the boxes so they would pierce the can, and nails were also driven through the boxes at places where they were not needed to ruin the contents.

Under direction of Haywood, the witness declared, he joined various fighting units of the army to spread I. W. W. doctrines among the soldiers.

Woodrow Wilson Receives Permission To Cast Absentee Vote in Princeton

TRENTON, N. J., Oct. 24.—Former President Woodrow Wilson will not be disfranchised in New Jersey because he no longer lives in this State. This was the ruling today by the Mercer County Board of Elections, which considered the former President's application for a ballot under the absentee voters law.

Several former New Jersey residents were barred from voting by the board because it was clear they had abandoned that State as their residence. An opinion obtained from the Attorney General read that under a decision of the Supreme Court in 1888 the residence of the voter was determined by the voter's intention.

The board, in its decision, pointed out that Mr. Wilson had made application to vote from his former residence, 10 Nassau Street, Princeton, and that it was obvious that, even though he was now a resident of Washington, D. C., he wished to vote in this State.

It was announced that his ballot would be forwarded to him and that he would no doubt cast his vote here as usual. Mrs. Wilson made no application for a ballot, and her voting status was not considered.

No. 10 Nassau Street, Mr. Wilson's legal residence, is a one-room apartment over a grocery store, across from the university dining hall. Due to his prolonged illness, which has kept Mr. Wilson confined for the greater part of the last three years, he has not returned to his Princeton "home" to vote. The room is now occupied by a student at the university.

"All the News That's Fit to Print."

The New York Times.

THE WEATHER.
Fair, slightly warmer Thursday; Friday, fair, warmer; moderate winds, becoming south.
For full weather report see Page 23.

VOL. LXXII....No. 23,713. NEW YORK, WEDNESDAY, DECEMBER 27, 1922. TWO CENTS [illegible]

HARDING MAY OPPOSE BORAH PARLEY PLAN IN STATEMENT TODAY

President Expected to Answer Through Press Written Question as to His Attitude.

LODGE TO SPEAK IN SENATE

Raising of Point of Order May Exclude Borah Amendment From Naval Bill.

FARM GROUP STRONG FOR IT

Agricultural Sections of West, Converted From Isolation Policy, Advocate Economic Aid for Europe.

Special to The New York Times.

WASHINGTON, Dec. 26.—On the eve of the Senate's assembling after the Christmas recess the interest of political Washington is centred in Senator Borah's amendment to the Naval Appropriation bill authorizing President Harding to call an international conference to consider reduction of land armament and the economic ills of Europe. The prospects are that most of tomorrow's session of the Senate will be given up to discussion of the Borah proposition.

The prevailing interest was augmented today by a hint from the White House that the President would have a statement to make to the press tomorrow. It became known that this hint was the outcome of a written question submitted to the President as to whether the Borah amendment with pending reservations would be acceptable to the Administration. No intimation was given as to what line the promised Presidential statement would take, but the hint has whetted curiosity to a marked degree, as it is realized that the President's views are certain to have an important bearing on the Borah proposal.

Officials Circles Cool to Plan.

Everything that has come from Administration sources since the Borah proposal was offered goes to show that there is no cordiality toward it on the part of important officers of the Government. There has been no direct or authoritative statement of the Administration's views, but nothing has occurred to put a new aspect on the sentiment attributed to advisers of the President that it would not be the part of wisdom for the United States Government to take the initiative in offering its help in an effort to bring Europe out of its economic quagmire.

The position of the Administration is understood to be that it is the part of the European powers concerned and not the part of the United States to suggest an international conference aimed at an adjustment of Europe's troubles. There are several specifications which illuminate this attitude, all going to make out a case against Administration sentiment with the manner in which Senator Borah is trying to accomplish his end.

Today brought out indications of the line-up of part of the Senate on the Borah amendment. The most interesting of these was that representatives of the agricultural sections of the Middle West and the Far West intend to stand by Senator Borah. While Senator La Follette, leader of the new radical-progressive group, has failed to commit himself, two of his most earnest followers, Senators Ladd of North Dakota and Brookhart of Iowa, are among the most enthusiastic supporters of the international conference idea. With them will be Senator McNary of Oregon, one of the few Republicans who supported the League of Nations Covenant. He said today that he had received telegrams from a farm organization and some individuals urging him to vote for the Borah amendment. Not only would he vote for it, said Mr. McNary, but he would make a speech in support of it.

The positon of Brookhart, McNary, Ladd and others from the West is particularly significant. It reflects the new realization among farmers that their troubles are bound up with those of Europe. The strong opposition in farming sections of the West to any participation by the United States in European affairs, which had such an influence in the defeat of the Versailles Treaty with its inclusive League Covenant, is undergoing a rapid revision through the permeating knowledge that as long as unsettled conditions prevail there Europe will have no money to buy American farm products. Senator Capper, head of the bipartisan farm bloc, was one of the first to see this trend and to reflect it in advocating economic assistance as a plank in the farm bloc platform.

Lodge to Speak on Borah Plan.

Senator Lodge is down for a speech on the Borah resolution in the Senate tomorrow. A statement to that effect today from Mr. Lodge's office aroused much interest. Mr. Lodge is Chairman of the Committee on Foreign Relations, the committee which would deal with additional legislation for holding an international conference at the instance of the United States, and it is expected that what he will say will in some measure reflect the views of President Harding with respect to what Senator Borah seeks to accomplish.

Although the Administration's attitude toward suggestions of an attempt by this Government to bring about an adjustment of Europe's troubles appeared to have been pretty well understood, there seems to be division of opinion among Administration supporters in the Senate, and this has produced some confusion as to the President's present position. Senator Lodge himself is credited with being opposed to the adoption of the

Continued on Page Three.

Picture Is Sent by Wireless By London Inventor's Device

Copyright, 1922, by The New York Times Co.
Special Cable to THE NEW YORK TIMES.

LONDON, Wednesday, Dec. 27.—The Daily Mail this morning publishes a photograph transmitted by wireless a distance of 100 yards from one building to another by means of a wireless apparatus invented by T. Thorn Baker.

A specially prepared photograph was placed on the wireless transmitter and within three minutes an actual photographic record was obtained in the receiving instrument, the whole operation being automatic throughout, without the intervention of a human operator.

Results as yet, though surprisingly good, are not perfect. The wireless photograph published by The Daily Mail is coarse-grained and blurred, but it is easily recognizable as that of a man on skis assisting a less experienced woman skier.

GERMANY DECLARED IN WILLFUL DEFAULT

Britain Overruled in Reparation Board Vote on Question of Wood Deliveries in 1922.

BIG VICTORY FOR FRANCE

Paris Sees Great Significance in Italo-Belgian Swing on Eve of Premiers' Conference.

PARIS, Dec. 26 (Associated Press).—France gained an important victory in the Allied Reparation Commission today when the commission by a vote of 3 to 1 declared Germany in voluntary default in her wood deliveries for 1922.

France, Belgium and Italy voted in favor of the declaration, while Great Britain cast her ballot against it.

The decision of the commission was immediately communicated to the allied Governments for their action. It may have a vital effect on the reparations problem if France can retain the support of Italy and Belgium when the reparations questions is discussed at the meeting of the Premiers on Jan. 2.

The lone vote cast against the declaration by Great Britain was in accordance with British policy, which has been opposed to declaring Germany in default, in the fear that such action might have a disastrous effect on the already precarious state of German finance.

France is considered to have scored an important point by reason of the fact that the decision of the commission was arrived at on a majority vote. France had been alone for a long time in the contention that Germany could be placed in voluntary default by a simple majority vote. Italy's support of France in the balloting came as a surprise and as an indication that Premier Mussolini is swinging over to the French view in the reparations controversy.

Germany has carried out more than 60 per cent. of its schedule of wood deliveries for this year. When the German experts were before the commission several weeks ago they announced that Germany had been unable to deliver more than she had and that the deliveries for the future must be greatly reduced.

There was much comment tonight over the fact that Great Britain had declined to vote in favor of declaring Germany in default, in view of the approaching meeting of the Premiers. Although the deliveries of wood in themselves are of less importance than other matters connected with reparations, the French point out that today's decision is of real value to France's position on reparations, since it reverses the order of things and places Great Britain in an isolated position on the issue.

Some of the French observers affected tonight to see in the vote an indication that France, Italy and Belgium may present a united front before Great Britain on the question of reparations at the coming meeting here of the Premiers.

BERLIN, Dec. 26 (Associated Press).—Negotiations between Germany and France over the French demand for the delivery of 80,000 tons of pure nitrogen on reparations account have reached a deadlock.

Experts from both countries took part in conferences on the question during the past week at which it was developed that the German Government holds the delivery of this quantity impossible, inasmuch as the German production of nitrogen is already far below the domestic requirements. French and German fertilizer interests are expected to confer soon on the possibility of a compromise.

It is announced that the recent strike

Continued on Page Three.

REDS HERE JUBILANT; CLAIM GREAT STRIDES TOWARD REVOLUTION

Go Forward With New Enthusiasm, Convention Cables Moscow Headquarters.

BOAST OF THEIR IMMUNITY

Say They Might Come Under Ban in Some States, but Are Safe in New York.

DEMAND LOAN FOR RUSSIA

Workers' Party Executive Includes Leading Domestic Communists and Anarchists.

The Workers' Party of America closed its second national convention yesterday at the Labor Temple, 243 East Eighty-fourth Street, by sending a telegram to Moscow notifying the Communist International that it had devoted itself to "constructive work of building a powerful revolutionary movement in America."

In support of its program for the establishment of a Soviet Government in the United States and the "dictatorship of the proletariat" the convention issued an appeal to the revolutionary elements of the country to rally under the party banner and go forward "to the victory of the American social revolution under the leadership and guidance of the Communist International."

On the ground that they were keeping within the law and that the Federal Government had no grounds on which to prosecute them, the delegates discussed communism without restraint. They were careful to avoid the agitation of violence or armed insurrection, pointing out that there was no tangible proof that such tactics were endorsed by the party. Singing the "International" and cheering for the Workers' Party, the convention, which has been in session three days, adjourned late in the afternoon. The several hundred radicals that filled the hall were elated that they had escaped any action by the Department of Justice, which was represented at the meetings.

Cable to Communist International.

The last business of the convention was the unanimous decision to send the following cablegram to the Communist International at Moscow:

"Second national convention Workers' Party sends greetings to Communist International. Convention reports with joy absence of all factionalism. Convention devoted itself to constructive work of building a powerful revolutionary movement in America. All reports indicate greater influence of party in actual struggles of workers. We go forward with new strength and enthusiasm. Long live communism and the International."

The machinery of the convention functioned yesterday with little discussion, the most important developing on the question of appointing committees to "awaken the women to full class conscience." One woman delegate resented the smiles of the men delegates when this matter was brought up, declaring that such actions were "driving the women to feminism." W. Mollenhauer of Detroit said that "You can never make much out of the housewoman, for all she is good for is to stick at home with the frying pan and darn socks." The "flappers," he said, were also hopeless. The matter was finally sent to the Executive Committee with instructions to act favorably.

The delegates followed up their revolutionary program of yesterday with a declaration for "political unity of all revolutionary elements."

Call to Revolutionary Groups.

"The achievements of the Workers' Party since its first convention one year ago," said the resolution, "conclusively demonstrate it to be the rallying centre of the revolutionary elements in the political struggle of the American labor movement. This surely must now be apparent to all those militant elements that still remain outside its ranks.

"We call upon all the revolutionary elements still affiliated with the Proletarian Party, the Socialist Party and similar organizations to join the Workers' Party.

"We now say join the Workers' Party

Continued on Page Five.

Greek Prince Will Visit America Soon; Andrew to Join His Brother Christopher

Copyright, 1922, by The New York Times Company.
Special Cable to THE NEW YORK TIMES.

LONDON, Dec. 26.—Prince Andrew of Greece, who owes his life, as he thinks, to the British Government, talked freely of his plans to THE NEW YORK TIMES correspondent tonight.

"I have some money which I managed to bring out of Greece with me," he said, "but for the moment I am undecided whether to live in England or elsewhere. While I think out that and other problems I am going to visit my brother [Prince Christopher] in America. I shall leave here with part of my family early in January and hope to spend three months at Palm Beach, Florida."

Prince Andrew appeared to feel little bitterness about his arrest. After resigning his command he sent a report on the Anatolian campaign, accusing one of his military superiors.

"Soon after," he said, "there came the revolution, and, having assurances that I was not required to remain in Athens, I went to Corfu, where my home is, and where my wife and children had just arrived from England. While there I wrote to the military authorities at Athens, saying I desired to resign my commission. The reply was that the resignation was accepted, and that I was free to remain in Corfu.

"Shortly afterward, without a word to any one, a vessel was sent for me. I was taken to Athens and lodged in two rooms in a private dwelling as a prisoner, with a police officer always at my door. Well, I do not complain; it might have been much worse, and I am alive, thanks a thousand times to the British Government, which has done so much for me."

The Prince has not yet decided whether to appeal against his sentence of banishment.

"I have ample documentary material for an appeal," he said, "and when the right time arrives I hope to publish the facts. Then the people of my country can judge for themselves whether I was rightly convicted. At present all the evidence that reaches me is convincing that the Greeks as a whole disagree with what has happened. I believe I can say without egotism that the nation is in sympathy with me, and I am confident that, when hot passion and political prejudice have subsided somewhat and my statement of my case is placed before them, the people will decide in my favor."

The Prince emphatically repudiated any intention of visiting ex-King Constantine.

Trade Under Tariff Encourages Harding; Hoover Expects Early Exports of Gold

Special to The New York Times.

WASHINGTON, Dec. 26.—At today's regular meeting of the Cabinet President Harding was interested and pleased, according to what was said at the White House afterward, by information given to him concerning the effect of the new customs tariff on the trade of the United States.

Exact figures were not available, but the President was informed that there had been increases in both exports and imports. What appeared to give the most satisfaction to him and the Cabinet was that the incomplete figures at hand showed that exports of agricultural products were increasing.

Secretary Hoover informed the Cabinet that the trade situation was such that there was a prospect that the United States would shortly begin to export gold. This gold will be shipped mainly to Europe, to take care largely of what was described as invisible exchange. This term applies, in a broad sense, to expenditures by American tourists and the necessity for American gold shipments to cover such things as freight charges and insurance rates.

At the Department of Commerce it was said this afternoon that the information imparted to the Cabinet today followed along the lines of statements made in the annual report of the Secretary of Commerce for 1922. In that report Secretary Hoover said that our gold stocks amounted to about $3,077,000,000 with our surplus over legal necessities and the preservation of a reserve of security "to somewhere over $780,000,000."

Mr. Hoover said that while this was an asset, it would be more advantageous to us, if it were in active use abroad.

"The automatic tendencies in our international trade and financial relations are, however, setting strongly toward rectification of this whole situation without artificial action," he continued. "There is a steady increase in the ratio of imports over exports of goods, as indicated by the decrease in the average monthly balances in our favor over the last two and one-fourth years."

After quoting figures to show that at the end of December, 1920, the average monthly balance in our favor was $274,674,811, and for the three months ended Oct. 1, 1922, was $51,633,542, Mr. Hoover said:

"At this rate we would, theoretically, reach a balance in the movement of goods in another few months."

He went on to explain that economic movements did not proceed on time schedules, but "it would, at least, appear that the invisible exchange is able to take care of commodity balances and that we are reaching the end of the gold import stage of war readjustments." Continued trend in the general direction evident, added Mr. Hoover, would soon produce gold exports even in the face of payments on account of allied debts.

The Department of Commerce expects to have illuminating figures of imports and exports on Jan. 15. These will cover the period since the new tariff law went into operation.

GIGANTIC OBELISK IS FOUND AT ASSUAN

It Is 133 Feet Long and Weighs 1,168 Tons, Three Times That of Heaviest Previously Known.

BUT WAS NEVER ERECTED

It Reveals the Great Ingenuity of the Egyptian Engineers of 4,000 Years Ago.

Copyright, 1922, by The New York Times Company.
By Wireless to THE NEW YORK TIMES.

LUXOR, Egypt, Dec. 26.—A brief item in the continental papers recently announced the discovery of a gigantic obelisk at Assuan on the Nile, south of Thebes. This is not as important as the discovery of the Tutankhamen tomb but is nevertheless of great interest. THE NEW YORK TIMES correspondent can give the first reliable account of this discovery through the courtesy of Captain Engelback, chief inspector of antiques in the department of Upper Egypt.

Captain Engelback said the Assuan antiquities were greatly enriched by this monument, which is not only most impressive but absolutely unique.

Throughout the ages the top portion of this immense obelisk in granite on a hill in Assuan was known, as it was exposed to view for about twenty-two meters of its length sloping into a vast chipheap. The trouble had never been taken to clear away the débris until when in the Winter of 1920 King Fuad, who takes a real interest in antiquities, visited this quarry and expressed a desire to see the obelisk completely exposed to view. This was done by the antiquities department and a complete report will be published by that department early in the new year.

The obelisk, which is still attached to its granite bed, is 133 feet long, 14 feet wide at the base and tapers to 8 feet at the small end. The weight, had the obelisk been extracted, would be 1,168 tons, which is triple the weight of the largest obelisk known to have been erected—that of Queen Hatshepsut at Karnak in Upper Egypt.

Captain Engelback acknowledged that it seems incredible, but added that the ancient Egyptian engineers moved heavier and more awkward blocks, such as the Colossi at Thebes, which were transported far from the South, while the huge broken Colossus of Rameses II. in the Rameseum, which was brought to Assuan, must have weighed almost as much.

This obelisk now unearthed at Assuan was cut from the parent rock by a deep, narrow trench running around it. There is every reason to suppose the trench was bashed out by blows from balls of dolerite, which is a tough greenish stone allied to diorite, of which hundreds were found in the course of the excavating of this obelisk.

Thus they had a tool, durable and efficient, but easily lost. By experiment it can be demonstrated that the work with such tools would have taken about a year. Presumably each dolerite was attached to a hammer which was lifted and bashed down by several workmen under the supervision of foremen with whips.

When the work was about half finished it was abandoned owing to fissures in the granite, which made it unable to stand the tremendous strains due to the great length of the obelisk. It was not abandoned without a most searching examination and it was finally realized that all the work done of bashing out the obelisk was useless as it was manifestly impossible to erect it.

It is apparent from different measurements on the granite that several attempts were made at different periods to complete it before the final rejection of the idea, but as it was not the habit of the ancient Egyptians to associate themselves with failure, there is no evidence as to which Kings ordered the respective attempts.

This destroys the historical value, but the obelisk is most interesting to engineers as showing how the ancient Egyptians, who were ignorant of all tools except rollers and levers, were able to move a brittle mass weighing 1,168 tons.

The numerous tourists who have seen this obelisk since it has been excavated declare it appealed to them more than the tombs and temples because of its majesty and its story of the boundless ingenuity of these remarkable Egyptians of forty centuries ago.

SCIENTISTS UPHOLD EVOLUTION THEORY

Leaders in That Field Unanimously For It, Council of Association Says.

FREE TEACHING DEMANDED

Convention Is Opened at Cambridge With More Than 2,000 in Attendance.

Special to The New York Times.

CAMBRIDGE, Mass., Dec. 26.—The scientific world is convinced of the truth of the evolution theory, it was strongly affirmed today in a formal statement issued by the Council of the American Association for the Advancement of Science, whose convention began here with between 2,000 and 3,000 of the leading scientists of America in attendance.

Denying that the theory of evolution was "a mere guess," the council asserted that it was thoroughly established and that there were no doubters among scientists of note.

The council considered it necessary to issue this statement because of what was deemed the wide misrepresentation of a paper on evolution read several months ago before the association by William Bateson, an eminent English scientist. He is a strong supporter of the theory of evolution, but maintained that the factors which caused evolution were in doubt. It is alleged that fundamentalists and other anti-evolutionists quoted him as a scientist who did not believe in evolution, and that attempts had even been made to array the American association against Darwin.

Limit on Teaching Deplored.

The statement read:

"Inasmuch as the attempt has been made in several States to prohibit in tax-supported institutions the teaching of evolution as applied to man, and

"Since it has been asserted that there is not a fact in the universe in support of this theory, that it is a 'mere guess' which leading scientists are now abandoning, and that even the American Association for the Advancement of Science at its last meeting in Toronto, Canada, approved this revolt against evolution, and

"Inasmuch as such statements have been given wide publicity through the press and are misleading public opinion on this subject, therefore,

"The Council of the American Association for the Advancement of Science has thought it advisable to take formal action upon this matter, in order that there may be no ground for misunderstanding of the attitude of the association, which is one of the largest scientific bodies in the world, with a membership of more than 11,000 persons, including the American authorities in all branches of science. The following statements represent the position of the council with regard to the theory of evolution:

"1. The council of the association affirms that, so far as the scientific evidences of the evolution of plants and animals and man are concerned, there is no ground whatever for the assertion that these evidences constitute a 'mere guess.' No scientific generalization is more strongly supported by thoroughly tested evidences than is that of organic evolution.

"2. The council of the association affirms that the evidences in favor of the evolution of man are sufficient to convince every scientist of note in the world. The evidences are increasing in number and importance every year.

"3. The council also affirms that the theory of evolution is one of the most potent of the great influences for good that have thus far entered into human experience; it has promoted the progress of knowledge, it has fostered unprejudiced inquiry and it has served as an invaluable aid in humanity's search for truth in many fields.

"4. The council of the association is convinced that any legislation attempting to limit the teaching of any scientific doctrine so well established and so widely accepted by specialists as is the doctrine of evolution would be a profound mistake, which could not fail to injure and retard the advancement of knowledge and of human welfare, by denying the freedom of teaching and inquiry which is essential to all progress.

"EDWIN GRANT CONKLIN, Chairman;
"HENRY FAIRFIELD OSBORN,
"CHARLES B. DAVENPORT,
"Committee."

The association at its first general session tonight in the Walker Memorial Building at the Institute of Technology was welcomed by Mayor Curley of Bos-

Continued on Page Two.

IZAAK WALTON HOUSE BOUGHT AS MEMORIAL TO JULIEN T. DAVIES

"Compleat Angler's" Cottage to Be a Shrine for All Fishermen, Including Americans.

ENDOWMENT IS PLANNED

Fund for Upkeep of Historic Structure at Shallowford, Eng., Is Under Way.

WILL ASSEMBLE A LIBRARY

Devotees of Rod and Creel Here to Aid in Gathering Books on Their Favorite Diversion.

A movement to restore and preserve the cottage of Izaak Walton, prince of anglers, at Shallowford, England, begun by Mayor T. A. Dunn and other officials of Walton's birthplace, Stafford, is to be carried on in this country through friends and former legal and business associates of the late Julien Tappan Davies, attorney and trustee of the Mutual Life Insurance Company.

This was disclosed yesterday coincidentally with news that an offer made by relatives and friends of Mr. Davies to purchase the cottage had been accepted by Mayor Dunn and his committee appointed to consider the future of the great angler's home. It is the hope of the American sponsors of the fund to obtain enough money to endow the structure, place in it a library of piscatorial lore and make it a shrine for followers of the rod and creel the world over.

The cottage, six miles up the river from Stafford, is a timber-framed building with thatched roof. According to tradition, it was the favorite resting place of the great fisherman when he was whipping the brooks and rivers for fish. There also, according to persistent tradition, Walton mused upon his book "The Compleat Angler."

Was Gift to Charity.

When Walton died, in December, 1683, his will directed that the cottage be given to the Corporation of Stafford for the assistance of the worthy poor and various other philanthropic purposes. At a later date the cottage was assigned as part of the revenue of the King Edward VI. grammar school of Stafford, but, owing to the lapse of time, the building has become dilapidated, and the Stafford County Education Committee, though sympathetic, is without funds to renovate and keep the dwelling as a link to the great disciple of angling.

A brief notice in a London weekly, which caught the attention of Major Archibald G. Thacher of Barry, Wainwright, Thacher & Symmers, New York attorneys, resulted in the idea of American help in the restoration, and also of making the rehabilitation a memorial to Mr. Davies, who was a keen fisherman. The London publication reported that Mayor Dunn and other officials were seeking to raise a fund of £500 to rehabilitate the cottage and an additional £50 to purchase it.

"Fishermen and sportsmen, both in the United States and England, will, I am sure, be glad to have an opportunity of contributing for the preservation of such an interesting relic of 'the Prince of Anglers,'" wrote Major Thacher, who served in the World War, to Mayor Dunn.

"My late father-in-law, Mr. Julien T. Davies, was a great sportsman and fisherman, and I am sure that were he alive he would wish to enjoy the privilege of contributing to such an admirable object. May I, therefore, enclose draft for £5 to your order, 'In memory of Julien T. Davies, American fisherman and sportsman'?

Fisherman Led Cortege.

"An incident occurred at the cemetery immediately before Mr. Davies was buried which was of such a picturesque and touching character and so reminiscent of his fondness for angling, that one of his partners included the following description of that incident in a most touching and beautiful memorial written of Mr. Davies, in the following language:

"'An old fellow of the vicinage, with fishing basket—not the creel—on his arm, and a [illegible]—not a rod—over his shoulder, and in typically homely attire, was, to all appearance, returning from some neighboring trout stream. After a significant pause he turned and preceded the hearse to the grave, and then with

Continued on Page Six.

Town Hall's Banker-Preacher Arrested; Is Accused of Selling Worthless Bonds

Victor H. Arnold, who has been preaching Sunday mornings in the Town Hall, was arrested last night at his Bayside home on a Federal warrant in which thirty-one charges are made, among them using the mails to defraud and being a fugitive from justice. He was taken before United States Commissioner Michael McGoldrick in Brooklyn and held in $25,000 bail, which he was unable to produce. Later he was taken to Raymond Street Jail to await examination, set for Jan. 7. It was alleged by Federal officers that Arnold had been indicted in Madison, Wis., on charges involving the sale of worthless bonds to the amount of $750,000.

Arnold characterized his arrest as a "frame-up." He said that he had resigned in the latter part of 1919 as President of the Madison Bond Company of Madison, Wis., which he says he founded. According to the authorities, Arnold said he then went to Chicago and began to lecture on Christianity, that he still owns a large block of stock in the bond company, and that after he left it a new Secretary and other officials were elected, who are responsible for the company's troubles. The authorities say Arnold explained that the new officers were indicted, but never were brought to trial, and he went to Washington to get the Attorney General to push the indictments, but the cases are still pending.

It is alleged that the Madison Bond Company issued $1,000,000 in worthless bonds guaranteed to pay interest at 7 per cent. and that of these about $750,000 were sold all over the country.

On Nov. 5 Arnold leased the Town Hall for $100 each Sunday to preach on "The Spirit of Truth." For seven Sundays he spoke on the same text, paying the expenses himself and making up part of them from the collections. At some of the services he was heckled, but he always managed to silence his questioners.

He is said to be a life member of the Art Institute of Chicago and a member of the Union League Club of Chicago. When he first began his services here he said his one hope was "to advance the spirituality of the individual by directing the person to the teachings of Christ."

Mrs. Arnold and her three daughters were in a luxurious hall of the large house they occupy in Bayside last night when she told the story of her husband's rise and his present predicament. She insisted that a "political ring in Madison was jealous of her husband, and was doing all in its power to undo him."

"I have been trying to raise the bail to get my husband out of jail," she said, "but we are penniless. My husband telephoned me from the jail tonight that perhaps he can do some good while there."

Only One Complaint in a Day Prosecutor's New Low Record

Only one complaint was received in the District Attorney's office yesterday, breaking a record of many years, according to District Attorney Banton. Approximately 35,000 complaints are received in a year, he said, and as many as 200 are filed in the Complaint Bureau in a day.

The lone complaint, from a man who alleged that he had been defrauded in the purchase of an automobile, was received just as the office was about to close for the day.

LITTLE GIRL SLAIN IN MIDST OF TOYS

Pretty Theresa McCarthy, 10 Years Old, Found Shot Dead in Her Home.

MURDER PUZZLES POLICE

Body Discovered by Mother—No Weapon Nor Sign of Intruder.

Theresa McCarthy, a pretty ten-year-old girl, was found dead with a bullet hole in her breast in the midst of her toys on the floor of the dining room of her home, at 562 Morgan Avenue, Greenpoint, last night.

Her murder puzzled the best detectives in Brooklyn. They could find no motive for the killing, or indication as to how the person who did it gained entrance to the house. There was no sign that the girl had been ill-treated.

The only clue that came to them after hours of investigation was the story told by a playmate of Theresa's, Charles Nell, 13 years old, of 296 Nassau Avenue, who said that a man in a sailor hat had followed them on the street one day. How the man got into the house unless Theresa admitted him they were at a loss to explain, for there were no marks to indicate that an entrance had been forced.

The fact that a window was found raised a few inches in the kitchen led them to believe that possibly the man might have got out that way to the yard a few feet below. But no fingerprints were found on the window sill. It would not have been possible either for the bullet to have entered this way.

Theresa was known in the neighborhood as "the little vamp," because of her pretty face and dark eyes. She was a favorite with every one. She lived with her mother, Mrs. Pauline McCarthy, who had been separated from her husband for nine years and who supported herself and the child by working in a factory at Kingsland Avenue and Sutton Street, near by. There was also a boarder in the house, Benjamin Prenderville, who worked in the Brooklyn Post Office until 5:30 o'clock last night.

The husband, Edward McCarthy, a veteran of the war, lived with his sister, Mrs. Mary Corbett, at 91 Driggs Avenue. Despite the long separation there was friendliness between him and his wife and he was very fond of his daughter. He gave Theresa Christmas presents every year and on Christmas Day there was a family gathering at Mrs. Corbett's, at which McCarthy gave the little girl a sled. They all had dinner together and were very happy.

Left Alone in House.

Yesteray morning Mrs. McCarthy went to work early, leaving Theresa in bed. There was no school and no reason why she should get up early, so she told her mother she would get her own breakfast and not to worry about her. Some time after her mother had gone she apparently got up and had bread and milk, for there was a bowl on the table, and then she played around the apartment, clad in her little shirt and petticoat. Her Christmas toys interested her so that she did not want to go out right away and roller skate about the neighborhood with the other children, who always looked for her and made her one of their leaders in their games.

What happened after that nobody has been able even to guess. Only her little pet dog, shut in the bathroom, knows. No gunshot was heard by others in the house, nobody heard a scream, there was no sign that the door had been forced open by burglars.

When Mrs. McCarthy left her work and reached the street she looked around for Theresa, for the little girl used to take her dog and skates to meet her mother nearly every day. There was no sign of her yesterday and, somewhat worried, Mrs. McCarthy hurried on

Continued on Page Four.

ARREST DR. M'KOIN, REPUTED KLAN HEAD, AS MER ROUGE SLAYER

Physician Who Accused Murdered Men of Seeking His Life Held in Baltimore.

HIS EXTRADITION SOUGHT

Louisiana Governor Declares There Is Ample Ground for Ordering His Detention.

KU KLUX ISSUES STATEMENT

Denies Part in Murders—Federal Agents Say They Know Lake Dynamiters.

Special to The New York Times.

BALTIMORE, Dec. 26.—Dr. B. M. McKoin, former Mayor of Mer Rouge, La., was arrested this afternoon at Brady Institute, Johns Hopkins Hospital, where he has been taking a post graduate course. The arrest was made in compliance with a request from Governor Parker of Louisiana, which asked that the former Mayor be held for the Louisiana authorities in connection with the recent alleged Ku Klux Klan murders at Mer Rouge.

Dr. McKoin asserted that he was not a fugitive from justice and that he came to Baltimore on Oct. 1 to take a course in urology under Dr. Hugh Young at the Brady clinic. He insisted that he knew nothing of the murders of Richards and Daniels and that he left the town after he had been shot at one night as he was returning from attending a false call.

"I am practically ruined financially," he continued. "Physician friends of mine are providing the money to enable me to study here. My friends advised me to leave because my work required me to go into rural communities much at nights. Shot at once from ambush and just missed, I was told that I could not protect myself from such attacks.

McKoin Tells of Threats.

"The trouble, so far as I was concerned, began six years ago when I was elected Mayor of the town for a period of two years. I did not want the position but the best people of Mer Rouge wanted me to run. They elected me and I did my best to stop the association of white men with negro women, gambling and other evils. Mer Rouge is a town of between 750 and 1,000 people. It is surrounded by a prosperous farming community. You know how things are in a small town when any change is attempted. One-half is with those who are in. The other half is against them.

"When I had finished my first two years I received a letter telling me not to run again. After such a threat, of course, I had to run. I was elected. I finished my second term in 1920. Since then there has been some disorders at various times. Last Summer some of the men who were opposed to me used to come out in front of my house and fire off their guns and shout. It frightened my wife and children and I asked that it be stopped, but it wasn't stopped."

Dr. McKoin then told of how he had been called by a false message to attend an aged negro woman who had not asked for him, and how he had been shot at in his car on returning home. Federal agents who examined his car after he left Mer Rouge hold that the shots which punctured the car would have killed the driver, and that because Dr. McKoin escaped unhurt, the shots must have been fired from within the car. After relating that, following this occurrence, he had received a letter telling him that "they would get me the next time," he continued:

"It was then, after my friends had told me that I could not practice medicine, make my calls and protect myself from such night attacks as that, that I got out. I received this letter on Friday and I left Mer Rouge on Tuesday. That was last August. While I know nothing about the death of Richards and Daniels, the attack of the mob on those men and on J. L. Daniels, W. C. Andrews and C. C. Davenport occurred after I left. I do know the men."

"Were they identified with you when you were Mayor?" he was asked.

"No, not especially," he answered.

Denies He Is Klansman.

"All I know is that both men who were killed were on the bad side—the side of the bootleggers, gunmen and men who kept negro concubines," he continued. "I had fought that element while I was in the Mayor's chair and had a hard time doing it.

"Just before I left Mer Rouge a boy of good family was shot in the back there. What did the Sheriff and the Governor do? The case was dismissed, after a jury filled with bootleggers and the vicious element declared the alleged murderer innocent.

"Now, however, when a bootlegger and some one else is killed the Governor joins in the investigation. This affair, in my opinion, will decide whether the decent or good element of the town will control. The town has a reputation for being rough."

He asserted that lawlessness was a common occurrence at Mer Rouge and that he was among those who started to clean up the place. The result, he said, was a hard battle with bootleggers, moonshiners and men of bad reputation.

"Were you identified with any church?" he was asked.

"Yes; I was a deacon in the Baptist Church."

"Were the church people with you when you were Mayor?"

"Yes, generally."

"Was the Ku Klux Klan active in the neighborhood?"

"Well, they used to parade around a great deal with their robes and their masks on, but I never knew of anything like this that they did."

"Are you a member of the Ku Klux Klan?"

Dr. McKoin refused to answer the question.

[illegible]

Howard Carter and A.C. Mace after they had broken through the wall of the sealed chamber of Tutankhamen's tomb on February 16, 1923.

"All the News That's Fit to Print."

The New York Times.

THE WEATHER.
Fair, slightly warmer Thursday; Friday, fair, warmer; moderate winds, becoming south.
For full weather report see Page 23.

VOL. LXXII....No. 23,687. NEW YORK, FRIDAY, DECEMBER 1, 1922. TWO CENTS

GREEKS TAKE STEPS TO ARRAIGN PRINCE; ARMY CHIEFS SEIZED

Evidence Against Andrew Collected—Rebels to Join in Putting Him on Trial.

TWO GENERALS ARRESTED

Dousmanis and Valettas Taken and the Former Commander-in-Chief Is Sought.

EX-MINISTERS DIED BRAVELY

Pope Will Protest—Italy Threatens Break—Constantine Planning to Come Here.

ATHENS, Nov. 30 (Associated Press).—The following official statement was issued today:

"General Dousmanis, former Chief of the General Staff, and General Valettas, former Chief of Staff in Asia Minor, have been arrested, and a warrant has been issued for the arrest of General Papoulas, former Commander-in-Chief of the army in Asia Minor.

"The trial of Prince Andrew (brother of former King Constantine), who commanded an army corps at the time of the Sakaria operations, begins next week."

Inquiry into responsibility for the Anatolian disaster continues, and the prosecution of General Papoulas and other officials was due to new evidence said to have been found.

The Commission of Inquiry has forwarded the report of its investigations into the actions of Prince Andrew during the campaign to the Revolutionary Committee, which, in conjunction with the Government, will make arrangements for his trial.

Leaders Met Death Jauntily.

The six Cabinet Ministers executed here last Tuesday went courageously, even jauntily, to their deaths. [illegible]

[illegible]

Refused to Be Blindfolded.

The death sentence was delivered by the court-martial on Tuesday, and was communicated to the condemned men, who had previously been removed from the Averoff Prison, where they had said farewell to their relatives. [illegible]

[illegible]

When the order to fire rang out all fell simultaneously and physicians said that death in each case had come instantly.

The bodies were removed to a near-by cemetery, where relatives attended to the burial rites. Only a small crowd saw the executions.

Prince Andrew on Trial Monday.

LONDON, Nov. 30 (Associated Press).—A dispatch to the Exchange Telegraph from Athens quotes the Greek newspaper Eleutheros Typos as saying that the trial of Prince Andrew will begin next Monday.

A dispatch to The Daily Mail from Athens, referring to impending new trials of former officials and others, says it is not likely that any further death sentences will be imposed. [illegible]

Britain acted without consulting her allies in withdrawing her Minister from Athens, Prime Minister Bonar Law informed the House of Commons today in answer to a question. [illegible]

"In taking this action his Majesty's Government were actuated by the general consideration that it is contrary to the practice of civilized governments to put ministers on trial and execute them on account of the failure of their policy."

This statement evoked loud laughter and cheers, in which Mr. Lloyd George and the other Ministers in the late Government joined.

The Prime Minister added that the executions were carried out by a company.

Continued on Page Three.

Pray for Fuel and Water At Thanksgiving Service

Special to The New York Times.

CAPE MAY, N. J., Nov. 30.—At the union Thanksgiving service in the First Presbyterian Church prayers were offered by the pastor, the Rev. George Hillman of the Methodist Episcopal Church for both fuel and water. It has not rained in lower Cape May County in many weeks and the coal situation is acute.

Forest fires have destroyed much firewood. Wood is bringing as high as $16 a cord.

REPORT FIFTY KILLED IN MEXICO CITY RIOT

Police Pour Machine-Gun Volleys Into Parade Protesting Against Water Famine.

CITY HALL FIRED BY MOBS

Rioters Re-Form for Attack at Night and Federal Troops Are Ordered Out.

MEXICO CITY, Nov. 30.—Seventeen persons are known to have been killed, and other estimates of dead run as high as fifty, with anywhere from a dozen to one hundred wounded, when police fired machine gun volleys late today into a parade protesting in front of the City Hall against the water famine.

Rioting continues tonight and Federal troops have been ordered out.

It is impossible to determine the exact number of casualties, as there were 2,000 persons in the parade, and of these at least 300 penetrated into the City Hall enclosure, where they came into the direct line of fire as the police opened the machine gun volleys.

[illegible]

Mexico City's lack of water during the past eight days has caused great suffering to the whole population, with the result that a spontaneous organization was formed today to parade through the main street to the City Hall. [illegible]

[illegible]

IGNORANCE ON NAVY HERE PIQUES LONDON

Britain Scraps 16 Ships Under Treaty and Is Surprised Over the Denial Here.

LONDON, Nov. 30.—Considerable surprise has been caused in naval circles here by a dispatch from Washington attributing to the State Department a statement that it was unaware that any country signatory to the Washington naval limitation treaty had already begun the scrapping of battleships.

All the British battleships except four condemned by the schedule of the treaty to immediate destruction are already either in the shipbreakers' hands or on the way there. Those already sold to the shipbreakers are the Commonwealth, Dreadnought, Bellerophon, St. Vincent, Inflexible, Hercules, Indomitable and Temeraire. Six others rendered useless for further warlike service are the Neptune, Orion, New Zealand, and Monarch, Conqueror and Princess Royal, and two more, the Agincourt and Erin, will be rendered useless by the end of the year. [illegible]

GEM-STUDDED RELICS IN EGYPTIAN TOMB AMAZE EXPLORERS

Art Treasures Fill 2 Sealed Antechambers, Reached Through Blocked Passages.

GILT STATUES AND BEDS

Portraits and Hunting Scenes Painted on Funeral Paraphernalia of Tutankhamen.

ONE ROOM YET UNOPENED

This Is Thought to Contain Mummy of a Monarch Who Ruled 3,270 Years Ago.

Special Cable to THE NEW YORK TIMES.

LONDON, Nov. 30.—The Cairo correspondent of The London Times in a dispatch to his paper describes how Lord Carnarvon and Howard Carter unearthed below the tomb of Rameses VI, near Luxor, two rooms containing the funeral paraphernalia of King Tutankhamen, who reigned about 1350 B. C., the discovery of which was announced yesterday. He says:

"A sealed outer door was carefully opened, then a way was cleared down some sixteen steps and along a passage of about twenty-five feet. A door to the chambers was found to be sealed similarly to the outer door, and as on the outer door had been, and, as on the outer door, there were traces of reclosing.

"With difficulty an entrance was effected and when at last the excavators managed to squeeze their way in an extraordinary sight met their eyes, one that they could scarcely credit.

"First they saw three magnificent state couches, all gilt, with exquisite carving and the heads of Typhon, Hathor and a lion. On these rested beds beautifully carved and inlaid with ivory and semi-precious stones and also innumerable boxes of exquisite workmanship.

Contents of Some of the Boxes.

[illegible]

Wreaths and Rolls of Paper.

"There were some remarkable wreaths still looking like evergreen, and one of the boxes contained rolls of paper, which are expected to render a mass of information.

"A further chamber revealed an indescribable state of confusion. Here furniture, gold beds, exquisite boxes and [illegible]

Continued on Page Two.

James R. Mann Dies in Washington Home After Week's Illness, Ending in Pneumonia

Special to The New York Times.

WASHINGTON, Nov. 30.—Representative James R. Mann of Illinois, for nearly twenty-six years a member of the House, and during most of that time a leader of the Republican Party, died at his home here at 11:15 o'clock tonight.

Mr. Mann was 66 years old and had been ill since Friday. Not until yesterday was his condition considered serious. His colleagues had been informed that he was suffering from a severe but not serious cold, but last night pneumonia developed. He had a sinking spell this afternoon, but rallied and for a time was thought to be much improved. A second sinking spell tonight ended with death.

For a quarter of a century James R. Mann, or "Jim," as he was known on both sides of the House, had been a dominating figure in the House. He was a leader in hundreds of parliamentary battles, and his ability was recognized by foes as well as friends. [illegible]

Yesterday he sent word to Mr. Mondell, the majority floor leader, that if his vote was needed to pass the Ship Subsidy bill he would risk a trip to the Chamber. Mr. Mondell refused to risk Mr. Mann's health, and a pair was arranged with Representative Sabath.

[illegible]

Mr. Mann was born on a farm near Bloomington, Ill., Oct. 20, 1856. He was a graduate of the University of Illinois and the Union College of Law, Chicago. His wife was Miss Emma Columbia, of Champaign, Ill.

Mr. Mann is the second member of the House to die since Congress was convened in extraordinary session on Nov. 20. The other was Representative Nolan of San Francisco.

CLEMENCEAU MOVED AT TOMB OF LINCOLN

Placing a Wreath on Grave, He Says He Came to Get "New Strength, New Powers."

ANGERED AT CAMERA MEN

Says His Reason for Going to Baltimore Is to Study Terrapin—Denies He Is on Egg Diet.

Special to The New York Times.

SPRINGFIELD, Ill., Nov. 30.—Georges Clemenceau observed Thanksgiving Day by visiting the home of Lincoln and laying a wreath upon his grave, and outside the tomb he spoke with great emotion of the spirit of the man he came to honor.

[illegible]

Angered at Camera Men.

The veteran French statesman was highly indignant over an incident that he considered a desecration of Lincoln's tomb. [illegible]

[illegible]

Continued on Page Seven.

W. G. ROCKEFELLER DIES OF PNEUMONIA

Nephew of John D., Stricken on Monday, Suffered Relapse Wednesday.

IN MANY CORPORATIONS

Elected Only Last Tuesday a Director of the Consolidated Textile Company.

William Goodsell Rockefeller, son of the late William Rockefeller, nephew of John D. Rockefeller and brother-in-law of James A. Stillman, died at twenty minutes before 10 last night of double pneumonia at his home, 292 Madison Avenue. Mr. Rockefeller returned from his office Monday complaining of a chill, and his physician ordered him to bed.

[illegible]

Lawson's Prediction.

Thomas W. Lawson, then writing a sketch of the Rockefeller connections, was one of those who made such a prediction. [illegible]

[illegible]

Continued on Page Two.

HARVEY IN 6 POINTS SUMS UP AMERICA'S 'NATIONAL POLICY'

In Manchester Speech He Gives His Formula for Our Internal and External Position.

FOR A CONCERT OF EUROPE

To Avoid Needless and Entangling Alliances, but Preserve Blessings of Peace.

ALL NATIONS' RIGHTS EQUAL

Declares Our Foreign Policy Should Always Be Inspired by Love of Freedom.

MANCHESTER, England, Nov. 30.—Ambassador Harvey, speaking tonight at the Thanksgiving Day banquet of the Anglo-American Society of Manchester, to the toast of "our cordial relations," said:

"A very few words would comprise a comprehensively adequate response. The relations of Great Britain and the United States ought to be cordial and they are. They should continue to be cordial, and they shall. What more need be said? If I were wise I should now take my seat, but who other than a craven will pay heed to prudence when he may yield to temptation?"

He then, in the course of his speech, outlined what he said might be considered the "national policy" of the United States in these words:

"First—To foster the strength of the Republic by just legislation and economy at home.

"Second—To preserve to the nations of the world the blessings of peace.

"Third—To strive to cultivate and maintain a concert of Europe.

"Fourth—To avoid needless and entangling alliances.

"Fifth—To acknowledge the equal rights of all nations.

"Sixth—The foreign policy of the United States should always be inspired by love of freedom."

Improving Trade Conditions.

[illegible]

Says We Want All to Prosper.

[illegible]

Continued on Page Three.

To Open Old Croton Aqueduct During Repairs on the Catskill

Special to The New York Times.

CROTON, Nov. 30.—Orders have been issued to prepare the old Croton aqueduct, which has not been used for five years, to convey water to New York City.

Employes who look after the old tunnel have been informed that the water from the Croton reservoirs is to be turned into it again. Since the United States declared war against Germany the original Croton aqueduct, opened in the '40s, has not been used. Water has been conveyed through the so-called new Croton aqueduct and the Catskill aqueduct.

Aqueduct employes are told that the temporary reopening of the original Croton tunnel will be necessitated because of repairs to the new Catskill aqueduct.

ACCUSE EACH OTHER OF BECKER MURDER

Husband of Woman Whose Body Was Found in Ash Pit Says Friend Killed Her.

ADMITS HE KNEW OF CRIME

Auto Repair Man Declares Innocence—Anna Elias Held as Material Witness.

District Attorney Edward J. Glennon of the Bronx obtained partial confessions yesterday from Abraham Becker and Reuben Norkin, who are under arrest in connection with the murder of Mrs. Becker, whose body was found on Wednesday in a vacant lot in the Bronx.

Mrs. Becker was killed, according to her husband's confession, by Norkin. Becker admitted that he was an accessory after the fact in concealing the crime. Norkin admitted that he had furnished the shovel to bury the dead woman last April, but denied that he participated in the killing.

[illegible]

Norkin Accuses Husband.

[illegible]

Continued on Page Ten.

Lost Football Prestige Leads President And Professor of Geneva College to Resign

Special to The New York Times.

BEAVER FALLS, Pa., Nov. 30.—The rift that has been brewing at Geneva College over the failure of the varsity football team to win glory on the gridiron has caused Dr. Archibald A. Johnston, President, and Dr. Robert C. Colwell, Professor of Mathematics and Radio, to resign. [illegible]

[illegible]

PRESIDENT MOVES TO BLOCK RADICALS PLANNING FOR WAR

With Wallace and Old Guard Leaders, He Frames Program for Relief of Farmers.

BITTER FIGHT IN PROSPECT

La Follette Group Purposes to Attack All of Harding's Policies in Congress.

WILL BEGIN WITH SUBSIDY

Intends to Force Its Own Candidate on Republicans in 1924 or Form Third Party.

Special to The New York Times.

WASHINGTON, Nov. 30.—President Harding and the conservative Republican leaders will be brought into a bitter struggle with the radical progressive forces in the regular session of Congress beginning Monday, in the opinion of observers who have been watching the movements of Senator La Follette and his group promoting the progressive movement.

[illegible]

Republican Division Predicted.

[illegible]

Foresee a Liberal Party.

[illegible]

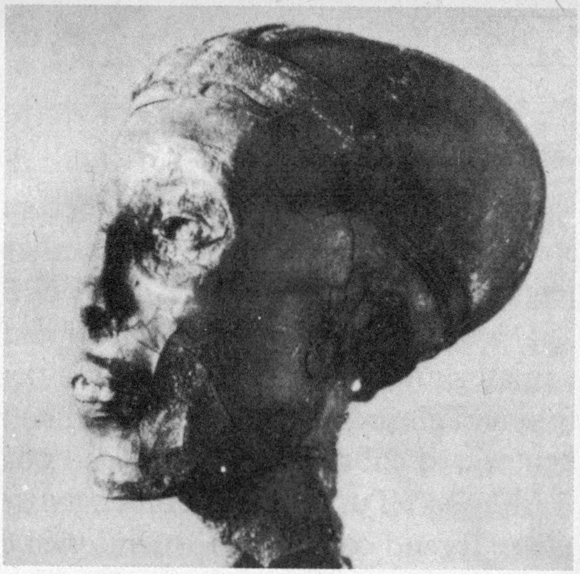

Tutankhamen's mummified head.

The back of the gold-plated throne.

A mirror-case in the form of the sign of life.

"All the News That's Fit to Print"

The New York Times

LATE CITY EDITION

Weather: Fair, very cold today and tonight. Chance of snow tomorrow. Temp. range: today 24-14; Sunday 33-26. Full U.S. report on Page 30.

VOL. LXXII....No. 23,765. NEW YORK, SATURDAY, FEBRUARY 17, 1923. TWO CENTS In Greater New York | THREE CENTS Within 200 Miles | [illegible]

ESSEN IS COWED AFTER WOUNDING OF TWO SOLDIERS

Fight in Beer Hall Causes the French to Turn Out a Stronger Military Display.

CITY NOW WITHOUT POLICE

Chief Arrested, Men Disarmed and Records Seized—Frequent Clashes Elsewhere.

JAIL FOR 2 BURGOMASTERS

Electric Plant Director Is Fined 5,000,000 Marks—Berlin Supplies Funds for Strikers.

Special Cable to THE NEW YORK TIMES.

DUESSELDORF, Feb. 16.—Every day is adding more and more to the casualty list of the Ruhr occupation.

Last evening in a beer hall at Essen two French soldiers were slightly, and one German policeman gravely, wounded.

At Gunkenrath a French sentinel fired on and killed a German workman who was trespassing on the railroad track.

At several points last evening sentries and posts fired shots as warnings and with every rifle discharged the tension is growing.

The affair at Essen was the most important as affecting the situation in the town. It began, as trouble may at any time begin, trivially enough. Eight French soldiers and two Belgians went into the beer house and called for drinks about 9:30 in the evening. As usual the landlord refused to serve them and the soldiers, as has become their habit, began to draw beer themselves. In protest the landlord called in the German policeman on duty at the door, and, according to all accounts of both the Germans and the French, this policeman entered excitedly with his revolver in his hand crying "Hands up!"

At once the affair which had been a burlesque became serious. The French soldiers instead of obeying such a peremptory order began to draw their revolvers. Then the German fired. Before he could be overpowered he had wounded two men slightly and it was not till he fell with a bullet through his body that he stopped firing.

Attracted by the noise the German police patrol entered at that moment and prevented further fighting.

Police Headquarters Raided.

Today the affair had an aftermath. With armored cars and machine guns a detachment of French troops rode through the town and wheeled sharply into the police barracks before it was known what was intended. They arrested the chief of police, disarmed eighty men in the station and took possession of all records.

Everywhere throughout town patrols have been moving about all day, and as if in warning to the nationalist trouble makers, the French are displaying their strength.

Yesterday the town was silent, depressed and suspicious. Today it is cowed. The French have the whip hand and even the most ardent nationalist must admit it.

All through the province the measures of the French for repressing organized resistance and propaganda are increasing in severity. Over half the newspapers in the Ruhr have now been suspended for one cause or another, police who do not salute, being arrested in batches, and with every new batch the penalty is being increased.

To all this tightening up the Germans are making as yet no new reply. The telephones of Düsseldorf, Essen and several other places are still suspended.

At Bochum the municipal employes today struck for four hours as a protest against the arrests which have been made in the town and against the requisitioning of automobiles. The only return to work was at Duisburg, where the tramway employes have been granted a 110 per cent. increase in wages at a time when the mark is improving by leaps.

Yesterday for the first time the effect of the export prohibition order became evident. As fewer freight trains are leaving the district fewer are coming in, and from 200 the number out and in, has fallen to about 40. If that falling off continues a food shortage, which always threatened, may become a reality, and both the French and Germans are doing their utmost to deal with the situation when it arises, each with the hope that their efforts will rally the masses to their support. The Germans are organizing storage and distribution centres as if for a siege, and at the same time the French are accumulating all the food they can in the district. The number of military trains has been largely increased and food is being brought from France far in excess of what is needed by the troops.

To counter all this effort to obtain local support among the workers the Germans have now nearly completed their arrangements for payment of workers forced out of employment by the prohibition of exports. Big firms are prepared themselves to stand a loss, but to small firms the Government, through the Employers' Association and the Reichsbank, is prepared to give all the help that is needed. The total wages roll which it is estimated will have to be met is something like 50,000,000 gold marks a month, and the Government, which in November last asked for a moratorium in reparation payments, seems now prepared to pay this sum to workmen in order to support resistance to the French. So far there has, however, been little or no closing down, and except at the coalpits where little or nothing is being done except for repairs and local consumption work, the Ruhr seems almost normal.

Quick Retaliation by French.

ESSEN, Feb. 16 (Associated Press).—Following the wounding of two French soldiers by German security police in a café brawl last night, Essen was the

Continued on Page Three.

89 M. P.'s Ask Harding's Aid; 'One Hope of Saving Europe'

By Wireless to THE NEW YORK TIMES.

LONDON, Feb. 16.—Signed by eighty-nine Labor and Co-operative members of the British Parliament, the following cablegram was sent to President Harding today:

"America with Britain unwittingly made France's present destructive action possible. We appeal for American co-operation today as the one hope of saving Europe."

Among those who have signed the message are Arthur Henderson, George Lansbury, R. E. Buxton and John Hodge.

$500,000 GEM THEFT SUSPECT ARRESTED

"Marshall" Held as Leader of Gang That Robbed Mrs. Schoellkopf at Drinking Party.

CAUGHT ON MONTREAL TRAIN

Another Arrest Here Said to Have Furnished Clue—Companion Also in Custody.

Inspector John D. Coughlin at Police Headquarters last night announced that the debonair "Marshall," alleged leader of the gang that robbed Mrs. Irene Schoellkopf of $500,000 worth of jewelry in an apartment at 64 West Fifty-second street aerly on the morning of Jan. 1, had been arrested yesterday on a train between Schenectady and Troy. The arrest was made by Detectives Daly, Horan and Buckley of Inspector Coughlin's staff. They caught "Marshall" when he was attempting to return from Montreal and took him to a house at 75 Lancaster Street, Albany, which he said was his home, to look for the stolen jewels. The detectives reported to Inspector Coughlin by telephone from the Lancaster Street house that they had not found the booty.

The man alleged to be "Marshall" was traveling under the name of M. D. Biddulph. According to the police, his full name is Matthew Darian Biddulph. The police say that he is an ex-convict, and that he is known to the police all over the country under the aliases of R. H. Matthews, R. H. Harrison and John F. Derby. According to the police, his photograph is No. 17,555 in the Rogues' Gallery at San Francisco, and he has been arrested many times, and convicted several times.

Inspector Coughlin said the man was wanted in Los Angeles and San Francisco on the charge of passing worthless checks.

Search of the records at Police Headquarters last night showed that "Marshall" had been arrested for passing a worthless check at the Yale Club in New York City in 1917, but had got off with a suspended sentence.

"Marshall," when arrested, said he was 27 years old and gave his occupation as traveling salesman and actor. Under the name of Biddulph, Inspector Coughlin said, the man had had some success as a moving picture actor, appearing in Universal photoplays. By a coincidence, the last film in which he is known to have appeared was called "Wanted at Headquarters," in which he played a "heavy" part—in other words played a movie villain. This was in 1919.

Companion Also Arrested.

The detectives arrested with "Marshall," a man who identified himself as George F. Daley of 83 Clinton Street, Albany. As far as known, Daley had no connection with the Schoellkopf case, but the police are holding him to investigate why he was traveling with "Marshall." Daley is said to be a New York billposter, with an address in the vicinity of Broadway and 82d Street.

The arrest of "Marshall" and Daley followed a few hours after Horan, one of the detectives who made these arrests, had locked up a man named Charles Curtis in New York. Horan and his partner, Detective Owens, have been detached from all other duty to work exclusively on the Schoellkopf case for several weeks. In the line-up at Police Headquarters yesterday morning, Horan and Owens recognized Curtis, who had been arrested as a suspect in another case, as a man they had been looking for as a friend of one of "Marshall's" alleged confederates in the Schoellkopf robbery.

Curtis was released from the charge on which he was first held, but Horan immediately rearrested him on the charge of suspicion of burglary in another jewel theft—the robbery of Mrs. Lillian Myers of $50,000 worth of jewels in her apartment at 300 West Forty-ninth Street on July 21 last. Curtis is believed to have given the information on which Horan and the other

Continued on Page Six.

ANDERSON ENRICHED BY REALTY TRADING, IS STORY TO PECORA

Prosecutor Quotes Him as Saying $24,700 Came, in Currency, From Deals.

CONTRADICTS HIS AFFIDAVIT

Report to Anti-Saloon Directors in 1919 That Money Came From Loans Is Recalled.

GRAND JURY MOVE HINTED

Inquiry Will Be Pressed "in Some Other Way," Brackett Is Warned in Letter.

In a letter to ex-Senator Edgar T. Brackett, counsel for William H. Anderson, State Superintendent of the Anti-Saloon League, Acting District Attorney Ferdinand Pecora yesterday indicated that unless Mr. Anderson answered questions relating to the source and expenditure of the publicity fund of $24,700, he would take Grand Jury action. Mr. Pecora's letter was in reply to a reiteration by Mr. Brackett that Mr. Anderson should not submit replies to questions pertaining to the fund, details of which Mr. Anderson professes to have withheld from the Board of Directors of the League.

Intimating that he questioned the accuracy of statements made by Mr. Anderson, Mr. Pecora disclosed that Mr. Anderson had asserted he had obtained the money through realty investments negotiated by a friend at a time when he was earning $4,000 a year as an official of the League in Maryland. Mr. Pecora quoted Mr. Anderson as saying that the profits were in excess of $24,700, the sum which he alleged he had loaned the League here for its work when the necessary expenditures exceeded the income. Mr. Pecora pointed out that Mr. Anderson was unable to give the location of any of the realty and declined to divulge the name of his investor friend. Mr. Anderson told the Acting District Attorney that he had received the profits in currency, which he placed in his safe rather than in a bank, according to the letter to Senator Brackett.

Text of Pecora's Letter.

Mr. Pecora's letter follows:

Feb. 16, 1923.

Hon. Edgar T. Brackett, 120 Broadway, New York City.

Dear Senator Brackett:

Much as I regret your adherence to your advice to Mr. Anderson to refuse to answer certain questions which I have asked him as to the sources from which he obtained the sum of $24,700.00, which he claims to have expended on behalf of the Anti-Saloon League during the years 1913 and 1914, and details of such expenditure, I recognize fully your unquestioned right to advise him as his counsel in such manner as you may deem to be in accordance with his own interests.

You express the view that it would seem grotesque to base any prosecution of Mr. Anderson on the facts which have been shown. You also recognize that the ascertainment of the sources from which Mr. Anderson obtained the $24,700, and the methods by which he expended the same, properly comes within the scope of the inquiry which this office is making in so far as light may be shed on the question as to whether the representations which Mr. Anderson made to the Directors of the league in connection therewith are true or false.

In connection with his expenditure of $24,000, Mr. Anderson has declared to me, among other things, that the monies were paid out by him in currency from time to time to certain persons whose identities he will not disclose; that these payments were made for publicity work on behalf of the league; that he has no vouchers or written records of any kind which would show the respective dates and specific amounts of such payments, and that he cannot from memory give such data; that he cannot produce a single copy or piece of printed matter that was used in such publicity work; that all of said monies came from his personal means which he did not keep in any bank or other such depositary, but which he kept in a safe in the office of the respective headquarters of the league in the States of Maryland and New York; and that he made such expenditures upon his own initiative and judgment; and without his having consulted the Board of Directors of the league in New York with regard to them.

Tried to Trace Money.

In view of the unusual circumstances under which, according to his own statements, Mr. Anderson made

Continued on Page Four.

Idaho Assembly Bars Japanese From Leasing Any Lands There

BOISE, Idaho, Feb. 16.—The Assembly of the Legislature, by a vote of 54 to 6, today passed a measure to prohibit the leasing of lands in the State to Japanese. The measure, according to its author, Representative Gillis, while aimed primarily at the Japanese, is applicable to all aliens.

Speaking to the Assembly, Representative Gillis said he feared an influx of Japanese and other aliens to Idaho through refusal of the Federal Government to re-lease land now occupied in Washington, and because of other States passing anti-leasing laws.

ENGINEER AMBUSHED AND SLAIN AT DOOR

Earl Remington of Los Angeles, Who Made Planes in War, Is Found Dead in Driveway.

WIFE ASLEEP IN THE HOUSE

Victim, Shot as He Stepped From Automobile, Met Death He Had Feared.

LOS ANGELES, Feb. 16.—Earl Remington, wealthy electrical engineer, found dead from gunshot wounds in the yard of his home here early today, had lived in fear of death for the last week, according to his wife, who was so prostrated with grief that she could not be seen until late today.

Two persons took active parts in the slaying of Remington, according to police conclusions announced late tonight.

Mrs. Remington said her husband had been acting strangely and showed extreme nervousness. Noises outside the house, particularly at night, seemed to distress him, she said. Remington had offered their home, which is in an exclusive residential district, for sale, the widow stated, but had instructed her never to permit any stranger to enter the house.

Although Remington telephoned to his wife yesterday that he was going to their ranch near Chino and would not return until late, it has been established, according to the police, that he did not go to the ranch.

Detectives are attempting to trace his movements yesterday in the hope of finding some clue to the slaying. They stated they had found two friends of the dead man who said they saw him at 5 o'clock yesterday afternoon.

That Remington was slain by some one having a grudge against him is the opinion expressed by the detectives.

Whether an attempted burglary of the office of the safe company of which Remington was the head, on Oct. 15, 1922, had anything to do with the engineer's death also is being investigated. Two of the company's safes were broken into, according to a report, but nothing of value was taken. The police are working on the theory that papers may have been taken at that time which were used later in a blackmailing plot against Remington.

Remington evidently was murdered at about last midnight. A dozen neighbors heard the fatal shot, and his wife lay sleeping within a few feet of him; but the body was not found until 6 o'clock this morning, when Charity Dawson, a negro maid, started downstairs to light the gas heating plant of the house at 1,409 South St. Andrews Street, a fashionable neighborhood.

There was a trail of blood on the driveway and a riddled leather portfolio which Remington had carried. The maid called Mrs. Remington, and the whole neighborhood was soon aroused by their screams.

Remington left his offices early in the afternoon for a trip to his Chino ranch. He was not seen thereafter by either employes or family until his body was found. He rang up his wife at 3:30 P. M. and told her he was going to Chino, according to the maid.

Remington, the police believe, drew up in his Ford coupé at the side of his house, perhaps at the order of his assailant. He stepped around to the back of the car, shifting the leather portfolio now high, now low, in front of his body in an effort to shield himself.

There was a loud report, perhaps two. One charge from the shotgun tore its way to the engineer's heart.

As he staggered away from the machine he fell on his back, arms spread out.

Mrs. Remington, according to the maid, did not hear the report of the gun. As her husband lay dying she was asleep in a bedroom in the northeast corner of the house, directly above the driveway. From her window she could have looked down on the struggle.

Neighbors playing cards heard the shots but thought they were automobile engines backfiring, or tires exploding. If the Remington dog had not been chloroformed for rabies about two weeks ago, the engineer might still be alive, according to the maid. She believes the dog might have awakened the family. Remington had no children.

"The motive may have been robbery, it may have been revenge," said Detective Sergeant Cline after talking with Mrs. Remington.

Remington was Vice President of the International Electric Protective Association, and had a wide reputation as a safe and bank designer.

Aviation was his sporting diversion, and he was adept at stunt flying. During the war he organized and was general manager of an aviation company here.

Charge Hawaiian Coolie Labor Plot.

Special to The New York Times.

WASHINGTON, Feb. 16.—Charges were made today by the Executive Council of the American Federation of Labor that for two years there had been an intensive agitation for the importation of 50,000 Chinese coolies into the Hawaiian Islands, where they would be placed under bond making them "debt slaves" for five years or less if they became rebellious. The council instructed the Federation's legislative representatives to do all in their power to prevent any enactment of laws that would in any degree open the gates to this character of immigration.

SENATE APPROVES BRITISH DEBT BILL; FINAL VOTE, 70-13

46 Republicans, 24 Democrats Favor It—Borah Among the Four Republicans Opposed.

BITTER DEBATE TO FINISH

Many Assail "British Victory," but Glass Wins Applause by Recalling Allies' Sacrifices.

ONLY ONE AMENDMENT

Settlements With Other Allies Must Have Congress Approval—Bill Now Goes to Conference.

Special to The New York Times.

WASHINGTON, Feb. 16.—The Senate passed the British Debt Refunding bill tonight by a vote of 70 to 13, forty-six Republicans and twenty-four Democrats voting to ratify the settlement as agreed to by the Debt Funding Commission, while nine Democrats and four Republicans were recorded in favor of repudiating the settlement.

The final roll-call was ordered at 7:20 o'clock tonight. The Administration victory was much more impressive than had been anticipated, it having been predicted that between fifteen and twenty Senators would oppose the bill when the vote on passage was reached.

The measure passed with only one amendment—that proposed by Senator Robinson of Arkansas, which gives to Congress the right to pass on settlements that may be arrived at in the future with other debtor nations. An amendment to equalize the interest rates and require Great Britain to pay the same interest as the United States itself pays on the loan was defeated, 61 to 21.

It is expected that the House will promptly accept the Robinson amendment and that the bill will be in the hands of the President early next week.

All efforts to amend the bill with regard to interest rates or in other important particulars were signally defeated. An amendment proposed by Senator Harris of Georgia, which authorizes the appointment of three Democrats on the Funding Commission, would undoubtedly have carried, but was withdrawn when the Republican leaders promised to give this matter early consideration when it is presented to the Senate in the form of an independent bill. The Republicans appear as anxious as some of the Democrats to have the minority share the responsibility of adjusting the more than $11,000,000,000 debt now due this country by its former associates in the European war.

Sharp Debate Continued All Day.

Eight lively hours preceded the passage of the bill. At times the debate was spirited to the point of bitterness, but the clean-cut Administration victory was never in doubt. The defeat of the Hitchcock amendment to maintain the British interest charges at a rate as high as rates paid by this Government and a speech by Senator Glass of Virginia broke the back of the opposition. The impassioned plea of the Virginia Senator for favorable action and his fervid defense of Great Britain came near the close of the long day. When Senator Glass concluded it appeared for a minute or two as if the session might have to suspend while Senators, Republicans as well as Democrats, pressed forward to shake his hand and congratulate him.

The leaders of the opposition were La Follette, Reed of Missouri, McKellar, Heflin, Trammell and Norris, while Smoot, Lenroot, Glass and Underwood commanded the defending forces. La Follette made the longest of all the speeches, a carefully prepared utterance in which he denounced Secretary Mellon, ridiculed the President and assailed the majority membership of the Finance Committee for what he charged was its undue and unwarranted haste in rushing the bill to a final vote.

The last day arguments of the opposition were based principally on the claim that the United States, in agreeing to fix the interest Great Britain will pay at 3 per cent. for the first ten and 3½ per cent. for the remaining fifty-two years, had, in fact, canceled what they claimed was approximately $1,666,000,000 of the interest charges.

La Follette Ridicules Harding.

Opening the debate, Senator La Follette recalled the White House dinner of a year ago, which was attended, among others, by J. Pierpont Morgan, Charles H. Sabin and Secretary Mellon, all of them, declared the Wisconsin Senator, of the international banking group.

Continued on Page Five.

TUT-ANKH-AMEN'S INNER TOMB IS OPENED, REVEALING UNDREAMED OF SPLENDORS, STILL UNTOUCHED AFTER 3,400 YEARS

KING TUT-ANKH-AMEN,
wearing the crown and royal vestments, as he appeared to his contemporaries. From a multi-colored decoration on the walls of the tomb of Huy, his Viceroy, discovered some years ago near the tomb of the King.
Courtesy Metropolitan Museum of Art.

KING IN NEST OF SHRINES

Series of Ornate Covers Enclose Pharaoh's Sarcophagus.

WHOLE FILLS LARGE ROOM

Mortuary Chamber Opens Into Another Room, Crowded With Great Treasure.

EXPLORERS ARE DAZZLED

Wealth of Objects of Historic and Artistic Interest Exceeds All Their Wildest Visions.

Special Cable to THE NEW YORK TIMES.

LUXOR, Egypt, Feb. 16.—This has been, perhaps, the most extraordinary day in the whole history of Egyptian excavation. Whatever any one may have guessed or imagined of the secret of Tut-ankh-Amen's tomb, they surely cannot have dreamed the truth as now revealed.

The entrance today was made into the sealed chamber of the tomb of Tut-ankh-Amen, and yet another door opened beyond that. No one have yet seen the King, but to practical certainty we know that he lies there close at hand in all his original state, undisturbed.

Moreover, in addition to the great store of treasures which the tomb has already yielded, today has brought to light a new wealth of objects of artistic, historical, and even intrinsic value which is bewildering.

It is such a hoard as the most sanguine excavator can hardly have pictured, even in visions in his sleep, and puts Lord Carnarvon's and Mr. Carter's discovery in a class by itself and above all previous finds.

Official Opening Sunday.

Though the official opening of the sealed mortuary chamber of the tomb has been fixed for Sunday, it was obviously impossible to postpone until then the actual work of breaking in the entrance. This was a job involving some hours of work, because it had to be done with the greatest care, so as to keep intact as many of the seals as possible, and also to avoid injury to any of the objects on the other side which might be caused by the falling of material dislodged.

All this could not be done on Sunday while the official guests were kept waiting in the singularly unpleasant atmosphere of the tomb, so an agreement was made with the Egyptian authorities by which the actual breaking through of the wall should be done in their presence today.

Consequently, Howard Carter was very busy inside the tomb all morning with Professor Breasted and Dr. Alan Gardiner, whose assistance has been invaluable from the beginning of the work of examining seals and deciphering and copying inscriptions of all kinds. They had finished by noon, and the tomb was closed till after luncheon, at which Lord Carnarvon, Mr. Carter and Lady Evelyn Herbert entertained all those invited to be present today.

Official Story of Inner Tomb.

It was after 1 o'clock when the official party entered the tomb, and the operation was begun which was to result in such astounding discoveries, of which I am able to give the following authoritative description.

Today between the hours of 1 and 3 in the afternoon the culminating moment in the discovery of Tut-ankh-Amen's tomb took place when Lord Carnarvon and Howard Carter opened the inner sealed doorway in the presence of Lady Evelyn Herbert, Abdel Hamid Suliman Pasha, Under Secretary of Public Works; Pierre Lacau, Director General of the Antiquities Department; [illegible] William Garstin, Sir Charles [illegible] Mr. Lythgoe, the curator of the Metropolitan Museum of Art of New York; Mr. Winlock, [illegible]

GOV. REILY RESIGNS PORTO RICO OFFICE

Tells President Ill Health Forbids Him to Resume Executive Duties.

HAD BEEN LONG UNDER FIRE

Offended by His Inaugural Address, Unionists Made Many Charges Against Him.

WASHINGTON, Feb. 16 (Associated Press).—The resignation of E. Mont Reily as Governor of Porto Rico was received at the White House early this evening, but no announcement was made concerning it, although there was every indication that it would be accepted.

The text of the cablegram of resignation, as made public at the White House, follows:

Hon. Warren G. Harding, President of the United States:

On account of very serious injury while in the States, my trip to Porto Rico prostrated me, and I have been confined to my bed since, not being able to resume my official duties. My physicians inform me it will be several months before I can recover and I must have complete change and rest, free from all care. This being the case, I feel that I should resign and look after my health first.

I would like for my resignation to become effective April 1, believing that by that time I will be able to travel, and if I am not can be taken to a hospital here until I am able to do so.

In offering my resignation, I cannot do so without expressing to you and Secretary Weeks my appreciation of the unfailing loyalty and support you have both continually given to me in my arduous and trying work here.

Your recent statement to me that you were for me 100 per cent. had its echo in the great demonstration tendered me on my return, and shows that the work of your Administration in Porto Rico has not been in vain, but has been appreciated. It was a complete vindication of our American policies instituted in the islands two years ago.

A delegation composed of men of all political parties called on my Secretary yesterday, requesting that I withhold my resignation until you could be communicated with. I have notified them my resignation was irrevocable. Ninety per cent. of the people of the Island are for you and the things you stand for, and are pleading that no backward step be taken in

Continued on Page Five.

GOETHALS DEMANDS COAL FOR UP-STATE

"We Want Action, Not Conferences," He Says in Message to Federal Fuel Distributer.

SEIZURE IS THREATENED

Insists Shipments to Canada Be Diverted—People Will Get Coal, He Asserts.

General George W. Goethals, State Fuel Administrator, serving notice on the Federal Fuel Distributer that "we want action, not conferences" for the relief of suffering localities in Northern New York, suggested in two telegrams yesterday immediate authorization by the Federal officials of drastic relief measures.

Diversion to up-State towns of coal now moving to Canada, priority of New York shipments over shipments to Canada and seizure of cars en route to Canada were some of the measures suggested.

"The people in that part of the State are going to get coal," General Goethals asserted in making public the telegrams. "I am awaiting action from Washington on the telegrams. In case I don't get it, I am not saying what I am going to do."

The seizure of one car of coal consigned to Canada for use of the Saratoga Springs Hospital was authorized yesterday by the shipper, John F. Bermingham, President of the Lackawanna Coal Company. General Goethals called this to the attention of F. R. Wadleigh, Federal Fuel Distributer, in one of his telegrams and asked why the Government could not require the Delaware & Hudson Railroad "to supply our needs."

Reports from Mr. Kilmer to the State Fuel Administration offices yesterday were that people up-State were "on the point of taking coal off the tracks." The people were ready "to take the law in their own hands," he stated and added that "no juries in the afflicted communities would ever vote for conviction."

Predictions of epidemics from influenza and pneumonia unless coal arrived at some of the up-State points today were made by Mr. Kilmer.

General Goethals told reporters that priority must be given both to an emergency shipment of 20,000 tons, which is required immediately, and to future regular allotments.

Schools at many points in the Saratoga district have been closed for lack of fuel, reports to the State Fuel Administration said. Two schools in Corinth have been closed, and unless some coal arrives before Monday, or the school authorities can get some wood, the high school also will close. The school at Schuylerville was ordered closed yesterday for an indefinite period because of the lack of fuel.

Louis Cohen, a landlord of 514 West 152d Street, was sentenced to thirty days in the workhouse in the Court of Special Sessions yesterday for failing to supply sufficient heat and hot water for the house at 522 West 146th Street.

Probation officers reported that the building was badly in need of repairs. Window panes were out and doors were loose, they said, and the temperature recently had been several degrees below the legal minimum.

Mrs. Bertha Becker, who owns a building at 524 West 151st Street, was fined $250 on a similar charge in Special Sessions.

Won't Stop Coal to Canada.

WASHINGTON, Feb. 16.—The proposal for an embargo on anthracite exports, especially to Canada, has been carefully considered and definitely abandoned, it was said today at the White House.

In the view of high Government officials an embargo would have no material effect on the coal shortage which is being experienced in sections of New York and New England.

Doctor and Chauffeur Killed When Train Wrecks Ambulance at Jersey Grade Crossing

A fatal grade crossing accident occurred last evening at Hackensack, N. J., where a train running forty miles an hour, on the New Jersey and New York branch of the Erie Railroad, smashed into an ambulance, crushing a hospital interne and a chauffeur to death. James Reape, 38 years old, of 99 Nassau Street, Brooklyn, the chauffeur, was instantly killed. Dr. Louis Nishawitz, 25, of 830 Kelly Street, the Bronx, an interne at the Hackensack General Hospital, was mortally injured. His skull was fractured and his left leg and right arm were cut off. He died in the hospital half an hour after the accident. The ambulance was wrecked.

Dr. Nishawitz lost his life in the performance of his duty, as he was answering a call to take a sick woman to the hospital from her home on Hudson Street, Hackensack. After the accident a second ambulance was sent for the woman, but the delay had been fatal, and she was dead on its arrival.

The accident occurred about 5:50 P. M. at the Essex Street crossing. The train was a Haverstraw express, carrying commuters from New York.

Owing to a sharp curve south of Essex Street, the engineer could not see the crossing until he was close to it. The crossing gates should have been lowered, but were not. John Burke of Pearl River, N. Y., the gate tender, said the gates were frozen and out of commission. According to Burke, he stood in the middle of the road and swung a red lantern, but the ambulance driver did not heed. Burke was arrested on a technical charge of manslaughter.

Dr. Nishawitz was the son of Max Nishawitz, a shoe merchant in the Bronx. The physician was a graduate of De Witt Clinton High School and the Long Island College Hospital.

Harding Threatens to Cut Shipping Fleet Unless Congress Passes the Subsidy Bill

WASHINGTON, Feb. 16.—The Administration Shipping bill was restored tonight to its former place as the unfinished business of the Senate, after having been laid aside since early in the week to allow consideration of the British debt settlement legislation. This was done on motion of Senator Jones of Washington after advocates of the measure had demonstrated their superior strength by voting down, 38 to 30, a motion by Senator Robinson of Arkansas to adjourn.

The vote on adjournment was not regarded as an accurate test of the strength of the forces supporting and opposing the Shipping bill, as several Senators on both sides were absent.

Opposition of the shipping measure are expected, when the Senate meets tomorrow, to counter with a proposal to lay the bill aside again in favor of the Capper Truth-in-Fabrics bill, and it was considered possible that a test vote on the merchant marine legislation may result.

Although the future of the subsidy bill in the Senate has not been clearly indicated in the face of claims and counter-claims on the possibility of its passage, it was said at the White House today that President Harding would not call a special session of Congress to consider the merchant marine situation if the Shipping bill should fail.

Mr. Harding was said to feel that the necessity for action looking to a solution of the shipping problem had been clearly demonstrated, and to have reached the decision that if the Shipping bill is not enacted the Government will proceed at once to take such steps as will diminish in a very great degree the present losses of the Government's fleet.

Detailed reports on the operation of Shipping Board vessels, showing net losses on individual voyages running as high as $100,000, had been studied by the President and his advisers, it was said, and the consensus of opinion was that the losses would be wiped out under the necessary economics which would follow the return of the shipping to private ownership.

"All the News That's Fit to Print."

The New York Times.

THE WEATHER.
Fair, slightly warmer Thursday; Friday, fair, warmer; moderate winds, becoming south.
For full weather report see Page 22.

VOL. LXXII....No. 23,774. NEW YORK, MONDAY, FEBRUARY 26, 1923. TWO CENTS In Greater New York | THREE CENTS Within 200 Miles | FOUR CENTS Elsewhere

FRENCH SEIZE MORE RHINE TERRITORY; TIGHTEN BLOCKADE

Occupy Intervals Between the Bridgeheads of Mayence, Coblenz and Cologne.

BRITISH ALMOST CUT OFF

Export Restrictions Begin to Be Felt as Ruhr Concerns Are Forced to Close.

65,000,000 MARKS SEIZED

Raid Troops Quit Bochum After Taking Office Furniture Delivery of Which Was Refused.

Special Cable to THE NEW YORK TIMES.

DUESSELDORF, Feb. 25.—The French this morning advanced troops into all the intervals which separate the bridgeheads of Mayence, Coblenz and Cologne.

These bridgeheads, which were occupied as one of the conditions of the armistice and are to remain in occupation under the peace treaty for fifteen years from the commencement of the execution of the treaty, formed three separate semi-circles having each a radius of thirty kilometers. Between them there was in each case a short space at the base of the arc and naturally a wider space at the extremity. It is these intervening spaces which have now been occupied, making the zone of occupation a continuous stretch of thirty kilometers east of the Rhine.

The reason for this extension of occupation is the necessity of having a definite line for customs control. So long as the arcs were not contiguous it was difficult for the French to establish the customs and export license systems which have been prepared. The situation arose in which firms on the right bank of the line, but just outside the thirty kilometer radius, were entirely outside the control.

British Almost Cut Off From Germany.

One of the most curious results of the extension is that the British bridgehead at Cologne will be almost cut off from Germany by the French troops, which will surround it on each side. They have filled the gap between the Coblenz and Cologne bridgeheads, and having in their possession also the Düsseldorf area they cut the British off from contact with unoccupied Germany everywhere except at the crown of the arc.

The Germans will undoubtedly protest against the new occupation as being a further infringement of the Versailles Treaty. Its defense by the French is that it is a necessary part of the penalties which are being applied because of failure to fulfill the treaty terms. According to information here the operation was carried through without any incident.

In the Ruhr the situation is developing very slowly along the expected lines. The effect of the restriction of the export of coal and manufactured goods is tardily beginning to make itself felt. Unemployment is increasing as one after another of the smaller firms with small resources close down. Most of the steel plants are continuing at full pace, but other metal working and die works are closing.

At Witten there are between 11,000 and 12,000 unemployed out of a working population of 70,000, and though this figure is in excess of the average, it is significant of what is happening generally.

Koenigswinter and Limburg Occupied.

By Wireless to THE NEW YORK TIMES.

DORTMUND, Feb. 25.—The French made a dramatic military move at 4 o'clock this afternoon. Advancing by land and water, they occupied Königswinter on the right bank of the Rhine nearly opposite Bonn.

French marines landed from a fishing steamer, while colored colonial troops entered from the land side. A British eye witness vouches for the color of the colonial troops and vividly describes the suprise of Königswinter at finding itself occupied after more than four years immunity.

The French also occupied Limburg, well known to many members of the American Army of Occupation. Limberg lies just beyond the nearest Berlin point reached by the American army.

According to a tip from Düsseldorf, Dortmund is to be strafed tomorrow on a big scale. Police Headquarters is to be surrounded by tanks, cavalry and machine guns and the Security Police are to be disarmed as was done in Essen. Dortmund is enjoying its customary Sunday night quiet.

French Raid on Bochum Explained.

By Wireless to THE NEW YORK TIMES.

BOCHUM, Feb. 25.—The French scare in Bochum is over today, the punitive expeditionary forces having apparently been withdrawn to surrounding villages.

Their whirlwind descent on the city, particularly the wholesale arrest of officials and the ransacking of the Chamber of Commerce headquarters, is considered the most serious reprisal yet inflicted in the Ruhr. The French official version of the shooting affray is that the crowd had seized a French interpreter and beaten him, and the shots were fired into the crowd to liberate him from its clutches.

The French version of the ransacking and alleged looting of the Chamber of Commerce is that they needed office furniture, delivery of which was refused, so that they were forced to help

Continued on Page Three.

Soviet Troops Suppress Petrograd Workers' Riots

LONDON, Feb. 25.—Serious disturbances are reported among the unemployed in Petrograd, says a dispatch to the Exchange Telegraph from Copenhagen. Red troops who were trying to quell disorders were received with shouts of "We had rather be shot down than starve to death."

The dispatch adds that the officers had great difficulty in preventing the troops from joining the unemployed.

SEE RUSSIA BACKING LITHUANIA FOR WAR

Tchitcherin's Visit to Minsk Is Accepted in Paris as Evidence of It.

ANOTHER APPEAL BY POLAND

She Will Ask the Allies Today to Recognize the League's Polish-Lithuanian Frontier.

By EDWIN L. JAMES.

Special Cable to THE NEW YORK TIMES.

PARIS, Feb. 25.—The action of Lithuania, a nation of 2,000,000 people, with an army of three divisions, in defying Poland, a nation of 18,000,000, with thirty divisions in her army, might appear at first glance to be laughable. But it is not laughable. It is importantly serious. It is serious because George Tchitcherin, the Soviet Foreign Minister, is in conference today at Minsk with representatives of the Kovno Government.

Lithuania would not dare hurl defiance at Poland if she were not urged on by Russia, and if she did not count on Russia's help. So far as the chances of war are concerned, the Eastern European situation is far more perilous than that in the Rhineland. And it is to be noted that at both danger points, Angora and Kovno, the Russians are busy.

By a coup which was arranged by the Kovno Government the Lithuanians seized the port of Memel, the subject of dispute between Germany and Lithuania, and the Allies, as the best way out of the situation, gave Lithuania title to the territory on condition that Poland have the right to use the port. The Lithuanians took over the district, and the first thing they did after the allied troops departed was to expel the Polish representative put there by the Allies to watch over Poland's interests.

Russia had all along favored Memel's going to Lithuania. But did she admit that the Allies' decision was the proper one? Not at all. She has protested in long notes that the Allies have not done the right thing in giving Poland the right to use the port of Memel, and has urged Lithuania to pay no attention to that provision of the settlement.

But it is in the Vilna territory that the big difference exists between Poland and Lithuania. The Council of the League of Nations divided the Vilna district between Poland and Lithuania and Poland proceeded to occupy her share. There was fighting for several days, but before greatly superior forces the Lithuanians went back where they belonged. Lithuania at once telegraphed to Geneva, complaining that the Poles had gone too far—a statement which has been shown to be false. The same day Tchitcherin sent notes to Warsaw, Kovno and elsewhere saying that Poland and Lithuania by the Treaty of Riga had no right to allow a boundary line to be drawn by a third party, especially since that party was the League of Nations, but that Russia was ready to fix the line for them. The allied diplomats know that Russia is bringing pressure to bear on Lithuania to fight to get back Poland's share of the Vilna region and carry out the threat which the Lithuanian spokesman made before the Council of the League in Paris on Feb. 2 to use force to prevent the execution of the League's decision.

Poland fears trouble with Russia. Allied statesmen are divided in their opinions as to the sincerity of Trotzky's recent threat to use the Russian army; but the Poles, being nearer the danger, take the situation more seriously. The Council of Ambassadors tomorrow will receive a note from Warsaw asking that body, as representing the Allies, to give formal recognition to the frontier between Poland and Lithuania as laid down by the League, and Poland will also ask the Allies formally to recognize the line between Russia and Poland. Both these requests will be made to lessen the danger of unpleasant incidents along the border.

It is believed in Paris that the success or failure of the French in the Ruhr will have an important effect on developments in Eastern Europe. Whichever way Russia might turn in her hostile acts, west or south, she would run into allies of France—allies who might well seek help from France. If France succedes in the Ruhr, she will naturally be in a position, both morally and materially, to promise more aid against the Russian rush than if she fails; for that would mean moral discredit abroad and increasing need of strong forces on her own frontiers.

WARSAW, Feb. 25.—Everything is calm in the neutral zone of Memel, except in the vicinity of Landvorovo, where Lithuanian irregulars attacked the Poles, wounding four, but were repulsed.

Last night at Smolniki the Lithuanian and Polish military delegates discussed the situation, the Lithuanian officers asserting their readiness to negotiate the boundaries of the neutral zone and pledging no hostile acts during the conference.

The conversation will continue today and tomorrow, when the Poles will make an effort to release the two officers arrested with General Carton de Wiart, who are held in Kovno.

ROBS RICH MAIL CAR, ELUDES 10 RIFLEMEN IN GRAND CENTRAL

Daring Thief Escapes Through Park Avenue Tunnel, Chased by Trackwalker.

VALUE OF BOOTY UNKNOWN

Car, Sealed Inside and Out, Arrived With One Pouch Gone, One Rifled.

HIS METHOD A MYSTERY

Guards and Clerks Failed to See Robber—Probably Boarded Train Up-State.

A daring robber stole a package of registered mail from a heavily guarded mail train just in from Chicago at Grand Central Terminal yesterday and escaped after a chase through the Park Avenue tunnel, during which he had to drop a pouch of mail he was trying to carry away.

The value of the stolen package could not be learned. Inspector Kinzel, who has charge of the investigation begun by the Post Office Department, said he did not know the value. The package was about a foot square, and was addressed to a foreign port. Depending on the nature of its contents, it might have been worth either a small or a huge sum. The pouch of mail saved contained articles valued at hundreds of thousands of dollars. In addition to the pouch, a second package was dropped by the robber in his flight, and was recovered.

The authorities are mystified to account for the ability of the robber to enter the mail car that was robbed. Like all the other cars in the train, it was found to be locked, with both the inside and outside seals intact, when it was "officially" opened after the arrival of the train at Grand Central. Another puzzling feature of the affair is that an hour and a half elapsed between the discovery of the robbery and the discovery of the robber trying to escape in the tunnel a few blocks from the train. Whether he had any accomplices to assist him in getting into the train or in concealing himself immediately after the robbery was discovered is being investigated.

Boarded Train Up-State.

It is believed that the thief boarded the train at Albany or Harmon, the only stops made by the train between Buffalo and New York. As the train is surrounded by guards armed with rifles when it stops to exchange its steam locomotive for an electric motor at Harmon, it is regarded as more likely that he got on during the shorter but less guarded stop at Albany.

The train carried ten guards with rifles. It was due at Grand Central Terminal at 5:15 o'clock yesterday morning, but was delayed over two hours, getting in at 7:40. The train is officially known as United States mail train No. 32.

When the train drew up at its platform on one of the three lower level tracks reserved for mail trains in a special part of the station, the armed guards got out and surrounded the cars while the local mail clerks proceeded to open each car. On entering the second car from the front of the train, and making a check of its contents, the clerks found that one pouch was missing, that another pouch had been slashed with a knife and that two packages were missing from the second pouch. A quick search of the entire train, which consisted entirely of registered mail addressed to foreign ports and worth millions, disclosed that nothing else had been taken.

No One Saw the Robber.

The robbery was immediately reported to the Post Office Department and the Department of Justice. Post Office Inspectors and Department of Justice operatives hurried to Grand Central Terminal, but could find no clue to the robber, either inside or outside of the raided car. Statements were taken from members of the train crew, the mail clerks, the guards and mail handlers at the station, all of whom declared that they had seen nothing of the robber and knew nothing of the robbery.

About 9:30 o'clock, however, Edward Coyne, a track walker in the Park Avenue tunnel, saw a man walking north along the tracks at Fiftieth Street. Coyne was 50 or 100 feet back of the man. The stranger apparently knew his way among the dangerous electrically charged wires in the tunnel as well as Coyne, for he was walking ahead as briskly as he could, in view of the heavy mail pouch he was carrying. He was dragging the pouch along with one hand, while he carried two packages in another.

The track walker at first thought that the stranger was a mail clerk who was

Continued on Page Two.

Skull of an Ape Found in Island of Jersey; Resembles One Believed 500,000 Years Old

By Wireless to THE NEW YORK TIMES.

LONDON, Feb. 25.—A prehistoric skull, which is almost entirely without forehead, has been found in St. Ouen, a village in Jersey, by workmen who were digging at the rear of a building. It is probably that of a female, and may date from an earlier period than the famous Rhodesian skull found at Broken Sill in 1921. This was estimated by Sir Arthur Keith, President of the Royal Anthropological Institute, to be 100,000 years old.

There is, however, a much older skull, the one discovered in Java twenty-nine years ago, and known as the Pithecanthropus Erectus, or erect man ape. This skull is reckoned to be 500,000 years old, and there is a possibility that the Jersey skull, which resembles that found at Java, may date from the same remote period in the world's history.

The skull is to be sent to London for examination by Sir Arthur Keith.

BATTLE ICE BARRIER TO GET COAL TO CITY

Tugs Work All Day and Night to Supply Dealers' Empty Bins Here.

24-HOUR DELIVERIES BEGUN

Fuel Is Rushed to Needy as Soon as It Is Received—Mild Weather Gives Hope.

Coal movements across the ice-clogged Hudson continued all day yesterday and throughout the night, although under great difficulties. Officials of the State Fuel Administration spent the day wandering about the waterfront to watch the progress of the tugs that were battling their way through the floes with coal barges and inspecting the bins of dealers to get a line on the city's reserve supply.

Although the results of the Sunday efforts to get coal across the river were characterized as "disheartening" by the fuel officials, the rise in temperature was a welcome factor. "It has given us a breathing spell," said one of General Goethals's aids at the coal office last night. "We are not losing any on the amount of coal that is being brought across and we are making an appreciable gain because of the saving in coal that the warmer weather brings about. A few more days of the same kind of weather will let the city build up a little surplus and then we can get through the winter all right.

"There is still, of course, the danger of a real blizzard. Such a thing would leave the city in a serious condition. The situation would be greatly helped if the people would only use substitutes now. There is plenty of soft coal here, but they will not burn it."

Start Night Deliveries.

The trans-harbor transportation efforts yesterday were described by the same official as "a shocking task." The wind and tide brought a great deal of ice down the river to a point opposite the city. At many points the river was covered from one shore to the other with masses of ice cakes.

Tugs that were attempting to fight their way into the piers on the New York side were having a hard time. One tug, of the most powerful type, which ordinarily could handle several barges without difficulty, found it almost impossible to bring a single bargeload of coal into 125th Street.

From now on, the fuel officials said, the tugmen and the dealers would work nights and Sundays to make deliveries. This step has been necessary at different times since the critical period began, but it had not been necessary before the harbor tangle to make it part of the regular program.

Most all of the big dealers have already begun to use night shifts to speed up deliveries. The widespread shortage makes it necessary for trucks to carry half a ton or a ton sometimes several miles, when ordinarily a full load would be carried. Now the trucks are kept on hand twenty-four hours a day and coal is rushed out to fill orders as soon as it is received.

A member of the State Fuel Administration said that an inspection of the bins of several of the big dealers yesterday disclosed that they were literally "scraping the floor" to send out the last pound of coal to consumers. It became known that among the steps that the administration is keeping in mind if the situation becomes more acute is the cutting down of the allotment in emergency cases to 100 pounds. Half a ton is allowed now under these emergency orders, which are first checked up by police and health department officials to see whether real emergencies exist.

Westchester in Straits.

Frederick Coykendall of the Cornell Steamboat Company, said that since Saturday tugs of his company, serving the piers between Edgewater and the Lackawanna piers, had moved all of the cars that had been loaded. He said that the movements were greatly hampered because of the ice conditions, but that his tugs were getting every barge load across.

T. W. Brockman of Morgantown, W. Va., officer of a coal mining company that produces what is called "the Sewickley seam" coal, said last night that he had 100 carloads of the coal now in this city on tracks of the New York Central and that it would be sold at a price "greatly less than the poorest grade of anthracite." Mr. Brockman said that many carloads were being sold in the city every day through the Superior Fuel Company, Room 1026, Woolworth Building, and that he had letters from hotel and apartment owners to the effect that the coal had given great satisfaction. He said that the coal, although classified as bituminous, gave out no objectionable gases and that it was not as highly volatile as most bituminous.

Westchester County is now suffering from a real coal famine, according to reports last night from Mount Vernon. Dr. Elmer A. Sheets, County Fuel Administrator, is trying to relieve the situation by the transportation of coal from one town to another. In the last week the shortage has been so acute that many Westchester residents have been forced to cut down big shade trees for fuel. In several of the towns in the outlying districts schools have had to close for lack of coal.

In Mount Vernon the police have been selling coal in 100-pound lots and it is common to see big limousines drive up and their occupants alight to get in line for the distribution. Fuel Administrator Sheets received word yesterday that Sing Sing prison had only a few days' coal supply of coal.

The Taxpayers' Alliance of the Bronx made public yesterday resolutions which had been sent to President Harding asking that he present to Congress a measure for the taking over of the mines by the Government and that the price of coal mined under Government control be fixed to include "reasonable prices for the coal unmined plus the cost of mining and the reasonable transportation cost to places or zones of distribution."

HIS HERETIC THRONE IN PHARAOH'S TOMB

Cleaning Reveals the Sun Rays of the Abandoned Faith Shining on Tut-ankh-Amen.

OLD BEAUTY IS RESTORED

Experts Renew Original Colors and Designs of Treasures, Revealing Fine Workmanship.

The Times (London) World Copyright, by Arrangement with the Earl of Carnarvon.

Special Cable to THE NEW YORK TIMES.

LUXOR, Egypt, Feb. 25.—Despite the appalling interruptions of the last week, Mr. Lucas and Mr. Mace managed to do a lot of work in the workshop in the Seti II. tomb, and it is now possible to give a number of details of various beautiful objects from the tomb of Tut-ankh-Amen before they are finally packed, to reappear at some probably remote date in the Cairo Museum.

The shop itself is not more than eight or nine feet wide, a mere square tunnel driven into the hillside, the walls of which are the usual yellowish white, covered with large unpainted figures in incised relief. They reflect the light well, and for the first twenty or thirty feet the light is good enough. After that, however, as you penetrate the heart of the hill, the light fails, and a close inspection of any article is only possible with the use of an electric torch, for there is no electric installation. Down both sides run lines of tables, or larger objects, in orderly array, with a narrow pathway down the middle.

The table nearest the light on the left is devoted to Mr. Mace's jig-saw puzzles. It was here he labored over the disintegrated fragments of the King's robes and deduced the facts already communicated of the King's evident youthfulness from the small size of the collarette, &c. It is now spread on the same table and is even a more intricate conundrum than the King's corselet, and it is astonishing how far Mr. Mace has already gone toward a solution of the collar. Except for a piece of the back it has been reconstructed and shows a very rich pattern of concentric rings and rectangular plaques of vari-colored faience of deep blue turquoise and red and yellow.

The body of the corselet is made of wedge-shaped, or more accurately pear-shaped, links of faience laid on gold. Below the collar and let into the body of this truly royal fabric resembling a chain of mail is a superb design stretching across the King's chest representing a scene in which King Tut-ankh-Amen is being introduced by the hawk-headed god Horus to the great Amen. The whole thing is extremely effective, and when it has been properly treated to bring out the colors it will be as beautiful a thing as is to be seen in any museum.

Beauty of Throne Is Restored.

Immediately beyond this table is the famous throne, and none could have believed how marvelously, under expert treatment, the brilliance of the original colors has been restored.

When first examined the exposed fleshy parts of the figures of the King and Queen on the back were supposed to be carnelian, but it is now seen to be of semi-opaque glass of a glorious deep sang de boeuf red. The Queen's headdress, of the finest inlaying of brilliant royal blue, is magnificent. All the colors stand out with the same vividness, and the modeling of the King and Queen with the sun above shooting down its rays, each ray ending in a hand, according to the well-known design, is very good.

[What the correspondent here describes is remarkable, and it is almost equally remarkable that he does not point out its significance. The "sun above shooting down its rays, each ending in a hand," is a representation of Aten, the sun-disc god of the "heretic" faith established by Khu-n-Aten (Amenhotep IV.), the father-in-law of Tut-ankh-Amen. It was this faith that Tut-ankh-Amen abjured, to restore the old Amen faith, at the same time changing his name from Tut-ankh-Aten to Tut-ankh-Amen. The throne found in the tomb, it would now appear, is that on which he sat as a "heretic" King, at the heretic capital, Khut-Aten, and not that he occupied at Thebes at the time of his death in the orthodox Amen faith. That this throne was permitted to exist after the heretic faith had been abandoned, and even more, that it, and not his "Amen" throne, was buried with the King, is a fact which leaves room for explanations that might enlarge our slender knowledge of the history of this King. It is also curious that figures of the hated heretic King, Khun-Aten, described by the correspondent further on, should have been allowed to go into the tomb.]

On the reverse of the back of the throne is a boldly modeled tier of uraei or cobras crowned with sun discs and impressively lifelike.

On the opposite side of the pathway beyond a couple of tables with covered

Continued on Page Four.

ANDERSON CHARGE BRINGS SHARP REPLY BY ROCKEFELLER JR.

League Head Accuses Fosdick of Plotting With "Wets," Tammany and Republicans.

DEFIES WEALTHY GIVERS

"I Am Guilty, Too," Says Rockefeller, if Allegations of Conspiracy Are True.

WANTS GIFT SOURCES SHOWN

Declares He and Father Believe Public Accounting Should Be Made of Expenditures.

A conspiracy has been formed, backed by the liquor interests, Tammany and "wet" Republican machine politicians, to influence the legal proceedings now pending against him, William H. Anderson, State Superintendent of the Anti-Saloon League, declared yesterday morning in an address in Trinity Methodist Episcopal Church at Albany, N. Y. Alluding to Raymond B. Fosdick, representative of the Rockefellers in their benefactions, as a "de facto stool pigeon," Mr. Anderson said he did not intend silently to submit to being destroyed by the power of the Rockefeller money wielded through a hostile employe.

Mr. Anderson told his hearers that if necessary the League would appeal for increased subscriptions to make up the loss caused by the defection of the Rockefeller, in the event it was impossible to obtain help from such friends of the prohibition cause without having to accept the dictation of Mr. Fosdick.

In a statement sent last night from Ormonde Beach, Fla., John D. Rockefeller Jr. replied to Mr. Anderson, declaring that if Mr. Fosdick were guilty he was equally so, for he approved of all Mr. Fosdick had done. He added that he believed all the accounts of the Anti-Saloon League should be made public.

Mr. Anderson's Charge.

In his Albany address Mr. Anderson said:

"An assumption of perfect propriety of motive and action on the part of the office of the District Attorney of New York County does not obscure the fact that the activity of that official, even though he be innocent of any such intent, is being utilized in perhaps the most gigantic and vicious conspiracy ever framed against a man engaged in prohibition work to blacken him in advance of, and to influence the result of, formal legal hearing on the merits of charges.

"While I am the immediate target, the assault upon the good faith of the League Board, representing the churches, the effort of the "wets" to have the League declared a political committee, the resolution in the Legislature to suppress it entirely and the effort to repeal 'dry' enforcement legislation make clear that the underlying purpose is to destroy, not in New York alone, but nationally, the agency of the militant churches which whipped the liquor traffic when that traffic was entrenched, and which, unless it can be discredited and its power broken, will also root out the outlaw traffic. And it is no accident that these things all 'broke' at the same time in New York.

Charges Threefold Conspiracy.

"In this conspiracy are not merely the criminal liquor interests alone. But Tammany, which now controls the higher offices of city and State, and also the 'wet' Republican machine politicians are back of it. And there are other influences. In addition there are involved the 'wet' financial interests which have used as a de facto stool pigeon a 'wet' talking, personally hostile employe of the John D. Rockefellers, themselves staunch friends of prohibition. The power and scope of the influences interested in 'getting' me are the best proof both of the effectiveness of my work and the failure of ordinary methods to eliminate me.

"The activity of the District Attorney's office is of minor importance compared with the viciousness of the accompanying non-official effort to rob me of the benefit of the doubt, to befog the issue, to suggest suspicion, to smear me up, to scare the "drys," to propagandize the general public into assuming that a mere investigation is evidence of guilt, and so to convict me in the public mind as to destroy my future usefulness to the league, even though it is impossible to convict me under an indictment, if one is returned.

"Unfortunately for him, Raymond B. Fosdick, Rockefeller representative, without his knowing that fact, was the only

Continued on Page Six.

Week's Rally Against Klan to Start in Chicago Tonight

Special to The New York Times.

CHICAGO, Feb. 25.—An "All Nations Rally" against the Ku Klux Klan, with a program of six nightly mass meetings at the Coliseum, will be started tomorrow night under the auspices of the American Unity League.

Governor Parker of Louisiana, who instituted the Mer Rouge inquiry, and former Senator Percy of Mississippi will be the speakers tomorrow. Governor Smith of New York and Bishop Gallagher of Detroit are on the program for other meetings to be held through the week.

DROPS TWINS, LEAPS 3 STORIES FROM FIRE

Mother and Babies Plunge From Roaring Furnace to Street in Early Morning Blaze.

WOMAN AND ONE BABY DEAD

Father and Second Child Not Expected to Live—Firemen Rescue Many.

Flames crept from the basement of the tenement at 747 Tenth Avenue up stairways and airshafts to the four floors above just after 1 o'clock this morning, swept through the hallways and cut off a number of tenants who, roused by smoke or the cries of persons in the street, sought to run from their apartments.

A mother, penned in her flat, with flames at every door and window, flung her infant twins to the street and leaped after them. The father fell unconscious as his wife disappeared. Firemen carried him out. The mother and one baby died soon after they had reached hospitals. The father and the other child may not survive.

John Healy and his wife, who live on the third floor with their 11 months old twins, Anna and Marion, jerked open their front door, only to leap back as a burst of flame confronted them. They ran to one window after another, only to find that flames licking up from the second floor made egress impossible. Meanwhile, as the frantic couple raced around seeking some means of escape, the fire swept along carpets and over the furniture until the whole place was full of flame. The infants were wailing, death was drawing close, and suddenly, Mrs. Healy, able to bear it no longer, ran to a front window with the infants, whom she had been trying to cuddle against her breast to keep the acrid smoke from them.

The window panes had splintered, the sash was afire with flame, and Mrs. Healy, thrusting her arms far out, murmured a prayer and let first one child and then the other drop. Then she jumped after them.

Caught in Backdraught.

Patrolman Stark of the West Forty-seventh Street Station had discovered the blaze before the Healy family was forced to jump. He ran to a corner and sent an alarm, then hastened back, jerked open the front door and was flung off his feet by a backdraught.

Patrolman Daly of the West Sixty-eighth Street Station and James Dawson, a member of the sporting staff of THE NEW YORK TIMES, passed the building in time to see Stark fall in the flame-lit hallway and lie still. Daly and Dawson, followed by Albert Sauppes, who lives in the neighborhood, shielding their faces against the intense heat, plunged into the hallway and dragged the policeman out.

Then the trio plunged back through flame and smoke and began helping out women and children who were milling in panic in the halls in imminent danger of being burned to death. When they finally had to give over their attempts at rescue, Dawson and Daly were unhurt, but Sauppes had burns and cuts which needed the attention of an ambulance surgeon.

When firemen reached the building they found the upper-floor windows filled with screaming people, begging them to hurry. They ran a seventy-five-foot ladder up against the front wall and Fireman Reilly of Truck 4 made his way to the top. Despite swirls of flame that burned against his hands and face, he stuck to his post until all those visible at top windows were out. Then he clambered down and slumped on the sidewalk, hands and face badly burned.

Victims Taken to Hospital.

Fireman Arthur Corey of Engine 54 was another who was burned severely while sticking at windows long enough to get out some of those who had been cut off. He and Reilly were rushed to Roosevelt Hospital in an ambulance.

Father Francis Corcoran had run from the Roman Catholic Church of the Sacred Heart around the corner from the tenement, which is between Fiftieth and Fifty-first Streets, when he heard the clattering engines. He got there just after Mrs. Healy had tossed her children from the window and jumped after them. The four Healys were carried tenderly to a doorway by onlookers. There Father Corcoran bent over them long enough to administer the last rites, after which three of them were taken to Roosevelt Hospital with all possible speed, while the other, the baby, Marion, was taken to Polyclinic Hospital, where she died. The mother died at about the same time.

The basement of the building is occupied by the Glendale Social Club. Firemen were unable to say whether the blaze had started in their quarters or just outside them, nor had they determined the origin of the fire.

SENATE SUSPICION OF WORLD COURT MEANS LONG DELAY

Harding Proposal to Join Is Regarded as Doomed Until December at Least.

SHARP FIGHT IN PROSPECT

Borah Unconvinced—Wants a Tribunal on Supreme Court Principles.

OTHER MEMBERS ADRIFT

Cannot See How America Can Accept Court Without Embracing League.

Special to The New York Times.

WASHINGTON, Feb. 25.—The first reaction of the Senate to President Harding's request for the Senate's sanction to his proposal that the United States Government become an active party to the League of Nations World Court of Justice is that the proposal is too important to be acted upon in the short time remaining for the present Congress, which will end a week from today. Having had a chance to consider the President's recommendation overnight, Senators were generally of the opinion today that it was out of the question to bring the proposal to a vote before the final adjournment.

It was late yesterday afternoon when the President's message reached the Senate, and that body adjourned after it had been read in executive session. Some Senators said today that they had not had time even to read, let alone study, the explanatory letter from Secretary Hughes which accompanied the message.

In the crowded hours of the closing week of a Congress there are many pressing matters to require attention. Friends of the Administration in the Senate were willing to concede that these could not be put aside to give way to the consideration of a new project, especially one that affected an association of the United States with the League of Nations, whose enemies in the Senate are still militant.

Active Opposition in Sight.

Sufficient evidence is not at hand to give an adequate idea of Senate sentiment toward the President's proposal. A night of sleeping on it did not make Senators better prepared than they were yesterday to commit themselves as to what course they would take. Enough is known, however, of the effect of the proposal on certain Senators to justify the prediction that it is certain to precipitate a spirited contest, which could not be concluded in the short space of a legislative week.

On Tuesday the Committee on Foreign Relations will meet at the call of its Chairman, Senator Lodge, to consider the President's message and the explanatory letter from Secretary Hughes. The probability is that the committee will defer action until the next Congress, which is not likely to assemble until December.

Doubt was expressed today that the committee would vote to report the proposal to the Senate for a place on the executive calendar, where it would rest until the new Congress convenes. As the Senate is a continuous body, it will not be necessary for the President to present the subject again to the new Congress.

Borah Not Won Over.

Some idea of the attitude toward the proposal on the part of the Senators who do not love the League of Nations is afforded by Senator Borah's brief comment today.

"If this can be worked out to give us in fact an international judicial tribunal governed by law and based on the principles of the United States Supreme Court, I will support it, said Mr. Borah. "But I have not yet been able to see that it will work out that way, although I will be very glad to have Mr. Hughes show me."

As the proposal was placed before the Senate by the President's message and the Secretary of State's letter, it contemplates reservations to the separate protocol creating the world court of justice so as to enable the United States Government to have representation in both the council and the assembly of the League of Nations for purposes connected with the court exclusively. The executive communication indicated that the governments which are parties to the protocol have been sounded and will be ready to make concessions in the form of reservations so as to permit the United States to have a voice in the League's administrative and legislative bodies in the selection of judges of the court and in all matters pertaining to its administration. But before making the United States a signatory of the protocol, President Harding desires the Senate to give its sanction.

It is this proposal of entering into an association with the League of Nations, if only for a limited and non-political purpose, that gives pause to some, perhaps many, of the Senators who were bitterly opposed to the ratification of the League covenant. As the position of certain of the irreconcilable group was outlined today, the point which they are unable to grasp is how can the United States be a member of a court which depends for existence on the League of Nations and whose decisions the League alone is to enforce, and yet not be a member of the League? The point was made today that Secretary Hughes's explanatory letter was silent on that subject.

Another possible objection that may arise in the minds of Senators, according to suggestions heard, was that with no code of laws to guide it the World Court of Justice does not have the status of a judicial tribunal but merely the status of an arbitral tribunal. The United States Government is a party to

American Husbands Win First Place In a Canvass of 20,000 French Women

PARIS, Feb. 25 (Associated Press).—The Woman's Weekly Eve recently in one of its issues asked its readers two questions. The first of these was what occupation they would prefer their husband to follow, and the other, if not French, from what nationality they would choose a husband.

Nearly 20,000 replies were received on the second question, and in these nearly 14,000 women voted that they would choose an American for their helpmeet. France's allies made a poor showing on this question. Italy received only about 2,000 votes, while England received only 1,800. No other nation, aside from the United States, Italy and England, passed the 400 mark. The list closed with Turkey, for whose subjects 18 women voted they had a preference.

On the question of the occupation of a husband the manufacturer led the van with 9,000 votes. He was followed by the scientist with 3,000, the banker with 2,000 and the moving picture actor with 1,000. No other trade or profession reached the four-figure mark. The aviator was ninth on the list, with 360 ballots, and the pugilist twelfth, with 141. No votes were received from women who would have army or navy officers or State employes as their husbands.

'Flu,' Pneumonia and Accidents Crowd New York's Hospitals to Overflowing

The city hospitals are much overcrowded as a result of the prevalence of pneumonia and influenza. The hospital authorities said yesterday that other cases due to the severe weather conditions this Winter, such as ice and snow accidents, also had contributed to the overcrowded conditions.

Wards M and L in the surgical division at Bellevue have been assigned for the use of pneumonia and influenza patients. A steady increase in the number of cases has led the hospital staff to install extra cots. The cots have been placed along a wide aisle at one side of the wards. Wards A and B in the Bellevue medical division also are used exclusively for pneumonia and influenza cases.

Visitors to all of the wards housing influenza cases are required to wear special hospital gowns, to prevent the spread of the disease. The patrolmen on duty about Bellevue have been instructed to be especially watchful to prevent smoking in the wards.

Miss Spear, night Superintendent at Harlem Hospital, said last night that all of the medical wards in the hospital were greatly overcrowded as a result of the many influenza cases. The surgical wards also were crowded, she said, because of an exceptionally large number of accidents in the icy streets, including automobile mishaps and injuries to persons falling on slippery pavements.

New York Hospital also is crowded, it was said last night. The authorities said there were no vacancies in the institution. Patients attended by New York Hospital ambulance surgeons are being taken to Bellevue immediately after treatment.

Officials said that when there was no more room in Bellevue Hospital cots would be placed in all the available space in New York Hospital.

"All the News That's Fit to Print."

The New York Times.

THE WEATHER.
Fair, slightly warmer Thursday; Friday, fair, warmer; moderate winds, becoming south.
For full weather report see Page 23.

VOL. LXXII....No. 23,775. *** NEW YORK, TUESDAY, FEBRUARY 27, 1923. TWO CENTS In Greater New York | THREE CENTS Within 200 Miles | FOUR CENTS Elsewhere

SMITH ASKS LAWS TO BEGIN THE WORK OF REORGANIZATION

Urges in Message to Legislature Abolition of Many Offices, Regrouping of Others.

AS MEASURE OF EFFICIENCY

No Business, He Declares, Could Survive With Hodge-Podge Officials Such as State Has.

NOW IS TIME FOR ACTION

And Constitutional Enactments Can Follow—Bills Are Soon to Be Introduced.

Special to The New York Times.

ALBANY, Feb. 26.—Not content to await the consummation of his plans for general reconstruction of the State Government through the slower process of constitutional amendment, Governor Smith sent a special message tonight to the Legislature recommending the abolition of several useless bureaus or agencies and the consolidation of others by means of legislation which can be passed at the present session if the lawmakers take kindly to the Governor's proposal.

About 100 such agencies which are now independently administered will be scrapped or co-ordinated with some major department of the State Government if the Governor's recommendations are followed. In this process many useless offices will be abolished, resulting in considerable saving to the State and a higher degree of efficiency in the Administration, according to persons at the Capitol who are in a position to judge.

"If you can carry out these recommendations we will have taken the first long stride toward accomplishing the final consolidation contemplated by the constitutional amendments which have already passed the Senate, and which I assume will shortly receive the approval of the Assembly," the Governor said in his message. "In the main these statutory changes follow the principles of the recommendations made to me by the non-partisan Reconstruction Commission which I appointed in 1919. They have been carefully studied and are based upon a wide field of experience."

Bills to carry out Governor Smith's recommendations are now being prepared. It was said tonight that there would be at least twenty bills and might be as many as thirty. Introduction of these measures, it was said, would probably begin Monday and continue throughout the week. After the message had been read in the Senate and the Assembly tonight it was ordered printed and referred to the Judiciary Committee in both houses.

Proposes Laws Now to Save Time.

The Governor points out in his message that the changes he recommends in his message are not to be regarded as substitutes for the constitutional amendments upon which there has already been action taken by the Legislature. But those measures would require the sanction of a Legislature with a different Senate and could not be submitted to the voters for ratification before the general election in 1925, and could not be made operative through the enactment of legislation before the Legislature meets in 1926.

He urges in the message that the statutory changes he recommends may readily be adjusted to the broader scheme of constitutional reorganization which has in view the grouping of all the activities now performed by 187 departments, bureaus and commissions under nineteen main divisions, the permanency of which would be guaranteed by provision in the organic law of the State.

The Motion Picture Censorship Commission, bills for the abolition of which are already pending, and the Board of Port Wardens, the scrapping of which as useless has been urged by many Governors, head the list of a dozen or more boards or bureaus which under the Governor's recommendations would be legislated out of existence.

Creation of a new department of public works to take over all the public works and engineering functions of the State from more than a dozen agencies that are now performing them; a co-ordination of the welfare and institutional activities of the State, involving the abolition of the Patrol Board and the Probation Commission and the transfer of their functions to the Prison Commission, and the bringing together under the control of the Conservation Department of two score or more of commissions and agencies that now supervise small parks and places of scenic, scientific or historic interest which the State has taken over are other salient points made by the Governor.

What He Wants Abolished.

The Governor's message in full is as follows:

"To the Legislature:

"In the annual message which I sent to you on Jan. 30 I stated that it would be desirable, pending the final adoption of the constitutional amendments which are to bring about a permanent reorganization of the State Government, to bring about certain statutory consolidations of scattered departments. My present message has for its purpose the recommendation of changes which can be made as soon as your honorable body passes the necessary legislation.

"If you carry out these recommendations we will have taken the first long

Continued on Page Four.

Senator Johnson Facetious Over Joining World Court

Special to The New York Times.

WASHINGTON, Feb. 26.—Senator Johnson of California commented ironically today on President Harding's proposal of American participation in the World Court of Justice. He said:

"If we now do what is asked, the situation is this: We are wholly out of the League. We are in part of the League. By reservations we are out of the part of the League we are in. The part of the League we are in, and from which by reservations we get out, functions as a part of the League with our assistance.

"In the language of a great editor of the West, 'All of which is partly true.' We are not going into the League of Nations at this session of Congress."

CAN'T RUN THE RUHR, FRENCH NOW ADMIT

But Will Withdraw Troops Only When Germans Co-operate Fully in Production.

BERLIN PUTS OUT FEELERS

Swiss Emissary Told by Poincare That Germany Must Deal With Allies Direct.

BY EDWIN L. JAMES.

Copyright, 1923, by The New York Times Company
Special Cable to THE NEW YORK TIMES.

PARIS, Feb. 26.—Many of those who concede that France will win the Ruhr fight against Germany—that is, that Germany will sue for terms—nevertheless ask the question "What can France get out of the Ruhr, even if the Germans back down, since she has discovered she cannot run the great workshop against the will of Directors and workers?" I will endeavor to give the answer of French officials to this question.

It is an essential part of French conception of the situation that Germany's backdown must include an agreement on the part of the Berlin Government to do its best to put the workshops back to production, to urge the miners to dig coal, the railroad men to run trains and the industrials to operate their factories. Without that promise the French will maintain their cordon around the Ruhr, cutting it off from the rest of Germany.

Will Credit Taxes to Reparations.

When Germany shall have promised to set the Ruhr back to work, the French intend to collect taxes on coal and manufactured products to the amount Germany collected, or had promised to collect and credit this amount to reparations. In the meanwhile Germany should have accepted new reparation terms providing new payments and new periods of payment.

When she shall have fulfilled the conditions imposed and continued payments until the French deem she has shown good faith—and this is likely to be a matter of some years—the French will consider turning the Ruhr back to Germany, with reservation of the right to go back whenever Germany defaults.

This plan differs from the original French Ruhr plan and may undergo other changes, but it represents the way the French figure today. They have come to realize that they cannot make the Ruhr pay so long as the German's resistance keeps up. They are counting on the deprivation of the Ruhr riches to persuade Germany to agree to operate the Ruhr for partial profit under the Reparations Commission.

Sounding Out the French.

PARIS, Feb. 26 (Associated Press).—The French Government has received intimations, of a vague and indirect nature, that the German Government desires to negotiate a settlement of the reparations issue, it was declared in responsible quarters here today.

The most important of these suggestions appears to have been made through M. Dubois, a Swiss financier, who came to Paris last week avowedly charged with a mission as a friendly neutral to sound Premier Poincaré as to the possibility of opening conversations for a reparations agreement.

Premier Poincaré's reply to every suggestion is understood to have been that the German Government must come out into the open and talk plainly, and directly with the Reparation Commission or with the allied Governments, and that efforts made through outside private persons, or even neutral Governments, could not, under the circumstances, be the basis for negotiations.

The official impression here is that Germany is endeavoring to draw out for

Continued on Page Three.

SENATE DEMOCRATS RALLY TO HARDING ON THE WORLD COURT

But Republicans Condemn His Proposal to Join or Show Lukewarm Feeling.

KING MOVES ACCEPTANCE

Enough Votes to Pass It, but Action Appears Certain to Be Blocked.

UP IN COMMITTEE TODAY

Bitter Enders to Fight It There—Harding Relies on Public Sentiment.

Special to The New York Times.

WASHINGTON, Feb. 26.—Democratic Senators began today to get behind the recommendation of President Harding that the United States Government associate itself with the League of Nations World Court of Justice. Republican Senators condemned the President's proposal, or gave it cautious endorsement, or, for the most part, said they preferred to defer comment.

More than ever it became apparent that there is not the slightest chance that the Senate will take action on the proposal in the present Congress, which will expire by constitutional limitation next Sunday.

Tomorrow's meeting of the Committee on Foreign Relations to consider the President's recommendation of an immediate sanction of American participation in the world court is likely to be negative. At the most, the committee might agree to report the President's recommendation to the Senate, but this would not mean that the Senate would act. Opposition intermixed with uncertainty is too marked to permit a vote to be taken by next Sunday.

While Democratic Senators are not overlooking the opportunity to play a little politics in relation to the President's proposal that the United States associate itself with the League of Nations to a limited degree it became apparent that the greater number of them are ready to take up the President's recommendation at once and give it hearty support. There was a partisan tone to the comment of Democratic Senators; they could not resist the temptation to take a fling at a Republican President endorsing a child of the League of Nations. But they showed themselves to be for the proposal on its merits and practically invited the Republicans to bring it up for final action.

Harrison for Quick Acceptance.

Senator Harrison of Mississippi, one of the most persistent critics of President Harding's policies, said:

"I am in favor of discharging the Committee on Foreign Relations unless it acts on this matter immediately. The will of the people must be obeyed. It is an eleventh-hour conversion, but I am glad to see the Administration right on one issue."

Meanwhile the Republican leaders seem to be at sea as to the course to pursue. They do not deceive themselves into the belief that the Senate can be expected to act before final adjournment, granted that the party in the Senate should determine to stand by the president. Their concern comes from endeavoring to determine whether it is wise at the present moment to take any position whatever on the subject, with the knowledge that most of the opposition to the President's recommendation would come from the Republican ranks.

At that, it appears to be evident that with the greater number of Democrats ready to join the greater number of Republicans—some of the latter reluctant adherents to anything pertaining to the League but loyal to the Administration—the sanction of the Senate could be obtained if the question could be brought to a vote.

Thirty Republican Votes Needed.

Two-thirds of the Senate are necessary to give American adhesion to the protocol for the establishment of the League's Court of Justice. That means sixty-two of the ninety-six members. All except four or five of the thirty-seven Democrats are believed to be favorable to endorsing the Republican President's stand for the court, while the remaining thirty or more votes, it is contended in some quarters, would be found in the ranks of the fifty-nine Republican Senators, most of whom would be willing to follow the President's lead.

Senator Lodge, the Republican floor leader, at whose instance the Committee

Continued on Page Two.

60,000 Tons Aid City's Depleted Coal Bins; Big Shipments Arrive as Ice Blockade Ends

The fuel situation in this city has greatly improved within the last forty-eight hours, officials of the State Fuel Administration declared yesterday. Continuance of the warm weather has made it possible to break the blockade on the New Jersey side of the Hudson, and with less coal being consumed the reserve is steadily growing.

More than 60,000 tons of domestic anthracite came across the river to the city on Sunday, according to Harry T. Peters, Assistant Fuel Administrator. Of 127 barges that had been held up in New Jersey because of the heavy ice floes 125 barges were moved. This was said to be about twice the normal supply reaching New York daily. The barges averaged 500 tons each, and most of them were towed over by the Cornell Transportation Company. Shipments in large quantities continued to arrive all day.

The shortage on Long Island has been greatly relieved during the last day or two. On Saturday the Long Island Railroad took 171 cars across and on Sunday 237 cars. Reports received at the office of Samuel J. Drummond, District Fuel Administrator for Brooklyn, were to the effect that several barge loads of coal had been received there Sunday and yesterday. Two boatloads consigned to the Commonwealth Coal Company were anchored at the Gowanus and Wallabout Canals, and two carloads consigned to the same company were taken to the freight yards of the Long Island Railroad in Long Island City. Boatloads of anthracite have arrived at Newtown Creek, Greenpoint and the Gowanus and Wallabout Canals. The Cullen Fuel Company, Coney Island, notified Mr. Drummond that it had 1,200 tons of substitutes for sale to persons who needed fuel.

To help out the situation in Westchester County the Consolidated Gas Company has shipped 350 tons of coke to the Westchester Lighting Company at Mount Vernon. Francis A. Stratton, President of the company, announced that it was being sold in 40-pound lots. The use of public schools for social functions in Mount Vernon has been suspended until the fuel shortage ends.

Solomon Gave Airship to Queen of Sheba; Her Son Flew in It, Ancient MS. States

Copyright, 1923, by The New York Times Company.
Special Cable to THE NEW YORK TIMES.

LONDON, Feb. 26.—There has just been brought to light in an ancient manuscript the statement that Solomon gave to the Queen of Sheba "a vessel wherein one could traverse the air [or wind], which Solomon had made by the wisdom that God had given unto him."

This statement is quoted by Colonel Lockwood Marsh, Secretary of the Royal Aeronautical Society, in the opening of his preface to "Bibliotheca Aeronautica," to be issued in a few days. The text is taken from an ancient Abyssinian manuscript, "The Glory of the Kings," translated by Sir E. Wallis Budge, Director of Egyptian Antiquities in the British Museum, in his book "The Queen of Sheba and Her Only Son Menyelek," published last year.

"This ancient manuscript has, of course, been translated many times," said Colonel Lockwood Marsh to press representatives, "but the statement about Solomon's airship apparently escaped the notice of the reviewers, and it has been left to a flying enthusiast like myself to discover and proclaim it. Solomon lived in the tenth century B. C., so it is quite the earliest reference to flying extant and as such will be added to our records."

Many theosophists believe there were airships a million years ago in lost Atlantis, but as a book describing these airships was not published until 1896 and the theory was based on astral clairvoyance Colonel Lockwood Marsh prefers to regard this reference to Solomon's airship in the dawn of civilization as the earliest one.

There are other references to flight in Abyssinian sacred writing, and there is a long description of the miraculous way in which the Queen of Sheba's son Menyelek left Solomon, journeying to his mother's country. "No man hauled his wagon, and whether it was men, or horses, or mules, or loaded camels, each was raised above the ground to a height of a cubit." A cubit, according to the ancient Egyptians, measured about twenty inches, but elsewhere it is recorded that over the Red Sea they were lifted up three cubits, "and every one traveled in the wagons like an eagle when his body glideth above the wind."

PHARAOH'S TOMB IS CLOSED TILL AUTUMN

Discoverers Cover It With Sand for Protection Until the Work Can Be Resumed.

TOURISTS WATCH SEALING

Everybody Who Saw It Was Impressed by the Egyptians' Great Faith in a Hereafter.

The Times (London) World Copyright, by Arrangement with the Earl of Carnarvon.

Copyright, 1923, by The New York Times Company.
By Wireless to THE NEW YORK TIMES.

LUXOR, Egypt, Feb. 26.—Howard Carter and Mr. Callender closed today the tomb of Pharaoh Tut-ankh-Amen and labored throughout the day to assure the dead Egyptian monarch a quiet rest until work can be resumed next Fall.

The whole morning was taken up with blocking the door and clearing from the well the appartus accumulated there during the past three months. An interested crowd of tourists watched process. This afternoon the work of filling in with sand and rubble was started and it is not expected to be finished before tomorrow evening.

The filling in of the entrance to the tomb is being done by a couple of score of boys and men under overseers, who run backward and forward in an endless chain discharging basket after basket of sand and rubble into the shaft, from which emerge a huge cloudlike smoke as from a great fire. It was an extraordinary spectacle, rendered all the more curious by the fact that while the digging out a tomb is an ordinary experience this is probably the first time that any of those present had ever assisted at the filling in of a tomb containing an ancient king.

Farewell Visit to the Tomb.

It was impossible not to be moved on paying a farewell visit to the wonderful death chambers of Tut-ankh-Amen, knowing that in a few hours the work of shutting up the tomb would be begun. The large ante-chamber, with its bare, undecorated walls of pale pinkish yellow, is now emptied of all its precious contents, and seemed bleak and desolate.

To the left as one enters the end of the chamber, behind a wooden barricade, lay trays containing two lovely alabaster vases, a black wooden swan and a heap of blackened fibrous matter which was once a rush basket, with some bones found lying on the floor of the sepulchral chamber. These bones have not yet been examined, but they are believed to be the bones of some quadruped animal, conjecturally the remnants of something sacrificial. Close by, also behind the wooden rail, is a boarded patch low down on the further wall. It shows the entrance hole made by the robbers into the annex, and has been temporarily shut.

At the opposite end of the chamber, that is, on the right as one enters, stand conspicuously the two black and gold statues of the King, one on each side of the wide, gaping entrance to the sepulchral chamber. At some places on these statues pitch was used for bituminizing and seems to have run, and here and there superficial cracks are observable. These are minor flaws, however. As they stand the two figures are very striking, and when properly treated they will be magnificent.

Sight of Tabernacle Is Dazzling.

As one approaches the entrance to the sepulchral chamber the light gleams on the face of a screen, which seems almost to choke the entrance, of brilliant turquoise blue faience inlaid in gold sea, the thing with which the whole surface of the tabernacle is covered, producing a dazzling effect.

The floor of the sepulchral chamber is more than three feet lower than that of the ante-chamber, without any steps or anything to break the drop down over the rock ledge. The best way to get in its to sit on the floor and dangle one's legs and let oneself drop in like a boy sliding off a wall. Caution is needed, however, not to bump into the gilded structure in front, the lower part of which is covered with planking to guard against accidents.

When you land you find yourself on the right hand almost at the corner of the room and you wriggle round the angle of the tabernacle to find that the room in this dimension, that is from north to south, is not more than eleven feet or twelve feet long. On your left is the splendid front and closed doors of the shrine with their belts and staples. On the right is another doorway which opens into the treasure house. I have already described all the articles

Continued on Page Six.

ROCKEFELLER BUYS $1,100,000 TAPESTRY

John D. Jr. Announces Acquisition of Fifteenth Century "Hunt for the Unicorn."

FRENCH PRESS INDIGNANT

Editors Quote Alleged Agreement by de la Rochefoucauld to Keep Treasure in France.

Six of the rarest tapestries of medieval France, woven bits from a dimming past, but bright themselves despite their centuries of age, have been purchased by John D. Rockefeller Jr. for $1,100,000, and unless complications develop soon will be hung on the walls of the Rockefeller home in West Fifty-fourth Street.

The tapestries are the series depicting the "Hunt for the Unicorn," a famous piece of work which for years was in the Castle of Verteuil in France, the seat of the family of La Rochefoucauld. The news that Mr. Rockefeller has acquired them prompted some speculation, since the French press for the last few months has been up in arms about the whereabouts of the art treasures. One Paris newspaper has stated that the present representative of the family, Count Gabriel de la Rochefoucauld, had promised that the tapestries never were to be taken from France.

The six relics of gone time when peasant fingers still retained the highest skill of the weaver's art first reached this city early in November last. They were placed on exhibition in the Anderson Galleries. Admittance to the room where the tapestries were displayed was by card only. Then they suddenly were withdrawn and no one, at least among the general public, knew until yesterday whither they had been taken.

"Unknown American" First Suggested.

There was a report at the time that an "noknown American" had bought the six pieces for $1,000,000 but no one at the Anderson Galleries could be found to substantiate this. The tapestries, it developed, had been brought to the United States by Edouard Larcade, Vice President of the Syndical Chambers of Curios and Fine Arts of Paris. It was said that Mr. Larcade had purchased the tapestries as a speculation, but it was thought that he was merely here acting as an agent. He left New York at about the same time the tapestries disappeared, and so details, and even confirmation, of the reported sale to an American buyer could not be obtained from him.

Whether any friction had developed in the customs over the importation of the pictures could not be ascertained last night.

An official statement issued late yesterday on behalf of Mr. Rockefeller, who is at Ormond Beach, Florida, was as follows:

"The tapestries in question were exhibited last Fall in the Anderson Galleries. Later they were taken to London. A few weeks ago they were purchased in London by an agent of John D. Rockefeller Jr., and have now been shipped to this country, although the report that they are hanging in his home is incorrect for the reason that they have not yet been released by the customs authorities.

"Before purchasing them, Mr. Rockefeller had what he considered to be responsible assurances that their sale was duly authorized by their owner. Mr. Rockefeller had no information as to any understanding between the owner and the French Government concerning conditions under which these tapestries might be removed from France."

Metal Thread Interwoven.

As nearly as antiquarians can place the manufacture of the tapestries they seem to have been removed from their primitive looms in 1460, but there exists some difference of opinion as to the strict accuracy of this date. At least, it is known definitely that they were woven by order of Jean I. de la Rochefoucauld and his wife, Marguerite de Barbezieux. In the execution of the tapestries a metal thread was employed here and there, greatly enhancing the brilliancy of the effect.

When the tapestries were completed the six phases of the pursuit of the unicorn were placed on the walls of Verteuil Castle, where they were kept cold and dimly lighted and admirably tended for more than four centuries. The great care expended on the tapestries was quite evident to those who had opportunity to view them at the semi-

Continued on Page Seven.

PECORA OPENS FIGHT TO HAVE GRAND JURY INDICT ANDERSON

Moor and Fancher Testify on $24,700 "Confidential Publicity Fund."

WILL HEAR WOMEN TODAY

Miss Odell and Miss Hill Will Be Called When Hearing Is Resumed.

ROCKEFELLER JR. ASSAILED

Anti-Saloon League Superintendent Says Endorsement of Fosdick Evades Issue.

The January additional Grand Jury began an investigation yesterday afternoon into the allegation that William H. Anderson, Superintendent of the Anti-Saloon League, presented a fictitious bill for $24,700 to the league for "confidential publicity promotion."

When the Grand Jury convened at 2 P. M., Dr. George Caleb Moor, pastor of the Madison Avenue Baptist Church and Secretary and Director of the League; Bertram H. Fancher, Vice President of the Fifth Avenue Bank and Treasurer of the League; Miss Maude M. Odell, Mr. Anderson's confidential assistant, and Miss Mary Hill, head bookkeeper and Assistant Treasurer of the League, were waiting to be called as witnesses. They had been subpoenaed last Saturday to appear before the body. The subpoena served on Dr. Moor also commanded him to produce certain papers which had not been turned over to Mr. Pecora at the time he began his preliminary inquiry.

It developed that a subpoena had been left for Dr. Burrell at the study adjoining his church, but it could not be learned whether the clergyman received the subpoena when he appeared at the church Sunday morning to deliver the sermon.

Dr. Moor was called before the Grand Jury about half an hour after Acting District Attorney Pecora had entered the room. He remained inside for more than half an hour, and later Mr. Fancher was called. Mr. Fancher remained with the Grand Jurors less than half an hour. He came out with Mr. Pecora, who announced that the Grand Jury had adjourned for the day, but that Miss Odell and Miss Hill would be called at the resumption of the inquiry this afternoon.

Before the proceeding began, Mr. Pecora was asked if he intended to demand an indictment against Mr. Anderson, and he replied:

"Certainly. That is my purpose of going before the Grand Jury. It would be absurd to think that I would go there just to entertain the Grand Jurors."

It was reported that in the event that Dr. Burrell did not appear before the Grand Jury before the close of the inquiry in the latter part of the week, the body would make a report on the testimony to a Judge in General Sessions without waiting for his evidence.

Replies to Mr. Rockefeller.

Mr. Anderson made public two statements based on an address he made in the forenoon to the Ministers' Association of the Reformed Church, in which he attacked John D. Rockefeller Jr., Raymond B. Fosdick, whom he described as a "Rockefeller employe," and Acting District Attorney Ferdinand Pecora.

The attacks were founded on statements made by Mr. Rockefeller, Mr. Fosdick and Mr. Pecora in connection with the Acting Prosecutor's preliminary inquiry into the charge against Mr. Anderson, which ended a week ago. Mr. Anderson, in the opening paragraph of his second statement, declared that Mr. Fosdick, "having failed to crush me into silence by the anonymous use of the influence of the Rockefeller money, evidently now seeks to finish the job by use of a direct statement by Mr. Rockefeller, which does not even squarely touch let alone meet the issue."

The reference to Mr. Rockefeller was based on Mr. Rockefeller's reply Sunday to Mr. Anderson's attack on Mr. Fosdick as a friend of the "wets" in an address which Mr. Anderson made that day in the Trinity Methodist Episcopal Church in Albany.

Assails Acting Prosecutor.

Mr. Anderson's first statement contained the attack on Mr. Pecora. He charged that a plot was on foot against the Board of Directors of the League "because it could not be scared into repudiating me." He also described as "wanton brutality" the statement of Acting District Attorney Pecora that if Dr. David James Burrell, President of the League, and who is pastor of the Marble Collegiate Church, Fifth Avenue and Tweny-ninth Street, was not too ill

Continued on Page Five.

Proposes a 6 Per Cent. Tax on All Amusements in State

Special to The New York Times.

ALBANY, Feb. 26.—From $5,000,000 to $7,000,000 annually in additional revenue is expected from a tax on sports and amusements, proposed in a bill introduced tonight by Assemblyman Miller, Republican, of Genesee.

The proposed tax would be levied at the rate of 6 per cent. on gross receipts at theatrical performances, concerts, baseball games, prizefights, running races, wrestling matches and amusements of every character for which an admission fee is charged.

Mr. Miller said tonight that his bill would go through as it had endorsement of both the Democratic and Republican leaders in the Assembly.

SUSPEND POLICEMEN AFTER 2 OUTRAGES

First Victim Beaten and Left Unconscious After Dispute With Two Bluecoats.

MAN SHOT THROUGH DOOR

After a Row Over Gasoline for Commandeered Taxi—Suspension Ordered by Deputy Leach.

Policemen Walker G. Harrington and James McFadden, both attached to the Astoria Station, were suspended from duty last night following a fight in front of the saloon of Patrick McGovern, Twelfth Street and Grand Avenue, Astoria, and a shooting. Harrington, at the time of the fight, was in citizen's clothes, and McFadden was in uniform.

The suspension followed an investigation by First Deputy Police Commissioner John R. Leach into the shooting of Daniel Doyle of 411 Astoria Avenue, an automobile mechanic, who was wounded in the head, and the beating of William Montanus, a bricklayer, of 357 Twelfth Avenue, Astoria, whose skull is believed to have been fractured. Montanus was hurt in front of the saloon and Doyle was shot as he was closing the door of a garage at Grand and Thirteenth Avenues a few minutes later.

McGovern said that the two policemen drove up to the front of his place in a taxicab. Montanus, who was standing at the door, apparently knew one of the occupants of the taxicab and spoke to him. After a few minutes' conversation there were blows. As McGovern ran to the street the fight ended, he said, and the two policemen jumped into the taxicab, leaving Montanus unconscious on the sidewalk.

According to witnesses, the two policemen then rode in the taxicab to a garage at Grand and Thirteenth Avenues, got out and demanded that Doyle give them gasoline. Doyle filled the tank of their car and then an argument ensued.

Details are lacking as to just what followed. The policemen are said to have followed the garage man into his place and the row continued. Doyle, it was said, succeeded in getting the two policemen to the street again, and as he was pushing the door shut he was shot in the head.

The policemen then disappeared. Soon after several detectives from Hunts Point appeared on the scene in response to telephone messages. They questioned several persons in addition to Doyle. After both injured men had been removed to St. John's Hospital in an ambulance, the detectives went to the Astoria station where, it was said, they found Policemen Harrington and McFadden.

The detectives refused to say anything about their conversation with Harrington and McFadden, nor would the police give out any information as to the manner in which Doyle and Montanus came by their injuries.

It was learned, however, that soon after the appearance of the detectives at the station, Deputy Commissioner Leach was sent for. Mr. Leach arrived at the station, where for a time he was closeted with Harrington and McFadden and the detectives. An hour after his arrival Mr. Leach announced that he had suspended both policemen from duty pending a full investigation of the shooting and the alleged attack on Montanus.

FRENCH BUDGET HELD UP.

Chamber Votes Provisional Credits as Debate Grows Hotter.

PARIS, Feb. 26 (Associated Press).—The Chamber of Deputies today voted provisional credits for the Government of 1,879,000,000 francs for March. This action was taken because the 1923 budget is still being debated and a balance between expenditures and receipts has not yet been attained.

The Chamber also voted 1,354,000,000 francs for March and April expenditures, chargeable to Germany. This question brought out a sharp debate over charges of waste in the reconstruction of the devastated regions.

Gasoline Price Is Put Up 1 1-2 Cents; Wholesale Tank Wagon Rate Now 24 1-2 Cents

The Standard Oil Company of New York yesterday announced an advance of 1½ cents a gallon in the wholesale price of gasoline in New York and the New England States, the territory served by the company. This follows an advance announced by the Standard Oil Company of New Jersey last week. The wholesale tank wagon price quoted by the New York company is now 24½ cents. A similar advance also was announced in naphtha to 23½ cents a gallon.

Advances in gasoline prices were announced in other sections of the country. In Ohio the price was increased 1 cent a gallon yesterday, to 23 cents retail. In some of the South and Southwestern States advances of a cent a gallon also were announced.

These advances, according to trade advices, are in line with a policy of the larger companies to bring the price of refined products more in accord with the price of crude oil, which has advanced sharply since the beginning of the year. The advances in crude, it was stated, cut down the margin of profit, and to offset this gasoline and other products are being advanced. Predictions were made in the trade that another advance in the price of mid-continent crude oil is expected within the near future. If Midcontinent is again advanced, Wyoming crude is expected to follow, as these two grades have moved in unison since the beginning of the year.

BRONX CONTRACTOR SLAIN IN HIS CAR; WOMAN SUSPECTED

Frederick Schneider Shot to Death at Wheel—Companion Fled From Auto.

FARMER HEARD TWO SHOTS

When He Saw Woman Leave Spot He Notified Police—Pistol Found Near Victim.

DECLARED NOT A SUICIDE

Impossible From Position of Body, Says Medical Examiner—Owner's Two Chow Dogs in Death Car

Frederick Schneider, wealthy Bronx contractor, was shot to death in his automobile late yesterday afternoon at a lonely spot on Sea View Avenue. Thirty detectives are hunting for a woman who hurried away from the automobile as it stopped with the dead man's hand on the wheel. Two other women, with one of whom he had lived for ten years and the other his real wife, with whom he had remained on friendly terms although they were separated, are aiding the police in their search for the woman supposed to have killed him.

An early theory that Schneider might have committed suicide was destroyed by the physical evidence. District Attorney Edward Glennon announced last night that the authorities unquestionably were dealing with a murder. Admittedly it was one of baffling circumstances, the slayer having picked a deserted spot, and having avoided any living witness to the actual crime except two chow dogs, Schneider's inseparable companions, who were barking over the body when the police reached the car.

Money and Checks in Pocket.

Robbers were eliminated when a bank book in which was a large sum in currency and checks was found in the dead man's pocket. Relatives and confidential employes joined in denying rumors that Schneider had business troubles, insisting that he had made a million dollars in the past few years, having obtained many of the biggest excavating jobs in his home borough. Likewise they said that while Schneider had suffered some delays and extensions of time on one of his biggest contracts because of labor troubles several years ago, he had no enemy either among his own workers or among union men who might conceivably have sought his death.

It was 5:45 yesterday afternoon when Schneider's touring car, close curtained as a shield against the drizzle, came to a stop about two feet from the Clason Point trolley tracks in Sound View Avenue near Rosedale Avenue, its nose pointed toward Clason Point, a snow bank separating the car by several feet from the sidewalk. At that same instant Nicholas Fuelner, in the house on his farm paralleling the road, but three blocks inland, lifted his startled head at the sharp reverberation of two shots. His view unobstructed, Fuelner could see the car at a standstill, its doors closed and the curtains shielding the interior from view.

Saw Woman Hurry Away.

It was Fuelner, too, who saw a woman hurrying away toward Westchester Avenue. Whether he actually saw the woman get out of the car or first noticed her after she had picked her way across the snowbank and started along the sidewalk the police refused to tell. At any rate, Fuelner knowing that his own house and the Clason Point Military Academy, a quarter of a mile from where the touring car had come to a standstill, were the nearest habitations, was certain that the sound of shots had come from the automobile whence emanated the sharp barking of dogs.

Fuelner sent word to the Simpson Street police station and Patrolman James Doyle soon made his way to the motionless car. He opened the right forward door, to be met by the snarls of the two chows, Hulu and Zulu, on the rear seat. But Doyle had no time for the dogs. Slumped over the wheel was the body of a big, powerfully built man about 46 years old. The man's left hand, in a heavy driving glove, rested on the wheel. His right hand was in his coat pocket, pressed against the other glove. Close to the front door the policeman had opened lay a .38 calibre pistol, the butt almost touching the door when it was closed, the barrel pointing toward the dead man. Doyle picked up the pistol and found one shiny chamber empty, as if the owner had been in the habit of carrying the trigger on that empty space to avoid accidental discharge. The other chambers of the cylinder were filled, two with cartridges that had been fired and the barrel was fouled from very recent firing.

Two Bullet Wounds in Head.

Next Doyle noticed that there were two bullet wounds in the man's head and that he was unquestionably dead. One bullet had been fired through the right ear. The other had been fired into the back of the head at the base of the brain. Either well might have caused instant death. There was no slug in the car, no hole through body or curtain or windshield, so apparently neither bullet had come out.

Following routine, Doyle sent a call to Fordham Hospital for an ambulance and presently Dr. Schlosser came, wrote "Dead on arrival" in his case book and went away again. Meantime Doyle had notified the desk lieutenant and [illegible] reserves from the Simpson Street station hurried around to make the [illegible] hurried search of the region.

Acting Captain Henry Bruckman, in charge of the detectives of the [illegible] Division, got there soon after. [illegible] man saw that he had a [illegible] ahead of him and [illegible] picked men to [illegible] for all possible [illegible]

"All the News That's Fit to Print."

The New York Times

THE WEATHER
Cloudy and colder today; Tuesday fair and cold; northwest gales.
Temperature yesterday—Max., 43; Min., 39.
For full weather report see Page 24.

VOL. LXXIII....No. 24,068. NEW YORK, MONDAY, DECEMBER 17, 1923. TWO CENTS In Greater New York | THREE CENTS Within 200 Miles | FOUR CENTS Elsewhere

OBREGON ATTACKS REBELS IN PUEBLA, OPENING OFFENSIVE

President Hurries Back From the West to Lead Army Against de la Huerta.

CAPITAL WILL BE DEFENDED

Loyal Forces Establish a Base at Apizaco—Hard Fighting Is Expected Soon.

REPORT OF A REBEL SPLIT

Generals Are Said to Be Trying to Oust de la Huerta—Socialist Regime Ended in Yucatan.

MEXICO CITY, Dec. 16 (Associated Press).—A trap has been sprung on the de la Huerta forces which this morning entered Puebla, evacuated by the Federal troops last night.

Directing an advance from Apizaco (twenty miles north of Puebla), where he arrived this afternoon, President Obregon launched an attack upon 1,000 rebel troops.

According to a War Department announcement, an engagement is expected soon, and belief is expressed that success would result.

Federals to Hold the Capital.

Special to The New York Times.

MEXICO CITY, Dec. 15 (via Laredo, Texas), (Delayed).—General Arnulfo Gomez, commander of the Federal garrison in Mexico City, denies the rumor that Mexico City will be evacuated.

"Mexico City may be tranquil," he said today, "as the Government has not a thought of leaving the capital so long as we have one soldier. The people will have all guarantees, and will not be in danger. Our soldiers are old veterans, tried in battle, and have the highest ideals of duty."

General Gomez laughs at the idea that the city may be in danger and states that unpleasant surprises are in store for the rebels.

President Obregon left Mexico City this morning to review the Federal troops who are advancing on Vera Cruz. The President arrived in Mexico City on Friday evening.

Owing to the defection of General Maycotte, commander of the forces in the State of Oaxaca, in company with the Governor of that State, Manuel Garcia Vigil, the Federal troops were obliged to evacuate the city of Puebla, the third largest city in the republic. The revolt of General Maycotte was entirely unexpected, as he had been assisting in forming plans for suppressing the revolt. Maycotte left Mexico City the early part of the week to take part in the campaign against Vera Cruz.

Reports from Irapuato, according to El Universal, are that the advance of the Federal troops has continued. The Federal troops, the paper says, are the best equipped body of troops ever seen in Mexico.

President Obregon, according to El Universal, when asked about the campaign to take the city of Guadalajara, stated the difficulty was not in capturing the city and driving the rebels into the open, but to surround Guadalajara so that the rebels would be unable to leave.

The troops under Estrada's command burned a large bridge over the Larma River to prevent the advance of the Federal Army.

General Romulo Figueroa, who started the first revolt in the State of Guerrero, was killed on the road from Teloloapam to Toluca, according to telegrams received here.

It is rumored that the Mexican Senate is unable to act on the claims commission or other parts of the convention between Mexico and the United States owing to the lack of a quorum.

Flores Threatens to Take the Field.

Copyright, 1923, by The Chicago Tribune Co.

MEXICO CITY, Dec. 16.—It is reported here that General Angel Flores, on the west coast, may go out at any time. His attempt to bring about a compromise between Adolfo de la Huerta and President Obregon has proved a failure, and now he stands to take the field and attempt to pacify the country. General Flores is the strong man of the west.

Messages published in the Grafico state that Sinaloa, Lower California, Sonora and Nayarit (on the Pacific) are in perfect peace. All forces have remained loyal to the Government.

Reports from Esperanza Station, on the Mexican Railway, state that the rebels have dynamited the large city oil tank containing 3,000 barrels of oil.

Dissension in Rebel Ranks.

EL PASO, Dec. 16.—The El Paso Times received today the following telegram from Francisco Torreblanco, private secretary to President Obregon:

"On board Presidential special train, Apizaco, Tlaxcala, Dec. 15.

"After reviewing the troops engaged in operations against the City of Guadalajara, where the rebel divisional commander, Enrique Estrada, is active, and giving the necessary instructions for the campaign, President Obregon returned to Mexico City. After a few hours in the capital, the President journeyed to Apizaco, where he spent the day reviewing the troops about to attack the forces of the rebel General Guadalupe Sanchez.

"The first formal fighting probably will occur Sunday or Monday, and all probabilities indicate the rebel forces will be completely routed. The republic generally remains quiet and no branch of the public service has been inter-

Continued on Page Five.

Reconstruction of Rheims May Be Completed in 5 Years

RHEIMS, France, Dec. 16.—The Rheims Co-operative Society for the Reconstruction of Rheims held a general meeting today under the Presidency of the Marquis de Polignac.

The Marquis in outlining the fourth year of the work of the society said that 180,000,000 francs had been spent in Rheims during the present year and that if the State was able to continue its aid in the work the reconstruction of Rheims should be completed within five years.

FIND AMERICAN DATE RECORDED 613 B. C.

First Calendar in the West Set by the Highly Civilized Mayas of Yucatan.

AN EINSTEIN AMONG THEM

Dr. Spinden of Peabody Museum Discovers Ancient Scientist Knew Relativity Theory.

A story of remarkable intellectual adventure and scientific achievement was told yesterday in a statement issued by the Peabody Museum of Harvard University. It revealed the discovery of the first two dates in American history, as the result of the recent expedition to the peninsula of Yucatan in Central America, headed by Dr. Herbert J. Spinden of the museum's scientific staff.

The first date discovered was Aug. 6, 613 B. C., according to our present system of counting time. This date marked the first day in the record of time by the Mayas, that highly civilized race of Indians who inhabited Yucatan and other parts of Central America for centuries before Columbus discovered the New World. The second date—Dec. 10, 580 B. C.—marked the formal beginning of the marvelous Mayan day-by-day calendar, based on scientific observations, which was kept intact for 2,000 years.

Discovery of these dates followed Dr. Spinden's studies of the dates on the monuments in the ancient Mayan cities. He has been able to adduce scientific proof of his day-by-day correlation of the Mayan calendar in our system of counting time to correspond with the oldest recorded dates in the Mayan system. According to the announcement from the museum, Dr. Spinden's achievements have been a great triumph for the American school of archaeology against German, French and Spanish savants, who advanced an entirely different theory to account for the Mayan dates.

Mayas Ahead of Einstein.

That a surprising intellectual power existed in Central America before Columbus discovered America is emphasized in the announcement from the museum. Dr. Spinden, in a supplementary statement, adds the striking theory that the Mayas anticipated Einstein in the discovery of the theory of relativity, and that they used this theory in calculating their calendar. According to Dr. Spinden, the Mayas were a wonderfully advanced race in mathematical and astronomical genius.

About 1,300,000 Indians in Mexico and Central America still speak the Mayan languages. Their ancient native culture exhibits the highest aboriginal development found upon the American continent. They surpassed all other American Indians in their architecture, their calendar and their system of hieroglyphics.

Dr. Spinden has spent years studying the Mayan hieroglyphics and the dates on the monuments showing the Mayan system of counting time. He has written a history of the Mayan arts and has done much research work for the Peabody Museum, which for many years has specialized in Central American research.

The museum points out that scientists have been fascinated by the puzzle of the Mayan dates since the time of Alexander von Humboldt, and that Dr. Spinden's solution of the problem required great patience and ingenuity.

"These positive and perfectly defined points in chronology, the earliest dates in New World history," says the announcement from the museum, "probably fell within the working years of one of the world's first scientists, the unknown mathematical and astronomi-

Continued on Page Six.

POINCARE AGREES WITH LIMITATIONS TO BERLIN PROPOSAL

Reserves Right to Consult Allies and Bars Treaty Revision as Subject.

WILLING TO DISCUSS RUHR

Insists Germany Still Violates Treaty as Regards Military Control Clause.

MARX SEES TRIALS AHEAD

Stresemann Talks of Humiliations—Sees No Need of Control Board.

Copyright, 1923, by The New York Times Company.
Special Cable to THE NEW YORK TIMES.

PARIS, Dec. 16.—Premier Poincaré's written reply to the note submitted yesterday to the French Government by Dr. von Hoesch, the German Chargé d'Affaires, was dispatched this evening by the Quai d'Orsay to the German Embassy. M. Poincaré telephoned the draft of the reply to Brussels last evening and the Belgian Government expressed itself as entirely in accord with the French viewpoint.

It is understood that the document, which Wilhelmstrasse is now studying, will permit the further conversations which the German Government strongly desires while at the same time again laying down those points on which neither France nor Belgium considers it possible to give way.

As regards reparations, M. Poincaré declares there can be no question of taking matters relating thereto from the hands of the Reparation Commission, empowered to deal with them under the Peace Treaty, and revision of which can neither directly nor indirectly be considered.

Regarding the Ruhr and Rhineland there can be no question of restricting the powers of the Interallied High Commission or of the Franco-Belgian authorities. Apart from these questions of principle France is quite ready to discuss the establishment of a modus vivendi in the Ruhr and Rhineland, which may re-establish normal economic conditions.

The French note mentions one point which is not included in the written statement submitted to M. Poincaré yesterday by Dr. von Hoesch. The French [illegible] recalls the fact that the Interallied Disarmament Commission of Germany has not yet been able to resume its activities. So long as this is the case, he adds, the Reich cannot pretend that it is loyally executing the clauses of the Versailles Treaty.

Ready to Listen, Says Premier.

PARIS, Dec. 16 (Associated Press).—The French Government has accepted, with limitations, the German proposals submitted by Herr von Hoesch, Chargé d'Affaires, concerning conversations Germany desires to enter into with France, as well as Belgium, on the Ruhr and Rhineland questions.

Passive resistance having apparently ceased in the Ruhr, Premier Poincaré declares that he is always ready to confer with an official representative of the German Government on all questions which this Government wishes to bring before him; at the same time he remarks that he regards such questions as of equal interest to the Allies, and therefore the French Government reserves the right of concerting with them before replying.

With respect to reparations, the French Government, as it has frequently declared, will never consent to take that question out of the hands of the commission instituted by the treaty, nor consider any regulation not strictly conforming with the treaty.

Concerning the Rhine and the Ruhr, the reply says, the French Government has nothing to change in the views already set forth; it cannot agree to take matters out of the hands of the Franco-Belgian authorities in the Ruhr, nor of the Interallied High Commission in the other occupied territories.

As to the establishment of a modus vivendi in either of these regions, M. Poincaré is fully disposed to listen to suggestions from the Berlin Government and communicate them, if circumstances admit, with his opinion to competent authority. He will, notably, accept any discussion on prolongation of the agree-

Continued on Page Three.

Greek Republicans Win in Two Provinces; Capital Is Monarchist in Orderly Election

Copyright, 1923, by The Chicago Tribune Co.

ATHENS, Dec. 16.—The Republicans scored sweeping successes today in Macedonia and Thrace, but were weak in Athens. Tranquillity marked the election day.

ATHENS, Dec. 16 (Associated Press).—The long postponed elections are taking place today throughout the country. Thus far there have been no reports of disturbances.

The newspapers today print a statement by Premier Gonatas to the effect that if the Liberals win and ex-Premier Venizelos is returned it will be the duty of the King to endeavor to persuade Venizelos to assume the Premiership.

M. Gonatas is reported to have begged the King yesterday to disregard rumors concerning an upheaval or a coup d'état, as the Government had taken measures to make such an eventuality impossible.

Special to The New York Times.

WASHINGTON, Dec. 16.—Balkan diplomats in Washington today ridiculed the news report from Rome to the effect that the armed forces of Rumania and Yugoslavia might be sent against Greece if young King George II. were dethroned and a republic established as a result of the Greek Parliamentary elections being held today.

Copyright, 1923, by The New York Times Company.
Special Cable to THE NEW YORK TIMES.

VIENNA, Dec. 16.—Among the many political refugees now in Vienna are certain ex-Ministers of Greece, of whom two were imprisoned and about to be sentenced to death at the time the other Ministers were executed, but were able to escape through the intervention of the allied powers, especially England and Italy.

These politicians yesterday addressed a protest through foreign representatives here against the elections which are being held in Greece today and against the terrorism which they say prevails in Greece.

The protest maintains that the Greek elections are fraudulent and that the results will be entirely contrary to the wishes of the people, oppressed by the revolutionary army and deprived of their rights as citizens.

Borah Denies Candidacy For President on Any Ticket

WASHINGTON, Dec. 16.—Senator Borah of Idaho "is not a candidate for the Presidential nomination of any party," he said today in discussing a prediction of Frank E. Johnesse at Boise, Idaho, last night that he would soon announce his candidacy for President on the Progressive ticket.

A dispatch from Boise last night quoted Frank E. Johnesse, State Chairman of the Progressive Party, as predicting the announcement of Senator Borah's candidacy within ninety days.

He declared that the Senator recently told him in Washington that he could run on the Progressive platform, "railroad plank and all," and if things shaped up right would accept that party's nomination for the Presidency.

SEE M'ADOO BEHIND PLANS OF RADICALS

Republicans Say Deal to Make Smith Commerce Chairman Is for His Benefit.

AID TO LA FOLLETTE ALSO

Move Would Help His Third-Party Project by Curbing Rail Legislation, They Say.

Special to The New York Times.

WASHINGTON, Dec. 16.—Republican leaders are charging tonight that the plans of the Radicals and Democrats to upset the Senate organization by electing Senator Smith Chairman of the Interstate Commerce Committee is intended as a move to benefit Senator La Follette in his plans to form a third party and get a radical railroad bill reported, and that it also is fostered by the McAdoo followers in the Democratic Party.

This is one of the outstanding features of the situation as Congress begins the third week of its session with neither Senate nor House fully organized by the appointment of its standing committees.

The whole purpose of the Radical-Democratic move, it is argued, is to form a campaign issue for McAdoo and La Follette and place President Coolidge and the Conservative Senate Republicans in the attitude of supporting the railroads. Republican leaders fear that the move may lead not only to tying up legislation on railroads but will form the real issue for McAdoo, and give La Follette arguments to stir up the radical States of the Northwest.

According to Republican leaders, the McAdoo followers in the Senate are hopeful that, with Senator Smith at the head of the committee, they will be able to report out a railroad bill which will strengthen McAdoo in the West. The bill they hope to report, it is said, would carry out McAdoo's plans and would be approved by him as reflecting the kind of legislation which he thinks ought to be enacted into law to curb the railroads.

Would Defeat Rail Measure.

Such legislation the McAdoo followers know cannot be passed, because there would be enough conservative Democrats in the Senate who would not vote for a railroad measure which would seriously disturb present conditions.

It is declared that Senator Underwood, who is opposed to the McAdoo ideas about what should be done to the railroads, would vote against the kind of bill the McAdoo followers want to see reported. That, it is asserted, would place Underwood clearly before the country as a conservative and give McAdoo the ammunition he is seeking to back his claims as a Progressive on railroad legislation.

Democrats who are in the plans to make Senator Smith Chairman say that a radical bill cannot be passed in Congress, but they want to put the conservatives in the position of defeating it. Such a development, they say, would allow McAdoo to announce that he and his friends favored the railroad bill. It would be a strong appeal, his followers say, if he could go to the country with such an argument.

Friends of Senator Underwood have become aware of the plans of the McAdoo forces, and if they have enough strength in the Senate they may balk the plans of the Radicals in both parties to capture the chairmanship of the Interstate Commerce Committee with the ultimate idea of playing politics next year with railroad legislation.

The effect of the move, it is declared, would be to defeat all railroad legislation.

The plan of the insurgents for tomorrow's procedure in the Senate is for the La Follette group to vote for Senator Howell of Nebraska on the first ballot, for Senator Couzens of Michigan on the second and for Senator Smith on the third ballot. The Old Guard announces that it will vote for Senator Cummins until the end. Tonight it is declared that the only possible way to stop a La Follette triumph appears to be for two Democrats to flop to Senator Cummins, and that, Democratic leaders say, will not happen.

Congress Still Unorganized.

The Congress enters tomorrow on its third week still unorganized, and without having accomplished anything whatever in the way of legislation. Hundreds of bills have been introduced, but no move has been made in either house, so far as legislation of major importance is concerned. The Senate has confirmed a few Presidential nominations, among them that of Frank B. Kellogg, as Ambassador to Great Britain. This is the sum total of what Congress has done in the first two weeks of its session. The house is expected to finally ratify its committee assignments tomorrow.

It is now certain that Congress will not get down to work until after the Christmas holidays. Both houses are

Continued on Page Four.

MELLON REVEALS TAX LAW CHANGES IN DRAFT TO HOUSE

Normal Tax on First $4,000 Income Would Be 3 Per Cent., 6 on the Remainder.

EARNED INCOME CREDITED

Surtaxes Would Run From 1 Per Cent. on $10,000 to 25 Per Cent. on $100,000.

ASSETS SALE LEVY LIMITED

Secretary Refers to "Most Favorable Public Reception" in Sending Draft to Green.

Special to The New York Times.

WASHINGTON, Dec. 16.—A summary of the tax legislation advocated by the Treasury Department was sent today by Secretary Mellon to Acting Chairman Green of the Ways and Means Committee. Mr. Mellon expresses the opinion that the Administration's program "appears to have met with a most favorable public reception." He says that a complete draft of a bill has been prepared and is available for the consideration of the committee. Only the summary, however, is made public at this time.

In his summary of the proposed legislation, Secretary Mellon gives the changes in surtax rates which the Treasury advocates, and also includes recommendations for simplification of the tax laws. Under the proposed law, unearned income would be taxed 25 per cent. more than earned income, such as salaries; surtaxes would begin at 1 per cent. of net income from $10,000 to $12,000, and the maximum surtax would be 25 per cent. on incomes of $100,000 and over.

Secretary Mellon does not propose an elimination of capital gains and capital losses, but recommends a change in the present law which would limit deductions for losses to 12½ per cent. of the loss on the sale of property held for profit more than two years. Other recommendations by the Treasury for simplification of the tax laws were contained in a memorandum accompanying the letter to Representative Green.

It is understood that the new law as proposed by the Treasury will be made the basis of the Administration efforts to have a satisfactory tax measure reported to the House by the Ways and Means Committee.

The Secretary's letter reads:

"Washington, Dec. 16, 1923.

"Dear Mr. Green:

"Under date of Nov. 10, 1923, I wrote you setting forth a comprehensive program of tax reduction. This program appears to have met with a most favorable public reception. I understand from my recent conference with you and Representatives Treadway and Hawley that it is the desire of your committee that its work upon tax revision may be commenced without delay and the subject be given the full consideration its importance demands.

"With this end in view, the Treasury has prepared a complete redraft of the Revenue act, which embodies in detail my previous recommendations for tax revision and for the simplification and clarification of the administrative provisions of the law and which, in accordance with your suggestion to me at our conference, is herewith transmitted to your committee. There is also now available for the use of your committee a comparative print of the Revenue act of 1921 and the proposed new Revenue act, showing every change in the proposed act over the old act. Explanation of the reasons for these changes will be given your committee as desired. In addition I enclose a short summary of the substantial changes embodied in the draft.

"I with to express to you and to your committee my appreciation for the prompt consideration which you are giving to this important measure.

"Very truly yours,
"A. W. MELLON,
"Secretary of the Treasury.

"Hon William A. Green, Acting Chairman, Committee on Ways and Means, House of Representatives, Washington, D. C."

Summary of Proposed Changes.

A summary of the substantial changes in the Treasury draft of the proposed Revenue act from the Revenue act of 1921 as submitted by Secretary Mellon to Mr. Green follows:

"1. Earned income, defined as wages,

Continued on Page Four.

DR. PARKS FLOUTS VIRGIN BIRTH DOCTRINE AND DEFIES BISHOP TO TRY HIM FOR HERESY; EPISCOPAL LIBERALS RALLY TO HEATON

MODERNISTS WILL FIGHT

Church Union Takes Up Case of Rev. L. W. Heaton in Texas.

HAVE COLLECTED A FUND

Pamphlet With Evidence for Defense Will Be Sent to 10,000 Episcopal Clergymen.

COUNSEL WILL BE ENGAGED

Modernists Will Carry Case, if Necessary, Up to the General Convention.

The Rev. Lee W. Heaton, rector of Trinity Episcopal Church, Forth Worth, Texas, who is facing trial for heresy in denying the Virgin Birth of Christ, will be defended by the Modern Churchmen's Union. This organization composes about 500 Protestant Episcopal clergymen who recently reaffirmed their conviction that the Bible should be interpreted in the light of science and made a plea for liberal views and freedom of worship.

The union has brought Mr. Heaton to New York; has raised $1,000 to fight his case; has printed the evidence and will forward 10,000 copies to Episcopal Bishops and clergymen. Counsel will be engaged for Mr. Heaton, and if necessary his case will be carried up to the General Convention, which is the Supreme Court of the Episcopal Church.

"We will take up any cause in the interest of freedom and truth," said the Rev. Dr. Stuart L. Tyson, honorary vicar of the Cathedral of St. John the Divine, and Vice President of the Modern Churchmen's Union. "There is not a man of the 500 members of our union who is not going to stand by Mr. Heaton."

Charge Based on Sermon.

The charge against Mr. Heaton is based on a paragraph in a sermon on Palm Sunday on "What Is Truth," in which he said:

"Consecrated Christian men differ much in their interpretation of the ancient creeds, and each succeeding generation must reinterpret for itself 'the faith once for all delivered to the saints.' For instance, there are those who cling with unquestioning minds to the doctrine of the Virgin Birth as a statement of physical fact, while others have been [illegible] to analyze it and have discovered new spiritual truths that transcend what the form of words thus so imperfectly express. There are those among us who believe that Jesus was in all things and in every way both God and man; the incarnation of God and the son of Joseph. This is my own opinion, and there is room in the Church for those who must reconcile theology with religion."

The evidence in the case was made public at a conference in the parish house of St. George's Episcopal Church, in Stuyvesant Square, between Dr. Tyson and Mr. Heaton, who was accompanied by his senior warden, Dr. John D. Covert, a Fort Worth physician. Dr. Tyson declared that the attitude of Mr. Heaton was identical with that of Bishop William Lawrence of Massachusetts. "But instead of taking a man like Bishop Lawrence," he said, "it is proposed to take this young man from the Southwest for a test case." He called attention to the importance of the coming trial, and said that the last Episcopal heresy trial, twenty years ago, was that of the Rev. Dr. Algernon S. Crapsey on the same charge.

Defense Fund Collected.

"Bishop Moore of Dallas has stated that this Heaton case is the beginning of a concerted movement to cleanse the Episcopal Church of Modernism," said Dr. Tyson. "And let me say right here that Mr. Heaton did not actually deny the Virgin Birth.

"News of the action of Bishop Moore reached here, and we telegraphed Mr. Heaton to come North. Mr. Heaton arrived here ten days ago, and since then

Continued on Page Two.

Dr. Reisner Sees No Good In Doctrinal Disputes

"Doctrinal discussions between fundamentalists and modernists do not prove anything or do any real good to the cause of religion," said the Rev. Dr. Christian F. Reisner in his sermon last evening at Chelsea Methodist Church, 178th Street and Fort Washington Avenue.

"It gives occasion for the slackers to sit idly by with the excuse that 'leaders do not agree,' when it is only the loud-mouthed would-be leaders who make the noise while real disciples are building up audiences and doing constructive work," said Dr. Reisner. "The real test of doctrinal correctness is not words and phrases, but results shown in effective helpfulness," he continued. "The great leaders like Wesley did not waste their time quibbling about doctrinal terms, but they went out into the highways and hedges and worked transformation in the lives of those people."

DR. GUTHRIE STIRS THRONG BY DEFENSE

Crowd Overflows St. Mark's to Hear Him Justify Pagan and Eurythmic Rituals.

TAKES HIS CRITICS TO TASK

Scores Fundamentalists and Holds Up the Ancient Greeks for Emulation.

Dr. William Norman Guthrie, who has been called to account by Bishop Manning for unorthodox services at St. Mark's-in-the-Bouwerie, vigorously defended his position yesterday morning. While he was speaking, crowds surged outside the church doors in a vain effort to catch his words. At the conclusion hundreds of parishioners surrounded their rector and congratulated him. His address was characterized as "an outstanding piece of oratory."

Similar scenes occurred at the conclusion of the afternoon service, at which Miss Amy Lowell recited from her poems. It was estimated that 2,500 went down to St. Mark's yesterday, of whom about 1,900 found accommodation. Women predominated, but the congregation also included Greenwich Village artists and writers, working men from Dr. Guthrie's club, peddlers, and Orientals from the neighborhood.

At the outset Dr. Guthrie said he would explain not only his position but the conference at Synod Hall last Thursday, when he was summoned before Bishop William T. Manning of the Episcopal Diocese of New York on account of the symbolic dancing in St. Mark's and the parish hall. He went on:

"I want to say before I enter the substance of my sermon, which is devoted to 'The Holiness of Hellas,' that if I believed of what we are doing in St. Mark's the things that many of our critics believed, why, I should be more offended, perhaps, than they, since I have devoted the whole of my life's work to labor for beauty, order and reverence.

Called "Son of the Devil."

"I was born in the church. I was no convert. To be fanatical about my Mother—I know her weaknesses and I know her strength, and though I may be fiercer in my distress than some of my critics, though I think it hard to beat the appellation 'son of the devil,' as one of my critics called me in a letter—I should at least want, before I undertook to discuss the matter at issue, to understand. I should want to know what the facts are. I should want a definition of terms before I went mad. That much Greek training I do have, for it is to the Greeks we owe this training to insist on knowledge of facts and definitions of terms and corrections of mental images before discounting them. Socrates, at least, made this very successful at Athens. The story is familiar to every one. But because it became familiar to Socrates, it does not prove that it is practiced by the majority of Americans. We are so much in a hurry that we are not always accurate and careful.

"But I may say in regard to my fundamentalist and constructive critics that they seem to have forgotten the Scriptures. If the Archangel Michael durst not bring a railing accusation against Satan, when he knew he was Satan, but only remarked: 'The Lord rebuke thee,' which would seem to mean, 'May God make it evident to thee thou art in error,' I cannot see what they have to say. Surely my fundamentalist and conservative brethren should remember the parable of our Lord Jesus Christ about the tares in the wheat. Tares are fake wild wheat, as you know: 'Let them grow together until the harvest, lest happily while ye gather up the tares, ye root up the wheat also.'

The greatest thing the Protestant Episcopal Church ever did in the United States was to undertake deliberately to split and actually to lose more than 30,000 members and a vast amount of valuable church property when she preferred to stand by the liberty and initiative of Dr. Dekovi, who wanted to introduce the Oxford movement. He stood alone, but the Protestant Episco-

Continued on Page Two.

DOFFS CHURCH VESTMENTS

Rector of St. Bartholomew's Dons Academic Gown to Speak.

VOICE BREAKS WITH FEELING

Amazes Congregation by Vigorous Attack on Conservatives in Episcopal Church.

PREDICTS LIBERAL CONTROL

Declares That Modernism in House of Bishops Will Soon End Present Domination.

The Rev. Dr. Leighton Parks uttered a dramatic rallying cry for the Modernists yesterday morning in St. Bartholomew's Episcopal Church when he stripped off his priestly vestments, entered his pulpit in the gown of a doctor of theology, defended denial of the doctrine of the Virgin Birth and challenged Bishop William T. Manning to bring him to trial for heresy.

The venerable rector, manifestly deeply stirred, proclaimed his freedom in a voice that broke at times. Again he became so tense in his denunciation of the Fundamentalists that his brow was wet with perspiration and his congregation, leaning forward to catch every word, gasped as he drove home his points. Dr. Parks was particularly severe on the choice of an obscure Texas rector for trial by an ecclesiastical court, asking insistently why some one like Bishop Lawrence of Massachusetts had not been chosen, and answering that if such a thing were done "it would split the church to its foundations."

His hearers were deeply moved when Dr. Parks touched on his long and intimate connection with them in their joys and sorrows and, referring to the pastoral letter of the House of Bishops with its implication that the Modernists were not honest, asked why his congregation should believe in Bishop Manning, relatively a stranger, rather than himself.

Dr. Parks Congratulated.

At the end of the services Dr. Parks was the centre of a Modernist demonstration, in which he was showered with congratulations, but his sermon and the manner of it, while the outstanding event of the day, was not its only development in the Episcopal doctrinal strife. It was disclosed, as another evidence of the determination of the liberal element to show fight, that the Modern Churchmen's Union had taken up the cudgels for the Rev. Lee W. Heaton of Forth Worth, the Texas pastor whose selection as the defendant in a heresy trial Dr. Parks had denounced.

The extent of the controversy and the degree in which it is occupying the minds of churchmen were evidenced further by its choice as the topic of sermons in many other pulpits. The Rev. Dr. Percy Stickney Grant in his Church of the Ascension, for example, denounced the Bishop's pastoral letter and defended the scholarship of those who dissent from the doctrine of the Virgin Birth. The Rev. Dr. William P. Merrill at the Brick Presbyterian Church decries the approaching debate on "Fundamentalism and Modernism" between a Baptist and a Unitarian, saying that neither "extremist" represented the liberal view of the evangelical liberals, and a number of other preachers ranged themselves on one side or the other of the dispute.

Takes Off Cassock.

There was nothing to foreshadow the sensational address of Dr. Parks at St. Bartholomew's. Before going into the pulpit he wore the accustomed cassock, surplice and stole of an Episcopal priest. He disappeared from the chancel just before the time to preach. When he returned and ascended the pulpit he appeared in a plain black academic gown. He called attention himself to his unusual dress and said he appeared thus in order to speak simply "as a Doctor of Theology."

The text he had chosen was I. Corinthians, iv:2: "Moreover it is required in stewards that a man be found faithful."

Dr. Parks had his curate read the pastoral letter that has become the storm centre of the controversy, and then said:

"I did not wish to call your attention to this, but I am required by the canons of the Church to see that it is read to this congregation. Inasmuch as that letter implies that there are pastors preaching from their pulpits dishonestly I find it necessary to enter an emphatic protest.

"I have laid aside the accustomed vestments worn by a clergyman and I have put on an academic robe that I may come before you to instruct you as a doctor of theology, and that I may drive out any erroneous doctrine.

"It is very questionable whether this letter has any legality at all. There is much in it that may commend itself to any man or woman. But there are several things that ought to be seriously considered in this crisis the bishops have brought upon the Church.

"One of these is the questioning of the integrity of our clergy.

"Are the bishops the sole defenders of the doctrine of the Church? If they are, then I have no right to speak to you, and all you have to do is to listen to

Clemenceau Hurt as Auto Strikes a Tree; Ex-Premier's Face Is Cut by Flying Glass

ST. GERMAIN-EN-LAYE, France, Dec. 16 (Associated Press).—Georges Clemenceau, France's War Premier, was severely hurt in an automobile accident while driving along the Paris road.

His face was cut by glass from a broken windshield and he was brought to the hospital here. The surgeons found it necessary to put in several stitches, after which the former Premier proceeded to his Paris home, where he arrived some hours later than had been expected. Apparently he was little the worse for his mishap.

His chauffeur suffered more serious injuries and remained in the hospital at St. Germain.

M. Clemenceau was returning from a visit to old friends, including the famous painter, Claude Monet, at Giverney, dashing along the fine, smooth road beloved of autoists, known as "The Forty Sous Road." Another machine preceding that in which the former Premier was driving, on reaching the crossroad, was suddenly confronted by a third machine emerging from a side road. The driver threw on the brakes instantly, bringing the car to a dead stop, and Clemenceau's chauffeur, to avoid a collision, jammed his brakes down hard and his machine skidded into a tree.

The front of the machine was badly damaged and the glass splintered. M. Clemenceau, as usual, was seated beside the driver. He was cut on the forehead, nose and lip, and Dr. Coutelas, a friend, who was riding inside the limousine, was severely cut also.

A passing automobile took the injured men to the St. Germain Hospital, where six stitches were necessary to close the wounds in each case. M. Clemenceau lost a good deal of blood, but as soon as his injuries were dressed he continued on his way home.

M. Clemenceau's brother, alarmed at the news of the accident, hurried around to the former Premier's apartment in the Rue Franklin and found Clemenceau calmly reposing.

"All the News That's Fit to Print."

The New York Times.

THE WEATHER.
Fair, slightly warmer Thursday; Friday, fair, warmer; moderate winds, becoming south.
For full weather report see Page 22.

VOL. LXXIII....No. 24,230. • • • NEW YORK, TUESDAY, MAY 27, 1924. TWO CENTS in Greater New York | THREE CENTS Within 200 Miles | FOUR CENTS Elsewhere

HOUSE PASSES THE TAX BILL 376 TO 9; MELLON STUDIES IT, MAY NOT ASK VETO; COOLIDGE SIGNS THE IMMIGRATION BILL

RENDIGS REPORTED TO HAVE CONFESSED ON FIXING OF JURIES

Sentence of Juror Convicted of Perjury in Fuller Case Is Postponed.

BANTON HINTS SENSATION

District Attorney Says Important Developments May Be Expected.

FALLON WANTS TRIAL NOW

Lawyer Indicted in Fuller Jury Case Aided in the Defense of Rendigs.

Developments of a sensational nature growing out of the conviction last week of Charles W. Rendigs for perjury, were forecast last night by District Attorney Joab H. Banton. Rendigs was found guilty of swearing falsely that he did not know Edward M. Fuller, bankrupt bucketeer, or his attorney, William J. Fallon. Rendigs at the time was being examined for the jury at Fuller's third trial in General Sessions. He voted throughout the balloting for acquittal. Fuller was a partner with W. Frank McGee in E. M. Fuller & Co. Fuller and McGee are now at Governors Island, confined for contempt of court in failing to produce certain papers in the Federal Court.

Mr. Banton would not make known the nature of the events at hand, saying that his lips were sealed for the time being. But it became known that the developments in prospect involved Fallon, who appeared as Rendigs's chief counsel at his recent trial. It was also learned that last Saturday Rendigs was taken from the Tombs and questioned for seven hours by Assistant District Attorney Hugo Wintner. In the Criminal Courts Building it was reported yesterday that Rendigs had made a confession involving a number of other persons in the buying of [illegible].

Fallon and Rendigs [illegible] Federal indictments, alleging that Fallon gave and Rendigs accepted bribes totaling $2,500 in 1922 for Rendigs's vote of acquittal in the trial of Durrell, Gregory & Co., Inc., bankrupt stock brokers, and others. They were acquitted.

Fallon Appears in Court.

Fallon appeared yesterday in the Criminal Court Building shortly after General Sessions Judge Alfred J. Talley had deferred Rendigs's sentence until Monday and had announced that he would see to it that the June Grand Jury, meeting next Monday, would receive as its first case perjury evidence against two witnesses at the Rendigs trial. Fallon left the building after declaring he did not believe Rendigs made any confession, an opinion in which associate counsel Leonard A. Saitkin concurred.

Within an hour after Fallon had left a group of men hurried to the Criminal Courts Building in quest of him. They said they were anxious to find him. They would not answer a question as to whether they represented a bonding company. It could not be learned whether the bonding company had decided to surrender Fallon on the Federal charge. Rendigs and Fallon were released in $5,000 bail each in that case to await trial.

Though he said he was compelled to withhold the announcement he had contemplated making during the afternoon, Mr. Banton made no secret of the fact that momentous events in the Rendigs-Fallon case were at hand and that the Federal authorities were keenly alert to the impending developments. He would not say whether Fallon was being sought.

At 4 o'clock Mr. Banton said he hoped to be able to make the announcement in half an hour. But when he left his office at 5 o'clock he said he was not yet in a position to speak. During the evening he informed reporters that the announcement might be made momentarily and that he hoped to be able to unseal his lips shortly.

"For the obvious reason that it would obstruct the cause of justice I cannot answer any questions," he replied when pressed for information as to whether Rendigs had made a confession and whether Fallon was involved in the developments predicted.

In the Federal Building, Assistant Prosecutor Millard yesterday accepted the challenge made by Fallon during the Rendigs trial. Fallon demanded an immediate trial of the Federal indictments against him, intimating the case was being delayed because he could not be convicted. Mr. Millard said he was ready to place Fallon on trial as early as next Monday.

Besides the sentence that would be imposed in event of conviction in the Federal Court, Rendigs is confronted with the possibility of a sentence of from ten to twenty years in Sing Sing because of his conviction by a General Sessions jury.

Fallon was indicted July 10, 1923, by the Federal Grand Jury on the charge of bribing a juror in the case of stock brokers tried for using the mails to defraud customers. Rendigs, the juror, was also indicted. Both were accused of conspiracy to obstruct justice and of handling bribes amounting to $2,500. It was alleged the bribery was for Rendigs' vote as a juror in the trial of Durrell, Gregory & Co., Inc., and others. Fallon was attorney for Alfred de W. Blum, one of the defendants. Rendigs was Juror No. 3. The jury was impaneled Oct. 5, 1922. On Nov. 17 it returned a verdict of not guilty. This exonerated even six defendants who had offered no defense.

In the Fallon-Rendigs case, the Federal Grand Jury returned three indictments. It was charged that on Oct. 5, 1922, the day the jury was impaneled, Fallon gave Rendigs $1,500 in cash and

Continued on Page Six.

Coolidge Is Unrecognized On Stroll in the Capital

Special to The New York Times.

WASHINGTON, May 26.—Joining the throngs that turned out for the first sunny afternoon in several days, President Coolidge took a long walk through the streets of Washington today, traversing the business and shopping districts. For him the trip was sightseeing as well as an effort to shake off the cold that has clung to him tenaciously for two weeks or more during a rainy period unusual for the capital city in May.

Few of the pedestrians whom he passed recognized the President, who seemed greatly interested in things along the route and did a lot of "window shopping" during the trip.

At crossings policemen cleared the way if they saw the President in time, but Mr. Coolidge himself took a survey up and down the intersecting streets before crossing.

REICH CABINET OUT; MARX MAY RETURN

President Ebert to Consult Party Leaders Today on Formation of New Government.

BREAK WITH MONARCHISTS

Middle Parties Decide to Ignore Them When They Insist on Tirpitz as Chancellor.

By T. R. YBARRA.

Copyright, 1924, by The New York Times Company.
By Wireless to THE NEW YORK TIMES.

BERLIN, May 26.—The German Government resigned late tonight. President Ebert accepted its resignation. The members of the Marx-Stresemann Cabinet are to continue, however, to discharge their duties for the present.

President Ebert tomorrow will confer with the party leaders regarding the formation of a new Government. In political circles the belief is freely expressed that the present Chancellor, Dr. Marx, has an excellent chance of being called upon to form the next Government.

Previous to the Government's resignation conferences between the Government coalition parties and the Nationalists were fruitless, largely because the Nationalists persisted in pushing forward Admiral von Tirpitz as a candidate for Chancellor and making their acceptance of the Dawes report subject to such extreme conditions that the coalition refused even to answer the Nationalist proposals.

All Day Duel Inconclusive.

Throughout the day the duel between the Government coalition parties and the Nationalists to see whether they could agree on forming the next Government went on but up to a late hour tonight no definite result had been reached.

This evening the Nationalists after a long and stormy session went before the meeting of the representatives of the three Government parties—Centre, German people's party and Democrats—with the ultimatum that they would cooperate with the coalition in forming the Government provided acceptance of the Dawes report were made conditional on the following points:

Agreement by the Entente to evacuate the Ruhr; abrogation of the "Micum" agreements; immediate return to their homes of Germans exiled from the Ruhr and the release of all those imprisoned in the Ruhr by the French and Belgians.

In addition, the Nationalists made the cryptic demand that the German Government must sign nothing representing "another Versailles."

To many these conditions look as if the Nationalist representatives were doing their best to make their cooperation in the Government impossible. It looked as if they preferred being in opposition, yet, in case their demands were rejected by the Government coalition of being able to tell the members of their party that they had wished to cooperate in forming the new Government, but had been rebuffed.

This line of thought had already occurred to many here when the Nationalists proposed Admiral von Tirpitz as Chancellor, since he seems so utterly impossible except from the extreme Nationalistic viewpoint that the idea leaped instantly into people's minds that he was proposed only in order that he might be rejected by the coalition.

Doubt Nationalist Unity.

Observers watching today's duel between the coalition and the Nationalists are inclined to believe that even if Dr. Hergt and other moderate Nationalists, who favor qualified acceptance of the Dawes report, succeeded in swinging their fellow Nationalists to entering the new Government they would not be able to hold their party to a friendly attitude toward the coalition and that within a short time more than half the Nationalists would secede from such an unnatural union and throw in their lot with the Voelkisch extremists of the

Continued on Page Four.

BOY WITNESS JAILED ON PERJURY CHARGE IN TRIAL OF HOFFMAN

Harry Edkins, Friend of the Defendant, Arrested on Order of Judge Tiernan.

DEFIANT ON THE STAND

Prisoner Smiles at Him as He "Forgets" Testimony He Gave Before Grand Jury.

STATE TO REST TODAY

Sixty-nine Persons Have Testified in Prosecutor's Effort to Fix Murder on Film Operator.

Harry Edkins, 17 years old, former reel boy in the Palace Theatre at Port Richmond, S. I., was locked up in the Richmond County Jail yesterday afternoon on a perjury charge after he had left the witness stand in the trial of Harry L. Hoffman, motion picture operator, for the murder of Mrs. Maud A. Bauer.

Edkins was one of thirty-five witnesses called during the day by District Attorney Albert C. Fach. He was taken into custody outside the courtroom by Under Sheriff Peter J. Finn on an order issued by Judge J. Harry Tiernan, who is presiding at the trial. The Judge ordered that the boy be removed immediately to the county jail, and it was not until he had been placed in a cell there that news of the arrest became public. Not even District Attorney Fach knew about the arrest until some time after it had been made. During a recess of the court Hoffman learned of it, but made no comment, it was said.

While the boy was on the witness stand repudiating statements he was alleged to have made before the Grand Jury which returned the first-degree murder indictment against Hoffman, the accused man frequently smiled encouragement to him, twirling a long, yellow pencil the while.

When the boy first [illegible] District Attorney Fach in the investigation which led to Hoffman's indictment, he was alleged to have professed little knowledge of events in connection with Hoffman's conduct immediately before and after the killing. Later he was called as a witness before the Grand Jury.

Subsequently the boy again was interrogated by the District Attorney and was alleged to have made statements to the prosecutor which were in conflict with his previous testimony before the Grand Jury. Mr. Fach then brought him before the body again and he was said to have repeated his new statements.

The boy, following further investigation by Captain Ernest L. Van Wagner, head of the Staten Island Detective Bureau, and Detective Sergeant George F. McGann, was called to the District Attorney's office a third time, and was said to have admitted that on the day following the killing of Mrs. Bauer, Hoffman told him, in the projecting room of the Palace Theatre, where they were employed, that he (Hoffman) was under suspicion by the police as the murderer.

Told of Hoffman Talking of Hair Cut.

Young Edkins also was alleged to have told the District Attorney that Hoffman had been called to the telephone on the afternoon following the murder and when he came back to the projecting room Hoffman remarked that Mrs. Hoffman, wife of the accused man, had just told him that the police suspected he was the murderer. The boy was alleged to have further stated that as Hoffman made this remark he said, "I'm going out to get my hair cut, and then I'll surely be railroaded." Mr. Fach again took the boy before the Grand Jury, where he was said to have repeated this statement.

The importance of this testimony by the boy, it was said, lay in the fact that at the time Hoffman told young Edkins that he was under suspicion as the slayer the police really had no evidence on which to direct suspicion against anybody. Hoffman first came to the attention of the police on March 30, five days after the killing, as the result of a letter which had been received by Captain Van Wagner in Police Headquarters in St. George, and in which Hoffman's name was mentioned.

About a week after Hoffman's indictment the boy was arrested as a material witness, held in $10,000 bail by Judge Tiernan and committed to the West Side Prison in Manhattan, so that he would be removed from Hoffman's influence. Later he was discharged from custody on a writ of habeas corpus obtained in the Supreme Court.

The boy is undersized and has shift-

Continued on Page Ten.

VICTOR HERBERT,
Who Died Suddenly Yesterday.
From his latest portrait, a miniature by Mrs. F. Enid Stoddard, which was to have been presented to him by the Irish Musical Society next Sunday.

VICTOR HERBERT DIES ON WAY TO PHYSICIAN

America's Leading Composer of Light Opera Stricken With Heart Attack.

SAMUEL LOVER'S GRANDSON

Born 64 Years Ago in Dublin, He Swept This Country With His Melodies.

Victor Herbert, American composer and one of the world's first composers of light opera, died of heart disease yesterday afternoon at 4 o'clock. He fell as he was walking up the stairs at 57 East Seventy-seventh Street to visit his physician, Dr. Emanuel Baruch, and in a few minutes he was dead.

His health apparently had been of the best up to yesterday afternoon an hour or two before his death. He had luncheon at the Lambs Club and had an engagement later in the afternoon to meet Samuel F. Kingston, manager for Florenz Ziegfeld. Mr. Herbert had written much of the music for the next production of the Follies and was up late on Sunday night assisting at a rehearsal.

After luncheon Mr. Herbert fell ill and went to his home at 321 West 108th Street, instead of going to the Ziegfeld office. He continued to feel great discomfort, but was not alarmed about his condition. Instead of sending for his doctor, he decided that he was well enough to go there himself. He left his automobile unassisted, but weighing over 250 pounds the extra effort of walking up the stairs caused him to collapse on the way.

Seemed in Best of Health.

Mr. Herbert was 64 years old. Full-faced and florid, he seemed to be in vigorous health, and his friends had been telling him that he was looking younger and better than he had in years. He was working harder than he had been at any period of his career. Besides writing much of the music for the Follies, he was working on an overture for the motion picture, "Janice Meredith," which will be presented in June. In addition to writing the music, rehearsing it, conferring with producers, planning other work and leading an orchestra at the Cosmopolitan Theatre, he had been active in fighting the battle of the Society of American Authors, Composers and Publishers to prevent radio companies from broadcasting copyrighted music without paying for it.

In this work he was concerned more with the interests of younger composers than with his own, because his income from his long line of successful operas and songs was very large. In this campaign he appeared last month before the Senate Patents Committee and was a picturesque witness.

"I have heard one of my compositions, 'A Kiss in the Dark,' played eight or nine times in one night over the radio," he said. "They play and play that ad nauseam. How can you expect anybody to buy it in printed form?"

Wrote on High Stool.

No matter how much rehearsals, conferences and meetings took up his time, he always sat up for several hours a day on a high stool before a high desk, writing the melodies which had so taken lovers of light opera in this country and abroad season after season. No other composer has ever had such an output of popular successes. His place in light opera has been such that his biography would almost be a history of light opera in America.

The news of his death took the theatrical district by surprise. He was a frequenter of the Lambs Club and spent much of his time in and near Times Square. For more than a generation he had been one of New York's best known men and the number of his personal friends ran into the thousands. Of the hundreds who saw him nearly every week, nearly all had been deceived by his high color and his youthful appearance and heartiness. All this made the shock a great one. There was no topic discussed last night in the theatre section, except the death of Victor Herbert. In all groups there were men who had known him intimately. There was sorrow both for the loss of a picturesque and engaging personality and of a man whose output of music kept on the average half a dozen theatres going, and was heard nightly in millions of homes on the piano, the phonograph and radio.

His Last Composition.

The last composition by Mr. Herbert to be played was the music of "Romeo, Juliet, Johnny and Jane," in "Round the Town," on the Century Roof.

One of the characteristics of the composer that was emphasized on all sides last night was the cleanness of all his

Continued on Page Three.

GLASS, IF PRESIDENT, WOULD RESIGN OVER BONUS VETO, HE SAYS

Senator Declares That He Would Get the Votes to Sustain His Action or Quit.

ARRAIGNS ADMINISTRATION

And Says Democrats Must Advance Constructive Issues, Including League of Nations.

SAYS HE IS FOR M'ADOO

And Doubts Latter's Strength Will Swing to Himself—Upholds Mellon Tax Plan.

Special to The New York Times.

PHILADELPHIA, May 26.—Senator Carter Glass of Virginia, a former Secretary of the Treasury, asserted here today that if he were President, and the soldier bonus bill were passed over his veto, he would resign.

Speaking before the Women's Democratic Luncheon Club, in the ballroom of the Bellevue Stratford, Senator Glass scored the whole Republican Administration. He said:

"I have respect for President Coolidge, and I sympathize with him because of his frightful legacy. I have said that if ever I should become President—" At this point the several hundred attending the luncheon applauded so vigorously that the speech was interrupted.

When he was able to continue Senator Glass said:

"As I said, if I were President, and I should find the Treasury menaced by an unjust obligation of $4,000,000,000, such as the soldiers' bonus, and I could not summon enough votes from my party to sustain my veto, I would resign."

Ridicules Pepper's Plan.

Senator Glass ridiculed the world court plan of Senator Pepper. He attacked the alleged corruption of Republican officials and declared that if an investigation had been made of Secretary Mellon's Bureau of Internal Revenue, "the investigators would have found something."

"I told the Senators it would be silly to insist upon an examination of Mr. Mellon's tax returns," he explained. "I know that Mr. Mellon personally is honest and has good sense. Senator Watson said he did not mind an investigation of Mr. Mellon's tax returns and refunds.

"Of course he did not. He knew that everything would be all right there, but when it was proposed to investigate the Internal Revenue Bureau, Mr. Watson said it was time to call a halt. He said President Coolidge was the leader of the party, and such an investigation might hurt him. Of course the investigators would have found something if they had gone ahead."

Wants Democrats for League.

The Senator declared that the Democrats must not base their Presidential campaign solely upon a criticism of the Republican Administration, but that they must have constructive issues to place before the people. These issues he defined as a revision of taxation and entry into the League of Nations.

Referring to the World Court plan of Senator Pepper, he said:

"If I were disposed to treat such grave matters with levity, I would say that Senator Lodge had changed his tactics—heretofore he has been throwing sand in the eyes of the people, while now he is throwing Pepper."

The Senator began by defending the character of the investigation conducted by the Senate into the alleged abuses in the Republican Administration.

"Judge Gary," he said, "recently stated that Congress should be abolished. Not all of the Eugene Debses who ever existed have constituted as real a menace to popular government as this gentleman when he says Congress should be abolished," he declared.

Mr. Glass then said that even the President and Secretary Mellon had objected to the Senatorial investigation. He said that at the end of the Wilson Administration the Republicans had instituted fifty-one inquiries without discovering any corruption, and had even gone so far as to "lift the coverlet" on the sickbed of President Wilson to see if he was able to perform his duties as Chief Executive.

He complained that the whole criticism of the Congressional investigation by the Republican leaders and the press

Continued on Page Seven.

EXCLUSION LAW IS SCORED

President Calls That Part of Act "Unnecessary and Deplorable."

WOULD VETO IT IF ALONE

Accepts Measure Because of Its Good Features and Because Comprehensive Law Is Needed.

SENATE LEADERS PLEASED

Alien Quotas of 2 Per Cent. Based on the 1890 Census Go Into Effect on July 1.

Special to The New York Times.

WASHINGTON, May 26.—The Immigration bill, with its provision for Japanese exclusion, was signed today by President Coolidge.

In a statement given out soon after he had signed the bill the President explained that he had approved the bill because it had many desirable features and a comprehensive act was necessary at this time, but that he would have vetoed it if Japanese exclusion had stood alone.

The President's Statement.

The President's statement follows:

In signing this bill, which in its main features I heartily approve, I regret the impossibility of severing from it the exclusion provision, which in the light of existing law affects especially the Japanese.

I gladly recognize that the enactment of this provision does not imply any change in our sentiment of admiration and cordial friendship for the Japanese people, a sentiment which has had and will continue to have abundant manifestation.

The bill rather expresses the determination of the Congress to exercise its prerogative in defining by legislation the control of immigration, instead of leaving it to international arrangements. It should be noted that the bill exempts from the exclusion provision Government officials, those coming to this country as tourists or temporarily for business or pleasure, those in transit, seamen, those already resident here and returning from temporary absences, professors, ministers of religion, students, and those who enter solely to carry on trade in pursuance of existing treaty provisions.

But we have had for many years an understanding with Japan by which the Japanese Government has voluntarily undertaken to prevent the emigration of laborers to the United States and in view of this historic relation and of the feeling which inspired it it would have been much better, in my judgment, and more effective in the actual control of immigration, if we had continued to invite that cooperation which Japan was ready to give and had thus avoided creating any ground for misapprehension by an unnecessary statutory enactment.

"Unnecessary and Deplorable."

That course would not have derogated from the authority of the Congress to deal with the question in any exigency requiring its action. There is scarcely any ground for disagreement as to the result we want, but this method of securing it is unnecessary and deplorable at this time.

If the exclusion provision stood alone, I should disapprove it without hesitation, if sought in this way at this time. But this bill is a comprehensive measure dealing with the whole subject of immigration and setting up the necessary administrative machinery. The present quota act of 1921 will terminate on June 30 next. It is of great importance that a comprehensive measure should take its place and that the arrangements for

Continued on Page Two.

Weeks Gets First Refusal Of Veteran to Take Bonus

Special to The New York Times.

WASHINGTON, May 26.—The first refusal of a veteran of the World War to accept the bonus under the Soldiers' Adjusted Compensation act was received by Secretary Weeks today.

In a letter to the Secretary a former Second Lieutenant who went through the battle of Chateau-Thierry with the Twenty-third Infantry, but whose name the War Department declined to make public, requested that his name be dropped from the mailing list of the applications for the bonus. His letter follows:

"The service of my country in time of war is not of a kind that can be rewarded by a gratuity from Congress. I wish to have my name removed from the mailing list of the applications for the recently enacted soldier bonus."

SENATE ADOPTS NEW CAMPAIGN GIFT LAW

Passes Borah Amendment Requiring Statements From All Committees Every Ten Days.

BOTH PARTIES SUPPORT IT

Walsh Suggests That an Investigating Committee Sit as During the Campaign of 1920.

Special to The New York Times

WASHINGTON, May 26.—An amendment to the Postal Salary bill which would require the publication of campaign contributions every ten days by all committees, local, State and national, while the forthcoming Presidential race is in progress, and also provide other means for obtaining full publicity as to the identity of contributors, corporations or individuals, and the size of the gifts made, was submitted today by Senator Borah and adopted by a vote of 55 to 0.

The Postal Salary bill is now before the Senate and a vote may be reached tomorrow, with the chances strongly in favor of adoption. It is the hope of Senator Borah to have a similar bill enacted by the House before adjournment.

Senator Borah said that he considered the adoption of legislation of this sort, before Congress adjourns, as a supplement to the other laws covering the reporting of campaign contributions, of vital importance to the country. Just before he offered his amendment, in the form of two proposed sections to the Postal Salary bill, he asked that a quorum of the Senators be summoned.

Senator Robinson of Arkansas, the Democratic floor leader, joined with Mr. Borah in urging adoption of the amendment. He expressed the view that the "most effective way to prevent corrupt practices is to enforce absolute publicity."

During the debate Senator Robinson also made the charge that Postmasters and certain other Federal appointees in a number of instances had been solicited for contributions to campaign funds. He said that he could name one State where, during a certain period, every Postmaster had been "required" to make such a contribution, although this was in violation of the laws. He hoped that the adoption of the proposals made by Senator Borah would help to cure this evil.

Text of the Proposed Law.

The two sections of the Postal Salary bill as offered by Senator Borah read as follows:

Section—That all committees, local, State or national, and all persons or parties having any part or share in the election or in the campaign for the election of members of Congress and all officers or officials of the Government of the United States, shall publish at the end of each ten days a financial report of the contribution received by, or for the account of, the committee, or person, or party, or candidate, directly or indirectly, with the name, residence and official position, if any, of each contributor and the amount of his contribution, directly or indirectly, and at the end of each campaign for election of such members of Congress or officers or officials of the Government of the United States, shall publish a complete and detailed financial statement giving the names of each contributor and the amount of his contribution together with the amount of any deficit incurred in the campaign, and such committee or party shall thereafter publish at the end of each month the amount received by it from each contributor, directly or indirectly, to make up the deficit.

Such report and financial statement, together with the copies of circulars used in soliciting contributions and the names of all solicitors of all campaign funds shall be filed with the Clerk of the House of Representatives and the Secretary of the Senate and shall also be open to inspection by the public.

Section — Every person, including every member of the committee, offending against the foregoing section shall be deemed guilty of a misdemeanor and shall, upon conviction thereof, be imprisoned not more than one year or fined not to exceed $5,000 or by both such fine and imprisonment.

Senator Borah said he was anxious to make his proposal as far-reaching as

Continued on Page Five.

LESS CRITICAL OF TAX BILL

Mellon Is Inclined to Favor It As the Best Available Now.

HOUSE ASSERTS LEADERSHIP

All Parties Declare Tax Measure Is Theirs—Call Mellon Plan a "Gold Brick."

SECRETARY UNDER ATTACK

"If He Cannot Administer the Bill and Bonus, Let Him Resign," Says Green.

Special to The New York Times.

WASHINGTON, May 26.—The conference report on the 1924 tax reduction bill was approved in the House of Representatives this afternoon by a vote of 376 to 9. Two hours later the bill was sent to the White House, where the measure's advocates expect President Coolidge to sign it.

On receiving the bill President Coolidge sent it immediately to the Treasury Department for report, analysis and recommendations. At the Treasury Department it was said the report could be made in a very short time, probably by tomorrow or the next day.

Further study by Secretary Mellon has convinced him, it is said, that the bill is more acceptable than the present law, or the carrying into effect only of a [illegible] reduction on income taxes [illegible] would result if the President [illegible] law and the veto were sustained.

Secretary Mellon does not approve the bill as it came to him today, but he is inclined to accept it as preferable to no revision of the revenue law. It was said that while the Secretary still held to his original views on taxation he was not inclined to go so far as to recommend that the President veto the measure. He feels that this is the best revision possible in a Congress where the Republicans have only a nominal majority, and is now reported willing to accept temporary revision and have the Administration continue its demand for reduction in the high surtaxes in the coming campaign.

The impression is that the President will follow the same line of reasoning in the tax bill as he did in the immigration bill. He will approve it because of some desirable features, and make his record for the campaign and a platform declaration by pointing out objectionable features.

As passed, the bill provides a 25 per cent. reduction in income taxes payable this year, a lowering of the surtax rates, the abandonment or modification of most of the miscellaneous and excise taxes, and a 25 per cent. reduction on earned income of $10,000 or less.

Revised Treasury estimates submitted by Chairman Green of the Ways and Means Committee today set the tax reduction for the present year at $268,000,000, made up of $232,000,000 through the 25 per cent. reduction and $36,000,000 through the reduction in excise taxes for the last six months of 1924. The tax reduction through the bill was estimated at $361,000,000 for the fiscal year ending June 30, 1925, and at about $100,000,000 for the fiscal year ending June 30, 1926.

Only 15 in Whole Congress Opposed.

The nine negative votes cast this afternoon included those of Representatives Fenn, Merritt and Tilson of Connecticut, Mills and Wainwright of New York, and McFadden of Pennsylvania, Republicans who voted against the bill on its passage, and Representatives Hill of Maryland, Phillips of Pennsylvania and Moores of Indiana, Republicans, who voted for the bill when it passed the House on Feb. 29, by a vote of 406 to 80.

In that former vote Representatives Bachrach of New Jersey, Republican, and Howard of Nebraska, Democrat, voted against the bill, but they voted for the adoption of the conference report today.

The bipartisan character of the vote favoring the adoption of the conference report was illustrated by the fact that 187 Democrats, 186 Republicans and three Independents, Berger, Kvale and Wefald, joined in this majority.

Taking into consideration the Senate vote of 60 to 6 approving the conference report last Saturday, 436 men in Congress have now voted for the bill, while only fifteen have opposed it. This result leads to the conclusion that a vote to override a Presidential veto would not be difficult if Mr. Coolidge decided not to affix his signature.

Debate on the conference report consumed only an hour and a half. The stage was set and the outcome so confidently anticipated that the heated controversies that might have occurred over the ditching of the Mellon plan and the introduction of the publicity features were missing.

Opponents of the Simmons rates and of opening tax details to Congressional committees denounced these scathingly, but the sparks did not fly as they would had the vote been closer.

The sentiment of the House on the bill demonstrated itself when Republican Floor Leader Longworth, defending himself against past criticisms for compromises, was cheered lustily by both sides when he asserted that to have insisted on the Mellon plan or nothing

Commits Suicide With Auto Exhaust Gas By Starting Engine in Sealed Garage

Walter B. Kenaga, 37 years old, a stenographer of 60 Northern Avenue, committed suicide yesterday morning by locking the doors and windows of a small garage at 185th Street and Amsterdam Avenue, starting the engine of his automobile, lying down under it and breathing carbon monoxide gas until he died. He wrote a farewell note as he lay dying. This is the first suicide of this kind which has been reported in this city.

Kenaga had quarreled with his wife and he told her yesterday morning at 8 o'clock over the telephone that he was going to jump off Brooklyn Bridge. Apparently he changed his mind on entering the garage and decided to kill himself by breathing carbon monoxide, which has recently caused many deaths by accident in small garages.

As he lay dying Kenaga scribbled a note to his wife. Pencil and paper were found in his hand when the garage was forced open at 11 o'clock in the morning.

"I can't write much more. I'm dying," was the last line. The rest of the letter was not made known.

Old Record Gives Noah's Age as 64,800 Years, But Only to Cover a Long Gap in History

Special to The New York Times.

PHILADELPHIA, May 26.—A Babylonian account of the life of Noah, giving his age as 64,800 years, and thus making the 969 years of Methuselah pale into insignificance, is the basis of a theory advanced by Dr. Howard Chiera, Professor of Assyriology at the University of Pennsylvania, to account for the extreme longevity of personages in early history.

In a paper submitted to the Crozer Theological Seminary, Dr. Chiera tells of the recent discovery of a four-sided prism, inscribed in the Sumerian language, giving a list of the kings who ruled in Babylonia from the creation to the time of Hammurabi. The prism gives the names of eight kings who ruled in the 241,200 years (according to the Babylonians), preceding the flood. The prism, now at Oxford University, in the comparison it affords with the lives of Old Testament patriarchs, Dr. Chiera believes, "will help us toward filling many gaps in the history of ancient Babylonia."

The eight kings who ruled within a period of 241,200 years are paralleled by another list, discovered, not long ago, according to Dr. Chiera, of ten kings whose rule covered 432,000 years.

"Did the Babylonians really believe that their ancient heroes had lived for such incredibly long periods of time?" Dr. Chiera asked. "They certainly did not. But they knew that the world was much older than the date corresponding to 4,000 B. C., which was the Hebrew figure. They had historical records going further back than that date and they pushed the date of the creation as far back as they could.

"But they did not have sufficient historical and traditional records to fill up a gap in their history which would extend into hundreds of thousands of years. To avoid confessing their ignorance of history they had either to invent names for their supposed patriarchs or stretch the lives of the personages they knew to make them cover the whole period.

"They resorted to the latter alternative as the one which did the least violence to facts, hence the exceptional longevity of the Babylonian heroes.

He also pointed out that the Jews were faced by the same problem and it was necessary to multiply the average length of human life by ten.

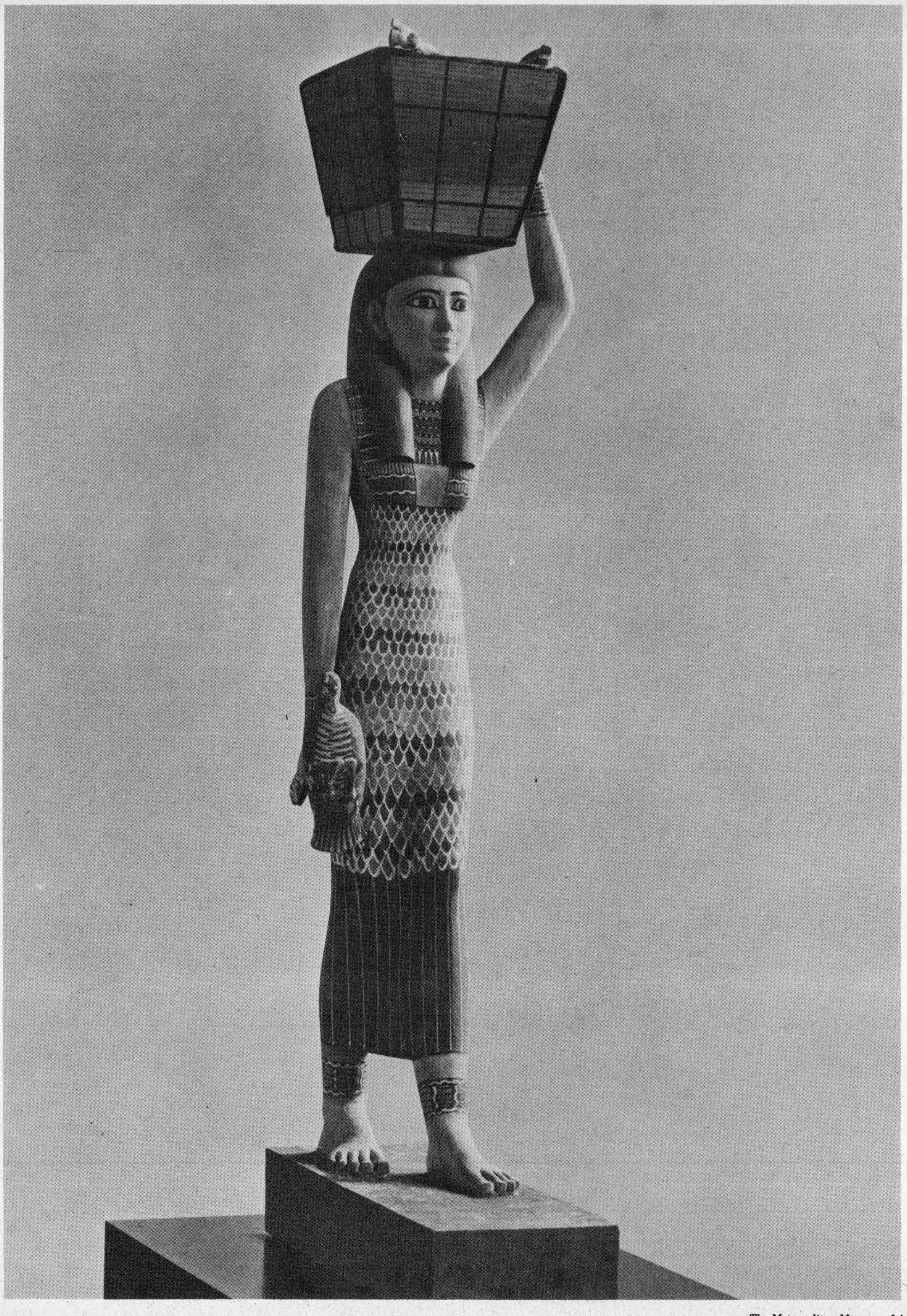

The Metropolitan Museum of Art

The funerary model of an offering bearer, showing that women's fashions have not changed that drastically since 1991 B.C.

"All the News That's Fit to Print."

The New York Times.

THE WEATHER.
Fair, slightly warmer Thursday; Friday, fair, warmer; moderate winds, becoming south.
For full weather report see Page 22.

VOL. LXXIII....No. 24,108. * * * NEW YORK, SATURDAY, JANUARY 26, 1924. TWO CENTS In Greater New York | THREE CENTS Within 200 Miles | FOUR CENTS Elsewhere

THIRD EXPEDITION TO SCALE EVEREST PREPARES TO START

The New York Times Will Tell and Picture Here News of Attempt to Reach the Top.

FULL RIGHTS ACQUIRED

Frequent Bulletins of Progress to Be Rushed From Base for World-Wide Publication.

CONFIDENT OF SUCCESS

With Improved Apparatus and Experience of Previous Attempts Climbers Expect to Attain Summit.

Special Cable to THE NEW YORK TIMES.

LONDON, Jan. 25.—By arrangement with the Mount Everest Committee, organizer of the third expedition for the ascent of the highest mountain in the world, The London Times has undertaken to distribute throughout the world all news dispatches, pictures and special articles dealing with the expedition, which will set out from the lower Himalayas in March. With special equipment and a personnel made familiar with the difficulties of the undertaking by two previous attempts, the climbers confidently expect this year to reach the summit.

Distribution of the news and pictures of the attempt will be made in the United States and Canada through THE NEW YORK TIMES, which has acquired from The London Times the exclusive right of publication there, of all dispatches, special articles and photographs sent out by the expedition.

Special Arrangement for News.

Under the terms of this arrangement, readers of THE NEW YORK TIMES and all other newspapers subscribing to the service will learn of the progress of this third attempt to scale the world's highest peak as soon as readers in London or on the European continent. All news of the expedition is to be published simultaneously in every large city in the world in frequent news bulletins, which will be virtually official, as The London Times's arrangement with the Mount Everest Committee gives it exclusive access to all news and pictures at the source.

Already The London Times has perfected an extraordinarily complete organization, especially for the speedy transmission of all news direct from the expedition. News and photographs illustrating the expedition's progress will be carried by native runners from the base of operations in the wilderness to the nearest telegraph head. From that point they will be sent to the special correspondent of The London Times at Simla, who will relay them to London, whence they will be transmitted to THE NEW YORK TIMES office. In the case of photographs, publication in London will be so arranged as to be practically simultaneous with that in America.

Government Aiding Expedition.

The Mount Everest personnel of this third expedition is now practical complete. Brig. Gen. the Hon. C. G. Bruce, C. B., will again lead the expedition. The second in command will be Major E. F. Norton, D. S. O., who accompanied the expedition of 1922. Other members of this year's expedition who also made the attempt in 1922 are George Leigh Mallory, T. Howard Somervell, Captain J. B. L. Noel and Captain Geoffrey Bruce of the Sixth Gurkha Regiment, and Captain C. J. Morris of the Third Gurkhas.

New members of the expedition include N. E. Odell of the Imperial College of Science, Bentley Beetham, A. C. Ervine, J. V. Hazard, Major R. W. G. Hingston of the Indian Medical Service, and E. O. Shebbeare of the Indian Forest Service. Captain Geoffrey Bruce was a member of the climbing party which reached a height of 27,250 feet in the 1922 expedition. Major Norton, Mr. Mallory and Mr. Somervell were members of the earliest high climbing party which reached a height of 27,000 feet.

The climbers in this year's expedition will be equipped with oxygen apparatus, modified in the light of the 1922's experience. Major Norton will be in command of the high camps.

Captains Bruce and Norris and Mr. Shebbeare have been given leave by the Government of India to accompany the expedition as transport officers. Major Hingston, who is now in charge of the R. A. F. hospital at Bagdad, has been similarly released from duty to accompany the expedition as medical officer and naturalist. Captain Noel, who made the cinematographic record of the 1922 expedition, will again be official photographer. With the consent of the Government of India and of the Dalai Lama of Tibet, the expedition will leave Darjeeling toward the end of March and will follow the same route as the 1922 expedition along the Chumbi Valley, by way of Kampa Dzong to the Rongbuk valley, where they will establish a base camp at the end of April. The renewed assault upon the peak will probably start toward the end of May.

Confident Hope of Success.

Climbers and men of science hope that the expedition, fortified by the experience gained in 1921 and 1922, will succeed in its great task. The first expedition, of 1921, under command of Colonel Howard Bury, was really a reconnoitring party for the second expedition, which attacked the mountain in the following year. The object which Bury and his party set themselves was to discover whether there was a practicable

Continued on Page Six.

6,000 Tokio Police to Guard Imperial Wedding Today

TOKIO, Jan. 25 (Associated Press).—The police were completing today elaborate preparations to guard the Prince Regent and his bride at the wedding ceremony tomorrow.

Six thousand policemen were detailed to the route over which the couple will approach the Imperial Palace. Gendarmes are assisting in keeping Tokio clear of suspicious characters. Radicals and other persons considered dangerous are being rounded up and will be held until after the wedding.

The imperial marriage has been made the occasion of amnesty affecting forty thousand prisoners, whose sentences will be lessened. The prisoners include the assassin of Premier Hara and Captain Amakasu, who was convicted of killing Sakaye Osugi, a Socialist leader, and Osugi's family in the excitement after the great earthquake.

The ceremony has been set for 10 A. M.

COOLIDGE STANDS ON TAX BILL MERIT

He Believes Congress Will Become Convinced That the Mellon Plan Is Soundest.

$103,000,000 LOPPED OFF

Committee Drops Levies on Admissions Up to 50 Cents, Telegraphs and Telephones.

Special to The New York Times.

WASHINGTON, Jan. 25—President Coolidge, it was said by a White House spokesman today, believes that the Administration tax bill is gaining support in and out of Congress, as the substitute proposals are analyzed and compared with the economic features of the bill recommended by Secretary Mellon. The impression received by the President from conferences and reports coming to him from the country at large is that the prospect for the enactment of the Administration bill, without substantial changes, is growing better constantly.

Mr. Coolidge is hopeful that the bill will not be made a partisan measure and that members of Congress will support it without thinking of such consideration. He welcomes such support, it was said, as he does not desire to take credit for the bill but hopes that credit will go to those who vote for it, and that final action in Congress will be taken on the merits of the proposal, regardless of political leanings.

It was pointed out that the effects of the different substitute proposals had not been analyzed by experts. When these analyses are made and comparison is reached with the Administration bill, the President believes that none of the other bills will show anything like the degree of relief from taxation provided in the Administration bill, and that such analyses will tend to break down the opposition in Congress.

Party Leaders in Dilemma.

Republican leaders in Congress are greatly worried over the refusal of Mr. Coolidge to consent to amendments increasing the surtax rates over those in the Mellon bill. They had hoped that the President, if he did not consent to these changes, would become less aggressive in his espousal of the Mellon schedules. The President has become stronger in his support of the Mellon bill as its support by Republicans in Congress has begun to grow weak and wavering.

In view of the difference between the majority party in Congress and the President, the opinion is expressed that taxpayers are beginning to examine carefully the relative merits of the bills. That the Administration bill is gaining in this comparison is the belief of the President, despite the apparent purpose of the Republicans in the House to amend its surtax provisions.

It was said today by prominent Republicans that 50 or 60 per cent. of their party adherents in the House were prepared to vote against a 25 per cent. maximum surtax. Chairman Green of the Ways and Means Committee and Floor Leader Longworth joined in saying that they had received no overtures from the Democrats. "But," said Mr. Longworth, "I am optimistic."

The Republican Steering Committee will meet tomorrow and is expected to discuss the outlook for the tax bill.

Reductions of more than $103,000,000 were made by the committee today in

Continued on Page Two.

ENRIGHT LAUNCHES NEW FLYING SQUAD TO DEAL WITH VICE

Liquor Traffic Suppression Also in Hands of Special Service Division.

INSPECTORS LOSE POWER

Combating Crimes of Violence Only Duties Left to the Rank and File.

ALL MUST WEAR UNIFORMS

And None but a Designated Raider May Enter a Resort—Order Is Effective Today.

Police Commissioner Richard E. Enright in a memorandum to Chief Inspector Lahey last night revolutionized the department's methods in dealing with vice, gambling and the enforcement of the Volstead act.

He took the duty of suppressing these three phases of crime from the uniformed force entirely, and particularly from the precinct vice squads, and delegated it to the Special Service Division, under Deputy Chief Inspector Samuel Belton.

This move called for the transfer of one district inspector, three deputy inspectors, eleven captains, seventeen lieutenants, twenty-three sergeants and 330 policemen. Of these, thirteen lieutenants, one sergeant and 184 patrolmen who formerly were assigned to plain-clothes work in inspection districts are sent to precincts.

The change will become effective at 8 o'clock this morning. Inspection district commanders, who formerly were held responsible for the cleanliness of their districts, will become administrative heads of the uniformed men under them. They and their staffs must appear at all times in full uniform both in their offices and in public.

The order to the Chief Inspector also strikes a blow at individual action on the part of uniformed policemen, without previous consultation with their superiors, in enforcement of the laws against vice, gambling and bootlegging. Commissioner Enright ordered that no uniformed member of the force, from inspector of a district down to a patrolman, shall enter any place in quest of evidence of a violation of any of these offenses, whether he is in uniform or in plain clothes. In fact, all, except a unit of one deputy chief inspector, one deputy inspector, four captains, ten lieutenants, twenty-nine sergeants and 250 plain clothes detectives of the newly organized Special Service Division will confine their activities to the enforcement of city ordinances and coping with crimes of violence.

Special Squads Increased.

The Commissioner explained that under the new scheme the Special Service Division, which has been increased by four captains, five lieutenants, twenty-three sergeants and 135 plain clothes men, none of whom was connected heretofore with inspection district work, "will work in relays throughout the various inspection districts, and, when necessary, a larger force can be quickly mobilized in any district to clean up any local condition which may threaten the welfare, peace and good order of the community."

The Commissioner intimated that it was his belief that in this way there would be no possibility of collusion on the part of any of the men assigned to duty with the Special Service Division and "those living on vice, gambling and violation of the Volstead act," as no member of the force could guarantee what those who might follow them through a district would do in regard to the suppression of resorts.

The Commissioner made no mention of it, but the impression around Headquarters, when his statement was made public, was that the whole scheme is an attempt to eliminate the possibilities of graft on the part of policemen on posts and others in winking at resorts of whose existence they could not but learn. The fact that the Special Service Division had been increased by thirty-two superior officers, ranking from captain to sergeant, was taken to mean that these will be used as "shoo-flys" to watch the men on posts, in addition to the plain-clothes men under them, and to see that they report their suspicions of the existence of illegal resorts to the captains, who, under the new order, must forward such information in wax-sealed envelopes to Commissioner Enright at his office. In cases where an emergency appears to exist for more urgent action, the captain or inspector to whom such a report is made must

Continued on Page Four.

Preaches 22,000th Sermon, Nearing Wesley's Record

LONDON, Jan. 25.—John Wesley's record of having preached 27,000 sermons is being approached by Canon Hay Aitkin, aged vicar of Norwich Cathedral, now in his eighty-third year, who has ascended the pulpit to deliver sermons for the 22,000th time. Canon Aitkin began preaching at the age of 17.

Since 1900, when he became attached to Norwich Cathedral, he has conducted seven to ten missions each year. He plans to continue his mission work for a year or so longer, after which he will continue his pulpit work at the Cathedral.

Never, he says, has he preached from a written sermon and not once has he delivered a sermon written by any one else. He became aide de camp to Moody in 1875 and for many years preached in England and America.

DR. STRATON PLANS BIG RELIGIOUS HOTEL

To Be Part of a Great "White Temple," He Says, Providing a Spiritual Centre.

FOR TRUE CHRISTIANS ONLY

Meanwhile Mr. Potter, His Unitarian Opponent, May Build an Apartment House.

Dr. John Roach Straton, pastor of Calvary Baptist Church, West Fifty-seventh Street, announced last night that his Board of Trustees and Deacons is favorably considering a proposal to tear down the present building and erect on its site a new church capable of seating 5,000 and housing a choir of 500. In addition, it is planned to build over and around the church at the same time a 20-story Christian hotel, where, according to Dr. Straton, "solid men and women can rest in peaceful fellowship without the unwelcome attentions of the scarlet woman and the lounge lizard."

The pastor of Calvary Church is now defending the fundamentalist cause in a series of public debates with the Rev. Charles Francis Potter, pastor of the West Side Unitarian Church. By a coincidence it became known last night that Mr. Potter intended to proceed along somewhat similar lines. The Unitarian Church plans to build a 14-story apartment house on the vacant lots between 109th and 110th Streets, near Broadway, which adjoin the church itself. Dr. Straton said last night that he had great hopes of converting Mr. Potter to his cause, but, failing that, he would attempt to win him over by offering him the general management of his Christian hotel, which probably would be named Mizpah House.

Dr. Straton estimates the cost of the new building at $5,000,000. One of the largest architectural firms in New York, he said, already had laid the blue prints before the Board of Trustees, but he said that he did not feel at liberty now to disclose the firm's name.

Planning a Spiritual Centre.

The church part of the edifice will be named the White Temple. It is intended to devote the second and third floors to the executive offices of what Dr Straton last night said he hoped would become the greatest spiritual centre in the United States.

Strict rules will be drawn up for the guests of the Christian hotel. Calvary Church will see that a Bible is placed in every bedroom, parlor and other rooms. Only those who are known to be true Christians will be welcome guests. Precautions will be taken against the possible introduction of liquor into the building and there will be no dancing or secular music. Preference will be given to those who hold fast to the Fundamentalist cause, it was indicated.

Dr. Straton last night outlined the rebuilding scheme on which it is proposed to act within the next few weeks.

"You must understand," said Dr. Straton at his home at 62 East Seventy-seventh Street, " that the plan is as yet tentative. The greatest city in the world ought to have the greatest soul winning church in the world. I have been laboring here for six years and I have fought the good fight against those who did not want the church I did, and now, at last, I shall see the practical realization of my great dream.

"Our trustees and deacons are strong and powerful men. They are in complete accordance with me about this great new building. They realize that it has been clearly demonstrated that there are thousands who have both money and a strong sense of religion, and that, I think, is an important factor, in the idea under consideration.

"We want to build up a great people's church. All branches of our church work have grown so rapidly that our housing conditions have become acute. Our present building is old-fashioned. In order to meet the demands of those who are active in the work at Calvary Church we propose to put up a new twenty-story building with a cathedral effect. It will probably be along the lines of the Woolworth Building, for with a little alteration a decidedly church effect could be given to that building.

Church May Use All the Space.

"Ultimately, I believe our work will so grow that we shall have the biggest Christian centre in New York, and perhaps in the world, so that we might take over the whole of the twenty stories to house our preachers, experts, executives, teachers and the like. To begin with, most of the stories will be used as a hotel, or possibly for apartments, but they will be so constructed

Continued on Page Ten.

ANDERSON REVEALS NEW MYSTERY MEN AND ADMITS DECEIT

Gave $20,000 He Got From 'King' to 'Mann' and Two Others for Publicity, He Says.

NEVER SAW THEIR OFFICE

All Four Persons Named in Forgery Trial Gone Away Long Ago, Accused Declares.

TWO STORIES IN CONFLICT

Jury Is Told the One About Mortgages to Raise Loans to Aid Dry League Was Untrue.

William H. Anderson, Superintendent of the Anti-Saloon League, on trial for forgery, admitted under cross-examination yesterday that he had told two different stories of the origin of the $24,700 publicity fund around which the case revolves. In addition he added three more mysterious figures to his gallery of aids. The first was "Henry Mann," described as a publicity agent, who directed the spending of the $24,700 and was not asked to account for his disbursements or his results. The others were his assistants, "Green" and "Johnson." The publicity agent, it developed, was a friend of "John T. King," the mysterious stranger who is now said by Anderson to have supplied the $24,700.

Anderson had told this narrative on the witness stand on Thursday. The fund, as he told it, came about through the generosity of "King," the utter stranger who showered Anderson with gifts of cash and then dropped out of sight. Anderson testified that it was due to "King"—still unidentified beyond being 45 years old and the owner of a black mustache—that he had the money with which to finance a confidential publicity campaign for the league.

Out of the campaign came a debt from the league to Anderson of $24,700, according to the defendant, and it was to liquidate this debt that he accepted O. Bersall Phillips offer of a "fifty-fifty" split on commissions. Anderson, under further cross-examination yesterday, reiterated this story.

Differs From First Story.

With this again on the trial record, Chief Assistant District Attorney Ferdinand Pecora asked Anderson if he had not told the board of the Anti-Saloon League that he raised the money by mortgaging his Baltimore home and by pledging his insurance policies. Anderson's memory was poor on that point, and Mr. Pecora produced a letter by Anderson to the board saying that the money was thus raised, and making no mention of "King."

Anderson, however, scored a point when he testified that the indebtedness had been investigated by a special committee appointed by the league. This committee, he said, and the minutes of the league supported him, found nothing blameworthy about the matter. The committee was composed of the Rev. Dr. David James Burrell, President of the league; Truman H. Baldwin and Dr. Duncan. Anderson said that Dr. George Caleb Moor of the Madison Avenue Baptist Church, Secretary of the league, joined the committee later. The report was signed by Dr. Burrell, Mr. Baldwin and Dr. Moor. Mr. Baldwin, who did most of the investigating, is dead.

Mr. Pecora drew from Anderson the three additions to the cast of the case. They proved to be as little known as "Mr. King." The first was "Henry Mann," who, according to Anderson, was the publicity man who directed the campaign which cost $24,700. Anderson said he remembered that "Mann" was 30 or 35, had light hair, but was not blonde or brunette, worked for "King" at one time and never gave or was asked for a receipt for the money he spent or on an explanation of how he was spending the money.

Publicity as Trail Blazer.

Anderson testified that he knew "Mann" had an office somewhere down-

Continued on Page Three.

COOLIDGE PREPARES TO END OIL LEASES AND PROSECUTE IF EVIDENCE WARRANTS; SINCLAIR LENT FALL $25,000 IN BONDS

THE PRESIDENT IS AROUSED

Feels That Facts Already Given Point to Criminal Action.

QUICK INDICTMENT HINTED

Defense of Fall in the Face of Doheny's and Others' Testimony Is Awaited.

CANCELLATION IS CERTAIN

President Will Move Cautiously, but Realizes Evidence of Fraud Is Very Strong.

Special to The New York Times.

WASHINGTON, Jan. 25.—President Coolidge is prepared to announce within a few days his intention to annul the naval oil lease contracts on the completion of the inquiry by Department of Justice officials, which is expected to lead to a presentation to a special Grand Jury.

That the inquiry before the Senate Public Lands Committee has developed testimony that needs explanation and probably already has furnished sufficient evidence for use of the Department of Justice to prepare an indictment, is the opinion of Administration leaders who have been following the case and who are greatly worried over the political effect it already is having on the Coolidge Administration, in no way connected with the making of the leases.

Although President Coolidge has been advised to announce his intention to cancel the leases, he does not wish to make such a statement until ex-Secretary Fall at least has had an opportunity to answer the accusations made against him and to give some explanation of the several loans made to him, now asserted by those appearing before the committee to have reached $193,000.

It is believed that the President will be able early next week to assure the public that the Department of Justice is ready to present an indictment to a special Grand Jury, charging fraud in the making of the leases. On such an action, the President, it is said, feels that he will be justified in announcing his decision to cancel the leases.

To Avoid Prejudgment.

The view of the President is that as an executive officer he should not prejudge the case, which has not yet been put in shape for action by the proper Federal officers.

When the Teapot Dome inquiry assumed the phase of criminal action early this week, the President ordered an observer to watch the course of events and to review the testimony, so as to be prepared without delay to take whatever action might be necessary to protect the interests of the United States and to punish any one guilty of wrongdoing.

The first thing of importance in the mind of the President is to punish any one who committed fraud in the making of the leases, as when this is done the leases almost automatically cancel themselves, as fraud in their consummation vitiate the contract between the Government and the private oil companies holding the valuable leases.

That Mr. Coolidge is proceeding in an orderly way, but not without a full sense of importance of the transacation and its effect on the public, was made clear today by a spokesman for the President, who also asserted that the Cabinet had gone over the situation

Continued on Page Two.

Mr. Fall Stays in Bed All Day; No Word From Him Till Monday

Special to The New York Times.

WASHINGTON, Jan. 25.—Former Senator Albert B. Fall spent the day in bed, under orders, it is stated, of his physician.

Mr. Fall is a guest of Colonel J. W. Zevely, Harry F. Sinclair's personal attorney, at his apartment at 2,029 Connecticut Avenue.

It is stated that he has been ill for some time, that this was the reason for his trip to Florida, and that it was on advice of his physicians, on account of the high temperature and fatigue from his recent journeys that Mr. Fall remained in bed. It is related also that an old throat infection has returned.

The former Senator sent out word to inquirers that he would have nothing to say about the Doheny testimony on oil leases before he appeared at the hearing on Monday.

REPUBLICAN ORGAN URGES PROSECUTION

Guilty in Oil Leases Should Be Punished, Says Paper Run by National Committee.

LOOKS FOR 'ULTIMATE GOOD'

And Holds Integrity of Harding Administration Is Not Involved—Blames War Waste.

Special to The New York Times.

WASHINGTON, Jan. 25.—The National Republican, of which George B. Lockwood, Secretary of the Republican National Committee, is editor and owner, with John T. Adams Chairman of the committee, and others, says editorially in this week's issue that "the guilty in the oil reserve leases ought to be punished."

"The disclosures in the Fall case are in a sense discreditable to the United States Senate and to the Harding Administration, for Senator Fall was a member of both," says the editorial. "They do not, however, involve the integrity of the Senate or of the Harding Administration as a whole. Guilt is personal and dishonesty is a characteristic that has been noted in men of all parties; there will never be a political party in which all its members charged with official responsibility may be depended on not to betray their trust. Every act committed by any official in violation of the laws he has sworn to uphold, every betrayal of trust by whomsoever committed, should be prosecuted with a view to the punishment of the guilty.

"It is unfortunate that the orgy of graft and waste during our own recent war period was so widespread that the very magnitude of the task of prosecuting all the guilty persons and concerns has prevented the infliction of punishment befitting the crimes. It is interesting to note that some of the statesmen on Capitol Hill who regarded such scandals as our billion dollar aircraft fiasco with entire equanimity are now quivering with outraged virtue over the Teapot Dome transaction. That, however, is one of the advantages of party government—the party of opposition can always be depended on to view with a sufficient amount of indignation the offenses of rascals in other parties.

"Ultimate good will come out of the exposures in the Fall case—to the betterment of legislation and administration. It is not when crimes against the people are exposed and punished that there is cause for apprehension, but when they are hidden and protected, as was done so generally during the period of the war, when billions of dollars, contributed by the people at a time when four million men were making the supreme sacrifice of military service, were wasted in a riot of extravagance and worse without parallel in the history of the world."

FALL MINE LEASE QUESTIONED.

Senate Committee Asked to Investigate Oklahoma Grant.

OKLAHOMA CITY, Jan. 25.—A resolution was introduced in the upper house of the Oklahoma Legislature today by Senator Feuquay asking that the United States Senate Committee investigating the Teapot Dome oil lease hear testimony also in regard to a lead and zinc mining lease granted by A. B. Fall, while he was Secretary of the Interior, to the Eagle-Picher Mining Company in the restricted Quapaw Indian lands in Northeastern Oklahoma.

The original lease on the Indian land expired in 1920, 1921 and 1922, according to Senator Feuquay, and it was on the last renewal, during Mr. Fall's term of office, that the charges are based.

The resolution declared that it is "currently rumored" that the lease on the Quapaw land was made to the Eagle-Picher Company at a "lesser price than that offered by other responsible bidders."

The resolution also requests an investigation into the alleged transfer of $25,000 in Liberty bonds, which Harry F. Sinclair was declared by W. G. Wahlberg, his secretary, to have given to Colonel William Zevely in 1922. The resolution seeks to determine if there was a connection between this alleged payment to Zevely and rumor current during the 1922 Gubernatorial campaign in Oklahoma that Sinclair had helped finance the campaign of J. C. Walton.

ZEVELY TELLS OF LOAN

Made After Oil Grant, Bonds Being Sent to Bank Fall Suggested.

UNSECURED NOTE WAS GIVEN

Sinclair Counsel Says $10,000 More Was Given to Finance Fall's Russian Trip.

EXPLAINS VISIT TO RANCH

Witness Declares Sinclair Went to Three Rivers to Discuss Osage Indian Lands.

Special to The New York Times.

WASHINGTON, Jan. 25.—Further evidence of a sensational nature involving the relations of ex-Secretary Fall with the principal owners of the Doheny and Sinclair oil interests was developed today when J. W. Zevely, intimate friend and personal attorney of Harry F. Sinclair, informed the Senate committee investigating the Teapot Dome oil case that in June or July of last year Mr. Sinclair had loaned $25,000 in Liberty bonds to Mr. Fall.

Mr. Zevely said he did not know what Fall did with the proceeds of the bonds, but he had heard that he wanted the money to buy some ranch properties near Three Rivers, N. M. Several months subsequent to the transfer of the bonds Fall gave a note to Zevely which the latter said he thought bears interest at the rate of 6 per cent. He indicated that the loan was made without security.

While the committee was examining Mr. Zevely Representative Morehead of Nebraska introduced a resolution in the House calling for cancellation of the Teapot Dome lease, on the ground that it was "corruptly obtained."

Thought Loan "Nothing Unusual."

Mr. Zevely testified that there was nothing unusual, to his way of thinking, about the loan to Mr. Fall. He explained that Fall told him he wanted some money to buy "one or two small ranches," and when he put the proposition up to Mr. Sinclair the latter instructed him to let Fall have the money when he wanted it.

Subsequently, in June or July last, Mr. Zevely said, Mr. Fall was ready for the money and Sinclair told G. D. Wahlberg, at that time his confidential secretary, to give Zevely "$25,000 or $30,000 in bonds." The bonds were sent at Fall's request to a bank in El Paso, Texas, with instructions to the bank to credit them to the account of Mr. Fall.

It was asserted by Mr. Zevely that it was during a visit he made to the Fall ranch in New Mexico in the late Spring or early Summer of last year that Fall told him he needed some money to buy "one or two" small ranch properties near Three Rivers. He went to Three Rivers at the instance of Mr. Sinclair to ask Fall if he would accompany Mr. Sinclair as an attorney on a trip to Russia, where Sinclair was going in connection with certain Russian oil properties which Sinclair hoped eventually to obtain. Fall received $10,000 expense money for that trip, and Mr. Zevely added that he supposed he also received a fee.

Call on Fall Only Friendly.

There was nothing significant about his recent trip to New Orleans, said Mr. Zevely. Fall wanted somebody to talk to, and as Zevely was an old friend, he wired Zevely to come to New Orleans, and, added Mr. Zevely, "I was glad to go." Among other things, he said, he and Mr. Fall discussed the Senate investigation. He described it as "a sort of general discussion as to what the trend of things would be and what was going on."

Referring specifically to the lease of the Teapot Dome to Sinclair, Mr. Zevely said that Mr. Sinclair and himself visited Fall at Three Rivers in December, 1921, to confer with Fall, who was then Secretary of the Interior, regarding certain properties in the Osage Nation section of Oklahoma. He said he was not certain, but he thought Sinclair asked Fall whether or not he was going to lease the Teapot, and Fall replied that the matter was under investigation.

In the February following Mr. Sinclair submitted a proposition to Fall for the lease of the Wyoming Naval Reserve.

It was recalled today that the visit of Sinclair and Zevely to Three Rivers was made soon after the time Edward L. Doheny says he made his $100,000 loan to Fall, and that the negotiations for the leasing of the California fields to Doheny and the Teapot to Sinclair were started at about the same time. Doheny testified that he made his loan, which bears no interest, and is unsecured, on Nov. 30, 1921. Immediately thereafter Sinclair and Zevely appeared at Three Rivers to confer regarding the promotion in the Osage Nation country.

Zevely Says He Acted Only as Lawyer.

Mr. Zevely, in beginning his testimony, said that he was a native of Muskogee, Okla., at present temporarily domiciled in Washington. He was in the service of the Department of the Interior from 1896 to 1902 or 1903 as an inspector under Secretaries Bliss, Hitchcock. For four or five

Clothes on Mummy Show Women's Styles Have Not Changed in Egypt in 2,642 Years

LUXOR, Egypt, Jan. 23 (Associated Press).—Dr. Robert Mond, the English Egyptologist, who during the past week has been engaged in clearing the space behind the Rameseum, or mortuary temple, of Rameses II. in the region known as Sheikh-Abd-El-Qurna, to remove the rubble for his intended excavation of the tomb of Ramose, an official of the heretic King Khu-n-aten, has made some interesting finds. These are three mummies, of which two are in an excellent state of preservation. The third, possibly the body of a soldier killed in one of the wars of ancient Egypt, is in a bad state.

The first two mummies proved to be the bodies of a goldsmith and his wife, a priestess of Amonie, of the twenty-fourth dynasty, 718 B. C. When the mummy of the priestess was unwrapped, it was found that under the outer wrappings her clothing of fine linen, now browned by age, had been laid, neatly folded, upon the body. There was a long robe, piped with green, with a V-shaped opening in front and holes for the arms, fringed around the hem; then an outer garment with a hole for the head and several fringed veils. Strangely, it was seen that at various places the garments had been darned.

As each garment was unfolded and held up to the bright sunshine the native diggers broke out into loud exclamations, declaring them identical in form and arrangement to those worn by the fellaheen women of today. Mlle. Baud of the excavation mission at Thebes of the French Institute Archeological of Cairo, who was present, donned the robes, which were in excellent condition, and the contention of the diggers was found to be correct.

Round the neck of the goldsmith were four amulets of steatite, and on his breast, upon a leaden symbol of hawk's wings outspread, a faience scarab with hieroglyphics painted on it. A particularly fine scarab of black basalt, painted with hieroglyphics of yellow, was found on the breast of the goldsmith's wife.

Two papyri, one in perfect condition and the other damaged, were discovered with the bodies.

37 Die in Illinois Coal Mine Blast; Phoned They Were Safe, Then Perished

JOHNSTON CITY, Ill., Jan. 25—Thirty-seven miners are dead, six are seriously injured and badly burned, and eight others are suffering from burns about the head and body received in a mine disaster which occurred here this afternoon.

Among the dead were Herbert McCullough, mine manager, and Jesse Ford, mine boss.

Fifteen of the rescued, who were trapped with the dead and injured, were carried out by rescuers. Practically all of their clothing had been torn off and the hair on their bodies singed, but they were not seriously hurt.

The men near the entrances escaped easily, but those in entries 9, 10, 11 and 12, in the depths of the colliery where the actual explosion took place, were farthest from means of escape and they suffered the full horrors of the terrific blast.

Hundreds of men volunteered to go down into the mine after four Johnston City physicians announced their intention of braving the poisonous gases of the inner recesses. Waiting in the zero cold outside, relatives and workers were completely enveloped by clouds of dense, black smoke coming from the shaft. Ambulances from Herrin and Johnston City were lined up outside, and as each body, borne on a stretcher, was brought out of the smoky shaft, the waiting crowds pushed forward, fearful that it might be some relative.

Following a terrific explosion in the McClintock coal mine, operated by the Crerar Clinch Coal Company, more than a score were trapped in the workings with fire raging about the entries to their place of refuge.

Throngs of frenzied men, women and children gathered about the entrance to the mine. Rescue teams worked valiently in shifts of six men each in attempts to reach the imprisoned miners. The men were in entries Nos. 8 and 9, which are rooms opening off the main entry. These entries had been battened off from the main sections by the rescue workers, and other parts of the mine cleared of gases.

Following the explosion twenty miners escaped uninjured. Three hundred and ninety others working on the 230-foot level were not affected. Those who were trapped at first established telephone communications with the surface and reported that they were safe. Soon afterward they failed to answer calls from above ground.

The rescue workers brought one of the dead, mangled beyond recognition, and four of the injured to the surface soon after they entered the mine.

After hours of arduous work on the part of the volunteer rescue teams to aid the organized crews of Williamson County, the last of the injured was brought to the surface. All received medical aid in hospitals here and in Herrin.

"All the News That's Fit to Print."

The New York Times.

THE WEATHER.
Fair, slightly warmer Thursday; Friday, fair, warmer; moderate winds, becoming south.
For full weather report see Page 22.

VOL. LXXIII....No. 24,284. •••• NEW YORK, SUNDAY, JULY 20, 1924. Including Rotogravure Picture Section in two parts—Magazine and Book Sections in Rotogravure. FIVE CENTS In Manhattan, Bronx and Brooklyn | Elsewhere TEN CENTS

FRANCE WINS POINT AS ALLIED CONFEREES NEAR AN AGREEMENT

Committee on Sanctions Concedes Her Right to Take Separate Action if Berlin Defaults.

REPARATION BODY TO DECIDE

But It Can Give Judgment Against the Reich Only After Consulting Agent General.

GERMAN LOAN SAFEGUARDED

Bondholders Are to Be Assured of Priority on All Resources of the Fatherland.

LONDON, July 19 (Associated Press).—The committee of the allied conference in charge of sanctions in the event of Germany's default under the Dawes scheme this morning unanimously agreed to assure to investors in the loan to Germany priority on all German resources.

The committee also unanimously agreed to preserve all the rights enjoyed by the nations which signed the Treaty of Versailles.

These two issues stood in the way of the negotiations of the conference yesterday, and the agreement on them, it is believed, will expedite the work of achieving a general agreement on the Dawes plan.

A Concession to Herriot.

The agreement on the preservation of the rights of the signatories to the treaty was a concession to Premier Herriot of France, and in effect it preserves to France the right to take separate action. It enables M. Herriot to live up to the pledge he gave to ex-Premier Poincaré that all the French rights under the treaty would be maintained.

After Committee No. 1, in which these debated issues had been causing delay, had reached an agreement, the French Premier authorized a statement that he was highly pleased with the progress of the conference.

The agreement reached in regard to Germany's default greatly diminishes the power with which the British proposed to invest the agent general of reparations and trustee for the bondholders.

Reparation Commission Retains Power.

The Reparation Commission has been agreed upon as the proper authority to adjudge Germany in default, but, in making such a decision, the commission must take the advice of the agent general and representative of the shareholders in the German loan. It is not stipulated that the representative of the shareholders is the trustee for the bondholders under the Dawes plan.

By the terms of the agreement the initiative for declaring Germany in default must be taken by the Reparation Commission after advice has been given by the agent general and his colleagues.

Berlin Rages Against Sanctions.

Copyright, 1924, by The Chicago Tribune Co.

BERLIN, July 19.—The German Government, it was learned from an official source today, cannot accept the French, British and American compromises which recognize the fundamental right of the Allies to take territorial sanctions in the future for Germany's failure to fulfill the Dawes reparations plan.

As all confidential public information from London indicates the acceptance by the conference there of the sanctions article, consternation entered the German camp, the shock echoing through Wilhelmstrasse. Until tonight Germany's policy concerned itself chiefly with obtaining the evacuation of the Ruhr as fundamental to the Reichstag's accepting the Dawes plan. From now on, it is predicted, Germany will concentrate on demanding that the Allies drop territorial sanctions.

The Nationalists and other opponents of the Government party are jubilant over reports that the conference demands territorial sanctions in the future. The Nationalists believe that puts a lever in their hand to upset the Government. Their relation will be to rally all forces opposed to the Reichstag's acceptance of the Dawes plan. These forces until now had been in the minority, but some popular slogan for a popular cause is likely to give them a majority.

Says British Repudiated Pledges.

BERLIN, July 19 (Associated Press).—Calling for rejection of any interpretation of the Dawes report by the London conference which provides for arbitrary territorial sanctions under Article XXII. of the Treaty of Versailles, the Zeit, the organ of Dr. Stresemann, the Foreign Secretary, expresses rank displeasure with the drafts of memoranda now under consideration by the conference.

"Both the French and English drafts as now constituted," the paper says, "fundamentally recognize the right of territorial sanction, in flagrant contradiction of the English point of view set forth in the note of Aug. 11, 1923.

"These questions are of such paramount importance and, further, are calculated to disturb the German public to such an extent that their ultimate disposition will in no small measure determine the German Government's attitude toward the experts' report."

German official apprehensiveness is feeding on the supposition that France in future would retain a free hand in the event of German default and could proceed to impose sanctions which the Germans say would be in contradiction to the letter and spirit of the Dawes report.

So far the London conference has provoked only desultory comment, and much of this is inspired by the familiar partisan spirit. The German Nationalist organs and Reichstag Deputies see Germany confronted with fresh dictation, and warn the Government of their avowed opposition to any agreement

Continued on Page Three.

Greek Cabinet Falls; Held Office Since March

ATHENS, July 19 (Associated Press).—The Greek Cabinet, headed by Premier Papanastasion, has fallen.

A Government crisis in Greece has been threatening since the early part of June, when General Condylis and M. Tsouderos, respectively Minister of War and Finance, resigned, General Condylis accusing the Government of encouraging communism. It was believed at the time that other resignations would take place and every effort was put forth by Government leaders to avoid the resignation of the Cabinet.

The Cabinet of Premier Papanastasion was formed in March to succeed the temporary Ministry headed by Premier Kafandaris.

HUGHES IN LONDON, PRAISES DAWES PLAN

He Declares American Sentiment Is "Strongly" Behind Experts' Proposals.

HIS VISIT IS "UNOFFICIAL"

Insists That He Comes as Head of Bar Association, Not Secretary of State.

Special Cable to THE NEW YORK TIMES.

LONDON, July 19.—Secretary Hughes arrived here today, a little bronzed after a pleasant trip on the Berengaria. His visit to London while the allied conference on the Dawes report is in session is merely a coincidence, his arrangements to attend the Bar Association convention here having been made before the conference was convoked. But it is regarded as a happy coincidence.

Mr. Hughes was emphatic in his statements to all interviewers that his visit was unofficial and personal, and that he came as President of the American Bar Association and not as Secretary of State.

"The American people and the American Government," he said, "are much interested in the putting into effect of the Dawes report, for we in the Government regard it as a sound basis for the economic recuperation of Europe. We are assured that American sentiment is strongly behind the Dawes report and believe that its execution is of the greatest consequence for the future peace of the world."

Premier MacDonald will come to town from Chequers in order to dine with Mr. Hughes tomorrow evening at Crewe House, where the Secretary is staying as the guest of Ambassador Kellogg.

"American influence, which is thus strengthened, is making itself felt in the conference," is the way in which one London paper tonight attempts to summarize the one essential fact of the situation. The Sunday Times pays tribute to Mr. Hughes in an editorial which closes with these words:

"He could not find himself in England at a more opportune moment."

SOUTHAMPTON, England, July 19 (Associated Press).—Pressed for his views regarding the Dawes plan, Secretary Hughes, on his arrival here today on the Berengaria, said:

"American sentiment is very strongly behind the Dawes report as it now stands, and we believe that prompt execution of that report is of the greatest consequence."

In a statement to newspaper men Secretary Hughes emphasized the fact that his visit to England was unofficial and personal. Regarding the Dawes report, however, the Secretary said: "We are very much interested in having it put into execution.

"We hope it will be found possible to have that effect given to it at an early date," he continued. "We consider it affords a sound basis for the economic recuperation of Europe."

Asked whether he considered that the Dawes plan could be modified and yet have the full effect which he apparently hoped from it, Secretary Hughes replied: "That is a discussion into which I am afraid I cannot enter."

Speaking of the approaching Bar Association meeting, Mr. Hughes said:

"My visit here is entirely unoffical and personal. I am here as President of the American Bar Association. Members of this association are looking forward with pleasure to enjoying the hos-

Continued on Page Three.

FOES OF FOREIGNERS SLEW MAJOR IMBRIE; HUNDREDS ARRESTED

Photographing of Teheran 'Miracle Fountain' Apparently a Pretext Used by Fanatics.

CALLED HIM A BAHAIST

Native Press Had Been Inciting Demonstrations Against the Foreign Element.

PERSIA PROMISES REDRESS

Government Sends Regrets to Washington—State Department Orders Inquiry.

TEHERAN, Persia, July 19 (Associated Press).—Vice Consul Robert Imbrie of the United States, who died yesterday after he had been beaten by a fanatical mob as he and an American named Melin Seymour were photographing a sacred fountain, was buried today, the entire diplomatic corps attending the funeral.

The tragedy was the culmination of recent anti-foreign and particularly anti-British activity which had been shown in the native press and elsewhere and which the Government appears unable to check owing to the lack of laws controlling such incitement by the press.

The fountain where Imbrie was beaten and where Seymour, described as an oil driller, suffered serious injuries at the hands of the crowd, is supposed by the natives of the city to have been the scene a few days ago of a miracle and ever since huge crowds have been making pilgrimages to it.

Impressive Funeral Held.

Copyright, 1924, by The Chicago Tribune Co.

TEHERAN, Persia, July 19.—A temporary funeral for Major Robert Imbrie was held today in the American Church, the body being taken from the police hospital with military music and under a very large guard. It will be taken to America when Mrs. Imbrie is ready.

The church was packed to suffocation. Among those present were Prime Minister Serdar Sepah and the members of his Cabinet, the Court Minister of Ceremonies, all the members of the Persian Parliament, all the foreign legations, including the Afghan and Turkish, except the Russian, and practically the whole European colony. The dejection, particularly of the Persians, was marked.

All signs point to the barbaric murder playing an important part in Persia's internal politics.

Melin Seymour, the other American who was beaten, said today that he felt better. He is well attended at the police hospital by European and Persian doctors, who predict his recovery.

Hundreds of arrests have been made. Major Imbrie is mourned by all.

State Department Begins Inquiry.

Special to The New York Times.

WASHINGTON, July 19.—Confirmation of the death of Major Robert Imbrie at the hands of a mob of fanatical natives was received by the State Department today in a cable message from Joseph S. Kornfeld, Minister to Persia. Pending an inquiry which the department has begun by direction of Under-Secretary Joseph Grew, Acting Secretary of State in the absence of Secretary Hughes in Europe, no formal action to obtain redress will be taken by the United States Government.

The State Department gave this paraphrase of the report from Teheran:

"A telegram from the American Minister at Teheran, Joseph S. Kornfeld, dated evening, July 18, states that Vice Consul Imbrie succumbed at 3 o'clock in the afternoon to the shock following an assault by a mob which practically cut him and beat him to death.

"The Minister reports that for some days throughout the city there had been denouncements of Bahaists, a religious sect, and many religious demonstrations. It appears that at 11 A. M. the Vice Consul, accompanied by Seymour, a prisoner in the consulate, stopped their carriage in front of one of these demonstrations and it was alleged that the Vice Consul had taken pictures. The mob rushed upon him, crying out that he was a Bahaist and though the servant of an American missionary cried out that he was the American Consul, the mob took no heed of the statement, dragged the Americans from their carriage and attacked them savagely.

"The Minister adds that Seymour's

Continued on Page Thirteen.

Mrs. Willard Cleared of Baby's Murder; Policeman Gilles Also Acquitted by Jury

MAYS LANDING, N. J., July 20.—The extraordinary tactics adopted by the prosecution in exhibiting the dead body of an infant in the courtroom failed to bring about conviction of Mrs. Pearl Willard and John J. Gilles, tried here for murder. Both were acquitted by a jury early this morning.

The jury took the case at midnight after the first night session in a capital case ever held in Atlantic County. It returned its verdict about 1:30 A. M., and the defendants regained their liberty after having spent several months in jail.

Mrs. Willard and Gilles, a former New York policeman and a boarder in the Willard home in Atlantic City, were charged with having killed Mrs. Willard's five months-old daughter, Doris. Mrs. Willard denied that the body of an infant found by a ragpicker near her home in an old mattress was hers. She stuck to that denial throughout her ordeal on the witness stand when she testified in her own behalf.

It was because of her denial that the body was that of her child that Assistant Prosecutor Hinkle induced Justice Campbell to consent to the introduction of the embalmed body "for purposes of identification."

The spectators in the courtrom, most of whom were women, cheered as the foreman announced the verdict. Mrs. Willard, who had maintained a stolid demeanor throughout the trial, except once when she fainted, gave vent to shouts that were unintelligible but unmistakably joyous.

Eugene G. Schwinghammer, who defended Mrs. Willard and Gilles, was one of the first to congratulate her. Mr. Schwinghammer built his case on the doubt as to the identity of the child shown in court and stressed the disappearance of Mrs. Willard's husband, who fled the State about the time the body was found and who still is sought in connection with the case.

When the summing up was over and the jury had been charged, Mr. Schwinghammer, who had been without sleep most of the five days of the trial, staggered to the Judge's private chambers and there collapsed from sheer exhaustion. A physician revived him, and he was able to remain for the verdict.

SAYS HIS 'DEATH RAY' COULD STUN ARMIES

But Defense, Declares Inventor Matthews, Is Chief Purpose of Electrical Beam.

WILL SELL ONLY TO BRITAIN

Englishman, Who Arrived Here on the Paris, Is Going Blind as a Result of His Experiments.

H. Grindell Matthews, British wireless telephone expert and the inventor of what he says has been miscalled the "death ray," arrived here yesterday on the French liner Paris. In the experiments which led up to the invention he lost the sight of his left eye and says he is gradually losing the sight of the other one.

He wears spectacles with heavy tinted lenses to keep out the injurious rays.

Mr. Matthews said that the purpose of his visit was not to make money but to look up certain electrical records and to try to rest himself back to health. He said that he wished it to be clearly understood that he had not come to sell his invention to the United States Government as he would dispose of it only to Great Britain. Overtures had been made to him by France and the Governments of four other countries to purchase the secret of his invention, he said, but he had declined them all.

Has Been Using One Kilowatt.

"My invention," he said, "has been incorrectly called a death ray. It is an electrical beam which I have demonstrated to be of hitherto unknown character. I use a one-kilowatt power, but there is nothing to prevent the increase to fifty kilowatts or more. With a maximum range of sixty-five feet I have stopped motor engines and killed a rat and a mouse and lighted an incandescent lamp. In these experiments I used a six-inch beam, the apparatus for which could be carried easily on a motor lorry.

"After the first demonstration of my invention I was offered £1,000 by the British officials for another test, which I have not yet given. When I have rested I intend to return to England and give another and more powerful demonstration of the electrical beam on Flatholm Island in the British Channel, where I have already placed the parts of a bigger machine ready to be assembled when I arrive there.

"They are carefully guarded by two of my assistants who know the secret of the beam, and in case anything happens to me they will carry out the experiments. There has been a good deal of ridicule cast upon my invention and silly stories fathered upon the 'wonderful beam,' as they called it, but I am confident that some day I shall be able to give out certain technical information about it that will convince electrical experts that I have discovered a new force."

Could Fire or Stun a City.

Mr. Matthews was asked if his electrical beam had sufficient force to destroy New York in time of war.

"The beam is more of a defensive than an offensive device," he replied, "and the country possessing it would be immune from attack by another power. I firmly believe that it could be used to destroy an army or to stun it, as I have demonstrated by first stunning and then killing the mouse in my experiments in England. Stunned by the electric beam, an enemy army could easily be captured, and its use would speedily put an end to wars. An airplane could carry the beam easily, fly over a city and set it on fire or stun the population so that the place could easily be captured.

"Within the next three or four months the device will be developed to project the beam four or five miles. It travels as fast as light—186,000 miles per second. The beam consists of ether vibrations similar in a way to the wireless wave, though it employs a wave length which is radically different. Its form is complex and is a combination of five characters."

Cannot Explode Magazines.

When asked if he had patented his device, Mr. Matthews said that it was impossible for him to do so because it would disclose his secret. Any technical discussion of the invention would do the same thing, so that he could only speak of the electrical beam, as he preferred to term this discovery, in a general way. Although the beam could damage cities and stun armies, he said that it could not explode magazines on warships at sea because they were what he called in radio language "earth-bound," or grounded and surrounded by metal.

R. K. Bartlett, who came over with Mr. Matthews, explained that the inventor had been experimenting with electricity since he was 10 years old and that fifteen years ago he made the original experiment with wireless telephony. Mr. Bartlett said that during the voyage Mr. Matthews had a nervous breakdown, which, in his opinion, was due to the fact that since 1915, when the experiments with the electrical ray or beam were begun, he had worked until 3 or 4 o'clock every morning.

When asked if his electrical ray was of the same nature as that used by a German inventor for stopping airplane motors, Mr. Matthews said that the German ray caused a partial short circuit of the magneto. "Mine kills the engine," he added.

Mr. Matthews will stop at the Hotel Vanderbilt for two weeks while he is making his electrical researches.

DRUG AGENTS SEIZE 2 IN ELEVATED FIGHT

One Federal Worker Battles With Four Peddler Suspects on Train.

HE IS BADLY BEATEN

Clings to One Man—Another Arrested at Station—Passengers in Panic.

Two alleged drug peddlers were arrested by Federal narcotic agents yesterday afternoon after a battle which commenced on the Twenty-third Street uptown station of the Sixth Avenue elevated, was carried on while an uptown train was speeding between the Twenty-third and Thirty-third Street stations and was finished on the Thirty-third Street platform. Scores of women and children on the train were terror-stricken as one lone Federal narcotic agent fought with four alleged drug peddlers. One of them was dragged to the station and placed under arrest at Thirty-third Street; the other arrest was made by other agents at the Twenty-third Street station. Three suspects managed to escape.

The two men arrested were taken to the West Thirtieth Street police station, where they described themselves as Jose Celazauez, 343 West Thirtieth Street, and Juan Capasoti, 225 West Twenty-fifth Street.

The Federal agents and police got about ten ounces of narcotics, whcih the alleged peddlers are said to have thrown from the elevated train windows. The agents say they recovered $49 in marked money which was used in the purchase of the narcotics.

Under the direction of Agent Harry D. Smith, the Federal men had been negotiating with the alleged peddlers for more than a week for the purchase of a considerable amount of drugs. Yesterday was agreed upon as the date for the "buy." The place selected was the Twenty-third Street station of the elevated. At the appointed time Agents Smith, George Coyle and four others came to the platform dressed in rough clothing to allay the suspicions of the alleged drug traffickers.

According to Agent Smith, the purchase money for the drugs was passed to Celazauez, who then told Smith that the drugs would be delivered when the next elevated train pulled into the station. When the train came in the drugs were passed out of the train, and the agents prepared to board the train and arrest the men on board. The guard on the car on which the alleged peddlers were riding shut the gates too quickly, however, and only one agent, Coyle, was able to get on board.

Coyle at once went into the car and attempted to place the four men who were suspected under arrest. They immediately raised the cry of "pickpockets" and commenced to fight Coyle. A battle followed in which Coyle was badly beaten. The train was crowded with passengers, among them scores of women and children. They screamed and tried to get out of the way of the struggling men. The motorman sounded the emergency whistle, and police on duty on Sixth Avenue rushed to the Thirty-third Street station to intercept the train.

When the train reached the station Coyle still retained his hold on one man, who afterward said he was Capasati. He had difficulty in identifying himself to the police, as did Agent Smith and his assistants, who had hurried in a taxicab from Twenty-third Street to Thirty-third Street.

Some of the agents and police searched the elevated structure and street between the two stations and packages of drugs, amounting in all to ten ounces, were found scattered along the route.

The marked money which was used in the purchase of the drugs was found on the Thirty-third Street station.

CHURCHILL SARCASTIC OVER OUR DEBT POLICY

Says We Demand 'Uttermost Farthing' From Britain and Then Bar Her Goods.

Special Cable to THE NEW YORK TIMES.

LONDON, July 19.—Winston Churchill, speaking as a guest at the dinner last night at the Hotel Cecil of the Society of Planters of Malaya, said: "Our American friends have demanded the uttermost farthing of the debt which we incurred on behalf of our allies during the course of the great common struggle against Germany."

On the other hand, he continued, the United States had erected enormous barriers of tariffs which prevented payment in goods and service. He said he felt strongly that, however severely Britain's obligations were judged, the British were under no obligation to supply their American friends with rubber at a loss.

MANY CHEER DAVIS ON TRIP TO MAINE TO REST AND WORK

Candidate Reaches Island Home of C. D. Gibson, Where He Will Draft His Acceptance.

PLANS LARGE USE OF RADIO

Deeply Impressed by Convention Broadcast, He Wants His Speeches Widely Spread.

ACCEPTANCE TO BE SHORT

Most of His Addresses Will Be Brief as Possible—He Extols Shaver as Silent Man.

Special to The New York Times.

DARK HARBOR, Me., July 19.—Greeted along the route by groups of enthusiastic Democrats who wished him success, John W. Davis, Democratic nominee for President, arrived here at noon today for a ten-day vacation at the Summer home of Mr. and Mrs. Charles Dana Gibson on Seven Hundred Acre Island.

Mr. Davis, who appeared in excellent health and spirits, was accompanied by Mrs. Davis and Frank L. Polk, former Acting Secretary of State, the latter rejoining his family, who have a Summer home at Islesboro, the large island off which Seven Hundred Acre Island is situated. Others in the party were Mr. and Mrs. J. M. Nye and Harold McCarthy and George Zengerle, Mr. Davis's two secretaries, who will help him in his correspondence and possibly in the drafting of his acceptance speech, if Mr. Davis decides to reduce his ideas on campaign issues to writing before his return to New York.

Mr. and Mrs. Gibson met Mr. and Mrs. Davis on their arrival at the dock at Dark Harbor, Islesboro, after an hour's steamer trip from Rockland, the railroad terminal. They drove in horse-drawn surreys across the island of Islesboro and went by motor launch to the Gibson home. Mr. Gibson had been reported suffering from a grave illness, but his physician, Dr. D. E. Larabee, pronounced it nothing serious, and Mr. Gibson met the Davis party in person.

Just before leaving for Seven Hundred Acre Island Mr. Davis explained that the chief purpose of his trip was rest and recreation, but that he expected to do some work in connection with campaign plans and arrangements and on his speech.

Acceptance Speech to Be Short.

Mr. Davis said he expected to keep his acceptance speech as short as possible.

"I agree with those who hold that no souls are saved after the first twenty minutes," he said, smiling, indicating that he intended to keep his campaign speeches down to a minimum of length compatible with the presentation of the issues he will discuss.

Mr. Davis also indicated that he expected to use the radio a great deal in representing his views to the people of the country.

"The radio has been the most important development in the last fifty years," he said. "It will make a great change in campaigning. I thought the motion pictures would be an important adjunct to campaigning, but the pictures do not compare with the radio in effectiveness."

The broadcasting of the proceedings of the Democratic National Convention which nominated him apparently made a strong impression on Mr. Davis. In conversation with reporters it was agreed that at least 10,000,000 persons must have listened to the convention proceedings by radio at one time or another. It was evident that Mr. Davis expected to reach many more thousands of persons by radio than otherwise would be possible. The time of his acceptance speech at Clarksburg, W. Va.—8 o'clock in the evening of Aug. 11—was fixed almost entirely with a view to reaching the largest possible number of radio listeners.

Mr. Davis declined to talk politics or to comment upon the remark of William M. Butler, Republican National Chairman, that he did not agree with Mr. Davis's definition of a progressive as synonomous with a Democrat.

"Mr. Shaver [Clem L. Shaver, the new Democratic National Chairman] will have to do the replying to Mr. Butler, if any is done," Mr. Davis said. "I don't believe, though, that you will get much out of Shaver. He is as careful of his words as most persons are with dollar bills."

Mr. Davis added that it might be an advantage to have a National Chairman who did not do much talking, and indicated complete satisfaction with the

Continued on Page Two.

Davis Engages Throat Expert To Accompany Him on Tours

Special to The New York Times.

WASHINGTON, July 19.—Dr. J. Richardson, a throat specialist, has been engaged by John W. Davis, Democratic nominee for President, to accompany him on his speaking campaign, which will carry him into most of the States.

Dr. Richardson made several similar trips as physician to William H. Taft when the latter was a candidate for President in 1908, and in the 1912 campaign.

SHAVER TAKES HOLD AS CAMPAIGN CHIEF

Will Act as Democratic Chairman, at Cordell Hull's Request, Until Formally Elected.

PARTY POLICIES DISCUSSED

Governor Bryan Will Be Notified Aug. 18 at Lincoln of His Nomination.

Special to The New York Times.

WASHINGTON, July 19.—Plans for making the Democratic national campaign this year a thorough one were discussed today by Clem L. Shaver, Acting Chairman of the National Committee, with Cordell Hull, the retiring Chairman, and other Democratic advisers.

Mr. Shaver formally took charge of the affairs of the committee, and Mr. Hull announced that all debts had been paid and there was a comfortable surplus in bank. While Mr. Shaver will not become actual Chairman until his election by the committee, which will meet in Clarksburg Aug. 11, he was requested by Mr. Hull to relieve him today so that the latter might go on a vacation.

Mr. Shaver went over with Mr. Hull the personnel of the National Committee headquarters and details of the organization, which is declared to be in better shape here and throughout the country than at any other time in recent years.

Mr. Shaver discussed plans of the campaign and policies with Mr. Hull, Senator Harrison, George H. White, a former Chairman of the National Committee, and Daniel C. Roper, one of William G. McAdoo's pre-convention managers. This conference decided to bring into the campaign, if possible, all the managers of the pre-convention candidates for the Presidential nomination. These men will be asked to serve as members of the Executive Committee and in other capacities. It is understood that Mr. Roper will take an important part in the campaign and that David L. Rockwell, Mr. McAdoo's chief manager, also has offered his services.

Mr. Shaver sent a telegram to Governor Charles W. Bryan, nominee for Vice President, asking him to fix the time and place for the notification meeting. It was announced later that the notification will be held in Lincoln, Neb., on Aug. 18.

It was definitely decided by Mr. Shaver that the headquarters of the National Committee will be continued here and its facilities increased to take charge of all shipments of literature and the conduct of the speaking engagements. Campaign headquarters will be maintained in New York and Chicago, while there will be regional headquarters in two or three other cities of the West and one in a Southern State.

Mr. Shaver left for his home in West Virginia, but will return here Monday to complete the organization and arrange the personnel of the office force. No decision has been made as to Vice Chairman or other officers of the committee, Mr. Shaver said.

In announcing his retirement as Chairman, Cordell Hull said:

"Clem L. Shaver of West Virginia will perform the duties as Chairman of the Democratic National Committee for and instead of myself from this date.

"I am greatly pleased to know that my successor as Chairman of the committee is an exceptionally able man with much successful political experience. The management of the coming campaign could not be placed in abler or safer hands. Mr. Shaver is a man of great energy, fine judgment, and is scrupulously conscientious. I confidently predict for Mr. Shaver a highly satisfactory administration and for the Democratic Party a sweeping victory under his guidance as official head of the party organization.

"It is a source of satisfaction to me to be able to turn over the organization free from all debt, which includes the payment of some $235,000 of old obligations. A balance of several thousand dollars is on hand. There is also some pride in the knowledge that I am able to turn over to him a highly developed organization which is ready to functioin in each essential line from this day forward."

WHEELER WILL RUN WITH LA FOLLETTE; HITS RIVAL TICKETS

Accepting Nomination for Vice President, He Links Davis and Coolidge With "Wall Street."

INSISTS HE IS A DEMOCRAT

But Charges That Party Ignored the "Call of Millions in Economic Distress."

$2,000,000 FUND IS SOUGHT

New Yorker to Be Financial Director—Party Will Take "Progressive" Label.

Special to The New York Times.

WASHINGTON, July 19.—Senator Burton K. Wheeler of Montana formally accepted today the nomination as the Vice Presidential candidate on the ticket headed by Senator Robert M. La Follette of Wisconsin.

"I am a Democrat, but not a Wall Street Democrat," declared Mr. Wheeler in his letter of acceptance. He charged the Democratic Party with ignoring the call of millions in economic distress and declared there was no choice between Davis and Coolidge, whom he characterized as the candidates of reaction and the "privileged interests."

In conclusion he said he would do his best "to help make this, my country, safe for democracy." Senator La Follette later issued a statement expressing his gratification and declaring Mr. Wheeler's candidacy would strengthen the Progressive ticket in every State in the Union.

Immediately following the receipt of the letter from Senator Wheeler in which he stated that he would make the race, the Progressive leaders assembled here and proceeded with their plans to carry on the fight.

The decision of Senator Wheeler to align himself with the Independent movement aroused great enthusiasm among the Progressive chieftains. They predicted that this combination of Republican and Democratic Progressive leadership would sweep the country.

Late this afternoon, just as the day's meeting of the National Committee for Progressive Political Action was about to come to an end, Senators La Follette and Wheeler appeared and made a few remarks. They received an enthusiastic welcome.

Text of Letter of Acceptance.

Senator Wheeler's letter of acceptance, addressed to William H. Johnson, head of the sub-committee that tendered the nomination, was as follows:

After careful consideration I have concluded to accept the honor your committee so generously conferred on me by tendering to me the nomination for Vice President as the running mate of the Hon. Robert M. La Follette, candidate for President of the United States.

I have had no desire, as you know, to become a candidate for any office in the approaching election, but have decided that it is my duty to accept your call because it appears to me that by so doing I can best serve the highest interests of the American people.

I regret exceedingly that the Democratic Party in the recent National Convention in New York so completely lost sight of the fundamental principles of democracy and ignored the great economic issues of the present hour. It has wantonly abandoned an opportunity for great public service that never before was so clearly within its reach and so certain to lead to success.

While the farmers of the entire nation are facing bankruptcy, labor unemployed, business depressed and a large majority of our citizens suffering from sinister exploitation, the Republican and Democratic Parties in convention ignored the call of the unorganized millions who are the victims of the present economic disorders and chose leaders whose training, whose sympathies and whose social and political association are with the great predatory interests.

Assails Coolidge and Davis.

Every Democratic leader in and out of Congress has proclaimed the Democratic Party free from the taint of Wall Street and has blamed with some degree of truth the financial interests centred there, but whose ramifications extend far beyond, for the corruption in the Republican Administration and for the discriminatory legislation against the common people of America.

What are the people to think when these same men in convention assembled select as the standard-bearer of their party an attorney who represents these interests, who lives and associates with them, and who typifies all that big business stands for, just as much and just as truly as does the Republican nominee?

In this situation I find myself unable to support either the Republican candidates, who frankly admit their reactionary standpat policy, or the Democratic candidate, who may claim in well chosen phrases that he is a Progressive, but whose training and constant association belie any such pretension.

Between Davis and Coolidge there is only a choice for conservatives to make. The uncontrolled, liberal and Progressive forces must look elsewhere for leadership.

This is a time when every one who claims to be a Progressive must show his colors, must support the candidacy of Robert M. La Follette and the genuinely Progressive program, or else forever disclaim any pretense to Progressive political action. It is our duty to our country to give [illegible] Progressive and liberal forces [illegible]

Catholic Church Denies Its Sacraments To French Women in Decollete Attire

Special Cable to THE NEW YORK TIMES.

PARIS, July 19.—The Catholic Church, despite the fact that only recently Cardinal du Bois failed signally in a similar effort, has declared war on women's décolleté attire. The battle cry appears this week in the Semaine Religieuse, published by Clermont Ferrand, and the general orders are as follows:

"The ever-growing indecency of the modes of women's costumes, which are suppressing sleeves and increasing the décolleté style, and the disregard with which certain women enter church in a costume unworthy of a Christian, and even dare to approach the holy altar, obliges us to call on priests to publish the following advice:

"Immodesty in dress, which is always reprehensible, is particularly so in holy places; it is for this reason that all persons appearing in insufficient costume and exposing themselves shall be invited to leave the church.

"The sacraments must be refused to all women and girls who present themselves at confession or at the holy altar in indecent costumes—décolleté corsage or sleeves not covering the elbows.

"Concerning the refusal of the holy eucharist, the priest, without saying why, must pass before the incorrectly dressed woman without giving her holy communion.

"The priest of a person who has thus been refused communion and who can later find occasion to give her paternal aumonition must never fail to perform this act of charity."

The Paris papers, commenting on the orders this afternoon, recall the vain effort of the Cardinal of Paris to increase the volume of material in women's costumes, with the result that there was a drop in church attendance at the French capital.

Greek Vanity Case of 500 B. C. Is Found In Tomb Unearthed in Southern Russia

ODESSA, July 19 (Associated Press)—One hundred and sixty ancient Greek tombs of striking design and rare archaeological interest have been unearthed in the dead city of Olyva, near here, by Professor Semenov Zusser, a distinguished Russian archaeologist.

Among the articles found in the tombs was a small linen bag containing a mirror and believed to be the forerunner of the present-day vanity case. In the bag there also were a rouge-stick for the lips and a charcoal pencil for the eyebrows. The bag was found in a woman's grave with tufts of false hair and a number of silver bracelets, earrings, beads and other jewels.

In other tombs were discovered pottery of exquisite workmanship, multi-colored vases, amulets, knives and various articles of bronze and copper, all in a perfect state of preservation.

The excavations, which have been in progress for many months, thus far have yielded more than 1,700 articles of surpassing antiquarian interest.

Olyva, which means "merry," was once a centre of Greek learning, culture and trade, and flourished about 500 B. C. Later it became known among Russians as the "Pompeii of the Black Sea."

Greek emigrants from Asia Minor selected Olyva, Herodotus records, because "it is free from malaria, and its air is pure and transparent as crystal." From a thriving, prosperous port for the rich goods of the East, it became in the course of centuries a pauper colony existing solely on the revenue from occasional traders. Originally the population of the city worshipped the Greek gods, in whose honor they erected temples. Today [illegible] ruins, and the [illegible] by Professor Zusser are [illegible] witnesses to its past greatness.

"All the News That's Fit to Print."

The New York Times.

THE WEATHER
Unsettled today; showers this afternoon; tomorrow partly cloudy.
Temperature Yesterday—Max. 80, min. 61.
For weather report see next to last page.

VOL. LXXIII....No. 24,292. NEW YORK, MONDAY, JULY 28, 1924. TWO CENTS In Greater New York | THREE CENTS Within 200 Miles | FOUR CENTS Elsewhere

LOEB 'MASTER MIND' OF FRANKS SLAYING, ALIENISTS REPORT

Leopold His Mental Slave in Burglaries, Arson and Murder, Defense Specialists Assert.

LONG DREAMED OF CRIME

Murder Plot Was Formed While Returning From Robbery of Loeb's Fraternity House

LACK NORMAL EMOTIONS

Both Mentally Irresponsible From Early Youth, Psychiatrists Find—Had No Sentiment.

Special to The New York Times.

CHICAGO, July 27.—Richard A. Loeb was the "master mind," Nathan F. Leopold Jr. was a mental slave, according to the psychiatric report, based on their examination of the slayers of Robert Franks by Dr. Karl M. Bowman of Boston and Dr. H. S. Hulbert of Oak Park, defense alienists, which was made public tonight.

From early youth the two have been mentally irresponsible, the report states, and early this mental failing swerved into the pathway of crime. Petty thefts led to burglaries on a large scale, to setting houses on fire. Then it led to death plots. And always it was Loeb who led Leopold, who gloried in being the follower, the alienists assert.

There was no sentimentality in their search for the "supreme adventure" of killing of a fellow human being. Often the thought entered into the mind of Loeb of killing Leopold, and Leopold believed that some day he might kill Loeb.

But if either did that, half the thrill would be missing. There would be none to share it, and there was no great glory in killing if no one else knew—if there was no one else to admire.

Discussed Killing Loeb's Brother.

When the idea of the combined crime of kidnapping and murder came to them last Fall, the first plan was to kill a mutual friend, Richard Ruben, but the boy's father might not come across with a large enough ransom, they thought, so they abandoned him.

They thought of "Tommy" Loeb, Richard Loeb's brother. They even talked of making their own fathers victims of the plot which should satisfy the torturing craving to kill some one. But that would be too close to home. They were practical, not sentimental.

First in the list of emotions that moved these two to kill was the pleasure to be gained from the act, the report sets forth. Notoriety was secondary, though the added thrill of seeing the details of their crime, of seeing "lesser minds" running about seeking a solution in vain, and knowing all the time that they alone held the key to the mystery, was a mighty urge. Lastly, there was the money.

Last Fall, when the thought of killing a boy first came to them, the two had gone to Ann Arbor, armed with burglars' tools, and had entered and robbed Loeb's fraternity house. On the return journey the plan which resulted in the death of Robert Franks seven months later began to crystallize. Loeb did the planning.

Ever since babyhood, almost, he had had dreams of being a master mind of crime. He had dreamed of himself behind prison bars and had found the fantasy not unpleasant because he was being looked at in his cell by an admiring world. The murder was to be just such a crime as the pair had talked of in their flights of imagination.

Neither Afraid to Die.

Reading the story of a criminal who kidnapped a little boy and held him in a padded room of the attic in the boy's home, the alienists reported, set the germ of the Franks murder in Loeb's mind. "I think this started me off on the whole thing," he told his examiners.

Intellectually superior to the average youth, the two are emotionally far below normal, and Loeb especially is almost devoid of emotions, according to the alienists. Loeb, in actual physical encounter, is cowardly. Yet he is of the type that sets off into certain danger, perhaps involving loss of life, without a tremor of fear.

Either Leopold or Loeb would die on the gallows without any more feeling than they displayed when killing Robert Franks, in the estimation of their examiners.

Would Loeb go through with the killing of another boy, provided he were released and had reason to believe he might escape punishment? He would, he says, if he were sure he could get the money. But the money is the lesser motive.

"I killed because I wanted to," is his reason.

In describing the actual act of striking young Franks, Loeb said:

"He was hit on the head several times. He bled. * * * I got great excitement, great heart beating which was pleasant. I was cool and self-possessed. I had quite a time quieting down Leopold. I cooled him down in five minutes after we got him [Franks] into the back seat, thinking him still alive.

"'He bled,' Leopold said. 'This is terrible. This is terrible.' I told him it was all right and laughed and joked, possibly to calm myself, too."

Leopold has done what he has because he acknowledges no other law than his own desire. Loeb acted because, though he recognized the rights of others, he believed himself so superior to them that he didn't need to obey them.

Loeb play-acted. He pretended to himself and to others. He called himself a bootlegger, flourished a pistol, told tales of shooting up a saloon, just to impress a girl. He pictured himself as the detective as well as the criminal.

Continued on Page Two.

Train and Auto in Collision; Engine Wrecked, Four Die

PHILADELPHIA, July 27.—One man, two women and a boy were killed and five other persons were injured when a Reading train crashed into an automobile tonight at Willow Grove Park crossing, on the outskirts of the city.

Those killed were Mrs. Morris Stein, Mrs. Helen Morningstar, the latter's son, Jerome Morningstar, and George Maxheimer, engineer of the train. Four of the injured are badly hurt.

Witnesses said that Mrs. Julius Stein, who was driving the automobile, became confused as she approached the crossing or that the brakes of her car failed to hold. Application of the emergency brakes by the engineer caused the rails to spread, derailing the locomotive, tender and two cars. The locomotive turned over on its side and was wrecked. None of the passengers was hurt.

The Steins and Morningstars, who were related, had just started for a drive through the country.

FLIERS TO HOP OFF AGAIN WEDNESDAY

World-Girdling Squadron Will Go to Kirkwall as First Stopping Point.

NAVAL CHAIN NEARLY READY

Lieut. Smith Expects Favorable Weather—Ice Fields Predicted for Them Off Greenland.

By Wireless to THE NEW YORK TIMES.

HULL, England, July 27.—The plans of the six American world fliers for the resumption of their journey home are now complete. Tomorrow the floats which have been fitted to the three airplanes at Brough will be tested in the Humber estuary, and the start for Kirkwall will be made Wednesday.

A new type of compass, invented and made in this country, has been installed in the machines to overcome oscillation.

Lieutenant Lowell H. Smith stated this evening that Major H. C. Davidson, air attaché at the American Embassy in London, already is in Kirkwall, the fliers' first stopping place, making arrangements for the escort of American naval ships, which, Lieutenant Smith is informed, will include an American cruiser expected to arrive off Scotland within the next few hours. The naval escort will be at hand between Kirkwall and Rejkyavik, Iceland, and also from there to Greenland, Newfoundland and America.

"We expect that Boston will be our first place of call if we succeed in reaching America," Lieutenant Smith said. "We have taken the most painstaking measures to insure our success, even to suitable clothes for the climate we have to pass through. In my judgment, everything, including the weather, will be in our favor. Our worst and most perilous stretch will be between Greenland and Labrador, but we shall have cruisers, destroyers and various other types of naval boats to help us, and shall do no flying in darkness.

"On the way North to Kirkwall, we shall keep to the coast. The Italian airman will not fly with us, but will follow in our wake, and we shall help him all we can with supplies and repairs from our bases."

Lieutenant Smith in his reference to the Italian airman was speaking of Lieutenant Locatelli, who is flying from Pisa to Spitzbergen, along the route of the Americans, in preparation for his attempted expedition to the North Pole by air next year.

HALIFAX, N. S., July 27 (Associated Press).—The special American torpedo-boat destroyer division, under Commander Russell Willson, which is on its way to Labrador to meet the army fliers homeward bound from their round-the-world flight, swung quietly at anchor today awaiting sailing orders from the cruiser Milwaukee, which tonight was nearing Hawkes Bay, Newfoundland.

While the weather yesterday was clear and hot, today the sky was overcast and the air chilly. Fog was reported hovering seaward. No information has come through from the north as to weather and water conditions in and around Labrador, Greenland and Iceland. Seafaring men here express the belief that the destroyers will meet some ice fields, especially off Greenland, the waters of which are to be patrolled for the safety of the fliers.

Naval air service officers on the Milwaukee will survey Hawkes Bay to find an anchorage for the planes, and after establishing it will proceed to Cartwright Bay and thence to Indian Harbor for the same purpose. Because of the necessity of these surveys and

Continued on Page Five.

BANDITS KIDNAP GIRL, HOLD UP THREE AUTOS ON LONG ISLAND ROAD

Young Woman Torn Screaming From Escort and Taken to Woods in Robbers' Sedan.

RESCUED AFTER A BATTLE

One Highwayman Is Caught and the Other Wounded as He Disappears in Flight.

ONE OF THEIR VICTIMS SHOT

Captive Forced to Drive Car to Jamaica, Where He Is Held in $75,000 Bail.

William Steffen, a 21-year-old Manhasset youth, was held in $75,000 bail in Jamaica yesterday charged with being one of two auto bandits who held up three different automobile parties on lonely roads outside Jamaica within an hour late Saturday night.

In the first of the three raids Henry Steger of Ridgewood, Queens, was shot through the knee. In the last, Helen Scheffield of Bayside, 17, was abducted but later rescued in a woods where a second bandit escaped after being wounded by police gunfire. Police said they had since learned his name.

Both Miss Scheffield's rescue and Steffen's arrest were largely due to the quick thinking of the girl's escort, Albert Wilson of Flushing. Wilson and Miss Scheffield were motoring along the East Alley Road when they were overtaken by a speedy sedan at Little Neck Road, back of Creedmoor, a short distance from Queens Village. The sedan forced them to the side of the road, and the couple found themselves covered by revolvers in the hands of two young men they said wore white handkerchiefs across the lower parts of their faces.

Couple Forced to Alight.

Brought to a stop, the bewildered young people were forced to alight and, while one of their captors stood guard, the other appropriated their valuables. Wilson yielded $17. Miss Scheffield parted with two schoolgirl rings, a new bracelet and a vanity case.

The hold-up men, with an exchange of looks, began to quicken their movements, but not, Wilson observed with misgiving, with apparent intention of departing. One reached into Wilson's car and removed the key from the ignition switch. The other man stepped roughly between Wilson and Helen Scheffield. Wilson squared off, but the confederate pinned him from behind, threw him aside, and then jumped to the assistance of the man who was wrestling the girl into the sedan. Wilson sprang up, only to be halted by a blaze of revolver shots fired into the ground at his feet. The sedan shot into a dirt lane, which tunneled through a woods, and disappeared with the screaming girl.

Wilson found a telephone in a farmhouse several furlongs further on, where his alarm was relayed to Patrolman Henry J. Tideman on duty at a police booth in Queens Village. Jotting down the directions the frantic young man cried out to him over the wire, Tideman started to the rescue in a motor he commandeered from Charles H. Evanson of Ozone Park. Tideman and Evanson picked up Wilson at the entrance to the woods.

Guerrilla Car Located.

Evanson drove full speed through the twists and turns of the sylvan trail, the car rocking from side to side, and after about a mile the headlights suddenly picked up the guerrilla car, standing under the trees some fifty yards ahead. Two dim figures were just pushing a slight girlish figure in a light colored dress into the car.

The two figures seemed to run in front of their car. Revolvers flashed. Bullets began whistling past the pursuers. Tideman let himself out on Evanson's runningboard, and, hanging by one hand, leaned far out to return the fire. One of the defenders ran. Evanson threw on the brake enough for Tideman to jump off. Steadying himself, the policeman loosed one quick burst at the fugitive plunging into the underbrush. There was a sharp cry of pain, Tideman recalled, a stumble, then the man got back into his stride and vanished.

His companion took to the woods in the other direction but was caught by Tideman, who subdued him after a sharp fight. Lined up in the glare of the headlights he proved to be Steffen, police said.

Miss Scheffield was hysterical, her dress torn in the struggle she had made against her abductors. She was taken to her home in Evanson's car, while Tideman with drawn revolver forced Steffen to drive to Jamaica.

At Jamaica, Tideman found that two other parties had been made the victims

Continued on Page Six.

Supposed Bell Clapper From Babylon Proves to Be Sceptre of a King of Ur

PHILADELPHIA, July 27.—What Babylonian scholars have regarded as the clapper of a bell since it was found at Nippur in 1907 has proved to be a priceless treasure—the bronze sceptre of King Dungi of Ur, who ruled in 2270 B. C., the University of Pennsylvania Museum announced.

The sceptre was found by the archaeologists of the University Museum. It was supposed to be a bell clapper with a broken shaft. It weighs ten ounces and is six inches in length, with cuneiform inscriptions at the enlarged end. When the bronze piece was held as though it were suspended in a bell none of the scholars could read the inscription. The object was placed in the vault at the museum with other Babylonian material for further study, remaining there seventeen years.

Recently when Dr. Leon Legrain, curator of the Babylonian section, was cleaning the collection he chanced to pick up the supposed clapper and hold it as though it were a blackjack. In this position the cuneiform was decipherable. He instantly recognized the word "Dungi." Then began the task of deciphering the entire inscription, which states that it is the royal sceptre of the ruler of Ur. This is followed by the name of the King, Dungi.

Mrs. Ferguson Second to Klan's Man in Texas; May Run Off in Final Primary for Governor

DALLAS, Texas, July 27.—The probability that a woman would contest in the run-off primary on Aug. 23 for the Democratic nomination for Governor against the Ku Klux Klan candidate developed tonight when Mrs. Miriam A. Ferguson of Temple, the first woman candidate for Governor in the history of Texas, took the lead over Lynch Davidson of Houston for second place in yesterday's Democratic primary.

Judge Felix Robertson of Dallas, who was endorsed by the Klan, continued to pile up a lead for first place.

The count for the three leaders announced by the Election Bureau at 6 P. M. was as follows: Felix Robertson, 91,155; Mrs. Ferguson, 72,419, and Lynch Davidson, 68,502.

Senator Morris Sheppard, seeking re-election, had a majority of 73,128 over Fred W. Davis of Austin, Senator Sheppard having 117,141 to Mr. Davis's 44,013. John F. Maddox, the third Senatorial candidate, had received 20,368 votes.

Returns still were meagre in the Congressional race, but the incumbents probably all had been renominated.

For Lieutenant Governor, W. C. Edwards, publisher of The Denton Record and Chronicle, had a lead of 3,148 over Barry Miller of Dallas.

Mrs. Ferguson is the wife of ex-Governor James E. Ferguson, who was impeached by the State Senate on Sept. 22, 1917, when ten of twenty-one charges against him were sustained. The ten charges had to do with monetary affairs, the principal being that he used $5,600 of State funds to pay a personal note.

Governor Ferguson was violently opposed to the Ku Klux Klan. In 1918 he opened a campaign for the office from which he had been removed, and formed the American Party in opposition to the Democratic organization. He was defeated.

In February, 1922, ex-Governor Ferguson announced the dissolution of the American Party, proclaimed his return to the Democratic fold and announced his candidacy for the seat in the United States Senate then held by Charles A. Culberson. One of the bitterest political fights in the history of Texas followed. The State law in Texas provides that a Democratic candidate must certify that he supported the party's candidates in the last election. Mr. Ferguson could not do this, but his wife could, and she entered the race. At the time he said:

"If it should develop that the committee arbitrarily bars my name I will continue on the stump for my wife, explaining to the people of Texas that I will be her private secretary if she is elected, with full privileges of the floor of the Senate."

Earl B. Mayfield, the Klan candidate, led the primaries, with ex-Governor Ferguson more than 20,000 votes behind.

CHEAP TAXIS SEND CITY ON A JOY RIDE

Tremendous Demand for Cabs Yesterday by Cooperative Parties at 4 Cents a Mile Each.

GO TO PARKS AND BEACHES

Cut-Rate Company Reports an Epidemic of Punctures—War on Dishonest Chauffeurs.

New York City taxied yesterday as if that method of transportation were mandatory. The demand for taxicabs operating on the cut-rate scale of 20 cents a mile or 10 cents a half mile began when parties of five or six, starting out to enjoy the Sunday holiday, discovered that entire groups could ride for the 20-cent flat fare.

The discovery that five men in a 20-cents-a-mile taxicab could ride a half mile at the rate of 2 cents each and a mile at the rate of 4 cents each resulted in a record Sunday demand for taxicabs. The 20-cents-a-mile cabs were in greater evidence than on any preceding day since the taxicab cut-rate war began.

Cabs of all the operating companies that have slashed rates were seen anywhere and everywhere. Taxi riders visited Central Park in greater numbers than ever before.

In the course of a band concert on the Mall of Central Park parties of taxi riders passed back and forth two or three times. Taxicabs of the 20-cent operators were hired by riders who wished to visit Coney Island and the Westchester beaches on Long Island Sound.

Prefer Taxi to Roller Coaster.

At Coney Island a party, upon finding that it was cheaper to ride in a taxicab than on a roller coaster for the same distance, stuck to their cab. Parties of five and six in taxicabs were seen as far out as Long Beach and Patchogue.

One of the taxicab operators said the cooperative riders greatly outnumbered the single passengers using taxicabs yesterday.

The taxicabs of the Mogul Checker Cab Corporation, the United States Cab Corporation and the Luxor and Premier taxicab companies were in great demand, because the cabs of those operators are the ones that have posted the 20-cents-a-mile rates on the sides of the cabs.

"Last night we totaled receipts of four taxicabs operating on the night shift and found that the amount was $83.60," said Jerome T. Davis, sales manager of the Luxor Cab Manufacturing Company. "The same cabs earned a total on the day shift of $48.35, or a total of $131.95 for the entire twenty-four hours. That is an average of $32.99 for each of the four taxicabs, as against $23 they earned formerly at the higher rate, which resulted in from 50 to 60 per cent. 'dead mileage.'

An Epidemic of Punctures

"Our cabs have increased their revenue in a most gratifying manner despite what seems to be an epidemic of tire trouble. Our cabs have been crippled repeatedly by punctures from tacks and nails. We are at a loss to explain why we should encounter such an epidemic at this time."

The Commissioner of Licenses, according to Mr. Davis and other 20-cent operating companies, has promised to deal rigidly with drivers found guilty of fraudulent practices. A case was discovered by a taxicab patron who rides from Broadway and Seventh Avenue to Twenty-second Street between Eighth and Ninth Avenues nightly when he goes home. Before the rate war started he was accustomed to pay 50 cents for the trip, approximately one mile. Last Friday night he entered a cut-rate taxicab and was charged 33 cents for the trip. Saturday night he entered supposedly a 20-cent-a-mile taxicab and the driver demanded 60 cents.

When the passenger protested against that charge the driver called his attention to a sign which read, in diminutive letters, "This cab is not operating at," and in large display letters, "20 cents a mile." When the passenger threatened to report the driver to the company, the chauffeur answered by saying he owned his own cab and that he had to make a living, so he would charge what he pleased.

"Then I'll report you to the Commis-

Continued on Page Two.

DAVIS SPEECH TOUR BEGINS ABOUT SEPT. 1

Nominee Completes Acceptance Address—Starts Back From Maine Wednesday.

WILL SCAN CAMPAIGN PLANS

Friends Tell Him La Follette's Campaign Will Seriously Hurt Coolidge in the West.

Special to The New York Times.

DARK HARBOR, Me., July 27.—John W. Davis, Democratic nominee for President, will have his personal campaign headquarters "in the saddle" after the first of September, and until that time will have his base in his home at Locust Valley, L. I., except for a short visit to his former home, in Clarksburg, W. Va., to deliver his acceptance speech on Aug. 11.

Mr. Davis indicated this today. Although no details of his campaign trips have been arranged, it is considered certain that he will start his speaking campaign soon after Sept. 1.

Greatly rested by his stay at the home of Mr. and Mrs. Charles Dana Gibson on Seven Hundred Acre Island, Mr. Davis probably will leave here for New York on Wednesday. He had intended to return on Thursday, but there are so many details of campaign organization and methods requiring his attention that he has about made up his mind to return a day earlier.

Acceptance Speech Completed.

The nominee completed the tentative draft of his acceptance speech last night. This will be sent to New York to be put into type before his return, and probably will be revised and corrected in the proof before it is given out in advance to newspapers and press associations.

Mr. Davis received today a letter from Clem L. Shaver, Chairman of the Democratic National Committee, reporting progress in the formation of a campaign organization. Mr. Shaver will have complete charge of the direction of the campaign, as Mr. Davis considers it his task to present the case of the national ticket to the people. The nominee, however, will have a large part in determining the campaign organization, methods and policies at the start, and it is expected that these matters will be settled after his return to New York and before his departure for Clarksburg, which probably will be on Saturday, Aug. 9.

Friends of Mr. Davis who have visited him during the last week have been greatly encouraged by the developments since the national convention. The nominee has been informed that a hasty survey of the situation has indicated that the La Follette ticket will have great strength in the Middle West and that President Coolidge is not at all likely to have a majority of the electoral college.

Supporters of Mr. Davis have expressed belief that a growing realization of the probability that Senator La Follette may carry enough States to throw the election into the House of Representatives will tend to bring increasing conservative support to Mr. Davis, on the theory that he, and not President Coolidge, is the only candidate who will have a chance to get a majority of the electoral vote.

Mr. Davis Attends Church.

Accompanied by Mr. and Mrs. Gibson, Mr. and Mrs. Davis again attended Christ Church today. Being a Presbyterian instead of an Episcopalian, Mr. Davis left the church after the sermon, while Mrs. Davis remained for communion.

The Rev. Dr. S. S. Drury, of St. Paul's school, Concord, N. H., preached on the necessity of becoming "soldiers of Christ."

"The reason why we are not real soldiers of Christ is because we are materialists," Dr. Drury said. "A materialist is not one who does not believe in the spiritual; he is one who puts God in second place."

"I wonder if we are ever going to be near Jesus Christ as long as we worship the security that lies in our strong boxes. The reason we are not actual disciples of Jesus Christ is because we worship things. We are acquisitive and we worship things, and we put ideals in second place. The thing that amazes me is the lack of principle in prosperous America."

Mr. Davis's visitors today were Colonel William A. Gaston and Arthur Lyman of Massachusetts, and Cyrus H. K. Curtis, the publisher. Mr. Curtis, who has a Summer home at Camden, made a social call on Mr. and Mrs. Davis.

SOCIALISTS NAME THOMAS AS HEAD OF STATE TICKET

Former Assistant Pastor in Fifth Avenue Church Is Nominated for Governor.

SOLOMON IN SECOND PLACE

Congressional Choices Left to State Committee and Local Organizations.

BAR OLD PARTY NOMINEES

Resolutions Condemn the Ku Klux Klan and Mobilization Day Movement.

The Rev. Norman Thomas, former assistant pastor of the Brick Presbyterian Church in Fifth Avenue, was nominated as candidate for Governor by the State convention of the Socialist Party in Finnish Hall, Fifth Avenue and 127th Street yesterday. The whole ticket named by the convention, which adjourned last night after having been in session for two days, was:

Governor—The Rev. NORMAN THOMAS, Manhattan.

Lieutenant Governor—CHARLES SOLOMON, Brooklyn.

Secretary of State—FRANK R. CROSSWAITHE, a negro, Manhattan.

State Controller—Mrs. THERESA B. WILEY, Schenectady.

State Treasurer—FRANK EHRENFRIED, Buffalo.

Attorney General—LOUIS WALDMAN, Manhattan.

State Engineer and Surveyor—Professor VLADIMIR G. KARAPETOFF of Cornell University.

There was a long fight over requiring Socialist Party nominations for Congress in districts where there was no candidate endorsed by the Conference for Progressive Political Action. A resolution eventually was adopted permitting the State Executive Committee with the district organizations, to decide whether or not a Socialist candidate shall be named. In no event, however, are the Republican or Democratic candidates for Congress to be endorsed by the Socialist Party.

This action, it was pointed out, would apply in the case of Major F. H. LaGuardia. Should he be nominated for Congress by the Republicans he would not receive the support of the Socialist Party, but it need not necessarily name some one to run against him. Should he cut loose from his past Republican affiliations and become a candidate on the La Follette ticket he would then be eligible for endorsement by the Socialists.

Mr. Hillquit Declines.

Louis Waldman was named Chairman of the convention at yesterday's session and Fred A. Sander of Syracuse Vice Chairman, replacing, respectively, Algernon Lee and Charles P. Noonan, who served at the opening session Saturday.

As soon as the nominations were reached Municipal Court Justice Jacob Pankin presented the name of Morris Hillquit as the gubernatorial candidate. Mr. Hillquit promptly declined.

"Your leader must be one who can give his whole time and attention to the campaign and I cannot," he said. "It also would be ill advised for me to accept, as I was your representative at the Cleveland meeting of the Conference for Progressive Political Action and I would not give our opponents the chance to say that I was using that movement to further my own political preferment."

Mr. Thomas was then named by St. John Block and the nomination was made unanimously.

Before Mr. Solomon was nominated as the candidate for Lieutenant Governor, the name of Harriot Stanton Blatch was presented. Mrs. Blatch's name was withdrawn after the reading of a telegram from her in which she said she could not accept.

A contest over the nomination for Attorney General developed between Mr. Waldman and Darwin J. Meserole of Sullivan County, who, it was said, had refused to accept a nomination for the Supreme Court bench because he expected to be named at the convention yesterday. He received eleven votes to twenty-one for Waldman. Mr. Hillquit and H. D. Wilcox of Elmira were both placed in nomination and both declined to be candidates.

A resolution was adopted which "calls attention to the grave danger of the development of a pernicious and dangerous militarism embodied in the plans for a so-called 'Mobilization Day.'"

"We declare," the resolution read, "that this mobilization is part of the program of militarism that is gradually eating away the opposition of the people

Continued on Page Three.

Russia Faces Sugar Famine With Failure of Beet Crop

MOSCOW, July 27.—Soviet Russia is confronted with another famine in the form of an acute sugar shortage, due to the failure of the beet root crop in Ukrainia. While it is not of the same proportions as the threatened wheat famine, seven of the largest factories in the Kief and Kursk districts have been forced to suspend work owing to lack of raw material.

The Government has arranged to receive large quantities of refined sugar from abroad, including the United States, and to safeguard the public interest the Government will regulate the supply and price of the sugar.

The re-establishment of sugar refineries such as existed before the war, in contemplation by the Government for some time, has been abandoned until next year.

SENATOR LODGE ILL, IS OPERATED UPON

Reported in Serious Condition From Bladder Trouble in Cambridge Hospital.

STRICKEN IN NAHANT HOME

Latest Public Appearance Was at the Cleveland Convention, Where He Suffered Rebuff.

Special to The New York Times.

BOSTON, July 27.—A sudden and unexpected operation was performed on Senator Henry Cabot Lodge today at the Charlesgate Hospital in Cambridge for the removal of an obstruction in the bladder

Tonight, being 74 years old, he is in a serious condition, but his physicians believe he will pull through. Dr. John H. Cunningham, the Back Bay surgeon who operated, made this statement:

"It is a serious situation. I believe Senator Lodge will be all right, but nothing much can be told for another twenty-four to forty-eight hours.

To that declaration, made early in the evening not long after the Senator had come off the operating table, Dr. Cunningham added at 11 o'clock tonight:

"Everything is satisfactory."

Senator Lodge's ailment was said to be one not uncommon in men of his age and one of which his physicians had been aware for some time. But the unexpectedly acute stage which came without warning this morning had become so serious by the time Dr. Frederick Winslow of 275 Clarendon Street, Back Bay, had arrived at his bedside at Nahant that he at once entered into consultation by telephone with Dr. Cunningham, who was at his Summer home in Wareham.

Dr. Cunningham advised that the patient be removed to the Charlesgate Hospital at once and agreed himself to hasten thither ready to operate at once if that should be found imperative.

Senator Lodge, accompanied by his son, Henry Cabot Lodge Jr., was driven to the hospital from Nahant in an automobile, declining to go in an ambulance, although his suffering was acute. The Senator displayed a degree of courage that aroused the admiration of those attending him and cheerfully submitted himself to preparations for surgical treatment.

It was nearly 5 o'clock this afternoon when Dr. Cunningham, with Dr. Winslow, also in the operating room, began to operate. Within a short time after the Senator had been wheeled to a bed he regained consciousness and it was then that the surgeon announced the gravity of the patient's condition and made known his inability to forecast the outcome with certainty.

A second operation may be necessary before the patient can be discharged, it was said, but this possibility, not unusual in such cases, is not of itself considered a menace. The prognosis in Senator Lodge's case, his physicians said, would depend very largely on his vitality and recuperative power. In this respect his chances are considered excellent for a man of his age, particularly in view of the undaunted spirit in which he faced the ordeal.

News that Senator Lodge's illness, of which some of his intimates had known in a vague way, had reached the stage where immediate surgical measures were necessary was communicated only to a few relatives and close friends. Later it came with a shock to the general public in Boston and its suburbs with the appearance of early editions of Monday's newspapers.

Even with the most favorable progress it is expected that Senator Lodge

Continued on Page Three.

Coolidge Plans to Finish Speech This Week; George Harvey Consulted Often Recently

WASHINGTON, July 27.—Concentrated effort will be applied by President Coolidge this week to his notification address in the hope that he may be able to complete it by the end of the week or by early next week at the latest.

The notification ceremonies still are eighteen days away, but Mr. Coolidge would like to be able to place the prepared address in the hands of newspaper editors at least a week in advance of delivery.

Executive business has lessened considerably since the adjournment of Congress, but it still requires so much attention that about the only time the President will have to work on his speech is the early morning before his day's engagements begin and portions of the afternoons. His secretaries plan to restrict his engagements somewhat this week to afford him more time.

Much of the work preliminary to the address already has been done, and Mr. Coolidge is almost ready to start the writing of the speech. It was learned today that George Harvey, former Ambassador to Great Britain, has had several conferences recently with the President, but whether these related to the notification address has not been disclosed.

Sunday was spent very quietly at the White House. The President and Mrs. Coolidge, with their son John and Frank W. Stearns, attended services at the First Congregational Church, where the Coolidges worship, and listened to a sermon by the Rev. Arthur C. Hill of Glasgow, Scotland, a visiting minister.

Mrs. Coolidge and John took a short automobile ride late in the day, but the President was unable to join them because of a conference he held with Acting Secretary Grew of the State Department, the subject of which was not announced.

MACDONALD PRESSES TO HAVE THE FRENCH EVACUATE THE RUHR

Herriot Said to Have Decided to Defy Poincare and Consider Early Withdrawal.

HE POSTPONES HIS RETURN

Full Conference to Discuss Invitation to Germans Today, Probably on Equality Basis.

AMERICANS WILL EXPLAIN

Resent Interpretation of Bankers' Action as Effort to Advance Their Political Views.

Special Cable to THE NEW YORK TIMES.

LONDON, July 27.—The interallied conference will resume active work tomorrow after a week-end that was for most of the delegates a welcome interval for rest and reflection. Naturally informal conversations have been continued wherever the delegates met, but it will not be clear until tomorrow whether the chances of agreement are much greater than they were on Friday. Hope is expressed that the conference will be over by the end of this week.

At the plenary session to be held tomorrow afternoon the question of inviting the German representatives to come immediately will be considered, and it is probable that the decision the conference will take on this matter will be largely determined at the preparatory meeting of the heads of delegations which will be held at 10 Downing Street in the morning.

The proposal to invite the Germans now is regarded as a sign that there is hope of the Allies reaching an agreement within the next day or two on the questions still in dispute. Premature optimism is, however, to be discounted.

Indications that the question of the military evacuation of the Ruhr may also be dealt with seriously in this conference have aroused some disquiet in French circles. Premier MacDonald is reported to have expressed to Premier Herriot his desire that the military evacuation of the Ruhr should be completed by next January, when the British occupying forces are expected to leave Cologne.

Report Herriot Has Decided.

The diplomatic correspondent of The Daily Telegraph writes:

"During the week-end the whole outlook of the allied conference has undergone a remarkable and welcome transformation, largely due to the decision of Premier Herriot to ignore the threats of the Nationalist opposition in France. M. Herriot has agreed that the German Government, subject to the approval of the plenary conference, should be invited to send its delegates to London forthwith, and that on such main issues as measures for restoring the financial and economic unity of Germany, or in other words, the economic evacuation of the Ruhr, the German delegates should enjoy the right of free discussion with the Allies on the proposed agreements that the early military evacuation of the Ruhr to follow upon economic evacution should be considered by the allied Governments and discussed by the occupying powers and Germany.

"It required a good deal of courage on the part of M. Herriot to act as he has acted, for these decisions of his have been preceded by an informal ultimatum in regard to three points conveyed to him on behalf of M. Poincaré, in which M. Herriot was warned that he must expect the most stubborn opposition if he did not adhere to the following among other three conditions: (a) Germany should not be admitted to the conference on terms of equality; (b) the principle of dilution of the German personnel in the Rhineland by means of allied railway men should be maintained; (c) no definite dates should be fixed for economic evacuation.

"The decision to meet the Germans on the main issues on what is virtually a footing of equality was largely prompted and determined by conversations which M. Herriot and M. Clementel had with Secretary Hughes and Secretary Mellon during the second half of last week, more particularly with Mr Hughes.

"M. Herriot's attitude toward Germany was fully supported by Sir Cecil Hurst and M. Fromageot, who composed the special commission appointed on Thursday.

"M. Herriot's second decision, namely, that as to the military evacuation of the Ruhr, was provoked by a letter from Ramsay MacDonald in which the latter on behalf of the British Government suggested to his French colleague in the friendliest manner that the moment had now come when the question of military evacuation of the Ruhr might be raised, since it would be difficult to justify it after economic evacuation had ceased."

The First Committee, which deals with the question of default, will meet tomorrow morning and may possibly have something to report to the plenary session in the afternoon.

At this session the completed report of the Second Committee on the economic evacuation of the Ruhr will also be discussed.

Secretary and Mrs. Hughes spent part of the week-end with Lord and Lady Astor at Cliveden, and this morning motored to Chequers, where they lunched with Premier MacDonald, returning to London later in the day. The American Ambassador was also of the party.

American Attitude To Be Made Clear.

LONDON, July 27 (Associated Press).—Important developments relating to the part the United States has played in the Interallied Conference are expected when the experts who have been dealing with the questions of defaults and sanctions

"All the News That's Fit to Print."

The New York Times.

THE WEATHER
Warmer and unsettled today; tomorrow, probably showers.
Temperature yesterday—Max., 52; Min., 37.
For weather report see Page 33.

VOL. LXXIV....No. 24,517. NEW YORK, TUESDAY, MARCH 10, 1925. TWO CENTS in Greater New York | THREE CENTS Within 200 Miles | FOUR CENTS Elsewhere in the U. S.

REPUBLICANS WIN FIGHT TO DEMOTE SENATE RADICALS

Most Democrats Refrain From Voting as the La Follette Group Is Dropped.

TEST VOTE IS 36 TO 13

Then the Regulars' Committee Assignments Are Put Through by 64 to 11.

BORAH BACKS INSURGENTS

Warns His Party That Its Action Will Spell Disaster to Republicanism.

Special to The New York Times.

WASHINGTON, March 9.—After a battle that raged all day, the Republican regulars of the Senate, aided first by the hands-off attitude of most of the Democratic Senators, and later by their supporting votes, put through this evening the selections they had made of Chairmen and members of committees for the Sixty-ninth Congress, in which the La Follette Senators were dropped to the bottom. action followed a warm contest centring around the action of the regular Republicans in depriving Senator Ladd of North Dakota of a chairmanship and demoting him with the other insurgents.

Senator Borah led the assault on the committee organization program proposed by the majority of his own party. He had begun his contest on Saturday and then caused a postponement of consideration of the committee list until today. His critical remarks on party management at that time were intensified by what he said this afternoon. He was obviously angry when he repeated his warning that the course of the Senate's Republican majority in attempting to inflict punishment on those nominal Republicans who had followed La Follette in the Presidential campaign last year meant trouble for the party.

Last year's election, Mr. Borah declared, was not a victory for the Republican Party but for Calvin Coolidge. The party, he added, was in bad repute with many Republicans in the Northwest and other Western Senators who voted for Coolidge without favoring the party to which he belonged.

The course of the Democrats was outlined by Senator Robinson, the minority floor leader. This battle within the Republican ranks was none of the Democracy's business, he held. The Republicans controlled the Senate; therefore let them assume the responsibility for selecting committee Chairmen and the Republican members of committees. The Democrats would hold aloof and merely record themselves as "present" when the affair concerned a fight in the Republican ranks.

Democrats Answer "Present."

That plan of campaign was adhered to by most of the Democratic Senators when votes were taken. They answered "present" when the question was whether Senator Stanfield of Oregon, regular, or Senator Ladd, La Folletteite, should be elected Chairman of the Committee on Public Lands and Surveys. When the vote was taken Mr. Stanfield got 36 votes, one from a Democrat, and Mr. Ladd 13, two from Democrats, while 25 Democrats and Messrs Stanfield and Ladd voted "present." Three Democrats voted for Senator Jones of New Mexico.

Senator Norris of Nebraska, Mr. Borah's chief lieutenant, made a point of order that with seventy-nine Senators voting Mr. Stanfield could not win with only thirty-six votes. He was overruled by the Chair and decided not to contest the decision.

That finished the fight, and the complete committee slate, assigning Republicans, Democrats, the sole Farmer-Laborite and the insurgents to committee places went through by a big vote, with most of the Democratic Senators sponsoring it.

Senator La Follette, who is in Florida, was put forward in one instance as deserving of better treatment at the hands of the Republican committee-makers, but there was no serious effort in his behalf, although his third party movement in 1924 came in for considerable discussion. The whole contest practically concerned the displacement of Senators Ladd, Brookhart of Iowa and Frazier of North Dakota.

Vote to Displace Ladd.

The vote on the motion to elect Senator Stanfield Chairman of the Committee on Public Lands and Surveys in place of Senator Ladd was as follows:

FOR STANFIELD—36.

Republicans—35.

Bingham,	Gooding,	Pepper,
Butler,	Hale,	Pine,
Cameron,	Harreld,	Reed (Pa.),
Cummins,	Jones (Wash.),	Sackett,
Curtis,	Keyes,	Schall,
Deneen,	McKinley,	Shortridge,
du Pont,	McLean,	Smoot,
Edge,	McNary,	Spencer,
Ernst,	Means,	Wadsworth,
Fess,	Metcalf,	Watson,
Gillett,	Moses,	Willis.
Goff,	Oddie.	

Democrats—1.

Bruce.

FOR LADD—13.

Republicans—8.

Borah,	Howell,	Norbeck
Couzens,	Johnson (Cal.)	Norris.
Fernald,	McMaster,	

Democrats—2.

Copeland, Wheeler.

Farmer-Labor—1.

Shipstead.

La Follette—2.

Brookhart, Frazier.

FOR JONES OF NEW MEXICO—3.

Democrats—3.

Glass, Heflin, Walsh (Mont.)

The twenty-five Democrats who voted "present" were Senators Ashurst, Bay-

Continued on Page Four.

British Adopt Summer Time As a Permanent Institution

LONDON, March 9.—The Government has adopted Summer [Daylight Saving] time as a permanent institution.

There was a private bill before the House of Commons to make Summer time permanent, fixing the yearly period from the beginning of April to the end of October. Sir William Joynson-Hicks, Secretary of State for Home Affairs, announced today that the Government would allow a free vote on the bill and adopt and carry it through as a Government measure.

This means that the bill is certain to become a law.

FIND ROYAL TOMB OF 5,000 YEARS AGO

Americans at Giza Open the Sepulchre of King Sneferu, 3000 B. C., or One of His Circle.

AT BOTTOM OF DEEP SHAFT

Alabaster Coffin and Many Objects Visible—Great Importance Attached to Discovery.

Copyright, 1925, by The New York Times Company. By Wireless to THE NEW YORK TIMES.

CAIRO, March 9.—The Ministry of Public Works issued the following communiqué today:

"The Harvard-Boston expedition working among the Giza pyramids has found an important tomb. The burial chamber is at the bottom of a 150-foot shaft which passes through fissured rock and is not oversafe and possibly will need strutting before the work of clearing can continue. No detailed examination is yet possible, but a plain rectangular alabaster coffin is visible with a number of poles, the tops whereof are covered with gold foil.

"By the side of the coffin is a plank, or at least something resembling a plank, with inlaid inscriptions, among which the Cartouche of Sneferu, first King of the Fourth Dynasty (about 3000 B. C.) and predecessor of Cheops, is distinguishable. Presumably the body within the tomb is of some member of Sneferu's family or one of the high officials, or conceivably that of the King himself.

"The floor of the tomb is covered by a quantity of objects, including alabaster bowls, a copper basin or ewer and remains of heavily gilded chairs. As all the wooded framework of the furniture has disappeared, the ornamentation is very fragile and the task of extraction and preservation will be long and delicate."

Dr. Reisner, head of the expedition, is at present in America and the good fortune of the discovery has fallen to the lot of his assistant, Allen Rowe.

Egyptian and European officials of the Antiquities Department attended the opening yesterday. The great depth of the tomb shaft and the dangerous condition of its sides render inspection by the public impossible.

Budge Believes It Is King's Tomb.

Copyright, 1925, by The New York Times Company. Special Cable to THE NEW YORK TIMES.

LONDON, March 9.—News of the discovery of the tomb at Giza, announced today, was received by Egyptologists in London tonight as of the highest importance. The unusual depth of the shaft is regarded by Sir Wallis Budge, formerly keeper of Egyptian antiquities at the British Museum, as reason for believing the tomb may prove to be of King Sneferu.

Dr. Alan H. Gardiner, on the other hand, is not prepared to indulge this belief in view of the fact that Sneferu hitherto has been supposed to be buried at Medum, where one of his pyramids stands.

Dr. Budge expressed the opinion that the shaft made it "quite likely" the tomb is that of the King. Also, he made a comparison between this and the discovery of the tomb of Tut-ankh-Amen.

"The world, he said, "will remember the excitement caused by that discovery and the joy of finding gilded chairs and couches inlaid with blue glazed porcelain. But these things blinded people to the fact that we have not recovered one historical fact from that tomb. Tut-ankh-Amen was a King of no importance, but in Sneferu we have certainly one of the master builders of Egypt, who may possibly be bracketed with Usertsen III. and Thothmes III. as founders of the empire.

"It is a piece of very good fortune that the discovery was made by careful excavators. From the particulars given it is quite clear this is not the tomb of an ordinary individual, and with a shaft 150 feet deep which is filled with concrete and cement instead of ordinary

Continued on Page Three.

ASK COUZENS TO PAY $10,000,000 IN TAXES; HE CHARGES REVENGE

Treasury Heads Reopen His Sale of Ford Stock, Analyzing Valuation.

DISCIPLINE, SAYS SENATOR

He Lays Demand to His Activity in Investigation—Mellon Upholds Action.

STEEL TAX LOSS ALLEGED

Committee Counsel Contends War Amortization Benefited the Corporation by $21,478,513.

Special to The New York Times.

WAHINGTON, March 9.—James Couzens, formerly one of Henry Ford's associates in the Ford Motor Company, and one of the country's wealthiest men, who now is senior Senator from Michigan, charged on the floor of the Senate this afternoon that in retaliation for the Senate investigation, which he has been conducting into the Bureau of Internal Revenue, the Treasury is now trying to force him to pay between $10,000,000 and $11,000,000 in taxes over and above those he paid when he sold his holdings in the Ford Company to Mr. Ford in 1919.

A letter personally given to him last Saturday by David H. Blair, Commissioner of Internal Revenue, was produced by Senator Couzens. It warned him that, since he had less than a week to come within the statute of limitations in the case, he must sign a waiver or submit to the assessment. Mr. Couzens told the Senate that he had flatly refused to sign such a waiver.

With this letter he displayed to the Senate a memorandum, also presented by Mr. Blair, which stated that although Daniel C. Roper, Internal Revenue Commissioner under the Wilson Administration, had valued the Ford stock at $9,000, it was actually worth then only $2,500, and that because of this striking difference of $6,500 in value, Mr. Couzens and other minority stockholders now owed the Government $35,000,000 in addition to the approximate $20,000,000 which they paid when they turned over their holdings five years ago.

Mellon Explains Memorandum.

Secretary Mellon of the Treasury stated officially tonight that the memorandum came to the Treasury from a "responsible person," and that as the Treasury could not investigate before the statute of limitations expired four days hence, Senator Couzens was asked to sign the waiver, as other minority stockholders had done. Having learned that Senator Couzens had said this afternoon that he would not sign the waiver, it would probably be necessary, the Secretary observed, to "make an arbitrary assessment, but before this assessment is levied Senator Couzens, as any other taxpayer, will be given every opportunity he may desire to present the facts to the bureau."

Coming so quickly after the disclosures by the Couzens committee that tax adjustments running into the millions had been made by the Internal Revenue Bureau with the Atlantic, Gulf and West Indies Steamship Corporation and that a tax deduction of almost $600,000 was under consideration for William Boyce Thompson, Chairman of the Ways and Means Committee of the Republican Party in 1920, the statement by Senator Couzens electrified the Senate in the midst of the debate on the reorganization of that body.

Secretary Mellon stated today that the compromise with the Atlantic, Gulf and West Indies Steamship Corporation was not an actual refund, but that the Government has settled for $1,280,000 and a judgment against the Shipping Board of $1,351,000 in lieu of taxes of $9,913,841 because the company could not pay more, and if the Government had insisted on its full rights it would have received nothing. The Secretary denied that he had ever had an interest in the concern. The matter of "the other taxpayer mentioned Sunday," evidently meaning William Boyce Thompson, he said, was yet in abeyance.

Defends Copper Men's Payments.

Another statement issued tonight by the Secretary said that valuations of the copper companies had been made in 1919, and on this basis taxes were paid for 1917 and 1918, but that when a question arose of how these valuations would affect future taxes there was a revaluation of all copper properties. However, he added that since the taxes of 1917 and 1918 had been paid the Treasury Department had decided not to reopen them.

Senator Couzens, in making his charges, said flatly that because he had the "temerity to dare to criticise a Republican Administration or a Republican Cabinet officer, they propose immediately when things get too warm to penalize that Senator to the extent of $10,000,000 and $11,000,000." He compared the course of the Government toward him

Continued on Page Six.

Kipling Is Seen as Adviser of Baldwin As Premier Voices Peace Plea of His Cousin

Copyright, 1925, by The New York Times Company. By Wireless to THE NEW YORK TIMES.

LONDON, March 9.—Rudyard Kipling as adviser of the Prime Minister of Great Britain in the governance of the country is the interesting picture outlined today. Mr. Kipling is Stanley Baldwin's cousin, and it is known that their relations are close and frequent.

Attention has been drawn to the almost extraordinary similarity in tone and argument between Mr. Baldwin's brilliant speech in the House of Commons on Friday and that of Mr. Kipling delivered on Feb. 20. Both appealed for peace and good-will in solving the difficulties of the time, and, while the oratorical methods of the poet and the politician differed, both struck an identical note.

Mr. Baldwin, as a practical politician, found the opportunity to translate words into acts by solving the political levy bill, affecting trade unions, at the risk of offending a large section of his supporters. Governmental acceptance of the measure, in the eyes of the Labor Party, would have been almost a declaration of war between classes.

The Laborites were already embittered by the suspension of one of their members, David Kirkwood, under circumstances which they regarded as unjust and typical of Tory arrogance and of the determination of the Conservatives to use their great majority in Commons without scruple.

The most moderate of the Conservatives agreed that the Deputy Speaker who "named" Mr. Kirkwood had been somewhat over hasty and that the offense committed by the member from Dumbarton was incommensurate with the penalty imposed upon him, which penalty, besides suspending him from Parliament during the remainder of the session, would have resulted in docking his salary over the same period. Ramsay MacDonald, as leader of the Labor Party, tabled a motion of censure on the Deputy Speaker.

Today the Prime Minister made a gesture of conciliation, which it is hoped will soothe the ruffled feelings of the Labor members and contribute toward the spirit of peace and good-will both he and his cousin, Rudyard Kipling, invoked.

Mr. Baldwin, addressing Mr. MacDonald, offered to ask the House to rescind the resolution suspending Mr. Kirkwood if the Labor leader would withdraw the motion of censure. After some exchanges of opinion, the arrangement was practically agreed to and will be confirmed tomorrow.

I. R. T. FIGHTS M'AVOY IMPROVEMENT COSTS

Won't Pay $4,000,000 Yearly Unless Fare Is Raised, Counsel Declares.

SCOUTS RECEIVERSHIP TALK

Believes Earnings Will Wipe Out Deficit—Nicholson Opposes Fare Increase.

James L. Quackenbush, counsel for the Interborough Rapid Transit Company, declared yesterday that the company would appeal to the courts if required to pay its share for the improvements recommended by Justice John V. McAvoy in his report to the Governor. He added, however, that there would be no receivership for the company unless the courts held that it must add $4,000,000 a year to its expenses without obtaining any additional revenue.

Mr. Quackenbush said that talk of a receivership was absurd, but reiterated his assertion that the company must have a higher fare if it was required to carry out the McAvoy recommendations. These require among other things the lengthening of station platforms at an estimated cost of $11,000,000 to the company, if it is required to pay half of the expense.

Corporation Counsel George P. Nicholson, in a statement declaring an increased fare unnecessary, called upon the Interborough yesterday to give up the subways it is operating if it cannot comply with the terms of its contract. He asserted that the subway was being operated at a profit and that the company's difficulty came from using subway profits to pay deficits on its elevated lines.

Called Receivership Talk Absurd.

"Having got $10,500,000 of new capital from Interborough stockholders after the readjustment of 1922, which money enabled the Interborough to go on, a voluntary receivership or any talk of a voluntary receivership is absurd," Mr. Quackenbush said.

"With our expected earnings for March, April and May we hope to wipe out the Interborough's deficit in the present fiscal year, and it is quite likely that we shall do so.

"In the event of the company being forced to put through the recommendations made by Justice McAvoy regarding its service, there will be no involuntary receivership until the highest court shall have said this company must add $4,000,000 a year to its expenses without getting any additional revenues. This is the amount which would be needed to carry out the McAvoy recommendations for improvements to the Interborough's service, and it cannot be forthcoming unless we are permitted to charge a higher fare. In any case, I should resist a receivership of either kind."

When asked if he cared to state what rate of fare the company regarded as adequate for the purposes mentioned, Mr. Quackenbush, who had not mentioned this matter in his statement to the Governor and Legislature, called attention to the brief he submitted to Justice McAvoy.

Suggested 7-Cent Fare.

According to this the cost of carrying a passenger in the Interborough subways was 5.71 cents, on the Interborough elevated lines 6.83 cents and on the combined system 5.96 cents. Mr. Quackenbush explained that actual cost eliminated both city and company profit, but did include all interest and sinking fund requirements on both company and city bonds. He suggested a 7-cent fare in his brief, and expressed the opinion that this would wipe out the company's accumulated deficits under the contract and pay the annual return of 8.75 per cent. on the city's investment in the subways.

In discussing the Interborough's memorial to the Governor and Legislature asking for an increased fare, Mr. Nicholson said that the company had dissipated its assets in the past by paying extravagant dividends, aggregating 92½ per cent. in the five years from 1914 to 1918 inclusive, or $32,375,000 on a capital of $35,000,000. He declared that the Interborough's financial difficulties had come, not through its contract with the city, but through its own acts and the necessity of paying elevated deficits out of subway profits.

CALL POLICE TO END FREE SPEECH RALLY

Series of Assaults on Various Governments Halted When Soviet Is Assailed.

COUNT KAROLYI ABSENT

Fearing He Might Break Pledge, He Sends Regrets to Meeting in His Behalf.

The attempt of one speaker to say harsh words about the present Government of Russia caused boos, hisses and a general uproar last night which finally put an end to a protest meeting at Town Hall on the political prisoner question, at which it was promised that Count Michael Karolyi was to be the chief speaker.

Count Karolyi, who was allowed to enter this country on promising to engage in no political activities, did not attend the meeting, but a long list of speakers attacked the Governments of England, the Irish Free State, the United States, Italy, Spain, Germany, Esthonia, Yugoslavia, Hungary and India.

These attacks were well received. There was great applause when Norman Hapgood attacked the State Department and declared the United States Government to be "the most in need of moral enlightenment of any Government on earth."

But when the last speaker, B. Charney Vladeck, ventured his first criticism of the treatment of political prisoners by the Soviet Government of Russia, he was smothered by bellows and hisses from all parts of Town Hall.

"They are attempting to suppress all—" began Vladeck, but his sentence died away in a roar from all sides. Several men and women jumped to their feet on the main floor and in the gallery and sought to reply to the few phrases which Vladeck had been able to enunciate.

Tries to Quell Disturbance.

One of Chairman Hapgood's long arms shot up in a stop-traffic gesture. Nothing stopped. Puzzled, he shot both arms into the air. The noise grew louder than ever. He turned a shocked expression in this direction and that and broke into a speech which turned out to be a soliloquy. It did not travel beyond his own ears, if it traveled that far.

After a long spell of disorder there was a lull and the man who did not entirely approve of the course taken by the Soviet Government tried to make a new start, but he was again drowned by shouts and attempts to reply.

Chairman Hapgood walked about, wringing his hands and scratching his head, and at length forgot that the purpose of the meeting was to protest against persecuting people for their political opinions. He called on the police to throw out the men and women who were standing up for their causes in various parts of the house. The police could not hear this demand for the suppression of free-for-all speech. Mr. Hapgood finally leaped down from the platform and strode to the back of the hall, where four policemen were looking on indifferently.

"Please throw out four or five of the worst disturbers," requested Mr. Hapgood, "and then the meeting can go on."

Meeting Ends in Uproar.

The policemen moved into the aisles and watched for individual disturbers. Most of three hours of speechmaking had been devoted to attacking the police and civil authorities of other countries for suppressing political activity and speechmaking, and this move to call in the New York police to deal forcibly with persons who differed from the platform opinion was received with indignation. There was a chorus of hisses from nearly half the audience, but no disturber stood out sufficiently from his neighbors to be picked out for special action by the police.

After half an hour's triumphant assertion of the right not only of free speech but of simultaneous speech by as many persons as felt like it, the meeting broke up, still in an uproar.

The star of the evening, according to advance notices, was to be Count Karolyi, but he stayed away and sent a letter to the effect that his friends advised him that he would be violating his parole to the State Department if he attended the meeting.

Before the meeting the Count's lawyer and representatives of the International Committee for Political Prisoners sought in vain to get the State Department to interpret Count Karolyi's agreement for him. The State Department took the position that it was presumptuous on the part of the Count to ask the State Department to act as his legal adviser.

"He knows what is meant by his promise," wrote William R. Castle Jr., chief of the Division of Western European Affairs, to Karolyi's New York lawyer, "and what fairly may be taken to be political activities."

GOVERNMENT OPENS TEAPOT DOME SUIT; SECRECY ADMITTED

Pomerene Declares Sinclair and Fall Perpetrated Big Fraud Under Cover.

TESTIMONY BACKS CHARGE

Finney Testifies Fall Ordered Silence—Navy Oil Chief Says He Was Kept in Dark.

COL. STEWART NOW AT SEA

Witness to Canadian Deal Goes to Latin America—Two Others in France Won't Return.

Special to The New York Times.

CHEYENNE, Wyo., March 9.—The Government's suit for the cancellation of the Teapot Dome naval oil reserve lease to the Sinclair oil interests was called in the Federal Court at 10 o'clock this morning.

That the battle is to be a fight to the finish was indicated before the first session was an hour old. The Government bluntly charged that Harry F. Sinclair, head of the oil interests bearing his name, and former Secretary of the Interior Albert B. Fall were conspirators in one of the greatest frauds ever practiced on the Government, and that the Teapot Dome reserve was secretly and fraudulently transferred to Sinclair's control, the consideration being Liberty bonds exceeding $233,000 in value.

Coincident with the beginning of the trial it was admitted by representatives of the Standard Oil Company of Indiana that Colonel Robert W. Stewart, the Chairman of the board of that company, is now outside the jurisdiction of the American courts, somewhere on the Atlantic, bound either for Mexico or for South America.

The admission that Colonel Stewart is safely outside the process-serving zone was made by John D. Clark, Vice President of the Standard Oil Company of Indiana and assistant to the Chairman of the Board. Mr. Clark admitted that he gave the information with reluctance, explaining that Colonel Stewart is "southbound" on a business deal so important that the company desired to keep his movements secret.

Uncertain as to Stewart's Return.

Mr. Clark said Col. Stewart would not return until the business was completed and that may be a month or longer. The trial in Cheyenne is expected to last not longer than four weeks.

"Will Colonel Stewart return in time to take the stand and tell what he knows about the Continental Trading Company deal?" Mr. Clark was asked.

"He will return when the business that has made his presence in Mexico and South America necessary is concluded," Mr. Clark replied.

When Owen J. Roberts of counsel for the Government was informed concerning Colonel Stewart he said:

"I am not surprised. It looks now that Stewart, like Blackmer and O'Neil, who are in France, will not be available as a witness when we reach the all-important Continental Trading Company phase of the case. His quitting the country leaves only Mr. Sinclair in American jurisdiction, and if what I hear is true Mr. Sinclair may be expected to refuse to tell what he knows about that deal when he takes the stand. We shall, of course, put Sinclair on the stand, but we will be powerless if he refuses to talk on the ground that to do so might incriminate him."

As for Blackmer and O'Neil, the correspondent of THE NEW YORK TIMES is able to state that neither has any intention of returning to the United States at any time in the near future.

In fact, Mr. Blackmer, who is Chairman of the board of the Midwest Refining Company, and Mr. O'Neil, a former President of the Prairie Oil and Gas Company, may never return to their native land. This statement is made on the authority of their counsel, George Gordon Battle of New York. Mr. Battle, who arrived in Cheyenne this morning, was in conference with his clients in Paris two weeks ago.

"Mr. O'Neil may never return to the United States and it may be that he will make France his permanent home," said Mr. Battle.

"How about Mr. Blackmer?" Mr. Battle was asked.

"He may also decide to reside permanently in France" he replied.

The two sessions today were largely devoted to reading into the record official correspondence and orders relating to the Teapot Dome negotiations. For-

Continued on Page Six.

'Ma' Ferguson Signs Act Prohibiting Masks in Texas

AUSTIN, Texas, March 9.—A bill prohibiting the wearing of masks in public was signed today by Governor Miriam Ferguson. It provides severe penalties for persons entering in public buildings, churches or private residences while masked.

The bill was a Democratic Party pledge of the last campaign and resulted mainly from flogging parties staged by masked bands in Texas during the last few years, Representative Holbrook, author of the bill, explained.

One section of the law, which becomes effective immediately, declares it unlawful "for any secret society or organization or a part of the members thereof, masked or disguised, to parade upon or along any public road or any street or alley of any city or town in this State."

ROB WOMAN IN HOME OF $40,000 IN GEMS

Trail Mrs. Beatrice Perkins and Milton Abbott, Her Escort, From Cafes to Apartment.

BEAT HER AND BIND BOTH

Hold-Up Similar to a Series Beginning With Dot King Case —No Clues Found.

Mrs. Beatricec Perkins, 25, wife of Benjamin F. Perkins, owner of the Colonnade Club at 16 East Fifty-third Street, was trailed to her studio apartment at 168 West Fifty-eighth Street at 3 o'clock yesterday morning and brutally beaten by three masked robbers, who broke into her home and robbed her of nearly $40,000 worth of jewelry.

The three men, who followed her from a restaurant, bound and gagged Mrs. Perkins and her escort, Milton Abbott, 32, a cotton broker, of 522 West End Avenue, and a relative of the late Lyman Abbott. Abbott, who made no resistance, was tied with strands torn from a bed sheet. Mrs. Perkins, who screamed when one of the bandits impatiently stuffed her bejeweled finger in his mouth and began working the rings loose with his teeth, was beaten over the head with a revolver, punched and knocked down and threatened with torture if she failed to reveal where all her jewels were.

Mrs. Perkins kicked one of the bandits in the stomach. His handkerchief mask, concealing the upper part of his face, fell off and she saw a gray-haired man with a flat nose.

Robber Pulls the Trigger.

"I'll give it to you good now," he menaced her, and pulled the trigger of his pistol, but there was no explosion.

The robbers bound her to a chair, stuffed a gag in her mouth and then threw some pillows over her face. Gathering up the jewels, they ran out. Mrs. Perkins, faint from loss of blood, slowly extricated her hands and reached a pair of scissors. She cut her bonds and then freed Abbott, who ran to get a taxicab, saying he was going to see Arnold Rothstein, insurance broker, who would get detectives busy on the case.

Mrs. Perkins called her husband on the telephone, but failed to reach him. Then she summoned her mother, next door. A doctor bandaged up the young woman, who was hysterical.

The attack on Mrs. Perkins was one of a series of crimes against women perpetrated by thugs who frequent the white light district's cabarets and supper clubs and who pick their victims from among the conspicuously bejeweled patrons. The series of crimes began two years ago with the murder of Dot King, or Keenan, in her home at 144 West Fifty-seventh Street, within a stone's throw of the Perkins home. A year ago Louise Lawson, a model, was strangled in her apartment at 22 West Seventy-seventh Street. Recently Miss Avonne Taylor, an actress, was attacked in her apartment at 414 Madison Avenue and robbed of $15,000 worth of jewels. On New Year's Eve Mrs. William J. Fox was robbed and beaten in the elevator of her home at 885 West End Avenue. Jewels worth $25,000 which she was wearing were torn from her.

A robbery similar to that of the Perkins case was that if Miss Edith Bobe, costume designer, who, together with Robert L. Hague and a housemaid, was bound last September at 158 East Sixty-third Street and jewelry and furs valued at $50,000 were carried off.

About six weeks ago Mrs. Perkins sprained her ankle and was taken to Roosevelt Hospital. Owing to her singular habit of wearing her jewels in bed she was nicknamed by the nurses "The Sleeping Beauty."

"My daughter always wears her

Continued on Page Two.

REPUBLICANS REFUSE TO JOIN SMITH NOW FOR INCOME TAX CUT

Reject Governor's Conference Offer and Declare Delay Is Necessary.

KNIGHT ISSUES STATEMENT

Majority Will Pass Appropriation Bills and Await Governor's Action.

SMITH PREPARES ANSWER

Highway Bills Recalled at Colonel Greene's Request—$2,000,000 to Be Saved.

Special to The New York Times.

ALBANY, March 7.—The Republican majority controlling the Legislature refused tonight to join Governor Smith in his efforts to bring about a 25 per cent. reduction in the State income tax, declined to confer with him on the subject and delayed giving a definite answer on what their final attitude would be until the appropriation bills had been passed and the Governor had acted on them.

As if to give a hint of what the Governor has in store for his opponents in the statement he is preparing to show how his tax-cut proposal can be carried out, Colonel Greene, his Superintendent of Public Works, set in motion machinery for reducing highways appropriations and providing at least part of the sum which would be necessary to lower the income tax.

As the Assembly was getting ready to adjourn just before midnight, Assemblyman Hutchinson, Republican chairman of the Ways and Means Committee, offered a concurrent resolution recalling two highway appropriation bills totaling approximately $15,000,000 from Governor Smith. The resolution was adopted unanimously. The Senate had adjourned but it will concur tomorrow.

These are the bills which were recalled from the Governor last week, held in the Assembly for two days and then returned to the Executive without being reduced. The Governor had asked that the bills be recalled and reduced to aid in bringing about a reduction in the income tax.

The action taken by the Assembly, according to Speaker McGinnies, was requested by Colonel Greene.

According to reports at the Capitol tonight, these measures will now be reduced about $2,000,000 at the request of the Highway Department.

Assemblyman Hutchinson said he did not know the exact amount which the Highway Department wanted taken out, but that he had heard the sum named as ranging from $1,000,000 to $3,000,000.

Republicans Delay Answer.

Instead of attending what was to be the final conference with the Governor on his proposal and giving a decisive answer on what their final action would be, the Republicans issued a statement through Senator Knight giving their reasons for delay.

While still insisting that they were not opposed to an income tax reduction if it were possible without harm to the interests of the State, they stuck to the position they have maintained from the start—that there is no way of cutting appropriations to allow a reduction in the income tax.

Senator Knight, leader of the upper house, as spokesman for the majority in both houses, issued the statement about the time the night session began.

"We favor tax reduction so far as it is possible," Senator Knight said. "If there is any way in which tax reduction can be accomplished along sane, economic lines, we stand prepared to do all within our power to bring about such curtailments. We oppose tax reductions now which will be sure to cause tax increases next year."

Denies Rejecting Smith Proposal.

While some persons at the Capitol were inclined to regard the statement of Senator Knight as a thinly veiled refusal to entertain the Governor's proposal, the Senator himself insisted that no such meaning should be read into it.

"We are not turning down the Governor's proposal," he said in reply to a direct question. "The statement is nothing more or less than what it purports to be—a frank declaration that we could not intelligently discuss the topic of tax reduction until we know what our major appropriation bills are going to be when they pass from the Legislature to the Governor and what the Governor is going to do with them."

There is every likelihood that both houses will take action on the appropriation bills before the end of the present week. But even at the best, with a reasonable allowance of time for the Governor to consider the manifold items in the two measures, ten days or a fortnight probably will elapse before he will be in a position to announce his action.

Earlier today strong intimations were forthcoming from the Republican leaders that they would defy the Governor—who has threatened, in the event of an unfavorable reply, to take his case to the people—and turn down his proposal outright. With the arrival of the lawmakers here tonight the tone changed and the Knight statement was handed out.

The Governor, when he was informed of the statement and its contents, declined to make any comment. He is at work on a statement of his own in which he expects to show conclusively that the proposed reduction in the income tax can be granted without any harm to the legitimate interests of the State. He will cover the ground he went over with the Republican leaders in the conference he held with them last week.

Senator Knight's statement said:

"In his annual message to the Legislature Governor Smith described the State as a great corporation and com-

Curzon Undergoes a Serious Operation; Reported as Well as Could Be Expected

LONDON, March 9 (Associated Press).—Marquis Curzon of Kedleston, Lord President of the Council, underwent a serious operation this morning. A brief statement was issued describing it as "quite successful." The extremely serious nature of the operation, however, was emphasized by another bulletin issued tonight, which reads:

"Marquis Curzon has been visited throughout the day by Sir Harry Bruce-Porter and Sir John Thomson-Walker (both noted physicians and surgeons). They expressed the opinion that the Marquis had borne the shock of the operation as well as could be expected and that the patient's strength was being well maintained.

"They will see the patient later tonight and, unless some change occurs, no further report will be issued today."

The exact nature of Lord Curzon's ailment has not been disclosed. He had a collapse several days ago and is reported to have also suffered from hemorrhages.

Among the many prominent persons to inquire as to his condition was Lord Stamfordham, in behalf of the King, who sent a message of sympathy.

His Majesty himself, according to tonight's report, is going on "very well indeed," but, owing to the treacherous cold winds, has not ventured out, and the date for his departure for his Mediterranean cruise has not yet been fixed.

Charles Page Perin and His Wife Separate; Lawyers Discuss Her Demand for $250,000

Reports from Milwaukee that Mrs. Charles Page Perin, who formerly was Miss Jeannette Bean of that city, was separated from her husband and that a divorce was contemplated were confirmed yesterday by Mr. Perin, who is an engineer at 40 West Fortieth Street and is socially prominent.

While reluctant to discuss the matter, Mr. Perin, when shown a dispatch from Milwaukee which said that the chief point of contention between the two was a demand by Mrs. Perin for a lump sum settlement of $250,000, admitted that this was true.

"The matter," Mr. Perin said, "is in the hands of attorneys representing Mrs. Perin and myself. Now that it appears to have been made public by some one there is, I suppose, no use in pretending that it is not true."

Mrs. Perin could not be found last night. It was said that she was in Washington.

The Perins were married in France in January, 1919. Both had been married before. Mr. Perin's first wife died about ten years ago. He had then gone to India and to China on engineering enterprises and was in India when the World War broke out.

After the armistice Mr. Perin returned to England and to France. In Paris he met Mrs. Jeannette Bean Dickson, who was nursing wounded French soldiers and had had charge of that work in the Toul sector. They were married on Jan. 9 and soon set sail for India, to which country Mr. Perin was returning. After a brief stay there Mrs. Perin returned to France, and Mr. Perin followed her a few months later. They came to this country by separate ships.

Friends of Mr. Perin said last night that while he was eminent in his profession and commanded large fees for his services, such a lump payment was quite impossible, and that he could offer only annual payments. Mrs. Perin was said to have declined to agree to this. The matter was then placed in the hands of attorneys.

Mr. Perin is 63 years of age and his wife is 56. They are without children, but Mrs. Perin has a son and a daughter by her previous marriage.

The Metropolitan Museum of Art

Mummy labels, once decifered, greatly help in the identification of the carefully preserved mummies.

"All the News That's Fit to Print."

The New York Times.

THE WEATHER.
Fair, slightly warmer Thursday; Friday, fair, warmer; moderate winds, becoming south.
For full weather report see Page 22.

VOL. LXXIV....No. 24,590. NEW YORK, FRIDAY, MAY 22, 1925. TWO CENTS In Greater New York | THREE CENTS Within 200 Miles | FOUR CENTS Elsewhere in the U. S.

CAPITAL DISPLEASED BY WAR DEBT TALK OF CITIZENS ABROAD

State Department Unfavorably Impressed by Remarks Deprecating Our Funding Moves.

FEAR CONFUSION AS RESULT

Statements of Otto H. Kahn and Representative Green Are Subjects of Particular Interest.

PAINLEVE TELLS PLANS

Says France Must Balance Budget, Stabilize Floating Debt and 'Improve Financial Position.'

Special to The New York Times.

WASHINGTON, May 21.—The Administration leaders who are seeking to obtain a funding of the French wartime debt are not a little concerned over cable dispatches which quote prominent Americans abroad as deprecating the steps which have been taken recently, through instructions sent to Ambassadors and Ministers, to bring about funding negotiations by the foreign countries that have not as yet taken that step.

Reports of these addresses and statements, as well as a rumor that a prominent citizen may take a trip to Europe soon to discuss a middle-course funding program with French statesmen, have been called to the attention of the State Department, and while no formal statement has been made it has not been difficult to sense the unfavorable reaction.

Report of Kahn Address Causes Stir.

The attention of Administration officials has been attracted particularly to a cable dispatch which represented Otto H. Kahn, the New York banker, as apologizing, in an address in Paris, for the steps which have been taken by the State Department, and as stating that the reported pressure actually was being brought to bear by politicians who do not represent the American nation.

The same dispatch represented George W. Wickersham, former Attorney General, and James W. Gerard, former American Ambassador to Berlin, who are in France, as offering explanations and attempting to apply the soft pedal.

Newspaper dispatches also have been sent to Paris, it is said, which sought to picture President Coolidge as taking the lead in urging a speeding up in funding negotiations, not because he believed in such a course, but because he wished to placate Chairman Borah of the Senate Foreign Relations Committee and win Senator Borah's support for domestic legislation in the next Congress.

Another newspaper today carried a dispatch from London picturing Representative William R. Green, Chairman of the House Ways and Means Committee, as among those who doubted that France could make any payments on her wartime debt to the United States at this time.

The attitude of the Administration is that speeches and statements of this kind by Americans who have gone abroad in unofficial capacities are unfortunate and serve only to muddle up the situation, bring about misunderstandings and interfere with the Administration's plans for running the Government.

Fear Confusion Abroad.

It is contended that when citizens, some of whom have been prominent in the Government service in the past, make statements such as have been reported, it necessarily results in confusion among the foreign peoples and serves to put obstacles in the way of the orderly process of governmental activities.

If the Administration could have its way such speeches and statements would be brought abruptly to an end during deliberations over the debt-funding negotiations. Apparently, however, there is no chance of misinterpreting the Administration feeling.

"The explanations" about which reports come from Paris and other foreign capitals are attributed, in part, to advocates of American participation in the League of Nations and some financial interests who are favorable to reduction or cancellation of the French debt. It is feared that a continuation of the situation will serve to arouse again a false hope in the minds of foreign peoples that these debts will be canceled, although there is no intention on the part of the Administration to change from its policy of seeking a settlement under which the foreign nations will recognize that eventually the war debts must be paid in full.

It was recalled here today that a somewhat similar situation had been faced while the Dawes plan was under discussion abroad, when it was feared that France might make extreme demands which would prevent ratification.

Senator Borah, who for some time has been urging a speedy settlement of the French debt problem, also was reported as intensely interested in the dispatches concerning the speeches by citizens abroad. He was represented as supporting the Administration in criticizing the attitude of individuals in making "explanations." The Senator refused to make a statement today, but probably will express his views in some detail soon.

Denial was made today that Assistant Secretary Dewey of the Treasury had any intention of discussing the foreign

Continued on Page Two.

Underwood & Underwood.
The Rev. Dr. Charles R. Erdman.
New Moderator of Presbyterian General Assembly.

CALLS CONFERENCE ON EXTRA SESSION

Governor Summons Legislative Leaders to Decide on State Parks Program.

DEFENDS FISCAL POLICY

He Replies, in Syracuse Speech, to Attacks of Mills and Miller.

Special to The New York Times.

ALBANY, May 21.—A special session of the Legislature to enact measures to carry out the State's park program appeared likely today, when Governor Smith summoned legislative leaders and representatives of the various State park commissions to confer with him at the executive chambers next Tuesday at 11 o'clock.

"This conference," the Governor said, "will be for discussing an extraordinary session of the Legislature to carry out the mandate of the people as indicated by the adoption by a million majority last Fall of the park bond issue."

In his letter of summons the Governor stated that he was anxious to see whether an agreement could be reached so that the subject might be disposed of without further controversy.

The legislation involved is a measure to provide for the use of $6,000,000 from the $15,000,000 bond issue authorized by the voters last November. The Thayer bill, providing for such an appropriation, was passed by the Legislature, but was vetoed by the Governor on the ground that it placed unnecessary restrictions on the activities of the various park commissions.

Should an agreement be reached a special session would not be required, but recent developments indicate that the Republicans and Democrats are far apart on the park question.

Soon after the Governor vetoed the Thayer bill with the comment that it apparently was amended by the Republicans with the purpose of allowing every State Department "to dip into the park funds" and while the Legislature was still in session there was talk of an extra session for the adoption of a State park program denuded of the provisions forced through by the Republican majority.

This plan seemed to have been forgotten, however, until this week, when the differences between the Governor and the Republicans were again brought to the surface by Attorney General Ottinger, who, in censoring the use of funds by Robert Moses, head of the Long Island Park Commission, asserted that Governor Smith's veto of the Thayer bill had deprived the people of the State of the immediate use of park lands.

Both Governor Smith and Mr. Moses issued rejoinders describing the Attorney General's attack as political propaganda. The Governor's calling of the legislative leaders for a council is looked on here as a determination on his part to smoke out the Republicans, put them on record as to where they stand on the park question and show the voters that he is not to blame for a lack of legislation which will allow the acquirement of additional park lands with funds authorized by the bond issue.

The legislative leaders summoned to

Continued on Page Three.

DR. ERDMAN ELECTED BY PRESBYTERIANS; DEFEAT FOR BRYAN

Pacific Fundamentalist Chosen Moderator by 470 Votes on Second Ballot.

DR. McAFEE CHIEF RIVAL

Commoner Is Glum as Ovation Is Given to Princeton Theological Professor.

MACARTNEY LOOSES SHAFTS

Militant Fundamentalist Attacks Modernist Views at General Assembly Session.

Special to The New York Times.

COLUMBUS, Ohio, May 21.—The Rev. Dr. Charles R. Erdman, professor in Princeton Theological Seminary and pastor of the First Presbyterian Church of Princeton, N. J., a pacific Fundamentalist, who was supported by all the Modernist and liberal elements, was elected Moderator of the Presbyterian General Assembly which opened its 137th meeting here today.

Dr. Erdman defeated the Rev. Dr. Lapsley A. McAfee of Los Angeles, the official candidate of the militant Fundamentalists, whose slogan has been to purge the Church of all with modernistic leanings. The new Moderator's policy, as indicated by past utterances, will be one of conciliation toward the Modernists but opposition to heresy.

The vote was regarded as a defeat for William Jennings Bryan, retiring Vice Moderator, who broke with his militant Fundamentalist associates yesterday, and announced that he favored the election of Dr. W. O. Thompson, retiring President of Ohio State University. The extreme Fundamentalists refused to follow Mr. Bryan, and today Dr. Thompson also rejected the support of the Commoner and announced at the afternoon session that he was not in the race.

Dr. Erdman Wins on Second Ballot.

Dr. Erdman was elected on the second ballot, receiving 470 of the 950 votes of the Assembly. A majority of 454 was necessary to elect. Dr. McAfee received 420 votes. On the first ballot Dr. Erdman had 420 votes, Dr. McAfee 372, Dr. H. C. Rogers of Kansas City 112 and Dr. William L. McEwan of Pittsburgh, 2. On the second ballot all but 16 of Dr. Rogers's following deserted him. Dr. McEwan received one complimentary vote on the second ballot.

The refusal of Dr. McEwan, a militant Fundamentalist, to become the candidate of his party was a severe blow to the extremists, whose defeat was attributed to this fact and to Mr. Bryan's support of Dr. Thompson.

Mr. Bryan was silent and grim when applause for Dr. Erdman rocked Memorial Hall for two minutes after the latter's election was announced. He applauded feebly when Dr. Erdman was led to the platform and joined in the singing of the Doxology.

It was a dramatic moment when Dr. Erdman was escorted to the platform and shook hands with Dr. Clarence E. Macartney, the retiring Moderator, his bitterest ecclesiastical enemy, who defeated him last year for the Moderatorship by eighteen votes.

Dr. Erdman Asks Patience.

Referring to speeches by those who nominated and seconded the three candidates, Dr. Erdman said it was obvious that no great differences "divide us as an assembly."

"We want to feel that we are one great court of the Lord," he said. "I plead with you to be patient and to support me with your prayers. I shall allow you to exercise Christian charity, but I want us to believe that there is not one man here who is not absolutely loyal to the Divine Lord and Master whose presence we wish to acknowledge."

Dr. Erdman was placed in nomination by Dr. Herbert B. Smith of Los Angeles, who referred to him as "the best loved man in the Presbyterian Church today." He recalled Dr. Erdman's twenty years as Professor of Practical Theology at Princeton and his score of years on the Board of Foreign Missions. The three

Continued on Page Five.

Divers Find Pottery in Hunt for "Lost City," Whether Roman or Modern Experts Can't Tell

Copyright, 1925, by The New York Times Company.
By Wireless to THE NEW YORK TIMES.

ISLAND OF DJERBA, Tunis, May 21.—A flurry of excitement was caused on board Count de Prorok's ship, "The Elpis, when the tense expectancy which greeted the return of each diver exploring the bottom of the sea for the "Lost City" was rewarded today with slight fragments of pottery covered with marine incrustations.

The rough field examination, which is all that it is now possible to make, however, fails to reveal any convincing evidence that the pieces are ancient. They are unfortunately of a type and form of undecorated pottery common to both the Roman and the modern Arab world. Pending study by experts and the discovery of corroborative evidence in the shape of walls or other such solid proof of the city's existence the pottery is regarded as possibly ancient but probably modern—especially since its presence at the bottom of the sea may be due to shipwrecks in recent centuries, as pottery has long been and still is one of the chief articles of export of the Island of Djerba.

Six divers exploring different parts of a section a half mile long of the channel all reported seeing much pottery, most of which is solidly incrusted in the bottom of the sea, necessitating the use of a hammer to break off pieces. They brought up fourteen fragments, several of which are fifteen inches long with mouths and handles intact, forming parts of large urns and amphorae. They are all covered with beautiful marine growths, giving them splotches of color, green, purple, while, with incrusted shellfish, waving seaweed and some sponges attached.

It is these strange sea changes which make the work of discovering the city—if it exists—especially difficult, for the action of the water during centuries is likely to have disguised the ruins beyond recognition. For this reason an especial effort is being made to guard against optimism.

Four other divers explored another area in the Gulf of Bouprara reported to be the site of the "Lost City" and while one's hopes are roused by reports of seeing stairsteps, further investigations showed that the observer had apparently been mistaken by the natural formation.

Despite the disappointments and difficulties, which are proving greater than anticipated, the work continues to have all the excitement and interest of deep sea fishing on a glorified scale. One diver, who ventured in the water when the current was flowing five knots, was swept off his feet and his lifeline rope was caught by rocks. Quick action in hauling him up saved him, though he returned to the ship greatly weakened by the undersea battle. Such attempts will not be permitted in the few days remaining for exploration.

Beebe Studies Fish at the Bottom of the Sea; Swarms Darken Water as He Sits on Reef

By WILLIAM BEEBE.
Copyright, 1925, by The New York Times Company.
By Independent Wireless via New Orleans to THE NEW YORK TIMES.

S. S. ARCTURUS, May 21.—The New York Zoological Society's oceanographic expedition has been at anchor for five days off Cocos Island, north of our return course from Panama to the Galapagos. We left Panama, after coaling and revictualing, May 12.

It was the absolutely clear water that brought us here, where we have just about completed our submarine photography. This has been one of the greatest features of our work. We had carefully planned for an under-water study of sea life, but our expectations have been far exceeded by results.

Descending from fifteen to thirty feet among the marvelous coral reefs off Cocos in our diving helmet, we have been able comfortably to watch fish life with greater facility than bird life may be observed ashore.

Professor W. K. Gregory and myself dived all day yesterday, first oiling ourselves thoroughly, as we have found that that permits a longer stay under water. Then standing or sitting among gigantic mushrooms of coral, we do not have to seek out fish, as they come in swarms, in all their brilliant tropical colors, to investigate the diver.

At times the water is literally darkened by the clouds of fish that sweep around one down the coral avenues. We have not yet devised a means for making notes undersea, but the habits of the vast population make such an impression that very little escapes us. Professor Gregory is as enthusiastic as I am, and as surprised that such a simple method has apparently not been used before for serious scientific collecting. I consider this one of the most important discoveries of the expedition.

Among the strange fish are many sharks, but they are apparently harmless. We take all possible precautions against large sharks and morays, but the greatest precaution seems to be to remain motionless. When we descend we often carry with us a wire cage into which we may retreat if sharks or morays become belligerent.

Before anchoring here we trawled in the unsounded waters north of Cocos and made rich hauls.

This island is an extreme contrast to the barren Galapagos, being heavily wooded and sparkling with lovely cascades falling through a thick jungle.

Cocos is the site of buried treasure, for which many exploring parties have searched. Legends even connect the buccaneers with Cocos, and we find abandoned tombs and excavations left by treasure seekers. However, this counter attraction has meant no distraction from our oceanographic work.

Every night the Arcturus is invaded by hundreds of gannets, which fly to our decks and obligingly regurgitate rare fish.

The tension engine, that is part of our trawling and dredging equipment, has again prevented the loss of gear in an emergency, and I extend congratulations to Charles Yates of the technical staff of Harrison Williams (chief patron of the expedition), to whose sagacity we are indebted for this engine.

INDICT BABY FARMER FOR MANSLAUGHTER

Authorities Also Investigate Identity of Dead Infant, Which May Be Angerer's.

RESEMBLES MISSING CHILD

Found in Ashcan Near Woman's Home After Anonymous Tip to Police.

Mrs. Helen Augusta Geisen-Volk was indicted for first degree manslaughter in one case yesterday, and last night Assistant District Attorney William F. Ryan said an effort would be made today to determine whether an unidentified infant, found dead two weeks ago in an ash can in East Seventy-ninth Street, was Steven Angerer, last seen by his father more than two months ago.

No trace of the Angerer child has been found in the intensive investigation into the infantorium which Mrs. Geisen-Volk maintained at 235 East Eighty-fifth Street. The decision to inquire into the identity of the ash can baby was made when information indicated to Mr. Ryan that it had physical characteristics like those of the Angerer baby.

The unknown baby was found in a leather bag, and about its small form a copy of a German newspaper had been wrapped. The date of its finding coincides with the time when William Angerer, father of the missing child, was becoming insistent that Mrs. Geisen-Volk produce his boy. He had called at the infantorium and had been given an infant which he claimed was not Steven. Finally he communicated with the District Attorney's office, and on his complaint Mrs. Geisen-Volk was indicted Wednesday for baby substitution, being held in $35,000 bail.

The decision to exhume the body of the ashcan baby from Potter's Field and have Dr. Otto H. Schultze, Medical Assistant on the District Attorney's staff, examine it for indications that it was the Angerer child, came as the result of an anonymous tip to the authorities.

Last Wednesday night, it was said, a man who refused to reveal his identity telephoned to Richard Gonzales, an attaché of the Homicide Bureau at the Criminal Courts Building.

This man said that a woman living in a city close to New York had told him that she had deposited a "bundle" in an ash can in East Seventy-ninth Street. According to the man's statement to Gonzales, she took a leather bag from the infantorium with instructions to "throw it away somewhere outside of the immediate neighborhood."

Detective Investigates.

At first, Gonzales did not place much credence in the story, but when he and Detective John Markey began to check over records they decided to put the matter before Mr. Ryan. The investigators found that the ash can infant had two front teeth and light hair, items in the description furnished to the police by Angerer. Mr. Ryan, in order to further check up, called in Captain Arthur Carey, in charge of the Homicide Bureau, and Detective Fred Winkelman.

Just what the policemen discovered was not disclosed last night. An order for exhumation probably will be sought today and the examination by Dr. Schultze and Dr. Charles Norris, Chief Medical Examiner, probably will be conducted tomorrow.

The indictment of Mrs. Geisen-Volk was voted in connection with the death of William Winters, 6 months old, of 1,342 Third Avenue. An autopsy performed on the infant's body last week disclosed that the child's skull had been fractured. The indictment will be handed up today to Judge John F. McIntyre in General Sessions. The indictment was returned after only two witnesses had been examined yesterday. Others had testified on Wednesday, when the indictment charging baby substitution was returned.

The witnesses called before the additional May Grand Jury yesterday were George F. Krum, an undertaker, of 1,025 First Avenue, who buried the Winters baby from the Geisen-Volk place, and James McEvey, an employe of the Morgue, who testified that he had identified the Winters baby as the one exhumed in Calvary Cemetery.

Before the Grand Jury returned its graver accusation, Mrs. Geisen-Volk appeared before Judge McIntyre and through her attorney, Newman Levy of 7 Dey Street, entered a plea of not

Continued on Page Six.

AMERICANS INVADE ONTARIO FOR BEER

Hosts Cross Into the Border Cities as 800 Resorts Begin Selling New Beverage.

DETROITERS FIND NO "KICK"

Women Go Along Also—Toronto Has Quiet Day, but Ottawa Throngs Celebrate.

Special to The New York Times.

TORONTO, May 21.—Curiosity rather than thirst prevailed at most of the 300 resorts of the Province of Ontario which began dispensing 4.4 beer today for the first time since the war. None of the dispatches from all parts of the Province admitted any rush for the stronger beverage except in Kitchener, where one hotel having a permit was overwhelmed during its temporary monopoly, and in Ottawa, whose citizens never let the bartenders rest.

In addition to the 300 permits under which beer was sold today, 400 more have been issued, and it is estimated that when all are certified, 1,600 hotels will be licensed. In Toronto alone seventy-five hotels are dispensing the beer.

The border points, notably Windsor, opposite Detroit, entertained many visitors from the United States, although the ferries were not crowded, and there were apparently more spectators than drinkers when the first bottle was opened at 7 o'clock this morning.

The real "invasion" began tonight, however, with every table in all the hotels and restaurants of Windsor and Walkerville and in the roadhouses between the two cities reserved, mostly by Detroiters. The taprooms of the hotels were crowded all the afternoon, chiefly by Americans, and the general opinion was that the new brew was just as represented, a non-intoxicating, palatable beverage.

Rollicking Throngs in Ottawa.

While Toronto took the day philosophically, the news from Ottawa told a different story. "Beer sufficient to flood every street in the Dominion's capital," dispatches said, "has been gurgling down thirsty throats since 7 o'clock this morning in every section of the city."

Despite a drizzling rain, queues lined up at the Ottawa saloons and every one in them seemed anxious to be the first to sample the brew. Some of the more enterprising places gained a full hour's start under the law by reverting to Standard instead of Daylight Saving Time.

A milling, shouting, rollicking throng was to be found in every Ottawa "beverage room," where bartenders of both sexes, even little girls, were frantically filling and refilling the never-ending stream of glasses.

The New Wellington Hotel had the honor of being the very first to open its doors for the relief of the thirsty. The proprietor was amply rewarded, as by noon he had sold more than 2,400 bottles and business was still rushing, not a chair having been vacant at the tables, where the law requires the beer must be served.

The proprietor of the Castor Hotel had his permit brought to him specially from Toronto by a member of the Legislature and boasted of his "real friend" as he dashed around the drinking room with a tray. Restaurants and stores also obtained permits and began service.

Since this was Ascension Day, a religious holiday on the Quebec side, many residents of that Province crossed the line.

Toronto Takes the Day Calmly.

There was no wild rush for the new beer in Toronto this morning. It may have been that the 8 o'clock opening hour was inconvenient for the working man, who had to be on his job at that hour.

The sale did not begin on time, because the permits had been sent through the mails, and consequently it was not until the letter carrier had arrived that the bartenders could get busy.

Still another obstacle presented itself in that a large proportion of the hotels were getting their deliveries only this morning, and they had not received their supplies.

Toronto accepted the inauguration of the sale of beer without the slightest attempt to make a holiday of it. At none of the many hotels was there the slightest indication of better business than usual.

James A. McCausland, a member of the Provincial Parliament and a "wet"

Continued on Page Seven.

KOENIG AND WOODS SAY FUSION MUST BE REPUBLICAN POLICY

Tammany and Hylan Stand or Fall Together, Chairman Tells Republican Rally.

CALLS THEM ACCOMPLICES

Declares if Wigwam Deserts the Mayor It Will Only Be 'Turning State's Evidence.'

WOODS ATTACKS SINNOTTS

Cites Rise in City Government Cost, and Asks if Misrule Has Been Worth It.

Every thought of a straight Republican ticket in the Mayoralty campaign this year must be abandoned, Chairman Samuel S. Koenig of the New York County Republican Committee told members of that organization at its regular monthly meeting last night at Bryant Hall, Sixth Avenue near Forty-second Street.

He said a straight Republican ticket at the present crisis in the city's affairs would be as inadequate to meet the situation as would "the substitution of one Tammany man for another" in the Mayor's office. He pleaded warmly for the nomination of a "Citizens" ticket behind which all elements determined to see the city redeemed from misrule could unite.

The same sentiments were voiced by Colonel Arthur Woods, who was Commissioner of Police in the Mitchel Administration, and who addressed the meeting in his capacity as Chairman of the Executive Committee of the Republican Advisory Committee which for some months has been laying plans for the coming fight against Tammany.

The remarks of Chairman Koenig and Colonel Woods were warmly applauded by committee members who filled the big hall. Colonel Woods failed to say anything specific regarding the management of the Police Department, with which he is so closely familiar, under Hylan and Enright. He contented himself with a general attack along the familiar Republican lines upon the Hylan Administration, its wastefulness, its inefficiency and insincerity, winding up with some stinging references to the Sinnotts and their relations with their kinsman in the City Hall.

One portion of Mr. Koenig's brief remarks, made when he introduced the speaker of the evening, brought the audience to its feet.

Links Tammany and Mayor.

"Tammany," he said, "may be willing at this juncture to turn State's evidence against its accomplice, Mayor Hylan. But Tammany and Hylan must stand or fall together."

Many women attended the meeting, one of the largest in a long time. The remarks of Colonel Woods were broadcast over the Hotel Majestic radio station.

Chairman Koenig in his introductory remarks praised the work of the Advisory Committee, declaring it had fully justified its creation.

"In exposing the shortcomings of the Hylan-Tammany Administration it has performed a great public service," he said. "As a result, the Tammany leaders are greatly worried and talk is heard of refusing renomination to Mayor Hylan—as if that would wipe out the wrongs of seven years of Tammany misrule.

"Let not the people be fooled. Whatever Hylan is, Tammany is its partner. Tammany men occupy all the public offices. The organization in every instance supported the so-called Hylan policies, whether in the Board of Estimate, in the Legislature or in the city or State campaigns, and jointly they fooled the people on subways and the other issues. Hylan and Tammany must stand or fall together.

"There seems to be a belief in some quarters that with Hylan out, Tammany will become purified and the people will come into their own. Let them dream on! It is true that Tammany in its anxiety to retain control of the city is willing to throw overboard, if necessary, its partner, although it is my opinion it will not do it.

"However, the attitude of Tammany Hall is not unlike what we witness in our criminal courts. Having been caught by the people of the City of New York, Tammany is now willing to turn State's evidence against its accomplice, and is pleading for immunity and for another chance, promising to reform under new management and is offering to bring

Continued on Page Four.

Gloves Worn by Pall-Bearer For George Washington Found

Special to The New York Times.

WASHINGTON, May 21.—The gloves worn by Richard Key Watts of Maryland when he was a pallbearer at the funeral of General George Washington were found by Harry M. Sieber, an amateur collector of this city, while driving in the country near Rockville, Md., this afternoon. Mr. Sieber found the old gloves in the home of a family named Wallace, who claimed to be lineal descendants of the man who wore them 126 years ago.

The gloves are in a good state of preservation, are of black kid, with white kid cuffs, edged with black. On the cuff of each is written in faded ink: "Part of mourning for General G. Washington, R. K. Watts."

At the same time Mr. Sieber recured the gloves he purchased a miniature of Richard Key Watts, a handsome, fair-haired man. The Watts family is well known in Maryland, and the middle name of the owner of the gloves identifies him, it is said, with the family of Frances Scott Key, the author of "The Star-Spangled Banner."

$10,000,000 AIR LINE FOR FREIGHT FORMED

Ford, Wrigley, Curtiss and Wright Interests Said to Be Back of Enterprise.

NEW YORK-CHICAGO ROUTE

Service Eventually to Be Nation-wide—No Stock Offered for Public Sale.

Special to The New York Times.

CHICAGO, May 21.—Interests believed to be representing William Wrigley Jr., Marshall Field 3d, Edsel Ford, the Curtiss Aeroplane and Motor Company and the Wright Aeronautical Corporation combined today at a meeting of thirty-five men in the Drake Hotel to organize the National Air Transport, Inc. The company will open a commercial air line early in the Fall between New York and Chicago.

Colonel Paul Henderson, Second Assistant Postmaster General of the United States, in charge of the air mail service, will resign from his present post Monday to become general manager of the National Air Transport, it was announced at the meeting.

Colonel Henderson will ask that his resignation become effective August 1, after the Government night air service between Chicago and New York has been opened.

The new company will transport freight and express, but no passengers. Its present plans embrace only the Eastern route, but other routes will be mapped to the South and West, making Chicago the hub of the mail express. While a definite schedule has not as yet been proposed, it has been decided that the company planes will leave New York about 9:30 P. M., fly over a lighted airway, and arrive in Chicago at approximately 5 o'clock in the morning. Direction of the lanes will be by radio.

No Public Sale of Stock.

The company is capitalized at $10,000,000. The delegates to today's meeting offered $5,000,000, it was learned, but only $2,000,000 was accepted. No stock will be offered for public sale.

Howard E. Coffin of the Hudson Motor Car Company, Detroit, Mich., was elected President of the company; Clement E. Keys, Curtiss Aeroplane and Motor Company, New York, was made the Chairman of the Executive Committee. Other officers elected, all of whom were present at the meeting, are: First Vice President, Charles L. Lawrence, Wright Aeronautical Corporation, New York; Second Vice President, Wayne Chatfield Taylor, representing Marshall Field 3d and Glore, Ward & Co., Chicago; Third Vice President, Eugene W. Lewis, Industrial Bank, Detroit; Secretary, Carl B. Fritsche, right hand man of Edsel Ford, Detroit; Treasurer, John J. Mitchell, Illinois Merchants Bank, Chicago; counsel, Chester W. Cutshell, New York, and William P. McCracken, Chicago.

Directors or others interested in the enterprise include William A. Rockefeller, Jeremiah Milbronk, Leonard Kennedy and Trowbridge Calloway of New York, John Hays Hammond of Washington, William Metzger, Harold H. Emmons, George M. Holley and C. F. Kettering of Detroit, Phillip K. Wrigley, Charles F. Glore, Robert L. Lamont and Lester Armour of Chicago, C. T. Luding-

Continued on Page Two.

New Postoffice Planned for Times Square; Present Quarters Outgrown, Kiely Says

Postmaster J. J. Kiely announced yesterday at a luncheon of the Broadway Association at the Hotel Astor that plans were under way for the construction of a new postoffice to serve the Times Square district. He said that the present building at Thirty-eighth Street west of Seventh Avenue was crowded with the mail traffic, and incapable of the expansion necessary to keep up with the postal facilities required in the rapidly growing section.

The project is not yet in definite shape, Mr. Kiely said, but plans will soon be taken up with the Postoffice Department in Washington. The new building, he said, would have far greater facilities than the present one and would probably be located in the district somewhere west of Eighth Avenue.

"All you need to do to see what is required in the near future in this district," he told the members of the association, "is to go along Seventh and Eighth Avenues in Times Square and notice the new buildings going up and the great crowds coming out of the present buildings. We must keep abreast of a growing section."

Major Gen. Charles P. Summerall, commander of the Second Corps Area, another speaker at the luncheon, told his hearers that this country stood on the verge of a great development in commercial aviation, which is sure to come. He said merchants and business men should interest themselves in this project. One of the things that should be done soon, he said, was to select large sites on the outskirts of the city for use as landing places for inter-city commercial aviation. The high cost of real estate would prevent landing fields near the centre of the city, he said.

Louis Wiley, a director of the association, was toastmaster. He told of the work for civic improvement undertaken by the organization since its founding.

Other speakers were George L. Slawson, President of the association; Colonel Jefferson De Mont Thompson, its first President, and Chief Chaplain Thomas E. Swan of the Second Corps Area, who delivered the invocation. Music was provided by Ernie Golden's Hotel McAlpin Orchestra.

AMUNDSEN PLANES HOP OFF ON FLIGHT TO THE NORTH POLE

Leave Kings Bay, Spitzbergen, at 5:15 P. M. in Effort to Reach Top of Earth.

EACH CARRIES THREE MEN

Veteran Explorer Commands One and Lincoln Ellsworth of New York the Other.

TRIP MAY TAKE 8 HOURS

Several Halts Are Likely and Some Time May Be Consumed in Locating True Pole.

The North American Newspaper Alliance announced last evening through The Associated Press that it had received a dispatch from Kings Bay, Spitzbergen, stating that the two flying boats of the Amundsen-Ellsworth polar expedition hopped off there at 5:15 o'clock yesterday afternoon for the North Pole. The dispatch said that each plane carried three men.

Get Full Weather Reports.

OSLO, Norway, May 21 (AP).—Captain Roald Amundsen's polar expedition, which had been delayed at Spitzbergen because of unfavorable weather conditions, had to hop off late this month or early in June, in the opinion of M. Hesselberg, director of the Oslo Meteorological Station, which collected and forwarded information regarding the weather to the north for the benefit of the explorer.

M. Hesselberg said today that he expected the fog conditions to become appreciably worse after the first week in June and that an attempt after that time might risk disaster to the airplanes.

A meteorological station aboard the expedition steamer Fram received weather reports thrice daily by radio from Oslo, Paris, London, Leningrad and Siberian stations. Reports were also relayed from Canada, the United States, Iceland and Greenland.

The station on the steamer was under the direction of M. Bjerkness, representing the Royal University of Oslo. The Russian and American reports were usually received within a couple of hours. They were immediately decoded and placed in the hands of Mr. Bjerkness, who collated the information for Captain Amundsen.

Even while the flight is on, Captain Amundsen will receive weather reports by radio and his two planes are equipped with instruments by which it will be possible to make observations from high altitudes.

London Eager for News.

Copyright, 1925, by The New York Times Company.
Special Cable to THE NEW YORK TIMES.

LONDON, May 21.—Great interest is aroused here by the news that Amundsen has started his flight for the North Pole and the outcome of his gallant attempt is eagerly being awaited. Amundsen with his two airplanes had been waiting at Kings Bay, Spitzbergen, for favorable weather. He had planned to start at 4 o'clock because at that time the sun would be moving across the sky in such a way that for twelve hours no shadows from wings or the flying boats would fall on the solar compass.

Accompanying him are two flight lieutenants in the Norwegian navy, Ruserlarsen and Dietrichson, who were attached to the British Royal Air Force during the war.

Amundsen is well ahead of his two Polar flight rivals, Captain MacMillan, the American explorer and Grettir Olgarsson, the young explorer of Vancouver who will attempt to reach the Pole by airship. The latter will leave Liverpool soon.

Constantine Dumbrava, a young Rumanian explorer, is in London preparing for a voyage to the North Pole. Dumbrava, who has received the support of the Royal Geographical Society and the Société de Geographie de France, will start from Upernivik, the most northerly port of Greenland and proceed to Itna, where he will establish a base and also a wireless station, which will enable him to communicate with most European and American stations. He will then continue his journey by sledge by way of the Smith Channel.

First of Three Expeditions.

The first of the three expeditions to attempt a comprehensive survey of the North Pole and the surrounding country this Spring and Summer is that headed by Captain Roald Amundsen, who achieved the honor of being the first man to discover the South Pole. The second expedition will be undertaken by British explorers who will use a dirigible for their dash to the Pole. The third is the All-American McMillan-United States Navy Expedition, which, like Amundsen, will use two airplanes in its attempt to fly over and about the Pole.

Amundsen originally laid plans for the present polar flight in 1923 but met with financial reverses and was compelled temporarily to abandon the project. He made a lecture tour of this country and enlisted the aid of Lincoln Ellsworth, a well-known explorer and aviator, and through him a syndicate of seven prominent men raised about $100,000, half of the estimated expense of the trip. The balance was raised in Norway.

Two "mother" ships, the Fram and the Hobby, were sent from Norway and berthed at King's Bay, Spitzbergen, arriving there on April 13, with two Dornier Wal metal planes, fifty-five feet long, with a wing spread of seventy-five feet. Each plane has two Rolls-Royce motors and two propellers and is equipped with sleds for landing on the ice as well as pontoons for landing on water.

Amundsen's original plan provided for a continuation of the expedition to Nome, Alaska, after the Pole had been

"All the News That's Fit to Print"

The New York Times

LATE CITY EDITION

Weather: Fair, very cold today and tonight. Chance of snow tomorrow. Temp. range: today 24-14; Sunday 33-26. Full U.S. report on Page 30.

VOL. LXXIV....No. 24,635. +... NEW YORK, MONDAY, JULY 6, 1925. TWO CENTS In Greater New York | THREE CENTS Within 200 Miles | FOUR CENTS Elsewhere in the U. S.

WAGNER AND FOLEY LOOM AS CANDIDATES TO OPPOSE HYLAN

Both Put Forward as Probable Choice of Tammany for the Mayoralty.

OLVANY DELAYS DECISION

Organization in No Hurry to Break With Mayor, Who Has Places to Fill.

CANVASS IS COMPLETED

Reports of District Leaders as to the Sentiment for Hylan Received by Tammany Chief.

Supreme Court Justice Robert F. Wagner and Surrogate James A. Foley are coming to the front as probable candidates for the Mayoralty to be put forward by Tammany to displace Mayor Hylan for the Democratic nomination for the head of the city ticket.

Neither is an active aspirant for the nomination, it was said yesterday, but the opinion among prominent Tammany leaders is that either could defeat Mayor Hylan for the nomination if the Mayor should decide to enter the Democratic primaries after being informed that he would not be the choice of the organization. It is the belief also in Tammany that either Justice Wagner or Surrogate Foley would be a strong candidate at the election if Mayor Hylan should decide to run independently, and that either, because of his past record, would be likely to get strong independent, and perhaps Republican, support.

Tammany, represented by George W. Olvany, its leader, has so far made no definite decision as to whether it would oppose Mayor Hylan's renomination, it was learned from a well-informed Tammany leader. Judge Olvany, it was said, was still delaying a definite decision, which, according to the best information obtainable, is likely to be postponed for another two weeks.

The belief in Tammany is that the delay in breaking with the Mayor, if a break is to come, is largely for reasons of expediency. Mayor Hylan has important appointments to make, including the members of the new Board of Appeals and three Justices of the Court of Special Sessions. Tammany and the Brooklyn Democratic organization, it was said, would like to get some of those places, if possible, and in any event is in no hurry to begin a war on Mayor Hylan and jeopardize the places held by Tammany men in the Hylan Administration any sooner than it must.

Strategy in Delay.

A certain strategic advantage was said by Tammany men to be gained by keeping Mayor Hylan and his supporters uncertain as to whether the Tammany organization would support him or not. If refused support for renomination by Tammany and Democratic organizations in other boroughs, Mayor Hylan must then make up his mind whether he will make a contest in the Democratic primaries, run for Mayor independently or retire. One view expressed by opponents of the Mayor was that keeping him guessing until the last minute possible would make his entrance into the primaries less likely and prevent his getting a start on the formation of an organization to support him as an independent candidate.

Practically all the Tammany Assembly district leaders were at Tammany Hall on Saturday for the Fourth of July celebration of the Tammany Society. While few would discuss the possibility of the organization turning down Mayor Hylan, it was significant that the conversation of practically all was based on the assumption that this would probably be done.

It was among the Tammany district leaders that the sentiment for Justice Wagner and Surrogate Foley was most apparent, and there also was considerable support for Senator James J. Walker, Democratic leader of the State Senate, whose boom was launched by the visit of a large delegation to Tammany Hall last Thursday.

Olvany's Canvass Completed.

The canvass undertaken by Judge Olvany to ascertain the sentiment concerning Mayor Hylan was said to have been completed. As is customary, the Tammany canvass has been conducted along organization lines, the election district captains reporting to each district leader and each leader reporting in person to Judge Olvany. As these reports have been oral, probably no one but Judge Olvany knows just what the canvass has disclosed, but it is believed that the organization sentiment shown has been largely against the Mayor.

Judge Olvany is understood also to have asked whether those districts in which strong Hylan sentiment existed would go for the Mayor against an organization candidate if some one else were nominated. He was said to have been assured that even these districts would give a plurality for the organization candidate.

The canvass of the district leaders was said to have failed to show even one who would support Mayor Hylan against a candidate of the organization if a candidate such as Justice Wagner or Surrogate Foley were selected. It was said that Judge Olvany would have practically undivided organization support for any generally acceptable candidate he might choose, and that such leaders as Deputy County Clerk Thomas M. Farley, who announced he favored Mayor Hylan's renomination, and Dock

Continued on Page Two.

Labor's Aid in Traffic Safety Arranged by Green and Hoover

WASHINGTON, July 5 (AP)—By agreement between Secretary Hoover and William Green, President of the American Federation of Labor, arrangements have been made to bring labor organizations generally into service in an attempt to reduce traffic casualties.

Mr. Green, inquiring as to the work of the National Conference on Street and Highway Safety, which held its first session last Fall, suggested to Mr. Hoover that central labor organizations all over the country receive the reports of the conference.

Secretary Hoover, accepting, also proposed that the labor organizations should arrange to hold local meetings for discussion of the safety methods under study by the conference. A policy of having labor representatives serve with Municipal Governments and civic associations in working to improve conditions also was outlined.

URGES COMPETITION IN ANTHRACITE FIELD

Trade Board Asks Congress to Act for Adequate Supply at Reasonable Cost.

PRICE CONTROL IS OPPOSED

Periodic Publication of Facts Suggested—Strike Threats Add Interest to Report.

Special to The New York Times.

WASHINGTON, July 5.—The establishment of more effective competition in the anthracite coal industry to provide the public with an adequate supply at fair prices is recommended to Congress and price regulation is opposed by the Federal Trade Commission in a report made public today.

The railroad coal monopolies, it was asserted, have controlled more than two-thirds of the output of the anthracite fields, and wholesale and retail dealers have joined with producers in pyramiding prices at the expense of the consumer.

The commission reports that the output has remained at a stationary level for several years, despite the high prices obtainable and the heavy demand. It is stated that the Department of Justice has met with some success in its efforts to keep up competition in the industry, and it is recommended that further steps be taken to prevent a recurrence of high premium prices.

The report has attracted unusual interest because of the threats made recently that the miners of the bituminous coal fields would go on strike if demands for heavy wage increases were refused by the operators.

Strike Threats Stir Fear of Shortage.

A shortage in the bituminous coal supply, caused by a strike, would bring an increase in the demand for anthracite, over normal, and the result would be acute shortage of coal of all kinds.

The threat of a strike in the anthracite fields is also present, and a tie-up imminent. The wage contract of the anthracite miners expires on Aug. 31 and the anthracite miners have already formulated their demand for a 10 per cent. increase in wages and the recognition of the check-off by the operators.

This situation, as well as the threat by John L. Lewis, President of the United Mine Workers of America, of calling out the bituminous miners if the operators of that industry continue alleged violations of their contracts, has been called to the attention of President Coolidge. The joint scale committee of the anthracite fields are to meet soon in Atlantic City and the labor issues in the coal fields may then come to a head.

Under the most favorable conditions the supply of anthracite in certain seasons has seldom kept pace with the demand because of the limited amount which has been mined by the companies in control of the anthracite fields. The commission's report is accepted as expressing the viewpoint that development of the anthracite fields has been kept down in an unwarranted manner by the companies in control.

"In spite of steadily increasing prices and large untouched coal land reserves of the railroad companies, some of which at the present rate of production would last more than a hundred years," the report says, "the output has remained comparatively stationary for a number of years."

Hindered by Lack of Information.

The commission feels that more information as to the actual conditions in the coal industry should be obtained and placed before the public. The sugges-

Continued on Page Twelve.

SHORT CIRCUIT BURNS HUGE BRIDGE GIRDER; STOPS B. M. T. TRAINS

Rapid Transit on Williamsburg Span Declared Unsafe Till New Beam Is Put In.

ALL TRAFFIC OFF 3 HOURS

Emergency Trolley and Bus Service Installed to Handle B. M. T. Passengers.

REPAIRS BY NOON TODAY

Late Fourth of July Homebound Crowds Delayed—Arrangements for Today.

A fire on Williamsburg Bridge, caused by a short circuit, early yesterday morning stopped all traffic over the bridge for three hours. A girder, partly consumed by the intense heat, was so weakened that engineers of the Department of Plant and Structures declared that the bridge was unsafe for the passage of the B. M. T. rapid transit trains and their operation will not be resumed until the replacement of the girder, which is expected to be some time after noon today.

The fire took place at 2:45. Vehicular and pedestrian traffic was resumed three hours later and the operation of the surface cars, which are run by the city, soon afterward. William Wirt Mills, Commissioner of Plant and Structures, offered to William S. Menden, President of the B. M. T., the use of the bridge cars, and "block" tickets were issued to the B. M. T. passengers, entitling them to free transfer to the bridge cars and to the B. M. T. subway in Manhattan. This process was reversed for passengers going from Manhattan to Brooklyn.

Buses to Aid Service.

Special arrangements for the accommodation of the thousands of passengers who cross the bridge daily in B. M. T. trains were announced by the company for this morning or until the resumption of its regular service. The company will augment the bridge car service by buses and will put into effect shuttle service in the Centre Street loop and issue emergency transfer tickets to enable passengers to continue to their destination by B. M. T. lines without paying an additional fare.

The company's announcement of its emergency arrangements follows:

All trains of the Canarsie line will run to the Marcy Avenue station of the Broadway (Brooklyn) elevated; all Broadway elevated trains of the Jamaica line during rush hours will run to Hewes Street only, and a shuttle service will be operated in the Centre Street loop between Essex Street and Chambers Street.

By courtesy of Commissioner William Wirt Mills, the city's bridge local line will honor block tickets issued by the B. M. T. to passengers at Marcy Avenue, Hewes Street or Essex Street, so that passengers can ride over the Williamsburg Bridge by making these two transfers.

In addition, the B. M. T. on Monday morning will run its buses between Hewes Street at Broadway in Brooklyn, and Essex Street, Manhattan, and block tickets will be accepted on the buses for the ride between these two points. When block tickets are issued at Hewes Street, they will be honored for passage to the Williamsburg Bridge Plaza on the B. M. T. trolley lines in Broadway.

All Chambers Street trains of the Myrtle Avenue line and some of the trains on the Jamaica-Chambers Street line will be discontinued and additional service on each of these lines will be operated to Park Row, where special transfer tickets will be issued to passengers desiring to use the Broadway (B. M. T.) subway in Manhattan. These transfers will be accepted at the City Hall station and also at Chambers Street. Similar transfer tickets will be issued at the City Hall and Chambers Street stations to passengers desiring to go to Brooklyn via trains from Park Row.

Heat Fuses Power Cables.

The fire caused the firemen considerable difficulty. The "dry standpipe" along the bridge was connected with high pressure hydrants and three lines of hose attached in a "Siamese" connection, but fear of the high voltage in the power cables prevented the firemen from turning on the water for ten min-

Continued on Page Two.

History of Egypt Carried Back 14,000 Years; Relics of Earliest Art Found Near Asgut

By Wireless to THE NEW YORK TIMES.

LONDON, July 5.—A continuous view of successive civilizations in Egypt, carried back some 14,000 years, is provided as a result of the discoveries of the British School of Archaeology in Egypt, says Professor Sir Flinders Petrie, writing in The London Times. During the last Winter, he says, the work of the school was devoted to excavating the remains of the earliest civilization, known as the Badarian civilization, so-called from the name of the district which is south of Asyut.

Discoveries there by Mrs. Guy Brunton and Miss Caton Thompson confirm the theory that this civilization, he said, was the foundation of much that is seen in well-known prehistoric times.

"Ivory work of combs and spoons," writes Professor Petri, "slate palettes for grinding malachite, eye paint, glazed stone beads and some kind of pottery continued to these later times, but the finest pottery, conspicuous for its thinness and finish, is confined to the Badarian period, and the style of the statuettes is also distinctive.

"It had been already noted that the workmanship of flint implements was like that found in the Fayum region and across to Palestine. Miss Caton Thompson therefore searched north of Fayum and found many settlements of this age. These settlements extend down the desert slopes to a level which was covered by the lake since about 12,000 B. C., and this gives the minimum age for the Badarian civilization.

"This, in turn, will imply a date for subsequent prehistoric work rather earlier than hitherto assigned.

"Dating by the level of the Nile, which gradually raised its mud bed nearly five feet in a thousand years, is of value for determining historic times.

"The colossi of Amen-em-hat III at Biahmu had their courtyards under the high Nile by 3000 B. C., and therefore the twelfth dynasty must have been before that age, as the Egyptians themselves stated.

"Thus, owing to the discoveries in the field and the researches following on these, we now have a perfectly continuous view of successive civilizations of Egypt carried back some 14,000 years.

"The source of these Badarian arts must be referred to some centre in common with the solutrian age of Europe, wherewith they were contemporary, and which shared the same styles of flint work.

"Probably the Caucasus was the home of both these branches of culture."

WOMAN DIES IN FIRE; BABY SAVED BY TOSS

Rescuers Catch Infant Flung From a Fire-Escape Ladder by Father.

TWO PYROMANIACS SOUGHT

Alcohol-Soaked Rubbish Found After a Second Blaze—Fireman Proves a Hero.

A woman was burned so badly that she died later in a hospital, several firemen were overcome by smoke and more than fifty persons were driven to the street by a fire that burned from the cellar to the top floor of a four-story tenement at 429 West Fiftieth Street, early yesterday morning. A search for two pyromaniacs was begun by Fire Marshal Thomas P. Brophy after an incendiary fire had been started in another tenement house, at 20 West Sixty-fifth Street, several hours later.

Rubbish soaked with alcohol was found in a vacant apartment in the building where the second fire started. The carpet on the stairway also was soaked with alcohol. One tenant of the second building reported that she had seen two men running away soon after she was aroused by smoke and the crackle of the flames.

The first fire was at 3:30 o'clock in the morning. So rapidly did the flames eat their way from the cellar to the top floor that Mrs. Mary Legg, 50, was trapped in her bed in an apartment on the fourth floor. She was unconscious when lifted from her burning bed by a fireman. At the City Hospital, where she was taken, it was found that she was terribly burned on the face, hands and body. She died there later in the afternoon.

Makes Perilous Trip Up Ladder.

John White, driver of Hook and Ladder 4, carried Mrs. Legg from the building. An aerial ladder was raised to the roof and White, jumping off his truck, climbed up the ladder while it was being put in place. He knew that precious moments might be lost.

He clung to the topmost rungs while the ladder was still swaying and swinging toward the side of the building. With a space of two or three feet still between the ladder and the building, White swung himself out and dropped astride the window sill. He found the room filled with smoke. He dropped on his hands and knees and crawled along the floor where the smoke was the least dense. In that way he explored several rooms before he came to the bedroom where he found Mrs. Legg.

The bed clothes were afire. Mrs. Legg lay in a stupor, in a ring of fire that was slowly eating its way through the flimsy bed linens. White pulled her out of the bed and dragged her to the window where the aerial ladder was now propped against the wall. Unaided he lifted his helpless burden over the window ledge. Bracing himself he slid down the ladder, carrying Mrs. Legg to the street.

White was near collapse when other firemen ran to his assistance. Mrs. Legg was treated by an ambulance surgeon and removed to the City Hospital.

Firemen Thomas Bohan and George Russell of Engine Company 54 were overcome by smoke while fighting the fire. Their comrades rescued them and took them to the street, where they received first aid treatment. Drs. Bonanno and McDaniels of the City Hospital worked over the two firemen for ten minutes before they could revive them. Bohan and Russell were sent back to their company's quarters. Fireman Thomas Raisen was overcome by smoke, but responded quickly to first aid treatment and remained at his post.

Fireman James Walsh of Hook and Ladder 40 was cut on the hand by broken glass, but was able to continue his work.

Several Daring Rescues.

Several daring rescues were made before the building was cleared of all its tenants. The fire spread so rapidly that many tenants hardly had time to flee to the fire-escapes. George Clardy and his wife, when aroused by the shouts of warning and the clatter of the fire apparatus, gathered up their five children and led them to fire-escapes in the

Continued on Page Six.

REMOVE 41 BODIES FROM BOSTON RUINS

While Digging Goes On Police Capture Four Looters, Wounding One in Scuffle.

SEARCH FAR FROM ENDED

Some of the Injured Likely to Die—Governor Fuller Orders Swift Inquiry.

Special to The New York Times.

BOSTON, Mass., July 5.—Forty-one bodies, of whom thirty-three in all had been identified, had been recovered at a late hour tonight in the ruins of the Pickwick Club building on Beach Street.

Although more than 200 rescue workers were removing the débris throughout the day, not a body was recovered from early forenoon until 6 o'clock tonight.

As the flood of electric lights once more illuminated the scene new groups of victims were found among the tangled mass of timbers, iron beams, bricks and plaster. Every moment brought forth evidence of other victims still more deeply imbedded in the wreckage.

Firemen, elevated road workmen and employes of the city Public Works Department comprised the crew that labored in the ruins of the five-story building, which sent scores to death or serious injury when it collapsed early yesterday morning.

The flood lights created a picture resembling the stage of a theatre without curtains. The scene was one of cross-sections, showing portions of rooms still hanging from the back walls of the wrecked building, with some furniture still in place and pictures hanging on the wall, while beneath the workers continued the task of recovering bodies.

The balconies filled with spectators were real balconies, the fire escapes of the surrounding buildings, and one side, overlooking the whole area, was the Olympia Theatre with its signs completing the stage picture.

The authorities refused tonight to estimate the probable number of dead in the calamity. It has been impossible to check up on the total of merrymakers at the club. Some of the sixteen injured, now in the hospitals, are likely to die.

The Identified Dead.

The list of the identified dead is as follows:

ALEXANDER, BENJAMIN, Police Inspector, Dorchester.
COCHRANE, WILLIAM D, 28, Malden.
CONGDON, JAMES, 45, waiter, West End.
DE LUCA, Mrs. PAULINE, 35, South End.
DUFFY, JOHN, 30, singer and former boxer, Back Bay.
FLANAGAN, EDWARD S. "NEDDY," 29, Malden.
GLAVIN, HENRY J., 40, waiter.
GLENNON, JAMES F., 28, Roxbury, manager of the club.
GRAHAM, ARTHUR M., 28, Jamaica Plain.
GROSSMAN, WILLIAM J., 36, West End.
HALLORAN, Patrolman PAUL, 33, Dorchester.
HENDERSON, STUART, Milton.
JORDAN, Mrs. EDITH, 28, Somerville.
KEEGAN, LORETTA, 30, Cambridge.
LANZER, J., alias SARGE PENTA, 25, Boston.
LAWSON, MARGARET "PEGGY," 27, Brookline.
LONGOBARDI, JERE, 38, North End.
McEACHERN, Mrs. CECELIA, 22, Roxbury.
McLAUGHLIN, JOHN J., 30, South End.
McLEAN, FRANCIS J. Jr., 19, Malden.
MARR, W. H., 30, U. S. coast guard cutter Mohave.
MOORE, MAY, address unknown.
MURPHY, MARGARET, 20, Roxbury.
MURRAY, WILLIAM, 35, West Somerville.
NIXON, Miss, New York City.
O'DONNELL, BARTHOLOMEW, 24, South End.
PAULSEN, CARL JR., 23, Roxbury, taxi driver.
PHANEUF, JOSEPH G, address unknown.
SCALES, JOHN J., 21, Roxbury, singer in the club cabaret.
SMITH, JOSEPH, Providence.
STERN, MRS. DORIS, 24, 60 Sumner Ave., Brooklyn, N. Y.
TILLO, FRANK, 28, Chelsea, boxer.
VARA, FRANK "TEDDY," South End.
WILSON, Miss ESTHER, Roxbury.

While the work of recovering bodies was going on the officials of city and State were preparing to begin inquiries concerning the disaster. District Attorney Thomas C. O'Brien was at the scene most of the day and tomorrow he will present to the Grand Jury the evidence he has gathered.

Tonight Governor Fuller announced that he had ordered the Commissioner of Safety, A. F. Foote, to make an investigation of the collapse and report to him at once.

All the other night clubs in the city have been closed pending inspection of their buildings.

TWO KIDNAPPED MEN FOUND NEARLY DEAD CHAINED TO A TREE

Held for Eleven Days in Tennessee Mountains, They Say—One Was in Liquor Feud.

WERE MOVED EACH NIGHT

Kidnappers Thus Evaded Large Posse Scouring the Mountains for the Missing Pair.

LONG FIGHT OVER STILLS

But Both Declare They Do Not Know Their Assailants or Why They Were Seized.

CHATTANOOGA, Tenn. July 5—Dr. W. D. Mason, veterinary surgeon and Lawrence Bowman, alleged feudist, an aid of Federal prohibition agents, who had been missing for ten days, were found chained to a tree on Signal Mountain today by Jim Thomas, mountaineer. Sam Godsey, Deputy Sheriff, alleged leader of a feud clan, said that the men's disappearance was a frame-up.

Sheriff Tom Selman said that the story appeared dubious to him and that he would go to the bottom of the affair. It had been thought, since the two men disappeared and their automobile had been found covered with blood, that they had been the victims of a feud, in which the Bowman family had been opposed to the Godsey clan.

Both men were alive but in serious condition due to their long exposure and insufficient nourishment. They were brought to the city in an ambulance.

Mason and Bowman, after being sufficiently revived, stated that they had been set upon the night of their disappearance by five hooded men, carried off from Dr. Mason's car and chained to a tree. Each night they were blindfolded and removed to another place, they stated.

As the two men were found on a spot that was previously searched by a posse, it is believed that the men were moved each night to a section of the mountain that was searched on the previous day by the posse to prevent their discovery.

Although very thirsty, Bowman was able to talk, according to Thomas, but Mason did not speak. Bowman said that it had been four days since Mason had eaten, having become angry at being held captive and refused to eat and drink on one occasion. The captors then grew angry with Mason, Bowman stated, and refused either to feed him or give him water.

Thought Man Was an Apparition.

The men were found when Thomas, accompanied by his 9-year-old grandson and a German police dog, was seeking hogs that had escaped from his farm. He was amazed, he stated, when he saw Bowman, his face covered with a heavy growth of beard, and thought he was an apparition.

"I first asked him if he was thirsty," Thomas stated. "With an oath, he replied, 'Yes.' I always carry water on my horse, as it is impossible to secure water on the mountain due to the long drought. I fetched him a bottle of water which he grabbed at greedily. I succeeded in twisting it from his frenzied grip after he had taken about three swallows, as I feared the effects might kill him.

"I then turned my attention to Dr. Mason who was lying in a stupor, and Lawrence said he had not spoken all morning. I forced the mouth of the bottle through his lips and allowed the water to go through his teeth.

"Presently he began to show signs of life and began sucking at the bottle. I let him have about three or four spoonsful, but was afraid to give him any more.

"Leaving my little grandson with the men I rushed off to the nearest telephone. I couldn't find the Sheriff's telephone number, so I communicated with Joe Willis's stable, from where ambulances were secured for them.

"I then realized that I shouldn't have left the boy alone, for the bandits might have come back and killed him as well as spirited the men away. However, nothing like this occurred, the men having been frightened away.

"Bowman told me that they usually kept guard over them some distance away. From where I found them a creek runs only a short distance away. The sun beat down upon them unmercifully, while gnats, mosquitos and other insects preyed on their bodies.

"Dr. Mason's wrists were badly cut by the handcuff, which I severed with a saw and file I secured at the home from where I called the ambulance. The handcuffs were fastened to the chain, which was wrapped around the tree. Mason was chained the tightest,

Continued on Page Three.

Strike Sabotage Delays President Calles's Train

Special Cable to THE NEW YORK TIMES.

MEXICO CITY, July 5.—El Universal publishes a dispatch from Gomez Palacios, Durango, saying railway men tried to wreck the train of President Calles. The engineer noticed the bearings of his engine were getting heated and he was compelled to slow down the train several times. A complete examination was made, when the bearings were found to be full of iron filings.

President Calles by wire ordered the instant dismissal of the foremen of the roundhouses at Gomez Palacios and Lerdo, where the engine had been overhauled. Strikes at the shops began last week.

ASK MARRIAGE BAN ON ALL THE DIVORCED

Episcopal Organization Calls Proviso Favoring "Innocent Parties" Unscriptural.

MANNING AIDS MOVEMENT

Big Increase in Divorce Record Cited in Petition to the New Orleans Convention.

The Sanctity of Marriage Association launched a movement yesterday to bar absolutely the marriage of divorced persons in the Protestant Episcopal Church. The association announced that it was sending a petition for the repeal of the one proviso by which innocent parties in divorces based on infidelity have been allowed to remarry, to the General Convention of the Episcopal Church for presentation at the triennial convention in New Orleans in October. The petition attacks the proviso on the ground that it is unscriptural and contrary to the practice of the early Christian Church.

The Sanctity of Marriage Association is headed by the Rev. Dr. Milo H. Gates, vicar of the Chapel of the Intercession, Trinity Parish, and its Executive Committee includes, among others, Bishop William T. Manning, Bishop Frederick Burgess of Long Island and Bishop Paul Matthews of New Jersey.

The proviso to the canon forbidding the remarriage of divorced persons is as follows:

"This canon shall not be held to apply to the innocent party in a divorce for adultery; provided, that before the application for such remarriage a period of not less than one year shall have elapsed after the granting of such divorce; and that satisfactory evidence touching the facts in the case, including a copy of the court's decree, and record if practicable, with proof that the defendant was personally served or appeared in the action, be laid before the ecclesiastical authority, and such ecclesiastical authority, having taken legal action thereon, shall have declared in writing that in his judgment the case of the applicant conforms to the requirements of the canon; and provided, further, that it shall be within the discretion of any minister to decline to solemnize any marriage."

Bans Provided by the Canon.

The canon itself is:

"No minister, knowingly after due inquiry, shall solemnize the marriage of any person who has been or is the husband or the wife of any other person living from whom he or she has been divorced for any cause arising after marriage. Nor shall it be lawful for any member of this Church to enter upon a marriage when either of the contracting parties is the husband or the wife of any other person then living from whom he or she has been divorced for any cause arising after marriage."

The association gives the following seven reasons why in its judgment the one "exception" should be repealed:

"Because nowhere in the New Testament is there a single word in support of remarriage of either party after 'putting away' during the lifetime of the other.

"Because nowhere either in the Old or the New Testament is there any assumption, much less assertion, of the modern theory that adultery, or any other sin, ipso facto, dissolves a marriage, which is not a mere contract but a state or condition.

"Because nowhere in the history of the first three centuries, when the Church was suffering persecution and was free from all entanglements with the State, can there be found a single author who interprets the exceptive clauses of St. Matthew about 'putting away' as reason for remarriage during the life of the other party.

"Because nowhere since the fourth

Continued on Page Twelve.

BREAK IN RIFF LINE ALARMS THE FRENCH; PICK NEW GENERAL

Paris Admits Collapse of East Morocco Front, Following Desertion of Loyal Tribes.

LYAUTEY DEMANDS TROOPS

Marshal Declares He Will Not Accept Responsibility Unless Offensive Is Started at Once.

FEZ SAFE, PAINLEVE SAYS

War Office Issues Reassuring Statement, but It Shows Steady Gains by Rebels.

Special Cable to THE NEW YORK TIMES.

PARIS, July 5.—The situation on the Moroccan front has taken so serious a turn the French Government today felt it necessary to warn the country of the exact state of affairs, going even so far as to intimate that recent developments have rendered obligatory a retreat of French forces along a large section of the front.

Premier Painleve himself discussed the situation extensively, declaring the Cabinet intended to designate tomorrow an army chief who will take complete charge of military operations, thus enabling Marshal Lyautey to concentrate his efforts on nullifying the propaganda with which Abd-el-Krim has won to his side in the last few weeks four tribes previously faithful to the French. The leading possibilities for this post are Generals Targe, Weygand and Duport.

"However disagreeable may be the defections and however great be the demand on the efforts and heroism of our soldiers," said M. Painlevé, "I repeat solemnly that Fez is absolutely safe and has nothing to fear from Abd-el-Krim's warriors."

Marshal Lyautey has informed the French Government that unless it provides enough troops to begin an immediate offensive against the Riffians he will not accept responsibility for the situation which develops. Even more than a new leader the Government realizes what is needed in Morocco is more men, plentifully equipped; armored cars, airplanes and especially good riflemen and skirmishers.

French Line Is Opened.

An official communiqué issued by the Cabinet today announces that tribes formally faithful to the French went over suddenly to the enemy, thus opening a vast hole in the front through which Abd-el-Krim could hurl a violent offensive against French regulars. The regulars, declares the communiqué, are placing themselves in the best possible position to repulse the enemy and make him pay heavily for his aggression. The communiqué then continues as follows:

"It is highly important public opinion should not be at all disturbed by episodes inevitable in colonial warfare wherein defections always more or less accompany military operations. It must not be forgotten that the present operations in Morocco are confronted by difficulties which render them different from operations previously conducted in the same country or operations in Europe. On the one hand our adversaries are much better armed than they were six years ago, their attacks are more numerous and better coordinated on a much more extended front, and they know how to utilize, especially in certain regions, advantages of terrain and defense measures such as trenches, shelters, barb wire, &c.

"On the other hand, tactics of a modern army, notably concentration of forces for striking decisive blows, if employed too systematically, produce isolation of faithful tribes and consequent defection, following which occurs an increase of infiltration of enemy contingents.

"We must therefore not be astonished or alarmed if over so vast a front difficulties of the character described above should necessitate retirement in some localities and reorganization and reconcentration of forces in order that they might organize a more vigorous counter-offensive."

Offensive Urged to Stop Desertions.

Mussulman authorities, says a message from Fez, declare that only a lightning offensive can prevent further disaffection among the tribes. In an effort to counteract this spirit, the French today counter-attacked in several places along practically the whole front. North of Ouezzan they used heavy artillery and airplanes to bombard enemy villages, and the official communiqué states they profoundly demoralized the enemy.

Further east another mobile column made a night march against Teroual, which was reached despite stubborn resistance. In the upper Leben Valley a stern fight has gone on all today with the French on the offensive and the important position of Bab Taza recaptured. Bou Halima also has been relieved after heavy fighting with hand grenades. The communique adds with a certain indefiniteness as to actual position that the French troops engaged "in front of Taza" with important enemy forces belonging to three separate fighting bands which are being slowly [illegible] back.

Yesterday and today for the first [illegible] the French censor has slightly [illegible] the veil on the seriousness of the [illegible]tion. The Temps correspondent [illegible] that disaffection of the tribes [illegible]

2 New Police Trucks Ready With Squads To Cope With Fires, Wrecks and Riots

A new police emergency service—the first of its kind in the world—will begin operation in Manhattan, the Bronx and Brooklyn tomorrow morning, it was learned in Police Department circles last night. The service will start with two new emergency trucks, of a special type, built by the White Motor Truck Company, at a cost of about $14,000 each.

One of the new trucks, garaged at the West Thirtieth Street Station, will serve Manhattan and the Bronx; the other, located at the Poplar Street Station, Brooklyn, will serve Brooklyn and Queens. Each truck, in charge of a Police Lieutenant, will carry a specially trained personnel, consisting of three sergeants and twenty-one patrolmen.

The new service will combine the duties of a rescue squad, pulmotor truck, riot platoon, first aid and motor patrol squad. Each of the trucks, in its territory, will attend all fires of over two alarms, riots, train wrecks or automobile collisions in which a number of persons are injured or imperiled.

Fully equipped the new trucks will cost more than $20,000 each and provide New York City with a police emergency service said to be unequaled anywhere. The trucks are enameled in dark blue and bear in gold letters: "Police Department Emergency Service." Each is capable of speed of more than sixty miles an hour, the average gait at which they are expected to travel.

The equipment carried by the trucks includes 12 fire axes, 2 pulmotors, 6 acetylene torches, one life line, one rope cannon, 8 stretchers, 6 hydraulic jacks, 6 searchlights, 4 cot beds, 6 camp chairs, one full medical chest of complete surgical equipment, 8 gas helmets, 6 blankets, special clothing for injured and personnel, and many items of minor importance.

Voorhis's Office Is Under Jersey Apple Tree; To Stay at Old Home Until He Is 96 on July 27

Special to The New York Times.

POMPTON LAKE, N. J., July 5.—John R. Voorhis, President of the Board of Elections in New York City, and Grand Sachem of the Tammany Society, who came here to recuperate from an illness and to celebrate his ninety-sixth birthday at the place where he was born, has opened an office of the Board of Elections beneath an apple tree.

The venerable Tammany leader is the guest of Albert Van Saun, a farmer and Justice of the Peace, who lives on the Newark-Pompton Turnpike, between Pompton Plains and Pompton Lake.

Yesterday Mr. Voorhis unloaded a box of books and writing material on a pine table, strategically placed in back of the barn and underneath an apple tree. He said that his office would function here for the month or so that he remained.

In a house that once stood across the highway from the Van Saun farm Mr. Voorhis was born. Although he has no relatives here, he comes back regularly to the scene of his early days. He will be 96 years old on July 27.

Section 1

"All the News That's Fit to Print."

The New York Times.

THE WEATHER
Showers and cooler today; unsettled and cooler tomorrow.
Temperature yesterday: Max., 92; min., 67.

Section 1

VOL. LXXIV....No. 24,592. • • • NEW YORK, SUNDAY, MAY 24, 1925.

Including Rotogravure Picture Section in three parts—Magazine and Book Sections in Rotogravure. FIVE CENTS In Manhattan, Bronx and Brooklyn | Elsewhere TEN CENTS

SAY DEBTOR STATES BREAK AGREEMENT ON POST-WAR LOANS

Washington Officials Take a Firmer Tone in Demanding Settlement of the Full Amount.

OTHER CLAIMS PUT FIRST

All Debtor Countries, Except Yugoslavia, Paying Reconstruction Credits, but Ignore U. S.

BELGIUM CITED AS EXAMPLE

£8,000,000 to Great Britain and Nothing Here—War and Post-War Debts on Same Footing.

Special to The New York Times.

WASHINGTON, May 23.—A note of greater firmness was sounded in governmental circles today in comment concerning allied war-time and post-war indebtedness to the United States. The flat statement was made informally, but nevertheless authoritatively, that with the possible exception of Yugoslavia, all the nations which borrowed money from the United States Treasury for post-war purposes, chiefly reconstruction, had violated an obligation to this Government to treat it on a parity with all their governmental creditors in liquidating these obligations. In the face of that understanding, these post-war borrowers, it was asserted, had been making payments to other creditors when they were as greatly obligated to pay the United States.

The plain speaking which came today was the obvious outcome of comment by prominent Americans in this country and Europe in the interest of having the United States cancel its war claims against borrowing Allies or, at least, suspend for the present its policy of pressing its allied debtors for settlement. The unofficial attitude of debtor nations, and especially the reports that France claimed that there was a distinction between political debts and commercial debts, with the construction placed upon this contention that the United States should cancel the political debts, or those contracted by the Allies for prosecuting the war, is supposed to have added to the spirit of resentment that flared up in official quarters today. This resentment was more obvious than it was last week when it came to the surface in a way showing unmistakably the temper of the administration.

Violation of Agreement Charged.

It was apparent from what was said that the Government is angry over comment intended to be critical of its policy of pressing "courteously but firmly" for arrangements looking to the payment of allied obligations to the United States. Enough was disclosed to show that the Government feels that its position is being misrepresented abroad. But more important was the flat accusation that most of the allied Governments which obtained money for post-war purposes from the United States Treasury had been guilty of violating a guarantee, given by all of them, that there should be no discrimination against the United States in favor of other creditor countries when payments were made in liquidation of these loans.

It was further declared that as far as war debts were concerned there was absolutely no distinction ever recognized by this Government in the obligation of these nations to repay the United States. All the war-debtor nations, it was said, are governed by the same American law as far as collections are concerned, this law being the Debt Funding act, which provided for the creation of the Debt Funding Commission, the body which arranged with the British and other debtor Governments to liquidate wartime obligations to this nation. The obligations, according to the statement made, were just as absolute in the case of one nation as in the case of another.

With that statement as prefatory, it was pointed out that there was a distinction between war debts and post-war debts of allied nations to the United States in that in making advances to allied countries for post-war reconstruction and relief measures the United States obtained a stipulation from each debtor nation that there should be no discrimination against the United States in favor of other Governments advancing money for similar purposes. Such advances were made, in addition to the United States, by Great Britain and other Governments. In spite of the guarantee obtained by the United States, however, it was asserted, some of these post-war debtors were paying interest to government creditors but not paying a cent to this Government. In that course, according to what was said, these nations have discriminated against the United States and thereby violated their obligation to this Government.

Yugoslavia the Only Exception.

In specifying Yugoslavia as being an exception to the Governments which have not lived up to the obligation given to the United States, the qualifying statement was used that this was "generally speaking." While there was an apparent indisposition to go over the list of post-war debtor countries in detail, with a view to making clear the manner in which each had failed in its understanding with the United States, it was said that, leaving out Yugoslavia and speaking generally, all the foreign Governments to which this Government had advanced money for post-war purposes had made payments of at least a portion of their relief debts to other governmental creditors, and furthermore were paying interest on their other governmental funded indebtedness. This agreement, it was stressed, did not apply to war debts, each of which was on its own basis with each creditor nation at liberty to deal on terms satis-

Continued on Page Twenty-one.

Five Florida Men Convicted of Peonage

PENSACOLA, Fla., May 23 (AP).—Five Calhoun and Bay County turpentine producers were convicted in Federal Court today of violating the law against peonage by arresting, holding and returning negro turpentine workers to a condition of peonage against their will.

In a sealed verdict the jury found M. B. Davis, naval stores producer, guilty on twelve counts, and Charles Land, Cary Whitefield, William Proctor and Frank Daniels guilty on the same number of counts for aiding and abetting Davis. Sentence will be imposed next Friday. The defendants said an appeal would be taken.

The date for trial of five others indicted for the same offense will not be set, it was stated, until after sentence had been imposed on the men convicted today. The others indicted are Alfred Land, turpentine operator and brother of Charles Land; Sheriff Charles Lake, Judge William T. Chafin, County Attorney Henry V. McClellan, Deputy Sheriff Thomas Cason and W. White, commissary manager for Davis.

RETREAT FROM FIGHT ON PRESBYTERY HERE

Chester Presbyterians Decide Not to Ask General Assembly to Exscind New York Body.

PENSION PLANS DISCUSSED

Commissioners Endorsed Proposal to Erect a Monumental Church at the National Capital.

Special to The New York Times.

COLUMBUS, Ohio, May 23.—The fight of the Presbytery of Chester, Pa., to exscind, or excommunicate, the Presbytery of New York, which promised to be one of the important issues at the 137th General Assembly of the Presbyterian Church, will not occur, it was learned today.

The militant Fundamentalist majority of the Chester Presbytery has been persuaded to agree that no good would come of endangering the peace of the General Assembly by insistence on its declaration that the Presbytery of New York has been "guilty of long-continued disloyalty to the doctrinal standards of the Presbyterian Church" and "persistently disobedient to the mandates of the General Assembly."

Instead of pressing its overture the Chester majority has decided, it is reported, to stand behind a mild and innocuous measure calling for a committee or commission to investigate the New York situation.

Two reasons have been advanced for the change in the plans of the Chester Presbytery. The first was the election of Dr. Charles R. Erdman, a Pacifist Fundamentalist, as Moderator, which made it clear to the extremists that the assembly, as a whole, was anxious for unity and impatient of ecclesiastical warfare. The second reason was the presence here of a determined minority of Presbyters from Chester who were ready to wage a vigorous campaign against the overture from their own Presbytery in the interest of peace and harmony in the church.

To Raise $15,000,000 Pension Fund.

Will H. Hays, arbiter of the motion picture industry, who is Chairman of the Laymen's Committee on Ministerial Pensions, received a warm welcome when he presented the report of his committee and announced that the new pension plan would be inaugurated April 1, 1926. In the meantime a fund of $15,000,000 will be raised by Mr. Hays's committee, which has been enlarged to include Andrew W. Mellon, Secretary of the Treasury, as treasurer, and Frederick W. Weyerhauser of St. Paul, Minn. Other members are Robert Lansing, former Secretary of State; John Willis Baer, Pasadena, Cal.; Richard B. Mellon, Pittsburgh; Nathan G. Moore, Chicago; A. H. Whitford, Buffalo, N. Y.; T. N. Jarvie, New York City, and Senator William B. McKinley of Illinois.

Contributions to the pension fund are to be voluntary, the equivalent of 10 per cent. of the pastor's or church worker's salary being paid into the fund every year. The beneficiary of the fund pays 2½ per cent. and the employing organization 7½ per cent. of the premium. The pension is to be paid when the recipient is 65 years of age, and is to be one-half of the average yearly salary for thirty-five years of service.

After explaining that the pension plan had the approval of the foremost actuaries in the United States, who declared it to be as nearly perfect as it was possible to make it, Mr. Hays said he was interested in it "as an essential step in the preservation and development of the world's one essential industry—for religion is the one essential industry of the world."

"For a life of service the average material compensation of preachers in America is less than that paid our alien

Continued on Page Twenty-four.

HUNDREDS KILLED IN SEVERE QUAKE THAT ROCKS JAPAN

More Are Injured and Thousands Are Made Homeless in North of Main Island.

TOYO-OKA IS DESTROYED

Two Hundred Are Reported Dead There—Fire Sweeps Through Town.

FAMOUS KINOSAKI DAMAGED

But Large Cities in Area Are Said to Have Suffered Little Harm.

TOKIO, May 23 (AP).—More than 200 persons are believed to be dead at Toyo-Oka and several hundred injured at Kinosaki Springs because of an earthquake and fire this morning. It is not believed that any foreigners are victims.

Tsuiyama, near Toyo-Oka, was reported in flames, but no damage has been listed east of Kinosaki Springs.

Police at Kyoto report that ten persons are dead and many were injured in Fumihama, where numerous houses collapsed. Kinosaki Springs was reported to be burning, also, and a forest fire was said to be raging near the Springs.

The Maizuru Naval Station, fifty miles from Toyo-Oka, is preparing for relief work. The destroyer Enoki and the cruiser Kasuga have been ordered to the scene.

Troops from Fukuchiyama, thirty-seven miles from Toyo-Oka, are reported antraining for the stricken town to maintain order there.

The authorities here have not yet been able to obtain accurate estimates of the number of casualties or the amount of damage done.

The most accurate reports obtainable tonight estimated that more than 10,000 persons had been left homeless.

An airplane from the Asahi a Tokio newspaper, relayed reports that the fire at Toyo-Oka continued to rage late today and the whole town seemed virtually destroyed.

OSAKA, May 23 (AP).—Fully 200 houses were reported as collapsed and numerous fires were raging today in the vicinity of Toyo-Oka, a town of 7,700 population, eighty miles northwest of Osaka, as the result of an earthquake which sent terrified residents into the streets, fearing a repetition of the Tokio disaster of 1923.

Unverified reports from the Tajima district now state that it is believed that the heaviest loss of life occurred at Kinosaki Springs, where it is said all the buildings were wrecked, burying many persons. Fires starting immediately completed the ruin.

The estimates of dead in the town of Toyo-Oka vary between 100 and 200. Two-thirds of the town was destroyed, including all of the large buildings. Rail traffic will soon be restored, it is expected.

The earthquake, according to meteorological reports, was a horizontal vibration of nearly three inches, which is a record for the past thirty years. The temblor was continuous and lasted several minutes.

Reports received here by the vernacular newspaper say the Toyo-Oka Post Office has collapsed and the railroad station burning. Military airplanes have been dispatched to the area affected to investigate the extent of the damage.

Tajima Province, in which the temblor was centred, is a thinly populated area. The important industry in the section is sericulture, the damage to which has not yet been estimated.

Panic in Stricken Area.

Copyright, 1925, by The New York Times Company.
Special Cable to THE NEW YORK TIMES.

LONDON, May 23.—The greatest earthquake in the Osaka area of Japan for thirty years shook the town of Toyo-Oka and the surrounding area at 11 A. M. today, fragmentary news reporting eighty dead in Kuniyama and Fukuchi alone, indicating a considerable death total in all.

In Toyo-Oka the town is burning up and 10,000 natives are fleeing in a panic.

A special dispatch to The Evening News from Tokio gives the following details of the Japanese earthquake:

"Many big office buildings are cracked and damaged and smaller buildings were brought down. Reports from the affected districts are only fragmentary, as telegraphic communication is interrupted.

"It is reported to have been the greatest earthquake in the region for thirty years. The worst of the danger is over in Osaka, Kyoto, Kobe and Nagoya, which did not take fire, but the cities are in the wildest confusion. Every one is in the streets, afraid to re-enter the buildings.

"The greatest damage was done at the seaport of Toyo-Oka on the Japan Sea, in the Province of Tango. There fires are raging and the city is doomed, its population of 10,000 being in full flight.

"At Toyo-Oka the railway station and 200 houses collapsed, fire breaking out immediately and trapping many of the

Continued on Page Two.

28 Breton Seamen Perish As Seas Upset Lifeboats

Copyright, 1925, by The New York Times Co.
Special Cable to THE NEW YORK TIMES.

PARIS, May 23.—Twenty-eight brave Breton seamen lost their lives this afternoon when a sudden, violent tempest arose, driving the fishing smacks St. Louis and St. Pierre, of Kerity, Penmarch Harbor, toward the land and finally overturning them.

With the shore lined with anxious relatives, two lifeboats were launched in the raging waters and picked up the men desperately clinging to the wreckage of their ships only to capsize with their heavy burden.

A dozen fishing craft bore swiftly down on the scene of the disaster, but could save only nine of the twenty-four lifesavers while all twelve of the fishermen were drowned. Tonight Captain Berrou, who commanded one of the lifeboats, died from exposure.

ABDUCTED GIRL SLAIN; SUSPECT IS CORNERED

Winthrop (Me.) Posse Discover Aida Heyward in Cottage Just Vacated by Man.

HIS VICTIM WAS STRANGLED

Posse Reports Having Fugitive Surrounded—Woman He Shot May Also Die.

AUGUSTA, Me., May 23 (AP).—Word that Harry A. Kirby, wanted in Winthrop in connection with the murder of Miss Aida Heyward, has been surrounded in Portland, was received here tonight at the office of the State Highway Police.

Special to The New York Times.

WINTHROP, Me., May 23.—The body of Miss Aida Heyward, who was abducted on Tuesday night by a man who shot her aunt, Mrs. Emma M. Towns, and set fire to their cottage on Lake Maranacook, was found today hidden in another cottage on the lake about a mile and a half from her former home.

Only partially clad, the body lay between two mattresses on a bed on the second floor of a cabin at Pine Point, which is owned by Miss L. Jane Gray, a school teacher of Watertown, Mass. Apparently the girl had been attacked and choked to death. A protruding tongue showed she had been strangled.

The police are already on the track of Harry A. Kirby, of Watertown, Mass., who had occupied the cottage where the body was found until late last night, when he suddenly left town. He hired the place two weeks ago from Miss Gray, who had been a schoolmate of his wife, and obtained employment in a factory here.

Last night Kirby went to the home of Ted Bearce, on the road half a mile from the lake shore, and said he wished to engage a room. He said he had been occupying the Gray cottage, but "wouldn't stay there another night for $1,000." He said he had an engagement to meet Fred H. Moulton of Lexington, Mass., brother-in-law of Miss Heyward, at 9 o'clock this morning.

Kirby did not appear at any such appointment. Instead, in the course of the forenoon Postmaster Earl D. Jones received a postcard from him saying he had gone to Augusta and asking that his mail be forwarded to that city. Mail for Kirby was sent to Augusta and at the same time State policemen set a watch at the Augusta postoffice and began a systematic search of the city.

Evidence of Desperate Struggle.

The body was found by Charles Towle, Representative in the Maine Legislature; S. Lee Woodman, former Deputy Sheriff, and Dr. Carl J. Bates of Winthrop.

These three, with others, had been making a canvass of cottages along the twenty-mile shore of Lake Maranacook. The Gray cottage, however, had been overlooked because it had been occupied.

Today, Towle, Lee and Dr. Bates found the gray cottage locked. They broke in, made a quick search, and on a bed on the upper floor found the body of the missing woman. Chairs had been piled atop the mattress, which had been placed over the body.

Everything about the room was in disorder, indicating that Miss Hayward had put up a desperate battle with her assailant, to save herself. A rope was found in the room.

News of the discovery of the body aroused the townspeople to a high pitch of excitement. Many vowed vengeance upon the brutal perpetrator of the murder. Officials hastened to the scene. With the party were County Attorney Southard, Detective James R. Wood of Boston, Sheriff Cummings, Chief Sanborn of the State Highway Division, and a score of others, including newspaper men.

A call had been sent to the nearest Medical Examiner, and after making a cursory examination of the body, the party awaited his arrival.

Sixty Armed Men Search for Kirby.

A posse of sixty armed men, however, has begun ranging over the countryside in the belief that Kirby has taken to the woods. A description of him broadcast throughout New England tonight was as follows: 35 years old, dark complexion, small bristling mustache, wearing Norfolk coat, low shoes and brown sweater.

It was learned that Kirby first came to Winthrop three years ago but when his wife received a legacy, they moved to Old Orchard, where Mrs. Kirby now resides.

Mrs. Towns, who was shot twice by the man who abducted her niece and burned their home late Tuesday night, was still in such a serious condition at the hospital tonight that the authorities were afraid to tell her of Miss Heyward's fate. They rely upon her to identify the murderer when he is apprehended.

Special to The New York Times.

BOSTON, Mass., May 23.—Miss L. Jane Gray of Watertown, a teacher at the West Junior High School, said tonight she was the owner of the cottage at Lake Maranacook in which the body of Miss Aida Hayward was discovered. While she did not know the victim, Miss Gray stated she was a school chum of the wife of Kirby, who is being sought in connection with the death.

The teacher said she permitted Kirby and his wife to use the cottage last year and again in April of this year.

Gerard Denies Talking on Debt Collection; Says State Department Listed Him Wrongly

By EDWIN L. JAMES.

Copyright, 1925, by The New York Times Company.
Special Cable to THE NEW YORK TIMES.

PARIS, May 23—Former American Ambassador to Germany James W. Gerard has asked THE NEW YORK TIMES today to quote him as saying he was improperly included in the State Department's list of Americans abroad who had been talking too much about America's debt collection.

Mr. Gerard said he was of the opinion that any American citizen had the right to express his opinion about any issue, but that in the present instance he had not so indulged.

"The only interviews I have given since reaching Europe," he said, "have been interviews denying statements sent to a New York newspaper by its Paris correspondent, charging that I had been 'talking' about the French debt. As I have not 'talked,' and am therefore neutral on this question of 'talking,' it is not without interest to examine this problem of the discussion of a nation's foreign policy by its citizens. I think there is a distinction between one who 'talks' to a foreign Government, or even in a foreign country, purporting to represent either his Government or the sentiments of his own country, and a mere discussion by our citizens among themselves and even publicly, on the question of our foreign policy, whether with reference to debts or anything else.

"When I was in Berlin I suffered much from volunteer diplomats, and the volunteer ambassador should be thoroughly discouraged and effectively sat upon. But I am sure our President, whose foreign policy thus far has, to my mind, been so notably successful, does not mean through his 'spokesmen' to forbid American citizens to discuss any phase of governmental policy, whether foreign or domestic."

HIGH WIND HITS CITY; FALLING FENCE KILLS FATHER AND CHILD

Trees Uprooted, Canvas Tops Ripped From Buses and Autos Blown Adrift.

MANY WINDOWS BROKEN

Man Is Drowned When His Boat Is Upset in Lake Hopatcong—His Companion Saved.

TWO HEAT PROSTRATIONS

Earlier Hailstorm Brings Relief, but Causes Damage to Crops in Suburbs.

Yesterday's sultry weather was dissipated with sudden fury just before 7 o'clock last night when a wind that was almost a tornado hit New York and swept so fiercely through the city that automobiles with brakes set were sent scurrying before it, canvas tops were ripped from the double-decked Fifth Avenue busses, plate glass and thinner windows were shattered by the hundreds, trees were uprooted and a child was killed when a fence was tossed over in the lower West side.

The outskirts of the city and some of its suburbs got relief several hours earlier when the forerunner of the heavy wind brought hailstorms that peppered Saturday afternoon pleasure seeking crowds.

The beaches suffered, particularly with the second onslaught of wind, which whirled up great clouds of stinging sand and gave thousands of New Yorkers a taste of wild weather in a desert.

On the waters hereabouts were many small craft, some of which had exciting scurries for shore when clear skies darkened, and then a big blow came up, whipping smooth surfaces into angry waves and threatening to capsize every small boat in its path.

Charles Gemar, 65 years old, of 320 Pichenor Avenue, South Orange, N. J., was drowned in Lake Hopatcong, near Dover, N. J., when the boat in which he was sailing with a companion was overturned by the sudden descent of the storm. The companion clung to the overturned boat and was rescued by Miss Grace Douglas, who saw his plight and put out in a sailing skiff. Efforts to recover Mr. Gemar's body were unsuccessful.

The Weather Bureau reported a maximum wind velocity of sixty-four miles an hour for the evening storm, to which it allotted a duration of about ten minutes. The storm caused the temperature to drop from 91 degrees to 74 in a few minutes. The Weather Bureau thermometer at 4:30, while the hailstorm was going on in upper Manhattan, registered at Battery Place a temperature of 92 degrees, which marks the hottest in its records for any May 23. It does not, however, set a new record for the month.

Caught by a Fence

George Westley Whitney of 508 West Twenty-first Street and his two-year-old daughter, Olga Virginia, were the victims of the storm in West Twentieth Street. They were walking eastward on the north side of the street while the wind was at its height. They were passing a fence sixty feet long and twelve or fourteen feet high that encloses a lot next to the garage of the Fullerton Trucking Company at 531 West Twentieth Street. In the lot motor trucks and other gear of the trucking company are kept.

The couple were about opposite the middle of the fence when, without warning, there came a sudden crack like a pistol shot, a forty-foot section of the fence lurched forward, and in another moment was a mass of splintered and twisted timbers on the street. Dense clouds of dust arose from the wreckage and were whirled off in the wind.

Most of those who heard the noise did not know there were people caught in the wreckage, as all had been busy seeking shelter. But two passersby, Jack Kelly of 822 Washington Street and Rudolph Christensen of 206 Ninth Avenue, had seen the father and daughter before the crash came. Calling help they rushed to the wreckage and began to pull it aside in the spot they thought the pair would be.

As they pulled the beams and crosspieces aside, they found the father with his arms clasped around the child. Both were unconscious. His scalp was torn over the forehead. Both were covered with blood. They were carried to a garage across the street, where they received first aid.

Then John Long of 500 West Twen-

Continued on Page Twenty-six.

AMUNDSEN NOT HEARD FROM IN 61 HOURS; EXPERTS BELIEVE HE LANDED FROM PLANE; SAY THERE IS NO INDICATION OF DISASTER

MacMillan Is Ready to Hunt Amundsen Party If Needed, Changing His Exploration Plans

BOSTON, May 23 (AP).—All the plans of the Captain Donald B. MacMillan Arctic expedition will be subordinated to the relief of Roald Amundsen if Amundsen is not heard from before the MacMillan ships, Bowdoin and Peary, leave this country late in June.

Captain MacMillan made this announcement this afternoon just prior to departing for his home in Maine. He said the relief of Amundsen would be made the main object of his expedition, and that his original plans would be entirely secondary to finding the Norwegian explorer.

Captain MacMillan believes the chance of finding Amundsen in Northern Greenland will be good. If when the MacMillan expedition reaches Etah in August the Amundsen party has not been heard from, MacMillan will dispatch airplanes to old Fort Conger, where he thinks it possible Amundsen may be found.

At Fort Conger there are three small huts, a big coal mine and game is plentiful. Captain MacMillan said musk oxen, seals, reindeer, Arctic hares, ducks and ptarmigan would afford sufficient food.

Contrary to published statements, there is no cache of food at Cape Columbia, but there is a small cache at Ward Hunt Island, twenty miles west of Cape Columbia. The existence of this cache has been known hitherto only to Captain MacMillan, who left it there in 1909, with the idea that it might possibly be of use to Admiral Peary in his polar expedition.

The cache contained oil, tea, biscuits and pemmican, the supplies being sufficient to last five men for a week.

Commander MacMillan thinks Amundsen's best chance of rescue would be to make for Fort Conger, which was the headquarters of the Greely expedition in 1881-1883. The location is on Franklin Bay, approximately 400 miles from the Pole.

PREPARE FOR THRONG AT EVOLUTION TRIAL

Little Town of Dayton, Tenn., Seeks Tents and Pullmans for Crowd.

GRAND JURY TOMORROW

And Trial of Professor Scopes Is Likely to Begin Next Month.

Special to The New York Times.

DAYTON, Tenn., May 23.—This thriving little city of 2,500 people nestling at the foot of Walden's Ridge, a chain of picturesque foothills of the Appalachians, awaits with eager anticipation the coming of Monday morning and the calling together of the Rhea County Grand Jury for a special term ordered by Judge John T. Raulston of the Criminal Court. This jury will investigate charges filed against John Thomas Scopes, Dayton High School teacher, that he taught his pupils principles which are in violation of the recently enacted statute forbidding teachers in schools "supported in whole or in part by the public school funds" to teach "any theory that denies the story of the Divine creation of man as taught in the Bible, and to teach instead that man has descended from a lower order of animals."

If Professor Scopes is indicted it will be followed by what is expected to be the most sensational trial in the State's recent history, and which is scheduled to bring to Dayton William J. Bryan of Florida to assist in the prosecution, with Clarence Darrow of Chicago and Dudley Field Malone of New York coming to defend the young educator, who states that he is "ready to fight, and, if need be, die, for that which he conceives to be right."

That the conclusion of the lower court may be disposed of by the Supreme Court in December, in time that the teachers of Tennessee may be advised as to their status under the act when the Fall terms open, Judge Raulston has under consideration a special June term of the Criminal Court to try Professor Scopes, if he is indicted. The regular term coming in August would preclude the case being passed upon by the higher courts until after the schools had gotten under way.

Trial Expected to Draw Throngs.

Meanwhile, Dayton is preparing for the trial of the case with the expectation that the Grand Jury will hold the teacher for the Criminal Court, where, under the law, he would be subject to a fine of $100 to $500 for each offense, if convicted. Thousands of outsiders are expected to be on hand for this trial, including some of the prominent educators of the country. Requests for reserved seats have been received from several college presidents, and the belief is that the Rhea County Court House, seating about 1,000 persons, will be inadequate to entertain the spectators.

Representative Cordell Hull, whose district includes Rhea County, will be requested to obtain from the War Department, if possible, a supply of tents to house visitors who cannot find other

Continued on Page Twenty-two.

COOLIDGE TAKEN ILL, RECOVERS QUICKLY

Combination of Heat and Cantaloupe Causes a Brief Attack of Indigestion.

KEEPS ON WITH HIS WORK

Attended by White House Physicians, He Cancels Engagements; Takes Mayflower Trip.

Special to The New York Times.

WASHINGTON, May 23.—President Coolidge suffered a slight attack of indigestion today in his office, a few hours after breakfast.

The attack, while intense for a time, was of short duration, but the President accepted the advice of his physician, Major J. F. Coupal, canceled his engagements and remained in his study.

The President spent a restless night, it was said, due to the change in the weather and the sudden appearance of the hottest weather Washington has experienced this early in May for many years. He took his usual morning walk, had breakfast at 8 o'clock and went to his office about 9 o'clock.

The heat wave was sharply felt in the President's office, the sun pouring in through the south windows.

A few minutes after his arrival he began to suffer and he returned to the White House, where his physicians, Major Coupal and Lieut. Commander Joel T. Boone, attended him. The ailment quickly yielded to treatment and the President wished to return to his office. But he consented to remain in his study until he started for the usual week-end trip down the river on the Mayflower at 2:30 o'clock.

He walked up to the gangplank without aid and stood on the bridge as the yacht moved away.

Lays Attack to Fruit.

Mrs. Coolidge had gone on a shopping tour and when she returned to the White House she found the President in the hands of the physicians and apparently recovered. He told her that there was nothing the matter, and ascribed the attack to his having eaten cantaloupe at breakfast for the first time this season. After lying down for a short time the President went to his study, where he continued some of his routine work and conferred with Senator Borah.

Senator Borah had been sent for earlier in the day, it was believed to confer about the debt situation.

This is the first indisposition that has affected the President this year. He says that he does not eat heavy meals, but is known as a "reliable eater," with a healthy appetite. He had a similar attack last December when he went to Chicago and earlier in that year suffered from rose fever, to which he is subjected, and which is likely to recur any time now.

Generally speaking, the President enjoys the best of health and keeps himself in trim by walking morning and night and daily exercise on his electric horse. He has the wiry constitution of his mountain ancestors.

There is evidence that the President is slightly run down at present and that he greatly needs a long vacation such as he will take for the first time in two years the latter part of next month.

Accompanied by his two physicians, President Coolidge took his usual week-end trip down the Potomac. Those in the party besides Mrs. Coolidge included Attorney General and Mrs. Sargent, Secretary and Mrs. Hoover, Senator and Mrs Butler and H. L. Stoddard.

A radio dispatch was received from the Mayflower early this evening stating that all on board were well.

"White Court" in Readiness.

SWAMPSCOTT, Mass., May 23 (AP).—"White Court," which will be the Summer home of President Coolidge here, has passed through the hands of decorators and is now ready for occupancy. The twenty-six-room porticoed mansion, reconditioned, is spick and span and cheery, in readiness for the President's first real vacation in two years.

The dining and other rooms have been entirely renovated according to a general scheme. The rooms in which official callers will be received are differently decorated from those in which the President and Mrs. Coolidge will meet personal friends and live. Hangings, upholstery and wall paper have been done over.

THIRD DAY BRINGS NO NEWS

Pole Seekers May Have Abandoned Planes and Taken Land Route.

MAY NOT HEAR FOR WEEKS

Great Difficulties Will Be Met if They Try for Greenland, Experts Say.

TALK OF ARRANGING RELIEF

Navy Is Asked at Washington to Assist, but Says There Is No Need Yet.

The North American Newspaper Alliance announced through The Associated Press at 9:30 o'clock last night that no news had been received from the Amundsen-Ellsworth North Pole Expedition.

The Alliance further announced that the weather at the Spitzbergen base of the expedition continued perfect, with moderate temperature, Summer sunlight, no wind and ice-free seas.

Fifty-seven hours have elapsed since the explorers flew from Spitzbergen.

Sixty-one hours had elapsed at 1:15 o'clock this morning since the explorers flew from Spitzbergen at 5:15 P. M. on Thursday (12:15 P. M. New York time)

No Anxiety in Copenhagen.

Copyright, 1925, by The New York Times Company.
By Wireless to THE NEW YORK TIMES.

LONDON, May 23.—Dispatches from Copenhagen state there is little or no anxiety felt there regarding the Amundsen expedition. Amundsen increased his benzine supply to such an extent that he had to discard his wireless apparatus, and news from him cannot be expected until he is either back at Spitzbergen, if the flight is successful, or, in the contrary event, until he and his companions make their way across the ice to North Greenland. One dispatch says:

"While awaiting news it is worth remembering that it would take five hours for a wireless message from the expedition's ship Fram to reach Copenhagen, five retransmissions being necessary.

"Those whose Arctic experience and other expert knowledge warrant an expression of opinion appear to think the absence of news of Amundsen's return to Spitzbergen indicates that he either has landed at the Pole or that he has discovered intermediate land where he has descended for investigation, and may therefore have encountered difficulties in reascending or found it necessary to wait for better flying conditions.

"Captain Godfrey Hansen doubts that Amundsen would attempt to land, and believes he would remain a-wing, flying at the Pole until he ascertained all that was possible and then would drop a Norwegian flag and commence to return."

British Speculate on Results.

British geographers are waiting with anxiety for news of Amundsen, though they have no special knowledge of his flight. For some years relations between Amundsen and the Royal Geographical Society have not been close, and he did not inform it of his plans for the polar trip.

From one point of view his venture is regarded here more in the nature of a feat of travel than anything else. He planned to make such a short stop at the North Pole that, even if successful, it would be quite impossible to make many observations of scientific value. At the same time, it is regarded as probable that by the mere fact of traversing to the polar regions he would be able to bring back interesting information.

In the first place, he should be able to throw much light on the controversy concerning the existence of undiscovered land in the polar basin. It is possible that low-lying land, covered, it is presumed, with ice and snow, might not be detected from a rapidly moving airplane, but if there were land with any elevation it must be identified. Even Greenland, in the districts covered with a permanent ice field, has such a rugged rock formation that snow and ice cannot rest on it, and bleak, bare rocks crop out through the prevailing white of the snow.

Secondly, even a rapid flight to the Pole and back will determine a point much discussed by meteorologists, the so-called "inversion" of the temperature of the air—that is, the belief that in the polar basin the higher stratum of air is warmer than the lower in consequence of the latter being continually cooled by the ice-floes. Such an inversion, if it exists, must have an important effect on air currents and would help to explain meteorological phenomena.

Explorations in both Arctic and Antarctic regions in the past have been very helpful to weather prophets, but of course in an ordinary expedition using sledges it has been possible to carry on observations over a considerable period.

Another point of the flight which is attracting attention here is the way the airplane engines will behave. The two used are 370 horsepower Rolls-Royce IX Eagle type, and if they succeed in getting to the Pole and back it will be great proof of their reliability. A similar make of engine has just achieved a triumph in the success of Lieutenant Aviator Edmund Thieffery of the Bel-

To Sell Candy and Gum in New Subways; Transit Board Gives Permit Under New Law

The sale of candy, gum and other merchandise will be resumed in the city's newer subways. The Transit Commission announced yesterday that it had approved applications by the Interborough Rapid Transit Company and the Brooklyn-Manhattan Transit Corporation for permission to exercise the vending privileges at all the stations of their rapid transit lines for the sale of such articles as are commonly sold on railway newsstands. The privilege is expected to add about $150,000 a year to the revenues of each company.

The action of the commission was taken under the provisions of the Nicoll-Clayton act, passed by the last Legislature and signed by Governor Smith, which eliminated from the Rapid Transit act the clause prohibiting the sale of anything but newspapers and the display of any advertising in the stations of the subways built under the dual contracts. The Interborough Company has also filed an application for permission to sell advertising space in all its subway stations, as it does in the stations of the original subway, but the commission will consider the application for the advertising concession separately.

In approving the applications of the two companies the commission reserved the right of revocation and specified that vending might be carried on only under such rules and regulations as it might prescribe. The commission also specified that the location of all vending and weighing machines should be subject to its approval and should in no case interfere with passengers or employes or interfere with the heating, lighting, ventilation or proper appearance of a station.

It is expected that a number of station newsstands, which were closed when the commission enforced the contract provision against the sale of candy and other merchandise except periodicals, will be reopened.

The Bettmann Archive

Lincoln Ellsworth, who financed and accompanied Roald Amundsen on his flights to the North Pole by airplane and dirigible.

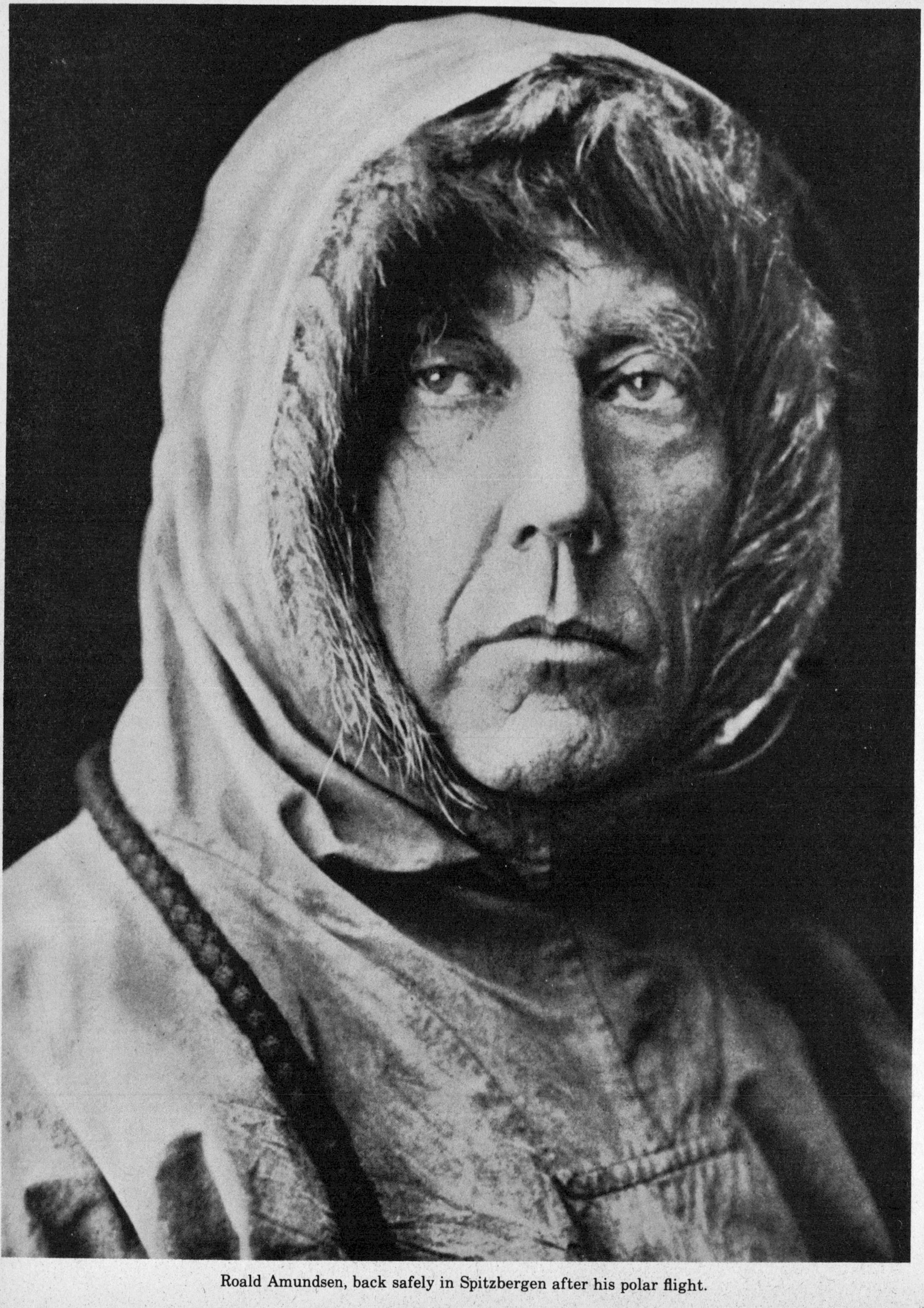

Roald Amundsen, back safely in Spitzbergen after his polar flight.

"All the News That's Fit to Print"

The New York Times

LATE CITY EDITION

Weather: Fair, very cold today and tonight. Chance of snow tomorrow. Temp. range: today 24-14; Sunday 33-26. Full U.S. report on Page 30.

VOL. LXXIV....No. 24,618. • • • NEW YORK, FRIDAY, JUNE 19, 1925. TWO CENTS In Greater New York | THREE CENTS Within 200 Miles | FOUR CENTS Elsewhere in the U. S.

BRITISH AND FRENCH SECURITY POSITION MADE CLEAR IN NOTES

Exchanges on German Proposal Show Frank Explanation and Understanding.

BRITAIN TO DEFEND FRANCE

And Use Influence to Compel Observance of Continental Arbitration Treaties.

WON'T GUARANTEE THEM

France Reserves Right to Fight for the Protection of Poland and Czechoslovakia.

By EDWIN L. JAMES.

Special Cable to THE NEW YORK TIMES.

LONDON, June 18.—A clear idea of the work being done by the British and French Governments toward the establishment of a more stable political status in Europe is given by the publication tonight of the German proposal for a Rhine compact made last February to the French Government and the French reply on behalf of the Allies, which was delivered in Berlin the day before yesterday, with the notes exchanged between Paris and London on the subject.

In the exchanges between Paris and London, in which frank explanations were made and understandings reached, the British Government declined to guarantee any frontier other than that of the Rhineland, or arbitration treaties entered into among the European powers generally, but added that in principle England was ready to use her influence to oblige the signatories of such of these treaties as she approved to observe their promise to resort to arbitration.

France, on the other hand, expressed readiness to arbitrate all issues with Germany except the provisions of the Versailles Treaty. She reserved the right to use armed force, if necessary, for the protection of Poland and Czechoslovakia.

The German proposals and French answer agree closely with the forecasts which have been given in THE NEW YORK TIMES.

Berlin proposed treaty arrangements based on a Rhine compact entered into by Germany, England, France and It and completed by arbitration treaties and treaty pledges against war, all to take the form of commitments by the contracting powers toward the Government of the United States as trustee.

In answer the French accept the general idea of a Rhine compact and of an agreement to arbitrate all issues between Germany and France on certain conditions, among which are the entry of Germany into the League of Nations, an understanding that none of the treaty rights now held by the contracting parties are affected, that Belgium be included and that Germany make arbitration treaties with her other neighbors. The German suggestion to make Washington trustee was dropped in the French note.

Points Left Open Considered.

While the texts of both notes leave many points open, the correspondence between Paris and London shows that they have been considered. Several tentative drafts of the reply to Berlin given in a White Book issued by the British show the full meaning of the proposed arrangements. One notable point the British make plain, that they are not willing to agree to general arbitration of all issues which may arise between England and other signatories, so this has led to the plan for separate arbitration treaties, France being ready to arbitrate all issues with Germany, except the provisions of the Treaty of Versailles.

On this point of treaty enforcement the British Foreign Office note of May 19 made plain, and the French later agreed, that there must not be isolated action, but rather that machinery must be set up for deciding differences and whether they justified sanctions. Mr. Chamberlain recommended that the League Council be called on for this task.

On May 22 M. Briand replied that what the French meant was that they should not in the proposed treaties give up any rights they held under the Treaty of Versailles. He stated that France was willing to arbitrate any issue except a clear violation of a treaty obligation, in which case coercive action could be taken only in accord with the provisions of the treaty violated. M. Briand stated that the reason for not including the names of Poland and Czechoslovakia in the note to Berlin was to aid the Reich statesmen in dealing with their public opinion, but that, nevertheless, the French intended to take the position that any attack on Poland would mean a treaty violation calling for sanctions. As M. Briand put it:

"If, for example, Germany were to violate the arbitration treaty with Poland, Great Britain could not automatically be drawn in to a greater extent than she was involved in the first place by the guarantee which she has given in the arbitration treaty, and in the second place, by her capacity as a member of the League of Nations. In return France could not be deemed to violate the Rhineland compact if she should be called upon to help Poland."

M. Briand in several notes recognizes Mr. Chamberlain's stand that Britain will do no advance military guaranteeing of any line except the Rhine line, and in his note Mr. Chahberlain on May 22 says:

"In placing the whole guarantee compacts and agreements under the auspices

Continued on Page Four.

Britain to Have Penny Post And Better Phone Service

LONDON, June 18.—Great Britain is to return to penny postage, equivalent to the two-cent rate in America, and there is to be improvement of the country's antiquated telephone service, according to Sir W. L. M. Thompson, Postmaster General.

"I do not like to see this country standing tenth or eleventh in the list of telephone-using countries of the world," declared the Postmaster General. The telephone system in England is under Government control. Recently there has been some improvement in the service because of the installation of automatic exchanges.

The return of penny postage is promised within the life of the present Parliament. The present rate is 1½ pence (3 cents) for ordinary letters, imposed as a war measure.

BRITAIN WILL HOLD PEKING TO ACCOUNT

Chamberlain Tells Commons British Lives Will Be Protected.

REGRETS THE CRISIS THERE

Shanghai Peace Conference Breaks Up—Mob There Said to Have Called for War.

Special Cable to THE NEW YORK TIMES.

LONDON, June 18.—Alarm lest the agitation in China should become anti-British rather than anti-foreign was expressed by Mr. Lloyd George in the debate over the Chinese disturbances in the Commons today. He urged the Government to be sure that other powers acted in concern with them in any action which might be taken in China, and was reassured by Mr. Chamberlain, who declared that this has been in his mind from the start.

The evening resolved itself less into a debate on the Government's handling of the Chinese situation than into a discussion as to the causes of the disturbances. Labor speakers held that terrible industrial conditions in Shanghai were mainly responsible for the outbreaks. The Foreign Secretary, while admitting that there was much room for improvement in this respect, declared that the disturbances were assignable in the last analysis only to the break up of the Central Chinese Government.

He announced that England is approaching other powers to expedite the approaching Chinese tariff conference provided for by the Washington conference with a view to finding the real solution of all of China's troubles.

The debate was opened by C. P. Trevelyan, ex-Minister of Education in the Labor Government. Evidence, he said, had been given by American missionaries that the Shanghai crowds were fired upon without provocation, and that it is the Government's duty, after securing the lives of its subjects, to bring home the responsibility for the tragedy.

The Chinese felt that they were being governed by economic exploiters and the powers evidently realize that extra-territoriality in China is eventually doomed. He asked whether the forthcoming conference on Chinese tariffs could not be extended to cover the question of extra-territoriality. The root cause of the trouble, he concluded, is the rule of forty-nine of the greatest cities of China by foreigners.

Mr. Chamberlain said that the evil conditions in Shanghai are admitted and that the British Government no later than June 10 had pressed for the adoption of humane regulations by the Shanghai Municipal Council. However, an elementary sense of perspective would show that the present troubles originated in the break-up of the centralized autocratic Government and the substitution of rudimentary, fermenting Westernism.

British Must Be Protected.

To deal with the resulting turmoil, the Washington conference had done its best, he said, to organize the interested powers. They agreed to help China and composed their own differences as the first step, but China has proved more difficult to help than had been expected. Her disorganization had increased and it has been difficult to find any Government there to deal with. Therefore, a watching though not a valueless policy had alone been possible.

The very first and only immediate step, said Mr. Chamberlain, was to protect British lives and property and to hold the Chinese Government responsible for injury to either. But the causes of the trouble were more than the strike in a Japanese factory. General poverty and insecurity, owing to civil wars, had

Continued on Page Eight.

"DR." FAIMAN RECITES DEAL WITH SHEPHERD FOR POISON GERMS

Astounding Story by Head of Chicago Medical 'University' Consumes Whole Day.

SAYS HE TAUGHT ACCUSED

Gave Him Detailed Instruction on How to Put Germs Into Human Body, He Charges.

FIRST PRICE WAS $200,000

Suave Young Medico Tells How He Knew of Billy McClintock and Was to Benefit by His Death.

Special to The New York Times.

CHICAGO, June 18.—The dapper young witness whom everybody in the Shepherd trial has disowned, Charles C. Faiman, took the stand today at the order of the Court and told in a dispassionate, low voice, a story of the long-planned and deliberate murder of "Billy" McClintock by means of typhoid germs which he furnished. On whether or not the jury believes his story depends the fate of William D. Shepherd.

He is an unpleasant person, this smiling blond young man of twenty-five, who adds to his name the degrees of Ph. B., M. D., and LL. D. which he says he obtained at various colleges in his short career. His eyes are shifty, under a bald forehead back through the middle of which runs a line of carefully plastered hair. It is reddish hair and curls a little over his ears, above side-whiskers. A dainty mustache, pointed at the ends, adorns his upper lip. His face is plump and pale, his lips full, and his teeth very white.

He talked into his lap a good part of the time he was relating his dealings with Shepherd, in a voice so low that words could hardly be distinguished by persons twenty feet away. Judge Lynch frequently told him to raise his voice, and finally the smoothly purring electric fan above his head was turned off, so that even that slight sound might not interfere. Sometimes he would turn toward the jury and talk directly at them, but those furthest away sat on the edge of their chairs and cupped their ears.

It was a story worth hearing, for he told blandly how he instructed Shepherd in the administration of typhoid bacteria, told him how to prepare cultures, bargained with him for "two hundred grand"—$200,000—and finally reduced his terms to $100,000. He spoke glibly of the effect of typhoid on the system, the various unpleasant ways in which it causes death, and the difficulty of detecting it until eight or ten days after infection.

Defense Fails to Shake Story.

The apprehension of State's Attorney Crowe that Faiman would change his story, which led Mr. Crowe to disown him as a witness, proved unjustified, and made evident the State's strategy in having him called by the Court so that Crowe could cross-examine him. Faiman admitted that he had lied in his first denials of any dealings with Shepherd, but the story he told today was a smoothly running narrative, and when court adjourned, the strenuous efforts of the defense to break it had not been successful. They did prove him to be an unprincipled rascal, but there were those on the State's side who argued that this made his tale all the more plausible. The State seemed more pleased today than at the close of any previous day since the case opened.

When William Scott Stewart took Faiman in hand and brought out the unsavory details of his short but spectacular career, they were so bizarre that his replies caused ripples of amusement in the court room, until Mr. Crowe twice demanded that order be preserved, and Judge Lynch twice threatened to clear the room. Most of this took place when he was examined about his school, the National University of Sciences, in which young Faiman, Ph. B., M. D., and LL. D., but without a license to practice any of the things he taught, admitted giving instructions in everything from veterinary surgery to embalming.

Faiman Dresses for the Occasion.

Faiman astonished those in the court room by changing his clothes between sessions. In the morning he was attired in a neat blue suit, tan shirt and darker tie, extremely neat and immaculate. After lunch he arrived in a tan suit, with a blue shirt and a blue tie.

Judge Lynch began the questioning of Faiman, and brought out that Faiman received a letter from Shepherd in October or November of 1923 requesting in-

Continued on Page Five.

Radium Killed Woman, Relatives Declare; She Is Seventh Watch Dial Painter to Die

Special to The New York Times.

ORANGE, N. J., June 18.—Mrs. Sarah T. Maillefer of 174 Main Street, East Orange, died today in St. Mary's Hospital, where she had been a patient for a week, suffering from what the Essex County physician said was a "pernicious type of anaemia."

Mrs. Maillefer was employed at the United States Radium Corporation's factory and was engaged in painting luminous radium dials on watches. She is the seventh employe of the company to die after exhibiting similar symptoms. Relatives assert that her death was caused by "radium poisoning."

Professor Edwin E. Leman, chief chemist of the corporation, died ten days ago after thirteen years continuous working with radium.

Some weeks ago Mrs. Maillefer's parents started suit against the radium corporation, alleging that it was responsible for the illness of Mrs. Maillefer and her sister, Marguerite Carlough.

The sisters shared the same room at home and had worked together for six years. Miss Carlough has been ailing for eighteen months from the same type of pernicious anaemia, according to physicians at the hospital, where she has been confined for several months.

County Physician Martland, after performing an autopsy on Mrs. Maillefer today said that laboratory tests would be made to determine whether radium was directly responsible for her death. The tests will take about six weeks.

The dead woman's parents said that three years ago she was stricken with what was then believed to be an attack of rheumatism and became lame. Soon afterward she experienced trouble with her spine. They contend radium phosphate was the cause of the trouble. Three weeks ago, they said an X-ray photograph was made and the physicians declared that Mrs. Maillefer was suffering from poisoning caused by constant exposure to radium.

Unions to Levy Half-Cent Tax Per Member in Education Drive

Forty-one international labor unions have voted to finance an educational campaign among working men and women, according to a statement issued yesterday by Spencer Miller, Secretary of the Workers' Educational Bureau of America. These unions have decided to tax themselves to the extent of one-half cent per member in order to complete the $50,000 budget needed this year by the bureau.

The program of the campaign includes the printing of a pamphlet series and of the "Workers' Bookshelf," which already contains some twenty-five books on labor subjects. The bureau will also organize lectures, study classes and will support Summer schools and various labor institutes.

TO RUN, HYLAN SAYS, M'COOEY AT HIS SIDE

Mayor Declares Himself Out for Nomination, Regardless of Party Leaders.

'CAN'T STOP ME,' HE ADDS

Guest of McCooey on Madison Club Outing, Announces He Is Ready for Fight.

With his political sponsor, John H. McCooey, Democratic leader in Brooklyn, looking on and listening, Mayor Hylan reiterated yesterday his determination to become a candidate for a third term regardless of how the leaders of his own party felt about it.

"I am a candidate for renomination and shall be to the finish," Mayor Hylan said. "If there is to be a fight, I am ready for it. Nothing can stop me from running except the Great Power above."

The Mayor pointed to the blue sky overhead as he uttered the last sentence. He was standing in the bow of the steamer Mandalay, on her way to Bear Mountain on the annual outing of the Madison Club in Brooklyn. This is the headquarters of the regular Democratic organization of the Eighteenth Assembly District in Kings, the district of which McCooey is the de facto leader and executive member. The occasion this year marked the twentieth anniversary of the founding of the club and also was the celebration of the sixty-first birthday of Leader McCooey.

Mayor Hylan could scarcely have chosen a more dramatic setting for delivering his ultimatum to politicians of his own party intent upon his elimination as a candidate to succeed himself in his present office.

Hylan Guest of McCooey.

McCooey, who was the Mayor's host on the outing, was standing by his side. Surrounding him on all sides were Brooklyn Democrats, a majority of them members of Mr. McCooey's district organization, but many hailing from other districts in Kings. McCooey came fresh from conferences on the Mayoralty situation with Governor Smith at Albany, where he is known to have delivered as his ultimatum that until a stronger candidate could be produced he would stand by Mayor Hylan.

When the Mayor made his statement to a group of reporters he had been in protracted conference with the Democratic chieftain of his home borough, whose support will be necessary if the Mayor is to realize his ambition to serve three terms as Mayor of New York.

Mayor Hylan was the central figure of the excursion and virtually the whole show. The McCooey outing this year was far from joyful. It was pronounced a very tame and lifeless affair by some of those who went along. In the crowd on the boat were scores of Democrats from the Mayor's home borough who are bitterly opposed to the renomination of Mayor Hylan. Arthur Somers, who is McCooey's close friend and the only President the Madison Club has had during the twenty years of its existence, is one of the strongest opponents of Mayor Hylan in his home borough. He has been talked of as an opposition candidate for Mayor in the event that Hylan should run as an independent.

That Mayor Hylan had not overlooked anything that might lend strength to the impression that he could bank on the support of McCooey to the end, although many persons have suggested that the Brooklyn leader had his tongue in his cheek when he expressed his undying determination to stand with the Mayor, was apparent to observers aboard the Mandalay.

While the steamer was making its way up the river the Mayor stood in the bow of the boat where all could see him in close conversation with the Brooklyn leader. Later he went to the dining room and had luncheon with Mr. McCooey. After the meal the two emerged and were walking the upper deck together, when McCooey proceeded to make the most politically of the Mayor's appetite.

"Some of the Mayor's opponents," he told newspaper reporters, "are saying that his health is not so good. Well, if a big appetite is a proof of good health, let me say I personally saw the Mayor eat two big bowls of clam chowder, two big slices of steak with all the trimmings, pie, ice cream and coffee.

"Any man who can digest a meal like that must be in fine physical condition. There is no doubt about the Mayor enjoying splendid health."

2,000 on the Outing.

The Mandalay got under way from the Battery a little after 9 o'clock yesterday morning. About 2,000 followers of McCooey were on the passenger list. A band was playing on the upper deck. A few minutes before the gang plank

Continued on Page Eight.

LA FOLLETTE DIES IN CAPITAL HOME; LAUDED BY HIS FOES

Final Attack of Heart Disease in Early Morning Is Fatal to Insurgent Leader.

"AT PEACE" HIS LAST WORDS

Family Are at Bedside When End Comes While He Strives to Speak.

COOLIDGE PAYS TRIBUTE

Special Wisconsin Election to Fill Senator's Seat Deemed Likely Next Summer.

Special to The New York Times.

WASHINGTON, June 18.—Senator Robert Marion La Follette, leader of the Republican Progressives and an independent candidate for the Presidency last year, died in his home here at 1:21 P. M. today from heart disease, which had been complicated by attacks of bronchial asthma and pneumonia.

He had been seriously ill for a month, and a day or two ago his heart began to weaken so much that his family realized the end was not far off. Last night he was in a grave condition, and when he suffered an unusually severe heart attack at 8 o'clock this morning he was not able to survive it.

An official statement by the Senator's physician revealed that Mr. La Follette had been a sufferer from angina pectoris for ten years and that he knew when he attempted the Presidential campaign last year what the consequences might be, but despite that fact and the additional one that he had had pneumonia the previous Winter he depended on his splendid vitality and fighting spirit to take him through.

The death of the Senator is fraught with tremendous political significance, for with his passing is removed from American life by far the strongest opponent of what are termed by political radicals "the predatory interests," and apparently there is now no one to succeed him as the organizer of a third party which would oppose the policies of the conservative elements of the two major political organizations.

Conscious of the End.

Regardless of their political convictions, public men in Washington were inclined this afternoon to look on the death of Senator La Follette as a distinct loss to the country. Many of them disagreed with him on basic principles, but they regarded his public career as one which brought to the fore great issues which required solution and discussion not only by Congress but by the people of the country at large.

Strikingly different from his vivid life, the Senator's death was peaceful. He had been in bad health since last November, but on last Friday he became very ill, and on Sunday, his seventieth birthday, he began to fail rapidly.

Coughing spells of violence accompanied his illness and these gradually took what strength his weakened heart had left him. This morning he lay quietly awaiting the end. He knew that he was about to die, and at one time turned to his son-in-law, George Middleton, the playwright, and said:

"Well, George, I am going to take a long, long rest this time."

At another time he called his devoted son Robert to his bedside and said:

"Bob, I am at peace with all the world, but there is a lot of work I could still do. I don't know how the people will feel toward me, but I will take to my grave my love for them which has sustained me through life."

These were the last audible words the Senator spoke, although several times later he vainly rallied his fast failing strength in an effort to say something to his family. Just before he died his lips moved, but what he endeavored to say could not be heard. Immediately afterward he lapsed into unconsciousness and in a few moments he was dead.

President's Letter to Widow.

One of the first perons in Washington to send condolences to the widow of Senator La Follette was President Coolidge, whose message follows:

THE WHITE HOUSE,
Washington,
June 18, 1925.

My dear Mrs. La Follette:
The news having just reached me of the death of Senator La Follette, I wish to extend to you and your family the sympathy of myself and Mrs. Coolidge. As you know, I presided over the Senate for a considerable period while he was a member of that body and so came to know of his great ability and untiring energy. He has left behind him a great concourse of friends who will, I know, do every-

Continued on Page Six.

AMUNDSEN BACK SAFE IN SPITZBERGEN; PLANES LANDED 150 MILES FROM POLE; SHORTAGE OF FUEL FORCED RETURN

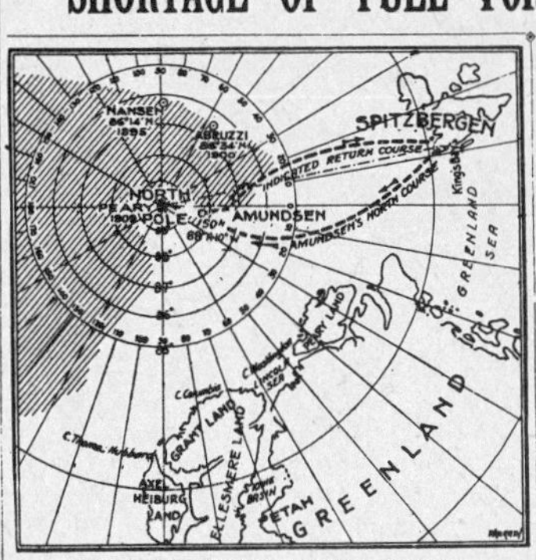

AMUNDSEN'S ROUTE NORTH AND BACK.

The Course Taken by the Norwegian Explorer's Two Airplanes on the Trip North From Spitzbergen to Within About 150 Miles of the North Pole. The Shaded Portion Marks the Area MacMillan Plans to Study.

FLEW BACK OVER THE ICE

Explorers Dropped Into the Sea and Were Rescued by a Fishing Boat.

PLANES ICELOCKED IN NORTH

Water Lane Froze After Landing, Balking Efforts to Reach Pole and Endangering Return.

ONE MACHINE LEFT THERE

Expedition Sighted No Land in the Far North—New Attempt May Be Made.

By EDWIN L. JAMES.

Special Cable to THE NEW YORK TIMES.

LONDON, Friday, June 19.—Captain Roald Amundsen and his comrades returned to Spitzbergen yesterday, exactly four weeks after he left in his attempt to reach the North Pole by air. Meanwhile no news of any kind had been received from him.

The most interesting feature of Captain Amundsen's trip was his observations from the air at a distance of less than 150 miles from the North Pole, which showed no land in sight. [An unconfirmed Associated Press report from Oslo last night said that Amundsen got within "about 100 miles" of the Pole.] This raises the point of whether or not there is land at the Pole or whether the northern end of the earth lies under sea.

It is apparent that had fate not dealt the intrepid explorer a head wind he would have come within a few miles of the Pole, if not have reached it in his daring flight. He covered a thousand kilometers in his airplanes and it is estimated here that with no wind, or a favorable wind, he would have easily covered the 200 more which would have taken him to his goal.

The feature of the absence of land in the polar regions is especially interesting in view of the discussions of the rights of the nations to claim the land which may be found.

Returns as Searchers Were About to Start.

Commenting on the return of Captain Amundsen, The London Times says editorially:

"Yesterday afternoon welcome news reached London that at 1 o'clock in the morning Captain Amundsen and his six companions had arrived safely at King's Bay, Spitzbergen, the point from which he started on May 21. After an absence of just a month, during which fears that they must have been lost grew steadily, all cause for anxiety is at an end.

"On Tuesday, less than forty-eight hours before the return of the wanderers, two seaplanes sent out by the Norwegian Government to help search for the missing men were on the point of beginning the journey northward from Spitzbergen. It is to be hoped that both in their case and that of Commander Donald B. McMillan, the American explorer who set out independently on the same mission Wednesday their start may have been delayed.

"Meanwhile the message Captain Amundsen himself gives is a thrilling account of the flight, the happy termination of which justifies the confidence which he has from the first expressed in the successful issue of the daring enterprise. The first man to take a vessel from one end of the Northwest passage to the other, the first to reach the South Pole and now the first to attempt a seaplane journey to the North Pole, he has been favored in all adventures with good luck. More than once he has come back out of the unknown when to all intents and purposes he had been given up as lost.

Covered 625 Miles in 8 Hours.

"But not even luck could have carried him safely through these trials and perils unless he had been backed by unfailing confidence and personal initiative and driving power as well as consummate knowledge and judgment in dealing with each crisis as it arose.

"In the first stage of the voyage from which he has now returned the two flying boats covered a distance of 625 miles in eight hours before being compelled, with the half store of petrol consumed, to come down for the purpose of getting their bearings on a water lane cutting through the ice since no more solid landing place was available. But for the contrary winds he could have gone another 120 miles further.

"Observations during this part of the flight showed an area of 100,000 kilometers, up to 88.30 degrees north, with no sign of land, and they came to the conclusion that no land is likely to be found further north on that side of the Arctic Ocean.

"The fact that when they tried to rise from the water lanes they found at first both flying boats frostlocked, speaks volumes for the energy and resourcefulness which enabled them in the end, despite this alarming mischance, to make their way back to Spitzbergen. If they failed in this primary object of reaching the Pole they have at least added to the checkered story of polar exploration another chapter of gallant endeavor in the face of difficulties and dangers that to ordinary men would be insurmountable. [illegible] escape from a graver [illegible] with a feeling of ad-

MRS. J. P. MORGAN HAS SLEEPING SICKNESS

Blood Transfusion Aids Patient, Whose Condition Is Reported Encouraging.

HUSBAND AT THE BEDSIDE

Stricken After Church Service —3 Physicians at the Home —3 Cases Reported Here.

Mrs. J. P. Morgan, wife of the banker, was stricken with sleeping sickness following church service last Sunday, but her condition was reported yesterday to be encouraging. Specialists and nurses, however, remained at the bedside last night in the Morgan home at Matinecock Point, East Island, Glen Cove, L. I.

A blood transfusion was resorted to early yesterday morning, when Mrs. Morgan's condition gave cause for anxiety. The operation was satisfactory and she began to mend at once, the turn for the better becoming more marked as the day progressed. A bulletin on her illness, issued at the office of J. P. Morgan & Co., Broad and Wall Streets, at 3:30 P. M., said:

"Mrs. J. P. Morgan throughout the day maintained the improvement and the outlook is encouraging."

The final bulletin of the day on Mrs. Morgan's condition made public by Martin Egan of J. P. Morgan & Co. was as follows:

"At 10:30 P. M. Mrs. Morgan's condition was much improved. She had a good day and it looks quite encouraging."

During the services on Sunday in St. John's Episcopal Church, Glen Cove, Mrs. Morgan appeared to be in good health. Upon her return to Matinecock Point she developed preliminary symptoms of sleeping sickness. Mr. Morgan was cruising in Long Island Sound in his yacht Corsair, and when his wife failed to respond to initial treatment he was summoned home by wireless. He has been at the bedside constantly since his return, with his two daughters, Mrs. Paul G. Pennoyer and Mrs. George Nichols.

Four physicians were in charge of the blood transfusion operation. Those who gave their blood were brought from New York with extra nurses. In order to perform the transfusion it was necessary to requisition some supplies from the Glen Cove Community Hospital, to which Mr. Morgan recently gave $50,000. Physicians on duty yesterday at the home were Dr. Henry S. Patterson and Dr. J. J. Tierney of New York and Dr. Edward Jessup of Roslyn, L. I. Dr. Patterson is Mrs. Morgan's personal physician.

Townsfolk Are Anxious.

Mrs. Morgan is very popular among the townsfolk of Glen Cove, and they

Continued on Page Eleven.

$1,000,000 OF ESTATE TO GUINEVERE GOULD

George J. Gould Heirs Agree to End "Old Animosities and Legal Scandal."

NEW JERSEY SUITS TO STOP

Settlement Is Allowed Pending Outcome of Action by Jay Gould Heirs Against Estate.

All the heirs of George J. Gould, who for a year have been in litigation in the New Jersey Chancery Court for the recovery of property due them individually from the estate, have reached an amicable agreement out of court, it was announced yesterday to Vice Chancellor Backes at Newark.

Harold A. Content, attorney for the Edith Kingdon Gould estate, presented the application for confirmation of the agreement to the court.

"This settlement," he said, "has been reached in an effort to do away with the old animosities and to avoid the legal scandal which has characterized the long-drawn out Gould controversies in the New York courts for the past generation. In thus arriving at a settlement each and every one of the litigants have made a personal sacrifice to a certain extent of their contentions, but for the first time in years the members of the George J. Gould family are amicably reunited."

Vice Chancellor Backes confirmed the settlement, but provided that before the property may be distributed security for the money involved must be furnished pending the outcome in New York of the suit brought against George J. Gould by his brothers and sisters for a surcharge of $80,000,000 from the estate of their father, Jay Gould. This, it was stated, would protect the $15,000,000 estate of George J. Gould for whatever verdict is reached in the New York case.

Under the terms of the agreement, which are said to have been promoted largely by Jay Gould, the tennis star, Mrs. Guinevere Sinclair Gould, second wife of George J. Gould, will get $1,000,000 in Liberty bonds which her husband cabled to her just before his death in Paris. The other heirs had previously insisted Mr. Gould was incompetent mentally when he made this gift. The settlement of the Liberty bonds does not affect the claim of Mrs. Guinevere Gould and her three children in a $4,000,000 trust fund established for them in George J. Gould's will.

Gives Up Claim on Paintings.

Mrs. Guinevere Gould relinquished her claim on five valuable paintings given to her in his lifetime by Mr. Gould, but which were claimed by the heirs of Edith Kingdon Gould, his first wife, as having been left to him by their mother for use only while he lived. The settlement gave these paintings and the contents of the Edith Kingdon Gould homes at Lakewood and New York to the Edith Kingdon Gould estate, worth about $700,000.

The Edith Kingdon Gould estate relinquished its claim against the George J. Gould estate for $1,900,000 of Pacific Express stock, alleged to have been profits in a transaction Mr. Gould made in his first wife's name.

Jay Gould relinquished a claim of $890,000 against his father's estate which he claimed was money lost by Mr. Gould from a trust fund left for the young man by his grandfather, Jay Gould, and agreed to pay into his father's estate $142,000 represented by claims of the estate for money advanced to him. There were $240,000 of these claims, but all save $71,000 Jay Gould had declared previously represented gifts from his father.

After Vice Chancellor Backes had confirmed the settlement, George W. Wickersham and Ralph E. Lumm, attorneys for Mrs. Guinevere Gould, applied to Vice Chancellor Backes for $50,000 for each of her three children for support

Continued on Page Three.

Missionary Blinded on an Errand of Mercy; Loses Sight of an Eye in African Sandstorm

Dr. Howard Buchanan, medical missionary for the United Presbyterian Board of Missions in the Sudan, came home yesterday on the President Harrison after an absence of seven months, blind in one eye and almost blind in the other because he would not seek shelter in an African sandstorm while he was hurrying to aid a mission station stricken with fever.

"It's just the sort of thing that happens sometimes," he said as he stood on the pier with his wife and two children, who accompanied him, and a group of friends, but the latter made it clear that Dr. Buchanan's mishap was not the sort of thing that happens often.

Dr. Buchanan and his family were the only white persons in a hamlet on the White Nile, 300 miles south of Khartum, in [illegible] Africa, when word [illegible] from the south [illegible] mission station was stricken with fever and that he must come at once.

As he and the guide pressed south, the sky darkened, and both knew its portent. It was the mansur, or duststorm of the Sudan. The native begged Dr. Buchanan to seek shelter, but he refused, and then the sky was black and the storm was upon them. An hour later the storm was over, the sky clear and the sun shining. But Dr. Buchanan did not see it. He was led to his destination, his friends said, and there, ignoring his own misfortune, he administered to the sick missionaries. Ophthalmia, which might have been averted by treatment, set in, and now all he can see is a glimmer of light. He went to Philadelphia, his home, hoping something can be done there to save the vision of his remaining eye.

The Bettmann Archive

Roald Amundsen (far right) and the members of his Polar flight crew, being decorated for valor.

"All the News That's Fit to Print"

The New York Times

LATE CITY EDITION

Weather: Fair, very cold today and tonight. Chance of snow tomorrow. Temp. range: today 24-14; Sunday 33-26. Full U.S. report on Page 30.

VOL. LXXIV...No. 24,656. NEW YORK, MONDAY, JULY 27, 1925. TWO CENTS In Greater New York | THREE CENTS Within 200 Miles | FOUR CENTS Elsewhere in the U. S.

W. J. BRYAN DIES IN HIS SLEEP AT DAYTON, WHILE RESTING IN EVOLUTION BATTLE; HAD SPOKEN CONTINUOUSLY SINCE TRIAL

LARGE EFFECT IN POLITICS

Democrats Divided as to How Bryan's Death Touches Party.

GREAT CREATOR OF ISSUES

Fear Had Arisen, However, That the Commoner Would Cause a Religious Schism.

HAD PREMONITION OF DEATH

Bryan Felt His Strength Was Waning at the Convention Here a Year Ago.

By RICHARD V. OULAHAN.

Special to The New York Times.

WASHINGTON, July 26.—Practically deserted during this heated season of those politically prominent, there were few in Washington this evening who had been associated with William Jennings Bryan or had known him during his active career since he came here a young Congressman from Nebraska in 1893, thirty-two years ago.

For that reason it cannot be said, in the sense of widespread knowledge of it, that Mr. Bryan's sudden death created a sensation in the national capital. But to the meagre number of those here tonight whose public life had brought them into close contact with the great Commoner the news of his passing came as a distinct shock. That was apparent from their exclamations when they were informed of the tragic happening in the little Tennessee town where he so recently fought his last battle for principles in which he believed and to the promotion and defense of which he devoted every bit of his abundant energy.

The death of Mr. Bryan was entirely unexpected in Washington, but that he was not in the best of physical condition and had feared for some time that his days were numbered was disclosed by a fellow Nebraskan, also a Democrat, Gilbert M. Hitchcock, former Senator, who was Chairman of the Senate Committee on Foreign Relations when Mr. Bryan was Secretary of State.

Spoke of Death at Convention.

Their official duties during the rather brief period of Mr. Bryan's tenure in the Cabinet interlocked, and years before then they had been on the most intimate professional and personal terms through the fact that Mr. Bryan was the editor of The Omaha World-Herald, owned by Mr. Hitchcock. But in more recent times they were bitter personal opponents in the leading rôles they played within the Democratic Party.

When he had recovered from the distinct shock that the news of Bryan's death caused him, the former Senator said that, on reflection, it was not so surprising, as he recalled that during the Democratic National Convention in Madison Square Garden last year Mr. Bryan had told his fellow members of the Committee on Resolutions, when they were engaged in the bitter contest over the matter of including a denunciation of the Ku Klux Klan in the party platform, or omitting reference to it, that he felt that his life was fast coming to an end.

"I think he had a premonition," said Mr. Hitchcock. "He could not any longer stand fatigue. I served with him on the Committee on Resolutions during the convention and he told us in committee that this would be the last convention he would attend. He seemed to have a feeling that he would not live. He had overtaxed himself so much. Evidently the struggle in Dayton during the hot weather was too much."

That the premonition of an early death had been in Mr. Bryan's mind prior to the Democratic convention a year ago was indicated by Mr. Davis, who disclosed that his former chief had written to him about two years ago with reference to obtaining a plot of ground in Arlington for the last resting place of Mrs. Bryan and himself. Mr. Davis at

Continued on Page Two.

© Underwood & Underwood.

WILLIAM JENNINGS BRYAN,

Who Died Suddenly Yesterday Afternoon at a Friend's Home in Dayton, Tenn.

BRYAN IS EULOGIZED, EVEN BY OPPONENTS

Leaders of Varying Political and Religious Beliefs Join in Tributes.

HONORED FOR SINCERITY

Governor Smith, Mayor Hylan and John W. Davis Among Many Praising Him.

Political friends and foes of William Jennings Bryan, Modernists and Fundamentalists, were shocked and saddened by the news of his death last night.

His immense vigor and activity during the last few weeks heightened the surprise caused by his death. He was thought to be hale and hearty enough to be the leading champion of the causes of Fundamentalism and prohibition for many years to come.

The political and religious enemies of the old crusader spoke with feeling last night in expressing their regret at his sudden death. Those who had fought him for three generations respected him as a foe for his sincerity and for his fighting qualities. His followers in religious and political battles were stunned by the news of his sudden death. The drys regarded him as the greatest living champion of prohibition and the Fundamentalists looked to him as their national chief and hoped that the man who played so great a part in putting prohibition into the Constitution would eventually succeed in safeguarding the literal word of the Bible by legislation.

Governor Alfred E. Smith said: "I heard of the death of Bryan with a great deal of regret. He was a vigorous American and even those who disagreed with his ideas had a great regard for him."

Mayor Hylan said: "I regret very much to hear of the death of Colonel Bryan. I have known Colonel Bryan for a great many years and always held him in high esteem. I believe that he has always been sincere in any cause he espoused."

John W. Davis, Democratic candidate for President at the last election, said at his home at Locust Valley, L. I.:

"The depressing news of Mr. Bryan's death must prove a great shock, not only to his friends but to the country at large. I am most deeply grieved by it.

Continued on Page Three.

ARLINGTON BURIAL ASKED FOR BRYAN

Military Service in Spanish War Entitles Him to Rest in Hallowed Soil.

HAD REMARKED ITS BEAUTY

Funeral Arrangements Will Be Made Today by Ben G. Davis, His Secretary for Many Years.

Special to The New York Times.

WASHINGTON, July 26.—Arrangements are being made for the burial of Colonel William J. Bryan in Arlington National Cemetery.

Immediately after the death of her husband at Dayton, this afternoon, Mrs. Bryan sent a telegram to Ben G. Davis of Takoma Park, Md., former chief clerk of the State Department and an intimate personal friend of Colonel Bryan, stating that the latter had died while asleep and requesting Mr. Davis to make arrangements for his interment at Arlington. Mr. Davis was unable to communicate tonight with Major Robert P. Harbold of the office of the Quartermaster General of the Army, who is in charge of the cemeterial division.

After conferring with the superintendent at Arlington and with attachés in Colonel Harbold's office, Mr. Davis sent a telegram to Mrs. Bryan asking for further particulars with respect to her wishes and informing her that he will take up the matter with the War Department tomorrow. Colonel and Mrs. Bryan are both entitled to burial at Arlington under the Federal law which permits interment there and in other national cemeteries of all who have served in the army, navy and marine corps, or the volunteer forces of the United States, and their wives.

Led Nebraska Infantry.

Colonel Bryan is entitled to burial at Arlington by reason of his service in the Spanish-American War. He raised the Third Regiment of Nebraska Volunteer Infantry in May, 1898, for service in the war with Spain and became its Colonel. After serving in that war, he came to Washington and made possible the ratification of the Treaty of Peace which had been negotiated by the American commission at Paris.

The treaty was in danger of being defeated by Democratic votes but Colonel Bryan exerted his influence and swung them into line so that he could make "imperialism" the issue in the subsequent national campaign. When laid away under the oaks at Arlington on the green Virginia hills with the placid Potomac below, Colonel Bryan will rest, after life's fitful fever, with many of the distinguished dead of the Nation. It is there that the American Unknown Soldier, now the mecca for distinguished visitors from all parts of the world, is buried.

Will Lie With Many Famous Dead.

On the slopes of the hill, near the old Lee Mansion, at Arlington, are the graves of Major L'Enfant, the French engineer who planned the City of Washington, General "Phil" Sheridan, Admirals Porter and Farragut, General Crook, the great Indian fighter, former Secretary of State Gresham, Generals Lawton, Wright, Hazen, Myers, Meigs, Belknap and many others. The latest distinguished army officer to be interred there was the late Major Gen. Nelson A. Miles.

Until recently Admiral George Dewey

Continued on Page Two.

APOPLEXY CAUSES HIS DEATH

Had Said He 'Never Felt Better' on His Return From Church.

SPOKE TO 50,000 SATURDAY

Full of Zeal to Take Cause to Country, He Was Thrilled by Crowds on Last Journey.

WIFE WAS APPREHENSIVE

Feared Anti-Evolution Fight Was Overtaxing His Strength, but Now Bears Loss Bravely.

Special to The New York Times.

DAYTON, Tenn., July 26.—William Jennings Bryan died suddenly of heart disease while he slept this afternoon at the residence of Richard Rodgers here.

Apparently in perfect health, full of plans to make a nation-wide fight for laws protecting the Bible against the teaching of evolution, Mr. Bryan went to his room for a nap after a hearty meal.

At 2 o'clock Mrs. Bryan's housekeeper, Mrs. C. Stevens, passed through Mr. Bryan's room and he said cheerfully: "I think I'm going to get a good sleep." Soon after 4 o'clock, Msr. Bryan, who was in a wheelchair on the porch, became nervous over her husband's failure to awaken and asked William H. McCarney, the family chauffeur, to rouse him.

Mr. McCartney shook Mr. Bryan gently but got no response. He realized something was wrong and called a neighbor, A. B. Andrews, who summoned Dr. A. C. Broyles and Dr. W. F. Thomison. The doctors said that Mr. Bryan had been dead about twenty minutes. Death occurred about 4:45 o'clock. They said the cause was apoplexy, accompanied by a cerebral hemorrhage.

Dr. Broyles said that the clogging of veins in the neck indicated that death was not caused by heart dilation, the opinion of Dr. Wallace of Chattanooga, who examined Mr. Bryan on Friday. The Commoner was 65 years odl.

Physicians were then summoned. They found that Mr. Bryan had been dead for some minutes. Death occurred at about 4:45 o'clock.

Refused to Take Vacation.

His death came as the greatest possible shock because Mr. Bryan himself and every one else believed that he had passed through the Dayton ordeal without suffering the least detriment to his health through the heat, fatigue and excitement.

"I never felt better in my life," the veteran orator said time after time today and yesterday, when the friends he had made at Dayton called on him.

"The fight that we have made here will be transferred to a greater scope," he said, referring to movements in several Southern and Western States to enact anti-evolution or Bible-protecting legislation.

Mr. Bryan had lost weight during the trial and his face was pale and lined, but the zest of battle had been awakened in him and the ardent spirit of the old crusader did not permit him to consider the need of rest. Many of his friends advised the former Secretary of State and three times candidate for President to take a vacation and recruit his strength.

"No," he replied, "we must strike while the iron is hot." Following this principle, he had been speaking incessantly at Tennessee meetings since the conviction of Scopes. He planned further speeches in Tennessee, and had in mind a speaking tour of many States in behalf of this cause into which he threw his heart more fully than he had into any other.

His Last Triumphant Journey.

He told his friends during and after the Scopes trial that no cause has ever stirred him to the bottom of the heart like this one, not even the cause of peace before 1917 or the cause of free silver twenty-nine years ago.

Less than twenty-four hours before his death, the Commoner spoke to a great crowd at Winchester, Tenn. He was in fine form. He delivered a stirring speech and took delight in the applause and in the evident affection and admiration in which the crowd held him.

Returning from Winchester last night, Mr. Bryan's train was like his famous election special of 1896. From the rear platform he made speech after speech at each stop, and the crowds cheered him wildly and kept the train until its schedule was thoroughly disjointed.

At the town of Cowan Mr. Bryan spoke for twenty minutes. He electrified his hearers, as he has seldom failed to do in his public career of thirty years. He represented the conviction of Scopes as a great victory for the cause of Christianity, and a staggering blow to "the forces of darkness." Never had Christian and crusading zeal of this old warrior of the ancient faith burned more fiercely than during two or three days preceding his death.

His trip, which turned spontaneously into a rear platform speaking tour, covered more than 200 miles on Saturday. At 10 o'clock in the morning yesterday

Continued on Page Two.

ABD-EL-KRIM OFFERS TO NEGOTIATE PEACE; PETAIN TO RETURN

Marshal Expected Back in Paris to Confer on Deal With Moors.

RIFF CHIEF ASKS PLEDGE

Wants Assurance of His Country's Independence as Condition of Conference.

SELECTS TANGIER FOR IT

His Tribesmen Prepared to Kill Their Women and Children and Die Fighting, He Says.

Special Cable to THE NEW YORK TIMES.

PARIS, July 26.—The most significant development of the Moroccan situation today is an announcement of Marshal Pétain's intention of return to Paris within the next ten days. Entire direction of the operations in the field was given him only a few days ago and it is generally believed here that he would not be leaving the scene of action unless he felt the crisis had been resolved and the end of the war was definitely in sight.

In well-informed quarters the conviction even prevails that Marshal Pétain is not to present the Government with a plan of campaign when he returns, but with a peace plan which he has been able to develop as the result of his personal contact with the situation.

Abd-el-K[illegible] Offers to Parley.

Special Cable to THE NEW YORK TIMES.

TANGIER, July 26.—Abd-el-Krim informs me that he has replied to the Franco-Spanish note which stated that the terms of peace which the French and Spanish Governments were prepared to offer him were at his disposal if he wished to consult them.

Abd-el-Krim [illegible] he is prepared to [illegible] with France and Spain on condition that before the negotiations are opened he shall receive solemn assurance that the Riff will enjoy independence. In a separate communication he demands that the negotiations shall take place at Tangier.

I am informed that if France and Spain agree to these two stipulations Abd-el-Krim is prepared to cease hostilities and enter upon immediate negotiations for permanent peace.

The French and Spanish Governments will probably receive Abd-el-Krim's reply tomorrow.

It is not difficult to surmise the main lines of the peace terms which Spain and France are willing to offer Obd-el-Krim. These main lines are in a measure independence for the Riff under the sovereignty of the Sultan and under the authority of the Khalifa of the Spanish zone, with the proposed title of Emir for Abd-el-Krim; rectification of the French protectorate frontier by granting the Riffs facilities for procuring and growing grain and other foodstuffs, assistance in introducing home rule in the Riff and a semblance of disarmament of the tribes.

What Riff Chief Hopes For.

The press of Europe and Morocco has lately published very diverse accounts of what Abd-el-Krim himself demands, but as a matter of fact Abd-el-Krim has never stated any definite terms. He has from time to time as a measure of propaganda told journalists who visited him and has announced to the tribes that he will insist upon the cession of Tetuan Laraiche and Arsella, and only intends to leave in possession of the Spaniards Ceuta, Melilla and the smaller presidios.

At times his successes have almost made such demands possible, but that day has passed and even his most enthusiastic followers realize that all that today is beyond his reach. For some months it has been an open secret that Abd-el-Krim has abandoned all claim to Tetuan and other towns, the capture of which he had promised the Jabala as a means of procuring their assistance.

In return for the abandonment of Tetuan he speaks of demanding an indemnity of 25,000,000 Spanish pesetas. He bases his claim on the ground that when after the Spanish War in Morocco in 1859 the Spaniards consented to evacuate Tetuan they received an indemnity of that amount from the Sultan. The Riff leader argues that as the Spanish Government agreed by treaty to abandon Tetuan in perpetuity and since has reoccupied it he can justly demand the return of the sum extorted from his country on that occasion.

The difficult point in the peace negotiations must turn upon the measure of independence which Abd-el-Krim is to enjoy. It is not only difficult from his personal point of view, but still more so because it is the only subject on which he made definite promises to the Riff tribes. All other subjects of negotiation are for him and him alone to settle, but this question of independence is shared by all. He has definitely promised the tribesmen not to negotiate peace except on the understanding that independence of the Riff is assured. It was the only price by which he could obtain their full-hearted cooperation.

Realizes His Limitations.

Complete independence, however, is impossible, partly because of existing treaties but more from the fact that Abd-el-Krim and his Riffians are not

Continued on Page Five.

Treviso Statue Declared To Be by Michelangelo

TREVISO, Italy, July 26 (AP).—Officials of the Venetian Art Academy have announced that a terra cotta statue found some time ago by Eugenio Loschi, a public employe, is the work of Michaelangelo.

The statue is about 24 inches high. Loschi will present it to the Vatican through the local Bishop.

The recent discovery in the Vatican of seven terra cotta statuettes by Michelangelo led Loschi to request art experts to come to Treviso and examine the object he had found.

INQUIRY THREATENS PUBLIC LAND SCANDAL

Senate Committee Will Begin Delving Soon Into Alleged Maladministration.

WIDESPREAD CHARGES MADE

Allegations Against Park Service and Forestry Bureau to Have Full Airing.

Special to The New York Times.

WASHINGTON, July 26.—The Senate Committee on Public Lands, the committee which exposed the Teapot Dome and Elk Hills Naval Reserve Oil leases, is going hunting again. This time it is going to investigate the administration of the public domain, the Forestry Bureau and the national parks. According to some members of the committee the investigation is expected to develop a situation which will parallel in interest the sensational developments of the naval oil hearings. The committee will act under a Senate resolution passed near the close of the last Congress and its authority is virtually unlimited.

Governor Pinchot of Pennsylvania, a former Chief Forester of the Government, a few days ago gave out a statement warning the "friends of the forest service" that an assault against that Government bureau is about to start. The Governor did not mention the Senate, but it is known that he had the Public Lands Committee in mind. And the national forest question is going to be thoroughly investigated. For instance, Senator Cameron of Arizona is authority for the statement that of the more than 136,000,000 acres of public land in the Federal forest reserve more than 90,000,000 acres are treeless. There is one forest in Arizona, it is charged, 13,000,000 acres in extent, that never has had a tree on it since the beginning of the world.

The administration of the forest reserve, as well as the public domain, the latter 186,000,000 acres in extent, has, it is alleged by certain Western Senators, worked great injury to the stock raising business.

The cattle industry, it is asserted, has almost touched bottom, and one of the main subjects of the inquiry will be to find a way, if possible, to resuscitate this business.

In one Western town, it was pointed out, bank failures, due mainly to the crisis in the cattle industry, involved bank losses exceeding $10,000,000. There are scores of other towns, it is asserted, which have been proportionately hard hit for the same reason.

Cattlemen who a few years ago were reputed wealthy, some of them millionaires, are now poverty stricken, according to stories current in legislative circles. A case cited is that of a man who six years ago was said to be worth more than $1,000,000. Recently this man accepted a job as an assistant sergeant-at-arms of a Western State Legislature.

One other case is that of a cattleman who had been listed as among the wealthiest men in his community. He is now running a little adobe hotel in a town of less than 300 population.

Questions Midwest Company's Deals.

It is asserted that these are but samples of thousands of other cases involving men who were mainstays of the great cattle business a few years back.

The homesteading features of the public domain administration will be another phase of the inquiry, as will also the disposition of mineral and oil lands, other than those included in the naval reserves.

One feature of the oil part of the investigation is expected to involve the Salt Creek (Wyo.) holdings of the Midwest Refining Company, a subsidiary of the Standard of Indiana. Salt Creek adjoins Teapot Dome, but it is a vastly richer field than the Sinclair lease.

Senator Walsh of Montana, a member of the committee, said recently that there is no more important duty facing

Continued on Page Five.

SINNOTT FIRM HIRES MAX STEUER TO SUE ON BOND EXPOSURES

Lawyer Says Libel Actions Will Be Brought Against Craig, Kerrigan and Newspapers.

SEES "VENOM" IN CHARGES

Declares Recent Published Statements Require That Proceedings Be Brought.

WON'T HALT INVESTIGATION

"Let Them Go Ahead," Is Controller's Comment—Wants Chance to Get Hylan on the Stand.

Announcement that the bonding and insurance firm of Sinnott & Canty would bring libel actions against Controller Charles L. Craig, Deputy Controller Charles F. Kerrigan, and those newspapers which have published statements from either of them regarding the investigation of alleged relations between the firm and the Mayor's office, was made yesterday by Max D. Steuer, attorney for the members of the firm.

Mr. Steuer said that he had at first advised the members of the firm, the head of which, J. Paul Sinnott, is a brother of John F. Sinnott, Mayor Hylan's secretary and son-in-law, not to bring suit because he sought to keep them out of a political controversy into which he believed Mr. Craig and Mr. Kerrigan were seeking to force them. Mr. Steuer added that recent published statements by Mr. Craig and Mr. Kerrigan were "so much more veromous" that he had determined that the best interests of Sinnott & Canty required that an action be brought and that the facts be developed in court.

Mr. Craig and Mr. Kerrigan, neither of whom had been served with notice of any action yesterday, declared that no libel action would be permitted to interrupt their investigation. Mr. Craig declared that he would welcome the opportunity to have the members of the Sinnott & Canty firm and Mayor Hylan examined on the witness stand.

Steuer Issues Statement.

Mr. Steuer's statement, announcing the determination to bring libel actions, follows:

"When the articles instigated by Controller Craig and his deputy, Charles Kerrigan, first began to appear in the press, the firm of Sinnott & Canty conferred with me concerning their rights against the individuals who instigated them and the press that continued to publish them. I advised Messrs. Sinnott & Canty then that upon the facts as submitted by them, the articles were clearly libelous and that for the damage by them sustained each of the defendants could be compelled to answer.

"Nevertheless, I suggested that they abstain from commencing any actions because of the fact that the claim would immediately be put up that the suits were brought solely to aid the present City Administration in anticipation of the coming primaries and election.

"Solely because of my insistence, they abstained not only from commencing suits, but from demanding that criminal prosecutions be instituted. With each separate publication they submitted to me a statement of the facts as they claimed them to be and as investigation actually indicates they are. On each occasion, however, I adhered to the view that I first expressed, and although they became more and more desirous of putting their version before the public, I advised against it, seeking to keep them out of a political controversy that seemingly Mr. Craig, Mr. Kerrigan and others were attempting to force Sinnott & Canty into.

"The recent publications, however, are so much more venomous, encouraged very likely by the previous silence of these men, that I have finally determined that the best interests of Sinnott & Canty make necessary the immediate commencement of actions against Mr. Craig, Mr. Kerrigan and the various newspapers that have seen fit to publish these articles maliciously calculated to deceive the public and to grievously injure the firm as well as the individuals whose names figure therein.

"In consequence thereof, I have advised my assistants to immediately cause process to be served upon Mr. Craig, Mr. Kerrigan and each of the newspapers in which these articles appeared, and such process is now out for service.

"The only place, in my opinion, where the real facts can be developed satisfactorily is the courts, and at the earliest moment the plaintiffs will seek a

Continued on Page Five.

Coolidges Take Little Space In North Shore 'Who's Who'

Special to The New York Times.

SWAMPSCOTT, Mass., July 26.—Very modest is the manner in which President and Mrs. Coolidge and their son John Coolidge are listed in the 1925 issue of Who's Who Along the North Shore, distributed yesterday. Their names appear under the Cs as follows:

Coolidge, President and Mrs. Calvin, Swampscott, Little's Point, White Court. Winter residence, Washington, D. C., the White House. President of the United States. (Mrs. Coolidge was Grace A. Goodhue.)

Coolidge, John, with President and Mrs. Coolidge (son), Swampscott. Student at Amherst College.

BUCKNER TO BARGAIN WITH DRY VIOLATORS

Prosecutor Will Ask for Fines for Small Offenders Who Plead Guilty.

JAIL FOR THOSE WHO FIGHT

Drive Planned to Clear Docket of 2,000 Cases for New Campaign in the Fall.

United States Attorney Emory R. Buckner will open his second drive on the overcrowded liquor calendar before Judge Edwin L. Garvin in the Federal Court today. This campaign, he said, would be in the nature of a bargain sale and those of the 2,000 petty offenders who pleaded guilty would be fined and those who stood trial and were convicted would be recommended for a jail term. He said he expected to clear up the 2,000 cases in the coming week, after which he would take up the fifty padlocking cases which were ready for presentation.

To accommodate the expected crowd of owners and employes of speakeasies Mr. Buckner cut departmental red tape and has had his own force remove the chairs and tables from the special court room. When Mr. Buckner undertook to have the custodian of the building remove the chairs and tables he found that the order would have to travel by a roundabout way to Washington for official sanction and then be returned for the further approval of a Judge.

"I have told Judge Garvin that I think it is in the public interest and in the interest of prohibition enforcement to clean up these 2,000 small cases on the basis of a July clearance bargain sale," he said. "I have recommended, and I hope he will approve, the imposition of fines running from $50 to $100 upon all who plead guilty, and jail sentences upon all who stand trial and are convicted.

No Bargains in the Fall.

"We want to clear ourselves of all stock of this character and we hope to open in the Fall with an entirely new line of prohibition goods. We shall discontinue the five and ten-cent counter in accordance with the policy which has been in effect since I took office, so far as new cases are concerned, and we will deal only, generally speaking, in the padlock for the retailer and jail sentences for the bootlegger, the wholesaler, the importer, the manufacturer, and the financial backer.

"Prohibition enforcement will get nowhere in this district until the owner of the retail establishment finds himself padlocked on the outside, and until the man who supplies him with liquor finds himself padlocked on the inside.

"The policy of stopping petty arrests and concentrating upon the men higher up and those actively engaged in the bootleg trade, which I put into effect five months ago, has been cordially approved by Gen. Lincoln C. Andrews.

"The thousands of petty arrests which have been made in this district during the past few years have so swamped Federal machinery as to render it impossible to wage a concentrated and sustained war against the rum-runners and bootleggers and manufacturers. The Federal officials have been trying to run a marathon on tanglefoot flypaper. The piling up of thousands of arrests and the collection of hundreds of thousands of dollars' worth of fines, calling them 'convictions,' make a very impressive 'record,' but from the standpoint of law enforcement are nothing but a farce.

Explains His Plans.

"This farce has been aggravated by the absolute necessity of dealing with these petty offenses only on a fine basis, as there has not been any remote possibility of trials before juries and jail sentences for the smallest fraction of them. It is a little short of compounding with crime for the Government to take this dirty money and call it rigid enforcement of the prohibition law.

"An arrest is the beginning and not the end of law enforcement. Until Federal officials look only at the end of a prosecution and not at the beginning of a prosecution, we shall make no headway in dealing with the formidable and vexatious problem of prohibition in this district.

"When Judge Garvin cleans up the 2,000 petty liquor cases to be brought before him this week there will be no more cases of that type, generally speaking, so long as I am in office. I am not picking and choosing prosecutions according to whim or caprice, or attempting to repeal the law in part and enforce it in part. I am simply picking and choosing prosecutions in accordance with the number of Judges, the number of assistants and the number of clerks which are provided by the Federal Government, and my oath of office not only justifies but actually compels me to employ this limited machinery in the manner which will peg out the greatest advance in the enforcement of the prohibition law, while at the same time enabling me to enforce other laws with equal regard.

"I cannot, in justice to the rest of my job, devote more than 25 per cent. of my equipment to the enforcement of the prohibition law, and I want to make this 25 per cent. produce the greatest results which it is capable of producing rather than merely to keep it conspicuously busy milling around with a mob of petty violators of the Volstead act."

Palestine Explorers Find Chambers in Rock That May Prove to Be the Tomb of David

Special Cable to THE NEW YORK TIMES.

JERUSALEM, July 26.—Discovery of what it is hoped may prove to be the long-sought tomb of David was announced today by the Rev. J. Garrow Duncan of the Palestine Exploration Fund.

The Rev. Mr. Duncan states that the excavations at Ophel brought to light on the western side a series of underground rock-cut chambers comprising a large central room, with five smaller chambers, five feet square, branching from it. The southernmost room, which is fifteen by sixteen feet in size, leads into two rooms, each fifteen by eight feet. These again lead into similar narrow chambers, each with smaller chambers cut into its walls.

Toolmarks on the walls are of the Iron Age period and not earlier than 1200 B. C. There is a similar series of rock chambers and galleries on the eastern side of Ophel, entered from the face of a rock scarp under the Jebusite east city wall and closed by a curious stone door. It is considered not improbabl that this constitute David's tomb, and the probability is that both sets of parts constitute a series of royal tombs. Its series is much abused by later usage, first as an olive press and as store rooms in the Byzantine period, then as cisterns by Arabs.

Gladstones, Angered at Attack on Father, Call Capt. Wright "Liar, Coward and Fool"

Special Cable to THE NEW YORK TIMES.

LONDON, July 26. — Viscount Gladstone and Henry Neville Gladstone, sons of the late Liberal statesman W. E. Gladstone, have written to Captain Peter Wright, author, calling him "a liar, coward and fool."

Mr. Wright, in a recent volume of impressionist sketches entitled "Portraits and Criticisms," declared W. E. Gladstone "founded a great tradition since observed by many of his followers and successors with such pious fidelity — in public to speak the language of the highest and strictest principle and in private to pursue and possess every sort of woman."

Viscount Gladstone addressed a letter to Mr. Wright saying, "Your garbage about Mr. Gladstone in 'Portraits and Criticisms' has come to our knowledge. You are a liar. Because you slander a dead man you are a coward, and because you think the public will accept inventions from such as you, you are a fool.

The following line was added by H. N. Gladstone: "I associate myself with this letter."

Mr. Wright has replied to the Gladstones with a letter in which he repeats his charges against the late statesman. He says, among other things:

"I attributed to Mr. Gladstone the character of a hypocrite in matters of sex. I have evidence of his conduct as good as any that exists about events in the past. I wrote what I did write on the authority of the late Lord Milner.

"To use Milner's own phrase, Mr. Gladstone was 'governed by his seraglio.' This foible had considerable political effect. One affair turned Mr. Gladstone from being a friend of Turkey and an enemy of Russia, as he was in the '50s, into being a friend of Russia and an enemy of Turkey, as he was in the '80s.

"All the News That's Fit to Print."

The New York Times.

THE WEATHER
Fair today and tomorrow; slight change in temperature.
Temperature yesterday—Max., 75; min., 68.
For weather report see next to last page.

VOL. LXXIV....No. 24,670. NEW YORK, MONDAY, AUGUST 10, 1925. TWO CENTS In Greater New York | THREE CENTS Within 200 Miles | FOUR CENTS Elsewhere in the U. S.

LEWIS DASHES HOPE OF NEW COAL PARLEY; SCORNS ARBITRATION

Writes Warriner That Only Way to Peace Is Granting Wage Increase and "Check-Off."

IRONIC UPON ARBITRAMENT

Refers to Disappointment of Miners With 1920 Award and Compliments Foe.

STRIKE PROSPECT GROWS

Coolidge Is Reported Surprised at Development, Which May Cut Short His Vacation.

Special to The New York Times.

ATLANTIC CITY, N. J., Aug. 9.—Hopes for an early resumption of the anthracite wage parleys were dashed today by the reply of President John L. Lewis of the United Mine Workers of America to the recent letter of Samuel D. Warriner, Chairman of the Anthracite Operators' Conference, who declared that despite the breaking off of relations he was hopeful "that means will be found to compose the differences between us and avoid a suspension."

Mr. Lewis in his letter to Mr. Warriner indicated that only an abandonment by the operators of their opposition to wage increases and the check-off would bring the miners into conference again. In well chosen words, ironically polite, the miners' chief rejected Mr. Warriner's suggestion of arbitration.

Challenged by Mr. Warriner to justify his earlier statement that the miners opposed arbitration because of the "anthracite operators' well-known policy of keeping close to an arbitrator," Mr. Lewis said he referred "to the arbitration proceeding of some years ago when the final decision of the arbitrator was changed between twilight and dawn."

In 1920 the miners expected a wage increase of 27 per cent from President Wilson's arbitration commission. They received 17 per cent.

Mr. Lewis added nothing to his letter in the way of explanation. "It speaks for itself," he said when questioned. It could not be learned whether developments of the last 24 hours had decided the tone of the reply, which it was earlier reported would be as conciliatory as that of Mr. Warriner.

Mr. Lewis's Letter.

Here is Mr. Lewis's reply:

Ambassador Hotel, Atlantic City, N. J., Aug. 8, 1925.

Mr. Samuel D. Warriner, Chairman, Anthracite Operators' Conference, 437 Chestnut St., Philadelphia, Pa.

My dear Mr. Warriner:—

I acknowledge your favor of the 6th instant. I do not desire to quibble over the fine shades of meaning affecting words and involved phrases. It remains that your Atlantic City conferees informed the mine workers' representatives, including myself, that they would reject any demand that would disturb the factor of mine costs. In addition, they rejected the request for full recognition of the union for some other mysterious reason. Your letter confirms the position of your committee. Be it so. We do not have any inclination to further argue when judgment has been given. I will be glad to hear from you when you abandon this position.

I note your reference to my previous comments upon arbitration. I can well understand your natural irritation in the premises. I referred, of course, to the arbitration proceedings of some years ago when the final decision of the arbitrator was changed between twilight and dawn. You might, if you wish, accept the reference as a compliment from the mine workers to a skillful adversary.

We really do not care to arbitrate. Thanks for the offer. We know that you think the medicine would be good for us, but frankly, we have little faith in your diagnosis. It will be long before we recover completely from your previous arbitration treatment, and until we do we will modestly decline to accept your prescription. Very truly yours,

JOHN L. LEWIS, President.

Strike More Likely.

The prospect of a strike of 155,000 mine workers upon the expiration of the present agreement on Sept. 1 was heightened by the Lewis letter. The Federal authorities have made it plain that they intend to take no hand in the situation unless an emergency is created after a strike is called. Secretary of Labor Davis is due from Europe on Aug. 25, a week before the expiration of the anthracite agreement. If he deems it wise, he may, acting unofficially, arrange a conference of mine workers and operators, but the time will then be short and it it feared here that it would be too late to reach an agreement and avoid a suspension Sept. 1.

Governor Pinchot of Pennsylvania, as Chief Executive of the State in which all the hard coal mines are located, may, if he wishes, call both sides to a conference at Harrisburg. That is apparently the only possibility of getting the disputants together in time to frame an agreement and avert a walk-out.

A strike is certain, according to the miners, unless the anthracite operators, as Mr. Lewis states bluntly in his letter, abandon their position of "no wage concessions and no check-off."

The unionists believe that a strike will win for them some of the demands which were adopted late in June at the convention of the three anthracite districts. These include a wage increase of 10 per cent. for contract miners, a dollar a day for day men, payment for certain "dead work" and the free furnishing of pneumatic drills and compressed air to operate them.

To grant the miners' demands, according to Mr. Warriner, would add $100,000,000 annually to the coal production bill of the operators and would mean between $1 and $2 a ton additional...

Continued on Page Two.

Severe Earthquake in Smyrna Razes Village, Damages Others

CONSTANTINOPLE, Aug. 9 (AP).—Severe earthquake shocks on Thursday and Friday in the Villayet of Smyrna razed one village and badly damaged several others.

The loss of life is believed to have been small, but many persons were injured.

PARIS, Aug. 9 (AP).—A Havas dispatch from Smyrna says that one entire village was destroyed and that several persons were injured during earthquake shocks Saturday night and today at Hamadieh and Denizli.

In the latter place the railway station was destroyed and a number of houses collapsed.

The shocks occurred between 10 o'clock Saturday evening and 8:30 o'clock Sunday morning.

ROB SUBWAY BOOTH, GIVE OUT CHANGE

Two Hold-Up Men Serve Early Morning Passengers in Times Square Station.

STEAL A DAY'S RECEIPTS

Agent, Bound, Butts Off Receiver With His Head and Gives Telephone Alarm.

Members of early-morning dance or supper parties starting home on the Seventh Avenue subway yesterday morning received change from an armed hold-up man in the busiest booth in the Times Square station. None knew of the presence of the robber, however, for in every respect he acted the part of the cashier or change agent and handed out the proper amounts even when bills that might have tempted his cupidity were thrust under the window.

In the booth was another robber, who swept the night receipts of the booth into a canvas bag, and John Duncan, 45 years old, 185 Concord Street, Brooklyn, the change agent of the Interborough Rapid Transit Company. Duncan's hands were securely tied behind him and he was powerless to move, even if he had been inclined to ignore the muzzle of a pistol that kept digging at his back to remind him to keep still.

The daring hold-up was perpetrated in Booth 4—the first booth approached by passengers entering the Times Square station through the street entrance at the northwest corner of Forty-second Street and Seventh Avenue. Only a small volume of travel was filtering through the turnstiles. It was 3 o'clock in the morning.

Caught at Turnstiles.

Duncan had been on duty since 7 o'clock in the evening. The receipts from the Saturday night theatre crowds were large. The change agent, who was about to be relieved, opened the side door of his booth just a crack, saw no one and decided to seize that opportunity to harvest the crop from the row of turnstiles in front of his booth.

He had unlocked one after another of the battery of turnstiles, emptied them of their nickels, which he dumped into a canvas bag, closed the money receptacle of the last turnstile and was just starting back to his booth when he found himself face to face with two armed men, according to the story told by Duncan to detectives of the West Forty-seventh Street Police Station.

Duncan said the men covered him so quickly that he believed they must have been hiding behind the change booth. One of the armed men approached the change maker so closely that he seemed to be about to confide a secret. Speaking in a low voice, he ordered Duncan to get back into the booth instantly without making any noise.

So quietly did the robbers go about their business and so deftly did they juggle their pistols that they kept Duncan covered without attracting attention from passengers entering or leaving the subway station. The intruders probably were taken for inspectors as they followed the change maker into the booth and closed the door.

Bind Agent's Hands.

Once inside the booth, one of the armed men whipped out a jack knife and cut off a length of the window sash cord

Continued on Page Five.

ONE DEAD, MANY HURT AS RIVAL FACTIONS CLASH IN BERLIN

Stahlhelm Group Attacks Reichbanner Members on Way to Republican Rally.

SHOT STARTS BATTLE ROYAL

Bloodshed Marks Opening of Celebration of Weimar Constitution Anniversary.

BIG PARADE AT TREPTOW

Contingent From Austria and 50,000 Provincial Delegates Already in Capital.

By LINCOLN EYRE

Copyright, 1925, by The New York Times Company.
Special Cable to THE NEW YORK TIMES.

BERLIN, Aug. 9.—One member of the Stahlhelm, a reactionary organization, was killed and a number of members of the Stahlhelm and the Republican organization Reichsbanner were wounded in a clash this afternoon between Monarchists and Republican groups during the preliminary celebration of the anniversary of the adoption of the German Constitution.

A detachment of the Reichbanner, marching through Kurfuerstendamm, Berlin's residential section, en route to a big Republican demonstration, was attacked by the reactionary group. The Reichsbanner leader, who tried to check the Stahlhelm forces' advance by firing shots into the air, later fired into the crowd which refused to halt, killing a member of the Stahlhelm.

Police Stop Free-for-All Fight.

Several members of both sides were injured in the free-for-all fight which followed before the police broke it up. The Reichsbanner leader surrendered to the police.

In Treptow, which is a suburb of Berlin, 150,000 Republican militants paraded across the common in military formation, drilling like veteran soldiers. President Hoersing of the Reichsbanner addressing the crowd, reported the membership in this Republican protective organization as now numbering 3,000,000, all of whom, he said, were potential soldiers should the republic be forced to fight for its existence.

Already provincial delegations, more than 50,000 strong, including a contingent from Austria, have arrived in Berlin to swell the ranks of the Reichsbanner League. And on this occasion, unlike that of President von Hindenburg's inauguration, the black, white and red flag of imperialism is conspicuous by its absence, while the banner of the republic is everywhere to the fore.

The Republican press stresses the "Bigger Germany" character of this celebration, supposedly commemorative only of the creation of the Weimar Constitution six years ago.

"Living Symbol" of Pan-Germanism.

Writing in the Democratic Vossische Zeitung, Georg Bernhard, Germany's foremost Liberal publicist, qualifies the presence of the Austrian delegation as a "living symbol of the Pan-German significance of the Republican colors, black, red and gold." He continued:

"These colors are not only the standard of Germany's political unity but of German culture and Germanism as well. Wherever Germans live, either as individuals abroad or in masses on foreign soil, there the colors of the young republic must demonstrate the cultural community and intellectual union of all who speak and think in German."

The Berliner Tageblatt observes:

"It would be self-deception to pretend that German Republicans approach the anniversary of their Constitution this year happy and content. Certainly the republic stands fast, but it is not the republic we aspired to when, six years ago, the great work of the Democrats, the Democratic Catholic Centre and the Socialists arose out of the chaos which was the heritage of the old régime.

"For the first time since then there is a Government of the Right at the helm, and in the Presidential election the opponents of the republic were victorious. Yet since they have been in power the Right parties have had to pursue the foreign policy that killed Rathenau, and by offering voluntary renunciation of Alsace-Lorraine they have gone much further than any Democratic Government did.

"Moreover, a Nationalist Minister of the Interior issues invitations for the celebrations of the republic's birthday and on the palace of President von Hindenburg and the public buildings occupied by Nationalist Ministers there will fly the German Republican colors—black, red and gold."

Average Age in New York State Has Risen From 24 Years in 1840 to 30 Years Now

Special to The New York Times.

ALBANY, Aug. 9.—Under the caption "We Are Getting Older," the current issue of Health News, issued by the State Department of Health, declares that "the estimated average age of our people now is 30 years and 2 months, whereas eighty-five years ago we were barely out of our 'teens.' The following table of the average age of the population of New York is based on returns from the Federal census:

Year.	Average Age.
1840	24 years 6 months
1850	24 years 7 months
1860	25 years 4 months
1870	26 years 7 months
1880	27 years 6 months
1890	28 years 6 months
1900	28 years 7 months
1910	28 years 11 months
1920	29 years 8 months
1925 (est.)	30 years 3 months

"The figures given must not be interpreted as indicating the number of years by which the span of life has actually been lengthened," the article says. "These facts may be gleaned from another source; namely, from so-called life tables. Unfortunately for this State, we have no tables for the earlier years. We shall, therefore, compare the 'expectation of life'—the number of years a new-born baby was expected to live in 1901 (the first year for which we have these data)—with 1910 and 1920:

EXPECTATION OF LIFE.

Year.	Males.	Females.
1901	45 years 7 months	49 years 2 months
1910	47 years 11 months	51 years 11 months
1920	52 years 10 months	55 years 8 months

"Thus in only twenty years the expectation of life at birth has increased for males by 7 years and 3 months; for females, by 6 years and 5 months.

"Two factors have exerted the greatest influence upon the age composition of this State as well as of most of the other States in this country—immigration and the advance in preventive and curative medicine. Progress in public health work has increased the duration of life of the people, and therefore raised its average age. On the other hand, immigration has retarded the normal aging process, by adding every year to our population thousands of young persons from overseas. If the purpose of present restrictive immigration laws is carried out the average age of the people in the future will mount even at a higher rate than it has in the past."

Find Urn and Bangles in Rhodesian Ruins; Experts Says They May Be 10,000 Years Old

Copyright, 1925, by The New York Times Company.
Special Cable to THE NEW YORK TIMES.

JOHANNESBURG, Aug. 9.—An ancient copper urn, containing five thick copper bangles, supposedly taken from the legs of dead slaves, has been found among the wonderful terraced ruins of Ivanga, in Southern Rhodesia. When exposed to the air the urn crumbled into dust.

The find is said to be of first importance archaeologically. The age of the urn, which was found ten feet deep under alluvial soil and which is the only man made article ever found in these terraced ruins, is estimated by the finder to be from 8,000 to 10,000 years.

The Ivanga district is noted for its ruins, which cover an area of sixty by forty miles. They consist of the remains of stone buildings, aqueducts and terraces. No clue has hitherto been obtained regarding the builders of these ruins.

South Africa has long been a centre for archaeological research and has yielded important discoveries in the last few months. Many scholars are inclined to look upon the region as the cradle of humanity as a result of the recent discovery there of a skull of a native who died a few weeks ago which corresponds entirely to the famous Boskop skull, one of the most primitive known.

The Taungs area is particularly rich in fossils of archaeological and anthropological importance and is now being combed for data by several expeditions.

The Rhodesian skull found at Broken Hill, considerably further north than Taungs, has been taken by some students to show the migration south of the ancestors of man from the equatorial regions of Central Africa to the open forests and short grass plains of South Africa.

ASK YOUNG TO HEAD AIRWAY COMPANY

Promoters of $50,000,000 Corporation Expect Dawes Plan Organizer Will Accept.

HAMMOND TELLS OF PLANS

Great Air Liners Would Serve Chief Cities of Country and Go Abroad.

Special to The New York Times.

SWAMPSCOTT, Mass., Aug. 9.—Plans of John Hays Hammond Jr., Herbert Satterlee of New York and General Clarence B. Edwards to establish a daily air service linking the chief cities of the United States and ultimately to create a transatlantic dirigible system were revealed in detail today by Mr. Hammond.

If this company, known as the Airways Corporation, obtains a lease of the Los Angeles, requested of the Government for experimental purposes, the plans contemplate a dirigible daily schedule between New York and Chicago to be covered in twelve hours. The proposed rate of mileage is 10 cents, or $75 for the trip from New York to Chicago.

If using the Los Angeles in the experimental stages proves successful, the company purposes to extend the system with faster ships to include Boston, Pittsburgh, Detroit, Chicago, Omaha and St. Louis. A second route takes in Southern cities and goes as far as Havana.

Owen D. Young May Head Company.

The promoters have outlined the program to Owen D. Young of the General Electric Company and the genius in the Dawes plan, and requested him to become head of the $50,000,000 corporation. He has the proposal under consideration and reports are that he will accept if the Government acts favorably in leasing the Los Angeles and in the enactment of air navigation legislation.

"The dirigible railways proposed by us will not be in competition with the railroads," Mr. Hammond explained today. "We have discussed the scheme with the heads of the leading railroads and they welcome the running of a daily air service between the chief cities of the United States. They say it will relieve them of some of the great expense of maintaining fast trains, which are not paying.

"If the Government cooperates to the extent of leasing the Los Angeles to us and manning it with naval officers for the experimental stages our company plans to build airships double the capacity of the Los Angeles and faster. Our plans call for ships of 5,000,000 cubic feet, capable of carrying 100 passengers with baggage and fifty tons of freight of a perishable nature.

"The Los Angeles is not fast enough nor of proper carrying capacity ofr final commercial use. What we ask of the Government is to aid us in the experimental stages so that we can determine whether if the air route were developed with faster ships and more comfortable ones we could afford to go ahead and expend the $50,000,000 it is estimated will be required to build a dirigible air service to connect the chief cities in this country.

"Of course a greater capitalization will be necessary to carry out our ultimate plans to place commodious ships in the transatlantic service. The development of service to Europe will come only after it is shown that the ships will pay interest from 8 to 10 per cent. on the money invested in American air development.

Cities Offer to Build Masts.

"Already two cities, Omaha and Chicago, have offered to build mooring masts which cost about $250,000 and provide other loading facilities. We are greatly encouraged with the offers of municipal and private assistance already made if our plans are carried out with the cooperation of the Federal Government.

"We would use the Los Angeles only between New York and Chicago. The travel between these two office is the largest in the country and if the service proved successful then our company would extend the route, with new and better ships, to Omaha and St. Louis and cover Boston, Detroit, Buffalo and Pittsburgh. The distance to Chicago from New York by air is 750 miles and our charge would be 10 cents a mile, or $75, which is not much in excess of the Pullman and passenger rates on fast trains between these two points. The distance of the extended route to include the eight cities mentioned would be 2,800 miles.

"Our plans ultimately propose to have all these cities connected with service to Atlanta, Havana and Panama, making a route of over 4,000 miles. If these

Continued on Page Three.

BROWNING GIRL QUITS CINDERELLA ROLE

Leaves Foster-Father for Lure of Movie Job and 'Literary' Offer.

OMITS TO SAY A GOOD-BYE

Realtor Says He Is Amazed but Admires Her—Will Never Adopt Another.

Edward W. Browning, wealthy real estate broker, announced last night that Mary Louise Spas Browning, the young woman he adopted in the belief that she was 16 years old and not 21 years, as she really is, had left his custody. He said that she had accepted an offer to enter the movies and to write her story for publication.

The realtor said that an agent, who said that he represented a movie firm and also could get her story into print, made the offer yesterday afternoon to the girl in the home of Robert H. Dunnet, 1,151 East Ninety-first Street, Canarsie, Queens. Mr. Browning had placed the girl in the home of Mr. Dunnet, a business associate, pending his application tomorrow to Surrogate Daniel A. Noble to have the adoption set aside on the ground that Mary Louise had misstated her age in the adoption papers.

Mr. Browning said he had tried to persuade the young woman not to accept the offer, but that she had finally decided to take it. Mr. Browning said that he had spent $20,000 in his effort to make the young woman his foster-daughter and a companion to Dorothy Sunshine Browning, 9 years old, who was adopted five years ago. He said the sum included the cost of forty frocks which he purchased for her.

Tells of Agent's Visit.

"The agent telephoned me at the Kew Gardens Inn," said Browning. "He told me that he would like to help me out of my difficulty, and after some conversation I invited him over for dinner last night. He came and had dinner and talked. He outlined what he had in view for Mary and I told him that I thought it would be better for him to await the outcome of the proceeding looking to annulment of the adoption. Then he left."

Mr. Browning said that he had the agent's offer on his mind when he arose yesterday morning, and after thinking it over he decided that perhaps it would be wise to move the girl out to the Dunnet Summer home in Rockville Centre, L. I. He was opposed to taking this step, but if it were to save the girl annoyance—as he thought—he would motor her out to the Long Island town.

With this idea in mind, Browning telephoned to Mr. Dunnet, and when the business associates joined him at the Kew Gardens Inn they got into their machines and went out to Rockville Centre. Mrs. Laura G. Dunnet, mother of Mr. Dunnet, said that she would be glad to open her home to Mary Louise for the time being. After riding about Brooklyn to prevent persons from following them, the motorists went to Canarsie.

In the meantime Mary Louise, with Mrs. Dunnet, the little daughter of the Dunnets, and two trained nurses employed by Browning, had remained in the frame dwelling there in seclusion. The shades of the house were drawn and the neighbors were unaware who was there.

According to Miss Virginia Martin, who was employed by Browning to be her companion, the girl passed the morning in and out of hysteria. The threatened loss of her future with the millionaire caused her to spend Saturday night in almost unbroken tears. Yesterday morning she cheered up a trifle and began to move about the house, scribbling literary ventures on a small pad.

Mr. Browning and Mr. Dunnet reached the house shortly after 2 o'clock. The agent had arrived before them. So had word that Mary Louise was in the house. A crowd had gathered so great that Mrs. Dunnet appealed to the police. Two mounted policemen were sent around and took up a patrol that lasted until 7:30 o'clock last night.

According to Mr. Browning, the discovery that the agent was already trying to persuade Mary Louise to leave occasioned him distress.

"He repeatedly told the girl that he could obtain her a position in the motion picture industry, and that he could also provide her with an opportunity

Continued on Page Two.

CORNERED BY POLICE FOR MURDER BLAST, SCHWARTZ ENDS LIFE

Chemist, in Farewell Note to Wife, Admits Killing Man in California Cellulose Plant.

HE ALLEGES SELF-DEFENSE

But Authorities Say He Lured Barbe, a Wanderer, to Death in $200,000 Insurance Plot.

PLANNED FLIGHT TO MEXICO

Slayer Had Maps and Ticket, but Manager of Oakland Apartment Revealed Hiding Place.

Special to The New York Times.

SAN FRANCISCO, Aug. 9.—Cornered today in an Oakland apartment, where he had been hiding since the explosion he contrived after the murder of an itinerant laborer in the Pacific Cellulose Company's plant at Walnut Creek, Charles Henry Schwartz shot and killed himself.

The chemist and head of the company who, in an attempt to perpetrate a $200,000 insurance fraud, had lured the wanderer into his laboratory and murdered and mutilated him in the hope that the charred corpse would be named as his own, had been the object of a nation-wide search for nine days following the blast that wrecked his factory on July 30.

The murderer sent a bullet into his brain at the Nottingham Apartments, 446 Forty-first Street, Oakland. Detectives from Berkeley and Oakland, acting on special information, had the place surrounded, but the sound of the shot as they attempted to force the door to his apartment apprised them beforehand that they had been cheated out of their quarry alive.

On a table near his body was a death note addressed to his widow, Mrs. Alice Schwartz, 5,901 Rockbridge Boulevard, Berkeley, in which he made a full confession of the murder.

Mrs. Schwartz, who, since the murder, has been dry-eyed and insistent that the body found in the laboratory was that of her husband, could not be reached today. She sent word through her attorney that she had no statement to make.

That the chemist sought to escape into Mexico at a propitious time was evident from a map showing all the railroads and highways of that country and a Pullman ticket to Barstow, both found in Schwartz's effects.

A suitcase and briefcase, fully packed, further indicated that the chemist was ready for instant flight.

Apartment Manager Gave Clue.

It was through C. W. Hayward, manager of the apartment house where Schwartz sought refuge, and N. B. Edmunds of Berkeley that Schwartz was located.

On Thursday morning, July 29, the day that the "too perfect crime" was executed, Schwartz appeared before Hayward.

"I want to rent an apartment and I will be here tonight," he told the manager.

Hayward said that he had known Schwartz casually for more than two years under the name of Harold Warren. He readily gave the man an apartment.

The next morning at 4 o'clock Schwartz stumbled into the place, limping, bruised and visibly disturbed. He awoke Hayward.

"I have had trouble with the police in Santa Clara," he said, excitedly. "I was in an automobile accident there and there was booze in my car. There were three men with me. What happened to them I don't know. But I escaped with a sprained ankle. I will have to lay low for a while."

From then on Schwartz did not leave the apartment. Occasionally he walked furtively through the hallways, but always first making sure that no one was outside his door. He took all his meals with the Hayward family, and, although usually nervous, he never lost his characteristic bravado.

On several occasions at the table he discussed volubly the Walnut Creek explosion, always urging the theory that the body was that of Schwartz.

Several days after Schwartz's arrival, Hayward grew suspicious. He told Ed-

Continued on Page Seven.

'Too Hot to Talk,' Says Dawes, But He Tells a Fish Story

OMAHA, Neb., Aug. 9 (AP).—When newspaper men met in his car here Vice President Dawes, on his way to Chicago at the conclusion of a Western vacation, they found him in his bare feet, collarless, "breaking in" a new pipe and decidedly ruffled.

When he greeted C. W. Delamatre, an Omaha attorney and his former college classmate, Mr. Delamatre suggested that he talk with the reporters first.

"It's too darned hot to talk," Mr. Dawes replied.

The Vice President warmed up to fish stories, however, and told one of his own about a fish two feet long he had caught on his trip.

RADIO AIDS SEARCH FOR EVELYN HOBBS

No Trace of Girl Who Left Her Park Avenue Home Saturday With Only $25.

HAD BEEN ILL FOR A YEAR

Mother Is Near Breakdown as Police, Parents and Friends Fail to Trace Her.

Evelyn Jacqueline Hobbs, the 18-year-old society girl who left her home at 911 Park Avenue Saturday morning for a hike in Westchester County, had not returned last night, and her father, Elon St. Clair Hobbs, a lawyer, said no word had been received from her either at his home here or his country home at Twin Lakes, Conn., where her brothers and sister are staying. He said he felt sure, however, that she would return home this morning.

Miss Hobbs's disappearance was reported to the police on Saturday, and yesterday a general alarm was broadcast by radio. As nothing has been heard of her and as her movements have not been traced since she walked out of her home, her father was very much alarmed.

Mrs. Hobbs, who had been resting at a hotel here after caring for her daughter during a long illness, returned to the Park Avenue home on Saturday afternoon, and Mr. Hobbs said that after talking with her he felt that his daughter's absence might be explained by the fact that she knew her mother would be away over the week-end and had decided to take advantage of this to go for a walk in the country. She had been ill for so long that he thought she simply forgot that her parents would be worried when she did not return.

Thought Nurse Was With Her.

Mr. Hobbs took the blame for her disappearance upon himself, for he heard her leave the house, but as he was in bed he concluded that the nurse who had been caring for the girl must be with her. Later he found she had left without saying a word to any one.

"Mrs. Hobbs was away at the time at a hotel in the city," he said, "for she was worn out from caring for our daughter during her long illness and thought she would rest better in a hotel, where she could be completely isolated. She returned home yesterday afternoon and she came to the conclusion that Evelyn had merely gone away for the week-end because her mother was also away. We are sure we will hear from her tomorrow."

Mrs. Hobbs was on the verge of a nervous breakdown, he said, and should be in bed, although she would not rest until she heard from her daughter. Although the police were notified and Mr. Hobbs and his friends did everything they could to trace the girl's movements, nothing was learned to indicate where she went after leaving the apartment house. The elevator man was the last one to see her, for he was dozing on a bench early in the morning when Miss Hobbs asked him to help her open the heavy door leading to the street.

She had been in ill health for a year, her father said, having left school because of her weakness. For several months she had suffered from tonsilitis, and an operation for removal of her tonsils was performed at her home a short time ago. Since then she had been constantly attended by a nurse.

Miss Hobbs had only $25 with her when she went away, for her father had given her $20, with which she planned to do some shopping, and at the time

Continued on Page Three.

Chandelier of 1766, Missing for 87 Years, Is Found Hidden in Attic of St. Paul's Chapel

Hidden away in an attic the great crystal chandelier which hung in St. Paul's Episcopal Chapel, Broadway between Fulton and Vesey Streets, until 1838, was found last Spring, it was learned yesterday, when the work of restoring the interior of the church began. It is planned to utilise this chandelier in the new scheme of decoration and the other smaller chandeliers if they can be found.

The great chandelier was laid away in the attic when the chapel was last renovated. The twenty-four smaller chandeliers were given to various churches. The present location of some of them are known, and an effort is being made to discover the others and have them returned.

"It is hoped that many of the original ones may be returned through the cooperation of the churches which have had them in their possession," said a statement issued yesterday from the office of Trinity Parish, Fulton and Church Streets, of which St. Paul's is a part.

St. Paul's is the oldest building of worship in New York City, it having been erected in 1766. Arrangements have been completed to restore the interior as nearly as possible to its original form when George Washington worshipped there.

The work of restoring the church has begun with the chancel. It is under the direction of Thomas Nash, architect for Trinity Parish. Because the whole interior is to be restored to the Colonial Gregorian style the coloring of the chancel will be white, gray and gold—rather than dull brown and gold, which are the present colors.

Two rows of pews have been removed together with the floor underneath, and this space is to be tiled to match the rest of the floor. When this flooring was taken up the beams were found to have been laid directly on the ground when the building was erected in 1766, and were in perfect condition. The earth underneath these cedar beams is probably that of the original wheat field in which St. Paul's was built.

RICHMOND REVOLTS; ANTI-HYLAN TICKET TO ENTER THE RACE

Judge J. H. Tiernan Announces He Will Run for Borough President There.

CURLEY QUITS THE MAYOR

Assistant Corporation Counsel Will Be a Candidate for District Attorney.

WALKER IDOL AT BALL GAME

Has Picture Taken With Babe Ruth—Hylan Denies Charge of Disloyalty to Smith.

Democrats in the Borough of Richmond, regarded as a veritable Hylan stronghold, raised the banner of revolt yesterday against the renomination of Mayor Hylan for a third term. The smallest of all the boroughs, Richmond was the first to decide to place in the field a local ticket in opposition to the prospective nominees on the Hylan ticket who have not as yet been named.

The uprising against Mayor Hylan in Richmond will mean that in every borough where the regular Democratic organization is nominally pledged to the Mayor for a third term the Tammany-Bronx Democratic entente behind the candidacy of Senator James J. Walker will have organized local support for their candidates. The prevailing opinion in the Borough of Richmond is that the Mayor will be smothered on primary day by the organized opposition in that borough. Shall Governor Smith or W. R. Hearst lead the Democratic Party in City and State, will be the clear-cut issue upon which the battle will be waged in Richmond.

The nominal leader of the anti-Hylan Democratic faction in Richmond is Bertram G. Eadie, who is Chairman of what is known as the regular Tammany organization of Staten Island. Mr. Eadie is a prominent Richmond lawyer. The real leader, however, is J. Harry Tiernan of Tompkinsville, County Judge and Surrogate of Richmond. He is looked upon as beyond doubt the most powerful figure in the Democratic organization of the borough. He made it known yesterday that he would turn his back on the position he now holds and enter the Democratic primaries as a candidate for Borough President of Richmond against John A. Lynch, the incumbent, who will be a candidate for re-election on the Hylan ticket, although his term on the bench has four years more to run.

Curley Also Quits.

Announcement was made also that Assistant Corporation Counsel Thomas F. Curley, who received his present appointment from the Hylan Administration, had quit the Mayor and would become candidate for the nomination for District Attorney against District Attorney Albert C. Fach, who has been slated to run for renomination on the Hylan ticket.

The announcement of the revolt in Staten Island, which was easily the biggest development of the day, fell like a bomb in the Hylan camp. David S. Rendt, the Democratic borough leader, who all through the recent conferences of the Big Five stuck to Hylan and was regarded as more strongly committed to the Mayor than any of the other leaders, evidently is in for a big fight. The news of the Richmond development came about the time when the Tammany-Bronx entente's candidate for Mayor, Senator James J. Walker, was being lionised by the baseball fans at the Yankee Stadium, where he was photographed with Babe Ruth and Colonel Jacob Ruppert, President and owner of the Yankees, after 20,000 spectators had cheered and applauded the candidate for several minutes as the "Father of Sunday Baseball." Senator Walker was sponsor in the upper house at Albany of a bill which made professional baseball on Sunday possible.

The revolting Democrats of Staten Island will open headquarters and take steps to place their ticket officially in the running today. Their fighting base will be in the Hugo Building at St. George. A Walker headquarters will be opened simultaneously in Brooklyn in the Albee Theatre Building, on De Kalb Avenue, while the anti-Hylan and anti-Connolly Democrats in Queens, another borough included in Mayor Hylan's triple alliance, will mobilize for action at a meeting to be held for organisation purposes tomorrow.

Resent Rendt's Action.

Bertram G. Eadie, the anti-Hylan leader in Richmond, made this statement last night:

"The rank and file of the Democratic Party on Staten Island feel that a great injustice has been done to them in the attempt made by David S. Rendt to deliver them to Mayor Hylan for a third term.

"Judge Tiernan did not consider entering the fight against Hylanism until W. R. Hearst issued orders that Tammany Hall must renominate the Mayor. The order was taken by Judge Tiernan's supporters to mean that Hylan's renomination would result in the ruin of the Democratic Party in the whole city.

"The thing that clinched the decision on the part of Judge Tiernan to go into the fight on Hylan came with the designation of Senator James J. Walker as Tammany's candidate. Senator Walker is held in high esteem on Staten Island and has a very big following here.

"During the leadership of Thomas F. McGinley, he repeatedly announced his

"All the News That's Fit to Print"

The New York Times

THE WEATHER
Generally fair today; tomorrow cloudy and cooler, possibly showers.
Temperature yesterday—Max. 80, min. 69.
For weather report see Page 38.

VOL. LXXIV....No. 24,680. NEW YORK, THURSDAY, AUGUST 20, 1925. TWO CENTS in Greater New York | THREE CENTS Within 200 Miles | FOUR CENTS Elsewhere in the U. S.

FRENCH NOW COMING TO ARRANGE DEBT WITH WASHINGTON

Mellon Announces Mission Will Sail for This Country in September.

MOVE BY ITALY IS EXPECTED

Six Nations to Date Have Contracted to Repay $5,000,000,000 Advanced.

CREDIT IS OPEN TO BELGIUM

Large Loan to France Also Is Being Considered by Bankers Following Refunding Settlement.

Special to The New York Times.

WASHINGTON, Aug. 19.—Now that the funding of the Belgian debt has been successfully completed, the eyes of the American Debt Commission and the Treasury are turned toward France and Italy, who, American officials earnestly hope, will exert every effort to join with the six nations that have arranged settlements of their obligations to the United States.

French Commissioners are expected here in September. Secretary Mellon made the announcement this afternoon that he had been informed that the Frenchmen would sail about the middle of next month. Nothing of an official nature has been received from Italy outside of the cablegram Mario Alberti sent Under Secretary Winston a day or so ago, saying he had been made head of an Italian agency to deal with Italy's debts and assuring Mr. Winston he would do all he could to promote an agreement. But Rome dispatches of this afternoon optimistically reflecting that nation's attitude toward the Belgian settlement make Treasury officials believe Italy is about to do something.

Members of the Debt Commission take the position that France and Italy are not entitled to special indulgence, no promises having been made regarding separate consideration of their pre-armistice and post-armistice debts which would warrant the moral obligation felt in the case of King Albert's country. It is believed they will insist they must have easy terms on first payments of their debts, and will drive hard, too, for the same terms on accrued interest granted Belgium, which, in calculating this interest for reaching the principal for funding purposes, was permitted 4¼ per cent. from the armistice to December, 1922, and 3 per cent. thence to June, 1925, whereas Great Britain was charged 4¼ per cent. to the date of her funding.

It is not thought here that the two nations will feel in a position to demand a lower rate of interest than 3½ per cent. on the debt, because that is the rate for previous settlements.

What France and Italy are expected to stress most are pleas for a moratorium, and it is thought probable that they will urge that the easy payments permitted Belgium for ten years on her post-armistice obligation really amount to a moratorium itself. Members of the American commission seem now in no way inclined to think about giving France or Italy a moratorium, although the desire not to be unduly harsh may result in arranging light payments at the opening stages of payments. It is further intimated that there is no thought of cancellation of any part of the interest charges.

It was learned this afternoon that some pressure was brought to bear on the Belgians in the way of suggesting that they come to an agreement as soon as possible, and it was also stated that France and Italy had been notified that failure to come forward with proposals would militate against their countries should they desire to obtain foreign loans in the United States in the near future.

With the funding of the Belgian debt, six nations have made arrangements with the United States for payment of more than $5,000,000,000 of the $12,000,000,000 due her through war loans to twenty countries. These six nations have agreed to fund a total of $5,213,309,000, and to pay an aggregate interest charge of $7,097,094,285, making a total payment to the United States of $12,310,403,285.

The principal as funded, the interest to be paid and the total payments are shown in the following table:

	Principal.	Interest.	Total.
Belgium—	$417,780,000	$310,050,000	$727,830,000
Finland—	9,000,000	12,695,055	21,695,055
Great Britain—	4,600,000,000	6,505,965,000	11,105,965,000
Hungary—	1,939,000	2,754,240	4,693,240
Lithuania—	6,030,000	8,501,940	14,531,940
Poland—	178,560,000	257,137,550	435,697,550
Total—	$5,213,309,000	$7,097,094,285	$12,310,403,285

On May 15, 1925, the five nations other than Belgium which had already funded their debts had made some payments. The following table shows the amounts then due on their debts and the payments on principal and interest:

	Debt.	Prin. Paid.	Int. Paid.
Great Britain—	$4,554,000,000	$46,000,000	$275,320,000
Finland..	8,910,000	90,000	538,650
Hungary.	1,958,412	9,672	29,303
Lithuania	6,030,000	....	90,450
Poland...	178,560,000	....	....
Total..	$4,749,458,412	$46,099,672	$275,968,403

On May 15, 1925, the total indebtedness to this country of the twenty nations totaled $12,151,238,393, of which $10,556,804,223 was in principal and

Continued on Page Six.

Caillaux Finds in Paris Mint Early American Medal Dies

Copyright, 1925, by The New York Times Co.
Special Cable to THE NEW YORK TIMES.

PARIS, Aug. 19.—On a tour of inspection of the French Mint yesterday, Finance Minister Caillaux came across a series of dies for what are known as the "American Medals," which date back to the time of Louis XVI.

They were made at the request of the United States Government, which had no mint at the time capable of making appropriate medals to commemorate the War of Independence.

These dies include excellent likenesses of George Washington and Benjamin Franklin. There is also one of the Battle of Cowpens, and a Lafayette medal. The best of all is said to be that of Paul Jones.

M. Caillaux intends to have a new series of medals struck from these eighteenth century dies, which are still in perfect condition.

V. F. LAWSON DIES FROM HEART ATTACK

Publisher of Chicago Daily News Expires Suddenly in His Home.

EDITED PAPER 49 YEARS

Was a Founder of The Associated Press—Active in Many Lines.

CHICAGO, Aug. 19 (AP).—Victor F. Lawson, editor and publisher of the Chicago Daily News, died at his home here tonight after an illness of two days.

Mr. Lawson had suffered heart attacks in recent years from overwork, and an attack of myocarditis with acute dilation, which came yesterday, proved fatal at 10 o'clock tonight. His nearest relative, his niece, Mrs. Clark N. Tavenee, of Chicago, summoned when it was plain his illness had become grave, was at his bedside.

Mr. Lawson would have been 75 years old next month. Earlier in the year, and two or three times in the last decade, he had suffered attacks which kept him confined for a few days, but after brief rests he resumed his vigorous activities, refusing to turn over the burden of direction of The Daily News to his staff.

Victor Fremont Lawson gained fame and fortune by his foresight in anticipating the success of a low-priced paper. His Daily News was the first Western paper to make a success at the one-cent price.

He later gained hosts of friends in the newspaper business when his foresight again came to the front and enabled him to supply hundreds of publishers and smaller newspapers with print paper during the paper shortage of wartime days.

Mr. Lawson was one of the most influential publishers in the United States. He was one of the founders and always a leader in the affairs of The Associated Press, being one of the most vigorous advocates of cooperative news gathering. He was President of the Illinois corporation from 1894 till 1900. He had been a member of the Board of Directors of the present organization continuously since November, 1900.

Mr. Lawson learned the rudiments of the newspaper business on a newspaper in which his father had an interest. He began early to acquire the experience which later enabled him to develop one of the most successful and widely read newspapers on the continent.

He was born in Chicago Sept. 9, 1850, the son of Iver and Meling H. Lawson. Mr. Lawson Sr., who helped to found the Republican Party in Illinois, was a great admirer of John C. Fremont, then a popular hero because of his part in the conquest of California, and he named his son Victor Fremont Lawson. Mr. Lawson completed his schooling at Phillips Academy, Andover, Mass. His father, who came to Chicago from Western Norway, founded, with others, The Scandinavian and was elected to the City Council and the State Legislature.

At the death of the elder Lawson the son assumed charge of the interest of the estate in the publishing business. He was thus engaged when Melville E. Stone, establishing The Chicago Daily News, rented quarters in the Scandinavian office. The first issue of The

Continued on Page Eight.

SHIP BLAST DEAD 36; LIST GROWS HOURLY; BAD BOILER BLAMED

Three Investigations Started As Undertaking Wagons Roll From Hospitals.

ONE ORDERED BY HOOVER

Pitiful Scenes Enacted in the Naval Training Station Wards Among Scalded Excursionists.

35 ARE STILL IN DANGER

Crowd of 10,000 Throngs Pawtucket, R. I., Stations When Survivors Return From Newport.

NEWPORT, R. I., Aug. 19 (AP).—Thirty-six persons had lost their fight for life tonight, twenty-four hours after they had been enveloped in a flood of steam let loose from the bursting boiler of the excursion steamer Mackinac bound for Pawtucket, R. I., as she steamed through Narragansett Bay.

There are still left in the Naval Training Station and Newport City Hospital thirty-five persons. Naval physicians said that several, perhaps all, of their patients might die.

The death list grew by the hour. Every attendant at the Naval Hospital, where most of the victims were taken, was on duty and worked ceaselessly. As many of the patients as could be removed were taken to the Newport Hospital, where twenty-five volunteer nurses, many of whom saw service overseas, attended them in wards filled with flowers brought from the gardens of Newport's society leaders.

Naval physicians found new deaths in the accident wards on almost every visit. Hospital officials stated that the number of dead would probably reach fifty.

Three Investigations Started.

A defective boiler was ascribed as the cause of the disaster by Oscar A. Heltzen, Assistant Attorney General, who said the State Attorney General's department would investigate to determine whether there was criminal culpability and what, if any, persons were responsible for the conditions which caused the fatalities.

"When the State investigators inspected the Mackinac's exploded boiler they found it was an old one, deteriorated by wear and thinned down in certain places," said Mr. Heltzen. "What occurred at the time of the explosion was a rupture of the plate in the cross drum extending from the right-hand side of the firebox to the centre of the boiler alongside of the longitudinal seam.

"The longitudinal seam was very thin and the opening was six or seven inches wide, extending upward to the rear of the drum. It appeared that from time to time the boiler had been subjected to extensive repairs by the addition of new bolts and patches.

"The repairs may be evidence that the boiler was in a weakened condition. It has been intimated to the Attorney General's department that an inspection should have determined this condition by the use of hydrostatic or hammer test.

"There appeared next to the longitudinal joint a sign of discoloration for a distance of two and a half feet. This is a suggestion of an old break. An old crack appeared beyond the break made at the time of the explosion. This crack has a splitting appearance instead of a tearing one, which, in the opinion of the State officials, is significant in that in the case of a regular explosion a wide bursting would have taken place, whereas in this case the opening followed the weak spot.

"At the edge of the sheet of metal it is plain to be seen how thin it had become."

Federal Authorities Act.

Federal steamship inspectors and the Newport police started independent investigations. United States Senator Jesse H. Metcalf asked Secretary Hoover to start an immediate inquiry.

Captain George McVay, Commander of the vessel, and George Kelly, General Manager of the Blackstone Valley Transportation Company, owners, were among those who accompanied the investigators over the craft.

Boiler Inspector Richard F. Bailey said that the Mackinac's boilers were

Continued on Page Eight.

New Club in London Launches Campaign To Make the British a Nation of Fliers

Copyright, 1925, by The New York Times Company.
By Wireless to THE NEW YORK TIMES.

LONDON, Aug. 19.—When the London Light Aeroplane Club was formally opened today, England's most expensive sport made its official bow. The membership of this unique club is restricted to 100, but the list, which runs the entire social scale from dukes to butchers, is already full and scores of applicants are clamoring to get in.

While the desire to learn to fly for its sporting possibilities no doubt prompted many to join, the British Government attaches much greater importance to the club, which is the first of six to be established in Great Britain. Sir Philip Sassoon, who officialy opened the club as Under Secretary of the Air, declared the ideal of the club is "to make a nation of airmen" for any future emergency.

Mrs. Elliott Lynn, famous English athlete, who was the first member to take the air in a tuition flight, said, upon descending, that the women of England were equally determined to make Great Britain a nation of "air women" as well.

Sir Philip Sassoon called on the nation to build up a big reserve of air pilots and popularize flying by developing the "air sense" so necessary to the achievement of the club's ideal. "It is up to you," he told the assembled members, "to help the Government to wean away the airplane from its association with war, by making it a powerful agent for civilization and peace."

Mrs. Lynn was enthusiastic over her first lesson. "I think this new movement will attract a host of women," she said, "and may quite easily lead to the establishment of a veritable army of women pilots. Flying is very easy to learn and certainly easier than driving a car. I think women should make good as pilots of light airplanes, as they have made good as drivers of motor cars."

The opening of the club today was singularly appropriate, for it was the anniversary of the first British reconnaissance flight in the World War on Aug. 19, 1914. The club is equipped with little aerial runabouts or moths of sixty horsepower and fitted with every possible fool-proof appliance to reduce the dangers of flying to an absolute minimum.

The British Government is backing the light airplane movement, but has called on its wealthy subjects to lend their financial support in the interest of the nation. Sir Sefton Branckner, Director of Civil Aviation, who postponed an air trip to Egypt long enough to be present today, asserted the movement was "of greatest importance to Great Britain," being, as it is, a thoroughly organized campaign to train a vast army of airmen for any war which may come in the future.

FIND AMAZING RELICS OF MAYAS' EMPIRE

Tulane Expedition Discovers Several Ancient Cities in Central America.

TOMB HAS RARE PORTRAITS

Proof Found That Dentistry Was Practised—Great Engineering Feats Done.

Special to The New York Times.

NEW ORLEANS, La., Aug. 19.—Bringing with them a pure descendant of the ancient Maya Indians, Frans Blom and Oliver La Farge, comprising the first Tulane Middle American expedition, arrived here tonight from a six months' exploration trip into Mexico and Guatemala reporting one of the most astounding series of archaeological discoveries ever made by a single expedition.

Discovery of three huge centres of Maya culture, each a distinct cluster of ruined cities containing a tremendous quantity of monuments carved with dates and other important hieroglyphs; unearthing of a large tomb containing the bones of some mighty Maya ruler, on the walls of which sepulchre were found nine portraits in low relief, each more beautifully artistic than any Maya paintings previously discovered; proof that the Empire Maya area extended 1,000 miles further westward toward the Pacific Coast of Mexico than has been hitherto known; discovery that the modern descendants of the Maya, despite the religious influence of thousands of Catholic missionaries in Mexico, still worship the pagan idols of their ancestors on the far-off and obscure mountain tops; proof that the Maya race possessed dentists possibly more skillful than modern molar experts, and absolute conviction that the Maya Indian could compete with any race in the world in the art of making beautiful pottery—this outlines the work accomplished by the Tulane explorers.

Descendant of the Mayas.

The scientists brought with them Tata, a full-blooded descendent of the Mayas. He will remain in New Orleans for a fortnight while attempts are made to induce him to divulge the secret customs and rites of his famous ancestors. His Spanish name is Lazaro Hernandez. He cannot speak a word of English. Among his tribe he is respected for his so-called supernatural powers of curing and causing ills. He might be termed, therefore, a "medicine man."

It is doubtful if a previous archaeological party ever suffered such body and nerve-racking hardships as did the first Tulane expedition. Messrs. Blom and La Farge crossed faint Indian trials over which the feet of white man probably had never trod. They slowly bored their tortuous way through wild jungles, while a squad of Indians cut a swath for them with machetes. They climbed and descended almost perpendicular peaks. They visited tribes of Indians who still use the bow and arrow for weapons and whom they were warned not to visit "if you want to get out alive." They escaped death by the narrowest of margins a dozen times. And yet the only weapon they carried was a small .22-caliber special rifle for shooting small birds and other provender.

However impenetrable the jungle and insurmountable the obstacles, the Tulane explorers pushed steadily on, so that at the end of their journey they tabulated the following:

1. Covered 1,250 miles on horseback.
2. Traveled 2,500 miles by water and 1,000 by railroad.
3. Discovered studies and brought back data on twenty-four new cities.
4. Discovered and photographed seventy-three new carved monuments.
5. Brought to light thirty-two new inscriptions, most of them dates.
6. Discovered virtually that the Maya civilization comprised many sub tribes.
7. Filled out many heretofore puzzling gaps in Maya history.
8. Cemented a close friendship between

Continued on Page Six.

MONGOLIA BANISHES ANDREWS EXPEDITION

Charges American Scientists Engaged Military Suspects and Stirred Propaganda.

ANDREWS TELLS NEW FINDS

Director in Peking Reports Traces of Earliest Human Type Ever Discovered.

URGA, Mongolia, Aug. 19. (AP)—The Mongolian Government has ordered the third Asiatic expedition of the American Museum of Natural History, under the leadership of Roy Chapman Andrews, to cease its exploration and scientific work and to leave Mongolian territory, alleging that Mr. Andrews has violated the terms of his agreement with Mongolian scientific organizations.

The Mongolian Government further alleges that besides carrying out his scientific work in the domains of paleontology, geology and zoology, Mr. Andrews's expedition also has engaged in topographical observation work and has employed a number of persons held suspicious, in a military sense.

Mr. Andrews also is accused of carrying on political propaganda and stirring up to Mongolians against the "Red Bolsheviks."

Reports Human Traces Centuries Old.

PEKING, Aug. 19. (AP)—Stone implements and weapons of a race of men who lived thousands of years ago among sand dunes on the shore of a lake which has since been swallowed up by the Gobi Desert, and who discovered the eggs of the dinosaur countless ages before these were introduced to the civilized world two years ago by Roy Chapman Andrews, have been found far in the interior of Mongolia by the expedition of the American Museum, Mr. Andrews, disclosed here today.

That these primitive men knew of the eggs left by the dinosaur, the giant reptile that roamed the Asiatic uplands some 10,000,000 years ago, is proved by the fact that they neatly bored the shells and made ornaments of them, Mr. Andrews said. They used for the same purpose the shells of a gigantic ostrich, long since extinct.

In this discovery Mr. Andrews believes his expedition has uncovered traces of the earliest type of men yet discovered. He has named them the "Dune dwellers of Shabarack Ussu," using the name of the site of the find.

"In these dune dwellers," he said, "we believe we have found the earliest type of man in his development from ape."

Mr. Andrews, who has been in Peking several days, was on the eve of his return to the expedition, which he left about 300 miles northwest of Kalgan, the original jump-off point for the expedition in Northwestern Chihli Province, in China. (This locates the present encampment of the expedition in Southeastern Outer Mongolia.) Since entering Mongolia last Spring the party has traversed more than 4,000 miles, penetrating as far as the Altai Mountains, in far Western Mongolia.

Forty More Dinosaur Eggs Are Found.

The scientist-explorer described other rare finds, including traces of other primitive humans, forty more dinosaur eggs to add to the collection of twenty-five brought out of the Gobi two years ago and skeletons of two men who came after the Stone Age humans but before the Mongolian race peopled the upper Asiatic plains.

The American scientists also found the skulls of two animal types, which Mr. Andrews believes illustrate the evolution of animal life from the reptile to the mammal stage. These were primitive beasts about the size of rats, and their skulls, fossilised, were found embedded in a rock formation which is dated two or three million years before the age of mammals.

The new finds of dinosaur eggs show many different types, some small and quite smooth, others large. One nest of twelve eggs was found neatly ar-

Continued on Page Four.

FIND 'RADIO ROOF' ENCIRCLES WORLD AND CAUSES 'FADING'

Naval Experts Locate Ionized Region 100 Miles High, Deflecting Broadcast Waves.

ACCOUNT FOR 'DEAD AREAS'

Secretary Wilbur Announces Result of Experiments as Vital to Progress of Science.

TWO WAVES DISCOVERED

One Is "Horizontal," Traversing World Surface—The Other "Vertical," Rebounding From Sky.

Special to The New York Times.

WASHINGTON, Aug. 19.—The existence of a radio deflecting roof in the higher levels of the earth's atmosphere, accounting for "fading" and "skip distances" in broadcast reception, has been established by investigations conducted by the Naval Research Laboratory at Bellevue, D. C., in association with the Carnegie Institution of Washington.

Secretary Wilbur, in announcing today the results of the experiments, also brought out a second point: the demonstration that there are two waves in broadcasting and transmission.

One of these waves, known as the "horizontal wave," arrives by way of the earth and the other, the "vertical wave," by way of the sky "layer" or "ceiling," an ionized region varying in height above the earth, according to atmospheric conditions, and generally over 100 miles high.

The horizontal wave moves along the earth's surface till it slides off tangentially into the ether. The vertical wave, striking the undersurface of the sky ceiling is deflected downward, hitting the earth at distances which depend upon the angle of impact upon the ceiling.

After striking the earth again, these rebounded waves are deflected upward at an angle, again strike the sky ceiling, rebound and continue this process around the world. It is this process that creates the so-called "skip distance."

Secretary Wilbur said that the Navy Department was not yet ready to announce in detail the result of the experiments, but that with the confirmation of the "radio roof" theory he felt, because of its importance to the radio world, scientists and radio engineers should have the benefit of a preliminary announcement immediately.

The experiments are continuing, he said, but the results already stand as "the nearest approach to the key to unsolved problems of radio that has yet been made." Though the chief benefit at present will be to commercial radio telegraphy, the eventual achievement will be the building of a high frequency transmitting station for $60,000 "that will give better service and longer range than the present high-power stations costing $2,000,000, while the cost of operation will be correspondingly reduced."

Wilbur Tells of 'Skip Distance' Quest.

Secretary Wilbur's announcement was as follows:

"Investigations conducted by the Naval Research Laboratory, in association with the Department of Terrestrial Magnetism of the Carnegie Institution of Washington, have resulted in confirming the theory of an ionized region in the higher levels of the earth's atmosphere.

"From observations made, it appears that the plans of maximum density, in popular language, the ceiling of the sky, lies at a varying distance above the surface of the earth, rising and falling as atmospheric conditions vary.

"This layer, the conception of which originated independently with Heaviside in England and Kennelly in the United States, is known in the scientific world as the Kennelly-Heaviside layer. It acts as a deflecting surface to electro-magnetic waves, under which they are guided around the world in a very similar way to that in which whispered sound waves run under the domes of the Capitol at Washington and of Saint Paul's Cathedral in London.

"The results attained are based upon an analysis of the phenomenon known as the skip distance, checked by a simple mechanical device by means of which the effective distance of the deflecting layer may be actually measured.

"In the pioneer work of short wave length transmission, it was the experience that signals could be picked up at

Continued on Page Three.

More City Primary Petitions This Year Than Ever Before

More designating petitions for a primary election were filed Tuesday than ever before, George W. Conklin, deputy chief clerk of the Board of Elections, declared yesterday. He said there were 50 per cent. more petitions than for the municipal election four years ago, and that the number of signatures was much greater.

Twenty clerks were put at work to tabulate the list of candidates and count the signatures. Mr. Conklin said the big task before the board was arranging to print two million primary ballots, 25 per cent. more than ever before.

MANY BULLETS FLY IN LONG THIEF CHASE

Two Policemen and a Negro Hit in Battle After a Drug-store Hold-Up.

SHOTS RATTLE IN BROADWAY

Dozens of Automobilists Join Midtown Pursuit—Firemen Aid Hunt for One Suspect.

A wild automobile chase through the midtown district after three negroes who had held up a drug store at Ninth Avenue and Forty-first Street ended early this morning with the shooting of two policeman and one of the alleged robbers and the capture of another.

The third robber was believed to be hiding on the roof of a building in Thirty-third Street, near Ninth Avenue, and nearly 100 policemen, detectives and firemen surrounded the place and were still searching it more than an hour after the shooting. Several hundred shots were fired during the chase.

The chase after the robbers who fled in a Ford Sedan wound dangerously through the streets for several miles. The police fired many shots at their quarry and were answered by volleys from the fleeing car. Many motorists joined in the pursuit, which at one period extended along a crowded section of Broadway.

The two injured policemen were Patrolman Harold S. Moore of the Special Service Division and Patrolman Harry Nichols of the West Sixty-eighth Street Station. Both were taken to the French Hospital. Moore was said to be in a serious condition with a bullet wound in the abdomen. Nichols's chest a few inches from the heart was grazed by a bullet from the pistol of the robber. His condition was not serious.

Negro Critically Wounded.

The wounded negro was taken to Bellevue and was in such a serious condition that detectives were unable to question him. He was not expected to live. The other negro was held at the West Sixty-eighth Street station, where he was said to have admitted the robbery of the drug store and to have told of laying plans for it in a café in Harlem. He gave his name as John Wages of 125 West 142d Street.

Due to the uproar over the chase and the efforts of all available police to surround the tenement where the third robber was said to be in hiding, the police were unable to provide the details of the drug store hold up. It was said that only a small sum had been obtained by the robbers.

The robbery took place a short time after midnight. Patrolman Frank O'Brien of Traffic B, who was off duty saw the robbers leave the drug store just after they had held it up as he passed on his way to visit a friend. As the three negroes jumped into their automobile putting their pistols into their pockets, O'Brien called to them to halt. They laughed and sped away turning west of Forty-first Street.

O'Brien commandeered a passing automobile and started the chase. The patrolman standing on the running board of the pursuing car fired several shots at the robbers as their automobile turned the corner at Tenth Avenue on two wheels and headed north. Two robbers in the rear seat kept up a fire to the rear.

The two cars sped up Tenth Avenue at more than forty miles an hour with persons dodging as the shots fired by the policemen and the robbers flew about. Many cars joined in the chase behind the car in which O'Brien was riding.

Patrolman Simon Knapp of the West Sixty-eighth Street Station was on duty at Amsterdam Avenue, a continuation of Tenth Avenue at Sixty-first Street, wand when he saw the robbers' car ap-

Continued on Page Three.

HYLAN ATTACKS WALKER'S RECORD ON HOME RULE ACT

Reply to Opponent's Platform Is Charge He Let Amendment Be Changed and Voided.

DEFENDS HIS OWN RECORD

Says Senator's Issues Are Only What the Administration Has Fought For.

HITS SMITH BOND POLICY

Asserts He Will Fight Helping Railroads Finance Abolition of Grade Crossings.

In a reply to Senator James J. Walker's declaration of principles, Mayor Hylan charged the Tammany candidate for Mayor yesterday with responsibility as Senate leader for permitting the Citizens Union to make a change in the home rule constitutional amendment, which led to it having been declared void by the courts.

Mayor Hylan declared Senator Walker's declaration constituted an endorsement of his Administration. He said the people knew his position on transit, and knew that he was pledged to the five-cent fare and pledged to bring about the desirable transit conditions for which Senator Walker "professed" to stand. The Mayor also asserted that, like Senator Walker, he was for the elimination of grade crossings, but at the expense of the railroads and not of the taxpayers. He declared that he would oppose the proposal to issue $300,000,000 in State bonds to finance the railroads' share of the expense, as favored by Governor Smith.

The Mayor's statement, which was interpreted as his "declaration of principles" for the campaign, follows:

I ask the newspapers which have been hostile to me to print in full my reply to Mr. Walker's declaration.

I find nothing new in the Walker declaration of principles. It is a substantial endorsement of the present City Administration, which has fought for such principles and done everything humanly possible to carry them out.

I stand now, as I have stood since I have been in the office of Mayor, upon every plank of the Democratic city platforms of 1917 and 1921.

Asserts He Is "Regular."

I do not have to accentuate my democracy. Actions speak louder than words. I am the regularly designated candidate of a majority of the Democratic counties of the City of New York. Mr. Walker has been designated by a minority of the counties of the City of New York.

He speaks of municipal ownership and operation, including buses and free transfers. I do not have to make any such statement. No one knows better than he who fought hardest in the City of New York and at Albany for these very things. The people know by my actions that I have at all times insisted upon a transit program to give safe and adequate service, free from the control of private traction interests; that I have already started a new subway system to be operated at a five-cent fare and that I am pledged to bring about the desirable conditions for which Mr. Walker professes to stand.

I am for the elimination of railroad grade crossings. But I am for such elimination at the expense of the railroads and not at the expense of the people. I shall oppose in the future, as I have in the past, the attempt to make a gift of about $300,000,000 of the people's money to the railroads, with no compulsion upon the railroads to pay back the people's money other than "when practicable," which means not at all.

I am for the creation of new arteries of traffic. The Board of Estimate and the Police Department have studied this problem carefully. Expedients adopted have prevented utter traffic chaos from overtaking us. The construction of vehicular tunnels, street widening, introduction of arcade streets, express highways, laying out of spacious boulevards in unmapped areas, the diversion of vehicular traffic from congested central avenues to water-front areas (the repaving of First and Tenth Avenues has been carried on with this thought in mind), as well as a wide variety of police arrangements, from the one-way street to the traffic tower, are all embraced in our plan. There has been only one drawback to the immediate inauguration of all our suggested devices for traffic relief and that has been the capacity of the City of New York to finance them. Within the limits of that capacity we have proceeded.

Cites Schools Built.

I do not have to profess what I will do for the schools. Every one knows the heritage of neglect which was mine on Jan. 1, 1918, as they well know the hindrances to immediate school construction which the war created. On June 30, 1925, there had been constructed and opened for the children 155 new public schools. At the opening of the Fall term this year thirty-seven additional school buildings will be ready for occupancy. This means a total of 192 new school buildings with sittings for [illegible] pupils, aggregating an cost [illegible], exclusive of sites. We have done more for the public schools in the

Gov. Smith Denounces Carrying of Weapons; Never Needed One Here, He Says at Hearing

ALBANY, N. Y., Aug. 19 (AP).—Governor Smith warned against gun-carrying today when he heard appeals for clemency for three men convicted of murder and awaiting death in the chair during the week of Aug. 25 in Sing Sing Prison.

"I have walked in the lower sections of New York for years," the Governor said, "and have never felt the need of a weapon. A man usually carries a gun for a purpose."

Earl Carroll, New York theatrical producer, appeared for Julius Willis Miller, known as "Yellow Charleston," Bronx negro, convicted of the shooting of Baron Wilkins, a wealthy negro, also of the Bronx. Mr. Carroll, who flew in an airplane from New York City to Albany for the hearing, described himself as a former cellmate of Miller in the tombs when the theatrical man refused to give bail after his arrest for producing a show alleged to be indecent. Mr. Carroll's plea that Miller had shot in self-defense, and testimony that the negro had carried a gun with him when he had appealed to Wilkins for money, drew the admonition against use of weapons from the Governor.

To the theatrical man's assertion that he believed Miller was not sane, the Governor retorted that no condemned man went to the electric chain in New York State unless alienists believed him sane.

Representative John J. O'Connor of New York City, Miller's two small children, and his sister were at the hearing.

Ambrose Ross, convicted of the murder of Ernest L. Whitman, a bond salesman, in the Bellmore Bank robbery in Nassau County in April, 1924, will get a stay of execution, the Governor indicated, when Nassau County officials said they would agree. The cases of two other men, convicted with Ross, are being reviewed by the Court of Appeals.

Clemency was asked also for John Durkin of the Bronx, who was convicted of first-degree murder in the killing of Detective Timothy Connell of the New York police.

The Governor gave no indication that he would intervene in any case with the exception of that of Ross.

Mail Carrier Saves Man From Subway Death; Holds Him Down as Train Roars Over Them

A letter carrier's bravery and quickness of wit saved the life yesterday afternoon of Sam Thomas, about [illegible] years old, a negro truck driver, who lives at 237 South Street. Thomas was in the Times Square subway station shortly before 3 o'clock when he jumped or fell in the path of an approaching express train. While the crowd of several hundred which was on the platform gasped in horror a mail carrier jumped to the tracks and tried to get the man out. Seeing that he had not time to lift Thomas from the track, the rescuer threw him flat and held him in the well between the track while the express passed over.

John Eaton, motorman of the train, had put on his brakes when he saw the pair, but the train did not stop until two cars had passed over the men. Thinking both had been killed, the crowd was intensely excited, but in a few minutes the letter carrier got out from under the train carrying the negro. Neither was injured.

In the excitement the rescuer disappeared without giving his name, but several bystanders noted his number, and he was later identified as John J. McBride of 1,285 East Twenty-seventh Street, Brooklyn. When located last night McBride at first denied all knowledge of the incident, but finally admitted that he had done "something of the sort." He is twenty-four years old and has a wife and two small children.

Thomas was let go after being treated for shock by Dr. Hemerich of the New York Hospital.

Ruins of what were thriving centers of Mayan culture were found in Mexico. Archaeologists believe that if properly excavated, hundreds of hidden Mayan cities could be found.

The Chichen Chob (Prison) that was recently found. It is thought to be the most perfect existing unit of ancient Mayan architecture.

"All the News That's Fit to Print."

The New York Times.

THE WEATHER
Cloudy and cooler today; possibly morning showers; tomorrow fair.
Weather Yesterday—Max. 84, Min. 70.
For weather report see next to last page.

VOL. LXXIV....No. 24,681. NEW YORK, FRIDAY, AUGUST 21, 1925. TWO CENTS in Greater New York | THREE CENTS Within 200 Miles | FOUR CENTS Elsewhere in the U. S.

COOLIDGE APPROVES BELGIAN DEBT TERMS BY FORMAL SIGNING

Document Is Returned to Washington to Await Action by Congress.

LENIENCY IS EXPLAINED

Wilson Signed Pledge to Belgium When She Threatened to Quit Peace Conference.

FRENCH FIND MORAL FACTOR

Recall That Wilson Agreed Germany Should Pay for All War Damage in France.

NORTHAMPTON, Mass., Aug. 20 (AP).—President Coolidge tonight approved the Belgian debt settlement.

The agreement, rushed from Washington to Swampscott in a special mail pouch, was brought from the Summer White House to Northampton in a White House automobile by E. C. Geisser, personal stenographer of the President.

Mr. Geisser was here when the President arrived from Plymouth, Vt., for an overnight stay.

The President's signature to the agreement leaves the next step, so far as the American Government is concerned, up to Congress, which, under the provisions of the act creating the Debt Funding Commission, must ratify all settlements.

Immediately after the President had signed the agreement Mr. Geisser left for Swampscott so as to have the document placed in the mail pouch, which was to go forward to Washington tonight from Swampscott.

French Debt a Distinct Problem.

Special to The New York Times.

WASHINGTON, Aug. 20. — When France moves to arrange a settlement of her debts to this country her claims will be considered as a question distinct from any agreement made with other nations. Precedents will not govern the situation nor will France be permitted to point to other settlements as examples which should be followed. In other words, France will stand single and alone in the eyes of the World War Foreign Debt Commission, and the sole question on which the funding will be consummated will be the French capacity to pay.

As a basic policy the commission has decided that each nation must make its claims only on its own merits and not use persuasive arguments that because another country received preferential treatment this rule should be followed. Special favors will be granted to no nation unless that nation is able to demonstrate its right to such indulgences.

The rule laid down paves the way to meet French arguments that because Belgium was kindly treated—and there is no concealment whatever that she was—France can demand comparable terms. Even should some nation prove she could lay claim to a moral obligation, something like that incurred by Woodrow Wilson, the commission would consider this claim as a new issue.

But, it was said at the Treasury today, France is not in the same position as was Belgium, for no promises were made to her that German reparations would be accepted in lieu of her prearmistice debt. The same thing, it was said, applies to Italy.

Since the settlement of the Belgian debt terms, great interest has been created in just what the promise of Woodrow Wilson amounted to regarding the acceptance of reparations to aid Belgium in discharging the obligations held against her.

Wilson Commitment in Writing.

This Wilson agreement, which was signed also by Mr. Lloyd George and Georges Clemenceau, was embodied in a letter to Paul Hymans, the Belgian Foreign Minister, under date of June 16, 1919, and stated that the United States, France and Great Britain would be willing to accept German bonds turned over to the Reparation Commission.

Mr. Wilson sent this letter to the Senate and House of Representatives Feb. 22, 1921, covering it with a recommendation that it be concurred in. But as by that date President Harding was nearly ready to take office and the League of Nations had been badly battered in the Senate, the transmission of the document amounted to little more than a turning over of the policy toward foreign debts to the new Administration. Nothing was done about the matter.

The letter sent by Mr. Wilson to Congress reads:

To the Senate and House of Representatives:

I herewith call your attention to an agreement with Belgium made by the British and French Premiers and myself, which is embodied in the following letter:

"June 16, 1919.

"M. Hymans,
"Ministre des Affaires Etrangères,
"Hotel Lotti, Paris.

"Sir: The reparation clauses of the draft Treaty of Peace of Peace with Germany obligate Germany to make reimbursement of all sums which Belgium has borrowed from the allied and associated Governments up to Nov. 11, 1918, on account of the violation by Germany of the Treaty of 1839. As evidence of such an obligation Ger-

Continued on Page Four.

Savings of Berlin Waiters Set Pace for All Classes

By Wireless to THE NEW YORK TIMES.

BERLIN, Aug. 20.—Waiters in the cafés and hotels show the biggest increase in savings deposits of any class of laborers in Berlin, according to the latest statistics from savings banks.

Lawyers, doctors and dentists also show greater prosperity in the last three months, but their savings per capita are lower than those of waiters.

The total deposits in Berlin savings banks amount to 80,000,000 marks and are showing a steady increase despite the alleged adverse economic conditions indicated by the decreased accounts of skilled and unskilled laborers.

Civil Service employes, who last year were credited with 25 per cent. of the entire savings deposits, have now dropped to 15 per cent.

SAYS HUMAN BRAIN EMITS RADIO WAVES

Prof. Cazzamali of Milan Declares They Can Be Harnessed for Distant Communication.

AND CODED LIKE WIRELESS

Long Series of Tests Was Made With Hypnotized Subjects in Insulated Metal Chamber.

Special Cable to THE NEW YORK TIMES.

PARIS, Aug. 20.—That the human brain is capable of the emission of radiographic waves, which, harnessed and reduced to a code, will create a method of communication between distant minds as perfect as that developed by wireless telegraphy, is the conclusion reached by Ferdinando Cazzamali, an Italian scientist, who is Professor of Neurology and Psychiatry at the University of Milan.

His theory, resulting from his investigation of the so-called radiographic waves of the brain, is significant in that it purports to reveal a scientific basis for the whole phenomenon of telepathy.

Professor Cazzamali's conclusions will be published in the forthcoming number of the Revue Metaphysique. Advance pages of his report, made public today, have aroused the world of French science to an intense pitch of interest. His investigation covers a period sufficiently long to convince the scientists that his conclusions cannot be dismissed as superficial or based on purely accidental evidence.

Ever since 1912 science has been endeavoring to prove that the human body, under certain conditions, is able to emit the radiations on which the whole theory of telepathy has been based without concrete proof. Given these radiations, the next step was to prove that a system of communication similar to that of wireless telegraphy could be developed between cerebral organisms situated at distant points.

Sounds Like Radio Signals.

Professor Cazzamali asserts that he has discovered radiographic waves of the brain through experimenting with subjects in a hypnotic state. He had built an insulated metallic chamber where the subject could remain several hours without any sense of fatigue. This chamber was so constructed as to render possible absolute electromagnetic isolation. He then erected four sets of receivers such as are used in wireless telegraphy.

As subjects he employed victims of nervous maladies whose mental faculties were easily excitable, neurasthenics, epileptics and especially an Italian clairvoyant, Mlle. Maggi. Locked up in the metallic chamber, the subject was put in a hypnotic state, with the face turned toward the wireless receiver.

Then followed a stimulation of the mental faculties of the subject, the experimenter listening to the reactions through a wireless headpiece attached to his ears. Professor Cazzamali declares that he heard through the headpiece sound waves similar to radiotelegraphic transmission sounds which ceased immediately upon the awakening of the subject from the hypnotic state and recommenced each time that the subject was put to sleep again.

When the hallucinations of the subject became more intense, the experimenter, through the receiver, could hear whistling sounds and soft modulations like those produced across the muted strings of a violin or cello, these modulations also ceasing as soon as the subject, either spontaneously or through the will of the experimenter, returned to the normal state. The cerebral radio sounds

Continued on Page Six.

BISHOP KIDNAPPED BY CHINESE BANDITS; 5 WOMEN ALSO TAKEN

The Rev. H. W. K. Mowll of Toronto, His Wife and 6 Others Are Captured in Szechwan.

HINT OF CANTON BLOCKADE

Joint British-Japanese Move Is Discussed to Prevent Further Boycott of Hongkong.

OUR ATTITUDE CONSIDERED

America Would Not Oppose Operation to Keep Ports Open, London Paper Thinks.

LONDON, Aug. 20 (AP).—Eight British missionaries, including five women, were kidnapped on Aug. 6 by Chinese bandits, report cable dispatches received tonight by the Church Missionary Society from Munyang, Province of Szechwan, China.

Among those in the hands of the bandits are Bishop H. W. K. Mowll, formerly Dean of Wycliffe College, Toronto, and his wife.

All members of the party were reported to be safe and being well treated by the outlaws.

Mowll's Plight Excites Toronto.

Special to The New York Times.

TORONTO, Ontario, Aug. 20.—Excitement has been caused in church circles here by dispatches reporting the capture by Chinese bandits of Bishop H. W. K. Mowll. Friends of the Bishop say that he was on a holiday in the hills where the bandits flourish.

Of English birth and education, Bishop Mowll first was associated with Wycliffe College in 1913, when he became a tutor. He was later appointed a professor and from 1919 to 1922 served as Dean. In 1922 he was named by the Archbishop of Canterbury as assistant Bishop for West China.

Dr. Howard's Captors Surrounded.

PEKING, Aug. 20 (AP).—Dr. Harvey J. Howard, the American who was captured some time ago by bandits in Manchuria at the same time that they killed Morgan Palmer of New York State, has been located in a bandit camp about forty miles from Fuchow-Hsien.

A Chinese prisoner released by the bandits recognized a photograph shown him as that of Howard. He said that Howard was being treated well pending payment of the ransom demanded by the bandits.

Troops are reported to have surrounded the district, making the escape of the bandits impossible, but owing to the desire to avoid placing Dr. Howard in jeopardy through an attack, they are being held back and negotiations for the release are proceeding.

British Aroused Over Hongkong.

By T. R. YBARRA.

Special Cable to THE NEW YORK TIMES.

LONDON, Aug. 20.—Coincident with the sudden return of Foreign Secretary Austen Chamberlain to London to tackle the Chinese situation a report arose tonight that the "Red" Government of Canton has as its real object nothing less than the wiping of Hongkong, Britain's great Oriental emporium, off the commercial map.

This is the true meaning of the boycott rules issued by the Canton authorities against British shipping, according to a report current here.

It is pointed out that the new regulations issued by Canton forbid the transporting of goods from Canton to Hongkong, and as the bulk of the Hongkong interior, trade comes from there, the effect on British business firms is already serious.

Moreover, the Canton Government insists upon the right of searching foreign ships, which is a breach of international law, it is held here. It also forbids the export of food and raw material, which the British call a violation of existing treaties.

Great Britain is the country most affected by these acts of the Canton Government, but other powers, especially Japan, are also involved.

Vice Admiral Sinclair, commanding the British China naval station, has arrived at Canton on the flagship Petersfield to protect British and other foreign interests. It is understood, however, that he has not received direct instructions so far from his Government on how to act in the emergency which has arisen.

Naval Action With Japan Discussed.

Great Britain and Japan have considered here the likely development of the Canton situation. There is accordingly a good deal of speculation in diplo-

Continued on Page Six.

John McCormack Buys a Home in Ireland, Where He Will Retire When He Reaches 50

By Wireless to THE NEW YORK TIMES.

LONDON, Aug. 20.—John McCormack, the Irish tenor, has bought a beautiful home in Ireland, to which he will retire in about nine years—when he is 50.

"I shall retire at 50, and from now on shall come to London each year to sing in Albert Hall," he said. "However, I emphatically refuse to broadcast. I tried it once in New York and disliked it thoroughly."

The new home is in picturesque Curragh of Kildare.

Many years ago Mr. McCormack bought a lucky black boy figure at the sale of the late Sir John Murray Scott. He gave it to an old London friend who runs a well-known restaurant in Soho, London's French quarter, and now intends to claim the figure for his Irish home.

Mr. and Mrs. McCormack and two children, Cyril and Gwendoline, are occupying the Essex home of Lord D'Abernon, the British Ambassador to Berlin.

"Everybody is happy in Ireland," said McCormack with a half-serious smile and added: "Except those out of office, Ireland is all right and safer than England."

Eating Sprayed Fruit Kills One And Makes 2,000 Ill in Jersey

Special to The New York Times.

HAMMONTON, N. J., Aug. 20.—Over two thousand cases of "devil's grippe," as a new malady which has struck this section has been designated, have been reported by physicians in this part of the State within the last three weeks. Most of the cases are in Camden County.

Dr. A. S. McCallum of Barrington said he had treated 500 victims and Dr. Russell S. Magee of Audubon said he had treated 200. The complaint is laid to eating unwashed fruit which has been sprayed to combat the Japanese beetle.

Marian Lyons, 5 years old, of Audubon, who ate peaches which had been so sprayed, died on Tuesday night, and Earl Marshall, 11, of Mapleshade, is seriously ill in the West Jersey Hospital, Camden, after eating sprayed grapes.

MARVELS IN TOMB OF MAYA MONARCH

Tulane Explorers Found Figures of King and High Priests on Walls.

MYSTERY CITY DISCOVERED

Temples Found Where Priestly Astronomers of Ancient Race Made Their Observations.

Special to The New York Times.

NEW ORLEANS, Aug. 20.—Further details were revealed today of the discoveries made by Frans Blom and Oliver La Farge of the first Tulane Middle American expedition, who reported on their return here last night the results of six months' exploration of Maya ruins in Guatemala and Mexico.

The explorers added today to their first account of their discoveries, which included the ruins of three huge centres of Maya culture. Many hieroglyph monuments, proof that the Maya domain extended further westward toward the Pacific than had been supposed; examples of beautiful pottery and examples of astounding engineering feats, a description of the burial place of "King X," the unidentified monarch whose tomb and bones they unearthed at Comalcalco, surrounded by stucco relief portraits of a beauty unparalleled among previous finds.

Dr. William Gates, director of the Tulane Department of Middle American Research, met the explorers at Villa Hermosa and the party proceeded to Comalcalco. They were the first archaeologists to visit the ruins since Charney, a French writer, who gave a fantastic description of it back in the '80s and termed the ruins "as big as those at Palenque."

The Tomb of "King X."

The Tulane men soon satisfied themselves that Charney's report was greatly exaggerated and that he had seen little save a few mounds with temples on them, overlooking entirely the most important feature of the ancient city. Mr. Blom discovered a remarkable plaza formation, similar to the one he discovered at Uaxactum a year ago. This was the first real astronomical observatory of the old Mayas to be unearthed.

Here the mounds and pyramids had been constructed in such a relative position to one another that the priests could ascend the main mound and, sighting over three mounds in the foreground, make scientific astronomical calculations. It was from such points that they determined when eclipses of the sun and moon were due to appear, knowledge which enabled them to exercise power over the Indians, who feared the terrifying occurrences. The Comalcalco observatory, however, is not so well arranged as that of Uaxactum.

The tomb of "King X" was found in the main mound. It consisted of a small room, nine feet long and seven feet wide. The explorers entered by the roof, which had caved in. Four square pillars were still standing upright on the floor. These, Mr. Blom believes, must have supported a small wooden table on which the body of the King, clothed in his finest ceremonial garments, lay. A number of human bones littered the floor about the pillars. More than 300 perforated sea shells, punctured at the ends with painstaking care as if to form a necklace, were scattered among the bones.

The most important discovery in the tomb, however, rested on the north, south and east walls. Large blocks of hieroglyphs were inscribed on each and each bore perfect portraits of three men molded in stucco relief. On the east wall the figures were slightly better executed than on the others. Evidently the figure in the centre was that of the dead King and the others those of the highest of the high priests. The sun, entering from the open wall on the west, cast its dull glow on the face of the ruler's portrait late in the afternoon. It was at this hour, undoubtedly, that the burial ceremony took place. The Maya rulers had their tombs prepared many years in advance of their deaths.

The faces of the figures and their headdresses had been carefully molded. The state of preservation was almost perfect.

"I am convinced," said Mr. Blom, "that here we have found nine stucco portraits so far unparalleled in Maya research. They are without a doubt the most beautiful examples of Maya portrait art ever found."

The Tulane explorers attempted to guard the tomb until the local and Fed-

Continued on Page Six.

J. A. FOSTER SLATED TO HEAD DRY FORCES IN NEW YORK AREA

Divisional Head at Philadelphia Expected to Take Charge Here Sept. 1.

MERRICK TO GO TO BUFFALO

Andrews Is Known to Have Drawn Slate, but He Refuses to Confirm Shift.

NEW CHIEF CALLED FIGHTER

Veteran of Internal Revenue Bureau Has Name for Hard-Fisted Enforcement.

Full charge of the task of drying up the New York area has been delegated to John A. Foster, Divisional Prohibition Director for Philadelphia, according to reports current here and in Washington yesterday. Direct confirmation of the slating of Foster for the New York post in the reorganized prohibition enforcement agencies was not obtainable. But one man in direct touch with the authorities at Washington said he had every reason to believe Foster was the man.

According to the report the designation of Director Foster was determined upon at the conference of dry officers held in Washington on Wednesday at the order of Brig. Gen. Lincoln C. Andrews, Assistant Secretary of the Treasury in charge of prohibition enforcement.

R. Q. Merrick, who for two years has directed the work for this territory, is to be transferred to Buffalo, it was said. In his new post Mr. Merrick will have full sway over the fight against rum running over the Canadian border. He will direct an intensive patrol from Buffalo along the border to Rouse's Point and will cooperate with the Coast Guard in the rum war on the lakes.

Expected to Take Charge Sept. 1.

The reports dealing with the contemplated change in the dry régime for this district placed the time of Foster's assumption of control as Sept. 1. Whether there will be wholesale shifting of field agents in this territory could not be learned last night.

The statement that Foster would exchange Philadelphia for New York in the prohibition work was put up to General Andrews in Washington yesterday. He declined to confirm the report. It was learned, however, that he had completed his slate for the reorganization of the divisional prohibition chiefs and would submit it today for approval. In connection with General Andrews's unwillingness to discuss the Foster change specifically, it was pointed out that it had been his intention to announce the changes en bloc.

As far back as mid-July Foster was reported as destined to shift his activities to this city. He is a veteran of the Bureau of Internal Revenue and is known for his stern and thorough methods. It was then said that if Foster moved over to New York his post at Philadelphia would be filled by William G. Murdock, now State Prohibition Director for Pennsylvania. Mr. Murdock, it was said, would hold a post in the reorganized service similar to the post which Foster is said to be slated for here.

Mr. Foster has investigated liquor conditions in Massachusetts and in Ohio and it was his work which Washington officials said led to the breaking up of liquor rings in both States. He was sent into Philadelphia when the Federal officials decided on a vigorous campaign to end the illicit distribution of industrial alcohol. Foster is a Bostonian by birth.

When he took charge of the Philadelphia staff of agents he began a housecleaning the first week in his new job. As the first fruits of his reorganization eight prohibition agents were dropped by Commissioner David H. Blair of the Bureau of Internal Revenue. There were nine agents whom Foster decided must go. He asked for their resignations and all refused. While his message to the Commissioner was on the way, one of the agents changed his mind and resigned. At that time Director Foster said that he planned to investigate the activities of every agent in his jurisdiction. No further resignations of members of his staff were demanded.

Captain Carmine Takes Charge.

Captain George C. Carmine took command of the New York district of the Coast Guard yesterday. He succeeded

Continued on Page Two.

M'COOEY WARNS TIGER NOT TO CROSS BRIDGE; WALKER IN HOME DISTRICT RALLY BACKS '5-CENT FARE WITH A SEAT, NOT A STRAP'

WOULD KEEP TAMMANY OUT

Hylan Rally in Brooklyn Revives McCarren's Old Slogan.

MAYOR ARRAIGNS HIS FOES

Begins an Active Fight Against His Enemies in His Own Borough.

SEES TAMMANY DICTATORS

Says Traction Interests Back Organization—Blames Opponents for Transit Delay.

The old-time slogan of the Brooklyn Democracy, "The Tiger Must Not Cross the Bridge," was revived yesterday by John H. McCooey, Brooklyn Democratic leader, in a speech introducing Mayor Hylan at a meeting of the Kings County Democratic Executive Committee at its headquarters, 4 Court Square.

Lamenting the death of Charles F. Murphy, which he declared had deprived Tammany of its greatest leader, Mayor Hylan attacked George W. Olvany, leader of Tammany, and Sheriff Edward J. Flynn, Democratic leader of the Bronx, as tools of Wall Street and the traction interests, and charged that the movement to defeat him was started because the city, in the event of his reelection, would have its own municipally operated subway system. The Mayor also asked if, in the event of his defeat, the city was to be opened to vice and gambling and if revenue was again to flow from these sources.

The meeting of the committee was closed and Mr. McCooey's remarks were made public afterward as he recalled them, while Mayor Hylan's speech to the committee members was made public in its entirety.

The meeting of the committee was said to mark the beginning of an aggressive campaign for the Mayor in his own borough. The Mayor's friends, it was said, had been somewhat disturbed by the reports of the inroads being made there by Senator Walker and the rest of the city ticket. Mr. McCooey, however, seemed to feel that the organization was entirely loyal to the Mayor, and devoted much of his energy to urging the district leaders to get out a large vote for the Mayor.

Recalls McCarren Fight.

In his talk introducing the Mayor, Mr. McCooey recalled the warfare of twenty-one years ago between Tammany and the late Senator Patrick H. McCarren, then the Brooklyn Democratic leader, and said that a "somewhat similar" situation existed now, in view of the fact that Tammany and its allied Bronx organization were opposing Mayor Hylan, and the Democratic organizations of Brooklyn, Queens and Richmond were supporting him.

In telling of this after the meeting, Mr. McCooey reminded newspaper reporters of the slogan of that time, which had existed even earlier, when Hugh McLaughlin was the Brooklyn Democratic leader. It also was said that Mr. McCooey had a "compact" with Mr. Murphy, under which agreement Tammany was not to interfere in purely Brooklyn political affairs, but Mr. McCooey had no such continuing agreement with Judge Olvany.

Mr. McCooey urged the leaders of the Brooklyn Democratic organization to work hard for the Mayor, and expressed confidence that they would carry Brooklyn for him by a large majority.

The revival of the old "bridge" slogan was interpreted differently by members of the committee. One cynical veteran's comment was that when Senator McCarren was leader the Brooklyn Bridge was the only ready method of access to Brooklyn from Manhattan, while now there were a number of subway tunnels. He added that, from what he had heard of the Walker organization in Brooklyn, Tammany must be

Continued on Page Two.

Walker Denies He Opposes The Rockaway Boardwalk

Senator James J. Walker, Tammany candidate for Mayor, denied yesterday in a letter to Frank X. Sullivan, his Queens campaign manager, reports that, if elected, he would hold up the construction of the proposed Rockaway Boardwalk.

"Of course you know that rumors to the effect that I am opposed to the Boardwalk at the Rockaways are nothing but political propaganda of my opponents and that there is not a scintilla of truth in these reports," Senator Walker wrote. "I think that this is a great improvement to the Rockaways and that it is of vast importance to all the people of our city."

LYONS REACHES CITY; ASSAILS WATERMAN

Says All the Republicans Want of Rival Are His Fountain Pen and Check Book.

TELLS OF HIS URGE TO RUN

Two Hundred Supporters Cheer Candidate at Station, Then Hold Informal Parade.

Met by about two hundred enthusiastic friends and a seven-piece brass band at the Pennsylvania Station on his return from a hurried trip to Florida last night, former Secretary of State John J. Lyons, candidate for the Republican nomination for Mayor, characterized Frank D. Waterman, designee of the organization leaders, as a "knockdown" candidate, put up only to be defeated, and related how he had felt the call to run himself to give the Republicans of the city an opportunity to avoid betrayal and defeat.

The welcome home of Mr. Lyons was somewhat marred by his missing connection at Washington and arriving at a quarter past 7 in the evening instead of at half-past 2 in the afternoon, the time at which he had originally been expected.

Mr. Lyons was met at the train by John C. Lewis, his campaign manager; Arthur B. Murtha, Frederick E. Goldsmith and other friends as the band upstairs struck up "Hail, Hail, the Gang's All Here."

First Parade of the Campaign.

Mr. Lyons smiled and shook hands with his friends and was conducted to a waiting automobile and driven to the Hotel McAlpin. It was the first parade of the campaign, preceding that for Senator Walker, Tammany candidate, by half an hour.

There were seven or eight automobiles in the Lyons procession, a policeman in a department Ford and the band leading the way. Nearly a hundred of his adherents followed Mr. Lyons into the McAlpin, where his headquarters will be opened today, and attended an informal reception in the Blue Room.

"My friends," said Mr. Lyons, "I am certainly gratified by this reception. I assure you that it was unexpected, and even when informed of it by a member of the committee at Manhattan Transfer, I did not realize that there would be such a gathering of my friends and such enthusiasm shown.

"Last Friday, just as I was ready to start on a combined business and vacation trip to Florida, I was sitting with a party of friends. It was getting to the last days in which something could be done toward running in the Republican primaries. Something seemed to take hold of me. It seemed as though it were the call of duty to stick. It seemed to me that it was the time to strike, if any one was to strike at all.

"The committee named to nominate a candidate for Mayor had put up a 'knockdown' ticket. I refer to Mr. Waterman, the head of the ticket. I felt it to be my duty to give the members of the Republican Party throughout the city an opportunity to say whether they wanted a ticket headed by a man about whom they knew nothing and about whom they had not been consulted, or by a man who had been of some service to his party.

Saw Party Going on the Rocks.

"I have given thirty years of service to my party and my city, which I love. I thought of Mr. Waterman, who does not know the city or its people, and I realized that the so-called party leaders were leading us on the rocks.

"So I said to my friends, 'Boys, go ahead; I'll stand pat.'

"I had to leave for Florida to keep an engagement, previously made, but within two working days, I am informed, my loyal friends obtained not merely the 1,500 signatures legally required for the petitions designating me as a Republican candidate, but more than twice that amount.

"That spells encouragement. That means success for me in the primaries. I want to tell you that nothing but God Almighty can keep me from running in the primaries.

"I wish to say nothing against Mr. Waterman, to whom I give my most kindly and generous thought. But Mr. Waterman is being used to fill a breach in the situation after the supposed leaders had failed to get any other candidate to stand up and make a fight.

"There were plenty of candidates, but evidently they were not properly persuaded or lacked courage.

"So Mr. Waterman was selected to fill the breach. What they wanted of Mr. Waterman was his fountain pen in one hand and his check book in the other. Let him lock up the check book and he will find out how popular he will be."

RED FLARES FOR WALKER

Old Neighbors Cheer for 'Jimmy' as He Opens Primary Fight.

CITES RECORD AT ALBANY

Candidate Says He'll Stand on That and Not Be a "Caddy for a Windmill."

McKEE AND BERRY SPEAK

Tammany Designees Enthusiastically Received in a Torchlight Parade.

Senator James J. Walker went down among his neighbors in Greenwich Village last night and opened his campaign in the Mayoralty primaries in a fashion that recalled the picturesque methods of old-time political fights—red flares, a torchlight parade, a band, and the hall packed with the people who called him by his first name.

Among his own, Senator Walker started out to deliver "just a talk in the kitchen to the neighbors." But before he ended he promised to "make my voice heard even in Brooklyn" and said that he would make his fight on his sixteen years' record at Albany.

"That's a record of action," he said, as he stepped to the edge of the platform, "that's a record of action, and let me tell you there's no blather shifting on that. I'd rather stand on that record than caddy or understudy for a windmill."

The 1,500 persons jammed into the auditorium of old Public School 3, Grove and Hudson Streets, burst into a roar of applause. There were cries from all parts of the hall for Walker to "Give it to him, Jimmie," and to "Let him know where he gets off."

Standing at the lip of the stage, the slender, youthful looking Tammanyite smiled out at the neighbors. He brushed back his hair impatiently. He motioned time and again for silence, but the crowd kept up the din. Finally he made a mock move as though to turn away and order came back.

For Five-Cent Fare With a Seat.

"And, listen," he said. "It seems to be a habit to talk about car fares. Well, get this right, now, and then go out and spread it around: I'm for the five-cent fare. I have always been for it and I will be for it always. I'm for the five-cent fare with a seat, and not for the five-cent fare with a strap. There's a difference."

Walker, who had said that he would not formally open his campaign in last night's speech, spoke for about thirty minutes. Before he entered the hall and received an enthusiastic welcome his running mates on the Tammany ticket had briefly addressed the meeting. They, too, received a striking welcome from the audience and at the end of the meeting were forced to join Senator Walker on the steps of the school while a thousand or more persons filed past to shake the candidates' hands.

City Judge Joseph V. McKee, candidate for President of the Board of Aldermen, who spoke first, stirred the meeting when he paused in the course of his speech and, in a deeper tone, solemnly pledged himself, Walker and Major Gen. Charles W. Berry, candidate for Controller, to the five-cent fare. In his speech Judge McKee attacked the record of the Hylan-McCooey candidate for Aldermanic President, William A. Cokeley of the Bronx. He recalled that Cokeley had been the right-of-way agent for the Boston & Westchester Railroad some years ago, and said that Bronx residents still remembered that.

General Berry also discussed the five-cent issue. He said the public was not getting "five cents worth of service nowadays" and said that if Walker were sent to the City Hall "a nickel in the subway will get you more." General Berry, a physician and for many years on the Board of Health, assailed Mayor Hylan's claims for greater health in the city. He said that the personnel of the Health Department "is bright, but they are hampered by obstructionist tactics by persons higher up."

Demonstration Begins Early.

The Village's demonstration to its favorite son began at 7 o'clock, when hundreds began to gather at the headquarters of the Huron Club, the regular Democratic organization, at Broome and Hudson Streets. Lieutenants of Dan Finn, leader of the district, and a lifelong friend of Senator Walker, lined up the club members, and about fifty taxicabs were parked in Broome Street and in Hudson Street.

Members of the Huron Club bustled up and down the street [illegible] red flares, Roman candles and bombs. Hundreds of the women in the district appeared early at the clubhouse and they were seated in the taxicabs, with American flags. Every machine and, it seemed, every house in the line of march was plastered with Walker posters. "Walk with Walker," said some of them. "Win With Walker" called others, and still others told all who were

Broker's Wife Ends Life at Long Beach Home; Says in Note She Is Sorry to Cause Trouble

Special to The New York Times.

LONG BEACH, L. I., Aug. 20.—Mrs. Carlie Aline Sibley Didrichsen of 25 Fifth Avenue, Manhattan, wife of Ferdinand Van Zandt Didrichsen, a stock broker of 15 Broad Street, committed suicide today by taking veronal tablets in her Summer apartment at 335 East Boardwalk. A quarrel with her husband was said to have been the cause.

She was found in her bedroom in the rear of the apartment by her husband and John Thompson, the superintendent of the apartment house, and had been dead for several hours. By her side were two empty bottles labeled "veronal" and a third from which all but six tablets had been removed.

She left two notes, one to her husband, which read: "Dear boy. Sorry to cause you trouble, good-bye." The other, addressed to the superintendent, read: "Sorry to cause you all this inconvenience. I appreciate all you have done. Cordially yours——."

The local police said that Mr. Didrichsen had informed them that he and his wife had a disagreement last night and that he left to spend the night in New York lest his presence aggravate the quarrel. He went to business in the morning and when he called the apartment here on the telephone and received no answer feared trouble and came down to investigate.

He knocked on the door of the apartment but there was no answer. He found the superintendent and the two tried to force the door, for Mr. Didrichsen had left his key in New York. When this effort failed they climbed a fire escape in the rear and through a window that opened on the bedroom.

Mr. Didrichsen jumped into the room first and discovered the body of his wife. He was badly stricken over the event, and when the City Physician and the police arrived, was unable to talk to them for nearly an hour. The City Physician, Dr. George Reiss, pronounced the death a suicide.

The couple had no children. In the Social Register Mr. Didrichsen is recorded as a veteran of the World War. Mrs. Didrichsen was 34 years old.

"All the News That's Fit to Print."

The New York Times.

THE WEATHER
Fair, with slowly rising temperature, today; showers tomorrow.
Temperature yesterday—Max. 59, min. 50.
☞For weather report see Page 32.

VOL. LXXV....No. 24,727. NEW YORK, TUESDAY, OCTOBER 6, 1925. TWO CENTS In Greater New York | THREE CENTS Within 200 Miles | FOUR CENTS Elsewhere in the U. S.

COOLIDGE SEES SIGNS OF WIDE PROSPERITY ON TRIP TO OMAHA

Industrial and Agricultural Activity in Evidence All Along His Route.

CONFIDENT IT WILL GO ON

Friendly Crowds Greet the President and Present Floral Gifts to Mrs. Coolidge.

LEGION CONVENTION OPENS

Seven Thousand Veterans Attend, While 50,000 Visitors Throng Omaha's Streets.

Special to The New York Times.

ST. LOUIS, Oct. 5.—President Coolidge's train arrived here on schedule time this evening and after being switched from the Baltimore & Ohio tracks to the Wabash Railroad proceeded on its way to Omaha, where Mr. Coolidge will address the American Legion convention tomorrow. The President and Mrs. Coolidge waved adieu to several hundred persons who gathered in the railroad yard to get a glimpse of them.

The 900-mile run from the national capital was made in an unostentatious manner, and no attempt was made to drum up crowds at the few stops the special train made.

Leaving Washington last night at 6:20 o'clock, the President's train was run as the first section of the Washington-St. Louis train. It was made up of what Colonel Walter V. Shipley, General Passenger Agent of the Baltimore & Ohio in Washington, declared "the last word in Pul[illegible] equipment." The President and Mrs. Coolidge, Mrs. Drain, wife of National Commander Drain of the American Legion; Major Coupal, the President's personal physician; Erwin C. Geisser, his private secretary, and a Secret Service guard occupied the last car on the train.

Other military and naval officers, including Major Gen. Lejeune of the Marine Corps, Captain Adolphus Andrews of the Mayflower, the President's yacht, senior naval aid; Colonel Cheney, the President's military aid, and Secretary Sanders occupied quarters in the adjoining stateroom car.

Sees Evidence of Prosperity.

President Coolidge appeared well satisfied with the evidence of industrial and farm prosperity he saw on every hand in his day trip through Indiana. Government reports have indicated an era of good times, with little unemployment and favorable crops. Agricultural Indiana verified the reports as to an improved condition among the farmers. The corn fields appeared to be bounteous in their yields. The small towns were not without industrial activity. The smokestacks poured forth smoke indicative of production. All along the route farmers drove to the stations in automobiles.

As the train passed through Indiana and skirted St. Louis, prosperity became more patent in the thousands of mills, which at that hour were discharging their workmen.

President Coolidge saw nothing in the outward signs to weaken the opinion of the Administration that a long season of industrial progress is ahead. He believes that there can be no developments in the months to come that will retard the steady industrial movement. The prosperity in the manufacturing areas is creeping into the farm section. The result is that the President cannot see anything except satisfactory conditions.

If industrial content exists President Coolidge feels confident that there will be no reaction against the Republican Party next year, as good times rebound to the credit of the party in power just as bad times hurt the party's fortunes.

The President and Mrs. Coolidge had their meals in the public diner. Mr. Coolidge's appetite is good and he enjoyed his customary steak and vegetables at today's meals on the trip across West Virginia, Ohio, Indiana, Illinois and part of Missouri.

The first stop on the trip last evening was at Keyser, W. Va. A good-sized crowd greeted the train, but the President did not go out on the platform during the short stop.

Through Twenty-three Tunnels.

In the run during the night the Presidential train was hauled by what is said to be the largest mountain type locomotive in the world. Twenty-three tunnels lay in the path of the train through the Alleghanies, but so well did the railroad officials lay their plans that nobody on the train experienced the slightest inconvenience. The President told Colonel Shipley this morning that he was unaware that he had passed through so many tunnels.

There were short stops at Grafton and Parkersburg, W. Va., during the late night and early morning, and at Chillicothe, Ohio.

The special did not enter the Cincinnati passenger station, but skirted around the city.

The first stop of the forenoon today was North Vernon, Ind. A good-sized crowd greeted the President and Mrs. Coolidge there. Surging around the rear end of the train, the crowd demanded that the President and his wife come out, and when they appeared on the platform they were warmly greeted.

One of the crowd called out that "if Jim Litchfield were home he would

Continued on Page Six.

Boston Postoffice Fortified As Crime Wave Sweeps City

BOSTON, Oct. 5 (AP).—In view of recent hold-ups and murders in and around Boston, postal authorities here are taking extra precautions and Police Commissioner Herbert Wilson has been asked to cooperate in protecting Federal property.

The main postoffice in the Federal Building and each of the eighty-three branches have been turned into miniature fortresses, with expert rifle and pistol men as guards, Postmaster Roland M. Baker said today.

Postoffice receipts are being transported in steel-armored trucks, each manned by four men, three of whom are experts with the pistol. Every postoffice clerk serving at an open window is armed with an army revolver.

FASCISTI WELDING LABOR AND CAPITAL

First Decisive Step Taken in the Legal Establishment of Compulsory Arbitration.

SOCIALISTS ARE LEFT OUT

Fascist Trade Unions and the Employers' Confederation Agree to Act Together.

By Wireless to THE NEW YORK TIMES.

ROME, Oct. 5.—An agreement of the greatest importance not only in its effects on the future of Fascismo but also of labor was reached today between the Confederation of Fascist Trade Unions, representing some 2,000,000 organized Fascist workers, and the Confederation of Industry, representing almost the whole of the Italian employers of labor. Each organization agreed to deal exclusively with the other in all matters appertaining to what is needed in the disputes.

By this agreement, in other words, the Socialists, who for over thirty years have monopolized the right to speak in the name of and to defend the workers' interests, see themselves completely put out of any participation in labor disputes, their monopoly being transferred to the Fascist trade unions.

The Italian press predicts that [illegible] agreement will be the death warrant of Italian Socialism, which henceforth must cease to be an active force in Italian politics.

Important as the agreement is on its face, its value assumes even greater importance when it is considered as the first step in important legislative measures soon to be presented in Parliament and instituting compulsory arbitration for the settlement of labor disputes.

It is mainly an effort to substitute for the Marxian theory of class war the Fascist ideal of collaboration of classes by training workers to the idea that production is not the result of their own work only but is the outcome of concerted efforts under all categories of human activity. To obtain this change of thought among the workers, however, it was necessary first to clear the ground of socialist organizations, which, being founded on and permeated with the theory of class war, resolutely barred the way against the attainment of any such ideal.

Accord Obtained by Farinacci.

ROME, Oct. 5 (AP).—The new labor agreement in Italy was brought to fruition by Deputy Farinacci, Secretary of the Fascist Party, but the principles motivating it have been espoused for many months by such experts as Minister of Justice Rocco in accord with general lines laid down by Premier Mussolini.

The kernel of these principles is that the old idea of socialist labor unions has proved a failure because it was based on the theory of a class struggle to obtain the rights of the workingmen, whereas the Fascist principle, its exponents say, is that the best results can best obtained by class cooperation.

The Fascist idea is that class struggle amounts to cutting off the nose to spite the face, whereas class cooperation means proper recognition not only of the rights of manuel labor but also those

Continued on Page Ten.

Americans Unearth Temple of Ashtaroth, Where Saul's Armor Was Hung as Trophy

PHILADELPHIA, Oct. 5 (AP).—The Temple of Ashtaroth, renowned in the Old Testament as the sanctuary of the Philistines and the edifice in which King Saul's battle armor was hung as a trophy of the Israelites' defeat at the battle of Gilboa, has been found. A cablegram notifying the Museum of the University of Pennsylvania in this city that the university expedition to Beisan (the ancient Bethshan), in Palestine, had unearthed the structure, was received today from Alan Rowe, field director.

The announcement of the find followed a cable of Sept. 30, saying that the expedition had discovered an image of the goddess Ashtaroth, deity of the Philistines, with a shrine, bronze serpents, doves and similar objects used in the cult worship.

The cablegrams were brief, but the Temple of Ashtaroth was described as an oblong structure of three columns to each side. Within its cornerstone the excavators found a casket or foundation deposit containing, among other objects, ingots of "electrum," a mixture of gold and silver. Detailed descriptions of the valuable find are expected by the first mail from Palestine, Dr. G. B. Gordon, Director of the Museum, said tonight.

The site of the excavations was selected in 1919 by Dr. Gordon after careful surveys, permission then being obtained under the British mandate for the exclusive exploration of the site of the Acropolis by the University of Pennsylvania Museum's expedition. The expedition entered its fourth season of work at Bethshan on Sept. 1. In former seasons' work on the Acropolis, or tell, the expedition dug through eight periods of occupation, each civilization being represented by a layer of ruins and foundations.

It is quite probable, Dr. Gordon stated, that the expedition would unearth evidence showing that the Temple of Ashtaroth was destroyed by King David, for Old Testament chronology records his capture of Bethshan, following his ascending the throne in succession to Saul. The possibility of finding the actual armor of King Saul, which the Book of First Samuel declares was deposited in the temple, Dr. Gordon said was remote.

1926 CITY BUDGET RISES $25,000,000 TO $425,000,000

Preliminary Figures Include Teachers' Increase and Five Million More for Police.

HIGHER TAX RATE UNLIKELY

Greater Valuation of Property to Keep Levy Down—State Tax Is $1,600,000.

MAYOR HYLAN IS ABSENT

Adheres to Plan to Let Men Who Will Run City Next Year Bear Budget Burden.

New York City's budget for the year 1926 will approximate, if it does not exceed, $425,000,000, which is $25,000,000 in excess of the budget figures for the current year. Despite that large increase it is believed that because of the great appreciation in assessed property valuations it will not be found necessary to increase the tax rate for the coming year.

That information came from authoritative though unofficial sources at the close of an executive session of the budget making committee of the Board of Estimate yesterday. The meeting was held behind locked doors in a committee room of the City Hall. It was learned further that no matter how relentlessly the Board of Estimate later may ply the pruning knife upon the several municipal departmental estimates, legislation which is mandatory in character will force the totals to the figures named.

Estimates for twenty-one of these departments were under primary consideration and the examiners reported that substantial reductions were visible in only six.

Figures Only Tentative.

The meeting was mainly to acquaint the members of the committee, the personnel of which is identical with that of the Board of Estimate, with the preliminary estimates of the departments whose requests for appropriations are already in hand. The Budget Committee is composed of the Mayor, the Controller, the President of the Board of Aldermen and the five Borough Presidents.

The 1925 budget amounted to $399,618,885.44 after it had survived the final pruning process, but the actual expenditures of the city for this year aggregated more than $400,000,000 through the issuance of special revenue bonds and tax notes to meet additional expenditures.

According to Tammany members of the budget-making body, the prospective increase of $25,000,000 for the coming year will be chiefly mandatory in character, due to charges imposed by the State, to increases caused by the necessity of carrying a greatly enlarged personnel in the Police Department and a similarly increased force under the jurisdiction of the Board of Education, made necessary by the large number of new schools. The State tax alone, according to one official, will be $1,600,000 greater than this year, while there will be also an enormous increase in the debt service of the city through the redemption of bonds and the payment of interest on the extensive school building program and other large public improvements.

Mayor Hylan did not attend the meeting. Apart from the announcement that he was detained at home suffering from a slight cold, his arrival at the City Hall later in the day gave color to the surmise that he intended to adhere to his determination, announced soon after his primary defeat, to let the men who will have to run the administration next year without him bear the burden of the 1926 budget making. In the budget committee meeting the Mayor was represented by Joseph Haag, assistant to the Mayor, and by Augustin Kelly, Mayor Hylan's executive secretary.

The largest request for increases came from Commissioner Enright of the Police Department. He asked for a total of $43,615,322.65, an advance of $5,663,218.63 over the figures for 1925. Virtually all of this, it was pointed out, is necessary to meet the salaries to be paid the men

Continued on Page Thirteen.

Grand Jurors Denounce Federal Hospital Where 1,000 Insane Veterans Are Confined

Special to The New York Times.

WASHINGTON, Oct. 5.—Alarmed over conditions at the Government Hospital for the Insane, known as St. Elizabeth's, where 1,000 war veterans are confined, the outgoing Federal Grand Jurors filed today with Justice Bailey in Criminal Court a report in which they suggest that Congress authorize the President to appoint a commission of investigation.

At the same time the Grand Jury returned an indictment charging William McIntire and Irwin R. Sweeney, attendants at the hospital, with manslaughter in connection with the death of William Green, who died July 17, 1924, from a beating he is said to have received at the hands of the defendants because he objected to having his hair cut.

The jurors made a personal inspection of the hospital, its staff, equipment and grounds. The first thing complained of in the report is the overcrowding of patients, which, it is inferred, are packed in like sardines in a box. The hospital houses a total of 4,000 patients. Rooms intended to accommodate twenty single beds contain forty beds, the report avers, with the result that the inmates so crowded have no privacy at all. The total number should be reduced at least 1,000, the jurors declare.

Conditions in Howard Hall, where Green was confined, "are particularly bad," the report avers. This building contains the "bull pen," a space for recreation, where the most dangerous and the almost normal patients get a little exercise together.

"In Winter," says the report, "conditions in Howard Hall must be even worse than in mild weather, as during cold months the inmates cannot, because of the cold, long remain in the open court (bull pen), their only place of recreation. After examining conditions in Howard Hall the members of the Grand Jury "could readily believe the statement of the guard who said: 'If a man went to Howard Hall with a perfectly sound mind he would be hopelessly insane in less than three years. If I were an inmate I would go crazy in less than a year.'

"We recommend that another recreation ground be provided inside the wall surrounding this hall and that those patients only mildly afflicted be at all times entirely separated from those hopelessly insane; also that harmless games of all kinds be provided to divert the minds of the patients.

"In the main part of the hospital conditions seemed much better. It has been well said that 'fun is the best medicine,' and for weak-minded people it should be supplied in abundance.

"Among the witnesses who were summoned and appeared before us, including present patients of the hospital, former inmates and others well acquainted with the present inmates, many expressed the belief that there are many persons now confined there who are not now and never were insane, but who have been sent there from ulterior motives. Like stories have been in circulation in Washington for a long time, and, whether true or not, they are unquestionably injuring the hospital in the estimation of the people of this city, and some steps should be taken to clear up the situation.

"We suggest that the commission of investigation act in conjunction with the Superintendent and medical staff of the hospital in carefully investigating every case there, to the end that full justice may be done to each."

JEWELERS ROBBED AS CROWDS PASS BY

Five Men Force Shopkeeper and Three Clerks Into Rear Room, Bind and Gag Them.

$55,000 LOSS FROM SAFE

Hold-Up on 6th Av. Near 14th St. Unnoticed Outside Shop in Evening Rush Hour.

John Linherr, proprietor of a jewelry shop at 193 Sixth Avenue, and his three clerks were preparing to close the shop at 5:30 P. M. yesterday while scores of persons were passing the place and thousands were walking through Fourteenth Street, a half block away.

They had the safe opened and were placing in it trays of rings, earrings, bracelets and watches when a touring car stopped at the curb and five young men entered carrying a bag.

The four jewelers looked up at five pistols, they told the police later.

"Get into the back room and be quick about it," said one of the armed men. "Make it snappy."

As the four jewelers started, four pistols were pressed against their sides by four of the intruders, while the fifth followed slowly.

William Roseley of 114 Seventh Avenue, a clerk, was the last in line. As they neared the door of the rear room he grasped the pistol pressed against him and grappled with the robber who held it. A blow on the head with the butt of the pistol of the man behind forced him to release his hold. He was dragged into the rear room.

Then as the jewelers were forced into chairs by four of the robbers they saw through the open door that the fifth man had taken off his coat and was standing behind the counter, as if he were a clerk.

The door was closed then. The four jewelers were tied to the chairs and gagged with their handkerchiefs. Their pockets were emptied of $65 in cash, and then the four men went back into the shop.

Ten minutes later Patrolman Lynch of the Charles Street Station, who had passed the store a quarter of an hour previously, passed it again and looking in was surprised to find the door open but no one in sight.

Curiously he stepped into the door and called Linherr's name. Getting no response he walked to the rear of the shop and found the four men tied to the chairs.

Lynch released them, and sent for an ambulance surgeon to attend Roseley, who had received a scalp wound. Linherr and his two other clerks found the safe had been emptied, probably into the bag the five young men carried. The safe's contents, Linherr told the police, were worth about $55,000.

On the floor was found a diamond brooch worth about $750. It was bent as if it had been stepped on as the five men were leaving.

The cash register contained $460, but it was untouched.

The police were told the stock was insured for $50,000.

Thirty-five taxicab drivers and automobile mechanics were in a more or less friendly dice game in a garage on East Fourteenth Street, near Shore Road, Sheepshead Bay, early yesterday, when three masked, armed men entered and commanded them to put all the money on the table.

The money was mostly in coins and small bills. One of the hold-up men looked at it, it was learned later, and sniffed:

"What do you fellows do for a living?" he asked.

"We're chauffeurs," was the answer.

"H'm," was the robber's comment. "Take your money back. We're not cheap stick-up men. We're looking for a big game round here. This isn't it. Take your money back and keep quiet until we drive off."

Curtis Suller, 41 years old, of 263 West Thirtieth Street, was shot in the left side of the abdomen on Tenth Avenue, between Thirtieth and Thirty-first Streets, last night shortly after three men had stopped him and Miss Betty King, 30, of 78 Ninth Avenue.

One man, the police were told later, wrested a handbag from Miss King and ran, pursued by Suller, whereupon one of the two other men fired at him. The three men disappeared.

Patrolman Russell Smith had Suller taken to French Hospital, where it was said his condition was serious, and took Miss King to the West Thirtieth Street Police Station for questioning.

The shooting occurred a block and a half from the spot where, a week ago, Stanley Brozio, 14 years old, was shot and killed by warring gangsters, in the presence of his mother, who was wounded. There have been fourteen other shootings and slayings in that vicinity in the last six months.

REGISTRATION LIGHT ON THE FIRST DAY

151,291 Qualify to Vote in Mayoralty Race, Compared With 162,208 in 1921.

MANHATTAN LOSES 9,950

Brooklyn Decrease Is 4,088—Queens Gains 2,958, Bronx 136 and Richmond 27.

Registration of voters yesterday, the opening day, was exceedingly light for a Mayoralty year. The first day's figures showed a falling off of more than 40,000 from the first day last year and almost 11,000 below the first day returns in 1921, the last year of a municipal election in this city.

Registration by Districts.

The following table shows the returns from last night's registration by Assembly districts, with borough and city totals and with corresponding figures from the registration of 1921, when a Mayor was elected; 1922, when there was a State election, and from last year's Presidential election:

Manhattan.

A.D.	1921.	1922.	1924.	1925.
1	2,403	2,406	2,750	2,314
2	1,798	1,779	2,197	1,637
3	2,992	2,482	3,022	2,494
4	1,912	1,944	2,429	2,316
5	3,046	2,511	2,883	2,007
6	2,112	2,125	2,553	2,068
7	3,182	2,849	4,153	2,990
8	1,706	1,621	1,874	1,435
9	3,396	3,136	4,701	3,395
10	2,807	2,303	3,602	2,284
11	3,248	2,703	3,773	2,729
12	3,446	2,796	3,527	2,728
13	2,767	2,316	3,027	2,156
14	2,615	2,433	2,747	2,062
15	3,316	2,567	4,379	3,011
16	3,289	2,822	3,228	2,337
17	2,553	2,128	2,655	1,855
18	2,603	2,236	2,625	1,914
19	2,515	2,071	2,509	1,940
20	1,743	1,522	1,858	1,203
21	2,341	1,954	2,588	1,720
22	3,029	2,564	3,160	2,349
23	3,801	3,260	4,471	3,726
Total..	62,620	54,528	70,711	52,670

The Bronx.

A.D.	1921.	1922.	1924.	1925.
1	3,335	2,728	3,331	2,526
2	4,058	3,117	4,706	4,254
3	2,468	2,407	2,836	2,264
4	2,444	2,006	2,564	2,044
5	2,876	2,516	3,113	2,202
6	2,046	1,702	2,882	2,643
7	2,568	2,024	2,664	2,046
8	3,699	3,316	6,050	5,651
Total..	23,494	19,816	28,146	23,630

Brooklyn.

A.D.	1921.	1922.	1924.	1925.
1	2,297	2,022	2,599	2,143
2	2,591	2,429	4,171	3,907
3	1,638	1,356	1,254	1,173
4	2,369	1,940	2,140	1,616
5	3,287	2,678	3,290	2,503
6	2,408	2,168	2,654	1,966
7	1,943	1,514	1,854	1,491
8	1,638	1,388	1,537	1,404
9	2,497	2,242	3,728	3,024
10	3,092	2,493	3,319	2,815
11	3,366	2,701	4,029	3,026
12	3,218	2,845	3,450	2,778
13	1,571	1,383	1,415	1,223
14	1,559	1,445	1,613	1,341
15	1,773	1,381	1,642	1,270
16	2,544	2,310	3,289	2,673
17	2,974	2,374	3,552	2,544
18	3,044	2,755	4,583	3,705
19	1,423	1,298	1,409	1,116
20	3,576	3,050	3,434	2,734
21	3,537	2,857	4,904	3,874
22	3,417	2,915	4,113	3,350
23	1,756	1,603	1,911	1,622
Total..	57,406	49,147	65,940	53,318

One election district missing.

Queens.

A. D.	1921.	1922.	1924.	1925.
1	2,406	1,977	2,623	2,209
2	2,223	1,786	2,540	2,283
3	2,229	2,023	3,080	2,360
4	2,508	2,248	4,942	4,083
5	2,912	2,504	4,671	4,068
6	2,363	2,090	3,224	2,610
Total..	14,861	12,628	21,060	17,819

Richmond.

A. D.	1921.	1922.	1924.	1925.
1	2,192	1,737	2,843	2,127
2	1,635	1,348	1,650	1,727
Total..	3,827	3,085	4,493	3,854

Recapitulation.

Boroughs.	1921.	1922.	1924.	1925.
Manhattan..	62,620	54,528	70,711	52,670
Bronx	23,494	19,816	28,146	23,630
Brooklyn ...	57,406	49,147	65,940	53,318
Queens	14,861	12,628	21,060	17,819
Richmond ..	3,827	3,085	4,493	3,854
Total.....	162,208	139,204	190,350	151,291

In Manhattan every Assembly District showed a decrease from the first day's

Continued on Page Three.

BIG BAKING MERGER FACES AN INQUIRY BY THE GOVERNMENT

Justice Department Will Ascertain if $400,000,000 Deal Violates Anti-Trust Laws.

ONE UNIT ALREADY ACCUSED

Complaint Against Continental Company to Federal Trade Board April 13 Disclosed.

CAUSES ROW IN COMMISSION

Thompson and Nugent Say Others Neglected Duty—Coolidge Is Asked to Remove Them.

Special to The New York Times.

WASHINGTON, Oct. 5.—Strong intimation was given at the Department of Justice this afternoon that the proposed new $400,000,000 bakery merger will be placed under scrutiny for the purpose of determining whether any phase of the deal falls within the purview of the anti-trust laws.

Department officials refused to comment on the merger beyond informally authorizing the statement that they intend to look into the matter.

The Federal Trade Commission was equally reticent, as a commission, with respect to the steps taken yesterday to effect the merger through the incorporation at Baltimore of the General Baking Corporation, but Commissioner Huston Thompson and John F. Nugent disclosed the fact that complaint was made on April 13 last by the commission against the Continental Baking Company, which is proposed to be taken over in the new merger. This complaint was never made public.

Commissioners Thompson and Nugent, who are a minority of the Trade Commission, scored their colleagues, Commissioners Van Fleet, Humphrey and Hunt, for withholding the issuance of the complaint, pointing out that under the law the respondents are allowed thirty days in which to reply. Commissioner Thompson stated that instead of making reply the Continental Baking Company asked for an informal hearing before the commission's Board of Review.

Removal of Board Majority Asked.

Prior to the issuance of the joint statement of Commissioners Thompson and Nugent, announcement was made by Basil M. Manly, Director of the People's Legislative Service, that he had written to President Coolidge urging him to demand the immediate resignation of "those members of the Federal Trade Commission who have by their neglect of duty permitted the formation of the bread trust."

"This trust," said Mr. Manly, "to be known as the General Baking Company, has just been incorporated in Maryland to take over the Ward and Continental Baking Corporations, and many other unnamed companies engaged in the production of bread, flour, condensed milk and other commodities used in baking.

"It will have 157 huge bakeries and will control the price of bread in every important city in the United States. The price paid for the shares of the General Baking Company, $225 a share, is equivalent to $1,350 for each share of the original stock, which was split up six to one in 1922 by stock dividends.

"This original General Baking Company stock sold for $2 a share in 1916. This is an indication of the outrageous profits that have been made by the constituent members of the bread trust."

In his letter to the President Mr. Manly said:

"I am informed that Commissioners Thompson and Nugent have consistently urged action against the bread trust.

"Without access to the official records of the commission, it must be inferred that the majority members, namely, Commissioners Van Fleet, Hunt and Humphrey, have used their power to suppress the investigation and protect the trust.

"If the records of the commission confirm this inference, it would appear to be clearly your duty to demand the immediate resignations of the Commissioners who have been guilty of this gross negligence."

In his statement in behalf of himself and Commissioner Nugent Commissioner Thompson said:

"The courts have held that the Clayton act was intended to arrest the creation of trusts, &c., in their incipiency and before consummation.

"I cannot see how we can now follow out that thought when from newspapers accounts this huge combine has already

Continued on Page Two.

Railroad Indicted for Transporting Beer; Warrants Out for Lehigh Valley Officials

SYRACUSE, N. Y., Oct. 5 (AP).—Seventy-two indictments, including the first ever returned in this section of the country against a railroad for transporting liquor, were handed up to Judge Frank Cooper in United States Court today by the Federal Grand Jury which has been in session here for two weeks.

The feature of the presentment is the indictment of the Lehigh Valley Railroad for transporting two carloads of beer without a permit and without keeping the proper records. Warrants for the arrest of company officials were issued immediately and will be served by the United States Marshal this week, so that the defendants can be arraigned in Auburn before adjournment Friday night.

The Syracuse enforcement office asserts the beer was not properly labeled and that the records required by law were not kept.

Any shipment of beer or other alcoholic liquors over the Lehigh Valley Railroad lines was made without the knowledge of the operators of the contents, the Lehigh Valley Railroad management here declared yesterday in a statement concerning the indictment returned at Syracuse.

"The management was aware of the inquiry being conducted by the United States District Attorney at Syracuse," said the statement, "and had cooperated with his office in this connection, placing all available records at his disposal and offering to produce any other which had been, or might be, requested.

"The railroad had accepted the shipments, which were labelled 'cereal beverage,' without the slightest indication that they were not correctly billed or that they were not entirely lawful shipments."

Confidence was expressed by the railroad officials that the company "would have no difficulty in proving its innocence and good faith in this matter."

Stresemann's Sudden Illness Forces Conference Delay

LOCARNO, Oct. 5 (AP).—Dr. Gustav Stresemann was taken suddenly ill today, and the plenary session of the security conference fixed for tomorrow has been postponed.

Because of the reported plot against the life of Dr. Stresemann and Chancellor Luther, the announcement that the Foreign Minister was confined to bed aroused fears that some such attempt had actually been made.

The German spokesman repudiated such rumors and explained that the Locarno climate had affected Dr. Stresemann's throat and caused a slight fever. After a consultation of physicians it was decided to ask the Allies to postpone tomorrow's regular session until the afternoon, when the Minister would probably be able to be present.

PATROL BOAT'S S O S STIRS RADIO TURMOIL

Leaking Craft Quits Spot Where She Is Reported Sinking as Vessels Hunt.

HEADS FOR ATLANTIC CITY

Meanwhile Criss-Cross Radio Calls Try to Trace Dry Navy Vessel With Broken Engine.

An S O S call from the Coast Guard boat 101 of the prohibition navy caused a commotion among ships off the New Jersey coast last night, and they went to her assistance from every direction, although the distressed vessel started limping to port on one engine, with a flooded compartment, leaving no word for the anxiously searching ships. How she got into trouble nobody knew last night.

Some time after Captain William Ridgeley of the Coast Guard at Atlantic City had heard that the 101 was safely on her way home and had himself gone home to bed, ships were circling about the spot where the vessel was supposed to be, and one of them sent word to another:

"I think she's sunk."

At 12:30 this morning the disabled boat was headed safely for Atlantic City under her own power. A message from the CG-183, one of the boats sent out from Atlantic City, received at the Coast Guard Station there shortly before 1 o'clock, said that the CG-101 was carrying a lot of water, but was doing well and all was O. K. She was then about eighteen miles from the New Jersey resort and was expected to reach port at 3 A. M. A wireless from the G 183 said that the radio operator of the C. G. 101, when he feared the boat was sinking, inadvertently gave the wrong position in his call for aid.

The first word from the 101 came shortly after 8 o'clock. It was picked up by the steamship Porto Rico and flashed to other ships in the vicinity and was picked up by land stations. The message was simply an S O S and gave no information as to what was the matter. When Captain Ridgeley received the message he sent out the Coast Guard cutter Seneca and two other small boats.

Search Waters Without Avail.

In the meantime the ships at sea had started to bear down on the position given by the 101, which was about 125 miles south of New York, and almost directly off Cape May. The Seneca soon got within reach of the Porto Rico, and the two ships, when about eight miles apart, kept each other advised of their positions and circled about looking for the disabled boat. They could not see her, but once the Porto Rico sent word that the 101 had been sighted, only to correct the message by saying that it was another ship, and that there were several vessels near by.

The naval radio was trying frantically to communicate with the Seneca all this time without being able to get a reply, and on land there were fragmentary messages picked up indicating that out in the night another marine tragedy was being enacted. There was almost total lack of communication between the shore and the ships at sea, and how the message from the 101 reached Captain Ridgeley, telling him that the ship was safe, despite a leak, and was proceeding to her base, without any of the near-by ships learning that their worst fears were unfounded, was still a mystery last night.

Radio broadcasting was stopped when the first S O S was received. At 11:24

Continued on Page Eight.

GERMANY AGREES TO JOIN THE LEAGUE; RHINE DEAL SPEEDED

Commission of Jurists at Locarno Starts Work on Security Provisions.

LONDON DRAFT AS BASIS

Separate Arbitration Treaty Is to Be Made by France and the Reich.

AMICABLE SPIRIT IS SHOWN

At British Suggestion No President Is Named and Formality Is Dispensed With.

By EDWIN L. JAMES.

Special Cable to THE NEW YORK TIMES.

LOCARNO, Oct. 5.—Seven long years after the nations' countless cannon roared the final salvo of the hymn of hate on the bloody battle lines where millions had died the statesmen of the principal countries of Europe met here today for the official purpose of trying to arrange that it shall not happen again.

Europe has come to Locarno to declare peace.

The technical reason for the conference is the draft of a Rhineland compact which shall give protection to France. But the conference may mean more than that if it succeeds. It may mean a real end of the World War. If those leading the Locarno conference have their way, out of it will come a political status of Europe quite different from the alignment which has been but faintly successful since the armistice.

Since then Europe has had an allied camp strongly dominant, with the former enemy countries, particularly Germany, on the outside. The Allies have decided what was to be done in Europe, and Germany has had to accept or oppose as best she could. She made efforts to build up a rival camp. She tried the Treaty of Rapallo with the Russians. The result has been sorry indeed, and now for the first time since the war there is a conference where there is no distinction of conquerors and conquered, but where England, France, Germany, Belgium and Italy are meeting as equals to see what can be done politically for Europe.

Germany to Enter League.

Today they agreed on the opening of the conference that there should be a Rhineland compact and that Germany should enter the League of Nations. If an agreement can be had on terms of Franco-German arbitration it is possible that the League Assembly will hold a special session in January to admit Germany to membership and assign to her a place on the Council.

As Austen Chamberlain put it today:

"We are here to seek to trace mutual relations which will be on a happier footing than they have been for the last several years. We are here to get away from the antagonisms of the great conflict and lay foundations for peace in the future."

As Dr. Stresemann said:

"We are all here on an equal footing, and Germany wants to show she needs permanent peace as much as other nations."

In this effort the Rhineland compact, it is hoped, will be regarded as symbolical in removing some danger of war from the most dangerous spot in Europe, and not as another application of the Treaty of Versailles.

At the opening meeting today, after the exchange of courtesies, the Germans took the lead in proposing immediate consideration of the Rhineland compact. Mr. Chamberlain suggested that the work be begun on the basis of the drafts prepared by the allied and German experts in London last month. It was found that immediate agreement could be had on the principle of a treaty by which France and Germany would accept mutually arbitration of all differences and in which England—and Italy if she wishes—will guarantee the arrangement to the extent of promising to come immediately to the military aid of either country when a victim of aggression.

It was tentatively decided that the Rhineland compact on broad principles would be one treaty, while a technical arbitration treaty between France and Germany alone would be another document. The Germans admitted formally their entrance into the League as a part of the bargain.

The French tried to raise at once the issue of security compacts between Germany on the one hand and Poland and Czechoslovakia on the other, but that was shelved for the moment by Mr. Chamberlain, who thought the best plan was to proceed first with the Rhineland treaty.

It was then voted to name a jurist commission to consider technical parts of the Rhineland treaty, and they began work this afternoon.

One important development of the day outside the conference was a statement by Mr. Chamberlain that he was perfectly willing to aid in the discussion of security compacts between any nations here. It is believed this statement was made in agreement with the Germans and to signify that treaties between Berlin and Warsaw and Prague will be discussed.

On all sides here one gets the impression of the vast political significance of the work undertaken. Germany comes back into good society. In the future she will be at the table in European conferences and she will be free instead of handcuffed—that is, if Locarno [illegible]

"All the News That's Fit to Print"

The New York Times

THE WEATHER
Rain and colder today; tomorrow fair; southwest and west winds.
Temperature yesterday—Max., 59; min., 50.
For weather report see next to last page.

VOL. LXXV....No. 24,758. NEW YORK, FRIDAY, NOVEMBER 6, 1925. TWO CENTS in Greater New York | THREE CENTS Within 200 Miles | FOUR CENTS Elsewhere in the U. S.

COOLIDGE MESSAGE WON'T ASK ACTION ON THE COAL STRIKE

It Will Merely Urge the Enactment of the Coal Commission's Recommendations.

THESE INCLUDE ARBITRATION

President to Follow a Policy of 'Hands Off' Unless Emergency Forces Drastic Measures.

CHOICE SOFT COAL $19 HERE

Brooklyn Dealers Find Little Demand for Substitute Even With Anthracite at $23.50.

Special to The New York Times.

WASHINGTON, Nov. 5.—In his message to Congress, on which he consulted Speaker-designate Longworth today, President Coolidge will not ask any drastic action to bring an end to the coal strike. Neither will he recommend to Congress any revolutionary legislation to deal with strikes in general. He will devote a portion of his message to the coal problem, however, and will suggest the enactment of some of the recommendations made two years ago by the Coal Commission.

The essential feature of these recommendations was that providing for the creation of a special commission to further conciliation and arbitration when the employes and employers fail to adjust their difficulties.

According to those who know the President's position, this is all that he will do regarding the coal strike. Of course a long cold spell may bring about a condition where public interest will compel the President to take further action. At the present time his attitude is to keep his hands off the coal strike, believing that public sentiment will be formed for legislation that will lead to laws which will make strikes in public necessities impossible.

Won't Ask Radical Legislation.

Mr. Coolidge does not intend to recommend any radical legislation in his message, according to those who have conferred with him. He will deal in a conservative way with taxation, farm legislation, railroad consolidation and recommend the adoption of the World Court protocol.

It is becoming clear as the time for the convening of Congress approaches that the President is going to do all he can to bring the warring wings of the Republican Party together. The very fact that he has frequently consulted Senator Borah and seems to rely greatly on his advice has led some World Court proponents to feel that the President does not intend strongly to exert his influence to get the Senate to adopt the protocol. Senator Borah has been an opponent of the Court and there is no indication that he has modified his position.

The fact that the President has summoned Senator Borah to the White House is accepted by Republican leaders as a part of the President's plan for conciliation within the party. It is said that the President will follow out the plan by conferring with other Congressional leaders with the idea of bringing about harmonious action if possible on his program.

Hoover Urged as Mediator.

ROCHESTER, N. Y., Nov. 5 (AP).—Although realizing that actual intervention by President Coolidge in the present anthracite strike is not legally possible, Representative Meyer Jacobstein, believing that the President, through Herbert C. Hoover, Secretary of Commerce, might bring about a solution of the difficulties between the miners and the operators, tonight sent the following telegram to the White House:

"Hard coal situation serious enough to warrant intervention. Why not offer the services of Secretary Herbert C. Hoover as mediator?"

Senator James W. Wadsworth Jr. said today there was nothing the President could do in the present situation except "hope for peace."

"There is no legislation on the statute books giving the President authority to intervene in a situation like this," said the Senator. "The legislation recommended by the Coal Commission, headed by John Hays Hammond, was not enacted by Congress. So what is left for the President to do?"

Dealers "Pirates," Eltz Says.

George J. Eltz, Commissioner of the Coal Merchants' Association and representing the coal trade on the State Coal Commission, warned the public yesterday not even to try to buy what stove size anthracite remained on sale here. He said the supply was practically exhausted, and that the prices being asked were out of reason.

"From what some of the small dealers are asking, they must be pirates," Mr. Eltz said, "and I am advising those in need of coal not to buy anthracite at all."

Speaking in the absence of Major Gen. Charles W. Berry, Chairman of the commission, who left for a rest at Atlantic City over the week-end, Mr. Eltz held out new hopes on coke. Mr. Eltz all along had pronounced coke an ideal substitute for anthracite, preferable to soft coal. Coke had been bid up, however, and was scarce at $17 and $18 a ton. Mr. Eltz said there seemed to have resulted a falling off in the buying, but

Continued on Page Four.

Mayor Alone Votes 'No' On Daughter Taking His Post

Copyright, 1925, by The New York Times Co.
Special Cable to THE NEW YORK TIMES.

LONDON, Nov. 5.—Miss Lucy Dales has been elected Mayor of Dunstable. There was only one dissentient vote, and that was cast by her father. Councilor Dales has been himself Mayor for one year, and his daughter presided as Mayoress for him, but he strongly opposed her taking office on her own account.

Asked if he wanted the job for himself, he replied:

"Oh, no. I have had enough and would not be Mayor again on any account."

Pressed hard for reasons for his vote against his daughter, he at length said:

"I object out of sympathy for her. She already has had as much responsibility as a woman should carry. I am afraid her health will not stand the strain."

FRENCH BUY STOCKS AS FRANC GOES DOWN

With Monetary Unit at 25.40 to $1, Orders Overwhelm Brokers on Bourse.

IS LOWER THAN LIRA HERE

Painleve to Tell Financial Plans Tomorrow—Lottery Bond Proposal Is Outlined.

Copyright, 1925, by The New York Times Company.
Special Cable to THE NEW YORK TIMES.

PARIS, Nov. 5.—The French franc took a new slump today when early this afternoon it sold for 123 to the pound and 25.40 to the dollar.

Before the opening of the Bourse the franc held firm at 24.70, but as soon as trading began started upward, reaching 25.22 to the dollar at the 2 o'clock closing. After uncertainty over a couple of hours it strengthened toward the end of the day, the 5 o'clock trading being on the basis of 25 francs to the dollar.

The Bourse presented a rather wild scene. French Government securities sold off, but French industrials held well. Of course securities based on foreign values followed exchange.

An interesting angle on the Bourse operations was the discovery today of the sale of more sterling and dollar securities than were available for deliveries, this situation arising through the limitations placed on the import of foreign securities.

Bank Statement Discouraging.

The Bank of France statement today was discouraging and perhaps had to do with the sales of francs. Not only did the end of the month business settlement make heavy calls on the Bank of France, but during the week 1,450,000,000 francs new advances were made to the Government, bringing these advances to within 600,000,000 of the legal limit of 32,000,000,000.

Note circulation showed an increase of 1,333,000,000, making the total circulation slightly over 48,000,000,000 or within 3,000,000,000 of the legal limit of 51,000,000,000. Discounts by the Bank allowed an increase of 870,000,000 francs.

Replying to a question by former Minister Loucheur as to when the Chamber might expect the Government's financial projects, Premier Painlevé this afternoon stated he hoped to lay them before the Finance Commission on Saturday.

Former Finance Minister François Marsal today explained the principles behind a bill for a national lottery bond issue, favored by the Republican group in the Senate as a means of meeting the nation's financial difficulties.

The issue, he says, should not be an ordinary lottery, but interest should be paid on the bonds; the Treasury should not be loaded with extensive maturities and care should be taken to diminish the impression among the public that it is a game of chance.

The details of the plan provide for a State loan with a 6 per cent. annuity divided into two parts, 3 per cent. being paid to bondholders as interest and 3 per cent. used to constitute prizes

Continued on Page Six.

MUSSOLINI SAVED FROM DEATH PLOT; 4 MEN UNDER ARREST

Would-Be Assassin, a Socialist Ex-Deputy, Is Caught in Act of Aiming Rifle.

AUTO READY FOR ESCAPE

His Driver and Secretary and a General High in New Masonic Body Are Seized.

DISSIDENT LODGES CLOSED

Party Is Ordered Dissolved—Premier Warns Throng of 100,000 Against Taking Reprisals.

Copyright, 1925, by The New York Times Company.
By Wireless to THE NEW YORK TIMES.

ROME, Nov. 5.—A plot to shoot Premier Mussolini yesterday, during his Armistice Day speech to thousands of citizens gathered before the balcony of his office at the Palazzo Chigi, was disclosed today.

The Premier owes his life to the quick wit of the manager of the Hotel Dragoni, whose windows face those of the Palazzo Chigi, and the prompt intervention of the police, who arrested a former member of the Italian Parliament who had a rifle trained on the balcony onto which Signor Mussolini was to step a few moments later.

The former Deputy under arrest is Tito Zaniboni, a member of the Unitarian Socialist Party, who entered the Chamber in 1921. A powerful automobile at the back entrance of his hotel, with which Zaniboni intended to seek safety after shooting Signor Mussolini, was also discovered by the police and its driver was taken into custody.

Later the police in Turin arrested the retired General Luigi Cappello, one of the moving spirits in Freemasonry's fight against Fascism. Though his share in the plot is not yet clear, it is alleged that he was preparing to flee toward the French frontier.

Last night Zaniboni's private secretary, a man named Quaglia, was arrested. He works on the staff of an extreme Opposition paper here.

Demand for Room Roused Suspicion.

Zaniboni, who recently returned from France, where he frequented anti-Fascist circles, took a room at the Hotel Dragoni, which faces the Palazzo Chigi, the seat of the Ministry of Foreign Affairs. He asked with great insistence to have a room with windows overlooking the balcony from which Signor Mussolini habitually speaks to Roman citizens on all great occasions.

His anxiety to have that particular room aroused the hotel manager's suspicious, who, in view of Zaniboni's anti-Fascist record and the fact that Signor Mussolini was scheduled to speak from the balcony of the Palazzo Chigi that very day, informed the police of his fears.

When the police, who knew from other sources that a plot was being hatched against the Premier, burst suddenly into Zaniboni's room afterward they found the Socialist former Deputy at the window with a military rifle trained on the spot where he expected the Premier would appear at any minute.

The arrest of General Cappello and the other suspected persons followed.

Measures Taken to Avert Reprisals.

As soon as the tangible evidence of a plot against Signor Mussolini's life was in the hands of the authorities, the Government ordered the immediate occupation of all Masonic lodges throughout Italy belonging to the so-called Freemasonry of the Palazzo Giustiniani, to which General Cappello belonged. This is the dissident Masonic movement which broke away from the Scottish Rite Freemasonry and started in opposition to the latter body.

The Government also ordered the immediate dissolution of the Unitarian Socialist Party, to which Zaniboni belonged, and suspended the publication of its official organ, the newspaper Giustizia.

These measures, it is understood, were taken partly to forestall Fascist anger which would have broken out dangerous-

Continued on Page Six.

607 Issues Traded In, 2,718,360 Shares Sold In Broadest Market in Exchange History

More separate issues of common and preferred stocks were traded in yesterday on the New York Stock Exchange than on any other five-hour day in the institution's history. The total was 607, or about five-eighths of the total number of issues listed. Sales for the day were 2,718,360 shares, slightly smaller than for the previous day.

The market lost ground moderately, but there was no hint of nervousness about it and nothing but the usual profit taking incident now and then to such big and broad markets brought about the declines. The features were the steel, copper and motor shares. Some good sized advances were established in particular issues, but others, in which speculation has been rampant, lost several points of their recent gains.

The average of twenty-five representative railroad shares at the close showed a decline of .67, while the industrials declined .85. The entire market, as measured by fifty representative issues of all sorts, lost .81 for the day.

The reaction, if it could be called such, was the first in fourteen days of trading, during which the averages have advanced each day, with many of the more volatile issues gaining from ten to fifty points. The average gain of the industrials in this fourteen-day period has been more than twelve points.

The news of the day was considered generally good. It included an optimistic review of the automotive industry and the increase of the regular dividend rate or the payment of an extra dividend by several well-known corporations. One of the extras was $7 in cash by the Brooklyn Union Gas Company. The fact that there was no change in the rediscount rate of the Federal Reserve Bank after the close of the market probably will play a part in today's trading. It had not been generally expected, but nevertheless Wall Street in such a speculative period as the present always has a weather eye out for unexpected happenings which might rock the market.

The extreme breadth of the market of 607 shares is attributed to the fact that many people in all sections of the country are now buying stocks and that their wants, for their own particular reasons, are multitudinous. The Stock Exchange tickers kept well up to the market most of the day.

Gilt Inner Coffin of Tut-ankh-Amen Found; Bears His Likeness and Gold Ornamentation

Copyright, 1925, by The New York Times Company.
Special Cable to THE NEW YORK TIMES.

CAIRO, Egypt, Nov. 5.—The gilt inner coffin of Pharaoh Tut-ankh-Amen, built to the shape of the young King and bearing an exquisite representation of him, has been uncovered by Howard Carter and his associates.

This was revealed in an official announcement today telling of the progress at the tomb since work began on Oct. 12. When the outer sarcophagus was opened, the communiqué says, a second sarcophagus was disclosed, bearing on top a representation of the god Osiris and entirely covered from head to foot with painted designs and glass of many colors on a surface of gold with a marble background. On the body of this second sarcophagus were painted figures of Nechbet, the goddess of Upper Egypt, and Buto, the goddess of night.

After the second sarcophagus was scientifically examined and lifted out the cover was removed and it revealed the gilt-covered human-shaped inner coffin, but the details of its design were covered by a linen shroud which adhered closely. About it was an exquisite necklace, and flowers were tied to the head bandage and were reposing on the breast. The head of the coffin was uncovered and the likeness of the young Pharaoh was seen.

After photographing the contents of the second sarcophagus, the necklace and linen shroud were removed, revealing the beautiful coffin covered with gold ornamentations of marvelous workmanship, but, unfortunately, most of the detail is covered with a black glutinous layer from the libations at the original funeral ceremonies.

The most important part of the work now is the removal of this glutinous layer and the lifting of the human-shaped coffin from the second sarcophagus, to which it is closely sticking, owing to the libatiounal deposit.

MRS. CLARK ARRESTED AT HUSBAND'S GRAVE

Seized After She Shrinks From Hooded Klansmen Burying Victim of Hammer Murder.

DRAGGED, WEEPING, TO JAIL

Cowen, Her Admirer, Held Without Bail for Murder—No Bail for Woman Either.

Special to The New York Times.

HILLSIDE, N. J., Nov. 5.—After being dragged struggling and weeping from the automobile which brought her from Evergreen Cemetery, where her murdered husband had been buried with the rites of the Ku Klux Klan this afternoon, Mrs. Priscilla Kent Clark was subjected to a 3-hour examination by the Hillside police and then taken to the Union County jail at Elizabeth. She was arraigned as a material witness and held without bail.

Joseph Cowan, her alleged admirer, was arraigned before Recorder James Dowd in Hillside Police Court on a charge of the murder of William J. Clark tonight, Chief of County Detectives John A. Galatian announced at 10:45 o'clock. Cowan was held without bail, Chief Galatian said.

"I told him," Chief Galatian said, "that he had better pray for God to forgive him, and he answered, 'How can God forgive me?'"

The Chief would not say whether or not there had been any sort of confession.

Mrs. Clark made the trip to Elizabeth in an automobile driven by County Prosecutor Abe J. David. Before starting she was permitted to go to her home at 218 Pennsylvania Avenue, in the garage of which Clark was beaten over the head with a hammer shortly after midnight last Monday, receiving injuries from which he died two hours later. Mrs. Clark wept constantly as she changed her clothes in the house, all exits of which were guarded by policemen.

Mrs. Clark's automobile was closely followed on its trip to Elizabeth by another in which, handcuffed between two detectives, sat Cowen, who sought, the police declare, to induce her to elope with him the night her husband was killed.

Masked Klansmen at Funeral.

More than 500 persons gathered in Evergreen Cemetery this afternoon for the murdered man's burial. Lined up, awaiting the arrival of the funeral procession from the undertaking rooms of Joseph H. West in Newark, were thirty-five hooded members of the Essex County Ku Klux Klan, of which Clark was a member. About half were women and none unmasked during the services.

Mrs. Clark collapsed at the service in Newark and was carried to a limousine, the chauffeur of which was a Union County detective. Although they expected no effort by Mrs. Clark to escape, policemen said they were taking "no chances."

Acting on a request of Samuel Clark, the murdered man's father, the Newark police supplied an escort as far as the city line. He did not want, he said, to "get the same dose" as his son. What he meant by this remark, he did not say.

As the funeral cortège drew up in front of the lot where Clark was to be buried, his widow saw the masked and hooded figures of the Klansmen who stood rigid and silent in a semi-circle. She drew back behind the half drawn curtain of the automobile and refused to leave it or to approach the grave.

The white robed Klan contingent moved forward while prayer was offered by the Rev. O. A. Browning, pastor of the Dutch Reformed Church at Avon Avenue and South Tenth Streets, Newark. He quoted from Bryant's Thanatopsis, but made no reference to the unusual nature of the scene nor to the circumstances under which Clark met his death.

Then came the Klan service, conducted by a man who said he was the Rev. Joseph R. Jack but who refused to give his address or the name of the church with which he was affiliated. As he started speaking a cross about four feet high, which was covered with oil-soaked material, was ignited. It blazed for a time and was still flaming when the body was lowered into the grave.

"I don't want any one to think the Klan is trying to get advertising by ap-

Continued on Page Twelve.

CHAPMAN LOSES NEW TRIAL APPEAL

Supreme Court Decides Against Bandit Doomed to Die Dec. 3 for Killing Policeman.

EXPECTED NO MORE, HE SAYS

"Won't Hang," Says Chief Counsel—"Must Serve Federal Sentence First."

Special to The New York Times.

BRIDGEPORT, Conn., Nov. 5.—The Connecticut Supreme Court of Errors today rejected the appeal of Gerald Chapman for a new trial on the charge of murdering Policeman James Skelly of New Britain. The "super-bandit" has been condemned to die on Dec. 3.

The decision text of 4,000 words, filed here, was written by Chief Justice George W. Wheeler of Bridgeport and concurred in by all the Associate Justices. It was made public tonight.

Chapman's only hope now is in a reprieve by the Governor to permit the case to be taken to the United States Supreme Court, and that is conceded to be a forlorn hope.

Chapman's appeal was from the verdict of guilty brought in by the jury which tried him in Judge Newell Jennings's session of the Superior Court at Hartford last Spring.

Guilt Proof Declared Conclusive.

"There is no error," concludes the Supreme Court's decision, after reviewing the facts and the alleged errors in the case.

"The result of our consideration and reflection has led us to the fixed opinion that the verdict reached by the jury was the only verdict which reasoning minds could reasonably have reached upon this evidence," reads the decision. "Seldom is a charge of this character so completely and conclusively proved.

"The record shows that in fact the accused had under our rules of law a fair and impartial trial and that he was accorded all the rights which our law gave him.

"It is difficult to conceive of a case where a reversal should be granted upon a refusal to order a change of venue after the case has been tried, every right of the accused protected and a fair and impartial trial accorded him."

As to the defense contention that there was error in the drawing of jurors' names, the decision says:

"It does not appear that the rights of the accused were unfairly prejudiced by the manner in which the panel was drawn."

On the claim of error because Judge Jennings refused to segregate witnesses, the decision says:

"There is nothing which tends to indicate in the slightest degree that the denial of the motion to segregate the witnesses operated to the disadvantage of the accused, or that the trial Court exercised his discretion unreasonably."

Nitroglycerin Incident Reviewed.

Chapman's counsel charged error because, during the examination of a witness by State's Attorney Hugh M. Alcorn, when three bottles of nitroglycerin were introduced, three men supposed to be guarding the prisoner and said to be in the employ of the State's Attorney stood up in the court room in a manner to create a prejudicial atmosphere and to indicate that Chapman was a desperate character.

On this point the decision says:

"No request was made to the Court to caution the jury, investigate the incident or rebuke the State's Attorney or any one else for the responsibility of the incident. Nor does it appear that the men were officers, or in the employ of the State's Attorney. The record relieves the State's Attorney of all responsibility for the incident."

Upon the claim that State's Attorney Alcorn appealed to the passion, prejudice and partiality of the jury, the decision says:

"It is quite true that the arraignment of the accused was a severe one, but no more so, we think, than was reasonably permissible in view of the evidence and the record of the accused, practically admitted or undisputed, and especially in the light of the argument of counsel for the accused."

The Court pointed out that the nature of counsel's argument for the accused required a vigorous reply on the part of the State's Attorney.

Time Table Evidence Upheld.

The decision says that the State's Attorney's arguments for a conviction do not fall in the category of "improper" arguments, nor was there any "flagrant

Continued on Page Ten.

BOND AMENDMENT BELIEVED SAFE, BUT MAJORITY IS FALLING

Returns Still Missing From 629 of a Total of 4,711 Districts Outside City.

DELAY CAUSES DISCUSSION

But Figures Yet to Come, It Is Believed, Could Not Defeat the Proposal.

OTHER MAJORITIES BIG

Grade Crossings 204,755 in Lead; Short Ballot, 314,879—Judiciary, 403,927.

Returns from up-State on Constitutional Amendment No. 1, the $100,000,000 bond issue proposal, which kept dribbling in during the day, had brought the majority for that measure down last night to 72,087. There still remained to be heard from 629 election districts out of a total of 4,711 up-State. In this city all the 3,073 election districts with the exception of one have reported their vote on the Constitutional amendments.

The total included in last night's report was 919,190 votes in the affirmative and 847,103 votes in opposition to the proposed bond issue for public improvements. The majority for the amendment in this city, steadily reduced as up-State returns have been coming in, was 291,625.

Complete returns from almost one-third of the counties up-State are still missing, according to the tabulated returns of The Associated Press. Albany Broome, Chautauqua, Chenango, Clinton, Essex, Herkimer, Monroe, Oneida, Onondaga, Otsego, Rensselaer, Rockland, Saratoga, Suffolk, Warren and Washington have sent returns with one or more election districts missing. In many instances the vote on the Constitutional amendments in the missing districts, according to up-State dispatches, have been locked in the ballot boxes by the local election board and may not be heard from until the official canvass is made.

Slow Returns Arouse Comment.

The slowness with which returns were coming in was a matter of comment in some quarters. Even though the districts to be heard from are all in rural sections where there was strong opposition to the proposed bond issue, it is not believed that the returns, when opened, will wholly overcome the present plurality for the amendment. One county, Hamilton, however, has failed so far to report any vote on the bond proposal and other constitutional amendments.

In the counties of Nassau and Suffolk on Long Island, there has been great paucity in the reports on the vote cast for the amendments. The other districts which have failed to report are largely in the rural sections of the State.

Nassau County's vote on the amendments is expected to be made known in Mineola today when the Board of Canvassers completes the tabulations begun in the County Clerk's office yesterday.

The absence of figures on the amendments is explained as due to the lack of interest in them when the returns were first tabulated in the election districts. Persons who then reported the figures unofficially concentrated their attention, it was said, on the vote for local candidates and for the charter and did not wait to get the vote for the amendments. Further, it was explained, election officers in several districts misdirected the official returns to Town Clerks instead of to the County Clerk, who had to send for them, otherwise the complete vote would have been announced yesterday afternoon.

Returns on Bond Issue Amendment.

Here follows a table giving the latest returns last night on the bond issue proposal:

County.	Yes.	No.	E.D. Missing.
Albany	[illegible]	18,832	56
Allegany	772	9,571	0
Broome	764	5,331	73
Cattaraugus	2,906	11,349	0
Cayuga	4,536	12,650	0
Chautauqua	3,080	12,635	1
Chemung	7,950	11,787	0
Chenango	311	2,081	29
Clinton	261	774	42
Columbia	3,402	6,550	0
Cortland	1,017	7,575	0
Delaware	1,667	11,244	0
Dutchess	7,985	7,320	0
Erie	40,172	28,774	0
Essex	2,127	4,530	1
Franklin	1,848	4,971	0
Fulton	1,876	6,484	0
Genesee	1,223	4,856	0
Greene	1,402	3,865	0
Hamilton	......	......	11
Herkimer	2,197	7,104	2
Jefferson	4,326	11,085	0
Lewis	1,504	4,853	0
Livingston	1,394	5,165	0

Continued on Page Two.

MISS MARY LEWIS.
Singer who has risen from cabaret to the Metropolitan Opera Company.

EX-FOLLIES SINGER TO STAR IN OPERA

Mary Lewis to Sing Mimi in 'La Boheme' at Metropolitan in January.

STUDIED ONLY THREE YEARS

Debut in Vienna After Year's Training—Acclaimed There as 'Greater Than Jeritza.'

Mary Lewis, a 25-year-old American girl from Little Rock, Ark., who heard grand opera sung for the first time in her life only five years ago, has been engaged, it was announced by the Metropolitan Opera Company yesterday, to sing star parts this season. She probably will be heard first in January in the rôle of Mimi in "La Bohême."

Miss Lewis broke all traditions by making her début in Vienna in 1923, a little more than one year after she had first taken up the study of grand opera and, according to cables from Vienna, she was acclaimed as "greater than Jeritza."

She sang in public at the age of 5 years in the choir of the Methodist Church at Dallas, Texas. During the next eleven years she sang and played the violin and pipe organ in church at Dallas and Little Rock. Her musical career outside the church began six years ago when she ran away from her home in Little Rock to appear in the chorus of the traveling musical show "Reckless Eve." Two years ago she was a star of Ziegfeld's "Follies."

On her return a month ago from successes in Europe, the statement was made that the Metropolitan Opera Company planned to engage her for appearances a year from now. The Chicago Opera Company, however, made Miss Lewis an offer to sing there in important rôles this season. This changed the situation. Two weeks ago the Metropolitan Opera Company gave the young American singer an audition, and yesterday the contract was signed. Miss Lewis said that it called for her appearance in star parts only. She has a repertoire of fifteen.

Resume of Her Career.

Her unprecedented rise in six years from chorus girl to Metropolitan star is briefly told as follows:

1919—Ran away from home to join the chorus of the "Reckless Eve," road show, which stranded in San Francisco. Sang in a cabaret in San Francisco.

1920—Went to Hollywood and acted for six months in Christie comedies. Came to New York on June 1, got a place in the chorus of the Greenwich Village Follies and was promoted from chorus girl to prima donna before the show opened. Heard grand opera for first time at a matinee.

1921—A leading singer with Ziegfeld's Follies.

1922—Singing in the Follies. Studied under Thorner, teacher of Rosa Ponselle and Galli-Curci. Studied French and Italian.

1923—Sang at Monte Carlo. Made her début in grand opera at Vinna as Marguerite in "Faust."

1924—Sang five weeks in London and toured England for three months and a half. Sang with five other principals of the British National Opera Company at 10 Downing Street.

1925—Made a great hit in Paris in the leading rôle of "The Merry Widow." Signed with the Metropolitan.

In less than three years after hearing grand opera for the first time Miss Lewis was singing Marguerite in Vienna.

"The first opera that I heard was 'Madame Butterfly,' said Miss Lewis yesterday afternoon at the Metropolitan. "I was in the Greenwich Village Follies at the time and went with another girl to the Metropolitan one after-

Continued on Page Eight.

Our Women Losing Beauty and Intelligence, As Homely and Dull Multiply, Says Biologist

MILWAUKEE, Wis., Nov. 5 (AP).—American women are losing their beauty, and intelligence will be next to go, as beauty and intelligence go together, Albert E. Wiggam, biologist and author, of New York, told the Wisconsin Teachers' Association today.

The expression "beautiful but dumb," as applied to women, is nonsense, he said. A thousand beautiful women have more intelligence than a thousand homely women, he declared, adding that there are exceptions "both ways."

"The more intelligent, beautiful women are allowing the less intelligent and less beautiful to have nearly all the children. If it keeps up, the next generation will be both homely and dumb," Mr. Wiggam said.

He asserted it takes three college women to produce one baby, and that during the same time one homely woman with little education will produce two or three. Only about half of America's college women ever marry and the average college-bred married woman has but two children, he added.

1,000,000 PERSONS RELIEVED OF TAXES IN $300,000,000 CUT

Ways and Means Committee Also Raises Exemption for Family Heads to $3,500.

DEPENDENT AGE EXTENDED

Earned Income Deduction Will Remain as in the Present Tax Law.

SURTAX MAXIMUM IS 20%

Normal Rates Will Run From 1½ to 5 Per Cent. in Tentative Bill.

Special to The New York Times.

WASHINGTON, Nov. 5.—Exemption through reductions of more than 1,000,000 persons from the Federal income tax, a tentative agreement that $300,000,000 should represent the total reduction, the increasing of personal exemptions for single men from $1,000 to $1,500, and of married men from $2,500 to $3,500, and extending up to the age of 21, where they are attending school, the exemption now extended for children up to the age of 18, were among the steps taken by the House, Ways and Means Committee today in rounding toward its final form the income tax reduction bill.

Fix Tentative Normal Rates.

More than $200,000,000 of the $300,000,000 total the committee decided should be devoted to reducing normal and surtaxes. The committee tentatively fixed a new normal tax rate of 1½ per cent. on the first $4,000 of income, 3 per cent. on the second $4,000 and 5 per cent. on the balance, and agreed that the maximum surtax should be 20 per cent., this to be imposed on incomes above $100,000.

The committee agreed, too, that the provisions of the present law allowing a deduction at 25 per cent. on earned income up to a certain point should remain, but it was not settled whether the present limit of $10,000 on income considered earned should be raised or left where it now stands.

The sweeping changes settled upon were made behind closed doors and no intimation of the votes upon the various steps or the partisan sentiment of committee members was disclosed. It appeared, however, that with the exception of one or two Democrats every one seemed to be well satisfied.

Viewed from the outside, the indications were that there had been concessions all around, for while the Administration had, at least for the time being, obtained its desired maximum surtax, the Democrats had in turn gained their point on substantial increases in exemptions.

It must be noted, too, that if the agreement to devote $200,000,000 to surtaxes and normal taxes is adhered to there is virtually no chance that the Administration can carry out its wish of wiping the estate tax off the books, the repeal of which would entail about $100,000,000.

Garner Gains His Points.

The increased exemptions were the pets of Representative Garner, the ranking Democratic member of the committee, and it seems apparent that his generalship played a part in persuading the committee to sanction them. He has said that more than 1,000,000 persons would be put in the exempt class through the changes he advocated, and Chairman Green said after the meeting that he thought this was a correct estimate.

The Treasury had wished to use $140,000,000 for reduction of normal and surtaxes, and had included no provision for retention of the earned income clauses or increase of the exemptions.

Should the committee decide to go further in the earned income provision and raise the maximum limit the $200,000,000 allocated would be greatly increased. Under the present law all income of $5,000 and under is automatically "earned," but to have the remaining $5,000 permitted under law considered as "earned" the taxpayer must prove his claim in this regard. What the committee is now considering is whether or not to make the limit larger than $10,000.

When the last revenue bill was being written the Administration asked for an increase in the limit on earned income on the theory that professional men and others were entitled to 25 per cent. exemption on whatever they had actually earned in contrast to wealth that should come to them from other sources. Congress at that time would not agree to this request and set $10,000 as all that should be deemed earned.

While the maximum surtax was fixed today at 20 per cent. on incomes of above $100,000, which contrasts with the present maximum of 40 per cent. on above $150,000, no other part of the scale of surtaxes was voted on. The graduated scale has not been worked out and it will be left to a subcommittee after further progress has been made with the bill. Under present law the 1 per cent. of the surtaxes applies at $10,000-$14,000.

The normal rates approved by the committee differ from those of the Treasury, which were 1 per cent. on the first $3,000, 7 per cent. on the next $1,000, 3 per cent. on the next $4,000 and 5 per cent. on the remaining income. The present rates are 2 per cent. on the first $4,000, 4 per cent. on the following $4,000 and 6 per cent. on the balance.

Agreement that $300,000,000 shall be employed for tax reduction is tentative, and it may be that the completed bill will show a larger amount. Before the

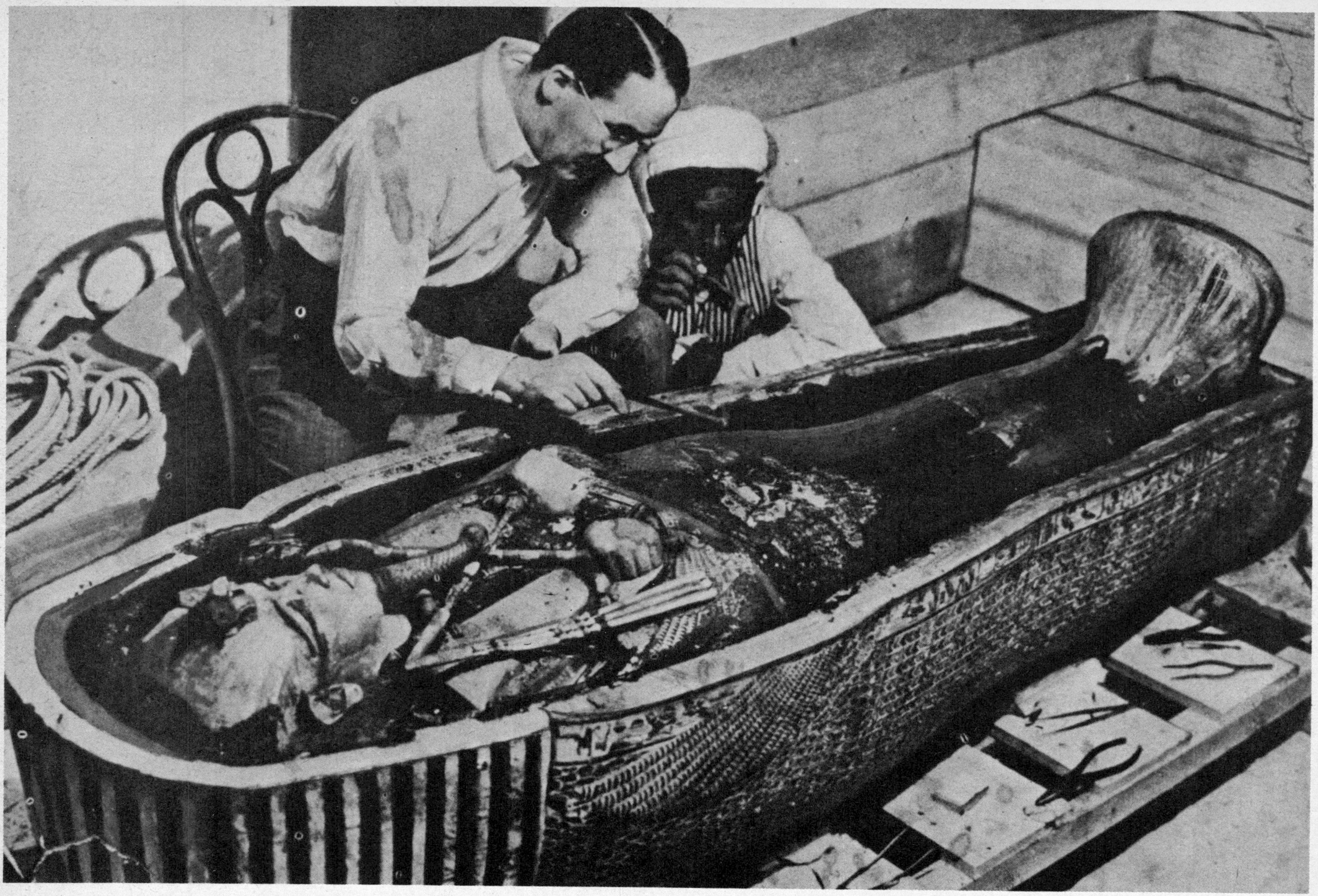

When Howard Carter excavated the tomb of King Tutankhamen, he discovered an ancient Egyptian plaque which was decifered to read: *Death shall come on swift wings to who toucheth the tomb of the Pharoahs.* Within ten years of the opening of the tomb, fourteen people connected in some way with the opening, died in a mysterious manner. Here Carter is shown studying King Tut's mummy.

"All the News That's Fit to Print."

The New York Times.

THE WEATHER
Partly cloudy and colder today; fair and warmer tomorrow.
Temperature yesterday—Max. 50, min. 43.
For weather report see next to last page.

VOL. LXXV....No. 24,768. ••• NEW YORK, MONDAY, NOVEMBER 16, 1925. TWO CENTS in Greater New York | THREE CENTS Within 200 Miles | FOUR CENTS Elsewhere in the U. S.

FRANCE SEES TEST OF LOCARNO POLICY IN COLOGNE DECISION

Government Has Support of Majority in Trusting Germany's Good Faith.

HITCH MIGHT MEAN UPSET.

Preparations for Evacuation Go On, With Ambassadors Drafting a New Note Today.

BERLIN OPPOSITION FAILS

Nationalists Are Badly Split Through Hindenburg's Condemnation of Their Position.

By EDWIN L. JAMES.

Special Cable to THE NEW YORK TIMES.

PARIS, Nov. 15.—It is a far cry from the occupation of the Ruhr to the evacuation of Cologne. Since the French and Belgians marched into the heart of Germany's industrial region, nearly three years ago, to the new decision of the Allies to begin to free the Cologne zone on Dec. 1, there has been a great change in European politics and, in the circumstances, this means a change in France's policy. This change is measured by the distance between Poincaré's policy of strict enforcement of the Treaty of Versailles and Briand's declaration yesterday that the present policy of France was one of close cooperation and collaboration with Germany.

While this change represents a shift in the policy of statesmen who are not always exactly in line with public opinion, it is nevertheless true that a majority of Frenchmen are perfectly willing to try the policy, which in the last analysis may be said to be that Frenchmen, having seen the impossibility of keeping a great nation like Germany disarmed if she wishes to arm, have now turned to the effort to persuade her she does not need to arm and that such a policy could not bring the expected results.

Of course, the Locarno treaties enter into this situation in both directions, for at one and the same time they give France the assurance of protection against a German revenge effort and also let Germany know in advance against what difficulties she would run in such an effort. That is the hard and cold foundation upon which Briand, Chamberlain and Luther as well as Stresemann hope to build a new political situation in Europe.

Failure Might Reverse French Policy

In very large measure the success of the new effort depends on Germany. Failure of the Reich to carry out its part of the Locarno bargain would cause an enormous reaction in France and give the French Nationalists ammunition with which they might well be able to change France's foreign policy back into the old Poincaré-Millerand channels. For just as in Germany there is a Junker faction against the Locarno plans and spirit, there is the same opposition in France, and indeed in France the Nationalists may be said to be more strong than in Germany.

It would be a mistake to suppose there is unanimous enthusiasm in France for the new policy based upon trust in Germany. It rather represents a studied decision based on the feeling of a majority of Frenchmen that in view of the results of the opposite policy the new plan is worth giving a fair trial. There are many misgivings and many doubts in France, and it is for Germany to say whether they grow or decrease.

Certainly when Briand and Chamberlain arrange a special session of the Conference of Ambassadors in order to give Luther and Stresemann ammunition against the German Nationalists they show evidence of wishing to do their utmost to help the spirit into which the German Government leaders entered at Locarno. When they made the reservation that the Cologne evacuation would be gradual over two months they took a step to satisfy French public opinion, which would doubt the wisdom of giving up the guarantee before Germany had carried out her disarmament promises. If she makes good no one can doubt that British troops will be out of the first bridgehead by Feb. 1.

Tomorrow the Ambassadors will draft a note to Germany, giving details of the proposed plan for the Reich's regaining full control of Cologne and its vicinity.

French Comment on Cologne.

The French press today behaves as might be expected. The Government and moderate papers generally praise the move as showing the Allies' good faith, while the Nationalist press condemns the move as misplaced generosity. The Gaulois says:

"When Cologne is to be evacuated before Germany has fulfilled the disarmament conditions. That is a fine prize for blackmailing the German Nationalists against the Luther Cabinet. This will encourage the Junkers to new tricks to get back [illegible] hasten the evacuation of Coblenz and Mayence."

Pertinax finds the Allies insincere. "Since we are adopting the Locarno policy, why not say so? Why not say this: We are giving up efforts to disarm Germany. But do not let the Government tell France that Cologne is being evacuated because Germany is disarmed."

The Petit Parisien observes:

"This shows a manifestation of the Locarno spirit which is now modifying

Continued on Page Three.

Hunter College So Crowded It Turns Down 300 Students

Crowded conditions at Hunter College, the city's institution of higher learning for girls, will cause the rejection of several hundred applications for admission for the term beginning February, 1926, according to Dr. George S. Davis, President of the college.

"The facilities of this institution are so inadequate when the large number of students requesting an opportunity for a collegiate education is considered that it will be impossible to admit more than 200 new students next February for the Spring term," the President said yesterday.

"Yet 500 students have already signified their desire to enrol! here, and this is only the middle of November. We will, in all probability, receive several hundred more applications by the end of the term, in spite of the fact that of those who have already applied for admission 300 virtually have been turned down."

HOLDS $300,000,000 IS TAX CUT ENOUGH

Green, Ways and Means Chairman, Thinks Treasury Right in Setting Limit.

CAUTIONS ABOUT BUSINESS

Recession in Trade by 1928, He Says, Might Cause Government Deficit.

Special to The New York Times.

WASHINGTON, Nov. 15.—Chairman Green of the Ways and Means Committee announced today his decided opposition to increasing the amount of the 1925 tax reduction bill beyond the $304,000,000 already applied by his committee. His declaration was something of a surprise, because Mr. Green has been credited with looking favorably on a total tax reduction approximating $350,000,000, but he said flatly that the Treasury was entirely justified in demanding a reduction of not more than $300,000,000.

Chief among the reasons actuating Mr. Green in his decision was the uncertainty of business conditions in 1928, for, he said, while in that year the full effect of the contemplated reductions would be first felt by the Government, a slackening of business conditions would mean a revenue loss of $50,000,000 and, a general depression would mean a drop in receipts of $100,000,000.

Although reiterating his conclusion that Treasury estimates were ultra conservative and the calculation of the surplus much too low, Chairman Green refused to sympathize with the Democratic attitude that the bill could be carried to $500,000,000 by spreading the payment of the public debt over a longer period. The present system of paying the debt quickly looked forward to a possible emergency, he stated, and if there were a larger surplus it could be applied to the debt or some other use, such as a building program.

Expects Complete Bill This Week.

"The work of preparing the new revenue bill is drawing to a close and it is expected that it will be finished this week, or at least before Thanksgiving," said Chairman Green in his statement. "The main features of the bill have been completed and given out to the press. While the action with reference to these matters was not beyond recall, up to this date no change has been made, and at this late date it is not likely that any will be made.

"There remain matters of form and the administrative features, upon both of which a subcommittee and the members of the drafting bureau are still at work. While these subjects are not as important as the provisions of the bill which have been announced, they are extremely complicated and technical, and require the most careful examination. For this reason the work upon them must necessarily proceed slowly.

"The Treasury estimates of the surplus in the future have intentionally been made very conservative on the basis of the maximum expenditures and the minimum receipts. My opinion is, and has been, that the amount of surplus thus determined is much too low, and the returns for each month are strengthening this opinion. As a con-

Continued on Page Four.

BORAH WOULD WIDEN BAN ON SUBMARINES TO END WAR ITSELF

With Senator Swanson, His Democratic Colleague, He Endorses British Move.

WANTS WORLD AGREEMENT

But Demands the Outlawing of War as an Institution as a Basis of Campaign.

LORD LEE JOINS APPEAL

He Says Britain Still Holds to Washington Proposal—Veterans Ask Parliament to Act.

Special to The New York Times.

WASHINGTON, Nov. 15.—Senator William E. Borah of Idaho, Chairman of the Committee on Foreign Relations and one of the outstanding figures of the Senate in the consideration of problems of armament, strongly endorsed tonight the campaign that has begun in Britain for the abolition of submarines.

Senator Borah said he was in hearty sympathy with the war on submarines declared by British public leaders, including Lady Astor, Chairman MacKinnon of Lloyds and Lords Cecil, Parmoor and Sydenham, as a result of the loss of the British submarine M-1 soon after the sinking of the America submarine S-51, both with a heavy toll of lives.

The Senator added that the campaign against the submarine should be much broader in scope and include also an attack on war as an institution.

Senator Claude A. Swanson of Virginia, ranking Democratic member of the Foreign Relations Committee, also went on record in an interview tonight against retention of the submarine if that can be achieved by an agreement among the nations of the world.

Senator Swanson, who also is ranking Democratic member of the Naval Affairs Committee and has devoted several years to the study of naval matters, expressed the opinion that more than half the value of submarines in time of war had been taken away by resolutions adopted at the Washington arms conference.

Borah Demands Attack on War Itself

Senators Borah and Swanson both said they had read with exceeding interest the dispatch from London printed in THE NEW YORK TIMES this morning setting forth the views of British public leaders in favor of scrapping submarines.

"The sad disaster to the M-1 will have some compensation if it starts a crusade against the very existence of the submarine," said Senator Borah.

"I am in hearty sympathy with the suggestion of those who seemed disposed to start this world-wide campaign. I would like to help the cause.

"But, of course, the campaign must have a wider scope than that. So long as war is recognized as a legitimate method of settling international controversies, some kind of cruel and brutal weapon will have to be used and, when the war is on, its most destructive weapon will be the first chosen.

"Let us make the attack, therefore, upon the institution of war itself as an institution and outlaw it by a common agreement among the nations of the earth. Let there be an agreement among the civilized nations that war is itself a crime. That is the basis of their fight.

Swanson Recalls Conference Plan.

Senator Swanson recalled the fact that during the Washington Conference the British delegation had proposed the abolition of the submarine as an implement of war and that Secretary Hughes, as chairman of the American delegation, had declared that the American Government was seriously impressed with the British proposal.

"If the agreements reached in the Washington conference are lived up to," said Senator Swanson, "the submarine, so far as five of the great powers is concerned, will be robbed of much of its efficacy as a weapon for use in time of war.

"That conference agreed to a treaty in relation to the use of submarines and stated with clarity and force the existing rules of international law which condemned the abhorrent practices followed in the use of submarines against merchant vessels.

"The conference adopted a treaty by

Continued on Page Ten.

Gen. Sarrail, Arriving in Paris, Rebuffs His Successor's Attempt to Discuss Syria

Special Cable to THE NEW YORK TIMES.

PARIS, Nov. 15.—General Sarrail has come back to Paris to meet the storm of criticism and defend his administration of France's mandate in Syria before a Parliamentary Commission. When he was asked by the Government to come and give this full report on the situation his recall was not ordered in such definite fashion as to indicate he would not return. But this morning one of the first persons the returning General met on the station platform was his successor, Senator Henry de Jouvenel. Their meeting at once took a dramatic turn.

"You should not have troubled to come to meet me," were the General's first words. De Jouvenel made a courteous reply and wished to fix an hour when he could discuss the situation as he was anxious to have all opinions. General Sarrail barked back:

"You have sent Reiffye back there. He can inform you."

Reiffye was the civil adviser to the High Commissioner whom Sarrail dismissed and whom de Jouvenel has reinstated.

At this outburst De Jouvenel stepped back. "As you like," he said, "but I have considered it my duty to seek information everywhere and have sought the advice of Generals Gouraud and Weygand, your predecessors."

"Well, that should be enough," was Sarrail's rejoinder.

Politely though coldly de Jouvenel insisted, and grudgingly, a rendezvous was made. It was of course secret as was the conversation the returning General had during the morning with Premier Painlevé. His explanations of a more public nature will be given before the Parliamentary commission this week.

To the press the General's statements were terse. He was far from pessimistic, he said. Only determination was needed to straighten things out. Then he hastened to add that in Syria he was only the executive agent and hinted other interests were at work which perhaps were more responsible than his administrtion for recent troubles.

Tut-ankh-Amen Mummy Laden With Jewels; It Has Gold Stalls on Its Fingers and Toes

By Wireless to THE NEW YORK TIMES.

CAIRO, Egypt, Nov. 15.—The mummy of Tut-ankh-Amen is loaded with rare and precious jewels, an official communiqué issued tonight reveals. It wears sandals of gold and has stalls of gold on all the finger and toe nails. It declares that the body is in a much emaciated condition.

The communiqué, which covers work at the tomb up to Nov. 13, confirming the main lines of the dispatches to THE NEW YORK TIMES, says:

Howard Carter commenced the examination of the mummy on Nov. 11. This had to be carried out with the mummy in situ, since it could not be removed from the coffin without injury. The outer surfaces of the mummy's wrappings, which were in a most fragile condition, were first strengthened by means of a thin coating of paraffin wax, after which Professor Derry made a longitudinal incision extending from mask to feet.

The outer coverings being turned back, exposed the next layers of wrappings, which proved to be equally carbonized and decayed. In these circumstances any orderly unwrapping was manifestly impossible.

As the work proceeded a large number of interesting and beautiful objects were gradually revealed. At each stage of the proceedings photographic records were taken.

Among the objects found were amulets and collarettes, a superb gold dagger with a crystal handle, bracelets of intricate workmanship, a large number of finger rings of diverse materials and designs, some having scarabs bearing the Kings' names for their bezels; a second dagger, larger and even more beautiful than the first, several large inlaid pectorals, beadwork ornaments, gold circlets, &c.

So far the work of uncovering the mummy has proceeded to the exposure of the lower part of the body and limbs. According to the opinion of anatomical experts the evidence so far revealed that there is no doubt the body is that of a male, not yet adult. The body is much emaciated and carbonized. On the feet are golden sandals and on each toe and finger are golden stalls. Up to the present there is no trace of documents. Both the right and left forearms are loaded with magnificent jewels. The jewelry discovered so far on the King, who lies in the coffin, is made of heavy solid gold, and is far beyond anticipation. Work of such delicate nature must necessarily proceed slowly. The cleansing and restoration of these wonderful objects will be continued as soon as the examination of the mummy is finished. For this reason, and in order that they may be transferred to the Cairo Museum in the quickest possible time, for exhibition, visits to the tomb are suspended till the work is completed.

I understand that the gold coffin weighs so much that it took eight men to lift it. Although the communiqué states that no documents have been discovered, I have reason to believe that a wonderful specimen of the Book of the Dead lies in the coffin. There is besides every indication that a number of discoveries are still to be made in chambers of the tomb not yet opened.

REPUBLICANS READY TO START A REVOLT

Waterman League Acts This Week to Make Itself Permanent Party Organization.

CITY LEADERS UNDER FIRE

Wadsworth Involved by Discontent in Brooklyn Under Livingston's Rule.

Republicans who are up in arms against the leadership of their party in this city before long may have a banner of revolt under which to rally. Announcement was made yesterday that the Waterman's Business Men's League would hold a meeting late this week to consider ways and means to convert that organization from a mere campaign agency and establish it on a permanent basis with units in every Assembly district, and, if possible, every election district.

After a long succession of defeats in Mayoralty and other local elections there is deep dissatisfaction with the Republican leaders among disinterested members of their party throughout the city. It is no exaggeration to say that a spirit of revolt is brooding and that it extends to virtually every Assembly district in the five boroughs. Although up to the present time no Republican actively identified with the work of the party has been found to take the initiative in a fight on the party leaders, the consensus of reports which reach political observers indicates that the situation is only waiting upon some one with the courage and the means to assume the leadership.

So far most of the grumbling among Republicans has been directed against Samuel S. Koenig, leader of the Republican organization in Manhattan. But in Brooklyn, where Jacob A. Livingston is the executive head of the Republican organizations, the situation is said to be fully as bad and discontent with the leadership fully as rife as in Manhattan.

If the leaders in Bronx, Queens and Richmond have escaped open criticism so far, it is said to be due to the fact that those boroughs are less important units in the city organization and not because the voters feel that the leaders in those boroughs acquitted themselves of their task in the recent election with any more credit to themselves than did Mr. Koenig and Mr. Livingston.

Joseph H. De Bragga, for instance, veteran leader of the Republican forces in Queens, which, with the new influx of voters from Manhattan and Brooklyn, is becoming a promising field for the Republican Party, lost everything. According to Republican workers in that borough Mr. De Bragga is pretty much of a stranger at the headquarters of his own organization in Long Island City. Party men from the borough, when they want to confer with their leaders, most of the time must go to Brooklyn, where Mr. De Bragga holds a job in the courts.

W. J. Wells Heads League.

At the head of the Waterman Business Men's League, which is composed exclusively of Republicans who, until the time of the Waterman campaign, had never been asked actively to identify themselves with the work of their party, is William J. Wells, general manager of R. H. Macy & Co.

"I am not at the present time authorized to speak for the league and am speaking only for myself," Mr. Wells said. "I think there is great need for a change in the Republican organizations in this city. We saw them function in the recent election and became convinced that the Republican Party has no organization worth the name in the City of New York.

"What little the party has in the way of an organization is a flimsy structure which does not function at all except a few weeks before an election and then only in a half-hearted fashion.

"I think there is reason as well as a demand for another organization if the Republican Party is not willing to maintain its organization on an effective footing and conduct its work according to methods that are modern and can win the approval of business men.

"It is my own personal opinion that we ought to find out what strength we can command and how far we can go

Continued on Page Two.

COUSIN OF HARDING, GIRL OF 15, MISSING

Mother, Wife of a Bank Official Here, Fears She Was Kidnapped and Starts Search.

LEFT HER HOME ON FRIDAY

Girl Phoned in Evening She Was Going to Movies With Friend, but Did Not Return.

Isabel Bennett, 15 years old, of 500 West 165th Street, a second cousin of the late President Warren G. Harding, was reported yesterday as missing from home since Friday, and her mother said she believed it was possible the girl was kidnapped.

The mother, Mrs. Frank Bent, wife of an official in a downtown bank, was divorced from Isabel's father, John B. Bennett, a first cousin of Mr. Harding, in Cleveland, Ohio, last June. Dispatches from Cleveland said Mr. Bennett, an automobile salesman employed by the William Bennett Motor Company, left that city four months ago.

Mrs. Bent reported Isabel's disappearance Saturday morning, but the police kept it secret until last night. She said that her maid told her Isabel got a telephone message Friday afternoon from a girl named Sara Cohen and went out immediately to join her. Mrs. Bent said she herself was then at a hospital, visiting a sick friend, but at 6 o'clock she received a telephone call from her daughter who said she and Sara Cohen intended to go to a motion picture and that she would not be home for dinner.

Mrs. Bent said she was not worried when Isabel did not return by 10 o'clock because she had a key to the apartment and often came in from similar excursions at later hours. She and Mr. Bent retired at 11 o'clock with the girl still absent, she said, but she became worried a few hours later when she awoke and found Isabel had not come in. In the morning she reported her daughter's absence to the West 152d Street Police Station.

Girl Large for Her Age.

Detective Hauptmann, who was assigned to the case, reported that he sought to find a Sara Cohen, with whom Isabel said she went to the movies. He said he found two girls of that name in the neighborhood, but both said they were not acquainted with Isabel. No girl of that name has been reported missing. Hauptmann was unable to learn whether Isabel had attended a motion picture theatre in the neighborhood.

Isabel was described as large for her age—5 feet 7 inches tall. She is blond, with straight bobbed hair, blue eyes and a fair complexion. When she left home she wore a dark blue cloth coat with squirrel fur trimming, a blue hat trimmed with silver braid, a black silk dress, black shoes and light-colored stockings.

Until last June she was a pupil of Drew Seminary at Carmel, N. Y., where she had been for five years. Since then, her mother said, she has been studying professional dancing of the ballroom variety at several studios in the city, but spent most of her time at home.

Mrs. Bent said her daughter was fond of parties and often went to them with young men acquaintances, but said she was sure the girl had had no love affair.

"She told me everything, and I would have known if there was anything like that," said Mrs. Bent. "There is only fifteen years difference in our ages and we were more like sisters than mother and daughter. I am sure she hasn't gone away with any one. More likely she may have been lifted into an automobile and carried away by some one."

Mrs. Bent obtained a divorce from Mr. Bennett in June and was married a few months later to Mr. Bent. She said the girl's father has not communicated with Isabel.

The police investigated yesterday a report that Isabel had gone to a dance at a boat club at the Harlem River

Continued on Page Eight.

FIND PHILISTINE FORT BURNED BY DAVID FOR DEATH OF KING SAUL

Excavators Uncover Battleground of Egyptians on Top of Hill of Beth-Shan.

BIBLE HISTORY CONFIRMED

Monument of Rameses II. Tells of Hebrews' Sojourn and of Early Religions.

OBJECTS FROM STONE AGE

Figures of Goddess Ashtaroth Also Discovered in Mountain of Archaeology in Palestine.

The excavation of forts and battlegrounds where Saul and David fought the Philistines is described by Alan Rowe, field director of the Palestine expedition of the University of Pennsylvania Museum of Philadelphia, in a report which was made public here yesterday by Dr. George Byron Gordon, Director of the Museum.

Fortresses successively occupied by the Egyptians, Philistines and Israelites have been unearthed on the top of the hill of Beth-Shan near the Jordan, laying bare the wall on which the Philistines hung the body of Saul. The interior of the wall is blackened by an ancient conflagration believed to have been set about 1,000 B. C. as part of the revenge for the death of Saul, which was wreaked on the Philistine city by David after he conquered it. A quantity of baked clay objects belonging to the cult of Ashtaroth have been collected among the remnants of a building which is apparently the temple of Ashtaroth, in which, according to I. Samuel, the armor of King Saul was hung.

Figures of the goddess Ashtaroth were found in association with quantities of Egyptian objects, indicating that the temple was originally erected by the Egyptians, who held the hill of Beth-Shan for several centuries before it was seized by the Philistines, who in turn were dispossessed by the Israelites.

The excavation, which is being pressed by 200 workmen, is illuminating the rise of the goddess Ashtaroth, who was apparently introduced originally by the Egyptians into Palestine and Syria, where she was worshiped for centuries. The Greeks are believed to have taken her over and worshiped her as Aphrodite.

Go Back to the Stone Age.

The excavators, in two previous seasons, stripped off several layers of the débris of civilizations which occupied the Beth-Shan in later times, before they exposed the Egyptian-Israelite-Palestine complex. The top layer was Arab. Under that were relics of the Crusaders, who made a strong point of this hill when they held Palestine. At an earlier level were remains representing the great Arab movement of conquest. Christian, Roman and Greek layers were beneath this. Then came the evidences of the Hebrew conquest about 2,900 years ago. The Egyptians go back to about 3,200 years ago. Layer after layer of earlier civilizations are still to be explored, for the cultures that lie on top of the hill go back through the Bronze Age to the Stone Age.

As a strong point on the highway between Asia and Africa, the hill was always a stragetic location, with the capital of the Jezreel and Jordan Valleys near it. Each successive location has left behind it a layer of building materials, pottery, tools, weapons and other imperishable or slowly perishable objects. Century after century these deposits have solidified into the structure of the hill until there are in places 150 thicknesses of relics of ancient human habitation.

So far the expedition has only touched the surface of this massive archaeological quarry, but much of interest relating to Biblical lore and to the early movements of races and religions of Syria has come to light. One of the great finds has been a large engraved stone monument erected by Rameses II, which contains the first information outside the Bible about the sojourn of the Hebrews in Egypt.

Confirms Account in Exodus.

In spite of the plagues, the destruction of Pharaoh's army in the Red Sea and the other stirring events of the sojourn in Egypt, as described by the Hebrew

Continued on Page Eleven.

Bellboy Has Half-Hour Career as Bandit; Robs 2 Taxi Drivers of $9.50 and Is Caught

Half an hour's career of crime late Saturday night resulted in Leo Fayette, 16 years old, of Watertown, N. Y., netting $9.50, the proceeds of holding up two taxicab chauffeurs, being arrested a few minutes afterward and then held in $23,000 bail on three charges of robbery and violation of the Sullivan law.

In explanation to the police the lad said he turned hold-up man in order to obtain money for medical attention.

The two taxicab chauffeurs both identified the boy after he had been arrested at 143d Street, near Third Avenue. He had $15.75 and a loaded revolver in his pocket, the police say.

Fayette said he was employed as a bellboy at the Hotel Hamilton, Seventy-third Street near Columbus Avenue, and since his arrival here had been living with his brother, Cleophus, at 2,081 Grove Street, Brooklyn.

According to the police, he engaged a taxicab at 142d Street and Third Avenue and ordered the driver, Anthony Ferraro, to drive him to 144th Street. He stopped the cab between St. Ann's and Brooks Avenues, and then held up Ferraro at the point of a revolver, taking $5 from him.

As the lad walked away Ferraro went to look for a policeman. In the few minutes that elapsed before he found one, Fayette hailed a cab driven by Alexander Rice and told Rice to drive to 142d Street. When the cab had gone a block or two the lad stopped it, covered Rice with his revolver and took $4.50 from him.

Fayette remained in the vicinity, the police believe, looking for another victim. He was seen by Ferraro, who had picked up Patrolman Kurner. He was arrested and taken to the Alexander Avenue station.

Arraigned before Magistrate Albert Vitale in the Morrisania Court yesterday morning, he was held for the Grand Jury.

Paris Drops 'Wave' for 'Swirl' In Trend Toward Long Hair

PARIS, Nov. 15 (AP).—Permanent swirls are now to the fore. The permanent wave has been discarded and all fashionable hairdressers are advertising the swirl.

Skilful hairdressers can place the hair permanently in upward curves and conceal neck and head lines which do not harmonize with prevailing fashions. But the swirl requires longer hair than the prevailing modes and is regarded by many fashions experts as the first step back to long hair.

This new style in curliness is especially in demand among women with square heads and phrenological bumps which do not lend themselves to the lines of beauty for which artists and modistes are always striving.

Extremely youthful women with perfect heads do well with the short shingle and can plaster their hair back straight like a college sophomore. But heavy women, especially elderly women, have to try some other style, and the swirl seems to be the most satisfactory.

METHODIST BOARD ATTACKS GOV. SMITH

Declares His Proposed Candidacy for President Is "Astonishing Effrontery."

WARNS SOUTH AGAINST HIM

Cites "Tammany Defiance" on Liquor Issue and Walker's Prizefighting Connections.

Special to The New York Times.

WASHINGTON, Nov. 15.—The Board of Temperance, Prohibition and Public Morals of the Methodist Episcopal Church has issued a statement attacking Governor Smith of New York as a candidate for President and criticizing Mr. Walker's connection with prizefighting legislation. The statement is as follows:

"Press reports state that Mayor-elect Walker of New York City is to make a southern trip in the interest of Tammany, and presumably in the interests of Governor Al Smith. The South will be interested to know Mr. Walker's connection with New York's odorous prizefighting game and with those elements in New York which are doing their best to murder American standards of morality.

"The advancement of Governor Al Smith as a proposed Presidential candidate is, in view of the circumstances of the last campaign astonishing effrontery, and there is no doubt it will so appear to the South. Mr. Walker, who will experience a courteous hospitality not given to Mr. McAdoo's Southern delegates at the New York convention, need not be misled thereby into believing that the South will support the country's foremost political champion of the liquor interests.

"The South has come into a new and wonderful prosperity which is the fruit of two generations of careful, intelligent conservation of the merits of the pre-war civilization and of devoted industry for fifty lean years. It has kept the faith and now has the sympathy and understanding of the entire country in the difficulties which are rapidly being cleared away, a sympathy no less than Southern pride in Northern industry and economic achievement.

"Let the South remember the defiance by Tammany of the Democratic decision rendered by the South, West and a large portion of the East that the liquor traffic shall not be legalized and protected in its exploitation of the American people. Let it remember the propaganda which is systematically organized to incite to crime in the South and West in order that the prohibition law may be overthrown by these criminal activities. Let us remember that Governor Al Smith and his friends were the first political group in America to introduce a religious issue into a convention of a political party, an atrocious thing to do in a country where all religions stand upon the same basis.

"The effort to make it appear that Governor Smith's opponents are 'prejudiced' against his religion is as false now as it was then. To an American they have more respect for a good Catholic than they have for a bad Protestant. But they will never accept as a President a man whose conduct of

Continued on Page Two.

WALKER INCLINES TO TAMMANY MAN FOR POLICE HEAD

He Feels the Organization Should Take Responsibility for All City Government.

FRIENDS SOUND WARNING

But He Thinks Frawley and McCue, District Leaders, Right Type for the Place.

TRANSIT POLICY STILL OPEN

Mayor-Elect, Unlike Hylan, Will Hear Commission's Plea for Unification Plan.

Special to The New York Times.

MIAMI, Fla., Nov. 15.—A member of Tammany Hall, perhaps a district leader, is being considered for appointment as Police Commissioner of New York City by Mayor-elect James J. Walker, it was learned today.

While the selection of a Tammany man is by no means certain, Senator Walker having been advised against it, he has told friends that he is not sure a Tammany man should not be named and responsibility for the administration of the police department placed on the Tammany organization as it will be for the rest of the city government after Jan. 1.

James J. Frawley and Martin C. McCue, both Tammany district leaders, have been mentioned by Senator Walker as men in the organization of the type he believes would make an acceptable Police Commissioner. He has told friends he believed that neither of these two, each of whom formerly served in the State Senate, would be influenced either by policemen seeking promotion or preferment in the department or by politicians seeking favors.

Would Mark Change in Policy.

The appointment of a Tammany man to head the Police Department would be a departure from the policy of Charles F. Murphy, whose political strategy during the last years of his leadership was to keep control of the Police Department as far removed from Tammany Hall as possible. It was Mr. Murphy's belief that success for the organization in New York City elections could be threatened seriously only by a police scandal.

Friends of Senator Walker have advised him to "play safe" on the police question by appointing a politically independent citizen or an army officer of the type of Major Gen. Summerall, and have warned him that the choosing of a Tammany member would probably alienate popular and newspaper opinion. The suggestion has also been made that he should appoint a business man. But Senator Walker, so far, has been disinclined to name either a business man or a soldier.

Since his trip South the Mayor-elect, according to his friends, has become inclined to believe that Tammany should accept responsibility for the administration of the Police Department and not try to "duck" it. He has told them that it seemed to him inconsistent to try to "sell" Tammany to the rest of the country, as he did in his recent speech in Atlanta, as a progressive and courageous political organization and then by the appointment of an outsider to admit that it had no one capable of handling the police situation in New York City.

Senator Walker, it is said, also believes that the Chief Inspector of the Police Department should have somewhat more power than he now has, and should be, in effect, a Chief of Police, with a civilian head over him. It is not likely, however, that he will go to the length of increasing the Chief Inspector's powers by legislation of the Municipal Assembly, but will merely make some one more completely responsible for the handling of the uniformed force.

He will make no decision as to the Police Commissioner and other appointments until after his return to New York City, which from present indications will be about Dec. 1. He will then consult George W. Olvany, Governor Smith and other leaders of Tammany.

Senator Walker today had his first real rest since his arrival in Miami on Friday. He passed most of the day at the home of his host, Charles F. Flynn, managing director of the Miami-Biltmore, at Coral Gables. His plans for this week are indefinite, as his visit here is purely for a vacation, but he expects to go on a fishing trip tomorrow or Tuesday.

WALKER TO TAKE UP TRANSIT.

Will Confer With Commission on Return From the South.

There is every assurance that the aloofness that has marked the relations between Mayor Hylan and the State Transit Commission will be absent from the Administration of his successor. This is said to be the situation despite the opposition, repeatedly voiced by Mayor-elect James J. Walker in speeches he delivered during the campaign, to the so-called "unification" plan of the Transit Commission. This plan would involve the taking over by the city of all the transportation lines within the municipal borders at a valuation to be agreed upon by the commission, the city authorities and the transit corporations and their consolidation into one all-inclusive municipally controlled transit system.

It is learned that soon after his return from the South, the Mayor-elect will confer with the Transit Commission, which is engaged in preparing for

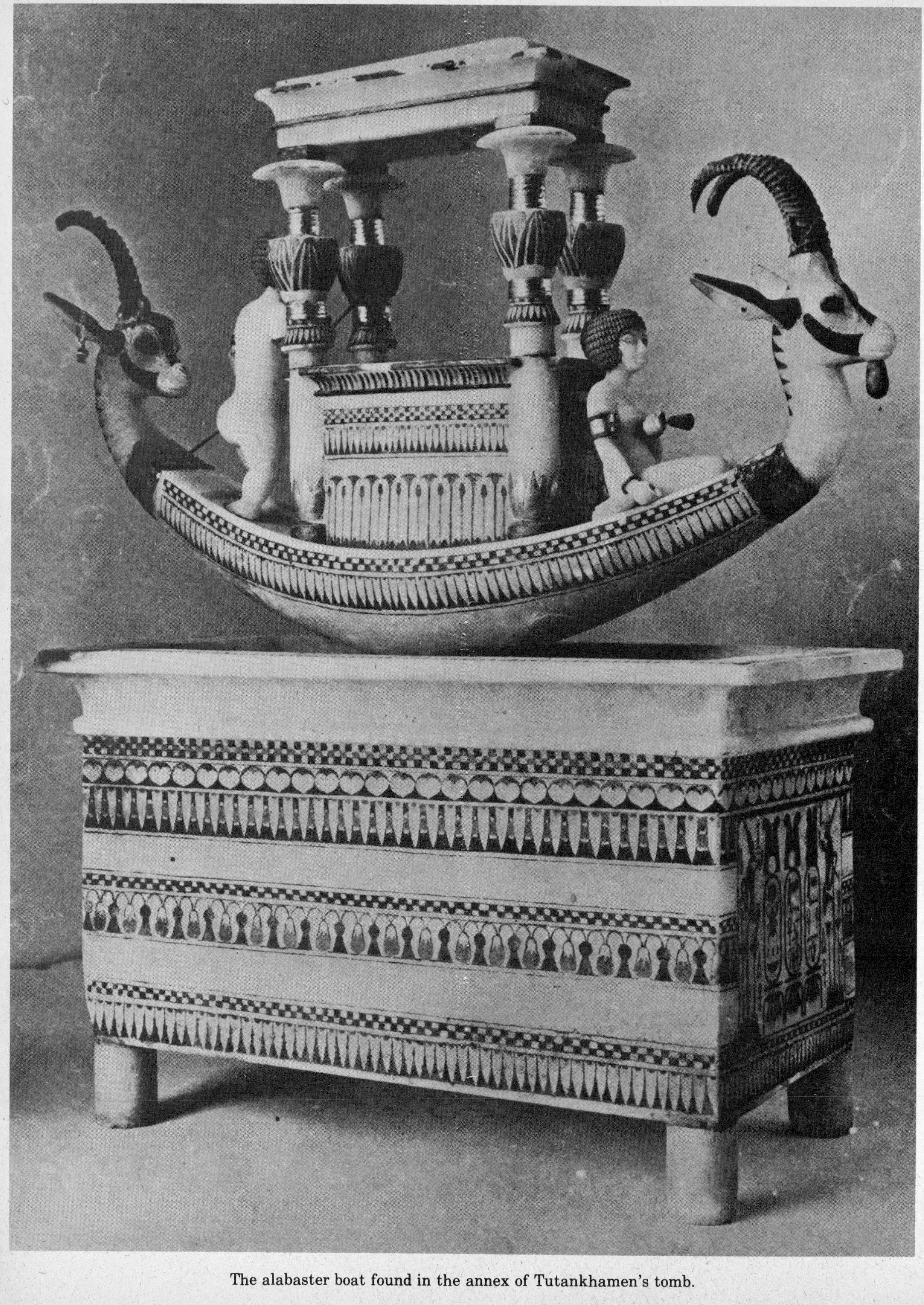

The alabaster boat found in the annex of Tutankhamen's tomb.

"All the News That's Fit to Print."

The New York Times.

THE WEATHER
Cloudy and warmer, probably showers, today; tomorrow showers.
Temperature yesterday—Max., 64; min., 42.
For weather report see Page 45.

VOL. LXXV....No. 24,943. NEW YORK, MONDAY, MAY 10, 1926. TWO CENTS In Greater New York | THREE CENTS Within 200 Miles | FOUR CENTS Elsewhere in the U. S.

BYRD FLIES TO NORTH POLE AND BACK; ROUND TRIP FROM KINGS BAY IN 15 HRS. 51 MIN.; CIRCLES TOP OF THE WORLD SEVERAL TIMES

BALDWIN STRATEGY IS WINNING STRIKE FOR GOVERNMENT

Aggressive Action Keeps Vital Services Going as Unions Balk at "Trump Cards."

THOMAS'S TALK SIGNIFICANT

Both Sides Spend a Quiet Sunday, While London Sees Another Food Convoy.

FOOD PRICES KEPT DOWN

Only Rise Allowed Is for Milk—Incoming Cargoes Are Unloaded and Distributed.

By T. R. YBARRA.

Copyright, 1926, by The New York Times Company. Special Cable to THE NEW YORK TIMES.

LONDON, May 9.—The essence of strategy is robbing the enemy of his freedom of action. If that axiom be transferred from the domain of warfare to that of strikes it must be admitted tonight that so far the British Government, led by Premier Baldwin, has robbed leaders of Britain's great general strike of their freedom of action.

At the close of the sixth day of this gigantic industrial struggle it becomes increasingly apparent that even if the British Government has not won the game yet it has consistently forced the play.

From the very outset of the great strike, at midnight last Monday, most of the aggressiveness recorded has been contributed by those seeking to crush the strike. Each day brings increased railway service. Each day shows a more efficient organization of the Government's emergency food distributing services. Each day has shown a bigger enrollment of volunteers in every branch of strike breaking. Each day has shown hesitation on the part of the strikers to play their trump cards.

They have not tried to smash the great food distribution organization of the Government. They have not called out the "second line of defense" and the "third line of defense." Will they? That is the question, asked in a constantly growing tone of skepticism by those who have lived through these first six days of one of the greatest industrial crises in the entire history of the world.

Thomas Adds to Skepticism.

Tonight this skepticism received decided impetus from J. H. Thomas, the noted labor leader, who has been consistently against extremist measures in the fight to find a panacea for British labor grievances. Speaking at Hammersmith, a London suburb, Mr. Thomas made statements which, as befits a conservative trying to please the moderates without infuriating the extremists, partook largely of the nature of those "weasel words" which so infuriated the late Theodore Roosevelt in the heyday of his acrimonious political combats.

Nevertheless, stripping the speech of all its diplomatic "I don't want to displease anybody" quality, there are in it statements which clearly imply that the general strike is not going exactly as its instigators hoped and that, therefore, Moderates like Mr. Thomas are beginning to hope that the dawn of conciliation is approaching. The most striking statement in Thomas's speech is:

"If the people who talk about a fight to a finish carried it out in that sense the country would not be worth having at the end of it."

"I have never disguised and I do not disguise now that I have never been in favor of the principle of the general strike," said Mr. Thomas. "No one will disagree, however, that the fundamental principle of trade unionism is not only the right for men and women to organize, but the essential part of that legal right is collective bargaining. The workers have no right to say to the employers, 'You must negotiate under the threat of a strike,' but it is equally right and just that the workers should not be asked to carry on negotiations under the threat of a lockout.

"From the start I deliberately went in to get peace. Let there be no mistake about that, and in spite of all that has been said I repeat that it is the duty of both sides to keep the door open.

Extols Workers' Solidarity.

"The response to the appeal of the Trades Union Congress has been the most wonderful, the most marvelous demonstration of solidarity the world has ever seen and has staggered your opponents.

"All attempts to raise the constitutional issue are not only wrong, but

Continued on Page Five.

Strikers Urged 'to Stick to It' If 'Further Steps' Are Needed

LONDON, May 9 (AP).—C. T. Cramp, President of the National Union of Railwaymen, addressing a strikers' meeting in London today, warned that it might be necessary "to take further steps" to gain that for which they were fighting. He said:

"We have entered this fight as railwaymen because we realize that if the miners' standards of living is depressed below the present level, it would not be long before the remainder of the organized workers would find themselves in the same position."

If it were necessary to take further steps to uphold the things which they now required, he asked his hearers to "stick to it," remarking:

"If I am going into a scrap I prefer to scrap with both hands and not with one tied behind my back."

BALFOUR DENOUNCES REVOLUTION INTENT

He Calls Upon Britons to Save "the Civilization of Which They Are the Trustees."

SAYS NATION FACES RUIN

Declares Success of the Revolt Would Put a Minority of Extremists in Power.

Copyright, 1926, by The New York Times Company By Wireless to THE NEW YORK TIMES.

LONDON, May 9.—The Earl of Balfour declares the general strike to be an attempt at revolution "which would bring ruin, swift, complete and irresistible upon this country," in a statement upon the industrial conflict which appears in tonight's issue of The British Gazette, the official Government organ.

"From such a fate," concludes Lord Balfour, "may the courage and resolution of our countrymen save the civilization of which they are the trustees."

Lord Balfour's Statement.

The text of Lord Balfour's statement is as follows:

"Two hundred and thirty-eight years have passed since a revolution occurred in this country, whose object was to secure the supremacy of parliamentary government and the traditional liberties of our people. Through eight generations it has proved successful.

"But we are now threatened, it seems, with a revolution of a very different kind, and it behooves us seriously to consider what would be its actual results were it, unhappily, to succeed.

"Its methods are being practiced before our eyes; they are to deprive the people of food, transport, employment and a free press. The conveniences of civilized life, which long have been counted among its necessities, are in some cases to be immensely diminished, in others to be brought to an end.

"Personal security is to be threatened; industry is to be seriously hampered, even when it is not wholly stopped. Willing workers are to be kept in idleness; anxious purchasers are to be kept in want; perishable food is to rot in port. All the wheels of social life are to be clogged.

"Such are the methods of the revolutionary movement. What, then, are its objects?

"The nominal object is to maintain unchanged existing conditions of the miners' remuneration as regards hours of work and rates of pay. Now, there is no man who does not heartily share this desire; but neither is there any man who has read the coal mines report who thinks it can be satisfied under existing conditions.

"Were the revolution to succeed tomorrow, the country would suffer, but the miner would not gain.

"No revolution in Great Britain, however triumphant, is going to diminish foreign competition in neutral markets; no revolution is going to hasten the changes recommended by the commission in the methods and organization of the mining industry; no revolution is going to compel the mine owner indefinitely to carry on his industry at a loss. Revolutionary methods would be completely powerless except for evil.

"On the other hand, their power for evil is beyond calculation. All strikes, all lockouts are costly both to employers and employed.

"But neither in fact, nor, I believe, in law, is the course advocated by the trades unions a strike in the proper sense of the term. It is what I have called it—an attempted revolution.

"Were it to succeed, the community would henceforth be ruled not by Parliament, not by the Parliamentary Labor Party, not by the rank and file of the trades unions, not by the moderate members of the Trades Union Council, but by a relatively small body of extremists, who regard

Continued on Page Five.

WETS NOW DEMAND SENATORS SUMMON GARY, ROCKEFELLER

In Brief Filed Today With the Committee They Call for Noted Drys' Testimony.

AIM OF GIFTS CHALLENGED

End of Anti-Trust Prosecution Is Charged When 'Big Business' Allied With Prohibition.

WAYNE WHEELER ATTACKED

Subpoenas Are Urged for Counsel of Anti-Saloon League and the Congress Members in Its Pay.

Special to The New York Times.

WASHINGTON, May 9.—A demand that the Senate Judiciary Committee reopen its prohibition hearings and subpoena Wayne B. Wheeler, John D. Rockefeller Jr., Judge Elbert H. Gary and others and ask them to disclose the sources of the great sums expended by the Anti-Saloon League, is made in a brief which will be filed tomorrow by the wets.

Denouncing Mr. Wheeler for not "keeping his word" to appear as a witness at the recent hearings, the brief declares the anti-prohibitionists wish to question him about the $35,000,000 he has asserted was used by the drys in their fight for the Eighteenth Amendment.

The wets assert that Mr. Wheeler should be forced to tell about contributions by Mr. Rockefeller, Judge Gary and other captains of industry and also "as to the significance of the strange phenomenon that after the alliance of the Anti-Saloon League and big business to keep up a continuous ferment or smoke screen over prohibition, anti-trust prosecutions suddenly ceased."

Members of the House and Senate who have admitted that they are on the League's payroll should also be summoned, as well as Dr. Ernest H. Cherrington of the World League Against Alcohol, who like Mr. Wheeler, escaped cross-examination by Senator Reed, the wets insist.

"Let us have the whole story of prohibition propaganda and prohibition politics as well asthe sordid story of prohibition itself," the brief states.

Attack Centred on Reformers.

There is a review of the testimony given at the hearings, but it is upon Mr. Wheeler that the fire is centred.

Declaring that prohibition is costing the United States $500,000,000 annually in direct enforcement and loss of revenue, the wets contend that this is too heavy a price, "even to keep the unctuous Mr. Wheeler—quite voluble enough in the open forum but silent as a clam when it comes to testifying under oath before this committee—in a lifetime job as a parasite upon misguided religious and industrial organizations, and as a super-Government in his own divine right."

Mrs. Ella Boole, President of the Women's Christian Temperance Union is severely criticized for refusing to reply to questions as to whether it would be better to sell mild alcoholic beverages in the open or to allow them to be made at home in the presence of children.

Dr. E. C. Dinwiddie, while described as a man who has earned his living for twenty-seven years as a professional reformer, is complimented as "the highest type of professional dry."

Prohibition has brought in its wake increased drunkenness, secret drinking, deaths from alcoholism, corruption in Government, extensive bootlegging and a widespread use of the still in the home, the wets assert in the brief. Women and children are drinking today, there is an army of rum-runners and moonshiners, denatured alcohol can be easily renatured and prohibition has been an utter failure from a temperance standpoint, the brief adds.

The example of Canada, which sells liquor under Government regulation, is contrasted with conditions in the United States where the public morale has been broken, the modificationists assert.

Reopening of Hearing Unlikely.

In spite of the strenuous nature of the plea for a reopening of the hearings, the request of the wets probably will go unheeded. The Senate subcommittee is 4 to 1 dry, Senator Reed of Missouri, being the only modificationist upon it.

So arid is the committee that there also seems to be no chance that it will favorably report any of the bills which would authorize a modification of the

Continued on Page Twelve.

Only 147 Workless in Paris, Says French Labor Minister

TOURS, France, May 9 (AP).—There are only 147 unemployed persons in Paris, whereas London before the strike there had 800,000 and Berlin 450,000, Minister of Labor Durafour said at a banquet inaugurating the Tours exposition week.

France's birth rate, the Minister asserted, hardly varied from 1913 figures of 192 births for each 10,000 of population, whereas German statistics for the same units of population were 283 in 1913 and 200 in 1926. England, he said, shows 238 in 1913 and 186 in 1926.

"We have done this by organizing against infant mortality," the Minister affairmed, "which, although 13 per cent. before the war, had fallen to 9 per cent. in 1925. Therefore we must not despair. Our percentages of births equal Germany's and surpass England's."

NO TRACE OF WARD; FAMILY IS ALARMED

Brother, Fearing Foul Play, Asks Police to Broadcast Alarm for Missing Man.

SEARCH ON IN THREE STATES

Trenton Police Suspect Ruse in Abandoning His Car—Race Tracks to Be Watched.

The police began a search for Walter S. Ward yesterday at the request of his brother, Ralph D. Ward, who reported his disappearance to the Missing Persons Bureau at Police Headquarters. Mr. Ward said that his brother, who was acquitted three years ago of the murder of Clarence M. Peters, had not been seen or heard from since last Wednesday and that his family feared foul play.

Captain John Ayres, in command of the Missing Persons Bureau, broadcast a confidential alarm for Ward, with his description, among all the police stations in the metropolitan district. Detectives working on the case said last night that they had no clue to Ward's whereabouts, and had no idea whether he had been killed or had disappeared for some reason known only to himself.

No Clue in Abandoned Car.

Ward's automobile was found in Trenton, N. J., last Friday morning, with the windshield broken and a large stone on the front seat. There was neither anything in the car nor any witness to clear up the mysterious circumstances under which the machine had been abandoned.

Ralph Ward told Captain Ayres that at the time his brother disappeared he had been on a business trip to Baltimore on behalf of the Electruck Corporation of 532 West Forty-sixth Street, of which Walter S. Ward is President. Ralph Ward did not know, he said, whether his brother had reached Baltimore and was on his way back or was driving to Baltimore when the car was abandoned.

To reporters who called at his home, 1,010 Fifth Avenue, at Eighty-second Street, Ralph Ward said:

"Walter went to Baltimore early in the week, but came back to New York and was seen here on Wednesday. He went away again in his car and was to have returned home again on Thursday, but we have not seen him since Wednesday."

Thinks It Was Second Trip.

"Was he going to Baltimore on his second trip?"

"I believe so," replied his brother.

"On business?"

"Presumably."

"Have you any clue to what has become of him?"

"Absolutely none," said the brother. "We have no idea what has become of him or where he is."

"Do you think that violence is indicated?"

"Yes, that is the only possible explanation."

Ralph Ward said that the family intended to investigate to see whether Walter might have had an enemy who could have had a motive for attacking him.

At Walter Ward's home, 30 West Seventieth Street, it was said that the missing man's wife was too ill to see reporters. A physician was in attendance on her yesterday morning. Ralph Ward told the police and reporters that his sister-in-law had been "prostrated" by her husband's disappearance.

George S. Ward, former head of a bakery chain company, and father of Walter and Ralph Ward, has been in the South for some time but is expected back soon, it was said at his home.

The Ward family is said to have engaged private detectives to search for

Continued on Page Ten.

PEARY'S OBSERVATIONS ARE CONFIRMED

Flight Is Favored by Sunlight and the Absence of Fog; Sun Compass Functions Perfectly

LEAK DEVELOPS IN PLANE'S OIL SYSTEM NEAR POLE

But Byrd Insists on Going On, Overruling Pilot Bennett—Commander's Nose and Fingers Frozen in Zero Temperature

By WILLIAM BIRD.

The New York Times Correspondent With the Byrd Expedition.

Copyright, 1926, by The New York Times Company and The St. Louis Post-Dispatch. By Wireless to THE NEW YORK TIMES.

KINGS BAY, Spitzbergen, May 9.—America's claim to the North Pole was cinched tonight when, after a flight of fifteen hours and fifty-one minutes, Commander Richard E. Byrd and Floyd Bennett, his pilot, returned to announce that they had flown to the Pole, circling it several times and verifying Admiral Peary's observations completely.

They were favored by continued sunlight, and there was never the slightest fog, enabling Commander Byrd to use his sun compass and bubble sextant and obtain the most accurate observations possible. There were three magnetic compasses in the plane, but all of them deviated eccentrically after reaching high latitudes. Bennett declared that when he was piloting the magnetic compasses were wholly useless and would swing almost a quarter turn, returning very slowly.

Take Turns in Piloting.

Without the sunlight, navigation would have been almost impossible. Bennett and Commander Byrd alternated in the piloting, Bennett refilling the gasoline containers while the Commander piloted and navigated.

Commander Byrd found that the Bumstead sun compass worked perfectly, even when held in the hand, so when he was in the pilot's seat he held the control stick in one hand while he got his direction from the sun compass held in the other.

When they were within sixty miles of the Pole the oil system of the right-hand motor began leaking badly and it seemed necessary to choose between proceeding with two motors or attempting a landing to make repair

Bennett For Landing, Byrd Refuses.

In the neighborhood of the Pole numerous stretches of smooth ice were visible and a landing was favored by Bennett, but Commander Byrd, remembering his difficulties in starting at Kings Bay, vetoed this proposal.

Both agreed, however, to continue the flight to the Pole even if they went on with only two motors. To their surprise, the right-hand motor continued to work effectively, despite the ruptured oil tank, and when the Fokker returned to Kings Bay all three motors were hitting perfectly.

Chantier's Men Embrace Fliers.

The Josephine Ford, after making three circles over Kings Bay, landed at the take-off runway and taxied to her original starting position.

Commander Byrd and Bennett hurried a mile and a half to the shore, where a motor boat rushed them to the Chantier. The crew aboard her went wild with joy, waving flags and their caps. Many of the crew completely broke down with emotion, and with tears streaming from their eyes embraced the fliers.

Commander Byrd's nose and several fingers were frozen while he was taking observations in zero temperature (Fahrenheit) above the North Pole, but treatment here speedily restored circulation, and the Commander is all right now.

At 8 o'clock this morning, Greenwich Time [11 P. M. Sunday, New York Daylight Saving Time], the Norwegian radio station at Stavanger reported that heavy static was interfering with further transmission of The New York Times dispatches from Spitzbergen. These dispatches will be published tomorrow. Commander Byrd's story will be told in New York exclusively in The New York Times.

LIEUT. COMMANDER RICHARD E. BYRD, U. S. N.

The American Naval Aviator Who Flew Yesterday to the North Pole and Back.

Coolidge Sends 'Heartiest Congratulations'; Glad That Flight Was Made by an American

Special to The New York Times.

WASHINGTON, May 9.—President Coolidge received the first details of Commander Byrd's successful flight to the Pole from a radio message sent by THE NEW YORK TIMES to the Mayflower, which is cruising tonight in the lower Potomac River.

The message, sent by the Washington Bureau soon after 5 o'clock, furnished the President with all the details known at that time. In reply he radioed:

"Thanks for your message."

Later Mr. Coolidge sent by radio the following comment:

The President sends his heartiest congratulations to Commander Byrd on the report that he has flown to the North Pole. It is a matter of great satisfaction that this record has been made by an American.

The fact that the flight seems to have been accomplished without mishap demonstrates the high development of the art in this country. That it was made by a man trained in the American Navy is a great satisfaction.

CALVIN COOLIDGE.

It is well known that the President was very anxious that the flight should be made, and, although there had been some adverse criticism of the proposal, Mr. Coolidge gave his approval to the plans.

First News of Byrd's Great Feat As It Reached The New York Times

Whole Population of Kings Bay, Including the Members of the Amundsen-Ellsworth Party, Out to Welcome the Aviator.

From Staff Correspondents of The New York Times.

Copyright, 1926, by The New York Times Co and The St. Louis Post-Dispatch. By Wireless to THE NEW YORK TIMES.

KINGS BAY, Spitzbergen, Sunday, May 9, 6 P. M. Greenwich Time (2 P. M. New York Time). — Lieut. Commander Richard E. Byrd, U. S. N., leader of the Byrd Polar Expedition, returned from his flight to the North Pole in the airplane Josephine Ford at 4:20 this afternoon, Greenwich Time (12:20 P. M. New York Daylight Time).

The Commander reached the North Pole. He started at 12:50 o'clock this morning, Greenwich Time (8:50 P. M. Saturday, New York Time), which is full daylight at this time of the year in the Arctic, so that his flying time on the dash to the Pole and back was fifteen and a half hours.

[Some error in the wireless transmission of these figures is possible, according to later dispatches to THE TIMES, which state that the commander's total flying time was 15 hours 51 minutes. This is 21 minutes longer than the elapsed time here indicated. It is, however, possible, that the hour 4:20, recorded as marking the commander's return, was the moment at which the returning plane was sighted.]

The Josephine Ford had as its pilot on the trip Floyd G. Bennett, the American pilot of the Byrd Expedition.

The two were welcomed on their return by Captain Roald Amundsen, Lincoln Ellsworth and the entire crew of the airship Norge, now awaiting her chance to fly over the North Pole from Spitzbergen to Alaska, and the entire Summer population of Kings Bay, all of whom had been asleep when the airplane took off fifteen hours previously.

BYRD FAMILY PROUD OF FLIER'S SUCCESS

Governor of Virginia Declares His Brother Never Would Give Up—Mother Rejoices.

Special to The New York Times.

RICHMOND, Va., May 9.—Richmond received its first information of the successful polar flight of Lieut. Commander Richard Evelyn Byrd about 3 o'clock this afternoon, when a message saying the flier had "returned safely" was received by Governor Harry F. Byrd by telephone. The flier's mother, Mrs. Richard Evelyn Byrd, was at the executive mansion when the message was received.

"I am tremendously gratified," Governor Byrd said, "and proud to hear of my brother's success in reaching the Pole."

"Dick has always been so lucky all his life that he believes he will come through, even though ninety-nine of a hundred chances might be plainly against him. I am proud of him. He has always been such an adventurous fellow, we are somewhat relieved, though proud, that he has made the flight. If he had not, and believed there was a ghost of a chance to do so, he would try again as soon as possible."

This one day of the year dedicated to mothers, the message flashed across the frozen miles, brought happiness and comfort to Virginia's "first mother," Mrs. Richard Evelyn Byrd—

Richard E. Byrd flew to the North Pole and back.

"All the News That's Fit to Print."

The New York Times.

THE WEATHER
Cloudy and cooler today; tomorrow fair; fresh north winds.
Temperature yesterday—Max. 61, min. 50.
For weather report see Page 54.

VOL. LXXV....No. 24,944. NEW YORK, TUESDAY, MAY 11, 1926. TWO CENTS In Greater New York | THREE CENTS Within 200 Miles | FOUR CENTS Elsewhere in the U. S.

BYRD SAW NO SIGN OF LIFE NEAR THE POLE, NEITHER BIRDS NOR SEALS; FLEW 2,000 FT. UP; NORGE READY TO GO, DELAYED BY WEATHER

INFORMAL PARLEYS STARTED IN BRITAIN TO END THE STRIKE

Formula Is Sought to Satisfy Both the Government and the Unions.

LABOR CAUSE IS SAGGING

Many Men Are Returning to Work, While the Government Steadily Improves Services.

NEWSPRINT IS TAKEN OVER

Government Also Commandeers a Printing Plant Beside That Used for Labor Organ.

By EDWIN L. JAMES.

Copyright, 1926, by The New York Times Company.
Special Cable to THE NEW YORK TIMES.

LONDON, May 10.—There are now going on informal conversations looking to the finding of a formula which will permit the ending of the British general strike. Neither the Government nor the Trades Union Council officially are represented, but those undertaking the effort are in touch with both sides.

While secrecy surrounds these talks, it is evident that they are centring about the coal industry and there is a report that they hope to persuade the miners that their best chances lie in the ending rather than the continuance of the strike. Should it be possible to satisfy the miners of this the way might be opened for the strike leaders to rescind the general strike order, which would fulfill the essential condition Prime Minister Baldwin makes for the resumption of negotiations with the trades unions.

This does not mean any weakening of the Government's determination to show that a general strike cannot be used to force the Government, but the idea back of the effort is that a way can be found to end the struggle without carrying it to the exhaustion stage. It may be that the next few days will mark an advance in the endeavor to arrange a method for ending the strike.

It is the idea of these intermediaries that if the struggle can be ended in the way they plan, there will remain clearly the issue aroused by the difficulties in the coal industry with what has been called the constitutional strike banished into limbo.

Says Sir Herbert Samuel Is Active.

The London Times will say tomorrow morning:

"There need be no difference of opinion about the value of the conversations, informal and unofficial, but none the less important, which have been taking place since the return of Sir Herbert Samuel on the future of the coal mining industry.

"That industrial problem, already half forgotten in the great industrial struggle which has succeeded it, will remain to be settled whenever the general body of the trades unions restores the only condition on which negotiations are possible.

"It is all to the good that men of peace in every relation with the mining industry are looking ahead to the restoration of order and fully recognizing that the essential preliminary should be considering how best to get to work when once the general strike is abandoned.

"The miners and mine owners alike should welcome the effort, for popular sympathy with their common difficulties runs some risk of disappearing under the present conditions. It was high time that the economic issue resulting in the deplorable but legitimate strike should be revived and plainly distinguished from the illegal and intolerable challenge to constitutional government."

May Call Dole Receivers.

If any of the strike leaders say they have not shot their last bolt the same may be said for the Government. Today the Cabinet discussed at length a proposal to call to work the million and more workers who have been receiving doles from the Government. The proposal was to the effect that these men be summoned to go to work as needed or forfeit the sustenance the Government has been supplying them.

The move was suggested on the ground that since the general strike represents a fight between the striking unions and the public, the public has a right to get something in return for the many millions of pounds it has been paying out for years to workers because there were no jobs for them. Since jobs exist now it is argued that the idle workers have only to fill them.

It is reported that the proposal had the support of Lord Birkenhead and Winston Churchill, but, however, the Cabinet took no decision, reserving the matter for future discussion.

The Government also had before it

Continued on Page Four.

Four Killed, Twenty Injured In British Railroad Accidents

LONDON, May 10 (AP).—The first serious railroad accidents since the beginning of the strike occurred today, causing four deaths and the serious injury of about twenty others.

At a point near Edinburgh, a passenger train manned by a volunteer crew collided with a freight train. Three passengers were killed and a number hurt.

Another accident occurred at Cambridge, one person being killed and two injured.

A third occurred north of Newcastle, several persons being injured.

JUDGE PARKER DIES IN HIS AUTO IN PARK

Democratic Nominee for the Presidency in 1904 Succumbs at 73 to Heart Disease.

ON WAY TO COUNTRY HOME

Only Recently Recovered From Pneumonia, He Was Riding Through Central Park.

Alton B. Parker, former Chief Judge of the Court of Appeals and Democratic nominee for President in 1904, died yesterday afternoon of heart disease while riding in his automobile through Central Park, en route to his country home in Esopus. He was 73 years old, and had only recently recovered from an attack of bronchial pneumonia.

Judge Parker had been ill for a week with a severe cold and had been under the care of Dr. Martin DeForest Smith at his city home in the Hotel Ambassador. His condition was not considered serious and because of his anxiety to get to his country home and recuperate there, Dr. Smith gave his permission for the trip to Esopus by automobile.

Judge Parker had been in the habit of making frequent trips to Esopus to indulge his interest in horseback riding and motor boating. The Parker country home is located on the west bank of the Hudson River, just out of Kingston, and has a private dock for motor boats.

On leaving the hotel, warmly wrapped against the chill of Spring, Judge Parker directed his chauffeur to drive through Central Park. He seemed in fairly good health when the journey began and chatted with his wife, Mrs. Amy Campbell Parker, and his nurse, Mrs. Ruth Belles.

Falls Dead in Auto.

As the automobile neared the reservoir in the park Judge Parker gasped suddenly, half stood in the car and then fell back. The chauffeur turned the car around and hastened back to the Ambassador.

With his wife not knowing whether he was dead or just unconscious, Judge Parker was carried to his apartment. Dr. Smith said that Judge Parker must have died immediately. He said the cause of death was heart disease and that it could not have been foreseen.

According to Colonel Walter Scott, a friend, Judge Parker was in excellent spirits Sunday afternoon and spoke to Colonel Scott of the joy he felt in the prospect of going to his Esopus home. Colonel Scott said that Judge Parker expressed regret at the death of former Governor Benjamin B. Odell, whom he knew well, and displayed great interest in the British strike situation. Colonel Scott said that Judge Parker had no inkling that his illness was in any way serious and discussed plans for riding his favorite mount in the country roads as soon as he recovered a little more strength.

Judge Parker is survived by his widow, a daughter, Mrs. Charles Mercer Hall, wife of a Bridgeport, Conn., clergyman, and two grandchildren, Mary and Parker Hall. Mrs. Hall is the daughter of Judge Parker and his first wife, Mrs. Mary Louise Schoonmaker Parker, whom he married in 1873 and who died in 1917. He married the present Mrs. Parker three years ago.

The funeral will be held tomorrow at noon at St. Thomas's Protestant Episcopal Church, Fifth Avenue and Fifty-third Street, which Judge Parker attended. The Right Rev. Ernest M. Stires, Bishop of Long Island, formerly rector of this church, will officiate. The interment will be in the Parker family lot at Kingston.

The list of those invited to act as honorary pallbearers is as follows:

Charles E. Hughes, John W. Davis, Nathan L. Miller, David Hunter Miller, Colonel Walter Scott, Morgan J. O'Brien, Delancey Nicoll, John W.

Continued on Page Ten.

$10,000,000 PLOT TO SMUGGLE LIQUOR IS CHARGED TO SIX

Prominent Men of Port Chester Indicted for Operations Since October, 1923.

SAID TO OWN BOATS, TRUCKS

Landed Cargoes by Daylight at Private Docks and Gave Bribes, It Is Alleged.

ALL ARE FREE UNDER BAIL

Emil Wormser of New York Called "Central Figure in Gigantic Organization."

Emil Wormser, said to live on Riverside Drive and reputed to be wealthy, and five other men said to have been his lieutenants in an alleged liquor conspiracy representing an investment of at least $10,000,000 and involving men prominent socially and in business in Port Chester, N. Y., were made defendants in a five-count indictment handed up, sealed, by the Federal Grand Jury last week and opened yesterday.

Irving M. Austin, one defendant, was formerly President of the Port Chester Chamber of Commerce, which he helped to organize. He lives at 510 Westchester Avenue, Port Chester, and is now a real estate operator, with interests in New York and Florida. Edwin Studwell, President of the Port Chester Country Club and owner of the Port Chester Transportation Company, is mentioned in the indictment as having permitted rum runners to use his private docks, but was not made a defendant because of his testimony before the Grand Jury.

The alleged liquor syndicate is charged with having operated since October, 1923. It is said to own a fleet of speed boats, each capable of landing 800 cases of liquor every trip, and to have owned also a large number of motor trucks which, well guarded, distributed the liquor the boats landed.

Others Not Directly Involved.

With the exception of Austin, the business men of Port Chester who were said to have been involved were not concerned directly with the purchase and sale of the liquor alleged to have been imported and distributed in this country. Their only connection with the alleged conspiracy lay in their consent to the use of their private landings, for which, it is said, they received liberal compensation.

Others indicted with Wormser and Austin are Edward Siegel, cigar store operator at 164 North Main Street, Port Chester; Harry Lawson of Atlantic City, Chris Berg of 111 Pioneer Street, Brooklyn, and Robert Olsen of 120 West Forty-eighth Street, Manhattan.

An informant told United States Attorney Emory R. Buckner, and others have since corroborated the statement, that the operations of the alleged conspirators were matters of common knowledge throughout Port Chester. It was later said by others that on more than one occasion speedboats came in and unloaded in broad daylight with citizens looking on, but afraid to interfere because of men who stood by "twirling revolvers in their fingers."

The method, Mr. Buckner said, was to arrange for the purchase of liquor abroad, have it transported to rum row and there landed "over a way made smooth by bribery, threats and corruption."

Mr. Buckner was unable to say where the liquor had been transported by the trucks or how distributed. A statement given out yesterday at Mr. Buckner's office read:

"The indictment names but does not indict the following men because of testimony given by them before the Grand Jury: Edwin Studwell, whose docks were used; Joseph Elton, alleged chief lieutenant and confidential secretary of Wormser and also alleged dummy president of several of Wormser's corporations; John Tief, captured skipper of one of Wormser's boats, and Frank Roberts, a wholesale coal dealer of Port Chester, whose docks were used."

Workers Were Strangers.

Wormser is described by Mr. Buckner and his aids, who conducted the investigation together with under-cover men, as having been the "carefully guarded central figure in a gigantic organization." So cautious were the few principals, according to the investigators, that the underlings seldom knew one another. All of the defendants had been arrested and released in bail before the indictment was made public.

Wormser and Lawson were arrested recently in the Federal Building, where they had gone in the interest of two

Continued on Page Fourteen.

6 Per Cent. of Nation's Fires Laid to Careless Smokers

ATLANTIC CITY, N. J., May 10.—Rudolph P. Miller, head of the National Fire Protection Association, in an address today before that organization's thirtieth annual convention at Haddon Hall, declared that 6 per cent. of the nation's fires in 1925 were caused by careless smokers.

"Other careless practices," he said, "added another 4 per cent., bringing the total number of fires due to carelessness to 10 per cent."

Miller, formerly Superintendent of Buildings in Manhattan, made a plea for stricter zoning restrictions, and asserted that fire hazards could be lessened by legislation limiting buildings in which dwellings and business places are combined. Records of the New York City Fire Department for a five-year period showed that 50 per cent. of the city's fires were in buildings of this type, he said.

GOV. SMITH SIGNS NEW HOUSING BILL

He Stresses Need of State Bank in a Statement Approving the Republican Bill.

SEES DOUBT ON FINANCING

Expresses Hope That Law Will Wipe Out Old, Unsanitary Tenements in This City.

Special to The New York Times.

ALBANY, May 10.—Governor Smith late today approved the Republican Housing bill, which has been before him since the Legislature adjourned. In an explanatory statement filed with the new statute the Governor more than intimated that the measure was not all that it ought to be.

The bill signed by Governor Smith was enacted as a compromise after the Republicans had declined to pass a bill drafted by Julius Henry Cohen, counsel for the State Housing Commission, who has given years of study to the housing situation and remedial legislation. The principal difference between the Housing Commission bill and the Republican bill is that the latter meaure makes no provision for a State housing bank, as provided for in the commission's bill, but substitutes a State Housing Board with no banking functions.

"Our old friend, Mr. Politics, put his nose in the door, and the majority party in control of the Legislature conceived it to be their duty to have a bill that they called their own. Although left to themselves they initiated nothing, and the Housing Commission's bill was referred to as a socialistic move," Governor Smith said in his explanatory statement. "Of course, nobody took that seriously, not even the men that said it."

Defends Commission Bill.

The Governor declared that the commission bill would have facilitated the borrowing at a minimum rate of all the money necessary, and that it presented a complete program for quasi-building operations for housing purposes.

Governor Smith's statement, in part, follows:

"The bill as finally enacted leaves some of the financial problems in doubt, but in its main features it recognizes, as I had originally suggested, the limited dividend companies as the basic element, giving to them, under rigid regulation by a State housing board, the right to condemn land needed for large-scale operations, such as are necessary to achieve cheap construction. Rents are regulated and limited. Public aid to those projects is in the form of tax exemptions, positive as to certain kinds of State taxes and permissive in the case of local taxation. Federal tax exemptions for these securities is in doubt, but is to be sought through Congressional action.

The Housing Board which the bill creates has broad powers of regulation and control over the companies operating under the act, and has other responsibilities of study and planning that should prove vitally important in making progress in city planning and general housing development.

"We must make a beginning in the attack on the entrenched system of constructing housing for speculative purposes only, and having reached the conclusion, as evidenced by this bill, that the State has a responsibility in the matter, earnest cooperation between the State and local agencies who can aid in practical ways, and those who can and will finance such undertaking, should soon establish results.

"This legislation is not perfect, nor do I believe we have said the last word on the subject, but honest effort on the part of all those connected with

Continued on Page Twenty-two.

NORGE LOADED TO SAIL

Start Was Planned for This Morning When the Weather Was Calm.

SUPPLIES FOR TWO MONTHS

A Possible Return by Siberia Instead of Alaska Is Contemplated.

VIKING FEAST GIVEN CREW

Men Carry an Odd Assortment of Mascots, Medals and Amulets—All Confident.

By FREDRIK RAMM,
New York Times Correspondent Aboard the Norge.

Copyright, 1926, by The New York Times Co. and The St. Louis Globe-Democrat.
By Wireless to THE NEW YORK TIMES.

KINGS BAY, Tuesday, May 11.—The start of the Norge for the North Pole, which had been set for 1 o'clock this morning, has been delayed on account of a local wind.

All preparations have been made for the polar flight. The engines, envelope and steel constructions have been overhauled, and the engines supplied with a fresh cooling mixture consisting of water and 30 per cent. glycerine.

Captain Amundsen, Mr. Ellsworth, Colonel Nobile and Lieutenant Riiser-Larsen have discussed navigation and agree that the wireless direction finder for terrestrial navigation is best suited.

All Equipment on Board.

All personal equipment has been brought aboard, skiis, arms, sleeping bags and four tents, and all stores are stowed astern, consisting of biscuits, dried milk, chocolate and pemmican sufficient to last two months on a basis of 400 grams for each person daily.

Many mascots are aboard, including Colonel Nobile's terrier, which is clothed in three woolen coats. The portraits of the Norwegian King and Queen presented to Captain Amundsen on his departure on his third Fram expedition, and also a framed four-leafed clover presented by Major Scott, hang in the navigation car. The Italians have also a picture of the Madonna.

The weather last night was calm and the sun bright, and it was believed this was the prevailing condition in the polar basin generally, hence the early start was planned under the most favorable weather conditions possible.

When we have passed the Pole, American stations will keep in touch with the Norge, helping us to determine the course. Though there may be fine weather at the Pole, we must be prepared for unfavorable weather when approaching America, the Bering Straits being known for difficult conditions. This is an added reason why there is some doubt that the airship will actually reach Nome.

Crew Discuss Return Route.

The Norge's crew are discussing the prospective time of their return to Europe after the flight. Captain Wisting of the ship Maud says the first ship for Nome leaving Seattle will be at the beginning of June, returning the beginning of July. If the airship does not reach Nome, but lands on the north coast of Alaska, it will not be possible to pass by land, but the crew must wait for later ships. In this case they could not be back in Europe before the beginning of November.

The expedition now shows only smiling faces, Amundsen, Ellsworth, the whole airship crew and the residents of Kings Bay; but perhaps the most happy is Colonel Nobile. He says the experience has been better than he dared to hope. Cold offers no danger; indeed, the temperature, 10 below zero, centigrade, is the best possible, for the airship's lifting capacity is then so great that she can take 1,000 kilos of petrol. He says:

"I consider this quantity necessary for the flight. This temperature prevails in the early morning, when we plan to start. We Italians will do the best we can if compelled to leave the airship to continue afoot, but this is the last thing we will have to do, Amundsen, Ellsworth and Riiser-Larsen agree, even if all three engines stop. We might be unable to repair them if there was a strong headwind.

Can Float Without Engines.

"But even if all the petrol were consumed it would be foolish to leave the Norge, as with all ballast, equipment and engines removed we could remain drifting in the air one month.

"It may be possible to reach Nome, but it is probable we may not go further than the north coast of Alaska.

"It is preferable to descend on the earth rather than on the sea. If the weather is dead calm this will be easy by stopping the engines, trimming the airship completely and making a slow descent by careful release of the gas. The airship's safety when descending is dependent entirely on the strength of the wind.

"The following Italians will accompany us: Cecioni, Arduino, Pomella, Carratti and Allessandrini."

Colonel Nobile has received telegrams from King Haakon, King Victor Emmanuel and the Italian Air Under Secretary, and also numerous telegrams from members of other expeditions.

Spanish Fliers Make Hop to Philippine Islands

MANILA, May 11 (AP). — Captains Loriga and Gallarza, the Spanish aviators, flying from Madrid to Manila, landed safely at Aparri today from Macao, China, with but one more hop ahead to reach their destination.

MANILA, May 10 (AP).—American destroyers have been dispatched from the China coast to patrol the China Sea between Hong Kong and Aparri, Luzon, to aid the Madrid-to-Manila Spanish fliers, Captains Lorriga and Gallarza, in case they meet with an accident on their flight from Macao to Aparri.

Two American airplanes flying from Camp Stotsenburg tomorrow morning will meet the Spaniards at Aparri and escort them southward. At Camp Stotsenburg a dozen other planes will join the escort to Manila.

Governor General Wood plans a reception for the European visitors.

MAKING ARCTIC HISTORY.

By RUSSELL D. OWEN,
Staff Correspondent of The New York Times.

Copyright, 1926, by The New York Times Co. and The St. Louis Globe-Democrat.
By Wireless to THE NEW YORK TIMES.

KINGS BAY, Spitzbergen, Tuesday, May 11.—While Kings Bay rejoices over the return of Commander Byrd, preparations are being rapidly completed for the departure of the airship Norge for the North Pole. The motor crankshaft, which broke after leaving Vadso, has been replaced; the gas in the ballonets has been changed and the side of the rudder replaced. The wire on the rudder had broken, and instead of repairing it, it was thought better to replace the rudder. Supplies have been loaded, including provisions and sleds. The sleds are beautiful examples of Northern craftsmanship, light and flexible, and they can carry heavy loads.

Now that one expedition has come to a successful end, excitement is high over the beginning of another great adventure to the north. They constitute two great dramas being enacted here, where so many unsuccessful departures for the Pole have been witnessed. Men stand in groups discussing them, and they go through their daily tasks mechanically.

More Northern history has been written this week than in many years together. Commander Byrd dropped from the blue sky, happy and triumphant, and soon the Norge will swing from her hangar and rise, ponderously but smoothly, toward the ice-bound mysteries of the other side of the Pole. With the one happy outcome thus far, every one feels that this year the Arctic is conquered. Confidence abounds, though the Norge's crew felt sure of success even before this.

A Merry Viking Feast.

Great events are occurring in the silence of this great white amphitheatre of Kings Bay. Saturday night the men of the Norge, who had been through the terrific strain of their long trip from Italy, made merry for hours with a typical Viking meal. The big mess hall was hung with flags, and at the long table Captain Amundsen and Mr. Ellsworth sat, facing Colonel Nobile and the great bulk of Lieutenant Riiser-Larsen, the Norwegian pilot. With them were the ladies of Kings Bay society, where social distinction and rivalries are as keen as on Fifth Avenue. With the leaders of the expedition were the smiling Korgen, the slim Omdal, the chunky, genial figure of Captain Wisting, and all the Italian and Norwegian officers and mechanics, who had been laboring so hard in preparing for the Norge's arrival.

Perhaps so many varied costumes never were seen about a festive board, for some came in dungarees and others in unaccustomed business suits, fitting tightly about figures accustomed to woolen shirts. Trousers were tucked into high boots or drooping about uncomfortable street shoes, while a few Norwegian officers were in natty uniforms and the Italians brilliant with gold braid. The only dinner coat graced the smiling Dr. Schaefer, who after nine years liv-

Continued on Page Twelve.

BYRD SAW MANY GOOD LANDING PLACES

Observed Stretches of Smooth Ice—Too Busy to Drop the American Flags He Carried.

THE RETURN CAME AT THE END OF AN ANXIOUS DAY

Amundsen Embraced and Kissed American Rival, Crying "Magnificent! Wonderful!"—Crowd Hoisted Fliers on Shoulders.

By WILLIAM BIRD.
The New York Times Correspondent With the Byrd Expedition.

Copyright, 1926, by The New York Times Company and The St. Louis Post-Dispatch.
By Wireless to THE NEW YORK TIMES.

KINGS BAY, May 9, 8:30 P. M., Greenwich Time, 4:30 P. M. Sunday, New York Time (Delayed in Transmission.—The successful trip of Commander Byrd was made on a bee-line from Amsterdam Island to the Pole, thence a bee-line to Verlegen Hook, New Friezeland, thence west to Amsterdam Island and home. He did not follow the identical course on the return because he wanted to be sure to hit Spitzbergen, but the navigation was perfect.

He saw not a single sign of life after entering the icepack, which begins immediately north of Amsterdam Island and apparently touches Verlegen, reaching much further southward than usual. No birds, seals, polar bears, nor traces of them were seen, neither any indication of life throughout the course.

Commander Byrd established an exploring record by not dropping flags. When he reached the Pole he was too busy taking observations and worrying about the leaking oil tank to think about flags, although he had a hundred small and several large American flags stored in the plane.

Commander Byrd flew at an average height of 2,000 feet outward and 3,000 on the return, making extra speed on account of the light load.

Both fliers arrived in good condition. Bennett is fatigued on account of the continuous strain of the previous days, when he slept little. Once aboard the Chantier both took hot baths and were rubbed down by Captain Brennan.

Commander Byrd does not agree with Captain Amundsen's and Mr. Ellsworth's conclusions about the absence of landing places in the polar region. He says they saw plenty of stretches of smooth ice where a ski-shod plane could safely alight, and they brought back a photograph demonstrating the possibility of landing and flying thereabouts.

The Chantier is the scene of wild rejoicing tonight. All the crew are happy and many have gone ashore to spend their first hours of recreation since leaving New York. Kings Bay affords no amusements, but the Chantier brought a movie apparatus and is giving entertainments in the other expedition's mess hall, inviting the whole population.

Fliers Sleep the Clock Around.

Copyright, 1926, by The New York Times Company and The St. Louis Post-Dispatch.
By Wireless to THE NEW YORK TIMES.

KINGS BAY, Monday, May 10, 10:30 A. M., Greenwich Time (6:30 A. M., New York Time).—Although protesting that he was not fatigued Commander Byrd retired early after his return last night and slept the clock around, Floyd Bennett, his pilot, doing likewise. In the exhilaration of their success they had not realized to what extent their muscles and nerves had been strained by their ten days of unremitting labor to prepare the expedition.

Kings Bay rubbed its eyes this morning after its all night celebration, wondering whether it were true or not that the little band of Americans which wriggled their ship into the harbor ten days ago in a snowstorm and rafted ashore through the grinding ice had already flown to the Pole and returned. All express the most intense admiration for Commander Byrd's accomplishment and wonder at the absolute perfection of his navigation which took his plane to the Pole without the slightest deviation from the course. On his return, according to calculations made this morning, the plane still had gasoline and oil enough for five and a half hours more of flight.

Plan Test Flights Over Spitzbergen.

The entire expedition is taking a day off today, but tomorrow the crew will begin regathering material for the return. The Chantier's boilers must be cleaned, and this will take from a week to a fortnight.

Meanwhile the Josephine Ford, while probably doing no further exploring, will be taken up for one or more test flights over Spitzbergen especially to obtain more data about ski construction. Both Commander Byrd and Bennett agree that skis are the only feasible landing gear for polar work but think those used in the first flight had insufficient surface and that the design can be improved.

Bennett is enthusiastic about the possibilities of Arctic flying and he predicts it will soon be a common occurrence for planes to traverse the polar regions, alighting and soaring at will.

By RUSSELL D. OWEN.
Staff Correspondent of The New York Times.

Copyright, 1926, by THE NEW YORK TIMES Company and The St. Louis Globe-Democrat.
By Wireless to THE NEW YORK TIMES.

KINGS BAY, May 9, 6 P. M. Greenwich Time, 2 P. M. New York Time (Delayed in Transmission).—This is a great day

"All the News That's Fit to Print."

The New York Times

THE WEATHER
Fair today; tomorrow fair and warmer; fresh northwest winds.
Temperature yesterday—Max., 58; min., 47.

VOL. LXXV....No. 24,945. NEW YORK, WEDNESDAY, MAY 12, 1926. TWO CENTS in Greater New York | THREE CENTS Within 200 Miles | FOUR CENTS Elsewhere in the U. S.

THE NORGE FLIES OVER NORTH POLE AT 1 A.M.; REPORTS HER FEAT TO TIMES BY WIRELESS; GOING ON OVER ARCTIC WASTES TO ALASKA

EFFORTS FOR PEACE ACTIVE IN LONDON; BOTH SIDES SILENT

Baldwin Waits Until a Late Hour for an Important Message From the Unions.

EXPECTED THIS FORENOON

Strike Leaders in Session Most of Day and Night, With MacDonald Exploring Situation.

MORE MEN ARE CALLED OUT

Meanwhile the Government Reports Still Further Progress in Maintaining Services.

By T. R. YBARRA.

Copyright, 1926, by The New York Times Company
Special Cable to THE NEW YORK TIMES.

LONDON, Wednesday, May 12.—Though the Government and the strikers continued to face each other in full battle formation throughout yesterday, the eighth day of Britain's great general strike, there were signs that the dove of peace was hovering somewhere in the immediate neighborhood. Up to a late hour last night, however, nobody had quite located the bird. Many insisted, nevertheless, that they had distinctly heard the soft whirring of its wings.

They stuck to their assertion despite the declaration in last night's British Worker, the strikers' official organ, that today more workers will join the great strike—the molders and shipyard workers, members of the Amalgamated Engineering Unions and the General Engineering Unions. The strikers' organ also said that instead of "dribbling back to work," according to the Government's statement, the workers are "standing like a rock and more are coming out."

There were also two statements in the official Government communiqué last night which did not partake of the generally rosy hue pervading the bulk of the official statements. One was: "There is as yet little sign of a general collapse of the strike." The other was the admission that the Trades Union Council "is believed to be making efforts to call out certain trades still at work."

Peace Rumors Still Persist.

But these and other similar reports current during the eighth day of the strike could not down the rumors of imminent peace.

The General Council of the Trades Union Congress met last night at strike headquarters to "explore the position with a view to leaving no door shut that could be opened." The meeting was attended by Ramsay MacDonald and J. H. Thomas, who came from Parliament for the purpose. After the meeting had been in session for some hours Mr. MacDonald and Mr. Thomas hastily returned to the Commons, their arrival giving rise to the hope they might have something to announce. They found, however, that the Commons had concluded its sitting.

They went back to the meeting, which lasted until 1:35 o'clock this morning. No announcement was made at its conclusion, but it is understood that there was a spirited discussion between Mr. MacDonald, Mr. Thomas and other members of the Parliamentary Labor Party who are moderate in their views and Ernest Bevin and other leaders of more extreme opinion.

One of those stated to have been active during the day in the interests of conciliation was Ramsay MacDonald. One of the most moderate of the labor chiefs, in addition to visiting the miners' executive and the General Council of the Trades Union Congress today, MacDonald sent the following message to The British Independent, a mimeographed makeshift newspaper run by university students:

"I welcome most heartily your efforts for conciliation. This dispute ought never to have happened, and had the problem in the dispute been handled with ordinary care and common sense there would have been neither a lockout nor a strike.

"On one thing I can give the nation confident assurance. The general strike in support of the miners was never meant as and even now is not a strike against Parliament, the Government or the Constitution. For purely war propaganda purposes the Government says it is.

"Good-will and calm heads will in the end prevail. We are working literally night and day that that may be soon."

It was certainly apparent during the day that something was going on beneath the surface, that it was some-

Continued on Page Five.

'Cop Evangelist' to Retire After 25 Years on Force

Detective Alfred Smith of the Missing Persons Bureau, known as the "cop evangelist," will retire from the force on June 1, after a service of twenty-five years. He will receive an annual pension of $1,250.

In the intervals of his work of seeking missing persons for the last fifteen years Smith had devoted much time to preaching the Gospel in Chinatown, on the Bowery and in the Eighth Avenue Gospel Mission at 290 Eighth Avenue. He will continue at the head of his Bible class under Miss Sarah Gray at the Gospel Mission.

Smith is 55 years old and lives at 62 East Eighty-seventh Street. His son, Robert, is employed in a Wall Street brokerage house and his daughter, Gertrude, is at college.

RAIL LABOR BILL PASSED BY SENATE

By 69 to 13 the Upper Branch Accepts the House Measure Without Amendment.

HARD FIGHT FOR CHANGES

Curtis Fails to Get Commerce Board Power Over Wages—Coolidge's Approval Expected.

Special to The New York Times.

WASHINGTON, May 11.—The bill to abolish the Railroad Labor Board and permit railways and their employes to settle disputes over wages and working conditions by mutual agreement was passed by the Senate by a vote of 69 to 13 late this afternoon. As the Senate approved the bill in identically the same form it passed the House no conference will be necessary and the bill will become law when the President affixes his signature.

Before the Senate passed the bill it was stated at the White House that it was not an Administration measure. The President, it was said, was interested in it to the extent that he believed it would work well because a majority of the railroad managers and employes favored it. But it was also understood that he did not entirely approve the bill as passed, he having suggested that it be amended so as to protect the public interest.

The detailed vote follows:

FOR THE BILL—69.

Republicans—39.

Borah,	Howell,	Robinson (Ind.),
Butler,	Johnson,	Sackett,
Cameron,	Jones (Wash.)	Schall,
Couzens,	LaFollette,	Shortridge,
Cummins,	Lenroot,	Smoot,
Dale,	McMaster,	Stanfield,
Deneen,	McNary,	Wadsworth,
Edge,	Means,	Warren,
Ernst,	Metcalf,	Watson,
Fess,	Norris,	Weller,
Frazier,	Nye,	Willis.
Gillett,	Oddie,	
Gooding,	Pine,	
Harreld,	Reed (Pa.)	

Democrats—29.

Ashurst,	Glass,	Sheppard,
Blease,	Harris,	Simmons,
Bratton,	Heflin,	Steck,
Broussard,	Jones (N. M.),	Stephens,
Bruce,	Kendrick,	Swanson,
Copeland,	McKellar,	Trammell,
Dill,	Mayfield,	Tyson,
Edwards,	Neely,	Walsh,
George,	Overman,	Wheeler.
Gerry.	Pittman,	

Farmer-Laborite—1.

Shipstead.

AGAINST THE BILL—13.

Republicans—9.

Bingham,	Keyes,	Norbeck,
Curtis,	McLean,	Phipps,
Hale.	Moses.	Williams.

Democrats—4.

Bayard,	Robinson (Ark.).	Underwood.
Ransdell,		

Provisions of the Measure.

The bill, which was agreed upon last year by most of the railway executives and heads of the four brotherhoods, and which the President endorsed in principle in his message to Congress, provides:

1. That the railroads and employes shall establish adjustment boards to arrange disputes.

2. That the President shall appoint, with the consent of the Senate, a board of mediation of five persons, none of whom has a pecuniary interest on either side, to intervene when the adjustment boards fail.

3. That boards of arbitration shall be created when both parties consent to arbitration.

4. That when the above methods fail the Board of Mediation shall notify the President, who may appoint an emergency board to investigate and report to him within thirty days. For thirty days after the report has been made there shall be no change in the

Continued on Page Twelve.

FIRST MESSAGE EVER RECEIVED FROM THE NORTH POLE

By FREDRIK RAMM.
New York Times Correspondent Aboard the Norge.
Copyright, 1926, by The New York Times Company and The St. Louis Globe Democrat.
By Wireless to The New York Times.

NORTH POLE, Wednesday, May 12, 1 A. M. (on Board the Dirigible Airship Norge)—We reached the North Pole at 1 A. M. today, and lowered flags for Amundsen, Ellsworth, and Nobile.

LATER, 3.30 A. M.—Lowering the three flags, Norwegian, American and Italian, when the Norge was over the North Pole, was the greatest of all events of this flight. Riiser-Larsen's observations showed that we were over the Pole. The Norge descended and speed was reduced, when the flags were lowered over the wastes whose edges gleamed like gold in the pale sunlight, breaking through the fog which surrounded us.

Roald Amundsen first lowered the Norwegian flag. Then Ellsworth the Stars and Stripes; finally Nobile the Italian flag.

The airship's 1 A. M. time (Norwegian time), was 8 o'clock on Tuesday night, New York daylight time.

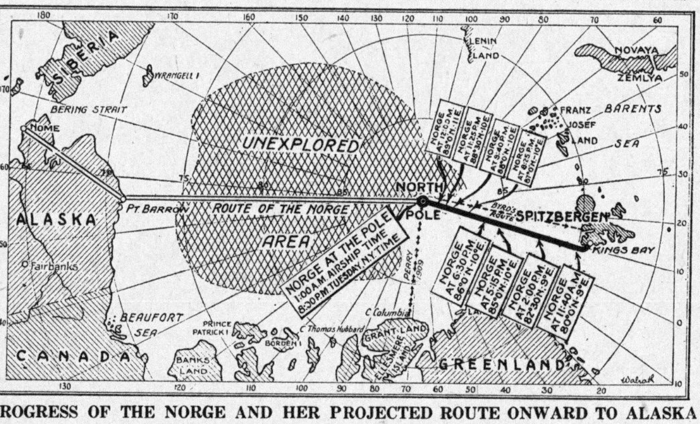

PROGRESS OF THE NORGE AND HER PROJECTED ROUTE ONWARD TO ALASKA

Here is shown the route covered, according to the last wireless reports from the Amundsen-Ellsworth-Nobile airship Norge, which sailed from Kings Bay, Spitzbergen, at 10 o'clock yesterday morning, Norwegian time (5 A. M. New York daylight time) to fly over the North Pole, and her probable course onward toward her ultimate destination, Nome, Alaska.

The hours given in the hollow squares on the map show the position of the Norge at the times stated. The figures are Norwegian time, which is five hours ahead of New York daylight time. The thick black line shows the course the airship has already covered; double line shows her probable future course to Nome. Dotted lines show the routes taken to the Pole by Lieut. Commander Peary in 1909 by dogsled, and by Lieut. Commander Byrd by airplane on Sunday last.

Norge Sails Straight Into the Golden Glow of the Morning Sun, A Silver Creature of the Air, Moving With Grace and Quiet Dignity

Kings Bay Cheers and Weeps as the Giant Dirigible Starts Down the Fjord Accompanied by Commander Byrd and Bennett in Their Polar Airplane, a Striking Contrast in Arctic Exploration—Colonel Nobile Says That the Wind Is His Only Concern—Expedition May Spend Sixty Hours on the Trip to Alaska.

By RUSSELL D. OWEN.
Staff Correspondent of The New York Times.
Copyright, 1926, by The New York Times Company and The St. Louis Globe-Democrat.
By Wireless to THE NEW YORK TIMES.

KINGS BAY, Spitzbergen, May 11.—At 9 o'clock this morning, Greenwich time, or 5 A. M. New York time, the Norge, of the Amundsen-Ellsworth-Nobile expedition, started for Point Barrow, Alaska.

Straight into the morning sun, a tiny speck soon lost in the golden glow of the north, the dirigible disappeared on her journey across the Pole and into the unknown wilderness of the Arctic.

The giant airship, like a silver creature of the air, rose slowly and gracefully from the hands that held her and with her motors humming sailed swiftly down the fjord, following the path Commander Byrd had taken in his spurt to the Pole. She turned over across the bay and rose over Cape Mitre. Then her black silhouette was lost in the sun.

There was rush and swift action to Commander Byrd's departure and the tense hazard of his quick take-off, but the Norge's departure was tremendously impressive because of the ponderous grace and quiet dignity of the great ship, lifting her immense burden from the ground and sailing into the unknown like a liner of the air. There were power, endurance and swiftness all embodied in her action.

Cheers and Tears at Departure.

Those below the floating fabric raised their hats in the air or flung up their arms in farewell, some cheering and a few moved to tears by the tenseness of the moment which saw their comrades departing on the greatest Arctic feat ever attempted. The air voyagers will spend at least sixty hours in Arctic regions never seen by man and at the end face the greatest hazard, when they may be forced to land the dirigible without assistance from the ground, something never done before.

All the day before Kings Bay was in a fever of preparation, the men of the expedition assembling equipment, packing provisions and small things for comfort, and making sure that nothing was overlooked. Mechanics swarmed over the dirigible, grooming her as though she were a race horse. Every bolt, stay, control wire and girder was gone over carefully. The full tanks were minutely examined, all pipes were overhauled and all instruments tested.

The big motors raced as they received their final turnovers, the immense green curtain near the end of the hangar billowing out in the gale created by the propellers. The new motor was put in splendid condition. Commander Gottwaldt tinkered over the wireless, making sure that the batteries and all the connections were in good condition, for on his direction-finder much depends.

Crew Spurts at Tasks.

There had been uncertainty all day as to the time of departure, but late at night it was announced that the start would

Continued on Page Two.

NORGE SAILS OVER VAST ICE DESERT

Start Made From Kings Bay at 9 A. M. Greenwich Time and Course Is Laid Due North

VOYAGERS SEE POLAR BEARS AND SEALS BELOW

Gentle Wind, Clear Skies and Temperature A Few Degrees Above Zero Accompany Fliers on First Reach to Pole.

By FREDRIK RAMM.
New York Times Correspondent Aboard the Norge.
Copyright, 1926, by The New York Times Company and The St. Louis Globe-Democrat.
By Wireless to THE NEW YORK TIMES.

ON BOARD THE DIRIGIBLE NORGE, KINGS BAY, Spitzbergen, May 11.—The airship Norge, carrying the Amundsen-Ellsworth-Nobile expedition on its flight across the Pole to Nome, Alaska, started today at 10 A. M. Norwegian Time (9 A. M. Greenwich Time, 5 A. M. New York Time).

Make 66 Miles an Hour at Start.

ON BOARD THE DIRIGIBLE NORGE, Flying Poleward, May 11, 11:40 A. M. Norwegian Time (10:40 A. M. Greenwich time, 6:40 New York Time).—We are north of Danes Island, 80 degrees latitude, 9 east longitude. The weather is bright, with the lightest breeze from the south-southeast. The temperature is minus 7 degrees centigrade (19 degrees above zero, Fahrenheit). Our altitude is 425 meters (1,394 feet) and our speed is 107 kilometers (66 miles) an hour. The edge of the ice pack is a few kilometers north of Danes Island. We have sighted seals on the ice. Our motors are running perfectly and we are not feeling cold.

[Later] We are now in latitude 81.12. Our speed is 100 kilometers [62 miles] an hour. The weather is bright with a light easterly breeze. The temperature is minus 10 degrees centigrade (14 degrees above zero, Fahrenheit) and our altitude is 530 meters (1,732 feet).

Espy Polar Bears on Ice.

ON BOARD THE DIRIGIBLE NORGE, Flying Poleward, May 11, 2 P. M., Norwegian Time (1 P. M. Greenwich Time, 9 A. M. New York Time).—We are now in latitude 82.30, longitude 9 east. Our altitude is 560 meters (1,836 feet). The temperature is minus 9 degrees centigrade (15.8 degrees above zero, Fahrenheit). The weather stays clear, with a light southeasterly breeze. The air pressure is 730.

In the sea some lanes are covered with new ice. All the time we have used the left and back motors. Lieutenant Riiser-Larsen has been navigating, assisted by Captain Gottwaldt. Ellsworth has been measuring the atmospheric electricity. Our better speed is due to our new altitude, where the conditions are more favorable.

We have now lost all sight of land and the ice changes the whole aspect. We see several great polar bears and can discern white fish in the small openings in the ice. One meteorological report from the Stavanger radio promises that fine weather will continue far on the other side of the Pole.

All of us are naturally in the highest spirits. We are now eating our first meal and discussing how to celebrate Ellsworth's forty-sixth birthday tomorrow.

View of Ice Desert Most Beautiful.

ON BOARD THE DIRIGIBLE NORGE, Flying Poleward, May 11, 5:15 P. M. Norwegian Time (4:15 Greenwich Time, 12:15 New York Time).—We are now in 85 degrees north latitude 10 east longitude, and heading directly north at a speed of 87 kilometers and a height of 610 meters. A gentle south wind is blowing and the weather is clear. The temperature is minus 12 degrees centigrade (9.8 degrees above zero Fahrenheit) and the barometer stands at 727 millimeters.

We have now flown over the ice a long time. Despite our great height we can clearly see how the ice is cracking and screwing.

The low temperature has as yet had no effect on us. The whole view of this desert of ice is indescribable and most beautiful.

All are well.

Speed North Under Clear Sky.

ON BOARD THE DIRIGIBLE NORGE, Flying Poleward, May 11, 6:30 P. M. Norwegian Time.—We are now in 86 degrees of latitude, 10 degrees east longitude. Our course is due north and our speed is 92 kilometers (57 miles) an hour. We are 570 meters above the ice. A light south-southwest breeze is blowing and the skies are entirely clear. The temperature is minus 12 degrees centigrade [9.8 degrees above zero Fahrenheit] and the barometer stands at 727 millimeters.

Weather reports, which are constantly being received, continue to be favorable. The left engine has been stopped and the right set going. All are well.

The Pole Four Hours Ahead.

ON BOARD THE DIRIGIBLE NORGE, Flying Poleward May 11, 8:25 P. M. Norwegian Time.—We are now at 87 d

The *Norge*, the famous dirigible that Roald Amundsen flew over the North Pole.

"All the News That's Fit to Print."

The New York Times.

THE WEATHER
Cloudy, probably showers today and tomorrow; southerly winds.
Temperature yesterday—Max. 71. Min. 53.
For weather report see Page 31.

VOL. LXXV....No. 24,948. ••• NEW YORK, SATURDAY, MAY 15, 1926. TWO CENTS in Greater New York | THREE CENTS Within 200 Miles | FOUR CENTS Elsewhere in the U. S.

NO WORD FROM NORGE, MISSING TWO DAYS; MAY BE ADRIFT IN POLAR STORM OFF ALASKA; BYRD PREPARES FOR A SEARCH BY AIRPLANE

PILSUDSKI CONTROLS CAPITAL OF POLAND; LOYALISTS OUTSIDE

Battle for the Possession of Warsaw Expected Today With 20,000 in Fight.

CONFLICTS IN THE CITY

Meanwhile Varied Stories of Whereabouts of President and Cabinet Are Circulated.

RUMORED FLIGHT IN PLANE

Lithuanians Take Advantage of Polish Turmoil and Invade Vilna.

By Wireless to THE NEW YORK TIMES.

DANTZIG, May 14.—The Polish Government is concentrating troops at Skierniewice, about fifty miles southwest of Warsaw and at the junction of the railroads from Posen and Silesia, for a march on Warsaw, which is still firmly held by Marshal Pilsudski.

Two regiments of infantry and one cavalry regiment are moving toward the Marshal's aid from Vilna, his home town.

Tomorrow is likely to see a pitched battle outside the gates of Warsaw between the insurrectionary and Government forces, in which some 20,000 men may be engaged with light and heavy artillery, tanks, armed automobiles and aircraft.

That is the substance of reports collected here from various sources and through roundabout channels.

Direct communication between Dantzig and Poland, either by telephone, telegraph or railroad, have been severed for twenty-four hours. Air service between the Free City and Warsaw is also suspended. The Polish machines employed on this route have been commandeered by Pilsudski. The usually lively auto traffic across the frontier into the Polish main highways has ceased altogether, owing to the drivers' fears that the cars and trucks would be requisitioned by the Polish military authorities.

Aerial Battle Over Warsaw.

There was an aerial battle over Warsaw this morning, according to a Polish merchant residing here, who crossed the frontier afoot at Dirschau. He learned from a Polish staff officer there that the Government planes bombed the Saxon palace on the bank of the Vistula River, where Pilsudski's headquarters are established.

Subsequently the Government's planes were attacked by pursuit machines flown by rebel pilots. One of the Government bombers was shot down. The damage done at Pilsudski's stronghold was reported very slight.

While news from the provincial centres is unreliable, it is evident that all Poland is potentially in a state of civil war, even though no bloodshed has been recorded outside of the capital.

Warsaw is temporarily tranquil, but any move by the Government to contest Pilsudski's control there will provoke a fresh conflict. Conservative estimates place the dead among the soldiers on both sides at fifty and the wounded at more than 200.

The Polish consulate here confirmed the killing of General Zeligowski, the conqueror of Vilna.

Whereabouts of Cabinet Unknown.

What has become of Witos's Cabinet cannot be ascertained. President Wojciechowski is still believed to be residing in Belvedere Palace, situated at the extreme western edge of the city. Except at a point where its spacious gardens break abruptly down to the Vistula, the palace is hemmed in by insurgent troops.

By this river retreat several of the Ministers succeeded in escaping under cover of the darkness last night, going by motorboat to Skierniewice to aid in the concentration of the loyal forces.

General Razwadowski, a bitter opponent of Pilsudski, has been given supreme command. The new Minister of War has issued an order to the army denouncing Pilsudski as a traitor to the fatherland.

Efforts to reach a compromise by negotiations have been shattered thus far by Marshal Pilsudski's refusal to speak with Premier Witos's Cabinet whose unconditional resignation is demanded as a preliminary to a truce. The Mrashal is evidently confident that he has the bulk of the army and the civilian population behind him.

Pilsudski Counts on Labor.

He counts on the labor unions, who are among his strongest adherents, to

Continued on Page Four.

British Stationery Office Now Becomes an Open Shop

Special Cable to THE NEW YORK TIMES.

LONDON, May 14.—The British Government's Stationery Office is no longer a union shop. The non-union volunteers during the strike are to be retained, and although the union men will be taken back as opportunity offers, they will be required to recognize that the Stationery Office is now open shop.

The Federation of Wholesale News Agents and the Associated Wholesale News Agents also have decided to become open shops, but will make no change in the wages and hours in effect before the strike.

BALDWIN PROPOSES COAL PEACE TERMS

He Also Announces Ending of the Rail Strike With a New Agreement.

CRISIS NOW NEARING END

Men Are Returning to Posts, With Services and Industries Nearing Normal.

By T. R. YBARRA.

Special Cable to THE NEW YORK TIMES.

LONDON, May 14.—Prime Minister Baldwin brought himself an ovation this afternoon in the House of Commons by making a two-fold announcement of a nature calculated to arouse high hopes that Britain will soon fight her way back to normal, despite the terrible crisis through which she has just passed.

The first part of this announcement was to the effect that the employes of the British railways and of the London underground railway, omnibu and tramway systems were returning to work as a result of agreements already signed between the underground, omnibus and tramway employes and their employers, and about to be signed between the railway companies and the railway workers.

The second part of Mr. Baldwin's announcement was that, having decided that the coal mine owners and coal miners were in hopeless disagreement, he had himself framed a set of proposals aimed at ending the coal dispute which he would submit to the coal disputants for them to ponder during the week-end.

Both statements were received with relief by the House of Commons, especially the second one, since if the Premier's proposals are accepted it will mean the end of the coal crisis, which precipitated the general strike.

MacDonald Honors Premier.

Former Premier Ramsay MacDonald asked the Premier to preside personally over the discussion of his proposals, thus giving renewed evidence of the confidence which Mr. Baldwin inspires alike among the adherents and opponents of the strikers.

David Lloyd George, the other Opposition chieftain, also expressed satisfaction at Mr. Baldwin's statements and seconded Mr. MacDonald's suggestion that the Premier preside over the coming discussions.

"Otherwise," added Mr. Lloyd George, "I am afraid they will not be guided to a satisfactory conclusion."

Thereupon the House adjourned for the week-end, which gives infinitely greater promise of enjoyment than the last one when the black shadow of the general strike darkened Britain.

Coal Terms Are Outlined.

The Prime Minister's proposals for settling the coal dispute, which has proved of such terrible gravity, are embodied in a letter addressed to Evan Williams and Herbert Smith, representating respectively the coal owners and the coal miners.

The first proposal is a general one for the adoption of all practical means for improving the organization of the industry and increasing its efficiency in accordance with the recommendations of the Royal Commission. The Government sets out the legislative and administrative measures it proposes to take. The additional financial assistance it offers the industry is a grant of £3,000,000 to be used primarily in aid of wages during the period that the National Wages Board with an independent Chairman is framing a national wages agreement to govern the principles on which the general wage rates shall be ascertained in each district and deciding the minimum percentage of the basis that shall be paid.

Subsistence wages are not to be reduced in any district where at present they are 45 shillings a week or less. The Government proposes that pending the decision of the Wages Board the miners shall accept for a number of weeks, at present unspecified, a reduction in the minimum wages, other than subsistence rates, in all districts. The amount of this reduction is not

Continued on Page Twelve.

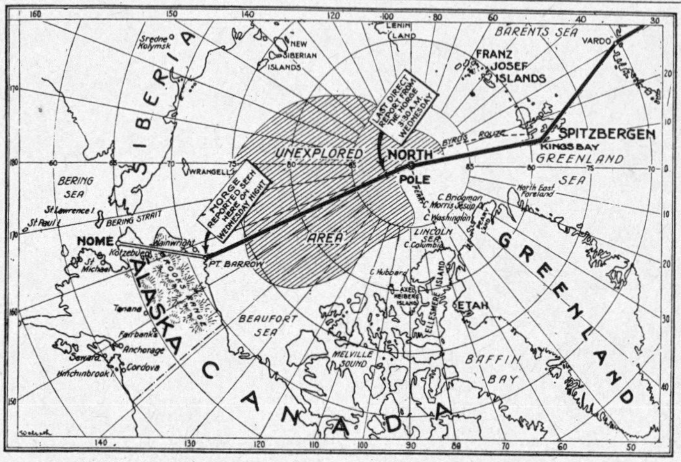

WHERE THE NORGE WAS LAST REPORTED AND HER SUPPOSED COURSE.

This Map Shows the Norge's Course to Point Barrow Where She Was Last Seen on Wednesday Night, Apparently Turning Inland Toward Nome, and the Alaskan Radio Stations Where Watch Is Being Kept For Her.

ADVANCES THEORIES FOR NORGE'S SILENCE

Dr. Goldsmith Thinks It Unlikely That Airship Is Caught in "Dead Spot."

SHE MAY BE OVER LAND

Radio Expert Says Many Calls in Alaskan Air Would Weaken Dirigible's Signals.

It is conceivable but not probable that the Norge has run into a "radio dead spot" in the Arctic, according to Dr. Alfred N. Goldsmith, Chief Broadcast Engineer of the Radio Corporation of America.

"The dirigible if she remained in a position high above the ground would not be affected by 'dead spots,' which are generally caused by the nature of the ground," he explained. "However, on long waves, that is, above 600 meters, and I understand the Norge is using 900 meters, it has been found that moist ground is more favorable to transmission over long distances. But in the case of the Norge, while it is in the air, the physical ground should not play an important part. An airship's transmitter is not connected directly with the earth, but generally the frame of the ship or the engine is employed as the ground contact. With such a system the signals are reflected from overhead.

"It may be that the Norge's messages broadcast between Norway and the Pole were favored by a good reflecting layer in the sky, and for that reason they covered the distance from the Pole to the receiver at Spitzbergen. Since the dirigible passed the Pole it may have encountered a reflecting layer unsuited to radio transmission, and for that reason the range has been greatly reduced.

"Another explanation for the silence is that the Norge is now flying overland, which we know absorbs radio signal strength and reduces the effectiveness of the waves. On the trip from Kings Bay to the Pole the ship flew chiefly over ice, which would be a much better condition for radio.

"It may be that Amundsen is drifting over the unknown area and that the wind is not right to operate the propellers which drive his radio generator. He probably would consider it unwise to consume gasoline just to operate the radio generator while everything was all right and the ship was drifting on an exploration cruise.

"If the ship had been forced to land the radio range would naturally be greatly reduced, and it may be if the ship has landed that there is no means of driving the generator. Futhermore, an improvised aerial and ground would have to be constructed and this would require insulators if the transmitter was to have a fair range.

"There is a possibility that the Norge is sending in an effort to reach the Alaskan stations, but with so many transmitters up there calling the dirigible, it has no opportunity to have its fainter signals heard. However, I am inclined to believe that Amundsen is just drifting over that territory with the wind and that his driving propellers are temporarily resting."

"Off for Pole With a Zoom"; Byrd Describes His Hop-Off

He Pictures Emotions of the Fliers as They Set Course for the North—Wondered if They Would Come Back—Commander Freezes Face and Hands Taking Observations.

The second instalment of the story of his dash to the North Pole written by Commander Richard E. Byrd and radioed from Kings Bay, Spitzbergen, is given below. In his first instalment, published in yesterday's TIMES, Commander Byrd told of the obstacles encountered when the expedition reached Spitzbergen and of their hard work to get the great Fokker plane ashore. In the present instalment he carries his narrative through the actual start for the North Pole.

In tomorrow's issue THE TIMES will publish the third instalment of Commander Byrd's narrative telling of his flight to the North Pole.

By LIEUT. COMMANDER R. E. BYRD,
Leader of the Byrd Polar Expedition.

By Wireless to THE NEW YORK TIMES.

KINGS BAY, Spitzbergen, May 14.—When it came to repairing the broken parts of the plane, and so forth, we were glad to avail ourselves of the coal company's machine shop, and it is a pleasure here to record my appreciation of the kindness of the manager, Mr. Smithmeyer, and Mr. Kise.

When we got ashore we found some misunderstanding had arisen about motion-picture rights, and for the first day none of our camera men were allowed ashore. This was straightened out later to everybody's satisfaction, but meanwhile our resourceful operators had taken possession of a stray iceberg which was anchored near our landing place and from there had a splendid view of the whole operation of putting the plane ashore.

The men worked all night on the plane to get the motors ready to taxi her up the hill opposite the great Amundsen-Ellsworth hangar. We had decided to take off down the grade toward the water.

Carpenter Gold, "Chips," as we called him, and the hardest working man of the expedition, built a house near the plane of Celotex, and so the cook with gasoline stoves was able to supply food and hot coffee at all hours.

I knew we must get off before the middle of May, as the weather is likely to be calm and clear of fog up to that time, but foggy and uncertain after that. There was great need to accomplish the preparations as soon as possible.

Big Plane Ready to Fly.

Bennett and the crew got the motors going and the skis on in record time, and after lunch we were ready to taxi up to the hill. We had on the plane our largest and, we thought, strongest skis. We got the plane started with considerable difficulty, but when once under way the powerful motors pulled it easily over the snow. We went half way up the hill and turned for the taxi-off.

The skis did not look any too strong when we got them on the great plane, and I was worried about them. Sure enough, we found upon examination one ski was split and one of the landing-gear fittings torn loose. Things looked black. If the strongest ski would crack up with the light weight of the practically empty plane, what would happen with a double load? To pass briefly over a lot of detail, we changed the gear-fitting and put on what we thought were the next strongest skis and proceeded to repair the first broken ski. Chips worked all night and accomplished the repairs.

I had come to have more respect for the snow, so we

Continued on Page Three.

BYRD MAY ATTEMPT SEARCH EXPEDITION

Says He Will Fly to Assist if Norge Is Forced Down in Arctic Wilds.

ORDERS PLANE MADE READY

Norwegian Aero Club Head Thinks Dirigible Is Down in Alaska.

By WILLIAM BIRD,
The New York Times Correspondent With the Byrd Expedition.

By Wireless to THE NEW YORK TIMES.

KINGS BAY, Spitzbergen, May 14.—When Commander Byrd heard tonight from THE NEW YORK TIMES that the report of the Norge's arrival in Alaska was not confirmed and the airship was therefore overdue, he immediately ordered the Josephine Ford made ready for a possible rescue expedition.

He believes that if the Norge is forced down in the unexplored area the party must attempt to proceed on foot to Cape Columbia, which would be a terrific effort, particularly for the Italians, untrained in Arctic work. He declared that he would certainly fly to Columbia, to make excursions into the unexplored area to search for the Amundsen party, alighting if possible on the polar ice to render assistance.

Preparations to re-embark the Josephine had been begun after today's flights, but were halted.

Kings Bay was struck with gloom after last night's rejoicings, the few Italians remaining here radioing to their compatriots aboard the Heimdal, which left at noon, urging them to return.

Thinks Norge Has Landed.

By Wireless to THE NEW YORK TIMES.

OSLO, May 14.—Rolf Thomassen, President of the Norwegian Aero Club says he believes the Norge has landed somewhere in Northern Alaska.

It can hardly be doubted, he said, that the airship was observed off Point Barrow, but the fact that no real wireless communication has been established with Northern Alaska stations seems to indicate that the airship has not been south of the Alsakan mountain chain.

The fact that the airship's wireless station was not heard from in the last twenty-four hours, he thinks, shows that the Norge probably has landed, thus putting the wireless out of business. It is quite possible there will be no news from the expedition before a ski party from the expedition reaches an Alaskan outpost.

Thomassen believes there is no dan-

Continued on Page Two.

NORGE MAY BE BUCKING BERING SEA WIND

Capt. Heinen Thinks Dirigible Can Still Keep Going for 70 Hours—Falsely Reported at Nome.

MANY COURSES BELIEVED AT NOBILE'S COMMAND

Skill of Navigator Expected to Avert Disaster From Craft Whose Whereabouts Is Unknown 46 Hours After Sighting at Point Barrow.

The whereabouts of the dirigible airship Norge of the Amundsen-Ellsworth-Nobile expedition was unknown at 3 o'clock this morning, ninety-four hours after the start of the flight from Spitzbergen and forty-nine hours after she was last reported seen at Point Barrow, Alaska.

The Norge had covered the distance of 2,000 miles across the Arctic from Kings Bay to northern Alaska in forty-one hours, but in forty-nine hours had failed to cover the remaining distance of 750 miles from Point Barrow to Nome.

The Norge's radio had been silent since the fragments of messages from the airship were received by three Alaskan stations.

A storm has been raging over the Bering Sea and part of northern Alaska, perhaps blocking the Norge from Nome. This might have forced her descent either in the interior or on the coast of Alaska.

A false report that the Norge had arrived safely at Nome reached New York at 10 o'clock last night and caused a considerable stir before it was withdrawn as unconfirmable. The report originated with the Federal Telegraph Company in San Francisco, which received it by land wire from its Seattle office.

Inquiries in every quarter having communication with Nome showed that no other agency had received such a rumor, and that it probably originated in a mistranslated word over the wire.

Captain Heinen Is Sure of Safety.

Captain Anton Heinen, the famous airship navigator, said yesterday that, in his opinion, the Norge was riding in a circle with a storm and would probably pass near Wrangel Island, over the coast of Siberia into the Bering Sea, and travel up from the south to Nome.

Captain Heinen calculated that the Norge arrived at Northern Alaska with more than half the gasoline with which she started from Spitzbergen and would be able to continue in motion for 70 hours longer, using a single engine.

"I would not begin to worry about her until Monday," he said.

May Have Bucked a Storm.

According to the German expert on air navigation, still another course was open to Captain Amundsen, Colonel Nobile and Lincoln Ellsworth in case they were being beset by a storm.

Colonel Nobile, the navigator of the Norge, might be heading her into the storm and using his engines just enough to hold her stationary, while waiting for the storm to abate. According to the German navigator, the Norge could hold herself stationary against an ordinary storm for two days or longer, without cutting heavily into her reserve of gasoline.

The fact that the four stations which caught messages from the Norge at 4 o'clock on Wednesday morning (New York Daylight Saving Time) were all at coast points, either in the Bering Sea or on the Pacific Ocean, indicated that the radio signals from the Norge probably traveled over water, making it probable that the airship was then over the southern Arctic.

The fact that signals from her were intercepted as she sought to get into communication with a Siberian station gave color to one of the theories advanced—that she was running along with a storm which was whirling about the direction of Siberia.

Theories on the Norge's Course.

In the absence of any knowledge of the position of the Norge when another morning dawned yesterday without word from her, those who still had faith that she had come to no harm advanced several reasons for their belief.

If a storm had blocked the Norge from Nome for the time being, she might have gone out of her course to avoid the centre of the disturbance. She might have fought the storm, as far as her fuel permitted. She might have shut off her engines and drifted with the object of conserving fuel and resuming her flight at the end of the storm. Colonel Nobile might be drifting with the wind toward Nome when it was favorable and anchoring against it when it came from the wrong direction.

Between Point Barrow and Nome there lies a great mountain range, with peaks considerably over a mile in height, rivers and vast stretches of Arctic prairie. If the Norge should find herself in trouble while over the Brooks [Endicott] range of

Section 1

"All the News That's Fit to Print."

The New York Times.

THE WEATHER
Cloudy today, possibly showers this morning; tomorrow fair.
Temperature yesterday: Max. 73, Min. 54.

Section 1

VOL. LXXV....No. 24,949. NEW YORK, SUNDAY, MAY 16, 1926. Including Rotogravure Picture Section in three parts—Magazine and Book Section in Rotogravure FIVE CENTS In Manhattan, Bronx and Brooklyn | Elsewhere TEN CENTS

NORGE SAFE IN ALASKA AFTER 71-HOUR FLIGHT; FORCED DOWN BY FOG AND ICE FORMING ON SHIP; CROSSED NORTH POLE, FOUND NO NEW LAND

FIRST WORD OF NORGE'S SAFETY SENT TO THE TIMES

By LINCOLN ELLSWORTH

American Leader of the Amundsen-Ellsworth-Nobile Transpolar Expedition.

By Wireless to The New York Times.

WITH THE NORGE, AT TELLER, Alaska, May 14, Via Nome, May 15.—The Norge landed on Thursday, May 13, at 8 o'clock in the evening, Alaska time (3 A. M., Friday, New York daylight time), at Teller, 91 miles west of Nome, after 71 hours of flight (from Kings Bay, Spitzbergen, and across the North Pole). The program of the expedition was thus realized. The Norge will be demounted here. All the crew are safe. LINCOLN ELLSWORTH.

THE AIRSHIP WHICH FLEW OVER THE TOP OF THE WORLD.

BYRD FILMED THE TOP OF THE WORLD

Commander Relates How He and Bennett Reached Their Goal—Shook Hands at Supreme Moment.

LEADER SALUTED IN HONOR OF PEARY AND THE NAVY

Fliers Wondered When Motor Trouble Came if They Should Try to Land, but Decided to Make Pole First and Take Chances Afterward.

By LIEUT. COMMANDER R. E. BYRD,
Leader of the Byrd Polar Expedition.
[THIRD INSTALMENT.]

By Wireless to THE NEW YORK TIMES.

KINGS BAY, Spitzbergen, May 15.—The trap-door in the bottom of the plane gave a fine method for taking the wind drift and I found, as I had expected, that I could tell to within a degree the angle that the wind was taking us off our course.

We had been able to do that on the first transatlantic flight and I knew we could do it even better by sighting on the ice. When the angle of drift is obtained, it means that the exact direction in which the plane is going over the ground is known.

Fog is the great enemy of the air navigator, for it is impossible, while flying over fog, to tell in what direction the plane is going or the extent of the wind drift. The wind drift indicator also gives quite accurately the speed the plane makes over the ground which, on account of the wind, may differ from the speed of the plane through the air.

Calculated Speed Frequently.

I found myself extremely busy. On the average I calculated the drift and speed once every three or four minutes and when I found any change in the drift made the corrections for the course on the sun compass and then checked Bennett on the new course. I wrote a note to Bennett asking him to do his utmost to keep on the course prescribed, for I knew that should the sun stay with us we could steer on almost an exact line to the Pole. Without the sun our course would be very doubtful, for when nearing the Pole from all but one direction the compass does not point north and no one knows exactly in what direction it does point. It is not so steady as it is in other parts of the world. I had on the plane a magnetic compass as large as that used by some big sea-going ships and it was far more reliable than a smaller one would have been. If the weather was rough we would be able to steer with it, though not a perfectly straight course as can be done when the weather is calm. With the sun compass I could tell when Bennett was off his course.

No Currents or Bump in Air.

I was astonished at the accuracy of his steering. Luck was with us. There was not a bump in the air, no upward and downward currents that tilt the plane and throw the compass to spinning. The sun was bright and we had a wonderful view of the formidable ice pack. It was covered everywhere with snow and criss-crossed with pressure ridges like a crazy quilt. The constant movement of the polar ice pack causes ridges and opens leads of water, but we saw very few such leads that had not recently been frozen over, with the fresh snowless ice looking greenish against the white snow around them.

Some of these frozen leads, probably older than the others, had a layer of snow over them and looked as flat as a table, but I knew them for dangerous sirens. They gave the appearance of affording an excellent landing, but they were very probably too thin to hold the plane, which, in landing, would crash through to destruction.

We were flying now at 2,000 feet and the temperature was eight degrees above zero or twenty-two degrees below freezing. No wonder none of the ice was melting into pools of water.

Byrd Both Pilots and Navigates.

After about three and a half hours of flying it became advisable to pour some gasoline into the tanks from the five-gallon cans we carried. We were well established on the course, so I took the wheel to pilot, give Bennett a short rest and enable him to fill the gasoline tanks from the loose cans. I did not put much faith in the magnetic compass, so I held the sun compass in my left hand and piloted with my right. After fifteen or twenty minutes Bennett was ready to take the wheel again. He wrote on his pad that we had burned thirty-two gallons of gas an hour since starting the motors. That was two gallons an hour more than we calculated on, so I was somewhat apprehensive about trying to make Cape Morris Jesup after leaving the Pole. However, we were averaging a good speed, about ninety miles an hour, and there were 480 gallons of gasoline left as well as some that was used for heating up the engines before starting, so it looked as if we would have enough gas to make it back to Kings Bay.

While I had been piloting I took the time to examine the

Continued on Page Four.

OSLO AND ROME REJOICE AT NEWS

Norwegian Capital Roused to Great Excitement by the Norge's Success.

ITALIAN CITY GOES FRANTIC

Impromptu Celebrations Start—Nobile Cables Trip Was Like a "Dream."

OSLO, Norway, May 15 (AP).—News of the arrival of the Amundsen-Ellsworth dirigible Norge at Teller, Alaska, caused great excitement here.

Because of the period of suspense when the fate of the Norge was unknown, interest in the expedition has been most intense and news of the fortunate outcome was received joyously.

United States Minister Swenson has sent greetings and congratulations on the expedition's success to Nome.

Another congratulatory message was sent by Frederick Herman Gade, Norwegian Consul at Chicago, who is here on leave. Before renouncing his American citizenship in 1911 Mr. Gade was Mayor of Lake Forest, Ill., and was a close friend of Roald Amundsen.

Mr. Gade first introduced Amundsen into the United States and has supported him in all his expeditions.

Rome Mad With Enthusiasm.

By Wireless to THE NEW YORK TIMES.

ROME, May 15.—The news that the Norge had arrived safe in Alaska, published in Rome today in mid-forenoon, produced a great spontaneous explosion of popular joy. The city where the Norge was built assumed a holiday appearance. Huge crowds poured into the streets, flags were flown from every window, the historic bells atop the municipal building on the capital pealed joyfully and at night the city was illuminated. Thousands of citizens improvised enthusiastic demonstrations outside the windows of Premier Mussolini at the office of the Foreign Ministry.

The King, Premier Mussolini and Colonel Nobile's wife were the first to be informed of the happy news. Both the King and Mussolini immediately had their congratulations conveyed to Mrs. Nobile. Shortly afterward she received a radiogram from her husband dispatched from Alaska, announcing his safe arrival and saying the journey had been "like a dream."

Even before the newspapers could print special editions announcing the Norge's reappearance Rome's population was made aware of the fact by

Continued on Page Two.

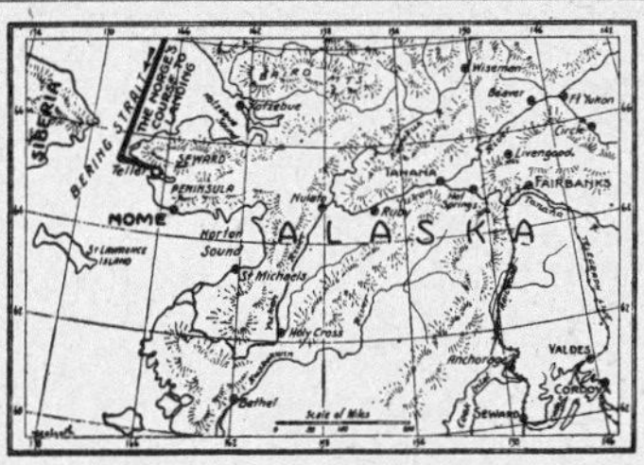

Where the Norge Landed in Alaska and Her Course in Bering Strait.

Washington Acclaims Norge's Feat; Army Radio Brings News from Teller

Admiral Moffett, Chief of Navy Aviation, Declares Exploit Justifies Airships and Predicts Arctic Route—Secretary Wilbur Hints New Naval Dirigible May Explore Arctic.

Special to The New York Times.

WASHINGTON, May 15.—First news of the arrival of the Norge at Teller, came to Washington this morning in a message to the Chief Signal Officer of the Army from the Army radio station at Nome.

The contents of this message were made public in the following statement at the War Department:

The office of the Chief Signal Officer is in receipt of a message from Nome, Alaska, to the effect that the Norge is at Teller, Alaska, about seventy-five miles northeast of Nome.

Communication bewteen Nome and the Norge was established at 11 P. M., May 14, Alaska time.

The message to the Chief Signal Officer was sent from Nome to Fairbanks, in interior Alaska at the head of the Government Alaska Railway, by Army radio; from Fairbanks to Valdez, Alaska, by Army land line; from Valdez to Seattle by Army cable, and from Seattle to Fort Douglas, Utah, to Fort Leavenworth, Kan., to Washington, by Army radio.

Moffett Sees Airship Justified.

Rear Admiral William A. Moffett, Chief of the Bureau of Naval Aeronautics, declared in a statement here this afternoon that the success of the Norge comes at an opportune time to justify America's faith in lighter-than-air craft, which he believes is particularly suited for use in the polar regions.

He expressed the opinion that large airships would be used in the future for commercial routes across the polar regions, linking Europe and the Far East.

"The Bureau of Aeronautics and Naval Aviation are delighted at the news that the Norge has been located so close to the terminus of her great flight," Admiral Moffett declared.

"At no time have we lost confidence in the ability and resourcefulness of Amundsen, Ellsworth and Colonel Nobile, and in the suitability and capability of their lighter-than-air craft for this momentous task.

"The selection by Amundsen of a lighter-than-air ship for polar exploration was the result of very mature judgment founded upon long experience in Arctic and Antarctic exploration. The scarcity of landing fields for airplanes and the extreme roughness and irregularity of the ice packs covering the polar region make the use of heavier-than-air craft in this region in their present stage of development a daring adventure.

"On the contrary, a lighter-than-air ship possessing the ability to remain in the air without power and to descend slowly and vertically if a landing is desired is particularly suited for use over the top of the world. The evenness of temperature and the absence of marked land elevations between Spitzbergen and Point Barrow materially reduced the hazard of the flight from the weather standpoint.

Predicts Air Route Over the Arctic.

"Overseas and polar flying, where weather influencing land characteristics are absent, is the logical element of the lighter-than-air ship. Storms and extremes of weather are less severe in the polar regions than in some of our own Northwestern States, and for this reason the large airship will be utilized in the future where advantage is taken commercially of the Arctic route for transport between Europe and the Far East.

"The success of the Norge comes at an opportune time to add material justification to America's faith in the lighter-than-air ship and her policy of continuing the development of this

Continued on Page Four.

QUEER RADIO PICK-UP STIRS WIRELESS MEN

Seemed to Indicate Norge Was Adrift Again, but There Was a Simple Explanation.

JUST SIBERIA ON THE AIR

Explaining What Was Heard From the Norge on Wednesday in Storm Before She Landed.

A message received yesterday afternoon by the Puget Sound naval headquarters from the navy wireless station at St. Paul Island, in the Pribyloffs, caused a temporary sensation in many cities because at first glance it was interpreted as indicating that the Norge, after arriving safely at Teller, Alaska, had broken away in a storm and was drifting to sea.

This would be improbable as much of the airship's gas was released in descending and the process of deflating and demounting her was probably well under way by yesterday afternoon.

The message from St. Paul Island read as follows:

Following intercepted on approximately 920 meters, continuous wave strength two, at 8:45 A. M.: "Quite terrific gale northeast drifting — [words lost] probable latitude eighty—ten one sixty—zero zero—[words lost]. Roger Dog George." Signals sound more like bubbling are than valve. Interference from radio beacons. Unable to work with Nome yet.

A little study of the picked up fragments, supplemented by information obtained in possession of THE NEW YORK TIMES soon provided a simple explanation of the message, which would indicate that it had nothing to do with the present situation of the Norge.

Navy radio operators in Alaska, as told in Saturday's dispatches, overheard early on Thursday morning fragments of a message from the Norge indicating that she was trying to establish communication with Station RDG, which is at Sredne Kolynsk, in Siberia. At the request of THE NEW YORK TIMES the Soviet Government of Russia on Friday sent out requests to all radio stations in Siberia to listen for the Norge, then missing, and immediately to communicate any information they had regarding any messages heard previously. "Roger, Dog, George" is the wireless version of the call "R. D. G.," and "bubbling" signals are characteristic of the Russian wireless stations.

With these facts in mind, it seems most probable that fragments overheard yesterday at St. Paul Island formed part of a message sent out by Station RDG at Sredne Kolynsk, rather than that they came direct from the Norge or had reference to any new difficulties the airship was experiencing. The

Continued on Page Two.

ICE HURLED BY PROPELLER PUNCTURED SHIP

Norge Faced Critical Moment When, Lost in Fog, Material for Patching the Pierced Skin Ran Out.

SEEKING TO CLEAR MIST, SHE RAN INTO SNOWSTORM

Sighted Point Barrow and Then Land Was Suddenly Shut Out—She Turned South to Bering Strait and Thence Made Way to Teller.

By FREDRIK RAMM.
New York Times Correspondent Aboard the Norge.

By Wireless to THE NEW YORK TIMES.

WITH THE NORGE, AT TELLER, Alaska, May 14, via Nome, May 15.—The Norge, now safely landed at Teller, Alaska, left Kings Bay on Tuesday, May 11, at 8:55 A. M. Greenwich Time (4:55 A. M., New York Daylight Time), with a load of twelve tons, including gasoline.

Before leaving Amsterdam Island, by magnetic compass, land bearing and sun compasses, we set a course true north, following the meridian of the Kings Bay wireless station. For later control we used the radio direction finder.

We had bright sunshine except for the last hour before reaching the Pole. There was no special interest in this part of the flight, as the territory had been explored already by the Amundsen-Ellsworth expedition of 1925.

Our course was continuously checked by the radio goniometer and by longitude observations when the sun was in a favorable position.

Heretofore the speed of the ship was controlled by direct measures and by latitude observations.

Sun Confirms Arrival at Pole.

The sun's position was favorable to ascertain our arrival at the Pole at 2:30 A. M. the following morning [Wednesday]. Here we went down to a low height and slowed down the engines. Captain Amundsen, Lincoln Ellsworth and Colonel Nobile dropped their countries' flags, mounted banner-like on steel-pointed rods. These rods steered themselves vertically into the ice and remained standing.

The crew took off their caps during the ceremony, and it was a beautiful sight to see the flags against the glittering snow. We circled around the Pole and then set our course for Point Barrow.

All Gaze Ahead for Unknown Land.

Now all were gazing for possible land ahead 2,000 kilometers (1,240 miles) never seen by human eyes. At 7 A. M. the Ice Pole was reached and its inaccessibility broken. [The Pole of Inaccessibility or Ice Pole is the centre of the polar ice pack, considered the most difficult point on earth for man to reach. The Pole of Inaccessibility is about 400 miles south of the North Pole in the direction of Alaska, its position being 83 degrees 50 minutes north by 160 degrees west.] Everybody shook hands warmly and all wore bright smiles.

Meet Fog, Snow and Hoar Frost.

There was plenty of fog further on, obliging us to go very high. Frequent openings in the fog, however, allowed us to view a wide area on both sides. There was no land. There were thick clouds overhead which later closed up with the fog underneath, obliging us to proceed slowly.

We went on in the fog and our excitement began. We went down low but it was snowing. We tried the zone directly above us, but the hoar frost had started to settle and the outside metal parts and ropes grew thick with ice.

The fog was too high to pass over without too much loss of gas. Therefore we tried different heights. The meteorologist was always watching the temperature and the forming of ice. We found no height without this danger, but chose one of the least dangerous altitudes.

Ice Makes Holes in Air Balloons.

Ice formed on the engine gondolas and rigging and dropped off in pieces and was then caught by the propellers and shot through the ship, together with the pieces of ice formed on the propellers themselves.

These were very exciting hours, the crew being engaged continuously in patching up holes in the fabric covering the keel and all the air balloons. The gas bags fortunately had been strengthened to meet this eventuality, but we could not know if our precautions had been sufficient.

Therefore, watching the ice pack beneath us was no longer platonic but was mingled with the thought, How could we walk on it?

Conditions Grow Better.

At last conditions grew better. We could pass under the clouds. Our course was kept by magnetic compasses, continuously changing as the elevation altered. Now and then the sun

When the tomb of a king of Ur who ruled in the fourth millennium B.C. was discovered it was found that over 70 of his retainers and their wives were killed and buried with him to accompany him. Here is a sketch of the position the skeletons were found in.

"All the News That's Fit to Print."

The New York Times.

THE WEATHER
Generally fair today and tomorrow; not much change in temperature.
Temperature yesterday—Max. 52, min. 34.
For weather report see Page 45.

VOL. LXXVII....No. 25,555. **** NEW YORK, THURSDAY, JANUARY 12, 1928. TWO CENTS In Greater New York | THREE CENTS Within 200 Miles | FOUR CENTS Elsewhere in the U. S.

SMITH'S NAME UPPERMOST AS PARTY LEADERS GATHER FOR THE HARMONY DINNER

DRYS DISPOSED TO WAIT

Will Avoid Clash for the Present at Least, It Is Expected.

McADOO NON-COMMITTAL

But Says He Made No Pledge Not to Mention Governor's Candidacy.

CITIES BID FOR CONVENTION

Contest at Capital Meeting Appears to Lie Between Detroit and San Francisco.

Special to The New York Times.

WASHINGTON, Jan. 11.—The strength of Governor Smith of New York among leaders from many sections of the country was sharply emphasized today as more of the National Committeemen arrived here for the meeting of the Democratic National Committee tomorrow, which will be followed in the evening by a big Jackson Day dinner.

The "dry hosts" of the party have not, up to this time, attempted openly to stir up discord. W. G. McAdoo and other outstanding drys who are opposed to the candidacy of Smith or any man bearing the so-called "wet label" kept away from the pre-meeting gatherings at the Mayflower Hotel, and word was passed around that they will avoid making any trouble, at least until after the dinner tomorrow evening has been permitted to go down into history as an event marked by harmony.

The Smith backers are doing everything in their power to bring about peace accomplishing this end chiefly by avoiding loud claims of supremacy and by taking the position that any city selected for the convention will be suitable to them whether it is in so-called wet or dry territory.

It was stated also by some of the Smith adherents that the Governor's friends were not seeking to have the convention rules changed so that a majority would nominate in fact, they declared, they wanted the two-thirds rule to stand so that Governor Smith, if nominated, would win the honor over the same route that other Democrats have traveled.

This, for the moment at any rate, is proving sound strategy and is making an appeal to some of the leaders who have been doubtful as to whether they should join the Smith band wagon.

Rivalry for Convention City.

The National Committee will take up the selection of a convention city tomorrow. The choice appears to have narrowed down to Detroit, Chicago, San Francisco and Cleveland.

National Committeeman Comstock, for the City of Detroit, was exhibiting a check for $125,000 and said that Detroit also would pay the rent of the auditorium and possibly meet some of the other expense.

San Francisco, through National Committeeman Dockweiler, is promising anywhere from $200,000 to $250,000 in cash and a hall. Colonel George Buckingham, in behalf of Chicago, will guarantee expenses up to $125,000, but is not ready to give any cash into the National Committee treasury.

Earlier in the day Cleveland was considered a dominant contender and rumor was that a fund of $150,000 would be raised and a hall thrown in, but tonight there were reports that the Cleveland boom was not so strong as at first indicated.

If this proves to be a fact, the real fight is expected to be between San Francisco and Detroit. Backers of Detroit were talking tonight of raising their bid to $175,000, although the additional $50,000 had not then definitely been subscribed. The promise of $200,000 or more by San Francisco was alluring to the National Committee, which has a considerable deficit, and if it were not for the fact that San Francisco is a long way west it is said there would be little doubt of the outcome.

Any City Suits Smith Men.

The handicap under which Detroit labors is the fact that it has been liberally advertised as wet by reason of its proximity to the Canadian border. This is said to have ended the city's chances for the Republican Convention and might have the same effect now, it is stated, if some other city more centrally located than San Francisco was making a generous cash offer.

Committeeman Dockweiler was doing his best today to turn the tide to San Francisco. He gave a luncheon to the National Committeewomen, at which a royal time for all was promised if the convention went to the West Coast.

The best prediction leaders had to offer tonight was that the choice now appeared to lie between Detroit and San Francisco. The Smith forces, which were dominant in the early in-

Continued on Page Two.

Duce Gets Legacy for Charity And Abruzzi Mountain Eagle

ROME, Jan. 11 (AP).—Premier Mussolini has fallen heir to two unexpected presents—one a fortune of 5,000,000 lire [about $250,000] and the other a splendid eagle captured in the Abruzzi Mountains.

The fortune has been bequeathed in trust to Il Duce by the will of Signora Cortella di Castellazzo Dorba, whose husband was an Italian General, and is to be devoted to charitable purposes.

The Premier is instructed by the terms of the will to set aside 1,000,000 lire for the foundation of a new Fascist hospital in Rome; 500,000 each for funds for the protection of needy artists and the education of poor boys; 400,000 for the Jewish colony at Milan; 200,000 each for the war blinded and for developing cancer relief.

Signor Mussolini, after admiring the eagle, bestowed it on the Rome "zoo."

THOMAS HARDY, 87, NOTED WRITER, DIES

Dean of English Literature Had Been Ill Since He Took Cold Dec. 12.

SPENT HIS LIFE IN WESSEX

Countryside Made Famous in Novels and Poems Was Place of His Birth and Death.

Copyright, 1928, by The New York Times Company By Wireless to THE NEW YORK TIMES.

LONDON, Jan. 11.—Thomas Hardy, regarded by many as the greatest English writer of his time, died at his home in Dorchester shortly after 9 o'clock tonight. He was 87 years old and had been ill for several weeks, but his condition was reported as improving within an hour of his death, when a sudden seizure set in.

Hardy's illness began with a chill and he took to his bed Dec. 12. Chances for his recovery were greatly retarded by the unusually severe weather, but his naturally robust condition enabled him to make a long fight. Almost to the last he was able to read and converse and yesterday signed with his own hand a check to the Royal Literary Fund.

Nursed by Wife and Her Sister.

He was nursed throughout his illness by Mrs. Hardy and her sister, who is a professional nurse. His brother and sister, who live near by, were constant visitors, as well as Sir James Barrie and S. C. Cockerell, Hardy's literary executor.

Among the last things read to Hardy were some poems by Walter De La Mare. He also maintained his interest in the day's news to the last.

It is known that he wished to be buried in the Hardy family vault at Stinsford, a tiny village outside Dorchester, which appears as "Mellstock" in "Under the Greenwood Tree." He was seldom seen recently in Dorchester or the lanes near his home, where for so many years it was his habit to go walking—his favorite exercise.

One of his last public appearances was made a few months ago when he laid the foundation stone for the new building of the Dorchester Grammar School, an institution founded by one of his ancestors and whereof he himself was Governor until recently. It is a long time since he last took his place on the bench of the Magistrates in Dorchester.

Born In Scene of His Novels.

Thomas Hardy was born on June 2, 1840, in a thatched cottage in Upper Hampton, three miles from Dor-

Continued on Page Twenty-seven.

COUNTRYMEN CHEER LINDBERGH AS GUEST IN THE CANAL ZONE

Army and Navy Officers and Employes and Their Families Bestow Their Plaudits.

HE SEES CHILD SWIMMERS

In Speech He Predicts Air Line Between United States and Panama Soon.

WILL HOP TO COLON TODAY

There Spirit of St. Louis Will Be Tuned Anew for Flight to Venezuela.

By C. H. CALHOUN,
Special Correspondent of The New York Times.

Copyright, 1928, by The New York Times Company. Special Cable to THE NEW YORK TIMES.

BALBOA, Jan. 11.—Colonel Charles A. Lindbergh spent today with his own people in the Panama Canal Zone, in which he was whirled through a program of entertainment almost at an airplane rate. The speed limit of eighteen miles an hour in the Canal Zone towns was lifted and with motorcycle policemen leading the way, the flier's car, often making forty miles an hour, soon made up the time lost on account of a late start.

Although scheduled to leave the American Legation at Panama and proceed to the Canal Zone at 9 A. M., it was after 9:30 when Colonel Lindbergh bade good-bye to the American Chargé d'Affaires, John F. Martin, whose guest he had been while in Panama. The airman left the legation accompanied by Captain John Downes, marine superintendent of the canal, who was representing Colonel Harry Burgess, Acting Governor of the Zone; Commander Harold Bemis, representing Rear Admiral H. H. Christy, commandant of the Fifteenth Naval District, and Colonel Samuel G. Shartle, representing General William S. Graves, commanding the Panama Canal Department of the army, all of whom were members of the reception committee of Panama.

Greeted by Americans.

Panaman police escorted the party to the Canal Zone line, Colonel Lindbergh riding in the car of the Governor of the canal. He was driven to the Canal Administration Building, where he was received by Colonel Burgess and conducted to a balcony where he was introduced to hundreds of American school children assembled below.

A large number of canal employes and their families surrounded the children and when Colonel Lindbergh appeared a great and joyous shout arose. Introducing the guest of honor, Colonel Burgess said: "Ladies and gentlemen and children of the Canal Zone: Sometimes our dreams come true. For many months we have dreamed of and hoped for the coming of the great Lindbergh. Now that dream has been realized and I am pleased to present Colonel Lindbergh."

The crowd gave a rousing cheer and applauded, then paused as if waiting for an expected speech. But Colonel Lindbergh only smiled and bowed and made the characteristic gesture that has come to indicate no speech is forthcoming.

Cheers Hospital Patients.

Returning to his car through cheering lines of canal employes, Colonel Lindbergh was intercepted by a girl who presented to him an airplane model made of flowers. The flier bowed, shook hands with the girl and thanked her and passed the plane to one of his aides. Thence his route led through the beautifully parked grounds of Ancon Hospital, where he passed the first of many patients in pajamas, the majority of them soldiers, lined up alongside the way. Colonel Lindbergh's car slowed up as he saluted them.

At the entrance to the hospital he was received by Colonel George E. K. Wurzel, the superintendent, who conducted him through the wards. Never was there a hospital more

Continued on Page Three.

Movies of New Plane Carrier Cut in Theatres In Line With Navy Policy of Guarding Secrets

Motion picture theatres, which expected to display last night a news reel film showing the new $45,000,000 aircraft carrier Saratoga under way, received peremptory instructions by telegraph from Universal Pictures, the distributer of the film, to cut it drastically. The order directed the complete elimination of certain airplane views of the new vessel which displayed fully the broad flying deck built to accommodate eighty-three planes.

While the telegram from the distributers did not say so, managers thought that the order was broadcast at the request of the Navy Department.

At one theatre, the Fifth Avenue Playhouse, the order was received just as the film was about to be displayed. The picture was quickly removed and cut, leaving only those views taken from tugs and other surface craft and the shore.

Special to The New York Times.

WASHINGTON, Jan. 11.—Officials of the Navy Department professed ignorance tonight of any request transmitted to news reel companies to recall all airplane views of the airplane carrier Saratoga leaving Philadelphia. But it was suggested that the distributers may have recalled the pictures of their own accord, being aware that the department does not want air views taken of the Saratoga. Permits were given to photographers to make pictures of the craft from tugs, officials explained, but none for pictures from the air, as the flying deck contains seventy Government secrets, such as the new arresting gear for airplanes.

The attitude of the department was outlined to the companies in advance, but if any broke faith, it was admitted, no legal authority exists to recover the objectionable pictures. Only a request for their recall could be made. Arrangements for the photographers were in the hands of the Philadelphia Naval District, and it was said tonight that no word had been received of anything objectionable in connection with photographing the Saratoga.

Lieutenant Charles B. Gary, who issues photographic permits, said all the movie reel representatives were aware that the department does not wish any pictures of the Saratoga or Lexington taken from above their decks.

UR KING'S RETAINERS FOUND IN HIS GRAVE

Wives and Servitors Had Been Killed to Accompany the Monarch in Death.

FIRST HINT OF THE CUSTOM

Discoveries in Tomb Show Chaldean Civilization Superior to Egyptian in 3,500 B. C.

Copyright, 1928, by The New York Times Company. By Wireless to THE NEW YORK TIMES.

LONDON, Jan. 11.—The recent announcement of the discovery of the grave of a King of Ur by the joint expedition of the British Museum and the University of Pennsylvania was followed today by news of a discovery scientifically more important and intrinsically much more interesting and one which throws a new and grim light on royal burial customs in Mesopotamia 6,000 years ago.

The body of the King himself was not discovered, probably having been stolen by tomb robbers not very long after the burial. But there was evidence in plenty not only that this is truly a royal tomb but that when the King of Ur passed to his ancestors he took with him to the shades not only his war chariot and the asses which had drawn it, his gaming board and dice, but also his grooms, his servitors, his musicians and his wives.

What the investigators found was not a tomb, but a hecatomb, the mummied relics of a massacre.

A similar custom prevailed in the earliest days of Egypt, but that it was followed in Mesopotamia was unknown until the spade brought to light this tomb "with gold-bedecked women of the harem laid out in ordered rows apart from musicians and servants at their task, and men on guard," to quote the report of the discoverers. "It has supplied definite information absolutely new to science and affords material for theories still more far-reaching."

Woolley Tells of Discoveries.

Special to The New York Times.

PHILADELPHIA, Jan. 11.—Details of the discovery of the most remarkable grave found thus far in Ur of Chaldees were contained in a report by C. Leonard Woolley, director of the expedition, which the University of Pennsylvania gave out tonight.

A magnificently decorated chariot and harp, gold and silver vessels, an exquisite toilet set and various other treasures yielded by the grave serve to illustrate the extraordinary degree of material civilization which Mesopotamia enjoyed more than 5,000 years ago and how far it was in advance of contemporary Egypt, according to the director.

The grave was found after an area of some forty by seventeen feet had been uncovered. The first object to come to attention was the harp, decorated with gold, lapis lazuli shells and plaques engraved with mythological scenes. Of the next discovery, the chariot, Mr. Woolley wrote:

"We had never hoped to recover from the salt-laden soil of Iraq the design of things so perishable as these. Now, for the first time, we can realize the extraordinary richness of the furniture which a Sumerian King might possess in the middle of the fourth millenium before Christ.

"The chariot had been drawn by two asses, and at the head of each ass lay the groom, as if still holding the reins, while a third groom lay by their side.

Bodies Are Huddled Up.

"The whole group reminded one of the description that Herodotus gives of the funeral of a Scythian King, although whether here the animals and the men had been impaled as in Scythia or merely killed and permitted to lie in their places there was no evidence to show.

"On three sides of a 'clothes chest' and under the offerings piled against it, we found human bodies, not properly laid out for burial, but huddled up as if death had overtaken them suddenly. The body at the chest seemed to be that of a person of some standing, for around its forehead was a frontlet of beads of gold and lapis and two lengths of gold chain, while gold earrings were on the ears. Perhaps the keeper of the wardrobe carried on his duties to another world."

Mr. Woolley explained that five other bodies lay in a shallow trench near the chariot and a sixth body on

Continued on Page Twelve.

NEW KELLOGG NOTE REJECTS BRIAND PLAN

Tells French Minister America Does Not Favor Limiting Treaty to Aggressive War.

HOPES FOR AN AGREEMENT

But Wants Assurances From Other Powers That They, Too, Will Sign the Compact.

Special to The New York Times.

WASHINGTON, Jan. 11.—France will be invited to give further consideration to the proposal for a multilateral treaty renouncing war as an instrument of national policy, in a note decided upon today after a conference between Secretary Kellogg and Paul Claudel, the French Ambassador.

The communication was also the subject of a conference between Secretary Kellogg and Chairman Borah of the Senate Foreign Relations Committee, who is understood to be in complete accord with its terms.

It informs the French Government that the United States cannot enter into the treaty for peace without adequate assurances from many other countries that they, too, are prepared to become signatories, and that it does not view with favor the position of Aristide Briand, the French Foreign Minister, for its scope to be restricted to wars of aggression. It nevertheless acquaints France with the hope of this Government that, although the two Governments stand apart on these two propositions, from the basis already laid down negotiations can proceed out of which some mutually satisfactory arrangement may emanate.

It is not being accompanied by a draft treaty embodying the ideas of Secretary Kellogg for a multilateral treaty. This has been suggested by M. Briand but has not found favor here.

Just what form the treaty basis now being sought may take is too early to predict, but it is the intention of the State Department and French Embassy to continue conversations in the light of the note to M. Briand. At the same time negotiations will be carried on in Paris. Myron T. Herrick, the American Ambassador, will sail Sunday to resume his post and plans to confer with Secretary Kellogg before leaving. He will be informed in detail of the situation, so as to be in position to use his good offices in direct conversations with the French Foreign Office.

The subject of renewal of the Root arbitration treaty, which expires by limitation Feb. 27, it is understood did not enter extensively into the discussions today between Secretary Kellogg and Ambassador Claudel. The latter was informed that a reply to the French note concerning that convention probably would not be transmitted until after Mr. Kellogg returns from Havana.

CECIL ATTACKS OUR STAND.

Doesn't Know What Renunciation of War Proposal Means.

Copyright, 1928, by The New York Times Company. By Wireless to THE NEW YORK TIMES.

LONDON, Jan. 11.—The American proposal for renunciation of war was criticized in a speech to the League of Nations Union at Sheffield tonight by Lord Cecil, who wanted to know exactly what it meant.

"I am all for the outlawry of war," he said. "I have listened with great sympathy and approval to the proposal of the President of the United States that we should renounce war as an instrument of international policy. That is an admirable policy, but I want to know exactly what it means. I do not want to put unnecessary difficulties in its way, but I want to know whether it means renunciation of war as an instrument of national defence. I cannot believe that it does. It must, if you are going to talk sense at all, mean renunciation of war only for all aggressive purposes.

"But we are told that is exactly what is not intended because it is said it is impossible to find which is the aggressor. Therefore you must renounce war altogether.

"If you want to establish a real system of peace between nations you have, broadly speaking, to do what you have done with individuals. You have got to establish an international court of justice which can say who is guilty and who is innocent, and you have got to have something in the nature of a police force to see that the law is obeyed.

"And where you want renunciation or outlawry of war the first condi-

Continued on Page Five.

COOLIDGE WILL URGE PAN-AMERICAN AMITY AT HAVANA CONGRESS

Speech to the Delegates May Furnish Cornerstone for Better Understanding.

CORDIALITY TO BE KEYNOTE

No Prospect Is Visible of Outcropping of Irritation Against the United States.

INTERVENTION TO COME UP

But Neither Nicaraguan Nor Mexican Questions Are Likely to Be Stressed Formidably.

By RICHARD V. OULAHAN.
Special to The New York Times.

WASHINGTON, Jan. 11.—When President Coolidge departs from Washington on Friday for his first venture outside the territorial boundaries of the United States he will be undertaking a journey that may have an important, and some suggest a momentous, bearing on the foreign relations of his Government.

His visit to Havana to address the opening session of the Sixth International Conference of the American States, while it may be devoid of spectacular features, will be a supreme friendly gesture which may furnish the cornerstone of a new and better understanding between this country and the countries to the south of us which comprise the area commonly designated as Latin America.

Those who make a study of such subjects find it impossible to overlook the possibilities of the President's brief stay at the Cuban capital while the conference of American States, better known by its unofficial designation as the Pan-American Congress, is in session. No people are more appreciative of courtesies and recognition of this character than those of Latin America, but a situation prevails which makes it difficult to predict whether the President's visit, no matter how gratifying to the nations which will participate in the international gathering, will be translated into terms of better understanding of the position this Government has taken toward some of the Latin-American States.

Cordial Keynote Expected.

Will it merely be a flash in the pan, a momentary arousing of good feeling likely to fade away after the conference gets down to an analytical discussion of the relationship of the great Republic of the North to the smaller republics of this hemisphere?

The prospects are that the President's arrival at Havana and his address at the opening session of the Pan-American body, with delegations from twenty-one American States in attendance, will have an extremely good effect in establishing a cordial feeling, which will give the keynote of the meeting. There is no visible prospect of any outcropping of irritation directed at the United States and its Latin-American policy.

Necessarily there will be an undercurrent of resentment due to the conception which some of the Latin American nations have formed of the attitude of the Washington Government toward their part of the world, but the opportunity will be presented of dissipating the clouds of political misunderstanding which have hung over the Western Hemisphere for a long time.

A chief fundamental of the suspicion and, to put it mildly, the dislike toward the United States existing in certain sections of Latin America is our present course in Nicaragua. There is reason to believe, however, that this will not come to the surface in any formidable way, although the possibility of some forensic outburst over the Nicaraguan situation cannot be overlooked.

The Nicaraguan Question.

But it should be kept in mind that the present occupation of Nicaraguan territory is with the consent and approval of both political factions of that perturbed land, and the delegates of Nicaragua in the Havana conference will reflect that consent and approval instead of be-

Continued on Page Four.

Mrs. Coolidge Goes to Mother in Northampton To Spend Day by Sick Bed on Eve of Cuba Trip

WASHINGTON, Jan. 11 (AP).—In the face of a six-day journey to Havana, Mrs. Coolidge left Washington tonight for Northampton, Mass., to visit her mother, Mrs. Lemira Barrett Goodhue, who has been ill with influenza.

She decided to make the trip before leaving for Cuba, although Mrs. Goodhue's condition was said to have developed no serious turn. Mrs. Coolidge will spend a full day with her mother, returning to the capital on Friday morning.

Accompanying her were Lieut. Commander Joel T. Boone, a White House physician, and John J. Fitzgerald of the White House Secret Service staff. Her trip will necessitate four nights on the train in succession, since on Friday and Saturday nights she will be en route with the President to Key West, Fla., where they will embark on the battleship Texas early Sunday morning for the crossing to Havana.

Before her departure today Mrs. Coolidge took time personally to supervise the arrangements for the funeral of Miss Katherine Wynne, the maid who served her in the White House for more than four years and had served Mrs. Harding and Mrs. Wilson.

Pending arrival of Miss Wynne's relatives, Mrs. Coolidge went to the undertaking establishment and ordered White House palms placed there for the services. Flowers from the White House greenhouses have been sent to the funeral home daily.

NORTHAMPTON, Mass., Jan. 11 (AP).—News that Mrs. Calvin Coolidge was coming to this city to visit her mother before sailing for Cuba came as a surprise to her friends here tonight.

Dr. Elmer H. Copeland, personal physician of her mother, who has been attending Mrs. Goodhue since she was taken ill Dec. 11, admitted that his 78-year-old patient had not been making as satisfactory a recovery from her attack of influenza as desired.

Mrs. L. L. Campbell, friend of the President's wife, declared that her visit would "do Mrs. Goodhue more good than any doctor could."

MRS. SNYDER WINS A STAY UNTIL TOMORROW MORNING; NEW PLEA FOR GRAY TODAY

WRIT ISSUED IN CIVIL SUIT

Delay Granted to Decide if She Is Needed for Insurance Hearing.

WARDEN'S ACTION IN DOUBT

He Has Said He Would Not Act, but Order Is Held Binding by Justice Levy and Hazleton.

FEDERAL APPEAL FOR GRAY

Plea for Him and Woman to Be Made on Constitutional Grounds Today.

Supreme Court Justice Aaron J. Levy granted a stay of execution last night to Ruth Brown Snyder until tomorrow at 10 A. M. on the plea of her lawyers, Edgar F. Hazelton and Dana Wallace, that her presence is needed as a witness in the litigation over the insurance of $95,000 left by her husband, Albert Snyder, whom she was convicted of murdering. Application will be made to the Federal court today for a stay in behalf of her and Henry Judd Gray on the ground that his constitutional rights were violated.

Justice Levy granted the stay to allow further time in which to hear argument on the necessity for Mrs. Snyder's presence as a witness. The lawyers made their appeal on behalf of the child, Lorraine Snyder. They argued that she was a ward of the court; that she was the ultimate beneficiary of the insurance and that her rights were jeopardized if she were deprived of the testimony of her mother.

Action of this kind has been threatened by lawyers for Mrs. Snyder in the past, although no precedent exists for postponing a death sentence because of the alleged necessity for the presence of a witness in a civil case.

It could not be learned whether Justice Levy's stay, in the event it was recognized, would act also to delay the execution of Gray, set for tonight, it being within Warden Lawes's discretion to carry out the sentence of the Court of Appeals within the week ending Saturday.

Justice Levy's order was served on Warden Lawes at Sing Sing at 2 o'clock this morning, according to The Associated Press. Warden Lawes, in accepting service of the order, said he would "act after consultation with the proper authorities." The order was served by Frank Bambara, a clerk in the office of Mr. Hazleton.

Stay May Fail of Purpose.

The stay of the woman's execution may fail of its purpose. When told that such a move had been planned, Warden Lawes said he would probably disregard such an order, unless he received direction to the contrary from his superiors. Warden Lawes disregarded two Supreme Court orders yesterday, both directing him to allow visitors to see Mrs. Snyder. He held that those court orders were invalid.

Mr. Hazelton said last night that there was no chance that the Warden would fail to heed the mandate of the court and postpone the execution.

"The Supreme Court has again and again granted stays of execution and no Warden has ever been known to ignore them," he said. "He would be in contempt if he did so, and most seriously in contempt.

"No stay of execution has ever been granted before on this ground in the history of the criminal law, but, of course, the Warden has nothing to do with that. He has nothing to do with the grounds on which a court order is granted.

"We made our motion for the stay of execution on the ground that the Supreme Court has certain inherent, equitable powers which cannot be taken away by the Legislature or by any provision of the Penal Code. We have applied in behalf of Lorraine Snyder, an infant, a ward of the State and a ward of the court. That court is required to protect the rights of that infant with a jealous eye. That child is the sole owner of all the rights in the insurance policies involved in this case, the mother having assigned her interests to the child last October. If the mother be dead the child has no testimony to offer in her behalf to contradict the claim of the insurance company that the policies were fraudulently obtained, and therefore we ask that the stay of execution be granted until the case be tried."

Would Ask Stay for Appeal.

"If the case is tried and appealed, would you ask for the stay of execution during the appeal?" he was asked.

"Certainly," he replied. He added that it was impossible to foresee the length of time the stay of execution must continue, if his contention was sound.

"The stay is legally binding on Warden Lawes of Sing Sing Prison," Justice Levy said later at his home, 201 West Eighty-ninth Street, even though the Warden may think "it has not that effect. But it does not affect the case of Gray," he said.

"The stay was granted on an appli-

Spain Will Restore to Cuba All Independence Relics

Copyright, 1928, by The New York Times Co. Special Cable to THE NEW YORK TIMES.

MADRID, Jan. 11.—Primo de Rivera, the Spanish Premier, today announced a decision to return to Cuba all relics and trophies of the war of independence found in the Spanish museums.

This action was determined on in the spirit which the present Directorate wishes to foster for the removal of all reminders of the past of armed encounters with countries which are now friendly.

The Government desires to efface any remembrances which might be susceptible of hindering the present excellent relations between Spain and Cuba.

Among the first relics to be returned is the flag of Cespedes y Borges, the Cuban patriot, the first symbol of the island's independence, which is now in the Artillery Museum at Madrid. This flag was wrested from the Cubans by Spanish troops at Yara in 1868.

MARINES KILL 14 IN NICARAGUA FIGHTS

They Defeat Two Attempts of Sandinistas to Ambush Them—Airmen Account for 9.

OUR MEN TAKE SAN ALBINO

Haiti Bandit-Fighter Assumes Command—Bogota Press Protests to Coolidge.

By HAROLD N. DENNY,
Staff Correspondent of The New York Times.
Copyright, 1928, by The New York Times Company. By Tropical Radio.

MANAGUA, Jan. 11.—Two attempts during the past twenty-four hours to ambush columns of United States marines moving into position for their expected general attack on the rebel forces of General Augustino Sandino were broken up with losses to Sandinistas, according to reports to Marine headquarters here today.

The first clash occurred yesterday afternoon when Sergeant Satterfield, a Lieutenant in the Nicaraguan National Guard, ran into fifty bandits at Cuje, a few miles northwest of Quilali. Five of Sandino's men were killed in the brief, sharp action, which resulted in the dispersal of the Sandinistas.

The second attempt was made this morning and was defeated from the air by Lieutenant C. F. Schilt, who distinguished himself last week in the removal of several wounded men from the front line by airplane.

Lieutenant Schilt was heading a group of fighting planes which were cruising over the fighting zone this morning while a column of marines headed by Captain Roger Peard was moving from Quilali to Jicarow. Lieutenant Schilt saw the bandits, who, he estimated, numbered 200. They were lying in wait on Sapotillal Ridge, scene of the recent ambush of Captain Richal's column. Schilt led his group toward the rebels, dropping bombs down upon them and raking them with machine guns.

When Captain Peard and his men arrived they found nine bandits dead. They buried them.

Major Archibald Young, who made a notable record against bandits in Haiti, has assumed command of the forces facing Sandino.

Lieut. Col. B. S. Berry, Chief of Staff of the Second Marine Brigade, which is commanded by Colonel Louis Mason Gulick, left here by airplane today to survey conditions in the combat zone.

New York Peace Body Leaves.

MANAGUA, Jan. 11 (AP).—Colonel Gulick declared today that airplanes

Continued on Page Four.

F. P. Dodge Willed $15,000 to Devoted Nurse; Woman Broken in Health by Long Service

A voluntary gift of $15,000 from the estate of Francis Phelps Dodge to Miss Laua Kjeldsen, who attended Mr. Dodge constantly during eight years prior to his death when he was an invalid, and who contracted tuberculosis because of her devotion to her duties, was disclosed in the appraisal of the estate filed yesterday by Deputy Tax Commissioner Stephenson. The estate of Mr. Dodge, who died Jan. 14, 1926, was valued at $1,539,356 gross and $1,408,604 net.

William Church Osborn, one executor, said in an affidavit that Mr. Dodge's inability to leave his bed was due to a disease of the joints, and that because of the care given by his nurse, who gave up her vacations in the interest of her patient, Mr. Dodge had considered making her a beneficiary in his will, or of paying her a certain sum, but died before he could do so. She had received only $50 a week and after his death, although tuberculosis prevented her from taking employment, she made no claim against the estate because of her professional relations with Mr. Dodge. For this reason Mr. Osborn said that the heirs had agreed that the $15,000 payment was just.

The appraisal shows the bulk of the estate consisted of $1,235,761 in securities, the largest holdings being 2,913 shares of the Washington Water Power Company worth $381,603, and 1,476 shares of the Fajardo Sugar Company common stock. He also owned $145,000 in Liberty bonds. The estate included $286,145 which he had power to dispose of under the will of his father, the Rev. Dr. D. Stuart Dodge. His will gave a third of the estate to each of his brothers, Walter Phelps Dodge and Clarence Dodge, and divided the other third among the three children of his deceased brother, Walter Guy Dodge. The will left $50,000 to the Beirut Syrian Protestant College, of which his father was long the head, and $10,000 to Teachers College.

"All the News That's Fit to Print"

The New York Times

THE WEATHER
Cloudy and warmer today, rain to night; colder tomorrow.
Temperature yesterday—Max., 37; min., 24.
For weather report see Page 30.

VOL. LXXVII....No. 25,587. NEW YORK, MONDAY, FEBRUARY 13, 1928. TWO CENTS In Greater New York | THREE CENTS Within 200 Miles | FOUR CENTS Elsewhere in the U. S.

HOOVER COMES OUT FOR THE PRESIDENCY ON A PLATFORM OF COOLIDGE POLICIES; ENTERS OHIO PRIMARY; BARS ANY BIG FUND

CITY TO NEGOTIATE FOR ELEVATED ROAD IN FIGHT ON I. R. T.

Seeks an Operating Alliance With Owners as Part of Plan to Seize Subways.

STOCKHOLDERS ARE UNEASY

Fear Contest Over Fares Will Result in Voiding Manhattan Line Lease.

UNTERMYER LAUDS WALKER

Asserts Mayor Is in Dead Earnest and With Proper Support by Public Will Get Relief.

Transit officials of the City Administration and the Transit Commission plan to enlist the aid of the owners of the Manhattan elevated lines in their fight to prevent the Interborough Rapid Transit Company, which operates the elevated under a lease, from collecting a seven-cent fare on both systems.

The plan to form an alliance with the elevated owners, as divulged yesterday, is part of the larger scheme, which involves seizure or recapture of the subway lines if the Interborough puts the higher fare into effect. The city, it was learned, hopes to effect an agreement with the Manhattan stockholders, whereby the elevated lines would be turned over to the city for operation with the subway system in order that the two systems might be continued as one in operation.

Information has reached the authorities that the principal owners of the Manhattan are greatly concerned over the Interborough's increased fare move, feeling that the probable effect of it would be the repudiation of the Manhattan lease, with the consequent return of the elevated lines to them for operation.

Sees Violation of Contracts.

Samuel Untermyer, the Transit Commission's special counsel in charge of the unification efforts and counsel for both city and the State in the forthcoming [illegible] fare litigation, declared yesterday in a guarded statement that the Interborough's contract with the city "has for years been flagrantly violated." While not admitting in so many words that the authorities planned to seize the Interborough lines under the default provisions of the contract, he agreed with city officials who favor that move that the actual putting of an increased fare into effect would be a violation of the contract which would entitle the city to take over the lines forthwith. He said he did not believe the Interborough would be foolhardy enough to put the increase into effect over the ruling of the Transit Commission.

The plans of the city and the Transit Commission, it developed yesterday, were now in definite shape. The program includes court action of a temporary nature to restrain the Interborough from raising the fare and practical steps looking to the elimination of the Interborough from the transit situation entirely.

The move to obtain an understanding with the Manhattan owners is part of the practical end of the program. In the event the city is enabled to take over the Interborough system on the ground of default the I. R. T. will be left with the elevated lines alone. At present these lines are not earning the 5 per cent. which the Interborough has to pay to the Manhattan owners under their lease of the property.

Fear Voiding of Lease.

It is understood that the Manhattan interests were fearful lest the Interborough's attempt to increase the rate of fare provided in the contract with the city would be construed as a breach of the contract. Should the Interborough be left with merely the elevated lines to operate, it was figured, the company would probably go into receivership and the courts would void the Manhattan lease.

The present owners of the Manhattan are not the original owners who operated the elevated lines long before the Interborough came into being with the construction of the first subway. The present owners have no facilities for operation and would be greatly embarrassed if forced to take the lines back.

The elevated system, however, is regarded by the city authorities as an important part of the rapid transit facilities of the city and cannot be abandoned without serious congestion in the subways resulting. To guard against the possibility of service on the elevated being halted, therefore, some of Mayor Walker's advisers favor an arrangement whereby the Manhattan interests would turn the elevated lines over to the city.

To Start Negotiations Soon.

It is understood that negotiations with this end in view are to be undertaken probably before the end of this week. The city officials, it was said last night, would urge that the elevated lines would have to be torn down within a few years anyway and that it would be to the interest of the Manhattan owners to cooperate with the city at this time, since they could then expect more favorable terms. It is planned eventually to substitute subways for the present elevated lines.

Although the Interborough's lease on the elevated lines runs for 999 years, it is inevitable, it was pointed out, that this lease would be voided

Continued on Page Eleven.

'Big Stick' of Kipling's Pen Is Defied by Rural Council

TICEHURST, England, Feb. 12 (AP).—Rudyard Kipling's pen looks more like a big stick than it does a sword to the Ticehurst Rural District Council.

In a dispute regarding flood damages to Kipling's Burwash property, the author recently wrote the council that, although he was "extremely adverse to litigation," he would place the matter in the hands of his solicitors unless the council soon made amends. After reading the letter to his colleagues, Chairman Spring-Rice declared:

"We can see the big stick which Kipling has waved at us, and I consider it most uncalled for."

The council then unanimously adopted a resolution denying all responsibility.

CLUB DANCER TRIES TO DIE IN PARK LAKE

Vainly Fights Off Young Man Who Breaks Ice to Swim to Her in the Darkness.

CARRIED PICTURE OF LOPEZ

Mlle. Roseray, a Night Club Performer, Refuses to Explain Her Act.

Mlle. Simone Roseray, Paris dancer starring at the Casa Lopez night club, Fiftieth Street and Broadway, was rescued against her will from drowning in the lake in the middle of Central Park early yesterday morning by Thomas Moore, 25 years old, a security company investigator, of 22 Post Avenue, who broke his way through the ice as he swam toward her.

A photograph of Vincent Lopez, orchestra leader and proprietor of the night club where she began a contract a week ago, was found among her belongings after she had been taken to the Lexington Hospital, a private institution in Lexington Avenue near Fifty-seventh Street. Detectives said words of endearment, in French, were written on the photograph.

Restored to consciousness after Dr. J. M. Blank of 15 Central Park West had worked over her for nearly three hours, the dancer would give only her name and occupation to detectives of the Arsenal Station, declining to tell why she had jumped into the lake or to reveal the names of friends or relatives, saying it would only "embarrass them."

Knows of No Romance.

Lopez spent yesterday at New Rochelle and his partner, Eugene Geiger, who occupies an apartment with him at 200 West Fifty-seventh Street, said late in the afternoon that he did not believe the orchestra leader knew of the affair.

"No, I don't know if there was any romance between the two," Geiger said, "but if there was, it was very secret, because there was nothing to show on the surface. Besides, I know Lopez was interested in another girl. Whether that had anything to do with the occurrence, I don't know."

Geiger said he had tried to see the dancer at the hospital to ascertain when she might be able to resume her appearances at the night club, but she had refused to see him. He added that she was suffering from shock and submersion. The hospital Superintendent declined to discuss Mlle. Roseray's condition.

The dancer's rescuer, who also was taken to the hospital suffering from chill, was discharged yesterday afternoon. Moore's family, talking over the telephone, said they had "heard something" about the rescue, but did not know the details, "as Tom hasn't come home yet."

Moore and a companion, John Reagan, of 141 West Ninety-fourth Street, were driving through Central Park toward Fifth Avenue at 4:30 A. M., when they heard screams from the direction of the lake. Without even slipping off his coat, Moore jumped from the car, ran to the edge of the lake and started out on the thin ice. He had gone only a few et when he crashed through. Breaking the ice ahead of him with his hands, he threshed his way

Continued on Page Eight.

LINDBERGH LEAVES HAVANA AT 2:26 A.M. FLYING TO ST. LOUIS

Hops Off by Moonlight on 1,250-Mile Trip, Which Concludes His Tour.

THRONG SEES HIM START

And Cuban Band Plays a March for His Plane—Takes Sandwiches as Only Food.

TOOK UP CUBAN PRESIDENT

He Piloted Machado and Pan-American Conference Delegates in Nine Flights Yesterday.

By The Associated Press.

HAVANA, Monday, Feb. 13.—Colonel Charles A. Lindbergh hopped off at 2:26 o'clock this morning on his return trip to St. Louis.

Eager to see the "Lone Eagle" start on his flight of about 1,250 miles to his home port of St. Louis, spectators began arriving at Columbia Field at 1:15 o'clock.

His route is from Havana to Key West, Fla., the only hop over water. Then he will go along the Gulf of Mexico to a point directly south of St. Louis and then turn directly north.

The moon rose soon after 1 o'clock, and arrangements were being made for the flight, although the Spirit of St. Louis was still in the hangar.

Colonel Lindbergh arrived at the field at 1:50. He was accompanied by the United States Ambassador, Noble Brandon Judah.

The Spirit of St. Louis was taken out of the hangar immediately after Colonel Lindbergh's arrival.

The flier walked about the field looking for a suitable place from which to take off. He announced he would start as soon as possible.

As the Spirit of St. Louis appeared on the field, accompanied by twenty-five attendants, the Cuban band struck up a spirited march.

Soon after 2 o'clock, Lindbergh started the plane's motor.

"The motor sounds perfect," he announced.

Before starting, Colonel Lindbergh stowed several sandwiches in the plane.

He decided to taxi the plane the whole length of the field to the far end from the hangar. He would then be able to take off in the face of the wind and have the whole length of the field before him.

Lindbergh appeared rested and smiling. Mrs. Judah arrived at the field with the flier and the Ambassador.

As the flier taxied down the field an automobile preceded him to show the way over the bumpy ground.

FLIER BUSY ON LAST DAY.

Takes Ninety Passengers Into Air in a Series of Flights.

By RUSSELL OWEN.

Special Cable to THE NEW YORK TIMES.

HAVANA, Feb. 12.—Colonel Charles A. Lindbergh made another Presidential convert to aviation today when he took up President Machado of Cuba for his first airplane ride. The President was as pleased as a child, and when he came down seemed eager to go again.

While he was in the air in a big three-motor Fokker of the Pan-American Airways, which plies between Key West and Havana, he could not keep still and walked up and down the aisle talking to his wife and members of his Cabinet who were in the party and looking out of the windows.

President Machado was much delighted with the view of the National Palace from the air and the old Spanish forts, which form such a picturesque part of Cuban scenery. Once he stuck his hand out of a window in the plane and laughed like a boy when the wind slammed it back against the casing.

It was a busy day for the "flying Colonel," for he took up most

Continued on Page Three.

Olympic Crowd Rebels When Swiss Ski Race Utterly Exhausts Youths on 20-Mile Trail

ST. MORITZ, Switzerland, Feb. 12 (AP).—Popular feeling was aroused to a high pitch at the utter state of exhaustion of the young soldiers finishing the twenty-mile military patrol ski race today and may cause an elimination of the event from future Winter Olympic sports.

France, it is understood, is preparing to present a motion to eliminate the race at the next meeting of the International Olympic Committee.

The rules provide that contestants, carrying a rifle, rations and other field equipment, must be soldiers in active service. Many of the nations with military service requirements of a year or eighteen months had mere youths of 20 and 21 years in the event.

Gendre, a French youngster who collapsed three miles from the finish and was carried on the shoulders of his comrades the rest of the way, is reported to be delirious and to have a high fever tonight. He is a slender youth of 20. The Finns recovered quickly from the effects of the long hike and were up and around after a few hours of rest.

Norway won the event, with Finland second and Switzerland third. Two of the four members of the Finnish team collapsed after crossing the finish line and had to be carried tot a hotel, where hot grog and other stimulants were administered.

Some of the youthful soldiers dropped exhausted in the mountain passes and others staggered over the finish line to fall headlong in the snow.

Norway's winning time over the twenty-mile course, in which the difference of altitudes between the start and finish at some points was 3,000 feet, was 3 hours 50 minutes 47 seconds. The hardy men from the Northland, fresh and erect, finished, singing the national anthem of Norway at the top of their lungs, five minutes ahead of the Finns.

Clear, Crisp Weather Draws Throngs to Seaside Resorts

Yesterday's clear, crisp weather sent city dwellers in thousands to near-by resorts. Coney Island, the Rockaways, Asbury Park and scores of other places along the seaboard were thronged. A crowd estimated at more than 100,000 at Coney Island caused the Police Department to detail about fifty additional traffic policemen for duty.

A continuous stream of automobiles passed over the Cross Bay Boulevard and Beach Channel Drive to the Rockaways throughout the day and Asbury Park accommodated an unusually large number of visitors. Atlantic City reported the largest Lincoln Day crowd in its history.

The coldest hour of the day in this city was at 7 o'clock when the temperature was 24 degrees. At 4 o'clock in the afternoon the mercury had risen to 37. According to the Weather Bureau forecast last night, today should be warmer, with rain probably this evening and tomorrow.

FIND QUEEN'S TOMB AND RICH ART IN UR

U. of P. Excavators Bare Gold Crowns and Rings, Vases and Other Sumerian Treasures.

ARCHES OLDEST EVER FOUND

Date to Fourth Millennium, B. C., Director Says—Attendants Lie With Queen.

Special to The New York Times.

PHILADELPHIA, Feb. 12.—From the tomb of a Sumerian Queen just discovered in Ur of the Chaldees by the joint expedition of the University of Pennsylvania and the British Museum have come contributions to archaeology and the history of architecture that may rival in importance the secrets given up by the tomb of King Tut-ankh-Amen in Egypt, a report received here from C. Leonard Woolley, director of the expedition, today indicated.

Besides the rich treasures surrounding the body of the Queen, Shub-ad, whose name appeared on a cylinder seal worn on her head with two crowns, the excavators brought to light what are declared to be the oldest arches ever discovered.

The tomb of the Queen adjoined that of a King, which was discovered recently and with which were found the bodies of his grooms, servitors, musicians and wives who had been slain to accompany the King into the next world.

Each of these tombs had a doorway, above which was a true arch of baked bricks. The chambers were vaulted with arches, of which a few rings still remained.

Date Put at 5,000 Years Ago.

Director Woolley said that the oldest previous arch known to archaeologists was that found over a drain at Nippur, a Babylonian city, dating back to the third millenium, B. C.

Excavation of the tombs in Ur reveals," the director said, "that corbel vaulting, the true arch and the dome all were familiar to the Sumerian builder and were carried out both in brick and stone in the fourth millenium, B. C."

Archaeologists in charge of the expedition have concluded, on the basis of the evidence they found, that the robbery of the King's tomb adjoining was done by the persons who buried the Queen, and done at the very time of her burial, probably 5,000 years ago.

Queen Shub-ad's tomb had evidently been left undisturbed by the vandals. The director described it as follows:

"The main interest here centred in the tomb itself. There were vessels of clay and copper, stone and silver, many of them broken and distorted, but others wonderfully preserved. At the other end, on a wooden bier, at the head and foot of which were crouched the bodies of attendants, lay the bones of the Queen, Shub-ad.

Marvelous Headdress.

"The Queen's headdress, worn originally over a great wig, was a marvelous sight as it was laboriously disengaged from stones and earth. Coil after coil of gold ribbon surrounded the hair. Above these and across the forehead ran a frontlet of lapis and carnelian beads, from which hung heavy rings of gold.

"Higher up was a wreath of large gold mulberry leaves hanging from another string of beads, and above this another wreath of leaves resembling willow leaves, with large gold flowers, whose petals were inlaid with lapis and white shell.

"Under the edge of the ribbon hung enormous gold earrings, and towering over the top of the head was a golden ornament like a Spanish comb, shaped like a hand with seven fingers, each of which ended in a gold flower.

"The Queen wore a tight-fitting necklace of lapis and gold and a cloak entirely covered with beadwork, vertical rows of beads in gold and lapis, carnelian and agate, with a border of beads set in horizontal groups of ten and fringed with dangling gold rings.

"The cloak was fastened on the right shoulder with three gold pins with lapis heads, and by the fastening were amulets—two goldfish and one of lapis—a lapis fringe of a re-

Continued on Page Four.

SMITH TO OPPOSE AN EVASIVE PLANK ON PROHIBITION

Friends Expect Him to Fight a Straddle if He Is to Be the Candidate.

FOR CONSTRUCTIVE STAND

He Would Expect the Party Declaration to Set Forth His Views, Supporters Say.

HE NEVER URGED REPEAL

But Has Advocated Right of States to Fix Non-Intoxicating Alcoholic Percentage.

By W. A. WARN.

Special to The New York Times.

ALBANY, Feb. 12.—No mild or evasive plank on prohibition for the Democratic national platform will have the approval of Governor Smith, in the event he should be the choice of the Houston convention for the Presidential nomination. No plank merely pledging the party to law enforcement, following the pattern of other Presidential years since the Eighteenth Amendment has been in force, will pass muster with him. That is what his friends are saying.

There has been no departure by the Governor from the policy of aloofness he has adopted for himself and consistently pursued with regard to the activities in which his friends throughout the country are engaging, to clinch what now appears to be his firm hold on the Democratic nomination.

Even though they believe now that it is nearly a foregone conclusion that he will be picked at Houston, the Governor consistently has declined to be drawn into any full discussion of national policies or the prospect of the nomination coming his way, and this in the face of much pressure brought to bear on him to toss his hat into the ring and give public expression to his views on questions that will figure prominently in the campaign this year.

For a Constructive Platform.

But in recent weeks, especially before the meeting of the Democratic National Committee and the Jackson Day Dinner in Washington last month, the Governor discussed with some of his friends and advisers in advance the contents of his letter, read at the dinner, which formed his first public expression upon matters having a bearing on the Presidential fight.

According to friends and advisers, the Governor strongly feels that in order to do justice to the opportunity that will come to it to win a victory this year, the party should provide a platform constructive from beginning to end; upon prohibition as well as upon all other questions of national import.

While there is no desire on the part of Governor Smith or his friends unduly to feature the prohibition question in the platform, the Governor is said to feel that if he should run it must be on a platform containing a prohibition plank that would leave no room for suspicion that he had sought to evade that issue, controversial though it be even within his own party. Consequently the Governor is credited with a determination to have the prohibition plank, in the event that he should be the standard bearer, set forth the views he has consistently expressed since prohibition in its present stage has been a topic of public discussion.

His Record for Enforcement.

The Governor, despite his approval of the repeal of the State Prohibition Enforcement law in 1923, has always strongly advocated rigid enforcement of the Volstead law, not only by Federal enforcement officials but by the peace officers of the State and of localities.

In connection with this it was recalled that after President Coolidge had summoned the Governors of the several Commonwealths to Washington for a discussion of ways and means for better prohibition enforcement throughout the country, Governor Smith was the only Chief Executive of a State to follow up the decisions reached at that gathering by calling together a council of public prosecutors and peace officers for the purpose of impressing upon

Continued on Page Two.

Klan to Establish National Headquarters Near Large Catholic Church in Washington

Special to The New York Times.

WASHINGTON, Feb. 12.—The Ku Klux Klan is to establish a new national headquarters in this city at 1,723 Rhode Island Avenue, Northwest, which is separated by only one residence from St. Matthew's Church, one of the most imposing Roman Catholic edifices in the capital. The property is but two squares from Dupont Circle, around which are grouped many of Washington's fashionable residences, including the mansion which President Coolidge occupied during the recent renovation of the White House roof and attic.

Arrangements by the Ku Klux Klan for leasing the property were made a few days ago with Miss Laura Harlan, a real estate agent here. She said today, however, that she had no detailed information as to the plans of those with whom the lease was negotiated.

The lease, which will expire in the Fall unless renewed, she added, has not yet been returned to her. It was sent to Atlanta following the call of the persons wanting the property, who saw her sign as the real estate agent.

The residence belongs to the estate of former Representative Richard Wayne Parker of New Jersey, and has been vacant since his death. It is a substantial old house, semi-detached, and was built some fifty years ago. Its construction is of brick, there are four floors and about twelve rooms.

None of the klan's officials could be reached here for details of plans for moving the national headquarters into the building.

Text of Secretary Hoover's Letter to Ohioans Announcing Candidacy for the Presidency

Special to The New York Times.

WASHINGTON, D. C., Feb. 12.—The text of Secretary Hoover's letter to his Ohio supporters is as follows:

Feb. 12, 1928.

Colonel Thad. H. Brown, Columbus Ohio.

My Dear Colonel Brown: I have received through you and others requests from very many Republicans of Ohio that I permit my name to be entered in the Presidential primaries of that State. I do so.

I shall be deeply honored by whatever support the people of Ohio may decide to give me at the Republican National Convention. I shall be glad to serve the American people through the Republican Party in any way that I can in finding constructive solution to the many problems which confront our country.

My conviction that I should not strive for the nomination and my obligations as Secretary of Commerce preclude me from making any personal campaign. I must rely wholly upon my friends in Ohio to conduct it and to conduct it in a fair manner and with steadfast regard for Republican success in the State and the nation. It is my special desire that expenditure of money shall be strictly limited and rigidly accounted for.

If the greatest trust which can be given by our people should come to me, I should consider it my duty to carry forward the principles of the Republican Party and the great objectives of President Coolidge's policies—all of which have brought to our country such a high degree of happiness, progress and security.

Yours faithfuly,
(Signed) HERBERT HOOVER.

CRITICIZED OFFICIAL RAIDS A PUBLISHER

But Westchester Prosecutor Denies It Is in Retaliation Against Brady Press.

TRIP TO EUROPE ATTACKED

Rowland Planned to Go Abroad Again for Prisoner—Won't Tell Why He Seized Books.

Books and accounts of Terence A. Brady of Yonkers, whose newspapers have been attacking District Attorney Arthur Rowland of Westchester County for planning a second trip to Europe to bring home a criminal, were seized in Mount Vernon last Thursday at the instance of District Attorney Rowland, it was learned yesterday.

Mr. Rowland said yesterday that the books and accounts had been seized because of a complaint made to his office and that the attacks on him had no bearing on the case.

"I am not at liberty to divulge the nature of the complaint at present," Mr. Rowland said. "I have no malice or enmity against Mr. Brady. The attacks on me have not annoyed me in any way and have nothing to do with the matter. It is unfortunate that the complaint came at such a time as to suggest that it was a retaliatory act on my part."

The attack by the Brady newspapers, which are The Yonkers Sunday Record, The Yonkers Star and The Mount Vernon Star, began on the announcement of Mr. Rowland that he planned to go to Europe personally to bring home a prisoner, John Wenzel of Yonkers, who is under arrest in England on a charge of stealing bonds from his wife.

The Brady newspapers criticized the District Attorney on the ground that his duties required his presence in the county; that he had no authority outside of Westchester, and that the duty of bringing home criminals from foreign parts should be performed by ordinary peace officers. Mr. Rowland went abroad a year ago on a similar mission, which, according to the Brady newspapers, involved a waste of the money of Westchester County taxpayers. In their campaign against him the Brady newspapers referred to the official as "Westchester County's seagoing District Attorney."

Terence A. Brady said he did not know the cause of the seizure of his

Continued on Page Ten.

NAVY TUG HITS ROCK; 5 OF CREW MISSING

The Mohave Smashes Her Hull on a Ledge Outside of Boston Harbor.

RESCUE SHIPS SPEED TO HER

Fourteen Men Taken Off, Six Others Reach Shore in Boat.

Special to The New York Times.

BOSTON, Mass., Feb. 12.—Five members of the crew of the navy tug Mohave are missing as the result of the craft striking on Harding's Ledge off Point Allerton late this evening while she was returning to Boston from Provincetown. Six others reached shore in a dingy and the remaining fourteen were rescued by naval vessels.

A big hole was smashed in the tug's bow by the collision in the darkness and water began to pour in. The radio operator at once sent out S O S signals and Admiral Andrews, commander of the naval district, started all available craft to the scene.

Thanks to this swift action, Patrol Boat 242 was able to reach the Mohave and take off the survivors. Because of the near-by rocks no attempt was made to salvage the Mohave, and with the waves breaking over her bow it was feared that she would probably become a total loss.

According to survivors, the Mohave struck with a tremendous crash just before 9 o'clock. She was carried high on the rocks and her hull was ripped for several feet.

Most of the crew were in their bunks when she struck, the impact hurling them on the deck. Wearing meager attire, the men rushed out and were drenched by the high waves breaking over the tug.

Two men were found to have disappeared overboard. After a few minutes the radio apparatus went dead and the commander of the tug, Boatswain Powers, sent three sailors off in a punt to carry news ashore of the disaster. Soon after they put off they shouted for help, and six more of the crew lowered a dingy and started on a vain hunt for them.

The six men in the dingy came ashore later on Nantasket Beach but those in the punt have not been seen since. Late tonight the rescue force was still hunting for them in the near-by waters.

When the first S O S messages from the Mohave were picked up, naval officials said that they were confronted with an unusual accident and with the fate of the lost S-4 still fresh in their minds made all haste to render aid.

Admiral Andrews ordered the navy tug No. 71 to proceed at once to Point Allerton while the Coast Guard vessels 78, 244 and the Dix departed on the same mission.

Later the navy destroyer Maury left the Navy Yard for the scene.

Other vessels which raced to the assistance of the Mohave were the Bushnell, mother ship of the S-4, and the naval tug Sagamore, which steamed out from Provincetown.

The names of the six men who reached Nantasket on the dinghy are Charles Thompson, Clifford Alexander, Francis Sliney, Edgar Townsend, Richard Connelley and James Colbert.

Meanwhile the Coast Guard crew at Point Allerton had been notified by telephone of the wreck. They launched a surfboat and were forced to go by way of the Gut to reach the tug.

WRITES TO OHIO BACKERS

'Shall Be Glad to Serve the American People,' Secretary Says.

INSISTS ON A FAIR FIGHT

Believes He Should Not Strive for Nomination and Will Make No Personal Campaign.

HE'S WELCOME, SAYS WILLIS

Senator Ready for Knockdown Battle—Hoover Soon to Enter Other State Contests.

Special to The New York Times.

WASHINGTON, Feb. 12.—Herbert Hoover, Secretary of Commerce, tossed his hat into the ring today when, in a letter to Thad Brown, leader of his Ohio supporters, in which he consented to have his name entered in the Republican Presidential primaries in that State, he announced that if nominated and elected he would carry forward the principles of the Republican Party and "the great objectives of President Coolidge's policies."

Mr. Hoover writes that his conviction that he should not strive for the nomination and his obligations as Secretary of Commerce preclude him from making any personal campaign, and he must rely wholly upon his friends in Ohio to conduct it. He says he wants the campaign conducted "in a fair manner," and emphasizes his desire that "expenditure of money shall be strictly limited and rigidly accounted for."

The decision by Mr. Hoover to get out in the open and fight was generally accepted in political circles here as the most important development in the pre-convention campaign since President Coolidge made his "I-do-not-choose" statement at Rapid City in August. It is expected that the Secretary's message to Mr. Brown will be accepted by his backers in all parts of the country as a signal to go into action in his behalf.

"Perfectly Welcome," Says Willis.

Senator Frank B. Willis, who will appear as a favorite-son candidate in Ohio and whose attitude in refusing to permit Hoover to appear as a second-choice candidate is held to be in part responsible for the bitter party contest which is now certain in that State, had just returned from delivering a political address in Utica, N. Y., when the Hoover message was made public.

"Oh, very well," said Mr. Willis. "He's perfectly welcome to come in. I have been known to the people of Ohio for about thirty years. I know them and they know me. He will find out at the close of the primary contest whether he has been correctly advised by those assuming to be his friends."

Despite Mr. Hoover's expressed hope that the fight in Ohio will be carried on with "steadfast regard for Republican success in the State and in the nation," there is every indication that the campaign leading up to the primary election on April 24 will be marked by such warfare as the party has not known since 1912. Senator Willis in a recent statement following Representative Burton's first suggestion that Mr. Hoover enter the Ohio contest said that it would be no kid glove affair and, in effect, that he intended to call a spade a spade.

Complete Hoover Ticket in Ohio.

Hoover candidates for delegates and alternates will be entered in each of the twenty-two Congressional districts of Ohio and for the seven delegates-at-large. Each district elects two delegates, thus giving a total of fifty-one, and the Hoover campaigners are going to battle for them all.

There is held in Ohio also a State-wide preference vote, which, however, is not legally binding on any of the delegates after the first ballot in the convention. While a final decision has not been made, it was indicated tonight that the Secretary, now that he was in the battle, would try to win this preference vote as well.

In 1920, when Leonard Wood contested the Ohio delegates with Warren G. Harding, the General won nine of them but was defeated by about 15,000 ballots in the preference vote. The backers of Hoover feel confident that they will win the preference vote and also get at least twenty of the district delegates and the seven delegates-at-large. To the Hoover forces thus are virtually conceded twelve delegates, including six from the three Cleveland districts, four from the two Cincinnati districts and two from Toledo.

Burton May Head Hoover List.

It is expected here that Representative Burton will head the list of Hoover candidates for delegates-at-large. The name of William Cooper Procter of Cincinnati, who was in command of the Leonard Wood campaign in 1920, has been suggested as another candidate for delegate-at-

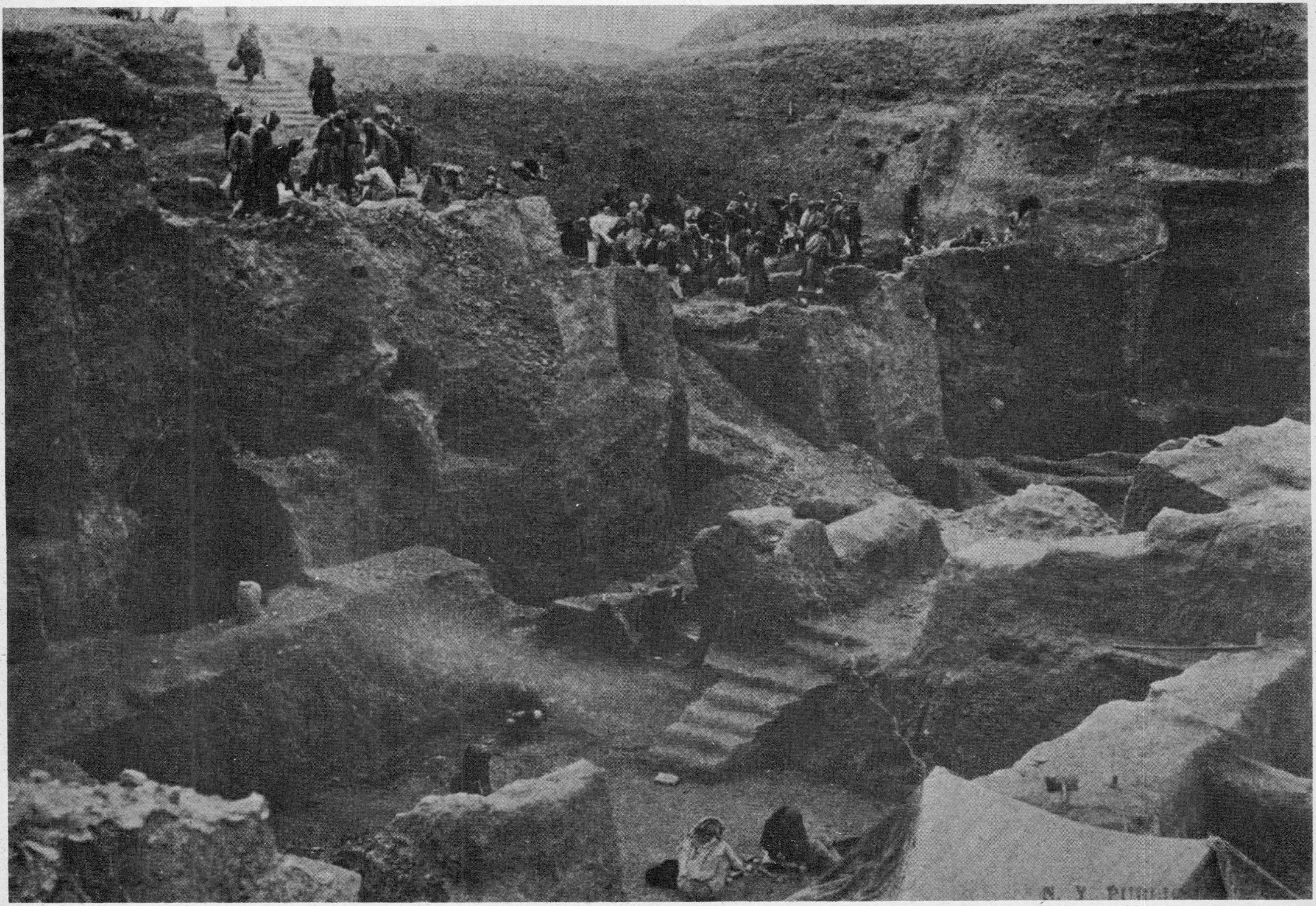

Excavation at the site of the King of Ur's tomb.

Section 1

"All the News That's Fit to Print."

The New York Times.

THE WEATHER
Cloudy, with rising temperature, today, followed by rain or snow.
Temperature yesterday—Max., 39; min., 26.
For weather report see Page 27.

Section 1

VOL. LXXVII....No. 25,614. * * * * NEW YORK, SUNDAY, MARCH 11, 1928. Including Rotogravure Picture Section in two parts—Magazine and Book Sections in Rotogravure. FIVE CENTS In Manhattan, Bronx and Brooklyn | Elsewhere TEN CENTS

HAYS SENT MELLON $50,000 OIL BONDS TO COVER 'GIFT' TO PARTY; WERE SENT BACK

SECRETARY BARES 'TRICK'

Writes to Walsh When Pratt Records Reveal 'Andy' Notation.

THREE OTHER NAMES SHOWN

'Weeks,' 'Butler,' 'du Pont' on Mysterious Memorandum Put Before Committee.

NEW CONTINENTAL TRAIL

Pratt Got $25,000 of the Canadian Concern's Bonds—Hipsley Has Few Data.

Special to The New York Times.

WASHINGTON, March 10.—Revelation before the Senate oil inquiry committee today of the word "Andy" in the handwriting of the late John T. Pratt of New York City, written in the right hand corner of a memorandum relating to Mr. Pratt's contribution of $50,000 to the Republican National Campaign deficit of 1920, led to the announcement tonight by Andrew W. Mellon, Secretary of the Treasury, that in the late Fall of 1923 he had received $50,000 in Liberty bonds from Will H. Hays, the 1920 Chairman of the Republican National Committee, to whom Harry F. Sinclair turned over in November, 1923, Liberty bonds to the value of $260,000.

Mr. Mellon, in a letter to Senator Walsh of Montana, declared that when he received the bonds he had no knowledge of Mr. Hays's purpose in sending them to him, and that a few days later when the matter was explained by Mr. Hays he returned the bonds to him. Subsequently, he added, he made a contribution of $50,000 to be applied to the deficit.

Mr. Hays told Secretary Mellon that the bonds were part of an allotment turned over to him by Mr. Sinclair, and at that time suggested that Mr. Mellon hold the bonds and contribute an equal amount to the National Committee.

In other words, the Secretary, had he accepted the suggestion of Mr. Hays, would have made a "fake" contribution, such as James A. Patten, the Chicago grain operator, admitted on Thursday having made. Mr. Patten's so-called "trick" contribution was only $25,000, or half the amount asked of Mr. Mellon.

Same Program With Pratt.

The same program was followed in the case of Mr. Pratt, and his gift was down for $50,000. Mr. Pratt accepted the bonds, Mr. Hays testified before the Senate committee, but subsequently returned bonds to the amount of $50,000, which Mr. Hays said he gave back to Mr. Sinclair.

The Senate committee today traced $25,000 of the Pratt allotment of the Continental Trading Company, out of the profits of which the Government charges Sinclair gave to A. B. Fall, his co-defendant in the Teapot criminal actions, more than $230,000. The other half of the bonds which Mr. Hays says he gave to Mr. Pratt remain unaccounted for. Mr. Pratt died in June of last year.

The fact that Mr. Hays sought to have Mr. Mellon, who was a Cabinet colleague of his when Mr. Hays was Postmaster General, stand for one of the "fake" contributions to the deficit was suggested to the committee when E. De T. Bechtel of New York, counsel for the Pratt estate, handed to Senator Walsh a small card on which Mr Pratt noted that he had sent $50,000 to the late Fred W. Upham of Chicago, then Treasurer of the Republican National Committee. At the bottom of the card and written in pencil appeared four names. They were "Weeks," "Andy," "Dupont" and "Butler."

Will Now Question Butler.

Immediately, the curiosity of the committee was aroused. Senator Nye and Senator Walsh recalled that when on the witness stand last week, Hays admitted giving $75,000 of Sinclair's bonds to General du Pont to be applied to a committee note in the Empire Trust Company, New York; another $25,000, Mr. Hays added, had gone to the late Secretary of War, John W. Weeks, while $60,000 he said had been sent to Mr. Upham.

He did not at the time name Mr. Mellon or "Butler."

Senator Walsh said tonight that he had sent a telegram to ex-Senator William M. Butler of Massachusetts, Chairman of the Republican National Committee, asking him to appear before the Senate committee on Tuesday, as he was anxious to know what if anything Mr. Butler knew of the Sinclair bonds. Senator Walsh also said that he felt it would be necessary to recall Mr. Hays and ask him why he omitted to inform the committee that he had sent $50,000 of the bonds to Mr. Mellon.

Immediately following the disclosures before the committee today, Senator Walsh sent a transcript of the testimony in which the word "Andy" was mentioned to Secretary Mellon. With the transcript went a note in which Senator Walsh asked the Secretary if there was anything he

Continued on Page Twenty-two.

Parked Autos Keep Firemen From West 49th Street Blaze

Firemen, responding last evening to an alarm sent in from Eighth Avenue and Forty-ninth Street, found that automobiles were parked so tightly together in the street that they could not get within 100 feet of the blaze. The fire was in the basement of a five-story tenement at 316 West Forty-ninth Street.

An effort was made to move some of the cars, but the owners had locked the doors and windows before parking. The firemen were forced to run hose lines under the parked cars to the basement of the building. They had further trouble in getting two extension ladders into position.

Sixteen families in the building were driven out by the smoke. No one was hurt.

RADIO RISES TO LEAD IN BIGGEST MARKET

Gains 12¾ Points in Turnover of 398,500 Shares as General Motors Yields 2 Points.

WEEK SETS TRADING RECORD

16,278,900 Shares Dealt In, Swelled by 2,200,630 in Heaviest Saturday's Business.

With Radio Corporation furnishing a fresh sensation as General Motors was staggering under a wave of profit-taking, the New York stock market yesterday wound up the greatest week of trading in its history. Radio closed with a net gain of 12¾ points, while General Motors ended the day with a net loss of 2 points. In eight consecutive trading days this marked the first recession.

General Motors yielded its leadership to Radio in the day's advance after a brief struggle at the opening, but it finished a close second in volume of turnover. General Motors, with transactions totaling 396,000 shares, and Radio, with 398,500 shares changing hands, accounted for more than one-third of the aggregate business on the Stock Exchange in the busiest Saturday since that institution was established.

Old Record Is Smashed.

Sales of all stocks amounted to 2,200,630 shares, a gain of 397,920 over the Saturday record of 1,802,710 shares established on Feb. 18. Although no official hourly records are kept, it was believed by stock market veterans that yesterday's turnover was the heaviest for any two-hour period since stock trading began in New York.

In the week ended yesterday there was dealt in on the Stock Exchange a total of 16,278,900 shares, against the previous record of 15,628,870 shares in the week ended Dec. 3, 1926. Of last week's total business 2,431,500 shares were in General Motors, a turnover for one stock that has rarely been exceeded by any other issue in that time. Old-time followers of the market could not recall yesterday when any issue had been the focal point of such heavy trading in recent years or when, in all Stock Exchange history, a stock issue of the size of General Motors had staged such a spectacular advance as it has since the uprush began on Friday, March 2.

Althoug supplanted temporarily by Radio as the market's bellwether, General Motors continued yesterday to monopolize a large share of trading interest. With the speculative appetite whetted by the remarkable advance of Friday, orders for General Motors had piled up overnight in such volume that it was ten minutes after yesterday's opening before the confusion could be cleared away

Continued on Page Twenty.

ALL SAVED ON LINER, BUT 3 RESCUERS DIE WHEN BOAT CAPSIZES

Coast Guardsmen Lose Lives After Thrilling Rescues in Small Craft Through Raging Seas.

PASSENGERS AVOID PANIC

Some Suffer From Cold and Hunger—Tell of Tedious Vigil After Crash on Rocks.

VESSEL MAY BE TOTAL LOSS

Waves Pound the Robert E. Lee Off Manomet Point, With Three Officers Watching on Cutter.

Special to The New York Times.

BOSTON, Mass., March 10.—After hours of heroic rescue work, during which three Coast Guardsmen from Manomet lost their lives, all of the 150 passengers and the 113 members of the crew on the stranded steamer Robert E. Lee were taken off safely shortly after noon today.

The tragedy which took the lives of the three Coast Guardsmen occurred when a crew of eight men from the life saving station at Manomet Point were thrown into the water by the capsizing of their boat. One was drowned, another died ten minutes after he was rescued and a third died of exposure aboard the Paulding. A fourth was reported so severely affected by the immersion and exposure that he may not recover.

The steamer was still held fast on the rocks where she had grounded off Manomet Point last night while on her way from Boston to New York during the gale.

The passengers were taken off the vessel in surf boats manned by Coast Guardsmen, and transferred to the 125-foot patrol boats Bonham and Active, and the CG-176, which had been sent from the Boston Navy Yard this morning.

Women and Children Taken First.

Though some of the passengers had spent a night of discomfort on board the steamer, they were confident of being rescued and were in good spirits when they stepped ashore at Plymouth Rock. Seven of the passengers were put aboard the Coast Guard cutter Red Wing, and decided to return to Boston in that vessel. They were landed at the navy yard this afternoon.

Captain Robinson of the Lee came to Boston this evening. He left three of the ship's officers aboard the Coast Guard cutter Tuscarora standing by the stranded vessel.

The passengers who landed at Plymouth said those who had staterooms on the lower deck of the liner were forced to the upper decks when the water which had leaked in flooded their rooms.

Twenty-five women and children were first taken from the stranded steamer. The steamship officials had arranged to have a fleet of buses to carry the passengers to Boston.

The first bus left for Boston at 1:30 this afternoon. It was followed by several others, which left Plymouth at ten-minute intervals. The passengers were brought to the South Station here and those who wished to go on received tickets for the New York train. The steamship passage money was refunded to others who remained here.

The first passengers landed on the pier at Plymouth showed some signs of suffering from exposure and hunger and they were taken to the Plymouth Rock House, where the Red Cross provided for their comfort.

The entire rescue work was made under the most perilous circumstances, and the relief boats were in constant danger from the high seas. Life savers from the Sagamore station who had put out for the wreck last night, were forced to return. As no news had been sent out regarding their return it was at first feared they had gone down. The men of the crew, with three others, put out again for rescue work today.

Liner George Washington Stands By.

The steamship George Washington of the Eastern Steamship Line ar-

Continued on Page Twenty-three.

Shifting of Mountainside Kills 200 in Brazil; Sleeping Santos Families Buried in Homes

By The Associated Press.

RIO JANEIRO, March 10.—Sudden shifting of a side of Mount Serrat, in the centre of the City of Santos, State of Sao Paulo, Brazil, crashed thousands of tons of earth and rocks without warning onto a section of that place this morning and left a dead and dying toll estimated at more than 200.

Houses and buildings in the path of the slide were crumpled and buried, their occupants apparently not discerning the impending disaster until it was too late to escape the huge avalanche.

Tonight, while 2,000 men were engaged in rescue work in the stricken area, there were indications that the slide on one side of the mountain had weakened the dirt on still another side, and there was fear that another catastrophe in an adjoining district was impending.

Mount Seratt, with a moderately high peak, is situated practically in the centre of Santos, Brazil's principal coffee port, with residences and business buildings spread around it on three sides.

While details as received here are comparatively few it was said that the avalanche occurred just before dawn at 5:20 this morning. Although there had been previous warnings of a possible shifting of the side of the mountain there had been no indication that any such danger was immediate. Coming as it did, it undoubtedly caught many residents of the stricken area asleep.

Dispatches to the Buenos Aires papers said sixteen houses were completely crumpled and buried; other estimates were even higher. Between three and four million cubic yards of earth are said to have shifted, completely burying to a depth upward of forty feet, an area whose bounds were in places as far distant as a hundred yards from the old base of the mountain.

SANTOS, BRAZIL, March 10.—Late today eighteen bodies had been taken from the debris of the alvalanche which crashed down the side of Mount Serrat at dawn today burying, it is believed, 200 beneath it. Three others were found alive and were rushed to hospitals.

Work was frantic tonight in an effort to recover others buried beneath the mass of earth and rocks, some of whom, it is believed, may have escaped death. Mobility of the sliding earth, which was still shifting tonight, however, hindered work.

BYRD'S PLANS FOR HIS SOUTH POLE EXPEDITION; A $500,000 VENTURE TO MAP AN UNKNOWN CONTINENT, WITH NEWS COMING DIRECT BY RADIO TO THE TIMES

Wilbur Bans Outside Loops Save by Special Authority

Special to The New York Times.

WASHINGTON, March 10.—Fear that young and enthusiastic but relatively inexperienced naval aviators may attempt outside loop-the-loop led Secretary Wilbur today to issue an order against such flying except by special authorization of the Navy Department.

Lieutenant Al Williams, crack navy speed pilot, recently performed the dangerous feat and a few days later a naval aviator at Hampton Roads was reported to have duplicated it.

Called upon to explain, however, he said he did not know he had executed an outside loop.

CONFESSES 2 MEN SLEW CANTON EDITOR

McDermott, Ohio Life Prisoner, Declares Streitenberger and Mazer Shot Mellett.

CLEARS LENGEL AND RUDNER

He Admits Witnessing Murder, but Insists Attackers Did Not Mean to Kill Victim.

Special to The New York Times.

YOUNGSTOWN, Ohio, March 10.—Floyd Streitenberger, former city detective of Canton, and Louis Mazer, an underworld character, fired the shots which on July 16, 1926, ended the life of Don R. Mellett, editor of The Canton Daily News, while the latter was parking his automobile in his garage.

This "confession" was made by Patrick Eugene McDermott, serving a life sentence in the Ohio Penitentiary, according to a copyrighted article published by The Youngstown Vindicator and specially released to THE NEW YORK TIMES. Both Streitenberger and Mazer are serving life sentences in the State Penitentiary at Columbus for their participation in the crime.

If McDermott's confession is true, it clears up the mystery which has surrounded the Canton editor's death in so far as the actual perpetrator of the crime was concerned. McDermott was sentenced to the penitentiary without hope of pardon. He admits that he was with Streitenberger and Mazer when the fatal shots were fired, and says the murder was the culmination of a carefully laid plot.

Speaks to "Free His Mind."

This is the first time since his arrest and incarceration that McDermott has made any statement regarding the crime other than to deny knowledge of it or participation in it.

The authorities are inclined to believe his story is true. The confession was made to a Vindicator reporter in the presence of P. E. Thomas, Warden of the penitentiary.

At the time of the murder the city detective force of Canton was under fire by The Canton News.

McDermott, in his confession, said he had nothing to gain and simply wanted to free his mind. He absolved S. A. Lengel, former Police Chief of Canton, from any participation in the crime, and Ben Rudner of Massillon, formerly identified with Canton's underworld and now serving a life sentence in connection with Mellett's death. Rudner is reported to be the son of a wealthy man.

McDermott said he did not believe either Streitenberger or Mazer intended to kill Mellett, but only meant to scare him. On the night of the killing both had .38 calibre revolvers.

"I promised Mazer I'd never talk and I didn't until now, when everything is ended," said McDermott. "It was a matter of principle with me." McDermott says he did not know Mellett was killed until he read it in the newspapers the next day and he immediately left Canton.

Former Chief Lengel was recently freed at Lisbon, Columbiana County, on a directed verdict by the presiding Judge. He had previously been tried and sentenced to a life term, which he had started to serve.

Tells of Volley From Ambush.

McDermott said that the attack on Mellett was the outcome of a plot to frighten the editor. Streitenberger, Mazer and he met by appointment on the evening of the murder, and after driving around town went to Mellett's home, where they concealed themselves in the vicinity of the garage.

When Mellett came home from a party and had parked his automobile the two men opened fire on him. McDermott said that a volley was fired and Mellett fell.

He said that he first met Mazer in the Atlanta Penitentiary and was introduced to him by Ben Rudner. Rudner was serving time for bootlegging, while McDermott was in for grand larceny.

Following the crime, McDermott said, Rudner, Mazer and he were

Continued on Page Nineteen.

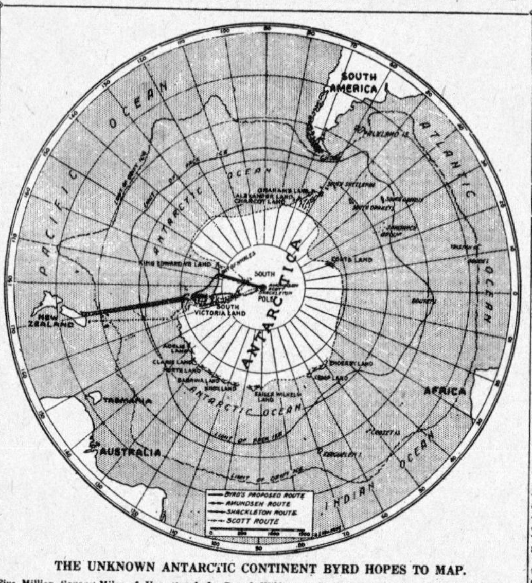

THE UNKNOWN ANTARCTIC CONTINENT BYRD HOPES TO MAP.

Five Million Square Miles of Unexplored, Ice-Bound Wilderness, Broken on One Side Only, So Far, by the Trails of Amundsen, Scott and Shackleton.

MINER'S WIFE TELLS SENATORS OF WOES

Had to Choose Between Shoes and Food at Company Store, Mother of 8 Says.

BRINGS BABY TO HEARING

Her Husband Was Discharged Because She "Talked Too Much" to Investigators.

Special to The New York Times.

WASHINGTON, March 10.—A declaration made before the Senate Commerce Committee by R. L. Wildermuth of Columbus, Ohio, General Manager of the Lorraine Coal and Dock Company, that if a representative of the United Mine Workers of America tried to organize Logan County, West Virginia, "the miners would mob him," caused a spirited colloquy in the coal hearing this afternoon, ending in sharp criticism of Mr. Wildermuth by Senator Gooding of Idaho, who is presiding.

A few moments later a scene from the home life of a Pennsylvania coal mining village was enacted when a miner, C. E. Barr, testified he had been discharged by the Pittsburgh Coal Company because his wife had told the Senate Subcommittee, which recently visited Pricedale, Pa., that her children were without shoes and stockings because there was not sufficient income to pay for them.

He was followed by his wife, a gaunt but neatly attired woman, who sat at the common table with a year-old blue-eyed girl—Eva Matilda—the youngest of eight children, and the first infant in recent years, if ever, to face a Senate committee across the table.

Coal Company Protests.

Their presence and testimony without cross-examination, followed by adjournment for the day, brought a vigorous protest on behalf of the Pittsburgh Coal Company by H. F. Baker, President of the Pittsburgh Terminal Coal Company, who hurried to Chairman Gooding while all were standing ready to leave and declared it was unfair to let the Barrs go until they had been cross-examined.

For several minutes he engaged in heated objections to the procedure, saying it was not right to let their story go out unchallenged. There were indications that the committee would permit the cross-examination Monday.

Prior to these incidents legislation to relieve conditions for the whole mining industry was declared by Senator Gooding to be the purpose of the committee in holding its present investigation. This came while John W. Searls of West Orange, N. J., President of the Pennsylvania Coal and Coke Company, as a witness, said he believed present conditions would improve with efficient management.

Senator Gooding told Mr. Searls the coal industry was basic and "has

Continued on Page Twenty-four.

Congress Leaders Doubt Adjournment Before June 1

WASHINGTON, March 10 (AP).—Republican legislative pilots are generally of the opinion that President Coolidge is optimistic in his belief that Congress can wind up its session by mid-May.

They conceded today that adjournment then would be possible, but as they viewed the legislative field, with much work still to be done, adjournment at or near June 1 was regarded as about the best that could be expected. That would enable the lawmakers to get away before the political conventions.

Of the leaders, Tilson, the Republican floor manager in the House, was about the only one who seemed to share the President's hope for a May 15 adjournment.

BOY FOILS ATTEMPT TO WRECK L. I. TRAIN

Finds Five-Foot Timber Wedged Under One Rail and Lying on the Other at Valley Stream.

Special to The New York Times.

VALLEY STREAM, L. I., March 10.—What appears to have been an attempt to wreck a Long Island passenger train on the West Hempstead Division near the Merrick Road crossing in this village last Thursday night, was revealed today. The Valley Stream police have been investigating the incident ever since it was reported to them a few minutes after the discovery. They thought it best to withhold all information until today.

The attempt, which was made by wedging a piece of heavy timber under one rail, allowing it to lie on top of the other, was discovered by an 11-year-old boy, Justin Loeffler, the son of Mr. and Mrs. John Loeffler of Merrick Road as he was walking along the track on his way home last Thursday evening.

He immediately realized the danger and attempted to remove it. His strength proved insufficient, however, and he ran along the track 100 yards to the watchman's shanty at the Merrick Road crossing. Walter Haff, who was on duty there, did not at first believe the boy's story, but after a few minutes of desperate urging by the boy, placed a red lantern in the middle of the tracks to halt the southbound train that was due in a few minutes and hurried to the spot.

Man and boy together removed the timber, which was about five feet long and three inches thick, a scant ten minutes before the arrival of the train from Mineola, which bore few passengers. But trains running in the opposite direction were heavily loaded with homeward-bound commuters on the single track line.

According to the watchman, who first examined the piece of timber, and Patrolman Richard Thompson of the Valley Stream Police Depart-

Continued on Page Three.

MAYOR TO LET PUBLIC DECIDE STRIKE BLAME

Orders All Moves by Union and I. R. T. in Writing and Ends Secret Mediation.

18 MORE MEN ARE OUSTED

Amalgamated Says Skilled Men Are Being Forced to Quit by Humiliating Tasks.

Mayor Walker figuratively washed his hands of responsibility for a subway strike yesterday, following a conference with leaders of the Amalgamated Association of Street and Electric Railway Employes. The Mayor stipulated that from now on both union leaders and the Interborough Rapid Transit Company must communicate with him by letter, in order that the communications may be published and the public may judge who is responsible in the event of a strike.

Having been turned down by the Interborough heads in his request that the company refrain from dismissing any more Amalgamated employes, the Mayor is understood to have told the union leaders that whether there is a strike or not is up to them. The union heads do not want a strike, but admitted to Mayor Walker yesterday that they may be forced to order a walkout because of the Interborough's policy.

Brotherhood Ousts Eighteen.

Eighteen men were expelled from the Brotherhood of Interborough Employes yesterday. Under the terms of the contract between the company union and the company their employment ceased automatically.

Ten of these men, Mayor Walker was told, were expelled after they had resigned. According to the union men the ten were ordered to report to the Lenox Avenue and 147th Street yards. They were lined up and a pail and a large sponge were handed to each man. They were assigned to clean the lavatories which the 2,000 strike-breakers held in readiness for a strike have been using.

According to union officials, the company's new policy is not to dismiss the Amalgamated workers, but to humiliate the skilled employes by requiring them to do the work of porters and thus compel them to quit.

Mayor Walker was plainly incensed by reports which reached him during the day. He was evidently convinced that the company is determined to force the Amalgamated to call a strike, and, although the union leaders still indicated a desire to avoid an open war with the I. R. T., Mayor Walker feared last night that the company's policy would result in an unauthorized strike.

The extent of such a strike was admittedly problematical. The Amalgamated has refrained from issuing a strike call because they could not be sure of winning. In the opinion of city officials in touch with the situation. Yet the best information the authorities have is that 5,000 or 6,000 men still belong to the A. F. of L.

Continued on Page Twenty-one.

WILL START IN SEPTEMBER

May Be Gone Nearly Two Years, but Will Be in Touch by Radio Daily

FROM ICE CAP TO NEW YORK

Struggles of the Best Equipped Expedition of Modern Times a Breakfast-Table Story.

WHAT THEY PLAN TO DO

Party of 55 Men, 3 Airplanes, 75 Dogs, With Tractors and Special Ice Ship to Reveal Antarctic Wonders.

By RUSSELL OWEN.

The Byrd Antarctic Expedition, which will attempt by means of airplanes to reach the South Pole and, what is more important, to lift some of the veil of mystery which lies over 4,600,000 square miles of that unexplored wilderness, will leave New York late in August or early in September.

On the wooden ice-ship Samson, three airplanes, 75 dogs and a personnel of pilots, scientists and crew of fifty-five altogether, including a member of the staff of THE NEW YORK TIMES, will sail for the Ross Ice Barrier to spend from three to fifteen months in the frozen South. It will be the most complete and expensive expedition that ever went into the Antarctic, and, because of its planes, will be able to explore scores of thousands of miles of territory never before seen by man.

News to Come to The Times.

From the time the expedition leaves New York until it returns it will be in touch with home, Commander Byrd and others telling of its difficulties and accomplishments by means of short-wave radio messages sent direct to THE NEW YORK TIMES. Thus, for the first time, it will be possible to follow, day by day, adventures and discoveries in the wild Antarctic, where every day is a struggle for existence and every extended journey threatens the lives of those who make it.

By an arrangement antedating even Commander Byrd's historic flight to the North Pole, exclusive rights throughout the world to this great story of his new expedition to the Antarctic have been acquired jointly by THE NEW YORK TIMES and The St. Louis Post-Dispatch, which, through the agency of Current News Features of New York and Washington, will share it with a selected group of newspapers in the United States and elsewhere throughout the world. As in the North Pole flight, the stories of this expedition, written by a staff correspondent of THE NEW YORK TIMES will appear in New York in THE TIMES alone. They will be sent by radio at frequent intervals, sometimes every day, giving a connected and dramatic narrative of what is going on in a land of mist and snow, 2,300 miles from the nearest inhabited territory.

Plans of the Expedition.

Commander Richard Evelyn Byrd, leader of the expedition, who has been at work on the plans for this journey of exploration ever since he returned from his North Pole flight, interrupting his preparations only to fly the Atlantic, does not know yet just how long a time will be required to fly over the territory he wishes to map. He hopes to reach the ice barrier about Dec. 16, but if he is delayed by the pack ice which lies outside Ross Sea, and which extends for hundreds of miles, it may be the first part of January before he can begin the work of establishing his first base.

The Antarctic has a way of upsetting the best-laid plans, but if Commander Byrd is fortunate he may be able to make his flights and get out before Winter weather sets in early in March and closes the line of retreat. If not, he will Winter, with about twenty-five men, on the ice barrier, sending his ship back to New Zealand, and continuing his exploration when Spring makes it possible. In that case he will spend fifteen months in the Antarctic, of which six months are the long night, when little can be done.

If the Long Night Overtakes it.

During this entire period, however, communication will be maintained with THE TIMES. Two complete short-wave radio sets will be taken with the expedition, one for use on the ship and another for use on

The South Polar plane, the *Floyd Bennett*'s landing gear consisted of skis instead of wheels.

The snowdrift that sheltered the *Floyd Bennett* from the worst of the winter storms.

"All the News That's Fit to Print."

The New York Times.

EXTRA—7 A. M.

THE WEATHER—Colder today, probably snow flurries.

VOL. LXXIX....No. 26,242. ****** NEW YORK, FRIDAY, NOVEMBER 29, 1929. TWO CENTS In Greater New York | THREE CENTS Within 200 Miles | FOUR CENTS Elsewhere Except 7th and 8th Postal Zones

COMMANDER BYRD OFF ON FLIGHT TO THE SOUTH POLE; RADIO REPORTS "ALL IS WELL" AT 6:30 A. M., 8 HOURS OUT; PASSES SLEDGE PARTY ON THE TRAIL AND DROPS MESSAGES

NANKING AND MUKDEN AT ODDS ON POLICY AS HOSTILITIES CEASE

Manchuria's Yielding Ignored by Chiang, Who Offers Reds New Counter-Proposal.

APPEALS SEEN AS GESTURE

Tokio Sees China Completely Beaten and Danger Over as Soviet Withdraws.

POWERS APPROACHED BY US

Envoys to Five Nations Propose Joint Action Under Kellogg Treaty if Situation Warrants.

By HUGH BYAS.

Wireless to THE NEW YORK TIMES.

TOKIO, Nov. 28.—The end of the Chinese resistance in Russia is the important fact emerging from the medley of reports reaching Tokio today. Edwin Lowe Neville, American Chargé d'Affaires, called on Baron Shidehara, Foreign Minister, at 6 o'clock last evening, and communicated a dispatch he had received from Washington. The Foreign Office declines to indicate the nature of Secretary Stimson's proposals, or Japan's views on them, but the collapse of Chinese resistance ends the situation which had aroused Secretary Stimson's anxiety.

The ease with which the Russians drove 12,000 Chinese troops from Manchuli in Western Manchuria, added to the financial strain of maintaining armies on a war footing, has forced Mukden to cancel its action of July and consent to the reinstatement of a Russian manager and submanager of the Chinese Eastern Railway. Nanking has been reluctantly compelled to acquiesce in Mukden's surrender, since Mukden had decided to make terms with Moscow anyhow.

Nanking press telegrams announcing that Russia's terms are being conceded add the curious statement that China will ask the United States and Germany to mediate, while the Chinese Minister to Tokio states that China is appealing to the League of Nations. In the Japanese view, direct negotiation with Russia is the better course, since Russia is not a member of the League and the United States has not recognized Russia. These reports appear to be intended to divert the Chinese public's attention from the surrender, although China is doubtless prepared for direct negotiations.

The Japanese are probably relieved that the necessity of international action has been removed. They would have joined the other Kellogg pact powers in issuing a warning, but they have always believed the matter had best be settled by the Chinese and Russians themselves.

The news from Manchuria confirms the Japanese anticipation that the Russians did not intend an invasion. The Russians apparently have not occupied any Chinese towns and are back in their own territory. They have given the Chinese a severe slap, humiliated them by disarming 10,000 troops, and scared Mukden into a settlement all by a relatively small operation which led to no entanglements.

Direct Negotiations Reported.

SHANGHAI, Friday, Nov. 29 (AP).—The North China Daily News, a British newspaper here, published a statement this morning purporting to be from local Russian Tass Agency sources stating that the Chinese commission of Foreign Affairs at Harbin had inaugurated negotiations between Mukden and Moscow seeking settlement of the Chinese Eastern Railway dispute, "on the express authority of both Nanking and Mukden Government officials."

"More War" Forecast.

MUKDEN, Friday, Nov. 29 (AP).—The Russian wireless station at Habarovsk broadcast a statement last night saying conversations between Moscow and Mukden looking to settlement of the Chinese Eastern Railway controversy still were proceeding, but that there would be "more war."

The radio announcer, commenting upon the Manchurian situation, said: "The Chinese Manchurian Army has suffered heavy losses but Russia has no faith in Chang Hsueh-liang's word, as his forces are still fighting. Therefore, Russia must prepare for more war."

Chang Hsueh-liang is Governor of Manchuria.

Nanking Counter-Proposal.

NANKING, Friday, Nov. 29 (AP).—The Nationalist Government has

Continued on Page Four.

Incendiaries Start 19 Fires In Siskiyou National Forest

GRANTS PASS, Ore., Nov. 28 (AP).—Records in the hands of officials of the United States forest office here today revealed that nineteen of the latest fires reported in the Siskiyou National Forest were of incendiary origin.

Several of these blazes were giving rangers serious trouble, but two, located almost directly on the Oregon-California line, were being held back.

A brisk wind from the Pacific last night swept inland various forest fires in Southwestern Oregon. Stands of virgin timber were being devastated.

The Shumate logging camp in the Port Oxford district was reported in danger of destruction, and advices from that front said families were fleeing from their cabins with their personal belongings.

POLLING OF SENATE CHEERS INSURGENTS

They Figure Strength Enough to Dominate Coming Session and Carry Tariff Program.

FOUR BLOCS IN THE PARTY

But Coalition of Progressives and Democrats Is Estimated as Outvoting Old and New Guards.

Special to The New York Times.

WASHINGTON, Nov. 28.—Confident of their ability to retain the balance of power among the Senate Republicans, the insurgents are prepared to continue their drive against the industrial rates of the Smoot-Hawley tariff bill when the measure is again taken up some time next week, a few days after Congress convenes for its regular session.

During the breathing space since the Senate adjourned on Friday, the members of the Republican "New Guard," who are determined to continue their efforts to keep these rates from being cut materially, have made further informal overtures to the insurgents, but without success.

The formation of the Senate's Republican "freshmen" and some Old Guardsmen into a recognized bloc has in no way dismayed the party's insurgents. In fact, the insurgents are positive in predicting success for the program they mapped out before the extra session was begun in April, that is, material benefits for agriculture through increased tariff duties on imported farm products and a reduction of the industrial rates wherever believed to be discriminatory against the farmer.

Time for Reckoning Strength.

This week the insurgents have been counting noses to see if the situation has changed to any extent. Today they said they were able to demonstrate on paper that they were still in command.

They maintained that they still control the Senate through the Democratic-progressive Republican coalition and that they were strong enough numerically to make an important wedge in their own party.

One man who is familiar with the situation and is watching it closely said tonight that the Republican party in the Senate was being "factionalized" through putting all those legally registered as Republicans into their proper groups. So far, it was pointed out, there were four Republican "columns."

First, there are the so-called Old Guardsmen; secondly, the progressives or insurgents; thirdly, the "freshmen," who, with some temporarily shifting Old Guard members, call themselves the "New Guard," and fourthly, the "half-ways," as one might call the Old Guardsmen who for the moment have joined with the "freshmen."

How Various Senators Stand.

Continuing his comment, this observer said:

"In their own ranks the Young Guardsmen are counting, for the time being, Senators Cutting of New Mexico and Capper of Kansas, who have been voting with them.

"Senators Couzens of Michigan and Johnson of California, each of whom calls himself 'a one-man bloc,' are being numbered with the Young Guard. Senator Couzens seems to be somewhat sympathetic with the 'New Guard,' but he has not been with them all the time.

"In the Old Guard are listed Senator Baird, the successor of Senator Edge of New Jersey, as well as

Continued on Page Twelve.

BUCKNER CENSURES HARVEY FOR PUTTING MOORE BACK ON JOB

Prosecutor of Connolly and Seely Demands Engineer Be Tried as Sewer Grafter.

CITES EVIDENCE IN CASE

Stirred by Failure to Get Reply to Protest Sent Eight Days Ago Urging Action.

QUEENS PRESIDENT RETORTS

Asks Why Charges Were Not Pressed Before and Wants a Formal Complaint.

Emory R. Buckner, special prosecutor in the Queens sewer graft scandals, and George U. Harvey, Borough President of Queens, the two leading figures in the uncovering of the "sewer ring" and the overthrow of the old political régime in that borough, crossed swords yesterday over Mr. Harvey's action in restoring Clifford B. Moore to duty at $8,000 salary as assistant borough engineer.

Indignant at the failure of Mr. Harvey either to acknowledge or act upon a letter of protest delivered eight days before, Mr. Buckner initiated the conflict by making public the letter, which charged that Moore was a co-conspirator in the graft scandals along with former Borough President Maurice E. Connolly, Frederick Seely, former borough engineer in charge of sewer design, and the late John M. Phillips, sewer pipe "czar."

The special prosecutor asserted that Moore escaped indictment as a party to the conspiracy only because the evidence did not appear until the Connolly trial was under way. He insisted that the record of the trial clearly showed Moore's part and pointed to a prevailing opinion of the Brooklyn Appellate Division affirming Connolly's conviction, which held that the engineer acted "in furtherance of the conspiracy" as a "co-conspirator" himself.

"The fact that Mr. Harvey has not acknowledged the letter makes me wonder who is back of Moore," Mr. Buckner said as he gave out copies of his letter.

Invites Action By Buckner.

Stung by the implications of the missive, Mr. Harvey, who has himself won two major campaigns and a primary fight by associating his opponents with the "sewer ring," at once struck back at the special prosecutor. Informed that the letter had been made public, he pointed out that Mr. Buckner had been charged with the duty of bringing all official wrongdoing in Queens before the grand jury.

"Why did Mr. Buckner not bring this matter to the attention of the grand jury at that time?" he demanded, and added an invitation to the special prosecutor to bring formal complaint against Moore "if he is so anxious in this matter."

Mr. Harvey's explanation of the return of Moore to the payroll on Nov. 19 was that his leave of absence had expired and no charges were legally pending against him, former Borough President Bernard M. Patten having failed to take action on accusations for which the engineer was suspended after Connolly had resigned.

The Borough President's statement evoked from Mr. Buckner the response that since the real evidence against Moore appeared after the Connolly trial had started he could not have been made a co-defendant, and the trial of Moore alone on a charge of conspiracy would have been idle. Taking under consideration the matter of preferring formal charges to Mr. Harvey against Moore, but pointing out that the Borough President had ample authority to start the action himself, Mr. Buckner said, "I want to see what Harvey will do. He must answer to the people of Queens, not me."

Moore Indicted Twice.

Although Moore was not indicted as co-conspirator with Connolly and the others, the special grand jury in Queens under Mr. Buckner's direction did indict the engineer for verifying a false State income tax return. He was charged with reporting only his income from the borough in 1926 and omitting additional receipts of over $60,000. Subsequently he pleaded guilty, served thirty days in the workhouse and paid a fine of $1,000. He was also indicted by the Federal grand jury for failing to file Federal

Continued on Page Fourteen.

Byrd, as He Flies, Remembers Those He Left in New Zealand

Wireless to THE NEW YORK TIMES.

LITTLE AMERICA, Antarctica, Nov. 28.—As the moment neared for his start for the Pole, Commander Byrd thought of his men who were turned back from the Barrier last February to winter at Dunedin, N. Z., and by wireless, flashed to THE NEW YORK TIMES station in New York, to be relayed to the Antipodes, this message:

New Zealand Contingent,
Byrd Expedition:

As we take off flying for the Pole, I send the best of good wishes to you and the Tapleys.

I want you all to know that you are playing just as important a part as any one of us down here. BYRD.

(H. L. Tapley, Ltd., are Commander Byrd's representatives in New Zealand.)

FOKKER LAYS CRASH TO HUMAN FAILURE

Says Huge Plane Should Not Have Been Taken Up When in Poor Working Order.

STRESSES SAFETY FACTOR

20,000 Visit Scene of Wreck on Long Island—Two Inquiries by Officials Under Way.

Anthony H. G. Fokker declared yesterday that the crash of his huge thirty-two passenger monoplane, which destroyed two homes in Carle Place, Long Island, on Wednesday afternoon, was due to a failure of the human element in aviation. The disaster should have been avoided, he said as he stepped from the gangplank of the White Star liner Homeric after a tour of the aviation industry of Europe.

"There was no necessity of taking the craft up without having everything in good working order," he said. "The failure of the second engine on the same side as the one which was left idle at the take-off resulted in loss of control before the plane had attained sufficient altitude and speed. There is no doubt that this type plane can be brought to a safe landing regardless of the failure of one or two engines, if flying under normal conditions and at safe altitude.

"Such accidents as this prove that no matter how safe and airworthy a plane may be it can be wrecked at any time by failure of the human element."

Mr. Fokker then declared that he would conduct personally an investigation of the accident. He voiced regret at the loss of his $110,000 plane, and emphasized the additional aggravation of its having been responsible for the destruction of other property which may account for an equal figure.

At Roosevelt Field George Gardner, the local inspector of the Aeronautics Branch of the Department of Commerce, spent the day investigating the crash of the huge Fokker monoplane and that of James Pisani, the private flier who was killed an hour earlier when his plane plunged into a street not more than a mile from the scene of the Fokker disaster. No details of the inspector's findings were revealed. His report will be forwarded to Major Clarence M. Young, his chief in Washington.

District Attorney Edwards of Nassau County also investigated the crash. After a conference with the officials of Roosevelt Field he announced that he would try to have all experimental flights restricted to the air over unsettled country or the landing area. He added, however, that the crash would not be a case for the grand jury, as no criminal negligence was apparent.

Pilot Still in Hospital.

Meanwhile the pilot of the Fokker, Marshall Boggs, also a Department of Commerce inspector who is on leave to compile engineering data on the Fokker plane for commercial interests, remained in the Nassau Hospital. It was said that his injuries were slight. His mechanic, Harry McDonald of the Fokker company, had recovered sufficiently to be removed to his home at Hasbrouck Heights, N. J.

Throughout the day more than 20,000 persons visited the scene of the Fokker crash and fire, accord-

Continued on Page Thirteen.

START IS MADE AT 10:29 P. M. NEW YORK TIME

Climax of Year's Work of the Expedition Comes at 3:29 o'Clock in the Afternoon of Little America's Thanksgiving Day.

BALCHEN IS PILOTING THE BIG PLANE

Two Others With Them, One at the Radio—Airmen Must Climb to 12,000 Feet to Top Mountains on 1,600-Mile Dash to Pole and Back.

By RUSSELL OWEN.

Wireless to THE NEW YORK TIMES.

LITTLE AMERICA, Antarctica, Nov. 28.—A huge gray plane slipped over the dappled Barrier at 3:29 o'clock this afternoon [10:29 P. M. New York time] the sun gleaming on its sides, reflected in bright flashes from its metal wing and whirling propellers. With a smooth lifting movement it rose above the snow in a long, steady glide.

Commander Byrd had started on his 1,600-mile flight to the South Pole and back. With him were Bernt Balchen, flying the plane; Harold I. June at the wireless, and Captain Ashley C. McKinley, photographer, surveyor and general utility man.

Just before the take-off, Dr. Lawrence Gould, head of the geological sledging party now nearing the Queen Maud Mountains, reported by radio that "good flying weather" lay ahead of Commander Byrd at the edge of the Polar Plateau.

Once in the air, as if liberated from the clinging influence of earthly things, the great plane became suddenly light, a true bird of the air. With its three motors roaring their deep song it turned southward and was gone into the wilderness of space over a land of white desolation.

This will be a historic flight over the rolling Barrier, through gaps in towering mountains, where the wind whirls in buffeting eddies, and on over that lonely Polar Plateau, the loneliest spot on earth, where somewhere is a tiny invisible point which, with all his navigator's cunning, Commander Byrd is attempting to reach.

Weather Just Right at the Start.

Byrd's flight came today, as does everything here, with thrilling effect. Here, more than anywhere else, flying depends on the weather, and the genius of the winds brooding over the mysterious heights above us had been idly stirring the conflicting elements into shifting winds and clouds which blocked the way.

Then, as if by magic, a deep hush spread over the rolling plain, shining cream and rose colored under the flowing rays of a sun so bright in this translucent atmosphere that it seemed to fill half the sky. It was as if nature said, "I have done my part now; there is peace before you."

In the glittering silence of such a day, for morning, noon and midnight are all the same, men scurried busily about, intense with excitement. They knew that the moment had come for which they had worked for more than a year, in black isolation and in cold that seared and burned, in winds that shrieked and hid the earth in a shroud of numbing and bewildering drift.

There was elation in their quick movements, confidence and eagerness. If they could have done so, they would have pushed the heavy plane off the ground with their own determination.

Mechanics hurriedly looked with skilled and careful eyes where the huge metal machine rested on the snow like a ponderous, big, confident bird. It looked so strong, so graceful, even in its bulky outlines, so strange in this environment, as if in itself it had the will to conquer.

How different riding this machine from the way men have toiled with aching bodies and troubled minds over the treacherous surface of the snow, above which this great creature soars so easily!

Long Wait That Is Now Over.

It is hard to believe, as it wheels in graceful curves with long sweeping dips of its wings, that it is not a conscious entity. One never tires of watching it. Is it because it is so out of place here or because in this lost land it becomes a prehistoric denizen of the air, this its natural abiding place which by accident we have discovered?

It had come through so many hazards, had been watched with such jealous care. For 10,000 miles it had been transported, through tropics where the sun scorched it and the sea tried vainly to corrode its metal members. It had been lifted and dropped into the holds of ships and to docks, hauled ashore in sections on a crumbling shelf of ice with disaster momentarily ahead and then left to hibernate a long Winter night while the cold closed in around it.

Then the day came when it was brought up into the light, a complete machine, put together with blistered fingers and long hours of toil and, with its engines growling a note of satisfaction, had taken the air to soar in its own element.

Well Prepared for the Flight.

All this some of those watching the big plane made ready for the flight thought of as they stood by. How much it meant to all who have lived here and worked for this day can hardly be imagined by those back home, who can never picture this land as it really is, cold, beautiful, but treacherous and implacable in its resistance. This seemed the way to conquer it.

The plane had been loaded for the flight long before the hour came when the word was given to start. Men had stowed away in its big cabin food and clothing, extra cans of fuel to be poured into the fuselage tank; sleds had been tucked away in the tail for use if, by some mischance, the plane faltered on the way and sought a resting place far inland.

Byrd Watched All Preparations.

Over all the preparations Richard Byrd watched, wrapped in his fur clothing that will keep him warm when taking sights through an open window in temperature far below zero.

The tiny tables on which he will do his navigating were in place, and his instruments, the sextant securely in its case, the compass lashed in a corner where it is free from deviation.

The radio operator, his chunky figure also wrapped in fur, face smiling above the thrust-back hood with its rim of soft brown fur, had tested his instruments, made sure that all the means of keeping camera, with its paraphernalia, over which he will work so rapidly

COMMANDER RICHARD E. BYRD.
Leader of the Antarctic Expedition, Who Is Now in Flight With Three Companions Toward the South Pole.

LATEST MESSAGE FROM BYRD

"All is well with the Byrd plane" was the brief message that Commander Byrd's base at Little America flashed to The New York Times at 6:30 oclock this morning.

As this message was received the radio contact with Little America faded out, and no more was obtainable before this late edition of The New York Times went to press.

From the Commander's airplane, as it sped toward the South Pole, The New York Times radio station last night and early this morning had been receiving frequent messages up to 3:20 A. M. These messages were signed by Harold I. June, the radio operator on the airplane and were routed through Little America, the expedition's base.

Soon after that hour the Byrd plane reached the neighborhood of the Queen Maud range of mountains where an elevation of 10,000 to 12,000 feet was necessary to carry the plane southward. No message came from the plane while this stage of the flight was on, and later daylight coming in the zones northward caused a fading of signals from Little America, as is customary at that hour.

The last clear message that came from Little America before the brief flash telling that all was well, was rceived at 5:15 A. M., New York time. It said that the plane's signals had not then been heard for an hour.

EARLIER MESSAGES FROM PLANE.

Wireless to THE NEW YORK TIMES.

AIRPLANE FLOYD BENNETT, in flight toward the South Pole, 4 P. M. [11 P. M. New York time], Nov. 28.—Flying well over the Geological party's trail. Just passed Forty-five Mile Depot [Depot No. 1 established by the Supporting Party late in October.] Motors fine. JUNE.

4:30 P. M.—We passed the snowmobile [abandoned after an unsuccessful test of Antarctic travel several weeks ago, on the trail southward, some eighty miles from the base] at 4:25 o'clock. JUNE.

5 P. M.—We have made a hundred miles at 4:50 P. M. JUNE.

5:30 P. M.—Flying well. Motors fine. Now at the Crevasses. JUNE.

[The Crevasses are eleven miles beyond Depot No. 3, shown on the map on Page 3.]

7 P. M.—Flying well. Motors fine. About 100 miles from Gould's Geological Party on trail. JUNE.

[Professor Gould's Geological Party was last reported at Depot No. 6 on Nov. 25, and was then making good progress south.]

8:20 P. M.—Reached Gould party 8:15. JUNE.

[The plane carried radio messages for the Geological Party on the trail and it was planned to drop them with a parachute. In the package of messages was also a packet of photographs of the mountains of the Queen Maud Range made by Captain McKinley on Byrd's previous flight a few days ago. These, it is hoped, will help Dr. Gould in his geological work, when he reaches Depot No. 8, shown in the map on Page 3, at the mountains.]

The aviation pilots conferring in the library in Little America. From left to right: Dean C. Smith, Alton N. Parker, Commander Byrd, Bernt Balchen and Harold June.

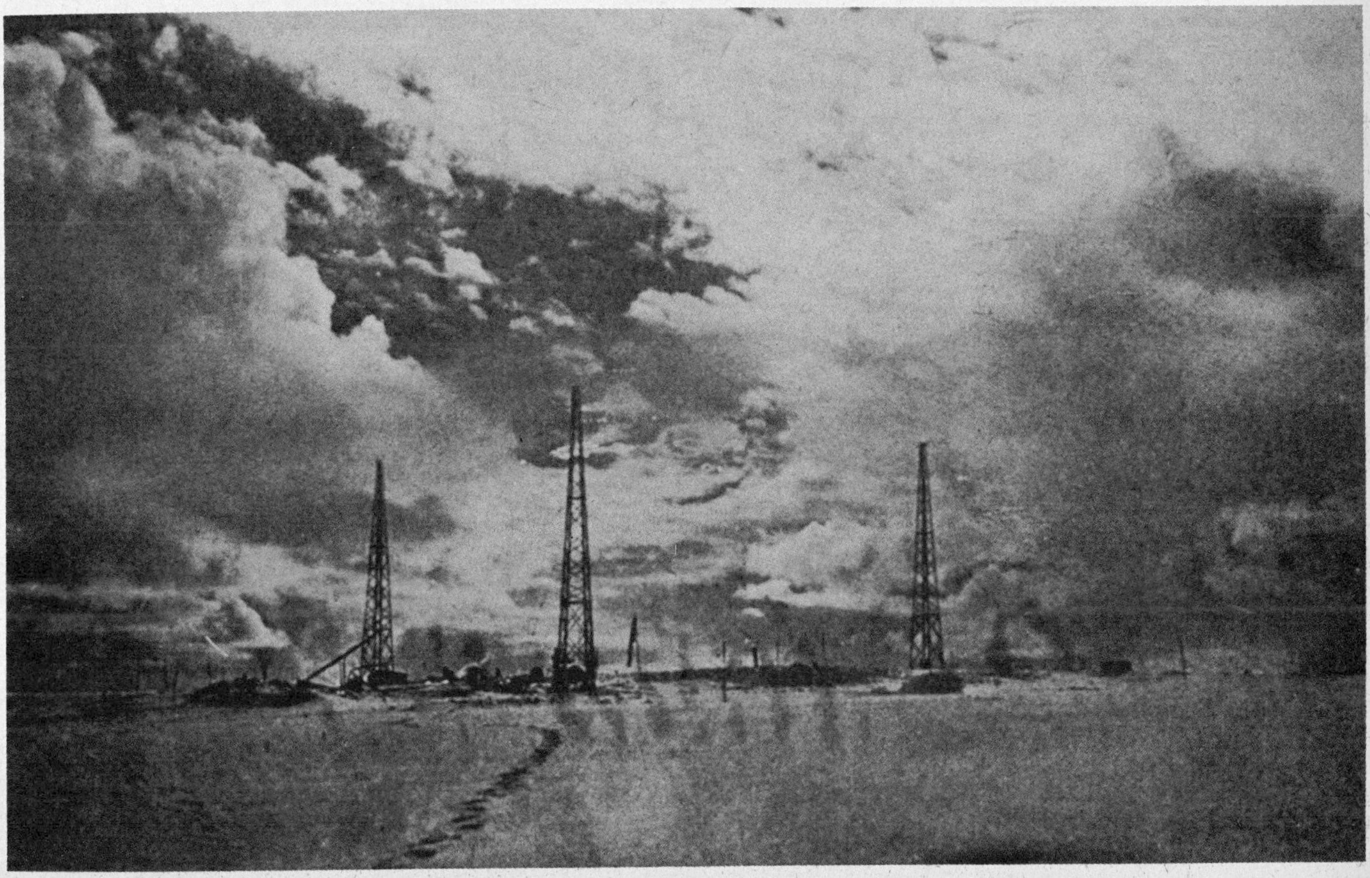

Little America, entirely snowed under, with only the radio towers, flag and smokestack showing.

Commander Byrd at the entrance of the hole leading to the administration building of Little America.

"All the News That's Fit to Print."

The New York Times.

THE WEATHER
Fair and continued cold today; tomorrow cloudy and warmer.
Temperatures yesterday—Max. 30, min. 20.
U. S. Weather Forecast—For details See Page 38.

VOL. LXXIX....No. 26,243. + * * * * NEW YORK, SATURDAY, NOVEMBER 30, 1929. TWO CENTS In Greater New York | THREE CENTS Within 200 Miles | FOUR CENTS Elsewhere Except 7th and 8th Postal Zones

BYRD SAFELY FLIES TO SOUTH POLE AND BACK, LOOKING OVER 'ALMOST LIMITLESS PLATEAU'; DROPS FOOD, LIGHTENS SHIP ON PERILOUS TRIP

WOMAN HEARD CRASH IN HOTEL AT THE TIME ROTHSTEIN WAS SHOT

Says She Saw Man With Angry or Agonized Look Near McManus's Room.

UNCERTAIN ON HIS IDENTITY

Mrs. M. A. Putnam, "Surprise" Witness for State, Attacked by the Defense.

RAYMOND TELLS OF BIG BET

Testifies He Won $40,000 From Rothstein on One Card—Admits That They Had a Quarrel.

A fragile woman with gray hair, but a schoolgirl complexion, took the stand yesterday in the Criminal Courts Building to aid the State in its effort to convict George A. McManus of the murder of Arnold Rothstein. In clear tones she identified herself as Mrs. Marian A. Putnam of Asheville, N. C., chief of the surprise witnesses for the prosecution.

Loosening the gray squirrel collar of a broadtail fur coat, she said that she had been a guest at the Park Central Hotel on the night of Nov. 4, 1928, when Rothstein received a bullet wound which caused his death two days later. She added that she had registered at the hotel on Oct. 30.

Assistant District Attorney George N. Brothers, urbane in manner and soothing of voice, asked her to tell what she had heard and seen that night. Mrs. Putnam turned her thin face toward the jurymen and folded her hands, asparkle with four diamond rings. Quietly she told how she had heard a "crash" and had seen a man walking down a corridor on the third floor, leading from Room 349, part of a suite hired by McManus.

Saw Agony or Anger in Face.

She had looked at the man's face. It bore the imprint of agony or anger. He had his hands clasped over his abdomen as he followed her down the carpeted passageway. Mrs. Putnam said she locked the door of her room and said nothing about the episode even the following morning when she learned of the shooting.

On through the events of the evening Mr. Brothers led the witness. She told a straightforward story under the prosecutor's questioning and now and then a faint smile curved her tight lips. Mrs. Putnam settled more comfortably in the witness chair and slipped out of the heavy fur coat. As she replied to the questions she smoothed the lace ruffles at the wristbands of her black velvet dress and adjusted the cream-colored lace fichu at her neck.

She completed her story and then James D. C. Murray, attorney for the defense, began his cross-examination. The slow-moving lawyer, his grizzled hair somewhat rumpled, favored the witness with a prolonged stare before he started his questions. Suavely but searchingly he delved into Mrs. Putnam's past. His questions were blunt, but were met with composure by the witness.

Raymond Tells of Winnings.

She made impeaching admissions with a detached calm that almost equaled the perfect poise which had been displayed shortly before by another witness, Nathan (Nigger Nate) Raymond. Raymond, who told how he had won $40,000 from Rothstein when the slain man drew the deuce at high card, admitted that he probably had been guilty of a faux pas—the expression was his own—when he asked Rothstein to give him I. O. U.'s for $200,000 he had won.

During the cross-examination of Raymond the defense developed that he had quarrelled with Rothstein in a taxicab subsequent to the poker game. Raymond said that he had no recollection of any blows having been struck.

When Raymond left the stand the defense sought to have stricken from the record all testimony regarding the poker game. Mr. Murray told the court that the prosecution had failed to carry out its promise to show that the game gave McManus the motive for the murder. Judge Nott refused to grant the motion.

Mrs. Putnam admitted that she had been registered at the Park

Continued on Page Fourteen.

Byrd Lauds Radio Amateurs For Help in Message Relays

LOS ANGELES, Nov. 29 (AP).—A congratulatory message sent by Commander Richard E. Byrd just before the start of his flight over the South Pole, was read today at the convention of the Pacific division of the American Radio Relay League.

The message, received by B. E. Sandham, Los Angeles amateur short wave radio operator, read:

"Greetings from Little America to the radio amateurs of the Pacific division. Am glad for this opportunity to acknowledge the big debt our North and South Pole expeditions owe to the amateur radio operators.

"I wish to thank them for their helpfulness and to express my admiration of the high sense of honor they show in handling messages.

"It is radio that has made this expedition possible.

"Cordial good wishes in which all of Little America join.

"RICHARD BYRD."

WINTER GRIPS NATION; MERCURY AT 20 HERE

Icy Blast Sweeping Out of the Northwest Kills 9, Spreads Damage, Blocks Shipping.

BLIZZARDS RAGE IN WEST

One Frozen to Death in New York and No Let-Up in the Frigid Wave Is Seen.

Winter came howling out of the northwest and the Arctic wastes yesterday, bringing blizzards to the Western States and Canada, hampering shipping on the Great Lakes, and holding the West, the Middle West, the East and many Southern States in the grip of sub-freezing temperatures.

It was the frigid season's first general offensive, and it scattered death, suffering and property damage widely. White River, Ontario, which usually claims the distinction of recording low temperatures, shared with Thief River Falls, Minn., first place on the icy list yesterday, both communities recording 26 below zero. At least eight persons died in the North Central States as a result of the sudden zero snap, according to the Associated Press. New York City added one death to the list. Fears were felt for the safety of hunters caught unprepared for the severe cold in the Minnesota woods. Near the cradle of Winter, where a 30-mile gale was driving a blizzard over the Saskatchewan Lakes, the fate of fifty fishermen, pushing northward on a 50-mile trip, was in doubt. The fishermen had been gone for three days.

Cold to Continue Here Today.

New York had an uncomfortable sample of Winter, and last night the local Weather Bureau gave practically no hope of a let-up today in the cold temperatures.

This city felt its lowest temperature of the season at 10 o'clock last night when the thermometer registered 20 degrees above zero, 12 below freezing. Even the maximum temperature at 9:30 A. M. was only 30 degrees, or 2 below freezing. The average temperature for the day was 26 degrees, compared with a normal Nov. 29 reading of 39. The coldest Nov. 29 on record occurred in 1872 when the thermometer registered 15 degrees.

The cold here was aggravated by a biting northwest wind, blowing at thirty-eight miles an hour. The city's firemen were put to their first severe test of the season in what was a busy "fire" day in Manhattan, the Bronx and Brooklyn. Up to 9 o'clock last night the number of fires for the day totaled thirty in Manhattan, ten in the Bronx and forty-three in Brooklyn.

Fair Weather Forecast.

Although the barometer in the New York Weather Bureau was rising last night, indicating fair weather for today, the cold snap will continue, according to the official forecaster, and the thousands of football spectators who will swarm into the Yankee Stadium for the Army-Notre Dame game this afternoon will have to wear their warmest clothes and wraps.

"Fresh northeast winds and continued cold" was the prediction for today. At the Weather Bureau it was even considered possible that today might be a little colder than yesterday.

A woman on Staten Island was New York's addition to the list of victims of the cold. She was Mrs. Gladys Todd, 53 years old, who was found dead in the back yard of her home, at 4 Schrenkheisen Place, Mar-

Continued on Page Twelve.

FIRST MESSAGE EVER SENT FROM THE SOUTH POLE

By Commander Richard E. Byrd

WIRELESS TO THE NEW YORK TIMES.

ABOARD AIRPLANE FLOYD BENNETT, in flight, 1:55 P. M. Greenwich mean time [8:55 A. M. New York time], Friday, Nov. 29.—My calculations indicate that we have reached the vicinity of the South Pole, flying high for a survey. The airplane is in good shape, crew all well. Will soon turn north. We can see an almost limitless polar plateau. Our departure from the Pole was at 1:25 P. M. BYRD

The difference in the times mentioned in this dispatch, that is between 1:55 P. M. in the date line and 1:25 P. M., given by the Commander as that of his departure from the South Pole, is probably accounted for by the lapse between the writing of the dispatch by the Commander and its coding and sending by the wireless operator, Harold I. June. Greenwich time is five hours ahead of New York time and twelve hours ahead of time at Little America.

The Commander's last sentence was evidently added after he began to fly away from the Pole; the first part written before he left there.

CAPITAL DISPLAYS KEENEST INTEREST

President, Waiting News, Is the First in Washington to Hear of Byrd's Success.

OFFICIALS LAUD FLIGHT

Admiral Hughes Says the Commander Is a Worthy Successor to Admiral Wilkes.

Special to The New York Times.

WASHINGTON, Nov. 29.—President Hoover, who had waited anxiously all day for word of the progress of the daring flight to the South Pole, was the first person in Washington, outside of the staff of The New York Times bureau, to learn of the successful flight of Commander Byrd to the South Pole and back to the base at Little America.

The word was flashed to the White House tonight from the Washington Bureau of The New York Times. It was transmitted to the President before dinner by Secretary Walter H. Newton.

All day the President had asked for word of the progress of the flight and late in the afternoon had indicated his deep interest. When the news was taken to him, the President expressed his delight over the successful outcome.

Official Washington expressed the most intense relief and the greatest delight at the successful termination of the flight.

Admiral Charles F. Hughes, the Acting Secretary of the Navy, was among the first to be informed.

"We are greatly pleased at the success of Commander Byrd's flight," he said. "He is a worthy successor to Admiral Wilkes, the American naval officer who first discovered the Antarctic Continent."

Earlier in the day Admiral Hughes had said:

"The Navy Department is intensely interested and, knowing Commander Byrd, we are thoroughly confident that he will return successfully."

Davison Congratulates Expedition.

F. Trubee Davison, Assistant Secretary of War for Aeronautics, declared the success of the flight demonstrated again the value of aircraft.

"The flight of Commander Byrd and his brave companions to the South Pole," he said, "is another epic in the annals of the achievements of heavier-than-air craft and proves once again the value of the airplane in exploration of unknown areas where distances can be traveled in hours which under ordinary forms of transportation would require weeks and months. On behalf of the War Department and the Army Air Corps, I wish to congratulate the Byrd Antarctic Expedition. Their achievement will be lauded by Americans the world over."

Major Clarence M. Young, the Assistant Secretary of Commerce for Aeronautics, declared the Byrd flight was simply another demonstration of the "limitless purposes which aviation can serve."

"The flight to the South Pole and back was surely a major accomplish-

Continued on Page Three.

President Sends His Congratulations to Byrd, Saying Spirit of Great Adventure Still Lives

Special to The New York Times.

WASHINGTON, Nov. 29.—After being informed tonight of Commander Byrd's successful flight to the South Pole and back to the base at Little America, President Hoover gave to The New York Times the following message of congratulations on behalf of himself and the American people, to be transmitted by radio to Commander Byrd:

Commander Richard E. Byrd,
Little America:

I know that I speak for the American people when I express their universal pleasure at your successful flight over the South Pole. We are proud of your courage and your leadership. We are glad of proof that the spirit of great adventure still lives.

Our thoughts of appreciation include also your companions in the flight and your colleagues, whose careful and devoted preparation have contributed to your great success.

HERBERT HOOVER.

BYRD'S FEAT STIRS ENTHUSIASM HERE

Victorious Flight Hailed With Tributes to Commander's Daring and Foresight.

With the reception of news from Little America of the return of Commander Byrd and his companions from their flight over the South Pole, explorers, aviators, aeronautical designers and builders whose names are known throughout the world of aviation and scores of others offered their congratulations to the Commander and expressed their enthusiasm over the success of his efforts.

Some of these comments follow:

Anthony H. G. Fokker, designer of the plane in which Commander Byrd crossed the Atlantic—I didn't expect anything but success from Byrd and Balchen. The Commander is an excellent organizer and Balchen is a fine pilot. With all the qualities fliers need for such an expedition, they have proved the unquestioned value and possibility of the airplane.

Mayor Walker—That's marvelous news. I can sum up the way I feel about it in a single sentence. I knew Dick Byrd would do it. He has made another great contribution to scientific advancement and world knowledge. The American flag will certainly look great down there. I know I speak for the people of this city when I say that we rejoice with him and his intrepid companions in this epoch-making exploit. We will await his return to New York with impatience, so that the city can give him the welcome he so richly deserves. New York City has honored Commander Byrd before. It is glad to honor him again, for it feels that in a very real sense he is one of us.

Lieutenant Governor Herbert H. Lehman—It is glorious news. Commander Byrd's successful flight to the South Pole will go down in history as one of the greatest of human exploits. Its success is all the more noteworthy because achieved in the face of great obstacles after the most painstaking preparation. The nation whose flag he has now carried to the uttermost ends of the globe rejoices with him and his gallant crew for the success they have

Continued on Page Four.

BYRD'S FAMILY GETS NEWS OF FLIGHT

Virginia Governor at Capitol Gets News and Mother Hears It at Winchester.

Special to The New York Times.

RICHMOND, Va., Nov. 29.—Although he knew that his brother, Commander Richard Evelyn Byrd, intended to hop to the South Pole "about this time of the year," Governor Harry F. Byrd said in his office tonight that no one in the family or any one else had known exactly what day the plane Floyd Bennett would leave the base.

Commander Byrd's mother, Mrs. Richard E. Byrd Sr., and Thomas Byrd, his brother, received news of the successful flight at their home in Winchester.

Governor Byrd flew to Richmond late today from Norfolk to get news of his brother. He had been at Chapel Hill for the Virginia-Carolina football game on Thanksgiving Day and stopped in the capital to be the guest of Governor O. Max Gardner of North Carolina. Accompanying Governor Byrd in another plane was Colonel Willard D. Newbill of his staff.

From the Executive Mansion the Governor relayed news of the flight to his mother at Winchester.

When Commander Byrd duplicated his top of the world feat by flying over the South Pole at the very bottom of the world his mother, thought it "glorious" and was "thrilled to death," she said tonight.

"I was in Washington when we heard Dick had hopped off," she said. "My son Tom drove up there to get me when I phoned him and we went back to Winchester to wait for news. The New York Times called me about 6 o'clock but said they would not release the news generally until later.

"Dick had sent me a Thanksgiving radio message a few hours before they hopped off, 'We are off.' We were very uneasy, but I was never so happy in my life as when we heard he had landed safely back at Little America. We really were quite uneasy because this flight seemed more hazardous than anything he ever tried. Nobody knew anything much about Antarctica.

"When Tom heard Dick had gone over safely he said he was 'tremen-

Continued on Page Two.

BRITISH APPLAUD FLIGHT AS TRIUMPH

Thrill Over Byrd's Feat Puts Polar Land Dispute in the Background.

NEWS EAGERLY AWAITED

German Press and People Followed Commander's Course With Keen Interest.

Special Cable to The New York Times.

LONDON, Saturday, Nov. 30.—Great Britain watched Commander Byrd's progress over the Antarctic wastes to the South Pole and his return as a magnificent adventure, and what claims he may make to any rich coal or mineral deposits over which he has flown or staked with the American flag is an issue that is exciting no comment here.

Even the publication by New York newspapers of a summary of the State Department's answer to the British Government's year-old note concerning sovereignty over the Antarctic lands, which was read here as clearly indicating that the United States does not intend to abandon its claims based on earlier discoveries by American explorers, was not allowed to distract attention from Commander Byrd's performance or to cause a controversy almost on the eve of the five-power naval parley in London.

Hailed as Byrd Triumph.

The Daily Chronicle outstripped its London rivals this morning by alone printing a full account of Commander Byrd's South Pole flight, as transmitted to it by The New York Times and associated newspapers. The remainder of the London newspapers were able in their final editions to announce only the bare fact of the aviator's epoch-making flight, with full acknowledgment of the source of their information.

The feat, therefore, was hailed here not only as a personal triumph for Commander Byrd and his three companions, Balchen, June and McKinley, but as an outstanding feat in newspaper organization.

Stupendous as is the accomplishment of a flight of 1,560 miles over the frozen wastes to the South Pole and back in 18 hours and 55 minutes in itself, it has been brought home more vividly to the public mind here by the fact that within a few hours of Commander Byrd's return to his base on the Ross ice shelf, at 10:10 o'clock London time last night, the leading newspapers of the world were able to reproduce the story of the exploit.

It has not escaped notice that scientific development, from the short-wave radio to the finer details of aircraft construction, have been pressed into use on this occasion.

Scientists, aviators and public men on every hand are expressing admiration for Commander Byrd's initiative and courage in carrying out successfully a flight which for scientific results may stand alone.

Commander Byrd had been flying over twelve hours before the British

Continued on Page Four.

CROSSES GLACIER PASS AT 11,500 FEET

Commander Takes Chance and Plane Roars Upward Amid Swirling Drift Out Through Gorge to Tableland

FLYING TIME FOR THE WHOLE CIRCUIT ABOUT 18 HOURS

With Two New Ranges Discovered, the Four Air Argonauts, Guided by Chief, Turn Back to Wild Welcome at Base Camp.

By RUSSELL OWEN.

Wireless to The New York Times.

LITTLE AMERICA, Antarctica, Nov. 29.—Conqueror of two Poles by air, Commander Richard E. Byrd flew into camp at 10:10 o'clock this morning, having been gone eighteen hours and fifty-nine minutes. An hour of this time was spent at the mountain base refueling.

The first man to fly over the North and South Poles and the only man to fly over the South Pole stepped from his plane and was swept up on the arms of the men in camp who for more than an hour had been anxiously watching the southern horizon for a sight of the plane.

Deaf from the roar of the motors, tired from the continual strain of the flight and the long period of navigation under difficulties, Commander Byrd was still smiling and happy. He had reached the South Pole after as hazardous and as difficult a flight as has ever been made in an airplane, tossed by gusts of wind, climbing desperately up the slopes of glaciers a few hundred feet above the surface.

Radiant Airmen Borne in Triumph.

His companions on the flight tumbled out stiff and weary also, but so happy that they forgot their cramped muscles. They were also tossed aloft, pounded on the back and carried to the entrance of the mess hall.

Bernt Balchen, the calm-eyed pilot who first met Commander Byrd in Spitzbergen and who was with him on the transatlantic flight, came out first. There was a little smudge of soot under the nose, but the infectious smile which has endeared him to those who know him, was radiant.

He was carried away and then came Harold June who, between intervals of helping Balchen and attending to fuel tanks and lines and taking pictures, found time to send the radio bulletins which told of the plane's progress.

And after him Captain Ashley McKinley was lifted from the doorway, beaming like the Cheshire cat because his surveying camera had done its work all the way.

Dumped Food of Forty-five Days, But Not Fuel.

Men crowded about them eager for the story of what they had been through, catching fragments of sentences. It had evidently been a terrific battle to get up through the mountains to the Plateau.

"We had to dump a month and a half of food to do it," said Commander Byrd. "I am glad it wasn't gas. It was nip and tuck all the way."

"Yes," chuckled Balchen. "Do you remember when we were sliding around those knolls picking the wind currents to help us and there wasn't more than 300 feet under us at times? We were just staggering along, with drift and clouds and all sorts of things around us."

When the plane approached the mountains on the way south, Commander Byrd picked out the Livingston Glacier, a large glacier somewhat to the west of the Axel Heiberg Glacier, as the best passageway.

Swooping Upward Through Swirling Drift.

The high mountains shut them in all around as they forced their way upward, Balchen, conserving his fuel to the utmost, coaxing his engines, picking the up-currents of air as best he could to help the plane ride upward.

Clouds swirled about them at times, puff-balls of mist driven down the glacier; drift scurried beneath them; it was a wicked place for an airplane to be, hemmed in by the wall of the towering peaks on either side.

This was the time when they had to lighten ship and Byrd, looking around for what could best be spared, decided to dump some food. There was a dump valve in the fuselage tank, but he had determined to go through and did not know what winds he might face at the top of the glacier. So food was thrown overboard, scattered over the ridged and broken surface of the Livingston Glacier.

"It is an awful looking place," Commander Byrd said.

Over the "Hump" and Vast Panorama Unfolds.

They finally reached the hump at an elevation of 11,500 feet, as indicated by the barograph, although it might have been a little more, because of the difference in pressure inland.

But there was little space under the staggering plane, buffeted by the winds that eddied through the gigantic gorge. Once at the top, Balchen could level off for a time and then gain altitude.

Then there came into view slowly the long sweep of mountains of the Queen Maud Range, stretching to the southeast, and the magnificent panorama of the entire bulwark of mountains along the edge of the Polar Plateau.

Beheld Tinted Slopes of Myriad Mountains.

"It was the most magnificent sight I have ever seen," Commander Byrd said. "I never dreamed there were so many mountains in the world. They shone under the sun, wonderfully tinted with color, and in the southeast a bank of clouds hung over the mountains, making a scene that I shall never forget."

Over the plateau the Commander set his course for the pole. They had had a beam wind all the way in to the mountains which

"All the News That's Fit to Print."

The New York Times.

THE WEATHER.
Fair, slightly warmer Thursday; Friday, fair, warmer; moderate winds, becoming south.
For full weather report see Page 23.

VOL. LXXIX....No. 26,245. **** NEW YORK, MONDAY, DECEMBER 2, 1929. TWO CENTS in Greater New York | THREE CENTS Within 200 Miles | FOUR CENTS Elsewhere Except 7th and 8th Postal Zones

BYRD BEGINS HIS OWN STORY OF POLAR FLIGHT; TOOK CHANCE ON CLEAR WEATHER AND FOUND IT AT MOUNTAIN PASSES WHERE SEVEREST TEST CAME

CONGRESS REOPENS TODAY WITH SENATE STILL SPLIT BADLY

Regular Session, Convening at Noon, Faces Long Program Uncertainly.

COMMITTEE POSTS AN ISSUE

Democrats Aiding Insurgents to Put La Follette on Finance Body of Upper Branch.

TAX CUT FIRST IN ORDER

House Will Act After President's Message Tomorrow—Senate Taking Up Vare Case and Tariff.

Special to The New York Times.

WASHINGTON, Dec. 1.—The first regular session of the Seventy-first Congress will open tomorrow, following the special session which completed farm relief legislation, but adjourned ten days ago with a tariff bill still pending, the Republican party in the Senate divided into uncompromising groups and the majority leadership in that body surrendered to a coalition of insurgent Republicans and Democrats.

A tax reduction resolution and appropriation bills in the House, and the Vare case and tariff bill in the Senate are the chief subjects awaiting early attention as Congress begins the long session, which is expected also to devote much time to consideration of measures intended to stimulate industry and aid in the maintenance of prosperity. The Senate will also be asked to ratify a naval limitation treaty if one is negotiated at the London conference, which meets in January.

Vice President Curtis and Speaker Longworth will call the two branches to order at noon and both bodies will immediately adjourn, after appointing committees to notify the President of their readiness to receive his message.

The message, the first from President Hoover to be devoted to general subjects and matters dealing with the "state of the Union," will be read by clerks in both branches Tuesday. Mr. Hoover has decided not to follow the example of President Wilson, and adopted on one occasion by President Coolidge, of appearing in person before Congress.

Budget and Other Messages to Come.

The President's annual budget message probably will be presented on Wednesday. Secretary of the Treasury Mellon's annual report also is scheduled for submission to Congress on that day. Other departmental and bureau reports will be transmitted at different times during the week.

Organization of committees will receive attention on both sides of the Capitol. The House during the special session set up only such committees as were necessary to transact the business then pending, namely, the Ways and Means, Agriculture, Rules and Accounts, and Appropriations bodies. While there will be but few changes in the chairmanships from the last Congress, a number of vacancies must be filled and there will be a change in the ratio of party strength in the committees to match the increase in the Republican House majority.

The Republican Committee on Committees of the House is to meet Tuesday and will report recommendations for assignments a few days later.

Inasmuch as the Senate is a continuing body, its standing committees do not require reappointment. The death of Senator Warren, however, leaves a vacancy in the chairmanship of the Appropriations Committee, which is to be filled by the transfer of Senator Jones of Washington from the chairmanship of the Committee on Commerce. This will lead to several shifts in the chairmanships of other committees.

The death of Senator Burton of Ohio and the resignation of Senator Edge of New Jersey to become Ambassador to France have left a number of vacancies which must be filled.

There is a lively contest for the Edge vacancy on the Finance Committee. The insurgent Republicans are demanding the place for Senator La Follette of Wisconsin and the Democratic-insurgent coalition may go into action to obtain it for him if the Republicans assign it to some one else. Senator La Follette's father held a place on this committee for many years, but since his death the regulars have seen to it that the radical group had no representation on this powerful body, which has charge of the tariff and tax measures.

Control Shifted to the West.

Control of the Republican Committee on Committees in the Senate has been shifted from the East to the West with the recent naming of Senator Capper of Kansas as a mem-

Continued on Page Seventeen.

Pickford-Fairbanks Visit Cut By Proposed Chinese Boycott

Special Cable to THE NEW YORK TIMES.

SHANGHAI, Dec. 1.—Because of local agitation in favor of boycotting Mary Pickford and Douglas Fairbanks, who will arrive here from Singapore Dec. 10, their projected stay has been shortened from four days to one. The boycott is advocated because a Chinese sequence of the film, "The Thief of Bagdad," is declared to be derogatory to the dignity of the Chinese race.

A popular movement has been launched here to demand that the government, after the intended abolition of extraterritoriality on Jan. 1, order the customs not to permit the landing of individuals in China unless they sign a pledge to submit to Chinese laws and courts.

This movement is being backed by the Chinese members of the Shanghai Municipal Council.

SING SING CONVICT SLAIN AS 100 LOOK ON

Reuben Kaminsky, 17, Stabbed as He Stands in Ranks With 1,700 Others.

FOUR PRISONERS SEIZED

Victim Is Said to Have Informed on One of Group Placed in Solitary Confinement.

Special to The New York Times.

OSSINING, N. Y., Dec. 1.—As 1,730 dull gray figures stood in line in the gathering twilight in the old prison yard at Sing Sing prison this evening, preparatory to returning to their cells in the new prison on the hill, Reuben Kaminsky of Brooklyn, one of the youngest convicts in the prison, was mysteriously stabbed to death. As the boy, who was only 17 years old, fell from his place in the line a dozen guards rushed to the spot, but already a cold, immobile silence had settled over the long lines of men. A hundred convicts must have seen the slaying, but none of them would give the authorities any clue to the slayer, his weapon or the motive.

Several hours later, following an investigation, Warden Lewis E. Lawes ordered Jacob Burakoff, another convict from Brooklyn, and three other men who were in the line into solitary confinement pending the outcome of further inquiry. Burakoff, who is also 17, and Kaminsky were companions in a Brooklyn hold-up for which they were both serving sentences, and prison records show, according to Warden Lawes, that Burakoff was arrested on information supplied by Kaminsky after the latter had been arrested.

The prison whistle had just announced the end of the Sunday afternoon recreation period. The men were drawn up in single file in long rows across the yard. In another moment they would start to file, one by one, through the gate into the yard of the new prison. The guards had taken their places at the ends of the lines and about the gate. Sergeant of the Guard Frederick Vetter turned just in time to see Kaminsky fall. The boy had made no outcry, but when Vetter reached him he found that he was bleeding from five stab wounds, one in the left cheek, one under the left arm and three in the chest.

Dies on Operating Table.

With the aid of another guard Vetter carried the wounded prisoner to the hospital, where he died on the operating table about fifteen minutes later. He was unconscious when Vetter reached him and was able to give no information regarding his assailant. Back in the yard other guards made a hurried search of the men nearest Kaminsky, but found no trace of a knife or other weapon.

All the wounds apparently had been made by the same weapon, presumably a knife, prison physicians said.

Warden Lawes, who had been away for the day but returned to the prison shortly after the stabbing, ordered an immediate investigation. He said that he was convinced from the nature of the wounds that whoever stabbed Kaminsky had been standing in front of him. Prisoners in the leather factory use knives in their work, he said, and knives are supplied the men in mess hall during meals, but they are contraband in the prison and there is a severe penalty for any convict found with one. As a disciplinary measure, Warden Lawes canceled tonight's showing of the annual prison show, "Good News." The show was given for convicts last night and will be given for the general public tomorrow.

Burakoff denied any knowledge of the stabbing, but the warden ordered him held for further questioning. Meanwhile a search of the cells and the men who were in the line at the time of the stabbing failed to reveal any further evidence. Prison physicians said that the wounds had been inflicted by a knife with a blade at least two and one-half inches long. The only knife which was found in a thorough search of the men and the cells was a small jack-knife which the warden said could not have inflicted the wounds. This knife was found in the cell of a prisoner who,

Continued on Page Two.

NAVY PARLEY HANGS ON SIZE OF FLEETS IN MEDITERRANEAN

French Plans Will Not Allow Britain to Maintain Force Equal to Two Powers.

ITALY TAKES PART IN CLASH

Mussolini's Call for Parity With France Upsets Calculations for Auxiliary Craft.

AMERICA TO BE INVOLVED

Conference Threatened With Failure if United States Delegates Refuse to Join European Issue.

By EDWIN L. JAMES.

Special Cable to THE NEW YORK TIMES.

LONDON, Dec. 1.—It is now perfectly plain that the hardest problem which will confront the five-power naval conference will be the sea strength in the Mediterranean. Not only will that issue involve the naval forces of France and Italy as between themselves but, even more important, it will involve the position of Great Britain.

There is one big reason why Britain does not wish to consummate a definite arrangement with the United States prior to the conference and that is, she wishes to remain in a position to control the Mediterranean in a manner to enable her to protect her most important lines of communication in that sea.

While the government as a whole has not yet formulated publicly its Mediterranean policy for the conference, the Admiralty and the Foreign Office wish Britain to have a two-power fleet with regard to all nations other than America. In other words, Britain may be found to demand a strength in cruisers, destroyers and submarines equal to that of Italy and France combined.

Seeing that London is pretty close to agreement with Washington on the tonnage of the various classes of warships and seeing that an agreement with Japan is not expected to be immensely difficult, it would seem that the chances of the conference reaching a definite five-power treaty on naval limitation depends on the settlement of the Mediterranean business.

Demands of France and Italy.

Were France and Italy to accept for cruisers, destroyers and submarines the same ratio they accepted for capital ships, namely, roughly one-third of the British and American strength, it is plain that Britain would maintain the position of dominance she wishes. But that result will not be attained because France is not going to accept limitation of her cruisers, destroyers and submarines to one-third of the tonnage in those classes which England and America are ready to accept, and Italy demands the same sea strength as France.

Now, France and Italy have no capital ships worth speaking of, nor do they desire to build any. There may be an effort made to argue that Britain's capital ships will give her what she seeks in the Mediterranean, since, counting capital ships, her fleet tonnage will remain as great as the French and Italian fleets combined, and if France and Italy have relatively large fleets of auxiliary craft. Of course, one cannot tell how far this argument will go with the statesmen, but certainly the Admiralty will contest it and will stand for a safely supreme position in auxiliary ships.

As for cruisers, the French have, counting those which are less than twenty years old and those under construction, just about one-third of the tonnage of 340,000 which would be acceptable to Great Britain. But the French contend that, somewhat like the United States, they are behind in cruiser building, and that their naval plans call for a good deal of additional construction. It would

Continued on Page Nine.

Gov. Roosevelt Greets Byrd, Telling of Thrill Over Feat

Special to The New York Times.

ALBANY, N. Y., Dec. 1.—Governor Roosevelt has sent a message from Warm Springs, Ga., to Commander Byrd at Little America congratulating him on his flight over the South Pole. Guernsey T. Cross, secretary to the Governor, made the message public tonight, as follows:

"I am thrilled by your latest achievement, but knew all along that you would pull it off. My congratulations to you and whole party, in which the family joins."

CHAIRS FLY IN ROW AT STRIKE MEETING

Communist Issue Starts Clash Among 300 Municipal Subway Construction Workers.

SCORES IN FIST FIGHTS

Many Receive Bruises and Black Eyes—Left Wing Insists on a General Walk-Out.

The injection of communism into a mass meeting of nearly 300 subway construction workers precipitated a clash yesterday afternoon in Royal Hall, 85 East Fourth Street. Fists, chairs and water glasses were used as weapons as scores of workers belabored each other.

Although no serious injuries were reported, there were plenty of black eyes and bruised noses, and several men were cut by chair rungs, while many others emerged from the free-for-all with body bruises and torn clothing. No arrests were made, most of the workers having left the hall when two patrolmen appeared in response to a hurry call sent out by the custodian of the building.

The meeting was called by the International Subway, Tunnel and Compressed Air Workers' Union to discuss the question of calling a general strike of the 15,000 laborers employed on the city's new subway system. About 600 members of the union have been out on strike on two Bronx sections of the subway system for about three weeks.

Left Wing Action Threatened.

It was said last night that a "left wing" group of the union, which met in a near-by hall after the meeting broke up in confusion without taking action on the general strike question, would meet tonight to press plans for calling such a strike immediately. This group asserted that the union's executive committee refused to grant its spokesmen a hearing on their demand for prompt action.

The disorder began when James Moran, until recently president of Local 63 of the subway workers' organization, was berating Communist interference and defending the American Federation of Labor from attacks contained in leaflets distributed among the men. John McQueen, the new president of the local, suggested that he was "out of order." Mr. McQueen said later that his purpose was not to contradict Moran, but to cut his speech short so that the meeting might proceed.

Mr. Moran's reaction to the suggestion was a blow aimed at Mr. McQueen's jaw. John F. McPartlan, secretary-treasurer of the union, rose to protest and some one punched him. In an instant the hall was in an uproar. Most of the men made a rush for the single exit at

Continued on Page Sixteen.

International Newsreel Photo.

COMMANDER BYRD TAKING BEARINGS.
This Photograph, Taken on One of His Earlier Flights, Shows the Polar Explorer Using the Sextant in Plotting His Course.

MORGAN'S ESTATE TO BE YACHT CLUB

Syndicate to Spend $1,500,000 Converting Cragston-on-the-Hudson Near West Point.

CHAMBERLIN TO BE AIR AIDE

Speedboats and Planes to Give 30-Minute Service to City From Historic Property.

Cragston-on-the-Hudson, the estate of the Morgan family, on which slabs mark the graves of Molly Pitcher and many soldiers of the Revolutionary War, has been acquired by a syndicate of yachtsmen who plan to convert the place into the Cragston Yacht and Country Club, it was announced yesterday by Charles W. Hickernell, who is secretary of the new club with offices at 37 Wall Street. More than $1,500,000 will be expended for the project, which includes conversion of the estate into a club with golf and tennis facilities, provision for yachts and amphibian airplanes and a clubhouse.

For fifty-seven years the Morgan family has invested huge sums in horticulture and landscape architecture on the estate. It has been a show place of the East for many years. The members of the elder family of Morgans used it as a country home, and the late Mrs. J. Pierpont Morgan Sr. lived there from the death of her husband until she died in the mansion in November, 1924.

733 Acres in Tract.

The tract, which comprises 733 acres between Bear Mountain and West Point, was bought by the father of the present head of the Morgan family in 1872. It has been chosen as the site of the new club because of its historic value, the beauty of its landscape and its accessibility by water to New York. An effort has been made for years, it was explained, to establish a complete country club in connection with yachting activities, but because the cost of deep-water shore frontage has been too great to permit the buying of extensive properties, many plans have been abandoned. Since the advent of the high-speed yacht and seaplane, however, this acreage, less than fifty miles from the centre of business, has been brought within commuting distance of the city. J. Pierpont Morgan, the elder, commuted from the estate in his yacht for years.

The price and conditions of the sale of the estate were not revealed. It was learned, however, that a previous sale had been made, with special restrictions, on April 10 last year to another syndicate headed by Colonel Evan Shelby of New York, who was not reached last night.

Membership in the new club is restricted by invitation, and applications are to be approved by the directorate, which includes:

F. Calvin Demarest, president
C. W. Hickernell, secretary
Lee Buckingham, vice president
Charles F. Chapman
Henry W. Pope
E. C. Huntington Jr.
John F. Sanderson
Lady Archer-Shee
E. Arthur Carter
Fred C. Reynolds
R. McManamy Jr.
W. S. Hawkins
Judge W. W. Dey
McClelland Barclay
L. C. Stowell
J. C. Demarest

Club Engages Chamberlin.

Many technicians have been retained for the conversion of the estate into a club. Clarence D. Chamberlin is to direct the aviation activities, Devereux Emmet will supervise the golf course architecture, and other architects will lay out the tennis courts, equestrian paths and swimming pool. The landlocked harbor of the estate is well suited to an-

Continued on Page Thirteen.

MOORE SUSPENDED; HARVEY TO TRY HIM

Queens President Removes the Engineer Who, Buckner Held, Was Guilty With Connolly.

GIVES NEW EXPLANATION

Now Asserts Moore Went Back to Job on 'Probation' While His Aide Was Investigating.

Borough President George U. Harvey of Queens announced yesterday the suspension of Clifford B. Moore, consulting engineer in the Connolly administration, who was restored to duty as assistant borough engineer two weeks ago. Moore will be placed on trial before the Borough President on charges of neglect of duty, incompetency and conduct unbecoming a public official.

Although Mr. Harvey in his announcement insisted that he was following an orderly procedure from which he had refused to be "coerced," his decision was taken to be a victory for Emory R. Buckner, special prosecutor of the Queens sewer graft scandals, who had demanded the termination of the engineer's career in public office. Mr. Buckner charged that official records showed Moore to be a co-conspirator in corruption with former Borough President Maurice E. Connolly and Frederick Seely, former engineer of sewer design, both of whom have been convicted of conspiracy to defraud the city.

From last Thursday until yesterday the Borough President took the position that he was unable to prove the accusations against Moore and that the engineer, according to competent advice, had a right to return to work. It was Mr. Buckner's duty, the Borough President had insisted, to take charge of any action that might be initiated against Moore.

Demands Buckner Act.

In his announcement yesterday Mr. Harvey again demanded that the special prosecutor proceed criminally against the engineer by presenting evidence to the grand jury and characterized Mr. Buckner as being "remiss in his duty." The Borough President explained that his determination to suspend and try the engineer followed an investigation undertaken by Commissioner of Public Works John J. Halleran. He also declared that Moore had merely been permitted "to resume his title for a probationary period pending the investigation."

This was the first intimation which Mr. Harvey had given during the public controversy that the engineer was on probation or that any qualification had been attached to his restoration to duty. When Mr. Buckner on Thursday made public his letter of protest after it had remained unanswered for eight days, the Borough President in his comment at that time also failed to mention Mr. Halleran's investigation.

Mr. Harvey's statement yesterday followed a meeting at his home in Flushing of Mr. Halleran, Borough Secretary Frederick Sasse, Frank Lee Donaghue, Deputy Commissioner of Highways, and John Holley Clark Jr., Mr. Harvey's legal adviser, but the Borough President asserted that Moore had been suspended on Saturday.

Statement by Mr. Harvey.

Mr. Harvey's statement follows:

Clifford B. Moore, assistant engineer, was ordered suspended by me at the close of business Saturday, Nov. 30, 1929, pending the trial and hearing of charges. Speci-

Continued on Page Twenty.

FELT THAT FLOYD BENNETT'S SPIRIT 'FLEW WITH US'

Commander Recalled Comrade on North Pole Dash Who Died While Preparations Were Being Made for Southern Flight.

CLOUDS MELTED TILL SUN SHONE ON PEAKS

Passing Unmapped Ridges West of Air Route, Dropping Supplies to Sledges, Airmen Grimly Faced Big Climb Over Glacier Wall.

By COMMANDER R. E. BYRD,
Leader of the Antarctic Expedition.

Wireless to THE NEW YORK TIMES.

LITTLE AMERICA, Antarctica, Dec. 1.—On our flight to the South Pole sunshine was necessary. Not only must the eye of our surveying camera be able to record the mountains and other Antarctic phenomena at great distance, but also we must avoid finding clouds over the mountains, obscuring the glacier passes by which we hoped to dodge through the 15,000-foot peaks that fringe the great South Polar Plateau.

Flying down here with a cloud-covered sky is like flying in a world that has turned to milk. There is nothing to check on. Horizons disappear and there is no way to tell where the snow begins, how rough the surface is, nor even how high we are above it.

The altimeter records inaccurately on account of rapid changes in the sea level barometer, and there are bigger barometric changes in the Antarctic than anywhere else in the world. With such weather, navigation would be uncertain, landing impossible. Visibility down here is like the little girl with the curl—very good when it is good and terrible when it is bad.

Weather at Plateau the Chief Concern.

To have sunshine for 800 miles in this country of changeable weather is more than one can expect. But for the success of our flight it would be absolutely necessary that the mountains around the Plateau should not be cloud-covered.

Several hours before our departure Bill Haines got a weather report from the geological party which convinced him that the flying conditions were O. K. over the Plateau. The weather was not so important here as it was there. That is why we did not wait for ideal conditions for our departure.

In flying across the ocean, for example, one can fly through clouds and even storms with impunity, but when the course goes over mountains whose peaks tower higher than the plane can fly, good visibility is required to get between the peaks over the glaciers.

Heart Goes Out to Men at Departure.

We had long felt that we might have to make several attempts before we could get the proper combination of circumstances. When we took off with our heavy load, clouds partly covered the sky. There was, however, a rim of green on the horizon to the south and we knew that it would be clear beyond.

As the skis left the snow, all I could see in that white bowl beneath us was the little group of my shipmates throwing their hats into the air—wild with joy that at last we were headed poleward.

A warm glow of affection for those fellows went through me. For weary months they had undergone hardships and sacrifices for this moment. They had given us our great opportunity and they were unselfishly glad.

Rock From Bennett's Grave Weighted Flag.

My mind shot back to an exactly similar scene in the Arctic Spring, May 9, 1926, when Floyd Bennett and I rose from the snow at Spitsbergen and headed north-poleward. Many of the fellows who were in the cheering crowd at Spitsbergen were below me now. Each of them was Floyd Bennett's friend. And there beside me sat Bernt Balchen at the wheel.

It had been the three of us—Bennett, Balchen and myself—who had set out on this job two years ago, and the three of us would be together at the finish, for we knew that Floyd Bennett's spirit flew with us.

He had selected the Ford plane, prepared it and flown it, and had helped with our early plans, so that his genius and his friendship were with us helping us to reach our goal.

The last thing we put in the plane was a stone that came from Floyd's grave at Arlington. We weighted with it the American flag that we proposed to drop on the South Pole.

Out Into Sunshine on Air Trail to Pole.

The plane had circled now and hit the Gilbert Grosvenor air trail, which by midnight we hoped to extend to the South Pole. In a few moments we emerged from the confusing bowl of milk over the take-off into sunshine that stretched ahead to the horizon.

A thousand feet beneath us we picked up the dog team trail. It is only with the sun in certain positions that the trail can be seen from the air. Now it was a faint broken thread that we lost time and again but managed to pick up each time with the Bumstead sun compass.

A strong easterly breeze forced us to head 10 degrees to the left of the course to allow for this wind and so the plane crabbed along toward the south with its nose pointed well to the left of the trail.

We had constantly to check the course by the drift indicator, an instrument through which the ground is sighted to ascertain the amount the wind has caused the plane to drift from the true direction.

Sun-Blazed Peaks Like Erupting Volcanoes.

We enjoyed the first few hours of the flight when we had time to look around for flying over this mysterious Barrier never loses its fascination. Shortly after we passed the crevassed area, 150 miles from Little America, we sighted the mountains to the westward. [Seen on a previous trip to the Queen Maud Mountains.]

Again I was struck with the majesty of these ranges. We saw one great mountain mass end and another one, unaccounted for on the maps, begin to the south and run toward the Beardmore Glacier.

Great white glaciers flowed into the Barrier and about a hundred

Public Service Commission to Investigate Traffic Congestion on Long Island Railroad

Special to The New York Times.

ALBANY, Dec. 1.—A general investigation to determine whether the Long Island Railroad Company is able to care adequately for the traffic it would naturally gain in the next five years was ordered today by the Public Service Commission. The hearing will take place at the New York City office of the commission, 120 Broadway, on Dec. 23 at 11 A. M.

The matter was taken up by the commission on its own initiative. Representatives of the railroad, municipalities, boards of trade and Long Island civic organizations generally will be invited to attend the hearing.

No inquiry into the reasonableness of the rates charged by the Long Island is contemplated at this time. The present and future adequacy of the service the railroad is giving between points on its railroad and New York City is the sole object.

It was stated by the commission that at a recent hearing before it, on complaints of commuters who sought additional trains, and in reply to inquiries as to future expansions and betterments, the representative of the Long Island Railroad gave no adequate answer.

"The railroad is not able at the present time," the commission's statement read, "so the commission was informed, to offer any plans for relief in the near future from the congested conditions, claiming that it cannot put on any more trains, and further alleging that it cannot get them into the Pennsylvania Station in New York or the Brooklyn station during the rush hours. The company has proffered no general plan as to what it will be able to do in the next four or five years. No suggestions have been offered by it as to relief from existing conditions, which, it is believed, will become worse in the future.

"The commission enters into a general investigation of the plans of the railroad for its development and expansion during the next five years with a view to obtaining a detailed program from the company designed to meet the conditions of even greater congestion, which will undoubtedly exist at the end of that period in the Long Island territory."

"All the News That's Fit to Print."

The New York Times.

THE WEATHER
Cloudy and colder today; tomorrow warmer, with rain or snow.
Temperature yesterday—Max., 36; min., 25.
U. S. Weather Forecast—For details see Page [illegible]

VOL. LXXIX....No. 26,246. NEW YORK, TUESDAY, DECEMBER 3, 1929. TWO CENTS In Greater New York | THREE CENTS Within 200 Miles | FOUR CENTS Elsewhere Except 7th and 8th Postal Zones

STIMSON SENDS TO RUSSIA REMINDER OF PEACE PACT; FRANCE AND BRITAIN JOIN

CITES WAR MOVES IN CHINA

Calls on 53 Other Signers to Marshal World Opinion for Treaty.

FIRST REAL TEST FOR PACT

Identical Note Also Delivered to China—Tone Is Informal and Persuasive.

PARIS IN COMPLETE ACCORD

Delivers Our Note to Moscow and One of Its Own—London Will Act With Us.

Special to The New York Times.

WASHINGTON, Dec. 2.—The United States has appealed to Russia and China, in the name of the general pact for the renunciation of war, to avoid warlike measures in Manchuria and adjust their dispute in that region over the Chinese Eastern Railway by pacific means, and has notified fifty-three other nations of its move.

In announcing today that the appeal had been transmitted to both governments, Secretary Stimson disclosed that the United States, as sponsor of the anti-war treaty, had again taken the initiative in urging its observance by those party to it, and in so doing had appealed to world public opinion for support.

The appeal to Russia and China referred particularly to Article II of the Kellogg Treaty, which binds them to use only pacific means in the settlement of disputes; recalled that last July when the controversy first arose in Manchuria both governments, in response to a communication from Secretary Stimson, gave public assurance that neither would resort to war unless attacked; and expressed the "earnest hope" of the United States that they would refrain or desist from measures of hostility.

In conclusion, it warned Russia and China that the respect with which they were held in the world will depend upon the manner in which they carry out their "sacred promises."

Other Countries Approached.

The move was not made without careful preparation through diplomatic exchanges with other governments particularly interested in the Far East, namely, Great Britain, France, Italy, Germany and Japan. There had developed as a result of these interchanges, Mr. Stimson said, a "community of view with regard to the fundamental principles."

The United States not only united these five governments in order to send nearly identical communications to Russia and China, but notified the forty-eight other parties to the Kellogg treaty of its course and the opportunity they had to join in the appeal.

As a result it is already assured that other governments will take action along the line of the United States and that there will be seen a great marshalling of public opinion in the civilized world in support of the Kellogg Treaty in its application to the Manchurian crisis. Assurances were received late today that France and Great Britain were acting in support of the American thesis, and similar moves are expected on the part of many other powers.

The significance of this goes far beyond the controversy over the Chinese Eastern Railway into the status of international relations generally and conceivably may have an important bearing upon the London naval conference.

The marshalling of world opinion behind the anti-war treaty will, it is believed, demonstrate that that compact is a reality. That the Kellogg treaty as a living force should give a great impetus to the movement for naval reduction has been admitted in many capitals. Although Mr. Stimson said that the recent events in Manchuria could not be permitted to pass without notice or protests by the governments party to the multilateral treaty, the stand the United States has taken is interpreted as one directed as much for general international relations in the future as for the Manchurian difficulty of the moment.

Note Is Persuasive.

The communications sent to Russia and China by the United States were notable for the care in which any impression of exerting pressure was avoided. The dominant note was one of an effort at friendly persuasion

Continued on Page Four.

Wang Will Quit Nanking Post; Takes Blame for China's Woes

Special Cable to THE NEW YORK TIMES.

SHANGHAI, Dec. 2.—C. T. Wang, Foreign Minister, today notified President Chiang Kai-shek in an interview in Nanking of his determination to resign, which he reiterated in a speech at the Foreign Office, declaring himself responsible for the deadlock in the negotiations with Japan, and for the Sino-Soviet impasse, and stating that the question of extraterritoriality was too difficult.

Though General Chiang, in the usual face-saving manner, has earnestly asked Dr. Wang to retain his post, it is believed here that he is slated for early retirement, because some head must be offered to save the face of the government over the Manchurian débâcle, and because many Kuomintang party organizations have been passing resolutions demanding Dr. Wang's resignation and punishment, blaming him for the invasion of Chinese territory and slaughter of Chinese by Russians, causing loss to the nation's dignity.

MOSCOW IS SILENT ON STIMSON'S MOVE

Peace Efforts Thought Belated and Unnecessary in View of Mukden's Capitulation.

JAPAN REFUSES TO JOIN

Considers Russia and China Need No Outside Help to Settle Manuchruian Dispute.

By WALTER DURANTY.

Wireless to THE NEW YORK TIMES.

MOSCOW, Dec. 2.—Obstinate silence was maintained in official circles here regarding Secretary Stimson's communication about Manchurian affairs to the signatories of the Kellogg pact. So far as Moscow is concerned, it might not have been received at all, to judge from the absence of information or comment.

In point of fact, Moscow doubtless considers that the American Secretary's suggestion has become obsolete, because it was made prior to Mukden's acceptance of the Soviet terms for negotiations now proceeding more or less briskly at Khabarovsk in Eastern Manchuria.

Should a reply be made, it will doubtless express the same viewpoint as the reply to the belated—though naively pre-dated November 14—proposal of Nanking to negotiate. In short, it will say that as the Soviet is now discussing the Manchurian question directly with the party principally concerned—namely, Mukden—it thanks the Secretary for his good offices, but finds them no longer necessary.

Not the least interesting phase of this curious little piece of Oriental diplomacy is that all three parties most closely connected with the Manchurian imbroglio, the Soviet, Mukden and Japan, all have equally good reason not to wish outside intervention, whether that of Nanking, the United States or the League of Nations. Especially, perhaps, Japan, which may well hope to get certain advantages in regard to railroad tariffs and freight shipment—to say nothing of other political or economic benefits—from the Soviet-Mukden agreement, if it can be reached.

At present best-informed opinion in Moscow considers the prospects of such an agreement fair enough, despite efforts on the part of Nanking and others to put a finger in the Manchurian pie. No matter what may be believed or asserted in London or Washington, your correspondent has good reasons to be convinced that Red troops occupy no considerable area of Manchurian territory—if any part at all—and certainly are not conducting, or for the moment contemplating, offensive action.

Japan Cold to Suggestion.

By HUGH BYAS.

Wireless to THE NEW YORK TIMES.

TOKIO, Dec. 2.—Reports that Washington proposes again to remind Russia and China of their Kellogg pact obligations coincide with cumulative evidences that the dispute is ended.

Manchurian envoys are now in Russian territory meeting a Russian representative to complete arrangements for restoring the status quo on the Chinese Eastern Railway. Baron Shidehara, Foreign Minister, saw the Soviet and Chinese Ministers this morning. If, as is generally assumed, he reminded them of their obligation under the Kellogg pact, M. Troyanovsky, the Russian envoy, could have answered that the episode

Continued on Page Four.

Representative Disavows Wife's Debt for Furs; Wins Suit on Plea of Forbidding Credit Buying

By The Associated Press.

WASHINGTON, Dec. 2.—The husband who gives his wife money to pay cash instead of having her buy on his credit won today in a decision by the District of Columbia Court of Appeals, which excused Representative George Huddleston of Alabama of liability for a $245 debt for furs bought by his wife.

The Alabaman had said he gave Mrs. Huddleston $75 in cash each month for her personal expenses and had forbidden her to pledge his credit. She purchased the furs on credit, nevertheless, making a small payment on a coat and fox scarf costing $253.

Judgment in favor of the husband was rendered in the Municipal Court and the fur merchant sued out a writ of error. Justice Charles H. Robb in today's decision said it would tend "to check extravagance, one of the most pronounced modern evils, and at the same time protect husbands who, in good faith, have made such provisions for their wives as their means and station in life warranted from debts thoughtlessly and needlessly contracted and often beyond the capacity of the husband to pay."

"Moreover," the decision continued, "it does not require the discernment of a Solomon to appreciate that the unauthorized purchase of goods by a wife whose husband has adequately provided for her inevitably will have a tendency to disturb and possibly disrupt their conjugal relations."

As for the merchant who makes such a sale as involved in the case, the Appeals Court held he must learn whether a wife has authority to pledge her husband's credit.

$160,000,000 TAX CUT PRESSED IN HOUSE AS CONGRESS MEETS

Way Paved to Pass Resolution in Short Order Under Businesslike Procedure.

VARE CASE TANGLES SENATE

Move Declaring the Pennsylvania Seat Vacant Will Be Taken Up Today.

By RICHARD V. OULAHAN.

Special to The New York Times.

WASHINGTON, Dec. 2.—The outstanding feature of an otherwise drab opening today of the first regular session of the Seventy-first Congress was the introduction by Representative Willis C. Hawley of Oregon, chairman of the Ways and Means Committee, of a joint resolution to speedily fulfill the Hoover administration's promise of a tax cut of $160,000,000.

The resolution would cut the corporation tax from 12 per cent to 11 per cent and reduce the normal income tax levy by 1 per cent.

The proposed slash will apply only to 1929 income, on which the taxes will be due in 1930.

The measure was referred to the Ways and Means Committee, which will make a prompt report, so that the House, followed by the Senate, can act quickly and send the resolution, which will have the effect of law when signed by the President, to the White House before Congress recesses for the Christmas holidays.

Senate in Session Nine Minutes.

The Senate was in session nine minutes, the House barely more than an hour. Both adjourned out of respect for Senator Francis E. Warren of Wyoming, last Union veteran to sit in Congress, dean of the Senate and chairman of the Senate Appropriations Committee. Senator Warren died after adjournment of the extra session.

The first annual message of President Hoover will be read in the Senate and House tomorrow.

The House assembled at noon after what amounted to a holiday of nearly six months. The Senate began the first sitting of the regular session at the same hour, but its holiday had lasted only for the brief period since it adjourned the extra session on Nov. 22, a week ago last Friday.

Gloomy skies from which rain, intermingled with sleet, poured steadily, were symptomatic of the lethargic and spiritless return of the Senate. In the House, however, an atmosphere of jollity prevailed. The Representatives laughed heartily when a messenger from the other end of the Capitol announced solemnly that the Senate was ready for the transaction of business.

The prolonged laughter was symptomatic of the reaction of the people's representatives to the failure of the Senate to pass the tariff revision bill after it had it under consideration for months during the extra session.

While the Senate was working on the measure, or supposed to be working, the House was merely going through forms of legislative activity. It had completed its business before Summer began, and has been waiting ever since for the Senate to catch up with it.

Both Houses took a recess on June 19, the Senate until Aug. 19 and the House until Sept. 23, but when the House reassembled it found there was no prospect that the Senate would get through with the tariff bill for a long time.

So the handful of Representatives who had returned to Washington would solemnly meet twice a week and on each occasion would immediately adjourn for three days at a time, as the Constitution permits one House to do without the consent of the other.

Tariff Bill Faces Stormy Path.

Today, in the House much time was taken up calling the roll of members. Perfunctory business was transacted. Representative Garner, the Democratic floor leader, made a speech of ten minutes. The income tax reduction bill was introduced without comment and the House then adjourned

Continued on Page Three.

FIRST SNOWSTORM CLOGS CITY TRAFFIC; NEW COLD WAVE DUE

Four-Inch Fall Makes Streets Perilous, Causing Skidding Mishaps and One Death.

PLANES KEPT AGROUND

30,000 Commuters on Staten Island Delayed—Sweepers Mobilized in All Boroughs.

The first snowstorm of the season dealt New York a blow yesterday, hampering air and street traffic, causing one death and many minor accidents, giving the city's millions new discomforts in overtaxed subways and slippery streets, and sounding the call for the city's army of street cleaners to muster for its first snow battle.

Four inches of snow, mixed occasionally with sleet, fell between 10:25 A. M. and 6:45 P. M. The snow brought with it a slight rise in temperature, giving the city some relief from the cold wave that had gripped it for several days.

One death in Chappaqua and another in Paterson, N. J., marked the descent of the storm in the metropolitan area. Mail and commercial aviation at suburban airports was at a complete standstill, all mail destined to be carried by plane being brought into or sent out of the city for a considerable distance by train.

'Much Colder' Tonight.

More snow was expected to fall some time during the night. The snowstorm will end today, the Weather Bureau said, but tonight will be "much colder." The temperature yesterday averaged 31, reaching its high mark of 36 degrees at 9:45 A. M., after having been down to a minimum of 25 above zero or seven below freezing at 3:30 A. M.

Cold weather prevailed from the Rocky Mountains to the Atlantic seaboard and penetrated deeply into the South. The stormy weather that hit New York was considerably more violent in the Great Lakes region and along the Newfoundland coast.

Many Great Lakes vessels were battling to keep afloat in what was one of the worst storms on these inland waters. Several vessels were reported in distress, more than a score were overdue at the Soo locks, and Lake Superior was strewn with more wreckage than has ever been seen there before.

The storm pounded the Newfoundland coast, as well as Central and Western Canada, and at St. John's, N. F., the fate of three freighters and a dozen schooners was in doubt.

Shipping in New York was not affected, but gales that are customary on the Atlantic at this season are expected to cause some delays in the arrival of various ships.

All coastwise traffic entered the port of New York on time. Ferries kept up a normal schedule between Manhattan and Staten Island, South Ferry and Brooklyn, New York and New Jersey. Last night the upper bay was fairly clear, offering normal visibility, but there was a slight fog in the lower bay, insufficient, however, to cause any serious delay to shipping. Sandy Hook reported light fog off the coast with only a moderate Winter wind. No distress calls from ships were received here.

Skidding Truck Kills Man.

The skidding of automobiles, trucks and horse-drawn vehicles on the slippery streets of the city caused many accidents, one of them fatal, as well as traffic tie-ups.

Rocco Mazza, 65 years old, of 1,239 Franklin Avenue, the Bronx, died in Lincoln Hospital of injuries he received when a truck skidded in the snow at East 163d Street and Third Avenue and struck him. The police found the brakes of the truck in good condition and did not hold the driver, Joseph Alman of 628 East 141st Street.

Policeman Samuel Cohen of Traffic G saw the truck careening eastward down the steep incline and halted all traffic to give it a clear passage. As the truck neared Third Avenue however, it swerved sharply

Continued on Page Seventeen.

BYRD TELLS OF DARING CLIMB IN PLANE OVER JAGGED PEAKS TO POLAR PLATEAU; WON BY SCANT MARGIN, THE POLE AHEAD

House Sends Message Congratulating Byrd; Acclaims Skill and Courage in Polar Flight

Special to The New York Times.

WASHINGTON, Dec. 2.—Congratulations of the House of Representatives were sent to Commander Byrd at Little America today by Speaker Longworth in compliance with a resolution unanimously adopted soon after the House convened. The resolution, introduced amid applause by Representative Moore of Virginia, was as follows:

Resolved by the House of Representatives, That the Speaker is requested by means of the radio to convey to Commander Richard E. Byrd and his associates the congratulations of the House on their recent successful flight over the South Pole, which was marked by such unerring skill and dauntless courage, and to express its confident hope that the further activities of the expedition under the able and brilliant leadership of Commander Byrd will greatly contribute to the world's scientific knowledge.

TELL HOW ROTHSTEIN SHIELDED ASSASSIN

Policemen Testify That Gambler Would Not Even Say if He Was Shot in Hotel.

REVOLVER SHOWN TO JURY

Detective Asserts It Was Found Near McManus's Window—Mrs. Putnam on Stand.

The determination with which Arnold Rothstein, conscious that he faced death, refused to tell who had shot him or where he received his wound was described yesterday at the trial of George A. McManus for the murder of the gambler. The defendant heard the story of Rothstein's silence with the same immobility he has shown since his trial began.

A slender young physician, who found Rothstein lying wounded in a service lobby of the Park Central Hotel, said that the patient had shaken his head when he asked how he had been injured. A timekeeper, who had pillowed the wounded man's head, said Rothstein had muttered "I won't tell you."

A tall, uniformed policeman, who had stood beside the huddled figure, had asked for the identity of the assailant. He had jotted in his police notebook—"Rothstein said 'I won't tell you.'" A veteran detective, one who had known "A. R." well, had bent low over the suffering man and put the all-important questions.

Refused to Tell Detective.

"What happened to you, Arnold?" Detective Patrick Flood had asked.

"I've been shot," said Rothstein, gazing up at the officer.

"Who shot you?"

"I won't tell you."

"Were you shot in the hotel?"

"Please don't ask me any more questions."

The detective said that he had tried again, when Rothstein was lying in Polyclinic Hospital awaiting the operation for the removal of a .38 calibre bullet from the groin. Rothstein managed to smile faintly. This time he did not reply. He merely placed his right index finger on his mute lips.

McManus, at his attorney's table in the room in the Criminal Courts Building, watched the witnesses as they told of their vain efforts to discover the identity of the man who, according to the State, shot Rothstein in Room 349 of the hotel on the night of Nov. 4, 1928. Now and then he shifted his gaze to watch the snow drifting down outside.

Weapon Produced at Trial.

Even when the alleged murder weapon, a blue-barreled Colt, was produced, the defendant held himself apart from the proceedings. The re-introduction of Rothstein's clothing, formally placed in evidence yesterday, found McManus, an arm hitched comfortably over the back of his chair, looking on with less outward interest than the average spectator on the public benches.

The revolver was shown for the first time in the trial during the examination of Detective Flood. The witness said that the weapon had been picked up fifteen feet from where five unexploded shells had been found in Seventh Avenue. The shells, he swore, had been found in the street directly under the windows of Room 349.

The location of the shells and the pistol was a strong point for the State. The defense, outside of the court room, has maintained that the weapon and the ammunition had been found 185 feet north of the windows of the suite. This distance would be too great for a throw from the room, the State's contention being that the Colt was tossed through

Continued on Page Twenty-six.

LABOR TO SOCIALIZE LONDON TRANSPORT

Minister Tells Commons That Government Has Decided to Apply Public Ownership.

NEWS CREATES SENSATION

But Quick Action Is Considered Unlikely on Laborites' First Really Socialist Expression.

By CHARLES A. SELDEN.

Special Cable to THE NEW YORK TIMES.

LONDON, Dec. 2.—For the first time since it came into power as the result of the Labor party's victory at the polls last May, the MacDonald Government today declared itself officially in favor of a Socialist scheme within the popular understanding of what the term "socialism" means, so far as public ownership of transportation facilities is concerned.

The announcement was from Herbert Morrison, Minister of Transport, in reply to a question in the House of Commons and the abbreviated bulletin form in which his reply first emerged from the Parliament buildings to the general public created a great sensation in London. There was momentary fear on the part of the Conservatives and momentary hope on the part of the radicals that at last the Socialist Government was really going to carry out the policies for which one part of the country damns it and the other part blesses it.

The Welfare Measures.

Although the various welfare measures, such as pension bills and unemployment acts, already introduced by the government are really socialistic in the sense that they take by taxation from those who have to give to those who have not, they none of them have that hallmark of socialism as popularly understood which is implied in the words "public ownership." Hence they have been criticized by the opposition in and out of Parliament merely as unwise and uneconomic.

But today a Cabinet Minister actually used the words "public ownership" and there was a shudder. It was a needless shudder, however, for as it turned out the expression was quite academic and had no more immediacy than the expression "Dominion status for India," which all British Governments and parties have been using for the last twelve years without any intimation as to whether such status should be granted a year hence or a century hence. So, apparently, it is with the public ownership of London's transportation systems.

The question which provoked the discussion came from a Labor member who asked if the government was now in a position to state its policy concerning the London traffic situation.

In the course of his reply, which he said was authorized by Prime Minister MacDonald, the Minister of Transport said that the government was convinced that no lasting solution of the dual problem of congestion of the streets and proper travel facilities for the public would be found unless further steps were taken for the elimination of unnecessary and uneconomic competition.

Sees Unification Essential.

A far-reaching measure of unification under public control was essential to progress, Mr. Morrison said, and there was little doubt that elimination of the present wasteful competition would result in sufficient revenue being obtained from the several undertakings at the present level of fares to attract new capital and to provide for the steady and progressive development of the whole traffic system.

It was after this allusion to the attraction of new capital that the Minister of Transport made his re-

Continued on Page Twelve.

COMMANDER STAKED ALL ON UNKNOWN GLACIER PASS

Pointing Upward Amid Buffeting Winds and Clouds Hiding Dangerous Ridges, Fliers Came to Limit With Their Load.

"FOOD OVERBOARD!" THE CHIEF COMMANDED

Again and Yet Again Supplies Went Down Till Craft Labored Over Top With a Few Hundred Feet to Spare—Clear Sailing Then Over Flat Plateau.

This is the second instalment of Commander Byrd's story. Yesterday he described the take-off from Little America and the easy flight to the mountains. There the severest test of the polar trip was encountered, and how it was met he tells today.

By COMMANDER R. E. BYRD,
Leader of the Antarctic Expedition.

Wireless to THE NEW YORK TIMES.

LITTLE AMERICA, Antarctica, Dec. 2.—We had headed for Axel Heiberg Glacier. We knew that Amundsen had reported the highest point of the pass there 10,500 feet high, with towering peaks on each side, but would they be so close together that air currents would dash us to the ground, hovering as we would be with our heavy load near the absolute ceiling of the plane, near the altitude where the controls of the plane no longer function?

To the right was another great glacier we had seen on our base-laying flight. It looked passable. But was it? It appeared wide enough. Were there mountains beyond that would block us—over which we could not fly?

The top of the pass was partly cloud covered. Would Axel Heiberg Glacier be entirely cloud covered? Clouds so frequently hover around the tops of these mountains, even on the clearest days.

Fog Forming While Fliers Conferred on Course.

The sun on the bare, vertical rocks sends up warm currents which, striking the cold above, formed fog while Bernt Balchen and I conferred. Would we choose the unknown glacier?

If we should fail to get over and have to turn back down the glacier to select another pass we could not reach the Pole. The gas would be too low. We would have to turn back to Little America. It seemed a flip of the coin. We decided to stake success on the unknown glacier to the right.

The white clouds around the mountains that bounded the top of the pass to the right and left merged with white in the centre of the pass. Was it snow or clouds, and, if clouds, could we fly above them? Would the clouds stretch over the plateau to the South Pole, making flying impossible?

Danger of Collision With Cloud-Hidden Peaks.

We would have to keep out of clouds while dodging around among the mountains, for in the clouds we would almost certainly collide with a peak. Soon we had passed near our little cache of food and gasoline more than a mile above it. It was, of course, too tiny to be seen from our altitude.

When we had landed at that base the mountain ridge running in an easterly and westerly direction about four miles south of it loomed above us from the snow as a very large mountain. Now we could see behind it, and to the south, southeast and southwest were great towering peaks that made our base mountain look like a pigmy. We realized forcefully then how very little indeed the foot traveler sees.

Now below us was the ice line of the Great Glacier. For a distance it was terribly crevassed, cracks running parallel, looking like a great washing board—not a good landing place.

Awed by Huge Shapes Carved by Ice of Ages.

The mountain peaks and formations that were in our view now were awe-inspiring in their majesty, terrible in the colossal shapes that had been carved into extraordinary jagged and rounded forms by ice cutting through them for the untold years that the bottom of the world has been in the clutches of an ice age.

As we eagerly looked around we felt very insignificant and small among these lofty and eternal peaks which, since the childhood of mankind, have symbolized its aspiration. Everywhere we looked was some formation probably no living thing had ever before seen, for this area, the coldest on the earth, is dead.

McKinley and June Struggling for Pictures.

But there was little time for such thoughts. Our plane was a busy plane—a great contrast to our lifeless surroundings.

There was McKinley with his great aerial camera, elated at his opportunity to record for geography the unknown things about him, snapping picture after picture and panting from his strenuous efforts in the rarefied air of our high altitude—the air bumps throwing him about as he aimed his fifty-pound camera through the window.

But all of it didn't prevent him from looking around and smiling at us occasionally. Good old Mac, an invincible, straight-shooting fellow to whom one can't help becoming attached.

There was Harold June cranking away at his moving-picture camera to get a panorama of the mountains or dashing over to the radio to report our position.

Calmly Testing Gauges at Critical Moment

The critical time has come now, the moment we had discussed a thousand times. What had been our gasoline consumption? Would we have enough left to reach the Pole? Would we have too much aboard to climb over the hump?

Calmly, even tranquilly, Harold stands examining the gauges of the five gas tanks in the great wing. Then he unscrews the cap of the tank in the fuselage and measures, with a graduated stick, the gas left in that tank.

Then he cuts open some of the sealed five-gallon tins, dumps the gas into the tank so that we can throw the tins overboard.

"All the News That's Fit to Print."

The New York Times.

THE WEATHER
Cloudy, warmer and probably rain this morning; tomorrow, warmer.
Temperature Yesterday—Max. 39, Min. 31.
For weather report see Page 45.

VOL. LXXVII....No. 25,615. *** NEW YORK, MONDAY, MARCH 12, 1928. TWO CENTS In Greater New York | THREE CENTS Within 200 Miles | FOUR CENTS Elsewhere in the U. S.

SCIENTISTS ACCLAIM TRIP OF BYRD TO SOUTH POLE; FORESEE GREAT RESULTS

MAY BARE MANY SECRETS

Fossil Search Expected to Reveal 'Life Bridge' of Geologic Ages.

WAY OF FLORA AND FAUNA

Dr. Smith Hopes Byrd Can Peer Under Antarctic Ice and Solve Age-Old Riddles.

PRAISE EXPEDITION PLANS

Savants of Smithsonian, Geographic and Other Bodies Commend Careful Preparation.

Special to The New York Times.

WASHINGTON, March 11.—The plans of Commander Richard Evelyn Byrd for his South Polar expedition have gripped the imagination of scientists, who hope his $500,000 venture to map an unknown continent as large as or larger than the United States will be productive of data of far-reaching scientific value.

The Antarctic, it was pointed out today by men of science well qualified to make such a declaration, undoubtedly holds the key to the solution of many scientific problems, not the least fascinating of which is the distribution of plant and animal life in widely separated parts of the world.

One of the greatest riddles of science awaiting solution is the question whether Antarctica—the almost mythical name by which the South Polar continental mass is known—was the great crossroads of the ancient world. The hope was expressed by scientists that the Byrd expedition might bring back fossil specimens that would solve this question and show more definitely whether Antarctica is all that remains of a "continental bridge" across which land animals and land plants traveled between the African and South American continents in early geologic periods.

Look to Fossils for Answer.

Scientists of the Smithsonian Institution, the National Geographic Society, the Carnegie Institution of Washington and the United States Geological Survey indicated that they were hopeful that the scientific staff of the Byrd expedition would be successful in uncovering fossil remains capable of answering this question.

"What wonders would not stand revealed," said Dr. Waldo L. Smith, curator of marine invertebrates of the National Museum, "if we could lift off the Anarctic ice cap and see what lay beneath?" He added the hope that "it may be given to the Byrd expedition to peer beneath the surface of the ice, to find a geologic outcrop, and to unlock some of the unsolved riddles of animal life."

Dr. David White, senior geologist of the Geological Survey, emphasized the importance of endeavoring to solve the question of the earlier relations of the Antarctic continent to the continents of Africa and South America and even the Australo-Indian archipelago.

Dr. White pointed out that there were peculiar and characteristic land flora and fauna in South Africa and South America that were identical. The evidence indicated, he asserted, that these plants and animals could not have traveled from one of these continents to the other by any route north of the Equator. The question for science to solve, he asserted, is whether there was a land route, or bridge, in one or more geologic periods by which land animals and plants could pass freely between Africa and South America via Antarctica.

Dr. White joined with other scientists in voicing the hope that the Byrd expedition would succeed in obtaining geologic outcroppings of a character which might unlock some of the secrets of nature bearing on this important scientific question.

Careful Preparation Commended.

The care with which Commander Byrd has planned his expedition, which will be the best equipped of modern times, embracing fifty-five men, three airplanes, seventy-five dogs, tractors and a special ice ship, as set forth in the announcement of his plans in this morning's NEW YORK TIMES, has deeply impressed scientists, who, when interviewed today, pointed out the importance of such an expedition to those interested in geology, geography, meteorology, geodesy, terrestrial magnetism, oceanography, cartography and plant and animal life.

Wholly aside from the broader scientific phases of the Byrd expedition were two aspects in particular that appealed to the imagination of scientists here, the plans for utilization of two of the latest and most valuable handmaidens to modern achievement—the airplane and radio.

It was pointed out that by means of the airplane, with good fortune smiling on his flights, Commander Byrd would be in a position to cover thousands of miles of the vast Antarctic continent, only a small part

Continued on Page Five.

Reports of a Marauding Bear Excite Village of Nanuet

Special to The New York Times.

NYACK, N. Y., March 11.—The village of Nanuet, near here, is excited over the reports of a bear which is said to have been seen at least a dozen times within the past fortnight.

The bear, according to Police Judge Raymond Fisher of Nanuet, has been seen five times within the past week near the ice pond of O. Keiser, east of the village. The animal is believed to have raided garbage pails outside several homes. The bear is described as at least three feet tall.

Game Warden Everett Knapp said today that there was a closed season on bear in Rockland County and that the law makes no provision for shooting the animal even if it attacks some one. He added, however, that a bear never attacked a human being unless driven to a corner to protect itself. The Warden thinks the bear may have wandered here from the Catskills.

FIND OLDEST TOMB KNOWN OF UR KING

Pennsylvania-British Museum Excavators Come On It 40 Feet Underground.

GUARDS LAY AT OPEN DOOR

Barbaric Gold and Stone Objects Are Dug Up in Discovery Closing Season's Work.

Special to The New York Times.

PHILADELPHIA, March 11.—On the eve of suspension of excavation work in Ur of the Chaldees until next season the archaeologists of the joint expedition of the University of Pennsylvania and the British Museum have discovered a royal tomb that is described as "architecturally remarkable and probably the oldest we have found," in a report received at the university today from C. Leonard Woolley, director of the expedition.

The tomb, like others found by the expedition, had been looted centuries before by grave robbers, but in despoiling the last resting place of the royal Chaldean the thieves nevertheless left behind some unique and valuable objects. Dr. Woolley declared that, in spite of the rich discoveries made by the archaeologists at Ur in the last six years, "the richest part of the ancient cemetery is yet to be dug."

Work will be resumed next season with increased vigor on the excavation of the courtyard of the great Temple of the Moon God, Nannar, which was buried beneath thousands of tons of earth when King Nebuchadnezzar about 600 B. C. raised the floor of the building to the level of the terrace of the ziggurat.

Dr. Woolley described the excavation of the newly discovered tomb as unusually difficult because it lay beneath forty feet of hard mud.

Cut Into by Grave Above.

"When we found the tomb," he said, "the guards lay at the open door and the chambers were empty of all save what robbers had overlooked when they plundered the grave thousands of years ago, but it well repaid excavation, for it was in many ways the most interesting that we have yet found.

"Probably it is the oldest tomb we have found. The modern surface has here been denuded far below the ancient level, yet the floor of the tomb lies at a depth of no less than forty feet, and the grave of King Meskalam-dug, which lies high above it,

Continued on Page Ten.

'REIGN OF TERROR' IN THE COAL REGION TOLD BY SENATORS

Brutality, Shooting Into Schools and Break-Down of Morality Charged in Report.

COAL AND IRON POLICE HIT

Victims Carrying Scars of Beatings Discovered 'Everywhere' in Pittsburgh District.

UNIONS' LOYALTY PRAISED

One Relief Society Is Assailed for "Slimy Trail" and Is Linked With Reds Here.

Special to The New York Times.

WASHINGTON, March 11.—A story of conditions in the coal fields in and around Pittsburgh and in Central Pennsylvania, which are declared to amount to a "reign of terror" in one section, is related in a report made public today by a subcommittee of the Senate Interstate Commerce Commission, which recently made a tour in the regions where a bitter strike has been in progress for almost a year.

The report is severely critical of housing conditions and tells of shootings into school houses, immorality, alleged brutality by strikebreakers and by the Coal and Iron Police maintained by the operators, activities of the I. W. W. and of the Ohio and Pennsylvania Relief Society, which, it was declared, had headquarters "identical with the Communists' headquarters at 43 East 125th Street, New York City."

The members of the subcommittee were Senators Gooding, Chairman; Pine, Wheeler, Wagner and Metcalf.

Find Many Victims of Beatings.

"Everywhere your committee made an investigation in the Pittsburgh district," the report declares, "we found Coal and Iron Police and deputy sheriffs visible in great numbers. In the Pittsburgh district your committee understands there are employed at the present time between 500 and 600 Coal and Iron Police and deputy sheriffs. They are all very large men, most of them weighing from 200 to 250 pounds. They all are heavily armed and carry clubs usually designated as a 'blackjack.'

"Everywhere your committee visited they found victims of the Coal and Iron Police who had been beaten up and were still carrying scars on their faces and heads from the rough treatment they had received. Your committee found more or less evidence of bootlegging in the places visited and, in one community especially, it seemed as if the morals of that community had been broken down entirely

"Everywhere your committee visited in the Pittsburgh district they found the slimy trail of an organization known as the 'Ohio and Pennsylvania Relief Society.'

"The more suffering and distress your committee found, the more sure it was to find the Ohio and Pennsylvania Relief Society, active, offering food and clothing to the distressed miners and at the same time preaching its doctrine of disloyalty, the breaking of injunctions by mass picketing, and the destruction of the organization of the United Mine Workers of America, together with the destruction of the Government itself.

"At first the union mine workers accepted relief from the Ohio and Pennsylvania Relief Society, but upon learning that its object was to destroy the union and next the Government, they all refused to accept assistance from the agents of this dangerous organization.

Calls Relief Society Disloyal.

"Your committee found that the Ohio and Pennsylvania Relief Society had held meetings in the Pittsburgh district in which a special effort was made to organize the young boys and girls into an organization known as the 'Young Patriotic Workers of America.'

"In no place did your committee find where the Coal and Iron Police or the deputy sheriffs, although they

Continued on Page Six.

Fords Experimenting on Metal Dirigibles Of Huge Size for Ocean Passenger Service

By The Associated Press.

ATLANTA, March 11.—The Atlanta Journal said today in an interview with Edsel Ford, President of the Ford Motor Company, that the Fords as a private experiment are investigating metal dirigibles and their possible use for ocean passenger service in the belief that planes would not be feasible for that purpose.

Mr. and Mrs. Ford are at Warm Springs, Ga., the guests of Detroit friends who reside there in Winter.

As for "flivver" planes of the type in which Harry Brooks dropped into the ocean two weeks ago, Mr. Ford was quoted by The Journal staff correspondent as saying the company never intended such planes for mass production.

The manufacturer was quoted as revealing plans of the Ford company to build two-seaters of safe and stable construction intended primarily as training planes.

"Unless people know how to fly," The Journal quoted Mr. Ford, "it is useless to talk of mass production of planes. Until a large number of persons do know how to fly, they will require pilots and, consequently, larger planes."

The Journal said Mr. Ford was reluctant to discuss the dirigible project, prefacing all his references with adequate qualification as if his information came from experts.

It was Mr. Ford's own opinion, however, that transatlantic air passenger service was now practicable. But Mr. Ford explained, The Journal continued, that experiments were not being conducted by the company, but by the Fords themselves, and were directed chiefly toward a metal craft, larger than those now in use, and a ship which in no case would catch fire in the air.

"I am told," Mr. Ford was quoted, "that the efficiency of dirigibles is increased as their size is increased, while exactly the opposite holds true of airplanes."

Mr. Ford was quoted as saying long-distance planes might be impractical at this time, although his company intended the new two-seaters for popular use.

The two-seater, Mr. Ford said, would not feature the circular motor, but would use a four-cylinder, air-cooled motor of about eighty horsepower, the cylinders so placed in opposite pairs that they balanced, an important feature in the elimination of vibration.

CONGRESS MEMBERS LEAD HOOVER FIGHT

Men in Both Houses Are Directing Organization for Him in Home Districts.

HE WILL NOT TAKE STUMP

Strategy Planned Is for State Groups to Meet Attacks Such as That by Willis.

By RICHARD V. OULAHAN.

Special to The New York Times.

WASHINGTON, March 11.—The attacks made on Secretary Hoover by Senator Frank B. Willis in speeches in Ohio will not cause Mr. Hoover to make a speech-making campaign in that State prior to the Republican National Convention. Nor will Secretary Hoover make a campaign in Indiana in the interest of his candidacy for the Presidential nomination.

In making known these decisions of Mr. Hoover, supporters of his add that, while he may make some speeches prior to the National Convention, he has no intention of going out of Washington to do so.

The strategy of the Hoover campaign, according to what is told in informed quarters, is to leave its management in the various States in which he will make a contest for the Presidential preference or National Convention delegates, or both, to those who have volunteered to work for his nomination.

Hooverites here assert that no national headquarters of the Hoover campaign has been or will be established prior to the Kansas City convention, according to present determination, and that Mr. Hoover will take no active personal part in the effort to make him the choice of his party for President.

Costs Are Kept at Minimum.

Those in a position to know what is being done in behalf of Secretary Hoover's Presidential aspirations are authority for the statement that work for him is being done at a minimum of expense and that this policy will be continued. One estimate of the amount of money spent so far in his political interest is $30,000, which is contrasted with the hundreds of thousands of dollars expended in the Wood and Lowden pre-convention campaigns in 1920.

Some of the workers for the Hoover cause have been aroused over published statements that the campaign for his nomination is being conducted from a central national headquarters and that the "old Harding crowd" is lining up behind him.

Among those mentioned by his critics as being part and parcel of the Hoover campaign is Will H. Hays, who was Chairman of the Republican National Committee in the contest which resulted in the election of President Harding and whose recent testimony before the Senate Teapot Dome investigating committee about his transactions with Harry F. Sinclair in connection with overcoming the Republican deficit of the 1920 campaign has aroused widespread criticism.

In this connection, the statement is made that Mr. Hays cannot work actively in Mr. Hoover's behalf, for the reason that his contract with the moving picture producers of America provides that he shall not participate in politics.

It is denied also that Hubert Work, Secretary of the Interior, who was Republican National Committeeman for Colorado, has been appointed National Campaign Manager for Mr. Hoover. Secretary Work, it is explained, is doing everything he can in Mr. Hoover's interest, but is not directing any national Hoover organization nor has he been designated as Chairman of the so-called Hoover board of strategy.

Has Many Backers in Congress.

According to some of those on the inside of the Hoover cause, Secretary Work is one of a good many people in Washington who are anxious to have Mr. Hoover nominated for President, and what he is doing in Mr. Hoover's behalf has the sympathetic cooperation of Postmaster General New, Secretary Jardine and

Continued on Page Two.

BROTHERS SEIZED IN $500,000 FRAUD

Pair Arrested in Atlantic City Are Accused of Swindling Stock Investors in Toronto.

WERE TRAILED FOR MONTHS

Cheated Clients by Switching Stock, Police Say—Both Give New York Addresses.

Special to The New York Times.

ATLANTIC CITY, N. J., March 11.—Charged with obtaining $500,000 from investors of Toronto by fraudulent stock transactions, two brothers, who described themselves as Milton and Ira Janis, were arrested here this afternoon by Pinkerton detectives, who have trailed them for months, and Atlantic City policemen.

The arrests were made at the request of Edward H. Lockwood, counselor for Sir Harry Armstrong, British Consul General in New York, representing the Canadian Government.

Milton Janis said he was 30 years old and lived at 10 Watkins Place, New Rochelle, N. Y., and his brother described himself as being two years older and living at 385 West End Avenue, New York.

The police say that when they entered the hotel room where the brothers were staying, Milton tried to hide in a closet, and that the men offered them $5,000 each on the way to the police station to be allowed to escape.

Pair Trailed From Miami.

George A. Archer, an agent of the Pinkerton National Detective Agency, said that he trailed the brothers here from Miami, after having followed them through various States for a considerable time. He said that their operations in Canada extended over a period of above five years.

In Toronto they conducted the Toronto Securities Company at 65 Adelaide Street. The Police Department in that city became suspicious of their operations, he said, when complaints began to come in. Before they could be arrested, he said, they fled from Canada.

Archer declared that his agency was retained in November, 1927, and that he trailed the pair to Chicago, Miami and other cities. He said he believed the brothers at one time operated in Northern New Jersey and that one of their methods of obtaining money was by substituting worthless stocks for valuable ones deposited with them.

They will be arraigned before United States Commissioner Herbert R. Voorhees tomorrow.

Both men were well dressed and had considerable money in their possession.

Will Ask Extradition.

Special to The New York Times.

TORONTO, Ontario, March 11.—"It is the best news we have heard in a long time," said A. Rogers, legal secretary to the Attorney General's department, when informed that Milton and Ira Janis were under arrest at Atlantic City, charged with fraud. Mr. Rogers said that the Crown alleged that these two men obtained fully $500,000 in Canada last year by selling stock known as "Dominion Lead."

"We say it was a company without a mine," said Mr. Rogers.

The Janis brothers operated under the name of the Toronto Securities Company, with offices in Montreal, Winnipeg, London and Windsor. On Oct. 4 last the police raided the offices of the company, but it was learned that the Janis brothers had sold out just the day before to another concern, McLean, Smith & Co., which also figured in the courts. The Janis brothers were reported to have crossed the ocean and Immigration officials were advised to keep a sharp lookout for them. Mr. Rogers said the Department would institute extradition proceedings at once.

At 585 West End Avenue, the address given by Ira Janis, it was reported that a Mr. and Mrs. Janis had occupied an apartment there for about a week shortly before last Christmas.

BRIAND SEES HOPE OF MAKING TREATY TO DOOM ALL WAR

He Tells Correspondent of the Times European Nations Want Our Help on It.

BELIEVE IT CAN BE DONE

Efforts Will Now Be Made to Get Negotiations Down to a Practical Basis.

RESERVATIONS ONLY SNAG

Recognition of Right to Punish Aggressor, Even Though We Abstain, Is Desired.

By EDWIN L. JAMES.

Special Cable to THE NEW YORK TIMES.

PARIS, March 11.—What are the chances of the conclusion of the anti-war treaty which has been proposed by the American Secretary of State?

On the train coming from Geneva to Paris today I asked M. Briand for an answer to this question, with the idea that the reply of the French Foreign Minister might indicate the latest developments regarding Mr. Kellogg's plan, which it is known was discussed unofficially, but none the less seriously, by the Foreign Ministers gathered in Geneva the past week.

"There is every possibility of the conclusion of this treaty suggested by the United States, provided we can find a formula which is fair and square," said the French Foreign Minister. "I am convinced we shall be able to find it. And such is the sentiment of other European nations."

M. Briand added that since he was about to reply to Mr. Kellogg's latest note he preferred not to give a detailed interview on the situation at this time.

European Position Outlined.

However, from his frank and free personal discussion of the matter I am able to give a sketch of the European position as it stands after the Geneva meeting. And it may be taken for granted that M. Briand's reply, which will be an effort to get the negotiations on a more definite basis, will represent pretty closely the ideas of the other Foreign Ministers concerned.

At the outset it can be said that from the statements of M. Briand as well as from the statements of other ministers, it is quite clear that the European Governments feel they can go quite as far as the American Government in practical application of Mr. Kellogg's idea to make a compact against war as an instrument of national policy. They emphasize the word practical, and by that they say they indicate the necessity they feel in respect of their existing commitments in making any new commitment.

One finds two dominating opinions on the matter. First there is an overwhelming expression of the great desirability of obtaining America's cooperation in the world effort to maintain peace, and Mr. Kellogg's move is welcomed as indicating a growing desire on the part of the American people to do more than they have done. Secondly, one finds on all sides a desire to make a treaty amounting to something different than a general pious declaration.

Object of First Briand Proposal.

As the French explain their position, when M. Briand made his first proposal he intended, in view of the relations between the United States and France, to create a movement of opinion in the two countries for banishing war between them. Mr. Kellogg then suggested making the treaty multilateral.

The French consider that they replied in the affirmative in principle,

Continued on Page Four.

BORAH URGES PARTY REFUND OF 'SINISTER' OIL MONEY; GOT NO BONDS, SAYS BUTLER

SENATOR SEES A 'STIGMA'

Wrote Chairman Butler That Sinclair Gifts Had 'Ulterior Purpose.'

SUGGESTED 'DOLLAR DRIVE'

He Has Reply to Plea, but Withholds It, Indicating It Is Unsatisfactory.

WALSH HAS WORD OF BONDS

Chairman Telegraphs He Never Received Securities or Gifts From Hays or Sinclair.

Special to The New York Times.

WASHINGTON, March 11.—Senator Borah revealed today that he had appealed to Chairman William M. Butler of the Republican National Committee to take steps to purge the party of the "stigma" of "oil" money. The Senator made public a letter which he had written to the Chairman March 5.

The Idaho Senator has received an answer to his letter, but refused to make it public, intimating that it was not entirely satisfactory.

The appeal from the Senator suggested that every cent of "oil" money paid into the Republican Committee coffers to help wipe out the 1920 deficit be returned to the persons who supplied it. He felt that "the whole transaction" had in view "an ulterior and sinister purpose" and suggested a new money drive for contributions "of $1 up" to clear the party of "this humiliating stigma."

Mr. Butler in a telegram sent from Boston today to Senator Thomas J. Walsh, of the Senate committee investigating the Continental Trading Company angle of the Fall-Sinclair Teapot Dome lease, declared that he never received any bonds or any contributions from Will H. Hays, Chairman in 1920 of the Republican National Committee, or from Harry F. Sinclair, who, in the latter part of 1924, turned over to Hays $260,000 in Liberty bonds of the first issue, to be applied to the liquidation of the Republican deficit of the 1920 Presidential campaign.

Mr. Butler became Chairman of the National Committee in 1924, succeeding John T. Adams, who in turn had succeeded Mr. Hays.

Mr. Butler's telegram to Senator Walsh reads as follows:

Boston, March 11, 1928.
Hon. Thomas J. Walsh, United States Senate, Washington, D. C.

I never received any bonds or any contribution from Will H. Hays and Mr. Sinclair, and I have no records or memoranda under my control relating thereto or concerning contributions to the Republican National Committee during 1922 and 1923. I have never met Mr. Sinclair and do not know him. In accordance with your request I will attend the meeting of the Public Lands and Surveys Committee on Tuesday, March 13.
(Signed.) WILLIAM M. BUTLER.

Pratt Note Bore Name "Butler."

The name "Butler" was written on a card which John T. Pratt left as a record of the fact that he had contributed $50,000 to the 1920 deficit, and this led to the assumption that the person referred to by Mr. Pratt, who died last June, was Chairman Butler of the National Committee, and the intimate friend of President Coolidge. The other names noted by Mr. Pratt were "Weeks," "du Pont" and "Andy."

Mr. Hays testified two weeks ago that of the Sinclair bonds he gave $75,000 to General T. Coleman du Pont, to be paid on a committee note in the Empire Trust Company, New York; $25,000 to the late John W. Weeks, who was Secretary of War in the Cabinet of President Harding, and for a time in the Cabinet of President Coolidge; $50,000 to Mr. Pratt and $60,000 to the late Fred W. Upham of Chicago, who was the Treasurer of the National Committee in the campaign of 1920.

Secretary Mellon, in a letter to Secretary Walsh printed in this morning's NEW YORK TIMES, disclosed that he had made a gift of $50,000 to the 1920 Republican deficit, and that at about that time he made that contribution he received from Hays $50,000 in Liberty bonds, which Mr. Mellon said Hays subsequently informed him came from H. F. Sinclair.

These bonds, the Secretary said, he promptly returned to Hays. Whether or not Hays returned them to Sinclair or used them to finance "fake" contributions elsewhere, is a question the committee will put to Mr. Hays when he is recalled as a witness, possibly Tuesday.

Borah's Letter to Chairman.

Senator Borah's letter to Mr. Butler reads as follows:

United State Senate, Washington, March 5, 1928.
Hon. Wm. M. Butler, Chairman Republican National Committee, No. 77 Franklin Street, Boston, Mass.
My dear Mr. Chairman:

The investigation of the oil scan-

40th Anniversary of Blizzard To See Rising Mercury Today

Instead of the blizzard and zero temperature which New York confronted forty years ago this morning, the city will have today mostly cloudy weather with a rising temperature and probably rain this morning, the Weather Bureau announced last night. Today is the fortieth anniversary of the historic blizzard of 1888.

Rain today would help to melt away the snow that remains, but it would cause a cessation of operations by the 10,400 men and the 1,299 vehicles that were working yesterday to clear the streets, according to the Street Cleaning Department. Most thoroughfares have been cleared and were being flushed yesterday. Cost of the snow removal, it was estimated, will be $400,000. Of those employed 8,200 were jobless men, who received 50 cents an hour.

The minimum temperature yesterday was 31 degrees at 6 A. M., and the maximum 39 at 5:30 P. M.

MAYOR IN BILL ASKS FULL TRANSIT POWER

Wants State Board Abolished and City Put in Control of Unification Plan.

AS A STRIKE WEAPON, TOO

Measure to Be Offered at Once Would Aid in the 7-Cent Fare Fight.

Mayor Walker plans to move this week to abolish the Transit Commission and transfer its powers to the city's Board of Transportation, the members of which are appointed by him. A bill to accomplish this is being drawn and will be introduced in the Legislature at the Mayor's request.

Such a measure, if Mayor Walker could obtain its passage, would place in his hands a strong weapon with which to deal with the threatened strike on the lines operated by the Interborough Rapid Transit Company, the Mayor believes. It would also result in transferring to his appointees the preparation of a transit unification plan and would strengthen the city's position in opposing the Interborough's efforts to obtain a 7-cent fare.

Mayor Walker and Samuel Untermyer, the Transit Commission's special counsel, have discussed the proposal and Mr. Untermyer is understood to be friendly to the plan although a bill transferring the Transit Commission's powers to the city board would conflict sharply with his bill for a Board of Transit Control. The Untermyer bills, having been turned down by the Republican leaders in the Legislature, however, it was hinted that the commission's attorney might accept the Walker bill as a substitute, which, although not advancing his own unification plan, would permit of closer cooperation between him and the city authorities in working out a transit solution.

Members Said to Favor Plan.

In discussing the proposal, Mr. Untermyer is understood to have told Mayor Walker a few days ago that even the members of the Transit

Continued on Page Three.

Trapped Dog Swims 8 Hours in Flooded Cellar After Suspicious Fire at Pocantico Hills

Special to The New York Times.

TARRYTOWN, N. Y., March 11.—The Tarrytown Fire Department now has as hardy and as worthy a mascot as can be boasted of by any department in the country. Its name has not been decided upon yet, because it is difficult to find a name fitting a collie who can swim eight hours trapped in a flooded cellar—flooded, indeed, by the department itself in an unsuccessful effort to save the house.

It was 3 o'clock this morning when Thomas Pyle happened to look out of his widow in Pocantico Hills and see the house next door, owned by Ernest Conrad, in flames. He sent in an alarm to the Pocantico Hills Fire Department and then rushed over, broke down the door of the burning building and roused the owner, his wife and four children. All of them escaped in their night clothes.

Presently the apparatus arrived, to be joined in a few minutes by an engine from North Tarrytown and the Hilltop Engine Company from the near-by estate of John D. Rockefeller. Despite the efforts of the men the house was destroyed.

Later this morning an investigation was started into the cause of the fire. Mr. Pyle saw the blaze on the outside of the building, and there have been several fires thought to be of incendiary origin in Westchester County during the last year or so.

This afternoon when discussion was still going forward some one heard a faint bark from under the pile which was the Conrad house. He investigated, then called the Tarrytown Fire Department. Firemen cut through the charred floor and discovered the collie lying on top of the furnace, which by that time was a foot or so out of water. The animal was wrapped in blankets and taken to Tarrytown, where its new owners figured that it had been swimming from five to eight hours before the water receded sufficiently to allow its resting on the top of the furnace.

Miss Miller to Embrace Hinduism Tomorrow; Will Be Married to Ex-Maharajah Saturday

By Wireless to THE NEW YORK TIMES.

BOMBAY, March 11.—Miss Nancy Ann Miller, the American fiancée of the ex-Maharajah of Indore will arrive at Nasik at dawn tomorrow for the picturesque ritual of her conversion to Hinduism. She changed her plans at the eleventh hour so as to hold the ceremony Tuesday for the purpose of eluding an army of photographers and newspapermen. The former Maharajah may have had the same object in view when he engaged all the available hotel accommodations.

The ceremony will be in two parts. The actual religious ritual will be performed at Gangapur, five miles from Nasik on a bank of the sacred River Godaveri where the benediction will be given by the Jagadura Shankaracharava of Karwir Pith, acknowledged the head of Orthodox Hinduism.

Later he will deliver an address on the importance of converting foreigners to Hinduism. Miss Miller herself is expected to speak also. It is reported that a film will be taken of the "shudi" part of the ceremony for the purpose of giving the widest publicity to the event from a religious standpoint.

Meanwhile, Nasik, which is a city of the holiest of Hindu associations, is divided by demonstrations of sympathy and [illegible] organized by meetings and [illegible] propaganda. Sectional feeling is clearly shown, the orthodox being against the reformers, the Brahmins against the non-Brahmins and the depressed classes against the upper classes.

Some of the Brahmins regard it an outrage to their faith that an infidel should be brought into the fold in the sacred city, while the reformers and Arya Samajists, though a small minority regard it as a rare opportunity for carrying the war to the enemy's camp.

The conflict of views promises to make the conversion a far livelier affair than was generally expected, especially as thousands are flocking to Nasik.

BARWAHA, India, March 11 (AP).—The wedding of Miss Miller and the former Maharajah of Indore will be held Saturday at the latter's residence at Darya Mahal, in the midst of a small jungle near here.

The arrangements for the wedding are nearing completion. The customary marriage procession is to be omitted, but the program provides for lavish festivities and illuminations. The bridal couple have been leading a quiet life on the Darya Mahal estate.

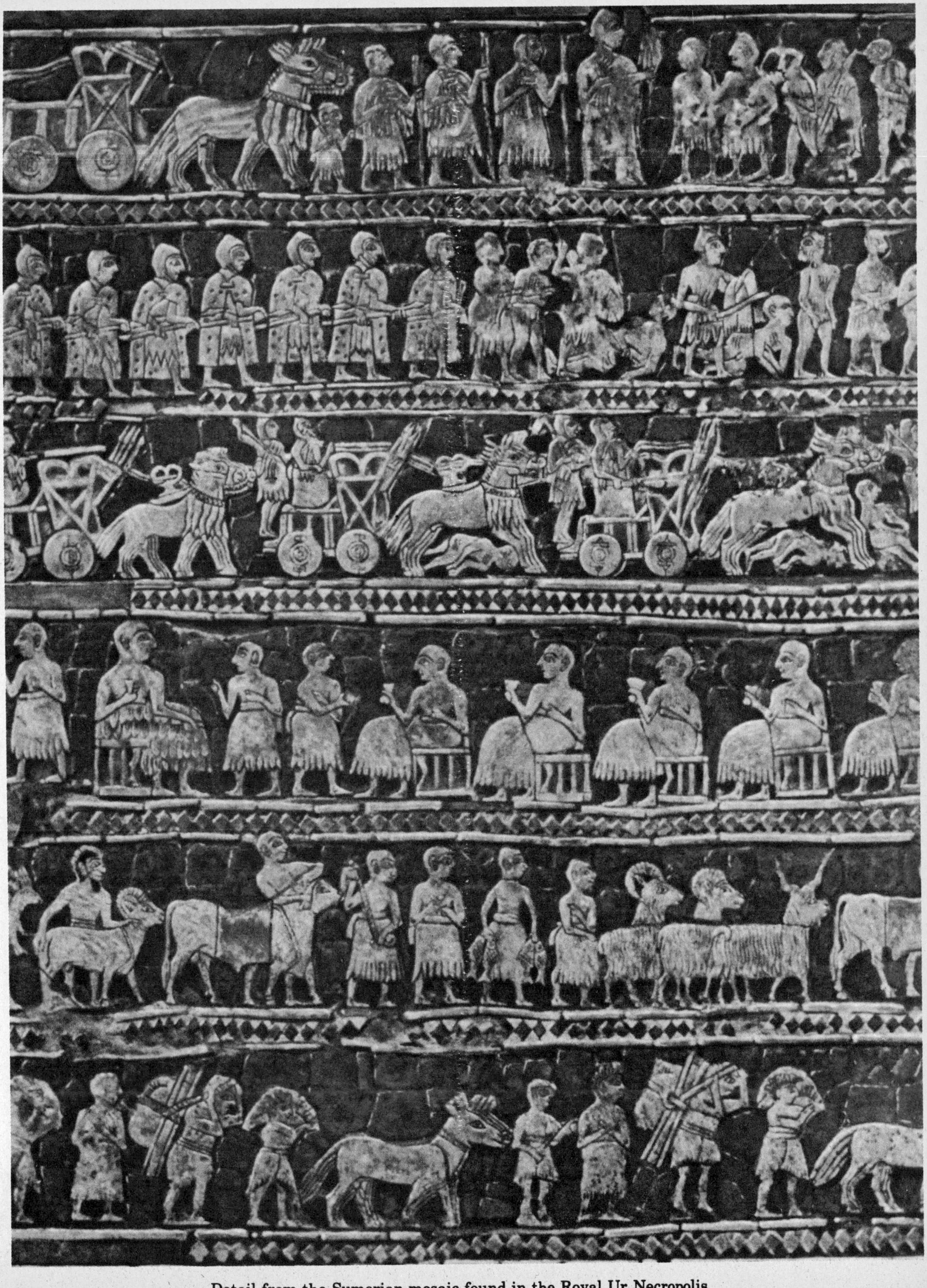

Detail from the Sumerian mosaic found in the Royal Ur Necropolis.

"All the News That's Fit to Print."

The New York Times.

THE WEATHER
Partly cloudy and colder today; tomorrow fair.
Temperature Yesterday—Max. 71; Min. 56.
U. S. Weather Forecast—For details see Page 30.

Copyright, 1928, by The New York Times Company.

VOL. LXXVIII....No. 25,841. **** NEW YORK, WEDNESDAY, OCTOBER 24, 1928. TWO CENTS In Greater New York | THREE CENTS Within 200 Miles | FOUR CENTS Elsewhere in the U. S.

COOLIDGE IS HOPEFUL OF A NAVAL PARLEY IF ACCORD IS ALTERED

Thinks Concessions by Paris and London Might Bring Limitation Meeting Before 1931.

BONCOUR PLAN IS REVIVED

Washington Would Consider Flexible System—Cold to Having Gibson Confer in Geneva.

FRENCH CLING TO ACCORD

Britain's Stand on Land Arms Pleases Them—Both, However, Would Discuss Modification.

Special to The New York Times.

WASHINGTON, Oct. 23.—President Coolidge hopes that France and Great Britain will modify their naval agreement if developments make it advisable and believes that such a move might lead to a successful conference on limitation of naval armament.

Since the two-party agreement has met with opposition partial or complete in Japan, Italy and the United States, the President sees the possibility of the minority countries making further concessions. Unless Great Britain and France do so there is little hope, in his opinion, of any progress being made toward an international agreement on naval limitation in the near future.

The very fact that France modified her original position in the compact with Great Britain, the details of which were made public officially in London and Paris yesterday, leads the President to hope that terms may be offered that may lead to a conference before 1931, when the Washington treaty expires.

Cold to Talk of Gibson Mission.

Suggestions in press dispatches from Europe that the United States might designate Hugh Gibson, Ambassador to Belgium, to discuss the naval limitation situation with the Foreign Ministers of Great Britain and France at the next meeting of the Council of the League of Nations in Geneva fell on cold ground here.

No such suggestion, it was stated, had been made officially and indications were that the United States would not resort to such a course.

Officials contended that a meeting of the Council of the League would not be a satisfactory occasion for such a conference, and that the United States was content to state her case before the Preparatory Commission of the League as a duly constituted body to deal with such matters.

Since Great Britain and France transmitted the outlines of their naval limitation accord to the American Government and the United States replied rejecting the arrangement, it was said no communication had been received from the London or Paris Government on the subject.

If any step is now contemplated on the part of either Great Britain or France, it was added, no inkling of it has reached here.

Officials read with interest in the White Book and Blue Book as made public in London and Paris last night that France had at first expressed a preference for an agreement along the lines of flexible categories which was put forward informally by M. Paul-Boncour of the French delegation to American naval advisers at the meeting of the Preparatory Commission last year. The possibility of some such formula was suggested by the United States in the recent note rejecting the Anglo-French accord as a basis of discussion.

It was declared today on high authority that when the American note was written it was not known here that France had made such a proposal to Great Britain. That such was the case, it was argued, tended to confirm opinion here that France might be ready to consider naval limitation in the future on some such basis. The United States, it was reiterated, would be ready to consider the subject along that line.

By EDWIN L. JAMES.

Special Cable to The New York Times.

PARIS, Oct. 23.—Now that the Franco-British naval understanding has been told about in a hundred or more printed pages comprising the British White Book and French Blue Book, the question naturally arises, "What becomes of the agreement?"

One hears it said on many sides that since the two diplomatic books both end with America's refusal to accept the plan the matter is ended once and for all. Such an opinion will probably turn out to be a very sorry prognostication.

Future developments will in all likelihood show that the accord is not dead. It has received a considerable setback from the standpoint of putting it into quick operation, but we shall hear from it again.

What interests the French above all in the business is Great Britain's agreement not to oppose the French attitude on trained reserves, which is the keystone of the French position on limitation of land armaments. As the British White Book made very plain, indeed, M. Briand obtained this concession from Sir Austen Chamberlain in return for French support of what London described as a concession on the British position of naval limitation.

Not even the most nationalistic Frenchman dreams of a French fleet

Continued on Page Four.

Soldier of the Revolution Was Ancestor of Hoover

Special to The New York Times.

WASHINGTON, Oct. 23.—One of Herbert Hoover's ancestors was a New York Revolutionary soldier, Frank B. Steele, Secretary General of the Sons of the American Revolution, said today when he approved the application of Theodore Hoover of Palo Alto, Cal., brother of the Republican candidate, for membership in the society.

The great-grandfather of Huldah Minthorn, mother of Herbert Hoover, was Jacobus Wynne (Winne), a soldier in the First Regiment, Ulster County (N. Y.) Militia, of which Colonel Johannes Snyder was commander.

Jacobus Winne was also a member of the Sixth Regiment of the Dutchess County (N. Y.) militia.

GEO. B. M'CUTCHEON DIES AT A LUNCHEON

Novelist, 62, Has Heart Attack as He Chats With Members of Dutch Treat Club.

WON FORTUNE ON NOVELS

Author of "Brewster's Millions" and Twoscore Books Sold "Graustark" for $500.

George Barr McCutcheon, author of "Graustark," "Brewster's Millions" and many other novels, the many editions of which aggregated more than 5,000,000 volumes and yielded one of the largest fortunes ever won by an American writer, died suddenly of heart disease yesterday at a luncheon of the Dutch Treat Club at the Hotel Martinique, Broadway and Thirty-second Street. Mr. McCutcheon was a guest at the luncheon. He was 62 years old.

In the company of novelists, short-story writers, newspaper men and cartoonists, many of whom he had known for years Mr. McCutcheon had been giving reminiscences, telling his plans for the future, describing his expedition of the day before with Mrs. McCutcheon to Fifth Avenue stores to buy rugs for their new apartment, when he was stricken. He excused himself from table at the end of the second course and walked from the second-floor dining room, down two flights of stairs, to the washroom in the basement. Hotel attendants there found him in a state of collapse.

Some of his friends of the Dutch Treat Club telephoned the office of Mr. McCutcheon's physician, Dr. Walter L. Niles, of 893 Park Avenue, and called an ambulance from New York Hospital. When Dr. Bell from New York Hospital arrived Mr. McCutcheon was dead. Dr. Dan H. Witt, associate of Dr. Niles, went to the Martinique. Mr. McCutcheon had been under treatment for heart disease for the past eighteen months.

Walter Trumbull, newspaper sports writer, and Clarence Buddington Kelland, short story writer, were among the first to reach the side of the novelist after the luncheon members had been notified. Among the 300 members of the Dutch Treat Club who were present at the luncheon were Rupert Hughes, Reinald Werrenrath, Tom Masson, Ray Long, Frederick A. Stokes, John O'Hara Cosgrave, Harold T. Webster and Clare Briggs.

Frank C. Dodd of Dodd, Mead & Co., publishers for Mr. McCutcheon, hurried to the hotel when notified of

Continued on Page Twenty-two.

MEDALIE FORECASTS WHOLESALE ARRESTS FOR FRAUD AT POLLS

Declares He Has Not Time for Court Action Against Illegal Registrants Before Nov. 6.

HARVEY'S CASE UP TODAY

Court Is Expected to Reject His Action to Force Use of Voting Machines in Queens.

650TH DISTRICT IS ADDED

Aldermen Approve $264,865 for Ballots, New Machines and Copies of Vote Books Without Bidding.

Declaring that insufficient time remained before election day to check fraudulent voting effectively by court action alone, George Z. Medalie, Special Assistant Attorney General, served notice yesterday that the work of his 230 deputies and agents had uncovered frauds which would lead to wholesale arrests at the polls on Nov. 6.

Persons against whom evidence of fraudulent registration has been obtained, Mr. Medalie said, would be arrested if they attempted to cast ballots. The arrests, he said, would be made on warrants to be issued as the result of Grand Jury indictments under a recent State law, on warrants to be issued by magistrates, and by direct action of his assistants and deputies in their capacities as peace officers.

Another District Is Added.

While Mr. Medalie was issuing his warning, the Board of Elections wrestled again with the problem of providing voting facilities to handle the increase in registration. It added another new election district to the 649 already authorized and obtained from the Board of Aldermen permission to let without bidding a $130,000 contract for 2,970,000 ballots and sample ballots for use in Queens, Bronx and Richmond. The aldermen also authorized a similar letting of a contract for 100 additional voting machines, to cost $84,865, and another for the purchase of 650 photostatic copies of registration signature books for use where election districts are split. The cost of these was estimated at $50,000.

Edward J. McGowan, clerk of the Board of Elections, explained that the shortness of time before election day made it impossible to submit the work for public bidding.

The creation of the new district, established by splitting up the twenty-fifth election district of the Third Assembly District in Manhattan, required another special meeting of the board, the fourth since last Friday.

Harvey Case in Court Today.

The validity of the board's action in limiting the use of voting machines to Manhattan and Brooklyn, and using paper ballots in Queens, Richmond and the Bronx, will be tested in the Supreme Court today when Justice Ingraham hears the petition of John H. Clark Jr., counsel for Alderman George U. Harvey, for a writ of mandamus to compel the use of machines in Queens. The motion will be opposed by Assistant Corporation

Continued on Page Eight.

Solomon's Walls Bared in City Joshua Won; Temple Also Uncovered on Hazor Acropolis

Wireless to The New York Times.

JERUSALEM, Oct. 23.—Professor John Garstang, the archaeologist, has just arrived in Jerusalem bringing interesting discoveries from Hazor, situated in Northern Palestine along the main highway to Damascus. The excavations there, patronized by Sir Charles Marston, were carried out by Professor Garstang under the auspices of the Liverpool Institute of Archaeology.

Hazor is known historically from references to it in Egyptian and Biblical history. Its capture by Joshua at the close of his campaign was his last great achievement before settling the land of Canaan.

The present site has two parts. First, a great "tel," or mound, marking the Acropolis, and, second an open space 1,000 meters long and 600 wide, apparently used as a camping ground. Because of its situation on the highway from Damascus to Egypt at the junction of the main road to Tyre and Sidon, the place probably was used by travelers also as a camping ground during the wars.

The camp enclosure is protected by earthen ramparts similar to those at Misrefeh in Central Syria. Such camps are also found in Turkestan and on the frontiers of Egypt where they are attributed to the Hyksos invaders who overran Egypt. The Hazor excavations confirm this view, for most of the evidence found of occupation of the camp was of the Middle Bronze Age, from 2000 to 1600 B. C. At a date not yet determined but in the late Bronze Age, between 1600 and 1200 B. C., occupation of the camp site totally ceased. Signs of fire indicate that it was destroyed. Further occupation of the area was confined to the Acropolis.

The first Israelite period, from 1200 to 1000 B. C., is thinly represented in the Hazor finds and it is doubtful whether there was considerable inhabitation of the place by them in that time. In the age of Solomon the city again sprang to life. Numerous buildings belonging to that period and also a wealth of domestic and other objects were found.

The Old Testament states that Solomon repaired Hazor. The walls of his period were found resting on the top of the former Canaanite ramparts. The date of the walls is attested by a sign similar to the well-known Masonic emblem. In one part of the Acropolis there was found a large building supported by monolithic columns. Nine were found by traces to have a height of more than two meters each. On the best side, the southern end, of the Acropolis a building was discovered resembling a temple or other public structure, with huge doorways and a central court leading to chambers around it.

The city defenses were repaired in that period and these were traceable in the higher level where they stood upon the previous Canaanite ramparts.

The city apparently was destroyed about 700 B. C. There is no trace of continuous occupation thereafter, Professor Garstang says. He believes the Acropolis is much older than the camp enclosure and probably dates to the time of the patriarchs.

Girl, 10, Revealed as Newark Baby 'Kidnapper' By Boy's Realistic Tale in School Story Hour

Through the narrative powers and vivid realism of Albert Berner, 10 years old, of 120 Elizabeth Avenue, Newark, an exciting police hunt for the supposed kidnapper of a seven-months-old child ended uniquely in a Newark school yesterday.

Dorothy Maclear, 10, of 52 Hunter Street, Newark, to whom Albert assigned a leading rôle in his classroom recital, was revealed, according to the police, as the person responsible for the mysterious four-hour disappearance of John Clay Chaney, infant son of Mr. and Mrs. John Chaney of 1,189 Broad Street, Newark, on Monday afternoon.

John had vanished from his baby carriage on the front porch of his home about 1:30 P. M. on Monday. Four hours later the baby was found a mile away from home, lying in a doll carriage in front of a house at 83 East Bigelow Street, occupied by Mrs. Esther Hamilton. Mrs. Hamilton was at a complete loss and so were the police to solve the riddle.

The baby was returned to its home on Monday evening, but the police record still lacked the name of its supposed kidnapper. And that was where Albert Berner, raconteur par excellence, stepped in.

Yesterday, during the story-telling hour in the 3A grade in Newark's Miller Street Public School, Albert was called upon. At a desk near him sat Dorothy.

Albert's story opened confidently with "Once upon a time." Deftly the narrator unwound the thread of his plot of a baby that was taken from its home and of a girl who was seen later wheeling the baby in a doll carriage. "That girl," said Albert, working up to his climax, "was Dorothy Maclear." The startled teacher telephoned to the police.

The police said later that Dorothy admitted having taken the baby to play with. Dorothy's story was that she had taken a doll carriage from the store of Abraham Appel at 132 Sherman Avenue and, finding no doll to put in it, had helped herself to John Chaney, according to the police. The girl wheeled the baby around until after dusk, then, becoming tired, left him at the Hamilton home.

Albert told the police that on Monday night he had heard his father reading aloud a newspaper account concerning the Chaney child. He said he remembered having seen Dorothy on Monday afternoon playing with "a live baby" in a doll carriage, but kept silent until yesterday afternoon.

WALDMAN DEATHS AGAIN HELD ACCIDENT

Police After Second Inquiry Stick to Original Theory of Children's Fall.

WORKMEN TELL OF TRAGEDY

Describe the Mother's Frantic Efforts to Save Sons—Norris Investigation to Go On.

The second police investigation into the deaths of Terrence Waldman, four and a half years old, and his brother, Benjamin, fourteen months old, heirs to the Benjamin Guggenheim fortune, who were killed last Friday afternoon in a fall from the roof of the sixteen-story Hotel Surrey, 20 East Seventy-sixth Street, was virtually closed yesterday. Again the detectives characterized the tragedy as an accident.

However, Dr. Charles Norris, Chief Medical Examiner, announced yesterday afternoon that he had issued subpoenas for seven witnesses and would question them this afternoon in his office in the Municipal Building. Dr. Norris emphasized that he was conducting the investigation without any theories as to how the two children met their death, but merely with a desire to find out the truth and place the facts on his records.

Mother Not Questioned.

The detectives have been unable as yet to question Mrs. Milton S. Waldman, mother of the children, who is in a state of collapse under the care of a physician. They plan to do so later. Dr. Norris said Mrs. Waldman would not be among those he would question this afternoon. He said he would interview Mrs. Waldman when she had improved sufficiently to be able to make a statement.

Dr. Norris said that the circumstances of the deaths of the children made a complete investigation imperative "in justice not only to the public but to Mrs. Waldman as well." He also explained the police were not to be blamed for the quick removal of the children's bodies after they had fallen from the roof, saying they had acted with the permission of a clerk in his office.

Workmen Tell Tragedy.

The conclusions of the detectives were largely based on statements made yesterday by a woman and two men to Deputy Inspector Arthur S. Carey and Detective William I. Jackson of the Homicide Squad. Those making the statements were Ann McCormick, a maid employed by Mrs. Cornelius B. Love, occupant of the penthouse on the Hotel Surrey roof, cousin of Mrs. Waldman; Liberator Maceri of 73 Merritt Street, Long Island City, bricklayer's helper, and Alexander Hill of 31 Atlantic Street, Jersey City. The two men were working on a scaffold on the fifteenth floor of the Professional Building, directly across from the Surrey.

They saw Mrs. Waldman and the children on the Surrey roof. Maceri told Inspector Carey he saw Mrs. Waldman with the youngest child in her arms near the roof parapet, and the other child's head appear above the top of the stone coping. He said he then saw the children plunge downward, saw the mother's frantic efforts to save them and heard her screams. He said he turned and shouted to Hill.

Hill corroborated Maceri's recital. Both told of hearing Mrs. Waldman shout to the maid: "Get my child. He has fallen over the roof." They quoted the maid as replying, "Which child?" and Mrs. Waldman's reply, "Both—both have fallen over." They said the women then screamed and Mrs. Waldman collapsed.

At the Hotel Plaza, where Mrs. Waldman has an apartment it was said she had been removed to a sanitarium. Dr. Newton B. Waller of 53 East Eighty-second Street, who is treating Mrs. Waldman, said last night that Dr. Norris had been invited to take Mrs. Waldman's statement whenever he was ready. He said Mrs. Waldman was still very hysterical and extremely nervous.

DECLARES NORRIS WILL SHIFT TO SMITH

Omaha Leader Says Senator in Saturday Speech Will Call Progressives.

LIKELY TO SWING NEBRASKA

Norris in Tacoma Says Hoover Speech Here Repudiated Progressives on Power Issue.

Special to The New York Times.

OMAHA, Oct. 23.—Senator Norris of Nebraska will come out for Governor Smith in a speech here Saturday night, according to an announcement made today by Joseph Koutsky, City Commissioner and President of "the Progressive League for Alfred E. Smith," under whose auspices the Independent Republican will speak.

Democrats have asserted and Republicans have practically conceded that if Senator Norris actually supported Smith the Democrats would carry this State.

Mr. Norris has expressed satisfaction with Governor Smith's stand on farm relief and water power, and it is upon these issues that he is expected to support the New Yorker. According to reports thousands of Nebraska voters have been awaiting Senator Norris's speech before deciding how they will vote.

Mr. Koutsky, President of the Progressive League for Smith, is a lifelong Republican and has polled the largest vote for City Commissioner of any candidate.

A wide radio hook-up is being arranged for Saturday night's speech.

Senator Critical of Hoover Speech.

TACOMA, Wash., Oct. 23 (AP).—Senator George W. Norris of Nebraska said here today that Hoover in his New York address last night had by his position on hydroelectric power repudiated all the Progressives who have supported him in the past.

Senator Norris is in Washington urging re-election of Senator C. C. Dill, Democrat.

"Mr. Hoover has made himself clearer on the power issue than in any of his earlier speeches," Senator Norris said. "He is repudiating Nye, Brookhart, Borah, myself and all the other Progressives who have supported him in the past."

Shift Had Been Expected Here.

Reports that Senator Norris of Nebraska would come out for Governor Smith and sound a call to all Progressives were current in local Democratic circles yesterday.

While no official confirmation of the report could be obtained at Democratic National Headquarters, there was no denial of it and it was generally accepted as authentic. It has been known for many days that strenuous efforts were being made by the supporters of Governor Smith to induce the influential Senator from William Jennings Bryan's old State to come into the Smith camp, and with more or less expectation that the move would succeed.

A few days ago Senator John J. Blaine declared for the Governor. Senator Blaine is looked upon as the de facto leader of the La Follette forces in Wisconsin. Senator Norris, while not occupying quite the same position of power within the Republican organization of his own State, will nevertheless be in a position to exert far-reaching influence in Nebraska, even though Adam McMullen, the Republican Governor of the State, who prior to the Kansas City convention took active part in the agrarian revolt, since has come out for Mr. Hoover.

Many days ago, before it was known what course Senator Norris would determine upon as the campaign was approaching its final stage, leaders in the Smith camp were a unit in declaring that in the event he should come out in support of Governor Smith the eight electoral votes of Nebraska would be found in the Democratic column on election day.

The joint influence of Senators Norris and Blaine is expected by Democratic leaders here to bring thousands of Progressive votes in the farm States to the support of Gover-

Continued on Page Fourteen.

SMITH TO HIT BACK AT HOOVER CHARGE OF 'STATE SOCIALISM'

Prepares an Answer on Eve of Intensive Tour of Three New England States.

EAGER TO ENTER DEBATE

Nominee's Friends Say He Has Successfully Fought the Same Attack in the Past.

FINAL DRIVE OPENS TODAY

Program Includes a Boston Speech Tonight and Parades Through Many Cities Tomorrow.

From a Staff Correspondent of The New York Times.

ALBANY, Oct. 23.—Governor Smith will leave here for Boston tomorrow morning to open what he calls the "battle of the Atlantic seaboard." He is ready to throw all his efforts into the final drive which his associates say will carry the fight even more directly than heretofore to his Republican opponent for the Presidency, Herbert Hoover.

The Governor is eager to meet the Hoover charge that his policies constitute State socialism. His answer will be pushed to the front in the political battle.

Bearing out reports of the intensity of this last phase of the campaign, Governor Smith today indicated a virtual tour of three New England States. There will be ten-minute stops at Springfield and Worcester, tomorrow before he arrives in Boston where a parade will precede his speech.

The next day he will lead an automobile procession from Blackstone, Mass., through Rhode Island towns into Providence. There will be another parade in the course of a two-hour visit to Hartford that afternoon, and stops will be made later at Waterbury, Derby-Shelton, New Haven, Bridgeport and South Norwalk, Conn., on a return journey to New York City.

Governor Smith did not hear Mr. Hoover's New York speech over the radio, but he read it this morning. There was no doubt of his reaction to it. He himself stated that he would make a reply and the only question here was whether it would come in his speech tomorrow.

Governor Eager for Debate.

For several weeks now the Governor has sought a debate along definite lines with his opponent. He has flung questions at the Republican candidate which he asserted could not be passed along to other leaders of the party. Confronted now with Mr. Hoover's attack upon his own policies, he has found it to his liking, according to his friends, and he will not be slow in answering.

His whole attitude as to his coming speeches was indicated in a press interview today.

"Do it as fast as you can," he said, cutting questions short with the remark that he had much work before him.

"Governor, were you interested in that part of Mr. Hoover's speech where he said he wanted to keep the Government from competing with private enterprise and then listed your policies for the solution of the water power, farm relief and prohibition problems as being State socialism?" he was asked.

"I noticed that," the candidate replied.

"When are you going to talk on his speech?"

"I don't know."

"You will, though, won't you?"

"Oh, yes."

"Have you been called a Socialist before?" was asked.

"Yes, sir," the Governor answered crisply.

On that final note which ended

Continued on Page Twenty.

Briton Gets 'Messages' After Radio to Mars, But He Says He Must Wait to Decode Them

By The Associated Press.

CHISWICK, England, Wednesday, Oct. 24.—Dr. Mansfield Robinson, who sent a wireless message to Mars early this morning, said at 4 o'clock that he had received certain messages, but would have to wait until they were decoded.

Dr. Robinson was at the laboratory of his scientific friend, Professor A. M. Low, trying to pick up signals from Mars on a high-powered radio set.

LONDON, Wednesday, Oct. 24 (AP).—Dr. Robinson, who is a psychic devotee, addressed his wireless dispatch to Compararu, the big-eared woman of Mars, through the big station at St. Albans.

The call was sent out at 2:15 A. M. and the engineers at St. Albans listened on a 30,000-meter wave length for a reply, but up to 3:30 had received none.

Since, however, communication between London and St. Albans at this hour of the morning is about as easy as communication with Mars, it might be premature to say that the listeners have nothing to report.

It was understood that Dr. Robinson also intended to listen for a reply at his home in Royden, Hertfordshire. The Daily Express sent a reporter there late last night, but he found the house dark. On the front door was pinned a paper bearing the word "Out." Nothing daunted, the reporter knocked at the door until Mrs. Robinson came to it and said:

"If you have come about that message, I know nothing. I have refused to have any experiments in the house while I am in it.

"My husband has gone to London. I do not know whether anybody there will encourage him, but there will be no foolishness around this house."

Then she closed the door.

HUGHES IN FIRST SPEECH CALLS HOOVER BEST FITTED TO FILL THE PRESIDENCY

SAYS CHOICE IS AS TO MEN

Praises Smith as Governor, Points to Rival's National Service

AND WORLD-WIDE TRAINING

Election of Republican Nominee, He Says, Is the Way to "Buttress" Our Prosperity.

WET FIGHT HELD "A SHAM"

He Declares Democratic Policy Endangers Tariff Protection for Farmers and Industries.

Special to The New York Times.

ST. JOSEPH, Mo., Oct. 23.—Capping the climax of the Republican drive to insure the eighteen electoral votes of Missouri for the national ticket, Charles Evans Hughes, Secretary of State under Presidents Harding and Coolidge, and the Republican standard-bearer twelve years ago, pleaded the cause of Herbert Hoover before a capacity audience this evening in the City Auditorium here.

Large delegations were present from St. Louis, Kansas City and Northwest Missouri.

The primary question in the Presidential campaign, Mr. Hughes said in his speech, is as between men rather than issues.

"The question is between Smith and Hoover, and I decidedly prefer Hoover," he asserted.

Sees Hoover as "Better Equipped."

Reviewing at length Mr. Hoover's career as an engineer and in the public service, Mr. Hughes frequently emphasized the opinion that Hoover "is the better equipped man for the office of President."

He declared that, although Governor Smith undoubtedly had the most comprehensive grasp of New York State affairs of any man, the Democratic candidate's viewpoint was of Albany rather than of Washington. It would take one term in office to place him on a parity with Mr. Hoover's present knowledge of national affairs, he said.

Northwestern Missouri is emphatically dry, compared to the reputedly wet St. Louis, and Mr. Hughes's declaration that any increase in the alcoholic content of liquor would be contrary to the Constitution, met with applause. Cheers greeted his statement that the fight over the prohibition issue in the campaign was a "sham battle."

Mr. Hughes delivered his address twice in the evening, because of the radio situation. His auditorium speech was concluded at 9 o'clock and was broadcast over a limited area by KFEQ, a local station. It was not possible to obtain a national hookup at this time and immediately following the original speech, he delivered it again at a local studio, with connections that would enable it to be heard all over the nation.

Makes Comparisons for a Choice.

ST. JOSEPH, Mo., Oct. 23 (AP).—The question in the coming election is whether Herbert Hoover or Alfred E. Smith is the better equipped to hold the Presidential office, said Mr. Hughes in making here tonight his first speech of the campaign.

"We have a choice between two men," Mr. Hughes said. "It is not merely a question as between two parties. It is not merely a question as to what qualifications one or the other of these two men has, considered alone, or as compared with some one else. The primary question is, Which one, for this highest office, is the better of these two men?

"The question is between Smith and Hoover, and I decidedly prefer Hoover."

Stresses Prosperity and Security.

Mr. Hughes asserted that the voters were called on to determine what were the policies that would make for the prosperity and the security of the country. He added:

"The way to buttress our prosperity, to give every one, employer and employed, producer and consumer, a feeling of greater security as he looks forward to the next four years with all their uncertainties, to secure the most earnest effort under competent leadership to deal with all the economic difficulties that confront us, is to continue the policies of the Republican Administration under the Presidency of Herbert Hoover."

Mr. Hughes reviewed at length Mr. Hoover's career as an engineer and in the public service. The question of choosing between the two major candidates, he said, should be dealt with "in the American spirit."

"I have no patience with bigotry," he affirmed. "I confess that I am intolerant of intolerance. I denounce every effort to bring any question of religion into this campaign. We have enough troubles in this country without introducing into our political

Continued on Page Three.

Smith Gets His First Vote From Republican Absentee

Governor Smith has already received his first vote for President and the ballot was that of a Republican. It was cast in California, home State of Herbert Hoover, the Republican nominee for President, but it will be counted in Ohio, for it was an absentee ballot marked and sent in yesterday by George H. Pinard of Cleveland, Ohio, who is living temporarily at San Jose, Cal., where he is Secretary of the Smith-Robinson Club. The information was received and made public yesterday by the Democratic National Committee, with the following statement from the year's first Smith voter:

"This is the first time I ever voted the Democratic ticket. I have been a voter for a great many years and always have voted the Republican ticket, but this time my vote went for Al Smith."

NEW YORK OVATION HEARTENS HOOVER

He Returns to Washington, Confident He Will Carry the State.

LUNCHES WITH PRESIDENT

Coolidge Has No Political Speeches Scheduled Between Now and Election Day.

Special to The New York Times.

WASHINGTON, Oct. 23.—Greatly encouraged in his belief that he will carry New York State, Herbert Hoover returned to Washington today for a busy period before he starts for California next week. He had looked for a hearty welcome in New York City but his friends say he had not expected such an ovation as that he received at Madison Square Garden.

This morning his desk was piled high with telegrams from all parts of the United States in which the senders congratulated him on his "Garden speech," a great many of them declaring it to have been the best "vote getting" utterance he has made since his nomination.

Soon after his return Mr. Hoover went to the White House, where he was the President's guest at luncheon. The campaign and its progress were discussed but no reference was made, it was said, to speeches by the President for the Republican ticket and the impression is that none will be made.

Subsequently the White House spokesman announced the President had no speeches on his schedule between now and election day. His next speech, as the program now stands, will be his memorial address in Arlington on Armistice Day.

Sees Gains in East.

Mr. Hoover was asked, after leaving the White House, if there was any probability that the President would make a political speech.

"You will have to ask the President," he replied.

When asked his opinion of the political situation, Mr. Hoover's answer was, "There's nothing to worry about."

The Eastern situation is steadily improving, in the opinion of Mr. Hoover and his Massachusetts Avenue headquarters staff. Yesterday in New York Mr. Hoover received first-hand information as to conditions in Massachusetts, Rhode Island, New Jersey and Connecticut as well as in New York.

In every instance the information was optimistic, his informants de-

Continued on Page Ten.

"All the News That's Fit to Print."

The New York Times.

Copyright, 1929, by The New York Times Company.

THE WEATHER
Cloudy and colder today; tomorrow, rain or snow.
Temperatures yesterday—Max. 55, min. 39.
U. S. Weather Forecast—For details see Page 46.

VOL. LXXIX....No. 26,259. NEW YORK, MONDAY, DECEMBER 16, 1929. TWO CENTS In Greater New York | THREE CENTS Within 200 Miles | FOUR CENTS Elsewhere Except 7th and 8th Postal Zones

PLANE OVER OCEAN IN NON-STOP FLIGHT, SPAIN TO URUGUAY

Larre-Borges of Uruguay and Challes of France Hope to Break Distance Record.

SIGHTED OVER WEST AFRICA

Turn Out to Sea After Making 650 Miles to Rio de Oro in Five and a Half Hours.

BRAZIL FIRST DESTINATION

Route Is Then Down West Coast to Montevideo and Beyond If Their Gas Holds Out.

Special Cable to THE NEW YORK TIMES.

MADRID, Dec. 15.—Major Tadeo Larre-Borges of Uruguay and Lieutenant Challes of France left Seville at 12:40 P. M. today in an attempt to fly the South Atlantic to Brazil and beyond. They were sighted over Casablanca, Morocco, three hours later.

The fliers made an excellent start in fine weather, although they carried a heavy load of 4,150 liters (1,100 gallons) of gasoline and 200 liters (210 quarts) of oil. Their plane is a dual-control Breguet land biplane with a 600-horsepower motor. They carry wireless equipment and special pontoons were installed. In addition, they carry two collapsible boats.

Before the departure Lieutenant Challes estimated that their trip would take fifty hours.

[London reported the fliers due to turn out to sea from the African coast at 1:30 A. M. Monday, European Time, which was 8:30 P. M. Sunday in New York.]

As supplies the fliers carried three roast chickens, fruits, chocolate, water and four bottles of champagne.

Five Successful Predecessors.

SEVILLE, Spain, Dec. 15 (AP).—The two aviators who left here today were embarked on the great adventure of an attempted non-stop flight to South America over a route where five successful expeditions have preceded them but where several have failed.

Major Larre-Borges was seeking to fulfill a long-held dream of linking Montevideo, capital of his native Uruguay, to the Spanish motherland by a single flight. His French co-pilot, Lieutenant Challes, is a Frenchman with a distinguished record of other long-distance flights.

The start was made from the Tablada airdrome. Friends of the aviators assembled to see the take-off, and many signed their names on the wings of the plane. The fliers also received numerous messages for delivery to officials and residents of Argentina.

They left here at 12:40 P. M. (7:40 A. M. Eastern Standard Time) and at 3:25 P. M. flew over Casa Blanca, Morocco. In the first three hours of their flight they had covered nearly 300 miles. They were favored with good weather over the first stage of their flight and tonight had a moon nearly full to light their way down the tropical coast.

Reports received here last night forecast clear weather for the flight along the Cape Verde Island route. The fliers' friends expected them to take that route, crossing the South Atlantic to Natal, Brazil, and fly thence to Bahia and Rio de Janeiro. Montevideo is their ultimate destination.

Hope to Pass Montevideo.

The aviators intended to skirt the western shores of Africa as far as Cape Jubi in Southern Morocco and then head out across the Atlantic. They expected to pick up the South American Continent in the vicinity of Natal, Brazil, and would then follow the coastline to Montevideo, if their fuel lasts. There was even talk of pushing further if conditions proved favorable, in an effort to set a new world distance record.

The plane used for the flight is a dual control French Breguet with a 450-horsepower Lorraine motor. The French flag is painted on the rudder, and the Uruguayan flag on the fuselage. The machine was sealed by the Royal Aero Club of Andalusia yesterday after successful trial flights.

The fliers took about 1,400 gallons of gasoline. The plane has a wing surface of forty-six square meters. It carried a radio set with two antennae. Two small motors under the wings of the machine supply electricity for the radio. Both Larre-Borges and Challes are skilled pilots.

The last successful flight from Europe to South America was that of Captain Arturo Ferrarin and Major B. Del Prete in July, 1928. They set a new world record, later broken by Dieudonne Coste, of 4,600 miles in flying from Rome to Brazil in fifty-nine hours.

If the Uruguayan aviator maintains an equal speed he should reach the

Continued on Page Three.

Urge British Revival Of Coastal Shipping

Special Cable to THE NEW YORK TIMES.

LONDON, Dec. 15.—A plan to reopen Britain's derelict ports and stimulate coastal shipping with a view to reducing unemployment was advanced by shipping and industrial interests in a report issued today.

Many small ports, some of ancient origin, which once did a flourishing trade, now are in danger of becoming obsolete not because they are no longer required but because the policy of competitive agencies like the railways has been to divert natural traffic to artificial channels, the report says. In some instances the decay of ports has actually been encouraged, it is asserted. The employment of seagoing motor barges, the report suggests, might bring such ports into commission again, and the development would be in line with motor-driven traffic on the roads and possibly would result in an equally striking expansion of trade.

BYRD BASE SOUNDING PLUMBS 1,600 FEET

Camp on Barrier Is Proved to Be Afloat on Waters of Bay With a Floor of Clay.

SIPLE DRILLS THROUGH ICE

Boy Scout Bores 18 Feet With Aid of Two Others—Geologists Push 17 Miles Eastward.

By RUSSELL OWEN.

Copyright, 1929.
By The New York Times Company and The St. Louis Post-Dispatch. All rights for publication reserved throughout the world.

Wireless to THE NEW YORK TIMES.

LITTLE AMERICA, Antarctica, Dec. 15.—The first sounding made near the base camp of the Byrd expedition shows that we are indeed floating. Through a hole in the ice at the head of Ver-sur-Mer Inlet, only about 150 yards from our front door, a sounding of 1,600 feet was obtained. That is a long way to the bottom.

It is hoped that a series of soundings around the Bay and in crevasses south of the camp may be made so that something more definite may be learned about the possible presence of land near here. Something must hold this Barrier or the Bay of Whales would have disappeared long ago.

Sounding is hard work where the old ice remains and eighteen feet of it were penetrated before the water was reached.

Device Operated by Siple.

This sounding was done by Paul Siple, the Boy Scout, and Victor Czegka, our machinist. A sled had been fixed up to hold a reel, the framework for it being made by Arnold Clark, our fireman, on a forge set up on the Barrier surface.

When it was ready, Paul started to dig a hole through the ice. For the first five feet Tom Mulroy helped him by burning oil and using gasoline torches. A long pipe was then used, and for hours he tapped away, scooping up the broken ice chips with a tin can.

When the pipe had gone down as far as it would reach and the bottom of the ice was not reached, Czegka put together two pieces of angle iron, making a drill twenty feet long. Czegka worked down through the last three feet and when the drill went through it nearly jerked from his hand.

The sounding line was then let down through the hole and after dropping 1,590 feet brought up against the bottom. It showed a clay floor at this part of the bay.

Czegka has made a device for bringing up samples of the bottom

Continued on Page Four.

'MISSING LINK' SEEN IN FIND NEAR PEKING; SCIENTISTS STIRRED

Ten Skeletons and a Skull in Perfect Condition Hailed as Ancestors of Man.

HELD GREATEST DISCOVERY

Dr. G. Elliot Smith Sees Piltdown and Java Finds Outrivaled by That in Chinese Cave.

CANADIAN LED EXCAVATORS

Rockefeller Foundation Cooperated —Scientists Now Studying Bones Believed 1,000,000 Years Old.

Special Cable to THE NEW YORK TIMES.

LONDON, Dec. 15.—The discovery in a cave near Peking of the fossilized bones of ten men, who possibly lived 1,000,000 years ago, as reported by scientists representing the Rockefeller Foundation and the Geological Survey of China, is held here to excel in interest all previous findings of this kind.

Of paramount importance is the discovery of a perfect skull, now in the possession of Dr. Davidson Black, a Canadian paleontologist, which, it is asserted, bears characteristics showing that even at the beginning of the ice age there existed men with the power of thinking and who, unlike the "ape men," walked erect.

From the fact that the ten skeletons lay huddled together in the cave, found in a field at Chou Outien, thirty miles from Peking, the scientists hold that they led a community life.

Believed the Ancestor of Man.

According to the Peking dispatches, the deduction made by scientists there from the discoveries is that the Java ape man is relegated definitely to a minor position in man's ancestry. The "Peking man," in fact, is believed to be a direct ancestor of the present human race.

"Every authority in Peking who has seen the skull," says a dispatch to The London Daily Telegraph, "unhesitatingly describes the discovery as epoch-making and outrivaling all previous discoveries, including the Piltdown man and the Neanderthal man."

The Chinese insisted that a Chinese excavator named Pei Wen-chung be permitted to accompany Dr. Black's party, and it was he who actually exposed the matrix containing the skull in the limestone cave. The field was first surveyed in 1927 by Dr. J. G. Anderson, Swedish geologist, in company with Dr. Grainger, paleontologist of the American Museum of Natural History in New York.

Dr. Anderson, continuing his investigation later with Dr. Bohlin, also of Sweden, who is now a member of Dr. Sven Hedin's expedition, discovered a tooth of the Peking man, the first finding in connection with this type of ancient man.

Calls Discovery the Greatest.

Dr. G. Elliot Smith, London anthropologist, in an interview tonight declares the discovery attributed to Dr. Black must be regarded as the most important discovery of the remains of ancient men ever made. He said:

"In the case of the ape man in Java there was recovered simply a tantalizing fragment of a skull, with three teeth and a thigh bone, and with no certain knowledge that the leg bone was part of the same individual as the fragment of skull.

"In the case of the Piltdown man there was simply a fragment of skull and a piece of jaw. Hence, the discovery in China of the remains of no fewer than ten individuals belonging to a primitive type which may be as

Continued on Page Ten.

Detective, Demoted in Vitale Dinner Hold-Up, Hunts Seven Robbers to Redeem Himself

Arthur C. Johnson, the first grade detective who was demoted and suspended by Commissioner Whalen for his failure to resist the seven robbers who held up the guests at the dinner to City Magistrate Albert Vitale on Dec. 7, is working night and day to find the robbers and thus redeem himself, it was learned last night.

Johnson, reduced to patrolman after the unlucky dinner, is having an enforced lay-off while he awaits a police trial for allowing the robbers to hold him up and take his revolver and also for his presence as a guest at a social function where, according to Mr. Whalen, he was associated with persons known to have police records. He is employing this time, on his own responsibility, searching parts of Harlem and the lower east side in hope of learning the identity of the gunmen who invaded the dinner in the Roman Gardens at Southern Boulevard and East 187th Street and got $5,000 from the two score guests.

Meanwhile District Attorney McGeehan of the Bronx is conducting an independent investigation of the hold-up. In the past two days he has questioned about ten of the guests. He did not announce their identity, but it was learned that neither Magistrate Vitale nor former Magistrate Michael N. Delagi, the host at the dinner, was among them. Those whom he questioned, he said, denied reports published last week that loot taken from the diners had been returned. He also disclaimed information which would support a rumor that the robbers' raid had been in reprisal for the failure of certain political leaders to obtain results from an alleged campaign fund of $10,000.

A reply from Magistrate Vitale to a letter of inquiry from Chief Magistrate William McAdoo concerning the dinner hold-up is expected by the chief magistrate today.

U. S. Steel to Acquire Atlas Portland Cement For Common Stock Valued at $31,320,000

The United States Steel Corporation has offered to acquire the Atlas Portland Cement Company through an exchange of stock. The entire transaction will involve 180,000 shares of United States Steel common stock in return for the outstanding stock, entire assets and good-will of the cement company. The Steel Corporation will also assume the liabilities of the cement company. These facts became known yesterday through a letter sent by the Atlas company to its stockholders, informing them of the offer.

The Steel Corporation's offer of 180,000 shares of its common stock amounts practically to an exchange of stock on a basis of one share of Steel for five shares of Atlas. Beyond its common stock the Atlas company's liabilities are said to be negligible. The preferred stock was recently retired, and there is no bonded indebtedness. Most of the liabilities will consist of accounts payable and other small items, it was said.

Common stock of the United States Steel Corporation closed on the New York Stock Exchange on Saturday at 174, making the total value of the shares offered for the cement company $31,320,000. The cement company has 899,211 common shares outstanding upon which regular dividends at the rate of $2 a year have been paid since June, 1925.

This acquisition marks the second purchase by the Steel Corporation in four months. Terms for the purchase of the Columbia Steel Corporation of San Francisco have been agreed upon.

It is not known whether the Atlas purchase was included in the $250,000,000 expansion program for the next three years which was announced by the Steel Corporation on Saturday. It was understood, however, that the major part of this money was to be spent on expanding properties already owned by the company.

The letter to the Atlas stockholders, which was signed by John R. Morron, president of the company, asserts that officers of the company consider the offer very favorable and urges the stockholders to deposit their holdings as quickly as possible to speed the plan.

A special meeting of the stockholders has been called for Dec. 28 for formal ratification. But further statements in the letter indicate that this ratification is a formality, for it says that already a majority of the stockholders have announced their approval of the merger, and the directors have already voted to accept the terms of the Steel Corporation.

An important development in the fight of the cement companies for higher tariff rates against foreign cement is seen by some in this proposed extension of the Steel Corporation's interests. The preliminary tariff schedules included an increased rate for cement, but in the recent tariff disputes in the Senate this has not been definitely assured.

FOX TRUSTEES PLAN A HOLDING COMPANY

Loew's, Inc., Would Be Included in Consolidation and the Dividend Rates Maintained.

EARNINGS ESTIMATE RISES

More Than $33,000,000 for Year Indicated Now—Fox's Plan for Merger Scrapped.

Consolidation of all the Fox holdings, including Loew's, Inc., into a new holding company, and the maintenance in the interim of regular dividend rates on the stock of the affected companies, are the two things which have been definitely decided by the trustees appointed by William Fox to control his interests, it was learned yesterday. Letters to the holders of the bulk of the short-term obligations of the company announcing these plans were mailed on Saturday, it is understood.

According to an authoritative source the letter said that the original plan of Mr. Fox to consolidate his holdings into the Fox Film Corporation had been found impractical at this time, and had therefore been abandoned for the idea of a new holding company. Last September the stockholders of Fox Film Corporation approved an issue of an additional 4,000,000 shares of Class A stock of the company.

Earlier Provisions Scrapped.

When this change was effected, the directorate of the company was to be increased from eight to twelve and the Class A stockholders, who at present have no voting power, were to have the election of five members of the enlarged board. It was also provided that if less than $1 was paid in dividends for four consecutive quarters the Class A stockholders were to have the election of nine of the twelve members, until dividends had been restored to the $4 a year basis, the present disbursement.

It was learned yesterday, however, that no new certificate of incorporation had been filed and none of the newly authorized stock has been issued, and that therefore the voting plan for Class A stockholders has not become operative. The trustees have no intention of going through with the plan of enlargement of the capitalization of the company, it is understood, but in formulating the plans for the holding company arrangements are said to be included for a wider participation of the Class A holders of Fox Film Corporation in the management of the company.

Earnings Estimate Raised.

The matter of dividends, which has been the subject of much speculation since the trusteeship was established, was said to be a subject not affected by the present position of the companies. It was pointed out that all of the short-term obligations, totaling $91,000,000, were not expenditures of the capital of the companies involved but were merely obligations accumulated in contracts for the purchase of assets. The authority for this statement also said that since the estimated earnings of the companies in the Fox holdings had been computed and announced as being about [illegible],000,000 for the year, more detailed reports had been received by the trustees which indicated that the earnings had been underestimated.

He said that in compiling the estimate West Coast theatres had been estimated at $3,500,000, whereas later figures indicated that the year's gross from these properties would be well above $6,000,000. Loew's, Inc., has also earned better than $10 a share on a first quarter of its fiscal year, which began Sept. 1, which indicated a total for the year of close to $14,000,000, he said, while the com-

Continued on Page Fourteen.

PONTIFF BEATIFIES 136 ENGLISH MARTYRS

British Prelates and Prominent Catholic Laymen at Colorful Ceremonies in St. Peter's.

RELICS VENERATED BY POPE

He Is Carried in State Into the Basilica for Rites Before a Huge Crowd.

By ARNALDO CORTESI.

Wireless to THE NEW YORK TIMES.

VATICAN CITY, Dec. 15.—With the spectacular rites prescribed by Vatican ceremonial procedure, the beatification took place in St. Peter's basilica this morning of 136 English martyrs who lost their lives in defense of their faith in the period between the reigns of King Henry VIII and Charles II.

This afternoon the Pope, surrounded by his ecclesiastical and military courts, was carried in state on the sedia gestatoria into St. Peter's, there to venerate the newly beatified martyrs and their relics, which were exposed on the high altar.

Both ceremonies were watched by many English ecclesiastics and laymen, who came to Rome especially for the occasion. Among the clergy were Cardinal Bourne, Archbishop of Westminster, and the Archbishops of Cardiff, Birmingham and Liverpool. Among the laymen were numerous descendants of the newly beatified martyrs and members of the most representative Catholic families in England.

Cardinal Dougherty of Philadelphia, who was in Rome in connection with the Pope's sacerdotal jubilee celebrations, participated in the ceremonies.

300 in the Original Group.

The process of the beatification of this group of English martyrs, which was the largest ever beatified at a single sitting, was begun in the middle of the nineteenth century under Pope Pius IX. They then numbered about 300. Some were immediately rejected, while others were beatified singly or in groups of twos or threes at various times.

A month ago, when the Congregation of Rites held its final sittings in the presence of the Pope, 260 candidates for beatification still remained. The Pope decided that full proofs of martyrdom had not been obtained for 124 of their number, with the result that only 136 were beatified today. The process of the beatification of the others will be continued and it is possible they also or most of them will be beatified shortly.

Of the first group beatified today, sixty-five were priests, thirty-five laymen. Of the clergy twenty-one were Jesuits, eight Benedictines, two Franciscans, one Minimite hermit. The others were secular priests. There were also three women and one Knight of Malta.

Two of the martyrs were put to death under Henry VIII, eighty-five under Queen Elizabeth, fifteen under James I, sixteen during the Cromwellian period and eighteen under Charles II. They were all held, after scrupulous investigation by the Congregation of Rites, to have died as martyrs for their faith and are credited with the minimum number of miracles necessary for their beatification.

The beatification proper occurred this morning and was conducted with the traditional ceremonial. At 10 o'clock Cardinal Laurenti, prefect of the Congregation of Rites, followed by other Cardinals and prelates forming part of the Congregation of Rites entered St. Peter's in a procession and took seats in the

Continued on Page Six.

HIPPODROME TO GO; 83-STORY BUILDING TO RISE ON ITS SITE

1,100-Foot Tower, Topping All but Proposed Empire State, Will Supplant Theatre.

TOTAL COST $30,000,000

Fred F. French Operators Buy Property at 43d St. and 6th Av. for $7,500,000.

WILL TAKE TITLE ON MAY 1

Purchasers Said to Be Negotiating With Department Store to Take Space—Offices to Be Included.

The Hippodrome, occupying the block front on the east side of Sixth Avenue between Forty-third and Forty-fourth Streets, has been sold for approximately $7,500,000 to the Fred F. French Operators, Inc., who announced yesterday that they would erect an eighty-three story skyscraper on the property. The total cost of building and land will be about $30,000,000.

Title to the property will be taken by the French company next May 1 at which time the store leases and the lease on which the theatre is operated will expire.

According to the French announcement the skyscraper will be about 1,100 feet high, compared with the projected Empire State Building's 1,300 feet, including a tower for anchoring dirigibles, which former Governor Smith and associates are to build on the site of the old Waldorf-Astoria Hotel Fifth Avenue and Thirty-fourth Street.

Will Top Chrysler Building.

The French skyscraper, to be called the Hippodrome Building, will be higher than the 1,030 feet Chrysler Building near completion at Forty-second Street and Lexington Avenue, now the highest structure in the world, and the new Manhattan Company Building which rises in Wall Street to a height of 925 feet. It will far overtop the Eiffel Tower, rising 984 feet above the streets of Paris, and the Woolworth Building, 792 feet high.

The new skyscraper will be designed with stores and offices, it was announced. When reports that Wanamaker's was negotiating to lease the basement and first five floors of the building were brought to the attention of William L. Nevin, chairman of the board of trustees of Wanamaker's in Philadelphia, yesterday, he said there was "absolutely" no basis for the reports which he described as "a lot of hot air."

The sale of the Hippodrome to the French interests is the third sale of the property since 1925, each transaction showing an advance of many thousands of dollars in the price. The parcel, which is considered one of the largest and finest plots adjacent to Times Square available for immediate improvement with a structure capable of carrying a tower of great height, was purchased by the French Company, which built Tudor City in East Forty-second Street, from Frederick Brown, operator. Mr. Brown purchased the realty from the Keith-Albee interests last January for a reported price of about $6,000,000.

Purchased by Keith-Albee.

The Keith-Albee interests took the Hippodrome over in 1923, remodeled it and operated it in conjunction with the owners, the United States Realty and Improvement Company. After operating the house for two years the Keith-Albee interests decided to purchase the property and in April, 1925, paid the United States Realty and Improvement Company about $5,000,000 for it.

Since then the structure, on a plot fronting 200.10 feet on Sixth Avenue

Continued on Page Twelve.

VITAL NAVAL TALKS START WITH THE JAPANESE TODAY IN MOVE TO END SUSPICION

TWO DELEGATIONS TO MEET

Visitors Will Be Assured No Hard and Fast Deal Has Been Effected.

4-DAY MEETINGS LIKELY

Whole Situation of Cruisers and Call for End of Submarines Will Be Canvassed.

CRUISER RATIO A PROBLEM

Wakatsuki Says He Will Insist on 70 Per Cent of Tonnage of Largest Powers.

By RICHARD V. OULAHAN.

Special to The New York Times.

WASHINGTON, Dec. 15.—Japan's delegates to the London Naval Armament Conference arrive in Washington tomorrow for a stay of four days, and the diplomatic conversations between the five naval powers preliminary to the conference will enter the intensive stage.

Much or little may depend on what takes place between the Japanese delegates and Secretary Stimson and his associates of the American conference delegation, but at the very least each will obtain an intimate understanding of the viewpoint of the other. Especially will Secretary Stimson and his colleagues be able to give the Japanese emissaries a picture of what is in President Hoover's mind concerning reduction in cruiser and submarine strength and his willingness to go the limit in advancing the principle of submarine abolition if an opening for suggesting that radical departure is offered.

Delegates Meet Tomorrow.

Arrangements have been completed for members of the Japanese delegation to meet the American delegates at the State Department Tuesday afternoon. The conference will continue on Wednesday, and if necessary on the following day, when the Japanese delegates are scheduled to leave for New York.

The Japanese delegates also will have an opportunity to confer with representatives of the other naval powers participating in the conference at London, the Japanese Ambassador, Katsuji Debuchi, having extended invitations to Sir Esme Howard, British Ambassador; Paul Claudel, French Ambassador, and Nobile Giacomo de Martino, Italian Ambassador, to attend the dinner which he is giving Tuesday evening in honor of the Japanese delegation.

The five weeks that remain before the London conference assembles are likely to be a period of pessimism as to the outcome. Every aspiration of each of the five naval powers is apt to be cited as a reason which forbids any common agreement on naval disarmament.

It is to be expected that when the conference gets down to business each nation will advance its major claims to preference. These major claims are given much prominence in the unofficial preliminary comment on the situation. It always has been so on such occasions. What is overlooked is that if each nation were determined to make no concession from its original program, there would be no necessity for holding an international parley.

The whole object of the conference is to see if the conflicting views of the various participants cannot be harmonized in the light of frank exchanges of views influenced by a common purpose to do something for the peace of the world and relieve nations of the heavy burden of preparation for war.

Anglo-American Plan Suspected.

It is evident that in the minds of the French and Japanese, and possibly in the minds of the Italians, there exists a suspicion or conviction that the United States and Great Britain have entered into a preliminary arrangement for naval armament reduction and limitation which they will seek to force upon the other powers. A curious aspect of this condition is that, at the outset of the informal conversations between the British and United States Governments looking to holding a disarmament conference, there was plenty of evidence they had the whole-hearted sympathy and good wishes of the three remaining naval powers.

The object of these conversations was to ascertain whether the United States and Britain would be able to adjust the differences between them which caused the Geneva naval conference of 1927 to fail. Unless these differences could be adjusted in a way to insure possible success of another naval disarmament effort, it

School Children Sing Carols To Hoover at White House

By The Associated Press.

WASHINGTON, Dec. 15.—About fifty youngsters from a Washington school sang Christmas carols for President and Mrs. Hoover in the White House today.

The children had taken pains to learn their songs perfectly and when their teachers asked that they be permitted to sing for the President the request was readily granted.

The President, with Mrs. Hoover, came down from their private apartments on the second floor to the East Room, where the carols were sung.

FIRM BUT FAIR RULE PLEDGED AT AUBURN

Dr. Christian Will Open Industries Today and Start Restoring Normal Conditions.

MEALS IN MESS HALL AGAIN

Unemployed Convicts Will Get Exercise and Deserving Will Retain Their Privileges.

Special to The New York Times.

AUBURN, N. Y., Dec. 15.—After surveying conditions at Auburn Prison since his arrival here last night to take charge, under Governor Roosevelt's orders, as acting warden, Dr. Frank L. Christian, superintendent of Elmira Reformatory, announced tonight the régime which would be followed while he is in control.

He will put into effect here the system he has employed so successfully at Elmira, a system combining fairness to prisoners with strict military discipline. The Mutual Welfare League, for the present, will not function.

Colonel George L. Chandler, appointed by Governor Roosevelt to make a full inquiry into the riots and the general conditions at the prison, began his inquiry in Syracuse tonight by consulting with officers of the State troopers who took part in suppressing the outbreak.

Will Reopen Shops Today.

Dr. Christian, in outlining his plans, stated that tomorrow morning he would open the prison and, so far as possible, operate the institution under normal conditions. Work in the shops and industrial and other departments will be resumed under the conditions that prevailed before the riot.

The hundreds of unemployed convicts will be taken out into the air for recreation periods after being cooped up in their cells for three days.

He has assigned the guarding of the prison walls to 100 State troopers who will serve in relays. All the prison guards will be taken from the walls and used inside.

A systematic period for the recreation of the unemployed convicts will be established. Instead of the usual milling around, they will have a chance to exercise in an orderly manner under the supervision of guards. All prisoners will have their meals in the mess hall in the usual manner.

Dr. Christian has discussed the situation with Warden Jennings and the force of guards. He has explained to them just what he will

Continued on Page Sixteen.

Maurice Falk Sets Up $10,000,000 Fund For Philanthropic Uses as Memorial to Wife

Special to The New York Times.

PITTSBURGH, Pa., Dec. 15.—A gift of about $10,000,000 for charitable purposes, to be expended through a philanthropic foundation established as a memorial to his wife, was announced today by Maurice Falk, capitalist.

The fund will be known as the Maurice and Laura Falk Foundation. It will be organized at once, and will begin operations early in 1930.

The life of the foundation is restricted to thirty-five years. Within that time the entire fund, both principal and interest, must be expended in projects intended to serve the public welfare.

Broad powers of discretion are given the managers of the foundation to make grants for the promotion of educational, religious, charitable, philanthropic and public interest. It is understood that Mr. Falk has made no restrictions regarding the work in which the foundation may engage.

Seven managers have been named by Mr. Falk to administer the fund. This board, which has the power to fill its own vacancies, is composed of Leon Falk Jr., E. T. Weir, I. A. Simon, Frank B. Bell, Nathan Jacobs, Eugene B. Strassburger and A. E. Braun. Announcement will be made soon of the director and staff.

In the agreement establishing the foundation Mr. Falk expresses the belief that it is the duty of one who through good fortune has accumulated wealth beyond his personal needs to regard the remainder as a trust to be expended for the benefit of mankind.

In his latest gift Mr. Falk carries on the policy, initiated in his earlier benefactions, of making this distribution during his own lifetime.

The Falks have long been known for their interest in philanthropy. The $900,000 Falk clinic and dispensary, which is to be a part of the medical centre of the University of Pittsburgh, is the combined gift of Maurice Falk and his brother, the late Leon Falk.

Maurice Falk has for years devoted much of his time and effort to philanthropic undertakings, and has been identified with many public projects.

"All the News That's Fit to Print."

The New York Times.

THE WEATHER
Fair and slightly warmer today; tomorrow cloudy.
Temperature yesterday—Max., 56; min., 38.
U. S. Weather Forecast—For details see page 30.

VOL. LXXIX....No. 26,325. •••• NEW YORK, THURSDAY, FEBRUARY 20, 1930. TWO CENTS In Greater New York | THREE CENTS Within 200 Miles | FOUR CENTS Elsewhere Except 7th and 8th Postal Zones

NAVAL PARLEY HALTS FOR A WEEK AT CALL OF AMERICAN LEADER

Stimson's Suggestion to Await New French Delegation Wins Approval of Others.

ITALY REITERATES DEMAND

France Contends Grandi Bases Request for Parity on False Measures of Fleets.

ROBINSON AIRS OUR VIEWS

Senator Tells Correspondents of American Desire to Avoid European Political Compacts.

The texts of the Italian statement on naval needs and of the speech of Senator Robinson in London yesterday are on page 19.

By EDWIN L. JAMES.

Special Cable to THE NEW YORK TIMES.

LONDON, Feb. 19.—The London Naval Arms Conference adjourned today for one week. This step was taken because of the absence of the French delegation, due to the governmental crisis in Paris.

It is understood that the decision to adjourn until next Wednesday, by which time it is hoped the French delegates will have returned, was taken on the initiative of Secretary of State Stimson, who assumed the position that negotiations between the English and American delegates as well as among other delegations in the absence of the French might cause irritation.

Suggestion Quickly Approved.

The suggestion of the chief of the American delegation was made this morning and was approved early in the afternoon by Prime Minister MacDonald and soon afterward by the Japanese and Italians. The adjournment was announced at 5 o'clock. In the meantime, it was announced officially, there will be no meetings of delegates, official or otherwise.

Secretary Stimson went to his country place at Stanmore today and will remain there until next week. The experts, however, will continue here some of their consultations on purely technical matters.

The Italians issued a statement today on their position, reiterating their demand for parity with France. The declaration contained nothing new.

Dino Grandi, chief of the Italian delegation, and Admiral Sirianni will leave for Rome tomorrow morning. It is said Foreign Minister Grandi will return on Monday for the resumption of the conference. Their purpose in going to Rome is to confer with Premier Mussolini on the situation regarding Italy's demand for naval parity with France.

In French quarters it was said tonight that the naval figures given by the Italians in their public statement were incorrect. The French say their actual tonnage is more than 600,000, or approximately double the Italian tonnage, instead of 10 per cent greater, as the Italians maintain.

Americans Less Enthusiastic.

The adjournment of the conference today appears to have been taken in an atmosphere of unhappiness bordering on pessimism. It has been noticeable that the American delegates have lost much of the optimistic enthusiasm which marked them up to this week. Even if the French were present the conference would still face difficult days. Not that there is any doubt that a limitation treaty will be written, but the statesmen have made too many political promises which they find themselves unable to carry out. Both the British and Americans misjudged the French stand, as they now are quite willing to admit.

Especially does one sense the idea that many delegates, especially the Americans and British, fear the week's postponement of activity will cause the conference to lose popularity. It is likely to get off the front pages of newspapers, and when it resumes must work hard, it is believed, to regain its position in popular consideration.

Robinson Airs Views.

Before the American correspondents, who entertained the American delegation at lunch today at the Savoy Hotel, Senator Robinson made a speech which contained much food for comment. He had prepared a speech which had been approved by Secretary Stimson and had been cabled to Washington for release by the State Department. Therefore that speech might be considered a statement on behalf of the American delegation.

But, in starting, the Senator prefixed some remarks outside the set speech. He said the conference had reached the stage where some dele-

Continued on Page Eighteen.

Pistol Sales in Last 7 Months Trebled Over 1928 Period

Special to The New York Times.

WASHINGTON, Feb. 19.—Despite the nation-wide campaign to restrict the sale of firearms, there was almost a three fold increase in the purchases of pistols and revolvers during the first seven months of the current fiscal year, according to a report issued today by the Bureau of Internal Revenue.

Collections of excise taxes on the sale of these weapons totaled $272,555 in the seven months ended Jan. 31, compared with $94,011 for the same period of the previous year, an increase of $178,544.

The Commerce Department reported that exports of these firearms had decreased. It was taken for granted by officials, therefore, that the large increase in sales was for domestic use.

LOOK TO CHAUTEMPS TO FORM A CABINET

French Expect Doumergue Will Call Radical-Socialist Leader to Be the Premier.

LEFT ALLIANCE IS SOUGHT

Party Leaders Rule Out Collaboration With Right Groups in Forming Ministry.

By P. J. PHILIP.

Special Cable to THE NEW YORK TIMES.

PARIS, Feb. 19.—Two solutions for the French political crisis were offered to President Doumergue today by party leaders whom he called into consultation at the Elysées Palace. One was that the formation of a definitely Left Cabinet should be attempted, and the other that an effort should be made to form a cabinet of what is called the "Republican Concentration"—that is, in which the Radical-Socialists would be the predominating party, but would include with them all the Republicans as far to the Right as the party controlled by André Mignot, who was M. Tardieu's Minister of War.

It is expected that as a result of this advice the President tomorrow morning will ask Camille Chautemps, leader of the Radical-Socialist Party in the Chamber, to form a new government. M. Chautemps will have to make a decision as to whether he will try to make a purely Left Cabinet with the support of the Socialists or whether he will attempt the alternative of a Moderate Cabinet with Centre and perhaps some Right support, but with the expectation of encountering sooner or later the hostility of the 100 Socialists whose votes combined with those of the Right may at any moment wreck his enterprise.

Tardieu Next in Order.

If M. Chautemps fails the President then, it is believed, will ask M. Tardieu to form another Ministry, in which the Radicals could not very well refuse to participate if they themselves had failed to form a Cabinet. The Republican Concentration would then have its Centre somewhat to the Right, although the inclusion of the Radicals, which it is understood M. Tardieu would be perfectly willing to accept, would give it a stronger Left flavor than the Cabinet which was defeated on Monday.

That, however, is a situation which will arise only if M. Chautemps fails as M. Deladier failed last October to form a Left government.

It is no secret that among the Radical party leaders the regret at the outcome of Monday's vote is as great as it is among the supporters of the former government. They realize that the present is no time to come forward with a program for the solution of the four questions which they will have to face—settle-

Continued on Page Sixteen.

FIVE ANTI-DRYS URGE END OF PROHIBITION; STATE RULE ARGUED

Channing Pollock and Owen Johnson Denounce Dry Law at the House Hearing.

G. M.-P. MURPHY FOR REPEAL

Declares He Knows No Leader in Business Who Is Not a Violator.

'CHURCH LOBBY' ATTACKED

Wickersham Was Associated With It, Says H. B. Joy—Stayton Asserts Saloons Multiply.

Special to The New York Times.

WASHINGTON, Feb. 19.—Prohibition was denounced and arguments for it replied to in the testimony of five prominent advocates of repeal or modification who testified at the House Judiciary Committee's "dry hearings" today.

Channing Pollock, playwright, of New York, declared prohibition "led people to orgiastic excesses, filled us with a sense of being watched and filled us with the fear of a logical extension of that kind of legislation."

Grayson M.-P. Murphy of New York, broker and director of many banking, commercial and transportation companies, declared that virtually without exception he knows no one who observes the law.

Henry B. Joy, former president of the Packard Motor Car Company, criticized the law enforcement commission, which, he said, represented "the marriage of vast church influence and the Anti-Saloon League, which had been consummated through the creation of the Wickersham Commission." Pointing out that William Howard Taft had prophesied prevailing conditions in two letters written twelve years ago, the witness stated that "today civil war is upon us."

Stayton Argues Repeal.

William H. Stayton, chairman of the board of directors of the Association Against the Eighteenth Amendment, who has marshaled much of the testimony presented for the wets in their first hearing by Congress, declared the repeal of the Eighteenth Amendment as the aim of his organization.

Owen Johnson, one of the founders of the Authors' League, widely known as a writer and the representative of the Authors' and Artists' Committee of the association, suggested a referendum on the prohibition question.

The session was presided over by Representative George S. Graham, chairman of the committee, himself identified as a wet, and was attended by some 300 persons, most of them standing all day in the comparatively small committee room. There were, in addition, about thirty reporters in the room, measuring 30 by 60 feet. Behind a curved desk on an elevated platform were a score of committeemen.

Reciting his opinions of the public attitude regarding law and respect for the Constitution in its changes during the last decade, Mr. Pollock extended a brief statement into almost an hour's testimony.

Drinking, aside from the bit of wine in which he and his family always have indulged, did not interest him, he said, but the enforcement of prohibition at this date, which he believes could not even be accomplished by force, would be a "triumph not of law, but of tyranny."

Says Law Cannot Be Enforced.

His observations of the public, gained by delivering more than 1,000 lectures and mingling with some 300,-

Continued on Page Thirteen.

Agents Arrest Another Alleged Bootlegger Just Outside the Senate Office Building

Special to The New York Times.

WASHINGTON, Feb. 19.—The arrest of a second bootlegger suspect in the vicinity of the Senate Office Building revealed today that prohibition agents have been working secretly in the shadow of the Capitol for some time.

The man is William David Goldberg, whom agents brought into police court today, charging that he had been caught near the office building while transferring a package of liquor from an automobile. His arrest occurred yesterday hardly two hours after George L. Cassidy, known as "the man in the green hat," had been taken into custody.

When Goldberg's car stopped near the Capitol, he got out with a package under his arm, the agents said. When they closed in on him, he dashed his package to the pavement, breaking six bottles of alleged gin, of which they were able to save about a gill for evidence.

Goldberg waived arraignment and was held for the grand jury on charges of transportation and possession of a gill of whisky. A woman companion, who gave the name of Ida Decklebaum, was released when the District Attorney's office declined to make out papers against her.

The agents explained that their ready spotting of Goldberg was due to a tip they had received that the man was to make delivery to the Senate Office Building.

Cassidy, "the man in the green hat," was caught in much the same manner earlier in the afternoon, and immediately made a protest, declaring he had been "framed."

Senator Wheeler issued a statement today citing Cassidy's seizure as another reason why the Senate should investigate prohibition and its enforceability, as sought in a resolution which he has introduced.

Senator Jones of Washington suggested an investigation to determine where Cassidy was going when arrested.

"I think we ought to know more about Cassidy," said Senator Jones. "Certainly we ought to know where he was going in the office building. However, we are not detectives, and I do not know how to find out."

Mercury Climbs to 56, High Record for Feb. 19

New York got a premature taste of Spring yesterday as the weather broke its second record in four days. Last Sunday, and again on Monday, the thermometer dropped to 7 degrees, the coldest temperature on record this season. And yesterday, just to show its versatility, it took a running jump in the opposite direction. At 2:40 P. M. it reached 56 degrees, which was the warmest in the Weather Bureau's records for Feb. 19. The previous high record was 53 degrees on Feb. 19, 1909.

Further surprises are in store if the Weather Man keeps his promise. The forecast is "warmer today."

DRY ISSUE IS THRUST ON REPUBLICAN CLUB

Group of Members Ask National Organization Here to Vote on Repeal Move.

SLAP AT HOOVER SEEN

Bitter Fight Expected on the Petition—Dr. Butler and Coudert Among Signers.

The prohibition issue, which threatens to split the Republican party in this State, was again put forward yesterday when fifteen members of the National Republican Club, the leading party organization in the city, called for a special meeting of all members on March 10 to vote on a resolution urging Republican members of Congress to vote for the repeal of the Eighteenth Amendment and the restoration of States' rights in the control of the liquor traffic.

The petition for the special meeting was presented by Frederic R. Coudert Jr., Republican nominee for District Attorney last Fall. Signers of the petition in addition to Mr. Coudert are Dr. Nicholas Murray Butler, president of Columbia University; Frederick C. Bellinger, Millard H. Ellison, Sidney Harris, Norman Johnson, Arthur H. Kuhn, J. J. Lesser, J. Edward Lumbard Jr., former State Senator Courtlandt Nicoll, William M. K. Olcott, former Assemblyman Phelps Phelps, Jehial M. Roeder, Martin Saxe and William Bell Wait. Under the club's by-laws, any ten members have the right to a special meeting on demand to the recording secretary.

Move Is Resented.

The injection of the prohibition issue into the club, which defeated a similar resolution two years ago, was resented bitterly by many of the club members. Richard W. Lawrence, president of the club, is a strong supporter of President Hoover and is opposed to passage of the resolution on the ground that it would be interpreted as a slap at the President for the prohibition enforcement activities of the National Administration. Agitation of the issue also is believed to impair the chance of electing a Republican Governor and cause a further division in the party, already in none too good shape for a State campaign. The club is a national institution and has many out-of-town members from all sections of the country. Conservative members expressed the fear that adoption of the resolution would bring about the resignation of many dry members.

The anti-dry resolution introduced two years ago was defeated by a combination of drys and organization Republican members who, although opposed to prohibition in its present form, believed that neither the club nor the party had anything to gain by putting the club on record in favor of the repeal of the Eighteenth Amendment. An attempt will be made to bring about a similar combination for the defeat of the resolution this time.

Some feeling among the dry and conservative members also was expressed because Mr. Coudert, Dr. Butler and their associates did not introduce the resolution at the club's regular monthly meeting Tuesday night, in which case it would have been referred to the club's committee on national affairs, of which former United States Senator William M. Calder is chairman. The call for a special meeting was construed as indicating that the sponsors of the resolution were willing to go over the heads of Mr. Lawrence, the president, and Senator Calder to avoid the possibility of the resolution being buried in committee.

Uphold States' Rights.

The resolution, as made public by Mr. Coudert, follows:

Whereas the existence of the Eighteenth Amendment to the Constitution of the United States is disruptive of our Federal system in that it is destructive of the rights of the States so effectively described in Lincoln's platform in the following words:

"The maintenance inviolate of the rights of the States, and especially the right of each State

Continued on Page Thirteen.

GRAND JURY ACCUSES HIGHEST OFFICIALS IN NARCOTIC BUREAU

Reports to Washington From Here Falsified at Their Orders, Presentment Charges.

ASKS COMPLETE SHAKE-UP

Sees Dereliction by Agents and Evidence of Collusion With Big Drug Sellers.

FINDS AN ADDICT IN SQUAD

Tuttle to Report to Mellon on Testimony Against Colonel Nutt and Blanchard.

The January Federal grand jury, which for seven weeks has been investigating the illegal drug traffic, filed a presentment yesterday charging local narcotic agents with misconduct, incompetence and dereliction and with having regularly falsified their reports to Washington as a result of an order to do so, telephoned to the New York office by William C. Blanchard, Assistant Deputy Commissioner of Prohibition in charge of narcotics.

The presentment touches the highest narcotic enforcement official in the United States when it sets forth that the Assistant Deputy Commissioner testified that, in telephoning the order to "pad" the monthly reports to the Washington office, he "did not approve of it, but was acting under orders from the Deputy Commissioner." The Deputy Commissioner of Prohibition, who is the head of narcotic law enforcement throughout the country is Colonel L. G. Nutt of Washington, who was a witness before this grand jury.

"We are of the opinion that the usefulness of certain of the men attached to the New York office is at an end," the presentment continues, "and that the situation calls for a complete reorganization from top to bottom."

Copies Go to Mellon.

The report carefully avoids the use of the name of any official or agent. It refers to Colonel Nutt, Mr. Blanchard and to George W. Cunningham, agent in charge of the local Federal narcotic office, by title only. The presentment itself, however, explains that the actual testimony, on which it based its findings, includes names and dates, and the report suggests that a summary of this testimony be sent to Secretary of the Treasury Mellon. It urges also that copies of the presentment be forwarded to the United States Attorney General. United States Attorney Tuttle said he would mail the copies last night.

The grand jurors concluded that there were strong indications of collusion between some local narcotic agents and the "men higher up" in the narcotic traffic, and pointed out that on more than one occasion the small dispenser of drugs was caught while the more important law violators escaped easily.

The presentment declares that one local narcotic agent is known to be a drug addict but remains on the government payroll. It hints at other drug users on the narcotic force and suggests greater safeguards "as to protecting and checking stocks of seized narcotics."

"In the last two days of this investigation," the presentment sets forth, "we have had much testimony concerning a customs agent and have heard him testify. We think that the evidence is such that, with the permission of the court, a summary of it should be placed before his superiors with a view to drastic action."

The grand jury expressed the opinion that the narcotic laws should be amended and admitted the conviction that the drug traffic could never be suppressed through "local prosecution alone." The menace, it de-

Continued on Page Three.

I. R. T. Moves to Silence Subway Turnstiles; New Device Will Be Tried at Grand Central

The clacking of Interborough subway turnstiles, mounting in the rush hours to a machine-gun staccato, will be transformed into a gentle clicking sound if a new device perfected by the company proves successful in tests authorized yesterday by the Transit Commission.

The device, representing the company's contribution to the current anti-noise campaign, will soon be installed on one of the turnstiles at Grand Central Station, where its operation will be checked by company engineers and Transit Commission experts. The installation cost for experimental purposes will be from $500 to $800, but it will cost only $20 per turnstile to install the device for general use. The commission has authorized the company to charge the experimental cost to maintenance account.

In recommending the tests the commission's engineers reported that the use of the device entailed no question of royalty payments by the company, since the device would not be patented by the Interborough or any of its employes. In the past the commission has objected to payment of royalties, charged as joint operating costs under the contract between the city and the company, to Interborough employes.

If the device proves successful the company plans to use it on all turnstiles on its subway division. The new mechanism, it was said, is constructed of different material than that now in use. The tests about to be started will show not only whether the present noisy operation can be eliminated, but also whether the device will stand up under the heavy punishment inflicted by the daily subway traffic.

BYRD PARTY ON SHIP HOMEWARD BOUND; CITY OF NEW YORK LOADED OVER NIGHT; POLAR PLANE LEFT AT ANTARCTIC BASE

Chronology of the Byrd Expedition

1928.

Aug. 25—The bark City of New York left New York.

Oct. 10—Commander Byrd and his party sailed from Los Angeles on the whaler C. A. Larsen.

Dec. 2—The City of New York and the Eleanor Bolling left Dunedin, N. Z., for the Antarctic.

Dec. 14—The City of New York started through the ice pack; the Bolling returning to New Zealand.

Dec. 25—The expedition arrived at the Ice Barrier.

1929.

Jan. 6—Permanent base established at Little America.

Jan. 16—Commander Byrd made his first Antarctic flight, exploring 1,200 square miles.

Jan. 31—Commander Byrd saved Roth, aviation mechanic, from drowning when part of Barrier cliff collapsed.

Feb. 18—Commander Byrd explored 40,000 square miles of unknown territory by plane.

March 8—Larry Gould, Bernt Balchen and Harold June flew to the Rockefeller Range for geological studies.

March 19—Commander Byrd flew to their rescue and found their plane wrecked.

March 22—Commander Byrd and geological party returned safely to Little America.

Oct. 15—Supporting sledging party started south on a base-laying trip.

Nov. 4—Geological party started 400-mile sledge trip to Queen Maude Mountains.

Nov. 10—Supporting party returned to Little America.

Nov. 18—Commander Byrd made a base-laying flight to Queen Maude Mountains.

Nov. 28—Commander Byrd and three companions started for the South Pole at 10:29 P. M. (New York time).

Nov. 29—Commander Byrd wirelessed THE NEW YORK TIMES from the South Pole at 8:55 A. M. (New York time); returned to his base at 5:10 P. M.

Dec. 5—Commander Byrd discovered a new mountain range as he explored 35,000 square miles of unknown territory.

Dec. 21—President Hoover signed bill, commissioning Commander Byrd a Rear Admiral.

Dec. 26—Geological party found a cairn containing Amundsen relics of eighteen years before.

1930.

Jan. 19—Geological party arrived back at Little America, having discovered coal outcroppings on Mount Nansen.

Feb. 7—The City of New York completed passage of ice pack on way to bring the expedition home.

Feb. 18—The City of New York reached the Bay of Whales.

Feb. 19—The expedition left for home.

SUN LIGHTS EARLY SAILING

Ross Sea Fog Clears as Vessel Leaves Bay of Whales at 9:30 A. M.

BYRD SALUTES HIS CAMP

Deserted Aircraft Stand on Hill of Barrier—Men Get Year's Mail as They Depart.

BARK SCARRED BY THE ICE

Skipper Tells of Fight in Storm to Reach Expedition, There 13 Months and 25 Days.

By RUSSELL OWEN.

Wireless to THE NEW YORK TIMES.

ABOARD THE BARK CITY OF NEW YORK, ROSS SEA, Antarctica, Feb. 19.—Admiral Byrd's ship, the City of New York, left the Bay of Whales at 9:30 o'clock this morning [4:30 P. M. New York time].

The night had been raw and cold and the bay covered with a dispiriting fog. But with the coming of the sun, the mists were swept away and those who had lived for more than a year on the Barrier and those who had come to take them home had a final glimpse of the white cliffs gleaming white and forbidding in the sun.

The last hours since the ship arrived have been so busy, so much has been going on in the rush to get materials aboard, that they seem like days. It is really only a short time since her masts were seen above the frost smoke that covered the harbor last evening and she moved in half concealed, the ghost of a ship, until she neared the edge of the ice and we could see her.

What a delirious moment, one of those moments when one stands quietly almost without thought for the happiness of it.

The weather beaten and ice sheathed ship, glistening in the fading sun, meant letters and home and the way back to civilization.

Ship Greeted "Almost Diffidently."

She came on up to the ice dock at the west side of the bay, where a little group of men waited for her, for she was far ahead of her schedule, and as she neared them an arm was waved, almost diffidently, and somebody waved back from the ship. Then, as she came closer, a voice called across the water.

A little nearer and we could distinguish the faces of men we knew, Captain Melville on the bridge, who had taken his ship safely through one of the worst passages an Antarctic ship ever had; Bendik Johanssen, mate and ice pilot, who had picked the leads through the pack; man after man who had been on the trip down last year and who had stuck to the ship to bring the expedition home.

Oh, it was good to see them, to see new faces and hear new voices! It had actually happened! We were going home!

The ship was no sooner alongside the ice than gear which had been piled there was tumbled aboard. It came over the side in a steady stream, records and scientific gear first, then personal baggage and finally the other things which piled up in the 'tween-decks hold until it was full to the hatch.

All night the loading went on and by breakfast this morning it was finished except for a few things which did not long delay the ship.

There was need for haste, for the season is getting late and the ice pack has not disappeared this year.

Mail Interrupts Breakfast.

Breakfast was a sadly interrupted meal, because the mail was distributed then. There were bags and bags of it. It had been piled in Admiral Byrd's cabin to keep it dry, and it seemed as if there would be no end to the amount of letters and bundles.

Some of them had been sorted into bags and men staggered away from the door with bags they could barely lift.

What a mail day! There will never be another like it for most of us. And even then there was not time at first to read; men grabbed a handful of letters, scanned the handwriting on them hurriedly and then stuck them in their pockets until the ship could be at sea and there would be time to look them over at leisure, at least for those who would not be seasick. And most of us

BLAST TOLL NOW 11; GRAND JURY TO ACT

Full Reports of Four Inquiries Into Elizabeth Explosion to Be Placed Before Body in May.

EMPLOYES ARE QUESTIONED

Break Found in Pipe Outside of Alcohol Plant—New Fire on Standard Property Quelled.

Special to The New York Times.

ELIZABETH, N. J., Feb. 19.—Four of the persons injured Tuesday afternoon in the explosions at the Bayway Refinery of the Standard Oil Company died today, bringing the list of those killed in the disaster to eleven. Of the fifty-seven victims in the various hospitals six were reported as still in a critical condition.

While the authorities were checking the names of the dead and injured, announcement was made that four separate investigations had been started to determine the cause and place responsibility for the three explosions. The results of the investigations, according to Prosecutor Abe J. David of Union County, will be placed before the regular May term of the grand jury.

The list of dead follows:

CORNELIUS, GEORGE, of 747 Jefferson Avenue, Elizabeth.
SULLIVAN, JOHN L., of 543 Marshall Street, Elizabeth.
LUKASICWICZ, JOSEPH, of 451 Bond Street, Elizabeth.
CROFT, CLARENCE, of 97 West Thirty-fifth Street, Bayonne.
ROBERTSON, GEORGE, of 119 Union Road, Roselle Park.
HALLIDAY, HOWARD A., of 169 West Fiftieth Street, Bayonne.
CROSS, ARTHUR, of 21 Union Avenue, Union.
BONNAN, DOMINIC, of 604 Fourth Avenue, Elizabeth.
LUBAS, JOHN, of 24 Atlantic Street, Elizabeth.
DUFFY, WILLIAM, of 63 Garrison Avenue, Bayonne.
CASEY, WILLIAM, of 528 Grier Avenue, Elizabeth.

New Fire on Property.

A spectacular but apparently trifling blaze started in another part of the Standard Oil property at 8:15 o'clock tonight when a column of flame 100 feet high suddenly flared

Continued on Page Eight.

TO GRANT AUTHORITY FOR PAY RISE HERE

Legislature Will Approve Today Reopening of Budget for Policemen and Firemen.

CITY OFFICIALS CENSURED

Dunmore Calls Roosevelt's Attitude on County Government 'Hypocritical.'

By W. A. WARN.

Special to The New York Times.

ALBANY, Feb. 19.—Senator Knight and Speaker McGinnies announced tonight that a bill would be passed tomorrow by the Legislature, with the aid of an emergency message from Governor Roosevelt, authorizing New York City officials to reopen the city budget and include a sum not to exceed $5,000,000 to allow increases in salary for 20,000 policemen and firemen.

The referendum approved by the voters of New York City last Fall provided salary increases only for first-grade patrolmen and firemen. The city officials had planned to include a sufficient amount in the 1930 budget to increase the pay of officers and lower-grade members of these two departments, but the item was overlooked when the budget was prepared.

Controller Berry came to the Capitol today and, on behalf of Mayor Walker, urged the Republican leaders to pass the bill speedily. Corporation Counsel Hilly and other city officials also told the Republican leaders that Friday would be the last day in which the budget could be reopened. Governor Roosevelt is expected to sign the measure as soon as it reaches his desk tomorrow afternoon.

While the Republican legislative leaders agreed to pass the bill, they issued a statement censuring New York City officials for their oversight.

"The bill authorizing the city of New York to include in the 1930 budget a sum not exceeding $5,000,000 to provide increases in salaries of the uniformed officers of the police and fire departments will be reported from the Cities Committee and will be submitted for passage to the Legislature tomorrow. Because of an inexcusable oversight the city officials failed to include this sum in the budget already made up."

Dunmore Criticizes Roosevelt.

Governor Roosevelt was described as "hypocritical" in his attitude on up-State county legislation by Assemblyman Dunmore, Republican leader of the lower house, on the floor today. The attack on the Governor followed opposition expressed by Mr. Steingut, the minority leader, to a bill increasing the salaries of supervisors of Otsego County.

"I think we should go a little slow in saddling more expenses on the shoulders of the taxpayers in the up-State counties and it might be well to make a study of the home-rule law," Assemblyman Steingut said. "The Legislature never seems to hesitate in passing up-State legislation, but it always seems to be suspicious of New York City bills."

Mr. Dunmore retorted that at the end of the last week more than 50

Continued on Page Four.

Rear Admiral Byrd was warmly welcomed to New York. Here he is shown being escorted up Broadway, amid throngs of enthusiastic admirers.

"All the News That's Fit to Print."

The New York Times.

THE WEATHER
Mostly fair today and tomorrow; little change in temperature.
Temperatures Yesterday—Max. 83, min. 67.
U. S. Weather Forecast—For details see Page 31.

Copyright, 1930, by The New York Times Company.

VOL. LXXIX....No. 26,445. **** NEW YORK, FRIDAY, JUNE 20, 1930. TWO CENTS In Greater New York | THREE CENTS Within 200 Miles | FOUR CENTS Elsewhere Except 7th and 8th Postal Zones

BYRD AND HIS MEN ACCLAIMED BY CITY; WILDLY CHEERED IN BROADWAY PARADE; WALKER BESTOWS MEDALS OF MERIT

MOVE FOR REPRISALS IN FRENCH CHAMBER IF OUR DUTIES STAND

Deputies Favor Ending Most-Favored-Nation Treatment Unless We Heed Protest.

UNANIMOUS BACKING LIKELY

Even Leaders Most Eager to Hold Our Friendship See Drastic Move Justified.

PLEA TO HOOVER EXPECTED

Our State Department Declines to Comment Pending Receipt of Official Representations.

By P. J. PHILIP.
Special Cable to THE NEW YORK TIMES.

PARIS, June 19.—Suppression of most-favored-nation treatment for the United States and wholesale discrimination against American imports into France was urged today on the French Government by the tariff committee of the Chamber of Deputies in the event that all efforts should fail to obtain reductions in the new American import duties on French goods.

The committee met in the morning at the same time that the French Minister of Commerce, Pierre Etienne Flandin, was laying before the Cabinet his report on the effect the Hawley-Smoot act will have on French commerce with the United States. The results of the committee's deliberations were set forth in the following communiqué:

Committee's Statement.

The Committee on Customs of the Chamber, after having attentively examined the consequences of the increase in customs duties decided upon by the United States, notes with regret:

First, that the new American tariffs, imposed on the most active branches of production, will appreciably reduce French exports to this great, friendly country.

Second, that they will seriously aggravate the difficulties which generalized economic nationalism places on international exchange.

Third, that because of the injury done to their commercial balance, those countries which have debts to pay to the United States will incur great risk to the exchange value of their national money.

The committee deems it necessary that the French duties on American goods should be adapted to the same régime as is imposed on French exports to the United States. The committee urges that the government make immediate representations to the President of the United States to obtain such decreases in the American tariffs as may be necessary for the maintenance of French exports.

In the event this intervention fails to yield results, the tariff committee would insist upon the suppression of the clause according most-favored-nation treatment to the United States, believing it illogical to accord beneficial treatment to that country without obtaining any compensation through reciprocal concessions such as are accorded by other nations.

Stand Causes a Stir.

This pronouncement by the tariff committee produced a considerable stir in the Chamber today. It was regarded, however, with general approval. Even those Frenchmen who are most anxious for a continuance of friendly relations with the United States are unwilling to accept any longer a situation in which, they say, the United States lays claim to every commercial advantage and accords none.

All the countries with which France deals, it was pointed out, accord in exchange for most-favored-nation treatment certain specific advantages to certain French products. The recent commercial treaty with Germany was cited, and it was pointed out that immediately on the signing of this treaty the United States demanded equal privileges with Germany.

It is not expected that the United States will depart from its traditional tariff policy, but the recommendation of the tariff committee to the French Government that the highest instead of the lowest scale of French tariffs be imposed on American goods if no concessions are obtained is likely to have almost unanimous support. The legal position, however, will have to be examined by the government, which is expected to act with due deliberation. Undoubtedly, however, official representations to President Hoover will be made within the next few days.

Criticize Embassy Statement.

The Paris press today devotes its attention to the American Embassy's defense of the new law. While the figures in the embassy statement are not challenged, the statement itself is criticized in some quarters for

Continued on Page Seven.

New Manhattan Phone Books Include 285,000 Changes

Delivery of 1,715,000 copies, or about 350 truckloads, of the Summer issue of the Manhattan telephone directory is under way, and 750,000 copies will be in the hands of Manhattan subscribers by tomorrow, the New York Telephone Company announced yesterday.

The new directory contains more than 285,000 changes in names, addresses and telephone numbers. The book comprises approximately 460,000 listings, and includes three new exchanges: Andrews for a part of the financial district, Tompkins Square in the Fourteenth Street district and Tillinghast for a part of Harlem.

BANK RATE TO 2½%; STOCKS RISE AGAIN

New York Reserve Makes Rediscount Charge Lowest in System's History.

MARKET UP 3 TO 15 POINTS

Reactionary Influences Shaken Off After Steady Decline of Three Weeks.

The lowest rediscount rate in the history of the Federal Reserve System was established yesterday by the Federal Reserve Bank of New York when the directors voted to reduce the charge for member bank borrowings to 2½ per cent.

The announcement of the new rate was not made until after the close of the stock market, but in the meantime stocks had made a broad and vigorous rally, shaking off reactionary influences after an uninterrupted decline of three weeks. Stocks that had declined daily from 3 to 15 points went up suddenly, canceling all losses recorded in Wednesday's sweeping break, with a small margin to spare. The market's abrupt about-turn was ascribed in Wall Street, in the absence of a better explanation, to internal technical conditions. Brokers' loans decreased $211,000,000 in the last week, yesterday's report disclosed.

The new rediscount rate, which will go into effect this morning, will replace a charge of 3 per cent established on May 1 when the Bank of England and the Bank of France lowered their rates to 2 per cent and 2½ per cent respectively. The local Reserve Bank now shares with the Bank of France the distinction of having the lowest discount rate in the world. It is a distinction that banks expect to be short-lived, however, for further reductions in rates of leading European central banks are regarded as certain to follow yesterday's action here.

The cut took Wall Street by surprise. Such an action had been discussed a few weeks ago, when open market rates for bankers' bills dropped below 2½ per cent. As the reduction was not made then it was assumed that the banking authorities did not intend to send the rate below the previous low mark.

In the meantime, bill rates had fallen to an asking price of 2⅛ per cent. Following the announcement of the bank rate reduction a further slash was made effective in bill rates, making the open market quotations 2⅛ per cent bid, 2 per cent asked, for all maturities up to 90 days; 2¼ bid, 2⅛ asked for four months' bills, and 2⅜ bid, 2¼ asked for five and six months' paper.

Bill Rates Lowest in Six Years.

These rates are the lowest in six years and offer American business the opportunity to finance its projects at a cost that has been available only at rare intervals.

The reduction of the rediscount rate in New York to 2½ per cent, as in the five previous reductions that carried down the charge from 6 per cent last Fall, was primarily to stimulate business and the bond market, in the understanding of the financial community. But leading bankers said the depressed state of business was already sufficiently well known and had been rather overemphasized than minimized lately. The cut, they said, was amply justified by open market rates for credit and should ultimately have a salutary effect in stimulating trade.

Bankers have for some time held that a strong bond market was the first prerequisite of business improvement. Cheap money, they contend, offers the most powerful stimulant to the bond market available. The New York Reserve Bank's action gives assurance, it is said, that the low price of credit is to continue. Banks, faced with the difficulty of profitably employing their funds elsewhere, must ultimately turn to the bond market for an outlet.

The action was, in a measure, foreshadowed by a reduction from 2¼ to 2⅛ per cent in the rate at which the local Reserve Bank would purchase bankers' acceptances, announced earlier in the week.

One early result of the reduction

Continued on Page Nineteen.

BROOKLYN MAN SHOT IN AUTO AS POLICE HUNT QUEENS SLAYER

Insurance Man Badly Wounded by "Wild-Eyed" Assailant at His Carroll Street Home.

GUNMAN ELUDES SEARCHERS

New Note in Killings, in Writing of Supposed Murderer, Lists Seven for Death.

KILLING RUMOR STIRS BRONX

But Search There Reveals No Body—Several Suspects Freed, Asylum Clues Fail.

While the police were searching Queens and Nassau Counties last night for the mysterious slayer of two men, Morris Horwitz, 50 years old, an insurance man, was shot and seriously wounded by "a wild-eyed, crazy-looking man," as he sat in his sedan in front of his home at 1,287 Carroll Street, Brooklyn, at 10:30 o'clock last night, talking to his wife, who was seated on the porch.

The gunman escaped on the run, disappearing into an automobile driveway between Brooklyn Avenue and Kingston Avenue. Although a strong police guard was thrown around the district, efforts by armed searchers with powerful flashlights failed to discover him.

Horwitz was taken to the Crown Heights Hospital, Lefferts and Brooklyn Avenues, suffering from a gash in the forehead, inflicted by the gunman with the butt of his pistol, and from a bullet which entered his shoulder, penetrated a lung and lodged in his abdomen.

Able to Give Description.

During an interval of consciousness at the hospital Horwitz, who is president of the Municipal Underwriters, Inc., an insurance firm at 26 Court Street, Brooklyn, and also has an insurance office of his own at 186 Joralemon Street, Brooklyn, gave Detectives Edward McNamee and William Riley of the Empire Boulevard station a description of his assailant. He said the man was about [illegible] feet 4 inches tall, weighed about [illegible]30 pounds, wore a dark suit but no hat, had blond hair and was "wild-eyed, as if he were crazy."

Horwitz was leaning out of the right front seat window of his machine, chatting with his wife, Rose, when the man approached. Without warning, he flourished a pistol, and said, "Move over to the steering wheel and start the car and keep going. If you don't, I'll shoot you."

The thug then entered the car and took a front seat beside Mr. Horwitz. Apparently dissatisfied at the slow actions of the insurance man, the stranger struck him on the forehead, then placed the barrel of the pistol against his victim's shoulder and fired.

Second Shot Goes Wild.

While Mrs. Horwitz screamed, the man fled, firing a second shot, which went wild. He ran east on Carroll Street to Brooklyn Avenue, turned north and ran half a block to one of the dark alleys leading to the garages in the rear yards of the neighboring houses and disappeared.

Two acquaintances of the wounded man, Al Zalb, a real estate man, and his brother, Leon, a glassware salesman, both of 377 Montgomery Street, approached in their car as the gunman fired his second shot.

They pursued on foot, but lost the trail at the alley entrance. Then they ran back to the wounded man and rushed him to the hospital.

Horwitz's son, George, 10 years old, was asleep in his bedroom on an upper floor of the three-story house in which they live. A son, Benjamin, 25 years old, a lawyer, and a daughter, Ruth, 14 years old, were away from home at the time of the shooting.

Late last night, while the police were still searching the neighborhood, officials said they had not found any clues to connect the gunman with the supposed madman who is being sought in Queens and Nassau Counties as the slayer of two men in somewhat similar circumstances.

A police alarm brought Deputy Chief Inspector Vincent J. Sweeney, in charge of the Brooklyn detective division, and a score of detectives as well as uniformed policemen and the police emergency squad, from the Empire Boulevard station.

The police sought to get into communication with the wounded man's business partner, Benjamin Herman, to see if he could give any information on whether or not Horwitz had any enemies. They did not know Herman's home address but obtained his telephone number. They were unable, however, to reach him.

New Murder Note Received.

Another letter containing a cabalistic list of seven persons marked for death, in the handwriting of the man who says he murdered two men

Continued on Page Eight.

Lindbergh Congratulates Byrd By Phone, Meets Him Monday

While Rear Admiral Byrd was telling the story of the expedition in an interview with newspaper men at the Biltmore yesterday afternoon an aide whispered to him: "Colonel Lindbergh is on the wire."

Admiral Byrd went to an adjoining room to talk to the flier. It was announced later that Colonel Lindbergh had congratulated Admiral Byrd on the success of his expedition and his scientific achievements. He made an appointment for a private meeting at the Biltmore at 11 o'clock Monday morning.

SAYS G. O. P. GAVE FUNDS CANNON USED

Caraway Tells Senate He Thinks That Jameson Passed on the National Committee's Money.

DEFENDS BISHOP'S RELEASE

Reports of Concessions "Lies," He Declares—Presentation of Report Closes Incident.

Special to the New York Times.

WASHINGTON, June 19.—Chairman Caraway of the lobby committee, in presenting to the Senate today a committee resolution on the case of Bishop James Cannon Jr., said that he thought that when E. C. Jameson, New York insurance man, gave to the Church leader $65,300 to fight the Presidential candidacy of Alfred E. Smith in Virginia, and an almost equal sum to other organizations, "he was passing out the money of the National Republican Committee."

"I may be mistaken," Senator Caraway said, but he emphasized his belief.

The Senator denied any special concessions had been given to Bishop Cannon, who was relieved from testifying about his financial and political affairs when he protested they were no concern of the committee and refused to answer questions. Such reports, the Senator declared, were "lies," adding that "there have been more assertions made that arose from utter ignorance of what did not occur or were prompted by malicious lying than about any other incident I know of."

"It is intimated," said the Senator, "and I am not defending it, or making the charge; I say that it was made in insinuation, at least on the floor of the House, that Bishop Cannon misappropriated the funds. That may be true, but we are not a grand jury. We uncovered several things that we did not pursue."

The reference of the intimations was to a recent speech of Representative Tinkham, who, on the floor of the House, attacked Bishop Cannon.

Walsh's Stand Is Set Forth.

The resolution as adopted at an executive session of the five lobby committee members, was reported as follows:

> Resolved, that it is the sense of the committee that it should not insist upon answers to questions propounded to Bishop James Cannon Jr. Senator Walsh of Montana dissents to this order only because of doubt raised as to the authority of the committee under the resolution pursuant to which it is acting.

Accompanying this resolution was the transcript of the Bishop's testimony, including the questions he declined to answer.

Presentation of the report was believed at the Capitol to have officially closed the incident. Vice President Curtis told newspaper men that he did not intend to present the case to the District Attorney for possible contempt action, adding that if Senator Blaine of Wisconsin, carries out

Continued on Page Seventeen.

50,000 AT CITY HALL FETE

Mayor Lauds Explorer as a Humanitarian and Leader of Men.

N. Y. U. DEGREE CONFERRED

Admiral Dons Cap and Gown—Dr. Brown Cites Him as Poet, Scientist, Man of Learning.

LEADER VOICES GRATITUDE

Acknowledges Roar of Throng as Family Looks On—Salutes Richmond Blues Battalion.

As an old hero whom New York takes repeated pleasure in welcoming because his charm and exploits remain forever new, Rear Admiral Richard E. Byrd was greeted by Mayor Walker at City Hall yesterday in what was the climax of the city's reception program.

About 10,000 persons in the grandstands and in and about City Hall, with another 40,000 in the immediate vicinity, joined in this tribute to the explorer. The platform from which the Mayor extended the welcome in behalf of the people of the city was crowded with distinguished guests, while the entire scene was one of bright color, joyous music and warm sentiment, marked repeatedly by tumultuous applause of the spectators and their cheers.

Paying due regard to Admiral Byrd's scientific achievements, it was as a humanitarian, as a great leader of men, as an inspiring example to the youth of the land that the Mayor welcomed the explorer and bestowed the city's medal of merit.

Standing calm and erect before the crowd in his immaculate white uniform, with his face tanned from his sojourn in the Canal Zone en route from the Antarctic, Admiral Byrd heard himself extolled by the Mayor as the man who had brought the North and South Poles together and as one who, by his courage, devotion to his calling and determination to grasp the secrets of the universe, had added glory to his country and enhanced the scope of human knowledge.

Mother and Wife Present.

Proudest of all in the audience which witnessed this eulogy were Mrs. Eleanor Bolling Byrd, the Admiral's mother, and his wife, who, each carrying a bouquet of flowers, stood with faces glowing a short distance from the spot at which the Mayor spoke.

No less proud was a group of Virginians headed by Governor Pollard, who had come to New York to participate in the welcome. They, too, occupied places close to the Mayor.

The first to greet Admiral Byrd on his arrival at City Hall, however, was his son, Richard E. Byrd Jr., and his daughters, Evelyn Bolling Byrd and Katherine Byrd. They were among the early arrivals and were taken to the Mayor's reception room to await the arrival of their father. Here they met the children of Joseph V. McKee, President of the Board of Aldermen, who with Mrs. McKee, were among the guests on the reviewing stand.

With "sincere and very deep gratitude" Admiral Byrd accepted the

Continued on Page Two.

Times Wide World Photo.
HOME AGAIN AFTER NEW CONQUESTS.
Rear Admiral Byrd Saluting New York From the Deck of the Macom.

BYRD IS PROUDEST OF ADVANCING FLAG

In Summing Up Achievements He Puts First the Claiming of Vast New Land.

TELLS SCIENTIFIC FINDINGS

Reveals That 12 of His Men Offered to Stay in Antarctic to Found Weather Station.

As objectively as an outsider, Rear Admiral Richard E. Byrd summed up yesterday the accomplishments and scientific discoveries of the expedition into Antarctica.

The outstanding achievements, to his mind, were the claiming of new land and mountain ranges of more than 125,000 square miles for the United States, and the discovery of carbonaceous material in the Queen Maud Mountains, including the probability of vast deposits of coal and possibly metals. He admitted, however, that these have no immediate value.

Aboard the City of New York, as he discussed the expedition informally while waiting until it was time to dress for the reception committee, the Admiral seemed, at first glance, the same [illegible] and youthful figure. Closer inspection, however, belies the youthful appearance. There are lines of responsibility and worry in the returning Admiral's face today and threads of gray in the dark hair.

On the way up the bay, all informality was gone and he was the naval officer in crisp white uniform taking command of that monstrosity, a mass interview. Again in the afternoon at the Biltmore he submitted to the questioning of newspaper men, and again took command of the interview, steering into the channels he desired.

"A Matter of Providence."

It was the accomplishments of his associates about which he told, and it was the safe return of every man of which he was "glad above all else." Here, too, he declined the honors and said it was "a matter of Providence," although it was "surprising the number of dangerous situations which passed without mishap." This was his story:

"In the field of geology we investigated one of the most important points, geologically speaking, left in the world, the Queen Maud Mountains, about 300 miles from the South Pole. We sent out a dog sled party under Dr. [Lawrence] Gould. They discovered carbonaceous material at 5,000 feet and other material which proved that Antarctica was once tropical or semi-tropical. We investigated the newly discovered Rockefeller Mountains and found them to be granite and some of the oldest in the world.

"In meteorology two men from the United States Weather Bureau, [William C.] Haines and [Henry T.] Harrison, took thousands of observations at temperatures of 60 and 70 below zero. These balloon runs continued all Winter. These are important because this climate affects the

Continued on Page Three.

5 MILES OF CROWDS CHEER EXPLORERS

Half Million Along Parade Route Send Up Din That Dazes Antarctic Veterans.

30,000 MASS AT BATTERY

Many Perch on Ledges of Office Windows—Elevated Station Used as Grandstand.

It was from the packed and sizzling sidewalks of New York that Admiral Byrd and his companions received the ovation yesterday which told them better than could the speeches of the dignitaries of the admiration of the city for their accomplishments and its joy at their safe return.

The acclaim poured out spontaneously from the throats of more than a half-million persons who lined the five-mile route over which they passed through the city. It had been matched only by the welcome to Colonel Lindbergh three years ago on his triumphant return from Paris.

Yesterday's reception was one in which all New York took part. Those who gave it ranged from the Mayor and other high officials to prisoners in the Tombs, who waved and shouted through the barred windows as Byrd sped by, and were rewarded with a cheery wave of the explorer's hand in return.

30,000 at the Battery.

Hours before the landing of Admiral Byrd and his companions the people of the city were getting ready to greet him. Long before noon the crowds were trooping to the Battery for a first glimpse of the polar heroes until some 30,000 finally had gathered there and in the streets leading to it.

The seawall was fringed with a dense mass and the windows and ledges of buildings looking down on the scene, from the Whitehall Building to the custom house, gradually became packed. The crowds had begun coming while the leaden sky showed a threat of rain, and they were still standing patiently when the clouds had melted and the sun was beating down.

The booming of a thirteen-gun salute on Governors Island was the signal which turned the reception from formality to an enthusiastic torrent of public acclaim. The eyes of the thousands along the Battery wall turned in the direction of the Statue of Liberty, and the first ticker-tape floated down from the Whitehall Building.

It was exactly 11:30 A. M. when the salute was fired. In front of the Whitehall Building waited 300 Boy Scouts in their khaki uniforms. They represented all boroughs of the city and five States, and were accompanied by a crack bugle and drum corps from Erie, Pa., home city of Scout Paul Siple, a member of the Byrd Expedition.

Vendors of peanuts and candy, flags, pictures of Rear Admiral Byrd, books describing his career and cigarette cases bearing his likeness,

Continued on Page Three.

HARBOR SHRIEKS WELCOME

Los Angeles Gleams in Sky as Craft Cluster About Polar Ships.

PAPER BLIZZARD LET LOOSE

Crowds Pack Route to City Hall—Admiral Shares Honors With His Aides.

BUSINESS MEN HAIL HIM

He Is Guest at Two Functions—Party to Be Received by Hoover Today.

A page of pictures of Rear Admiral Byrd's homecoming will be found on Page 5.

Rear Admiral Richard E. Byrd came home from the end of the earth yesterday and New York cheered him and honored him and took him to its heart as an old friend returning from new adventures and new conquests.

It was a homecoming that would have quickened the pulse of a Nelson or a Farragut, but he insisted on sharing it with the sunbronzed men who had braved the bleak silences of Antarctica with him while he was preparing for his flight to the South Pole and back.

Nearly two years he had been gone, but New York had not forgotten him. The city's millions remembered the day he rode up Broadway, hailed as the conqueror of the North Pole. They remembered his gallant transatlantic flight, which came so near a tragic end, and they lifted up their voices as they have for no man since Colonel Charles A. Lindbergh captured their imagination by his solo flight from Roosevelt Field to Paris three years ago.

In the wild cacophony of the welcome they accorded Admiral Byrd and his gallant band were blended joy at his return with every member of his expedition safe and well, admiration for his achievement, honor and respect, and, no doubt among the boys that lined his path, more than a little hero worship.

Glorious as was New York's attempt to erase the memory of the long, dreary days and nights in the limitless land of ice 17,000 miles away, it left Admiral Byrd and his followers tired out at the end of the day.

The Byrd party left the Pennsylvania Station on a special train at 2 o'clock this morning for Washington, where they will be received at the White House as the nation's heroes.

Whole Nation Hears Welcome.

Radio carried the speeches of Mayor Walker, Grover A. Whalen and other official greeters to all the country and to foreign lands as well in the greatest hook-up ever arranged for a returning hero's reception. It carried, too, the throaty voice of the city's "Hello," but it could not convey the color and the motion of the pageant on the water, in the air and on the sidewalks of New York.

For the crowds that hailed him Admiral Byrd had a message. He had claimed for his country and theirs, he said, unexplored lands east of the British possessions in Antarctica, rich in carboniferous deposits, indicative of "enormous quantities of coal." He had added 125,000 square miles to the map of the world and added considerably, with the help of the experts with him, to the total of the world's knowledge of biological, geological and meteorological conditions at the bottom of the earth.

From the moment he stepped off the deck of his flagship, the three-masted bark City of New York, to the deck of the city's welcoming tug Macom at Quarantine amid a deafening din of sirens and steam whistles of seventy-odd craft until the day was done, Admiral Byrd was swept along at the will of the crowd with his fellow-explorers excepting one. One man, too modest to face the crowd, remained on the ice-battered old veteran of the Antarctic and smilingly waved adieu as the Macom pulled away. He was George Black, supply officer of the expedition.

Reunions Forced to Wait.

For the rest, separated from their kinsfolk for many long months, reunions had to wait, although some there were aboard who were anxious to see for the first time children born since they started on their

Kingsford-Smith Plans to Refuel in the Air, Allowing Flight Here Against Strong Winds

Wireless to THE NEW YORK TIMES.

BALDONNEL AIRDROME, DUBLIN, June 19.—In order to avoid a possible fuel shortage on his westward transatlantic flight, which was again delayed today by strong westerly winds, Major Charles Kingsford-Smith intends refueling in the air off the American coast, if the necessary preparations are completed in time.

"I had provided for a start only when the adverse winds over the Atlantic averaged less than fifteen miles an hour," said Major Kingsford-Smith. "With any greater wind I should not have enough fuel to reach my destination. By refueling in the air, however, I could start against a headwind averaging as much as twenty miles an hour. Assuming we have to meet such conditions, the petrol would last to within a few hundred miles of Maine, then we could take on more fuel in the air."

To carry out the refueling operation the wireless operator will be provided with a hammer and chisel to punch a hole in the top of the main tank for the insertion of a fuel line.

"My great hope is that preparations can be made in America in time to permit refueling in the air," said the Major, "because in that case the chance of getting away without further delay will be enormously improved."

Officers of the Irish Free State Air Force learned with interest today of the report that former Squadron Leader Wynne-Eyton is contemplating using Baldonnel as the starting point for a solo flight across the Atlantic in a "Puss" Moth plane, but nothing more is known here beyond the indirect news from London.

Representatives here of the Fokker Company, builders of the Southern Cross, and other American representatives of Major Kingsford-Smith, said yesterday that no arrangements for refueling over the ocean had been made. The difficulties of such a plan were pointed out, and pilots here said that, though not impossible, it lacked all probabilities of success.

"It is hard enough to make the contacts over an airport, to say nothing of finding a plane moving at 80 or 100 miles an hour over the open ocean," one pilot said.

"All the News That's Fit to Print."

The New York Times.

THE WEATHER.
Fair, slightly warmer Thursday; Friday, fair, warmer; moderate winds, becoming south.
For full weather report see Page 22.

VOL. LXXIX....No. 26,347. **** NEW YORK, FRIDAY, MARCH 14, 1930. TWO CENTS In Greater New York | THREE CENTS Within 200 Miles | FOUR CENTS Elsewhere Except 7th and 8th Postal Zones

NINTH PLANET DISCOVERED ON EDGE OF SOLAR SYSTEM; FIRST FOUND IN 84 YEARS

LIES FAR BEYOND NEPTUNE

Sighted Jan. 21 After 25 Years' Search Begun by Late Percival Lowell.

SEEN AT FLAGSTAFF, ARIZ.

Observatory Staff There Spots It by Special Photo-Telescope —Makes Thorough Check.

ASTRONOMERS HAIL FINDING

The Sphere, Possibly Larger Than Jupiter and 4,000,000,000 Miles Away, Meets Predictions.

By The Associated Press.

FLAGSTAFF, Ariz., March 13.—In the little cluster of orbs which scamper across the sidereal abyss under the name of the solar system there are, be it known, nine instead of a mere eight, worlds.

The presence of a ninth planet in the retinue of the sun, long suspected, was definitely announced here today by Dr. V. M. Slipher of the Lowell Observatory, who headed a group of eminent astronomers whose groupings in the Milky Way with telescopes and cameras located the new-found sphere.

Way out beyond Neptune, tagging bashfully behind its brothers, the new planet's exact whereabouts, size and age are still unknown and it has not even a name.

Its presence was mathematically predicted years ago by the late Dr. Percival Lowell, noted scientist, who founded the observatory here, partly for the very purpose of identifying it. Other astronomers, notably Dr. W. W. Campbell, director of Lick Observatory, verified Dr. Lowell's calculations.

Reward of Long Search.

Today the faith in those calculations was rewarded by an announcement by Dr. Slipher that the new planet had been "sighted" Jan. 21 by an extremely delicate photographic lens developed for the search. Announcement was withheld, Dr. Slipher said, "until we were absolutely sure."

The discovery revealed that the planet is forty-five times as far from the earth as the earth is from the sun. Although its size has not been definitely determined, it is believed it may be bigger than Jupiter, largest member of the solar family, which is 1,200 times larger than the earth; and, said the announcement, it is at least no smaller than the earth. Astronomically the discovery is regarded as the greatest since the location of Neptune, eighth member of the solar system, in 1846.

The astronomers who participated in the discovery are C. O. Lampland, E. C. Slipher, J. C. Duncan, K. P. Williams, E. A. Edwards and T. B. Gill.

Until some one entitled to do so gives the sphere a name, it is to be known as "the trans-Neptunian planet."

First notice of the body was made by C. W. Tombaugh, photographer at the observatory, who saw a tiny spot on one of his plates. With this revelation, investigations were intensified and the scientists soon determined they had come upon the long-sought planet.

Announcement of Discovery.

Announcement in connection with the discovery was made at the observatory as follows:

"The announcement is made by the Lowell Observatory at Flagstaff of the discovery of a celestial body whose rate and path among the stars indicates a new planetary member of the solar family beyond the outermost known planet, Neptune.

"Twenty-five years ago Dr. Percival Lowell, who founded Lowell Observatory, began a mathematical investigation for a planet beyond Neptune. The probability of locating such a body, however, was difficult and involved enormous and intricate computations.

"In 1914 he announced as the result of his calculations the possibility and distance of the predicted body in a large memoir, a Lowell Observatory publication.

"The search of the skies directed by Dr. Lowell's theoretical work was begun by photography in 1905 and has been continued to the present time. The use was made of the best available instruments, the search

Continued on Page Fourteen.

New Planet Compared With Earth and Neptune

Size:
Earth—8,000 miles in diameter.
Neptune—32,000.
New Planet—8,000 or more.

Distance from Sun:
Earth—One astronomical unit.
Neptune—Thirty astronomical units.
New Planet—About fifty units.

Speed of Revolution:
Earth—19 miles a second.
Neptune—3½ miles a second.
New Planet—From 1 to 2 miles a second.

Time of Revolution:
Earth—One year
Neptune—146 Earth-years (entire revolution not yet observed).
New Planet—Probably 300 to 600 years.

Note—These figures on the new planet are tentative, based upon computations of astronomers here on the Flagstaff announcement.

M'DONALD RALLIES NAVAL CONFERENCE

Prime Minister Devotes Whole Day to Talks With Heads of All the Delegations.

BRIAND DECIDES TO REMAIN

French Leader Says He Will Cooperate to Bring About Successful Conclusion.

By EDWIN L. JAMES.
Special Cable to THE NEW YORK TIMES.

LONDON, March 13.—After yesterday's relapse, the naval conference had a slight rally today when faced by the danger of the failure of the whole proceedings, and Prime Minister MacDonald, heartened by his victory over the Tory motion for a vote of censure, canceled all formal meetings and devoted himself to a supreme effort to save the negotiations. One after another he conferred with the heads of all the delegations, and tonight it was stated officially that the efforts of the Prime Minister, with whom Secretary Stimson was cooperating, were being turned upon the Italians to try to bring them to a position the French would accept.

Foreign Minister Briand, at the solicitation of both Mr. MacDonald and Mr. Stimson, withheld his statement intended to show why France thought the conference should adjourn, and now M. Briand, who last night was talking about going home, assures every one that in a full spirit of cooperation he will remain so long as necessary to bring the conference to a successful conclusion.

Credit for the new lease on life for the conference must go to Mr. MacDonald, who apparently realized last night that unless something strenuous were done the conference might as well be called off. After a consultation between M. Briand and Mr. Stimson this morning, Mr. MacDonald saw both the head of the American delegation and the head of the French delegation and then after talking to the chief of the Japanese asked Foreign Minister Grandi of Italy to come to see him at the House of Commons. It is said that this meeting, coupled with the Stimson interview with Signor Grandi, caused the Italian Foreign Minister to wire a résumé of the situation to Premier Mussolini in Rome.

Before the French flat refusal to accept parity with Italy, it is understood that with the French agreeing Mr. MacDonald suggested to the Ital-

Continued on Page Four.

PROHIBITION HAILED BY STAGG AS CHECK ON POST-WAR YOUTH

Chicago Athletic Director Is Chief Dry Witness in Session Ending in Committee Row.

DRY MEMBER ASSAILS WET

Celler Is Accused of "Insulting" Mrs. Peabody by Charging She Prompted Speakers.

ADJOURN FOR COOLING OFF

Sherwood Came Under Fire by Attacking Anti-Dry Leaders as "Fanatics."

Special to The New York Times.

WASHINGTON, March 13.—Amos Alonzo Stagg, veteran director of athletics at the University of Chicago, testified before the House Judiciary Committee today to the improved status of the nation's youth under national prohibition.

Mr. Stagg, who headed the list of dry witnesses at today's hearing on the various modification bills, said to the committee:

"In my judgment, since prohibition has been put into effect, hundreds of thousands more children have had a fairer start in life than existed in pre-prohibition days. With the breakdown of the home life and with all the complexities of new opportunities for being misled, I tremble to think what this revolt of youth might have led to were prohibition not in operation."

Mr. Stagg's testimony was a feature of the day's session, which ended in an acrimonious exchange between members of the committee over a charge that Mrs. Henry W. Peabody, who organized the testimony of twenty-two women yesterday, had coached her witnesses. The charge, made by Representative Cellar of New York, stirred up such a heated dispute that Representative Graham, the chairman, finally adjourned the hearing to let his colleagues "cool off."

Mr. Stagg in his evidence contrasted his own early environment with that of the boys and girls of today. In the old days, he said, saloons were a substitute for most of the common diversions of today. Now, he added, a drunken man is seen "only occasionally."

Mr. Stagg denied that drinking was a serious problem in the great Middle Western universities, and added:

"I happen to know that 30,000 or more of us coaches are preaching and practising total abstinence."

Following his testimony, Coach Stagg was complimented by Representative La Guardia, who said:

"Yours is the most sincere, most telling statement I've heard on your side of the case."

Sherwood Calls Wets Fanatics.

Coach Stagg's testimony followed that of Carlton M. Sherwood, executive secretary of the Citizens' Committee of One Thousand for Law Observance, which includes prominent persons throughout the country.

Mr. Sherwood opened with the statement that "the wets have become the fanatics," and devoted much of it to reading telegrams from professional and business men replying to testimony given for the wets by Grayson M.-P. Murphy of New York that he knew no bankers or business men who do not drink.

During cross-examination of this witness, the wets made a determined effort to show that Mr. Sherwood could not speak authoritatively for the committee, inasmuch as some of its members are known to favor modification of the existing laws.

Charles M. Hay, a lawyer of St. Louis, who was defeated for Senator

Continued on Page Three.

Union League Club Votes Wet, 1,196 to 109; 70 Per Cent Call for Repeal of the Dry Law

The Union League Club, the oldest and most conservative Republican organization in the city, has voted wet by a little more than 90 per cent. This was made known last night at a meeting of the club, when the result of a questionnaire among its members was reported. There are approximately 1,800 members in the club and 1,324 replies were received. Of these, 932, or 70 per cent, favored repeal of the Eighteenth Amendment; 264, or 20 per cent, favored modification of the Volstead act; 109, or 8½ per cent, were opposed to repeal of the amendment, and 19, or about 1½ per cent, were non-committal. This gave a total of 1,196 on the wet side, as against 109 favoring prohibition in its present form.

Announcement of the result was made to the press by Alfred E. Marling, president of the club, and Linson L. Lewis, secretary. The questionnaire was initiated by the club's committee on public affairs on motion of George B. Wightman and was sent out by Mr. Lewis. The revelation of anti-prohibition sentiment among its members followed expression of similar sentiment in the National Republican Club and in the New York Young Republican Club's reorganization committee.

The Young Republican Club, the committee of which recently declared for State control of the liquor traffic, will send out a questionnaire to its 2,500 members, it was announced yesterday. The club is expected to act on its committee's report next Thursday.

The questionnaire follows:

1. Do you favor the continuance and strict enforcement of the Eighteenth Amendment?
2. Do you favor a modification of the Volstead law to permit light wines and beer?
3. Do you favor the repeal of the prohibition amendment?
4. Do you favor the Republican party going on record in its platform as favoring repeal of the Eighteenth Amendment?
5. Do you favor governmental control of liquor along the lines of the Quebec plan?
6. Do you use intoxicating liquor?

GRUNDY GROUP ROUTS COALITION IN SENATE

Industrial Combination Holds to Tariff on Sugar and Cement by 2 Votes of 47 to 38.

PENNSYLVANIAN ASSAILED

Grundy Is Called a "Collector of Revenue to Elect Republicans, up to White House."

Special to The New York Times.

WASHINGTON, March 13.—The new Senate combination, chiefly representing industrial States, which marked its grasp of power in tariff making by increasing the duty on sugar and cement was able today to rout the coalition of insurgent Republicans and Democrats, when, by decisive votes, the Senate refused to reconsider its action on these commodities. Both motions to reconsider were offered by Senator Nye, of North Dakota, and were rejected in each instance by a vote of 47 to 38.

This action leaves a duty of $2 a hundred pounds on Cuban sugar and $2.50 on world output as against the present duties of $1.76 and $2.20, respectively. Cement retains a duty of 6 cents a hundred pounds, whereas under the present tariff law it is on the free list.

Coalition leaders now think the Old Guard, led by Senator Grundy and supported by the sugar, lumber and oil interests, is in control of the tariff bill now approaching final consideration after the hardest fight in two decades.

Senators Watson and McNary conferred with President Hoover today, telling him that the Senate would dispose of the pending bill in another week and that four weeks would be consumed by the conference committee. They said that the bill should become a law by the end of April. Adjournment can be taken by the middle of June, these leaders told the President. The Senate has still to act upon Muscle Shoals, the transfer of prohibition enforcement to the Department of Justice and the annual supply bills.

The coalitionists entered today's contest confident of winning enough votes to obtain reconsideration and reduced rates. The triumph of the new combination left them without hope of carrying out their program of limited tariff revision with farm rates, but on a parity with industrial protection. While there is some disposition among the insurgent Senators to vote against the bill because of the heavy sugar and cement duties, the Old Guard say that they cannot retrace their steps and reject the results of their efforts to raise farm products rates to the highest in history. The bill, when passed by the Senate, will probably set some of the highest rates ever had by industry and put a tariff wall around farm products.

Grundy Denounced as "Collector."

Senator George, of Georgia, while discussing late today a motion to make the wool duty applicable to an article containing 15 per cent of wool, denounced Senator Grundy and the alliance between the worsted and wool manufacturers. He asserted that Senator Grundy collected the revenues to elect those from the low even up to the White House. Senator Grundy sat silent during this arraignment.

After the defeat on sugar, Senator Harrison, of Mississippi, in a sharp half-hour speech chastised members of his party and especially Senator Thomas, of Oklahoma, for not remaining loyal to the principle. Senator Thomas defended his attitude and said that he had been outvoted by the coalition when he offered a motion to limit tariff revision to the Borah resolution, which confined it to farm products.

In his speech Senator Harrison said:

"I have tried to adhere to certain principles in the consideration of the

Continued on Page Twelve.

MAYOR RUFFU SEIZED ON 14 GRAFT CHARGES

Atlantic City Executive, Freed in $28,000 Bail, Is Confident Trial Will Vindicate Him.

$313,000 INSURANCE CITED

Conway, Building Supervisor, Is Held on Five Extortion Counts —Gives $10,000 Bond.

Special to The New York Times.

ATLANTIC CITY, N. J., March 13.—Mayor Anthony M. Ruffu Jr. was arrested late this afternoon on fourteen indictments charging him with violating Section 32 of the Criminal Code by awarding insurance and other city contracts to companies in which he was financially interested.

He was later released on bail of $2,000 on each indictment or a total of $28,000, for pleading tomorrow.

The indictments were returned at Mays Landing early in the afternoon before the representatives of the Prosecutor's office had returned to this city with the indictments. Word had reached the Mayor and as soon as the weekly City Commission meeting was over he hurried to the office of Charles C. Babcock, his personal attorney, in the Guarantee Trust Building immediately below the offices of the County Prosecutor. With him were Joseph A. Perskie, City Solicitor, and Assistant City Solicitor Anthony J. Siracusa.

Bench Warrant Issued.

Upon receipt of information as to the grand jury's action, County Judge William H. Smathers issued a bench warrant for the Mayor's arrest, and a constable notified him in the office of Mr. Babcock.

With his counsel, the City Solicitors and City Commissioner Joseph A. Paxson, the Mayor went to the chamber of Judge Smathers, where he was formally notified of the indictments. Mr. Babcock moved for permission to allow the Mayor to furnish bail for himself. Judge Smathers replied that, as a matter of justice, he believed that the Mayor should furnish surety bonds.

The Mayor inquired if the court would accept Commissioner Paxson as bondsman, and Judge Smathers replied that if the Commissioner could qualify he would be acceptable. The bonds were signed and the Mayor released.

It was announced by Prosecutor Louis Repetto that the Mayor would be arraigned before Judge Smathers in Common Pleas Court at Mays Landing at 10 A. M. tomorrow.

The Prosecutor added that the trial would be held over until the May term of court, and that the $28,000 bail would be continued until that time.

$313,000 Policies Involved.

Of the fourteen indictments against Mayor Ruffu, ten were for his actions as "broker and agent" in the placing of insurance, two for the placing of insurance in companies in which he was a "stockholder," and the other two true bills for the placing of city insurance in companies in which he was both "stockholder and director."

The separate indictments in which he is charged with acting as "broker and agent" and the amounts involved are:

Atlantic City Fire Insurance Company	$5,000
Atlantic City Fire Insurance Company	4,600
Atlantic City Fire Insurance Company	5,000
Fidelity Insurance Company	6,300
Atlantic City Fire Insurance Company	10,000
Seaboard Fire Insurance Company	2,500
Fidelity Insurance Company	10,000
Atlantic City Fire Insurance and Seaboard Company	10,000
Seaboard Fire Insurance Company and Fidelity Insurance Company	7,500
Atlantic City Fire Insurance Company (three policies)	42,000

The two policies which Mayor Ruffu was indicted for placing in concerns in which he was a "stockholder" are:

Fidelity Insurance Company	$12,500
Fidelity Insurance Company	16,000

For placing insurance in the following companies, in which he is ac-

Continued on Page Nine.

'TRUSTY' KILLS GUARD, THEN DIES IN BREAK AT TRENTON PRISON

Fells Another Keeper With Lead Pipe, Takes Pistol and Shoots a Third.

FLEES TO CELL UNDER FIRE

Lifer Found Dead With Shot in Head After a Siege of Tear Gas Bombs.

POLICE ON WATCH OUTSIDE

But Other Prisoners Make No Move to Bolt—Colonel Stone Ends All 'Trusty' Privileges.

Special to The New York Times.

TRENTON, N. J., March 13.—Convict Charles F. Evans, 29 years old, a "trusty" in the New Jersey State Prison, where he was serving a life sentence for killing a Hoboken policeman in 1918, made a desperate bid for liberty tonight that cost his life after he had killed one prison guard and slightly wounded two others.

Evans's attempted jail-break caused brief but tense excitement throughout this city. Residents, upon hearing the wild shriek of the prison's siren and seeing police reserves and firemen mustering from all sections of the city to form a cordon around the prison, believed at first that a general prison riot had started. The excitement, while it lasted, was heightened when the crowd of from 4,000 to 5,000 spectators outside the prison walls heard the staccato of many pistols being fired and when their eyes smarted occasionally from exploding tear bombs. During the uproar, which lasted only a half hour, none of the 1,615 convicts in the prison made an attempt to escape.

The dead guard was Frank Butcher, who leaves a wife and two children.

The wounded guards are:

SOREN, THOMAS, lacerated scalp and possibly a fractured skull, as a result of a blow on the head by Evans with a blackjack; in St. Francis Hospital.

GORDON, ERNEST, superficial bullet wound in the shoulder; also in St. Francis Hospital.

Body Found in Cell.

Evans's body was found in an empty cell in the north section of the prison where the shooting took place. He had died of a bullet through the head, but whether he had committed suicide or had been shot by a guard was undertermined, pending an autopsy today by Dr. Charles H. Mitchell, Mercer County physician. Although first reports were that Evans had turned a pistol on himself, Dr. Mitchell late tonight expressed the opinion that the convict had been shot by a guard. Gordon told reporters that he had shot Evans.

Evans, whose home was in Springfield, Ill., was a desperado whose record included deserting from the navy in 1918, escaping from prison at Deer Island, Mass., and according to his own confession, he killed a Jersey City baker on Thanksgiving Day, 1918. He entered the prison here in January, 1919.

Tonight, as a result of Evans's futile and costly attempt to escape, Colonel Edward B. Stone, warden of the prison, announced that he would immediately withdraw all privileges from "trusties." An investigation was begun by William J. Ellis, State Commissioner of Institutions.

Evans was a cell runner as well as a "trusty" in the prison and had the freedom of the prison corridors. He was regarded as a model prisoner.

Shortly after 6 o'clock tonight Soren was making one of his regular inspection tours of No. 2 wing, in the southern part of the prison. His

Continued on Page Two.

VITALE REMOVED BY COURT OVER THE ROTHSTEIN LOAN; SCORED FOR INCOMPETENCE

CORRUPTION COUNT QUASHED

But Appellate Justices Find Magistrate Was Grossly Careless.

DECISION IS UNANIMOUS

Holds $19,940 Note Tended to Put Him in the Power of the Gambler.

VITALE SILENT, HURRIES OFF

No Proceeding for Disbarment Expected, as Court Does Not Mention It.

Albert H. Vitale was removed as a city magistrate yesterday by a unanimous decision of the Appellate Division of the Supreme Court. The verdict was returned by the court an hour after the magistrate's trial for judicial misconduct had ended.

The five justices found Vitale guilty on one of the two charges which the Bar Association made the basis of its petition for his removal. By unanimous opinion the justices dismissed the second charge leveled against the jurist. The ousting of Vitale marked the first time in thirty years that a magistrate has been unseated.

Mr. Vitale received the verdict without outward emotion. He refused to discuss the decision. Max D. Steuer, his attorney, likewise was silent, saying merely, when asked whether he would appeal, that he would not discuss that for the present.

The act that cost the magistrate his position was his acceptance of a loan of $19,940 from Arnold Rothstein, murdered gambler, which, when exposed during the Mayoralty campaign by Representative F. H. La Guardia, involved the magistracy in "a loathsome scandal." The count which was dismissed against Vitale for lack of evidence was his discharge of Charles Fawcett, a Rothstein henchman, after the prisoner had confessed his guilt to the arresting officer.

Incompetency Seen in Fawcett Case.

The opinion of the court, as read by Presiding Justice Victor J. Dowling, did not permit the magistrate to go scot-free on that case, however. The magistrate's handling of the matter, said the presiding justice, convicted him of "gross carelessness, inattention, ignorance and incompetency."

Although the court had power to disbar the former magistrate, as well as remove him, the opinion contained no suggestion of disbarment. It was understood that inasmuch as the Appellate Division had omitted this, the bar association committee would take no further steps in the matter.

The decision was announced at 12:15, exactly an hour after the presiding justice and his associates—Edward R. Finch, John F. McAvoy, James O'Malley and Francis Martin—had retired to formulate the opinion. An hour of summing up by both sides had preceded the retirement. Mr. Steuer had admitted that his client had been "indiscreet" in accepting the gambler's money, but he defended his conduct in the Fawcett proceedings. George Z. Medalie, prosecuting for the bar association, had denounced Vitale on both charges.

Presiding Justice Dowling in announcing the decision spoke as follows:

"At the outset, I desire to express the appreciation of the court for the courtesy and fairness with which this case has been conducted on both sides. It is a very important matter both to the respondent and the community. It has been approached by both sides in the proper spirit of responsibility, and the court has endeavored to cooperate as a matter of justice both as to the respondent and to the community in obtaining a speedy decision by this method, which, while it has involved a great deal of extra labor upon the court, has been cheerfully met and discharged in the public interest, and I thank all of the gentlemen involved for their conduct of the case.

Corruption Evidence Insufficient.

"Taking up the second charge, which is that of Fawcett, treating the charges in the order that they have been presented to the court by the proof, we unanimously find that in the Fawcett case the respondent was guilty of gross carelessness, inattention, ignorance and incompetency. We find, however, that there

4-Day New York-Paris Service By Ship and Plane to Be Tried

By The Associated Press.

HAVRE, March 13—Shortening the Atlantic steamer journey by a full day is to be tried by utilizing airplanes between here and Queenstown.

Late this Spring a test will be made from the Irish port here, with a twelve-passenger plane. From here the air trip could be continued to Le Bourget, making about five hours for a trip that usually takes a day and a half.

The object is to establish four-day service between New York and Paris, via Queenstown. Such a schedule, Queenstown port authorities believe, would encourage more boats to call there, so they are cooperating in establishing the air relay.

CRAIN AND THOMAS HIT AT MAGISTRATES

Prosecuter Says Half of Felony Cases Are Discharged and Asks a Special Court.

SEES EXTORTION BY 'FIXERS'

Socialist Leader Accuses 11 Jurists of Irregularities and Charges Tammany Influence.

The grand jury which in January began an investigation of bail bonding and other evils in the magistrate's courts of Manhattan ended the questioning of witnesses yesterday. It was announced that at 11 o'clock this morning the body would hand up a presentment of about 2,300 words to Judge Koenig in General Sessions.

It was reported that the presentment, which will be handed to the court by Joseph P. Day, the foreman, would contain suggestions for legislation and changes in the courts' regulations to bring about improvements in conditions surrounding the acceptance of bail bonds, the elimination of "steerers" for lawyers, so-called "fixers" pretending mysterious influence in the courts, and the breaking up of corrupt alliances between court attaches and hangers-on.

Thomas Gives Views.

Norman Thomas, Socialist party leader, was among the last eight witnesses questioned yesterday by the grand jury. Before entering the grand jury room Mr. Thomas issued a statement giving his views on the magistrates' courts. The statement asserted that a copy of the court calendar of Magistrate George W. Simpson, dated July 14, 1925, showed that the names of prominent Tammany leaders had been jotted down alongside cases scheduled for hearing on that date. The leaders' names, the statement declared, were in handwriting alleged to be that of Magistrate Simpson.

Among the names appearing on the calendar, Mr. Thomas said, are "Ahern" and "Hamill," each of which has been jotted down twice; "Jim Day," "Healey," "McCooey," "McManus" and "Farley." The name "Hamill," it is said, appears in one instance opposite a case involving Nicoasia Brothers, Inc., opposite which the name "Hirschfield" also appears. Mr. Thomas said that the name "Hamill" was for leniency or "fixing" the case, while the name

Continued on Page Two.

Society Must Sell Washington Irving House; Funds Lacking to Make It a Patriotic Centre

The National Patriotic Builders of America, organized by Mrs. William Cumming Story, honorary president general of the Daughters of the American Revolution, to buy the Washington Irving house at the southwest corner of Irving Place and Seventeenth Street as a centre of patriotic and good citizenship work, has been compelled to give it up for lack of financial support. This was disclosed yesterday when Supreme Court Justice Townley signed an order permitting the society to sell the house to Louis Sobel, a realty man, for $65,000, which includes the assumption of mortgages for $37,000.

The petition for permission to sell the property was signed by Mrs. Story, who said the society had bought the Irving home to preserve it in connection with "the encouragement of patriotism and American ideals in citizens and prospective citizens." She said that the organization has not been self-sustaining and that the members have been compelled to assume the financial burden.

"We have been endeavoring for some months to sell the property and this is the only offer we have received," said Mrs. Story. "If we do not sell there is danger of a mortgage foreclosure."

While the petition declared that the surplus after payment of the society's debts will be used to further its work elsewhere, Mrs. Story said last night that the debts would use all the money received. They are listed at $28,795, of which $13,500 is due Mrs. Story, who took a third mortgage as security.

"We expect to occupy the Irving house as our headquarters for some time yet, possibly for a year or so," said Mrs. Story, who explained that the contract of sale will give the society this right.

Announcement of the purchase of the Washington Irving house from Algernon S. Boll was made by the society in August, 1927. A drive for $250,000 to aid the society in carrying on its Americanization work in the quaint little house associated by tradition with the closing years of Irving's life was started in May, 1928, but was not successful.

Sergievsky Sets Record at 143.9 Miles an Hour In Seaplane With 'Pay Load' of 4,400 Pounds

Captain Boris Sergievsky, flying the Hornet-powered Sikorsky which ten days ago set a world's altitude mark for seaplanes carrying a two-ton load, yesterday brought another record back to the United States. Speeding at an average rate of 143.9 miles an hour, he drove his big twin-engined plane carrying a "pay load" of 4,409 pounds of metal twice over the 100-kilometer course between Execution Light off Port Washington, L. I., and Fairfield, Conn., once with the wind and then back again against the stiff breeze.

The former record was 130.1 miles an hour and was made by Richard Wagner of Germany two years ago with a Dornier Wal. The speed test took place in the morning, and in the afternoon Sergievsky took the same plane aloft for an attempt at the altitude record for seaplanes carrying a 1,000-kilogram load, or about 200 pounds more than a ton. His indicated altitude was well over the previous mark of 20,961 feet made in November, 1928, by Franz Kneer in Germany with a Junkers seaplane. Sergievsky's altimeter went out of commission at 12,000 feet, but the official instrument installed in the plane by Major Luke Christopher, secretary of the contest committee of the National Aeronautical Association, kept ticking along. The markings on this instrument indicated an altitude of well over 20,000 feet, but the exact height will not be known until the instrument has been calibrated at the Bureau of Standards in Washington.

Today mechanics will install special tanks, and tomorrow, weather permitting, Sergievsky will attempt to break the 500-kilometer record with a 2,000-kilogram load.

He left North Beach, Queens, at 10:30 A. M. yesterday for his speed test and flew to Fairfield, where Major Christopher was stationed.

Sergievsky came down low over the water as he crossed the starting line at Fairfield, and made the thirty-one miles to Execution Light at two miles a minute. He turned sharply, his left wing tip almost touching the water, and swung back by the marker at terrific speed, his two 525-horsepower engines wide open and his metal propellers turning at 2,000 revolutions a minute.

At 11:30 he was back again on the sheltered waters off North Beach.

Sir Douglas Mawson and his companions prepare to go ashore at MacRobertson Island, formerly unexplored territory.

"All the News That's Fit to Print."

The New York Times.

THE WEATHER
Generally fair and colder today; tomorrow fair and colder.
Temperatures yesterday—Max. 42, min. 32.
U. S. Weather Forecast—For details see Page 28.

VOL. LXXX....No. 26,653. **** NEW YORK, WEDNESDAY, JANUARY 14, 1931. TWO CENTS in Greater New York | THREE CENTS Within 200 Miles | FOUR CENTS Elsewhere Except 7th and 8th Postal Zones

GENEVA SEES REFORM IMPERATIVE TO SAVE WORLD'S GOLD BASIS

League Group Hits at Tariffs, Trade Barriers and Policy of Maintaining High Wages.

STATE BANK POWER URGED

Report Insists That Central Institutions Must Be Free to Cooperate Fully.

WOULD CUT RESERVE RATIO

Commission Says Reduction Is in No Way Likely to Weaken the General Credit Structure.

By CLARENCE K. STREIT.

Special Cable to THE NEW YORK TIMES.

GENEVA, Jan. 13.—Radical reforms are recommended to meet the fundamental changes which the gold standard systems have undergone in the gold delegation's draft report on the distribution of gold, which was prepared for it by the League of Nations Secretariat's financial section as a basis for its discussion. How far the delegation will adopt or modify this draft depends on the results of the debate over this very controversial question going on since yesterday in meetings which the delegation is holding here behind closed doors. The discussion so far is understood to have led to only minor changes in its text.

The document, although not representing the delegation's final views, gives the first definite indications of the general lines on which it is working. It is regarded as especially important as showing the diagnosis and the remedies which the Secretariat's financial section, as a result of the delegation's previous discussions, evidently believes represents a basis of an agreement. The draft report as a whole is also believed to represent the views which the British, at least, are willing to accept.

Asks Power for Central Banks.

The main thing on which the draft report insists is the need for legislation giving central banks greater power and freedom of action—above all, the liberty to cooperate. It gives an important rôle to the International Bank at Basle as a means of carrying out the gold policy which it recommends in this regard.

It holds that purely monetary reforms are insufficient, however, to assure the best distribution of gold and the proper functioning of the gold standard. Stressing the underlying need of a smooth free flow of capital being accompanied by a smooth free flow of goods and services, it attacks tariffs and other artificial barriers to trade, as well as the policy of trying to maintain high wage levels in some countries—the reference apparently being to the United States. It goes so far as to state that adherence to the gold standard "at once implies and necessitates adherence to an international economic system."

The first part of the report, examining the existing distribution of gold, ends with these conclusions: "We do not consider, therefore, that undue importance should be attached either to the actual distribution of gold today or to recent gold movements. We believe that the difficulties which those movements have involved will gradually disappear as later the effects of the disturbance caused by the war and the subsequent period of currency inflation and stabilization work themselves out."

Leaves Distribution Aside.

The report explains that it does not deal with the problem of redistribution, declaring this requires "a radical policy" which "may prove beneficial, but on the problem of its opportuneness we do not consider any general rules can be framed."

After explaining at length "the monetary reforms and banking principles necessary to secure optimism in the distribution of gold," the report ends with this paragraph:

"The application of these principles can only be expected if the central banks are allowed the necessary freedom of action—a freedom which will be, we consider, assured by the legislative changes we have suggested. The freedom to which we attach special importance, however, is the power to cooperate, for the measures we have mentioned imply close cooperation of the central banks at an early date with a view to preventing developments which may ultimately cause disequilibria, and at a later stage, if for one reason or another the disturbance has not been avoided, with a view to localizing that disturbance and securing that necessary correctives are put into opera-

Continued on Page Ten.

15 Billions Invested Abroad By Americans, Despite Slump

WASHINGTON, Jan. 13 (AP).—Hard times have not stemmed the flow of American money and tourists abroad. Wilbur J. Carr, Assistant Secretary of State, told the appropriations committee in hearings on the State supply bill reported to the House today that American investments in foreign countries in 1930 were estimated at $15,000,000,000, or about $1,000,000,000 more than in 1929.

Passports issued in 1930 reached the record figure of 209,211, an increase of over 15,000, he said. In 1914 the department issued 20,000 passports to Americans traveling abroad.

SIGNS OF REVIVAL NOTED BY MITCHELL

National City Bank Chairman Reports Gradual Trend to Return of Prosperity.

SEES NEW STATE OF MIND

Reveals Readjustment of National City Company Holdings to Cost or Market Value.

Admitting that the past year has been one of repeated disappointments because the scope of the economic disturbance was not at first fully comprehended, Charles E. Mitchell, chairman of the National City Bank, in his annual message to stockholders, made public yesterday, assured them that a "multitude of corrective influences are gradually restoring conditions to a return of prosperity."

"At the moment there is little basis for a prophecy of speedy recovery, but judging by past experience it would seem that the volume of business has fallen as low as it is likely to go, that replacements may be expected at least to maintain the present level, and that as the industries take the measure of the conditions with which they have to deal, a general revival of activity will gradually develop," he wrote.

Mr. Mitchell compared the present depression with that of 1920-1922 and pointed out that both were alike in that in addition to the usual influences characterizing a downward trend of the business cycle they were intensified by the "enormous derangements resulting from the war."

Business Stronger Now, He Says.

The business structure of the country is much stronger now, however, than it was in 1920-1922 or during any previous crisis, and is ready to function more promptly and with greater efficiency than after any other crisis, Mr. Mitchell declared.

The past year has been one of debt-paying on a great scale, Mr. Mitchell found, "which necessarily means curtailment of purchases and a check upon enterprise, but also means that when this policy has run its course new and sustained buying power will appear in all markets."

"Gradually the new conditions will make themselves felt," he wrote. "A new state of mind will also be developed, more sane and constructive than which ruled in the boom period. This attitude of mind is likely to be reflected in the bond and security markets even before the industrial recovery is perceptibly under way."

Meanwhile the National City Company, the securities affiliate of the National City Bank, has completed a sweeping readjustment of its inventories, Mr. Mitchell revealed. Security holdings have been marked down to cost or market as of Dec. 31, 1930, whichever was the lower, and the sugar properties of the com-

Continued on Page Fourteen.

$36,000,000 BONUSES BY BETHLEHEM STEEL ARE ATTACKED IN SUIT

Excessive Payments Charged in Action for Accounting, Refund and Injunction.

PREJUDICE LAID TO SCHWAB

Grace and P. A. Rockefeller Among 19 Directors and Officers Named.

FAVORITISM ALSO ALLEGED

Four Stockholders Act but Wall St. Group Is Said to Back Them—Ruling in Jersey Likely Today.

An unprecedented action said to be backed by a Wall Street group was begun yesterday in Court of Chancery at Newark to compel an accounting of and refunding of any part determined to be excessive of $36,000,000 distributed as bonuses to high officials of the Bethlehem Steel Corporation in a period including the war and post-war booms. The complainants ask that further bonus payments be restrained pending disposition of the injunction motion.

The defendants comprise officers and directors or former directors of the Bethlehem Steel Corporation. They include Eugene G. Grace, president; Charles M. Schwab, chairman; Percy A. Rockefeller, William C. Potter, Grayson M.-P. Murphy and Alvin Untermyer, directors, and thirteen others. The Bethlehem Steel Corporation, a New Jersey Corporation, is made a formal party defendant.

The action is brought in the name of four stockholders, one of whom holds 500 shares and the others nominal amounts of Bethlehem stock.

Injunction Is Asked.

The action was filed by George W. C. McCarter of McCarter & English of Newark, as counsel for the complainants. Mr. McCarter asked Vice Chancellor John H. Backes for an order requiring the defendants to show cause why the payment of bonuses should not be enjoined and restraining the further payment of bonuses pending determination of the injunction motion. The defendants are also required to show cause why, pending disposition of the suit, they should not be restrained from disposing of their stockholdings in the corporation, excepting subject to the rulings of the court.

The clause as to stockholdings was inserted with the object of insuring that these securities might be available to meet the claims of the complainants should the latter be successful in their suit.

Vice Chancellor Backes reserved decision on the application and took the complaint with him to his home in Trenton. He was to read the papers last night and announce today whether he would grant a preliminary injunction.

Mr. McCarter, in representing the four stockholders, is acting for the firm of House, Holthusen & McCloskey of 11 Broadway. Appearing as counsel for the complainants in addition are William S. Stuhr of Jersey City, Victor House, George V. A. McCloskey and Henry F. Holthusen.

The complainants are Camillus Berendt of Hoboken, holder of 16 shares; James E. Riley of New York, holder of 30 shares; Benjamin Glickfeld of New York, holder of 500 shares, and David Tait of Hackensack, N. J., holder of 10 shares.

Filing of the action followed the

Continued on Page Seventeen.

Sikh Kills Officer's Wife, Slashes Children; Boasts Gandhists Join Army to Slay British

Special Cable to THE NEW YORK TIMES.

LAHORE, India, Jan. 13.—A Sikh ex-soldier today attacked and fatally slashed the wife of Captain A. G. C. Curtis of the British army with a sword and then cut down her two children. Captured in the hills tonight, he made an amazing confession of disaffection in the Indian army.

Adherents of Mahatma Gandhi's Congress party, the Sikh told the police, early last year joined the reserve battalion of a Punjab regiment for the express purpose of killing British army officers. No opportunity, he said, arose during his three months of service, and following his discharge he received a three months' jail sentence for his activities with the Congress volunteers.

He said he regretted he had not been shot after today's outrage, and declared there were plenty of men in his village prepared to commit similar crimes.

Mrs. Curtis was sitting on the veranda of her bungalow in the British cantonment when the Sikh, shouting, "I am a Congress wallah," dashed at her. Mrs. Curtis's left arm was almost severed in warding off his first sword stroke. His second blow fell between the fingers of her right hand, splitting the hand to the wrist.

Rushing outside, where the two Curtiss girls, 7 and 5 years old, were playing with a bicycle, the Sikh cut down one with a blow on the head, but her heavy topi, or Indian helmet, saved the child from instant death. Upon the other girl he inflicted severe wounds in the head and leg.

Then he dashed into the open country, where he was chased and captured by servants.

Mrs. Curtis died in a hospital, following the amputation of her arm.

On Dec. 9 a Captain of the Tenth Battalion, Punjab Regiment, and an Indian sergeant were murdered by a lance corporal who afterward committed suicide in the Lahore cantonment.

Mawson Discovers New Land in Antarctic; Aides Fly Off Ship as Ice Blocks Passage

By Sir DOUGLAS MAWSON.

Copyright in the United States by THE NEW YORK TIMES. World copyright reserved. Reproduction in whole or part forbidden.

Wireless to THE NEW YORK TIMES.

ABOARD S. S. DISCOVERY, Jan. 9.—Yesterday evening, after crossing D'Urville Sea the Discovery arrived off Cape Robert, which was the extreme western point of the lands seen by Admiral D'Urville in 1840.

Passage further to the west is effectively blocked by a shoal area upon which are innumerable large, grounded bergs, holding the pack.

Extending to the northwest from this locality, both Wilkes and D'Urville some ninety years ago reported the existence of a sheer walled ice barrier, extending about 180 miles. With a view to the further investigation of this blockage to east and west traffic, and to delineate the coast line in the blocked area, Lieutenant S. A. Campbell and Flying Officer E. Douglas ascended in a plane. They observed new land extending westward from Cape Bickerton toward the eastern extremity of the land sighted by Captain John K. Davis in the Aurora in 1912, and then named Wilkes Land.

No floating barrier of ice tongue was within their range of vision in the blocked area, it being apparently entirely occupied by grounded bergs and firmly consolidated pack ice. Thus, nothing has yet been seen of the floating barrier of ice which existed in 1840.

We are now on our way around the north end of this blockage, but owing to a serious invasion of pack ice into the D'Urville Sea we have been pushed back far east in an endeavor to break through from coastal water to the open sea.

This evening progress through the pack has been satisfactory, and we hope to emerge into open sea tomorrow. For some days the weather has been ideal.

Sir Douglas Mawson, the noted English explorer, started last November with a group of scientists to continue his topographical and oceanographic explorations in the Antarctic.

BUYING OF LIQUOR AS EVIDENCE TO END

Dropping of Quest for "Private" Violators Also Disclosed as Supply Bill Is Reported.

IN WOODCOCK TESTIMONY

But House Wets Start Fight on $2,369,500 Rise in Dry Fund for 500 Additional Agents.

Special to The New York Times.

WASHINGTON, Jan. 13.—The government has ceased all activities looking to the apprehension of "private violators" of the prohibition laws and is preparing to eliminate the practice of having dry agents buy liquor to get evidence of violations.

This was disclosed today when the stenographic report of the committee hearings on the increased prohibition enforcement appropriations was made public in the House simultaneously with the introduction of the Department of Justice supply bill for the fiscal year 1932.

Colonel Amos W. Woodcock, director of the Prohibition Bureau, told the Appropriations Committee of the policy change during his testimony on Dec. 8, when he said:

"We are directing our forces against commercial violations, against the traffic in intoxicating liquors. We are not making any effort to apprehend private violators of the law. There are so many constitutional difficulties that the task would be impossible."

Colonel Woodcock insisted that with the increase in personnel, provided in the bill at his request, he could make headway against traffickers in liquor, and that once they were under control the prohibition problem would be largely solved.

The prohibition enforcement item in the bill totaled $11,369,500, an increase of $2,369,500 over the amount appropriated last year. Practically all of the increase would be applied to adding 500 agents to the bureau's staff.

On the subject of purchasing liquor for evidence, Colonel Woodcock testified at the hearing that since he took office on July 1, $31,940.45 had been spent by agents for this purpose. Then he declared that the "buy-yourself-a-drink" method of enforcement would be ultimately eliminated.

However, he regarded the tapping of telephone and telegraph wires as justified in trapping commercial violators.

"Wet Bloc" Prepares Long Fight.

While there is no question that the increased appropriation asked by Colonel Woodcock will be voted by this Congress, the wets in the House and Senate are forming their lines in the hope of registering a worthwhile opposition.

With the report of the Wickersham Commission on the prohibition problem expected to be made public in the next few days, the House wets gave notice today of their intention to fight the increased appropriation for prohibition enforcement.

Furthermore, the so-called wet bloc in the House is not only determined to call for record votes on all prohibition legislation at this session, but is also planning to hold a caucus here before March 4 with the newly elected wet members of the Seventy-second Congress to map a program for the next session.

Black Urges New "Solidarity."

The proposal to call this wet caucus was disclosed today by Representative Loring M. Black, Democrat, of New York, who, it was said, was

Continued on Page Thirteen.

REPUBLICAN APOLOGY DEMANDED BY SMITH

"Bar Room" Circular Used Against Norris Is Denounced as Based on Hoax Here.

NEVER ISSUED STATEMENT

His Demand on National Committee Is Read at Nye Inquiry by Senator Wagner.

Special to The New York Times.

WASHINGTON, Jan. 13.—A letter from Alfred E. Smith, Democratic Presidential candidate in 1928, to Senator Wagner of New York was read before the Nye campaign fund investigating committee today. The letter demanded from the Republican National Committee "an apology and reparation" for permitting Robert H. Lucas, its executive director, to circulate 800,000 copies of the so-called "Al Smith-Raskob barroom" circular in Nebraska and other States during the Congressional campaigns last year.

Ex-Governor Smith denied that he had ever made a statement used in connection with the circular, and said that he felt entitled to have 800,000 copies of his denial given publicity equal to that accorded the circulars which Mr. Lucas had had distributed.

The circular to which ex-Governor Smith took exception was part of the anti-Norris "literature" distributed by Mr. Lucas in Nebraska in the Senatorial campaign when Mr. Norris was opposed by ex-Senator Gilbert M. Hitchcock, Democrat. Mr. Lucas has testified that he paid for the activities out of his own pocket, using part of $4,000 lent to him by a bank here on the security of a $50,000 special fund which the Republican National Committee maintained in the bank.

Republican National Committee officials, including Senator Fess, its chairman, and Mr. Lucas, refused to comment on Governor Smith's letter tonight.

TEXT OF SMITH LETTER.

The letter was read before the Nye committee at the suggestion of Senator Wagner, a member of the committee. It follows:

New York, Jan. 8, 1931.

Dear Bob:

I have been following the testimony before the Nye committee concerning the cartoon entitled "Al Smith-Raskob Idea of Happiness." The text of it has been laid before me.

I find that the whole cartoon hinges on the following statement: "To my mind the Democratic party will soon be in control and will make this a happy as well as a prosperous nation. The Democratic party is always looking for the common good and opposing oppressive laws and sumptuary legislation."

This statement which purports to come from me as of Aug. 21 was never issued by me. At that time in August, the Joel Parker Association of Newark, N. J., was holding an annual reunion and dinner. I refused the invitation to attend the dinner, but on Aug. 19 some over-enthusiastic admirer of mine sent a telegram to the association and signed my name to it.

My first knowledge of it was when I saw the newspaper headlines quoting me. I made careful investigation among my own staff, and found it had not emanated from my own office, nor any one

Continued on Page Six.

HOOVER ASKS NATION TO GIVE $10,000,000 FOR RED CROSS AID

Sum Imperative for Agency to Relieve Crisis in Drought Area, He Says.

PAYNE URGES "EMERGENCY"

$15,000,000 for Food in Relief Bill Causes Deadlock of Conferees in Congress.

ISSUE UP IN SENATE TODAY

House Rejects Item by 215 to 134 After Sharp Fight by La Guardia and Democrats.

Special to The New York Times.

WASHINGTON, Jan. 13.—President Hoover appealed to the American people today to contribute a fund of $10,000,000 to the American Red Cross to be applied to the relief of destitute sufferers in the drought areas of the country. This amount the President described as the minimum that will be needed.

The drought-relief problem presented the greatest peace-time emergency ever faced by the Red Cross, National Chairman John Barton Payne said in a statement following the President's appeal. He asserted that, with calls for aid increasing, "the peak of the emergency is not yet in sight."

The Red Cross appeal preceded the deadlocking of House and Senate conferees late in the day over an additional $15,000,000 for food loans which the Senate voted into the $45,000,000 drought relief appropriation bill. The Senate conferees will report the impasse to the chamber tomorrow.

The House sent the bill to conference by a 353-to-4 vote, defeating by 215 to 134 a motion to concur in the Senate's $15,000,000 proposal.

THE PRESIDENT'S APPEAL.

The text of the President's appeal follows:

The White House,
Washington, Jan. 13, 1931.

To my fellow-countrymen:

There must be a very material increase in the resources of the American Red Cross to enable it to bear the burden which it has undertaken in the drought area and smaller communities over twenty-one States during this Winter. Within the last ten days the Red Cross has had to increase the rate of expenditures to an amount greater than during the entire preceding four months.

The American Red Cross is the nation's sole agency for relief in such a crisis; it is meeting the demand and must continue to do so during the remainder of the Winter.

The disaster reserve of the Red Cross which was pledged to this emergency last August is not sufficient to meet the increased demands. It is imperative in the view of the experienced directors of the Red Cross that a minimum of at least $10,000,000 be contributed to carry the relief program to completion.

The familiarity of this situation, due to months of press reports of its progress, should not blind us to the fact that it is an acute emergency, nor dull our active sympathies toward our fellow-countrymen who are in actual want and in many cases will lack the bare

Continued on Page Twelve.

Azores Repudiates Mysterious Radio Report Saying Mrs. Hart's Plane Fell Into the Ocean

By The Associated Press.

HORTA, Island of Fayal, Azores, Jan. 13.—Information received late tonight from Sao Miguel Island revealed that neither residents of the island nor its wireless station had heard anything of the American seaplane Tradewind, which left Bermuda for the Azores last Saturday with Mrs. Beryl Hart and William S. MacLaren and since has been unreported.

Horta's only information of the plane was a roundabout dispatch from New York saying the Mackay Radio Company had picked up a message from the liner President Garfield telling of a Sao Miguel broadcast to the effect that the Tradewind had fallen into the sea about twenty miles off the island.

Villagers were said to have seen the plane diving for the water, but the Sao Miguel wireless station, to which the report was attributed, informed the government tonight that the object which fell was only a rocket fired from a British cruiser engaged in gunnery practice near by.

Admiralty officers ordered the destroyer Ibo to the spot when they first learned of the rumor but withdrew it after hearing from Sao Miguel.

LISBON, Jan. 13 (AP).—A bit of hope for the safety of William S. MacLaren and Mrs. Beryl Hart was dashed here tonight after Portuguese Admiralty officials had ordered an eager search on receiving reports from New York that the seaplane Tradewind was alleged to have fallen into the sea off Sao Miguel Island, in the Azores.

A message received here yesterday from the liner President Garfield by the Mackay Radio Company said the Sao Miguel radio station in the Azores had broadcast the following:

"Understand airplane Tradewind fell in sea about twenty miles off Mosteiros Point, St. Michael's [Sao Miguel] Island. All ships advised to keep a lookout and report this station if anything seen."

Mrs. Cora Mansfield and Mrs. Georgia Gwynne, mother and sister of Mrs. Hart, took on new hope when the message was relayed to them at their apartment at 206 East Sixty-ninth Street.

Washington Memorial Bridge Is Name of New Hudson Span

Selection of the name, "George Washington Memorial Bridge" for the new suspension span across the Hudson River, between Fort Washington Park, Manhattan, and Fort Lee, N. J., was announced yesterday by the Port of New York Authority. This designation was chosen, according to John F. Galvin, chairman, as most historically appropriate for a monumental structure in a location with which the name of George Washington is intimately associated.

Many suggestions were considered by a special committee, consisting of Commissioners George R. Dyer, George deB. Keim and Howard S. Cullman. There was a strong feeling that the simple title "Hudson River Bridge" would be sufficiently descriptive, but it was finally agreed that something more historically significant was desirable.

MAYOR ACTS TO FREE 71 IMPRISONED GIRLS

Offers Hilly's Services in Getting Writs for Victims of Illegal Sentences.

MISSING VICE DECOY FOUND

Harry Levy, Trapped in New Orleans, Says Policeman Gave Him Money to Flee.

The arrest of Harry Levy, described as a much more important stool-pigeon than Chile Mapocha Acuna, who has already caused the suspension of twenty-seven policemen, was reported to Commissioner Mulrooney by the police of New Orleans yesterday. Levy, known also as Reiss, was said to have declared that he had been receiving money to live on and travel from Patrolman James J. Quinlivan of the West 100th Street station, one of those already under suspension on frame-up charges.

While Attorney General Bennett still had under consideration a plan by which to free 71 girls illegally committed as wayward minors, an independent action in behalf of Philomena d'Angelo, one of them, was instituted.

Mayor Walker took up the plight of the seventy-one girls, and following a conference held at City Hall announced that Chief Magistrate Corrigan would visit Bedford Reformatory and offer the services of the Corporation Counsel to apply for writs of habeas corpus "where the facts or the law warrants such action to meet the ends of justice."

At the conference were, beside the Mayor and Mr. Corrigan, Corporation Counsel Arthur J. W. Hilly, William J. Cahill, Bill Drafting Commissioner; Police Commissioner Mulrooney and a representative of the committee of fourteen.

Attack on Kresel Denied.

Besides the first intimation that the sudden disappearance of stool-pigeon wanted for questioning might have been prompted by policemen, developments in and outside of the investigation offices where preparations were being made for a public hearing tomorrow included a denial by District Attorney Crain that the appointment of Max D. Steuer as special prosecutor in the Bank of United States inquiry was a move aimed at Mr. Kresel.

In Brooklyn Mrs. Catherine Parker Clivette forwarded to Presiding Justice Edward Lazansky of the Appel-

Continued on Page Two.

CITY INQUIRY FACES OPPOSITION BY WARD; MINORITY UNDECIDED

Westchester Leader Has So Far Refused to Back Proposal or to Instruct Delegation.

DOWNING ASSAILS PLAN

"Fair-Minded Investigation Is Precluded" by Resolution's Language, Democrat Says.

ASSEMBLY REFERS MEASURE

Sends It to Committee Without Debate and No Action Is Expected for a Month or More.

By W. A. WARN.

Special to The New York Times.

ALBANY, Jan. 13.—While Democratic leaders in the Legislature opened fire today on the concurrent resolution, sponsored by the Republican majority, for a sweeping legislative investigation of the New York City Administration, including all the courts as well as the political organizations within the city, it developed today that there is widespread dissatisfaction among leaders of the Republican State organization with the proposal.

With the narrow working majority of only one vote in the Senate, temporarily at least, wiped out through the absence of Senator Nelson W. Cheney of Erie, who has gone South for his health, and a working majority of only five in the Assembly, dissension in the Republican ranks would present a rather vexing problem to the leaders of the Republican majority unless the differences are ironed out.

It was learned today that such a powerful Republican chieftain as William L. Ward of Westchester, with two Republican members in the Senate and five Republican members in the Assembly, so far had withheld his support from the New York City probe proposal. It had been supposed that Chairman W. Kingsland Macy had won Mr. Ward over to support of the inquiry, but apparently this supposition was erroneous.

Word came also that Clarence King, the Republican leader in Onondaga was of the same frame of mind. There are three members of the Assembly and one Senator from Onondaga, all Republicans.

Measure Goes to Committee.

It would be hazardous to predict at this early stage to what extent the dissatisfaction of these and other leaders in the Republican State organization will be reflected in the Senate and Assembly when the time comes for final action on the Hofstadter-Story resolution, which was introduced at the session last night. The resolution was read in the Assembly today and referred to the Ways and Means Committee without comment from the floor.

Last year Speaker McGinnies of the Assembly came out openly against a proposal to investigate the affairs of New York City. While it is known that he regards as doubtful the political advantage of the investigation now in contemplation, he is in line and prepared to use his undoubted influence in the lower house to see the resolution through there.

Senate Leader Knight, it is known, will adopt a similar course in the upper house.

In the meantime it will be left to the chairman to iron out differences among the leaders of his organization up-State and prepare the way for harmonious action in the Senate and the Assembly.

"Must Now See It Through."

The proposal to investigate New York City was adopted at a meeting of the executive committee of the Republican State Committee held here a week ago last Saturday. It was stated then that the action of the executive committee had been by unanimous vote.

It is learned, however, that before the vote was called for several leaders who sat in had expressed themselves as doubtful with regard to the political effect and timeliness of the measure. In fact, it was stated today, no one showed an enthusiasm in connection with the proposal with the exception of Chairman Macy himself.

Now that the resolution already has been put in, it is the opinion of the legislative leaders that the Republicans must see it through, as a backward step would involve loss of prestige more detrimental to the party than the effect of even an investigation that, like the investigation of the Meyer committee in 1921, should fail to bring results to justify it.

There were indications today that the Democrats, who find it somewhat embarrassing to come out in direct opposition to the resolution, might get around it by making

"All the News That's Fit to Print."

The New York Times.

Copyright, 1931, by The New York Times Company.

THE WEATHER
Generally fair today; tomorrow cloudy and warmer.
Temperatures yesterday—Max. 27, min. 18.
U. S. Weather Forecast—For details see Page 25.

VOL. LXXX....No. 26,663. **** NEW YORK, SATURDAY, JANUARY 24, 1931. TWO CENTS In Greater New York | THREE CENTS Within 200 Miles | FOUR CENTS Elsewhere Except 7th and 8th Postal Zones

GOVERNORS ADVISED TO FIGHT IDLENESS WITH JOB INSURANCE

Seven States Represented as Albany Conference Called by Roosevelt Opens Sessions.

ECONOMIC EXPERTS HEARD

Majority Favor Establishment of Unemployment Reserve Fund by Industry.

AID FROM STATES URGED

Professor Leiseron Calls Charity for the Unemployed a Subsidy for Employers.

By W. A. WARN.

Special to The New York Times.

ALBANY, Jan. 23.—Unemployment was brought immediately to the front today when the conference among Governor Roosevelt and the Chief Executives or representatives of six other industrial States opened. They purpose to formulate a plan of joint action for dealing with such an economic emergency as now exists, should it recur.

At the first session a number of economic experts described various phases of the problems the Executives have met to consider. Tomorrow and Sunday will be spent in studying in an analytical way the material submitted today. This presented a wide range of opinion as to the advisability and plan and scope of insurance against unemployment. The preponderance of opinion appeared to be in favor of mandatory insurance, with the States contributing to the funds.

While the name of President Hoover was not mentioned references were made to alleged lack of preparation by the administration at Washington to meet the present unemployment emergency.

Governor Roosevelt Presides.

Governor Roosevelt presided and began by saying that while the area of the seven States represented constituted only a little more than 5 per cent of the entire area of the country, 32 per cent of the nation's population lived in them and paid 46 per cent of the income taxes collected. These States also contained 49 per cent of all wage earners, who received 52 per cent of all wages paid.

Under the circumstances, there was justification for looking at the seven States as presenting the front line in the fight on unemployment and unstabilized industry.

Those executives, or their representatives, present beside Mr. Roosevelt were Governors Larson of New Jersey, Cross of Connecticut, Ely of Massachusetts and Case of Rhode Island; Dr. Charles Reitell, director of the Greater Pennsylvania Commission, and Samuel P. Bush, chairman of the Ohio State Commission on Unemployment, representing Governor White of Ohio, who will not arrive until tomorrow.

Lieut. Gov. Lehman, adviser of Governor Roosevelt in matters of economic, financial and industrial import, sat with him. Mrs. Roosevelt and the wives of some of the other Governors had seats in the Executive Chamber and Miss Frances Perkins, State Industrial Commissioner, was present, but took no part in the discussions. The conference lasted all day with an hour's intermission for luncheon served at the Capitol.

Discuss Employment Reserves.

Unemployment was taken up under the heading of "unemployment reserves" and the speaker dealing with the subject with the greatest thoroughness and the least shyness was Professor William Leiserson of Antioch College. He is also a member of the Ohio State Unemployment Commission and was identified with the drafting of the report of the Wainwright Commission on workmen's compensation submitted in Governor Hughes's régime.

Unemployment insurance, he said, would be nothing more nor less than an extension of workmen's compensation systems in effect in most of the States.

"Workmen's compensation is not paid out as damages for injuries in industrial employment," he explained. "It is in payment for lost time. Unemployment and the consequent loss of wages cannot be eradicated. The risk must be considered.

"In the case of some of our industries, commonly called public utilities, the Supreme Court of the United States has made a ruling rendering it compulsory on such corporations to make provision for obsolescent or wornout machinery. Is there any reason the same should

Continued on Page Three.

Texas Town's Citizens Fast To Provide Food for Poor

By The Associated Press.

LUBBOCK, Texas, Jan. 23.—Containers bearing the inscription "I was hungry and ye gave me to eat" were placed on counters and in offices for a city-wide fast day here today to aid the poor.

Residents were asked to go without all or part of their meals and to give the money which would have been spent for food.

The voluntary fast day was suggested by the Rev. Dr. John C. Granberry of the Texas Technological College Faculty.

Estimates were that from $1,000 to $3,000 was contributed.

BILL TO 'DRY' CAPITAL TAKEN UP BY SENATE

Howell, Urging His Measure, Asserts Washington Is "Bootleggers' Sanctuary."

DIPLOMATIC WHISKY FLOWS

Servants Buy It Freely, He Says—House Passes Supply Bill for 500 More Dry Agents.

Special to The New York Times.

WASHINGTON, Jan. 23.—Chief interest in the prohibition battle shifted today to the Senate when that body voted by 39 to 29 to take up the Howell bill, designed to strengthen enforcement in the national capital and make the city a model for testing the enforceability of the Eighteenth Amendment.

Senator Howell pictured Washington as a "sanctuary of bootleggers," and declared that one liquor dealer here was arrested on fifty-four charges in a single year.

Other developments today included the introduction by Senator Copeland of New York of a bill recommended by the Wickersham Commission, to repeal the law which limits physicians to the amount of whisky they may prescribe and to abolish the requirement of specifying the ailment for which the liquor is prescribed.

In the House, Representative Charles L. Gifford, a dry Republican of Massachusetts, warned the wets that they should cease trying to embarrass the drys and should offer some concrete plan to improve the situation or be prepared to lose the full wet strength in the next Congress.

The House passed the State, Justice, Commerce and Labor Departments supply bill, which had been a storm centre of the wets' attack for a week, and sent it to the Senate. The measure provides for a total of $135,789,000 for the departments for the fiscal year, setting aside $11,363,000 for the Prohibition Bureau to enable it to increase the number of dry agents from 1,400 to 1,900.

Hoover Is Told of Protests.

The political aspects of President Hoover's position continued to hold the attention of Republican politicians, who sought to analyze the effect of his message, transmitting the Wickersham report, and the subsequent "interpretation" of it that was made by close friends of the President.

President Hoover was told today of the receipt of messages protesting against the interpretation that had been put upon his message by those of his advisers who declared he had not closed the door to revision of the Eighteenth Amendment.

One message expressed the opinion

Continued on Page Four.

SENATE RENEWS WAR WITH THE PRESIDENT OVER POWER BOARD

Names of Three Commissioners Are Sent Back to Committee by a Vote of 45 to 32.

COURT TEST MOVE UPHELD

Walsh Resolution Directing Quo Warranto Proceedings Referred to Norris Committee.

MITCHELL BACKS HOOVER

Holds Appointments Are Valid, Since White House Was Notified of Confirmation.

Special to The New York Times.

WASHINGTON, Jan. 23.—The Senate, continuing its struggle with President Hoover and his nominees to the Federal Power Commission, today adopted by a vote of 45 to 32 a motion by Senator Walsh of Montana to recommit the names of Chairman George Otis Smith, Marcel Garsaud and Claude L. Draper to the Interstate Commerce Committee, which approved their nominations before the Senate confirmed them in office, Dec. 20 and 21.

Following the vote, Senator Walsh pressed for action in court against the commissioners, notice of whose cofirmation President Hoover has declined to return. Upon Senator Walsh's motion, the Senate unanimously referred to the Judiciary Committee a resolution directing the District Attorney of the District of Columbia to institute quo warranto proceedings to ascertain if the three commissioners were lawfully in office.

Soon after the Senate had recommitted the names President Hoover gave out the text of an opinion by Attorney General Mitchell, taking a position contrary to that of the Senate.

Mitchell Upholds President.

In holding that the President was within his constitutional rights in appointing the commissioners after he had been notified by the Senate that it had confirmed the nominations, and that they were legally holding office, the Attorney General summarized his convictions as follows:

"I cannot escape the conclusion that, fairly construed, the rules of the Senate contemplate that where it orders notification of the Senate's consent to an appointment to be forthwith transmitted to the President, without waiting for the expiration of the period for reconsideration, that action is intended as a deliberate expression to the President of the Senate's unqualified consent to the immediate appointment, and that it amounts to a decision by the Senate, not under suspension of its rules but in accordance with them, to place reconsideration beyond its power if the President should act and make the appointment before a request of the Senate for a return of the papers reaches him."

Before the vote was taken on the motion to recommit, Senators Walsh and Norris denounced the three commissioners for dismissing Charles A. Russell, solicitor, and William V. King, chief accountant of the commission, from service after the commission held its first meeting.

Senator Watson, Republican floor leader, and Senator Jones, Republi-

Continued on Page Six.

Paris Evolves Adaptable Frocks and Suits; Cotton Gowns in Styles for Leaner Purses

By The Associated Press.

PARIS, Jan. 23.—Practicality for poor pocketbooks is the watchword of small couturiers at whose showings late today were exhibited fashions for modern matrons who want frocks capable of being worn in half a dozen different ways.

The suit ensemble idea, adapted to everything from street to evening wear, marked the showings, while the two-color idea permitting interchange of coats and dresses was a definite feature of Spring modes.

The suits shown today depart widely from the old skirt and coat idea. Plain or print frocks of small pattern, with matching coats or coats of plain material, were shown. The coats varied from short Eton jackets to seven-eighths length. The skirts featured stitched-down pleats, releasing fullness below the knees.

Even dresses for the evening are designed for a double purpose. Several models shown had short coats making them adaptable for late afternoon wear.

Frocks for restaurant wear, with light yokes or bodices encrusted on dark crêpe skirts, were shown with matching short coats. Not quite so practical weer dinner pajamas of scintillant pailletes on dull crêpe or silk mesh. The pajamas were made with trousers so full that the mannequins displayed them with whirling steps to demonstrate that they were not wearing skirts.

Color combinations were brown and beige, gray and rose, and black, and a water-green shade called seafoam.

Cotton frocks for débutantes instead of the lustrous silk they ordinarily wear were exhibited. One of American buyers' favorite houses displays linen, cotton, organdy and dotted Swiss frocks for every occasion. Even for social butterflies cotton is the smartest raiment in a year marked by uncertain financial conditions. The new frocks are reminiscent of grandmother's garb.

There are bright-hued ribbon belts on the new evening frocks, some of them trimmed with bright glass buttons. Dance dresses for young girls have unusually high necklines, both front and back, and are often finished with lace-edged berthas or small capes.

As yet waistlines, skirt lengths and sleeves have undergone no change. Evening gowns continue to reach to the instep with an occasional very short train shown. Daytime dresses are from twelve to fourteen inches from the floor. Waistlines are fitted to the normal curve of the body on frocks for young and slender figures.

Canadian Premier Soon to Visit Washington; St. Lawrence Development May Be Discussed

Special to The New York Times.

WASHINGTON, Jan. 23.—R. B. Bennett, Prime Minister of Canada, will arrive in Washington Jan. 31 for an "unofficial" visit of several days, according to notification given by the Canadian Legation to the State Department today. Although no formal program has been arranged for him, it is expected that the Prime Minister will call upon President Hoover, Secretary Stimson and other officials.

Whether Mr. Bennett has any special purpose in view was not stated in the communication to the State Department, and the Canadian Legation did not amplify its statement that the visit will be merely unofficial.

In the past, other Prime Ministers of Canada have made unofficial visits here and found such occasions opportune for discussing informally with American officials problems of joint concern to the two countries.

It will, therefore, come as no surprise should Mr. Bennett discuss tariff, prohibition enforcement and other questions which are of immediate interest to the two governments.

OTTAWA, Jan. 23 (Canadian Press)—The visit of Premier Bennett to Washington will be the first which he has made to the United States capital since he became Prime Minister.

While there is no mention of it in the brief announcement handed out today, it is generally assumed the St. Lawrence project will be the subject of discussion between President Hoover and Mr. Bennett. Before leaving for the Imperial Conference Mr. Bennett informed the United States Government he would be prepared to take up the waterways question shortly after his return from London.

At present there is no Canadian Minister in Washington and no definite indication of the probable appointee is available here yet.

MAWSON FINDS LAND IN ANTARCTIC FLIGHT

British Explorer on Daring Trip Before Storm Sees Great Stretch in East Territory.

FINDS COSMIC RAYS STEADY

Variation Had Been Expected Near the Magnetic Pole—Rare Specimen of Penguin Visits Ship.

By SIR DOUGLAS MAWSON.

Wireless to THE NEW YORK TIMES.

ABOARD THE S. S. DISCOVERY, in the Antarctic, Jan. 21.—On the eve of a bad break in the weather on Sunday, when our ship was approximately at Lat. 64:30 degrees S. and Long. 116 degrees E., Flight Lieut. S. A. Campbell and I made an aerial reconnoissance.

The clouds, which were developing fast, limited our view, but we could discern along the southern horizon what appeared to be high land, upon which clouds were forming under the influence of a northerly warm, moist wind. This formation extended to the east and west in about latitude 66.

The plane got safely back and aboard just in time to escape serious trouble on account of the rising sea and snow, which soon even obliterated the view of adjacent bergs.

As this locality is of special interest and apparently near extensive land, we are awaiting a clearance in the weather, which fortunately now appears to be near at hand.

During several days of continuous snowfall and a heavy swell from the northwest, The Discovery has remained in the ice pack. We made use of the opportunity to conduct some scientific work and to transfer to the bunkers aft a large quantity of coal which had been carried in the forward water-tight compartments.

Rare Penguin Pays Visit.

Crab-eater seals and sea leopards are abundant in the pack hereabouts. In the early evening hours they leave the ice and forage in the sea, appearing again about 6 in the morning to bask all day on the floes. A few emperor penguins and a great number of 1-year-old Adelie penguins are always in sight. Older Adelies are away at the rookeries on the coast, busy with their young families.

Today R. A. Falls, our ornithologist, captured a remarkable Adelie penguin on which most of the plumage which is normally white, is black. An Albino specimen, opposed to this melanistic type, was taken some days ago.

We have also had frequent visits from all the well-known varieties of antarctic flying birds. Consequently, though the thick weather limits us in certain directions, the scientific staff is kept busy.

The Geiger Mull of ultra gamma radiation apparatus is always a source of interest. Its registering tube is embedded in a very massive block of lead, sufficiently thick to cut off all Roentgen rays, but through it pass those recently discovered penetrating rays which reach the earth from outer space.

It was thought possible that a greater concentration of this interesting phenomenon might be a feature of the region near the magnetic poles. But A. L. Kennedy, our physicist, who has made frequent tests throughout the voyage, has failed to discover any appreciable variation in this cosmic bombardment.

Mawson Found Land Before.

Sir Douglas Mawson, the British explorer, served on the staff of Sir Ernest Shackleton's Antarctic expedition in 1907, was leader of the Australasian Antarctic expedition of

Continued on Page Eight.

SEEK CRADLE OF RACE IN AMERICAN JUNGLE

London and New York Museums Back Trip to Secret Region of Central America.

RELICS AND RUINS ABOUND

Mitchell-Hedges, the Noted Explorer, Found "Tons" of Objects Last Year, He Says.

Wireless to THE NEW YORK TIMES.

LONDON, Jan. 23.—Frederick A. Mitchell-Hedges, the English explorer, disclosed today the details of a forthcoming expedition to Central America, to be conducted jointly by the British Museum and the Museum of the American Indian of New York, on which he hopes to unearth a wealth of material proving the existence of an age-old culture, hitherto unsuspected, on the American continent, and to gather data that may change the entire scientific conception of the Central American aborigines.

The goal of the expedition is hidden in almost impenetrable jungles, guarded by well-nigh inaccessible mountain ranges. Mr. Mitchell-Hedges declined to divulge the exact geographical location of this remote corner of the world, which he thinks may prove to be one of the cradles of mankind, beyond saying that it is in the region of Mosquitia, almost bordering the Caribbean Sea and the Republic of Honduras. He visited the region last year with Lady Lillian Richmond-Brown, as head of an expedition promoted by the Museum of the American Indian, and brought back 1,100 specimens of pottery, vases and figurines.

Mr. Mitchell-Hedges plans to sail next week for New York on the White Star liner Adriatic to complete the financial arrangements for the second expedition, of which he will be the leader. He said that this will be the first time that the British Museum will join the United States in American exploration work. The famous British institution and the Museum of the American Indian will share all the finds of the expedition.

Tells Plans in Interview.

In an interview today with a correspondent of THE NEW YORK TIMES, he said:

"In the region are to be found traces of a culture of antiquity totally unexpected. It dates from the time of Ur of the Chaldees or even earlier—about 3000 to 4000 B. C. What we will find there may change the entire scientific conception of the aboriginal races of Central and South America.

"Our expedition proposes to penetrate a certain region marked on the maps of today as unexplored, in order to conduct the excavation work. Within my knowledge the region contains immense ruins never yet visited, as well as Indian tribes of whom practically nothing is known. I have every reason to believe also that we will find fossilized remains both of prehistoric animals and fish.

"Exploration of this country from the air is useless in this instance, because the ruins I speak of are absolutely invisible from an airplane.

"I shall visit again the same place where I collected last year the specimens that are now in the Museum of the American Indian in New York to continue the work I started there. Up to now we have touched only the fringe of a territory that may be worth exploring over a large area. Here we have already located the site of an ancient city and a cenote, or sacred well, where the previous specimens were obtained.

"On our last expedition we found a number of caves after trekking through dense jungles. Unlike the

Continued on Page Two.

BUTLER URGES BOARD TO STUDY WAR DEBTS WITH VIEW TO SLASH

We Are the Chief Sufferers, Educator Tells League Association Convention.

PAYMENT HELD IMPOSSIBLE

Millions in Cash Gained Means Billions in Value Lost, He Declares at Chicago Meeting.

HE WANTS US TO TAKE LEAD

American "Isolation" Ridiculed by Dr. Jenkins—Prof. Shotwell Says We Are Pledged to Disarm.

Special to The New York Times.

CHICAGO, Jan. 23.—Urging the American people to demand that Washington take steps for the formation of an international commission to restudy the war debt question in the light of world depression, Dr. Nicholas Murray Butler, president of Columbia University, while speaking tonight before the League of Nations Association, implied that the time had come when the staggering indebtedness incurred by European nations in the world struggle should be reduced or wiped out.

Declaring that this country was the chief sufferer by the war debt settlement, Dr. Butler further asserted that while millions of dollars were being brought across the sea, to be lodged in the Federal Treasury, tens of millions were being paid by the American farmer, the American wage earner, the American business man and the American investor through destruction of values, loss of markets and disruption of trade.

"The time has now come," he said, "when the people of the United States may justly ask to be quickly relieved of the burden which the war debt settlement has put upon them, without any regard whatever to the effect of that settlement upon those nations which are among our debtors."

Britain's Stand on Debts Lauded.

Concerning war debts Dr. Butler said:

"On Aug. 1, 1922, the British Government, through a dispatch signed by Lord Balfour, addressed these words respecting war debts to the representatives of France, Italy, the Serb-Croat-Slovene State, Rumania, Portugal and Greece:

" 'It is true that many of the allied and associated powers are as between each other creditors or debtors or both, but they were and are much more. They were partners in the gratest international effort ever made in the cause of freedom; and they are still partners in dealing with some at least of its results.

" 'Their debts were incurred, their loans were made, not for the separate advantage of particular States, but for the great purpose common to them all, and that purpose has been, in the main, accomplished. * * * The economic ills from which the world is suffering are due to many causes, moral and material * * * but among them must certainly be reckoned the weight of international indebtedness, with all its unhappy effects, upon credit and exchange, upon national production and international trade. Peoples of all countries long for a speedy return to the normal, but how can the normal be reached while conditions so abnormal are permitted to prevail?'

"These sober and well-weighed

Continued on Page Thirteen.

Envoy to Nicaragua Called To Washington for Parley

Wireless to THE NEW YORK TIMES.

MANAGUA, Jan. 23.—The American Minister, Matthew E. Hanna, and General Douglas C. McDougal, in command of the Nicaraguan National Guard for the past two years, have been called to Washington to confer with Secretary of State Stimson in order that the United States Government may gain a more intimate knowledge of Nicaraguan affairs and be in a better position to cooperate with the Nicaraguan Government.

Mr. Hanna and General McDougal will leave Managua by Pan-American Airways Sunday, and their plane is due in Miami on Tuesday. From there they will proceed to Washington by train.

DAISY DE BOE GUILTY ON ONE THEFT COUNT

Los Angeles Jury in Tearful Court Room Asks Mercy for Clara Bow's Ex-Secretary.

SHE COLLAPSES AT VERDICT

Former Employer Also Weeps at Home and Hints at Aiding in Plea for Probation.

Special to The New York Times.

LOS ANGELES, Jan. 23.—Amid sobs from nearly all the women in the crowded court room, the jury which for two days had deliberated on Miss Daisy De Boe's guilt or innocence, this afternoon returned a verdict of guilty on one of thirty-five counts of embezzling money from the accounts of Clara Bow, screen star, for whom she was secretary. The jury added a request for leniency.

The conviction was for diverting money from Miss Bow's bank account. Under the verdict Miss De Boe may be sentenced to from one to ten years in San Quentin prison. She may also receive probation if she applies for it. Her hitherto unbroken coolness broke as the verdict was read and her wails resounded through Judge William Doran's court room.

"If they were going to convict me at all why did not they convict me of everything?" she cried before bailiffs took her to the county jail for the night.

Weeping Upsets Bailiffs.

Three of the five women jurors wept openly as they were polled. Other women in the crowd dabbed at their eyes and choked up.

The bailiffs were too amazed at the flow of tears to succeed in restoring order promptly. During the polling of jurors spectators clambered and pushed their way to positions to where they might see, many standing on the backs of seats.

Flashlights boomed all over the room as the convicted girl buried her head in her hands at the counsel table and cried inconsolably. Her sister, Mrs. Grace Black, was unable to comfort her.

Judge Doran set Monday morning for passing sentence. Nathan Freedman, counsel for Miss De Boe, did not indicate whether he would file notice of appeal at the time of sentencing or take the other course possible for liberating his 26-year-old client by filing application for probation.

Under California criminal law a jury's recommendation for leniency is without legal or binding force on the sentencing judge, but may be of considerable weight in a probation proceeding.

The verdict represented a compro-

Continued on Page Two.

Three Killed When Ten-Ton Cornice Plunges Seven Stories From Jackson Heights Building

Three men were killed and two others seriously injured late yesterday afternoon when a ten-ton stone cornice, being put in place on an apartment house at Eighty-third Street and Polk Avenue, Jackson Heights, Queens, slipped and fell.

Two men were standing on the stone as it broke loose, a third was on a scaffold directly beneath it, the fourth was carried along by the falling mass and the fifth man was struck by the débris as it crashed to the ground, seven stories below.

The Dead.

FELICETTI, DOMINICK, 35 years old, of 1,024 Sixty-fourth Street, Brooklyn.

SINOVITCH, JOHN, of 272 Dahlgren Place, Brooklyn.

JOSEPH NICASTRO, 40, of 23-30 Beaumont Avenue, the Bronx.

The Injured.

NAWATHNIG, FRED, 54, Frank Court, Gerritsen Beach; contusions of the right shoulder and hip and internal injuries; St. John's Hospital, Queens.

WALISKE, JOHN, 43, of Cauldwell Avenue, the Bronx; internal injuries and lacerations of the scalp; St. John's Hospital.

Police Inspector John J. Gallagher and Leo Heffernan, Assistant District Attorney, after questioning David Slote, the contractor, and officials of the Fillmore Garden Corporation, owners of the apartment house, said they believed the mortar holding the bricks on which the cornice had been set had not hardened sufficiently. They will continue their investigation today.

Sinovitch and Nicastro were standing on the cornice helping to swing it into place on the roof when the huge stone slipped. It crashed through the scaffold on which Felicetti was standing, killing him outright. Nawathnig, who was standing on planks one story below, was struck but fell clear. Waliske was hit by fragments of the stone.

An unidentified passerby narrowly escaped death as the wreckage buried itself in the soft earth a foot from him. His dog was hit, however, and died in his arms a few minutes later. The man walked on, cradling its body in his arms, and refused to give his name. The emergency squad from the Hunters Point Precinct arrived later, followed by two ambulances from St. John's Hospital. Sinovitch and Nicastro died on the way to the hospital.

MARCUS GETS WRIT TO BLOCK INQUIRY ON BANK BY STEUER

Investigator's Right to Serve as Bennett Aide Challenged as He Asks Indictments.

ORDER HALTS EXAMINATIONS

Lawyer Must Show Cause Monday Why Subpoenas Should Not Be Quashed.

14 WITNESSES ARE CALLED

Grand Jury Hears Six, Including Herbert Singer and an Aide of Broderick's.

Officials of the closed Bank of United States moved yesterday to oust Max D. Steuer as Assistant Attorney General in the investigation of the affairs of the bank a few hours after Mr. Steuer, acting as Assistant District Attorney, had appeared before the grand jury in an effort to obtain indictments against the bank officials.

The action against Mr. Steuer was in the form of an order obtained from Justice Richard P. Lydon in the Supreme Court by Bernard K. Marcus, president of the bank, and Saul Singer, executive vice president, seeking to disqualify Mr. Steuer from examining them in public.

The order, obtained through Charles H. Tuttle, attorney for Mr. Marcus, and Emory R. Buckner, attorney for Mr. Singer, requires Attorney General Bennett to show cause why subpoenas issued for the bank officials by Mr. Steuer through Mr. Bennett shall not be vacated and quashed. The order is returnable on Monday and will be served on Mr. Bennett this morning. Mr. Marcus is under subpoena to appear before Mr. Steuer on Tuesday.

Order Halts Examinations.

In their petition for the order Mr. Marcus and Mr. Singer, through their attorneys, challenged also Mr. Steuer's right and qualification to serve in the capacity of assistant to Mr. Crain. The order does not affect, however, Mr. Steuer's position as Assistant District Attorney, but if confirmed will make it impossible for him to conduct the State's end of the bank inquiry.

Until Mr. Bennett shows cause why the order should be vacated Mr. Steuer will be unable to examine Mr. Marcus and Mr. Singer in the investigation under the Martin act.

Fourteen witnesses, including employes of the bank and examiners for the State Banking Department, were called by Mr. Steuer to appear before the grand jury yesterday. Six of them were heard, among them Mr. Singer's son, Herbert Singer, president of the Bolivar Development Corporation, which played a part in the oft-mentioned $8,000,000 transaction in which the Bank of United States is alleged to have paid to itself with its own money a debt to that amount owing it by its affiliates, the Bankus Corporation and the City Financial Corporation.

Herbert Singer is connected with the law firm of Isidor J. Kresel, attorney and director of the bank and special counsel in the Appellate Division's inquiry into magistrates' courts.

Mr. Kresel, whose name has been mentioned frequently at the Attorney General's hearings on the bank's affairs conducted by Mr. Steuer, has called upon Attorney General Bennett to give him an opportunity to be examined immediately by Mr. Steuer to refute "baseless statements" made concerning his part in the affairs of the bank.

Mr. Steuer and Mr. Bennett conferred yesterday on Mr. Kresel's request after Mr. Bennett had discussed the matter by telephone with Samuel Seabury, presiding over the magistrates investigation. Mr. Bennett let it be known that he may make his reply to Mr. Kresel public today. It was understood that Mr. Kresel will be permitted to testify at an early date, although Mr. Bennett stated that he had not yet made up his mind on Mr. Kresel's request.

Held Steuer Disqualified.

In their petition to the Supreme Court Mr. Marcus and Mr. Singer contended that the investigation by Mr. Steuer in his capacity as Attorney General is illegal, and that he has made himself guilty of a misdemeanor in making public the proceedings of his examination of officers and directors of the bank.

The petition declared that Mr. Steuer is disqualified from serving as Assistant Attorney General in the bank investigation because he has been and still is the principal counsel for a large committee of depositors and stockholders of the bank, because he has announced his purpose to see to it that the officers and directors are held financially liable and because "before such committee and before mass meetings of

Mawson's Gipsy Moth seaplane, being swung over the side of the ship before a flight over unexplored lands.

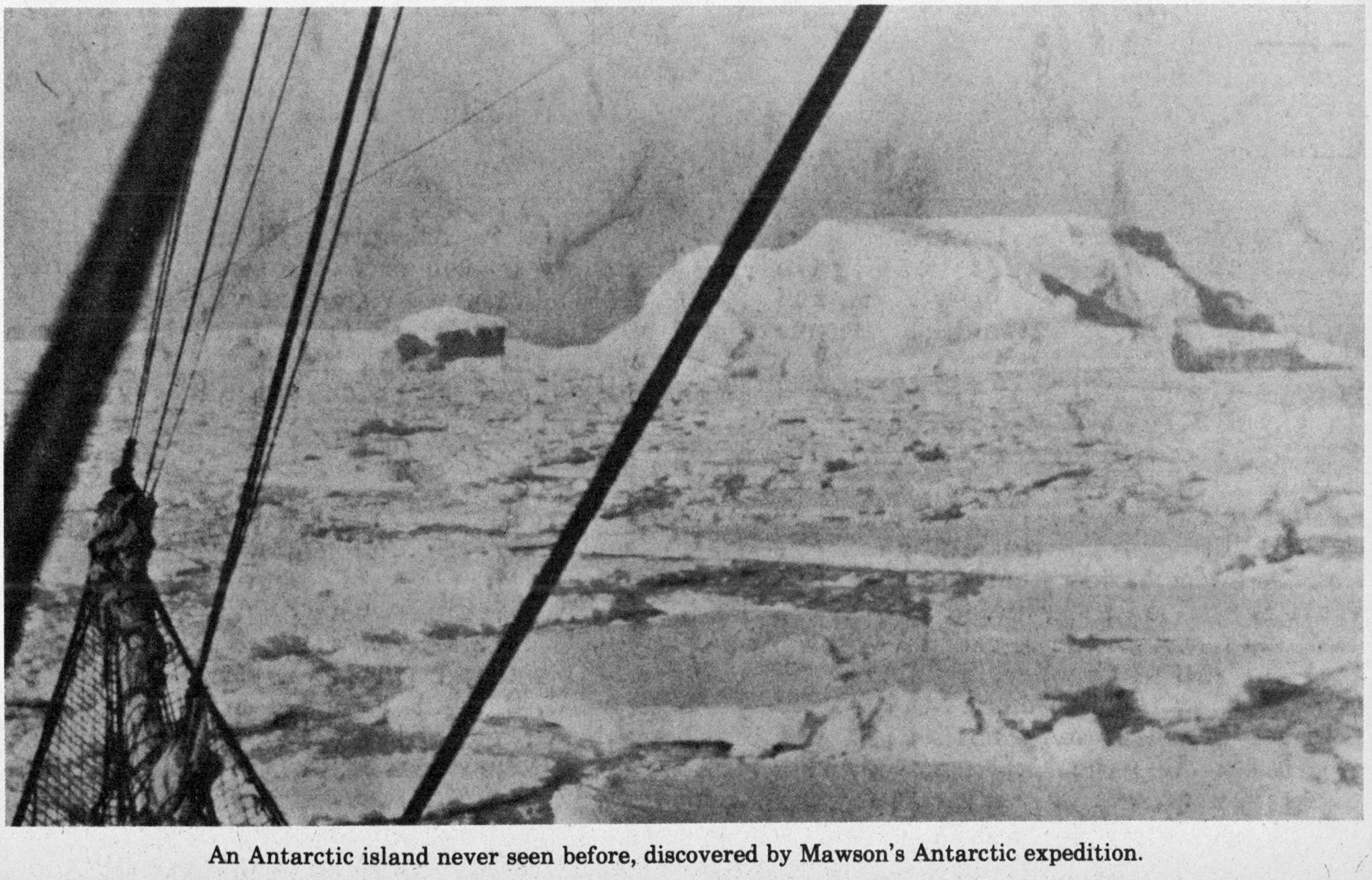

An Antarctic island never seen before, discovered by Mawson's Antarctic expedition.

"All the News That's Fit to Print."

The New York Times.

THE WEATHER

Rain today, colder at night; tomorrow partly cloudy.
Temperatures yesterday—Max. 46, min. 42.
U. S. Weather Forecast—For details see Page 42.

VOL. LXXX....No. 26,688. * * * * + NEW YORK, WEDNESDAY, FEBRUARY 18, 1931. TWO CENTS In Greater New York | THREE CENTS Within 200 Miles | FOUR CENTS Elsewhere Except 7th and 8th Postal Zones

51 POLICE BANK ACCOUNTS SUBPOENAED IN WIDE HUNT FOR 'HIGHER-UPS' IN GRAFT

600 BANKS GET SUMMONS

All 'Tenderloin' Officers Are Named in Sweeping Order by Seabury.

OTHER CITIES CANVASSED

Clearing House and Brokers to Be Asked to Help Trace Vice and Speakeasy Tribute.

FEDERAL INQUIRY PLANNED

Income Tax Bureau to Study Returns of 'Collectors' Banking Huge Sums.

Pushing his hunt for the "higher-ups" who may have benefited from the speakeasy collections and the other forms of police graft revealed thus far in the Appellate Division inquiry into magistrates' courts, Harland B. Tibbetts, special counsel, sent subpoenas to 600 banks yesterday calling for the accounts of fifty-one police officials and will send 600 more today to brokerage houses.

The fifty-one policemen named in yesterday's batch included one inspector, one deputy inspector, nine captains and one acting captain, thirty-seven lieutenants and two acting lieutenants. All are stationed in either the Third or Sixth Division, and the fifty-one will be under fire from another angle in the subpoenas to be served today.

Meanwhile United States officials in New York, it was learned, have been actively watching the reports of policemen with large bank accounts and quietly planning investigations of their own to discover whether the policemen have been paying proper income tax returns.

First Perjury Trial Opens.

A jury was selected before Judge Nott in General Sessions yesterday to try Leigh Halpern, a former vice squad member, on a charge of perjury. He is the first of seven policemen indicted on perjury charges growing out of disclosures of "framed" vice arrests to go on trial. His case and that of his partner, Daniel Sullivan, were the result of an investigation by Chief Magistrate Corrigan of charges made by Rose Davies and Marion Godfrey.

Referee Samuel Seabury was in Albany yesterday arguing a private case before the Court of Appeals, and although he is expected to return to New York today, the next public hearing was tentatively scheduled for tomorrow. The nature of the evidence to be presented at that time was not disclosed by Mr. Tibbetts.

The blanket subpoena sent out yesterday was different in form and wider in scope than any heretofore sent out.

It required all persons receiving it to produce "all transcripts of accounts, in whatever branch of your institution said accounts may have been or may be; all deposit and withdrawal slips; all photostatic copies, if any, of checks cashed; all drafts; all signature cards; all loan liability accounts; all contracts for hire of safe deposit boxes and all records showing visits to such safe-deposit boxes of each of the individuals named."

The previous blanket subpoena, which named 158 individuals, brought in the information that Patrolmen James T. Brady and Robert E. Morris had holdings in the neighborhood of $40,000 each, that Lieutenant John W. Kenna and his mother, Mrs. Anna Kenna, had made deposits of about $237,000 in six years and that the wife of James J. Quinlivan had also made deposits totaling more than $57,000 in four and a half years.

Wide Data Demanded.

The new one differed from the old in that it called for five additional types of records. These are the drafts, signature cards, loan liability accounts, safe deposit contracts and the records of visits to the boxes.

The subpoena further ordered: "In responding to the foregoing subpoena you are requested to make a thorough search of your files and records for the names of the persons indicated. Personal response to the subpoena is required in respect to all names appearing in your records. In the event, however, that some or all of such names do not appear in your

Continued on Page Eleven.

Senate Votes to Reinstate Two Expelled Midshipmen

By The Associated Press.

WASHINGTON, Feb. 17.—The Senate passed a bill tonight to direct the reinstatement in the Naval Academy of two midshipmen who were dismissed for escorting into the academy mess hall two girls masquerading in men's clothing.

The midshipmen are Lawrence L. Myatt of Massachusetts and Miller S. Burgin of Florida.

Senators Walsh, Democrat of Massachusetts, and Fletcher, Democrat of Florida, sponsored the resolution.

INQUIRY FUND VOTED; BLOCK STILL HOLDS

Senate Adopts Budget With $250,000 Item, but Fight Leaves Resolution in Air.

KNIGHT SLATED AS HEAD

Hofstadter Retires as Prospective Chairman If and When City Investigation Is Ordered.

By W. A. WARN.

Special to The New York Times.

ALBANY, Feb. 17.—By a bare majority of 26 to 25, the Republicans in the Senate today won the first skirmish over the proposal to launch a legislative investigation into the conduct of the New York City Government under the Walker régime, including the administration of justice in some of the courts within the city.

The conflict came on the $250,000 appropriation for the legislative contingent fund, embodied in the budget with the view of using the money to defray the cost of the inquiry. After a determined attack by the Democratic minority to eliminate the item, the Republicans retained it by a straight party vote; whereupon the two main budget bills for $293,000,000 were adopted, receiving the unanimous support of Republican and Democratic Senators.

With the decks thus cleared for action in the Senate on the Hofstadter-Story resolution to set up the machinery for the proposed inquiry, Republican leaders of the Legislature were still in doubt regarding the wisdom of bringing the measure out tomorrow.

It faces the prospect of being beaten in the end through the defection of William L. Ward's two Republican Senators from Westchester, whose votes, with the Democrats a unit in opposition, would be essential for its adoption.

A spokesman for W. Kingsland Macy, chairman of the Republican State Committee, said that if the orders from headquarters were obeyed, the resolution would be voted on in the Senate tomorrow, despite the menacing outlook.

Committee Fails to Meet.

It was noticed, however, that the Senate Finance Committee, which has preliminary custody of the measure, held no meeting during the afternoon, a departure from usual

Continued on Page Nine.

DELAY ON BONUS BILL CRUSHED IN SENATE; HOOVER SEES AIDES

Senators Force Smoot to Agree to Report Bill From the Committee Today.

MELLON WILL BE HEARD

Stories of Compromise Proposals Are Heard After the Conferences at White House.

REED FOR SPREADING LOANS

But President Is Told That He Will Get the Measure Before the Week-End.

Special to The New York Times.

WASHINGTON, Feb. 17.—Advocates of the veterans' bonus loan bill, by swift and determined attacks on what they declared was a program of administration leaders in the Senate to delay action, today forced Senator Smoot, chairman of the Finance Committee, to agree to report the measure tomorrow, after Secretary Mellon and General Hines of the Veterans' Bureau have explained to the committee the financial aspects of the House measure.

Conferences were held at the White House tonight by Senators and treasury advisers to consider a compromise plan that would lessen the immediate financial drain upon the government. While modifications of the bill probably will be offered in the Finance Committee by Senator Reed it is believed that they will be rejected and that the Senate by Friday will pass the House measure unamended.

The Senate debate was spirited and at times personal, Republicans and Democrats stating that they would tolerate no delay and declaring that the Senate should act by Friday night, thus removing any possibility of the President killing the bill by a "pocket" veto.

Amendments Face Opposition.

Suggestions of amendments that might delay passage were swept aside by Senator Couzens and others, who, while believing that the interest rate of 4½ per cent should be reduced, are unwilling to jeopardize prompt passage by considering a reduction.

Suggestions of a possible compromise were heard late tonight after Senator Reed and Senator Smoot had conferred with President Hoover on the Senate situation.

Senator Smoot told the President that the bill would be sent to the White House before the end of the week without material change, and that its advocates were strong enough in the Senate to override a veto.

Senator Reed's mission was to discuss with the President the effect of amendments which he will offer. He may offer an amendment providing that the loans shall be made in four periods of a month each, and that banks may make the loans instead of the treasury.

Ogden L. Mills, Under Secretary of the Treasury; Walter E. Hope, Assistant Secretary, and General Hines saw the President later.

Talk of Compromise Persists.

These conferences led to reports that Senator Reed would sponsor amendments before the Finance Committee, which, if agreed upon, would make the bill acceptable to President Hoover.

Senator Reed said, however, that

Continued on Page Two.

Vanderlip's Profit in Auburn Auto $3,000,000 By Sensational Rise of the Stock This Year

As a result of the sensational rise in the stock of the Auburn Automobile Company, which advanced yesterday to a high for 1931 of 205, compared with a low of 101½ in January, Frank A. Vanderlip, former president of the National City Bank, has a paper profit in the stock of from $3,000,000 to $5,000,000, according to estimates made in Wall Street.

In an interview given to The Associated Press in Los Angeles Monday, Mr. Vanderlip, who is now a special partner in the Stock Exchange concern of Baker, Harden & Weeks, admitted that he had been heavily interested in Auburn, almost since the company was started. He made his last purchase of the stocks, he said, at 105, or 100 points less than yesterday's high.

Mr. Vanderlip and his associates are credited generally with the ownership of one-fourth of the 173,475 shares of Auburn stock outstanding. This block, at yesterday's top figure, was valued at $8,000,000, about half of which represents market appreciation during the last month.

The Cord Corporation, a holding company, is said to own 50 per cent of the Auburn stock. Owing to the small floating supply of the stock, there have been frequent rumors that a technical corner existed in the issue. After touching yesterday's high price, the stock declined sharply, in sympathy with a general market reaction, to 188¾, a loss of 10¼ points for the day.

Auburn sold as low as 60¾ last November. Several large bear operators are reported to have lost heavily in the issue's sharp advance.

It has been reported for several days that the business conduct committee of the New York Stock Exchange is watching the trading in Auburn shares by certain houses particularly interested in the stock, in order to ascertain whether transactions in the shares for the last few months have conformed to the standards of the institution. No general questionnaire, however, has been sent out to the members of the Exchange.

Byrd's Little America Will Be Occupied As Base for Polar Study by 27 Nations

Special to The New York Times.

WASHINGTON, Feb. 17.—Little America, Rear Admiral Byrd's base in the Antarctic, may be occupied again if a proposed international plan for meteorological, electric and magnetic research, approved by President Hoover, is entertained by the government.

A resolution authorizing an appropriation of $30,000 for the participation of the United States with twenty-six other nations in the "second polar year" was voted favorably by the House Foreign Affairs Committee today.

From Aug. 1, 1932, to Aug. 31, 1933, the participating countries, through nearly fifty stations, plan to gather information as to the elements that surround the earth, chiefly at its polar extremities.

Plans for the international research, which is also to be participated in by Soviet Russia, were explained to the House committee by John A. Fleming of the department of terrestrial magnetism of the Carnegie Institution in Washington.

Mr. Fleming explained that in 1882 the leading nations joined in observing the "first polar year" and sent scientists to the ends of the earth to make observations.

The project for rehabilitating Little America comes from New Zealand, he said, where it is proposed that a station be established by Norwegian whalers who venture that near the South Pole in whaling seasons.

The United States has been asked to outfit and man two stations, one near Fairbanks, Alaska, and another near Refuge Harbor, in northeast Greenland. Argentina has agreed to establish a station at New Year's Island, off the southernmost tip of South America. Brazil also will establish an observatory in the South Polar region. France hopes to establish a station in the extreme South Indian Ocean. Russia will plant her station in the Arctic, while other nations will have stations over the globe.

Secretary Stimson, in a representation to the committee, said the Departments of Commerce, the Interior and Agriculture, the Postoffice Department and the Navy are interested in the plan where it touches their various services.

DEMOCRATIC CHIEFS OPPOSE WET STAND

Both Wets and Drys in Senate and on Committee Object to Raskob's 'Showdown' Now.

WAGNER INSISTS ON REPEAL

In Senate Speech He Advises Party to Adopt Plank as in Line With Wickersham Report.

By RICHARD V. OULAHAN.

Special to The New York Times.

WASHINGTON, Feb. 17.—Yesterday's flurry within the Democratic ranks of the Senate, which brought to the front a marked opposition among Southern Senators to having the prohibition question considered at the coming meeting of the Democratic National Committee with a view to demonstrating party policy concerning it, had a significant reaction today in the apparent sympathetic response among Democratic Senators from other sections.

The impression was gathered that a good many Democratic Senators of wet proclivities felt that it would be a serious error to have the National Committee undertake to map out a policy at its special meeting here on March 5.

Such a course, it was maintained, was the business of the national convention, but, aside from that, any placing of the party on record fifteen months before the convention would kindle controversy to the detriment of party morale and harmony.

Raskob Said to Seek "Showdown."

The call for the meeting issued by John J. Raskob, chairman of the National Committee, has been very generally interpreted as suggesting that it was intended to consider the adoption of a set of party principles, including what was described today as a "show-down" on the prohibition issue now, instead of waiting for the National Convention in 1932.

The impression is widespread among prominent Democrats here that if that was Mr. Raskob's intention he will abandon it prior to the meeting of March 5. A considerable number of national committeemen and committeewomen from States accounted as wet in sentiment, as well as the generality of wet Democratic Senators, no less than those of dry leanings, were represented as opposed to bringing up the issue at this time.

Wagner Advises Repeal Plank.

Today's output on the prohibition question in the Senate was comprised mainly in a speech by Senator Robert F. Wagner, Democrat, of New York, in which he analyzed the Wickersham report, to the conclusion that it marked "the beginning of the end" of prohibition, and for this reason advised that the Democratic party in 1932 should advocate repeal of the Eighteenth Amendment.

Arguing that "fear of the saloon" kept the Wickersham commission from recommending repeal, he declared that "concurrent action" by the States to prevent the return of the saloon "would meet every ultimate requirement laid down by the commission."

Also appearing to contend that political parties should declare without delay how they stood on the wet-dry issue, he said:

"Now that the issue has become sharp and clear, we hear the political counsel of silence. We are told there is more harmony in evasion.

"Perhaps there is, but there is no genuine lasting cohesion except that of common faith in a significant

Continued on Page Three.

FINAL CITY TAX ROLL IS UP $578,548,612

Real Estate Is Assessed at $18,806,166,924, Personalty at $356,350,090 for 1931.

BIG SLASH IN ESTATE ITEM

$450,811,845 Cut Held to Show Haphazard System—41,000 Protests Were Filed.

New York City's taxable real estate is valued for assessment purposes at $18,806,166,924 for this year and personal estates at $356,350,090, according to the final figures announced yesterday by James J. Sexton, president of the Department of Taxes and Assessments. The total is $19,162,517,014. Deductons and exemptions of all sorts from the tentative assessment figures announced last October amounted to $623,328,228. Taxable propery increased this year by $578,548,612 over last year.

When the tentative assessment valuations were announced last October they caused a flood of protests which reached about 41,000 by the middle of November, the last date for filing protests. In Manhattan 12,220 protests were filed. Brooklyn sent in 15,800; Queens, 5,600; the Bronx, 6,500, and Richmond, 900. The tax department held hearings on 27,000 protests to determine whether the assessment valuations should be lowered or retained.

Hearings were held on 9,500 protests from Manhattan, 8,000 from Brooklyn, 3,500 from Queens, 5,500 from the Bronx and 500 from Richmond. The number of protests and the hearings they required gave the department one of the busiest years in its history.

Personalty Shows Big Drop.

The arbitrary methods used by the tax department in valuing personal property for assessment purposes are shown in the fact that deductions amounting to $450,811,845 were made after protests had been filed. Last October the taxable personalty was set at $807,161,935, but it dwindled to $356,350,090 on the final tabulation. George W. Adee, deputy in charge of the personal bureau, said the appraisers had no accurate information upon which to base their estimates of the amount of personal property any one possessed. A man's wealth is judged by the neighborhood in which he lives and similar haphazard methods, assuming that if the valuation is excessive the owner will "swear it off," Mr. Adee said. Mayor Walker is opposed to the levying of this tax, and some months ago a movement was on foot to abolish it. After some discussion of its evils, however, the matter was dropped.

Personal estates showed a decrease this year, compared with last year. The total decrease was $24,089,540, and was distributed over Manhattan, the Bronx and Richmond. In Manhattan the decrease was $27,464,950. Increases in Brooklyn and Queens, however, brought the total decrease to $24,089,540. Mandatory tax exemptions, such as those for property used for church purposes, amounted to $1,145,198,130. This sum included about $25,000,000, consisting of tax valuations placed upon uncompleted buildings not ready for occupancy on Dec. 15, 1930. The courts held that a law exempting this class of property from taxation was constitutional.

Manhattan real estate was valued for tax purposes at $9,485,832,565 this year, compared to $9,093,001,835 last year, a net increase of $392,830,730. In the Bronx the real estate

Continued on Page Thirteen.

PENNSYLVANIA LINES SPEED CONSTRUCTION; TO SPEND $175,000,000

Atterbury Announces Decision to Rush Electrification, New Stations and Other Work.

REDUCES 4-YEAR ESTIMATE

Says Program Will Be Pushed to Completion in Two and a Half Years.

SEES EMPLOYMENT AIDED

Declares Conditions of Labor and Finance Are Favorable Now for Expansion.

Plans calling for the total expenditure of $175,000,000 and the completion within two and a half years, instead of four, of the extensive program of improvements, such as electrifying lines and building new passenger stations, begun a little more than a year ago by the Pennsylvania Railroad, were announced yesterday by W. W. Atterbury, president.

Mr. Atterbury pointed out that the proposals "to go forward with redoubled energy" on the improvements would involve "very large expenditures" for labor which would be of great benefit to the unemployment situation.

Mr. Atterbury's Statement.

His statement, in full, follows:

"The Pennsylvania Railroad, a little over a year ago, embarked upon an extensive program of improvements. The plan called for an expenditure during the year 1930 of about $90,000,000, but actually $106,000,000 of construction work was done.

"It had been planned that the remainder of the work would be spread over a period of four years. However, the Pennsylvania Railroad has come to the conclusion that now is the time to go forward with redoubled energy, and it has accordingly decided, instead of carrying out this work in a period of about four years, to complete it, if possible, within approximately two and a half years.

"The plans in hand call for improvement items totaling in cost some $175,000,000.

"It is our view that commodity prices are now at a level, and the efficiency of labor is so great that these improvements can now be definitely contracted for on exceptionally favorable bases. Furthermore, at a time like the present, with reduced traffic, the work can be done with much less interference from the movement of passing trains which, of itself, would constitute a definite economy.

"This is, accordingly, an exceptionally favorable time to push to conclusion the plans in hand.

"The improvements contemplated will involve the use of upward of 150,000 tons of steel; the purchase of 240 electric locomotives; the electrification of eighty passenger cars, and, in addition, there will be very large expenditures for labor which will be of great benefit to the unemployment situation.

Lists Rail Projects.

"The projects which will now be pushed forward to completion are:

(a) Electrification of the remaining portions of all the lines of track between New York and Washing-

Continued on Page Four.

Mawson Finds Big Open Sea in Antarctic; Water Is So Cold That Fish Are Frozen in It

By SIR DOUGLAS MAWSON.

Wireless to THE NEW YORK TIMES.

ABOARD S. S. THE DISCOVERY, in the Antarctic, Feb. 12.—Yesterday The Discovery pushed through an area of slack pack ice into a splendid sea of open water leading south. In these ice-encircled waters a strong southerly wind had worked up a considerable sea.

After establishing contact with land we followed the coast south all day. Late in the afternoon, in the shelter of an enormous tabular berg, our airplane was got up and further geographic observations were made, while a marine station was run from the ship. We were then in an extensive region of shallow sea ranging from 100 to 250 fathoms deep.

Here the water was uniformly cold. Howard found the bottom of the water the coldest yet recorded by our expedition, namely 28.30 degrees Fahrenheit. Large numbers of small fish floated past the ship, dead and apparently frozen.

Hurley sculled the pram into some remarkable grotto formations sculptured in grounded bergs and obtained a striking photographic record. From Lat. 67.43 degrees S. and Long. 69.20 degrees E. the coast takes a sharp turn south with open water along the coast until past the sixty-ninth degree of Latitude. Then it comes back slightly north, extending east to meet the land ice slopes seen from our airplane on Feb. 9. The land is entirely covered by ice.

This inland ice sheet was observed to reach an elevation of 4,000 feet at no great distance inland. From such heights it descends in a series of undulations, finally to the sea level. It is fringed for the most part by horizontally disposed floating extensions which advance several miles over the waters before truncation by periodic carving of tabular bergs.

The existence of this ice-locked sea extending beyond the sixty-ninth degree of Latitude S., was an interesting discovery. Very strong winds descending from the land ice slopes feature this neighborhood and appear to be responsible for driving the pack away from the coast.

ALFONSO FIGHTS FOR CROWN AS ARMY BACKS BERENGUER IN MOVE FOR NEW CABINET

Rembrandt's 'Anatomy Lesson' Slashed by Vandal in Museum

Special Cable to THE NEW YORK TIMES.

PARIS, Feb. 17.—Rembrandt's famous painting, "The Anatomy Lesson," in the Rijks Museum in Amsterdam, was seriously damaged today by a fanatical Hollander, who slashed it with a hachet.

The man, who refused to give any explanation, was immediately arrested and tonight was examined by alienists. He is 33 years old. He entered the museum quietly and attacked the picture at a moment when the museum guards were some distance away. He apparently had no intention of stealing the painting, for the slashes were evidently delivered with intent to damage. Five rents were made, one almost a foot long.

With "The Night Watch," another of Rembrandt's great paintings, "The Anatomy Lesson" is one of the most popular with visitors to Holland. Experts have pronounced it one of the most valuable paintings in the world.

WHITE LOSES POST AT GRACE CHURCH

Resignation Offered on Jan. 15 Accepted Following Clash on Companionate Marriage.

WARNED NOT TO AIR VIEWS

But Aide Ignored Dr. Bowie's Advice and Sought Church Trial on His Beliefs.

The resignation of the Rev. Eliot White as a member of the auxiliary staff of Grace Church, Broadway and Tenth Street, was accepted Monday evening by the Rev. Dr. W. Russell Bowie, the rector, it was learned yesterday.

In connection with his views on marriage Mr. White has demanded a Church trial from Bishop Manning, asking "either ultimate conviction, with whatever penalties it may involve, or else open exoneration." So far, Bishop Manning has ignored Mr. White's challenge.

The termination of Mr. White's connection with Grace Church came as a result of his advocacy of companionate marriage in a chain of circumstances precipitated by his invitation to Judge Lindsey to address the New York Churchmen's Association on Dec. 1.

Declaring that the name of Grace parish should not be linked with the idea of companionate marriage, Dr. Bowie issued a brief statement last night as an official announcement of the acceptance of Mr. White's resignation. Further comment on the matter was refused at the church. The statement follows:

"Grace Church, in view of its exceptionally high standard for marriages which take place in the parish, and in view of its provision that only those are married by its clergy who express their purpose 'to enter a life-

Continued on Page Six.

GUNS TRAINED ON MADRID

Troops Held in Barracks After the King Rejects Cabinet List of Foes.

ROYALISTS CHOSEN INSTEAD

All but Three Are Selected—Former Premier May Take Office Today.

THREAT OF GENERAL STRIKE

Socialists Ready to Act—Police Suppress Minor Disorders in the Capital.

By FRANK L. KLUCKHOHN.

Special Cable to THE NEW YORK TIMES.

MADRID, Wednesday, Feb. 18.—King Alfonso astounded Spain yesterday by reversing his decision of the day before and deciding to fight for his crown and seems early today to have won the first round in his battle.

Leaders of all the Monarchist parties agreed last night, after a five-hour meeting, to form a new government under General Damaso Berenguer, who resigned Saturday.

News of the decision of the Monarchists, which came at 1 o'clock this morning, made dimmer the prospect of a military dictatorship, the only other solution left to the King, which still remains a possibility if any hitch occurs in the present plan.

The Berenguer Government, if formed, as seems practically assured, will include the Count de Bugallal, the head of the Conservative party; Juan de la Cierva, Conservative, the father of the Autogiro's inventor of the same name; Belito y Musito, Francisco Cambo, the Count de Romanones, the Liberal leader; the Marquis de Alhucemas, the Duke of Maura, and the former Minister of Finance in the previous Berenguer Cabinet, Julio Wais.

Army Support Is Seen.

General Berenguer's presence in the Cabinet which has been proposed to King Alfonso is an indication that the army is prepared to back the monarch, whose moves probably will include the election of an ordinary Cortes (Parliament), which would modify the Constitution to some extent.

Señor Wais took an incomplete list of the proposed government to the palace at 1 o'clock this morning and on leaving said:

"It appears likely that a government will be formed, although I have not completed the list at present. Since we will have to agree on all the members it is possible the government will not be announced today."

It is also reported, however, that the new Cabinet may take office this afternoon. Three Cabinet members are still to be chosen.

The Marquis de Alhucemas, in a statement to the press, said:

"We are all disposed to put ourselves at the complete service of the King."

Republicans Infuriated.

The Republicans are as angry as they are amazed by King Alfonso's change of front—his surrender to their demands one day and his refusal to even treat with them the next.

However, what matters now is whether the Republicans will set in motion the machinery for a general strike, which has long been prepared, or mark time for a more favorable opportunity to overthrow the monarchy by force.

Señor Sanchez Guerra, according to his friends, is a broken old man this morning and verging on a nervous breakdown. If he had shown greater strength yesterday morning, it was said by some, the chances are that he would have won his point with the King, but, weakened in health, he received King Alfonso's decision not to hold a constituent Cortes (constitutional convention) without a protest. When Señor Alvarez came along later it was too late—the monarch had made up his mind to fight it out.

Army Ready for Action.

The Spanish military machine was standing with weapons at hand, ready to march into the streets of Spain's cities last night to save the crown for King Alfonso if he asks it.

Two military garrisons near Madrid—the Alcala Henares and the

"All the News That's Fit to Print."

The New York Times.

THE WEATHER
Cloudy today and tomorrow; not much change in temperature.
Temperatures yesterday—Max. 45, min. 32.
U. S. Weather Forecast—For details see Page 25.

VOL. LXXX....No. 26,693. ****+ NEW YORK, MONDAY, FEBRUARY 23, 1931. TWO CENTS In Greater New York | THREE CENTS Within 200 Miles | FOUR CENTS Elsewhere Except 7th and 8th Postal Zones

PERUVIANS MOBILIZE PLANES AND RESERVE TO CRUSH REBELLION

Troops Move South Against Arequipa Garrison as Fliers Reconnoitre.

CENSORSHIP VEILS FACTS

Santiago Hears Rebels Hold the Entire South, but Lima Says Outbreak Is Limited.

INSURGENTS ON TRIAL TODAY

One Court Will Hear Evidence on 39 Seized and Another Will Review Their Cases.

By The Associated Press.

LIMA, Peru, Feb. 22.—Airplanes and reservists were mobilized today to quell an uprising in Southern Peru which has arisen to menace the government of Provisional President Louis M. Sanchez Cerro.

With a strict censorship in effect, it was impossible to confirm reports that the entire southern half of the country was in revolt against the régime of Colonel Sanchez Cerro, who himself is a revolutionary President, but the government admitted in an official statement that the large city of Arequipa was captured by rebellious troops Friday night and that several loyal officials had been killed in defense.

The Arequipa rising followed by only a few hours a revolt at Callao, the port of Lima, just outside the capital, in which some sixty persons were killed before the movement was suppressed and thirty-nine were arrested for court-martial.

Today government airplanes took off from Lima to fly over Arequipa and survey the situation, while 1,600 reserves between the ages of 21 and 30 were called into active service for sixty days. They will be incorporated into regiments of the second military region, Lima and Callao.

In addition, loyal troops from Cuzco, Puno, Juliaca and Tacna were said to be marching on Arequipa to crush the rebellion.

Several Loyalists Killed.

When the revolt began at Arequipa several loyal officers were killed, including Lieut. Col. Gamarra, the divisional commander, and Captain Gomez Sanchez, while a number of enlisted men also died.

As soon as it learned of the trouble the Central Government at Lima immediately shut off traffic to Mollendo, the seaport for Arequipa, and also closed the Mollendo airport to anything except government traffic.

The movement at Callao was sponsored by adherents of Augusto B. Leguia, the former President, who was deposed by the August revolution and now is in the national penitentiary at Lima.

It was understood, however, that the Arequipa rising had no connection with Señor Leguia and instead was declared to fulfill the August revolution.

This Arequipa revolt is starting in the same area as that which made Colonel Sanchez Cerro Provisional President in August. The President at that time was a Lieutenant Colonel in the army and he began a revolt at Arequipa which soon resulted in the overthrow of the Lima Government and his installation in the National Palace amid wild acclamation. His régime has been marked by much trouble and dissension, accentuated by the economic distress which has afflicted Peru as well as the rest of the world.

Meanwhile the government is preparing for an early trial of the thirty-nine prisoners arrested after Friday's revolutionary attempt at Callao. The trials probably will be started tomorrow. Among those under arrest are General Pedro Pablo Martinez and Colonel Cesar Zorilla Lujan.

Death Sentences Doubtful.

Although those found guilty could be sentenced to death, according to the military code, all indications are that the convicted will receive sentences of twenty years in the penitentiary.

It is learned reliably that two tribunals will be appointed. One, consisting of four high officers, will hear the cases and pronounce sentence, and their action will be confirmed or appealed by five other officers acting as supreme justices.

It was stated here that southern garrisons were invited by Arequipa rebels to join them but refused, remaining loyal to the Lima Government. Puno and Juliaca troops, after reiterating their adhesion to Colonel Sanchez Cerro, are said to have marched on to Cuzco, joining there the loyalists who also had refused to join the revolt.

The troops of Cuzco, Puno and

Continued on Page Seven.

Sidney Franklin Gored Again In Fight With Bull in Mexico

By The Associated Press.

NUEVO LAREDO, Mexico, Feb. 22.—Sidney Franklin of Brooklyn, the only known American matador, was gored through the right leg and painfully injured this afternoon by the fourth bull in an exhibition here today.

The American fainted and was carried from the arena. Marcial Lalanda, Spanish matador, killed the bull, but before the next fight was concluded Franklin returned to the ring, receiving an ovation. He killed the sixth bull, and Mexican admirers proclaimed him "very brave" and "bold."

During the first encounter a sword plunged at the bull was flung into the air by the enraged beast and struck a spectator in the thigh, badly wounding him.

During the third fight another sword was hurled from the lunging bull and narrowly missed an American girl in the audience.

ATTACK ON M'DONALD LAUNCHED BY MOSLEY

Bid for Power Seen in a New Manifesto Urging Restrictions on British Parliament.

TORIES AND LIBERALS AID

New Plan for "Social-Fascism" Calls for Cancellation of War Debts and Tariffs.

Special Cable to THE NEW YORK TIMES.

LONDON, Feb. 22.—Sir Oswald Mosley, aristocrat of the Labor party, who has been called the British Hitler, has thrown down the gauntlet to Prime Minister MacDonald and is making a bold bid for the dictatorship of Great Britain.

"Fed up," as he says, with the "old gangs" of party politicians and convinced the present Parliamentary system is inadequate to deal with Britain's industrial crisis, Sir Oswald is preparing a new policy of national reconstruction.

In a few days he will appear at the head of a group of young reformers of all parties pledged to the establishment of a restricted form of dictatorship with enormous powers, largely superseding Parliament. Their policy, according to the new manifesto, which is expected to be issued Tuesday, will be social-fascism based on tariffs with sweeping financial changes, including the cancellation of war debts.

Plans Nation-Wide Campaign.

Hitherto Sir Oswald has been aiming at reform of the Labor party from within. Now he is going to "ginger it up" from outside. As soon as the manifesto is completed and published, Sir Oswald and a number of lieutenants drawn from the extremists of the Liberal, Labor and Conservative parties will start a nation-wide campaign in search of recruits.

As this campaign will be directed against the MacDonald Government, Sir Oswald's resignation or expulsion from the Labor party is expected hourly. It is said he has received pledges of support for a new group in Commons from seven parliamentarians, including his wife, Lady Cynthia, and John Strachey. Outside Parliament, Sir William Morris, automobile manufacturer, is said to be his principal backer.

Mr. Morris, before leaving England for Buenos Aires last week, made a strong attack on what he termed the "shams of party politics," which he said had disgusted and discouraged British industrialists and hampered reconstruction. This happens to be the main line of Sir Oswald's

Continued on Page Eleven.

ONLY 3 MAJOR BILLS LEFT FOR CONGRESS; NAVY FUND DROPPED

Bonus Loan, Following Veto, Muscle Shoals and 'Lame Ducks' Measures Remain.

TREATY FLEET PLAN DEAD

Hale Abandons Program for $90,000,000 Appropriation for Warship Construction.

NO FEAR OF A FILIBUSTER

With Eight and a Half Legislative Days Remaining, Extra Session Menace Has Vanished.

Special to The New York Times.

WASHINGTON, Feb. 22.—With the adoption of practically all the supply bills and the virtual disappearance of the spectre of an extra session, Congress has left eight and a half legislative days of the present session before the final adjournment, now considered certain, on March 4.

While the second deficiency bill is still before the Senate and the navy supply bill is yet to emerge from conference, there is no indication of a filibuster on either.

In the remaining days three controversial questions must be decided, the promised veto of the veterans' bonus loan bill, the "lame duck" resolution sponsored by Senator Norris, and the conference report on Muscle Shoals.

Hoover Preparing Bonus Veto.

President Hoover has completed the first draft of his veto message on the bonus loan bill and it is now being revised so that it will be ready for Congress not later than Thursday.

In the opinion of opponents of this measure there has been no appreciable shift in the attitude of Congress. A canvass made by Senate leaders indicates that there will be a switch of four votes to sustain the veto, including Senator Watson, Republican floor leader.

This would give twenty votes to sustain, while thirty-three are necessary, provided the full Senate vote is cast. In the House the final estimate is that not more than sixty votes will be cast to uphold the President. Only thirty-nine opposed adoption of the bill.

There are many points of disagreement in the navy bill passed by the Senate Saturday, but the conferees meeting tomorrow are expected quickly to reach an agreement and present their report before the end of the week.

There will be no further difficulties respecting naval matters as the House leaders agreed last week not to present a bill for naval construction under the treaty. Senator Hale of the Naval Affairs Committee was ready to report a bill to the Senate carrying $90,000,000, but the decision of the House leaders and the opposition of Senator Borah to the expenditure for treaty naval construction has led him to abandon his plans.

Of the other major questions to be disposed of, the most important, as affecting Republican policy, is the Muscle Shoals bill, since it involves the issue of government operation of a public utility. The compromise adopted in conference provides for government operation of the power plant and the leasing to private enterprise of the nitrate plant.

The former provision satisfies the advocates of public operation and the opposition is somewhat appeased by the provision that the nitrate plant

Continued on Page Two.

Indians Give Gandhi Sole Power to Arbitrate; He Summons Conference of Congress Chiefs

Special Cable to THE NEW YORK TIMES.

NEW DELHI, Feb. 22.—Mahatma Gandhi telegraphed tonight all over India for Nationalist Congress leaders to come here as quickly as possible.

The round-table delegates, Sir Tej Bahadur Sapru, Srinivasa Sastri and M. R. Jayakar, profess the greatest optimism regarding the events of the past week, declaring quite frankly that Gandhi had never been more open to reason or readier to consider practical politics. In government circles and the European non-official community, however, there is by no means the same measure of cheerfulness.

Congress members are less concerned with India's future constitution than with whether Bhagat Singh, sentenced to death for the murder of Captain Saunders at Lahore, can be saved from the gallows and on the immediate release of their companions from jail. Until these matters are settled it is useless to expect any intelligent participation, even by the best brains of the Congress, in the resumption of the task started at St. James's Palace.

Yesterday the second contingent of round table delegates returned on an Italian mail steamer and lost no time in endorsing the manifesto issued by the first party to return.

NEW DELHI, India, Feb. 22 (AP).—Sweeping powers to make any decision in behalf of the All-India National Congress in his dealings with the Viceroy were given to Mahatma Gandhi today by a formal resolution of the working committee, which is the cabinet of the Congress.

Today's action also would appear to set at rest recurrent rumors that there is a split in the opinions of the working committee. There had been reports that some of the more moderate members disagreed with Gandhi's views and were in favor of peace at any price.

Three Convicts Killed in Break at Joliet; 14 Escape From Arizona Prison Into Desert

Special to The New York Times.

JOLIET, Ill., Feb. 22.—In a break for freedom from Joliet penitentiary early today, three convicts from Chicago ran into an ambuscade of prison guards armed with machine guns and were shot to death in the darkness.

Warned by the burst of gunfire, accomplices outside, who were awaiting the convicts in two cars, sped away from the prison toward Chicago, pursued by prison cars, but they escaped.

Those killed were Joseph Norkiewicz, 30 years old, who was serving from one to ten years for larceny; Julio Chileno, 39 years old, a confidence man and suspected leader of the plot, who had served terms also in the Maryland and New Jersey penitentiaries, and Alvin Kilmon, 33 years old, convicted on six robbery charges and serving from one to twenty years.

For three weeks the prison authorities had been aware that some of the inmates were plotting to escape, but, not knowing the author of the plot, Warden Harry Hill ordered twenty guards to night patrol duty outside the wall. Within the east cell block, housing some of the trusted prisoners, five men were planning the final details of a scheme to bring them liberty. All five had been detailed for some months to early morning duty in the kitchen.

Their opportunity came at 3 o'clock this morning. Awakened by guards, they shuffled in line down the yard to the kitchen.

As usual, one guard, Frank Lambert, was left in charge of them. Norkiewicz and Chileno armed themselves with butcher knives. All five rushed the guard. With knives at his throat, Lambert dropped his club and permitted his captors to thrust him into a refrigerator.

They improvised a ladder of long sticks used to push bread pans into the ovens, climbed to the wall and let themselves down by a cable made of tin cans, bits of chain and other materials. As the last of the three started down this cable, the hidden guards started firing.

FLORENCE, Ariz., Feb. 22 (AP).—Scaling a twenty-foot wall while a guard's back was turned, fifteen

Continued on Page Fourteen.

GUNS SOUND PRELUDE FOR CHICAGO PRIMARY

Attempt Made on Life of Candidate—Two Workers Beaten, Two Kidnapped.

POLICE HUNT FOR CAPONE

Legionaires to Join 70,000 Watchers in Guarding Polls in Tomorrow's Mayoralty Fight.

Special to The New York Times.

CHICAGO, Feb. 22.—Police, deputy sheriffs and government agents are hunting tonight for Al Capone, public enemy No. 1 and reputed contributor of $150,000 to Mayor Thompson's primary campaign fund, who was reported to have returned here to direct the activities of his gangsters at the primary polls Tuesday.

Although Capone apparently has avoided his usual haunts on the South Side and in Cicero, it is reported that he is in hiding at a place where he can see to it that his interests at the polls are looked after.

Capone is due to appear in the Federal court Wednesday to answer an old contempt-of-court charge. The police have a warrant issued months ago by Judge John H. Lyle, charging him with vagrancy.

One of the indications of Capone's presence was that Frank Rio, his personal bodyguard and a helper of City Sealer Dan Serritella, alleged Capone lieutenant and member of Mayor Thompson's cabinet, gave assurances to the Thompson headquarters during the day that the First Ward, or "Loop" district, would be "delivered" for Thompson on Tuesday.

Rio has been accused of the murder of a policeman and served a prison term with Capone in Philadelphia for carrying concealed weapons.

Lyle Dispenses with Guard.

The three leading candidates for the Republican Mayoralty nomination continued today their attacks on one another. Judge Lyle for the last twenty-four hours has been under constant surveillance by two motorcycle policemen. This evening he turned on them.

"Go back to Chief Alcock," he said, "and tell him not to worry about me. Tell him to do his worrying about "Al" Capone. There are two warrants out for Capone which I issued and neither has been served. Tell Alcock to get service on those warrants. I'll take care of myself. I have done it so far in this campaign. Capone and his gangsters are cowards and they wouldn't attack me."

Mayor Thompson made his principal speech before a Negro audience at the Eighth Regiment Armory. He told them that Negroes will "go in the front gate" at the world's fair if they help keep him in office. If his opponent was elected they would go in the back gate or not at all.

Outbreaks in Two Wards.

CHICAGO, Feb. 22 (AP).—Pre-primary violence ran rampant in Chicago tonight. Two sluggings, two kidnappings and an attempt upon the life of a candidate for Alderman were reported to officials as they rallied an army of 70,000 persons for a guard against fraud and disorder in tomorrow's voting, the result of which will decide whether Mayor "Big Bill' Thompson or Judge Lyle is to be the Republican nominee for next Mayor of Chicago.

The disturbances were centred in the Eighth and Thirtieth Wards. In the Eighth Theodore Clifford, candidate for Alderman, told the police

Continued on Page Three.

CITY AND NATION PAY WASHINGTON TRIBUTE

Lord Grey on Radio Declares England Sees George III Was Wrong in 1776.

THRONGS OUT FOR HOLIDAY

Hoover Worships in First President's Pew — Liberty Bell Sounded in Philadelphia.

Viscount Grey, Great Britain's wartime Foreign Secretary, speaking over the radio from London yesterday, helped America celebrate the 199th anniversary of George Washington's birth. He told the nation that George Washington was one of the world's truly great men and said that Britons now view the Revolution in a new light.

The broadcast was heard here distinctly because of excellent atmospheric conditions. It was one of the features in the observance of the holiday which was celebrated also by many thousands of motorists who took advantage of the fine weather to drive to countryside and to beaches, enjoying breezes that hinted warmly of approaching Spring.

There were formal exercises to mark the day, but there will be even more today. Most of the city's stores and all of its schools are to remain closed until tomorrow morning to permit the populace to take part in them or to stay at home and hear them over the radio.

1,400 Leave by Planes.

Air-minded week-enders are not unusual, but their number over this particular holiday was by far the greatest since the beginning of commercial aviation. At Newark Airport extra planes were put into service to Boston, Washington, Miami and the West. They carried 373 passengers out of the metropolitan district yesterday, bringing the week-end total to 1,400, a new record.

Viscount Grey came out of Fallodon to speak to the American people, and his talk was heard here and in Canada, over the network of the Columbia Broadcasting Company. He spoke extemporaneously, because of his failing sight, and he spoke slowly. The burden of his speech was that the new generation of Britons does not regard American revolutionists as rebel upstarts, but places the blame for the war on the poor statesmanship of George III and his advisers.

Called "A Very Great Man."

"I have been asked, as president of the English Speaking Union in Britain to say something on this, the anniversary of the birth of George Washington," said Lord Grey. "I cannot say what is adequate and all I should like to say in the time that is available, but I do most genuinely and willingly wish to pay my tribute to the memory of a very great man. George Washington's place in history is established; his fame is secure; his work endures. He is one of the men justly called 'great' and one of the men to whom that word is justly applied.

"Few men achieve great success in public services and still achieve it without being spoiled by it. George Washington was one of those few. * * * George Washington fought a very successful war, but at the end of it the object for which he had fought was just as clear to his eyes and dear to his heart as it was at the beginning. Victory and success never clouded his vision. Personal power, personal success had never been his objects in the struggle and they never

Continued on Page Twelve.

WHITE MAN CROSSES THE ARABIAN DESERT FOR THE FIRST TIME

Bertram Thomas Travels 850-Mile Expanse of Mysterious Waste of Ruba-el-Khali.

TREK FRAUGHT WITH PERIL

Closest Secrecy Maintained to Escape Murder by Tribes Guarding Vast Stretch.

AREA HAS BIBLICAL HISTORY

May Have Been Home of Shuhites —Explorer Foiled by Hostile Natives in Previous Effort.

Special Cable to THE NEW YORK TIMES.

BAHREIN, Persian Gulf, Feb. 22.—Ruba-el-Khali, or the Great Southern Desert of Arabia, has at last yielded up its secrets. The news has been received here that Bertram Thomas, explorer and Orientalist, who left Dhofar in December, has crossed what was one of the greatest unexplored sections of the world to Dohah El Katar Peninsula, which he reached yesterday.

No white man had previously crossed this "no man's land," which extends 650 miles from north to south and 850 miles from east to west, and it is doubtful whether any Arab had done so. Only a few white men have ever seen even the fringes of this region.

Mr. Thomas, former Finance Minister and Wazir to the Sultan of Muscat, early last year journeyed 200 miles into the interior and then was obliged to turn back.

Owing to the hostility of the tribes living on the borders of the desert to every kind of penetration by Europeans, he had to make his plans with the greatest secrecy. The danger of death, whether by murder or by starvation, was assuredly great, and only by taking a multitude of precautions could Mr. Thomas avoid "raising" the country ahead of him and thus arousing hostility at his point of entry into the desert.

Thus far Mr. Thomas has not communicated the details of his discoveries, which the geographical world is awaiting with the greatest interest.

Desert Long a Riddle.

Dr. D. G. Hogarth, in his work "The Penetration of Arabia," wrote of Ruba-el-Khali: "Such an expanse is vast enough to hide many secrets * * * There may be an important central lake * * *; there may be unknown tracts of fertility and nomad or settled tribes of which no rumor has reached us. Or there may be none of the things, but only sand or rock."

Before the war the fringes of this region were viewed by several explorers, and during the war St. John Philby skirted its northern boundary and told of encountering a native who said he had crossed the great sand from south to north. Captain R. E. Cheesman also recently penetrated a short distance into the unknown territory. However, until the expedition of Mr. Thomas the vast, uncharted area remained intact.

It is mainly the sterility of the "Empty Quarter," as it is called, which has blocked penetration, and many superstitions about it have grown up among the Bedouins. They regard it as djinn infested and de-

Continued on Page Nine.

Thief Grabs Theatre's Cash Amid a Broadway Crowd

Boldly reaching through a window of the cashier's booth in front of the Strand Theatre on Broadway just north of Forty-seventh Street, a youth grabbed a roll of bills and made off at top speed late last night while a long queue of movie fans waited at another window of the booth to buy tickets for the midnight show.

A uniformed doorman and two or three men in the line who had seen what had happened chased the thief north on Broadway but were impeded in the pursuit by the sidewalk crowds. The fugitive ran into the subway station at Fiftieth Street and got away.

Reports spread that the theatre had been held up and detectives hurried to the scene. The theatre management said that only about $200 had been taken.

POLICE MOVE TO HALT BANK BOOK INQUIRY

Counsel Will Sue to Restrain Seabury From Examining Wund on His Accounts.

OTHERS PLAN COURT FIGHT

Contend Investigator Has Failed to Link Police Money to Subject of Inquiries.

A concerted attempt to halt the search for police graft being made by Referee Samuel Seabury in the Appellate Division inquiry into the lower courts was foreshadowed yesterday when Herman L. Falk, attorney for Charles A. Wund, a policeman with bank accounts showing deposits of $83,000 in less than six years, said he planned to ask, tomorrow or Wednesday, for a court order exempting his client from further examination concerning his financial affairs.

"I believe," Mr. Falk said, "that a great many attorneys for other police will probably follow my example," but it was learned that a fight on the investigation from another angle was being prepared on behalf of police inspectors, captains and lieutenants named in the most recent subpoena for bank accounts and brokerage house records.

Meanwhile, Mr. Seabury went ahead with plans for three public hearings this week, on Thursday, Friday and Saturday, at which he intends to reveal that other policemen have large financial resources.

Six Banked $500,000 in Five Years.

The accounts of six police thus far examined in public have revealed aggregate deposits in about five years of nearly $500,000. The accounts of James T. Brady and Robert E. Morris, plain-clothes men attached to headquarters, showed that each had accumulated about $40,000.

James J. Quinlivan was shown to have handled about $57,000, while his partner, William M. O'Connor, was known to have turned over more than $10,000.

Lieutenant John W. Kenna of the Third Division, with his mother, Mrs. Anna Kenna, the records showed, made total deposits of $237,000. Wund, a plain-clothes man, also in the Third Division, had deposited $83,000, and his account, like Kenna's, showed heavy withdrawals in hceeks to persons unidentified and for purposes undetermined.

It was on Wund's examination that this phase of the investigation struck its first snag. Wund refused to answer Mr. Seabury's questions on the ground that the investigation was ex-

Continued on Page Thirteen.

Alcohol Poisoning Killed 625 in City in 1930; Dr. Norris Puts Total Liquor Deaths at 1,295

The annual report of Chief Medical Examiner Dr. Charles Norris, made public yesterday, shows that alcohol poisoning killed 625 persons in New York City in 1930; and that, in all, about 1,295 deaths were caused either directly, or indirectly, by liquor. These figures, Dr. Norris pointed out, covered only such cases as came to the attention of his office.

"There are probably hundreds of alcoholic deaths we never know of," he said. "Physicians conceal them by putting other causes on death certificates. They do this to spare disgrace to families of the dead persons, for insurance and for a dozen other reasons.

"There is no reliable method of checking up, and it is useless to try to make any comparison of the present number of alcohol deaths with the numbers in the days before prohibition."

The report indicates that wood-alcohol deaths increased from fifty-eight in 1929 to seventy-five last year, or about 40 per cent. Several of these deaths were attributed to the drinking of automobile anti-freezing solutions.

Autopsies established also, the report says, that poisonous denaturants employed by the government in its efforts to stop the diversion of industrial alcohol were responsible for many deaths.

Manhattan had eighty fewer deaths from alcohol poisoning last year than in 1929, the report shows, and about 80 per cent of these occurred on the east side from Brooklyn Bridge to Houston Street. Most of these deaths were in Bowery "smoke shops."

But Brooklyn, with 144 deaths last year, was 14 ahead of its 1929 total, while the Bronx, with 22 deaths, and Queens, with 11, equaled their records of the year previous. Only one such death was recorded on Staten Island.

Manhattan had fifty-six deaths from wood alcohol, Brooklyn had thirteen, the Bronx five and Queens one.

POLICE OPEN DRIVE ON ALCOHOL GANGS TO HALT KILLINGS

Detectives Search Speakeasies and All Underworld Haunts in City for Gunmen.

INSPECTOR LEADS MAN HUNT

No Trace Found of Abe Wagner as Mother Prepares for His Brother's Funeral.

GUN BATTLE IN DANCE HALL

One Gangster Killed, Another Is Wounded in Shooting in Crowded Brooklyn Resort.

With a record-breaking week of six gang killings behind them and with a gang war in progress, detectives scoured the dens and dives of the east side yesterday and last night under orders to bring in all criminals who could shed light on the recent series of murders.

Detectives in the east side and Bro..x precincts, where, on Friday night and Saturday, Al Wagner, John (Aces) Mazza and John Franzone were killed, were called in from their days off and started on a systematic hunt through low speakeasies, cheap restaurants and disreputable night resorts for gangsters. Their object was twofold: to prevent a second battle in the gang war and to get information concerning the crimes already committed.

There was a personal as well as a professional motive for their efforts, for one of the six dead of the past week was Detective Christopher Scheuing of the East Twenty-second Street station. Mindful of the warning by Commissioner Mulrooney not to be caught with their guns inaccessible, as Scheuing was caught, the detectives went out prepared to shoot if necessary.

Sullivan Leads Man-Hunt.

Yesterday's man-hunt was started personally by Acting Deputy Chief Inspector John J. Sullivan, in command of New York detectives, who spent the morning at Police Headquarters.

Inspector Sullivan ordered a rigid search for crooks and gunmen, but he made it clear afterward that he had not ordered a general round-up of suspicious persons and that his orders did not imply a revival of the strong-arm methods employed two years ago by Commissioner Whalen.

"No places are going to be smashed up and no people are going to be arrested without good reason," said Inspector Sullivan. "We are after the criminals and we are not after anybody else. I have not ordered any general round-up. The detectives are simply following out the program of keeping after the criminals."

The homicide squad, under Lieutenant Martin, added its forces yesterday to those of the East Thirty-fifth and East Fifth Street detectives investigating the feud between the Mazza and Wagner gangs over alcohol territory on the east side, which resulted in two of the killings Saturday morning. They again visited the Hatfield House Hotel at 103 East Twenty-ninth Street, where Al Wagner was shot, and the restaurant at 15 First Avenue, in front of which Mazza fell under a rain of bullets.

They encountered the blank wall of silence which normally surrounds gang affrays.

Harry Brown, said by the police to have been an associate of the Wagners, and who was severely wounded when rival gangsters broke into the Hatfield House and killed Al Wagner, still refused in Bellevue Hospital yesterday to tell who had done the shooting. He was stronger as the result of a transfusion of blood from his sister.

Despite his serious condition, Brown was transferred yesterday from the emergency ward, on the ground floor facing the river, where an enemy easily could attack him through the windows, to the prison ward, which is well guarded. At 3 A. M. yesterday his wife, small, pretty and red-haired, went to the hospital and engaged a private nurse for him.

The police had found no trace last night of Abe Wagner, who they believe was the special target of the rival gangsters and who escaped, though wounded, in the battle in which his brother was killed. Nor had any more bodies been found on outlying refuse dumps or in vacant lots, as they had expected on the strength of reports that two other members of the Mazza gang had been killed and taken away.

Plea for Truce Answered.

Mrs. Pauline Wagner, mother of the Wagner brothers, waited in vain yesterday in her flat at 19 Rutgers Place, beside a plain black coffin in which lay the body of Al Wagner, for word from the missing Abe. She had appealed for her son's enemies to call a truce for to-

Bertram Thomas, the first white man to cross the Arabian desert.

"All the News That's Fit to Print."

The New York Times.

Copyright, 1931, by The New York Times Company.

THE WEATHER
Fair today and tomorrow; not much change in temperature.
Temperatures yesterday—Max. 40, min. 26.
U. S. Weather Forecast—For details see Page 31.

VOL. LXXX....No. 26,696. **** NEW YORK, THURSDAY, FEBRUARY 26, 1931. TWO CENTS In Greater New York | THREE CENTS Within 200 Miles | FOUR CENTS Elsewhere Except 7th and 8th Postal Zones

THOMAS TELLS HIS STORY OF ARABIAN DESERT TREK; FOUND 7-MILE SALT LAKE

CROSSING REQUIRED 58 DAYS

Only 13 Arabs Completed 900-Mile Camel Trip With Daring Briton.

GIVES HINT OF BURIED CITY

Explorer Hears From Bedouins That Vague Trail Is Old Caravan Track to Ubar.

LONDON HAILS BRAVE FEAT

General Cox Points Out Young Orientalist Succeeded Alone Where Others Had Failed.

By BERTRAM THOMAS.

Special Cable to THE NEW YORK TIMES.

BAHREIN, Persian Gulf, Feb. 25.—My camel journey of 900 miles across the great Ruba-el-Khali or Unknown Desert of Southern Arabia took fifty-eight days. On thirteen of those I halted and on forty-five I marched, averaging eight hours a day in the saddle.

I traveled in an Arab kit, but otherwise as an undisguised Christian. I carried a prismatic compass, sextant and navigation instruments for mapping purposes.

My starting point was Dhofar, on the central South Arabian coast, with an escort of thirty Arabs and forty camels. I arrived at Dohah, on the Persian Gulf, with an escort of thirteen Arabs and eighteen camels, having progressively reduced my forces as the early menace of Hadramaut raiders was left behind.

Crossed Frankincense Country.

My route lay north over the Oara Mountains, 3,000 feet in altitude, through the frankincense country of the Bible, across the steppe I explored last Winter, to Shisur, then westward into the unknown. For 100 waterless miles, skirting the southern edge of the sands, was a mighty bulwark of red, fringed with dunes, the habitat of the ostrich and antelope. The ostrich is now extinct, but antelope were plentiful, and I am bringing a young calf to England.

In Lat. 19 degrees N. and Long. 52.30 degrees E. I came upon numerous deeply cut caravan tracks in patches of the steppe running across our path, evidence of centuries of usage in bygone times. The Bedouins call it the road to Ubar, their legendary city of the prehistoric Addites.

In the course of the ages the sands have encroached to the southward. Hereabouts Urbar, according to the local tribesmen, lies buried beneath them—the Atlantis of the Ruba-el-Khali Desert. The country now is a borderland 100 miles from the sea and 1,000 feet in altitude, strewn with seashell fossils.

Proceeding northwest, I encountered the phenomenon of singing sands, a deep, sustained booming caused by wind action among the sand cliffs, resembling the notes of a ship's siren. At Lat. 19 degrees N. and Long. 45 degrees E. I turned northward and so continued through the midmost heart of the sands. I encountered a sandstorm which my small cinecamera and one aneroid did not survive.

Dispensed With Tent's Weight.

I carried no tent, from considerations of weight, although night temperatures averaged 50 degrees, falling to 40 on occasions, and actually below it on Lat. 23.40 degrees N., where I discovered a lake of salt water seven miles long. West of my line of march the sands were reported rising in altitude and waterless. East of it the sands were falling and water extremely plentiful, a veritable subsurface lake so brackish in parts, however, that it was undrinkable by man and sometimes even by camels.

The prevailing winds were northerly and there was slight rain in the northern marches. The entire area is sand to the northward to the twenty-third parallel, with the aneroid falling gradually to 250 feet. Its moods are as varying as the ocean's, the stormy mood characterizing the south, moderating to the northward to unruffled calms. North of the twenty-third parallel the altitude falls to the sea level and the

Continued on Page Twelve.

British Anthem to Stand as Is; Snowden Says Only Tune Counts

Wireless to THE NEW YORK TIMES.

LONDON, Feb. 25.—A controversy concerning the suitability of the words of the British national anthem was recognized in the House of Commons today, when the government was asked if it would consider advising a more appropriate stanza for public occasions under State auspices.

"In a matter of this sort," replied Philip Snowden, Chancellor of the Exchequer, "tradition is everything. The government does not propose to do anything about it."

A Conservative questioner asked if Mr. Snowden approved the words of the second stanza, which he repeated, as follows:

"Confound their politics. Frustrate their knavish tricks. On Thee our hearts we fix. God save us all!"

Mr. Snowden said "The words are not the anthem. The real thing is the tune, which is played in honor of the King."

MEYER CONFIRMED ON RESERVE BOARD

Surprisingly Small Number of 11 Votes Cast Against Him, With 72 in His Favor.

TWO MAKE FINAL ATTACKS

Brookhart and Frazier Reiterate Charges, but Even Heflin Votes for Nominee.

Special to The New York Times.

WASHINGTON, Feb. 25.—By a vote of 72 to 11 Eugene Meyer Jr. of New York was confirmed this afternoon by the Senate as governor of the Federal Reserve Board. The only surprise in the outcome was in the small number of opponents—four insurgent Republicans and seven Democrats.

On the other hand, forty-two Republicans, twenty-nine Democrats and Senator Shipstead, the Farmer-Labor member, voted for Mr. Meyer. He even commanded the support of Senator Heflin, a violent opponent of Federal Reserve Board policies. Counting the pairs, there were only fourteen Senators opposed to the nominee.

Only two speeches were made against confirmation.

Brookhart Makes an Attack.

Senator Brookhart in his final assault charged that Mr. Meyer was a "Wall Street" man and unfriendly to the cause of agriculture. He said that as head of the War Finance Corporation, as later as Farm Loan Commissioner, or head of the Farm Loan Board, Mr. Meyer was supposed to be a great friend of agriculture, but had failed to use more than a small fraction of the resources placed at his command under the laws creating those organizations to aid the credit position of the farmers.

Senator Brookhart talked nearly two hours, repeating many of the charges which he had before made against Mr. Meyer as a representative of Wall Street.

Senator Frazier took much the same line, expressing the belief that Mr. Meyer was allied with financial forces which did not have at heart the best interests of the farmers.

The openly voiced opposition to Mr. Meyer was so limited that an hour and a half before the time set for

Continued on Page Five.

EUROPE IS HOPEFUL OF NAVY AGREEMENT; HENDERSON IN ROME

Italy Enthusiastically Greets British Ministers—Talks Will Begin Today.

PARIS LOOKS FOR SUCCESS

Bases Belief on Reserve of the Italian Press and Reaction to Menace to Peace.

LONDON RESTRICTS OUTLAY

Discussion in Commons Shows Britain Is Cutting Costs—Berlin Uneasy at Moves.

The eyes of Europe's four greatest nations turned to Rome yesterday where Britain's officials arrived to seek an Italo-French naval accord.

Paris felt highly optimistic, after the negotiators' success there.

London's high hopes were shown in Commons, where it was stated that naval expenditures this year would be very low.

Berlin's reaction was one of uneasiness based on the feeling that Britain had made concessions to France to get her to yield.

HENDERSON REACHES ROME.

By ARNALDO CORTESI.

Wireless to THE NEW YORK TIMES.

ROME, Feb. 25.—Arthur Henderson and A. V. Alexander, accompanied by Robert L. Craigie and A. Selby, arrived in Rome this evening and were greeted at the station with marked cordiality by Foreign Minister Dino Grandi, Minister of the Navy Giuseppe Sirianni and the British Ambassador, Sir Ronald Graham, and also a great number of officials of the Ministries of Foreign Affairs and of the Navy, who participated in the previous negotiations for the limitation of naval armaments.

The program for this evening had been left open, since it was thought they might wish to hold a preliminary meeting with Signor Grandi as soon as they arrived, but they expressed a desire to rest after their fatiguing journey since they were not pressed for time in Rome because they intend to remain here at least two days. They accordingly drove to the British Embassy, where they will reside during their stay as guests of the Ambassador.

Because of the uncertainty concerning the intentions of the British Ministers it has been impossible to lay down beforehand a definite program for tomorrow. It has been decided, however, that they have their first contact with the Italian officials in a conference tomorrow morning at Signor Grandi's office at the Palazzo Chigi.

May Return to Paris Friday.

Their further movements will largely depend on what happens at that first meeting and on the turn the negotiations take. They will be received by Premier Mussolini probably tomorrow afternoon or the following morning. If the negotiations are as successful as every one here hopes, they may return to Paris Friday.

Italian official circles still are somewhat uncertain whether to be elated or downcast by the sudden appearance in their midst of the British Foreign Secretary and the First Lord of the Admiralty. They do not yet know whether the visit means that France has accepted the so-called Craigie proposals or whether it means that France has rejected them and they may have come to Rome in order to attempt to wrest further concessions from the Italian Government.

If the former hypothesis is correct it is not believed there will be any

Continued on Page Ten.

War Against Ibn Saud Threatened in Arabia Because Viceroy Hanged Chief Sheik of Asir

Special Cable to THE NEW YORK TIMES.

BEIRUT, Syria, Feb. 25.—There is a strong likelihood of a new revolt in Arabia, this time against King Ibn Saud of the Hedjaz. War rumors have started in Southern Arabia because Ibn Saud's Viceroy in Asir hanged a prominent tribal leader.

Some time ago Ibn Saud occupied the small Asir district lying between the Hedjaz and Yemen, which has been the cockpit for intertribal warfare. Ibn Saud sent to its capital a Viceroy, who discovered the chief of the sheiks of the Maharrassa tribe was communicating secretly with Imam Yehia of Yemen with the view of starting a revolt against Ibn Saud.

The Viceroy immediately had the old sheik hanged, causing great excitement among the tribesmen, who are declared to be on the verge of revolt. It is reported Imam Yehia intends intervening, which portends war between the Hedjaz and Yemen should he take such action.

Reports from Bagdad indicate that Ibn Saud is not very friendly toward the pan-Arab federation proposed by the Premier of Iraq. The present negotiations for a treaty between Iraq and the Hedjaz refer only to neighborly relations, including the extradiction of fugitives.

Ibn Saud, King of the Hedjaz and Sultan of the Nedj, is the leader of the "fundamentalist" sect of Moslems. His followers are known as Wahabis. He is able to muster an army of more than 50,000 tribesmen, so has been able to crush revolts of disgruntled sheiks.

Wireless Messages Received and Typed By a Machine Demonstrated in Detroit

Special to The New York Times.

DETROIT, Feb. 25.—The first demonstration of a radio typewriter invented by Glen W. Watson, with which messages typed on a transmitter are received in typewritten form at any distance from the sender, was given here today by Mr. Watson.

The speed of sending and receiving, it was said, is limited only by the ability of the operator, since the machine's capacity is set theoretically at 1,200 letters a minute.

Representatives of the Federal Government, the Michigan State police and the press watched a bank of typewriter keys operated in one room while a typewriter electrically operated in another room picked up the radio waves and automatically typed the message on paper.

The essentials of the mechanism are two identical revolving contact arms, electrically driven and synchronized, each passing in revolution over insulated segments.

Each segment of the sending mechanism is connected with a key of the sending typewriter, and a similar connection is made of the segments at the receiving end with the receiving typewriter.

Contacts on the sending segments release short-wave radio impulses through the usual radio apparatus, and these impulses, picked up by the receiving radio apparatus, are converted into battery impulses strong enough to operate the receiving typewriter. So long as the revolving contact arms are perfectly synchronized the only possible mistake in sending must be charged to the typist, or to a static crash, which would, however, only misspell one word by as much as one letter.

Synchronization of the revolving contacts, or switches, is automatically controlled. A commercial sending set of this kind can be made to weigh not more than fifteen or twenty pounds, Mr. Watson said, and with the multiple variations in short-wave radio impulses every owner of a sending and receiving apparatus can be independent of all others on the Watsongraph.

The secret of the device lies in the perfect synchronization of two disk motors. These revolving disks contain the letters of the alphabet along their edge. All the letters pass a point or indicator. A thousand miles away a similar disk is revolving at precisely the same speed. The letters are in the same relative position.

The operation at the receiving end is automatic. As soon as the connection is made with the sending end, by simply tuning in as you would on an ordinary radio, the message is received on a roll of paper, printed identically as sent out.

The device can be used to great advantage on police cars, the inventor said, as the messages can be sent in utmost secrecy without using a code. This is done by changing the letter position on both the receiving and sending sets so that both synchronize.

CAPONE PUT ON TRIAL; COURTROOM GUARDED

Thousands Besiege the Chicago Federal Building as Gangster Answers Contempt Charge.

ALL WHO ENTER SEARCHED

Government Contends That Defendant Was Not Ill When He Did Not Heed Summons.

Special to The New York Times.

CHICAGO, Feb. 25.—The Federal Government pressed its contempt of court case against Alphonse Capone, Chicago's foremost "public enemy," with a trial today that brought thrills to every clerk and stenographer in the Federal Building and disappointment to thousands who beseiged the street entrances, unable to gain admittance.

Federal Judge James H. Wilkerson, who sentenced "Scarface Al's" brother Ralph to three years in the penitentiary for income tax fraud, is hearing the case.

Against the contention of the defense that Capone was "a dangerously sick man" in March, 1929, and could not answer a subpoena to come from Florida to testify before the grand jury without endangering his life, the prosecution built up its case. It rested at the end of the day and the defense will go on tomorrow.

Witnesses testified that Capone had attended the Hialeah races, taken airplane and steamer trips to the Bahamas and was a spectator at the Sharkey-Stribling fight during his purported "six weeks' confinement in bed."

Sleek, well groomed and well fed, Capone appeared little perturbed by the proceedings. With an air of complacency he settled his bulk of 235 pounds in his chair at the counsel table. A platinum watch-chain, studded with diamonds, crossed his waistcoat, and pearl-gray spats and a white silk handkerchief in his coat pocket set off his rich blue suit.

Capone Dodges Photographers.

He had entered the closely guarded court room secretly, however, to avoid photographers. City police, mounted and on foot, surrounded the building and Federal officers were on watch inside as precaution against possible gun-play at the gang leader's appearance. The few persons allowed in the court were searched for weapons.

John M. Coroneas, a policeman from Hialeah City, Fla., was the first Federal witness to combat Capone's illness plea. An affidavit from Capone's physician, Dr. Kenneth Phillips, which gained a stay for the grand jury appearance from March 12 to March 20, 1929, stated that Capone was convalescent from "broncho-pneumonial pleurisy, with fluid effusions in the chest." Dr. Phillips first attended Capone on Jan. 13.

Coroneas testified to having seen Capone at the races Jan. 18, 1929.

"I walked over to the ticket office and waited for him," said the policeman. "I said, 'Hello, Al'; and he said, 'Hello,' handing me a $10 bill."

Coroneas told of seeing the gangster fifteen or twenty times at the race track until it closed on March

Continued on Page Seventeen.

ANDERSON WARNS OF GRAVE DRY PERIL

Conditions Worse Than Causes of Civid War Menace Nation, He Tells Merchants Here.

EXPLAINS HIS CONTROL PLAN

But Wickersham Aide Would Keep Prohibition Until New System Is in Effect.

The immense revenues derived from the illegal liquor trade by the lawless elements now "threatens our social peace and security," in the opinion of Colonel Henry W. Anderson of Richmond, Va. Already conditions are such as to be "a serious menace to the health of present and future generations and a challenge to orderly government," he said here yesterday.

Colonel Anderson painted his picture of lawlessness in a speech at a luncheon of the members' council of the Merchants' Association at the Astor. He explained the plan for liquor control which he—as a member of the commission—had advocated in a codicil to the late Wickersham report.

Saying that he was "opposed to repeal—even under the present conditions," Colonel Anderson remarked that 'the field is now clear for the establishment in the United States of a sound and effective system of liquor control." It should be kept clear until such a system can be established, he maintained.

In introducing the speaker Lincoln Cromwell said that the association would remain nonpartisan—but law-abiding—on the subject of prohibition. But the several hundred guests vigorously applauded such phrases of Colonel Anderson's as "this is certainly not prohibition," and "interference with the personal liberty of the individual." Another member of the commission, Miss Ada L. Comstock, was present, but she made no address.

Sees Peril to National Health.

"Present conditions as to the illegal traffic in and use of intoxicating liquors, often of inferior quality," Colonel Anderson said, "is a serious menace to the health of present and future generations and a challenge to orderly government. The immense revenues derived from this source by the lawless elements of society threaten our social peace and security. These conditions must be met We have eliminated the legalized saloon. We must go further and eliminate the bootlegger and other agencies of this traffic by depriving them of their profits and bringing into action against them the irresistible forces of economic law.

"It is essential that this be done promptly. The whole world is in a state of economic and social unrest. America cannot expect to escape these conditions. We are now facing the necessity of far-reaching social and economic adjustments. At a former period in our history, when the strain upon our structure was much less severe than it is today, the prolonged agitation of the inflammable question of slavery under intemperate leadership on both sides threw us into an unnecessary war. So to-

Continued on Page Sixteen.

PHYSICIANS ACCUSED IN HUGE LIQUOR RING, BROKEN UP IN 14 RAIDS

Only 47 Listed as Conspirators, Though 396 Are to Be Cited to Federal Grand Jury.

SOLD THEIR PRESCRIPTIONS

$3,000,000 a Year Syndicate Is Said to Have Paid $1.35 Each for Whisky Blanks.

MANY DRUGGISTS INVOLVED

Round-Up by 100 Dry Agents in the Three Boroughs Includes Seizures in 12 Stores.

What was described as the largest liquor-prescription syndicate ever uncovered in the United States was believed to have been broken up yesterday when agents of Horace J. Simmons, special Treasury Department agent of this district, aided by 100 picked men of the staff of Andrew McCampbell, prohibition administrator, arrested more than thirty persons in fourteen simultaneously conducted raids in Manhattan, the Bronx and Brooklyn.

The syndicate, which is said to have done a $3,000,000-a-year business for the last six or eight years, diverting medicinal liquor by the illegal use of prescriptions, had been aided in its operations, according to Mr. Simmons, by about 1,000 physicians and at least 400 druggists.

In the complaints on which warrants for the arrests were issued, forty-seven physicians in Manhattan and the Bronx are named as conspirators. None of the physicians was actually named a defendant in the present action, but Mr. Simmons, whose men found 1,432 signed prescriptions in one of the raids, said a Federal grand jury would receive the names of 396 physicians who have already been involved, he said, in the conspiracy, as well as the names of druggists also said to be involved.

Twelve Stores Raided.

Twelve of the raids, in which as many prisoners were taken, were made on stores in the three boroughs. Agents said they seized anywhere from one to five cases of whisky in each store.

One of the prisoners, Morris Sweetwood, who has served a term in Atlanta Penitentiary with Emanuel (Nannie) H. Kessler, so-called "King of Bootleggers," was arrested in the Alba Hotel, which was known as the Hotel Harding, 203 West Fifty-fourth Street, before Dutch Schultz, Bronx beer-runner, was said to have been shot last month in the Club Abbey, which is in the hotel.

Sweetwood, who is said by Simmons to have deserted the prescription racket several months ago along with his former partner, was arrested on the charge that he sold a case of liquor to Mr. Simmons's agents on Nov. 20.

He has been under surveillance ever since and when the raid was made yesterday on a search warrant issued by Francis A. O'Neill, United States Commissioner, agents said they found twenty-five cases of whisky in Sweetwood's room.

They also arrested Abe Miller, described as the manager of the hotel, and Dr. A. G. De Marco and Harry Gratske, after the additional discovery of a ten-gallon barrel of spirits, five gallons of alcohol and twelve one-gallon jugs of liquor.

The head of the syndicate, it is charged, is Nathan Bernstein, who

Continued on Page Seventeen.

Sheppard Offers a Bill to Ban Fruit Juices; Would Amend Dry Law to Prevent Their Sale

Special to The New York Times.

WASHINGTON, Feb. 25.—Senator Sheppard of Texas, co-author of the dry law, introduced an amendment to the Volstead act today to place concentrated fruit juices under the ban of the prohibition law by striking out the clause under which the California grape growers assert they have authority to market their concentrates.

No provision of the law has aroused more controversy over its interpretation than the one which Senator Sheppard would remove. Under this provision, the wets maintained, fruit juices and cider could be sold, with no responsibility attaching to the seller if such fruit juices later turned into beverages containing alcohol.

The clause in the Volstead act reads:

"The penalties in this act against the manufacture of liquor without a permit shall not apply to a person for manufacturing non-intoxicating cider and fruit juices exclusively for use in the home, but such cider and fruit juices shall not be sold or delivered except to persons having permits to manufacture vinegar."

The Wickersham Commission on Law Enforcement and Observance recommended the deletion of this provision.

"It is my opinion," Senator Sheppard said, "that the sentence my bill eliminates does not permit, and cannot be properly construed to permit, the manufacture of intoxicating cider and fruit juices in the home."

"Inasmuch as great difference of olpnion prevails as to the meaning of this sentence," he continued, "I am introducing a bill to eliminate it in order to remove any possible source of controversy.

"Manufacturers of non-intoxicating cider and fruit juices for use in their homes or elsewhere are not required by any part of the Volstead act to obtain permits and this sentence has served only to create a conflict of opinion and widespread misunderstanding as to what it really means."

NEW BIDS FOR THE WORLD; COURT DELAYS DECISION; EMPLOYES SEEK TO OWN IT

Clause in Pulitzer's Will That Court Is Asked to Void

Surrogate Foley's difficulty in deciding The World case lies not only in the injunction the elder Pulitzer laid upon his sons to carry on the papers he had established, but in an absolute prohibition he made in his will against the sale of the enterprises by his heirs.

In this clause the elder Pulitzer, after authorizing his trustees to sell and dispose of stock in the Pulitzer Publishing Company, owner of The St. Louis Post Dispatch, which he founded and which his son, Joseph Pulitzer, is now managing successfully, said:

"This power, however, is limited to said stock of the Pulitzer Publishing Company and nothing in my will shall be taken to authorize or empower the sale or disposition by the trustees of any stock of the Press Publishing Company, publisher of The New York World newspaper. I particularly enjoin upon my sons and my descendants the duty of preserving, perfecting and perpetuating The World newspaper in the same spirit in which I have striven to create and conduct it as a public institution from motives higher than mere gain."

WORLD EMPLOYES ACT TO PURCHASE IT

$650,000 Pledged at Meeting Called to Draft a Program to Mutualize Papers.

OUTSIDE AID GIVEN QUICKLY

$100,000 From Man "High in the Service of This State"—Morale of Staff Praised.

A desire among the 2,800 employes of the Press Publishing Company to prevent the extinction of The Morning, Sunday and Evening World, to which many of them have given a lifetime and upon which all have depended for their livelihood, took the form yesterday of a cooperative project "to take over the operation of The World newspapers and maintain the tradition of Joseph Pulitzer, the founder."

The project was launched yesterday morning in the news department, and gathered momentum and enthusiasm in other departments all day, until in the evening a meeting of all employes of all departments was held at the Hotel Astor, at which it was announced by James W. Barrett, city editor and temporary chairman of a mutualization committee, that pledges of $650,000 to a fund for the purchase of the papers by the employes had already been made, and that an attempt to enlist additional outside financial support would be made this morning.

It was the expressed hope of the employes' committee to be able to determine the possibility of mutualization of the newspapers by 11 o'clock this morning, when Surrogate Foley is scheduled to announce whether he can release Pulitzer's sons, Herbert, Joseph and Ralph, from their father's injunction twenty-

Continued on Page Two.

LONG HEARING IN COURT

Volunteer Counsel Asks That World Workers Be Allowed to Run It.

PLEA MOVES SURROGATE

But He Points Out That His Duty Ends With Applying Law to the Case.

PROMISES DECISION TODAY

Figures of Decline Presented by Pulitzers Questioned—Other Competitors Coming In.

The fate of The World and The Evening World still hung in the balance last night.

Surrogate James A. Foley delayed until today his decision on the application of Herbert, Ralph and Joseph Pulitzer, to set aside a provision in their father's will forbidding them to sell the newspapers and for approval of a contract they have signed to transfer the ownership of the publications to Roy Howard of the Scripps-Howard newspaper chain.

At the same time there entered into the dramatic struggle of the interests competing for control of the newspapers which Joseph Pulitzer created, still another factor—the employes of those newspapers.

The Surrogate's announcement that he would wait until 11 o'clock this morning before deciding the legal issues involved, was made after a second hearing, held in the Hall of Records. It was taken as an indication that he would grant the right of the heirs to sell but wanted first to satisfy himself that the Scripps-Howard offer was the best obtainable.

Paul Block Puts In a Bid.

At the hearing, Paul Block, publisher of The Brooklyn Standard Union and other newspapers, appeared, tired looking and worn after a race across the continent to try to wrest the newspapers from Mr. Howard. Mr. Block submitted a bid, in writing, for the purchase of The World, morning, Sunday and evening editions, at a figure said to top Mr. Howard's offer of about $5,000,000. The exact amount was not revealed.

The employes of the Pulitzer newspapers, led by James W. Barrett, city editor of The World, made a dramatic entrance into the proceedings when they appeared in a group at the hearing and asked, through their counsel, Gustavus Rogers, for ten days' delay in which to raise sufficient capital to take over the properties on a cooperative basis.

Mr. Rogers said that Adolph S. Ochs, publisher of THE NEW YORK TIMES, had suggested sale of the newspapers to the employes on such a basis as a possible solution of the problem faced by the Pulitzers when he was approached by them as a possible purchaser. Incidentally the lawyer challenged the accuracy of Herbert Pulitzer's estimate that the newspapers had lost $1,900,000 last year.

When the proceedings ended, Max D. Steuer, attorney for Mr. Block, told newspaper men that if his client succeeded in buying The World Mr. Block would be willing to give the employes of the newspaper forty-five days in which to raise the capital to take it off his hands.

At a meeting last night of World employes at the Hotel Astor it was announced that $650,000 had been pledged toward purchasing the newspapers for the employes. Included in this sum was $100,000 from a man "very high in the service of this State."

More Competitors Appear.

Despite the statement of the Pulitzer brothers that there was no hope of resuscitating the newspapers their faither left them to conduct "beyond the thought of mere gain," new bidders entered the field during the day.

Charles E. Kelley, attorney for Frank E. Gannett, owner of a chain of newspapers, attended the hearing and said afterward that his client, who is in Florida, was "interested" in the prospective sale. William Griffin, publisher of The New York Enquirer, a Sunday afternoon newspaper, announced that he would submit a bid to the Press Publishing Company, publisher of The World, through his attorney, Daniel F. Cohalan.

Rumor, meanwhile connected the

"All the News That's Fit to Print."

The New York Times.

Copyright, 1931, by The New York Times Company.

LATE CITY EDITION
THE WEATHER—Fair and somewhat warmer today; tomorrow rain.
Temperatures yesterday—Max. 53, min. 37.
U. S. Weather Forecast—For details see Page 35.

VOL. LXXX....No. 26,760. ***** NEW YORK, FRIDAY, MAY 1, 1931. TWO CENTS In Greater New York | THREE CENTS Within 200 Miles | FOUR CENTS Elsewhere Except 7th and 8th Postal Zones

CRAIN WORST PROSECUTOR IN 25 YEARS, MOLEY SHOWS BY REVIEW OF THE RECORDS

FELONY CONVICTIONS DROP

Charts Reveal Failure of Crain in Cases on Which He Asked to Be Judged.

LESSER PLEAS ACCEPTED

Gradual Breakdown in Office Since Days of Jerome Is Found by Expert.

MILLINERY RACKET BARED

Employers Hesitantly Tell of Payments as Recipient Glowers at the Hearing.

The administration of criminal justice in New York County started on a downward path when Tammany Hall took control of the District Attorney's office in 1916 and fell to its lowest point under the present administration, according to evidence presented yesterday to Samuel Seabury at a public hearing in the removal proceedings against District Attorney Crain.

The testimony was given by Dr. Raymond Moley, Professor of Public Law at Columbia University and an authority on criminal jurisprudence, in support of charges of inefficiency brought against Mr. Crain by the City Club.

Milliners Tell of Racket.

Dr. Moley's statistical analysis of the achievements of the District Attorney's office under the administrations of William Travers Jerome, Charles H. Whitman, Edward A. Swann, Joab H. Banton and Mr. Crain overshadowed in significance the dramatic testimony of the morning session when three frightened milliners told of the tribute levied upon them by racketeers.

Under the threatening eye of Tough Jake Kusman, who fell heir to the racket developed by Jacob (Little Augie) Orgen, when the latter's life was brought to an abrupt end by a gangster's bullet three years ago, the milliners told their stories hesitantly. The names of Arnold Rothstein, slain Broadway gambler, and Thomas (Fatty) Walsh, his bodyguard, who was shot and killed in Miami, Fla., fell reluctantly from their lips.

All these underworld figures were linked by them to the millinery racket which Mr. Crain had said he investigated thoroughly without obtaining an indictment. Evidence was also presented that before Mr. Crain marched Kusman before his Committee of Public Safety as a specimen of the genus racketeer, Kusman had committed an assault upon an employe of a hat manufacturer, but that this escaped the District Attorney's notice until two weeks ago, when Mr. Crain began an investigation of a complaint by the victim of the attack.

Moley Finds Prosecutor Lax.

Through this phase of the hearing conducted by John Kirkland Clark, chief counsel to Mr. Seabury, and Henry J. A. Collins, making his début as an interrogator, Mr. Crain smiled and seemed satisfied with the explanation of Samuel Untermyer, his counsel, that it was "no business of the District Attorney." His face took on a graver appearance when Jacob Gould Schurman Jr., another of Mr. Seabury's staff, called Dr. Moley.

Then, confronted by graphic evidence of what is alleged to have been his failure in the form of graphs and charts resting on an easel beside the witness chair, the District Attorney slumped lower and lower in his chair and his thin white hand drooped listlessly from the arm rest. Many in the court room looked with sympathy at the white-haired prosecutor, who after a lifetime in the public service was being accused as the most inefficient Tammany District Attorney in the present century.

The yardstick by which he was measured, however, was of his own choosing, for in answer to a question he propounded to himself at an earlier hearing he had said he wanted to be judged, not on his record in minor cases, but upon his effectiveness in prosecuting the "graver crimes," among which he listed homicide, grand larceny, burglary and robbery. Dr. Moley's analysis of records therefore was restricted to crimes in these categories.

Dr. Moley's charts indicated that

Continued on Page Twenty-two.

DO-X to Leave Canaries Today, Resuming South American Trip

By The Associated Press.

LAS PALMAS, Canary Islands, April 30.—Captain Friedrich Christiansen, commander of the giant German flying boat DO-X, announced tonight that he planned to leave on a flight to South America tomorrow morning at 8 o'clock [5 A. M., New York Daylight Saving Time].

His first destination will be Rio de Oro, on the West African Coast. The crew, the commander said, will be transferred to Gando Bay three hours earlier to prepare for the departure.

The DO-X left Altenrhein, Switzerland, on Nov. 5, 1930, on the first leg of a trip to South America. At Lisbon, less than a month later, the plane's left wing was destroyed by a sudden blaze in the auxiliary tanks, and it was not until Jan. 31 that the huge craft was able to fly to Las Palmas.

RYAN AIDES BOUGHT LOTS AT SCHOOL SITE

Testify at Higgins Inquiry They Did Not Act Till After City Acquired Queens Land.

BERRY CHARGES A "LEAK"

Declares Three to Five Times Assessed Value Has Been Paid for School Plots.

Joseph Miller Jr., secretary of the Board of Education, and Morris Warschauer, assistant secretary, testified yesterday that they had joined Francis T. McEneny, chief examiner of the Board of Aldermen, in investing in 200 lots in Queens three blocks away from a school site authorized for purchase by the Board of Estimate.

Their testimony was given before Commissioner of Accounts James A. Higgins and Leonard Wallstein, special corporation counsel, appointed by Mayor Walker to investigate condemnation procedure, and was heard by representatives of the City Affairs Committee. Controller Berry, the first witness, spent four hours testifying, and said he had flatly refused last May to buy any more school sites because leaks on their location that apparently could not be stopped had increased their price beyond all reason.

As soon as Mr. Warschauer took the witness chair Mr. Wallstein subjected him to a barrage of questions concerning his relatives and their names. The witness said he had access to information on the location of school sites that had been approved by the Board of Education, since it was his duty to go with members of the committee on buildings and sites to point out sites on city maps.

"Have you ever, either alone or with others, or with a corporation, acquired property or options on property with the intention of selling it to the city for school purposes?" Mr. Wallstein asked.

"Absolutely not," was the reply.

"Are you interested in any corpora-

Continued on Page Nineteen.

BUSINESS MEN VOTE GREENE COUNTY WAR ON DIAMOND GANG

Bipartisan Mass Meeting, With Names Kept Secret, Adopts Resolution Backing Bennett.

SHOW GIRL NOW HUNTED

Troopers Seek Marion Roberts as a Woman Is Linked With Torture of Cider Peddler.

'SHAKE-DOWN' IS DISCLOSED

Witnesses Tell of Demands for Tribute—Diamond Takes Turn Toward Recovery.

From a Staff Correspondent of The New York Times.

CATSKILL, N. Y., April 30.—A pledge of support to Attorney General Bennett in his efforts to imprison Jack (Legs) Diamond for life and break up his gang in Greene County was voted by representative business men in the county seat here tonight at a mass meeting in the Chamber of Commerce rooms.

The meeting adopted a resolution calling on citizens to tell the State investigators, sent here by the Governor last Monday, all they know of the gang's threats and extortion methods. It appears now that resentment against the gang has become general since its leader started recently to "put the finger" on legitimate business.

The presence at the meeting of business men representing both major parties seemed fair evidence that political differences would not greatly interfere with the Attorney General's investigations and that in the interests of business party lines might be forgotten.

None Speaks but All Vote.

Before the meeting started, the chairman stipulated that reporters were not to take notes nor to mention the names of any of the men attending the meeting.

He said that the Chamber of Commerce had received many complaints from boarding house owners who had fallen under the oppression of the racketeers and that unless the organization took some steps to show that it was behind the Attorney General in the drive against the gangsters, the racketeers would spread out and have the whole county under subjection.

He called upon other speakers to voice their opinion, but his request was followed by a strange hush. Not one of the 100 men present accepted the invitation.

Finally, one grim-jawed man, who looked like a banker, moved adoption of the resolution which had been prepared in advance, and by a rising vote it was unanimously adopted.

Resolution of the Chamber.

The meeting lasted only a few minutes. The resolution was as follows:

Whereas the grand jury of Greene County is in session and the court has charged them especially with reference to the activities of racketeers in this county; and

Whereas the Attorney General of this State, with the force at his command, is assisting our grand jury in inquiring into such racketeering activities and the crimes being committed in connection therewith; therefore be it

Resolved, That, the Catskill Chamber of Commerce pledges itself and its members to the support of the Attorney General and

Continued on Page Twenty-one.

Stocks Score Broadest Advance of the Year; Issues Long Hammered by Bears Lead Rally

With selling pressure suddenly withdrawn, the stock market turned about sharply yesterday and staged the widest advance of the year, to the discomfiture of the most aggressive "bear party" of which Wall Street has any recollection.

Stocks which had been driven down relentlessly for weeks and which in many instances had been carried to the lowest levels of three or four years were the first to rebound, their gains ranging from 2 to 8 points. Auburn Auto, long a spectacular market performer, leaped forward more than 30 points and closed at 213 with a net advance of 24½ points on the day. This meant an aggregate appreciation of more than $4,500,000 in the company's outstanding shares.

United States Steel, which broke more than 9 points in Wednesday's furious selling movement, recovered 4¾ points of that loss and closed at 120 after duplicating its previous low of 115. Ingersoll Rand had a net gain of 14¼ points, Allied Chemical 6⅛, J. I. Case 8¾, Southern Railway preferred 14½, New York Central 4⅛, Worthington Pump 6⅛, American Telephone and Telegraph 3⅞ and Atchison, Topeka & Santa Fe 6.

The combined averages of The New York Times indicated that the advance was the most extensive since Dec. 16. Fifty stocks showed an average net gain of $6.19, twenty-five industrials $10.06 and twenty-five rails $2.32. Before the rally got under way the industrials, early in the day, reached the lowest level of the year.

Wall Street offered a variety of explanations for the recovery. Obviously, there was extensive covering by speculators who have been short of the market and they began to take in their commitments as if at a given signal at about 11 o'clock. From then until the close prices advanced steadily and often sensationally. Brokers said that "bargain hunters" in large numbers had been attracted by the low prices.

Transactions on the Stock Exchange amounted to 3,334,642 shares, comparing with 3,187,020 on Wednesday.

The bond market displayed pronounced strength under the leadership of domestic issues.

Di Robilant Rescued, Dazed and in Rags; His Mate Dying After 18 Days in Jungle

Special Cable to The New York Times.

SAO PAULO, Brazil, April 30.—Just before noon today a tiny river steamer struggling against the swift current of the Paraná River dropped anchor and swung to in answer to frantic signals coming from the bank, where two figures, one standing, the other prostrate on the ground, beckoned for help.

Lowering a small boat, an officer and two sailors rowed to shore and took the two ragged figures aboard. On returning to the steamer the captain attempted to identify the two rescued men, but they not knowing Portuguese, great difficulty was encountered. After several minutes of delay an Italo-Brazilian member of the crew was summoned and through him the pair were identified as Count di Robilant, the missing Italian aviator, and his mechanic, Mauranta Quarenta.

Count di Robilant, although greatly weakened by eighteen days of wandering through the forest, still was able to walk and respond to questions, but his mechanic, who was injured when their plane crashed, lapsed into a coma after boarding the steamer.

The steamer resumed its course upstream, landing the aviators at the village of San José, an isolated town on the Paraná River, 100 miles from the landing place of the plane. The aviators were moved ashore, lodged in a hotel and doctors summoned. They said the mechanic was near death and Count di Robilant was suffering from loss of blood from scratches received while passing through the dense underbrush.

It is impossible to communicate by wire with San José, and the old radio on the steamer sent out the first news of the rescue.

Count di Robilant's face and hands were a mass of blood and cuts. His clothes were torn to shreds. His skin was tightly drawn over his face and hands. He lost twenty pounds in his struggle to reach the exterior, having lived on wild fruit.

Details are scant, due to Count di Robilant's lack of knowledge of Portuguese and the territory where he was found is inhabited by Indians

Continued on Page Two.

KING MUST UNDERGO OPERATION ON EYE

Dr. Wilmer Finds Cataract Has Seriously Affected the Left Optic of Siam's Ruler.

GETS DEGREE AT CAPITAL

Royal Couple Has Crowded Day, Including Trip to Mount Vernon by the Queen.

Special to The New York Times.

BALTIMORE, April 30.—King Prajadhipok of Siam was told by Dr. William Holland Wilmer today that it is "absolutely necessary to remove the cataract over the left eye to save his sight." His decision was reached after an examination lasting an hour at the Wilmer Eye Institute of Johns Hopkins Hospital.

Dr. Wilmer found the cataract on the right eye had not increased. Its condition was about the same as it was when the patient was first examined here in 1924, before he became King. The left eye, however, had not responded to treatment, and its condition had become more serious.

Dr. John M. Wheeler of New York, who will perform the operation in about ten days or two weeks, will come here tomorrow for consultation with Dr. Wilmer.

Leaving Washington accompanied by a number of men of his entourage, and riding in the automobile of President Hoover, the King arrived at the Wilmer clinic shortly before noon. He had asked that his visit be made unofficial and personal. He wore a derby hat, while his attendants wore silk hats. The Queen was not in the party, having gone with Mrs. Hoover for a boat ride to Mount Vernon.

As the several cars carrying the King and those accompanying him swung into the drive of the Hopkins hospital grounds, patients looked down from porches, and nurses and physicians and attachés stood on the lawns and sought an opportunity to see a reigning King.

While undergoing the examination, the King sat in a chair which had been occupied by Presidents Cleveland, Roosevelt, Taft and Harding and by J. Pierpont Morgan, all of whom had been Wilmer's patients. As several tests had been made in Siam and the results forwarded to Baltimore, Dr. Wilmer was familiar with the case. The King was smiling cheerfully as he left the hospital.

In the King's party were Prince Svasti, his uncle and father-in-law; several of his staff and Rear Admiral Henry V. Butler, his American naval aide. After the examination he and members of his party were entertained at luncheon by Dr. and Mrs. Wilmer at their home. Afterward the party returned to Washington.

Should Regain His Vision.

By Dr. IAGO GALDSTON,

Executive Secretary of the Medical Information Bureau of the New York Academy of Medicine.

(Written especially for The Associated Press.)

The cataract of the eye for the removal of which King Prajadhipok of Siam has come to the United States, while not presenting a serious surgical problem, is interesting from the medical point of view in that it should occur in so young a man.

King Prajadhipok is 38 years old. Cataracts among the aged are rather common.

Both eyes of the King are affected. The cataract in the left eye, which has been developing for six years, is now ripe for removal. The cataract in the right eye is not yet ready for surgical treatment. There is no way of getting rid of cataracts except by operation.

The term cataract is used to indi-

Continued on Page Three.

FUNCHAL IS SHELLED; LISBON LANDS MEN

Three Columns Said to Be Moving on Capital, With Third of Island Held.

REBELS CLAIM A VICTORY

Say They Repulsed Loyalists at Santa Cruz—End of Dictatorship Is Forecast.

Special Cable to The New York Times.

LISBON, April 30.—Troops of the Portuguese punitive expedition have made landings at several places on the island of Madeira after a bombardment following the breakdown yesterday of negotiations with the rebels who have held Funchal for a month.

A heavy offensive was ordered after the Minister of Marine, Rear Admiral Magalhaes Correa, refused an offer of conditional surrender proffered on behalf of the revolutionaries by the Bishop of Funchal. A strong bombardment was laid over the enemy's position by warships and airplanes, and afterward landings of men were effected.

The principal land position taken up was at Machico, fifteen miles northeast of Funchal, where the rebels retreated and left prisoners in the hands of the punitive forces.

Rebel leaders have refused several ultimatums to surrender unconditionally.

After informing the government of a second mediation offer by the Bishop of Funchal, the Minister of Marine radioed the government a long report which said a reconnoissance was made also at Calheta under the protection of the destroyer Vouga. The rebels were put to flight, leaving prisoners in the hands of government troops.

The note continued that nowhere did the rebels offer resistance. Another detachment landed without needing the warships, which were ready to cover the landing, and landing parties occupied their positions according to plans worked out in advance. No casualties were suffered by the government.

Tell of Repulsing Loyalists.

FUNCHAL, April 30 (AP).—The rebel junta declared in an official statement tonight that it had successfully repulsed an attack of the Portuguese Government loyalist expeditionary force, prevented a landing on the island, and had taken a number of prisoners.

"Two enemy detachments of approximately 300 men armed with machine guns," the statement said, "attempted to land on the beach at Santa Cruz under cover of the fire from two warships which bombarded our position for forty minutes.

"After an engagement lasting an hour the enemy retired in disorder, leaving war material and a number of prisoners in our hands.

"Great enthusiasm prevails throughout the island over the victory. Our troops were brilliantly led by distinguished officers, including Major Frazao and Captain Martelino."

Government Claims Success.

LISBON, April 30 (AP).—Reports from Funchal to the Portuguese Government late tonight said that Government forces had landed on the island and that the rebels were retreating into the interior, hotly pursued by the loyalists.

One-third of the island, the reports stated, is already in the hands of the expeditionary force and three columns are marching on Funchal, after occupying Sao Vincent, Camara do Lobis and Machico.

The retreating rebels, according to

Continued on Page Twelve.

SOUTH CHINA SECEDES IN A NEW REBELLION; NANKING WON'T FIGHT

Canton Taken in Bloodless Coup in Kwantung and Possibly Four Other Provinces.

CAPITAL BELITTLES MOVE

Holding Country Could Not Stand Another War, Nationalists Will Take No Action.

CHANG STANDS BY NANKING

Manchurian Leader Arrives for People's Convention—Other Northern Generals Steadfast.

By HALLETT ABEND.

Special Cable to The New York Times.

SHANGHAI, April 30.—While delegates from farflung provinces are arriving hourly at Nanking for the People's Convention, scheduled to open next Tuesday, and while workmen are feverishly busy decorating the auditorium for the convention with bunting, flags and loyalist mottoes, it is learned that a bloodless coup has been engineered in Canton by which Kwangtung Province virtually declares its independence of the Central Government, joins the Kwangsi rebels and thus offers a challenge for civil war.

But there will be no Spring war in China this year, because Nanking will not fight. This was learned definitely tonight from the highest government circles, who declared that, even if the admitted Canton coup resulted, in fact, in the rumored secession of Yunnan, Kweichow and Fukien Provinces and their joining the Kwangsi rebels, those provinces would be permitted to go their own way until time taught them their error.

Nanking Officials Flee.

It is definitely confirmed that General Chan Chai-tong has seized control not only of Canton but all Kwangtung in a move inimical to Nanking. General Chen Ming-chu, the Nanking Government's main supporter in the South, has fled to Hongkong, accompanied by Finance Commissioner Fan Ki-mo and other officials loyal to Nanking. General Chan Chai-tong, fully controlling the military, is understood to have agreed with Pai Tsung-hsi, Chang Fa-kwei, Li Tsung-jen and other leaders of the Kwangsi rebels upon a widespread secessionist movement, currently reported to include the five southern provinces.

These reports receive the color of reality by the official admission of the Nanking Government that the entire Fukien Provincial Government has resigned and the former members are proceeding to Shanghai by sea. The reason for the resignation was that the provincial treasury has been empty for months past and the government was, of course, unable to function without funds.

The Canton Central Kuomintang supervisory committee, supporting General Chan Chia-tong, issues a declaration of thousands of words denouncing the Nanking régime and virtually declaring independence. It accuses Minister Soong of the misuse of Nanking Government funds and General Chiang Kai-shek of using anti-Kuomintang elements to suit his own purposes. It denounces General Chiang as high-handed and demands the release of Hu Han-min and General Li Chai-sum.

It is announced that Hsu Hung-chi is heading the military branch and

Continued on Page Ten.

ROOSEVELT CALLS HOOVER AND REGIME REACTIONARY; HAILS SWING TO DEMOCRATS

TERMS RULE TIMOROUS

Holds National Machine Is Geared to Pace of Fifty Years Ago.

TALKS HERE OVER RADIO

Declares People Look to His Party to Lead Way Back to Basic Principles.

PRAISES SMITH'S RECORD

First Utterance on Nation-Wide Conditions Since He Loomed for Presidency in 1932.

Governor Roosevelt assailed the Hoover Administration in Washington as reactionary and opposed to fundamental governmental reform, in an address last night at a dinner of the New York Young Democratic Club at the Hotel Astor.

The Governor, who is looked upon as the outstanding probability as his party's candidate for President in 1932, assailed the national policies of the Republicans and declared that the people of the nation were looking to the Democratic party to lead the way to a restoration of the basic principles upon which the government was founded.

Speaking to a group that contained several of the more important political leaders of the city and State, the Governor did not mention the Hoover Administration by name, but he left no doubt of his meaning when, referring to the Democratic achievements in this State, he said:

"We have not reached the ultimate goal in all these lines, but I feel that the people of this State realize how greatly we have progressed toward that goal, and that by continuing us in power they will see these great reforms accomplished. And as in this State, so it is in the nation—from the conservative and reactionary party now in power in Washington, from the timid counsels of the aged, from the selfish grasping of the powerful few who control actions from behind the scenes, the people all over these United States are looking to our party to lead them into the broad road that leads to the real democracy of which our forefathers dreamt, to the real government of the people, by the people and for the people, which Lincoln pleaded for, but which his party has since filed in the archives of the past, only to be dragged out and quoted for campaign speeches and Memorial Day addresses."

Only Recent Talk on National Politics

The Governor's excursion into the national political field, in a speech which was broadcast on a wide National Broadcasting Company hookup, marked the first time since the movement to nominate him for President has assumed formidable dimensions, that he has taken up countrywide political conditions. In the past Mr. Roosevelt has avoided national in favor of the State topics, but in his talk at the dinner he used the record of the Democratic party in the State under former Governor Smith and himself as a symbol of what he asserted could be accomplished by it in the nation.

His expression of confidence that the people of the country were ready to rally to the Democratic banner to oust the "reactionary" party in power, had at least a partly Tammany setting, as among the invited guests were John F. Curry, Tammany chieftain; several Tammany legislators and officeholders, as well as John H. McCooey, Brooklyn Democratic leader, and numerous others high in the counsels of the city party.

Speakers Foresee Victory.

A note of confidence for Democratic victory in 1932 marked the utterances of all the speakers at the dinner. The Governor was received with a burst of applause when he arose to speak. One enthusiastic guest hailed him as the next President, but in his confusion shouted "Hurrah for the President of the next United States."

The Governor did not actually deliver at the dinner several of the paragraphs in his set speech dealing with national politics. He was asked later if this was intentional, but he laughed and said he did not even know he had left the paragraphs out and declared the speech as prepared for publication was intended as a

Pleas to Oust Bishop Cannon Go Before College Today

By The Associated Press.

NASHVILLE, Tenn., April. 30.—"Communications," asking the resignation of Bishop James Cannon Jr. will be laid before the College of Bishops of the Methodist Episcopal Church, South, which meets here tomorrow, Bishop J. M. Moore, Atlanta, secretary of the college, said tonight.

Bishop Moore declined to say whether the "communications" were letters or petitions.

"I can only say that they will be laid before the college."

Bishop Cannon had declined earlier to comment on proposals that he resign and that he waive his succession rights to the college presidency.

HOOVER DEFENDED IN RETORT TO BORAH

Congress, Not the President, Is to Blame for Expenditures, Says Representative Wood.

SENATE BONUS VOTE CITED

Billion Outlay Was Twice 10-Year Budget Savings, Says Appropriations Chairman.

Special to The New York Times.

WASHINGTON, April 30.—Responsibility for the increase in governmental expenditures lies at the door of Congress, and the President cannot properly be blamed, Representative Will R. Wood, chairman of the Appropriations Committee, declared today in replying to assertions made yesterday by Senator Borah that the executive branch of the government was plunging the country into extravagances and that Congress had reduced the budget recommendations.

Much of the blame for heavy expenditures was placed by Mr. Wood on special groups in the nation, which, he said, demanded that Congress support legislation to which the President was opposed.

Senator Borah, Representative Wood observed, had helped to pass the veterans' bonus loan measure over President Hoover's veto, had supported unsuccessful efforts to pass legislation dealing with Muscle Shoals and had advocated the debenture plan for agricultural exports.

Sees No Answer in the Budget.

"I fear that Senator Borah's statement does not present the real view of the growth of government expenditures," Mr. Wood declared. "That growth does not lie in the difference between Congress and the Executive over the budget. The budget is a more or less pro forma recommendation to Congress of expenditures under previous legislation or authorization acts of Congress, and the Executive is helpless once this legislation is passed.

"I think if Senator Borah would examine the authorization bills which have been passed by Congress over the opposition of the Executive, and the legislation which calls for expenditures in excess of that recommended by the Executive, he will find that Congress has an infinitely larger

Continued on Page Twenty-three.

Roosevelt's Mother Is Stricken in Paris; He Delays Departure on Vacation Trip

Governor Roosevelt postponed his departure for the South yesterday when he learned in a transatlantic telephone conversation that his mother had been stricken with influenza and was in a hospital in Paris.

The Governor had completed all his plans to leave for a vacation in Warm Springs, Ga., tonight. As soon as he received word from his aunt, Mrs. D. D. Forbes, who accompanied, his mother, Mrs. James Roosevelt, on her trip abroad, he canceled his reservations and said that he would stay in the city until he had received some reassuring word from Paris.

The Governor said that his mother, who is 76 years old, apparently was suffering from an ordinary attack of influenza. There was nothing to indicate as yet, he said, that she was in a serious condition. However, he said, he did not want to go to Warm Springs during a possibly dangerous period in her illness, as he wanted to remain where he could have close communication with Paris.

Mrs. Roosevelt and Mrs. Forbes, her sister, sailed for Europe on April 10 and planned to spend about two weeks abroad. The first news of her illness came in a cablegram from Mrs. Forbes and then the Governor called his aunt on the transatlantic phone. Mr. Roosevelt will keep in close touch with Paris and if improvement in his mother's condition is recorded he will leave for his vacation about Monday.

The Governor, an only son, and his mother are deeply attached and Mr. Roosevelt showed yesterday his distress at the news of her illness. Friends of the Executive intimated that if Mrs. Roosevelt was seriously threatened there was a possibility that he might hurry to Paris to see her.

Special Cable to The New York Times.

PARIS, April 30.—Mrs. James Roosevelt, mother of Franklin D. Roosevelt, Governor of New York, who has been ill for several days, was resting comfortably tonight at the American Hospital. Nurses in attendance answering inquiries, said tonight, "Mrs. Roosevelt is very much better."

"All the News That's Fit to Print."

The New York Times.

LATE CITY EDITION
THE WEATHER—Fair today; warmer tomorrow, followed by showers at night.
Temperatures yesterday—Max. 56, min. 47.
U. S. Weather Forecast—For details see Page 39.

Copyright, 1931, by The New York Times Company.

VOL. LXXX....No. 26,763. * * * * * NEW YORK, MONDAY, MAY 4, 1931. TWO CENTS In Greater New York | THREE CENTS Within 200 Miles | FOUR CENTS Elsewhere Except 7th and 8th Postal Zones

AHRENBERG REACHES GREENLAND IN PLANE TO SAVE COURTAULD

Flies From Iceland, but Lands at Angmagsalik, Short of Base Camp, Due to Ice on Wings.

BRITISH FLIERS DRIVEN BACK

Two Go Inland Seventy Miles Over Ice Cap Before Mist Halts Their Attempt.

FIND NO TRACE OF WATKINS

Leader of Expedition and 2 Aides Believed Further On in Search—Fears for Their Fate Scouted.

By CAPTAIN PERCY LEMON.
Wireless Officer of the British Arctic Air Route Expedition.

Special Cable to THE NEW YORK TIMES.

ANGMAGSALIK, Greenland, May 3.—Captain Albin Ahrenberg landed from his monoplane at the settlement here at 4:30 P. M., Greenwich mean time [12:30 P. M. in New York].

He had left Reykjavik, Iceland, at 11:15 A. M. [7:15 A. M. in New York].

Weather conditions were excellent for the flight.

Flight Lieutenant D'Aeth, accompanied by Quintin Riley, flew toward the ice cap yesterday, but owing to mist had to turn back after going seventy miles. They failed to see anything of the sledging party under H. G. Watkins, which evidently was further in.

[The plane used in this flight in an attempt to rescue Augustine Courtauld, the member of the British Arctic Air Route Expedition marooned on the inland ice cap, was one of the expedition's repaired machines.]

Rescuers Near Their Goal.

Special Cable to THE NEW YORK TIMES.

LONDON, May 3.—The parties engaged both by land and air in the work of rescuing Augustine Courtauld from his predicament on the Greenland ice cap are tonight within striking distance of their goal.

Captain Albin Ahrenberg with two companions and a load of much-needed gear in his Junkers seaplane had tonight, according to a dispatch from Angmagsalik, arrived there safely at the end of a long and dangerous flight across the North Atlantic from Malmoe, Sweden.

At the same time news reached London that one of the recently repaired Moth airplanes attached to the Watkins expedition had made a reconnoitering flight from the base camp toward the ice cap, but owing to encountering mist had been compelled to return after covering seventy miles, or roughly half the distance separating the base camp and Courtauld's isolated refuge amid the eternal snows.

The two British airmen, Flight Lieutenant D'Aeth and Riley, who made this flight, reported that they could see no trace of Watkins and two companions, who since April 21 have been making a laborious 150-mile journey with dogs and sledges over the broken glaciers toward the ice cap.

It is estimated that Watkins is nearer Courtauld's little meteorological station than the daring pilots in the Moth plane could get yesterday, and the fact that the searchers were not sighted has given no grounds for uneasiness here. They are well supplied with provisions for a search lasting to the end of the month.

The first news of the British reconnoitering flight came briefly from Captain Percy Lemon, radioist of the Watkins expedition, and was dated at the base camp at 10:10 P. M., Greenwich Time, Saturday.

False Reports Repudiated.

The publication in certain newspapers of reports about the British Arctic Air Route Expedition which are "inaccurate and in some cases without foundation" led to the issuance tonight of the following announcement signed by Stephen Courtauld, chairman of the expedition, and Captain Ralph Rayner, honorary secretary.

"Watkins with two companions left the base camp on April 21 to search for the ice cap station [at which Augustine Courtauld is marooned], taking with them dogs, sledges and food for five weeks. They need not return to the base camp, therefore, until the end of this month.

"They are naturally not in communication with the base camp, but it is entirely misleading to describe them as 'lost.' They are following a route which has been traversed at

Continued on Page Three.

Quake Startles Mid-England And Scores for a Golf Putter

Wireless to THE NEW YORK TIMES.

LONDON, May 3.—No one was more astonished by an earth tremor which shook a large area in East Lancashire today than an elderly golfer on the Chorlton links. He was taking his stance for a putt when suddenly he saw his opponent's ball, lying near the cup, start to move—and trickle in!

About breakfast time thousands of alarmed people in various districts of Manchester and Broughton, part of Salford, rushed from their homes as chimney pots began to fall, but no serious injuries or damage were reported.

In the mining areas there were many, as earth tremors in this part of the world are unknown, who rushed to the pitheads believing that a severe subterranean explosion had occurred, while in the Manchester Children's Hospital a ceiling fell.

The shock lasted from five to forty seconds.

CHINA FACES CRISIS AS UNREST SPREADS

Disaffection Inside Nanking Circles Revealed by Effort to Impeach Chiang.

REBELS CLAIM 685,000 MEN

Say 17 Generals Back Them—British Order Cruiser to Nanking as Treaty Parleys Fail.

By HALLETT ABEND.
Special Cable to THE NEW YORK TIMES.

SHANGHAI, May 3.—A demand for the impeachment of Chiang Kai-shek, President of the Nanking Government, on charges of dictatorial usurpation of authority in connection with the arrest of Hu Han-min, President of the Legislative Yuan, and General Chiang's subsequent complete vindication, were disclosed late tonight when a series of documents were issued in Nanking.

The attempted impeachment of the President of the National Government, it is disclosed, was backed by four members of the Control Yuan.

The second document is Chiang Kai-shek's reply, excusing his conduct and asking the Central Executive Committee to investigate. The committee replied, expressing surprise at the charge and the belief that the Control Yuan had not properly considered the circumstances. The committee also addressed a communication to the Control Yuan, declaring that the latter was misled by sentiment into an improper procedure.

Another of the documents was a telegram from General Wu Ti-chen to Canton, urging the people and the leaders there to forget their differences and strive their utmost for national unification.

Rebels Claim Large Force.

General Chan Chia-tang and the Canton rebels announce today that they do not desire to overthrow the Nanking Government, nor do they intend to overthrow the rule of the Kuomingtang party, but they aim solely at ousting General Chiang Kai-shek, T. V. Soong and others of the régime. They charge that the present leaders are usurping power and strangling Kuomingtang activities. Aiming at unity, the Cantonese leaders publicly invite to Canton all members of the Central Executive Committee of the Kuomingtang who are now residing in Nanking.

The Shanghai International Settlement headquarters of the rebellious faction issued today a list of seventeen Generals, with collective forces of 685,000 men, who, they say, have already pledged active assistance to

Continued on Page Ten.

PRESIDENCY CONTEST CENTRES ON BRIAND; GERMANY THE ISSUE

Foes of French Foreign Minister Rally for Attack on His Attitude to Customs Union.

CAMPAIGN GETS UNDER WAY

Laval Strikes Keynote in Program Speech, but Briand Awaits Chamber Debate.

PREMIER STANDS FOR PEACE

He Is Believed Logical Successor in the Foreign Office if Briand Is Elected.

By P. J. PHILIP.
Special Cable to THE NEW YORK TIMES.

PARIS, May 3.—With a program speech by Premier Pierre Laval such as is customary on the eve of the reassembly of Parliament, there began today in France a week of political movement which is certain to be of the greatest interest and consequence.

It may have for a result the election of Aristide Briand to the Presidency of the Republic, from which post he would be able to direct his country along the paths of peace and international cooperation which he has sought to follow as Foreign Minister for the past six years.

It may have a quite different outcome, for opposition to M. Briand is not just personal. It is opposition which derives from political doctrine and from nostalgia for that military glory which has always characterized the French people.

The touchstone of the situation will be reached Thursday, when, in the Chamber of Deputies, debate will be provoked on the attitude which France has taken and will take with regard to the proposed customs union between Germany and Austria.

That proposal by the German Government has from the first, as perhaps it was intended it should, been regarded in France as a deliberate challenge on what could be made to seem a minor issue to the whole structure of the Treaty of Versailles. It is held simply preliminary to others which will be made later.

These are seen as moves against fulfillment of reparation payments under the Young plan and against the terms of Germany's disarmament if next year's disarmament conference does not result in some general measure of arms limitation such as was foreseen in the preliminary paragraph to that part of the Treaty of Versailles which laid down Germany's military, naval and air status.

That paragraph reads:

"In order to render possible the initiation of general limitations of armaments in all nations, Germany undertakes strictly to observe the military, naval and air clauses which follow."

France Calls It Political.

While in some other countries the proposed customs union has been considered from only its legal and economic aspects, in France from the outset it has been regarded as essentially a political first step by Germany toward revision of the territorial and other conditions of the Treaty of Versailles. The attitude which the Foreign Minister and the government will take, and the probable results of that attitude, are therefore considered of the very gravest importance. It is no secret that most of the present government's majority and several of M. Briand's fellow-members in the Cabinet consider the fact that Germany

Continued on Page Nine.

Aviator Starts From Tokyo for America; Yoshihara Will Stop in Siberia and Alaska

Special Cable to THE NEW YORK TIMES.

TOKYO, Monday, May 4.—Seiji Yoshihara took off from here at 10:10 this morning (9:10 P. M. Sunday, New York time), on the first stage of a flight to San Francisco.

It was with the most elaborate ceremonial and publicity that Yoshihara left Haneda Airdrome on this trip to America by way of the Aleutian Islands, Alaska and Canada.

The first lap will take him to Numasaki, twenty miles north of Sabishiro Beach, where Harold Bromley started last year.

The 27-year-old flier arose at 4 A. M., prayed to the gods of Japan for success, and then flew his Junkers plane to the airdrome, where a bustling scene was evolving in the presence of several collateral imperial princes and foreign diplomats.

After the Rising Sun flag was hoisted by a pretty girl, American, Russian and Canadian representatives made speeches and a message from President Hoover was read.

The trip was toasted in consecrated wine, a song specially composed for the flight was sung and the flag was then hauled down and handed to the airman, who will take it to the United States. Then his motor roared as Yoshihara took off, circling Tokyo and heading north.

TOKYO, Monday, May 4 (AP).—Alone and without radio, the "Lindbergh of Japan," as he is often called, started in a light, open seaplane on a good-will trip to America, carrying to President Hoover a message from the Japanese magazine publisher, Seiji Noma, backer of the flight.

He hoped to complete the first stage of the journey today to Numasaki, 368 miles north of Tokyo. The next jump would take him 297 miles further north to the extreme tip of Hokkaido Island. Then his itinerary calls for flights over the Kurile Islands to Petropavlovsk, Siberia, over the Bering Sea to the Aleutians, and after several stops to Seward, Alaska. From there he would fly southward to Seattle, then to San Francisco. He would then go to Washington.

The young flier speaks English poorly, but is better versed in German. He expressed confidence of completing the flight without mishap despite the gales which swirl from the Arctic Circle and the fog which during May obscures the Aleutian Is-

Continued on Page Fourteen.

FRENCH FAVOR PACT FOR WHEAT SOLUTION

Laval Stresses Hope of a World Accord, Urging Cooperation on Other Products as Well.

BID TO CHADBOURNE BACKED

Government Economic Advisers Support Movement to Have Him Tackle Wheat Issue.

By CARLISLE MacDONALD.
Special Cable to THE NEW YORK TIMES.

PARIS, May 3.—The optimism regarding the possibility of a solution of the world wheat problem which has been evidenced by the disclosure of the movement to obtain the services of Thomas L. Chadbourne as a sort of world wheat dictator was reflected today by Pierre Laval, the French Premier, in a significant political speech before the Independent Socialists of the suburb of La Courneuve.

Without actually referring to the decision of the United States Government to be officially represented in the world wheat conference opening in London on May 18, the head of the French Government emphasized the point that developments, encouraged by the results of the recent wheat meetings in Europe, now justified the hope that the delicate question might be brought within the scope of an international accord.

Although it would of course be impossible to attempt to indicate what line of action prompted M. Laval's remarks, it is nevertheless known that some of the most important economic advisors within the government feel that Mr. Chadbourne should be asked to tackle the wheat issue.

Man Outside Field Favored.

As explained in yesterday's message, the French have already adopted for their own wheat problem what they call the "little Chadbourne plan," and its success, together with the successful termination of the international sugar negotiations, has led to the belief that a strong personality entirely outside the wheat question is now needed to bring the widely divergent wheat exporting and importing nations into an international agreement.

For that job it is felt that an American should be chosen, since by common consent the crux of the whole matter is admitted to be in the United States and its huge excess of wheat. There is also a feeling that the right American could influence Canada, whose attitude toward the projected world agreement is of equal importance.

Encouragement for those who are now trying to bring the wheat problem down to the point of active negotiations is therefore being derived from certain passages in Premier Laval's speech.

"We must have respect for treaties, since they remain the surest guarantee against the recurrence of war," he declared. "However, we must also admit that peace cannot be well-founded nor enduring unless it is based upon close economic cooperation among peoples.

"It is said that the efforts of the League of Nations along these lines have met with failure. I do not think we should contemplate giving up a work which, after all, must be the outcome of time. We must rather renew our efforts with added force and profit by the experiences gained.

"There is, for example, the question of grain, especially wheat, in the Eastern European countries, which, following conferences in Geneva, Paris and Rome, gives hope for an eventual accord.

"The creation of an international

Continued on Page Seven.

FOREIGNERS BUY BACK $500,000,000 BONDS

Low Prices Caused "Unparalleled" Homeward Movement Last Year, Says Dr. Klein.

OUR PROFITS ABROAD FELL

But Short-Term Loan "Exports" Set New Mark, Lamont's Aide Discloses in Radio Address.

Special to The New York Times.

WASHINGTON, May 3.—A "terrific, unparalleled" movement by foreign bankers in 1930 to repatriate foreign bonds, which had fallen in many instances to "absurdly low levels" on the American market, carrying purchases of the kind in the year to about $500,000,000, was described tonight in a radio address by Dr. Julius H. Klein, Assistant Secretary of Commerce.

Dr. Klein spoke over the Columbia Broadcasting System, discussing the importance of the meeting of the International Chamber of Commerce which begins here tomorrow. He took his figures from an advance summary of the department's "balance of international payments" for 1930 which has been prepared for the use of the delegates.

He referred to the international chamber as having an "impressive record of getting things done, constructive things that mean business," and declared that it had started the movement which led to the adoption of the original Dawes plan for German reparations, at its meeting in Rome in 1923.

There is no doubt, he added, "that the world is desperately in need of just that kind of practical, result-getting help at once."

In his "pre-view" of "invisible" exports and imports Dr. Klein said that the American money market exported last year a record volume of short-term capital to industrial and other borrowers abroad. This totaled $443,000,000.

"Here is another big asset which foreigners derived here. The proceeds of foreign bonds and stocks floated in the United States during 1930 gave foreigners new capital amounting to about $905,000,000," he said, and went on:

"An 'all-time record' was established in a type of international transaction that is not often discussed. That was in the so-called "repatriation" of foreign bonds. Here is the situation: In 1930 the prices of foreign bonds in this country fell, in scores of cases, to absurdly low levels. Foreign bankers and others found that there was not the usual heavy demand for money on the part of business men, because of the depression, so they used their surplus funds to buy up the foreign bonds which had become so absurdly cheap on Wall Street. We call that "repatriating" foreign bonds.

"That movement was very quiet, but it was terrific, unparalleled. The exact total of our sales of foreign bonds to foreigners in 1930 is not yet determined, but it will probably be between $400,000,000 and $500,000,000.

"So you see we imported several hundred of millions of long-term capital during 1930, at the same time that we were so furiously busy exporting short-term capital. You could almost say that we borrowed on long-term from foreigners and lent the proceeds to them on short-term, an amazing reversal of the trend of recent years."

Preliminary estimates, Dr. Klein said, indicate that the foreign nations received from tourist expenditures by Americans and immigrant remittances from this country about

Continued on Page Four.

Washington Recognizes Arabian Kingdom; Our Trade With the Hejaz and Nejd Growing

Special to The New York Times.

WASHINGTON, May 3.—The State Department announced tonight that the United States is extending full diplomatic recognition to the dual kingdom of the Hejaz and Nejd and its dependencies in Arabia. Notification of this action is being communicated through Ambassador Dawes to the Hejazi Minister at London.

"The kingdom of the Hejaz and Nejd and its dependencies," the department points out, "has been recognized by nearly all of the principal governments of Europe and it has entered into treaty relations with several of these governments.

"In extending recognition on its part to the government of King Ibn Saud the United States takes cognizance of the actual existence of that government during a considerable period of time and of the successful maintenance within its borders of political and economic stability."

The dual kingdom of the Hejaz and Nejd and its dependencies includes all of the Arabian peninsula except the Arab States of the Persian Gulf, the British settlement and protectorate of Aden and the kingdom or imamate of Yemen at the southwestern end of the peninsula. The capital of the Hejaz is Mecca, while that of the Nejd is Riyadh.

Since the introduction in 1926 of the automobile in the Hejaz and Nejd, used chiefly in carrying pilgrims to Mecca, there has been a large demand for American automotive products. With the establishment of closer relations it is believed that the American share in these imports will considerably increase. Other imports from the United States consist chiefly of kerosene, pumps and miscellaneous machinery.

No consideration is being given at present to the appointment of an American Minister to Jeddah, as that would require action by Congress. Relations will therefore for some time continue to be conducted through the Hejazi Minister at London.

The department indicated that there had been no recent consideration given to the diplomatic recognition of Afghanistan.

SEABURY WILL SCAN BANK DATA OF HEADS OF ALL CITY BUREAUS

To Subpoena Accounts of Their Families Also When Inquiry Starts, Probably Next Week.

PLANNING OF SCOPE HELD UP

Hofstadter Is Expected Back Tomorrow to Help Set Up Investigation Machinery.

CRAIN ASKS $10,000 FUND

Wants as Much to Prepare Defense Charts as Dr. Moley Received—Schieffelin Warns on Leaks.

The bank accounts of the heads of virtually all city departments will be examined by Samuel Seabury, counsel of the Hofstadter legislative committee, it became known yesterday. Subpoenas have not yet been issued, but they will be soon after the inquiry, as yet in its early stages, gets fully under way.

The financial data to be examined will include not only those of the commissioners and deputy commissioners but of members of their families. Many of these bank records have been scrutinized before during the investigation of the magistrates' courts by Mr. Seabury and the investigation of the Ewald case by Hiram C. Todd as special Deputy Attorney General.

Hofstadter Back Tomorrow.

Senator Samuel H. Hofstadter, chairman of the legislative investigation, will not return from vacation until tomorrow, and the scheduled conference between him and Mr. Seabury will be postponed. Assemblyman Hamilton F. Potter of Suffolk County, vice chairman of the committee, will visit its headquarters in the State Office Building at 80 Centre Street today and will confer with Mr. Seabury.

Senator Hofstadter will see Mr. Seabury tomorrow or Wednesday, and it then will be determined when to call a meeting of the committee to arrange a definite course of procedure and set up machinery for the private hearings, which will precede those to be held in public.

A clash between the Republican and Democratic members of the committee is expected over the private hearings. The Democrats on the committee will fight for representation on any subcommittees that may be established and there will be opposition, possibly to the extent of an appeal to the courts, against the reported plan of Senator Hofstadter and Mr. Seabury to have the private hearings before Senator Hofstadter alone. It also is likely that some of the city officials will contest the right of Mr. Seabury to question them in private and contend that they have the right to demand examination at a public hearing.

As Mr. Seabury intends to go to Washington the middle of the week to attend the meeting of the American Bar Association, it is quite probable that no meeting of the legislative committee will be held until next week. Assemblyman Abbot Low Moffat, the only New York City Republican member of the committee besides Senator Hofstadter, also is on vacation, and it was said at his home that he would not return until May 12.

Warns of Interference.

A warning that any interference with Mr. Seabury would impair the investigation by making it possible to suppress important evidence and to get necessary witnesses out of the

Continued on Page Six.

Megan Lloyd George on Radio Says Welsh Were Here First

The legend of Prince Madoc, who, the Welsh say, discovered America, was discussed yesterday by Megan Lloyd George, member of the House of Commons and daughter of former Premier David Lloyd George, in the first of a series of international travel broadcasts over the Columbia Broadcasting Company's network, from London.

Miss Lloyd George told how Madoc, compelled by civil strife to leave his native land, sailed westward in 1170 and reached a new land, whose products and inhabitants were unlike those of Europe. This land is assumed to have been America.

"It is certainly true," she declared, "that many hundreds of thousands of Welshmen have discovered America since." She added that a distinguished American had estimated this number and their descendants at 6,000,000.

FALL ACCEPTS JAIL; TO MAKE NO APPEAL

Decides Not to Carry His Doheny Bribe Conviction to Supreme Court.

GOT YEAR AND $100,000 FINE

Ex-Secretary's Announcement Is Climax of His Long Fight on Oil Scandal Charges.

By The Associated Press.

EL PASO, Texas, May 3.—Albert B. Fall, former Secretary of the Interior, announced today he would not appeal to the United States Supreme Court from a District of Columbia Court sentence of one year in jail and $100,000 fine.

He was sentenced after conviction of accepting a bribe from E. L. Doheny, oil magnate, in connection with oil leases during the administration of President Harding. The District of Columbia Court of Appeals recently upheld the conviction and sentence.

From his ranch home at Three Rivers, N. M., Mr. Fall said he was wiring his attorneys in Washington to take no further action in the case.

Found Guilty Oct. 25, 1929.

Albert B. Fall was found guilty on Oct. 25, 1929, of accepting, when Secretary of the Interior under President Harding, a bribe of $100,000 from Edward L. Doheny, Los Angeles oil operator. In consideration for this bribe, the government charged, Mr. Fall leased to Mr. Doheny the Elk Hills naval oil reserve in Southern California.

Mr. Fall, who was the first member of an American Cabinet to be convicted of a felony by a jury, was sentenced to a year in prison and $100,000 fine by Associate Justice William Hitz of the Supreme Court of the District of Columbia. In imposing sentence Justice Hitz gave consideration to Mr. Fall's weakened physical condition.

The former Secretary had been brought to the court room in a wheel chair and had collapsed once during the trial. Had he been in normal health, Justice Hitz said, the sentence would have been the maximum provided by law—that is, three years in prison and a fine three times the amount of the bribe, or $300,000.

Mr. Fall appealed from the decision to the Court of Appeals of the District of Columbia, but that court upheld it unanimously in a decision handed down April 6 last.

The bribery charge against Mr. Fall was one of the many civil and criminal prosecutions growing out of the exposure of the oil lease scandals

Continued on Page Two.

Biggest Crowds of Year Flock to Resorts; Sun Tempts a Few to Brave Wind for Swim

Bright skies and warm sunshine lured thousands of New Yorkers to the seashore yesterday, and most of the resorts reported the biggest crowds thus far this season.

Although a biting wind was blowing out of the northwest and the average temperature for the day was 4 degrees below normal, many persons appeared on the beaches in bathing suits. A few even ventured into the surf, but they did not stay long.

The highest temperature was 56 degrees at 4 P. M. Thereafter it dropped rapidly. By 9 P. M. it was down to 47 and still descending. However, the Weather Bureau promised rising temperatures and continued fair weather for today.

The Jersey coast resorts from the Highlands to Atlantic City enjoyed midsummer crowds and many concessions opened for the first time this year. Highways were jammed with automobiles and boardwalks crowded with promenaders. Hotel men at the resorts said business was well ahead of the corresponding period of last year.

At Coney Island the crowd was estimated at more than 250,000. The amusements at the island did a good business, as did the vendors and refreshment stands along Surf Avenue and elsewhere. Evidence that the economic readjustment had affected even the hot sausage business was seen on all sides, the frankfurter, roll and dab of mustard that formerly sold for ten cents being advertised everywhere for five.

The crowd at Long Beach numbered more than 20,000. There, as at Coney Island, few visitors appeared on the beach. But in the Rockaways crowds said to number more than 50,000 included many parties on the sand and a few bathers. Scores of visitors lined the shore of Jamaica Bay fishing for flounders. But the water was rough and there were few catches.

Edward B. Wolf, 17 years old, who had just built a new sailboat, decided to give it a trial spin in the Hudson yesterday. Off 125th Street the boat capsized. John Sweeney, 30 years old, of 577 West 130th Street, rescued Wolf and he was taken to Knickerbocker Hospital and treated for submersion. Later he was sent home.

TWO NATIONS READY TO RAISE DEBT ISSUE IN CAPITAL THIS WEEK

German and British Chamber Delegates Want Matter Taken Up Despite Our Attitude.

NO POLITICS, SAYS THEUNIS

Council of the Chamber Approves International Action to Stabilize Silver Values.

GERMAN MADE PRESIDENT

Prof. Angell Tells Foreign Policy Association We May Be Forced to Cut on War Debts.

Special to The New York Times.

WASHINGTON, May 3.—Reparations and war debts are expected to come prominently before the congress of the International Chamber of Commerce at its meetings beginning tomorrow, despite the indications given by the administration that its policies in these matters are unchanged and that it will pay no heed to any agitation of the subject in the chamber.

Both German and British delegates are understood to be prepared to make a strong effort to obtain supporting sentiment in favor of reductions of reparations and debts.

Abraham Frowein, a leader of the German delegation, said today that his group would probably raise the question, adding his belief that reparation payments are based on an uneconomic basis which is upsetting the whole European trade structure. He said the system is founded on "economic fallacies" and pointed out that in the first three months of this year Germany has exported about 560,000,000 gold marks (approximately $133,280,000), which he said was almost fatal to her import trade.

British Want Issue Studied.

The British delegation, of which Sir Arthur Balfour is chairman, gave out no direct statement but, according to information from an authoritative quarter, it feels that the question of revising reparations and debt payments might well be a subject of deep study.

Assurance was given, however, by George Theunis, president of the chamber, that there will be no attempt to treat any question on a political basis.

Important action was taken on the silver problem in advance of the Congress today, when the council of the chamber passed on to the Congress a resolution asking international action for stabilization of silver values in the interest of world trade.

The council also confirmed the election of a German, Franz W. Mendelssohn, to be the next president of the chamber. He is a private banker and a descendant of the famous composer. He was unable to come to the meeting and will broadcast a speech from Germany on Saturday.

Not to Open Russian Debate.

Another point clarified today was that the British delegation does not favor opening of discussion on Russian trade, a sentiment previously attributed to it. It was said the delegation feels that little can be accomplished by such discussion at this time, and that the result would be only unnecessary publicity of Russia's economic workings.

M. Theunis submitted to a general interview immediately after the adjournment of the council, or governing body of the chamber, at the headquarters of the Chamber of Commerce of the United States. It was the first press conference held by him.

"These matters which we are to discuss," he said, "are questions of trade and not questions of politics. We are seeking, as 'free men' or men freed from political ties, to work out the numerous problems that confront us."

This statement by the spokesman for the chamber was interpreted as a reassuring reply to a statement from official sources here last week that the government would take no official cognizance of criticisms in the chamber of its tariff, debt or other policies.

Council Acts on Silver.

The meeting of the council was private, the only meeting of the Congress to be held behind closed doors. According to M. Theunis, there was little or no discussion of any of the controversial subjects to be taken up later in open sessions.

The council adopted without change a resolution on silver previously drawn by the executive committee, which will be considered at a group meeting on Tuesday afternoon. It reads:

"The executive committee of the International Chamber of Commerce, having considered the deplorable effect of the fall in the price of silver on the economic situation of China, and the consequent reduction of

Augustine Courtauld, (second from right) a member of the British Arctic Air Route Expedition, volunteered to remain alone at the meteorological station in the interior of Greenland. After five months he was dug out by H.G. Watkins, (second from left).

"All the News That's Fit to Print."

The New York Times.

LATE CITY EDITION

THE WEATHER—Showers today; tomorrow generally fair, showers at night.
Temperatures yesterday—Max. 63, min. 55.
U. S. Weather Forecast—For details see page 31.

Copyright, 1931, by The New York Times Company.

VOL. LXXX....No. 26,767. ***** NEW YORK, FRIDAY, MAY 8, 1931. TWO CENTS in Greater New York | THREE CENTS Within 200 Miles | FOUR CENTS Elsewhere Except 7th and 8th Postal Zones

COURTAULD IS FOUND SAFE ON THE GREENLAND ICE CAP; FOOD DROPPED FROM PLANE

RESCUED BY WATKINS PARTY

British Scientist on Way to Camp After Winter in Wilderness.

AHRENBERG BRINGS NEWS

Courtauld, Well, Walks Behind Sledge—Group May Take 8 Days to Reach Base.

WEGENER WILL BE SOUGHT

Swedish Aviator Radios He Will Go Further Inland to Find German Explorer.

By CAPTAIN PERCY LEMON.
Wireless Officer of the British Arctic Air Route Expedition.

Wireless to THE NEW YORK TIMES.

WATKINS BASE CAMP, via Angmagsalik, Greenland, May 7.—Augustine Courtauld is safe. Captain Albin Ahrenberg's plane flew into the ice cap at 12:19 P. M. today, and after going about 100 miles an observer saw the Watkins's sledging party five miles to the south. Going nearer, Captain Ahrenberg saw four men and knew that all was well. [H. G. Watkins, leader of the British Arctic Air Route Expedition, set out from the base camp three weeks ago with two companions to search for Courtauld, meteorologist, marooned on the ice cap.]

The Watkins party is returning with Courtauld. He is quite well and walking behind the sledge. The plane dropped letters, two sacks of seal meat and one sack of food for the men. The dogs appeared well and will be greatly encouraged by the fresh meat, but as the surface of the ground is soft the party may take eight days to return. There is ideal weather with a bright sun and no wind, but they appear to have had snow recently. The ground temperature is about 5 degrees Fahrenheit.

Praises Ahrenberg.

The flight reflects great credit on Captain Ahrenberg's navigation in most difficult conditions over the ice cap, with no landmarks and nothing to indicate the drift. Returning, he dropped the welcome news to Andrew Stephenson's party.

A further flight to drop food to the Watkins party will not be necessary. They took food for five weeks and will be back at the base in under four. Food for them was taken today only for prolonging the search if necessary.

Another flight will be made in two days, however, to drop luxuries and take photographs. There is great rejoicing here.

Details of Rescue.

By SVEND CARSTENSEN.

Special Cable to THE NEW YORK TIMES.

COPENHAGEN, Friday, May 8.—From radiograms received in official quarters here in the last few hours from Angmagsalik and conversations with some of the most eminent Greenland explorers, including Dr. Lauge Koch, it is now possible to give a fuller account of the last dramatic moves leading up to the discovery that Augustine Courtauld is alive and well.

Captain Ahrenberg left the Watkins base camp shortly after noon yesterday in his Junkers monoplane carrying three companions and ample provisions not only for the Watkins sledging party, which since April 21 had been trudging across the inland ice field in search of Courtauld's hut, but sufficient "iron rations" which would enable the party in the plane to get back to the base camp near Angmagsalik in the event of a forced landing being made on the ice cap.

The Swedish flier started the hop with two objectives in view. The first was to find the Watkins party, comprising the leader of the expedition and two aides, and provision it for a more extensive search for Courtauld. The second was to try to locate Courtauld's hut, roughly 150 miles inland on the ice cap at a position given by him on a map as Lat. 67 degrees 3 minutes N. and Long. 41 degrees 49 minutes W.

Captain Ahrenberg had been in the air about three hours, climbing steadily to an elevation of more than

Continued on Page Twelve.

Britain Licenses Manufacture Of 100 Tanks for the Soviet

Special Cable to THE NEW YORK TIMES.

LONDON, May 7.—The diplomatic representatives in London of the various European countries informed their governments today that the British Government had issued a license to Vickers-Armstrong, Ltd., permitting it to manufacture for shipment to the Soviet Government 100 military tanks. The reported cost is $3,000,000.

According to the report of the transaction, it has been conducted under the rules laid down by the convention for the international trade in arms reached at Geneva in 1925. This requires an order in writing from the prospective importing government and a license to the manufacturer from the government in whose country the munitions are made, with a report of the transaction to the Secretariat of the League of Nations.

REDISCOUNT RATE CUT TO 1½%, RECORD LOW

Federal Reserve Bank Here Takes Drastic Action to Force Money Into Trade.

BONDS EXPECTED TO RISE

Member Banks Due to End All Interest on Demand Funds—Flow of Gold Abates.

The Federal Reserve Bank of New York reduced yesterday its rediscount rate to 1½ per cent, the lowest rate for member bank borrowing ever established by any central bank. The new rate, which becomes effective today, supersedes a rate of 2 per cent, which has been in effect since Dec. 24.

The reduction had been expected in Wall Street for the last two weeks as a result of steps which the Reserve Bank had taken to prepare the market. These steps included three successive cuts in the bill-buying rate of the Reserve Bank, forcing as many reductions in the open market yield rates on bankers' bills, and the lowering on Wednesday of the rediscount rates of the Federal Reserve Banks of Boston and Philadelphia to 2 and 3 per cent respectively.

Ogden L. Mills, Under Secretary of the Treasury, attended the meeting of the directors of the Federal Reserve Bank yesterday, and participated in the discussions which led to a reduction in the rediscount rate. The recent reductions in money rates are expected to have an important bearing upon the large financing program with which the United States Treasury is faced.

The entire program is viewed by bankers as a new and aggressive campaign devised by the Federal Reserve authorities with two main objectives: first, the deflection of the flow of gold from this market and toward London, and second, the stimulation of a market for foreign and domestic bond issues here.

Flow of Gold Slackens.

The first purpose has already achieved some success. The movement of gold from France to this country, which began just prior to the first steps taken by the Reserve,

Continued on Page Five.

REPARATION ACTION IS ASKED BY GERMAN IN WORLD CHAMBER

Bergmann Says Solution Is Still to Come and Points to the Slump as a Reason.

BRITON TAKES LIKE STAND

Henry Bells Asks Americans to Be 'Kinder'—Attacks on the War Debts Applauded.

SILVER INQUIRY AGREED ON

Agricultural Group Adopts Resolution for World Control of Farm Products.

Special to The New York Times.

WASHINGTON, May 7.—A definite statement of British and German sentiment that the United States should yield from its uncompromising position on reduction of war debts was made today in a group meeting of the International Chamber of Commerce.

Agreement was reached by all delegations interested in silver except the British that a resolution be passed by the chamber asking the governments of the world to take up immediately a study of this problem. The British are expected to agree tomorrow and so end a contentious issue.

A third development was the presentation by a special group of a resolution recommending world-wide control of agricultural production and distribution. Consideration of the proposal was marked by attacks on the Federal Farm Board and on the immigration policy of the United States as a deterrent to consumption of agricultural products.

Group Takes Up War Debts.

Reduction of war debts came up in a group meeting of the congress for the study of international settlements and movements of capital.

Dr. Carl Bergmann, former German Secretary of State for Finance, who based his speech on a report to the chamber by Dr. Bernhard Dernburg, former Finance Minister of Germany, said: "The problem of reparations is not yet definitely settled. It still awaits a complete and final economic solution."

Henry Bell, director of Lloyd's Bank of London, included in a brief speech many of the foreign criticisms of the United States as a creditor nation, saying he believed this country does not realize the responsibilities this position entails, and suggested that "a rather larger, a rather kinder, a rather better attitude might be taken."

Both stressed the fact that they were speaking as individuals, but the applause following their remarks was ample confirmation of the attitude of their associates.

Traylor Thanks the Speakers.

Melvin S. Traylor, Chicago banker, whose criticisms of the Stock Exchange created a stir earlier in the week, was presiding as chairman of this meeting. He thanked both speakers for their frank exposition of their positions.

These speeches were considered generally as greatly strengthening the proposed fight by the British and German delegations for adoption of a resolution in which the chamber would recommend a revision of the reparations and debt settlements, but opponents of such action, including most of the American delegation, held to their ground.

It is generally believed the American delegation will not forsake its opposition without some word that the administration has changed its own position, and the Americans

Continued on Page Twenty-two.

New Avenue From 42nd to 59th St. Urged To Cut Through Radio City on Three Levels

A proposal submitted yesterday to the Board of Estimate undertakes to reduce Radio City to an element in a larger scheme of general city planning, according to the proponents of the development.

This scheme calls for a new north and south avenue between Fifth and Sixth Avenues, extending from Forty-second Street to Central Park, and running through Radio City. It also calls for an open square in front of St. Patrick's Cathedral, reaching west to the new avenue. Thus it eliminates from the Rockefeller development as projected—the work on which is about to be begun—most, if not all of the northernmost of the three blocks of the Columbia University leasehold between Forty-eighth and Fifty-first Streets, which, it is said, constitutes the basic real estate of the enterprise.

Direct action by the City Government is the essence of the proposal, and the sponsor for it is the Fine Arts Federation of New York, of which Joseph H. Friedlander is president. This is a group representing various architectural organizations and professional bodies.

Peter J. McGowan, secretary of the Board of Estimate, who received the proposed plans for the new street, said the proposal would be considered by the Board of Estimate at its meeting one week from today, and then probably would be referred to John F. Sullivan, City Planning Engineer. Mr. McGowan recalled that about thirty years ago a somewhat similar project was put forward calling for the construction of an elevated street between Sixth and Seventh Avenues at the level of the first stories of buildings.

The proposal is put forward, it is explained, to take advantage of a strategic moment. In the first place, it is calculated to capitalize for the city's future good the intense public interest in and the active discussion of the plans for the projected Rockefeller Radio City. In the second place, it is proposed to seize the last opportunity before that vast project goes into the construction stage to make sure that it coordinates with and does not block more far-reaching schemes for the improvement of the region which is the very heart of Manhattan.

The Fine Arts Federation's recommendation, which calls for definite

Continued on Page Eighteen.

1,000 POLICE GUARD BRIAND AT DEBATE

Precautions Follow Anonymous Threat as Attack on His Entire Policy Opens.

CHAMBER ASSAILS UNION

But Chance of Foreign Minister for Presidency Is Held Chief Issue at Stake.

By P. J. PHILIP.

Special Cable to THE NEW YORK TIMES.

PARIS, May 7.—There have never been at any time so many policemen on guard outside the Chamber of Deputies and the Ministry of Foreign Affairs as today, when the debate began on France's foreign policy and especially on the attitude which has been and will be taken by Foreign Minister Aristide Briand with regard to the proposed Austro-German customs union.

Almost 1,000 men in blue were gathered in the short distance between the Chamber and the Quai d'Orsay, which is M. Briand's residence as well as his office. Hundreds stood grouped in side streets and on the riverside, while every one who approached the Chamber or the Ministry was closely scrutinized and immediately requested to move along.

The reason for these most unusual precautions lay, it is stated, in the fact that an anonymous message was received today at the Foreign Ministry intimating clearly that M. Briand's life was in danger.

No Chances Being Taken.

Whether the message came from some one who knew that a plot was being formed against him or whether it was just a vague warning of some nervous person is not sure. It may even have been a hoax. In the circumstances, however, and with the passions of the Royalists stirred up as they have been against M. Briand, who has been their most formidable enemy, neither Premier Laval as Minister of the Interior nor the Prefect of Police, Jean Chiappe, liked to take any chances. They apparently seriously believe the Foreign Minister's life is in danger.

Not only round the Chamber but along the boulevards this evening large forces of police were massed at subway stations, apparently with the aim of preventing a demonstration by extreme nationalists.

Toward 6 o'clock a crowd of about 300 young Royalists, mostly students of the law school, gathered in the Boulevard St. Germain but were dispersed. About half of them formed their ranks again and tried to get near the Chamber. Their procession was again broken up and about sixty were arrested. They were all released later in the evening.

Within the Chamber the debate was serious and calm. Every one is of the opinion that what is being debated is not in reality what is to be done about the proposed Austro-German union but whether M. Briand will be elected next week as President of the Republic.

That this is so is regretted by many, for even the election of the Foreign Minister to the higher post would indicate in no clear way what France's policy is or will be toward Germany and whether peace is to be maintained by insistence on a strict observance of the treaties of peace or by a gradual incorporation of these imposed terms in a wider and voluntary accepted organization.

No Settlement Seen.

That issue has never been settled, and in this Chamber it cannot be. For most of those who tomorrow or on Saturday will vote for M. Briand still hanker after the policy of Ray-

Continued on Page Ten.

WOMAN DEFIES NYE IN CANNON INQUIRY

Treasurer of Anti-Smith Fund Refuses to Answer Senators' and Blocks Hearing.

FACES CONTEMPT CHARGE

Warned, She Maintains Silence Except to Challenge Committee's Power.

Special to The New York Times.

WASHINGTON, May 7.—Miss Ada L. Burroughs, treasurer of the Virginia anti-Smith committee in 1928, today bluntly challenged the authority of the Nye campaign fund committee to investigate expenditures by Bishop James Cannon Jr. in the Virginia campaign against ex-Governor Smith of New York and refused to answer any questions regarding the use of money contributed to the Bishop for that purpose.

Appearing before the committee, she submitted a carefully worded protest, based on legal grounds, and stood continuously on that statement. To almost every inquiry she responded in an almost inaudible voice: "I decline to answer," or "I have nothing to add to my statement."

Bishop Cannon, central figure in the investigation, sat at the committee table, two feet away from Miss Burroughs, his eyes riveted upon her. He held his crutches close to his chin as he posed for photographers, to whom he said "you are wasting your films again." His one utterance was when he asked if his protest of last night would be incorporated in the record, to which Chairman Nye replied, "if there is no objection by a committee member."

Miss Burroughs, a middle-aged woman, who wore a black dress and horn-rimmed spectacles, probably will be cited to the Senate for contempt, Senator Nye indicated after the session. The committee will actually decide next week whether she will be brought up under contempt proceedings, as were Harry F. Sinclair and Thomas F. Cunningham. Committee members said tonight they saw no other course.

"There seems nothing for the committee to do but call the attention of the Senate to the refusal of Miss Burroughs to answer its questions and ask the Senate to proceed against her," Mr. Nye said.

The committee will probably draft a report and file it with the secretary of the Senate. Nothing further can be done until the Senate reconvenes.

Manifestly nervous, Miss Burroughs demurred at giving her name and address before she read her statement. Senator Nye demanded these particulars twice, and finally Senator Dale, Republican, of Vermont, exclaimed: "Before we proceed, I want to know who this witness is."

Her statement closely followed that sent to the committee by Bishop Cannon last night. It said Miss Burroughs had been "legally advised" that the Senate lacked jurisdiction for the inquiry. She declared she had not knowingly violated the corrupt practices act nor fraudulently converted any campaign funds to her personal use. The investigation, she asserted, would be a violation of her personal rights.

When Senator Nye asked if she prepared the statement, she started to refuse to answer and then said she prepared it with legal advice. Senator Dale asked that the question be repeated, because Miss Burroughs obviously did not understand. "Any one knows some lawyer did it," he commented.

After she left the stand Miss Bur-

Continued on Page Seven.

SCHOOL AIDES ADMIT WIDE REALTY DEALS; RYAN ASKS INQUIRY

McEneny, $6,500 a Year Examiner, Tells of Holdings Involving Big Profits.

SOME IN NEIGHBORS' NAMES

Warschauer Says He Bought Queens Land Before Approval of Near-by School Site.

CRITICISM AROUSES RYAN

He Upholds Efficency in the Schools and Wants Graves to Conduct Investigation.

Morris Warschauer, assistant secretary of the Board of Education, contradicted yesterday his previous testimony about ownership of land in Queens near a school site by admitting under examination by Leonard Wallstein that he had become interested in the purchase before the Board of Estimate had authorized acquisition of the site on March 25, 1926. Warschauer's salary was $6,000.

Under examination by the Special Corporation Counsel, he also contradicted testimony by Francis T. McEneny, chief examiner of the Board of Aldermen in several particulars. Previously Mr. Warschauer had maintained that he did not become interested in the property until after March 25, 1926, setting the date on which he was first approached concerning it as some time in May of that year. He testified yesterday that he obtained $2,200 to aid McEneny with the purchase from George Wise, employer of his brother Emil.

McEneny, whose salary was $6,500, gave striking testimony concerning a large number of real estate transactions in which he was interested. He was led through the involved steps of his real estate dealings by Mr. Wallstein. Among other deals he testified that he had obtained an interest in property in Springfield, in Queens, worth $67,600 with a personal investment of only $980, raising the remainder through Joseph Miller Jr., secretary of the Board of Education; Mr. Warschauer and Mr. Wise.

Asks School Inquiry.

Stung by the recent criticism of the city's elementary schools expressed in the report of the City Affairs Committee of the National Republican Club, President George J. Ryan of the Board of Education announced last night that he had asked Dr. Frank P. Graves, State Commissioner of Education, to make a thorough and impartial study of the city schools. His statement read:

"In view of irresponsible charges that have been made from time to time with respect to the efficiency of the New York public schools, I have this day asked the State Commissioner of Education, Dr. Frank P. Graves, to make a thorough survey of the public schools in New York City.

"The children in the public schools of the city of New York have scholastic records of which their parents may well be proud. For years they have led the entire State in the matter of passing regents' examinations, which are a test of educational efficiency administered by the State Department of Education.

"Those of us who know the facts feel that the schools of New York City are thoroughly efficient. In order that all the facts may be developed impartially I have called

Continued on Page Two.

POLICE SLAYER CAPTURED IN GUN AND TEAR GAS SIEGE; 10,000 WATCH IN W. 90TH ST.

CROWLEY SHOT FOUR TIMES

Trapped in Apartment, He Fires Out Windows at 150 Besiegers.

MULROONEY DIRECTS FIGHT

One-Minute Barrage Laid Down Before Police Attack—Girl Found With Slayer.

HE ADMITS KILLING HIRSCH

Rudolph Duringer, Also Caught, Confesses He Murdered Dance Hall Hostess in Bronx.

Vanquished after a two-hour siege which turned a quiet west side neighborhood into a battle-front, Francis (Two-Gun) Crowley, 20 years old, wanted for two murders, lost his gangland bravado and surrendered to detectives yesterday at 6 P. M. in a rooming-house hideaway at 303 West Ninetieth Street.

With him were his confederate, Rudolph Duringer, wanted for participation in the slaying of Virginia Brannen, dance-hall hostess, and 16-year-old Helen Walsh, who was with Crowley when he shot and killed Patrolman Frederick Hirsch near North Merrick, L. I., early Wednesday.

One hundred and fifty heavily armed policemen fought for two hours to capture the slight young man, 5 feet 3 in height and hardly more than 100 pounds in weight. Before the desperado ceased firing from the two automatic pistols which gave him his nickname, and was seized by detectives in a room that reeked with tear gas and powder fumes, hundreds of shots had been fired at him by the besiegers.

Crowley was wounded, though not seriously. Duringer and Miss Walsh were injured slightly by what might have been either flying plaster or grazing bullets. The walls which had protected the three fugitives were literally riddled in the two-hour bombardment. Bits of plaster were scattered through the rooming house as far as the hallway two floors below the scene of the firing.

Duringer Admits Killing.

At Police Headquarters, where Duringer and the girl were questioned, it was said that Duringer confessed to killing Miss Brannen, saying that his motive had been jealousy. Miss Walsh, who regained her composure and asked for a cigarette, admitted that she had been with Crowley when he shot Patrolman Hirsch, and by her statement, according to detectives, clinched a first degree murder case against him.

Even when captured, Crowley still had hopes of shooting his way to freedom, the police declared. His two automatic pistols, which he said he had thrown away, were found in his trouser legs, with the barrels thrust down his socks and the butts clasped by his garters. Had the guns not been found, the youth, who had been described as one of the most dangerous killers, might have conceivably shot his way to freedom while he was being taken to Bellevue, accompanied only by a detective and the ambulance surgeon.

Had he not been captured, the youthful gunman confessed, he planned also to kill another policeman who, he believed, might capture him. His intended victim was Detective Thomas J. Sheehan of the Alexander Avenue station, the Bronx. Crowley had seen Sheehan last Sunday while the latter was driving across the Queensboro Bridge and had planned to kill him then, but had given up the idea because the detective was accompanied by his family. By a coincidence, Detective Sheehan was detailed to ride in the ambulance that took Crowley to the hospital.

The battle was carried on with rifles, shotguns, service revolvers and sub-machine guns. For two hours after Crowley had been located at the rooming house by Bronx detectives, working "to break the case" because the youthful, swaggering gunman had also shot and wounded one of their comrades a month ago, the policemen and Crowley fired at each other through the windows and walls of the two-room suite in which the killer, Duringer,

Continued on Page Three.

What and Whose Is the Ether? Canada's High Court Won't Rule

OTTAWA, May 7 (By the Canadian Press).—The Supreme Court of Canada has no intention of attempting to decide for scientists whether the ether exists and if so, what it is.

This was made clear at the hearing of the radio case this afternoon when Charles Lanctot, counsel for Quebec, questioned the existence of the ether, the theoretical medium by which radio waves are supposed to be transmitted.

After stating that scientists disagreed as to the ether, Mr. Lanctot said:

"It all goes to show that knowledge of this subject is very limited."

"It all goes to show we will be very careful to limit our answers to the questions to matters of present-day knowledge," said Chief Justice Anglin.

"It also goes to show how difficult it will be for you to demonstrate that the ether and the waves in it are property," said Justice Smith.

CLUE THAT HIS GANG SHOT DIAMOND FOUND

Slugs Used Match Those in Wall of His Beer Depot, Ballistics Expert Reports.

HIS WIFE DEFIES INQUIRY

State Physician Says Gangster Is Recovering—Medalie Plans Federal Jury Action Here.

From a Staff Correspondent of The New York Times.

CATSKILL, N. Y., May 7.—Evidence tending to show that Jack (Legs) Diamond was shot down by members of his own gang on the veranda of the Aratoga Inn in Cairo a week ago Monday morning was adduced today from the report of Captain William A. Jones, ballistics expert, who has appeared in several celebrated trials, including the Becker case.

Mrs. Alice Schiffer Diamond, wife of the gang leader, refused on the advice of counsel to testify before the Greene County grand jury, "on the ground that it would tend to incriminate and degrade" her.

Attorney General John J. Bennett Jr., who is investigating the Diamond gang's criminal operations in this area, had hoped that Mrs. Diamond would disclose some of her husband's activities. She was resubpoenaed for appearance Monday.

Dr. Stanley Alderson of Albany, designated by the State to examine Diamond in the Albany General Hospital, looked the gangster over and decided that he should be "well on the road to recovery within two weeks, unless something unforeseen occurs." This confirms the report yesterday by Dr. Thomas Holmes of Delmar, who has been attending Diamond, that the gang chief had cheated death again.

A motion is to be heard by Supreme Court Justice Brewster in Schenectady tomorrow for Diamond's re-

Continued on Page Four.

Marshal French's Diary Reveals Bitterness Over Britain's 'Neglect' of Her Army in War

By The Canadian Press.

LONDON, May 7.—"The only thing that surprises me is that the British Empire finds any men to fight for her. * * * There is never a word of hope or encouragement from any source—nothing but grousing and complaining."

This bitter entry is taken from the diary of Field Marshal the Earl of Ypres, who as Field Marshal Sir John French commanded the British expeditionary force at the outbreak of the great war and commanded the British Army on the Western Front until the end of 1915. He died in 1925.

The entry is produced in the book on the life of the Earl of Ypres, by his son, Major Gerald French, published today. On his own account Major French says:

"To put the matter in a nutshell, throughout the whole period of his service in command of the British expeditionary force my father was severely handicapped by lack of support and undue interference at home."

Marshal French resigned his command in December, 1915, and returned home to be raised to the peerage as the Earl of Ypres. During his term as commander the chief events were the retreat from Mons, the battle of the Marne and the subsequent advance to the Aisne; the transfer of the expeditionary force to Flanders; the desperate fighting in the Autumn of 1914, generally called the first battle of Ypres; the second battle of Ypres in April, 1915; the abortive operations near Festubert a few days later and the important victory in the region of Loos in September.

The Manchester Guardian concludes its review of the book:

"French is not amongst the world's greatest soldiers, but he stands high among soldiers of the great war, which was singularly barren of genius in high places. * * * So long as men do not forget the old 'Contemptibles,' they will not forget the man who led them."

20 Dead, $2,500,000 Loss in Fires in Japan; Health Resort Razed, Three Cities in Peril

By HUGH BYAS.

Wireless to THE NEW YORK TIMES.

TOKYO, May 7.—Fires which broke out today, after a long dry spell, in several parts of Japan, whipped by high winds, spread disastrously, resulting in the loss of twenty lives and damage estimated at $2,500,000.

Yamanaka village, a hot springs resort on the slope of Mount Fuji, was destroyed. Owing to the destruction of the postoffice, only the scantiest details are available.

The Yamanaka fire was first observed at 2:30 o'clock this morning. The wooden houses were as dry as tinder after a long spell of rainless weather, and the flames, fanned by a vigorous wind, flew from house to house, leaping narrow streets and a little river flowing through the town. Large rambling Japanese inns, more than twenty in number, built entirely of wood around courtyards and gardens, quickly became raging furnaces. Guests, awakened from sleep, barely escaped amid scenes of great confusion.

The Yamanaka fire brigade was unable to cope with the conflagration, which spread with alarming speed and fury until the whole village was burned to ashes.

The inns were relatively empty, owing to the earliness of the season. The largest party at any of them was one of 100 primary school children making an educational tour. It is not possible to estimate the number of casualties, but more than 100 persons were believed to have been injured, many seriously, while trying to escape.

Help was sent from the neighboring towns of Fuki-Kanazu and Kanazawa, where those who escaped were taken. Fortunately for the 300 homeless villagers, tonight is fine and warm.

A smaller fire at Shirokane, a suburb of Tokyo, though quickly extinguished, caused six deaths. Fifty houses in the city's Chinatown, including the Chinese Consulate, were burned at Yokohama. Another fire swept the Chinese quarter of Toyama City. Several forest fires also were reported.

Section 1

"All the News That's Fit to Print."

The New York Times.

Copyright, 1931, by The New York Times Company.

THE WEATHER
Showers and thunderstorms today; tomorrow cloudy and cooler.
Temperatures yesterday—Max. 73, min. 58.
U. S. Weather Forecast—Page 12, Section 7.

Section 1

VOL. LXXX....No. 26,769. **** NEW YORK, SUNDAY, MAY 10, 1931. Including Rotogravure Picture Section in two parts—Magazine and Book Sections in Rotogravure. TEN CENTS

WEGENER GIVEN UP AS LOST IN GREENLAND'S ICE FIELDS; THREE AIDES FOUND SAFE

LEADER GONE SINCE NOV. 1

German Set Out for Coast With Native and Dogsled, but Never Reached It.

LEFT SCIENTISTS BEHIND

Relief Party Reaches Them, to Find They Thought Wegener Safe at Base Depot.

AHRENBERG IS HELD BY FOG

Will Drop Luxuries to Courtauld and British Party on Way Back From Ice Cap.

Special Cable to THE NEW YORK TIMES.

WEST STATION, Kamarujuk, Greenland, May 9.—Hope for Professor Wegener, leader of the German Greenland expedition, was finally abandoned today when word was received by wireless from the central station that the relief expedition, upon its arrival there yesterday from the west coast, found the others of the expedition well but learned that Professor Wegener started back for the west station on Nov. 1, since when no word has been heard of him.

Dr. Weiken and Dr. Holzapfel, who led a relief expedition as soon as the weather permitted, found Dr. Georgi, Dr. Loewe and Dr. Sorge, the three who had wintered at the central station, in good health, but were greeted with the dismaying words:

"Why, no. The chief left on Nov. 1 with one dog sled and one Greenlander. We supposed he had reached the coast."

The relief party had taken a portable wireless set and immediately reported the tragic fact here.

Ahrenberg to Fly Inland Again.

By CAPTAIN PERCY LEMON,
Wireless Officer of the British Arctic Air Route Expedition.

Wireless to THE NEW YORK TIMES.

WATKINS BASE CAMP, via Angmagsalik, Greenland, May 9.—The flying weather is now bad, with low clouds and fog coming from the sea, but it may be clearing.

If the weather is fine, Captain Albin Ahrenberg, in his Swedish plane, will fly in over the ice cap again tomorrow and drop luxuries such as cigarettes to the Watkins party, which is returning with Augustine Courtauld to the base camp. They do not need food, as they took a five weeks' supply and will be back in under four weeks from their start.

We are now busy getting seals and sharks for the return of the extra dog teams.

The Swedish plane may attempt to pick up a mesage from Watkins tomorrow with a hook.

After this flight, in order to economize on fuel, one of our expedition's two Moth airplanes will always be used.

Fate Long in Doubt.

Doubt as to the fate of Professor Alfred Wegener, who headed a party into the interior of Greenland last year in the interests of meteorological research with a view toward the possible establishment of an air route, existed throughout the Winter.

His expedition had established two bases, on the eastern and western coasts of Greenland, and Professors Wegener, Loewe, Sorge and Georgi, with snow sledges, huskies and full equipment, finally succeeded, after several failures, in establishing a central meteorological station 250 miles inland.

No direct word had been heard from that station, prior to the foregoing dispatch, since the last of Dr. Wegener's dispatches, dated Oct. 2, was printed in THE NEW YORK TIMES on Oct. 26.

Dr. Wegener had made his way to the central station after starting in mid-September from the westerly station with Dr. Loewe, to bring supplies to Dr. Georgi and Dr. Sorge. The latter two had served notice that unless they received supplies, of which they were in dire need, they

Continued on Page Twenty-six.

Barrie, 71, Smokes on Birthday; Lipton, 81 Today, Is Cruising

Wireless to THE NEW YORK TIMES.

LONDON, May 9.—Two noted Britons are celebrating birthdays this week-end. Sir James Barrie, 71, today left his Adelphi Terrace flat to buy himself a birthday present of tobacco. The author of "My Lady Nicotine" walked into the Strand, vanishing down Fleet Street, and when he returned the reason for his walk was seen. A pipe was in his mouth and a trail of smoke behind.

Sir Thomas Lipton will spend his eighty-first birthday tomorrow cruising around the south coast in his yacht, Erin. He has been sailing for more than a week and may spend the rest of the month that way. He will soon be honored by the exclusive Royal Yacht Squadron when his name is put forward for membership.

DOUMERGUE LIKELY TO OPPOSE BRIAND

French President Pressed to Be Candidate Again to Defeat the Foreign Minister.

LATTER STILL IS HESITATING

Demands Support by Centre as Well as the Left—Will Decide Tomorrow.

By P. J. PHILIP.
Special Cable to THE NEW YORK TIMES.

PARIS, May 9.—Before he will permit his name to be put forward as a candidate for the Presidency of the republic at next Wednesday's election, Aristide Briand has stipulated that he must have the assurance of the support of the Centre parties as well as the Left. His decision, therefore, has been postponed until Monday, and it is still uncertain either that M. Briand will be a candidate or that, if he does consent, he will be elected.

It may happen, if he does obtain and accept the invitation of a majority of the Left and Centre parties, that he will find himself opposed by the strongest candidate he could possibly have against him, Gaston Doumergue, present President, whose seven-year term of office comes to an end on June 13.

Until within the last twenty-four hours M. Doumergue has declared himself definitely opposed to re-election. He has said he wanted to spend the rest of his life in greater peace than has been his lot since 1924 at the Elysée Palace. In the past few days, however, he has been subjected to a storm of argument from many sides to the effect that he should accept renomination even if he did not remain in office for a complete term.

Move to Beat Briand.

These arguments, of course, are advanced by those who for one reason or another are opposed to M. Briand's being elected President and fear that he will be if he has against him only such weak candidates as Paul Doumer, President of the Senate, and Jean Hennessy, Deputy.

Since yesterday those closest to the President declare his opposition to re-election has distinctly weakened, and they go so far as to declare that he will finally stand against M. Briand, or perhaps just permit his can-

Continued on Page Sixteen.

6,000 POLICEMEN, LED BY THE MAYOR, AFOOT, CHEERED FOR 5 MILES

Walker and Paraders Greeted by Enthusiastic Crowds From Battery to 62d Street.

HE JESTS WITH ONLOOKERS

Admirers Evade Guards to See Him, Shake His Hand or Ask for Autographs.

YEAR'S HEROES REWARDED

Honor Medals Are Given to 11 for Bravery—11 Go to Relatives of Men Killed on Duty.

Mayor Walker, on foot, led the annual police parade five miles up Broadway and Fifth Avenue yesterday, while hundreds of thousands who watched the brilliant spectacle from sidewalks and windows applauded. It was a personal triumph, although 6,000 of New York City's "finest" also came in for their full share of admiration as they swung along in perfect time to the music of many brass bands.

Fair skies and a brilliant sun made a perfect day for the parade, which had been postponed the Saturday before on account of rain.

Wearing cutaway coats, the Mayor and Police Commissioner Edward P. Mulrooney doffed their silk hats often as the crowds cheered. All along the line of march, from the Battery up Broadway to Twenty-third Street and up Fifth Avenue to Sixty-second Street, Mayor Walker was greeted by spectators with shouts of encouragement.

Parade Starts at Noon.

He arrived at the Battery five minutes ahead of time. The parade started at noon. In the man-made canyon of lower Broadway Mayor Walker and the head of the parade were greeted with the characteristic shower of ticker tape and fluttering paper.

Sidewalk constituents shouted such sentiments as, "How are the dogs, Jimmy?" "Hey, Jimmy, how are you?" and "Do your feet hurt, Jimmy?" to all of which the Mayor responded with a wave of his high hat and a smile.

A bootblack, wearing clownish evening clothes, danced out of Prince Street to the side of the Mayor and shouted:

"How are you, Jimmy?"

"All right, Tony," the Mayor shouted back, pointing to his own striped trousers. "I'll give you the pants later."

When a woman at White Street threw a sprig of apple blossoms at the Mayor he remarked:

"I thought they were lilies at first."

At Prince Street a Negro longshoreman, who said he was Clarence Hines, 303 West Fifty-fourth Street, ran out waving an American flag to meet Mayor Walker. He said he had taken the day off in order "to see Jimmy." He was delighted when the Mayor grasped his hand and permitted him to walk by his side for a few paces.

Marchers Stop for Rest.

When the parade halted at Ninth Street to permit the Mayor to rest, he lighted a cigarette. After a three-minute pause the order to march was given, the Mayor threw away his cigarette, and with mock sadness said:

"I'll be back to get you."

During a second pause at Twenty-third Street the Mayor had another smoke. When someone asked him how he was enjoying himself, he replied:

"The further I go the better I like it."

To a spectator with a German ac-

Continued on Page Thirty.

Queen Helen Is Hastening Back to Bucharest; Reported She Will Return to King Carol Today

Special Cable to THE NEW YORK TIMES.

BUCHAREST, May 9.—Queen Helen, who left Wednesday evening to visit her sister, Princess Olga, in Belgrade, will return early tomorrow morning, it was officially announced today. The report that she would participate with Carol in the review of tomorrow's big military parade gave rise to rumors of a reconciliation.

The estranged pair have not appeared at a public ceremony together since Carol's return to Rumania. There has been talk of a possible reconciliation since Carol's recent meeting with his brother-in-law, King Alexander of Yugoslavia. No official confirmation has been obtainable.

BUCHAREST, May 9 (AP).—It is reported here that King Carol and Queen Helen will appear together in a grand stand tomorrow with Crown Prince Michael to review a military parade celebrating the fiftieth anniversary of the enthronement of King Carol I.

Although the police denied the story, it was reported today that they had uncovered a plot to assassinate the King, arresting a man who had concealed himself under the grand stand with a loaded revolver.

The prospective reconciliation between the King and Queen is believed to have originated Monday when King Carol met King Alexander of Yugoslavia in a motorboat on the Danube. Carol, the story goes, gave his brother-in-law, the Yugoslav King, a message for Queen Helen, proposing the terms of the reconciliation.

The Queen left hurriedly for Belgrade after an invitation from King Alexander and Queen Marie, who is Carol's sister.

"Sheer Merit" of Michelson Praised by Sir James Jeans

By The Associated Press.

PASADENA, Cal., May 9.—Sir James Hopewell Jeans, noted British astronomer, who for two weeks has been here studying in the environment of the late Dr. A. A. Michelson's last experiments, said tonight:

"He was one of the outstandingly great scientists of our age and gained his world-wide reputation by sheer merit and the uniform excellence of his work.

"Nothing satisfied him but the best, and all his experiments were conducted with an extreme and meticulous care, which endows them with lasting value.

"Perhaps his two greatest accomplishments were his invention of the interferometer for measuring the sizes of the stars and his determination of the velocity of light. The interferometer probably is the most ingenious instrument known to science, while his determination of the velocity of light is perhaps the most careful and exact scientific experiment ever performed."

A. A. MICHELSON DIES; FAMOUS SCIENTIST

Nobel Prize-Winner Succumbs to Cerebral Hemorrhage at 78 in California.

MEASURED SPEED OF LIGHT

Experiment Paved Way for Einstein Theory—Last Work of Checking Error Finished.

By The Associated Press.

PASADENA, Cal., May 9.—Dr. Albert A. Michelson, 78 years old, who measured the speed of light and was one of the greatest scientists of modern times, died here at 12:55 P. M. today.

Death came quietly to the man whose work made it possible to know the distance of the stars.

It came just after the success of what he called his "last experiment," the most precise and extensive in physics—the exact determination of the speed of light.

Paralysis was the cause. The frail scientist took to his bed here just after the last instruments were in place, and the first measurements started in his mile-long vacuum tube at Irving Ranch, near Santa Ana, about sixty miles from here.

Since the first week in March, Dr. Michelson had been confined to his home here under the watchful care of his wife and two physicians. Hope for his recovery was given up on May 1, when the doctors found the creeping paralysis beyond their skill. Death was hastened by a cerebral hemorrhage on Thursday.

Suffered Breakdown Two Years Ago.

Two years ago he suffered a breakdown, and complete rest was ordered for him. He lost partial use of his lower limbs, but he won back strength by hikes in the foothills and a new hobby of sketching. Then he began an intensive study of problems of his last experiment at the laboratory here as research associate of the Carnegie Institution of Washington.

Month after month he attacked difficulties involved in the construction of the mile-long vacuum tube at Irvine ranch. This was his third test of the speed of light. Many years ago he completed laboratory experiments that fixed light velocity at 186,173 miles a second.

That furnished the astronomical yardstick by which measurements of things in the universe is made. A light-year is derived from Michelson's work as the distance light travels in a year, or six million million miles.

Eight years ago Dr. Michelson made his second test, with revolving mirrors flashing light beams back and forth between Mount Wilson and San Antonio Peak, a distance of twenty-two miles. He then determined the speed of light to be 186,213 miles a second.

Realizing the tremendous importance that precision of this measurement plays in astronomy and physics, Dr. Michelson determined upon a third test. He concluded certain errors might exist in the instability of the atmosphere between the mountains, and determined that the test of precision should be made in a vacuum.

Physicists throughout the world looked upon him as their dean. Professor Albert Einstein was pleased to refer to Professor Michelson as the master who awakened in him the concept of the theory of relativity.

Burial May Be at Arlington.

Special to The New York Times.

WASHINGTON, May 9 (AP).—Charles Michelson said tonight that his brother, Dr. Albert A. Michelson,

Continued on Page Three.

STIMSON LAYS DOWN BASIS OF OUR POLICY FOR LATIN AMERICA

Secretary in Radio Address States We Will Not Use Army or Navy to Collect Debts.

PROTECTION FOR CITIZENS

They Will Receive Such Safeguards as Are Due Them 'Under Law of Nations.'

OUT OF NICARAGUA IN 1932

Washington by "Foresight and Courage" Seeks Cordiality on This Hemisphere, He Says.

Special to The New York Times.

WASHINGTON, May 9.—In an address on the foreign relations of the United States, Col. Henry L. Stimson, Secretary of State, tonight outlined our policy with respect to Latin-American countries and served notice that the government would not use its army and navy to collect debts from foreign nations.

Secretary Stimson's address, broadcast in The Washington Star's national radio forum by the Columbia Broadcasting System, reviewed the extent and character of the machinery of our diplomatic intercourse, and while it mentioned State Department activities concerning the Kellogg peace pact, the World Court, the London naval conference of last year and other outstanding international matters, its most significant features were devoted to the dealings of the United States with Latin America.

As if in answer to criticisms to his recent notice to Americans in the interior of Nicaragua that the United States could not undertake to protect them, the Secretary declared that the government would look after the protection of Americans wherever they were, and that "we are not departing from American traditions."

Defines Stand as to Our Citizens.

Colonel Stimson explained that in spite of what he termed "outlaw activities" in Nicaragua, all American soldiers would be removed from that country by the Autumn of 1932, and indicated that this policy of letting the people of Latin America manage their own affairs would be extended to the other nations to the south of us. At the same time he declared that "we have no intention of removing from American citizens in Nicaragua the protection which American citizens in foreign lands are entitled and accustomed to receive under the law of nations."

All the counsel and assistance to which Americans were entitled under the law of nations would be given to them where their investments and claims abroad were imperiled, Colonel Stimson said, but he made clear that the Hoover Administration is adhering to the principle enunciated by Elihu Root when Secretary of State that our armed forces would not be employed for debt collection purposes.

Colonel Stimson's statement on the policy of the Hoover Administration toward Latin-American countries was construed here as designed to clarify his recent message to the American Minister at Managua, reading as follows:

"In view of the outbreak of banditry in portions of Nicaragua hitherto free from such violence, you will advise American citizens that this government cannot undertake general protection of Americans throughout that country with American forces. To do so would lead to difficulties and commitments which this government does not propose to undertake."

At the time there was much favor-

Continued on Page Two.

Army Chiefs Agree to Cut Cost of Service In Conferences With Hoover on the Rapidan

From a Staff Correspondent of The New York Times.

ORANGE, Va., May 9.—President Hoover was told by high War Department officials, after conferences at his Rapidan camp today, that further economies could be made in the military establishment without impairment of the service. Details were not disclosed.

Mr. Hoover was accompanied on his week-end trip, as planned, by Secretary of War Hurley, General Douglas MacArthur, Chief of Staff, and others in key positions throughout the department, and by Representative Will R. Wood of Indiana, chairman of the House Appropriations Committee, who has pledged himself to a program of rigid economy in the next Congress.

Soon after their arrival at the camp, at 10:30 this morning, the President asked the military chiefs to confer with the idea of seeing if they could make savings in the next budget. He laid particular stress on the idea that any cuts must be made without impairment of the service and gave them to understand that the decision would be left primarily in the hands of those charged with the national defense.

He remained out of this conference, seating himself under a tree and working out his Memorial Day speech. He called another after luncheon and economy was discussed for two hours. He and Mr. Wood were present. After that some of the participants went fishing. Mr. Hoover made the largest catch. The conference was resumed this evening.

The President also asked that attention be given to the matter of public works under the Chief of Engineers to see where economies might be effected without retarding the ambitious program of river and harbor development and flood control upon which the government has embarked.

STUDY OF WAR DEBTS AND REPARATIONS URGED BY WORLD CHAMBER TO AID TRADE; TARIFF AND ARMAMENT CUTS FAVORED

Views of Chamber on Arms, Debts and Tariff As Set Forth in General Resolution Adopted

Special to The New York Times.

WASHINGTON, May 9.—The general resolution adopted here today by the International Chamber of Commerce contained the following paragraphs:

1—The International Chamber has repeatedly emphasized the fact that war is the greatest barrier to social and economic progress, and the establishment of higher living standards is dependent primarily on the maintenance of peace. The chamber commends the efforts being made by the governments of the world to reduce armaments to the lowest possible limit, and urges not only that there should be no relaxation of this effort, but rather that it should be redoubled. The attainment of this objective would relieve the peoples of all nations of heavy burdens of taxation.

2—International obligations have been made definite in amount and in terms as between nations. The integrity of such obligations is always fundamental to the maintenance of international credit and to the expansion of commerce and industry. The observance of this essential principle, however, is not inconsistent with an impartial examination of the effects of these obligations on international trade, if warranted by changed economic conditions, such examination to be based on the principles laid down by the International Chamber of Commerce at its congresses.

3—National and international trade should be encouraged by the removal of every obstacle possible. Tariffs should not discriminate unfairly between nations. Embargoes should be exercised only against dumping or other unfair practices. The machinery provided by some countries for the adjustment of tariff inequalities should be utilized without delay, and all nations should unite in an effort to remove all unjustifiable restrictions.

BUSINESS CONGRESS ENDS

The Integrity of National 'Obligations' Upheld in Resolution.

FLEXIBLE TARIFFS BACKED

Such Provisions Held Valuable Even If Criticism Is Leveled at Our Duties.

HOOVER WINS ARMS POINT

But W. H. Booth Says Americans Never Asked for a Ban on Re-examining Debts.

Special to The New York Times.

WASHINGTON, May 9.—An avenue for reopening the question of reparations and war debts was provided in the closing session of the congress of the International Chamber of Commerce today, with the adoption of a resolution advocating an examination of the effect of international "obligations" on world trade "if warranted by changed economic conditions."

The resolution also inferentially advocated abolishment of high tariff walls through a recommendation that world trade be forwarded "by the removal of every obstacle possible."

A third provision endorsed activities leading toward the reduction of world armaments, and two other sections advocated, respectively, the divorce of government from business and the holding of government expenditures within budget estimates.

Resolution a Compromise.

The resolution embodying these provisions was frankly a compromise between demands by some foreign delegations for an expression by the chamber in favor of debt reductions and lower tariffs, and the opposition of the Hoover Administration against action on such so-called political topics by a convention of business men.

The final draft of the resolution was drawn by the American delegation, headed by Silas H. Strawn, this morning, after days of study and conversations with the German, French, British and Italian delegation leaders had made it obvious that the congress of the chamber could not be adjourned without some expression of opinion on the outstanding topics of discussion during the last week.

In its phraseology, the resolution was as mild as possible, and nowhere did the expressions "reparations" or "war debts" occur, in deference to the feelings of the Washington Administration, but there was no doubt of the intent of the resolution. Regardless of its wording, it was agreed that it paved the way for further agitation for a revision of the reparations and war debts settlements.

Had the American delegation been solidly aligned against the inclusion of statements on war debts and tariffs in the resolution, it was agreed that they might not have been placed there, but within the delegation there was a division of opinion which disturbed friends of the administration throughout the conference.

This division was emphasized today when Willis H. Booth, honorary president of the chamber, who gave the chief seconding speech for the resolution, said:

"Relative to the question of international obligations, I desire to state in behalf of the American delegation that it has never opposed the suggestion that any nation should not feel free to ask a re-examination of these debts on the basis of the underlying principles upon which they have been settled."

Met Hoover on Disarmament.

The consensus among the delegates appeared to be that Germany and Great Britain, whose delegations were most anxious to have an expression on debts and tariffs recorded, had made clear gains to that end, as against the desires of the Hoover Administration, which clearly has represented itself as opposed to any mention of these subjects.

On the other hand, the administration scored with the paragraph devoted to disarmament, as this was one topic which would have been left untouched had not President Hoover in his speech at the opening of the congress pointed out that world armaments exact $5,000,000,000 annually from the nations of the world.

It was generally agreed that the

Continued on Page Twenty-seven.

SENATORS CRITICIZE CHAMBER'S ATTITUDE

Versailles Treaty Changes Needed Ahead of Tariff and Debt Cuts, They Say.

BORAH EXPECTED TO RETORT

Shipstead Calls Delegates' Action Political—Hatfield Assails Barnes's Initiative.

Special to The New York Times.

WASHINGTON, May 9.—One reaction to the resolution adopted by the International Chamber of Commerce on the debt and tariff problems came from Senator Shipstead, Farmer-Laborite of Minnesota, a member of the Senate Foreign Relations Committee, who suggested that the "internationalists" discuss the revision of the Versailles Treaty, since they had entered upon a discussion of other political questions.

A similar belief was expressed by another Senator, who held that the economic problems of Europe could not be settled until the Versailles Treaty has been made less severe. He said that it was conceived when its framers were still under the influence of war passions.

Out of respect to the foreign visitors several Senators declined to comment on the resolution but will do so later.

Senator Borah, chairman of the Foreign Relations Committee, it is believed, will attempt to show the European critics how they can settle the economic problems by other means than getting the war debt reduced by the United States and our tariff rates lowered.

Shipstead Comments on Arms.

Senator Shipstead said that the meeting of the International Chamber had been more political than economic in character; that opinion in the United States was opposed to any further debt reduction, and that many here looked with disfavor on the heavy armaments in Europe,

Continued on Page Twenty-seven.

MENDELSSOHN ASKS WORLD COOPERATION

New President of Chamber Says Well-Being Cannot Be Isolated in One Country.

BROADCASTS FROM BERLIN

Sees Great Chances for Business Leaders to Convert Earth's Riches to Use of Mankind.

Special to The New York Times.

WASHINGTON, May 9.—Franz von Mendelssohn, who became president of the International Chamber of Commerce at noon today, stressed the interdependence of the nations and advocated the application of "practical idealism and sober imagination" to the problems of the world-wide depression in an inaugural address which he delivered from his home in Berlin via radio to the delegates to the chamber's congress, which closed its session here today.

Dr. Mendelssohn spoke in English after delivering a brief greeting to his countrymen at the congress. His speech was transmitted over the ocean by a short-wave system and rebroadcast in America by the National Broadcasting Company.

Dr. Mendelssohn frankly conceded that "business is in extraordinary straits," but added that "equally extraordinary are the possibilities given to the leaders of business to release it from these straits."

Will to Communal Service.

Dr. Mendelssohn cordially greeted his predecessors in his new office, and expressed his glad acceptance of the presidency of the International Chamber. He then recalled the congress in Boston in 1912, in which, among many other Germans, Dr. Gustav Stresemann, actively participated. He said that now there is more need than ever before to pay heed and render service to the community, and went on:

"You gentlemen, who have assembled in large numbers in Washington, are living witnesses of the will to such communal service," he added. "My voice, as that of a single individual coming across the ocean, is weak and feeble, but I remind you that other voices are making the same appeal, those of all the many men and women of the industrial employer class, who, in spite of all their efforts, have lost their business or see that it is in distress; all the efficient workers whose jobs are threatened and, last but not least, the 20,000,000 unemployed in the world at the present time.

"All these are complaining bitterly, and their complaints would become accusations if all was not done in a common effort to provide work again for these in search of it and to give the destitute a share in the good things of this life.

Interdependence of the World.

"The economic interdependence of the world is more strongly expressed in the universality of the world economic crisis than in the exchange of our wares, the movement of our ships, the means used for disseminating news, without which our con-

Continued on Page Twenty-nine.

"All the News That's Fit to Print."

The New York Times.

LATE CITY EDITION

THE WEATHER—Cloudy, warmer, possibly showers early today; tomorrow fair, warmer.
Temperatures yesterday—Max. 52, min. 47.
U. S. Weather Forecast—For details see Page 47.

VOL. LXXX....No. 26,773. ***** NEW YORK, THURSDAY, MAY 14, 1931. TWO CENTS In Greater New York | THREE CENTS Within 200 Miles | FOUR CENTS Elsewhere Except 7th and 8th Postal Zones

WEGENER GAVE UP HIS LIFE TO SAVE GREENLAND AIDES; LEFT SO FOOD WOULD LAST

FOUGHT WAY TO THEM FIRST

Reached Central Station With No Supplies After a Forty-Day Trek.

RESTED ONLY DAY AND HALF

Then Set Out for Coast With Native With the Temperature 65 Degrees Below Zero.

SLEDGE FOUND ON ICE CAP

Lay Ninety Miles From Depot, With Skis Upright in Snow, 42 Miles Away—Body Is Sought.

Special Cable to THE NEW YORK TIMES.

BERLIN, May 13.—Details which partially explain how Professor Alfred Wegener, leader of the German expedition there, met death in the icy wastes of Greenland last November were received here today by wireless from the expedition's central station on the ice cap. The heroism of the leader, who lost his life in saving that of his comrades, is evident despite the cryptic style of the message, which follows:

CENTRAL STATION, Greenland, May 12.—Professor Wegener, Dr. Loewe and the Greenlander Rasmus arrived here on Oct. 30 after a forty-day trek from the coast. They had three sledges, twenty dogs and no provisions. The last bit of provisions had to be dumped six miles from here owing to the poor going.

It was all that was left of a sledge party of fifteen which had left the coast on Sept. 21 with two tons of provisions and equipment. Continual snow and ice forced all but one of the Greenlanders to turn back. The daily jumps fell as low as three miles and less toward the end of the haul.

Three Pushed On.

Dr. Wegener, Dr. Loewe and Rasmus pushed on, determined at least to reach the 125-mile point [the central station is 250 miles from the coast], since Dr. Georgi and Dr. Sorge had sent a message earlier that they would depart from the centre on Oct. 20 unless provisions arrived.

But Dr. Georgi and Dr. Sorge had not dared to start owing to the deadly cold, which hung around 65 degrees below zero, Fahrenheit; so Professor Wegener and his companions pushed on ever further. Upon their arrival at the centre all of Dr. Loewe's toes were frozen and later they had to be amputated there.

Dr. Sorge and Dr. Georgi had taken to a snow cave, finding a tent insufficient protection. With the help of an oil lamp they had kept the temperature as high as 5 to 10 degrees above zero, Fahrenheit, inside throughout the Winter.

Professor Wegener, perceiving that provisions could be stretched to feed only three until the end of May, departed again for the coast, accompanied by Rasmus, after a day and a half of rest. He took two sledges and seventeen dogs and 270 pounds of food for men and dogs. The two men, on skis, hoped to average twelve miles daily.

The rescue expedition found Professor Wegener's sledge ninety miles from the centre, having passed his skis stuck upright in the snow forty-two miles nearer the coast. This is the last any one knows of him.

The scientific program will be continued, Dr. Georgi remaining alone here while Dr. Sorge undertakes to find Professor Wegener's body.

Fate Like That of Scott.

The news from the centre of Greenland, revealing perhaps as well as ever will be known how Dr. Alfred Wegener, leader of the German Greenland Expedition, met death in the fearful cold, places that disaster in the list of heroic tragedies of exploration in the frozen wastes.

The revelation of how Professor Wegener pushed on in the face of 65 degrees below zero weather in order to save food for his comrades is reminiscent of the futile struggle against death of Captain R. F. Scott on his march from the South Pole in 1912. Months afterward the frozen bodies of Captain Scott and the two companions who died with him were found huddled in their tent, eleven miles from a cache of

Continued on Page Twelve.

Ban on Ticker Tape Showers On Visiting Notables Urged

There will be no more showers of ticker tape and torn telephone books as returning heroes ride up the canyon of Lower Broadway to receive the city's greetings, if the New York Board of Trade has its way. At its monthly meeting at the Pennsylvania Hotel yesterday the board urged the Mayor and all business organizations to cooperate in substituting "a more suitable and dignified" welcome.

"It is a poor tribute to a great personage to empty a waste basket over him," said the committee which proposed the resolution, which also pointed out the fire hazard from paper lodging on the roofs and in the crevices of buildings and the expense of removing the litter from the streets.

SPAIN TO CONFISCATE EX-KING'S PROPERTY

Republic Will Seize Private Holdings Pending Inquiry Into Conduct Back to 1923.

PRIMATE LEAVES COUNTRY

Cardinal Is Now Expected to File Protest Instead of Receiving Reprimand.

Special Cable to THE NEW YORK TIMES.

MADRID, May 13.—Under cover of resentment against monarchist provocations Spain's provisional republic tonight dropped all semblance of good-will toward the exiled King Alfonso and ordered the confiscation of his personal property throughout Spain.

It was announced when the new government came into power that the Crown properties would become the public's, but that the King's personal lands, palaces and assets in his own name would be respected and he be allowed to dispose of them as he desired.

The reason for the change in attitude as given in the government decree tonight is Alfonso's "tyrannical" attitude as monarch and his failure to uphold the Constitution.

King Alfonso is reported to be an extremely wealthy man and on his own private account had several palaces and owned interests in many business enterprises throughout Spain.

Decree Is Retroactive.

The decree is so worded that any property in Spain which the King may have disposed of since his departure on April 14 also would be seized. It says:

"Whereas the former King of Spain, Don Alfonso de Bourbon, exercised tyrannical powers during his reign and in 1923 broke his oath to uphold the Constitution, the government has the right to repair these wrongs, proof of which has been foud in documents discovered in the royal palace in Madrid. Therefore the Minister of Finance is authorized to seize the three palaces in Madrid, Santander and San Sebastian and all their contents, including the personal property of the King and royal family and all the King's interests and investments in Spain.

"No bill of sale can be issued by

Continued on Page Thirteen.

BAKER WILL DIVIDES $75,000,000 FORTUNE; SON GETS $60,000,000

Transfer to Heir of Securities Before Death Said to Have Reduced Huge Estate.

TESTAMENT IN 5 PAGES

$5,000,000 Each Goes to Two Daughters and Twelve Employes Receive Bequests.

LIBRARY GIFT OF $250,000

Washington Cathedral Gets a Like Sum—Women's Exchange and Tuxedo Hospital Aided.

With the filing for probate yesterday in Surrogates' Court of the will of George F. Baker it was revealed that the estate of the banker and philanthropist is valued at about $75,000,000, as against estimates ranging from $150,000,000 to $500,000,000. Mr. Baker died on May 2 at his home, 258 Madison Avenue, after a brief illness, in his ninety-second year.

It was said, however, that more than a year ago Mr. Baker transferred a substantial portion of his holdings of the bank stock, said to have been about 10,000 shares, to his son, and it is assumed that in a similar manner he had transferred many of his other holdings.

The high estimates of the size of the estate were based upon Mr. Baker's supposed holding of 22,000 shares of the stock of the First National Bank of New York, which even now is valued at about $3,500 a share, and his known large holdings of United States Steel Corporation and certain railroad stocks.

Will in Simple Terms.

The will was brief and its terms simple, the entire fortune being bequeathed outright. More than $60,000,000 of it was left to the banker's only son, George F. Baker Jr., who also was named executor. Two daughters, Mrs. Howard B. St. George of Kingston, Surrey, England, and Mrs. W. Goadby Loew of New York City, each received $5,000,000. In addition they and their brother receive certain personal bequests. Miss Florence J. Loew, a granddaughter, receives Mr. Baker's Tuxedo, N. Y., country estate. Twelve employes and servants get legacies of $25,000 to $1,000.

Although he had been noted throughout his long career for his philanthropies, known to have exceeded $15,000,000, Mr. Baker's will made only four such bequests for a total of $550,000. He left $250,000 to the New York Public Library and a like sum to the Protestant Episcopal Cathedral Foundation of the District of Columbia to be devoted to the erection of an addition to the Washington, D. C., cathedral, to serve as a memorial to his parents, George E. and Eveline S. Baker. Legacies of $25,000 each were left to the New York Exchange for Woman's Work and to the Tuxedo (N. Y.) Memorial Hospital.

The five-and-a-half page will was signed May 21, 1930. Attached to it was a one-page codicil, dated April 14, 1931, less than three weeks before Mr. Baker's death. The codicil revoked a $2,000 legacy to a servant who had left his employ.

Inheritance Taxes Reduced.

Based on a valuation of $200,000,000, the inheritance taxes would have enriched New York State by $31,000,000 and the Federal treasury by more than $7,000,000. The $75,000,000 valuation will reduce materially the taxes that must be paid. The actual security holdings of the

Continued on Page Nineteen.

Snowden Is So Ill Premier Seeks Successor; J. H. Thomas Is in Line for Exchequer Post

Special Cable to THE NEW YORK TIMES.

LONDON, May 13.—Philip Snowden, Chancellor of the Exchequer, is so seriously ill that it is extremely unlikely that he will be able to conduct the Labor Government's fight for the finance bill incidental to his budget through the House of Commons.

The reports of his ailment vary from serious bladder trouble to cancer. Whatever it is, his condition is so serious that his successor as the head of the British Treasury is already being considered by Premier MacDonald.

So far as fitness and special training are concerned, William Graham, president of the Board of Trade, would be the logical appointee as Chancellor of the Exchequer, who is next in rank to the Prime Minister. But politics may demand the appointment of James H. Thomas, now Minister of Dominions, because of his high standing with the trade-union element of the Labor party.

LONDON, May 13 (AP).—While Chancellor of the Exchequer Snowden was confined to bed for a few days under his doctor's orders, The Daily Herald tonight quoted Mrs. Snowden in what it described as "the first interview by television in history."

The interviewer and Mrs. Snowden were visible as well as audible to each other, although one was in The Herald's office and the other at 11 Downing Street.

Asked about the Chancellor's health Mrs. Snowden told the reporter:

"He has had rather a set-back this week, I'm afraid. But I do not think it is serious. However, it has temporarily deprived him of use of his legs to some extent.

"He started his political work again too soon by making a supreme effort to be in his place to introduce the budget. But I believe he will soon be quite better."

Senor Pico, Spokesman for President Uriburu, Tells Argentina's Present State and Outlook

By OCTAVIO S. PICO,
Minister of the Interior of Argentina.
By Cable to the Editor of THE NEW YORK TIMES.
(Translation.)

BUENOS AIRES, May 13.—In the name of his Excellency the President of the Provisional Government, I am making the following statement to you:

The Provisional Government is developing its administrative and social policy in accord with the clear and definite ideas that inspired the revolution, and is keeping all its actions within the existing constitional and legal regulations.

All the political parties are preparing to participate in the elections that are to be held Nov. 8, and at this time are engaged in the work of organization preliminary to all electoral campaigns.

The army and the navy have displayed the greatest firmness and patriotism in supporting the Provisional Government and are maintaining their discipline intact and their faith in the intention of fulfilling the noble and disinterested aims of the revolution.

The sane and virile forces that contributed to the success of the revolution continue to support the government. The financial and administrative readjustment is being effected according to the outlined plan, in spite of the difficulties caused by the world crisis and the mistakes of the deposed administration.

The task of working out the definite budget is on the eve of being finished, and, judging by the estimated resources and the régime of economy that has been instituted, we may be assured that the fiscal year will be closed without a deficit, although the administration pays on the dot, without a single delay, the service of the domestic and foreign debt.

LIQUOR THIEVES BEAT SALVADOR'S ATTACHE

Dr. Leiva Felled by Raiders on His Surprising Them in the Legation at Night.

STIMSON SENDS "REGRETS"

Secretary Assures Diplomat Every Effort Will Be Made to Capture Assailants.

Special to The New York Times.

WASHINGTON, May 13.— Señor Dr. Don Carlos Leiva, Chargé d'Affaires and counsellor of the San Salvador Legation here, was beaten early today in a battle with burglars whom he discovered in the act of stealing liquor from the legation.

In the attack Dr. Leiva was felled by a blow from a pistol, but, although seventeen stitches were taken in his head, his condition is said not to be serious. At Emergency Hospital, to which he was taken, he received assurances from Secretary Stimson that intensive efforts would be made to capture his assailants.

When Dr. Leiva entered the legation early this morning, after playing cards at a friend's house, he saw a man sitting on the steps leading to the second floor. The intruder snapped a flashlight in Dr. Leiva's face, at the same time commanding him to "Stick 'em up!"

Although he saw a revolver gleaming, Dr. Leiva strode up the stairs and grasped the thief, who had risen to meet him, by the throat. The struggle which followed was furious, the combatants pushing and pummeling each other down the stairs and up and down the hall.

The bandit shouted for "Pete," and a second man appeared and joined in the struggle. Suddenly Dr. Leiva was struck over the head with the butt of a pistol and two shots were fired at him, but went wild. The bandits then fled.

Stimson Sends Note of Sympathy.

With blood pouring from his head, Dr. Leiva staggered from the legation and reached a store across the street. There the night manager telephoned police headquarters and took Dr. Leiva to a physician. After receiving treatment Dr. Leiva was taken to the hospital.

Secretary Stimson sent him the following note:

"I was shocked to learn of the injuries which you suffered last night, and I hasten to extend to you an expression of my regret. I assure you that the police will make every effort to apprehend the offenders.

"I trust that you will recover promptly and I want you to know that you have my deepest sympathy."

Walter Thurston, chief of the Latin-American division of the State Department, and Captain Joel T. Boone, President Hoover's physician, called at the hospital to be certain that the patient was as comfortable as possible.

As a result of the attack, Secretary Stimson has begun an investigation directed at the District of Columbia police to ascertain if envoys are receiving the protection to which they are entitled under international usage.

Seventeen Cases Removed.

Although the legation decided not to bring the matter officially to the attention of the State Department, Mr. Stimson took official cognizance of the incident.

It is a serious thing, he said, when the diplomatic representatives of other countries who are entitled to diplomatic immunity and protection

Continued on Page Two.

'POLICY KING' SEIZED; BANKED $1,251,556

Miro Is Arrested on Perjury Charge at Court Hearing—Denied Some Accounts.

HUGE PROFIT IN 4 YEARS

Two Lawyers Are Accused of Failing to Protect Clients—Vice Policeman Ousted.

Henry Miro, who was the banker for one of many Harlem policy games, was arrested yesterday on a charge of perjury and held in Tombs prison in bail of $15,000, after he had denied before Referee Samuel Seabury in the Appellate Division inquiry that he had opened three of ten bank accounts in which deposits of $1,251,556 had been made in four years.

The arrest, unexpected and swift, was asked by Assistant District Attorney James J. Daly when the hearing resumed after the noon recess. A short affidavit charging Miro with perjury was signed by Detective James Finn on information furnished by Irving Ben Cooper of the investigation staff, who questioned Miro, and Magistrate Adolph Stern in Tombs Court held him for hearing Friday. A grand jury, however, will take up the case today.

Another open hearing was set for today, at which the activities of Wilfred Brunder, another operator of the policy game, will be taken up. As this was made known yesterday, it was learned that Brunder, who lived at 357 Edgecombe Avenue, had vanished. His bank accounts, however, said to be larger than those of Miro, will be put in evidence anyway.

Began as a Laborer.

Miro testified that he landed in the United States from Porto Rico in 1916, and, being comparatively penniless, began work as a common laborer. This, he said, he continued until 1924, when he took up gambling. He married in 1925, he said, and in 1926 became a banker in what he insisted upon calling the "numbers" game. This activity he discontinued in 1928, he said, and since then had made his money gambling—"cards, dice, horses, fights, any place to make a bet."

From 1927 through 1930 the bank accounts, ten of them in various names, but all in the branch of the Bank of United States at 116th Street and Lexington Avenue, told a graphic tale of the rise of Henry Miro. All but two of the accounts were "thrift accounts." These were under the names of "E. M. Martin," Enrique Martin, Jose Casanova, Jose Jiminez, Victor Martin, Jose Miro, Henry Miro, and still another as Enrique Martin. The two checking accounts were both under the name of Enrique Martin.

In the Henry Miro account, $10 was deposited and neither withdrawn nor augmented until the Bank of United States closed. Miro denied opening or having had anything to do with accounts in the names of Casanova, Jiminez or Victor Martin. But all three paid accumulated interest into an account under the name of Enrique Martin, which he owned as his. On one occasion $1,000 had been withdrawn from one account and deposited in the Enrique Martin account on the same day.

In 1927, in the checking account of Enrique Martin, the only operative one of that year, $14,170.82 was deposited.

In 1928 in all accounts $235,258.80 was deposited. That was his last year in the "numbers" game, Miro testified, but in the following year all of his accounts carried a total deposit

Continued on Page Two.

ARMY OF 4,000,000 BY DRAFT PROPOSED AS WARTIME PLAN

Unified Civilian Control of All Industry in Program of War Department.

CONSCRIPT LABOR OPPOSED

Chief of Staff Presents Details to War Policies Body—Churches Against Such Preparedness.

CUT IN ARMY POSTS FOUGHT

Members of Congress Are Aroused by President's Suggestion to Reduce Military Expenses.

Special to The New York Times.

WASHINGTON, May 13.—Emergency War Department plans for the mobilization of an army of 4,000,000 men through conscription and for the maximum operation of necessary industries under the guidance of civilians were described today by General Douglas MacArthur, Chief of Staff, to the War Policies Commission.

The Commission, under the chairmanship of Secretary of War Hurley and composed of Cabinet heads and four members each of the Senate and House, reconvened after a long recess to continue a study of "taking the profit out of war," authorized by a resolution of Congress.

General MacArthur outlined what heretofore has been regarded as a more or less secret program for wartime action, but he coupled his exposition with pleas for education of the public designed to make it continually realize that war is a tragic experience which should be the last defensive resort of a nation. He asserted, however, that "a reasonable preparation for defense is one of the best guarantees of peace."

In conflict with the army plan, a statement protesting against the elaboration of a war program as tending to "create suspicion and fear among the nations of the world and diminish, rather than increase, the security of the United States," was presented by the administrative committee of the Federal Council of Churches of Christ in America.

Asserting that the "supreme need of the world" was to make the Briand-Kellogg peace pact effective, the church statement said:

"We regard the adoption by Congress in times of assured and prolonged peace of detailed and comprehensive plans for the potential, complete and instantaneous wartime control by the United States Army of the country's industrial, commercial and transportation system as fraught with grave dangers to our country.

"The United States will more surely establish its own security by exalting the significance and authority of the institutions of peace, which will also provide security for all the nations, and by working wholeheartedly for drastic reduction of armaments by all nations, including our own, than by perfecting extensive and elaborate war plans for itself alone."

Frederick M. Payne, Assistant Secretary of War, preceded General MacArthur as a witness. He described his peacetime duties as the formulation of wartime procurement plans, which would be turned over to a civilian organization for administration in event of war. War Department operations, he stated, would be generally limited to army supply.

"Whatever governmental control is

Continued on Page Four.

DOUMER DEFEATS BRIAND FOR FRENCH PRESIDENCY; WINS ON SECOND BALLOT

EARLY MARGIN IS NARROW

Foreign Minister Quits Race After Failure to Obtain Majority.

RESULT LAID TO RADICALS

Their Support Wavers, Though They Had Been Expected to Vote for Briand.

DOUMER IS SELF-MADE MAN

Of Humble Origin, He Began as a Boy as Apprentice to an Engraver.

By P. J. PHILIP.
Special Cable to THE NEW YORK TIMES.

VERSAILLES, May 13.—Paul Doumer was elected and Aristide Briand was beaten when Parliamentary France today in the Palace of Versailles decided who should be President of the French Republic for the next seven years.

On the first ballot M. Doumer, President of the Senate and so second ranking citizen in France, received 442 votes against 401 for M. Briand. With more than 50 votes for other candidates, neither had the requisite clear majority of 51 per cent of the total votes cast and so there had to be a second ballot.

But M. Briand would not consent to stand again. He withdrew and his place was taken by Senator Pierre Marraud. It was a kind of a forlorn hope of the Radical and Left parties, for after that first vote every one was convinced that nothing could shake the position of the 74-year-old veteran, who twenty years ago was himself defeated in a Presidential election. By 504 votes to 334, M. Doumer was elected and declared President of the Republic for the next seven years.

Doumer of Humble Origin.

Despite his years, the new President is robust and vigorous. He is a man who has risen from humble origin, as have so many others of France's most prominent statesmen.

At the age of 14 he was apprenticed as a medal engraver in Paris. In his leisure he continued his studies, took a degree at the Sorbonne and at 20 was a teacher of mathematics in the College of Mende. He might still have been a schoolmaster if a throat weakness had not compelled him to abandon that career.

His political and other friends helped him to the editorship of a provincial newspaper and so to political life. In 1889 he was elected a Deputy for the Aisne Department, and though he has known defeat he has been in politics ever since.

For a time he was Governor General of France's rich colony of Indo-China. Later as President of the Chamber of Deputies and then of the Senate, he rose to the highest position the republic has to offer.

Such is the man who on this momentous day defeated the best known and widely respected living Frenchman in a contest for the votes of their fellows in the country's Parliament.

It was a day of intense excitement and political feeling. It was also a day of tragedy in many ways, for M. Briand's defeat is far more than M. Doumer's success. When M. Briand accepted the invitation of his friends to become a candidate, they, at least, were certain he would be elected. If he had doubts he concealed them. He felt it was his duty to accept when all those who through good and bad fortune had supported him had asked him to accept this crown of his career.

Three Precedents.

The defeat of M. Briand overshadowed every other event of the day. To explain it one must delve deep into the psychology not only of the French people but especially of the French Parliament. There have been, even in the short history of the Third Republic, several illuminating precedents, of which three defeats, that of M. Pams by Raymond Poincaré, that of Georges Clemenceau by Paul Deschanel and that of Paul Painlevé by Gaston Doumergue, are all of the same character.

If reasons must be given they are likely to be found in the traditional opposition of Parliament as a whole to the presence at the Elysée Palace of any one who is likely, either by intellect or by popular appeal, to

Continued on Page Three.

Giant Cunarders May Be Named For Princesses, Breaking Rule

Special Cable to THE NEW YORK TIMES.

LONDON, May 13.—A ninety-year-old tradition of the Cunard Line, all of whose vessels have been christened with names ending in "ia," is to be broken, it is understood, when the 73,000-ton vessel now being built for the Atlantic service in John Brown's yard on the Clyde and her sister ship come to be named.

It is reported that the vessel, now in an advanced stage of construction and now known as "No. 534 Cunard," will be named the Princess Elizabeth, and her sister ship, the Princess Margaret Rose, after the two daughters of the Duke and Duchess of York. It is possible that King George will perform the launching ceremony of the Princess Elizabeth next Spring.

LABOR STARTS DRIVE TO HALT WAGE CUTS

Federation Says Reductions Mean Loss of Buying Power and More Unemployment.

APPEALS TO ALL WORKERS

Bankers Are Blamed and Violation of Hoover Conference's 'Understanding' Charged.

Special to The New York Times.

WASHINGTON, May 13.—The executive council of the American Federation of Labor today denounced wage-cutting policies as contributing to a continuation of unemployment and announced that it would issue an appeal to workers, organized and unorganized, to "resist to the fullest extent."

"The executive council," the statement read, "in giving consideration to a number of administrative problems, gave special attention to the unemployment situation and to the attempt which, apparently, certain banking interests and certain employers are making to bring about a general reduction in wages.

"Obviously, the situation is serious. Unemployment has steadily increased. The stress of almost two years of increasing unemployment is being more keenly felt. Suffering and distress prevail, while social unrest is steadily increasing. There are strong indications that we are facing a third Winter of distressing unemployment.

Says Purchasing Power Is Cut.

"Notwithstanding this loss of earning power on the part of millions of working men and women, a number of employers are attempting to further reduce the purchasing power of the masses of the people through the imposition of wage reductions.

"The Goodyear and Goodrich tire companies have announced substantial reductions in wages. The significant fact related to this proposed reduction in wages is that automobile and automobile tire manufacturing industries must depend upon a high purchasing power on the part of the masses of the people if a market is to be found for their prod-

Continued on Page Four.

Widow, 72, Succeeds Weehawken Mayor; Trades Broom for Gavel for Good of Party

Mrs. Clara E. Grauert, 72-year-old widow of Emile W. Grauert, who at the time of his death on April 20 had completed twenty-one years as Mayor of Weehawken, N. J., was sworn in last night at the Weehawken City Hall as her husband's successor.

Mrs. Grauert, who is said to be the second woman Mayor in the State of New Jersey, and who says she has spent her life "being just a housewife," was surprised at her selection and abandoned her broom and doffed her apron on Tuesday to prepare herself for the new rôle when she was informed that such action was necessary to save her husband's political organization, the Republican party in the township, from fractional strife.

Still taken aback by the suddenness with which the honor had been thrust upon her, Mrs. Grauert found when she reached the town hall that she had forgotten her glasses. She borrowed a pair from a police lieutenant to sign the oath of office, which was administered by the township clerk, Leo Carroll.

"I have no intention of pursuing a program of political reform," Mayor Grauert announced. "If I can continue to serve Weehawken until the expiration of the term at the end of this year as well as my husband did I will be more than satisfied." She will give special attention, however, to the playground system, she said, since it was one of her husband's keen interests.

A small woman of slight build, Mrs. Grauert will be relieved of as much of the burdensome part of her office as the town committee can arrange. She is not new to her task, however, as it often fell to her lot to assist her husband in recent years. She is a graduate of the Hoboken Academy and the University of Leipzig in Germany.

Although she is a member of many clubs, Mrs. Grauert has not attended their meetings for a long time, she revealed, because she had been too busy keeping house at 21 Bonn Place for her husband and their son, E. Robert. "But I have no apprehension about women in politics," she declared. "They are just as capable as the men are."

"All the News That's Fit to Print."

The New York Times.

LATE CITY EDITION
WEATHER—Fair today; tomorrow slightly warmer, probably thunder showers.
Temperatures yesterday—Max. 84, min. 72.
U. S. Weather Forecast—See next to last page

VOL. LXXX....No. 26,852. **** NEW YORK, SATURDAY, AUGUST 1, 1931. TWO CENTS In New York City | THREE CENTS Within 200 Miles | FOUR CENTS Elsewhere Except 7th and 8th Postal Zones

GLOBE FLIERS QUIT MOSCOW ON A FLIGHT OF 3,000 MILES; CUT DOWN POST-GATTY LEAD

NEXT STOP TO BE IRKUTSK

Herndon and Pangborn Face Storm Danger Across Asia.

WILL LAND TWICE IN SIBERIA

Pilots Hope by Longer Hops to Be Ahead of Post-Gatty Time at Khabarovsk.

RUSSIANS GIVE THEM AID

Fuel Arranged For All Along Route — Soviet Officials Entertain Pair.

By WALTER DURANTY.
Wireless to THE NEW YORK TIMES.

MOSCOW, July 31.—"Sure we've got a chance of beating Post and Gatty—in fact, we are confident of beating them," were almost the last words of Hugh Herndon Jr. before departure this afternoon at 5:32 Moscow time [11:32 A. M. New York Daylight Time], just twelve hours behind their predecessor's schedule.

American correspondents assembled to see them off, share their optimism for two reasons—first, the greater cruising radius of the Miss Veedol, which should give them two stops, at Irkutsk and Khabarovsk, to four for Post and Gatty, Novo-Sibirsk, Irkutsk, Blagovestchensk and Khabarovsk, across Russian, and second and more important, that both being pilots and navigators, they can "spell" each other for brief intervals to get sleep. They sit side by side in the cockpit, whereas Post and Gatty were in different compartments, the former piloting up above and the latter navigating below, with a speaking tube for communication.

Anyway, Herndon and Pangborn were much fresher on arrival here at 11:52 this morning [5:52 New York time] than Post and Gatty as they jumped down from their crimson monoplane and ran shouting toward the airfield headquarters. Strangely enough, no one saw them land. The correspondents who had been waiting since early dawn were now lying half asleep in the shade of the hangars and the airfield force was occupied with its own business when the red plane swooped from the city side instead of from the opposite direction as expected, made a curve, landed in the middle of the field and taxied up toward the hangars.

Found Way by Cathedral.

The fliers said later they did not spot the airfield at first but located the golden dome of the cathedral, made straight for that and then circled over the river, the Kremlin and the central squares until they saw the field to the northwest.

They made a good trip from Berlin, but ran into fog for about three hours between the Koenigsberg region and the Russian border, which they crossed exactly where they planned—in the region of Begossova, on the Moscow-Riga Railroad—thanks to their Ritchie aperiodic compass and Sperry false horizon apparatus. Their maps were not any too good in alone the fog, but their instruments held them right on line. Both were clean-shaved and Herndon was wearing a chamois jacket and Pangborn a slate-colored sweater.

First they made a tour of the field in a bus to estimate the load for the runway. The field is a kilometer across, but a diagonal gives 150 meters more, so they decided to take a full load of 5,000 pounds of gasoline—Post and Gatty assured them it and the oil were of good quality—and got their machine loaded right away.

The Misses Gillis, daughters of an American specialist here, one of whom, Fay, has an American pilot's license, offered the fliers a quick luncheon in their apartment, barely a stone's throw from the field, but the Russians had arranged a celebration luncheon in the Grand Hotel and they thought they could spare the time. Unlike Post and Gatty, they sampled the "wine of the country," vodka, and pronounced it excellent, but they took only mineral water, chicken, bread and fruit with them when they left.

Show No Signs of Fatigue.

At the luncheon they produced American cigarettes, "fresh from the factory by transatlantic air mail,"

Continued on Page Three.

British Are Planning to Break Record Made by Boardman

Special Cable to THE NEW YORK TIMES.

LONDON, July 31.—With the arrival of Russell Boardman and John Polando at Istanbul, preparations are being pushed here for an official British attack on the coveted world's long-distance air record.

A new long-range monoplane manufactured by the Fairey Aviation Company was handed over today to Royal Air Force pilots, Squadron Leader O. R. Gayford and Flight Lieutenant D. L. G. Bett, who have been chosen to make the attempt.

Tests will be made at Cranwell, in Lincolnshire, and afterward a preliminary flight will be made to Egypt. The main attack on the record, it is understood, will be made with a flight from Cranwell to Cape Town. The great circle course on that route is 5,900 miles.

FLIERS' OWN STORY OF TRIP TO ISTANBUL

Boardman and Polando Found Night Crossing of Alps in a Haze Was the Hardest.

FOUGHT FOG MUCH OF WAY

They Praise Navigation Instruments—Wined and Dined in Istanbul After Long Sleep.

Russell Boardman and John Polando, who completed a record flight on Thursday from New York to Istanbul, describe their adventures in the following dispatch:

By RUSSELL BOARDMAN AND JOHN POLANDO.

Special Cable to THE NEW YORK TIMES.

ISTANBUL, July 31.—After several weeks of tedious preparation, getting together the best possible equipment, making gasoline and oil consumption tests with our Wright J-6 motor and load tests with our Bellanca monoplane and installing the latest night flying instruments, we decided we were ready to attempt our flight from New York to Istanbul. When we heard from Dr. Kimball on Monday evening that prospects of fine weather were excellent we decided to fuel our plane with a view to start in the early morning of Tuesday.

We immediately went to the flying field that evening and put in 718 gallons of gasoline and twenty-one gallons of oil. Our food consisted of two roast chickens, some sliced bread and butter wrapped in wax paper, two thermos bottles of black coffee, two gallons of water, some chocolate bars and chewing gum.

At 4 A. M. Tuesday we were at Floyd Bennett Field. [All times given are Eastern Standard.] At 5 o'clock we took off down the 4,200-foot concrete runway. Despite its great length, we would have been unable to get into the air had not officials in charge of the field of the airport removed some telephone standards which run along this road at right angles to the airport runway.

Thanks to their help, we were able to obtain an excellent take-off. We proceeded across Long Island to the

Continued on Page Three.

DOYLE KEPT IN JAIL; DECISION ON APPEAL IS PUT OFF TO AUG. 10

Highest Court in State Hears Seabury's Plea to Uphold Sentence for Contempt.

IMMUNITY ISSUE PRESSED

Counsel Stakes Inquiry's Fate by Demanding a Ruling on Power of Committee.

STRATEGY PARLEY ROUTED

Curry and Steuer Quit Hotel When Process Server Arrived Night After Phone Call to Lake Placid.

From a Staff Correspondent of The New York Times.

ALBANY, N. Y., July 31.—Confronted today by Samuel Seabury's plea for a ruling on the powers of the Hofstadter committee to grant immunity from self-incrimination, the Court of Appeals allowed itself ten days for deliberation and left Dr. William F. Doyle in jail awaiting its decision.

The State's court of last resort reserved decision on the former veterinarian's appeal from a thirty-day sentence for contempt for refusing to tell the joint legislative investigating committee with whom he split his fees. An adjournment was taken then until Aug. 10, by which time Doyle will have served half his term.

Doyle Kept in Jail.

"What happens to my client in the meantime?" Samuel Falk, Doyle's attorney, asked Benjamin N. Cardozo, chief judge of the court, in chambers after the hearing.

"He stays where he is, of course," replied the white-haired jurist who presided during the argument before the full bench of seven judges.

The issue of the committee's power under a joint resolution lacking the signature of Governor Roosevelt to set aside constitutional guarantees against self-incrimination by promising immunity from future prosecution has been ignored by the lower courts, and until today Mr. Seabury, the committee's chief counsel, had not pressed it.

It is on the power to force testimony from witnesses, whom the courts might otherwise excuse from testifying, that Mr. Seabury is relying to remove the lid that he believes is hiding widespread graft and corruption in the Tammany-controlled government of New York City. He is prepared, it is known, to ask Governor Roosevelt to call the Legislature in special session to confer that power by law if he is beaten in the courts.

Sees Fate of Graft in Balance.

Standing before the bench from which he resigned fifteen years ago to run unsuccessfully for Governor, Mr. Seabury made an eloquent plea to the court "not to put bribery and corruption on a preferred list of crime." As he concluded he turned and looked at the portrait of his great-uncle, which hangs upon the richly carved oak-paneled walls almost opposite a picture of himself.

"There are in this State and in this country," he declared, "hundreds of thousands of young men and women whose character has not been warped; whose high purpose and public spirit have not yet been deadened by cynicism; who still believe the fight against bribery and corruption is not an empty and futile battle.

"Tell them by your decision that the bribe-giver and bribe-taker are immune from having their acts disclosed and you kill that conviction on the part of those to whom I refer,

Continued on Page Five.

British Party Crosses Greenland Ice Cap In Arctic Wastes Never Before Seen by Man

Special Cable to THE NEW YORK TIMES.

LONDON, July 31.—A telegram received tonight from James M. Scott, a surveyor with the British Arctic Air Route Expedition to Greenland, stated that a party consisting of himself, Andrew Stephenson and Lieutenant Martin Lindsay, also surveyors, had successfully accomplished their journey from the base camp at Angmagsalik across the Greenland ice cap.

They picked their way to the southwest coast of Greenland and are now at Ivigtut.

The three members of the British Arctic air route expedition, now at Ivigtut, left their base camp at Angmagsalik on July 1 to begin the 460-mile journey across the ice cap. They left the base with three sledges, twenty-seven dogs and provisions for a six-week journey and expected to average little more than thirteen miles a day. If their time is computed at thirty days, they beat the estimate somewhat, averaging fifteen and one-third miles a day.

The object of the trip was to enable Stephenson to estimate the width of the coastal mountain strip and to check the position of the higher mountains. Except at the point where Nansen attempted to cross the cap in 1888, the inside edge of the coastal mountain strip traversed by the party has never before been seen by man.

H. G. Watkins, leader of the expedition, in his last dispatch, dated July 13, said Scott's party would have to depend on aneroid barometer and hypsometer reading for finding the altitude and general slope of the ice cap if it expected to travel more than thirteen miles a day.

The expedition has been in Greenland since July 26, 1930, prepared to remain there for fourteen months to map an air route from Britain to Canada.

Gunmen Wound Two in Crowded Street; Shots Scatter East Side Children at Play

While Police Commissioner Mulrooney, tense with indignation at the shooting of five children by gangsters Tuesday evening, was directing his forces in a war on slayers yesterday, the criminal world replied with two more ruthless shootings.

One resulted in the instant death of a Brooklyn clothing manufacturer almost on his own doorstep and within sound of his family.

The other resulted in the probably mortal wounding of a petty east side racketeer and another man, who was thought at first to have been merely a passer-by but later was said to have been in the car with the racketeer.

Yesterday's shootings came simultaneously with the institution of extraordinary police measures to control crime, and with additional offers by private agencies to supplement police activity with so-called vigilante efforts.

Early in the day Mr. Mulrooney announced that the city would be protected by bands of four detectives, armed with repeating shotguns, and touring the city in relays day and night, twenty-four hours a day, in fast cars. One such band will be on duty at all times in each of the sixteen detective divisions in the city. Until now the practice has been to maintain patrols only from 6 P. M. to 6 A. M. One member of each group of detectives will be chosen for marksmanship.

Following out Commissioner Mulrooney's orders to shoot gangsters and other gunmen "above the waist," one of the special police squads, assigned to patrol the Harlem streets last night, captured four Negro robbers in a Harlem drug store after a pistol battle in which three of the men were wounded, one seriously.

The second of the earlier shootings yesterday in many respects was a startling parallel to Tuesday's outrage, and it, too, occurred in a crowded east side street only four blocks from the scene of the children's tragedy. The police said that only the fact that the killer in this case used a pistol instead of a shotgun saved children playing in the street.

The similarity of the two crimes was so marked that detectives investigating, with no apparent progress, the Tuesday night murder,

Continued on Page Fourteen.

SCACCIO CONVICTED IN QUICK VERDICT

Catskill Jury Finds Diamond Gangster Guilty of Assaulting and Torturing Farmer.

CAHILL SEES TURN OF TIDE

Prosecutor Now Hopes to Punish "Legs" When He Is Tried Again in September.

From a Staff Correspondent of The New York Times.

CATSKILL, N. Y., July 31.—Prison bars loomed for John (Garry) Scaccio, former bodyguard of Jack (Legs) Diamond, when a jury in Greene County found him guilty this afternoon, after a trial of six days, of the assault and torture, last April 16, of Grover Parks, cider hauler of Cairo. The jury reached its verdict in forty minutes on a single open vote. Justice F. Walter Bliss set next Wednesday for sentence.

Scaccio stands to get not less than ten years nor more than twenty. Only the twitching of his lips in his masklike face showed his reaction to the verdict. He even attempted a twisted smile as he stood up to give his pedigree.

The staff of Attorney General Bennett was jubilant over the verdict. They saw it as "the turn of the tide" in favor of law and order here. They now feel that they have a better chance of putting Diamond behind the bars when he goes to trial in September on the kidnapping indictment growing out of the Parks assault.

"We find the defendant guilty as charged in the indictment," was the verdict delivered by Gerhardt Launer, Athens farmer.

"Mr. Foreman, did you find the defendant actually had a pistol in his possession at any time during the commission of this crime?" asked the court.

"We did," was the answer that spelled an additional five to ten years for Scaccio.

On the assault verdict and on the special pistol count the clerk polled each individual juror. The affirmatives fairly crackled. If there was any fear in the hearts of the jurors, their voices gave no indication of it. They were a more open, clearer eyed and more determined group than the jurors that turned Diamond loose in Troy.

Judge Bliss thanked them in behalf of the people of Greene County. Scaccio mumbled his pedigree to Jones while his counsel pleaded that sentence be put over until Wednesday. Deputy Attorney General John T. Cahill was instructed by Judge Bliss to file before that time an information showing the previous convictions against Scaccio. The gangster is a second offender, having been arrested nine times.

"The people of Greene County have reason to be proud not only of this verdict but of the spirit in which it was reached and pronounced," said Harry Epstein, Deputy Attorney General. "It was perfectly evident from the manner of the individual jurymen that they had no doubt of the guilt of this defendant. They were men of courage and their decision shows that the turn of the tide against the gangster has come in Greene County."

Scaccio's alibi, offered by Mrs. Anna Talamo of Brooklyn, his sister-in-law, and Gerlando Casesa, a pastry cook of Brooklyn, was broken by witnesses called in rebuttal by Mr. Cahill. Patrolman John Fitzsimmons of Catskill, who had seen Scaccio on at least a hundred previous occasions, testified he saw the gangster in the village speakeasy with Diamond and others of the gang just before midnight of April

Continued on Page Fourteen.

COURT ORDERS JURY TO REINDICT CAPONE

Wilkerson Points Way to Bring Severe Penalty to Bear Under the Jones Law.

ALLOWS NEW TAX CASE PLEA

But Is Dissatisfied With Liquor Consiracy Punishment for Which Gangster Bargained.

Special to The New York Times.

CHICAGO, July 31.—In a surprise court session this forenoon Federal Judge James H. Wilkerson permitted "Scarface" Alphonse Capone Chicago's "public enemy," to substitute a plea of not guilty for one of guilty to income tax dodging, but ordered that the gang chieftain be indicted again with his sixty-eight co-defendants on charges of conspiracy to violate the prohibition law, the new indictment to embody specific charges and heavier penalties. The latter move was looked upon as an effort to bring to bear upon the defendant the Jones law, which carries a penalty of five years' imprisonment and $10,000 fine.

Capone was not in court, the judge having instructed his attorneys that the defendant's presence would not be required.

Although the hearing on the gangster's motion for a withdrawal of his pleas of guilty had been set for 2 o'clock this afternoon, Judge Wilkerson summoned counsel to his court at 10 A. M., and without asking whether George E. Q. Johnson, the United States District Attorney, consented, allowed the motion to withdraw on the income tax plea. The tax case was continued until Sept. 8, to be set for trial probably the latter part of that month.

Demands That Another Jury Act.

"As to the conspiracy case," said Judge Wilkerson, "the ruling is reserved and the motion (to withdraw the plea of guilty) taken under advisement and continued for disposition until Sept. 8.

"The matters covered by the indictment should be presented to another jury. In the enumeration of overt acts the defendant and others are charged with substantial offenses within the period of the statute of limitations for which a heavier penalty is provided than that possible under the conspiracy indictment.

"The court will not believe, unless it is forced to do so, that the language of this indictment was chosen, without probable cause, merely for the purpose of creating the impression that this defendant has been a flagrant lawbreaker over a long period of time. This is a matter which must be inquired into fully."

The court then addressed the grand jury, which had filed in, and instructed it in virtually the same language.

The statement of Judge Wilkerson indicated that if the government had sufficient evidence against Capone and his sixty-eight co-defendants to link them with the crimes of manufacturing and transporting beer, as the overt acts of the conspiracy indictment charge, they should also be indicted under the Jones law.

5,000 Offenses Were Charged.

The court's statement with respect to the "language" of the conspiracy indictment and the impression it creates apparently referred to the charge that defendants conspired to commit 5,000 offenses against the dry laws.

Special prohibition agents who developed the conspiracy case are doubtful whether they can link Capone directly to offenses such as the manufacture, sale or transportation of beer within the statute of limitations. The only overt act set forth within the three-year statute

Continued on Page Fourteen.

PARIS AND NEW YORK PLAN $250,000,000 CREDIT TO BRITAIN

Joint Advance by the Federal Reserve and Bank of France Is Expected Today.

GOES TO BANK OF ENGLAND

Paris Paper Says This Is First Time We Acted on Equal Footing in Credit Deal.

BRITISH BOARD ASKS CUTS

Saving of $500,000,000 Yearly in Budget Seen as Necessary to Avert a Crisis.

By P. J. PHILIP.
Special Cable to THE NEW YORK TIMES.

PARIS, July 31. — Arrangements were finally discussed here today and will, it is understood, be made definite tomorrow for the extension to the Bank of England of a credit of £50,000,000 (about $250,000,000) jointly in equal proportions by the Bank of France and the Federal Reserve Bank of New York.

The terms of this agreement were outlined last week-end during the visit to Paris of Sir Robert Kindersley of the Bank of England and were discussed by him in later conferences in London. He returned to Paris today and had a second interview with Clement Moret, governor of the Bank of France. It is understood that this time an agreement was reached, the transatlantic telephone being used during the evening to discuss the terms of the credit with the directors of the Federal Reserve Bank of New York.

Bankers Will Meet Today.

A meeting of representatives of the principal Paris banks which will participate in the advance has been convoked for tomorrow morning at the Bank of France, where they will be informed of the conditions of the contract. It is understood a statement will be issued afterward giving an outline of the agreement.

"What is interesting in this great credit operation," says the Matin, commenting on today's events, "is that for the first time in the history of credit France and the United States will be cooperating on an equal footing."

It was expected when Sir Robert Kindersley made his visit here last week-end that the agreement would be concluded. In London, however, there have been two somewhat contradictory currents of opinion. Some circles at the Bank of England opposed accepting direct help from the Bank of France, but government circles held the credit was essential if financial conditions in London were to be made convenient for the war debt conversion project which Chancellor of the Exchequer Snowden has had in view for some time and to which he referred in his speech yesterday.

Cheaper Money Required.

If the conversion project is to be put through successfully, with its consequent huge saving to the treasury, money must be made cheaper than at present. Toward this objective the arrangement being made with the Bank of France and the Federal Reserve Bank of New York is considered an important step, though, in view of the large drain in the past few weeks on the English gold reserve, it is thought that it will be some time before the Bank of England will be able to lower its discount rate.

The proposals of the Bank of France which were given to Sir Rob-

Continued on Page Two.

HOOVER SUGGESTS GERMANY BUY OUR WHEAT AND COTTON ON LIBERAL CREDIT TERMS

Idea of Loan on Their Art Is Resented by Germans

Special Cable to THE NEW YORK TIMES.

BERLIN, July 31.—The report from Paris that a syndicate of France's principal art dealers would offer Germany a loan of $40,000,000 on the security of the old masters now in German museums has aroused a storm of indignant protest. The whole idea is scouted as preposterous and impracticable.

What rankles most deeply, however, is that the national monetary need should be taken advantage of for laying hands on German cultural treasures that money cannot buy. What is resented most fiercly is the condition that the masterpieces when pledged would be transported to Paris, to be on view there until the loan was repaid.

But even if German museums and private collectors were willing to give up highly prized possessions, it is pointed out, their acquiescence would be nugatory, since a law of the Reich forbids exportation of its principal art treasures.

REICHSBANK RAISES RATE TO 15 PER CENT

Charge of 20 Per Cent Is Put on Collateral Loans in Plan to Reopen Banks.

TWO INSTITUTIONS HELPED

Government Takes Control of Dresdner Bank and Danat Bank Sells Stock.

Special Cable to THE NEW YORK TIMES.

BERLIN, July 31.—The central committee of the Reichsbank tonight raised the discount to 15 per cent and the rate for loans on collateral to 20 per cent.

It was also announced that in all probability the private banks would resume full activities on Wednesday. Only the savings banks, which owing to their mortgage investments have been unable to raise their liquidity so as to meet all eventualities, will still be subjected to restrictions.

Agricultural organizations opposed the raise in the discount rate, pointing out that the farmers are unable to pay increased interest rates, but they were told that the raise is necessary in connection with the full reopening of the banks. The raise now decreed has been demanded by the critics of Dr. Hans Luther's policy. A minority of economists advocated a raise to 20 or even 30 per cent.

It was also announced tonight that the German Government will subscribe 300,000,000 marks ($71,400,000) of new preferential stock of the Dresdner Bank, virtually buying control of the institution, which, with its present capital stock of 100,000,000 marks ($23,800,000) and its reserves of about 34,000,000 marks ($8,192,000), ranks second among the large German private banks. It is virtually certain that the bank's governing board, which is to meet tomorrow, will accept the proposal,

Continued on Page Two.

Cannon Predicts Renomination of Smith; Bishop Warns Democrats It Means Defeat

Special to The New York Times.

WASHINGTON, July 31.—Declarations by two dry leaders today warned the Democratic party against nominating a wet candidate on a wet platform in the 1932 Presidential campaign.

Bishop James Cannon Jr. of the Methodist Episcopal Church South predicted that former Governor Smith would "in all probability" be the Democratic nominee or might consent to the naming of Governor Roosevelt, also "committed to prohibition repeal," and asserted that neither would be supported by dry Democrats.

F. Scott McBride, general superintendent of the Anti-Saloon League, stated that there would be no wet plank in the 1932 Democratic platform unless the delegates to the convention become so "Tammanyized" that "the destruction of their party means less to them than the approval of a handful of wet millionaires who are hungry for the blood-tainted profits to be gained from the return of legalized liquor traffic."

In a statement issued after he had departed for Europe, Bishop Cannon said that Mr. Smith, "the titular leader of the Democratic party, who fully realizes that he received around 15,000,000 votes for President," had recently declared in The Princetonian that "both political parties will have to take a definite stand on prohibition in the next Presidential campaign," and had advocated the home-control plan of John J. Raskob, chairman of the Democratic National Committee, as "the most important suggested."

Declaring that Mr. Smith and Mr. Raskob would "probably control enough votes to write their anti-prohibition views into the platform" and would "insist upon making prohibition the dominant issue," the statement concluded:

"If so, 1928 will be repeated in 1932, with the majority of the electoral votes of the South cast against any wet candidate."

SACKETT INFORMS BERLIN

Move Is Described as One Other Way of Aiding Reich Recovery.

NO RESPONSE MADE AS YET

Washington Thinks Cotton Proposal Is More Likely to Be Accepted of the Two.

VIEWED AS A "HAPPY IDEA"

Farm Board's Burden of Carrying Surpluses Would Be Lightened by Plan.

By RICHARD V. OULAHAN.
Special to The New York Times.

WASHINGTON, July 31.—President Hoover has undertaken another effort to help Germany in her present economic and financial stress. It is in the form of a "suggestion" to the German Government through Frederic M. Sackett, Ambassador at Berlin, that if Germany should so desire, the Federal Farm Board would sell it substantial amounts of wheat and cotton on liberal credit terms.

No response has come from the German Government, which is supposed to be engaged in attempting to ascertain what the reaction of its agricultural population would be to the wheat proposal. Under recent German Government regulations, which have severely restricted the importation of wheat, there has been a heavy increase of production in German territory and any large American importation might come into competition with the German domestic wheat output.

The State Department did not issue any formal communiqué, but in response to questions it was said there that Ambassador Sackett has suggested to the Germans that perhaps it might be of help to Germany if the Federal Farm Board would sell on liberal credit terms substantial amounts of its holdings in wheat and cotton. However, the department added, neither the Farm Board nor the government has yet received any requests from Germany along these lines.

Should the suggested deal eventuate it will serve the double purpose of helping Germany and American agriculture, especially cotton growers in this country.

Cabinet Considered Proposal.

The proposal has been urged upon the administration by farm organizations. There is no official acknowledgment that it has the sanction of President Hoover, other than the inference to be drawn from what came from the State Department about Ambassador Sackett's part in it. Every effort has been made heretofore to give the impression that the suggestion had received mere casual consideration in administration circles and never had progressed beyond the stage of being considered "a happy idea."

It became known tonight, however, that the matter had been considered by the Cabinet and had produced a profound impression among its members. It was discussed also this week at frequent conferences between President Hoover and William R. Castle Jr., Acting Secretary of State, and Ogden L. Mills, Acting Secretary of the Treasury.

Among some of those informed persons who knew of the secret move of the administration the idea prevailed that if the German Government accepted the proposal there would be an immediate and perhaps sensational rise in commodity prices in the markets of this country.

Opinion in informed quarters in Washington tonight is that the proposal with reference to wheat will not be acceptable to the German Government but that the cotton proposal may be acceptable in the interest of obtaining plenty of raw material for German textiles and thus accelerating industry.

Material Aid to Germany Seen.

The fundamental of the "happy idea" is that the Farm Board will not only be able to dispose of large amounts of its surplus of wheat and cotton, but that long-term credits will be extended to Germany should she choose to buy, and that this procedure will be of enormous help in the effort to adjust the perturbed financial and economic situation in that country.

What credit terms Germany would ask for should the proposal be ac-

"All the News That's Fit to Print."

The New York Times.

LATE CITY EDITION
THE WEATHER—Partly cloudy and cooler today; tomorrow partly cloudy.
Temperatures yesterday—Max. 93; min. 74.
U. S. Weather Forecast—See next to last page.

VOL. LXXX....No. 26,859. ****++ + NEW YORK, SATURDAY, AUGUST 8, 1931. TWO CENTS In New York City | THREE CENTS Within 200 Miles | FOUR CENTS Elsewhere Except 7th and 8th Postal Zones

DARK AGE CRUELTY CHARGED IN SYSTEM FOR DEPORTATIONS

Wickersham Report Declares Practices 'Unconstitutional, Tyrannic, Oppressive.'

FAMILIES ARE SEPARATED

Laws Carried Out 'Without Simplest Discretion'—Evils 'Inherent in Procedure.'

ALIEN APPEALS BODY URGED

Two Members Dissent From Report Based on Study by Baltimore Lawyer.

Special to The New York Times.

WASHINGTON, Aug. 7.—Practices comparable to the ruthless cruelty and inhuman despotism of the Dark Ages were charged against the immigration officials of the Labor Department in the tenth report of the Wickersham Commission, which was issued at the White House today.

The report severely criticized the deportation system, declaring that "unconstitutional, tyrannic and oppressive" methods sometimes were employed.

Many persons have been separated permanently from their families in violation of the "plainest dictates of humanity," through the administration of certain of the immigration laws which Labor Department officials have carried out without either deviation or the simplest discretion, it was asserted.

Two members of the commission, Colonel Henry W. Anderson of Richmond, Va., and former Justice Kenneth Mackintosh of the Washington State Supreme Court, dissented sharply from the findings and refused to sign the report.

Mr. Anderson said that the indictment was so severe that he could not concur in it without a more thorough investigation than that which was made. Most of the report was a survey by Reuben Oppenheimer, Baltimore attorney, which was adopted as the commission's own finding.

Colonel Anderson objected not only to the conclusions of Mr. Oppenheimer, but likewise to the latter's basic recommendation that a quasi-judicial body from the Department of Labor be set up to hear deportation appeals.

Mr. Mackintosh said he could not agree to the "general indictment of a purely administrative branch of the government, based in a large measure upon the failure to follow usual judicial procedure."

Nine Agree with Findings.

The nine members who signed the report, however, showed that they had been convinced by the findings of Mr. Oppenheimer. In the seven pages taken up with their own language the majority commissioners said there could be no doubt that too much despotism had been practiced in handling deportation cases, adding that this had contributed materially to the general problem of law enforcement by keeping aliens in a constant state of apprehension as to their security in this country.

"This apprehension," said the report, "is constant, for no foreign-born resident of the United States, whether he has been naturalized or not, can ever be sure that he will not suddenly be made the subject of an administrative process, carried on without his knowledge by telegraph between an inspector in the field and a bureau in Washington, which will find some irregularity in his entry or in his conduct, break the personal and property ties which he has established in the United States and return him to the country from which he came, where he will not be welcome and where he has already found the conditions of life too hard to endure. * * * This situation prolongs and deepens the immigrant's insecurity and delays his mental and moral stabilization in the country which he is seeking to adopt."

In this connection the commission hastened to exonerate the foreign-born in the United States from the general charge that they have been responsible for a disproportionate share of the crime in the United States. The report said that statistics and facts found by the commission failed entirely to bear out such an assumption.

Evils "Inherent in System."

The "despotic, tyrannic and oppressive" practices which the commission described, both in its own language and by adoption of Mr. Oppenheimer's, have accumulated during the development of immigration regulation and have become inherent in the system itself, the report said. During this development, the immigration authorities of the Department of Labor have been allowed to become detectives, prosecutors and judges "three functions

Continued on Page Seven.

Wilkins Abandons Polar Trip For This Year, His Wife Says.

By The Associated Press.

COPENHAGEN, Aug. 7.—Lady Wilkins today informed the newspaper Berlingske Tidende that her husband, Sir Hubert Wilkins, would not attempt to reach the North Pole this year in the submarine Nautilus.

Instead, she said, he will try out the submersible under the ice in the vicinity of Spitsbergen and will return in about a month to Bergen, where the vessel will remain during the Winter.

LINDBERGHS START FOR TIP OF ALASKA

Take Off for Point Barrow as Clearing Weather Ahead Is Reported at Aklavik.

'SPOKEN' FROM THEIR GOAL

Radio Flashes Guidance to the Speeding Plane—Also Sighted at Herschel Island.

By The Associated Press.

POINT BARROW, Alaska, Aug. 8.—The Point Barrow radio station at 1 A. M., Eastern Standard Time, contacted the plane being flown by Colonel Lindbergh from Aklavik and sent out weather conditions in this vicinity. The weather is clearing, with a thirteen-mile-an-hour southwest wind.

Within a few minutes a message from Herschel Island, about 180 miles northwest of Aklavik, said the plane had been sighted there at 12:30 A. M. (Eastern Standard Time). It had taken about two hours for the flight to that point.

Set Out as Fog Lifts.

AKLAVIK, Northwest Territory, Aug. 7 (AP).—Starting the last half of their vacation trip to the Orient, Colonel and Mrs. Charles A. Lindbergh took off from this Arctic trading post today at 7:30 P. M., Pacific Standard Time (11:30 P. M., Eastern Daylight Saving Time) for Point Barrow, on the tip of Alaska, 536 miles away.

Clearing weather permitted the flying couple to leave after being grounded for three days and two nights, the longest halt since they left Washington, D. C., ten days ago on their flight to Tokyo.

Early today reports were received of fog lying over Point Barrow and along the rim of the Arctic Ocean there, but clearing winds later blew the mists away and Lindbergh made his decision to hop in the afternoon.

As the plane has averaged about 105 miles an hour on previous hops it was thought they would reach the northernmost American settlement in about five hours.

May Land Beside Fuel Ship.

Three-quarters of an hour before hopping off Colonel Lindbergh boarded the plane and warmed the motor up, taxiing about in the waters of Peel Channel, while his diminutive wife sat in the office of the radio station on shore, receiving greetings from Point Barrow.

Enthusiastic over the messages of good wishes for a safe and speedy trip from residents of the most Northern Alaska community, she sent a short message of appreciation.

The United States Coast Guard cutter Northland, carrying a gasoline supply intended for the Lindberghs at Point Barrow, is blocked by ice about 100 miles away, and there is a possibility the Lindberghs may fly direct from Aklavik to the Northland and refuel alongside the ship.

While the Lindberghs waited improvement in weather they tested and checked their plane and its radio equipment. Mrs. Lindbergh spent considerable time with the Aklavik

Continued on Page Three.

HOOVER DECLARES WINTER PROBLEM OF IDLE WILL BE MET

"Whatever Situation Is," President Promises Relief by Previous "Successful" Methods.

CLOSE SURVEY REVEALED

Executive Has Been Consulting Business and Labor Leaders for Three Weeks.

JOB CANVASS UNDER WAY

Public and Private Construction Facts Are Gathered to Appraise Measures Required.

Special to The New York Times.

WASHINGTON, Aug. 7.—President Hoover made the confident declaration today that the unemployment situation next Winter, "whatever it may be," will be met by an adaptation of the same methods with which he said the situation was successfully handled last year.

The President told how he had been engaged for three weeks, with other members of his administration, in a study of the unemployment problem and of relief measures likely to be necessary with the coming of the cold weather.

While he did not say so, it is known that the President and his advisers are anxious to have a plan ready before December with which to forestall the possible enactment of "dole" legislation by the next Congress. He has been told by observers that, unless a workable project is in progress by the time Congress meets, a flood of "socialistic" proposals is probable.

The President said today that the first fact to be determined is the probable volume of the load to be carried through another season, and to that end the various bureaus of the government are engaged in a study of the experiences of last year. These reports are not yet complete, he said.

An appraisal also is being made of such action as is now in progress, the President said, and of the relief facilities that will be available next Winter.

Text of Mr. Hoover's Statement.

President Hoover said in his statement:

During the past three weeks I have been engaged, together with members of the administration, in a study of the problems of unemployment and relief likely to confront us over the coming Winter and the organization necessary to meet the situation. While improvement in the situation in many directions seems promising, the problem, whatever it may be, will be met.

With the organized cooperation of local and State and Federal authorities, and the large number of relief and charitable organizations, the problem was successfully handled last Winter. We shall adapt organization methods in such manner as may be necessary for the coming Winter.

The first of the facts to be determined is the probable volume of the load of distress which will need to be provided for. The various breaus of the government are engaged in an exhaustive study of last Winter's experience of all organizations, the average number of persons in distress and their locations.

Further examination is being made of the probable load during next Winter. The economic changes during the year will materially improve certain areas and others may

Continued on Page Four.

Three Army Airplanes Crash in Midair; Pilots of Two Leap Safely in Parachutes

Special to The New York Times.

SELFRIDGE FIELD, Mount Clemens, Mich., Aug. 7.—Two Selfridge Field pilots escaped with minor injuries today after leaping about 4,000 feet with their parachutes following a three-plane collision in the air. The pilot of the third plane flew back to Selfridge Field and landed safely, despite a damaged propeller.

The three planes were flying in formation with fifteen others when the wing of a plane piloted by Kenneth W. Mosher, a Ninety-fourth Pursuit Squadron reserve officer, tipped into the propeller of the plane piloted by Lieutenant Richard Crabb, another Reserve Squadron officer. Mosher's plane then crashed into the plane of Lieutenant Robert W. Burns of the Seventeenth Pursuit Squadron.

The planes of Mosher and Burns were destroyed. As planes began to fall the pilots leaped. They landed in a farm field a half mile from where the crash occurred.

Mosher's back was wrenched in landing and Burns was cut on the nose in fighting clear of the brace wires before leaping. The Burns plane crashed into the front yard of a farm home, severing a limb from a tree.

The Mosher plane fell in the Clinton River, within 150 feet of where Junior Carney of Mount Clemens was shooting blackbirds from a rowboat. The boy said he heard an explosion just after the plane hit the water. Cottagers ran panic-stricken into their cottages as they saw the wreckage fall.

Lieutenant Crabb flew back to Selfridge Field.

Today's flight, composed of planes of the Seventeenth and Ninety-fourth Squadrons, was led by Lieutenant Norris Harbold.

"It was a pleasant sensation drifting down," Lieutenant Burns said. "I could look up and see Mosher drifting down above me. He waved his hand to signify he wasn't hurt."

Indians Shadowed Dickey to Orinoco Source; Explorer Decides White Tribes Are Myths

By DR. HERBERT S. DICKEY.

Wireless to THE NEW YORK TIMES.

SAN FERNANDO, Upper Orinoco, Aug. 7.—The age-old guess of the map makers that the Orinoco River rises in the Parima Mountains has proved to be a good one. It does rise in those mountains, but not very near where the cartographers have placed it. No one has guessed or suggested that the Orinoco flows elsewhere than in Venezuela. We know that we have every available map as well as every geography and atlas in the world against us, not excepting those published in Brazil. Yet, unless we are the victims of a colossal mistake, one persisted in after a number of careful astronomical observations, the Orinoco washes many miles of Brazilian river bank, far up on its upper reaches, beyond where no white men other than ourselves have been. Naturally, our astronomical findings on this point will not be given out until after one of our geographical societies has the opportunity to check them.

We have just returned from the Ventural River after a wild-goose chase after Indians. We found none, nor traces of them. And it was the same on the upper reaches of the Orinoco, excepting that here there were traces in abundance. We found Indian houses recently abandoned, we found hastily and recently constructed bridges by which Guaharibos had crossed the streams. We saw no Indians, white or otherwise.

We were compelled to leave our heaviest boat at the celebrated Guaharibo Rapids. We left it in the care of two members of the crew. Two days after our departure upstream, several hundred Guaharibos appeared on the banks of the river and with brandishing of weapons and bellicose cries frightened our two

Continued on Page Four.

DIAMOND CASE GOES TO THE JURY TODAY

Defense in Opening Indicates It Will Try to Supply Alibi for Gangster.

CITES HOSPITAL DATES HERE

An Aide, Scared and Balky, Is Forced to Admit He Took Beer Orders From Racketeer.

The government's case against Jack (Legs) Diamond and Paul Quattrocchi, his aide in the beer and liquor trade in Greene County, was closed and the defense opened yesterday in Federal court at 3:35 P. M. The defense and the summing up addresses are expected to be completed by 3 P. M. today. How much time the charge will take is not known, but the jury will probably begin deliberation not later than 5 o'clock.

Thirty-two witnesses in all were called by Arthur H. Schwartz, the 28-year-old prosecutor, to bear out the promise he made in his opening that the government would prove that Diamond and Quattrocchi conspired to solicit orders for and distributed intoxicating liquor in Greene County and that they had a 1,500-gallon alcohol still in Catskill in violation of the prohibition law. The trial started Tuesday.

Diamond's attorneys have not indicated how many witnesses they will call, nor would Daniel H. Prior, the gangster's chief counsel, say whether Diamond will take the stand. It is generally believed he will not. Quattrocchi, however, will take the stand and will call on at least four character witnesses.

An indication of the nature of Diamond's defense may be gleaned from the first move made by his attorneys yesterday, when they read into the record reports from the Polyclinic and Metropolitan Hospitals, where he was a patient from Oct. 12 to Dec. 31, 1930, after he was shot in the chest and the lungs in the Monticello Hotel. Some of the government evidence on the conspiracy count includes these dates. After the hospital records were read, court adjourned until 10 A. M. today.

Witness Appears Frightened.

Nick Fusco, beer runner for Diamond and before that beer runner for Cagliones, who had more or less of a monopoly in Greene County before the appearance on the scene of the New York gangster, was the outstanding government witness yesterday. He seemed to be afraid of Diamond or Quattrocchi, or both. It showed in his testimony, in his uneasiness, in his squirming. He was harried and forced into many contradictions by both sides before he left the stand.

One thing was certain by the time Fusco's experience was over: that Diamond's reputation as a leader and a "big shot" in racketeering is considerably inflated; that he is, or was, a petty beer peddler at best. Fusco's testimony revealed that when he was not running beer for Diamond, he had to do housework, trim the lawns, cut the hedges and whitewash the trees on the gangster's place in Acra—all for $30 a week. When he asked for an increase, he got a promise.

Diamond, troubled by the heat as well as the damaging government testimony, kept dabbing at his thin lips with a handkerchief. The furrows seldom smoothed out on his tall forehead, and his thinning black hair was damp with perspiration. Mrs. Diamond sat through the afternoon session with another woman and fondled a boy about 3 years old, said to be Diamond's nephew. Diamond, asked during recess, as he stood in the corridor, if the boy was his nephew, threw his skinny arms

Continued on Page Fourteen.

3 GANGSTERS NAMED AS CHILD'S SLAYERS

Witness Says Men Who Shot From Auto in 107th St. Were Coll's Aides.

ARRESTS EXPECTED SOON

Informer Describes Fusillade as Part of Feud Between Rival Narcotic Peddlers.

The names of three of the gunmen who were in the automobile driven through East 107th Street on the evening of July 28, when five children were sprayed with bullets, one having been fatally shot, were obtained yesterday by the police from an eyewitness to the shooting.

The informer was said to be Joseph Mucciolo, 20 years old, of 355 Pleasant Avenue, who was seized on a burglary charge by Detective Andrew O'Connor of the East 126th Street police station, and was arraigned before Magistrate Stern in the Harlem Court. The burglary charge was dismissed.

Early this morning Joseph Bendinelli, 21, of 442 East 115th Street, was arrested and held on a charge of robbery by Detectives O'Connor, McLaughlin, Smith and Grippen, who are working exclusively on the case. Bendinelli will be questioned today. The detectives refused to give any information in connection with the arrest other than to say that Bendinelli has a police record. He was charged with the robbery of an A. & P. grocery store at 1,258 Madison Avenue on Aug. 5.

Mucciolo was questioned at length by the detectives and Assistant District Attorney Thomas Dyett, and it was said he furnished valuable information. He told the police that the automobile from which the shots were fired had as its passengers, "Trigger" Mike Coppola, a man named Grecco and a third called "Louis." He also described the car and gave the license plate number. He informed the detectives that he knew by sight the man at the wheel of the automobile, but he could not give his name.

Four in Coll's Gang.

All four, according to the informant, are members of the Vincent Coll gang. He said that with the exception of the chauffeur the others in the car took part in the shooting, the victim of the gunmen escaping. The story of Mucciolo, corroborates in part information the detectives obtained from Anthony Trobino, 21, of 307 East 119th Street, who was questioned at length on Thursday by detectives from the East 104th Street stations.

Trobino is believed to be the man who was the target for the shots that hit the children. The detectives were reticent over what they learned from Trobino. They are said to have learned that the gunmen in the automobile had set out to find Joey Rao, lieutenant of Coll. Rao, according to the police informer, worked at one time with a narcotic seller named Rock. When Rock had a disagreement with Coll, it is said, Rao joined Rock and supported him, in opposition to Coll.

With this information the detectives asked the police of Jersey City to help locate Rock. It was said that Rock had friends in Jersey City and was a frequent visitor there. The Jersey City detectives reported that Rock was seen frequently, both in Jersey City and Union City, in company with Vannie Higgins, gangster and racketeer.

The police also said that Coppola was arrested about a year ago on a charge of shooting Rao in front of the Pompeii Restaurant, 116th Street and Third Avenue. At the time Rao refused to press a complaint and the charge was dropped.

Police Commissioner Mulrooney and

Continued on Page Fourteen.

100 SUBPOENAS OUT AS SEABURY HUNTS PROTECTED GAMING

Tammany Club Heads Called After Study of Police List of Suspected Resorts.

McGUINNESS ARREST SIFTED

McLaughlin to Be Asked to Tell of Raid Which Preceded His Resignation.

GANG INQUIRY IS PRESSED

Police Officials Face Examination on Methods Used to Curb Thugs and Racketeers.

Nearly 100 subpoenas for members and records of political and social clubs which sought injunctions against the police were sent out yesterday by Samuel Seabury, counsel of the Hofstadter legislative committee.

The issuance of these subpoenas followed comparison of the list of organizations which sought injunctions furnished the preceding day by Corporation Counsel Arthur J. W. Hilly, with a list of clubs suspected by the police of permitting gambling which had been compiled by Mr. Seabury's assistants. Among the subpoenas were some for political leaders and persons suspected of being gangsters, who are expected to appear for questioning next week at the committee's headquarters in the State office building.

McGuinness Arrest Sifted.

During the day the committee subpoenaed the records of the Bridge Plaza Court, Brooklyn, in connection with the arrest in March, 1927, of Former Alderman Peter J. McGuinness on a charge of bookmaking, of which he was acquitted. Mr. McGuinness, who is Democratic leader of the Fifteenth Assembly District, is now Deputy Commissioner of Public Works in Brooklyn. His arrest with about 150 others took place in his political clubhouse in a raid by the police anti-gambling squad.

The subsequent resignation of George V. McLaughlin as Police Commissioner was attributed in some quarters to dissatisfaction among Democratic leaders with the raid on this and other political clubs, but this was denied at the time by Mr. McLaughlin. It is expected that Mr. McLaughlin will be called as a witness within a week.

Deputy Chief Inspector John J. Hennessey, in command of the police in the Bronx, was questioned by Philip W. Lowry, assistant counsel, regarding methods used to keep track of known gangsters and criminals. Other police officials will be examined on steps being taken to check racketeering.

Highway Witness Recants.

The investigators encountered an apparent change of mind in a witness. He is Harry B. Greene, head of the H. B. Greene Contracting Company, who appeared voluntarily two weeks ago with information regarding bidding on the West Side express highway. On his first appearance Mr. Greene was questioned by William G. Mulligan, assistant counsel, and gave some information regarding bids on construction of the highway. According to the investigators he appeared to be dissatisfied with the treatment of his bids.

Mr. Greene since has been recalled three times for further questioning. His attitude had changed and, according to the investigators, he not only failed to give further data but recanted some of his previous testimony. Mr. Seabury is now seeking to obtain some records and documents concerning the bids from Mr. Greene.

Disclosure of the attitude of Mr. Greene revealed that Mr. Seabury is

Continued on Page Five.

Walker Is Silent on Report His Funds Are Under Inquiry.

By The Associated Press.

S. S. BREMEN AT SEA, Aug. 7.—Mayor James J. Walker of New York, on his way to Germany for his health, declined today to comment on reports that his bank accounts were being inspected by the legislative committee headed by Samuel Seabury, which is investigating city affairs.

"As to the report that my bank and brokerage accounts have been subpoenaed" he said, "I must respectfully refer you to the legislative committee and Judge Seabury."

The Mayor spent a restful night, visited the captain on the bridge today and posed for pictures. He interested himself in a pico of students on the tourist deck for permission to use the ship swimming pool. He is tanned and looking rested.

BERLIN DROPS PLAN TO CURTAIL IMPORTS

Regular Trading Firms Are to Get Exchange Needed to Carry On Business.

OUR TRADE WAS AFFECTED

Automobiles, Chemicals, Textiles and Foods Would Have Been Shut Out.

Special Cable to THE NEW YORK TIMES.

BERLIN, Aug. 7.—Germany tonight abolished the restrictions on foreign exchange which had threatened to impede American imports, such as chemicals, automobiles and textiles. Instead of enforcing an embargo on certain kinds of goods by refusing to grant the exchange for payment, the government, under a new decree, has provided that demands of exporters and importers for exchange to be used in the course of their ordinary business shall be granted by the Reichsbank without restrictions.

While in view of the limited reserves of exchange left over from the July runs it was thought there must be a curtailment of imports, the government decided to heed the insistence of the Ministry of Economics and overcame the resistance of the Reichsbank to a change in the ordinance which has upset the nation's import trade to an unparalleled extent and has threatened to bring reprisals by other countries.

The decree placing the exchange traffic under the supervision of the Reichsbank remains in force, however, and importers, while free to obtain as much exchange as they want, will still be compelled to explain for what purpose it is to be used in order to prevent the flight of capital under the cover of fake imports. No newly formed firms of importers will be permitted to get such exchange.

Americans Had Been Anxious.

American exports to Germany would have been seriously affected by the rationing ordinance had it remained in full effect. The United States commercial attaché had received complaints and inquiries from many sides, indicating much anxiety on that score. While the government did not reveal the list of goods for the import of which only limited exchange, or no exchange at all, was to be granted, experiences during the first days of rationing showed that among those categories were American chemicals and automobiles and other so-called luxury commodities; certain foodstuffs, notably cereals and fruits, and textiles, especially bathing suits.

Twelve big firms in Cologne which had been importing vegetables and fruits announced that they would be compelled to close their doors immediately unless the exchange restrictions were relaxed today. It was realized also that barring of foreign goods would be interpreted as a violation of trade agreements, especially by France, which was selling mostly

Continued on Page Two.

King Albert Dictates Foreign Policy in Crisis; Silences All Political Writers in Belgium

Special Cable to THE NEW YORK TIMES.

BRUSSELS, Aug. 7.—King Albert returned from Switzerland yesterday to preside over an important Ministerial Council held at the palace this afternoon, when Belgium's attitude toward the Hoover plan was discussed.

It is understood that the King indicated his intention of directing foreign policy, as is his habit in times of national crisis, and requested diplomatic writers on newspapers to keep their silence until international problems are settled.

The King also recommended drastic reductions in expenditures, a policy he has advocated ever since the war.

BRUSSELS, Belgium, Aug. 7 (AP).—King Albert, interrupting his holiday in Switzerland, sat in today on a Cabinet meeting which discussed details of the Hoover moratorium plan as applied to Belgium.

Unofficially it is said that Belgium is prepared to sacrifice approximately $6,300,000 in German payments as against $21,000,000 which she would not receive if no special alterations were made in the Hoover plan

One difficulty is the unwillingness of Great Britain to admit a moratorium for this year's annuity of the Belgian and Congolese reconstruction loans, equivalent to $4,000,000. Also, Germany has not yeet agreed to continue the annual mark settlement payments, totalling $5,000,000.

Belgium still insists on German payment in kind, at least to the extent of $6,000,000, representing payments under contract.

FARM BODY REJECTS REICH OFFER TO BUY ITS SURPLUS COTTON

But 'Alternative' of 'Direct Buying' on Basis of New Dollar Credits Here Is Suggested.

WAR CLAIM FUNDS BASIS

Besides Unacceptable Terms of German Proposal, Deletion of Price Minimum Is Factor.

CHANGE IN POLICY IS SEEN

Despite Official Denials, a Shift From Sales of Last Year Crop to 1931 Crop Is Noted.

Special to The New York Times.

WASHINGTON, Aug. 7.—The Federal Farm Board today rejected the offer of the German Government to purchase 600,000 bales of the board's surplus cotton holdings with an option on an additional 200,000 bales, but advanced an alternative proposal.

While the terms offered by Germany were unacceptable to the board and many of the conditions were regarded as "beyond the ability of the board to comply with," the board suggested that direct buying of the commodity would be made possible through the efforts of the Treasury Department to provide Germany with dollar credit here by expediting the payment of awards on certain German claims.

Germany's proposal, which was transmitted to the State Department yesterday by Ambassador Sackett and immediately referred to the Farm Board, provided that three years be allowed to pay for the 600,000 bales with interest at 4½ per cent. The price of the cotton was to be based on the monthly average prices of the New York Cotton Exchange or upon the monthly average prices of the Cotton Exchanges at New York, Bremen and Liverpool.

Deletion of Minimum Price.

In its reply to the State Department, the Farm Board pointed out that the original suggestion of Ambassador Sackett, five weeks ago, provided for a minimum price, but that since that time the price of cotton had fallen and the German Government had "necessarily" eliminated the minimum price feature from its offer.

Then the board stated that "an alternative" course had been offered by a "new possibility" in the effort now being made by the Treasury to expedite the payment to German nationals of amounts due them under awards made during the past few years by the Mixed Claims Commission on claims growing out of the World War. Awards have also been made by the same body to American claimants.

Text of the Farm Board's Reply.

The Federal Farm Board's answer to the proposal from the German Government was as follows:

The Farm Board has given careful consideration to the German offer to purchase cotton. The board is desirous of facilitating assistance to Germany and to the American cotton producer by expanding his immediate markets.

Many conditions of the German offer are beyond the ability of the board to comply with. It is, therefore, unable to accept the offer under the present proposed terms.

In addition to other difficulties, the original suggestion of Ambassador Sackett five weeks ago provided for a minimum price which would have contributed materially to stabilizing the price of cotton and would have made it possible for the board to offer participation to the holders of new crop cotton.

The fall in prices since that time, due in part to the situation in Central Europe, has necessarily led to the elimination by the German Government of that feature of its offer.

However, a new possibility has arisen in this whole question, which offers an alternative course. The purpose of the discussion has been, in effect, to assist the Germans in securing the foreign exchange necessary to provide immediate supplies.

The effort now being made by the Treasury Department to expedite payment to German nationals under awards of the arbiter of certain German claims, if successful, would place the German bank in possession of an even larger amount of dollar exchange than the value of this proposed transaction in cotton and would enable German business to make its purchases directly from the producers and the trade in the normal way.

Policy Declared Unchanged.

Officials of the Farm Board, as well as of the State Department, through which the decision of the board was communicated to the Bur-

"All the News That's Fit to Print"

The New York Times

LATE CITY EDITION

Weather: Fair, very cold today and tonight. Chance of snow tomorrow. Temp. range: today 24-14; Sunday 33-26. Full U.S. report on Page 30.

VOL. LXXX....No. 26,864. ****+ NEW YORK, THURSDAY, AUGUST 13, 1931. TWO CENTS In New York City | THREE CENTS Within 200 Miles | FOUR CENTS Elsewhere Except 7th and 8th Postal Zones

CUBAN REBELLION SPREADS AS THOUSANDS JOIN RANKS; 15 ARE KILLED IN SKIRMISH

WHOLE INTERIOR IN ARMS

Leaders Are Believed to Be Organizing for a Major Battle.

FORAYS MADE ON HAVANA

Wires Are Cut and Attemtps Are Made to Destroy Oil Wells and Water Reservoir.

REBEL 'PRESIDENT' IS HERE

Dr. D. M. Capote Chosen Before He Left Cuba—Local Junta Formed, Headed by Him.

Special Cable to THE NEW YORK TIMES.

HAVANA, Aug. 12.—Despite the strictest censorship, news filtering into Havana indicates that the entire interior of the island is a boiling pot, with thousands already under arms against the government.

With absolute lack of news from revolutionary headquarters and without definite knowledge of the location of the leaders it is impossible at present to predict either success or failure of the revolutionary movement. However, those who have studied the situation are of the opinion that the rebel forces will attempt to gain control first of Oriente, Camaguey and Santa Clara Provinces, where it is known that they have many sympathizers. Once in possession of these strategic points, the island could be divided into two sections, the lower end under the domination of the rebel forces, with comparative ease.

Fifteen Are Reported Killed.

Government military headquarters issued a report tonight that about 200 rebels commanded by Justo Luis Pozo were encountered by a detachment of Federals under command of Captain Aran late this afternoon in the vicinity of Ceja del Negro, Pinar del Rio Province, and routed after a brief skirmish.

Fourteen revolutionists were killed, twenty-six prisoners taken and a large amount of arms and ammunition captured, according to authorities. One Federal was killed.

The balance of the rebel band fled into the hills, an ideal place for guerrilla warfare on account of the mountain brush, deep ravines and generally rough country. It is said that this section of Pinar del Rio Province was a favorite spot of rebel bands in the days of the war of independence.

Official reports of many minor encounters of government troops with rebels both in Piñar del Rio and Santa Clara Provinces indicate that the revolutionists are still very active.

Reports are that former President Mario G. Menocal, Colonel Carlos Mendieta and Dr. Mendez Penate are heading the insurrection forces in the provinces of Oriente, Camaguey and Santa Clara, respectively, and that major operations will begin as soon as their organizations are complete.

Menocal Experienced as Rebel.

Whether or not this is the campaign plan of the rebels, it is pointed out that General Monocal not only has had experience in the field as a revolutionist, but during his administration as President put down a revolt of the Liberal party in 1917. It is said he personally directed every military movement of the Federal forces during the rising.

For this reason, it is generally believed, contrary to the government opinion that the rebellion will be put down within a few hours, the movement under way has the earmarks of a well-planned organized effort, having sufficient backing to give it at least a fair chance of victory.

General Menocal asserted in his proclamation calling on the people to take up arms, that he expects and has reason to believe that many of the armed forces of the nation will come over to his side. The government has branded this as mere propaganda, but it is known that the Opposition has many supporters throughout the island.

Any Leader Welcomed.

The administration of former President Menocal from 1913 to 1921 is not regarded as absolutely exemplary, although it is admitted by his worst enemies that he made splendid efforts during his first term. However, the dissatisfaction of the people

Continued on Page Four.

Manila Fears Colorum Plot Against Rich Natives Today

Wireless to THE NEW YORK TIMES.

MANILA, Aug. 12.—Outposts of the Philippine Constabulary were heavily reinforced today in preparation against a generally rumored uprising of Colorums scheduled for tomorrow, which is "Occupation Day."

This outbreak was originally scheduled for July 4 but was nipped by prompt action; hence the next American holiday, according to popular report, was chosen to signal the movement.

Reports from Nueva Ecija, which is the centre of the disturbance, say that the uprising is not aimed at Americans but at rich Filipinos, who are charged with oppressing the poor.

Officers of the constabulary admitted the gravity of the situation today but asserted that everything was in readiness to quell an uprising.

WHITE-COLLAR CLASS LIBERATED BY SOVIET

Engineers and Others Put on Same Footing With Workers, Stalin Ally Asserts.

ALL TOLD TO FORGET PAST

Y. E. Rudzutak, Explaining Speech of Red Leader, Says Classless Society Is at Hand.

By WALTER DURANTY.

Wireless to THE NEW YORK TIMES.

MOSCOW, Aug. 12.—Important light was thrown tonight on Joseph Stalin's recent speech by Y. E. Rudzutak, who ranks next to Premier Molotoff as M. Stalin's closest coadjutor and outdates M. Molotoff as a member of the Communist Political Bureau. M. Rudzutak addressed the Society of Technical Engineers "to explain the position of the higher technical personnel in carrying out the points raised by Stalin."

M. Rudzutak said the keynote of M. Stalin's speech as far as engineers were concerned was the statement, "The working class of the Union of Socialist Soviet Republics must create its own industrial and technical intelligentsia." The new and complicated process of nation-wide industrialization, he said, had made high technical knowledge and executive efficiency absolutely necessary.

Cites Need of Competent Men.

The foundations of Socialist industrialization, he said, were already laid and its form and scheme had taken shape, but all this was inadequate without persons competent to run it. The speaker briefly reviewed historical events—the civil war, when a large section of the technical intelligentsia did not believe in the victory of the proletariat; then the later period of class war and the inception of Socialist industrialization.

The great difficulties encountered at first, he said, prolonged the doubts of the intelligentsia, and the period was characterized by damaging and treasonable activities on the part of some engineers, "who still looked back at yesterday instead of facing the facts of today." Now that was past, he continued, and it was

Continued on Page Eleven.

FARM BOARD ASKS PLOWING IN COTTON TO AVERT 'DISASTER'

Wires Governors of 14 States to Abandon 4,000,000 Bales Now Growing.

WILL HOLD ITS SUPPLY

Also Will Urge Cooperatives Not to Sell Stocks Before July 31, 1932.

CROP FORECAST DEFENDED

Agricultural Department Declares Private Calculators Overestimated Boll Weevil Damage.

Special to The New York Times.

WASHINGTON, Aug. 12.—The Federal Farm Board tonight took another drastic step to stabilize cotton prices, when it wired the Governors of fourteen cotton-producing States and urged them to lead a movement for abandoning much of the cotton now growing in the fields and thus eliminate an excess production which threatened "direct disaster to cotton-producing States and indirect distress to the nation."

The board suggested that the Governors immediately "mobilize every interested and available agency" in their respective States, including farmers, bankers, merchants, landowners and all agricultural educational forces "to induce immediate plowing under of every third row of cotton now growing."

A "major operation of this kind rather than attempts at lesser measures is now needed," said the message.

The hope was expressed that by these means 4,000,000 bales of an estimated production of 15,584,000 might be destroyed, and in return for such cooperation offered a pledge not to sell the 1,300,000 bales owned by the Cotton Stabilization Corporation before July 31, 1932, and to urge cotton cooperatives under its dominance not to sell their stocks in that period.

Thus it was estimated that 3,000,000 bales carried over from last year by the corporation and cooperatives would be withheld from the market and a total of 7,000,000 bales thereby be taken out of the 1931 market.

Admits Defeat of Program.

If the action counseled is not taken, the board predicted in the telegram, signed by Chairman James C. Stone, the Fall may find America holding 24,500,000 bales of cotton, including this year's crop and the carryover from last year, of which only 13,000,000 could be absorbed in the whole market and 11,000,000, virtually a year's production, to be carried into 1932.

The Farm Board virtually admitted defeat of its stabilization program when it stated that its efforts "have been outweighed by continual excess production and continually increasing surplus."

The step was taken after a day filled with conferences of the Farm Board and after the Department of Agriculture had issued a detailed defense of its crop forecast totaling 1,500,000 bales more than private forecasts, which served on Monday to break the cotton market to the lowest level since 1905.

This forecast was taken as evidence of the helplessness of the Farm Board to overcome natural conditions, for bumper crop prospects were found, despite the fact that the Farm Board had been able, through its educational work, to obtain a 10 per cent reduction in cotton acreage planted this year.

Alexander Legge, former chairman of the Federal Farm Board, was

Continued on Page Thirteen.

Germans Find Greenland Ice 8,850 Ft. Deep; Prove Island Like Gigantic Ice-Filled Bowl

Wireless to THE NEW YORK TIMES.

WEST STATION, German Greenland Expedition, Aug. 12.—From the reflection from the bottom of the ice of the artificial earthquake waves produced by blasting, Dr. Sorge and his companions at the central station, at Lat. 72 degrees N., an altitude of 9,850 feet and a distance of 248 miles from both the east and west coasts, have measured the ice there to be 8,850 feet thick.

Twenty-five separate measurements were taken during twelve days of work and 396 pounds of explosives were used, the biggest blast taking 163 pounds.

In the marginal zone Dr. Brockamp and Dr. Herdemerten measured thicknesses of 2,296 to 2,952 feet at an altitude of 5,900 feet, fifty-eight and one-half miles from the west coast. Altogether there were fifty-four blastings on a north-south line.

Special Cable to THE NEW YORK TIMES.

BERLIN, Aug. 12.—Reports from the German Greenland expedition of its measurement of the inland ice by blasting fulfill predictions of the late Professor Alfred Wegener, leader of the expedition, who perished on the ice cap during the Winter, for the facts confirm his conception of Greenland as a bowl filled with ice.

Rimmed by mountains up to 6,560 feet and higher, the "bowl" inside drops down to 984 feet, with an enormous mass of ice overlying it from 3,280 to 9,840 feet in height.

According to Dr. Wegener's theory, this huge weight of ice, in the course of millions of years was lowered into the interior of Greenland, but if the ice cap, as now indicated by the observations of the expedition, is in process of melting, the land should gradually rise again from the semi-fluid interlayer on which, according to Dr. Wegener and other geologists, the earth crust floats.

The method of measuring the thickness of the ice by measuring the rate of artificially induced seismic waves was perfected at the Geophysical Institute at Goettingen. Such waves spread uniformly in all directions. Reaching the rock, they are reflected and from the time taken to return to the starting point, the thickness of the ice which they have passed through can be calculated.

CITIES PLAN RELIEF WITH NO FEDERAL AID

Report to Hoover Shows That 227 Communities Will Meet Winter Demands.

SPECIAL SESSION OPPOSED

A. F. of L. Council Asks Immediate Adoption of 5-Day Week to End Unemployment.

Special to The New York Times.

WASHINGTON, Aug. 12.—Administration leaders became more confident of being able to meet the unemployment situation this Winter without any form of Federal "dole" when President Hoover was told today by Allen T. Burns, executive director of the Association of Community Chests and Councils, that this organization will be able "wholly" to undertake the burden of relief.

The President was told by Mr. Burns that organizations had been completed in 227 cities, that their plans were going forward actively and that more communities were being heard from daily. The organizations in every city had reported "complete confidence" that, in cooperation with municipalities and other local agencies, they will be able to meet whatever situation develops in the coming months.

The White House announced the report from the director of Community Chests and Councils. It was considered as a major bulwark in the confidence of the President and his economic advisers that the relief problem will be met through community initiative.

President Hoover continued today his studies of the situation, determined to have a plan for relief ready before Congress meets in December. He has been told by some of his closest advisers that a plan must be ready to ward off a flood of socialistic legislation which might result in the enactment of a "dole," which the administration will exert every influence to prevent.

Hoover Confers With Gifford.

The President discussed the general business outlook, with its promise for employment or threat of more unemployment, at a breakfast conference this morning with Walter S. Gifford, president of the American Telephone & Telegraph Company. They talked over their coffee cups for a long time. It was the second such conference the President has had with Mr. Gifford within ten days.

The administration still holds tenaciously to its policy against wage reductions, despite the threat of even greater unemployment.

Rumblings of the activities of those who seek outright Federal relief have been heard. Senator Blaine of Wisconsin, insurgent Republican, has sent a communication to the President, insisting on a special session of Congress to enact relief legislation.

Representative Patman of Texas and other members of Congress also have urged the President to call a special session.

To prevent agitation of this kind and an attempt to enact "dole" legislation, President Hoover is formulating his plans, with the primary purpose of prompt relief for the unemployed and their families.

Rail Employment Rose in May.

Employment on Class I railroads increased in May to the highest point of any month this year and was only behind the total of last December.

According to figures given by the

Continued on Page Thirteen.

SCHOOL BUDGET RISES $5,953,963 FOR 1932

Board Sets Record Estimate at $146,338,848—Increase Laid Largely to Depression.

1,447 NEW TEACHERS ASKED

$30,000,000 for Buildings and Sites—All Expenditures in Year to Reach $212,000,000.

New York City's school budget for 1932, calling for an expenditure of $146,338,848.48, was adopted yesterday by the Board of Education in the form of a proposed departmental estimate subject to approval by the Board of Estimate. It represents an increase of $5,953,963.14 over the budget for this year, and is the largest budget ever adopted by the Board of Education.

Added to the estimated budget, debt-service expenditures and expenses incurred by other city departments for school purposes will bring the total cost of elementary and secondary education in this city for 1932 to approximately $212,000,000.

An increase of $2,938,189 is asked for the day high schools, where the register in the Fall of 1932 is expected to exceed the register of March, 1931, by about 20,000 pupils. The budget committee believes this increase is due largely to the economic depression, which has caused more young persons than usual to remain in school. To care for this increase, about 1,000 additional teaching positions have been provided.

New School Plans Approved.

At its semi-monthly meeting, the board also approved plans for the erection of Public School 242 at Flatlands Avenue and East 100th Street, Brooklyn, at an estimated cost of $303,800, and approved plans for an addition to Public School 79 at 147th Street and Fifteenth Drive, Whitestone, Queens, at an estimated cost of $346,000.

A contract for the general construction of Public School 129, College Point, Queens, was awarded to E. Waters & Co. for $873,973.

The total estimate for 1932 includes a general school fund of $125,769,684.81, a special school fund of $20,444,662.67, as well as $24,501 for retardation survey and $100,000 for the Bureau of Child Guidance.

The city will be asked to contribute $98,683,987.06 to the total budget and the State and Federal Governments will be asked for $47,654,861.42. The city figure is about $4,200,000 more than in 1931 and the amount expected to be derived from State and Federal funds is about $1,700,000 more than this year's figure.

The board also estimated that about $30,000,000 would be spent during the year for acquisition of school sites and enlargement and construction of new schools. This amount, however, is not included in the departmental budget estimates.

In addition to the increase in teaching positions in the high schools, sixty-seven additional positions are provided for the day industrial high schools. These will provide for the full organization of the new Industrial High School for Girls in Brooklyn this Fall and for partial organization of the new Samuel Gompers Industrial High School for Boys, to be opened in the Bronx in the Fall of 1932.

The board also repeated a request for a Summer evening high school, to cost about $22,500.

"The raising of the compulsory ed-

Continued on Page Two.

DIAMOND GETS LIMIT, 4 YEARS, $11,000 FINE; TROY TRIAL SEPT. 15

Gangster Is Released in $15,000 Bail for Appeal on Dry Law Conviction.

TWO YEARS, $5,000 FOR AIDE

Quattrocchi's Counsel Pleads for Clemency—Prosecutor May Seek His Help.

NEW PROSECUTION URGED

Court Points to Trial Evidence of Jones Act Violations and Advises Further Inquiry.

The maximum sentence of four years' imprisonment and a fine of $11,000 was imposed in Federal court yesterday on Jack (Legs) Diamond by Judge Richard J. Hopkins of Kansas, who presided at the five-day trial of the gangster last week on charges of conspiracy and violation of the prohibition law.

Paul Quattrocchi, owner of the Hollywood Inn in Cairo, who was Diamond's lieutenant in the beer and liquor trade in Greene County, was sentenced to two years' imprisonment and fined $5,000. He was convicted on the conspiracy count, but was acquitted on the other. Both men announced that they would appeal and were released in bail.

Diamond took it hard. So did his wife. Every muscle of his thin body was taut as the moment for sentence drew near. Mrs. Diamond leaned forward. The gangster's face was livid and the jaw muscles flexed with nervous tension. His hair, neatly brushed when he entered the court room, became disordered as he passed his hands through it nervously.

Court Room Was Filled.

Court opened at 10 A. M. A crowd was in the corridor, but the doors were closed when all the seats were filled. No one was allowed to stand. Diamond, dressed in gray, the powder of a fresh shave heightening the whiteness of his drawn face, sat down at the counsel table. Quattrochi came in a few minutes later.

The erstwhile associates did not speak to one another. Quattrocchi took a seat a few feet behind his former chief, then shifted to the other side of the table. He had accused Diamond last Sunday, after the trial, of having "double-banked" him. They did not look at one another during the proceedings, nor did they meet after sentence was pronounced.

Counsel for Diamond argued that the second count of the indictment—the prohibition violation, having to do with operation of a 1,500-gallon alcohol still in Greene County—did not properly allege a crime. Judge Hopkins, however, held that the indictment was sufficient.

Herman S. Schwartzman, counsel for Quattrocchi, asked for a new trial for his client.

"At this time," he said, "defendant Paul Quattrocchi moves for a new trial on the ground that the District Attorney had knowledge that witnesses were being tampered with during the trial, to the prejudice of the defendant Paul Quattrocchi; that he failed to ask for the withdrawal of a juror and to have a mistrial declared."

"I had no knowledge that the tampering with witnesses had anything to do with Paul Quattrocchi," retorted Arthur H. Schwartz, Assistant United States Attorney. "I refuse to state on whom the burden of guilt was to be placed and can state only

Continued on Page Two.

CURRY ON STAND TOMORROW; SEABURY SAYS HE CAN SHOW DOYLE ASKED TAMMANY AID

LEADER AGREES TO TESTIFY

Seabury Asserts He Will Prove That Chief Was Approached on Stay.

ASSAILS FALK IN COURT

Calling of Public Hearing of Committee Ends Clash Over New Doyle Writ.

SPECIAL SESSION PLEA UP

Request to Go to Roosevelt After Meeting to Question Veterinarian on Bribes.

Proof that Dr. William F. Doyle turned to John F. Curry, leader of Tammany Hall, while seeking a justice of the Appellate Division to grant him a stay of a thirty-day contempt sentence will be offered to the Hofstadter legislative committee at a public hearing tomorrow, Samuel Seabury, counsel, said yesterday.

Mr. Curry will be a witness at the meeting which was called yesterday by Samuel Hofstadter, chairman, to permit Dr. Doyle to purge himself of the contempt charge and also formally to request Governor Roosevelt to call a special legislative session to enact a measure granting the committee power to confer immunity on witnesses.

The Tammany leader will be questioned about the telephone call which went from his apartment in the Park Lane Hotel to Lake Placid, where Justice Henry L. Sherman has his Summer home, on the evening before Justice Sherman signed a stay for Doyle which was presented to him by Ilo Orleans, partner of Samuel Falk, Doyle's counsel.

Seabury Makes Charge in Court.

The statement that Doyle or his counsel or agents, had been in touch with Mr. Curry before the telephone call went out from the Park Lane apartment was made by Mr. Seabury in the course of an argument before Supreme Court Justice John F. Carew.

The argument was on a show-cause order by which Mr. Falk sought to compel the committee to assemble forthwith and permit Dr. Doyle to make the explanation which would remove the contempt sentence. Holding that the motion of Mr. Falk should be denied, Mr. Seabury explained that everything possible had been done to arrange a meeting of the committee tomorrow.

He declared, however, that at the same meeting at which Doyle was to be heard, he wanted the presence of a "material witness" whom he had been unable to locate, and he stated that the witness was Mr. Curry.

"This waiting for Mr. Curry is none of my affair," interjected Mr. Falk.

"I have asked the counsel for Dr. Doyle to get in touch with Mr. Curry and tell him his presence is desired," Mr. Seabury said.

When Mr. Falk demurred again, Mr. Seabury continued: "They got in touch with him before and they can get in touch with him again. I say that some one connected with Doyle did get in touch with Curry."

Justice Carew, holding over Mr. Seabury's objection that he had the power to order the legislative committee to assemble, adjourned further argument until Friday, after which Mr. Seabury said to newspaper men:

"I am prepared to prove that Doyle got in touch with Curry while he was seeking a stay. I want to get the whole story of the telephone calls from Curry. I am sure he will be willing to tell about it."

Telegram Sent to Curry.

While Mr. Hofstadter was spending the afternoon getting in touch with Republican members of the committee who are out of town, Mr. Seabury located Mr. Curry at the United States Hotel in Saratoga. There he sent him his telegram:

"Joint legislative committee desires your presence as a witness on Friday Aug. 14, at 10 A. M., in the County Court House. Can I count on your presence at that time? Will telephone you at 7:30 this evening unless I hear from you in the meantime. If you prefer to have a subpoena served upon you please indicate when and where service should be made."

Meanwhile, Mr. Hofstadter told Senator John J. Dunnigan, spokesman for the Democratic minority on

Seabury Confident of Making Doyle Testify on Split Fees

The belief that Dr. William F. Doyle will be eventually forced to tell with whom he split fees received while practicing before the Board of Standards and Appeals, even if he succeeds in purging himself of contempt tomorrow, was held yesterday by Samuel Seabury, counsel to the Hofstadter legislative committee.

If the contempt sentence is lifted tomorrow, Doyle will be placed under subpoena to appear before the committee at a future date. Then, should the special session of the Legislature pass the immunity enactment, Mr. Seabury indicated, he will again seek to force the veterinarian to disclose the disposition of part of his fees.

WALKER IS HONORED AS FRIEND IN BERLIN

City and Reich Extend Greeting at Luncheon Given by the Schurz Association.

NO PLACE TO REST, HE SAYS

Finds City Has No "Depression of Hospitality"—Will Broadcast Overseas Tonight.

Special Cable to THE NEW YORK TIMES.

BERLIN, Aug. 12.—Mayor Walker of New York was a luncheon guest of the Carl Schurz Association today and easily carried off the speaking honors.

Chief Mayor Heinrich Sahm in a speech of welcome dwelt on the adverse changes which had come over Berlin and the Reich since Mr. Walker's previous visit four years ago. He explained that if he spoke in a manner not customary on such occasions it was not only because of the seriousness of the time but because he was speaking to an avowed friend of Germany, a man whose popularity had extended across the ocean to Berlin.

"Friendship is most appreciated in a time of need," he added, "and Germany so treasures the friendship of America, from which Germany could learn nothing more valuable than confidence in the future."

Anton Erkelenz, president of the Carl Schurz Association dwelt on the historical and fruitful inter-relations of the two countries, the debt of Germany to America for inspiration before the war and guidance and help in rebuilding and rationalizing her industry since the war. This debt had been deepened, he added, by the boon of the holiday year, for which he gave deep thanks to President Hoover and the services of Ambassador Sackett.

Then Mayor Walker stood up, a lithe figure but the physical antithesis of Chief Mayor Sahm, who is 7 feet 2 inches in height and is called "Long Henry."

No "Depression of Hospitality."

His speech was a mingling of humor and seriousness.

He expressed his thanks for the way he had been received in Berlin and his gratification, as an American citizen, in the praise bestowed on President Hoover. "But if I could have had my own way," he said, referring to the last election, "Mr.

Continued on Page Twelve.

Chile to Cease Deposits Against Foreign Debts, Completing Moratorium as Crisis Grows Worse

By The Associated Press.

SANTIAGO, Chile, Aug. 12.—The Chilean Cabinet recommended to Congress the suspension of service on the foreign debt, making the partial moratorium declared last month complete.

It was held that because of the shortage of funds this interest on foreign debts, now deposited locally in accordance with the original moratorium declaration and amounting to about $13,000,000 for the remainder of the year, should be discontinued.

Payment of interest on the internal debt and on short-term notes was suggested, however.

Government expenditures for the last five months totaled $52,440,000, the Cabinet announced, but estimated receipts were only $33,000,000. Expenditures included $17,040,000 for debt service.

The announcement warned that rigid economy would be necessary, and that the 1932 budget must not exceed $84,000,000.

Chile decided on July 15 to declare a moratorium on the foreign debt, planning in the meantime to deposit the amounts due with local banks in Chilean currency instead of gold, holding that it could not spare gold because of the economic crisis.

This prevented the depletion of the Central Bank's reserves and was intended to keep away the danger of a collapse of Chilean currency, but the local deposits were to be considered evidence of the government's good faith and intent to pay foreign creditors when it was able.

Since then the country has been beset by political troubles, ending with the fall of President Carlos Ibañez and the formation of a new government, and the economic crisis has grown worse instead of better.

Cornwallis's Surrender Will Be in Pageant; Yorktown Board Ends Controversy on Scene

Special to The New York Times.

RICHMOND, Va., Aug. 12.—The scene depicting the surrender of the British Army under Cornwallis to General Washington at Yorktown Oct. 19, 1781, will be included in the pageants to be presented during the Yorktown sesquicentennial celebration Oct. 16-19, the Congressional commission in charge of the celebration decided today, the 150th anniversary of Lord Cornwallis's occupation and fortification of Yorktown, the setting of the final act of the Revolutionary War.

The announcement of the decision by S. Otis Bland, secretary of the commission, ended four weeks of controversy, during which attacks and defenses of the propriety of presenting the surrender scene came from many parts of the country.

When proposals that the commission delete the surrender scene from the pageants became known, their origin was reported in some quarters to have been in a State Department suggestion that the scene would offend England and in the army's traditional policy of avoiding participation in scenes hostile to countries with which America is at peace.

The commission was accused of sidestepping the issue two weeks ago when it declared final action would be postponed until an opinion was obtained from trustees of the Yorktown Sesquicentennial Association, a citizens' cooperating agency.

The executive committee of the association met Saturday and refused to give an opinion, throwing full responsibilities for the pageants on the commission, although Dr. W. A. R. Goodwin of Williamsburg, president of the association, had led the fight for deletion. It was his view that the pageants should depict the triumph of ideals of liberty and justice and democratic institutions, rather than of physical force.

Representative Bloom of New York was a leading advocate of staging the surrender. He ridiculed the idea that it would offend British sensibilities.

"All the News That's Fit to Print"

The New York Times

LATE CITY EDITION

Weather: Fair, very cold today and tonight. Chance of snow tomorrow. Temp. range: today 24-14; Sunday 33-26. Full U.S. report on Page 30.

VOL. LXXXI....No. 27,020. ***** NEW YORK, SATURDAY, JANUARY 16, 1932. TWO CENTS In New York City | THREE CENTS Within 200 Miles | FOUR CENTS Elsewhere Except 7th and 8th Postal Zones

CITY POLICE WARNED OF REDUCTION IN PAY AS ECONOMY MOVE

Commanders, Reading Letter From Head of Benevolent Society, Suggest Voluntary Action.

19,000 MEN ARE AFFECTED

Some Contend Acceptance Would Be Less Onerous Than Legislation by City.

OTHERS ARE INDIGNANT

Mass Meeting to Be Held to Decide on Action—Rise Followed a Referendum in 1929.

A warning has been spread generally through the Police Department that its members of all ranks may have to accept salary reductions as a result of the city's financial difficulties, and the rank and file of the men have been advised that it may be wise for them to accept the cuts voluntarily rather than to wait for legislative action, it was disclosed last night.

Discussion of some such possibility has been going on in the back rooms of police station houses throughout the city recently. Added vigor was given the rumors in talks by the commanding officers of the various precincts and special squads to their subordinates on Thursday.

At that time, in some precincts, at least, the commanding officers advised the men that a pay reduction was inevitable and that they would be better off if they took it voluntarily than if they waited until it was forced on them. It was pointed out that a voluntary cut might be less in extent and shorter in duration than one imposed by legislation.

These warnings were accompanied by the reading of a letter sent out by Patrolman Joseph P. Moran, president of the Patrolmen's Benevolent Association, which hinted at the possibility of a general cut and pledged the efforts of the association to "every honorable means to protect the 1932 salaries."

Letter to Commanders.

The text of the letter follows:

"The Patrolmen's Benevolent Association feels that you should know that the New York State Conference of Mayors has adopted the following:

" 'Whereas the State and municipalities are confronted with serious deficits in government funds due to the abnormal but necessary increases in expenditures for home and work relief and by decreases in revenues derived from taxes and other sources, and

" 'Whereas, by reason of lower costs of living and the increased purchasing power of the dollar today, it appears that statutory salary increases are not only unjustified but reasonably may be disregarded without inflicting a hardship on the recipient; now therefore be it

" 'Resolved, That, to meet the present emergency and at the same time not impair the efficiency of public service, we approve the suggestion and recommend immediate action by the State Legislature that a three-year moratorium be declared on all salary increases made mandatory by State and local laws.'

"Whether we are to forfeit now a part of the pay provided in the budget will depend upon the measure of cooperation given by policemen of all ranks to save what the city and the people have been quite willing to give for difficult and perilous police duty in the metropolis. Our delegates have been informed of the situation with a view of cooperating with all other ranks and using every honorable means to protect the 1932 salaries.

"Fraternally,
"JOSEPH P. MORAN."

Mass Meeting to Be Held.

A mass meeting to discuss the subject will be held within a few days under the auspices of the Patrolmen's Benevolent Association. At that time it is expected that definite schedules covering suggested voluntary pay cuts will be advanced for the consideration of the men.

In the innumerable discussions which have been raging throughout the department since the Moran letter brought the talk out into the open, voluntary acceptance of a temporary reduction of 10 per cent has been most frequently debated.

This figure was said by its proponents to be less than would probably be slashed from the police payrolls if action were taken independently by the city authorities, and at the same time was held up as large enough to effect a substantial economy and thus win popular favor for the men.

At the present time first-grade patrolmen receive annual salaries of $3,000. Sergeants are paid $3,500,

Continued on Page Five.

2,000,000 Pilgrims Kiss Feet Of St. Francis Xavier in India

By The Associated Press.

GOA, Portuguese India, Jan. 15.—The embalmed body of St. Francis Xavier, who died in 1552, was replaced in its silver sarcophagus today after having been exposed for forty days, during which 2,000,000 pilgrims from all over the world filed past it and kissed the feet in the Church of Bom Jesus.

Thousands of miracles were reported to have occurred during the forty days. The church officials will publish a list of them after verification.

BANKS COOL TO PLAN OFFERED BY WALKER

Financiers Silent After Parley, but Demand for More Drastic Steps Is Indicated.

MORE SLASHES IN OUTLAYS

Park Extension Fund Reduced $22,500,000, but Return to a Liberal Policy Is Pledged.

In order to facilitate the borrowing of sufficient funds to enable the city to meet current expenses and maturing obligations between now and May 1, when tax collections begin, Mayor Walker submitted yesterday to spokesmen for the city's leading banks his program of "the most rigid economy compatible with the necessities of the city," together with a summary of the steps already taken toward its fulfilment.

The report to the banking group was made behind closed doors in the office of Controller Charles W. Berry, who, with the Mayor and Charles F. Kerrigan, assistant to the Mayor, presented the city's viewpoint. The banking group, headed by Thomas W. Lamont of J. P. Morgan & Co., included Arthur M. Anderson and George Whitney, two other Morgan partners; John McHugh, chairman of the Chase National Bank's executive committee; Winthrop W. Aldrich, also of the Chase National Bank, and Charles E. Mitchell, chairman of the board of the National City Bank.

First of Series of Talks.

The only statement regarding the conference was made by Mr. Kerrigan, speaking for Mayor Walker. He indicated that the conference was the first of a series to be held on the loan desired by the city, but declined to say what progress, if any, was made toward ironing out the city's financial troubles.

"We had a pleasant talk," he said, as he emerged from the one-hour meeting. "Mayor Walker reviewed the retrenchment measures taken to date and we agreed to resume our discussions within a day or two."

Mayor Walker declined to discuss the conference, as did Controller Berry. Mr. Lamont, who headed the smiling group of bankers who emerged from the conference room, dismissed questioners with a wave of his hand.

"We respectfully refer you to our hosts, the Mayor and the Controller," he said.

It was indicated from other sources that the bankers, while conceding that the icty had taken some steps in the direction of economy, were far from satisfied that much more could not be done along the line of "prudent" administration of the city's affairs. In financial circles confidence was voiced that the city would be aided in meeting maturing short-term obligations, but it was predicted that the necessary funds would either be doled out as required or that steps would be taken to renew or extend some of the maturities, probably at an interest rate of 6 per cent.

Mayor Walker, it is understood,

Continued on Page Four.

DIVERSION OF FUNDS DEFENDED BY FARLEY; 'NOW WILL TAKE ALL'

Sheriff Tells Committee He Made Grave Error in Giving Up Any Accruals.

CLERK ADMITS "ERASURES"

Testifies He Thought His Books Would Be Neater—Lays Taking of Interest to 'Depression.'

CULKIN FACES GRAND JURY

Crain Also Orders Action Against City Marriage Clerk—Hastings Appeal Is Argued.

Claiming a right to the interest on official funds, Sheriff Thomas M. Farley told the Hofstadter Committee yesterday that he would go right on taking it, making certain in the future that he got it all instead of a mere fraction of the total.

His attitude seemed to bespeak irritation with himself for not getting it all before, and gratitude to Samuel Seabury, chief counsel to the investigating committee, for calling the matter to his attention. Although he admitted he was not entitled to a penny of the principal of funds entrusted to his care, he declared he would go to the Court of Appeals to defend his title to the interest upon them.

While the Sheriff was making his somewhat surprising declaration, District Attorney Crain was directing Harold W. Hastings, one of his assistants, to put the transactions of former Sheriff Charles W. Culkin before a grand jury next week. Mr. Seabury has charged that Culkin committed embezzlement by converting more than $25,000 in interest on official funds to his personal use.

McCormick Also Faces Charges.

Mr. Hastings also was instructed by the District Attorney to seek grand jury action in the case of Deputy City Clerk J. J. McCormick, who, in attempting to explain bank deposits of $168,000, estimated that he received about $16,000 a year in gratuities from couples he had married in the course of his official duties.

The Appellate Division meanwhile granted permission to Mr. Seabury to carry his fight to put Dr. William F. Doyle in jail again to the Court of Appeals on his contention that the former veterinarian in denying that he split fees with public officials committed perjury, but did not purge himself of contempt.

The Appellate Division in Brooklyn, before which the committee's counsel appeared at noon, reserved decision on his plea that it sweep aside all legal technicalities and permit him to force State Senator John A. Hastings, a friend of Mayor Walker, to answer a subpoena. Supreme Court Justice Byrne of Brooklyn has ruled already that Senator Hastings must do so, but the Brooklyn Senator blocked a move of the committee to cite him for contempt by appealing to the higher court and obtaining a temporary injunction.

Crowd Storms Farley Hearing.

Returning after his argument before the Brooklyn court to conduct the scheduled public hearing, Mr. Seabury found a line of from 1,000 to 1,500 men and women in the rotunda of the County Court House, waiting for the day's proceedings to begin. He was greeted with cheers and handclapping.

Before Farley took the witness stand to defend a practice which Mr. Seabury contends was grand larceny,

Continued on Page Four.

Nebulae Speeding 15,000 Miles a Second Into Space Discovered by Mt. Wilson

Special to The New York Times.

WASHINGTON, Jan. 15.—Discovery of two spiral nebulae or "island universes" in the constellation of the Gemini, which apparently are moving away from the earth at the rate of about 15,000 miles a second, was announced today through the Carnegie Institution.

These objects, presumably vast star systems comparable to the great Milky Way system itself, represent the farthest reach up to now of human observation into outer space. Their speed of recession is about 3,000 miles a second faster than that of the most distant nebulae previously photographed.

This discovery, which was made by Dr. Milton Humason of the Mount Wilson Observatory in California, is regarded as adding further confirmation to one of the strangest phenomena ever observed in the heavens. The explanation of this is in dispute among astronomers, and is largely responsible for the presence of Dr. Albert Einstein and Dr. Wilhelm de Sitter of Holland in Pasadena this Winter.

The speed and direction of a luminous object in the heavens can be calculated from the shifting of lines in its spectrum. If these lines shift toward the red end of the spectrum it means that the object is moving away from the earth. If they shift toward the blue end, it means that the object is moving toward the earth. The speed is determined from the extent of the shift.

Three years ago Dr. Humason and his colleague, Dr. Edwin Hubble, made the astonishing discovery which proved that the 'shift" was a reliable criterion, that the "island universes" were moving outward at enormous speeds and that the speeds were in ratio to their distance away. This was found to hold good for all those nebulae whose distance could be calculated by independent methods, such as observations of variable stars which could be detected on photographs of the "island universes."

Last Summer the observations were carried about four times farther into outer space by the development of a method of calculating the distance of nebulae by their luminosity. This gave a check on those great star clusters which are so far removed that there was no hope of detecting in them any variables or clusters of variables.

The distances are so vast that the results are given in parsecs, a parsec

Continued on Page Three.

ROSENWALD WILLED CHARITY $11,000,000

He Continued His Philanthropies by Bequest to His Family Charitable Corporation.

5 CHILDREN SHARE REST

Estate Above $20,000,000—W. F. Lessing and Mrs. Marion Stern Are Executors.

Special to The New York Times.

CHICAGO, Jan. 15.—The philanthropy of Julius Rosenwald is to continue under the terms of his will, which was drawn in the last week of his life.

The will, filed today in the Probate Court, leaves the bulk of the estate to Mr. Rosenwald's five children and charges them with carrying on his philanthropies in an $11,000,000 gift to the Rosenwald Family Association, a charitable corporation organized shortly before his death.

The will was admitted to probate by Judge Henry Horner. In an application for letters testamentary the value of the estate is estimated to be "in excess of $20,000,000," with real estate holdings of $250,000. The exact amount has not been determined, though close associates have estimated Mr. Rosenwald's holdings in Sears, Roebuck & Co. at 1,000,000 shares, which have a market value of $33,000,000. He was known to have other holdings.

Announcement of the creation of the family corporation was made on Christmas Eve, thirteen days after the will was drawn. Mr. Rosenwald provided that a part of the $11,000,000 be used for the Museum of Science and Industry, which he founded. Executors are allowed two years to turn over the fund.

Five Children Share Equally.

The remainder of the estate is to be divided equally among the five children—Lessing Rosenwald, Mrs. Adele R. Levy of New York, Mrs. Edith R. Stern of New Orleans, Mrs. Marian R. Stern of Highland Park and William Rosenwald of Elkins Park, Pa. The will states that other provisions have been made for Mrs. Rosenwald.

The will was drawn by Leonard M. Reiser and Hugh Sonnenschein of the law firm Sonnenschein, Berkson, Lautmann, Levinson & Morse. Mr. Reiser, Mr. Sonnenschein and Dr. Herbert Pollack, who attended Mr. Rosenwald, were the witnesses. Mr. Reiser and the law firm of Lederer, Livingston, Kahn & Adler filed the will. The document consisted of three pages.

The executors are Mrs. Marion R. Stern and Lessing Rosenwald. Mrs. Stern and Mr. Reiser appeared before the court. Judge Horner granted a private hearing in chambers. After Mrs. Stern said her father had died Jan. 6 and told how the will was drawn at his orders it was admitted to probate.

The executors are to give bonds for $40,000,000. The widow and the children filed their consent to probate and expressed satisfaction with the terms.

The family association is distinct from the Julius Rosenwald Fund, created by gifts of the philanthropist. The latter fund at one time had $30,000,000. It is conducted by a separate body of trustees.

The text of the will is as follows:

I, Julius Rosenwald, residing and domiciled in the city of Chicago, county of Cook and State of Illinois, being of sound and disposing mind and memory, do hereby make, ordain, publish and declare

Continued on Page Eight.

JAPAN REPLIES TO US, PLEDGING 'OPEN DOOR'

Tokyo Glad It Can Rely on Our "Support" for Its Efforts on Peace Treaties.

CHINESE DRIVE BACK FOES

Hold Tahushan, Rail Centre in Manchuria—Enemy Retreats at Many Points.

By HUGH BYAS.

Special Cable to THE NEW YORK TIMES.

TOKYO, Saturday, Jan. 16.—Japan's reply to the note of the United States invoking the Nine-Power Treaty in the Manchurian conflict was handed to Ambassador W. Cameron Forbes at 11 o'clock this morning.

The document will find a place in the State Department's files as a graceful example of a communication written because a formal note requires a formal answer and not because there is anything new to say. It repeats that Japan regards the Open Door as a cardinal feature of Far Eastern politics, but regrets that its effectiveness has been seriously diminished by China's condition.

Japan "takes note" of Secretary Stimson's intimation that the United States does not recognize any matters brought about by means contrary to the Kellogg Pact and answers as follows:

"It might be the subject of an academic doubt whether, in a given case, the impropriety of the means necessarily and always voids the ends secured, but as Japan has no intention of adopting improper means that question does not practically arise."

The note adds that treaties must be applied with due regard to actual conditions and the present state of China is not what the Washington treaty contemplated.

Mr. Stimson's suggestion that the last vestige of China's administrative authority has disappeared in Manchuria is answered by the statement that the local administration collapsed because Chang Hsiao-liang's officials fled, and their replacement was a necessary act of the local population.

With an eye to the future, the note continues:

"The Japanese Government cannot believe the Chinese people are incapable of self-determination."

Text of the Note.

TOKYO, Saturday, Jan. 16 (AP).—The Japanese note, addressed to Mr. Forbes follows:

I have the honor to acknowledge receipt of your Excellency's note of Jan. 8, which has had the most careful attention of this government.

The Government of Japan is well aware that the Government of the United States could always be relied upon to do everything in their power to support Japan's efforts to secure full and complete fulfillment in every detail of the treaties of Washington and the Kellogg treaty for the outlawry of war.

They are glad to receive this additional assurance of the fact.

Open Door Policy Upheld.

As regards the question which your Excellency specifically mentions of the policy of the so-called Open Door, the Japanese Government, as has so often been stated, regard that policy as a cardinal feature of the politics of the Far East and only regret that its effectiveness is so seriously diminished by the unsettled conditions which prevail throughout China.

In so far as they can secure it, the

Continued on Page Six.

Persian Vizier Regally Feted in Moscow; Hippodrome Races Recall Splendor of Old

Wireless to THE NEW YORK TIMES.

MOSCOW, Jan. 15.—It was like a scene from an old storybook at the Moscow Hippodrome today when the Russians entertained their Oriental guest, Timoor Tash, Minister of Court or Grand Vizier to the Persian potentate, Shah Riza Khan, a tough soldier who rose from non-commissioned rank to sit on the Peacock Throne.

"A visit of courtesy and friendship" they call it, when Timoor Tash, the brains of the Persian State, comes to Soviet Moscow, whose watchword is "Asia for the Asiatics." Not long ago the Soviet Foreign Commissar, Maxim Litvinoff, made a similar visit to the Turkish dictator, Mustapha Kemal Pasha, and soon the Turkish Premier, Ismet Pasha, is to come here.

It was dark when the racing began this afternoon at 5:30, and there were electric lights around the track. It was bitter cold with a small, bright crescent moon.

The Persian visitors and their Russian hosts, with foreign diplomats, sat in a glass-sided box in the grandstand, open in front. Beside Timoor Tash, there was the Cossack General Budenny, like a Timoor Tash's sovereign, once a sergeant in a royal army and today a famous general and probably the most popular man in Russia.

Below sat a crowd of several thousand, seemingly indifferent to the cold. And on the wide track trotters skimmed like swallows with their wheeled sulkies, their roughed shoes biting into the hard snow and their drivers with fur caps and incongruous gay silk shirts over heavy coats. The horses were hooded and blanketed until they began the preliminary canter for the flat racing or the trial breather for trotters.

It was all so strange and unfamiliar that the immense round white fur hats of two Turkoman horsemen among the crowd seemed not at all grotesque. They and a group of Caucasians with pinched waists and flaring coattails fitted harmoniously into the picture.

DR. BUTLER ASSAILS 'STUPID ISOLATION' IN PLEA FOR LEAGUE

Counter-Offensive Against Foes of Adherence Is Begun by League of Nations Union.

HOLDS 'WAR IS STILL ON'

Columbia's President Urges the Public to Demand End of Debt and Reparation Problems.

WICKERSHAM LAUDS COURT

Compares It to Our Supreme Tribunal—Davis and Baker Messages Read at Philadelphia.

The text of Dr. Nicholas Murray Butler's address is on Page 8.

From a Staff Correspondent.
Special to The New York Times.

PHILADELPHIA, Jan. 15.—A counter offensive against the drive of "isolationists" in the Senate to keep the United States out of world affairs, combined with a demand for a more active policy and wider cooperation by this country in world reconstruction, was begun today by the League of Nations Association in session here.

Participating in the movement were George Wickersham, president of the association; Dr. Nicholas Murray Butler, president of Columbia University; Newton D. Baker, John W. Davis and other prominent advocates of American adherence to the League of Nations.

Dr. Butler and Mr. Wickersham were among the speakers. The contributions of Mr. Baker and Mr. Davis were in the form of letters read at the annual dinner of the association tonight. Mrs. Woodrow Wilson, guest of honor at the dinner, received a warm ovation.

The League advocates received encouragement in a joint message from Viscount Cecil and Lord Grey as officials of the League of Nations Union.

A message was read from Ignace Paderewski, pianist and former Premier of Poland, reaffirming his "faith in Woodrow Wilson's immortal ideals" and in the future of the League.

The British statesmen wrote that "1932 may well prove to be a turning point in League history," and that upon the success of the forthcoming disarmament conference in Geneva will depend not only the future of the League "but the ultimate salvation of civilization as we know it."

Speakers emphasized this point, together with the need of a more active policy by the United States in strengthening the machinery for world peace, the removal of tariff and trade barriers, the solution of the war debt and reparation problems and the promotion of substantial disarmament.

Hoover Blamed for Delay on Court.

The intention attributed recently to President Hoover to lay aside consideration of foreign affairs pending solution of important domestic problems was deplored. Manley O. Hudson, Bemis Professor of International Law in the Harvard Law School, demanded that such a policy be amended on the question of ratification of the World Court protocol, to the end that America may at once become a member of that tribunal.

The Geneva disarmament conference and the Manchurian situation were the subjects of special discussions.

Both Mr. Wickersham and Dr.

Continued on Page Eight.

H. P. Fletcher Asks Congressional Backing For Dawes Post, but Hoover Turns Deaf Ear

Special to The New York Times.

WASHINGTON, Jan. 15.—Henry P. Fletcher, former Ambassador to Mexico, who has been conspicuously discussed as the successor to General Dawes as Ambassador to Great Britain, will not be appointed to that post, according to friends who have urged his selection on the President.

Political leaders expect that if the post, which Mr. Fletcher much desired, is refused him, he will become active as a candidate to succeed Senator Davis of Pennsylvania whose term expires in March, 1933.

Support of the Vare forces is said to have been assured Mr. Fletcher should he enter the campaign, as well as that of the Association Against the Prohibition Amendment. He would run as a wet.

Senator Reed of Pennsylvania urged the appointment of Mr. Fletcher early this week but found that the President had virtually decided on another person. The understanding is that the appointee will be outside the diplomatic service and that he will be a prominent Western business man. Mr. Fletcher had sent the following telegram to Pennsylvania members of the House.

"I would sincerely appreciate your willingness to unite with other Republican members of our Congressional delegation earnestly urging upon the President my appointment to succeed General Dawes as Ambassador to London. Please consult or notify Dr. Temple if you are willing to join. Pennsylvania has not had the London post since before the Civil War."

Representative Temple, ranking Republican member of the Foreign Relations Committee, found that all his colleagues favored Mr. Fletcher. He was prepared to send a letter to the President to that effect but held it back when told of the President's decision.

Smith Says Decision on Race Won't Be Made in Rail Depot

By The Associated Press.

BOSTON, Jan. 15.—Alfred E. Smith, New York Democratic leader, left Boston for New York today after having participated last night in the opening of the Democratic drive for campaign funds at a dinner which was attended by 2,000 New England Democrats.

Mr. Smith visited this morning Frank J. Donahue, chairman of the Massachusetts Democratic Committee, and Mrs. Daniel Lynch of Albany, N. Y., both of whom are ill in hospitals here.

As the former New York Governor departed he was asked the question, "Have you decided to be a Presidential candidate, Governor?" Mr. Smith answered, "When that decision is made it will not be in a railroad depot."

RECONSTRUCTION BILL PASSED BY THE HOUSE

$2,000,000,000 Finance Measure Is Adopted by a Vote of 335 to 55.

DEMOCRATS USE CLOTURE

Opposition of Progressive Group, Led by La Guardia, Futile—Measure Goes to Conference.

Special to The New York Times.

WASHINGTON, Jan. 15.—The reconstruction finance corporation measure, providing for emergency financing to the extent of $2,000,000,000 for banking institutions, building and loan societies, railroads and agriculture and regarded as the backbone of the administration's program for economic relief, was passed in the House late today by a vote of 335 to 55.

Thus the first portion of the President's program took a long stride forward, as a measure of generally similar tenor was passed by the Senate Monday night, and the few differences between the two bills are expected to be adjusted in conference within the next few days. Confidence was expressed tonight that the final bill will become law by the end of next week.

The House also agreed to confer with the Senate on the bill providing for additional capital for Federal land banks. The House measure was adopted before the Christmas holidays, but the Senate raised the amount from $100,000,000 to $125,000,000.

Plans were announced today by Senator Watson for early action on the depositors' relief and home building loan bills.

Quick Agreement Expected.

Quick adjustment of the differences between the House and Senate finance reconstruction measures was forecast when it was found that the two were substantially alike. The only disagreement is expected to be over the provision of the House bill to allow notes and exchanges secured by the Reconstruction Finance Corporation to be rediscounted at Federal Reserve banks, which the Senate voted against. The Senate also attached a "rider" to its bill, providing that an additional $50,000,000 be lent through the Secretary of Agriculture to farmers for crop production. Repeated attempts to include this provision in the House bill were met with points of order, sustained by the chairman.

The House measure provides, however, that $50,000,000 of the original $500,000,000 capital shall be allocated for loans to agricultural and live stock credit organizations.

Party lines were obliterated in the House vote. The only group that maintained its identity was the small

Continued on Page Two.

CENTRING ON RELIEF, PRESIDENT REFUSES TO TALK CANDIDACY

Ban on Politics at White House Follows Enthusiasm of Party Chiefs Calling Earlier in Day.

BURKE REVEALS DECISION

After a Second Visit to Hoover He Obeys New Order, but Says Primary Drive Will Go On.

OKLAHOMA IS PROMISED

Hurley Forecasts Pledged Delegation—Mrs. Carter Tells the President Kansas Is for Him.

Special to The New York Times.

WASHINGTON, Jan. 15.—Although President Hoover today put a ban on discussion of his candidacy for renomination with his callers, his friends went ahead with plans to elect Hoover delegates to the Republican National Convention and to enter him as a candidate in States having preferential primaries, wherever this course seemed to be advisable.

Cognizance of the statement by Postmaster General Walter F. Brown on Thursday that the President would stand for renomination was taken at the White House early in the day by Theodore G. Joslin, secretary to the President.

"The President is giving his undivided thought and attention to the problems concerning the country and to the relief program that is before Congress," Mr. Joslin said. "He just refuses to see any one on personal politics or to discuss personal politics."

Soon after Mr. Joslin issued this statement James Francis Burke, counsel of the Republican National Committee, appeared at the executive offices. Mr. Burke, talking freely with newspaper men, said that he had come to Washington to discuss the steps to be taken to bring about the President's renomination and to assist in laying the groundwork for the campaign.

"Pledging" of Oklahomans.

Mr. Burke then went into a conference with Mr. Brown and Colonel Patrick J. Hurley, the Secretary of War, who are regarded as two of the President's most trusted political advisers. This conference lasted nearly an hour, and at its end Mr. Hurley said that the Oklahoma delegation to the national convention would be "pledged to Mr. Hoover."

Colonel Hurley explained that Oklahoma did not have a direct primary but would elect its twenty-five delegates at a convention. He added that it was certain that they would be for Hoover.

After seeing the President later in the day, Mr. Burke slightly modified his earlier utterances. Apparently reading from a memorandum, he said:

"I had a very pleasant chat with President Hoover on many current matters, but he has put a ban upon political talks of every kind. He is avoiding all partisan party discussions and devoting himself entirely to his reconstruction program and leading the country back to prosperity."

Mr. Burke explained that he had to catch a train and was in great haste. He paused at the door of the executive offices and added:

"All this, however, is not preventing his friends from being active throughout the country."

Kansas Report Pleased Hoover.

The President's decision not to discuss politics with his callers seemed to be somewhat disarranged by the visit of Mrs. Jonathan B. Carter, vice chairman of the Kansas Republican State Committee, whose appointment was arranged before Mr. Joslin had let it be known that the President was not discussing personal politics with his callers.

Mrs. Carter said she had reported to the President on conditions in her State. Asked if she had discussed politics, she said:

"I certainly assured him that his Kansas friends were going to stand by him."

Mrs. Carter added that she had assured the President that prospects were bright for him in Kansas. She was asked if Mr. Hoover seemed pleased.

"He certainly was," she replied.

The White House announcement that the President had placed a taboo on discussion of his candidacy by those who visited him was interpreted for an hour or two in some quarters as indicating just a possibility that the President might decide not to run. The President's friends, however, were emphatic in disclaiming that the White House attempt to "soft-pedal" further candidacy talk at this time had any such meaning.

The President's friends, as stated by Mr. Burke and confirmed by other supporters of the President, will continue their plan to organize

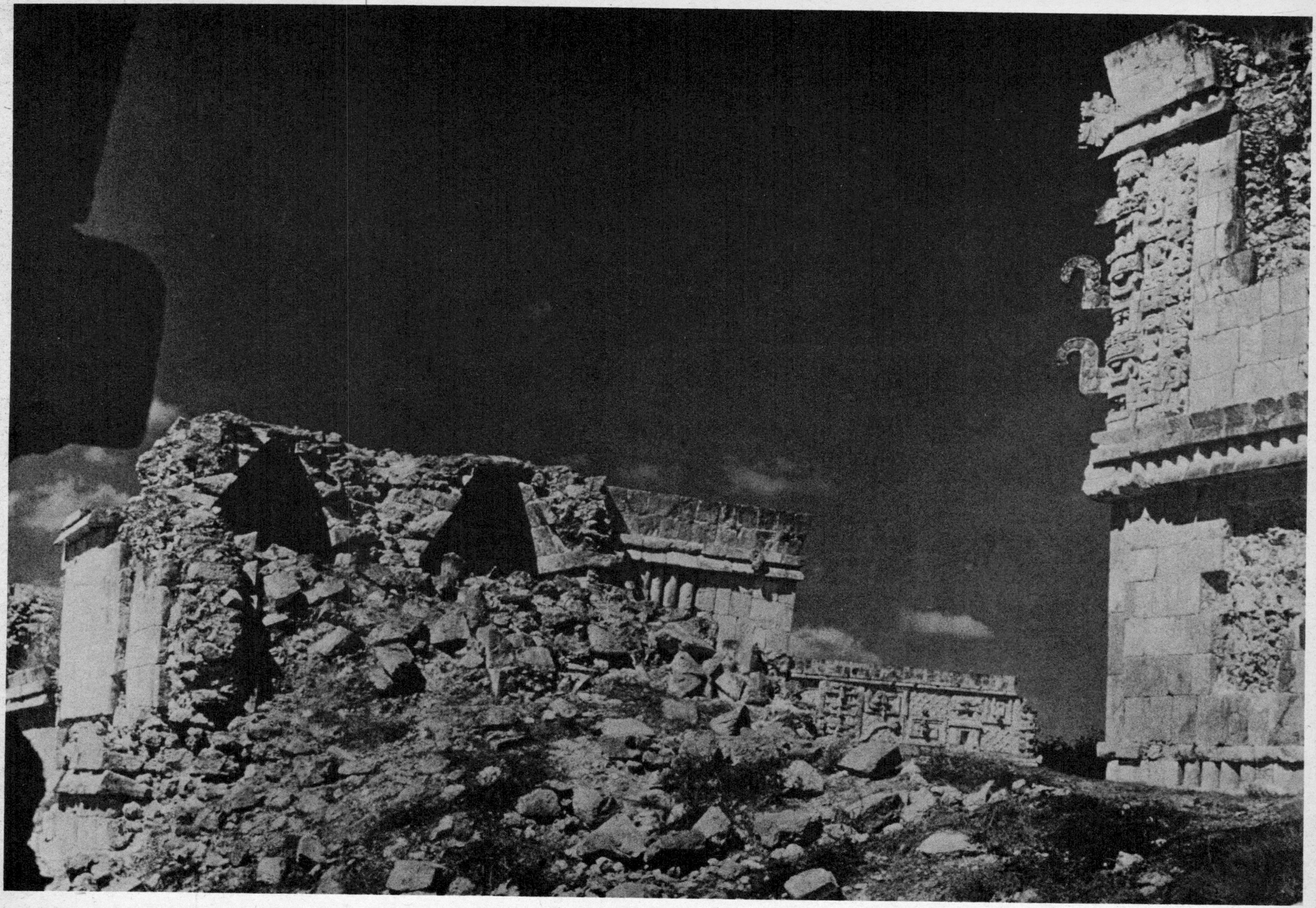

Ruins of Mayan tombs similar to those in which great treasures of gems and ornaments were discovered.

"All the News That's Fit to Print."

The New York Times.

LATE CITY EDITION

THE WEATHER—Clear today, colder tonight; tomorrow fair and colder.
Temperatures Yesterday—Max., 47; min., 38.
U. S. Weather Forecast—See next to last page

Copyright, 1932, by The New York Times Company.

VOL. LXXXI....No. 27,022. ****+ NEW YORK, MONDAY, JANUARY 18, 1932. TWO CENTS In New York City | THREE CENTS Within 200 Miles | FOUR CENTS Elsewhere Except 7th and 8th Postal Zones

CHINA WILL DEMAND SANCTIONS BY LEAGUE AGAINST JAPANESE

Nanking Also Will Ask Parley of Nine-Power Pact Signatories on Manchuria.

BREAK WITH TOKYO SEEN

Foreign Minister Chen Said to Favor Severance of Diplomatic Relations.

CHINESE FORCE WIPED OUT

500 Irregulars in Manchuria Are "Almost Entirely Annihilated" by Japanese Troops.

Wireless to THE NEW YORK TIMES.

SHANGHAI, Jan. 17.—With the Nanking Government functioning and its financial difficulties temporarily overcome, China has decided to take more definite measures against Japan.

Dr. Fu Ping-chang, Vice Minister of Foreign Affairs, announced that China would invoke Article XVI of the League covenant when the League Council reassembles Jan. 25, and also would ask the signatories of the Nine-Power treaty to convene and consider the Sino-Japanese dispute.

Consideration also will be given by the Chinese to the possible severing diplomatic relations with Japan, but although some members of the government strongly favor it no decision has yet been reached. Dr. Fu asserted severance of diplomatic relations appeared inevitable, but that the government so far was unable to reach complete agreement on the point.

Foreign Minister Eugene Chen was represented as believing severance of relations was the only effective way of ending the Sino-Japanese deadlock, but one section of the government opposed this action owing to the grave consequences.

The prospects of the "Big Three" returning to Nanking are growing brighter.

General Chiang Kai-shek, who at present is at Hangchow, will receive Nanking leaders after his long silence. Wang Ching-wei, Left-Wing leader, who had been ill in a hospital here for many weeks, has left for Hangchow to see General Chiang Kai-shek, and important results are expected from the conference to be held today.

[Hu Han-min, now at Canton, is the other member of the so-called big three. He is strongly opposed to co-operation with General Chiang.]

Toll in Manchuria Still High.

Special Cable to THE NEW YORK TIMES.

MUKDEN, Jan. 17.—Japanese suppressive measures continue throughout Manchuria. The week's toll in lives is more than fifty Japanese and 300 Chinese, labeled "bandits."

The Japanese, under cover of the interim Chinese Government, are controlling the northern section of the Peiping-Mukden Railway and are directly controlling 80 per cent of Manchuria's total railway mileage both as regards operation and financing. In spite of repeated public assurances of the political and territorial integrity and sovereignty of Manchuria, the Japanese continue to hold actual though unseen control of governmental agencies.

On this head the general Chinese bitterness has not decreased, but, in the opinion of foreign business men, Manchuria as a whole will become a better place to transact profitable business in the future, provided the Japanese maintain the open door.

The apparent Japanese intention to establish an actually, though not technically, independent Manchuria would not greatly change the situation, as Manchuria since the Chinese Revolution was only nominally under the Nanking Government and has had separate revenues, currency and government.

Japanese railway guards surprised 500 Chinese irregulars twenty-five miles south of Mukden, near the Mukden-Dairen Railway, and engaged them in a forty-minute battle. The details of the fight are not known. A bulletin said the Chinese were "practically annihilated, with no Japanese casualties."

South Manchuria Railway guards today surprised 300 bandits besieging the village of Tiehling, north of this city, and killed forty. One Japanese was wounded. The Japanese column, seeking to avenge the heavy Japanese casualties at Chinhsi last week, continues on its way toward the Jehol border. These troops are combing the district for Chinese troops.

Town Near Kirin Bombed.

LONDON, Jan. 17 (AP).—An Exchange Telegraph dispatch from Har-

Continued on Page Ten.

Liner Caronia to Be Broken Up, Ending Long Atlantic Career

Special Cable to THE NEW YORK TIMES.

LONDON, Jan. 17.—The Cunarder Caronia is being sold to a shipbreaker, it was learned from Plymouth tonight, and her long and useful career on the Atlantic is over.

Like her sister ship, the Carmania, the 20,000-ton Caronia has reached an age at which even the most famous liners must give way to newcomers. Both were built in 1905. The Carmania is already in the wreckers' hands, and it is expected that the Caronia will soon join her.

If the two liners had been continued in the Atlantic service it would have necessitated a complete overhauling, which in the present situation of the Cunard Line is not regarded as worth while.

4 EUROPEAN NATIONS ON BRINK OF DEFAULT

$600,000,000 American Money Invested in Austria, Bulgaria, Greece and Yugoslavia.

GRADUAL STEPS EXPECTED

"Standstill" Accords Believed Likely, Putting Off Admission of Inability to Repay.

By JOHN MacCORMAC.

Wireless to THE NEW YORK TIMES.

VIENNA, Jan. 17.—Several of Hungary's neighbors are likely to follow her example, declaring their partial or complete inability to meet their foreign obligations, including $600,000,000 in American money invested in Central Europe outside Germany, it is indicated by Premier Mouchanoff's hint a few days ago that Bulgaria would have to declare a moratorium unless she received early foreign aid. The events of the next few weeks at Geneva will go far to determine how many defaults will take place and when.

The countries over which, judging from known facts or the statements of their public men, the dark shadow of such a necessity is brooding, appear to be Austria, Bulgaria, Yugoslavia and Greece.

Austria's vitality is still drained by the Creditanstalt, and her savings banks have been seriously embarrassed by hoarding of schillings. Bulgaria has been successively crippled by peace treaties, earthquakes and argicultural depression. Greece was hard hit by the fall of the English pound. Yugoslavia's troubles have been accentuated by her annual budgetary loss of $8,000,000 through the suspension of German reparation payments.

Frank Admissions Unlikely.

Few Eastern European countries are likely to follow Germany's example with her war debts and boldly declare their inability to pay their foreign debts. The admission of this inability will be made step by step, disguised where possible under "standstill agreements," which are only an admission by foreign creditors that they can expect nothing at present but promises of payment in the future.

Austria took the first step with the Creditanstalt short and intermediate term debts and the second step last week with reduction of the amortization rate on her $20,000,000 of other bank debts from 15 to 5 per cent quarterly.

In Hungary, although the transfer moratorium applies only to two-thirds of her foreign obligations, it is a serious question whether the service on any but League of Nations loans and treasury obligations can be met in anything but pengoes.

Yugoslavia met a run on its banks by restricting the withdrawal of deposits and has been able to keep the

Continued on Page Eleven.

LONGER DEBT HOLIDAY NOW AIM OF EUROPE IN LAUSANNE PARLEY

Paris Expects Nations Will Ask Another Year and Give Like Relief to Germany.

ORIGINAL PLAN IS UPSET

Britain Regarded as Backing France in Stand Against Final Reparations Action.

BERLIN FORESEES A DELAY

But Bruening Will Demand Settlement of Issue by Midsummer or Early Autumn.

By P. J. PHILIP.

Special Cable to THE NEW YORK TIMES.

PARIS, Jan. 17.—The Lausanne reparations conference is likely, it is believed here, to see an exact reversal of what happened last June when President Hoover made a demand on all Germany's reparations creditors that they grant her a moratorium for one year. In return he undertook to obtain from Congress a similar moratorium for America's debtors.

At Lausanne, as the situation is seen here, America's debtors will demand from the President another year's extension of that moratorium for themselves, and in return will undertake to give a similar extention to Germany.

That will give a further eighteen months for full consideration of the reparations problem and the position of Germany. It will in reality postpone until Dec. 15, 1933, any further payment by France or England of the annuities due under their debt settlements with the United States.

Likely to Appeal to Hoover.

At Lausanne there will be no American representative present to receive this proposal. Apparently the assembled debtors will address themselves to the author of the present moratorium. In a very marked way the President's concern for the situation in Germany, which caused him last June to take direct and energetic action, will therefore be made to react in Washington. The Lausanne conference, at which no American will be present, will be in reality a conference to demand the adjournment of all debt payments, in which the United States has the largest single stake.

When it was first planned, it was not expected the Lausanne conference would take quite this aspect. But it is not yet completely certain what will be done. Nothing final will be decided until after the British Cabinet formulates its plans this week. But it is increasingly evident in Paris that unless the British Government takes a very different attitude from that which is expected and one, too, which must be opposed to that of France, no other course is open.

The present French Government, backed not only by the French press but by a very large majority of opinion in the country, can be expected absolutely to refuse any clean-slate proposition for Germany unless there is a definite undertaking that the slate is going to be cleaned all round.

It is not just Premier Laval, War Minister Tardieu and Finance Minister Flandin who are of that opinion. Edouard Herriot, Radical-Socialist leader, has voiced it. Almost all Radicals endorse it, and there are very few Deputies, except perhaps the Socialists, who would dare go before their constituents next April with the proposal that reparations should be wiped out unless they feel more sure than they do today that

Continued on Page Eleven.

Gems and Gold Ornaments in Mexican Tomb Likened in Richness to Tut-ankh-Amen's

Wireless to THE NEW YORK TIMES.

MEXICO CITY, Jan. 17.—Recent archaeological discoveries at Monte Alban, in the State of Oaxaca, are hailed as unequaled in this hemisphere and probably rivals anything yet unearthed even in Egypt, and they appear to be increasingly marvelous as reports from the axcavators continue to reach this capital.

Alfonso Caso, the head of the expedition working at Monte Alban under the direction of the Ministry of Education, says that alongside a number of tombs uncovered in the last few years there has been found another with an entrance nearly 40 meters across, covered with priceless treasures in diamonds, jade, turquoise, gold and silver ornaments.

He also asserts that the tomb's walls, apart from hieroglyphics at present undecipherable, are decorated with such magnificence in jewelry that the total value of his discovery is incalculable.

The treasures, as they are extracted by a small army of laborers working fourteen hours a day, are being stored at the Oaxaca branch of the Bank of Mexico and when the task of cataloguing them is completed they will be exhibited publicly. So far the general public has been refused access to the precincts of the ruins in order to avert possible robberies.

Señor Caso believes his discoveries date from around the sixteenth century, and that when burying their chiefs the Indians held great fear that their resting place might be violated. He believes also that after the burial of most of those whose remains have now been found the Indians closed the tomb so tightly they believed it could not be opened, and buried others from a hole in the roof, which was sealed by an immense boulder, hieroglyphically carved.

Señor Caso considers his recent find much more valuable than the treasures unearthed under the patronage of the Carnegie Institute at Chichen Itza in the State of Yucatan.

One of the skulls found at Monte Alban is decorated with a mosaic of turquoises, with a stone knife in the nose. The knife is believed to represent a war trophy of some invincible Mixtec captain. Some of the

Continued on Page Ten.

ROOSEVELT MEN CITE SMITH'S INACTIVITY

No Signs Are Seen of Preparations to Enter Primary Fights Against the Governor.

ALASKANS FOR ROOSEVELT

South Dakota State Convention Today Also Is Slated to Endorse Him.

Special to The New York Times.

WASHINGTON, Jan. 17.—Despite reports of a growing estrangement between Governor Roosevelt and former Governor Smith of New York Mr. Roosevelt's supporters here have seen no indication that Mr. Smith intends to enter a primary fight in any State for delegates to the Democratic National Convention.

This was learned here tonight after the Roosevelt group here had received assurances that the first delegates to the convention to be elected, the six from Alaska, would be pledged to New York's Governor. The Alaska Democrats will hold their convention Friday. J. J. Connors, national committeeman from the Territory, has been in touch with the Roosevelt leaders and has assured them that they can count on the support of the delegation.

The next delegates to be elected will be the sixteen from Washington on Feb. 6. The Washington State committee endorsed Mr. Roosevelt, and the purpose in calling an early convention was to instruct the delegates to vote for him under the unit rule.

South Dakota to Act Today.

The South Dakota Democrats at their State Convention tomorrow are expected to endorse Roosevelt, and to vote to put him in the primaries in that State as the organization candidate. The primaries will be held on May 3, and on or before March 3 Mr. Roosevelt will have to file written consent and approval of the delegates selected to run on his ticket.

The North Dakota State Committee took similar action last week, but probably will meet opposition from Governor William H. Murray of Oklahoma, who is likely to be a candidate in the primaries, as he is in South Dakota. With the Democratic organizations in these two States for Roosevelt, the New Yorker's supporters believe that he can win both contests, even though he is from the East and Governor Murray is a Middle Westerner.

There is a strong feeling here that the Democratic nomination for President will be decided by the results in the fourteen States electing delegates by direct primaries, not putting in this category New York, which elects the district delegates by direct primaries and the delegates-at-large at a State convention.

From the point of view of the Roosevelt supporters, the time has been reached when Mr. Smith, if he is to make any primary contest for delegates, must make some move in preparation, of which they would learn.

Eyes Are on Pennsylvania.

One of the States in which Mr. Smith's open candidacy might be hurtful to Governor Roosevelt is Pennsylvania, with seventy-six delegates, which will have a preferential primary on April 26. Governor Roosevelt, who was in Philadelphia yesterday for the wedding of his son, was accompanied by friends who talked with some of the Pennsylvania Democratic leaders, including Joseph F. Guffey of Pittsburgh, who

Continued on Page Seven.

AUTO LIABILITY RATE INCREASED IN STATE

Underwriters, Citing Greater Hazards, Also Announce Rise in Damage Insurance.

SOME REDUCTIONS HERE

Operators Involved in Accidents Must Pay From 10 to 50% Advance in Premiums.

Citing increased motive power, greater use of automobiles in adverse weather, highway congestion and increased "family" use of cars, the National Bureau of Casualty and Surety Underwriters announced yesterday increased rates for automobile public liability and property damage insurance in New York State. George S. Van Schaick, Superintendent of Insurance, has approved the changes.

While the rates are raised generally up-State, in the New York suburban area and in Richmond, they are reduced in the four other boroughs of New York City. The reductions are from $103 to $102 in the case of public liability and from $30 to $27 in the case of property damage rates.

In granting this approval, Mr. Van Schaick required the companies to pledge observance of rules on commissions and expenses approved by the National Convention of Insurance Commissioners.

An important modification in the rating of private passenger car business involves the elimination of the present so-called merit rating plan and the substitution of a demerit rating plan. Formerly a discount of 10 per cent was allowed to those who had owned and operated a car for not less than two years and had not been involved in an accident involving bodily injury or damage to the property of another during a period of twenty-one months ending three months prior to the effective date of the policy. Such discount was not allowed if the assured had his operator's license suspended or revoked for having been convicted of driving while intoxicated, reckless driving or leaving the scene of an accident without stopping to report.

Increase Following Accidents.

Under the new plan persons involved in accidents in the same period, where the cost of such accidents exceed $50, or who are convicted of driving while intoxicated, failing to stop and make a report following an accident, reckless driving or commiting a felony involving the use of an automobile, are charged increases in premiums of 10, 25 or 50 per cent, according to the category in which they fall. In this manner automobile owners whose operation of vehicles constitutes them a substandard class are required to pay proportionately higher premiums.

The statement says the underwriting loss of stock casualty companies on automobile public liability insurance increased from a national total of $4,000,000 in 1929 to $14,000,000 in 1930. The National Bureau of Casualty and Surety Underwriters attributes this increase not to more unsafe driving, but to the following causes:

"There has been a substantial increase in the horse-power of practically all models of automobiles during recent years. This has been particularly true with regard to the lower-priced vehicles, and it is found that the experience statistics underlying the new insurance rates indicates that the largest increase in rates was justified for this class.

"There has been within recent years a material increase in the number of miles of highways, together with an even more substantial in-

Continued on Page Three.

Hoover Picks Grew as Envoy to Japan; 'Career Man' Will Succeed Forbes Soon

Special to The New York Times.

WASHINGTON, Jan. 17.—President Hoover has decided to appoint Joseph C. Grew, Ambassador to Turkey, to be Ambassador to Japan, succeeding W. Cameron Forbes, who will soon return to the United States. Ambassador Grew is a "career man" in the diplomatic service and is regarded as eminently fitted for the important post at Tokio in the present difficult situation.

Jefferson Caffery, Minister to Colombia, is mentioned for appointment as Ambassador to Turkey.

Former Senator Lawrence C. Phipps of Colorado has been urged upon the President for appointment as Ambassador to Great Britain.

Some Senators are confident that Mr. Phipps has an excellent chance for this appointment. One of the President's confidants said tonight that the post would go to a Western man who is not connected with the diplomatic service.

TOKYO, Monday Jan. 18 (AP).—Ambassador Forbes notified the Japanese Foreign Office today that Joseph C. Grew probably would succeed him. It was unofficially understood that Mr. Grew would be acceptable to the Japanese Government. He is held friendly to Japan.

Joseph C. Grew has had a distinguished diplomatic career. He entered the service in 1904 as a clerk in the consulate at Cairo.

After holding minor posts he went to Berlin two years before the World War as secretary of the embassy. Later he held a post in the State Department.

He attended the pre-Armistice negotiations at Versailles as secretary to the American delegation. In January, 1919, he was named Minister to Denmark, and two years later was transferred to Switzerland. In 1927 he became Ambassador to Turkey.

STATE REPUBLICANS FACE BIG PROBLEM ON DRY LAW STAND

Leaders Are in Quandary Between Hoover's Position and That of Party Wets.

DRY BOLTERS STILL ACTIVE

Fear Is Expressed That They Might Put Out a Candidate and Repeat 1930 Tactics.

NO HELP IN REFERENDUM

If National Party Submitted the Question, Extreme Drys Would Oppose the Mandate.

By W. A. WARN.

Special to The New York Times.

ALBANY, Jan. 17.—While prohibition appears too delicate a subject with the Republicans to have been discussed at any of their conferences held last month, it is causing more worry in party circles than any other. The Republican leaders are well aware that the time will soon be at hand when the question of what stand the party shall take on the wet and dry issue in the State election this year will force itself upon them.

The question which is harassing them and will call for a solution in advance of the Spring convention is whether they should yield to insistent pressure from national party leaders in Washington and by a sharp change of front place the organization in this State in line with the anti-repeal stand of President Hoover, whose renomination is viewed as a foregone conclusion, or remain in line with the 1930 program in order to hold the wet Republicans in New York City and the counties up-State with large cities, such as Erie, Monroe, Onondaga, Oneida, Albany and Rensselaer, depending upon the candidacy of Mr. Hoover to bring the 1930 bolters back into the party fold.

It is not expected that a decision will be reached at the conference to be held here Tuesday by members of the Executive Committee of the Republican State Committee, although on this occasion a majority of the "best minds" within the party, including the Republican National Committeeman, Charles D. Hilles, and W. Kingsland Macy, State Chairman, will be seated at the council table. The Executive Committee is pretty evenly divided between wets and drys.

Drys Plan No New Measure.

The meeting will be held for the purpose of perfecting a legislative party program for the session now in progress at the Capitol. As was pointed out by one of the leaders, it does not appear probable that prohibition will come before the lawmaking body this year, at least not as a major legislative topic, although half a dozen wet measures already are pending, with more undoubtedly to come.

So far there is no indication that the extreme drys, represented by the Anti-Saloon League and the Woman's Christian Temperance Union, are at all eager to exploit what dry sentiment there may be in the Senate and Assembly by seeking support for a State prohibition enforcement bill, and there is even doubt whether, under the circumstances, they would be able to find in either branch wholehearted sponsorship for such a measure.

It may be regarded as the irony of fate that the Legislature, controlled by the Republicans in both its branches, should be so set against dry legislation, since the extreme

Continued on Page Five.

World Spent $36,000,000,000 In Ten Years on New Housing

Special to The New York Times.

WASHINGTON, Jan. 17.—A total of $36,000,000,000 was expended throughout the world by governments and private interests in the construction of homes and living quarters from 1920 to 1930, according to estimates of Charles F. Stephenson of the Foreign Construction Division of the Department of Commerce. He based the figures on reports sent from abroad and statistics of construction in the United States.

"Although a large part of these expenditures cover what might be called extraordinary housing construction, to distinguish it from normal housing requirements," he said, "there is still urgent need for more homes to house satisfactorily the millions of people now residing in unsuitable quarters."

REMOVAL OF PERRY SOUGHT BY SEABURY

He Writes City Court Justices That Chief Clerk Evaded and Falsified on Bank Accounts.

INQUIRY SHOW-DOWN NEAR

Future at Stake, Committee Meets in Albany Tonight to Map Fight for Extension.

Samuel Seabury has initiated ouster proceedings against another Tammany officeholder, it became known yesterday as the Hofstadter Committee prepared to ask the Legislature for longer life and additional funds for its investigation of New York City Government.

This time Mr. Seabury's charges are aimed at Harry C. Perry, chief clerk of the City Court and until recently the Tammany leader of the Second Assembly District. They are contained in a letter from Mr. Seabury to Chief Justice Edward B. La Fetra.

The letter, written by Mr. Seabury as a private citizen rather than as chief counsel to the joint legislative investigating committee, which will meet in executive session in Albany tonight to plan its future course, was sent to Justice LaFetra Saturday together with a transcript of the evidence affecting Perry.

Pointing out that the testimony "establishes the continuous existence of professional gambling" at Perry's political club, Mr. Seabury accused the erstwhile district leader with evasion and falsification regarding the sources of his large bank accounts. He charged too that Perry had "commercialized" his control of city funds to strengthen his own credit at the bank and expressed surprise that no action had yet been taken "although upward of three months have elapsed since the testimony was taken."

To Map Fight for Inquiry.

Meanwhile it became known that Senator Samuel Hofstadter, chairman of the investigating committee, has summoned its members to meet in executive session to be held before the meeting of the Legislature in Albany tonight.

Senator Hofstadter would not discuss the purpose of the meeting but from other sources it was learned that the future of the investigation is at stake. Authorization will be sought and undoubtedly voted by the Republican majority, it was said, for a request to both houses of the Legislature for more time and more money to finish the committee's work.

The joint resolution which created the committee carried with it an appropriation of $500,000 and set Feb. 1, 1932, as the date for the filing of its report. The approach of the time for reporting to the Legislature finds the committee only about half way through its task with most of its

Continued on Page Two.

Police to Teach Safety to Motor Fleet Heads; Course, Starting Feb. 1, Aims to Cut Mishaps

With the primary purpose of preventing accidents, the Police Department will begin on Feb. 1 a course on street safety and problems of traffic regulation for traffic managers, safety directors, superintendents and supervisors of fleets of motor vehicles operating in New York, it was made known yesterday by Police Commissioner Mulrooney.

The course will be given in the traffic and safety school of the Police Academy, 400 Broome Street, from 10:30 A. M. to 1 P. M., and will be under the general supervision of Deputy Chief Inspector John J. O'Connell, dean of the academy. Invitations to enroll will be sent out today to representatives of concerns using large fleets of commercial vehicles. Taxicab company officials will be asked to attend a later course.

Commissioner Mulrooney explained that police activities in safety work had been extended in many directions. Monthly reports have been made to the city schools, which have served as a basis of safety educational work among children.

While these increased activities have greatly helped reduce accidents, Mr. Mulrooney said it was felt that further improvement would result from the new course. He hoped, he said, that the instruction given the executives responsible for the safe operation of large fleets would be the basis of intensive campaigns among their drivers.

Experts will present all phases of traffic problems and general discussions will follow. Applicants will be assigned to the sessions according to the order in which acceptances are received. Applications are required to be presented by Jan. 21. In addition to Commissioner Mulrooney, speakers will be First Deputy Commissioner Philip D. Hoyt and Thomas W. Rochester, police chief engineer.

BANKERS WITHHOLD ASSURANCE OF LOAN ON WALKER PROGRAM

Additional Economies Demanded in Three-Hour Conference at C. E. Mitchell's Home.

PROGRESS AS TO $32,500,000

Financiers Likely to Advance Money Needed Wednesday—New Parley Set for Today.

FARE ISSUE TO FORE AGAIN

Bankers Dwell on Need to Make City Revenue Projects Self-sustaining and Subways Are Chief of These.

The most comprehensive retrenchment program Mayor Walker has been able to formulate to date was submitted yesterday to spokesmen for the city's leading banking houses and failed to elicit from them any definite assurance that they would lend all or any part of of the $150,000,000 needed to meet short-term obligations maturing between now and May 1.

There were indications, however, that the banking groups would see their way clear to handle the city's $32,500,000 short-term obligation maturing on Wednesday, or even the total of about $80,000,000 maturing at various dates this month. Their attitude on these maturities may be crystallized at another conference tentatively set for today.

As to municipal short-term obligations which mature in February, March and April, the attitude of the bankers will probably not be settled until after several more meetings with city officials. What that attitude will be, it was said, will depend largely upon what additional economies, retrenchments and new revenue sources the city will be prepared to lay before them.

Mayor Walker submitted his enlarged economy program at a three-hour conference held in the home of Charles E. Mitchell, chairman of the board of the National City Bank, one of the eight houses with which the loan negotiations are being carried on. With the Mayor were Charles F. Kerrigan, his assistant; John H. Delaney, chairman of the Board of Transportation, and Controller Charles W. Berry. Besides Mr. Mitchell, the banking group included Thomas W. Lamont and Arthur M. Anderson of J. P. Morgan & Co., and representatives of the Chase National Bank.

Participants Are Reticent.

None of those who attended the conference would give a hint of what was discussed.

"Tomorrow is another day," was Mayor Walker's only comment, as he referred all questions to the banking group.

"There is nothing to be said," was the way Mr. Lamont put it. "Ask the Mayor."

From Mr. Mitchell came word, in response to a written query, that "the issue is not settled." Later, when asked if this meant the existence of a deadlock between city officials and the bankers, he sent a note declaring that "there is no deadlock."

As the situation stood at the close of the conference Mayor Walker and his associates are to present to the bankers some time before Wednesday their views on additional economy measures discussed at the meeting. Although none of those at the conference would talk about the subject, it is understood that these were concerned with the matter of making the city's revenue-producing enterprises as nearly as possible self-sustaining.

The conference was by far the longest of the three which Mayor Walker has attended thus far. It dealt, it is understood, not only with the proposed program of retrenchment and economy but also with the general fiscal policies of the city. The five-cent-fare issue, although cloaked in the language of financial diplomacy, was necessarily discussed because of its outstanding importance in any analysis of methods by which municipal revenues might be substantially increased without undue delay.

Delaney at Conference.

The presence of Mr. Delaney at the conference was interpreted as an indication that the rapid transit issue, including the fare question and the possible revision of the city's short-term bond method of financing new subway construction, was under consideration. In this connection it was recalled that the bankers, in a statement issued a week ago, stressed their belief that the city "must make every effort, wherever possible, to transform existing enterprises which today are not self-supporting into ones that carry themselves and thus

Continued on Page Two.

"All the News That's Fit to Print"

The New York Times

LATE CITY EDITION

Weather: Fair, very cold today and tonight. Chance of snow tomorrow. Temp. range: today 24-14; Sunday 33-26. Full U.S. report on Page 30.

VOL. LXXXI....No. 27,231. Entered as Second-Class Matter, Postoffice, New York, N. Y. NEW YORK, SUNDAY, AUGUST 14, 1932. **** Including Rotogravure Picture, Magazine and Book Sections. TEN CENTS

WIFE AND PAUL BLOCK LIKELY TO TESTIFY IN MAYOR'S BEHALF

Mrs. Walker and Publisher Expected to Aid City Executive at Hearing Tomorrow.

BASIS FOR APPEAL IS LAID

Mayor Has an Issue to Take to United States Supreme Court, Lawyers Declare.

HAS A TWELVE-HOUR SLEEP

Spends Week-End Relaxing at Home of A. C. Blumenthal—Seabury Ready to Play More Active Part.

By F. RAYMOND DANIELL.

Special to THE NEW YORK TIMES.

ALBANY, Aug. 13.—With the removal proceedings against Mayor James J. Walker only half completed, it appeared today that three witnesses might be summoned to corroborate the explanations the Mayor has offered to Governor Roosevelt.

They are the Mayor's wife, Mrs. Janet Allen Walker; Edward Stanton, his former secretary, and Paul Block, the newspaper publisher, who opened the trading account from which Mr. Walker derived $246,000 in profits without investing anything.

It is possible there will be others before the hearings are over. Mr. Walker, in explaining that the $10,000 letter of credit which an employe of the Equitable Coach Company bought for him was really purchased with a common fund to which he and his friends subscribed, has named Miss Evelyn Wagner, his stenographer, and Hector Fuller among those who can corroborate his story.

Lays Basis for Court Fight.

Upon the number of witnesses called by the Mayor depends the time when the hearings before the Governor will be concluded. If, as some observers believe, the Mayor intends to wage a final fight in the courts, it is possible that he will rest his case on his own testimony, without calling any corroborative witnesses. In that case the eight charges remaining against him probably could be disposed of by Monday night.

Regardless of when the hearing before Governor Roosevelt is concluded, no final decision on whether he shall be removed is expected before Friday, when the Governor has been ordered to appear before Supreme Court Justice Staley to show cause why he should not be prohibited under the home rule amendment from exercising powers that never before have been challenged.

The show-cause order was obtained by George Donnelly, secretary of the Bronx Chamber of Commerce, who insists that his interest is only in protecting the home rule act. John J. Curtin, the Mayor's legal adviser, has disavowed knowledge or responsibility for the move.

Both Mr. Curtin and Mr. Walker, however, by their repeated protests against the procedure being followed by Governor Roosevelt, have indicated that they are laying the groundwork for an appeal to the courts on the question of jurisdiction in the event of Mr. Walker's removal. They have challenged the Governor's right to accept "the minutes" of the Hofstadter committee as legal evidence, and they have insisted that Samuel Seabury, Mr. Walker's chief accuser, call witnesses and try his case against the Mayor all over again.

Some observers believed also that Mr. Walker, in his impassioned plea at the first session of his hearing for the privilege of cross-examining his accusers, was laying the basis for an appeal to the Federal courts on constitutional grounds. In claiming a "vested interest" in the proceedings and alleging a monetary value to his elective office, lawyers said, he was creating the basis of an appeal to the United States courts to step in and save him from being deprived of his property without due process of law.

Governor to Speed Ruling.

While the Governor, as a matter of courtesy between the elective and judicial branches of the government, has indicated that he will take no action in the Mayor's case until after Friday's argument on the writ of prohibition, it is known that he does not intend to withhold decision indefinitely. It is his intention, it has become known, to dispose of the case and let the courts debate his jurisdiction afterward.

The question raised by Mr. Donnelly is different from that which is believed to be contemplated by Mr. Walker and his counsel, a law partner of John J. Glynn, former Governor Smith's nephew. Donnelly claims that the home rule amendment nullifies the power of removal given to the Governor in the City Charter, which provides that the Mayor may be removed in the same man-

Continued on Page Three.

Next President Faces Term 43 Days Short of 4 Years

By The Associated Press.

WASHINGTON, Aug. 13.—A prospect of less than four years in the White House faces the Presidential candidate elected in November.

Herbert Hoover or Franklin D. Roosevelt, after beginning the term of President on March 4 next, may be forced to relinquish that high position forty-three days short of the four-year term. A new inauguration date, Jan. 20, is in prospect.

Shortened terms for the President and members of Congress will be brought about by the adoption next year of the "lame duck" amendment to the Constitution. Fourteen States already have ratified it.

5TH AV. COACH GROUP SEEKS BUS MONOPOLY

Surface-Car Subsidiary Plans Acquisition of Harlem Road and Motorization of All.

WIDE SYSTEM IN PROSPECT

Linking of "Outlaw" Crosstown Routes Would Be a Part of Proposal for Manhattan.

The New York Railways Corporation is preparing to submit to the Board of Estimate in the Fall a comprehensive plan of bus operation in Manhattan, including motorization of its own surface-car system, acquisition and motorization of the surface-car lines of the New York & Harlem Railroad on Madison and Fourth Avenues and the linking of all motorized lines with the crosstown routes now under "outlaw" operation.

It is expected that the stockholders of the New York Railways Corporation, at a special meeting called for Sept. 13, will approve a plan for acquisition of the New York & Harlem lines, under a long-term lease or by outright purchase. The New York & Harlem stockholders are expected to approve the transaction soon afterward. The deal will then go to the Transit Commission for approval.

Since the Fifth Avenue Coach Company owns the stock of the New York Railways Corporation and the New York Central Railroad holds more than 75 per cent of New York & Harlem stock, approval of the plan seems a foregone conclusion because the directors of the two stockholding corporations already have agreed upon virtually every detail of the plan.

Decision Awaited in Test Case.

The New York Railways Corporation now has pending in the Board of Estimate its applications for bus franchises to cover seven crosstown routes and the important crosstown and longitudinal routes upon which it now operates trolley cars. Action on these petitions has been held up pending disposal of a test case on the validity of Fifth Avenue Coach Company operation on many of the company's existing lines.

The Appellate Division, on Sept. 27, will hear argument on an agreed statement of facts and a Court of Appeals decision is expected to follow soon thereafter. The court action was begun at the insistence of Aldermanic President Joseph V. McKee, who asserted that the status of the parent company should be cleared up before its subsidiary received any franchise.

The revised bus system to be proposed to the Board of Estimate in the Fall, if approved, would give a virtual monopoly of bus transportation in Manhattan to the Fifth Avenue Coach Company, which owns all of the New York Railways stock and which, in turn, is controlled by the Omnibus Corporation of Chicago.

Consummation of the deal whereby

Continued on Page Seven.

$1,500,000 LIMIT SET BY CAMPAIGN CHIEFS TO ELECT ROOSEVELT

Farley and Aides Fix Budget at One-third of Amount Spent on Drive for Smith.

MEET ON FUND THIS WEEK

Parley of National Committee on Oct. 1 Is Regarded as Democratic Innovation.

TOUR OF COUNTRY CHARTED

Governor Will Start Sept. 12 Taking In Middle West, Pacific and Northwest States.

The sum of $1,500,000, less than one-third the amount spent by the Democrats in the effort to elect former Governor Alfred E. Smith President in 1928, was set yesterday as the tentative amount to be disbursed by the Democratic National Committee in its campaign to elect Franklin D. Roosevelt.

Mention of this sum followed a conference among Evans Woollen, the Indianapolis banker recently named as chairman of the finance committee; James A. Farley, national chairman, and Frank C. Walker, treasurer, at the headquarters in the Biltmore Hotel. Jesse H. Jones of Texas, a friend of Speaker John N. Garner, nominee for Vice President and a member of the Finance Reconstruction Corporation, also conferred with the group.

Mr. Farley announced that a meeting of the national committee would be held here about Oct. 1 to check up on the progress of the campaign. This will be an innovation in Democratic campaign management, but Mr. Farley, who will complete his conferences with the State chairmen tomorrow, explained that the decision to call the national committeemen together was a natural sequence to the gathering of the State chairmen. He added that he expected the meeting of the national committee to be of great value in determining whether the Democratic plan of campaign was progressing satisfactorily at the time when it would enter its critical stage and whether there were weak spots in any of the States which proper and energetic management might eliminate.

To Confer on Fund Raising.

A meeting of the finance committee will be held here on Wednesday, at which time a more definite decision on methods of raising money will be reached. Mr. Woollen said he had some ideas on raising a campaign fund but was "too freshly on the job" to make them public.

Mr. Woollen, however, was willing to discuss the situation in Indiana, concerning which he said:

"The Democrats of Indiana are confident of success. They are confident notwithstanding the State has not gone Democratic in a Presidential election for forty years except when the Republicans were split between Taft and Roosevelt. Their confidence is seemingly supported by polls and other tests. The backbone of the Republicans in the State has been the farmer, and he is in ugly mood.

"I share the general confidence of the Hoosier Democrats as to the outcome both in the State and in the nation."

Indicating that he expected to keep within a budget of $1,500,000, Mr. Farley said:

"We realize the difficulty of raising money at this time. We hope to keep within the amount we set out to collect."

Mr. Farley and his associates ex-

Continued on Page Twenty.

U. S. Wins Olympic Eight-Oared Title; Japanese, Americans Share Swim Honors

Special to THE NEW YORK TIMES.

LONG BEACH, Cal., Aug. 13.—The undefeated University of California crew won the Olympic eight-oared championship on Alamitos Bay today, with Italy second, Canada third and Great Britain fourth. The Americans triumphed by the narrow margin of one foot.

A throng of 80,000 lined the 2,000-meter course as the California oarsmen successfully defended the title won at Amsterdam in 1928. The winning time was 6:37 3-5. Italy was clocked in 6:37 4-5, Canada in 6:40 2-5 and Britain in 6:40 4-5.

In other events of the final rowing program, Great Britain captured the championship for four-oared crews without coxswain, while the United States pair of W. E. Garrett Gilmore and Ken Myers of the Bachelors Barge Club, Philadelphia, triumphed in the double sculls.

In the competition at the Los Angeles swimming stadium America's stars scored again. Miss Helene Madison of Seattle annexed her second Olympic title by taking the 400-meter free-style event in the world's record time of 5:28.5, while in the high-platform dive a clean sweep was registered by the Americans when Harold (Dutch) Smith, Mickey Riley Galitzen and Frank Kurtz placed one, two, three, respectively.

Yoshiyuki Tsuruta of Japan was victorious in the 200-meter breast-stroke final, retaining his title. Kusuo Kitamura won the 1,500-meter swim, clipping more than 39 seconds off the Olympic record.

Hungary's water polo team was declared Olympic champion by the International Swimming Federation. The unbeaten team received a score of 8 for the round-robin series, with Germany second and the United States third.

Complete details of yesterday's Olympic events in Sports Section.

BALLOON UP 17 MILES GAUGES COSMIC RAYS

Record of Unmanned German Bag Upsets the Theory of Constant Intensity Gain.

FRAGILE DEVICES USED

Photographic Plates Register 14 Times Above the Altitudes Recorded by Prof. Piccard.

Special Cable to THE NEW YORK TIMES.

STUTTGART, Germany, Aug. 13.—Professor Erich Regener of the Stuttgart Institute of Technology has succeeded in sending up an unmanned balloon to the altitude of 92,000 feet (nearly 17½ miles) with special apparatus for measuring and registering cosmic rays in the stratosphere. After several hours the balloon landed safely in the Welzheim Woods outside Stuttgart without damage to its fragile devices.

This set a remarkable record for altitude in measurement of the cosmic ray. The previous mark was made by Professor Auguste Piccard, Swiss scientist.

[Professor Auguste Piccard ascended in a balloon on May 28, 1931, to an altitude of 52,462 feet, breaking a record of 43,000 feet made in an airplane].

Examination of the photographic plates and other registering devices, which, like an artificial brain, explored altitudes far above any that living beings have ever attained, showed surprising results that are reported to disprove scientific theories on the rays in the stratosphere.

The photographic plates showed that, contrary to theory, the intensity of the cosmic rays does not keep on increasing within the stratosphere in ratio to altitude at the same rate as in lower strata of the atmosphere. Between the altitudes of 39,000 and 85,000 feet, Professor Reneger's device registered the intensity of the cosmic rays fourteen times at regular intervals, while Professor Auguste Piccard in his stratosphere flight succeeded in taking only one measurement, and that at a much lower altitude.

Intensity Diminishes.

Up to 39,000 feet the intensity of the ultra rays increased rapidly, but from there on to 85,000 feet, where the last registration of their intensity was made photographically, the increase of the intensity of the rays was much slower, until at last it was comparatively insignificant.

On the eve of Professor Piccard's second stratosphere flight, Professor Regener's balloon brought down from its phenomenal flight evidence from spheres which Professor Piccard never hopes to reach. It was after several failures that Professor Regener's experiment was successful.

He used two balloons, bound together, each with a diameter of six and one-half feet. They were made of specially elastic rubber, since, owing to reduced air pressure, their diameter at the peak altitude expanded to twenty-three feet.

The temperature within the small gondola containing the registering devices was maintained throughout the flight at 86 degrees.

Piccard's Ascent Is Delayed.

Wireless to THE NEW YORK TIMES.

ZURICH, Switzerland, Aug. 13.—Unfavorable weather prevented Professor Piccard from making an ascent in his balloon today, and this and other factors caused him to postpone the attempt until next Wednesday or Thursday.

He learned that the 200 soldiers on whom he must depend to keep back the crowds of sightseers would not be available tomorrow, since Swiss Army regulations do not allow mobilization on Sundays. On Monday and Tuesday his assistant will be absent because of some experiments he has under way in Brussels.

Crowds of sightseers have been

Continued on Page Fifteen.

MARCONI HARNESSES ULTRA-SHORT WAVES

'Bending' of Currents Surmounts Earth's Curvature, Formerly Bar to Such Transmission.

EPOCHAL ADVANCE IS SEEN

American Radio Scientist Says Achievement May Rank With Discovery of Wireless.

By The Associated Press.

ROME, Aug. 13.—Guglielmo Marconi has made another advance in the science of radio communication by "bending" ultra-short radio waves which heretofore he had been unable to transmit through obstacles, he disclosed today.

From his yacht Elettra, in the Gulf of Aranci, he sent a message to his life-long collaborator, the Marchese Luigi Solari, announcing that he had sent messages on 57-centimeter waves from Rocca di Papa to Capo Figari, in Sardinia, a distance of 167 miles. He used portable reflectors, communicating clearly both by radio telegraph and radio telephone. The messages were sent only one way because no transmitting apparatus had been taken to Capo Figari.

Today's discovery permits transmission on ultra-short waves in such a manner as to overcome the earth's curvature. This, said Senator Marconi, was proof that the ultra-short wave was not definitely limited by all obstacles.

See Great Steps in Discovery.

His associates attributed great importance to the discovery because heretofore it had been possible to use ultra-shortwave communication only between two points in a line of vision. The waves would not pass through houses, trees and similar objects. Senator Marconi had been trying for a year to "bend" the waves.

Experts here said that if he had overcome the obstacle of the earth's curvature he could overcome other obstacles, thus greatly extending the possibilities of ultra-short wave communication. This method, they said, eventually would revolutionize radio transmission, for it was infinitely cheaper and simpler than methods in use at present.

The inventor has been pushing his experiments recently to apply them in a first installation for Pope Pius between the Vatican and the Pontiff's Summer home at Castel Gandolfo.

Senator Marconi granted a transatlantic radio interview to The Associated Press a year and a half ago, in the course of which he hinted at experiments which would be of great importance to radio transmission. He did not disclose their nature then, but he probably was thinking at the time of the discovery he announced today.

Step Called "Wonderful Thing."

Charles W. Horn, general engineer of the National Broadcasting Company and one of the leaders in development of international radio communications, said in regard to the Marchese Marconi's announcement:

"If the press reports correctly interpret Signor Marconi's achievement, the inventor has done a wonderful thing, something not believed possible heretofore, and an achievement that will rank with his original development of wireless. It is also possible that he has developed some new principle unknown to radio engineers in this country."

It was the belief of the scientific world, Mr. Horn said, that ultra-short waves had characteristics similar to those of light and therefore could not be "bent" or curved, although they could be transmitted around or over obstacles by reflectors or other devices.

Mr. Horn said he would withhold further opinion until he had communicated with Signor Marconi or had an opportunity to study the new

Continued on Page Five.

H. I. HARRIMAN GIVES RECOVERY PROGRAM; URGES BEER AT ONCE

U. S. Chamber of Commerce Head Declares a Revival Is Clearly Under Way.

TAX REFORMS DEMANDED

Twofold Sales Levy Advised—25 Per Cent Cut in Costs of Government Sought.

PROHIBITION AN OBSTACLE

Brew Tax of $6 a Barrel and Later Modification or Repeal Proposed Over Radio at Capital.

The text of Mr. Harriman's address is printed on Page 2.

Special to THE NEW YORK TIMES.

WASHINGTON, Aug. 13.—An immediate change in the Volstead act to permit sale of non-intoxicating beer, with $6 a barrel tax, followed by prompt repeal or modification of the Eighteenth Amendment, was advocated tonight by Henry I. Harriman, president of the Chamber of Commerce of the United States, in an address over the Columbia Broadcasting System, setting forth "the obstacles which confront economic recovery."

Reviewing the slightly upward trend of recent weeks, Mr. Harriman declared that "after three years of travail and devastating depression" there were "definite indications of reviving activity." Many fundamental factors appeared in a better light, and fear was "slowly giving way" to hope.

Confidence was "the starting point of all business enterprise," he pointed out; but before a full return to prosperity could be achieved "many fundamental changes in our way of looking at things and of doing things must be recognized and put into effect."

Eight Steps Toward Recovery.

To facilitate economic recovery Mr. Harriman made these further suggestions:

1. Abolition of the excessive cost of government by reducing at least 25 per cent all governmental budgets, with an amendment to the Constitution authorizing the President to veto single items in appropriation bills.
2. Overhauling of our whole system of taxation, with consideration by Congress of a manufacturers' sales tax and by local governments of a retail sales tax "as a partial substitute for the over-heavy burden upon real property and certain classes of productive industry."
3. Application of spread employment and part-time work to all classes of workers.
4. Elimination of increasing governmental competition with private productive enterprise, such as operation of barge lines, hotels, sawmills, retail stores, dairy farms and the sale of electricity and gas.

Easing of Trust Laws Urged.

5. Modification of anti-trust laws where their effect has been to block constructive cooperation, and modification of the Federal Trade Commission act to the same end.
6. Fair trial of the domestic allotment plan for wheat, cotton and tobacco.
7. Legislation to provide for a minimum capital of $50,000 for State and national banks, extension of branch banking within State limits, establishment of a liquidating corporation to enable depositors in closed banks to recover at least

Continued on Page Two.

French Soldier and Italian Arrested on Border as Spies

Wireless to THE NEW YORK TIMES.

PARIS, Aug. 13.—On the Italian frontier, which has drawn attention in the past few days because of the magnitude of the Italian air and naval manoeuvres, two men were arrested yesterday on a charge of espionage. One of them is a young French soldier who is a native of Monaco and the other an Italian workman.

When arrested in Peiracava after the discovery of a letter written by the soldier in which a good deal of secret information was divulged, they declared they were working for a consular officer of a foreign nation in Peiracava.

HOME LOAN BANKS LIKELY IN 2 WEEKS

Fort Says Organization Is Nearly Completed, but No Sites Have Been Chosen.

HOOVER WORKS OUT DRIVE

Chapin Says 'Business Men Are Going to Like' New Plan for Attack on Depression.

Special to THE NEW YORK TIMES.

WASHINGTON, Aug. 13.—President Hoover turned today from the consideration of politics, which had engrossed him for more than a week, and again took up plans for a further drive on the force of the business depression.

Seeking to get plans for the forthcoming conference of business leaders from the Federal Reserve districts, the President called in Secretary Chapin. After the conversation Mr. Chapin said that the President had evolved "a very definite and fine plan."

"Speaking as a business man," Mr. Chapin said, "I think the business men of the country are going to like it."

Mr. Hoover's purpose, generally, is to call business and industrial leaders from the twelve Federal Reserve districts to the capital and plan with them the utmost use of the weapons which the last Congress set up to fight the depression. He was about ready today to announce the date for the meeting.

The President also called in Secretary Hyde to discuss plans for setting up a chain of agricultural credit banks over the country, as provided at the last session of Congress. The government is about ready to begin designating the localities of these banks. Floods of application for their location have been received at the Department of Agriculture.

Speed on Home Loan Banks.

In addition, the prospect that Home Loan Banks might be established within a fortnight to carry out the last phase of the President's major relief program became a probability today as Franklin W. Fort, chairman of the Home Loan Bank Board, announced that most of the problems of organization were nearing a solution.

At the same time Mr. Fort appointed two administrative assistants to important posts. William E. Murray, former assistant to Secretary Hyde, was named secretary of the board, and A. R. Gardner, now with the Reconstruction Finance Corporation supervising applications for loans by building and loan associations, administrative assistant.

Although planning for the establishment of the mortgage discount banks, of which eight to twelve are authorized to handle mortgages on homes valued at less than $20,000, has reached an advanced stage, Mr. Fort again said today that no bank sites had been selected.

"No definite conclusion has been reached as to any district or the loca-

Continued on Page Two.

HITLER DEMANDS OFFICE AS DICTATOR; HINDENBURG BARS IT

Nazi Chief Refuses Secondary Post, Asking Power of 'Mussolini After March on Rome.'

EMERGENCY DECREE READY.

Prussian Police and Special Detective Squads Prepare to Crush Any Outbreak.

ADVANCE ON BERLIN DENIED

Future Action of Fascist Forces Uncertain—Threat of Defeat Faces von Papen.

By FREDERICK T. BIRCHALL.

Special Cable to THE NEW YORK TIMES.

BERLIN, Aug. 13.—Today, on the thirteenth day of the month in which the German Republic was founded thirteen years ago, negotiations between the present German Government and Adolf Hitler, Austrian house painter, who conceived a great movement for the regeneration of Germany and created out of it a private army with 13,500,000 votes behind it, have reached their climax.

Tonight whether law and order shall prevail in this republic or whether it will be plunged again into the turbulence that marked its beginning depends very much on the whim of this same Hitler and the strange aggregation of semi-fanatics who surround him and are trying, as there is good reason to believe, to goad him to extremes to which he alone probably would never proceed.

All Compromise Refused.

For today Hitler in interviews, first with the German Chancellor, whom he hopes to replace, and afterward with the venerable President, whose personality counts for more in Germany than any other single factor, refused all compromise aimed at giving him and his followers only a share in the government and demanded the Chancellorship for himself and full power in the government for his associates.

He told the President that he sought "precisely the same power Mussolini exercised after the march on Rome." When this demand was rejected and he was bidden by President von Hindenburg to think of his duty and responsibility to the Fatherland, he went away silent.

What the next move of the Nazis will be is known tonight only to themselves. There is always a possibility of their carrying to their logical conclusion the Italian Fascist tactics they have already adopted, although it can be said positively after a thorough investigation that reports repeated from New York of "masses" of Nazis concentrated outside of Berlin in preparation for a march on the city are not true so far, nor is there any serious expectation of such an attempt at present.

On the other hand, there is every ground for the assertion that the authorities are kept informed well in advance of any Nazi move and it is generally understood that a decree placing the whole of Germany in a state of emergency is already prepared and even signed, ready for issuance the moment it is needed.

Police Concentrated.

Dr. Franz Bracht instructed the Prussian police today to concentrate all forces to fight terrorism. In all the big cities special detective squads equipped with the most modern facilities for investigating crimes are to be permanently held in readiness to be rushed to the scene of political assaults and murders. Local police of small communities have been ordered immediately to advise these central squads as soon as anything happens.

After the calm of yesterday, events moved swiftly today. Last night Hitler flew in from Munich, landing at Tempelhof Field, whence he motored to a lodging previously arranged for in the home of a friend. There Count Helldorf and Captain Roehm, two of the leaders of his private army, found him and reported the result of their afternoon interview with Chancellor von Papen.

They brought an invitation from the Chancellor to Hitler to have luncheon with him today and afterward call on von Hindenburg. Hitler's acceptance was telephoned to the Chancellor, who in turn informed the President.

This morning the National Socialist chieftain first saw General von Schleicher at the Reichswehr Ministry. There is reason to believe that he there received good advice that fell on deaf ears, for he did not heed it. Thence he motored to the Chancellery. The mere rumor of his coming had attracted a crowd of about 1,000 persons to its front on the Wilhelmstrasse.

In the crowd were many Nazis, both in uniform and in civil dress, ready to make a demonstration, but this had been foreseen and the car that brought him drove in through a

Continued on Page Nine.

Hoover to Fish in Chesapeake Bay for Rest; Leaves Capital Today on Government Boat

Special to THE NEW YORK TIMES.

WASHINGTON, Aug. 13.—President Hoover plans to leave Washington tomorrow afternoon aboard a small inspection boat of the Department of Commerce for a few days of fishing and rest in Chesapeake Bay.

The cruise is to be strictly for rest and will be the first time, other than the brief week-end respites at his Rapidan camp, that President Hoover has taken a rest since his trip to Puerto Rico and the Virgin Islands a year ago last March.

The President passed up his visit to the Rapidan camp this week-end. He seldom cancels one of these trips, but because of his desire to clear away routine matters on his desk and to be at the dedication ceremonies at the Gibbons monument tomorrow he remained in Washington today.

Only a few close friends will accompany the President on what the White House said would be a "stag" party. Another boat will carry the regular detail of Secret Service men.

Mr. Hoover's main desire, other than to rest, is to get in a few days of deep-sea fishing. He enjoys the short-lived tussles with the bass and trout of his own Rapidan River fishing reserves, but likes even more the difficult task of landing the big salt water denizens. The only vacation of more than three or four days at a time that Mr. Hoover has taken since entering the White House was spent in deep-sea fishing off the Florida keys.

The name of the boat on which the President will sail was not made known at the White House this afternoon, nor the names of his guests. The trip was said to have been decided upon quickly, and arrangements had not been completed tonight.

Whatever boat he takes will be equipped with radio, so the President can keep in close touch with his office in Washington. His interests now are twofold, taking in both the effect of his economic measures on the country and the reaction to his candidacy by the electorate.

Irish Boycott of English Goods Planned Here To Fight Tariff Barrier Against Free State

Plans for a campaign looking toward a boycott of British goods in this country in retaliation for England's tariff wall against Ireland, which grew out of the dispute over Irish land annuities, were made yesterday at the first session of a two-day convention in the Hotel Astor of an organization known as the Irish Race. More than 700 supporters of President Eamon de Valera came from many parts of the United States and Canada to attend the convention, which is sponsored by The Irish World, a newspaper, the publisher of which, Thomas J. Ford, was named permanent chairman.

After the delegates heard speeches denouncing England, committees were appointed to draft plans for the boycott campaign. It was indicated also that the convention would sponsor a campaign for the payment of the American soldiers' bonus out of the war debts due this country from England.

In delivering the keynote address, John T. Hughes, a Boston attorney, told the delegates that "the English politicians" think they are going to weaken the Irish by the agricultural duties on Irish exports "but they are deluded, because the Irish people in America, Canada, Australia and South Africa are going to stand behind the Irish in Ireland and help them."

England, he added, is going to feel the return blow not only in Ireland but in all these other places. He declared that agents of various European manufacturers are already in Dublin soliciting Irish trade "and they're going to get it."

Mrs. W. A. King of Ironton, Ohio, compared President de Valera to George Washington, but she said it was harder for de Valera to set up a republic than it was for Washington, because the American patriot had the protection of the Atlantic Ocean, "while the Irish Sea affords no such protection." Another speaker was Assistant District Attorney Clare Gerald Fenerty of Philadelphia.

Last night the delegates attended an Irish ball. Their business sessions will end today.

Section 1

"All the News That's Fit to Print."

The New York Times.

LATE CITY EDITION
WEATHER—Partly cloudy, cooler today; tomorrow partly cloudy.
Temperatures Yesterday—Max., 84; Min., 67.

Section 1

Copyright, 1932, by The New York Times Company.

VOL. LXXXI....No. 27,245. Entered as Second-Class Matter, Postoffice, New York, N. Y. NEW YORK, SUNDAY, AUGUST 28, 1932. **** Including Rotogravure Picture, Magazine and Book Sections. TEN CENTS

REVIVAL PROGRAM BEGUN WITH MOVE TO SPREAD JOBS; A. F. OF L. BACKS THE DRIVE

COUNCIL GROUP MEETS

Teagle Will Use Coast Model in Appeals to Employers.

UNIFORM ACTION SOUGHT

Industrialists Will Be Called On by Committees in Every Reserve District.

GREEN PRAISES PARLEY

Fort Is Cheered by Responses From 20 States to His Plea to Halt Foreclosures.

Special to THE NEW YORK TIMES.

WASHINGTON, Aug. 27.—A nation-wide drive, organized along the lines of war-time Liberty Loan campaigns, for spreading available employment to more workers in all industries was launched today as the nation's business and industrial committees started a new offensive against the depression.

Less than twenty-four hours after the committees, in conference here, had set up a central council at the instance of President Hoover, a subcommittee headed by Walter C. Teagle, president of the Standard Oil Company of New Jersey, had laid its plans, adopted a slogan and gone to work. The battle cry was "Job security by job spreading."

Simultaneously, the American Federation of Labor, through its president, William Green, hailed the work-spread movement as the greatest step toward solving the unemployment problem.

"The recommendation of the conference that working time in all lines of industry be reduced so that the amount of work available may be spread among a larger number of workers should be accepted and supported by employers and employes in all lines of industry," Mr. Green said.

Leaders in the new campaign for recovery had further cause for encouragement today in the responses to the proposal for a sixty-day suspension of foreclosures on home-loan mortgages which was vigorously urged by Franklin W. Fort, chairman of the Home Loan Bank Board, in a speech before the conference and in telegrams to State Banking Superintendents.

Similar telegrams in the nature of orders had been sent to receivers for national banks by J. W. Pole, Controller of the Currency.

Answers received today from twenty State banking superintendents promised fullest cooperation.

Teagle to Follow Western Plan.

Meanwhile Mr. Teagle's "coordinating committee," as he called it, was planning such a campaign as would "make a real dent in the whole unemployment problem." Its work will be to bring about uniformity of action by the twelve Business and Industrial Committees in the Federal Reserve districts, and will be patterned after a drive now being carried out successfully in San Francisco and other West Coast cities through the Twelfth District committee headed by R. H. Kingsbury, president of the Standard Oil Company of California.

Members of he committees will call upon employers whose businesses are similar to their own, suggesting that jobs be given a larger number of workers by reducing the working time of those now employed full time. Thus committee members, through their own familiarity with problems of employers in a certain business, may offer suggestions on how to spread work most effectively, but there will be no dictation of how an employer shall accomplish the result.

"We are not trying to sell any definite plan," Mr. Teagle declared. "We are not going to talk the six-hour day or the five-day week. Our purpose is to get all employers to take on additional workers and to so adjust the hours of all that by the end of a given period, whether one month or three months, all workers will have worked the same amount of time.

"We hope to make this a movement to which all employers of labor will subscribe, and we think that if the move is successful it will at least prevent a further increase in unemployment."

The meeting of the Teagle committee was attended by the heads of

Continued on Page Two.

$3 Advance in Cotton Leads New Upswing in All Markets

Led by cotton, which advanced $3 a bale in response to the heaviest demand in several years, all the financial and commodity markets extended their recent gains sharply in yesterday's trading.

The wide advance in cotton was something of a market sensation. It brought the net gain for the week to $7.50 a bale. Since July 9, when the extreme lows were reached, the gain has amounted to $20 a bale.

In the stock market yesterday's gains ran from 1 to 4 points, with interest concentrated in the public utilities. The volume on the Stock Exchange exceeded 2,201,000 shares. About 140 stocks went into new high ground for the year. The maximum advances in the bond market ranged from 3 to 10 points. Wheat was up 1⅛ to 1⅞ cents a bushel on the day.

Details of all markets will be found in Section 4.

$10,000,000 IS SOUGHT TO AID HOME OWNERS

Broderick Will Apply for That Amount to Preserve Small Mortgages in State.

TO DELAY FORECLOSURES

He Notifies Fort He Will Call on Closed Bank Receivers for 60-Day Moratorium.

Application will be made to the Federal Loan Home Bank when it opens for business here about Oct. 15 to help refinance $10,000,000 worth of mortgages, most of them on small homes and apartments, it was announced yesterday at the offices of State Superintendent of Banks Joseph A. Broderick.

The announcement was made after Mr. Broderick had telegraphed Franklin Fort, chairman of the Home Loan Bank Board, in Washington, that he would cooperate in the request that receivers of closed banking institutions in this State refrain from foreclosing on mortgage obligations for sixty days. Mr. Broderick in his telegram to Mr. Fort said he was fully in accord with the principle of not foreclosing on these mortgages, that the banking department had been practicing this principle and that the superintendent intended to cooperate in every way possible. Mr. Broderick's telegram was in reply to one Mr. Fort sent, which read in part as follows:

"We hope to have the Federal Home Loan Banks open and doing business on or before Oct. 15, after which date substantial relaxation in the mortgage loan market should develop speedily. In the meantime, we feel that foreclosure should be prevented wherever possible.

Foreclosure Delays Asked.

"We therefore request you to instruct the receivers or other liquidators of closed institutions under your jurisdiction to withhold or delay foreclosure proceedings for at least sixty days, thus offering chance

Continued on Page Two.

FARM STRIKE GRIP TIGHTENS ON IOWA; DES MOINES NOW HIT

Seizures Block Council Bluffs Milk Supply as Pickets Are Roused by State Leader.

HE BLAMES REPUBLICANS

Charging 'Deflation of Farmer,' He Denounces Federal Agencies and Calls for 'Action.'

SHERIFF HUNTS RED CLUES

Grand Jury Inquiry Set—Siege Centre Shifts to Capital—Parley of 15 Governors Proposed.

By LOUIS STARK.

Special to THE NEW YORK TIMES.

COUNCIL BLUFFS, Iowa, Aug. 27.—While the law-enforcement authorities in this area were gambling against time to avoid bloodshed in the farmers' rebellion, the large dairies, against whom the strike is directed, served an ultimatum today that they would not negotiate on higher milk prices until the blockade was lifted.

The picketers and their leaders took the notice under advisement, but in the meantime they kept patrolling four highways leading into Omaha, across the Missouri River from here, and stopping milk and provision trucks.

The confiscation of a truckload of twenty-two cans of milk on Highway 34 this morning and the halting of private automobiles by pickets made a tense situation more acute.

Sheriff Calmly Avoids Force.

Sheriff P. A. Lainson of Pottawattamie County, who was advised of the confiscation of the truckload of milk destined for this city, declared calmly that he would not be tempted to use a display of force "such as you are used to in the East when you have strikes."

He kept his 112 deputies in this city ready for use in emergency, but indicated that his policy, made after consultation with the State Attorney General, was to "let public opinion take care of the picketers after they learn what peaceful picketing really amounts to."

The Sheriff, who served in the Rainbow Division, is well supplied with machine guns, tear-gas bombs, baseball bats and pickhandles. If necessary he will be able to call upon four units of the National Guard which are returning here from Camp Dodge tomorrow.

Farm Leader Rallies Pickets.

Picket lines were thinned this morning because of the rain, although the morale of the pickets was strengthened by the visit of Dennis Ryan of Corning, State director of the Farmers' Union and a member of the farmers' holiday movement to stop marketing until prices are higher.

Mr. Ryan, a veteran of farmers' campaigns, aroused cheers in the ranks of the overalled pickets on Route 34, several miles from this city, when he declared that the holiday movement would soon enlist a million farmers in Iowa, Nebraska, the Dakotas, Missouri and Oklahoma.

Sloshing ankle deep in mud at the side of the road and gulping a breakfast of ice cream—they had been picketing all night—the dishevelled farmers listened approvingly to Ryan's attack on "Wall Street, the Chicago Board of Trade, the meat packers, the Department of Agriculture and the Federal Farm Board," on whose

Continued on Page Twenty-six.

New England and Canada to Draw Thousands For Eclipse Wednesday; City Will Be on Watch

Millions of persons all over the nation will stare skyward next Wednesday afternoon to witness the greatest show the heavens have to offer, an eclipse of the sun.

The total eclipse, that beautiful and wonderful spectacle when the glittering circle of the sun is gradually but completely obscured by the moon, will be visible in the United States only in parts of New England, but some kind of an eclipse can be seen all over the country and as far south as Northern South America.

In New York, the city's millions will be able to view through their smoked glasses and strips of developed photographic film—the best devices for filtering the blinding light of the sun, a 95 per cent eclipse. In Washington, President Hoover, weather permitting, should be able to watch the small dead disc of the moon gradually obscure about 89 per cent of the flaming bulk of the sun.

Sweeping across the earth with tremendous speed, the shadow of the moon will drape many Canadian communities in a brief 100 seconds of daytime darkness and then dash on across portions of Maine, Vermont, New Hampshire and Massachusetts out into the Atlantic.

In the 100-mile swath cut across New England thousands of persons, including hundreds of scientists and photographers, are expected to gather. Provincetown and Chatham and the whole tip of Cape Cod, Salem, Mass., and Cape Ann, Portsmouth, N. H. and Concord, Portland, Saco and Freyburg, Maine, and Montpelier, Vt., are a few of the favored communities that lie in the 100-mile belt of totality.

The band of shadow, sweeping out of the north, will darken the White Mountains. Mount Washington is on the exact centre line of the path of totality, and the little town of Wolfeboro on Lake Winnipesaukee will be swathed in the moon's shadow.

Boston just misses the favored-city status, but thousands of its citizens are expected to travel the few miles necessary to enter the area of totality, and the highways and transportation facilities, it is believed, will be crowded with thousands of amateur astronomers.

The path of the moon's shadow includes much of the New England lake, mountain and seashore vacation region in its course, and pleasure resorts and hotels are prepared for a rushing business. Many persons who will view the eclipse are

Continued on Page Eighteen.

STATE LEGION ASKS FOR BONUS AT ONCE

Votes Overwhelmingly for It After Booing Davison's Defense of Hoover.

SESSION ENDS IN UPROAR

But Censure of Administration Is Defeated—End of Dry Law Also Is Demanded.

The American Legion of the State of New York demanded immediate payment of the Federal bonus, totaling more than $2,000,000,000, by a vote of 499 to 138 yesterday as its annual convention came to an end in Brooklyn.

It took this action at the climax of an exciting and at times wildly disorderly session in which Legionaires and guests in the galleries hooted and howled down Assistant Secretary of War F. Trubee Davison and high officials of the Legion itself who pleaded against the bonus, and greeted the mention of President Hoover's name with catcalls.

It overwhelmingly defeated a resolution which in effect censured the Federal Administration for forcibly expelling the Bonus Expeditionary Force from Washington, although only after a debate in which the President, while his name was not mentioned, was condemned so immoderately that the orator was forced to forego further personalities.

Flushing Doctor Is Commander.

It carried on for six and a half hours in an intermittent pandemonium of cheers, jeers, hisses, applause, catcalls and boos, which caused several threats to clear the galleries, but when the convention finally adjourned late in the afternoon it had accomplished several important pieces of business besides voting for the cash bonus.

One of these was the election of Dr. George J. Lawrence, a gynecologist of Flushing and former medical officer in the Rainbow Division, as State commander for the coming year, together with subordinate officers.

Another was the tumultuous adoption by viva-voce vote of resolutions calling for the immediate and unconditional repeal of the Eighteenth Amendment, immediate modification of the Volstead act and the rescinding of all appropriations for prohibition enforcement.

Davison Braves Opposition.

Mr. Davison's address came early in the day, before the bonus proposal was before the convention, and the storm of disapproval which it called forth set a noisy pace for the rest of the long session. Mr. Davison is a candidate for the Republican nomination for Governor of New York, but he knew in advance that his speech would displease many of his hearers. He is an aviation veteran of the World War, but he spoke as a member of the Hoover Administration and the War Department and his speech was a fiery one.

He brought on the first outburst by a frank statement that he was opposed to the bonus. He followed it with sensational statements concerning the Bonus Expeditionary Force, which he said had been composed, at the end, largely of non-service hoodlums under Communist influence equipped with forged army discharges ground out on a hidden printing press. He defended the conduct of the army in its eviction of the bonus army and paid tribute to the wisdom of President Hoover in the affair.

Through it all, and through the

Continued on Page Sixteen.

'MA' FERGUSON GOES AHEAD OF STERLING

Acquires Margin of 3,000 Over Governor as Count Progresses in Texas Run-Off.

MILLION VOTES ARE POLLED

Two Wets and One Dry Lead for the Three Places for Congressman-at-Large.

By The Associated Press.

DALLAS, Texas, Aug. 27.—Mrs. Miriam A. ("Ma") Ferguson swept into a narrow lead over Governor R. S. Sterling in the race for the Democratic Gubernatorial nomination late tonight in tabulation of the vote in today's run-off primary.

Returns to the Texas Election Bureau from 229 out of 254 counties in the State, including ninety-two complete, gave Mrs. Ferguson 398,838, Sterling 395,648.

Taking the lead in the first tabulation of returns, Governor Sterling at first steadily forged ahead. As boxes from the Ferguson strongholds in rural districts reported, however, an early lead of nearly 22,000 soon was lost.

Governor Sterling's strength appeared to be fairly well distributed over the State, except in East Texas, the oil field territory, where Mrs. Ferguson appeared to dominate.

Much opposition to Governor Sterling appeared in East Texas during the campaign as a result of his declaration of martial law in the oil fields to assist in enforcing proration of production.

Officials of the Texas Election Bureau predicted that the total vote would be 1,000,000 or more, which would smash all records for elections in this State. The vote in the July primary was 967,928.

In three contests for Congress at Large, two men classified as "wets" and one as a "dry" led, although the prohibition question was not emphasized in the campaign.

Late returns gave:

Place No. 1—George B. Terrell, 383,584; Pink Parrish, 314,751.

Place No. 2—Joseph W. Bailey, 425,460; J. H. Davis, 300,569.

Place No. 3—Sterling P. Strong, 390,382; Joe Burkett, 322,638.

Organizations favoring repeal of the Eighteenth Amendment endorsed Terrell, Bailey and Burkett. Strong is a former Texas State superintendent of the Anti-Saloon League.

In the only district Congress race W. D. McFarlane led George W. Backus, 12,806 to 11,532 on incomplete returns. They sought the seat of Representative Guinn Williams of Decatur, who did not run for re-election.

In the July primary Mrs. Ferguson received 402,328 votes, or 41.55 per cent of the total. She predicted Mr. Sterling's defeat by about 150,000 votes in the run-off.

Governor Sterling got 296,383 votes in the first primary, equivalent to 30.62 per cent of the total. In 1930 he ran behind by about the same number of votes, but in the second primary defeated Mrs. Ferguson.

Much depends on the distribution of the 220,391 votes polled by Tom F. Hunter, a dark horse candidate, who ran third in the first primary. Mr. Hunter, who plans to be a candidate in 1934, refused to take sides, and both the Ferguson and Sterling forces exerted efforts to capture his bloc of votes.

Mrs. Ferguson has served one term as Governor and has been a candidate for the office on four other occasions.

Democratic nomination in Texas is tantamount to election.

East Greenland's Inland Slopes Ice-Covered; Danish Explorers in Airplanes Solve Mystery

Special Cable to THE NEW YORK TIMES.

REYKJAVIK, Iceland, Aug. 27.—The mystery of Greenland's eastern mountains has been solved by Dr. Lauge Koch, Danish explorer and chief of the Danish Government's East Greenland Expedition, who has just reached here after a daring flight yesterday from Greenland to Akranes, Iceland.

With the help of airplanes Dr. Koch has established the fact that the inland slopes of the East Greenland mountains are sheathed with impenetrable ice in Summer and Winter. Only the rocky ridges and peaks project through the ice-cap, according to Dr. Koch, who hitherto had believed the inland slopes might be ice free, like the coastal ranges.

Dr. Koch brought with him the first news of this Summer's researches by the Danish scientists in East Greenland. Twenty men in three stations, all equipped with wireless, will Winter in Greenland, while eighty of their companions are expected at Reykjavik soon aboard the expedition's ship.

"Our mapping flights have been successful beyond all expectation," said Dr. Koch in a preliminary report of his work. "The flights have had three different objects—first, to see the hitherto unexplored portions of the ice-cap; secondly, to accomplish an extensive mapping of the ice-free coastal districts, and finally, to explore the entire coast from the air.

"Altogether our planes have flown 24,000 miles, working often in cold far below zero and at heights up to 15,000 feet. Yet we have had not one mishap, proving that the planes and men have been of the right kind for Arctic flights.

"On previous expeditions I have learned to know the eastern slope of the East Greenland mountain range, which is unbroken by any fjords. The western slopes, however, were unknown until now. We expected to find large areas ice free, but, surprisingly, we found them ice-covered with only isolated peaks of rocks protruding from their white surface.

"We further expected to find an extensive ice-free grazing district for the musk-ox of East Greenland, but the area of suitable land is considerably less than had been expected."

JAPAN WOULD BLOCK CENSURE BY LEAGUE AND AVERT A BREAK

Hopes to Forestall Action by Recognition of Manchukuo Before Assembly Convenes.

MISSION CONDEMNS TOKYO

Report Rejects Self-Defense Plea and the Theory That Natives Set Up New State.

CHINA FEARS NEW CONFLICT

Evacuation of Chapei Continues as Japan Emphasizes Its Warning Against Boycott Terrorism.

By HUGH BYAS.

Special Cable to THE NEW YORK TIMES.

TOKYO, Aug. 27.—The government knows definitely that the narrative portion of the report of the League of Nations inquiry commission on Manchuria will impugn two of the main points in Japan's juristic case.

These are that the army's action in September in seizing Mukden, Manchuria, and other cities following alleged tearing up by Chinese soldiers of a section of railway was self-defensive, and that the establishment of the new State of Manchukuo was self-determined.

The government, therefore, has worked out a policy to meet the situation foreseen at Geneva. It considers that it has a mandate to leave the League if necessary, but, meantime, it is steering a course intended to clarify the issue and make it easier for the League to avoid a break.

The critical moment is not expected before the Assembly meets, probably in November. The commission will take its report to Geneva. Two weeks then will be necessary for printing and study before the Council takes it up. The Council afterward will refer it to the special committee of nineteen, which, in turn, will report to the Assembly.

Time Given for Reflection.

This process allows time for reflection on Japanese recognition of Manchukuo, which will be a fait accompli before mid-September. The draft treaty between Japan and Manchukuo is now in the hands of the Changchun Government and Foreign Minister Hsieh Chien-shin of Manchukuo is in Mukden conferring with General Nobuyoshi Muto, the Japanese administrative chief in Manchuria. As soon as they have signed the treaty, it will be submitted to the Tokyo Privy Council for ratification.

It is believed here that nothing that the League can do will reverse the fait accompli and that the issue is reduced to whether Japan is to be censured by the League in terms that will compel her withdrawal. If Geneva merely endorses Secretary Stimson's doctrine of non-recognition of any situation brought about in contravention of treaties, Japan will not object.

Indifferent to Others' Action.

Officials said today that Japan did not care if Manchukuo were never recognized by any other government.

Qualified foreign observers agree that Japanese public opinion will support withdrawal from the League if that is the price of recognition. Nationalists, with their "Back to Asia" slogan, would welcome withdrawal as giving Japan a freer hand. The bulk of influential opinion here is moderate, and would, when the

Continued on Page Five.

Pinchot Is Reported Planning To Race Davis for the Senate

Special to THE NEW YORK TIMES.

PHILADELPHIA, Aug. 27.—Reports from Harrisburg indicated today that Governor Pinchot was seriously considering making a third attempt this Fall to win a seat in the United States Senate.

The impression was that neither the Governor nor anybody else expected Senator Davis to retire as the Republican nominee because of Mr. Pinchot's demand that he do so, based upon Mr. Davis's indictment in connection with an alleged lottery conducted by the Moose lodge, and it was believed that the Governor would enter the campaign as a proponent of prohibition.

In this event, he would not be expected to link his Senatorial fight with the Presidential campaign of Governor Roosevelt, although it had previously been thought that he would back the New Yorker.

COURT READY TO RULE ON WALKER HEARING

Decision Expected Tomorrow on Right of Governor to Remove the Mayor.

APPEAL IS HELD CERTAIN

Judge Could Hold Proceedings Illegal but Refuse to Stay Them, Observers Say.

By F. RAYMOND DANIELL.

Special to THE NEW YORK TIMES.

ALBANY, N. Y., Aug. 27.—A judicial determination of Governor Roosevelt's power to remove Mayor Walker was expected to precede the reopening of the Mayor's hearing before the Governor Monday night in the Executive Chamber of the State Capitol.

Supreme Court Justice Ellis J. Staley was reported today to be spending the week-end working on his decision in the two suits that have been filed to test Mr. Roosevelt's jurisdiction in the case. His ruling was expected Monday.

Observers point out that it would be possible for Justice Staley to rule in favor of the Mayor on the legal points involved, and at the same time decline to stay the proceedings on the ground that the courts have no power to interfere in an Executive proceeding, as such action might be more embarrassing for the Governor than the writ of prohibition which the Mayor and George Donnelly, secretary of the Bronx Chamber of Commerce, are seeking in separate suits.

Protracted Court Fight Seen.

During the argument by John J. Curtin, attorney for Mr. Walker, and Assistant Attorney General Henry Epstein, who appeared on the Governor's behalf, Justice Staley asked what effect a ruling on the law and a refusal to interfere would have.

In the brief which he filed in support of his argument, Mr. Curtin predicted that New York's affairs would be thrown into such a state of chaos by a removal of the Mayor without a

Continued on Page Nine.

Troops Oust Baquerizo as Ecuador's President; Loyal Forces Mass to End the Revolt at Quito

Special Cable to THE NEW YORK TIMES.

GUAYAQUIL, Ecuador, Aug. 27.—The government of Dr. Alfredo Baquerizo Moreno was overthrown today by part of the Quito garrison, supported by civilian partisans of Naptali Bonifaz, who was disqualified last Saturday as President-elect because he was said to be a Peruvian.

While telegraphic communication with Quito is under censorship, reports arriving from the northern district indicate that only two regiments are supporting the Bonifazistas and that the two other Quito regiments are retiring to Rio Bamba, where Minister of War Sotomayor has his headquarters and is concentrating eight regiments to march on Quito.

Four other regiments also promise to support the Baquerizo Government, and many civilian volunteers are ready to reinforce the regulars. Congress is disorganized, owing to the exodus of many anti-Bonifaz members. The Guayaquil delegation is expected to arrive here this evening on the first train to reach this city from Quito since the revolt started.

Earlier reports said Congress was reconsidering the disqualification of Señor Bonifaz, who would otherwise have become President of the republic on Sept. 1 since he received a popular majority in the last election. At the time of the disqualification of Señor Bonifaz, the army announced it would support Congress and the Constitution.

A train bound south from Quito is being held for an unannounced reason at Bucay, which is about 145 miles south of the capital and 45 miles west of this city.

The newspaper Universo states that troops from Tulcan, near the Colombian border north of Quito, and Riobamba, 100 miles south of Quito, are marching on the capital against the Bonifaz partisans. Some troops have already left this port, and groups of citizens here are offering their services to put down the rebellion, but they are being refused arms.

GUAYAQUIL, Aug. 27 (AP).—President Baquerizo took refuge today in the Argentine Legation at Quito as affairs there grew hazardous, according to an official announcement.

ROOSEVELT ASSAILS HOOVER AS INSINCERE ON DRY LAW; 100,000 IN JERSEY HEAR HIM

SCORES 'PUSSY CAT' WORDS

Statement of President 'Was Made to Mislead,' Governor Asserts.

DEMANDS OUTRIGHT REPEAL

Quotes Democratic Platform to Refute Charge Party Is for Return of Saloon.

HAILED BY CROWDS ON WAY

Huge Hague Rally at Sea Girt Follows Motor Parade From the Holland Tunnel.

The text of Governor Roosevelt's speech is printed on Page 20.

From a Staff Correspondent.

Special to THE NEW YORK TIMES.

SEA GIRT, N. J., Aug. 27.—Demanding outright prohibition repeal as a social and economic necessity, Governor Roosevelt told a throng, estimated at 100,000 persons today that President Hoover and the Republican party were attempting a "circus stunt" to appeal to both wets and drys.

Hailed by the huge gathering of New Jersey Democrats as "the next President," the Democratic candidate charged President Hoover with using "meaningless" and "pussy-cat" words in a vain effort to please both sides in his speech of acceptance. He called the Republican plank "ambiguous and insincere," and contrasted with it the direct call for repeal in the platform of his own party.

But it was on the contradictory positions of Vice President Curtis and President Hoover that the Governor trained his heavy batteries. He recalled his last campaign, when he ran for Governor of New York against Charles H. Tuttle, a wet, with Caleb H. Baumes, a dry, the Republican candidate for Lieutenant Governor, and said the Republican candidates this year were in the same position.

Governor Gets Warm Welcome.

The Democratic candidate for President received a warm welcome at the traditional rallying point for the New Jersey Democracy. Mayor Frank Hague of Jersey City, Democratic leader of the State, had his cohorts out in force, and it was a show similar to those put on for Alfred E. Smith and John W. Davis when they were the candidates of the Democracy for the White House.

Governor A. Harry Moore presented the Democratic candidate to the throng and lauded him in terms which were unusually optimistic about the chance for the Democratic slate to capture the electoral votes of New Jersey in November. State Chairman Harry E. Heber made a similar prediction on the trip down.

Mayor Hague led the fight for former Governor Smith at the Chicago Democratic Convention, and the turnout today was designed to display to the leaders that New Jersey would do its best for the Democratic ticket. James A. Farley, national chairman, came here with a party of leaders from the West to give them a demonstration of Mayor Hague's methods of stirring political enthusiasm.

Governor Roosevelt was well received on the trip to and from the "Summer Executive Mansion" as well as at the rally itself. The crowd was said to be practically the same as that which assembled for former Governor Smith in 1928, and, while Governor Roosevelt did not appear arouse it to the same pitch as did Mr. Smith four years ago, it gave this year's candidate a long cheer. His demand for prohibition repeal and his attacks on the Hoover and Curtis positions especially captured the favor of the big throng.

The Governor made his prohibition repeal demand here after a long motor trip from New York City as part of a very busy week-end which is taking him back to New York and thence to Westhampton for the night. He will return to Albany tomorrow to resume the hearing on Mayor Walker Monday night.

The large crowd which gathered to greet the Presidential nominee represented a typical "Hague rally." Although the Jersey City Mayor remarked that the audience contained between 200,000 and 250,000 persons, impartial observers estimated that there were no more than 100,000 present.

While the vast throng milled about

Continued on Page Twenty.

"All the News That's Fit to Print."

The New York Times.

LATE CITY EDITION
WEATHER—Rain today, tomorrow; colder this afternoon and tonight.
Temperatures yesterday—Max., 69; min., 56.

Copyright, 1932, by The New York Times Company.

VOL. LXXXII....No. 27,295. Entered as Second-Class Matter, Postoffice, New York, N. Y. NEW YORK, MONDAY, OCTOBER 17, 1932. * * * * TWO CENTS In New York City | THREE CENTS Within 200 Miles | FOUR CENTS Elsewhere Except in 7th and 8th Postal Zones

PAPEN SAYS REICH CAN PAY CREDITORS ONLY IN GOODS; WANTS TRADE BARS LIFTED

TO PLEAD AT WORLD PARLEY

Asking Payment While Keeping Tariffs High Called Bad Logic.

NO HINT OF MORATORIUM

But the Chancellor Indicates Expansion of Standstill Agreement Is Needed.

FINDS TRANSFER FETTERED

Addressing Industrialists, He Defends New Import Quotas as Safeguard to Farming.

By GUIDO ENDERIS.
By Cable to THE NEW YORK TIMES.

BERLIN, Oct. 16.—Chancellor Franz von Papen warned Germany's private foreign creditors today that obligations to them could be paid only by sale of goods and that to make this possible trade barriers would have to be lifted.

In a significant speech before Westphalian industrialists at Paderborn he emphasized that the German Government would seek to impress this point on creditor nations at the coming world economic conference.

Discussing the government's political and economic program at length, the Chancellor announced that while previous repayment of $1,000,000,000 of foreign private debts suggested impressive testimony of Germany's economic virility, withdrawal of further credits in the present situation could not be countenanced, as it would involve serious convulsions of her economy.

Wants Consolidation of Debts.

Lieut. Col. von Papen forecast as indispensable the consolidation of Germany's long and short term foreign and private indebtedness beyond the scope fixed in the "German credit agreement of 1932," which expires next March 1. But aside from this he gave no intimation of how the government would intervene in present private commitments between foreign creditor banks and the German debtors committee.

There was nothing in his statement to permit an inference that the government would proclaim a private debt moratorium before thoroughly canvassing the situation with the foreign creditors. A promise to this effect, it is well known, was given to Albert H. Wiggin as chairman of the foreign creditor bankers committee by the Bruening Government when the present standstill agreement was initialed.

"Our creditors abroad," the Chancellor said, however, "can reckon on repayment of Germany's foreign indebtedness only if they are prepared to take German commodities in payment, and this presupposes they are willing to open their trade frontiers to our goods. To expect repayment of debts while confronting us with trade barriers suggests both crass and indefensible violation of all economic logic.

"With export prospects thus lightened, the burden of 20,000,000,000 marks [about $4,750,000,000] of private debts still owed abroad will be made tolerable and will not longer constitude a paralyzing factor in our national economy."

Disappointed Over Ottawa.

Chancellor von Papen expressed disappointment over the results of the Ottawa conference, and believed they were hardly conducive to promoting an international revival of trade. "But we must not give up hope," he added, "that the world conference will succeed in showing the path to world-wide economic improvement."

One of the most important problems confronting the conference, he said, is suggested in the existing confusion and impediments imposed on international money transfers, now hopelessly fettered by complicated exchange restrictions which are obstructing private initiative the world over.

Defending his government's import quota policies, the Chancellor said these had not been conceived in a spirit of reprisal, but had been dictated by the urgent necessity of conserving German agriculture. The opposition to them abroad, he believed, will disappear once it is

Continued on Page Ten.

Catholic Clergymen Tell Papen Economic Program Aids Reds

By The Associated Press.

BERLIN, Oct. 16.—A group of Catholic clergymen and the chairman of the Westphalian Workers Association have addressed an open letter to Chancellor von Papen charging that certain provisions of his economic program "give Communism a chance" instead of private initiative as intended.

The letter expressed fear that bloody uprisings might occur and said:

"At no time, not even during the months of breakdown, have we noted such deep unrest and embitterment among the workers. Mr. Chancellor, you can not serve the Fatherland on the present road."

The letter said the economic program, which was intended to spread employment among more workers and permitted salary adjustments for that purpose only, had altered workers' protection in the social institutions of Germany.

LOWER TARIFF URGED BY 180 ECONOMISTS

Open Petition Sent to the White House Asks the President to 'Eliminate Inequalities.'

DECLARES HE HAS POWER

Reduction of 'Excessive Duties' Are Asserted to Be 'Essential to World Recovery.'

Special to THE NEW YORK TIMES.

WASHINGTON, Oct. 16.—An open petition signed by 180 economists was presented to President Hoover today urging him to use his official power, under the flexible tariff provision, to "eliminate the inequalities" of the Hawley-Smoot tariff act, "especially those which are causing retaliation abroad."

The petition, which was made public by Professor James C. Bonbright of Columbia University, takes issue with the main points of Mr. Hoover's Des Moines speech on the tariff and its relation to agriculture and the depression and declares that the farmer and laborer would be better off with reduced tariff rates.

Each of the signers of the statement signed the petition of May 4, 1930, to the President, asking him to veto the Hawley-Smoot bill, then nearing a final vote in Congress. There were 2,000 signers to that appeal.

"More signatures are coming in every hour," Professor Bonbright said today. "It has not been possible to present the statement to the entire list of signers of the petition of two years ago.

"The response of the first signers clearly demonstrates a hearty, nationwide support of the position we take among leading economists and authorities on the tariff."

TEXT OF THE PETITION.

The petition to President Hoover read:

On May 4, 1930, we joined in a petition presented to you as President of the United States, respectfully urging the veto of the Hawley-Smoot tariff bill.

The petition was signed by the leading American authorities on

Continued on Page Four.

TAMMANY EXPECTED TO BACK M'KEE TODAY IN BUDGET ECONOMY

Likely to Go Along on Slashes After Bankers' Warning on New Financing for City.

ACTING MAYOR SET TO FIGHT

In Position at Final Hearing to Ask Roll-Call on Each Item to Put Tammany on Record.

BIG DROP IN TAX PAYMENTS

Grimm Says Study Shows Manhattan Alone Will Be $30,000,000 Behind at Present Rate.

Whether or not the Tammany-controlled bloc in the Board of Estimate will go along with Acting Mayor McKee in a budget-reduction program sufficiently drastic to persuade the city's leading bankers to float new security issues and establish new credits essential for transacting municipal business on a cash basis will be determined this morning at an executive meeting of the board called for 10 o'clock.

John F. Curry, Tammany leader, and his principal political allies and advisers were reported in conference last night in an effort to shape a budget policy that would satisfy the banking groups and yet not imperil their own prospects in the Mayoralty campaign.

The bankers, who saw the city through a major financial crisis in January, relying on a Board of Estimate resolution pledging strict economy and retrenchment, have notified Controller Charles W. Berry that they are unwilling to extend further aid unless that pledge is at once fulfilled.

Final Hearing on Budget.

The executive meeting is to be followed by the final public hearing on the tentative budget for 1933. Mr. McKee is ready to press his economy program to the fullest—ready, if necessary, to go through the huge budget book line by line, armed with resolutions calling for specific reductions. He is in a position to demand a roll-call vote on each item, placing the members of the Tammany-controlled bloc squarely on the record, so that responsibility may be fixed for any consequences which might ensue because of failure to make the 1933 budget many millions lower than that for 1932.

Among taxpaying groups and in financial circles confidence was voiced that Tammany and its allies would not run the risk of jeopardizing city payrolls and the proper performance of essential municipal functions by holding out against drastic budget reductions. It was predicted that the organization leaders would pass the word to their spokesmen in the Board of Estimate to go along with the McKee program or submit an equivalent one of their own.

Although the bankers decline to discuss the situation for publication, it is known that their recent notice to Controller Berry of their unwillingness to lend the city more money was virtually a repetition of a similar warning given last August, about a week before former Mayor Walker resigned. At that time Controller Berry took the matter up with the Board of Estimate at an executive session called at his request, insisting that prompt steps should be taken toward drastic budget reductions for 1933, and warning his colleagues that unless advances could be had from the banks the Sept. 15 payrolls would be imperiled.

The necessary funds were ob-

Continued on Page Two.

Earth's Age Ten Billion Years, Says Einstein; Figure More Than Doubles Other Estimates

Special Cable to THE NEW YORK TIMES.

BERLIN, Oct. 16.—Professor Albert Einstein in a lecture here tonight on cosmic space said one of its salient characteristics was that it was not static but in a process of expansion. This, he said, had been established by the most recent astronomical research, especially by admirable observations made at Pasadena, Cal., on the so-called Doppler effect—the displacement of spectral lines in light received from distant stellar bodies.

"The measurement of these displacements shows that outer spiral nebulae are moving away from us at a speed of 12,500 miles a second," he said. "That is the rate at which our universe is expanding. It has been expanding for, say, 10,000,000,000 years. Now that is quite a tidy bit of time.

"But when you consider it is only ten to a hundred times longer than the beginning of life on the earth, and when it is added that our planet very probably saw the very beginning of this expansion of universal space, then the question arises: What was universal space like before it started expanding? But to that we have as yet no answer."

The lecture had been announced as a "popular" exposition, and Dr. Einstein did not employ any mathematical formulas. He drew only a few simple diagrams on the blackboard. He spoke simply and lucidly, with felicitous, homely illustrations of the more difficult points.

It is necessary to conceive of bodies before one can conceive of space. "Space is merely a summary term for the possible relations of bodies in space and time, and these relations depend on gravitational fields." "'Curvature' as applied to space is an unfortunate term. Curvature should be conceived of as lying in the time component of the space-time continuum."

These and other "explanations" of Dr. Einstein's were delightfully unintelligible to many of his listeners.

The successful measurement of the withdrawal of outer spiral nebulae from the earth, the professor said, not only had given information on the nature of universal space but also had made it possible to determine by means of observed data the mean density of the distribution of matter in space. This density, he said, was approximately one hydrogen atom per cubic meter.

He emphasized the necessity of a

Continued on Page Eleven.

BOTH PARTIES HAIL HUGE REGISTRATION

2,334,131 Voters Qualify, Indicating Keenest Election Interest in City's History.

DEMOCRATS SEE VICTORY

Mayoralty Candidates Called to Court Today in Legal Test of Nominations.

Registration in the city for the November election, which totaled 2,334,131, breaking by 305,000 the record of 2,029,618 set in 1928, was regarded yesterday as an indication of an extremely heavy vote for the Democratic national and State tickets on Nov. 8.

With harmony restored within the ranks of the Democratic organizations in the city, the heavy vote expected for Roosevelt and Lehman would be of advantage as well to John P. O'Brien, candidate for the one-year Mayoralty term at stake at the polls, it was contended by the Democrats.

The registration on Saturday, the last day for qualifying to vote in November, was so heavy that a number of registration booths did not close until well after midnight. The final figures for the city, which were not available until 3:30 yesterday morning, were printed in the final edition of THE TIMES.

Hoey Sees Record Victory.

James J. Hoey, campaign manager for Surrogate O'Brien, issued a statement claiming a record plurality for the Democratic ticket in November, on the basis of the registration figures.

The figures mean, Mr. Hoey said, "that the well-organized forces of Democracy are united and working in perfect harmony to get out a huge vote for Governor Roosevelt, Colonel Lehman, Senator Wagner, Judge O'Brien, and all their associates on the ticket."

Republican leaders also expressed pleasure in the heavy registration, with Lewis H. Pounds, Republican Mayoralty candidate, contending that the independent and so-called "silent voters" would protest at the polls the present City Administration.

"The national election has something to do with it, of course," Mr. Pounds said, "but the tremendous registration shows the enormous interest being manifested by the people in the State and especially the municipal election.

"It is indicative that the independent and dormant vote has come out more freely this October than in years because of the tremendous interest in the municipal government."

The last-day rush brought 746,536 voters to the registry booths, carrying the city total for the six-day period far beyond the record set in 1928, when the contest between Herbert Hoover and Alfred E. Smith for the Presidency brought out, all over the nation, a heavier vote than ever before.

Tammany Workers Active.

This year is the first in the history of the Greater City that the voters have been called on to express their preferences for President, Governor and Mayor at the same election, and the desire on the part of a great number of independent and casual voters to vote for or against one of the many candidates in the field was regarded as having contributed to the unusually heavy registration.

In addition, Tammany did its best to get out the vote, hoping that a plurality of imposing proportions might be recorded in the city for its

Continued on Page Two.

MACY PICKED STEUER BECAUSE OF FATHER

Member of Lawyers' Committee Says Chairman Admitted Friendship Swayed Him.

REPORT CLEARS NOMINEE

Citizens Union Scores "Deal" Made in an Atmosphere of "Selfish Intrigue."

W. Kingsland Macy, Republican State chairman, told an investigating committee of the County Lawyers' Association, it became known last night, that his party's endorsement of City Court Justice Aron Steuer, after his nomination for the Supreme Court by Tammany Hall, resulted from Mr. Macy's friendship for Max D. Steuer and was not part of a political deal.

This was revealed by Peter Gatens, who with former Supreme Court Justice James A. Delehanty was appointed as a subcommittee by the judiciary committee to investigate the circumstances under which Justice Steuer and State Senator Samuel Hofstadter received simultaneous bipartisan nominations for high judicial office.

The sub-committee's report exonerating Justice Steuer from participation in a political deal has been adopted by the judiciary committee and will be presented to the directors of the association at their meeting this afternoon. A second subcommittee appointed to look into Senator Hofstadter's nomination by the Democratic organization, which as chairman of the joint legislative committee he is still investigating, will make its report on Wednesday.

Heard Curry and Koenig.

Mr. Gatens said the subcommittee of which he was a member examined John F. Curry, leader of Tammany Hall; Mr. Macy, Samuel S. Koenig, New York County Republican leader; Justice Steuer and his father, Max, before rendering its report to the judiciary committee, which is headed by William C. Breed.

"We decided that there was no possibility of there having been a deal," said Mr. Gatens, after hearing Mr. Macy and Mr. Koenig. Mr. Macy explained that after the Bank of United States failure, when the Republican party was considering legislation for banking reform, he consulted many lawyers in search of advice. Of all those he saw, he told us, Mr. Steuer, who was serving as a Special Deputy District Attorney, was the best informed and most helpful.

"Mr. Macy informed us that he resolved then that if the opportunity ever presented itself to do anything to help Mr. Steuer he wanted to do it. On three different occasions, he said, he spoke to Mr. Koenig about it. He was deeply aggrieved to think that any one suspected anything sinister about the Republican endorsement of Justice Steuer.

"We called Mr. Koenig before us and he confirmed what Mr. Macy had said about his anxiety to do something for Mr. Steuer. I think the whole furore sprang from the fact that Justice Steuer is Max Steuer's son. After we had heard the statements of the Republican leaders and after Mr. Curry had denied that there was any deal, we reached the conclusion that there was no reason for further inquiry, although Mr. Steuer appeared before us also."

Mr. Gatens said Supreme Court Justices Isador Wasservogel, Edward J. Glennon, Alfred Frankenthaler and Richard P. Lydon spoke in the most glowing terms of Justice

Continued on Page Two.

Bulgaria Bars 2 Returning for Death Penalty; Exiled Ex-Ministers Must Wait for Amnesty

Special Cable to THE NEW YORK TIMES.

SOFIA, Oct. 16.—Bulgarian officials today refused to let two former Cabinet Members enter the country to meet sentences of death which had been passed on them for alleged subversive activities. They are MM. Athanasoff and Stoyanoff, members of the Cabinet of the late Premier Alexander Stambulisky, who fled the country after their leader was overthrown and assassinated in 1923.

At the request of the Sofia authorities the Yugoslav Government had rounded up forty Bulgarian refugees. Yesterday guards started with them for the frontier. Six of the party were under sentences of death and the others had long terms of imprisonment awaiting theem.

They reached the frontier town of Zaribrod today. Nearly all of them were arrested immediately and taken to prison in motor lorries. The two former Ministers, however, were sent back into Yugoslavia. As long as amnesty had not been granted to them, they were informed, they would not be permitted to re-enter Bulgaria. The amnesty law is expected to pass in the Chamber on Oct. 28.

The former Cabinet members protested against this action, demanding they be arrested with the others. They pointed out that Bulgaria had demanded their surrender by the Yugoslav authorities. The Bulgarian police, however, insisted that they turn back.

The Bulgarian Agrarian party had made great preparations for a demonstration to mark the return of MM. Athanasoff and Stoyanoff, but it was suppressed by the police, who garrisoned all the stations from the frontier to Sofia. Twelve Agrarian Deputies, including the Vice President of the Sobranje, who tried to reach the frontier, were turned back to Sofia by mounted police, who threatened them with carbines.

ROOSEVELT TO STATE ANTI-BONUS POSITION IN PITTSBURGH TALK

He Will Offer Plan Wednesday for a Wartime System to Aid Needy Veterans.

HOOVER TO BE CRITICIZED

His Stand Toward Ex-Soldiers and Cleveland Speech, Also, to Be Discussed on Tour.

PROGRAM FOR TRIP IS SET

Governor Confers With Advisers—He Starts Tuesday With Day of Campaigning for Lehman.

Governor Roosevelt will announce opposition to immediate cash payment of the soldiers' bonus in an address at Pittsburgh on Wednesday, it was learned yesterday.

At the same time he is expected to link to his disapproval of bonus payment a program calling for relief for destitute war veterans, with machinery similar to the draft boards of World War days.

The Governor will make this address on the second day of his coming tour, which starts Tuesday morning from Albany.

While the program for relief to be offered along with opposition to cash payment of the bonus has been kept a secret, it is suggested that the Governor will propose that the boards which would be set up would see to it that needy veterans who had an active war service would be assured of relief during the depression.

In this way, it is felt by the Governor's managers, veterans' groups which would otherwise find a grievance in a flat bonus refusa would have their opposition to the Democratic candidate somewhat tempered.

It is also indicated that in his discussion of the question the Governor will take President Hoover's Administration to task in respect to veteran relief measures and have something to say about the ousting of the "B. E. F." from Washington.

The Governor's bonus speech has been practically completed, although it will not be fully assembled until a few hours before he speaks in Pittsburgh.

Governor Lays Plans for Trip.

From a Staff Correspondent.

HYDE PARK, Oct. 16.—Governor Roosevelt spent many hours today with his research advisers in mapping out the program of speeches for his tour.

Among those who worked with him were Professor Raymond Moley of Columbia, Professor R. G. Tugwell, Adolph Berle, Samuel I. Rosenaman, Supreme Court justice, and General Hugh Johnson. They went over data and whipped into shape the manner of expression of some of the views the Governor will voice on national problems.

The Governor received few visitors, William H. Woodin, financier, being the only person of prominence who called.

Mr. Rosevelt seemed undisturbed by the "fighting" Hoover speech of last night in Cleveland. He was understood to be planning no comment on the criticisms until he made an occasion to do so during his trip.

Governor Not to Change Tactics.

While the charge has been made by Mr. Hoover or in his behalf on several occasions that the tactics of Democratic campaigners are unfair, the Governor does not intend to shift from the type of offensive that has been waged.

He is believed to be taking the view that the Republicans are making a

Continued on Page Three.

Gov. Roosevelt, Fearon, McGinnies to Confer Oct. 27 on Relief Session of the Legislature

Special to THE NEW YORK TIMES.

HYDE PARK, N. Y., Oct. 16.—With the voters expected to ratify the proposed $30,000,000 bond issue for State unemployment relief on Nov. 8, Governor Roosevelt announced today that on Oct. 27 he would confer in Albany with Lieut. Gov. Lehman, Senator Fearon and Speaker McGinnies of the Assembly to determine whether a special session of the Legislature would be necessary to make the funds available.

Harry L. Hopkins, chairman of the temporary emergency relief administration, which handles the State's relief program, also will be present.

In some quarters there has been a disposition recently to believe that a special session will not be necessary. The opinion has been voiced that the relief administration will have enough cash in November to give assurance that relief will continue in the normal course until the regular session of the Legislature meets early in January.

It has been pointed out that while commitments of the State to localities for its share of the relief work might consume all the money available, actual payments will not have to be made for several weeks. For that reason some officials feel that the State will have enough relief cash to carry over until the regular session can make appropriations from the bond issue.

A final decision cannot be made, however, until a checkup has been made just before the Oct. 27 conference. The Governor and the legislative leaders are insistent that nothing shall be left undone to prevent a breakdown in the relief machinery.

The Governor and the Republican leaders are confident that the voters will approve the bond issue. It has the support of both major parties and it is being advocated by prominent social welfare workers.

HOOVER APPEALS TO NATION FOR 'NEIGHBORHOOD' RELIEF; BAKER SEES 'CALL TO DUTY'

Davison to Tour State in Plane, With Wife Acting as His Pilot

F. Trubee Davison, Republican candidate for Lieutenant Governor, who is doing his campaigning by airplane, will fly about 1,000 miles this week to keep his speaking engagements in the State. Mrs. Davison will pilot the plane most of the time.

Early this morning the Davisons will take off in their Loening amphibian from Glen Cove, L. I., for Auburn, where Mr. Davison will address a luncheon meeting. He will speak tonight at Cortland. Tomorrow he will be in Norwich at noon, in Syracuse at night.

On Wednesday Mr. Davison will have luncheon in Utica with Moses G. Hubbard, Republican candidate for Attorney General, and that night he will address a rally at Babylon, L. I. On Thursday he will fly to Seneca Falls and Wellsville. He will be in Hornell on Friday and will speak here Saturday.

$183,481,502 SPENT FOR RELIEF BY CITY

About 2,000,000 Persons Aided in 3½ Years—Third of Total Used in First Half of 1932.

775,967 NOW ON THE ROLLS

Taylor Report Excludes Cost of Health Activities and of Private Charity Work.

Between Jan. 1, 1929 and June 30, 1932, public relief agencies in New York City aided about 2,000,000 persons and spent a total of $183,481,502, it was disclosed yesterday, when Frank J. Taylor, Commissioner of Public Welfare, made public statistics he had compiled and submitted to Acting Mayor McKee.

This sum, which was exclusive of amounts spent by charitable organizations and by the city in health activities, was about equal to two-thirds of the New York State budget of 1929 ($268,463,989); more than the budgetary expenditure of the city of Detroit in 1929 ($152,841,000); and about $5,500,000 more than the State of New York spent on ordinary disbursements in 1926 ($178,016,047).

More than $50,000,000, or nearly one-third of the total spent in the three and one-half year period, was dispensed in the first six months of 1932. This is believed to indicate that the total expenditures for 1932 may reach $100,000,000, or three times the amount spent in 1929.

Total on City Relief Roll 775,967.

A chart explaining the statistics puts the total number of men, women and children now receiving relief in New York City at 775,967. This number is about equal to the 1928 census figures for Boston, St. Louis or Baltimore, or to the combined population in 1928 of Newark and Jersey City.

The chart shows that with one exception—blind relief, which is limited by legislation to a maximum of $200,000 annually—every relief function has shown a steady increase since January, 1929.

At the beginning of that year there were five such functions—Veteran Relief, the Municipal Lodging House, Dependent Children, the Board of

Continued on Page Eight.

JOINT PLEA OVER RADIO

The President Summons 'Great Heart of People' to Meet Distress.

COMMUNITY AID 'ONLY WAY'

Proud That Each Has Accepted Task, He Says in Urging All Who Are Able to 'Give.'

BAKER VOICES CONFIDENCE

'Mute Appeal' of Children Will Be Answered, He Holds—Gifford Also Speaks.

Special to THE NEW YORK TIMES.

WASHINGTON, Oct. 16.—Opening a series of nation-wide radio programs for the welfare and relief mobilization of the Winter of 1932-33, President Hoover tonight appealed in a speech broadcast from the White House, to each community to meet its own needs.

Expressing confidence that the nation would respond generously, the President closed his appeal with the statement:

"I wish my last word to you to be the word 'Give'."

Brief addresses were also delivered by Newton D. Baker, former Secretary of War, who is chairman of the mobilization committee, and Walter S. Gifford, who acted as chairman of the President's Organization for Unemployment Relief. Their speeches were delivered from Cleveland and New York, respectively, and were carried, as was the President's talk, over the National and Columbia nation-wide hook-ups.

A musical program was provided from Washington by the United States Marine Band.

THE PRESIDENT'S ADDRESS.

The President, who was the first to speak, said:

The purpose of this appeal this evening is to summon again the great heart of the American people. We must make our material provision for the support of our charitable and character-building institutions. We must provide to the utmost extent for the local community support to the increased distress over the country.

I take profound pride in the fact that my countrymen have accepted the responsibility, each in his own community, to meet this need. That is the only way to meet it effectively—in the neighborhood itself, where the need is known.

The normal burden has been easily met in the past, and in the past two years we have responded to the unusual burden.

This personal sense of obligation and the desire to give have added to these community funds a wealth of human sympathy that has meant much indeed to those who have received aid from them. Not only have their material needs been supplied, but a friendly hand has added a precious warmth besides.

I have confident faith that the overwhelming majority of our people will not allow themselves to be tempted into doing less than their uttermost to a cause so charged with civic duty and so rich in appeal to every generous instinct of their hearts.

For the past two Winters this campaign for community funds for relief was carried on by committees, which I have organized specifically for that purpose. This year the National Association of Community Chests has taken the responsibility of organizing the work of voluntary giving in every community. They represent the cooperation of all these agencies. The funds they gather will be disbursed in relief through these existing agencies, upon an agreed division of the work. Thus the appeal for funds is centred locally in the one group, in order to simplify and expedite their collection.

In closing, let me say that no richer blessing can fill your own hearts than the consciousness on some bleak Winter's evening that your generosity has lighted a fire upon some family's hearth that otherwise would be black and cold and has spread some family table with food where otherwise children would be wanting. I wish my last word to you to be the word "give."

Mr. Baker's Address.

Ex-Secretary Baker's address from Cleveland was as follows:

"Modern psychologists agree that

Continued on Page Eight.

"All the News That's Fit to Print"

The New York Times

LATE CITY EDITION

Weather: Fair, very cold today and tonight. Chance of snow tomorrow. Temp. range: today 24-14; Sunday 33-26. Full U.S. report on Page 30.

VOL. LXXXII....No. 27,299. Entered as Second-Class Matter, Postoffice, New York, N. Y. NEW YORK, FRIDAY, OCTOBER 21, 1932. **** TWO CENTS In New York City | THREE CENTS Within 200 Miles | FOUR CENTS Elsewhere Except in 7th and 8th Postal Zones

THREATS TO VOTERS' JOBS ARE CHARGED BY ROOSEVELT AS INDIANAPOLIS HAILS HIM

100,000 CHEER NOMINEE

Republicans Pictured as Preaching Panic to Wage Workers.

CANNOT SUCCEED, HE SAYS

Prosperity Will Be Restored Despite Hoover's 'Ruinous Policies,' He Asserts.

THRONG SETS STATE RECORD

Rousing Welcome Bolsters Democrats' Predictions of a Sweep in Indiana.

The text of Governor Roosevelt's speech is printed on Page 16.

By JAMES A. HAGERTY.

INDIANAPOLIS, Ind., Oct. 20.—Indianapolis turned out today to give a rousing welcome to Governor Roosevelt which went far, in the opinion of observers, to bear out the predictions of the party leaders that he would sweep the State.

A crowd estimated at nearly 100,000, one of the largest in the history of the city, gathered in Monument Circle to hear him speak from the balcony of the Hotel English. A parade two miles long, with floats and banners, preceded his speech, and many thousands of men, women and children lined the streets and cheered him as he drove at the head of the procession from the railroad station to the hotel.

The outpouring of so great a throng of voters, among which women were conspicuous by their numbers, was accepted as an answer to the attempt the large business interests of the State have been making within the last two weeks to reverse what seems to be the political current. Stories are told that by a threat of stoppage of whatever industries are running in the event of Governor Roosevelt's election, the prospect of an extension of unemployment has been held before the voters.

Threats to Jobs Denounced.

Governor Roosevelt, who touched on this attempt of the Republican campaign management to revive the tactics of the first McKinley-Bryan campaign in his Pittsburgh speech last night by charging that the Republicans were trying to create a panic by "spreading the gospel of fear," went further along this line today.

In a talk to the members of the Indiana Democratic State organization he asserted that the Republicans were trying to intimidate voters by threatening them with the loss of their jobs and telling their employes that his election would result in going to the "demnition bow-wows."

The Governor declared that this attempt would fail for two reasons, first, because there had been Democratic Presidents and the country had not gone to the dogs under them, and, secondly, because there was a Republican President at present and everybody knew of the unfortunate business conditions during his administration.

Thomas D. Taggart Jr., national committeeman; R. Earl Peters, State chairman, and other party leaders who saw the Governor told him that there was no doubt that he would carry the State. Estimates of the plurality for the Democratic national ticket ran as high as 275,000. In 1928 President Hoover carried the State by 287,000.

They also told Mr. Roosevelt that Paul V. McNutt, candidate for Governor, would win from Raymond S. Springer, Republican, and that Fred Van Nuys, Senatorial candidate, would defeat Senator James E. Watson, veteran Republican who is running for re-election.

It was admitted by Republicans that Governor Roosevelt probably would carry the State, although they asserted that there had been a recent swing back of disgruntled Republicans and a prospect that some of the employes of the large industrial plants might be brought to support the Republican national ticket. According to the Republican viewpoint, Senator Watson stands about an even chance of re-election.

In his speech from the balcony of the Hotel English, Governor

Continued on Page Sixteen.

Hoover Denies 'Dime's Interest' Outside the Nation in 15 Years

By The Associated Press.

LOS ANGELES, Oct. 20.—President Hoover, in a telegram to C. C. Teague, head of the Republican campaign in Southern California, declares that he has not "had a dime's interest" in any activity outside the United States during the last fifteen years.

The telegram, made public today, was in response to an inquiry from Mr. Teague, who informed the President that oil workers in California were receiving political pamphlets charging that he opposed a tariff on oil because of ownership of foreign oil wells.

The President said:

"I have your telegram stating that Democratic agents, despite all proof to contrary, are still circulating misleading statements through their fields that I have been opposed to relief of oil industry because of my supposed interest in foreign oil and that I opposed the tariff on oil. This is the usual type of politics.

"I have not in fifteen years since I entered public service had a dime's interest outside the United States of any kind, including oil. I supported the oil tariff in the revenue bill and signed that bill. Without the support I gave I do not believe it would have received sufficient votes from non-oil sections to have been carried."

ROOSEVELT DISTORTS FACTS, SAYS MILLS

Governor Guilty of 'Inaccuracies' in Speech on Federal Finances, Treasury Head Declares.

BILLION INCREASE DENIED

Makes Public Letter From Fearon, Charging Candidate Fought State Economies.

Special to THE NEW YORK TIMES.

WASHINGTON, Oct. 20.—Charging that Governor Roosevelt, in his references at Pittsburgh last night to Federal finances, was guilty of "extraordinary inaccuracies and distortions," Secretary Mills presented in a statement tonight the administration's reply. He called the speech of Mr. Roosevelt "amazing" and showing a complete lack of understanding of the realities.

At the same time Mr. Mills made public a communication from George R. Fearon, majority leader and Temporary President of the New York State Senate, in which that Republican leader alleged that expenditures in New York had increased rapidly under Mr. Roosevelt and added that the best estimate now was that New York State was facing an actual deficit of $100,000,000 in the fiscal year.

In the course of his statement Mr. Mills remarked:

"The Governor complains of the Republicans seeking to arouse fear among the people as a result of his election, but how can he expect anything but fear in the face of the financial record of the Democratic House of Representatives? How can he expect that fear will do anything but grow when he himself, in discussing the fiscal policy of the Federal Government, deals in terms of fiction rather than fact and, worst of all, when for campaign purposes

Continued on Page Thirteen.

MELLON URGES NEED OF ELECTING HOOVER IN TALK IN ENGLAND

Tells English Speaking Union the Only Issue Here Is That of Discontent.

FEARS DELAY IN CHANGE

Points to a Waiting Time of Four Months if the Country Changes Leadership.

DEFENDS ADMINISTRATION

Ambassador Thinks High Tariffs and Empire Accords Will Aid People of Both Nations.

The text of Ambassador Mellon's speech is printed on Page 12.

Special Cable to THE NEW YORK TIMES.

MANCHESTER, England, Oct. 20.—Appearing before the English Speaking Union of Manchester today, Ambassador Andrew W. Mellon made it plain to a British audience that in his opinion the American people should re-elect President Hoover. Most of his address was devoted to a statement of the reasons for his belief that this would be the wise course.

He declared that the Presidential campaign in the United States was not being fought on any issue other than that of discontent with the present economic conditions and a desire for better times under whichever candidate seemed most likely to bring back prosperity.

"In the final analysis," he said, "the real question to be decided in the coming election is one of leadership rather than of issues. The electors are called upon to determine whether Democratic or Republican leadership is better qualified by experience and methods of approach to shoulder the responsibilities of government at this critical moment in the world's history and meet the problems which will arise in the years immediately ahead.

Calls It Unfortunate Issue.

"It is a solemn decision. Not only will it determine whether new men shall be substituted for those now directing the nation's policies but it means also that if the country should vote for a change of administration there will be a waiting interval of four months during which the United States and, to a certain extent, the world also will mark time until the new administration takes charge next March.

"It is a situation that is causing much concern to thoughtful Americans, regardless of what their affiliations and desires in the present election may be. It is doubly unfortunate, therefore, that this election should be decided, not on the merits of some important policy, but rather on the vague general issue of discontent.

"Many people blame President Hoover and his administration for the calamities which have overtaken America and the world. It would be just as reasonable to blame the Governor of Massachusetts for the low price of textiles or the Governor of Minnesota for the low price of wheat."

In regard to prohibition, Mr. Mellon said both parties wished to do away with "the illicit liquor traffic and the resulting lawlessness that has come in its train."

He said both major parties had cooperated in enacting emergency legislation designed to lead the way out of the economic slump, but he declared that "aside from this, the President has had to fight every inch of the way." He reminded his hearers that he had served with Mr.

Continued on Page Twelve.

Germans Attack Award of Medal to Herriot; Editor Calls Premier a 'Dangerous Enemy'

Special Cable to THE NEW YORK TIMES.

BERLIN, Oct. 20.—The presentation of the Goethe Centenary Medal to Premier Herriot in Paris yesterday by Dr. Leopold von Hoesch, the retiring German Ambassador, has produced a deal of astonishment here.

This astonishment was deepened when it became known today that President von Hindenburg had awarded the medal to the French Premier for his writings on Goethe and Beethoven as early as last August. Why the award was not made public then and why it has not been presented until now are questions as yet unanswered.

The nationalist press is displeased. "Whoever may be responsible for this curious act of courtesy, nationally minded Germany has precious little understanding for such a gesture at this most inappropriate time," says the Boersenzeitung. "That M. Herriot takes a literary interest in Goethe is commendable, but it does not alter the fact that this Radical Socialist is a more dangerous enemy of Germany than the most fervid avowed French chauvinist."

Much the same opinion is voiced by the Deutsche Tageszeitung, which suggests that at the time of the medal's bestowal last Summer the Wilhelmstrasse was shutting its eyes to M. Herriot's political anti-Germanism.

"This appreciative judge of German cultural values, this admirer of Goethe and Beethoven, makes it his political goal to keep their native country in a degrading position of inferiority and deny her rights that France accords to any Negro State," the paper declares.

"There is no covering up the fact that Franco-German relations have become worse. The more amicable contacts of the past prove to have been illusory. France showed us an amiable face as long as we were satisfied with mere show.

"The existing tension is the result of France's unwillingness to receive Germany in the circle of great powers with equal rights, and this animosity is rooted in the Versailles mentality, which has not yet been overcome, and the war guilt lie.

"It is regrettable that against this lie not even the present Reich Government has found plain enough words—that, indeed, Germany's moral struggle is not pressed with all the intensity, passionateness and consistency that it demands."

MANCHURIAN REBELS STRIKE AT JAPANESE

Cause Losses and Throw Foes on the Defensive by Attacks on Three Strongholds.

WRECK KILLS 13 RUSSIANS

Insurgents Derail and Burn a Train—Soviet Kerosene Shipment Destroyed.

Special Cable to THE NEW YORK TIMES.

HARBIN, Manchuria, Oct. 20.—The Japanese army in North Manchuria was thrown on the defensive today when the rebels started vigorous attacks against the most important Japanese military centres.

A Japanese official announcement admits losses when the insurgents attacked Chiamussu in the lower Sungari River area, where 480 Japanese soldier-settlers arrived a few hours later, expecting to establish a farming colony.

The forces of Wang Teh-Lin, long dormant, assaulted Ninguta (150 miles southeast of Harbin) and also harassed Hulan, across the Sungari from Harbin.

The east line of the Chinese Eastern Railway was the scene of a disastrous wreck for the second time this week, when bandits derailed a train. At least thirteen Russian refugees were killed and the train was burned. Sixteen carloads of kerosene and five of benzine, the property of the Soviet Naphtha Syndicate, were destroyed.

A Manchukuo announcement of a plan to establish a customs station at Fularki (about twelve miles west of Angangki) is taken to indicate that the authorities expect the Manchouli-Barga region to remain in rebel hands a long time.

Peaceable Outcome Sought.

By HUGH BYAS.

By Wireless to THE NEW YORK TIMES.

TOKYO, Oct. 20.—The War Office said today the Manchurian headquarters of the Japanese Army was continuing its efforts to effect a political solution of the Manchouli situation.

Military authorities agree that no reason exists to suspect that Russians are backing Hsu Ping-wen, the Chinese commander whose force seized the Manchouli area and who is holding as hostages some 270 Japanese and twelve Koreans. On the contrary, the Soviet officials are endeavoring to relieve the hostages.

While necessary military measures will be taken if General Hsu continues to hold the Japanese prisoners, the press admits that the difficulties, both geographical and climatic, are serious.

Hsieh Chieh-shih, Manchukuo's Foreign Minister, is fully occupied with entertainments. Yesterday was spent in formal calls and in attending an imperial luncheon and a gala fête at a theatre. This morning he visited the imperial mausoleum and this afternoon attended a municipal reception.

This evening he was at the Foreign Office for dinner. Tomorrow he will hunt ducks in the imperial gardens and afterward attend a students' meeting. The Minister seems overcome with the warmth of his welcome.

The attempt of the Japanese to round up the Chinese insurgents who have been operating in the region between the South Manchuria Railroad and the Korean border is probably the reason for the renewed boldness of the Chinese insurgents in Northern Manchuria.

Dispatches from Mukden have indicated that all available troops had been gathered for this drive.

LAWYERS REJECT 4 OF BENCH SLATE

Led by Seabury in Stormy Fight They Disavow Hofstadter, Steuer, Leary, Genung.

2 INDEPENDENTS ENDORSED

Senator "Shopped Around" for Post When Kept Off State Ticket, Says Investigator.

The New York County Lawyers' Association, after a two-hour debate interrupted by prolonged cheering, heckling and hissing, disavowed last night the bipartisan Supreme Court candidacies of City Court Justice Aron Steuer and State Senator Samuel H. Hofstadter.

Going further than any of the other bar associations of this city, the county lawyers also disavowed Municipal Court Justice George L. Genung, the Republican nominee, and President Justice Timothy A. Leary of the same court, the nominee of the Democrats.

When the meeting broke up near midnight, the members had enthusiastically endorsed the two independent candidates, Bernard S. Deutsch and George W. Alger, and had pronounced S. John Block and Matthew M. Levy, Socialist candidates for Supreme Court judgeships, qualified, and left only Supreme Court Justice Richard P. Lydon of the Tammany and bipatrisan ticket with its approval.

In their disapproval of Justices Steuer, Leary and Genung the members of the association ran directly counter to the recommendations of their own board of directors and followed the leadership of Samuel Seabury, who, fighting alone, swayed the meeting against a number of Tammany speakers.

Meeting Overflows Hall.

Long before the session was due to open, the little auditorium of the association at 14 Vesey Street was filled to capacity and the hall outside had begun to fill with the overflow. Charles A. Boston, president of the association, remarked from the chair that he had never seen so large a gathering of the members before and expected he would not soon again.

The meeting got under way with the usual transaction of prepared business, which included a speech from Chief City Magistrate James E. McDonald on the progress and affairs of the magistrates' court.

A tremor of expectation ran around the gathering when Terence J. McManus, secretary, read the list of recommendations that had been worked out at a meeting of the board of directors during the afternoon. The recommendations were that:

Judge Cuthbert W. Pound be approved for Chief Judge of the Court of Appeals; Justices Lydon, Leary, Steuer and Genung be approved. Mr. Deutsch and Mr. Alger were recommended to the membership as exceptionally qualified and their election was recommended. Mr. Block and Mr. Levy were recommended as qualified, and of Mr. Hofstadter the directors recommended that his candidacy be disapproved.

Former Municipal Court Justice Jacob A. Panken, the Socialist candidate seeking election as the opponent of Judge Pound, they recommended to be not qualified for the high judicial post.

This precipitated the first combat. The vote was viva voce, and Mr. Boston, on a close vote, ruled that the directors' recommendation re-

Continued on Page Eleven.

RAIL PRICES SLASHED; STEEL MEN PREPARE FOR A BUYING RUSH

Huge Orders Expected as Cut of $3 a Ton Follows Parley With Carrier Heads.

MILLS MOVE TO REOPEN

Employment of Thousands in Chicago Area Is Predicted—Cleveland Hails Change.

EXPECT PROMPT REACTION

Pittsburgh and Birmingham Plan for Quantity Production—First Reduction in Ten Years.

In the hope of inducing the railroads to place orders which have been long deferred the principal steel producers announced yesterday that the price for standard steel rails had been reduced to $40 a ton from the $43 figure, which had been in effect since October, 1922.

The Carnegie Steel Company, one of the principal subsidiaries of the United States Steel Corporation, announced that the reduction was already in effect. Similar reductions were announced in other centres, notably Chicago.

Eugene G. Grace, president of the Bethlehem Steel Corporation, said yesterday afternoon: "As in the past, whatever price of rails we find being made by competitors we will, of course, meet." Similar information was given by other producers.

Large Orders Expected.

It became apparent yesterday that the luncheon conference held on Wednesday by Myron C. Taylor, chairman of the United States Steel Corporation, with executives of nine large Eastern railroads was the forerunner to the price readjustment. According to the impression in steel trade circles, the railroads are about to place large orders for steel rails and other products required to replenish exhausted stocks and to carry out repair programs.

Some estimates place the potential buying demand of the railroads at several hundreds of millions of dollars. The lower price for steel rails undoubtedly will encourage a more active demand, it was pointed out. A great deal of steel besides rail is needed by the carriers, however, and the buying program believed to have been set in motion will result in a sharp expansion in steel operations as well as in an enlargement of shop operations by the railroads themselves.

The executives of the principal Eastern roads have hesitated to express themselves with respect to their steel needs. It is believed, however, that they will enter the market shortly for rails and other products in considerable volume.

Steel producers say that there is no intention of putting into effect a general reduction in prices. They have thus far stubbornly resisted requests for lower prices. Recently the tendency has been to discourage price concessions in all lines. It happens that steel rails, which are a special product, are not surrounded with the same competitive conditions that apply to other steel products.

The new rate of $40 a ton for steel rails represents the first cut in a decade. Prior to 1922 the price varied from a low of $33 a ton to a high of $55. In recent years rail prices have been investigated by government agencies.

Other Centres Meet Cut.

Special to THE NEW YORK TIMES.

PITTSBURGH, Pa., Oct. 20.—A reduction of $3 a ton in the price of steel rails, announced today in New York, the first in ten years, is expected to break a deadlock between

Continued on Page Two.

German in Andes Measures Cosmic Rays At 20,000 Feet, Record Terrestrial Height

Special Cable to THE NEW YORK TIMES.

BERLIN, Oct. 20.—The German Andes Expedition, which recently discovered grandiose Inca remains in the theretofore unknown Quitarasca Valley, has performed new mountaineering feats netting scientific data of much value.

A cablegram from Jungay, Peru, dated Oct. 18 reports:

"Overcoming great difficulties, Hoerlin and Drs. Kinzl and Borchers have succeeded in climbing the central summit of Hualcan, 6,100 meters [about 20,000 feet] high.

"Hoerlin remained at the summit eight days for the measurement of cosmic rays—the highest terrestrial station where these were ever taken. Despite bad weather we succeeded in making measurements at relay stations on the descent to the base camp. We hope the results will be of special value for research in cosmic radiation.

"Hein and Erwin Schneider have conquered Hualcan's main summit, 6,200 meters [about 20,340 feet] high. Kinzl has traversed the east face of the Cordillera Blanca. Dr. Borchers and Hein have made a photogrammetric survey of a large part of a hitherto almost unknown mountain range."

The object of the German Andes expedition is to combine mountain conquest with scientific research. Herr Hoerlin and Herr Schneider were members of the party that climbed Tchopikalki, about 21,650 feet high, last August. They also were in the party that climbed Huascaran, 22,000 feet high, and have the distinction of having been the first men to climb Jonsong Peak in the Himalyas.

$1,785,301 ADDED TO BUDGET, MAKING TOTAL $558,406,601; 'RACKET' CHARGED BY M'KEE

Steps by Which Budget Cut Of $72,959,696 Was Reached

The following tabulation shows the chief steps by which a reduction of $72,959,696.24 was obtained in the 1933 budget as proposed for adoption.

1932 budget	$631,366,297.97
1933 proposed budget	558,406,601.73
Decrease	$72,959,696.24
Subway bonds taken out of budget	$49,750,000
Board of Transportation salaries and expenses taken out of budget	5,765,353
Total	$55,515,353
Surplus from Teachers Retirement Fund used as credit against budget debt service	$3,815,156
Surplus from City Retirement Fund used as credit against budget debt service	400,000
Total	$4,215,156
Total taken out of budget by new methods	$59,730,509

The remaining items going into the total of $72,959,696.24 listed as a saving include $16,717,385 removed by the budget director and various transfers of city funds.

ESTIMATE BOARD VOTES

Ignores Acting Mayor's Proposals for Savings of $12,500,000.

HE SCORES HOSPITAL FUND

Indicates $1,000,000 Restored for Temporary Workers Is to Aid Political Favorites.

LIMOUSINES ARE LEFT IN

Public Hearing on Thursday—Schedules Can Now Be Cut but Not Increased.

The Board of Estimate formally approved yesterday the budget as proposed for adoption with a total of $558,406,601.73, which may not be increased but may be cut in further public hearings. Acting Mayor Joseph V. McKee charged that a political "racket" was responsible for $1,000,000 of $1,785,301.33 put back into the budget during the session, which makes the decrease from this year's budget $72,959,696.24.

Controller Charles W. Berry, who applied for a $35,000,000 loan from the Chase and National City Banks recently, informed the bankers yesterday that the city had money enough to last through this month without additional loans. Before visiting the bankers the Controller said there had been no change in the city's financial situation. He did not clarify why his application for $35,000,000 was still standing if the city did not need the money.

Instead of taking up the remaining economies suggested by Mr. McKee, which totaled about $12,500,000, the Board of Estimate turned its attention yesterday to increasing the budget. The items it restored included $1,000,000 for temporary help in hospitals, $600,000 for custodial service in the Education Department, $36,000 for the Museum of the City of New York, $33,299 for the city's free employment agency, $115,263.93 in mandatory expenses for the Supreme Court in all boroughs and $738.40 to equalize pay rates of per diem employes in the Manhattan Borough President's office.

Though the board also voted to include $561,928 in additional items for the Board of Education, this sum was not counted by the Budget Director as a budgetary item. His explanation was that the entire amount would be met from accruals in the department, though the accruals had theoretically been slashed to the bone before the tentative budget was presented. With this addition, the total restored in the budget stands at $2,347,229.33.

Clash on Hospital Funds.

The first clash came when Aldermanic President Dennis J. Mahon moved for the restoration of $1,000,000 cut from the $8,000,000 payroll for temporary help in the Hospitals Department. Dr. J. G. William Greeff, Commissioner of Hospitals, told the board that the loss of $1,000,000 meant the dismissal of 500 graduate nurses earning $500,000 a year and the dropping of 700 other positions. He said the nursing staff would be reduced by 20 per cent and the cleaning of wards and care of patients would be curtailed. In response to Mr. McKee's question, Dr. Greeff said the words temporary help were not accurate in describing these employes.

Dr. Greeff explained that the temporary force was made up from persons who applied at the hospitals for work. If they were qualified, he said they got the jobs. He said that about half the $8,000,000 appropriation went for nurses.

"And anybody that is qualified can go to Bellevue and get a job?" the Acting Mayor asked.

"As far as I know," the hospital head replied.

"Well, you ought to know," Mr. McKee snapped. "You're the Commissioner. Don't you know that this $8,000,000 or $9,000,000 which is being asked is to cover employes that are handed to you by political leaders? Isn't that a fact? One of your deputy commissioners told us that these men were put to work after they had presented cards from their political leaders. This has been a racket and is being particularly abused this year.

"If you had people doing the work as they should, without politics, you could take $1,000,000 out of the budget," the Acting Mayor told Dr.

Continued on Page Eighteen.

BERRY INSISTS CITY HAS FUNDS FOR NOV. 1

He Confers With Mitchell and Aldrich, However, and Gives Them Data on Budget.

THEY WILL STUDY NEEDS

Deny Any Commitment on the Controller's Request for a Loan of $35,000,000.

Following the meeting of the Board of Estimate yesterday Controller Berry conferred with Charles E. Mitchell, chairman of the National City Bank, and Winthrop W. Aldrich, president of the Chase National Bank, at the offices of the Chase Bank. Mr. Berry discussed the city's budget with the bankers and turned over to them data upon the budget as it stood at the close of the last day on which increases could be voted.

At the close of the meeting the Controller told reporters that the city had sufficient funds to carry it over the first of next month, while the bankers said that they had made no commitments, present or future, of any kind, but had merely taken the information supplied them by the Controller to study it for the next few days.

The Controller's statement that the city had sufficient funds to meet its needs until after Nov. 1 served to relieve some of the suspense that had surrounded the city's financial position. In his letter to Mr. Aldrich on Oct. 13, which was made public last week in connection with the appearance of Mr. Mitchell and Mr. Aldrich before the Board of Estimate, Mr. Berry had applied for loans aggregating $35,000,000, of which, he stated, $20,000,000 was needed today, $10,000,000 on Monday and $5,000,000 on Oct. 28.

Whether the funds Mr. Berry is now relying on to carry the city through the rest of this month have been on deposit with the banks all

Continued on Page Eighteen.

Old-Time Torchlight Parade in Times Square To Mark Roosevelt's Return From the South

An old-fashioned torchlight parade across Forty-second Street and through Times Square is planned to mark Governor Roosevelt's return from his Southern campaign trip, it was revealed at Democratic National Headquarters, where it was said that nothing of the sort had taken place in New York since the days of Grover Cleveland.

Announcement of the program for the reception was made by Eddie Dowling, chairman of the Stage and Screen Division of the Democratic Campaign Committee, who said that every Democratic club in the city, as well as many notables of the stage, would march in the parade carrying torches and banners.

The Governor's train is due at Grand Central at 8 P. M. on Oct. 27. The torchlight procession will form there and escort him to the Hotel Astor, where he is to attend the pre-election dinner in his honor. Mr. Roosevelt, according to present plans, will ride at the head of the parade in an open, horse-drawn barouche, with the Democratic leaders of all five boroughs following in similar conveyances.

The line of march as announced yesterday will be west on Forty-second Street to Times Square and thence northward on Broadway to Forty-fifth Street. A large delegation from Jersey City, headed by Mayor Frank Hague, will be massed in Times Square.

At the dinner which is to follow the parade, it was said, Speaker John Nance Garner and Governors Moore of New Jersey Ely of Massachusetts and Cross of Connecticut will be seated on the dais with Governor Roosevelt. Others who are expected to be there are Lieut. Gov. Herbert H. Lehman, Surrogate John P. O'Brien and Senators Robert F. Wagner and Royal S. Copeland.

"All the News That's Fit to Print"

The New York Times

LATE CITY EDITION

Weather: Fair, very cold today and tonight. Chance of snow tomorrow. Temp. range: today 24-14; Sunday 33-26. Full U.S. report on Page 30.

VOL. LXXXII....No. 27,315. Entered as Second-Class Matter, Postoffice, New York, N. Y. NEW YORK, SUNDAY, NOVEMBER 6, 1932. **** Including Rotogravure Picture, Magazine and Book Sections. TEN CENTS

HOOVER AND ROOSEVELT END CAMPAIGNS, GOVERNOR AT BIG TAMMANY RALLY HERE, PRESIDENT WITH A SPEECH AT ST. PAUL

NEW DEADLOCK SEEN IN REICH POLL TODAY; NAZI LOSSES LIKELY

Result Is Expected to Prevent Return to Parliamentary Rule, Letting von Papen Carry On.

HITLER MAY DROP 50 SEATS

With Decline in Centrist Vote Also Anticipated, Bi-Party Coalition Is Improbable.

NATIONALISTS DUE TO GAIN

They and Communists Should Add to Representation—Socialists Again Face Defections.

By FREDERICK T. BIRCHALL.

By Cable to THE NEW YORK TIMES.

BERLIN, Nov. 5.—Tomorrow's election whereby it is intended to remove the Damocletian sword that was suspended over the von Papen Cabinet while the last Reichstag existed will in all probability achieve that purpose.

In other words, it is expected to eliminate any possibility of the formation of a coalition which might present to President von Hindenburg the alternative of a return to parliamentary government. Thus his "presidial" Cabinet could carry on indefinitely with or without a Reichstag hopelessly divided.

Such a situation is what both the President and the Cabinet desire, and all indications are that they will get it.

In the last Reichstag the von Papen Cabinet had the support of less than 5 per cent of the membership. Moreover, there was always the possibility of the National Socialists and Centrists forming a working combination, presenting the President with an accomplished fact and demanding a government based thereon. Such a combination would have given them a Reichstag majority of twenty-four and the demand would not have been easy to refuse. It would probably have involved the installation of Adolf Hitler as Chancellor.

Nazis May Lose Fifty Seats.

That prospect seems to have disappeared. The most reliable indications are that the Nazis will lose from thirty to fifty of the 230 seats they now possess and that the Centrists will lose some of their seventy-five, their Bavarian allies, however, probably retaining their twenty-two.

The lost seats, save those vanishing entirely through diminution of the total vote—the German electoral system provides one seat for every 60,000 votes obtained—are expected to go to the Nationalists and Communists.

The country is getting tired of the Nazis. They had their chance last August when President von Hindenburg offered a share in the government to Herr Hitler and he refused it, and their performances since have intensified the disgust then experienced by their moderate supporters, while enhancing the disappointment of their more radical followers. The moderates are due to vote Nationalist or stay at home and the radicals will veer to the Communists.

The Centrists are slated to lose a large Jewish vote, which resents their flirting with the Nazis and the clumsiness whereby they permitted the more acceptable von Papen government to be rejected by the Reichstag without giving it a chance to show what it could do. It is not an immense vote in comparison with Germany's millions, but it should reduce the Centrist representation somewhat.

Nationalists Expect Gains.

The Nationalists, who had thirty-seven seats in the last Reichstag, will probably increase their representation. The Cabinet, which largely reflects their views, is regarded as not having made a bad record, and they should gain as a result. It is not likely to do them much good, but it will be of importance in preventing the Nazis and Centrists from obtaining a majority without taking them in a development scarcely conceivable.

The Socialists probably will lose some seats because of their ineptitude. They have also had their chance and muffed it and their program comprises a continuation of large expenditures in social service that the country feels it cannot afford.

The very transit strike that is tying up Berlin today and inflicting hardships on thousands of workers shows that the Socialists no longer control a large part of their own following. It is the Communists and Nazis who are running this strike, largely to demonstrate the decline of the Socialist power, and the demonstration is not unheeded.

Thus there looms once more, in the opinion of the most experienced observers, a Reichstag worse split and more hopeless than the last.

In all likelihood, the only two-party combination possible as a result of the election which could command a

Continued on Page Eight.

Major Sports Results

Football—A powerful Army eleven swamped Harvard, 46 to 0, in the Harvard Stadium before 48,000 persons. In New York, Fordham triumphed, 14 to 0, in its intersectional clash with St. Mary's while 32,000 looked on, and N. Y. U. conquered Georgia, 13 to 7, at the Yankee Stadium. Columbia eked out a 7-6 victory over Navy at Annapolis. The largest crowd of the season in the East, 70,000 persons, saw Pittsburgh beat Pennsylvania, 19 to 12, at Philadelphia. Scores of other important games:

Brown	10	Holy Cross	7
Cornell	40	Albright	14
Princeton	53	Lehigh	0
Providence	46	C. C. N. Y.	0
Wesleyan	13	Williams	6
Rutgers	7	Lafayette	6
Michigan	7	Indiana	0
Ohio State	20	Northwestern	6
Purdue	37	Chicago	0
Notre Dame	24	Kansas	6
Nebraska	14	Iowa	13
Tulane	20	Georgia Tech	14
So. California	27	California	7
Washington	18	Stanford	13

Racing—Adolphe Pons's Swivel won the $40,000 added Pimlico Futurity, defeating J. E. Widener's Golden Way by a length to earn $62,430. Swivel paid $24.90 to win.

Details in Sports Section.

MINISTRY APPROVES MUSSOLINI AMNESTY

Decree Affecting Criminals and Political Offenders Is Sent to King for His Signature.

THOUSANDS WILL BENEFIT

Those Sentenced for Minor Acts Against the Fascist Regime Will Be Released.

By ARNALDO CORTESI.

By Wireless to THE NEW YORK TIMES.

ROME, Nov. 5.—The Italian Cabinet today approved Premier Mussolini's amnesty decree, which was immediately sent to King Victor Emmanuel's country residence at San Rossore for the royal signature. The decree probably will be published tomorrow, as soon as it receives the King's approval.

The amnesty is reported to be the most liberal and most comprehensive ever drafted in the Kingdom of Italy. It reduces the sentences for many crimes and shows leniency to those condemned for anti-Fascist crimes. Thousands of prisoners will benefit.

Those guilty of minor anti-Fascist crimes will be freed from prison and sentences for major political crimes will be reduced. The commutations are less liberal for second offenders and political exiles.

Exiles Not Likely to Benefit.

ROME, Nov. 5 (AP).—The names of the prisoners affected by Premier Mussolini's amnesty will be announced when the King signs the decree. It was considered unlikely that the amnesty would be extended to anti-Fascists living abroad, such as former Premier Francesco Nitti, who lives in Paris, and Count Sforza.

The government's communiqué said the amnesty would not be total because "there are some necessary limitations regarding recurrent offenders and offenders at large."

Among other anti-Fascists abroad are Signor Nitti's nephew, Francesco Nitti; Captain Lusso and Nathan Roselli, who made dramatic escapes from the Lipari Island prison in 1929.

The amnesty was Mussolini's gift on the occasion of the Fascist decennial. He promised it five years ago and again on Oct. 25 last when he said "the act would be a sign of strength rather than one of weakness."

The news came as a great relief to hundreds of families who have relatives confined on the Lipari Islands. There are about 1,000 prisoners on the two islands. They were sent there charged with conspiring against the government, for outbreaks against the régime, for membership in the Communist party or for other political reasons.

It was problematical whether the two men who tried to assassinate Mussolini would enjoy freedom. One of these, General Zaniboni, was sentenced to thirty years in prison when he was discovered with his rifle trained on Premier Mussolini from a hotel window in 1925. The other, Gino Lucetti, received a similar sentence for throwing a bomb at the Premier's automobile in 1926.

Few Restrictions on Lipari.

Lipari, the largest island of the Lipari group of volcanic isles north of the eastern coast of Sicily, holds many of the leading political prisoners of Italy. The prisoners are not confined to a jail but are allowed to roam at will on a large area of the island.

Francesco Nitti, a nephew of the former Italian Premier, escaped with two others from Lipari in 1929. In his book, "Escape," he wrote that on his arrival the government aban-

Continued on Page Five.

400 ELECTORAL VOTES GOING TO ROOSEVELT, FORECASTS INDICATE

Composite Opinion of 200 Observers Is That He Will Carry Thirty-nine States.

SOUTH, WEST RATED SOLID

Analysis Puts Thirty States With 300 Electoral Votes as Sure for the Democrats.

NINE STATES GIVEN HOOVER

California, Massachusetts, New York and New Jersey Doubtful, With Trend to Roosevelt.

By ARTHUR KROCK.

The composite opinion of nearly 200 usually well-informed political observers in the several States is that Franklin D. Roosevelt will be elected President next Tuesday with from 400 to 450 electoral votes. Their preponderant view is that he will carry at least 39 States with a total of 438 electors.

This estimate is the net of final reports from all parts of the country received yesterday by THE NEW YORK TIMES. In each instance anonymity was promised to the observers, since a number of them are affiliated with the Republican party, either as State organizers and leaders or as editors who have been urging and hoping for President Hoover's re-election.

They were asked three questions: How their State would probably vote on the Presidency; how it would vote in local contests for the Senate, the House and on the Governorship; and whether there had been a change in the last weeks or days fundamentally affecting the outcome.

In tabulating their replies, this method is used: Where the observers are united in an opinion the State is set down as Democratic or Republican; where one opinion is preponderant, the State is marked as "probably" Republican or Democratic.

Nearly all of those taking part in the symposium are commonly considered experts in forecasting political results. Many of them, as party leaders, are, during campaigns, in daily touch with their chairmen in the various counties and districts. They do not rely on newspaper or magazine straw polls but take soundings on their own account. They should be able to hear a landslide coming. Each of them conferred with many others before dispatching his conclusions.

Their composite opinion is that, from the standpoint of electoral votes, the landslide will arrive on Tuesday. The result, contrasted with their prediction, should provide a test for the forecasting abilities of the experts.

The successful candidate for the Presidency must have 266 electoral votes. The following are, by agreement of the contributors to this symposium, assigned to Governor Roosevelt:

Alabama	11	Nevada	3
Arizona	3	New Mexico	3
Arkansas	9	No. Carolina	13
Florida	7	North Dakota	4
Georgia	12	Ohio	26
Idaho	4	Oklahoma	11
Illinois	29	So. Carolina	8
Indiana	14	South Dakota	4
Kentucky	11	Tennessee	11
Louisiana	10	Texas	23
Maryland	8	Virginia	11
Mississippi	9	Washington	8
Missouri	15	West Virginia	8
Montana	4	Wyoming	3
Minnesota	11		
Nebraska	7	Total	300

States Where Opinion Differs.

The prevailing opinion, where the experts are in dispute, is that Governor Roosevelt will carry these States:

California	22	Oregon	5
Colorado	6	Rhode Island	4
Kansas	9	Wisconsin	12
Mass.	17		
New Jersey	16	Total	138
New York	47		

The prevailing opinion, where the experts are in dispute, is that the President will carry the following States:

Connecticut	8	N. Hampshire	4
Delaware	3	Utah	4
Iowa	11		
Michigan	19	Total	49

The unanimous opinion of those whose views were sought in the following States is that the President will carry them:

Vermont	3	Pennsylvania	36
Maine	5		
		Total	44

Giving Mr. Hoover the benefit of both the certainty and the doubt of these political prophets, he would have a grand total of 93 electoral votes, or six more than Alfred E. Smith had four years ago. This would amount to a violent landslide of the suffrage, particularly since the Republicans have a normal majority of several millions of votes in the United States.

It would not necessarily, however,

Continued on Page Twenty-seven.

Texas House Attacks Hoover For Likening Crisis to Civil War

By The Associated Press.

AUSTIN, Nov. 5.—A resolution attacking President Hoover's speech at Springfield, Ill., yesterday and calling on all "who sought, accepted or hold office as a Democrat" to vote the Democratic ticket from "top to bottom" was adopted today by the Texas House of Representatives, 83 to 11.

The action was not final because of a motion to reconsider and spread on the journal.

The resolution referred to Hoover as the "Acting President" and quoted him as likening the present economic situation to the Civil War period. Citizens of Texas were "reminded" of the "bayonet-enforced Republican rule one time foisted on the people of the Lone Star State."

Criticizing the President's Springfield address, the resolution stated: "We condemn the veiled threat to arouse sectional strife among our people and to return to our State carpetbag Governors. And to prevent this we respectfully urge the citizens to vote a straight Democratic ticket in order that the great principles of Democracy may survive."

DEMOCRATS PREDICT CONGRESS CONTROL

But Republicans Count on Holding Their Own by "Many Surprises."

32 SENATE SEATS AT STAKE

And 435 Will Be Decided in the House—Wets Expect to Control Both Houses.

Special to THE NEW YORK TIMES.

WASHINGTON, Nov. 5.—As Tuesday approaches, leaders of both the Democratic and Republican Congressional campaigns officially express the utmost confidence in the outcome of the election, the Democrats prophesying extensive gains, the Republicans asserting that they will hold their own. Private expressions of Democratic leaders, however, seem to carry a greater weight of personal conviction. Besides the President and the Vice President of the United States, thirty-two Senators, 435 members of the House and thirty-four Governors are to be elected.

Wet leaders confidently assert that the next Congress will have a majority in favor of submitting repeal of the Eighteenth Amendment. The more enthusiastic champions believe that a sufficient number of drys will shift in the session of Congress meeting in December and vote to revise the Volstead act permitting the sale of beer.

Surveys by the Wets indicate that at least fifty-nine members of the new Senate will be favorable to a repeal resolution. Indications are, they say, that five Senators, now wavering, will go along with the verdict of the electorate in November and give the resolution the necessary two-thirds vote. Wet leaders assert that 294 members of the next House, four more than necessary to pass the resolution, will be for repeal.

Appeal for Democratic Congress.

In a joint pre-election forecast issued by Senator Swanson of Virginia, chairman of the Democratic Senatorial Committee, and Representative Byrns of Tennessee, chairman of the Congressional Committee, the country is told that only through the election of a Democratic President can full cooperation between the Executive and legislative branches of the government be achieved, and a harmonious and effective program looking to the restoration of economic stability put into effect.

"Everybody knows that the next

Continued on Page Thirty-three.

Russian Ship Battled 3,000 Miles of Ice To Establish New Route Through the Arctic

By The Associated Press.

TOKYO, Nov. 5.—The Soviet icebreaker Siberiakov III arrived at Yokohama today after successfully negotiating the first Arctic passage between Europe and Asia in a single season.

The Siberiakov threaded her way laboriously from Archangel on the White Sea to the Bering Strait in six weeks, although she smashed two propellers against the ice in the venture and had to make the last stages under sail.

It was the climax of high adventure for Dr. Otto Schmidt, director of the Leningrad Arctic Institute, and his crew of sixty-five, among whom were three women. Dr. Schmidt and several associate scientists called on Premier Makoto Saito of Japan today and received the official's congratulations.

The Russians said their feat demonstrated the practicability of Summer water communication between Europe and Far Eastern Russia in the event other methods of travel were impossible.

The Siberiakov left Archangel, Western Russia's northern outpost, on July 28. She battled ice floes along more than 3,000 miles of Arctic and tributary waters, reaching the Bering Strait on Sept. 10 in an almost helpless condition.

A Soviet trawler was summoned and towed the Siberiakov from the Bering Strait to Yokohama. Besides the crew there were scientists, movie camera men and newspaper men aboard. One of the women was a geologist and the others were members of the crew.

The northern passage across European and Asiatic Arctic oceans has been negotiated only twice before. A Swedish expedition made the passage in 1872, spending one Winter ice-bound. The Roald Amundsen vessel Maud spent the Winters of 1918 and 1919 in northern ocean ice, going from Europe to Asia.

THE PRESIDENT SUMS UP

Holds Democrats 'Trick' Nation by Stirring Up 'Protest' Vote.

LISTS 21 RECOVERY STEPS

He Concludes That Real Issue of Campaign Is the Crisis—Assails 'Fictions' of Foes.

SCORES RIVAL AT MADISON

Addressing 12,000 at University, He Says Roosevelt Has Failed on Gangster Problem.

President's speeches in St. Paul and Madison, Wis., Pages 30, 31.

Special to THE NEW YORK TIMES.

ST. PAUL, Minn., Nov. 5.—President Hoover in his final major speech of the campaign here tonight declared that the great issue before the people was the problem of overcoming the industrial and commercial crisis. He contended that he had presented a comprehensive program to overcome the depression, and declared that a Democratic victory would mean a year's delay in bringing about decisive action. This, he held, would mean stagnation at a critical point.

His address was a summing up of the issues and the record as he sees them. In it he criticized Democratic acts in the House of Representatives, attacked policies and utterances of Governor Roosevelt and denounced what he declared to be a campaign of misrepresentation by his opponents.

He defended the protective tariff and again asserted that his opponents were sponsoring ideas which strike at the foundation of the republic.

Taking notice of the address of Governor Roosevelt last night, he quoted his rival as saying that "I have been scrupulously careful to engage in no personalities, no unfair innuendoes, no baseless charges against the President of the United States."

He added:

"I would recommend that any one interested in this statement should read Governor Roosevelt's speeches from the beginning of this campaign.

"I have been compelled to take the unprecedented action of calling attention to a few of them. I have been also compelled to frequently call attention to statements being put out through the Democratic National Committee and their agencies, which amount to positive calumnies. In no case has the Democratic candidate disavowed this action of his official committee or agencies. He has naturally profited by silence."

Strenuous Day of Speaking.

Reports circulated in Ohio that the Farm Board spent lavishly on expense accounts had just come to his attention. These were untrue, he said.

The President made his speech in the St. Paul Auditorium, thus closing a strenuous two-day swing of day

Continued on Page Thirty.

Secretary Chapin 'Theoretical' Head of Nation As Most of the President's Cabinet Campaigns

Special to THE NEW YORK TIMES.

WASHINGTON, Nov. 5.—Were an emergency to arise today in the affairs of the Federal Government there would be no legal head of the government here to direct the various agencies or to sign official papers.

President Hoover is away on his Western campaign trip; members of his Cabinet whose succession is provided by law and in this order—Vice President, Secretary of State, Treasury, War, Attorney General, Postmaster General, Secretary of the Navy and Secretary of the Interior—are also out of the city in the interest of Mr. Hoover's candidacy, or for private reasons.

The law which provides the order of succession was passed by Congress on Jan. 19, 1886, years before the Departments of Agriculture, Commerce and Labor were created, and the heads of the three departments, therefore, are not legally authorized to act in the absence of the other Cabinet members.

Only two secretaries are in the city today, Mr. Chapin of Commerce and Mr. Doak of Labor. Theoretically, some observers say, Mr. Chapin, because his department has precedence over the Labor Department, is the acting head of the government. But, according to the act of 1886, there is no legal head.

Secretary Stimson apparently wondered about the situation yesterday when he prepared to leave for the week-end. He jokingly told reporters at his press conference that Theodore G. Joslin, one of President Hoover's secretaries, "would head the government during the President's absence."

Mr. Stimson is spending the week-end at his Long Island home and could be easily reached in case of emergency.

REPUBLICANS FIGHT TO HOLD THE STATE

Macy Predicts Vote Outside of This City Will Give Plurality to Hoover and Ticket.

DISPUTES RIVALS' CLAIMS

He and Aides Say Democrats Will Not Gain Control of the Legislature.

After one of the most intensively fought campaigns in the history of the State, all surface indications support the Democrats' claim that Franklin D. Roosevelt, their Presidential nominee; Herbert H. Lehman, their candidate for Governor; Robert F. Wagner, who is seeking a second term in the United States Senate, and other candidates on their State ticket will win by towering pluralities on Tuesday.

The Democratic campaign managers say that Mr. Roosevelt, Mr. Lehman and Senator Wagner, with their running mates on the State and national tickets, not only will carry this city by unprecedented pluralities but will run far ahead of President Hoover and the Republican candidates on the State and national tickets in the counties outside of New York City.

Mr. Roosevelt as a candidate for Governor two years ago accomplished a feat with no recent precedent when he came down to the Bronx with approximately 175,000 plurality. The Democratic campaign managers last night expressed confidence that he would duplicate that feat, that Mr. Lehman, the Gubernatorial nominee, would run not far behind Mr. Roosevelt in his up-State vote, and that Senator Wagner might run ahead of both Mr. Roosevelt and Mr. Lehman outside of the city, due to the fact that his Republican opponent, George Z. Medalie, is little known up-State.

Trend in New York City.

From every indication the New York City pluralities for the Democratic candidates will be great. The Republicans have expressed hopes of bringing their candidates to the city line with pluralities large enough to offset those polled by their opponents in the five New York City counties. City pluralities of 800,000 or more were predicted last night by Democratic observers.

Chairman W. Kingsland Macy in an election-eve statement claimed a plurality of 400,000 to 500,000 for President Hoover north of the Bronx and on Long Island, outside this city. This is the highest estimate of the up-State plurality for the party made by any Republican leader. Even if the Democratic claims for the city should prove high, there is every indication that the Republican pluralities up-State would be swallowed up by the Democratic pluralities here.

The Democratic claims include a clean sweep for all their candidates for the House of Representatives in New York City districts as well as for their candidates for the State Senate and Assembly. Up-State they expect to make sufficient gains to capture control of the Legislature, obtaining for Mr. Lehman, in the event of his election, a law-making

Continued on Page Thirty-one.

PROTEST VOTE TO CUT O'BRIEN PLURALITY

Election as Mayor Certain, but Tammany Concedes He Will Run Behind Ticket.

600,000 MARGIN FORECAST

Hillquit Is Expected to Poll a Large Total—Many Will Write In Name of McKee.

The Mayoralty contest virtually came to an end last night without, in the opinion of political observers, ever having actually started.

The names of three candidates, John Patrick O'Brien, Democrat; Lewis H. Pounds, Republican, and Morris Hillquit, Socialist, will be on the voting machines and the name of Joseph V. McKee, the Acting Mayor, will be written in by many voters.

The election is for a one-year term, beginning at noon on the 1st of January, 1933, and ending a year from that date, the period representing the unexpired term of James J. Walker, resigned.

Result Sure From First.

The election of Judge O'Brien appeared to be assured as early as Oct. 6. On the afternoon of that day the Court of Appeals decided that a Mayoralty election must be held this year, and in the evening the members of the Democratic county committees of the five boroughs gathered in Madison Square Garden and ratified the selection of Judge O'Brien as the party nominee, a selection made late that afternoon at a conference of leaders at the Hotel Plaza.

The gathering at the Garden heard the "withdrawal" from the race of Mr. Walker, recited in a wireless message to the hall from the former Mayor, still aboard ship on his way back here from Europe.

Mr. McKee, a resident of the Bronx, had become Acting Mayor by virtue of his post as President of the Board of Aldermen and had fought in the courts for the right to keep the job until the end of the Walker term without an election.

The belief existed at the time that had Tammany nominated Mr. Walker, in defiance of its Presidential nominee, Governor Roosevelt, that Mr. McKee, with the support of his county leader, Edward J. Flynn, would have run independently.

The Socialists had already nominated Morris Hillquit, who, as the party's nominee for the same office in 1917, had finished a very close third to Mayor John Purroy Mitchel and ahead of the late William M. Bennett, the organization Republican nominee.

Two days after the Democrats nominated Mr. O'Brien the Republicans, in a meeting at Mecca Temple, nominated Lewis H. Pounds, 72-year-old Brooklyn civic worker, who had been President of the Borough of Brooklyn in the Mitchel administration and later State Treasurer.

Judge O'Brien, nominated by the Democrats, started in the city employ thirty-one years ago, working his way up through the Law Department to the post of Corporation Counsel. He was elected Surrogate of New York County in 1922, a post he has held since then.

Tammany has been accustomed in

Continued on Page Thirty-four.

22,000 CHEER IN GARDEN

Governor, Wildly Hailed, Calls Fears for the Nation Baseless.

SAYS COUNTRY ASKS CHANGE

Smith, Backing Him and Ticket, Scores Republican Record at Washington and Albany.

ASSAILS DELAY AND EVASION

Party Is Confident of Sweep—Roosevelt Makes Last Plea at Poughkeepsie Tomorrow.

Speeches of Gov. Roosevelt and ex-Gov. Smith are on Pages 32, 33.

By F. RAYMOND DANIELL.

The two great leaders of the Democratic party stood with arms about each other's shoulders in Madison Square Garden last night and delivered the valedictory addresses of the 1932 campaign.

They were Governor Franklin D. Roosevelt and former Governor Alfred E. Smith, who, envisioning victory, predicted the return of happy days.

All the factions and elements that make up Tammany Hall were present occupying boxes rather than platform seats. Old hatchets had been buried and Edward J. Flynn, the Bronx leader who supported Governor Roosevelt at Chicago, had smoked the pipe of peace with John F. Curry and John H. McCooey.

Their Mayoralty nominee, Surrogate John P. O'Brien, had just pledged for them the undivided loyalty of the organization for the party's nominees in the State and nation, declaring that he wanted no votes from those who did not vote for Mr. Roosevelt, Speaker John N. Garner, Senator Robert F. Wagner or Lieutenant Governor Herbert H. Lehman.

An Eight-Minute Demonstration.

The evening's oratory stretched over a period of two hours and a half and no candidate was omitted from the program. When Mr. Roosevelt and Mr. Smith stood together before the crowd there was frenzied cheering. For eight solid minutes the demonstration continued. The crowd in the balconies, the boxes and on the floor of the great sporting arena waved flags, cheered and tossed confetti in a demonstration that had in it emotion and perhaps a little hysteria.

It was the sight of Mr. Smith standing, with a happy smile upon his face with one arm about the shoulders of the man who won the nomination he sought to win again this year, and the other around his friend, Colonel Lehman, that provoked the heartiest outburst of the evening.

There had been other moments of enthusiasm, but there was none to equal this. The nearest approach was perhaps when the "Happy Warrior," after a characteristic attack on the entire Republican administration, said:

"Well, finally, after this long, black night of sorrow, and sickness, and stress, and storm, they make no account of that stewardship, but in the panic that they now find themselves in, facing complete collapse, they hand us a campaign of fear, of threat, and of intimidation. They can be steward no longer.

"The American people on Tuesday, next, will relieve them of that responsibility, and we will put it into the capable hands of Roosevelt, Garner, and a Democratic Congress."

Has No Bitterness.

Delivering one of the last major addresses of his campaign for the Presidency, Governor Roosevelt told the great throng which had begun assembling at 4:30 yesterday afternoon that he preferred to remember the battle as one that was characterized by hard fighting rather than with bitterness.

"The greatness of America," he said, "is grounded in principles and not on any single personality. And I for one shall remember that, even as President."

He spoke of the lessons the depression had taught—that "extravagant advantage for the few ultimately depresses the many," and "while the families upon our farms are in want, there can be no safety for the families of the workers in our cities."

The Governor, who said he felt like one standing at the "gates of vic-

Continued on Page Thirty-two.

"All the News That's Fit to Print."

The New York Times.

LATE CITY EDITION
WEATHER—Much colder and snow today; tomorrow fair and cold.
Temperatures Yesterday—Max., 55; min., 46.

VOL. LXXXII....No. 27,326. Entered as Second-Class Matter, Postoffice, New York, N. Y. NEW YORK, THURSDAY, NOVEMBER 17, 1932. * * * * + TWO CENTS In New York City | THREE CENTS Within 200 Miles | FOUR CENTS Elsewhere Except in 7th and 8th Postal Zones

PRESIDENT WILL NOT REQUEST CONGRESS TO SUSPEND WAR DEBT PAYMENTS DEC. 15; FURTHER STUDY DEPENDS ON ROOSEVELT

HOOVER BACK IN CAPITAL

Congress Is Unanimous Against New Delay, He Is Informed.

PAYMENT HELD ESSENTIAL

Then He Would Consider Urging Revival of Funding Commission on Successor.

POWERS' MOVE A SURPRISE

Senators Are Told Debtor Nations Might Better Have Asked Re-examination First.

Special to THE NEW YORK TIMES.

WASHINGTON, Nov. 16.—President Hoover indicated to visitors today that he would not recommend to Congress a suspension of the war debt payments due Dec. 15 as requested by Great Britain, France, Belgium and other countries. The decision was reached, it was said at the Capitol, after Mr. Hoover had been informed of the almost unanimous opposition to a further moratorium reported among members of Congress.

The administration, it was declared, will not even move in favor of a revival of the debt funding commission to study the capacity of the debtor nations to pay, unless President-elect Roosevelt, in the forthcoming conference with President Hoover, favors such a course. In other words, the present debt terms will not be disturbed, nor any plan recommended to Congress by this administration, unless such a program is acceptable to Mr. Roosevelt.

New Moves Hinge on Payment.

In his discussion of the debt situation, President Hoover was represented as insisting that the payments due Dec. 15 should be met before he would consider urging upon his successor the creation of a commission to consider revision of the debt funding terms. If the debtor nations default on next month's payments, this administration, it was said, would abandon the promotion of a program to restudy their capacity to pay, Republican Senate leaders declared.

President Hoover repeated today that he was opposed to cancellation, but expressed the belief that this country would obtain commercial advantages if the debts were reduced. He made it clear, however, that inasmuch as his administration would end March 4, he would not attempt to impose an important policy upon the incoming administration unless such a program coincided with Mr. Roosevelt's plan to deal with the foreign debts.

The President told Senators that he was very much surprised that the foreign countries should ask for a suspension at this time, holding that their case would have been better received by Congress if they had asked for a restudy, and had not made the re-examination follow upon a suspension of the interest payments next month.

Held Out for Payment or Default.

The situation as interpreted by Senators is that the debtor countries must meet their December obligations or default, and can hope for no leniency from the present Congress.

Democratic leaders were of the opinion that President-elect Roosevelt would not consent at this time to a restudy of the capacity of the debtor nations to pay. The policy of the new administration, in the belief of Democratic Senators, will be to throw the debt question into an international conference, which will consider not only the debts, but reciprocal tariff treaties and other economic factors held to be impeding world recovery.

The revived debt problem constituted only one subject discussed by President Hoover with the constant stream of callers at the White House offices after his return there at 8 o'clock this morning.

Among the visitors were Secretary Mills, who discussed the war debts and the budget, but declined to describe his conversation with the President; Secretary Stimson, who had luncheon at the White House, and Senator Reed of Pennsylvania.

Stimson Again at White House.

Secretary Stimson returned to the White House offices late this afternoon accompanied by Harvey M. Bundy, Assistant Secretary in charge of finance, and conferred with the President for more than an hour. He

Continued on Page Four.

Head of Grange Urges War Debt Breathing Spell And Cuts if Powers Buy Our Farmers' Products

By The Associated Press.

WINSTON-SALEM, N. C., Nov. 16.—Louis J. Taber, master of the National Grange, at a grange meeting here today said:

"The grange has declared again and again their belief that these are honest debts, that they should be paid and that any reduction places an added and unfair burden on the taxpayers of the United States.

"The collapse of many nations in Europe, the drop in commodity prices, the depreciation of foreign currency, the erection of tariff barriers and world disintegration compel the reconsideration of this whole debt problem in the light of world stability and world peace. We have a right to collect just debts, but we do not have the right to put great nations of the world into involuntary receivership or to add to the present international confusion.

"Agriculture has a very large stake in the foreign debt settlement. We cannot tolerate the acceptance of agricultural commodities from foreign nations in payment of these debts. We cannot ask that the products of labor or manufacturing be accepted at the present time. Foreign nations do not have sufficient gold for immediate payment; therefore postponement, reconsideration or readjustment of this problem becomes imperative to prevent further world collapse.

"We suggest that there be no cancellation, but that there be a short period of postponement of interest charges, and that during that period our debtor nations in Europe be given a credit of from 10 to 20 per cent debt reduction on all purchases of agricultural products in the United States which can be moved at a price which will allow a marginal profit to the producer."

LAMONT HOLDS DEBTS FAIR BUT IMPOSSIBLE

Payment Would Choke Channels of World Trade, He Says, Urging Economic Peace.

ASSAILS TARIFF BARRIERS

Capitalistic System Must Be Revised, but Not Abandoned, He Tells Educators.

Thomas W. Lamont of J. P. Morgan & Co. characterized the war debts as "perfectly just but impossible" yesterday in an address before the Conference of Universities, held at the Waldorf-Astoria under the auspices of New York University and attended by men and women representing colleges, universities and other institutions of learning in thirty-two countries. Yesterday was the second day of the three-day conference.

Mr. Lamont made this statement in an analysis of the causes of the depression, which he attributed to the World War and the subsequent economic warfare throughout the world. The remedy for present conditions, he said, was in rebuilding the capitalistic system and in seeking economic as well as political peace; not in changing our economic system to adopt either socialism or communism.

Sir James Arthur Salter, former director of the Economic and Finance Section of the League of Nations, declared that the present economic system must be transformed gradually into a system based on collective planning, without, however, replacing the present system altogether.

Edwin Francis Gay, Professor of Economic History at Harvard, who spoke at the same session as Mr. Lamont and Sir James, defended American universities against critics who have assailed the tendency to offer business and other utilitarian courses in recent years. Mr. Lamont presided at this session, the topic for which was: "The University and Economic Changes."

Mr. Lamont said that economic warfare in Europe since the World War had been more destructive than the war itself. The Versailles treaty, he declared, had set up new States on economic lines, and had brought "a militant peace filled with resentments." He thought the struggle over German reparations had helped bring Europe to the verge of bankruptcy, with war budgets and taxation going up alarmingly.

The United States, he continued, had taken the lead in erecting tariff barriers which now "prevent the very exchange of goods and facility of commerce which are essential to the restoration of world prosperity." Nationalism had grown all over the world, with every country trying to save itself, regardless of the rest of the world.

During our boom years, he went on, this country adopted "a very contradictory trade policy," of trying to sell goods abroad but buying as little as possible from abroad, forcing us to lend foreigners the money to pay us for our goods, these loans approximating $5,000,000,000 from 1923 to 1929.

"American banks and bankers," he

Continued on Page Eleven.

CHAMBER MAY BALK PAYMENT BY FRANCE

Deputies Are Likely to Refuse to Vote Credits if Plea for Delay Is Not Granted.

HERRIOT'S POWER DOUBTFUL

If Premier Uses Pressure, He Will Be Asking Reversal of Post-War Policy.

By P. J. PHILIP.

By Cable to THE NEW YORK TIMES.

PARIS, Nov. 16.—If Congress, as is reported here probable, refuses to grant the French request for a postponement of the Dec. 15 debt payment, there is every likelihood that the Chamber of Deputies will in turn refuse to vote the necessary credits to enable the government to pay.

And so there will arise the strange situation of a deadlock between the legislative assemblies of the two countries, with both Executives powerless to do anything. France's 600 Deputies will be ranked in order against America's 96 Senators, while Premier Herriot, President Hoover and the French and American financial and business world wait for one or the other to give way.

A short canvass of leaders of groups and parties in the Chamber today indicated that unless the government puts extreme pressure on its followers, and perhaps even so, the majority will stand firm by the unilateral reservation that the Chamber adopted when it ratified the debt agreements on the night of July 21, 1929.

Doubtful About Credits.

Some of the leaders prudently said the decision of the Chamber would depend entirely on how the question was presented and others were convinced that M. Herriot's government, if still in office a month hence, would not be able to obtain the necessary credits unless there were such wholesale abstentions as would make the vote almost ridiculous.

It is recalled that the debt settlements were ratified by a majority of only eight, the figures being 300 against 292. On the same day the Chamber almost unanimously adopted a resolution that declared that "except through the regular accomplishment of the obligations of Germany" and "exclusively by the sums that Germany shall pay to France." the payments to the United States and Britain could not be made.

So if the government is compelled to ask the Chamber for the necessary credits to make the December payment it will be equivalent to asking it to reverse its vote and to abolish the policy that France has firmly held to ever since the war.

For the moment it is being emphasized here that all France and the others are asking is a delay in the payment and it is argued that direct justification of that request is to be found in the Hoover-Laval memorandum issued at the conclusion of the interview between the President and the Premier on Oct. 25 of last year.

M. Laval's own newspaper, Le Moniteur, drew attention to this circumstance Monday, when it republished, with several lines in black type, part of the text of that communiqué. The quotation was as fol-

Continued on Page Four.

Girl Slain in Ice Age Found in Minnesota; Apish Mongol Maid Lived 20,000 Years Ago

By WALDEMAR KAEMPFFERT.

ANN ARBOR, Mich., Nov. 16.—Twenty thousand years ago, when late Neanderthal men were hunting in Assyria, and Egypt was a wilderness inhabited by equally primitive savages, a 17-year-old girl, who had something of the Mongol and something of the ape about her, was killed and perhaps thrown into a glacial lake in what is now Ottertail County, Minn. It was not the crime but the victim that held the attention of the National Academy of Sciences at the third and last session of its Autumnal meeting, held at the University of Michigan. For this Minnesota girl is one of the most important anthropological discoveries ever made in America, so far as both her antiquity and her type are concerned.

Dr. A. E. Jenks of the University of Minnesota told how a gang that was building a highway last year through the dried silt of what had been the bottom of the lake had unearthed some of the girl's bones. He recovered more last Summer. Near her was an antler dagger, but this was probably hers and not the weapon with which she had been killed. The shell pendants that she wore on her head and around her neck and the shell apron that hung from her waist also were found, although not intact.

In her shoulder blade is a nick that mutely testifies to her murder. In his reconstruction of a 20,000-year-old crime Dr. Jenks advanced the theory that she was shot from the front through the right lung and probably through the heart by an arrow that left its mark on the shoulder blade. Or perhaps it was a spear that killed her.

Was she in a canoe or on a raft or on the ice when the end came? Even the anthropologists at the meeting, more concerned with the girl as a specimen than as the subject of a be-

Continued on Page Fifteen.

FRANCE JOINS REICH, WITH AID OF BRITISH, TO PUSH PUBLIC WORK

Nations to Study, Finance and Execute Rail Electrification Plans Throughout Europe.

AIM AT SAFE INVESTMENT

Use for Idle Funds and Relief of Jobless Sought in Project of Economic Commission.

Wireless to THE NEW YORK TIMES.

PARIS, Nov. 16.—Hope of supplanting the old German system of Mitteleuropa in its economic aspects by international cooperation was raised here today by announcement that a Franco-German accord for a European consortium for the construction of public works throughout Europe had been reached at a meeting of experts in Berlin.

According to Raymond Patenôtre, French Under Secretary of State for National Economy, who attended the meeting, the Franco-German Economic Commission also agreed to enter the consortium scheme, which will be financed by bankers in France, Great Britain and Germany through bonds issued in European markets. M. Patenôtre, outlining the project which he said was expected to begin practical operation next Spring, expressed great optimism over the prospects of a Franco-German renewal of confidence in the economic field. He emphasized the spirit of collaboration exhibited by Chancellor von Papen and other German officials with whom he had conferred.

Traced to Berlin Visit.

M. Patenotre traced the project back to the visit of the late Aristide Briand and ex-Premier Pierre Laval to the German capital last year when the Franco-German Economic Commission was created. The accords just reached represent the conclusion of the work of a fourth subcommittee of this commission on which France was represented by Max Hoschiller and R. Coulondre and Germany by Dr. Andreas Hermes.

The accord provides for the creation of three separate consortiums for cooperation with foreign countries in the execution of public works.

The first consortium will be Franco-German only and confined to technical study.

The second consortium, an Anglo-Franco-German one, will deal with the financing of the programs in various foreign countries. It has been agreed that bonds will be offered in London and Paris and eventually in Berlin and that 40 per cent will be floated in London, 40 per cent in Paris and 20 per cent in Berlin. All details are now being studied by bankers of the three countries, who are preparing strong guarantees for investors, for one advantage of the project, it is hoped, will be to afford firmly secured investment for a large amount of idle capital in European countries. The project also aims to reduce unemployment throughout the Continent and allow modernization of public services in countries now paralyzed by the economic depression.

Plan to Electrify Railways.

"A third consortium has also been outlined in Berlin," said M. Patenôtre. "This consortium would be charged with putting through a program of electrification of railways in several countries such as Poland, Rumania, Iraq and Portugal. The maximum capital to be devoted to this program has been set at 17,000,000,000 francs [about $666,400,000], but full details of this proposal will be worked out at a conference scheduled for the second half of February in Paris."

The French Under-Secretary ex-

Continued on Page Four.

ROOSEVELT UP AGAIN, WORKS AT BALANCING BUDGET OF THE STATE

Sharp Economies Planned to Pave Way for Lehman and Meet $80,000,000 Deficit.

INCREASE IN TAX RETURNS

Saving of $10,000,000 in Appropriations Listed as Another Helpful Factor.

Special to THE NEW YORK TIMES.

ALBANY, Nov. 16.—Having promised in the Presidential campaign to readjust Federal fiscal affairs, Governor Roosevelt today pledged himself to present an "absolutely balanced budget" for the State of New York to Governor-elect Herbert H. Lehman.

"The budget will be balanced," he said. "There will be big economies. The final details, of course, will not be available until I come back from Warm Springs and we hold the budget hearings."

With the national fiscal picture requiring considerable retouching in the face of a growing deficit, Governor Roosevelt, as President-elect, would offer no indication of the course he expects to follow when he goes to Washington March 4. It was explained that the intricacies of a Federal budget needed first-hand investigation, and until that opportunity specific remedies would not be suggested.

The Governor made it clear, however, that before he departs from Albany Jan. 1 he will suggest ways and means for wiping out the State's threatened deficit of $80,000,000.

Receives the Correspondents.

For the first time since last Friday the Governor was up and dressed today for his 4 o'clock talk with the correspondents. Seated at a bridge table in his high-ceilinged bedroom on the second floor of the Executive Mansion, he appeared completely recovered and in more than his usual good humor.

He talked freely about the State budget, on which he will labor as soon as he returns from his annual visit to Warm Springs.

While the Governor did not touch on the subject of the new Washington administration, it has become apparent that the possibility of revenues from legalized beer may play an important part in Federal budgetary problems. The Democrats in Congress may set out at the short session to initiate some items of their own budget plans.

Estimates among Democratic leaders are that the legalization of beer with a tax of $8 per barrel would bring to the Federal Government a revenue of about $350,000,000 annually. The figure is based upon the theory that consumption would be akin to that of the days immediately preceding the time when the Volstead act became law.

It is believed that such a revenue raising possibility will play a big part in Congress when the drive for immediate modification is begun at the short session.

To Phone Hoover Soon.

The war debts, brought again to the front by the requests of debtor nations for a renewed study and suspension of the payments due Dec. 15, cast a long shadow over fiscal affairs at Washington. For that reason the coming conference between President Hoover and President-elect Roosevelt will have a domestic as well as an international significance.

It is expected that within a day or two Governor Roosevelt, as he stated in his reply to the President's

Continued on Page Three.

M'KEE BREAKS OPENLY WITH TAMMANY; ASKS CRUSADE FOR A 'DECENT' REGIME IN SPEECH TO STATE'S TRADE LEADERS

City Tax Collections $17,368,223 Under Last Year; 150,000 Protests on Realty Assessments Are Filed

As protests against assessed valuations on property reached a total of about 150,000 for the five boroughs yesterday, the Finance Department reported that tax collections for the last half of this year were $17,368,223 behind last year's collections for the same period.

Up to yesterday the department had collected $241,898,486 of the 1932 tax levy of $535,534,293. Taxes in arrears, listed separately, amounted to $63,314,302. For the same period last year the city collected $259,266,709 in current taxes and $60,691,684 in arrears. The tax levy for 1931 was $514,146,082, or more than $20,000,000 lower than this year's levy.

Tax collections for the first half of this year's levy were more than $18,000,000 behind the 1931 collections for the same period.

Manhattan was responsible for $14,850,000 of the tax deficiency for this year. Brooklyn had unpaid taxes amounting to $1,409,000 and the remainder was scattered among the three remaining boroughs. A large part of the amounts collected in arrears was in "distress taxes" resulting from the foreclosure of property.

James J. Sexton, president of the Department of Taxes and Assessments, said last night that the protests against assessed valuations were about 30,000 more than the total filed last year. In Manhattan 70,000 protests were filed and 50,000 came from Brooklyn. Hearings on these appeals begin on Monday in Manhattan and a week from Monday in Brooklyn. The dates of hearings in the other boroughs have not been set. Tax officials estimate that 100,000 hearings will be held.

RAINEY EXPECTS BEER AT THE SHORT SESSION

Changing Mind After Talks With Returning Members, He Now Urges Speed.

237 HOUSE VOTES INDICATED

Survey Shows 19 More Than Majority for a Brew Bill, 70 Others Doubtful.

Special to THE NEW YORK TIMES.

WASHINGTON, Nov. 16.—The movement for beer at the approaching short session of Congress had reached such proportions today that Representative Rainey of Illinois, majority leader in the House revised his opinion regarding the prospects and virtually predicted that modification was close at hand.

Mr. Rainey had said only yesterday that he saw little or no chance for a change in the present Congress. He thought that since many members of this House had been elected on dry platforms they should and probably would hold to that stand.

But as he studied further the sentiment of returning House members Mr. Rainey changed his mind and today not only expressed the view that beer legislation was possible in the "lame duck" session, but said that he would not oppose advancing it on the calendar.

"If it can be done at the short session it might as well be done," Mr. Rainey said. "The quicker the better. Both parties are pledged to alter the dry laws. If there is to be a change during the prospective extra session it might as well be done during the short one. It would be wise to raise the needed revenue as soon as possible.

Fess Doubts Early Change.

"I have not had a chance to make a thorough canvass, but two or three members with whom I have talked tell me a beer bill can be put through at the December session."

From the Senate side of the prohibition controversy came the expression of Senator Fess of Ohio that he did not believe the short session would amend the Volstead act to legalize beer, but that he was sure the incoming Congress would because of the Democratic platform.

"But I see no reason why a submission resolution should not pass this Winter," he said, "for both parties put some part of it in their platforms. What I would prefer when the question comes up is to submit it to the States in such form as to include a 'constructive submit.'

"I mean by that to assure dry States Federal protection and to also insure against the return of the open saloon."

Senator Fess added that he thought the beer problem would be carried to the Supreme Court for final decision.

A study today by THE NEW YORK TIMES, based on the vote on the O'Connor-Hull beer-for-revenue bill at the last session and changes in positions of individual members as made known since, indicated in the House a probable vote of 237 for beer at the short session, 19 above an actual majority of the House membership.

—With the sentiment of this number

Continued on Page Ten.

SUIT PLANNED TO CUT $17,000,000 IN BUDGET

Citizens Commission Seeks to Transfer That Amount to Subway Account.

A BLOW AT FIVE-CENT FARE

Tammany, Fearing Loss of Power, Now Turns to Slashes in Pay of Exempt Classes.

Plans are well under way for the filing of a taxpayer's suit to transfer from the 1933 budget to the account of the city's independent subway system the item of more than $17,000,000, representing interest and amortization on rapid transit securities issued and to be issued on account of construction of the new network, it was ascertained yesterday.

The litigation, which was foreshadowed at the recent budget hearings of the Board of Estimate, probably will be sponsored by the Citizens Budget Commission, whose spokesman, George A. McAneny, pleaded in vain with the board to strike the items from the budget on its own initiative. Because the Board of Aldermen has no power to cut a debt service item from the budget, the right to bring a suit matured when the Board of Estimate adopted the annual budget schedules about a week ago.

It is probable, however, that filing of the suit may be delayed until after the Aldermen have formally adopted the budget. This would mean that the court battle would be waged during the Mayoralty term of Surrogate John P. O'Brien, leaving his administration to cope with any financial or political embarrassment which might follow.

Ease Load on Taxpayer.

Elimination of the $17,000,000 item from the 1933 budget would remove that much load from the taxpayer during the coming year and augment a saving now under consideration by Tammany leaders who are considering a plan to have the Board of Aldermen strike from the 1933 schedules a sum representing a cut of approximately 10 per cent of all salaries over $5,000 in exempt positions.

This particular salary cut was advocated in a resolution adopted during the budget hearings of the Board of Estimate. No action was taken by that body, however, because of an opinion given by Corporation Counsel Arthur J. W. Hilly, declaring that the Aldermen had the sole power of making the reduction.

The filing of the suit will constitute another assault upon the five-cent fare on the city's new subway system. The nickel fare has already been imperiled, in the opinion of transit experts, by the recent action of the Board of Estimate in substituting a policy of fifty-year subway bonds for the plan of four-year issues sponsored by John H. Delaney, chairman of the Board of Transportation. If the litigation results in striking the $17,000,000 interest charge from the 1933 budget, it may leave the incoming city administration faced with the political perils inherent in the danger that the five-

Continued on Page Two.

CITY 'SICK' OF MACHINE

Election Proved Spirit of Protest Is Abroad, Acting Mayor Says.

DENIES PERSONAL AMBITION

Pleads for Support of Any One Who Will Carry On Fight for Municipal Reforms.

HIS ATTACK IS UNEXPECTED

Had Asked to Be Excused From Speech Before State Chamber —Tammany Is Silent.

Text of Acting Mayor McKee's address last night is on Page 2.

Acting Mayor Joseph V. McKee broke with Tammany Hall last night on the issue of "decent government."

His declaration of war, in which he declared himself and the citizens of New York to be "sick and tired" of present conditions in the city government, was made unexpectedly before bankers, merchants, and business men at the 164th annual dinner of the Chamber of Commerce of the State of New York, at the Waldorf-Astoria.

Without attempting to lay down his specific course for the future, he told his hearers that the time had come for a crusade to purify the city government, and he asked them to cooperate with him in this undertaking. His voice trembled at times with indignation. At others it was husky with emotion.

He declared that he had been finally moved to action by recent occurrences in Board of Estimate meetings. This was taken to refer primarily to the "gagging" on Tuesday of John H. Delaney, chairman of the Board of Transportation, when he sought to plead for $52,000,000 in short-term bonds to finance subway construction. Mr. McKee protested at the time, and warned the board that he would join Mr. Delaney in seeking "other forums."

Leaders Are Silent.

Tammany's reaction last night to Mr. McKee's speech was that of interest, but silence.

John F. Curry, leader of Tammany Hall, listened to a brief resumé of Mr. McKee's remarks when reached over the long-distance telephone in Washington and said he had no comment to make.

John H. McCooey, Brooklyn Democratic leader, indicated that he would rather wait until he had read Mr. McKee's address in full, but that it was doubtful whether he would have any comment even then.

Because of the way in which it was delivered, Mr McKee's speech had something of th effect of an exploding bomb on the orderly program that had been planned for the dinner. Mr McKee had attended only as a guest, and upon the express condition that he should not be required to make a speech.

James Brown, president of the State Chamber of Commerce, referred, however, to the numerous ballots of protest "written in" for the Acting Mayor on election day, commented pointedly to the charges that the Tammany machine had prevented other protest ballots from being cast, and asked Mr. McKee to rise for a moment, if only to accept the greetings of the audience.

Greeted by Applause.

Mr. McKee rose and, after the applause had died down, said that because of conditions in the city government he had decided to speak after all. Declaring that he had always tried to do what he believed to be right in his political life, regardless of political expediency, he insisted that he was seeking no preferment for himself in seeking to start a reform campaign, but that he did seek support for "any individual" who might advance the cause of good government.

His auditors interrupted him with frequent applause, leaving no doubt as to their sympathy with his stand. No one, however, would hazard a guess as to what the political effect of his action might be.

The first opinions voiced were that the Acting Mayor had pitted himself against Tammany, although he studiously refrained from naming

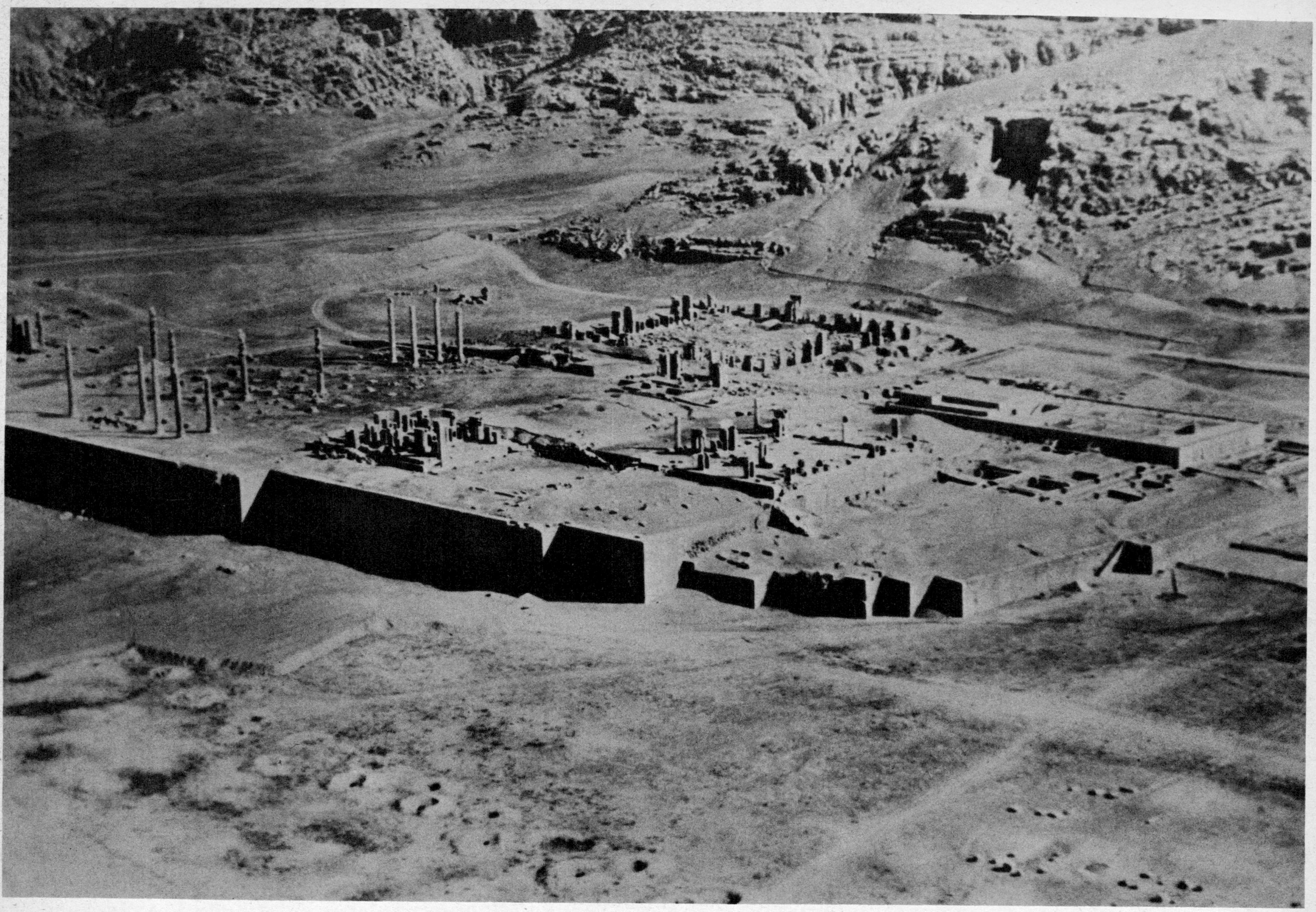

Air view of the terrace of Persepolis, built by Darius the Great, who ruled ancient Persia from 521 to 486 B.C.

"All the News That's Fit to Print."

The New York Times.

LATE CITY EDITION
WEATHER—Fair, mild today; cooler tonight; tomorrow fair.
Temperatures Yesterday—Max., 61; min., 48.

VOL. LXXXII....No. 27,393. Entered as Second-Class Matter. Postoffice, New York, N. Y. NEW YORK, MONDAY, JANUARY 23, 1933. **** TWO CENTS In New York City. | THREE CENTS Within 200 Miles | FOUR CENTS Elsewhere Except in 7th and 8th Postal Zones

PALACES OF XERXES AND DARIUS DUG UP IN PERSEPOLIS RUINS

Chicago University Excavators Find Rich Art in City Fired by Alexander the Great.

SCULPTURES MAGNIFICENT

Covered for 2,500 Years, They Are as Fine in Color and Quality as When First Chiseled.

STONE-AGE VILLAGE FOUND

These Two Discoveries Are Hailed by Scientists as Chapters in Rise of Man From Savagery.

Special to THE NEW YORK TIMES.

CHICAGO, Jan. 22.—After digging two years into the black lime soil of Persepolis, ancient capital of Persia, University of Chicago archaeologists have uncovered two rich chapters of the story of man's rise from savagery. Dr. James Henry Breasted, director of the Oriental Institute at the university, made public today reports of "great and important" discoveries prepared by Dr. Ernest Herzfeld, field director of the institute's Persian Expedition.

Under twenty-six feet of rubbish and masonry from the Persepolis palaces, which were fired in 330 B. C. by Alexander the Great during a drunken debauch, the excavaters have discovered a wealth of magnificent sculpture, dating back to Cyrus the Great, which is hailed as containing the earliest specimens of art ever discovered in Asia.

Within two miles of this find, the scientists unearthed a primitive Stone Age village about 5,000 years old, in a state of preservation said to surpass previous discoveries of the period.

Hailed as "Greatest" Find.

"The discovery at Persepolis is one of the greatest and most important in the history of archaeological research," Dr. Breasted said. "It not only far surpasses any archaeological disclosure ever made in the history of such research in Persia, but there has never been any discovery like it anywhere in Western Asia since archaeological excavation began there almost a century ago.

"Persian civilization and Persian art were the great composite mosaic of the life of the earlier Orient which culminated in Persian culture, but since that day the country has been so swept by one devastating invasion after another that its most splendid and impressive monuments have almost all disappeared or been so badly wrecked that they are practically lost.

"Hence, when a great body of Old Persian sculpture like this, which almost doubles the known volume of the work of art is recovered, the value of such a treasure is priceless."

That the Persians were skilled engineers was established by the scientists in their operations at the palaces. They discovered beneath the terrace and extending beyond it a vast drainage system, which carried off water flowing down the mountain side. These tunnels were drilled through solid rock and an explorer can walk through them great distances without bowing his head, Dr. Breasted disclosed.

Important Inscriptions Included.

Under the leadership of Dr. Herzfeld, professor of Oriental archaeology of the University of Berlin, and reputedly the world's foremost specialist in Persian archaeology, the Oriental Institute's expedition found a series of wall sculptures, which, if set together, would form a vast panel of reliefs five or six feet high and almost 1,000 feet long. The carvings, described as "unparalleled in beauty and refinement of detail," include a series of historical inscriptions of importance, which Dr. Herzfeld has not had time to decipher, because of an attack of malaria.

The walls of the palaces, built by Darius and Xerxes, and overlooking a mighty plain circled by mountains, were of sun-dried brick, but the colonnade halls, windows and great doors were of black stone polished like ebony.

On this black stone is represented a magnificent durbar, or conclave, of official Persians and their relatives, the Medians, with the Emperor drawn up to receive Ambassadors of twenty-one subject nations bearing gifts to the ruler after the fashion of the Wise Men of the East of more than three centuries later.

The array of imposing panel sculpture was found between two pretentious staircases leading like an inverted V to what was a vast state audience hall situated on a terrace 1,500 feet long and 1,000 feet

Continued on Page Three.

Atlantic's Thunderstorms Are Located by Use of Radio

By Science Service.

LONDON, Jan. 16.—The positions of large thunderstorms in Europe and the North Atlantic can now be determined by radio apparatus in the British Isles independently of weather reports.

This is announced by R. A. Watson Watt of the British Department of Scientists and Industrial Research.

Atmospherics produced by the thunderstorms are so exactly analyzed by cathode ray oscillographs that with two radio stations working in cooperation it is possible to calculate trigonometrically the positions of the storms to within about a hundred miles.

The American Navy is experimenting with the system.

BOLIVIANS STORM CHACO FORT 3 DAYS

Paraguayans Report 1,200 of Foe Have Fallen in an Attack on Nanawa.

KEY TO REGION'S CONTROL

La Paz Hopes to Split Road System That Gives Enemy Defense Advantage.

By JOHN W. WHITE.
Special Cable to THE NEW YORK TIMES.

BUENOS AIRES, Jan. 22.—One of the fiercest battles in the Chaco war has been raging since Friday at dawn in the vicinity of the Paraguayan Fort President Ayala, which the Bolivians know as Port Nanawa.

The Bolivians have been trying to capture this position for three months. They made several attacks on Sunday and Monday of last week, which the Paraguayans repulsed. The attempt was renewed with new determination at daylight Friday with a force the Paraguayan communiqués place at 5,000 men, supported by a heavy artillery barrage and assisted by several airplanes reconnoitring the Paraguayan positions.

The battle continued all day Friday and Saturday, with the Bolivians making repeated unsuccessful attacks against Paraguay's heavily fortified outposts.

Asuncion dispatches tonight say the battle continued today with the Paraguayans continuing to inflict heavy losses on the enemy. The Paraguayan War Minister's communiqués say the Bolivians are suffering heavy losses, but do not indicate the number of casualties.

One Paraguayan newspaper this morning published an unofficial report that the Bolivian losses in dead and wounded total 1,200, but this is unconfirmed.

Defenders Were Prepared.

The Paraguayans, expecting a renewal of the offensive against Nanawa, had reinforced the garrison and increased vigilance, so were not surprised by Friday's attack. La Paz dispatches say the offensive is designed to separate the Paraguayan northern and southern armies and that the Bolivian War Office authorities expect Nanawa to fall soon.

Although Paraguay is heavily outnumbered by the Bolivian armies, it has an advantage in better roads behind its line of forts and has been moving troops northward and southward as needed, holding Bolivia at bay in both the Saavedra and Corrales sectors.

Bolivia hopes, by capturing Nanawa, to prevent continuance of these tactics, as it would then be in

Continued on Page Four.

CHINESE UNIFYING ARMIES IN ANSWER TO JAPAN'S THREAT

Military Leaders Assemble at Nanking to Work Out Plans for Defense.

PEOPLE GIVE FOR PLANES

Unions and Others Ask for Sacrifices to Resist the Invaders in Jehol.

FACTIONS DROP QUARRELS

Tuan Chi-jui Announces His Loyalty to Regime—Feng Yuhsiang's Aid Sought.

Special Cable to THE NEW YORK TIMES.

SHANGHAI, Monday, Jan. 23.—China's reply to the increasing Japanese threat in North China and to the warning uttered Saturday by Count Uchida, Japanese Foreign Minister, has assumed the form of an intensified national effort. There is to be a hurried assembly of military leaders at Nanking where a policy of resistance is likely to be formulated and support assured to Chang Hsiao-liang in his defense of Jehol and Hopei.

A most important secret conference was proceeding in Nanking early today between Chiang Kai-shek, Chang Hsiao-liang and Finance Minister Soong, who was hastily summoned from Shanghai yesterday. Measures of resistance following Geneva's admission that conciliation is impossible, are believed to be the subject. Other military leaders are assembling at Nanking and it is understood they will work out a policy of resistance and assurance of support for Chang Hsiao-liang in Jehol and Hopei.

Meanwhile remarkable manifestations of a growing national spirit are visible in the leading cities in the face of the crisis. Movements have been launched to obtain funds with which to purchase airplanes, which is now the chief public obsession in view of Japanese use of these craft.

One hundred Shanghai street unions today broadcast a message asking the Chinese to skip a meal on Jan. 28, the anniversary of the Japanese action in the Chapei suburb of the city last year and to contribute the money to the national salvation fund.

Hangchow organizations have petitioned the provincial government to institute a general scheme of amusement taxes, automobile and rickshaw taxes, rental levies, deductions of official salaries and city collection funds to swell the war treasury. A provincial lottery is also proposed to obtain money to buy airplanes.

Tuan Pledges His Loyalty.

Marshal Tuan Chi-jui, head of the Anfu party at Peiping, arrived at Nanking this morning and received a warm welcome. He immediately conferred with General Chiang Kai-shek, who afterward issued a statement urging the nation to support the government in a united program against Japanese aggression. It is understood that Tuan Chi-jui, whose organization has been regarded as pro-Japanese, gave assurance that he was patriotic and was not planning an insurrection against Chang Hsiao-liang as Japanese propaganda had intimated.

Nanking was thrown into a fever of excitement later by the sudden arrival from Peiping by airplane of Chang Hsiso-liang, who immediately was closeted with Chiang Kai-

Continued on Page Four.

Paderewski Says Machines Destroy Culture; Blames 'Crazy' Production for the Depression

By The Associated Press.

LONDON, Jan. 16 (by Mail).—Ignace Paderewski, pianist, who has been in England to fulfill musical engagements, sees the machine destroying beauty and culture.

"I see everywhere the same tragedy," he said. "The countries which I have known so well in the past, in prosperous times, are all facing the almost insoluble problems, overproduction and unemployment.

"I do not believe that these problems can be settled in a short time. It may take generations, perhaps, for matters altogether to adjust themselves.

"Who can tell the way out? It is not human nature that is at fault. That is, as it always has been, mainly good. Man has created something that has got beyond him. The machine, apart from displacing its creator, has in general destroyed something which is the most important factor in the life of civilized man, beauty and the sense of profession.

"Production has been simply crazy. In America, which I have seen so often, they have overproduced in every direction until there is no market. They made four or five million more automobiles than they could sell. They needed about six billion barrels of oil a year, and they produced ten billion, until the whole industry is almost ruined."

In music, he believed, the effects of "the uncontrolled machine" are the same as elsewhere.

"There was a short period when the phonograph stimulated the general interest in music," he said, "and had a good effect. That period has now passed.

"As for the effect of the mechanical age directly on musical composition, I am no fortune teller, but I am afraid we are now in a very arid period of culture. Maybe there will be a return to absolute simplicity. There are at least signs of that."

Ferryboat Crashes Into Battery Wall in Fog; Orizaba, Off Course, Rips Brooklyn Pier

A dense fog covered New York harbor late yesterday afternoon, delaying ferryboats from five to twenty minutes on their regular runs and causing two accidents.

The Ward liner Orizaba, bound in from Progreso, Vera Cruz and Havana, lost her way and crashed into the pier of the Red D Line at Montague Street, Brooklyn, at about 5:30 P.M.

At approximately the same time the Staten Island ferryboat Tompkinsville, Manhattan-bound from St. George, drifted into the Battery Park seawall after narrowly escaping a collision with the excursion boat Bear Mountain and a customs cutter that loomed in her path.

The ferryboat was virtually undamaged, but about fifteen feet of planking protecting the seawall was ripped away. There was considerable excitement among the 1,100 passengers on the Tompkinsville, and one woman, thrown from her feet by the impact, was slightly injured. There was no panic, however, and twenty minutes later, when the boat pulled into her slip, most of the passengers were laughing about the mishap.

The woman injured was Mrs. Celia Brooks, 38 years old, of 3,108 Darby Street, Brooklyn. She and her husband, accompanied by a woman friend, were returning from Staten Island in a car, one of the twenty-nine aboard the ferry. A sudden screeching of whistles, followed by the clanging of bells in the engine room, and a vibration that made the whole boat tremble, apprised them that something was wrong. All three leaped out of the car and started along the line of cars toward the bow.

The vibration did not last long. The engines stopped and the boat drifted almost imperceptibly. But as Mr. and Mrs. Brooks and their friend neared the foremost car in the line the ferryboat drifted head-on into the sea wall. There was a sharp crunching sound as timbers lining the wall were splintered. Mrs. Brooks was thrown from her feet. One hip was injured and her

Continued on Page Three.

ELISABETH MARBURY DIES IN 77TH YEAR

Noted Leader in Theatrical, Literary and Political Life of City and Nation.

AGENT OF GREAT AUTHORS

Told in Book of Meeting Famous Persons—On Democratic National Committee.

Miss Elisabeth Marbury, noted leader in theatrical, literary, political and civic life, died of a heart attack at 5:33 A. M. yesterday at her home, 13 Sutton Place. On Thursday she had undergone a minor operation on a leg, from which she was supposed to have suffered no ill effects. She was in her seventy-seventh year.

With Miss Marbury at the end were her servants and her physician, Dr. A. W. Dunn. She was in seemingly good health until shortly after 2 o'clock yesterday morning, when a coughing spell occurred. Soon she sank into a coma from which she never recovered.

At the direction of Cardinal Hayes, a special mass will be celebrated for Miss Marbury at 8 A. M. today in St. Patrick's Cathedral by Mgr. M. J. Lavelle, the rector. Funeral services will be held at 10 A. M. tomorrow in the cathedral. Mgr. Lavelle will celebrate a high mass of requiem. Burial, which will be private, will take place in Woodlawn Cemetery.

Prominent Democratic national, State and city officials will attend the funeral. Mayor John P. O'Brien will head the list of honorary pallbearers, and it is expected that Gov. Lehman and other State officials will attend. The Tammany Hall executive committee will attend in a body, in accordance with an order issued by Leader John F. Curry. Sections of the cathedral will be reserved for members of the various societies of which Miss Marbury was a member.

Miss Marbury is survived by two nephews, Frank Marbury of Orange, N. J., and John Clinton Work, who lives at Indian Head, near Marbury, Md., a town named after one of Miss Marbury's ancestors; a niece, Mrs. R. L. MacDuffie of Boston; five grandnephews, F. Marbury MacDuffie of 347 East Fifty-seventh Street, John MacDuffie of Boston, Ross and John Marbury of Florida and John Clinton Work Jr. of 242 East Sixty-second Street, and a grandniece, Miss Cecily Work of the last given address.

An Unusual Career.

As Democratic National Committeewoman for a number of years, as authors' agent and adviser to young talent, as a war worker and a woman leader, Miss Marbury out of a full life created an unusual career for herself.

She was born in New York on June 19, 1856, daughter of Francis Ferdinand and Elisabeth McCoun Marbury. Her father was a prominent lawyer. When she was a young girl she often sat in her father's office, she later wrote, reading Blackstone's Commentaries and studying case after case. Her familiarity with questions concerning international copyrights, plagiarisms and piracies she later found invaluable as a representative of authors and as a play broker.

Miss Marbury represented authors from all parts of the world, and in her memoirs, entitled "My Crystal Ball," she recounted her relations with poets, statesmen, dancers, Generals, playwrights, politicians,

Continued on Page Fourteen.

BORAH SAYS BUDGET CAN'T BE BALANCED

We Must Adjust Currency First and Stabilize Prices, the Senator Contends.

SALES TAX CALLED 'CRUEL'

Touching People 'Least Able to Pay,' It Would Aggravate Our Present Malady.

Special to THE NEW YORK TIMES.

WASHINGTON, Jan. 22.—Arguing for reflationary adjustment of the currency to meet advantages held by countries off the gold standard, Senator Borah today assailed proposals for imposition of a sales tax.

In a statement discussing our present economic distress, the Idaho Senator declared that the Federal budget could not be balanced until the currency question was settled and prices stabilized.

A sales tax would be "iniquitous," a "cruel proposal," in the light of "diminishing profits," he said, and would decrease purchasing power.

All taxes have increased to such an extent that, taken together with interest and taxes, the "income of the nation is about zero," he added.

"Traveling in Vicious Circle."

"The question of balancing the budget is again being urged," Mr. Borah said. "I venture the opinion that the budget will not, and cannot, be balanced except on paper, and that briefly, either now or under the incoming administration, until we settle the currency question. It cannot be done any more than you can build a house upon a receding sand-bar.

"With commodity prices near the bottom and still slowly falling; with the purchasing power of the masses near the minimum and still diminishing; with taxes increasing in amount but diminishing in returns; with the value of the dollar depreciating and taxes responding accordingly, there is no such thing as balancing the budget, except on paper and temporarily.

"The proposal has been made to cut government expenses $500,000,000. That is a wise proposal. It is then proposed to raise $500,000,000 by increase of taxes, the sales tax. That is a cruel proposal in the light of diminishing profits, falling prices and decrease of purchasing power. At a time when underconsumption is a malady which menaces our whole social structure, there can be no justification for aggravating the malady.

"If we cannot stabilize prices, to lay on a sales tax which strikes at those least able to pay is to accentuate the fall in prices and decrease purchasing power. We are traveling in a vicious circle toward economic collapse.

Calls for Reflation "Adjustment."

"In 1929 the national income was about $85,200,000,000, in 1932 about $37,500,000,000. Our national income now is about equal to the taxes of the people, city, State and national, together with the interest falling due on private indebtedness. We have already reached the point where, measured against interest and taxes, the income of the nation is about zero.

"To put a tax on the poorer people, until we have done something to raise and stabilize the prices of commodities, is not wise from an economic standpoint, and socially it is an iniquity.

"At the present time we are on the gold standard in this country. The rest of the world, except France, which, owing to certain reasons not necessary to discuss

Continued on Page Two.

DANGER IN INFLATION OF UPSETTING PRICES ANEW, MILLS SAYS

Treasury Secretary Argues Against Proposed Manipulation of Currency.

DISPUTES 'GOLD SHORTAGE'

World Stock Gained From 1929 to End of 1932—Money in Credit and Deposits Ample.

RISE IN PRICES DESIRABLE

But Needed Impulse Will Come in Removing Bars to Trade and Industry, He Asserts.

By OGDEN L. MILLS.
Secretary of the Treasury.
Copyright, 1933, by NANA, Inc.

WASHINGTON, Jan. 22.—The precipitous fall in prices that has taken place during the course of the last three years has given rise to all manner of economic maladjustments. The price levels, not only for commodities, but for rents, services, &c., are so out of line, both in domestic and world markets, as to reduce to a minimum the exchange of commodities, out of the production and exchange of which the civilized world makes a living and derives its wealth.

As price relationships become distorted so that exchange of goods does not proceed freely, production soon exceeds consumption and is increasingly dammed up. Prices fall further. Commercial and industrial stagnation follow and we are confronted with the paradox of poverty in the midst of plenty.

In the meanwhile, with an enormously contracted volume of business and a very much lower price level, the burden of payments of debts piled up during the preceding period of expansion and high business activity becomes unbearable. Debtors of all classes, governments, corporations and individuals seek relief from a weight that has become crushing.

Impulse to Alter Currencies.

Since depressed, disordered and declining prices appear, on the surface at least, to be the most disturbing factor affecting trade and industry, and since prices are expressed in terms of money, which is the medium through which the exchange of goods is effected, there is a very natural tendency to look upon our currency system as the key to the situation, and to jump to the conclusion that currency can be so manipulated as to relieve the only too obvious ills from which the world is suffering.

This is the basis for the talk of inflation of which we hear so much these days. In its crudest form inflation is visualized as the process of pumping out currency in one way or another, the assumed effect of which rests on the simple conception that the level of prices will have a fixed relationship to the volume of currency in circulation.

But this conception, even as applied to "money" in the broadest sense, is altogether too simple. Money in the modern world consists of currency only to a very small extent. Money, particularly in the United States, consists of credit of all kinds, but principally of that form of credit known as a bank deposit. Currency in circulation amounts to less than $5,600,000,000; bank deposits to about $43,000,000,000.

But even the volume of bank

Continued on Page Seven.

Six City Employes to Be Shot In Sevastopol for Grafting

By The Associated Press.

SEVASTOPOL, Russia, Jan. 22.—Six employes of the city financial department today were sentenced to be shot for an "economic counter-revolution" that took the form of large-scale grafting.

Headed by the first assistant chief, all the accused were former officers or soldiers of White Guard armies who catered to private dealers and speculators by reducing high taxes these classes should have paid the city, taking bribes in the form of produce and manufactured goods. The leader was sentenced to a year of hard labor and six others, including a woman, to varying prison terms.

BRITAIN IS DIVIDED OVER DEBT POLICY

MacDonald Is Said to Oppose Starting With Refusal to Pay Before Revision.

WORLD PARLEY SUGGESTED

Britons See Opportunity to Take Up Economic Problems After They Win Settlement.

By CHARLES A. SELDEN.
Special Cable to THE NEW YORK TIMES.

LONDON, Jan. 22.—Although definite consideration of the Washington invitation to discuss war debts cannot begin before tomorrow's special meeting of the Cabinet, there already are two views as to what the British point of departure for the negotiations should be.

One is that it must be understood from the beginning that the payment due next June is not going to be made under any circumstances and that discussion of future payments or a single payment must be based on an entirely new agreement for a greatly reduced total. Supporters of that policy contend such a course was indicated by the British notes last December, explaining the conditions under which payment was made then.

MacDonald Is Conciliatory.

It is understood Prime Minister MacDonald personally disapproves this course as being too abrupt and involving an implied threat at the start of the Washington discussions of a future default if their outcome is not satisfactory to Britain. Such an attitude, in the opinion of those who oppose it, would also mean for Great Britain the loss of some of the American good-will she won by not defaulting in December.

Mr. MacDonald is as desirous as any member of his Cabinet of wiping out all war debts or, failing that, reducing them as materially as reparations were reduced at Lausanne. But he would go about it by more conciliatory methods and take as the point of departure the existing debt situation as it is understood by the United States Congress and government and not, as many Britons now consider it, fixed by their own determination to pay no more on the old terms.

One outcome of this question of what is Britain's best way of approach to the United States may be for Prime Minister MacDonald himself to head the delegation to Washington. In that case Stanley Baldwin, Lord President of the Council, would remain at home and as Deputy Premier would assume government leadership in the House of Commons.

In many political quarters Mr. Baldwin is considered the best man for the Washington job because of

Continued on Page Two.

Spain Brings 59 Royalists Home for Trial After the Escape of 29 Others From Africa

By The Associated Press.

MADRID, Spain, Jan. 22.—Fifty-nine Monarchists, exiled to the African penal colony at Villa Cisneros, were being hurried to Madrid tonight to stand trial in connection with the rebellion of last August.

They arrived at Puerto Santa Maria, near Cádiz, this morning on a tugboat which was under the close surveillance of a gunboat.

In groups of three the deportees were permitted to land under the vigilance of guards. Then they proceeded to the railroad station, where friends and relatives were allowed to greet and embrace them.

They complained about being guarded and being forced to travel third class, but all appeared comparatively happy. They said they did not learn of the escape on Jan. 1 of twenty-nine of their number, who landed a few days ago at a Portuguese port, after days of hardship on several small vessels, until authorities at Villa Cisneros began an investigation of the escape.

On Jan. 2 it was revealed that twenty-nine out of one hundred and thirty-two royalists imprisoned at Villa Cisneros, on the west coast of Africa, had escaped on a small Franch barque and that Spanish naval vessels and airplanes were in hot pursuit. For days afterward it was reported that a diligent search was being made and Republican officials in Madrid expressed their determination that they should be recaptured. Nevertheless the little vessel eluded all this professed vigilance and arrived fourteen days later at Lisbon with a tale of hardships and hunger in their flight.

Although the prisoners now in Spain to face trial say they knew nothing of the flight of their companions until they were questioned, those who reached Portugal said selection was made among the refugees on a basis of courage previously displayed.

SENATORS CONFER WITH ROOSEVELT ON FEDERAL RELIEF

La Follette and Cutting Take Up $500,000,000 Bill and Report 'Sympathetic Hearing.'

CABINET IS BEING SHAPED

President-Elect Is Seeking a Balance in a Liberal and Conservative Alignment.

OLDER MEN TO THE FRONT

Glass, Hull and Walsh Are Now Outstanding in Consideration at Warm Springs.

By JAMES A. HAGERTY.
Special to THE NEW YORK TIMES.

WARM SPRINGS, Ga., Jan. 22.—The first callers on President-elect Roosevelt after his arrival at Warm Springs this morning were Senators Robert M. La Follette of Wisconsin and Bronson Cutting of New Mexico, two of the leading members of the Progressive Republican group who supported him for election.

The Senators came from Washington by train to Atlanta, motored from there and had dinner with Mr. Roosevelt at his cottage.

Both Senators denied afterward that they had discussed Cabinet appointments with the President-elect and declared that their conference was about legislation for unemployment relief and mainly about the bill which Senator La Follette has introduced to appropriate $500,000,000 for that purpose.

"The committee, of which Senator Cutting and I are members, wanted to give the President-elect a résumé of the testimony taken by our committee," Senator La Follette said, "and to discuss with him the legislative procedure that should be taken in what Senator Cutting and I regard as a critical and desperate situation.

"The Governor gave us a very attentive and sympathetic hearing. So far as his general attitude was concerned, it was very gratifying.

"We both feel that the Federal Government must grant aid and that the bill which grants $500,000,000 errs on the side of conservatism. The fiction of loans to be deducted from future highway funds has vanished. The Federal Government must step in and take part of the load."

Asks "Direct Appropriation."

Asked if he thought $500,000,000 would be sufficient, Senator La Follette replied:

"I think it would be a good start. There must be a direct appropriation by the Federal Government."

He added that he intended to press for the passage of his bill at the present session.

Senator Cutting, asked about dispatches from Washington to the effect that a place in the Cabinet, probably Secretary of the Interior, had been offered to him, replied:

"Nothing to that."

The Senators left the Roosevelt cottage at 9:30 P. M. and returned to Atlanta by automobile to catch a midnight train for Washington

The presence of the Progressives who continued a discussion they began last week in Washington, was construed as indicating with certainty that Mr. Roosevelt would have a Republican of their type in his Cabinet and as corroborating reports that Senator Cutting would be Secretary of the Interior.

For Conservative-Liberal Balance.

Mr. Roosevelt's conference with the Senators, leaders of the younger Progressive group, also seemed to show a desire on his part to retain Progressive support during his administration, and his invitation to them was regarded as part of a balancing process by which Mr. Roosevelt hopes to avoid a break with either conservatives or liberals.

By his agreement with President Hoover to receive a representative of the British Government for a discussion of the war debts immediately after his inauguration, Mr. Roosevelt pleased the conservative leaders of his party and the business and financial interests generally, but this step did not meet with the approval of many of the Progressives, particularly those opposed to cancellation or any considerable revision of the debts downward.

By his inspection of the power and nitrate plants at Muscle Shoals in company with Senator George W. Norris of Nebraska, another Republican Progressive, and Senator Clarence C. Dill of Washington, one of the Democratic liberal group, and by his announcement that he intended to put the plants to practical use with the help of Congress, Mr. Roosevelt took a

The Metropolitan Museum of Art

Relief from the monumental stairway of the palaces of Persepolis.

"All the News That's Fit to Print."

The New York Times.

LATE CITY EDITION
WEATHER—Cloudy today; tomorrow rain or snow, warmer.
Temperatures Yesterday—Max., 36; Min., 30.

Copyright, 1933, by The New York Times Company.

VOL. LXXXII....No. 27,400. Entered as Second-Class Matter. Postoffice, New York, N. Y. NEW YORK, MONDAY, JANUARY 30, 1933. **** TWO CENTS In New York City. | THREE CENTS Within 200 Miles | FOUR CENTS Elsewhere Except in 7th and 8th Postal Zones

ROOSEVELT AND LINDSAY FIND A BASIS FOR BRITISH DEBT 'MEETINGS' IN MARCH, BUT ENVOY EXPECTS WIDE DIFFERENCES

TWO CONFER FOUR HOURS

Call Talk 'Satisfactory' in Brief Statement at Warm Springs.

AGREE ON ARRANGEMENTS

President-Elect Believed to Hold to Bargaining and to Have Made No Promises.

AMBASSADOR IS HOPEFUL

'Good Effort' Will Be Made to Get Together Despite Clash of Views, He Says.

By JAMES A. HAGERTY.

Special to THE NEW YORK TIMES.

WARM SPRINGS, Ga., Jan. 29.—A satisfactory agreement on arrangements for discussion of the British war debts at Washington early in March was reached today by President-elect Franklin D. Roosevelt and Sir Ronald Lindsay, British Ambassador, at a conference in Mr. Roosevelt's cottage on the slope of Pine Mountain.

Sir Ronald was at the "Little White House" for four hours, virtually all of which time was passed in conversation with the President-elect, the two having luncheon alone to enable them to continue the discussion.

The British Ambassador, who had been interviewed by newspaper correspondents at 11 o'clock, just before he left the cottage of William Moore, where he had passed the night, for the Roosevelt cottage, declined to answer further questions when he left by automobile for Atlanta at 3 o'clock in the afternoon.

Issue Statement in Longhand.

Instead, Sir Ronald handed to the newspaper men a joint statement by Mr. Roosevelt and himself, written in longhand. The statement follows:

The British Ambassador and Mr. Roosevelt have had a wholly informal and unofficial but very satisfactory conversation concerning tentatively the arrangements for the coming meetings in Washington. It is hoped that it will be possible to start these meetings early in March.

Nothing of the details of the discussion could be obtained from Mr. Roosevelt, and, as no others heard it, information obtained from members of the President-elect's party was wholly speculative.

There was said to be good grounds for belief, however, that Mr. Roosevelt had not abandoned his idea that the war-debt situation might furnish opportunity for bargaining.

Belief also was expressed that the President-elect, in his talk with the British Ambassador, whom he has known as a friend for years, had made no definite promises and that the conversation had concerned largely how the negotiations for a revision of the British debt would be started, probably including a statement by the Ambassador of the position of his government in desiring a large reduction or even cancellation and an explanation by the President-elect to Sir Ronald of his attitude for transmission to the British Government.

Speculate on Word "Meetings."

The use of the plural in the phrase "coming meetings in Washington" in the statement issued by Mr. Roosevelt and Sir Ronald led to the supposition that this might mean that there had been an agreement that British representatives would discuss with representatives of the United States economic questions concurrently with the war-debt negotiations. It appeared later that this was not necessarily an accurate inference and that the use of the word "meetings" referred to the series of discussions on the war debts, which will take place with Mr. Roosevelt soon after he becomes President.

Today's discussion is expected to result in a clarification of the attitude of the new administration when Sir Ronald conveys the result of his talk with Mr. Roosevelt to his government. He left Warm Springs seemingly hopeful that his talk with the President-elect might be of great help toward solving one of the world's most perplexing problems.

A report that Mr. Roosevelt had extended an informal invitation to

Concessions in Return for Reduction in War Debt Urged in Referendum of United States Chamber

Special to THE NEW YORK TIMES.

WASHINGTON, Jan. 29.—Recommendations of a special committee of the Chamber of Commerce of the United States for modification, under certain conditions, of the wartime debts of European nations to this country have been ratified by overwhelming votes by the member organizations of the chamber, it was announced today. The committee took a definite stand against cancellation and held that debtor nations should make concessions so that American goods would receive entry to their markets on a fair competitive basis.

The proposals of the committee and the results of the referendum follow:

1. Further postponement of payments on the governmental debts due the United States should be authorized by Congress on a temporary basis in the case of those debtor countries showing inability to make present payments. For, 1,834; against, 89.
2. Congress should give authority for negotiation of a modified agreement that will promote the best interests of the United States upon a debtor country showing material changes in the bases of its existing debt agreement with the United States. For, 1,791; against, 100.
3. Any modification of an existing debt agreement should be conditioned upon definite provisions for such treatment of our trade by the debtor country as will assure access of American goods to its markets on a fair competitive term. For, 1,743; against, 146.
4. Any modification of an existing debt agreement should be conditioned upon reduction in expenditures for armament. For, 1,568; against, 292.
5. Proposals for the United States to cancel war debts owed it by other governments should be rejected. For, 1,826; against, 44.

BRITON URGES RISE IN VALUE OF SILVER

Sir Robert Horne, in Broadcast From London, Says Low Price Perpetuates Trade Slump.

HOPES FOR ACTION HERE

Ex-Chancellor of Exchequer Believes Britain and United States Can Aid Recovery.

Many Britons believe the larger use of silver as a supplementary currency to gold will aid stabilization in many parts of the world, said Sir Robert Horne, former British Chancellor of the Exchequer, in a talk from London yesterday which was rebroadcast in the United States over a National Broadcasting Company network.

Sir Robert spoke under the auspices of the International Radio Forum.

His talk as received here was in part as follows:

"The whole world is in a condition of confusion unparalleled in our experience. All mankind is in deep distress, and how perplexing it all is! Nature is yielding her fruit more generously than ever before. Man is more competent than at any previous period of history. Science and invention have supplied more devices for increasing the production of wealth than the most ardent dreamer ever fancied.

"And yet multitudes of deserving people in every country are enduring poignant and bitter hardships while politicians and statesmen strive continuously, but with no apparent success, to rid their countries of the haunting nightmare of unemployment.

"While there is much in our present condition that is puzzling, certain things are obvious enough. The trade of the world has shrunk to a skeleton of what it was, and the export trade of every nation has declined in a startling degree.

Internal Production Slump.

"Similarly, internal production has withered in most countries. It reached its peak in 1929. In that year world production was 47 per cent above that of 1913. In 1932 it is back at the figure of 1913 in spite of the vast expansion of the machinery of production which, since that date, has taken place.

"These conditions sufficiently explain the appalling statistics of unemployment in the world today.

"The man who lives on the soil can no longer buy from the manufacturer. He in his turn finds his trade so constricted that he cannot meet his establishment charges and he shuts down. Unemployment stalks like a malevolent spectre alike through country lanes and city streets, and it is lasting so long that the world is almost numb with despair.

"The British Government has declared its intention to employ all reasonable measures to raise wholesale commodity prices. I shall not elaborate this matter further be-

Continued on Page Two.

HEARS ROOSEVELT INVITES M'DONALD

London Expects Lindsay to Bring Bid for Visit Here of Prime Minister.

SECRET MESSAGE AWAITED

Premier Denies Report That He and Stanley Baldwin Are Controlling Negotiations.

Special Cable to THE NEW YORK TIMES.

LONDON, Jan. 29.—The debt talks between Ambassador Sir Ronald Lindsay and President-elect Roosevelt have aroused keen speculation here regarding the exact purport of the invitation which resulted in the Ambassador's flying visit.

A rumor reached London late tonight to the effect that Sir Ronald had been charged with conveying to Prime Minister MacDonald a personal and pressing request to visit the United States in March as head of the British debt delegation. In circles in close touch with the Prime Minister it is expected such an invitation will be included in a confidential dispatch on the conversations at "the Little White House" in Warm Springs, Ga.

The Ambassador presumably will put his dispatch in code for London as soon as he reaches Washington from Atlanta.

Cable dispatches tonight from Warm Springs suggest the British and United States views on debts still are widely divergent and that "stiffening of the British attitude," which Mr. Roosevelt is reported to have been concerned to observe, does in fact exist. In the circumstances, therefore, it is felt doubtful whether Mr. MacDonald, with all his experience of round-table conferences and appeal to sentiment, could present the British case in any more favorable light than the financial experts who are advising the Cabinet.

MacDonald Denies Report.

Mr. MacDonald's only excursion into the debt controversy today was to describe as "all rubbish" the report appearing in a Sunday newspaper in the effect that Mr. Roosevelt's invitation to send a mission to Washington was considered by Stanley Baldwin and Mr. MacDonald without consulting the Cabinet. The report added that they drafted a reply and were keeping the whole thing in their own hands, and that the country might find that Mr. Baldwin had decided to send himself to Washington again. The Daily Mail asserts tonight that the government, until it hears from Sir Ronald, has only a vague idea of Mr. Roosevelt's attitude.

"For instance, it is not known definitely whether he favors striking a bargain in return for debt revision, nor how much the United States' reported demand for Britain's return to the gold standard and new tariff agreements favorable to the United States are being used as propaganda for the benefit of opinion across the Atlantic."

A Cabinet meeting is being held

Continued on Page Two.

DALADIER FORMING CABINET IN FRANCE; ASKS SOCIALIST AID

War Minister Seeks Basis for Parliamentary Majority and Man for Finance Post.

HITLER FAVORED IN REICH

Will Visit Hindenburg Today and May Get Chance to Head Party Ministry.

HIS FATE UP TO CENTRISTS

100,000 Republicans at Rally in Berlin Voice Their Readiness to "Mount the Barricades."

By P. J. PHILIP.

Wireless to THE NEW YORK TIMES.

PARIS, Jan. 29.—Edouard Daladier, Minister of War in Joseph Paul-Boncour's Cabinet, has been asked by President Lebrun to undertake the task of forming a Cabinet and finding a parliamentary majority. Almost all those whom the President consulted yesterday and this morning advised him that M. Daladier was the best choice at the moment.

M. Daladier's principal difficulty is to find a majority. If, as appears certain, he seeks the support of the Socialists, this will automatically alienate the votes of the Right and Right Centre. If he tries to do without the Socialists it is doubtful that he will find sufficient support in other quarters to form a stable majority.

His first effort will certainly be to obtain the full cooperation of the Socialists. Tomorrow he is expected to ask them to share the responsibilities of government. There is a considerable body of opinion in Leon Blum's party favorable to this course. They believe the only way to preserve a Left government and to avoid a return of Right influences in the form of a government of national concentration is to abandon their policy of non-participation.

Socialists Are Cautious.

Most Socialists, however, remain unconvinced that this is the proper course. Although the Socialists are willing enough to support the Radicals if and when they are in a position to push the latter forward in the direction in which the Socialists want to go, they are still unwilling to take the responsibility of a closer alliance.

It is the fact that twice within six weeks a break has occurred between the Radicals and the Socialists that makes the present situation so difficult.

M. Daladier, who accepted the invitation to try to form a Cabinet this afternoon, has spent his time since then visiting and receiving visits from the presidents of the two chambers and all the leaders of his own Radical party. Former Premier Edouard Herriot, one of the first to see him, promised his full support. However, Mr. Herriot's action Friday night in supporting the Paul-Boncour Government against the Socialists in exceptionally warm terms has rendered him suspect to many.

It is M. Daladier's choice of a Finance Minister that will finally indicate the character of his Cabinet. But before he reaches the point of naming any one there must first inevitably be somewhat lengthy discussions with and among the Socialists. The first contact was made with M. Blum late this evening, but M. Blum of late has consistently shown himself more moderate than his party.

In this whole question of Cabinet forming there is not and will not be any question of foreign policy or debts. Whether M. Daladier or another finally forms a cabinet, he will be bound in the same way as M. Paul-Boncour was by the vote of the Chamber of Deputies on the debts issue. That is to say, he will be restricted in his conversations by the same formulae of no payment without a conference and no payment beyond the amount received from Germany.

Budget Immediate Issue.

It is the budget and the budget alone which is occupying attention, and behind the problem of the budget there lies the greater issue of which section of the Chamber, which is evenly divided into three main groups, is to have control.

All the orators and the press of the Right are campaigning for another National Concentration Cabinet, in which the Radicals would be controlled by the Right. Un-

Continued on Page Five.

Petition to Recall Gov. Rolph Approved by Grange Leaders

By The Associated Press.

SACRAMENTO, Jan. 29.—Leaders of the California State Grange said today that a petition seeking recall of Governor Rolph on the general charge of "incompetency" had been approved by grange attorneys and would be rushed to the printers tomorrow.

The action followed adjournment of the State Legislature's first-half session. The Legislature will reconvene Feb. 28.

The recall movement was initiated by George H. Sehlmeyer, State Master of the Grange, who said he had been urged by members to provide for circulation of a petition, which will need about 166,000 signatures to qualify.

Sheridan Downey, attorney for the Senate special committee investigating alleged irregularities in the State Government, has been in Los Angeles rounding up witnesses to testify as to the State's dealings in land and purchases.

SARA TEASDALE, POET, FOUND DEAD

Body Discovered in Bathtub of Her Fifth Av. Apartment—Despondent Over Illness.

DOCTOR REPORTS SUICIDE

But Medical Examiner Awaits Autopsy Today—She Won Pulitzer Prize for Verse.

Sara Teasdale, whose lyric poetry had won her widespread recognition, was found dead yesterday morning in her apartment at 1 Fifth Avenue. She was lying in a bathtub filled with warm water, but whether her death was caused by drowning, a stroke or heart disease will not be known until today, when an autopsy will be performed by the Medical Examiner.

Her body was found soon after 9 o'clock by Miss Rita Brown, a nurse, who had been attending her since last September, when she returned from London suffering from the effects of pneumonia. Her condition was complicated by a nervous breakdown from which she had not recovered. She was 48 years old.

Miss Brown summoned Dr. Frederick R. Bailey of 103 East Seventy-fifth Street, who, with Dr. Dana Atchley of the Presbyterian Hospital, had been attending Miss Teasdale since her return from England. Dr. Bailey, in notifying the Medical Examiner's office of her death, reported it a suicide.

Had Been Despondent.

This version of her death gained further credence when Miss Brown told Assistant Medical Examiner Henry Weinberg that Miss Teasdale had been extremely despondent in the last few days and frequently questioned her about the various methods of committing suicide. The nurse said she had attempted vainly to change the subject, but Miss Teasdale had insisted upon discussing it.

Although she did not believe Miss Teasdale had committed suicide, Mrs. Joseph Wheless of 780 Riverside Drive, a sister, admitted the poet had been in exceptionally poor spirits recently and had feared she might suffer a stroke. She complained of high blood pressure, Mrs. Wheless said.

"She called me to her apartment yesterday," Mrs. Wheless continued, "and gave me power of attorney over her affairs. She seemed to fear she would become incapacitated and unable to care for them herself."

Dr. Weinberg withheld the issuance of a death certificate and ordered the body transferred to the morgue for an autopsy. He said he was not convinced Miss Teasdale had taken her life, although the evidence of the nurse and the physician who had been attending her seemed to point in that direction.

Even if tests should prove that Miss Teasdale had drowned, Dr. Weinberg said, it would not mean necessarily that she had committed suicide. A heart attack or slight stroke might have rendered her unconscious, he explained, and she might have drowned accidentally.

Former Husband a Trade Expert.

Miss Teasdale's former husband, Ernst B. Filsinger, a foreign trade expert and writer, was reported to be in Africa. They were married in St. Louis in 1914 and were divorced in Reno in 1929. They had no children. Mr. Filsinger, a former vice president of the Royal Baking Powder Company, is a foreign trade consultant for several leading American concerns.

Miss Teasdale was born in St. Louis on Aug. 8, 1884, the daughter of John Warren and Mary Elizabeth Willard Teasdale. She first attracted attention in 1907 by a vol-

Continued on Page Four.

50,000 SOVIET REDS WILL DIRECT DRIVE TO SOCIALIZE FARMS

100,000 Tons of Grain Will Be Used to Spur Collectivization in North Caucasus.

TRACTORS ALSO PROVIDED

Aim Is to Win the Peasants and Produce Results in Rural Regions.

MOVE ELECTRIFIES PARTY

Russian Communists Thrilled by Measures That Are Expected to Reawaken Country.

By WALTER DURANTY.

Wireless to THE NEW YORK TIMES.

MOSCOW, Jan. 29.—With the introduction this month of two measures of action to win the villages to real socialization—the formation of a political department in the machine-tractor stations and the "mobilization" decree in the North Caucasus—the coming Spring will witness a decisive struggle on the agrarian front.

Events have shown that the mere form of collectivization is not sufficient—that the old individualist spirit remained in the new organizations and often gained strength by the sheer fact of greater unity.

During the past fortnight the writer has asked a number of prominent Communists why the steps now projected were not taken earlier. Some said that the material equipment had been inadequate hitherto, others that there had been an insufficient personnel, but Joseph V. Stalin gave the fundamental reason—that the Communist party as a whole had been hypnotized by the Socialist form but had neglected its spirit and substance.

Kremlin to Direct Drive.

Every one felt that there was something wrong with the collectives, but no one quite knew what, or what to do about it. Now the central committee of the party has given the lead, and for the first time rural collectivization will be really taken in hand by a strong force of Communists with full powers and a proper supply of machinery, seed, fertilizer and, if necessary, food, under the direct control and eye of the Kremlin.

In the coming two months there will be thrown into the North Caucasus drive 50,000 Communist "actives" with a reserve fund of 100,000 tons of grain and all the needed tractors, plows and supplies to organize and invigorate the Socialist cause. It is difficult to exaggerate the effect of these new decisions upon Communist opinion here.

The first days of the recent Communist sessions gave a pessimistic impression, which has always found a loud echo among resident foreigners, most of whom, for easily understandable reasons, are neither sympathetic to the Bolshevist aims nor yet convinced that when the Bolsheviki say Socialism they mean Socialism, not a hybrid of Socialism and capitalism.

Then in quick succession came the machine-tractor political department, Joseph Stalin's speech of Jan. 11 and the Caucasian "mobilization" decree. Here at last was the "lead" and concrete action for an attack. Sentiment changed overnight, as did the spirit

Continued on Page Four.

Base to Handle Entire Fleet Is Sought at San Pedro, Cal.

By The Associated Press.

SAN PEDRO, Cal., Jan. 29.—Naval officers announced here today that investigation of possible sites and costs for a base at San Pedro Harbor sufficient to handle the entire United States fleet has been ordered by the Navy Department.

Immediate acquisition of a site in the harbor was recommended by Admiral Richard H. Leigh, Commander-in-Chief of the United States fleet, and the Navy Department has commissioned Rear Admiral T. J. Senn, Commandant of the Eleventh Naval District, and Commander H. A. Jones, new Naval Reserve chief here, to conduct the study.

Prime factors of the enterprise were given as enhanced security for the nation in war and economy and convenience for the fleet.

"The need of base facilities should not be confused with a navy yard," said Admiral Leigh. "We already have too many navy yards."

SPITALE AND BITZ JAILED IN A MURDER

Gang Aides in Lindbergh Case Accused of East Side Killing After Mysterious Arrest.

BOTH ARE FOUND ARMED

Police Act for Safety on Tip Shooting Is Threatened in Mott St. Restaurant.

Stone walls and iron bars separated Salvatore Spitale and Irving Bitz from their enemies yesterday. The two "square-shooting gangsters," chosen by Colonel Charles A. Lindbergh to negotiate with the kidnappers of his infant son, were prisoners in the Tombs, seemingly for their own good.

Officially the record showed that Spitale and Bitz, to whom the police turned for help in investigating the murders of Jack (Legs) Diamond and Charles (Vannie) Higgins, were charged with homicide and carrying pistols without permits. Behind the official version, however, lay a tale which inquiry among detectives finally brought to light.

About 9 o'clock Saturday night Lieutenant Henry Hanley, in charge at the Elizabeth Street station, received a telephone call. An anonymous voice informed him that unless the police hastened to the Red Devil Restaurant at Broome and Mott Streets, two blocks from Police Headquarters, there would be another murder for Commissioner Mulrooney to list in his annual report. Some one was about to be "bumped off," the anonymous caller warned.

Search Reveals Pistols.

Detectives Alexander McKittrick, John Phillips and Henry Fitzsimmons were sent to the restaurant. Almost every table was occupied, but in a corner the detectives saw the bulky frame of Spitale and the milder, smaller figure of Bitz. They occupied a table for four and seemed to be expecting guests to fill the vacant chairs, for their hats and coats were piled upon them as if to mark them as reserved.

Detective Phillips promptly covered the two uncomfortable diners with a pistol partly concealed in his pocket. Fitzsimmons hastily searched Bitz while McKettrick took care of Spitale. The somewhat sensational incident caused

Continued on Page Three.

Mexican Farmers Find Huge Buried Castle; Building 158 Feet High Covers 2.47 Acres

Special Cable to THE NEW YORK TIMES.

MEXICO CITY, Jan. 29.—Hitherto unknown marvelous archaeologic ruins are reported to have been discovered on the San Felipe Ranch, about twenty miles from the celebrated centre at Chichén Itzá, in the State of Yucatan, according to a reliable source.

Telegrams announcing the find say field laborers came upon the ruins when preparing the land for the next crops.

So far an immense castle has been located, spread over an area of one hectare [2.47 acres] and fifty meters [158 feet] high. Local authorities express the opinion that further excavations will show it to be surrounded by an entire city.

The latest discovery is believed to have been buried by the Cacique Nachi Cocom to preserve it from the vandalism of the early conquerors of Mexico.

It has been estimated that within 100 miles of Mérida, the capital of Yucatan, are located the ruins of more than 100 Maya cities. Some of these, as, for instance, Chichén Itzá, have been partly restored, but many of them either have lain buried for centuries or, once discovered, have been left to be swallowed again by the lush growths of the jungles.

The predominant characteristic of the important Maya structures is that they are built upon an artificial elevation. The walls are usually of great thickness, elaborately carved outside with warriors or animals, and sometimes adorned inside with vividly colored murals. Nearly all the buildings are of white limestone and sometimes single blocks weigh several tons.

The Mayas had no beasts of burden and these blocks frequently had to be hauled for great distances through the jungles. The carving was done usually with bird bones or calcite chisels worked in water on the rock.

The castle mentioned in the dispatch is characteristic of all large Maya cities. Such castles served as temples. It was upon their summit that captive warriors were sacrificed to the god of war while the populace of the city looked on from below.

YOUNG ASKS NAME NOT BE CONSIDERED FOR A CABINET POST

Sends Request to Roosevelt After Report He Might Be Secretary of State.

FARLEY BUSY IN CAPITAL

On Way to Warm Springs, He Sees Glass on Treasury Offer and Other Party Leaders.

PLACE FOR HULL LIKELY

Norman Davis Strongly Mentioned for Ambassador to London to Aid in Coming Parleys.

Special to THE NEW YORK TIMES.

WASHINGTON, Jan. 29.—Owen D. Young, who has been prominently mentioned for Secretary of State in the Roosevelt Cabinet, has written a letter to the President-elect at Warm Springs, Ga., informing him that he cannot be considered for a Cabinet position.

This information was made known here today by Democrats in the confidence of Mr. Young. According to them, he was prompted to send such a message to Mr. Roosevelt, now making up his Cabinet, because he understood that the latter had seriously discussed him for Secretary of State with leading Democrats with whom he had consulted about Cabinet timber. It was emphasized that Mr. Young had not received an offer of the post.

Mr. Young, it is asserted, gave the same reasons that he offered when, early last year, he withdrew his name from consideration as a possible Presidential candidate. He felt that he could not allow his name to be considered for a Cabinet place, partly because of business affairs and for personal reasons.

Hull's Name Comes to Fore.

Senator Hull of Tennessee was mentioned tonight as a possibility to head the Roosevelt Cabinet as Secretary of State, while some Democrats thought that the final selection might be either Newton D. Baker or Bernard M. Baruch.

The composition of the Cabinet may become a more serious task than it has appeared heretofore, due to the attitude of Mr. Young and the reported indecision of Senator Glass with respect to acceptance of the Secretaryship of the Treasury. Should Mr. Glass finally decline the offer made to him last week, two of the most important places in the Cabinet would be open, with the possibility that no selections might be finally made by Mr. Roosevelt for these places until late in February.

Senator Glass may have sent his decision to Mr. Roosevelt today. Senator Glass had an hour's conversation during the afternoon with James A. Farley, chairman of the Democratic National Committee. The meeting was held to learn, if possible, Mr. Glass's final decision.

Mr. Farley stopped off here for three hours on his way to Warm Springs, where he and Colonel Louis Howe will go over with the President-elect the situation respecting Cabinet and Ambassadorship places. Mr. Farley declined to say whether the Senator had accepted the proffered appointment. Some of Mr. Glass's friends say that he will accept in case Mr. Roosevelt still persists in his becoming a member of his Cabinet.

Farley Also Sees Hull.

The fact that Mr. Farley also visited Senator Hull gave rise to the belief that the discussion with the Tennessee Senator also dealt with a Cabinet place.

Democrats who figure in Mr. Roosevelt's advisory board said that Senator Hull would be in the Cabinet, but that the probability was that he would be either Secretary of the Treasury, in case Mr. Glass declines the appointment, or Secretary of Commerce.

Senator Hull refused to say whether he would or would not accept a Cabinet place. He avoided the question of a Cabinet offer by saying that he was busy formulating a Democratic program.

"Senator Hull is one Democrat who will be in the Cabinet," a Roosevelt intimate said, however.

Probable Line-Up Reported.

According to well-informed Democrats, the probable line-up of the Cabinet, so far as tentatively agreed upon, will be as follows:

SECRETARY OF THE TREASURY—Senator Carter Glass of Virginia.
ATTORNEY GENERAL—Senator Thomas J. Walsh of Montana.
SECRETARY OF COMMERCE—Senator Cordell Hull of Tennessee.
POSTMASTER GENERAL—James A. Farley of New York.

Continued on Page Three.

"All the News That's Fit to Print."

The New York Times.

LATE CITY EDITION
POSTCRIPT
WEATHER—Rain, warmer today; colder tonight; tomorrow cloudy.
Temperatures Yesterday—Max., 44; min., 33.

VOL. LXXXII....No. 27,421. | Entered as Second-Class Matter, Postoffice, New York, N. Y. | NEW YORK, MONDAY, FEBRUARY 20, 1933. | TWO CENTS In New York City. | THREE CENTS Within 200 Miles | FOUR CENTS Elsewhere Except in 7th and 8th Postal Zones.

GERMANY IS UNEASY ABOUT HINDENBURG; FEARS HE IS WEARY

President Is Reported to Be in Good Health, but Strain on Him Causes Worry.

RARELY SEEN IN PUBLIC

Receives Few Save Intimate Friends—Consults His Son and Papen on Politics.

NEW GERMANY IS FORMING

Nazi Progress Toward Fascism Goes On Unchecked—Control of All Publicity Seized.

By FREDERICK T. BIRCHALL.
Wireless to THE NEW YORK TIMES.

BERLIN, Feb. 19.—Outside official circles in Germany, in which the subject is taboo for journalistic purposes, certain apprehensions are beginning to be expressed regarding the continued good health of the venerable and respected President of the Reich.

Undoubtedly these have their origin in the remarkable series of political developments of the last two months and are motivated by fear lest this continued somersaulting should prove overmuch for even the most rugged constitution and mentality to endure at the advanced age of 85.

It should be stated at the outset that all the official information available on this point under the new governmental régime—which, incidentally, is more notable for its reticences than for its frankness in all matters of fact—is wholly reassuring. Nor has there been anything recently in the rare public appearances of the aged President to confirm the forebodings confidentially whispered in quiet corners.

Stood for Hours at Parade.

It was only a few weeks ago that President von Hindenburg stood for hours at a lighted window in his temporary apartment in the Chancellery while a seemingly endless procession of torchbearing Nazis and Stahlhelm members passed before him, shouting "Heil!" and laughing, as excited as children by the flags, bands and singing with which they were thus inaugurating, as they saw it, the new Third Reich—the Year One of the Nazi kingdom of heaven.

The attention of the marchers was focused rather on the neighboring lighted window at which Adolf Hitler stood, drinking in this renewed acclaim of his supporters. The great Reichspresident had become secondary.

The fact could scarcely have failed to arouse some misgivings in that silent figure. His hand went up in salute as his favorite colors passed him—not as often as the hand of that other figure, his rival attraction. He scarcely seemed as interested as usual. But when some one pushed a chair forward that he might sit during part of the long ordeal, he is said to have spurned the proffered ease indignantly. Throughout the long hours he stood there until the procession had faded out, seeing it to the end.

Other Recent Appearances.

Since then the President has appeared once in public—at a riding tournament—and twice at dinners, respectively official and friendly, the one a formal function at which the new Cabinet met the diplomatic corps and the other a dinner given by the Papal Nuncio, at which it has been the President's custom to appear as an annual guest. On neither occasion did his fellow-diners note anything more than that the old Field Marshal wearied a little more easily, perhaps, than he once did.

In the diplomatic corps, moreover, there is current a story that an old friend, who is also a doctor, representing a neighboring republic, was calling on the President recently, and on hearing him good-naturedly berate his advancing years asked to test his pulse. After which the doctor exclaimed: "With such a pulse, Herr Reichspresident, you should live to be 150!"

However, less than ever does the President see many persons save his intimates. Detesting public appearances and devotedly loving home life, he deals as little with politics as his high office permits.

Son Constant Companion.

His constant companion is his only son, Colonel Oskar von Hindenburg, a product of the old army and supposedly devoted to it. His next favorite is undoubtedly Vice Chancellor Franz von Papen, whom he trusts absolutely in political matters and who is his mouthpiece in the present Cabinet, in the framing of which the former Chancellor bore the principal part.

Nevertheless, despite the favorable

Continued on Page Six.

Cuba to Fine Foreigners Not Registered by Feb. 28

By Air Mail to THE NEW YORK TIMES.

HAVANA, Feb. 19.—All foreigners living in Cuba who have not registered with the Department of Interior prior to Feb. 28 will be subject to a fine of from $5 to $30, according to a new government ruling.

Compulsory registration was put into effect by a Presidential decree of April 19, 1932. The period of registration has been extended several times.

Only a small percentage of the estimated 500,000 foreigners in Cuba have applied for registration. This is caused largely, it is said, by the financial condition of many thousands here, particularly Spaniards and natives of the West Indies, who are unable to pay the $1.45 required as well as the cost of photographs that must be presented.

The registration cards will be valid for five years.

BOETTCHER SAFE; FATHER GETS NOTES

Immunity Pledge Answers Kidnappers' Missives Enclosing Messages From Son.

POLICE ALLOW PROCEDURE

But Press Own Search With Federal Agent Entering Case —Denver Citizens Arm.

By The Associated Press.

DENVER, Feb. 19.—Claude K. Boettcher, father of Charles Boettcher 2d, kidnapped Denver broker, said tonight that he had received communications which he was satisfied were from the captors of his son. He added that they contained notes undoubtedly penned by the 31-year-old victim, who was kidnapped from the driveway of his home a week ago tonight as he and his wife returned from a party.

Mr. Boettcher said that the communications convinced him that his son, held for $60,000 ransom, was alive and well.

He did not comply with the kidnappers' demands contained in the letters, but dispatched an answer pleading for time and better directions, he said.

Revealing that the communications were received through the mail two days ago and answered immediately, he said it was now feared that the reply had gone astray because it had not been acknowledged. He guaranteed immunity from police interference if the kidnappers would again contact him.

Police Won't Interfere.

Because of the position of the Boettcher family in Denver, his guarantee of protection to the kidnappers would probably be rigidly observed, the police said, although Chief Albert T. Clark said that investigation of the case would not be relaxed. He said that he had not seen the letters.

Police Commissioner Carl S. Milliken joined Chief Clark in denying knowledge of the notes. He said, however, that the interests of the Boettcher family in the case would be fully protected.

From the moment the young man disappeared into the darkness with his captors there was no word of him until receipt of the notes, the police continuing their investigation unaware that the communication had been made.

Mr. Boettcher's Statement.

In a statement tonight Mr. Boettcher told of receiving "many ransom notes," and continued:

"Some of the notes, I am convinced by certain enclosures, among

Continued on Page Three.

ROOSEVELT DRAFTS HIS DEBT PROGRAM FOR PARLEY TODAY

Spends Day Conferring With Advisers in Preparation for Meeting With Lindsay.

SEES BARUCH AND MOLEY

Talks to Woodin, House and Lehman Also—Still Against Outright Cancellation.

ENVOY'S SHIP DUE AT 1:30

Sir Ronald Expected to Bring a Proposal for Immediate World Economic Conference.

In preparation for another conference on war debts today with Sir Ronald Lindsay, British Ambassador, President-elect Roosevelt conferred yesterday with his economic advisers at his home, 49 East Sixty-fifth Street.

The list of Mr. Roosevelt's callers was regarded as significant. During the afternoon he talked with Bernard M. Baruch, an authority on finance. Mr. Baruch is believed to be slated for chairman of the American delegation to the World Economic Conference, and he may be named as a special representative of the President at the discussion of world economic problems which is expected to take place simultaneously with the negotiations for revision of the British war debts.

Others with whom Mr. Roosevelt talked during the day were Professor Raymond Moley, his chief adviser on economics; Colonel Edward M. House, veteran in foreign affairs and confidential adviser to President Wilson, and William H. Woodin, president of the American Car and Foundry Company, who probably will be appointed Secretary of the Treasury if Senator Carter Glass refuses the appointment, as he is expected to do. Other callers were Professor Rexford G. Tugwell, Charles W. Taussig, president of the American Molasses Company; Governor Lehman, Ogden Reid, publisher of The New York Herald Tribune, and Louis A. Johnson, National Commander of the American Legion.

Envoy Arrives Today.

These conferences at the Roosevelt home were linked with the sudden invitation extended by Mr. Roosevelt through the State Department for the British Ambassador to call on him immediately on his arrival from England before proceeding to Washington.

The Majestic, on which Sir Ronald is returning, is due to dock at 1:30 this afternoon at Pier 59, Hudson River, at West Seventeenth Street. The Ambassador will be met at the pier by Gerald Campbell, British Consul General, who will accompany him to Mr. Roosevelt's home.

No date has been set for the beginning of the war-debt negotiations, but it is possible that a decision on the date may be reached today. Mr. Roosevelt has no knowledge of what message Sir Ronald will bring back from his government, but there is a belief that he may have a proposal for an immediate world economic conference to which all nations would be invited.

Apparently matters are moving swiftly to an arrangement for the war-debt negotiations. Professor Moley flew to meet Mr. Roosevelt at Miami on the latter's return from his fishing cruise and conferred with the President-elect on Vincent Astor's yacht there. It is understood that Mr. Roosevelt, as President, intends to participate

Continued on Page Two.

Japan Held Manchuria Part of China in 1904, Documents in British Foreign Office Show

Wireless to THE NEW YORK TIMES.

LONDON, Feb. 19.—Japanese diplomatic documents have just been brought to light in London proving that at the time of the Russo-Japanese War Japan insisted on keeping Manchuria "an integral part of China."

In the dusty archives of the British Foreign Office has been found a Japanese note to Russia, dated Feb. 5, 1904, expounding the same arguments that China is using against Japan today. The note speaks of the "repeated refusal of the Imperial Russian Government to accept the obligation to respect the territorial integrity of China in Manchuria," and also declares that China's integrity "has been menaced by prolonged occupation of that province by Russia."

The London Times published a letter yesterday from the well-known publicist, Augur, carrying the revelations a stage further. After Japan had broken diplomatic relations with Russia, the French Minister to Tokyo, M. Harmand, transmitted to Paris an explanation given him by Baron Komura, then Japanese Foreign Minister. One sentence of the report quoting Baron Komura follows:

"Japan desires that Russia should recognize Manchuria as an integral part of China. Provided such a declaration is forthcoming, Japan is prepared to allow Russia complete liberty of action in that province."

Commenting on the present situation Augur writes:

"Today it is precisely on that point that Japan holds out strongest against the viewpoint held at Geneva. It refuses to admit Manchuria is a part of China. Why?"

These revelations have stirred diplomatic circles here, and were used against Japan with damaging effect in a London Times editorial yesterday on the League's report.

Pastor, 34, and Trustee, 68, Come to Blows In Long Beach Church and Are Arrested

Special to THE NEW YORK TIMES.

LONG BEACH, L. I., Feb. 19.—The Rev. Felix G. Robinson, pastor of St. John's Lutheran Church-by-the-Sea, and Charles W. Ackerman, vice president of the church board of trustees, were booked at the police station here this morning on charges of assault, following a row in the edifice.

What led to the row, how many blows were struck and who struck them, how the fracas was stopped—all these details the principals and members of the congregation refused to discuss. There was an unconfirmed report that the quarrel had its origin in a discussion of financial matters.

The row took place in the church, according to the police. A telephone call was received at the station house from an excited woman member of the congregation shortly after 10 A. M., about a half hour before the pastor was to open the Sunday service. He had chosen for his sermon the subject, "What the Church Ought to Be."

Patrolman Gus Koberstein was sent to the church. He found several women members rather excited and most of the men engaged in trying to smooth matters over. Mr. Ackerman, a large man with gray hair and mustache who owns a hat and clothing firm in Fifth Avenue, Manhattan, was bruised and bleeding from cuts on the face.

Patrolman Koberstein took the minister, who was unmarked, and Mr. Ackerman before Sergeant Thomas Moore, who was on desk duty. Each made charges of assault against the other, and then Mr. Ackerman was taken to Long Beach Hospital. The record shows that Dr. L. L. Bean treated the merchant for lacerations of both eyes, contusions over the right eye and lacerations of the forehead.

The minister was to have entered the pulpit at 11 A. M., but the police were unable to find City Judge J. Charles Zimmerman in time to release him and Mr. Ackerman. It was 1 P. M. before the judge appeared, took the pleas of "not guilty" from both sides and released the defendants on their own recognizance for hearing Tuesday.

In the meantime there was no

Continued on Page Three.

THREE BOYS DROWN UNDER ICE IN BRONX

Four, Walking on River Near the Zoo, Fall In—One Is Saved by a Youth.

2 BOATS SINK WITH POLICE

Ladder Laid on Ice Crashes Through—Seven Rescued in Recovering the Bodies.

Three young boys were drowned yesterday afternoon in the Bronx River, about four blocks north of the entrance to the Bronx Zoological Park, when the thin ice on which they were walking gave way beneath them. A fourth boy also plunged through the ice, but was rescued by an unidentified youth who dragged him ashore by the hair.

The rescuer, drenched to the skin, applied a few moments later at the Fire Alarm Telegraph Bureau, 1,100 East 180th Street, for permission to dry his clothes, explaining that he would not dare go home in that condition lest his mother learn he had disobeyed her orders in venturing near the river.

The boys drowned were Ralph Mazzaca, 12 years old, of 1,813 Victor Street; Frank Gramnara, 10, of 1,801 White Plains Avenue, and Michael Theorio, 12, of 1,712 White Plains Avenue. All lived in the Bronx and attended Public School 34, at 1,830 Amethyst Avenue.

Their companion who was rescued, Anthony Borello, 14, of 1,811 Victor Street, is a student at the same school.

Section of Ice Gives Way.

Borello said they were walking over the ice, Gramnara and Therio in front and he and Mazzaca behind, when there was a loud crunching and Gramnara and Therio disappeared. He and Mazzaca rushed forward immediately, Borello said, and tried to rescue them, but as they neared the jagged hole through which the two had plunged another section of ice gave way and they, too, were struggling in the water.

Borello said he was able to swim a little and tried to help Mazzaca but a strong current carried the other boy away. He clung to an ice floe, Borello said, until his rescuer reached him and dragged him ashore.

Meanwhile, from the river bank, several persons had seen the accident and hurried to summon aid. The Bronx Park police station was notified and soon two police radio cars and two emergency crews arrived.

Policemen Fall in River.

Patrolman Joseph Sheehan, who arrived in the first radio car, saw a boy's hat floating in the open water and started out toward it. But a few feet from the shore the ice gave way under him. He struggled back to the river bank after getting a thorough ducking.

With the arrival of the first emergency truck, a ladder was stretched out over the ice toward the open water and Patrolmen John Hughes and George Kieg climbed out along it. Hughes, who was nearest the end of the ladder, reached for the hat and picked it up. But he could find no trace of the missing boys. He was about to turn back when the ice gave way beneath the ladder and he and Kieg were hurled into the water. Both policemen clung to the ladder and, with the aid of others, dragged themselves back to shore.

Realizing the futility of attempting to work on the thin ice, Sergeants Kavanaugh and Egan, in

Continued on Page Eight.

MERCHANTS FIGHT TO REFORM CHARTER

Offer Own 8-Point Plan for Revision, Like Seabury's, and Map Drive for It.

ONE COUNCIL, FEW BOARDS

Proportional Voting Is Urged and Legislation Will Be Asked to Legalize It.

The Merchants Association announced yesterday that it had adopted an eight-point plan for revision of the New York City charter and that it would make a determined fight for the adoption of its proposals.

The plan in general is in line with the principal recommendations made by Samuel Seabury, counsel to the legislative investigating committee, in his report to that body.

The eight points, as presented by the association, follow:

The establishment of a single-chambered council to exercise the policy-determining function of the Mayor, the Municipal Assembly, the Board of Estimate and Apportionment, the Board of Aldermen and the Sinking Fund Commission.

To be truly representative of the people this council should be elected by proportional representation.

It should preferably be elected from the present boroughs upon a fixed quota basis.

The Mayor and Controller should be nominated by petition, and elected at large by the proportional representation method of voting as applied to the selection of a single official, otherwise called majority preferential voting.

The ballots for municipal elections should bear no party designations.

The number of independent city departments should be reduced to ten from sixteen.

Provision should be made for appropriation and capital outlay budgets to be prepared by the executive.

The task of conforming the administrative and other features of the charter to the above proposals within a reasonable fixed period should be imposed as a duty upon the council.

The association announced also that in order to remove any doubt as to the constitutionality of proportional representation it would seek a constitutional amendment giving specific authorization for that method of voting.

Report on Program.

The report of the committee, in support of the eight-point program, was as follows:

The city has at present one individual and four bodies possessed of some policy-determining or legislative functions—the Mayor, the Municipal Assembly, the Board of Estimate and Apportionment, the Board of Aldermen and the Sinking Fund Commission. Neither logical nor practical reasons exist for the continuance of all this machinery. It scatters responsibility, makes difficult the passage of needed measures and discourages public interest in governmental affairs, while it in no way promotes efficiency or safety.

It is recommended, therefore, that all of this machinery be replaced by a single council of approximately twenty-five members, which shall exercise all of the policy-determining functions of the city government.

The plurality system of election

Continued on Page Nine.

HOUSE WETS COUNT UPON REPEAL TODAY; PUSH RATIFICATION

Rainey Says Resubmission Will Pass by 20 Votes Above Two-thirds Majority.

CONVENTION ACTION NEXT

Steps Are Taken Toward Law for State Machinery of Ratification.

WYOMING VOTES OWN ACT

Meanwhile Anti-Prohibition Eastern States Poise for Race as First to Ratify.

Developments on Repeal.

Representative Rainey, Democratic floor leader of the House, predicted an excess of twenty votes over the two-thirds necessary when the House takes final action today on submitting to the States the amendment to repeal prohibition.

Steps were taken in the House toward legislation by Congress defining the method of setting up State conventions to pass on ratification.

Wyoming took the lead among the States in providing for a convention in a bill signed by Governor Miller. Four per cent beer also was legalized.

Other States, among them New York, New Jersey, Massachusetts and Maryland, mapped plans for a race to be the first State to ratify repeal.

House Wets Are Mustered.

Special to THE NEW YORK TIMES.

WASHINGTON, Feb. 19.—Since the adoption of the Senate's prohibition repeal resolution by the House tomorrow was regarded by Democratic and Republican leaders as a certainty, steps were taken today to bring forward legislation paving the way for the machinery for ratification by State conventions. Indications are increasing that such legislation may be enacted before the present session of Congress adjourns March 4 to make prompt action by the States possible.

A check-up tonight disclosed that virtually all wets will be on hand for tomorrow's vote in the House on repeal. The absentees, in the main will be drys. Representative Rainey, the Democratic floor leader, predicted tonight that there will be at least twenty votes in excess of the two-thirds majority required for adoption of the resolution.

Although Speaker Garner has said that Federal legislation providing for ratifying conventions in the States would not be considered, if at all, until the next Congress meets, it was learned tonight that the question of seeking such legislation at this session will come before the House Judiciary Committee this week.

Saving in Time Is Seen.

Inasmuch as no constitutional amendment has ever been submitted to conventions, as provided by the prohibition repeal resolution, there is a widespread feeling in Congress that action on ratification would be expedited by Federal legislation laying down at least the broad principles to be adhered to by States in constituting the conventions.

Otherwise, some members contend, much time would be lost by State Legislatures in working out convention formulas, and the Governors might hesitate to call special sessions of the Legislatures because of the expense entailed.

Representative La Guardia is drafting a bill embodying the con-

Continued on Page Two.

Catholics Use Anglicans' Site In Error for Bahaman Church

By The Canadian Press.

NASSAU, Bahamas, Feb. 19.—A Roman Catholic church has recently been built at High Rock, Island of Andros, on land belonging to the Church of England, it was revealed here today. The error was discovered shortly after the construction of the building.

In an exchange of correspondence between the Prefect Apostolic of the Roman Catholic Church in the Bahamas and the Lord Bishop of the Church of England here, the latter states:

"We are absolutely sure of your good faith, and we consider that you took all reasonable steps to ascertain that your title was valid. This being so, we have resolved that to exercise legal rights would be contrary to Christian charity and have decided to take no action in the matter."

SLAY WOMAN, 2 MEN IN MIDTOWN RESORT

Two Thugs Open Fire Without Warning on Couple Standing at Bar in 52d St. Speakeasy.

BARTENDER ALSO KILLED

Pistol Unused in Coat of One Victim—Money in Cash Register Is Untouched.

Three persons, one of them a woman about 30 years old, were slain without warning at 2:45 o'clock this morning while they were standing about the bar of a resort known as "Porky Murray's Speakeasy" at 267 West Fifty-second Street, two doors west of the Guild Theatre, by gunmen who fired a fusillade of shots.

There were two gunmen, according to information obtained by the police from persons in the vicinity. How they entered the resort, which occupies the ground and second floors at the address, was not determined, since the front door was locked when the police arrived. A window opening on the rear yard was open, however, and it was believed that through this the murderers escaped. Probably also through it, the police said, they were able to enter and surprise the victims.

The bodies of the woman and a man, who is believed to have been her escort, were found on the floor before the bar in the rear of the dining room on the ground floor. The body of another man, said to have been the bartender of the resort, was slumped behind the bar. None was immediately identified.

The suddenness with which the attack was sprung was illustrated by the finding of a fully loaded revolver in the inside breast pocket of the escort's coat. Although the pocket's position afforded easy access to the weapon, it had not been disturbed in an attempt to draw it.

Nor did robbery appear to have played a part in the triple crime, for the cash register, investigators found, had not been rifled although it contained the evening's receipts. The bodies did not appear to have been molested, apparently having fallen in the hail of bullets where they were found.

The woman was shot through the head, the escort squarely in the body. This led the police to believe that the man and woman, rather than the bartender, were the principal objects of the gunmen's fire. From the positions of the bodies it was apparent that the three were talking together when the murderers opened fire, the police said.

The shots were heard by persons on the street outside the resort, which is near Eighth Avenue, and by neighbors in the row of brownstone three-story dwellings west of the theatre. They notified the West Sixty-eighth Street station.

JAPANESE DECIDE TO QUIT THE LEAGUE; JEHOL DRIVE READY

Tokyo Cabinet Votes to Act as Soon as the Assembly Adopts Rebuke.

FIGHTING DUE TOMORROW

Foreign Office Hints That Offensive Will Open as the Geneva Assembly Meets.

TROOPS SWARM TO FRONT

Japan Has Big War Machine on Jehol Border—Shanghai Fears Naval Blockade.

By The Associated Press.

TOKYO, Monday, Feb. 20.—Japan has decided to secede from the League of Nations if the League Assembly adopts its proposed condemnation of Japan's activities in Manchuria, it was learned today from a high official source.

Foreign Minister Yasyua Uchida has cabled this decision to Japan's delegation at Geneva, it was stated.

Only the time and manner of withdrawal remained undecided, this source said.

Authoritative sources tended to confirm these reports, which rose after the Cabinet had met in another session to discuss the move.

Following the meeting, Premier Makota Saito and Foreign Minister Uchida went together to the Palace and reported the decision to the Emperor. It was learned that the findings would be submitted to the Privy Council later in the day.

A Foreign Office spokesman said, "That Japan must withdraw from the League was decided long ago—the only questions remaining were when and how."

Expects Prive Tomorrow.

The spokesman said it would not be surprising if the opening of the offensive in Jehol, the Chinese Province which Japan seeks to add to Manchukuo, would coincide with the session of the League of Nations Assembly on Tuesday.

He added that the government might address to the Nanking and Peiping governments demands that Marshal Chang Hsiao-" "'s Chinese regulars be immediately withdrawn from Jehol to a neutral zone to be established on both sides of the Great Wall.

This was deemed necessary, he continued, "to minimize the danger if Japan is compelled to extend the operation southward from the Great Wall." Such an extension would not be done unless absolutely necessary, he said.

After consulting with Prince Saionji, last surviving member of the council of the Genro, Premier Saito said yesterday that even if the Japanese delegation withdrew from the League of Nations as a result of the Manchurian dispute, that action would not necessarily mean that Japanese secession from the League was imminent.

[Recent dispatches from Tokyo have shown there is a sharp division of sentiment over the issue of secession from the League. The army element desires to break away, but strong elements in the Cabinet and political parties have counseled against such a course. Leading newspapers have opposed it. Premier Saito's visit to Prince Saionji was a consequence of this division of opinion, and apparently the last of the Genro has thrown his vast influence against precipitate action.]

The Premier added that it had not been decided whether to instruct the Japanese delegation to leave Geneva immediately after issuing a counter-statement to a report of the League, which condemned Japanese policy in Manchuria and recommended that member nations of the League continue to maintain non-recognition of the Japanese-sponsored State of Manchukuo.

The counter-statement is expected to be made public at Geneva tomorrow.

Ready to Fight in Jehol.

PEIPING, Feb. 19 (AP).—Marshal Chang Hsiao-liang, military leader of North China, today sent a telegram to the Chinese delegation at Geneva saying that "we have categorical orders from the central government to resist" a threatened Japanese invasion of the Chinese Province of Jehol.

The Marshal returned today with T. V. Soong, Finance Minister of the Nationalist Government, from an inspection trip to Jehol. The message to the Chinese delegation to the League of Nations said, in part:

"Determination of the government and the people of China to resist the Japanese invasion has crystallized in a concentration of forces for that purpose. My visit

Continued on Page Five.

Frescoes of Fatimid Period Found in Egypt; First Specimens of This Type of Moslem Art

Wireless to THE NEW YORK TIMES.

CAIRO, Feb. 19.—An important discovery of medieval Moslem art in Egypt, consisting of several beautiful frescoes of the Fatimid period from the tenth to the eleventh century, has been made by Dr. G. Wiet, director of the Egyption Government's Arab Art Museum, near the famous Abul Saoud Mosque at Cairo, where many decorations in strong relief of the Tulunid period were unearthed several months ago.

It appears from the position of the frescoes that there must be a cupola there whose inner walls are covered with paintings. A preliminary examination indicates that they portray figures sitting in Oriental fashion. One of these, representing a young man holding a cup and wearing a white robe with red flowers, still retains its vivid coloring.

At intervals are decorations of foliage in white, black and red in perfect harmony, and figures of animals and birds. Each scene is framed by a black band studded with small white disks like pearls on a black background.

Paintings of the Fatimid period are often mentioned in historical texts, but the frescoes just discovered are the first specimens found. All are worthy of a place among other Fatimid antiquities, such as rock crystals, ceramics and wood sculptures, legacies of the mighty sovereigns of medieval Egypt.

The paintings are particularly important because, besides those found at Samrra, they are the only specimens known of this type of Moslem art. They are now being transported to the Arab Art Museum at Cairo.

"All the News That's Fit to Print."

The New York Times.

LATE CITY EDITION
WEATHER—Rain today; tomorrow fair; temperature unchanged.
Temperatures Yesterday—Max., 47; min., 40.

VOL. LXXXII....No. 27,472. Entered as Second-Class Matter, Postoffice, New York, N. Y. NEW YORK, WEDNESDAY, APRIL 12, 1933. PP TWO CENTS In New York City. THREE CENTS Within 200 Miles | FOUR CENTS Elsewhere Except in 7th and 8th Postal Zones

FARM LEGISLATION SHARPLY DEBATED IN BOTH CHAMBERS

Senator Long Denounces the Roosevelt Program, Asserting Bankers Are in Power.

SMITH URGES INFLATION

Robinson of Arkansas Backs President as Accomplishing Most of Any Executive.

MORTGAGE BILL SPEEDED

House Adopts Special Rule for 8-Hour Limit on Talk as the Republicans Shout 'Gag'!

Special to THE NEW YORK TIMES.

WASHINGTON, April 11.—Tempestuous debate of two hours' duration marked consideration of the administration's farm relief bill in the Senate today and the emergency farm mortgage bill in the House.

Senator Long was the storm centre in the Senate, denouncing every feature of the Roosevelt program thus far enacted, while Senator Robinson of Arkansas, the Democratic leader, replied with a vigorous defense of the administration.

In the House the Republicans charged that the administration was applying the "gag rule" as the body adopted a special rule to make the mortgage measure the business before the House, with a debate limit of eight hours and no amendments except of committee origin.

Black Hits at "Influences."

While the farm relief bill was technically the subject of debate in the Senate, the atmosphere became highly charged on the Democratic side when Senator Black charged that powerful influences were at work to defeat his thirty-hour-week bill, once passed by the Senate but being held up by a motion to reconsider filed by Senator Trammell.

Senator Trammell replied with some heat to what he took as a personal criticism, and Senator Long then stepped into the debate.

Reading a speech by Senator Smith yesterday, in which the latter voiced doubt as to the efficacy of the pending farm relief bill, Senator Long asked:

"Since it appears that the agriculture bill will be of very little use anyway, why can't we concentrate on the thirty-hour-week bill?"

Senator Smith in reply renewed his promise to support the administration's bill, but added:

"We should have addressed ourselves to expansion of the currency. Now here we go with a bill to raise farm prices when it is notorious that the people who must buy haven't enough money to buy farm products.

Switching to the Conservation corps, he declared it was "tantamount to saying that, with other surpluses, we have a surplus of human beings in the United States, and added:

"Mr. President, I am looking for some one to introduce a bill to enforce birth control in order to get rid as nearly as possible of a portending increase in population."

Long Assails Ezekiel.

Concluding with a reference to "those who live in comparative wealth and are clothed in purple and fine linen," Senator Smith said that these "cannot write an agricultural bill for me."

This gave Senator Long his cue. After an attack on Mordecai Ezekiel, credited with partial authorship of the farm relief bill, terming him "one of that clique we were going to kick out of office when we got in," Senator Long continued:

"We came along here with the currency deflated, with the banks breaking, the purchasing power in the hands of the masses practically gone, and in order to get legislation to correct this tragedy of events we have allowed the same clique to fortify themselves with a great bunch that did not dare to show their faces here when Herbert Hoover was President, when they worked behind the veil.

"We have allowed even the partners of Morgan & Co. to come in here and attach themselves to this clique which is drawing the laws, and they have set us up a situation that is two-fold more the son of hell than what we promised to put out in the election on the eighth day of last November.

"Parker Gilbert from Morgan & Co., Leffingwell, Ballantine, Eugene Meyer, every one of them are here, and whatever you try to concoct—I do not care whether it is from the genius of the Senator from California or the chairman of the Banking Committee, the Senator

Continued on Page Two.

Teheran-Caspian Road Ready; Crosses Pass at 10,000 Feet

Wireless to THE NEW YORK TIMES.

TEHERAN, Persia, April 11.—The new road from Teheran to the Caspian Sea at Deh Nov has now been finished, forming the shortest route to the sea. Crossing a pass in the Elburz Mountains at an altitude of nearly 10,000 feet, it is one of the highest roads in the world. It is of Persian construction throughout.

Teheran, which is about seventy miles south of the Caspian Sea with the Elburz Mountains between, has hitherto been forced to depend on motor roads to the ports of Pahlavi and Meshed Sar to obtain outlets to the sea. The road from the capital to Pahlavi, which is northwest of it, is about 235 miles long; that to Meshed Sar, which is northeast, is about 195.

ROOSEVELT DEFERS DEPOSIT GUARANTEE

Banking Bill Held Up After Word He Wants Further Study of Insurance Idea.

SEES GLASS AND WOODIN

President Also for More Restricted Branch Banking—May Redraft Bill.

Special to THE NEW YORK TIMES.

WASHINGTON, April 11.—President Roosevelt was reported today to be opposed, but not irrevocably, to bank deposit insurance as provided in the revised Glass banking bill. His position was so reported in Senatorial circles after a twenty-minute conference with Senator Glass and Secretary Woodin at the White House.

While the White House vouchsafed no definite comment it was said that the President was still studying the problem and had not definitely decided whether or not the banking situation would be improved if some form of deposit insurance were enacted. The demand for insurance, which differs only slightly from the earlier proposal for a government guarantee, is so great that some administration officials thought the President might accept a compromise.

In case the President should make any concessions to those advocating an insurance of bank deposits, he will not support legislation that requires the government to back up the insurance plan. Such backing, his advisers say, must be entirely by Federal Reserve System and the member banks.

President Roosevelt was said by Democratic leaders in the Senate to be opposed to permitting branch banks in States where the law permits, but favored only county-wide branch banking.

"Debasing of Currency" in Issue.

In connection with the discussion in Senatorial circles of the insurance of deposits, the President and Secretary Woodin were quoted as having said that they were against "debasing the currency or any radical monetary changes."

Those advocating the remonetization of silver said that the President had never given them any assurance that he favored inflation via the silver route. In fact they are convinced that all the administration will do in this respect will be the naming of an American delegate to the World Economic Conference who is sympathetic with the silver cause.

Congressional leaders reacted immediately to the White House con-

Continued on Page Three.

SHOALS OPERATION PROVIDED IN BILLS; EARLY ACTION SEEN

Both Chambers Get Measures and House Starts Hearings on Roosevelt Plan.

BOARD TO DIRECT PROJECT

Tennessee Valley Authority Is to Have Power to Acquire Lands and Alter Plants.

NORRIS SEES QUICK START

Construction of Cove Creek Dam First Move—Wide Sale of Fertilizer and Power Mapped.

Special to THE NEW YORK TIMES.

WASHINGTON, April 11.—President Roosevelt's plan for development of the Tennessee Valley through the operation of the huge facilities of Muscle Shoals and improvement of the Tennessee River was introduced in the Senate and House today. Steps were taken for early passage of the measure. Before the bill had been read by the membership of the House the Military Affairs Committee had begun the first of brief hearings by which they hope to present it to the House next week.

Chairman McSwain of the Military Affairs Committee said that extended hearings would not be necessary, "because there are tens of thousands of pages of printed information taken at previous meetings."

Two separate measures were introduced, one by Senator Norris and the other in the House. Representative McSwain and Representatives Hill and Almon of Alabama each offered a bill for the project, but the three bills were identical in language and were presented simply as a gesture of recognition of the continuous efforts of the two Alabama Representatives for Federal operation of the $181,000,000 nitrate and munitions plant.

The principal difference between the two measures is in the House provision for an immediate appropriation of $10,000,000 and issuance of $50,000,000 bonds to bear an interest rate of 3 per cent, the funds to be used to construct Cove Creek Dam and Dam No. 2. The Norris bill, on the other hand, provided for a study of Dam No. 2, and then a bond issue, if necessary. The amount of the bond issue is not fixed.

Would Set Up Authority.

Both measures would establish a board of three members appointed by the President, which would be known as the Tennessee Valley Authority of the United States.

The phraseology of the two bills differs somewhat, but in fundamental matter both are so nearly alike that those familiar with the drafts predicted there would be no trouble at all in agreeing to the slight changes.

Senator Norris said today that he probably would offer an amendment defining transmission lines as common carriers, to be regulated by the Interstate Commerce Commission.

Tennessee and Alabama both will benefit through operations of the gigantic plant. Five per cent of the gross income from sales of power generated in each State will be paid to the respective State treasuries, while the bills specified that the home office of the authority be adjacent to Muscle Shoals, in the

Continued on Page Two.

Man-Made Cold, 459.1 Below Zero, Fahr., Created by Magnetization in California

By The Associated Press.

BERKELEY, Cal., April 11.—Officials of the University of California announced today that the coldest man-made temperature yet attained, 459.1 below zero Fahrenheit, had been reached by experiments at the university. This achievement of Professor W. F. Giauque, assisted by C. F. Nelson, a mechanician, and D. P. MacDougall, research assistant, was accomplished by use of a magnetic cycle process which Professor Giauque developed.

The mark reached is within .25 degree centigrade of the absolute absence of heat. The temperature is infinitely colder than that of liquid helium and considerably lower than any point yet obtained by processes involving previously known methods of refrigeration. Experimenters generally have held that attainment of practical zero is essential to solution of numerous scientific problems.

Among the theories advanced are those that the practical absence of heat is necessary as a preliminary to creation of a perfect vacuum; that new low temperatures can be applied to manufacture of a super-steel and that this research will contribute to the study of the structure of the atom.

The substance cooled by Professor Giauque was gadolinium sulphate octahydrate, a compound of gadolinium, a metallic element discovered in 1880. The magnetization process extracts from this substance the heat generated in it when it is magnetized and demagnetized.

By ammonia refrigeration and other customary cooling processes Professor Giauque reaches a temperature of about 306.4 degrees below zero Fahrenheit, at which point the magnetic cycle begins. The heat generated by magnetizing and demagnetizing is drawn out of the substance by liquid helium which surrounds it. The substance then is isolated from the helium by a high vacuum. The magnetic field is decreased and this action further cools the substance.

Professor Giauque states it should be possible to continue even closer to the absolute zero mark.

Shaw Tells America It Must Lead To Save Civilization From Ruin

First We Must Scrap Constitution, He Declares in Address in Crowded Opera House—Takes Pains Not to Give Offense to Hearers on Brief Visit Here.

The text of Mr. Shaw's speech is printed on pages 14 and 15.

George Bernard Shaw told an audience which filled the Metropolitant Opera House last night that it is up to the United States to provide leadership to save civilization from the ruin which previous civilizations have met in the history of the human race.

He proposed that this country scrap its Constitution, which he termed "anarchic," and build a new Constitution based on purely American needs; that it nationalize the banks and destroy the power of the financiers, and that it wipe the slate clean of the war debts.

Mr. Shaw gave a doleful description of the present American picture. He said that our widespread unemployment spelled the breakdown of the capitalistic system, that our farmers were in revolt, that our employers had become members of the proletariat subservient to the financiers and that the financiers, whom he called our real masters, had run the country "into the ditch."

The main hope he saw for our future was that the typical 100 per cent American of the past was giving way to a new type. He thought this type might develop into a "100 per cent statesman" and might pull America and the rest of the world out of the ditch.

President Roosevelt, he said, represented this new type in American political life. He linked to President Roosevelt's the name of William Randolph Hearst, remarking that they were "both violently against the Constitution." He warned that President Roosevelt at the end of his term would be as "great a disappointment as Mr. Hoover," unless he is able to govern without being handicapped by Congress and the Constitution.

The 76-year-old Irish dramatist and political propagandist was

Continued on Page Fifteen.

MEYER IS LEAVING HIS RESERVE POST

Resignation of Governor of Board, Tendered 10 Days Ago, Accepted by Roosevelt.

WAITS CHOICE OF NEW MAN

Wall Street Hears Walter W. Stewart, Central Banking Expert, Is Being Considered.

Special to THE NEW YORK TIMES.

WASHINGTON, April 11.—That Eugene Meyer tendered his resignation as a member and governor of the Federal Reserve Board to President Roosevelt about ten days ago and that it had been accepted with the understanding that he would remain in office until his successor was chosen became known here tonight.

Mr. Meyer, who has served the government almost continuously since 1917, was appointed governor of the Federal Reserve Board on Sept. 16, 1930, by President Hoover. He is said to feel that, as a member of the former administration, he should withdraw so that, in the light of changed fiscal policies, the President would be free to appoint his own choice to the post.

While criticism has been directed at Mr. Meyer by members of both parties, high administration officials have made it known informally that they do not support them and feel that the government will suffer a severe loss when he finally gives up active service.

For some time there have been reports that Mr. Meyer wished to resign and speculation as to his successor, should he give up his post. Among those who have been prominently mentioned is Adolph C. Miller of San Francisco, now vice governor of the board and one of its original members. President Roosevelt and Mr. Miller and their families have long been close friends, the intimacy dating back to the wartime days, when Mr. Roosevelt was Assistant Secretary of the Navy.

Aided in Banking Reform.

Mr. Meyer was born in Los Angeles in 1875 and since his college days has been a student of banking. In late years, when not in Washington, he has lived at Mount Kisco, N. Y.

In the recent banking emergency as governor of the Federal Reserve Board he cooperated with the administration in working out the program for putting the banking structure back on a sound basis. He has long advocated a unified banking system which would bring all commercial banks under supervision of the Federal Government.

Mr. Meyer had acquired a fortune by the time he was 40 years old. He first appeared as an official of the government when he was appointed adviser on non-ferrous metals on the advisory commission of the Council of National Defense in 1917. President Wilson selected him as a member of the War Industries Board and the National Committee on War Savings and he was named a director of the War Finance Corporation in April, 1918, and made its managing director in January, 1919.

This agency did much to aid the agricultural and live stock industries. Mr. Meyer accomplished its liquidation without loss to the government.

He resigned that post when the corporation ended its active services in 1920, but was reappointed by President Harding in 1921 and by President Coolidge in 1925 to

Continued on Page Eight.

BRITISH LORDS PASS SOVIET IMPORTS BAN

Government Can Apply It if Trial of Six Engineers Today Is Held Unfair.

BREAK BELIEVED LIKELY

Case Is Said to Hinge on Forced Confession—Embassy to Send Out News.

Wireless to THE NEW YORK TIMES.

LONDON, April 11.—A bill empowering the government to prohibit the importation of Russian goods passed all stages in the House of Lords tonight, thus endorsing the action of the House of Commons in its effort to obtain a fair trial tomorrow for the British engineers accused of sabotage in Russia.

Viscount Hailsham, Minister for War, said the government hoped to make the Soviet realize how seriously the question is regarded here and that this country is behind its government.

Lord Passfield expressed anxiety that threats might have an adverse effect upon the fate of the accused but Viscount Cecil interjected that no threats would be issued until it was evident that ordinary diplomatic representations would not influence the Soviet.

Lord Hailsham's observation was that Lord Passfield's speech was "singularly ill adapted to its professed purpose of saving the engineers."

Courts Held Organs of Power.

There is much comment on an incident in the House of Lords tonight when Lord Hailsham read a translation of a passage from a book written in 1927 by the present Soviet Minister of Justice, which admitted the "Soviet courts are organs of the State power."

"When a man is before a Soviet court," Lord Hailsham proceeded, "and any question of State policy is involved, the question which the court has to determine is not whether the man is guilty, but whether it is in the interests of the State administration that he should be convicted and sentenced. How can a man rely on justice which is administered by such a court based on such principles?"

Whichever way the Moscow trial may go, and there is grave uneasiness, it is felt in diplomatic quarters that relations between Britain and Russia are ended, at any rate for the life of the present government. It is unlikely that any further passports for Russia will be issued and a number of widely advertised "holiday tours" have been canceled.

Mr. Strang, the Chargé d'Affaires in Moscow since Ambassador Ovey was recalled, will be in court during part of the trial and members of the embassy staff will be in constant attendance with a stenographer. A daily message will be transmitted to London from the embassy for the benefit of those newspapers to which the Soviet has refused visas.

Thorntons Long in Russia.

The Daily Sketch publishes an interview with a relative of Thornton, one of the arrested Britons, who says his real name is Leslie and not William Henry, as stated in Moscow. According to the informant Leslie Thornton's family for more than ninety years conducted a huge woolen mill employ-

Continued on Page Thirteen.

SCHWARZ OUSTED AS REICH CONSUL; ASSAILS HITLER

Ordered to Quit 'for Political Reasons,' Official Here for 4 Years Is 'Honored.'

HE EXPECTED THE ACTION

Liberal Says His Views Are at Odds With 'Bigoted Policies' of New Regime.

NAZIS MORE RESTRAINED

Dislocation of Business, Hostile World Opinion and Davis's Visit Are Held Responsible.

For the first time since he became virtual dictator of Germany, Chancellor Adolf Hitler reached out across the ocean yesterday and dismissed a German official who has refused to embrace the new political dispensation in Germany. The victim was Dr. Paul Schwarz, who for four years has been the German Consul in this city.

Shortly before the consul closed his office late yesterday afternoon he received a cablegram from the Foreign Office in Berlin informing him that "for political reasons you will have to take an immediate leave" and be placed "at the disposal of the government." Dr. Schwarz immediately wired his reply in the form of the requested resignation.

To newspaper men assembled in his office last night, Dr. Schwarz explained that to be placed "at the disposal of the government" meant to be put on the shelf for an indefinite period. He said his polite dismissal was not unexpected, as he was an ardent republican and democrat. He proclaimed himself "an enemy of the Hitler régime," and said that under no circumstances would he consent to give it his approval.

Plans to Remain Here.

He expects to remain in this country, feeling there is no room for him and those like him in Germany under the Hitler government. The consul added that he might reenter the Consular Service in the event of a governmental change in Germany, but he was pessimistic as to the possibility of any early change.

"I feel honored, for I am the only German Consul to be dismissed by Hitler so far as I know," Dr. Schwarz said after handing out a typewritten statement explaining his forced resignation.

Dr. Schwarz pointed out that while he was the first German official to be compelled to quit, his dismissal was preceded by the voluntary resignation of Ambassador von Prittwitz, who, Dr. Schwarz said, declined to serve under Hitler.

The genial, portly consul is widely known in New York and has been very popular with newspaper men, who have been used to meeting him on official occasions and at receptions of German notables in this city. The last distinguished visitor he met in his official capacity was Dr. Albert Einstein, on the latter's recent visit to New York. Dr. and Mrs. Einstein were guests at tea at Dr. Schwarz's home at the Hotel St. Moritz. Last night Dr. Schwarz declined to comment on the possibility that his entertainment of Dr. and Mrs. Einstein might have been responsible for his dismissal.

"Dr. Einstein is a friend of mine

Continued on Page Fifteen.

American Missionary Held For $500,000 in Manchuria

Wireless to THE NEW YORK TIMES.

MUKDEN, Manchuria, Wednesday, April 12.—Dr. Niels Nielson, 58 years old, an American missionary from Minneapolis, was kidnapped last night by bandits, according to word received here today from his wife, Mrs. Anne Nielson, at Siuyen, about 100 miles southeast.

Ransom of $500,000 is demanded.

Dr. Nielson, a medical missionary of the Danish Lutheran Church, has been in China four years.

American Consular authorities here are making efforts in his behalf and Japanese cooperation is promised.

M'CORMICK GUILTY, RESIGNS CITY POST

Marriage Clerk Convicted of Failing to Report Income—Cleared on 2 Charges.

JUROR TO BE PROSECUTED

Ousted Man Faces Contempt Action for Not Revealing He Knew Lawyer.

Within an hour after Federal Judge John C. Knox had opened a sealed verdict, in which James J. McCormick, Tammany leader of the Twenty-second Assembly District, had been found guilty late Monday night of having failed to file income tax returns for 1929 and 1930, Michael J. Cruise, City Clerk, announced yesterday that McCormick had resigned as his deputy in charge of the Marriage License Bureau.

The jury, made up of only eleven men, decided in the same verdict that the defendant, represented by John A. Bolles, Republican leader of the same Assembly district, had not been guilty of a willful attempt to evade and defeat the income tax law during the years in question, when he received $69,000 in tips from bridegrooms.

Juror Held in Contempt.

As soon as the verdict had been read, Thomas E. Dewey, Chief Assistant United States Attorney, asked Judge Knox to hold Herman M. Goldsmith of 38 Fort Washington Avenue, in contempt of court for having willfully withheld truthful answers during his examination a week ago, when the trial began, as to his qualifications as a juror.

Until Monday morning Goldsmith had served as Juror No. 5. At that time he was excused by stipulation of Mr. Dewey and Mr. Bolles, when it was discovered that he had been a member of the latter's political club three years ago.

The prosecutor will file an information this morning against Goldsmith, whose assigned counsel, John Cashin, will oppose citation for contempt of court on the ground that his client had not understood questions put to him.

Judge Knox, who could send McCormick to jail for a maximum term of two years and fine him $10,000, announced after hearing the verdict that he would impose sentence next Monday, and continued the convicted man in bail of $5,000.

"There was ample evidence," he said, "to warrant a conviction on all four counts."

In announcing McCormick's resignation as Deputy City Clerk, Mr. Cruise said:

"Mr. McCormick submitted his

Continued on Page Eight.

Test Due Today on Lea Bill for 10% Wine; House Committee Called to Decide Fate

By The Associated Press.

WASHINGTON, April 11.—Behind closed doors tomorrow, the Lea bill to legalize wine of 10 per cent alcoholic content by weight will stand trial before the Ways and Means Committee.

Chairman Doughton late today issued a call for his committee to meet in executive session, at which time it will decide whether the measure will be subject to hearings and put through the regular legislative course, or whether it will be shoved into the background.

The wine bill is sponsored by Representative Lea, Democrat, of California, and has the backing of the California delegation as well as Representatives of other wine-producing States.

Mr. Lea wrote stringent regulations into his measure. Should the 10 per cent wine be legalized, he would confine the sale to use with meals in hotels, restaurants or other public eating places, and homes. He would not permit the sale of sweet wine.

A tax of 20 cents a gallon would be levied, placing wine, it is contended, alongside the present 3.2 beer and wine bill as a procurer of revenue.

The Lea bill was the measure agreed upon by Representatives of the wine-growing States after Senator McAdoo of California inserted the 3.2 wine provision in the beer bill.

Wine growers generally opposed the McAdoo provision, holding that it would be difficult to make a wine of such low alcoholic content, and that it would hurt the chances of the Lea bill. Makers of wine tonics, however, lent support to the 3.2 provision.

The measure before the Ways and Means Committee would apply only to naturally fermented wines, which generally run between 12 and 13 per cent alcoholic content by volume, and thus would come well within a provision for 10 per cent by weight. Fortified wines would not be permitted.

The method of legalization for the wine would be to amend the Volstead act along the lines of a present provision, which permits farmers and others to make up to 200 gallons of fermented juices a year.

O'BRIEN WILL NAME MAN FROM FORCE TO HEAD THE POLICE

Chief Inspector O'Brien and Sullivan, His Aide, Now Favored as Commissioner.

McCOOEY BACKS LATTER

Curry Is Said to Have Been Urged Strongly to Throw Support to Policeman.

MAYOR STILL UNCERTAIN

"Have Had No Word Yet," He Replies to Inquiries—Mulrooney Says Good-Bye to Men.

Edward P. Mulrooney brought thirty-seven years of service in the Police Department to a close yesterday when he handed his resignation as commissioner to Mayor O'Brien. He expects to assume his new duties today as head of the State Beer and Wine Control Board, to which he has been appointed by Governor Herbert H. Lehman.

Asked last night who Mr. Mulrooney's successor would be, the Mayor said:

"I have had no word on that yet. I haven't done a thing all day from the drop of the hat but take up one thing after another. I don't know if I will have word tomorrow or not, but I will give the matter immediate attention."

Asked if the new police head would be a civilian or a member of the uniformed force, the Mayor replied:

"There has been no conclusion on that as yet."

O'Brien or Sullivan Likely.

Choice of the new Police Commissioner lay between Chief Inspector John O'Brien and Assistant Chief Inspector John J. Sullivan last night, according to reliable information in political circles. Deputy Chief Inspector Thomas P. Cummings, commanding all uniformed forces in Brooklyn, was eliminated from consideration late yesterday, it was reported, after Democratic Leader John H. McCooey of Brooklyn swung his support to Inspector Sullivan, who is also a Brooklyn resident.

The offer of the post was to be made first to Chief Inspector O'Brien, it was said. If he declines it, it will next be offered to Inspector Sullivan. Because of poor health, the Chief Inspector is considered unlikely to fill the vacancy, leaving Inspector Sullivan virtually alone in the field. He holds the position from which Mr. Mulrooney rose to the Commissionership, which ranks higher than the post held by Deputy Inspector Cummings.

Inspector Sullivan has been in the Police Department since Dec. 30, 1902, and has spent most of his time in Brooklyn. He holds four departmental commendations. Promoted to sergeant in 1913 he became a lieutenant in 1918 and rose to captain six years later. He was made a deputy inspector in 1925, commanding all Brooklyn detectives, and two years later was made full inspector.

Sullivan's Record Notable.

When Mr. Mulrooney was appointed Police Commissioner, Inspector Sullivan was elevated to the post vacated by Mr. Mulrooney, Assistant Chief Inspector. He commands the entire detective division and is second in rank in the uniformed force only to Chief Inspector O'Brien. Former Police Commissioner Grover Whalen called Mr. Sullivan "one of the outstanding detective commanders in the country." As a commander he was as active as he had been during his days as a policeman. He usually presides at the morning line-up in Police Headquarters, questioning criminals and instructing his subordinates.

In September, 1932, Inspector Sullivan collapsed at the line-up one morning from overwork. After a short rest he resumed his duties, and has been in good health since that time. He is fifty-three years old and lives at 84 Eighty-sixth Street, in the Bay Ridge section of Brooklyn. Thomas Wogan is Democratic leader of the district in which Inspector Sullivan lives.

While Deputy Inspector Cummings seemed to be in the lead for the appointment yesterday, political observers held that his association with Kenneth Sutherland, Democratic leader of Coney Island, would hurt his chances. Relations between Mr. McCooey and Mr. Sutherland, they pointed out, were not as close as they might be. Inspector Cummings lives at 3,561 Bedford Avenue, in Mr. Sutherland's district.

Although Mayor O'Brien had not said the choice of a new police head would be confined to police offi-

Continued on Page Five.

"All the News That's Fit to Print."

The New York Times.

LATE CITY EDITION

WEATHER—Fair and warmer today; tomorrow fair.

Temperatures Yesterday—Max., 55; min., 42.

Copyright, 1933, by The New York Times Company.

VOL. LXXXII....No. 27,489. Entered as Second-Class Matter, Postoffice, New York, N. Y. NEW YORK, SATURDAY, APRIL 29, 1933. TWO CENTS In New York City. | THREE CENTS Within 200 Miles | FOUR CENTS Elsewhere Except in 7th and 8th Postal Zones.

SENATE PASSES INFLATION-FARM BILL BY 64-20; INDUSTRY CONTROL BILL PERMITS PRICE FIXING; THREE NATIONS TO ACT TO STABILIZE EXCHANGE

CENTRAL PARK PLAN PRESSED AS SHEEHY REBUFFS ITS CRITICS

He Tells Them at Hearing He Cannot Promise Sport Field Will Not Be Permanent.

BUT CALLS IT 'TEMPORARY'

School Officials and Others Back Reservoir Project as Meeting Needs of Youth.

CIVIC GROUPS OPPOSE IT

Urge "Beauty and Tranquillity" Be Not Marred—Issue Not Yet Closed, Litchfield Warns.

Disregarding growing protests by organizations and individuals who have been fighting for years to save the city's parks from encroachments, John E. Sheehy, newly appointed Park Commissioner, announced yesterday that he would proceed at once with his plans to convert the thirty-four-acre site of the abandoned lower reservoir in Central Park into a series of baseball diamonds and athletic fields. He would "give no guarantee" against the permanency of those features.

Commissioner Sheehy arrived at his decision immediately following a public hearing on his plans at Park Department headquarters in the Central Park Arsenal, Sixty-fifth Street and Fifth Avenue. He had listened to more than a score of spokesmen arguing for or against his plans.

Advocates of the plan, largely from the public schools and neighborhood and church organizations, frequently insisted that the Park Commissioner give definite assurance of the permanency of the athletic and playground features he is introducing into Central Park. They demanded all the accessories that go with athletic fields.

"We want showers and lockers," was the demand of the spokesmen.

Civic, art, landscape and other organizations opposed the athletic fields contemplated by the new commissioner on the ground that they had no place in the park, and that they would certainly become permanent despite Mr. Sheehy's announcement that they were intended to be only temporary.

Says 40,000 Will Watch.

When it was pointed out that the ten contemplated baseball diamonds would furnish recreation for only 200 players to the exclusion of every one else, and especially small children and their mothers for whom a sunken meadow had been planned by a committee of the New York Chapter, American Society of Landscape Architects, Commissioner Sheehy shot back this rejoinder:

"After all, there will be baseball leagues in the park with 40,000 to 50,000 watching them."

"How many?" asked William Bradford Roulstone, more incredulous than he had ever been in the course of his bitter fight that forestalled Mayor Hylan's effort to place an art centre in the park.

"Forty to fifty thousand," repeated Commissioner Sheehy.

"Saints save us, if that's what we're planning to do," said Mr. Roulstone.

At that point Nathan Straus Jr., president of the Park Association of New York City, intervened to suggest that the Park Commissioner did not mean to say that he would erect grand stands in Central Park to accommodate 40,000 to 50,000 spectators. Mr. Sheehy explained that he had not meant to convey the impression that he contemplated building stadia.

At the end of the hearing, held from 10 o'clock till noon, Commissioner Sheehy was asked whether he would disclose his next step.

"I intend to proceed with my original plan for utilizing the park reservoir site immediately," he replied.

Can't Guarantee for Future.

Asked whether he favored development of the reservoir tract ultimately in accordance with the plans designed by the landscape architects' committee headed by A. F. Brinckerhoff, Mr. Sheehy explained that so far as he personally was concerned he favored those plans.

When asked whether the baseball fields and athletic facilities would be temporary, he said: "They will be temporary as far as I myself personally am concerned, but I can't guarantee for the future."

Mr. Sheehy reiterated his statement, in opening the hearing, that by temporary use he meant until such time as funds become available for the more comprehensive architects' plan for the reservoir.

The first of the ten baseball diamonds contemplated will resound to the crack of ball and bat and the shouts of players and umpires with-

Continued on Page Six.

Clocks Should Be Set Ahead For Daylight Time Tonight

Before retiring tonight millions of Americans and Canadians will advance their clocks one hour, for Daylight Saving Time will become effective at 2 A. M. tomorrow. The lost hour will be recovered Sept. 25, when the daylight saving period will end.

More persons than ever before will use daylight time this year in the United States and Canada, according to the Merchants' Association of New York, although the time will be observed in only thirteen States this year, as compared with fifteen last year. However, large gains in Maine, where the area of observance virtually will be doubled, and gains in Canada have more than offset the population loss caused by the defection of Florida, last year represented by Pensacola, and of Minnesota, where last year business men belonging to the chambers of commerce in St. Paul and Minneapolis observed the time.

In New York State, Rochester, Syracuse and Binghamton are the only large cities not in line.

MILKY WAY STARS FOUND IN FLIGHT

Dr. Ross Gunn Tells Physicists His Tests Back Theory of an "Exploding" Universe.

PROOF OF ETHER CLAIMED

Prof. D. C. Miller Asserts He Has Traced Drift—Transparency of Alkali Metals Told.

By WILLIAM L. LAURENCE.

Special to THE NEW YORK TIMES.

WASHINGTON, April 28.—Evidence that the stars and constellations in our own Milky Way galaxy, of which our solar system is a relatively insignificant part, are running away from each other at a uniform speed of three miles a second from the centre of gravity of the galaxy was presented today before the meeting of the American Physical Society by Dr. Ross Gunn of the Naval Research Laboratory.

His data, Dr. Gunn added, agreed with the observational data made by Dr. Edwin P. Hubble and others at Mount Wilson Observatory, showing that the distant nebulae are receding from us and from each other at the explosive speed of 15,000 miles a second, and thus offered independent proof that the universe as a whole is "exploding."

Basing his calculations on previously observed velocities of recession of the hot stars in our galaxy, known as B-type stars, Dr. Gunn said he found that not only did these hot stars recede, but that all the other stars and constellations in the galaxy did likewise.

Applying the figures for our galaxy to the figures previously obtained by other observations of Dr. Hubble, Dr. Gunn found that they corresponded to within a very small percentage of error.

Uniform Recession Shown.

Both sets of calculations showed, Dr. Gunn said, that the rate of recession was uniform throughout the universe, increasing with distance at the rate of 100 miles a second for each million light years, so that the furthest galaxies so far observed, at a distance of 150,000,000 light years, should recede at the previously observed speed of 15,000 miles a second.

This figure checks exactly with that obtained by Dr. Hubble by measuring the observed shift of spectrum lines toward the red, a shift known to increase at a definite rate when an object is receding.

From his data Dr. Gunn evolved a new hypothesis, reconstructing the beginning of the universe. Some time about 5,000,000,000 years ago, he held, the universe was but one immense supernebula, in a very gaseous state, revolving at terrific speed. As it kept whirling around it broke up into smaller fragments in the course of about 100,000,000 years.

These fragments, which made up the galaxies, island universes, constellations, suns and stars, were asymmetrical in the distribution of their heat energy; that is, one side was necessarily much hotter than the other side, just as a piece from a hot baked potato is much hotter on the side that came from inside the potato than on the surface of the skin.

Star Heat Divided.

For this reason each star, Dr. Gunn reasoned, had one half which was about twice as hot as the other half.

Now, this extra heat, by the known laws of radiant energy, would be radiated away in two directions. Part of it, by far the largest part, would be radiated away in the surrounding space, while the other part would keep going toward the cooler part of the

Continued on Page Six.

IOWA TROOPS RULE FARM RIOT AREAS; MOB BLOCKS A SALE

Martial Law Is Declared In Plymouth County, Where Judge Was Abducted and Beaten.

CROWD ROUTS DEPUTIES

Officers Are Forced to Stop Denison Foreclosure and Governor Sends Militia There.

COURTS SPLIT ON NEW LAW

State Act Aimed to Help Debtors Is Upheld and Held Unconstitutional in Decisions.

Special to THE NEW YORK TIMES.

LEMARS, Iowa, April 28.—Martial law was established here today under a proclamation by Governor Clyde Herring and the arrival of 250 National Guardsman as a result of the attack yesterday on District Court Judge C. C. Bradley by farmers who demanded that he refuse to sign foreclosure papers.

Other State troopers were ordered to Denison, Iowa, sixty miles from Sioux City, after 800 farmers had attacked six State agents, a Sheriff and forty special deputies when they attempted to conduct a foreclosure sale on J. F. Fields's farm.

The crowd stopped the sale after a fight in which many were slightly injured.

Governor Herring's martial-law order covered all Plymouth County.

Terming the attack on Judge Bradley "a vicious and criminal conspiracy and assault upon a judge while in discharge of his official duties, endangering his life and threatening a complete breakdown of all law and order," he authorized the troops to work beyond the borders of the county if necessary.

"The public peace and good order will be preserved upon all occasions and throughout the county, and no interference will be permitted with officers and men in the discharge of the duties under this order," the proclamation read.

Doubts Crowd All Farmers.

The Governor declared he believed Sioux City hoodlums were in the crowd that attacked the judge. He urged the newspapers not to be too quick in describing the assailants as all farmers. Talk of "Red" agitators was also heard.

In Lemars rumors of outside help for the farmers was not taken seriously. Persons who saw a hundred or more men sweep into the court room of Judge Bradley while court was in session, who saw the jurist slapped and choked and otherwise maltreated before a noose was placed around his neck, asserted that many in the crowd were recognized as farmers from O'Brien, Primrose and Sioux Counties.

"It seemed to be a crowd without direction," said one observer, "moving under the impulses of mob psychology. The members had gone into the court to demand that Judge Bradley refuse to sign any more foreclosure actions. When he declined to promise that on oath the mob seemed to move mechanically about seizing him."

This observer said that the plague of drought and grasshoppers had well nigh ruined farmers in this section before the low prices of farm products in the last year or two added to their troubles.

Meanwhile Judge Bradley, suffering only slight effects of the manhandling by the mob, presided over a routine court session. He said he had not recognized any of those who seized him, although he had been on the district bench for many years.

The troops are under command of Colonel Golden C. Hollar. The men carried full field equipment and are quartered for the time being in the armory.

Courts Differ on Law.

By The Associated Press.

DES MOINES, April 28.—Constitutionality of Iowa's emergency debtor's relief law was both upheld and denied by district courts today.

District Judge A. P. Barker, in a ruling at Muscatine, upheld the constitutionality of the law passed by the recent Iowa General Assembly, but earlier in the day Judge W. E. Dingwell, at Winterset, had held the same law unconstitutional in several mortgage foreclosure actions brought before the Madison County District Court.

The law provides for continuance of all mortgage foreclosure actions until March 1, 1935, on request to the court and also gives the court custody of the property during the period of continuance with authority to direct the application of rents, profits and income.

State Income Tax Receipts To Equal Those of Last Year

Special to THE NEW YORK TIMES.

ALBANY, April 28.—For the first time since 1930 State income tax collections this year will not show a drop from the preceding year.

Mark Graves, president of the State Tax Commission, announced today that the present returns will equal the $30,858,000 mark of last year. To date the State has collected $29,198,591. In the boom period income tax collections totaled $78,000,000.

"The number of paid tax returns received in the calendar year 1932 was 238,834," the Tax Commission statement said. "The number of returns filed this year to date is 150,294. It is estimated that 25,000 additional returns will be filed during the year, making a total for this year of 175,294 returns."

Governor Lehman in his executive budget estimated the income tax for this year at $31,000,000.

LABOR PROTECTION ASKED IN RAIL BILL

Union Chiefs Demand Provision for Men Losing Jobs by Operation Economies.

TO FIGHT IN COMMITTEES

Meantime, Eastman Conditions Taking Coordinator's Post on Final Shaping of Measure.

Special to THE NEW YORK TIMES.

WASHINGTON, April 28.—The administration's railroad legislation, providing for a Federal coordinator of transportation to direct and if necessary to force more economical operation, is not acceptable to organized railway labor, George M. Harrison, acting chairman of the Railway Labor Executives' Association, said today in demanding adequate protection of the union workers.

In his statement, issued after a meeting of the association called to consider the legislation, Mr. Harrison assailed the proposed setting aside of the anti-trust laws and other Federal and State statutes, which he said was "merely to permit monopolized railroads to gather unjust and unearned profits."

The labor executives plan to carry their fight to Senate and House committees with a demand that provision be made for railroad workers thrown out of employment by elimination of services and facilities in the interests of economical operation.

Eastman Approached on Post.

Publication today of the text of the administration measure again brought to the fore the name of Interstate Commerce Commissioner Joseph B. Eastman as the outstanding candidate for the office of Federal Coordinator.

He has been "sounded out" on the proposition by some of President Roosevelt's economic advisers and is understood to regard the bill as satisfactory as it now stands but to condition his acceptance of the post on the final form of the measure.

He is said to feel that he could accept the responsibilities only if he received a "free hand" to work out the complicated railroad problem according to his own judgment, subject to the limitations which include judicial review of the coordinator's decisions by the full commissions.

Objections Made by Unions.

In stating the position of organized railway labor on the bill, Mr. Harrison said:

"We are thoroughly opposed to the prospective railroad legislation. We see no justification for drastic reductions of essential transportation service in order that unearned interest may be paid on idle capital.

"Communities deprived of adequate and competitive rail transportation will be further depressed. Thousands of railway workers will be added to the breadlines. Economic recovery will be retarded by this further deflation of business and labor.

"Communities, shippers and employes threatened with irreparable losses, should be able to prevent the passage of such a law as now proposed. But, at least, the organized railway employes will do all within their power to have written

Continued on Page Five.

RECOVERY ACT DRAFTED

National Board Would Rule Output, Hours and Markets.

TRUST LAWS TO BE WAIVED

Trade Associations Would Seek to Correlate Production and Demand in Each Line.

SPUR TO BUYING AN AIM

Proponents Admit Idea Is Daring—Moley and Warburg Are Said to Endorse It.

By LOUIS STARK.

Copyright, 1933, by The New York Times Company.

WASHINGTON, April 28.—The "national industry recovery act," a bill that envisages complete control of industry through a national board modeled after the War Industries Board, is being hurried for submission to the President next week, it was reported today.

The tentative draft of the act, which has just been completed, sets aside the anti-trust laws and the Federal Trade Commission act, empowers the national board to designate any industry as one affected with a public interest, permits price fixing under government supervision for the period of the emergency, and agrees to a plan of self-organization of industry through trade associations.

Designed to stabilize industry, and to bring about increased employment and an enlarged purchasing power, the tentative bill follows out in detailed form the first outline of the plan set forth in a Washington dispatch to THE NEW YORK TIMES on April 14.

The general outlines of the measure have been submited to Raymond Moley, Assistant Secretary of State, who early endorsed the idea behind it, and to James P. Warburg, New York banker, who is active in plans concerning economic recovery. Mr. Moley and Mr. Warburg, according to those in charge of the proposal, expressed enthusiasm when the plan to stimulate manufactures and increase employment were placed before them.

Backers Admit Plan Is "Daring."

Admitted by its proponents to be a "daring" and "audacious" plan to further industrial recovery, the scheme sets up a board consisting of seven members, headed by the Secretaries of Commerce and Labor. The others are to be spokesmen for commerce, finance, labor, agriculture and the public.

The plan sanctions the formation of industrial and trade associations which shall work with the national board to correlate production with demand, establish prices of commodities at fair levels and stabilize markets.

Each trade association will have on its governing board a representative of the supreme body of seven. Before the government, through the national board, can approve prices and trade arrangements set up by the trade associations the national body must be in complete possession of the facts, which will be obtained through its own agents and through the data submitted by the trade association.

The government's agent on the Trade Commission body will be the liaison officer, while the national board will be the umpire or the court of last resort in making effective or revising the decisions arrived at by the trade association.

Loans, Not Subsidies Provided.

Loans but no subsidies are provided for private industry, according to the revised plan. The national board will be empowered to certify to the Reconstruction Finance Corporation any plant that may require a loan.

It is expected that such loans would be repaid quickly, once the plan achieves its result of the stimulation of purchasing power and the opening of factories, mines, mills and workshops to idle employes.

A higher price level which will be sanctioned by the act, it was said, will encourage banks to pour into industry the credit now frozen in their vaults because of the continuing downward spiral of commodity prices.

Under the Fred I. Kent plan, the

Continued on Page Five.

Points in the Farm-Inflation Bill

Special to THE NEW YORK TIMES.

WASHINGTON, April 28.—The farm relief bill, as passed by the Senate, clothes President Roosevelt and his assistants with virtually dictatorial powers in his discretion for the regulation of currency and agriculture.

The bill is divided into three parts, providing:

DIRECT AGRICULTURE RELIEF.

The President and the Secretary of Agriculture are authorized to use one or all of three methods to raise farm values as follows:

1. Domestic Allotment—To determine the consumption of wheat, cotton, corn, hogs, dairy products, tobacco, rice and beet and cane sugar; to license producers and processors so that only domestic consumption requirements shall be sold in the domestic market at prices equal generally to the average in 1909-1914, and to collect a tax from processors to pay the cost.

2. To lease marginal lands and withdraw from production sufficient acreage to cut production of agricultural commodities to domestic needs.

3. To guarantee cost of production to farmers.

An amendment providing that the 2,500,000 or more bales of cotton held by farm credit agencies as collateral for crop production and other purposes should be withheld from the market until the Spring of 1934 was adopted.

FARM MORTGAGE RELIEF.

To refinance through voluntary arrangements with mortgagors farm mortgages at interest rates of 4½ per cent through the issuance of bonds, the interest of which would be guaranteed by the government.

INFLATION.

Authorizing the President to use three methods of raising the dollar values of commodities.

1. By increasing Federal Reserve credits by a maximum of $3,000,000,000.

2. By issuing up to $3,000,000,000 of Treasury notes, secured not by gold, but solely by the credit of the United States. This money would be used to buy back government securities.

3. Devaluing the gold content of the dollar by as much as 50 per cent, with additional authorization for the President to establish, at his discretion, a fixed ratio of silver to gold and to provide for the unlimited coinage of silver at that ratio.

HERRIOT SAYS TALKS SAVE TRADE PARLEY

In Final Messages Here, He Holds Roosevelt Avoided a "Tower of Babel."

PLEADS FOR COOPERATION

Former Premier Is Honored at French Chamber Dinner—Sails at Noon Today.

The text of M. Herriot's speech here last night is on Page 2.

Edouard Herriot, former premier of France, returned to New York yesterday after conversations with President Roosevelt on world economic problems had been closed and, in a farewell address at the Waldorf last night, declared that important progress had been made toward their solution. He will sail for France at noon today on the Ile de France.

M. Herriot spoke before an audience of distinguished French and Americans under the auspices of the French Chamber of Commerce in the United States and Franco-American societies.

Denies France Is "Egoist."

He denied that France was "an international egoist," pledged that France would join with England and the United States in efforts for world peace and hailed a movement to restore a suffering world in which politics and morality would never be separated.

Political agreements were not enough, he declared, but a sense of security and stability must be passed down to the family and to the individual before political tranquillity could be restored.

"We must reconstruct the world on a new moral basis," he said. "We must rebuild it upon a basis of justice, law and liberty."

Finally, he brought the whole assemblage to its feet with a toast to Mr. Roosevelt as "a great President directing a great people."

Sees World Parley Saved.

It was the last of a series of statements and interviews, which he gave yesterday in Washington and New York and in which he declared that the conversations in Washington had gone far to forward the objects of the economic and monetary conference to begin in London June 12, and declared that the London conference might well have degenerated into a "Tower of Babel" had not President Roosevelt taken this step.

He further declared that the conversations had made the London

Continued on Page Two.

PLAN TO STABILIZE CURRENCY, TARIFFS

Great Britain, France and United States Will Seek Action Before London Parley.

JOINT STATEMENT ISSUED

Roosevelt and Herriot Refer to Understanding 'of the Realities of the Situation.'

Special to THE NEW YORK TIMES.

WASHINGTON, April 28.—Edouard Herriot, envoy of France, left Washington today after his conferences with President Roosevelt bearing an olive branch but leaving behind him a few significant words on the French idea of what constitutes political security. Prime Minister Bennett of Canada continues here for another day, and the Italians and Argentines are due here next week.

What possible differences of opinion there may be between Mr. Roosevelt and M. Herriot revolve around their point of view as to how far this country can commit itself through diplomatic channels to consultative pacts, and to the definition of what is an aggressor nation.

It is believed that Mr. Roosevelt must have told M. Herriot that both these subjects were extremely delicate flags to wave before the Congress of the United States. As to an embargo, the President would have power under pending legislation to join in such an action.

Joint Statement Encouraging.

The well-known American practice of refusing to commit this country to foreign decisions may have been reflected in a statement issued by M. Herriot just before leaving when he said that the solidarity of nations must "find guarantees" and when he referred to the desire for freedom "and the organization of France."

A joint statement issued by the President and M. Herriot, however, carried the encouragement that both governments "are looking with like purpose at the main problems of the world and the objectives of the World Economic Conference." The disarmament conference was not mentioned.

In a second joint statement on war debts an understanding "of the realities of the situation" was referred to, and it was said that further conversations will be continued in Paris and Washington, which carries out the avowed intention of the President to discuss these debts separately with each

Continued on Page Two.

SWEEP FOR THE FARM BILL

Authority for Inflation Voted in Measure to Raise Prices.

BONUS PAYMENT IS BEATEN

Amendment Is Adopted to Accept $200,000,000 in Silver on War Debts.

NEW CURRENCY FOR BONDS

Thus Treasury Will Meet Maturities—Farm Mortgage Refinancing Is Approved.

Special to THE NEW YORK TIMES.

WASHINGTON, April 28.—In an overwhelming response to the administration's recommendations, the Senate today adopted the Thomas inflation amendment to the farm relief bill and then quickly passed the farm relief measure itself, after voting down the resurrected proposal for immediate payment of the veterans' bonus.

Meanwhile, the Senate adopted an amendment to the Thomas amendment, sponsored by Senator Hayden and approved by the administration, permitting the acceptance of as much as $200,000,000 of silver, at a maximum rate of 50 cents an ounce, in payments on the war debts.

Four decisive roll calls were taken with the following results:

The Thomas amendment, adopted—64 to 21.

The bonus amendment, defeated—60 to 28.

The Hayden amendment, adopted—53 to 32.

The farm bill, passed—64 to 20.

Measure Goes to the House.

The bill will go before the House Monday. That body has passed the farm relief bill proper and the farm mortgage relief sections as separate bills. It has not yet considered the inflation measure, which originated in the Senate. In anticipation of the House's asking a conference on the bill, Vice President Garner tonight named Senators Smith, Fletcher, Thomas of Oklahoma, Wagner, McNary and Walcott as conferees.

The bill now incorporates three alternative plans for giving direct relief to agriculture, a program of refinancing farm mortgages at interest rates of 4½ per cent, and the inflation amendment.

In addition, the measure authorizes the withholding from the market until the Spring of 1934 of all stocks of government-owned cotton and includes a plan to permit cotton growers to take options on these stocks at present low prices in return for a reduction of acreage. Under the latter plan, the grower would be compensated on an advance in price by selling the optioned cotton.

In the inflation amendment are four major authorizations under which the President could, although he has not indicated he will use all the authority, inflate the currency by many billions of dollars.

Inflation Authorizations.

The inflation amendment authorizes:

(1) Expansion of Federal Reserve credits by $3,000,000,000.

(2) The issuance of Treasury notes to a maximum of $3,000,000,000.

(3) Reduction of the gold content of the dollar by as much as 50 per cent, with additional authority to fix a definite ratio between silver and gold and provide for the unlimited coinage of silver.

(4) Acceptance of payments on the war debts in silver.

Some of these sections of the bill were added after the original draft was presented, particularly the silver monetization authorization, but it has been emphasized that no amendment was adopted without the administration's approval.

On the three major roll calls an average of only 23 votes were cast against the stand taken by administration leaders.

Only in the last hours of debate today did Senator Robinson of Arkansas, the Democratic floor leader, make an announcement on a question which has been the basis of much speculation, namely, that the inflation amendment is primarily a plan for refinancing obliga-

Continued on Page Four

"All the News That's Fit to Print."

The New York Times.

LATE CITY EDITION
WEATHER—Showers tonight or tomorrow; temperature unchanged
Temperatures Yesterday—Max., 80; Min., 61

Copyright, 1933, by The New York Times Company.

VOL. LXXXII....No. 27,545. Entered as Second-Class Matter, Postoffice, New York, N. Y. NEW YORK, SATURDAY, JUNE 24, 1933. P TWO CENTS In New York City. | THREE CENTS Within 200 Miles | FOUR CENTS Elsewhere Except in 7th and 8th Postal Zones

GENERALS PROCLAIM INDEPENDENT STATE IN NORTHERN CHINA

Chiefs in Area Neutralized in Truce With Japan Set Up Capital at Tangshan.

NANKING IS DENOUNCED

Appeal Is Made to Populace of Hopei Province Against Nationalist 'Dictatorship.'

TRUCE BREACH CHARGED

Japan Accuses China of Letting Regular Soldiers Take Towns in Demilitarized Area.

By HALLETT ABEND.

Special Cable to THE NEW YORK TIMES.

SHANGHAI, June 23.—A declaration of independence for the North China area neutralized under the truce with Japan was issued today by a group of renegade Chinese Generals.

These chieftains, among whom are Generals of considerable note, including Ho Yu-peng, former Finance Commissioner of Chihli Province (now Hopei); Li Chi-chun and Hsi Yu-shan, are in command of considerable forces of North China troops. Their armies resisted for a time the Japanese invasion southward from the Great Wall boundary of Jehol, but when they were overwhelmed, instead of retreating they remained behind the advancing foes.

General Ho sent a circular telegram today to the populace of Hopei Province, in which the neutral area lies, denouncing the "dictatorship" of the Kuomintang (Nationalist party) and calling attention to the "independence" of the demilitarized zone under "the self-governing armies of North China."

The Generals announced that the capital of the new government would be at Tangshan, about seventy miles north of Tientsin.

Significantly, the Japanese high command in North China charged today that the Chinese authorities had broken the terms of the truce signed at Tangku on May 31 by allowing regular soldiers to enter the demilitarized zone and occupy two villages.

Talks Are Blocked.

Conversations between Japanese and Chinese officials concerning the future of the neutral zone had been carried on for several days following Chinese allegations that the Japanese were violating the truce by allowing 6,000 Manchukuo soldiers to enter the zone from Manchukuo. These talks, however, were stalemated today, as both sides professed to be unable to foresee the outcome of the independence movement.

[The area that is reported to have declared its independence is larger than the State of Connecticut, and lies between the Great Wall and a 250-mile line that passes ten miles north of Peiping and thirty miles north of Tientsin to the coast of the Gulf of Po.]

General Feng Yu-hsiang, in revolt against Nanking, continues in control of Chahar Province.

The American and British mission headquarters in Shanghai were telegraphically informed that because of a sudden advance toward Central Szechwan by Communist armies, mission workers had evacuated the cities of Pachow, Kwangyuan, Paoning and Futsunyi Pachow and Kwangyuan were captured by Reds immediately after the missionaries fled.

Transport Train Attacked.

By The Associated Press.

TOKYO, Saturday, June 24.—A dispatch from Shanhaikwan to the newspaper Nichi Nichi Shimbun said fighting had briefly flared up in the North China zone, with a clash between a Japanese transport train and 500 Chinese between Tsunhwa and Fengjun.

After several hours of fighting, the dispatch said, the Chinese fled. The Japanese lost six killed.

The Japanese command considered the incident isolated, with Chinese authorities not responsible.

1,000 Communists Killed.

By The Associated Press.

CANTON, China, Saturday, June 24.—One thousand Communists were killed in Southern Kiangsi Province in a three day battle against Kwangtung Province troops, said Canton Government military authorities today.

The Kwangtung forces lost 200 officers and men.

Confirmation of reports that Manchukuo troops were filtering back into the North China demilitarized zone was given Wednesday by foreign observers, who have long forecast an independence movement in that area under Japanese auspices.

Heavier Element Is Transmuted From a Lighter One by Science

Neutron, 'Weighed' by Prof. E. O. Lawrence, Proves Lighter Than Its Component Parts—Deuton, Split in Attack on Gold Atom, Yields Enormous Energy.

By WILLIAM L. LAURENCE.

Special to THE NEW YORK TIMES.

CHICAGO, June 23.—Remarkable news from "scouting expeditions" into the "no man's land" of matter, the interior of the atom, was reported here today at the meeting of the American Association for the Advancement of Science.

The reports were delivered at a symposium on nuclear disintegration.

One of them contained the news that science has at last succeeded in building a heavier element out of a lighter one.

Another told of the bold assaults of science on some of the strongest citadels of matter, the nuclei of atoms of gold and of platinum, with the ultra-modern "big Berthas" among atomic artillery.

The projectiles were the "deutons," hearts of the recently discovered heavy hydrogen atom, known as hydrogen 2. Against lighter elements, such as lithium, these projectiles are irresistible. But against the heavier elements it seems to illustrate the case of the irresistible force meeting an immovable body.

So strong are the inner fortifications guarding the atom of platinum and of gold, the scientists reported, that these powerful projectiles are themselves bounced back, broken into component parts, without causing any damage to the targets.

In cracking up, however, the projectile yields up enormous amounts of energy locked up within it, part of the vast store of atomic energy, so great, it is estimated, that the atomic energy in a glass of water would be enough to drive the Mauretania across the Atlantic and back again. That is, if science could only find a way to unlock "the cosmic cupboard," as Sir Arthur Eddington calls it.

In this case the amount of atomic energy yielded up by the smashing of the "deuton-gun" when hurled against gold and platinum amounts to 7,500,000 electron-volts. This in itself constitutes an important scientific discovery, showing for the first time by how much energy the elements in the deuton, consisting, it is believed, of a proton and a neutron, are held together. Every

Continued on Page Seven.

CHINA ACTS TO MEET WIDE FLOOD PERILS

With Millions in Danger and Cities Inundated Nanking Calls Emergency Parley.

RIVERS CONTINUE TO RISE

Yellow River's Dikes Weaken and People Go to Temples and Offer Incense.

Special Cable to THE NEW YORK TIMES.

SHANGHAI, June 23.—With the flood peril to millions of people increasing hourly in the valleys of China's two greatest rivers—the Hwang (Yellow) and Yangtse—the government at Nanking sent out a call today for an emergency national conference on flood prevention.

Representatives were summoned from the provinces of Hupeh, Hunan, Kiangsu, Kiangsi and Anhui, where are the lowlands into which flood waters have already broken, inundating cities and devastating thousands of acres of farmland.

The Legislative Council created a conservancy commission of eleven members and appropriated $150,000 for works to check the floods.

Meanwhile, in ancient temples throughout the enormous threatened area, great crowds, hearing of the menace, were praying and burning incense, and in some places Buddhas were being hauled through the streets by formal processions in order that all inhabitants might intercede for safety from the torrents.

The Yellow River dikes at Kaifeng, protecting the old channel to the south, continue to show signs of crumbling and returning the stream to the channel it left in 1852, along which millions of people now dwell.

The Yangtse at Hankow had reached today a stage nearly forty-five feet above normal, and the current had attained a rate of seven miles an hour, with the apex of the flood expected tomorrow.

Some hope that repetition of the great disaster of 1931 would be avoided in the Yangtse Valley was given, however, by the fact that the Yangtse's rise at Hankow was nine inches yesterday and one foot daily for the preceding three days.

Far up the river, in the West China province of Szechwan, the flood waters were reported as having begun to recede and the weather was fair.

More Wheat May Be Needed.

By The Associated Press.

WASHINGTON, June 23.—China's twin terrors—the Yangtse and Yellow Rivers—again threaten to flood valleys with a population of more than 40,000,000 and create an even greater market for American surplus wheat supplies than was contemplated when the recent Reconstruction Finance Corporation loan of $50,000,000 was made to the Chinese Government to buy wheat and cotton.

These two rivers flow through China's granary. Two years ago, they flooded their basins and left millions homeless and in want. At that time the United States government sold China 15,000,000 bushels of wheat valued at about $9,000,000. This was used largely as wages for

Continued on Page Six.

JOHNSON PERMITS BASIC PRICE CODES BY BROADER POLICY

Industries May Agree Not to Sell Under Cost of Production, He Says.

BUSINESS FEARS ALLAYED

Government Would Regulate Timber Destruction Under Pact With Lumber Trade.

Special to THE NEW YORK TIMES.

WASHINGTON, June 23.—Permission for a modified form of price-fixing in "air competition codes" formulated under the National Industrial Recovery Act appeared to the administration today as the best way out of its first serious difficulty with business over the program for industrial control.

Obviously in answer to the demands of industrial management that it be allowed to share in the first fruits of recovery along with labor, General Hugh S. Johnson, administrator of the act, disclosed that he had amended his policy against price-fixing to allow agreements within an industry to the effect that it will not sell for less than the cost of production.

Meanwhile, the purpose of the government to regulate under the National Recovery Act the 500,000,000 acres of forest land in the United States was revealed. The intention is to prevent destructive competition. President Roosevelt is reported to have directed steps by which the lumber interests would submit a code to the recovery administration.

Licensing Power in Reserve.

General Johnson sought to allay the fears of business leaders that the drastic licensing provisions of the Recovery Act would be applied as a general policy in enforcing it. While still holding to the idea that the licensing clauses constitute the "pistol in the hip pocket" to enforce control, General Johnson evidently wanted to assure industrialists that he does not intend to be quick on the trigger.

The administrator's reference to the policy of price-fixing was looked upon as another evidence of a conciliatory attitude.

"In these codes it will be proper for industry to say that it will not sell below cost of production," General Johnson told questioners, "but if they use the code to fix extortionate prices, I should have to step in immediately in conformance with the law."

Earlier in the week General Johnson, elaborating upon a statement of President Roosevelt, left the impression that price-fixing would be banned for the time being. He explained then that the prime purpose of the Recovery Administration at this time is to return men and women to normal employment.

In keeping with this impression, he sent out a bulletin to the ten unidentified largest industries of the country, asking that they trim their codes down to the bare essentials of minimum wages, maximum hours and enforcement agreements, leaving price-fixing and all such "refinement" to a later date.

With the development of this attitude on the part of the Recovery Administration and its transmission in more practical ways to industrial leaders, a protest went up from business against demands to increase payrolls without compensatory considerations in the way of

Continued on Page Four.

$8,000,000 IN WORKS APPROVED BY CITY

Estimate Board Acts After Conferring With Wagner on Expected Federal Aid.

QUEENS PARKWAY VOTED

Completion of the Express Highway Also Is Provided —4,000 to Get Work.

The Board of Estimate cleared the way yesterday for highway improvements estimated to cost more than $8,000,000 and which Mayor O'Brien said would provide a substantial number of jobs.

The board voted to vest title to all the land required for Grand Central Parkway in Queens by July 1. The cost of acquiring the land is estimated at $3,000,000. The actual construction cost to be borne by the State is estimated between $3,000,000 and $4,000,000. The parkway will provide work for 1,650 men on the relief payroll immediately. Before completion it is estimated that between 4,000 and 5,000 men will find work on it.

Completion of the west side express highway at a cost of $1,184,-878 was also voted by the board. The unfinished link runs between Thirty-eighth and Forty-sixth Streets. When it is completed the highway will run along the Hudson from Canal Street to Seventy-second, where it joins Riverside Drive.

Wagner Confers With Board.

The board went over its improvement program with Senator Robert F. Wagner during the day. Senator Wagner told the members that the city could expect a substantial share of the Federal funds authorized under the Industrial Recovery Act. After the session, Mayor O'Brien was enthusiastic over the prospect of getting large projects started without delay.

"Our discussion with Senator Wagner was very profitable to the board, since we obtained an insight into the workings of the Federal Recovery Act," the Mayor said. "Senator Wagner was hopeful that Federal funds might be advanced shortly to equip our schools and hospitals. These buildings have been finished, but they cannot be placed in operation without furniture and equipment. While there was some question about obtaining Federal funds for this use, I think the Federal authorities will advance the money."

Adoption of the resolution applying to the Queens Parkway was marked by the opposition of Borough President Samuel Levy of Manhattan, who cast his two votes against the measure. He explained that every project undertaken at the expense of the city at large placed about 53 per cent of the cost on his borough. For that reason he opposed the parkway. Deputy Controller Arthur Philbin voted against Mr. Levy's express highway link, apparently in retaliation, but the matter went through.

In approving the Grand Central Parkway, the board committed the city to no expense this year. While the land will cost about $3,000,000, court delays in acquiring it will defer payment until next year at the earliest. The State is using its own

Continued on Page Five.

Reich Party Prisoners Must Pay for Own Keep

Wireless to THE NEW YORK TIMES.

BERLIN, June 23.—Communists and other political prisoners interned in concentration camps in Wuerttemberg are to be forced to defray the expenses of these camps, those of ampler means being compelled to furnish the cost of maintaining their fellow-prisoners.

The authorities of the State have imposed a levy totaling 100,000 marks (currently about $29,700) on a number of relatively wealthy camp inmates. The measure is justified on the ground that the political prisoners are collectively liable for their keep and that those who can must pay for those who cannot.

Similar action is foreshadowed for the concentration camp in Breslau, where Edmund Heines, the city's police president, told the inmates that the large pension of Hermann Luedemann, Socialist former Governor of Lower Silesia, would be applied to furnishing better camp fare. Herr Luedemann, who was transferred there today, was put to work digging ditches.

ALLOT $400,000,000 FOR STATES' ROADS

Recovery Plans Set in Motion Provide $22,330,101 for Work in New York.

ARMY ASKS $135,000,000

Program for Reconditioning Posts and National Cemeteries Is Put Up to the Board.

Special to THE NEW YORK TIMES.

WASHINGTON, June 23.—The gigantic public works phase of the national recovery program was set in motion today with allotment of $400,000,000 in road funds to States and Territories, and submission by the War Department of a $135,000,-000 program for reconditioning army posts and national cemeteries.

The road funds will become available July 1, as specified in the Recovery Act.

The announcement of these allotments and the War Department plans followed an all-day conference at the offices of the public works administration.

In making public the road allotments, Colonel Donald Sawyer, Public Works Administrator, gave out also a complete schedule of rules and regulations covering use of the funds. In addition to technical provisions, these rules provided:

1. All projects must be initiated by the States in the same manner as other Federal-aid projects.

2. Not more than 50 per cent of funds apportioned to any one State may be used outside municipalities; not less than 25 per cent must be used on extensions of the Federal-aid highway system into and through municipalities, and not more than 25 per cent may be applied to secondary roads until provision has been made for completion of at least 90 per cent of the initial Federal-aid highway system.

3. The right is reserved to require construction of roads desired by the Coordinator of Transportation to replace branch-line railroad service.

4. Preference in purchasing ma-

Continued on Page Four.

Plane Drops Anti-Nazi Leaflets on Berlin; Press Stresses Vulnerability to Air Raids

Wireless to THE NEW YORK TIMES.

BERLIN, June 23.—The Telegraphen Union News Agency, which is close to the government, issued a bulletin to its subscribers this evening with the warning, "This must be run on the front page as an extra by all newspapers, with the heading 'Red Air Test Over Berlin.'"

The bulletin read:

"This afternoon a foreign plane of a type unknown in Germany appeared over Berlin and dropped handbills abusing the German Government in the district containing the government offices and in the eastern region of the city.

"Since the air police, who promptly gave the alarm, have no planes of their own and the private planes at the airport were less speedy than the foreign one, which appeared suddenly, the latter was able to escape unidentified.

"This occurrence illuminates the strikingly untenable position that Germany is now in. Aircraft of a type heretofore not seen in Germany can unimpededly fly over German Government buildings and drop handbills—tomorrow, perhaps, gas or explosive bombs carrying death and destruction."

By The Associated Press.

BERLIN, Saturday, June 24.—A streamer headline reading "Down With the Unbearable Chains of the Treaty of Versailles" appeared today in Chancellor Hitler's newspaper, the Völkische Beobachter, a few hours after the police had reported that an unidentified foreign plane had flown over the city dropping handbills that insulted the government. The treaty denied an air force to Germany.

"Every bird is allowed to protect its nest," the Völkische Beobachter said. "Only Germany, with clipped wings and pulled claws, must sit idly by while its nest is befouled."

The entire Berlin press directed its editorial comment this morning against Germany's helplessness in the air.

By The Associated Press.

LINZ, Austria, June 23.—An airplane without distinguishing marks flew over Linz this afternoon scattering leaflets denouncing the Dollfuss régime and proclaiming that new aggressive Nazi measures would commence within a few days.

CONFERENCE IS HANDICAPPED BY INDECISION OVER POLICIES, BUT MACDONALD IS HOPEFUL

SENATORS BACK BARUCH

Democrats in Capital Put Domestic Gains First of London Aims.

BAR TARIFF CUTS NOW

Group Also Favors Deferring Currency Steps Until Prices Rise Under Industry Act.

COMMITMENTS OPPOSED

Wheeler Assails Stabilization at Present—Calls Pittman's Plan for Silver Insufficient.

Special to THE NEW YORK TIMES.

WASHINGTON, June 23.—While the American delegates to the World Monetary and Economic Conference have been advancing a program in London, Democratic Senators have been conferring here on conditions for putting the administration's domestic economic program into successful operation.

The conferences have centred chiefly on Bernard M. Baruch.

Some Senators who exchanged ideas in these meetings are convinced that the Industrial Control and Farm Relief Acts, in the drafting of which Mr. Baruch had a hand, will fail of their purpose if tariff duties are lowered and an agreement is entered upon to stabilize currencies at this time. The view expressed was that nothing would be done at the London conference along these lines.

The dominant opinion of Democratic Senators here is that the domestic program enacted in the last session of Congress must be thoroughly tested under present conditions. They hold that to stabilize the dollar now and make agreements with foreign nations to lower tariffs would make it impossible to increase commodity prices and raise wages.

An increase in the exchange value of the dollar, they contend, would work against exports, would stimulate the entrance of foreign goods manufactured on cheap wage scales abroad, and would interfere with the successful operation of both the Industrial Control and Farm Relief Acts.

Views to Be Submitted to Moley.

It is understood that such views will be contained in the document Mr. Baruch is sending to Assistant Secretary of State Moley at London for consideration of the American delegates. The prospective trend of this document, and the privately expressed opinion of many Democratic Senators, is that the World Economic Conference is being held at an inopportune time for this country, and that nothing in the way of important international agreements can be hoped for until some time later.

Senator Wheeler of Montana today expressed the view held by many Senators in saying:

"It seems apparent that it is absolutely impossible for this country to agree upon any tariff reduction until we find what the legislation passed in the last session of Congress is going to do toward raising commodity prices and wages in this country.

"Likewise, with our going off the gold standard and with the adoption of possible inflationary measures, no one can say definitely at this time where the dollar should be stabilized. While our export trade is increasing and business generally on the upturn, the stabilization of currencies can wait until there is a stabilization in commerce.

"In my opinion, the only thing the conference can do at this time is to work out an agreement on the remonetization of silver. The program outlined by Senator Pittman will be of little benefit. He is still treating it as a commodity and not even as a favorite commodity. His plan absolutely disregards the resolution which was passed by the Senate urging the American delegation to stand for remonetization of silver."

Tariff Treaty Action Doubtful.

It was argued by some tariff experts that the World Economic Conference would have a difficult task to make any effective international agreements on tariff. These experts say it would require many years to dissolve the most-favored-

Continued on Page Two.

British-Soviet Parley To Seek End of Clash

Special Cable to THE NEW YORK TIMES.

LONDON, June 23.—British and Russian statesmen will meet Monday to discuss the position created by the imposition of the British embargo on Russian imports and possibly arrange the release of Leslie C. Thornton and William MacDonald, British engineers, whose imprisonment in Moscow was responsible for the embargo.

Maxim Litvinoff, the Soviet Union's delegate to the World Economic Conference, and his wife were guests of Prime Minister MacDonald at luncheon at 10 Downing Street today. Subsequently it was announced M. Litvinoff had agreed to meet Sir John Simon, Foreign Secretary, Monday.

There have been no further conversations between the Russians and United States delegates though it is known several of the Americans are anxious that a basis for American recognition will be found before M. Litvinoff returns to Russia early next week.

PARLEY IS CRIPPLED, PARIS PRESS HOLDS

American Refusal to Take Up Stabilization Called a Deadly Blow.

SENTIMENT IS UNANIMOUS

Opposition Deputies Start a Move to Ask Suspension of London Negotiations.

Wireless to THE NEW YORK TIMES.

PARIS, June 23.—The United States delegation's definite refusal to consider currency stabilization at the World Economic Conference has produced what the semi-official newspaper, Le Temps, calls tonight "a deplorable impression on France."

The French press unanimously agrees today that the American monetary thesis directly contradicts France's official position and hence that nothing important or useful can be expected of the conference. Many papers, in fact, express inability to see why the conference should have been called in the first place.

"The American delegation seems to exclude definitely all possibility of useful work by the conference," writes C.-J. Gignoux in La Journee Industrielle. "Finance Minister Bonnet's speech and the American note are exactly at variance."

Le Temps Sees Impasse.

"It is hard to see," says Le Temps, "what fruitful work can still be accomplished at London as long as the situation created by the present attitude of the United States continues. The defeat of the monetary truce plan makes it necessary to continue the work of the conference with the greatest prudence."

"The London conference has lost its raison d'être," says the leading editorial in Le Journal des Débats. "The two conditions which would make it useful are lacking. There has been no solution of the war-debt problem or that of the instability of the dollar and pound. The conference can only now go on talking without obtaining any results."

Pertinax says the American statement dealt "a mortal blow to the conference." Stephane Lauzanne in Le Matin writes that the United States has "torpedoed" the conference. L'Intransigeant calls it "a missed opportunity," while Camille Aymard in La Liberté refers to it as "a murder party."

The adjournment of the conference until de facto stabilization of currencies now off the gold standard has been effected was demanded in a motion presented to the Chamber of Deputies tonight by a group headed by Rene Dommange, Paris Deputy. All measures that the conference might take would be "vain and precarious" unless the United States agreed to stabilize the dollar, M. Dommange said. His motion calls on the government to ask for immediate adjournment of the parley.

A similar resolution was adopted tonight by the National Federation of Agricultural Associations.

HE SEES 'LITTLE SETBACK'

British Leader Asserts Lack of Stabilization Does Not Block Work.

REBUKES GLOOMY PRESS

Prime Minister Asks Writers at Parley to Ignore Many Rumors of Failure.

FRENCH FOR QUOTA TRUCE

Paris Proposal Would Permit Nations to Keep Prohibitions on Some Imports.

By FREDERICK T. BIRCHALL.

Special Cable to THE NEW YORK TIMES.

LONDON, June 23.—With currency stabilization temporarily removed from the discussions, the commissions, committees and subcommittees of the World Economic Conference continued work today, debating problems of a minor nature. The solution of even these problems is largely dependent upon an agreement about stabilization, when one is discovered. Nevertheless, some progress is made by discussion now.

However, the fact cannot be escaped that the conference is largely marking time pending the arrival of that happy day when, with full information, the instructions of distant governments permit it to go ahead and really vital issues can be tackled. Meantime, its proceedings are largely technical and exceedingly dull. Delegates hailed the hour of their relief tonight with unconcealed satisfaction.

Week-End Holiday Adopted.

Tomorrow not a commission, not even a subcommittee will meet. The day after is Sunday, so it can be accepted that the World Economic Conference has adopted the insidious British habit of week-ending, in which nothing will be done before Monday morning.

Prime Minister MacDonald is at Chequers with a small party of chosen guests. Finance Minister Bonnet of France has gone to Paris. Dr. Hendryk Colijn, president of the economic commission, has flown to Holland, and most of the Americans are in the country, whence dull care has succumbed to golf, with scarcely a qualm.

Today was notable for only one incident: In mid-afternoon, when things were dullest, there appeared in the Geological Museum press room no less a personage than the president of the conference, Ramsay MacDonald himself. The British Prime Minister went there, as he speedily made apparent, on a mission of admonition and rebuke for certain reports about the proceedings which he regarded as "discouraging the conference."

French Cooler to Parley.

Naturally enough, his action, rather than to allay rumors, had the effect of starting another crop as to the reasons for his quite unprecedented incursion, one of them being that the present Franco-British understanding regarding the ratio between the dollar and the franc had been somewhat jeopardized by yesterday's determination to put dollar stabilization into the background. There was no confirmation that this was an unreasonable theory, but it is a fact that the French feeling toward the conference has become noticeably cooler.

The correspondents crowded around Mr. MacDonald and he spoke pointedly and emphatically.

"You journalists always are tapping for propaganda and rumors," he said. "I hope you will steadily resist both at this gathering. We have now come to the end of the second week of our work. Those who follow previous international conferences know that the end of the second week is the time when pessimism begins to show itself.

"An international conference is of necessity a slow-working machine; we have difficulties of language difficulties; we have difficulties that arise on account of the conflicting interests of various nations, and so on. Those difficulties always are at their maximum after a conference has been going about a fortnight.

"Therefore pessimism or doubt or clouded mind comes. The dele-

Continued on Page Two.

"All the News That's Fit to Print."

The New York Times.

LATE CITY EDITION
WEATHER—Thunder showers today, tomorrow; temperature same.
Temperatures Yesterday—Max., 78; Min., 67.

Copyright, 1933, by The New York Times Company.

VOL. LXXXII....No. 27,549. Entered as Second-Class Matter, Postoffice, New York, N. Y. NEW YORK, WEDNESDAY, JUNE 28, 1933. P TWO CENTS In New York City. | THREE CENTS Within 200 Miles | FOUR CENTS Elsewhere Except in 7th and 8th Postal Zones

$35,000 WAS PAID TO DAVIS TO PROMOTE CHILE LOANS, OTTO H. KAHN TESTIFIES

THEN A PRIVATE CITIZEN

Guaranty Company Was Linked With Kuhn-Loeb in Flotation.

LOANS WERE SORE SPOT

They Were Firm's Only Foreign Advances to Default, Kahn Tells Senate Committee.

BALANCE SHEETS SHOWN

Concern's Assets Dropped From $120,402,103 in 1929 to $66,974,845 in 1931.

Special to THE NEW YORK TIMES.

WASHINGTON, June 27.—Otto H. Kahn, one of the partners in the private banking firm of Kuhn, Loeb & Co. of New York, told the Senate Banking and Currency Committee this afternoon that Norman H. Davis, Ambassador at Large, received two fees amounting to $35,000 in 1925 for promoting Chilean loans.

Both fees, Mr. Kahn testified, were paid to Mr. Davis by the Guaranty Company of New York. One of $25,000 was for services in connection with a loan of $20,000,000 to the Mortgage Bank of Chile, negotiated in 1925, and another of $10,000 was in connection with the negotiation of a second loan of $20,000,000 to the same concern.

"My firm contributed nothing," Mr. Kahn testified. "The syndicate contributed, as part of the syndicate expenses, $15,000, and the Guaranty Company contributed $10,000. Afterward the second business was done, and Mr. Davis received another fee of $10,000; so that his total fees received were $35,000."

The syndicate to which Mr. Kahn referred consisted of the Guaranty Company and Kuhn, Loeb & Co., and the two loans of $20,000,000, in connection with which it was testified that Mr. Davis had been paid the two fees, were part of a series of five loans totaling $90,000,000 which the syndicate made to the Mortgage Bank of Chile between 1925 and 1929.

Davis Then Private Citizen.

Mr. Kahn testified that Mr. Davis was a private citizen at the time he rendered the services for which the fees were paid.

Anticipating that he would be interrogated about the Davis fees, he took the precaution to obtain from J. R. Swann, president of the Guaranty Company, a memorandum on June 2 relative to the services for which Mr. Davis was paid. This memorandum asserted that Mr. Davis in 1925 had informed the Guaranty Company that the representative of the Chile Mortgage Bank had consulted with him with regard to placing a loan in New York.

Mr. Swann added that Mr. Davis "wished to know if we would be interested in considering it, to which we replied in the affirmative."

The revelations concerning the Davis fees came at the end of a sultry day of testimony during which Mr. Kahn, suave and dapper, dressed in a blue serge suit, polite and ready with his answers at all times, had testified regarding the general banking practices and ethical code of Kuhn, Loeb & Co.

The Senate Office Building, in which he had been testifying since 10 o'clock in the morning, was being drenched by a torrential rain in a terrific storm, during which thunder and lightning punctuated his testimony concerning Mr. Davis.

Mr. Kahn smoked a cigarette calmly and, after telling generally of the Chilean transaction, asked that Benjamin J. Buttenwieser, another partner of Kuhn, Loeb & Co., be heard regarding the more intimate details of the $90,000,000 that had been lent to the Chilean company.

Chilean Loan a "Sore Spot."

When Mr. Pecora suddenly plunged into the Chilean transaction, which will be gone into further when Mr. Kahn resumes the witness stand tomorrow, the latter immediately exclaimed that this particular transaction was a "very sore spot."

The five loans, four of them for $20,000,000 each and the other for $10,000,000, had been sold to the

Continued on Page Thirteen.

Ganges Island Is Gone From a Pacific Group

By The Associated Press.

TOKYO, June 27.—Ganges Island, shown on maps of the Pacific Ocean at 30.57 degrees North Latitude, 154.10 degrees East Longitude, has disappeared, according to Japanese naval surveyors who have just completed an extensive hydrographic cruise amid the Magellan Archipelago.

Ganges Island is shown near the steamship route from Yokohama to Honolulu, about a quarter of the distance from the Japanese port. The total distance is 3,445 nautical miles.

The Magellan Archipelago, which includes Ganges Island, extends from the Southern Japanese island about half way to Hawaii. The numerous islands are scattered between 20 and 30 degrees North Latitude and 130 and 170 degrees East Longitude.

REPEAL TRIUMPHANT IN TWO MORE STATES

West Virginia Is First in the Southern Tier to Give Wet Vote.

TWO TO ONE AGAINST DRYS

California Supporters of Repeal Are Piling Up a Big Anti-Prohibition Majority.

Repeal Vote Developments.

West Virginia yesterday became the fifteenth and California the sixteenth consecutive States to vote for repeal of the prohibition amendment.

By a big majority West Virginia elected a wet slate to ratify repeal at a State convention July 25.

In California, the lead for repeal was more than 3 to 1, with the hitherto dry area of Los Angeles going strongly wet.

Wet Tide Turns South.

By The Associated Press.

CHARLESTON, W. Va., June 27.—Bone dry for twenty years, West Virginia voted tonight to cast off prohibition.

The wet tide, surging below the Mason and Dixon line for the first time, added the Mountaineer State to the fourteen others which have voted to ratify the Twenty-first Amendment.

With 1,718 precincts out of 2,338 reporting, the vote stood at 186,742 for repeal and 110,508 against.

The repealists gained as ballots from the industrial centres rolled in, offsetting the stanch prohibition stand of the hill dwellers and farmer folk in the less populous areas.

Repeal started strongly in early returns with a 2-to-1 trend. That

Continued on Page Sixteen.

REPEAL IS RATIFIED AT ALBANY SESSION, HAILED AS HISTORIC

Smith and Root Assert State's Action Will Give Impetus to War on Prohibition.

ROOSEVELT IS ACCLAIMED

Honored as Pioneer in Fight—Dry Act Held Object Lesson of Minorities' Power.

Special to THE NEW YORK TIMES.

ALBANY, June 27.—New York's ratification of the Twenty-first Amendment to the Federal Constitution, repealing the Eighteenth, was unanimously voted today by the 150 delegates to the State convention.

The Twenty-first Amendment, if approved by thirty-six States, will end national prohibition after a trial of thirteen years.

The action taken today was hailed as an historic event of national as well as State significance by such champions of repeal as Elihu Root, former Governor Smith, Governor Lehman and Representative James W. Wadsworth, all delegates.

Another pioneer in the fight for repeal, Dr. Nicholas Murray Butler, who had been elected a delegate, but is now in Europe, sent a cablegram from Paris in which he welcomed the end of prohibition as the beginning of true temperance. The cablegram was read into the record by Mr. Smith after he had assumed the gavel as presiding officer.

Speedy repeal of the Eighteenth Amendment was predicted by several prominent speakers, who declared that New York's action would lend impetus to the movement in other parts of the country.

Root Predicts Dry Rout.

Mr. Root predicted that the drys would not be able to hold the thirteen States necessary to block repeal, while Representative Wadsworth went even further.

"We shall secure repeal, quite possibly within the calendar year," the latter said. "If not, we will have it by the middle of next Winter."

Mr. Root, Mr. Smith and Representative Wadsworth all emphasized that today's convention was giving to the people of the State their first opportunity to be recorded on the question of national prohibition. All declared, moreover, that this opportunity should have been afforded in 1918, before the State voted to ratify the Eighteenth Amendment.

Mr. Root and the former Governor asserted that, unless the lesson of prohibition had been lost on the people, it should warn them against letting organized minorities take control of the government and to make certain that ratification of future amendments should be not by legislative action but by conventions created by direct vote.

The spaces set aside for visitors in the Assembly Chamber were filled by a distinguished audience long before the convention was called to order, about half an hour behind the scheduled time.

There was delay because of the belated arrival of delegates from New York City, arriving on a special train, and of Postmaster General Farley, who was coming on from Michigan to sponsor the nom-

Continued on Page Sixteen.

Electrical 'Ladder' 550 Miles High Explores the Outer Ionosphere

New Radio Device Is Described by Bureau of Standards Scientists—Clue That 14.6 Meter Wave Length Could Carry Message to Stars Is Reported at Chicago.

By WILLIAM L. LAURENCE.
Special to THE NEW YORK TIMES.

CHICAGO, June 27.—An electrical "Jacob's Ladder" on which man can climb to the outer reaches of the "ionosphere" 550 miles up and map out with delicate measuring tools the unexplored regions in the three shells of radiant energy surrounding our planet was described today before the Institute of Radio Engineers, meeting here as one of the forty affiliated societies in the Summer session of the American Association for the Advancement of Science.

The new "ladder" records automatically the electrical state, or ionization, of the three upper layers around the earth beyond the stratosphere and determines their distances. With this new tool it is hoped not only to gain much new knowledge about radio transmission and reception but also to chart other regions in that cold land of mystery above the clouds. For example, it is hoped to measure for the first time the earth's magnetic forces up to distances of several hundred miles.

The new "ionosphere" measuring rod, another step in man's conquest of space, was described before the institute by T. R. Gilliland of the United States Bureau of Standards, Washington. Three other Bureau of Standards scientists, L. V. Berkner, S. S. Kirby and D. M. Stuart, described other recent studies on the "ionosphere," which includes layer E, F-1 and F-2 and their application to radio transmission.

The institute also heard Dr. Karl G. Jansky of the Bell Telephone Laboratories present further evi-

Continued on Page Eleven.

GUARANTEE OPPOSED BY STATE BANKERS

They Plan to Seek Change in Glass-Steagall Law on Deposit Insurance.

FEAR 'POLITICAL CONTROL'

G. V. McLaughlin, Elected Head of Association, Urges Uniform Code by Banks Themselves.

From a Staff Correspondent.

BOLTON LANDING, LAKE GEORGE, N. Y., June 27.—The State Bankers' Association in convention today adopted a resolution opposing the deposit insurance provision of the new Glass-Steagall Act.

Permission given by the law to the Federal Deposit Corporation to make unlimited assessments against the capital funds of member banks, according to the resolution, might mean the confiscation of bank stockholders' funds, and would remove incentive for good management and sound banking practices. The association advocated an amendment to limit the maximum liability of any bank for any year.

Another resolution adopted pledged cooperation with the government and public to create a stronger banking system. Appointment of a committee was authorized to make recommendations for the correction of provisions in the new law which might prove unsound and unworkable.

The committee will be appointed by George V. McLaughlin, president of the Brooklyn Trust Company, who was elected president of the association today. Mr. McLaughlin was formerly State Superintendent of Banks.

Other officers elected were: Vice president, William L. Gillespie, president of the National Commercial Bank and Trust Company, Albany; treasurer, A. B. Wellar, treasurer of the Ithaca Trust Company.

Discussion of Deposit Guarantee.

Discussion of the deposit guarantee section of the new Federal law occupied the greater part of the day's sessions. G. Tracy Vought of the law firm of White & Case, New York City, delivered a comprehensive analysis of the Glass-Steagall Act, in which he characterized the insurance provision as a "disastrous mistake."

Mr. Vought "hoped" that politics would not enter into the selection of the two administrators of the permanent Deposit Insurance Corporation, to be appointed by the President as associates of the Controller of the Currency in its management. He expressed the fear that in some States, not New York, banks which were not members of the Federal Reserve System would find it too easy to obtain certificates of solvency enabling them to join the permanent fund.

"Most important of all," he said, "is that the entire capital resources of the member banks are committed to insure the depositors of the other banks in the plan from losses which they otherwise might incur. Every bank which remains in the Federal Reserve System or which comes into this insurance corporation is unlimitedly liable to prevent, up to the insured amount, losses to depositors in other banks resulting from insolvency of such other banks.

"This is an appalling liability. It is easy to conceive that the stockholders might prefer voluntary liquidation of their bank to its assuming this liability."

Recalling previous experiments in

Continued on Page Fourteen.

30-CENT WHEAT TAX TO START ON JULY 9

Tugwell Announces Processing Levy on Millers Despite Rise in Prices.

ADDS HALF CENT TO BREAD

Wheat Continues to Soar in the Chicago Pit, Crossing $1 Mark for 1933 Delivery.

Special to THE NEW YORK TIMES.

WASHINGTON, June 27.—Despite the quotation of dollar wheat on the Chicago Exchange and even higher prices elsewhere, the Agricultural Adjustment Administration announced today its decision to apply a processing tax of 30 cents a bushel on wheat milling, effective July 9.

The Acting Secretary of Agriculture, Mr. Tugwell, made the announcement with the approval of President Roosevelt. From that day on bakers will pay $1.38 more for a barrel of flour and the consumer will pay about a half a cent a loaf more for bread.

These prices assume that the full amount of the processing tax will be passed on to the consumer. Officials of the adjustment administration contend, however, that the present prices for bread and flour are not warranted by the price of wheat and processers and manufacturers may be required to absorb at least a part of the tax.

June 15 Price Level Set.

In deciding on the maximum tax under the Agricultural Adjustment Act, the administration selected June 15 prices as representing the normal current level. This was not disclosed in the proclamation, in which Mr. Tugwell stated merely that he had ascertained what the maximum processing tax should be "from available statistics of the Department of Agriculture."

The law provides that the maximum tax should represent the difference between the current farm price for wheat and the average of that received from August, 1909, to July, 1914. The average for the latter period was established by the department to be 88.4 cents a bushel, while on June 15 it was about 60 cents a bushel.

The law does not require that the farm price paid on the date the processing tax goes into effect be used in determining the amount of the tax, but leaves this largely to the discretion of the Secretary of Agriculture. Disregard of the prevailing increased prices for wheat amounts, therefore, to a finding by the Secretary that the present high level is abnormal.

The law also requires that the processing tax be placed in effect at the beginning of the marketing year, which for wheat is July 1. But the law gives the Secretary the right to proclaim when the beginning of the crop year will be, and it was according to this privilege that July 9 was set as representing the earliest date by which the new administrative machinery could be set up.

Wallace Touring Grain Belt.

Secretary Wallace is making a tour of the grain belt urging growers to comply with the stipulation necessary to become eligible for sharing in the benefit payments of $150,000,000 to be raised by the processing tax. Growers are required under the terms of a contract with the Secretary to agree, if required, to reduce their present acreage by 20 per cent in 1934.

It is possible that no reduction in acreage will be required, but agreements must be made, in advance of benefit payments, to reduce up to

Continued on Page Thirty-eight.

COTTON INDUSTRY OPPOSED BY LABOR ON ITS TRADE CODE

40-Hour Week Urged at Industrial Act Hearing—Green Wants Standard of 32.

MACHINERY CURBS ASKED

G. A. Sloan Sees End of Child Labor—Tire Firms Seek to Exempt Fabric Plants.

Special to THE NEW YORK TIMES.

WASHINGTON, June 27.—Leaders of capital and labor in the cotton textile mills sat down today with representatives of the consuming public to obtain approval of a model code for the administration of the National Recovery Act, with the expectation of returning millions to employment in American industry in general.

The textile manufacturers laid before General Hugh S. Johnson, the Industrial Administrator who presided in opening the meeting, their proposals for a 40-hour work week and a minimum weekly wage of $11 for the North and $10 for the South. Immediately, labor announced that it stood ready to fight for a shorter week, and objections to other points by a minority of the industry were foreshadowed.

Hailed as one of the most significant assemblages in the history of this country, it was the first open hearing on a code of fair competition as provided for in the Industrial Recovery Act. Eight hundred spectators heard the terms of the code, upon which two-thirds of the textile industry has agreed, outlined to General Johnson and his aides.

National Labor Stand Seen.

The purpose of labor to approach a thirty-hour-work week in all American industry through the agency of the Recovery Act was evident. William Green, president of the Federation of Labor, will be called as a witness in the public hearing tomorrow.

The Federation, he said today, was prepared to suggest that a maximum of thirty hours be established in the textile code, although thirty-two hours would not be looked upon with disfavor. The proposed forty-hour week would not accomplish the results contemplated by the administrators of the act, he said, and a minimum wage of even $14.40 a week would be too low.

Already amassed against Mr. Green's prospective proposal is a voluminous record made today by the textile manufacturers. That record is replete with statements and statistical data to the effect that a work week of forty hours is the most desirable for the industry. A shorter week would drive small cotton mills out of business, causing additional unemployment that would more than offset any possible gains, the textile manufacturers argued.

George A. Sloan, president of the Cotton Textile Institute, one of the framers of the proposed code, estimated that as presented today it would put 100,000 men back to work. Robert Amory of Boston, another textile manufacturer, predicted that the full normal employment of the industry would be a reality within sixty days. W. B. Anderson, representing the Southern mills, predicted there would be an actual shortage of cotton mill labor in the South. All agreed that the minimum wage requirements of

Continued on Page Eight.

25% GOLD RESERVE ENOUGH, PARLEY'S EXPERTS DECIDE; BRITAIN WON'T PEG POUND

GOLD AS COINAGE OPPOSED

Committee Would Limit It to Reserves and to Foreign Payments.

FRENCH BLOC THWARTED

Chamberlain Balks at Binding Stabilization—Five Nations Agree to Act in Common.

SUGAR CURBS WIN FAVOR

But the Deadlock Holds on Wheat—Moley Arrives in London After Midnight.

Trade Parley Developments.

The plan to set a figure of 25 per cent for gold reserves of central banks was approved yesterday by a subcommittee of the World Economic Conference, which also resolved that gold should be withdrawn from general circulation as money.

France, Holland, Italy, Belgium and Switzerland conferred on measures to defend the gold standard against American reflation plans. Britain refused to aid them by attempting at present to peg the pound to the franc.

Efforts for a wheat reduction agreement were postponed in view of the changed situation caused by the market rise.

Germany promised to make at least part interest payments on long-term debts.

Professor Moley arrived in London by steamer and train, having abandoned his plan to fly from Ireland. He explained that after giving information to the American delegation he would return next week with information for President Roosevelt.

MacDonald Seeks Speed.

By FREDERICK T. BIRCHALL.
Special Cable to THE NEW YORK TIMES.

LONDON, June 27.—Although today brought new, distinct steps in the process of clarification of issues through which the World Economic Conference is passing, Prime Minister MacDonald has evidently decided more rapid progress can be made toward definite decisions. He has called for tomorrow a meeting of the conference bureau to consider progress, at which, it is announced, a report will be made of developments to date and consideration given to coordinating and expediting "the great mass of work now in committee."

Today's actual developments were somewhat overshadowed by the attention paid to the topic that is invariably uppermost in the minds of the delegates—stabilization of the present monetary systems, particularly the relation of the pound to the dollar and the pound to the franc and other European currencies still attempting to cling to the gold standard. Yesterday's attacks on the Dutch guilder, which, however, recovered somewhat today, have intensified French and Swiss anxieties and brought the matter again prominently into the foreground.

Gold Countries Meet.

The five principal European countries that still adhere to gold held a meeting led by France and Holland and discussed the situation but reached no formal decision beyond the expression of a general desire to act in common for the maintenance of their interests. The conversations yesterday between Georges Bonnet, French Finance Minister, and Neville Chamberlain, British Chancellor of the Exchequer, on the same subject with special reference to the ratio between the franc and the pound at present under de facto stabilization are understood also to have been inconclusive. Mr. Chamberlain is believed to have been reluctant to bind Great Britain to continued stabilization by agreement, although he disclaimed any intention of deliberate inflation.

The fact is that over all these side conferences hangs the uncertainty about what will be done about the dollar. It is recognized that President Roosevelt's refusal to agree at this time to even approximate and temporary stabilization is inevitable in view of the policy he has adopted to meet the crisis at home and that until he has raised prices, particu-

Continued on Page Two.

Deputies Tie Hands Of French Delegates

Wireless to THE NEW YORK TIMES.

PARIS, June 27.—As a result of a second vote tonight by the Chamber Finance Committee the French Government will be unable to act with a free hand at the World Economic Conference when questions of international tariff reductions arise.

The government sought full powers to modify customs duties by decree. These powers were refused by the Chamber's Finance Committee several days ago, but Minister of Commerce Serre appeared before the body this evening a second time to explain that the government only wished to exercise special authority during the imminent Parliamentary Summer vacation.

The committee, however, decided that negotiations must be subject to ratification by Parliament after the Summer holidays.

NATIONALIST PARTY DISSOLVES IN REICH

Hugenberg's Lieutenants Join Hitlerites as He Submits Cabinet Resignation.

NAZIS LIMIT MEMBERSHIP

Archbishop of Canterbury, at London Meeting, Appeals for Tolerance to Jews.

Special Cable to THE NEW YORK TIMES.

BERLIN, June 27.—Dr. Alfred Hugenberg, Nationalist Minister of Economics and Agriculture, sent his resignation as a member of the Hitler government to President von Hindenburg tonight.

It had not been accepted up to 9 P. M., when telephonic communication with Neudeck, in East Prussia, where the President is sojourning, was broken off to allow him to retire at his accustomed hour.

Dr. Hugenberg's resignation was his reply to the Nazis' demand that his party should voluntarily dissolve, and the Nationalist leader made his continuance in office conditional on his party's being allowed to remain intact.

No sooner had he signed his request to be relieved of office and transmitted it to Dr. Otto Meissner, State Secretary to President von Hindenburg, to be relayed to the President, when his political lieutenants hastily called a party conference and after less than an hour's deliberation voted to dissolve the moribund Nationalist group, which has been parading under the label of the National Front and to march bag and baggage into the Nazi camp.

Think He May Remain.

Since their action exonerates Dr. Hugenberg of the stigma of having deserted his party and relieves him of the odium of having surrendered to the Hitlerites, it is inferred tonight that he may still be induced

Continued on Page Four.

Chinese Squadron of Five Vessels Deserts; Believed Going to New 'Independent' Zone

Wireless to THE NEW YORK TIMES.

SHANGHAI, June 27.—After an attempt was made today to assassinate Admiral Shen Hung-lieh, commander of the Northeast Squadron of the Chinese Navy, the entire squadron of five vessels deserted.

It was observed sailing northward around the Shantung Peninsula, and it is conjectured that it is proceeding to Chinwangtao, in the area demilitarized in the Chino-Japanese truce. It is believed that it may join the Chinese Generals who last week declared the region to be independent of China and set up their capital at Tangshan.

Admiral Shen, who is also Mayor of Tsingtao, remains ashore. He is left in command of only three small antiquated ships.

Tsingtao is quiet and there are American and Japanese warships in the harbor.

General Feng Yu-hsiang, leader of a revolt against the Nanking Government in Chahar Province, Inner Mongolia, is reported to have received $400,000 from the faction of Hu Han-min in South China. He is said to have given $100,000 of this to General Liu Kwei-tang, who joined forces with Manchukuo in February after being forced out of Shantung Province, and who now announces his allegiance to General Feng.

Twenty-six other and less well-known Generals also announce that they are joining the Feng revolt.

The Northeast Squadron consists in the cruisers Hai Chi, built in 1897, and Hai Shen, 1898; the destroyer Hsiao An, 1912; the aircraft carrier Chen Hai and the training ship Cheng Ho, 1911. The cruisers displace 4,300 and 2,950 tons, respectively.

Shantung Province, at whose principal port, Tsingtao, the deserting fleet was stationed, has itself been an uncertain factor in the North China situation. Its Governor, Han Fu-Chu, though nominally serving the Nanking Government, has shown great independence

Washington Yields to League in Chaco War As the Quickest Means of Achieving Peace

Special to THE NEW YORK TIMES.

WASHINGTON, June 27.—For what was said to be the first time in diplomatic history, the United States today renounced jurisdiction in a Western Hemisphere dispute in favor of the League of Nations.

The Commission of Neutrals, appointed under Pan American Union peace machinery to mediate in the Chaco dispute between Paraguay and Bolivia, gave out a statement this morning, after a long meeting, announcing its withdrawal from any further participation in the settlement of the quarrel.

The statement said in part:

"Experience has shown that if there is more than one centre of negotiation confusion and lack of agreement are the inevitable results. The commission therefore feels that it can best contribute to peace on this continent by withdrawing from the negotiations. Thus negotiations can be centred in Geneva, if other peace agencies will take a similar attitude, allowing the League committee to work with universal support for peace.

"The neutral commission also feels that its action * * * clearly demonstrates to the American nations the necessity for them to deal effectively at the next Pan American conference with the fundamental problem of the preservation of peace and order in this hemisphere. * * *

"Should both countries agree at a later date to appeal to the countries that have formed the neutral commission, for further good offices in seeking to establish peace between them, their petition will, of course, be considered with care and sympathy."

The move was not unexpected. Since the Bolivian Minister to the United States, Dr. Enrique Finot, sailed for Europe recently to lay his country's case before the League, some members of the neutral commission were in favor of disbanding, while others wanted to continue in existence, in the apparent feeling that the League mediators would not be successful.

It is understood that the United States, Cuban and Mexican representatives were in favor of disbanding, while the Uruguayan and Colombian members desired to continue the commission.

"All the News That's Fit to Print."

The New York Times.

LATE CITY EDITION

WEATHER—Fair today and tomorrow; rising temperature.

Temperatures Yesterday—Max., 76; min., 67.

VOL. LXXXII....No. 27,597. Entered as Second-Class Matter, Postoffice, New York, N. Y. NEW YORK, TUESDAY, AUGUST 15, 1933. P TWO CENTS In New York City. | THREE CENTS Within 200 Miles | FOUR CENTS Elsewhere Except in 7th and 8th Postal Zones

UNTERMYER LEADS ALBANY TAX FIGHT; SCORES CITY WASTE

Demands O'Brien 'Clean House' and Then Fight for a 'Fair Share' of State Levies.

CALLS FOR RELIEF INQUIRY

Agrees to See Lehman After Mayor and McCooey Back His Entire Program.

REPUBLICANS ARE BITTER

Continued Delay in Presenting an Acceptable Program Fans Hostility in Assembly.

Text of the Untermyer letter on city finances is on Page 2.

Samuel Untermyer, special financial adviser to the O'Brien administration, will present to Governor Lehman in Albany today a new program to obtain immediate funds for relief and early restoration of the city's credit.

Mr. Untermyer stepped into the breach when city officials were apparently without a single idea to solve the city's financial problem. His suggestions were advanced yesterday at a conferenec attended by Mayor O'Brien, Democratic Leader John H. McCooey of Brooklyn and the Democratic legislative leaders, Assemblyman Irwin Steingut and Senator John J. Dunnigan.

Mr. Untermyer proposed immediate action by the city to meet the accusation that its government was conducted wastefully and extravagantly. With these charges unrefuted, he declared, the city could not expect immediate relief from the Legislature. He suggested that the State assume the burden of providing funds for city relief, either directly or through having the Legislature provide means whereby the relief burden might be met.

For Home Relief Inquiry.

The special counsel also urged that the State be asked to make an investigation without delay into charges that political favoritism had operated in the distribution of home relief and unemployment relief funds. He also proposed the creation of a committee to investigate city expenses.

"Clean house and demand the restoration of the city's credit," he demanded in summing up his program. After these steps had been taken, he maintained, State taxes should be reapportioned to restore the city's credit.

Following the conference, all of Mr. Untermyer's proposals received the endorsement of those present, and he was authorized to present the city's latest program to Governor Lehman in Albany this morning, if an appointment could be made. He agreed to represent the city.

The Untermyer plan provides that the Legislature shall provide funds for city relief work temporarily, pending permanent restoration of the city's credit. It also provides for the immediate local enactment of a five-cent tax on each taxicab ride. These things accomplished, the Legislature would recess for thirty days while city economies were being worked out. Permanent relief would then be provided.

Mr. Untermyer included himself on the city economy committee and recommended that five other members be chosen from the civic organizations that have studied the budget. The committee within fifteen days after it had been formed would report to the Legislature on economies that could be made.

Would Protect 5-Cent Fare.

After the suggested economies have been carried into effect the Legislature would be asked to reapportion State taxes so that a greater part would be paid to the city. In that manner, Mr. Untermyer held, the city could restore its credit permanently and at the same time maintain the five-cent subway fare.

He said his program would defeat the plans of bankers and transit companies for an increased fare next year. While admitting that the report that such an increase was planned had received circulation, Mr. Untermyer said he did not believe it.

The State taxes in which the city should have a larger share, in Mr. Untermyer's opinion, are the income, gasoline and motor vehicle taxes. Proceeds from all three are now rebated to municipalities on the basis of the assessed valuation of real estate, New York City, contributing the lion's share of these

Continued on Page Two.

£8,600,000 in Death Duty Paid by Ellerman Heirs

Special Cable to THE NEW YORK TIMES.

LONDON, Aug. 14.—The estate of Sir John Ellerman, shipping owner, has been provisionally proved at £17,224,000, the largest the Inland Revenue authorities have ever had to deal with. The whole of this sum is in cash and government securities.

The death duty already paid exceeds £8,600,000.

The figure for the estate, according to The Daily Mail, includes none of the vast interests Sir John had in shipping and many other enterprises. The final total is expected to be about £30,000,000.

Sir John Reeves Ellerman had a controlling interest in six or more major British shipping companies at the time of his death, July 17.

CHINA FLOOD COVERS 10,000 SQUARE MILES

Yellow River Continues to Overflow—150,000 Already Made Homeless.

STREAM PUSHES TO SOUTH

Frantic Efforts Pressed to Prevent It From Returning to Its Former Bed.

By HALLETT ABEND.

Wireless to THE NEW YORK TIMES.

SHANGHAI, Tuesday, Aug. 15.—More than 50,000 Chinese are homeless and destitute as a result of the floods of the Yellow River in Honan and Hopei Provinces, and more than twice that number, it is believed, are destitute in Shantung Province, making the total number of homeless more than 150,000.

A vast region between Kaifeng and Lanfeng, in Honan Province, and Chenchiao, in Hopei, to the north, is under water. and many rescue boats have capsized in the turgid waters. For seventy miles from Chengchow, about fifty miles west of Kaifeng, to Kwangsu, southward of Chengchow, and to Kunghsien, on the west, no land is visible. The Peiping-Hankow Railway's bridge foundations are endangered.

[The flooded region described above is more than 10,000 square miles in area and does not include the perhaps even greater flooded region in Shantung Province or the other areas along the great course of the Yellow River that have been inundated.]

Frantic Efforts Made.

Reports from the Kiangsu-Honan border describe the frantic efforts being made to prevent the flood waters from returning to the old bed of the Yellow River, abandoned by the stream in 1852.

From Minchiuan, on the Lunghai Railway, east of Kweiteh, in Honan Province, flood waters are pouring into the city of Lin Ho, sixty miles east of Kaifeng, and are flowing toward Northern Anhwai Province. They are likely to join the Hwai River, which flows under the Lunghai Railway into the lakes north of Nanking.

An inspection of the old riverbed, once heavily diked, revealed ten serious breaks in the dikes, and attempts are being made to repair them before the flood arrives.

Thousands Believed Lost.

By The Associated Press.

SHANGHAI, Aug. 14.—Several thousand persons are believed to have been drowned by the rampant Yellow River, the flooding waters

Continued on Page Eight.

DRESS UNIONS VOTE STRIKE OF 60,000; NRA SEEKS PEACE

Efforts to Reconcile Clash Over Code Fail—Walkout Tomorrow Likely.

WHALEN IS 'NOT NEUTRAL'

Demands Fair Wages and End of Sweatshops—Publicity on Code Complaints Barred.

The local NRA movement faced last night its first major problem, a threatened strike of 60,000 dressmakers, after having recieved earlier in the day the support of 800 persons representing practically every field of business and civic activity here.

Coincidentally, the NRA executive committee adopted a resolution safeguarding concerns under investigation, but providing that proved violators of the President's Agreement and the details of their cases might, "in the discretion of the committee," be made public.

The strike of the dressmakers was decided upon last night by a vote of 12,146 to 463 in a referendum conducted by the joint board of the Dress and Waist Makers Union and the International Ladies Garment Workers' Union.

Meanwhile the employers in the National Dress Manufacturers Association decided by a unanimous vote to sign the President's Agreement. Their meeting in the Hotel New Yorker was addressed by Grover A. Whalen, head of the New York recovery drive, and Earl Dean Howard, deputy administrator of the National Recovery Administration, who has been in charge of negotiations preliminary to the adoption of codes in the needle trades.

New NRA Interpretation.

Another development was a new interpretation of the National Recovery Administration rules by Mark Eisner, who is in charge of the local interpretation bureau. He said that although the Merchants Association and the State Chamber of Commerce had been designated by the NRA to grant stays to worthy concerns seeking relief under one clause of the President's agreement, other representative trade organizations generally had jurisdicition to perform the same function.

That a larger strike vote was not cast by the dress workers last night was due to the fact that the referendum was confined largely to Manhattan and Brooklyn, according to Julius Hochman, president of the joint board of the Dress and Waist Makers' Union.

The strike vote affects workers in New York City and suburban communities of New Jersey and Connecticut. In New York 60 per cent of the workers are women, and in New Jersey the percentage of women is even higher, according to Mr. Hochman.

Union Chairmen Meet Tonight.

A secret meeting of the local chairmen has been called for tonight in Webster Hall, Eleventh Street and Third Avenue, to set the date for the strike, and in union circles it was reported last night that the strike would be called tomorrow. Mr. Hochman and David Dubinsky, president of the International Ladies' Garment Workers' Union, will address the local chairmen. According to Mr. Hochman, a strike is practically inevitable, despite the efforts that have been made by the local NRA organization to avert the clash.

Mr. Hochman said he had been informed that the National Associa-

Continued on Page Thirteen.

Marconi Short Wave Heard Over Mountains, Proving Solid Objects Do Not Block Rays

By The Associated Press.

ROME, Aug. 14.—Communication with ultra short waves only a foot and a half long through or around physical obstacles was reported here today before the science department of the Royal Academy by Guglielmo Marconi, noted Italian wireless inventor.

In a series of tests conducted between the inventor's yacht Elettra in the Tyrrhenian Sea and inland Italy, Signor Marconi said, both radiophone and radiotelegraph messages had been exchanged with the experimental station at Santa Margherita, 94 miles inland.

Even with the Elettra anchored at Porto Santo Stefano, 161 miles from Santa Margherita, faint code messages on a 60-centimetre wave were picked up on the yacht, despite two intervening mountainous promontories, indicating that the short waves were not hindered by such opaque objects.

Twenty-five watts of power were used, Signor Marconi said, in a newly developed short wave combined transmitter and receiver. He added that he hoped through the development of more sensitive apparatus to be able to bring about further important advancements in radio communication.

This latest announcement by Signor Marconi would indicate that the heretofore generally accepted theory that ultra short waves are limited to the range of vision does not hold altogether true.

Engineers had believed that these waves would travel only as far as the eye could see from the top of a high building, at the most sixty miles. They also believed that such opaque objects as buildings and mountains had the same effect on these waves as would be in the case with a searchlight or other form of light beam.

This condition, they believed, was due to the fact that the tiny waves were so close to the light spectrum that their action was similar.

Opera Will Be Given at Stadium In New Bid for Public Interest

'Madame Butterfly' to Be Presented at City College Next Monday With Tickets at 25 Cents to $1—Experiment Is an Innovation for the Philharmonic Orchestra.

In an effort to stimulate public interest in a season none too successful financially, the management of the concerts by the Philharmonic-Symphony Orchestra at the Lewisohn Stadium will experiment with the production of opera, it became known yesterday. The first presentation will be Puccini's "Madame Butterfly" next Monday evening.

The Stadium authorities were influenced in making this decision, it is understood, by the success of popular-priced opera at the New York Hippodrome during the last ten weeks.

Giuseppe Bamboschek, formerly of the Metropolitan Opera and more recently of the Hippodrome, will conduct the performance on Monday night, according to present plans. Anne Roselle of the Philadelphia Grand Opera Company will have the role of Cio-Cio-San and Dimitri Onofrei, a member of the Hippodrome company, will be in the rôle of Pinkerton, the leading tenor part. A selection for the important baritone rôle, that of the Consul, has not yet been made, but Claudio Frigerio, formerly of the Metropolitan, probably will appear in the rôle. The orchestra will be the Philharmonic-Symphony.

The present Stadium season will close on Wednesday evening, Aug. 23. "Madame Butterfly" will be the only operatic presentation this season. But the production is considered important because it marks a definite shift in policy that may continue in future seasons.

The furthest that these concerts have gone toward meeting the operatic masterpieces in the past has been the presentation of excerpts, either with soloists or chorus or both. Outside of spectacles like those offered by various dance groups, which have met considerable public response at the Stadium, the concerts have devoted themselves exclusively to the symphonic répertoire.

It will be an innovation for the

Continued on Page Four

OGBURN QUITS POST, WARNING JOHNSON

Consumers' Interests Are Not Being Properly Safeguarded, Sociologist Declares.

'NO FEUD' WITH CHAIRMAN

But He Feels Program Will Fail Unless Price and Purchase Indexes Are Developed.

Special to THE NEW YORK TIMES.

WASHINGTON, Aug. 14.—Charging that consumers' interests were not being adequately protected under the national recovery program, Professor William F. Ogburn of the University of Chicago resigned today from the Consumers Advisory Board.

In a memorandum to General Hugh S. Johnson, the Recovery Administrator, Professor Ogburn denied that there had been a feud between himself and the chairman of the consumers' board, Mrs. Mary H. Rumsey.

He again declined membership on the Central Statistical Board, to which he had been transferred without his advance knowledge.

The sociologist had called to see General Johnson today at the latter's request. He waited for some time, and when the Recovery Administrator, without seeing him, left for the White House, Professor Ogburn turned his memorandum over to General Johnson's secretary. He is to leave for Chicago tomorrow.

In the memorandum Professor Ogburn indicated that the NRA was moving in the direction of the cartelization of industry, and pointed out that "the voices of the consumers will undoubtedly be loud in the coming years on this issue, as is shown from the German experience with cartels."

Mr. Ogburn declared that unless indexes of prices and of purchasing power were developed in connection with the NRA program, consumers would not be protected and the movement would be endangered.

He took occasion to criticize a committee of which General Johnson's wife was recently made chairman by Mrs. Rumsey: the complaint committee.

In this connection he said that during his absence and without his knowledge complaints of consumers were relegated to "a group inadequately equipped to learn the facts of costs and prices, which are the topics of most complaints."

Ogburn's Memorandum.

The memorandum reads:

General Hugh S. Johnson,
Director, National Recovery Administration,
Washington, D. C.

Dear General Johnson:

When I called to see you Saturday and offered my resignation you asked me to remain. In view of all of the circumstances, however, I have decided I can best serve the consuming public and NRA by withdrawing, thereby leaving you free to effect such reorganization of the consumers' unit of NRA as you may desire.

May I say at once, however, that there is no personal feud between myself and the chairman of the Consumers' Advisory Board? Also, I scarcely need emphasize that I am not interested in "holding a job" for myself as the headlines of the press indicate. I came to Washington at some sacrifice in order to do my

Continued on Page Twelve.

MULROONEY WANTS CRIMINALS EXILED

Use of Lash and 'American Devil's Island' Proposed at Senate Racket Hearing.

MARTIAL LAW SUGGESTED

Lawes Says President Should Control Situation Pending Change in Constitution.

A wide variety of weapons for use in a nation-wide war on organized crime was proposed yesterday to United States Senator Royal S. Copeland's subcommittee investigating racketeering.

Edward P. Mulrooney, chairman of the State Alcoholic Beverage Control Board and former Police Commissioner, advocated public application of the lash and exile to a criminal colony like the French "Devil's Island" for habitual offenders.

Warden Lewis E. Lawes of Sing Sing favored modified martial law by Presidential proclamation pending adoption of a constitutional amendment and legislation eliminating State lines so far as the war on criminals is concerned. He said he could stamp out racketeering in sixty days if he were a Mussolini.

Others for Milder Measure.

Most of those who appeared at the committee's first hearing, which was held in the auditorium of the Association of the Bar of the City of New York, favored measures less extreme, such as tightening up existing statutes and broadening the police power of the Federal government, especially in kidnapping cases.

A central Federal bureau of crime detection along the lines of the popular conception of Scotland Yard seemed to be favored by Senator Copeland. Many of the police officials welcomed the idea of a Federal agency to "cooperate" with them, but expressed no great enthusiasm at the prospect of being superseded by Federal agents in the investigation of local crimes.

One proposal that was advanced by the local Federal Bar Association, which was represented by Robert Daru, chairman of its committee on racketeering, already has been submitted to General Hugh S. Johnson, Administrator of the National Recovery Act, it was learned.

Would Use NRA as Curb.

This plan is to have a clause inserted in codes of fair competition granting the Federal Government the right, upon complaint from any responsible source, to require business men to explain extraordinary expenditures for "entertainment" and similar otherwise unexplained items.

By this means, according to sponsors of the idea, the reluctance of business men to testify against racketeers in the face of threatened reprisals might be overcome. District Attorney Crain, who urged that prosecuting officials be given the power to subpoena witnesses and examine them under oath, and Grover A. Whalen, head of the New York City NRA campaign and former Police Commissioner, both said the reluctance of business men to help themselves was one of the most serious obstacles to effective prosecution of racketeering.

Two men prominently identified with President Roosevelt's admin-

Continued on Page Three.

URSCHEL ABDUCTOR CAPTURED IN TEXAS ON A LONELY RANCH

Bailey, a Man of Many Crimes, Including the Kansas City Massacre, Is Taken.

PLANE'S COURSE GAVE CLUE

Oil Man's Alertness Solved Case—A Dozen Others Are Held by Federal Agents.

Special to THE NEW YORK TIMES.

DALLAS, Aug. 14.—Harvey J. Bailey, alleged leader in three of the most sensational crimes in many months, and a dozen other persons were under arrest tonight here, in St. Paul and in Denver as the Department of Justice realized its first major triumph in the recently undertaken war against kidnapping and racketeering.

Trapped as he slept, with a machine gun and an automatic pistol beside his cot in the backyard of a lonely ranch seven miles south of Paradise, Texas, Bailey was captured without resistance by a party of Federal agents and Dallas and Fort Worth police.

On him was a "substantial sum" of the $199,620 in marked $20 bills paid as ransom by the family of Charles F. Urschel, wealthy Oklahoma oil man who was held prisoner on the ranch for nine days last month. Urschel's fingerprints were found on a bed, a bench and a drinking glass in a shack on the ranch.

Also Kansas City Gunman.

Bailey has also been identified positively by several witnesses as the operator of the machine gun which murdered four peace officers and Frank Nash, ex-convict, in front of the Union Station in Kansas City, the Federal agents announced. He was a leader in the Memorial Day jailbreak from the Kansas penitentiary at Lansing, in which eleven convicts escaped.

The round-up of Bailey and five companions on the Wise County Ranch took place early Saturday but was kept secret by the Federal agents, who hoped to trap other members of the gang.

The arrest of George Bates in Denver followed today and four other suspects were being held in St. Paul, but those most eagerly sought, Wilbur Underhill, leader of the Lansing break, and George Kelly, are still at large.

Urschel's Alertness a Factor.

Urschel's alertness during his nine-day imprisonment made possible the round-up of the gang, it became known today. He noticed that every morning and late afternoon an airplane passed over the shack in which he was held. But one Sunday afternoon it failed to appear, and he made a mental note of the date.

After his release near Norman, Okla., Federal agents began a systematic check of all airline schedules in an attempt to identify the plane, The Associated Press reported from Fort Worth, Texas. At first they thought he had been hidden in Southern Oklahoma, but their check-up proved this to have been impossible.

They decided that it must have been on the American Airways route between Amarillo and Fort Worth, probably nearer the latter city. Then they interviewed pilots and ground-radio operators and learned that on the day Urschel had missed the plane the pilot had swerved from his course because of bad weather.

This left a comparatively small area, which was carefully searched with binoculars from the air and also from the ground. Because of the number of high-powered cars

Continued on Page Three.

Destroyer Going to Cuba Sets Canal Speed Record

Special Cable to THE NEW YORK TIMES.

BALBOA, C. Z., Aug. 14.—Under orders to proceed to Manzanillo, Cuba, to protect American lives and property, the destroyer Sturtevant set a record today when she completed transit of the Panama Canal and arrived at Cristobal five hours seven minutes after having left Balboa.

The Sturtevant cleared Cristobal at 12:35 P. M. She is in command of Lieut. Commander E. R. Henning and has 110 men, including a complement of marines, aboard.

The cruiser Richmond started transit of the canal before noon under Rear Admiral W. S. Crosley, commanding the Special Service Squadron, accompanied by the destroyer Overton.

DESTROYER RETIRES AS CUBA IS CALMER

Washington Withdraws the Claxton, Leaving Only the Taylor in Havana Harbor.

SHIPS' PRESENCE USEFUL

Linked to End of Violence —Welles Indicates New President Is Popular.

Special to THE NEW YORK TIMES.

WASHINGTON, Aug. 14.—With conditions in Havana quieter today, the Navy Department announced tonight that the destroyer Claxton had been ordered to leave Havana and go to the naval base at Guantanamo. Thus, only the destroyer Taylor was left in Havana Harbor.

The most critical stage of the Cuban revolution, in the opinion of State Department officials, passed off in relative quiet late last night and early this morning. The avoidance of more widespread mob violence and looting was attributable at least in part, it was believed, to the presence in Havana Harbor of the United States destroyers.

The moral effect of the presence of these two small vessels far outweighed the potential power of the American forces, as there are only about seventy men on each ship. The need for the presence of any ships is virtually at an end, it was said. State Department officials denied any further warships had been requested to proceed to Cuban waters.

Denies Richmond Is Going.

"Reports indicating that the Richmond is proceeding to Cuba are without foundation," Secretary Swanson said today. "The Richmond is now en route through the Panama Canal from Balboa to Colon, on the Atlantic side, where she will await whatever orders the Navy Department will issue."

The Richmond is a cruiser and flagship of the Special Service Squadron in the Caribbean. In addition to the crew of bluejackets, the cruiser carries a marine guard of about seventy men.

No question of recognition by the United States of the de Céspedes government arises, Jefferson Caffery, Assistant Secretary of State, said today. After a careful study of the procedure in Cuba, the State Department decided that the change in personnel of the government had been carried out along thoroughly constitutional lines. The United States takes the position that no change in government has taken place, but merely that new office-holders have taken the governmental positions under the Cuban Constitution.

Unofficially, the view is taken here that the de Céspedes govern-

Continued on Page Ten.

Taxi Fleet to Give 25% Refund on Fares In Test to Operate on 15-Cent-a-Mile Basis

Reduction of taxicab rates to 15 cents a mile, notwithstanding the recent refusal of the Police Department to license 15-cent meters, will be undertaken this week by a group of independent operators, it was announced yesterday.

Otto Gutfreund, president of the Taxicab Industry Service Bureau, Inc., and Sidney Rogers Lubin, his counsel, declared that a test fleet of low-rate cabs would be sent out from the W. J. & S. Garage, 309 West Ninety-seventh Street, probably tomorrow. These will carry the present 20-cents-a-mile, or 15 and 5 meters.

A sign on the cab, however, will announce a 25 per cent refund, so that the passenger will pay only three-fourths of the amount appearing on the meter.

Should police order the test cabs off the streets, the sponsors of the low rate will take court action, on the ground that the Police Department has no authority to prescribe a minimum fare, Mr. Lubin stated.

Mr. Gutfreund said that rate reductions in Chicago and Cleveland have resulted in doubling the business done by taxicab owners. He declared that the independent operators, were generally of the opinion that the same result would follow here, but had been unable to put the lower fare into effect because of the ban on low-rate meters.

Deputy Police Commissioner Felix Muldoon, who refused on Aug. 3 to sanction the new meters, said at the time that it would be best to defer action on the plan until after a code is adopted by the taxicab industry under the National Recovery Act. If a minimum rate were fixed in such a code it might make the low-rate meters obsolescent almost as soon as they were installed, he pointed out.

An effort by the independents, through Mr. Lubin as counsel, to obtain a writ of mandamus in Supreme Court was blocked by an adjournment until next month. The adjournment was ordered on a similar plea by the Corporation Counsel's office that a code might be adopted.

NEW CABINET TAKES CONTROL IN HAVANA; LABOR ENDS STRIKE

Army Tightens Control and Violence Subsides While the City Resumes Activities.

PRESIDENT GETS OVATION

De Cespedes Pleads for United Nation to Prove 'Capacity for Self-Government.'

AMERICANS WIN APPLAUSE

Welles and Naval Officers Hailed at Cabinet Ceremony—Students Hunt Machado Officials.

By J. D. PHILLIPS.

Special Cable to THE NEW YORK TIMES.

HAVANA, Aug. 14.—A new Cuban government, headed by President Carlos Manuel de Céspedes, began to function this morning as the Cabinet was sworn in at 11 o'clock at the Presidential Palace.

In his first address as President, Dr. de Céspedes peaded for a united nation and said bitter passions of conflict would be put aside and Cuba would work to establish peace so as to "leave no doubt of our capacity for self-government in the future."

Meanwhile, Havana began to take on a more normal appearance as the general strike was broken. At noon today street cars and buses started to operate. Business houses began to open cautiously.

Normal Operations Today.

This morning only cafés opened although they had little to serve because of the lack of deliveries. In the afternoon many merchants opened their establishments with what clerks appeared to work, and it is expected the city will resume normal business operations tomorrow. The dock workers are expected to go back to work tomorrow and undoubtedly the other unions will gradually follow, as the basis for the entire movement was really the presence in office of President Gerardo Machado and the other grievances were subordinate.

There was continuous broadcasting this morning telling of the new régime and appealing to the public to remain calm. The laboring classes especially were appealed to by leaders in commerce and industry to return to their jobs immediately so that all the wheels of transportation and industry could be placed in motion for the welfare of the nation as a whole.

The army in Havana and in the interior tightened control today to prevent further looting of homes and businesses belonging to Machado adherents. The first frenzy of the people had spent itself during the past two days, however, so that little rioting occurred in the city today. But the hunt for members of La Porra, the Machado murder squad, went on and four more were killed.

The United States destroyers Claxton and Taylor, which arrived here early this morning, lay at anchor in Havana harbor all day. At 7:30 o'clock tonight, however, the Claxton departed.

President Gets Ovation.

President de Céspedes arrived at the Palace shortly after 10:30 o'clock this morning on his first visit to the President's official home since his inauguration yesterday. He immediately went out on a second floor balcony accompanied by his aides and smilingly bowed for several minutes as a great crowd surrounding the Palace gave him an ovation.

Then going indoors, the President signed the decrees necessary for each Cabinet appointment, after which the oath of office was administered to each official, who took his place behind his chair at the Cabinet table. Dr. de Céspedes advised Secretary of Justice Saladrigas that he was to fill the office of Secretary of State ad interim.

This correspondent and another foreign correspondent were the only press representatives to witness the ceremonies of signing the decrees and administering the oaths. The salons were immediately cleared of the few persons who had attended the ceremonies and the first Cabinet meeting of the new régime began.

United States Ambassador Sumner Welles, accompanied by his military attaché, Colonel Thomas N. Gimperling and Lieut. Commanders George T. Howard and Kenneth Lloyd-Jones, commanders of the United States destroyers Taylor and Claxton, visited the palace shortly before noon. Mr. Welles chatted informally with all secretaries. The crowd roundly applauded the United States diplomatic and naval officials as they left the palace.

The new Cabinet greatly strengthens the de Céspedes go-

Continued on Page Ten

NRA MEMBER U.S. WE DO OUR PART

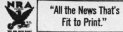

"All the News That's Fit to Print."

The New York Times.

LATE CITY EDITION
WEATHER—Partly cloudy today, tomorrow; temperature unchanged
Temperatures Yesterday—Max., 72; min., 49.

Copyright, 1933, by The New York Times Company.

VOL. LXXXIII....No. 27,652. Entered as Second-Class Matter. Postoffice, New York, N. Y. NEW YORK, MONDAY, OCTOBER 9, 1933. P TWO CENTS In New York City. | THREE CENTS Within 200 Miles | FOUR CENTS Elsewhere Except in 7th and 8th Postal Zones

CRILE ADVANCES LIFE RAY THEORY AS MEDICAL BASIS

Says Wave-Lengths, as in Radio, Emanate From Body and Set Its Course.

FUTURE DIAGNOSIS GUIDE

'Tuning In' for Assurance of Health or 'SOS' Predicted At Surgeons' Session.

NEW CONTROL IN PROSPECT

He Now Looks to Applying Physical and Chemical Laws to Modify Radiations.

By WILLIAM L. LAURENCE.
Special to THE NEW YORK TIMES.

CHICAGO, Oct. 8.—The processes of life and the mystery of mind and matter involve a mechanism very similar to a radio set, depending for their growth, development and functioning on a definite series of radiations of various wave lengths, emanating from the living substance of the body.

This, in essence, was reported today at the opening of the Century of Progress congress of the American College of Surgeons by Dr. George W. Crile of Cleveland, who addressed a gathering of eminent surgeons from all parts of this country and abroad at the Hall of Science on the exposition grounds.

The medical man of the future, Dr. Crile said, would "tune in" on the living body as one does now on the ordinary radio. By "listening in" to the short-waves and the long-waves, transmitted by the various organs, he would hear the "symphony" played by the living organism and would determine the rhythms of the "dance of life."

Long before there was any outward evidence of disease, the physician-radio-engineer of the future would thus be enabled to tell by the "reception" of the "life-waves" whether they were playing a melody of health or whether they were signalling an SOS.

Effects of Rays on Body.

The life rays, Dr. Crile added, have a range of wave-lengths from the ultra-violet, through the visible spectrum, down to the infra-red. These rays are generated and emitted during life and change with the state of activity of the protoplasm.

They are increased during malignant processes, such as cancer, and by such drugs as thyroxin and caffeine, and are decreased by anesthetics and narcotics.

The short wave-lengths emanated by the body, Dr. Crile stated, have the power to modify atoms and to build up organic compounds; that is, the power to create protoplasm or living matter. A long wavelength does not possess the power of modifying an atom and is thus incapable of producing a living thing.

"It is a proper balance of the infra-red, the visible, and the ultraviolet radiations that makes possible the building up of the dynamic mechanism which we call protoplasm," Dr. Crile said.

"On this conception, protoplasm is no more mysterious than is a combustion engine. In either case the energy depends upon oxidation in the course of which solar energy is released.

"It now appears probable that when we wish to increase the activity of the brain, for example, it is necessary to alter the wave-lengths so as to increase the percentage of the short-wave radiation within the brain, and this is done by increasing the oxidation within the brain by the action of the thyroid gland and the adrenal gland."

Life as "A Series of Explosions."

It is being established now, Dr. Crile continued, that there is a great similarity between the chemical behavior of nitro-explosives, such as dynamite, and that of the nitrogen compounds found in protoplasm. Life, in other words, is in itself a form of "explosion," or series of explosions.

"As radical researches have progressed," Dr. Crile said, in discussing the "advancing frontiers of medicine," "it has become increasingly evident that the phenomena of life, like the phenomena of the inanimate world, are dependent upon physical and chemical laws—that is, that protoplasm is not a specialized structure requiring special laws for its control.

"Advancement in the biological sciences must, therefore, in the future depend upon the fundamental sciences of physics and chemistry.

"Already a rapid penetration into the mysteries of protoplasm has been made by the application of physical and chemical laws, and we

Continued on Page Four.

393 Miles an Hour Flown By Italian for a Record

By The Associated Press.

ANCONA, Italy, Oct. 8.—A new air-speed-record over a 100-kilometer course of 393.33 miles an hour was established by Lieut. Col. Guglielmo Cassinelli, officials reported today.

The flier is second in command of the high-speed school at Desenzano, where Lieutenant Francesco Agello last Spring made a world record of 426½ miles an hour on a five-lap course.

Lieut. Col. Cassinelli's machine was a Macchi seaplane, powered with a 2,400-horsepower Fiat engine similar to Lieutenant Agello's Red Bullet, holder of the triangular course record between Ancona, Pesaro and Falconara.

Major Pietro Scapinelli, probably using the Red Bullet with a lighter motor, expects to try for the Bleriot Trophy for a plane flying 300 kilometers at a speed of more than 375 miles an hour next Sunday.

AMPHIBIAN PLANE SETS WORLD MARK

De Seversky Drives Craft 177.79 Miles an Hour at Charity Air Pageant.

WOMAN SURPASSES MEN

Mrs. Kenyon Wins Trophy—An 11,000-Foot Parachute Jump Nearly a Tragedy.

Special to THE NEW YORK TIMES.

ROOSEVELT FIELD, L. I., Oct. 8.—With 50,000 persons on the grounds of this airport and many more occupying every vantage point and in parked cars, the national charity air pageant ended this afternoon.

A world's speed record for amphibian planes was set by Major Alexander P. de Seversky, veteran of the Russian Imperial Air Force, who lost a leg in the world war. In the SV-1 of his own design, with a 325-horsepower Wright engine, he averaged 177.79 miles an hour.

Amateur pilots, army bombing and pursuit planes, racing fliers, parachute jumpers and autogiro pilots thrilled the audience. The Seventh Regiment, New York National Guard, 1,000 strong, under command of Colonel Ralph Tobin, lent an added military note.

Major de Seversky took off the amphibian low-wing monoplane from the water at Glenn Curtiss Airport, North Beach, Queens, and came in over the field in mid-afternoon.

Sweeping in from the west he made the first run at 175.63 miles an hour. Swinging around in the eastern sky, he came back at 179.87 miles an hour, according to the electric timing device. Once more he shuttled from west to east at 176.14 and then roared down the final run at 179.53 miles an hour.

First Test in New Category.

A new category for records for amphibians was established last June by the Federation Aeronautique Internationale. Under the rules, the take-off and landing must be from water before and after the runs over the land. Seversky's was the first official trial in the new category.

James R. Wedell of Patterson, La., in his Wedell-Williams, in which he set the world's landplane record at 305 miles an hour last month, tried to better that mark. After covering the three-

Continued on Page Three.

GERMANY APPEALS TO DAVIS FOR AID IN ARMS DISPUTE

Geneva Delegate Asks Him to Arrange Conference With French on New Differences.

BERLIN EXPLAINS DEMANDS

Foreign Office Denies Seeking Equality, Only Weapons for 'Training Purposes.'

By The Associated Press.

GENEVA, Oct. 8.—Norman H. Davis, United States delegate to the disarmament conference, is expected to arrange a conference between the representatives of France and Germany in which they can thresh out their armament differences.

A request that he use his good offices to arrange such a conference was made today by Dr. Rudolf Nadolny, German representative, when he called on the American Ambassador at Large shortly after his arrival in Geneva.

Captain Anthony Eden, British Under-Secretary for Foreign Affairs, also arrived here today and conferred with Mr. Davis.

Peace of Europe Menaced.

On the eve of the disarmament conference, observers find the situation grave for the peace of Europe but not desperate.

The outstanding event of the past week, regarded as an encouragement to success, is Germany's move to be admitted on a basis of equality and frankness into five-power conversations with Great Britain, France, the United States and Italy.

The statesmen assembled here are awaiting results of the British Cabinet meeting tomorrow which is expected to decide whether Britain will back France in her decision that there must be no rearmament of Germany and that there must be a period of trial after which Germany would be allowed certain armaments.

Mr. Davis found Dr. Nadolny conciliatory and wishing to reach a disarmament agreement. Dr. Nadolny said he wanted particularly to talk with the French and asked Mr. Davis to arrange such a meeting.

Franco-German Accord Vital.

The American delegates realize that a Franco-German understanding is essential if disarmament is to get anywhere.

Tomorrow's meeting of the steering committee of the conference probably will be devoted to a speech by Arthur Henderson, president of the conference, summarizing the efforts to conciliate the theses.

Both the British and the Americans, who are hostile to the idea of adjournment, expect that the forthcoming week will permit constructive Franco-German conversations.

A French spokesman said France stood solidly by the disarmament accord reached in Paris and added that he was confident the British Cabinet would stand by France. France believes Germany is building armaments secretly and wants a control of armaments to determine Germany's exact military strength before approving new armaments.

Germany Explains Demands.

Wireless to THE NEW YORK TIMES.

BERLIN, Oct. 8.—The German Foreign Office explained today its disarmament policy as follows:

"It is wholly erroneous that Germany demands parity with France after the expiration of five years. All Germany wants after five years

Continued on Page Nine.

Stars' Invisible Rays Photographed By New Aluminum Mirror Device

Cornell Astronomers, 8,000 Feet Up on Arizona Peak, Use Process Developed at Ithaca to Obtain Record of "Blue Rainbows."

By The Associated Press.

ITHACA, N. Y., Oct. 8.—The "blue rainbows" of nearly 100 stars, made by their ultra-violet rays, have been caught with a new aluminum mirror by Cornell astronomers and physicists on top of an 8,000-foot mountain peak in Arizona.

This announcement, made public tonight, indicates that one of the "blind sides" of radiation from all stars has been opened on a grand scale for observation by scientists.

The invisible rays, all of them a blue darker than anything the eye can detect, are reflected by the mirror to photographic plates. The photos record the light as spectra, or rays broken into bands of blue of varying hues, which merge into one another the same as the colors of the visible rainbow.

These color bands appear as straight lines, standing side by side, like pickets in a fence. Each line is an unmistakable sign of some temperature or some electrical condition in the distant star. Each shows the condition and the action of either masses of molecules or masses of the still smaller atoms.

Each indicates also what kind of substance these molecules and atoms are made of. All the lines reveal conditions which do not appear in the visible light of stars.

The precise meanings of these blue rainbow lines have been learned in laboratories, where the ultra-violet spectrum of light has been under close study for years. But it has not been easy to get clear pictures of the ultra-violet spectrum of stars.

This invisible light is absorbed by the silver which ordinarily has been used for astronomical mirrors. But aluminum reflects it to a high degree, and makes it easier to get good ultra-violet images.

The mirror was developed by R. C. Williams of the Cornell physics department. So promising were the tests here that the National Research Council and the Heckscher Council financed an expedition to Arizona. S. L. Boothroyd, Professor of Astronomy, headed a party including Mr. Williams, R. W. Shaw, George Sabine and H. C. Ketcham. They set up their instruments on Schultze Peak, about fifteen miles from Flagstaff.

DALADIER PLEDGES DEFENSE OF FRANC

Bars Devaluation and Says if Budget Balancing Plan Is Rejected He Will Quit.

INSISTS ON ARMS CONTROL

Asks at Party Session Why Reich Protests Peace Aims While Nazis Drill for War.

By P. J. PHILIP.
Wireless to THE NEW YORK TIMES.

VICHY, France, Oct. 8.—With France and Europe listening, Premier Edouard Daladier at the closing dinner of the congress of his party here today made it clear that he did not consider himself master of events.

Devalorization of the franc—that was for Parliament and the country to decide.

Disarmament—that was for Germany to determine.

For himself, for his government and for his party, he confined his clear announcements to this:

His government, backed by the Radical Socialist party, will, when Parliament resumes on Oct. 17, present a financial program that will insure the safety of the franc and complete re-establishment of financial stability or "France will have another government."

France's Stand on Arms.

Moreover, France will not disarm by a single rifle without a sincere and loyal international agreement which organizes progressive disarmament assured by the establishment of permanent, automatic control.

The Premier kept returning again and again to the question of finance. He did not spare his predecessors who had converted a Treasury surplus of 17,000,000,000 francs into a deficit by the time the Left parties came into office sixteen months ago. In that sixteen months, he contended, much has been done to redress the alarming situation, but the last obstacles are still to be overcome.

His audience of nearly 3,000 militant Radical Socialists from all over the country heard almost in silence the warning that he conveyed in half a dozen different phrases that unless the budget were balanced, unless the Chamber responded to the government's plea and unless there were real economy and real sacrifice the only course would be for the franc to join the dollar and the pound and seek again its economical level.

Will Strive to Cut Deficit.

The present government and the Radical Socialist party, he emphasized, will not take the responsibility for a new devalorization of the franc. If their plans for balancing the budget are rejected he will give way to those who reject them, he said. Meanwhile the struggle must go on. The government will strive, he said, to fill up the deficit of 6,000,000,000 francs that it inherited. It will admit no other policy and no other possibility. If it fails, he declared, it is for others to do what they can.

That was the main theme of the Premier's speech. For the rest he gave his party members every kind of assurance that wisdom lay with them and their leaders, but he did not promise them victory.

To Germany M. Daladier held out a small olive branch in much the same way as former Premier

Continued on Page Nine.

COAL PEACE MOVES SLOW IN STARTING

Steel Institute, Including the Owners of Captive Mines, to Meet Here Tomorrow.

OVERTURE MADE BY UNION

Labor Officials Expected to Bring Pressure on Strikers to Return to Work.

Special to THE NEW YORK TIMES.

WASHINGTON, Oct. 8.—President Roosevelt returned this evening from a short boating trip on the Potomac to find no perceptible progress so far in the settlement of the labor troubles in the captive coal mine fields, the principal problem up for administration consideration at present. Meager reports received here during the day indicated few definite moves on the part of either miners or employers to begin negotiations ordered by the President in his statement last night.

It was learned that the directors of the American Iron and Steel Institute will meet in New York on Tuesday to receive the formal communication laid down by the President yesterday. The large steel companies represented in the institute own the captive mines, employing 100,000 men, who are on strike.

The first step toward starting negotiations came from the labor side, according to reports here. Phillip Murray of Pittsburgh, vice president of the United Mine Workers, sent a telegram to Thomas Moses, president of H. O. Coke Company, immediately after he had learned the result of President Roosevelt's conference yesterday with the steel officials, General Hugh S. Johnson and Donald R. Richberg. It is understood here that Mr. Murray offered to start negotiations at once.

Ambiguity Is Charged.

Considerable conjecture was heard today as to whether the strikers in the captive coal mine fields will return to work tomorrow in accordance with the President's recommendation yesterday. In coal circles there was some discussion of possible ambiguity in the White House statement issued last night.

It was said that the apparently studied omission of the two major issues, from the miners' point of view—recognition of the United Mine Workers and acceptance of the check-off—might leave the individual miners uncertain as to their course. It was taken for granted that much pressure would be brought by the officials of the union to get the men to follow the President's instructions.

The charges of ambiguity apparently revolve around paragraphs 2 and 7 of last night's statement. Paragraph 2 said:

"The workers in every captive mine can choose their own representatives for the purpose of collective bargaining."

According to labor sources here, John L. Lewis, president of the United Mine Workers, is fully authorized to represent the captive mine workers. One of the points at issue with the employers has been their unwillingness, until recently, to treat with Mr. Lewis on the ground that they were not convinced he represented their employes. They insisted on treating with their own men.

Fall of Japanese Cabinet Is Threatened As Clash On Military Budget Grows Acute

By HUGH BYAS.
Wireless to THE NEW YORK TIMES.

TOKYO, Monday, Oct. 9.—The budget controversy between the Treasury and the army and the navy over the demands of the armed forces which again are exceptionally large has reached a most acute stage and the press is flooded with political speculations some of which anticipate the fall of the Cabinet.

The fighting services are demanding approximately 1,300,000,000 yen [currently about $360,750,000], a sum equal to an ordinary year's entire revenue. The Treasury is making stubborn efforts to reduce this to about 700,000,000 yen. The Treasury wants the navy demands of 430,000,000 yen for new construction cut to 230,000,000 and the army's special demands of 200,000,000 for Manchuria and 180,000,000 for new equipment cut to about 130,000,000 and 100,000,000 respectively.

The matter is now in the Cabinet's hands and two conferences of the "big five"—Admiral Makoto Saito, Premier; Korekiyo Takahashi, Finance Minister; Koki Hirota, Foreign Minister; General Sadao Araki, War Minister, and Vice Admiral Mineo Osumi, Navy Minister—have failed to bring about an agreement.

General Araki and Vice Admiral Osumi insist that the international outlook indicated in such salient facts as the United States Navy building program, Russian concentrations in Siberia, Great Britain's economic policy and Japan's isolation since quitting the League of Nations demands consolidation of the national defenses as a matter of urgency. The three others are credited in the newspapers with holding that Japan can economize on armaments by seeking diplomatic understandings with Russia, the United States and China as Mr. Hirota proposes. Further meetings of the "Big Five" are to be held.

Few observers expect the peremptory demands of the fighting services to be much reduced although the opposition is growing bolder and some newspapers even predict that a budget carrying excessive military figures will be rejected by the House of Peers.

BUY NOW TO SAVE, JOHNSON APPEALS; DRIVE OPENS TODAY

Better Times Are Here and Prices Are Going Higher, He Tells Consumers.

WARNS AGAINST SKIMPING

130,000 Merchants Here Are Pledged to Sell Goods at 'Fair and Square Prices.'

Special to THE NEW YORK TIMES.

WASHINGTON, Oct. 8.—Declaring that "better times are here," and that "prices are going up," under the stimulus of improved conditions, General Hugh S. Johnson, National Recovery Administrator, in a statement tonight, called upon all consumers to join in the "now is the time to buy" campaign which starts tomorrow. Payrolls cannot be maintained and new jobs created, he said, unless the consumer does his part.

"Industry and trade, cooperating with the government, under codes of fair competition or agreements with the President," said General Johnson, "have done and are doing their part. Hundreds of thousands of men, long idle, have gone to work and millions of dollars have been added to payrolls.

"These payrolls cannot be maintained and new jobs for other hundreds of thousands of workers cannot be made unless every consumer in the land does his or her part now.

Time to Save by Spending.

"The housewives of the country, the purchasing agents who spend 85 per cent of the family income, will realize that now is the time to buy, not only to save money but also because every dollar spent now is helping to keep the wage earner in her family on a payroll.

"For four years the American consumer has been skimping—putting off buying more than bare necessities until 'better times.' Better times are here. There is a new confidence abroad in the land. Men are going back to work. Industry is bringing into the market improved products held back for these better times. Merchants are restocking their shelves and warehouses.

"Better times always mean higher prices. Now is the time to buy for purely selfish reasons. Prices are going up. Buying now is an investment."

Fair Prices Pledged.

Pledges for the maintenance of fair prices are being received from all over the country, it was reported today at the headquarters of the NRA. In hundreds of letters and telegrams addressed to General Johnson increased advertising appropriations as well as new and improved products were reported by business men.

Samples of some of the communications received were quoted, with the names of the firms omitted.

The president of a great retail drug organization wrote:

"Beyond the mere fact of adjusting hours and wages, we are carrying out your other suggestion of making an extra effort to give the public up-to-date, fairly priced merchandise, and have increased our advertising expenditure over anything we have spent in the past three years."

A nationally known men's clothing manufacturer wrote:

"Our company is following

Continued on Page Six.

McKee Seeks to Join Suit Over Emblems on Ballot

Harry M. Durning, campaign manager for Joseph V. McKee's Recovery party, announced yesterday that Harold R. Medina, as counsel for the Recovery party, would seek permission today to intervene in the litigation now going on before Supreme Court Justice Cotillo over the rights of independents to emblems at the heads of their columns on the ballot.

John T. Dooling, chairman of the Tammany Hall law committee, had conceded in court that the independent groups were entitled to separate rows on the voting machines, but contended they were not entitled to use emblems. Mr. Medina is a former law partner of Mr. McKee.

Mr. Durning said wholesale confusion would result if the independents were not permitted to use emblems.

HILLQUIT, LEADER OF SOCIALISTS, DIES

An Organizer of Party in Its Present Form, He Was Often Candidate for High Office.

ACTIVE IN INNER COUNCILS

Delegate to Conferences, He Became a World Figure—Was 64 Years Old.

Morris Hillquit, lawyer, author and Socialist leader, died at his home, 40 East Sixty-sixth Street, shortly before midnight on Saturday. He was 64 years old. Despite an illness of many months, he kept at his work almost to the end. At his death he was national chairman of the Socialist party and his last act, several hours before he died, was the dictation of a letter to the executive committee of the party in Chicago dealing with party matters. Although his illness, for which he had undergone an operation early this year, entailed great suffering, he managed to devote time to writing his memoirs.

Mr. Hillquit became gravely ill after his strenuous work in the Mayoralty campaign of last year, when he headed his party's ticket and received the largest vote ever cast for a Socialist candidate in this city.

Body to Lie in State.

Present at his home at the time of his death were members of the family. News of Mr. Hillquit's passing was made known by his brother, Jacob Hillquit, who was associated with Mr. Hillquit's law firm at 19 West Forty-fourth Street. Besides his brother, he is survived by his widow, Mrs. Vera Hillquit, and their daughter, Nina Hillquit, and Lawrence Hillquit, a son.

The body will be moved from the Universal Chapel at 597 Lexington Avenue to the Debs Auditorium in the People's House, 7 East Fifteenth Street, tomorrow and will lie in state there until evening. A public funeral ceremony will be held on Wednesday, arrangements for which will be announced today. The body will be cremated.

Morris Hillquit was generally regarded as one of the most notable figures produced by the Socialist movement in the United States in the last four decades. While personalities like the late Eugene V. Debs were considered as perhaps

Continued on Page Seventeen.

RIVALS PUT O'BRIEN THIRD IN THE RACE; NEW TALK OF SHIFT

McKee and LaGuardia Backers View Mayoralty Fight as Only Between Them.

RESULTS OF POLLS CITED

Indicate Recovery Nominee in Lead—Heavy Registration Likely to Hurt Mayor.

MOVE TO DROP HIM HINTED

McCooey and Theofel Are Said to Favor a Substitution, but Curry Is Opposed.

By JAMES A. HAGERTY.

With the city election four weeks away, the indications yesterday were that the race for the Mayoralty would be between F. H. LaGuardia, Republican-Fusion candidate, and Joseph V. McKee, independent Democrat.

This view, of course, is not accepted by Tammany, leaders of which hope and expect to re-elect Mayor John P. O'Brien in the bitterest local political fight since Tammany Hall faced political attack by the County Democracy nearly two generations ago.

Though it is entirely too early to place Mayor O'Brien out of the running in view of the possibility of the Tammany candidate developing undisclosed strength and the organization drawing on secret resources, it is a fact that the supporters of Mr. McKee believe that Major LaGuardia is the man he will have to beat to be elected Mayor, and the leaders of the Fusion movement believe that their main battle will be with the ticket headed by the former acting Mayor. Both in the Fusion camp in the Paramount Theatre Building and at McKee headquarters in the Biltmore Hotel, it is the expectation of the leaders that Mayor O'Brien will finish third.

Polls Are Cited.

This belief that the Tammany entry in the Mayoralty sweepstakes will win neither first nor second place, which would be an unprecedented event in the city's political history, has been strengthened by the results of polls taken in various sections of the city, in most of which Mayor O'Brien has been third.

Although John F. Curry, leader of Tammany, is reported still to be confident that Mayor O'Brien can be re-elected, there has been a revival of the suggestion that Mayor O'Brien should be withdrawn and a candidate regarded as stronger be substituted. This would still be possible if Dennis O'Leary Cohalan, candidate for Supreme Court Justice, should decline the nomination given him by the convention last Tuesday night and Mayor O'Brien be named in his place by the committee to fill vacancies.

Chiefs Said to Want Shift.

John H. McCooey, Brooklyn leader, and John Theofel, Democratic leader in Queens, were said to believe a shift in the head of the ticket should be made and the suggestion is expected to come up today at a meeting of leaders. Mr. Curry is believed to be opposed to a change and there is the additional difficulty of getting another candidate. Former Governor Alfred E. Smith has been mentioned as the only man who could be substituted for Mayor O'Brien and almost certainly win, but there is great doubt that Mr. Smith would consent to run, even if the nomination should be offered him, as he said before Mayor O'Brien was nominated at the primary election that in no circumstances would he be a candidate.

Should a decision be reached to take Mayor O'Brien out of the race for Mayor, Mr. Cohalan would have to resign the Supreme Court nomination by Thursday or Friday night.

Interest in Surveys.

Particular interest is being shown by the campaign managers of all three Mayoralty candidates in the survey of The Literary Digest, which has gained a reputation for accuracy of forecast in the last three Presidential campaigns. The result of this poll is supposed to be secret, but information obtained by some of those politically interested is that the first results of the poll with Mr. McKee's name on the ballot showed Major LaGuardia receiving approximately 37,000 votes, Mr. McKee, 25,000, and Mayor O'Brien, 13,000.

These were said to have been the returns of the first few days last week and to have been almost entirely from Manhattan with no returns from the Bronx and Queens, where Mr. McKee is believed to be particularly strong. Returns received later in the week were said to have shown a gain for Mr. Mc-

Continued on Page Two.

Pact on Sugar Stabilization Is Scrapped, But Wallace Still Plans Domestic Crop Cut

By The Associated Press.

WASHINGTON, Oct. 8.—The proposed sugar stabilization agreement has been scrapped by the Roosevelt administration, following conferences between President Roosevelt and Secretary Wallace.

Little or no prospect was seen for revival of the pact, which would have assigned quotas to various producing interests.

Secretary Wallace, the President and other officials have been going over the proposed agreement for several days. Officials said that alternative proposals and modifications were considered and abandoned.

The Farm Adjustment Administration, however, plans to put through "immediately" marketing codes for the beet and domestic cane-sugar areas, Secretary Wallace said. Plans for limitation of production will probably be written into these, but the domestic codes would have no effect upon territorial and Cuban producers.

Developments in Cuba have probably had much to do with the decision to put an end to the efforts to arrive at an agreement which would have limited to about 7,000,000 raw tons the amount of sugar entering domestic commercial channels for the year beginning last July 1.

Secretary Wallace, in a statement, said:

"No action on the proposed sugar marketing agreement is practicable at this time because of changed conditions such as uncertainties regarding Cuban production, and because of difficulties of operation disclosed by further study of the proposed agreement.

"It is, however, proposed to put through immediately the beet sugar and domestic cane sugar marketing codes so far as may be feasible without the basic quota agreement. This does not mean that plans for limitation of production are abandoned."

From the time more than four months ago when drafting a basic sugar agreement began, it was evident that conflicting interests and the wide areas involved made the task a difficult one. President Roosevelt took a hand by directing Dr. John Lee Coulter of the Tariff Commission to approach the various groups with new proposals. Dr. Coulter did so, and representatives of all save Cuba finally approved the basic pact which has been discarded.

"All the News That's Fit to Print."

The New York Times.

LATE CITY EDITION
Mostly cloudy, with occasional showers and moderate temperatures today and tomorrow.
Temperatures Yesterday—Max., 74; Min., 63

Copyright, 1938, by The New York Times Company.

VOL. LXXXVII....No. 29,358. Entered as Second-Class Matter, Postoffice, New York, N. Y. NEW YORK, SATURDAY, JUNE 11, 1938. PP THREE CENTS New York City and Vicinity | FOUR CENTS Elsewhere Except in 7th and 8th Postal Zones.

YOUTH CONFESSES ONLY HE KIDNAPPED, KILLED JIMMY CASH

Insists Child Died Accidentally While Being Carried From His Home

TELLS OF PLANNING CRIME

Hoover Quotes Him as Saying He Wanted Money to Better Wife's Lot

Special to THE NEW YORK TIMES.

MIAMI, June 10.—While the sorrowing parents of little James Bailey Cash Jr. stood at his graveside here late today, Franklin Pierce McCall was transferred from Federal Bureau of Investigation headquarters to the county jail, following a full confession, according to J. Edgar Hoover, FBI chief, that he alone was responsible for the kidnapping and death of the 5-year-old son of the Princeton (Fla.) merchant.

The 21-year-old Princeton farm worker and former occupant of an apartment in the Cash home was transferred secretly to the jail, atop the twenty-five-story county court house, while a milling crowd of several hundred waited for his expected appearance in front of the building in which FBI offices are located.

He had been spirited across a near-by rooftop to a waiting automobile below, which made a quick run to the jail less than a block away.

Mr. Hoover declared that the case was closed so far as Federal investigation was concerned.

McCall steadfastly denied through hours of grilling that he murdered the boy, Mr. Hoover said. McCall insisted that the baby "was dead" after he had carried the child half a mile from the Cash home to his own house. He admitted planning the kidnapping three weeks in advance and visiting the Cash general store at Princeton the night of the kidnapping, to be sure the parents were busy and the way was clear for the crime, Mr. Hoover said.

He quoted the youth as saying he put three folded handkerchiefs over the face of the sleeping child, took him out of his bed and carried him through the rain to his house.

Two Others Escaped Fate

In the confession McCall said he first decided to kidnap the son of Charles Chambers, about the same age as the Cash child. Mr. Chambers owns a grove near Princeton. He eliminated that boy, however, because "he always was with his mother."

He also eliminated the grown son of Charles E. Eichenberger, Princeton grove owner, because the Eichenberger son was about the age of McCall and he feared he might cause too much difficulty.

At the court house, George Worley, State Attorney, assisted by Lawrence A. Truett, an Assistant Attorney General of Florida, was preparing evidence in the case to present to the grand jury next week. Mr. Worley said he would ask indictments for both murder and kidnapping, each a capital crime here.

At the jail McCall was a changed person from the bragging youth who was picked up by Sheriff D. C. Coleman only a few hours after the $10,000 ransom was paid by Mr. Cash for the safe return of his son. This afternoon he appeared to realize the seriousness of his crime. Sheriff Coleman expressed the belief that the youth would plead guilty when brought to trial.

The jailers removed all of McCall's clothes and carefully searched them. They took the laces from his shoes and his belt from his trousers, and put a guard at his cell door to present a possible suicide.

Summary of Confession

By The Associated Press.

MIAMI, Fla., June 10.—Here is Franklin Pierce McCall's eight-page confession in the Cash kidnapping case as summarized by J. Edgar Hoover in an interview:

"We have a full and complete confession from F. P. McCall admitting the kidnapping of the child, the death of the child and the placing of the body, as well as his previous statements that he wrote the ransom notes, collected the ransom, hid the money and disposed of the shoebox in which it was paid.

"He claimed he wanted the better things of life for his wife and himself and had been unable to get steady employment. About two weeks before the kidnapping he conceived the idea to kidnap some person in or about Princeton. The reason he chose some one there was because he had no automobile and so had to handle it within a narrow area.

"He considered three persons to kidnap

"First was the son of Charles Chambers, whom he eliminated because the child was always with its

Continued on Page Three

Eight Army Airmen Die in Crash; Illinois Accident Is Laid to Storm

Big Bomber, on Way to Colorado, Loses a Wing in 'Line Squall,' Chanute Field Officers Report After Investigation

Special to THE NEW YORK TIMES.

DELAVAN, Ill., June 19.—Eight army airmen were killed here today when a wing of a big bombing plane was torn off as they were about to make a forced landing in a farm meadow. The plane crashed from a height of about 400 feet and burned, scattering its wreckage and the bodies of seven of its occupants over a quarter of a mile of field.

The dead were:

Captain Richard D. Reeve, 36, of Wannakee, Wis.
First Lieutenant Norman H. Ives, 31, of Los Angeles.
Second Lieutenant Thomas B. Langben, 27, of Galveston.
Staff Sergeant Edward F. Murah, 32, of Denver.
Corporal William H. Housley, 30, of Stillwater, Okla.
Private Philip J. Truitt, 23, of Galax, Va.
Private Max Myser, 21, of Villa Grove, Ill.
Private George L. Huntsman, 23, of Kankakee, Ill.

For an hour before the crash the airplane had been flying through rough air currents, according to reports by its crew to the Air Corps radio station at Chanute Field, Rantoul, Ill. Presumably the pounding it had taken in flying through several small storms had weakened the essential structure and the pilots brought it down low to find a suitable field in which to land it.

While they were circling, a mile and a quarter northeast of Delavan, a line squall, which is an extremely violent type of thunderstorm, passed by. The plane was just beginning its glide toward a field when the terrific swirling winds of the squall struck it.

The wing fluttered away and the machine plunged to the ground, where its fuel tanks exploded into flame.

Parachutes attached to four of the bodies were partly opened, but the army investigating board, comprised of Major Roy W. Camblin, Captain Hugo P. Rush and First Lieutenant Samuel Stephenson, all from Chanute Field, said this did not indicate that any of the plane's crew had jumped. The 'chutes probably were opened by the impact with the ground, they explained.

After talking to a dozen farmers who saw the crash, Captain Rush said he was "reasonably certain" that one of the wings had torn away at the root and that it fell between 300 and 400 yards away from the rest of the machine.

"The crash must have been caused by weather," the captain said. "The plane might have been hit by lightning as some of the witnesses think, but planes have been hit before and little damage done. We think the fire occurred after the crash."

Carey Youle, the farmer who owned the field in which the plane fell, said he saw the plane circling the town just before the line squall arrived. He said that just as the high wind and rain struck the airplane, the wing separated from the cabin.

"It hit the ground and then it was just a sheet of flames," he said.

Floyd Glenn, a neighbor of Youle, said he was running toward his house trying to get to shelter before

Continued on Page Three

CZECH WARNS FOES OF DEEP DEFENSES

Staff Officer Says Invaders Would Lose Heavily—Tells of Machine-Gun Nests

By G. E. R. GEDYE

Wireless to THE NEW YORK TIMES.

PRAGUE, Czechoslovakia, June 10.—Major Rudolf Broz, an officer of the general staff, assured the nation in a radio broadcast this afternoon that an army invading Czechoslovakia would face a difficult task and suffer heavy losses.

"Our fortifications really consist of a chain of machine-gun nests that the enemy will encounter on crossing the frontier," he said.

[He also declared that these machine-gun nests extended far into the interior, The Associated Press reported.]

"Not only will he [the enemy] suffer heavy losses trying to break through this line but an attempt to overrun our country by a sudden push will dissolve itself into a series of individual battles.

Natural Defenses Cited

"Our artificial fortifications are supplemented by natural defenses on the frontier that dictate to the enemy in advance what roads he will have to take in order to force his way in. By the wise combination of natural and artificial obstacles and by the destruction of the enemy's communications, he will be compelled not only to delay his advance but to give battle at points most unfavorable to him.

"It is true that our fortifications will have to face a dangerous enemy from the air. It should not be forgotten, however, that such a minute target as a machine-gun nest reduces the danger from air attack to the minimum."

Representatives of Konrad Henlein's Sudeten German party today declined an invitation from Dr. Karel Englis, former Finance Minister and now Governor of the National Bank, to attend a meeting to organize a national subscription for the defense of the State. This subscription, which will be opened Sunday, is to be called the Freedom Fund.

Declining the invitation, the Senators' Club of the Henlein party sent Dr. Englis a sharply worded letter in which the Henleinists said they not only declined to take any part in the subscription but would produce constitutional and political grounds against it. They protested the fund because "it violates the financial laws" and seeks to obtain coverage for an extraordinary large expenditure for military purposes.

The country's poor economic situation, the Henlein deputies protested, does not permit the imposition of such an expense on the population.

Party Demands Studied

During the day government experts continued examination of the Henlein party's recent proposals and their comparison with the draft of the nationalities statute.

A story was cabled abroad tonight that the government had found a

Continued on Page Four

REBEL FLIERS SINK THREE MORE SHIPS

Four Eastern Spanish Ports Are Bombed by Planes of Italian and German Make

By The Associated Press.

MADRID, June 10.—Insurgent air raiders in planes of German or Italian manufacture continued today their methodical bombardment of four Mediterranean ports, destroying three British and French ships.

The bombers, two of which have teamed up, finished off the British freighter Thorpehaven, bombed three days ago at Alicante, and the French merchantman Brisbane, ablaze off Denia since her first bombing yesterday. They also sank a schooner of Spanish registry and, bent on crippling or stopping foreign shipping to government Spain, raided again the ports of Gandia, Alicante, Denia and Castellon de la Plana.

The British freighter Isadora, first attacked yesterday, sank following a new raid on Castellon early today when a bomb tore a big hole in her side. The Isadora settled to the bottom at her wharf, augmenting difficulties at the port, where many berths are now filled with sunken steamers.

At noon today two persons were killed and ten injured in a third raid on Castellon.

At Alicante a Non-Intervention Committee observer, alone on the Thorpehaven when two bombs struck her, escaped unhurt.

Strafe Ships Along Coast

Returning to their secret base, the two raiders shot at all schooners and fishing vessels they encountered along the coast. None was reported sunk.

Government leaders remained silent about plans to check the depredations, which they held injustified because the small towns had no known military objectives. It was believed the probable government counter-measures would hinge on any decisions taken in London and Paris to try to halt the forays.

The raiding aircraft have been repeatedly identified, officially and unofficially and by impartial foreign observers, as of German and Italian manufacture.

Dispatches from the coast said that a seaplane, possibly one of those that attacked Alicante, Denia and Gandia, swooped down on a sailing vessel off Javea, just below Denia, and dropped two bombs that missed the ship.

The British cruiser Penelope was to put into Gandia tomorrow to investigate the attacks.

U. S. Warship at Gandia

Gandia was first attacked two days ago, with the destruction of a dredger, warehouse and railroad property.

While Gandia port workers were still cleaning up the wreckage from the latest attack, the United States Destroyer Claxton steamed into the harbor at 9:40 A. M. today to take off Vice Consul Lee Worley, regularly stationed at Valencia, who had been ordered to Paris for an emer-

Continued on Page Four

ROOSEVELT OUSTS FOE OF GOV. BENSON IN MINNESOTA WPA

Christgau, Relief Chief, Held in Scorn Farmer-Labor Plan to Weed All Farms in State

CHARGED IT WAS POLITICS

Confusion Increases When His Organization Is Praised and Will Be Kept Unchanged

By TURNER CATLEDGE

Special to THE NEW YORK TIMES.

ST. PAUL, June 10.—President Roosevelt today had ousted Victor Christgau, hitherto ardent New Dealer, as Works Progress Administrator for Minnesota, and added another confusing element to one of the most baffling political scrambles ever experienced in this State, long used to unusual politics.

The ouster became effective last night, when Mr. Christgau, complying with a blunt demand of the President sent his resignation to Washington by air mail. The administrator told the President that no charges had been "preferred or proved" against him, and pointed to a record which had won for him a reputation in State Works Progress circles throughout the country.

The specific reason for the removal was understood both here and in Washington to be that Mr. Christgau had been constantly at odds with the State administration, now headed by Governor Elmer Benson, which came into power in a New Deal-Farmer-Labor coalition in 1936. Recently, Mr. Christgau refused to approve a weed eradication program sponsored by Governor Benson in which 2,000 or more WPA workers were to be sent out over the farms in the State's eighty-seven counties to pull weeds, particularly to deal with a scourge of "leafy spurge" and "creeping jenny."

Charged Political Design

Mr. Christgau contended that it was not so much the "spurge" and the "jenny" that Mr. Benson was after as the privilege of helping select the 2,000 workers for whatever aid it might give him in his race in the State primary for renomination, former Governor Hjalmar Petersen being his opponent.

The State WPA administrator was notified two weeks ago that an acting administrator was being sent here in his place. Up till then he had been backed at every turn by the Administration in Washington, even to his disapproval of the rural weed pulling project. His superiors, including Harry L. Hopkins, had asked him from time to time, however, to try to get along more agreeably with the Farmer-Labor State administration.

Except for the knowledge that the long-continuing dispute between the Governor and State WPA chief was at the bottom of it, the political implications of Mr. Christgau's ouster were not clear.

One group, for instance, held that it was a clear bid from the Washington Administration for another New Deal-Farmer-Labor tie-up in the Congressional races. Another felt that it was a successful attempt on Governor Benson's part to place the WPA behind his faction in his primary contest with Mr. Petersen. Yet both assumptions were discounted by the fact that Roy C. Jacobson, acting WPA administrator for Minnesota, announced upon his arrival here from Chicago a few days ago that the or-

Continued on Page Two

WAGE BILL IS SPED BY A COMPROMISE AIMED TO SUIT SOUTH

Final Agreement Is Expected Today, With Measure Going to the House Monday

'RIGID' CLAUSE SOFTENED

'Pale' Copy of Original Sets Up Boards to Decide as to 40-Cent Maximum

By LOUIS STARK

Special to THE NEW YORK TIMES.

WASHINGTON, June 10.—Conferees on the Wages and Hours Bill virtually agreed upon its major provisions today and, unless a hitch develops tomorrow, complete agreement will be announced and the bill will be submitted to the House on Monday.

Working under the spur of a desire to adjourn next week, the conferees held two sessions today, and when they adjourned until tomorrow Senators Ellender and Pepper said they believed there would be no trouble over the bill when it reached the floor.

The compromise draft was satisfactory to the Southern Senators who had intimated that they might filibuster against the measure if it contained a rigid provision that a minimum wage of 40 cents an hour might become mandatory in seven years.

This section was so scaled down with conditions today that it was said to be a "pale" copy of the original because of its exemptions.

The bill retains the House version of a minimum wage of 25 cents the first year and 30 cents the second. Having dealt with the "rigid" part of the bill in this manner, the conferees wrote in a "flexible" provision for creation of industrial wage boards to determine minimum wages up to 40 cents in those industries which, after hearings, appear able to afford rates above the 25-cent minimum.

Boards Would Start at Once

These boards would become operative once the bill is enacted and their findings would be put into effect as soon as decisions are issued. Thus it would be possible for wages up to 40 cents to be fixed in some industries in the first year of the act's operation and they would not have to wait two years until the rigid 25 and 30 cent provisions had been effected.

Exemptions would be provided for application of minimum rates above 25 cents through appeals to the wage boards, which would comprise representatives of industry, labor and the public.

In considering application for higher minima, the boards would have to consider several factors, such as local economic conditions, freight rates, value of services and the collective bargaining status of the employes.

An ingenious arrangement has been worked out to cover the case of concerns or industries which guarantee annual employment. Exemptions would be granted to these firms from the statutory hour provisions for certain seasons if they guaranteed 2,000 hours a year work to their employes.

Wages would be arranged by collective bargaining between the employers and employes.

The compromise provides for establishment of a maximum work week of forty-four hours the first year, forty-two hours the second year, and forty hours the third year.

However, the wage boards could

Continued on Page Two

Record of De Long and Arctic Ship Found After 57 Years on an Island Off Siberia

Wireless to THE NEW YORK TIMES.

MOSCOW, June 10.—A copper cylinder containing part of Lieut-Commander George Washington De Long's record of the Arctic expedition on which the explorer and most of his party perished fifty-seven years ago was found recently by a Soviet scientist on Henrietta Island, which Commander De Long discovered and named, Soviet officials revealed today.

Henrietta Island is one of the De Long archipelago of small islands north of Eastern Siberia far within the Arctic Circle. It was near there that Commander De Long's ship, the Jeannette, for which another island of the same archipelago was named, was crushed in the ice and sank on an attempt to reach the North Pole via Bering Sea in 1881.

Commander De Long and part of the expedition reached Siberia in a small boat, but all died except two who had gone ahead to hunt a settlement. Their bodies were found by other survivors and returned to the United States.

The copper cylinder was found by a biologist of the Soviet Arctic Institute stationed on Henrietta Island, who reported his discovery by wireless and asked advice on how to preserve the cylinder and its record until it could be sent to Leningrad. He said the cylinder's cap had come loose and that water had reduced the rolled-up record, written by Commander De Long, to a mass of pulp.

The lettering is still visible, the biologist reported, and it is hoped that with expert treatment much of the record will be deciphered.

The Jeannette sailed from San Francisco in 1879. She drifted in the Arctic ice for a year and ten months before she broke up. The party of thirty-three set out for land in three boats. One was lost. Another, containing Commander De Long, reached the mouth of the Lena River, but all the party, except two seamen, died of starvation.

The third boat, in charge of Lieutenant George W. Melville, also reached the Lena River and recovered the bodies of their companions, which were brought to New York for burial.

A diary written by Commander De Long was published in 1883 by his widow as "The Voyage of the Jeannette."

HAGUE TESTIFIES RED PLOTS FORCED BAN ON C. I. O. RALLIES; DENIES FREE SPEECH IS ISSUE

WPA Considers Plan for It to Buy Surplus Stocks of Men's Clothing

Sidney Hillman Confers With Officials on Idea to Spur Re-employment and Aid Industry—Garments Would Go to Needy

Special to THE NEW YORK TIMES.

WASHINGTON, June 10.—Sidney Hillman, president of the Amalgamated Clothing Workers of America, conferred today with WPA officials on a plan to handle surplus supplies of men's clothing. The proposal is designed to stimulate re-employment of idle clothing workers and help to stabilize the industry.

The meeting today was the second conference in the last few days, as Mr. Hillman had explained his idea in some detail previously to Harry L. Hopkins, WPA Administrator.

Mr. Hillman said tonight that he was hoping to reach an agreement with the WPA officials in ten days but he was unable to make public the exact nature of his proposal. It was learned, however, that the plan dealt with the large supplies of men's clothing and woolen goods now on the market.

In taking up the matter with the WPA officials Mr. Hillman presented to them an inventory of the entire clothing industry showing the amount of goods and clothes on the shelves of all factors in the industry.

"I do hope that something will be worked out to help the clothing industry from top to bottom," said Mr. Hillman. "Nothing specific has been agreed upon as yet. The idea is still only in a tentative stage.

"If something can be done to help the idle garment workers it seems to me that a way should be found whereby every part of the industry should also be assisted, from the wool factors to the manufacturers and retailers.

"To stabilize the industry through some plan which would permit the WPA to function would be a constructive achievement, it seems to me. I expect to confer again with the WPA officials next week."

By The Associated Press.

WASHINGTON, June 10.—The proposal that the government buy surplus clothing stocks would be

Continued on Page Eight

CONFEREES AGREE ON WPA FUND RISE

Would Also Keep Woodrum Curb, but Not Apply It to Added $175,000,000

Special to THE NEW YORK TIMES.

WASHINGTON, June 10.—Conferees on the Relief-Recovery Bill agreed in a brief session today to retain the $175,000,000 Senate increase in the WPA fund, theoretically voted to cover eight months on a pro rata basis, whereas the $1,250,000,000 voted by the House was intended to cover seven months.

The agreement retains the Woodrum amendment of the House bill, stricken out by the Senate, to require that funds be spread over the full appropriation period. The Senate's $175,000,000 increase would be freed from this restriction, however, and the President could use it in an emergency.

Representative Woodrum of Virginia, who piloted the bill through the House, said that separate House votes would be necessary on Senate amendments adding $212,000,000 for farm parity payments and granting the United States Housing Authority powers to borrow and lend to local authorities $300,000,000 more than its present $500,000,000 fund.

Housing Concurrence Likely

The House will probably accept the housing proposal readily, since it was considering it in a separate bill when the Senate added it to the relief measure. The proposal is part of the President's general relief-recovery program.

The farm parity payments may encounter House hostility, for the President has held that these should not be granted without provisions for raising the money. Such provisions must be initiated in the House, which will be in no mood to extend the session for the purpose, it is believed. Efforts to include such payments in the House draft failed.

Supporters of the Tydings "Anti-Politics" Bill, offered as a substitute for the defeated Hatch amendment to the Relief Bill, voiced the belief today that the Administration would not oppose it, since it has been amended to forbid political use not only of WPA money but of Federal highway and unemployment insurance funds granted to the States by the Federal Government.

Senator Barkley, majority leader, told reporters, however, that he saw no need for the bill because the powers of the campaign investigating committee which he sponsored were broad enough to cover the field fully.

Kentucky Contest a Factor

By The Associated Press.

WASHINGTON, June 10.—Broadening of the proposal for a Senate inquiry into any complaints of "politics in relief" followed an assertion by Senator Barkley that to restrict political activities by WPA administrative employes would prevent freedom of expression by Fed-

Continued on Page Two

LABORITES DESERT COUNCIL COALITION

Hollander Says Party Sees No Purpose in Continuing in Non-Existent Majority

For all practical purposes the coalition of Mayor La Guardia's supporters in the City Council no longer exists, Councilman Louis Hollander, Kings County chairman of the American Labor party, told 2,000 unionized laundry workers at a meeting in Brooklyn last night.

Accusing some members of the coalition of having "betrayed the principles of progressive government," Mr. Hollander said the Labor party bloc in the Council saw no virtue in continuing as the center of a "non-existent majority, some of whose members would fit better in the American Liberty League than in any progressive body."

"The sooner we let the public know that we of the American Labor party have constituted ourselves an independent unit, appealing for support on the basis of principle and not of expediency, the healthier it will be," the Councilman said.

Sees Ill Effect

The only effect of the coalition, he declared, was to fix in the public mind an idea that the Labor party was the dominant group in the Council, even though it could not count on the votes of its supposed allies, and thus to saddle the five Labor party members with responsibility for "much bad legislation."

"It is time for us to stop assuming responsibility for things we oppose," Mr. Hollander said. "We seek no monopoly in the presentation of sound bills. We are ready to support bills introduced by others if they are consistent with our program. We expect the same support from others. If we do not get it, our recourse will be to the people and we will let them know who is obstructing progressive legislation."

Give Party Stand

He spoke before members of Local 328 of the Amalgamated Clothing Workers of America, a C. I. O. affiliate, in the auditorium of Erasmus Hall High School. Mr. Hollander is international vice president of the union.

His exposition was intended to make clear to the members, as trade unionists and adherents of the American Labor party, the course the party is following in the Council.

Mr. Hollander, who did not single out any of his colleagues for specific criticism, said the Labor party bloc believed it important to take its place as a frank minority, committed to nothing but its own program. In appealing to others to support this program, the party would not resort to "horse trading or machine politics," the Brooklyn labor leader declared.

Michael Coleman, business agent of the union, presided at the meeting. Mr. Hollander formally presented a charter to the group and installed officers of the local headed by Jack Fitter, president.

DEFIES 'INVADERS'

Calls Thomas, O'Connell, All C. I. O. Chiefs Except Lewis 'Communists'

HE BACKS 'DEPORTATIONS'

Says Police Did Victims Favor—Takes Full Responsibility for Jersey City Policies

Transcript of Mayor Hague's testimony is on Pages 6 and 7.

By RUSSELL B. PORTER

Special to THE NEW YORK TIMES.

NEWARK, N. J., June 10.—Mayor Frank Hague of Jersey City, Democratic State leader of New Jersey and vice chairman of the Democratic National Committee, attacked the C. I. O. and allied groups involved in the Jersey City "free speech" fight as part of an "un-American" and "communistic" movement to overthrow this government and destroy all forms of religion, in two hours of testimony from the witness stand in the Federal District Court this afternoon.

The Mayor charged that all the leaders of the C. I. O., except John L. Lewis, national chairman, were Communists, and cited John Brophy, national director, in particular. He made the same charge against Norman Thomas, former Socialist candidate for President; Representative Jerry J. O'Connell, Montana Democrat, and Representative John T. Bernard, Minnesota Farmer-Laborite, all of whom were recently prevented from speaking on behalf of the C. I. O. in Jersey City.

He accused Morris L. Ernst, C. I. O. counsel; Roger N. Baldwin, director of the American Civil Liberties Union, and others who have been denied the right to speak in Jersey City, of the same thing.

Jersey City Called Spearhead

Insisting that there was no issue of free speech involved, the Mayor defended the denial of permits for street meetings on behalf of the C. I. O., the A. C. L. U. and allied groups not only on the ground of the alleged Communist nature of those organizations, but also, he said, because C. I. O. leaders had shown they intended to make a drive in Jersey City as the spearhead of an attempt against the government.

As proof of this, he asserted, Harry Bridges, West Coast C. I. O. leader, sent 500 "strong-arm men and killers" into Jersey City during the 1936-37 seamen's strike, and William J. Carney, C. I. O. regional director for New Jersey, threatened last November to send an "invasion" of 3,000 men into the city, "law or no law." He cited the record of the C. I. O. sit-down strikes in Detroit and elsewhere for "riots, bloodshed and disturbances" as further justification of his stand, in what he termed "war" with the C. I. O. against a "Red invasion."

Mayor Hague also defended the action of his police in the "deportation" from Jersey City of Mr. Thomas, Representative O'Connell and others, including C. I. O. organizers, on two grounds—association with radical groups and for their own protection against crowds which resented their activities. He defended the police as preserving law and order, and said they had wide discretionary power in such cases.

Although the police have followed the decision of the United States Supreme Court since last March, when it held unconstitutional a Griffin, Ga., ordinance similar to the Jersey City ordinance against distribution of leaflets on the public streets, the Mayor insisted they still have the right to stop such distribution if the leaflets themselves, or circumstances surrounding their distribution, might lead to public disorders.

Technical Witness for Foes

Subpoenaed as a witness by the C. I. O. in the suit brought before Federal Judge William Clark by the C. I. O. and the A. C. L. U. for an omnibus injunction against further interference with constitutional guarantees in the C. I. O. campaign to organize workers in Jersey City, the Mayor was technically testifying against himself as the chief defendant.

The direct examination, instead of being managed by his own counsel, was conducted by Dean Spaulding Frazer of Newark Law School, chief counsel for the plaintiffs. Never-

Continued on Page Eight

"All the News That's Fit to Print"

The New York Times.

LATE CITY EDITION
Cloudy and warmer; showers and colder at night. Tomorrow fair.
Temperatures Yesterday—Max., 61; Min., 45
Sunrise today, 6:27 A. M.; Sunset, 4:58 P. M.

VOL. XCV No. 32,059. Entered as Second-Class Matter, Postoffice, New York, N. Y. NEW YORK, FRIDAY, NOVEMBER 2, 1945. THREE CENTS NEW YORK CITY

HITLER ENDED LIFE IN BERLIN BUNKER, BRITISH FEEL SURE

Nazi Leader and Bride Slew Themselves Day After Wedding, Report Says

BODIES OF BOTH BURNED

Exhaustive Investigation of Many Eyewitnesses Cited in Detailed Account

The official British statement on the Hitler suicide, Page 3.

By RAYMOND DANIELL
By Wireless to THE NEW YORK TIMES.

BERLIN, Nov. 1—A British major said today that an exhaustive investigation had convinced the British authorities that Adolf Hitler and Eva Braun had died by their own hands in the Fuehrer's private bunker in Berlin on April 30, a few hours after a macabre wedding feast.

Intelligence officers who have questioned almost a score of important witnesses and sifted all the available evidence are as convinced as they can be, lacking the actual bodies, that Hitler and his mistress killed themselves. The spokesman was almost as certain that Martin Bormann, Hitler's still uncaptured deputy, was killed while trying to escape from the bunker with the last defenders on the day after Hitler had died. However, while the evidence was sufficient to convince the British, the Russians are still as skeptical as ever.

Why they should retain such strong doubts the investigator did not know. But the British, he added, have not completed their investigation or called off the search.

Say Woman Made Him Stay

The evidence indicated that, had it not been for his mistress' influence—she had her heart set on the reflected glory of dying with him in Berlin—Hitler might have followed his original plan of fleeing with his generals for a last stand in Bavaria. But he resisted all importunities to flee and went methodically about the business of self-destruction, arranging at his marriage feast for the slaughter of his pet Alsatian dog and making preparations to have his own and his bride's body burned. The conversation in his suite of the bunker during the wedding feast became so oppressive and morbid that, his secretary told the investigators, she could not stand it and excused herself early.

From April 22 until April 30, life in the bunker was pretty hectic. Hitler suffered periodic tantrums, charging and discovering new and old treacheries. He planned originally to leave for Berchtesgaden on April 20. At a staff meeting on April 22 he made it clear that he thought that the jig was up and he intended to remain in Berlin. Various people urged him to reconsider, but he heeded none.

On that day he had a nervous collapse. From that time on his physical health was poor but his mind seemed clear to his associates and he seemed even to achieve a relative calmness of spirit and an increased confidence in the outcome of the battle. Albert Speer, Minister of Armaments, visited him on the night of April 23 and heard in detail how Hitler planned to kill himself and have his body destroyed.

Married on April 29

By April 29 the absurdity of hoping for the relief of Berlin was borne in even on Hitler. That night he married his mistress. After the marriage feast Hitler shook hands with his old retainers and said good-by to them. This was about 2:30 A. M. on April 30. Some twelve hours later the transport office received orders to deliver 200 liters of gasoline to the Chancellery. At about that time Hitler and his bride again took leave of their faithful followers. It was the last time when they were seen alive.

Each then retired to his own apartment. Hitler shot himself through the mouth. Eva Braun, although she had a pistol, chose poison. A little later the two bodies were carried into the garden. Propaganda Minister Joseph Goebbels and Bormann acting as pallbearers. Hitler's body was wrapped in a blanket.

Both bodies were soaked with gasoline, which the sandy soil of the garden absorbed, and, in the

Continued on Page 3, Column 6

Four B-29's Fly From Japan To Washington Without Stop

Hop 6,554 Miles From Hokkaido in 27½ to 28 Hours—Weather 'Terrible,' Says General Armstrong, Leader

By The Associated Press.

WASHINGTON, Nov. 1—Four B-29s, carrying forty-three tired, happy men home from the war, completed tonight the first non-stop flight from Japan to Washington. The time of the lead plane was 27 hours and 29 minutes.

Brig. Gen. Frank A. Armstrong Jr., deputy commander of the Twentieth Air Force, led the flight home, landing at National Airport at 7:38 P. M., Eastern Standard Time. The distance was figured at 6,544 miles.

It was the Army's second attempt to make the trip non-stop. The first attempt, on Sept. 18-19, fell short of the goal because of constant adverse winds. That three-plane flight, led by Lt. Gen. Barney M. Giles, stopped at Chicago to refuel before coming on to Washington.

Both flights followed roughly the same route, the great circle course across the Pacific by way of Agattu and Kodiak, in the Aleutians, Sitka, Alaska, Fort St. John, Winnipeg, Detroit and thence southeastward across the United States.

General Armstrong, smiling through grime and two days' growth of beard, said the weather was "terrible" on this flight also, and that they did not know until they reached Kodiak, Alaska, whether they would make it. As it turned out, his plane landed with 800 gallons of fuel, enough for about three hours.

General Armstrong said the planes took off from the field near Sapporo, capital of Hokkaido, northernmost of the major Japanese islands, during a rain.

They had a helping tail wind up to about forty-five miles an hour part of the way, however, and made their best average ground speed of 290 miles an hour between Fort St. John and Winnipeg.

Lieut. Gen. Ira C. Eaker, deputy commander of the Air Forces, who was on hand to greet the airmen, said the flight was "primarily for the purpose of pioneering a new

Continued on Page 5, Column 3

Iraqi Says Finding Puts Dawn Of Civilization at 6000 B. C.

By Wireless to THE NEW YORK TIMES.

LONDON, Nov. 1—Archaeologists have unearthed in Iraq, 400 miles north of Ur, the site of the civilization of Abraham, the findings placing the beginning of civilized mankind between 5000 and 6000 B. C., 2,000 years earlier than previous evidence had shown, Dr. Naji al Asil, Director General of Antiquities for the Iraq Government, said here today.

Leader of the Iraq delegation to the United Nations Education Conference, Dr. al Asil disclosed that a team of archaelogists led by Seton Lloyd, an Englishman, and Fuad Safar of Iraq had been successful after two years' work in discovering positive evidence of the existence of this civilization seven to eight thousand years ago.

"We are able to verify the antiquity by the strata of the earth and ashes, by the shape, appearance and types of pottery and other relics unearthed," said Dr. al Asil. "Up to the present we believed that the civilization of Ubaid between five hundred and a thousand years before the Sumerian [discovered by Sir Leonard Wolley about fifteen years ago] was the beginning of civilized mankind. This newest discovery has put back the horizon of human civilization from 4000 B. C. to 6000 B. C."

The newest finds have been made at Hassuna, where Dr. al Asil said man for the first time 8,000 years ago began to cultivate the land, herd cattle, build brick houses and make pottery.

"We know that these first citizens were a peaceful community of farmers, builders and craftsmen," he said. "One of our most prized finds has been a sickle in a wonderful state of preservation. This 8,000-year-old farming implement must be the oldest instrument in the world."

The sickle, said Dr. al Asil, has a scythe of flint and is of perfectly carved and matched pieces of flint glued together with bitumen. He said the cutting edge was still sharp and as capable of cutting corn as it had 8,000 years ago.

"This sickle," he continued, "is more than a relic of great an-

Continued on Page 18, Column 5

SOVIET URGES RUHR BE INTERNATIONAL

U. S. and Britain Say Question Requires French Participation —Russians Would Share Area

By JAMES B. RESTON
Special to THE NEW YORK TIMES.

WASHINGTON, Nov. 1—The Soviet Union has told the United States and Great Britain that it favors internationalizing the Ruhr Valley, Germany's central industrial workshop.

France has been urging such a decision by the principal Allies for months, but has not been able to get the support of the United States or Great Britain.

It is understood, however, that Soviet officials raised the question at the Potsdam Conference and said they favored the idea of allowing an international commission to administer the Ruhr for the benefit of all Europe, including Germany and Russia. The reply of the American and British officials was that the question could not be discussed without France.

Washington and London Cool

Since then the Russians are understood to have repeated the suggestion through diplomatic channels and to have indicated that they should share in the occupation of the Ruhr Valley pending the creation of a commission to run it. This suggestion was not received enthusiastically in either Washington or London.

The Russian proposal at Potsdam and the reaction of the United States and Britain to it have interested the French. Gen. Charles de Gaulle has been pressing the Allies

Continued on Page 3, Column 4

Molotoff Spurns Newsmen's Plea To Ease Censorship on Reports

By BROOKS ATKINSON
By Wireless to THE NEW YORK TIMES.

MOSCOW, Oct. 31 (Delayed)—Acknowledging a statement criticizing the Soviet censorship written by the Anglo-American Correspondents Association in Moscow, Vyacheslaff M. Molotoff, People's Commissar of Foreign Affairs, informed a Foreign Office spokesman today that no reply was necessary. According to the spokesman, "in the opinion of Molotoff the association's letter in general was not solid and he did not find it necessary to give it his attention."

The letter, dispatched to Mr. Molotoff Oct. 20, put the Anglo-American Association on record as being opposed to the censorship of news dispatches for Great Britain and the United States. The letter declared that the Soviet Union was the only great Allied power that retained the wartime censorship. It added: "Censorship in peacetime of all dispatches relating not only to military affairs but to politics, economic, cultural affairs and every aspect of life in the Soviet Union destroys the value of foreign correspondence in a free world and has created general distrust abroad of all news emanating from the Soviet Union."

The letter said that Soviet censorship was "dictatorial and arbitrary" and charged that censors frequently had distorted the meaning of the messages by having altered the wording. It said that some censors were insufficiently familiar with the English language to understand the material submitted and that censors often were not informed on current events.

It also said that sometimes mes-

Continued on Page 4, Column 3

PALESTINE BANDS CRIPPLE RAILWAYS; 6 DIE IN OUTBREAKS

Tracks Are Cut at 50 Places —Pitched Battle Is Fought at Lydda Signal Tower

TRAIN HOLD-UP THWARTED

Blasts Rock Jerusalem—Stiff Curfew Is Imposed—British Blame Jewish Elements

By GENE CURRIVAN
By Wireless to THE NEW YORK TIMES.

LYDDA, Palestine, Nov. 1—All railroad traffic in Palestine is at a standstill today after a series of organized raids by terrorists who sabotaged communications and staged a pitched battle with the police and military. The casualty list stands at six dead and eight wounded.

[British sources in Jerusalem attributed the outbreak to Jewish elements, news services reported.]

Widespread terrorism started late last night and continued until the early hours of this morning. The most severe damage occurred here where a pitched battle was fought at the Lydda railroad junction, one of the most important in Palestine.

The raiding party, well armed and equipped with mines and other explosives, wrecked the railroad signal box, locomotives and train sheds and caused the deaths of one British soldier, one member of the Palestine police and two Palestinian railroad workers. In addition another Tommy, a member of the Palestinian police, and six members of the railway staff were wounded.

Tracks Cut in Fifty Places

Throughout Palestine railway lines were cut in fifty places along the coast from Acre to Gaza, between Haifa and Affule to the southeast, and between Lydda and Jerusalem. In all these cases parts of the tracks were blown away by home-made explosives. Late today there were still some explosions from time bombs.

In addition to these acts of violence, believed to be the most widespread and effective of any in recent history, two police launches were damaged by explosives in Haifa Bay and one sunk in Jaffa port within an hour. There was also a devastating blast in the consolidated oil refinery plant at Haifa where one man was killed. Late reports indicate that no dam-

Continued on Page 2, Column 3

BILL TO CUT TAXES BY $5,920,000,000 GOES TO PRESIDENT

Senate Almost Unanimously Votes Measure and Truman's Acceptance Is Indicated

DEEP '47 SLICE FORESEEN

Hope for $5,000,000,000 Drop for Individuals Voiced—12 Million Off Rolls in '46

By C. P. TRUSSELL
Special to THE NEW YORK TIMES.

WASHINGTON, Nov. 1—The Senate by an almost unanimous voice vote gave final approval to the $5,920,000,000 tax reduction bill today, completing Congressional action on the date which the Treasury Department had set as the latest that would assure full effect to the cuts by Jan. 1 to some 48,000,000 individual tax payers.

The bill, the first general tax-cutting measure to go through Congress in sixteen years, will be sent to the White House tomorrow for President Truman's signature, which he has virtually promised by pronouncing it a pretty good program.

Final adoption of cuts designed to reduce the taxes of individuals by $2,644,000,000 in 1946, of business by $3,136,000,000 during the fiscal year 1946-47 and give $140,000,000 of additional relief to both by repealing the automobile and boat "use" levy, came just a month after the program started through the Congress under Treasury recommendations.

12,060,000 to Go Off Rolls

An estimated 12,060,000 individuals in the lowest income brackets will be released from the tax rolls entirely as of Jan. 1.

Though the measure calls for reductions $920,000,000 greater than had been called a "safety" limit by Secretary Vinson, there were no qualms in the Senate today when it received approval after only forty minutes of debate.

Regrets were expressed by some members that $85,000,000 of tax relief to smaller corporations this year, which the Senate had approved, was eliminated during the adjustment of Senate and House differences.

Hope was expressed that another $5,000,000,000 might be cut from the taxes of individuals next year. It was contended that if the estimated $2,555,000,000 saved by corporations through repeal of the excess-profits tax were put entirely into increased wages, the

Continued on Page 34, Column 7

World News Summarized

FRIDAY, NOVEMBER 2, 1945

President Truman told delegates to the labor-management conference opening in Washington Monday that upon their success in solving this country's most pressing problem—a formula for real industrial peace—rested the confidence with which the world would accept our ability to help settle the world's problems. [1:8.]

Two unpublished reports were cited to prove that industry could raise wages without increasing prices. The CIO Executive Board referred to the findings of the Office of War Mobilization and Reconversion [11:2-3] and Secretary Wallace declared figures in his department showed that industry generally could increase pay 10 per cent next year and the automobile industry 25 per cent in two years. [1:6-7.]

The House passed and sent to the Senate an additional appropriation of $550,000,000 for UNRRA, but specified that none of the funds might go to nations preventing American correspondents from reporting freely. [4:5.] The Senate, by almost unanimous vote, completed Congressional action on the tax reduction bill. [1:5.]

Bernard M. Baruch urged an eight-point program of federally-supported scientific research as part of American preparedness to prevent Germany and Japan from devising some means for waging a third world war. [17:1.]

Japanese attempts to build Prince Konoye into a liberal leader and reviser of the constitution were repudiated by a spokesman for General MacArthur who said the former Premier was acting for the Emperor and the Japanese people would pass upon the final form of any new constitution. [5:1.]

The Netherland Government declared that any negotiations between Acting Governor van Mook and Indonesian independence leader Soekarno were unauthorized. [6:5.]

Britain has officially decided that on the basis of all known facts Hitler is dead. [1:1.]

Twenty-one German bank directors have been arrested in the American zone and may be tried as war criminals on charges of having worked closely with the Nazi party. [3:1.]

Moscow has informed Washington and London that the Soviet Union favors internationalization of the Ruhr, which the French have been demanding, and feels it should share in the occupation. [1:2.]

Foreign Commissar Molotoff rejected as "not solid" an appeal of British and American correspondents to end peacetime censorship and to permit free reporting for the sake of better understanding. [1:2-3.]

Britain's Labor government announced its intentions to nationalize all British air transport and to take over the empire's communications system. [1:7.]

Outbreaks all over Palestine, attributed to Jewish bands, resulted in six deaths, brought rail traffic to a standstill and damaged shipping and industry. [1:4; map P. 2.]

Greece finally obtained a new government when Panayotis Canellopoulis, leader of the Unionist party, became Premier. [4:8.]

Brazil's deposed President Vargas, his son-in-law and two close advisers announced their candidacies for the Senate. [3:8.]

One United Nations body ended its first meeting in Quebec while another opened its proceedings in London. The Food and Agriculture Organization pleaded for full support of its program by all governments [4:2], and Prime Minister Attlee told the Educational and Cultural Conference it must educate the world in the ways of peace. [2:6-7.]

Wallace Says Auto Makers Can Raise Wages 15% in '46

And Add Another 10% Rise in 1947, While Industry in General Can Raise Pay 10% in 1946 Without Increasing Prices

By RUSSELL PORTER
Special to THE NEW YORK TIMES.

WASHINGTON, Nov. 1—Secretary Wallace made public today a "confidential" report of his department's division of research and statistics, purporting to show that industry generally could raise wages 10 per cent in 1946 without raising prices, and that the automobile industry in particular could raise wages 15 per cent in 1946 and another 10 per cent in 1947 without raising prices.

The secretary made this statement to a group of newspaper men who ended here today a month's airplane tour of the country's industrial centers to survey the progress of reconversion.

He was asked to comment on President Truman's wage-price statement of Tuesday night, labor's demand for an increase of 30 per cent or $2 a day in take-home pay, and the proposal by Charles E. Wilson, president of the General Motors Corporation, that labor accept a forty-five-hour basic work week during the first few post-war years until the accumulated world-wide demand for goods is exhausted.

"As far as the general philosophy is concerned," said Secretary Wallace in reference to Mr. Wilson's statement on the need for greater productivity by labor, "his statement was fine, but as far as the automobile industry is concerned, I do not think it is sound.

"Improvements that have been made in the automobile industry are such that it could do better by the workers than Mr. Wilson's statement indicated. The automobile industry is in a better long-range position than most other industries to give its workers a substantial raise."

The Wallace report stated:

"It is apparent that present cost-price relationships are such throughout industry that a basic wage increase is possible without raising prices. For 1946 a general increase of 10 per cent is possible.

Continued on Page 11, Column 4

Spread of Greyhound Strike West of Chicago Is Forecast

The Greyhound Bus Company strike of 4,000 employes, which has halted operations of six Greyhound companies embracing all territory east of the Mississippi, may spread to other sections in the country, it was forecast yesterday by George Siff, president of Local 1202, Amalgamated Association of Street, Electric Railway and Motor Coach Employes of America, American Federation of Labor, one of the locals involved in the strike.

"If a settlement is not reached soon the strike may spread," Mr. Siff said, adding that employes of the Greyhound Southwestern and the Greyhound Northland "have disputes similar to ours."

The six Greyhound lines now involved in the strike are the Central, Pennsylvania, New England, Canadian, Illinois and Eastern. All six had contracts that expired Wednesday midnight. The strike was the climax of two months' negotiation for an agreement to replace a wage contract that expired at that time.

Union officials and company representatives met in Washington on Tuesday and Wednesday with the United States Conciliation Service, but no agreement could be reached. The union seeks a wage payment of 5.75 cents a mile for chauffeurs. The company has offered 5.4 cents for drivers in the East and 5.3 for drivers in the West. The union also is seeking a 30 per cent wage increase for garage and terminal employes, while the company offered a 10 per cent increase.

Company Stands by Offer

In his offices at Fiftieth Street, Jay L. Sheppard, vice president of Central and New England Greyhound Bus Lines, said: "The company has made what we consider a very generous offer in this case and that offer still stands."

Neither the union nor the bus company made any move yesterday to renew negotiations. Returning from the second session in Washington, R. W. Budd, president of Central Greyhound, and R. S. Sundstrom, president of Pennsylvania Greyhound, said that "the insistence on fifty-two hours pay for employes on a forty-hour

Continued on Page 8, Column 3

BRITAIN TO OPERATE ALL CIVIL AVIATION

Laborites Also to Nationalize Vast Telecommunications of Cable and Wireless, Ltd.

By HERBERT L. MATTHEWS
By Wireless to THE NEW YORK TIMES.

LONDON, Nov. 1- The Labor Government took new steps forward in its socialization program by announcing in Parliament today that civil aviation was to be state-owned and controlled and by disclosing its plans for nationalizing the great communications system, Cable and Wireless, Ltd.

All British air-transport services, all airports used for scheduled lines and all radio, meteorological and air traffic control services will be operated by the state, Lord Winster, Minister of Civil Aviation, told the House of Lords.

Meanwhile, in the House of Commons, Ivor Thomas, Parliamentary Under-Secretary for Civil Aviation, was telling members that "it is the object of the Government to make air travel a normal mode of travel for the masses and not a luxury for the few."

Lord Winster emphasized that the railway and shipping companies would have no financial share in the three proposed corporations. There will be one corporation for the British Commonwealth, North American and Far Eastern services. This will be operated by the British Overseas Airways Corporation, commonly known as the BOAC. A second corporation will serve internal and

Continued on Page 4, Column 4

Enterprise Will Be Preserved, May Be Berthed Here as Shrine

Special to THE NEW YORK TIMES.

WASHINGTON, Nov. 1—President Truman has approved Secretary Forrestal's proposal that the Enterprise be preserved permanently as "a visible symbol of American valor and tenacity in war, and of our will to fight all enemies who assail us."

Although it has not been decided where the Enterprise will be preserved and berthed, there was a possibility that she would go to New York City as Chairman Walsh of the Senate Naval Affairs Committee introduced a bill authorizing the Navy to transfer ownership of the carrier to the State of New York.

The Secretary proposed on Aug. 27 that the Enterprise, one of three surviving carriers of the seven with which we started the war, be preserved as a national shrine along with the old ships, the Constitution ("Old Ironsides"), the Constellation, the Hartford and the Olympia, which the Navy has saved from the scrap heap.

Mr. Forrestal said that the "Big E" most nearly "symbolizes and carries with it the history of the Navy in this war."

The Enterprise had one of the most active records of any warship in the Pacific war. She won a Presidential citation, participated in some twenty engagements, and her planes and guns destroyed nearly 1,000 enemy planes and her squadrons sank seventy-four enemy ships. She also survived six major hits from the enemy.

In urging Mr. Truman to authorize preservation of the Enterprise Mr. Forrestal wrote as follows:

"Time has accomplished what the enemy failed to do in four years of desperate and costly ef-

Continued on Page 4, Column 2

LABOR ROWS PERIL U. S. ROLE IN WORLD, TRUMAN ASSERTS

He Stresses Need for Success of Union-Management Parley in Talks With Delegates

THEY PLEDGE COOPERATION

Representatives of Both Sides Agree That Formula Must Be Found to End Disputes

By FELIX BELAIR Jr.
Special to THE NEW YORK TIMES.

WASHINGTON, Nov. 1—President Truman made it plain today to delegates to the labor-management conference, beginning Monday, that he regarded it as a definite milestone in his Administration and that its outcome might determine the leadership of this country in world affairs.

The President conferred at fifteen-minute intervals between 10 A. M. and noon with twenty-five of the delegates, seeing them in groups of four and five. He appealed to them for cooperation and asked them to speak frankly of any objections so that they might be remedied before the conference started.

He told the delegates that world leaders were looking to the United States to learn whether it could bring about economic stabilization on its home front. If that can be done, Mr. Truman added, then this country's position in world affairs will be strengthened immeasurably.

The President did not speculate on what would happen to American leadership if the conference failed.

Spokesmen for the delegate groups were unanimous in their insistence that a formula had to be found at the conference for peaceful solution of labor-management disputes.

John L. Lewis, president of the United Mine Workers, was among those who talked with the President this morning.

Delegates Pledge Cooperation

Generally, the representatives of both sides left the President's office after having pledged to enter the conference with an open mind, to cooperate in finding a solution for labor-management problems and to avoid controversial subjects at the sessions.

Mr. Truman told the delegates frankly of the problems facing his Administration and how concerned he was to bring about domestic economic stability. He asked them to be equally frank with him, especially whether they had any complaints on the agenda and organization of the conference.

If any complaints were voiced, they could not be learned from any of the delegates.

The President was told, mostly by labor delegates, how necessary it was to avoid at the conference matters of controversy, such as discussion of pending legislation.

If management got off on a tangent of amendments to the Wagner act or the Ball-Burton-Hatch bill, it was said, then labor would have a few things to say on demands for passage of the Full Employment measure as well as unemployment compensation, with the result that the conference would get nowhere.

Permanent Formula Urged

The President, too, adopted this theme in his discussions with management, asserting that the whole country would suffer unless both sides could bring to bear their respective abilities to work out a permanent formula.

Throughout the talks Mr. Truman stressed the common interest of both sides and the need for meeting whatever exigencies arose after the conference in the same spirit of general welfare.

The President repeated to the delegates his determination to avoid the pitfalls of inflation and deflation and said that this objective could be gained only if the conference succeeded.

The attitude of management was expressed by H. W. Steinkraus, president of the Bridgeport Brass Company, who said on leaving the executive office:

"We are determined to make the conference a success. There is no danger of this conference going off on tangents. I expect real accomplishments to come of it. After all, we both have so much in common, we shouldn't let minor differences interfere."

Leonard R. Hurtz, president of Paramount Creamery Company of Omaha, told how "the President wants us to find a program for

Continued on Page 10, Column 3

"All the News That's Fit to Print"

The New York Times

LATE CITY EDITION

Weather: Fair, very cold today and tonight. Chance of snow tomorrow. Temp. range: today 24-14; Sunday 33-26. Full U.S. report on Page 30.

VOL. XCVI...No. 32,430. Entered as Second-Class Matter, Postoffice, New York, N. Y. NEW YORK, FRIDAY, NOVEMBER 8, 1946. THREE CENTS IN NEW YORK CITY

U. S. TO RETAIN PACIFIC ISLES IF U. N. BARS TRUSTEE DRAFT; OPPOSES VETO ON SUCH PACTS

WAIVER IS OFFERED

Dulles Would Yield Right to a Negative Vote if Others Did Likewise

RUSSIANS, ARABS OPPOSED

Little Chance of Adoption Seen —But American Warns of Results of an Impasse

By THOMAS J. HAMILTON

Special to THE NEW YORK TIMES.

LAKE SUCCESS, N. Y., Nov. 7 —On condition that others would do likewise, the United States offered today to waive its right, as a state "directly concerned," to veto proposed United Nations trusteeship agreements.

John Foster Dulles, American member of the General Assembly's Trusteeship Committee, also served notice that if the United Nations did not accept the trusteeship agreements to be submitted by the United States for the Japanese possessions this country now occupies, the United States would continue "de facto control." Trusteeship agreements are those being submitted by nations administering non-self-governing territories to place them under the United Nations' aegis.

The United Nations Charter does not attempt to define who these states "directly concerned" may be, except that they must be selected by a two-thirds vote of the General Assembly. According to the prevailing opinion, however, the countries in the same area as the territory affected by the agreement, as well as the five great powers, all come within this category.

Britain, France Concur

The Soviet Union, which already has criticized the delay in establishing the United Nations trusteeship system, has served notice on Mr. Dulles that it will fight the United States proposal. The Arab countries, which thus would lose their veto over whatever arrangements are made eventually to bring Palestine under the United Nations trusteeship system, also are expected to oppose it.

Although Great Britain and France, the two leading colonial powers of the world, are in general agreement with the United States, the chances for acceptance of the American proposal are considered very poor.

There was nothing surprising about Mr. Dulles' statement to newspaper men after the committee meeting that if the American trusteeship proposals were not accepted the United States would continue to occupy the Japanese mandated islands. The United Nations Charter says specifically that, in the absence of approved trusteeship agreements, previous international engagements apply.

The United States simply has taken over Japan's rights under the League of Nations mandates, without the formality of a peace treaty. President Truman announced in Washington yesterday the terms of the trusteeship agreement for them that would be communicated "at an early date" to the United Nations Security Council.

A Morass Feared

Later, according to the President's statement, the United States will submit trusteeship agreements for "any Japanese islands for which it assumes responsibilities as a result of the second World War" —including, presumably, Okinawa, Iwo and any others that may be ceded to the United States when the peace treaty finally is written.

However, there is no question of the fact that, as Mr. Dulles told the committee, "in this trusteeship matter we can readily fall into a morass which will so entangle us that the trusteeship provisions of the Charter will never become operative."

"Let us frankly admit," he continued, "that the Charter provisions are awkward and ambiguous. They could give rise to prolonged controversy and lead to an impasse."

The eight trusteeship agreements

Continued on Page 4, Column 5

THE PRESIDENT RECEIVES MR. MOLOTOV

Mr. Truman with the Russian Foreign Minister at White House

The New York Times (Washington Bureau)

Molotov Calls on Truman, Has a 'Good Conversation'

By WALTER H. WAGGONER

Special to THE NEW YORK TIMES.

WASHINGTON, Nov. 7—President Truman, suffering from a cold, took time out from a restful day at the White House today to receive a social call from Vyacheslav M. Molotov, Foreign Minister of the Soviet Union.

The Soviet official was the President's only caller, Mr. Truman cancelling all other appointments at the request of his doctor and remaining "over in the house," according to Charles G. Ross, Presidential press secretary.

Upon leaving, Mr. Molotov, through his translator, told a group of news correspondents and still and newsreel photographers only that he had had "a good conversation with the President."

Asked, "What did you say to the President?" the Soviet official merely smiled, waved his hand and continued toward the door and his waiting car.

This was Mr. Molotov's third visit to the White House and his second with Mr. Truman. He called on President Roosevelt in 1942, and on April 23, 1945, he visited for half an hour with President Truman while en route to the San Francisco Conference.

Leaves Capital at 9 P. M.

Mr. Molotov was in Washington today to attend the annual party given by the Soviet Embassy in celebration of the anniversary of the 1917 October Revolution. He returned to New York this evening on the 9 o'clock train.

"It was purely a social conversation and politics did not enter into it at all," said Mr. Ross, after the Russian Foreign Minister had left. "He also said he had learned of the President's cold and he asked him how it was."

The President, Mr. Ross said, had answered that the cold was much better.

The White House press secretary also said that Mr. Molotov had told Mr. Truman that he was "very happy" at his reception in this country, and that he praised the Americans for being "delightful hosts."

Mr. Truman previously had sent a message of congratulations on the

Continued on Page 5, Column 5

BYRNES SEEKS END OF SNAG ON TRIESTE

Confers With Yugoslav Envoys —Italy Rejects Tito Offer to Trade Port for Gorizia

By JAMES RESTON

The Big Four Foreign Ministers Council, having failed to agree on many of the comparatively easy questions in the European peace settlements, will turn now to the tough question of Trieste.

Agreement on the future of this key Adriatic port has eluded the Foreign Ministers in their previous ninety-two meetings. When it came up in the first of the three meetings in New York earlier this week, the East-West split still existed and it was by-passed.

Yesterday Secretary of State Byrnes sought to break the deadlock by discussing the question privately with the Yugoslav Foreign Minister, Stanoje Simitch, and the Yugoslav Ambassador in Washington, Sava Kosanovitch. This meeting was friendly, but it did not produce any hope for an immediate solution.

Consequently, the Foreign Ministers Council will enter its ninety-third meeting this afternoon about where it was at the conclusion of the Conference of Paris last month. This is evidently true despite the statement of the Italian Communist leader Palmiro Togliatti that Marshal Tito had proposed a compromise under which the Yugoslavs would agree to allow Italy to keep Trieste as an autonomy if Italy would approve the cession of Gorizia to Yugoslavia.

United States representatives in

Continued on Page 3, Column 2

All Russia Marks 1917 Revolution With Round of Parades, Speeches

By DREW MIDDLETON

Special to THE NEW YORK TIMES.

MOSCOW, Nov. 7—Moscow and all Russia celebrated the twenty-ninth anniversary of the October Revolution today with parades and speeches.

Here in the capital, the focal point of the celebrations was Red Square, where for nearly an hour and a quarter thousands of troops, tanks, guns and cavalry paraded past Lenin's tomb. Premier Stalin, for the second consecutive year, was not in his usual place atop the tomb today, nor was he present at the meeting of the Moscow Soviet last night.

Marshal Leonid A. Govorov, victor at the Battle of Mozhaisk, took the salute from rank upon rank of soldiers marching or sitting their trucks, guns or horses.

In a long article by David Zaslavsky that appeared in Pravda, the Russian people were reminded repeatedly of the Soviet system's superiority over capitalism and of the Soviet Union's continued search for peace and security despite "the opposition of international reaction."

The parade through Red Square was an impressive display of men and weapons of the second World War as it was fought in Europe on the ground. Probably because of the weather, which was cloudy, no aircraft participated.

A vast crowd of civilians poured through Red Square on the tracks of the last tanks. Long rivers of humanity flowed through the streets of central Moscow to converge at the entrance to the square and surge past Lenin's tomb, carrying their banners with mottos glorifying industrial production and answering with deep-throated

Continued on Page 7, Column 1

MAYOR SET TO BALK TRANSIT WALKOUT; POLICE PLANS MADE

He Sends Word From Ranch in California He Will Not Tolerate a Stoppage

WORKERS BACK LEADERS

Agree to Meeting Next Week to Vote on Strike—Quill Sees Murray in Capital

By PAUL CROWELL

Mayor O'Dwyer is prepared to meet "head on" any strike called by the Transport Workers Union of America, CIO, on the city's unified transit lines as a result of the current controversy over retroactive pay rises and sole collective bargaining elections, it was disclosed yesterday. From his brother's ranch at El Centro, Calif., where he is recuperating, the Mayor has sent word to key city officials that he will tolerate no such stoppage.

Police Commissioner Arthur W. Wallander has already begun the process of setting up the elaborate machinery designed to meet a strike on the city lines when the TWU threatened a walkout last February.

The question of the legality of the retroactive pay rise, covering the period from July 1 to Nov. 4 is now before Supreme Court Justice James B. O'Malley for decision, but the TWU has demanded that it be made effective at once. The Board of Transportation has not yet acted on the recommendation of the Mayor's Advisory Transit Committee, favoring sole collective bargaining "negotiations" on the basis of employe elections.

The TWU has also demanded immediate favorable action by the board on that matter, and has been authorized by its joint executive board to call a meeting some day next week to take a strike vote.

A report that the TWU leadership plans to fix next Thursday as a strike deadline has been relayed to the Mayor, who is said to be ready to return to the city on short notice to take personal charge of the situation. In no event, it is understood, will it be handled by the city's newly created division of labor relations.

Quill Goes to Washington

A delegation of TWU officials, including City Councilman Michael J. Quill, international president of the union and Austin Hogan, president of the New York City local, went to Washington yesterday to confer with Philip Murray, president of the CIO, and other ranking CIO officials. The purpose of the trip was presumably to enlist their support of the TWU's strike threat. Assurance of such support was given by the Greater New York CIO Council, which denounced the Citizens Budget Commission for bringing the suit assailing the legality of any retroactive pay rise for the city transit workers.

At a meeting at TWU headquarters, 153 West Sixty-fourth Street, night workers on the city lines endorsed the action taken by the day workers on Wednesday, when the union leaders were authorized to call a meeting next week to take a strike vote. Both meetings also approved holding a mass demonstration at 11 A. M. tomorrow in front of the offices of the Board of Transportation at 250 Hudson Street.

In telegrams sent to Charles P. Gross, chairman of the Board of Transportation, and Commissioners William H. Davis and Frank X. Sullivan, Mr. Hogan asked that the retroactive pay rises be effectuated at once. The telegram also demanded that the board adopt immediately the sole collective bargaining election plan recommended by the Mayor's Advisory Transit Committee.

Mr. Hogan contended that it was understood by the Mayor and the union, when the committee was created last February, that it was to act as a fact-finding board "whose recommendations would be accepted in good faith by all parties." He advised the three commissioners that the labor section of the report, since the legality of its provisions has not been challenged either by Corporation Counsel John J. Bennett or counsel for the Board of Transportation, "is therefore as binding upon you as the wage section thereof."

The union's view on the binding force of the committee's recommendations is, however, known to be at variance with that held by

Continued on Page 16, Column 1

Penicillin Is Synthesized By Cornell Medical Team

Feat Follows Years of Effort by 38 Groups of Scientists—New Vistas Opened in Fight on Many Bacterial Diseases

By WILLIAM L. LAURENCE

The synthesis of penicillin as the climax of one of the greatest international cooperative efforts of its kind is announced today in Science, official journal of the American Association for the Advancement of Science.

The synthesis is regarded by chemists as one of the greatest achievements in biochemistry, duplicating in the laboratory what hitherto could be produced only by a living mold, penicillium notatum.

It was made possible by the unprecedented mobilization of scientific talent both here and in England during the war and comes as the culmination of five years of concentrated effort by thirty-eight teams of outstanding scientists, twenty-one in the United States and seventeen in England.

The final steps in the synthesis are the outcome of the intensive researches by the team at the Cornell University Medical College of the New York Hospital-Cornell Medical Center. Most of the preliminary work was performed by American and British chemists working under the joint auspices of the Committee on Medical Research, Office of Scientific Research and Development (OSRD), Washington, and the Medical Research Council, London.

The isolation in crystalline form of the active synthetic product and "the unequivocal proof of its identity with natural penicillin," of the type known as penicillin G, or benzylpenicillin, were achieved at the Cornell biochemical laboratories after the termination of the OSRD contracts, through the relentless pursuit of clues that had been discarded by most of the other teams working in the field.

The climactic experiments were carried out by Prof. Vincent du Vigneaud, head of the Cornell Department of Biochemistry, and Drs. Frederick H. Carpenter, Robert W. Holley, Arthur H. Livermore and Julian R. Rachele.

The present report in Science is

Continued on Page 26, Column 5

25 BILLION BUDGET IS GOP AIM, TAFT SAYS

Such a Cut in Federal Spending Would Mean a Big Slash in Taxes, Senator Asserts

Special to THE NEW YORK TIMES.

CHICAGO, Nov. 7—Senator Robert A. Taft, Republican, of Ohio, whose party will control the next Congress, said today that it should be possible to develop within two years a $25,000,000,000 Federal budget, a reduction of $18,000,000,000 from his estimate of the $43,000,000,000 budget for the present fiscal year.

The Senator, who is in line for the Senate majority leadership and chairmanship of the Finance Committee, foresaw a $30,000,000,000 transition budget for the new fiscal year, beginning July 1, 1947.

In the event of a $30,000,000,000 budget, the 20 per cent cut in individual income taxes for the calendar year 1947, as advocated by Representative Harold Knutson, Republican, of Minnesota, could be carried out, Mr. Taft told a press conference.

Mr. Taft's estimate of the present budget was $1,500,000,000 higher than the $41,500,000,000 set by President Truman in his revised figures for the fiscal year ending next June 30.

Taxes Called Too High

Taxes, though supportable at the moment "when we are on the upgrade," are too high when they absorb one-third of the national income, Mr. Taft asserted, in estimating Federal taxes at $40,000,000,000 and State taxes at $10,000,000,000.

"We are in an extraordinary inflative situation," he said, but when the "boom" period ends, present high taxes would be disastrous.

A $25,000,000,000 budget "would mean a tremendous reduction in taxes," Mr. Taft added.

Figuring in a budget of $25,000,000,000, the Senator said, would be $8,000,000,000 for the Army and Navy, leveling off from the present "war hangover" figure of $13,000,-

Continued on Page 19, Column 1

THREAT TO WORLD SEEN IN COAL STRIKE

Eugene Meyer, at Meeting Here, Warns of Global Effects of Crippling U. S. Production

By WILL LISSNER

The national coal strike now being threatened will cost the nation two million tons of fuel a day, a loss that will be felt in every phase of American production, threaten world recovery and condemn peoples abroad to serious deprivations, Eugene Meyer warned yesterday.

Mr. Meyer, president of the International Bank for Reconstruction and Settlement, told the Academy of Political Science, which opened a two-day annual meeting at the Hotel Astor here, that the international bank was playing the accelerating role in world recovery for which it was established but that "lending money alone will not supply the products" for which the world is starved.

Strikes in the United States have reduced the supply of many of the materials needed to restore a minimum of economic life abroad, he said, and a coal strike on top of them would prevent the maintenance of full production in this country, which requires every ton of coal that can be mined.

Full Production Held Vital

"I say emphatically," Mr. Meyer declared, "that the crucial importance of continuous full production for our own welfare and for that of mankind the world over cannot be exaggerated."

Prof. Jacob Viner of Princeton University, who frequently has been a monetary consultant of the Treasury, was another of eight speakers on the program. Professor Viner reported that the Soviet Union seemed to be embarked upon a foreign policy of "deliberate provocation" which deliberately courts the risk of war, and in view of that, he declared, "I urge frank and deliberate resort to dollar diplomacy."

We are in the most critical stage of diplomacy, Professor Viner said, and this requires that we throw

Continued on Page 13, Column 2

Bevin, Welcomed to City, Calls For Patience in Work for Peace

Officially welcomed by the city that is now host to the world's peacemakers, British Foreign Secretary Ernest Bevin declared yesterday that he was "not overly perturbed that we are not making peace too quickly."

"Ordinary people of the world," he said, "whatever their ideologies or political policies may be, have this in common—a burning desire and longing for permanent peace—that should inspire us to translate it into actual fact."

Speaking in the Council chamber at City Hall, where Acting Mayor Vincent R. Impellitteri extended New York City's welcome, Mr. Bevin made a plea for tolerance and patience in caring for a world that is in "a terrific fever."

"The world is not out of the hospital, so to speak," he said. "It hasn't reached the truly convalescent stage, much less arrived at a position of renewed health.

"I am fortunately not overly perturbed that we are not making peace too quickly. I believe that as we move further away from the war, acquire understanding and smooth out difficulties, with the proper exercise of patience and toleration, we will arrive ultimately at the true results."

The ceremony at City Hall capped the city's official reception for its distinguished visitor who arrived late last week aboard the Aquitania. Earlier, with noontime crowds jamming the sidewalks, Mr. Bevin and his wife rode at the head of a motorcade up Broadway from the Battery.

The police estimated that 100,000 persons watched the procession led by Troops A and B of the Mounted Police, the band and an honor guard from Fort Jay and the Police Department Band. Riding with Mr. and Mrs. Bevin in the first car was Grover Whalen,

Continued on Page 5, Column 2

LEWIS IS MOBILIZING 30 UNION LEADERS IN COAL SHOWDOWN

Presidents of His Bituminous Forces to Sit In on Sessions With Krug Starting Monday

OPERATORS MAY GET CALL

The Attorney General May Rule Early in Week on Legality of U. S. Reopening Contracts

By LOUIS STARK

Special to THE NEW YORK TIMES.

WASHINGTON, Nov. 7—The coal crisis in the current wage negotiations is expected to mount rapidly from next Monday to Friday as it became known today that John L. Lewis and Secretary J. A. Krug will meet face to face on Monday for the first time since the parley began on Nov. 1.

Mr. Lewis has called in the presidents of the thirty bituminous districts for the joint conferences.

The imminence of the crisis was indicated by this fact and by the decision of the United Mine Workers committee, and Capt. N. H. Collisson, Coal Mines Administrator, to defer further joint sessions until Monday instead of continuing tomorrow. Today's meeting was as unproductive as any since Nov. 1 when the sessions began.

All that has passed between the miners' committee and Captain Collisson has been preliminary. With the district presidents in Washington the meetings beginning Monday will be what are described as "real collective bargaining conferences."

The district presidents' committee will discuss any possible settlement terms that may result from the meetings.

Under Mr. Lewis' interpretation of the Krug-Lewis contract of May 29 last each side may give ten days' notice for a joint meeting to reopen the contract. Then fifteen days are allowed for negotiations. At the end of this period either side may announce that the agreement is at an end.

Although Mr. Krug insists that the contract was written for the duration of Government control of the mines, Mr. Lewis is expected to announce termination of the contract on Nov. 15 unless satisfactory progress has been made toward a new agreement. That gives the parties four days, beginning Monday, to speed up negotiations.

In the meantime Secretary Krug,

Continued on Page 13, Column 6

U. S. BROADCASTERS IN RUSSIA SILENCED BY SHORT-WAVE BAN

Moscow Asserts Its Own Heavy Winter Schedule Precludes Others' Use of Facilities

NETWORKS STUDY ACTION

Companies Differ on What Step to Take—State Department Watches Developments

By JACK GOULD

The Russian Government has silenced the correspondents of the American radio networks in Moscow by refusing to let them use short-wave facilities to relay their broadcasts to the United States.

The ban on the radio representatives was acknowledged here yesterday by the networks after it was learned that they had differed among themselves as to what course to follow in their efforts to resume news broadcasts from the Soviet Union.

The formal explanation made by the Russian Government was that its heavy winter schedule of short-wave programs precluded the allotment of time to the correspondents.

The networks noted, however, that in past years the advent of the winter season had not disturbed the schedule of the American correspondents. Ordinarily, it was said, the networks with regular correspondents consume at the most thirty minutes a day and often less.

First Halted on Oct. 7

One chain was understood to favor a formal representation to Moscow through the State Department. Two other networks were said to be pursuing a more moderate course, preferring to make further attempts to obtain a fuller explanation.

The State Department was known, however, to be following the developments closely.

The Moscow broadcasts were first cut off on Oct. 7, but the networks have not mentioned the fact on the air, presumably in hopes of restoring the pick-ups from the Soviet.

The network correspondents now assigned to Moscow are Richard C. Hottelet of the Columbia Broadcasting System, Robert Magidoff of the National Broadcasting Company and Edward Stevens of the American Broadcasting Company.

The Soviet's explanation that it did not have sufficient facilities for

Continued on Page 6, Column 5

World News Summarized

FRIDAY, NOVEMBER 8, 1946

The United States is ready to waive its veto right over trusteeship agreements if all other powers do likewise, John Foster Dulles, American member of the United Nations General Assembly's Trusteeship Committee, said yesterday. In the event agreements presented by Washington for control of former Japanese islands are not approved, the islands will remain under this country's de facto control, he added. [1:8.]

White Russia would have the United Nations impose strict economic sanctions on Franco Spain as well as break diplomatic relations. [3:1.]

Correspondents of American radio networks in Russia have lost the use of short-wave facilities to relay their news broadcasts to the United States. [1:5.]

Foreign Minister Molotov went to Washington to attend the Soviet Embassy celebration of the October Revolution. He called at the State Department and visited President Truman, who was suffering from a cold. [1:6-7.] Premier Stalin was absent from the Moscow ceremonies, featured by a Red Army parade. [1:6-7.]

The Foreign Ministers Council, having recessed for a day to permit Mr. Molotov to attend the Washington fete, will reconvene this afternoon and grapple with the real, unsolved issues of the Italian draft treaty, starting with Trieste. [1:7.]

Marshal Tito has offered to trade Trieste for Gorizia, Palmiro Togliatti, head of the Italian Communist party, reported after his return to Rome from a three-day visit with the Yugoslav leader. He said Marshal Tito stipulated Trieste must have sufficient autonomy to guarantee a really democratic government. [2:2, with map.]

New York City honored Foreign Secretary Bevin. At City Hall he said he was not overly perturbed by delays in peacemaking because "ordinary people, whatever their ideologies or political policies" have a common burning desire for permanent peace. [1:2-3.]

American business men and other foreign buyers with the necessary dollar credits were invited by General McNarney to buy in Germany. [8:3.]

Approval has been given to the British loan to Czechoslovakia, which was held up following the cancellation of American credits to Prague. [6:3.]

The United States, in a move to break the impasse caused by Russian objections that has prevented distribution of Japanese reparations, has invited opinions of ten other nations. [11:6.]

The crisis in the soft-coal wage negotiations is expected to mount next week when Secretary Krug meets John L. Lewis and thirty union district leaders. [1:4.] President Meyer of the International Bank warned the Academy of Political Science that the disastrous effects of a coal strike for "mankind the world over cannot be exaggerated." [1:3.]

Mayor O'Dwyer was said to be ready to fight a threatened strike on the city's transit lines over retroactive pay increases now before the courts. [1:1.]

"Strikes have become a national menace" and unless they are curtailed "the nation will sink into chaos and organized labor will perish," President Tobin told the members of the AFL teamsters union. [16:2-3.]

Synthetic penicillin has been produced at the Cornell University Medical College, culminating a five-year investigation in which British and American scientists cooperated. The synthesis is expected to open the way for the creation of new disease-fighting substances. [1:2-3.]

"All the News That's Fit to Print"

The New York Times

LATE CITY EDITION

Weather: Fair, very cold today and tonight. Chance of snow tomorrow. Temp. range: today 24-14; Sunday 33-26. Full U.S. report on Page 30.

VOL. XCVIII..No. 33,120. Entered as Second-Class Matter. Postoffice, New York, N. Y. NEW YORK, TUESDAY, SEPTEMBER 28, 1948. Times Square, New York 18, N. Y. Telephone Lackawanna 4-1000 THREE CENTS IN NEW YORK CITY

PEARY CACHE FOUND IN ARCTIC BY U. S. SHIPS ON RECORD TRIP; 1906 PAPERS BROUGHT BACK

SEALED IN A BOTTLE

Men in Helicopter Spot Cairn as Dark and Ice Threaten Expedition

PACK CRIPPLES A VESSEL

Two Others Set Northern Mark Under Own Power—Chart New Routes on Return

By MURRAY SCHUMACH

Special to THE NEW YORK TIMES.

WASHINGTON, Sept. 27 — A Navy and Coast Guard expedition has returned to the United States from the Arctic with handwritten records left in the Polar regions more than forty years ago by Commdr. Robert E. Peary, discoverer of the North Pole.

With the return of the American vessels to home ports, it has also been learned that the explorers found copies of documents cached in that vicinity by a British expedition of 1875-76. The original papers of this exploration were removed by Commander Peary in 1905, when he ordered the copies placed there that have now been found at Cape Sheridan, about 450 miles from the Pole.

Although the text of the papers was not made public, a man who saw parts of the notes said they were for the most part the usual evidence left by explorers of their presence in strange places.

"You might say," said this person, "that they were ancestors of the 'Kilroy was here' notes."

Find Made at Last Minute

The expedition was organized to resupply existing weather stations and to reconnoiter the area for the purpose of planning the construction of two new weather stations to be operated jointly by American and Canadian authorities.

While Commander Peary had first alluded to his own and the British papers in an account that he wrote for THE NEW YORK TIMES in 1911, there had been no more substantial proof of their existence, although original doubt had been dissipated in recent years.

A bottle in which these papers were enclosed was found under dramatic circumstances. Constant daylight was on the wane and ice packs were becoming increasingly threatening. An earlier attempt to locate the cache had failed. No more than two days were left before the expedition would have been forced to evacuate the area when the find was made.

By this time, however, the leaders of the expedition had already set one record. This expedition had pushed two of its three ships past Lat. 85 degrees N., or farther north than any vessel had gone under its own power.

New Channels Discovered

Finally, on the return trip, the expedition recorded still another achievement. Instead of heading for the safe waters by the route they had taken on the way north, the leaders of the expedition took to straits and channels believed never to have been navigated before.

Technically, the expedition was known as Task Force 80. It was made up of the Navy ice breaker Edisto, the Coast Guard ice breaker Eastwind and the Navy cargo vessel Wyandotte. On board these ships were more than 500 officers and enlisted men. Also participating were American and Canadian civilian experts and a few Canadian naval officers.

There were no sledges or huskies on this expedition and no Eskimos. Instead, each of the ice breakers had a flight deck aft with two helicopters that had inflated pontoons and plastic domes. Also on board were small landing craft.

The route taken north was not unusual. Peary had used it, calling it the "American route." The ships went through Davis Strait into Baffin Bay, then into North Water. From there they entered Smith Sound, which led to Kane Basin and Kennedy Channel, final-

Continued on Page 14, Column 2

WHERE EXPLORER'S CAIRN WAS FOUND

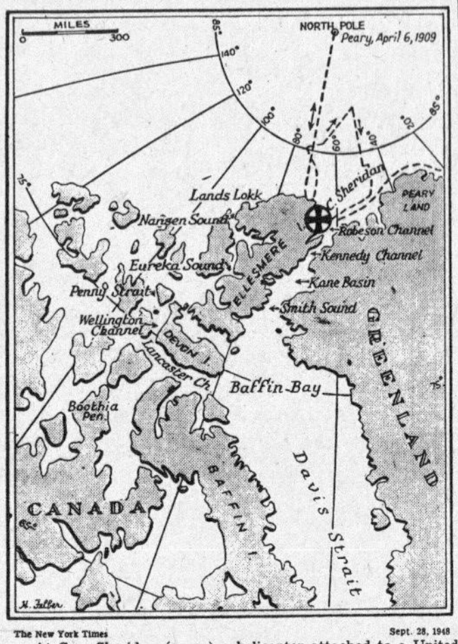

At Cape Sheridan (cross) a helicopter attached to a United States task force alighted and found papers left there by Commander Robert E. Peary, discoverer of the North Pole. Peary's route on his expedition to the Pole is shown by the dotted line.

CIO Teachers Union Called Subversive at U. S. Inquiry

By STANLEY LEVEY

The head of a New York technical school charged yesterday that the Teachers Union, CIO, was trying to organize trade schools with the objective of undermining the loyalty of their student-veterans "through control of their instructors and dissemination of subversive propaganda."

He was Col. William B. Campbell, executive vice president of the Radio Electronics School, 52 Broadway. He testified at the opening of an inquiry into the activities of the union and its parent organization, the United Public Workers, by a subcommittee of the House Committee on Education and Labor at the Federal Building, 10 Foley Square.

There were indications that the inquiry, which resulted from complaints to Fred A. Hartley Jr., chairman of the full House Committee, by the school's management, would be broadened into a thorough investigation of the extent of Communist infiltration into the local public school system and the New York Department of Welfare.

At the invitation of Irving McCann, counsel for the subcommittee, Andrew G. Clauson Jr., president of the Board of Education; Dr. William Jansen, Superintendent of Schools, and Raymond M. Hilliard, Commissioner of Welfare, will testify today. An estimated 5,000 members of the school system belong to the Teachers Union, while Local 1 of

Continued on Page 21, Column 2.

REGISTRATION HERE OFF TO SLOW START

Listings Lower Than First Day in 1944 in Every Borough Except Manhattan

Registration in the city for the November election got off to a surprisingly slow start yesterday, the first day on which the booths were open for voters to qualify.

While the totals ran higher than in minor election years, in every borough, except Manhattan, the registration was lower than it was on the first day in 1944, the last Presidential election year. Manhattan was 110 registrants higher than four years ago.

The total for the city for the first day, as tabulated early this morning, was 399,861, compared with 436,321 on the first day in 1944; 308,470 on the first day in 1946, a year in which a Governor

Continued on Page 17, Column 5

Hiss Sues Chambers for Slander; Calls Communist Charge 'False'

In an attempt to clear himself of the charge that he was a member of the Communist party, Alger Hiss, former high State Department official, filed a slander action yesterday in Federal Court against his accuser, Whittaker Chambers, now a senior editor of Time magazine.

Although the suit, charging defamation of character and asking damages of $50,000, was filed in the Maryland District Court, the complaint was given out here by Mr. Hiss, now president of the Carnegie Endowment for International Peace. Mr. Chambers, an avowed former Communist, lives in Carroll County, Md.

The complaint alleged that the "untrue, false and defamatory" accusations were made in a radio broadcast on Aug. 30 and were a repetition of Mr. Chambers' testimony in five appearances before the House Committee on Un-American Activities.

Mr. Hiss denied the charge under oath when he was called by the committee and dared his accuser to repeat it at a public forum where Mr. Chambers would not be immune from legal action.

Mr. Chambers did repeat it. A transcript of the broadcast was incorporated in Mr. Hiss' complaint. It reportedly contained several statements that the plaintiff asserted "damaged his professional reputation and office, brought him into public odium and contempt and caused him great pain and mental anguish."

The contents of the broadcast, Mr. Hiss charged, were designed to show him as disloyal and unfaithful to the United States, that he had betrayed his duty and had sworn falsely to oaths of office upon assuming various Government posts.

Asked at that time if he thought Mr. Hiss would sue for slander and libel, Mr. Chambers said, "I do not think so."

At his fourth appearance before the House committee, Mr. Chambers met Mr. Hiss in a dramatic

Continued on Page 21, Column 3

Indictment of Five Is Urged In Report on Atomic Spying

House Group Lists Two Scientists as in Bomb Project—Roosevelt Aware, Had to Guard Secret—Truman 'Inaction' Hit

By WILLIAM S. WHITE

Special to THE NEW YORK TIMES.

WASHINGTON, Sept. 27—Immediate indictment of five persons for wartime atomic espionage, spying alleged to have been directed by Russian diplomatic representatives, was recommended tonight by the House Committee on Un-American Activities.

Two of those accused were atomic bomb scientists when, as the Manhattan District Project, the operation was still under military control. They are Dr. Clarence F. Hiskey and Dr. John H. Chapin.

The others were Steve Nelson, an American Communist official from western Pennsylvania; Arthur Alexandrovich Adams, described as a professional and high-ranking Soviet spy now believed to be in Russia, and Marcia Sand Hiskey, Dr. Hiskey's former wife.

Still others, among them a man identified only as "Scientist X," were implicated by the committee to one or another degree. Of "Scientist X," it was said that he "should either be prosecuted forthwith or cleared."

The Truman Administration was accused of long and "completely inexcusable" lack of action against atomic spies despite a "complete record" of their activities which, it was stated, was made to President Roosevelt four years ago and later passed on to President Truman.

Mr. Roosevelt was by implication held not to blame for the absence of prosecutions, for, the committee said, court actions in wartime would have exposed what was then the capital secret of the very existence of the atomic bomb.

The committee's 20,000-word document was described as no more than an interim report in a continuing investigation which thus far had only "scratched the

Continued on Page 23, Column 6

The text of the House Committee's report is on Pages 22 and 23.

DEWEY REAFFIRMS WARNING TO WORLD AMERICA IS UNITED

Cautions Police States on Our Election—Hints at Seattle of Plea Over Iron Curtain

The text of Mr. Dewey's Seattle speech, Page 18.

By LEO EGAN

Special to THE NEW YORK TIMES.

SEATTLE, Sept. 27 — Governor Dewey today coupled a warning to foreign governments not to interpret the American political campaign as evidence of disunity with a promise to proceed with the speedy development of Western water-power resources. He expressed these views as he entered the Northwest in quest of electoral votes.

With Russia repudiating normal means of solving international differences, Mr. Dewey told a noonday audience in Portland, Ore., it was important that America's attitude be understood, both by totalitarian and by free governments.

"The attitude of the American people," he continued, "is that,

Continued on Page 18, Column 2

TRUMAN SAYS GOP WANTS SURRENDER OF PUBLIC'S RIGHTS

Republican 'Unity' Would Help Rich Not Poor, and Keep High Prices, He Tells Texans

The text of the President's Bonham speech, Page 20.

By W. H. LAWRENCE

Special to THE NEW YORK TIMES.

BONHAM, Tex., Sept. 27—President Truman declared today that the Republican leaders "don't want unity—they want surrender."

Climaxing his appeal for Texas' twenty-three electoral votes with speeches at Fort Worth, Dallas and here in the home town of former Speaker Sam Rayburn, the President replied for the first time to Gov. Thomas E. Dewey's opening campaign speeches promising that if elected he could bring "unity" to America.

The Chief Executive still did not mention his opponent by name, but his references were unmistakable. The Republicans, he said, wanted the kind of unity that "benefits the few at the expense of the many" while he, as President, was

Continued on Page 20, Column 1

World News Summarized

TUESDAY, SEPTEMBER 28, 1948

Britain will establish regional defense agreements "if we find in the end that we cannot proceed on a world basis, as we had hoped," Foreign Secretary Bevin told the United Nations General Assembly yesterday. "We must agree with whom we can agree," he said, adding that Britain would continue to rearm but would "never indulge" in aggression. Mr. Bevin detailed disputes and Soviet vetoes in answering charges leveled by Russian Deputy Foreign Minister Vishinsky. He regretted Russia's veto of the plan for control of atomic energy and declared that if an atomic war took place the blame must lie with Russia. [1:8.]

Mr. Bevin reaffirmed Britain's unqualified endorsement of the Bernadotte plan for Palestine, but Pakistan said that the East never would accept a sovereign state of Israel. [11:1.]

Poland's representative accused the United States of interfering in the administration of the United Nations and criticized Secretary General Lie for not having demanded an apology for spy charges made before a Senate committee. [12:6.]

The Western powers are expected to send to Mr. Lie today their formal request to place the Soviet blockade of Berlin on the Security Council agenda. [1:6-7.] In Berlin the City Council called for complete evacuation of all troops from Germany, an end of the blockade and a single currency. The Council asked that four-power rule of Berlin continue, with no power favored above the others, as long as Germany remained occupied. [1:7.] Ambassador Smith, after reporting to President Truman, said relations with Russia never were more serious [1:6-7.]

Combined military resources with which to meet a sudden emergency were studied by the defense ministers of the Western European Union. It was indicated that a successful defense was contingent upon supplies from the United States. [3:1.]

Against this background of political conflict representatives of twenty-one nations met in Geneva to try to stimulate East-West trade. [10:3-4.]

Governor Dewey warned foreign governments that despite the intensity of our political campaign "nothing will divide our country and nothing like a crisis will so unite us." In the Northwest he presented a nine-point conservation program. [1:4.] President Truman told Texans that the Republicans "don't want unity—they want surrender." [1:5.]

The immediate indictment of five persons, including two atomic scientists and a Communist official, on charges of wartime atomic espionage under the alleged direction of Soviet diplomats, was demanded by the House Committee on Un-American Activities. [1:4-5.] Another House group heard that the Teachers Union in this city sought to organize trade schools to undermine the loyalty of student-veterans. [1:2-3.]

Alger Hiss sued Whittaker Chambers for $50,000 damages for calling him a Communist in a broadcast of House committee testimony. [1:2-3.]

A cache of a Peary polar expedition with records of an earlier British party has been found and the papers brought to Washington. [1:1.]

BEVIN IN U. N. WARNS RUSSIA BRITAIN MAY TURN TO BLOCS; LAYS ATOM GUILT TO SOVIET

BRITISH STATESMAN ADDRESSING U. N.

Foreign Secretary Bevin speaking in Paris yesterday

Associated Press Radiophoto

CITES SECURITY AIM

Briton Says His Country Will Act Regionally if World Plans Fail

MOSCOW HELD TO ACCOUNT

Breakdown of Machinery for Peace Ascribed to Willful Obstruction of Minority

Excerpts from the address of Mr. Bevin are on Page 4.

By THOMAS J. HAMILTON

Special to THE NEW YORK TIMES.

PARIS, Sept. 27—In a powerful speech, the quiet tone of which underlined the gravity of the crisis between the Soviet Union and the Western powers, British Foreign Secretary Ernest Bevin announced today that the British Government would seek to establish regional defense agreements "if we find in the end that we cannot proceed on a world basis as we had hoped."

In his address to the United Nations General Assembly the Foreign Secretary did not refer to the breakdown of efforts to reach an agreement among the Big Four on the Berlin question which deepened even further the pessimism prevalent here since the General Assembly convened last week.

Cites Soviet Refusal

The Briton placed squarely upon Russia alone the responsibility for any eventual atomic war, citing the Soviet refusal to agree to the majority's wishes on the Atomic Energy Commission. He declared:

"This I must say with all the solemnity at my disposal. If the black fury, the incalculable disaster of an atomic war should fall upon us, all I can say is that one power, by refusing its cooperation in the control and development of those great new forces for the good of humanity, will alone be responsible for the evils which may be visited upon mankind."

Mr. Bevin's statement was interpreted as an announcement that Britain hoped to expand the nascent "Western Union"—which is to provide for mutual defense pacts between France, Belgium, the Netherlands and Luxembourg—to include most if not all the remaining democracies of Western Europe.

"We must agree with whom we can agree," Mr. Bevin solemnly told the Assembly, "work with whom we can work; understand and trust those who are willing to enter into trust and understanding with us."

Expects Structures to Grow

"It may be, after all, that if world government cannot come as we had hoped, out of these very regional structures to which we may now turn there may yet grow that world government for which humanity yearns and for which it has been striving and struggling for so long."

Mr. Bevin made it clear also that Britain would continue to rearm, declaring that "through no wish or fault of our own we have now been forced to turn from our work of reconstruction and to divert part of our resources to the production of munitions, which we had virtually abandoned in 1945."

"In our concern for the economic and social well-being of our people we came near to neglecting their safety, which we had hoped might have been secure in the hands of the United Nations," he declared.

With this he coupled the statement that the Western Union was not aimed at the Soviet Union, as Soviet Deputy Foreign Minister Andrei Y. Vishinsky charged on Saturday, but that the British Government had decided "to build a union—a Western Union—which can stand on its own feet and rally its own people against any aggression that may be launched against it, from wherever it may come."

"We are not suggesting an attack on anyone," said Mr. Bevin, adding that he wanted to quote the following "very solemn declaration" on the part of the British Government:

"If the Government of the Soviet Union is living in fear of any aggression by us on territory of the

Continued on Page 4, Column 3

West's Note on Berlin Goes To Security Council Today

By HAROLD CALLENDER

Special to THE NEW YORK TIMES.

PARIS, Sept. 27—A formal request of the Western powers that the United Nations Security Council discuss the Soviet blockade of Berlin may be sent to Secretary General Trygve Lie tomorrow, it was said tonight after United States Ambassador Lewis W. Douglas, Sir William Strang, permanent British Foreign Office Under-Secretary, and French Ambassador Rene Massigli had worked all day in drafting the request.

Identical notes from the United States, Britain and France will be delivered to Mr. Lie Tuesday at 3:30 P. M., thirty minutes after the Security Council is scheduled to meet, press services reported.]

It seemed likely that the appeal would be based on Chapter VII, Article 39, of the Charter, which provides that the Security Council shall determine the existence of any threat to peace.

Both in their note to Moscow yesterday and in their statement announcing their intention to go before the United Nations, the Western Foreign Ministers characterized Russian actions as a threat to peace. Officials predicted that in their letter to Mr. Lie, asking that the Berlin question be put on the agenda of the Council, the three Foreign Ministers would employ much the same language as that used in their statement yesterday.

French officials said that the request would include the suggestion

Continued on Page 3, Column 5

END OF OCCUPATION URGED BY GERMANS

People Want All Four Powers or None to Leave, Berlin City Council Declares

By EDWARD A. MORROW

Special to THE NEW YORK TIMES.

BERLIN, Sept. 27 — In a five-point declaration directed at the United Nations, the Berlin City Council today called for complete evacuation of the occupation troops from Germany as the only sure way of ending the present crisis and preventing recurrence of new ones.

However, the declaration emphasized that an overwhelming majority of the city's population wants the four-power rule of the city to continue so long as any part of Germany is occupied. There is an "emphatic desire on the part of the people" that none of the powers concerned occupy any position of precedence with regard to Berlin.

The declaration, which was

Continued on Page 5, Column 3

U. S. Moscow Envoy Sees Truman; Takes Grave View but Doubts War

Special to THE NEW YORK TIMES.

BONHAM, Tex., Sept. 27—Lieut. Gen. Walter Bedell Smith, Ambassador to Moscow, said tonight that he had reported to President Truman that United States relations with the Soviet Union had never been more "critical" than today, but later he changed the word "critical" to "serious" to indicate his belief that the United States was not "trembling on the brink of war."

The Ambassador, who had been flown from Washington to confer with the President on his election campaign train from Dallas to Bonham, said in a press interview that Mr. Truman agreed with his analysis of the Soviet situation.

General Smith, emphasizing that he was a soldier, not a politician, in dealing with a critical issue of foreign policy issue, said that while the Russians expressed great interest in the third party in this country, they wished to know what might be the effect on United States foreign policy if President Truman were replaced with Governor Dewey, the Republican nominee.

"We always answer in the negative, telling them that our policy is a considered policy supported by both parties and by about 90 per cent of the American people," the Ambassador said.

When reporters first asked General Smith about the state of United States relations with the Soviet Union he replied that they had "never been more critical since the beginning of the war."

"Is there going to be another war?" the ambassador was asked.

"That question is too deep for me to answer," he replied.

Then he was asked to define what he meant by "critical relations."

General Smith said that he would alter the word "critical" to "serious" because he did not think "we are trembling on the brink of war." He added that he thought the situation could be stabilized if the United States con-

Continued on Page 3, Column 2

"All the News That's Fit to Print"

The New York Times.

LATE CITY EDITION
Mostly sunny and seasonably cold today. Fair tomorrow.
Temperature Range Today—Max., 42; Min., 33
Temperatures Yesterday—Max., 56; Min., 41
Full U. S. Weather Bureau Report, Page 33

VOL. XCVIII. No. 33,280. Entered as Second-Class Matter, Postoffice, New York, N. Y. NEW YORK, MONDAY, MARCH 7, 1949. Times Square, New York 18, N. Y. Telephone Lackawanna 4-1000 THREE CENTS IN NEW YORK CITY

COURT DECREES END OF YONKERS STRIKE AS REFUSE PILES UP

Broad Injunction Forbids the City Workers to Continue Their 8-Day Walkout

STATE LAW CAUSES SNAG

Calls for Penalties if Men Are Rehired—Contractors Sought to Remove Garbage

By A. H. RASKIN

Armed with a Supreme Court order forbidding continuance of the Yonkers municipal employes' strike, officials of that city will make a new effort today to find ways of removing the eight-day accumulation of garbage, ashes and industrial waste before it becomes a threat to the health of Yonkers' 150,000 residents.

The outlook for immediate success was dim, even though the court order was one of the most sweeping ever issued in this state in connection with a labor dispute. It restrained the two striking unions from picketing, distributing circulars, gathering within three blocks of any city building or interfering in any way with the conduct of municipal operations.

The order, which remains in effect pending a hearing on a temporary injunction in White Plains Wednesday, was signed by Supreme Court Justice Frederick G. Schmidt of Port Chester at the request of Corporation Counsel John Galloway Jr. of Yonkers.

Peril to City Charged

The city contended that the strike presented a "grave and serious danger to the health, welfare, safety and convenience" of Yonkers citizens.

Edward Doyle, secretary-treasurer of Local 456 of the International Brotherhood of Teamsters, AFL, was served with a copy of the order shortly before midnight Saturday in a Yonkers restaurant. The police then directed members of the local to leave the round-the-clock picket lines they had been maintaining outside the Yonkers City Hall and the Department of Public Works garage.

However, members of the second union, Local 1025 of the United Government Workers, CIO, continued to picket without molestation. Process servers were unable to locate any responsible officer of that local, but they will be waiting at the Strand Theatre this morning when the 500 strikers gather for their daily report meeting.

There were hints last night that officers of the CIO group might stay away from the meeting and continue to make themselves scarce until Wednesday, thus making it possible for their members to maintain picket lines unbroken until the White Plains hearing. An alternative strategy under consideration in union circles was the taking over of picketing assignments by members of other American Federation of Labor or Congress of Industrial Organizations affiliates.

Unions Appeal to Washington

A complaint that the restraining order was so broad as to deprive the union members of their constitutional rights was telegraphed to Attorney General Tom Clark in Washington last night by Charles E. Hughes, chairman of the Joint AFL-CIO Non-Partisan Committee of Westchester County.

Mr. Hughes said "the ex parte use of the injunction" was a "very dangerous" backward step in labor relations. He added that the court order would not move any ashes or garbage, and reiterated his suggestion that the Yonkers city administration sit down with the two unions to work out a formula for putting the 500 discharged strikers back to work.

A similar suggestion was made by Emmett Burke, a member of the Yonkers Common Council, in telegrams to Mayor Curtiss E. Frank, Acting City Manager John A. Peterson and heads of the striking unions.

Mr. Burke recommended that all the workers be reinstated without penalty, that garbage be collected at the Polish Community Center, where a musicians' picket line helped precipitate the showdown between the city and the two unions; that an immediate meeting of the Common Council be called to canvass problems of wages, hours and Sunday and holiday pay, and that a board be set up to hear grievances of city employes as a means of preventing future strikes.

Mayor Frank said he saw no way under the Condon-Wadlin Law outlawing strikes of public em-

Continued on Page 16, Column 6

Price Curbs 3,800 Years Old, Babylonian Tablets Reveal

Yale Professor Translates Code That Ruled in Eshnunna Along the Tigris—Laws Were Found in Baghdad Museum

Special to THE NEW YORK TIMES.

NEW HAVEN, Conn., March 6—Price controls were used at least 3,800 years ago in the ancient Babylonian kingdom of Eshnunna, according to a translation of what is believed to be the oldest code of laws in the world, made public here today.

Tablets inscribed with the laws were discovered in the Iraq Museum in Baghdad last year by Albrecht E. R. Goetze, Professor of Assyriology and Babylonian Literature at Yale University, and director of the American School of Oriental Research at Baghdad. The tablets were said to be 200 years older than the Babylonian Code of Hammurabi.

Eshnunna flourished between 2000 and 1800 B. C., along the east bank of the Tigris.

The laws, which are similar to many of today's statutes, lead off with a price-control list of grain, wool and oil. The equivalent of bushels of grain was priced at one shekel of silver, or about one-quarter ounce of the white metal. The same price held for what would be twelve quarts of oil, or six pounds of wool.

The laws were not limited to commodities; they applied also to wages and services.

"The hire for a donkey is forty quarts of grain and the wages for its driver are forty quarts of grain," reads a translation which was in a recent issue of Sumer, a journal of the Iraq Department of Antiquities.

The code also regulated marriage dowries. In Eshnunna, young men had to pay "bride-money" to prospective fathers-in-law. In case of death of the bride, the father had to refund the money plus 20 per cent interest.

The criminal section of the code sets up a table of fines for various offenses.

"If a man bites the nose of another man and severs it, he shall

Continued on Page 13, Column 6

Nanking Paper Is Closed For Its Attacks on Chiang

By HENRY R. LIEBERMAN

Special to THE NEW YORK TIMES.

NANKING, March 6—The newspaper National Salvation Daily was suspended indefinitely and its publisher arrested by Nanking garrison headquarters today following the publication of two editorials demanding that President Chiang Kai-shek cease his alleged behind-the-scenes "manipulation" of political affairs and "go abroad."

The publisher, Kung Teh-po, was charged with "spreading rumors, slandering the Government, creating social disorder and alienating the feeling of high level government leaders." According to a garrison headquarters spokesman Mr. Kung's arrest was ordered by Gen. Tang En-po, commander of the Shanghai-Nanking area.

The newspaper had asserted that President Chiang's presence in Fenghwa in Chekiang Province, to which he retired on Jan. 21 made it difficult for the Acting President, Gen. Li Tsung-jen, to pursue a policy of either peace or war. It maintained that his continuing behind the scences influence rendered General Li's peace efforts suspect in the eyes of the Communists and that his lost prestige in the United States complicated the task of obtaining American aid should the Nationalists find it necessary to continue the war.

Special Courts Ended

The banning of the newspaper and the arrest of its publisher followed a decision of Premier Sun Fo's Cabinet yesterday to abolish the special criminals courts and "emergency criminal law" in accordance with General Li's "liberalization" program. It coincided with action taken by the military authorities in Shanghai in suspending the publication of all unregistered magazines and periodicals, especially those carrying "so-called inside stories."

Several members of the Legislative Yuan, which has adopted a resolution urging the Cabinet to implement all of General Li's "liberalization" program, immediately came to the defense of the Na-

Continued on Page 11, Column 5

MOSES DENOUNCES STATE BUDGET FOES

Radios From Caribbean That Dewey Highway Program Cannot Be Slashed

By LEO EGAN

Special to THE NEW YORK TIMES

ALBANY, March 6—Robert Moses, New York City construction coordinator, upbraided critics of Governor Dewey's fiscal program today for suggesting that funds for highway and parkway construction be reduced or eliminated. He said he could think of "nothing crazier."

Mr. Moses' assault on Dewey critics was broad enough to cover both the Republican insurgents from Westchester and Erie who have been clamoring for budget cuts to offset the need for a $168,-200,000 tax rise recommended by the Governor, and the Democrats, who have been contending that highway appropriations should be slashed and the savings used for school construction.

His statement was made in a radiogram from Jamaica, B. W. I. It came at a time when indications pointed to an effort some time this week to break the stalemate which has been holding up legislative action on both the Governor's $936,200,000 budget and his tax increase program.

The start of the drive to break the deadlock between the Legislature and the Governor may be hampered by the continued absence of Senator Arthur H. Wicks of

Continued on Page 4, Column 4

L.I.R.R. Cuts Non-Operating Crew 'To Stay Within Its Own Income'

The Long Island Rail Road confirmed last night statements made previously only by spokesmen for a labor union that the company had instituted heavy lay-offs among its non-operating personnel.

A terse statement issued by David E. Smucker, general manager of the line, said the necessity for the company to operate within "its own income" had made lay-offs among this category of employes imperative.

The statement made no mention—and a spokesman refused to fill in any details—of the number of workers laid off, or the savings involved in reducing the work force.

It was said, however, that the cut in the staff of workers in the repair shops would not result immediately in any curtailment in service, and that the safety factor was not involved.

The lay-offs came at the end of a week in which the 115-year-old railroad, which is reputed to carry the largest number of commuters of any line in the world, received an authorization to increase its rates, but was, nevertheless, forced to file a petition in bankruptcy in Federal Court.

A hearing scheduled for Friday before Federal Judge Harold M. Kennedy for the possible appointment of a trustee, or group of trustees, was suggested unofficially as the reason for the cut in a large part of the railroad's payroll.

Judge Kennedy was said to have asked for all necessary economies, pending the appointment of some kind of a trusteeship, and the Long Island apparently was hastening to comply.

The first word of the heavy lay-offs came Saturday from William J. McCarthy, president of Local 156, Long Island Rail Road System Federation, AFL.

Mr. McCarthy said that by Tuesday, some 500 craft workers will have been laid off at the Morris Park and Richmond Hill shops, which only last month had 1,500 men on their payrolls.

The union represents boilermak-

Continued on Page 16, Column 5

U. S. TO BAR SEARCH IN ITS GERMAN ZONE BY RUSSIAN TEAMS

Request to Recover Property Seen as Move to Strengthen Soviet Intelligence Net

WARNING GIVEN LAST YEAR

Britain Is Said to Have Joined in Announcing Restitution Work Would End April 30

By DREW MIDDLETON

Special to THE NEW YORK TIMES.

BERLIN, March 6—The United States will reject Marshal Vassily D. Sokolovsky's demand that Russian restitution teams be admitted into the United States zone, American military government officials said today. Marshal Sokolovsky's letter to Gen. Lucius D. Clay, United States Military Governor, released early this morning by ADN, the Soviet-licensed news service, purports to be a Russian attempt to speed recovery of matériel taken from Russia during the war.

Actually observers here see it as a Soviet attempt to strengthen the Russian intelligence network in the American zone. This network has been weakened by the forced withdrawal of the Soviet repatriation mission on Friday.

Beneath the haggling over the rights of various missions to operate in the western and eastern zones lies the hard fact of one of the most important intelligence campaigns of history.

Battle of Intelligence

One of the battles of this campaign ended in a draw last week when the Russian Repatriation Mission pulled out of Frankfort and two United States Graves Registration teams were ordered out of the Soviet zone.

Both the Russian and the American groups have, or perhaps had, legitimate business in each others portion of conquered Germany. But it is reasonable to assume that this business was much less important than the information that the groups returned to their respective chiefs.

American observers here believe that the Soviet demand to send fifteen "restitution officers" into the United States zone to inspect "German plants, archives, museums, picture galleries and private collections and to inspect relative documents" was another step in this intelligence campaign.

It is believed that Marshal Sokolovsky, who is more realistic than some of the political strategists sent him by Moscow, probably never thought the Soviet demands would be met. If this is true, he

Continued on Page 7, Column 4

THE PRESIDENT TRIES FOR A STORY

Mr. Truman interviewing Robert G. Nixon, president of the White House correspondents, at Key West yesterday. It was all in good fun. Associated Press Wirephoto

75-CENT BASE WAGE IN DANGER IN HOUSE

Leader in Committee Asserts Absence by Supporter Could Cut It to 55 or 60 Hourly

By ROBERT F. WHITNEY

Special to THE NEW YORK TIMES.

WASHINGTON, March 6—The Administration's bill to increase the the minimum wage requirement of the Fair Labor Standards Act from 40 cents an hour to 75 cents appeared to be in danger in the House Labor and Public Welfare Committee, a check of some members of the committee disclosed tonight.

The increase is one of the promises which President Truman made in his campaign and its possible serious modification points up President Truman's speech of a few days ago at the Jefferson-Jackson Day dinner of the Democratic party. He threatened to take to the stump in behalf of his program.

Developing tonight also were hints from leading Democratic sources in the Senate that the Administration might put off action on the President's civil rights program until the later days of the session despite what may happen in the filibuster which is tieing up the Senate.

The House Labor Committee ex-

Continued on Page 16, Column 4

Truman 'Interviews' Press As He Gaily Begins Vacation

By ANTHONY LEVIERO

Special to THE NEW YORK TIMES.

KEY WEST, Fla., March 6—President Truman "interviewed" Robert G. Nixon, president of the White House Correspondents Association, here this afternoon about the removal of Vyacheslav M. Molotov as Russian Foreign Minister.

Mr. Truman was having fun. He came here for a vacation and he began relaxing and plotting against White House correspondents even before his arrival.

When the chartered press plane arrived and the ladder was lowered, there was the country's new No. 1 reporter waiting. His gold pencil and the back of an envelope were ready.

"Where have you been?" demanded Mr. Truman as the first of the reporters started down. "Come on down. Where's the president of the White House Correspondents Association?"

"Here's the president now," reporters said as Mr. Nixon, of the International News Service, came down. The Chief Executive had seen him inaugurated last night as the association's new president at a dinner in Washington.

"Where's the band?" asked Mr. Truman. Voices hummed "Hail to the Chief."

"Yes Indeed," and "No, Too"

"What about Molotov, Mr. President?" asked President Truman.

"Yes, yes indeed, yes," replied President Nixon.

"All right," said Mr. Truman, apropos of nobody knew what.

"I agree," President Nixon commented expansively.

"And 'no' too?" asked President Truman.

"And 'no' too," added President Nixon, warming up. "On the other hand, perhaps I shouldn't comment on that. It is rather difficult to assay at the moment. We have the matter under considerable study."

All through the interview Mr. Truman made marks with his pencil on the back of his brown envelope. It was an interview that shed light only on the President's mood.

Mr. Truman also threw "What's new on Molotov" questions at Mer-

Continued on Page 5, Column 2

FOSTER AND DENNIS RETORT TO TRUMAN

Communists Say They Seek Peace, Are No Traitors—Take 'Jefferson, Lincoln' Roles

Two top leaders of the Communist party likened themselves yesterday to Lincoln and Jefferson as patriots fighting for peace and criticized President Truman for having called them "traitors."

William Z. Foster, chairman of the Communist party, U. S. A., and Eugene Dennis, general secretary, made public an open letter to the President. The letter was dated yesterday, indicating that it had been made public before its receipt by the President.

Mr. Dennis is one of the eleven Communist leaders now on trial in Federal Court. Mr. Foster was jointly indicted with them for conspiring to organize the Communist party to teach and advocate overthrow of the government by force, but his trial has been delayed on the ground of ill health.

"Dear Mr. President," the letter said. "Is the advocacy of peace treason? Is the moral climate of our country such that an appeal to reason becomes the basis for the charge of treason?

"So it would appear. One day you called a writer an s.o.b. because he dared criticize one of your aides for accepting a medal from the fascist Peron. Another day you termed traitors men who believe that war is not inevitable and that two social systems can coop-

Continued on Page 3, Column 3

World News Summarized

MONDAY, MARCH 7, 1949

Evidence will be presented to a Federal Grand Jury today against Valentin A. Gubitchev, Russian aide in the United Nations Secretariat, and Judith Coplon, a Department of Justice employe, who were arrested Friday on suspicion of espionage. [1:8.] United Nations officials were worried by the effect of the case on negotiations with the United States for a loan and for a definition of privileges and immunities for employes. [3:3-4].

The trial of eleven United States Communist leaders charged with teaching and advocating the overthrow of the Government opens in Federal Court today after seven weeks of preliminary argument. [3:5.]

Eugene Dennis, general secretary of the Communist party, who is one of the defendants, and William Z. Foster, chairman of the party, sent an open letter to President Truman protesting his allusion to them as "traitors." They likened themselves to Lincoln and Jefferson in advocating peace, assailed warmongering and criticized the proposed North Atlantic security pact. The President's characterization followed the appeal of the Communist leaders for their comrades to obstruct this country's efforts in the event of war with Russia. [1:7.]

The President flew to Key West, Fla., for a vacation until March 19 [1:6-7.]

Two Administration projects faced heavy going in Congress. A House committee was split over raising the minimum legal wage to 75 cents an hour and Senate leaders were considering a delay on the civil rights program. [1:5.]

Chairman George of the Senate Finance Committee said that the State Department must submit cost estimates on a North Atlantic pact [6:6] and must give details on the ECA's request for Marshall Plan funds before the Senate can act on the measures. [7:1.]

The NLRB ruled unanimously that a strike for a closed-shop clause in a union contract was illegal under the Taft-Hartley Law. [16:3.]

Striking municipal workers in Yonkers were ordered by a Supreme Court Justice to end their walkout and picketing, and to keep three blocks from any city building. Argument on a plea for a temporary injunction will be heard Wednesday. [1:1.]

Russia's request that restitution teams be permitted to enter the American zone of Germany will be rejected. United States occupation officials said. They explained restitution work had been ended last April, and felt that the demand was made for intelligence purposes. [1:4.]

Labor unions in Japan have opened a campaign of strikes against the Government's economic program, tended to implement reforms outlined by General MacArthur. [11:2.]

A Nanking newspaper that demanded that Generalissimo Chiang halt behind-the-scenes attempts to influence Chinese policy was suspended indefinitely and its publisher arrested. [1:2-3.]

Mexico, which long has barred foreign ownership of oil properties, granted to American interests headed by Edwin W. Pauley the right to drill wells in two states on a fee basis. [9:1.]

Index to other news appears on Page 22.

Mob Flips Coins to Pick Lyncher; Negro Saves Life by Dive in River

By The United Press.

OPELOUSAS, La., March 6—A 25-year-old Negro, kidnapped from the St. Landry Parish Prison and on the verge of being lynched, jumped into the Atchafalaya River today and escaped while the leaders of a mob matched coins to see who would be his executioner.

The man is Edward Honeycutt, who has confessed that he attacked a white woman three months ago. A fisherman dragged Honeycutt from the river, and he was rearrested by Marshal Kenneth Devillier of Krotz Springs, La.

Authorities took him to the "mob-proof" prison at Baton Rouge, the state capital. They said Honeycutt was "not harmed," but they refused to let anyone talk to him.

Sheriff Martin Guilbeau said there were two "and maybe three" automobiles filled with men in the mob that abducted Honeycutt. The Sheriff and a posse were so close on their heels that the kidnappers had to flee without looking for Honeycutt when he escaped from them.

An elderly jailer was tricked at midnight Saturday into letting three men snatch Honeycutt from the St. Landry Parish Prison, which was supposed to be "mob proof." The jail is on the top floor of the three-and-a-half-story court house building.

Three men came up in an elevator. Two of them complained to Jailer Henry Landry that their companion was drunk and making a nuisance of himself. They said they wanted him locked up.

The jailer opened the steel door between the elevator entrance and the prison. As he did so, one of the men smashed him across the arm with a pistol. Another grabbed his keys.

"And now get the hell out of here," one of the men snarled at Jailer Landry.

The jailer fled to a restaurant across the street and telephoned

Continued on Page 12, Column 7

GRAND JURY TO GET SPY CHARGE TODAY AGAINST U. N. AIDE

Presentation of Case Involving Gubitchev and U. S. Girl Expected to Take a Week

2D SOVIET PROTEST LIKELY

Admittance to Jail Is Denied to Two Russians Who Seek to Talk to Prisoner

By MURRAY SCHUMACH

The Government will explain today to a grand jury here why a Russian engineer attached to the United Nations staff and an American woman employed by the Department of Justice were arrested Friday evening on suspicion of espionage.

The Department of Justice said last night that it expected to spend a week presenting the case for indictments of Valentin A. Gubitchev, 32 years old, of 64 West 108th Street, and Judith Coplon, 27, an analyst in the internal security division of the Department of Justice.

Both prisoners are in jail. Gubitchev is being held in $100,000 bail and Miss Coplon in $20,000 bail. It was expected that in the course of the week Raymond P. Whearty, special assistant to the Attorney General, would ask the prisoners to appear before the grand jury. They have already been served with subpoenas. However, the prisoners can, on constitutional grounds of self-incrimination, refuse to testify before the grand jury.

FBI Is Analyzing Papers

The notes taken from Miss Coplon's purse when she was arrested with Gubitchev on Third Avenue between Fourteenth and Fifteenth Streets were being analyzed yesterday at the Federal Bureau of Investigation laboratory in Washington. These papers had been described previously as typed excerpts of restricted Government papers. Attorney General Tom Clark had said that though the papers related to national defense they were of little importance.

The Department of Justice said that since Mr. Whearty's presentation before the grand jury would be "a comprehensive outline of the facts," it would probably include at least a summary of the seized papers and perhaps the actual notes picked up after Miss Coplon and Gubitchev had been trailed through Manhattan for two hours.

Miss Coplon's lawyer, Bertram J. Adams, could not be reached yesterday for comment on his plans. So far as could be learned Gubitchev still was without counsel.

The fact that the Russian had no lawyer led to speculation in United Nations circles that Russia was using this device to emphasize its contention that Gubitchev was immune to arrest because he was attached to the United Nations. The Russian Ambassador, Alexander S. Panyushkin, demanded on Saturday that Gubitchev be released on the grounds of immunity.

U. N. Denies Immunity

Since then, Gubitchev has been suspended from his job by Trygve Lie and the United Nations' legal authorities have insisted that the question of immunity has no part in this case. The United Nations' contention is that Gubitchev had immunity only while he was working for the United Nations. In this instance, it was pointed out, Gubitchev was not doing United Nations work and had no immunity.

Because it was thought the issue of immunity might be raised in the future, it was said that the United Nations would have an observer at the proceedings in this case. The observer would have the added job of reporting to the United Nations so it could decide if Gubitchev's suspension should be lifted.

A United Nations spokesman elaborated on the procedure that prompted that organization to notify the Soviet delegation to the United Nations of Gubitchev's arrest. The explanation was that the organization had consulted with the United States Department of State before taking this step. Since the Soviet Government no longer has consulates here it was deemed proper, because Gubitchev is a Russian national, to notify the Soviet delegation of the arrest.

Some United Nations officials feared an incident that occurred yesterday at the Federal detention pen here might lead to another Soviet protest to the State Department.

In the afternoon, it was learned, admittance to the detention pen

Continued on Page 2, Column 6

"All the News That's Fit to Print"

The New York Times.

LATE CITY EDITION
Fair and warm today and tomorrow.
Temperature Range Today—Max.,85; Min.,63
Temperature Yesterday—Max.,85; Min.,61
Full U. S. Weather Bureau Report, Page 33

Copyright, 1949, by The New York Times Company.

VOL. XCVIII...No. 33,448. Entered as Second-Class Matter, Postoffice, New York, N. Y. NEW YORK, MONDAY, AUGUST 22, 1949. Times Square, New York 18, N. Y. Telephone Lackawanna 4-1000 THREE CENTS NEW YORK CITY

O'DWYER MEN MAP VIGOROUS CAMPAIGN ON REGIME'S RECORD

Joseph and Impellitteri to Join Forces With Mayor in a United Headquarters

HE PLANS 20 RADIO TALKS

Lehman Is Reported to Have Made Decision on Senate—To Announce It Soon

By WARREN MOSCOW

Combined headquarters for Mayor O'Dwyer, Controller Lazarus Joseph and Council President Vincent Impellitteri are being set up at the Commodore Hotel in preparation for what friends of the Mayor described yesterday as one of the most vigorous Mayoralty campaigns ever planned in the city.

For the last ten days a small headquarters has been operating informally at the Commodore. It will be expanded this week, starting today, and will be running full force shortly after Labor Day. Four years ago, while all three city-wide candidates operated from the Commodore, their campaign was not a joint one in financing or in direction.

This time, lending stress to the record of the O'Dwyer Administration during his last term, the three candidates will run as members of one team, with emphasis on the improvements carried out in the city.

Plans 20 Radio Speeches

The Mayor is understood to have committed himself to making at least twenty major radio and television speeches. His friends said he also plans visits every night to different neighborhoods, bringing home his record to the people. He will make one major speech a night after the campaign really gets under way in October.

In preparation for this, the group of advisers entrusted to run the campaign are understood to have amassed, and screened, information on the school building program, hospital construction, health work and other fields of activity in which they believe the administration has a good record.

They realize that the Mayor weakened his position by his long period of indecision over whether he would be a candidate for reelection, and believe that this ground will be regained during the campaign by listing the accomplishments in office of the O'Dwyer-Joseph-Impellitteri Administration.

A general campaign manager has been selected, though not announced, and soon all of the borough campaign directors will have been chosen. One of the Mayor's most important speeches, scheduled for relatively early in the campaign, will be outside New York, but aimed at the local situation. It will be delivered to a convention of the State Congress of Industrial Organizations at Saratoga Springs on Sept. 9.

Lehman Reported Decided

Meanwhile, former Gov. Herbert H. Lehman, still vacationing at Lake Placid, N. Y., was understood yesterday to have arrived at a final decision on his own candidacy for the Senate. The nominations of both the Democratic and Liberal parties have been offered to Mr. Lehman.

Mr. Lehman will return to New York at the end of next week, or the start of the following one, and will then communicate his decision to the political leaders of the parties.

Mr. Lehman has communicated his decision to no one outside his immediate family, and no authoritative information as to whether he had decided to run could be obtained. However, he has discussed the issues of his Senate race with a number of people. While none of them would say that Mr. Lehman had given an inkling of his plans, they are of the impression that he would be a candidate for the post vacated by the resignation of Robert F. Wagner.

The nominations for United States Senator will be made by the state committees of the various parties, the Democrats meeting here Sept. 15, and the Republicans in Albany on the same day. Should Mr. Lehman decline to be the Democratic nominee, Supreme Court Justice Ferdinand Pecora is one possibility for the post, and Laurence Steinhardt, Ambassador to Canada, is another.

On the Republican side, the situation is wide open, except that many in the party believe John Foster Dulles, who is now a Senator by interim appointment of Governor Dewey, should be persuaded to run for election. Mr.

Continued on Page 16, Column 5

Bones of Saint Peter Found Under Altar, Vatican Believes

Reported to Be in Urn Guarded by Pontiff—'Neutral' Experts Will Be Asked to Check Discovery Under Basilica

By CAMILLE M. CIANFARRA
Special to The New York Times.

ROME, Aug. 7—The bones of Saint Peter, "Prince of the Apostles," who, according to Christian tradition, was crucified in Rome during the second half of the first century A. D., are understood to have been found less than twenty feet below the pavement of St. Peter's Basilica.

Vatican archaeologists who directed the excavations have taken an oath of secrecy and are therefore forbidden to confirm or deny the discovery. However, statements made over a period of months by various persons in the Vatican are said to have supplied enough circumstantial evidence that the remains of Saint Peter have been recovered in the hypogeum, or subterranean cell, where tradition said he was buried.

This crypt was unearthed two years ago in the course of secret excavations in the Vatican Grottoes. The bones are being preserved in an urn closely guarded by Pope Pius XII himself, in the private chapel next to his study, Vatican circles said.

Officials have described the discovery as the most important contribution yet made to the history of the origins of Christianity in the West. They said that it confirmed traditions and legends reported by historians during the past 1,800 years about the life and work of the poor fisherman from Galilee who was said to be the most favored, trusted and authoritative disciple of Christ.

According to these officials, the discovery disposes conclusively of non-Catholic contentions that Peter never lived, that if he did he was never in Rome, that he was not therefore the founder of the Roman Catholic Church, and that the Bishop of Rome—the Pope—is not his successor.

The discovery, officials said, was

Continued on Page 3, Column 2

McCloy Names 7 to 'Cabinet' For German Occupation Role

By JACK RAYMOND
Special to The New York Times.

FRANKFORT, Germany, Aug. 21—John J. McCloy, High Commissioner for United States-occupied Germany, announced today the names of seven members of his "cabinet" in the United States High Commission for Germany, which is replacing the American Military Government as the United States occupation agency. Each of the Allied powers will have its commission. The chiefs of the commissions will constitute a Tripartite High Commission.

Today's appointees included Chester A. McLain as general counsel, the same post he holds in the World Bank from which he is at present on leave of absence, and James W. Riddleberger as director of the Office of Political Affairs, the equivalent of the post he has held since succeeding Ambassador Robert D. Murphy as political adviser in the Military Government.

Of the appointees made known today, only Mr. Riddleberger, Maj. Gen. James P. Hodges, United States Commissioner of the Military Security Board, and James E. King, executive secretary, held posts with Gen. Lucius D. Clay. The others, brought here by Mr. McCloy, are Harvey W. Brown, director of the Office of Labor Affairs and labor adviser in the Economic Cooperation Administration mission; Glenn G. Wolfe, director of the Office of Administration; Ralph Nicholson, director of the Office of Public Affairs, and Mr. McLain.

Mr. McCloy, who said he had hoped to announce subsequent designates to his staff in the near future, has yet to name a new director of economics, probably next to his own one of the most influential positions in his organization. He also has yet to announce who will succeed Maj. Gen. George P. Hays, present Deputy Military Governor, who, it is understood, will return to a strictly Army assignment some time in September.

It is conjectural whether Mr. McLain will stay here any length of time. He said the other day that

Continued on Page 4, Column 6

RISE IN RELIEF LOAD ONLY 1,293 IN JULY

Smallest Since Upswing Began in December—'Too Early' for Conclusions, Hilliard Says

The city's welfare case load increased for the eighth successive month in July, but the rise was the smallest since the upswing began last December, Welfare Commissioner Raymond M. Hilliard said in his monthly report yesterday.

Contrasting the increase of 1,293 cases in July with the peak increase of 6,339 cases in March, Mr. Hilliard said that while it was too early to draw any final conclusions, it was "significant" that for each of the four months since then "there has been a steady lessening in the rate of increase."

The report showed that in July 156,354 cases, or 310,924 persons, received assistance from the department, against 155,061, or 309,240 persons, in June.

Applications for assistance showed a decline of 3.65 per cent, to approximately 3,000 a week, but Mr. Hilliard said the decrease was "too small to warrant any significant conclusions."

The largest increase in the number of cases added to the rolls was for home relief and veterans' assistance, which accounted for almost two-thirds of the total increase, or 816 cases. Of the applicants accepted in this combined category 20.4 per cent lost their jobs because of temporary illness. Mr. Hilliard pointed out that virtually all these cases would be taken care of by the state next year

Continued on Page 16, Column 4

'Captain' of Dory Seized in Looting Of Craft at the Manhasset Bay Club

Special to The New York Times.

PORT WASHINGTON, L. I., Aug. 21—A visit by a prospective buyer to a 24-foot Jersey dory led today to the arrest of the craft's owner, William Frey, 21 years old, at the Manhasset Bay Yacht Club here today.

Booked on charges of assaulting the arresting detective and of unlawfully possessing two loaded pistols, the prisoner, who lived aboard the dory and described himself as a "yacht captain," still was being questioned tonight on a series of recent occurrences at the club. These included the looting of several boats at the club moorings and the mysterious burning of one to the water's edge.

In addition, the prisoner was being questioned on a recent $600 hold-up in the Beacon motion picture theatre in Port Washington, Inspector Stuyvesant A. Pinnell, in charge of Nassau County detectives, said.

It was the owner of the burned yacht, James B. Lambert of 22-37 Seventy-seventh Street, Jackson Heights, Queens, who brought about the arrest, the police said. He reported that in seeking a new boat, he visited Frey's craft and recognized among its equipment several articles that had been stolen from him.

With this information, Detective William Graeber went to the yacht club and inspected the dory at 2:30 o'clock this afternoon. He reported that he found a loaded pistol under one of the bunks, and that Frey then seized another pistol from beneath an opposite bunk.

The detective said he subdued the prisoner after a struggle and took him to the Roslyn police station.

Frey had moored his boat at the club under guest privileges. He is wanted in Westchester County on a bail-jumping charge involving the theft of an automobile, Inspector Pinnell said.

LUCAS THREATENS TO HOLD CONGRESS TILL THANKSGIVING

Senate Majority Leader Says It Cannot Rest Before It Decides on 'Vital Issues'

SEES THE 81ST DOING WELL

Speaker Rayburn Joins in View Final Record Will Be Good—Rent Fight Coming Today

By ROBERT F. WHITNEY
Special to The New York Times.

WASHINGTON, Aug. 21—The possibility of a Congress in session until Thanksgiving if it took that long for it to pass important legislation was suggested today by Senator Scott W. Lucas of Illinois, Democratic leader in the Senate.

Mr. Lucas' statement was in the nature of a threat. But most members of the Congress believe that in spite of the present legislative snarl adjournment may be reached by the middle of next month.

Later today Mr. Lucas and the Speaker of the House, Sam Rayburn of Texas, predicted in a joint broadcast that the final record of the Eighty-first Congress would be the most constructive in many years. In this the two Democratic leaders were not counting alone on the record of the first session, but were forecasting the accomplishments of next year's session.

"There are," said Mr. Lucas, "many important bills which must be brought up for action before we can take a rest—and we are not going to close up the doors of Congress until we have reached decisions on these vital issues, even if we have to stay in Washington until Thanksgiving time."

Money bills constitute the greatest log jam, especially in the Senate, and Mr. Lucas said he thought Congress would act in this session not only on appropriations but also on reciprocal trade agreements, minimum wage, basing point, higher executive pay, higher military pay and a farm price support bill.

The Senate leader mentioned Federal aid to education in his radio talk but did not predict it would be passed in this session. He said:

"I predict that the Congress eventually will approve a bill for Federal aid to education which will be satisfactory to Americans of all faiths."

The Senate has passed this bill, but in the House it is still in committee. A House bill drawn up by

Continued on Page 12, Column 4

WHERRY DECLARES DOLLAR PACTS NEED CONGRESS SANCTION

Senator Sees 'Desperate' Effort by Britain to Tie Economy to That of United States

PREDICTS MOVE WILL FAIL

Says Cripps and Bevin Will Propose Measures That Could Hit U. S. Living Standard

By H. WALTON CLOKE
Special to The New York Times.

WASHINGTON, Aug. 21—Senator Kenneth S. Wherry, Republican of Nebraska, and minority leader in the Senate, warned the Administration today that any major agreement resulting from the forthcoming United States-British-Canadian discussions on the British financial crisis would have to be approved by Congress.

Sir Stafford Cripps, British Chancellor of the Exchequer, and Ernest Bevin, British Foreign Secretary, are coming to the United States "in a desperate effort to tie the British economy to the United States," Senator Wherry said.

"When Britain wins world markets through efficiency, quality and competitive prices," the Senator declared, "her dollar shortages will disappear. Until her problem is attacked along that line there is no sense in pouring the taxpayers' money into a bottomless pit."

He predicted that any program agreed upon by the Administration that would "weaken our American economy and lower our standards of living will certainly be rejected by Congress."

The discussions among the top financial representatives of the three countries are scheduled to begin on Sept. 6. The purpose of the meeting, according to a joint announcement by the Treasury and State Departments, is to "discuss the balance of payment difficulties between the dollar and sterling areas and measures which could be taken to right the existing disequilibrium between the two areas, both in the long and short term."

John W. Snyder, Secretary of the Treasury, will preside at the discussions. Dean Acheson, Secretary of State, also will represent the United States. Representing the Canadian Government will be Douglas C. Abbott, Canadian Minister of Finance, and Lester B. Pearson, Canadian Minister of External Affairs.

"With the United States Gov-

Continued on Page 3, Column 8

World News Summarized

MONDAY, AUGUST 22, 1949

The Tito regime accused Russia yesterday of having sold out Yugoslav claims to Slovene Carinthia, in Austria, to further Kremlin interests. The Belgrade note, sixth in a series of bitter exchanges between the two countries, was issued in reply to a Soviet statement that Yugoslavia had been responsible for the loss of the territory. [1:8.]

In Germany, a Communist leader announced postponement of formation of an "All-German government" in the Soviet zone, a move that had been expected as a Russian reply to the coming establishment of a Western German Federal Republic. [6:2.]

John J. McCloy, United States High Commissioner-designate for Germany, announced the appointment of seven chief advisers who will serve on the Western Allied commission. Three of them worked under Gen. Lucius D. Clay. [1:2-3.]

The Christian Democratic Union, strongest party in the German Federal Republic, rejected the possibility of a coalition with the Social Democrats and reaffirmed its plans for a free-enterprise economy. [5:1.]

Any major agreements reached in the United States-British-Canadian monetary conference next month will have to be approved by Congress, Senator Kenneth S. Wherry warned. He predicted Congressional rejection of any program that would "weaken our American economy." [1:5.]

Britain will enter the Washington conference faced with the necessity of increasing dollar-returning exports from the sterling area by 40 per cent to meet the current dollar shortage and by 100 per cent after Marshall Plan aid is stopped, it was reported in London. [1:6-7.]

Some British trade unionists are hampering increased productivity through fear of creating unemployment, the Trades Union Congress reported, citing labor opposition to efficiency studies. [3:1.]

The struggle over the diminished dollar supply by members of the European Marshall Plan Council was held by Paris observers to be a potential turning point in European cooperation and recovery. [2:2.]

Raging forest fires in southwestern France claimed a high toll of lives, despite efforts by 20,000 soldiers and volunteers to control the week-old blaze. Flames were reported to have swept more than 100,000 acres. [1:6-7.]

The bones of St. Peter, the Apostle traditionally regarded as the founder of the Roman Catholic Church, have been discovered in a crypt below St. Peter's Basilica in Rome, according to Vatican reports. [1:2-3.]

In Washington, a joint statement by four Senators attacked the State Department's China policy. Citing the threat of Soviet conquest of Asia, the legislators urged that the United States immediately supply arms to the Nationalist forces. [1:7.]

The Senate Majority Leader threatened to keep Congress in session until Thanksgiving, if necessary, to complete important legislation. Most Congressmen believed, however, that adjournment might be reached by mid-September. [1:4.]

In this city, Democrats set up headquarters for the municipal ticket headed by Mayor O'Dwyer. The step was taken in preparation for what promised to be one of the most vigorous Mayoralty campaigns in New York history. [1:1.]

Index to other news appears on Page 22.

Dead Exceed 80 in Big Fires In Woods of Southern France

Blazes in Bordeaux Area Checked 10 Miles From the City—Soldiers Perish

The New York Times Aug. 22, 1949

Forest fires burned over a huge area in France's Gironde Department, taking a heavy toll. Fires also broke out in Correze Department (inset).

By MICHAEL CLARK
Special to The New York Times.

PARIS, Monday, Aug. 22—More than eighty persons have lost their lives in fires that have raged for several days through the forests of the Gironde Department in southwestern France.

The main blaze which approached to within ten miles of Bordeaux, has been contained on all fronts, the Ministry of the Interior announced early today. Estimates of the areas burned over were up to 125,000 acres of woodland.

The Ministry reported that sixty fire fighters, including twenty soldiers, had perished in line of duty and that others had been listed as missing or wounded.

A mortuary chapel was improvised in the Town Hall of Cestas, a village southwest of Bordeaux which for several hours yesterday had been threatened by flames from the timber 200 yards away.

[In the United States forest fires have swept out of control in Yellowstone National Park and in Idaho. Smoke jumpers were helping to fight the Yellowstone fires.]

Advices from Bordeaux list forty-one dead, all civilians, near the town of Saucats and forty military victims at Puch.

Eyewitness reports paint a pic-

Continued on Page 5, Column 2

British Need 40% Export Rise To Meet Their Dollar Deficit

By CLIFTON DANIEL
Special to The New York Times.

LONDON, Aug. 21—To meet its current dollar deficit the sterling area needs to increase its exports to the dollar area by something like 40 per cent, examination of official figures indicated today. To get along after 1952 without United States aid and still maintain its present level of dollar imports the sterling area would need to increase its sales to dollar countries by about 100 per cent.

These are among the basic facts that will confront the United States, British and Canadian Cabinet members when they meet in Washington next month to seek a solution for the sterling area's dollar shortage.

Absolute forecasts of the future trading position of the sterling bloc cannot be made because there are too many variable factors involved, but the following calculations give some notion of the magnitude of the problem of closing the dollar gap.

On the basis of figures for the first two quarters of this year the sterling area's exports to the dollar area are running between $1,600,000,000 and $1,800,000,000 a year, for 1949-50 the British Government has reported to the Organization for European Economic Cooperation in Paris that the sterling area will have a dollar deficit of about $1,518,000,000. A subcommittee of the OEEC has tentatively proposed over British protests that Britain should receive $850,000,000 from the United States aid funds in 1949-50.

That would leave a gap of $668,000,000 to be closed either by increasing exports to the dollar area or by cutting imports that the British and other Commonwealth governments already started doing. To close the gap by exports alone—as Paul G. Hoffman, chief of the Economic Cooperation Administration, has strongly suggested the European nations should try to do—might require an increase of as much as 41 per cent in the sterling area's dollar sales.

If the same set of conditions should prevail into 1952, which is

Continued on Page 3, Column 4

4 SENATORS ISSUE CALL FOR CHINA AID

McCarran, Bridges, Wherry, Knowland Say White Paper Is 'Whitewash of Do-Nothing'

By HAROLD B. HINTON
Special to The New York Times.

WASHINGTON, Aug. 21—Four Senators issued a joint call today for "immediate and adequate assistance for the free areas in China," and a policy of active cooperation with the countries bordering on China.

They pointed out that the Chinese National Government, even today, controlled a greater area of the country than it had after its first year of war with Japan. Despite the "chorus of doom," to which they said Secretary of State Dean Acheson had added his voice, "the Chinese Republic refuses to die," they declared.

Those who signed the joint statement were Senators Pat McCarran, Democrat, of Nevada, and Styles Bridges, of New Hampshire, and Republicans Kenneth S. Wherry, of Nebraska, and William F. Knowland, of California.

They undertook to refute some of the principal points made in the China White Paper, which the State Department released for publication on Aug. 5. They described the document as "a 1,054-page whitewash of a wishful, do-nothing policy which has succeeded only in placing Asia in danger of Soviet conquest with its ultimate threat to the peace of the world and our own national security."

The statement challenged the White Paper's thesis that the Na-

Continued on Page 6, Column 5

Pop-Bottle Barrage in Philadelphia Gives the Giants a Forfeit Victory

By JAMES P. DAWSON

PHILADELPHIA, Aug. 21—The Giants ran into a new high in excitement at Shibe Park today as they made off with a 9-0 forfeit victory when irate fans showered the field with a pop-bottle barrage.

Incensed over a decision by Umpire George Barr the Philadelphia fans voiced their displeasure to such an extent that Chief Umpire Al Barlick was forced to declare the New York club winner by forfeit in the second game of a double-header.

The thirty-four-year-old Ken Heintzelman had left-handed Leo Durocher's band with baffling simplicity to carve victory by 4 to 0 in the opener, reaching the Phils' high of six triumphs in a row.

The disorderly outbreak came at a time when the Giants were leading, 4 to 2, with one out in the upper half of the ninth. It was precipitated by Umpire Barr's decision that Richie Ashburn had missed a diving catch of Joe Lafata's line smash which went for a double, scoring Will Marshall from third.

Ashburn protested he had caught the ball and immediately Barr was the center of a vocal storm that came from players and fans alike. Lynwood Rowe, in there trying to keep the Phils' winning streak rolling, added his protest, claiming Umpire Lee Ballanfant, on third base, had motioned a catch. It was Barr's decision to make, however, and he stood adamant.

And, when the decision stood, fans among the 19,742 tossed bottles on the field, most of them landing in left and right field. For fifteen minutes the umpires waited while attendants kept busy removing the debris. Attempts to halt the demonstration through the loud-speaker were futile. Finally,

Continued on Page 17, Column 5

YUGOSLAVS CHARGE RUSSIAN DUPLICITY IN AUSTRIAN ACTION

Hold Moscow Double-Crossed Them in Dropping Aim on Carinthia in Big Four

BELGRADE ALLEGES TRAP

Retort to Soviet Accusations Details Actions by Stalin to Nullify Efforts

Excerpts from the Yugoslav note to Russia appear on Page 2.

By M. S. HANDLER
Special to The New York Times.

BELGRADE, Yugoslavia, Aug. 21—Yugoslavia accused the Soviet Government today not only of a double-cross but also of preparing a trap for the Yugoslavs that would justify such duplicity.

The charge was made in a reply to a Moscow note of Aug. 11 relating to the negotiations of an Austrian peace treaty and followed a Soviet rejoinder to a Belgrade communication dealing with alleged mistreatment of Soviet citizens in Yugoslavia.

Today's Yugoslav note dealt with the decision of the Council of Foreign Ministers at Paris to maintain the territorial integrity of Austria and to reject the Yugoslav demand for the integration of Slovene Carinthia into Yugoslavia.

The Soviet note of Aug. 11 threw the responsibility for the decision of the Council of Foreign Ministers on the Yugoslav Government, alleging that the Yugoslavs had sought to negotiate a settlement with the British and Americans behind the backs of the Russians and that, therefore, the Yugoslav Government must bear the responsibility for what happened at Paris.

Press Carries Reply

The Yugoslav reply, which was published this morning in the newspapers, told of the detailed negotiations over the Carinthia question from May, 1945 on, and concluded by repeatedly accusing the Soviet Government of double-crossing the Yugoslavs.

[According to the Yugoslav note, Vyacheslav M. Molotov, then Soviet Foreign Minister, informed a Yugoslav envoy that Russia was keeping the issue of Slovene Carinthia on the agenda of the Austrian treaty negotiations only as a bargaining point to obtain concessions from the Western powers on the issue of German assets in Austria.]

In substance, the Yugoslav note said the Yugoslav Government originally had been double-crossed by Generalissimo Stalin back in 1945 when, without informing the Yugoslav Government, the Soviet leader sent a letter to Karl Renner, Austrian Chancellor, promising Soviet support for Austrian territorial integrity.

The Yugoslavs said that their Ambassador to Moscow, Vladimir Popovitch, was able to get the text only after insisting upon it. The Yugoslav note said that the Austrians informed the Western powers of Premier Stalin's commitment and, as a result of this advanced knowledge, the Yugoslav case was lost from the very beginning.

Text of Stalin's Letter

The text of Premier Stalin's letter to Herr Renner, as contained in the Yugoslav note, read as follows:

"I thank my much respected comrade for your letter of April 15.

"I do not doubt that your cares about the independence, integrity and development of Austria are also my cares.

"I am ready to support, as far as possible, in extending every help that may be needed by Austria.

"Excuse me for this late answer."

The Yugoslav note traced the negotiations between Edvard Kardelj, Yugoslav Foreign Minister, and Andrei Y. Vishinsky and V. M. Molotov at the Council of Foreign Ministers at Moscow, in which the Soviet leaders, with the knowledge of Premier Stalin's commitment to Herr Renner, tried to persuade the Yugoslav representative to reduce his demands and seek a compromise.

The note went on to describe how the Soviet representatives in Paris and London continued to insist on Yugoslavs approaching the Western Governments with a compromise proposal, how the Yugoslavs finally reduced their demands, how the Yugoslavs reported all their conversations with the Western representatives to the Russians and how finally the deci-

Continued on Page 2, Column 3

"All the News That's Fit to Print"

NEWS INDEX, PAGE 95, THIS SECTION

The New York Times.

Copyright, 1950, by The New York Times Company.

LATE CITY EDITION
Rain and warmer today; cloudy and colder tonight and tomorrow.
Temperature Range Today—Max., 55; Min., 32
Temperatures Yesterday—Max., 44; Min., 24
Full U. S. Weather Bureau Report, Page 8; Sec. 1

Section 1

VOL. XCIX. No. 33,650. Entered as Second Class Matter, Postoffice, New York, N. Y. NEW YORK, SUNDAY, MARCH 12, 1950. Including Magazine and Book Review. FIFTEEN CENTS New York City / 50 Mile Zone | Elsewhere Twenty Cents

RESERVOIRS REACH HALF-FULL STAGE FROM LOW OF 33%

Rise Since Economy Program Began in Fall Is Credited Largely to Public Aid

CONSERVATION STILL VITAL

Clark Says New Gains Hinge First on Continued Savings, Next on Excess Rain

The Water Situation

The following figures as of 8 A. M. yesterday give the number of gallons of water in the city's reservoirs. The difference in the two days is the net after intake and the day's consumption:

Friday	124,775,000,000
Yesterday	126,501,000,000
Net Gain	1,726,000,000
Average daily gain needed to fill the reservoirs by June 1	1,544,000,000
Watershed rainfall	None
Next water holiday	Thursday

At normal consumption there remains eighty-four days' supply before pressure fails.

At present consumption there remains 112 days' supply before pressure fails.

Catskill and Croton reservoirs at capacity hold 253,136,000,000 gallons.

By ALEXANDER FEINBERG

Water in the city's reservoirs reached 50 per cent of storage capacity at 8 A. M. yesterday. When the conservation program began · October they were one-third full, but a year ago the watershed supply stood at 92.3 per cent of capacity.

The greatest single factor in the slow rise in the available supply, which sometimes fluctuated dishearteningly downward, was ascribed by officials to day-to-day curtailment in consumption.

"We hit the half-way mark right on the button," said Chief Engineer Edward J. Clark of the Department of Water Supply, Gas and Electricity. "The people of the city are pulling themselves out by their own bootstraps through conservation."

Mr. Clark pointed out that there was still a long way to go and pleaded for continued saving. The eleventh dry day will be observed on Thursday.

After losses were recorded in nine of eleven days the tide turned upward last Wednesday when heavy rains in the 1,000 square miles of up-State watershed brought a gain of 4,249,000,000 gallons to the reservoirs in the twenty-four hours ending at 8 A. M. Thursday.

Runoff Higher Than Estimate

An eventual runoff of 7,970,000,000 gallons was estimated at the time and the succeeding forty-eight hours saw this more than realized. In the twenty-four hours ending at 8 A. M. Friday the gain was 3,054,000,000 gallons and yesterday at 8 A. M. the accretion was 1,726,000,000 gallons, seven-tenths of 1 per cent.

The water level thus had risen, if haltingly, from its low of 84,643,000,000 gallons, 33.4 per cent of capacity, measured on Dec. 12, to 126,501,000,000 gallons at 8 A. M. yesterday, precisely 50 per cent of the 253,136,000,000-gallon capacity of the Catkskill and Croton reservoirs.

Heavy rains and slightly higher temperatures in midweek began to wash the snow that had lain on the mountains for several weeks into the quick-running streams that feed the reservoirs. The runoff continued despite two succeeding rainless and cold days. Yesterday snow was reported falling in the Catskills, brightening the outlook for further gains in the Schoharie and Esopus reserves.

Economy Major Factor

Continued gains depend on two variable factors, Mr. Clark said. One, and he emphasized that this was the most important, was no slackening in the water economy program, and the second was more than the normal amount of rainfall between now and June 1.

The chief engineer pointed out that the city was using 300,000,000 gallons less daily than before conservation and that this had saved 32,000,000,000 gallons.

As for the rains, Mr. Clark said, "we'll be very happy to have April showers in March this year."

Depletion of the reservoirs followed last year's drought, when rainfall was 8½ inches less than normal. One inch of rain will yield 12,000,000,000 gallons of water in storage, Mr. Clark pointed out, and thus 100,000,000,000 gallons were lost. In addition, he said, consumption has been climbing each year.

Chinese Red Troops Hold Tibet Village

By Reuters.

JAMMU, Kashmir, March 11—A force of 900 Chinese Communist soldiers from Sinkiang recently occupied the Tibetan village of Kakhajar, near the Chinese frontier, according to a statement today by Gulam Kadir Ganderbali, the Kashmir Government's chief administrative officer in Ladakh, bordering on western Tibet.

Mr. Ganderbali, who is here for consultations with his Government, said travelers from Lhasa, the Tibetan capital, reported that political conditions in Tibet had "considerably deteriorated" in recent months following the Communist victory in China.

BROCK PEMBERTON, PRODUCER, 64, DIES

Showman Who Put 'Harvey,' Other Hits on Broadway Is Heart Attack Victim

Brock Pemberton, producer, who had been a leader in the development of the American theatre during the last thirty years, died yesterday at his home, 455 East Fifty-first Street, of a heart attack. He was 64 years old.

Although he had been a cardiac sufferer for three years, Mr. Pemberton played the title role of "Harvey," as scheduled, for a week at Phoenix, Ariz., closing a week ago last night. And on his way back to New York he stopped at Topeka, Kan., to watch the performance there of another "Harvey" company. The play won the Pulitzer Prize in 1944.

He is survived by his widow, who was Margaret McCoy of East Orange, N. J., at their marriage in 1915, and a brother, Murdock Pemberton of this city.

Unlike most producers, Brock Pemberton remained actively in business until his death and had his biggest financial success during his last years, when he produced "Harvey." Before then, however, the slow-talking Kansan had made a big name on Broadway by bringing to Times Square many hits including the 1920 Pulitzer Prize winner, "Miss Lulu Bett."

Gave Noted Actors Start

In his shows appeared stars already famous and actors to whom he gave a first important opportunity. He produced plays of established playwrights and of writers who had been unknown.

His long producing career that began in 1920 and his habit of speaking his mind made him respected by all branches of the theatre. Theatre owners and brokers, actors and union leaders invited him to meet with them during controversies.

Among other shows produced by the tall, dignified former newspaper man were "Six Characters in Search of an Author," "Enter Madame," "Strictly Dishonorable," "Personal Appearance," and "Kiss the Boys Goodbye." His success was in the traditional pattern of the small-town boy making good in the big city.

During the war Mr. Pemberton was one of the founders of U. S. O. Camp Shows, Inc., and was on the board of directors of the American Theatre Wing. Despite his activity in theatrical organizations Mr. Pemberton found time this season to produce two shows, "Love Me Long" and "Mr. Barry's Etchings."

The son of Albert and Ella Murdock Pemberton, he was born at

Continued on Page 78, Column 3

BOYLE ASKS PARTY TO PRESS SENATORS FOR HOUSING BILL

Democratic Chief Telegraphs Leaders Foes Claim Votes to Beat Middle-Income Aid

BALLOT IS DUE WEDNESDAY

Measure Seeks Rental Building for $2,840-$4,425 Group—G.O.P. Substitute Favored

Special to THE NEW YORK TIMES.

WASHINGTON, March 11—William M. Boyle Jr., chairman of the Democratic National Committee, called on party officials throughout the country today to urge Senators to support the Administration's middle-income housing program.

In telegrams to members of the National Committee and state chairmen and vice chairmen, Mr. Boyle noted that opponents were claiming sufficient votes to defeat the measure on the showdown next Wednesday, when the Senate is scheduled to vote on the issue.

"I know that the majority of those who voted the Democratic ticket in 1948 are strongly in favor of this middle-income housing bill, and I hope that you and they will make their views known to the members of the Senate," he telegraphed. "I am counting on your support."

The pending bill calls for the creation of a $100,000,000 corporation that would make long-term loans to cooperatives at low interest rates for construction of housing designed to rent at a median rate of $69 monthly to families with incomes of $2,840 to $4,425.

Rival Bill Strongly Backed

A less liberal Republican substitute, sponsored by Senators Charles W. Tobey of New Hampshire and Irving M. Ives of New York, has strong support in the Senate.

Mr. Boyle in his telegram said:

"One of the great public services accomplished by the Democratic party which has won us widespread public trust and support has been the progressive legislation enacted in the field of housing.

"We must continue this record of achievement. * * * The real estate lobby and Republican opponents of this measure are claiming enough votes to block this bill. If they succeed, the resultant continued lack of decent homes for middle-income families will be a serious blow to the millions of Americans who have depended upon the Democratic party to carry out a successful housing program.

"The middle-income bill is based on the sound principle of locally operated cooperatives. These local co-ops will be assisted in planning and organization by self-liquidating loans from a corporation established by the new bill. This corporation will obtain funds from private investors to be loaned to the co-ops for actual construction.

"Those of you who have had experience with the Rural Electrification Administration program or with farmer co-ops know how much co-ops would be able to accomplish in the housing field."

The middle-income program has been under attack by the National Association of Real Estate Boards as "a vote-getting political vehicle." The organization is fighting it on the ground that it reflects a "growing tendency to make

Continued on Page 51, Column 1

Compromise Ends Airline Strike; Union Yields on Pay Rise Demands

By FREDERICK GRAHAM

The eleven-day strike of 4,600 maintenance and stores employes of American Airlines was settled yesterday when the Transport Workers Union, C. I. O., and the airline agreed to a compromise worked out by the National Mediation Board.

Under the terms of the agreement, some details of which remain to be worked out, the workers will start back to work at 7 A. M. today. Flight schedules, which had been reduced about 80 per cent, will be stepped up today and should be back to normal by tomorrow, a spokesman for the airline reported.

Union demands for a wage increase of 20 cents an hour were dropped, according to William Grogan, international vice president of the T. W. U., who explained the settlement. The airline did, however, agree to a job security clause in the contract and to the elimination of farming work out to sub-contractors when regular employes could handle it. The sub-contract work was one of the chief complaints of the union.

The issue of severance pay also was settled by compromise. The union had sought two weeks of severance pay for the first year, four weeks for two years and one week for each additional year up to eight. The airline finally offered and the union accepted one week's severance pay a year up to eight years.

Union demands for vacations and other so-called "fringe issues" will be considered at 10 A. M. tomorrow when representatives of the union and the airline meet with National Mediation Board officers at 120 East Forty-second Street.

The end of the strike came suddenly and at a time when it

Continued on Page 50, Column 3

U. S. Will Call Home 3 Aides in Hungary

By The Associated Press.

WASHINGTON, March 11—The United States will recall three military officers from the United States Legation in Budapest in accordance with a demand of Hungary's Communist Government.

The three probably will be ordered out early next week. Under the normal practice among nations, representatives of a foreign government who are declared personally unacceptable cannot be kept in a country regardless of how much their home government may disapprove of the action against them.

The United States officers whose removal was demanded in a note yesterday are Col. James B. Kraft, military attaché; Lieut. Col. John R. Hoyne, deputy military attaché, and Maj. Donald E. Griffin, deputy air attaché.

The Hungarian Government declared all these men persona non grata on the basis of testimony in the spy trial of Robert A. Vogeler, United States business man, who was convicted of spying and received a fifteen-year prison term last month.

EWING DENOUNCES HEALTH PLAN FOES

Accepting the Hillman Award, He Assails Stand by A. M. A. and Republican Leaders

By JAMES A. HAGERTY

Oscar R. Ewing, Federal Security Administrator, made a double-barreled attack yesterday on the leadership of the Republican party and the American Medical Association.

He charged "reactionary" Republican leaders with raising "the scarecrow issue of socialism," and asserted that the Medical Association was spending $3,000,000 to defeat President Truman's Health Insurance Plan which, he said, was designed solely to remove the financial barrier to adequate medical care.

Mr. Ewing spoke at a luncheon in the Century Room of the Commodore Hotel, at which he received the $1,000 annual award for meritorious public service of the Sidney Hillman Foundation. The award was presented by Jacob S. Potofsky, successor to the late Mr. Hillman as president of the Amalgamated Clothing Workers of America. It was the foundation's second award, the first having been bestowed a year ago on Senator Frank P. Graham of North Carolina.

In presenting the award to Mr.

Continued on Page 38, Column 3

POPE URGES FIGHT AGAINST GODLESS; FOR STABLE PEACE

Holy Year Encyclical Charts Program for All Catholics to Overcome Atheism

COMMUNISM HELD TARGET

Pontiff Condemns Arms Race in Plea for Wisdom and Justice by Statesmen

By CAMILLE M. CIANFARRA

Special to THE NEW YORK TIMES.

ROME, March 11—Pope Pius XII condemned today the policy and tactics of anti-Christian forces and enunciated a program of action for both the clergy and the faithful to counteract atheistic propaganda throughout the world.

The program, contained in an encyclical letter that will be known by its first two words, "Anni Sacri" (Holy Year), was directed to the Roman Catholic episcopate.

In an analysis of what Vatican circles said were the methods adopted by the Communists to undermine religion and discredit the clergy, the Pontiff declared that the root of present social unrest in many countries was the use of falsehoods as a political weapon.

The Pontiff remarked that he felt "anxiety and anguish" because the world lacked a "stable and solid peace." There is tension among many nations, he said, and as a result there is no trust. This, in turn, he added, has unleashed an armament race that sows fear in everyone's heart.

He Warns Statesmen

He reminded statesmen—the feeling in Vatican circles is that the Pontiff was here addressing himself mainly to the Soviet Union—that peace was the result of "wisdom and justice" while war was the offspring of "blindness and hate."

The Pope complained that the practice of religion was often neglected and actually forbidden by anti-Christian governments, while officially controlled newspapers aided the anti-religious campaign by insulting religious customs and by giving publicity to "basest obscenities" that were designed to corrupt the youth.

The Communists, he indicated, in an unmistakable reference to their policies, deceive the masses by false promises, foster hatred and rebellion, organize violence, disorders and lawlessness that ruin national economies and cause irreparable damage. This reference, Vatican circles said, was especially timely in view of the Italian Com-

Continued on Page 24, Column 2

World News Summarized

SUNDAY, MARCH 12, 1950

Belgium waited in a quiet but tense atmosphere for the results of today's referendum, in which about 5,500,000 voters are expected to indicate their choice on the question of whether King Leopold should be allowed to resume the throne. [1:8.]

A new Supreme Soviet was being elected in the U. S. S. R., and Soviet citizens went to the polling places to deposit their single-list ballots, following election-eve speeches on the Bolshevist "peace" theme by Politburo members; no Stalin speech was indicated in accounts. [1:7.]

The "anti-Christian" forces of communism were condemned in a Holy Year encyclical by the Pope, who called on Catholics everywhere to combat atheistic propaganda. The Pontiff expressed "anxiety and anguish" because there was no "stable and solid peace" and deplored the world tension, as a result of which there was a rearmament race that bred fear in everybody's heart. [1:5.]

A new United States political warfare effort to divide the peoples of Eastern Europe from their Soviet satellite governments was reported to be achieving a measure of success. It is being carried on primarily through Voice of America broadcasts affirming United States friendship for those "oppressed" by "imposed" Communist regimes. [1:6-7.]

United States diplomats from fourteen countries in the Middle East ended a four-day meeting in Cairo after a broad study of the means to promote stability, prosperity and peace in the region. A communiqué said these aims would receive substantial aid from President Truman's Point Four program to assist undeveloped areas. [32:2.]

In Berlin Allied intelligence officers felt certain that the Communist youth demonstrations set for May 28 would develop into the most serious Soviet attempt to seize control of the city since the end of the blockade. [4:6.]

The proposal by Secretary General Lie for a Security Council inquiry into which of the two rival regimes was entitled to represent China in the United Nations was said to be opposed by members of the Latin-American group of nations at Lake Success. [22:1.]

Economic Cooperation Administrator Hoffman said Britain faced the loss of $150,000,000 in Marshall Plan aid unless she cooperated with other Western European nations in the plan to lower trade barriers. [3:1.]

Republican Senator Joseph R. McCarthy of Wisconsin declared that when he resumed tomorrow his testimony on his allegations that the State Department rolls contained active Communists he would name a man now in "an important post." [36:3.]

Democratic party officials throughout the country were urged by the chairman of the Democratic National Committee to bring pressure on Senators to back the Administration's middle-income housing measure, which is scheduled to come up for a vote in the Senate on Wednesday. [1:3.]

New gains in the city's water reservoirs raised storage to 50 per cent of capacity. Officials praised the conservation efforts of the public but warned of the need for continued care in water consumption if a serious emergency next summer was to be averted. [1:1.]

A compromise ended the eleven-day strike of 4,600 maintenance and stores employes of American Airlines. [1:2-3.]

ON HAND FOR BELGIAN ELECTION

Princess Josephine Charlotte holding a bouquet and reaching for another at her welcome at the Brussels airport on her arrival from Switzerland on Friday. Associated Press Radiophoto

U. S. Seeks to Win Peoples In Satellites From Regimes

By WALTER H. WAGGONER

Special to THE NEW YORK TIMES.

WASHINGTON, March 11—In a political warfare maneuver to support its anti-Communist military preparation, the United States is pushing a propaganda campaign calculated to divide the peoples of Communist Eastern Europe from their Soviet satellite governments.

The effort is already many weeks old, but it has become recognizable lately as a thoughtfully deliberate program. Officials were able to confirm today that the distinction made by this Government between the "oppressed" peoples and their "imposed" Communist regimes was a major theme of United States political policy toward Eastern Europe.

Hardly a statement has been made, whether by Secretary of State Dean Acheson or any other spokesman of United States foreign policy, that has not affirmed the friendship of the people and Government of the United States for the peoples of the Soviet satellites, while at the same time denouncing in the strongest terms their leaders and their Governments.

Thus, when the United States broke off diplomatic relations with Bulgaria on Feb. 21, the note to the Bulgarian Government called attention in the first paragraph to the "deep interest and concern for the welfare and freedom of the Bulgarian people" felt by the United States.

And when, last December, this Government put an embargo on United States travel in Hungary, at the same time demanding the release of Robert A. Vogeler, the State Department made a point of the Hungarian Government's "systematic denial of fundamental human rights and freedoms to its own citizens."

These comments by the United States are designed obviously to be heard by the citizens of the countries under attack. And they are being heard, according to well-informed authorities.

The State Department's Voice of America broadcasts are carrying the United States views to the

Continued on Page 8, Column 1

VOTING UNDER WAY IN SOVIET ELECTION

Politburo Members' Speeches Press 'Peace Theme'—Stalin Is Not Heard

By The Associated Press.

MOSCOW, March 11—Soviet citizens heard tonight major political themes set out by Premier Stalin's top associates on the eve of the election of a new Supreme Soviet, or Parliament.

The Russians vote in a single-ticket election tomorrow.

Every member of the Politburo had spoken in the campaign for the election of the slate of Communist and non-party bloc candidates except its most important member, Premier Stalin. Tradition calls for him to speak on the night preceding the balloting as a climax to the campaign.

[No further mention was made in a dispatch nor was any Moscow broadcast of a Stalin speech heard by THE NEW YORK TIMES or news agencies. The Moscow Tass English-language night broadcast carried the text of Deputy Premier V. M. Molotov's Friday night speech. By 1 A. M., Moscow time, or 5 P. M., Saturday, in New York, voting was reported under way in the Soviet Far Eastern regions.]

Every Politburo member before him assured the people the big issue was the Soviet Union's policy of peace. In the light of these statements, many foreign diplomats predicted Russia would make some overture toward a new effort to settle the barbed problems dividing

Continued on Page 10, Column 1

1850 B. C. Murder Record Found; Modern Basic Law Used at Trial

Special to THE NEW YORK TIMES.

PHILADELPHIA, March 11—The oldest known record of a murder trial—a case dating back 3,800 years—has been found inscribed on a two-by-four-inch clay tablet recently unearthed in Iraq by archeologists from the University of Chicago and the University of Pennsylvania.

The composition, written in cuneiform script, tells of a prosecution in which three men were doomed to die and their feminine co-defendant set free in 1850 B. C. under a democratic process of law. It records the testimony given at the trial as well as the legal procedures followed by the Sumerians.

The tablet, it was announced tonight, was among several hundred excavated at Nippur, about 100 miles south of modern Baghdad, where an expedition has been digging since last November.

The cuneiform script in the Sumerian language—mankind's earliest known form of writing—was translated by Dr. Samuel Noah Kramer and Dr. Thorkild Jacobsen.

Essentially, they said, the Sumerian text records the story of the trial as follows:

"About 1850 B. C. three men killed another man, a temple official, and then informed his wife, Nin-Dada, that her husband had been killed. Strangely enough, she kept their secret and did not notify the authorities.

"The case was brought before the King, Ur-Ninurta, who ruled in his capital at Isin. The King turned it over for trial to the citizens assembly at Nippur which acted as a court of justice. In this assembly nine men arose to prosecute the three men and the woman as well. They argued that not only the three actual murderers should be executed, but also the wife.

"Two men in the assembly then spoke in defense of the woman.

Continued on Page 26, Column 2

FATE OF LEOPOLD TO BE FIXED TODAY IN BELGIAN BALLOT

5,500,000 Scheduled to Voice Their Opinion on Return in 5-Hour Voting Period

NATION QUIET AND TENSE

King Said to Be Determined to Let Decision Be Final—Says Regency Is at End

By SYDNEY GRUSON

Special to THE NEW YORK TIMES.

BRUSSELS, Belgium, March 11—The heated Belgian royal referendum campaign drew to a close tonight with unabated oratory and a last flurry of nightriders covering Brussels walls and pavements with posters and slogans for or against the return of King Leopold III to the throne.

On the eve of a vote that could end the long uncertainty over the future of the exiled monarch, the country was quiet but tense. No serious trouble was expected, but the authorities took no chances. They confined all military personnel to barracks. The Government issued an appeal for the nation to remain calm.

Belgium's 5,500,000 eligible voters will go to the polls between 8 A. M. and 1 P. M. tomorrow to vote "yes" or "no" to the question whether they favor the King's reassuming his royal prerogatives. The monarch has promised to abdicate if he receives fewer than 55 per cent of the votes.

King to Stand on Vote

Sources close to the King reported tonight that he was determined tomorrow's vote should end the long festering royal question once and for all. He was said to have told one of his closest advisers:

"In any event we are finished with the regency. I will remount the throne or Baudouin [the King's son] will go in my place."

There had been rumors both that Prince Baudouin would refuse the throne if his father were forced to abdicate and that King Leopold, if victorious, would abdicate "in the interests of national unity" after he had returned to the throne.

The King was said to have told these sources that there was no question of either possibility. In any circumstances, it was said the King intended to return to Belgium because he did not believe it would be proper to abdicate abroad should he be faced with that necessity.

The King's brother, Prince Charles, has been Regent for the last four and one-half years, although the 19-year-old Prince Baudouin is heir to the throne. At no time during the campaign has the Regent relaxed his determination to stay out of the public eye and play as unassuming a role as possible. He has become the forgotten man of the country.

Primate Favors Return

There was one major development today in the campaign on King Leopold's behalf. Joseph Cardinal van Roey, Primate of Belgium and Archbishop of Malines, authorized the release of a letter stating that for Roman Catholics "the royal question is not a free vote."

King Leopold is Belgium's "legitimate King" and because of this "he has the right to his sovereign powers," the letter stated.

Publication of the letter served to emphasize the Catholic Church's position on the royal question. It had been made clear earlier in the campaign in the Sunday sermons of priests throughout this 90 per cent Catholic country.

Leaders of the Socialist Federation of Trade Unions, which has 500,000 members, met to decide what strike action would be taken if the King attempted to return on a slender majority. No announcement was made after the meeting, which was unofficially reported to have decided to await a declaration of the King's intentions. The federation had previously threatened to call a general strike if the King came back.

The Socialists wound up their campaign against the King with mass rallies in all cities and larger towns. They posted a guard of 500 blue-shirted brawny young men around their Brussels headquarters to fight off any new attacks by Leopoldists against the building, which had been the scene of much of the violence of the campaign in the capital.

A huge banner saying "Vote no" hangs on the front of the building and student supporters of the King have made nightly attempts to rip it down. They tried new tactics

Continued on Page 3, Column 3

Sumerian tablets uncovered in Iraq proved to solve the classic problem of the triangle, 1700 years before Euclid.

"All the News That's Fit to Print"

NEWS INDEX, PAGE 79, THIS SECTION

The New York Times.

LATE CITY EDITION
Fair and much colder today; very cold tonight and tomorrow.
Temperature Range Today-Max.,34; Min.,20
Temperatures Yesterday—Max.,50; Min.,30
U. S. Weather Bureau Report, Page 13; Sect. 1

Section 1

VOL. XCIX. No. 33,587 | Entered as Second-Class Matter. Postoffice, New York, N. Y. | NEW YORK, SUNDAY, JANUARY 8, 1950. | Including Magazine and Book Review | FIFTEEN CENTS New York City / 50 Mile Zone | Elsewhere Twenty Cents

37 WOMEN PERISH BEHIND BARS IN FIRE AT IOWA HOSPITAL

All but One Are Mental Patients Confined in Old Building of Institution at Davenport

25 RESCUED, BUT ONE DIES

Firemen Hack at Windows as Victims Within Scream — Flames Spread Swiftly

Special to THE NEW YORK TIMES.

DAVENPORT, Iowa, Jan. 7 — Thirty-seven women, all except one of whom were mental patients, perished behind barred windows and locked doors as flames mushroomed early today through St. Elizabeth's psychiatric ward of Mercy Hospital, a Roman Catholic institution here. The toll reached thirty-eight with the death tonight of a 93-year-old woman who was among twenty-five who had been rescued.

Coroner C. H. Wildman said tonight that thirty-seven bodies, most of them burned beyond recognition, had been recovered from the debris of the building, one of five units of the hospital, the largest in this Eastern Iowa community.

All of the dead, and all but three of those rescued, were women. And of the sixty-two all but two were mental patients.

Among those who perished was Mrs. Anna Neal, 52 years old, of Davenport, a nurse and night attendant in the hospital.

Sister Mary Annunziata, Superior Mercy Hospital, said all of those rescued were treated for burns and injuries.

Illinois Tragedy Recalled

The catastrophe recalled a similar tragedy last April 8 at Effingham, Ill., where seventy-five persons, including twelve babies, died in a fire which spread swiftly through St. Anthony's Hospital. Many bedfast patients died in the flames.

The fire at Davenport started at 2:06 A. M. and spread so rapidly through the three-story, eighty-one-year-old brick structure—oldest of the buildings of the hospital operated by the Roman Catholic Sisters of Mercy—that by the time the first firemen arrived flames were pouring from windows.

Within less than half-an-hour the north wall of the building collapsed as the fire raced upward through an elevator shaft, a stairwell and a dumbwaiter shaft and quickly spread throughout the structure.

A number of the survivors escaped from the hospital through tunnels that connect the five buildings. A majority of the rescued, however, all barefooted and in night clothes, were escorted to the main hospital building through the pre-dawn cold.

107 Firemen Join in the Fight

Fourteen Davenport fire companies, aided by fire-fighting units from suburban Bettendorf and Green Acres and by all available policemen, battled the blaze for four hours before bringing it under control. A total of 107 firemen fought the flames.

Fire Lieut. Al Korando, in charge of the first units to arrive, said that when he came on the scene "fire was mushrooming through the building—it literally looked like hell."

Fire Chief Lester Schick, who reached the hospital seven minutes after the first alarm, said that he found flames already "spurting from the windows and the roof."

"It was horrible," said Chief Schick's assistant, Harry Lang, who beat his leader to the scene by a few seconds.

"We couldn't get into the building because of the intense heat, so we put up every ladder we could. But those windows were barred.

"Even as firemen stood on ladders, hacking frantically with axes at the window gratings, the heat cracked the glass and people inside disappeared into the flames before our eyes."

The first persons, aside from patients, to discover the fire were Murray Francis, orderly, and two nurse's aides, Mrs. Willard Bennett and Mrs. Gladys Oostendorf, who were in the main hospital building near-by.

Their attention attracted by the screams of patients, they rushed to the mental ward. Mr. Francis hurled himself against the locked main door to smash it open, and the three dashed inside and managed to rescue a dozen patients from the first floor before the fire, which apparently began on the second floor, had moved down.

James Stablein of Moline, Ill.,

Continued on Page 3, Column 2

A VIEW OF THE HOLOCAUST IN DAVENPORT

Flames and smoke issuing from three-story St. Elizabeth's Ward of Mercy Hospital
Associated Press Wirephoto

DEMOCRATS CLASH OVER TAX 'PACKAGE' OR EXCISE CUT FIRST

George Insists on Reductions in 'Luxury' Levies Promptly, With Reforms Later

OTHERS WANT SINGLE BILL

House Likely to Pass Omnibus Measure, but Senate Group May Split It in Two

Special to THE NEW YORK TIMES.

WASHINGTON, Jan. 7—Disagreement among key Congressional Democrats over tax revision procedure developed today as Senator Walter F. George of Georgia called for immediate reduction of excise rates, with other reforms to come later.

The chairman of the Senate Finance Committee thus split with Speaker Sam Rayburn of Texas, Representative Robert L. Doughton of North Carolina, chairman of the House Ways and Means Committee, and Senator Scott W. Lucas of Illinois, Senate majority leader, on the question of a single bill lowering the excises and compensating for the resultant revenue losses by other provisions.

President Truman also is believed to favor a one-package approach, while Republican leaders have been demanding that spending be slashed instead to offset the budgetary effects of immediate repeal of wartime excise increases. These rates cover twenty-odd so-called "luxury" items such as transportation, communications, furs and jewelry.

In advocating an omnibus bill Representative Doughton, whose committee originates tax legislation, has expressed the hope that no other rates would have to be increased but that sufficient revenue could be raised to compensate for excise cuts by closing legal loopholes in existing law and stepping up enforcement.

Senator George contended that excise reductions should be made without taking the time for an overhaul of the tax structure so business would know where it stood and to minimize the effects of customers stopping buying in anticipation of the cuts.

"I think we need reductions and readjustments in the whole tax structure,' Mr. George conceded. "It would be a mistake to put all the emphasis on elimination of excise taxes, although I am thoroughly committed to the view that the levies should be reduced immediately."

President Truman is expected to

Continued on Page 34, Column 4

Findings in Iraq May Revise History of the Human Mind

'Textbooks' Uncovered in Sumeria Tell of Solution to Classic Problem of the Triangle 1,700 Years Before Euclid

By ALBION ROSS

Special to THE NEW YORK TIMES.

BAGHDAD, Iraq, Jan. 7—The discovery here two months ago that schoolboys of the little Sumerian county seat of Shadippur about 2000 B. C. had a "textbook" with the solution of Euclid's classic triangle problem seventeen centuries before Euclid has resulted in a summons from the Iraqi Directorate of Antiquities to United States archaeologists.

[The classic problem is presumably the Pythagorean theorem that the square of the hypotenuse of a right triangle is equal to the sum of the square of the two other sides. It appears in the First Book of Euclid, proposition 47.]

The Director General of Archeology in Iraq, Dr. Naji al-Asil, has asked the American Schools of Oriental Research, the organization of leading archeological research institutes in the United States, for assistance in the translation, transliteration and scientific appraisal of 2,400 Shadippur tables uncovered during the last six excavation seasons, and particularly the last 200 excavated during the season just completed.

There is evidence that clay "textbooks" of the schoolboys of Shadippur contain an encyclopedic outline of the scientific knowledge of their time, which will necessitate a sharp revision of the history of the development of science and, accordingly, of the story of the development of the human mind.

The study of the tablets, in cuneiform writing and principally in the Sumerian language, will require several years, Dr. al-Asil stated.

Even now, the famous clay tablet on which the basic geometrical problem was presented about 4,000 years ago is so clear that it takes a layman back to

Continued on Page 28, Column 1

STATE DEPARTMENT SEEKS POLICY IDEAS IN CONGRESS' TRIPS

Members Back From Abroad Will Be Invited to Discuss Views on What They Saw

'GIVE AND TAKE' IS PLANNED

Move Is Seen as Deference to Charges of 'Iron Curtain' Between Two Branches

By WALTER H. WAGGONER

Special to THE NEW YORK TIMES.

WASHINGTON, Jan. 7 — The State Department has just initiated a plan for holding frank give-and-take discussions on foreign policy developments with the 130-odd members of Congress who have toured the world in the last several months.

This was learned today as Senator William F. Knowland, Republican, of California, one of the sharpest critics of Administration policy in the Far East, charged that the State Department was "lowering the Iron Curtain" between itself and Congress.

The department's program for taking up the issues of foreign affairs with legislators recently back from trips abroad, presumably with some ideas of their own on how the United States should conduct itself, has a two-fold purpose:

1. It should end or weaken the conviction among many members of Congress that United States foreign policy is made and conducted exclusively in the Executive Branch, without benefit of Capitol Hill consultation, and
2. It should prepare the ground for Congressional consideration of one of the most ambitious legislative programs ever to be sent to the Capitol by the State Department.

Congress to Get Proposals

Half a dozen key proposals will go before Congress this session, some to continue foreign policy programs already in effect, others to initiate new projects regarded by the Administration as essential elements in the carrying out of its plans and responsibilities in world affairs.

In the first category, for example, are the Economic Cooperation Administration and the funds it employs for the recovery effort, and the Mutual Defense Assistance Program, which received $1,314,010,000 for the current fiscal year and is likely to need that much or more in the next.

In addition, the Administration is still pressing for prompt action on the President's Point Four program for economic and technical assistance to under-developed areas of the world; and the International Trade Organization, a proposed United Nations specialized agency believed by the State Department to be the principal vehicle for increasing world trade generally and lessening the imbalance between this country and others.

Besides these cornerstones to United States policy abroad there are such proposals for relieving human misery and want as the bill for expanding the opportunities here for the Displaced Persons of Europe and the recommendation, still formative, for aiding through United Nations resettlement and work-relief projects the 750,000 refugees of the Palestine war.

Many, if not most of these face a critical audience in Congress. In anticipation of this, the State Department has undertaken its talks with the world-traveling legislators.

McFall Arranges Talks

The discussions, which, it is hoped, will encourage a free exchange of ideas among the participants, are being arranged by Jack K. McFall, Assistant Secretary of State for Congressional Relations.

Although Mr. McFall, a busy man these days, will take part in some of the talks himself, the State Department's representatives will in the main be the several Assistant Secretaries for the geographical areas: W. Walton Butterworth for the Far East; George W. Perkins for Europe (aided by Henry A. Byroade, Director of the German Bureau); George C. McGhee for the Near East and Southern Asia, and Edward G. Miller Jr., for the Inter-American states.

These are the officials whom Under-Secretary of State James E. Webb likes to call the State Department's "operating vice presidents." In addition, outside the geographical structure, there are the Assistant Secretaries of State for United Nations Affairs, Economic Affairs, and Public Affairs

Continued on Page 3, Column 6

Rain Aids City Water Supply But Curbs on Use Are to Stay

By KALMAN SEIGEL

New York's water supply showed its greatest gain yesterday since the beginning of conservation early last month. The increase was 1,981,000,000 gallons in the twenty-four hours ended at 8 A. M.

In putting out the welcome mat for the liquid bounty from heavy rains in the watershed, officials of the Department of Water Supply, Gas and Electricity warned the city's users against becoming "falsely optimistic" and went ahead with plans to enforce new curbs on recreational use as well as another bathless and shaveless day on Thursday.

Edward J. Clark, the department's chief engineer, said the rainfall in the city's watershed would yield an eventual run-off of

The Water Situation

The following figures as of 8 A. M. yesterday give the number of gallons of water in the city's reservoirs. The difference in the two days is the net after intake and the day's consumption:

Friday	92,385,000,000
Yesterday	94,366,000,000
Net gain	1,981,000,000
Watershed rainfall:	
Schoharie	1.11 inches
Esopus	1.23 inches
Croton	.44 inch

At normal consumption there remains about fifty-eight days' supply before pressure fails.

At present consumption there remains about seventy-seven days' supply before pressure fails.

Catskill and Croton reservoirs at capacity hold 253,136,000,000 gallons.

5,700,000,000 gallons, or about five days' supply. The net gain reported yesterday represented an increase of 0.8 per cent over the previous twenty-four hours.

Mr. Clark reported that storage rose from 92,385,000,000 gallons, or 36.5 per cent of capacity, to 94,366,000,000 gallons, or 37.3 per cent of capacity. Storage a year ago yesterday was 185,020,000,000 gallons, representing 73.1 per cent of capacity.

Terming yesterday's gain the greatest advance in storage since the beginning of the present con-

Continued on Page 51, Column 3

WINTER BLOWS IN ON 55-MILE WIND

Balmy Weather Ends Quickly Here—Conditions in West and South Improve

Loss of homes and other hardships brought on during the week by freakish weather still marked some sections of the South and Midwest yesterday. There were, however, indications that the situations in both these sections would improve rapidly in the next forty-eight hours.

Normal weather had returned also to this city and the northeast in general with falling temperatures and strong winds reported from most of the areas that had reported record high readings earlier in the week.

In this city, though it lacked the snow of many parts of upstate New York, the mercury, which had touched 62.3 degrees on Friday for a record, was down in the thirties most of the day despite almost constant sunshine.

To many in the city, as they pursued flying hats, the weather seemed even colder because of the high winds. At times the gusts reached fifty-five miles an hour, or gale intensity.

For today the Weather Bureau predicted that the winds and the cold air mass would bring temperatures here even lower than yesterday. In the suburbs readings between 10 and 15 degrees during the pre-sunrise hours were expected.

Though city airports were affected by the fog that accompanied the warm spell, other sections of the country were much more severely hit by freezing and floods for which they had not been prepared.

Floods in the Midwest made hundreds of families homeless The

Continued on Page 55, Column 1

HARMONY MEETING SET BY DEMOCRATS

Southern and Administration Wings to Gather at Raleigh—Taft Qualifies G.O.P. Plan

Special to THE NEW YORK TIMES.

WASHINGTON, Jan. 7—A significant move toward smoothing relations between the Southern and Administration wings of the Democratic party was projected today as a harmony conference was announced for Jan. 28 at Raleigh, N. C.

Plans for the meeting were disclosed in a statement which the Democratic National Committee distributed for Jonathan Daniels, publisher of The Raleigh News and Observer and Democratic National committeeman from North Carolina.

"All Southern Governors are being invited to attend this meeting, and we hope to mak a substantial contribution toward the achievement of the President's legislative program," Mr. Daniels said.

Vice President Alben W. Barkley is to be the principal speaker. Also invited are members of Congress and Democratic committeemen from the entire South; Charles F. Brannan, Secretary of Agriculture; Oscar L. Chapman, Secretary

Continued on Page 29, Column 1

Referendum on Saar Urged By West German Minister

By The Associated Press.

BONN, Germany, Jan. 7—The issue of the Saar boiled up again tonight between Germany and France. Jacob Kaiser, West German Minister for the Reunification of Germany, proposed a referendum to determine the political future of the Saar, a valley of 738 square miles thickly spotted with coal mines. Any other solution would endanger the accomplishment of European unity, he said, adding:

"It is unthinkable that some people try again to confront Germany with a fait accompli on the Saar."

His statement was made as Paris dispatches disclosed that Foreign Minister Robert Schuman planned to meet next week with Johannes Hoffman, President of the autonomous Saar Government, to work out closer economic and financial links between the Saar and France.

For generations the Saar, with about 1,000,000 people, has been controlled alternately by France and Germany. The valley was annexed to Germany after the war of 1870. The Versailles Treaty after World War I put the Saar under a League of Nations commissioner, but granted an economic link with France. But in 1935—after Hitler had organized a Nazi party there—the Saarlanders voted overwhelmingly in a plebiscite to return to Germany.

After World War II France proposed that the area be independent politically but be joined to France economically. It is now part of the French occupation zone. Three years ago Gen. Lucius D. Clay, then United States commander in Germany, protested what he called France's unilateral action in having thrown French customs guards about the Saar, in effect setting the area apart from the rest of the French occupation zone.

At Moscow in 1947, however, and later in London, British and United States Foreign Ministers agreed that the Saar should have a "special entity," with economic and military ties to France. Russia refused to agree.

The final status of the Saar depends upon the peace treaty that finally is written for Germany.

France, meanwhile, has proceeded toward the economic integration of the territory. In Oc-

Continued on Page 16, Column 3

WEST STUDIES PLAN FOR GERMAN PEACE

Acheson Initiates Move to End Legal Status of War —Many Questions Arise

By SYDNEY GRUSON

Special to THE NEW YORK TIMES.

BRUSSELS, Belgium, Jan. 7—On the initiative of Secretary of State Dean Acheson the United States, Britain and France have started formal studies of how to end the state of war with Germany. The three powers have reached an agreement in principle, according to information available here, that the legal relationship with Germany should be shifted from a war to a peace basis despite the fact that the "cold war" makes the conclusion of a peace treaty impossible.

Studies are being prepared independently by legal staffs in each of the foreign offices. Similar studies have been undertaken in the Netherland, Belgium and Luxembourg as a result of a request by the Benelux countries to be included in the forthcoming discussions.

Papers now under preparation are to be exchanged probably in a month or two. This is to be followed by a conference of legal experts early in the spring.

The Americans are understood to have hoped at the outset that the matter could be kept entirely on the plane of legal questions, but this has proved impracticable. It is now expected major policy decisions will have to be taken first.

The outstanding problems are the obligations to be assumed by the Bonn Government, the security and occupation of Western Germany and the status of Eastern Germany.

All the powers concerned are believed to agree the Bonn Govern-

Continued on Page 15, Column 1

Fox Nearly Ruins Essex Hunt Club; Riders Lamed, Prize Dog Is Missing

Special to THE NEW YORK TIMES.

PEAPACK-GLADSTONE, N. J., Jan. 7—Faces were as red as hunting coats at the exclusive Essex Fox Hound Hunt Club today as its members ruefully conceded, between applications of liniment, that a fox had successfully eluded the grimmest chase in local history and was still very much at large in the Somerset County hills.

Not only did this rocketing Reynard outdistance twenty huntsmen and two dozen hounds for twenty-two miles, leading them panting through Jersey villages and highway traffic, but he subjected the sportsmen to a final indignity. They lost their prize dog.

The futile fox-hunt started Thursday noon when Mrs. Charles Scribner Jr., master of the hounds, and William Chadwell, the club's head huntsman, led eighteen red-coated riders out across Mrs. Scribner's estate, Larger Cross Roads. In three hours two foxes were "grounded" as the "appointment" moved along on schedule.

But at 3 o'clock the sportsmen sighted a third fox and the real chase began. South across Route 28, through North Branch Station, across Route 29 and down the streets of Centerville raced the fox, dogs, horses and club members. Through fields, hedgerows and traffic the pace never slackened.

By 5:30 P. M. the pack had disappeared, having outdistanced their owners, while most of the latter retreated to their estates. Mrs. Scribner, Mr. Chadwell, Miss Diana Bowling of Greenwich, Conn., and James Kelly, the "whipper-in" of the hounds, pounded on.

After two hours more this

Continued on Page 62, Column 6

World News Summarized

SUNDAY, JANUARY 8, 1950

The State Department, seeking to meet Congressional objections that it is assuming full responsibility for the nation's foreign policy and to enlist support for its legislative program, has begun a program for frank discussions with members of Congress who recently returned from foreign trips. The department hopes to learn in this manner some of the ideas on foreign policy developed by these legislators and to persuade them that Congress is a partner in the formulation and execution of foreign policy. [1:8.]

Secretary of State Acheson has spurred a study by the United States, Britain and France on how to end the state of war with Germany although the stalemate with the Soviet Union makes it unlikely that a peace treaty can be concluded at this time. The three nations reportedly have reached agreement in principle that legal relationships with Germany should be put on a peace basis. [1:7.]

Replying to a State Department order closing Hungary's consulates in New York and Cleveland, the Budapest Government accused Washington of treaty-breaking and interference in Hungary's affairs. [23:1.]

The issue of the pace and extent of the "integration" of European economy as part of the program under the Marshall Plan was said to be creating sharp divisions of opinion between European and United States officials. [11:1.]

Thirteen evangelists of the Protestant Church of Christ, which began its activities in the Rome area a year ago, charged that they had been stoned and forced out of Castel Gandolfo and three other towns around Rome after priests had aroused the public against them. [1:6-7.]

An archaeological discovery showing that the schools of ancient Sumeria had clay "textbooks" with the solution of Euclid's classic triangle problem long before Euclid lived was expected to lead to a sweeping revision of the history of the development of science. [1:6-7.]

The Chinese Communist regime had no public official comment on the recognition accorded it by Britain, but pro-Communist newspapers in Hong Kong greeted the British action with satisfaction. [4:1.]

The question of tax revisions, which will become a leading issue in Washington following President Truman's budget message to Congress tomorrow, has led to disagreement among leading Democrats over procedure. Senator George urged immediate cuts in excise rates, with other tax reforms to be taken up later. Other key leaders favor an omnibus bill to take care of the whole matter. [1:5.]

All Southern Governors have been invited to a meeting to be held Jan. 28 in Raleigh, N. C., to consider ways of improving relations between the Southern and Administration wings of the Democratic party. [1:4.]

Senator Taft called for White House use of the emergency injunction under the Taft-Hartley Act against John L. Lewis to end the abbreviated work week of the coal miners. [44:3.]

A fire that swept a mental ward of Mercy Hospital, a Roman Catholic institution at Davenport, Iowa, took the lives of thirty-seven women, caught behind barred windows and locked doors. One of twenty-five rescued also died. [1:1.]

William A. Brady, theatrical producer, died at 86. [76:1.]

U. S. Evangelists Stoned in Italy; Charge That Priests Incited Mobs

By The Associated Press.

ROME, Jan. 7—Young evangelists of the Protestant Church of Christ said today they had been stoned out of Castel Gandolfo—summer home of Pope Pius XII—and three other towns near Rome where they had been working.

One of them said, "priests aroused the people against us." Italy's population is overwhelmingly Roman Catholic.

A Vatican source said priests in the area of the four towns had for several months complained that the evangelists of the Church of Christ were "teaching heresy." This source expressed doubt that the priests had aroused the townspeople against the evangelists.

[In Washington, Representative Ed Gossett, Democrat, of Texas, accompanied a group to the State Department on Friday to protest Italian treatment of the evangelical group, whose activities include operation of an orphanage at the town of Frascati.]

Nearly all of the thirteen evangelists, who include six young married couples, are from Texas and obtain most of their support from Texas Churches of Christ.

The group has now engaged an attorney in efforts to obtain renewal of visas to remain in Italy and written permission to operate their orphanage, which thus far they say they have been unable to obtain.

The group began its work in Rome and surrounding towns just a year ago. During the year it distributed $100,000 worth of clothing, food and medicine.

The entire operation, including salaries of the workers and maintenance of buildings and halls,

Continued on Page 20, Column 1

100TH ANNIVERSARY
"All the News
That's Fit to Print"
1851 1951

The New York Times.

LATE CITY EDITION
Fair and warmer today. Fair and continued mild tomorrow.
Temperature Range Today—Max., 64; Min., 43
Temperatures Yesterday—Max., 57; Min., 40
U. S. Weather Bureau Report, Page 16, Sect. 1

Section 1

VOL. CI..No. 34,259. Entered as Second-Class Matter, Post Office, New York, N. Y. NEW YORK, SUNDAY, NOVEMBER 11, 1951. Including Magazine and Book Review. FIFTEEN CENTS New York City 50 Mile Zone | Elsewhere Twenty-five Cents

PIER PANEL WEIGHS IMPARTIAL ARBITER FOR DOCK DISPUTES

Longshoremen of Both Groups Are Said to Favor Changes in Union Vote Procedure

PORT ACTIVITY IN SLUMP

Only 4,000 at Work—Lack of Truckers, Business Holiday, Overtime Pay Held Causes

By GEORGE HORNE

The state inquiry board investigating the port's longest waterfront strike may recommend a permanent disputes system for the dock workers including an impartial arbiter with strong powers.

With the strike over and the port slowly returning to normal, sentiment for a permanent arbiter or "czar" to settle recurrent waterfront troubles is growing among the longshoremen of the port, and it became known yesterday that Industrial Commissioner Edward Corsi favored such a solution. Mr. Corsi took over the twenty-five-day insurgent strike as a state problem a week ago and named a fact-finding board that has been meeting throughout the week. It will continue its search for causes and solutions on Tuesday.

Since it is known that the Industrial Commissioner favors the arbiter system for a management-labor area frequently plagued by disagreements, it can be assumed that the point has been discussed with board members.

Union Ratification Studied

Prof. Martin P. Catherwood of Cornell University is chairman of the board. Its other members are Msgr. John P. Boland of Buffalo and Dean Alfange, New York attorney. George J. Mintzer is counsel and Arthur Stark is secretary of the panel, which devoted last week to testimony on how the International Longshoremen's Association, A.F.L., negotiated and ratified a new contract with the New York Shipping Association.

The walkout was called off by the strike committee led by John J. (Gene) Sampson early Friday morning after a conference among the Sampson men, the state investigators and officials led by Mr. Corsi. A handful of locals sparked the uprising on Oct. 15 and have demanded a new contract negotiation, charging that the ratification vote was fraudulent.

A second basic solution to their problems also is being widely discussed among the longshoremen, including both factions in the intra-union dispute that cost shipping and foreign trading interests millions of dollars.

Union Changes Sought

This solution involves a change in union voting practices. A canvass of union men, taken in the last week, shows that they are genuinely dissatisfied with the voting system. This is true not only in the six striking locals that used the contract vote result as a war cry in the walkout, but among the majority of dock laborers who remained loyal to the union's president, Joseph P. Ryan, and the other international leaders.

Feeling among the men makes it

Continued on Page 53, Column 2

Major Sports News

FOOTBALL

Michigan State routed Notre Dame, while Cornell upset Michigan. Columbia beat Dartmouth and Princeton routed Harvard. Scores of leading games:

Army	27	The Citadel	6
Baylor	18	Texas	6
Boston U.	35	Oregon	6
Bucknell	21	Colgate	20
Columbia	21	Dartmouth	6
Cornell	20	Michigan	7
Ga. Tech.	34	V. M. I.	7
Holy Cross	39	Marquette	13
Illinois	40	Iowa	13
Maryland	40	Navy	21
Michigan St.	35	Notre Dame	0
Minnesota	16	Indiana	14
Nebraska	34	Iowa State	27
Ohio State	16	Pittsburgh	14
Penn State	32	Syracuse	13
Princeton	54	Harvard	13
Purdue	35	N'western	14
Rutgers	28	Brown	21
S. M. U.	14	Tex. A. & M.	14
Stanford	27	So. Calif.	20
Temple	34	N. Y. U.	6
Tennessee	60	W. and L.	14
Wake Forest	19	Duke	13
Williams	33	Wesleyan	7
Wisconsin	16	Penn	7

HORSE RACING

Oil Capitol, paying $31.40 for $2, won the $60,700 Butler Handicap at Jamaica.

(Details in Section 5)

Aide of Truman Gets Mutual Security Post

George M. Elsey
Associated Press

By W. H. LAWRENCE
Special to The New York Times.

KEY WEST, Fla., Nov. 10—President Truman announced today the transfer of his administrative assistant, George M. Elsey, 33 years old, to a top post in the new Mutual Security Administration, which coordinates the foreign economic and military aid programs.

Accepting with regret Mr. Elsey's resignation as a member of the White House staff, Mr. Truman took the unusual step of publicly urging Mr. Elsey to write for publication in the future an account of history in the making during the last decade as viewed from inside the White House.

"It has come to be the practice lately for people to write

Continued on Page 32, Column 1

EISENHOWER DENIAL OF '52 BID REPORTED

Taft Backer Asserts in Paris General Told Him Truman Made No Offer of Aid

By The Associated Press.

PARIS, Nov. 10—A friend of Senator Robert A. Taft quoted General of the Army Dwight D. Eisenhower today as saying there was "absolutely no truth" to the story that President Truman had offered to support the general for the Democratic nomination for President in 1952.

Representative George Bender of Cleveland, a Republican Representative at Large from Ohio, met with General Eisenhower today in company with three other House members—two Democrats and a Republican.

Mr. Bender was asked by The Associated Press if he had obtained any definite information from the general as to whether he was planning to run for the Presidency.

The Representative replied that he asked General Eisenhower directly whether there was any truth in the story published Thursday by THE NEW YORK TIMES that the President had offered to stand aside for the general and support him for the Democratic nomination.

"There is absolutely no truth in the story," Mr. Bender quoted General Eisenhower as saying.

The House member said the general told the four members of Congress that he had "one interest in life and that is in doing a job here."

Mr. Bender reported, however, that he received no direct answer

Continued on Page 57, Column 3

$11,500,000,000 CUT IN DEFENSE BUDGET NEXT YEAR STUDIED

Arms Leaders Thought to Fear Danger to Civilian Economy in High Spending Rate

FACTORY PROGRESS CITED

Production Believed to Insure Strength—$54,000,000,000 Called Pentagon Goal

By AUSTIN STEVENS
Special to The New York Times.

WASHINGTON, Nov. 10—Defense leaders are preparing to cut the next military budget as much as $11,500,000,000 below this year's. This is said to be possible without any fiscal hitch in the "orderly build-up" of United States forces and arms or interfering with the foreign military aid program.

The reasons for beginning a leveling off in armament outlays earlier than had been expected are twofold, according to Federal budget experts. One is that because of long "lead times" in the production of aircraft, tanks, ammunition and other "hardware" for the armed forces, funds already authorized by Congress cover much of the scheduled expension of the services and their weapons.

Of even greater significance, according to authoritative sources, is a growing awareness among defense officials that unless military demands are regulated and spaced, a "breaking point" in the civilian economy might result in the loss of public support for the long-term preparedness program.

Pentagon Drafting Budgets

Some of the strongest appreciation of the need for a stable economy is understood to be in the Pentagon itself, where the armed services are preparing their final budget requests.

There are indications, however, that the generals and admirals will not take quickly or quietly to the level-off philosophy. Long, hard wrangling is expected before the Defense Department can submit its 1953 fiscal year requests to the Bureau of the Budget.

The Defense Department is expected to place a complete budget before Congress in January, rather than the "one-line" request submitted last year in the President's over-all budget message. The detailed military budget was not completed until late April.

On another defense budget front, President Truman delegated today to Manly Fleischmann, Defense Production Administrator, the authority to approve borrowing from the Treasury by Government agencies participating in defense mobilization. This action, taken at Key West, where the President is vacationing, was described by aides as "largely technical" to relieve the President of routine approvals.

$54 Billions Expected

Although the figures are still tentative, it is expected that the combined spending authority to be sought for the three armed services and military aid under the Mutual Security Program will be not more than $54,000,000,000. This compares to the $65,500,000,000 authorized by the last session of Congress for the military and arms aid.

In round figures, the total spending authority in the Defense Department's hands, including foreign

Continued on Page 20, Column 1

Romans in Iceland Before Vikings, Expert Deduces From Old Coins

Special to The New York Times.

TORONTO, Nov. 10—A University of Toronto professor has discovered evidence that soldiers of the Roman Empire landed on Iceland as early as 300 A. D., at least 500 years before the Vikings discovered the island.

His discovery leads him to suggest that Iceland may have been found even 600 years before the Roman soldiers landed and that sailors of the Greek Empire may have roamed the Atlantic and known of North America in 300 B. C., about 1,800 years before Columbus.

Prof. Fritz Heichelheim, internationally known specialist in ancient economic history and ancient coins, told of his work in an interview. His findings are to be published in Antiquity, British archaeological journal.

This piece of history might never have been found if it had not been for an ancient German custom. When the Germans were lost or in trouble they buried coins in the belief that this might placate the gods who could help them.

About five years ago an ancient coin was turned up by tourists on a desolate stretch of Iceland coast. Soon afterward, two more coins were found at the same spot by natives.

The coins were minted during the period of three Roman Emperors, Aurelian, Probus and Diocletian, whose reign ended about 300 A. D. One of them was minted in a city called Cyzicus, on the Asiatic side of Lake Marmara near Gallipoli. The two others were issued later in Rome.

As Professor Heichelheim interpreted the find, the owner of the coins was a member of the Roman army, stationed first in the eastern Mediterranean area and then in the imperial guard in Rome. During

Continued on Page 44, Column 1

U.S., Upset by Crises Abroad, Leans to Granting More Aid

Gloomy Reports From London and Paris Said to Have Changed Theme of Debate From Need of Help to Its Extent

By PAUL P. KENNEDY
Special to The New York Times.

WASHINGTON, Nov. 10—Officials here are making no effort to conceal their concern over the mounting economic crises in France and Britain, particularly the former.

Debate on whether some sort of assistance is necessary to improve the dollar balance drains of the two countries, drains attributable largely to their defense building programs, appears to be diminishing rapidly. The increasing area of debate now seems to cover how the assistance will be supplied and how much of it will be necessary.

The gloomy speech made in the House of Commons Wednesday by Richard Austen Butler, Chancellor of the Exchequer, in which he called for greater austerity to stave off national bankruptcy, worried officials here. Reports that Vice Premier René Mayer, in charge of France's finances, will make an equally pessimistic speech to the French National Assembly next week have only intensified that worry.

Mr. Butler informed the British of a curtailment in imports amounting to about $1,000,000,000 or roughly 10 per cent of Britain's import total. Current reports are that France intends soon to cut her imports more drastically, proportionately, than Britain.

Such import cuts not only will lower the living standards of the nation but almost certainly will have an adverse effect, of a degree at present unpredictable, on the defense efforts of the two countries, officials here said.

United States officials concerned with the defense roles of the affected countries explained that Britain, for instance, depended on imports for about one-third of her total production.

To solve their similar problems.

Continued on Page 34, Column 3

INQUIRY HITS WASTE IN BUYING G. I. FOOD

Senators Again Charge Failure to Set Up Single Standard for Purchases by U. S.

Special to The New York Times.

WASHINGTON, Nov 10.—An "inexcusable failure" by the Departments of the Army and Agriculture to standardize their specifications for food bought for the armed forces is causing needless expense for the taxpayers, the Senate Armed Services Preparedness subcommittee reported today.

Nearly a year ago the subcommittee had gone into similar matters. It reported finding that little attention had been paid to its recommendations then beyond some "polite letter-writing."

This time it said:

"Our reports are not written as literary exercises. We expect our recommendations to be implemented or we expect to be shown the reason if they are not."

At issue were concededly dull matters—dried eggs and the precise manner in which holiday chicken should be served.

It was agreed that dried eggs had become an armed services breakfast item. Is was agreed, too, that on chicken days the troops loved chicken, and that they should have it in plenty.

The Senators complained, how-

Continued on Page 21, Column 1

SOVIET BLOC SELLS SEIZED ART IN U. S.

Hungary Establishes Monopoly for Peddling Objects Wrung From Middle Classes

By JOHN MacCORMAC
Special to The New York Times.

VIENNA, Nov. 10—The regimes of the "people's democracies" have worked out a new scheme to wring the last ounce of value from their expropriated middle classes.

In addition to deporting them from cities to farms and labor camps, where they must toil for bare subsistence twelve to fourteen hours a day, the governments are setting up organizations to purchase their possessions at confiscatory prices and sell them to the West, including the United States. This was done by the Russians in the Nineteen Twenties and by the Nazis with Jewish-owned property in the Thirties and Forties.

The Hungarian Government already has formed a Government monopoly for this purpose known as Artex, and it is reported that the Rumanian, Czechoslovak and Polish Governments may follow the example.

From May to July, about 50,000 members of the former middle class were deported from Budapest and other large Hungarian cities, and sent to labor camps or billeted with kulaks, wealthy farmers.

Continued on Page 42, Column 1

World News Summarized

SUNDAY, NOVEMBER 11, 1951

By a vote of 11 to 2 the steering committee of the United Nations General Assembly approved yesterday a resolution, introduced by Thailand, to recommend to the Assembly that it deny the Soviet request to put on the Assembly agenda the issue of Chinese Communist representation and that it bar discussion of any other proposals dealing with the same issue. Poland and the Soviet Union voted against the resolution and Yugoslavia abstained. [1:8.]

The United Nations is insisting in the Korean armistice parleys that the Communist foe guarantee against a build-up of his forces during the truce. Vice Admiral Joy, in a definition of the Allies' terms as the Panmunjom talks went on, also set out demands for a buffer zone, firm security for the United Nations forces and their rear areas and "quick and satisfactory" prisoner-of-war arrangements. [1:6.] Fighting action in Korea continued to be slight. [3:1; map P. 2.]

French troops in Indo-China launched a surprise one-day offensive that recaptured scores of villages and cleared 400 square miles of territory of Communist-led Vietminh forces. [1:7.]

The United States, Britain, France and Turkey gave the Arab states and Israel details of their preliminary plans to defend the Middle East against "outside aggression." The four-power statement sought "the cooperation of all interested states," but the appeal was confronted with Arab division and a skeptical Israel. [1:7.]

The growing economic crisis in both France and Britain caused grave concern in Washington. Officials, worried particularly by the French outlook, were debating how to extend United States aid and in what degree. [1:4-5.]

An $11,500,000,000 cut in the nation's military budget for next year is being planned by defense leaders, who felt that such a reduction from this year's outlay was possible without interfering with the "orderly build-up" of United States might. [1:3.]

A Republican Representative quoted General Eisenhower as saying that there was nothing to the report that President Truman had offered to support the general for the Democratic Presidential nomination. [1:2.]

The state fact-finding committee in the New York City dock strike was considering recommending a permanent arbiter for waterfront disputes. [1:1.]

Hungary was reported to have formed a government monopoly to buy the possessions of the expropriated middle classes at confiscatory prices and then to sell them to the West for badly needed dollars. Other satellite countries were said to be ready to follow suit. [1:5.]

Evidence indicating that the ancient Romans had landed in Iceland as early as 300 A. D. was reported. [1:2-3.]

NEWS BULLETINS FROM THE TIMES
Every hour on the hour
8 A. M. through Midnight
Except at 4 and 9 P. M. Today
WQXR AM 1560
WQXR FM 96.3

Index to other news appears on Page 95.

ALLIES TO DEMAND TRUCE FREEZE SIZE OF ENEMY'S ARMIES

Guarantee Also Asked Against Red Rearmament Following a Cease-Fire in Korea

ADMIRAL JOY LISTS TERMS

Negotiators Approach Meeting of Minds on Armistice Line, a U. N. Spokesman Says

Text of Admiral Joy's statement on truce conditions, Page 5.

By LINDESAY PARROTT
Special to The New York Times.

TOKYO, Sunday, Nov. 11—The United Nations will demand a guarantee from the Communists against reinforcement or rearmament of the Chinese and North Korean armies during a cease-fire as one of the conditions for a truce in Korea.

This was announced today by Vice Admiral Charles Turner Joy, senior Allied truce negotiator, as armistice talks by a military subcommittee continued at Panmunjom.

[The Associated Press said a United Nations spokesman had reported that the members of the subcommittee neared a meeting of minds at their session Sunday on a cease-fire line. He said certain proposals on the question had been "formalized" for consideration by the full truce delegations.]

Seek "Concrete Agreements"

The proposed guarantee apparently will be the keystone of the United Nations program for the third point of the agreed agenda for the truce talks, dealing with enforcement of the armistice once the shooting had halted.

"We require concrete agreements that will prevent a build-up of military forces beyond the level existing at the time the armistice is placed in effect," Admiral Joy's statement said. "This includes a proviso against the rehabilitation and refurbishment of existing forces whose combat effectiveness has been significantly reduced as a result of combat."

The terms made public by the head of the Allied delegation obviously were intended to prevent the enemy from using the truce to bring down new armies and supplies from Manchuria after the armistice had halted the United Nations air blockade of the Communists' lines of communications. It was the first indication that such a requirement would be sought.

Past Re-Equipping Cited

After the defeat of the North Korean Army, prior to the Chinese intervention, the Communist troops were reformed and re-equipped north of the Yalu River, then moved down into combat again. The United Nations terms would prevent the enemy from staging a similar maneuver, then ending the armistice with a sudden reinforced onslaught.

Issuing his declaration at a time when the subcommittee seemed to be bogged down after seventeen sessions in a dispute over location of an armistice line, Admiral Joy asserted:

"We intend to press vigorously for a full military armistice. Anything else would be totally unacceptable."

"We shall continue to use every weapon at our command, at the

Continued on Page 4, Column 1

French Drive Frees Big Indo-China Area

The New York Times Nov. 11, 1951

French troops seized Choben in a pincer movement (cross) aided by a paratroops' drop. Large-area map on Page 9.

By The Associated Press.

HANOI, Indo-China, Nov. 10—French forces lashed out from their Hanoi perimeter today and announced that they had driven Communist-led Vietminh forces from nearly 400 square miles of territory and sixty to eighty villages in a surprise one-day offensive.

A parachute drop soon after dawn resulted in the capture by noon of Choben, thirty miles southwest of Hanoi and the principal town in the rice-growing target area.

Bombers that dropped napalm, three French regimental combat teams and two battalions of Vietnamese soldiers pushed the attack. Many of the troops, following the bombers and para-

Continued on Page 9, Column 1

WEST GIVES DETAIL OF MID-EAST PLAN

Publishes 11-Point Tentative Defense Program—Reaction of Arabs Still Unclear

Text of four-power statement on Middle East, Page 16.

By WALTER H. WAGGONER
Special to The New York Times.

WASHINGTON, Nov. 10—Against a background of a divided Arab world and a highly skeptical Israel, the Western Big Three powers and Turkey made public today their preliminary plans for a defense program designed to secure the vital Middle East against "outside aggression."

The four sponsoring powers of a Middle East command—the United States, Britain, France and Turkey—delivered to Arab and Israeli diplomatic chiefs a statement of eleven "principles" on which the proposed defense organization would be created.

Again, following on the informal statements of intention by Secretary of State Dean Acheson and others, the four powers expressed their determination to press for a Middle East Command despite the grave obstacles to Middle East unity most officials knew existed.

"The defense of the Middle East is vital to the free world and its defense against outside aggression can be secured only by the cooperation of all interested states," the four-power statement said.

Egypt already has rejected such a program, however, and her Arab neighbors are right now wondering what course they should take in view of the Cairo action. The fact that they have not immediately

Continued on Page 17, Column 1

Army Cooks Up New Batch of Snow For 1,400 Veterans of Korea Cold

Special to The New York Times.

PINE CAMP, N. Y., Nov. 10—"That's the Army for you," is a lament not unknown to any military camp, but for 1,400 veterans of the Korean war it carried more than its usual icy meaning today.

For the veterans, having figured that the comparative security of Governors Island in New York Harbor would afford them well-earned bright lights and warmth, found themselves instead transferred to this encampment for winter maneuvers in near-zero temperatures.

The 1,400 men were sent back to the United States from Korea under the combat rotation plan. About a month ago they were processed through Camp Kilmer, N. J., and assigned to Pine Camp as replacements for the 278th Regimental Combat Team here. Before leaving Korea the men were permitted to express a geographic preference for an Army command in this country, and the 1,400 chose the First Army, with headquarters on Governors Island.

After arriving at Pine Camp the veterans found themselves considerably closer to Canada than to the bright lights of Broadway that they had visualized overseas. Complaints mounted a week ago when the temperature dropped to 10 degrees above zero, and reports circulated that marks of 30 and 40 below are not unusual here.

The complaints were intensified a bit later when the returned soldiers learned that they were scheduled to join in Exercise Snowfall, which begins after Jan. 1 with a total of 30,000 troops. For these winter maneuvers, the Eleventh Airborne Division will come to Pine Camp from Camp Campbell, Ky., and the Third Armored Cavalry Regiment will move northward from Fort Meade, Md.

For most of one winter month, the troops are scheduled to manu-

Continued on Page 9, Column 1

SOVIET LOSES MOVE TO KEEP RED CHINA A LIVE ISSUE IN U. N.

Question of a Seat for Peiping Barred From Paris Agenda, but May Be Revived

MALIK'S CHALLENGE MILD

Nearly 90 Rebuffs of One Plea Cited by Austin—Yugoslav Complaint to Be Heard

By THOMAS J. HAMILTON
Special to The New York Times.

PARIS, Nov. 10—The General (steering) Committee of the United Nations decided today to recommend that the General Assembly reject the Soviet proposal to place the question of the representation of Communist China on its agenda. For good measure the committee approved a further recommendation that this session of the Assembly refuse to consider any additional proposals to exclude representatives of the Nationalist Government or to seat those of the Communist regime.

These recommendations were contained in a resolution introduced by Thailand and approved by a vote of 11 to 2, the Soviet Union and Poland dissenting and Yugoslavia abstaining. The Soviet Union will have an opportunity to contest the recommendation when the Assembly considers it next week.

However, in the Security Council earlier in the day, Jacob A. Malik, representative of the Soviet Union, offered only a perfunctory challenge on this issue to Dr. T. F. Tsiang, the Chinese representative, who is President of the Council for November, and some delegates believe these are signs that the Soviet Union, whatever its motives, may not make much of a fight at this session on this issue.

Harping on China Opposed

In opposing inclusion of the item on the agenda, Warren R. Austin, United States representative, said Soviet proposals to seat Communist China had been rejected nearly ninety times in United Nations organs and declared exclusion of the item "would clear the way for the Assembly to proceed with the consideration of important problems before it."

Mr. Malik retorted that this showed that the United Nations organs had been wrong nearly ninety times. In any event, it is generally expected that if an armistice is concluded in Korea the Chinese Communist Government will be invited to send a representative to Paris to take part in discussion of a permanent settlement as well as other Far Eastern items. However, if the Assembly accepts the committee's recommendation, discussion of China's representation might be excluded.

Mr. Malik and Manfred Lachs, the Polish representative, also were defeated in their effort to have the committee recommend exclusion from the agenda of a Yugoslav item charging that the Soviet Union and Soviet satellites had committed hostile activities against Yugoslavia. The vote was 12 to 2.

Yugoslavia as Storm Center

Mr. Malik said the charges had been made by "agents provocateurs and slanderers" and had been filed in an effort to justify recent visits to Belgrade of United States generals, including Gen. J. Lawton Collins, Army Chief of Staff. However, he spoke only briefly and left most of the job of attacking the proposal to Mr. Lachs.

The Polish representative, alluding to the Oct. 27 issue of Collier's Magazine—whose account of a victory of the Western Allies over the Soviet Union in an imagined war is providing Communist delegates with material for constant attacks on the alleged aggressive aims of the United States—pointed out that Colliers had declared the war started with an attempted assassination of Premier Marshal Tito. He asked whether the editors of Colliers had inspired the Yugoslav charges or vice versa.

Mr. Lachs charged also that "thousands" of trains carrying American war equipment were crossing the Yugoslav frontier daily and ridiculed the idea that "tiny little Albania" was threatening Yugoslavia.

Mr. Lachs asserted also that the Yugoslav accusations were weak since they charged only two fron-

Continued on Page 13, Column 1

This section consists of 116 pages divided into three parts. Index is on Page 95. Society news begins on Page 92. The obituaries begin on Page 89.

100TH ANNIVERSARY
"All the News That's Fit to Print"
1851 1951

The New York Times.

LATE CITY EDITION
Cloudy and mild today. Some cloudiness, warm tomorrow.
Temperature Range Today—Max., 54; Min., 42
Temperature Yesterday—Max., 43; Min., 33
U. S. Weather Bureau Report, Page 7, Sect. 1

Section 1

VOL. CI. No. 34,308. Entered as Second-Class Matter, Post Office, New York, N. Y. NEW YORK, SUNDAY, DECEMBER 30, 1951. Including Magazine and Book Review. FIFTEEN CENTS New York City | Elsewhere 50 Miles Zone | Twenty-five Cents

U. S. STUDY SLATED TO EASE JOB LOSSES IN AUTO INDUSTRY

But Mobilization Chief Sees Hope Dim for Quick Way to Ease Detroit Plight

QUOTA RULING DEFERRED

Wilson Will Attempt to 'Shave' Materials From Other Work for Car Manufacturers

By PAUL P. KENNEDY
Special to THE NEW YORK TIMES.

WASHINGTON, Dec. 29—Charles E. Wilson, head of the Office of Defense Mobilization, said today he held out little hope to representatives of the automobile industry and officials of the auto workers' unions that the serious unemployment situation in the Detroit area could be alleviated in the near future.

He spoke to reporters after a day-long conference attended by high officials of the larger automobile companies, heads of the automotive unions and leading Michigan political figures. The conference was called to discuss the possibility of relieving the unemployment crisis by easing present and probable future curtailments in civilian automobile production.

Mr. Wilson said the only decisions he had reached as a result of the meeting were these:

1. To study the situation and see if he could "shave" from other programs in order to allocate more materials to the automotive group.
2. To appoint a task force composed of independent Government agencies and military departments to study the Detroit situation in order to determine if more defense contracts might be placed there quickly.

The task force, he said, will begin its work in Detroit next Wednesday. In any case, however, no decision will be reached before Jan. 12, when the allotment of materials for the second quarter of 1952 will be announced.

Continuing Study Planned

Mr. Wilson said the task force program would be a continuing one and, after the second-quarter allotment has been fixed, would study ways of alleviating the unemployment problem likely to be met in the third quarter.

Mr. Wilson said that nothing he had heard during the conference changed his belief that there was no way to avoid "substantial" cutbacks in production for the second quarter of 1952 except by "shaving" materials from defense and defense-supporting industries already asking for more "than we can give them."

In October, Mr. Wilson's office and the Defense Production Administration ordered in the first quarter of 1952 a 13.7 per cent reduction in automobile production beyond that of the last quarter of 1951 in which an estimated 1,100,000 cars were scheduled to be manufactured. The cutbacks were to be brought about by curtailment in metal allotments, particularly copper.

Predicts "Substantial" Cut

Earlier this week, Manly Fleischmann, Administrator of the Defense Production Administration, predicted a "substantial" cutback in the second quarter of 1952 beyond the 13.7 curtailment of the first quarter.

Mr. Wilson said that the automobile manufacturers had asked for more materials in the second

Continued on Page 26, Column 2

HEALTH BOARD HEAD

Dr. Paul B. Magnuson
The New York Times

PRESIDENT ORDERS U. S. HEALTH SURVEY

Magnuson to Head Commission to Scan Nation's Needs and Ways to Meet Them

By WALTER H. WAGGONER
Special to THE NEW YORK TIMES.

WASHINGTON, Dec. 29—President Truman created a fifteen-member commission today to determine within a year the nation's "total health requirements" and to recommend ways for meeting them in both the immediate and distant future.

Labeling the group a Commission on the Health Needs of the Nation, the President declared in a statement that the present world crisis made it particularly important that "we should seek to limit the drain upon our strength through illness and death."

He named Dr. Paul B. Magnuson, former Medical Director of the Veterans Administration, as chairman of the group and chose fourteen representatives of the medical profession, the American Medical Association, education and research institutions and farm, labor and consumer organizations to cooperate in reports and recommendations.

The selection of Dr. Magnuson was regarded as significant in view of the fact that he was dismissed last January from his Veterans Administration post following a long-standing dispute with Carl Gray, the agency's administrator, over the control of medical services.

It appeared to many observers that the President was making a new approach to safeguarding the country's health, which he has sought to accomplish in part by proposing a system of compulsory national health insurance.

Regularly, however, criticism of such a program has been sharp and persistent, especially by organized medicine itself. Congress, just as regularly, has defeated the President's proposals.

Mr. Truman did not refer specifically to Federal health insurance today, but did recall the "bitter opposition from some quarters" and the failure of his critics to come forward with what he could regard as adequate "counter-proposals."

By naming the commission at this time and giving it twelve

Continued on Page 16, Column 7

U. N. DROPS DEMAND FOR AIR INSPECTION OF TRUCE IN KOREA

But Allies Hinge Compromise on Red Concession on Other Terms for Armistice

PRISONER IMPASSE EASES

Foe Agrees to Yield Available Information on the Captives Missing From Roster

By LINDESAY PARROTT
Special to THE NEW YORK TIMES.

TOKYO, Sunday, Dec. 30—United Nations delegates negotiating for an armistice in the Korean war offered yesterday a sweeping new concession to the Communists, under which the Allies would forego aerial inspection behind the lines during the cease-fire.

The proposal, made by Air Force Maj. Gen. Howard M. Turner before a military subcommittee at Panmunjom, was on a "contingent basis," he told the Chinese and North Koreans. To close the bargain, the enemy representatives would have to accept in full a compromise Allied program eliminating a "built-in veto" over activities of neutral truce administrators and agree to troop rotation and limitation of airfield construction in North Korea.

"We have now conceded to your unreasonable views all that we can concede," General Turner told Chinese Gen. Hsieh Fang, senior Communist delegate to the subcommittee. "From this moment we have and shall have nothing further to propose."

Called 'Calculated Risk'

The new United Nations concession was offered, as has been the case on previous occasions, as the armistice sessions reached a deadlock, neither side apparently prepared to yield another inch in their debate over conditions for the truce. An Allied spokesman made it clear that it was put forward with some reluctance as a "calculated risk" in the interest of breaking the logjam.

Aerial inspection hitherto had been regarded as the principal assurance that the Communists would be unable to use the cease-fire as a breathing spell in which to build up air strength in Korea on newly constructed airstrips difficult to find or check by ground inspection.

There was no immediate indication, however, that the offer would be accepted. The Communists, it appeared, still intended to seek even more favorable conditions.

Calls for a Recess

General Hsieh called for a fifteen-minute recess to read the proposal. When he returned to the tent, he said:

"My impression after making a preliminary study is that, on the one hand, this is a step forward, but at the same time a stumbling block is left—namely your interference with our internal affairs, which has been consistently opposed by our side."

A broadcast by the Peiping radio interpreted General Hsieh's remarks as even stronger. The Allied plan, it reported him as having said, proposed "precisely what our side can't tolerate on the most important question of installations in Korea."

The Communists have insisted that North Korean sovereignty would be affected by any limita-

Continued on Page 3, Column 1

AIRMEN, RELEASED BY HUNGARIANS, SAFE AT BASE IN GERMANY

Fliers telling their commanding officer, Col. Park Holland, second from right, of their experiences in Communist prison, after their arrival at Erding, Germany. The airmen, left to right, are Sgt. James A. Elam of Kingsland, Ark.; T/Sgt. Jess A. Duff of Spokane, Wash.; Capt. John J. Swift of Glens Falls, N. Y.; and Capt. Dave H. Henderson of Shawnee, Okla. Associated Press Radiophoto

4 AIRMEN QUERIED 39 DAYS IN HUNGARY, 14 BY THE RUSSIANS

Freed Americans State They Were Held in Solitary but Were Not Mistreated

MILITARY SIDE STRESSED

Pilot, in Interview at U.S. Base, Tells of Losing Way—Forced Down by Soviet Fighter

By JACK RAYMOND
Special to THE NEW YORK TIMES.

ERDING, Germany, Dec. 29—The four released United States fliers said tonight they had been questioned for thirty-nine days while in solitary confinement after they had been forced down by a Soviet fighter plane in Hungary Nov. 19.

They were held prisoner first by the Russians and then by the Hungarians. [According to The Associated Press, the fliers said they had been questioned for fourteen days by the Russians.]

The airmen said at a press conference that at no time during the interrogation had they been accused of espionage. They were convicted earlier this week of having intentionally flown across the border and were freed yesterday upon payment by the United States of fines totaling $120,000.

In their interviews, the fliers said they had not been mistreated, although they had been interrogated repeatedly under trying conditions. At times they became "mad" and at times they considered their situation "black indeed," they said.

Pilot Kept Faith in U. S.

"Yet I had hope in my heart for I was a little man and I had hopes that they (the people and Government of the United States) would remember us as individuals," said Capt. Dave H. Henderson of Shawnee, Okla., the commander of the plane, veteran of the Pacific war and the Berlin airlift.

The other members of the crew—and they all looked in good health—were Capt. John J. Swift of Glens Falls, N. Y., T/Sgt. Jess A. Duff of Spokane, Wash., and Sgt. James A. Elam of Kingsland, Ark.

At one time during his imprisonment, Captain Swift tried to get word to United States officials in Budapest by cleverly and laboriously copying Russian words out of a book given to him by his jailers and handprinting a message on scraps of paper and scrip money. But the attempt failed when the Russians discovered a slip of paper bearing a message to United States officials in one of Captain Henderson's pockets.

Fliers Insist They Lost Way

The weight of the fliers' story was that they had become lost while on a routine flight from Erding to Belgrade, Yugoslavia, with a load of freight for the United States attache there.

They made it quite clear to their interrogators that theirs was a cargo plane with no one aboard but the crew and that the equipment they carried, such as an extra radio and blankets, and an extra parachute, was nothing more than the usual paraphernalia common to such aircraft.

The fliers were not permitted to talk to reporters until Samuel Klaus, assistant to the legal adviser of the United States State Department, had arrived here from Washington on a hurried trip by plane.

The airmen were questioned continuously throughout the day by State Department consular officials

Continued on Page 18, Column 3

YUGOSLAV DEFICIT IS PUT UP TO WEST

U.S., Britain and France Asked to Cover $189,000,000 Gap in Budget as Defense Aid

By M. S. HANDLER
Special to THE NEW YORK TIMES.

BELGRADE, Yugoslavia, Dec. 29—Boris Kidric, chairman of the Yugoslav State Economic Council, announced today that the 1952 budget would entail a deficit of 56,800,000,000 dinars ($189,333,333 at the new parity of 300 dinars to the dollar).

He added that the Yugoslav Government hoped this would be covered by loans, credits and grants in aid from the West.

An official source said later that the West meant the United States, British and French Governments and the International Bank for Reconstruction and Development. The three Western Governments concluded an agreement earlier this year to underwrite the Yugoslav Government's foreign trade deficit.

M. Kidric said in Parliament "we have a moral right" to expect this assistance from the West "because we are exposed to more difficulties than any other country in Europe today."

The chairman of the State Economic Council said the budget probably would arouse criticism in the West, but he insisted that the Yugoslav Government's requirements were modest compared with what other European countries, especially Britain and France, had received in aid from the United States between April, 1948, and the end of March, 1951.

M. Kidric said the 210,000,000,000 dinars earmarked for defense and the defense industries for 1952 represented 23.7 per cent of the national income and that this was regarded as an indispensable minimum for the main-

Continued on Page 5, Column 1

Falangist Denounces Waste And Official Abuses in Spain

By CAMILLE M. CIANFARRA
Special to THE NEW YORK TIMES.

MADRID, Dec. 29—Official abuses and the waste of public funds have been charged in a written statement submitted to the Cortes' Appropriations Committee by a Spanish Deputy, who also has appealed to Generalissimo Francisco Franco, Chief of State, to take drastic steps to achieve "more austere" state management that would halt the rising cost of living through sorely needed economies.

The author of the protest is Lieut. Col. Luis Serrano de Pablo, former Civil Governor of Zamora, and a member of the National Council of the Falange party because of his outstanding services to the Nationalist cause during the Spanish civil war. Considered one of the best Spanish pilots in that war, he now is air zone commander of the Atlantic base of Las Palmas, in the Canary Islands.

Colonel Serrano's 3,000-word philippic, which was dated Nov. 1, 1951, represented an attempt by a man who described himself as a loyal supporter of the Franco regime to cut down expenditures in the $540,000,000 national budget for the 1952 calendar year. The

Continued on Page 9, Column 1

HUMAN RIGHTS CASE ON FLIERS STUDIED

U. S. Sends Expert to Europe to Determine if Hungary Committed Violations

Special to THE NEW YORK TIMES.

WASHINGTON, Dec. 29—The State Department began today an investigation into the possibility that Hungary had violated human as well as diplomatic rights by the imprisonment of four United States fliers forced down over Hungarian territory by Soviet planes Nov. 19.

A State Department specialist in human rights violations was flown to Germany to question the four airmen, released by Hungary yesterday on the payment of their $120,000 in fines by the United States.

The official is Samuel Klaus of the State Department's legal adviser's office. According to Lincoln White, State Department press officer, Mr. Klaus "has legal experience and experience in human rights cases, and he has interviewed many people who have been involved in human rights cases behind the Iron Curtain."

Questioned about reports that the State Department had "gagged" the four airmen until Mr. Klaus arrived to question them, Mr. White said he knew of no such orders. Mr. Klaus "is not going as a censor, but to obtain information for the department," he added.

Consulates Get Deadline

The State Department meanwhile gave Hungary until midnight Monday to close its consulates in New York and Cleveland. The closing of the consular offices and a ban on travel by United States citizens in Hungary were ordered here yesterday in retaliation for the imprisonment of the four fliers.

Official notice went to the Hungarian Legation last night. A note sent to Dr. Emil Weil, Hungarian Minister here, repeated charges made by Secretary of State Dean Acheson yesterday that the Budapest Government "in this instance has again clearly failed to live up to the accepted standards of international practice with regard to the right of consular officers to exercise protective functions in behalf of nationals of their country."

"The detention of four Americans from Nov. 19, 1951, to Dec. 28, 1951, and the refusal by the

Continued on Page 10, Column 4

ELECTRICITY MADE BY ATOMIC REACTOR

Heat Removed by Liquid Metal Gives Power for Lights and Pumps of Building in Idaho

Special to THE NEW YORK TIMES.

IDAHO FALLS, Idaho, Dec. 29—Scientists have produced useful electric power from atomic energy for the first time, spokesmen for the Atomic Energy Commission announced here today.

Heat energy was removed from a breeder reactor by a liquid metal of a type not revealed and this energy produced enough steam pressure to drive a turbine.

The turbine, in turn, generated more than 100 kilowatts of power, which supplied a lighting system and operated pumps and other equipment.

This successful experiment, which wrote a new chapter in the history of the atomic age, took place in a modest brick and concrete building on the Snake River

Continued on Page 15, Column 1

SHIP OIL SHORTAGES CAUSE U. S. WORRY

Dearth, Most Severe on East Coast, Delays Departure of Marshall Plan Cargo

By GEORGE HORNE

A steadily increasing shortage of heavy bunker oil for seagoing ships is causing concern among Federal authorities and already has delayed one ship with Marshall Plan cargo.

There has been a "tight supply" situation in the residual grade of petroleum for some time, but the actual halting of a coal-laden Norwegian freighter in the port of Charleston, S. C., last week pointed up the serious problem.

The delayed vessel was the Silvana, loaded with Economic Cooperation Administration coal for Europe.

The Norwegian Embassy sent one of its major officials to the Department of State late in the week to seek a solution of the Silvana's plight, and the department passed the problem on to other official agencies. Efforts were being made yesterday to get enough oil for the delivery of the urgently needed coal. It was reported that the freighter was getting oil and would sail from the southern port during the night.

Leading market experts among the big oil companies said the bunker or residual oil shortage was most severe on the eastern sea-

Continued on Page 17, Column 6

World News Summarized

SUNDAY, DECEMBER 30, 1951

The four United States airmen released on Friday after having been held by Hungary since Nov. 19 said they had been subjected to intensive interrogation for thirty-nine days by the Russians and Hungarians but had not been mistreated. They explained that the questioners sought to obtain military data. [1:8.] The State Department launched an inquiry to determine whether Hungary had violated human rights by the imprisonment of the fliers. [1:7.]

The United Nations representatives, in an effort to break the deadlock in the Korean truce negotiations, offered to forego aerial inspection behind the battlefront during the proposed cease-fire and made some other concessions. [1;3.] Allied forces attacked to regain hilly ground near Korangpo. [2:2, with map.]

The Yugoslav Government hopes that the Western powers will help to make up a deficit of $189,000,000 in its 1952 budget. A Belgrade spokesman said Yugoslavia had a "moral right" to help from the West. [1:4.]

Generalissimo Franco's regime was criticized by a supporter for official abuses and waste of public funds. [1:5-6.]

Prime Minister Churchill went aboard ship to come to the United States for his conference with President Truman. [11:1.]

Mountainous waves, churned by winds of hurricane force, struck shipping and the coast of Europe from Spain to Denmark. Many ships were endangered by the severe storm and at least twenty-six persons were dead or missing. [1:8.]

Useful electric power has been produced for the first time from atomic energy, the Atomic Energy Commission announced. [1:5.] The American Association for the Advancement of Science saw a demonstration of a synthetic chemical capable of making soil fertile. [1:2-3.]

President Truman named a fifteen-member Commission on the Health Needs of the Nation. Headed by Dr. Paul B. Magnuson, the commission was entrusted by Mr. Truman with the task of finding a way to "limit the drain upon our strength through illness and death." [1:2.]

Defense Mobilizer Wilson said he had given little hope to the nation's leading automobile manufacturers who had appealed for help to relieve unemployment in the automobile industry by modifying the curbs on car production. [1:1.]

Index to other news appears on Page 27.

Synthetic Restores Soil Productivity In Hours Instead of Usual Years

By WILLIAM L. LAURENCE
Special to THE NEW YORK TIMES.

PHILADELPHIA, Dec. 29—A synthetic chemical that converts nonproductive into productive soil in a matter of hours instead of the years or generations required by present methods was demonstrated here today before the annual meeting of the American Association for the Advancement of Science.

The chemical, named Krilium, is not a fertilizer. It is a soil-conditioner that quickly restores the physical structure of the soil to the proper consistency, thus enabling plants to obtain the optimum amounts of oxygen, water and nutrients from the soil.

Extensive tests carried out during the last three years by the Monsanto Chemical Company and by approximately eighty soil scientists in various sections of the United States, indicate that the new chemical—the first synthetic soil-conditioner—will mark the beginning of a revolutionary era in agriculture, in which man-made deserts may be turned in a short time into blooming gardens and green acres.

The tests have shown, it was reported, that the chemical is a hundred to a thousand times more efficient in improving soil structure than compost, manure or peat moss, the only substances now available for this purpose. These substances, in addition to providing plant nutrients, also provide humus, the well-decomposed and more or less stable part of the organic matter of the soil, which serves to give the soil its proper consistency or structure.

These natural humus-producing substances, however, are not plentiful and large quantities must be used over a long period of time to restore worn-out soils to a state of productivity. Moreover, humus is destroyed within a matter of

Continued on Page 13, Column 1

Break in Gas Main Endangers Homes

A peril-fraught break in a high-pressure gas main under the pavement of Main Street in Kew Gardens Hills, Queens, just after noon yesterday tied up automobile and bus traffic on the principal artery from Jamaica to Flushing for almost three hours.

The unexplained mishap contributed also to a traffic accident in which a 5-year-old boy, crossing the street near his home a block from the main break, ran into the path of a light truck and was critically injured.

It was not until 5:30 P. M. that crews of the Consolidated Edison Company, aided by police and firemen of the emergency services, reached the valves on each side of the burst main and closed them off. It was expected that the twenty men

Continued on Page 17, Column 4

'Oldest' Proverbs Found in Turkey Prove Pointed Even in Modern Day

By WILLIAM G. WEART
Special to THE NEW YORK TIMES.

PHILADELPHIA, Dec. 29—Two large clay tablets, inscribed with what is believed to be the oldest collection of proverbs and maxims in man's recorded history, have been found amid the hundreds of Sumerian literary tablets and fragments in the Istanbul Museum of the Ancient Orient in Turkey.

Paraphrased versions of some of the proverbs are in frequent use today.

Among examples of the proverbs were these:

You say nothing about what you have found, you speak only of what you have lost.

A restless woman in a house adds ache to pain.

Discovery of the Sumerian "book" dating back some 3,600 years to the era of the famous Hammurabi dynasty was revealed today in a report received from Dr. Samuel Noah Kramer, internationally known Clark Research Professor of Assyriology at the University of Pennsylvania.

The new find antedates the Biblical book of Proverbs by more than 1,000 years, according to calculations made by Dr. Kramer. He has been in Turkey since late last summer, when he received a Fulbright award from the United States Educational Commission for nine months of archaeological research in Istanbul.

Dr. Kramer is devoting most of his time to the long-term Turkish-American project of restoring and translating ancient Sumerian literary documents, the oldest group of belles-lettres ever uncovered.

The major source material for this ancient and long-forgotten literature consists of several thousand tablets and fragments, inscribed in cuneiform script. Dating from 1800 B. C., they were excavated fifty years ago at Nippur, Sumer's cultural center for many centuries, by an expedition from the University of Pennsylvania.

Continued on Page 18, Column 3

Seas Batter Europe; 26 Dead or Missing

By The Associated Press.

LONDON, Dec. 29—Storms whipped up by hurricane winds roaring across the Atlantic lashed Europe's western coasts tonight and twenty-six persons were reported dead or missing.

Rough water raged from Spain to Scandinavia. The Atlantic was one vast boiling cauldron, from the Bay of Biscay to Britain.

Sixty-foot waves pounded over the coast of southern England. Hundreds of small boats lying at anchor were swamped. Even the giant Queen Mary arrived in port seventy-two hours late.

Most of the frequent radio calls from ships in distress came from the area off Land's End, the southeastern corner of England.

A dispatch from Spain said

Continued on Page 18, Column 5

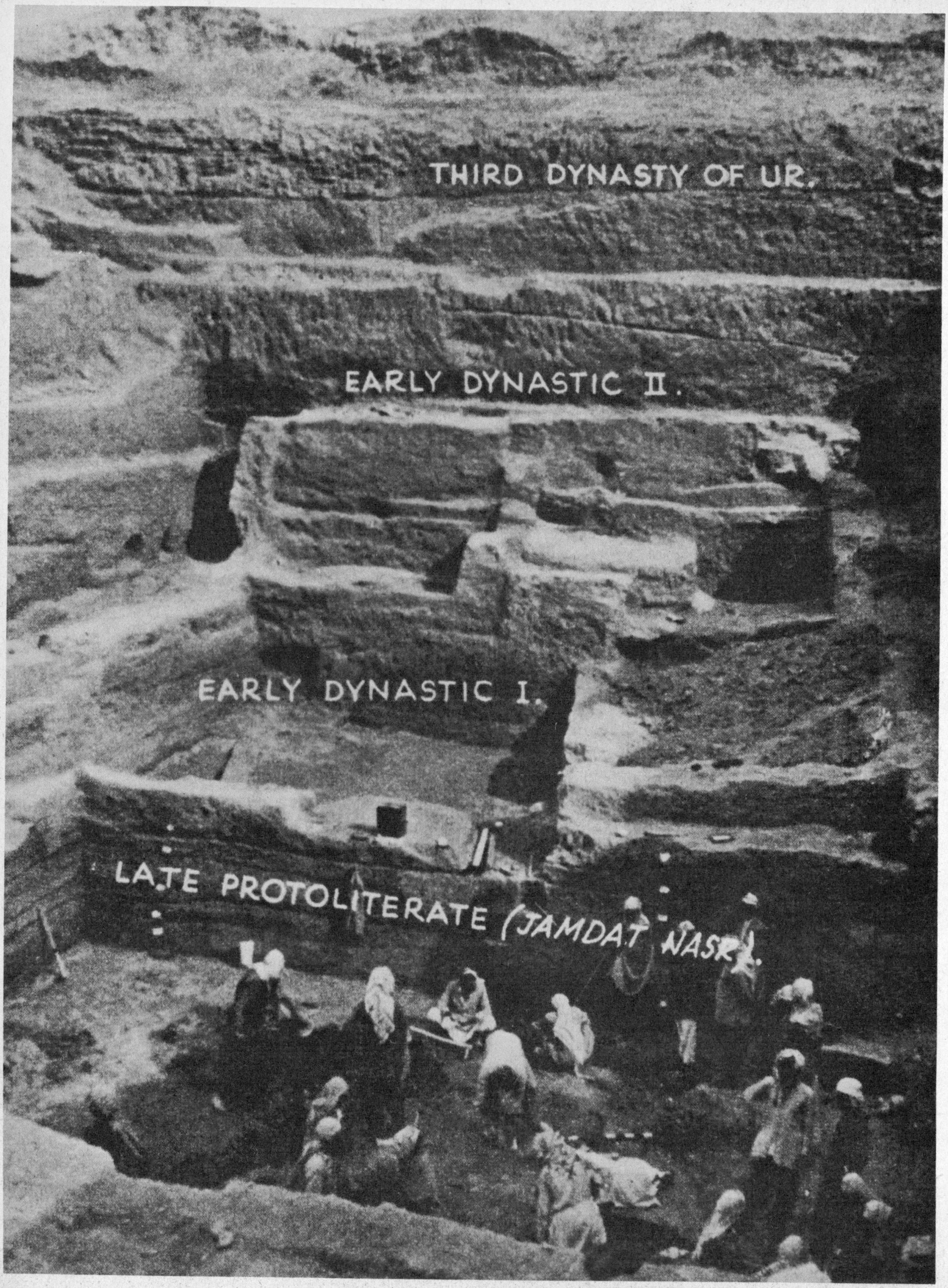

Excavations of the 4,000-year-old temple for Inanna, Sumerian goddess of love and war. The finding of the temple provides a vital key to understanding the history of the Sumerians.

"All the News That's Fit to Print"

The New York Times.

LATE CITY EDITION
Rain today; snow tonight. Clearing and colder tomorrow.
Temperature Range Today-Max., 42; Min., 30
Temperatures Yesterday—Max., 40; Min., 29
Full U.S. Weather Bureau Report, Page 8, Sect. 1

Section 1

VOL. CI No. 34,357. Entered as Second-Class Matter, Post Office, New York, N. Y. NEW YORK, SUNDAY, FEBRUARY 17, 1952. Including Magazine and Book Review. FIFTEEN CENTS New York City 50 Mile Zone | Elsewhere Twenty-five Cents

LA GUARDIA TO DROP 226 FLIGHTS A DAY; BANS FOREIGN RUNS

6,500 FEWER SEATS

Some Schedules Will Be Canceled, Others Will Shift to Idlewild

STEP TO CURB HAZARDS

Rickenbacker Committee Sets Changes, Which Are to Go Into Effect Immediately

The elimination of all overseas flights to and from La Guardia Airport and the reduction of domestic flights from the present peak load of 680 were announced last night by Edward V. Rickenbacker, chairman of the recently formed National Air Transport Coordinating Committee. The decision was made at a five-hour meeting of the committee.

The nineteen-man committee, which had met all day Friday, conferred from 2 to 7 P. M. yesterday in deciding on means to reduce the load at La Guardia. Use of the airport had risen from a normal 520 flights a day to 680 after the Port of New York Authority last week closed down Newark Airport as a result of the third air disaster in Elizabeth, N. J.

The members of the committee, Mr. Rickenbacker announced, agreed to reduce the flights at La Guardia by 226 a day, or to a point below the previous normal operations. The step was taken, he said, to stop the outcry of Queens residents that the facility was a hazard.

Warns on Other Closings

Pointing up the need for corrective action, J. E. Wood, vice president of the Air Line Pilots Association, warned members that not only did the remaining airports in the New York area face possible closing, but that "airports at practically every major terminal can also be suddenly closed."

"Another disaster such as those at Elizabeth," he said, "could very easily be the triggering action which would close every major air terminal in the country."

Mr. Wood added: "If this program does not work it is entirely possible a great many of us might not work either."

Serving on the committee with Mr. Rickenbacker, who is president and general manager of Eastern Airlines, were representatives of eighteen other organizations. These included ten industrial, union and Federal aeronautical agencies, among them the Civil Aeronautics Administration and the Civil Aeronautics Board, and eight airline companies.

Mr. Rickenbacker said the reduction would be prorated among the airlines using the airport, but the exact terms had not yet been decided. He added, however, that the plan would go into effect immediately, and would be in full force by March 1.

Eliminates 6,500 Seats

The new figure of 454 flights a day would reduce passenger traffic by 6,500 seats. In addition, the non-scheduled airlines that had shifted from Newark Airport to La Guardia agreed to discontinue the use of La Guardia. Other airports are being arranged for their use.

The plan will mean a wide rescheduling for commercial aircraft, bringing into use facilities as far north as Bridgeport, Conn., and as far south at Philadelphia. Some flights of scheduled airlines will be canceled, it was explained, some will be consolidated, and others will omit New York.

In the last group, it was said would fall such flights as the Boston-New York-Philadelphia and Boston-New York-Washington runs. The stop at New York on these flights would be eliminated, Mr. Rickenbacker said.

Four lines agreed at the meeting to take their international flights from La Guardia to the New York International Airport at Idlewild, Queens, Mr. Rickenbacker said. He said these companies were Colonial Airlines, Trans-Canada Airlines, Pan American World Airways and American Airlines.

Pan American operates between New York and Bermuda; Colonial to Bermuda and Canada, and the

Continued on Page 67, Column 4

One-Way Roads Set For Washington Sq.

By CHARLES G. BENNETT

Washington Square is due for a large measure of reconstruction under a $150,000 project slated to get under way late this spring under the direction of Borough President Robert F. Wagner Jr. of Manhattan and Park Commissioner Robert Moses.

When the job is completed, probably in the early fall, the congested two-directional roadway through the park will be replaced by two new roadways, one for northbound and the other for southbound traffic, and most of the playground and recreational spaces in the eight-and-one-half-acre area will be laid out differently.

As described by Harry W. Levy, deputy chief engineer of the borough works division of Mr. Wagner's office, a feature of the new layout will be a small sidewalk circling the Washing-

Continued on Page 68, Column 3

HOUSE TAX INQUIRY SUBPOENAS NUNAN

Two Other Former Officials, Olson and Bolich, Called—Ex-Collector's Fees Cited

By JOHN D. MORRIS
Special to The New York Times.

WASHINGTON, Feb. 16 — Joseph D. Nunan Jr. and two other New Yorkers, all former tax officials, have been subpoenaed by a House Ways and Means (King) subcommittee to testify here in an investigation of Federal tax collection operations in New York City.

This became known today in the wake of the Treasury's disclosure that it had granted Mr. Nunan special permission to represent nine clients in Federal tax cases after he had resigned as Commissioner of Internal Revenue in 1947. The subpoenas were served prior to yesterday's Treasury announcement, however, and were said to have no connection with it.

Mr. Nunan was subpoenaed for an appearance a week from Monday. Others subpoenaed were:

Daniel A. Bolich, former Assistant Commissioner of Internal Revenue, who resigned from the Federal bureau Nov. 19, giving ill health as the reason.

James B. E. Olson, who resigned last August as New York area supervisor of the Federal Alcohol Tax Unit.

The dates for appearances by Messrs. Bolich and Olson were not immediately determined.

[In New York, acting on advice of counsel, Mr. Nunan declined comment on the reports from Washington.]

Meanwhile records of a Senate investigating subcommittee linked one of the nine clients, Capitol Distributors Corporation of New York, with commissions paid to Mr. Nunan by the American Lithofold Corporation of St. Louis for printing business obtained by

Continued on Page 31, Column 1

HOUSE GROUP ASKS SPY DEATH PENALTY IN TIME OF PEACE

'Positive Steps' to Curb Soviet Agents Demanded in Report on Un-American Activities

TV INDUSTRY IS CAUTIONED

Warned Against Red Invasion —'51 Study Chides Hollywood as Lax on Communists

By C. P. TRUSSELL
Special to The New York Times.

WASHINGTON, Feb. 16—A formal plea to Congress to enact a law to punish by execution or life sentence espionage against the United States in peacetime as well as in war was filed today with the House of Representatives by its Committee on Un-American Activities.

"The statute of limitations," the committee added in its report for 1951, "would not then apply in espionage any more than it applies to other crimes carrying a capital punishment. * * * It is necessary that positive steps be taken to stem Soviet espionage. * * *

"It is felt that Congress must take the initial steps to ascertain what legislation is necessary to afford adequate protection. * * * In the course of such Congressional study it would be necessary to ascertain whether the existing laws relating to espionage have been properly enforced; and, if not, proper responsibility should be affixed."

The report criticized the motion picture industry for failing to move with sufficient firmness to weed out Communists, and termed Hollywood the Communists' greatest financial angel. The committee also warned the television industry against widespread Red infiltration.

Red Infiltration Expected

In the motion picture industry, the report said the committee had found that some 300 individuals, many at key points, had become Communists. Noting the effect of Hollywood on television, the committee hoped that its inquiries among film figures "will have a far-reaching effect and prevent a large-scale future Communist infiltration of the television industry."

"It is logical to assume that the Communists will endeavor to infiltrate television on a large scale because it is rapidly becoming an important entertainment medium in the United States," the committee asserted.

In education, the committee criticized the Massachusetts Institute of Technology for keeping on its faculty until recently Dr. Dirk J. Struik, Professor of Mathematics, who had been indicted in Massachusetts on charges of conspiring to overthrow the Government.

Then it assailed Prof. Kirtley F. Mather of Harvard and Harvard University itself because Professor Mather had written thirty ministers suggesting that they get acquainted with Professor Struik as "lovers of freedom" before he was brought to trial under the Massachusetts Anti-Anarchy Act.

"History alone will show how many of Professor Struik's students were led by him down the road to communism, from which they were unable to return until they had performed acts against their country and fellow citizens," the report commented.

In December the committee, after a thirteenth year of investi-

Continued on Page 4, Column 1

4,000-Year-Old Temple for Inanna, Key to Sumerians, Found in Iraq

Special to The New York Times.

CHICAGO, Feb. 16—A missing chapter of ancient history was written last month for modern-day scholars when a 4,000-year-old temple for Inanna, the goddess of love and war, was unearthed at Nippur, Iraq, by archeologists of the University of Chicago and the University of Pennsylvania.

Announcement of the discovery was made today by Donald E. McCown, field director and Associate Professor of Archeology at the Oriental Institute at Chicago. He described the unearthing of the temple and two other "finds" as "a rich haul" and "one of the most monumental discoveries made by a post-war archeological expedition."

The discoveries were made in one week by the universities' scientists at the Nippur site 100 miles south of modern Baghdad. The temple was unearthed on Jan. 22. On the previous day, Mr. McCown reported, hundreds of tablets of the oldest known language—Sumerian—were found in the scribal quarters adjacent to the temple site.

"Stacked like books against the wall of a scribe's home," the announcement said, "the tablets are expected to increase vastly the scholars' knowledge of Sumerian life and religion."

The third discovery, Mr. McCown was informed by cable, comprised three Sumerian statues from the Early Dynasty (2300 B. C.).

Mr. McCown said the discoveries were made as the archeologists were getting ready to close down their joint digging operations for the season. The expedition now has been authorized to extend their explorations until late March.

Discovery of the temple "came as a complete surprise to the archeologists," Mr. McCown said, as they were looking for temples of the family of the paramount

Continued on Page 66, Column 3

10 of Klan Seized by F. B. I. In Carolina in Flogging Case

Associated Press Wirephoto

Two F. B. I. men in Fayetteville, N. C., wear hoods and robes and display a whip they said was used in the flogging of a white man and white woman.

By PAUL P. KENNEDY
Special to The New York Times.

WASHINGTON, Feb. 16—The Federal Bureau of Investigation arrested ten former members of the North Carolina Ku Klux Klan in a series of raids around Fair Bluff, N. C., this morning on charges of kidnapping and flogging a 27-year-old white woman and a white man. The F. B. I. agents were assisted by the Sheriff and deputies of Columbus County, N. C.

The ten men, two of whom are former chiefs of police, were arraigned before Federal Commissioner T. L. Hon in Fayetteville, N. C., this afternoon and released on bond of $5,000 each for hearing Feb. 26 and 27. They were formally charged with violation of the Federal (Lindbergh) Kidnapping Act and also with violations of civil rights.

The violations allegedly took place last October and were part of a series of kidnappings and floggings in the Fair Bluff community that an F. B. I. spokesman described as among the most vicious yet investigated by the agency. The floggings, according to J. Edgar Hoover, chief of the F. B. I., were conducted by men hooded in Ku Klux Klan regalia.

According to Mr. Hoover, the ten arrested men were members of the Fair Bluff Klavern of the Klan, which was disbanded about three weeks ago. Bureau agents have been investigating the floggings since receiving reports that the

Continued on Page 12, Column 1

STIFFER U. S. POLICY ON CHINA STUDIED

Free Hand for the 7th Fleet and Opening for Nationalist Offensive Are Weighed

By WALTER H. WAGGONER
Special to The New York Times.

WASHINGTON, Feb. 16—The State Department has under study three limited but potentially important steps that might be taken to meet demands for a more affirmative policy toward Communist China and the Chinese Nationalist Government on Formosa.

Partly in answer to complaints that the present United States policy in that respect is negative and inadequate, and partly reflecting some official convictions that modification is called for, Far Eastern experts here are considering the following possible actions:

1. Clarifying the order to the Seventh Fleet to repel an attack by Chinese Communists on For-

Continued on Page 7, Column 1

World News Summarized

SUNDAY, FEBRUARY 17, 1952

France's National Assembly gave assurance early today that it would endorse the European army plan, subject to delay in West Germany's arming. Before the Assembly adjourned, Premier Faure won the Socialists to his side and got a 327-to-276 vote giving priority to his compromise resolution on the European army. A confidence vote was put off to Tuesday, with the prospect of Government success. [1:8.]

In London, where Secretary of State Acheson conferred with British Foreign Secretary Eden, American officials indicated there was no insurmountable obstacle to meet the French demand for Anglo-American guarantees against German defection from the European army project. [19:1.]

Premier Mossadegh of Iran agreed to renew oil negotiations with the World Bank after having declared that previous talks had revealed no room for agreement. [1:7.]

The United Nations truce delegates in Korea accepted the Communist post-armistice conference proposal, for recommendation to their Governments, with qualifications. They told the enemy group the Allied interpretation was that the conference would "exclude matters outside Korea" and that the term "foreign forces"—on the issue of withdrawing from Korea—included the Chinese Reds. The Communists are to reply. [1:6.]

In the Yangyang triangle, the one area of North Korea of any size freed from Communist control, the Koreans were said to be enthusiastic over free elections and self-government. [1:6-7.]

The State Department was giving careful study to three proposals that would tend to provide a more affirmative United States policy toward China. The proposals would give United States naval forces a freer hand in dealing with a Communist attack on Formosa and end the ban on Chinese Nationalist attacks against the mainland. [1:5.]

After much delay, Jordan, whose armed forces are kept in being with British aid, signed the Arab collective security treaty. [1:7.]

Queen Elizabeth II visited her grandmother, Dowager Queen Mother Mary, and the Duke of Windsor at Marlborough House. Rulers and statesmen were leaving London after King George's funeral. [24:3.]

The House Un-American Activities Committee asked Congress to enact a law meting out death to spies in peacetime as well as wartime. [1:3.]

The Federal Bureau of Investigation arrested ten former members of the Ku Klux Klan in North Carolina. The ten men, two of whom were former chiefs of police, were accused of kidnapping and beating a white man and a white woman last October. [1:4-5.]

A House subcommittee has subpoenaed Joseph D. Nunan Jr., former Internal Revenue Commissioner, to testify in an inquiry of the work of the New York City office of the Internal Revenue Bureau. [1:2.]

In this city airline officials announced the end of overseas operations at La Guardia Airport and the cutting of domestic flight operations. [1:1.]

NEWS BULLETINS FROM THE TIMES
Every hour on the hour
8 A. M. through Midnight
Except at Noon, 4 & 9 P.M. Today
WQXR AM 1560
WQXR FM 96.3

Index to other news appears on Page 87.

ALLIED TRUCE TEAM OFFERS TO SUPPORT KOREA PEACE TALKS

But Reds Are Asked to Accept U. N. Version of Enemy Draft for Post-Armistice Parley

LIMITED AGENDA IS URGED

Foe Is Told It Must Bar Issues Outside Peninsula—Exodus of Chinese Troops Sought

By LINDESAY PARROTT
Special to The New York Times.

TOKYO, Sunday, Feb. 17—United Nations delegates accepted today, with some qualifications, a Communist proposal for an international conference after the start of an armistice to make a lasting settlement of Korean problems.

Vice Admiral Charles Turner Joy, senior United Nations truce negotiator, told the Chinese and North Korean delegation at Panmunjom that the United Nations Commander would recommend the enemy plan to the governments concerned, but only if the Allied interpretation of the program, as the Communists had phrased it, was accepted by the enemy. He specified:

¶The Republic of Korea, virtually created by United Nations action, would have to be included among the governments to which the recommendations would be made.

¶A withdrawal of "foreign forces" would include all non-Korean forces. It has been conjectured that the Chinese, when the time came, might insist that their troops on the peninsula were "volunteers" serving under the North Korean flag, and were not in the "foreign" classification.

¶The United Nations would interpret the Communist call for a conference to discuss a "settlement of the Korean question, etc.," to exclude matters outside Korea.

Reds Promise to Answer

The Communists had indicated that they principally wanted to discuss at the international forum the status of the Chinese Nationalist regime on Formosa, which has been under the protection of the United States Seventh Fleet since the Korean war began.

Admiral Joy's answer was given to the Communists as soon as the full truce session opened this morning. North Korean Lieut. Gen. Nam Il, senior enemy delegate, immediately asked for a forty-minute recess to study the text.

Then, returning to the conference tent, the delegates adjourned until 10 A. M. tomorrow [8 P. M. Sunday, Eastern standard time], at which time the Communists said they would accept or reject the Allied qualifications.

The Communists' draft, when first handed over as a revision of their original, more detailed proposal, had appeared intentionally vague in its provisions. As Admiral Joy left the tent, he told correspondents he had felt compelled to make "a few remarks" to clarify the United Nations intentions.

Whether agreement could now be reached on the fifth and final item of the armistice agenda appeared still in doubt, however. At first glance, the enemy appeared to have left the door open for a discussion of a wide range of Far East issues, and the Allies to have insisted again on a limitation of debate to Korea.

Each side thus seemed to have

Continued on Page 3, Column 5

PARIS BACKS ARMY FOR EUROPE IF BONN DELAYS RECRUITING

VOTE IS 327 TO 276

Socialists Help Faure to Obtain Approval for Compromise Plan

FINAL VOTE DUE TUESDAY

Confidence Ballot Put Off—German Recruiting Now to Await Pact Ratification

By HAROLD CALLENDER
Special to The New York Times.

PARIS, Sunday, Feb. 17—The French National Assembly's endorsement of the European army plan was assured when adjournment was taken at 5 o'clock this morning after the Socialists had lined up with the Government in voting priority to a compromise resolution, which carried by 327 to 276.

But the long and difficult battle for this endorsement will not formally end until Tuesday, when the resolution will actually be adopted. This last delay was imposed by Premier Edgar Faure's decision early today to play safe by putting the vote of confidence, which permits absentee deputies to vote, instead of risking a vote with less than half the Deputies present.

Hence the vote of confidence, which was to have come Saturday but was abandoned for the final quest of a deal with the Socialists, will take place Tuesday with assurance of a Government success.

Schuman's Hand Strengthened

This hard-won parliamentary victory, which will have required a week's struggle, will enable Robert Schuman, French Foreign Minister, to attend the meeting of the North Atlantic Council in Lisbon next Wednesday with the backing of the French Parliament for his policy of a European army to embrace German units.

The draft treaty for this army, which has been under negotiation for a year, can now be submitted to the Atlantic Council according to plan and completed by subsequent negotiations by the foreign ministers of France, West Germany, Italy, Belgium, the Netherlands and Luxembourg.

The fact that the French Assembly's sanction for this part of the Atlantic defense program was belated, reluctant and qualified meant that the Assembly as a whole was cool toward it. Probably a majority disliked it with varying degrees of intensity, but accepted it because nobody had proposed any practicable alternative and the Assembly did not care to upset France's foreign policy or to impair the alliances it has produced.

[The North Atlantic Treaty Organization has agreed in theory that if Western German armed forces join a European army, an attack upon the Bonn Government's territory will be regarded as an attack on other members of the alliance, it was reported from Lisbon.]

French Recognize Dilemma

Widespread fear on both sides of the house was shown toward the rearmament of Germans, even under the safeguards provided by a European army under an Atlantic command and probably backed by United States and British guarantees.

Yet the idea of keeping the Germans unarmed indefinitely was rejected as impossible, as was the idea that France could take on the defensive burden that she hated to see the Germans assume. "Are we going to provide the twelve divisions that the Germans are to fill when 40 per cent of our trained officers are in Indo-China?" asked former Premier Paul Reynaud. To ask the question was to answer it.

The Assembly clearly felt that there was something wrong and ominous about any plan to arm Germans. But at the same time it felt that France was able, neither financially nor in terms of manpower, to fill the gap that would be left if the Germans were kept disarmed.

Indications that the United States and Britain might guarantee the fidelity of the German units to the European army brought some reassurance and may have helped win over the recal-

Continued on Page 22, Column 1

Jordan Signs Pact; Mid-East Link Seen

By ALBION ROSS
Special to The New York Times.

CAIRO, Feb. 16—The Kingdom of Jordan, whose armed forces are subsidized and armed by Britain and part of whose officers are British, signed the Arab collective security pact today after a long delay following signature of the pact by the other Arab states.

Much has been written in the press here recently about the possibility that some combination of the Middle East Command proposals, which the former Egyptian Government rejected shortly after abrogation of the British-Egyptian alliance in October, and of the Arab collective security pact program would become the basis for a solution of the Suez Canal base problem and a defense agreement for the Middle East. Two of the Arab nations' Parliaments, the

Continued on Page 13, Column 1

BREAK IN OIL TALKS IS AVERTED IN IRAN

Mossadegh Yields to Senate Pressure to Renew Parley With World Bank Mission

By The Associated Press.

TEHERAN, Iran, Feb. 16—After having declared that "no way is left for agreement," Premier Mohammed Mossadegh yielded to the demands of alarmed Iranian Senators today in agreeing to try for a last-ditch effort to negotiate an oil settlement with the International Bank for Reconstruction and Development.

The Premier had told the Senators that negotiations with a bank delegation that arrived here this week had broken down. The delegation, headed by Robert L. Garner, vice president of the bank, had come to try to get Iran's oil flowing again as a first step toward settling the country's dispute with Britain, from which the Mossadegh Government seized the industry.

The Iranian Parliament intervened for the first time since the delegation arrived. After urging another try at negotiations, Parliament named a five-man committee to meet with the delegation at Premier Mossadegh's residence this afternoon.

When news of the breakdown reached the Senate, informed sources said there were alarmed outcries and attacks against the Premier for not having consulted Parliament.

The Senators then appointed a committee to approach the Premier and demand that he try again to reach an accord with the bank delegates before they departed. The committee urged Mr. Garner to keep his delegation in Iran.

[The bank delegation met for three hours Saturday night with Premier Mossadegh and the Senate commission, but results of the talks were not disclosed.]

The mission this week offered Premier Mossadegh a face-saving

Continued on Page 15, Column 1

North Koreans Grasp Democracy Enthusiastically in a Freed Area

By GEORGE BARRETT
Special to The New York Times.

TOKYO, Feb. 16—In a "laboratory of democracy" in the only substantial slice of territory ever to be liberated for a long time from Iron Curtain control, the Yangyang triangle in North Korea, the majority of the populace has taken enthusiastically to free elections and education, and democratic self-government, according to findings of a special diplomatic committee of inquiry.

The survey, made quietly by a subsidiary group of the United Nations Commission for Korea in the 300-square-mile liberated triangle on the east coast of Korea just north of the Thirty-Eighth Parallel, and submitted to the headquarters of the world peace organization, indicates that most of about 64,000 North Koreans in this zone liberated more than eight months ago are thoroughly fed up with communism and are happy to put democracy into practice.

The people seem to need very little advice on what is the quick-

Continued on Page 3, Column 3

The New York Times Feb. 17, 1952
Yangyang area shown in black

"All the News That's Fit to Print"

The New York Times.

LATE CITY EDITION
Fair, mild today; becoming cloudy tonight. Showers likely tomorrow.
Temperature Range Today—Max., 53; Min., 34
Temperatures Yesterday—Max., 49; Min., 33
Full U. S. Weather Bureau Report, Page 39

Copyright, 1952, by The New York Times Company.

VOL. CI. No. 34,389. Entered as Second-Class Matter. Post Office, New York, N. Y. NEW YORK, THURSDAY, MARCH 20, 1952. Times Square, New York 36, N. Y. Telephone Lackawanna 4-1000 FIVE CENTS

DEWEY CLEARS WAY FOR PASSAGE TODAY OF CITY-AID BILLS

MEASURES READY

But Special Messages Are Needed to Permit Immediate Action

COMPROMISE IS REACHED

2½% Realty Tax Limit Agreed On—Action to Raise Pension Allowances Here Speeded

By LEO EGAN
Special to THE NEW YORK TIMES.

ALBANY, March 19—Governor Dewey agreed today, in conferences with legislative leaders, to clear the way for final legislative approval tomorrow of the $234,800,000 stop-gap financial program for the City of New York and thus to permit a final adjournment of this year's session of the Legislature immediately thereafter.

Mr. Dewey will send to the Legislature as soon as it convenes tomorrow a series of emergency messages permitting immediate consideration of the bills involved in the city program. Without these messages, the Legislature would be forced to wait an extra day before acting since some of the bills have been in final printed form for less than the three days required by the State Constitution.

Other Remaining Bills

Besides the bills involved in the city program, only two other measures of major concern remain to be disposed of before final adjournment. One is the proposal to require periodic inspections of automobiles, which has already received Senate approval and is awaiting action in the Assembly. The other is the bill providing for regulation of billboards along the Thruway, which has received Assembly approval and is awaiting Senate action. There are, of course, dozens of other bills dealing with other matters of limited interest on the legislative calendars.

The Governor's agreement to send the messages followed a compromise between spokesmen for the state and city administrations whereby two of the three proposed alternative constitutional amendments dealing with the limit on the city's real estate taxing powers will be dropped and only one put to a vote.

The original program called for adoption of all three alternative amendments this year with the understanding that when they came up again for reapproval next year only one would be selected for submission to the voters at the referendum required for all amendments.

The Three Proposals

One of the amendments provided for raising the city's real estate tax limit from 2 to 2½ per cent of the five-year average of full valuations. A second provided for continuing it at the present 2 per cent level. The third proposed an immediate increase, upon ratification, to 2.2 per cent with further automatic increases up to 3 per cent eventually. All three provided, in addition, for eliminating the city's right to impose a separate county tax on real estate.

Under the compromise agreement, only the 2½ per cent amendment will be approved tomorrow. The two others will be allowed to die. As a result, only the 2½ per cent proposal can be taken up for a second time next year and submitted to the voters in the fall of 1953. If it is approved, it will permit the city to collect a minimum of $100,000,000 in additional revenue from real estate taxation, starting with the tax levy of 1954.

City representatives had objected strongly to the 2 per cent proposal, which they regarded as putting the city in a worse plight than it is now. They preferred the 3 per cent amendment. But in order to eliminate the 2 per cent proposal they agreed to drop the 3 per cent one.

Meanwhile a measure that would increase Mayor Impellitteri's and other city employes' pension allowances was approved by the Assembly Rules Committee tonight. The bill had been passed previously by the Senate. The measure would credit time spent in the armed forces in computing pension allowances.

Lieut. Gov. Frank C. Moore, who represented the state administra-

Continued on Page 32, Column 4

Thruway Sign Curb Voted by Assembly

By WARREN WEAVER Jr.
Special to THE NEW YORK TIMES.

ALBANY, March 19—A bill that would authorize the State Thruway Authority to regulate the erection of billboards and other advertising devices along the cross-state expressway was approved today by the Assembly without debate. The vote was 108 to 40. The bill now goes to the Senate.

Sponsored by Assemblywoman Janet Hill Gordon, Republican of Chenango, the measure would prohibit all advertising devices within 500 feet of the Thruway pavement unless written permission from the authority was obtained. It also would empower the authority to change billboard regulations at any time.

Under the bill, the authority would be required, in formulating policies on allowing advertising, to consider the preserva-

Continued on Page 32, Column 6

TEN SUTTON JURORS PICKED, NOT SWORN

Chosen From 33 Veniremen, Group Still Faces Challenges —Defense Assails De Venuta

By MEYER BERGER

Ten prospective jurors were in the jury box in Queens County Court yesterday at the end of the second day of the bank robbery trial of William F. Sutton and Thomas Kling before Judge Peter T. Farrell.

There was no assurance that the ten men would remain in the box. Neither the state nor the defense had used any of the twenty peremptory challenges each has, but it seemed certain that some, if not all ten men, eventually may be challenged.

When yesterday's session adjourned at 4:30 P. M. a total of thirty-three talesmen had been examined. A prospective juror who had been sent to the box on Tuesday by Judge Farrell was excused yesterday so he could be at his son's confirmation March 29.

The Court intimated there may be night trial sessions to speed completion of a jury.

Though yesterday's session, like Tuesday's, was slow and yawn-inspiring, with snow-drip against the dark Long Island City factory background at the chamber windows, lawyers' questions to talesmen clearly indicated trial battle lines.

Assistant District Attorneys James P. McGrattan and William Kerwick made it evident that the state's case would rest in large degree on testimony by John De Venuta, an alleged Sutton-Kling accomplice. All three are charged with the $63,942 robbery at the Sunnyside Branch of the Manufacturers Trust Company in Queens two years ago. De Venuta has won a severance in the trial.

George W. Herz and James Mc-

Continued on Page 60, Column 5

TRUCE AGREEMENT ON PORTS OF ENTRY REACHED IN KOREA

Allied and Red Concessions on Points for Replenishment of Armies Speed Decision

AIRFIELDS, PIERS INCLUDED

Only the Soviet and Military Airbase Issue Left on Item 3 of Agenda, U. N. Aide Says

By LINDESAY PARROTT
Special to THE NEW YORK TIMES.

TOKYO, Thursday, March 20—Allied and Communist staff officers at Panmunjom reached agreement today on ten "ports of entry"—five behind the lines of each opposing army—through which replacements of men and equipment will be permitted to move after an armistice in the Korean war.

Final decision was reached after the United Nations delegates for the second successive day had presented a revised proposal closer to enemy views and the Communists had responded with some concessions. In North Korea the Communists agreed to make use of Sinuiju and Manpojin on the Yalu River as supply centers where neutral observers would be posted to assure that a period of cease-fire would not be used for a build-up of military strength.

Three other entry ports designated for the Chinese and North Korean armies were the Sinanju airhead, about half-way between the Thirty-eighth Parallel and the Manchurian frontier; Chongjin, on the Sea of Japan and the seaport of Hungnam—minus its inland railroad center of Hamhung.

Agree to Include Taegu

The enemy yielded to the Allied demand for Taegu as an entry port in South Korea and conceded that the "ports of entry" should include airfields and dock facilities in the neighborhood of designated cities, apparently withdrawing a proposal to limit the movement of neutral inspectors to city limits.

The senior United Nations staff member, Col. Andrew J. Kinney, emerging from today's session, told correspondents, "It looks as though everything was wrapped up except the Soviet issue and the airfields issue." The two major stumbling blocks to an agreement on agenda Item No. 3 thus far have been the Communist proposal to name the Soviet Union as one of the "neutral" nations to send armistice inspectors to Korea and the demand for permission to build military air bases without limitation in the north after a truce.

Besides Taegu, it was announced, the Communists accepted Pusan, Inchon, Kunsan and Kangnung as South Korean entry ports.

Colonel Kinney said that the "mechanical details" of the agreement still might take some days. The staff group still had to determine just what facilities for inspection would be allowed neutral observers in the designated areas and just how large the "entry port" zones would be.

Colonel Kinney presented the Communists with a large-scale map of the Kangnung district to illustrate the United Nations concept. On it were marked access roads leading to airfields and docks which the United Nations proposed should be made available to neutrals. The Communists invited Colonel Kinney to produce similar maps tomorrow of all the South Korean entry ports

Continued on Page 2, Column 2

Allied Reply to Soviet Note On Germany to Be Set Today

Eden, Schuman and Dunn Reported Ready to Agree on Answer at Parley in Paris—West Likely to Stress Free Voting

By HAROLD CALLENDER
Special to THE NEW YORK TIMES.

PARIS, March 19—It was expected tonight that a draft of the Western Powers' reply to the recent Soviet note proposing a peace treaty for a united Germany would be agreed upon tomorrow by Robert Schuman, French Foreign Minister; Anthony Eden, British Foreign Secretary, and James C. Dunn, United States Ambassador to France.

Officials here predicted the note would be an abridged version of that drawn up by the representatives of the United States, Britain and France in London and that it would raise chiefly the question whether Moscow would agree to free elections in all Germany and would admit to the Soviet zone the United Nations Commission on German elections.

A notable innovation in the renewed discussion of the German question was the consultation by the three Western powers with Dr. Konrad Adenauer, Chancellor and Foreign Minister of the West German regime, who is in Paris for this purpose and for the meeting of the Ministers Committee of the Council of Europe.

When the three powers' representatives have agreed on the reply they will propose to their governments, they will show it to Dr. Adenauer and take account of any suggestions he may make. Even in its present pre-sovereign condition, West Germany has thus virtually become one of the Western powers as a result of the policy of integrating it economically and defensively with the Western coalition.

It was expected that the Allied reply to Moscow would make it clear that the Western powers would not abandon their far-reaching program for defense and economic cooperation that has been expressed in the North Atlantic Treaty, the Schuman plan for a coal-steel merger in Western Eu-

Continued on Page 5, Column 1

BRAZIL IS ALERTED FOR RED OUTBREAKS

Troops Get Orders After Arms Dump Is Raided—Chief of Rio Command Would Quit

By SAM POPE BREWER
Special to THE NEW YORK TIMES

RIO DE JANEIRO, March 19—All Brazilian troops were reported alerted tonight for possible trouble from the Communists after an abortive raid on an army ammunition dump in Natal. No form of martial law apparently had been ordered.

Tension arose as the Brazilian Communist party was preparing to mark its thirtieth anniversary while the police were busy raiding its propaganda centers.

Another cause for disturbance was the resignation submitted yesterday by Gen. Euclides Zenobio da Costa, one of Brazil's outstanding soldiers, who is commander of the First Military Region (the Rio de Janeiro area). He resigned supposedly in protest over Communist infiltration of the armed forces.

The Communists scattered leaflets here today, urging "not one soldier for Korea" and calling on Brazilians to support the Soviet Union's plan for a five-power peace conference. In a raid yesterday the police broke up a propaganda center, arrested twenty-five persons and seized quantities of leaflets and equipment. However,

Continued on Page 15, Column 1

SPAIN MAY ASK U. S. FOR SECURITY PACT

Washington Told Granting of Bases Necessitates Firm Promise of Aid in War

By CAMILLE M. CIANFARRA
Special to THE NEW YORK TIMES

MADRID, March 19—The Spanish Government was understood today to have informed Washington that one of the basic premises for a successful conclusion of an agreement defining the terms of Spanish-United States collaboration should be a United States pledge to aid and defend Spain in case of aggression.

Whether Madrid would insist on a formal United States guarantee similar to the one binding signatories of the North Atlantic pact, or would agree to a formula merely implying it, well informed Spaniards said, would be decided after the arrival of Lincoln MacVeagh, the newly appointed United States Ambassador to Spain. Negotiations are to begin next week for conclusion of a bilateral agreement on economic and military collaboration between the two countries.

In outlining this suggestion, the Spanish Government was said to have pointed out that an agreement involving the use of Spanish naval and air bases by United States forces would mark, in effect, an end of Spain's policy of neutrality; that as a consequence this nation would be exposed to an

Continued on Page 5, Column 3

Volcano Rising From Ocean Off Northeast Tip of Luzon

To the South, Hibok-Hibok Spurts Again—Quake on Etna in Sicily Kills 3

Special to THE NEW YORK TIMES.

MANILA, March 19—A volcano erupting under the sea about seventy miles off the northeastern tip of Luzon has thrust its crater and cone an estimated 250 feet above the surface of the water.

[The South Philippines was shaken Wednesday night by an earthquake centering in the Mindanao Sea, where Hibok-Hibok Volcano on Camiguin Island showed renewed activity, said Associated Press dispatches.

[In Sicily three persons were killed and scores injured in a quake that shook the slopes of volcanic Mount Etna.]

The continuing eruptions of the volcano were seen today by observers in a United States Air Force plane. A plume of smoke and ash rose straight from the ocean to a height of several thousand feet. The plume was first sighted from a passing American steamer thirty-three miles away last Sunday.

Maj. Gen. Ernest Moore, commanding the United States Thirteenth Air Force at Clark Field, piloted the plane that flew during the day, with a crew of seven and accompanying newsmen, to the site of the phenomenon near what are known as the Didicas Rocks, on the east of the Babuyan Islands region. The flight determined that no loss of human life was involved since the nearest inhabited land in the Babuyan Islands is twenty miles westward.

The New York Times March 20, 1952

Volcanoes were active in the sea north of Luzon (1) and on the island of Camiguin (2).

The Philippine Government has alerted the near-by islands and all communities of the North Luzon coast against possible tidal waves should the eruptions become more violent.

General Moore took his plane in over the new volcano at 7,000 feet, approaching from the southwest and dropping to within 200 feet of the surface of the ocean and 300 yards laterally from the smoking cone.

The top of the volcano was gradually building itself out of the sea

Continued on Page 4, Column 4

Wilks Estate Is Put at 95 Millions, Third of It in One Checking Account

Mrs. Hetty Sylvia Howland Green Wilks, daughter of the late Hetty Green, noted woman financier at the turn of the century, left an estate of approximately $95,000,000 according to an accounting filed in Surrogate's Court yesterday. She died Feb. 5, 1951.

Mrs. Wilks, who was 80 years old, apparently had a habit of keeping things of value in unusual places, for, at the time her will was filed, attorneys said they had found it with four cakes of soap in a tin cabinet in her apartment at 988 Fifth Avenue.

Yesterday's accounting by the temporary administrators showed she had maintained two checking accounts, one at the Chase National Bank with a balance of $31,448,220 and the other at the New York-Fifth Avenue Bank with a balance of $4,545,601. She also had a cash balance of $2,304,540 with Green Estate, Inc., $650,000 in one safe deposit box and $8,908 in another.

The day before the probated will was discovered with the soap, an earlier will had been filed; it left the estate to Mrs. Wilks' brother, who in the meantime had died. As a result, the estate would have been distributed under provisions of the Intestacy Laws, passing to a cousin, Mrs. Emilie Keene Elmendorf Colles of 89 North Broadway, White Plains.

In the later will, which was probated, $5,000 was bequeathed to Mrs. Colles, and she filed objections to the probate. Objections also were filed by the Girl Scouts, who under an earlier will were to receive five one-hundredths of the residuary estate. The contestants, it was later reported, made a settlement whereby Mrs. Colles was to receive $140,000 and the Girl Scouts $50,000.

In their report yesterday the temporary administrators showed they had made payments of $2,062,-

Continued on Page 33, Column 4

WAGE BOARD GROUP PROPOSES 20C RISE TO STEEL WORKERS

Public Members Suggest Plan as Parleys Run Into Night in Effort to Avert Strike

PRICE INCREASE IS SLATED

Arnall Says That Companies May Get Two—Union to Act Today on Walkout Delay

By JOSEPH A. LOFTUS
Special to THE NEW YORK TIMES.

WASHINGTON, March 19—Public members of the Wage Stabilization Board proposed today a settlement of the steel dispute on terms reported to be worth about 20 cents an hour.

The proposal was made informally to industry and to labor members of the board, but it was uncertain whether either side would accept. It was lower than the labor members' asking price, and higher than the employer group has been willing to go. The public members need the support of one group or the other to get a majority vote.

The Wage Board's recommendations for settling the dispute are to be presented to the union and the industry tomorrow.

The board's own time table and the threat of a country-wide steel strike on Sunday night kept the members in conferences, formal and otherwise, far into the night. The Policy Committee of the United Steelworkers, C. I. O., has set a meeting for tomorrow to consider a new postponement of the strike deadline.

Chances for a delay were considered good, but whether the industry and the union eventually come to terms without a shutdown hinges largely on the question of price ceilings.

Industry Insists on Price Rise

The industry insists that the Government allow it to pass along all increases in labor costs in the form of higher steel prices.

Ellis Arnall, Director of Price Stabilization, told the Senate Banking Committee meanwhile that the steel companies would receive one price increase under the Capehart amendment, and possibly another under the "fair and equitable" formula, if needed after wage rises to permit the industry to earn 85 per cent of its average of the three best of the years 1946, 1947, 1948 and 1949.

Average hourly earnings in the steel industry are $1.81, exclusive of overtime. The cost of union's demands is variously estimated, but it would run well over 30 cents an hour.

Any recommended settlement is subject to different translations in terms of cents per hour. Industry members, for example, proposed yesterday that the board recommend a "package" they figured would cost the equivalent of 13.7 cents an hour of which 9 cents would be a straight wage increase, 4 cents in the form of paid holidays and 0.7 cents in vacations.

According to some calculations, six paid holidays would cost the equivalent of 3.2 cents instead of 4 cents. Other "fringe" items are subject to variables in the same way.

The board meeting tonight was the first it held "on the record" in the steel case since Sunday. Instead of the formal sessions, chairman Nathan P. Feinsinger, and the

Continued on Page 30, Column 4

EISENHOWER VOTE IN MINNESOTA HELD PUBLIC 'EXPLOSION'

HAPPY OVER RESULT

Associated Press Radiophoto

General Eisenhower after hearing outcome of the Minnesota voting at his headquarters near Paris yesterday.

POLL STIRS CAPITAL

Politicians View Result as More Significant Than Earlier Test

BLOW TO TAFT BID NOTED

But Headquarters of Senator Discounts Tally—Humphrey Scores an Easy Victory

By JAMES RESTON
Special to THE NEW YORK TIMES.

WASHINGTON, March 19—Professional politicians here were much more impressed today with General of the Army Dwight D. Eisenhower's showing in the Minnesota primary election than with his victory last week in New Hampshire.

Though Harold E. Stassen, former Minnesota Governor, ran ahead of the general by a margin of roughly 5 to 4, professionals here who are backing neither General Eisenhower nor Senator Robert A. Taft of Ohio agreed tonight that the casting of more than 100,000 write-in votes for the general was by far the most significant development of the Presidential primary campaign to date.

Senator Henry Cabot Lodge Jr. of Massachusetts, the Eisenhower campaign manager, issued the following statement on the Minnesota returns:

"The popular explosion for Eisenhower in the Minnesota primary confirms the vote in New Hampshire nd is a fitting sequel to the announcement by Gov. Alfred Driscoll of New Jersey [of support for the general]. It marks the most spectacular political upsurge within the Republican party since the day of Teddy Roosevelt. For the millions of us who are supporting Ike, this is the time t› redouble our efforts."

Organizers Opposed Drive

What impressed the politicians here was the fact that the general's write-in vote was achieved on a stormy day after less than a week of organization and despi.e the early efforts of the best political organizers in General Eisenhower's national headquarters to oppose the write-in campaign.

Thus, it was regarded here as a more spontaneous expression of popular support for the general than was New Hampshire and as another blow to the Taft candidacy.

The professionals also were noting two other points:

¶That the New Hampshire result could be interpreted as protest votes against Senator Taft whereas the Minnesota write-in vote was regarded as a more positive expression of Eisenhower's political strength;

¶That the so-called liberal vote in Minnesota that went to General Eisenhower and Mr. Stassen overwhelmed the more conservative voters who supported Mr. Taft and General of the Army Douglas MacArthur.

In addition to giving another great psychological boost to the Eisenhower forces, the Minnesota results also contributed to the frustrations that had existed within the Democratic party for the last few weeks as a result of President Truman's failure to decide whether to seek re-election.

Kefauver Gets Write-Ins

Senator Hubert H. Humphrey of Minnesota was the only Democratic candidate on the primary ballot, but Senator Estes Kefauver of Tennessee, who defeated Mr. Truman in New Hampshire, ran almost six to one ahead of the President in the Minnesota write-in contest.

Mr. Humphrey had run, however, as a stand-in for President Truman, although he told the President personally that in the event that Mr. Truman decided not to run again he (Mr. Humphrey) would not be antagonistic to the candidacy of Senator Kefauver.

The liberal leaders of the Democratic party were preparing tonight to increase their pressure on Mr. Truman to reach a decision fairly soon to run or get out of the race.

Their argument in favor of this course was that a conservative group within the Democratic party was improving its organization all the time and that the liberal ele-

Continued on Page 25, Column 6

EISENHOWER AIDES MAP DELEGATE BID

Court Action Is Seen Possible as Result of Strength in Minnesota Primary

By WILLIAM M. BLAIR
Special to THE NEW YORK TIMES.

MINNEAPOLIS, March 19—A write-in vote for General of the Army Dwight D. Eisenhower in the Presiaential preference primary Minnesota Presidential preference primary, running to more than 100,000 ballots, surprised political observers in the state today.

Following his smashing victory in the New Hampshire primary, the general heightened his Presidential prospects by capturing some 37 per cent of the Republican primary vote, on the basis of still incomplete returns, all on write-ins. This compared to about a 44.7 per cent vote for the "favorite son," Harold E. Stassen, former Minnesota Governor. Mr. Stassen ran a poor third in New Hampshire.

In the write-in, which was without parallel in Minnesota, Senator Taft of Ohio was far behind with 8.34 per cent of the Republican vote. The write-in caught the state, especially the veteran political leaders and the Eisenhower forces, completely by surprise.

With 3,550 of 3,769 precincts reporting—the unreported ones were in scattered and sparsely settled areas that could not affect the final outcome—the results were:

REPUBLICAN	
Harold E. Stassen	128,134
Gen. Dwight Eisenhower..*	106,788
Senator Robert A. Taft...*	23,966
Edward C. Slettedahl.....	21,339
Gov. Earl Warren.......*	5,173
Gen. Douglas MacArthur.*	1,536
DEMOCRATIC	
Senator Hubert Humphrey	98,704
Senator Estes Kefauver..*	19,783
President Truman ....*	3,602

*Write-in.

There were no clear-cut indica-

Continued on Page 24, Column 1

Prehistoric Tools Found in Mexico Place Man There 12,000 Years Ago

By SYDNEY GRUSON
Special to THE NEW YORK TIMES.

MEXICO CITY, March 19—Further proof of man's existence in the Western Hemisphere at least 12,000 years ago has been uncovered by Mexican archaeologists whose discovery was hailed today by a United States scientist as "the most important of its kind ever made in the Americas."

The proof consists of four ancient weapons found alongside the bones of an imperial mammoth, an extinct variety of elephant, uncovered near Santa Maria Tepexpan, about thirty-five miles north of Mexico City. The discovery was made near the spot where five years ago archaeologists found remains of a human skeleton dating back 10,000 years. Until the finding of the Tepexpan man, it had been generally believed that man was a comparatively new immigrant to the Western Hemisphere from Asia.

The four weapons, according to scientists here, have supplied final proof to destroy a long-held theory that human beings and the prehistoric animals that roamed the Western Hemisphere jungles could not have existed together.

Mexican archaeologists found two arrowheads made of obsidian (volcanic glass), a fragment of an obsidian knife and a scraper made of material resembling black onyx, which they believe was used by prehistoric man to skin his quarry so he could eat its meat.

The discovery was made by Prof. Manuel Maldonado Koerdel, Luis Aveleyra Arroyo de Anda and Dr. Pablo Martinez del Rio working on behalf of the National Museum of Mexico. Dr. Marie Louise Wormington of the Univer-

Continued on Page 14, Column 4

"All the News That's Fit to Print"

The New York Times

LATE CITY EDITION
Cloudy and cool with occasional light rain today and tomorrow.
Temperature Range Today-Max., 67; Min., 59
Temperatures Yesterday—Max., 62; Min., 59
Full U. S. Weather Bureau Report, Page 39.

VOL. CI..No. 34,484. Entered as Second-Class Matter. Post Office, New York, N. Y. NEW YORK, MONDAY, JUNE 23, 1952. Times Square, New York 36, N. Y. Telephone LAckawanna 4-1000 FIVE CENTS

UNION AND SYSTEM SEEK ACCORD TODAY ON CITY'S BUS SALE

Face Need to Adjust Pension and Seniority Demands to Retain the Franchise

STRIKE SEEN ON REFUSAL

Estimate Board's Hearing Set Next Monday on Awarding 5 Lines to New York Omnibus

By PAUL CROWELL

Representatives of the Transport Workers Union, C. I. O., and the New York City Omnibus Corporation will confer this morning with the Board of Transportation in an effort to iron out difficulties that threaten to upset the city's plan to sell its five Manhattan bus lines to the private operator.

The lines are the First and Second Avenue, Madison-Chambers Streets, York Avenue, Forty-ninth and Fiftieth Street crosstown and Sixty-fifth Street crosstown routes.

A company representative said yesterday that the remaining obstacle to the transfer was the union's insistence that it grant full seniority rights to employes of the city lines to be added to the company's payroll and provide for their benefit a pension arrangement equivalent to the present $1,500,000 funded pension plan under city operation.

Opposition to Two Demands

At an informal hearing before the Board of Estimate on June 10, John F. O'Donnell, counsel for the union, referred to the city pension plan into which employes of the five Manhattan lines have paid $750,000 in contributions in the four years following the city's purchase of the lines from the East Side and Comprehensive Omnibus Corporations in 1948, with the city paying an equal amount.

"Before we sign a contract with any private operator," he said, "we are going to see that money in the kitty."

The union is understood to be insisting that 347 of the 600 employes to be taken over by the private operator when the city lines are acquired be allowed to retain their seniority rights, dating in many cases back to the administration of former Mayor James J. Walker when the East Side and Comprehensive companies received their bus franchises.

Company officials were reported to be firmly opposed to the pension and seniority demands.

Tie-up of System Possible

Unless the city's understanding with the bus company is modified to permit the private operator to acquire the five lines without taking over any of the municipal employes, the wrangle over seniority rights and pensions could develop a strike situation on the entire New York City Omnibus system, embracing most of the longitudinal and crosstown bus routes in Manhattan.

The Board of Transportation is anxious to iron out the difficulties arising from the labor situation as speedily as possible because the Board of Estimate will hold a public hearing next Monday on a proposed franchise contract with the New York City Omnibus Corporation covering the five lines affected by the controversy.

Hearings also will be held on

Continued on Page 26, Column 8

City Forced to Take Another Rain Check

The celestial committee charged with providing week-end weather for the metropolitan area continued in a sullen and unreasonable mood yesterday. For the fifth week-end in the last seven, the weather was bad. Skies were gray and occasional rains fell.

The dank condition was discouraging. Sun worshipers could see their once golden-brown tans fading to a ghostly pallor. Baseball fans, instead of passing an afternoon amid roasted peanuts, soda pop and base hits, found themselves staring gloomily out the window at damp sidewalks.

Thus it was that yesterday most New Yorkers had too much time on their hands. They slept late, read the papers and watched television. And then took a nap. It was all very uninteresting.

SAWYER WELCOMES LINER COST INQUIRY

Derides Controller General for 'Silly and Untrue' Protest Over Subsidy Contract

Special to THE NEW YORK TIMES.

WASHINGTON, June 22—Charles Sawyer, the Secretary of Commerce, said in effect today that he would welcome an investigation of the contract by which the United States Lines had obtained the $78,000,000 superliner United States for $28,087,000.

"I don't want the taxpayer to lose one dime to which he is entitled," the Secretary declared in a letter continuing his dispute with the Controller General, Lindsay C. Warren, who has contended that the Government paid too much of a subsidy for the luxury liner, which was en route to New York today for her maiden voyage.

In a letter to Representative John F. Shelley, chairman of a special subcommittee of the Merchant Marine and Fisheries Committee, Mr. Sawyer accused the Controller General of making "silly and untrue" statements when he had appeared before the subcommittee last Tuesday.

The President Intervened

The United States, built at Newport News, Va., was delivered to the United States Lines on Friday. Shortly afterward President Truman ordered Attorney General James P. McGranery to take the necessary legal action to determine whether subsidy allowances paid by the Government had been excessive and to protect the Government's interests. The President said the ship had cost the Government "almost $78,000,000."

Mr. Warren, in a running feud with Secretary Sawyer, has estimated that the Government paid about $10,000,000 too much when it sold the giant vessel to the company for about $28,000,000. He has repeatedly said that the ship, built by the Government under a contract with the company, should not be turned over to the United States Lines until the company agreed to pay a greater part of the cost.

Secretary Sawyer, who has rejected Mr. Warren's protests, went ahead with plans for turning the vessel over to private hands and

Continued on Page 39, Column 2

EISENHOWER FORCES SEE INITIAL VICTORY ON CONTESTED SEATS

Feel They Can Win Motion to Bar Challenged Delegates From Voting on Disputes

1912 PARALLEL IS FACTOR

Reversal of Elihu Root Sought —General's Man Is Named to Credentials Committee

By JAMES A. HAGERTY

The first clash at the Republican National Convention between General of the Army Dwight D. Eisenhower and Senator Robert A. Taft, rival candidates for the nomination for President, is expected to come on a motion for a rule to prevent delegates whose credentials are challenged from voting on any of the contests.

Supporters of General Eisenhower believe they will have the votes to carry this motion, even with the Taft contestants, who presumably will be placed on the temporary roll by the Taft-dominated Republican National Committee, voting against it. The Presidential nomination may well depend on the adoption or defeat of this motion.

As a result of a check, leaders of the Eisenhower movement believe that in addition to delegates favoring the nomination of General Eisenhower they will have in support of this motion the majority of the delegates from the "favorite son" states—California with seventy votes, Minnesota with twenty-eight and Maryland with twenty-four—as well as scattering support from delegates nominally for Senator Taft but ready to leave him after the first ballot.

Credentials Aide Named

The Eisenhower leaders were encouraged yesterday by the election, at a meeting of the Michigan delegates at Flint, of George Shaffer, said to be a supporter of the general, as a member of the Credentials Committee of the convention.

They took this as an almost certain indication not only that they would have a majority of the forty-six Michigan votes for the motion but also that General Eisenhower would have the support of the majority of those votes for the nomination. Supporters of Senator Taft have claimed twenty-four Michigan votes.

In seeking establishment of a rule preventing contested delegates on the temporary roll from voting on any contests, the Eisenhower delegates will try to upset the ruling made by the late Elihu Root, temporary chairman of the 1912 convention.

At that time the title of seventy-two delegates supporting President William Howard Taft, father of the Senator, who was a candidate for renomination against Theodore Roosevelt, was in dispute.

T. R.'s Bolt Followed

Charles S. Deneen, then Governor of Illinois, moved that no delegates whose credentials were challenged could vote in the roll-call on the report of the Credentials Committee. This motion was tabled, 564 to 510, with the contested Taft delegates furnishing the decisive margin.

Mr. Root then ruled that contested delegates could vote on all contests except their own. The renomination of President Taft and the bolt of Theodore Roosevelt as the candidate of the Progressive party followed.

The contests at the convention this year involve Texas with thirty-eight votes, Louisiana with fifteen, Georgia with seventeen, Florida with eighteen and Mississippi with five, a total of ninety-three. There also are two contests in Nebraska and one each in Kansas and Missouri. The candidacies of General Eisenhower and Senator Taft are directly involved in the Texas, Louisiana and Georgia contests.

Although the Eisenhower supporters probably will not name a candidate for temporary chairman against Walter S. Hallanan, as the Theodore Roosevelt supporters did against Mr. Root, and no third party bolt is expected, the person picked to make a motion similar to that made by Mr. Deneen can hardly fail to point out the parallel between the coming convention and that of 1912.

The decision on convention tactics was reached by leaders of the Eisenhower movement several days ago. This decision was reflected in General Eisenhower's speech at Dallas Saturday night, when he attacked Taft supporters for an attempt to "steal" the Texas delegates. He said:

"The contested delegates at the

Continued on Page 11, Column 5

ASKS 4-POWER TALKS

The New York Times
Jakob Kaiser

CAPTIVE SCREENING IS RESUMED AT KOJE

45,000 Will Be Asked if They Wish to Return Voluntarily to Communist Territory

By The Associated Press

SEOUL, Korea, Monday, June 23—The United Nations Command announced today that screening of Communist prisoners of war and interned civilians was resumed on Koje Island today. The screening will determine whether prisoners wish to return voluntarily to Communist control or remain with the United Nations Command.

Brig. Gen. C. W. Christenberry, deputy chief of staff of the Eighth Army, told correspondents that the screening that was suspended April 29 was being resumed.

The Communist delegates to the truce negotiations at Panmunjom have bitterly denounced the Allied screening. The enemy demands the return of all prisoners—by force if necessary.

[At the United Nations, the Soviet Union, which holds the chairmanship of the Security Council for June, informed the delegates Sunday that it would give priority on the Council agenda to a United States demand for debate on a proposed inquiry into Communist charges of germ warfare by United Nations forces in Korea.]

No figures were available here on the number of prisoners and civilians to be screened. In a dispatch from Pusan, a correspondent said approximately 45,000 prisoners were to be screened for the first time.

General Christenberry announced that all prisoners would be given full orientation on the process and the consequences of the screening before they were asked seven ques-

Continued on Page 2, Column 3

ADENAUER FLOUTED BY AIDE WHO SEEKS SOVIET UNITY TALKS

Minister Kaiser Says Parley of Four Powers Is a 'Must' Despite Russian Deceit

DEFIANT ON EAST BORDER

Tells Refugees Reunification of Land Given to Poland Is Not Contemplated

By DREW MIDDLETON
Special to THE NEW YORK TIMES.

BONN, Germany, June 22—The great German debate on unity of the country against integration with the West took a startling turn today when Jakob Kaiser, Minister for All-German Affairs in Chancellor Konrad Adenauer's Cabinet, strongly supported calling a conference between the Western Allies and the Soviet Union on reunification.

Such a conference "must" be held, Herr Kaiser declared, despite Soviet deceit and cruelty, to decide whether the time is ripe for reunification of Germany.

Herr Kaiser's unqualified support for such a conference diverges sharply from the line of Chancellor Adenauer, which is that a conference would be useful only if it were clear that it could be successful from the German standpoint and that at present such a conference would delay ratification of the treaties binding Germany to the Western alliance.

Kaiser Talks to Refugees

But at Hanover, where he addressed 150,000 refugees, Herr Kaiser took a position very close to that of the French Foreign Ministry when he called for an early meeting to "clarify" the Soviet Union's intentions on German unity.

Herr Kaiser, who until he fled to West Germany was leader of the Christian Democrats in the Soviet zone, also abandoned the Government position in another important respect. He told the refugees that reunification as now contemplated did not include the territories east of the Oder and Niesse Rivers turned over to Polish administration at the Potsdam conference in 1945.

Dr. Adenauer and a number of other Government speakers over the last two and a half years have insisted on reunification of Germany within the borders of Jan. 1, 1937. These include the Oder-Neisse territories.

The Soviet Union in its notes on unity has opposed any change in the territories' status.

Herr Kaiser's speech came at an awkward time for the Government.

Dr. Adenauer is aware of the pressure that France, supported to some extent by Britain, is bringing to bear on the United States State Department to propose four-power

Continued on Page 6, Column 3

GERMAN BORDER INCIDENTS INCREASE

The New York Times June 23, 1952

A Russian-East German group kidnapped workers in disputed terrain near Schoeningen (1). The Russians charged officials had been shot at from an American-operated train at Babelsberg (2) and that United States planes had flown over Baltic coastal towns (3) and the southwest corner of the Soviet zone (4). Shaded line denotes the East zonal frontier.

Acheson Starts for Europe; Truman Gives Him Send-Off

By The Associated Press.

WASHINGTON, June 22—President Truman gave Secretary of State Dean Acheson a personal send-off tonight as the Secretary left by Presidential plane at 8:14 o'clock, Eastern daylight time, for important conferences abroad. Mr. Acheson will be away about sixteen days visiting countries of Western Europe and also Brazil.

President Truman told reporters that he wished Secretary Acheson luck on his latest mission.

"I always wish him a successful trip and he always has one," Mr. Truman told the reporters.

"That's what gets me through," Mr. Acheson observed.

Mr. Acheson took off from the Washington airport in President Truman's plane, the Independence, piloted by Col. Francis W. Williams, the Presidential pilot. The Secretary of State is due in London at 3 P.M. London Time (10 A.M., Eastern Daylight Time) tomorrow.

Mr. Acheson told reporters he would discuss "a number of things" in London with British Foreign Minister Anthony Eden and French Foreign Minister Robert Schuman.

He Praises Berliners

Later Mr. Acheson will spend a day in Berlin, where, he said, he expected to "pay tribute to the Berliners whose courage and tenacity in the face of great harassment has been admired by everyone in the free world."

He said he was going to visit "another brave and determined people" in Austria, a people who had been "patiently waiting for the independence promised them in 1943."

Mr. Acheson will conclude his trip with about sixteen appearances in Brazil, State Department officials said.

Mr. Acheson was accompanied by Mrs. Acheson, Dr. Philip C. Jessup, State Department ambassador at large; George W. Perkins, Assistant Secretary of State for European Affairs; Lucius D. Battle, a special Assistant Secretary, and Miss Barbara Evans, assistant to the Secretary.

President Truman drove from the White House, where he was enjoying a day at home with his daughter, Margaret, to wish Mr. Acheson farewell.

Statement by Acheson

Mr. Acheson, who arrived at the airport earlier, handed reporters the following statement:

"As you know, I am making a very quick trip to London, to Berlin and Vienna and from there to Brazil.

"In England, I shall be discussing a number of things with Mr. Eden and with the French Foreign Minister.

"I am also going to Oxford where an honorary degree is being conferred on me. At Mr. McCloy's (John J. McCloy, United States High Commissioner for Germany) suggestion, I shall spend a day in Berlin where a memorial library is being dedicated. This will give me an opportunity to pay tribute to the Berliners whose courage and tenacity in the face of great harassment has been admired by everyone in the free world.

"From there I am going to Vienna at the invitation of the Aus-

Continued on Page 8, Column 5

NEHRU LABOR PLAN STRESSES FREEDOM

Would Use India's Manpower on Local, Voluntary Basis in Contrast to Police States

Special to THE NEW YORK TIMES.

NEW DELHI, India, June 22—Prime Minister Jawaharlal Nehru announced today a plan designed to channel the vast manpower resources of the nation into constructive activities on a strictly "voluntary" basis.

The plan has been officially sponsored by the National Planning Commission, of which Mr. Nehru is chairman. It is drawn up on the premise that the five-year plan now before the country would not succeed without "willing, intelligent and effective public cooperation."

The two most important aspects of the plan are that no one would be forced to work against his will and that there would be the greatest measure of decentralization.

The plan as envisaged is expected to develop eventually into a huge people's voluntary organization that will become a fitting challenge to dictatorial governments that force regimentation on the people in executing their national plans.

The voluntary aspect has been specifically mentioned in a pamphlet giving details of the project, which has been drafted by Gulzarilal Nanda, one of the members

Continued on Page 3, Column 3

RUSSIAN SOLDIERS KIDNAP 40 GERMANS IN BORDER DISPUTE

Seize Workers at Gunpoint in Area Claimed by Both East and West Governments

3 INCIDENTS LAID TO U. S.

Soviet Charges Two New Air Space Violations and Firing of Shots From a Train

Special to THE NEW YORK TIMES.

BONN, Germany, June 22—Russian troops and East German police darted into disputed territory along the frontier between East and West Germany today and kidnapped forty West German workers.

The men were working on a branch line of the local railroad when, according to West German officials, they were surrounded by Russian soldiers and "Vopos" (People's Policemen) and forced at gunpoint to march to a house about 300 yards away on East German soil.

The incident occurred at Hohnsleben, south of Helmstedt in Lower Saxony. In the area in which the men were working, between Schoeningen in the British zone and Harbke, lies a power station just over the frontier in East Germany.

The men seized are employes of the Brunswick Coal Mining Company. Attempts by British and West German authorities to obtain their release failed.

Claimed by East and West

The area in which the men were kidnapped is claimed by East and West German authorities. For some time there have been rumors that the Russians desired to make a border "correction" there.

Such a "correction" would place a transformer station and water pipeline linked to the Harbke power station in East Germany.

The West German authorities say these installations are in the territory of the Federal Republic. The East Germans disagree.

Although there have been incidents up and down the frontier in recent weeks, this was the first major one in which Soviet soldiers were involved. It is also the first in which a considerable number of West German workers were seized.

Farther south along the border people living near Bad Hersfeld in the United States zone asked that units of the frontier guard of the Federal Republic be stationed permanently in their area.

Their appeal followed action by East German police. Friday these police moved the frontier some yards westward to include in East Germany two estates that formerly were West German property.

New Incidents Charged

By WALTER SULLIVAN
Special to THE NEW YORK TIMES.

BERLIN, June 22—The Soviet Union blamed the United States today for three more incidents in East Germany, all of which were alleged to have taken place last Thursday.

Two were called air space violations. The Russians now have made seven complaints in the last eight weeks that aircraft of the Western Allies have trespassed over East German territory. The third Soviet complaint today asserted that an East German policeman

Continued on Page 5, Column 1

Eisenhower Bars 3d Party Race If He Loses G. O. P. Nomination

Special to THE NEW YORK TIMES.

DALLAS, June 22—General of the Army Dwight D. Eisenhower said today that he would not accept a Democratic nomination for the Presidency or cooperate with any third party movement if he were defeated for the Republican nomination at Chicago next month.

Questioned on both points at a press conference before leaving here this morning for Nevada and Colorado, the general gave a flat "no" to questions about his availability for anything except the Republican nomination.

An Eisenhower supporter in Colorado suggested last week that if the Republicans nominated Senator Robert A. Taft of Ohio, the general should try to win the election without benefit of party support as did Theodore Roosevelt in 1912. The general brushed this aside.

Asked whether there was any truth to reports that he had been offered the Democratic nomination by President Truman in 1952, General Eisenhower referred his questioner to his book, "Crusade in Europe," in which he said that Mr. Truman had offered to back him for the Democratic nomination in 1948.

Later Don Whitehead of The Associated Press asked the general whether Mr. Truman had offered to back him for the 1952 Democratic nomination, and the general replied:

"He did not."

Last fall, Arthur Krock, the Washington correspondent of THE NEW YORK TIMES, quoted a "Northern Democrat" as saying that the general had been offered the Democratic nomination by the President during a trip he made home from Europe while commander of the Western European defense forces.

Mr. Krock, in commenting on the general's reply of today, said in Washington:

"I attributed to 'a Northern Democrat in an eminent public position' the report that Mr. Tru-

Continued on Page 14, Column 3

Taft Forces Charge Texas 'Smear,' Say Foes Imperil 2-Party System

By CLAYTON KNOWLES
Special to THE NEW YORK TIMES.

WASHINGTON, June 22—The National Citizens for Taft Committee charged today that supporters of General of the Army Dwight D. Eisenhower, in challenging Texas delegate elections, were seeking to "smear" Senator Robert A. Taft and "destroy our American two-party system."

With the Republican National Convention opening at Chicago July 7, the Taft forces told their side of the story in the Texas dispute, which involves thirty-eight seats, in full-page advertisements appearing tomorrow morning in more than a score of leading newspapers, including several in Texas.

"The badly licked Eisenhower managers render a disservice to their candidate, to the Republican party and to our country," the advertisement stated, "when they attempt to destroy our two-party system and smear Senator Taft.

"Even the New Dealers and the Fair Dealers never made any effort to besmirch his character. They knew that the American people know that Bob Taft, who has spent practically his whole adult life in public service, has brought to the American political scene the highest level of personal service, of patriotic activity and complete integrity.

"At a time when every right-thinking citizen wants to end corruption in Government and create a new atmosphere of decency and honesty, this effort to smear a great Republican and a great American should and will be repudiated."

A final decision on whether pro-Taft or pro-Eisenhower delegations will be seated has been referred to the Republican National Convention.

With preliminary hearings a week off, the Taft committee advertisement said the Eisenhower managers were "screaming 'we wuz robbed' because they know they have lost the fight."

They held that "the decision" against the Eisenhower forces in Texas had been "based on a faithful interpretation of the primary election laws of the State of Texas; and those laws have been upheld by the Texas District Court, the Supreme Court of Texas, the United States District Court and by the Supreme Court of the United States."

The Taft advertisement charged that these party rules, after being upheld by the courts, had been perverted in a "fraud" by Eisenhower managers who had solicited the attendance of Democrats at Republican precinct meetings, where the recommendations on delegates were made.

The advertisement said the Democrats had been told that they would not thereby be disqualified from their own party.

The Eisenhower people spread this word, by postcard and newspaper advertisements, the Taft people charged. They quoted postcards, which they said had been

Continued on Page 14, Column 6

Third Century Chapel Excavated On U.S. Embassy Grounds in Rome

By ARNALDO CORTESI
Special to THE NEW YORK TIMES.

ROME, June 22—The remains of a third century Christian oratory, or chapel, one of the very few extant within the limits of the ancient city of Rome, have been discovered in the grounds of the United States Embassy on the Via Vittorio Veneto.

The discovery awakened an intense interest in archaeological circles because, though it was known that other such oratories existed in the Imperial City, what news of them had come down to modern times was mainly of a literary nature. No other example is so incontrovertible and striking, in the opinion of experts who visited it, as the one that has just been found.

The remains of the oratory were discovered by workmen digging for foundations of a new garage in the grounds behind the Embassy building. The digging uncovered some ancient Roman walls that immediately drew the attention of archaelogists because they were situated in the area of the famous Horti Sallustiani, or Gardens of Sallust. These gardens were the property of the historian Sallust. He had acquired them from the heirs of Caesar.

The ancient remains were identified as a "cripto portico" or underground corridor, that got light from windows in the arches of the vaulted ceiling. The building was estimated to date from the first half of the third century A. D. and seemed to be connected with a stadium that formerly existed in the area of the Gardens. The Embassy changed its plans for the garage to permit the exploration and conservation of the ancient walls, which were covered with frescoes.

Prof. Michelangelo Cagiano de Azevedo, who teaches archaeology and history of Greek and Roman art at the Catholic University of the Sacred Heart in Milan, was called in by the Embassy to advise it on the most suitable method of restoring the frescoes. He was

Continued on Page 5, Column 6

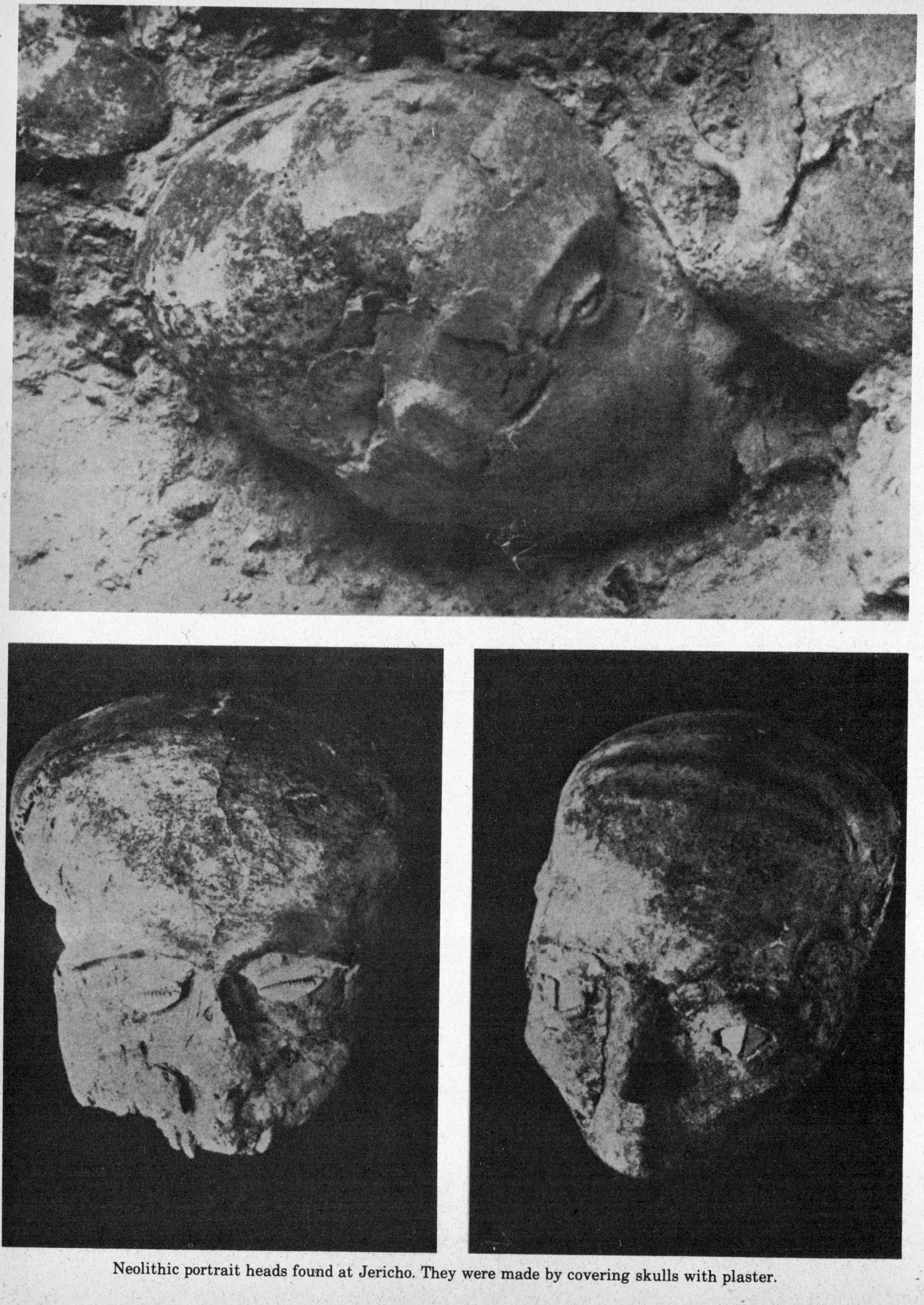

Neolithic portrait heads found at Jericho. They were made by covering skulls with plaster.

"All the News That's Fit to Print"

The New York Times.

LATE CITY EDITION

Partly cloudy today; slightly cooler tonight. Fair and mild tomorrow.

Temperature Range Today-Max., 56; Min., 45

Temperatures Yesterday-Max., 56.4; Min., 43.3

Full U. S. Weather Bureau Report, Page 40

VOL. CII..No. 34,778. Entered as Second-Class Matter, Post Office, New York, N. Y. NEW YORK, MONDAY, APRIL 13, 1953. Times Square, New York 36, N. Y. Telephone Lackawanna 4-1000 FIVE CENTS

CITY UNIONS GET AID OF HALLEY, WAGNER IN FIGHT ON BUDGET

Special Legislative Session to Be Asked to Upset Program Formulated by Dewey

HEARINGS TO START TODAY

Defeat of Mayor's Schedules, With Their Job Cuts, and of Transit Plan to Be Urged

By PAUL CROWELL

Manhattan Borough President Robert F. Wagner Jr., Council President Rudolph Halley and unions representing municipal employes all urged yesterday a fight by the city to obtain at a special session of the 1953 Legislature relief from alleged injustices contained in Governor Dewey's fiscal program for New York.

The Dewey program enacted by the Legislature called for a "higher fare" transit authority to take over the municipal transit lines and made the transfer of the lines to the new agency a necessary condition for the operation of statutes giving the city $50,000,000 of additional real estate taxing power and the right to impose by local law a $60,000,000 payroll tax on wages and salaries earned in the city.

Budget Hearings to Begin

Mr. Wagner and Mr. Halley, both of whom are regarded as possible candidates for Mayor in the city election next November, made their appeals on the eve of the first of three hearings to be held by the Board of Estimate on Mayor Impellitteri's 1953-54 executive budget of $1,528,812,795.

In his budget for 1953-54, the Mayor made no provision for gen... pay rises for city employes, deferred a $5,000,000 program of pay and job reclassifications and called for the dropping of 3,420 positions from the city payroll. He provided also for a cut of 500 in the number of new appointments to the police force, a cut of 200 in new Fire Department appointments and a reduction of 480 in the number of appointments to the Sanitation Department force. He also wrote off the attainment of a forty-hour week by July 1 for the 55,000 city employes now working a longer schedule.

Rejection of the Mayor's proposed budget, followed by action to get a special session of the Legislature to provide a fiscal basis for a budget responsive to city employes' demands for substantial pay rises, will be urged by city-employe unions at the first of the Board of Estimate hearings, scheduled for 10:30 A. M. today.

'March on Albany' to Be Urged

Mr. Halley and Mr. Wagner are expected to join in the appeal for rejection of the Mayor's budget and to urge that all citizens and organizations join with the Board of Estimate in a "march on Albany" to get relief at a special legislative session.

In a television broadcast from station WNBT, Mr. Wagner assailed the defense made by Governor Dewey of his fiscal program for the city in a radio-television broadcast last Wednesday. He agreed with Mr. Halley's accusation, made last week, that the Governor had indulged in half-truths and untruths in analyzing city-state fiscal relations.

"The Governor's talk," Mr. Wagner declared, "contained half-truths, quarter-truths and no-truths."

Contradicting Mr. Dewey's contention that his fiscal program

Continued on Page 21, Column 3

Letdown in Morale of Aides Found to Weaken U.S. Policy

Federal Employes Fear Tactics of Inquiries and Reprisals—Administration Discounts Possible Damage to 'Cold War' Effort

This is the first of three articles on the morale of Government employes as affected by the loyalty program, Congressional investigations and the change-over to a new Administration.

By W. H. LAWRENCE

Special to THE NEW YORK TIMES.

WASHINGTON, April 11—The Eisenhower Administration is faced with a morale problem among Federal employes that appears to be curtailing the efficiency of American diplomatic and propaganda efforts both at home and overseas at a critical moment in the "cold war."

It is a problem affecting many departments, but it is most acute in the Department of State and its related Voice of America operations that have been under fierce attack in Congress for many months.

The problem of sagging morale among Federal workers is not taken very seriously by the highest officials of the Eisenhower Administration, but reports from correspondents of THE NEW YORK TIMES both at home and abroad underline the grave potentialities of the situation.

One report from THE TIMES survey said that the morale of workers had been so undermined that "some of them believe that orderly processes of government have given way to a vendetta on a grand scale."

Fear of reprisals has become so widespread among Federal workers that NEW YORK TIMES correspondents, seeking information in Washington, New York and in several overseas centers of American activity, found that persons critical of the system were unwilling to be quoted by name in describing prevailing conditions.

Many of these employes regret the unwillingness of President Eisenhower and his top Cabinet aides to fight back against Senator Joseph R. McCarthy, Republican of Wisconsin, and other

Continued on Page 22, Column 3

Magsaysay Nominated to Run Against Quirino, His Ex-Chief

By HENRY R. LIEBERMAN

Special to THE NEW YORK TIMES.

MANILA, April 12—Ramón Magsaysay, former Defense Secretary who broke with President Elpidio Quirino's Liberal party in February, was nominated by a landslide convention vote today as the rival Nacionalista party's candidate for President in the election scheduled to be held in the Philippines next November.

Mr. Magsaysay, who is 45 years old, achieved a national reputation for honesty and efficiency in his military campaign against the Communist-led Hukbalahap outlaws. He bolted the Liberal party with a charge that its policies were hampering his efforts in fighting the Huks.

The Liberals have not yet held their party convention, but President Quirino is widely regarded as a candidate for re-election. Thus the outlook is for a bitter political battle between Mr. Quirino and a new national hero who formerly sat in his Cabinet.

Mr. Magsaysay was chosen as the Nacionalista standard bearer at a one-day convention held in the Fiesta Pavilion of the Manila Hotel. He received 705 votes compared with 49 votes for Senator Camilo Osias, majority floor leader in the Senate, the only other Nacionalista candidate for the Presidential nomination. One ballot was declared invalid.

Senator Carlos P. Garcia of Bohol Province in the eastern Visayan Islands was nominated as the party's Vice-Presidential candidate. He got 598 votes, and his opponent, Senator José C. Zulueta, got 149.

Mayor Arsenio H. Lacson of Manila was placed in nomination as a third Vice-Presidential contender, but he promptly declined.

Provincial delegations also named seventy-four favorite sons as prospects for eight Senatorial nominations under circumstances in which the party directorate is scheduled to make final choices later this week. Senators are elected at large in the Philippines,

Continued on Page 4, Column 5

RYAN IS SUMMONED TO HOGAN'S OFFICE

Pier Union Chief Must Appear Today—Prosecutor Silent on Reported Indictment

Joseph P. Ryan, president of the International Longshoreman's Association, A. F. L., has been ordered to appear at the office of District Attorney Frank S. Hogan at 10 o'clock this morning.

It was reported that Mr. Ryan had been indicted late Friday night by a New York County grand jury on a charge of misuse of union funds and that the call to the District Attorney's office was a result of this indictment.

There is, however, a legal provision against the announcing of an indictment before the apprehension of the person involved. Mr. Hogan's office refused any comment on the report of the indictment.

Mr. Ryan's attorney, Louis Waldman, said last night that he had been notified Friday to bring his client to the District Attorney's office this morning. He said he did not know whether an indictment had been returned against Mr. Ryan.

"That doesn't mean that it might not be true," he added.

Mr. Waldman said that he had visited Mr. Hogan's office with Mr. Ryan several times in the last week, when the investigation was apparently reaching its climax.

It's News to Ryan

Reached at his private club last night, Mr. Ryan said he knew nothing about the reports of the indictment.

"I don't know what the District Attorney wants to see me about," he said. "All I know is that he told my lawyer to have me down there tomorrow morning."

The reports said that the indictment of Mr. Ryan had been filed in General Sessions Court late Friday. Twice Mr. Ryan has refused to sign a waiver of possible self-incrimination, and Mr. Hogan has refused to allow him to appear before the grand jury without signing the waiver. On Feb. 3 Mr. Hogan charged that Mr. Ryan's action was blocking an important phase of his investigation into waterfront rackets.

The attempts to bring Mr. Ryan before the grand jury were an outgrowth of his testimony last Jan. 30 before the State Crime Commission, which revealed that in a variety of financial dealings the union chief had taken $241,097 out of his organization in the last five years. This included salary of $115,000 and such items as $12,494 to buy Cadillacs, $460 for a cruise to Guatemala, $1,332 for golf club dues and other charges, $478 funeral expenses for a sister-in-law and $10,774 for insurance premiums.

Mr. Ryan admitted that he did not keep his personal finances

Continued on Page 49, Column 4

City's Budget Crisis Straining Hospitals

By MURRAY ILLSON

New York's financial crisis is placing new strains on the city's municipal hospital system, already staggering under a burden of seemingly insoluble problems.

The recent disclosure that two new hospital units would have to defer their scheduled opening dates by at least six months has created serious concern among welfare and civic groups.

Even when these units do open to receive their first patients, shortages of personnel, particularly registered nurses, are almost certain to cause further delays and it may take many more months before the new plants are operating at full capacity.

The affected units are the 500-bed tuberculosis wing of the $40,000,000 East Bronx Municipal Hospital Center, whose opening date has been postponed until July 1, 1954, and the $6,500,000 addition

Continued on Page 24, Column 1

PROCEDURE FIXED BY ALLIES AND FOE ON CAPTIVE TRADE

Staff Officers Reach an Official Understanding on Exchange Set to Start in Week

U. N. PRISONERS ARE LISTED

Reds to Yield Ailing Men From 11 Countries—Clark Weighs Korea Truce Talk Bid

By The United Press.

TOKYO, Monday, April 13—United Nations and Communist staff officers completed an agreement at Panmunjom, Korea, today on details for an exchange of sick and wounded prisoners of the Korean war beginning next Monday.

The negotiators announced that an official "understanding" not requiring formal signed documents had been reached.

The Communist staff officers disclosed that wounded prisoners from Canada, Turkey, Greece, the Netherlands, the Philippines, South Africa, Australia and Colombia would be among the 600 Allied prisoners to be returned. The Reds had announced earlier that they would repatriate 450 South Koreans, 120 Americans, 20 British and 15 "miscellaneous" Allied troops.

Another staff session was scheduled for 11 A. M. tomorrow [9 P. M. Monday, Eastern standard time].

Clark Studies Parley Renewal

By ROBERT ALDEN

Special to THE NEW YORK TIMES.

PANMUNJOM, Korea, Monday, April 13—While Allied and Communist staff officers completed details here for an exchange of sick and wounded war prisoners, Gen. Mark W. Clark, United Nations commander, and his headquarters staff in Tokyo were studying an enemy proposal for renewal of the Korean armistice talks.

General Clark has said that the negotiations on the exchange of ailing prisoners would have to be completed successfully before resumption of the truce sessions could be considered. The negotiations have been in suspension since October.

At a staff officers meeting yesterday, the Communists said that April 20 was the date on which they would begin the delivery of 600 sick and wounded Allied prisoners, including about 120 Americans, to the United Nations in the Panmunjom neutral area. The Allies plan to deliver 5,800 Chinese and North Korean captives.

23 Vehicles in First Convoy

A convoy of twenty vehicles will leave Chonma, Korea, tomorrow, will be joined later by three other vehicles and will arrive in Kaesong, the Communist truce delegation headquarters six miles from Panmunjom, on Thursday, the enemy staff officers said.

The prisoners will be held in Kaesong for four days before they are exchanged.

This delay prompted Col. Willard B. Carlock, senior United Nations staff officer, to urge that transfer of the prisoners begin earlier, but the head of the Communist group, Col. Lee Pyong Il, said:

"We conceive that the date which our side told your side

Continued on Page 3, Column 5

1 Hat on Presidential 4-Hook Rack Gives Signal He's Working Within

But Lack of Any Could Mean He Just Didn't Wear One—Custom Left by Truman

By The Associated Press.

WASHINGTON, April 12—There is only one hat that ever rests on the hatrack outside the President's office, and that is the President's.

When President Eisenhower comes to his office in the morning from the White House residential wing, a messenger opens the door and takes his hat.

It is then carefully placed on top of the four-hook rack so that the brim rests on the top of the hooks.

The presence of the hat indicates that the President is in his office.

It is not an infallible sign, however, for some days the President goes into his office without a hat.

Harry S. Truman's hat was placed on the hatrack in similar fashion when he was the President.

There is a similar hatrack in the President's quarters within the White House, where a valet also places the President's hat atop the hooks.

Photographers got permission yesterday to take pictures of General Eisenhower's hat outside his office.

Associated Press Wirephoto

The President's hat

Associated Press Wirephoto

EISENHOWER DELIVERS PAN-AMERICAN DAY SPEECH: The President speaking at the Pan American Union in Washington yesterday. Listening to address, left to right, are Rafael Heliodoro Valle of Honduras, Luis A. Quintanilla of Mexico, Luis Oscar Boettner of Paraguay, Rene Lepervanche of Venezuela, U. S. Under Secretary of State Walter B. Smith and Ambassador John C. Dreier, U. S. representative to the Council of the Organization of American States.

Dulles Indicates Shift in Aid From Europe to the Far East

By The Associated Press.

WASHINGTON, April 12—John Foster Dulles, Secretary of State, has told Congress that the Eisenhower Administration may shift a substantial share of United States aid from Western Europe to the Far East.

Larger grants for Communist-threatened Indo-China and Formosa are contemplated, Mr. Dulles said, along with "perhaps a little more" in the Middle East. But he added in testimony made public today that this country's contribution to the military build-up of the North Atlantic Allies, to be considered this month in Paris, "could be considerably less" than now.

Advising against a "penny wise and pound foolish" policy in Indo-China, Mr. Dulles said that to provide more help to the French and their Vietnam allies over the next year or eighteen months might permit large cutbacks later. He asserted that a build-up of Chinese Nationalist forces on Formosa was "very important" to curb aggression by Red China and estimated that deliveries of military equipment to Formosa had lagged 70 per cent behind what was promised.

The Secretary, without giving figures, outlined Administration ideas about aid spending and foreign trouble spots in testimony before a House Appropriations subcommittee, which released printed copies today. Mr. Dulles testified on March 18, shortly before the visit here of French Premier René Mayer. M. Mayer is reported to have received assurances of United States backing for some fifty-seven new Vietnam commando-type battalions to fight Communist-led guerrillas.

A new foreign aid program for the 1954 fiscal year starting July 1 is expected to be ready next month, after a revision of the $7,600,000,000 Truman budget pro-

Continued on Page 15, Column 1

2 SENATORS WARN ON SOVIET 'PEACE'

Wiley and Humphrey Predict Senate Will Back Dulles in NATO Session in Paris

Special to THE NEW YORK TIMES.

WASHINGTON, April 12—Senator Alexander Wiley, Republican of Wisconsin, and Senator Hubert H. Humphrey, Democrat of Minnesota, made concurring statements today that the United States should beware of recent "peace gestures" by the Soviet Union. Both are members of the Senate Foreign Relations Committee, and Mr. Wiley is its chairman.

Mr. Wiley, in an interview, said one Soviet objective was to "split" the West while pursuing another—advancing into the Near East and building a bridge to Africa.

Indicating he believed there was growing public awareness that the Soviet Union might not be straightforward in its peace moves, he predicted that the Senate would give John Foster Dulles, Secretary of State, full backing when he went to Paris for sessions of the North Atlantic Treaty Council that start later this month. The meeting will discuss means of strengthening the West's defenses.

'Peace Blitz' Decried

Mr. Humphrey said that if the Soviet Union's new "peace blitz" could turn the United States from determination to complacency, the Kremlin would have "won a tremendous victory without firing a shot."

In remarks broadcast over Minnesota radio stations, the Democratic Senator said universal disarmament offered the only safe alternative to maintaining this country's armed strength.

"If Russia wants peace, let her agree to the universal disarmament proposal the United States has submitted to the United Nations—disarmament with effective universal inspection of development and use of atomic energy," Mr. Humphrey stated.

These comments came as René Pleven, French Foreign Minister, in Washington for conferences, was scheduled to meet with President Eisenhower at 8:30 A. M. tomorrow, and to discuss Western defenses with the Senate Foreign Relations Committee in closed session at 10 o'clock.

Senate plans, meanwhile, called for resumption of the debate tomorrow on one of the most controversial of domestic issues—the Administration-backed measure to

Continued on Page 16, Column 3

PARIS SEES NO NEED FOR 2-YEAR DRAFT

Also Tells NATO It Could Not Be Imposed—Rise in Defense Spending Held Unlikely

By HAROLD CALLENDER

Special to THE NEW YORK TIMES.

PARIS, April 12—In reply to the proposal of the North Atlantic military authorities that France should increase military service from eighteen months to two years, the French Government has said this is neither necessary nor possible.

The Government also has told experts of the North Atlantic Treaty Organization that in no foreseeable future can France spend on defense more than she has appropriated for this year—1,239,000,000,000 francs, or about $3,500,000,000.

These statements have been made in recent discussions here in the annual review of North Atlantic defense efforts being made by the international staff preparatory to the meeting of the North Atlantic Council in Paris April 23.

The experts agreed that no greater financial effort could be expected from France unless United States aid to her were increased. But the experts made the criticisms that experts always make of the internal financial instability in France that appears again to have reached a crisis stage marked by inflationary borrowing from the Bank of France to prevent the national treasury's running out of money.

The same criticisms are made by French experts, and French officials now seem more impressed than ever by the incongruity of chronic financial weakness in a country that aspires to play a leading role in European defense

Continued on Page 8, Column 1

Neolithic Skulls With Plaster Faces Found in 5000 B.C. Jericho Mound

By KENNETT LOVE

Special to THE NEW YORK TIMES.

JERICHO, Jordan, April 12—Seven human skulls upon which artists of the Neolithic Age modeled lifelike features with plaster have been unearthed in ancient Jericho.

They are relics of persons who died 7,000 years ago. But the men of the Neolithic culture, characterized by the use of polished stone tools, were relative latecomers to Jericho, one of the oldest cities in the world. Archaeologists have also found here the traces of men who lived in the Mesolithic Age, a period of transition between the Neolithic Age and the Paleolithic, or old Stone Age.

The skulls were uncovered ten feet below the present surface of a tell, a layered mound created by successive societies each building atop the debris left by predecessors, in a stratum containing implements of late Stone Age man at a pre-pottery stage of development.

Miss Kathleen M. Kenyon, director of the British School of Archaeology, who for two years has supervised joint excavations here with the American School of Oriental Research in Jerusalem, described the skulls as the "most important archaeological discovery in modern times." She said the sculpture on the skulls was "unique, one of the earliest known attempts at naturalistic modeling."

Miss Kenyon predicted the find would illuminate broad new regions in the religious, esthetic and civic life of prehistoric man.

The best preserved specimens were startlingly realistic. The artists of 5000 B. C. had given each skull a nose, mouth, chin, cheeks and ears and had made eyes with

Continued on Page 6, Column 5

EISENHOWER NAMES BROTHER TO FOSTER UNITY OF AMERICAS

Pennsylvania Educator to Tour Hemisphere as a Goodwill Envoy Seeking Solidarity

PRESIDENT ASKS STRENGTH

Speech Marking Pan-American Week Says Continent Cannot Find Security in Isolation

Text of Eisenhower address is printed on Page 13.

By WALTER H. WAGGONER

Special to THE NEW YORK TIMES.

WASHINGTON, April 12—President Eisenhower, in a dramatic bid for greater hemispheric solidarity, announced today that he had named his brother, Dr. Milton S. Eisenhower, to be his personal representative on a goodwill and fact-finding mission to Latin America.

The President disclosed his plan in an address before the Council of the Organization of American States, assembled to mark the beginning of Pan-American Week. The commemoration will reach its climax Tuesday with Pan-American Day.

The President said his brother's assignment would include taking to each of the several American Republics he visits "the most sincere and warm greetings of this Administration." On his return, Dr. Eisenhower will recommend to the President and the State Department ways "for strengthening the bonds between us and all our neighbors in this Pan American Union."

Capacity Audience on Hand

Mr. Eisenhower spoke for ten minutes before a capacity audience in the majestic Graeco-Roman Hall of Americans in the Pan American Union Building (the Pan American Union is the secretariat of the Organization of American States).

Present on the dais were the Ambassadors of the twenty-one member Governments of the Organization of American States and members of the Cabinet and of the official White House "family."

Although United States Presidents have addressed the Pan-American nations on similar occasions in the past—beginning with Theodore Roosevelt, who laid the cornerstone of the present building in 1908—the last such address was given by President Harry S. Truman on April 14, 1946.

Today thus gave President Eisenhower an appropriate opening for his Administration's campaign to mend what it regards as a deterioration of relations between the United States and its Latin-American neighbors since the end of World War II.

In a campaign address in Philadelphia last September, General Eisenhower described the Truman Administration's policy toward Latin America as "feeble" and said that "statesmanship can do better than that." A hint of the new Administration's line was also found in a speech Jan. 27 by John Foster Dulles, Secretary of State, who said that Latin America had been "neglected" by the United States in recent years.

Served in Two Administrations

Dr. Eisenhower, who is president of Pennsylvania State College and an authority on agricultural and economic development, has served in both the Roosevelt and Truman Administrations. He was director of information for the Department of Agriculture from 1928 to 1940 and land use coordinator from 1937 to 1942.

Dr. Eisenhower served for about four months in 1942 as director of the War Location Authority and as associate director of the Office of War Information until 1943. From then until 1950, he was president of Kansas State College, during which time he was named annually from 1946 to 1949 as United States delegate to the general conference of the United Nations Educational, Scientific and Cultural Organization.

The President in his address appealed for hemispheric strength against the enemies of both national freedom and economic stability. Without identifying either the Soviet Union or communism, he referred to "forces threatening this continent" that "seek to bind nations not by trust but by fear."

Declaring that "it is not possible for this hemisphere to seek security or salvation in any kind of splendid isolation," the President called for the mobilization of "spiritual, cultural and material" resources for the achievement of "an even better world."

For their part, he continued, the

Continued on Page 13, Column 4

One of the Jericho tombs showing a skeleton, table, bed, platter and vessels preserved from the neolithic period.

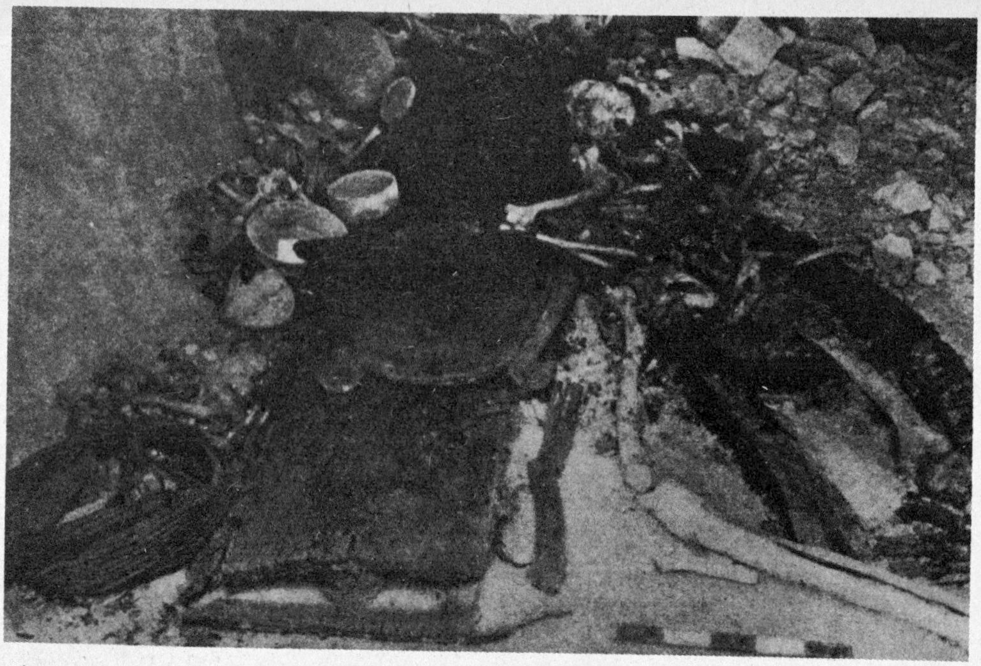

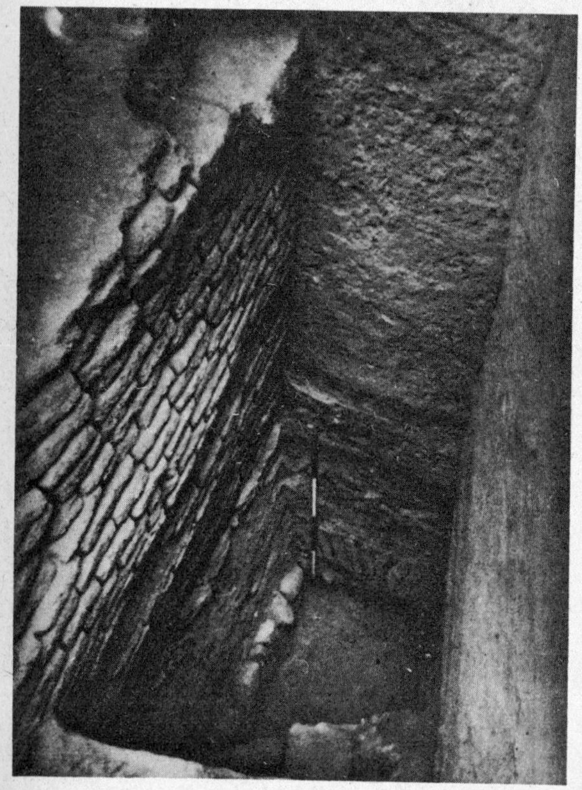

In the early Bronze Age, the walls of Jericho were destroyed by an earthquake. At the bottom of this pit a fallen wall can be seen with a new, reconstructed wall to the left.

The walls of Jericho are so early as to justify the claim that it is the oldest town in the world. Even earlier are the curved buildings, imitating tents.

"All the News That's Fit to Print"

The New York Times

LATE CITY EDITION
Fair and warm today. Partly cloudy and mild tomorrow.
Temperature Range Today—Max., 80; Min., 60
Temperatures Yesterday—Max., 78; Min., 57
U. S. Weather Bureau Report, Sect. 5, Page 12

Section 1

NEWS SUMMARY AND INDEX, PAGE 95

VOL. CIII . No. 34,952. Entered as Second-Class Matter, Post Office, New York, N. Y.

Copyright, 1953, by The New York Times Company.

NEW YORK, SUNDAY, OCTOBER 4, 1953. Including Magazine and Book Review.

TWENTY CENTS New York City and 20 Miles Zone | Elsewhere Twenty-five Cents

BRITAIN TO PRESS FOR SOVIET PARLEY ON HIGHEST LEVEL

Will Act Despite Failure of Moscow to Show Readiness for a Four-Power Meeting

LONDON HOPES FOR U.S. AID

Government Is Said to Feel Strengthened by Indications of Washington Policy Shift

By DREW MIDDLETON
Special to THE NEW YORK TIMES.

LONDON, Oct. 3—Britain will continue to sponsor a proposal for talks with the Soviet Union on the highest level. This became known today despite what is regarded here as the failure thus far of the Soviet Government to give the slightest hint that it might be prepared to accept such a proposal.

Some Government sources believe that this week's note from the Soviet Foreign Ministry dealing with the proposals for a meeting of foreign ministers at Lugano in Switzerland proved that the Russians were not now seriously considering a conference with the West.

But these sources do not make British policy. Prime Minister Sir Winston Churchill, who does, will persist, according to reliable reports, in seeking a meeting with Soviet Premier Georgi M. Malenkov and President Eisenhower.

The proposal could be raised anew by Sir William Hayter, the new British Ambassador in Moscow, when he presents his credentials to Vyacheslav M. Molotov, Soviet Foreign Minister, some diplomatic sources said.

Another possible channel of approach is through Andrei Y. Vishinsky at the United Nations. Selwyn Lloyd, Minister of State, returned to London from the United Nations meeting today and is to see Foreign Secretary Anthony Eden soon.

U. N. Channel Held Fruitful

The possibility that Mr. Lloyd might be instructed to ask Mr. Vishinsky about the talks is being discussed. In the past such approaches at the United Nations have occasionally proved more fruitful than the dispatch of diplomatic notes.

At any rate, representatives of the United States, Britain and France will meet here next week to begin drafting a reply to the latest Soviet note.

Sir Winston's determination is strengthened, it is understood, by the manner in which the United States Government has moved around to support some of his proposals on policy toward Moscow, first made in his speech to the House of Commons on May 11.

This change in the international attitude has been accompanied by the development of the talks into a serious political issue in Britain. When, in May, Sir Winston first suggested that "Russia has a right to feel assured that so far as human arrangements can run, the terrible events of the Hitler invasion will never be repeated," the State Department, in its first statement, ignored completely the Prime Minister's allusion to a guarantee for the Soviet Union.

Events in the United States have since convinced the British that the Administration has moved much closer to their view.

One of these was the speech of Secretary of State John Foster Dulles on Sept. 17 in which he said the Russian people were entitled to assurances against a repetition of

Continued on Page 2, Column 3

Dodgers Win, 7-3, Tie Series; Princeton and Penn Victors

The Dodgers evened the world series at two games apiece yesterday by defeating the Yankees, 7—3, before a new record Ebbets Field crowd of 36,775.

Duke Snider, Brooklyn centerfielder, blasted a home run and two doubles to lead his team to the most lopsided victory in its series history. Snider drove in four runs.

Billy Loes, 23-year-old righthander from Astoria, Queens, checked the Yankees with six hits through eight innings but was forced out in the ninth when the Bombers loaded the bases with none out.

Clem Labine, another righthander, struck out Phil Rizzuto and got Johnny Mize, the redoubtable pinch-hitter, on a short fly to center. Mickey Mantle then laced a single into right and Gene Woodling scored. Billy Martin tried to follow him home and was nipped at the plate.

The New York Times

HERO: Duke Snider, in club house after yesterday's game

Ed (Whitey) Ford, Yankee southpaw, who started and was relieved after yielding three runs in the first inning, was the loser.

FOOTBALL

Princeton defeated Columbia in the last minute and Penn beat Penn State. Scores of leading college contests:

Alabama	21	Vanderbilt	12		
Duke	21	Tennessee	0		
Georgia Tech	6	S. M. U.	4		
Harvard	16	Ohio Univ.	0		
Holy Cross	19	Colgate	6		
Illinois	33	Stanford	21		
Iowa	54	Wash. St.	12		
Kansas State	27	Nebraska	0		
L. S. U.	42	Boston Coll.	6		
Michigan	26	Tulane	7		
Mich. State	21	Minnesota	0		
Navy	55	Dartmouth	7		
Northw'n	33	Army	20		
Notre Dame	37	Purdue	7		
Ohio State	33	California	19		
Oklahoma	7	Pittsburgh	7		
Pennsylvania	13	Penn State	7		
Princeton	20	Columbia	19		
Rice	28	Cornell	7		
Rutgers	20	V. P. I.	13		
Wake Forest	18	Villanova	12		
Yale	13	Brown	0		

GOLF

United States professionals retained the Ryder Cup by beating a British team in England, 6½ to 5½.

HORSE RACING

Porterhouse, 7—1, owned by the Llangollen Farm, won the $117,575 Belmont Futurity. Artismo was second.

Details in Section 5.

A. F. L. BID FOR VOTE MAY BAR CONTRACT WITH RYAN DOCKERS

President's Fact-Finders Told Renewal of Strike Is Likely After 80-Day Injunction

By STANLEY LEVEY

The New York Shipping Association told a Presidential board of inquiry yesterday that until a clear-cut decision was reached on who represented striking Atlantic Coast dock workers, employers might be reluctant to sign a new agreement with the International Longshoremen's Association.

This statement, made as the board opened fact-finding hearings at the Governor Clinton Hotel as a preliminary to the issuance of an eighty-day no-strike injunction, was viewed as a strong indication that the dock tie-up, which began last Wednesday midnight, would be renewed when the injunction ran its course.

The inquiry panel, headed by David L. Cole, one of the country's leading mediators, took testimony from both the shipping association and the I. L. A. in open and closed sessions. Today the board will prepare a report for President Eisenhower, which will be used by Attorney General Herbert Brownell, possibly on Tuesday, in seeking an anti-strike ruling in a Federal court.

During the period of the injunction, the disputants would be expected to resume suspended negotiations, but at the expiration of the eighty days the union would be free to resume the walkout by 50,000 workers that has closed to commerce all ports between Portland, Me., and Hampton Roads, Va.

Counsel Notes 'New Factor'

The question of the prospects for pier peace within the eighty-day period was brought into the open by Mr. Cole in the course of questioning Joseph Mayper, counsel for the shipping association.

"If the strike is deferred for a reasonable period," asked Mr. Cole, "could the negotiations with the union conceivably lead to a settlement?"

"I don't know," replied Mr. Mayper after brief reflection. "We have a new factor in this situation, namely, notice from the American Federation of Labor of its prospective filing of a petition for a representation election among the workers."

The federation, which recently expelled the I. L. A. for failure to stamp out gangster control and influence and then chartered a rival longshore union of its own, informed shipowners and the National Labor Relations Board last week of its intention to contest the right of the I. L. A. to represent dock employes.

This step was what was bothering the shipping association. For when Mr. Cole pressed Mr. Mayper further on what effect the A. F. L. intervention would have on contract negotiations, the attorney said he was "not too sure." However, he expressed the hope that the representation question would be settled speedily and indicated that the association would petition the labor board to hold an election among employes.

In any event, Mr. Mayper told

Continued on Page 59, Column 3

Associated Press

NOT MISSING A WORD: Officials of the International Longshoremen's Association as they listened yesterday to Joseph Mayper, counsel for the New York Shipping Association, testify here before the President's inquiry board. Left to right, Harry Hasselgren, secretary-treasurer of New York local; Dan Donovan, vice president of Boston unit, and Patrick J. Connolly, executive vice president. Connolly will be spokesman for union members in various ports.

DEWEY MOVES FAY INTO DANNEMORA; TO CHECK VISITORS

Handcuffed Union Extortioner Driven to Prison 'Siberia' Near Canadian Border

WEEKLY REPORTS ORDERED

Governor Demands Names and Fingerprints of Callers—Wicks Link Is Assailed

By RUSSELL PORTER

Joseph S. (Joey) Fay, building trades labor leader and convicted extortioner, was transferred yesterday from Sing Sing to Clinton Prison at Dannemora, known in the underworld as "Siberia." The transfer was ordered by Governor Dewey. He also called for weekly reports on Fay's visitors.

Fay, wearing his prison gray uniform, was taken from Sing Sing at noon in an automobile with three keepers. He was handcuffed to one in the back seat, and another sat on his other side. The third drove the car on the 350-mile trip to Dannemora, which is in the Adirondack mountains near the Canadian border.

In Dannemora, Fay will be far less accessible to the New York and New Jersey politicians, labor leaders, contractors, raceway officials and others who have visited him at Sing Sing. A list of eighty-seven visitors since 1948 was made public Friday. It included Republican State Senators Arthur H. Wicks of Kingston and William F. Condon of Yonkers. Mr. Wicks has been acting Lieutenant Governor of the state since Thursday, following the resignation of Frank C. Moore. He also will continue as President of the Senate.

Publication of the list resulted from investigation of the Yonkers Raceway, after the Aug. 28 killing of Thomas F. Lewis, a Bronx union official. The raceway was shown to have paid large sums to union officials to insure "labor peace."

Fingerprints Are Required

The Governor's requirement of weekly reports on Fay's visitors calls for both their names and "basis of identification." Under prison regulations, it was understood, this requires fingerprints from visitors except for members of Fay's immediate family, his lawyers, members of the clergy and public officials. The Governor thus will be able to check on whether prison officials comply with regulations in registering other visitors.

Governor Dewey issued the transfer orders from his New York City office at the Roosevelt Hotel. After a meeting with his office staff and telephone talks with other advisers, the Governor issued this statement:

"I have today directed the Commissioner of Correction [Edward J. Donovan] to transfer Joseph Fay from Sing Sing Prison to Clinton Prison at Dannemora, N. Y. I have also directed that in the future the name and basis of identification of his visitors be transmitted weekly to the office of Counsel to the Governor [George M. Shapiro]."

The Governor's statement was made public by his executive assistant, Harry J. O'Donnell. Mr. O'Donnell said the Governor and Mrs. Dewey had left the hotel to attend a wedding in Pawling, their country home, and that the Governor would return here Monday.

Meanwhile Robert F. Wagner Jr.,

Continued on Page 64, Column 2

WEST DRAFTS REPLY TO MOSCOW ON TALK

Will Seek Clear-Cut 'Yes or No' Answer on a Lugano Meeting of Big Four Ministers

By WALTER H. WAGGONER
Special to THE NEW YORK TIMES.

WASHINGTON, Oct. 3 — The United States pressed ahead today in its effort to elicit from the Soviet Union a clear-cut "yes" or "no" to the Western Big Three proposal for a four-power foreign ministers meeting on German and Austrian problems.

In consultation with Britain and France, officials here were drafting a joint reply to the note received from the Soviet Government early this week. The Moscow communication, responding to the Western invitation to a foreign ministers conference proposed for Lugano, Switzerland, on Oct. 15, was found "evasive" and "dilatory" by the State Department. It left unanswered the question of whether the Soviet Government agreed to such a meeting, officials said.

There were no signs that Washington had changed its opinion that the proposed foreign ministers conference would accomplish all that a heads-of-government meeting could at this time. That seemed to remain the official view here, despite the persistence of reports that Sir Winston Churchill, British Prime Minister, still hoped for a meeting with President Eisenhower and Soviet Premier Georgi M. Malenkov.

The United States has never

Continued on Page 2, Column 5

INDIANS WIN RIGHT TO PUNISH CAPTIVES

Neutral Commission Provides Courts-Martial to Enforce Discipline in Korea Camps

By WILLIAM J. JORDEN
Special to THE NEW YORK TIMES.

TOKYO, Sunday, Oct. 4—The Neutral Nations Repatriation Commission adopted yesterday disciplinary rules that would permit the Indian Custodial Force to court-martial and punish prisoners of the Korean war in the custody of the commission.

Offenses for which the prisoners could be punished were listed as disobeying orders of the Indian guards and performing any act menacing the safety of the Indian troops or other persons acting for the neutral commission.

The courts-martial would be conducted by Indian authorities and would operate under India's Army Act of 1950. The rules specified that the prisoners could be tried for "any act prejudicial to the safety, good order or discipline of the camp or among the prisoners of war."

The rules were announced in an effort to tighten control of the prisoners who have refused to be repatriated. Three captives were killed and ten were wounded last week when Indian guards quelled demonstrations in the stockades in the neutral zone in Korea.

Nine Prisoners Missing

The Indian troops are acting as the guard force for the prisoners, who are being held in the custody of the neutral commission, consisting of representatives of India, Switzerland, Sweden, Poland and Czechoslovakia, pending an ultimate decision on their disposition.

The commission announced that nine of the more than 22,000 Chinese and North Korean prisoners who had refused repatriation were missing from the compound and were believed to have escaped. A count of the prisoners in the enclosure was made Friday after Indian guards had seen two captives attempting to escape the previous night.

Another announcement said that three prisoners had died, two of old ailments and the third of a ruptured liver, following their arrival in the demilitarized zone.

Arrangements for the courts-martial appeared to be an additional step in the efforts of the Indian guards to curb increasing violence displayed by the anti-Communist prisoners. The Indian troops twice last week resorted to gunfire to halt demonstrations in which the captives threw stones and tried to climb over barbed wire surrounding their enclosures.

The resorts to force prompted a strong protest yesterday from South Korea's acting Foreign Minister, Cho Chung Whan, who

Continued on Page 27, Column 3

SENATORS AROUSED BY AID STAFF CUTS

Bridges Declares an Inquiry Is 'Probable' on Stassen's Handling of Agency Trims

By C. P. TRUSSELL
Special to THE NEW YORK TIMES.

WASHINGTON, Oct. 3—Harold E. Stassen, Director of the Foreign Operations Administration, appeared today to be facing a Senatorial investigation into the procedures he has followed in carrying out Congressional demands for a sharp reduction in the personnel of his far-flung organization.

Senator Styles Bridges, Republican of New Hampshire and chairman of the Senate Committee on Appropriations, announced that such an inquiry was "probable" even before Congress returned from its adjournment in January.

There have been complaints, Senator Bridges said, that there has been "inept handling" of dismissals, resulting in "inequities" that have "impaired the efficiency of the organization."

He stated also that complaints had resulted from the manner of cutting down the agency's forces by about 25 per cent among the 1,700 officers and employes in Washington and reaching to about 50 per cent in Paris, where employment reached 2,700 at one time.

The complaints, Senator Bridges said, included incidents such as the following:

¶An employe submitted his resignation rather than take the apti-

Continued on Page 15, Column 1

Pleas to Register This Week Made by All Parties in City

By JAMES A. HAGERTY

Disturbed by the apparent lack of public interest in the New York City election, candidates and leaders of all political parties joined yesterday in appeals to potential voters to register this week and thus qualify themselves to vote in the election on Nov. 3.

Registration in the city and in Westchester County will start tomorrow and continue all week. The registration places will be open from 3:30 P. M. to 10:30 P. M. on Monday through Friday and from 7 A. M. to 10:30 P. M. on Saturday.

Registration elsewhere in the state in cities and villages of 5,000 or more population began on Friday and continued yesterday. This registration will continue next Friday from 10 A. M. to 10 P. M. and next Saturday from 7 A. M. to 10 P. M. Nonpersonal registration in other sections of the state began yesterday and will close next Saturday.

No political leader expects the city registration to reach the 3,528,968 mark for last year's Presidential election. But every effort will be made by the party organizations to get out a large registration that at least will approach the 2,808,594 total in 1950, a state election year in which Vincent R. Impellitteri was elected Mayor as an independent, and the 2,775,630 enrollment in 1949, the last regular city election year.

Reminders to the Voters

Sound trucks, spot television and radio announcements and house-to-house canvassing by party workers will be used to remind voters of their duty.

Declaring that the American free and secret ballot is a precious heritage denied to the peoples of the Soviet Union and its dominated countries, Mayor Impellitteri, candidate for re-election on the Experience party ticket, urged all qualified citizens to register. Citing the large registration for the Presidential election last year, he called for a similar registration this year, saying that "our local government is nearest to the immediate welfare of all of us."

"I urge all my fellow New Yorkers to consider the issues at stake in the present municipal campaign and the political character of the candidates presented to the people," he said. "And, having considered soberly the record of the past three years, I urge that the fullest possible proportion of the city's electorate register, so that they may vote in the election."

Warned by the light vote in the recent Democratic primary election and convinced that a sizable registration is essential for the election of Robert F. Wagner Jr., Democratic candidate for Mayor, and his running mates, Carmine G. DeSapio, the leader of Tammany Hall, has directed his district leaders to make unusual efforts to get out a heavy registration.

Similar instructions have been

Continued on Page 52, Column 4

HINCKS APPOINTED TO APPEALS COURT

President Names Connecticut Federal District Judge to Second Circuit Bench

Special to THE NEW YORK TIMES.

WASHINGTON, Oct. 3—President Eisenhower appointed today Judge Carroll C. Hincks, senior jurist of the Federal District Court for Connecticut, as Judge of the United States Court of Appeals for the Second District. Judge Hincks fills the vacancy left by the resignation in July of Thomas W. Swan, Chief Judge of the three-judge court.

Judge Hincks, a Republican, has been Federal District Judge in Connecticut since 1931. Before being appointed to this post by former President Hoover he had been a practicing attorney in New Haven and Waterbury.

He was endorsed for the Circuit Court appointment early in July by the Connecticut State Bar Association. Early in August, twenty-four well-known lawyers practicing in New York, Connecticut and Vermont, the states within the Circuit Court's jurisdiction, urged President Eisenhower to appoint Judge Hincks.

The recommendation was made in the form of a letter signed by the twenty-four attorneys. Among the signers were former Circuit Court Judges Swan and Learned Hand.

Judge Hincks was born in And-

Continued on Page 35, Column 1

Pope Proposes a World Legal Code To Penalize Unjust and Cruel War

By ARNALDO CORTESI
Special to THE NEW YORK TIMES.

ROME, Oct. 3—Speaking to the participants in the sixth International Congress on Penal Law, Pope Pius XII urged all civilized nations today to elaborate a code of international law that would punish persons responsible for unleashing an unjust war or for waging it with excesses in cruelty.

Nevertheless, he added what was interpreted as a criticism of the Nuremberg war crimes trials of Nazi leaders when he said that neutral judges should have a "decisive majority" in tribunals called upon to judge crimes of that sort.

The Pope was thought to be alluding to the Communist bloc when he said that agreement on war crimes might be difficult or impossible to reach with some nations.

"Whoever lives by injustice cannot contribute to the formulation of law," the Pontiff added, "and he who knows himself to be guilty will not propose a law that establishes his guilt and hands him over to justice."

He expressed the hope, however, that agreement even with such nations might be reached "bit by bit on essentials."

"The community of nations must reckon with unprincipled criminals who, in order to realize their ambitious plans, are not afraid to unleash total war," the Pope declared.

"This is the reason why other countries, if they wish to preserve their very existence and their most precious possessions, and unless they are prepared to accord free action to criminals, have no alternative but to get ready for the day when they must defend themselves. This right to be prepared for self-defense cannot be denied even in these days to any state. That, however, does not in any way alter the fact that unjust war is to be accounted one of the very gravest crimes that international law must proscribe, and the authors of it are in every case guilty and liable to punishment that has been agreed upon."

Even in a just and necessary war, the Pope continued, some acts are deserving of punishment. He mentioned mass shootings of innocent persons in reprisal for the behavior of an individual, massacres out of racial hatred, the horrors and cruelties of concentration camps, "liquidations" of human beings thought to be "not fit to live," mass deportations, force used against girls and wo-

Continued on page 24, Column 3

This section consists of 128 pages divided into three parts. The news summary and index will be found on Page 95. Society news begins on Page 91 and obituary articles appear on Pages 86, 87, 88 and 89.

Tools of Incas Are Reported Used In a Successful Brain Operation

By SAM POPE BREWER
Special to THE NEW YORK TIMES.

LIMA, Peru, Oct. 3—Two well-known Peruvian surgeons have performed a successful and virtually bloodless brain operation using only instruments of the Inca period, 2,000 years ago, according to a report published here.

The operation for removal of a blood clot from the left parietal region was performed in fourteen minutes on Sept. 22, and the patient was reported to have recovered completely. Before the operation he was unable to talk because of pressure on nerve centers after a heavy blow on the head.

The two surgeons, Francisco Grana Reyes, and Esteban Rocca, decided last July to try out the Inca technique after studying hundreds of ancient skulls with trepanning holes made in some cases with chisels and in others with saw edged knives of obsidian [volcanic glass]. After practicing on two bodies with both chisel and obsidian knives they decided to operate on a living patient with tools borrowed from the anthropological museum. The name of the patient was not revealed and neither doctor could be reached for comment today.

According to the newspaper El Comercio, the surgeons said the most remarkable feature of the operation was that it was almost completely bloodless, thanks to the use of an "Inca tourniquet," which they described as a bandage one inch wide wound tightly three times around the head.

Normally, it was explained, head operations involve profuse bleeding from the scalp but this tourniquet was found to prevent bleeding without causing ill effects.

One other head operation was said to have been carried out with Inca instruments by another pair

Continued on Page 65, Column 3

Outsiders Sought for School Board To End 'Cultural Inbreeding' Here

By GENE CURRIVAN

In a determined effort to rid the city school system of "cultural inbreeding" brought about by New Yorkers who apparently have the inside track on appointments, the Municipal Civil Service Commission has made a bid for talented "outsiders" to infiltrate the ranks and bring with them new ideas and perspectives.

The nation-wide summons was issued yesterday by Samuel H. Galston, director of the commission's examining division, who called attention to a forthcoming examination for the most important competitive position in the Board of Education—membership on the Board of Examiners, a post that pays $14,300 a year. It is one of the most searching and challenging examinations ever offered for a municipal post and one designed to test the mettle of those who feel qualified to participate in the selection of teachers, supervisors and administrators for the city's 730 schools.

The commission noted that because of the size and complexity of the school system, routine procedure had been established much to the disadvantage of "outsiders" seeking appointments.

"The same tendency with respect to placing supervisory and administrative procedures on a routine basis has carried over into the examination set-up," the report said. "'Insiders' who understand the examination set-up enjoy an evident advantage in taking an examination for any given position. Survey groups say that this has brought about excessive inbreeding, which has had a decidedly unwholesome effect on the school system."

The commission called attention to a report by the Mayor's Com-

Continued on Page 61, Column 1

Kamal el Malakh, a 34-year-old Egyptian architect was a director of works in the Antiques Department of Egypt. He was clearing a tourist road through the sand piled against the south side of the Cheops Pyramid when he noticed that a row of stone blocks had been uncovered. He surmised that these slabs might cover a hidden chamber. He hired stonecutters and subsequently discovered the 4550-year-old funerary boat. Here he is shown supervising diggers.

"All the News That's Fit to Print"

The New York Times.

LATE CITY EDITION
Fair, cooler today and tonight.
Increasing cloudiness tomorrow.
Temperature Range Today—Max., 70; Min., 57
Temperatures Yesterday—Max., 74; Min., 55
Full U. S. Weather Bureau Report, Page 59

VOL. CIII..No. 35,186. Entered as Second-Class Matter. Post Office, New York, N. Y. NEW YORK, WEDNESDAY, MAY 26, 1954. Times Square, New York 36, N. Y. Telephone LAckawanna 4-1000 FIVE CENTS

3 OFFICERS DISPUTE M'CARTHY CHARGE OF 'PHONY' CHARTS

Senator Calls Black Markings to Show Schine's Absences a Design to Deceive

MUNDT ALSO 'CONFUSED'

A Young Lieutenant Counters by Citing Shades of Trunks Worn by TV Boxers

Excerpts from transcript of the hearing are on Pages 16 and 17.

By W. H. LAWRENCE
Special to The New York Times.

WASHINGTON, May 25—A young Army lieutenant used televised boxing today to punch back at Senator Joseph R. McCarthy's attack on charts of the training camp absences of Pvt. G. David Schine compared with a norm.

Senator McCarthy, Republican of Wisconsin, charged the charts were "phony" and intended by the Army to deceive the television audience.

This was denied by three Army officers who testified today.

At issue before a Senate investigating committee were two large charts prepared by the Army to show that Private Schine was absent from Fort Dix, N. J., all or part of forty-three of his first seventy-five days in the Army, whereas the average private got passes covering only nine days during that period.

The passes for Private Schine were blocked out with black ink on the charts, while those for the typical private had black borders around white centers. Private Schine was an unpaid consultant to the McCarthy Permanent Subcommittee on Investigations before he was drafted.

Senator McCarthy said that this was the most dishonest and deceitful chart ever brought before his committee, and the committee's acting chairman, Senator Karl E. Mundt, South Dakota Republican, said it had confused and deceived him.

Lieutenant Employs Tactics

But the explanation was simplicity itself to First Lieut. John B. Blount, 26-year-old Korean war veteran and now aide to Maj. Gen. Cornelius E. Ryan, the commandant at Fort Dix, where Private Schine was a trainee.

"In my opinion, the reason that it was done was just for comparative purposes—just like in a prize fight on television. One of the fighters wears dark trunks and one of the fighters wears light trunks," Lieutenant Blount said.

There was an explosion of laughter from the crowded hearing room, in which Senator McCarthy joined. After the laughter subsided the Senator remarked that he could see "why you were selected as an aide to the general" and that he was not quite certain he wanted to ask the lieutenant any more questions.

The bickering about the charts, led by Senator McCarthy, highlighted the twentieth day of the hearings amid these other developments:

¶General Ryan said that Private Schine had left Fort Dix with a "superior" efficiency rating that placed him in the top 20 per cent of his company, but

Continued on Page 17, Column 5

Ethiopia's Emperor Lands Here Amid Noisy Welcome

The New York Times

Haile Selassie, Emperor of Ethiopia, Conquering Lion of the Tribe of Judah and Elect of God, puts finger to ear to soften din as he arrives on liner United States. At left is his granddaughter, Princess Sybel Desta, and at right, Richard C. Patterson Jr. of reception committee.

By PETER KIHSS

Haile Selassie of Ethiopia, Emperor of one of the world's most ancient territories, arrived here yesterday. He voiced the hope that—with American private investment—his country might swiftly develop modern opportunities. A dignified figure in a red-trimmed khaki field marshal's uniform with nine full rows of medals, he looked far younger than his 61 years. His thick black hair and beard had no touch of gray. His regal bearing made him seem taller than his 5 feet 4 inches. As the liner United States warped into Pier 86, West Forty-sixth Street, he brushed aside Ethiopian and State Department advisers who wished him to avoid answering

Continued on Page 8, Column 3

Humphrey Sees Budget Cut Of 5 Billion More Next Year

By RUSSELL PORTER

Secretary of the Treasury George M. Humphrey said here last night that the Administration had cut planned expenditures by more than $5,000,000,000 for the coming fiscal year beyond the $7,000,000,000 reduction in the present year.

This was regarded as a surprise for those who have been predicting an increase of $5,000,000,000 to $10,000,000,000 in defense spending this year. Reports had been published that Communist gains in Indochina had upset plans for material reductions. The Administration had been reported considering a request on Congress for new appropriations amounting to billions of dollars.

Mr. Humphrey spoke at a meeting on Government economy held by the Farm City Conference at Town Hall. His statement carried extra weight because he is a member of the National Security Council, which determines policy governing defense-spending.

Former President Herbert Hoover and Senator Harry F. Byrd, Democrat of Virginia, also spoke at the meeting. Mr. Hoover, who received a standing ovation, warned that pressure groups were trying to persuade Congress to spend $3,000,000,000 to $4,000,000,000 beyond present authorizations. Senator Byrd called for a moratorium on all new spending programs until the budget showed an actual surplus, unless there is a national emergency.

Mr. Hoover, Secretary Humphrey and Senator Byrd received awards from the conference for their work in behalf of Government economy. Each award consisted of a scroll and a clock. The conference is a nonpartisan

Continued on Page 20, Column 4

U. S. QUASHES CASE M'CARTHY CAUSED

Lorwin, Only Person Indicted From Among Senator's 81 Listed Targets, Is Freed

By LUTHER A. HUSTON
Special to The New York Times.

WASHINGTON, May 25—An indictment charging Val R. Lorwin, a former State Department official, with lying to a loyalty board about his alleged Communist affiliations was dismissed in Federal District Court today at the request of the Department of Justice.

Assistant Attorney General Warren Olney 3d, in charge of the Criminal Division, told Judge Edward M. Curran that the indictment had been obtained by misrepresentation.

Mr. Olney said the attorney who had presented the case to the grand jury had been suspended. The Justice Department later identified the lawyer as William Gallagher, a trial attorney in the Criminal Division since 1951. Mr. Gallagher was unavailable for comment.

The lawyer, Mr. Olney said, had made two erroneous statements to the grand jury. They were:

1. That the Government had two witnesses from the Federal Bureau of Investigation who would support the grand jury tesitmony of the single witness who had testified against Mr. Lorwin.
2. That it was not necessary to call Mr. Lorwin or his wife because they would plead the Fifth Amendment privilege against giving self-incriminating testimony.

Mr. Olney said that the Government did not have the additional witnesses. The record of the Loyalty Board hearings, he told the court, showed that Mr. Lorwin and his wife had testified at length and had vigorously denied communism. There was no basis for assuming that they would invoke the Fifth Amendment before a grand jury, he said.

Mr. Olney said it would be unfair to try Mr. Lorwin on an indictment obtained by "irregularities." Judge Curran then granted his motion to dismiss the case.

Mr. Lorwin was No. 64 on a list of eighty-one State Department employes accused of communism by Senator Joseph R.

Continued on Page 15, Column 2

Dulles Cites Danger Of Reds Near Canal

Text of Dulles statement on Guatemala is on Page 12.

By WALTER H. WAGGONER
Special to The New York Times.

WASHINGTON, May 25—Secretary of State Dulles said today that one purpose of the recent "massive shipment of arms from behind the Iron Curtain" to Guatemala might be the creation of a Communist bastion near the Panama Canal.

The Secretary declared at a news conference that the shipment delivered from Poland a little more than a week ago, which has been estimated at 1,900 tons, made Guatemala militarily dominant in the Central American region. Guatemala is about 800 air miles from the Canal zone.

Asked whether the arms could

Continued on Page 12, Column 3

INDOCHINA PLIGHT FORCING U. S. HAND ON STAND IN WAR

Military Situation Worsens—Native Troops Defecting—Cambodia Called Wobbly

Text of the Dulles remarks on Indochina is on Page 4.

By JAMES RESTON
Special to The New York Times.

WASHINGTON, May 25—The Indochina military situation is slipping faster than was expected and is now confronting the United States Government with the choice of an armistice or military intervention.

Secretary of State Dulles said at a news conference the prospect of moral sanction by the United Nations for military intervention by the United States and others in Indochina had improved.

The official reports on Indochina arriving here are even more depressing than the heavily censored news dispatches out of Hanoi and Saigon, Vietnam. They make these points:

¶A large part of the Tonkin Delta area, with a population of about 8,000,000, is under Communist occupation. For the time being, the French are comparatively secure in their ring of forts on the wide perimeter of the delta, but they probably will have to withdraw to a shorter perimeter to defend the Hanoi-Haiphong salient.

¶There have been defections among the native troops to the Communist side. Some of these contributed to the loss of Dienbienphu, where the French, ironically, got their fiercest support from the Germans fighting with the Foreign Legion. The Communist fifth column is an increasing worry, even in Hanoi and Haiphong.

¶The rich kingdom of Cambodia is politically wobbly. The young King Norodom Sihanouk is declared in these reports to be unreliable. At times he has shown some disposition to lead his forces, but at other times he is said to lean toward Son Ngoc Thanh, who was Premier under the Japanese, a Left-Wing (but not Communist) schoolmate of the King who has now taken to the jungle in opposition to the King.

¶France has made it clear to the United States that she is not prepared to reinforce the army in Indochina unless she has the assurance of United States intervention, and that she will be forced to accept whatever armistice she can get unless the United States agrees to participate in the war.

Confronted with this disturbing situation, France is more eager than ever to negotiate an armistice and both the United States and Britain have modified their positions.

Until now, the British have insisted on waiting until the end of the Geneva conference before taking any new political commitments in defense of the Southeast Asia area. Officials here now have the impression, however that, with the military situation deteriorating in Indochina, the

Continued on Page 2, Column 2

VIETMINH OFFERS REGROUPING PLAN

Calls for Large Withdrawal Zones in Indochina Truce—Bidault Is Back in Paris

By TILLMAN DURDIN
Special to The New York Times.

GENEVA, May 25—A simultaneous cease-fire everywhere in Indochina and withdrawal of the opposing forces into large zones was proposed here today by the chief Vietminh delegate.

In a speech at today's closed session of the Far Eastern conference Pham Van Dong, Vietminh Vice Premier and Foreign Minister, called for a cessation of hostilities "at the earliest possible date" over the whole territory of Indochina.

Georges Bidault, French Foreign Minister, left here tonight by train for Paris. His trip was decided upon suddenly and informed quarters related the journey to the Vietminh proposal and tomorrow's meeting of the French Cabinet to consider Indochina matters.

Pham Van Dong's proposal was the most concrete statement that has come so far from the Communist side on what the Vietminh favors with regard to reshuffling of troops and territories in Indochina.

Vietnamese Objects

The proposal drew an immediate objection from Nguyen Quoc Dinh, representative of the Vietnamese Government, who argued the result would be a partition of Vietnam.

There was speculation here tonight that the Vietminh proposal could be interpreted to mean the division of Indochina and represent a Vietminh preparedness to give up the south.

Conference sources, however, took the plan to mean simply that the Vietminh favored a regrouping into several large zones that in total would be roughly equal in size, population and strategic and economic importance.

Pham Van Dong's regroupment proposal provided that armed forces of the two sides would be given free passage through territory held by opposing forces in reaching regroupment areas and that authorities now administering areas would continue provisionally in control.

The Vietminh delegate also agreed in principle to a plan put forward during this afternoon's session by Anthony Eden, British Foreign Secretary, calling for officers of the two Indochina high commands to come to Geneva to assist in arranging a cease-fire and regrouping of forces.

Mr. Eden's proposal also asked that the conference get down to consideration of international supervision for an armistice.

Differences on the Indochina problem again cropped up at this

Continued on Page 2, Column 4

Bombing in Morocco Kills One, Injures 41

Special to The New York Times.

RABAT, French Morocco, May 25—A bomb apparently intended for Gen. Augustin Guillaume, retiring Resident-General in French Morocco, exploded in the main thoroughfare of Marrakesh today.

A French soldier was fatally injured and forty-one soldiers and civilians were hurt.

The explosion occurred this morning a few minutes after General Guillaume's car, at the head of an official procession, had passed on its way into the city. He is paying a farewell visit to the principal cities of the North African protectorate before relinquishing his office to Francis Lacoste, a civilian diplomat, whose appointment as Resident-General was announced Thursday.

The bomb outrage was believed to have been the work of nationalist - terrorists whose ex-

Continued on Page 8, Column 3

5 Per Cent Amusement Tax Is Voted by Estimate Board

Auto Use Levy Is Kept in Program to Add $29,800,000 for Budget—Council Gets Bill and Orders Hearing Tuesday

By CHARLES G. BENNETT

A 5 per cent tax on amusement charges was adopted yesterday by the Board of Estimate as the cornerstone of new financing estimated to produce $29,800,000 for the next budget.

The new tax, expected to yield $17,500,000, would hit a wide variety of activities, including admissions to theatres and baseball games, and dues paid to social, athletic or sporting clubs. Admissions to events run by religious, charitable and educational organizations would be, in the main, exempt.

The board approved retention of the $5 and the $10 automobile use tax, which it is believed will yield $8,800,000. Both this figure and that for the admissions tax are higher than previous estimates. The remainder of the new financing was provided through a re-estimate by Controller Lawrence E. Gerosa putting city revenues $3,500,000 higher than previously.

Action on the financial program was voted by the board in an executive session.

The amusement tax would take effect June 15, with the first returns due to the city by theatres and others paying it next Sept. 1. Thereafter returns to the city would be made four times a year—on March 1, June 1, Sept. 1, and Dec. 1.

A thirty-page bill embodying the new amusement tax, which in general would be applied to all activities covered by the Federal amusement tax, was introduced into the City Council at a brief meeting yesterday.

The bill was referred to the finance committee. It was announced that the committee would hold a public hearing on it next Tuesday at 10:30 A. M. The Council is expected to pass the bill Tuesday afternoon.

At the hearing the theatre

Continued on Page 34, Column 4

I. L. A. Put in Receivership; Dockers Here Vote Today

By A. H. RASKIN

The old International Longshoremen's Association was thrown into Federal receivership yesterday. Meanwhile, 25,000 dock workers prepared to vote today on whether the scandal-scarred union or its American Federation of Labor rival would rule in the Port of New York.

Patrick J. (Packy) Connolly, executive vice president of the I. L. A., reported that individual members had volunteered to mortgage their homes to pay off the union's $50,000 contempt fine and thus get it "out of hock." He said the union hoped to get the money together before the receiver actually took over at 10 A. M. today.

Raymond J. Scully, vice president of the State Bar Association, who was appointed receiver by Federal Judge David N. Edelstein, will file a non-Communist affidavit under the Taft-Hartley Act. As technical boss of the pier union, he must qualify under the labor law to protect the union's right to participate in today's crucial election.

His responsibilities will end as soon as the I. L. A. rounds up the $50,000 needed to satisfy the fine levied against it for its recent four-week strike.

A staff of 191 National Labor Relations Board officials from as far west as Denver will supervise the waterfront balloting at six polling places in New York and New Jersey. Twenty-five hundred policemen will be on duty at the three election centers in Manhattan, Brooklyn and Staten Island to see that there is no repetition of the violence that marked a similar poll here last December.

The voting, set to begin as early as 6 A. M. at three of the polling places, will end at 7 P. M. The count will get under way at

Continued on Page 22, Column 2

AUTHORITY OFFERS NEW L. I. R. R. PLAN

Agreement With Pennsylvania Calls for 20% Fare Rise, $58,739,000 for Refitting

Text of the Authority's letter to Dewey is on Page 26.

The state-created Long Island Transit Authority announced yesterday an agreement by which the Pennsylvania Railroad would resume running the Long Island Rail Road. It involved a twelve-year redevelopment plan including $58,739,000 in new car and other improvements. The plan would take effect with an average 20 per cent fare increase and a nine-year limitation on taxes.

Governor Dewey was understood to be ready to ask a special session of the Legislature, probably in mid-June, to amend the 1951 Railroad Redevelopment Corporations Law as needed.

Thereafter, all parties would formally adopt the agreement. The present bankruptcy proceeding in Federal Court in Brooklyn would be withdrawn, as would pending petitions for higher fare increases in the Interstate Commerce Commission and the state Public Service Commission.

Late this summer the Pennsylvania would take over with a new general manager and the 20 per cent fare rise. William Wyer, the present trustee, would be out of his job, and so would the authority, originally set up by state law March 31, 1951, to chart a new future for the line that went bankrupt March 2, 1949.

Pennsylvania Accepts Plan

The Pennsylvania Railroad has agreed to the plan. Its president, Walter S. Franklin, said it would cooperate fully and asked cooperation from the public and public authorities.

He promised definite improvement in service, but said it would take a year or more to show real progress. He expressed confidence that financing could be obtained for the new equipment.

There was no immediate comment from Mr. Wyer or the P. S. C.

Lawrence W. McKeown, Democratic leader of Nassau County, attacked the plan. He said it confirmed the "worst fears of commuters" by proposing to return the Long Island to Pennsylvania ownership and authorizing another fare increase. He urged that Governor Dewey be "bombarded" with protests.

The plan was submitted to Governor Dewey by George E. Roosevelt, chairman, and Tracy S. Voorhees, as unpaid members of the authority, and William W. Golub, counsel. Sidney H. Bingham, general manager of the New York City Transit Authori-

Continued on Page 26, Column 4

Passage Unsealed Near Pyramid Believed to Lead to Cheops' Tomb

15-Ton Stone Blocking Tunnel Is Cut—Egypt Hopes to Find King's Treasure

By KENNETT LOVE
Special to The New York Times.

CAIRO, May 25—An Egyptian archaeologist cut through six feet of limestone and five millenniums of history today.

The limestone blocked a newly discovered subterranean corridor that is expected to lead to the southern tomb of Cheops, builder of the Great Pyramid at Giza, whose mummy and funeral treasures never have been found.

If the corridor bears out its promise and leads to the tomb it will be "beyond all comparison the most important archaeological discovery ever made in Egypt," according to Kamal el Malakh, director of archaeological works for the Giza pyramids and Lower Egypt, whose workmen pierced the fifteen-ton limestone block sealing the corridor at 2 o'clock this afternoon.

The newly discovered passageway runs parallel to the south face of the Great Pyramid about twenty-five yards distant. The tomb is believed to be near the southwest corner of the pyramid.

The New York Times May 26, 1954

Site of the tomb (cross)

Since it never has been entered by thieves, who have looted most of the other tombs, Mr. el Ma'akh expects to find part of Cheops' remains, in addition to fabulous treasure of Egypt's greatest king. The existence of the tomb was revealed in hieroglyphics carved on a stone scarab found two years ago.

The corridor, which runs for 150 yards between the Great Pyramid and a row of Fifth Dynasty mastabas (oblong tombs with sloping sides), was discovered as a result of construction

Continued on Page 6, Column 4

T. W. U. PREPARES TRANSIT STOPPAGE TO BEGIN JUNE 14

Authority to Warn Employes on Dismissal as They Plan Vote on Strike Next Week

KLEIN DENOUNCES AGENCY

Charges His Colleagues With 'Union-Busting' in Rejecting Fact-Finders' Proposals

By LEONARD INGALLS

The Transport Workers Union, C. I. O., led by Michael J. Quill, moved yesterday to strike the city-owned subway, elevated and surface lines June 14.

Union officials fixed the date in protest against the repudiation by the Transit Authority of a fact-finders' formula for labor peace on the transit system.

The authority, meanwhile, prepared to warn its 44,000 employes of the consequences of a strike under the Condon-Wadlin law, which prohibits walkouts by public employes under pain of mandatory dismissal.

Counsel to the transit agency also was instructed to explore a possible State Supreme Court injunction against a strike.

As the lines were being drawn for the first major test of strength between the authority and the Quill union, Mayor Wagner warned that "a strike on our mass transportation system is unthinkable."

Expressing "deep concern" over the strike threat, Mr. Wagner noted that the city no longer had control over the transit system labor policies. Nevertheless, he said, he and Joseph E. O'Grady, the city's Commissioner of Labor, would keep the developments in the situation under constant study.

Report Set Off Crisis

It was a report by a fact-finding committee appointed by the Mayor that touched off the latest transit crisis. Mr. Wagner named the three-member group in January to head off a strike.

The fact-finders recommended a two-step hourly pay increase of 6½ cents now and 7½ cents next March 15, a two-year contract, recognition of majority unions as exclusive bargaining agents and an impartial arbitrator to settle disputes.

Although the T. W. U. had indicated an inclination to accept the recommendations, the Transit Authority voted 4 to 1 on Monday to reject them. Instead, it substituted its own scale of pay increases of 5 to 12 cents an hour and adopted a new set of labor regulations.

In addition to the wrath of Mr. Quill and the T. W. U., the authority's action also drew upon it yesterday a denunciation from Harris J. Klein, one of its members. Mr. Klein voted against the

"The finding of my four fellow members," he asserted, "is unrealistic, autocratic and typical union-busting technique.

"I do not think management can deal with labor with a bull whip and a comptometer machine," he said in urging a labor-relations program closely akin to the proposals of the fact finders.

By their action, Mr. Klein declared, his colleagues—Maj. Gen. Hugh J. Casey, chairman; Henry K. Norton, Douglas M. Moffat and William G. Fullen—were

Continued on Page 24, Column 8

Control of Central Up for Vote Today

BY ROBERT E. BEDINGFIELD
Special to The New York Times.

ALBANY, May 25—The venerable Tenth Regiment Armory on Washington Avenue here was clearing its vast drill shed today for the New York Central Railroad's annual meeting of stockholders.

That session, which will be convened at noon tomorrow by William White, Central president, is to decide whether fifteen men headed by Mr. White shall continue to manage the affairs of the giant railroad system. In opposition is a slate of fourteen men and a woman led by Robert R. Young.

[In New York, the Central failed in a last-minute effort to delay the annual meeting when the Appellate Division of the Supreme Court declined to act.]

Thomas J. Deegan Jr., vice

Continued on Page 45, Column 4

"All the News That's Fit to Print"

The New York Times.

LATE CITY EDITION
Cloudy, cooler today; showers likely tonight. Rain tomorrow.
Temperature Range Today—Max., 64; Min., 54
Temperatures Yesterday—Max., 74; Min., 57
Full U. S. Weather Bureau Report, Page 55

VOL. CIII.. No. 35,187. Entered as Second-Class Matter. Post Office, New York, N. Y. NEW YORK, THURSDAY, MAY 27, 1954. Times Square, New York 36, N. Y. Telephone LAckawanna 4-1000 FIVE CENTS

BLASTS ON CARRIER KILL 91, INJURE 200; HELICOPTERS FLY VICTIMS TO SHORE FROM THE BENNINGTON IN ATLANTIC

Associated Press Wirephoto

HELICOPTERS EVACUATE CASUALTIES: Four helicopters wait on deck of the aircraft carrier Bennington to fly injured seamen back to shore, a rescue technique perfected in Korean war. One elevator is below deck, apparently preparing to bring injured to helicopters. The plane with folded wings on left rear of deck is part of carrier's complement.

SHIP REACHES PORT

Explosions Cause Fire 75 Miles at Sea—Origin Unknown

By MURRAY SCHUMACH
Special to The New York Times.

QUONSET POINT, R. I., May 26—Explosions and fire aboard the aircraft carrier Bennington killed at least ninety-one men and injured more than 200 today.

It was one of the worst peacetime disasters in modern United States naval history.

The blasts originated on the deck below the hangar deck, the first one occurring at about 6:20 this morning. The hangar deck is just below the flight, or top, deck of the ship.

The 41,000-ton vessel was in the Atlantic about seventy-five miles south of Newport, R. I., when she was rocked by the explosions.

The carrier, escorted by the destroyer Ingraham, was on her way north to this naval air station from Norfolk, Va.

The Secretary of the Navy, Charles S. Thomas, who flew here from Washington to inspect the ship and talk to eyewitnesses, said the cause of the explosion was not known.

A court of inquiry will begin here tomorrow. According to Rear Admiral John M. Hoskins, commander of air activities here, the inquiry will "try to determine the cause of the accident; to learn if anyone was at fault and try to make sure that it never happens again."

Ambulances Stand By

From the first of three explosions, until the last man left the ship, the scenes often were reminiscent of wartime. Heroism was mingled with death as rescuers fought through smoke and bent steel to find comrades. The fire raged for about four hours after the explosions.

Helicopters made as many as a dozen trips out to sea to bring the critically injured to hospitals. Ten of the victims were on the critical list and some personnel were missing.

Long lines of ambulances were on the pier here before the carrier arrived, and later in the day many hearses occupied the same area.

While ranking Navy officers held conferences, hundreds of wives and parents sat tensely in a theatre here, waiting to learn if their men were alive.

Several theories advanced to explain the disaster were discredited during the day. Capt. William F. Raborn of Oklahoma City, skipper of the ship, suggested at first that a fuse magazine might have exploded. Later, however, he said a check had shown this to be unlikely.

The possibility of sabotage was discounted by Admiral Hoskins, but he added he could not dismiss this entirely until the investigation was concluded.

Other officers, including Captain Raborn, said they did not think the trouble began in the catapult room, which contains mechanism for launching planes.

At the time of the accident Captain Raborn was on the navigation bridge and the ship was

Continued on Page 16, Column 2

CHEOPS TREASURE, SHIP OF THE DEAD, FOUND AT PYRAMID

RELIC OF 2900 B. C.

Perfumed Funeral Craft in Deep Passage Is 55 Yards Long

By KENNETT LOVE
Special to The New York Times.

CAIRO, May 26—A perfumed ship built by a Pharaoh nearly 5,000 years ago to carry his soul to heaven was discovered today in a subterranean corridor beside a pyramid.

The ship, constructed and furnished by Cheops, was found in a limestone passageway next to his vast pyramid at Giza, south of Cairo.

Oars and a rudder sweep were placed in the gunwales as if ready for instant embarkation on a celestial voyage. Linen ropes were coiled on the deck of sacred sycamore and cedar wood. The hull of the ship, which is believed to be one of a pair, is fifty-five yards long.

The corridor in which it was found is hollowed out in the bedrock of a hill at the desert's edge overlooking the green Nile Valley. The ship has at least six decks and is estimated to be nine yards deep.

The discovery was described as explosive by Dr. Mustafa Amer, head of the Egyptian Department of Antiquities. The find, expected by authorities here to prove one of the most important in Egyptian archaeological history, was made by Kamal el-Malakh, 34-year-old Egyptologist and architect, who is director of archaeological work for Giza and Lower Egypt.

Mr. el-Malakh said there was no doubt that the ship had been built by Cheops, second king of the Fourth Dynasty, which lasted from 2900 to 2750 B. C.

Furniture and Artifacts

The importance of the find lies in the fact that it contains the first furniture and artifacts of Cheops' reign to be found. Except for the tomb of his mother, Hetep-Heres, discovered at the bottom of a shaft a short distance away in 1925, no other funeral chamber had been overlooked by robbers. All other pyramids have been plundered repeatedly since the world's first revolution of record overthrew the sixth Egyptian dynasty 2,500 years before Christ.

The funeral ship, which began evolving in prehistoric times, has been unearthed in many forms. The most magnificent ones were built around Cheops' time, but until today their contents could only be surmised.

Mr. el-Malakh penetrated into the corridor yesterday after his workmen had chiseled through one of the fifteen-ton limestone blocks that had sealed it from the weather and treasure-seeking ghouls through five milleniums. He had suspected that the blocks, uncovered three weeks ago in the construction of a tourist road circling the Great Pyramid, were the ceiling of a corridor leading to the southern tomb of Cheops. The tomb was mentioned in hieroglyphics found on a stone scarab two years ago.

The hole was enlarged enough this morning to permit the young

Continued on Page 4, Column 3

Anti-U.S. Plot Is Laid To 17 Puerto Ricans

By EDWARD RANZAL

Seventeen leaders of the terrorist Nationalist party of Puerto Rico were indicted here yesterday on charges of seditious conspiracy.

The indictment returned by a Federal grand jury stemmed from the shooting in Washington last March 1 of five Representatives in the chamber of the House. It also followed twenty-two years of violence by party members, who seek total independence for Puerto Rico.

In early morning raids Federal Bureau of Investigation agents arrested eleven of the defendants—four here, six in Chicago and one in Ponce, P. R. The remaining six are in prison, four in Washington in connection with the March 1 shooting, and two in Danbury, Conn., for contempt.

On the recommendation of United States Attorney J. Ed-

Continued on Page 14, Column 4

U. S. DETAINS SHIP FOR ARMS SEARCH

French Freighter at Panama Held on Report of Unlisted Weapons in Cargo

By WALTER H. WAGGONER
Special to The New York Times.

WASHINGTON, May 26—United States customs officials are inspecting a French merchant ship at the Panama Canal on suspicion that her cargo may include unlisted weapons.

The State Department, which announced this tonight, did not specify what the inspection of the vessel was expected to uncover.

Other United States officials made it clear, however, that recent reports of new arms shipments bound for Guatemala had prompted the Government to take new precautionary measures against Communist threats to the Western Hemisphere.

[Dispatches from Panama said the freighter was being detained on suspicion that she was carrying arms. A spokesman in New York for the French Line said he had been given to understand the ship carried "a few cases of hunting guns consigned from Belgium to a sporting goods outlet in a Central American country."]

Action Is Explained

After a careful study this evening of reports that the French Line merchant ship might hold a cargo of arms not listed on her manifest, the State Department issued the following statement:

"Before entering the canal the French Line merchant vessel S. S. Wyoming, which is now at Cristobal, is undergoing inspection by United States Customs inspectors to determine whether there has been a violation of customs regulations. The ship's manifest reflects a miscellaneous cargo comprised principally of machinery. Included are five boxes of sporting arms, but it is understood that no question is being raised about these.

"The inspection is being conducted with the knowledge and approval of the French Government and the French Line."

United States authorities said the inspection was to make certain that the machinery listed on the manifest was really machinery. They said it was not yet known what the destination or origin of the ship was. These questions are now being studied.

Officials pointedly separated the detention of the Wyoming from recent reports that two additional shipments of arms for Communist-dominated Guatemala were on their way from undisclosed Baltic ports. But they added that it was clear that certain information had reached the United States indicating that the cargo of the French vessel might contain more weapons than the five boxes of sporting arms.

The Government's alarm over the possibility of secret arms shipments to Guatemala developed suddenly about ten days ago when it was discovered that a

Continued on Page 6, Column 3

Nixon Urges Dewey To Seek Re-Election

By JAMES A. HAGERTY

Vice President Richard H. Nixon made an appeal last night to Governor Dewey to run for re-election in November.

Speaking at the $100-a-plate dinner of the Republican State Committee at the Waldorf-Astoria Hotel, Mr. Nixon said of Mr. Dewey:

"I don't know what his future plans are, but I would just like to say that I am among the great numbers of people in other states in America, interested in the cause of good government, who hope that he might continue to give the nation's most populous state the incomparable leadership he has given to it for the last twelve years."

Prolonged applause and cheers followed the Vice President's statement.

Mr. Nixon, whose speaking

Continued on Page 39, Column 6

M'CARTHY INQUIRY DISMISSES CASES OF HENSEL, CARR

Republicans Carry 4-3 Vote and Democrats Denounce It as 'a Slick Whitewash'

Excerpts from transcript of the hearing are on Page 20.

By W. H. LAWRENCE
Special to The New York Times.

WASHINGTON, May 26—Four Republican Senators outvoted three Democrats today to dismiss misconduct charges against H. Struve Hensel, Assistant Secretary of Defense, and Francis P. Carr, staff director for the McCarthy investigating subcommittee.

Joseph N. Welch, special counsel for the Army in its dispute with Senator Joseph R. McCarthy, called the decision "a stab in the heart."

Democrats denounced it as "a slick whitewash."

The action came at the close of the Army's presentation of its side of the case on the twenty-first day of public televised hearings before the Senate Permanent Subcommittee on Investigations.

Roy M. Cohn, counsel for the committee under Senator McCarthy, Republican of Wisconsin, was then sworn and will take the stand at 10 A. M. tomorrow to lead off the McCarthy side of the wrangle.

Senator Stuart Symington, Democrat of Missouri, threatened to appeal the committee's decision on the Hensel and Carr cases to the floor of the Senate. He said he would raise the matter also in the Senate Armed Services Committee, of which he is a member.

Motives Are Questioned

While the Republicans asserted their motion had been motivated by the lack of any evidence against Mr. Carr and Mr. Hensel, the Democrats charged that the real purpose of the move had been to relieve Mr. Carr of a requirement that he testify under oath as requested by Army representatives.

A Democratic motion to call Mr. Carr as the first witness on the McCarthy side was voted down, four to three, on straight party lines.

Mr. Carr had been accused by the Army of having participated with Senator McCarthy and Mr. Cohn in attempting by improper means to obtain preferential treatment for Pvt. G. David Schine.

Private Schine, a wealthy New Yorker, was an unpaid staff consultant to the McCarthy subcommittee before he was drafted last November.

Senator McCarthy had charged that Mr. Hensel "masterminded" the Army charges against the McCarthy staff to stop the subcommittee from investigating him. The Senator alleged that Mr. Hensel had acted improperly in organizing a private firm supplying shipping companies while he was a wartime Navy Department official.

Senator McCarthy specifically refused to withdraw his charges

Continued on Page 21, Column 1

PIER UNIONS' VOTE FAILS TO DECIDE CONTROL OF PORT

I.L.A. Takes Lead of 319 but Labor Board Must Rule on 1,797 Challenged Ballots

By A. H. RASKIN

For the second time in five months a fiercely contested National Labor Relations Board election failed last night to settle the interunion fight for control of the Port of New York.

The old International Longshoremen's Association, battling for its life against the combined assault of the American Federation of Labor, Governor Dewey and the Waterfront Commission, emerged from the balloting with a margin of 319 votes over its A. F. L. rival.

But the victor will not be known until the Labor Board disposes of 1,797 challenged ballots, a process that may take a month or more.

Twenty thousand dock workers participated in the balloting, which was conducted in an atmosphere of churchlike calm in contrast to the turbulence and bloodshed that forced invalidation of a similar poll last December.

The official result, as announced at 11 P. M. by Charles T. Douds, regional director of the Labor Board, gave the I. L. A. 9,110 votes to 8,791 for the A. F. L., with 1,797 ballots in dispute, 49 void and 51 against both unions.

Vote Is Increased

The new pier union, set up by the federation last September to bring honest unionism to the crime-steeped waterfront, bettered the record it made in the first election. At that time it ran 1,492 votes behind the I. L. A., with 4,399 ballots challenged.

Most observers expected, however, that a count of the disputed votes in yesterday's poll would guarantee victory for the I. L. A. Patrick J. Connolly, executive vice president of the old union, estimated that 1,500 of the challenges had been filed by the A. F. L. against I. L. A. stalwarts.

He demanded that the election results be certified without delay so the I. L. A. could negotiate a new wage agreement with the New York Shipping Association. He hinted at a new strike if the Labor Board engaged in protracted hearings before giving his union the green light to bargain with the employers.

No concession of defeat came from the A. F. L. John Dwyer, its port chairman, said he felt "very confident" the new union would get a majority of the challenged ballots and win the right to speak for all of the port's 25,000 dock workers. He made it plain that the A. F. L. had no intention of abandoning its drive to clean up the harbor, even if it did wind up on the short end of the final count.

Mr. Douds, who praised the vote as the "most orderly" he had ever seen, declared that it might take six weeks to two months to complete an investigation of the challenged ballots and decide which should be counted. Each union has five days in which to file objections to the conduct of

Continued on Page 55, Column 2

French Lean to Divided Indochina; Troops Quit Two Posts in Delta

Cabinet Gives Bidault Right to Seek to Compromise Red and Paris Plans

By LANSING WARREN
Special to The New York Times.

PARIS, May 26—The French seemed today to be moving toward acceptance of a partition of territory in Indochina.

The extent of the territory to be yielded to the Vietminh and the new line of defense depends on an international guarantee of the partition, in which the United States and other nations at the Geneva conference would join.

Georges Bidault, French Foreign Minister, returned tonight to Geneva, where the Far Eastern conference is being held. He was armed with the Cabinet's vote of confidence enabling him to seek a compromise between the new Vietminh proposal and the latest French plan for a cease-fire on the Indochina front.

The chances of obtaining this were said to depend on Allied solidarity to convince the Soviet bloc the Allies were united and that there would be no way of

Continued on Page 9, Column 3

Positions on Southern Rim Are Blown Up—Vietminh Pincer Drive Develops

By The Associated Press.

HANOI, Vietnam, May 26—French Union defenders of the Red River delta, menaced by an apparent Vietminh pincers advance, today blew up two of their posts on the southern rim of the delta.

As tanks, armored cars and planes furnished protective cover, the French evacuated and dynamited the posts at Thannhe and Doaithon, about sixty miles southeast of Hanoi. The posts, six miles southeast of Thaibinh, a market center, had been subjected to constant encircling maneuvers and harassing night attacks.

The pincers threat developed last night as Vietminh units, moving southeasterly along Route 41 from smashed Dienbienphu, suddenly struck off northeastward.

French Army headquarters here said bombers, from land and carrier bases, and fighter planes bombed and strafed the advancing column.

Military sources here believe

Continued on Page 8, Column

T. W. U. TO BATTLE FOR STRIKE RIGHT

Plans Suit on Condon-Wadlin Law—700 on Joint Board Unanimous for Walkout

By LEONARD INGALLS

Union preparations for a legal battle over the right of Transit Authority employes to strike were being made yesterday.

Michael J. Quill, president of the Transport Workers Union, C. I. O., defied the transit agency in its threat to seek an injunction against a walkout and to invoke the Condon-Wadlin Law, which makes dismissal mandatory for public employes who strike.

Rejection by the authority of fact-finding proposals that would have strengthened the T. W. U. as the representative of 34,000 of the agency's 44,000 employes led to the threat of a strike.

A strike at 12:01 A. M. June 14 was voted unanimously last night by 700 members of the union's local joint executive board at the Capitol Hotel. An open vote on the strike date during the next ten days by the rank and file was authorized. Plans for picketing at twenty-six places on the transit system during a walkout were made.

Earlier in the day, after a meeting of union lawyers, Mr. Quill announced that "there is considerable legal opinion that the Condon-Wadlin law has no application to the pending walkout by the T. W. U. in the New York City transit system."

The legal aspects of the situation were explored by Arthur J. Goldberg, general counsel of the Congress of Industrial Organizations, and John F. O'Donnell, general counsel of the T. W. U.

Another meeting was scheduled for June 4 and a union announcement said that the general counsels of all C. I. O. international unions would gather here then for "a council of war on New York State's anti-labor Condon-Wadlin Law."

The law was voted by the Legislature and approved by Governor Dewey in 1947. It has never been subjected to a major court test.

A spokesman for the Governor said yesterday that Mr. Dewey

Continued on Page 30, Column 2

Survivors Fight the Flames To Organize Instant Rescue

By WILLIAM M. FARRELL
Special to The New York Times.

QUONSET POINT, R. I., May 26—Rescue work aboard the aircraft carrier Bennington got under way almost simultaneously with the blasts and fire this morning. Sailors and marines were wrenched from sleep or routine tasks and plunged into the work of saving shipmates who lay burned.

The damage and injury were mostly in sleeping, dining and recreation areas, or in passages connecting such areas.

To reach the casualties, some of the survivors had to fight their way out of the blast-torn areas. Those who could get hold of mask-type breathing devices put them on, and worked for hours searching out and moving the injured. Others kept at the task as long as they could stand the suffocating atmosphere.

One of those who narrowly missed injury and helped to organize the rescue work was Marine Lieut. Carl Gage of Lynnfield, Mass. He and Capt. David Twomey, commander of the ship's detachment of marines, were asleep in their stateroom when the fire started.

They had barely awakened

Continued on Page 16, Column 6

Soviet Party Rising To a Par With State

Special to The New York Times.

MOSCOW, May 26—Parity or duality of the Communist party and the state in the Soviet Union has been growing.

Observers in the foreign diplomatic corps note, for example, that at the recent session of the Supreme Soviet, two important addresses of equal importance were delivered.

The first was that of Premier Georgi M. Malenkov to the Council of Nationalities. The second was that of Nikita S. Khrushchev, first secretary of the Communist party, to the Council of Union.

Although the meeting of the Supreme Soviet is what might be called a "Government" occasion, none the less the party secretary, Mr. Khrushchev, spoke on a basis of full parity with Premier Malenkov.

This parallel role of party and

Continued on Page 2, Column 4

CENTRAL VOTE IN; MEETING RECESSED

2,200 Stockholders Attend Noisy Session on Control—Count Starts Today

By ROBERT E. BEDINGFIELD
Special to The New York Times.

ALBANY, May 26—The noisy battle of the last eighteen weeks for control of the giant New York Central Railroad quieted today to a shuffling of a stack of 40,979 papers—representing votes.

That quiet, however, did not descend until 4:48 P. M., when the Central stockholders' meeting in the Tenth Regiment Armory here was recessed until Tuesday.

For the preceding four hours and forty-eight minutes some 2,200 Central shareholders had participated in a session more like a rousing political convention than an annual meeting of a century-old railroad.

It will be days, maybe weeks, before those shareholders and the ones who participated by proxy know whether they re-elected fifteen men to manage their $2,600,000,000 investment for the next year or elected an insurgent slate of fourteen men and a woman.

The count of proxies by the inspectors of election, three professors of law, will begin tomorrow at 9 A. M. in the Ten Eyck Hotel here. A tedious process, it will continue to 8 P. M. daily until completion. The professors are Robert W. Miller of Syracuse University, John Hanna of Columbia University and Covington Hardee of Harvard Law School.

The present board is headed by William White, 57-year-old

Continued on Page 41, Column 2

Student Body to Pay I.R.T. Melee Damage

Dismayed by last Thursday's disorder on the subway, the student body of the High School of Commerce has offered to pay for the damage.

The melee, which occurred on the I. R. T. subway trains and stations between the Van Cortlandt Park terminal and Ninety-sixth Street, involved hundreds of high school boys and girls. It occurred after a rain squall had forced cancellation of the school's field day in the park.

The day after the disorder representatives of the student government of the school, at 155 West Sixty-fifth Street, met with the principal, Vincent McGarrett, to discuss a plan of restitution. The proposal was then submitted to school's 2,000 students and overwhelmingly approved.

A spokesman for the Transit Authority said the principal damage was the smashing of electric

Continued on Page 27, Column 5

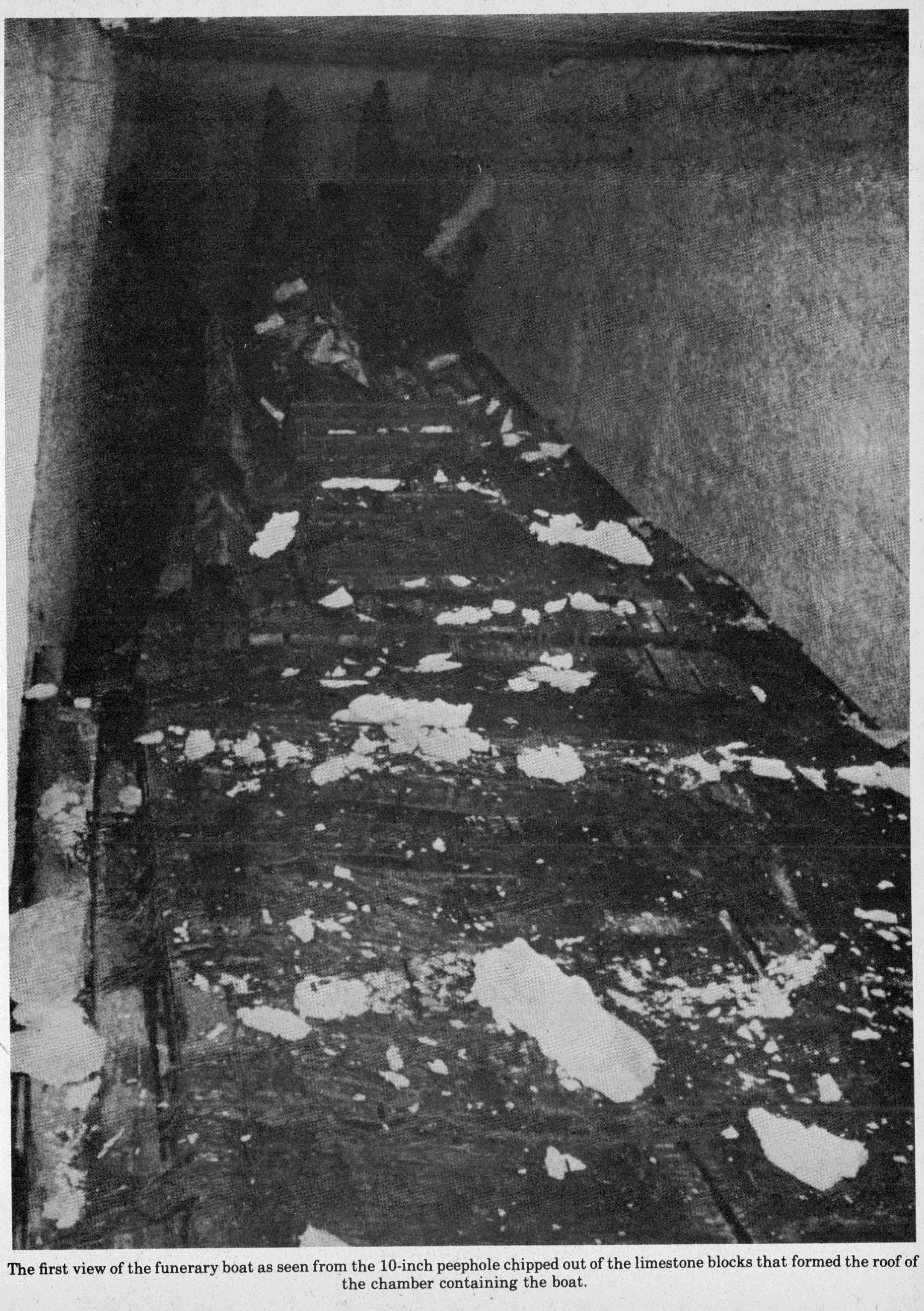

The first view of the funerary boat as seen from the 10-inch peephole chipped out of the limestone blocks that formed the roof of the chamber containing the boat.

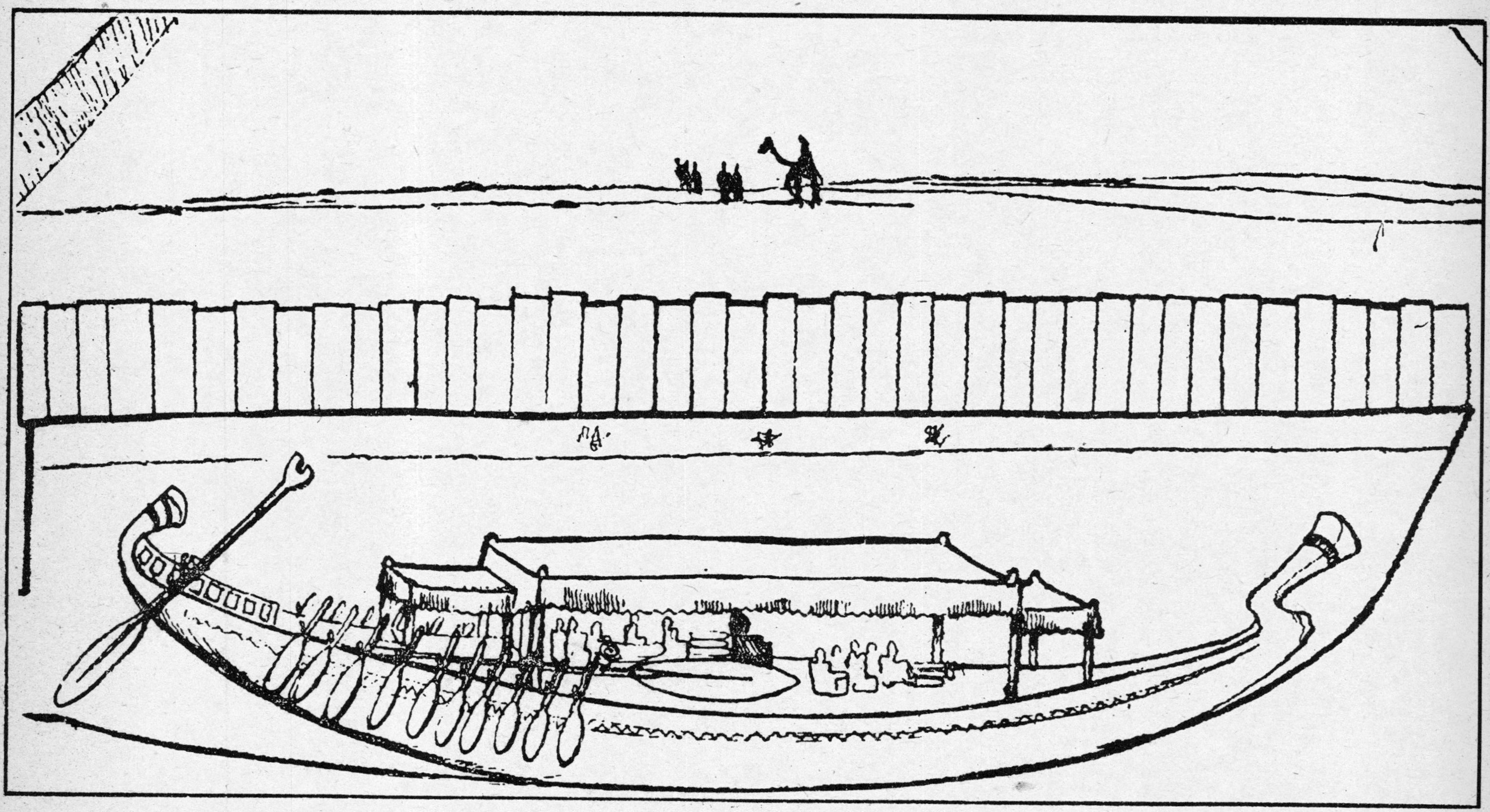

Kamal el Malakh's drawing of how the funerary boat appeared in Cheop's time.

"All the News That's Fit to Print"

The New York Times.

LATE CITY EDITION
Cool with occasional rain today.
Warmer with showers tomorrow.
Temperature Range Today—Max., 64; Min., 55
Temperatures Yesterday—Max., 62; Min., 57
Full U. S. Weather Bureau Report, Page 46

VOL. CIII . . No. 35,188. Entered as Second-Class Matter, Post Office, New York, N. Y. NEW YORK, FRIDAY, MAY 28, 1954. Times Square, New York 36, N. Y. Telephone LAckawanna 4-1000 FIVE CENTS

CARNEY SAYS PERIL IS 'GRAVER' TODAY THAN IN KOREA ERA

Admiral Finds That 'Imminent' Dangers in Indochina Crisis Are 'Increasing Swiftly'

PROMPT ACTION IS URGED

Speech Viewed as Advising U. S. It Must Be Prepared to Join in the Fighting

Text of Admiral Carney's talk is printed on Page 2.

By PETER KIHSS

The Navy's top-ranking officer asserted yesterday that the free world faced even "graver" alternatives in Indochina than those that led to the 1950 decision to fight in Korea.

Admiral Robert B. Carney, Chief of Naval Operations, said he was not predicting that a "holocaust" would come tomorrow, but he was "convinced that that 'tomorrow' can come far sooner than may be realized or sooner than we're ready to face up to."

He portrayed the Communist world as constantly adding to its resources and said, "The danger is imminent and it's increasing swiftly."

The admiral's statement was interpreted authoritatively here and in Washington as a new warning that the United States and its allies must be prepared for the possibility of joining the fighting in Indochina.

Admiral Carney hedged his statement by telling the National Security Industrial Association, at a luncheon in the Roosevelt Hotel, that there were "political and/or military" ways to organize resistance—and the decision must include "the whole-hearted consent of the populations that are involved."

Speech Is Called Grim

It was perhaps the grimmest Administration statement since Vice President Richard M. Nixon said last April 15 that it might not be possible for the United States to avoid sending troops to Indochina.

Admiral Carney in effect lined up with Admiral Arthur W. Radford, Chairman of the Joint Chiefs of Staff, who has been depicted in Washington reports as favoring any necessary intervention to prevent further Communist expansion in Indochina.

Admiral Carney's forum was an association of more than 600 companies, founded by the late James Forrestal, first Secretary of Defense and now providing thirteen standing advisory committees and sixty-five task committees to solve industrial problems submitted by the Defense Department.

A total of 256 persons attended, and C. C. Felton, regional vice president, who is vice president of Revere Copper and Brass, Inc., presided.

The Navy chief's speech had been cleared by both the Defense and State Departments in regular procedures. Asked later if he would verify that he was portraying the possibility of United States participation in the Indochina fighting, Admiral Carney limited comment to "Take it right from the speech."

Admiral Carney recalled that Americans repeatedly had had to

Continued on Page 2, Column 2

Pakistan Would Take Key Anti-Soviet Role

By JOHN P. CALLAHAN
Special to The New York Times.

KARACHI, Pakistan, May 27—Pakistan is willing to assume a key role in an anti-Soviet bloc provided the Western powers underwrite that role, a responsible Government official said tonight.

In effect, he added, that was the reply made recently to a British note to Prime Minister Mohammed Ali during the conference of South Asian Prime Ministers in Colombo, Ceylon, last month.

Pakistan is a week-old member of the United States-sponsored Middle East defense agreement.

Partners or allies in the group would be Burma, Ceylon and Indonesia, three of the five nations represented at the Colombo conference. According to the envoys from these countries, if they join with Pakistan, India, the fifth

Continued on Page 2, Column 2

New York Times Radiophoto. ©1954. The New York Times Company

SITE OF RARE FIND: Flanked by two uncut ceiling blocks, Kamal el-Malakh stands over the chamber where he discovered Cheops' craft. Yesterday he resealed opening with cement to keep out air pending further investigation.

Rock Holding Cheops' Ship Resealed to Aid Research

By KENNETT LOVE
Special to The New York Times.

CAIRO, May 27—Dr. Mustafa Amer, director general of the Egyptian Department of Antiquities, and his chief architect today described the discovery of a 5,000-year-old funeral ship of the Pharaoh Cheops as "beyond all others in importance."

He and Mohammed Mahdi, the architect, said the find, made by the director at Giza, Kamal el-Malakh, was "explosive" in the science of Egyptology.

Mr. el-Malakh resealed the ship today to prevent the cold night air of the desert from seeping into the chamber. He was fearful it would affect the furniture and the decks, numbering at least six, that still retained a faint odor of sacred sycamore and cedar wood mingled with incense.

He was apprehensive also, that sand might drift into the ghostly corridor, one of only two funeral chambers found so far that had apparently never been plundered by treasure-seeking ghouls.

The ship and a probable sister vessel to the west in the corridor, according to Mr. el-Malakh, are solar ships of the night, aboard which the ancient Egyptian rulers believed they could join the celestial caravan of souls journeying with the sun after death.

The ships, with their counterparts for the daylight part of the eternal voyages, were a central factor in the ancient Egyptian religion up to the Graeco-Roman period that began with the invasion by Alexander the Great in 332 B C.

Further investigation of the find near Giza will be delayed until the arrival of Dr. Zaki Iskander, chief chemist of the Department of Antiquities, who has been summoned from Upper Egypt. Dr. Iskandar will advise on the measures necessary to preserve the wood, which Mr. el-Malakh said, appeared to be in good condition.

It is likely the chamber will not be reopened until after the end of the Feast of Bairam, late next week, terminating the Fast of Ramadan.

Meanwhile Mr. el-Malakh is continuing his examination of the

Continued on Page 4, Column 4

THAILAND DECIDES ON APPEAL TO U. N.

Will Bid Security Council Help Bar Spread of Indochinese War—U. S. to Back Move

By A. M. ROSENTHAL
Special to The New York Times.

UNITED NATIONS, N. Y., May 27—Thailand's United Nations delegate said today his country had decided to ask the Security Council to help guard against a spread of the Indochinese war.

Thonat Khoman, who arrived from Europe on a consultation mission with Security Council members, said he expected the case to be put before the Council within less than two weeks.

[In Washington it was reported the United States had agreed to back the Thai move.]

Mr. Khoman said his country would ask the Council to dispatch observers from its Peace Observation Commission to Thailand to watch for signs that the war might spread into Thai territory.

The commission consists of fourteen members, including the United States and the Soviet Union. However, Mr. Khoman indicated his country was thinking of a five-member subcommittee that might include India, Pakistan, Sweden, Uruguay and New Zealand.

Question of Timing

The Thai delegate had been instructed by his Foreign Minister, Prince Wan Waithayakon, who is at the Geneva conference, to sound out opinion among the eleven Council members. Mr. Khoman gave the impression that the chief question to be settled now was one of timing—when the complaint of a possible threat to the peace would be put before the Council.

Mr. Khoman saw several Council members today and scheduled an appointment with Secretary General Dag Hammarskjold for 4 P. M. tomorrow.

Other Council delegates will meet with Mr. Khoman tomorrow and over the week-end. The attitude of most delegates was that it would be best to wait until they had talked with the Thai before making any statements. But the consensus was that there would not be any determined Western opposition to United Nations debate, such as the French put up last year when the Thais brought up the idea.

On Tuesday, Secretary of State Dulles said the United States would support an appeal for United Nations observers in the

Continued on Page 3, Column 2

BOARD WILL SEEK INJUNCTION TO BAR STRIKE BY T. W. U.

Move Ordered by Authority as It Defends View, Gives New Pay Rise—Union Votes

Statement by General Casey is printed on Page 46.

By LEONARD INGALLS

The Transit Authority decided yesterday to seek an injunction against the strike that the Transport Workers Union, C. I. O., has threatened to start June 14

To clarify its position in the labor dispute, the agency authorized its chairman, Maj. Gen. Hugh J. Casey, to issue a statement defending the authority's rejection of the major recommendations of a fact-finding committee.

General Casey denied in the statement that the authority sought to "destroy labor unions." He declared that acceptance of union contracts, the recognition of dominant unions as exclusive bargaining agents and an agreement to have an impartial arbitrator resolve labor troubles would be illegal.

The T. W. U., meanwhile, proceeded with plans for a strike of the 34,000 members it has among the authority's 44,000 employes.

In the first rank and file ballot on the walkout, 500 workers at the 147th Street I. R. T. repair shop voted unanimously to strike. Michael J. Quill, T. W. U. president, and other union officials met last night with the City C. I. O. Council to enlist the support of other unions.

Council Votes Support

At the council meeting, 200 delegates representing 500,000 workers in several industries, voted unanimously to support the transport workers in the dispute. After hearing a report from Matthew J. Guinan, president of Local 100, T. W. U., the delegates also adopted a program to "bring peace and stability to the transit industry."

The program included the calling of a mass meeting on June 9 of organized labor and all other persons interested in transit peace. It includes also the printing of 100,000 leaflets stating the transit union's position in the strike. These are to be distributed to C. I. O. members. A mass distribution of the leaflets at subway entrances during rush hours before the strike deadline likewise was proposed.

The delegates approved sending telegrams to the Transit Authority urging it to negotiate a contract in good faith with the T. W. U., and another to Governor Dewey. The Governor was urged to instruct the authority members he appointed to negotiate and sign a contract with the union "and thus obviate the necessity of a strike."

One member of the five-man authority was absent from yesterday's meeting. Harris J. Klein, who had denounced his colleagues for "union-busting," was in Albany on an unexplained mission.

The other members directed Harold L. Warner, the authority's

Continued on Page 46, Column 1

Guatemala Proposes Pact With Honduras

By SYDNEY GRUSON
Special to The New York Times.

GUATEMALA, May 27—Guatemala proposed to neighboring Honduras today that they immediately sign a pact of friendship and nonaggression.

The proposal apparently was aimed at countering increased fear in the hemisphere that Guatemala's recent purchase of about 2,000 tons of arms from Czechoslovakia had created a Communist menace to the safety of the Americas, and particularly the safety of Guatemala's neighbors.

Indications were that the Guatemalan Government, for the first time since the present crisis developed with arrival of the arms May 15, was seriously concerned that what it had always considered a war of nerves against it might turn into a shooting war.

Foreign Minister Guillermo

Continued on Page 7, Column 4

Justice Aide Quits; Brownell Ousts Him

By LUTHER A. HUSTON
Special to The New York Times.

WASHINGTON, May 27—William A. Gallagher, a trial attorney in the Department of Justice, made public today written instructions from his superiors directing him to disobey an order of a Federal Court.

He gave this as his reason for resigning this morning as Special Assistant to the Attorney General and as an attorney in the trial section of the Criminal Division.

The Justice Department, however, announced that a letter notifying Mr. Gallagher of his dismissal had been sent to him before the telegram of resignation reached the department. Mr. Gallagher said late this afternoon that he had not received the letter.

Attorney General Herbert Brownell Jr. said that Mr. Gal-

Continued on Page 15, Column 2

PIER VOTE BRINGS THREAT OF STRIKE

I. L. A. Urges Quick Count of Challenged Votes—Warns the Board on 'Kicking Around'

By A. H. RASKIN

The threat of a new dock strike hung over the harbor last night. It came in the wake of a second inconclusive election to determine union representation for the port's 25,000 longshoremen.

The old International Longshoremen's Association came out of the National Labor Relations Board poll Wednesday with a lead of 319 votes over its American Federation of Labor rival, but no winner will be certified until the board has disposed of 1,792 challenged ballots.

Capt. William V. Bradley, president of the old union, warned that it might not be able to keep its members at work if the board started "kicking us around like they did before." His reference was to the board's decision to deprive the I. L. A. of an indicated victory in a similar election last December on the basis of A. F. L. charges of intimidation and coercion.

"We want the board to count the disputed ballots right away and let us get down to negotiating a contract," Captain Bradley asserted. "For the second time the men have shown they want us to represent them; it is up to the board to stop fooling around. We think we can do a good job for the harbor if we are allowed to do so."

Board officials made it clear that they would move for an immediate injunction if a strike were called before either union had been given the green light to bargain with the New York Shipping Association. A four-week strike by I. L. A. members ended April 2 after the board had notified the old union that it would be barred from Wednesday's election unless it sent its members back to their jobs.

Isadore Katz, chief counsel for the A. F. L. pier union, said it

Continued on Page 45, Column 2

LAGGING PROGRAM STIRS G. O. P. WORRY ON FALL ELECTIONS

Threat to Passage of Major Items Is Expected to Spur President's Campaign Aid

Special to The New York Times.

WASHINGTON, May 27—Republicans are showing a growing apprehension over the outlook for President Eisenhower's legislative program and its correlative, the fall political campaign.

The evidence is that the President's program is, and has been for some time, in real trouble. Whereas a month or two ago Republican spokesmen were declaring confidently that a major part of the program would be approved the attitude now is more defensive, less confident.

The threat to the program has led General Eisenhower to consider making more appearances in marginal Congressional districts and states than he had planned. Republicans seeking reelection who feel they need his help are likely to be more cooperative in Congress if they see a chance of getting such help.

View Voiced by President

One illustration of what is going on was the White House visit yesterday of Representative George H. Bender, Republican nominee for Senator from Ohio. President Eisenhower, commenting on Mr. Bender's near-perfect record of supporting the Administration in Congress, said anyone who was for him was for his program.

On leaving the White House, Mr. Bender said:

"The President assured me he is coming to Ohio sometime this fall."

This was the first time an Ohio visit by the President was indicated. Mr. Bender, talking to news men, emphasized the content of the President's program, rather than what was happening to it. It is what the President stands for and the effort put into it that counts, he said.

Another illustration of the situation was the comments of farm state members of Congress after breakfast with the President yesterday. In effect, they put the President's farm price proposals on the retreat and compromise list for this session, although there was nothing on this from the White House staff.

At the Capitol, Senator Lyndon B. Johnson of Texas, the Democratic leader, implied that the Republican plan to adjourn Congress by July 31 either was nonsense or the Republicans intended to scuttle most of the Eisenhower program. He put the adjournment at Aug. 15 "at the earliest," if all phases of the program were to be considered.

While the President has shown no disposition to abandon his practice of staying out of local political fights as such, he is expected to continue the practice of the silent endorsement. This consists of traveling into a state for some civic or social function and having his favorite candidate at his side.

He did this in Kentucky last

Continued on Page 16, Column 4

The New York Times

IN FAVOR OF TRANSIT STRIKE: Maintenance men at the I. R. T. repair shop at Lenox Avenue and West 147th Street raise their hands in approval. Matthew Guinan, next to flag, president of Local 100, Transport Workers Union, C. I. O., had called for the show of hands.

COHN, TESTIFYING, DISPUTES STORIES OF ADAMS, STEVENS

Dare to Indict Him Made by McCarthy

Special to The New York Times.

WASHINGTON, May 27—Senator Joseph R. McCarthy today dared the Eisenhower Administration to indict him for admittedly receiving from Government employes secret information in violation of Presidential directives.

Speaking directly to the Senate Permanent Subcommittee on Investigations and to millions watching the inquiry on television, the Wisconsin Republican publicly invited his informers to continue to supply him with classified information and documents. He specifically included all 2,000,000 Government employes in the invitation.

His challenge to the Administration was set off by an assertion by Senator John L. McClellan, Arkansas Democrat, that he did not believe Senator

Continued on Page 14, Column 3

CARRIER DISASTER CALLED 'FREAKISH'

Carney Visits the Bennington, Is Puzzled by Blast Effects—Inquiry Board Meets

By JOHN H. FENTON
Special to The New York Times.

QUONSET POINT, R. I., May 27—Admiral Robert B. Carney, Chief of Naval Operations, visited the carrier Bennington today, a few hours after a Navy court of inquiry convened to investigate what he termed a "freakish" disaster.

The 45,000-ton carrier was racked by explosions and fire about 6:30 A. M. yesterday and suffered the loss of ninety-three men killed and about 200 injured. Of the injured, ninety-eight remain in hospitals, forty-six of them in critical condition.

Discussing the disaster with newspaper men, Admiral Carney said that "the fire had different characteristics from any I had ever seen before."

There were signs, he continued, indicating explosions without indicating heat, while at the same time, there were other spots that indicated inward pressure, "or vacuum."

"The part I saw was very badly torn up with freakish effects," he said. Structures and fabrics close together showed signs of heat on the former and none on the latter, he added.

Admiral Carney was accompanied by Vice Admiral Frederick W. McMahon, commander, Air Force, Atlantic Fleet. They spent about an hour aboard the Bennington, inspecting the wardroom area where most of the damage appeared to have been done.

Later, the two Navy officials visited and talked with injured men, both here and in Newport, where the more serious cases were taken. They shuttled between the points by helicopter.

Admiral Carney asserted that

Continued on Page 6, Column 3

Gang in Westchester Raids Another Home

Special to The New York Times.

WHITE PLAINS, N. Y., May 27—Four thugs shot their way into a fashionable home near Armonk, N. Y., tonight. They terrorized the wife of a toy manufacturer and disarmed the policeman sent to her rescue.

The gunmen ransacked the house, took an undetermined amount of cash and $5,000 in jewelry, and then fled in a Cadillac car driven by a woman. They escaped despite roadblocks hastily erected by the police departments of all central and northern Westchester County.

The police said the men were the same group of "party bandits" who had invaded isolated country homes in Westchester County for the last five week-ends. So far their loot has ranged from $82 to $15,000.

Sheriff John E. Hoy said the four men, between 25 and 35 years

Continued on Page 17, Column 1

CHARGES THREATS

Opens McCarthy Case—Swears Army Tried to Switch Investigation

Excerpts from transcript of the hearing, Pages 8 through 13.

By W. H. LAWRENCE
Special to The New York Times.

WASHINGTON, May 27—Roy M. Cohn swore today that the Secretary of the Army and his legal counselor had suggested that the McCarthy investigating subcommittee should turn its inquiries from the Army to the Navy and Air Force.

Mr. Cohn, chief counsel for the McCarthy group, thus contradicted the sworn testimony of Robert T. Stevens, Army Secretary, and John G. Adams, departmental counselor, who had declared this allegation to be false.

This conflict in testimony, which might lead to perjury action by the Justice Department, came on the twenty-second day of the inquiry into the Army-McCarthy dispute.

Mr. Cohn was the lead-off witness for the McCarthy side. Army witnesses have testified in support of the charges that the Senator and Mr. Cohn sought by improper means to obtain preferential treatment for Pvt. G. David Schine. Private Schine was an unpaid consultant to the subcommittee before he was drafted.

'Blackmail' Laid to Army

Highlights of the Cohn testimony were:

¶An assertion that Mr. Adams threatened to have Private Schine sent overseas if the McCarthy committee did not stop its investigations of Communists in the Army. Mr. Adams has denied this.

¶A reference to this as "blackmail." Mr. Cohn said that Mr. Adams had threatened to give publicity to the Cohn-Schine report, in an effort to discredit the McCarthy committee, if subpoenas were not canceled for Army "loyalty-security" board members. He declared that Mr. Adams later had conceded he would "stop at nothing" to halt the inquiry. This Mr. Adams has denied.

¶A contention that Secretary Stevens and Mr. Adams over a period of weeks had made several attempts to obtain Senator McCarthy's pledge of silence before they carried out plans to remove Maj. Gen. Kirke B. Lawton as commandant at Fort Monmouth, N. J., and dropped their plan only when Senator McCarthy served notice he would fight them publicly.

¶Contradiction of the testimony of Secretary Stevens, Mr. Adams and Maj. Gen. Cornelius E. Ryan, Fort Dix commandant, Mr. Cohn said the Army Secretary did ask Private Schine to come to his side during the taking of pictures at Maguire Air Force base in New Jersey on Nov. 17, 1953.

Use of 'Hostage' Charged

This was the incident that figured in the "cropped" picture prepared by the McCarthy staff early in this inquiry. An enlargement showed Secretary Stevens and Private Schine alone, whereas the original included other persons.

¶Allegations that all the pressure for stopping the Fort Monmouth inquiry came from the Army side, and did not arise from any suggestions by Senator McCarthy that he was ready to bow out of the inquiry.

¶An assertion that Mr. Adams called Private Schine "the hostage" more frequently than he used his proper name in conversations about what the Army might do for Private Schine if the McCarthy committee dropped its investigations of the Army. Mr. Adams has conceded he may have used the description "hostage" a few times, but only in a jocular vein.

There were reliable reports tonight that a decision had been taken to summon Francis P. Carr, subcommittee staff director, as a witness. Yesterday, when the subcommittee voted 4 to 3 on party lines to excuse Mr.

Continued on Page 13, Column 7

"All the News That's Fit to Print"

The New York Times.

LATE CITY EDITION
Warm with showers today. Clearing and less humid tomorrow.
Temperature Range Today—Max., 78; Min., 65
Temperatures Yesterday—Max., 74; Min., 55
Full U. S. Weather Bureau Report, Page 35

Copyright, 1954, by The New York Times Company.

VOL. CIII. No. 35,189. Entered as Second-Class Matter, Post Office, New York, N. Y. NEW YORK, SATURDAY, MAY 29, 1954. Times Square, New York 36, N. Y. Telephone LAckawanna 4-1000 FIVE CENTS

WHITE HOUSE CHARGES M'CARTHY BID TO GET SECRET DATA IS USURPATION; HEARING IN TURMOIL OVER SCHINE FILE

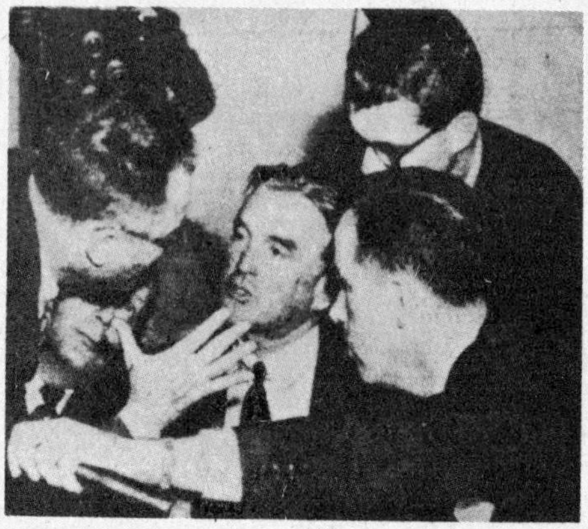

Associated Press Wirephoto

SUBPOENA STIRS CONFERENCE: A flurry of activity at committee table follows word that Senator McCarthy has been supboenaed to produce files on Pvt. G. David Schine. Left to right are Ray H. Jenkins, inquiry counsel; Senator Karl E. Mundt, acting chairman, who signed subpoena; Senator Stuart Symington, Senator Henry M. Jackson, with hand on microphone, and Robert Kennedy, right rear, the chief counsel for the Democratic minority.

SENATOR RETORTS

Again Defies Directive—Extends Charge of Treason to '21 Years'

By JOSEPH A. LOFTUS

Special to The New York Times.

WASHINGTON, May 28—The Eisenhower Administration challenged today Senator Joseph R. McCarthy's invitation to Federal employes to pass him classified information regardles of security regulations.

The Executive branch's responsibility "cannot be usurped by any individual who may seek to set himself above the laws of our land," said a White House statement personally approved by President Eisenhower.

The Wisconsin Republican retorted not only by renewing his invitation and promise to protect his sources but also by stretching his oft-repeated charge of "twenty years of treason" into "the past twenty or twenty-one years." This span would cover more than a year of the Eisenhower Administration.

He declared, moreover, that if an employe of the Executive branch had not rapped on Senator Karl E. Mundt's door one morning at 2:30 A. M. and given him information that the President would now block, Alger Hiss "might well now be an Assistant Secretary of State," instead of a Federal convict.

Even while making these statements in the Army-McCarthy hearings, the Wisconsin Senator declared he was casting no reflection on the President or his Attorney General, Herbert Brownell Jr.

Symington 'Astonished'

Senator Stuart Symington, Democrat of Missouri, declared during the exchange at the hearing that "if the Senator from Wisconsin is right, we have'nt got a good government, we haven't got a poor government, we just won't have any government at all."

"Finally," said the Missouri Senator, "I am getting a little astonished at the amount of defense that this Administration gets from the Democratic members of the committee and the abysmal silence on my right." The Republican members sit to the right of the Democrats at the subcommittee table.

Senator Charles E. Potter, Republican of Michigan, spoke up a little later, but not in defense of the Administration on this issue.

He declared his respect for President Eisenhower and calling him a great administrator and a great American. Then he told Senator Symington "it ill behooves a man who has been campaigning for the things that the President has stood for to tell us what we should do and how we should run our party."

The Administration challenge to Senator McCarthy was a statement in the name of Mr. Brownell. The White House press secretary, James C. Hagerty, issued it orally.

Mr. Hagerty said he had received both last night and today queries as to whether the White

Continued on Page 10, Column 4

Senators Seek to Determine Just What Work Schine Did

By W. H. LAWRENCE

Special to The New York Times.

WASHINGTON, May 28—Roy M. Cohn heatedly denied today that he and Senator Joseph R. McCarthy had used any improper means or sought any special favors from the Army in the case of Pvt. G. David Schine.

Mr. Cohn, the 27-year-old chief counsel for the Senate's Permanent Subcommittee on Investigations, underwent sharp cross-examination by Ray H. Jenkins, special counsel for the hearings, as he continued to contradict earlier testimony given by Army witnesses.

Efforts by the subcommittee to establish some quantitative

Excerpts from transcript of the hearing, Pages 6 through 9.

test of how much work Private Schine actually had performed for the subcommittee while he was on frequent authorized leave from Fort Dix, N. J., ran into several road blocks. They finally set off a fierce controversy between Senator McCarthy and Democratic members of the investigating group.

Private Schine, a wealthy New Yorker, was an unpaid consultant to the subcommittee before he was drafted last November.

The subcommittee at one stage found itself in the unusual position of subpoenaing its own files, containing documentary evidence of Private Schine's work, because Senator McCarthy, as the regular chairman, would not make them available. Later, when the subpoena was served and accepted, the Senator promised the information requested and the subpoena was canceled.

Democrats charged that the incident of the files demonstrated anew what they called Senator

Continued on Page 9, Column 1

FRANCE ADVANCES CALL TO 80,000 MEN TO HELP ASIA WAR

New Conscripts Will Replace Regulars Who Will Be Formed Into Units for Indochina

TOP POST OFFERED JUIN

Red River Delta Commander Hopeful as Reinforcements Arrive in Battle Area

By LANSING WARREN

Special to The New York Times.

PARIS, May 28—To facilitate the formation of a French reserve for Indochina, the Cabinet decided today to advance the draft normally starting in November. The conscripts affected will be called beginning in June.

The conscripts cannot be used in the war in the Far East without the approval of the National Assembly, but they can serve to replace the regular army men who will be assembled from the forces serving now in France, West Germany and North Africa. These latter will be formed as reinforcements for the Indochina war.

The call for conscripts next month was expected to raise about 80,000 soldiers, with another possible 80,000 to be called in December for advance service. Not all these men would be needed for replacements among the regulars who would be called to fight overseas in the special Indochina reserve. This reserve would be expected to number between 30,000 and 40,000 troops.

[In Hanoi, Vietnam, Gen. René Cogny said the arrival of reinforcements in the Red River delta had enabled him to envisage the future with optimism.]

The Cabinet did not determine on the appointment of a successor to Gen. Henri-Eugene Navarre, French Commander in Chief in Indochina. It is understood the Cabinet had sounded Marshal Alphonse-Pierre Juin, now commander of the Atlantic pact forces in Central Europe, as to whether he would accept a six-month assignment in Indochina with full powers in military and civilian affairs.

Juin Suggests a Substitute

Marshal Juin, however, is believed to have replied that he could not give up important work on which he is engaged for the Atlantic alliance at once. He suggested some commander who would be free immediately.

It is understood Marshal Juin did not definitively decline the offer to become commander in the Indochina war at a later date. Authorities were given to understand that he would be prepared to assume full responsibilities as commander if it should be decided to organize, in accordance with Allied decisions, an international expeditionary force for the defense of Indochina.

A large part of the Cabinet meeting was devoted to the decision of the Government to seize today's issue of the weekly newspaper Express. Rene Pleven, Minister of Defense, told the Cabinet the seizure of all copies of the paper had been ordered because it contained secret military information disclosed at a restricted meeting of the Cabinet Tuesday night. It is said the information related to an article purporting to reproduce particulars of Gen. Paul Ely's report to the National Defense Council

Continued on Page 2, Column 3

Clapp, Ex-Head of T.V.A., Is Named Deputy to Gulick

In $20,000 City Job, He Will Be a Management and Personnel Expert

By PAUL CROWELL

The appointment of Gordon R. Clapp, former chairman of the Tennessee Valley Authority, as a Deputy City Administrator was announced yesterday by City Administrator Luther H. Gulick.

Mr. Clapp, now living at Norris, Tenn., will move to New York soon. He will begin work in his new $20,000 post on June 15.

His assignment will cover two areas in the Division of Administration. One will deal with management problems of works and utilities, the other with personnel administration.

The appointment completes the staffing of the top positions in the division, which is headed by Dr. Gulick at an annual salary of $30,000. Charles F. Preusse is first deputy at $22,500 and Dr. John V. Connorton the second deputy at $20,000.

Mr. Clapp's duties will include management studies of such city agencies as the Department of

Associated Press

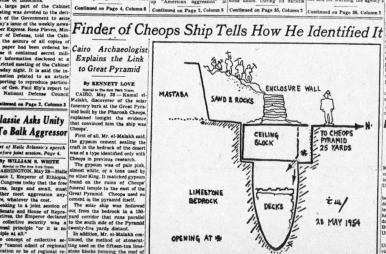

Gordon R. Clapp

Public Works, the Department of Water Supply, Gas and Electricity and the Board of Water Supply. His functions in connection with personnel administration, it

Continued on Page 11, Column 4

I. L. A. TUG MEN JOIN LEWIS' MINE UNION IN EAST COAST VOTE

Local 333 Here Is Nucleus of New Division Aimed at 45,000 Marine Workers

By STANLEY LEVEY

John L. Lewis won a foothold yesterday in the Port of New York.

The president of the United Mine Workers announced the formation of a United Marine Workers Division, composed initially of 9,000 East Coast tugboat, scow and barge workers, and staked out a claim to 45,000 such marine crewmen on the coastal and inland waters of the United States and Canada.

The nucleus of Mr. Lewis' newest appendage is the old Local 333, United Marine Division, of the old International Longshoremen's Asssociation. Since March 5 the 4,000 members of the local have been voting by mail ballot on whether to join forces with the mine union as an affiliate of the U. M. W.'s catch-all District 50.

Yesterday was counting day at the offices of Local 333. But three hours before the ballots had been tallied—and even as the envelopes in which they were mailed were being opened by a committee—Mr. Lewis' press representatives released a prepared announcement on the formation of the new division and the affiliation of the old I. L. A. locals.

When finally computed the vote was 1,857 for leaving the I. L. A. and joining the mine union, and 419 opposed. More than 1,600 members of the local apparently did not vote. In all, 3,942 ballots were sent out.

Merger Backed Elsewhere

Twenty-five hundred other tugboat captains and crewmen in Philadelphia, Norfolk, Va., and Wilmington, N. C., also were reported to have voted overwhelmingly for the merger with Mr. Lewis' union. Members of Local 933-4, composed of New York scowmen, and of Locals 933-5 and 933-1, composed of railroad and tidewater tugmen, also were voting on the question.

The locals seceding from the old I. L. A. had no part in last Wednesday's representation election between the old dock union and the rival American Federation of Labor pier group. In that balloting the I. L. A. had a margin of 319 votes, but 1,792 others were challenged and the processing of them will take at least six weeks.

The formation of the new marine division will give Mr. Lewis possession of a key group in the Port of New York. A strike of towboat crews, who man tugs that move most products in the harbor and that shepherd giant liners to their berths, could seriously affect the economy of the port.

There have been many reports that the old I. L. A. also ultimately would find a home in the mine union. During its darkest

Continued on Page 35, Column 2

U. S. and Five Others Insist Korea Vote Be Under U. N.

By THOMAS J. HAMILTON

Special to The New York Times.

GENEVA, May 28—The United States declared today that the fundamental issue in the Korean question was the supervision of elections by the United Nations. Five of the members of the organization supported the United States.

All six rejected the North Korean proposal, under which a joint North and South Korean commission to supervise elections would be "assisted" by a neutral nations commission.

In emphasizing this stand, Gen. Walter Bedell Smith, Under Secretary of State and head of the

Excerpts from remarks by Smith are printed on Page 2.

United States delegation to the conference on Far Eastern questions, said that "the United States did not come to Geneva to lend itself to the destruction of the United Nations."

General Smith charged that the Communists, in addition to denying that the United Nations had any authority or moral force to deal with the unification of Korea, were erecting "another iron curtain at Geneva" that was intended to shut out any constructive effort at the conference to attain its goals.

He charged that the North Korean proposal would permit "the imposed dictatorship of a minority of the Korean people still living in North Korea to obstruct forever the freely elected representatives of the great majority of the people in Korea."

General Smith declared that, despite a statement May 11 by Vyacheslav M. Molotov, Soviet Foreign Minister, in which the Russian charged that the United Nations flag was used to cover up "American aggression" in

Continued on Page 2, Column 5

JORDAN ABANDONS PALESTINE DEBATE

Quits Case in U. N. Council After Israelis Ask Her to Pledge to Obey Charter

By KATHLEEN TELTSCH

Special to The New York Times.

UNITED NATIONS, N. Y., May 28—Jordan withdrew today from discussions on Palestine in the United Nations Security Council.

The Amman Government's decision came in a brief communication to the Council. This obviously was Jordan's answer to recent Israeli demands that Jordan must commit herself in advance to accept the obligations for peaceful settlement of disputes laid down under the United Nations Charter.

The Jordanian communication was signed by Abdul Monem Rifai, Ambassador to Washington, who was invited to sit at the table during the Council's preliminary debates this month on how to handle the latest round of border disputes between Israel and Jordan. Jordan is not a member of the United Nations. Her charges against Israel were

Continued on Page 4, Column 8

TRANSIT PARLEYS CALLED BY MAYOR

Separate Sessions Planned Tuesday to Explore Crisis—2d Vote Backs Strike

By LEONARD INGALLS

Opposing sides in the city's transit crisis were invited yesterday by Mayor Wagner to meet with him Tuesday at City Hall.

Stressing the "imperative need for uninterrupted transit service," the Mayor asked for separate conferences with members of the Transit Authority and officials of the Transport Workers Union, C. I. O.

Labor advisers to the Mayor said the sessions would be exploratory, and that Mr. Wagner did not profess to have a formula for ending the dispute.

Meanwhile, a union plan to start a strike on the city-owned system June 14 at 12:01 A. M. continued to have unanimous support in the second day of rank-and-file voting. Authority officials proceeded with preparations for an injunction against a walkout and for warning the agency's

Continued on Page 36, Column 2

HIGHWAYS CHOKED AS HOLIDAY STARTS

Police in 24 States Open War on Speeders With Campaign to 'Slow Down and Live'

Highways in the metropolitan area were jammed yesterday as the vanguard of nearly a million families left the city by automobile to spend the three-day Memorial Day week-end elsewhere.

Mostly sunny weather swelled the number of tourists. The roads began crowding up by midday and were heavily traveled until late last night. Railroads, buses and airlines had a heavy passenger volume, with some lines setting new records.

The mild weather set off very heavy travel even though the weather forecast indicated a chance of thundershowers. Today is expected to be partly cloudy, warm and humid with scattered showers. The forecast for tomorrow is a chance of showers in the morning followed by clearing.

With the highways thronged, traffic casualties were expected to mount. The National Safety Council estimated that 35,000,000 automobiles would be on the country's roads and that, if past trends persisted, 340 persons would be killed. Last year the two-day week-end death toll was 241.

'Slow Down and Live' Drive

The roads were heavily patrolled, however, as state and local authorities sought to reduce the toll by showing extra severity toward speedy and reckless drivers. Twenty-four states, including eleven in the northeast, opened at 6 P. M. a "Slow Down and Live" campaign to curb excessive speed.

So far this year, despite an increase in travel, the nation's traffic death toll is downward. For the first four months deaths were 5 per cent below the corresponding period last year, according to the National Safety Council. The death toll in April, the third consecutive month to show a decrease, was 2,620, or 8 per cent below April, 1953.

The Memorial Day holiday opened the vacation season and the warm weather opened the swimming season. The beaches were expected to be thronged.

The New York Chapter of the American Red Cross, citing the fact that ninety-eight persons

Continued on Page 36, Column 4

Finder of Cheops Ship Tells How He Identified It

Cairo Archaeologist Explains the Link to Great Pyramid

By KENNETT LOVE

Special to The New York Times.

CAIRO, May 28—Kamal el-Malakh, discoverer of the solar funerary bark at the Great Pyramid built by the Pharoah Cheops, explained tonight the evidence that convinced him the ship was Cheops'.

First of all, Mr. el-Malakh said, the gypsum cement sealing the craft in the bedrock of the desert was of a type identified only with Cheops in previous research.

The gypsum was of pale pink, almost white, of a tone used by no other King. It matched gypsum found on the ruins of Cheops' funeral temple to the east of the Great Pyramid. Cheops used no cement in the pyramid itself.

The solar ship was hollowed out from the bedrock in a 150-yard corridor that runs parallel to the south side of the Pyramid twenty-five yards distant.

In addition, Mr. el-Malakh continued, the method of stonecutting used on the fifteen-ton limestone blocks forming the roof of the corridor, and the dimensions of the blocks were clear marks of the artisans of Cheops' reign, which was about 2850 B. C

Mr. el-Malakh noted that a projection of the rock bisecting the

Continued on Page 3, Column 3

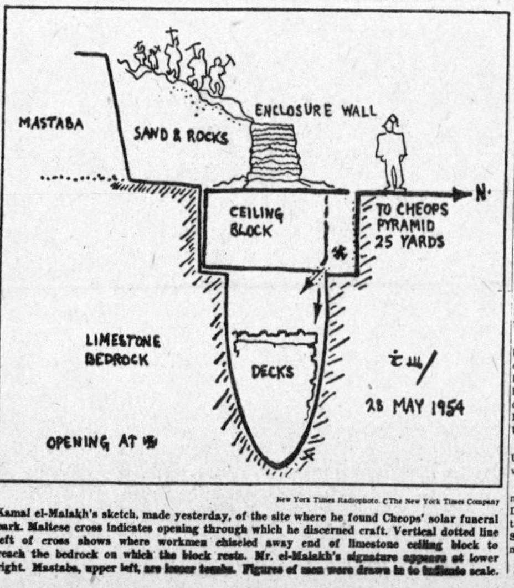

New York Times Radiophoto. ©The New York Times Company

Kamal el-Malakh's sketch, made yesterday, of the site where he found Cheops' solar funeral bark. Maltese cross indicates opening through which he discerned craft. Vertical dotted line left of cross shows where workmen chiseled away end of limestone ceiling block to reach the bedrock on which the block rests. Mr. el-Malakh's signature appears at lower right. Mastaba, upper left, are lesser tombs. Figures of men were drawn in to indicate scale.

Selassie Asks Unity To Balk Aggressor

Text of Haile Selassie's speech before joint session, Page 4.

By WILLIAM S. WHITE

Special to The New York Times.

WASHINGTON, May 28—Haile Selassie I, Emperor of Ethiopia, told Congress today that the free nations, large and small, must together meet aggression anywhere, whatever the cost.

Speaking to a joint session of the Senate and House of Representatives, the Emperor declared that collective security was a universal principle "or it is no principle at all."

The concept of collective security "cannot admit of regional application or be of regional responsibility," he said.

"Nowhere, can the call for aid against aggression be refused by any state, large or small," he added.

The Emperor, against whose

Continued on Page 4, Column 3

Dr. Bunche Cleared By Loyalty Board

By A. M. ROSENTHAL

Special to The New York Times.

UNITED NATIONS, N. Y., May 28—Dr. Ralph J. Bunche received a public and unanimous loyalty clearance today from a United States investigating board.

The six members broke the board's own strict-secrecy precedent to announce that after at least two days of hearings they had decided that there was "no doubt as to the loyalty of Dr. Bunche to the Government of the United States."

Dr. Bunche is Director of the United Nations Trusteeship Division.

Secretary General Dag Hammarskjold, who is known to have Dr. Bunche in mind for promotion to the new post of Under Secretary General, heard the news on his return from Europe

Continued on Page 10, Column 3

Two 'Party Bandits' Are Captured Here

Three men were arrested here yesterday and linked by the police to the wave of week-end robberies at fashionable homes in Westchester County.

Two of the men, the police said, are members of the gang of "party bandits" who for six weeks have spread terror over the Westchester countryside by invading secluded homes where they believed parties to be in progress.

The third man was described as the owner of the get-away car in which the bandits fled the scene of their latest crime, the home of Mr. and Mrs. Herbert L. Scofield in Armonk, N. Y. After that robbery Thursday night, police patrols throughout the county were strengthened, and 1,800 policemen were sworn in as deputy sheriffs so they could pursue

Continued on Page 11, Column 2

Lifting the first of the 15- ton limestone blocks that covered the roof of the chamber.

Looking down on the excellently preserved timbers of the 4550-year-old boat after the first roofing block had been removed.

"All the News That's Fit to Print"

NEWS SUMMARY AND INDEX, PAGE 47

The New York Times.

LATE CITY EDITION
Mostly fair and cooler today.
Fair and pleasant tomorrow.
Temperature Range Today-Max., 72; Min., 56
Temperatures Yesterday-Max., 79.2; Min., 63.1
Full U. S. Weather Bureau Report, Page 47

VOL. CIII No. 35,190. Entered as Second-Class Matter. Post Office, New York, N. Y. NEW YORK, SUNDAY, MAY 30, 1954. Including Magazine and Book Review. SECTION ONE TWENTY CENTS New York City } 50 Mile Zone { Elsewhere Twenty-five Cents

F.B.I. SEIZES 7 MEN AS RED OFFICIALS FOR CONNECTICUT

3 Arrested Here at Secret Meeting, 3 in New Haven, One in West Hartford

CONSPIRACY IS CHARGED

Agents Follow Trio to Art Studio in Harlem — 109 Rounded Up Since 1948

By RUSSELL PORTER

Seven more men were arrested in this area yesterday as Communist party leaders charged with conspiring to advocate the overthrow of the Government by force and violence.

The Federal Bureau of Investigation, which made the arrests, said all seven were officials or functionaries of the party in Connecticut.

It declared that two underground leaders and one open party leader were caught in a raid here. They were attending a secret party meeting in a rented art studio on the third floor of 38 Old Broadway in the West Harlem section. Three others were taken at their homes in New Haven and the seventh, who lives in Hartford, was seized in West Hartford.

The F. B. I. now has rounded up 109 party officials and functionaries since July, 1948. That was when the Government first moved against the party under the conspiracy section of the 1940 Smith Act.

Forty-six have been convicted, including five found guilty by a jury Friday in St. Louis. The first convictions were obtained here in 1949, when the party's eleven top leaders were found guilty after a nine-month trial. Eight party leaders disappeared after being indicted, but three have been caught.

Former Chairman Arrested

The F. B. I. had no addresses for the two underground leaders arrested here. They were:

Simon Silverman, 38 years old, known in the party underground as Sid Taylor, according to the bureau, and former state chairman of the party in Connecticut.

Robert C. Ekins, 46, a sculptor and World War II Army veteran; former party secretary for Connecticut.

The third person arrested here was Jacob Goldring, 39, of 28 Cottage Street, Trumbull, Conn., a college graduate who works as a carpenter. He is former state finance director, press director and former member of the party's state committee in Connecticut.

Those arrested in New Haven were:

Alfred Leo Marder, 32, of 323 Winthrop Avenue, who has been chairman of party sections in New Haven, Hartford-New Britain and Fairfield County.

Joseph Dimam, 34, of 19 Asylum Street, a machinist, who has been the party's secretary in New Haven and press director for Connecticut.

Sidney Sussman Resnick, 32, of 17 Gilbert Street, who has been the party's youth director for Connecticut and chairman of the Connecticut section of the Labor Youth League, which has been cited by the Attorney General as subversive.

The man arrested in West Hartford was James Sherman Tate, 43, of 2006 Main Street, Hartford, who has been a mem-

Continued on Page 25, Column 1

Major Sports News

BASEBALL

The Dodgers beat the Giants yesterday, 4—2, on Pee Wee Reese's two-run homer in the ninth inning. The blow, which came off Sal Maglie, enabled Carl Erskine to notch his fifth victory of the year. In Boston, the Yankees defeated the Red Sox, 10—2.

HORSE RACING

Cain Hoy Stable's Cherokee Rose defeated Open Sesame by a head in the $62,000 Coaching Club American Oaks at Belmont Park. Riverina was third and the favored Queen Hopeful fourth.

TRACK AND FIELD

Penn State, with 32½ points, won the intercollegiate championship at Randalls Island. Manhattan finished second with 25½ points.

GOLF

An Australian, Doug Bachli, upset Bill Campbell of Huntington, W. Va., in the British Amateur final, 2 and 1.

(Details in Section 5)

Finder of Cheops Ship Tells Own Story of Trip Into Past

Egyptian Archaeologist Describes Work on Corridor Holding Funeral Vessels —To Reopen It Briefly This Week

By KAMAL EL-MALAKH

CAIRO, May 29—It was my good fortune to become last Wednesday the first human being in nearly 5,000 years to look upon the solar ship of the night which Pharaoh Cheops built to take him on an eternal voyage through the heavens with the sun.

Cheops believed that the spirit image of the ship, hewn into the immovable rock of the desert, could rise in ghostly fashion from the fixed position of its material form and carry his soul in the company of the immortals journeying with the sun-god Ra.

He ordered architects, stonecutters, carpenters, munitioners and priests to make the vessel and furnish it for his eternal health and happiness. Then he sealed it, over the bedrock hull, with lintel roofing, built of fifteen-ton limestone blocks, joined and covered above and below with pink gypsum cement.

Cheops, like the kings before and after him, built two solar ships of the night—one for each of his royal titles of King of Upper Egypt and King of Lower Egypt. All dynastic kings bore dual titles after Menes, the first dynastic monarch, came from the south and united the two kingdoms around 3,200 years before Christ and about 450 years before Cheops.

I will find a second ship of the night a few yards west of the present discovery in the other half of the sealed subterranean corridor. Cheops' other solar ships, two for the day journey through the heavens and one for ghostly trips to the holy city of Abydos, in Upper Egypt, have long been known. Like all previous solar ships found, they had been stripped by grave-robbers long before any archaeologist saw them. The new discovery, beside Cheops' Great Pyramid and beneath ground trodden by multitudes for centuries, will prove to

Continued on Page 2, Column 4

MOSCOW SAYS U. S. INCREASES DANGER OF ATOM WARFARE

Statement Condemning Pool Plan of Eisenhower Seen as End of Negotiations

By HARRISON E. SALISBURY
Special to The New York Times.

MOSCOW, May 29—Soviet-United States discussions on atomic energy, it was apparent today, have come to a dead end.

Russia warned that there was a "growing threat of war with the use of means of mass destruction."

The conclusion that Soviet-United States talks, initiated last December following President Eisenhower's proposal for a pooling of atomic-energy resources for peaceful uses, have reached a stalemate was drawn by Western diplomats in Moscow after reading a Soviet declaration on atomic questions printed today in Pravda.

The Soviet statement not only made it evident that additional Soviet-United States discussions on the basis of the Eisenhower proposals were unlikely to produce any profitable results, but it went further. The statement warned that there existed in the world today a "growing threat of war with use of means of mass destruction of people" and that this threat was increasing.

New Talks Held Ruled Out

Western observers were particularly impressed that the Soviet statement did not merely express pessimism over President Eisenhower's May 19 statement that the United States was looking for a way to reach world-wide atomic agreement without Russia. The Soviet statement went on virtually to rule out the possibility of further Soviet-United States talks on the basis of President Eisenhower's December proposals.

The Soviet statement charged in effect that behind the facade of negotiations between the United States and Russia, Washington was actually laying the basis for international agreements designed to nullify genuine atomic control and give the United States a true atomic monopoly in the capitalist world.

Thus the Soviet position would appear to be that not only are negotiations with the United States on atomic questions fruitless on the present basis, but in the opinion of the Soviet Union they are creating even bigger atomic dangers.

The Soviet statement charged that when President Eisenhower talked about achieving an international atomic agreement without Russia, what he had in mind was some plan for organizing an "international cartel for atomic energy," or a "kind of atomic Marshall plan."

The Soviet statement, which bore the signature of "Observer," which is frequently used for important declarations in Pravda, said the United States was preparing to call an international meeting of nuclear physicists

Continued on Page 18, Column 5

Associated Press Radiophoto

A SAINT IS CANONIZED: Pope Pius XII sits on throne in St. Peter's Square during the ceremony at which Pope Pius X was canonized by Roman Catholic Church. Standing, second from right in foreground, among kneeling church dignitaries, is Gaetano Cardinal Cigognani, Prefect of Holy Congregation for the Rites, as he implores the Pope to sanctify Pius X.

INDOCHINA PARLEY BIDS 2 COMMANDS STUDY REGROUPING

Nine Powers in Geneva Agree to Summon Military Chiefs on Disposition of Units

VIETNAM TO TOP AGENDA

U. S. Insists Cambodia and Laos Be Treated Differently From the Third State

By THOMAS J. HAMILTON
Special to The New York Times.

GENEVA, May 29—The conference on Far Eastern affairs agreed today to ask the high commands in Indochina to negotiate here next week on the "dispositions of forces" throughout Indochina when a cease-fire is arranged.

The proposal, which was submitted by British Foreign Secretary Anthony Eden, provided that the military talks should begin with "the question of regrouping areas in Vietnam."

Although the proposal was adopted unanimously, the United States, Laos and Cambodia submitted reservations under which they stated that they were agreeing to it only on the understanding that Laos and Cambodia were in a status different from that of Vietnam.

Gen. Walter Bedell Smith, Under Secretary of State and head of the United States delegation, said the United States was agreeing to the proposal only on the understanding that the recommendations would not violate this principle, that they would provide for the withdrawal of Vietminh forces from Laos and Cambodia, and that the proposal was acceptable to all other delegates.

U. S. Reserves Position

He added that the United States, like other delegations, reserved the right to decide for itself whether any of the military experts' recommendations, regarding Vietnam as well as Laos and Cambodia, were "consistent with our firm positions." The Laotian and Cambodian reservations were less specific, but in the same spirit.

Reservations entered by the French Foreign Minister Georges Bidault were: First, France reserved her right to return to the question of Laos and Cambodia at the requisite moment; second, the question of controls and guarantees must be solved in the agreement here on Indochina; third, the military experts will work for the purpose and aims of the conference as a whole.

General Smith reiterated to the eight other delegates the United States view that the forces now "carrying on hostilities" against the Governments of Laos and Cambodia were foreign forces.

"It is essential that any settlement for Laos and Cambodia must provide for the complete withdrawal of these forces from both countries," General Smith declared.

"However, I do not view the proposal made by the United Kingdom as departing from the principle that Laos and Cambodia are in a different situation than Vietnam."

A British spokesman said later that Britain still wanted all Vietminh troops withdrawn from both Laos and Cambodia. He declared that Mr. Eden has submitted the proposal so that the military

Continued on Page 2, Column 3

2 Senate Leaders Deplore McCarthy Plea for 'Leaks'

By The Associated Press.

WASHINGTON, May 29—Two prominent Republicans spoke out today against Senator Joseph R. McCarthy's appeal to Federal employes to disregard security orders in giving him information. One of them was Senator William F. Knowland of California, the Majority Leader.

He said the Eisenhower Administration was just as anxious as Congress to catch traitors and that the Wisconsin Republican was on "dangerous and doubtful ground" in his controversy with the Executive Department.

The other, Senator H. Alexander Smith of New Jersey, in a statement dictated to his office here from Princeton, said he was deeply shocked by what he called "defiance of the Executive in this crisis."

"We cannot tolerate one-man government either in the Executive or in our legislative bodies, Mr. Smith asserted. He added that Senator McCarthy's stand was "beyond belief" and described yesterday's clash of statements as "an Executive-McCarthy contest" instead of an "Executive-Legislative" one.

Mr. Smith, one of General Eisenhower's earliest backers, is chairman of the Senate Labor Committee.

He also took issue with Senator McCarthy for denying some information in his subcommittee files to Democratic members of the group, the Subcommittee on Investigations. "Every member of that committee is entitled to access to all evidence and all information that the chairman is

Continued on Page 24 Column 1

CATAPULT LINKED TO CARRIER BLAST

2 Officers Say They Smelled Hydraulic Oil Burning at Time of Explosion

By JOHN H. FENTON
Special to The New York Times.

QUONSET POINT, R. I., May 29—Two key officers of the carrier Bennington reported today that they smelled "hydraulic oil" burning during a series of explosions that killed ninety-nine men last Wednesday morning.

Testifying at the Navy court of inquiry into the disaster, Comdr. Michael J. Hanley, flight officer of the Bennington, said that he had heard an "unusual noise" from the port catapult, or left-side plane launching machinery, just before the first explosion.

Commander Hanley said that his stateroom was "right under" the port catapult. From experience in a similar stateroom aboard the carrier Hornet, Commander Hanley said, he detected a "much louder noise than usual," following the launching of the last jet.

A moment later, there was a "hissing sound" and the room filled with dense, yellowish smoke. Within a moment, he felt the first of three rapid explosions.

Odor Traced to Catapult

Earlier, Comdr. Howard M. Avery, executive officer, had identified the odor as being associated with the catapult room. He added that he was certain it was not like that of exhaust gases from jet planes.

Explosions and fire racked the Bennington about 6:20 A. M., Wednesday, while the carrier was on training maneuvers some seventy-five miles south of this naval air station.

Thirty-seven of the 201 men who were injured remained in critical condition today. The death toll was expected to rise.

There were strong, but unofficial, reports that when the court reconvened next Tuesday morning, there might be evidence that a faulty safety valve on the port catapult actually triggered the explosions.

Chief Warrant Machinist Griley Goodman who was standing the watch in the No. 1 engine room, volunteered the information that he "lived next to that catapult," and that since last December it had sounded much different than it formerly did in launching. New shock absorber equipment was installed in December.

Mr. Goodwin made his observation at the invitation of the court. He said that the catapult made a "loud whine and a sort of jump." He added that "I don't like it." "The catapult had been

Continued on Page 27, Column 3

Anne O'Hare McCormick Is Dead; Member of Times Editorial Board

Pulitzer Prize Winner in 1937 Interpreted News in Her Column, 'Abroad'

Mrs. Anne O'Hare McCormick, a member of the editorial board of The New York Times, died yesterday at 6:50 P. M. in Doctors Hospital, which she entered as a patient on May 11. Her age was 72. She had lapsed into a coma in the late afternoon and did not regain consciousness.

At her bedside were her husband, Francis J. McCormick and a sister, Mrs. Paul Gill of 7 Gracie Square. Another sister, Mrs. James B. McCalley of Havana, also survives. Mr. and Mrs. McCormick made their home in the Carlyle Hotel.

Anne O'Hare McCormick's wise reportorial pen recorded and interpreted history in the world's most turbulent times. As a peripatetic correspondent, she brought light without heat to her readers out of increasingly complex national and international politics.

She was as much at home in the chancelleries of Europe as she was on the shell-pocked Greek mountainsides, and equally at home in the cratered desert of Israel as in the vast auditoriums during a national election campaign. In whatever part of the shrinking world her dateline put her, the sound, pungent

Arnold Newman

Anne O'Hare McCormick

reports of her conversations and observations won universal praise.

Mrs. McCormick's keen analysis and interpretation were crisp and markedly free of fuzziness and guesswork. In her early work for The Times in the Twenties she astutely recognized, long before most of her colleagues, the coming power of Mussolini.

Although partisan spokesmen

Continued on Page 44, Column 1

PIUS X PROCLAIMED AS SAINT BY POPE

400,000 Outside Vatican See Pontiff Conduct Ceremony Canonizing Predecessor

By HERBERT L. MATTHEWS
Special to The New York Times.

ROME, May 29—Giuseppe Sarto, Pope Pius X, was canonized today in one of the most grandiose ceremonies in the history of the Roman Catholic Church. The ancient ritual was held outside St. Peter's Basilica, permitting hundreds of thousands of persons to take part under the blue skies.

For Pope Pius XII it was a day of personal joy because, as he said in his eulogy of the new saint, "perhaps for the first time in the history of the Church, the formal canonization of a Pope is being proclaimed by one who once had the privilege of being in his service in the Roman Curia."

It had been feared that the ceremony would tax the Pontiff's strength too greatly, for he was desperately ill only a few months ago. It is true that the ritual established by Pope Urban VIII in 1634 and followed ever since was curtailed today to spare Pius XII, but the Pope seemed strong throughout.

There was color everywhere in St. Peter's Square—in the bright blue sky, on the line of Roman pines along the Janiculum, on the sunlit obelisk pointing upward from the midst of the crowd and over the whole towering mass of the largest cathedral on earth.

Throng Fills Big Square

How many thousands there were in the crowd, no one can say, but it is believed that 400,000 to 500,000 persons can crowd into this vast space.

Shortly after 5 P. M. the square was full as the deep tones of the Sistine Choir sang out "Christus Vincit" through loudspeakers, and choirs among the crowd and the pilgrims themselves responded. By 5:30, the Noble Guards were in their places on both sides of the throne, which had been set in front of the central portals of the church, just before the pillars. It was so placed that every person, wherever he stood, could see it. Above it hung a huge banner, now covered up.

Recitation of the Litany of the Saints a little after 5:30 heralded the fact that the procession had started from the bronze doors of the Vatican, led by regular clergy carrying the banners of their orders. Next came the heads of religious orders, bearing lighted candles. The air was so still and soft that the flames twinkled throughout the ceremony. Bishops filed in, hundreds of them, then Cardinals.

At 6:15 a great roar went up from the crowd. Pius XII had emerged from the bronze doors into the square sitting in his sedia gestatoria (the portable throne used for such ceremonies), supported on the shoulders of a dozen grooms and chairmen.

The procession of the Pontiff

Continued on Page 15, Column 3

Thailand Bids U. N. Set Up A Watch on Indochina War

Special to The New York Times.

UNITED NATIONS, N. Y., May 29—Thailand appealed today to the Security Council to take note of the dangers inherent in the situation in Indochina. She asked for the appointment of military observers to keep watch on developments there.

Without referring specifically to points at which the observers might be placed, the letter signed by Thanat Khoman, acting permanent representative of Thailand to the United Nations, implied that a logical point would be on that country's borders. Large-scale fighting has taken

Text of letter from the Thai delegate is on Page 3.

place repeatedly in the immediate vicinity of Thai territory, Mr. Khoman wrote, and there is in the view of his Government "a possibility of direct incursions of foreign troops."

The move, which had been forecast over the last several days, took the form of a letter addressed to the President of the Security Council, Sir Pierson Dixon of Britain. Under the rotation system by which the chairmanship of the Security Council changes according to alphabetical listing, the United States will assume direction of the Council Tuesday.

Because of the long week-end holiday at headquarters of the United Nations over Memorial Day, the only immediate consequence of the Thailand action is expected to be routine circulation of the request among the delegations. British circles said that it was unlikely that any Security Council meeting would be called before next week and that the decision as to a date would then be up to the United States.

Representatives of the Western powers were unanimous in commenting about the absence of any sense of urgency in the Thai communication. The consensus of reaction from the United States,

Continued on Page 3, Column 4

North Carolina Gives Scott Lead for Senate

By JOHN N. POPHAM
Special to The New York Times.

RALEIGH, N. C., Sunday, May 30—Former Gov. W. Kerr Scott held steadily to a slender lead early today in the Democratic primary returns for nomination to the United States Senate seat now held by Alton A. Lennon.

With only 250 precincts missing out of 2,027, Mr. Scott, a leading Southern liberal, had 261,656 ballots to 236,614 for Mr. Lennon. Mr. Scott's majority of approximately 51.5 per cent of all votes counted at that point indicated an unwavering trend that appeared to assure his election.

In this state, victory in the Democratic primary is tantamount to election.

There were five other contestants in the race, none of whom was within hailing distance of the two top contenders. Their total vote, however, made

Continued on Page 37, Column 3

AUSTRALIA KEEPS MENZIES IN POWER

Edge Over Labor May Be Cut From 14 to 6 in the Closest Vote in Nation's History

By ROY L. CURTHOYS
Special to The New York Times.

MELBOURNE, Australia, May 29 — The Liberal and Country party Government led by Prime Minister Robert Gordon Menzies has been returned to office for three more years with a reduced majority as a result of today's elections. It was the closest race in Australia's history.

There were so many keenly contested seats that the Government's majority may vary from two or three to six or seven seats.

The Labor Opposition, led by Dr. Herbert V. Evatt, has definitely gained four seats, but in seven or eight other divisions the Government and Opposition candidates were separated, when the counting ceased tonight, by only a few hundred votes, with many thousands more to be counted.

Seventy-eight per cent of the votes cast had been checked. Only the continuance of the count tomorrow can clarify the situation. All the Cabinet ministers have been returned.

Labor May Gain More

In the last Parliament the Government coalition held 68 seats against the Labor opposition's 53. The tentative status of the parties in the new house is: Government 64, Opposition 57, a reduction in the Government's majority from 14 to 6 after it has provided a Speaker who has only a casting vote.

The electors apparently weighed the prosperity and economic stability that four and a half years of Liberal Government have given Australia against the Labor party's promise of substantial additional social security benefits, and in the result they have struck a pretty close balance.

Norman Makin, former Ambassador to the United States, who was a member of the Government of the late Prime Minister Joseph B. Chifley, but lost his seat in 1949, won the South Australian division of Sturt from a retiring Liberal. But Frank M. Forde, former High Commissioner to Canada, who was deputy leader of the Opposition until 1949, failed to capture the Queensland division of Wide Bay for the Opposition.

Another former Labor Minister who returns to the House is Nelson Lemmon, who, as Labor Min-

Continued on Page 9, Column 3

French Aide Quitting Over Indochina Split

By LANSING WARREN
Special to The New York Times.

PARIS, May 29—Marc Jacquet, Under Secretary for the Indochina States, was reported to have handed in his resignation today, partly because of differences with Foreign Minister Georges Bidault on policy.

It was believed that the resignation would not be made public before Tuesday, when the National Assembly will begin a debate on Indochina.

M. Jacquet, a member of the Gaullist party, has long disagreed with the Government's stand on Indochina. He has favored direct negotiations with the rebel Vietminh and has hoped that such negotiations, rather than an international accord at the Geneva conference, would bring a solution.

Another major factor seen as leading to M. Jacquet's resigna-

Continued on Page 3, Column 1

"All the News That's Fit to Print"

The New York Times.

LATE CITY EDITION
Mostly sunny and cool today. Cloudy and milder tomorrow.
Temperature Range Today—Max., 52; Min., 38
Temperatures Yesterday—Max., 75; Min., 44
Full U. S. Weather Bureau Report, Page 47

Copyright, 1954, by The New York Times Company.

VOL. CIII..No. 35,139. Entered as Second-Class Matter, Post Office, New York, N. Y. NEW YORK, FRIDAY, APRIL 9, 1954. Times Square, New York 36, N. Y. Telephone LAckawanna 4-1000 FIVE CENTS

WILSON OUTLINES A PROGRAM TO BAR 'RISKS' IN MILITARY

Armed Forces Placed Under Same Standards Applied to Federal Civilian Employes

NO REDS TO BE DRAFTED

Order Is Outgrowth of Clash Between McCarthy and the Army Over Peress Case

By W. H. LAWRENCE

Special to The New York Times.

WASHINGTON, April 8—The Eisenhower Administration today put the armed forces under the general security risk standards already applied to civilian Federal employes.

Charles E. Wilson, Secretary of Defense, told the Senate Armed Services Committee the new military personnel security program was designed to "clean out and keep out" persons who were disloyal or "security risks."

The new directive, a result of the clash between the Army and Senator Joseph R. McCarthy, Republican of Wisconsin, provides that "known Communists" will not be drafted or accepted as volunteers.

Those who invoke the Fifth Amendment, which provides protection against self-incriminating testimony, and refuse to answer Army personnel form questions about alleged subversive affiliations or associations will not be accepted as volunteers.

Draftees who invoke the Fifth Amendment "will be accepted into the service and retained on nonsensitive assignments in the lowest enlisted pay grade permitted by law, pending completion of a thorough investigation."

Provides for Discharges

Discharges "under other than honorable conditions" were ordered for any persons whom it would be "inconsistent with the interests of national security" to keep in uniform.

Senator McCarthy's first big fight with the Army this year grew out of the fact that it granted an honorable discharge to Maj. Irving Peress, a New York dental officer who had refused, on Army personnel forms and before Senator McCarthy, to answer questions about his alleged Communist affiliations.

Mr. Wilson said he was ready to give "concrete assurance * * * that the matter of subversives, Communist sympathizers, or other security risks in the armed forces is being carefully worked out."

"Some changes have been made to prevent a repetition of previous mistakes," he said. "Some tightening up has been done to narrow to a minimum the time that we have to tolerate such individuals in order to make sure that we are operating in the national interests, being fair to individuals and at the same time not making it easy for draft dodgers.

"Other steps have been taken to remove any premium that these individuals might get because of their disloyal affiliations or sympathies upon being separated from the service."

There were suggestions from Senator John Sherman Cooper, Republican of Kentucky, and Senator Estes Kefauver, Democrat of Tennessee, that the new program did not provide adequate appeal machinery outside the

Continued on Page 10, Column 3

Tablets Antedating Homer Deciphered

Top, a photograph of one of the clay syllabaries, in which syllables are depicted pictorially. Below, a diagram of the characters. Tablet is about six and one-quarter inches long.

WIRETAPPING BILL IS VOTED BY HOUSE

But Chamber Rules Attorney General Must Get U. S. Court Approval to 'Listen In'

By C. P. TRUSSELL

Special to The New York Times.

WASHINGTON, April 8—The House of Representatives passed today, by a vote of 378 to 10, a bill designed to admit to Federal court trials wiretapped evidence against alleged spies and saboteurs.

To this extent it was a victory for the Eisenhower Administration, which had supported the measure. The two previous Democratic Administrations had failed to attain passage of the same fundamental program. However, the Eisenhower Administration, and especially Herbert Brownell Jr., Attorney General, suffered one setback.

Mr. Brownell had asked that complete control of wiretapped evidence be put into his hands. The House decided, by a vote of 221 to 166, that while the Attorney General could still certify that specific evidence was needed through the interception of communications, a Federal court judge would have to give approval before the wires could be tapped.

During the two-day debate, Mr. Brownell was said to be so firm in his call for sole control as the chief legal officer responsible for the country's internal security, that he would rather see the measure defeated than have final control go to the courts.

Voting Follows Party Lines

At one point in the fight, Representative Charles A. Halleck of Indiana, the Majority Leader, said that the Democrats did not like Mr. Brownell. Citing consistent expressions of faith in debate as to J. Edgar Hoover, director of the Federal Bureau of Investigation, Mr. Halleck proposed that the wiretapping authority be put into his hands.

Representative Ed Edmondson, Democrat of Oklahoma, jumped up to say that Mr. Hoover was on record as not wanting to have such a load on his shoulders. Mr. Halleck withdrew his proposal.

The debate showed that many members were reluctant to condone wiretapping, even under the drastic circumstances of foiling a Communist conspiracy. They asked one another to "forget" partisanship. However, the voting took distinct political lines.

Voting to give the courts the final say were 188 Democrats, who were joined by 32 Republicans and the House's one Independent, Frazier Reams of Ohio.

Continued on Page 12, Column 5

British Architect, in His Leisure Time, Solves the Script Riddle and Shows That Early Greeks Had Ability to Write

By SANKA KNOX

An ancient Greek script that for the last half century and longer has baffled archaeologists and linguists has been decoded finally—by an amateur. The riddle was solved by Michael Ventris, an English architect and leisure-time scholar of pre-classical scripts, who was a cryptographer during World War II.

Implications of Mr. Ventris' findings have stirred the archeological world, and, scholars assume, will be felt in other areas of learning before long.

The writing that Mr. Ventris deciphered on mud-colored clay tablets, sifted from the dust of a long-crumbled civilization in Greece and on Crete, is Greek from the pre-alphabet days 500 years before Homer.

It is a pictographic script, known as a syllabary, of the very time of the great heroes and heroic events of the Homeric epics. It comes from the days—mirrored dimly as yet in the now-deciphered evidence—of the people whom Homer, in the ninth century B. C., called Achaeans.

Immortalized by Homer

From the Achaeans, hundreds of years before Homer's time, came the company that the blind poet immortalized in song and story—Agamemnon, "king of men," and other heroic figures who peopled the "Iliad" and conquered Troy, manned the Argonaut under Jason and knew the travail of the "Odyssey."

And now with the decoding of the syllabary, the earliest Indo-European system of writing yet discovered, comes proof from the Achaeans that they were literate long before the Golden Age of Greece in the fourth and fifth centuries before Christ. It had been assumed for many years that Homer's Achaeans, who belong to the late Bronze Age, nearly 1,000 years before the Greek heyday, were illiterate.

Scholars now call this a false assumption. They point to the tablets found in Greece to prove that writing there went back to about 1500 B. C. The existence of the tablets was not known, however, until 1939, when they were excavated at Pylos. Few were aware of their existence, but the tablets became generally known when they were published twelve years later.

The first full details of the decoding of the script to be published in this country will appear in a day or two in an article written by Mr. Ventris for the scholars' publication, Archaeology.

Inspiration of a Schoolboy

Like Jean François Champollion, the great pioneer in decipherment who solved the riddle of the Rosetta Stone, Mr. Ventris first became fascinated by the mysteries of an ancient civilization as a schoolboy.

It was in 1935, at a lecture by Sir Arthur Evans, who told of his excavations in 1896 on Crete, an island south of Greece, where he found the first tablets to be uncovered. The young Ventris heard how the tablets had resisted all attempts of many scholars, who tried them without avail in a variety of languages—Hittite, Sumerian and Basque.

Mr. Ventris made the study of the tablets his avocation, and the first indications of success came just a few months ago. Champollion had a bilingual text—Egyptian and Greek—to pierce the secret of the ancient Egyptians. Mr. Ventris had no such "crib." His success is said to have come in some measure from modern advances in the science of crytography.

A more general story of the tablets also will be told tomorrow at 10:30 A. M. on a television program of the Columbia Broadcasting System by Casper J. Kraemer Jr., a professor in the Classics Department of New York University. The program, "Here is the Past," is created by

Continued on Page 18, Column 1

HARVESTERS RACE WIND IN THE WEST

Dust Bowl Conditions Grip Southeastern Colorado and Parts of 3 Other States

By SETH S. KING

Special to The New York Times.

LAMAR, Colo., April 7—Farmers in the croplands of southeastern Colorado were caught this week in a frantic race against the wind.

Most of their wheat was either lost entirely or was so badly damaged it would produce little or nothing, and they were now struggling to tie down their soil before what was left of it was snatched up and hurled across the Great Plains.

Until mid-February this area, consisting of the eight counties in the southeastern corner of the state, had favorable moisture condition.

But by early March vicious winds sprang up and began to buffet the exposed land, drying it out and tearing at the roots of the winter wheat, which had just begun to appear.

These winds continued steadily all last month and this week they were still pounding across the plowed fields and pasture lands.

Southeastern Colorado is not alone in this plight. Southwestern Kansas, to a lesser degree, has been hit in the same way. Sections of Texas and Oklahoma have also suffered, although in most parts of these two states, the damage to crops is heavier from lack of rain than from wind erosion.

In the Colorado area many of the sights that became familiar in the great Dust Bowl of the Nineteen Thirties have reappeared. For mile after mile the

Continued on Page 15, Column 2

CITY OFFERS BUSES FARE OR TAX DEAL FOR 1-WAY STREETS

Board Defers Change for 7th and 8th Avenues, but It Is Expected to Act April 29

By JOSEPH C. INGRAHAM

A fare rise to 15 cents or a bus franchise tax cut was indicated yesterday as the price the city would be willing to pay to convert Seventh and Eighth Avenues to one-way operation.

The controversy over the plan of Traffic Commissioner T. T. Wiley to restrict operations on those central Manhattan routes to one-way flow was aired at a two and one-half hour public hearing of the Board of Estimate.

While the board deferred decision until April 29 its members left little doubt that they favored the change but believed the New York City Omnibus Corporation was entitled to financial relief because it would lose some riders as the result of the new pattern.

The company is operating under an interim 13-cent fare that will expire April 30. Both the bus operators and the city contend they are in strong bargaining positions but will try to settle the matter amicably in a series of conferences before the deadline.

The city's position is that it can reduce the fare to the contractural rate of 5 cents if the company does not agree to waive its right to two-way operation on the avenues. The franchise does not expire until Dec. 27, 1958. The company contends that the Board of Estimate must set a fare sufficient to insure a reasonable return and hinted that it would go to court, if necessary, to get equitable treatment.

Tax Reduction Forecast

Before and after the public hearing Mayor Wagner conferred with representatives of the bus company and there were reports that a satisfactory formula would be evolved, with a reduction in the franchise tax the most likely compromise.

As administration leaders have indicated that eventually all main longitudinal routes in Manhattan would be made one-way, the tax cut is favored because it would provide a better long-range solution. However, yesterday's hearing was devoted solely to Seventh and Eighth Avenues.

Under the plan, which probably will go into effect the first week in May, Eighth Avenue and its continuation, Hudson Street, will be restricted to northbound traffic between West Broadway and Columbus Circle. Seventh Avenue and its continuation, Varick Street, will be southbound from the north end of Times Square (just below West Forty-sixth Street) to West Broadway.

At the end of the hearing Mayor Wagner left no doubt of his position when he said:

"I was for one-way avenues

Continued on Page 18, Column 6

WEST BIDS THE U.N. STUDY ALL PHASES OF PALESTINE CASE

It Opposes Arabs' Demand That Security Council Hear Jordanian Protest First

By A. M. ROSENTHAL

Special to The New York Times.

UNITED NATIONS, N. Y., April 8—The West urged the Security Council today to take a look at the entire Palestine situation. It called on the Council to try to get at the roots of Arab-Israeli tensions.

From Lebanon, Arab spokesman on the Council, came sharp opposition. Dr. Charles Malik, Lebanese delegate, insisted that the Council concentrate first on Jordan's complaint against the Israeli attack on the village of Nahhalin on March 28.

Dr. Malik said that it was asking the Arabs too much to ask them to agree to a wide-ranging debate as long as Israel continued her "aggression."

"You cannot at the point of the gun force the Arabs to enter into general debate or to sit around the conference table," Dr. Malik said.

For three hours, Council delegates fought without coming to a decision over whether they should allow a free-swinging debate or take up Jordan's charges first and separately and then Israel's counter-charges against Jordan.

Political Motivations

On the surface, the debate was technical. Actually, it was based on important political motivations. The West now takes the stand that the tensions in Palestine are so great that there is no point in continuing the complaint by complaint, piecemeal method of debate and that the Council should take an over-all look and attempt to find over-all solutions. The Israelis endorse that stand.

The Arabs are standing firm on the position that they are the aggrieved party, that they cannot sit down with aggressors until all aggression ends and they feel secure about the future and that it is the Council's duty to condemn Israeli attacks every time they occur.

Although no vote was taken today, most of the speakers lined up behind the general debate idea. They included the United States, Britain, France, the Netherlands, and Turkey. The West is expected to be able to gather the two more votes needed for a majority.

The Lebanese stand was supported by Andrei Y. Vishinsky of the Soviet Union and Dr. T. F. Tsiang of China. Mr. Vishinsky was in the chair and he backed appeals by Dr. Malik to postpone a decision until the Council meets again Monday afternoon.

The agenda, as it stands now, consists of two items.

One is the Jordanian complaint, submitted on Jordan's behalf by

Continued on Page 3, Column 3

PRISONER OF THE DUST: Merle Frazzee, owner of a farm in Colorado's dust bowl, inspects partly buried disk plow. His section was among those hardest hit by wind storms.

U. S., Canada Speed New Radar Network

Special to The New York Times.

WASHINGTON, April 8—The United States and Canada are going ahead with construction of a new radar fence across the Far North to forewarn both nations of approaching warplanes.

It is designed to give six hours' notice of an approaching attack on the United States.

This joint decision was announced simultaneously in Washington and Ottawa today by Charles E. Wilson, Secretary of Defense, and his Canadian counterpart, Brooke Claxton.

Mr. Wilson disclosed that preliminary work on the new early-warning barrier was "already well advanced." He said the plans had been approved by the Chiefs of Staff of both countries last November.

The fence will be strung

Continued on Page 4, Column 4

SENATORS CAUTION ALLIES ON U. S. AID

Knowland, Other Republicans Urge Delay—Dulles May Go Abroad on Indo-China Issue

By WILLIAM S. WHITE

Special to The New York Times.

WASHINGTON, April 8—Republican Senate leaders warned the Allies today that future foreign aid might depend on their willingness to join the United States in a common front in the Indo-China crisis.

The Eisenhower Administration itself was planning less blunt methods of persuasion.

John Foster Dulles, Secretary of State, was considering flying to London and Paris to appeal to the British and French to go along with his project for "united action" or "united will" against any Communist sweep through Indo-China and on over-all Southeast Asia.

The first response to this proposal in London and Paris had been chilly. Its implications have been accepted by some of the most responsible members of Congress as clearly meaning Allied military action, if necessary, to hold Southeast Asia.

Use of Force Considered

Several members spoke, in public or in private, of the possibility that United States sea and air task forces ultimately might be committed to the Indo-China theatre.

Such a use of force, which certainly would precede any conceivable commitment of ground troops, was said by one influential Senator to be among the "several alternatives" that could be considered under discussion in a great deal of preliminary planning against eventualities.

There was no suggestion that any such intervention was in any sense imminent or was more than one of the thus far academic possibilities.

For the moment, Washington's attention was focused on the Senate.

There, Senator William F. Knowland of California, Republican floor leader, gave to reporters an informal but vigorous statement intended to put great pressure on the French, the British and other associates of this country.

Knowland Warns Allies

Referring to dispatches reporting the rejection abroad, for the time at least, of Mr. Dulles' proposal for a united front, Mr. Knowland declared:

"Since some of the nations with which we are associated have been suggesting that they wait until after the Geneva conference before deciding how to respond to Secretary Dulles' inquiries regarding a collective action that would follow further aggression in Southeast Asia, I find there is a growing sentiment in Congress that perhaps Congress should delay until after Geneva before setting any final policy on appropriations in support of North Atlantic Treaty countries, particularly those that have dragged their feet so far as the European Defense Community is concerned.

"If they want to take a new reading based on Geneva maybe the Congress of the United States may determine it wants to take a new reading based on Geneva and on the Dulles inquiries."

At the Geneva conference, which is scheduled to open April 26, the United States, Britain, France and the Soviet Union propose to sit down with Communist China to discuss possible peace arrangements in Korea and Indo-China as well.

Senator Alexander Wiley, Re-

Continued on Page 2, Column 2

FRANCE WOULD LET OTHERS JOIN WAR IF TALKS COLLAPSE

Paris Drops Its Opposition to Having the Indo-Chinese Conflict Internationalized

STRESSES AID TO ENEMY

French Say Foe's Attacks on Dienbienphu Created New Battle Situation

By DANA ADAMS SCHMIDT

Special to The New York Times.

WASHINGTON, April 8—For the first time France has expressed a willingness to internationalize the anti-Communist front in Indo-China. She has made this conditional on failure of the forthcoming Geneva conference to end the hostilities.

This is a reversal of France's earlier position that, with the Vietnamese troops she is training and the planes, tanks and guns from the United States, she can do the fighting alone.

Allied diplomatic sources explained today that France would welcome an active part by other free nations if the Indo-China hostilities continued after the Geneva conference.

The disclosure of the change was indicated by French representatives in this week's consultations between the United States and other powers interested in Indo-China.

Since last Monday, the State Department has been carrying on what one diplomat called "a vast consultation" on Indo-China policy with France, Britain, Australia, New Zealand, Thailand, the Philippines, and the three Associated States of Indo-China—Vietnam, Laos and Cambodia.

The talks have shown general agreement that Indo-China must be saved, but disagreement as to methods and insistence on further clarification of United States intention, diplomatic sources said.

New Situation Created

The French took the position that the volume of the influx of war materials from China, revealed by intelligence reports during the last three months and now demonstrated in the battle of Dienbienphu, had created a new situation and opened a new phase in the war. In this new phase the French would accept the assistance of Allied powers on the fighting front.

The French command long had sought an all-out battle with the Communist-led Vietminh, believing this was the way to destroy the enemy. But at Dienbienphu, the French have been taken aback by the power of Vietminh artillery, of the Chinese-operated or directed anti-aircraft guns, and generally the extent to which the Vietminh have adopted the tactics of the Communist forces in Korea.

Intense artillery and mortar preparation has been followed by wave upon wave of infantry. Supplies for the troops are trucked in by the Chinese over newly developed roads to the Chinese border.

Under the circumstances, the French held that the Navarre Plan, adopted last September, was to a large extent out of date.

Only last Monday, Secretary of State Dulles in his statement to the House Foreign Affairs Committee referred to the Navarre plan. "There is no reason to question the inherent soundness

Continued on Page 2, Column 4

4 Arabs Walk Out At Rabbi's Remarks

Special to The New York Times.

WASHINGTON, April 8—A Government luncheon today to promote international amity fired Arab-Jewish enmity instead.

Representatives of four Arab nations walked out of a Shoreham Hotel ballroom in protest against a remark by an American rabbi, Dr. Norman Salit of New York, president of the Synagogue Council of America.

The speaker referred to "murders by Jordanians" as he digressed from the subject of a new postage stamp—designed to carry the symbols of faith and freedom around the world—into the delicate arena of Middle East politics.

Distressed United States officials offered instant apologies to no avail. Dr. Salit expressed his regret immediately after the incident.

Before the day ended, more formal measures were taken. Dr.

Continued on Page 3, Column 3

37 Die in Canadian Air Collision; British Comet Is Missing With 21

By The Associated Press.

MOOSE JAW, Sask., April 8—A Royal Canadian Air Force training plane rammed an airliner loaded with passengers today and thirty-seven persons were killed.

There were no survivors from this, Canada's worst airline disaster.

A recheck showed that thirty-six died in the crashed planes and one woman was killed on the ground when two engines and part of the burning cabin of the Trans-Canada Air Lines North Star liner plowed through a house and trapped her in it.

Among the victims were Rodney Adamson, 51 years of age, Progressive Conservative party member of Parliament, and his wife, and Pat Reid, 58, famous northland bush pilot, and his wife.

Thirty-one passengers, including five on company passes, and a crew of four were in the North Star en route from Montreal to Vancouver. The Harvard trainer was piloted by a British solo flier from a training field near Moose Jaw.

The North Star was Trans-Canada's flight No. 9 from Montreal to Vancouver via Toronto, Winnipeg and Calgary. It left Toronto four hours late early today, delayed by intense thunderstorms in western and northern Ontario. Several hours late, it was flying due west and the trainer was flying north.

[A British Comet jet airliner with fourteen passengers and a crew of seven was missing between Cairo and Rome and was presumed to have crashed in the Mediterranean. An air-sea search was under way. All Comets were grounded pending further information.]

Witnesses at Moose Jaw said the

Continued on Page 6, Column 4

"All the News That's Fit to Print."

The New York Times.

LATE CITY EDITION
Little change in temperature; showers and cooler in evening.
Temperatures Yesterday—Max., 89; Min., 71
Sunrise, 6:16 A. M.; Sunset, 7:40 P. M.

VOL. CIV—No. 35,421. Entered as Second-Class Matter, Post Office, New York, N. Y. NEW YORK, SUNDAY, JANUARY 16, 1955. Including Magazine and Book Review. TWENTY-FIVE CENTS

AMERICAS WEIGH ARMS FOR COSTA RICA; U. S. WOULD FURNISH FIGHTER PLANES; PRESIDENT OF PANAMA IS DISMISSED

BUDGET REFORMS SOUGHT TO CLARIFY U. S. COST PICTURE

Experts Ask Major Changes, With Spending Classified by Programs Involved

POLICY GROUP PROPOSED

Report Urges a Joint Capitol Body—President to Offer His Message Tomorrow

Special to The New York Times.

WASHINGTON, Jan. 15—The Committee for Economic Development urged today some major changes in the preparation and form of the Federal budget.

These changes, the committee said in one of its periodic reports on national problems, would give Congress and the public a clearer picture of proposed activities, their relative necessity and their cost.

The changes would include greater use of the "program budget." This would group spending proposals by functions and activities that are directed to the same policy goal instead of a budget breakdown by departments and agencies.

The committee is a nonprofit, nonpartisan economic research and education organization. The budget study was started more than two years ago.

President Eisenhower's Budget Message will go to Congress on Monday.

New Capitol Group Urged

Other changes recommended by the committee included:

¶Creation of a joint budget policy conference as a step toward coordinating expenditure decisions and revenue decisions in Congress. The joint conference would include several Congressional leaders and majority and minority representatives from the appropriations and revenue committees and the Joint Committee on the Economic Report. It would meet after the President had submitted the budget.

¶Improvements in Congressional procedures for considering expenditures and authorization for the President to veto individual items in appropriations bills. Under present law, the President must approve or reject an appropriation bill as a whole.

¶Establishment of a system of annual performance reports and periodic management audits of executive departments and large agencies, and the strengthening of the management staffs of the department secretaries.

Federal Outlay Rise Cited

The committee said that in the year ended June 30, 1954, the Government absorbed about 16 per cent of all the goods and services produced in the country, as against about 5 per cent in 1939 and only 1 per cent in 1929.

"With the Federal Government absorbing about one-sixth of all the goods and services produced in the country, the control of Government expenditures has become vitally important," the committee said.

"The manner in which the budget is prepared in the Executive Branch and the manner in which Congress considers the budget in making appropriations are at the heart of the problem."

The committee said that its proposals were aimed at these "principal weaknesses" in the budget process:

¶"The budget contains too

Continued on Page 71, Column 4

A Military 'Idlewild' To Open in Jersey

By RICHARD WITKIN
Special to The New York Times.

McGUIRE AIR FORCE BASE, N. J., Jan. 15—This airfield at the edge of Fort Dix, an uncongested fighter base in recent years, is about to become a major airline station—an Idlewild in uniform.

The Military Air Transport Service, a global airline, with routes penetrating far off the tourist beat, will begin scheduled operations here about April 1. The new service will make McGuire — named for Maj. Thomas B. McGuire Jr. of Ridgewood, N. J., a Medal of Honor hero shot down in the Philippines in January, 1945—the busiest military air terminus in the country.

Air Force and Army engineers have been working almost three years getting the field ready. They have been expanding runways, putting up a passenger

Continued on Page 66, Column 1

TO OUR READERS
In New York City and the Suburbs

Effective today the newsstand price of The New York Times Sunday edition in New York City and suburbs is 25 cents a copy.

Continuing and substantial increases in the cost of producing the Sunday Times make this new price necessary.

OTIS' ULTIMATUM GIVEN IN YONKERS

It Is: Cut Costs or Elevator Company Will Move—Similar Warning in Harrison, N. J.

By STANLEY LEVEY
Special to The New York Times.

YONKERS, Jan. 15—The Otis Elevator Company issued an ultimatum today to 2,100 employes and city officials. It said: Cooperate to cut costs or the company will move to a new plant in the Midwest.

The warning came from Le Roy A. Petersen, Otis president, and was delivered to an invited audience of 2,500 at the Brandt Theatre. A similar speech was made to a gathering of workers, their families and municipal authorities in Harrison, N. J., where the company operates another plant.

Otis has been part of this city's industrial fabric for 101 years. It has a local yearly payroll of $10,000,000 and is one of the community's major taxpayers. Word of the company's possible removal came as the city sought to regain its economic balance after the departure a few months ago of the Alexander Smith Carpet mills to a new location in the South.

Mr. Petersen did not base his appeal for lower production costs and reduced taxes on financial difficulties and poor business. In fact, he stressed that the concern was in a highly favorable economic position.

No Financial Difficulties

"These statements," he said, "should not be interpreted as indicating that the Otis Elevator Company has ceased to be a profitable company or is on the verge of becoming an unprofitable one.

"On the contrary it is anticipated that since our income is derived from a variety of sources * * * the annual report for 1954 will show an increase over the previous year in sales and earnings. In addition, it is believed that our backlog will assure a profitable level of operations in 1955."

The real problem, Mr. Peterson declared, is the increasing number of competitors who operate on a low-cost "hit-and-run" basis. Confronted with loss of its competitive position, he added, the company recently conducted an extensive study of all its operations. One of the conclusions was that:

"An annual saving in manufacturing costs of several million dollars could be secured by building a single plant to replace the Yonkers and Harrison plants and that this plant should be located in the Middle West near the geographical center of our elevator market."

Will Not Hesitate to Move

About half of this saving, he continued, could be achieved in the Yonkers and Harrison plants "providing we secure the enthusiastic and understanding cooperation of our employes and of the city authorities." But this must be forthcoming "with a minimum of delay," he said.

Otherwise, Mr. Petersen warned, "if we are unable to bring about a reduction in these costs in our present plants, we will have no choice but to transfer our manufacturing as soon as possible to a new Midwestern plant—and we will not hesitate to do so if it becomes clearly necessary."

Members of the audience sat through the talk quietly. There was scattered applause when the company president walked from the wings to a mid-stage lectern. There was no interruption of his speech and no visible reaction at its conclusion. His listeners filed quickly and silently from the big theatre.

Mr. Petersen offered no specific program for cutting costs. He said "concrete proposals" would be given this week to officials of Local 453, International Union of Electrical Workers, C. I. O., rep-

Continued on Page 77, Column 5

LODGE 'CONFIDENT' OF FLIERS' RELEASE BUT SOME DOUBT IT

U. N. Delegate and Senators Disappointed Over Failure to Win Liberty at Once

Special to The New York Times.

WASHINGTON, Jan. 15 — Henry Cabot Lodge Jr., United States representative to the United Nations, remained "confident" today, amid expressions of doubt and disappointment, that Communist China would release the eleven imprisoned American airmen.

Mr. Lodge expressed his optimism at Washington National Airport as he returned with the Secretary of State, John Foster Dulles, from a visit to the headquarters of the United States Strategic Air Command at Omaha, Neb.

President Eisenhower yesterday urged calmness in the face of "disappointment" over the failure of the United Nations Secretary General, Dag Hammarskjold, to win the immediate release of the airmen, held since the Korean war. The Secretary General returned this week from a mission to Peiping.

From Capitol Hill also came expressions of disappointment that the Hammarskjold mission had not produced immediate release of the fliers.

Secretary Dulles, as he stepped from an Air Force plane with Mr. Lodge, referred all questions about the prisoners to Mr. Lodge.

Disappointment Acknowledged

However, the fact that the two United States diplomatic officials had spent the last twenty-four hours on a trip together appeared to add significance to Mr. Lodge's remarks.

Ambassador Lodge said he was "confident" the prisoners would be freed, but declined to say when he thought the release would take place.

"Naturally there is disappointment that their immediate release was not effected," he added.

Both Mr. Dulles and Mr. Lodge said they had no "plans" to see President Eisenhower this weekend. Mr. Lodge added he expected to return to New York this afternoon.

He received an account of Mr. Hammarskjold's meeting with Chou En-lai, Premier and Foreign Minister of Communist China, soon after the United Nations official returned Thursday. He said he thought the United Nations Secretary General would make public a full and formal report.

Although they went to Omaha separately, Secretary Dulles, with State Department aides, and Ambassador Lodge returned this afternoon in the same plane. Another Air Force plane with Herbert Hoover Jr., Under Secretary of State, flew in from Omaha at the same time.

Secretary Dulles' trip to Omaha, though he had scheduled it six weeks previously, caught Washington by surprise. In fact

Continued on Page 14, Column 1

SOVIET AGAIN BIDS FOR GERMAN UNITY MINUS ARMS PACTS

Offers Parley, 'Normal' Bonn Ties if West Gives Way—U. S. Ridicules Proposal

By The Associated Press

MOSCOW, Jan. 15—The Soviet Union renewed its demands today for four-power talks on reuniting Germany and offered meanwhile to "normalize relations" with the Bonn Republic.

But it made both conditional upon Western rejection of the Paris accords for arming West Germany.

[A United States State Department spokesman ridiculed the Soviet offer. He called it another transparent effort by Moscow to block ratification of the Paris accords and predicted that it would have "no more success than the other efforts in this respect."]

Moscow warned that implementing the Paris accords to bring West German troops into the Western defense bloc would result only in "perpetuating the division of Germany," and that the Soviet Union would strengthen its ties with East Germany and build up a combined effort of its Eastern allies to counter the Western grouping.

These offers and warnings were contained in a "declaration of the Soviet Government on the German question" read to Western correspondents hastily summoned to a news conference by the Foreign Ministry press chief, Leonid F. Ilyichev.

Not a Diplomatic Note

The declaration was not made in the form of a diplomatic note to the Western powers and therefore its full significance was difficult to assess. It was part of the campaign the Kremlin has been carrying on for months to block ratification of the Paris accords.

The French National Assembly already has ignored such Soviet warnings and has adopted the accords. They are headed for the French Council of the Republic, or upper house, for almost certain final ratification.

It was evident that the new Soviet declaration was aimed specifically at West Germany's Parliament, which is scheduled to take up ratification of the accords soon.

"The German people must make their choice of which route they are going to take," the Soviet declaration said. "One way leads to reunification and normal relations with all the states of Europe. This way excludes the participation of one or another part of Germany in any military grouping directed against other states and could best be obtained by the inclusion of Germany in a European collective security system.

"The other way to which it [Germany] is drawn by the Paris agreements is a way of perpetuating the division of Germany and the establishment of militarism in

Continued on Page 31, Column 1

EX-CHIEF IS JAILED

Assembly Accuses Him After Plotter Tells of Remon Killing

By SYDNEY GRUSON
Special to The New York Times.

PANAMA, Jan. 15 — Ricardo Arias Espinosa, 42 years old, was sworn in as Panama's President today shortly after the National Assembly, meeting in a dramatic pre-dawn session, impeached and dismissed President José Ramón Guizado.

Guizado, 55, was named as one of the men back of the murder of President José Antonio Remon, who was killed by machine-gun fire at the Juan Franco race track here thirteen days ago. It was Guizado, as First Vice President, who succeeded President Remón. President Arias Espinosa had been Second Vice President in the Remón Administration.

A commission of the Assembly is expected to be named Monday to prepare formal charges against the accused former President. This evening Guizado was transferred from his home, where he had been under house arrest since Friday afternoon, to a prison in the heart of this city.

As the story behind the murder of President Remon reached its climax, the police began releasing many of the thirty persons held in connection with the murder. Among those released were Arnulfo Arias, another former President of Panama, a long-time political foe of President Remón, and Irving Martin Lipstein of New York.

Situation in Control

Mr. Lipstein, who had been on a holiday tour of Central America, arrived in Panama on Jan. 2, the day of President Remón's murder, and was arrested when he tried to leave the country. His story that he had been looking at ships going through the Panama Canal at the time of the shooting was verified.

The new Government, backed strongly by the police force that President Remón once headed, appeared to be in complete control of the situation. There were no extra policemen or soldiers in evidence in the streets here tonight.

That the police were ready to break the mystery of the Remón assassination had been evident for more than twenty-four hours, from the moment they surrounded the impeached President's home in the city's residential district, two blocks from the

Continued on Page 2, Column 3

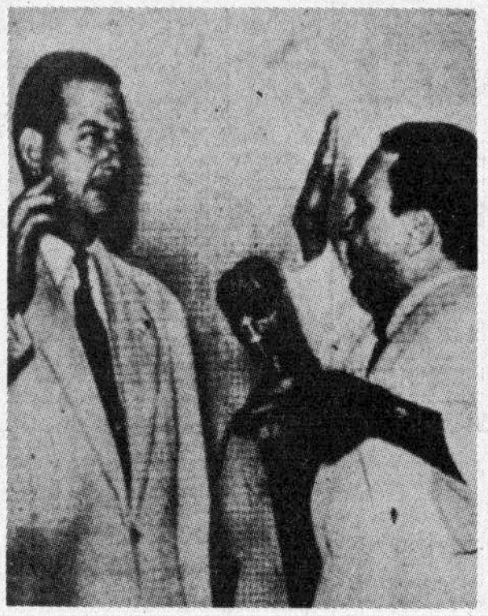

Associated Press Wirephoto (via U. S. Navy Radio)

PANAMA GETS NEW PRESIDENT: Ricardo Arias Espinosa, left, being sworn in by Assembly president, Meliton A. Graell.

Nehru Fights Andhra Reds In Whirlwind Speech Tour

By A. M. ROSENTHAL
Special to The New York Times.

VIJAYAVADA, India, Jan. 15—Prime Minister Jawaharlal Nehru appealed today for election support to prevent Andhra from becoming the first Communist-ruled state in India. The Indian leader has been making this appeal for the last two days as his ten-year-old plane carried him from town to town in Andhra.

The fight against the Communists in this state, a stronghold of the Communist party, will be taken to the election boxes beginning Feb. 11.

At least 110,000 persons came to Vijayavada from the countryside today. It was the biggest day of the year—a chance to see "Panditji" Nehru and to celebrate the rice harvest festival at the same time. Thousands of families, dressed in festival-time best, spent the night traveling by bullock-cart to see the Prime Minister, or to listen to his voice carried by loudspeakers to the crowd sitting on the police parade grounds.

Mr. Nehru, who faced a crowd of about 20,000 in Vishkhapatnam yesterday, did not give the people anything like an election pep talk. The only thing he said that came near being a promise was that the Government would try to end unemployment within ten years.

Perched on a bench on a fifteen-foot-high platform, Mr. Nehru slowly and quietly developed the theme that the battle against the British was as nothing compared with the battle ahead to achieve a Socialist state and lift up living standards. Those goals, said Mr. Nehru, can be reached only by a unified people—and the Communists are a force deliberately making for disunity.

Crowds Looking for Fun

A politicking fever has spread through this state and everbody seems to enjoy the filip of excitement it brings. All along the rutted back roads of Andhra fly the Commnist red flag and the spinning wheel banner of Mr. Nehru's Congress party. Almost every house has slogans painted on it and almost every village in this land of palm trees and green fields has its political rallies.

Both sides have brought their national leaders into the fight and they are making the Andhra the equivalent of whistle-stop tours, riding jeep or bicycle from one village square to another.

Each side is also keeping an eye out for entertainment value. In one village the Congress party paraded 100 pairs of yoked bullocks—the party symbol. Up and down the country roads traveling troupes of Communist song and dance men have put up platforms and lights and are giving political shows for the villagers who dearly love any kind of dramatic performance. Large crowds show up for the Communists and larger crowds for the congress.

But politicians who know

Continued on Page 28, Column 3

EUROPE'S ECONOMY FOUND VIGOROUS

Most Experts Call Outlook for '55 Favorable—Others Doubt Validity of Signs

By MICHAEL L. HOFFMAN
Special to The New York Times.

GENEVA, Jan. 14—European economic analysts and commentators, who take their time about such things, have by now given 1955 a pretty good once-over and found the prospects fine.

This season's end-year reviews and forecasts in various European countries leave the reader of any substantial number of them with the curious feeling that the pundits are looking for problems without being able to find them.

One of the most influential, Richard Fry, financial editor of The Manchester Guardian, acknowledged frankly that he could not find much wrong with the way things had turned out in 1954 in Britain.

From Belgium, Italy, Western Germany, Austria, Sweden and even France, long a laggard in economic growth, the reports repeat almost monotonously that production is up and expected to continue rising, agricultural productivity is up and expected to improve, unemployment is down

Continued on Page 4, Column 1

Secret Siberian City Linked to Uranium

By THEODORE SHABAD

A large Siberian city has arisen under unexplained circumstances in the last few years in one of the Soviet areas closed to foreign travel.

Redistricting data published recently in Moscow for the forthcoming election to the Supreme Soviet of the Russian Federated Republic not only list Norilsk, the booming city, as a centrally administered unit, but allot it a separate election district. Election districts in the Russian Republic usually have a population of about 150,000 persons each.

Norilsk is situated in the so-called Taimyr National District, an administrative area of northern Siberia that has been closed to foreigners, according to a recent State Department announcement. In the last Russian Republic elections in 1951,

Continued on Page 27, Column

COUNCIL IN SESSION

Colombia Offers Plan at Emergency Meeting Still On at 5 A. M.

By ANTHONY LEVIERO
Special to The New York Times.

WASHINGTON, Sunday, Jan. 16—The Council of the Organization of American States weighed early today a proposal calling upon the American republics to provide war material to Costa Rica to help her resist aggression.

Meeting in an extraordinary session that was still under way at 5 A. M., the twenty-one nation Council heard the United States pledge immediate military assistance in the form of armed aircraft as soon as the Americas' group approved Costa Rica's request for immediate aid.

Henry F. Holland, Assistant Secretary of State for Inter-American Affairs, the United States representative at the session, also offered fighter planes for sale to Costa Rica at "a laughable price." The Costa Rican Ambassador, Antonio Facio, said his country would provide pilots to fly the aircraft.

[The Costa Rican General Staff said loyal troops had defeated rebels in a three-hour battle at Santa Rosa, The Associated Press reported.]

Figueres Heads Troops

At 4:30 A. M., Ambassador Antonio Facio of Costa Rica said President José Figueres had assumed command of troops in the field.

The Council was acting on a draft resolution presented by Ambassador Cesar Julio Delgado of Colombia. This resolution, in its operative part, called upon the American republics' governments, "in position to do so," to "make available to the Costa Rican Government material of defense that she requires to defend herself against the attack of which she is a victim."

The resolution stated that action was urged on the basis of the Costa Rican plea for assistance and in view of reports received here from the O. A. S.'s investigating committee, now in Costa Rica.

It quoted the commission as saying that Costa Rica lacked planes or "necessary arms" to "defend herself against the attacks of foreign planes that are now arriving in the hands of the revolutionary forces."

Provision for Aircraft

Mr. Holland submitted an amendment shortly after 4:30 A. M. providing for the sale of planes to Costa Rica in addition to whatever other military aid might be rendered by the organization. The council recessed and then went into an executive session to consider this amendment.

The Council, scheduled to meet at 2 A. M., went into session at 2:35 A. M. because of the problem of calling the Ambassadors at that late hour.

Mr. Holland told the Council that if it voted to send aircraft, the United States would have them in Costa Rica today—Sunday. A decision of this kind would require a two-thirds vote of the Council and would be historic.

Never since the Rio de Janeiro Treaty went into effect on Dec. 3, 1948, had the O. A. S. voted military assistance to suppress aggression. The treaty has been invoked, however, to end disputes by negotiations on two previous occasions.

Secretary Holland disclosed that Costa Rica had requested the United States to send four F-47 fighter planes to repel invading aircraft. It was believed that they would be adequate to hold the rebels.

"My answer is that the Organization of American States is handling the problem, as it should be," said Mr. Holland. "We should continue to try to solve the situation, but within O. A. S."

"The United States cannot send the aircraft unless the O. A. S. decides that it should be done. If O. A. S. says yes, my Government will provide the planes," he added.

Secretary Holland said he was

Continued on Page 3, Column 1

Part of Little America Floats Away

Bay of Whales Gone, Byrd's Base Split in Ice Pressure

By WALTER SULLIVAN
Special to The New York Times.

LITTLE AMERICA, Antarctica, Jan. 14—The jest of yesterday proved to be fact today as the U. S. S. Atka arrived here.

The Bay of Whales, carrying with it the six Douglas DC-3's left here by the 1947 Byrd expedition, has gone to sea on two or more icebergs. The tent city where almost 200 men lived in 1947 has been split in two. Fragments of one tent are dangling from the face of the sheer ice cliff overlooking the Ross Sea.

What has taken place is a cataclysm of the Antarctic, the "calving" of the shelf ice. A triangular section of the continental icecap 600 feet thick and running sixteen miles inland from the former shoreline has cracked loose and floated away.

The jest that came true was made aboard the Atka during her approach to Little America. As a practical joke a message was fabricated indicating the Ross Shelf Ice had broken out far inland, carrying Little America with it. Although some of the earlier camps were spared, that, in essence, is what has happened.

The missing section formed the west side of the Bay of Whales. Flowing ice movements drove it against the east side of the bay during the years since man was last here in 1948. The impact not only cracked off the main triangular section to the west but knocked out a part of the eastern shore of the bay, destroying the air base of the 1947 Navy project led by Rear Admiral Richard E. Byrd and known as Operation High Jump.

The earlier Byrd camps at Little America appear to be intact and were visited today by helicopter. Nevertheless, Little

Continued on Page 17, Column 1

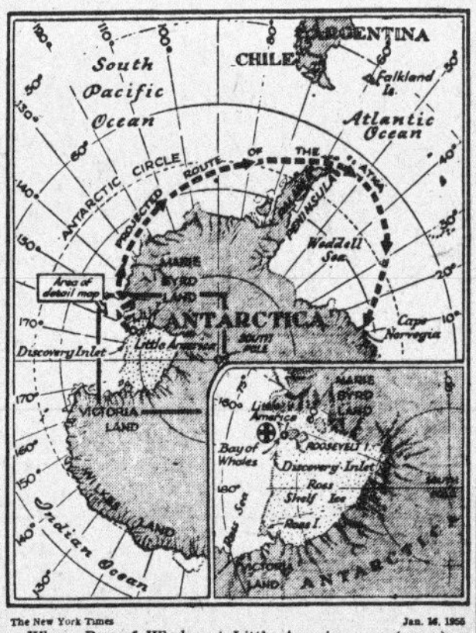

Where Bay of Whales at Little America was (cross)

"All the News That's Fit to Print"

The New York Times.

LATE CITY EDITION
Mostly cloudy with occasional rain today. Partly cloudy tomorrow.
Temperature Range Today—Max., 40; Min., 31
Temperatures Yesterday—Max., 32.7; Min., 14.8
Full U. S. Weather Bureau Report, Page 27

VOL. CIV..No. 35,427. Entered as Second-Class Matter. Post Office, New York, N. Y. NEW YORK, SATURDAY, JANUARY 22, 1955. Times Square, New York 36, N. Y. Telephone LAckawanna 4-1000 FIVE CENTS

4 CONVICTS GIVE UP TO CITIZEN GROUP AFTER 3-DAY SIEGE

Committee of Seven, Selected by Rebel Boston Felons, Arranges Surrender

HOSTAGES ARE RELEASED

'No Deals' Made, Editor Says—Prisoners Must Face Their Punishment

By JOHN H. FENTON
Special to The New York Times.

BOSTON, Jan. 21—Seven unofficial peacemakers walked without escort across a no-man's-land at the Massachusetts State Prison today and brought a passive end to a siege of four desperate convicts.

At 2:27 P. M., nearly eighty-three hours after the four had sworn that they would have freedom or die in the attempt, the men tossed guns and knives on a table and surrendered. The convicts themselves had named the negotiators.

Immediately, five guards who had been held hostage since 5 A. M. Tuesday, and six other convicts who had been caught in the swirl of events, were released unharmed.

Erwin D. Canham, editor of The Christian Science Monitor, as spokesman for the peacemakers, emphasized that there were no deals or conditions made in the surrender. He pledged his personal honor, and that of his colleagues, to work for better conditions in the prison.

Mr. Canham said that as far as he was concerned, the four would face court trial for their parts in the disturbance and be given such punishment as might develop. He said that their principal concern was "hope."

Quick Trial Promised

Governor Herter said the quartet would be tried quickly for their offense. Attorney General George Fingold said he personally would prosecute the cases. He did not specify what charge would be brought against the men. One possible charge—holding guards as hostages—could add twenty year terms to their already lengthy sentences.

Tonight, the four convicts were back in solitary confinement.

Theodore (Teddy) Green, 39-year-old bank robber and prison escape artist, wept near the end of the conference, Mr. Canham reported. He quoted the convict as saying:

"I've done a lot of bad things. Evil things. My only wish is that some time I might do a good thing. Like giving my eyes so that a blind child might see or my body so that men could understand disease better. Isn't there some way I could do something good?"

Two days ago, Green had wept as he turned down a plea by his daughter, Toby, 16, to "do the right thing."

The other rebelling convicts who capitulated were Joseph A. Flaherty, 32, rapist and associate editor of the prison magazine, "Mentor"; Fritz O. Swenson Jr., 31, a lifer on a second-degree murder charge, and Walter H. Balden, 38, former paratrooper and armed robber.

The full committee of seven had two conferences with the

Continued on Page 28, Column 2

7 on Lost Navy Plane Saved in Mid-Pacific

By The Associated Press.

HONOLULU, Saturday, Jan. 22—The Navy said early today the transport Fred C. Ainsworth had rescued all seven survivors of a twin-engined Navy amphibian forced down Wednesday night in the Central Pacific.

Only a few hours before the rescue the seven air men had transferred from their life raft to a thirty-three-foot lifeboat dropped by an Air Force plane. No further details were available immediately.

The lifeboat was about 665 miles northwest of Kwajalein, destination of the plane that developed engine trouble while flying from Johnston Island.

The survivors reported by a walkie-talkie dropped to them that there were no casualties, but some fever had developed.

The Ainsworth will bring the men on to Pearl Harbor, the Navy said, and should arrive

Continued on Page 7, Column 6

Winter's Coldest Day Brings Low of 14.8°

For the first time this year, the temperature yesterday dropped below 20 degrees, producing the coldest reading of the winter—14.8 at 7:50 A. M.

Moreover, the cold wave that has gripped the city for eleven days, with temperatures under 40 degrees, is due to continue today. The Weather Bureau forecast occasional rain with a high between 35 and 40.

Yesterday's high was recorded at 4:10 P. M., when the thermometer registered barely over freezing at 32.7 degrees. In Elizabeth, N. J., a temperature of 13 was the lowest for the date in a quarter of a century.

With a winter's low of 7 degrees in Ossining, N. Y., the ice of the Hudson River thickened for a half a mile out from shore. Sentries at Sing Sing Prison kept a constant watch near the prison dock for any prisoners who might try to scale the ten-foot fence in an attempt to escape over the ice.

LITTER DRIVE ADDS 200 TO CITY PATROL

Mayor Orders Budget Action at Once for $800,000 to Augment Sanitation Staff

By CHARLES G. BENNETT

The City Administration yesterday reinforced the present campaign to sweep litterbugs from New York's streets.

Mayor Wagner directed immediate budgetary authorization for 200 new sanitation patrolmen to bolster the Sanitation Department's existing fifty-man anti-litter staff. The 200 men will cost the city $800,000 a year.

Announcement of this development in the "clean city" drive was made by Budget Director Abraham D. Beame as Sanitation Commissioner Andrew W. Mulrain put in his departmental budget request for 1955-56.

Mr. Mulrain asked Mr. Beame at the budget hearing for $78,423,585 to cover routine appropriations for the fiscal year beginning next July 1. In addition, he sought supplemental items to be approved if the city was able to raise additional funds.

Smaller Force Accepted

Funds for "the litterbug squad," as well as $2,287,995 to extend alternate-side-of-the-street parking for an additional 1,285 curb miles, were requested in the supplemental schedules. The latter program applied to 925 curb miles at the end of 1954.

The Commissioner recalled that he had asked earlier this month for 1,000 sanitation patrolmen at a cost of $3,500,000. Although he said he was convinced that a force of this size was necessary for "rigid enforcement of the law," he said he would be willing to accept the smaller number "as a start" because of "the paucity of funds available."

Mr. Mulrain said the 200 additional jobs would give his department a roster of 13,600 men. The new special patrolmen, he explained, will be appointed as soon as possible from an assistant foreman's promotion list.

The anti-litter squad will wear blue uniforms with a "D. S." insignia on the collars and they may be armed, Mr. Mulrain said. They will have a short course at the Sanitation Training Center, 155 Ryerson Street, Brooklyn.

Cleaned Streets Soon Littered

"While our alternate-side parking program has enabled us to perform an efficient street cleaning job," Mr. Mulrain told Mr. Beame, "our work is very often nullified by the carelessness and indifference of many of our citizens. Soon after a typical street is cleaned, it becomes littered with discarded debris."

Mr. Mulrain's routine budget requests were $4,488,560 higher than his department's 1954-55 budget.

Eight city agencies put in requests for a total of $149,631,683 yesterday; an increase of $16,686,699 over their current appropriations. To date, sixty-eight of the city's 114 agencies have requested $226,581,880, of which $14,282,077 was in supplemental schedules.

The requests of the sixty-eight departments were $14,152,196 above current allocations in routine budgets and $28,434,273 higher in total requests, routine and supplemental. In all, 3,662 new jobs have been requested for

Continued on Page 6, Column 6

CONSUMERS' PRICES LOWEST SINCE '53, U. S. REPORT SHOWS

Index Also Drops 0.5% for the Entire Year—Food Costs' Decline a Major Factor

By CHARLES E. EGAN
Special to The New York Times.

WASHINGTON, Jan. 21—The United States Consumers Price Index last December dipped to its lowest level since May, 1953. It also showed a drop for the entire calendar year, for the first time since 1949.

Figures issued today by the Bureau of Labor Statistics showed a decline of one-half of 1 per cent from January, 1954 to December. The drop for the 1949 calendar year was 1 per cent.

Most of the decrease in consumer prices shown in the bureau's year-end check was reported caused by lower food prices. Declining food prices also accounted for the over-all dip in the index for the year.

The index, with 1947-49 prices equaling 100, stood at 114.3 at mid-December. It had reached 114 points in May of 1953, but by mid-December of 1953 had climbed to 114.9 points.

Although the recent drop has slight it attracted wide attention because declines have become rare since 1939. The rise in the Consumers Price Index has been continuous since then except for 1949 and 1954.

Food Costs Decline

A drop in food costs, notably for eggs, pork chops, chickens, lettuce and oranges, was the major influence on December's decline from the November index of 114.6 points. However, there also were other factors.

The report showed that prices were lower in December for transportation, apparel, reading and recreation, personal care, and the "other goods and services" category. Fuel, residential rent and medical costs were higher.

Egg prices last month were down seasonally about 8 per cent, according to reports in forty-three of the forty-six cities included in the index. Prices of pork chops dropped 5 per cent between November and December but ham prices rose slightly. Prices of frying chickens dropped about 3.5 per cent during the month and oranges averaged 8 per cent below November prices.

In its summarization, the Bureau of Labor Statistics said that the greatest month-to-month change in the average of all goods and services prices during last year had been 0.3 per cent.

The bureau made a special note of the fact that residential rents appeared to be leveling off for the first time since mid-1947.

Continued on Page 6, Column 2

Associated Press Wirephoto

U. S. CAPTIVES OF CHINESE REDS: These men playing cards are Air Force personnel held in Chinese jail. Photograph was brought to U. S. by U. N. Secretary General Dag Hammarskjold and released last night by the Department of Defense. It had no date. From the left: Daniel C. Schmidt of Scotia, Calif.; John W. Thompson of Orange, Va.; William H. Baumer of Lewisburg, Pa.; Wallace L. Brown of Banks, Ala., and Harry M. Benjamin Jr. of Worthington, Minn.

REBELLION ENDED, COSTA RICANS SAY

Field Chiefs Reveal Capture of 2 Key Towns—Bulk of Foe Reported Fleeing

By SYDNEY GRUSON
Special to The New York Times.

LIBERIA, Costa Rica, Jan. 21—Jubilant field commanders declared today that "the fight is over" after disclosing the fall of two key rebel-held towns to Government troops.

La Cruz, on the Inter-American Highway about five miles from the nearest point of the Nicaraguan frontier, was taken by Government forces yesterday afternoon. Puerto Soley, on Salinas Bay, four miles west of La Cruz, fell shortly afterward to the same troops.

Col. Francisco Orlich, the Government's northern commander, and Col. Rodolfo Quiros, chief of staff, said the bulk of the rebel force was fleeing across the northern border into Nicaragua. They said isolated pockets were cut off in the woods and mountains of Saint Elena Peninsula jutting into the Pacific Ocean west of Santa Rosa.

For all intents and purposes they agreed the war was over

Continued on Page 5, Column 2

Tachens Evacuation Begins; Americans Are Taken Off

By The United Press.

TAIPEI, Formosa, Saturday, Jan. 22—The evacuation of non-combatants from the Tachen Islands, including United States military advisers, nurses and civilians, has already begun, informed Chinese Nationalist sources disclosed early today.

A high Nationalist official hinted that the Chinese Nationalist Army would soon follow out of the Tachens. He said bitterly, "You don't have to guess (our intentions) now. Secretary of State John Foster Dulles has made it crystal clear the Tachen group is not vital."

[An Associated Press dispatch said a United States military observer team had already been withdrawn to Formosa.]

The Nationalist Air Force pressed attacks again today against Communist shipping along the mainland coast that might mean a Red invasion.

The staff of twelve nurses from the Nationalist hospital on Tachen were taken off.

High U. S. Officers at Taipei
Special to The New York Times.

TAIPEI, Formosa, Jan. 21—Top Chinese Nationalist officials here were silent tonight on reports from Washington that President Eisenhower was planning to ask Congress to approve use of the United States Seventh Fleet to evacuate the Nationalist garrison from the Tachen Islands.

Reports of a possible Tachens evacuation were accompanied here by the arrival of Vice Admiral Roscoe F. Good, Deputy Chief of Naval Operations for Logistics, for conferences. In his party were five rear admirals and Maj. Gen. A. E. Johnson, logistics specialist with the United States Joint Chiefs of Staff.

The visit of this group to Formosa was scheduled before the Communists invaded Yikiang Island, eight miles northwest of the Tachens, Tuesday.

About 10,000 regular troops are now stationed in the Tachens, 210 miles north of Formosa. But there are many civilians among the 15,000 persons living on the two Tachen Islands who would undoubtedly choose to accompany these troops if they withdraw.

Eisenhower Message Set

By ELIE ABEL
Special to The New York Times.

WASHINGTON, Jan. 21—Senate leaders were alerted today to expect a Presidential message on Monday asking "if-and-when" authorization for United States air and naval participation in the defense of Formosa.

A profound change in Far Eastern policy appeared in prospect. It evidently was discussed and approved today at meetings of the Cabinet and the National Security Council, but the White House remained silent.

Efforts in the United Nations to arrange a Strait of Formosa cease-fire received further high-level consideration here today when Sidney G. Holland, Prime Minister of New Zealand, visited the White House and the State Department.

These were the major developments:

¶Mr. Holland, after an eighty-

Continued on Page 2, Column 4

SENATE UNIT BACKS ASIA DEFENSE PACT

Foreign Relations Committee Votes 14-1—Ratification Next Week Indicated

By WILLIAM S. WHITE
Special to The New York Times.

WASHINGTON, Jan. 21—The Senate Foreign Relations Committee approved today the Southeast Asia Collective Defense Treaty. The vote was 14 to 1.

The Senate itself probably will consent to ratification—a constitutional process requiring a two-thirds majority of those voting—before next week is out.

The pact against Communist aggression in Southeast Asia, signed at Manila last Sept. 8, binds the United States and seven co-signers to these primary obligations:

¶To act together, each nation according to its own constitutional processes, "to meet the common danger" of any attack on the treaty area.

¶To consult together and to "agree on measures" of common action to meet any assault by way of subversion and infiltration.

Neither obligation is an automatic commitment to warfare by the United States in any and all circumstances of Asian trouble.

The understanding is general between the Administration and Congress that, if fighting broke out, Congress would be consulted before the United States became involved.

The sole dissenter in the For-

Continued on Page 2, Column 5

Iceberg Big as Long Island Noted In Atka's Antarctic Barrier Study

The New York Times Jan. 22, 1955

A huge iceberg (heavy line denoted by 1) cracked off from the Antarctic Icecap. West of the Little America harbor (2) another large section broke away. Discovery Inlet (4) has been erased. These phenomena were discovered while the Navy icebreaker Atka stopped at a point denoted by (3).

By WALTER SULLIVAN
Special to The New York Times.

ABOARD U. S. S. ATKA, Antarctica, Jan. 17—A section of the Antarctic icecap as large as Long Island has broken off and floated north, possibly in one piece, according to a survey completed today by this ship.

The operation gave some support to the contention that Antarctica sometimes produces icebergs more than 100 miles long.

Some of the scientists aboard this Navy icebreaker believe such icebergs divide into smaller bergs that may be as much as ten miles long. The Atka's survey threw new light on the processes involved.

The survey dealt with the ice cliff known as the Ross Barrier

Continued on Page 4, Column 3

Radio, TV Face Huckster Inquiry; Silver Charges $1,000,000 Racket

Television and radio advertisers, whose "pitchmen" often have irritated home audiences, may be prosecuted for unlawful practices.

Edward S. Silver, Brooklyn District Attorney, said yesterday that the methods of some of the electronic hucksters constituted a racket involving more than $1,000,000 a year.

The Kings County rackets grand jury will begin on Monday to investigate Mr. Silver's charges. Representatives of the seven local television outlets and sixteen radio stations have been invited to attend the grand jury session.

Mr. Silver said that he had requested County Judge Samuel S. Leibowitz to charge the grand jury after an investigation that lasted for eight months.

During the investigation, policemen and policewomen, posing as householders, responded to television and radio advertisements for products including sewing machines, vacuum cleaners and freezers and services such as upholstering and food plans.

The investigation, involving fifteen concerns, was directed particularly toward programs on which a response to an advertisement was followed by a visit to the potential customer's home by a salesman. Recordings have been made of telephone conversations leading up to the salesmen's visits and discussions in homes between the salesmen and the undercover police, Mr. Silver said.

According to the District Attorney, a typical high-pressure sales operation that was investigated worked as follows.

The pitchman demonstrated a sewing machine that was supposed to sell for $26.50. A prospective buyer, responding to the advertisement, would be visited at home by a salesman, who would discourage the customer from buying the advertised ma-

Continued on Page 8, Column 4

U. S. DISCOURAGES VISITS TO CAPTIVES

Says Relatives Must Travel to China at Their Own Risk—Calls Bid Propaganda

Special to The New York Times.

WASHINGTON, Jan. 21—The State Department tried today to dissuade relatives from visiting American airmen imprisoned in China. However, it will allow those who insist on accepting Peiping's offer to make the trip.

Most of the seventeen families concerned appear unwilling to go in any case. Not one passport application has so far been received in the State Department.

The Government denounced the Peiping proposal as a propaganda maneuver. It was, however, clearly reluctant to deny the interested families passports, lest the United States appear unmoved by their longing to see the imprisoned men.

Meanwhile, the American Red Cross said it would provide "supplemental financial assistance" to relatives who accepted the offer. The organization's headquarters said it would aid the relatives in "every appropriate way," including the financial assistance and suggested that the relatives who planned to go get in touch with their nearest Red Cross chapters.

Henry Suydam, State Department spokesman, asked for official comment on the offer Peiping had broadcast this morning, said the Government could not "in good conscience" encourage trips by United States citizens to Communist China.

He pointed out that the United States, which has refused to recognize the Peiping regime, could not offer its citizens the normal passport protections on the China mainland.

"World public opinion," Mr. Suydam said, "will judge the motives of those who, having it in their power and being under an obligation to end promptly the

Continued on Page 3, Column 6

RED CHINA OFFERS TO LET RELATIVES VISIT U. S. AIRMEN

Invitation Announced at U.N. and in Peiping Provokes a Mixed Reception

FEW FAMILIES FAVOR IT

Spokesman of Hammarskjold Reports He Has No Fear for Visitors' Safety

By LINDESAY PARROTT
Special to The New York Times.

UNITED NATIONS, N. Y., Jan. 21—Communist China has offered to open its doors to relatives of some of the detained United States prisoners of the Korean war.

Premier Chou En-lai during his talks with Secretary General Dag Hammarskjold of the United Nations, it was announced here today, indicated that the Communist Government would "provide facilities for relatives to visit" the men. Mr. Hammarskjold had gone to Peiping under a resolution of the General Assembly to work for the release of the Americans and other personnel of the United Nations.

Mr. Chou's offer, it was understood, was made after Mr. Hammarskjold had asked that steps be taken to reassure the families of the prisoners. The Chinese Red Cross, according to the announcement, was named by Mr. Chou as the agency that would make all arrangements necessary for the visit of the relatives to China and presumably for their travel and maintenance there.

The announcement of Mr. Chou's proposal to the Secretary General was made here simultaneously with a broadcast by the official Chinese radio in similar terms. The simultaneous release followed the pattern established for communiqués during Mr. Hammarskjold's conversations in Peiping.

Reaction at U. N. Is Mixed

Word of the Chinese offer brought mixed reactions at United Nations Headquarters.

One United Nations official, who asked that his name be withheld, said the move "might be a step" to the liberation of the captives soon.

[A check with relatives of the seventeen Americans as to whether they would seek to visit them in China, found most of the families dubious. In only three cases were relatives eager to go; and each of these raised the question of money. For the most part, the wives and parents of the prisoners were lukewarm, doubtful or opposed to going, often on the ground that it would not expedite the man's release. The families are scattered over thirteen states.]

A spokesman announced that Mr. Hammarskjold himself "has no doubt about the safety of those members of the families wishing to visit China to see their men."

His statement was made, it was stated, in answer to questions that arose over telegrams from the United States Air Force to relatives of the imprisoned men in the interval between the Secretary General's return from Peiping and the announcement of Mr. Chou's offer. Some doubt had been expressed, it was indicated, that the visitors would enjoy security behind the Iron Curtain.

Propaganda Maneuver Seen

Some delegates viewed the Chinese offer with scant optimism and saw good reason in the apparent reluctance of the State Department to endorse the visits of prisoners' relatives to China.

In Washington, a State Department spokesman announced that the "United States Government cannot of course in good conscience encourage those who may wish to go into an area where the normal protections of an American passport cannot be offered." The United States delegation at the United Nations, a representative said, has "no elaboration" on the State Department's statement to indicate whether or not passports would be issued to such prospective visitors as might apply.

Generally, the reaction among delegates here appeared to be that Mr. Chou had engineered a clever but perhaps cruel propaganda maneuver—clever in so far as it laid the onus of decision on the visits squarely on the United States authorities, cruel in so far as false hope of quick

Continued on Page 3, Column 2

"All the News That's Fit to Print"

The New York Times

LATE CITY EDITION

Mostly fair, cold today. Partly cloudy, not so cold tomorrow.

Temperature Range Today—Max., 31; Min., 20
Temperature Yesterday—Max., 33.4; Min., 22
Full U. S. Weather Bureau Report, Page 35

Copyright, 1955, by The New York Times Company.

VOL. CIV. No. 35,472. Entered as Second-Class Matter, Post Office, New York, N. Y. NEW YORK, TUESDAY, MARCH 8, 1955. Times Square, New York 36, N. Y. Telephone Lackawanna 4-1000 FIVE CENTS

DULLES DISCUSSES FIRM ASIAN STAND WITH EISENHOWER

Secretary Expected to Tell People U. S. Cannot Afford More Yielding to Reds

RADIO REPORT TONIGHT

Broadcast Likely to Indicate Strong Position on Islands but Leave Room for Talks

By DANA ADAMS SCHMIDT

Special to The New York Times.

WASHINGTON, March 7—Secretary of State Dulles conferred with President Eisenhower this morning on the need for a firmer stand by the United States and the free world in the Far East.

Mr. Dulles is expected to develop in a radio-television speech tomorrow night the theme that the United States and its allies cannot afford any more retreats in the Far East if they hope to prevent the Communists from continuing their expansion in Southeast Asia.

His speech will be broadcast by the Columbia Broadcasting System at 10 P. M., the American Broadcasting Company at 10:30 P. M. and the Mutual Broadcasting System at 11:30 P. M. Columbia will televise the speech at 11:15 P. M. The broadcasts will be made from a recording and films made earlier in the evening.

In his hour-long talk with the President, Mr. Dulles continued the report he began in an unscheduled visit to the White House yesterday a few hours after he had returned from a two-week visit to Southeast Asia.

He headed the United States delegation to the Southeast Asia Defense Treaty Organization conference at Bangkok, Thailand. He also reviewed Far East policy with United States Ambassadors in that area at Baguio, in the Philippines, and visited Burma, Cambodia, Laos, South Vietnam and the Nationalist Chinese Government on Formosa.

Likely to Leave Latitude

The Secretary is expected to indicate firmly in his broadcast the United States' determination to help defend the Quemoy and Matsu Islands, off the China mainland, if the Chinese Communists try to invade them.

At the same time, without going into detail, he is expected to leave himself latitude to engage in possible negotiations on these islands. At present, the possibilities of a "deal" leading to a cease-fire appear remote since neither the Communists nor the Nationalists are willing to discuss it.

Mr. Dulles has returned from the Far East apparently convinced of the unity of the fronts (1) in Korea, (2) in Formosa and the offshore islands, and (3) in southeast Asia. A Communist Chinese attack on any one of these fronts might be met advantageously by counterattacks on the other two fronts, in his opinion.

To maintain freedom to strike back where it would do the most good, he believes, the United States must concentrate its forces and not spread them thin in scattered garrisons.

Congress to Get Views

He expounded these views to the signatories of the Southeast Asia defense treaty at Bangkok, according to reports through diplomatic channels. He explained that under these circumstances the United States could not commit specific forces to Southeast Asia.

The Senate Foreign Relations Committee will hear a report from Mr. Dulles tomorrow morning, and the House Foreign Affairs Committee in the afternoon.

The chairman of the House group, Representative James P. Richards, Democrat of South Carolina, has said that he intends to question the Secretary on the prospects for a "deal" in which Communist China would get the Quemoy and Matsu Islands in return for a cease-fire pledge.

Mr. Richards believes this would be contrary to the intentions of Congress when it voted a joint resolution guaranteeing the defense of Formosa and the Pescadores Islands.

While other members of the two committees are also expected to question Mr. Dulles sharply, the consensus on Capitol Hill today was that the Secretary's work in Southeast Asia

Continued on Page 2, Column 4

The Atka Completes Antarctic Scouting Mission

Radiophoto to The New York Times (by Walter Sullivan)

Norman Bright of Dayton, Ohio, Air Force observer, wields a traveling bag as he taunts a sleepy seal in Admiral Byrd Bay and gets a violent reaction. The Atka, which has completed exploration of Antarctic, is moored to bay ice in rear.

Buenos Aires Gives U.S. Icebreaker Warm Greeting—All Aboard Except Penguins Are Pleased on Reaching Civilization

By WALTER SULLIVAN

Special to The New York Times.

BUENOS AIRES, March 7—The United States Navy icebreaker Atka arrived here today, concluding her Antarctic mission exactly two months after leaving Wellington, N. Z.

The Atka had scouted almost half the coastline of Antarctica looking for bases for future exploration and research.

The ship received a warm greeting as she steamed up the brown waters of the River Plate. Tugs dipped the blue and white flag of Argentina as their crewmen waved a welcome.

All except eleven aboard the Atka were happy to see the sunbaked streets of Buenos Aires. The exceptions were the ship's captive penguins—seven Emperors and four Adelies.

The birds drooped in the heat of the late-summer sun, and their keepers among the crew worried lest some die before their shipment by plane to the Washington Zoo could be arranged. So far the birds have come through without casualty since their capture in an unnamed bay on the Antarctic coast.

Perhaps the happiest man aboard was the captain, Comdr.

Continued on Page 3, Column 5

EDEN FOR DELAY IN FORMOSA TALK

Says Proper Basis Cannot Be Attained Now—Laborites Ask 3-Power Meeting

By DREW MIDDLETON

Special to The New York Times.

LONDON, March 7—Sir Anthony Eden indicated today that under present conditions an international conference on the Formosa situation was out of the question.

Shortly thereafter the Conservative Government and its Foreign Secretary were faced with a Laborite demand for an immediate attempt to arrange a three-power meeting with the United States and the Soviet Union on world disarmament.

These two developments did not represent cause and effect. They did reflect the preoccupation of both Government and Opposition with international conferences as a means toward easing world tension.

Sir Anthony, speaking at the airport on his return from a 16,000-mile tour of Asia and the Middle East, said that "unfortunately" the necessary conditions for a meeting on the Formosa problem did not exist. These conditions, he said, are basic understanding about the task of a conference and some agreement about its membership.

Dangers to Peace Seen

The British Government regards the situation in the Far East, specifically that concerning Quemoy and Matsu Islands, as potentially dangerous to peace.

Sir Anthony's pessimism about prospects for a conference and the reported stiffening of the United States' support for the Chinese Nationalists' retention of those offshore islands have dashed hopes that a settlement might be reached along lines suggested by Britain.

In official quarters there is vigorous assertion of the common objectives of the United States and Britain in the Far East and Southeast Asia. Both nations want peace and stability in those areas and neither advocates withdrawal from any vital position. The definitions of such positions differ, however.

The withdrawal of the Na-

Continued on Page 2, Column 5

SERVICES DIVIDED ON P. O. W. POLICY

Army and Air Force Split Complicates Move to Set Code for U. S. Captives

By ANTHONY LEVIERO

Special to The New York Times.

WASHINGTON, March 7—The Army and the Air Force are sharply divided on the indoctrination of war prisoners against Communist brainwashing techniques.

Their seemingly irreconcilable differences are complicating the Defense Department's effort to develop a unified policy of information, indoctrination and training.

To some officials it appeared that high national policy was involved and that the President might have to resolve it.

The Air Force has carried its more lenient attitude toward repatriated, brainwashed Americans into the planning of what to do about it in any conflict with Communist armies.

A secret, split report on the issue is on the way to Charles E. Wilson, Secretary of Defense. It was reported today that the Army and the Navy sided against the Air Force in maintaining that American prisoners of war must abide by the traditional position of giving the enemy nothing but name, rank and serial number.

The problem created many heartaches for the American people in the backwash of the Korean war. The Army began a series of courts-martial against those deemed to have aided the enemy or betrayed their country or their comrades. But the Air Force decided there would be no trials, and merely forced a handful of suspected men to resign.

The Air Force policy of no trials and the Army's policy of punitive action has stirred up a

Continued on Page 12, Column 4

U.S.-BRITISH MOVE ON SAAR IS ASKED

De Gaulle Kinsman Suggests Paris Ask for Intervention in Dispute With Bonn

By HAROLD CALLENDER

Special to The New York Times.

PARIS, March 7—A plea that the United States and Britain be asked to intervene in the dispute over the Saar territory between the French and West German Governments was made here today.

Jacques Vendroux, a Gaullist Deputy and a brother-in-law of Gen. Charles de Gaulle, introduced the plea in the National Assembly. His resolution proposes that the Government seek new assurances from Washington and London regarding the future of the Saar before the accord concerning that territory comes up for ratification in the advisory Council of the Republic March 22.

Some observers saw in the resolution a desire to postpone action on the Saar accord as well as on the other Paris agreements to arm West Germany and bring it into the Atlantic alliance.

There was no governmental reaction to this move tonight, but an implicit plea for the same

Continued on Page 8, Column 3

TITO TO DEVELOP ATOM FOR PEACE

Yugoslav Leader Says Nation Is Capable of Producing Own Nuclear Energy

By JACK RAYMOND

Special to The New York Times.

BELGRADE, Yugoslavia, March 7—President Tito projected Yugoslavia into the nuclear age on the domestic front today.

The Marshal told a cheering Parliament that Yugoslavia was now capable of producing nuclear energy. He said Yugoslavia had sufficient nuclear raw material in her own soil to supply her peaceful industry. Nuclear energy is not a monopoly of the big powers, he added.

The Yugoslav leader predicted that in the near future "that great invention of man's brain would serve for the achievement of prosperity for the peoples of our country."

The Marshal called for destruction of all existing nuclear weapons. He said he was for the use of nuclear energy only for peaceful needs. But, he added, "of course with effective international control that would prevent misuse of this high scientific work, no matter by which side."

Tart on Soviet Relations

Marshal Tito spoke tartly of Yugoslavia's relations with the Soviet-led Cominform bloc. He said that "normalization" with the Soviet bloc might have run its course short of good relations.

He attacked Vyacheslav M. Molotov personally, accusing the Soviet Foreign Minister of not telling the truth about relations with Yugoslavia. Marshal Tito said Soviet bloc leaders were falsely asserting that Yugoslavia was recasting the position she took when she broke from the Cominform in 1948.

The President said the publicly expressed attitude of the Eastern countries on "normalization" with Yugoslavia "created doubt in the full sincerity of statements given in direct contacts by the most responsible persons of those countries."

The Soviet-bloc leaders are telling their party members and their people that "we [the Yugoslavs] have now to some extent seen our errors and that we are trying to correct them, and similar nonsense," declared Marshal Tito.

"The formulation by Mr. Mol-

Continued on Page 6, Column 3

RUSSIANS' FAITH HEARTENS PRIEST

Ousted Clergyman Reports 'God Is Not Dead' in Soviet

By HARRISON E. SALISBURY

The Rev. Georges Bissonnette, Roman Catholic priest forced to leave Moscow last week, said yesterday that "God is not dead in the Soviet Union."

Father Bissonnette said on his arrival at Idlewild Airport that constant shifts in Soviet policy toward religion showed the inability of communism to cope with the steadfast religious faith of the Soviet people.

The dark-haired, soft-spoken 33-year-old priest walked down the ramp from the airplane with a light step and a beaming smile. He departed from Moscow by air Saturday morning after Soviet police officials had told him he must leave the country. He had been there twenty-five months.

"The officer at Ovir [the visa department of the Soviet civil police] gave me no reason," Father Bissonnette related. "He just said that my exit visa was ready and I could leave the country on March 2, 3 or 4. I left on the fifth."

United States Embassy offi-

Continued on Page 4, Column 3

Raid Warning Signals Revised; Fall-Out Peril Alters 'All-Clear'

Special to The New York Times.

BATTLE CREEK, Mich., March 7—New air raid warning signals for the United States and Canada were announced today by the Federal Civil Defense Administration.

The new system will supersede previous warning instructions and will be effective immediately in most areas. The announcement was made in a statement released at Civil Defense headquarters here in the name of Val Peterson, administrator of the agency.

The new signals are:

¶Alert—A steady blast of three to five minutes duration. This signal will be used to initiate evacuation of cities in most target areas. In most non-target areas, the signal will mean that the Civil Defense forces should mobilize.

¶Take Cover—A wailing tone or a series of sharp blasts of three minutes' duration. This signal will indicate that attack is imminent and that the public should take cover immediately.

There will be no all-clear signal, as in the past. Mr. Peterson explained that it had been eliminated because the hazard of radioactive fall-out would preclude bringing the public out of shelters in all areas simultaneously.

Instructions to come out of shelters, he said, would be given by radio, public address systems and through the police and Civil Defense wardens.

The United States and Canada agreed to the new warning signals, Mr. Peterson said, because they believed "the public can be more readily trained to recognize them and to take appropriate action in accordance

Continued on Page 5, Column 2

DOUBLE STANDARD IN STOCKS SCORED AT SENATE STUDY

Unlisted Issues Are Held to Have Advantage Over Ones Traded on the Exchanges

By BURTON CRANE

Special to The New York Times.

WASHINGTON, March 7—The Senate Banking and Currency Committee spent much of its time today on the over-the-counter market. This is where securities not listed on the exchanges are traded.

The committee, which is making a friendly study of the stock market, heard two stock exchange presidents insist that "the double standard in securities must be ended."

The interrogators, notably Senator J. William Fulbright, Democrat of Arkansas, chairman of the committee, seemed sympathetic to this view.

"I do not know whether we should have more regulation for the over-the-counter market or less for the registered exchanges," Ronald E. Kaehler, president of the San Francisco Stock Exchange, said.

He noted that since 1934 small companies had shown a disinclination to list their shares on the exchanges. To do so, he added, entailed heavy expense and more reports for the public.

In the over-the-counter market, prices and volume figures on stock traded are not made public. Only bids and offers by persons wishing to buy or sell are available.

Requirements Are Easier

Companies with issues in this market are not required to make the reports or follow other requirements of the listed companies. The unlisted concerns' officers, directors and large shareholders are not subject to restrictions on their trading.

[A detailed description of the over-the-counter market appears on page 36.]

On many points raised by the committee, Mr. Kaehler was in agreement with James E. Day, president of the Midwest Stock Exchange of Chicago.

At the end of today's session, Senator Fulbright was asked whether the committee would grant the request of Walter Winchell, columnist and broadcaster, to be heard. The Senator said that this was unlikely for the present.

On Friday, the committee heard testimony concerning Mr Winchell's television market tips. He replied with a statement to the press on Friday and in a broadcast last night asked for an opportunity to appear before the committee.

Senator Fulbright, who previously had seen no reason why he should call Mr. Winchell, said

Continued on Page 15, Column 1

False Alarm Gets Youth Year in Jail

A Brooklyn youth was sentenced yesterday to a year in the penitentiary for sounding a malicious false alarm of fire. It was the stiffest jail term ever imposed for the offense in this city.

A change last September in the New York Administrative Code increased the false-alarm punishment from a maximum of thirty days to one year. The maximum fine was increased at the same time from $100 to $1,000.

Magistrate Anthony Maglio in Bay Ridge Court imposed the sentence on John L. Mahoney, 19 years old, an unemployed seaman of 505 Seventy-seventh Street. The defendant had been arrested at 3 A. M. by Patrolman Raymond Rupelli, who caught him pulling the alarm in a box at Eighty-

Continued on Page 33, Column 2

HIGH COURT LIMITS SOVEREIGN RIGHTS

Ruling Against Nationalist China Restricts Immunity of Nations in Suits

By LUTHER A. HUSTON

Special to The New York Times.

WASHINGTON, March 7—A new judicial concept that limits the immunity of sovereign nations from legal action was announced today by the Supreme Court.

Justice Felix Frankfurter, writing the 4-to-3 majority opinion, held that a foreign government invoking the law of the United States in a suit could not use the legal immunity of a sovereign to shield it from counter-claims of American citizens.

Involved and overturned is an old legal principle stemming from English law. This holds that an action is not maintainable against a sovereign. In law, the sovereign is the king or ruling government of a nation.

The ruling was in a suit brought by the Republic of China to recover $200,000 deposited with the National City Bank of New York in 1948. The bank imposed two counter-claims for $1,634,432, based on defaulted Treasury notes of the Chinese Government.

The high court's decision reversed a judgment of the Second Circuit Court of Appeals at New York, which held that sovereign immunity barred the bank's counterclaims. The case was sent back to the Federal District Court, which also had dismissed the counter-claims. The lower court was ordered to reinstate the claims and rehear the case on that basis.

Justice Frankfurter was joined by Chief Justice Earl Warren

Continued on Page 10, Column 4

Anti-Crime Unit Backs Keating, Facing Wiretap Contempt Move

The New York Times

William J. Keating makes telephone call after refusing to tell the grand jury information sources on wiretapping.

By FOSTER HAILEY

The New York Anti-Crime Committee will stand behind its former counsel, William J. Keating, in his defiance of the grand jury investigating wiretapping.

Mr. Keating is facing a contempt of court citation for his refusal to divulge to the jury the source of his information on electronic eavesdropping. He is scheduled to be served today with papers to show cause before Judge Jonah J. Goldstein of General Sessions why he should not be adjudged in contempt.

The committee announced its support of Mr. Keating last night. Yesterday he had thrice declined to reply to jury questions after having been ordered on Friday to do so by Judge Goldstein.

The decision of the committee to support its $14,000-a-year counsel, whose resignation was accepted last Thursday, was made in a six-hour session at committee headquarters, 270 Park Avenue.

A statement issued at 10:30 o'clock by a spokesman for the committee said:

"Mr. Keating, while in this

Continued on Page 18, Column 3

WAGNER PLEDGES TO CONTROL RENTS IF STATE DOES NOT

He Warns Legislators City Will 'Take Steps' to Avert 'Abuses' by Landlords

PREFERS ALBANY CURBS

But Will Step In if Need Be —Legislature Defers Action Until Budget Is Passed

By CHARLES G. BENNETT

New York City is ready to take over the rent control field here if the state sees fit to abandon it, Mayor Wagner declared yesterday.

In a telegram to all members of the State Legislature from this city the Mayor said the city would also, if necessary, "take steps to prevent abuses by a small minority of unscrupulous landlords."

The city the Mayor told the legislators, prefers to have the state "do the job for all of the people" of the state. But, he contended, "we cannot permit profiteering, overcrowding and decreased services to be legalized."

Meanwhile, in Albany, Republican legislative leaders decided at a policy conference to defer action on rent control until the budget was passed. Most of the major budget bills are scheduled for passage in both Senate and Assembly Tuesday.

"My attention has been called to reports from Albany that the legislation being prepared to continue rent controls in New York City weakens rather than strengthens the present protection for the tenants," the Mayor wrote.

State the Proper Agency

"As I said in my statement to the Legislature on Feb. 9, there is no free market for housing in New York City at the present time or in the immediate foreseeable future. Continuation of controls is necessary. The proper agency to continue those controls is the State Government.

"But there must be controls in fact, rather than just in name. We cannot permit profiteering, overcrowding and decreased services to be legalized.

"I urge you, in my capacity as the elected representative of the 8,000,000 people of New York City, to do your utmost to see to it that the extension of rent control for New York City be on a basis that is fair and adequate.

"The City of New York is prepared to take over the rent control field if the state sees fit to abandon it, and to take the steps necessary to prevent abuses by a small minority of unscrupulous landlords. It prefers to have the state 'do the job for all of the people' of the state.

"It should not be forced to accept rent control laws which prevent the city from acting and at the same time do not furnish adequate and effective state controls."

Proposed rent control changes agreed upon by Republican leg-

Continued on Page 17, Column 3

MONOXIDE FUMES FELL 30 IN PLANT

Wind Blows Gases Back Into a Factory on Broadway

By JACK ROTH

Thirty persons were overcome by carbon monoxide fumes yesterday while working in a sportswear manufacturing plant in lower Manhattan. Sixteen were hospitalized, none in serious condition.

The freakish accident was attributed to a combination of a short exhaust stack from a steam boiler and strong winds that blew the fumes back through the stack and into the factory. The plant was that of Russ Togs, Inc., on the second floor of a twelve-story building at 580 Broadway. The stack jutted only four and a half feet into an air shaft.

At 10:45 A. M., according to Louis Russo, president of the corporation, the plant foreman, Ike Behar, 30 years old, reported that some of the girls working on sewing machines were feeling a "dizziness."

Mr. Russo said he turned to open some front windows in the factory, which occupies 10,000 square feet, and when he turned

Continued on Page 14, Column 5

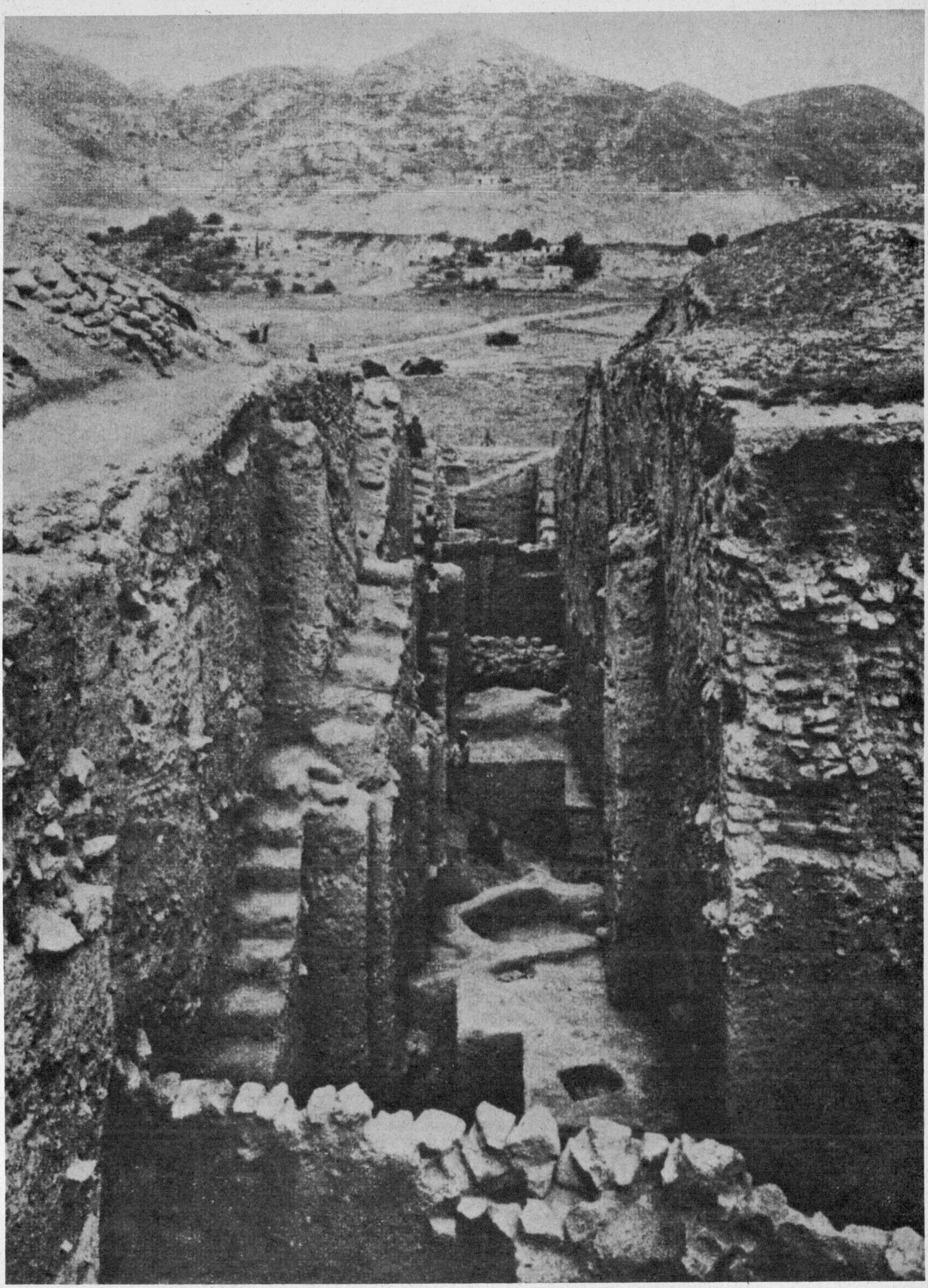

Jericho, as seen and excavated by Kathleen Kenyon, noted British archaeologist.

"All the News That's Fit to Print"

The New York Times.

LATE CITY EDITION
Mostly fair and warmer today.
Partly cloudy, warmer tomorrow.
Temperature Range Today—Max., 45; Min., 26
Temperatures Yesterday—Max., 33; Min., 18
Full U. S. Weather Bureau Report, Page 55

VOL. CIV...No. 35,473. Entered as Second-Class Matter, Post Office, New York, N. Y.

NEW YORK, WEDNESDAY, MARCH 9, 1955. Times Square, New York 36, N. Y. Telephone LAckawanna 4-1000 FIVE CENTS

DULLES WARNS RED CHINA FORCE WILL MEET FORCE; EDEN OFFERS COMPROMISE

REPUBLICANS WIN MAJOR REVISIONS IN ALBANY BUDGET

Legislature Cuts Harriman's Program by $16,800,000, Defeating Amendments

DEMOCRATS FOR INQUIRY

Thruway and Public Works Under Dewey Targets—G.O.P. Cries 'Smear'

By LEO EGAN
Special to The New York Times.

ALBANY, March 8—All of the major Republican revisions of Governor Harriman's budget were written into law today over Democratic opposition.

Before the final votes, Democratic plans to investigate the State Thruway Authority and the Dewey Administration's handling of the Department of Public Works were disclosed.

This brought a prompt Republican rejoinder that Mr. Harriman was attempting to ride into the White House next year on a campaign of threats, reprisals and smears.

Mayor Wagner of New York City was accused of collaborating in the campaign in the hope of being elected to the United States Senate next year in place of Herbert H. Lehman, whose term is expiring.

The Senate acted on nineteen of the twenty-seven budget bills. All but one were approved by unanimous vote after Democratic amendments to two had been defeated.

The Assembly approved seven of the bills that had passed the Senate. It will act on the twelve others tomorrow.

Beaten by Party Split

The bill that failed to get unanimous Senate approval provides for a single automobile license plate next year. The existing law would require two unless changed.

The vote was 51 to 6. The measure was not taken up in the Assembly.

The same Democratic amendments that had been beaten in the Senate by a party division were offered in the Assembly. They were rejected again on a similar division.

The amendments would have restored all but $4,900,000 of the cuts made by the Republican legislative majority in committee.

The one cut to which no objection was offered reduced state grants to county governments for highway construction. This item was included originally in the expectation that an increase in motor fuel taxes would take effect April 1. Later, the Governor agreed to defer the date to next Jan. 1.

Five of the seven bills that passed both houses became law

Continued on Page 19, Column 3

Stock Inquiry Told of Boom Psychology; Economist Recommends 100% Margins

Dr. Galbraith Asks Action to Bar 'Bust'—Market Off Up to 6 Points

By BURTON CRANE
Special to The New York Times.

WASHINGTON, March 8—Senators studying the behavior of the securities market heard today that, although stocks might not now be too high, the public was developing an all-too-familiar type of speculative hysteria.

Dr. John Kenneth Galbraith, Professor of Economics at Harvard University, said he believed that this boom psychology should be checked before it became dangerous.

[Prices of some leading stocks fell two to six points Tuesday in an unorderly fashion. The break, however, was not as extensive as those on Jan. 17 and Jan. 5, even though it rolled prices back to their lowest levels of this month. At the close, when prices were the weakest, the New York Stock Exchange's high-speed ticker tape was running nine minutes late.]

Associated Press Wirephoto

Prof. John K. Galbraith of Harvard testifying yesterday

Dr. Galbraith told the Senate Banking and Currency Committee that the margins, or down payments, on stock buying should be raised, perhaps gradually, to 100 per cent. He recom-

Continued on Page 12, Column 3

HOUSE UNIT, 26-11, VOTES TO RESTORE RIGID FARM PROPS

Agriculture Group Approves the Return of Supports to 90% of Parity

By WILLIAM M. BLAIR
Special to The New York Times.

WASHINGTON, March 8—The once-beaten bipartisan farm bloc bounced up today with a bill to restore high, rigid farm price supports.

By a 26-to-11 vote, the House Agriculture Committee approved a bill that the Administration will oppose at every turn.

Representative Harold D. Cooley, Democrat of North Carolina and committee chairman, predicted the House would pass the measure but other farm bloc members were not so positive.

In the Senate there is strong opposition to changing the flexible farm price system the Administration won last year after a bitter struggle.

Major provisions of the bill include:

¶Restoration of mandatory 90 per cent of parity price supports on the so-called "basic" crops of corn, wheat, cotton, peanuts, and rice for 1955, 1956, and 1957. The sixth "basic" crop, tobacco, continues under 90 per cent support in the Administration's program.

¶An increase in the price support on dairy products from 75 to 80 per cent of parity.

¶A national referendum by wheat growers on a two-price system for their crop.

¶An increase from $50,000,000 to $75,000,000 in Federal funds to subsidize milk consumption in public schools.

¶A two-year extension of the brucellosis eradication program for dairymen. The Government would expend $15,000,000 to repay farmers for destroying diseased cattle at a rate of not more than $50 a head.

Farm Income Down

Parity is a Federal standard designed to assure farmers a fair return on their products in relation to farm costs. It fluctuates with changes in various cost prices.

For more than a decade the "basic" commodities were supported at 90 per cent of parity. If farm prices on the six "basic" products fell below 90 per cent, farmers could dispose of their crops to the Government and receive the support price.

Last year, the Eisenhower Administration won the flexible system that permits supports at a range between 82½ to 90 per cent of parity. It argued that rigid price supports built up surpluses that the Administration now seeks to dispose of through a program of building new foreign and domestic markets.

The flexible system is geared to the theory of a higher support level to encourage production in periods of scarcity and a lower prop in times of over-production to discourage output and promote a shift to needed products.

Net farm income dropped 10 per cent last year. This com-

Continued on Page 14, Column 5

EXIT IS PROPOSED

Briton Would Give Up Quemoy and Matsu—U.S. Aims Lauded

By DREW MIDDLETON
Special to The New York Times.

LONDON, March 8—Sir Anthony Eden today urged a settlement of the Formosa crisis involving concessions by both sides and leading to discussion of China's representation in the United Nations. The political future of Formosa would also be discussed under the Foreign Secretary's plan.

Withdrawal of Generalissimo Chiang Kai-shek's forces from the Quemoy and Matsu Islands and Communist abstention from any attack on these islands or on Formosa and the Pescadores were the most important concessions proposed by the Foreign Secretary.

The United States, Sir Anthony emphasized in the House of Commons, desires an end of the fighting in the Far East. In pursuit of this, he added, Washington has restrained the Chinese Nationalists from attacking the mainland and has persuaded them to evacuate the Tachen and Nanki Islands.

Past Policy Exceeded

The Foreign Secretary's statement went well beyond past pronouncements of British policy. While it sought Nationalist abandonment of the coastal islands, it also impressed on Parliament the peaceful intentions of the Administration in Washington.

Sir Anthony indicated that Britain did not intend to stop trying to solve the Formosa problem, however her efforts might be received abroad, for without a solution, he warned, "the consequences may be very grave."

Although the Foreign Secretary warmly endorsed the United States' efforts to avert war in the Far East, his remarks demonstrated that British policy on the means of settlement remained unchanged. According to official sources, these means differ in timing, in scope and in extent of diplomatic preparation from those advocated by the United States.

The British will maintain the contacts already established with the Soviet Union and Communist China on the Formosa situation, Sir Anthony emphasized. These have not yet provided the necessary conditions for a big-power meeting on Formosa, but the Government will continue its efforts to establish such conditions and to prevent further fighting in the meantime, he said.

The Government's concern with the attitude of the other

Continued on Page 5, Column 4

Associated Press Wirephoto

GIVES REPORT: Secretary of State Dulles as he described the Far East situation on radio and television.

U. S. MIGHT CITED

But No Precise Stand Is Given on Offshore Isles by Secretary

Text of address by Mr. Dulles is printed on Page 4.

By ELIE ABEL
Special to The New York Times.

WASHINGTON, March 8—Secretary of State Dulles warned Communist China tonight that the United States was no "paper tiger."

The tiger analogy is a favorite of Communist propagandists, who depict the United States as snarling bravely enough but in the end backing away from a fight. Mr. Dulles suggested that the American tiger still had powerful teeth and claws.

He put Peiping on notice that a resort to force might be countered by "the greater force that we possess."

The United States, he said, has "new and powerful weapons of precision, which can utterly destroy military targets without endangering unrelated civilian centers." The Secretary evidently was referring to tactical nuclear weapons that can be fired from cannon or dropped from fighter-bomber planes on the battlefield, rather than the city-destroying hydrogen bomb.

But Mr. Dulles, in a broadcast speech, again left shadowy the precise response of the United States to an attack on the Quemoy and Matsu Islands off the south China coast.

Essential Ingredients

President Eisenhower will decide that question, he said, "in the light of his judgment as to the over-all value of certain coastal positions to the defense of Formosa, and the cost of holding those positions."

The Secretary of Defense, Charles E. Wilson, also deferred to General Eisenhower when asked at his press conference whether the United States would fight to prevent Communist capture of the offshore islands. Mr. Wilson's reply was that the President would know whether or not to defend these positions.

Mr. Dulles took his radio and television audience on a tour of the troubled Asian horizon, retracing his two-week trip to seven countries—Burma, Cambodia, Formosa, Laos, the Philippines, Thailand and Vietnam.

Brave words and patriotism alone, he said, cannot preserve

Continued on Page 4, Column 3

STATE G. O. P. SPLIT ON RENT CONTROLS

Leaders Fail to Agree Upon Party Plan—Compromise Program Is Offered

Special to The New York Times

ALBANY, March 8—Republican lawmakers were just about back where they started today on the thorny problem of rent control.

After a night and day of canvassing views of Republican legislators from various parts of the state, they were still unable to find agreement on a single party program.

As a result of a series of conferences, Republican leaders were now discussing a number of proposals. One of these would provide some tightening of controls in New York City and Buffalo but eliminate them entirely in two years.

The political reasoning behind the two-year extension reflects an attempt to avoid having the issue of expiration or renewal come up in 1956, a year when a President, a United States Senator and a full Congressional delegation will be elected.

Another suggestion would eliminate all controls outside of New York City but give counties or cities the right to recontrol accommodations within their boundaries if they desired.

This is being offered as a compromise between those who feel that rent control should be abandoned altogether upstate and those who believe it still is valuable in some localities.

Decontrol Is Permitted

At present, localities are permitted to decontrol, if they wish, but such action must be initiated by the local legislative body. Under the new plan, local action would be required only if controls were to be retained.

Two controversial proposals for relaxing controls have not been discarded, although they appear somewhat scarred by a kicking around from Thomas J. Curran, New York County Republican Chairman.

These involve decontrolling all two-family houses in which one occupant is the owner and permitting landlords to pass along to tenants in the form of rent increases any increases he incurs in taxes or operating costs.

The latter is designed in part to protect landlords against the effect of higher real estate taxes that will be levied in New York City if the Legislature approves Mayor Wagner's request for an increase in the tax limit.

Mr. Curran attacked both of these suggestions last week, saying that they would lead to another "rent spiral."

Governor Harriman signed today a bill extending the life of the Temporary State Commission on Rents until July 1, 1956. The measure also increased the membership of the commission from sixteen to eighteen, with the extra two to be named by the Republican legislative leaders.

Without the addition of two members, the replacement by Governor Harriman of three Republicans with Democrats would have deadlocked the two parties at eight members each. Under the new law, the Republicans will have a ten-to-eight spread.

Assemblyman Joseph F. Car-

Continued on Page 17, Column 5

Eisenhower Names Top Security Aide

Special to The New York Times.

WASHINGTON, March 8—President Eisenhower named Dillon Anderson today to be his Special Assistant for National Security Affairs.

Mr. Anderson is a 48-year-old practicing attorney from Houston. He was an Army officer in World War II and has been a consultant to the National Security Council since 1953. Mr. Anderson succeeds Robert Cutler April 1. It is the

Continued on Page 10, Column 6

DEMOCRATS PRESS SENATE TAX FIGHT

Johnson Seeks to Save Part of House Slash—Knowland Predicts Move Will Fail

By WILLIAM S. WHITE
Special to The New York Times.

WASHINGTON, March 8—Top Senate Democrats promised President Eisenhower today a quick showdown on the tax fight.

Senator Lyndon B. Johnson of Texas, the Democratic floor leader, arranged to bring the issue to the floor on Thursday and to seek a decisive vote by next mid-week.

He disavowed any Democratic intention to seek delay.

Mr. Johnson has been out of action for many days because of an operation and still must wear a steel backbrace. He returned to take personal command of the struggle with two purposes:

¶To come to the assistance of Speaker Sam Rayburn of Texas, who narrowly put a $20-a-person income tax reduction through that chamber over the President's vehement objections.

¶To find a means by which the substance of Mr. Rayburn's attempt could be preserved without alienating the Senate's fiscal conservatives among the Democrats.

The Senate Finance Committee, by vote of 9 to 6, has refused to approve the Rayburn plan. The decisive negative ballots were cast there by the committee's Democratic chairman, Senator Harry F. Byrd of Virginia, and his senior Democratic associate, Senator Walter F. George of Georgia.

The question now is what the Senate itself is to do—whether to go all, part or none of the way with the Democratic House

Continued on Page 13, Column 2

1,081 LINES TAPPED BY POLICE IN 1954

Adams Defends Practice—Keating Order Delayed

By FOSTER HAILEY

The New York City Police Department has not used wire-tapping to the extent many apparently believe, the Police Commissioner said yesterday. He defended the practice.

In 1954, said Francis W. H. Adams in a statement, the police listened in on 1,081 of New York City's 3,775,000 telephone circuits. All the interceptions were made under court order.

As a result of the intercepted conversations, 395 arrests were made, he said. Of these, 327 were on morals charges and sixty-eight for other crimes.

"It should be emphasized that while telephone interceptions may not lead to direct arrests, frequently they provide essential information concerning crime," the statement continued. "Arrest figures, therefore, do not provide the only criteria of the

Continued on Page 15, Column 4

HARRIMAN SCORES EISENHOWER POLICY

At Democratic '56 Strategy Dinner, He Says U. S. Has Retreated in Leadership

Text of the Governor's address will be found on Page 15

By DOUGLAS DALES

Governor Harriman charged last night that the Eisenhower Administration had been marked by a two-year "retreat from leadership."

The retreat, he declared, included military, economic and foreign policy matters and could be traced to appeasement of "go-it-alone" Republicans.

The Governor, often mentioned as a possibility for the Democratic Presidential nomination next year, leveled his strongest fire against the Administration's policy in Formosa. He called the "unleashing" of Chiang Kai-shek, the Nationalist China leader, "an incredible story."

Mr. Harriman's attack on the Eisenhower Administration was the highlight of a "1956 strategy" dinner at the Waldorf-Astoria Hotel given by the nationalities division of the Democratic National Committee.

One of the purposes of the dinner was to introduce Paul M. Butler of South Bend, Ind., the new Democratic national chairman, to political leaders in the East.

Conference of Governors

Before the dinner, Mr. Butler announced that he would call a conference of Democratic Governors in Washington in the spring. No date has been set.

He said there were enough electoral votes in the twenty-seven states with Democratic Governors to bring victory in the Presidential election. He was counting heavily, he explained, on the Democratic state administration to put over the 1956 national ticket.

The national chairman said the Governors' conference would have these objectives:

¶To give the Governors an opportunity to discuss with Congressional leaders problems and issues on which there should be mutual discussion.

¶To give the Governors an opportunity to exchange ideas on problems common to state administrations.

¶To establish a close working alliance between the Democratic National Committee and the Democratic state officials.

Mr. Butler said one of his aims as national chairman would be to give to Governors "more importance in the party structure" than they have had.

He reported that he had asked the eight former Democratic national chairmen to serve with him in an advisory capacity. All had agreed, he said. They include

Continued on Page 17, Column 1

CITY VOTES A BAN ON FAKE PISTOLS

Council Also Urges Increase in Subway Police Force

By CHARLES G. BENNETT

The City Council approved yesterday a local law banning the sale, manufacture or possession of toy or imitation pistols or revolvers that duplicate the actual weapons. Twenty members voted in favor of the law amending the Administrative Code. One abstained.

Councilman David Ross, Bronx, Democrat, warned his colleagues that the imitation weapons were "not toys." In 1954, he said, 108 hold-up suspects, all of whom had used imitation revolvers, were arrested here.

In another action, the Council approved a resolution calling on the State Legislature to pass pending measures that would ban the sale of .22-caliber bullets to teen-agers.

The Council also adopted unanimously another resolution requesting the Legislature to approve measures requiring the New York City Transit Authority to increase the subway police force from 523 to 1,000 men.

Council President Abe Stark took the floor to declare that crime in the subways—reflected in 40,000 official actions last year—was so bad that women and children did not dare to ride "during various hours of the day and night." Mr. Stark

Continued on Page 18, Column 5

Walls of Jericho Tumbled at Least 24 Times

Excavators Say First Barrier Fell Long Before Joshua

By KENNETT LOVE
Special to The New York Times.

JERICHO, Jordan, Feb. 26—Twenty-three successive walls of Jericho tumbled down long before Joshua's priests "blew with the trumpets" about 3,300 years ago. A team of British and American archaeologists has discovered the walls.

This season the archaeologists reached Jericho's earliest known town wall, built on bedrock and buried fifty feet deep beneath the layered debris of at least 7,000 or 8,000 years of history and pre-history.

Joshua attacked Jericho during the Israelite invasion of Canaan in the fourteenth century B. C. According to the Biblical account, the walls fell "down flat" after Joshua's army had marched around the city once a day for six days and seven times on the seventh day and "all the people" in Joshua's camp had "shouted with a great shout."

The excavation is expected to produce much information about

Continued on Page 2, Column 5

The New York Times (by Kennett Love)

Archaeologists uncover fortifications of Biblical town of Jericho, in what is now Jordan

BEVAN EXPULSION SOUGHT BY LABOR

Party Chiefs Map Discipline With Ouster to Follow

By THOMAS P. RONAN
Special to The New York Times.

LONDON, March 8—The Labor party's Parliamentary leaders moved today to obtain the expulsion of Aneurin Bevan from the party.

The eighteen-man "shadow cabinet," officially known as the Parliamentary Labor Committee, is headed by former Prime Minister Clement R. Attlee, leader of the party.

It will ask the Parliamentary Labor party to deprive Mr. Bevan of the whip. This would mean he no longer was recognized as a Labor member of the House of Commons.

If the Parliamentary Labor party, composed of the 293 Labor members of Parliament approves, its action will be reported to the National Executive Committee, the entire party's governing body.

Many members of the party believe that the committee would then proceed to expel the fiery Welsh radical from the party's ranks.

The drastic step by the shadow cabinet stemmed directly from Mr. Bevan's defiance of the leadership during the defense debate in the House of Commons last Wednesday.

At the end of the discussion,

Continued on Page 3, Column 3

The Jericho that Abraham might have seen, as recreated from the knowledge gleaned from Kathleen Kenyon's excavations of the ancient city.

"All the News That's Fit to Print"

The New York Times.

LATE CITY EDITION
Warm, chance of showers today.
Fair, not so warm tomorrow.
Temperature Range Today-Max., 75; Min., 55
Temperatures Yesterday-Max., 69.6; Min., 49.4
Full U. S. Weather Bureau Report, Page 49

VOL. CIV..No. 35,475. Entered as Second-Class Matter, Post Office, New York, N. Y. NEW YORK, FRIDAY, MARCH 11, 1955. Times Square, New York 36, N. Y. Telephone LAckawanna 4-1000 FIVE CENTS

HUMPHREY CALLS CUT IN TAX 'SILLY' AS BATTLE BEGINS

Bridges Backs the Secretary in Denouncing Democratic Program as 'Political'

DEBATE HIGHLY PARTISAN

Johnson Demands the G.O.P. Repudiate Official's Attack on the Party's Motives

By WILLIAM S. WHITE
Special to The New York Times.

WASHINGTON, March 10—The Eisenhower Administration and the Democratic Congress were involved today in a tax struggle amid perhaps the most bitterly partisan atmosphere of the President's tenure.

Senate debate on a bill by the Democratic leadership to cut the taxes on low incomes and repeal Republican tax relief for business and shareholders opened in a storm that went beyond the issue.

A vehement Republican-Democratic row involving Paul M. Butler, the Democratic National Chairman, and a remark he had made concerning the President's wife became a part of the proceedings.

The Administration's chief fiscal officer, George M. Humphrey, Secretary of the Treasury, denounced as "irresponsible," "political" and "silly" the new tax-cutting bill.

The top man in the Democratic leadership, Senator Lyndon B. Johnson of Texas, called on the principal Senate Republicans to repudiate Mr. Humphrey's accusations.

Republicans Challenged

Mr. Johnson suggested that the Republicans, in complaining that Mr. Butler had tried to involve Mrs. Eisenhower in politics by raising questions of her health, ought also to object to Secretary Humphrey's attack on the "motives" of the Democrats in the tax fight.

Senator Styles Bridges of New Hampshire, the senior Republican member of the Senate, arose to disavow two of the Humphrey charges but to endorse a third.

Mr. Bridges, chairman of the Senate Republican Policy Committee, declared from the floor:

"I certainly want to disassociate myself from two parts of that [the Humphrey attack on the Democrats]. I do not want to stand here and see sincere men called silly or irresponsible.

"But when they are called political, I think the Secretary has a pretty good name for it."

Almost overshadowed was the formal start of the tax debate.

Senator Harry F. Byrd of Virginia, a powerful conservative

Continued on Page 7, Column 1

Military Pay Rises Pass House, 399-1

By C. P. TRUSSELL
Special to The New York Times.

WASHINGTON, March 10—A $745,845,015 annual pay rise for 2,000,000 members of the military and related services was approved by the House of Representatives today. The vote was 399—1.

This was the House's response to an Administration move to correct a military situation that was becoming very serious.

The hard core of the armed forces was disintegrating. Civilian pay was coaxing to private industry men on whom the Government had spent from $3,200 to $275,000 to train as military experts, aground, under water and in the air.

The cost of this incentive pay program, it was conceded in House debate, was large.

Continued on Page 16, Column 3

2 PARTIES IN CLASH ON MRS. EISENHOWER

Congress Republicans Decry Butler Report of Illness—He Defends Remarks

Special to The New York Times.

WASHINGTON, March 10—Angry Congressional Republicans assailed Paul M. Butler, Democratic National Chairman, in concert today. They accused him of having involved the President's wife in politics.

Their criticism apparently reflected the President's indignation at Mr. Butler's suggestion that he might not run for re-election because of Mrs. Eisenhower's health.

Republican epithets running from "political bad taste" to "low and loathsome * * * scoundrel" were hurled at Mr. Butler.

In New York on Tuesday night Mr. Butler had declared a belief that the President would not seek re-election. He based this opinion, he said at the time, on conversations with various political leaders and "because of a personal situation in the Eisenhower household."

Statements Defended

He explained yesterday that in his reference to "a personal situation in the Eisenhower household" he had had in mind stories leaking from the White House that General Eisenhower was not happy there and a published United Press article that Mrs. Eisenhower was not well.

Today he further explained:

"All I referred to, in answer to questions by the press, were published reports which have appeared from time to time that Mrs. Eisenhower has not been in robust health, that her strength has been taxed by her official duties, and that her mother does not want her to live in the White House another four years. If these reports are true, I would think they would exert some influence on her husband.

"It seems to me that the Republicans who are criticizing me so violently for commenting on matters already reported in the press, are making a mountain out of a molehill. If their purpose is to persuade Mr. Eisen-

Continued on Page 6, Column 3

FEDERAL POLICIES ON CREDIT SCORED AT SENATE INQUIRY

Eccles and McCloy Condemn Easy Home Loans and Lack of Consumer Debt Curbs

By BURTON CRANE
Special to The New York Times.

WASHINGTON, March 10—Two prominent witnesses before the Senate Banking and Currency Committee joined today in attacking the Administration's liberal mortgage-lending policy and lack of control over consumer credit.

They also agreed that there were elements of danger in the recent sharp rise in stock prices

One witness was Marriner S. Eccles, for fourteen years chairman of the Federal Reserve Board under Presidents Roosevelt and Truman. The other was John J. McCloy, chairman of the board of the Chase National Bank of the City of New York. They testified in the committee's friendly study of the stock market.

Mr. Eccles not only attacked a seeming inconsistency between the Government's credit and fiscal policies, but also presented a plan for action. Its major feature was a proposal for dropping the rate of the tax on capital gains—profits from the sale of capital assets—as the holding period was lengthened and wiping it out eventually.

"There are soft spots in the economy," Mr. McCloy said. "I think the amount of mortgage debt, the methods of financing in connection with homes, have some elements of concern in them. I don't say it's a soft spot, but I am constantly wondering whether the level of consumer debt is healthy."

30 Billion in Consumer Debt

Robert A. Wallace, head of the committee's staff, said that the aggregate of consumer credit—which includes installment loans, charge accounts and personal loans—had risen in 1954 from $29,500,000,000 to $30,125,000,000.

"The consumer loan figure is high," Mr. McCloy said, "and creates some concern on my part. It is a fact that we haven't had any difficulty in the collection of consumer loans. They seem to be well maintained—but they weren't compromised in 1929, either. But the general level of debt is to me personally a matter of some concern."

Mr. Eccles called attention to the "paradoxical situation" of a booming stock market and "excessive construction activity" on the one hand and more than 3,000,000 unemployed and unused capacity in almost every field of production on the other.

There are estimates now, he said, that the gross national product—the sum of goods and services produced by the economy—for this year will approximate that for 1953—$364,900,000,000. But, Mr. Eccles added, the growth in the labor force, productive facilities and productivity should shove the gross national product $15,000,000,000 to $20,000,000,000 above 1953 without inflation.

He opposed further monetary

Continued on Page 12, Column 4

The New York Times (by Walter Sullivan). © 1955, The New York Times Company

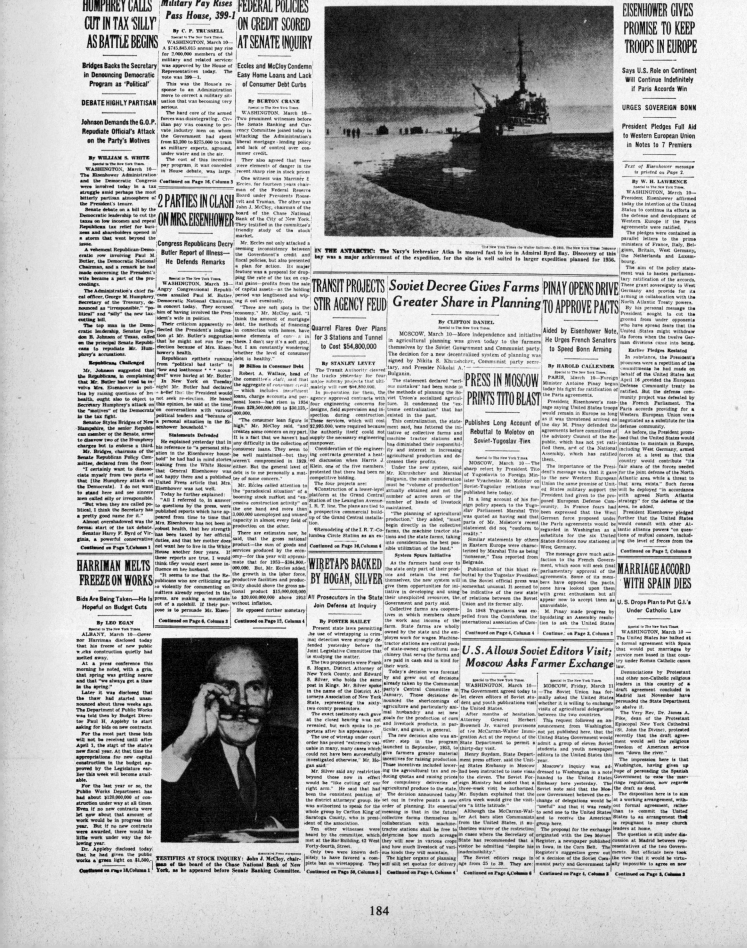

IN THE ANTARCTIC: The Navy's icebreaker Atka is moored fast to ice in Admiral Byrd Bay. Discovery of this bay was a major achievement of the expedition, for the site is well suited to larger expedition planned for 1956.

TRANSIT PROJECTS STIR AGENCY FEUD

Quarrel Flares Over Plans for 3 Stations and Tunnel to Cost $54,800,000

By STANLEY LEVEY

The Transit Authority cleared the tracks yesterday for four major subway projects that ultimately will cost $54,800,000.

In preparation for them, the agency approved contracts with four engineering concerns for designs, field supervision and inspection during construction. These services, which will cost $2,995,000, were required because the authority itself could not supply the necessary engineering manpower.

Consideration of the engineering contracts generated a heated discussion when Harris J. Klein, one of the five members, protested that there had been no competitive bidding.

The four projects are:

¶Construction of a lower-level platform at the Grand Central Station of the Lexington Avenue I. R. T. line. The plans are tied to a prospective commercial build-up of the Grand Central installation.

¶Remodeling of the I. R. T.-Columbus Circle Station as an ex-

Continued on Page 16, Column 4

WIRETAPS BACKED BY HOGAN, SILVER

All Prosecutors in the State Join Defense at Inquiry

By FOSTER HAILEY

Present state laws permitting the use of wiretapping in criminal detection were strongly defended yesterday before the Joint Legislative Committee that is studying the matter.

The two proponents were Frank S. Hogan, District Attorney of New York County, and Edward S. Silver, who holds the same post in Kings. Mr. Silver spoke in the name of the District Attorneys Association of New York State, representing the sixty-two county prosecutors.

The exact testimony each gave at the closed hearing was not revealed, but each spoke to reporters after his appearance.

The use of wiretap under court order has proved "extremely valuable in many, many cases which could not have been successfully investigated otherwise," Mr. Hogan said.

Mr. Silver said any restriction beyond those now in effect would be "like cutting off our right arm." He said that had been the consistent position of the district attorneys' group. He was authorized to speak for the whole group by Carlton King of Saratoga County, who is president of the association.

Ten other witnesses were heard by the committee, which met at the Bar Building, 42 West Forty-fourth Street.

Only two were known definitely to have favored a complete ban on wiretapping. They

Continued on Page 50, Column 5

Soviet Decree Gives Farms Greater Share in Planning

By CLIFTON DANIEL
Special to The New York Times.

MOSCOW, March 10—More independence and initiative in agricultural planning was given today to the farmers themselves by the Soviet Government and Communist party. The decision for a new decentralized system of planning was signed by Nikita S. Khrushchev, Communist party secretary, and Premier Nikolai A. Bulganin.

The statement declared "serious mistakes" had been made in the methods of planning the Soviet Union's socialized agriculture. It condemned the "extreme centralization" that has existed in the past.

This centralization, the statement said, has fettered the initiative of collective farms and machine tractor stations and has diminished their responsibility and interest in increasing agricultural production and decreased their profits.

Under the new system, said Mr. Khrushchev and Marshal Bulganin, the main consideration must be "volume of production" actually obtained and not the number of acres sown or the number of heads of livestock maintained.

"The planning of agricultural production," they added, "must begin directly in the collective farms, the machine tractor stations and the state farms, taking into consideration the best possible utilization of the land."

System Spurs Initiative

As the farmers hand over to the state only part of their produce and retain the rest for themselves, the new system will give them opportunities for initiative in developing and using their unexploited resources, the Government and party said.

Collective farms are cooperatives in which members share the work and income of the farm. State farms are wholly owned by the state and the employes work for wages. Machine-tractor stations are central pools of state-owned agricultural machinery that serve the farms and are paid in cash and in kind for their work.

Today's decision was forecast by and grew out of decisions already taken by the Communist party's Central Committee in January. Those decisions denounced the shortcomings of agriculture and particularly animal husbandry and set new goals for the production of corn and livestock products, in particular, and grain, in general.

The new decision also was another step in the program launched in September, 1953, to give farmers greater material incentives for raising production. Those incentives included lowering the agricultural tax and reducing quotas and raising prices for compulsory deliveries of agricultural produce to the state.

The decision announced today set out in twelve points a new order of planning. Its essential meaning is that in the future collective farms themselves in collaboration with machine-tractor stations shall be free to determine how much acreage they will sow in various crops and how much livestock of various kinds they will maintain.

The higher organs of planning will still set quotas for delivery

Continued on Page 4, Column 4

PRESS IN MOSCOW PRINTS TITO BLAST

Publishes Long Account of Rebuttal to Molotov on Soviet-Yugoslav Ties

Special to The New York Times.

MOSCOW, March 10—The sharp retort by President Tito of Yugoslavia to Foreign Minister Vyacheslav M. Molotov on Soviet-Yugoslav relations was published here today.

In a long account of his foreign policy speech to the Yugoslav Parliament Marshal Tito was quoted as having said that parts of Mr. Molotov's recent statement did not "conform to reality."

Similar statements by others in Eastern Europe were characterized by Marshal Tito as being "nonsense," Tass reported from Belgrade.

Publication of this blunt rebuttal by the Yugoslav President in the Soviet official press was somewhat unusual. It seemed to be indicative of the new state of relations between the Soviet Union and its former ally.

In 1948 Yugoslavia was expelled from the Cominform, the international association of Com-

Continued on Page 4, Column 4

PINAY OPENS DRIVE TO APPROVE PACTS

Aided by Eisenhower Note, He Urges French Senators to Speed Bonn Arming

By HAROLD CALLENDER
Special to The New York Times.

PARIS, March 10—Foreign Minister Antoine Pinay began today his fight for ratification of the Paris agreements.

President Eisenhower's message saying United States troops would remain in Europe so long as it was threatened arrived on the day M. Pinay defended the agreements before committees of the advisory Council of the Republic, which has not yet ratified them, and of the National Assembly, which has ratified them.

The importance of the President's message was that it gave to the new Western European Union the same promise of United States military support the President had given to the proposed European Defense Community. In France fears had been expressed that the West German force proposed under the Paris agreements would be regarded in Washington as a substitute for the six United States divisions now stationed in West Germany.

The message gave much satisfaction to the French Government, which soon will seek final parliamentary approval of the agreements. Some of its members have opposed the pacts, none have looked upon them with great enthusiasm but all appear now to accept them as unavoidable.

M. Pinay made progress by liquidating an Assembly resolution to ask the United States

Continued on Page 3, Column 2

U.S. Allows Soviet Editors Visit; Moscow Asks Farmer Exchange

Special to The New York Times.

WASHINGTON, March 10—The Government agreed today to let eleven editors of Soviet student and youth publications visit the United States.

After months of hesitation, Attorney General Herbert Brownell Jr. waived provisions of the McCarran-Walter Immigration Act at the request of the State Department to permit a thirty-day visit.

Henry Suydam, State Department press officer, said the United States Embassy in Moscow had been instructed to issue visas to the eleven. The Soviet Foreign Ministry had asked that a three-week visit be authorized. Mr. Suydam explained that the extra week would give the visitors "a little latitude."

Although the McCarran-Walter Act bars alien Communists from the United States, it authorizes waiver of the restriction in cases where the Secretary of State has recommended that a visitor be admitted "despite his inadmissibility."

The Soviet editors range in age from 25 to 39. They are:

Continued on Page 4, Column 6

Special to The New York Times.

MOSCOW, Friday, March 11—The Soviet Union has formally asked the United States whether it is willing to exchange visits of agricultural delegations between the two countries.

This request followed an announcement from Washington, not yet published here, that the United States Government would admit a group of eleven Soviet students and youth newspaper editors to the United States this year.

Moscow's inquiry was addressed to Washington in a note handed to the United States Embassy here yesterday. The Soviet note said that the Moscow Government believed the exchange of delegations would be "useful" and that it was ready to send one to the United States and to receive the American group here.

The proposal for the exchange originated with the Des Moines Register, a newspaper published in Iowa, in the Corn Belt. The Register's suggestion grew out of a decision of the Soviet Communist party and Government to

Continued on Page 4, Column 3

EISENHOWER GIVES PROMISE TO KEEP TROOPS IN EUROPE

Says U.S. Role on Continent Will Continue Indefinitely if Paris Accords Win

URGES SOVEREIGN BONN

President Pledges Full Aid to Western European Union in Notes to 7 Premiers

Text of Eisenhower message is printed on Page 2.

By W. H. LAWRENCE
Special to The New York Times.

WASHINGTON, March 10—President Eisenhower affirmed today the intention of the United States to continue its efforts in the defense and development of Western Europe if the Paris agreements were ratified.

The pledges were contained in parallel letters to the prime ministers of France, Italy, Belgium, Britain, West Germany, the Netherlands and Luxembourg.

The aim of the policy statement was to hasten parliamentary ratification of the accords. These grant sovereignty to West Germany and provide for its arming in collaboration with the North Atlantic Treaty powers.

By his personal message the President sought to cut the ground from under opponents who have spread fears that the United States might withdraw its forces when the twelve German divisions came into being.

Earlier Pledges Restated

In substance, the President's promises were a repetition of the commitments he had made on behalf of the United States last April 16 provided the European Defense Community treaty be ratified. But the defense community project was defeated by the French Parliament. The Paris accords providing for a Western European Union were negotiated as a substitute for the defense community.

As before, the President promised that the United States would continue to maintain in Europe, including West Germany, armed forces at a level so that this country would contribute "its fair share of the forces needed for the joint defense of the North Atlantic area while a threat to that area exists." Such forces will be deployed "in accordance with agreed North Atlantic strategy" for the defense of the area, he added.

President Eisenhower pledged further that the United States would consult with other Atlantic alliance powers "on questions of mutual concern, including the level of forces from the

Continued on Page 2, Column 6

MARRIAGE ACCORD WITH SPAIN DIES

U. S. Drops Plan to Put G.I.'s Under Catholic Law

Special to The New York Times.

WASHINGTON, March 10—The United States has balked at a formal agreement with Spain that would put marriages by service men based in that country under Roman Catholic canon law.

Denunciations by Protestant and other non-Catholic religious leaders in this country of a draft agreement concluded in Madrid last November have persuaded the State Department to shelve it.

The Very Rev. Dr. James A. Pike, dean of the Protestant Episcopal New York Cathedral (St. John the Divine), protested recently that the draft agreement would sell the religious freedom of American service men "down the river."

The impression here is that Washington, having given up hope of persuading the Spanish Government to ease the marriage regulations, now regards the draft as dead.

The disposition here is to aim at a working arrangement, without formal agreement, rather than to commit the United States to an arrangement that is repugnant to many church leaders at home.

The question is still under discussion at Madrid between representatives of the two Governments. But officials here took the view that it would be virtually impossible to agree on new

Continued on Page 3, Column 3

HARRIMAN MELTS FREEZE ON WORKS

Bids Are Being Taken—He Is Hopeful on Budget Cuts

By LEO EGAN
Special to The New York Times.

ALBANY, March 10—Governor Harriman disclosed today that his freeze of new public works construction quietly had melted away.

At a press conference this morning he noted, with a grin, that spring was getting nearer and that "we always get a thaw in the spring."

Later it was disclosed that the thaw had started unannounced about three weeks ago. The Department of Public Works was told then by Budget Director Paul H. Appleby to start asking for bids on new contracts.

For the most part these bids will not be received until after April 1, the start of the state's new fiscal year. At that time the appropriations for new capital construction in the budget approved by the Legislature earlier this week will become available.

For the last year or so, the Public Works Department has had about $120,000,000 of construction under way at all times. Even if no new contracts were let now about that amount of work would be in progress this year. But if no new contracts were awarded, there would be little work under way the following year.

Dr. Appleby disclosed today that he had given the public works a green light on $1,500,-

Continued on Page 18, Column 1

Associated Press Wirephoto

TESTIFIES AT STOCK INQUIRY: John J. McCloy, chairman of the board of the Chase National Bank of New York, as he appeared before Senate Banking Committee.

"All the News That's Fit to Print"

The New York Times.

LATE CITY EDITION
Fair and warmer today and tomorrow.
Temperature Range Today-Max., 51; Min., 30
Temperatures Yesterday-Max. 41.3; Min. 24.4
Full U. S. Weather Bureau Report, Page 59

VOL. CIV No. 35,493. Entered as Second-Class Matter, Post Office, New York, N. Y. NEW YORK, TUESDAY, MARCH 29, 1955. Times Square, New York 36, N. Y. Telephone LAckawanna 4-1000 FIVE CENTS

EISENHOWER SEES NO WAR NOW OVER CHINESE ISLES; WEST CHARTS BIG 4 TALKS

Active Consultation Begun On a Meeting With Soviet

Diplomats of U. S., Britain, France Hold Preliminary Talks—Bonn and Paris Suggest Deputies Weigh Agenda

By DANA ADAMS SCHMIDT
Special to The New York Times.

WASHINGTON, March 28—The United States has begun "quite active consultations" with Britain and France on plans for a meeting with the Soviet Union. West Germany will be included in the preliminary talks.

Henry Suydam, State Department spokesman, said the consultations, begun in a preliminary way last week, would be conducted through diplomatic channels here, in London, Paris and Bonn. They will go on "in a far more active state," now that France has completed ratification of the Paris agreements to arm West Germany, he added.

[Sir Anthony Eden, British Foreign Secretary, also said Monday that the Western Big Three were consulting.]

The first moves in the diplomatic exchanges were proposals by France and West Germany that the Western powers set up a working party on the level of deputies of the foreign ministers, diplomatic sources disclosed.

The United States representative in such a group probably would be Herbert Hoover Jr., Under Secretary of State. The time and place for the group's meeting remain to be worked out.

Mr. Suydam said "it would be natural" if the Western foreign ministers were to discuss plans for a great-powers meeting when they met at the North Atlantic Council session later this spring. The time and place of this meeting have not been set yet, but

Continued on Page 3, Column 3

ALARM DEPLORED

President Hears Reds Lack Build-Up Needed for a Major Attack

By W. H. LAWRENCE
Special to The New York Times

WASHINGTON, March 28—President Eisenhower does not share the view that war in the Formosa Strait is imminent.

He does not believe, as some military leaders do, that the Chinese Communists will begin a campaign to capture Matsu and Quemoy Islands about the middle of April.

The best political and military intelligence reaching the White House is that the Chinese Reds have not yet undertaken the kind of military and aviation build-up that would make an attack likely in the near future.

The President did not like stories published over the week-end that said his military advisers were satisfied that such attacks might begin by mid-April. They were said to be urging upon the President a definite declaration that he had decided that the United States would intervene militarily to prevent the capture of the Nationalist-held islands off the Chinese mainland.

The White House believes it is aware of the source of these stories, and treats them as "parochial," representing the view of only one man or one service.

Danger Not Discounted

It is the President's conviction that he has more information—both political and military—available to him than the source of last week's scare headlines.

He does not discount the danger in the Formosa Strait, but he does not think the Chinese Communists are ready for the major attack that would be necessary if they were to attempt to dislodge the Chinese Nationalists from Quemoy and Matsu.

Politically the President thinks the Chinese Reds would not launch such an attack on the eve of the African-Asian conference, scheduled to begin April 18 in Bandung, Indonesia.

In these conclusions, the President has the backing of the National Security Council and Secretary of State Dulles.

The President is still unwilling to say flatly whether the United States would go to war for the defense of Quemoy and Matsu under any and all circumstances.

He still sticks, in general, to

Continued on Page 2, Column 3

PRESIDENT'S PLAN FOR ROADS FOUGHT BY HIS APPOINTEE

Campbell, New U.S. Controller General, Terms the Program Financially 'Objectionable'

LEGALITY IS QUESTIONED

Weeks Puts Cost of Nation's Highway Needs in the Next 30 Years at 297 Billion

By RUSSELL BAKER
Special to The New York Times.

WASHINGTON, March 28—The Controller General, Congress' watchdog on Government spending, assailed the Administration's road building program today as financially "objectionable."

This newest attack on the President's highway plan came from Joseph Campbell, recently appointed by the White House over Democratic protests to head the General Accounting Office.

Mr. Campbell told a Senate Public Works subcommittee that the Administration's plans for financing the $101,000,000,000 program were legally dubious and could weaken Congressional control over highway building.

Making his first Congressional appearance since he was confirmed in his new job, Mr. Campbell said that the Administration's financing plans should be dropped. The program, like all Federal road projects, should be financed by Congressional appropriation, he added.

Outlay Put at 297 Billion

While the Administration bill was under fire in committee, Sinclair Weeks, Secretary of Commerce, sent the Senate a report outlining the country's future highway needs.

To maintain an adequate highway system for the next thirty years, the report stated, an estimated $297,100,000,000 must be spent by government at all levels. This would involve an average annual outlay of $9,900,000,000, or more than a 50 per cent increase over the $6,100,000,000 spent on roads last year.

The Administration bill would cover construction for the next ten years. About $70,000,000,000 of the proposed $101,000,000,000 would be paid by state and local authorities.

A Federal Highway Corporation would be created to issue up to $21,000,000,000 in 3 per cent bonds. This would constitute the major Federal contribution. Interest payments on the bonds would amount to about $11,500,000,000.

The President's program has been in political trouble since it emerged from the White House. Senator Harry F. Byrd, Democrat of Virginia and chairman of the Senate Finance Commit-

Continued on Page 21, Column 3

Harlan Assumes Supreme Court Post

Associated Press Wirephoto

John Marshall Harlan, newest Associate Justice of Supreme Court, is helped into robes by Robert Marshall, attendant.

By LUTHER A. HUSTON
Special to The New York Times.

WASHINGTON, March 28—John Marshall Harlan was sworn in today as an associate justice of the Supreme Court. The New Yorker became the eighty-ninth man to sit on the high bench since the Federal judiciary was established in 1789. His grandfather, also named John Marshall Harlan, was the forty-fifth. Justice Harlan, appointed from the Federal Court of Appeals for the Second Circuit, succeeds

Continued on Page 18, Column 5

HARRIMAN URGES LEGISLATURE PASS HOUSING PLAN NOW

Governor Outlines 8-Point Program, Seeks 170,000 Units Yearly Until 1965

By LEO EGAN
Special to The New York Times.

ALBANY, March 28 — Governor Harriman sent a special message to the Legislature tonight urging approval of an eight-point housing program before adjournment of the present session.

Almost all the legislation involved has bi partisan support. Some bills have been approved by both Senate and Assembly. Others have been approved in one house and are awaiting action in the other. Still others are scheduled for passage as soon as they have met constitutional requirements.

In urging approval of the program, Mr. Harriman told the Legislature that more than 2,000,000 residents of New York, roughly one-seventh of the total population, were forced to live in unsafe, dilapidated housing or in housing without adequate heating or sanitary facilities.

Construction of a minimum of 170,000 new housing units a year for the next ten years is needed to bring the state's housing supply up to adequate standards, the Governor declared. This construction rate is almost double last year's, when 90,000 units were built, and one-third higher than the record of 124,000 units completed in a single year, which was set in 1950.

Harriman's Program

The program recommended by the Governor called for enactment of legislation that would:

¶Permit families dislocated by slum clearance, rehabilitation or other governmental activities to move into public housing even though their incomes are above the maximums now fixed for admission. A bi partisan bill to accomplish this purpose has already been approved by committees of both Senate and Assembly and is awaiting action by both chambers.

¶Submit to the voters this fall a constitutional amendment authorizing annual state subsidies of $34,000,000 for public housing. This is an increase of $9,000,000 over the present limit. The amendment has already been approved in the Assembly and is awaiting Senate action.

¶Permit municipalities to lend up to 90 per cent of the cost of nonprofit or limited dividend private housing and to grant such housing partial exemption from real estate taxes. Leaders of both parties have agreed to this measure, but it cannot be brought to a vote before tomorrow because it has not been in final legislative form for three days.

¶Submit to the voters a proposition to make $50,000,000 of the housing bond issue authorized last year for state loans to nonprofit or limited dividend private housing companies. This

Continued on Page 22, Column 5

HOUSE UNIT VOTES RESERVE PROGRAM OF 2,900,000 MEN

Plan Would Employ 250,000 Teen-Agers Each Year—Draft Clause Rejected

By C. P. TRUSSELL
Special to The New York Times.

WASHINGTON, March 28—An Administration program to provide a military reserve of 2,900,000 trained men by 1960 was approved by a House of Representatives subcommittee today.

The 9-to-1 vote came after ten weeks of study and hearings in which service branches and most veterans' organizations participated.

The real Ready Reserve would use up to 250,000 teen-age youths a year. They could volunteer for six months of active service, in lieu of waiting for the two-year draft, and then continue with drills and periodic field training for seven and a half years.

All draftees and other servicemen also would face eight years of active and reserve service.

In the background was the fact that only about 700,000 of the millions of veterans of World War II and Korea had lived up to their reserve obligations. The new bill would make reserve training mandatory, but, it was held, it would not be too harsh.

48 Drills a Year

The reserve training would consist of about forty-eight drills a year, with two weeks of field training in the summer. If a trainee preferred, he could take thirty days of field training a year. If a trainee balked he could be called into active service for forty-five days a year, or he might be drafted for a two-year Selective Service assignment.

In all, the subcommittee approved much of the White House program. Reserve and service organizations appeared to be satisfied. All had played important roles in the decisions on the bill.

Two key provisions, however, were rejected by tie votes and left for the full committee on the Armed Services to decide, on or about April 18. They were these:

1. The question of drafting 17½ and 18-year-olds if they did not volunteer in sufficient numbers to create an effective National Security Training Corps requiring from 100,000 to 250,000 youth a year through a four-year program.
2. Returning to the President authority, in an emergency such as Korea presented, to call up a maximum of 750,000 Ready Reserves without getting special permission from Congress. Such Presidential power was rescinded by Congress in 1952.

Representative Overton Brooks, Democrat of Louisiana, subcommittee chairman, said he thought the full committee would approve these provisions. Mr. Brooks added that he was for

Continued on Page 12, Column 5

CITY SEEKS CURBS ON PORT AGENCY

Demands for Limit on Wide Condemnation Powers May Delay Vast Arterial Plan

By CHARLES G. BENNETT

Prospective costs of condemnation of land stood in the path yesterday of speedy approval by the Board of Estimate of vital parts of the $600,000,000 arterial highway program. The project has been put forward by the Port of New York Authority and the Triborough Bridge and Tunnel Authority.

As the board went into executive session yesterday morning on the subject, some of its members had serious doubts about giving the Port Authority the wide condemnation powers it seeks for the two major projects it will build.

These are a $220,000,000 twelve-lane double-decked suspension bridge across the Narrows, linking Fort Hamilton in Brooklyn with Fort Wadsworth on Staten Island, and the addition of a $19,300,000 six-lane lower deck to the twenty-four-year-old George Washington Bridge.

Of the $600,000,000 over-all arterial program, the Port Authority's share will exceed $300,000,000. The Triborough Bridge Authority will spend at least $100,000,000, including $93,000,000 for a Throgs Neck bridge across the East River. There also will be an outlay of about $200,000,000 in Federal-state financing of essential road links and approaches.

Board Members' Doubts

The principal doubts of some board members—doubts that must be resolved before the city's required approval will be given to the Port Authority proposals—were concerned with these points:

¶The wisdom of giving the Port Authority wide condemnation power without a checkrein by the Board of Estimate on final decisions for taking land. Some experts have put prospective condemnation costs as high as $80,000,000, of which half would be paid each by the city and the state.

¶The wisdom of giving up so large a quantity of land now yielding city taxes. Some estimates have put the probable tax loss at $1,000,000 a year.

¶The wisdom of forcing the reundertaking an annual added maintenance expense, put as high as $1,500,000, for lighting the new improvements and providing added policing and other services.

¶The wisdom of forcing the relocation of as many families as apparently is called for under present Port Authority plans. Rough estimates have put these figures at 7,500 to 10,000 families at the Bay Ridge end of the Narrows Bridge, 1,800 families

Continued on Page 20, Column 6

BYRD TO RETURN TO THE ANTARCTIC

U. S. Expedition Will Set Up Sites for Geophysical Study —Will Leave in November

Special to The New York Times.

WASHINGTON, March 28—The White House announced today plans for a new expedition to the Antarctic in November. It will be headed by Rear Admiral Richard E. Byrd, retired, who has made four previous trips to the Antarctic.

The purpose of the expedition, which will include several ships and aircraft, is to begin work on three observation sites needed for the United States' share in the program for the International Geophysical Year of 1957-1958.

The expedition will establish its main supply base in the Little America area. From there parties will depart by tractor trains in October, 1956, for a second station to be built in Marie Byrd Land. A third station will be built later at or near the South Pole from materials brought in by air over 700 miles of rugged mountain ranges and glaciers.

The White House announcement stressed that the expedition was purely scientific. It is part of an international effort, including scientists from the Soviet Union, to coordinate observations in earth sciences under the auspices of the International Council of Scientific Unions.

Admiral Byrd, brother of Senator Harry F. Byrd, Democrat of Virginia, was designated as officer in charge of the expedition. He will be the direct representa-

Continued on Page 13, Column 2

Johnson Says Right Wing Of G.O.P. Is 'Talking War'

By WILLIAM S. WHITE
Special to The New York Times.

WASHINGTON, March 28—The Senate Democratic leader, Lyndon B. Johnson of Texas, accused the right-wing Republicans today of "talking war." He warned against an "irresponsible adventure" in Asia.

The Republican leader, Senator William F. Knowland of California, countered with a demand to know whether the United States was now going to be sent "marching down the hill again in the face of Communist threats."

"The road of appeasement," he said, "is not the road to peace, but is surrender on the installment plan."

This brief Senate debate occurred almost on the eve of bipartisan foreign policy consultations at the White House. President Eisenhower has arranged to meet the Congressional leaders of both parties Wednesday and Thursday for discussions of the possibility of a Big Four meeting and the military situation in Formosa waters.

Senator Johnson promised that the Democrats would be ready to assist the President "with any advice and counsel that are at our command."

He declared he held "high hopes" that the conferences between the President and Congressional leaders would "brighten the prospects for the kind of peace we all want."

Mr. Johnson sought also to concentrate national attention on what he called "the key that will unlock the door that thus far has prevented the alliance of free nations from attaining its full strength"—the Paris agreements for bringing an armed West Ger-

Cont'nued on Page 6, Column 5

WEST FOR CENSURE OF ISRAEL ON GAZA

U. S., Britain and France Bid U. N. Act—Also Urge Steps to Ease Border Tension

By KATHLEEN TELTSCH
Special to The New York Times.

UNITED NATIONS, N. Y., March 28—The three major Western powers asked today that Israel be condemned for the attack last month on Egyptian forces in the Gaza Strip.

The recommendation was made in a joint resolution submitted to the Security Council by Britain, France and the United States. The Council's eleven members will meet on the case again tomorrow at 3 P. M.

In a second resolution, the three Western powers called on both parties to cooperate in carrying out the series of "practical measures" recently proposed by the United Nations' Palestine truce chief to reduce border friction.

Israel suggested changes in the text to include the idea that the truce supervisor, Maj. Gen. E. L. M. Burns of Canada, had listed infiltration from Egypt as "one of the main causes" of the present tension.

Propaganda by Cairo Alleged

It has been Israel's contention that the Cairo Government whipped up military and propaganda attacks against Israel for months before the Gaza clash. Thirty-eight Egyptians and eight Israelis died in the engagement. Israel also plans to raise in debate last Friday's raid by Egyptians on a wedding party in the Negev village of Patish.

The Western resolution to condemn Israel is expected to be approved by the Council, whose members have indicated they feel Israel should be censured. The resolution labels the attack a violation of the cease-fire ordered by the Council six years ago and also of the armistice agreement both parties signed in 1949 at the end of full-scale fighting in Palestine.

The measure calls on Israel to take all precautions to prevent such actions as the attack near Gaza. It also makes the point that no progress can be made toward permanent peace in the region unless both parties comply strictly with the armistice. It warns that "any deliberate violation" threatens this armistice.

Technically, the Council is

Continued on Page 10, Column 5

IZVESTIA ASSAILS ECONOMIC 'FOES'

Criticism on Consumer Goods Is Linked to Malenkov

By Reuters.

MOSCOW, Tuesday, March 29—The Soviet Government newspaper Izvestia today described persons who in the past put consumer goods ahead of the drive for heavy industry as "enemies of the people."

The article was published as speculation increased here about former Premier Georgi M. Malenkov after his absence last Saturday from a public function attended by other Soviet leaders.

It was Mr. Malenkov's first such absence since he resigned his post Feb. 8. Mr. Malenkov was associated with the campaign to step up production of consumer goods.

Izvestia also described the consumer goods advocates as "right-wing opportunists" and "capitulators." It said the Communist party had "cast out of the way" such persons when they attempted to put consumer goods before heavy industry during an earlier stage of the Soviet Union's development.

The trade union newspaper Trud also published an article on the economic controversy. It referred to the time when the Communist party waged a "violent struggle against class enemies and their agents" for the priority of heavy industry.

Such terms as "class enemies"

Continued on Page 5, Column 2

GRUNEWALD HELD GUILTY IN TAX FIX

Two Others Also Convicted, Two Are Acquitted Here

Henry W. Grunewald, Washington influence peddler and tax-fixer, was found guilty last night of a $160,000 tax-fix bribery. A Federal jury here also convicted two accomplices. Two other defendants were acquitted.

Grunewald, known variously as "The Mystery Man," "The Dutchman" and "Gravel-voiced Henry," broke into the spotlight in 1951 during a Congressional inquiry into scandals in the Internal Revenue Bureau. His conviction resulted from disclosures during that investigation.

Convicted with Grunewald were:

Daniel A. Bolich, former Assistant Commissioner of Internal Revenue. He is 54 years old and lives at 617 Second Street, Brooklyn.

Max Halperin, 69, of 390 West End Avenue, a tax attorney.

Max Steinberg, 58, of Beverly Hills, Calif., former group chief in the Upper Manhattan Division of the Internal Revenue Bureau, and Harry T. Scherm, 46, of Williston Park, L. I., a former agent in the same office, were acquitted. They had been charged with receiving a $40,000 bribe in the case.

Judge Archie O. Dawson fixed $30,000 bail for Grunewald, despite pleas by the prosecution that the defendant had money to

Continued on Page 20, Column 2

Javits Bolts G. O. P. On Key Labor Issues

By WARREN WEAVER Jr.
Special to The New York Times.

ALBANY, March 28—Jacob K. Javits broke with the Republican legislative leadership today on rent control and several key labor issues.

The Republican Attorney General endorsed a number of points in Governor Harriman's program, proposals that G.O.P. party leaders have been bottling up in committee throughout the session.

He took this stand at an "emergency" legislative conference held here by the State Congress of Industrial Organizations Council. Its aim was to mobilize legislative action on rent and labor measures.

In echoing several sections of the Democratic Governor's annual message of last January, Mr. Javits called for these things:

¶Continuing state-wide rent controls. The Republican bill

Continued on Page 23, Column 3

Youth Gang Invades High School; Two Pupils Beaten in Classroom

A band of teen-age boys forced their way yesterday into Evander Childs High School in the Bronx and beat two students in a classroom.

The attack was apparently in revenge for a fight last Friday in which a grudge between two students led to a free-for-all after classes two blocks from the building. The original quarrel was between a white boy and a Negro. Yesterday's raiders were Negroes and their victims were whites, but school officials and the police said it was not a "race fight."

The raiders struck and fled so quickly that there were widely varying versions of what had happened. The thirty-five boys and girls in the classroom and the teacher, who had her back to the class when the intruders entered, reported the size of the raiding party variously from five to eight members.

Original versions described the gang as holding the teacher at bay with a bayonet while they went about their vengeance. A calmer appraisal later developed that nobody had a bayonet or even a knife. The teacher, Mrs. Sophie Green, denied that she had been threatened. She said that by the time the sounds of scuffling caused her to turn from the blackboard the intruders were running out of the room.

The victims of the beating were Lawrence Capra, 16 years old, of 3216 Cruger Avenue, and Raymond Bisesto, also 16, of 666 East 224th Street, both the Bronx. The Capra boy was treated at Fordham Hospital for face cuts inflicted with an empty fiber scabbard. He then went home. Young Bisesto, who had a bloody nose, required no medical treatment and remained at school.

The police said both youths apparently had been victims of mistaken identity. Neither had been involved in Friday's fight, detectives of the Wakefield station reported.

The raiders, about 15 to 17 years old, entered about 10 A. M. They pushed aside John Basili, a monitor at the Barnes Avenue side door to the school, which fronts on Gun Hill Road. They wen to Room 252, where Mrs. Green was teaching a fourth-term history class. The door was open. The intruders walked in quietly, went directly to young Capra and Bisesto and began pummeling them.

The youth who carried the scabbard, about fifteen inches long and edged with metal, took several whacks at the Capra boy. As the teacher turned from the blackboard, one youth shouted to her: "You stay out of this!" Then the attackers ran from the building.

There was instant confusion,

Continued on Page 25, Column 4

Ex-President Guilty In Panama Slaying

Special to The New York Times.

PANAMA, Tuesday, March 29—Former President José Ramon Guizado was convicted early today of complicity in the assassination of his predecessor, President José Antonio Remon.

The National Assembly, sitting as a court, fixed the prison term for Señor Guizado at eight years. The vote for conviction as an accomplice in the slaying was 45 to 8.

The Assembly's deliberations were kept secret. Not even the Assembly secretariat was present. To insure secrecy the fifty-three-member Assembly met in the Supreme Court chambers on the third floor of the Palace of Justice instead of on the first floor in the Assembly chamber, which has many exits.

Colonel Remòn was slain Jan. 2 at a race track. Ruben O. Miro confessed the killing and implicated Señor Guizado.

"All the News That's Fit to Print"

The New York Times.

LATE CITY EDITION
Mostly fair, little temperature change today. Fair tomorrow.
Temperature Range Today-Max., 74; Min., 55
Temperatures Yesterday—Max., 72; Min., 56
Full U. S. Weather Bureau Report, Page 32

VOL. CIV..No. 35,560. Entered as Second-Class Matter, Post Office, New York, N. Y.

NEW YORK, SATURDAY, JUNE 4, 1955. Times Square, New York 36, N. Y. Telephone LAckawanna 4-1000 FIVE CENTS

TEACHERS TO GET $450 RISE IN PAY OVER TWO YEARS

40,000 Here to Receive $300 in '55-'56 and Additional $150 for '56-'57 Period

COST PUT AT $23,500,000

Increases to Take Effect on Each July 1—Salary Steps Cut by Estimate Board

By CHARLES G. BENNETT

The pay of New York City's 40,000 public school teachers will be increased by $300 in 1955-56 and by an additional $150 in 1956-57.

Mayor Wagner announced yesterday that his formula, which will cost the city $23,500,000 over the two-year period, had been agreed upon by the Board of Estimate in executive session.

The $300 increase will take effect July 1 of this year, and the additional $150 on July 1, 1956. High school teachers appointed before July 1, 1947, and all holders of a Master of Arts degree or its equivalent, will get $200 additional, split over two years.

The number of salary steps necessary to reach maximum pay were reduced from sixteen to fourteen.

At present salaries of teachers holding a Bachelor of Arts degree range from $3,450 a year to $6,750. Under the Board of Estimate's plan the range will be from $3,900 to $7,200.

For teachers with Master of Arts degrees the existing range is from $3,650 to $6,950. The new plan, when in effect, will place this range from $4,300 to $7,600.

Teachers Asked More

The teachers' own plan as submitted to the Board of Estimate called for a $450 across-the-board increase for all teachers in 1955-56, plus allowances for the higher degree. Its cost to the city was estimated at $26,000,000 additional in 1955-56.

The Board of Estimate's salary action received a mixed reaction last night from the major teacher groups. Some said they appreciated the increases and the projected cut in the number of salary steps necessary to reach maximum pay, but they were disappointed that certain features of their own proposals had been left out.

Charles H. Silver, president of the Board of Education, said the members of the board and Dr. William Jansen, Superintendent of Schools, were "fully aware that the new salary scales may fall short of what would represent proper compensation for our teachers and supervisors."

He noted, however, that the pay schedules represented many hours of discussion by top city officials. He said "the Mayor and his fiscal advisers gave us every cooperation for they too know the seriousness of this problem." Mr. Silver said he believed also that the Board of Estimate had made available the largest amount of money within the limits of the city budget.

The inadequacy of teachers' salaries, Mr. Silver declared, is "a continuing problem and we will work continuously to bring about a solution." He said he was gratified that Governor

Continued on Page 15, Column 2

A President Flies in 2-Engine Plane for First Time

Associated Press Wirephoto

President Eisenhower about to enter light plane yesterday for flight to Gettysburg

By W. H. LAWRENCE
Special to The New York Times.

WASHINGTON, June 3—For the first time in history, a President of the United States flew in a twin-engined aircraft. Until now Air Force and Secret Service regulations have required not fewer than four engines in a plane carrying the President. President Eisenhower made the 146-mile journey today to and from his Gettysburg, Pa., farm on his initial ride in a gleaming blue and white Aero Commander 560, an executive type of light plane, which retails for about $70,000. He called it "a lovely plane." The trip to Gettysburg required thirty-two minutes. The homeward journey was made in twenty-two min-

Continued on Page 4, Column 6

MAYOR SWEARS 14 IN GAY CITY HALL

Signs Tax Bills in Holiday Mood as He Prepares to Fly to Europe Tomorrow

Christmas arrived yesterday for many Democrats. For many it was somewhat tardy; for others it was six months early.

As City Hall swirled in unceasing activity on Mayor Wagner's last business day at his desk prior to his flying to Europe tomorrow, the Mayor ladled out fourteen judgeships and other city jobs as "bon voyage" gifts to the faithful.

It was a good day for it, too. City Hall, colorfully decorated in front for an afternoon scholarship award ceremony, was in a gay, holiday mood. All day candidates for appointment and legions of their friends milled about the building's corridors in restless anticipation of good things to come.

The Mayor had a practical matter of business to attend to, however, before he could distribute the largesse.

To keep the city's fiscal machinery oiled for the fiscal year beginning July 1—a year that will open before he returns from Europe—Mr. Wagner signed bills making some hitherto "temporary" taxes permanent and increasing others.

The new laws, sanctioned by the Legislature, made permanent the 3 per cent retail sales tax, yielding $210,000,000 a year; the compensating use tax, bringing in $800,000 annually, and the utility and conduit tax, returning $14,000,000 a year.

Another law signed by the

Continued on Page 15, Column 1

NEW PENN STATION SET IN BIG PROJECT

An agreement has been reached "on terms for building a new railroad station and the world's largest commercial building on the present site of the Pennsylvania Station."

This was disclosed yesterday by the Pennsylvania Railroad, which said the agreement was between the railroad and the real estate company of Webb & Knapp, Inc., headed by William Zeckendorf.

The railroad said the papers would be signed Tuesday when more detailed plans will be given.

WORLD CROPS DECLINE

F. A. O. Reports First Drop Since War in 1954-55

Special to The New York Times.

ROME, June 3—For the first time since the war world agricultural production failed to rise in 1954-55. This was reported today by the Committee on Commodity Problems of the United Nations Food and Agriculture Organization.

The trend was attributed by the committee to diminished yields in North America and the Near East. It cited acreage and marketing restrictions in the United States and poor crops in Canada and the Near East.

Western Europe, Latin America and the Far East gained.

SURPLUSES BILL SIGNED

Billions in U. S. Goods Now Available Free to Schools

WASHINGTON, June 3 (UP)—President Eisenhower signed today a bill to make billions of dollars of surplus Federal property available free to schools and hospitals.

The law, sponsored by the House Democratic leader, Representative John W. McCormack of Massachusetts, overturns a Defense Department order last year. It required that surplus goods be sold instead of being made available under the schools and hospitals donation program.

BOHLEN IS CALLED HOME

U.S. Envoy in Moscow Will Go to U. N. San Francisco Fete

MOSCOW, June 3 (AP)—United States Ambassador Charles E. Bohlen announced today he had been called to Washington for consultations.

Mr. Bohlen will take part in discussions at the United Nations anniversary meeting in San Francisco preliminary to a forthcoming four-power conference.

He plans to leave Moscow June 13 and arrive in Washington the next day.

Asian Peak Defeats Climbers

KATMANDU, Nepal, June 3 (AP)—A Swiss-German expedition abandoned its attempt to scale 26,810-foot Mount Dhaulagiri—the world's highest unclimbed peak—at 26,000 feet, a message reaching here said today. Mount Dhaulagiri, in Central Nepal, is the world's fifth tallest peak

UNION URGES FORD TO IMPROVE OFFER

U.A.W. Heads Cheered by Pay Decision but Unsatisfied Over Amount of Fund

By DAMON STETSON
Special to The New York Times.

DETROIT, June 3—Union negotiators pushed today for improvements in the Ford Motor Company's offer to make payments to laid-off workers.

Leaders of the United Automobile Workers, C. I. O., were heartened by the company's decision earlier this week to go along with the principle of supplementing unemployment compensation for workers who were laid off.

But they were far from satisfied with the amount of money that the company indicated it was willing to put into the fund from which such payments would be made.

Details of the plan, how it would be applied, qualifications for payment—all these factors were said to be under discussion as bargaining sessions continued here. Although developments of the last three days have been encouraging, union negotiators are said to feel that many further concessions must be made if a strike by 140,000 Ford workers is to be avoided on Monday.

A night negotiating session ended shortly before midnight. The negotiations are expected to go on throughout the weekend.

Talks With G. M. Go On

Meanwhile, negotiations continued between the union and the General Motors Corporation. But union pressure seemed to be concentrated on Ford. The General Motors contract does not terminate until midnight Tuesday, forty-eight hours after Ford could be struck.

General Motors and the union have scheduled talks for both tomorrow and Sunday.

The Ford company's willingness to make an offer of wage payments integrated with unemployment compensation was regarded as highly significant. Some observers here were saying that Walter P. Reuther, president of the union, had won his guaranteed annual wage battle.

Others, however, were not so sure, especially in view of the limited information available on what is going on. This limitation stems from the union-company agreement not to discuss developments at the bargaining tables. But leaks from various sources continue to confuse the picture.

Precise appraisals of the situation were difficult to make in view of the adamant refusal by top company and union negotiators to confirm or deny the flood of rumors about the talks.

The crux of the new offer put

Continued on Page 12, Column 7

2 Funeral Aides Seized at Track With Dead Man's $3,780 Tickets

By MEYER BERGER
Special to The New York Times.

MINEOLA, L. I., June 3—Here's a grim race-track story beyond any ever dreamed by Damon Runyon:

On May 26 Samuel I. Brandt of 41 Park Avenue, Manhattan, a retired lingerie manufacturer, went to Belmont Park Race Track in a car driven by his brother, Nathan, who lives at 1916 Avenue K in Brooklyn.

Nathan left before the eighth race that day. He took with him a $20-win pari-mutuel ticket on Kitty Lightner, a horse that was to run against eight others in the eighth. His brother stayed on.

When the eighth race ended, a little after 5 o'clock, Samuel Brandt crowded into the front seat of a limousine that carries horseplayers to, or from, the track to New York at $3 a head.

He sat between the driver, Eddie Charles, and a man identified only as an assistant coroner from Erie County, upstate. The car was barely out of the race-track parking lot when Mr. Brandt collapsed, slumped against the coroner.

He was taken to the track's little white-painted first-aid station. Dr. Phil Tuths, the track physician, and Miss Dorothy Mull, the nurse, bent over him. He had died of a heart attack. He was 62 years old.

Detective Robert Hennig and Patrolman R. Weston of the Nassau County police searched Mr. Brandt's pockets while the doctor, the nurse and Sgt. James Rabbit and Patrolman Sam Calhoun, Pinkerton men, looked on.

They found seven $100 bank-notes, one $50 bill, one of $10, a fiver, a $1 bill and 60 cents in change, a gold watch and chain, eyeglasses, several mutuel tick-

Continued on Page 33, Column 3

TRUMAN CHARGES REGIME 'BUNGLED' VACCINE PROGRAM

Implies G.O.P. Claims Credit for a Democratic Deed—Attends Cleveland Fete

By RICHARD J. H. JOHNSTON
Special to The New York Times.

CLEVELAND, June 3—Former President Truman charged the Eisenhower Administration today with "bungling" the Salk polio vaccine program.

Asked if he detected any politics in the handling of the program, he said:

"Well, this Administration disclaims anything that came out of the previous Administrations. This vaccine came from the March of Dimes and that came from President Franklin D. Roosevelt."

Mr. and Mrs. Truman arrived here shortly after midnight by train from Kansas City, Mo., to attend a fund-raising dinner for the Harry S. Truman Library, Inc.

Tonight's dinner was sponsored by a group of Ohio industrialists and Democratic politicians who have formed a committee to raise $75,000 toward the cost of the projected $1,750,000 repository for Mr. Truman's Senate and White House papers and mementos.

Heading the group for the $100-a-plate affair was Cyrus S. Eaton, a Cleveland industrialist, who, with a group of associates, recently formed the Ohio committee for the Harry S. Truman Library, Inc.

Mr. Truman, jaunty and sparkling in repartee, faced television cameras and reporters in a suite of the Cleveland Hotel.

Discusses Foreign Affairs

After giving his brief opinion of the Salk polio vaccine problem, Mr. Truman tossed off comment and "no comment" on a score of topics.

Mr. Truman was skeptical over favorable results from the projected meeting of the leaders of Russia, Great Britain, France and the United States.

"My idea of a Big Four meeting is one that would contribute to the peace of the world," he said. "I have no way of knowing what they are going to do because I don't have a Central Intelligence Agency any more.

"All I know is what I read in the papers—and I take that with a grain of salt."

He detected signs of easing in the cold war and he pointed to the Austrian peace treaty, the Russian wooing of Yugoslavia and the release by Communist China of four American flyers as evidence of this.

He replied to a number of questions on controversial matters of the recent past by declaring, "I'll discuss that in my memoirs which I'm now writing and I'd advise you to read them when they are published."

Mr. Truman is nearing the completion of his memoirs of public life. They will cover the period from Jan. 3, 1935, when he entered the Senate from Missouri, through Jan. 20, 1953, when he left the White House after slightly less than two terms.

Turning to the 1956 national

Continued on Page 34, Column 3

Moscow Sees Broad Effect In Its Yugoslav Agreement

Pravda Says It Has 'Tremendous' Impact for World—Settlement Is Held Bar to Belgrade Role in Atlantic Alliance

By CLIFTON DANIEL
Special to The New York Times.

MOSCOW, June 3—Pravda said today the Soviet-Yugoslav declaration had "tremendous significance" not only for the two signatory states but also for the world as a whole.

What that significance ultimately may be has been the subject of avid discussion and speculation in Moscow.

An unusual effort was exerted by the Soviet leaders to obtain a joint statement. The most powerful men of this country, the largest in the world, made a special journey to Belgrade, capital of a third-rate power.

On arrival, the chief of the Soviet delegation, Nikita S. Khrushchev, First Secretary of the Communist party, offered a profound public apology for wrongs done to the Yugoslav Communists. Then the Soviet representatives signed a document last night that in very large measure met the terms of the Yugoslav President, Marshal Tito.

Observers here naturally wondered whether in the extraordinary Soviet behavior there was some purpose larger than that of merely resolving the quarrel and whether the effects of the Belgrade declaration would not touch much more than relations with one country alone.

Certainly the declaration will be examined with great interest in the capitals of the other Eastern European Communist countries, especially that part relating to ideological and political autonomy.

The declaration said that the Soviet Union and Yugoslavia proceeded from several principles, among which was this: "Mutual respect for, and non-interference in, internal affairs

Continued on Page 3, Column 3

Red China Accord Likely, Indian Informs the British

By DREW MIDDLETON
Special to The New York Times.

LONDON, June 3—V. K. Krishna Menon, India's intermediary between Communist China and the West, predicted today that the recent release of four United States airmen might lead to settlement of outstanding issues. His efforts in Peiping were directed toward "lowering of tension," Mr. Krishna Menon said, and "American fliers or Chinese students are all items in that."

The Indian diplomat, who spent ten days in the Communist capital, arrived by air from New Delhi early in the afternoon. Soon afterward he met Prime Minister Eden and Foreign Secretary Harold Macmillan to discuss his exchanges with Premier Chou En-lai.

Mr. Krishna Menon will see Sir Anthony and Mr. Macmillan again Monday. Then he will fly to Canada to confer with Lester B. Pearson, Secretary of State for External Affairs and continue on to New York for a meeting of the United Nations Trusteeship Council. He is India's delegate to the United Nations.

Within limits the British are encouraged by the results of Mr. Krishna Menon's mission. They did not expect Mr. Krishna Menon to report any sudden alteration of Communist demands for the offshore islands of Quemoy and Matsu or Formosa, all held by Chinese Nationalist garrisons.

What they hoped was that Mr. Krishna Menon would make clear to Premier Chou the state of opinion in the Western nations and that simultaneously he would seek the views of the Premier on methods of reaching an over-all settlement with the West.

Mr. Krishna Menon and members of the Indian High Commissioner's office are cautiously

Continued on Page 3, Column 6

PEIPING ACCUSED ON PRISONER CODE

U. S. Aide Says Reds Violate Geneva Accord as Well as Truce in Holding Fliers

Special to The New York Times.

WASHINGTON, June 3—The general counsel of the Defense Department accused Communist China today of violating international law as well as the Korean armistice by detaining United States fliers.

The point was made by Wilber M. Brucker under questioning by the Senate Foreign Relations Committee. He said the 1949 Geneva conventions for the protection of war victims required repatriation of prisoners of war "without delay" after hostilities ended.

Mr. Brucker said the American airmen were "not strictly prisoners of war but are entitled to protection of prisoners of war" under the Geneva pacts. While "we don't have details of what has occurred in the last few days," he added, the United States position "was and is" that all the fliers held by Communist China have been illegally detained.

Communist China is not a party to the Geneva conventions but has indicated its adherence to the principles, according to Mr. Brucker. They are generally recognized as established international law.

Early Ratification Urged

The Pentagon's chief legal officer and other Administration witnesses, testifying at the one-day hearing, urged early Senate ratification of the four Geneva conventions. They are designed to modernize and in some respects broaden international law covering the treatment and protection of war prisoners and civilians in wartime. They also deal with relief of the wounded and sick in armies in the field.

The United States took a leading role in drafting the agreements at the 1949 Geneva Conference, attended by fifty-nine countries. Forty-seven, including the Soviet Union, have ratified the treaties.

Robert D. Murphy, Deputy Under Secretary of State, testified that the Soviet Union, by ratification, had "gained a propaganda advantage which it has been quick to use in recent international meetings."

"We know," he said, "that many nations have looked to us for an indication as to what they should do and have supported and acted favorably on the Geneva conventions in the expectation that we would do the same."

J. Lee Rankin, Assistant Attorney General, called the agreements "a humane step forward in the development of international law."

The State Department, mean-

Continued on Page 3, Column 6

SOVIET BLOC FEUD WITH TITO ENDED, KHRUSHCHEV SAYS

He Asserts Belgrade Accord Puts Finish to Seven-Year Period of Bad Relations

BULGARIA WELCOMES HIM

Moscow Party Chief in Sofia Declares Yugoslavia Keeps Clear of 'Imperialists'

By JACK RAYMOND
Special to The New York Times.

BELGRADE, Yugoslavia, June 3—Nikita S. Khrushchev, the Soviet Communist leader, said in Sofia, Bulgaria, today that the period of unfriendly relations between the Soviet bloc and Yugoslavia had ended.

Heaping praise on Yugoslavia in his first statement on the Soviet-Yugoslav joint declaration signed here yesterday, the Soviet Communist party's First Secretary also declared at a street rally: "We have seen that Yugoslavia did not abandon her sovereignty, but maintained her independence before the imperialists."

This allusion to Yugoslavia's relations with the Western powers, particularly her receipt of military and economic aid, recalled as well the early Cominform charges that Yugoslavia was a military base for "Western imperialist" powers.

These charges marked the high point of the feud that was started in June, 1948, when Yugoslavia was expelled from the Soviet-dominated coalition of Communist parties. The declaration signed yesterday by President Tito and Soviet Premier Nikolai A. Bulganin came at the close of negotiations to establish "normal" relations between Moscow and Belgrade.

Soviet Group Flies to Sofia

This morning, seven hours after a spectacular reception at which the Russians were hosts, Mr. Khrushchev, who headed the Soviet delegation, Marshal Bulganin and Anastas I. Mikoyan, a Soviet First Deputy Premier, flew to Sofia before returning to Moscow.

The Communist chief arrived at the airport with Marshal Tito in an open limousine that led the official convoy.

Wearing a rumpled blue suit and red tie, in contrast with the always spectacular uniform of Marshal Tito, Mr. Khrushchev was jolly as he walked down the line of foreign diplomats pumping hands vigorously.

"Good trip and good health," said Sir Frank Roberts, the British Ambassador, in Russian.

"Thanks for your good wishes," replied Mr. Khrushchev.

The Soviet leader bowed and shook hands enthusiastically with United States Ambassador James Riddleberger, with whom he had engaged in political repartee at Marshal Tito's officitl reception a week ago.

It was reported that Mr. Khrushchev intended to make a speech prior to his departing, but was induced to change his mind. The Yugoslavs are understood to have been annoyed by the speech Mr. Khrushchev had made upon his arrival here when he appealed for Yugoslav's return to the international Communist ranks.

Although a microphone and

Continued on Page 3, Column 2

African Cave Yields Fossil Proof Of Man's First Use of Tools, Fire

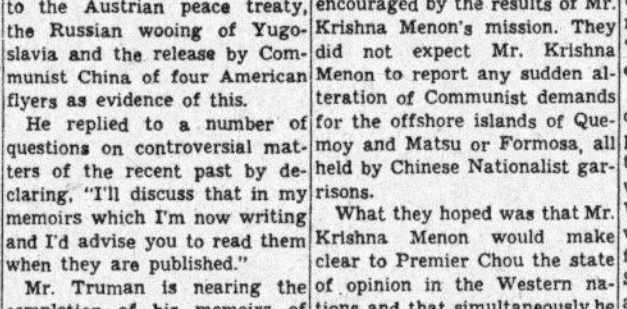

Left: A portion of what has been established as an adult right upper jaw, showing first and second molars, of an Australopithecus prometheus. Right: The newly discovered teeth, which in general shape match the known specimens.

By ROBERT K. PLUMB

A discovery in a cave in South Africa has clearly established a point on the evolutionary ladder at which man's ancestors first learned to use tools.

Word of the discovery was received here yesterday afternoon by the Wenner-Gren Foundation for Anthropological Research, 14 East Seventy-first Street.

The discovery definitely establishes for the first time that a creature known as Australopithecus prometheus lived during the time of and at the place of a very primitive stone "pebble culture."

Australopithecus prometheus (the "fire-giver") has been known since 1925, when it was described by Dr. Raymond A. Dart, head of the Department of Anatomy of the Medical School of the University of the Witwatersrand in Johannesburg. Many specimens of this very early man-ape or ape-man have been uncovered a series of

Continued on Page 7, Column 2

New Plan for Aiding Veterans' Survivors

By C. P. TRUSSELL
Special to The New York Times.

WASHINGTON, June 3—A thorough overhaul of benefits to survivors of service men was proposed by a special House committee today.

Months of study of the operations of five distinct programs had disclosed confusion, administrative duplications and serious inequities, the committee reported.

In thousands of instances, it asserted, widows and others were receiving more benefits than if the service men had remained alive and on active duty with their normal benefits added to basic pay. In other thousands of cases, the report said, the survivors were receiving less than was required for bare living standards.

The new plan was announced after an hour-long meeting of committee members with President Eisenhower yesterday.

Continued on Page 8, Column 4

"All the News That's Fit to Print"

The New York Times

LATE CITY EDITION

Weather: Rain likely today; cold tonight. Partly cloudy tomorrow. Temp. range: today 38-45; Monday 44-50. Additional details on Page 81.

VOL. CV..No. 35,732. Entered as Second-Class Matter, Post Office, New York, N. Y. NEW YORK, WEDNESDAY, NOVEMBER 23, 1955. Times Square, New York 36, N. Y. Telephone LAckawanna 4-1000 FIVE CENTS

6 LAWS TO ENABLE HOUSING REFORMS VOTED BY COUNCIL

Sweeping Program to Avert New Slums Scheduled to Be Established Jan. 1

KEROSENE HEATERS OUT

End to Overcrowding in Old Law Tenements Sought—Dwelling Code Set Up

By PAUL CROWELL

The City Council passed yesterday six local laws embodying one of the most sweeping housing reform programs in the city's history.

The measures, introduced at Mayor Wagner's request, were designed to implement a program conceived by his Administration early in 1954. They were designed to end over-crowding, prevent creation of new slums through substandard building alterations, end the use of kerosene heaters and other dangerous heating appliances and repair inadequate machinery for enforcement of building regulations.

A main objective of the Mayor's attack on improper housing facilities was the old-law tenement, constructed before 1901. About 1,500,000 persons are living in 53,000 such buildings.

The Mayor and his top advisers plan to have the program become effective by Jan. 1. The bills passed by the Council must receive approval of the Board of Estimate and be signed by the Mayor. The Jan. 1 goal was set to prevent the Legislature from pre-empting the field in 1956, thereby preventing the city from adopting its own program.

Summary of the Bills

The six bills passed by the Council were:

¶A measure setting up a City Multiple Dwelling Code with many provisions stricter than those in the State's Multiple Dwellings Law.

¶A measure requiring central heating and hot-water plants.

¶A measure incorporating into the new city code certain sections of the Building Code.

¶A measure outlawing kerosene heaters after specified dates. In the case of cold-water tenements, these were synchronized with the dates for mandatory installation of central heating and hot-water plants.

¶A measure reorganizing the Department of Housing and Buildings to centralize authority in the Commissioner.

¶A measure exempting from real estate tax for twelve years the value of improvements to substandard dwellings approved by the City Planning Commission for rehabilitation. The same measure would, by means of tax reductions to owners, amortize 75 per cent of the cost of improvements over a period of nine years.

Introduction of the bills followed preliminary interdepartmental conferences by agencies concerned with improvement of substandard housing. The Multiple Dwelling Code bill was introduced Nov. 16, 1954, and was the subject of nearly 100 hearings by the Council's welfare committee. These resulted in an amended version softening some of the more restrictive provisions.

Other bills in the program

Continued on Pag 16, Column 5

L.I.R.R. Raises Fare 7th Time Since 1947

By BERNARD STENGREN

Commuting will become still more expensive on Dec. 6 for those who ride the Long Island Rail Road.

The nation's largest commuter line told its 285,000 daily riders yesterday that a series of wage increases won this fall by railroad workers throughout the country made a fare rise imperative.

To meet the added costs, the following increases will go into effect at 12:01 A. M. on Dec. 6:

One-way tickets, 5 cents more; ten-trip tickets, 50 cents more; weekly tickets, 60 cents more; restricted monthly tickets, $2.30 more, and unrestricted monthly tickets, $3 more.

The increase is across the board, regardless of distance traveled. A railroad spokesman said a percentage rise would have put too heavy a

Continued on Page 24, Column 5

TRADE FAIR IN '57 SET FOR COLISEUM

First World Exhibition in U.S. Is Privately Organized but Government Endorsed

By PETER KIHSS

Mayor Wagner announced yesterday that the first United States World Trade Fair would be held in the new Coliseum April 14-27, 1957.

Expected to rank with the major Paris and Milan fairs, the exposition hopes to attract to the Columbus Circle structure up to 3,000 exhibitors, primarily foreign; 100,000 buyers, 90 per cent American; and 1,000,000 visitors.

The show is being privately organized by the Charles Snitow Organization of 331 Madison Avenue. Endorsements by the Federal, State and City Commerce Departments were officially announced at a luncheon in the Waldorf-Astoria Hotel.

Mr. Snitow reported discussions with representatives of forty-four countries here last April and May had elicited a "unanimous vote" in favor of the project.

Hopes to Hold Event Annually

Member countries of the Organization for European Economic Cooperation have appointed a liaison committee to receive information and convey suggestions. Represented on this are Belgium, Denmark, France, West Germany, Ireland, Italy, the Netherlands, Turkey and the United Kingdom.

The 48-year-old promoter said he expected to spend as much as $500,000 on the new project, with hope for enough profit to make it an annual venture.

The only predecessor in this country, he said, was a small-scale international trade fair in Chicago in 1950. With the end this year of Toronto's eight-year-old Canadian International Trade Fair, the new venture would be the only such large-scale project in the Western Hemisphere, Mr. Snitow said.

Mr. Snitow also is managing the International Automobile Show, which he said would run at the Coliseum next April 28 to May 26 to open the new hall along with two other shows. This is the successor to the International Motor Sports Show, which has been one of his past

Continued on Page 50, Column 3

Associated Press Wirephotos

AT YESTERDAY'S CABINET SESSION: On far side of table, starting from right, are Harold Stassen, Presidential Assistant; Agriculture Secretary Benson; Defense Secretary Wilson; President Eisenhower; Secretary of State Dulles; Postmaster General Summerfield, partly hidden; Secretary of Labor Mitchell; Budget Director Hughes and Defense Mobilization Director Flemming. At near side of table are, from front to rear, Ambassador Lodge, Interior Secretary McKay, Treasury Secretary Humphrey, Vice President Nixon, Attorney General Brownell, Secretary of Commerce Weeks and Secretary of Health Folsom. This was the first Cabinet meeting attended by the President since he was stricken with a heart attack.

BRAZIL'S LEADERS ASK MARTIAL LAW TO BAR PRESIDENT

Chiefs of the Armed Forces Back Step to Prevent Cafe From Resuming Office

HE SEEKS A COURT WRIT

But Congress Begins Action Toward Blocking His Move to End Virtual Arrest

By TAD SZULC

Special to The New York Times.

RIO DE JANEIRO, Wednesday, Nov. 23—Brazil's Congress began action early today toward imposing a state of siege throughout the nation for thirty days.

The purpose of this modified form of martial law would be to block the constitutional President, João Café Filho, from returning to the office he gave up following a heart attack.

Tank-supported troops and policemen have kept him incommunicado in his apartment building since Monday evening. But no charges have been made against him.

The siege measure was requested last night by Acting President Nereu Ramos. A message addressed to the Chamber of Deputies and the Senate invoked, without further elaboration, "the imminence of subversion of public order and grave internal commotion" and "the need to prevent and repress the subversive wave that threatens the constitutional order."

The chamber, which is sitting through the night, was expected to approve the request before adjourning. The Senate has scheduled a special 9 A. M. session to act on it. Acting President Ramos is expected to sign the measure later today.

Bill Blocks Court Action

A key provision of the bill strikes directly at Senhor Café's two petitions sent to the Supreme Court yesterday seeking injunctions to end his condition of virtual house arrest and to confirm him in Brazil's Presidency.

It provides specifically that, under the state of siege, the suspension of the writ of habeas corpus applies to the acts of Federal authorities. Thus the present caretaker Administration can effectively keep Senhor Café from returning to the political scene.

The Ramos message, delivered as the Army continued in control of Rio de Janeiro, was the latest development in Brazil's complex political crisis, now entering its third day.

It followed separate notes by the two chambers of Congress early yesterday declaring Senhor Café as "prevented" from resuming the Presidency. The Congress, dominated by Senhor Café's enemies and backed by the Army, which sent troops and tanks into this capital's streets on Monday, passed the disabling resolution in quick response to the President's announcement that he was well again and so was resuming office.

Last night the chiefs of the Brazilian armed forces issued an announcement pledging themselves to support the Ramos regime and guarantee Congress full freedom of decision. The announcement was signed by Lieut.

Continued on Page 10, Column 4

Flint Axes Found at Rome Traced to 200,000 B. C.

By PAUL HOFMANN

Special to The New York Times.

ROME, Nov. 22—The oldest Romans are now said to have been much older than Romulus and Remus. About 200,000 years before Rome's legendary founding in 753 B. C., the twins' ancestors hunted wild animals in this area, according to this theory.

This is the conclusion reached by a team of scientists of Rome University's Institute of Human Paleontology. On a promising clue the scientists have been digging on this city's outskirts for the last three months. They found what Prof. Count Francesco Pellati, president of the institute, described today as a prehistoric industry "unique in Europe."

Romulus was the legendary founder and first King of Rome. It is said he slew his brother after Remus had scornfully leaped over the wall of the city.

The important find is at Torre in Pietra, thirteen miles northwest of Rome's center. It consists of twenty-two hand axes, pear-shaped flint implements characteristic of the Lower Stone Age. These axes, known as coups de poing (literally, blows of the fist), were mingled with the fossilized bones of prehistoric elephants, rhinoceroses, hippopotamuses and hyenas.

Prof. Alberto Carlo Blanc, who took part in the excavations, speaks of a "prehistoric Pompeii." According to him, the early Stone Age men of this primitive settlement were driven off by ashes and a tidal wave of mud from a nearby active volcano. There are several extinct craters in the neighborhood. Lake Bracciano, a few miles north, is a result of a volcanic explosion.

The analogy to the highly civilized Roman city of Pompeii, buried by the eruption of Mount Vesuvius in A. D. 79, ends here. The excavations at Torre in Pie-

Continued on Page 6, Column 6

HARRIMAN ASSAILS G.O.P. POWER PLAN

Tells Oregon Rally Policy of Republicans Is Give-Away That Cuts West's Growth

By LAWRENCE E. DAVIES

Special to The New York Times.

MILWAUKIE, Ore., Nov. 22—Governor Harriman of New York charged today that the Republican party had a "firm and settled policy" of strangling the development of the West and giving away its natural resources.

He exhorted Western voters to resist by defeating an "absentee-owned" Republican party in 1956. He said that by "absentee-owned" he meant the party was dominated by powerful business interests of the East.

In press interviews and speeches, he pounded at "the phony partnership" that he said was represented in the controversial power policy of the Eisenhower Administration. He called it "domination of government by big business."

His actions all day were those of a Presidential candidate out trying to influence voters. But Mr. Harriman stuck to his "not an active candidate" description of himself. He said that he was going to be "scrapping with the Republican majority" in the New York Legislature to get legislation that was good for his state and would not have time next spring for anything else.

Praised by Morse

But an enthusiastic dinner crowd of about 500 persons here applauded heartily when Senator Wayne Morse, Oregon Democrat, said of Mr. Harriman and the 1956 Democratic National Convention:

"If in the course of historic events the mantle should fall on the great Governor of the State of New York the people of this country would be well represented in the White House."

Mr. Harriman foresaw a "fierce battle" in Oregon next year and urged the state to re-elect Senator Morse, whom he characterized as "one of the truly outstanding men in the United States Senate."

In his final talk of the day in this Portland suburban community, Governor Harriman urged voters of this region to insure the continuance of the Northwest dam building program begun in the first Franklin D. Roosevelt Administration by sending Democrats to Congress.

The development of the Pacific Northwest, he declared, "is not an issue of region versus region at all—it is fundamentally an issue of party against party."

"Every time you elect a Re-

Continued on Page 15, Column 4

PRESIDENT MEETS CABINET AT CAMP

Talks of Foreign Affairs and State of Union Message—Praises Work of Aides

By ALLEN DRURY

Special to The New York Times.

THURMONT, Md., Nov. 22—President Eisenhower told his Cabinet members today how much he had appreciated their "perfection of coordination and cooperation" when he was out of touch with them after his heart attack in Denver.

It was the first time he had seen the department heads together since mid-August, about six weeks before he suffered the attack. He met them this morning at Camp David, his Catoctin Mountain retreat, twenty-five miles from Gettysburg, and spent nearly two hours discussing the foreign situation and the annual State of the Union Message, which will go to Congress in January.

Later he authorized James C. Hagerty, his press secretary, to say that he had expressed his "gratitude and appreciation for the perfection of coordination and cooperation the Cabinet has maintained in carrying on the Executive business of the Government with the minimum of communication from the President while I was in the hospital in Denver."

John Foster Dulles, Secretary of State, reviewed the foreign situation as it stood after the breakdown of the recent Big Four foreign ministers' conference in Geneva. The Cabinet members then turned to the State of the Union Message, traditionally a full-scale review of Administration hopes and plans for the new Congressional session.

The President received addi-

Continued on Page 13, Column 2

New Group of Beria Aides Executed in Soviet Georgia

Special to The New York Times.

MOSCOW, Nov. 22—Five men have been executed and two others sentenced to life imprisonment on charges of having conspired to conceal the activities of Lavrenti P. Beria, late Minister of Internal Affairs.

A brief announcement this morning on the Tiflis radio said a former Georgian Minister of State Security was among those put to death after a trial in the capital of the Georgian Republic. The six other convicted men were identified as Georgian internal security officials.

[A Tiflis radio broadcast heard in London named six executed officials, according to news agency dispatches.]

This is the third series of executions linked with Mr. Beria since the former secret police chief was arrested on charges of high treason in July, 1953.

Mr. Beria and six accomplices were put to death Dec. 23, 1953, after having been tried in secret by a special tribunal of the Soviet Supreme Court. Among those executed with him were Vladimir G. Dekanozov, former Georgian Minister of Internal Affairs, and B. Z. Kobulov, former Deputy Minister in Mr. Beria's ministry.

Second Group Executed

In December, 1954, Viktor S. Abakumov, former Minister of State Security, and five officials of the ministry were also executed on charges of having conspired to commit treason with Mr. Beria.

In the meantime the Georgian Republic Government was reorganized after Mr. Beria's downfall. Valerian M. Bakradze was dismissed as Premier in September, 1953. Early last year Vilian S. Zodelava was ousted as First Deputy Premier of Georgia on charges of "nationalism."

The Tiflis radio reported Feb. 21 that "great harm" had been wrought by "Beria, that wastrel and enemy of the people."

The executions announced today were thought to reflect the Government's continuing campaign to eradicate the influence of Mr. Beria and his associates from the Georgian Administration, particularly the police.

In assessing the significance of today's announcement observers recalled that Premier Nikolai A. Bulganin and Nikita S. Khrushchev, party chief, had left the country for India accompanied by Gen. Ivan A. Serov, chairman of the Committee for State Security, during the concluding stages of the case against the seven Georgian officials.

Their absence, particularly that of General Serov, was interpreted as signifying the Government's equanimity about the situation. General Serov, who directs security affairs under the direct supervision of the Cabinet, took his post after Mr. Abakumov's execution and the liquidation of the Ministry of State Security.

Sentenced Officials Named

MOSCOW, Nov. 22 (AP)—The five executed Georgian officials were Nikolai M. Rukhadze, former Minister of State Security; Avksenty N. Rapava, former Minister of Internal Affairs; Shalva O. Tsereteli, former Deputy Minister of State Security,

Continued on Page 6, Column 5

BAGHDAD POWERS WIDEN ARMS PACT

Political and Economic Ties Are Included in Set-Up of Permanent Organization

By KENNETT LOVE

Special to The New York Times.

BAGHDAD, Iraq, Nov. 22—The five powers of the Baghdad Pact announced tonight the establishment of a permanent political, military and economic organization that will have its headquarters here.

The announcement came at the end of a two-day organizational conference attended by the Premiers of four countries of the Middle East—Turkey, Iraq, Iran and Pakistan—and the British Foreign Secretary.

The pact, which is being unofficially called the Middle East Treaty Organization, is linked with the North Atlantic Treaty Organization through Turkey and with the Southeast Asian Collective Defense Treaty through Pakistan. Thus it fills the Middle Eastern gap in the Western-sponsored "containment" pacts around the perimeter of the Communist bloc.

Premier Nuri as-Said of Iraq, chairman of the conference, said the "meeting was a complete success—more than we expected."

The delegations of the member countries included their Chiefs of Staff, the Foreign Ministers of Turkey, Iraq and Pakistan and the Iranian Minister of Industry.

The United States, which is

Continued on Page 3, Column 2

Factory Take-Home Pay at Peak As Consumer Prices Hold Line

By JOSEPH A. LOFTUS

Special to The New York Times.

WASHINGTON, Nov. 22—The United States Consumers' Price Index was unchanged from mid-September to mid-October, the Bureau of Labor Statistics reported today.

Factory workers' take-home pay over the same period rose more than 1 per cent to set a record, the Labor Department bureau said. Since prices paid by consumers were unchanged, the increase in take-home pay was reflected in increased purchasing power, which reached a high.

The stability of the over-all index was a source of gratification to fiscal officials, who are concerned with an inflationary potential in the economy. A rise in the index leads to a rise in wage rates, sometimes automatically. These in turn lead to further price increases and so on up the spiral.

The cost-of-living escalator clauses in major automobile contracts are due for their quarterly review this month. The wage rates which are covered by these contracts will not be changed because of the narrow range in which the index has moved.

The index in mid-October stood at 114.9 per cent of the 1947-49 average. This was 0.3 per cent higher than a year ago, but 0.4 per cent below the record reached in October, 1953. The base of 100 equals the price average in the 1947-49 period.

The take-home pay (wages after tax withholding) of the average factory worker has risen by more than $5 a month in the last year. In October the take-home pay of the average worker with three dependents was

Continued on Page 14, Column 4

Yemen Gives a U. S. Company First Oil and Mining Concession

George E. Allen Heads Group That Is to Have Exclusive Rights for Thirty Years

The kingdom of Yemen has granted to an American company the first oil and mineral concession in the nation's history.

The Yemen Development Corporation of Washington disclosed yesterday that it had signed a thirty-year agreement for exclusive exploration and development rights in the Middle Eastern kingdom. The agreement covers 40,000 square miles, or the northern two-thirds of the country except for the narrow coastal strip called Tihama.

All net profits are to be divided fifty-fifty with the Government of Yemen, which heretofore has largely been closed to foreigners. If commercial quantities of petroleum or minerals are not found within six years, the agreement can be voided.

Yemen is an absolute monarchy on the southern tip of the Arabian Peninsula. It is bordered by the kingdom of Saudi Arabia, site of some of the richest oil fields in the world, by the

The New York Times Nov. 23, 1955

A U. S. group has received from Yemen oil and mineral rights in the general area shown by diagonal shading.

Red Sea and by the British protectorate of Aden. The country covers approximately 75,000 square miles and has a population of about 5,000,000.

The chairman of the Yemen Development Corporation is George E. Allen, a friend of President Eisenhower and for-

Continued on Page 9, Column 4

Judge Rules U. S. Must Divulge Data Used in Denying Passports

By LUTHER A. HUSTON

Special to The New York Times.

WASHINGTON, Nov. 22—A Federal judge ruled today that the State Department must disclose the information upon which it bases a decision to deny a passport.

Judge Luther W. Youngdahl asserted in an opinion that "irreparable damage" was wrought by the use of information obtained from "secret informers and the faceless tale-bearer whose identity and testimony remain locked in confidential files."

Text of opinion on passports is printed on Page 12.

"When the basis of action by any branch of the Government remains hidden from scrutiny and beyond practical review, the seeds of arbitrary and irresponsible government are sown," Judge Youngdahl said.

He ordered the State Department to give a hearing within twenty days to Leonard B. Boudin, a New York lawyer. Mr. Boudin was denied a passport on the basis of evidence allegedly linking him with communism. The order directed that "the decision of the Passport Office must be substantiated by evidence contained in the record."

Mr. Boudin represented Dr. Otto Nathan, executor of the will of Dr. Albert Einstein, in a passport case earlier this year. Dr. Nathan was refused a passport because of alleged past Communist affiliations.

In Dr. Nathan's case the Federal Court of Appeals ordered a "quasi-judicial" hearing on his passport application. However, it did not define such a hearing. The State Department avoided the hearing by issuing a pass-

Continued on Page 12, Column 3

"All the News That's Fit to Print"

The New York Times

LATE CITY EDITION

Weather: Fair, very cold today and tonight. Chance of snow tomorrow. Temp. range: today 24-14; Sunday 33-26. Full U.S. report on Page 30.

VOL. CV . No. 35,760. Entered as Second-Class Matter. Post Office, New York, N. Y. NEW YORK, WEDNESDAY, DECEMBER 21, 1955. Times Square, New York 36, N. Y. Telephone LAckawanna 4-1000 FIVE CENTS

WILSON BUDGETS MISSILE PROGRAM AT RECORD LEVEL

Tells of Expansion Plans for Wonder Weapons in 35.5 Billion Spending Outlay

ATOM WARSHIP SLATED

Intercontinental Projectile With a Nuclear Warhead Is Likely in 5 Years

By ANTHONY LEVIERO

Special to The New York Times.

WASHINGTON, Dec. 20—Guided missile development and production will be pushed to a record-breaking $1,000,000,000 level, and the first atomic-powered surface warship will be ordered in the next defense budget.

Charles E. Wilson, the Secretary of Defense, confirmed today forecasts that the Administration would send to Congress a defense spending budget of $35,500,000,000, or about $1,000,000,000 more than current expenditures.

This budget for the 1957 fiscal year, beginning next July 1, will make a sharp shift from the old-fashioned shooting irons of World War II. Requests for conventional ammunition have been scratched out.

Instead the orders all along the research, development and production lines will be for wonder weapons—ballistics missiles to span the oceans, robot aircraft, nuclear-powered ships and aircraft, and the most advanced types of conventional airplanes.

Mr. Wilson estimated that the intercontinental ballistics missile, capable of carrying a nuclear bomb for a warhead and called the "ultimate weapon," might be attained in five years.

High Costs Are Stressed

He merely outlined the new budget, not wishing to anticipate President Eisenhower. But without giving details he told enough to herald the sharpest turn from conventional weapons since the first atomic bomb was tested in New Mexico in 1945.

Mr. Wilson gave his preview in a Pentagon news conference. The President will send the budget to Congress early in January. Secretary Wilson's main points were:

¶An appreciable part of the $1,000,000,000 increase in the proposed spending budget will be eaten up by the increased cost of wages and materials.

¶The Defense Department will seek obligational authority, as distinguished from the spending budget, for about $35,000,000,000, an increase of nearly $2,000,000,000. Obligational authority enables the department to make contracts for long-term

Continued on Page 16, Column 4

U. S. Asks 25 Million More To Widen Fight on Disease

Folsom Also Asks Grants for New Buildings and Training Personnel

By BESS FURMAN

Special to The New York Times.

WASHINGTON, Dec. 20—The Administration will ask Congress to increase its medical research funds by $25,000,000 next year.

The increase would provide expenditures "25 to 30 per cent" above this year's $97,800,000.

Marion B. Folsom, Secretary of Health, Education and Welfare, said today that legislation also would be asked to remove "the chief bottleneck" to research in the medical field. He proposed a bill for Federal grants in aid to combine medical school construction with the training of personnel needed to direct the new facilities.

Medical research programs cannot be expanded substantially, he suggested, without augmented facilities and trained researchers and directors to operate them. He said the proposed legislation would provide allocations on the basis of separate medical school projects.

The Secretary, in his first news conference as a Cabinet member, gave priority to medical research.

He said it was a field of great "appeal" to him, and that he

Continued on Page 25, Column 3

Associated Press Wirephoto

Secretary Marion B. Folsom during press conference.

DULLES CONFIRMS PLAN TO INCREASE FOREIGN AID FUND

Says Military Request Will Be Trebled, but Spending Rise Will Be Slight

The transcript of Dulles news conference is on Page 14.

By ELIE ABEL

Special to The New York Times.

WASHINGTON, Dec. 20—The Secretary of State confirmed today the Administration's plan to ask Congress for $4,900,000,000 in new foreign-aid money, 81 per cent more than the current appropriation.

But the actual rate of foreign-aid spending, John Foster Dulles said, will increase by only $200,000,000, from $4,200,000,000 to $4,400,000,000 in the fiscal year 1957, beginning next July 1.

In explaining the need for a greatly increased appropriation, he acknowledged that a foreign-aid program at the present scale had become a fixed part of national policy.

"Both the economic aid and the military aid will need to go on for a considerable period of time at about the present level," the Secretary said.

To keep this assistance moving in a continuous flow, the pipeline had to be replenished, Mr. Dulles said at his news conference this morning.

In confirming the foreign-aid increase reported last week-end, Mr. Dulles said that the requested appropriation for military assistance would run about $3,000,000,000. This is three times the amount voted by Congress during its last session.

Administration officials explained, meanwhile, the principal reason for the increase in military aid. They said it had been decided that expensive new weapons must be shipped to the nation's allies.

New Funds for Pipeline

The unexpected size of the Administration's foreign-aid request blew up a tempest at the Capitol that was not wholly abated by Mr. Dulles' explanation.

Mr. Dulles conceded that there had been a "genuine misunderstanding" at the White House briefing last Tuesday, when the Administration's program was outlined for Congressional leaders of both parties. The Secretary said he regretted it. The legislators, he said, were told that the rate of spending would remain about the same, but "apparently we did not get into the accounting aspects of the matter."

Mr. Dulles referred to the increased appropriation of new money to keep the pipeline for military supplies full although it would not be spent for several years.

This recollection was challenged by Representative John Taber of upstate New York, the ranking Republican of the House Appropriations Committee.

"We weren't told about it at

Continued on Page 14, Column 3

The New York Times

THE U. N. SOLVES A PROBLEM: José Maza, center, president of General Assembly, congratulates Leo Mates, left, of Yugoslavia and Carlos P. Romulo of Philippines after problem of seating those nations was resolved by a compromise yesterday at United Nations.

TENTH ASSEMBLY OF U. N. IS ENDED; DEADLOCK SOLVED

Vote Gives Yugoslavia Year of Security Council Term —Philippines to Get 2d

ACHIEVEMENTS ARE CITED

Atoms-for-Peace Plan and Entry of 16 New Members Are Singled Out by Maza

By THOMAS J. HAMILTON

Special to The New York Times.

UNITED NATIONS, N. Y., Dec. 20—The General Assembly elected Yugoslavia to the Security Council today in the final action of the 1955 session.

Under a compromise worked out last week, Yugoslavia will resign after one year and the Philippines will be elected for the remainder of the two-year term.

José Maza, President of the Assembly, declared in his closing speech that the United Nations had accomplished much in its first ten years but that "it will do much more in the years to come." This was the tenth annual session of the Assembly, which started work in London on Jan. 10, 1946.

In listing the achievements of the session Señor Maza placed two actions at the top: the Assembly's endorsement of the atoms-for-peace program and the admission of sixteen new members, bringing the total to seventy-six.

Señor Maza declared that the admission of the new members, which broke a deadlock that had prevented the approval of any applicant since 1950, would "inspire unfailing respect for the principles of the Charter."

Session Ends With Prayer

The session closed, as is now customary, with a minute of prayer and meditation. The eleventh session will open here on Sept. 18, 1956, unless the time or place is changed to avoid conflicting with the Presidental election in the United States next November.

Although the deadlock between Yugoslavia and the Philippines had lasted for thirty-five ballots, the arrangement for the split term made possible the election of Yugoslavia on the thirty-sixth and final ballot this morning.

However, the compromise aroused no enthusiasm, and there was no applause when Señor Maza announced that Yugoslavia, having received 43 out of 70 votes cast, was elected to succeed Turkey. Eleven last-ditch supporters continued to vote for the Philippines, and Sweden and Finland received one vote each.

There were thirteen absten-

Continued on Page 8, Column 3

U.S., Canadian Union Dues Exceed Half Billion a Year

By A. H. RASKIN

Unions in this country and Canada have a combined income of more than $500,000,000 a year, a research study disclosed yesterday. The year-long survey, compiled by the National Industrial Conference Board, represented the most comprehensive analysis ever made of union constitutions and dues structures. Only three unions, all racket-tainted, refused to cooperate with the private research agency in its study.

The board reported that a total of 194 unions with a membership of 17,500,000 collected a minimum of $457,000,000 annually in dues payments. No specific tabulation was made on how much more the unions received in initiation fees and assessments. However, James J. Bambrick, director of the study, said these payments would bring the total "well above the half-billion mark."

The report indicated that dues collections were divided almost evenly between the locals and their parent unions. The board estimated that per capita taxes to the internationals cost the locals $228,000,000 a year. This left the locals $229,000,000 with which to meet their own obligations.

The average dues payment for the individual union member was put at $26.14 a year. This compared with an average current factory wage of $78.69 a week. In some cases dues were as low as $1 a month. The highest scale reported was $25 a month for airline pilots earning more than $19,000 a year.

Initation fees varied from 65 cents to $250, with the top entrance charges enforced in the skilled trades. Seven unions were found to have constitutional prohibitions against initiation fees, and most were in the $2 to $5 range.

The survey covered 139 unions affiliated with the merged American Federation of Labor and Congress of Industrial Organizations, plus fifty-five independent

Continued on Page 32, Column 2

INSURANCE AGENCY RULES AUTO CLUB

Owns $20,500 Bond Issue That Controls Vote—Link Aired in Stormy Session

By BERT PIERCE

The control of $6,189,462 in assets by a $20,500 bond investment was described yesterday at a stormy annual meeting of the Automobile Club of New York.

The club has the assets, while the $20,500 in club bonds are owned by the Automobile Club of New York Agency, which deals in insurance.

The ties between the insurance company and the club were assailed by a group of members led by Irving Mariash, a lawyer. After a series of heated arguments he offered to buy the bonds to relieve the club of their dominating influence. They entail the voting power of one-third of the 327,000 members.

William J. Gottlieb, president of the club, refused to consider the offer. He is also president of the agency. He said that control of the club through the outstanding bonds was intended "to prevent an insurgent group, a few people with an axe to grind or larceny in their hearts, from taking over the assets and good-will of the organization."

Says Method Is Widely Used

He added that there was nothing illegal in the transaction and that this method of control was used by many of the automobile clubs throughout the country.

Leo T. Kissam, the club's general counsel, said that some of its directors had an interest in the insurance agency. Mr. Mariash, who is a former Professor of Law at City College, then asked why the bonds had not been paid off.

Mr. Kissam replied there was no obligation to pay off the bonds and that holders had not requested that they be paid off. Mr. Gottlieb declared that it was in the best interest of club members—"persons who joined the club for service as motorists and not to find fault with the policies of the organization."

Morris Iushewitz, secretary and treasurer of the New York City C. I. O. Council, then joined with Mr. Mariash in seeking to buy the bonds and was refused.

The power of the bonds lies in a transaction that took place in 1934 when the club obtained its charter from a privately owned membership corporation.

The bonds were issued with a specified voting power equal to that obtained by any third of the membership of the club.

The ownership of the bonds was brought into the limelight when Raymond W. Crossley, treasurer of the club, said the only outstanding indebtedness was the $20,500 in bonds owned

Continued on Page 26, Column 5

MENDES-FRANCE CRITICIZES NATO

Denies Council Charge Soviet Acts in Mideast and Asia Constitute New Threat

By HAROLD CALLENDER

Special to The New York Times.

PARIS, Dec. 20—Pierre Mendès-France took issue today with the statement of the North Atlantic Council Friday describing Soviet tactics in the Middle and Far East as "a new challenge to the free world."

The council's statement followed a speech by Secretary of State Dulles, who said a new "cold war" front had been opened by the Soviet Union in the Middle East.

M. Mendes-France, who was Premier and Foreign Minister last year and seeks the Premiership again, criticized the present Foreign Minister Antoine Pinay, for having signed the council's statement. His statements were contained in an editorial in his newspaper, L'Express.

The former Premier contended the Soviet Union was using its "growing productive capacity" for "economic expansion" of the same kind that the West had practiced in the last century and the beginning of this one. He contended this was no reason to increase Western armaments.

He described the recent Soviet bloc sales of arms to Egypt as a Soviet reply to "the unlucky Baghdad Pact, which constituted for the West a blunder of which we now see the consequences."

This pact, among Britain,

Continued on Page 6, Column 3

Mob Rips Down U. S. Flag In Jordan Anti-West Riots

Special to The New York Times.

JERUSALEM (Israeli Sector), Dec. 20—Anti-Western demonstrators tore down a United States flag today in the garden outside the United States Consulate in the Jordanian sector of Jerusalem. The crowd was driven off by Jordanian policemen, who have guarded the Consulate since it was stoned Saturday.

Consul General William E. Cole and members of his staff were in the Consulate, along with Americans who had been brought there for safety.

The demonstration was reported to have followed the funerals of three persons killed by Jordanian authorities in previous days while participating in rioting against Jordan's joining the Baghdad Pact. After the funerals today, crowds were said to have gone from one foreign consulate to another demanding that flags be lowered to half staff.

The leader of the demonstration was said to have shouted slogans in praise of Premier Gamal Abdel Nasser of Egypt and asking for arms to "fight Israel."

The demonstrators marched along a road past the United States Consulate. One group surged into the garden and bent the flagstaff over a wall into the adjoining street, and the flag was pulled from the staff.

Jordanian guards fired in the air and the demonstrators hurried on.

The American-supported tuberculosis hospital on Hebron Road was reported to have been badly damaged by a mob.

Crowds gathered also at the French and Turkish consulates. Patrice de Beauvais, French Consul Adjoint, drove a crowd from his home with a submachine gun. On the previous day he was struck with stones on the forehead.

Travelers coming to the Israeli sector of Jerusalem said the demonstrations in Jordan seemed more violent than was generally known in the outside world.

A crowd in Jericho was re-

Continued on Page 4, Column 5

BRITISH CABINET SHARPLY REVISED

Macmillan Treasury Head, Lloyd Foreign Secretary—Butler to Plan Policy

By DREW MIDDLETON

Special to The New York Times.

LONDON, Dec. 20—Harold Macmillan was named Chancellor of the Exchequer and Selwyn Lloyd replaced him as Foreign Secretary in a reconstruction of the Conservative Government announced tonight.

The announcement was made by Prime Minister Eden.

R. A. Butler, whom Mr. Macmillan succeeds as Chancellor of the Exchequer, is to be Leader of the House of Commons and Lord Privy Seal in the new Cabinet. Mr. Butler, who guided British economy from the clouds of 1951 to the intermittent sunshine of 1955, will be responsible for planning and carrying out the Government's legislative policy, a ministerial source said.

Sir Walter Monckton, regarded as a highly successful Minister of Labor, will take over Mr. Lloyd's job as Minister of Defense. His Labor Ministry will be assumed by Iain Macleod, until tonight Minister of Health.

Biggest Reshuffle Since War

These are the key changes in the most drastic governmental reshuffle the Conservative party has known since World War II. The new Cabinet is one on which Sir Anthony and Conservative rule will stand or fall in the four years before the next general election.

As reconstructed, the Cabinet averages 54 years and four months of age, four years and two months younger than the old Cabinet. But from the standpoint of a Government spokesman, the influx of eager, interested new ministers is its strongest recommendation.

The changes mark a departure from active politics of one of the builders of the present Conservative Government.

Viscount Woolton, organizer of the Conservative election victories in 1951 and 1955, has resigned as Chancellor of the Duchy of Lancaster. He has been replaced in the Cabinet by the Earl of Selkirk.

Queen Elizabeth has conferred an earldom on Viscount Woolton. Peerages have been bestowed on five other Conservative stalwarts.

Capt. Harry Crookshank, whose place as Lord Privy Seal and Leader of the House of Commons is being taken by Mr. Butler, becomes a viscount.

The offices of Lord Privy Seal, Chancellor of the Duchy of Lancaster and Lord President of the Council, held in this and the previous Government by the Mar-

Continued on Page 12, Column 3

FUND ENLARGING FORD STOCK SALE

Public Demand Lifts Offering to 10,000,000 Shares

So much interest has been shown in the pending first public sale of Ford Motor Company stock that the Ford Foundation has decided to enlarge the offering. It plans to put on the market next month not 6,952,293 shares, but more than 10,000,000.

This means that the fund will dispose of about 22 per cent of its holdings, instead of 15 per cent as announced on Nov. 6.

A registration statement covering the proposed stock offering is to be filed this morning with the Securities and Exchange Commission in Washington. If the offering runs to 10,000,000 shares or more, as was predicted last night in informed financial circles, the aggregate market value of the offering will exceed $600,000,000, making it the largest distribution of corporate securities ever made. At the time the Ford Foundation first announced its divestment plans, the indicated price of the stock was $60 to $70 a share, suggesting a market value of [illegible]00,000,000 to $500,000,000.

Demand was a major factor in the decision to increase the offering.

At the same time, marketing managers are pledged to make the distribution as wide as possible. No single purchaser will be permitted to subscribe to more than 200 shares of stock, it was said.

Eisenhower Returns To Capital for Yule

By EDWIN L. DALE Jr.

Special to The New York Times.

WASHINGTON, Dec. 20—The Gettysburg phase of President Eisenhower's convalescence ended abruptly today.

Largely because Mrs. Eisenhower wanted an extra day in Washington to prepare for Christmas, the President flew here a day ahead of schedule. He originally had intended to drive but when the weather proved perfect, took his personal plane instead. Mrs. Eisenhower followed the President by car.

In the background of the return, though the Eisenhowers had planned all along to spend Christmas in Washington, was the fact that the President's daughter-in-law, Mrs. John S. Eisenhower, was in the hospital awaiting her fourth child.

Mrs. Eisenhower stopped at

Continued on Page 26, Column 8

4 U. S. Planes Reach Antarctica, First to Fly In From the Outside

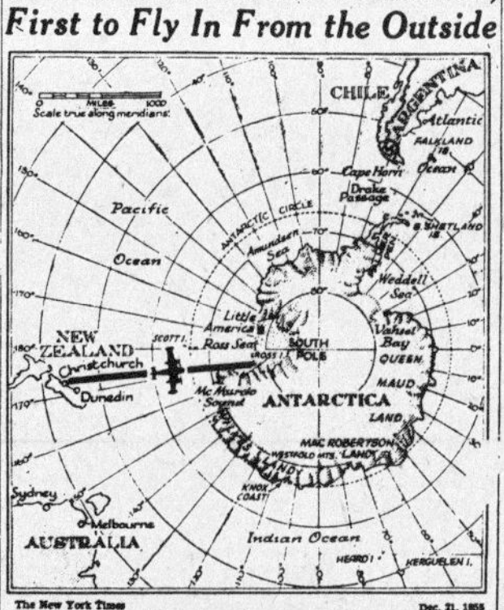

The New York Times Dec. 21, 1955

The line of the pioneering American flight to Antarctica

By The Associated Press.

AUCKLAND, N. Z., Dec. 20—Four United States planes flew from New Zealand to Antarctica today. It was the first time that planes had landed on the frozen continent from another land mass.

Mount Erebus, an active volcano towering 13,000 feet above the icy continent's landing strip, provided a guiding beacon on the last stages of the 2,400-mile non-stop flight from New Zealand's South Island.

Four other planes, all part of a United States expedition head-

Continued on Page 11, Column 1

Cocktail Party Bane Of U. N., Maza Says

Special to The New York Times.

UNITED NATIONS, N. Y., Dec. 20—Take it from an expert, the trouble with a United Nations General Assembly is the cocktail parties.

José Maza of Chile, President of the tenth annual session, which closed this afternoon, said at a press conference, that the receptions came in "torrents—sometimes three or four in a day."

"You have to drink the same Scotch or the same Manhattans and eat the same shrimps and talk to the self-same people," he commented.

This is not only "somewhat tiring to the President, who has to go, but undoubtedly to the delegates who do go," Señor Maza asserted.

The answer, the veteran Chilean diplomat suggested, would be smaller but longer receptions, "say on Friday aft-

Continued on Page 8, Column 5

6° COLD GRIPS CITY; LITTLE RELIEF DUE

Frigid Weather Is Prevalent Over Wide Area of U. S.

Winter, unwilling to wait for its official debut at 10:12 A. M. tomorrow, trod heavily on the mercury yesterday.

At 2 A. M. the temperature was down to 6 degrees at the Battery station of the Weather Bureau. This marked a low for the season. Before last night the low had been 16.2 degrees, recorded at 6:50 A. M. last Friday. At 3 A. M. today the mercury rose to 7 degrees.

The extreme cold was prevalent over a large part of the nation. It extended from the northern Great Plains east and from Maine South to North Carolina.

Here the temperature skidded from a high of 21.2 degrees at 12:30 A. M. yesterday. By 8 A. M. it was 13.4 degrees. Between 9 A. M. and 4 P. M. it fluctuated in the 15-to-17-degree range. By 5 P. M., when the crowds poured from office buildings into the biting air, the mercury was swinging downward again.

The freeze felt twice as bad because of the strong northwesterly winds that swept around corners and raced down the streets during the day. They averaged between twenty and twenty-five miles an hour, with gusts up to forty miles an hour.

The Transit Authority reported that the cold had affected

Continued on Page 22, Column 2

"All the News That's Fit to Print"

The New York Times.

LATE CITY EDITION
Condensation of U. S. Weather Bureau forecast:
Mostly fair and mild today.
Partly cloudy tomorrow.
Temp. range today: 52-32; yesterday: 47-38
Full U. S. Weather Bureau Report, Page 44

VOL. CV..No. 35,835. Entered as Second-Class Matter, Post Office, New York, N. Y. NEW YORK, MONDAY, MARCH 5, 1956. Times Square, New York 36, N. Y. Telephone LAckawanna 4-1000 FIVE CENTS

GOLDWATER SAYS 'BILL KECK' GAVE TO HIS CAMPAIGN

Sees No Reason Why Gift Should Disqualify Him as Lobby Inquiry Member

CONFUSION OVER NAME

Senator Believes Contributor Is Relative of Oil Man—Uncertain of Amount

By ALLEN DRURY
Special to The New York Times.

WASHINGTON, March 4—Senator Barry F. Goldwater, a member of the special Senate lobby investigating committee, disclosed today that he had received a campaign contribution from a member of the Keck family.

The Arizona Republican said he saw no reason why this should disqualify him as a member of the special committee.

[The United Press early Monday quoted Senator Goldwater as saying the contribution was from a "Bill Keck."

["He's the man I was acquainted with," he said. He added that the name of Howard B. Keck, president of Superior Oil Company of California, "does not ring a bell with me."

[Asked if his donor were related to Howard Keck, the Senator said:

["I think it's his father. I'm not sure. It might be his uncle or cousin. He must be related. It's the same name."

[Mr. Goldwater said he did not know whether "Bill Keck" was connected with Superior Oil.]

Howard Keck is a key figure in another Senate investigation of an attempt to give $2,500 to the campaign fund of Senator Francis Case, Republican of South Dakota.

Gift Made Three Years Ago

Senator Goldwater appeared on the American Broadcasting Company television program "College Press Conference." He said he could not remember the exact amount given to him by "Mr. Keck." But he said the records were on file with the clerk of the Arizona House of Representatives. The contribution was made three years ago, he said.

"If Mr. Keck likes the way I vote," the Senator declared, "he has a perfect right to give money to me. I have never known Mr. Keck to ask a favor of me * * *. If the C. I. O. United Auto Workers likes the way [Senator] Paul Douglas [Democrat of Illinois] votes, it has a right to give money to him."

The Senator added that he could "name you four or five Democrats who received contributions from Mr. Keck as well as Republicans."

Senator Goldwater is a member of an eight-man bipartisan committee created by the Senate to conduct a full investigation of any attempts to influence Senators and other Government employes.

Howard Keck had been a witness before another special Senate committee, a four-man group headed by Senator Walter F. George, Democrat of Georgia, in connection with the Senator Case episode. John Neff, a Ne-

Continued on Page 14, Column 7

Javits Is Available For Senate Contest

The New York Times
Jacob K. Javits

State Attorney General Jacob K. Javits yesterday eased the brim of his hat into the ring for a Republican nomination for United States Senator.

He insisted on the distinction that he was not "throwing" it in. The difference held political import.

Mr. Javits said he would consider it "my duty" to run this year for the seat of Democratic

Continued on Page 15, Column 5

EISENHOWER FACES BIDS TO CAMPAIGN

Hall and Knowland Agree He May Have to Add Tours to Assist Candidates

Special to The New York Times.

WASHINGTON, March 4—The Senate Republican leader and the chairman of the Republican National Committee agreed today that President Eisenhower might have to extend his personal appearances in the fall election campaign.

They asserted he might have to do this to help Republican candidates for Senator and Governor in doubtful states.

The President had said in his broadcast to the country Wednesday night on his candidacy that he hoped to avoid "whistle stopping" and keep "his personal traveling to the absolute minimum this year."

But Senator William F. Knowland of California and Leonard W. Hall, the G. O. P. chairman, said in separate television appearances that he might have to do considerably more than that because the coming campaign might be both "strenuous" and "hard-hitting."

Senator Knowland, appearing on the Columbia Broadcasting System's television program,

Continued on Page 15, Column 3

HARRIMAN TERMS PRESIDENT A DUPE OF KREMLIN DRIVE

Eisenhower-Dulles Policy Is Held Incapable of Checking Red Expansion in World

By RICHARD AMPER

Governor Harriman accused President Eisenhower and Secretary of State Dulles last night of unwittingly helping the Soviet campaign for world domination.

He charged that Mr. Dulles had abetted Communist propaganda by identifying this country with "militarism and colonialism" and had sought military pacts against communism to the neglect of economic and social aid to Near and Far Eastern countries.

Contending that the Republican Administration was incapable of meeting the new Soviet economic offensive, Mr. Harriman called for a "fresh start" and a "new approach that will electrify the people of the world" in the way the Truman Doctrine, Marshall Plan and Point Four aid to underdeveloped countries "checked the Soviets" and fostered unity in the free world.

He also charged that Mr. Dulles had given misinformation and "a dangerous misinterpretation" of Soviet strategy to a Senate committee.

Dulles Assailed Vehemently

The Governor, a possible candidate for the Democratic Presidential nomination, leveled a particularly vehement attack at Mr. Dulles in a speech at a dinner of the nationalities division of the Democratic National Committee at the Plaza Hotel.

He said the Soviet had made clear in 1952 its strategy of "peaceful co-existence" and reliance on economic, political and psychological weapons in the "cold war" but that the Eisenhower Administration had failed to take effective action.

"Worse than that, many of the Eisenhower-Dulles policies and actions unwittingly helped the Soviet campaign," he said.

"Mr. Dulles tarnished the good name of the United States with militarism. Mr. Dulles has an unquenchable passion for slogans—generally warlike—from 'massive retaliation' to 'brink of war.' And he has been flying around the world in the glare of publicity negotiating military pacts, with little attention to the peaceful aspirations of the people of the world for economic and social progress."

Mr. Harriman said Mr. Dulles often seemed to be "posing for the very picture the Kremlin is trying to paint of us."

The Governor attacked Mr. Eisenhower as well, saying:

"At Geneva the Soviets did not yield on a single issue of substance, but the President said

Continued on Page 24, Column 1

Associated Press Radiophoto

MONARCH OF JORDAN ACCLAIMED: Young King Hussein, center figure of three at left, being hailed by his subjects outside Royal Palace in Amman on Saturday. Demonstrators cheered the dismissal of Lieut. Gen. John Bagot Glubb.

SOCIALIST PARLEY REBUFFS MOSCOW ON UNITED FRONT

International Gives a Blunt 'No' to Communist Move for Political Cooperation

PRECONDITIONS ARE SET

Meeting in Zurich Demands an End of Dictatorship as a Prelude to Unity

By KENNETT LOVE
Special to The New York Times.

ZURICH, Switzerland, March 4 — Western socialism retorted with a blunt "no" today to communism's proposal for political cooperation.

The answer, given here by the Council of the Socialist International at the end of a three-day conference, said "the minimum precondition, even for the possibility of talks" was the abolition of the Communist dictatorship.

Communist attempts to revive the pre-war Popular Fronts with the Socialists were begun several months ago in Germany, France, Italy and other countries with overtures by Communist branches to the local Socialist parties.

The invitation was made officially by Soviet leaders last month at the twentieth Communist party congress in Moscow. It was reaffirmed in a congress resolution that proposed the elimination of the split in the working class movement and the restoration of businesslike contacts between the Communist and Socialist parties.

The forty-six delegates from seventeen European countries, plus Israel and Canada, also voted whole-hearted support of Israel in her conflict with the Arabs.

Arms for Israel Urged

The council called on Socialist parties "to urge insistently that Israel be provided with the necessary arms for self defense" and it castigated the West for "attempting to appease the Arabs."

A resolution urging progressive controlled disarmament as the world's most urgent problem, adopted on Friday, was the first of three major stands taken at the conference, including the reply to the Communists and the statement on the Middle East. However, the conference did not, as had been expected, make recommendations on German reunification.

The Socialist reply was made in two paragraphs, titled "Draft Statement on the Relations Between the Socialist International and Other Political Forces," that were unanimously approved by the delegates. The statement said:

"The changes of Communist

Continued on Page 8, Column 3

ADENAUER MAKES BADEN VOTE GAIN

But Christian Democrats Fail to Win Majority in Election of a State Parliament

By M. S. HANDLER
Special to The New York Times.

BONN, Germany, March 4—Chancellor Konrad Adenauer's Christian Democratic Union strengthened its position in today's election of a state parliament in Baden-Wuerttemberg. However, the party fell far short of the majority it received in the 1953 national elections.

Official election returns from all seventy constituencies showed that the Christian Democrats had polled 42.6 per cent, the Social Democrats 28.9 per cent, the Free Democrats 16.6 per cent, and the Refugee party 6.2 per cent. Minor parties shared the remaining 5.7 per cent.

In the 1952 state elections the Christian Democratic Union received 36 per cent of the votes. By comparison today's results represented an appreciable advance for the Chancellor's party, though it garnered far fewer votes than in 1953.

The 120 seats in the new Landtag (state parliament) will be occupied by fifty-six Christian Democrats, thirty-six Social Democrats, twenty-one Free Democrats and seven Refugee party Deputies.

The outgoing parliament included fifty Christian Democrats, thirty-eight Social Democrats, twenty-three Free Demo-

Continued on Page 10, Column 3

France Assures Her Allies Tie to West Will Stay Firm

By ROBERT C. DOTY
Special to The New York Times.

PARIS, March 4—Diplomats here of the United States and Britain have received assurances that French criticism of the two countries' leadership does not herald any weakening of France's loyalty to the Western alliance.

The assurances emerged from a week-end of diplomatic activity, including an unusual Sunday meeting between French Foreign Minister Christian Pineau and United States Ambassador C. Douglas Dillon. It was M. Pineau who kindled a diplomatic "brush fire" on Friday with a speech to the Anglo-American Press Association here in which he attacked alleged British and United States errors of tactics in the "cold war."

These events followed hard upon M. Pineau's speech:

¶Sir Gladwyn Jebb, British Ambassador here, saw Premier Guy Mollet yesterday to invite him to London next Sunday for talks with Prime Minister Eden.

¶Mr. Dillon and his principal aide made inquiries concerning the Pineau speech in conferences with Foreign Ministry officials Saturday.

¶Today, on his return from conferences with West German leaders in Bonn, M. Pineau asked Mr. Dillon to call on him at the Foreign Ministry.

It was understood on good authority that, in all these talks, French leaders reaffirmed their attachment to the Western alliance, whatever dissents they might enter to specific policies.

Speaking extempore on Friday, M. Pineau questioned the wisdom of United States-British tactics in placing emphasis on military matters with Middle and Far Eastern states.

Specifically, he criticized the

Continued on Page 3, Column 2

ISRAEL AND SYRIA IN A NEW CLASH

Arabs Kill Two Policemen in Their Patrol Launch on Sea of Galilee

Special to The New York Times.

TEL AVIV, Israel, March 4—Two Israeli policemen were killed today in an encounter with Syrian coastal positions in the northeast corner of the Sea of Galilee.

The Israelis said the Syrians had wounded and captured two other policemen and seized two boats.

Reports reaching the United Nations Truce Supervision Organization in Jerusalem from neutral observers on the spot confirmed the killing of the two policemen. The bodies and the two launches were returned to the Israelis this afternoon. United Nations observers on the Syrian side said there was no trace of any wounded Israelis.

Army headquarters here said there had been four policemen in the boat that the Syrians had attacked. The last radio message received from the craft shortly before 11 A. M. said all four occupants had been wounded.

The Israelis said another craft on the lake had witnessed the attack and had seen the Syrians drag the vessel with the four wounded ashore. The clash oc-

Continued on Page 6, Column 3

BRITISH SEE PERIL RISING IN MIDEAST

Glubb's Dismissal by Jordan Thought to Reduce Check on Arab-Israeli War

By THOMAS P. RONAN
Special to The New York Times.

LONDON, March 4 — British officials believe that the dismissal of Lieut. Gen. John Bagot Glubb as head of Jordan's Arab Legion has greatly increased the danger of an Arab-Israeli war.

Informed sources here said General Glubb had repeatedly warned Jordan, and indirectly other Arab nations, against becoming involved in a war with Israel.

As a military expert he had made it clear that he felt their position would be militarily hopeless in such a conflict. He had reiterated what Prime Minister Eden and other Western leaders have been saying: that the Arabs would forfeit the sympathy of Britain and other Western powers if they started a war with Israel.

Without General Glubb's restraining influence the Jordanians may be tempted to join with other Arab nations in an attack on Israel, it is feared here. In the Legion they have the best Arab force in the Middle East.

This is believed to be particularly true because the abrupt dismissal by King Hussein apparently was due in considerable measure to his desire to placate the extremists in Jordan. These extremists are believed to be not by any means averse to war.

Soviet Support a Factor

Another precipitating factor, it is said, may be the conviction of some influential Arabs that they can count on support from Moscow. Recent moves by the Soviet Union and its satellites to strengthen the Arabs militarily and economically have reinforced this belief.

General Glubb spent several hours with Sir Anthony today at Chequers, the Prime Minister's country residence, discussing his dismissal and the situation in Jordan and the Middle East generally. Earlier he had spent about an hour with Anthony Nutting, Minister of State for Foreign Affairs, at the Foreign Office covering the same ground.

After General Glubb's visit, Prime Minister Eden had conversations with Sir Walter Monckton, Minister of Defense, Mr. Nutting and other Foreign Office officials.

It is considered likely that Sir Anthony will reply to questions on the subject in the House of Commons tomorrow although Mr. Nutting is scheduled to make a statement there. Until then there will be no official comment on the subject or on today's discussions.

The Foreign Office has declined to elaborate on its comment Friday that the full facts that led to the dismissal are not known. But in well-informed quarters it is believed the desire to appease the extremists was a major reason and that another and possibly deciding factor was the 20-year-old King's increasing jealousy of the general.

The monarch was said to feel

Continued on Page 6, Column 5

Trough in Antarctica Spawns Hurricane Winds

A 1,000-Mile Chute in Icecap Sighted by Americans

By ANTHONY LEVIERO
Special to The New York Times.

WASHINGTON, March 4—The current United States Antarctic expedition has discovered a vast trough of ice, thousands of square miles in extent, in which the vilest weather in the world is spawned.

Hurricane gusts up to 200 miles an hour have been clocked in the chute between Victoria Land and Wilkes Land. The everlasting glacial ice also slides through the trough into the Indian Ocean.

Word of the expedition's geographic discovery, one of the most important this season, has just been brought back here by Dr. Paul A. Siple, geographer and deputy to Rear Admiral Richard E. Byrd. Admiral Byrd is in over-all command of the country's Antarctic work as part of the world research of the International Geophysical Year 1957-58.

Dr. Siple, a veteran of all the Byrd Antarctic expeditions, also said recent observations supported his belief that the Antarctic continental icecap was divided into two gigantic domes of ice, with perhaps some smaller satellite domes scattered around in the still unexplored regions.

The smaller of the two domes covers Marie Byrd Land—the eastern Pacific sector of Antarctica—and has an altitude of about 10,000 feet. The larger dome lies in the vast region between Wilkes Land and Queen Maud Land—the Australia-Indian Ocean sector—where the altitude is estimated at 12,000 feet.

It might be more accurate to describe these domes as separate icecaps; and one objective of future seismological tests is whether they are merely gargantuan plateaus of ice or primeval mountains buried under the glacial blanket.

Apart from its importance as a geographic feature, the trough noted by Dr. Siple is significant

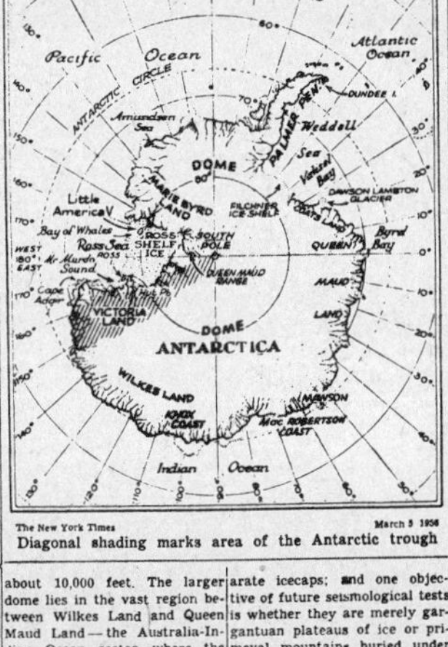

The New York Times March 5 1956
Diagonal shading marks area of the Antarctic trough

Siple Reports Gains by Byrd's Flights in Polar Area

for a number of reasons. It will provide data on the origin of winds that may affect weather in other parts of the world. Certainly the trough has a violent local effect on Antarctic weather.

And now new expeditions for the International Geophysical Year will know enough to stay out of the place and avoid the hardships suffered by the Australian Mawson Expedition of 1911-14 and the French expedition of 1950-53. Both of those groups had camped unwittingly at the bottom edge of the biggest air drainage ditch in the world.

"We got a little more of a peep into the Antarctic continent," said Dr. Siple, who flew once across the South Pole and once across the trough in his most recent trip. "The continent has this heaped-up dome we visualize as the Antarctic. As you get toward the center you find two lobes, one in the East Antarctic and one in the West Antarctic.

"The big section toward the Australia, Africa and Indian Ocean side is bigger, and goes up to quite a high elevation. We think of the continent as two, maybe more, gigantic icecaps. Until we get seismologists in there, we won't know whether they are great masses of snow

Continued on Page 7, Column 6

New State Parleys Seek Tax Cut Truce

By LEO EGAN
Special to The New York Times.

ALBANY, March 4—Governor Harriman invited Republican legislative leaders today to meet with him again tomorrow to discuss a compromise on income tax reduction.

The outlook for agreement was dim tonight. The principal dispute between the Democratic Governor and the Republican legislative majorities now involves the amount of revenue the state can afford to forego. Neither side seemed disposed to yield.

Because of the deadlock many members of the Legislature were predicting that there would be no general tax cut this year. A few were of the view that such an outcome would be a good thing for the state in the light of increases in expenses it faces next year.

It was disclosed today that a Republican-controlled Senate

Continued on Page 12, Column 2

Madrid Announces Wage Rise of 20%

Special to The New York Times.

MADRID, March 4—The Spanish Government announced today a 20 per cent nation-wide increase in wages, effective April 1.

In addition, a new increase will be put into effect on Oct. 1 that may be as high as 7½ per cent on today's wages, bringing the total increase for this year to 27½ per cent, a communiqué said.

In an effort to forestall a corresponding rise in the cost of living, the Government said it would reduce by nearly 50 per cent employers' contributions for social benefits now enjoyed by the workers. Under the Spanish syndicalist system those contributions amount, in effect, to an additional 25 to 50 per cent of the workers' wages, according to the branch of activity.

The purpose of that reduction, the communique ex-

Continued on Page 11, Column 6

POPE DENOUNCES RED 'PEACE' LURE

Warns World of 'Insidious' Pacts With 'Materialists'

Special to The New York Times.

ROME, March 4—Pope Pius XII warned the nations of the world today of the "lures of an insidious peace."

Although he named no specific power, he made it clear that he was replying to peace overtures made at the Twentieth Congress of the Soviet Communist party in Moscow last month.

Addressing diplomats of forty-two nations, the Pontiff said: "For militant materialism the time of 'peace' does not represent anything but a truce, a rather precarious truce, during which it awaits the social and economic collapse of other peoples."

The Pope put his listeners particularly on their guard against offers to promote peace by establishing economic relations or exchanging technical information with countries dominated by "materialism," Vatican parlance for the Communist bloc. This was seen as a reference to the Moscow congress' insistence on economic and technical cooperation between the Soviet Union and the West and neutral countries.

Economic and technical progress is useful and necessary, the Pope declared, but it must be subject to "higher spiritual needs." He urged nations to infuse their policies with spiritual

Continued on Page 4, Column 6

"All the News That's Fit to Print"

The New York Times.

LATE CITY EDITION
Condensation of U. S. Weather Bureau forecast:
Mostly sunny and mild today.
Cloudy and rain tomorrow.
Temp. range today: 52-37; yesterday: 46-30
Full U. S. Weather Bureau Report, Page 34

VOL. CV . No. 35,840. Entered as Second-Class Matter, Post Office, New York, N. Y.

NEW YORK, SATURDAY, MARCH 10, 1956. Times Square, New York 36, N. Y. Telephone LAckawanna 4-1000 FIVE CENTS

M'KAY TO RESIGN TO OPPOSE MORSE FOR SENATE SEAT

President Gives His Blessing to Move by G.O.P. to Oust Oregon Democrat

SECRETARY SCORES FOE

Asserts He Is Gunning for 'Left-Wingers'—Prepares for Hard Campaign

By LAWRENCE E. DAVIES
Special to The New York Times.

SALEM, Ore., March 9—Douglas McKay became a candidate today for the Republican nomination for United States Senator. He said he was gunning "for left-wingers and Socialists."

Mr. McKay expects to be the party's candidate next fall against his No. 1 political enemy, Senator Wayne Morse, now a Democrat after twice having been elected as a Republican.

The Secretary of the Interior flew unexpectedly to Portland after informing President Eisenhower of his intention to resign from the Cabinet and run for the Senate. He drove here after party conferences in Portland.

Shortly after 3 P. M. on this final day for filing nominations for the primary on May 18, he walked into the office of David O'Hara, Deputy Secretary of State, and signed the nomination papers.

'Made Up Own Mind'

"I have had my health checked and I'm ready for the hardest campaign in my life," he asserted.

[In Washington Mr. McKay received President Eisenhower's blessings for his political campaign.]

Mr. McKay declared that General Eisenhower had not asked him to make the race against Senator Morse.

"I made up my own mind," he said. "The important thing is to get some people back there who are Republicans, not Socialists and left-wingers. We can't be bothered with these fellows who block the way."

The 62-year-old Cabinet member's last-minute entry presaged one of the greatest no-holds-barred campaigns in Oregon history. He picked up the torch dropped by the late Gov. Paul Patterson, who died four days after announcing his candidacy for the nomination, in late January.

Since then four other have announced their candidacy for the Republican nomination. One of them, Lamar Tooze, a Portland attorney, dropped out this afternoon as soon as Mr. McKay

Continued on Page 8, Column 3

Fossil Research Questions Darwin Evolution Theory

Bones Found in 1872 Now Listed as Those of Man 10 Million Years Old

By ROBERT K. PLUMB

American anthropologists for a week have been quietly pondering what appears to be one of the most astonishing fossil discoveries ever made.

The find suggests that man was well along the process of evolution some 10,000,000 years ago. It suggests there is no connection between apes and man, ancient or modern. The discovery challenges the Darwinian dogma, in the opinion of Dr. Helmut de Terra, research associate in the Columbia University Department of Geology.

The new theory is that a double handful of fossil fragments found in northern Italy in 1872 are the bones of a human-like creature about 10,000,000 years old. The fragments include a lower jawbone complete with teeth.

A full account of the fossils and the theory they suggest was presented last Saturday by Dr.

The New York Times
Dr. Johannes Hurzeler

Johannes Hurzeler, curator of vertebrate paleontology of the Basle (Switzerland) Natural History Museum. He presented his report at a special meeting of

Continued on Page 7, Column 2

Stassen Calls Trade Curb Aid to U. S. in Missile Race

By CHARLES E. EGAN
Special to The New York Times.

WASHINGTON, March 9—Victory for the United States in the race to develop a long-range missile was linked today to this country's efforts to bar shipments of atomic materials to the Soviet Union. Harold E. Stassen, assistant to the President for disarmament, said that the outcome of the missiles race would depend considerably on keeping the strategic products out of Russian hands.

Appearing before a highly critical Senate Permanent Subcommittee on Investigations, Mr. Stassen defended the extreme security measures that the Administration has used to prevent public disclosure of details of international embargo lists at the subcommittee's hearings.

"There are fifty-four items that are embargoed but are not included on the list of products barred from shipment to Russia by our allies," the former head of the Foreign Operations Administration told the subcommittee.

"All fifty-four are products connected with atomic energy and which the Atomic Energy Commission is anxious to keep out of the hands of the Russians," he said. "Not only that, it would distress us if the Russians even knew we had certain materials."

Members of the subcommittee have been critical of what they termed the "persistent and arbitrary" refusal of the Executive Branch to make public the details of the international embargo list.

The international list, drawn up originally early in 1949, and modified considerably in 1954, includes items that fourteen allies in the free world agree should not be shipped to Soviet-bloc countries in Europe.

The list is divided into products against which there is a complete embargo, products that are limited as to the quantities

Continued on Page 20, Column 5

HOGAN SAYS THUGS SEEK UNION RULE

Drive to Control Teamster Council Is Charged—U. S. Widens Rackets Inquiry

By RALPH KATZ

District Attorney Frank S. Hogan asserted yesterday that "underworld forces are making a determined effort to capture control" of the Teamsters Joint Council here.

He made the charge at a press conference in which he declared that "the facts establishing this conclusion do not in themselves constitute evidence of a crime."

At the same time, Federal authorities announced a widened inquiry by a grand jury of charges of racketeering in the trucking and garment industries. Paul W. Williams, United States Attorney, said a special grand jury would be empaneled on Thursday in addition to a regular panel already looking into racketeering. He added that if necessary a third grand jury would be selected.

The Teamsters Joint Council is the governing body for fifty-seven locals in the metropolitan area of the International Brotherhood of Teamsters. The total membership is 125,000 among the international union's 1,300,000 members.

After Mr. Hogan had made his charge, Alfred J. Scotti, assistant district attorney, named John Dio Guardio—better known as Johnny Dio—and Anthony (Tony Ducks) Corallo as the underworld spearheads of the drive.

Says Thugs Back O'Rourke

He declared that they were supporting John O'Rourke for the presidency of the council. Mr. O'Rourke also has the support of James R. Hoffa of Detroit, international vice president of the union and president of the Central States Conference of Teamsters.

Mr. Hoffa recently arranged a mutual aid pact with the International Longshoremen's Association. That union was expelled from the American Federation of Labor in 1953 on charges of gang domination.

A $400,000 loan from the teamsters to the longshoremen has been held up because George Meany, president of the American Federation of Labor and Congress of Industrial Organizations, has indicated that the truck union faced suspension if it went through with the deal.

Mr. O'Rourke's efforts to dislodge Martin T. Lacey as president of the joint council here were highlighted by the chartering in Washington of six New York locals in time for the election last Feb. 14. Lacey forces contended the locals were "paper" organizations created to rig the outcome of the balloting in Mr. O'Rourke's favor.

Mr. Scotti declared that these

Continued on Page 36, Column 2

4 BANDITS SEIZE $20,293 PAYROLL

Submachine Guns Are Used—5 Other Robberies in City

Robbers taking advantage of the Friday pay day reaped about $36,000 yesterday in six hold-ups in the city. No one was injured, no shots were fired and all the robbers escaped.

The richest—and most spectacular—robbery was committed by a band of four men armed with two submachine guns and a shotgun. They made off with a $20,293 payroll at the La Guardia Houses project, Montgomery and Madison Streets, on the lower East Side.

At 7:30 A. M. two guards from the Tracer Alarm Protective Service drove through the main gate of the project with the payroll. It was for 250 employes of the Fleetway Construction Company, which is building the low-cost city project.

The guards were Elmer Canepa and Carmine Pacifico. As they stopped in front of a construction shack to unload the money, three men came through the Montgomery Street gate, disguised with comic spectacles and false noses.

Two of the thieves, armed with a shotgun and a submachine gun, ordered the guards out of their car. They grabbed the pay envelopes and dumped them into a burlap bag. A third man, with a machine gun, entered the shack and confronted Donald Barry, office manager.

"Don't touch that phone or I'll

Continued on Page 36, Column 1

Soviet Plans to Reform Farming; Aims to Eliminate Private Plots

By WELLES HANGEN
Special to The New York Times.

MOSCOW, March 9—The Soviet Union announced tonight a far-reaching program aimed at increasing farm production for the state and eventually eliminating privately owned plots on collective farms.

The members of the Soviet Union's 94,000 collective farms will henceforth receive the bulk of their income from work on the communally owned fields. The private plots and private livestock are to be progressively reduced to a point where they only "decorate" the life of the collective farmer.

The Communist party Central Committee and the Council of Ministers, two top policy-making agencies, issued 10,000 words of "recommendations" as the basis for drastic revision of the collective farm system. There was little doubt that the recommendations would be adopted in full throughout the country.

To make work on the collectives' lands more attractive the farms will be accorded wider initiative in planning production and establishing pay scales. The general meeting of each farm will henceforth have the final power to expel undesirable members and reduce the private plots of those who live on the farm but do not participate in the collective's work.

The farmers will receive monthly money advances up to one-half of the proceeds to be derived from their deliveries and sales to the state. Until now many farmers, especially on the poorer land, have had to wait till the end of the agricultural year before seeing the result of their work on collective fields.

The system of money advances is to be facilitated by the establishment of special transferable accounts with the State Bank of the Soviet Union and subordinate banks.

The practice of many farm members of consistently evading work on the collective fields is to stop. The farms are authorized to set a minimum number of days that every member must work on the collective land or

Continued on Page 6, Column 3

EISENHOWER WINS IN NEW FARM TEST; NIXON BREAKS TIE

Casts Deciding Vote to Block High Supports on Wheat—'Deals' Again Charged

By WILLIAM M. BLAIR
Special to The New York Times.

WASHINGTON, March 9—Vice President Richard M. Nixon cast a disputed deciding vote in the Senate tonight to give the Administration another victory on its farm policy. The vote was 46 to 45.

The Vice President's vote knocked from the Senate farm bill a restoration of rigid price supports on wheat. The vote supported the Senate's rejection yesterday of rigid supports on other crops.

Senator Albert Gore, Democrat of Tennessee, threw the Senate into a wrangle over the validity of Mr. Nixon's vote.

He contended that the Vice President had no right to vote in the situation, caused by a clerical error in an original tally. Vice President Nixon, backed by the Republican and Democratic leadership, cited the Constitution and precedents in rejecting the Tennessean's contention.

The dispute was the climax of a day of bitter debate that brought new charges that the Administration had engaged in "special deals" on corn and cotton to assure retention in farm law of a flexible price support system. Midwestern wheat state Senators, aided by Democrats, attacked what they said was "preferential treatment" for corn and cotton and a "rotten deal" for wheat.

Clincher Also Voted

After the vote on the amendment to strike rigid supports for wheat, Mr. Nixon announced the result as 46 to 45. Then, the Senate passed on to another roll-call vote to clinch the first victory. This was a move to reconsider the earlier vote and then table that motion. The Administration forces carried this clincher vote 46—41.

Senator Lyndon B. Johnson of Texas, the Democratic leader, got unanimous Senate consent for a recapitulation of the 46-45 vote. He told Mr. Nixon that the record of the teller showed a majority one way and the record kept at the majority desk showed a majority the other way on the amendment by Senator George D. Aiken, Republican of Vermont.

Mr. Nixon said he had been informed by the teller as the vote on the motion to lay on the table was under way "that apparently an error had been made in the announcement of the vote on the Aiken amendment."

As Mr. Nixon announced that the recapitulation showed a tie vote and before he could cast his deciding vote, Senator Gore interrupted to object that since no Senator could change his vote in a recount and because the Vice President had not voted in the first place, he could not vote to break the tie.

Mr. Nixon cited the Constitutional provision that gives the Vice President a right to vote if a tie occurs, the only Senate situation in which he can do so. He

Continued on Page 20, Column 2

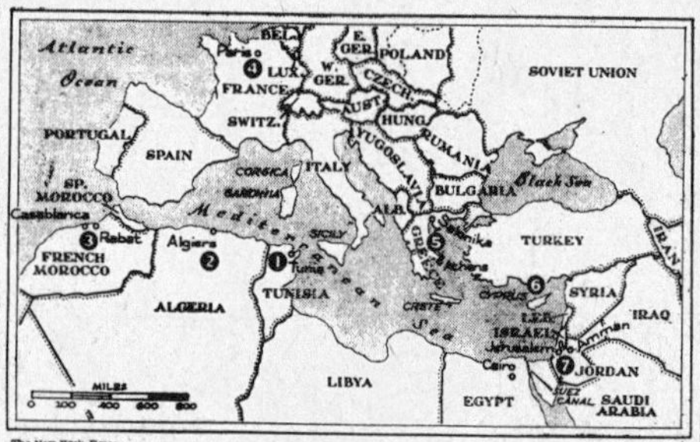

The New York Times March 10, 1956

TURBULENCE IN MEDITERRANEAN AREA: Frenchmen ransacked U. S. headquarters in Tunis (1) while mobs clamoring for independence in Algeria (2) rioted in Paris (4). French Morocco (3) marked its approach to independence. The British deportation of Archbishop Makarios from Cyprus (6) set off protests in Greece (5). A move to split Jordan (7) from Britain and ally her with Egypt, Syria and Saudi Arabia was set back.

TUNIS MOB SACKS TWO U. S. OFFICES

French Demonstrators Raid Consulate and Library—Loss Put at $20,000

By THOMAS F. BRADY
Special to The New York Times.

TUNIS, Tunisia, Saturday, March 10—A French mob wrecked the United States Consulate General and the United States Information Service library here last night.

A Tunisian Government spokesman charged the French police with "collusion and complaisance" in the rioting, in a press conference early this morning.

The destruction was accompanied by cries of "Down with America!" "Mendès-France to the gallows!" "Down with the Jews!"

Pierre Mendès-France is the former French Premier who promised internal self-government to Tunisia and began the negotiations that later led to it. He is now Vice Premier in the Government of Premier Guy Mollet. M. Mendès-France is a Jew.

No consular officers or employes were hurt except for the Tunisian guardian of the library, who suffered a minor head injury.

Damage Put at $20,000

The damage was estimated by consular officials at more than $20,000.

The pillaging of the two United States establishments, which States establishments, which are a quarter of a mile apart, occurred almost simultaneously at about 7 P. M. Morris N. Hughes, the United States Consul General, made an immediate and vigorous protest to Roger Seydoux, French High Commissioner in Tunisia. Mr. Hughes said M. Seydoux expressed profound regret and "sympathy."

French diplomatic and military officers conferred with Mr. Hughes until nearly 10 P. M. in an effort to determine exactly what was behind the mob's action. They discussed the possibilities that Communist agents had urged the rioters on but failed to establish any certain connection with communism.

The primary emotion of the mob seemed to be rage and fear inspired by the killing Wednesday night of two French farmers, the brothers Yves and Alber Thomassin, near El Aroussa about fifty miles southwest of here. The rioting began at the funeral of the victims, whose bodies were taken to a cemetery on the outskirts of Tunis for burial yesterday afternoon.

Americans Held Unpopular

The United States is generally unpopular among European residents in all of French North Africa. They charge Americans with pro-nationalist and anti-colonial sympathies and activities as well as commercial designs on French overseas possessions. Moreover, a report circulated among the rioters last night that guns of American manufacture had been found in the house where the Thomassins were killed.

Anti-American feeling among the French in Tunisia has been accentuated by the support the International Confederation of Free Trade Unions has given the nationalist General Union of Tunisian Workers. The confederation is regarded here as an American organization.

After the attack on the American Consulate General the mob also pillaged the offices of Le Petit Matin, a French-language daily newspaper, closely allied with the Neo-Destour party, the

Continued on Page 3, Column 3

Algerian Marchers Battle Police and Army in Paris

By HENRY GINIGER
Special to The New York Times.

PARIS, March 9—Algerians clashed with strong forces of the police and troops in Paris today and 2,700 were arrested. The violence occurred as 10,000 Algerians paraded in the shocked French capital in support of the revolt against France in their homeland.

Their goal was the French National Assembly, where the Government was asking for full powers to put down this revolt. Led by a young Algerian woman brandishing the green and white nationalist flag, the mile-long procession got as far west as the City Hall.

There the clashes occurred and the solid ranks of demonstrators were broken into small groups and dispersed.

Two Frenchmen were wounded by knife-wielding marchers.

It was announced tonight that all those arrested would be photographed and fingerprinted and their measurements filed for reference. The great majority were expected to be released, but some may be tried on charges of endangering the internal security of the state.

Strike Is a Surprise

The demonstration of Moslem strength was staged mainly by the illegal Algerian National Movement led by Hadj Messali, who is in forced residence in Angoulême in southwestern France. M. Messali's Nationalist Movement originated among Algerians living in France just after World War I and seeks full independence. It is in open rivalry with the National Liberation Front, which claims exclusive control over the rebels in Algeria. Some of these were also believed to have participated in the demonstration.

Today's disorders began suddenly in the morning with a surprise strike by Algerian workers throughout France. Response was spotty, ranging from 90 per cent of Algerian workers in some factories in Paris to almost none in others. It showed that M. Messali, despite his semi-isolation, still had considerable influence among Moslems in France and that his movement's clandestine system of spreading orders was working well.

Toward late morning Algerians from all over Paris and the suburbs began converging on the mosque on the Left Bank in the eastern section of the capital. Today being prayer day for Moslems, there was no attempt to halt the gathering.

Most of the Algerians were

Continued on Page 3, Column 2

MOLLET DEMANDS CONFIDENCE VOTE

Stakes Government on Plan for Algerian Reforms—Approval Indicated

By ROBERT C. DOTY
Special to The New York Times.

PARIS, Saturday, March 10—Premier Guy Mollet staked the existence of his Government early today in support of his demand for special powers to check the rebellion in Algeria.

M. Mollet asked for votes of confidence on four aspects of his bill conferring extraordinary military, economic, social and administrative powers on Robert Lacoste, Minister Residing in Algeria.

There appeared to be little doubt that when the balloting took place Monday the Assembly would vote overwhelmingly to give the Cabinet powers to restore order and initiate reforms in Algeria.

Two main tendencies emerged from the Assembly debate. The first was a desire on the part of Center and Right-Wing deputies to see the Left-of-Center Government firmly committed to a policy of unlimited application of force until order is restored. There were clear indications that this course will be followed.

Allies of France Prodded

The second important demand was for stronger diplomatic pressure to check Arab material and moral aid to the Algerian rebels and to obtain more effective support from France's allies. This was expressed by Maurice Schumann, Popular Republican Deputy and former Secretary of State for Foreign Affairs, when he said that Egyptian interference in Algeria would cease if France, Britain and the United States "with one voice" were to demand an end to it.

M. Mollet received valuable support for his program from Jacques Soustelle, former Governor General of Algeria.

M. Soustelle gave the most detailed account yet made public of the support given to the Algerian rebels by Egypt, by Libya and in the Spanish zone of Morocco.

He quoted from papers acknowledging receipt by the rebels of arms sent by Egypt. He described meetings in Libya at which rebel leaders urged ministers of the Libyan Government to speed the evacuation of the Fezzan region by French troops to clear it as a base for rebel operations in French North Africa.

He also told of regular allowance, of 200 to 500 pesetas a month given to rebels undergoing training in camps in Spanish Morocco.

Other speakers, mostly those of the Center and Right, brought support, and some embarrassment, to the Left-of-Center Government by stressing the need for the prompt application of force to end terrorism.

M. Mollet, with the other Socialists and Radicals of the Republican Front, was elected on a program for a quick peace of conciliation in Algeria. He sought, in his speech tonight, to re-focus the debate on the re-

Continued on Page 3, Column 6

Dulles Meets Nehru In Hope for Accord

By A. M. ROSENTHAL
Special to The New York Times.

NEW DELHI, India, March 9—John Foster Dulles and Jawaharlal Nehru, who see most of the world's problems differently, held a four-hour talk today. They tried to find common ground between themselves and their countries.

Both the United States Secretary of State, who is here for two days, and India's Prime Minister seemed determined to make a cool political situation as pleasant as courtesies could make it.

On his arrival from this week's Southeast Asia alliance meeting in Karachi, Pakistan, Mr. Dulles told news men at Palam Airport that the United States regarded Mr. Nehru as "one of the great men of the world today." This will surprise many Indians who have

Continued on Page 2, Column 6

BRITAIN DEPORTS CYPRUS PRELATE IN WAR ON TERROR

Expels Archbishop Makarios as Backer of Violence, Also Bishop and Aides

DESTINATION IS A SECRET

Island Terrorists Hit Back With Bombs—Greece Calls Envoy in London Home

Text of British announcement on deportation, Page 2

By BENJAMIN WELLES
Special to The New York Times.

LONDON, March 9—Archbishop Makarios, political and spiritual leader of Greek Cyprus and head of the anti-British movement there, was deported from the island today.

Simultaneously, the British authorities in the strategic colony arrested and deported Bishop Kyprianos of Kyrenia, the extreme right-wing, fourth-ranking prelate of the island; Papastayros Papa-Agathangelou, a Cypriote Orthodox priest, of Nicosia, the capital, and Polycarpos Ioannides, secretary to the Bishop of Kyrenia, which is in the Nicosia district. All were charged with actively supporting terrorism and violence.

So swiftly and suddenly were the deportations carried out that even close friends and associates of Makarios were said to be astonished. He was apprehended boarding an airliner for Athens and was whisked off with the others to a secret destination.

Evidence Against Them

An hour after the arrests, the Governor, Field Marshal Sir John Harding, announced that he had taken the action under the Emergency Powers Regulations.

The Governor said he acted "only after the most careful and deliberate consideration" and on reportedly incontestable evidence that the men were personally implicated in terrorism.

The Government learned tonight that Basil Mostra, the Greek Ambassador to Britain, has been recalled from London to Athens in immediate protest.

[In Athens and in Salonika, Greece, street crowds rioted in anti-British demonstrations. Cyprus reported bombings and British patrols were fired on. Britain has about 50,000 troops and police in the island.]

The Cabinet under Prime Minister Eden is understood to have weighed carefully probable repercussions of the Cyprus deportation order, particularly the potentially adverse effect in the United States, as well as in

Continued on Page 2, Column 4

JORDAN REJECTS CAIRO BLOC'S BID

King Balks at Condition He Drop British Subsidy

By SAM POPE BREWER
Special to The New York Times.

AMMAN, Jordan, March 9—The Arab "neutralist bloc" appeared today to have suffered a setback at the hands of Jordan's youthful King Hussein.

The Premier of Syria presented a new offer from Egypt, Saudi Arabia and Syria to take the place of Britain in subsidizing Jordan's defense forces on condition that Jordan drop the present British subsidy.

King Hussein turned down the offer in view of the conditions.

Since he dismissed Lieut. Gen. John Bagot Glubb March 1 as Chief of Staff of his army, King Hussein has been seeking every means to make it clear that he does not want to break with the British in defense cooperation.

The so-called neutralist bloc of Egypt, Saudi Arabia and Syria has been working to represent the Glubb dismissal as a victory for its point of view.

Today's message was a significant element in that situation.

The Syrian Premier, Said Ghazzi, landed at Amman airport just before 11 A. M. today in a Convair belonging to the Saudi Arabian Government. He came from the Cairo meeting of King Saud of Saudi Arabia, President Shukri al-Kuwatly of Syria and Premier Gamel Abdel Nasser of Egypt.

An earlier offer to take Brit-

Continued on Page 3, Column 3

"All the News That's Fit to Print"

The New York Times.

LATE CITY EDITION
Condensation of U. S. Weather Bureau forecast: Cloudy today with rain tonight. Rain tomorrow ending late in day.
Temp. range today: 58-50; yesterday: 65.3-48
Full U. S. Weather Bureau Report, Page 46

VOL. CV..No. 35,867. Entered as Second-Class Matter, Post Office, New York, N. Y. NEW YORK, FRIDAY, APRIL 6, 1956. Times Square, New York 36, N. Y. Telephone LAckawanna 4-1000 FIVE CENTS

THUG HURLS ACID ON LABOR WRITER; SIGHT IMPERILED

Victor Riesel, Columnist, Is Assaulted on Broadway at 3 A. M. Without Warning

BOTH EYES ARE INJURED

U. S. Attorney Calls Attack an Effort to Hurt Inquiry Into Industrial Rackets

By A. H. RASKIN

A thug hurled sulphuric acid into the face of Victor Riesel, crusading labor columnist, early yesterday morning. The attack damaged both eyes, and surgeons were not sure last night whether they could save his sight.

The assault came without warning an hour after Mr. Riesel had finished a broadcast condemning racketeering in the International Union of Operating Engineers. He said later he believed his denunciation of convicted extortionists in the union had provoked the attack.

United States Attorney Paul W. Williams called the acid-throwing a "black effort to intimidate witnesses" in his month-old investigation into industrial rackets in the metropolitan area. He said the writer, whose column appears in The New York Daily Mirror and 192 other newspapers, already had given the Justice Department "important information" on gangster methods in the trucking and garment industries.

The full facilities of the Federal Bureau of Investigation, the Police Department and District Attorney Frank S. Hogan's office were mobilized to seek out the assailant. But his identity remained a mystery, despite the posting of $14,000 in rewards.

Labor Chiefs Condemn Attack

George Meany, president of the American Federation of Labor and Congress of Industrial Organizations, expressed hope that "those responsible for this nefarious crime will be speedily apprehended and punished." David Dubinsky, president of the International Ladies Garment Workers Union, voiced a similar sentiment.

The 41-year-old columnist had just emerged from Lindy's Restaurant at Fifty-first Street and Broadway at 3 A. M. when a bottle full of acid was hurled across his forehead, eyes and nose. A slender, black-haired man in a blue and white lumber jacket stepped out of a doorway, threw the searing liquid, then walked calmly away in the direction of Eighth Avenue. No one made any attempt to stop him.

Mr. Riesel, a pint-sized, voluble man, with sandy red hair and a writing style that resembles Mickey Spillane's, has received scores of threatening letters and telephone calls in the fourteen years that he has been hammering away at Communists and racketeers in labor's ranks. However, he has always treated such threats as the work of "cranks" and has refused to be deterred from his anti-racket activities.

His father, Nathan, was head of a garment union local in this city and an active fighter for clean unionism. The elder Riesel died in 1947 of injuries attributed to a beating five years earlier by underworld elements.

The Post Hall Syndicate, which

Continued on Page 12, Column 6

COLUMNIST INJURED: Victor Riesel, victim of an attack yesterday in which acid was thrown in his face.

HOUSE APPROVAL OF FARM BILL SEEN

Democratic Conferees Also Expect President to Sign —Committee Votes Today

By WILLIAM M. BLAIR

Special to The New York Times.

WASHINGTON, April 5 — Democratic conferees today predicted quick approval in the House of Representatives of a farm bill that President Eisenhower would sign.

They displayed a jaunty attitude in the wake of the President's statement yesterday that he would not insist on perfection in a farm measure. However, they were divided on whether Republicans would move in the House to compromise the principal issue of rigid versus flexible price supports.

The Senate-House conference committee put the finishing touches on its farm bill this afternoon. The conferees will resurvey the measure tomorrow and take a final vote on the catch-all bill, which Ezra Taft Benson, the Secretary of Agriculture vigorously opposes.

The one major provision unresolved was whether the Administration's $1,200,000,000 soil bank should be compulsory or voluntary. Most conferees agreed that the soil bank should be voluntary. This measure would pay farmers to reduce surplus-producing areas.

The conferees said that a mandatory provision in the Senate farm bill was designed as a penalty section for violations.

Continued on Page 8, Column 5

HARRIMAN DEFERS DECISION ON CUT OF INCOME TAXES

Delay Stirs Belief Governor Is Being Influenced Against Veto of Republican Bill

By WARREN WEAVER Jr.

Special to The New York Times.

ALBANY, April 5—Governor Harriman pondered long and late today with the problem of whether to sign or veto the $40,000,000 Republican income tax cut, but he did not make up his mind.

The Governor spent all day conferring with his key aides on the income tax question. Shortly after 6 P. M. his assistant press secretary, Walter J. Mordaunt, announced that there would be no action today on the pending bill.

Last night in Rochester, Mr. Harriman told a press conference that he planned to sign or veto the tax cut measure today. An aide insisted today that the Governor had merely said he "hoped" to dispose of the question.

Thus, the calendar moved one day closer to the April 16 deadline for filing state income tax returns, with the taxpayers still not able to find out whether or not they will be entitled to a reduction in their taxes on 1955 income.

Leaders Under Pressure

The bill, which the Republican-controlled Legislature pushed through in the closing days of the session, provides for a reduction this year of only 15 per cent on the first $100 of tax and 10 per cent on the next $200, or a maximum forgiveness of $35.

In his deliberations on the measure, the Governor reportedly found himself torn between conflicting advice. His chief political lieutenants strongly favor approval of the tax reduction. His fiscal advisers insist that any reduction would be financially unsound.

Democratic state leaders have been under increasing pressure from county chairmen and other local officials. These officials insist that approval by Mr. Harriman of the tax reduction would be politically advantageous to them in an election year and cut some ground out from under the Republicans.

At the same time, the Governor's fiscal advisers in the division of the budget have been urging strongly that he veto the bill. They point to steadily increasing demands for state rev-

Continued on Page 22, Column 6

Transit Body Seeks To Retain Bus Lines

By STANLEY LEVEY

The Transit Authority is thinking in terms of keeping its money-losing bus lines—not of selling them to private operators.

This was indicated yesterday by Charles L. Patterson, authority chairman, who said he thought the agency's over-all surface system could be "put on a self-sustaining basis within three years."

As a further sign that the authority was reluctant to divest itself of the lines, Mr. Patterson said he and his associates had blocked out a $50,000,000 surface-system improvements program over the next five years.

This plan, which has already been suggested to the Board of Estimate, would be paid for out of the city's capital budget. It would entail almost

Continued on Page 22, Column 7

U.S. EAGER TO BEGIN ARMS REDUCTIONS

But Stassen Tells Gromyko Control and Inspection Must Be Set Up First

By BENJAMIN WELLES

Special to The New York Times.

LONDON, April 5 — The United States informed the Soviet Union today it was ready and willing to join in the first stage of an agreed world disarmament plan "as rapidly" as such a plan could be set up.

Provided a foolproof international control and inspection system can be created first, the United States is prepared to participate at once in "preliminary, partial conventional and nuclear disarmament," Harold E. Stassen, chief United States delegate, told the United Nations Disarmament Subcommittee.

Mr. Stassen cautioned that it would take "more than a year" to carry out the first, cautious stage of any world disarmament program—even with genuine Soviet cooperation. His combined promise and caution came during the eighth of sixteen current sessions of the five-nation subcommittee in which the United States, the Soviet Union, Britain, France and Canada are represented.

This was the seventy-seventh meeting in thirty months since the United Nations directed the

Continued on Page 6, Column 3

PRO-WEST REGIME IN CEYLON LOSING; OUSTER FORESEEN

27 Results Give Opposition 18 Seats, Kotelawala 4— British Bases at Stake

By A. M. ROSENTHAL

Special to The New York Times.

COLOMBO, Ceylon, Friday, April 6—Ceylon's ruling party is losing the national elections to a coalition pledged to the nationalization of plantations and the ouster of the British from air and naval bases here.

Returns from yesterday's voting, the first of three days of polling for a new Parliament, indicated an opposition landslide against Prime Minister Sir John Kotelawala's United National party.

Sir John's party was losing one seat after another that it had considered safe. Sir John still holds a mathematical chance of squeaking through, but his supporters were saying that those chances were disappearing fast.

Sir John's party arranged the voting so that "safe" districts would come up on the first day's balloting and start a bandwagon swing in its support. But the danger the Prime Minister faces now is that on Saturday and Tuesday, when the voting continues, the bandwagon will roll the wrong way.

Ninety-five seats are at stake and sixteen are being conceded by both sides to the Tamils of Indian descent. Of the remaining seventy-nine Sir John's party held fifty-four in the recently dissolved Parliament.

Trend Shows Quickly

Forty-two seats were at stake in the first day's balloting. Of the first twenty-seven decided, the opposition coalition won eighteen and the Government party only four. The rest went to independents, a splinter party and the Communists. One Communist was elected.

The worst blow to Sir John's hopes was the fact that seventeen Government party members in Parliament, including six Cabinet Ministers, were defeated.

The opposition party, called the People's United Front, is composed of a Trotskyite party, a strongly Buddhist group and a nationalist party called Sri Lanka (Ceylon Freedom party).

The leader of the coalition opposition is the head of the Sri Lanka party, Solomon West Ridgway Diaz Bandaranaike. Mr. Bandaranaike is a wealthy landowner who was a contemporary of Sir Anthony Eden at Oxford. He once was a Minister in a Cabinet of the United National party before he broke away.

Sir John is considered a strong friend of the West and is an outspoken enemy of communism. His defeat would be taken as a serious blow to Western prestige although the campaign was fought on national issues, not international ones.

Sir John himself defeated his opponent, a 22-year-old college student, but his majority was reported to be comparatively low.

The United National party has been drawing its strength from the middle class of Ceylon while the opposition concentrated on the villagers, discontended students and stanch Buddhists who want their religion to play more of a part in Government affairs. The opposition has also been

Continued on Page 4, Column 4

U. N. Chief Cautious on Mideast Trip

The New York Times

Dag Hammarskjold at his news conference here yesterday

By THOMAS J. HAMILTON

Special to The New York Times.

UNITED NATIONS, N. Y., April 5—Secretary General Dag Hammarskjold said today that his mission to the Middle East would be "just an episode on the long road" toward reduction of Israeli-Arab tension. He added that even the United Nations could not accomplish miracles. The Secretary General, who will leave tomorrow afternoon, said at a news conference that as "an agent of the Security Council" he would concentrate on arrangements to improve compliance with the armistice agreements between Israel and her four Arab neighbors. The Council voted unanimously yes-

Continued on Page 3, Column 2

100,000 MORE MEN TO GO TO ALGERIA

Lacoste's Plan to Reinforce Army to Crush Revolt Gets Endorsement of Mollet

By ROBERT C. DOTY

Special to The New York Times.

PARIS, April 5—Robert Lacoste, French Minister Residing in Algeria, won approval today for his plan to send 100,000 more French troops to Algeria to quell the rebellion there.

Premier Guy Mollet and others in his left-of-center Cabinet have long been united on the necessity for a major effort to re-establish order in the Algerian departments as a prerequisite to reform. But they have been reluctant to take the politically unpopular action of recalling reservists to meet M. Lacoste's demands.

Premier Mollet, in four days of study of the problem over the Easter week-end, reached the conclusion that it would be impossible to meet Algerian military needs with men already in the armed forces. In a three-hour conference with M. Lacoste, the Premier agreed that 30,000 men in the ready reserve would have to be recalled at once and up to 70,000 others would be mobilized during the coming months.

Most of Troops in Algeria

After having completed eighteen months of active service, French conscripts spend three years as ready reserves who may be recalled by a simple administrative decision. Thereafter, they enter the "first reserve," which may be mobilized only with parliamentary approval.

At last official report there were 330,000 French troops in North Africa, about two-thirds of them in Algeria. The new reinforcements would put the total for Algeria alone over the 300,000 mark.

[In Algeria itself, eighteen suspected rebels were shot and killed during an attempted escape from a stockade during an extremist attack on a French outpost in the Kabilya Mountains, French authorities announced, according to The United Press. The attack, against Maillot, seventy-five miles southeast of Algiers, appeared aimed at liberating the suspected rebels.]

The necessity for the present Socialist-directed Government to pursue a policy of force in Algeria has brought acute political embarrassment to M. Mollet. The Socialists and their allies of the Republican Front were elected on a program that included prominently a "peace-in-Algeria" plank and condemnation of those whose policies had led to previous recalls of French reservists for service in North Africa.

Today these themes are exploited only by the Communists, the Socialists' deadly rivals for working class allegiance. The

Continued on Page 3, Column 3

Saudi Arabia's King Is Reported Moving To Prevent a Revolt

By KENNETT LOVE

Special to The New York Times.

LONDON, April 5—Accounts of revolutionary ferment and counteraction in Saudi Arabia have been brought here by Middle Eastern diplomats and travelers.

King Saud, one of the few remaining absolute monarchs, is reported to be reviving the Ikhwan (Brotherhood), a fanatically religious tribal warrior force, as a precaution against increasing revolutionary sentiment.

Revolutionary activity is reported among officers in the Saudi Arabian Army, in the tiny middle class that is growing up under the impact of oil production, and in the illegal labor movement in the oil fields.

Last week, an Arabic-language broadcast from the Israeli radio reported the existence of a "Free Saudis Movement." This was described as a clandestine organization bent on overthrowing King Saud and his regime in favor of establishing a liberal government.

The Ikhwan was the empire-building force of the late King Ibn Saud, King Saud's father, in the first three decades of this century.

It brought most of the tribes on the Arabian Peninsula under Saudi authority and annexed vast desert areas. These included the Hedjaz, the Moslem holy land containing the pilgrimage cities, Mecca and Medina.

The Ikhwan was composed of adherents of the puritanical Wahabi movement of Islam, which they imposed throughout King Ibn Saud's desert domains. It lost importance with the pacification of the country in the Nineteen Thirties and still more with the development of a reg-

Continued on Page 3, Column 5

GAZA STRIP FIGHT RAGES 10 HOURS; U. N. WINS TRUCE

Egypt and Israel Accuse Each Other of Starting Battle— Cairo Protests to Council

ARAB DEAD PUT AT 33

Civilian Casualties Are Cited —Burns Issues Cease-Fire After Meeting Sharett

Special to The New York Times.

TEL AVIV, Israel, April 5—A cease-fire arranged by United Nations officials tonight appeared to have ended a flare-up in the Negev.

Agreement between Egypt and Israel halted ten hours of fighting along a ten-mile front of the Gaza Strip armistice line. A United Nations source in Jerusalem said the Egyptians reported forty-two dead and more than 100 wounded on their side.

[In a complaint to the United Nations Security Council, Egypt, charging Israel started the battle, said thirty-three civilians had been killed and ninety-two injured. In Cairo, a spokesman said forty-two Arab civilians had been killed in the area in two days.]

Army headquarters here said Israeli casualties were four soldiers and two civilians wounded, one severely.

The cease-fire was negotiated on the spot by Col. Robert Bayard of the United States, chairman of the Israeli-Egyptian Mixed Armistice Commission. The incident, in which artillery, mortars, machine-guns and rifles were used, was particularly dangerous in view of Israeli complaints that Egypt was massing troops and newly acquired Communist heavy armaments in the Gaza Strip.

Burns Asks for Cease-Fire

The United Nations source said the cease-fire was to have become effective at 6 P. M., but that shooting continued for another hour. Neutral United Nations observers on the spot have reported no incidents since 7 P. M.

The request for a cease-fire was made by the Chief of Staff of the United Nations truce supervision orgcnization, Maj. Gen. E. L. M. Burns of Canada, as reports came in of firing along the Gaza Strip armistice line.

Frontier villages and military positions were said to have been attacked throughout the day from Egyptian fortified positions with 120-mm. mortars and machine-guns. The Israelis returned the fire. One report said the Israelis used artillery.

General Burns' request for the cease-fire followed a meeting in Jerusalem with Foreign Minister Moshe Sharett. A Foreign Ministry spokesman said Mr. Sharett asked General Burns to call.

The spokesman said the Foreign Minister "placed the responsibility" for shooting in the previous two days and for the lives lost "squarely upon the shoulders of the Egyptians, who had obstinately refused to issue the cease-fire order as demanded by the United Nations."

The reference was to earlier cease-fire appeals by the United Nations. Four Israeli soldiers were killed in the attacks to

Continued on Page 2, Column 3

Capital's Blossoms Open; Spring Fulfills Promise Here

Associated Press Wirephoto

Delicate pink blossoms of Japanese cherry trees draw throngs to Tidal Basin, Washington

Easter Week visitors in Washington yesterday, many of them coatless, thronged the Tidal Basin for a view of the massed pinks and whites of the Japanese cherry trees. Many thousands of visitors are expected during the annual Cherry Blossom Festival. New Yorkers, who must wait another month for cherry trees to bloom at the Brooklyn Botanic Gardens and in Central Park, found vernal invitation enough in the warmest day of the year. The temperature reached 65.3 degrees just after 5 P. M. Experts at the Weather Bureau explained that the welcome change came about with the passing of the slight cold front that cleared away Wednesday's fog. Dry air followed, bringing spring's promise to the Northeast. With the dry air came cloudless skies for much of the day, and the sun got the chance it had been waiting for. So did the city's winter moles and school-less youngsters. It was a day for hopscotch on the sidewalk, softball and just walking or idling in the parks.

Boy, 7, Questioned, Freed in Fatal Fire

A pleasant but frightened 7-year-old tenement boy posed for an hour yesterday as an arsonist who set the East Bronx factory fire that killed six firemen and injured fourteen on Wednesday night.

Soon afterward, however, in a complete turnabout, he denied the entire story and was freed. Investigators said they believed the boy had no connection with the blaze. His mother, absent during the "confession," said the lad had been at home for hours before the fire began.

For more than an hour, however, the boy, described by the police as "a nice little kid," spun a long and imaginative account of his "crime" and attempted to buttress it with a spurious re-enactment near the rubble-strewn scene of the disaster.

It was his pathetic attempt

Continued on Page 22, Column 8

Bohlen Called Home For Talks on Soviet

By ELIE ABEL

Special to The New York Times.

WASHINGTON, April 5 — Charles E. Bohlen, United States Ambassador to Moscow, is coming home this week-end to join in a reassessment of Soviet policy in the light of the campaign to discredit Stalin.

Mr. Bohlen, now vacationing in Austria, is expected to spend a week or ten days in Washington, the State Department said.

At the same time, the department announced that Ambassador George Wadsworth was flying home from Saudi Arabia for consultations on the Middle East.

Officials indicated that they would discuss with Mr. Wadsworth not only the forthcoming negotiations with Saudi Arabia for renewal of the United States lease on the

Continued on Page 5, Column 2

Another Rome Catacomb Found; Beauty of Its Frescoes Is Hailed

By ARNALDO CORTESI

Special to The New York Times.

ROME, April 5—The discovery in Rome of a catacomb hitherto unknown to scholars was announced today by L'Osservatore Romano, the Vatican newspaper.

It is a small chamber measuring 158 feet by 89 feet, but it is remarkable for the number and beauty of the frescoed paintings that adorn it. The Rev. Antonio Ferrua, a Jesuit, who carried out the excavations on behalf of the Pontifical Commission of Sacred Archaeology, did not hesitate to affirm that "nothing like this has ever been found in any early Christian cemetery."

As remarkable as the number and the beauty of the frescoes is the wide variety of the subjects they represent. Some are subjects from the Old and New Testament but some are frankly pagan. Others represent scenes of life at the time when the catacomb was decorated.

The pagan subjects include the labors of Hercules, and Cleopatra finding death by holding an asp to her breast. The archaeologists made no effort to hide their amazement at finding such subjects chosen to embellish tombs of the early Christians.

Scenes from the contemporary life of ancient Rome include portraits of famous physicians adorning the tomb of a surgeon. The surgeon himself is depicted performing an operation.

The catacomb, which is not mentioned in any ancient text, is attributed by Father Ferrua to the early part of the fourth century. That it was not built before the fourth century can be deduced from its architectonic style, which is typical of the

Continued on Page 26, Column 6

"All the News That's Fit to Print"

The New York Times.

LATE CITY EDITION
Condensation of U. S. Weather Bureau forecast: Partly cloudy, not so cold today. Increasing cloudiness tomorrow.
Temp. range today: 50-36; yesterday: 37-32
Full U. S. Weather Bureau Report, Page 50

VOL. CV..No. 35,870. Entered as Second-Class Matter, Post Office, New York, N. Y.
NEW YORK, MONDAY, APRIL 9, 1956.
Times Square, New York 36, N. Y. Telephone Lackawanna 4-1000
FIVE CENTS

ISRAEL PROMISES DELAY OF 2 DAYS IN ANY REPRISALS

Premier Informs Burns Egypt Has 48 Hours to Pledge End of Bands' Forays

NEW ATTACKS REPORTED

Hammarskjold to Cut Short Rome Preparations for His Mission as Tension Rises

Special to The New York Times.

TEL AVIV, Israel, April 8—Premier David Ben-Gurion promised today that Israel would not strike back in retaliation at Egypt within the next forty-eight hours. The assurances were given Maj. Gen. E. L. M. Burns of Canada, chief of staff of the United Nations Truce Supervision Organization.

[Mounting Middle East tension caused Dag Hammarskjold, United Nations Secretary General, to cut short Rome preliminaries for his peace mission. He will hasten on to the Middle East, flying from Rome Monday evening, instead of Tuesday, as he had planned. He is to arrive in Beirut, Lebanon, early Tuesday.]

At a half-hour's meeting in Jerusalem, General Burns reportedly expressed the hope that Israel would not resort to counter-action against Egypt for a series of attacks by Arab bands last night in which four Israelis were reported killed and fifteen wounded.

Premier Ben-Gurion is understood to have told General Burns that his Government would give the United Nations Truce Organization a chance to obtain assurances from Egypt that she would refrain from hostile acts in accordance with the armistice agreement. The Premier said, however, that unless unequivocal assurances were obtained, Israel must reserve freedom of action.

Cabinet Discusses Crisis

The conference, at which Foreign Minister Moshe Sharett also was present, took place after the Israeli Cabinet discussed the crisis with Egypt. A United Nations announcement said the meeting took place at General Burns' request.

Meanwhile, the Government continued to make preparations for threatened full-scale warfare. The Cabinet adopted emergency regulations permitting the Defense Minister to requisition equipment and the Interior Minister to require all males over 15 to carry identity cards.

It was also decided to call a special meeting of the Knesset (Parliament), which is now in recess, to obtain authority for increased defense expenditures.

Late tonight a Foreign Ministry source in Jerusalem said "the Egyptian dictator's murder gangs are still at large."

Hand grenades were reported thrown into two houses in Shafir settlement twelve miles from the Gaza Strip at 9 o'clock tonight, wounding a child. At about the same time a motorcyclist traveling near Ein Hashofet was attacked and slightly wounded in the leg.

A woman was reported hurt by bomb splinters shortly before midnight when shots were fired

Continued on Page 4, Column 3

Compromise in U.N. Settles Atom Issue

By THOMAS J. HAMILTON
Special to The New York Times.

UNITED NATIONS, N. Y., April 8—The United States, the Soviet Union and India have agreed upon a compromise on the relations between the proposed atoms-for-peace agency and the United Nations.

This will be submitted tomorrow when twelve nations resume their negotiations in Washington on the draft statute, or articles of incorporation, for the agency.

The only other important issue that remains to be settled is the membership of the board of governors. If a compromise can be reached on that issue, the conferees will complete their work this week on the draft statute. The way will then be clear to call a conference of the more than eighty nations which are to participate in the agency.

Under the compromise, the

Continued on Page 8, Column 3

PRECISE U.S. POLICY ASKED IN MIDEAST

Survey of Area Finds Middle Course Often Mistaken for Indecisive Stand

Under the impact of new Communist tactics and nationalism, United States foreign policy is undergoing a reappraisal -- at home and abroad. Correspondents of The New York Times have obtained the views of foreign and American officials and other observers on the strong and weak points of United States foreign policy and their suggestions for its improvement. The findings are being presented in a series of regional reports, of which this is the second.

By SAM POPE BREWER
Special to The New York Times.

BEIRUT, Lebanon, April 8—Any American who travels in these times has to get used to being taken to task over United States foreign policy.

The bases of criticism vary with different areas and even inside an area critics do not agree on what the faults are or how they should be remedied. Still there are certain criticisms and suggestions that recur more often than others.

The traveling Americans, for their part, tend to feel that much of the trouble arises from the lack of any firm and definite policy rather than from the existence of a mistaken one.

In the Arab world and the rest of the Middle East, from Gibraltar to India and from the Black Sea down to the Sudan, the United States has unquestionably lost heavily in prestige and friendship in the last few years. In the Arab countries, at least, that trend is continuing.

The reasons given by critics vary but the best simple generalization might be summed up as "too much and too little." The United States has aided nation-

Continued on Page 3, Column 2

RUSSIA APPEALS ANEW TO FARMERS TO SPUR OUTPUT

More Products at Less Cost Called Only Way to Raise Standards of Living

By WELLES HANGEN
Special to The New York Times.

MOSCOW, April 8—The Soviet people were told today they must raise agricultural production drastically if they hoped to achieve a better standard of living.

The Communist party and Soviet Council of Ministers said the planned increase in real wages could be attained only if more and better farm products were produced at less cost. They declared the annual increase in population and industrial labor force created additional pressure for augmented farm output.

The two highest policy making organs of the Soviet regime cited these points in a 10,000-word appeal to farm workers and agricultural research scientists that covered the front page of every Moscow newspaper this morning.

The appeal appears to reflect the Soviet leaders' continuing dissatisfaction with results of the effort to spur farm production. They do not conceal their fear that fulfillment of the new five-year plan may be thwarted by the lag on the farms.

The call for increased agricultural production follows official proposals last month for reorganizing the collective farm system. Money incentives are being offered to persuade farmers to work more on communally owned land and less on their private plots.

Called Consumers Goods Key

Higher hourly output by city workers depends on increased deliveries of foodstuffs and agricultural raw materials to industrial centers, today's appeal said.

It told farmers that higher industrial output would mean more machinery for factories and farms and, eventually, more consumer goods, "which are equally necessary for working people in town and countryside."

The Central Committee and Council of Ministers acknowledged implicitly that the demand for farm produce was not being satisfied.

"We must aim at full satisfaction of the requirements of our country," they said. "This is all the more necessary now when, as a result of measures taken by the party and Government, a systematic growth of wages is being insured."

The appeal said "the main and chief thing" required for increasing real wages was farm production "in the necessary quantities of good quality and at reasonable prices."

The message conceded that the cotton and potato harvests last year had been "slightly lower" than in 1954, which was itself a drought year. It said the widespread corn cultivation spurred by Nikita S. Khrushchev, the

Continued on Page 10, Column 5

An Unexpected Late-Season Storm Once More Deposits Heavy Snow

Associated Press

IN CITY: Scene in Central Park South looking toward buildings on 59th Street. Park Department workers clear walks

The New York Times

IN SUBURBS: A fallen tree near Valhalla, N. Y. Many trees beginning to bud snapped and broke in the metropolitan area.

SOVIET CHIEFS SAY BRITISH CURB VISIT

Bulganin and Khrushchev See Program for Trip Limiting Contacts With People

Special to The New York Times.

MOSCOW, April 8—Nikita S. Khrushchev, Soviet Communist party chief, and Premier Nikolai A. Bulganin charged tonight they would be prevented from having close contacts with ordinary Britons when they visit Britain later this month.

In joint answers to questions from Tass, Soviet news agency, the Soviet leaders accused "certain forces" in Britain of having contrived to arrange their schedule so they would be unable to visit factories and enterprises, especially in Scotland and Wales, as they had requested.

Mr. Khrushchev and Marshal Bulganin expressed regret that the itinerary arranged by British officials would make it impossible for them to accept invitations from many ordinary Britons who, they said, had asked them to visit factories or homes.

The Soviet leaders' unusual

Continued on Page 10, Column 3

Governor and Mayor Join In Battle on Racketeering

Governor Harriman and Mayor Wagner, meeting here last night to discuss threats of industrial racketeering in the city, jointly resolved to "protect legitimate union and business activity."

Disturbed by signs that New York was in for a renewal of racketeering in some fields of business, the Governor and Mayor Wagner conferred for an hour at Mr. Harriman's city residence, 16 East Eighty-first Street, beginning about 8:30 P. M. A press aide for the Governor said the meeting had been suggested by Mr. Harriman in a telephone call last week to the Mayor, who was at that time in Florida on vacation. The Mayor arrived back in the city yesterday afternoon.

At the end of the meeting the two officials issued a joint statement declared that they had discussed "indications and threats" of a renewal in racketeering "in some phases of business" here. The brief statement closed with this pledge:

"We are determined to protect legitimate union and business activity and we will meet again on this subject in the near future."

The Governor and Mayor held their special conference after a series of warnings and predictions that the city was heading for trouble from underworld elements seeking to capture control of or invade both the garment and trucking industries.

Late last month United States Attorney Paul W. Williams warned that New York was on the verge of a "gangster invasion" of its garment and trucking industries. The Federal prosecutor said a Capone-era kind of gang control of these industries was imminent. The prosecutor

Continued on Page 17, Column 4

CONGRESS FACING FARM SHOWDOWN

Legislators Returning Today —Vote is Due Wednesday on Compromise Measure

By ALLEN DRURY
Special to The New York Times.

WASHINGTON, April 8—Congress returns to work tomorrow after a ten-day Easter recess. Its first major problem is the compromise farm bill, which could bring a Presidential veto.

The measure, carrying both the soil bank plan approved by the Administration and the high rigid price supports the Administration opposes, is scheduled for at House vote on Wednesday.

The House Republican leadership is expected to make a determined effort to send it back to a joint House-Senate conference with instructions to knock the rigid support provision out of the bill. If this move is defeated and the House approves the measure, it will then go to the Senate. If it survives there it will go to the White House, where its reception is uncertain.

Senator Allen J. Ellender, Democrat of Louisiana, chairman of the conference committee, predicted today that both houses and the President would approve the bill. If the President should veto it, "there will be no farm bill this year," the Senator predicted.

The Senator, appearing on the Columbia Broadcasting System's television program "Face the Nation," coupled this with another prediction: that if the President approved the bill, Ezra Taft Benson, the Secretary of Agriculture, might have to resign.

"If the President signs this bill," Mr. Ellender said, "I hope he [Mr. Benson] does resign, because he's never been in sympathy with price supports. He ought to resign."

Secretary Benson said yesterday that the bill in its present

Continued on Page 15, Column 5

ZONING PLAN NEAR ON STATEN ISLAND

Model Communities Are Part of Projected Development Soon to Be Announced

Staten Island is to be developed by zoning into several model communities that will provide semi-suburban living within the city.

The trend of the comprehensive rezoning of Staten Island, which has been on City Planning Commission drawing boards for a year and a half, was made public yesterday by James Felt, chairman of the commission.

The proposed rezoning of the entire sixty-square-mile Staten Island area is nearly completed, Mr. Felt said, and will be brought out soon for public hearings. Richmond Borough President Albert V. Maniscalco has been cooperating.

The rezoning, Mr. Felt said, will seek to keep Staten Island essentially a community of small homes by placing much of its land in low-density residential classifications.

Large apartment houses are to be confined to areas close to major transportation.

Sufficient land is to be reserved for business and retail needs. Industrial areas are to be laid out along the waterfront so that part of the population will work a short distance from home.

It is expected that construction of the Narrows Bridge be-

Continued on Page 18, Column 5

SPRING SNOWFALL HITS NORTHEAST; POWER CUT OFF

2.7-Inch Coating Takes City by Surprise—25 Inches Measured in Catskills

6 DEATHS LAID TO STORM

Hunt for 3 Marine Fliers Is Impaired—Phones Are Out and Travel Is Slushy

On the twentieth day of spring, a freakish snowstorm flung a surprise white mantle over the Northeast yesterday.

It cost at least six deaths, hampered a sea and air search of coastal waters here for three missing Marine fliers and darkened more than 100,000 homes by power failures.

The snowstorm ended here at 6:55 P. M. after a fall of 2.7 inches. It broke the city's 1.5-inch record for April 8, set in 1916.

Some suburban areas estimated considerably heavier falls. There were two to three inches in Nassau and in Connecticut's Fairfield County, three to seven in Bergen County, New Jersey, nine inches in parts of Westchester and a foot of snow in Rockland County.

Bearpen Mountain in the Catskills, near Prattsville, Greene County, reported twenty-five inches.

The snow was New York City's heaviest for spring since 6.5 inches fell on April 9, 1917. The only later spring storm surpassing it here dropped 3 inches on April 15, 1893.

Snowed April 18 in 1887

The latest measurable spring snow here was on April 18, 1887, with 2.1 inches. There have been snow traces—less than one-tenth of an inch—thrice in past Mays.

Fortunately for repair and snow-cleaning crews, yesterday's temperatures stayed either just at the freezing mark or above, so that the snow in the city streets melted rapidly to slush. The morning low was 32 degrees, the freezing point, at 3:50 A. M. The day's high was 37.5 at 12:01 P. M.

For today, the Weather Bureau predicted partly cloudy skies with the highest temperature near 50. It said at 2 A. M. today that tomorrow would be increasingly cloudy with no change in temperature, with a chance of rain tomorrow night.

Meteorologists here first warned the public about oncoming snow at 11 P. M. Saturday. A low-pressure center had developed over North Carolina early that afternoon and whistled north at twenty-five miles an hour.

At 12:55 A. M. yesterday snow began to mix with rain that had fallen all day Saturday for a total of 1.36 inches. Snow took over completely about 1:15 A. M., and thereafter a dismal day for robins was abetted by stiff west and northwest winds.

Trees just beginning to bud snapped and broke throughout the metropolitan area—thirty-eight toppling in Queens, nine in Richmond and scores more in the suburbs.

Good for Third Avenue Trees

But an expert at the New York Botanical Garden said the snow would provide "just wonderful" and lasting moisture for the oriental plane trees recently set out along Third Avenue.

Grass seeds, he said, wouldn't be hurt if they hadn't washed away; flower seeds might have to be watched a few days to see if they still germinate. Wet ground will delay other planting again.

The storm's death total included two Queens men. Charles Yost, 64 years old, of 101-02 Twenty-seventh Avenue, Elmhurst, a dishwasher, died shoveling snow at his home at 11 A. M. At 11:35 A. M., Henry Carpinelli, 65, a carpenter, of 114-30 124th Street, South Ozone Park, collapsed in his kitchen after a similar effort.

A man tentatively identified as Arthur Andrews, 26, an unemployed farm laborer, of Legion Avenue, Mattituck, L. I., was found lying coatless and dead alongside Route 25, a half mile west of Mattituck, at 2:15 P. M. The police tentatively ascribed his death to exposure.

The storm that whirled through New England took three lives. One man in Nashua, N. H., and two persons in Boston died while clearing snow.

Four police, Navy and Coast

Continued on Page 19, Column 8

U.S. Gives 25 Million To Turkey for Trade

Special to The New York Times.

WASHINGTON, April 8—The International Cooperation Administration announced today a $25,000,000 loan to Turkey and a new contract for agricultural education in India.

The I. C. A., the Government's foreign aid agency, said that the Turkish loan would help finance that country's importing of commodities and equipment needed in industry there.

The Indian project will draw on the long experience in agricultural education of four United States land-grant colleges to assist India in the development of its agricultural schools.

The agreement covering the loan was signed for Turkey by Ambassador Haydar Gork and for the United States by Samuel C. Waugh, president of the Export-Import Bank of Washing-

Continued on Page 3, Column 2

Radar Line Conquers Arctic Wastes

3,000-Mile Warning Net Rising Fast Despite Perils

By HANSON W. BALDWIN

A 3,000-mile, $400,000,000 electronic fence is rising rapidly in the frozen wilderness of the North.

Some 1,400 miles north of the United States-Canadian border, stretching from Alaska to inhospitable Baffin Island, this modern wonder of the world is being built to help protect the North American continent against enemy air attack. The radar project is known in contractors' jargon as "Project 572" but is more popularly called the D. E. W. or Distant Early Warning line.

Its economic effects on the North have been likened to those of the Yukon gold rush. The line itself has been compared, with both laudatory and critical intent, to the Great Wall of China.

A party of thirty-one United States and Canadian newspaper men was given the first public preview of the line in an extensive ten-day air trip that ended last week.

Their material, reviewed for security by the United States and Royal Canadian Air Forces, was released for publication last

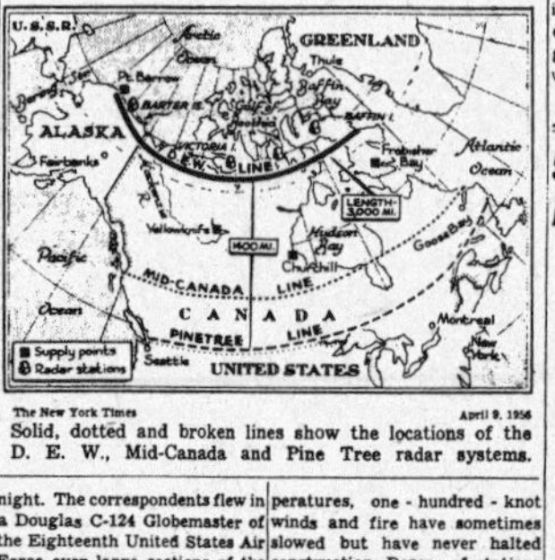

The New York Times April 9, 1956

Solid, dotted and broken lines show the locations of the D. E. W., Mid-Canada and Pine Tree radar systems.

night. The correspondents flew in a Douglas C-124 Globemaster of the Eighteenth United States Air Force over large sections of the line from east to west. They visited the three principal types of radar sites under construction or completed in Baffin Island, the Gulf of Boothia area, Victoria Island and northern Alaska.

The trip demonstrated that the immense difficulties of supply and construction in a winter wilderness, hundreds of miles beyond railheads and along the shores of frozen seas, were being overcome. Fifty-below-zero temperatures, one-hundred-knot winds and fire have sometimes slowed but have never halted construction. Dozens of stations are rising north and south of the seventieth parallel of latitude. Some are in places accessible only to aircraft and possibly never before trodden by men.

The line is far from finished but it is generally on schedule. Some stations should be completed this year and the entire project in about two years, the Air Force states. The D. E. W. line is a military project but it

Continued on Page 6, Column 3

5 Russians Go Home, Ending U. S. Asylum

By ALBION ROSS

Five of nine Soviet seamen given asylum in the United States last October returned to their homeland over the week-end in an apparent victory for the Soviet Union's redefection campaign.

The five men had been members of the crew of the Soviet tanker Tuapse captured in June, 1954, by a Chinese Nationalist destroyed off Formosa as a blockade runner.

Twenty of the crew had remained behind when their companions were repatriated to the Soviet Union and nine of these had been admitted to the United States.

The five seamen appeared Saturday afternoon at the New York International Airport, Idlewild, Queens, with reservations for the Scandinavian Airlines flight to Helsinki, Finland. They were sur-

Continued on Page 6, Column 8

Firemen Will Close Perilous Buildings

Fire inspection teams will swarm through the East Bronx next week and will close buildings in which they find serious fire hazards, Commissioner Edward F. Cavanagh Jr. said yesterday.

Other run-down areas of the city will get the same treatment in the near future, he added. The Commissioner spoke of the six men who were killed fighting a fire in the East Bronx last Wednesday night and declared he was "fed up" with having firemen killed in preventable fires.

He said the law did not give the Fire Department specific authority to close buildings. But he explained that this authority was implied in the fire-prevention clause of the City Administrative Code under which the department would shut buildings and let

Continued on Page 18, Column 2

"All the News That's Fit to Print"

The New York Times.

LATE CITY EDITION
Condensation of U. S. Weather Bureau forecast:
Becoming cloudy this afternoon.
Clearing tomorrow afternoon.
Temp. range today: 55-35; yesterday: 52.5-34.7
Full U. S. Weather Bureau Report, Page 62

VOL. CV...No. 35,871. Entered as Second-Class Matter, Post Office, New York, N. Y. NEW YORK, TUESDAY, APRIL 10, 1956. Times Square, New York 36, N. Y. Telephone LAckawanna 4-1000 FIVE CENTS

U. S. PROMISES TO OPPOSE MIDDLE EAST AGGRESSION; PLEDGES HELP TO VICTIMS

HIGH COURT BARS OUSTER FOR USING 5TH AMENDMENT

Orders City to Reinstate Dr. Slochower to the Faculty of Brooklyn College

5-4 RULING IN RED CASE

Due Process Violated, Jurists Find—Professor Faces Another Suspension

Texts of decision and dissents appear on Page 16.

By LUTHER A. HUSTON
Special to The New York Times.

WASHINGTON, April 9—The Supreme Court today denied New York City the right to dismiss a college professor for invoking the protection of the Fifth Amendment.

In a 5-to-4 ruling, the high court held that the "summary dismissal" of Dr. Harry Slochower, a teacher of German and literature at Brooklyn College for twenty-seven years, "violates due process of law."

[In New York, the president of Brooklyn College announced that Dr. Slochower would be reinstated on the faculty as the result of the court decision and then would be suspended on new charges of alleged "untruthfulness and perjury." It was estimated that Dr. Slochower would receive about $30,000 in back pay when he was reinstated.]

The Fifth Amendment to the Federal Constitution provides that no person shall be required to give self-incriminating testimony nor be deprived of life, liberty or property without due process of law.

Practice Is Condemned

"At the outset we must condemn the practice of imputing a sinister meaning to the exercise of a person's constitutional right under the Fifth Amendment," the majority opinion said.

"The privilege against self-incrimination would be reduced to a hollow mockery if its exercise could be taken as equivalent either to a confession of guilt or a conclusive presumption of perjury."

Dr. Slochower invoked the privilege against self-incriminating testimony when he was asked in September, 1952, at a Senate Judiciary subcommittee hearing, whether he had been a member of the Communist party in 1940 and 1941. On Oct. 6, 1952, he was dismissed under Section 903 of the New York City Charter.

That section provides for the automatic dismissal of any muni-

Continued on Page 17, Column 3

4 CAREER ENVOYS SWORN IN CAPITAL

Top State Department Aides First to Hold New Rank

Special to The New York Times.

WASHINGTON, April 9—The United States' first four Career Ambassadors, the diplomatic equivalent of five-star generals, took the oath of office today.

They were Robert Murphy Deputy Under Secretary of State; Loy W. Henderson, Deputy Under Secretary of State for Administration; H. Freeman Matthews, Ambassador to the Netherlands, and James Clement Dunn, Ambassador to Brazil.

The four men, designated as having rendered exceptionally distinguished service to the Government, become the United States' highest ranking career diplomats under the over-all command of John Foster Dulles, Secretary of State. They might, however, still be outranked in diplomatic service by political appointees. Under Secretary Herbert Hoover Jr., Mr. Dulles' first assistant at the department, is such an appointee.

Their special rank was created by the last Congress in accordance with recommendations made by a committee headed by Dr. Henry M. Wriston, president emeritus of Brown University, in the summer of 1954. The committee found that the rank and pay of the State Department's

Continued on Page 8, Column 3

Five Marines Die in Swamp During Parris Island March

Another Recruit Missing —General Pate at Scene for Personal Inquiry

Special to The New York Times.

WASHINGTON, April 9—A veteran Marine sergeant led seventy-five recruits in a floundering march in pitch darkness through a swamp near the boot camp at Parris Island, S. C. last night. Today five of the youths were dead and one was missing.

Circumstances surrounding the tragedy caused Gen. Randolph McCall Pate, commandant of the Marine Corps, and Brig. Gen. Carson A. Roberts, the Inspector General, to fly to Parris Island for a personal inquiry.

S/Sgt. Matthew C. McKeon of Worcester, Mass., a 31-year-old veteran of the Korean war, was placed in custody pending investigation by a court of inquiry. Early reports telephoned

The New York Times April 10, 1956
Site of the Marine base

from the camp indicated that Sergeant McKeon had marched his platoon into the swamp to punish them for an infraction of discipline.

A statement tonight by the Marine Corps made no mention of the report that the march was a disciplinary measure, and sur-

Continued on Page 19, Column 3

PRESIDENT OFFERS CIVIL RIGHTS PLAN

Calls for 6-Man Study Board and Special Justice Unit —Congress Is Hostile

Texts of Brownell letter and proposed bills, Page 20.

By WILLIAM S. WHITE
Special to The New York Times.

WASHINGTON, April 9—The Eisenhower Administration sent its civil rights program to Congress today. The proposals evoked cries of "politics" from right and left-wing Democrats alike, and less than all-out Republican backing.

The outlook tonight was strongly against any implementing legislation in this session. It appeared that any substantial action anywhere in the civil rights field was unlikely.

Southern Senators responded in tones ranging from annoyance to anger. Their view was that the Administration's plan went intolerably too far.

Liberal Democratic Senators joined their Southern conservative colleagues at only one point: both accused the Administration of offering a vote-catching pro-

Continued on Page 20, Column 6

Jobs Rise 500,000 For March Record; Earnings Hit Peak

Special to The New York Times.

WASHINGTON, April 9—Employment rose 500,000 from mid-February to mid-March. This put the total at about 63,100,000. It was 2,500,000 higher than a year ago and a record for March.

The number of jobless remained close to the level of the two preceding months at 2,800,000.

Estimates of total employment and unemployment were made by the Census Bureau, Department of Commerce, on the basis of a door-to-door sampling. The estimates include the self-employed, domestics, and farm workers.

The Bureau of Labor Statistics, Department of Labor, using payroll data only, reported that automobile industry lay-offs apparently had halted. A downtrend had started last fall.

The work week of factory production workers, which, normally remains unchanged or rises slightly at this time of year, declined from 40.5 hours in February to 40.3 in March.

Widespread wage gains, which in many cases reflected the rise in the minimum wage payable under the Fair Labor Standards

Continued on Page 24, Column 2

G.O.P. CHIEFS OPEN NEW FIGHT TO GET A 'GOOD' FARM BILL

Act After Eisenhower Says Compromise Measure Fails to Meet 'Test'

By WILLIAM M. BLAIR
Special to The New York Times.

WASHINGTON, April 9—President Eisenhower and Republican Congressional leaders plunged into a last-ditch fight today for an Administration farm bill.

They laid plans to revise a Senate-House conference committee measure that the President asserted today had failed to meet "the test of a good bill."

Their aim was to strike from the conference bill restoration of rigid price supports and other provisions the President contended would hurt rather than help farmers.

The major test of Administration farm policy, including existing flexible price supports, will come on Wednesday in the House. The Republican leadership will move to send the bill back to conference with instructions to House conferences to delete several provisions opposed by the President and Ezra Taft Benson, the Secretary of Agriculture.

Strong G. O. P. Vote Sought

Both sides predicted victory publicly but were privately apprehensive over the outcome of the showdown fight. The House last year adopted revival of rigid price supports by a vote of 206 to 201.

After a White House conference with President Eisenhower, House Republican leaders went to work to line up a strong Republican vote and woo big-city Democrats. They argued that the conference bill would increase consumer bread and butter prices. The Democratic-controlled House is divided 231 Democrats to 203 Republicans and one Independent.

Representative Joseph W. Martin Jr. of Massachusetts, Republican leader, indicated the line of attack when he told reporters at the White House that "basically we've got to work on some of the consumers."

The problem of instructions to the conferees will be threshed out at a meeting of House Republicans tomorrow. Mr. Martin said he expected a "goodly number" of Democrats to vote for Ad-

Continued on Page 21, Column 4

SOVIET PLANS AID FOR WEST EUROPE IF U. S. FUNDS END

Tells Nations in U. N. Group to Look Toward Moscow for Energy Needs

By MICHAEL L. HOFFMAN
Special to The New York Times.

GENEVA, April 9—The Soviet Minister of Foreign Trade invited Western European countries today to look to Moscow for their needs when dollar aid ran out.

In a major policy speech, Ivan G. Kabanov, the Soviet delegate to the United Nations Economic Commission for Europe, held out glowing vistas of an expanding Soviet economy, ready to supply Western Europe with just those things it lacks. He emphasized particularly the planned growth in Soviet production of coal and crude oil.

This was a shrewd stroke. In a speech prepared before hearing the Soviet discourse, Maurice Faure, French Secretary of State for Foreign Affairs, had stressed the increasing strain that French and other Western European industrial growth is putting on indigenous energy sources.

It is generally accepted that the supply of energy is the most important single problem for the rapidly expanding Western European industrial complex. The political disturbances in the oil-producing Middle East makes this painfully obvious.

Oil, Coal Rises Forecast

Mr. Kabanov said the Soviet Union would be producing 135,000,000 tons of petroleum by 1960. Western economists here are inclined to believe this is well within a practical range. Mr. Kabanov also said, without elaborating, that the Soviet's coal output would rise in the next five years by more than the total present British output. This is also regarded by independent economists as well within Soviet capabilities.

Mr. Kabanov urged Western Europeans to discard their restrictions on trade with the Soviet Union. He ridiculed the idea that restrictions on "strategic" items hurt the Soviet or slowed down its economic growth.

As an example, he cited some oil-drilling equipment recently sold by the Soviet to an American company. Oil-drilling equipment, Mr. Kabanov said, is considered "strategic" by the United States and can not be sold to the Soviet Union. The Russian said that the Soviet, which has complete state control of foreign trade, had no "strategic" lists.

Mr. Kabanov appealed for a "full normalization" of trade. He said that Western Europe's accounts were being balanced internationally only by "extraordinary" United States expenditures in Europe. He warned that they would not last.

CURB ON RUSSIANS DENIED BY BRITISH

London Says Soviet Leaders Can See Workers on Visit

By THOMAS P. RONAN
Special to The New York Times.

LONDON, April 9—The Foreign Office rejected today as "quite untrue" the two principal Soviet leaders' charge that their travels in Britain had been arranged to limit their contacts with the people.

"In the course of their travels through the country they will have plenty of opportunity, of which they will doubtless avail themselves, of seeing British people and their way of life," a Foreign Office spokesman said.

The Russian visitors-to-be, Premier Nikolai A. Bulganin and the Communist party chief, Nikita S. Khrushchev, told a Tass news agency correspondent in Moscow yesterday that the itinerary mapped by British officials had made it impossible for them to accept many invitations they had received from average British subjects.

Accusing "certain forces" in Britain, the Russians said also that they would be unable to visit factories and other enterprises, especially in Scotland and Wales, as they had requested.

The Foreign Office noted that arrangements for the visit had been gone over twice and accepted by the Russians. The Government is decidedly unwilling to

Continued on Page 11, Column 1

Frescoes in Newly Discovered Catacomb in Rome

Associated Press

These are the first photographs received here of fourth century frescoes found in a recently discovered catacomb in Rome. The upper picture shows the meeting of Christ and the Samaritan Woman at the well. In the lower picture a Roman surgeon is shown during an operation as colleagues look on. This fresco adjoins the surgeon's tomb. The frescoes range in subject matter from the Old and the New Testaments to the pagan.

Associated Press Radiophoto

HAMMARSKJOLD VISITS POPE: The U. N. Secretary General during his audience with Pope Pius XII at Vatican. Pontiff gave his blessing to Mr. Hammarskjold's mission.

EISENHOWER ACTS

Declaration of Policy Puts Constitutional Limit on Action

By EDWIN L. DALE Jr.
Special to The New York Times.

AUGUSTA, Ga., April 9—The United States Government pledged itself today to oppose aggression in the Middle East "within constitutional means." It said it would "support and assist" any nation attacked there.

The pledge came in the form of a brief statement issued here by James C. Hagerty, White House press secretary. He said it had "the full approval of the President." General Eisenhower came to Georgia for a week of golfing and work.

The statement said President Eisenhower and Secretary of State Dulles regarded the situation in the Middle East "with the utmost seriousness." It said the two men this morning in Washington had discussed "repeated incidents of hostility" in the area.

Support for U. N. Mission

Then the statement concluded with these principles of United States policy:

¶"The United States will support in fullest measure the mission of [Dag Hammarskjold] the Secretary General of the United Nations in the area" and trusts that all United Nations member countries, "particularly the states directly involved," will also support the mission.

¶"The United States, in accordance with its responsibilities under the Charter of the United Nations, will observe its commitments within constitutional means to oppose any aggression in the area."

¶"The United States is likewise determined to support and assist any nation which might be subjected to such aggression. The United States is confident that other nations will act similarly in the cause of peace."

The statement was issued against a background of new violence between Israel and her Arab neighbors, particularly along the Gaza Strip, held by Egypt.

Also in the background was the reported desire of the British Government for a firmer statement of United States policy in the Arab-Israeli crisis. Mr. Hagerty said, however, that the statement had not been issued because of any urgent rep-

Continued on Page 3, Column 1

Hammarskjold Sees Pope on Peace Aims And Flies to Beirut

Special to The New York Times.

ROME, April 9—Dag Hammarskjold had an audience with Pope Pius XII today before leaving for Beirut, Lebanon, on a Middle East peace mission.

[Mr. Hammarskjold arrived in Beirut early Tuesday.]

The Pope is understood to have stressed to the United Nations Secretary General that Jerusalem and the other places of Christendom in Palestine should be internationalized. He offered Mr. Hammarskjold the moral support of the Roman Catholic Church for his attempt to ease tension between Israel and the Arab nations.

According to Vatican sources, Mr. Hammarskjold, whose audience lasted less than half an hour, and the Pope also exchanged views on disarmament. Mr. Hammarskjold reportedly told the Pope that the Pontiff's warnings to the world on nuclear warfare had made a deep impression at United Nations headquarters and among member nations.

The Vatican position on the holy places in Palestine was outlined by the Pope in two encyclicals in 1948 and 1949. In the latter document, the Pope demanded for "Jerusalem and its surroundings" a juridical status "whose stability under present circumstances can only be adequately assured by the united effort of nations that love

Continued on Page 2, Column 3

ISRAELIS WIPE OUT SUICIDE BAND OF 5

Egyptian Raiders Penetrate to 15 Miles of Tel Aviv— Groups Still at Large

By HOMER BIGART
Special to The New York Times.

NIR GALIM, Israel, Tuesday, April 10—A five-man fedayen (suicide) band that penetrated within fifteen miles of Tel Aviv was surrounded and wiped out yesterday by Israeli border policemen in a dry creek bed just west of here.

That brought to nine the number of Arab marauders killed in a round-up of suicide bands that have slain seven Israelis since Saturday night. Up to midnight, twenty-four Israelis had been wounded. Four fedayen were captured.

[Egypt reported that an Israeli plane had flown over the Sinai Desert all the way to the Suez Canal Zone Sunday night and then had returned to its base.]

Fedayen bands were still at large early today. Shortly before midnight an Israeli policeman was injured an an ambush of a police car south of Beersheba. An irrigation pipeline was blown up at Beit Reyim on the Gaza Strip.

At Beeri, another settlement facing the Gaza Strip, one Israeli was killed and another injured in an ambush of a convoy. A tractor driver was injured at

Continued on Page 4, Column 3

Lysenko, Stalin's Protege, Out As Soviet's Scientific Chieftain

By WELLES HANGEN
Special to The New York Times.

MOSCOW, April 9—Trofim D. Lysenko, who once wielded Stalin-like power over Soviet biological research, has resigned as head of the All-Union Academy of Agricultural Science. His successor is Pavel P. Lobanov, a Deputy Premier in charge of agriculture.

Vladimir V. Matskevich, hard-working Minister of Agriculture who led the Soviet farm delegation on a tour of the United States and Canada last summer, succeeds Mr. Lobanov as Deputy Premier. Mr. Matskevich is known as a strong supporter of Nikita S. Khrushchev's panaceas for the Soviet Union's farm problem.

Academician Lysenko's resignation and the two new appointments were announced tonight by Tass, official Soviet news agency.

Observers here drew the following conclusions from the changes:

¶Soviet scientific research is being progressively divested of the men whom Stalin designated to enforce paralyzing orthodoxy in all fields.

¶Mr. Khrushchev, the Communist party chief, is further consolidating the critical agricultural sector of the Soviet economy.

The three-paragraph Tass announcement gave no indication what position, if any, Professor Lysenko would now hold. It said merely the Council of Ministers had accepted his request to be relieved of his responsibilities as

Continued on Page 10, Column 1

ASIA SURVEY FINDS NEED OF MORE AID

Some See Cut in U. S. Living Standard to Provide Help

Correspondents of The New York Times have obtained the views of foreign and American officials and other competent observers on the strong and weak points of United States foreign policy and their suggestions for its improvement. The findings are being presented in a series of regional reports, of which this is the third.

By A. M. ROSENTHAL
Special to The New York Times.

COLOMBO, Ceylon, April 9—The great challenge—and the great opportunity — facing United States foreign policy is communism's eager pursuit of nationalist movements all over the world.

The challenge springs from the fact that the Russians have grasped the enormous emotional and political drive behind what Asians like to call "the age of nationalism."

Not long ago, at one of those earnest diplomatic garden parties that make up a good deal of New Delhi's official social life, an Indian Foreign Office man was talking about a favorite topic—where the United States goes wrong.

"You don't seem to be able to realize that countries see the world in different ways, that

Continued on Page 3, Column 3

"All the News That's Fit to Print"

NEWS SUMMARY AND INDEX, PAGE 95

The New York Times

LATE CITY EDITION

Condensation of U.S. Weather Bureau forecast: Warmer today. Cloudy tomorrow, little temperature change.
Temperature range today: 81—61.
Temperature range yesterday: 75.6—58.7.
Full U.S. Weather Bureau Report, Page 95.

SECTION ONE

VOL. CV..No. 36,009. Entered as Second-Class Matter, Post Office, New York, N.Y. NEW YORK, SUNDAY, AUGUST 26, 1956. Including Magazine and Book Review. TWENTY-FIVE CENTS

STEVENSON SCORES 'BROKEN PROMISES' IN G.O.P. PLATFORM

He Says Rivals 'Have Done Just the Opposite' of What They Again Pledge to Do

PARTY ISSUES 'ANALYSIS'

25-Page Document Reviews Republican Planks—Sees Failure in Major Fields

Text of statement and analysis of G.O.P. platform, Pages 66-67.

By WILLIAM M. BLAIR
Special to The New York Times.

LIBERTYVILLE, Ill., Aug. 25—Adlai E. Stevenson today labeled the Republican platform for 1956 "one of the rarest collections of already broken promises in modern political history."

The Democratic Presidential nominee accused the Republicans of "huckstering" and "sleight-of-hand" and making "glib promises in fields where the Eisenhower Administration already has failed."

If voters compare the platforms of the Republican and Democratic parties, he asserted, they can draw only one conclusion:

"That the Republican party is still a standpat, do-nothing party; and the Democratic party is still a forward-looking party that sees a big job ahead and does not fear to undertake it."

His whiplash of the G. O. P. pledges was based on a twenty-five-page plank-by-plank "analysis" of the opposition platform. He said the analysis was prepared at his direction by the research division of the Democratic National Committee.

Confers With Kefauver

The committee's document was brought to Mr. Stevenson's country home near here. It dealt with every subject in the Republican platform from foreign policy to corruption in government.

It marked a take-off point on Republican policies for the candidate as he prepared to start on Monday a series of regional meetings with state and local party leaders. The meetings will serve to coordinate the national and local campaigns and gather information on special local or regional issues to thrust against the Republicans.

Senator Estes Kefauver of Tennessee, Mr. Stevenson's running mate, arrived to discuss plans for their campaign. He and Mr. Stevenson said they would woo the "Joe Smiths of the nation." This was a reference to the mythical American whose name came briefly before the Republican Convention as a prospect for Vice President. The Senator will accompany Mr. Stevenson on his regional tour.

Observing that voters usually had to wait a few years to see whether political parties carried out their platform promises, Mr. Stevenson asserted that this year "they won't have to wait."

The Eisenhower Administration's record, he said, "shows that they didn't intend to carry out their 1952 platform promises. In many cases they have done just the opposite of what they are now again promising the voters in this year's platform."

The national committee's analysis, he said, speaks for itself. But he directed attention to

Continued on Page 67, Column 2

Major Sports News

BASEBALL

The Yankees, despite Mickey Mantle's forty-fourth homer, lost to the Chicago White Sox, 4—2, at the Stadium yesterday. Phil Rizzuto, a dominant factor in Yankee successes since 1941, was released to make room for Enos Slaughter. The latter was obtained from the Athletics on waivers. The Dodgers lost to the Redlegs, 5—2, and the Giants climbed into seventh place by beating the Cubs, 6—0.

HORSE RACING

Paper Tiger, a 7-1 shot, defeated the favored Dedicate by a head in the $57,200 Saratoga Handicap. Conn McCreary rode the winner. Swaps finished seventh as Mahan won a stake race in Chicago.

TENNIS

Vic Seixas of Philadelphia and Hamilton Richardson of Westfield, N. J., advanced to the United States doubles final at Brookline. They will meet Lew Hoad and Ken Rosewall of Australia for the title today.

Details in Section 5

Eisenhower Calls His Shot a 'Louse'

Associated Press Wirephoto

President Eisenhower as he practiced chip shots yesterday

By RUSSELL BAKER
Special to The New York Times.

PEBBLE BEACH, Calif., Aug. 25—The President of the United States addressed the golf ball, brought the club back and swung it hard. The ball lofted high into the gray Pacific mist and, as the sea lions hooted, plummeted weakly on the fairway far short of the green. "That," said the President, normally a notorious abstainer from name-calling, "is a louse." This, pretty much, summed up his perform-

Continued on Page 64, Column 1

DE SAPIO TO JOIN STEVENSON DRIVE

Will See Finnegan This Week About Strategy in State—Power Held Unimpaired

By RICHARD AMPER

Carmine G. De Sapio and campaign aides of Adlai E. Stevenson, convention foes a week and a half ago, will join forces this week to plan their Presidential election battle for New York State.

The Tammany leader, somewhat rankled but still self-assured despite appraisals that he had lost prestige at the Chicago convention, said he would confer during the week with James A. Finnegan, campaign manager for the Democratic Presidential nominee, and Michael H. Prendergast, the party's New York State chairman.

Mr. De Sapio said he hoped to "blueprint" strategy and tactics on state and local levels to capture the major prize of New York's forty-five electoral votes for Mr. Stevenson in November.

His coming liaison with Mr. Finnegan supported the view that Mr. De Sapio and his organization were considered as important as ever even though he lost his battle to nominate Governor Harriman. He also wound up on the losing side of the Democratic Vice-Presidential contest. He supported Mayor Wagner and then Senator John F. Kennedy of Massachusetts against Senator Estes Kefauver of Tennessee.

Sees Mrs. Rosenberg

Mr. De Sapio already had made whatever peace might have been necessary with his recent foes in post-convention conferences with Mrs. Anna Rosenberg, co-chairman with Thomas K. Finletter of the New York State Stevenson for President Committee.

Mrs. Rosenberg announced that the committee and Democratic state and local organizations would operate autonomously in the campaign. The committee, she said, would have the same objective as the regular party organizations but would seek support from nonorganization Democrats and independent voters.

"There will be no interference with each other," she said. "The committee is going to dissolve on Nov. 6 [Election Day]. It is not a political organization."

She added that neither she nor Mr. Finletter was interested in maintaining a political organization—their only goal was electing Mr. Stevenson.

Whatever might be said of a

Continued on Page 71, Column 3

Nixon Is Planning A Moderate Tone In Campaign Talks

By GLADWIN HILL
Special to The New York Times.

LOS ANGELES, Aug. 25—Vice President Richard M. Nixon held his first campaign strategy conference as the Republican candidate for re-election today.

He met privately for two hours at the Statler Hotel here with a small group of members of Congress from California and other aides from the 1952 campaign who will assist him again.

Some salient features of the over-all Republican 1956 campaign as outlined by him at a news conference before the meeting, follow:

¶The campaign, starting the week of Sept. 17, will be essentially more defensive, moderate and constructive than that of 1952, basically because the Republicans are the incumbents rather than the challengers.

¶Mr. Nixon will be the principal Administration stumper, with President Eisenhower's participation centered in a few relatively "formal" appearances, not because of health but because of his position and responsibilities of office.

¶The major emphasis of Mr. Nixon's campaigning will be to help regain for the Republicans the majorities in both houses of Congress.

¶While the campaign's main theme will be Administration accomplishments and aims, the

Continued on Page 69, Column 1

Dr. Kinsey Is Dead; Sex Researcher, 62

By The Associated Press.

BLOOMINGTON, Ind., Aug. 25—Dr. Alfred C. Kinsey, who gained world-wide fame for his books on human sexual behavior, died today of a heart ailment and pneumonia. He was 62 years old.

The zoologist had been in ill health for six months. He was admitted to Bloomington Hospital Wednesday, but his condition had not been considered critical until last night.

Dr. Kinsey's illness had interrupted his busy schedule of travels to collect material for new sex-research projects—on men in prison, on Europeans and on animals.

His wife, Mrs. Clara Bracken McMillen Kinsey, one of his early students at Indiana University, was with him when he died. Also surviving are a son, Bruce, of Cleveland, and two daughters, Mrs. Robert Reed, wife of a physician in Colum-

Continued on Page 84, Column 5

RESERVE BARRING ITS AIRLINE PILOTS FROM FLIGHT DUTY

Fliers Protest as Air Force Orders the Move to Avoid Harming Industry in War

By JOSEPH DURSO

The Air Force has touched off a controversy by ordering its Reserve and Guard wings to ground all airline pilots to avoid any confusion in case of mobilization.

The order may cost the Reserve forces several hundred experienced pilots, many assigned to defending the nation's big cities. New York's 106th Bombardment Wing will lose seventeen pilots—the equivalent of a squadron—including its bomb group commander, a squadron commander and five flight commanders. And it promptly made a public call for fliers to fill its ranks.

The order is part of a wide screening of persons with critical civilian jobs who might be needed swiftly in "the kind of warfare that may confront the United States."

Its immediate effect, however, according to some officers, will be to cut units' operational ability. Most of the pilots involved were said to resent the prospect of quitting military flying and possibly losing pension rights and pay. And the Pentagon acknowledged last week that some members of Congress had inquired whether the airlines or the Air Force needed the pilots more.

Colorado Senator Inquires

According to Donald J. Strait, Deputy Assistant Secretary of the Air Force for Reserve Forces, one of the inquiries was from Senator Gordon Allott, Republican of Colorado. His state, like New York, is a major airline center and is also the headquarters of the Air Defense Command.

As a result of the inquiries from Congress, Mr. Strait said, Secretary of the Air Force Donald A. Quarles is now giving the order "another look."

Meanwhile Reserve and Guard wings throughout the country have begun screening their squadrons to remove the airline pilots "as soon as qualified reservists are available as replacements." About 170 men will be removed from the Air Guard's twenty-six wings, according to the Pentagon, but the number affected in the Air Reserve is not known. In any event, they are required to be out by Dec. 31.

The order stems from a memorandum of understanding in 1951 between the Secretary of Commerce and the Secretary of Defense. They agreed that in case of war the airlines would be needed to supply fleets of air transports for world-wide missions.

Last year the Armed Forces

Continued on Page 38, Column 3

U.S. FINDS GUNFIRE HIT PATROL PLANE; HUNT CALLED OFF

Bullet Fragments Discovered in Airman's Body—Fleet to Keep Watch Off China

By The Associated Press.

TOKYO, Aug. 25—Bullet fragments in a crewman's body confirmed tonight that a United States Navy patrol plane had been hit by gunfire before it plunged into the East China Sea off the Chinese mainland.

The sixteen crewmen of the four-engine P-4M Martin Mercator were under routine orders to fire back if attacked. But there was no indication whether they did before the crash early Thursday, Tokyo time, about 100 miles southeast of Shanghai.

[The Navy announced in Washington Saturday night that the search for survivors had been discontinued. However, the Seventh Fleet was ordered to "continue surveillance" of the area because of the possibility that more bodies might be found.]

Still unanswered were these questions:

¶How many planes attacked the patrol craft? Communist China announced a "Chiang Kai-shek plane" was damaged in an air action by a Communist plane in the area Thursday. But the Chinese Nationalists on Taiwan (Formosa) said none of their planes were near the scene at the time.

¶Did the plane explode in the air or when it hit the water?

¶Why was the wreckage found almost 200 miles north of the position the plane should have been in when the attack came?

Crash Injuries Caused Death

The finding that the plane had been hit was based on the examination of the body of Albert P. Mattin, aviation electronics technician 1/c, of Delta, Ohio. No other bodies have been recovered.

Capt. Earl Junghans, commander of the fleet air detachment at the naval air station at Iwakuni, Japan, said wounds on the technician's body contained metal fragments from gunfire. However, the airman died of multiple injuries suffered when the plane crashed into the sea, Captain Junghans added.

Officers said there was evidence the plane had burned. But they could not say whether it had caught fire in the air or burst into flames when it hit the water.

Captain Junghans said regular patrol operations would continue despite the incident.

The following items have been recovered from international waters in the East China Sea: the plane's wheels, two fuel tanks, two inflated life rafts, raft equipment, plane cushions and seats, parts of oil and fuel lines and personal items.

The Navy reiterated that the

Continued on Page 7, Column 1

Norwegians Will Explore Mountains in Antarctica

The New York Times Aug. 26, 1956

The site of Norway's proposed Antarctic base (cross)

By WALTER SULLIVAN

For the first time since Amundsen won the race to the South Pole in 1911, Norway plans to send an expedition into the interior of Antarctica.

The primary purpose of the venture will be to establish a station in Queen Maud Land, Norway's Antarctic claim, during the International Geophysical Year 1957-58. A number of nations are setting up bases at the bottom of the world during that period of world-wide scien-

Continued on Page 39, Column 1

Color Bar to Oust 100,000 Residents Of Johannesburg

By LEONARD INGALLS
Special to The New York Times.

JOHANNESBURG, South Africa, Aug. 25—More than 100,000 non-whites have been ordered to leave their Johannesburg homes in a new application of South Africa's segregation laws.

The residents of six areas have been notified that they must move out to make room for whites by Aug. 3 next year. Non-whites living in two other areas have been given until Aug. 3, 1958, to leave.

Orders have been issued under the Group Areas Act enacted by Prime Minister Johannes G. Strijdom's Nationalist Government in 1950. The act provides machinery under which the Afrikaner nationalist ideal of a society compartmented according to skin color would be achieved.

This latest move against non-whites has been denounced during the last week by opposition members of Parliament, members of the Transvaal Provincial Council and Johannesburg City Councilors as "a disastrous blow" to the property rights of non-whites. It has been called a manifestation of "the master race complex" and a move likely "to plunge the country into what will become the most serious

Continued on Page 30, Column 1

Stamford Freight Wreck Ties Up New Haven Railroad

The New York Times

Freight cars are scattered across the tracks on the Canal Street trestle in Stamford, Conn.

Service on the New York New Haven and Hartford Railroad was disrupted yesterday by derailment of a freight train at Stamford, Conn. From 8:30 A. M., when the mishap occurred, until early evening incoming trains were two to three hours late. Outbound trains operated irregularly and some were canceled. Until late afternoon all four main line tracks were impassable in Stamford at a point just west of the Canal Street bridge. Passengers in both directions were transferred between that point and South Norwalk—about ten miles—in forty buses. At 5:10 P. M. one track was reopened. Bus service then was discontinued and

Continued on Page 69, Column 3

DULLES RETURNS, HOPEFUL ON SUEZ

Secretary Urges That Egypt Make 'Indispensable' Move to End the Canal Crisis

By CHARLES E. EGAN
Special to The New York Times.

WASHINGTON, Aug. 25—Secretary of State Dulles expressed hope here tonight that Egypt would accept suggestions for international control of the Suez Canal.

Arriving from the Suez conference in London, the Secretary of State urged Egypt to "make its own indispensable contribution" to the peaceful solution of the crisis.

The Secretary's flight home was interrupted when an engine failed over the Atlantic, forcing him to return to the Azores and wait eight hours for another plane. He said he planned to talk by telephone with President Eisenhower at Monterey, Calif., and advise him of the progress made at the London meeting.

Secretary Dulles represented the United States in talks with twenty-one other nations considering problems raised by Egypt's nationalization of the Suez Canal Company.

Mr. Dulles said he would await President Eisenhower's return to Washington early next week before presenting to him a report in person.

He gave the following brief statements to the press after leaving his plane:

"The London conference on the Suez Canal set in motion pressures designed to lead to a fair and peaceful solution of the grave problems raised by the action of the Egyptian Government.

"Twenty-two nations met to consider how this waterway, internationalized in perpetuity by

Continued on Page 2, Column 3

Confederate Money Pays Off in Sweden

By FELIX BELAIR Jr.
Special to The New York Times.

STOCKHOLM, Sweden, Aug. 25—The credit of the Confederate States of America has been revived in Stockholm, but only briefly.

Several weeks ago a teller in a bank here paid out Swedish kroner—one of the harder currencies of Europe—when a bricklayer presented a $500 Confederate banknote.

The whole story came out when two small boys tried to pass a $500 Confederate bill bearing the identical serial number and happened to approach the same teller. Becoming suspicious, he called the police. Thereupon, all banks were alerted against money issued on the Richmond (Va.) Civil War Treasury.

The story as unfolded by the police goes back to last February. It was then that "an unidentified foreigner" was seen in a Stockholm public

Continued on Page 24, Column 5

NASSER WEIGHING AN APPEAL TO U. N. ON WEST'S TROOPS

Bid to the Security Council Would Cover Only British and French Movements

FULL SUEZ ISSUE BARRED

Egypt Said to Fear Broader Debate Would Recognize Dispute Is International

By OSGOOD CARUTHERS
Special to The New York Times.

CAIRO, Aug. 25—Egypt was reported today to be considering the possibility of seeking action by the United Nations Security Council against British and French troop movements in the Eastern Mediterranean.

The Government of President Gamal Abdel Nasser already has openly charged that these movements in the wake of the nationalization of the Suez Canal Company pose a threat to peace in the Middle East.

[Meanwhile in London, Hugh Gaitskell, leader of the Labor party, called upon the British Government to encourage non-Egyptian pilots to remain in their Suez Canal jobs.]

Political circles here said the Egyptians had begun canvassing United Nations officials and some of the members of the eleven-nation Security Council in the last twenty-four hours on the possibility of calling a special session to discuss the case.

Would Limit Issue

The sources that reported this new turn of events said Egypt would insist on confining a possible Security Council debate strictly to the question of British and French maneuvers. The Egyptians still are said to be somewhat wary of bringing the broader issue of the Suez Canal crisis before the United Nations lest such a move be interpreted as a concession by Egypt that the dispute is an international affair.

The Egyptians have made no effort to conceal their profound concern over British and French troop movements to the area. They consider these movements as a threat to use force unless Egypt bows to Western demands for international control of the Suez Canal.

The Egyptians have announced their determination not to accept any form of foreign control of the canal and have said they will fight to the bitter end any effort to impose such control by force.

According to these sources, the Government has made no formal request for Security Council debate on the subject. Consideration of this possible step still is in the preliminary stage, it was said. The Egyptians at present simply are making contacts to determine the wisdom of such a move, whether they could expect to have a good case to present to the Security Council and what chances they would have of gaining anything.

Nasser Noncommittal

President Nasser, meanwhile, still was keeping the lid of secrecy on Egypt's intentions regarding the five-nation committee that has been named by the London conference on Suez to bring here the Western proposals for settling the dispute. Diplomatic activity continued in Cairo at an intensive pace.

President Nasser talked for an hour and a half today with the Indonesian Foreign Minister, Ruslan Abdulgani, who stopped off here on his way home from the London conference.

Mr. Abdulgani said he had discussed with President Nasser the possibility of convening soon a conference of African-Asian nations similar to that held in April, 1955, in Bandung, Indonesia. The meeting would be called to discuss the Suez Canal crisis, he said.

Mr. Abdulgani voiced considerable optimism that settlement of the dispute would be negotiated peacefully. His country supported India's minority proposal to establish an international advisory board to watch

Continued on Page 2, Column 5

This section consists of 110 pages divided into three parts. The news summary and index will be found on Page 95. Society news begins on Page 86 and obituary articles will be found on Pages 84 and 85.

"All the News That's Fit to Print"

The New York Times.

LATE CITY EDITION
Condensation of U. S. Weather Bureau forecast:
Mostly fair today, cool tonight.
Partly cloudy and cool tomorrow.
Temperature range today: 78—64.
Temperature range yesterday: 80.1—70.2.
Full U. S. Weather Bureau Report, Page 43.

VOL. CV..No. 36,021. Entered as Second-Class Matter, Post Office, New York, N. Y. NEW YORK, FRIDAY, SEPTEMBER 7, 1956. Times Square, New York 36, N. Y. Telephone LAckawanna 4-1000 FIVE CENTS

NIXON WARNS U.S. AGAINST RELAXING VIGILANCE ON REDS

Tells Legion the Communists Are Spurring Subversion—Doubts End of Draft

DEFENDS ATOMIC TESTS

Chides 'Misguided' Who Urge 'Softer Line' With Soviet—Talk Moderate in Tone

By GLADWIN HILL
Special to The New York Times.

LOS ANGELES, Sept. 6—Vice President Richard M. Nixon warned today against the dangers of communism on both the international and domestic fronts.

In his first major appearance as a renominated candidate, he spoke in largely nonpartisan terms and with restraint in delivery. He gently chided "well-intentioned but misguided people" who would take a "softer line" against communism because of Soviet Russia's conciliatory "new look."

He told the concluding session of the American Legion's thirty-eighth national convention:

"All the evidence that has come to my attention shows that the Communists are stepping up internal subversion in the United States and other countries rather than reducing it. Now is the time to increase our vigilance—not relax it."

He noted that it was anyone's constitutional right to invoke the Fifth Amendment, which concerns immunity from self-incrimination, if questioned about knowledge of Communist activities. But such a person, he said, "forfeits any claim he might have to be an employe of our Government, Federal, state or local, and that includes our tax-supported schools."

Follows Stevenson

Mr. Nixon's stress on the Communist issue in the last two national campaigns and some resultant criticism had caused conjecture that he might soft-pedal the topic in this campaign.

The man who is expected to be the most active campaigner for the Republican ticket this fall appeared before the nonpartisan Legion just twenty-four hours after it had been addressed by Adlai E. Stevenson, the Democratic standard-bearer. Mr. Stevenson's theme was that the Republicans were fraudulently representing themselves to be the "peace" party and picturing Democrats as having an affinity for war.

Mr. Nixon drew a slightly smaller audience in the Shrine Auditorium than had Mr. Stevenson—although still about 5,000 people. But he got a somewhat more cordial reception, one

Continued on Page 10, Column 4

Associated Press Wirephoto

FIXED BAYONETS were in order yesterday as National Guardsmen escorted Negro students from the high school in Sturgis, Ky., after classes. The youths were slipped out a rear door and taken to their parents' automobiles.

TROOPS OPEN PATH IN KENTUCKY MOB FOR NEGRO PUPILS

Charge Crowd at High School in Sturgis—7 White Men Arrested in Fist Fights

By The Associated Press.

STURGIS, Ky., Sept. 6—National Guardsmen with fixed bayonets charged into a fist-swinging mob of 500 townspeople today to open a path for nine Negro youths entering Sturgis High School.

Fighting broke out when the Negro youths, who walked a mile to the previously all-white school, reached the building.

Seven men were arrested in the demonstration. They were released later after paying fines of $10 each on charges of breaking the peace.

No injuries were reported.

Yelling "Go home, Negro," the crowd surged around the students, trying to break through a ring of troops to reach the Negro youths.

In the melee a Guardsman took a revolver from his holster, stuck it against the head of the man nearest him and shouted:

"Get back or I'll shoot."

A state policeman in civilian clothing was assaulted by two men, one of whom was arrested later.

Later, Guardsmen with riot guns and fixed bayonets formed a protective wall around the Negro students as they left the school.

The crowd jeered the Negroes and hurled taunts at an estimated 100 white children who attended the school today. Someone shouted:

"Go on back in, you nigger-lovers. Why don't you go home with those niggers?"

The white children were not harmed.

Negroes Taken Home in Cars

More than thirty National Guardsmen formed a line from a side door of the school building to three cars in which parents of the Negro youths waited to take them home.

The crowd surged forward, but Guardsmen prevented anyone from reaching either the students or cars.

As the students and parents drove away, one man shouted:

"We'll get you niggers if it takes all year."

Just before the Negro students were let out the side door, troopers confiscated a shotgun being carried by an unidentified white man.

State police officers went into a conference after the Negro students were removed to discuss the possibility of setting up a guard around the Negro residential area tonight.

Col. Paul Smith, acting director of state police, and Don Sturgill, Deputy Safety Commissioner, left by plane to confer with Gov. A. B. Chandler in the state capital at Frankfort.

Mr. Sturgill said:

"If we can stop this here we feel we can stop it [the disturbance] anywhere else in the state."

As the Negro students were enrolling in the office of H. Earl Evans, principal, many white students began voluntarily to leave classes. Some were weeping. By noon, 175 of the 350 enrolled in the school had walked

Continued on Page 12, Column 2

British Parliament Summoned on Suez

By KENNETT LOVE
Special to The New York Times.

LONDON, Sept. 6—Sir Anthony Eden's Cabinet decided today to reconvene Parliament Wednesday in an emergency session on the Suez situation.

A Government statement said it was expected that the five-nation delegation discussing the Suez problem with Egypt's President would have completed its mission in Cairo by Wednesday. An authoritative informant said the Cabinet expected Prime Minister Robert Gordon Menzies of Australia, who heads the delegation, to return here Sunday or Monday.

Reports from the British Embassy in Cairo on the Menzies mission talks with President Gamal Abdel Nasser, which began Monday, have led to qualified pessimism here regarding the mission's chances

Continued on Page 2, Column 6

GLOOM OVERTAKES CAIRO CONFEREES ON SUEZ PROBLEM

Menzies Group Defers Parley With Nasser Pending Word From Home Governments

FINAL DEADLOCK DENIED

Spokesmen Omit Remarks About Optimistic Outlook for Success of Talks

By OSGOOD CARUTHERS
Special to The New York Times.

CAIRO, Sept. 6—An atmosphere of gloom all but extinguished tonight the spark of optimism that the talks on the Suez Canal crisis would succeed.

For the first time since the five-nation committee arrived last Sunday to discuss with President Gamal Abdel Nasser the Western plan for settling the dispute and to hear his views on the subject, there were strong indications that neither side had yet presented a formula for a compromise.

The talks between President Nasser and the committee, headed by Robert Gordon Menzies, Prime Minister of Australia, have been held in mutually agreed secrecy that has been rigidly observed by both sides.

Spokesmen for the Egyptians and the committee, made up of Australia, the United States, Iran, Sweden and Ethiopia, however, have been giving the impression up to now that the talks were getting somewhere. Reports by these spokesmen that the two sides were discussing various points of difference apparently were intended to give the impression that there was a chance of compromise.

New Meeting Uncertain

No such feeling was transmitted to reporters today.

No one could be found who would say that the situation had reached the point of final deadlock.

However, Mr. Menzies' committee met today without setting a date for its next meeting with President Nasser. It was decided that the committee would meet again tomorrow and "perhaps" the discussions with President Nasser would be resumed Saturday.

It was evident that the members of the committee wanted time to report to their governments and to the thirteen other powers that sponsored the proposal, introduced at the London conference by Secretary of State Dulles. They also were understood to be awaiting return advice from those governments.

The Western plan called for the establishment of an international control authority over the Suez Canal, whose operating company President Nasser nationalized July 26. The committee

Continued on Page 2, Column 3

PARIS HELD WARY OF FORCE ON SUEZ

French Said to Be Reviewing Drastic Policy in View of Opposition in Britain

By HAROLD CALLENDER
Special to The New York Times.

PARIS, Sept. 6—After a Cabinet meeting tonight it was said that French policy in the Suez crisis was about to take account of what were considered new factors.

In spite of reports here of the failure so far of the talks in Cairo resulting from the London conference on the Suez, there were indications that second thoughts were being entertained regarding the military operations for which France and Britain have been preparing.

These operations were said to be considered more difficult than had been assumed at first, while Britain's participation appeared more doubtful in view of the objections of the Labor party to any but defensive military action.

The basic assumption of French policy—that the Soviet Union would stand aside in case of war, Russia and the United States neutralizing each other—was reported to be held with somewhat less assurance than a month ago.

French Doubts Raised

The French never have intended that a reoccupation of Egypt should entail a risk of a world war. Doubts on this point resulting from Moscow's support of Egypt therefore led to a reappraisal, "agonizing" or not, of French policy.

The belief in political circles here tonight was that the French attitude had begun to be affected by three factors: the opposition to Prime Minister Eden's similar policy within Britain, the attitude of Moscow and reports published here that the United States was so determined on a peaceful solution of the crisis that it even would propose carrying the problem to the United Nations.

The French see the latter move as a way of burying the issue, at least until after the Presidential election in the United States.

The statement that the Cabinet was united behind a firm policy, which has followed most of its meetings since the Suez crisis began, was lacking from the authorized version of today's meeting given by Gerard Jacquet, Under Secretary for Information.

Few Questions Put to Pineau

But it was reported that not many questions had been put to Christian Pineau, the Foreign Minister, when he informed his colleagues of the talks in Cairo and of those he had in Paris yesterday with Selwyn Lloyd, British Foreign Secretary.

Nor was there any question yet of calling Parliament back into session, as Prime Minister Eden has done. But Sir Anthony did not receive from the House of Commons any such sweeping endorsement of a "strong" policy as the French Government received from the National Assembly before it adjourned Aug. 3 for the holidays. The Assembly adopted a resolution calling Gamal Abdel Nasser, President of Egypt, "a permanent menace to peace."

In taking what was described as a firm and energetic line, the French leaders, M. Pineau and Premier Guy Mollet, went beyond the attitude not only of the United States but even of Britain. They promised to impose upon President Nasser, by force

Continued on Page 3, Column 2

FRANCE CAUTIONS ALGERIAN REBELS

Lacoste Points to Build-Up of Forces to End War

By HENRY GINIGER
Special to The New York Times.

PARIS, Sept. 6—Robert Lacoste, French Minister Residing in Algeria, declared tonight that all the means to bring peace to Algeria were at hand.

In a statement to army officers and civil officials that was made public here, M. Lacoste said 200,000 men had landed in Algeria in the last three months. The total French forces there have been reliably estimated at 400,000.

The French spokesman warned the rebels, who have been fighting against French control for twenty-two months, that France's military effort was not temporary. He said the release of reservists would leave the number of troops unchanged and added that they would remain that way until calm had returned to the North African country.

The Ministry of National Defense recently promised to start releasing young reservists toward the end of the year. At the same time, it indicated that to compensate for this loss the length of military service prescribed for young recruits might be raised above the present limit, eighteen months. The possibility of military action against Egypt has introduced another element of uncertainty

Continued on Page 3, Column 3

STEVENSON SAYS G.O.P. FAILS LABOR

Lays Duplicity to Congress Leaders—Union Gives Him Stirring Reception

By LAWRENCE E. DAVIES
Special to The New York Times.

SAN FRANCISCO, Sept. 6—Adlai E. Stevenson denounced today the Eisenhower Administration's labor record.

Delegates to the machinists' international convention received his remarks with shouting, whistling, foot-stomping and marching. Associates of the Democratic Presidential nominee said it was the most enthusiastic demonstration so far in the campaign.

Mr. Stevenson, who appeared with his running-mate, Senator Estes Kefauver, accused Republican leaders of cheering President Eisenhower and then opposing in Congress the very things they had cheered for.

He said that "Mr. Eisenhower and a majority of Republicans, who talk feelingly now about the minimum wage law, opposed the raising of the minimum wage to one dollar." That action, however, was "put through with Democratic votes," Mr. Stevenson added.

Social Security Discussed

The Democratic nominee attacked the President on the social security issue also.

Mr. Stevenson declared:

"In his first State of the Union Message Mr. Eisenhower pledged himself to the principle that 'the individual must have safeguards against personal disaster inflicted by forces beyond his control.'

"But when the Democrats in the Eighty-fourth Congress took him at his word and offered these amendments to safeguard the worker against such 'personal disaster' he proclaimed them 'unwise and unwanted.' He threw the whole weight and power of his Administration into an all-out effort to defeat them."

The speaker added:

"Fortunately for all of us, his effort did not succeed. It failed because the Democratic majority in the United States Senate stood together and fought for their convictions."

Scores G. O. P. Foreign Policy

Turning to foreign policy, Mr. Stevenson charged that the Republicans "will be playing politics with peace in their campaign."

He departed from his prepared text and referred to Republican foreign policy statements by asking:

"Why don't they tell us the truth? Why don't they tell us that the menace of communism has been growing, that neutralism is spreading, that the realities are grim and that we can lose the cold war without even firing a shot?"

Instead, Mr. Stevenson said, the Republicans "sit complacently by and say all is well."

Such campaign tactics, he added, "seem to me lamentable, dangerous, insincere and putting political advantage, partisanship, far ahead of the ultimate understanding of the American people."

The arrival of Mr. Stevenson and Senator Kefauver at the Civic Auditorium was the signal for a prolonged demonstration by delegates to the quadrennial convention of the International

Continued on Page 11, Column 2

Rose Calls Javits Anti-Red; G. O. P. May Delay Choice

By LEO EGAN

Alex Rose, guiding genius of the Liberal party, came to the defense of State Attorney General Jacob K. Javits yesterday. In a voluntary testimonial he credited Mr. Javits with "a clear-cut anti-Communist record."

Reaction among Republicans to Mr. Javits' appearance on Wednesday before the Senate Internal Security Subcommittee in Washington was mixed. Among leaders upstate the view was widespread that his chances of winning the nomination for United States Senator had been damaged. Downstate leaders inclined to the opinion that his chances remained good.

So confused and contradictory were the views of influential Republican leaders that serious thought was being given to deferring the final selection of a candidate for a week. Those advocating this delay argued that it would allow a more reasoned appraisal of the political consequences of Mr. Javits' testimony.

Selection of a Republican candidate for the Senate seat being vacated by 78-year-old Herbert H. Lehman, Democrat-Liberal, is now scheduled to take place at a meeting of the Republican state committee in Albany on Monday. The election law requires that a choice be made no later than Tuesday.

Mayor Wagner of New York is scheduled to be nominated by acclamation as the Democratic candidate for the office at a state convention in Albany Monday. He is due to get the Liberal party endorsement on Tuesday at a convention in Manhattan Center.

Republicans could gain a week's respite by naming a "dummy" or "stand-in" candidate on Monday with the understanding that he would decline the nomination. They would then have until Sept. 17 to choose a substitute. This is a practice widely followed by all parties in the selection of local candidates, but is rarely used in the case of state-wide candidates.

The Javits testimony causing so much concern among Repub-

Continued on Page 14, Column 4

HARLEM OPPOSES STEVENSON TALK

City Democrats Say He Might Get Poor Reception There Because of Rights Plank

By RICHARD AMPER

Democratic leaders have found dissatisfaction with the party's civil rights platform plank so great that they deemed it inadvisable for Adlai E. Stevenson to speak in Harlem next week.

A suggestion for such an appearance by the Democratic Presidential nominee was turned down yesterday at a meeting of Mayor Wagner, Carmine De Sapio, Tammany Hall leader and Democratic National Committeeman, and some twenty-five Negro leaders from Manhattan, the Bronx, Brooklyn and Queens.

They met at a closed luncheon meeting at the Savoy Plaza Hotel.

They had gathered to pledge support to Mr. Wagner's candidacy for the United States Senate and to map a campaign for holding the Negro vote in the face of the civil rights issue. The Negro vote may be decisive in this year's Presidential election.

Mr. Stevenson is scheduled to appear next Monday at the Democratic state convention in Albany, where Mayor Wagner's

Continued on Page 11, Column 3

87 HURT IN CRASH OF EXCURSION SHIP

Swinging Span of Harlem Bridge Collides With Boat—2d Mishap in Month

By WAYNE PHILLIPS

Eighty-seven persons were injured yesterday when a sightseeing boat came to grief against the East 138th Street bridge over the Harlem River. It was second such accident in a month.

The captain of the boat contended that this time, however, it was the swing bridge that had struck the boat as the span was being opened. The bridge operator, on the contrary, said the current had carried the boat into the bridge.

Normally the Circle Line craft, Sightseer VIII, could have cleared the span—the Madison Avenue Bridge between Manhattan and the Bronx—without its being opened. But yesterday the bridge was being swung open for a tug and barge that were passing on the other side of the river.

25-Foot Gash in Sundeck

Metal legs that project downward for four feet at the ends of the bridge, to support them on the bridge abutments, ripped like a can opener through twenty-five feet of steel and glass on the boat's sundeck.

Most of the persons injured suffered minor cuts and bruises and were treated at the scene. But thirty-seven persons were taken to hospitals in ambulances. All but one woman, who suffered a possible concussion, were released after treatment.

In the accident at the same bridge on Aug. 8 thirty-three persons were injured. On that occasion the captain said the steering mechanism failed, the boat veered too close to a bridge abutment and the sundeck crashed into the underside of the bridge.

Both boats were part of a fleet that carry sight-seers, most

Continued on Page 44, Column 5

KIDNAPPED BABY DEAD NEAR HOME

Body of Ruotolo Girl Found in Lake at Hamden, Conn.

By RICHARD H. PARKE
Special to The New York Times.

HAMDEN, Conn., Sept. 6—The body of 6-week-old Cynthia Ruotolo, who was kidnapped Saturday from her carriage outside a village store here, was found today in a culvert of Lake Whitney, two miles from the store. Three boys who were fishing made the discovery. The body was wrapped in a transparent plastic bag and weighted with a rock.

The cause of death was not immediately established. The child apparently suffered a bruise on her head and appeared to have been in the water for several days, according to the police.

Mr. and Mrs. Stephen Ruotolo, the parents, live on New Road here. They have two other children, Gary, 8, and Susan, 20 months. Two others, a son and daughter, died in infancy. Mr. Ruotolo, 33 years old, is an $80-a-week salesman.

Mrs. Ruotolo, who is also 33, was taken to near-by New Haven late today for questioning. State Attorney Abraham S. Ullman said:

"I have just this statement to make: The baby has been positively identified by the mother."

Asked if anyone was in custody, he replied, "No." He then

Continued on Page 14, Column 6

Earth Peers at Mars, 35 Million Miles Away

Clues to Planet Are Sought on Closest Visit Since 1924

By ROBERT K. PLUMB

The great cosmic paths of Mars and the earth around the sun were closer last night than at any other time since 1924.

Plans for last night's observation of the planet had been made for many years. Observations from seventeen stations in ten nations were the climax of a series of studies of Mars extending over three weeks or more.

But overcast skies in the East last night and early today hid the planet from the naked eye.

The astronomers have concentrated on Mars as it neared, and they will follow it during the days and nights when it pulls away from the earth again as the two planets follow their eccentric orbits.

Elaborate plans have been made this year by an International Mars Committee to investigate dark markings and temperatures of the Martian surface, the intricate network of "canals," the motions of the satellites Phobos and Deimos, the diameter of Mars, and the possibility of vegetable life on the red planet.

The Mars committee was formed in 1954. That year Mars approached to within 40,000,000 miles of the earth. At its closest 1956 approach at 1 A. M., daylight time today the calculations showed, Mars should be about 35,120,000 miles from the earth.

During 1954, some 20,000 separate photographs of Mars were

Continued on Page 14, Column 3

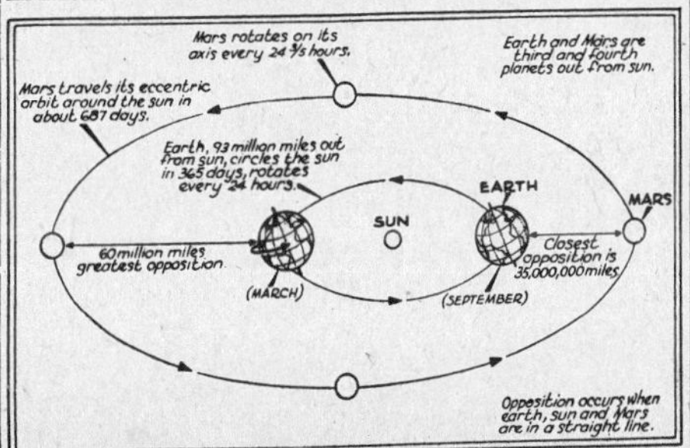

The New York Times (adapted from the National Geographic Magazine) Sept. 7, 1956

Earth and Mars, as they move around the sun, come to their closest point to each other (shown at extreme right of chart). Distances and sizes in diagram are grossly exaggerated.

View of the Qumran caves in the Judean Hills where the Dead Sea Scrolls were discovered in 1947.

"All the News That's Fit to Print"

The New York Times.

LATE CITY EDITION
Condensation of U. S. Weather Bureau forecast: Showers this afternoon, clearing and cooler tonight. Fair tomorrow.
Temperature range today: 80—68.
Temperature range yesterday: 87.2—68.4
Full U. S. Weather Bureau Report, Page 46.

VOL. CV . No. 35,923. Entered as Second-Class Matter, Post Office, New York, N. Y. NEW YORK, FRIDAY, JUNE 1, 1956. Times Square, New York 36, N. Y. Telephone Lackawanna 4-1000 FIVE CENTS

ARABS ASK CURBS IN U. N. PROPOSAL ON MIDEAST PEACE

Fight Plan for Hammarskjold to Continue Effort—Want Him to Avoid Peace Issues

SYRIA CHARGES 'POISON'

Settlement on a Mutual Basis Also Is Opposed — Israel Backs British Resolution

Excerpts from statements to the Security Council, Page 2.

By THOMAS J. HAMILTON
Special to The New York Times.

UNITED NATIONS, N. Y., May 31—Arab delegates hammered away today at a British resolution under which the Security Council would ask Dag Hammarskjold to "continue his good offices" in seeking a solution of the Palestine problem.

Egypt, Jordan, Syria and Lebanon concentrated their attack on two points.

One was the failure to state the exact authority to be granted to the United Nations Secretary General. They demanded that he should confine himself, as he did on his mission to the Middle East in April, to obtaining compliance with the Armistice Agreements, and should not take up issues involved in a peace settlement.

The other point to which they objected was the endorsement of a peace settlement "on a mutually acceptable basis." The Arab representatives charged that this would set up a new criterion and that the settlement must be made on the basis of United Nations decisions.

'Nothing But Poison'

Ahmed el-Shukairy of Syria went considerably farther than the other Arab representatives. He demanded the flat rejection of the resolution, which he said contained "nothing but poison, no matter how sugar-coated it may be."

Furthermore, he said that to obtain a settlement with Israel "we must begin from the beginning" and write off every United Nations resolution on Palestine since the partition resolution of Nov. 29, 1947.

"The establishment of Israel, its membership in the United Nations and all other resolutions will have to be revoked," he said. "Then, and only then, the United Nations can look forward to a solution on a 'mutually acceptable basis.'"

Mr. el-Shukairy and Abdel Monem Rifa'i of Jordan both said that, in addition to the United Nations decisions, the settlement must take into account the views of the "original inhabitants" of Palestine. In an earlier statement to the Council today, Mr. el-Shukairy said it was "common knowledge that Palestine is nothing but southern Syria."

The Arab delegates deferred their statements on the resolution until the afternoon in the hope that Sir Pierson Dixon, the British representative, who had already revised it once, would make further revisions to meet their objections.

Sir Pierson did not do so, but it was learned that he would make a statement to the Council tomorrow on the meaning of the

Continued on Page 2, Column 3

Dead Sea Scrolls Tell of Treasure

'Key' to Vast Riches Written on Copper Is Deciphered

By STANLEY ROWLAND Jr.

Two more Dead Sea scrolls have just been deciphered. They have surprised Biblical scholars by revealing clues to legendary buried treasure worth countless millions instead of dealing with Biblical subjects.

The information on the scrolls, found beside the Dead Sea in 1952, was announced yesterday by scholars in this country. The documents tell of hoards of fabulous value. If the treasure exists, it includes 200 tons of gold and silver.

Two hundred short tons of gold would be worth $204,000,000, based on present prices of $35 a troy ounce. Two hundred tons of silver would be worth $5,320,000, at present dealers' prices to manufacturers approximating 91 cents a troy ounce.

The announcement did not give the proportion of gold and silver. The weight estimates were computed by scholars in Jordan from amounts given in talents. Talents used to denote both weights and monetary amounts. In weight, a talent was 131.5 troy pounds.

Other treasure in the form of incense was also mentioned in the scrolls.

Scholars were quick to say that the treasure probably does not exist. So far, no way has been found to check the clues, because the topography of the land has changed since the first century A. D., when the scrolls were probably written. However, the

Continued on Page 21, Column 2

Courtesy of W. L. Reed The New York Times June 1, 1956

These scrolls, found in caves (cross on the map), tell of treasure buried in area between Nablus (1) and Hebron (2).

GRUENTHER SAYS SOVIET 'SMILES' MASK TRUE AIMS

Opposing Foreign Aid Cut, General Sees a 'Tougher' Future for NATO

By WILLIAM S. WHITE
Special to The New York Times.

WASHINGTON, May 31—Gen. Alfred M. Gruenther declared today that the Western alliance was approaching its supreme crisis in the face of dangerously powerful Soviet world propaganda.

He asserted that nothing the Russians had said or done in a new policy of "smiles, happy talk and receptions in the Kremlin" could justify the least reduction in United States assistance to the North Atlantic Treaty Organization.

On the contrary, NATO's supreme military commander stated, the next five years for that organization should be "tougher" because Soviet competition had become keener.

Thus, he said, NATO is in no sense "a community chest," for contributions to it are "simply contributions to our own survival."

General Gruenther testified as the final witness before the Senate Foreign Relations Committee in support of the full $4,900,000,000 authorization sought by President Eisenhower to carry forward and to extend the foreign aid program.

Several Democratic committee members described his presentation, which was made informally and without manuscript or notes, as the strongest and most persuasive yet heard in behalf of the Administration.

At the same time, John B. Hollister, head of the International Cooperation Administration, far less forcefully joined the Administration's effort to rescue the foreign aid bill from deep cuts recommended by the Foreign Affairs Committee of the House of Representatives.

Mr. Hollister told a news conference that the House committee's proposal for a $1,000,000,000 reduction in the $3,000,000,000 military aid aspect of the bill was "unfortunate."

He declined to apply to it such terms as "catastrophic" or "disastrous." He said, however, that such a cut would require a review of all current military planning.

He hit especially at a recom-

Continued on Page 8, Column 4

Associated Press Wirephoto

SUPPORTS FOREIGN AID PROGRAM: Gen. Alfred M. Gruenther, Supreme Allied Commander in Europe, testifying yesterday before Senate Foreign Relations Committee.

EISENHOWER FINDS NATION'S PRESTIGE AT POSTWAR PEAK

Says Policies Have Blunted Soviet Reliance on Force and Improved Outlook

UPHOLDS DULLES VIEWS

President Bids Citizens Unit Shun Complacency—He Hints Active Campaign

Transcript of remarks by the President is on Page 10.

By EDWIN L. DALE Jr.
Special to The New York Times.

WASHINGTON, May 31—President Eisenhower said today that "certainly the prestige of the United States since the last World War has never been as high as it is this day."

The three leading Democratic aspirants for President have charged the opposite repeatedly. Adlai E. Stevenson, Senator Estes Kefauver and Governor Harriman have said that United States world prestige and influence are declining.

Thus the President, addressing the campaign conference of the National Citizens for Eisenhower organization, crystallized a major campaign issue. He backed whole-heartedly the thesis of John Foster Dulles, his Secretary of State, that the world situation had improved and that policy shifts by the Soviet Union had helped to prove this.

The President cited the fact that "we have largely nullified [the Soviet Union's] reliance upon force and threat of force." The proof of this change, he said, is the fact that "it has gone to different kinds of influence."

He Decries 'Complacency'

The President touched on a variety of subjects in his extemporaneous fifteen-minute address. His main point was that "complacency" could not be afforded in the coming campaign.

Of his health, he said that the only way he knew now that he had been ill "is because the doctors keep reminding me of it." He hinted at a vigorous campaign. He said he would work to attain the goals of his Administration "as cheerfully, as energetically, as enthusiastically as it is possible for me to do."

But his remarks on foreign policy are likely to prove the most contentious.

Another evidence of over-all improvement in the world, he said, is that Soviet leaders "are more concerned with development of consumer goods, more concerned with the status and the frame of mind of the people." He noted that it now was possible for a Russian laboring man to change his job without official permission and said this "means progress."

The President conceded that "the goals we have set for ourselves have not been reached," either domestically or internationally. But he emphasized that "progress has been made."

In further defense of his foreign policy, General Eisenhower emphasized that "America has preserved its position as the friend of all." He said "we have not been drawn into the position of being so completely on one side of a quarrel—any quarrel—due to emotion or sentiment or anything else that we are in-

Continued on Page 10, Column 3

MOLLET CRITICIZED IN AFRICAN DEBATE

Some Chamber Speakers Say Program Is Too Liberal—Others Hold It Too Rigid

By ROBERT C. DOTY
Special to The New York Times.

PARIS, May 31—Premier Guy Mollet was caught between two fires today. On one side of him were those who thought his North African policy too liberal; on the other, those for whom it was not liberal enough.

At the opening of a crucial three-day debate in the National Assembly on general government policy, moderate and conservative spokesmen attacked the Government for alleged abandonment of essential French interests in Morocco and Tunisia.

From the other side of the Chamber, Pierre Cot, an ally of the Communists and one of the ablest orators in Parliament, urged the Government to abandon what he considered the policy of force in dealing with the Moslem rebellion in Algeria for one of negotiation. He warmly approved the Government's grant of independence to the former French protectorates of Morocco and Tunisia.

Despite these diametrically opposed views, there was little doubt that the Assembly would, in the end, give the Left-of-Center Mollet Cabinet a decisive vote of confidence on its general conduct of the nation's business. This result was expected because neither the conservative forces nor those of the extreme Left were strong enough to govern without the Socialists.

There were few surprises in the Right Wing strictures against the Government's policy in the protectorates. Jacques Isorni, an Independent, traced France's present difficulties there to the dramatic journey to Tunisia in July, 1954, by Pierre Mendès-France, who was then Premier.

M. Isorni said this, following upon what he called "abandonment" of Indochina by the Mendès-France Government, had been interpreted in North Africa as a sign of weakness.

He and other speakers expressed concern for the fate of

Continued on Page 3, Column 2

Export Guarantees In World Aid Plan Studied by Traders

By ARTHUR J. OLSEN
Special to The New York Times.

HAMBURG, Germany, May 31—International trading circles here are discussing the concept of a guaranteed export market. The idea is to substitute such a market for grants of aid and thus provide a potential answer to the long-term economic needs of underdeveloped countries.

The novel aid plan would have somewhat the character of a world-wide system of international commodity agreements. The single "commodity" subjected to international guarantees, however, would not be any one product but money.

Still in a theoretical stage, the new approach to the world economic development problem is undergoing scrutiny in the business community of this booming port city. Once a major terminal of European-Asian commerce, Hamburg has a profund stake in the re-establishment of its trading links with the East.

Advocates of the new approach would toss aside as inadequate and partly self-defeating all direct economic and financial aid now provided to underdeveloped

Continued on Page 6, Column 4

KOREA EXPULSION TIED TO REDS' BID

U. S. Used Peiping Request for Unity Talks to Effect Ouster of Neutral Units

Chinese and British notes and U. N. statement, Page 4.

By DANA ADAMS SCHMIDT
Special to The New York Times.

WASHINGTON, May 31—The United States used the Chinese Communists' "purely propagandistic" bid for new talks on Korea to win support for expelling the neutral inspection teams from South Korea.

Since 1954 the United States has wished to get these teams out of South Korea. Early today the United Nations Command ordered the six groups to leave on the ground that their Czechoslovak and Polish members had frustrated and distorted the operation of the armistice. The order was reported in late editions of The New York Times this morning.

When the Chinese proposal was received April 11, diplomats reported, the United States began a series of meetings at the

Continued on Page 4, Column 2

Soil Bank to Pay This Year For Crops Plowed Under

By JOHN D. MORRIS
Special to The New York Times.

WASHINGTON, May 31—Ezra Taft Benson, Secretary of Agriculture, put the new $1,200,000,000 soil bank into business on a limited scale today. He announced that "generous" payments would be available immediately to farmers who agree to withdraw land this year from production of cotton, wheat, corn, rice, peanuts and tobacco.

To qualify, farmers must reduce acreage planted to these "basic" crops below their Federal allotments. The aim of the soil bank is to discourage production of surplus commodities and bolster lagging farm prices and income.

Secretary Benson said farmers would be permitted to qualify by plowing under crops that "are not too far advanced." Payments also will be available in the relatively few cases where planting has not started.

[Prices received by farmers for their products increased 3 per cent between mid-April and mid-May, the Department of Agriculture reported. Details on Page 29.]

Some Pre-Election Benefits

The soil bank was the central feature of a compromise farm bill signed by President Eisenhower on Monday.

The measure directed the Secretary to put the bank into operation this year on land withdrawn from production of 1956 crops. But Congress denied the President's request for authority to make advance payments for 1957 withdrawals.

Secretary Benson had previously opposed a "plow-under" program. He told a news conference today, however, that there was "probably some justification for it," since farmers were not responsible for the delay in enacting the farm bill.

He said he could not estimate how many farmers would choose to participate or how much money would be spent this year.

Mr. Benson said the 1956 program was "designed to meet the time emergency," in view of the fact that most crops already had been planted. It will not be a fair test of the soil bank's effectiveness, he added.

It appeared likely that any pre-election benefits would be concentrated in the midwestern

Continued on Page 12, Column 6

MOSES BERATES 2 SLUM CLEARERS

Tells Developers of N. Y. U. Projects to Move Faster or Give Up Contracts

By CHARLES GRUTZNER

Robert Moses, impatient of delays on two slum clearance sites, will serve notice today on the developers to move faster or surrender their contracts.

The developers, beneficiaries of Federal and city subsidies totaling more than $18,000,000 in acquisition of the two sites, are the Washington Square Village Corporation and University Center, Inc.

The former has the contract for housing, a shopping center and expansion of New York University on 17.46 acres southeast of Washington Square. The University Center has the contract for the 9.44-acre New York University-Bellevue project from First to Second Avenue between Thirtieth and Thirty-third Streets.

Both projects have conventional mortgage financing and cannot, therefore, blame the Federal Government for their delays. Mr. Moses, as chairman of the Mayor's Committee on Slum Clearance, had replied last week to criticisms of construction delay on other slum clearance projects by saying the Federal Housing Administration was holding up mortgage insurance commitments to project sponsors.

City and U. S. Defray Costs

Mr. Moses expressed his impatience of the Washington Square Southeast and N. Y. U.-Bellevue project sponsors yesterday in the course of an inspection tour of a dozen Title I urban renewal projects in lower Manhattan.

Under Title I of the Federal Housing Act, the city acquires slum properties and sells them at a fraction of their cost to private developers, with the Federal Government paying two-thirds and the city one-third of the price difference.

It was 3:50 P. M. when Mr. Moses and a group of key assistants paused in front of a loft building on Wooster Street, where demolition had begun for the Washington Square Southeast project. The building dozed in the afternoon heat and there was no sound or sight of activity. The only employe of the wrecking company on the scene sat on a wooden box outside the building, a half empty quart beer bottle beside him.

"What sort of holiday is this supposed to be?" demanded Mr. Moses, walking up to the seated man.

"No holiday," was the reply. "I'm the watchman. Work stops at half past 3. Seven-hour day."

Mr. Moses counted up and down the street, the only one on which demolition had begun. Three small buildings down, and the razing of a larger one just begun. The city had turned over the property last October to the

Continued on Page 26, Column 5

Queen Takes Guards' Salute at Trooping the Color

Associated Press Radiophoto

Queen Elizabeth II takes the salute as the Grenadier Guards pass in review at Trooping the Color. At right is the Duke of Edinburgh and at left is Col. Sir Thomas Butler, commanding.

Special to The New York Times.

LONDON, May 31—The Queen and her people joined today to honor their past in the ancient, elaborate ceremonial of Trooping the Color. Riding side-saddle on Winston, a placid former police horse, Queen Elizabeth was the center of a faultless military pageant on the Horse Guards Parade. But, like her subjects and soldiers around her, the Queen was paying tribute to a rectangle of red silk heavily embroidered in gold. This was the color of the Third Battalion of the Grenadier Guards. The battle honors on it symbolized battles fought at long odds from Tangier in 1680 to Germany in 1945. There were 1,664 men and sixty-seven

Continued on Page 5, Column 7

Soviet Chiefs Bar Dancers' Visit Until U. S. Ends Fingerprinting

By JACK RAYMOND
Special to The New York Times.

MOSCOW, May 31—The three top men of the Soviet Union emphatically asserted today that no citizens of their country would go to the United States if they were forced to be fingerprinted.

They were discussing the United States law in connection with plans for the trip to the United States of the Moiseyev folk dance ensemble and other large Soviet cultural groups.

The attitude of the Soviet chiefs appeared to rule out definitely the scheduled performances of the Moiseyev troupe, which is due to leave for New York in the fall, unless the law is changed.

United States sources here disclosed that the Soviet Government had been informed that ninety members of the famous Soviet dance group could not be considered as official Government representatives.

According to United States law some Soviet citizens have been permitted to enter with documentation as official representatives. This has applied to entertainers, churchmen and small delegations.

However, United States officials told Soviet Embassy representatives in Washington, it became known here, that the size of the dance troupe precluded official status for all. They therefore would have to comply with fingerprinting regulations.

Soviet sources have complained about United States regulations on fingerprinting in the past. Definitive policy was made clear by Premier Nikolai A. Bulganin, Nikita S. Khrushchev, Soviet Communist party chief, and Vyacheslav M. Molotov, Foreign Minister, at a re-

Continued on Page 6, Column 4

450 New Cars Due For East Side IRT

By STANLEY LEVEY

The Transit Authority announced yesterday it was accelerating its IRT Division modernization program.

Charles L. Patterson, the authority's chairman, said earlier plans to purchase 250 subway cars for the East Side IRT line had been changed and that the order would be for 450 cars. This means an expenditure of $52,500,000 instead of $27,650,000.

Bids for the new cars will be sought early next month and contracts will be let in September. Delivery of the equipment—some of which may be air conditioned—will be completed in the spring of 1958, Mr. Patterson said.

The increased order is the third stage in the IRT modernization plan. The delivery of one earlier order of 400 cars will be completed in Sep-

Continued on Page 47, Column 2

Business Men Join To Back Harriman

By LEO EGAN

The president of the National Urban League announced yesterday the formation of a business men's committee to promote Governor Harriman's nomination for President.

Robert W. Dowling, who heads the league, is also president of the City Investing Company and the Citizens Budget Commission, Inc., of New York City. He will head the new Business Men for Harriman Committee.

His announcement signalized the start of an intensified pre-convention campaign on Mr. Harriman's behalf. Apparently it will stress the Governor's position on civil rights, particularly the integration of Negroes and whites in the public schools, and his efforts to encourage and stimulate small business.

Mr. Dowling said that, as president of the National Urban

Continued on Page 12, Column 1

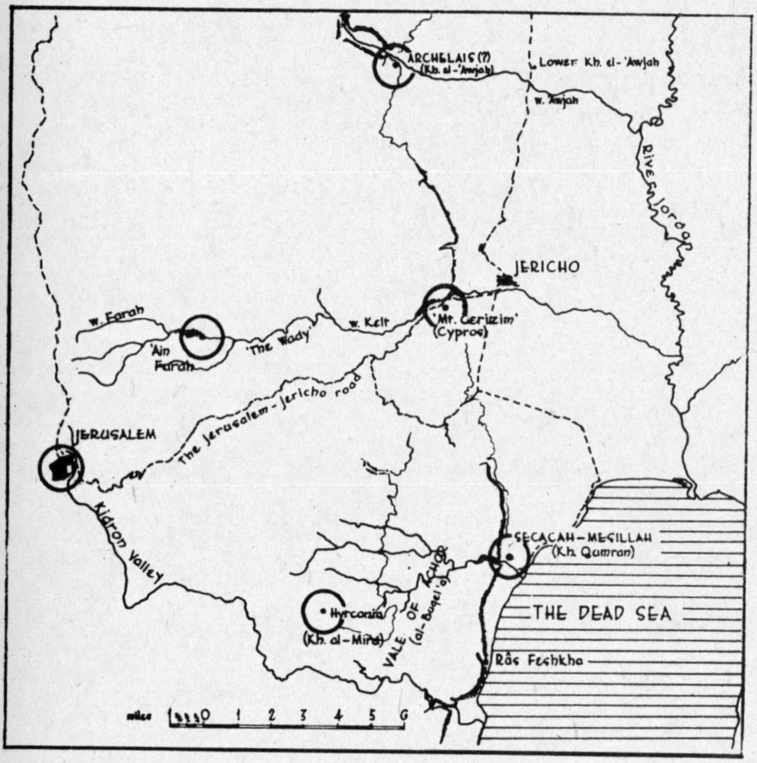

Qumran and the possible hiding places of the treasure of the Copper Scroll. This map shows the relation of Jerusalem, Jericho, the northern end of the Dead Sea and Khirbet Qumran.

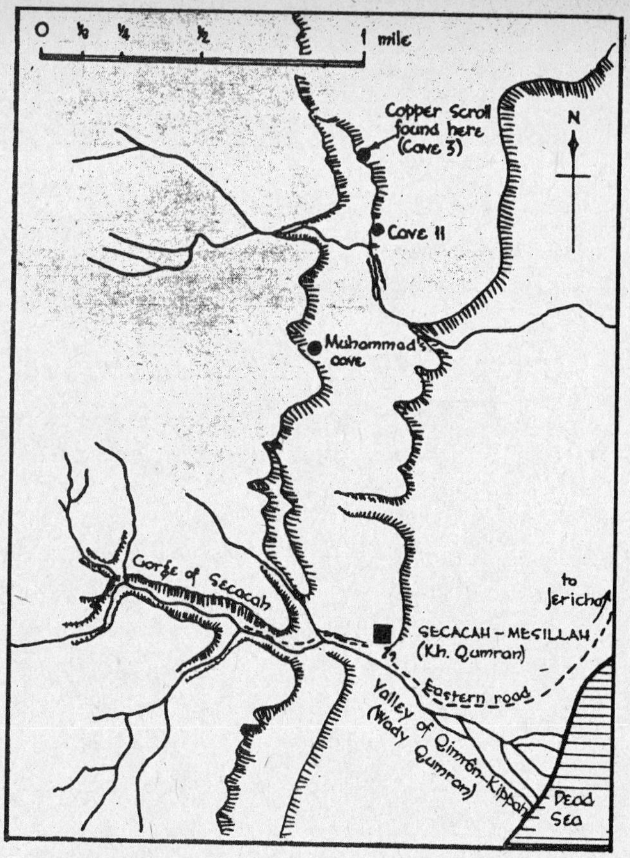

Qumran and the immediate neighborhood, showing Muhammad's Cave where the first Dead Sea Scrolls were found, and Cave III, where the Copper Scroll was found.

A plan of the Temple in Jerusalem, with the Kidron Valley to the east and the group of rock-cut tombs, including that of Zadok, which may possibly be that in which Christ was buried.

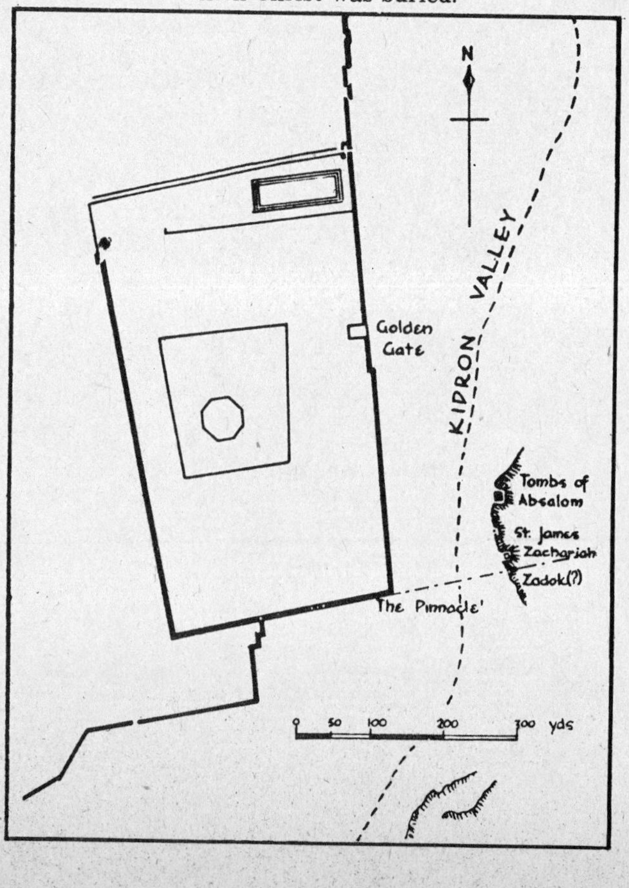

"All the News That's Fit to Print"

The New York Times.

LATE CITY EDITION
Sunny and warm today. Fair and warm tomorrow.
Temperatures Yesterday—Max., 72; Min., 48
Sunrise today, 5:54 A. M.; Sunset, 5:55 P. M.
Full U. S. Weather Bureau Report, Page 39

VOL. CVI..No. 36,040. Entered as Second-Class Matter, Post Office, New York, N. Y. NEW YORK, WEDNESDAY, SEPTEMBER 26, 1956. Times Square, New York 36, N. Y. Telephone LAckawanna 4-1000 FIVE CENTS

ISRAELIS KILL 50 IN REPRISAL RAIDS ON JORDAN POSTS

BASE IS BLOWN UP

Attackers Take Booty —Charge Pledge to U.N. Was Broker

By JOSEPH O. HAFF
Special to The New York Times.

TEL AVIV, Israel, Wednesday, Sept. 26—The Israeli Army announced early today that its troops had raided several Jordanian Army posts and a police station.

About fifty Jordanian policemen and soldiers were killed, a spokesman said. The police station, at Husan, was blown up.

The action, according to a United Nations truce team source, started shortly after 10 o'clock last night southwest of Jerusalem, not far from the scene of last Sunday's attack by Jordanian soldiers on a meeting of Israeli archaeologists. In that attack four persons were fatally injured and seventeen others hurt.

United Nations personnel, at their headquarters in the "no man's land" between Jerusalem's New and Old Cities, could still hear firing and other sounds of action at about 3 A. M. today.

[The announcement of the raids by an Israeli spokesman was unusual, the recent disclosures of Israeli raids having come from Arab sources.]

2 Armored Cars Set Afire

A communiqué issued shortly after 5:30 A. M. said:

"Several Jordan Army posts, including a company stronghold in the Husan area, were attacked and taken tonight by an Israeli Army unit.

"The Husan police station also was taken and blown up.

"Two enemy armored cars were set afire, and the enemy suffered approximately fifty killed.

"After accomplishing the task, our forces returned to their bases.

"Booty, including cars, heavy mortars, machine guns and rifles were brought back.

"This attack was carried out after Jordan soldiers killed four Israeli citizens in a murderous attack at Ramat Rachel, killed a woman in the vicinity of Moshav Aminadav and kidnapped and murdered a tractor driver of the kibbutz [settlement] Maoz Haim in the past three days."

Also referring to these raids and to the attack on the archaeologist's meeting, an Israeli

Continued on Page 3, Column 5

Brooks, Braves Win; No-Hitter by Maglie

Associated Press
Sal Maglie

The Brooklyn Dodgers remained a half-game behind the league-leading Braves as Sal Maglie defeated the Philadelphia Phils, 5—0, with a no-hitter at Ebbets Field last night. Milwaukee beat the Redlegs, 7—1, yesterday afternoon at Cincinnati as Warren Spahn hurled his twentieth victory.

The Redlegs were virtually eliminated from the pennant race. With three games to play, the Braves have won ninety-one and lost sixty contests. The Dodgers, with four games remaining on the schedule, have won ninetv and lost sixty.

Details on Page 37.

ANTARCTIC HEADS APPOINTED BY U.S.

Siple to Command Station at South Pole—3 Other Scientists Selected

By WALTER SULLIVAN

The United States has selected four scientist-explorers to head its outposts in Antarctica during the International Geophysical Year, 1957 to 1958.

The leader of the station to be airlifted to the South Pole will be Dr. Paul A. Siple, who first won fame when he went to Little America in 1929 as a Boy Scout. Dr. Siple has specialized in polar problems ever since and has accompanied almost all United States expeditions to Antarctica.

The scientific party at Little America V will be led by Dr. Albert Crary, a geophysicist who, in 1955, led a party that established a camp on T-3, a floating ice island in the Arctic.

The leader of the party to be set ashore in Vincennes Bay, near the junction of the Knox and Budd Coasts, will be Dr. Carl Eklund. He is perhaps best known for a memorable sledging journey he made in 1940-41 with Capt. Finn Ronne. Their 1,260-mile trek demonstrated that Alexander Island was in fact an immense island.

Ronne to Command Post

Captain Ronne, who is now on active duty in the Naval Reserve, will command the station on the Weddell Sea coast. On his last venture to Antarctica he led his own expedition to Stonington Island on the opposite side of Palmer Peninsula from the Weddell Sea.

The Pole station is expected to subject its occupants to conditions never before experienced by human beings. Only in one season—that of 1911-12—have men set foot at this remote point at the bottom of the world. They were the parties of Capt. Robert F. Scott of Britain and Roald Amundsen of Norway.

Since then several flights have been made over the Pole, but the conditions to be expected there during the six-month polar night can only be speculated upon.

Dr. Siple is also serving as deputy to Rear Admiral Richard E. Byrd, who is in charge of the United States Antarctic program. Dr. Siple has been lent for that job by the Army, where he is scientific adviser to the Chief of Research in the office of the Deputy Chief of Staff for Research and Development.

His party at the Pole will con-

Continued on Page 16, Column 4

PROCEDURAL FIGHT DUE IN U. N. TODAY ON CAIRO PROTEST

France to Oppose Inclusion on Agenda of Council—U.S. Holds Key to Suez Vote

By THOMAS J. HAMILTON
Special to The New York Times.

UNITED NATIONS, N. Y., Sept. 25—The Security Council's debate on the Suez question will open tomorrow with a procedural fight.

Although the final British position was not disclosed, France announced that she would vote against the inclusion on the agenda of the Egyptian version of the dispute.

The Egyptian counter-protest, submitted yesterday, accused Britain and France, together with some unidentified states, of actions threatening international peace and security and violating the Charter of the United Nations.

Bernard Cornut-Gentille, the new French representative, said to newspaper men today that "we definitely cannot accept" the charge of violation of the Charter.

British Opposition Seen

British spokesmen here and in London protested against the allegation. Therefore most United Nations delegates assumed that Britain, having taken the lead in bringing the Suez issue to the Security Council, also would vote against acceptance of the Egyptian counter-protest.

[Top leaders of the French and British Governments will confer in Paris Wednesday on the future course they will follow in the Suez crisis. Christian Pineau, French Foreign Minister, said the two nations would ask the Security Council to approve international operation of the canal.]

The British spokesman here contended that the wording of the Suez complaint, as submitted by Britain and France Sunday, was entirely objective. This accused Egypt of "unilateral action" in ending international operation of the canal, and asserted that this had been "confirmed and strengthened" by the Constantinople Convention of 1888, guaranteeing free passage to the ships of all nations.

Veto May Not Be Used

The Charter forbids the use of the veto on such decisions. The question tonight was whether Egypt, which is not a member, would get the seven votes necessary to include the item as a subheading under the general item, "The Suez Question."

The necessary majority for inclusion of the British-French item seemed to be assured, but the position of the United States may determine the fate of the Egyptian item.

After a day of strenuous diplomatic activity it appeared that Belgium and Australia, the most determined supporters of the British-French complaint, either would vote against the Egyptian request or abstain. An abstention would have the same effect as a vote against, since the Charter requires the affirmative votes

Continued on Page 2, Column 3

PIER UNION OFFERS TO DELAY STRIKE ON 2 CONDITIONS

Asks Retroactivity to Oct. 1 and Coast-Wide Accord for Month of Peace

By JACQUES NEVARD

The International Longshoremen's Association yesterday made a qualified offer of peace on the New York waterfront until Nov. 1.

The qualifications were designed to support the unaffiliated union's demand that current port-by-port contracts be replaced by some form of master accord for the entire Atlantic and Gulf Coast.

The union set two conditions as its price for extending by one month contracts scheduled to expire at midnight Sunday.

It asked the New York Shipping Association, which represents ship lines and contracting stevedores in the Port of New York and vicinity, to agree that any increases in wages and welfare payments be made retroactive to Oct. 1. Then the union said that, unless every Atlantic and Gulf employer organization agreed to similar retroactivity, "the deal is off."

2 Pleas Made to Union

That was the union's response to urgent pleas by Federal and city officials to keep the port operating until after a new waterfront jurisdictional election, to be held by Oct. 24.

The I. L. A. faces the third attempt by the International Brotherhood of Longshoremen, A. F. L.-C. I. O., to unseat it as bargaining agent for New York dockers. The brotherhood, which was chartered in 1953 by the former American Federation of Labor after the old union was expelled, failed in two previous elections.

Alexander P. Chopin, chairman of the New York Shipping Association, said that a committee of his organization would meet with I. L. A. representatives at 2:30 o'clock this afternoon. He said he could give no indication of the reception that awaits the union proposal because "any decision on retroactivity must be made by the conference committee."

'Outpost' Action Awaited

Employer associations in the other East and Gulf port areas have not yet responded to the union's demand that they, too, agree to retroactive wage and welfare payment increases. Their contracts, like those in New York, will expire on Sunday. In the past negotiations the "outports" have delayed settlements pending a New York agreement.

The union's decision to make a conditional acceptance of the no-strike pledge was taken at a closed meeting of its 200-member wage-scale committee in the Governor Clinton Hotel. Patrick J. Connolly, executive vice president, later handed out a typed statement of the terms after they had been sent to Mr. Chopin.

The statement did not include any reference to the other Atlantic and Gulf ports. Mr. Connolly added that in an interview later. He said the union's vice presidents from the other ports

Continued on Page 24, Column 4

EISENHOWER IN FARM TALK SCORES FOES' PLAN AS 'DECEIT AND MOCKERY'; STEVENSON ASSAILS FOREIGN POLICY

PERON CASE CITED

Democrat Is Critical of Milton Eisenhower in Latin Moves

Texts of Stevenson speeches will be found on Page 23.

By HARRISON E. SALISBURY
Special to The New York Times.

MIAMI, Fla., Sept. 25—Adlai E. Stevenson delivered tonight a frontal attack upon the Administration's foreign policy. He charged it had appeased Juan D. Perón in Argentina and encouraged Middle Eastern nations "to be ugly and threatening and to flirt with communism."

One of the principal targets of Mr. Stevenson's attacks as an architect and agent of Administration foreign policy in Latin America was Milton S. Eisenhower, brother of the President.

The Democratic nominee charged that Middle Eastern policy "is all too much of a piece" with the United States policy toward Perón in Argentina. He called the Administration's policy toward Perón "morally, politically and economically" off the track.

Perón was overthrown as President in a revolution last year.

Attitude Toward Perón Scored

Mr. Stevenson charged that "a member of the President's personal family" had assumed special responsibility for American policy toward Perón and that the United States had kept an Ambassador in Buenos Aires "because Perón liked him.

Roger Tubby, a Stevenson press representative, identified the "member of the President's family" as Dr. Eisenhower and the ambassador as Albert F. Nufer.

[The Associated Press reached Dr. Eisenhower at his Pennsylvania State University residence in Centre County, Pa. Dr. Eisenhower declined to comment on Mr. Stevenson's statements. He is president of the university, a post he will leave Monday to become head of Johns Hopkins University in Baltimore.]

Earlier Mr. Stevenson won applause in Little Rock, Ark., when he asked his audience, "as law-abiding citizens," to accept the Supreme Court decision for public school integration.

Later, speaking at City Hall in New Orleans, Mr. Stevenson charged that President Eisenhower had failed to remake the Republican party. He suggested that the party, instead, had "reshaped" the President.

In the original text of his address here Mr. Stevenson also included a charge that a "major accomplishment" of the Ambas-

Continued on Page 23, Column 3

Associated Press Wirephoto

STUBBORN CAMPAIGNER: Vice President Nixon, ill with a virus infection, pursued his campaign into the Southwest. He is shown in plane on way to Oklahoma City.

Kefauver Stresses Charge G.O.P. Aids Only Big Interests

By RICHARD AMPER
Special to The New York Times.

GRAND RAPIDS, Mich., Sept. 25 — Senator Estes Kefauver traveled 1,000 miles today in an attempt to swing Michigan to the Democratic cause. He pressed his party's charge that the Republicans served only big money interests.

"Over and over again the Eisenhower Administration has demonstrated that its heart does not lie with the plain ordinary citizen of America," went the theme of the Democratic Vice-Presidential candidate.

And over and over again he sounded it to the iron ore miner, farmer and small business man.

The Senator made a plane and auto tour across the upper Michigan peninsula through the furniture-making center of Grand Rapids in the midwestern part of the state.

He got as close to the grass roots as a mole, visiting such whistle-stop towns as Rudyard, with only several hundred population and Grand Rapids, with 200,000.

He brought to the little ore mining community of Ironwood in the extreme western part of the upper peninsula a sample of an era of campaigning that had passed it by.

The television age caught

Continued on Page 22, Column 6

NIXON, HIT BY 'FLU,' CONTINUES DRIVE

Both He and Wife Speak In Oklahoma City—Demand by Reuther Rejected

By WILLIAM M. BLAIR
Special to The New York Times.

HOUSTON, Tex., Sept. 25—Fighting a virus infection, Vice President Richard M. Nixon vetoed today his physician's advice against carrying his arduous campaign into the Southwest.

Although Dr. Malcolm C. Todd urged that he cancel his speech at Oklahoma City before flying into Texas, Mr. Nixon spoke for sixteen minutes to Oklahoma Republicans and pressed into service his wife Patricia. She made a brief political speech in his behalf.

Despite his ailment of virus influenza coupled with laryngitis, Mr. Nixon drafted and sent a rejection to a demand by Walter P. Reuther, president of the United Automobile Workers, that he commit himself and the Republican party to back legislation to gain a four-day work week.

"Mere artificial legislation will not accomplish" the task of gaining a four-day work week or a fuller life for Americans, Mr. Nixon wired the labor leader.

Joint Effort Called Need

The task, he went on, "is one that calls for the dedicated joint efforts of labor, management, government and research."

Mr. Nixon foresaw the four-day week and a life for Americans free of hard toil in a speech Saturday night in Colorado Springs.

In his telegram, the Vice President thanked Mr. Reuther "for your confidence in the Eisenhower ticket as evidenced by your assumption that President Eisenhower will be re-elected and the Republicans will organize the Congress in January, 1957."

Early this morning, as he prepared to fly to Oklahoma City, Mr. Nixon told newsmen that it was one of the "toughest times" in his career of public speaking.

"I thought I couldn't make it about half way through the speech," he commented in a husky voice.

Since leaving Colorado Springs Monday morning, he has been under constant treatment by Dr. Todd to stave off the illness. Dr. Todd said he was giving Mr. Nixon several kinds of medication, including antihistamines for a chronic hay fever condition and sedatives.

Mr. Nixon's effort to cover thirty-two states and 15,000 miles in fifteen days as the principal G. O. P. campaigner has

Continued on Page 21, Column 4

PEORIA BID SHARP

President Lays Farm Lag to Democrats—Predicts Upturn

Text of Eisenhower's speech is printed on Page 20.

By RUSSELL BAKER
Special to The New York Times.

PEORIA, Ill., Sept. 25—President Eisenhower assailed Adlai E. Stevenson's farm program tonight as a "mockery and deceit" for the farmer.

He told a nation-wide television and radio audience that the high, rigid price-support program endorsed by Mr. Stevenson was "a program for politicians, not farmers."

Making his major plea for the big Midwestern farm vote, the President pledged instead to continue his controversial flexible support policy.

He offered no innovations and no changes in the Administration farm program as it existed despite sharp Democratic criticism and polls indicating political unrest among farm voters.

Instead, he attempted to rebut Democratic criticism: to paint a bright picture of the present farm situation and to offer farmers more hope of "brighter peacetime prospects than they had had in years."

'Better Times' Seen

Thus he took sharp issue with Mr. Stevenson's contention that the Eisenhower Administration had produced a "farm depression." His speech was studded with optimistic phrases about the farm future and hard-bitten words for the Democratic opposition

This, the President's second major campaign address, predicted "better times for every farmer." The President asserted that his Administration had made a "good start" at solving the farm problem. His Administration has turned farm prices "back up without a war," he said.

"The toughest problems are giving way," he said. "The facts show good progress."

He blamed the Democrats' high, rigid price-support program for starting the price decline that began during the Korean war. He accused them of treating the farmer with "political expediency," of "politicking" at the farmer's expense and of a "fast-talking, slow-

Continued on Page 21, Column 1

STOCKHOLM IS PUT 19 MILES OFF LANE

Route Not Compulsory for the Liner, Lawyer Says

By RUSSELL PORTER

The eastbound Swedish liner Stockholm was about nineteen and one-half miles north of an eastbound lane provisionally recommended by the United States Government when she rammed the Italian liner Andrea Doria. This was conceded yesterday by the Stockholm's third mate, 26-year-old Ernst Carstens-Johannsen, who was in command of her bridge at the time of the collision.

The crash took place off Nantucket at 11:09 P. M. on July 25. Fifty lives were lost, mostly on the Doria. She sank the next day, but the Stockholm, her bow crumpled, returned to New York with more than 500 Doria survivors.

The Stockholm's third mate testified at pre-trial proceedings in Federal Court. Eugene Underwood of counsel for the Italian Line cross-examined him about a handbook for mariners issued by the United States Coast and Geodetic Survey.

When the witness testified that the Stockholm carried a copy of this book on its bridge, the lawyer quoted from its chapter on "routes and sailing directions — North Atlantic lane routes" as follows:

"The practice of following recognized routes across the

Continued on Page 42, Column 3

THIRD POLISH MIG FLIES TO DENMARK

Pilot Lands on Bornholm and Asks for Asylum

Special to The New York Times.

COPENHAGEN, Denmark, Sept. 25—Another Polish pilot has used the small Danish island of Bornholm in the Baltic to make good his escape from behind the Iron Curtain. He crash-landed his Soviet-built MIG-15 at the civil airport at the island's chief town of Ronne early today.

The pilot, who was unhurt, asked to be handed over to Danish authorities and demanded political asylum. He said he had escaped from a Polish air base. He showed a map indicating that the Ronne airport was equipped with a concrete runway. However, this is not yet finished.

The pilot, who was flown to Copenhagen for questioning, explained that he had broken away from a formation flight and dropped auxiliary fuel tanks to lighten his plane. He added that he reached Bornholm after a 20-to-25-minute flight and that he had been neither shot at nor pursued.

Danish Air Force specialists dismantled the plane, which will be taken to Copenhagen for further examination. It was said that the plane was fitted with extra radar equipment for all-weather flights.

Two Polish MIG-15's escaped to

Continued on Page 13, Column 4

First Call Made by Phone Cable to Europe

Line's Capacity Is 3 Times as Great as Radiotelephone's

By HOMER BIGART

The first telephone cable between North America and Europe was opened yesterday with ceremonies in New York, London and Ottawa.

Conversations were distinct and even, in contrast to the fading often experienced on radiotelephone. The $42,000,000 trans-Atlantic cable system, which took more than two years to build, can carry thirty-six voice messages at one time, about three times the traffic that radiotelephone circuits now transmit to Europe.

Cleo Frank Craig, chairman of the board of the American Telephone and Telegraph Company, picked up an ordinary black telephone in New York shortly after 11 A. M. and exchanged greetings with Her Majesty's Postmaster General, who was using an ivory white telephone in London.

"This is Cleo Craig in New York calling Dr. Charles Hill in London," he said.

For a fleeting but painful moment there was no answering voice. Mr. Craig repeated his signal.

Then: "Hello . . . Hello . . . This is Dr. Hill in London."

Dr. Hill came in clear and strong, as distinct as his accent would allow.

Their voices traversed the floor of the Atlantic on twin cables stretching 2,250 miles

Continued on Page 18, Column 3

The New York Times

Cleo F. Craig, chairman of American Telephone and Telegraph Company, making call to London and Ottawa. With him at ceremony were George C. McConnaughey, left, head of Federal Communications Commission, and Frederick R. Kappel, president of A. T. & T.

"All the News That's Fit to Print"

The New York Times

LATE CITY EDITION
Condensation of U. S. Weather Bureau forecast:
Sunny and pleasant today.
Fair and warmer tomorrow.
Temperature range today: 76—62.
Temperature range yesterday: 76—63.2.
Full U. S. Weather Bureau Report, Page 30.

VOL. CV..No. 36,008. Entered as Second-Class Matter, Post Office, New York, N. Y. NEW YORK, SATURDAY, AUGUST 25, 1956. Times Square, New York 36, N. Y. Telephone LAckawanna 4-1000 FIVE CENTS

HALL CALLS PERIL OF COMPLACENCY WORST G.O.P. FOE

Fixes Sept. 15 for the Start of Campaign, With Nixon Making First Trip

SEES A 'VIGOROUS' DRIVE

Chairman Says Eisenhower May Fly to Speak but Will Rule Out Whistle-Stops

By LAWRENCE E. DAVIES
Special to The New York Times.

SAN FRANCISCO, Aug. 24—The Republican National Chairman today fixed Sept. 15 for the probable start of the Presidential campaign. He also warned that "complacency" was the party's greatest enemy.

Leonard W. Hall, retained by President Eisenhower and the National Committee yesterday to direct the 1956 drive, indicated that his confidence in a victory was marred only by possible overconfidence among party workers.

Mr. Hall appeared at a news conference while thousands of delegates, alternates and visitors to the Republican National Convention were pouring out of the city by plane, train and automobile.

President Eisenhower was at the Cypress Point Golf Club on the Monterey Peninsula. Vice President Richard M. Nixon was back at the bedside of his stricken father, Francis A. Nixon, near Los Angeles.

Mr. Hall indicated that Vice President Nixon would begin his first campaign trip around mid-September. He said Mr. Nixon could be expected to wage a "vigorous" type of vote drive. He would not rule out the possibility of a whistle-stop campaign, through use of a train, by the Vice President, although the airplane certainly would be employed to a great extent.

Whistle-Stop Drive Out

The national chairman had had no opportunity, he said, to confer with President Eisenhower since his own re-nomination yesterday.

When it was suggested to Mr. Hall that the President might extend his campaign activities because of anger over attacks by the Democrats at Chicago last week, the chairman replied:

"He will make several nation-wide television speeches but will wage no whistle-stop campaign. That's all I can say at the present time. Except that I wouldn't rule out the possibility that he will fly out of Washington for some of the speeches."

Mr. Hall was reminded that he had said earlier in the week that the President would do as well against Adlai E. Stevenson, the Democratic nominee, this fall as in 1952, yet he had pledged the party yesterday to carry on the "toughest campaign" in its history.

Did this mean the Republicans were slipping?

"No," the chairman replied. "I hope every worker in the precincts will look on it as a tough campaign." He added that it was essential to get out the votes.

Was there any of the 1948 psychology present?

"I don't want it there," he said. "Our greatest enemy is complacency."

Would the Republicans con-

Continued on Page 6, Column 4

Eisenhower Plays 18 Holes on Coast

By RUSSELL BAKER
Special to The New York Times.

PEBBLE BEACH, Calif., Aug. 24—President Eisenhower celebrated his renomination today by playing his first full eighteen-hole round of golf since his operation.

Here for a long week-end of rest after his convention exertions, he was out on the tee by 9 o'clock this morning. His game went "pretty well," according to James C. Hagerty, White House press secretary.

In high spirits he went back to the Cypress Point Golf Club course after a midday rest to spend part of the afternoon riding about in a powered golf cart "heckling his friends," Mr. Hagerty reported.

The President, he added, felt "fine" after yesterday's campaign-like labor that kept him working until after 10 P. M. For the first time since his

Continued on Page 6, Column 5

WEINBERGER BABY FOUND DEAD IN L. I.

Hunt at Plainview Uncovers Body in Vines Near Home of Confessed Kidnapper

By MILTON BRACKER
Special to The New York Times

PLAINVIEW, L. I., Aug. 24—The body of Peter Weinberger, victim of kidnapping when he was 33 days old, was discovered here today.

It was found in a tree-enclosed thicket just west of Exit 37 of Northern State Parkway. The site was seven miles from the home of the baby's parents in Westbury and within three blocks of the home of the man charged with the July 4 abduction.

He is Angelo John La Marca, 31, of 22 Richfield Street, Plainview. Arrested at 2:30 A. M. yesterday, he was arraigned in Mineola this morning within a few minutes of the finding of the child's remains. Last night the police said he had confessed the kidnapping.

An unsmiling but superficially calm defendant, with a head of thick black hair and a smudge of a moustache, La Marca was held without bail for a preliminary hearing next Friday. He is the father of a boy, 9, and a girl, 5.

The suspect, wearing the green coveralls of a gas station mechanic, was charged with violation of section 1250, subdivision 2, of the penal code. The complaint alleged that he "did lead, take, entice away and detain a minor child, Peter Weinberger * * * with the intent to extort and obtain money and reward for the return of said child."

The penalty for the offense

Continued on Page 32, Column 2

PRICE INDEX RISES 0.7% TO A RECORD; IT MAY GO HIGHER

Food Cost Main Cause of 5th Upswing in Row—Wages to Go Up for Million

By JOSEPH A. LOFTUS
Special to The New York Times.

WASHINGTON, Aug. 24—The United States Consumer Price Index soared 0.7 per cent between mid-June and mid-July to a record for the second straight month.

The index compiled by the Department of Labor's Bureau of Labor Statistics rose to 117. That was 17 per cent above the 1947-49 average, which is the base of the index.

This latest increase was the fifth consecutive monthly rise and the third of unusual magnitude. The preceding rise also was 0.7 per cent; the one before that, 0.4 per cent. Apparently the trend has not ended yet, although food prices, the big item in the rise, are over their peak.

Democrats and labor leaders were quick to see political significance in a sustained rise in the price index in this campaign year.

Index rises such as these have an important impact on the stability of the economy. The accumulated increases of the last three months will give wage increases of 3 to 5 cents an hour to about 1,125,000 workers. The bulk of these—employed in automobile, aircraft, and agricultural implement plants—will get a 4-cent increase under the cost-of-living escalator clauses that are geared to the index.

Have a Dual Effect

These increases, at least theoretically, have a dual inflationary effect. First, they raise the cost of the products made in these plants and therefore the retail price, unless the manufacturers or retailers absorb the increases; second, they pour more money into the economic stream, thereby increasing the demand for goods and putting upward pressure on prices. There is a third factor: other employes demand matching increases.

For nearly three years the index had moved in a narrow range. The movement each month seldom exceeded 0.1 or 0.2 per cent.

Walter P. Reuther, president of the United Automobile Workers, said that "the latest spurt in the cost of living to an all-time high explodes Republican claims that the Eisenhower Administration has controlled inflation."

Senator George A. Smathers of Florida, chairman of the Democratic Senate Campaign Committee, said the rise proved that "the Republican prosperity they talk about is no more than skin deep." He predicted the price trend would be "reflected in the election returns."

Senator Theodore Francis

Continued on Page 13, Column 2

Clue to Statues of Easter Island Is Found

Heyerdahl Indicates Key to How They Were Erected

Dispatch of The Times, London.

OSLO, Norway, Aug. 24—How the huge statues of Easter Island were erected and transported—an archaeological mystery—may have been discovered by an expedition headed by Thor Heyerdahl of Kon-Tiki fame.

An experiment conducted by the expedition indicated that the ancient people who inhabited the island, in the Pacific west of South America, had mastered sculpture and knew advanced principles of transport.

A native chief, using a team of twelve men, showed the Heyerdahl party how, through the use of logs, stones and muscles, a large statue lying face down on the ground could be made to stand erect on a platform six feet high.

Mr. Heyerdahl said his expedition also had found "proof that at least some of the statues had been transported by sea and landed below precipices on the coast." He added that a large moon-shaped reed boat had been found carved on the chest of a statue that had been excavated.

The ship used by the Norwegian explorer on his expedition returned to Oslo today after a year's absence. On board the vessel, the Christian Bjelland, are a collection of ethnographical and archaeological material and about 57,000 feet of film.

Mr. Heyerdahl, who left the ship at Panama and flew back to Oslo, says the results of the expedition will probably give him two years of hard work. He plans to write a scientific record and a popular book, and to produce a film.

In 1947 Mr. Heyerdahl and five others had set off on a raft named Kon-Tiki from the coast of Peru in an effort to prove his theory that currents in the Pacific Ocean could have carried Indians of South America west-

Continued on Page 4, Column 6

Associated Press
Giant stone images dot the outer slope of the extinct volcano Rano Raraku on Easter Island

SUEZ COMMITTEE ASKS QUICK REPLY BY EGYPT ON TALK

5-Nation Group Sends Nasser Message as First Approach for Canal Negotiations

SECRECY IS EMPHASIZED

Menzies, at First Meeting of London Unit, Stresses Privacy of Deliberations

By EDWIN L. DALE Jr.
Special to The New York Times.

LONDON, Aug. 24—Representatives of the five nations selected to present to Egypt the plan for international operation of the Suez Canal met for the first time today. They constituted themselves the Suez Canal Committee.

Prime Minister Robert Gordon Menzies of Australia, chairman of the group, announced that it would keep its deliberations private and on the question of silence would "behave like Trappist monks."

It was learned, however, that Mr. Menzies paid an unannounced visit tonight to the Egyptian Ambassador.

He gave the Ambassador a message for President Gamal Abdel Nasser, asked that it be transmitted immediately and requested an early reply. The Ambassador agreed to send the message.

The committee expects an early reply from Egypt and will meet again, by Monday at the latest, to consider it.

The group was named by the eighteen nations at the Suez conference that supported the plan for the canal proposed by Secretary of State Dulles. It consists of Australia, Sweden, Iran, Ethiopia and the United States. The conference, which was called to cope with the situation developing from Egypt's nationalization of the private company that operated the canal, ended yesterday.

Shepilov Is Adamant

Shortly after the group met today Dmitri T. Shepilov, the Soviet Foreign Minister, held a press conference at which he said the committee of five had no status and was "quite outside the conference."

Mr. Shepilov also said the conference had been a "moral and political defeat" for the "forces" trying to render the Suez crisis "more acute" and aiming to impose on Egypt "demands of a colonialist character."

On the other hand Mr. Dulles, who left today by air for Washington, expressed confidence that the five-nation committee would succeed in its mission to achieve a solution of the Suez Canal dispute.

Egypt is expected to receive the five-nation committee. But her Government has stated repeatedly that the plan for international operation of the canal is unacceptable.

These were the other developments today in the Suez situation:

¶Loy W. Henderson, Deputy Under Secretary of State for the Administration and former Ambassador to Iran, arrived in London to serve as the United States member of the Suez Canal Committee.

¶Selwyn Lloyd, the British Foreign Secretary, said in a

Continued on Page 3, Column 2

Main Break Floods Wall St. Buildings; Bank Vault Cut Off

Water from a broken twelve-inch main under Wall Street flooded the basements of three buildings in the financial center yesterday. It disrupted traffic, inconvenienced hundreds of persons and caused considerable damage.

The break, which was discovered at 4:30 A. M., buckled a 50-by-30-foot section of the Wall Street roadway just east of Hanover Street. The police stopped automobile traffic on Wall Street from Hanover to Pearl Street and on Pine Street, one block to the north, from William to Pearl Street.

Water poured into the basements of the buildings at Nos. 60, 64 and 68 Wall Street before an emergency crew from the Department of Water Supply, Gas and Electricity could shut off the broken main and another twelve-inch and one six-inch main. The mains were shut off at 4:40 A. M. and the buildings were without water until 3:30 P. M., when the service was restored.

Possibly the flooding's highest point was in the sub-basement of the thirty-six-story building at 60 Wall Street, where it rose about fifteen feet. A day-long pumping operation by Fire Department apparatus was required to bring the water down to a two foot level.

The twelve-story building at 64 Wall Street was perhaps the

Continued on Page 31, Column 3

CITY CRIME AREAS TO GET MORE LIGHT

Plans Outlined to Improve Illumination of Streets to Meet Police Appeals

By CHARLES G. BENNETT

Improved street lighting is being planned by the city as a weapon in the fight against crime.

Acting on information from Police Commissioner Stephen P. Kennedy, the Department of Water Supply, Gas and Electricity is planning its program for new street illumination to include areas that have a high incidence of lawlessness.

Districts expected to come in for special attention include Central Park, Harlem and Greenwich Village in Manhattan; Park Slope, the Long Island Rail Road terminal area and Marine Park in Brooklyn, and Ozone Park and Long Island City in Queens.

Plans coordinated with the Police Department's recommendations have not been worked out for the Bronx and Staten Island.

The joining of street lighting to the fight on crime was disclosed before the City Planning Commission yesterday by Arthur C. Ford, Commissioner of Water Supply, Gas and Electricity.

The commission is holding departmental hearings at its Municipal Building offices on the 1957 capital budget. Mr. Ford asked for $20,116,530 in improvements to the water system, largely water main extensions and improvements to water supply sources, and $5,222,926 for new street lighting, all for 1957.

The total cost over the next several years of the water improvements Mr. Ford requested would be $70,541,530. The electrical improvements would cost $31,498,926.

Of the long-range street lighting allocations, $30,118,926 would cover the general illumination program that would take into

Continued on Page 13, Column 4

Dutch Royal Couple End Their Discord; Faith Healer Loses

By WALTER H. WAGGONER
Special to The New York Times.

THE HAGUE, the Netherlands, Aug. 24—Queen Juliana and Prince Bernhard announced today "the solution of difficulties" in the Dutch royal family.

The conclusion of a situation that had threatened to become an ugly crisis in the reigning House of Orange was the work primarily of a three-man commission named by the Queen and her Prince Consort June 28. In a communiqué made public at noon, the royal couple said the commission members "have reported their findings to us and given us advice."

"We express to them our sincere thanks," the statement continued. "Their advice has been a very valuable contribution to the solution of difficulties which had arisen. We now look forward to the future with confidence."

The statement was issued shortly after Queen Juliana and Prince Bernhard had left by plane for a short holiday on the island of Corfu with King Paul and Queen Frederika of Greece. They will return Tuesday.

It was clear both from the language of the communiqué and the official guidance to the press that there would be no abdication or other drastic and painful changes in the Dutch royal family.

The main element in the "solution" appeared to be the Queen's decision to end her relationship with a faith healer, 61-year-old Greet Hofmans. Prince Bernhard believed that Miss Hofmans had excessively and wrongfully influenced his wife.

"The Queen has decided to entertain no more relations either direct or indirect with Miss Hofmans," an official spokesman said. "This decision does not hold for a fixed period but indefinitely."

The Government spokesman said only that it was "possible

Continued on Page 4, Column 3

U. S. AIRMAN'S BODY FOUND OFF CHINA

Navy Also Reports Discovery of Parts of Craft Downed Near Mainland Coast

Special to The New York Times.

WASHINGTON, Aug. 24—The Navy announced tonight the recovery of the body of one of the sixteen crew members of the patrol plane attacked this week off the coast of Communist China.

The body was identified as that of Albert P. Mattin, aviation electronics technician 1/c, whose wife lives at the naval air station at Iwakuni, Japan. His father lives in Delta, Ohio.

The Navy said the body, two inflated life rafts, a plane wheel and fuel tanks had been found in international waters about 300 miles north-northeast of Taiwan (Formosa).

This was about twenty miles west of the plane's planned flight track, the Navy said.

In announcing the attack Wednesday, the Navy said the incident had taken place about 160 miles north of Taiwan and about thirty-two miles off the China coast.

The Navy announcement today would appear to place the site where the body was discovered east of the mouth of Hangchow Bay and about 100 miles southeast of Shanghai.

Search for Plane Extended

The search for the plane was said to have been expanded to that area after the Peiping radio had said that Chinese Communist fliers had attacked a "Chiang Kai-shek plane" there.

According to reports from the Navy destroyer that made the discovery, the wreckage had been damaged by fire. The Navy did not attribute this to gunfire, although the plane was presumed to have been shot down by Red Chinese fighter craft.

No survivors of the crew have been found, but the Navy said its search was continuing.

The Navy has said the plane, a P4M-Martin Mercator, was on a "routine patrol flight at the time of the attack." The Navy's statement was scheduled to have been released this morning. However, it was not made public until tonight after a day of checking with the State Department and White House officials in Monterey, Calif., where President Eisenhower is vacationing.

The text of the Navy statement follows:

"The body of a crew member of the Navy patrol plane, which disappeared Wednesday after reporting being under attack by unidentified aircraft, was found early today in international waters off the China coast amidst wreckage of the plane by the destroyer U. S. S. Dennis J. Buckley. It was identifed as that of Albert P. Mattin, whose wife resides at the Naval Air Station, Iwakuni, Japan.

"Also recovered by the destroyer at the same spot, approximately 300 miles north-northeasterly of Formosa, were two empty but inflated life rafts, a plane wheel and fuel tanks.

"The point at which the body

Continued on Page 2, Column 4

Stevenson Assails Eisenhower Record

By WILLIAM M. BLAIR
Special to The New York Times.

LIBERTYVILLE, Ill., Aug. 24—Adlai E. Stevenson set the tone today for the Democrats' plan to carry the election campaign fight directly to President Eisenhower.

He led off with a statement of faint praise of the President's speech in acceptance of the Republican renomination. Then Mr. Stevenson qualified that praise by asserting that "saying the right thing is not the same as doing it."

From his near-by country home, the Democratic Presidential nominee also took note of Vice President Richard M. Nixon's promise that the Republicans would carry the President's record to "every corner of the country."

"So are we," Mr. Stevenson said as he announced that his entire campaign would be run from Washington and named

Continued on Page 6, Column 2

The New York Times (by Neal Boenzi)
FLOODED BANK: Duncan MacLeod, building superintendent of 64 Wall Street, checks water depth in the main vault mechanism of the Bank of Montreal. The water, which came from a broken main, prevented operation of bank's vaults and stopped service on elevators.

U. N. Ousts a Soviet Translator Who Sought U. S. Plane Secrets

By KATHLEEN TELTSCH
Special to The New York Times.

UNITED NATIONS, N. Y., Aug. 24—A Soviet translator at the United Nations has been dismissed for attempting to obtain secret data on United States military aircraft.

The employe, Viktor Ivanovich Petrov, flew home yesterday without waiting for a formal discharge. The 31-year-old Russian was recruited in Moscow in 1953. He has been holding an $8,000-a-year job in the languages section.

His wife, Vladilena, and 6-year-old son, Alexei, were said to have left with him aboard a Scandinavian Airlines plane.

Today's announcement by the United Nations that Mr. Petrov had been "separated" from the international organization was made without warning. It came after Secretary General Dag Hammarskjold had been given information supplied by the United States Department of Justice in Washington. The data told how the Soviet staff member had tried without success to obtain secret specifications on planes from an employe of a United States aviation corporation.

Neither the employe nor the company was identified.

The findings from Washington were turned over to the Secretary General in the last few days by James J. Wadsworth, deputy United States delegate to the United Nations. Mr. Hammarskjold's "prompt action" was praised today by Henry Cabot Lodge Jr., top United States delegate, who was reached by telephone in California and told of the developments.

The Soviet staff member was described as tall and fair-haired. He lived with his family at 110 West Ninety-sixth Street. The

Continued on Page 2, Column 7

Jordan Tightens Tie To Nasser-Led Bloc

By SAM POPE BREWER
Special to The New York Times.

AMMAN, Jordan, Aug. 24—Jordan has taken another stride toward joining the "neutralist," or anti-Western, bloc headed by Egypt.

Heavy defense aid from Egypt, Saudi Arabia and Syria was arranged during the visit by King Hussein of Jordan and Maj. Gen. Ali Abu Nuwar, Army Chief of Staff, to Damascus at the end of last week, it is reported. The talks were also said to have resulted in agreement to intensify military cooperation.

President Shukry al-Kuwatly of Syria and King Hussein reported themselves in complete agreement on support for Egypt in the crisis over President Gamal Abdel Nasser's nationalization of the Suez Canal Company. That was a foregone conclusion. A report that Syria

Continued on Page 3, Column 6

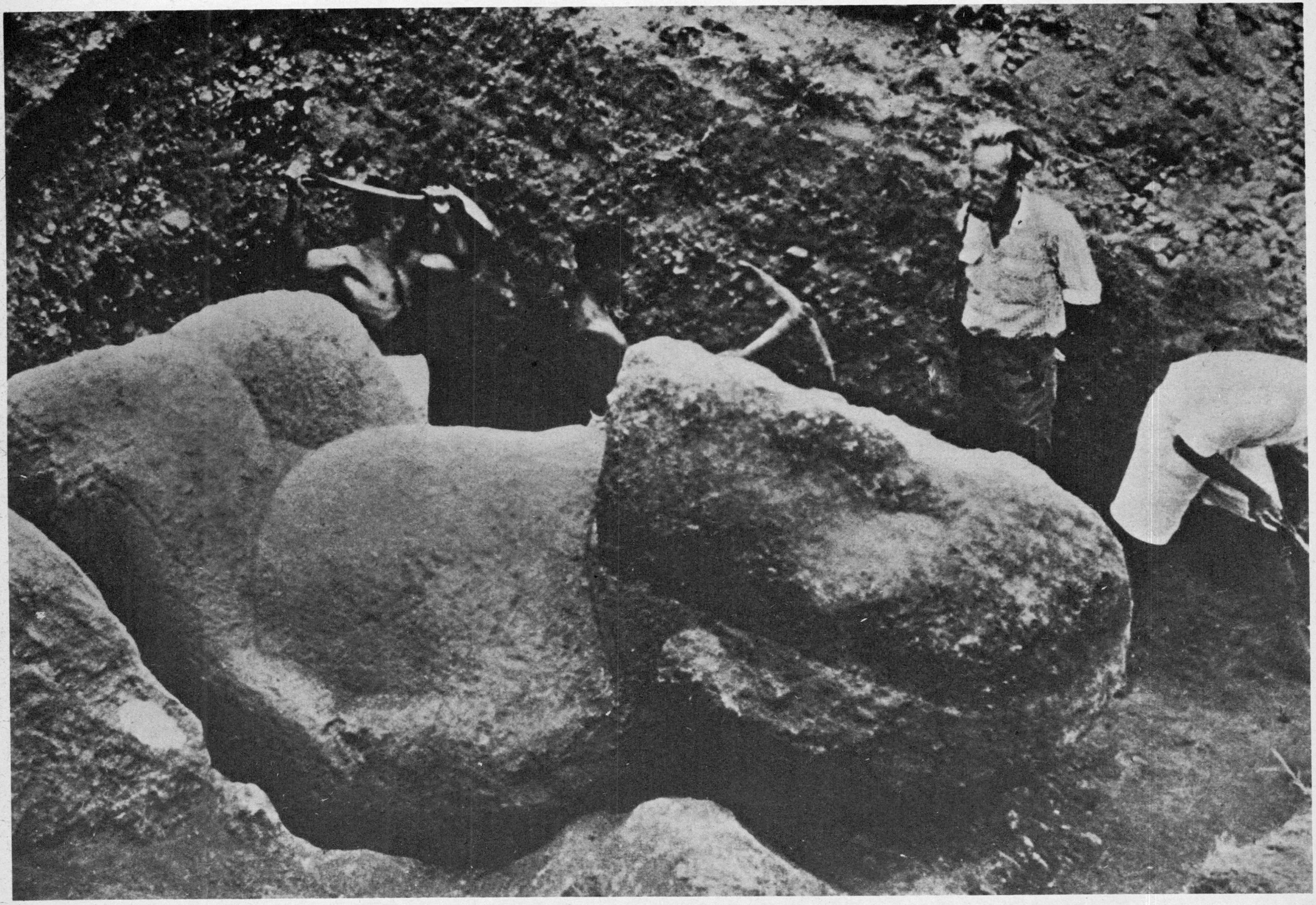

Uncovering a colossal statue on Easter Island.

"All the News That's Fit to Print"

The New York Times

LATE CITY EDITION

Weather: Partly sunny today; cool tonight. Chance of rain tomorrow. Temperature range: today 60-76; Tuesday 56-73. Details on Page 89.

VOL. CVI . No. 36,045. Entered as Second-Class Matter. Post Office, New York, N. Y. NEW YORK, MONDAY, OCTOBER 1, 1956. Times Square, New York 36, N. Y. Telephone LAckawanna 4-1000 FIVE CENTS

PRESIDENT ADDS WEST COAST TRIP TO HIS CAMPAIGN

Plans a Mid-October Flight to Washington and Oregon, With Minnesota Stop

TALKS ON TV TONIGHT

Before Leaving for Cleveland He Replies to Opponent on Schools and Civil Service

School message, memorandum on civil service, Page 14

By ALLEN DRURY

Special to The New York Times.

WASHINGTON, Sept. 30—President Eisenhower added another trip to his steadily expanding campaign itinerary today. The White House announced that he would fly to Minnesota, Washington and Oregon for a two-day visit in mid-October.

The announcement came a few hours before the President left Washington on a political foray that will take him to Ohio and Kentucky tomorrow. He is scheduled to speak informally in Cleveland at noon and make a nation-wide radio-television address from Lexington, Ky., tomorrow night.

Before leaving the capital, the President gave an indirect but pointed reply to the speech Friday night by his Democratic opponent, Adlai E. Stevenson. The President said he would ask Congress again next year for legislation to relieve the school shortage. Mr. Stevenson accused the Administration of neglecting the problem.

Answers on Merit System

And in answer to another Democratic charge—that the Administration had used the Civil Service system for political patronage—the White House released a statement by Philip Young, chairman of the Civil Service Commission. Mr. Young declared that the President had "specifically prohibited political considerations of any kind in appointments to Civil Service jobs."

[In Florida, Vice President Richard M. Nixon announced that he would visit fourteen states on a second campaign tour, starting Oct. 9.]

James C. Hagerty, the President's press secretary, outlined General Eisenhower's plans for the swing to the West Coast at an unusual Sunday afternoon news conference. He said the President was also considering trips to California, Texas and several other areas.

To Appear With Langlie

Mr. Hagerty said the President would fly to Minneapolis Oct. 17 for informal speeches there and in neighboring St. Paul. Then he will fly to Seattle for a state-wide radio-TV "discussion" with Gov. Arthur B. Langlie.

Governor Langlie is the Republican candidate for the Senate seat held by Senator Warren G. Magnuson, a Democrat.

On Oct. 18, the President will drive to Tacoma, where he will visit his brother Edgar and make a speech before going to Portland, Ore., for a nation-wide radio-TV talk that night.

He will be accompanied by Governor Langlie while in the State of Washington. When he crosses into Oregon he will be joined by Douglas McKay, for-

Continued on Page 14, Column 2

Dodgers Capture Pennant On Last Day of the Season

President and Stevenson Plan to See a Game of World Series

The Brooklyn Dodgers defeated the Pittsburgh Pirates, 8—6, at Ebbets Field yesterday and won the National League pennant on the final day of the season. The Dodgers will meet the Yankees, the American League champions, in the world series, starting on Wednesday at Ebbets Field.

Don Newcombe received credit for his twenty-seventh victory of the season for the Dodgers, although he needed help in the eighth inning from Don Bessent. Duke Snider hit two homers and made an outstanding catch in the seventh to shut off a Pittsburgh rally.

The Milwaukee Braves, who had been a game ahead of the Dodgers on Friday, beat the Cards, 4—2, in their final game at St. Louis and finished a game behind.

President Eisenhower will attend the opening game of the series and Adlai E. Stevenson, the Democratic candidate for President, will go to the game on Friday, when the competition will shift to the Yankee Stadium after the first two contests in Brooklyn.

Details on Pages 32-33.

The New York Times

SPECTACULAR CATCH by Duke Snider in the seventh.

G. O. P. RETAINING WISCONSIN LEAD; DEMOCRATS GAIN

Survey Shows Farm Unrest and Spotty Unemployment Are Having Influence

A Times Team Report

Four teams of New York Times reporters are making a pre-election grassroots survey of voter sentiment and trends in more than a score of states. A report will be presented on one state a day. This one is from a team composed of Clarence Dean, Tillman Durdin, Max Frankel, John D. Morris and William S. White, with Mr. White coordinating information and writing the team's report.

By WILLIAM S. WHITE

Special to The New York Times.

MILWAUKEE, Wis., Sept. 27—The Democrats are gaining in Wisconsin. But six weeks before the election all signs suggest that the state's twelve electoral votes will go for President Eisenhower again.

While the Democrats are unquestionably on the march, the vast preponderance of opinion—from both professional politicians and voters—is that they have too far to go to reach the summit in 1956.

This state has been traditionally Republican since the party was born in Ripon in 1856. Since then, Wisconsin has voted Republican in eighteen of twenty-five Presidential elections. Except for six occasions it has cast a heavier percentage of Republican Presidential votes than the national average.

Republicans Troubled

All the same, there are forces and currents here that trouble but do not deeply alarm Republicans. Perhaps the foremost factor lies in the widely accepted belief that the vote in November will be considerably below that of 1952. In that year, the total was 1,607,000 and General Eisenhower won by about 357,000.

In spite of some farm discontent and some spotty but not bitterly punishing unemployment, Wisconsin is in a mood of what the state's Germanic community calls "Gemuetlichkeit." This means, roughly, the comfort and contentment of one who, after a rich and satisfying dinner, sits in an overstuffed chair sipping his beer and watches television as the Milwaukee Braves win one.

The Republican leaders think that a light vote, proceeding from this relaxed state of mind, will help the Democrats. However, the Democrats see it almost precisely the other way. To an outsider the Republican view seems the sounder.

At all events, the following are the main points of a consensus of the probabilities. They

Continued on Page 15, Column 1

Eisenhowers Help Dedicate Greek Orthodox Cathedral

Associated Press Wirephoto

The President with Archbishop Michael at dedication ceremony yesterday in Washington

By The Associated Press

WASHINGTON, Sept. 30—The President and Mrs. Eisenhower helped dedicate St. Sophia Greek Orthodox Cathedral here today. They were presented with the highest award of the church—the Golden Medal of St. Andrew's. Before presenting the medals, Archbishop Michael, Primate of the Greek Orthodox Church in the Western Hemisphere, told General Eisenhower: "Your attendance of church services, Mr. President, has given the greatest example to all of us * * * especially to our youth."

Outside St. Sophia Cathedral, a crowd of about 1,000 stood behind police lines to watch the dedication ceremony, which followed a divine liturgy serv-

Continued on Page 22, Column 5

HUNGARIAN CHIEF JOINS TITO TALK; BULGANIN THERE

Gero and Premier Take Part in Yugoslav's Parley With Khrushchev in Crimea

TOPIC IS STILL A SECRET

Conference Seen as Attempt to Settle Ideological Rift Within Communist Bloc

Special to The New York Times.

LONDON, Sept. 30—Erno Gero, Hungary's Communist leader, and Soviet Premier Nikolai A. Bulganin went to Yalta today to join in talks with President Tito and Nikita S. Khrushchev.

The top-level conference is apparently an attempt to settle ideological differences still existing within the Communist bloc.

Mr. Gero, first secretary of the Hungarian Working People's (Communist) party, is the man who last July replaced Matyas Rakosi, a Stalinist who had a prominent role in the dismissal of Marshal Tito from the Soviet bloc eight years ago. Mr. Rakosi's ouster and his replacement by Mr. Gero were believed to have been Kremlin-inspired gestures to induce Marshal Tito to rejoin the Soviet community.

[An announcement in the Italian Communist party newspaper L'Unita said a delegation of prominent Italian Reds would visit Yugoslavia soon to study the "experience and achievements" of the country. This was seen as an indication that the Italian party might be supporting Marshal Tito in his current discussion with Soviet leaders.]

Reconciliation Held Aim

While the Soviet-Yugoslav rift has been healed to some extent, there have been no real signs of renewed friendliness between Yugoslavia and Hungary as a result of Mr. Gero's ascendancy. Although Mr. Gero ordered the release from prison of many Hungarians who had been sympathetic to Yugoslavia's leader, the two countries have remained divided.

Mr. Khrushchev, it is believed in diplomatic quarters, is eager to remove any frictions remaining between the Yugoslav and Hungarian leaders. Reports to London have indicated that the Soviet Communist party chief is now carrying on a fight with Old Bolsheviks in Moscow who have taken the position that the anti-Stalin crusade has gone too far.

In this struggle, according to reports, Vyacheslav M. Molotov and Lazar M. Kaganovich are believed to have challenged Mr. Khrushchev's "soft" policy. Mr. Molotov, former Foreign Minister and an old enemy of Marshal Tito, was removed from his top post in the Foreign Minis-

Continued on Page 3, Column 3

STEVENSON HOPES BUOYED BY TOUR

He Returns to Capital Sure of Gains—Starts Drive in East Tomorrow

By HARRISON E. SALISBURY

Special to The New York Times.

WASHINGTON, Sept. 30—Adlai E. Stevenson wound up a 7,500-mile campaign swing through the Midwest, border and Southern states today confident that he was making gains in his Presidential race.

It was 3:40 A. M. of a coolish Washington pre-dawn when Mr. Stevenson's plane touched down at National Airport after his first formal tour of the 1956 campaign.

But despite the hour and the grinding pace that had taken him through eleven states in eight days, Mr. Stevenson's step was bouncy and his mood was sparkling as he alighted from the plane.

With him he had a trophy acquired in a day of rousing campaigning in the Twin Cities area of Minnesota — a state where his chances of wresting away the eleven electoral votes won by General Eisenhower in 1952 were rated as excellent by observers.

The trophy was one from the

Continued on Page 16, Column 1

Wagner and Javits Spar in TV Talks, Plan Public Debate

By DOUGLAS DALES

On separate television programs, Mayor Wagner and Attorney General Jacob K. Javits traded blows yesterday in their campaign for the Senate.

Each candidate answered charges that had been made by his opponent.

The Mayor, interviewed on the Citizens Union "Searchlight" program over WRCA-TV, answered a charge by Mr. Javits that he was an "apprentice" unable to cope satisfactorily with foreign policy issues and that the Mayor's Administration had been one of extravagance.

The Attorney General responded to the Mayor's charge that he was no friend of the farmer, an allegation made by Mr. Wagner on an upstate tour Saturday.

Mr. Javits, appearing on WABC-TV at 1:30 P. M., goaded the Mayor again about not accepting a challenge to debate the campaign issues on television.

A half-hour later the Mayor accepted the challenge with a finalty that left nothing unanswered except details for the bouts.

"I'm willing to debate any of the issues at any time with anybody," Mr. Wagner said.

The Mayor laughed at the

Continued on Page 17, Column 1

INTEGRATION GAIN IN SCHOOLS NOTED

Survey of the South Shows 300,000 Negroes Are in Desegregated Districts

By BENJAMIN FINE

Special to The New York Times.

NASHVILLE, Tenn., Sept. 30—Integration is gaining slowly in the South.

An estimated 780 school districts and units now maintain racially mixed classes, a gain of about 200 districts over last year.

Approximately 300,000 Negro children, an increase of 50,000 over September of 1955, are going to school under integrated situations. And, what educators call just as significant, some 2,500,000 white pupils are attending classes with Negroes or are in school systems where Negroes are eligible to enter.

The term "integrated situation" is used by school officials to describe circumstances in which Negro children either attend mixed schools or are in school districts where such classes have been authorized.

The start of the third academic year since the Supreme Court outlawed segregation in public schools has seen much progress as well as serious set-

Continued on Page 20, Column 1

White House Is Expected To Continue Aid for Tito

By ALVIN SHUSTER

Special to The New York Times.

WASHINGTON, Sept. 30—President Eisenhower is expected to order United States aid to Yugoslavia continued despite President Tito's increased intimacy with Moscow. It had been generally thought that President Eisenhower would declare the Belgrade Government eligible for continued assistance before the Yugoslav leader's surprise visit to the Soviet Union.

This trip, to Yalta on the coast of the Black Sea, and other recent meetings between leaders of the two Communist countries are not regarded as sufficiently important to cause General Eisenhower to permit an end to all aid to Yugoslavia.

Congress has stipulated that unless the President decides by Oct. 16 that Yugoslavia is not a puppet of the Soviet Union, all United States assistance must cease.

Some Assistance Predicted

Some Government lawyers noted today, however, that the wording of the Congressional prohibition would not bar Presidential action after Oct. 16 to resume United States aid.

What seemed more likely today, however, was that President Eisenhower would make known his intention to continue at least some, if not most, of the Yugoslav aid programs before the deadline.

The President is known to be against any abrupt ending of the assistance programs, presumably accepting the view that such action might drive President Tito's government back firmly into the Soviet camp.

During the debate on the Mutual Aid Program in the Senate last July, President Eisenhower wrote that he would "deplore any abrupt mandatory cut-off involving the military aspects of our Yugoslav relationship."

Moreover, James W. Riddle-

Continued on Page 2, Column 5

U. S. HOLDING BACK ON AID TO EGYPT

Suez Crisis Brings Slowing of Projects Under Way—Experts on Home Leave

By OSGOOD CARUTHERS

Special to The New York Times

CAIRO, Sept. 30—The United States has applied the brakes to its aid program in Egypt because of the Suez Canal crisis.

Projects already under way are being slowed down as equipment from abroad becomes harder to get. At least twenty-five Americans are reported to be awaiting Washington's decision whether to return them from the United States to Egypt to fill key posts in the aid program.

The authorities of the International Cooperation Administration who are running the $42,750,000 assistance program say they are still on the best of terms with the Egyptians, from the ministerial level down.

There has been no public announcement here of a slow-down policy. However, even Egyptians friendliest to the United States in the nationalistic regime of President Gamal Abdel Nasser are ruefully aware that Washington's generosity has been caught in the whirlpool of international politics.

Both Sides Regretful

United States aid officials and Egyptians alike express regret that this should be so. For there had been visions that development projects, planned and started, would help pull the Egyptian masses out of their abject poverty.

It is apparent at the Cairo end of the Washington aid pipeline that the United States has suspended all plans for future assistance. Even the outlines of American policy regarding aid to Egypt seem to have become purposely vague.

It is clear that Washington is awaiting the outcome of the West's dispute with President Nasser over his nationalization two months ago of the Suez Canal Company.

In 1955 the United States allocated $40,000,000 to a development program for Egypt. Out of this amount, $7,500,000 was in the form of a long-term loan. The remainder was an outright grant. An additional $2,700,000 was allocated toward a program of technical assistance.

For 1956, the United States had earmarked $56,000,000 to help Egypt get started on the High Dam project at Aswan.

Continued on Page 4, Column 3

NEIGHBORS CHART PEACE IN ALGERIA

Tunisia and Morocco Press for 3-Nation Federation

By MICHAEL CLARK

Special to The New York Times.

ALGIERS, Algeria, Sept. 30—Proposals for a North African Federation were expected to emerge from discussions between Tunisian, Algerian and Moroccan leaders in Tunis in the latter part of October.

The Tunisian Premier, Habib Bourguiba, and Sultan Mohammed V of Morocco, have been trying separately to promote a negotiated settlement of the Algerian conflict, held to be a threat to the independence of both countries.

[The concept of Sultan Mohammed V of Morocco as a counterpoise to President Gamal Abdel Nasser of Egypt was reported to be capturing the imagination of the French.]

The Sultan's state visit to Tunis, to begin Oct. 21 or 22, will enable the two statesmen and their Governments to join in a concerted effort to find a basis for an honorable peace in Algeria.

The best evidence now suggests that Permier Bourguiba and the Sultan are not thinking in terms of mere home rule for Algeria. They are understood to prefer a solution based on Al-

Continued on Page 3, Column 3

Truck Strike Is On; 212 Concerns Sign

Long-haul truck drivers in the New York area halted operations of sixty-eight over-the-road shippers when they struck last midnight, according to the police. No picketing was reported.

Before the strike by the members of Local 707 of the International Brotherhood of Teamsters, 212 of the 280 trucking companies with whom the union has contractual dealings were reported to have signed a seventeen-point agreement with the union.

The 212 concerns are members of the Empire State Highway Transportation Association. The concerns, employing about 2,300 brotherhood members, represent two-thirds of the association's membership. The sixty-eight concerns that were struck employ about 1,100 union men. The cause of the dispute is

Continued on Page 18, Column 3

Pines 4,000 Years Old Found in California

Oldest Things Alive, Experts Say After Count of Rings

By WILLIAM L. LAURENCE

Pine trees more than 4,000 years old have been found growing in the upper timber line of mountains in eastern California.

Their great age, determined by the count of their tree-rings, makes them the oldest known living things, about 900 years older than the oldest dated giant sequoias of California.

The Methuselah-pines, which have already lived more than four times the age of the Scriptural patriarch, were discovered by Dr. Edmund Schulman, dendrochronologist of the University of Arizona Laboratory of Tree-Ring Research, and his assistant, C. W. Ferguson Jr.

A preliminary report on the discovery, made in the summers of 1954 and 1955, is presented by Dr. Schulman in a publication titled "Dendroclimatic Changes in Semi-Arid America," issued by the University of Arizona Press.

Dendrochronology is the science that uses tree-rings as "calendars" for past milleniums. To the relatively few experts in this rather recent scientific discipline, being developed at the University of Arizona, the number and patterns of the tree-rings tell not only the age of a tree but also of the variations

Continued on Page 24, Column 6

C. W. Ferguson Jr. of University of Arizona extracts core from ancient bristlecone pine

18 Suez Canal Users Reopen Talks Today

By KENNETT LOVE

Special to The New York Times.

LONDON, Sept. 30—All eighteen nations that supported the Western Big Three in the first phase of the dispute over the Suez Canal will be represented at the organizational conference of the Suez Canal Users Association opening here tomorrow.

A Foreign Office spokesman said the last few acceptances were delivered today. Two nations, Japan and Pakistan, will be represented only by observers with no commitment to join the association. Ethiopia has not said whether her delegate will be an observer or a participant.

The fifteen other nations have indicated they intend to join the users' association. Iran has made her adherence

Continued on Page 4, Column 5

"All the News That's Fit to Print"

The New York Times

LATE CITY EDITION
Condensation of U. S. Weather Bureau forecast: Rain and mild today; rain likely tonight. Showers likely tomorrow. Temperature range today: 51—44. Temperature range yesterday: 55—36.3. Full U. S. Weather Bureau Report, Page 75.

VOL. CVI..No. 36,117. Entered as Second-Class Matter, Post Office, New York, N. Y. NEW YORK, WEDNESDAY, DECEMBER 12, 1956. Times Square, New York 36, N. Y. Telephone Lackawanna 4-1000 FIVE CENTS

BETHLEHEM STEEL AND YOUNGSTOWN TO PUSH MERGER

Companies Will Act Despite U. S. Opposition—Assets Are Above 2.5 Billion

BROWNELL TO SEEK WRIT

Antitrust Suit Is Expected to Present a Historic Test of the Clayton Act

By JACK R. RYAN

Two of the nation's largest steel companies plan to merge in defiance of the Department of Justice.

The Bethlehem Steel Corporation, No. 2 in the industry, and the Youngstown Sheet and Tube Company, No. 6, announced yesterday an agreement under which Bethlehem would acquire Youngstown in exchange for Bethlehem common stock.

The Government immediately announced it would file an anti-trust suit to block the deal. The Department of Justice for more than two years has been outspoken in its opposition to the proposal, on the ground that it would tend to lessen competition in the steel industry.

The merger would be one of the biggest in the history of American industry, creating a company with assets exceeding $2,500,000,000.

The suit will also make history. A Government spokesman commented that it would offer a "significant" test of the application of the anti-trust laws. The outcome is likely to have a vital bearing on the merger trend in industry.

Steel Men Ready for Suit

The companies made it plain they were prepared for a legal battle. In their joint announcement here, Eugene G. Grace, chairman of Bethlehem, and J. L. Mauthe, chairman of Youngstown, said:

"The Department of Justice has advised the companies that it intends to sue to enjoin the proposed acquisition on the ground that it would violate the antitrust laws. The companies hope that the legal proceedings will be expedited and the question involved speedily determined by the courts."

In Washington, Attorney General Herbert Brownell Jr. issued a statement saying:

"In September of 1954 I announced that in my opinion this merger would violate Section 7 of the Clayton Act as amended in 1950. That section outlaws corporate acquisition of stock or assets of other companies 'where in any line of commerce in any section of the country the effect of such acquisition may be substantially to lessen competition

Continued on Page 64, Column 4

FARMERS REJECT A NEW CORN PLAN

Administration Loses Bid for More Acres, Lower Props

Special to The New York Times.

WASHINGTON, Wednesday, Dec. 12—Corn farmers rejected yesterday an Administration-backed plan that would have given them more acreage but lower price supports in 1957.

Returns from twenty-four commercial corn producing states in yesterday's corn referendum showed that the farmers favored retention of an acreage allotment program written in New Deal days.

The Administration's plan was considered a step in brushing aside the control programs of two decades and moving toward freeing farmers from crop restrictions. Administration officials contended that the old controls tended to build up surpluses and depress market prices.

Complete results from the twenty-four states showed that 61.2 per cent of the voting farmers favored the new program, which would have given them an expanded acreage base for the next three years but would have left price supports to the discretion of the Secretary of Agriculture. This was short of the 66.6 per cent vote necessary to put the Administration's proposal into effect next year.

The returns gave:

The new program, 257,857.

The present program, 163,227.

There were 17,745 challenged

Continued on Page 38, Column 1

Their Business Affiliations Are Under Investigation

Councilman James J. Murphy of Staten Island at City Council meeting yesterday.

Councilman Edward A. Cunningham of Bronx, who is latest to come under inquiry.

CITY COUNCIL ACTS TO EXAMINE ITSELF

But Isaacs Blocks Inquiry on Members for Week—Third Official Under Scrutiny

By CHARLES G. BENNETT

The City Council put in motion yesterday the machinery for requiring an investigation into the business dealings of all its members.

However, an objection by Minority Leader Stanley M. Isaacs, Manhattan Republican-Liberal, blocked immediate consideration of resolutions calling for the investigation.

But the Council's eleven-man Rules Committee, over Mr. Isaacs' negative vote, approved the resolutions, and Majority Leader Joseph T. Sharkey, Brooklyn Democrat, announced that the full Council would vote on them next Tuesday. A favorable vote on the inquiry proposal is expected.

Meanwhile Investigation Commissioner Charles H. Tenney's investigation of Councilmen having possible conflict-of-interest business dealings involved a third member of the Council—Edward A. Cunningham, Bronx Democrat.

The Cunningham Inquiry

Mr. Tenney disclosed that he was "looking into" the alleged business connection of Councilman Cunningham, chairman of the Council's Finance Committee, as counsel to a concern leasing a Bronx dump from the city.

At City Hall Mr. Cunningham said the operator of the dump, variously described as Anthony Rose and Michael A. Rose, had been his client "in private matters only," but never in any dealings with the city.

Two other Councilmen have come under the scrutiny of the Investigation Commissioner in connection with alleged business affiliations with concerns doing business with the city.

The two are Hugh Quinn, Queens Democrat, for his employment by the Triboro Carting Corporation, which had a snow removal contract with the city, and James J. Murphy, Richmond Democrat. According to a spokesman for the Todd Shipyards Corporation of 1 Broadway, Mr. Murphy has been associated with that company since July, 1940, as a special sales representative on private accounts. The company has done repair work on boats owned by city departments.

City Charter Provisions

The general tenor of Section 886 of the City Charter, under which Mr. Tenney is looking into the Quinn, Murphy and Cunningham affairs, is to bar City Councilmen and all other city officers and employes from holding jobs with persons or concerns having city contracts or doing business with the city for which payment is made from the city treasury.

Violation of the section is a misdemeanor and constitutes cause for removal from office.

The resolutions before the City Council yesterday were introduced jointly by Mr. Sharkey and Council President Abe Stark.

One called for the appointment of a special Council committee to study sections of the charter involving the duties and obligations of Councilmen, other city officials and city employes, and to recommend "any amend-

Continued on Page 45, Column 2

The New York Times (by Arthur Brower)

Councilman Hugh Quinn of Queens. His ties are being checked by several agencies.

Old Movie Taboos Eased in New Code For Film Industry

The film industry has revised and relaxed its code of morals and taboos for the first time since the code was adopted in 1930.

This action was announced yesterday by Eric Johnston, president of the Motion Picture Association of America, at a conference held at the association's headquarters, 28 West Forty-fourth Street.

The action on the code came after almost a year of study and countless consultations by a committee of film company executives appointed by Mr. Johnston. The revisions go into effect immediately.

The regulations are known familiarly as the "Hays Code" because of their adoption while the late Will H. Hays was president of the association.

Specific changes include elimination of the absolute prohibi-

Continued on Page 51, Column 5

STRAUSS OUTLINES ATOM POWER PLAN

Big Expansion Would Include New Reactors for Civilian Use and Release of Data

By ALVIN SHUSTER

Special to The New York Times.

WASHINGTON, Dec. 11 — Lewis L. Strauss, chairman of the Atomic Energy Commission, proposed tonight a major expansion in atomic power plants.

He suggested an eight-point program, including the construction of five "entirely new-type" power reactors for producing electricity for civilian use.

In a speech before the American Nuclear Society, Mr. Strauss also disclosed that the Government would soon make available for general use much secret technical information on the development and operation of power reactors.

'Bright Prospects' Noted

The results achieved in the last two years by Government and industry represent only a fraction of the "bright prospects for nuclear power development in the next five or six years, he declared.

Mr. Strauss said he was proposing steps to be taken without delay to assure the construction within the next six years of at least two large-scale and three small-scale reactors, all for civilian power.

They would be in addition to the eighteen civilian nuclear power plants planned for operation by 1962. These represent an investment by Government and industry of more than $650,000,000.

Mr. Strauss suggested that private industry have the first opportunity to build the new power plants. If it did not come forth with "acceptable proposals," he added, the commission should take "prompt and posi-

Continued on Page 23, Column 1

DULLES BIDS NATO USE MORAL FORCE TO COMBAT SOVIET

Also Stresses Defense Power but Opposes Resort to Arms to Right Wrongs

By HAROLD CALLENDER

Special to The New York Times

PARIS, Dec. 11—The trials and hopes of the Atlantic alliance, and ways of facing current crises, were discussed today by officials of the fifteen allied nations. The talks took place both within and outside the North Atlantic Council.

The talks touched on defense and its financing, the extension of collective consultation on foreign policies, the Suez Canal, the Soviet threat and even the value of moral force in international relations.

Secretary of State Dulles, who did the most talking in any single speech, placed approximately equal stress on what he called moral pressure and the military strength of the alliance.

Resort to Arms Opposed

Addressing the North Atlantic Council at its opening session, he seemed to rule out war as an instrument of national policy, saying that if a nation sought to remedy an injustice by using military force it risked a world war.

He urged reliance on moral pressure to overcome the power of Soviet despotism as expressed in Hungary, and he emphasized the "high ideals" of the United Nations and the North Atlantic alliance. His words were interpreted as an assurance to Moscow that the West would not make war to liberate even rebellious satellites.

Urging a "common Western policy," Dr. Gaetano Martini, Italian Foreign Minister, called for diplomatic cooperation outside as well as inside the Atlantic pact area. Christian Pineau, French Foreign Minister, proposed obligatory consultation on foreign policies.

Dr. Heinrich von Brentano, West German Foreign Minister, was expected to propose tomorrow an amendment to the North Atlantic Treaty or a formal agreement obliging signatories of the pact to consult other members on problems affecting the alliance.

NATO Cabinet to Be Suggested

Dr. von Brentano also was reported planning to suggest a special Atlantic pact cabinet of under secretaries of state to meet every two months to coordinate policies.

The question of financing the armed forces in Europe was raised by the British today in a meeting of British and United States foreign, finance and defense minister.

Britain plans to reduce her forces so as to cut her budget, but Continental nations, notably West Germany and France, have opposed a reduction of British or United States forces on the Continent.

Turkey was understood to have proposed to the council that the Baghdad Pact be strengthened.

Continued on Page 12, Column 3

Horvath Walks Out of U. N. Debate

The New York Times

Imre Horvath, Hungarian Foreign Minister, about to enter his car yesterday after leaving U. N. General Assembly.

Hungary in Grip of Strike; Workers Clash With Police

By JOHN MacCORMAC

Special to The New York Times

VIENNA, Dec. 11—A general strike went into effect today through most of Hungary. The stoppage had been called Sunday by the Budapest Central Workers Council before the group was outlawed by order of Premier Janos Kadar.

Reports from Budapest said part of the working staff turned up in a few factories in the capital. But as far as output was concerned, the strike, which was to run forty-eight hours, was fully effective.

This was obvious even from the Government's own statements over the Budapest radio. These were interspersed with appeals to workers to return to their jobs.

Instead, the workers demonstrated in the streets against the Soviet-controlled regime. They persisted despite the attempts to disperse them by the Kadar police, constituted mainly from the former political police force.

In the industrial suburb Ujpest policemen fired into a crowd, inflicting a number of casualties. In other cases, they used their rifle butts but were quickly surrounded and reportedly beaten by the crowds. When this happened, it was said, they called up Soviet tanks and armored cars.

Dispatches from Budapest, with which communications have partly been resumed, made it obvious, as did reports from fugitives who reached Austria, that the economy of Hungary had again been effectively paralyzed.

In the important factory towns of Gyor, Debrecen, Szolnok and Kecskemet, it was reported, no wheel moved. In the iron and steel center of Dunapentele, once called Sztalinvaros,

Continued on Page 2, Column 3

POLISH MOB RAIDS SOVIET CONSULATE

Arrest of Drunken Man in Stettin Sets Off a Spree of Window Smashing

Dispatch of The Times, London.

WARSAW, Dec. 11—Rioting in Stettin (Szczecin) last night culminated in an attack on the Soviet consulate.

From reports published here today the rioting appears to have begun with the arrest of a drunken man by a policeman. The policeman was attacked by what is described as a group of hooligans and the crowd that gathered soon blocked the Avenue of the Polish Army, one of the main streets.

Street cars were stopped and windows broken in several of them, and several more policemen were beaten up.

Workers Stop Rioters

At this stage the reports say, an attempt was made to organize a demonstration, "to the accompaniment of drunken songs and provocative shouts," and apparently with some success.

According to P. A. P., the Polish news agency, some of the rioters reached the Soviet consulate where they smashed windows and tried to break in.

The riot, it is said, was stopped after the local committee of the Polish United Workers (Communist) party had summoned workers from the Stettin shipyard, who with students and soldiers of the local military unit "dispersed the hooligans."

Arrests, described in the agency reports as "numerous," were made. The agency adds that "those guilty of the provocative brawls will be punished with the entire severity of the law."

Apart from having taken an anti-Soviet turn, the events in Stettin appear from the accounts in the Polish press to have been very similar to a riot at Bydgoszcz last month.

Radio Building Set on Fire

The trouble in Bydgoszcz was started by a group of "intoxicated hooligans" on a Sunday afternoon and finally culminated in the setting of a fire to a radio-jamming station and a neighboring building containing radio equipment. The local police headquarters was also attacked to shouts of "Long live Gomulka!" and the singing of the national anthem.

Wladyslaw Gomulka, Polish Communist party leader, has condemned the Bydgoszcz incident as the work of "social scum hostile to socialism and democracy."

Members of M. Gomulka's party believe that the vast industrialization of Poland has brought into the cities elements who have lost their country virtues without having acquired proletarian discipline.

BUDAPEST'S AIDES QUIT U. N. DEBATE ON HUNGARY ISSUE

Horvath, 'Rudely Offended,' Asserts He Will Boycott Assembly Discussion

ANTI-SOVIET MOVE GAINS

20 Lands for Condemnation —U. S. Weighs Support for Asian Proposal

Debate excerpts and text of revised resolution, Page 10.

By THOMAS J. HAMILTON

Special to The New York Times.

UNITED NATIONS, N. Y., Dec. 11—Imre Horvath, Hungarian Foreign Minister, walked out of the General Assembly this morning. He charged that his Soviet-supported Government had been "rudely and disgracefully offended" by the debate on the Hungarian issue.

Mr. Horvath said the Hungarian delegation would refuse to participate in the work of the current session of the General Assembly "as long as the discussion of the Hungarian question does not proceed in the spirit of the United Nations Charter."

Mr. Horvath, accompanied by Dr. Endre Sik, another Hungarian delegate, went from the basement committee room where the Assembly was meeting to the delegates' lounge. After discussing the situation briefly with V. K. Krishna Menon of India, he had a cup of tea, then left the building and disappeared.

Return Is Expected

Mr. Horvath's statement left the way open for him and his subordinates to return once the Hungarian question was disposed of. Hungary was not represented at any Assembly committee meetings today, but two representatives appeared this afternoon at a meeting of the executive board of the United Nations Children's Fund.

Henry Cabot Lodge Jr. of the United States told reporters he was glad to see Mr. Horvath go. He added that "it would save us a lot of wasted time if the others [the other Soviet-bloc delegates] stopped talking."

It was generally assumed that Mr. Horvath walked out because he expected an Assembly move to suspend or revoke his credentials. Cuba has been threatening to introduce such a resolution.

It is supposed that this will be the next move if the pending resolutions, which may be voted on tomorrow, do not result in the withdrawal of Soviet troops from Hungary, or at least the admission of United Nations observers to that country.

Sponsors of a resolution co

Continued on Page 11, Column 3

EGYPTIANS KIDNAP A BRITISH OFFICER

Act Follows Arrest of Eight Arabs in Port Said Area

By ROBERT C. DOTY

Special to The New York Times.

PORT SAID, Egypt, Dec. 11—Egyptians kidnapped a British officer at the point of his own gun here today.

The taxicab in which a witness said the officer had been driven off was found later slightly bloodstained, and with a gag and a piece of rope on the seat.

[The Associated Press said the Egyptian underground had informed allied military authorities that the officer had been killed. The War Office in London identified the officer as Lieut. Anthony Gerard Moorhouse, 20 years old, of the West Yorkshire Regiment.]

Lieut. Gen. Sir Hugh Stockwell, the allied commander, told a news conference that "patience is probably the best means of saving" the kidnapped officer. He said he had summoned the Egyptian Governor, Mohammed Riad, and "invited" him to use the Egyptian police to find and release the officer.

The kidnapping, the boldest action thus far by the Egyptians here, followed by a few hours a British raid resulting in the arrest of eight men believed to be Egyptian Army officers.

General Stockwell conceded that the kidnapping appeared to be a quick retaliatory action for

Continued on Page 12, Column 5

Physicist 'Creates' Universe in a Test Tube

Atom Gun Produces Galaxies and Gives Clues to Creation

By WILLIAM L. LAURENCE

Out of a small glass chamber, devised to study means for taming the explosive energy of the hydrogen bomb for peaceful uses, has come a new vision of creation. It offers for the first time experimental evidence of the possible origin of the infinite universe of stars and galaxies.

In the tests, electrified atomic particles, carrying both negative and positive electrical charges, were shot out of a thimble-sized "atomic gun" of special design, and subjected to a tremendous magnetic field. A 40-year-old atomic physicist of the Stevens Institute of Technology, Hoboken, N. J., was startled to observe the emergence of miniature analogues of the vast conglomerations of stellar bodies forming the universe as observed by astronomers.

The patterns emerging in the glass chamber out of the "atomic gun" included all the principal formations of the "island universes" observed to form the cosmos—the many-armed spiral nebulae, such as our own Milky Way, the "barred" S-shaped nebulae, as well as the giant ring-nebulae.

The spiral nebulae mark the early stage of the evolutionary process. The process continues then through stages showing fewer "arms," and as the nebulae grow older they gradually lose their spiral arms. In the later stages, they are ring-shaped.

The work was first done at the Livermore Laboratory at the University of California in the course of work on Project Sherwood, a project of the Atomic Energy Commission for converting the energy of the hydrogen bomb into controlled electrical power. The work is being carried out in three major centers, including Princeton University and

Continued on Page 22, Column 3

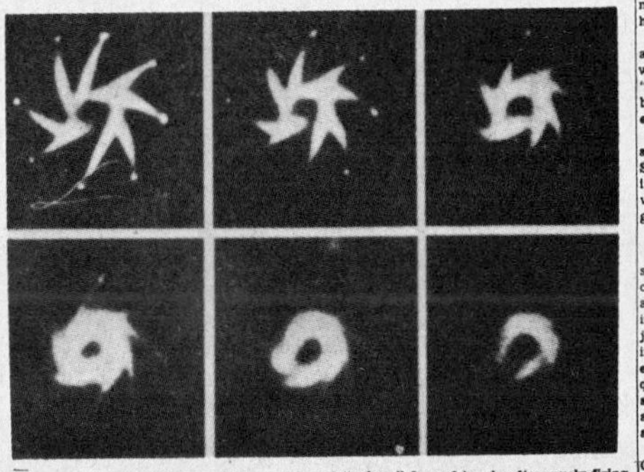

Sequence shows evolution of miniature 8-armed "galaxy" formed by simultaneously firing 8 "plasma guns." This simulates in fraction of second what would take billions of years.

"All the News That's Fit to Print"

The New York Times

LATE CITY EDITION
U. S. Weather Bureau Report (Page 58) forecasts: Mostly fair and seasonable today and tomorrow.
Temp. range: 70—57. Yesterday: 67.7—55.9.

VOL. CVII . No. 36,404. | NEW YORK, WEDNESDAY, SEPTEMBER 25, 1957. | 10c beyond 100-mile zone from New York City | FIVE CENTS

PRESIDENT SENDS TROOPS TO LITTLE ROCK, FEDERALIZES ARKANSAS NATIONAL GUARD; TELLS NATION HE ACTED TO AVOID ANARCHY

WEST AGAIN BARS SOVIET PROPOSAL ON MIDEAST TALK

U. S. Says Latest Moscow Note 'Cynically Distorts' American Actions

Text of U. S. note to Soviet will be found on Page 5.

By DANA ADAMS SCHMIDT
Special to The New York Times.

WASHINGTON, Sept. 24—The United States, Britain and France rejected today the latest in a series of Soviet bids for recognition of the Soviet Union's role in the Middle East.

A brief United States reply delivered in Moscow today said a Soviet note of Sept. 3 was "offensive in tone and cynically distorts United States objectives and actions in the Middle East."

It accused the Soviet Union of setting in motion "a chain of events leading to the present dangerous situation" by shipping large quantities of arms into the area.

U. S. Affirms Doctrine

The note warned the Soviet Union that the United States Government intended to carry out the national policy laid down in the Eisenhower Doctrine, which "regards the preservation of the independence and integrity of the nations of that region as vital to world peace and as vital, therefore, to its own national interests."

The doctrine, proclaimed in a Joint Resolution of the House of Representatives and the Senate on March 9, 1957, also affirmed the President's authority to use United States forces to aid any Middle East state that asked for help against aggression by a power controlled by international communism.

The Soviet Union's note had accused the United States of seeking to overthrow the Syrian Government and of generally fomenting trouble in the Middle East.

3d Rejection of Soviet Bid

It had proposed, for the third time, a four-power declaration renouncing the use of force in the area. Earlier Soviet proposals for such a declaration, all rejected by the West, were made Feb. 11 and April 19.

As interpreted by United States experts on the Middle East, these notes were meant to convey the idea that the four powers should meet to negotiate a settlement of their rivalries in the Middle East. The first of the notes even went into detail with a proposal for an embargo on shipment of arms to the area.

Because the Soviet Union has asserted its presence in Syria, and because there seems to be little the Western powers can do to reverse developments in

Continued on Page 5, Column 3

London and Bonn Rule Out Any Currency Revaluation

Britain Tells Monetary Fund Session She Will Draw $500,000,000 in Stand-By Credit From Export-Import Bank

By EDWIN L. DALE JR.
Special to The New York Times.

WASHINGTON, Sept. 24—British and West German spokesmen and the Managing Director of the International Monetary Fund said today that the question of exchange rates for the pound and the mark was "definitely settled." There will be no change.

At the same time, Britain, through Peter Thorneycroft, Chancellor of the Exchequer, announced she would draw "over the coming weeks" the $500,000,000 stand-by credit she arranged last winter with the United States Export-Import Bank.

In his speech at the annual meeting of the fund, Mr. Thorneycroft indicated that Britain was drawing the money to demonstrate to speculators that she had the resources to defend the pound.

Both the British and the West Germans emphasized that the recent huge flow of gold and dollars out of Britain and into West Germany had been based solely on speculation, not on basic factors in their foreign trading accounts.

Per Jacobsson, the Fund's Managing Director, said: "The growing knowledge that there will be no alteration in the value of either the Deutsche

Continued on Page 8, Column 5

SOLDIERS FLY IN

1,000 Go to Little Rock —9,936 in Guard Told to Report

The texts of Executive orders on troops are on Page 16.

By JACK RAYMOND
Special to The New York Times.

WASHINGTON, Sept. 24—The Army ordered all Arkansas National Guardsmen to report for Federal duty tonight and rushed 1,000 airborne troops of the Regular Army into Little Rock to preserve order.

The Regulars were members of the 101st Airborne Division, which won fame in World War II under the command of Gen. Maxwell D. Taylor, now Chief of Staff of the Army.

Maj. Gen. Edwin A. Walker, a much-decorated combat commander with a reputation for toughness, was put in command of the Regular Army contingent and the federalized Guardsmen in Arkansas. He is the commander of the Arkansas Military District.

General Walker's mission is to make sure that no one frustrates Federal Court orders that nine Negro pupils be admitted to Central High School.

Wilson Carries Out Order

Charles E. Wilson, Secretary of Defense, carrying out President Eisenhower's mandate, earlier had called the entire Arkansas Army and Air National Guard, totaling 9,936 men, into Federal service.

The Secretary of Defense and Wilber M. Brucker, Secretary of the Army, acted two hours after President Eisenhower's executive order authorizing "all appropriate steps" to make school attendance possible for the Negroes who had been admitted to the high school.

However, an Army spokesman said that it was planned to make "the absolute minimum demonstration of force necessary."

Immediately after Secretary Wilson signed the federalization call to the Arkansas Guard at 2:25 P. M., Secretary Brucker telephoned the office of Gov. Orval E. Faubus in Little Rock.

At the same time he sent a telegram to the Governor, explaining that President Eisenhower "desires" the personnel of the Arkansas Army and Air National Guard organizations

Continued on Page 14, Column 2

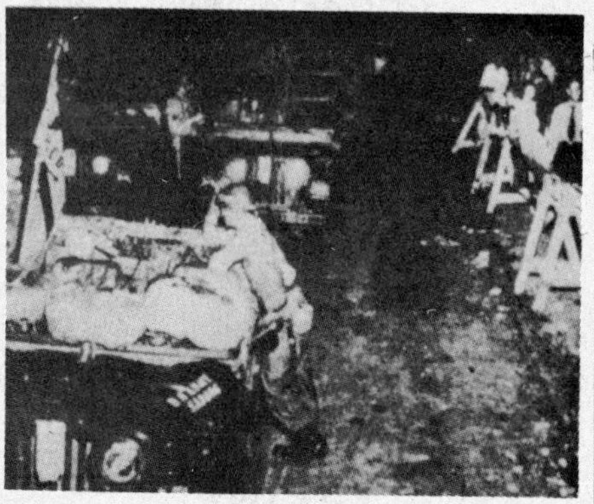

Associated Press Wirephoto

SOLDIERS IN LITTLE ROCK: Residents of Arkansas capital looking on last night as men of the 101st Airborne Division took positions outside the Central High School.

EISENHOWER ON AIR

Says School Defiance Has Gravely Harmed Prestige of U. S.

Text of President's address appears on Page 14.

By ANTHONY LEWIS
Special to The New York Times.

WASHINGTON, Sept. 24—President Eisenhower sent Federal troops to Little Rock, Ark., today to open the way for the admission of nine Negro pupils to Central High School.

Earlier, the President federalized the Arkansas National Guard and authorized calling the Guard and regular Federal forces to remove obstructions to justice in Little Rock school integration.

His history-making action was based on a formal finding that his "cease and desist" proclamation, issued last night, had not been obeyed. Mobs of pro-segregationists still gathered in the vicinity of Central High School this morning.

Tonight, from the White House, President Eisenhower told the nation in a speech for radio and television that he had acted to prevent "mob rule" and "anarchy."

Historic Decision

The President's decision to send troops to Little Rock was reached at his vacation headquarters in Newport, R. I. It was one of historic importance politically, socially, constitutionally. For the first time since the Reconstruction days that followed the Civil War, the Federal Government was using its ultimate power to compel equal treatment of the Negro in the South.

He said violent defiance of Federal Court orders in Little Rock had done grave harm to "the prestige and influence, and indeed to the safety, of our nation and the world." He called on the people of Arkansas and the South to "preserve and respect the law even when they disagree with it."

Guardsmen Withdrawn

Action quickly followed the President's orders. During the day and night 1,000 members of the 101st Airborne Division were flown to Little Rock. Charles E. Wilson, Secretary of the Defense, ordered into Federal service all 10,000 members of the Arkansas National Guard.

Today's events were the climax of three weeks of skirmishing between the Federal Government and Gov. Orval E. Faubus of Arkansas. It was three weeks ago this morning that the Governor first ordered National Guard troops to Central High School to preserve order. The nine Negro students were prevented from entering the school.

The Guardsmen were gone yesterday, withdrawn by Governor Faubus as the result of a

Continued on Page 14, Column 6

SOVIET ASSAILED BY LLOYD AT U. N.

Briton Suggests Arms Sent Arabs May Be Stocks for Future Bases

Excerpts from Lloyd's speech are printed on Page 4.

By THOMAS J. HAMILTON
Special to The New York Times.

UNITED NATIONS, N. Y., Sept. 24—Britain denounced today Soviet arms shipments to Arab countries. Selwyn Lloyd, British Foreign Secretary, suggested that the purpose might be to "pre-stock forward bases for the Soviet Union itself."

Mr. Lloyd told the General Assembly that Soviet arms had been delivered "on such a scale as to give some color to this suggestion." He added that Britain viewed the Syrian situation "with grave concern." In addition, he criticized Soviet policy throughout the area.

Mr. Lloyd devoted most of his speech to the Middle East and to disarmament. He did not say what action the Assembly should take on either subject.

However, he declared that Secretary of State Dulles, in

Continued on Page 4, Column 3

City Approves Plan By Wiley to Build Midtown Garages

By JOSEPH C. INGRAHAM

The Board of Estimate has approved in principle the program of Traffic Commissioner T. T. Wiley for garage construction in the heart of lower and mid-Manhattan.

The decision clears the way for a start on $24,000,000 of garages. It also settles a three-year dispute between Mr. Wiley and other city executives that has stymied off-street parking relief.

As a result, the first of the projects—a garage in the Herald Square area—will be on the board's calendar on Oct. 9. Eight other garages are to be centrally located in Manhattan and two in the busiest parts of the Bronx.

The Herald Square garage will be east of the Avenue of the Americas between West Thirty-fifth and Thirty-sixth Streets with entrances and exits on both streets. There will be space for 610 cars on eight levels accessible by ramps. Rates will be geared to "meet the heavy unsatisfied demand for short-time parking," Mr. Wiley said.

Rates proposed by the Commissioner would be 25 cents a

Continued on Page 25, Column 1

GOVERNORS URGE WHITE HOUSE TALK

Southerners Move to Set Up Mediation Machinery in Use of Federal Troops

By JOHN N. POPHAM
Special to The New York Times.

SEA ISLAND, Ga., Sept. 24—Southern Governors moved tonight to establish mediation machinery that would remove Federal troops from the South.

The Governors acted a few hours after the President had federalized the Arkansas National Guard.

Gov. Luther Hodges of North Carolina, chairman of the Southern Governors Conference in session here, announced that two proposals would be submitted to the resolutions committee of the conference for formal consideration tomorrow.

One is a proposal of Gov. Frank G. Clement of Tennessee to establish an informal committee of Southern Governors to seek a meeting with President Eisenhower in a search for a solution to the Little Rock school integration crisis.

The other is a request to the President to hold off the use of Federal troops and to agree

Continued on Page 16, Column 2

Troops on Guard at School; Negroes Ready to Return

By BENJAMIN FINE
Special to The New York Times.

LITTLE ROCK, Ark., Sept. 24—Troops from the Army's crack 101st Airborne Division, carrying carbines and billy clubs, took posts around Central High School tonight. They were here to see that court-ordered integration is carried out.

With police sirens wailing and headlights flashing, Army trucks loaded with soldiers roared into position. The soldiers represented about a quarter of the contingent of 1,000 crack troops of the division that was ordered to Little Rock by President Eisenhower to prevent mob riots and violence.

The first group of 500 airborne soldiers came to the city this afternoon from Fort Campbell, Ky., and a second group of 500 arrived by plane this evening. The bulk of the two groups bivouacked for the night in areas away from the school.

General Issues Order

Maj. Gen. Edwin A. Walker, commander of the Arkansas Military District, issued a formal order to the people of Little Rock not to collect in crowds and to let Central High School be integrated peaceably.

With the arrival of Federal troops, including some Negro soldiers who were not expected to be on duty at the school, Negro students were ready to try again to enter the high school.

A mob of 1,000 persons yesterday forced the city and school authorities to withdraw nine Negro students who had attended integrated classes for 3 hours and 13 minutes. The students did not try to enter the school today.

Mrs. L. C. Bates, president

Continued on Page 15, Column 1

CONGRESS IS SPLIT ON USE OF TROOPS

Johnston Calls for Faubus to Resist President but Others Hail His Move

By JOHN W. FINNEY
Special to The New York Times.

WASHINGTON, Sept. 24—Congressional reaction to President Eisenhower's decision to use troops in the Little Rock integration crisis ranged from angry denunciation to outright praise today.

Southern Senators sharply criticized the President and suggested he had exceeded his legal authority. Northern Senators supported the President, but some of them expressed reservations that the action was rather belated.

Expects Faubus to Act

Senator Olin D. Johnston, Democrat of South Carolina, suggested that Gov. Orval E. Faubus of Arkansas "stand up for states' rights" and force a showdown with the President by calling out the Arkansas National Guard on his own.

Senator Johnston, a former Governor of South Carolina, said if he were Governor Faubus, "I'd proclaim a state of insurrection down there, and I'd call out the National Guard, and I'd then find out who's going to run things in my state."

Asked by reporters whether he believed Governor Faubus would take such steps, Senator Johnston said, "I think he will and I hope he will."

Aiken Defends Move

Senator John L. McClellan, Democrat of Arkansas, said he believed such use of military force by the Federal Government was "without authority of law."

He said he was "very apprehensive that such action may precipitate more trouble than it will prevent."

Senator Richard B. Russell, Democrat of Georgia and leader of Southern opposition to the Civil Rights Bill in the last session, said that President Eisenhower's use of troops might "put Negro children in the white schools," but that it would "have a calamitous effect on race relations and on the cause of national unity."

On the other side of the issue, Senator George D. Aiken, Republican of Vermont, said the President "is undoubtedly with-

Continued on Page 17, Column 3

U. S. Cutters Conquer Northwest Passage

3 Coast Guard Craft First of the Nation to Make Transit

By JOHN H. FENTON
Special to The New York Times.

BOSTON, Sept. 24 — Two Coast Guard cutters were saluted in Boston Harbor today at the end of a successful mission to find a practical Northwest Passage—a route around the top of the North American Continent.

A third cutter, the Spar, proceeded directly to her home port at Bristol, R. I., to be welcomed there as the first United States vessel to circumnavigate the continent.

The cutters Storis, from Juneau, Alaska, and the Bramble, from Miami, Fla., put in here for their welcoming. They will continue their homeward voyages later in the week.

The three cutters were the first United States vessels to make the passage.

The shrill sirens of water-spouting fireboats and the deeper-throated whistles of other craft sounded a "well done" as the two bulky cutters made their way up the harbor.

Ranking Coast Guard officers and civil officials joined with members of families of the crews in a dockside welcome as the cutters tied up at

Continued on Page 10, Column 1

U. S. Coast Guard

Coast Guardsmen on the stern of the Spar view her sister cutters, Bramble, left, and Storis, during the transit of Simpson Strait. This was a difficult part of the voyage.

Rebel Chief Seized In Algiers Gunfight

By THOMAS F. BRADY
Special to The New York Times.

ALGIERS, Algeria, Sept. 24—The chief of the nationalist terrorist organization in Algiers was in the hands of French parachute troops today. The rebel leader, Saadi Yacef, 29 years old, had eluded capture in the crowded Casbah for more than two years.

With him was 24-year-old Miss Zorah Drif, an Algerian revolutionary, who was condemned to death in absentia by a French military tribunal.

A parachute colonel told reporters this evening that Mr. Yacef and Miss Drif had surrendered at 5:30 A. M. after the terrorist chief had wounded a lieutenant colonel and a master sergeant of a Foreign Legion parachute regiment. The colonel then told how he found a hideout high in the Casbah where he described how the

Continued on Page 4, Column 3

Price Index Up .2%; Sets Another High

By RICHARD E. MOONEY
Special to The New York Times.

WASHINGTON, Sept. 24—The United States Consumers' Price Index rose two-tenths of a per cent in August, setting another record. It was the twelfth consecutive monthly increase, but among the smallest of the twelve.

The Labor Department's Bureau of Labor Statistics reported today that the index rose in August to 121, using the price average in the 1947-49 period as a comparison base of 100. All the major categories of prices increased, but food and housing were the strongest factors.

The August index was 3.6 per cent higher than that of a year earlier. This meant that a typical city family paid $1.03 3/5 in August of 1957 for the goods and services that cost $1 in August of 1956.

The Commerce Department

Continued on Page 24, Column 3

Textile Union Gets 30 Days to Reform

By A. H. RASKIN

A scandal-tainted textile union was ordered yesterday to oust its two chief officers within thirty days or face possible suspension from the merged labor federation.

The ultimatum was given to the 40,000-member United Textile Workers by the executive council of the American Federation of Labor and Congress of Industrial Organizations.

It foreshadowed the fixing of a similar clean-up deadline today for the 1,400,000-member International Brotherhood of Teamsters and the 140,000-member Bakery and Confectionery Workers International Union.

The federation's Ethical Practices Committee has found all three unions guilty of violating the anti-racketeering provisions of the A. F. L.-C. I. O. constitution. The findings were based

Continued on Page 13, Column 1

"All the News That's Fit to Print"

The New York Times

LATE CITY EDITION

U. S. Weather Bureau Report (Page 54) forecasts: Mostly fair, little temperature change today, tonight, tomorrow. Temp. range: 64—50. Yesterday: 61.8—47.3.

VOL. CVII . . No. 36,623. © 1958, by The New York Times Company, Times Square, New York 36, N. Y. NEW YORK, FRIDAY, MAY 2, 1958. 10c beyond 100-mile zone from New York City. Higher in air delivery cities. FIVE CENTS

U.S. Satellites Find Radiation Barrier

Detect Intense Block to Space Traveler 600 Miles Up

By JOHN W. FINNEY

Special to The New York Times

WASHINGTON, May 1—United States satellites have detected a mysterious band of extremely intense radiation some 600 miles in space.

The radiation, 1,000 times more powerful than had been expected by scientists, raises a new obstacle to manned space flight. Scientists must now start redesigning future space ships to shield human passengers against the radiation.

The radiation is so intense that a space traveler would use up his weekly tolerance dose of radiation in one and a half hours. Scientists believe, however, that the radiation can be reduced to tolerable levels by enclosing the space travelers in a thin protective shield of lead.

The belt of intense radiation, which may stretch for several thousand miles into space, was discovered by the two Army Explorer satellites launched earlier this year. Both satellites were equipped with Geiger counters to measure the radiation, particularly from cosmic rays, in space.

The scientific findings obtained from the two satellites were described in detail for the first time today before scientists of the National Academy of Sciences and the American Physical Society. Later, the results were discussed at a news conference by scientists participating in the International Geophysical Year satellite program.

As a more encouraging sidelight, the satellites demonstrated that it was possible to develop space vehicles whose temperatures could be kept within tolerable limits for humans and

Continued on Page 6, Column 4

Associated Press Wirephoto

Dr. James A. Van Allen, at a meeting of scientists in Washington, tells of discovery of intense radiation belt.

Pravda Says Flight in Space Affected Laika's Heartbeat

By HARRY SCHWARTZ

Pravda has reported that the dog Laika revealed an unexpected effect of weightlessness when she was launched into space on Sputnik II last November.

While the satellite was being accelerated into orbit, Laika's heartbeat increased to about three times its normal rate, and then decreased somewhat even while acceleration continued. This had apparently been expected.

But then Pravda reports after acceleration ceased it took three times as long for Laika's heartbeat to return to normal as had been expected on the basis of tests on earth. During the tests the dog had been subjected to the same accelerations as she experienced in the satellite.

The Pravda report, in last Sunday's issue which arrived here yesterday, is the first comprehensive Soviet statement of scientific findings from the two Soviet satellites. It offers an explanation for the anomaly.

It suggests that in the experiments on earth the dog returned immediately to normal conditions once the effects of the experimental acceleration ceased. Within the satellite, however, the dog found herself in an unprecedented condition of weightlessness once the acceleration ceased. The weightlessness,

Continued on Page 6, Column 7

DULLES FORESEES A 'COLD WAR' CURB IN ARCTIC WATCH

Hints U. S. May Cut Flights of Strategic Bombers if Soviet Backs Plan

SAYS OFFER IS SINCERE

Reveals Private Meetings With Moscow Aides Here—Denies Gromyko Charges

Transcript of news conference is printed on Page 4.

By E. W. KENWORTHY

Special to The New York Times.

WASHINGTON, May 1—Secretary of State Dulles said today that an East-West agreement on an Arctic inspection zone might well be the turning point in the "cold war."

Mr. Dulles said at his news conference that if the Soviet Union would agree to a plan for such a zone and if international inspection disclosed no Soviet bomber and missile bases in the Soviet Arctic, the United States might reduce its flights of nuclear-armed bombers in the Arctic area.

Two days ago the United Nations Security Council debated a United States resolution calling for studies on Arctic inspection, on the ground and in the air, to guard against surprise attack across the polar region.

Soviet Rejection Recalled

Arkady A. Sobolev, the Soviet delegate, called the resolution a "diversionary maneuver." At a Moscow news conference, Andrei A. Gromyko, Soviet Foreign Minister, said the United States plan was a deceitful propaganda attempt to divert world attention from the "provocative" flights of American bombers. However, the United States plan won support not only from the non-Communist members of the Security Council but also from Secretary General Dag Hammarskjold.

Today Secretary Dulles walked into his news conference armed with a 600-word statement disputing the Soviet allegations.

The United States proposal was put forward "not as a maneuver, not as propaganda, but in a sincere effort to meet the admitted problems of a particular area," he said.

Private Talks Disclosed

As evidence of the sincerity of the United States move, Mr. Dulles told how last Saturday afternoon—three days before the Security Council debate—he met privately with Mikhail A. Menshikov, the Soviet Ambassador, and gave him a message on the plan, which had been authorized by President Eisenhower.

Mr. Dulles said that Henry Cabot Lodge, United States delegate at the United Nations, had had a similar meeting with Mr. Sobolev.

The Secretary said that the response of the two Soviet diplomats was not exactly heartwarming, though they had not used the extraordinarily violent phrases of Mr. Gromyko.

In his formal statement, Mr. Dulles conceded that the United States kept its bombers aloft at all times because it feared "the Soviets may launch a nuclear attack against us over the top

Continued on Page 4, Column 4

4 Pacifists Seized At Sea Off Hawaii

Special to The New York Times.

HONOLULU, May 1—Four pacifists intent on violating off-limits restrictions guarding the Einiwetok nuclear testing grounds were seized by the Coast Guard and arrested here today.

The four men, defying orders of the Atomic Energy Commission, the Navy and an injunction re-issued today by Federal Judge Jon Wiig, took their thirty-foot ketch Golden Rule out of the harbor and set sail for Einiwetok. A half-hour later, they were overtaken by a Coast Guard cutter and brought back to the Alai Wai Boat Harbor.

After a hearing at which the crewmen pleaded not guilty Judge Wiig ordered the men held in Honolulu City County Jail. They rejected bail on the ground that it was against their religious principles and will stand trial on Wednesday.

United State Attorney Louis B. Blissard swore out warrants for their arrest on

Continued on Page 7, Column 4

ARGENTINA HANDS REINS TO FRONDIZI

New President Is Sworn In—Nixon Misses the Oath—Peronists Demonstrate

By TAD SZULC

Special to The New York Times.

BUENOS AIRES, May 1—Arturo Frondizi, who three years ago was a persecuted Opposition politician, took office today as Argentina's first freely elected President in twelve years.

Vice President Richard M. Nixon of the United States, who traveled to Buenos Aires to attend the inauguration, missed it by twelve minutes.

Mr. Nixon, who arrived in the city yesterday, was delayed by heavy traffic in the streets and thick crowds inside the Congress building, where the ceremony began four minutes ahead of the scheduled time. However, Mr. Nixon heard part of the inaugural speech.

Difficulties Ahead

The inauguration may mark the end of the political upheavals that have shaken this nation of 21,000,000 inhabitants since 1930 and culminated successively in a decade of dictatorship under Juan D. Perón and in the revolution that ended it in September, 1955.

Nonetheless, immense difficulties face President Frondizi.

The inaugural speech and a series of incidents surrounding today's ceremonies were reminders that while Argentina had restored democracy she had not yet solved all the problems inherited from the recent past.

Addressing a joint session of Congress immediately after he and Vice President Alejandro Gomez were sworn in for their six-year term, President Frondizi said the economic situation of the country was "dramatic."

Most of his speech, which lasted an hour and twenty min-

Continued on Page 8, Column 4

LINCOLN SQ. PLAN UPHELD AS LEGAL BY APPEALS COURT

Protest Against Sale of Land to Fordham Fails—Work Expected to Start Soon

Text of court's decision will be found on Page 17.

By CHARLES GRUTZNER

The legality of the $205,000,000 Lincoln Square redevelopment project was upheld yesterday by the Court of Appeals.

The state's highest tribunal ruled in Albany that neither the State nor Federal Constitution had been violated in the resale to Fordham University of a campus site at a price less than what the city had paid to acquire it.

Opponents of the slum clearance project had contended that such a resale to the Roman Catholic institution involved a subsidy and therefore violated constitutional guarantees of the separation of church and state.

The decision rejecting this contention was unanimous. The opinion was written by Associate Judge Charles S. Desmond.

Way Apparently Cleared

The decision apparently cleared the way for an early start on the three-year job of relocating more than 5,000 families and business tenants from the thirteen-block area north and west of Columbus Circle. The Federal Government is contributing $28,000,000 and the city $14,000,000 toward slum clearance of the site.

Besides the Fordham campus, the project will include the construction of a new Metropolitan Opera House, Philharmonic concert hall, other edifices of the performing arts, private rental and cooperative housing, retail stores and a Red Cross headquarters.

Harris L. Present, lawyer for the plaintiffs, said last night he would "appeal with all deliberate speed" to the United States Supreme Court.

Early Start Foreseen

Sponsors of the proposed redevelopment said they expected to begin tenant relocation—the first step toward demolition of the old buildings and construction of the new—with a minimum of delay.

The sponsors said they would set a date to start relocation after their lawyers had studied the text of the opinion. Although the allegations of subsidy to a sectarian institution had involved only the Fordham campus site—the two blocks from Sixtieth to Sixty-second Street between Columbus and Amsterdam Avenues—the other sponsors also had delayed relocation.

The Court of Appeals accepted as a fact that Fordham was getting the site for about $3,500,000 less than what it cost the city. But the opinion held that this was not a subsidy because "what the city bought is not the same as what Fordham bought."

This finding sustained the contention of slum clearers that the value of slum properties is not

Continued on Page 17, Column 5

Mrs. Kross Accused By One of Top Aides On Outbreak in Jail

By JACK ROTH

A high official in the city Correction Department bitterly criticized his chief yesterday.

He charged that Commissioner Anna M. Kross had "deliberately misled the press" when she said in an interview that no correction officer had been injured in a disturbance in the Women's House of Detention Saturday night.

He said further that Mrs. Kross denied yesterday that she had told the detectives not to make an arrest, but a policeman in the Sixth Precinct insisted that Mrs. Kross had told detectives: "Don't make an arrest. I'll take care of the situation. This is my problem."

According to the Correction Department official, who asked not to be identified, three guards were injured in the disturbance.

"One was kicked in the stomach and was under a physician's care for two days," the official said. "A second had her eyeglasses broken and her uniform ripped and a third was slapped and pushed around."

It was learned that these correction officers had testified before a grand jury on Tuesday and that an indictment for assault was expected against some of the inmates.

When asked why she had said no correction officers were injured during the disturbance, Mrs. Kross said she "did not

Continued on Page 16, Column 2

POLITICS IS HINTED IN APALACHIN CASE

Reuter, in Final Report to Harriman, Theorizes Gang Discussed Lobbying

By PETER KIHSS

A state report said yesterday that the Apalachin, N. Y., gangland convention last Nov. 14 "presumably" met to discuss "lobbying, including political contributions," as well as to divide jurisdiction over illicit activities.

The report was the final one to Governor Harriman of Arthur L. Reuter, whose post as Acting Commissioner of Investigation ended Wednesday night. Mr. Reuter also cited "reasonable inference or speculation" that the gathering was a meeting of "the so-called Mafia."

Genovese Named

At least eight of the sixty-two or more participants, he reported, "are identified in various law enforcement agency files as leading members" of that reputed international criminal society. John C. Montana, former City Councilman in Buffalo, "is reputed to be high in Mafia circles in the Buffalo area," the report added.

The report gave dossiers on sixty-one participants, including Vito Genovese of Atlantic Highlands, N. J., "said to receive $20,000 weekly from Italian policy operation in New Jersey." Genovese, the report said, is also believed to have "a stake in the Monte Carlo lottery in Europe" and interests in four Manhattan clubs, among other operations.

Mr. Reuter said further state

Continued on Page 18, Column 8

Top Marine Sees a Threat To Corps in Pentagon Bill

By RUSSELL BAKER

Special to The New York Times.

WASHINGTON, May 1—The Marines went to the Capitol today and opened the first military beachhead against President Eisenhower's program to reorganize the Pentagon. Gen. Randolph McC. Pate, the corps commandant, conducted the assault.

General Pate began by telling the House Armed Services Committee that he "applauded" the President's "general objectives" and endorsed establishment of a centralized office to handle research and engineering.

But after these brief amenities, General Pate opened the first direct attack on the program that has yet come from any of the armed services.

He specifically opposed the President's bid for greater authority to transfer, consolidate and abolish service roles and missions. This is one of the central points of the program.

Purpose 'Not Clear'

He said the unified commands were "operating satisfactorily" and that the purpose of Administration proposals affecting them was "not clear" to him. These proposals are also central to the President's program.

He disagreed with the fundamental "philosophy" behind the reorganization.

"I'd like to see more decentralization in the departments rather than concentrating it in the Department of Defense," he told a questioner.

He viewed with "real apprehension" the prospect that an official less enlightened than the President might use the bill to "rationalize the Marine Corps out of a job," or give it "the bum's rush." The Administration has insisted there is no such intent.

To some observers it had seemed yesterday that Admiral Arleigh A. Burke, Chief of Naval Operations, came perilously close to mutiny when he gave highly qualified Naval backing to the program. General Pate left no doubts.

Wider Power Defended

The Administration, meanwhile, handed the committee a closely reasoned justification for broadening the power of the President and the Secretary of Defense to transfer, abolish or consolidate roles and missions. The committee, like General Pate, is also hostile to this plan.

The core of the debate is as follows:

Opponents in the committee and General Pate contend that the terms of the President's proposal would make it possible for some future Executive to render impotent whole military services by issuing a fiat that Congress would be powerless to countermand.

The Administration contends that it envisages no such sweeping application. It says it simply wants legal authority to back

Continued on Page 7, Column 2

MITCHELL EXPECTS TAX DECISION SOON

Sees a Determination in 30 to 60 Days—Terms a Cut Best Emergency Weapon

By EDWIN L. DALE Jr.

Special to The New York Times.

WASHINGTON, May 1—The Secretary of Labor said today that a decision on whether to "bolster the economy" by further Government action would have to be made in the next thirty to sixty days.

The Secretary, James P. Mitchell, said he would favor a tax reduction as the weapon if such a determination was made.

Mr. Mitchell's remarks at his news conference, added to a statement made in the Senate earlier this week by Senator Lyndon B. Johnson, Democrat of Texas, helped to keep alive the tax-cutting possibility.

However, there has been no discernible change in the position of President Eisenhower, who has called such a measure "emergency" action and has expressed his belief that the recession is "flattening out."

Today a wide variety of organizations testifying before the

Continued on Page 14, Column 4

HOUSE APPROVES PRESIDENT'S PLAN ON JOBLESS PAY

Southern Democrats Help to Defeat Their Party's Broader Bill, 223-165

SENATE GETS MEASURE

It Provides for 13 Weeks of Extra Benefits at Rates Ranging Up to $45

By JOHN D. MORRIS

Special to The New York Times.

WASHINGTON, May 1—The House of Representatives handed President Eisenhower a major victory today as it approved his plan for supplementary unemployment compensation to jobless workers.

Southern Democrats teamed with Republicans to vote down a much broader proposal of the Democratic leadership, 223 to 165. The Administration bill, with relatively minor modifications, was then passed by 370 to 17. It now goes to the Senate.

The approved measure calls for thirteen weeks of payments in New York and most other states at rates ranging up to $45 a week. Workers who exhaust their benefits in the current recession under the existing Federal-state unemployment insurance system would be eligible.

More than 3,000,000 may benefit if the bill is enacted in its present form. The cost, estimated at $800,000,000 would ultimately be paid either by the states or by a higher Federal tax on business concerns participating in the unemployment insurance program.

Senate Hearings to Start

The Senate Finance Committee expects to start hearings on the measure within about ten days. Prospects for favorable action there appear to be good.

The key vote in the House came on a proposal to substitute a slightly modified version of the Administration bill for the pending Democratic bill.

The $1,500,000,000 Democratic measure had been under heavy fire from President Eisenhower and others as a dole. Their main objection was to provisions for benefits to non-insured workers as well as those covered by unemployment compensation laws.

On the decisive roll-call, 163 Republicans and sixty Democrats voted to kill the Democratic bill and substitute the Administration plan.

Herlong Offers Motion

Seventeen Republicans and 148 Democrats opposed the move. The successful motion was made by Representative A. Sydney Herlong Jr., Democrat of Florida. He had active and coordinated support from House Republican leaders and Representative Howard W. Smith, Democrat of Virginia, as leader of an unusually large Southern conservative bloc.

It was apparent that the Democratic leadership had done little to keep Southerners in its camp.

One explanation, offered by Republicans and shared by some Democrats, was that the leaders were trying to make a political issue rather than win a fight.

"If I were running in a close district, I'd love to have this

Continued on Page 14, Column 3

U. N. Chief Appeals For Arms Talk Now

By LINDESAY PARROTT

Special to The New York Times.

UNITED NATIONS, N. Y., May 1—Secretary General Dag Hammarskjold renewed today his appeal to all nations to seize upon "any honest initiative by any government" to break the dangerous deadlock over disarmament.

Delay and detailed argument over the crucial disarmament issue gave him the feeling "that we may have missed the bus," he said, adding:

"We should not be too sure that the road will remain open for buses in the future."

The Secretary General made his remarks at a news conference to explain in part his surprise appearance Tuesday before the Security Council in behalf of a United States resolution calling for international inspection of the Arctic regions.

Continued on Page 2, Column 3

Associated Press Radiophoto

VIEW INAUGURAL PARADE: Newly inaugurated President Arturo Frondizi, left, and Vice President Alejandro Gomez of Argentina with Vice President Nixon in Buenos Aires.

Italian Cave Yields Ancient Art Gallery

By ARNALDO CORTESI

Special to The New York Times.

SPERLONGA, Italy, May 1—An archaeological find of outstanding importance has been made in a cave facing the sea on the Gulf of Gaeta, about halfway between Rome and Naples.

The cave must at one time have been a kind of art gallery, for pieces of fine ancient Greek sculptures have been found in such large numbers that the archaeologists have dubbed it "a mine of statuary."

No fewer than twenty-two marble heads have been found so far.

The twenty-two heads correspond to the same number of statues dating back to the last centuries before the Christian era and to the early part of the first century A. D.

The statues are of various sizes. Some are twice life size

Continued on Page 12, Column 4

Rogers Bids Public Back Courts Against 'Kill the Umpire' View

Special to The New York Times.

WASHINGTON, May 1—Attorney General William P. Rogers called on the public today to support the courts against a "kill the umpire" attitude.

"All Americans must keep in mind that our constitutional safeguards would have little lasting value in the hands of a subservient or timorous judiciary," he said.

In the Senate, meanwhile, a skirmish broke out on a bill to curb the Supreme Court and void some of its recent decisions.

Mr. Rogers spoke at an official ceremony celebrating Law Day, which was proclaimed by the President as a tribute to the American legal system. About 30,000 similar ceremonies were held around the country.

John Lord O'Brian, constitutional lawyer, also spoke on the need to support the courts.

"Periodically, even lawyers have to remind themselves that there can be no adequate protection of individual rights without the alert supervision of the courts," he said.

"It is the courts in this country that are the last bulwark against intolerance, passion and usurpation of power."

Mr. O'Brian said it was the particular "obligation of the bar to defend the courts against intemperate criticism." He warned that "irresponsible critics" of the Federal courts were "betraying the American tradition of fair play and toleration."

Mr. Rogers said:

"Many of the significant, and what today are regarded as the wisest and most profound, decisions of the courts were very

Continued on Page 16, Column 5

Dr. Vivan Fuchs at Shackleton Base, just prior to leaving for the South Pole. Dr. Fuchs and a party of eleven reached the Pole after travelling for fifty-six days over the 900 miles from Shackleton Base.

The South Pole: circled by oil drums and with the flags of the United Nations and the United States waving in the bitter wind.

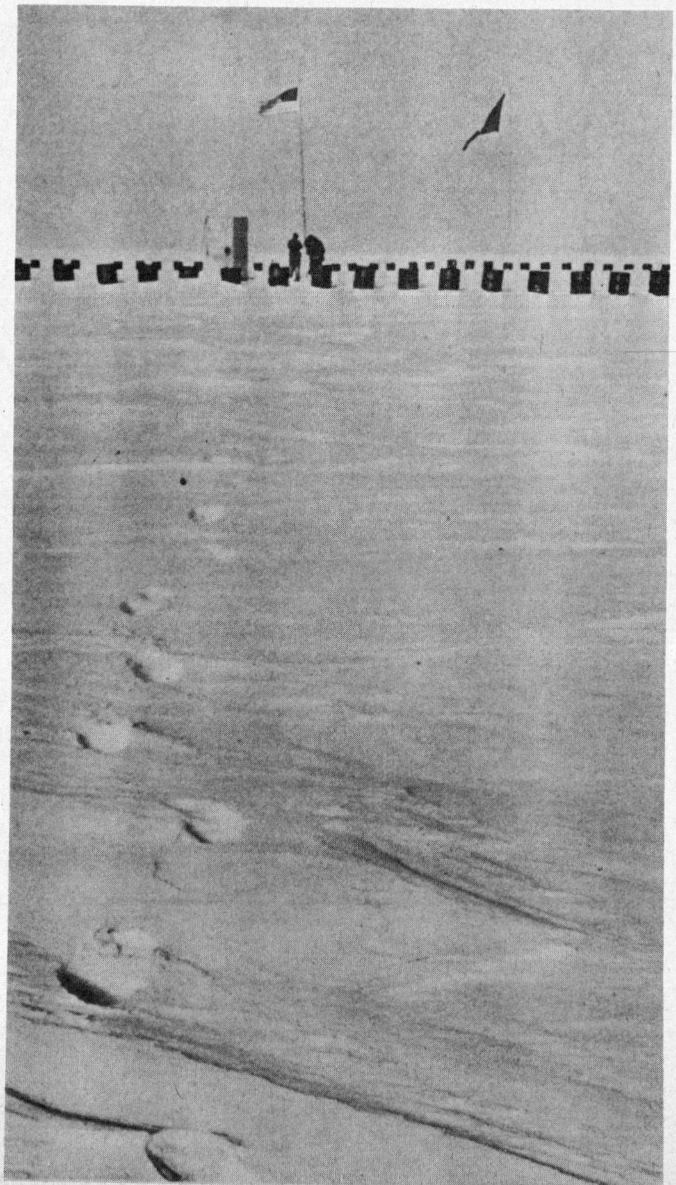

"All the News That's Fit to Print"

The New York Times.

LATE CITY EDITION

U.S. Weather Bureau Report (Page 38) forecasts: Mostly fair and mild today. Mild tomorrow, chance of showers.

Temp. range: 55.—40. Yesterday: 51.6—41.8.

VOL. CVII...No. 36,493.

NEW YORK, MONDAY, DECEMBER 23, 1957.

10c beyond 100-mile zone from New York City

FIVE CENTS

PRESIDENT TO GIVE REPORT TO NATION TONIGHT ON NATO

A Joint Eisenhower-Dulles Statement on Paris Talks Will Be Broadcast

SECRET PARLEYS URGED

Mansfield Says Only Thus Can East and West Attain Disarmament Accord

By E. W. KENWORTHY

Special to The New York Times.

WASHINGTON, Dec. 22 — White House and State Department officials were working today on the joint report President Eisenhower and Secretary of State Dulles will make to the nation tomorrow night on the North Atlantic Council meeting in Paris.

The broadcast, which will begin at 8:30 P. M., will be carried by major radio and television networks.

Tomorrow afternoon the President will light the traditional national Christmas tree in the oval behind the White House and deliver a Christmas message as part of the capital's "Pageant of Peace."

Eisenhowers at Church

Today the President and Mrs. Eisenhower attended divine service at the National Presbyterian Church.

State Department spokesmen could not say today whether the President and Secretary Dulles would take any notice of the speeches made yesterday before the Supreme Soviet (Parliament) by Nikita S. Khrushchev, Communist party leader, and Foreign Minister Andrei A. Gromyko.

In their speeches, the Soviet leaders denounced the proposals made by the NATO powers in Paris for the resumption of disarmament talks and reiterated Soviet conditions for new discussions.

The talks held last spring and summer in London by the United Nations Disarmament Subcommittee ended in deadlock. The allied communiqué last week looked to a resumption either within a United Nations framework or at a foreign ministers' meeting.

Proposals by Soviet

Yesterday the Soviet leaders said either way would result in nothing but "sterile" negotiations. They proposed a special session of the United Nations General Assembly or an international conference that would include all Communist and non-Communist countries.

Mr. Khrushchev also reiterated earlier Soviet suggestions for a heads-of-government meeting. This, he said, should be preceded by a meeting of

Continued on Page 3, Column 5

Associated Press Radiophoto

CHRISTMAS MESSAGE: Pope Pius delivering his annual message yesterday over new Vatican broadcasting station. Pontiff called upon "all rulers of men * * * to deter whoever should aim at disturbing the peace."

Pope Upholds NATO Aim Of Deterring Aggression

By ARNALDO CORTESI

Special to The New York Times.

ROME, Dec. 22—Pope Pius XII endorsed today in his Christmas message deterrence of aggression as a legitimate purpose of the North Atlantic Treaty. The world has "already experienced too much suffering" and deserves "a breathing spell," the Pope

Text of the Pope's message is printed on Page 4.

said in the message broadcast to the world.

He therefore urged the West neither to be overawed by Soviet earth satellites nor to reject any "approaches aiming at peace agreements."

The Pontiff endorsed deterrence of aggression only three days after a conference in Paris of the Atlantic alliance that decided to bolster the West's ability to deter aggression by basing missiles with atomic warheads on the territory of most of the European allies and Turkey. The conference also called for new discussions with the Soviet Union looking toward disarmament.

Without actually mentioning the North Atlantic Treaty Organization or the Soviet Union, the Pope made his point clear by dwelling on the duties that present international conditions placed upon "all rulers of men."

The Divine Law of harmony in the world, he said, imposes an obligation upon the rulers "to prevent war by means of suitable international organiza-

Continued on Page 4, Column 1

CONGRESS EXPECTS LENGTHY SESSION

New Problems and Host of Old Ones Pack Docket of Election-Year Meeting

By C. P. TRUSSELL

Special to The New York Times.

WASHINGTON, Dec. 22—In addition to the continuing rise of new and crucial problems, the second session of the Eighty-fifth Congress is facing a great load of unfinished business. Much of this backlog will be important legislatively and politically to the election-year session, which convenes on Jan. 7.

Moreover, much of the business left unfinished when Congress adjourned on Aug. 30 interlocks with the new problems. Such matters include budgetary decisions on possible expansion of spending, the missiles program that Congress thought was progressing well and Soviet advances in science. Also there are domestic programs of political import that were put aside in the getaway rush last summer.

Even with the new proposals coming up, members of Congress remain interested in programs that were deferred in the first session. However, they realize that the new matters might crowd out older programs that could mean re-election or defeat for some of

Continued on Page 10, Column 3

NASSAU, SUFFOLK FACING PROBLEMS OF SWIFT GROWTH

Need for Schools and Roads Imposes Heavy Tax Load—Political Role Magnified

By LEO EGAN

Nassau and Suffolk Counties are in a state of ferment these days as they try to assimilate the great wave of new population that hit them after World War II.

They must cope with political, governmental, social and other problems caused by extremely rapid growth.

In Nassau the population increased from 406,748 in 1940 to 672,765 in 1950 and to 1,180,000 in 1957, according to Federal censuses. Suffolk went from 197,355 in 1940 to 276,129 in 1950 and 528,836 in 1957.

For Nassau this represented a 190 per cent increase in population between 1940 and 1957 and for Suffolk a 168 per cent increase.

An increase of such magnitude imposed, and continues to impose, heavy strains on schools, highways, churches and community facilities of all kinds.

Main Difficulties Listed

These main problems face the counties today as they attempt to catch their breath during a lull in new housing construction and population influx:

¶Building and paying for school facilities adequate for their needs.

¶Developing highway arteries capable of meeting the needs for commercial, industrial and passenger transportation.

¶Minimizing the divisive effects of conflicts of interest between various groups of both pre-war and post-war settlers.

An inevitable effect of the tremendous growth that has taken place has been a magnifying of the counties' political importance.

Within recent weeks both L. Judson Morhouse, Republican state chairman, and Carmine G. De Sapio, the top political leader in the state Democratic party, have described the counties' role in next year's state election as "pivotal."

Democrats Make Gains

Both counties have been Republican strongholds in all the state and national elections since the end of World War II. In the recent local elections the Democrats, while losing, made spectacular gains.

Republicans attribute the Democratic gains to the popularity of local candidates and dissatisfaction with mounting local taxes, particularly those caused by school expansion. Democrats are hopeful they can continue to exploit local dissatisfactions to hold this year's gains in next year's elections.

In both counties the predominant economic group is the middle-class. Median and average incomes are substantially above the national average and even above the average for the metropolitan New York area.

The education level likewise

Continued on Page 14, Column 1

The New York Times (by Edward Hausner)

INVESTIGATE 'BUGGING': Assemblymen Anthony P. Savarese Jr., right, head of legislative committee, and John Monteleone, left, hold recording tape found behind Palm Garden, meeting place of motormen's union. With them are LeRoy C. Heinz, second from left, transit detective, and Howard F. Cerny, second from right, group's counsel.

CITY COLLEGES GET TECHNOLOGY PLAN

Board Proposes State Aid —Stronger Curriculum and Talent Hunt Asked

A plan to help the municipal colleges meet the need for more scientists, engineers and teachers was announced yesterday by the Board of Higher Education.

The plan was submitted by the board's six-member administrative council. Buell G. Gallagher, president of City College, is chairman.

The council said that municipal colleges were "strained to the breaking point" and urged increased state aid.

"There can be no considerable increase in the number of students trained for critical areas unless immediate steps are taken to provide additional teachers and new buildings," it said.

"Increased state aid would make possible the admission of larger numbers of students, better training for those we have and the extension of graduate and creative work in those areas where a pressing need now unmet exists."

The council's plan also calls for:

¶Eighty-three new teachers in the day sessions to strengthen instruction in the sciences, mathematics, engineering and liberal arts and to provide "adequate counseling that the

Continued on Page 21, Column 5

2 More M.B.A. 'Buggings' Admitted by Transit Aide

By EMANUEL PERLMUTTER

A Transit Authority detective yesterday disclosed two more places where the authority had hidden microphones to spy on the Motormen's Benevolent Association. These were a West Side social hall and the Times Square Hotel.

The authority conceded last week that it had "bugged" two M. B. A. meeting places at 864 Broadway and the Capitol Hotel.

Yesterday's admission was made by Detective LeRoy C. Heinz before the Joint Legislative Committee to Study Illegal Interception of Communications. Conducting the inquiry were Assemblymen Anthony P. Savarese, Republican of Queens, and John Monteleone, Democrat of Brooklyn.

Wagner Displeased

The disclosure produced a new expression of displeasure by Mayor Wagner. On Friday he had characterized the eavesdropping in the union's headquarters on Broadway as "reprehensible."

In an interview as he was leaving the Du Mont television studio at 205 East Sixty-seventh Street after a broadcast, Mayor Wagner said:

"I've been checking the law. If such an operation as planting a bug is legal, that law should be repealed."

Mr. Wagner added that he hoped to meet today with the authority's three members to discuss the eavesdropping. However, he said that he had not yet set the time and place for the meeting.

Charles L. Patterson, chair-

Continued on Page 15, Column 4

PROPOSED SUBWAY TO JERSEY SCORED

$500,000,000 Plan to Speed Commuter Travel Is Called 'Wasteful,' 'Monstrous'

The reaction to a new proposal for a Manhattan-New Jersey subway loop was almost unanimously unfavorable yesterday. The $500,000,000 plan is scheduled to be recommended this week by the Metropolitan Rapid Transit Commission.

The plan was called "disappointing," "wasteful," "monstrous." The nearest to commendation was a remark that the plan was "feasible."

State Attorney General Louis J. Lefkowitz said that a constitutional amendment might be necessary to get the money. That would put the matter off two years or more.

The ten unsalaried members of the commission—there are five each from New Jersey and New York—are believed to have agreed on the proposal that they will present to the Legislatures of the two states. The members will meet Thursday.

The plan is a modification of one announced last May. It was the work of Arthur W. Page, the commission's project director, who had conducted a lengthy survey of the rapid transit situation.

The Page report suggested a $400,000,000 expenditure for an

Continued on Page 15, Column 1

HARRIMAN WARNS QUILL AS WAGNER URGES PAY TALKS

Governor Calls the State's Condon-Wadlin Curb on Strikes 'Impractical'

PACT EXTENSION BACKED

Lefkowitz Suggests T.W.U. and Transit Board Mark Time for Two Months

By A. H. RASKIN

Governor Harriman lined up behind Mayor Wagner yesterday in demanding that there be no subway strike on New Year's Day.

But the force of the Governor's warning to Michael J. Quill, president of the Transport Workers Union, was blunted by a Harriman admission that he considered the Condon-Wadlin Act "impractical."

The ten-year-old state law requires the dismissal of Civil Service strikers. It also prohibits pay increases for three years to state or city employes rehired after a strike.

The Mayor himself gave a soft answer to the defiant telegram he received Saturday from Mr. Quill. The union chief had advised Mr. Wagner not to try to become a "second-rate Coolidge" with threats to smash a T. W. U. walkout.

Mayor Stands Pat

The Mayor told reporters that he was standing by his notice to Mr. Quill that he would "marshal the fullest resources of the city" to keep the subways running.

However, he added an expression of "sincere hope" that the Transit Authority and the Quill union would "sit down and bargain collectively" to negotiate a new wage agreement.

The T. W. U. strike threat grew out of an announcement by the authority that it could not negotiate until it got "clarification" of the impact of a bill being prepared by leaders of the Republican-controlled Legislature.

Shift in Control Sought

The bill, scheduled for passage next month, is intended to shift control over the designation of subway bargaining agents from the authority to the State Labor Relations Board. The independent Motormen's Benevolent Association, which ended an eight-day subway tie-up last Monday, has warned that it will sue to upset any agreement made with the Quill union before the bill becomes law.

The Mayor's statement indicated a strong possibility that the authority would renew contract talks with the T. W. U. this week. Charles L. Patterson, chairman of the authority,

Continued on Page 15, Column 5

PILLS TO COUNTER RADIATION SOUGHT

Use of Calcium Under Study to Combat Strontium

By JOHN W. FINNEY

Special to The New York Times.

WASHINGTON, Dec. 22 — The Atomic Energy Commission is investigating the possibility of giving populations anti-radiostrontium pills in the event of an atomic attack.

The commission also is studying the possible use of special fertilizers to neutralize radioactive debris from atomic reactor explosions, or possibly even from atomic attacks.

These two new possibilities of radiation countermeasures were disclosed in an interview by Dr. Willard F. Libby, the scientific member of the Atomic Energy Commission.

The two possible countermeasures would be aimed in particular at strontium-90, the dangerous, long-lived radioactive material produced in an atomic reaction. Chemically similar to calcium, strontium-90 tends to concentrate in the human bones, where it can cause bone cancer and leukemia.

Dr. Libby said that two apparently promising avenues for attacking strontium-90 have turned up in the commission's research into radioactive fall-out from atomic tests and the effects on radiation on the human body. The research is part

Continued on Page 6, Column 5

Reds Flock to Cairo For Anti-West Talk

By OSGOOD CARUTHERS

Special to The New York Times

CAIRO, Dec. 22—Delegations from the Communist bloc to the Asian-African People's Solidarity Conference arrived today from Moscow aboard a Soviet TU-104 jet airliner.

The announced aims of the conference, which starts Thursday, are to formulate a joint stand against imperialism and colonialism, against the manufacture, testing and use of nuclear weapons, for peaceful coexistence and for a number of other stereotypes of Soviet propaganda.

The Egyptians organized the conference on the nongovernmental level to promote solidarity among forty-four Asian and African countries, some of which are still under colonial domination. However, large Communist delegations appear

Continued on Page 8, Column 4

Hillary-Fuchs Race to South Pole Indicated

Associated Press

Sir Edmund Hillary

The Times, London

Dr. Vivian Fuchs

The New York Times Dec. 23, 1957

Solid and broken lines show the routes of Sir Edmund Hillary's New Zealand party, proceeding from Depot 700 (1) and of the British expedition, moving from Shackleton (2).

New Zealand Group Leaves Its Base Instead of Waiting for British Party —Each Has About 500 Miles to Go

By BILL BECKER

Special to The New York Times.

SCOTT BASE, Antarctica, Dec. 21—British and New Zealand exploring parties about 1,000 miles apart on opposite sides of the South Pole are apparently in a race to the bottom of the world.

The indicated race developed with Sir Edmund Hillary's decision to push on to the pole from his advance base about 500 miles away. A British group that started from the opposite coast of the Antarctic continent still has more than 500 miles to go.

The New Zealand conqueror of Mount Everest left his advance depot with a party of four last night, according to word radioed to this New Zealand base.

"I am sure that Sir Edmund intends to go to the pole," John Claydon, station leader at Scott Base, said.

He said that he thought Sir Edmund had informed the leader of the British expedition, Dr. Vivian Fuchs, of his intention.

If successful, the party will be the first to negotiate the trip on the surface since Roald Amundsen's group did it in December, 1911.

The original plans of the expedition called for Sir Edmund and his men to proceed only as far as Depot 700 and wait there until the Fuchs party arrived after passing the pole.

The New Zealanders reached that destination last Saturday after an amazingly speedy two-month journey by tractor-train and dog team.

Meanwhile, the British party has been beset by crevasses and bad weather and has yet to reach the British base of South Ice, only 270 miles from Shackleton Base, the party's starting point on the Weddell Sea.

The Weddell Sea is south of the tip of South America while the Ross Sea area, from which Sir Edmund's party began its trek, is south of New Zealand.

The nine-man British party got off to a late start Nov. 27,

Continued on Page 29, Column 4

Tired Britons Rebel Against Yule Tumult

By DREW MIDDLETON

Special to The New York Times

LONDON, Dec. 22—The British are becoming increasingly rebellious about Christmas. They think it is getting too big for St. Nick's britches.

The yearning for an old-fashioned Christmas is evident wherever men gather. And by old-fashioned they don't mean coaches outside Dickensian inns and the wassail of Olde England, but a little less of the great orgy of gift-giving, card-sending and frantic shopping that Christmas has come to be since 1945.

The blame is evenly distributed. There are some who think that every copy of Charles Dickens' "A Christmas Carol" should be bought and burned. One elderly clubman is convinced that the trouble all started with Prince Albert,

Continued on Page 4 Column 2

DRIVE TO TIGHTEN ALIEN LAW BEGINS

Apalachin Raid Leads to Call for Stiff Deportation Act

Special to The New York Times.

WASHINGTON, Dec. 22— The raid last month on a "crime convention" at the upstate New York hamlet of Apalachin apparently has set off a new drive for revision of immigration and naturalization laws. This drive, however, will be to tighten rather than soften the controversial statute, as has been demanded with little success for years.

On Nov. 14 New York State police surrounded sixty-five persons at a convention. The police called them racketeers, ranging from "small fry" to "big shots." The agenda of the convention has not been revealed. Whatever it was, the police and the Immigration Service got busy.

J. M. Swing, Commissioner of Immigration and Naturalization, called for an investigation of the records of those rounded up. It was taken as a new drive against persons possibly subject to deportation or a cancelation of their naturalization papers. Mr. Swing retorted, however, that it was merely an acceleration of a drive he started when he took office in 1954.

The possibility of Congressional action was disclosed today in correspondence between

Continued on Page 29, Column 9

Natural Obstacles Encountered by Polar Explorers

An area of heavy crevassing in the Polar glacier.

Sastrugi which man helped to form: a line of footprints in which the weight-compacted snow had formed a hard core eroded by the wind.

Looking like an aerial view of sand dunes, but in fact an area of snow *Sastrugi* (hard ridges of snow) photographed during Captain Scott's expedition.

"All the News That's Fit to Print"

The New York Times.

LATE CITY EDITION
U. S. Weather Bureau Report (Page 51) forecasts: Variable cloudiness today; fair, colder tonight. Cloudy tomorrow. Temp. range: 46—34. Yesterday: 48.9—33.8

NEWS SUMMARY AND INDEX, PAGE 51

SECTION ONE

VOL. CVII..No. 36,499. NEW YORK, SUNDAY, DECEMBER 29, 1957. TWENTY-FIVE CENTS 35c beyond 100-mile zone from New York City

U. S. TO CUT STAFF WORKING ABROAD ON TECHNICAL AID

Expected to Pare Drastically Number of Experts Now in Underdeveloped Lands

MOVE LINKED TO NIXON

Embassies Raise Warnings That Reductions May Turn Nations Toward Soviet

By E. W. KENWORTHY
Special to The New York Times.

WASHINGTON, Dec. 28—The Administration expects to cut sharply over the next two years the number of American technicians working on technical assistance projects in underdeveloped countries.

The planned cuts are still subject to adjustment, but overseas missions have been notified of the projected reductions in their areas.

The moving force behind the decision to reduce the American staff on technical assistance projects is Vice President Richard M. Nixon, according to officials in the State Department and the International Cooperation Administration.

Mr. Nixon, it is agreed, returned from his travels in the Far East and Africa convinced that there were too many Americans overseas, that they were too conspicuous and that they consequently often created resentment toward the United States.

Smith in Accord With Plan

James H. Smith Jr., the new director of the International Cooperation Administration, is reported to be in thorough accord with the reduction plan.

However, the United States diplomatic missions in those Middle East and Asian countries most vulnerable to Soviet economic penetration are deeply apprehensive over the effects of a cut in American technicians. They have made their fears known to the State Department and I. C. A. in blunt telegrams.

From the United States Embassy in Afghanistan came warning that a renunciation of obligations would disturb relations with Afghanistan; the United States intentions and sincerity would be open to question, and that Afghanistan would turn to the Soviet Union as the only alternative.

Warning Given in Ceylon

The United States Embassy in Ceylon cautioned against violating existing agreements, and pointed out to Washington that the Soviet bloc, which has been exploring possible economic projects with Ceylon, would be eager to furnish technicians to replace those withdrawn by the United States.

From American embassies in Iran, Iraq, Jordan and Nepal came similar protests and warnings.

Officials here are willing to admit that in some places—especially in the capitals of small countries—there are too many Americans, and that they have sowed resentment by their own tribal customs, their glaringly disparate living standards, their cars, their aloofness.

Nevertheless officials here maintain that technicians have contributed little to this situation and that a reduction in their number would not al-

Continued on Page 4, Column 3

Indonesian Premier Denies Hatta Charge

By TILLMAN DURDIN
Special to The New York Times.

JAKARTA, Indonesia, Dec. 28—Premier Djuanda denied today charges by Dr. Mohammed Hatta, former Vice President, that recent Government measures against Dutch interests in Indonesia had been taken without adequate planning.

The Premier conceded that the Government take-over of Dutch enterprises "would bring some temporary suffering" to Indonesians, but said that the Government's moves were based on previously prepared plans and decisions.

Premier Djuanda was answering criticisms contained in an article by Dr. Hatta that appeared this morning in Pedoman, Socialist party organ, and other newspapers. The former Vice President charged that the take-over of

Continued on Page 9, Column 1

ANTI-WEST DRIVES BACKED BY SOVIET

Pledge of Aid Given at Cairo Talk to Indonesia, Algerian Rebels and Jordanians

By OSGOOD CARUTHERS
Special to The New York Times.

CAIRO, Dec. 28—The Soviet Union offered its full backing today to all "movements for independence" from Algeria to Netherlands New Guinea.

The offer was made in the so-called anti-imperialism committee of the unofficial Asian-African Peoples Solidarity Conference here. This was the week-long session's third day.

The chief Soviet representative, Sharaf R. Rashidov, expressed concern for all those living under Western colonial rule or what he called imperialist domination.

'Struggle to Gain Freedom'

Pledging his country's support for anti-Western rebellions throughout the world, he declared:

"The Soviet Union has always been an ardent supporter of the common people in their struggle to gain freedom and the right to a better life."

Mr. Rashidov, his face beaming like a piece of fine mahogany carved in a perpetual smile, once again brought the Soviet Union to the center of the stage in the conference that appears to have dropped all attempts to conceal its pro-Communist leanings. He is president of the Presidium of the Supreme Soviet, or Parliament, of the Uzbek Republic.

The offer of Soviet support went to the Algerians, one of whose rebel leaders, Mohammed

Continued on Page 3, Column 5

WHITE HOUSE SAYS GAITHER REPORT FOUND U. S. STRONG

Hagerty Declares Published Versions Are 'Opposite' of Committee's Estimate

By JAY WALZ
Special to The New York Times.

GETTYSBURG, Pa., Dec. 28—The White House rejected today the idea that the United States "at this time" was weak in relation to the Soviet Union.

James C. Hagerty, White House press secretary, took vigorous exception to published reports that the Gaither committee of Presidential advisers had found the United States to be in a state of peril.

Such a finding was not in the secret report submitted to the President, Mr. Hagerty insisted, and the committee found "just the opposite."

He said the Gaither report was still "classified," and he held out no prospect that it would be made public.

Mr. Hagerty told a news conference that all the "factual material" on which the Gaither findings were based had been available to Congressional committees interested in military preparedness.

President to Give Estimate

In any event, he said, the President will give his estimate of the country's "military posture" in his State of the Union Message next month.

Mr. Hagerty talked with reporters after spending an hour with President Eisenhower this morning.

The President arrived at the family farm near here yesterday for a week of relaxation and work. He plans to work on the State of the Union Message over the week-end. On Monday and Tuesday he will receive key Administration officials for consultations.

The Gaither report, submitted recently to the President, contained findings and recommendations of a special Presidential committee.

It was originally headed by H. Rowan Gaither Jr., a San Francisco lawyer who was recently president of the Ford Foundation.

Report Was Guarded

The report had been one of the Administration's most carefully guarded secrets, and only a few copies are said to exist.

However, various versions of the contents have appeared in the press. These have reported the United States in or facing a state of great peril because of growing Soviet strength in new weapons.

In his comments on the report, Mr. Hagerty carefully distinguished between "at this time" and the future. He said

Continued on Page 8, Column 1

The New York Times

UNION LEADERS MEET: At Transport Workers Union session yesterday were, from the left: Daniel Gilmartin, Mark Kavanagh, Matthew Guinan, Frank Sheehan, Michael J. Quill and Ellis Van Riper. Mr. Quill, the president, holds recent copy of union paper emphasizing plan to strike unless contracts with the Transit Authority and bus lines are obtained. On the walls of office at Transport Hall are signs prepared in case a strike is called.

2d Nuclear Carrier To Lose Its Priority To Atom Submarine

By RICHARD AMPER
Special to The New York Times.

WASHINGTON, Dec. 28—The Administration's attempt to control spending and still meet modern defense needs was expected today to require a major shift in emphasis in naval power.

A Defense Department spokesman said that "in response to the needs of the times," the Navy would be forced to forgo construction next year of a second nuclear-powered aircraft carrier in order to build more nuclear-powered submarines.

This change in the development of the Navy arsenal, although representing an important shift in strategic policy, was said to be only temporary. It was understood to have been dictated by budgetary requirements and the need for submarine missile power, rather than by a new policy of permanently downgrading the role of the carrier.

The Navy had requested $290,000,000 in the military budget for the fiscal year 1959, which begins next July 1, to start laying the hull of a second atomic-powered carrier. But the Defense Department was reported to have turned down the request and was said to

Continued on Page 22, Column 1

REFUGEE PROGRAM EXPIRING TUESDAY

White House Says 38,000 Hungarians Entered U.S. Under Emergency Plan

Special to The New York Times.

GETTYSBURG, Pa., Dec. 28—The emergency program under which 38,000 Hungarians fleeing Soviet rule were brought to this country will end Dec. 31.

President Eisenhower announced this today from his Gettysburg farm, where he is spending a holiday week of rest and work.

The President expressed the hope that more Hungarian refugees might reach this country under provisions of an immigration law Congress passed last session.

Meanwhile James C. Hagerty, White House press secretary, told reporters that the President would again ask Congress to give parolee newcomers the status of permanent residents.

Of the 38,000 Hungarians reaching the United States under the Refugee Relief Act, only 6,130 have received immigration visas under the special provisions of that law. The others were admitted as parolees.

The President asked Congress

Continued on Page 12, Column 3

G.O.P. Bids City and State Apply Condon Act to Quill

By DOUGLAS DALES

The Republican leaders of the Legislature called upon Governor Harriman and Mayor Wagner yesterday to pledge the use of the Condon-Wadlin Act to prevent a strike on the subway on New Year's Day.

The Condon-Wadlin Law, enacted in 1947 as an aftermath to a Buffalo teachers' strike, is designed to prevent strikes among public employes. It sets up severe penalties for those who go on strike.

Assembly Speaker Oswald D. Heck of Schenectady and Senate Majority Leader Walter J. Mahoney of Buffalo asserted yesterday that New Yorkers were without the law's protection because Mayor Wagner, "with the tacit support of Governor Harriman, has deliberately nullified its application whenever the political allies and supporters of the Governor and the Mayor might be affected."

Labor Link Charged

Republican leaders in the past have charged that the Mayor and the Governor were under the domination of leaders of organized labor.

A city-wide transit strike has been threatened for Wednesday by Michael J. Quill's Transport Workers Union.

The legislative leaders said that the Condon-Wadlin Act would work in New York if the Governor and the Mayor had the "unequivocal determination" to enforce it.

They said that the picture of Mayor Wagner "cringing in the face of crude threats to call an illegal strike is hardly one to increase respect for law."

At Albany, a spokesman said that Governor Harriman would have no comment on the Heck-Mahoney statement. However, he pointed out that the Governor "has consistently stated that strikes by public employes cannot be tolerated."

On a television program last Sunday Mr. Harriman termed the Condon-Wadlin Law "impractical" and "unnecessary." It is unnecessary, he said, be-

Continued on Page 29, Column 5

MEANY CRITICIZES U.S. PROFIT REPORT

Tells Weeks He Gives False Picture and Understates Total by 3 to 4 Billion

By JOSEPH A. LOFTUS
Special to The New York Times.

WASHINGTON, Dec. 28—George Meany said today that Commerce Department reports had created "a false impression of corporate profits."

The president of the American Federation of Labor and Congress of Industrial Organizations made this assertion in a letter to Sinclair Weeks, Secretary of Commerce.

"Currently published profit pictures are understated by as much as $3,000,000,000 to $4,000,000,000," Mr. Meany wrote.

His letter raised a question about depreciation allowances that the department had been aware of, as indicated by an article in its October issue of The Survey of Current Business.

Direct Bearing Seen

Since depreciation allowances are written off as a current cost of doing business, Mr. Meany wrote, "the methods of depreciating assets have a direct bearing on reported costs and reported profits. When depreciation methods are changed, reported corporate profits are no longer comparable with each other.

"In 1947 and 1948, for example, corporations used straight-line depreciation, under the existing tax laws. The cost of an asset with a 'normal life' of twenty years was depreciated at a rate of 5 per cent per year. Since 1950 most of the cost of Government-certified defense-related facilities has been depreciated in five years—at a rate of 20 per cent a year.

"In 1954, the revenue law was changed to permit writing off about two-thirds of the costs of all new facilities in one-half the 'normal life' of the item.

"It is the rise in depreciation allowances, under these two provisions, that results in inflating the reported cost of doing business and understating reported profits, by comparison with previous years."

The situation should be corrected, Mr. Meany said, by the "regular preparation and publication of a depreciation adjustment series which takes into account the provisions for accelerated amortization in the 1950 tax revisions and the new method of depreciation contained in the 1954 tax changes."

The department agreed that such a change would reduce the profits ratios but it insisted that the decline would still be significant.

QUILL TURNS DOWN NEW OFFER OF 18C; STRIKE VOTE TODAY

Transit Authority Increases First Figure 5 Cents—Union Calls It Inadequate

SOME PROGRESS NOTED

T.W.U. Chief Still Planning Jan. 1 Tie-up—Bargaining to Gain Speed Tomorrow

By STANLEY LEVEY

The Transit Authority, trying to avert a New Year's Day subway strike, made a new offer yesterday of a wage increase of 18 cents an hour over a two-year contract period.

But Michael J. Quill, president of the Transport Workers Union, swiftly rejected the proposal as completely inadequate. He announced that his organization would go ahead with plans for a strike vote at a special membership mass meeting today. A walkout would begin at midnight Tuesday.

The new offer—the second in two days by the agency—was made during a bargaining meeting at the headquarters of city Labor Commissioner Harold A. Felix, 93 Worth Street. Negotiations began there Thursday, after Mayor Wagner told the authority and the union that neither he nor the people of the city would tolerate a transit strike.

Offered 13 Cents First

The first offer, made Friday and also promptly rejected, was for 13 cents an hour in two stages—8 cents the first year and 5 cents the second. The second offer raised the ante to 10 cents the first year and 8 cents the second.

The proposal to raise wages by 18 cents an hour was identical with an offer made by eight private bus companies to the T. W. U. Contracts covering 8,200 employes of these lines, which carry 2,500,000 passengers daily in the Bronx, Queens and Manhattan, also expire at midnight Tuesday. A failure to settle the subway dispute would also result in a bus strike, confronting New York with an almost complete transit shutdown.

Mr. Quill told the Transit Authority he would be glad to sit down and arrange for the posting of skeleton crews to guard and maintain delicate equipment in case of a strike. Such equipment would include power houses, maintenance of way machinery and bus maintenance gear.

No Narrowing Seen

Mr. Quill's immediate reaction was to notify the authority bargaining team, composed of Charles L. Patterson, chairman; Joseph E. O'Grady, in charge of labor matters, and E. Vincent Curtayne, financial expert, that the new offer had not appreciably narrowed the gap between the two parties.

But the new offer was regarded as progress by some observers. The negotiations were still alive, there had been movement and Mr. Quill would be able to carry to his union meeting today evidence that hard bargaining had produced an increase of 5 cents an hour between offers.

The expectation now is that strenuous negotiations will start tomorrow. No talks are scheduled for today. The hope is that a "final" package can be agreed

Continued on Page 29, Column 1

Discovery of Antarctic Island Is Reported

Ronne Asserts Land Underlies Section of an Ice Shelf

The following article was written by Capt. Finn Ronne, leader of the Weddell Station expedition of the United States National Committee for the International Geophysical Year. He reports from the base his expedition established early this year in Antarctica.

North American Newspaper Alliance.

ELLSWORTH STATION, Antarctica, Dec. 27—Our recent exploratory flights have resulted in what we consider several major geographical discoveries.

After several weeks of painstaking air and surface exploration we are able to announce that a huge island exists off the Antarctic Continent to the west of the Weddell Sea coast, below Cape Horn.

On present maps this expanse bears the name of Filchner Ice Shelf. From the west cape of Gould Bay the island extends 200 nautical miles to Lat. 80 degrees S.

The island's eastern escarpment near the Cape of Gould Bay at Long. 43 degrees W. has three embayments, the largest about fifty miles in depth. The snow-covered island extends to the west along the Weddell Sea coast for about 180 miles.

Its highest inland elevation, at Lat. 80 degrees S. and Long. 48 degrees W., has been recorded to be 3,200 feet above sea level.

When our five-man traverse party crossed the island their seismic soundings proved land underneath the ice shelf to be hundreds of feet above sea level. Many of the other contours of the island have still to be fully delineated farther westward. But they seem to tie in with the land in Catherine Sweeney and Lowell Thomas Mountains groups which Maj. James W. Lassiter and I first saw ten years ago at the base of Palmer Peninsula.

This huge new island discovery seems to limit the extent of the Filchner Ice Shelf from Moltke Nunatak to the east cape of Gould Bay, where the wide shelf terminates.

In many ways our other recent discoveries are even more challenging because they remain

Continued on Page 19, Column 1

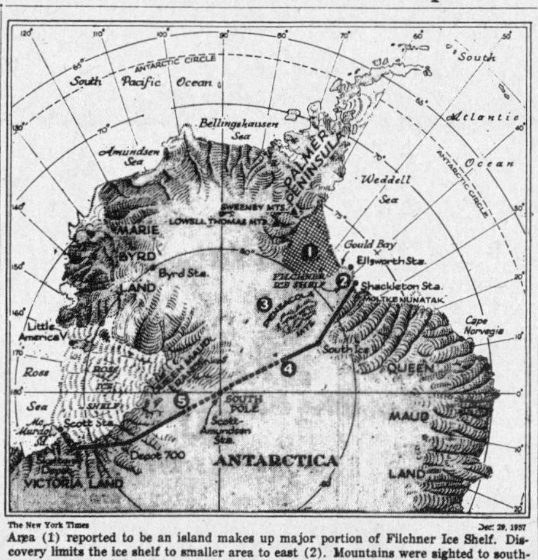

The New York Times Dec. 29, 1957

Area (1) reported to be an island makes up major portion of Filchner Ice Shelf. Discovery limits the ice shelf to smaller area to east (2). Mountains were sighted to southwest (3). Meanwhile, the parties of Dr. Vivian Fuchs (4) and Sir Edmund Hillary (5) were 400 and 240 miles from the Pole. Dotted lines mark remaining distances.

Soviet Nuclear Test Is Reported by U. S.

Special to The New York Times.

WASHINGTON, Dec. 28—The Atomic Energy Commission announced tonight that the Soviet Union was continuing its tests of nuclear weapons and had set off a shot today.

The explosion was the fifth reported by the commission since it announced that the Soviet had begun a series Aug. 23. The commission did not give the magnitude of today's device, saying only that it occurred at the "usual test site in Siberia" in the Asian northlands.

The commission first located the test site Oct. 10 as "north of the Arctic Circle" when it reported a small Soviet explosion on that date.

Today's explosion punctuated major pronouncements made by the Russians yesterday. They reiterated in Moscow their intention to boycott the meeting

Continued on Page 21, Column 4

Chattanooga Judge Urged to Step Down

Special to The New York Times.

NASHVILLE, Tenn., Dec. 28—The Tennessee Bar Association called today upon Judge Raulston Schoolfield of Chattanooga to step down from the bench while under investigation. It declared that if the charges against him were true he should be impeached.

The association, acting through its governing board, said also that Assistant Attorney General W. Corry Smith of Chattanooga and his staff should be permitted to withdraw from the investigation undertaken by the State Government.

At the same time, the executive committee of the State Judicial Council met to discuss charges before the Senate rackets committee that money had been used to influence decisions in Judge Schoolfield's court.

But the conference president,

Continued on Page 26, Column 6

Symington Will Seek Second Senate Term

By The Associated Press

CREVE COEUR, Mo., Dec. 28—Senator Stuart Symington announced today that he would seek re-election to a second Senate term next year.

The Missouri Democrat made the anouncement at his home in this St. Louis suburb.

Senator Symington, a critic of Administration defense policies, issued a statement reviewing his Senate record and pledging to continue to "work for the best interests of my state and nation in the future as in the past."

The 56-year-old Senator, who served under President Truman as Secretary of the Air Force, received 45½ votes from nine states for the 1956 Presidential nomination.

In his statement, Senator Symington said he had opposed such things as the Bricker

Continued on Page 35, Column 1

"All the News That's Fit to Print"

The New York Times.

LATE CITY EDITION

Weather: Periods of drizzle today; cloudy, warmer tonight, tomorrow. Temperature range: today 51-58; Thursday 60-68. Details on Page 73.

VOL. CVII..No. 36,505. © 1958, by The New York Times Company. Times Square, New York 36, N. Y. NEW YORK, SATURDAY, JANUARY 4, 1958. 10¢ beyond 100-mile zone from New York City FIVE CENTS

CIVIL RIGHTS UNIT BEGINS ITS WORK WITHOUT DISSENT

6 Commissioners Sworn In —Several Possibilities for Director Are Suggested

$200,000 FOR EXPENSES

Eisenhower Explains Duties of Federal Study Group in 'Very Broad Terms'

By ANTHONY LEWIS
Special to The New York Times.

WASHINGTON, Jan. 3—The six-man Civil Rights Commission was sworn in today and immediately got to work on its large and controversial assignment.

In its first official day, the commission:

¶Agreed on several possibilities for its key job, a staff director, and sent the names to the White House for the choice.

¶Met with President Eisenhower and then got the views of two of the President's chief assistants at lunch.

¶Drew $200,000 from a Presidential emergency fund to cover its first operating expenses in the absence of a Congressional appropriation.

Unanimity Is Stressed

The chairman of the commission, Dr. John A. Hannah, emphasized in talking with the press the atmosphere of cordiality and agreement that he said existed among the members as they got together for the first time.

"We got along very well," he said. He indicated that every decision made today had the endorsement of all six members.

This was of particular interest because the commission has three Southerners and three Northerners.

The Southern members are former Gov. John S. Battle of Virginia, former Gov. Doyle E. Carlton of Florida and Robert G. Storey, dean of the Southern Methodist University Law School. All are Democrats.

Those from the North are Dr. Hannah, who is president of Michigan State University, the Rev. Theodore M. Hesburgh, president of Notre Dame University, and J. Ernest Wilkins, an Assistant Secretary of Labor, who is a Negro and a native of Chicago. Father Hesburgh is an independent, the other two Republicans.

'Diplomas' Distributed

The members met informally with President Eisenhower for about half an hour this morning. Dr. Hannah said afterward that they had discussed the commission's job and that the President had cast the group's responsibility "in very broad terms."

Sherman Adams, the Assistant to the President, then administered the oath of office to the six men. President Eisenhower gave them what he called "their diplomas for their honorary doctorates."

At lunch the group met with Mr. Adams and Gerald E. Morgan, counsel to the President. The commission then adjourned to its own quarters, a suite of half a dozen offices in a small building less than a block from the White House.

The first business meeting lasted about two hours. There will be another a week from to-

Continued on Page 7, Column 2

Associated Press Wirephoto

PASSES OUT COMMISSIONS: President Eisenhower distributes certificates to members of Civil Rights Commission in Washington. From left: J. Ernest Wilkins, the Rev. Theodore M. Hesburgh, John S. Battle, Doyle E. Carlton, the President and Dr. John A. Hannah. The sixth member, Robert G. Storey, is behind the President.

AIR FORCE SETS UP 2 IRBM SQUADRONS

S.A.C. Units to Go Overseas With Thors and Jupiters by the End of This Year

By JOHN W. FINNEY
Special to The New York Times.

WASHINGTON, Jan. 3—The Air Force announced today the formation of the first two squadrons to be armed with intermediate-range ballistic missiles.

The Air Force indicated that the squadrons, after training, would be sent overseas by the end of the year. Presumably they will go to Britain.

The squadrons will come under the Strategic Air Command.

The 672d Strategic Missile Squadron was activated Jan. 1. It will be equipped with the Thor missile, developed by the Air Force.

The other squadron will be armed with the Jupiter, developed by the Army. It will be activated Jan. 15 as the 864th Strategic Missile Squadron.

To Train in California

Both missiles have a range of 1,500 miles and can carry thermonuclear warheads. Under a Defense Department decision of 1956, the Air Force has operational control of Intermediate Range Ballistic Missiles and of Intercontinental Ballistic Missiles, which are to have a 5,500-mile range.

The Air Force said the squadrons "will be in a training status and will not be equipped for some time." The units will train at the Ballistic Missile Training Center at Camp Cooke Air Force Base in Lompoc, Calif.

In indicating that the squadrons would go overseas this year, the Air Force noted that "it has previously been announced that the first operational IRBM units will be deployed overseas by December, 1958."

The Air Force referred to a statement by the Air Force Secretary, James H. Douglas, before the Senate Preparedness Subcommittee last month that "the Thor is being planned for deployment to the United Kingdom in 1958."

Gen. Lauris Norstad, Supreme

Continued on Page 5, Column 6

Hillary Reaches South Pole By 70-Mile Forced March

Dispatch of The Times, London.

SCOTT BASE, Antarctica, Jan. 3—Sir Edmund Hillary, conqueror of Mount Everest, reached the South Pole tonight after a forced march of seventy miles. He drove his train of tractors and his four New Zealand companions continuously for more than twenty-four hours on the last lap. When he finally decided at 8 P. M. New Zealand time (3 A. M. Eastern standard time) to halt for the night the round tower of the American station at the South Pole was in sight. The buildings of the base could be seen as a black blob on the snow two miles ahead.

[After a night's sleep, the New Zealanders finished their trip Saturday and joined seventeen Americans at the polar station, The Associated Press reported.]

The 38-year-old New Zealander's team thus became the third one ever to reach the South Pole by the overland route—and the first to do it in forty-six years.

The last group, led by Capt. Robert F. Scott of Britain, reached the Pole on Jan. 17, 1912. All of that party perished in a blizzard on the way home.

Captain Scott's group had lost in a race with a team led by Roald Amundsen of Norway, who arrived at the Pole on Dec. 14, 1911.

Polar Station Asleep

When Sir Edmund reached his polar destination tonight he had left only one drum of gasoline—enough for twenty miles. In his words, when he called Scott Base at 10 P. M.:

"We were cutting it rather fine due to the very soft snow experienced."

When the tired New Zealanders had turned in to bed within sight of their objective, no one at the polar station knew of their arrival. Conditions were misty and all the personnel at the polar station, including four newspaper correspondents from London, New York and San Francisco, slept.

Since all time zones converge at the pole, there is no real time. Arbitrarily, most Antarctic stations pick a time schedule, such as that of New Zealand, with which they are in frequent touch.

"Steering by the sun from earlier fixes we came bang on the base," Sir Edmund reported.

Continued on Page 6, Column 2

3 REPORTS MIRROR ECONOMIC DECLINE

New Claims for Jobless Pay a Record—Manufacturing Sales and Inventories Dip

By EDWIN L. DALE Jr.
Special to The New York Times.

WASHINGTON, Jan. 3—Three more Government statistical reports added details today to the picture of decline in the national economy.

New claims for unemployment insurance, an indicator of lay-offs, rose in the week ended Dec. 28 to a total of 550,995, the highest figure since the unemployment insurance system began in 1938. The previous high total was 460,000 in January, 1954.

The Commerce Department reported that sales of manufacturers, seasonally adjusted, had fallen 2 per cent in November, continuing a decline that began earlier in the fall.

Inventories Liquidated

Perhaps most important of all, manufacturers liquidated their inventories for the second month in a row, and by an amount greater than in any month since the 1954 recession. The decline, after seasonal adjustment, was $300,000,000, to a total of $53,800,000,000 at the end of November. This still left inventories higher by $1,600,000,000 than in the same month of 1956.

In another report today the Commerce Department said sales of wholesalers had fallen sharply in November.

[In New Jersey, the director of the State Division of Employment Security declared Friday that unemployment in the state was now greater than at any time since 1949 and that it might soon exceed the figures for that year. He placed the state's total unemployment at 175,000, 20,000 more than in mid-December.]

Holiday Week Noted

The statistics on unemployment insurance claims were reported by the Labor Department. Officials pointed out that the unemployment insurance system now covered far more workers than it had even as recently as the 1954 recession.

In terms of percentage, they said, the figure for Dec. 28 might not have been a record. They also noted that the holiday week might have had an artificially stimulating effect on the total.

None the less, the rise of 137,400 in this figure from the previous week, and 112,000 from the same week of 1956, was clear evidence of fairly heavy lay-offs.

The number of workers actually collecting unemployment insurance was reported at 1,954,200 in the week ended Dec. 21, compared with 1,201,265 in

Continued on Page 8, Column 4

STATE G.O.P. BACKS REFORM OF COURTS

Mahoney-Heck Support of Tweed Commission Aims Spurs Revised Plan

By LEO EGAN
Special to The New York Times.

ALBANY, Jan. 3—Republican leaders of the Senate and Assembly announced today their "wholehearted support" of the court reform objectives of the Tweed Commission.

In a joint statement, Senator Walter J. Mahoney of Buffalo and Assemblyman Oswald D. Heck of Schenectady listed these objectives as:

"1. Consolidation and unification of the major courts in the state and 2. Fixing responsibility for administrative controls."

In a second pre-legislative statement the two Republicans described Governor Harriman as inept, inefficient, vacillating, insincere, overly partisan and motivated by low-grade political expediency.

Senator Mahoney is the temporary president and majority leader of the State Senate. Mr. Heck is the Speaker of the Assembly. Both the Senate and Assembly are controlled by Republicans.

The Mahoney-Heck endorsement of the Tweed Commission's objectives appeared to assure favorable consideration by the Legislature of a constitutional amendment providing for court reform this year. A proposed amendment was approved in the Senate but defeated in the Assembly last year

Continued on Page 18, Column 2

SAVARESE URGES GRAND JURY STUDY TRANSIT 'BUGGING'

Legislator Sees Perjury as Possibility in Conflict of Views at Hearing

By RALPH KATZ

The possibility of a grand jury investigation into the "bugging" by the Transit Authority of the headquarters and meeting places of the Motormen's Benevolent Association was indicated yesterday.

Assemblyman Anthony D. Savarese Jr., chairman of the Joint Legislative Committee to Study Illegal Interception of Communications, said he would recommend an inquiry to the full committee.

Mr. Savarese disclosed his intention as the committee ended two weeks of hearings on the installation of a hidden microphone in the M. B. A. offices.

In another transit development, Mayor Wagner named a four-man union committee to seek a formula for permanent labor peace on the subway system, but the idea ran into a flurry of opposition immediately.

Committee Action Sought

At the "bugging" inquiry Assemblyman Savarese, Queens Republican, said he would convene the six legislative committee members in the next few days to consider turning over the minutes of the hearings to District Attorney Frank S. Hogan with the purpose of seeking grand jury action.

The decision came after another day of testimony in which witnesses were at variance with those who had preceded them. The closed hearings were held at 270 Broadway. Newsmen were permitted to question witnesses on the testimony they had given and to ask the committee what it had adduced.

Police Commissioner Stephen P. Kennedy, the principal witness at yesterday's session, said he had testified that the city police had not been "part and parcel" of the "bugging," or microphone eavesdropping, from its inception in November, 1955.

Testimony In Conflict

Contrary testimony had been given earlier by Chief John J. O'Rourke of the transit police.

"The Police Department was not 'part and parcel,'" Mr. Kennedy told reporters. "Let's have no nonsense about that. We are not interested in the merits of any labor issue. What we are interested in is to preserve law and order."

The Commissioner, however, defended the legality of the transit police eavesdropping. He said they were under a "reasonable apprehension" that a crime might be committed.

Asked why it had taken his department so long to come forward and place the respon-

Continued on Page 8, Column 4

Briton Offers U. S. Economic Merger

Special to The New York Times.

SAN FRANCISCO, Jan. 3—An "economic merger" of the United States, the British Commonwealth and Western Europe, with this country as "senior partner," was proposed today.

Sir David Eccles, President of the British Board of Trade and a member of the Cabinet, said some such program was necessary to meet the challenge of the Soviet Union with other than military weapons.

"We must make this merger or lose all," he warned. "For the warships, aircraft, bombs and bases will avail us nothing if our flanks are turned and our allies desert us on the economic field. Then efficient slavery would have defeated inefficient freedom." Sir David spoke at a

Continued on Page 4 Column 5

RUSSIA SEES CRISIS IN MIDEAST ENDING

Bulganin and Mikoyan Say That Is Why Rokossovsky Left Border Command

By WILLIAM J. JORDEN
Special to The New York Times.

MOSCOW, Jan. 3 — Soviet leaders said tonight that the danger of war over Syria appeared to have ended and that there had been a marked relaxation of tension in the Middle East.

Replying to questions by foreign correspondents at a Burmese Embassy reception, they agreed that this was the proper interpretation of the announcement made yesterday of the withdrawal of Marshal Konstantin K. Rokossovsky from his Transcaucasus command.

"You are very right," Deputy Premier Anastas I. Mikoyan told the newsmen. "You understand this very well."

Premier Nikolai A. Bulganin, standing next to Mr. Mikoyan, agreed.

Once an Official in Poland

Marshal Rokossovsky, one of the Soviet Union's top-ranking marshals, who was post-war Defense Minister of Poland until his ouster in November, 1956, was placed in command of the Transcaucasus Military District last October. The district consists of that part of the Soviet Union between the Black and Caspian Seas and extends southward to the Turkish border.

When the marshal was appointed, it was widely believed here that he had been sent to the Transcaucasus to dramatize and reinforce the Kremlin's position of that time of threatening to attack Turkey if Turk-

Continued on Page 2, Column 8

SOVIET BLOC AID TO 10 NATIONS PUT AT $1,500,000,000

U.S. Notes Communist Gain by Economic Offensive in Mideast and Orient

MORE OFFERS FORESEEN

Washington Total for Same 2½-Year Period in Area Placed at $900,000,000

Text of State Department's study is on Page 4.

By E. W. KENWORTHY
Special to The New York Times.

WASHINGTON, Jan. 3—The Soviet Union has agreed in the last two and a half years to provide ten underdeveloped nations with $1,500,000,000 in economic aid.

This estimate was made by the State Department today in a study of Communist economic penetration—prepared from reports by many sources, including United States overseas missions and the Central Intelligence Agency.

State Department officials were of the opinion that the economic offensive of the Soviet bloc had been effective and was likely to be intensified.

The study said that with few exceptions the Soviet bloc had begun the fulfillment of agreements "with considerable dispatch." Generally, programs have been carried out on schedule, according to the State Department.

Some Wary of Technicians

Certain underdeveloped countries were "wary" of accepting too many Soviet technicians because they recognized "the potential for subversive activities," according to the State Department report.

However, the behavior of Soviet bloc technicians "so far has given rise to few complaints," the State Department said.

From the Communist viewpoint, the success of the economic-penetration campaign will be measured by the fact that several underdeveloped countries have been satisfied enough with past performance to come back for more, United States officials said.

The study made public today has been the subject of considerable debate in the State Department and the International Cooperation Administration for the last month. There has been much dispute about how much information should be made public and how it should be presented.

Views Changed by U. S.

In the past some Administration officials have taken the position that the economic aid program of the Soviet bloc was trifling in amount compared to that of the United States, and ineffective.

This view has changed. Two weeks ago Secretary of State Dulles, in the broadcast report on the North Atlantic Council meeting in Paris, turned to President Eisenhower and said:

"Unless we do take it [the Soviet economic offensive] seriously, we can lose this struggle without ever a shot being fired."

The view here today was that the Administration had decided to make public the study on Soviet penetration to give hard

Continued on Page 4 Column 8

Polish Scientist Defects to U. S. in Quest for Freedom

Associated Press Wirephoto

Dr. Jerzy Leon Nowinski illustrating in Baltimore yesterday a discussion of the effects of stresses and strains on objects whose temperatures are subject to variation.

By The Associated Press

WASHINGTON, Jan. 3—A Polish scientist, Dr. Jerzy Leon Nowinski, has asked for and received asylum in the United States, Attorney General William P. Rogers announced today. Dr. Nowinski, a specialist in thermoelasticity, is expected to assist the United States missile program. Thermoelasticity is a field of mathematical theory dealing with stresses and strains on metals and other materials under varying temperature conditions. Dr. Nowinski came to this country last October to lecture at Johns Hopkins University and decided not to return home. His defection

Continued on Page 5, Column 4

Rome Crowds Denounce Callas; Physicians Say Her Voice Failed

By PAUL HOFMANN
Special to The New York Times.

ROME, Jan. 3—Motorized policemen were called out today to quell demonstrations against Maria Callas, the prima donna who infuriated Rome's lovers of opera by walking out of the gala performance of Bellini's "Norma" last night.

The performance was suspended when the soprano refused to continue singing after the first act.

Hundreds of protesters, many of them middle-aged or elderly men, gathered in front of the New York-born soprano's hotel today. They whistled and booed. They shouted "Down with Callas!" and other uncomplimentary remarks.

Policemen swinging truncheons charged the crowd repeatedly before order was restored. Old Roman music fans said with ill-concealed satisfaction that today's were the liveliest operatic riots since partisans of Verdi and Wagner fought more than half a century ago.

Throughout the city posters advertising last night's opening of the 1958 opera season and giving top billing to Miss Callas were covered today with such inscriptions as "We Don't Want Callas in Rome!"

The diva kept to her hotel suite all day. She was visited by several physicians who found her suffering from what one of them described as an "affection of the vocal cords." Tonight it was reported that she had no fever.

Giovanni Batista Meneghini, Miss Callas' husband, termed her ailment a "sudden tracheal complication." He said this condition, affecting the trachea, or

Continued on Page 3, Column 6

Computer Develops Capacity to 'Learn'

By ROBERT K. PLUMB

Evidence has been found that modern electronic computers may be able to "learn" from experience and get things done without being told exactly how.

Experiments suggest that an electronic computer might exercise judgment, in addition to exceeding the human brain in quickness of thought or extent of memory. They have been conducted by a young Harvard Medical School student on the International Business Machines 704 data-processing machine.

The results of a series of preliminary experiments on this scientific computer by the student, R. M. Friedberg, will be published in the January issue of The IBM Journal of research and development. Mr. Friedberg is a medical student who has had some recognition as a

Continued on Page 7, Column 5

British West Indies Begin a Federation

Special to The New York Times.

PORT-OF-SPAIN, Trinidad, Jan. 3—A new nation came into being today with the swearing-in of Lord Hailes as the first Governor General of the West Indies Federation.

Lord Hailes arrived in Trinidad for the first time this morning from Barbados aboard the Royal Navy frigate Troubridge. He drove in state through flag-lined and decorated streets, watched by thin lines of curious but not particularly enthusiastic spectators, to the Legislative Council chamber.

At 10:25 A. M. he was sworn in by the Chief Justice of Trinidad, Sir Joseph Mathieu-Perez.

Representatives of each of the ten federating units making up this new Caribbean nation—Trinidad and Tobago, Jamaica, Barbados, St. Lucia, St. Vincent, Grenada, Montserrat, St.

Continued on Page 2, Column 4

"All the News That's Fit to Print"

The New York Times

LATE CITY EDITION
U. S. Weather Bureau Report (Page 44) forecasts: Mostly fair today; cloudy tonight. Rain and mild tomorrow.
Temp. range: 38—15. Yesterday: 26.9—13.2.

VOL. CVII . . No. 36,521.

NEW YORK, MONDAY, JANUARY 20, 1958.

10c beyond 100-mile zone from New York City — FIVE CENTS

BRITAIN REQUESTS URANIUM FROM U.S. FOR ATOM POWER

A. E. C. Expected to Supply Enriched Fuel for Use in Future Reactors

BROADER PACT LIKELY

Washington Experts Doubt That Fusion Has Been Controlled in Tests

By JOHN W. FINNEY
Special to The New York Times.

WASHINGTON, Jan. 19—Britain has turned to the United States for uranium fuel to use in future atomic power plants.

Atomic Energy Commission officials disclosed that Britain had requested that the United States supply a substantial amount of slightly enriched uranium.

While no final decision has been reached, it is expected that the British request will be fulfilled as part of a broader agreement for closer atomic cooperation between the nations.

Nations Collaborating

In another area of atomic cooperation, commission sources predicted that official papers about to be released by the two nations would dispel the impression that Britain had scored a technological breakthrough in research on controlling the thermonuclear reaction of the hydrogen bomb.

For the last year the two nations have been collaborating on controlled thermonuclear research. They will disclose some of the results of their research this Friday.

In recent weeks, there had been repeated suggestions from British sources that Britain had taken the lead in the research and had momentarily produced a controlled fusion reaction in a small laboratory device.

Both Still Uncertain

Commission officials said the statements and scientific papers to be released by the two nations would demonstrate that neither country was clearly in the lead and that both were still uncertain whether they had produced a thermonuclear reaction in a laboratory.

One major research approach being pursued by both nations is to confine an electrified gas of heavy hydrogen (deuterium) in a magnetic bottle and heat it to temperatures of several million degrees. As the deuterium atoms apparently fuse under the pressure and heat, atom particles called neutrons have been detected.

Fission and fusion are the two phenomena by which atomic energy is used. In fission heavy atoms split into

Continued on Page 6, Column 5

VENEZUELAN EXILE ARRIVES: Dr. Rafael Caldera, opposition party leader, talks to reporters at Idlewild.

The New York Times

Venezuelan Regime's Foes Threaten a General Strike

By TAD SZULC
Special to The New York Times.

CARACAS, Venezuela, Jan. 19—Plans were made here this week-end for a school strike tomorrow and a general strike on Tuesday in a major effort to overthrow Venezuela's dictatorial regime. Reports of a general strike were circulated by leaflets and word of mouth in this rumor-swept capital. Workers in the oil fields were urged to join the walkout.

[Dr. Rafael Caldera, a Venezuelan Opposition party leader, arrived in New York Sunday night after having been exiled by the Pérez Jiménez regime. He predicted that the Venezuelan Government would be overthrown. Dr. Caldera said he was released on Christmas Eve after four months in prison, and received church asylum until his departure by plane.]

The general strike leaflets in Caracas were signed by the "Patriotic Junta," an underground organization of undetermined composition that has been attacking the Government since late last year.

Call for Open Demonstration

They set the strike for noon and called upon the people of Caracas to demonstrate at 1 P. M. at the downtown Plaza Silencio.

Other leaflets signed by the "Venezuelan Student Front" urged the school strike. Addressed to students, teachers and parents, the appeal said that beginning Monday, "nobody should attend classes until the tyranny of Pérez Jiménez is overthrown."

The reference was to Lieut. Gen. Marcos Peréz Jiménez, Venezuela's dictatorial President.

All students "from kindergartens to universities" were urged to strike and parents were asked to support the movement to "form a civic conscience in your sons."

Actually, the three universities of Caracas have not been reopened since the Christmas recess. The Government apparently fears that to bring to-

Continued on Page 12, Column 4

GUATEMALA CALM IN VOTE FOR CHIEF

Ballot for President Heavy —Congress May Have to Decide 4-Man Race

By PAUL P. KENNEDY
Special to The New York Times.

GUATEMALA, Jan. 19—Except for minor incidents, order prevailed today as Guatemalans queued in long lines to vote in one of the country's most important presidential elections.

The Provisional President, Col. Guillermo Flores Avendaño, said in an interview at noon there had been no reports of violence. He added that, while the army was prepared to cope with any demonstrations, he did not expect any difficulty during the voting.

Colonel Flores Avendaño said he believed the election would be so close Congress would have to decide the winner. The nation's election law provides the winner must receive a majority of all votes cast. If no one receives a majority Congress picks one of the two top vote-getters.

Four Candidates in Field

Four candidates were in the field. They were:

Mario Mendez Montenegro, a 47-year-old attorney who is the standard-bearer of the leftist Revolutionary party.

Col. José Luis Cruz Salazar, a 37-year-old army officer turned diplomat. He is the candidate of a coalition of six parties that are generally pledged to continue the program of President Carlos Castillo Armas, who was assassinated last July.

Gen. Miguel Ydigoras Fuentes, 62, who leads the National Democratic Reconciliation party. This represents the most conservative elements in the country, including the wealthiest landowners and business men.

Col. José Enrique Ardon Fernandez, the candidate of the small Nationalist Liberal Union. He is given no possible chance.

Congress Seats at Stake

Also at stake were thirty-three of sixty-six Congressional seats.

The queues of persons waiting to vote were appreciably longer than those of last October during the presidential election that was canceled because of fraud There was a feeling that the turnout might set a record for Guatemala elections. The largest previous vote was the 485,531 set in 1954 when Colonel Castillo Armas was elected,

However, the vote in the capital was running behind the 1954 figures at noon. Only 20,000 ballots has been cast, compared with 30,000 in the corresponding 1954 period.

Election officials said more

Continued on Page 12, Column 5

FRENCH TAKE GUNS OFF YUGOSLAV SHIP

Charge Arms Were Bound to the Algerian Rebels

Special to The New York Times.

PARIS, Jan. 19 — A 150-ton shipment of arms, which French officials said was destined for the Algerian rebellion, was seized aboard a Yugoslav ship that was stopped off Oran yesterday morning.

According to French dispatches received here, the freighter Slovenija out of Rijekya, Yugoslavia, was on her way to Casablanca, Morocco, and eventually New York, when two French escort vessels stopped her near the western Algerian port. There was no explanation as to whether the ship was in Algerian territorial waters when she was halted

[The French Ambassador in Belgrade will demand an explanation of the shipment, The Associated Press said.]

The ship was brought into Oran, where French inspectors discovered the arms in addition to other freight.

According to the manifest, the ship was carrying 3,286 cases of arms and munitions. French sources said the arms were to have been unloaded in Casablanca and then turned over to the Algerian National Liberation Front through an intermediary.

Among the weapons were said to be some for blowing up

Continued on Page 3, Column 6

Bulgarians Restrict Freedom of Writers

By ELIE ABEL
Special to The New York Times.

SOFIA, Bulgaria, Jan. 19—These are the days of reckoning for Bulgarian men of letters.

Pressed by the ruling Communist party, Bulgaria's leading novelists, poets and playwrights must recant their heretical ideas. The root heresy appears to have been their belief that with the shattering of the Stalin myth in 1956 and the downgrading a few months later of Bulgaria's "Little Stalin," Vulko Chervenkov, Communist authors could write pretty much as they pleased.

A surprising number slipped the halter of party control, to judge by the list of offenders published in the Communist press here. Some went so far as to condemn the Soviet Union for crushing the Hungarian revolt and to demand "complete

Continued on Page 4, Column 4

PRESIDENT OPENS G.O.P. VOTE DRIVE IN TALK TONIGHT

Eisenhower Chicago Speech and Nixon Address Here Will Be Televised

Special to The New York Times.

WASHINGTON, Jan. 19—President Eisenhower and Vice President Richard M. Nixon will share the Republican limelight on coast-to-coast television tomorrow night as the party opens an uphill fight to win the 1958 Congressional elections.

Some 40,000 Republicans at forty-four dinners in twenty-seven states and the District of Columbia will pay the party treasury from $10 to $100 a plate to see and hear their two leaders over closed-circuit television.

The thirty-minute program will also be presented nationally for home reception over the radio and television networks of the National Broadcasting Company, beginning at 9:30 P. M.

To Fly to Chicago

For his part in the program, the President will fly to Chicago tomorrow afternoon and speak before a dinner for 5,100 Republicans in Donovan Hall, near the Chicago Stockyards. The affair will be the biggest banquet ever served in Chicago. The scene is adjacent to the International Amphitheatre, both parties' favorite arena for National Conventions.

The President will be accompanied by Mrs. Eisenhower. They will spend the night at the Stockyards Inn and return to Washington Tuesday morning.

President Eisenhower's speech is scheduled to run slightly less than a quarter of an hour. He will be preceded by Mr. Nixon, speaking from a rally at the Sheraton-Astor Hotel in New York. The Vice President will speak less than ten minutes.

Party Luminaries to Talk

Each of the other forty-two dinners will be provided with a speaker from the party hierarchy—Cabinet members, Senators, Representatives, White House aides and well-known Republicans without portfolio.

The occasion is the fifth anniversary of President Eisenhower's first inauguration. From the practical viewpoint, however, the prime purpose of the dinners is to enrich the party treasury for the difficult fight ahead.

Republican political strategists admit privately that the party faces its toughest fight in years. The signs in the wind are last year's upset victory for the Democrats in Wisconsin's special Senatorial election, a sharp decline in the President's personal popularity as shown in the polls and an un-

Continued on Page 15, Column 4

CAPITAL EXPECTS ECONOMIC REVIEW TO BE OPTIMISTIC

President to Report Today —House Tax Chief Warns Slump May Force Trims

By ALLEN DRURY
Special to The New York Times.

WASHINGTON, Jan. 19—Congress awaits President Eisenhower's annual Economic Message tomorrow in the wake of a warning from the chairman of its major tax-writing committee of a possible need to reduce taxes.

The President is believed unlikely to mention either tax reductions or tax increases in his message, which is expected to paint a generally optimistic picture of the nation's economic condition.

Although the message was originally intended by Congress to present a factual presentation of this condition, political and economic factors make it almost obligatory for a President to draw an optimistic conclusion.

Has Projected Balance

General Eisenhower has already projected a balanced $73,900,000,000 budget for the 1959 fiscal year on the belief that business will pick up in the last half of 1958.

However, Representative Wilbur D. Mills, Democrat of Arkansas, chairman of the tax-originating House Ways and Means Committee, was considerably less optimistic today. He said that the economy was in a downturn that might last longer than the President's advisers thought.

Taxes may have to be reduced before the end of the year, Mr. Mills said, if the downturn is not halted.

Mr. Mills made his remarks on a television program prepared for WDSU-TV, New Orleans.

May Lift Burden

Before the year's end, he said, "it may be evident to all of us that the economy cannot come back from the depths to which it has fallen under existing rates of taxation. And we may be thinking at that time in terms of lifting some of those existing burdens, even though it would mean deficit financing."

Mr. Mills said he was not pessimistic, "but very frankly I question that the optimism manifested in the President's Budget message is thoroughly justified."

Representative Mills said that under these circumstances he would oppose any attempt to increase taxes.

"The worst thing that we could do when an economy is slipping," he said, "is to increase the burdens upon that economy that have perhaps contributed to its slipping. It's absolutely necessary that we think in terms—if we get into

Continued on Page 15, Column 6

Fuchs Arrives at South Pole; Hillary and Dufek Greet Him

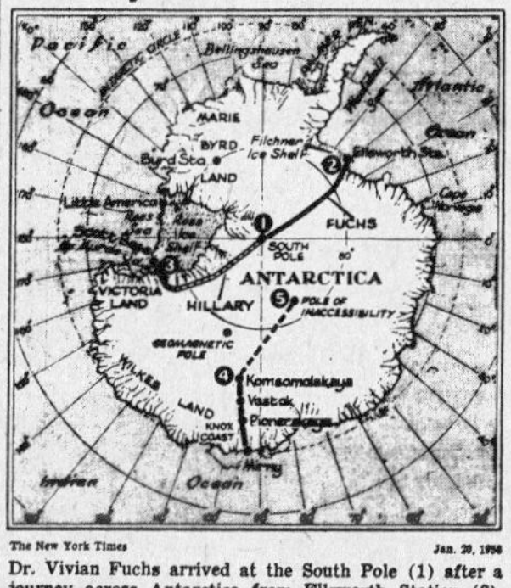

The New York Times — Jan. 20, 1958

Dr. Vivian Fuchs arrived at the South Pole (1) after a journey across Antarctica from Ellsworth Station (2). He plans to go to Scott Base (3). Russians have reached Komsomolskaya (4) on trip to Pole of Inaccessibility (5).

Special to The New York Times.

LONDON, Monday, Jan. 20—Trans-Antarctic Expedition headquarters announced early today that the main part of the Fuchs party had arrived at the South Pole.

The announcement, at 1:13 A. M. (8:13 P. M. Sunday, Eastern Standard time), said Dr. Vivian E. Fuchs reached the Pole late Sunday evening and was met by Sir Edmund Hillary. It did not state the time of his arrival, although it is known that it was several hours later than scheduled.

Thus Dr. Fuchs has achieved the first half of his trans-Antarctic trek in an eight-week battle against nature at its hardest. His original plan had been to arrive at the Pole by Christmas. His arrival brought release

Continued on Page 5, Column 1

Jobless Rise Here Found 50% Below Rate for State

Analysts Believe City's Fall-Off May Be Over—Apparel Pick-Up Forecast—Near-By Areas Are Harder Hit

By A. H. RASKIN

This city is less hard hit than the rest of the state by recession-born unemployment. Jobless lists in the five boroughs have gone up less than half as fast in recent weeks as those upstate.

State employment analysts believe that the fall-off in employment in the country's biggest city may be over. They anticipate no dramatic improvement, but they do not expect things to get worse unless a major economic tailspin develops on a national scale.

A survey of employment conditions disclosed those bright patches yesterday in an otherwise somber picture of job dislocation in the metropolitan area. The industrial communities of northern New Jersey showed the heaviest impact of the downturn, with no respite in sight.

In Passaic, where the combined weight of textile and aircraft layoffs has upset the job market, one worker in nine is idle. The situation is only slightly less acute in other Jersey cities. In New York and suburban areas of Long Island and Westchester the unemployment ratio is one in seventeen.

However, even in this city relief rolls are rising as some workers exhaust their state unemployment insurance rights and others fail to qualify for benefits under the insurance program. Extra financial aid for needy families is forcing a higher 1958 budget for the City Welfare Department.

New York's diversified economy is its chief bulwark against the kind of job decline that has afflicted other parts of the state and nation. The 3,500,000 jobs here cover almost every phase

Continued on Page 26, Column 1

Puerto Rico Migration Off; Recession in U. S. Is Cited

By PETER KIHSS
Special to The New York Times.

SAN JUAN, P. R., Jan. 19—A sharp decline in Puerto Rican migration to the mainland last year was attributed here today to effects of the economic recession in the continental United States. The Puerto Rican Labor Department reported that 37,704 more persons left this island for the continent last year than returned here. This was a 28 per cent drop from the net of 52,315 migrants for 1956.

About 65 per cent of the migrants are still believed to be settling in New York City. The problem created by this situation will be discussed at a joint migration conference of New York and Puerto Rican officials, which opens here tomorrow. The conference is the third since 1953.

The week-long parley was called by Gov. Luis Munoz Marin. Puerto Rico is again paying transportation and other limited expenses — something under $10,000.

Wagner Heads Party

Mayor Wagner will arrive Tuesday to head the New York delegation. His assistant, Stanley H. Lowell, led twenty New York participants who arrived tonight. They were the so-called middle echelon personnel from fifteen city agencies, along with State Rent Administrator Robert C. Weaver.

Ralph C. Rosas, director of the community organization for the Puerto Rican Labor Department in New York, said the 1957 decline in migration showed once again that job opportunities represented the main lure—or deterrent—of the mainland.

The Labor Department gave this picture of migration since World War II. The 1946 migration was 39,911, falling off to 24,551 in 1947 as demobilized soldiers enlarged the mainland labor supply. In 1948 it rose to 32,775, then sagged to 25,698 with the 1949 recession. Mainland activity rose with the Korean War and migration rose with it to 34,703 in 1950, 52,899 in 1951, 59,103 in 1952 and a record high of 69,124 in

Continued on Page 11, Column 4

MURRAY REJECTS RACE FOR SENATE

Action Points to Democratic Reshuffle of Candidates for High State Offices

By LEO EGAN
Special to The New York Times.

ALBANY, Jan. 19—Thomas E. Murray Sr. eliminated himself today as a possible Democratic candidate for the Senate.

The former member of the Atomic Energy Commission is now a consultant to the Joint Congressional Committee on Atomic Energy. He said that he intended to keep his activities free of any political implications.

His ban on a Senate race gave fresh impetus to speculation about a possible reshuffle of Democratic candidates for state offices. That is a subject Governor Harriman is reported to have discussed on several recent occasions with the other top leaders.

Changes Are Cited

Changes reported to be receiving the most consideration involve naming of Arthur Levitt of Brooklyn, the State Controller, for Attorney General, instead of for his present office, George M. Bragalini of Manhattan for Controller and some upstater for Lieutenant Governor in place of George B. De Luca of the Bronx, the incumbent.

The Controller and Lieutenant Governor are reported to be opposed to the plan to such a deep-seated degree that none of the top leaders has yet dared to approach them directly on the subject.

The reshuffle is reported to be the No. 1 item on the agenda of a conference to be held within the next two weeks by Governor Harriman, Michael H. Prendergast, Democratic State Chairman, and Carmine G. DeSapio, leader of Tammany and Democratic National Committeeman.

Seek Clean Sweep

In informal discussions of these three leaders the reshuffling has been represented to be one means of helping the party make a clean sweep of statewide offices at stake this year and helping Governor Harriman pile up a large re-election plurality.

The Governor, who won by only 11,000 votes four years ago, is said to be highly desirous of gaining a big margin this year to keep him in contention for the 1960 Presidential nomination despite his age. He will be 67 in the fall.

Another reason for the proposed reshuffle is a growing conviction in the party that it cannot find an upstater of sufficient stature to challenge Senator Irving M. Ives effectively.

Continued on Page 30, Column 3

Shorter Cars Asked By Region's Mayors

By PAUL CROWELL

Mayor Wagner has appealed to the automobile industry to help relieve traffic congestion by manufacturing shorter and narrower cars.

The request was made on behalf of the Metropolitan Regional Conference, of which the Mayor is chairman. The conference consists of the top elected officials of the immediate New York - New Jersey - Connecticut area.

In letters made public yesterday, the Mayor told the heads of five leading automobile companies that the long, wide cars now being turned out take too much curb parking space, shrink the facilities of parking lots and garages, force relocation of parking meters and increase congestion.

The Mayor's letters were sent to George Romney, president of

Continued on Page 30, Column 6

SENATE BILL ASKS FOR SCIENCE UNIT OF CABINET RANK

Democrats Urge Department to Unify Civilian Work—Would Put A. E. C. in It

PLAN FACING OPPOSITION

Would Drop Joint Congress Atom Panel and Set Up 2 New Technical Groups

By C. P. TRUSSELL
Special to The New York Times.

WASHINGTON, Jan. 19—A sweeping legislative program to coordinate and centralize all civilian scientific functions of the Government has been prepared for introduction in the Senate on Tuesday.

Its sponsors are Senator John L. McClellan, the Arkansas Democrat who heads the Senate Committee on Government Operations, and Senator Hubert H. Humphrey, chairman of that panel's subcommittee on reorganization. Mr. Humphrey is a Minnesota Democrat.

Subject to Change

The program, subject to change under the controversy certain to develop, will include proposals such as the following:

¶Creation of a new department with Cabinet rank to deal wholly with civilian science operations. This plan is expected to run into opposition from scientists within the Government who have sought freedom of action rather than a centralization of activities.

¶Absorption by the new department of the Atomic Energy Commission, now independent, "for administrative purposes."

¶Abolition of the Congressional Joint Committee on Atomic Energy, and establishment of permanent Senate and House committees to concentrate on science and technology.

The joint committee is planning to expand jurisdiction by setting up a panel to deal with the control of outer space.

Changes Widely Demanded

The proposals will be made in response to wide Congressional demands that there be absolute coordination of scientific and technological operations to meet the challenges presented in this field by the Russians. Both sides in the foreshadowed controversy in Congress will have much weight.

In giving advance notice of the proposed legislation, Senator McClellan said that he regarded the present draft as tentative, subject to "amendments, deletions, or additions." But, he remarked in effect, the thirty-page bill could lead to a showdown on what should be

Continued on Page 8, Column 6

2 KLANSMEN FACE CHARGES IN CLASH

None of Indians Who Balked Rally Are Arrested

Special to The New York Times.

MAXTON, N. C., Jan. 19—Two members of the Ku Klux Klan today faced charges of inciting to riot as the result of a clash between armed Indians and Klansmen last night. The Indians prevented 100 Klansmen from holding a rally.

The rally was called following rising tension between white segregationists and Indians in Robeson County. There are three sets of schools, restaurants and other facilities in the county—separate ones for whites, Indians and Negroes.

Trouble began a week ago when two crosses were burned on Indian property, following what the Klan considered relaxations in the race barriers.

Sheriff Malcom McLeod of Robeson County said today that he would seek the prosecution of the Rev. James W. Cole, the scheduled speaker at the meeting, and James Garland Martin of Draper, the one man arrested at the scene.

Martin was dragged from the bushes and arrested for drunkenness and carrying a concealed weapon last night. Mr. Cole, a Free Will Baptist minister who claims leadership of the Klan in the area, cautiously

Continued on Page 14, Column 1

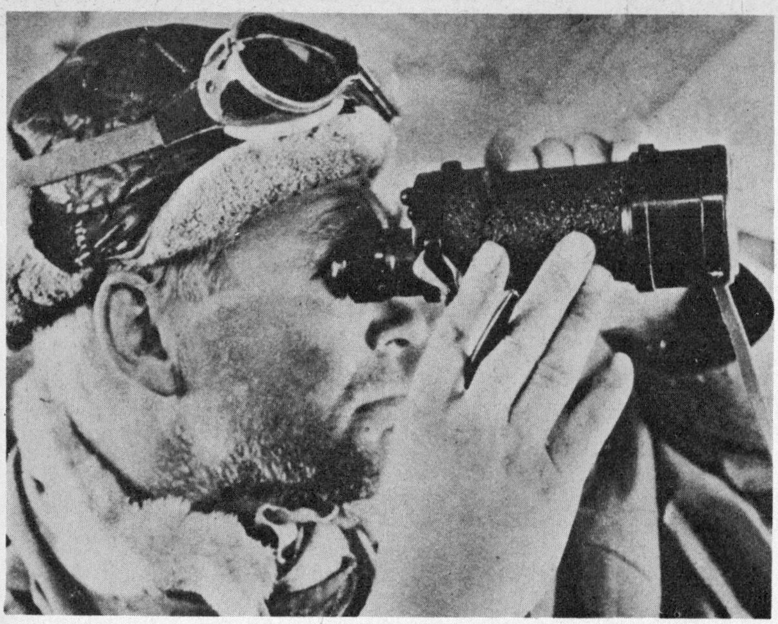

Dr. Fuchs surveying the Antarctic during a reconnaissance flight.

Dr. Fuchs and Sir Edmund Hillary shake hands during their long-awaited meeting at the South Pole.

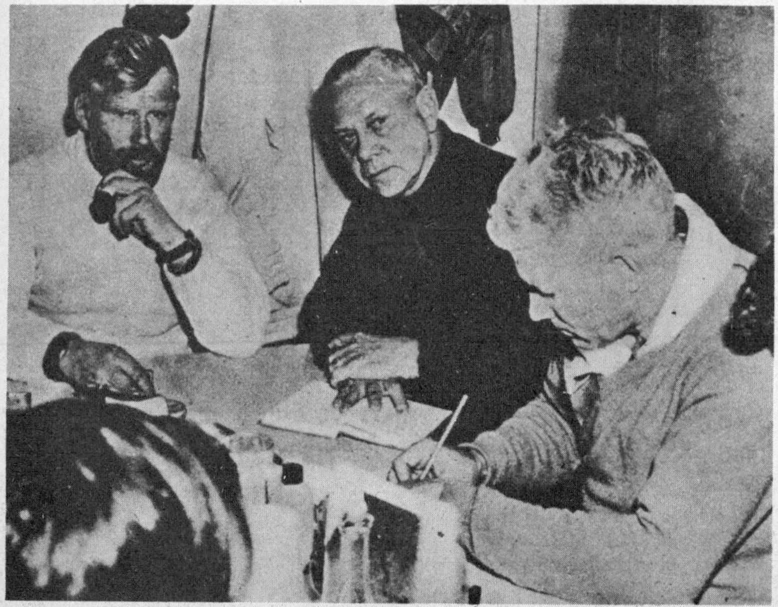

Dr. Fuchs (at left) holding a press conference at the South Pole on the day of his arrival.

"All the News That's Fit to Print"

The New York Times.

LATE CITY EDITION
U. S. Weather Bureau Report (Page 95) forecasts:
Partly cloudy today and tonight.
Mostly cloudy tomorrow.
Temp. range: 49—35. Yesterday: 46.1—39.

NEWS SUMMARY AND INDEX, PAGE 95 | SECTION ONE

VOL. CVII..No. 36,562. | © 1958, by The New York Times Company. Times Square, New York 36, N. Y. | NEW YORK, SUNDAY, MARCH 2, 1958. | 25c beyond 100-mile zone from New York City | TWENTY-FIVE CENTS

PRESIDENT FOUND FULLY RECOVERED FROM HIS STROKE

Speech Disturbance Gone, Neurologists Assert After One-Hour Check-Up

HEART TEST FAVORABLE

Report on Tooth Extraction Also Good—Eisenhower Says He Feels 'Fine'

By RICHARD E. MOONEY
Special to The New York Times.

WASHINGTON, March 1—President Eisenhower's physicians said today that he was completely recovered from the mild stroke he suffered in November. The President said he was feeling "fine."

A short report by three nerve specialists and the one-word report by the President himself were given to reporters at Walter Reed Army Medical Center.

General Eisenhower entered the hospital yesterday to have a tooth pulled and stayed overnight for a neurological examination and a check on his heart. James C. Hagerty, White House news secretary, said the medical reports on all three were favorable.

Reporters got the word from the President as he left the hospital shortly after noon to go home. Later in the day, he conferred at the White House with Secretary of State John Foster Dulles about the Soviet Union's new position on a summit conference. Mr. Hagerty had taken a copy of the new Russian note to the hospital for the President to read in the morning.

Hagerty Relays Report

The three neurologists who examined General Eisenhower this morning were among those who had attended him after the stroke. Their report was relayed to reporters by Mr. Hagerty in the hospital conference room, which doubles as a press room when the President is at the hospital.

The report said:

"The President underwent this morning at Walter Reed General Hospital a thorough neurological examination, including an electro-encephalogram [brain wave examination].

"The findings of these examinations were entirely normal. There is no evidence of any damage to his central nervous system.

"The President has completely recovered from the minor speech disturbance which he suffered on Nov. 25, 1957."

The examiners were Dr. Fran-

Continued on Page 46, Column 2

HOG RAISERS EYE A CONTRACT PLAN

Farmers in Midwest Study Move to Stabilize Income

By WILLIAM M. BLAIR
Special to The New York Times.

DES MOINES, Iowa, Feb. 25—Farmers in the Midwest corn-hog belt are considering a scheme some think may be the means of gaining the collective bargaining power and stable incomes they have sought so long. The idea is to produce hogs for meat packers under contract, rather than offer the hogs on the open market.

This is called vertical integration. It means putting under single control all the steps from growing the food to getting it into the consumer's market basket.

So much controversy surrounds the idea that a meeting here this week to discuss it attracted 600 farmers and livestock producers from all over the state.

The plan could provide more stable incomes, a Tama County producer acknowledged. But, he asked, "Will we become just hired hands, turning out pigs to specifications?"

His question posed the central issue of the controversy.

Pioneer farmers who put the plow to the prairies were integrators. They produced, processed and ate their own food.

The application of the old idea in modern agriculture goes far beyond the pioneers' use, and

Continued on Page 69, Column 1

Cardinal Stritch Is Named To a High Post in Vatican

First American to Lead a Sacred Congregation —To Head Missions

Text of Cardinal's statement is printed on Page 54.

By PAUL HOFMANN
Special to The New York Times.

ROME, March 1—Pope Pius XII today nominated Samuel Alphonsus Cardinal Stritch, Archbishop of Chicago, for the newly created post of Proprefect of the Vatican's Sacred Congregation for the Propagation of the Faith. In effect the Proprefect will be chief of Roman Catholic missions throughout the world.

Cardinal Stritch is the first American prelate to head one of the twelve congregations, or departments, of the church's central administrative machinery. His appointment came as a surprise to most high-ranking ecclesiastics in Rome and caused a sensation in church quarters.

The Pontiff's choice of a non-Italian Cardinal to strengthen the church's central administration was seen here as a further move toward "internationalizing" the Roman Curia, as the whole of the Vatican's administrative offices is called.

Associated Press
Samuel Cardinal Stritch

The Pope took the first step in this direction in 1940, when he gave non-Italian Cardinals a majority over Italians in his first consistory for the creation of new members of the Sacred College of Cardinals.

The nominal head of the Congregation for the Propagation of the Faith remains its present Prefect, Pietro Cardinal Fuma-

Continued on Page 54, Column 4

Recession and the People: No Panic, but Pinch Is Felt

By EDWIN L. DALE Jr.
Special to The New York Times.

WASHINGTON, March 1—Although there appears to be little outright suffering and no sense of panic, the 1957-58 recession has left its mark on the American countryside.

Generalizations about the recession are best derived from the statistics issued in New York and Washington. But its effects on people and towns and businesses sometimes escape the statistics.

Here are some glimpses of the recession in action—items that caught the eye of a reporter who has just completed a trip to the Chicago area, the Pittsburgh area and the Eastern part of Massachusetts.

Women Still Buy Hats

Officials here and there expect a rise in relief rolls soon if things do not get better. So far, however, welfare rolls have risen only modestly, except in unusual cases such as Saco-Biddeford, Me.

In the town of Ware, Mass., for example, where unemployment compensation claims are triple a year ago, only three cases have been added to the general relief load since Jan. 1.

Then there is the woman in Worcester, Mass., who makes women's expensive hats. Her business is booming.

The Exception and the Rule

There is the paradox of Kenosha, Wis., a town whose population is proudly announced as 54,368 as one enters the city. Its employment, unlike that of the nation as a whole, is over-

Continued on Page 66, Column 1

KNOWLAND URGES AID BUYING IN U.S.

Senate G.O.P. Leader Asks a Shift to Home Markets to Combat Recession

By ALLEN DRURY
Special to The New York Times.

WASHINGTON, March 1—Senator William F. Knowland asked President Eisenhower today to consider returning to home markets some of the foreign buying the Government was doing under the Mutual Security Program.

Mr. Knowland, the Senate Republican leader, told reporters his suggestion was an "anti-recession" proposal. The Californian said he had asked the White House, the Defense Department and the International Cooperation Administration, which handles foreign aid, to review the "offshore procurement" program with a view of giving more contracts to American producers.

The Senator's proposal came as the House Foreign Affairs Committee released more secret testimony on the aid program. The testimony was from Gen. Nathan F. Twining, Chairman of the Joint Chiefs of Staff, and Mansfield D. Sprague, Assistant Secretary of Defense for international security affairs, and their aides.

Both General Twining and Mr. Sprague devoted much of their testimony to explanations

Continued on Page 26, Column 5

Italian Bishop Guilty Of Defaming Couple

Special to The New York Times.

FLORENCE, Italy, March 1—The Most Rev. Pietro Fiordelli, Bishop of Prato, was convicted today of criminal defamation of character.

The Bishop was fined 40,000 lire (nearly $65) for a pastoral letter he wrote in 1956 describing marriages not celebrated in church as "scandalous concubinage" and persons so married as "public sinners."

The charges were brought by Mauro Bellandi, a Prato grocer, and his wife. They were the ones the Bishop had branded as sinners for their civil marriage.

The Rev. Danilo Aiazzi, a parish priest who read the Bishop's letter from the pulpit and published it in his parish bulletin, was acquitted of a charge of defamation of character.

Bishop Fiordelli was also

Continued on Page 13, Column 1

GARMENT STRIKE LOOMS IN 7 STATES AS TALKS CAVE IN

Union, Unprepared, Sets No Definite Date—Both Sides Hoping for a 'Miracle'

By STANLEY LEVEY

Negotiations to head off a general strike by 105,000 dress workers in seven Eastern states collapsed yesterday.

But the International Ladies Garment Workers Union set no definite date for the start of the industry's first major stoppage in a quarter century. The best indications were that the walkout would not come before Tuesday—if then.

The union's action in delaying its strike call had two explanations. One was that both labor and management hoped for a last-minute "miracle." To that end both sides promised to hold themselves in readiness for new talks at any time, even as they expressed deep pessimism concerning the possibility of a peace formula.

Union Lacks Halls

The second explanation—given by David Dubinsky, I. L. G. W. U. president—was that the garment union could not make final strike preparations until it had obtained enough halls to be used as strike headquarters. A new attempt to rent halls will not be made until Monday.

Louis Rubin, chief negotiator for the employers, said the industry had every intention of operating tomorrow and every other day until the workers were actually called out. After that, he asserted, all plants will be shut.

"We have never been up against a situation before where the union said it had no strike date," Mr. Rubin said with a look of puzzlement. "I guess they must be a little rusty. After all, we haven't had a strike in twenty-five years."

City Bid Rejected

Neither side appeared particularly receptive to the idea of enlisting the help of outside agencies to mediate the dispute. Last week Mayor Wagner offered the assistance of the city's Labor Department, headed by Commissioner Harold A. Felix. But there was no rush yesterday to accept the offer.

Both groups indicated they would continue efforts on their own to find a peaceful solution. Mr. Rubin said that while "it does not make good sense as of now to continue negotiations, perhaps with a little time there may be some thoughts or some action that can avoid a strike."

The main obstacle appeared to be a difference over economic matters. Mr. Dubinsky said the union had asked for a package estimated to cost 22 per cent. He reported that the I. L. G. W. U. had cut this to 15 per cent and that it stood ready to lower its wage demand in the same ratio—from 15 per cent to 10 per cent. The present average wage in the industry is $2.10 an hour.

However, the employers re-

Continued on Page 43, Column 1

U. S. JURY ORDERS WHITESIDE YIELD RECORDS ON MACK

Action Taken So F.B.I. Can Study Books—Lawyer and 3 to Appear Thursday

Special to The New York Times.

WASHINGTON, March 1—Thurman A. Whiteside was subpoenaed today to take before a Federal grand jury all records of his dealings with Richard A. Mack, Federal Communications Commissioner.

A Justice Department spokesman disclosed that subpoenas had been served on the Florida lawyer and three business associates.

The four were to have gone before a grand jury here Monday, but their appearances were postponed until Thursday at the request of Mr. Whiteside.

The postponements were confirmed by D. Malcolm Anderson, recently nominated as Assistant Attorney General in charge of the Justice Department's Criminal Division. Mr. Anderson said at his home in Pittsburgh that Mr. Whiteside's records had been subpoenaed because he had not come forward with them "as we would have desired."

Subpoena Explained

Dealings between Mr. Whiteside and Mr. Mack have become the focus of a House subcommittee investigating the Government's regulatory agencies. The Federal Bureau of Investigation is also looking into the Whiteside-Mack relationship.

The subpoenas do not mean that the Justice Department has any plans to seek an indictment in the case at this time. Mr. Whiteside's appearance will not be part of any formal presentation of a case to the grand jury.

Mr. Anderson said the grand jury would be asked to impound the records submitted and place them at the disposal of the F. B. I. "in aid of the investigation."

Those subpoenaed with Mr. Whiteside were Charles F. Shelden, secretary-treasurer of the Stembler-Shelden insurance agency in Miami; Josephine Reisenback, secretary-treasurer of Andar, Inc., a holding company, and Elizabeth G. Rissilla, president of Andar.

Whiteside Tells of Loans

Both Stembler-Shelden and Andar figured in the testimony given by Mr. Whiteside this week before the House Subcommittee on Legislative Oversight.

Mr. Whiteside, after tracing a series of loans he had made to Mr. Mack over many years, told the committee that he had given Mr. Mack a one-sixth interest in Stembler-Shelden in 1953. He said that share had earned Mr. Mack almost $10,000 since then.

Mr. Whiteside described Andar as an "inactive" holding company that he had reorganized with Mr. Mack as sole stockholder. He said it had paid "dividends" of $2,000 to Mr. Mack in 1957.

The committee was trying

Continued on Page 36, Column 1

SOVIET, IN SHIFT, PROPOSES FOREIGN MINISTERS MEET TO ARRANGE SUMMIT TALK

Russian Envoy Urges U.S. To Sign Friendship Pact

Menshikov Says a Bilateral Agreement Would 'Strengthen World Peace'—He Reveals Visits to Congress Leaders

By The United Press.

WASHINGTON, March 1—Soviet Ambassador Mikhail A. Menshikov proposed today that the United States and the Soviet Union sign a treaty of friendship and cooperation as a step toward "peace on our planet."

The proposal by the new Soviet envoy was one of several important points made in an interview and in an eight-page written reply to questions submitted by The United Press Feb. 7. His delay in replying suggested the statement had the full backing of the Government in Moscow.

Present "unsatisfactory" relations between the United States and the Soviet are not necessary, despite differences in their political and social systems, Mr. Menshikov said.

"In my opinion, the conclusion of an agreement of friendship and cooperation between the U. S. S. R. and the U. S. A. would serve to improve Soviet-American relations," he said, adding that it would be "a great contribution" and would "strengthen the world peace."

Soviet Premier Nikolai A. Bulganin has made a similar proposal. President Eisenhower turned it down, partly on the ground that such general pledges were already given when the two big powers joined the United Nations.

Mr. Menshikov's statement suggested the Kremlin was reviving the idea.

The Ambassador declared the Soviet sincerely wanted an "immediate settlement of the dis-

Continued on Page 2, Column 5

U. S. STUDIES NOTE

Moscow Aide to Call on Eisenhower and Dulles Tomorrow

By E. W. KENWORTHY
Special to The New York Times.

WASHINGTON, March 1—The Soviet Union has proposed that a foreign ministers' meeting be held in April to arrange a summit conference.

The Soviet proposal, which represented a partial accommodation to Western views on a heads-of-government conference, was contained in a four-page memorandum delivered in Moscow yesterday to the Ambassadors of the North Atlantic nations. It was reported that copies had also been given to the Ambassadors of the Soviet bloc and some neutral nations.

Officials said that the Soviet Union had obviously retreated from its former opposition to a foreign ministers' conference and was now prepared to hold a meeting limited to arranging the time, place and agenda of a top-level conference.

Basic Discussion Opposed

However, they indicated that the Soviet leaders were still opposed to any discussions of substantive issues by the foreign ministers. The United States and several of its allies have insisted that such discussion is necessary if a summit meeting is to produce positive results and not be merely a propaganda forum.

[Officials in London voiced the belief that the Soviet memorandum had improved the chances of holding a successful top-level meeting. France also expressed gratification at Moscow's latest action.]

The importance that was attached to the Soviet memorandum was manifested by the extraordinary round of high-level meetings in the State Department today of officials dealing with Soviet affairs and disarmament. In addition, President Eisenhower and Secretary of State Dulles conferred on the Soviet proposal.

White House Press Secretary James C. Hagerty took the memorandum to the President this morning at Walter Reed Hospital.

The news that Mr. Dulles

Continued on Page 3, Column 2

Lawyers Deplore F. C. C. Procedure In Deciding Cases

By ANTHONY LEWIS
Special to The New York Times.

WASHINGTON, March 1—The uproar over influence-peddling at the Federal Communications Commission has obscured so far the broader question that set off a Congressional investigation: How well are the regulatory agencies doing their job?

No one is in a better position to answer the question than the lawyers who regularly handle cases before the agencies. Their answer, sounded out in an informal survey, is a unanimous thumbs down on the F. C. C. and strong criticism of other agencies.

The lawyers seem less disturbed about the specific problem of influence at the F. C. C. than about the whole process of decision — the series of steps that ends, for example, with someone getting a television channel.

"It's a fraud on the public," one distinguished lawyer says.

He is one of several lawyers who have been discouraging clients from getting into the race for television channels.

"The heartache and the headache and the time are just not worth it," one man explains. Another says that the process at the F. C. C. is so irrational that "in self-respect" he can no

Continued on Page 37, Column 1

BATISTA INSISTING ON HOLDING VOTE

Determined on June Election Despite Spreading Revolt and Forecasts of Fraud

By HOMER BIGART
Special to The New York Times.

HAVANA, March 1—President Fulgencio Batista is determined to hold general elections June 1. He maintains this view despite a spreading rebellion in Oriente Province and a conviction widely held throughout Cuba that the election would be fraudulent and farcical.

President Batista needs the election to ease United States sensibilities about doing business with a regime that usurped power by military coup.

The election plan suffered a major blow last night when the Roman Catholic Episcopate of Cuba, headed by Manuel Cardinal Arteaga y Betancourt, issued a statement calling for a "government of national union that would prepare for the restoration of normal political life."

Appeal Is Rejected

President Batista, rejecting the appeal, said he would remain in office and hoped the elections would take place. The Government asked that publication and broadcast of the church statement be withheld, but the request was ignored.

General Batista's candidate is his obedient, colorless Premier, Andres Rivero Aguero, nominee of the four-party Government coalition.

Barred by the 1940 Constitution from seeking election to a second consecutive term, General Batista hopes to avoid having to go into exile by

Continued on Page 33, Column 1

300 Turks Are Lost As Ferry Overturns

Special to The New York Times.

ANKARA, Turkey, Sunday, March 2—More than 300 passengers were believed to have lost their lives when a ferryboat overturned and sank yesterday in an inlet of the Sea of Marmara.

Up to about midnight, 220 bodies had been recovered. There were thirty-nine known survivors of the about 370 passengers. The crew numbered at least twenty.

The scene of the capsizing, the Gulf of Izmit, is about thirty miles southeast of Istanbul.

The tragedy was caused by a sudden southeast gale that hit without warning as the ship, the 30-year-old Uskudar, was en route from the port of Izmit to the Turkish naval base at Golcuk across the gulf. According to witnesses who saw the accident from the village of

Continued on Page 11, Column 1

PERFECTED THOR SEEN IN 3 MONTHS

Air Force IRBM Is Reported Far Ahead of Schedule

By JACK RAYMOND
Special to The New York Times.

WASHINGTON, March 1—The Air Force expects to have the Thor, its intermediate-range ballistic missile, pronounced combat-ready by June and perhaps earlier.

This is far ahead of the schedule that calls for the United States to supply the 1,500-mile ballistic weapons for British bases before the end of the year.

An authoritative source also disclosed today that a proposal was under study at the Pentagon for establishing a long-range missile base in Alaska.

An IRBM there would cover much of Eastern Siberia. A 5,500-mile intercontinental ballistic missile from Alaska could penetrate deep into Soviet Asia.

Since the British bases will cover virtually all targets in European Russia, the Soviet Union would be confronted with the prospect of retaliation from

Continued on Page 19, Column 3

This section consists of 110 pages divided into three parts. The news summary and the index will be found on Page 95. Society news begins on Page 90 and obituary articles are on Pages 88 and 89.

Fuchs Completes 2,100-Mile Journey Across Antarctic on the 99th Day

Associated Press
Dr. Vivian E. Fuchs when he arrived at South Pole.

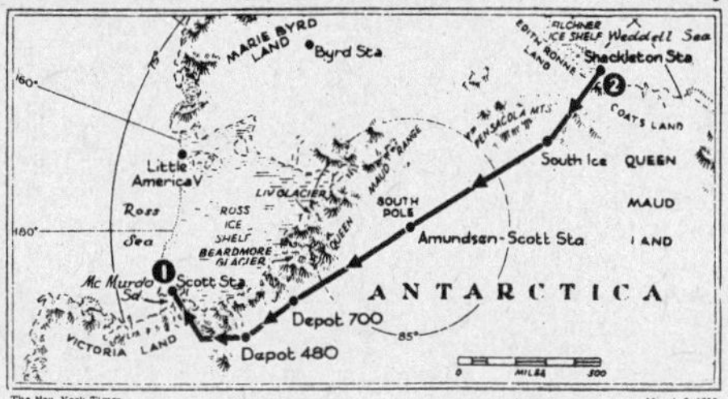

The New York Times | March 2, 1958

Dr. Fuchs's Antarctic expedition reached its goal at Scott Station on McMurdo Sound (1), after a ninety-nine-day journey across the icy waste from Shackleton Station (2).

By The United Press.

SCOTT STATION, Antarctica, Sunday, March 2—Dr. Vivian E. Fuchs and his British expedition arrived here today, completing man's first overland crossing of the icebound Antarctic Continent.

Dr. Fuchs and his eleven companions reached the station on McMurdo Sound at 1:47 P. M. (8:47 P. M., Eastern Standard Time, Saturday). Ninety-nine days ago they had left Britain's Vahsel Base at Shackleton Station on the Weddell Sea, 2,100 miles from McMurdo on the other side of the continent.

The expedition, which was sighted two hours before the arrival as it appeared over the white horizon, made the last twenty miles of its trek under clear skies and in comparatively warm weather. The temperature was about 10 degrees above zero Fahrenheit.

Dr. Fuchs's group was surrounded immediately by members of the New Zealand scientists stationed here and Americans from nearby Operation Deepfreeze headquarters.

The New Zealanders formed a small band and played martial music as the Fuchs Snocat vehicles rode into camp.

The Americans presented Dr. Fuchs with a cake baked for the occasion by chefs at the Deepfreeze camp. The cake was decorated with red, white and blue icing and had the flags of Great Britain and New Zealand.

Dr. Fuchs and his party had covered twenty miles in their last day's march. In the final leg of their journey they had been joined by Sir Edmund Hillary, New Zealand explorer and conqueror of Mount Everest.

They broke camp at 10 A. M. at White Island, where they had rested for the final push. The 50-year-old Dr. Fuchs radioed that he was on the way and was sighted a short time later coming over

Continued on Page 15, Column 1

"All the News That's Fit to Print"

The New York Times.

LATE CITY EDITION
U.S. Weather Bureau Report (Page 47) forecasts: Mostly fair today. Cloudy with a chance of showers tomorrow. Temp. range: 64—54. Yesterday: 69.6—56.1.

VOL. CVII..No. 36,645.

© 1958, by The New York Times Company. Times Square, New York 36, N. Y.

NEW YORK, SATURDAY, MAY 24, 1958.

10c beyond 100-mile zone from New York City. Higher in air delivery cities.

FIVE CENTS

ARMY STOPS WORK ON NIKE CHANGES; BLAST INQUIRY ON

Modification of Triggers Is Suspended at U. S. Bases After 10 Die in Jersey

NEW PRECAUTIONS DUE

Damage Claims Facilitated —Federal Aides Worried Over Effect on Europe

Text of the Army's statement is printed on Page 12.

By JACK RAYMOND
Special to The New York Times.

WASHINGTON, May 23—The Army announced today the suspension of its trigger modifications of Nike antiaircraft missiles throughout the country.

Such missile installations guard twenty-three major United States communities. Their warheads contain TNT, not nuclear materials.

The suspension came as a result of the explosion yesterday at a Nike-Ajax base near Middletown, N. J., in which ten persons were killed and considerable damage done to the surrounding area.

Hugh Milton 2d, Acting Secretary of the Army, ordered a full investigation to "determine the cause of the tragedy and to insure against such disasters in the future."

[In New Jersey, the Army opened its inquiry as a three-man board and a score of ordnance experts visited the Nike-Ajax launching base near Middletown. Brig. Gen. Charles B. Duff, acting commander of the First Region, Army Air Defense Command, told Gov. Robert E. Meyner that added precautions would be taken immediately.]

Procedures Outlined

The Army said that claims procedures had been outlined by Mr. Milton to Mayor Frank F. Blaidsell of Middletown Township and Governor Meyner, apparently by telephone from the Pentagon.

Officers on the staff of the Judge Advocate General flew to the Nike base this morning to facilitate the handling of claims from residents of the area whose property may have been damaged.

A team from the Army Corps of Engineers is also at the site to estimate the extent of the damage, the Army announced. It said a team of safety experts

Continued on Page 12, Column 4

PRESIDENT LOSES DEFENSE BILL BID

House Committee Rejects His Request for Changes

Special to The New York Times.

WASHINGTON, May 23—The House Armed Services Committee today rejected President Eisenhower's request for important changes in its compromise bill on Pentagon reorganization.

The committee gave details of its opposition in a report explaining the intent of the bill, which was approved earlier this week by a unanimous committee vote.

The President's latest suggestions, it stated, could not be written into law without opening the way for merging the services into an unmanageable "conglomeration."

The committee version of the bill is now ready for the House floor. The Administration has been studying amendments to be offered during later stages of the Congressional process, but it is possible that this fight to strengthen the bill may be delayed until it goes to the more sympathetic Senate.

The President's chief objection to the House version is that it fails to remove legal checks against Executive authority to transfer, merge or abolish individual service functions.

Specifically, the President objected to language specifying that the services shall be separately organized under the direction of the Secreary of Defense whose control shall be exercised "through the respective secretaries" of each service department.

To eliminate this provision, as

Continued on Page 12, Column 3

Curb Is Ordered for Jets Flying Below 20,000 Feet

Military Agrees Pilots on Non-Tactical Operations Will Use Instruments— Quesada Pushes Air Safety Drive

By W. H. LAWRENCE
Special to The New York Times.

WASHINGTON, May 23 — The White House announced tonight that the military services would put into effect tomorrow tighter controls on non-tactical jet flights below 20,000 feet.

The aim is to minimize risks of air collision pending completion of a more comprehensive modern Federal air traffic control system.

The new program was announced as air safety experts told Congressional investigators that because of equipment shortages little could be accomplished immediately under President Eisenhower's emergency five-point air safety program.

Elwood R. Quesada, White House aviation aide and former Air Force lieutenant general, announced the voluntary restrictions on military jet operations after a meeting of the Air Coordinating Committee.

General Quesada said that the military had agreed that all non-tactical jet flights would be made under instrument flying regulations if the flight plan called for a cruising altitude below 20,000 feet in an area through a designated Federal airway.

This restriction has no effect on tactical air operations, including practice alerts, or on any flights off the Federal airway system. It also permits special flights under visual flying conditions when authorized specifically by the Civil Aeronautics Administrator.

Principally affected by the new restrictions were student training flights, proficiency flights, itinerant travel, and administrative travel by jet aircraft. Flights planned above 20,000 feet would not be affect-

Continued on Page 14, Column 2

Lefkowitz Insists Mayor Sue Over Realty Frauds

By CHARLES G. BENNETT

Attorney General Louis J. Lefkowitz demanded yesterday that New York City sue to recover overcharges allegedly made by contractors in padded bills. The state official charged "widespread irregularities" in the city's scandal-torn Bureau of Real Estate and repeated his demand for a strong code of ethics for city employes.

Mr. Lefkowitz' demand came in connection with a new exchange of correspondence between himself and Mayor Wagner.

The Mayor wrote that he was willing that Mr. Lefkowitz or his aides examine Real Estate Bureau reports made by Investigation Commissioner Charles H. Tenney, but he said that the documents would have to be examined at Mr. Tenney's office, 50 Pine Street.

Copies Limited, Mayor Says

"The number of additional copies of such reports is extremely limited," the Mayor said.

To that Mr. Lefkowitz retorted in a new letter:

"It would be far more simple and would expedite matters no end if you will arrange to have these reports photostated and delivered to my office. I would be happy to pay whatever little expense may be involved."

On May 20, Mr. Lefkowitz requested that copies of the Tenney reports be made available to him. He asked particularly for the reports on the bureau's activities at the time of its connection with the Nassau Management Company, Inc.

In the same letter, Mr. Lefkowitz demanded that the city take court action "against those who are alleged to have con-

Continued on Page 19, Column 7

CITY G.O.P. DIVIDES ON COUDERT SEAT

Goodwin Is Designated but Faces Fight—Keating Assails Harriman

By RICHARD AMPER

Republicans in Manhattan's Seventeenth Congressional District set the stage yesterday for a primary battle over a nominee for the seat of Representative Frederic R. Coudert Jr.

Six of the nine leaders in the district designated Elliot H. Goodwin, 41-year-old lawyer, as the organization choice for the nomination. The three others stood firm for John V. Lindsay, a 36-year-old former assistant attorney general, who has vowed a primary fight.

The Seventeenth, which takes in the midtown and Park Avenue sections from 100th Street to Greenwich Village, is known as the "Silk Stocking" District. It was once considered to be "safe" for the Republicans.

But the primary winner will face Anthony B. Akers, the Democratic designee, who narrowly missed defeating Mr. Coudert in two previous Congressional races.

Dissatisfaction with the trend of Republican fortunes in the

Continued on Page 14, Column 5

Russians Report Finding Island Between Antarctic and Australia

Scientists Seek Data on Area —See It as Ideal Weather Station Outside Ice Pack

By WALTER SULLIVAN

The Soviet expedition ship Ob is reported to have discovered an island in the vast open sea area between Australia and Antarctica.

If confirmed, it will be a remarkable discovery. The site is 450 miles from the nearest land—the Vincennes Bay area of Antarctica. Present charts, based on meager soundings, show the ocean to be more than two miles deep in the area where the island is reported to be.

Sir Douglas Mawson, Australia's noted Antarctic explorer, has said the island is believed to have an area of eighteen square miles. The Russians reported it lay 1,150 miles east-south-east of Heard Island, in Latitude 59.5 degrees south, Sir Douglas told an American colleague in a letter.

Australian scientists have written to Moscow, asking for more information about the island and its suitability as a weather station. Sir Douglas noted that it lay in an ideal location for such a station. Not only is it in a great blank area on weather maps, but also it is outside the belt of Antarctic pack ice and thus would be accessible all year.

The New York Times May 24, 1958
The approximate location of reported island (cross).

The Australians maintained a station on Heard Island for sev-

Continued on Page 16, Column 3

INSURED JOBLESS REGISTER DECLINE FOR FOURTH WEEK

U. S. Credits Most of Drop to a Seasonal Pick-Up— Benefits End for Many

Special to The New York Times.

WASHINGTON, May 23—The number of workers receiving unemployment insurance registered its biggest drop of the year in the week ended May 10, the Labor Department reported today.

It was the fourth consecutive weekly decline. The four-week period marked the first time that insured unemployment had declined by more than usual for the season.

The department's Bureau of Employment Security said insured unemployment had declined by 93,300 in the one week to 3,101,500. In the four weeks, the reduction totaled almost 262,000.

[In Connecticut, Renato Ricciuti, State Labor Commissioner, announced that unemployed have reached 99,200, highest number for the state since 1949.]

Seasonal Gains Cited

The bureau said the greater part of the latest decline had stemmed from seasonal improvement in outdoor work and related activities.

It said that part of the decline was attributable to the fact that many unemployed workers were exhausting their rights to collect insurance, because they had been unemployed for long periods. They may still be unemployed, but they are not counted among the "insured unemployed."

For the week ended May 17, the bureau reported that the number of initial claims for unemployment insurance had dropped to the lowest since late November. Last week's claims numbered 359,200, a decline of 49,400. These figures correspond roughly to the number of new lay-offs.

Insured unemployment reports follow the initial claims report by one week.

In its most recent survey, the Government estimated total unemployment at 5,100,000 in mid-April.

7.4% Get Idle Pay

The insured unemployment figure for the week ended May 10 represented 7.4 per cent of the more than 40,000,000 workers covered by the system. In the previous week it was 7.7 per cent, and had been as high as 8.1 per cent. The previous largest weekly decline this year was 70,900 in the week ended May 3.

A year ago, insured unemployment was 1,373,200, or 3.4 per cent of insured workers.

All but four states reported smaller insured unemployment in the latest week. The largest reductions were in the state of Washington and California, where outdoor work was the big factor. Improvements in the automobile industry were factors in the two states with the next largest reductions—Michigan and Missouri.

The initial claims figure for the week ended May 17 reflected reductions in thirty-eight states and small increases in the remainder, the bureau said. California had the largest decline in this category, also, because of a slackening in lay-offs in the construction and food-processing industries.

Claims have declined in five of the last six weeks reported.

In April, 230,000 workers exhausted their benefit rights. In April, 1957, there were 115,000 exhaustions.

Eisenhower Greets Van Cliburn; Flies in Helicopter to Gettysburg

By FELIX BELAIR Jr.
Special to The New York Times.

WASHINGTON, May 23—President Eisenhower extended personal congratulations today to Van Cliburn, the tall, bushy-haired young Texan who won first honors in the international Tchaikovsky Piano Competition in Moscow a month ago.

The 23-year-old native of Kilgore, Tex., was accompanied to the President's office by his parents, Mr. and Mrs. Harvey Cliburn, and by Kiril P. Kondrashin, the Russian conductor who led the orchestra in Moscow when Mr. Cliburn played Tchaikovsky's First concerto.

While they posed for photographs in the President's office, General Eisenhower assured the pianist that he would have no difficulty with his concert appearances in this country after coming out on top in "that kind of ordeal over there."

The conductor told President Eisenhower through a State Department interpreter that he wanted to convey in behalf of the Russian people "their best regards and to say to you that they are very happy that the people of the United States have such a fine musician."

Young Cliburn had been invited by the President to come to the White House soon after the news came through that he had won the international competition in Moscow. He told

Continued on Page 17, Column 5

Associated Press Radiophoto

LEADERS IN ALGERIA: Dr. Mohammed Sid Cara, left, and Brig. Gen. Jacques Massu, right, are joint heads of new Committee of Public Safety for Algeria and Sahara. They are shown with Gen. Raoul Salan, the military ruler of Algeria, at Oran on Thursday.

REVISED AID BILL GAINS IN SENATE

Committee Adopts Measure That Restores Some Cuts —Would Ease Red Trade

By ALLEN DRURY
Special to The New York Times.

WASHINGTON, May 23—The Senate Foreign Relations Committee approved today a modified foreign-aid authorization bill. It cut military and defense funds by $235,000,000 and authorized the President to furnish economic assistance to any Communist-bloc nation except the Soviet Union, Communist China or North Korea.

In a final day of closed-door sessions, the Senators virtually rewrote many sections of the measure as it came to them from the House of Representatives.

The committee voted 14 to 1 for a total of $3,062,900,000 in new money to carry the mutual security program through the fiscal year 1959, which begins July 1.

The only dissenting vote was cast by Senator William Langer, Republican of North Dakota.

The total compared with $3,297,900,000 requested by the Administration and $2,958,000,060 allowed by the House. With carry-over funds of $644,092,500, it brought the total for the program in the 1959 fiscal year to slightly less than $3,707,000,000, compared with the President's original over-all request of $3,942,100,000.

Several Voice Votes

Today the committee in a series of informal voice votes made several major decisions.

It allowed to stand the President's requested ceilings for $1,800,000,000 for military assistance and $835,000,000 for "defense support" to the economies of friendly nations, but ordered a $235,000,000 reduction that the President might take from either figure at his discretion.

Thus, if he wished to increase direct military aid by that figure or any portion of it, he would have to reduce defense support by the same amount.

The committee approved an amendment making a major change in the Battle Act, which controls United States shipments to any nation that trades with the Soviet Union or Communist China.

The amendment was offered by Senator John F. Kennedy, Democrat of Massachusetts. It

Continued on Page 13, Column 3

Pflimlin Rejects New Call To Put de Gaulle in Power

By HENRY GINIGER
Special to The New York Times.

PARIS, May 23—Premier Pierre Pflimlin rejected tonight a renewed demand from dissident Algiers that Gen. Charles de Gaulle be called to power in France. In a bid for nation-wide support, Premier Pflimlin declared over national radio and television networks that "it would not be tolerable that a fraction of the nation should attempt to impose its will on the entire country."

Text of Pflimlin address will be found on Page 2.

But Algiers had what the Premier appeared dangerously to lack—a solid front. Military and civilian leaders in Algiers appeared more united and more intransigent than ever in their drive to bring down the present French Cabinet and replace it with one headed by General de Gaulle.

Some Favoring de Gaulle

If Premier Pflimlin himself gave no sign of yielding, a number of political elements in France did.

General de Gaulle, who is sitting at home in eastern France, twice has said he is ready to take power. An apparently growing number of conservatives, starting with former Premier Antoine Pinay, seemed willing to give it to him in a legal and orderly manner rather than run the risk of waiting for a bloody revolutionary tide that would forcibly sweep the general into office. There are also some liberals who paradoxically favor General de Gaulle.

Tonight, for the first time since a week ago Thursday, the calm of the French capital was broken by a short-lived demonstration of Right-Wingers on the Avenue des Champs-Elysees. A strong force of security troops quickly routed several hundred youths. About 100 of the demonstrators were arrested.

The Premier was adamant to-

Continued on Page 2, Column 4

2 LEBANESE QUIT POSTS IN CABINET

Defense and Communication Ministers Out—Beirut May Defer Plea to U. N.

By SAM POPE BREWER
Special to The New York Times.

BEIRUT, Lebanon, May 23—Lebanon's Cabinet showed cracks today at a critical time. Two members have resigned, for reasons not made public immediately. The resignations are not expected to cause a general Cabinet change.

Foreign Minister Charles Malik said that the resignations had not been caused by Beirut's decision to charge in the United Nations Security Council that the United Arab Republic was interfering in Lebanon's affairs.

[Dr. Malik charged that the Arab Republic was moving men and arms into Lebanon at "this very minute," The Associated Press said.]

Rashid Beydun, Minister of Defense, handed in his resignation yesterday but it was not acted upon. Today Premier Sami es-Solh accepted it, as well as the resignation of Bashir Osman, Minister of Communications.

Mr. es-Solh took over the Defense Ministry with the agreement of the Cabinet and of the defense chief, Gen. Fuad Shehab. The Minister of Economy, Kazem el-Khalil, took over the communications portfolio.

The security situation remained static. Moslem opposi-

Continued on Page 4, Column 4

Argentines Attack a Submarine And Say They May Have Sunk It

Frondizi Reports Navy Depth Charges Damaged Vessel Rumored to Be Soviet

Special to The New York Times.

BUENOS AIRES, May 23—President Arturo Frondizi announced today that an Argentine fleet might have sunk a foreign submarine Wednesday.

It was speculated that the vessel was a Soviet submarine, although neither Dr. Frondizi nor any other high official has suggested this publicly. This is the unofficial opinion of a majority in Government circles who commented, however.

President Frondizi announced at a hastily called news conference that an Argentine fleet of three cruisers and four destroyers sighted the submarine's periscope Wednesday in the Golfo Nuevo, 800 miles south of Buenos Aires.

The President said that when the submarine did not surface after a destroyer had dropped a depth charge, the four destroyers carried out four depth-charge attacks. Almost immediately oil slicks appeared on the surface and the supposition is, the President said, that the submarine either sank or escaped through the mouth of the gulf into the Atlantic.

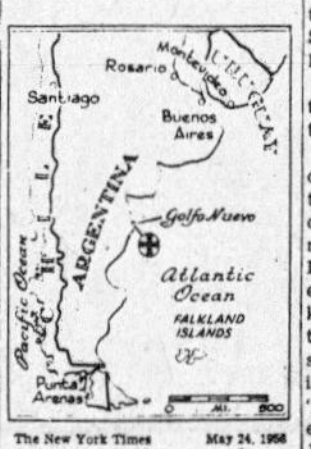

The New York Times May 24, 1958
Argentina's Navy may have sunk a foreign submarine in the Golfo Nuevo (cross).

The President said the fleet's underwater vibration recording devices had established the fact that the submarine was a high-velocity vessel. This, a retired naval officer commented, indicated that the submarine belonged to one of the great powers.

He added that of the great powers only the Soviet Union could conceivably be conducting

Continued on Page 18, Column 2

SALAN RECOGNIZES ALGERIAN JUNTAS, BUT RETAINS GRIP

General Appears to Strike at Pflimlin for First Time —Defines Groups' Role

AREA-WIDE BODY SET UP

Massu and Moslem at Head —Urge French at Home to Form Committees

By THOMAS F. BRADY
Special to The New York Times.

ALGIERS, May 23 — Gen. Raoul Salan, military ruler of Algeria, gave formal recognition today to a system of public safety committees, or juntas, established in Algeria since the anti-Paris uprising on May 13.

In a "statutory decision" headed "Committee of Public Safety" and signed by him, the general took the most revolutionary position he has displayed so far in the ten-day-old Right-Wing movement in this North African territory.

Today was the first time he appeared to strike at the Paris Government of Premier Pierre Pflimlin, which gave the general a mandate to assume full power here after the uprising.

The reason for General Salan's decree was the final constitution today of the All-Algeria Committee of Public Safety. It is under the joint presidency of Brig. Gen. Jacques Massu, chief of the parachute division that controls Algiers, and Dr. Mohammed Sid Cara, Secretary of State in the former Algeria Ministry of Robert Lacoste.

Gaullist Regime Urged

The all-Algeria committee's goal was defined as follows: "To permit the establishment of a government of public safety headed by General de Gaulle to promote and defend the profound reform of institutions of the French Republic."

Despite the revolutionary tone of the document, General Salan did not delegate any of his absolute powers to the committees in Algeria. He limited their function to that of liaison between the civilian population and the military command. The military command was specifically described as the "depository of civil and military powers."

General Salan said it was the committees' "sacred duty to be vigilant so that the will and the aspirations of the sovereign

Continued on Page 2, Column 7

INDONESIAN FINDS U. S. TIE IMPROVED

Envoy Expresses Optimism After Talk With Dulles

By E. W. KENWORTHY
Special to The New York Times.

WASHINGTON, May 23—Relations between the United States and Indonesia have taken a turn for the better, Dr. Mukarto Notowidigdo, Indonesian Ambassador, said today.

Dr. Notowidigdo spent twenty minutes with Secretary of State Dulles at noon and left the interview smiling.

"I am definitely convinced that relations are improving," the Ambassador told reporters.

United States and Indonesian officials have made statements that engendered resentment and distrust in the last several months. On one occasion, Mr. Dulles suggested that the "guided democracy" of President Sukarno might not square with the Indonesian Constitution and said that many Moslems in the islands were concerned over "the growing Communist influence in the Government of Java."

President Sukarno and other Indonesian officials, for their part, have suggested that the United States was giving at least moral aid to the forces rebelling against Jakarta rule.

This week, however, the United States made three moves that drew plaudits in Jakarta.

First, Secretary Dulles said in his news conference Tuesday that the civil war was an "Indonesian matter" for the Indonesians to settle and the United States hoped for the quick restoration of "peace and stability."

Second, the State Department

Continued on Page 9, Column 3

"All the News That's Fit to Print"

The New York Times

LATE CITY EDITION
U. S. Weather Bureau Report (Page 20) forecasts: Fair and pleasant today; fair tonight and tomorrow. Temp. range: 83—67. Yesterday: 83.0—70.0.

VOL. CVII . No. 36,722. © 1958, by The New York Times Company. Times Square, New York 36, N. Y. NEW YORK, SATURDAY, AUGUST 9, 1958. 10c beyond 100-mile zone from New York City. Higher in air delivery cities. FIVE CENTS

NAUTILUS SAILS UNDER THE POLE AND 1,830 MILES OF ARCTIC ICECAP IN PACIFIC-TO-ATLANTIC PASSAGE

U. S. Navy, from Associated Press

TIME OF DECISION: Officers of the Nautilus choose a place to submerge below ice for undersea voyage across Arctic regions. Standing at the right in the conning tower of the submarine is her skipper, Comdr. W. R. Anderson.

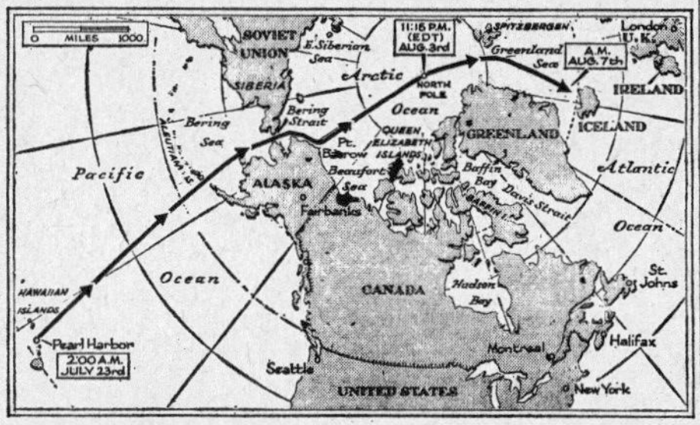

The New York Times — Aug. 9, 1958

NEW PASSAGE: Heavy line traces the Nautilus' route from Pacific to Atlantic Oceans

FOUR-DAY VOYAGE

New Route to Europe Pioneered—Skipper and Crew Cited

Text of Navy fact sheet, Page 6. The Citation, Page 7.

By FELIX BELAIR Jr.
Special to The New York Times.

WASHINGTON, Aug. 8 — History's first undersea voyage across the top of the world, a distance of 1,830 miles under the polar icecap, was disclosed at the White House today.

The trip was made in four days by the Nautilus, the world's first atomic submarine. The voyage pioneered a new and shorter route from the Pacific to the Atlantic and Europe — a route that might be used by cargo submarines. It also added to man's knowledge of the subsurface of the Arctic basin.

The voyage took the Nautilus under the North Pole. The overall trip began at Pearl Harbor July 23 and ended at Iceland Aug. 7.

Dives at Point Barrow

The Nautilus went under the icecap at Point Barrow, Alaska, and surfaced four days later at a point in the Atlantic between Spitzbergen and Greenland. She is now on her way to Western Europe.

The feat of the Nautilus, with 116 crewmen and scientific observers aboard, was revealed as President Eisenhower decorated the submarine's skipper, Comdr. W. R. Anderson, with the Legion of Merit. A Presidential Unit Citation—the first ever conferred in peacetime—went to the submarine, with a ribbon and special clasp in the form of a golden "N" to all who participated in the cruise.

The Presidential citation to Commander Anderson said that the Nautilus under his leadership had pioneered a submerged sea lane between the Eastern and Western Hemispheres. It added:

"This points the way for further exploration and possible use of this route by nuclear powered cargo submarines as a new commercial seaway between the major oceans of the world."

Skipper Tells Story

A few minutes after the award, Commander Anderson, admittedly "a little dazed" by the speed of events that brought him here overnight by helicopter and jet plane from Arctic waters, was telling his story of "Operation Northwest Passage."

News of the voyage reached the Capitol with electrifying effect. William F. Knowland of California, the Senate Republican leader, read a brief dispatch to the Senate and remarked:

"This should give us courage and remind us to have faith. It shows that this is no time to sell America short."

Senator Mike Mansfield of Montana, the Democratic acting

Continued on Page 6, Column 1

CHIEF OF U. N. GIVES A PLAN FOR MIDEAST

ASSEMBLY MEETS

Hears Call for Step-Up of Its Economic and Political Efforts

Hammarskjold and Munro statements are on Page 2.

By THOMAS J. HAMILTON
Special to The New York Times.

UNITED NATIONS, N. Y., Aug. 8—Secretary General Dag Hammarskjold proposed today that the United Nations step up its political and economic activities in the Middle East to stabilize the area.

Mr. Hammarskjold took the floor at the opening of the General Assembly's emergency special session on the Middle East to put forward his program. He had intended to present this proposal if there was a meeting of heads of government within the framework of the United Nations Security Council.

The principal provisions of his plan are:

¶A declaration by the Arab states reaffirming their adherence to the principles of mutual respect for each other's territory, non-aggression and non-interference in each other's internal affairs.

¶The continuation and extension of present United Nations activities in Lebanon and Jordan.

¶Joint action by the Arab states, with the support of the United Nations, in economic development. This would include arrangements for cooperation between "oil-producing and oil-transiting countries" and joint utilization of water resources.

Session Is Adjourned

Mr. Hammarskjold's statement was the outstanding development of the opening session, which lasted thirty-five minutes. The Assembly adjourned until 10:30 A. M. Wednesday to give foreign ministers of some of the eighty-one member nations time to get here.

Contrary to the general expectation, Arkady A. Sobolev, Soviet delegate, did not demand the admission of Chinese Communist representatives. However, he took the floor to repeat his denunciation of the presence of United States forces in Lebanon and British forces in Jordan, and again demanded their immediate withdrawal.

Henry Cabot Lodge of the

Continued on Page 2, Column 3

The New York Times

CALL TO ACTION: Dag Hammarskjold addressing the General Assembly.

U.S. LEADERS SPLIT ON MIDEAST AIMS

Eisenhower Action May Be Needed to Fix Policy for Assembly Debate

By E. W. KENWORTHY
Special to The New York Times.

WASHINGTON, Aug. 8—High-level differences of opinion have developed within the Administration over the strategy and tactics to be used in the United Nations debate on the Middle East crisis, officials indicated today.

The differences are being argued out thoroughly and amicably, and a concerted position will almost certainly be arrived at during the week-end, these officials said. Nevertheless, it was considered possible that President Eisenhower might have to make the final decision on the United States approach.

Dulles Remark Recalled

The differences were said to have become apparent soon after Secretary of State Dulles' news conference a week ago Thursday. At that conference he made it clear that the United States intended to meet the Soviet charge of United States and British aggression in Lebanon and Jordan with a counter-arraignment against the Soviet Union and the United Arab Republic on "indirect aggression."

Until the problems of indirect aggression are met directly and dealt with it will not be possible to create the atmosphere of political stability in the Middle East necessary for any attack on economic problems, Mr. Dulles said.

Almost immediately some

Continued on Page 3, Column 3

HOUSE VOTES BILL TO AID EDUCATION IN SCIENCE FIELD

Student Loans Raised in Place of Scholarships by 900 Million Measure

By BESS FURMAN
Special to The New York Times.

WASHINGTON, Aug. 8 — The House of Representatives adopted today a four-year, $900,000,000 bill to aid science education.

No money was shorn from the bill. But the scholarship provision, on which a compromise had already been made with President Eisenhower, was deleted.

The scholarship funds were shifted to the bill's loan provisions. This was accomplished in a standing vote of 109 to 78, on a motion offered by Representative Walter H. Judd, Republican of Minnesota.

The loan provisions of the bill were increased from $40,000,000 in the first year to $60,000,000 and from $60,000,000 in each of the three succeeding years to $80,000,000.

The final adoption was by voice vote, after a motion to kill the bill by sending it back to committee had been defeated in a roll-call vote of 233 to 139. The motion was offered by Representative Ralph W. Gwinn, Republican of Westchester.

The legislation now goes to the Senate, which has already scheduled to consider on Monday its own broader science-aid bill, sponsored by Senator Lister Hill, Democrat of Alabama.

Scholarships in Senate Bill

The Senate bill includes a four-year program totaling $70,000,000 for college scholarships. If that survives on the Senate floor, some compromise on scholarships will have to be worked out by House and Senate conferees.

As adopted, the House bill would cost an estimated total of $147,000,000 in the first year of operation.

It would provide:

¶Loans averaging $600 to more than 90,000 needy students, of which the Federal Government would pay a total of $60,000,000.

¶One thousand fellowships of $2,000 each to train college teachers, with reimbursement to universities for additional costs to expand graduate schools.

¶Grants to the states for scientific teaching equipment and laboratory improvement, totaling $60,000,000.

¶Grants to states to improve testing and guidance programs, $15,000,000, and $6,000,000 to set up teacher-training institutes in this field.

¶Grants to institutions to set up short-term institutes for foreign language teachers, to pay half the cost of permanent foreign language centers and stipends for those attending. This was estimated at a total of $4,500,000.

¶For research under the United States Office of Education on better educational use

Continued on Page 5, Column 3

VETO THREATENED ON PENSIONS BILL

Social Security Rate Rise Backed by White House but State Plan Is Fought

By JOHN D. MORRIS
Special to The New York Times.

WASHINGTON, Aug. 8—The Eisenhower Administration raised the threat of a veto today against a bill to increase Social Security benefits.

The measure, approved by the House, calls for a 7 per cent increase in Old Age and Survivors Insurance benefits and higher Social Security taxes to finance it. Those provisions were endorsed by Arthur S. Flemming, Secretary of Health, Education and Welfare.

But the Administration is "strongly opposed," Mr. Flemming told the Senate Finance Committee, to provisions that would increase the Federal Government's share in the cost of state relief programs.

Would Recommend Veto

"Suppose we passed the House bill, would you recommend a veto?" asked Senator Paul H. Douglas, Democrat of Illinois.

"I would," Mr. Flemming replied.

Mr. Flemming was the first witness at the opening of two days of hearings on the measure, which is scheduled for Senate action before Congress adjourns. He told the Senators that his views were those of the Administration.

The bill calls for increases in monthly cash benefits under the insurance program starting

Continued on Page 5, Column 2

Hogan Is Expected To Enter the Race For Senate Monday

By DOUGLAS DALES

A statement circulated yesterday by the New York Young Democratic Club indicated that District Attorney Frank S. Hogan had made up his mind to enter the race for the Democratic Senate nomination nearly a month ago.

Mr. Hogan yesterday scheduled a news conference for Monday noon to "issue a statement."

If, as expected, he then announces his entry, he will become the fifth declared candidate in the field.

Mr. Hogan's intentions were forecast in a summary of an interview conducted by a committee of the Young Democratic Club with Mr. Hogan on July 17. The summary was submitted to Mr. Hogan for revisions before its circulation among club members.

The summary indicated that Mr. Hogan was already making plans for the future operation of his office and that he expected to have a say in the selection of a successor.

His views on this were given as follows:

"When queried as to the

Continued on Page 14, Column 5

POLAR TRIP OPENS DEFENSE FRONTIER

U. S. Strategic Advantage Is Seen as Temporary—Soviet Effort Expected

By HANSON W. BALDWIN

A new ocean — the frozen wastes of the Arctic — has been opened to navigation and hence to naval utilization.

This is the meaning of the transpolar, under-ice voyage from Alaska to the Greenland Sea of the nuclear-powered submarine Nautilus.

The newest achievement of the Nautilus, which had already broken all records in submarine history, has immense strategic implications.

Last year the Nautilus made a five-and-one-half-day, 1,000-mile trip under the Arctic ice pack and clearly foreshadowed the shape of things to come.

The Arctic ice pack has hitherto prevented penetration of the Arctic Ocean except, with great difficulty, by foot or by air.

Ships Skirt Land

In certain seasons of the year when the ice pack recedes from the land, or thins out, surface ships have skirted the land masses bordering the Arctic, but their cruises have been short and difficult and they have never penetrated deep into the pack.

The submerged navigation of the Nautilus under the Pole and from Pacific to Atlantic means that utilization of the Arctic Ocean for military purposes is now possible for the first time in history.

Three military capabilities for Arctic submarine operations are immediately foreseeable.

Potentially the most important —in a strategic sense—is the utilization of the Arctic for the launching of guided missiles from submarines. The fleet ballistic missile, Polaris, a two-stage, solid-fuel rocket with a range of 500 to 1,500 miles, and a powerful thermonuclear warhead, is now under development. It has been designed for launching from a submerged submarine at considerable depths.

Nine nuclear-powered submarines, each much larger than the Nautilus and each capable

Continued on Page 6, Column 3

Nautilus' Skipper Helps to Mitigate A Snub to Rickover

By ANTHONY LEWIS
Special to The New York Times.

WASHINGTON, Aug. 8—The man largely responsible for construction of the world's first nuclear-powered submarine was not asked to the White House today to share her moment of triumph.

Some thought was given to inviting Rear Admiral Hyman G. Rickover to the ceremony for the Nautilus, White House officials said. But only "top brass" had been asked and it was decided no exception could be made for him.

The skipper of the Nautilus, Comdr. W. R. Anderson, proved in the circumstances to be as bold a navigator in Navy politics as in the waters under polar ice.

Commander Anderson went directly from the White House to Admiral Rickover's office in the Navy Building, a few blocks away. There he paid his personal respects on the slight, frail figure whose tough-minded drive made the Nautilus a reality.

For Admiral Rickover the of-

Continued on Page 7, Column 3

U. S. MAY REDUCE FORCE IN LEBANON

Token Removal of Marine Battalion Planned

By W. H. LAWRENCE
Special to The New York Times.

BEIRUT, Lebanon, Aug. 8—The United States tentatively plans to reload a marine battalion on ships next week in a "symbolic" gesture of withdrawal from Lebanon.

A responsible source said the decision to reduce the force on shore by about 2,000 men had been communicated to the Lebanese Government and to Gen. Fouad Chehab, armed forces commander and President-elect.

Before the marine unit is pulled out, a small detachment of Army engineers and truck personnel will be moved from Lebanon to the Turkish port of Iskenderun to improve facilities at the Atlantic alliance base at Adana, an important center of air striking power and supply for the United States operation in Lebanon.

The moves will have both political and military effects, it is believed. The political aims are both local and international.

Locally, leaders of the continuing insurrection against the Government of President Camille Chamoun have been insisting on speedy removal of United States troops as a condition for a cease-fire now that General Chehab has been elected. He will succeed Mr. Chamoun Sept.

Continued on Page 3, Column 2

Peronists Win Rule Of Argentine Labor

By JUAN de ONIS
Special to The New York Times.

BUENOS AIRES, Aug. 8—The Argentine Senate adopted today a controversial union organization law that virtually hands the labor movement back to Peronist control.

President Arturo Frondizi's Senate majority approved the text of a bill, passed by the Chamber of Deputies, without changing a word. It did so despite formal opposition to the measure by the Roman Catholic Church, business and professional organizations, nearly all of the press and the anti-Peronist labor unions.

The bill, which re-establishes the single General Labor Confederation, with the official right to speak for labor, awaits the President's signature only.

In eighteen of the bill's fifty-

Continued on Page 4, Column 7

Glennan, Ohio Educator, Named To Direct New U. S. Space Unit

Case Tech President Served on A.E.C. Under Truman—Dryden Picked as Aide

Special to The New York Times.

WASHINGTON, Aug. 8—T. Keith Glennan, a Cleveland educator and former member of the Atomic Energy Commission, is President Eisenhower's choice to head the new civilan space agency.

The President sent Mr. Glennan's nomination to the Senate today along with that of Dr. Hugh L. Dryden as Deputy Administrator of the agency.

Mr. Glennan is president of the Case Institute of Technology. Dr. Dryden is director of the National Advisory Committee for Aeronautics.

The National Aeronautics and Space Administration was created by an Act of Congress signed by the President ten days ago.

Mr. Glennan's appointment is believed to be noncontroversial. There may be some objection to the choice of Dr. Dryden, however, and this could delay Senate confirmation of the nominees.

If the Senate does not act

Associated Press

T. Keith Glennan

before Congress adjourns, both can be installed under recess appointments.

Members of the House Space Committee have criticized Dr. Dryden as presenting a program for the conquest of space that lacked "boldness, imagina-

Continued on Page 4, Column 3

Rackets Unit Asks Prosecution for 13

By ALLEN DRURY
Special to The New York Times.

WASHINGTON, Aug. 8—Senate rackets investigators voted unanimously today to ask the Senate to approve contempt-of-Congress citations against thirteen witnesses.

They include the president of the Carpenters Union and the reputed heir to Al Capone's gangland empire.

The action was taken by the Select Committee on Improper Activities in the Labor or Management Field. It acted in a closed meeting between morning and afternoon public sessions at which it heard witnesses give further testimony on associates of James R. Hoffa, president of the International Brotherhood of Teamsters.

Senator John L. McClellan, Democrat of Arkansas, the com-

Continued on Page 5, Column 6

479 Get Jaywalking Summonses But Public Is Hailed on Response

By BERNARD STENGREN

Pedestrians waited for traffic lights and motorists waited for pedestrians yesterday as the police began enforcing New York's new safety law.

High officials of the Traffic and Police Departments said they were gratified at the extent of compliance by drivers and walkers.

Traffic Commissioner T. T. Wiley said:

"My hat is off to New York. The reaction is wonderful."

He spoke after a tour of midtown Manhattan during which turning trucks waited for pedestrians and cab drivers not only waited but also shouted warnings to pedestrians starting to cross against lights.

John J. King, assistant Chief Inspector and head of the Safety Division, said that although some persons had argued, most had stopped when patrolmen admonished them about jaywalking.

There were, however, exceptions. Between 9 A. M., when enforcement began, and 4 P. M., when the police day shift ended, 479 summonses returnable for $2 were issued to pedestrians.

These included 255 in Manhattan, ninety-three in Brooklyn, ninety-eight in Queens, thirty-one in the Bronx and two in Richmond—where there is only one "Don't Walk" signal.

Twenty-two motorists who failed to give the right of way to pedestrians received summonses for that infraction, which was added Thursday to violations subject to "rigid enforcement."

In Manhattan, five were is-

Continued on Page 15, Column 5

"All the News That's Fit to Print"

The New York Times.

LATE CITY EDITION
U. S. Weather Bureau Report (Page 55) forecasts:
Showers and thunderstorms today; clearing tonight. Fair tomorrow.
Temp. range: 82—71. Yesterday: 76—71.

VOL. CVII . No. 36,726. © 1958, by The New York Times Company. Times Square, New York 36, N. Y. NEW YORK, WEDNESDAY, AUGUST 13, 1958. 10c beyond 100-mile zone from New York City. Higher in air delivery cities. FIVE CENTS

POWELL, LINDSAY WIN IN PRIMARIES BY WIDE MARGINS

Opponents of Both Concede Defeat in Contests for Congress Nominations

HARLEM VOTING HEAVY

Blow to Tammany Seen—Insurgent Beats Goodwin for Coudert's Seat

By LEO EGAN

Representative Adam Clayton Powell Jr. swamped his Tammany-backed adversary in yesterday's primary here to win a Democratic renomination for an eighth Congressional term.

City Councilman Earl Brown, who had been picked by Carmine G. De Sapio, the leader of Tammany, and by Harlem district leaders to oppose Mr. Powell, conceded defeat at 12:40 A. M. today.

In a statement issued after Mr. Brown had conceded defeat, Mr. De Sapio said last night that the Democratic party would unite and back Mr. Powell. He predicted that this would lead to an outstanding Democratic victory in the State in November.

At about the same time, Elliot H. Goodwin, the organization-backed candidate for the Republican Congressional nomination in the Seventeenth District, conceded defeat at the hands of John V. Lindsay, who was executive assistant to former Attorney General Herbert Brownell Jr.

Coudert Not in Race

The Seventeenth District covers most of mid-Manhattan and is frequently described as the Park Avenue or Silk Stocking district. It usually elects Republicans. Representative Frederic R. Coudert Jr., the Republican incumbent, was not a candidate for renomination.

At an early hour this morning, returns from 100 of the 143 election districts in the Sixteenth District gave Mr. Powell 9,573 votes to 3,475 for Mr. Brown.

Returns from 200 of the 219 election districts in the Seventeenth District, at the same hour, gave Mr. Lindsay 5,565 votes to 3,519 for Mr. Goodwin.

The Powell-Brown and Lindsay-Goodwin contests stirred an otherwise dull primary election within the city. Besides these two, there were twenty-seven contests for party nominations. In addition there were nine contests for Democratic district

Continued on Page 18, Column 2

2d U. S. Atom Submarine Crosses Pole; Skate Surfaces in Ice Gap and Reports

Associated Press
Comdr. James F. Calvert

The New York Times Aug. 13, 1958
The heavy line denotes the approximate route of the Skate

Special to The New York Times.

WASHINGTON, Aug. 12—A second United States nuclear submarine has sailed under the North Pole.

The Navy announced tonight that the crossing had been made by the U. S. S. Skate. She reached the pole at 9:47 o'clock last night, Eastern Daylight Time.

The Skate approached the pole from the east, the opposite way from the Nautilus. She sailed from New London, Conn., on July 30, passed between Iceland and Greenland to a point forty miles past the pole, where she is continuing under-ice explorations.

The Skate did not enter the Pacific. She will return under the polar icecap and thence to the Atlantic and New London.

The announcement of the Skate's trip said the submarine had surfaced in an ice gap near the pole and radioed home the news of her crossing. The Nautilus started on her trip at Pearl Harbor, went under the icecap at Point Barrow, Alaska, and did not surface until she was in the Atlantic.

The skipper of the Skate is Comdr. James F. Calvert, 38 years old, of Cleveland. He has been in command of the submarine since she joined the Navy as the fleet's third atomic-

Continued on Page 13, Column 2

U. S. BACKS MOVE IN LATIN AMERICA FOR A LOAN BANK

Step Is a Reversal of Policy—Dillon Cites the Reports of Officials After Tours

By E. W. KENWORTHY
Special to The New York Times.

WASHINGTON, Aug. 12—In a reversal of long-established policy, the United States gave its support today to the establishment of an Inter-American Development Institution.

The announcement was made by C. Douglas Dillon, Under Secretary of State for Economic Affairs, before the Inter-American Economic and Social Council of the Organization of American States.

In a brief statement, Mr. Dillon reminded delegates from the twenty-one American republics that Vice President Nixon, Secretary of the Treasury Robert B. Anderson, Dr. Milton Eisenhower and Secretary of State Dulles had all made recent trips to Latin America.

Cites Economic Studies

As a result of their reports and "our coordinated studies of the economic problems of the area," Mr. Dillon said, "the Secretary of State has authorized me to report to you that the United States Government is prepared to consider the establishment of an inter-American regional development institution which would receive support from all its member countries."

It is believed that the reversal of policy toward Latin America is largely the result of the Administration's decision to propose a regional development plan for the Middle East ir the United Nations debate beginning tomorrow. It is held here that the United States could hardly propose such a scheme for the Middle East while continuing to oppose one in this hemisphere.

The Latin-American countries have been urging the establishment of a hemisphere development bank ever since the Marshall Plan for Europe was set up in 1948.

The United States has steadily opposed it for a variety of reasons, political and economic.

Financing Questioned

For one thing, the United States preferred bilateral credit arrangements because it could then firmly control the dispensing of its loan funds for Latin-American countries.

Second, the United States Government had reason to believe that the Latin-American countries envisioned a fund financed almost entirely by the United States, since imports for capital development would have to be purchased for hard currency.

Third, the United States said that Latin America, in its search for investment capital, had access not only to private money markets here, but also to the United States Export-Import Bank, and the International Bank for Reconstruction and Development. Since last year, the Development Loan Fund of the International Cooperation Administration has also been available.

At the Buenos Aires Economic Conference last August, Secretary Anderson said that investment opportunities "throughout the free world are so numerous that all who seek investment capital must compete for it."

Flow of Capital Noted

"As the figures demonstrate, the Latin-American republics have been successfully competing and obtaining a sharply expanded flow of new capital funds," he added.

Mr. Anderson said that in the last decade more than 40 per cent of Export-Import Bank loans had gone to Latin America.

The Latin-American countries saw the problem somewhat differently. They saw themselves in a vicious circle. As raw material prices fell and costs of manufactured imports rose, they were caught in a balance-of-payments squeeze.

Their only salvation, they said, was regional development in order to reduce dependence upon imports. But many Latin-American countries were reaching the limit of their ability to service dollar loans for development.

They conceded that the new

Continued on Page 14, Column 6

PRESIDENT HERE TO GIVE MIDEAST ECONOMIC PLAN TO U. N. ASSEMBLY TODAY

The New York Times
HERE FOR U. N. MEETING: President Eisenhower as he arrived at Waldorf yesterday with Henry Cabot Lodge.

U. S. TO OFFER AID

May Give 100 Million for Regional Agency on Development

By THOMAS J. HAMILTON
Special to The New York Times.

UNITED NATIONS, N. Y., Aug. 12—President Eisenhower will propose a regional development agency for the Middle East when he addresses the emergency special session of the General Assembly tomorrow morning.

According to authoritative sources, the President will urge the establishment of an agency similar to the Organization for European Economic Cooperation, which helped distribute Marshall Plan aid for West Europe.

The United States will emphasize its willingness to make a substantial contribution, and will thus in effect challenge the Soviet Tnion to do likewise.

[According to Washington sources, the United States may offer a contribution of $100,000,000 toward a development fund.]

Eisenhower at Waldorf

The President arrived from Washington tonight and went to the Presidential Suite at the Waldorf-Astoria Hotel. He will be the first speaker in the Assembly session tomorrow morning, and will be followed by Andrei A. Gromyko, Soviet Foreign Minister.

The Assembly is scheduled to convene at 10:30 A. M., but United Nations officials indicated that it would be around 10:50 A. M. before it was called to order.

Authoritative sources said the President's address would be "constructive" and that, while he would not ignore the problem of indirect aggression, he would not mention inflammatory broadcasts by the Cairo radio.

Hammarskjold Proposal

In addition, the President is expected to make clear the United States' hope that Lebanon and Jordan, without being formally "neutralized," can be withdrawn from the tides of Arab nationalism that have recently overrun the Middle East.

Informed sources said that to this end the United States would support the proposal made Friday by Secretary General Dag Hammarskjold that the United Nations maintain its "presence" in both Lebanon and Jordan.

Mr. Hammarskjold suggested that the present United Nations Observation Group in Lebanon be continued and that the United Nations truce supervision orga-

Continued on Page 2, Column 3

Lodge Greets Eisenhower; 'Strong' Speech Predicted

By FELIX BELAIR Jr.

President Eisenhower arrived in New York last evening and took up residence in the Waldorf-Astoria Hotel. He immediately began putting the finishing touches on the major statement of United States policy on the Middle East that he will deliver today to the emergency meeting of the United Nations General Assembly.

The President arrived at the Marine Terminal of La Guardia Airport at 6:55 P. M. to be greeted by Henry Cabot Lodge, Ambassador to the United Nations, and Police Commissioner Stephen P. Kennedy. Formalities were held to a minimum as the President came down the ramp from his special plane, Columbine III, after an hour's flight from Washington.

Mr. Lodge shook General Eisenhower's hand warmly and told the President, who is expected to make a "strong" speech when he appears before the international forum this morning, that he was "so glad" General Eisenhower had come.

Poses With Lodge

Telling Mr. Lodge that he was "delighted" to see him, General Eisenhower posed briefly with the Ambassador for pictures.

While Mr. Lodge waited for the arrival of the President's plane, he told reporters that the fact that General Eisenhower was coming to the General Assembly's opening debate on the Middle East was a "very constructive development."

General Eisenhower kept to the Presidential Suite on the thirty-fifth floor of the Waldorf Towers during the evening. He conferred for about half an hour with Ambassador Lodge,

Continued on Page 2, Column 6

2 in Apalachin Case Jailed For Balking State Hearing

By HARRISON E. SALISBURY

Two participants in the Apalachin gangland convention were sent to jail yesterday for refusing to answer questions by the State Investigation Commission under a pledge of immunity. The witnesses were taken to civil jail on the orders of Supreme Court Justice Morris E. Spector and ordered held "until such time as you are willing to appear before the commission and answer such questions as may be propounded to you."

The two men are Frank Joseph Valenti, 46 years old, of Rochester, whose arrest record goes back to 1933, and Rosario (Russell) Mancuso, 51, of Utica, described as being in the concrete business.

Willful Refusal Charged

Valenti and Mancuso were charged with "willful and contumacious refusal to answer material and relevant questions" of the commission.

The gangland meeting was held last Nov. 14 in the luxurious hilltop home of Joseph Barbara at Apalachin, N. Y. Barbara has a long police record. A state police raid on his estate disclosed fifty-eight persons at the meeting, in addition to Barbara and his family. Many of the men had come from long distances. Many had police records. A half-dozen inquiries have been undertaken since that time in an effort to uncover the purpose of the meeting.

The action against the balky witnesses was ordered by Myles J. Lane, chairman of the commission. The two witnesses were questioned futilely in the morning as the commission opened

Continued on Page 19, Column 4

TRANSIT LOSS UP; '59 FARE IN DOUBT

Patterson Refuses Pledge on 15-Cent Rate as Deficit for Year Is 11 Million

By STANLEY LEVEY

The Transit Authority reported yesterday that it spent $11,097,309 more than it took in during the fiscal year that ended June 30.

The deficit exceeded by $1,000,000 what the agency had anticipated in a preliminary estimate two months ago. It was the first since the present three-man board took over three years ago and since the Transit Authority began operating the city transit in 1953.

Under the law, which requires the agency to be self-sustaining, the fare may not be increased until next Jan. 1. Charles L. Patterson, the chairman, made no promises yesterday that the 15-cent subway and bus fare could be maintained after the first of the year.

1959 Outlook Is Dire

The indications are that the agency will not be able to hold the line very long in 1959. The authority has announced that it will spend more money ($281,240,040) and lose more ($26,730,040) in the 1958-59 fiscal year than heretofore.

The surplus that the authority had accumulated has now shrunk to about $17,000,000. This year's expected deficit will wipe that out. Passenger revenues are continuing to decline as they have since 1948, when the fare first was raised.

The authority says there are

Continued on Page 19, Column 7

HOFFA IS TAUNTED ON HOODLUM AIDES

Inquiry Suggests Teamster Fears Them—He Denies It and Defends His Stand

By JOSEPH A. LOFTUS
Special to The New York Times.

WASHINGTON, Aug. 12 — Senate rackets investigators suggested today that James R. Hoffa was afraid to drop the ex-convicts on his union's payroll. He denied it.

Evidence was introduced to show that Mr. Hoffa had authorized the use of hundreds of thousands of dollars in Teamsters Union funds to defend officers accused of crimes and to pay their salaries while in prison. Some of these crimes were committed in their union capacities.

Mr. Hoffa, president of the International Brotherhood of Teamsters, said he was not going to "abuse his privilege" to take summary action under the union constitution. He implied that he saw nothing wrong in supporting his associates, even when they used their jobs to extort money from employers.

Asks for a Report

Senator Barry Goldwater, Republican of Arizona, a member of the Select Committee on Improper Activities in the Labor or Management Field, said he was convinced that the use of union funds to defend union members who got into trouble was a "general pattern" not confined to the teamsters.

He asked the committee staff to look into this and to submit a report.

Robert F. Kennedy, committee counsel, picked up where he had left off last week and read more names of teamster officials with long records of arrests and convictions. He asked Mr. Hoffa what he had done about them.

Challenged to Oust Group

In practically all cases the answer was "nothing," that Mr. Hoffa had been busy, that the men were entitled to trials under union procedure and that Mr. Hoffa would take care of things "in due course."

"Are you frightened of these people, Mr. Hoffa?" the committee counsel asked.

"I am not frightened of anybody, Mr. Kennedy," the witness replied in firm, measured tones, "and I don't frighten easily. I'm just not going around and abuse my privileges."

Mr. Kennedy declared that Mr. Hoffa "got fifteen of these people" in Detroit, and went on: "I say you're not tough enough to get rid of these people."

"The membership has the right

Continued on Page 17, Column 4

HOUSE APPROVES 2 CURBS ON COURT

Redefines Word in Smith Act and Stiffens Deportations

Special to The New York Times.

WASHINGTON, Aug. 12 — The House voted today to overrule Supreme Court decisions in two more areas of the law. With a handful of members on the floor, two bills were passed and sent to an uncertain fate in the Senate.

One measure would redefine the word "organize" in the Smith Act of 1940, which prohibits persons from advocating the violent overthrow of the Government and from organizing political parties to that end.

The second measure would provide a radically new method for judicial review of administrative orders to deport aliens from the United States.

Last June the Supreme Court held that, as applied to the Communist party, the word "organize" in the Smith Act covered only the organizing of the party as a whole. It limited the application of that part of the statute to those who took part in the reorganization of the Communist party in 1945.

The bill would expand the term to include "the recruiting of new members, the forming of new units and the regrouping or expansion of existing clubs, classes and other units" of the party.

The Supreme Court decision had virtually written the organizing provision out of the Smith Act because a three-year statute of limitations had long since run

Continued on Page 15, Column 4

Pill to Reduce Radiation Effects May Be Tested Soon on Humans

By HAROLD M. SCHMECK Jr.
Special to The New York Times.

BURLINGTON, Vt., Aug. 12—A pill said to be capable of halving the serious biological effects of a stiff dose of atomic radiation may be available soon for experimental use on human beings, a scientist said here today.

The compound has been tested widely in animals and is now undergoing toxicity studies. Dr. David G. Doherty of the Oak Ridge (Tenn.) National Laboratory, who reported on its progress, said at a news conference that he considered it among the most promising of several related compounds that have been under study for several years.

Dr. Doherty and Raymond Shapira reported on recent studies of the compound today at an International Congress of Radiation Research being held at the University of Vermont here.

From the experimental evidence with animals, Dr. Doherty said, it can be estimated that a one-gram dose of the compound could cut in half the radiation damage to an average person's blood and blood-forming system from a radiation dose of as high as 400 roentgens.

This is near the level of a single acute radiation dose that would cause death within thirty days to half of any group of persons irradiated. Dr. Doherty indicated that a dose of the compound higher than one gram would probably be too toxic for humans. He said he was hopeful that less toxic compounds could be developed.

The chemical seems to localize in the bone marrow and exerts its protective effect there. It is helpful primarily in protecting the blood and blood-forming organs, but not other body tissues.

If a compound does prove practicable for use in humans it would be valuable in some aspects of cancer treatment and as a preventive against undue radiation in industrial or wartime circumstances. The medication must be given in advance of the radiation. Its greatest effectiveness in animals has been seen when it is given less than an hour in advance, according to Dr. Doherty.

The compound is known as AET. Its full chemical name is S,2-Aminoethylisothiuronium Bromide Hydrobromide. Its po-

Continued on Page 12, Column 6

1,700 OF MARINES LEAVING LEBANON

Withdrawal Today Viewed as Move to Convince U.N. No Build-Up Is Planned

By SAM POPE BREWER
Special to The New York Times.

BEIRUT, Lebanon, Aug. 12—The first withdrawal of United States troops from Lebanon is scheduled to begin tomorrow morning.

Admiral James L. Holloway Jr., commander of operations here, announced today that one reinforced battalion of 1,700 Marines would board ship.

An informed source said the move would be a token withdrawal to emphasize coincidentally with the opening of the United Nations General Assembly debate in New York that the United States was not trying to build up its forces in Lebanon.

After tomorrow's embarkment, the total force left on shore will be approximately 9,000 Army troops and 3,000 Marines.

First Ashore, First to Leave

The first unit to leave is the one that came ashore first when the landings began on July 15. It is the Second Battalion, Second Marine Regiment.

The announcement was made on behalf of Admiral Holloway in a statement read by a United States Embassy spokesman. It did not indicate whether departures of other units were planned at present.

Rumors that some United States forces were to be sent into Jordan appeared tonight to be without foundation.

The embassy statement follows:

"Admiral Holloway recalled the statements of President Eisenhower and Secretary of State Dulles when United States forces landed in Lebanon in response to the request of the President and Government of that republic for assistance in maintaining the independence and integrity of Lebanon.

"It was stated at that time that the United States forces would remain only so long as desired by the Lebanese Government and in relation to the accomplishment of their mission.

"Admiral Holloway, after discussions with President Chamoun and the Commander in Chief of the Lebanese armed forces, Gen. Fouad Chehab,

Continued on Page 6, Column 6

Stamp Dealer Held In Red China Trade

By MILDRED MURPHY

A former president of the American Stamp Dealers Association was indicted in Brooklyn Federal Court yesterday for violating the Trading with the Enemy Act. He was charged with having smuggled valuable stamps from Communist China and having sold them at 100 per cent profit.

A six-count indictment handed up to Judge Matthew T. Abruzzo charged Kurt Weishaupt, the 45-year-old dealer, with importing the stamps from Shanghai. They were said to have been shipped to the United States from November, 1953, to February, 1957.

Mr. Weishaupt, who emigrated to this country just before World War II, was described yesterday by a colleague as prominent in his field with

Continued on Page 9, Column 5

MINISTERS STRESS EASING OF TENSION

Lloyd Leads Move to Avert New Mideast Aggravation

By LINDESAY PARROTT
Special to The New York Times.

UNITED NATIONS, N. Y., Aug. 12—Some Western allies of the United States pressed the Administration today to seek a solution of the Middle Eastern question without recourse to measures that would aggravate the "cold war."

Arriving at New York International Airport, Idlewild, Queens, Mr. Lloyd voiced the hope that the United States and British troops might be withdrawn from Lebanon and Jordan under a United Nations plan "without recriminations" and with justice to the Arab states.

Arriving at International Airport, Idlewild, Queens, Mr. Lloyd expressed the hope that the United States and British troops might be withdrawn from Lebanon and Jordan under a United Nations plan "without recriminations" and with justice to the Arab states.

Britain, it was understood, would "go a long way" to prevent the creation of an Arab

Continued on Page 3, Column 3

"All the News That's Fit to Print"

The New York Times

LATE CITY EDITION

Weather: Fair, very cold today and tonight. Chance of snow tomorrow. Temp. range: today 24-14; Sunday 33-26. Full U.S. report on Page 30.

VOL. CVII . No. 36,739. NEW YORK, TUESDAY, AUGUST 26, 1958. 10c beyond 100-mile zone from New York City. Higher in air delivery cities. FIVE CENTS

WARREN CALLS HIGH COURT FOR LITTLE ROCK DECISION; SESSION STARTS THURSDAY

SPECIAL TERM SET

Ruling on Integration Stay Likely Before School Opens

By ANTHONY LEWIS

Special to The New York Times.

LOS ANGELES, Aug. 25—Earl Warren, the Chief Justice of the United States, today called the Supreme Court into extraordinary session to resolve the school integration issue in Little Rock, Ark.

The court will convene at noon Thursday in Washington. It will hear oral argument and, in all likelihood, hand down a decision before the scheduled opening of Little Rock schools on Sept. 8.

The Chief Justice, who is here for the annual meeting of the American Bar Association, telephoned the clerk of the Supreme Court in Washington yesterday. The clerk issued the formal call for a special term this morning.

Lemley Order Is Issue

The action is in all respects most unusual. The Supreme Court has not met in special term since 1953, when it reconvened in June, just after the end of the regular term, to consider the case of the convicted atomic spies, Julius and Ethel Rosenberg.

The issue before the Supreme Court will be the order handed down by Federal District Judge Harry J. Lemley last June 21 canceling the Little Rock integration program until 1961. Judge Lemley based his order on the violence last year over the entry of nine Negro chiluren into the Little Rock Central High School.

Last Monday the United States Court of Appeals for the Eighth Circuit upset the Lemley order. But it stayed its own decision until the Little Rock school board could seek a review in the Supreme Court.

The National Association for the Advancement of Colored People promptly asked Justice Charles E. Whittaker to vacate the Court of Appeals' stay and also to hold up Judge Lemley's order. Only these twin moves

Continued on Page 18, Column 3

The New York Times

Chief Justice Earl Warren

LITTLE ROCK SETS DELAY ON SCHOOLS

Opening Put Off to Sept. 8—Faubus to Offer Bills to Legislature Today

By CLAUDE SITTON

Special to The New York Times.

LITTLE ROCK, Ark., Aug. 25—The school board announced tonight that it was postponing the opening of city schools pending action in the Central High integration controversy by the Legislature and the United States Supreme Court.

Virgil T. Blossom, school superintendent, said the term would begin Sept. 8 instead of a week from tomorrow.

He disclosed that an attempt was being made to integrate a second white high school. A 14-year-old Negro girl applied today for admission to Hall High, a new school in one of the best residential sections.

2 More Seek Admission

Mr. Blossom said another Negro boy and girl had asked to be enrolled at Central.

The Legislature meets tomorrow in special session to consider proposals by Gov. Orval E. Faubus to close Central if the Supreme Court orders officials to permit seven Negroes who attended last year to return.

All signs point to the swift passage of a six-bill package that will be introduced by administration leaders following the Governor's opening speech to a joint session at noon.

At a news conference Mr. Blossom said he would meet with the three new Negro applicants tomorrow, and decide whether they would be admitted.

However, he noted that a Federal District Court ruling

Continued on Page 16, Column 2

ALGERIANS WAGE TERROR IN FRANCE

Refineries and Shops Fired—7 Dead, 21 Injured

By HENRY TANNER

Special to The New York Times.

PARIS, Aug. 25—Large-scale and coordinated terrorism leaped from Algeria to Metropolitan France today, taking seven lives and leaving at least twenty-one persons injured.

About 2:30 o'clock this morning saboteurs struck simultaneously in Paris and at about twenty places between the English Channel and the Mediterranean. Their targets were gasoline storage facilities, a munitions factory, a railroad signal post and a plant producing military trucks.

Fourth Policeman Slain

The saboteurs killed three policemen and wounded one by machine gun fire when they tried to shoot their way into a police garage on Paris' Left Bank. They threw flaming gasoline torches into the garage in a futile attempt to set it afire.

A fourth policeman was killed a few moments later when the police, alerted by the attack on the garage, foiled an incendiary raid on a munitions factory in the Bois de Vincennes on Paris' east side.

At the same time saboteurs set fire to storage tanks in a big refinery in Moureplane near Marseilles. Fire-fighting units sought all day to control the blaze, which tonight, sixteen hours after the attack, led to an explosion wounding seventeen firemen, three seriously.

Continued on Page 10, Column 3

VIRGINIA RULING

Judge Advises Norfolk to Review Negro Integration Bids

Excerpts from the judge's message are on Page 17.

Special to The New York Times.

NORFOLK, Va., Aug. 25 — Negroes cannot be legally barred from white public schools because of racial tensions or isolation of the Negro child in a white student body, United State District Judge Walter E. Hoffman advised the Norfolk School Board today.

The judge referred back to the board "for further consideration" applications of all 151 Negro children seeking admission to white schools in September. The board last week denied all the applications. The judge asked the board to report on its review of the cases Friday.

Fifty-seven students have objected to the school board's rejections. Of these applicants, sixteen were denied for reasons the judge found "legally insufficient" today.

Their applications affect three white high school and two white junior high schools.

The racial tensions cited by the board in rejecting twelve applications were said to be in the Norview School District, part of an area annexed to the city in 1955. Bombings occurred in one section of the school district when Negro families first moved into a previously white residential area in 1954. No recent incidents have been reported.

Cited Little Rock Case

Judge Hoffman said the decision of the Eighth Circuit Court of Appeals in reversing United States District Judge Harry J. Lemley's two-and-a-half year stay in Little Rock desegregation "precludes further consideration of a plea of probable racial tension or racial violence as a sole legal excuse for denying an otherwise qualified Negro child admittance into a previously all-white school."

Whether the Supreme Court vacates or upholds the new stay of desegregation in Little Rock is "of no consequence" so far as the Norfolk case is concerned, Judge Hoffman said. The law, he added, is what the Eighth Circuit has expounded in reversing Judge Lemley.

On the question of social isolation of a Negro child, the judge observed that psychologists had testified isolation "is one, but only one, situation which may tend to deter the child." Expert testimony indicated the isolation might also

Continued on Page 17, Column 1

REDS LOSE 2 JETS IN QUEMOY CLASH; SHELLING GOES ON

Taiwan Reports 48 MIG's in Action Over Isle—Artillery Bombardment in 4th Day

Special to The New York Times.

TAIPEI, Taiwan, Tuesday, Aug. 26—The Chinese Nationalists said last night they had shot down two aircraft in a battle with forty-eight Communist planes over Quemoy.

Meanwhile, Communist shelling of the Quemoy island group off the South China coast continued for the fourth day. Communist artillery began a twenty-minute bombardment at 3 A. M., firing 850 rounds.

[The Nationalist Defense Ministry said Communist artillery had begun an eighteen-minute attack on Quemoy shortly after midnight and followed this by the 3 A. M. bombardment, The Associated Press reported.]

The Defense Ministry here said eight Nationalist Sabrejets engaged forty-eight Soviet-built MIG's over Quemoy an hour before dusk yesterday. The Nationalists suffered no damage, according to the announcement.

Red Landing Repulsed

Earlier, the Defense Ministry declared the Chinese Reds had tried unsuccessfully Sunday night to land on tiny Tungting Island, eighteen miles southwest of Quemoy. A communiqué said Nationalist warships intercepted and drove off a Communist naval unit in a gun duel.

[In Washington, President Eisenhower was believed to have discussed the situation in the Taiwan (Formosa) area during a White House meeting with Gen. Nathan F. Twining, chairman of the Joint Chiefs of Staff.]

Shore-based Communist artillery pounded fifty-square-mile Quemoy Island with about 6,000 rounds during the day yesterday. This raised the Defense Ministry's figure for the total of shells fired by the Red forces in three days of bombardment to more than 83,500.

Propaganda Fired

The Communists interrupted their periods of heavy shelling with lulls of several hours in which they shot several dozen rounds filled with propaganda leaflets. The leaflets, evidently intended to demoralize the Nationalist troops of the island's garrison, urged them to surrender or defect.

Late and unconfirmed reports said the air link between Quemoy and Taiwan had been cut, since the only airstrip on Quemoy was under Communist artillery fire. According to these reports, the Nationalist Defense Minister, Yu Ta-wei, flew to Quemoy Sunday night to survey the situation but was unable to land and had to return to Taipei.

A Defense Ministry communiqué said Nationalist warships sank two Communist motor torpedo boats, probably sank another and damaged five in Sunday's encounter with eight Communist PT boats in

Continued on Page 3, Column 2

ROCKEFELLER AND HARRIMAN PICKED; SENATE CHOICES REMAIN IN DOUBT, BUT DRIVE TO NAME WAGNER GAINS

DE LUCA SELECTED

Again Running Mate Of Governor—Mayor Still Bars a Draft

Harriman address excerpts and platform, Page 23.

By DOUGLAS DALES

Special to The New York Times.

BUFFALO, Aug. 25—The Democratic State Convention renominated Governor Harriman and Lieut. Gov. George B. De Luca by acclamation tonight.

The nomination of Governor Harriman touched off a fifteen-minute demonstration among the 2,286 delegates and alternates and several thousand Democratic partisans watching the proceedings from the balconies of the Memorial Auditorium.

Another demonstration following the seconding speeches was cut short after a minute of parading in the aisles. This was done to permit the Governor to start his acceptance speech at 9:30 P. M. to meet radio and television schedules. A twenty-minute demonstration followed the speech.

The nomination of Mr. De Luca was completed at 10:25 P. M.

The renomination of Mr. Harriman and Mr. De Luca was overshadowed as the two-day convention opened by discussion among leaders and delegates over the candidate for United States Senator.

Wagner in Limelight

Attention focused on Mayor Wagner of New York. Despite his reassertions today that his position was "unchanged" and that he would not yield to a draft, there was a growing suspicion that when the convention adjourns tomorrow night he will be on the state ticket.

If Mr. Harriman is successful in the November election, he is expected to make his third try for the Democratic Presidential nomination in 1960. He is 66 years old.

Mr. De Luca, a former Bronx County Judge and District Attorney, is 69.

The other chief prospects for the Senate nomination are Thomas K. Finletter, former Air Force Secretary; Thomas E. Murray, former member of the Atomic Energy Commission, and District Attorney Frank S. Hogan of New York County.

The Mayor conferred with Governor Harriman and Carmine G. De Sapio, Tammany leader, this afternoon, then left with Mrs. Wagner and their two children for a visit to Niagara Falls. On his return the Mayor conferred with Alex

Continued on Page 23, Column 1

Governor Harriman

The New York Times

Nelson A. Rockefeller

Keynoters Trade Charges As State Campaigns Open

Prendergast Asks Big Vote

By WARREN WEAVER Jr.

Special to The New York Times.

BUFFALO, Aug. 25 — The Democratic state chairman called today for a 400,000-vote majority as "an absolute minimum" for Governor Harriman in the fall election.

Michael H. Prendergast told the opening session of the party's nominating convention that a margin of 100,000 or 200,000 votes "will not be enough of a victory for us" in the light of the progressive Harriman Administration's record.

Four years ago Mr. Harriman defeated Senator Irving M. Ives by fewer than 12,000 votes, in one of the closest gubernatorial races in state history.

The Democratic state chairman characterized the Governor's political opponents as "the self-perpetuating clique of power-drunk bosses who dominate the Republican party's machinery, who have put it to work for selfish, narrow special interest, who have substituted the politics of the big lie for the policies of honest debate."

In his convention keynote

Continued on Page 22, Column 5

Heck Sees 'Mess in Albany'

By CLAYTON KNOWLES

Special to The New York Times.

ROCHESTER, Aug. 25—Former Gov. Thomas E. Dewey and Oswald D. Heck, Speaker of the Assembly, teamed today in delivering blistering attacks against the "mess in Albany" under the Democrats.

Mr. Dewey charged that Governor Harriman would leave "a blank record and an empty till." The former Governor addressed the Republican State Convention tonight shortly before Nelson A. Rockefeller was nominated for the Governorship.

Speaker Heck, convention keynoter, had accused Mr. Harriman earlier of "liquidation of the entire shining legacy inherited from his predecessor, Governor Dewey, and the Republican Legislature."

The keynoter, setting up the cry "Harriman must go," taxed the Democratic Administration with "confusion, vacillation and political caprice." He said that accomplishments claimed by the Democrats had been "conceived and initiated in twelve years of

Continued on Page 20, Column 6

FINANCIAL EXPERT NAMED G. M. HEAD

Donner to Succeed Curtice, Retiring Next Monday

By ROBERT E. BEDINGFIELD

The General Motors Corporation, the biggest manufacturing company in the world, has a new top management team.

Frederic G. Donner, 55 years old, has been named chairman and chief executive officer and John F. Gordon, 58, has been elected president.

Harlow H. Curtice, who became 65 on Aug. 15, will retire Monday as president and chief executive officer under the company's automatic retirement plan, after forty-four years' service.

Took Office in 1953

He had been top man at G. M. since Feb. 2, 1953, when Charles E. Wilson resigned to become Secretary of Defense in President Eisenhower's new Cabinet.

Mr. Curtice has been one of the highest-paid corporate executives in the United States. In 1957 he received in salary, director fees, cash and stock bonuses a total of $621,100.

While Mr. Curtice did not hold the post of chairman—that office has been held by Albert Bradley, 67, who also is retiring next Monday—he was the company's principal spokesman. His retirement came as no surprise either to Detroit or to Wall Street. It was announced by directors following a meeting here yesterday.

The board also announced a realignment of its top governing committees. It created a new finance committee and an executive committee to replace

Continued on Page 14, Column 5

EISENHOWER BACKS KNOWLAND'S RACE

Endorses Him for Governor in California Contest

Special to The New York Times.

WASHINGTON, Aug. 25 — President Eisenhower endorsed today the candidacy of his chief Senate spokesman for Governor of California.

In a letter to the Senate minority leader, William F. Knowland, the President said the California Republican soon would be waging "a political campaign on behalf of a philosophy of government in which we both believe."

The President said he was certain that the people of California were aware of the Senator's admirable qualifications, fine character and dedication to duty "and would want to utilize your services as Governor of that great state."

First Open Move

It was the President's first open move to influence the outcome of this fall's election, in which he is expected to play an increasingly active part. He announced last week that he would "probably have some things to say" during the campaign and personal appearances in half a dozen states are under consideration.

In endorsing Senator Knowland, General Eisenhower was bucking a California political trend to the Democrats that nonpartisan analysts have interpreted to mean almost certain defeat for the Republican gubernatorial candidate.

The Senator trailed his Democratic opponent, Attorney General Edmund G. Brown, by more

Continued on Page 19, Column 1

KEATING IS URGED

G. O. P. Leaders Press Representative to Seek Ives' Seat

Rockefeller speech excerpts and platform, Page 20.

By LEO EGAN

Special to The New York Times.

ROCHESTER, Aug. 25—Nelson A. Rockefeller, corporation executive and philanthropist, was nominated by acclamation tonight as the Republican candidate for Governor.

He delivered his acceptance speech shortly afterward to a cheering and enthusiastic crowd of 10,000. He promised to work twice as hard to win the election as he did to get the nomination.

Even while he was making his acceptance speech, there was confusion and uncertainty as to the identity of the candidate for United States Senator.

Look to Keating

There was a general assumption that Representative Kenneth B. Keating of Rochester would yield to pressure and accept. However, he was still holding out. Mr. Keating has been insisting that he would be more valuable as the ranking Republican member of the House Judiciary Committee. He was under heavy pressure all day to agree to run for Senator Irving M. Ives' seat. Senator Ives is not seeking re-election.

It started with a meeting Mr. Keating had this afternoon with L. Judson Morhouse, the Republican State Chairman. It continued throug a dinner with Mr. Rockefeller and became more intense later at a session with former Gov. Thomas E. Dewey.

A further conference between Mr. Keating and top state Republican leaders started after the convention session adjourned tonight.

The selection of a candidate for United States Senator will be the main business of tomorrow's concluding session of the Republican convention.

Administration Scored

In his acceptance speech tonight Mr. Rockefeller assailed Governor Harriman's Democratic Administration as a dismal failure. In this he echoed the views expressed earlier in the session by Mr. Dewey, Assembly Speaker Oswald D. Heck, the keynoter, and a half dozen others.

The box score of the Harriman administration should read, Mr. Rockefeller said: "No hits, no runs, but my what errors."

The newly chosen candidate was flanked by his wife, their five children and a daughter-in-law as he delivered his acceptance.

For noise and enthusiasm today's convention demonstration exceeded anything in recent Republican history. It bore evidence of careful staging.

One influential group of Re-

Continued on Page 20 Column 1

President to Take Newport Vacation

By FELIX BELAIR Jr.

Special to The New York Times.

WASHINGTON, Aug. 25 — President Eisenhower has chosen Newport, R. I., for a second time as a vacation spot.

He and Mrs. Eisenhower intend to leave Washington Thursday or Friday on his special plane, Columbine III, for the Quonset Naval Air Station in Rhode Island and there board the White House cabin cruiser, the Barbara Anne, for Newport.

The White House announcement stressed that the plans were only tentative and subject to cancellation should there be grave national or international developments.

Even more uncertain is the duration of the vacation. When asked why he could not say how long the President would be away, James C. Hagerty, the

Continued on Page 35, Column 2

City Greets the Nautilus With Cheers, Whistles, Fireboats and Helicopters

The New York Times

Harbor craft, aloft and afloat, give a hero's welcome to the nuclear-powered submarine as she nears the Battery

By MILTON BRACKER

The Nautilus sailed into New York yesterday under a mass of lowering gray clouds that seemed as impenetrable as the Arctic ice under which she cruised the first five days of August. But despite the brooding overcast, the rain-swept harbor provided a dramatic setting for a sea, air and land welcome that the atomic submarine's skipper called "absolutely overwhelming." Comdr. William R. Anderson shared the day's personal honors with Rear Admiral Hyman G. Rickover, the nation's leading expert on nuclear ship propulsion. But the captain of the Nautilus left no doubt about the principal subject of the celebration. "The hero in this case is the ship," he said. As the representative of President Eisenhower, Admiral Rickover boarded the Nautilus at the Narrows and was a passenger as she eased up the Hudson

Continued on Page 31, Column 2

"All the News
That's Fit to Print"

The New York Times

LATE CITY EDITION

Weather: Clearing today, turning cold tonight. Fair, cool tomorrow. Temp. range: today 62-44; Thurs. 73-52. Full U.S. report on Page 92.

VOL. CVIII..No. 36,999.

NEW YORK, WEDNESDAY, MAY 13, 1959.

10 cents beyond 50-mile zone from New York City except on Long Island. Higher in air delivery cities.

FIVE CENTS

SOVIET DEMANDS BIG 4 PARLEY SEAT POLES AND CZECHS

West Says No but Gromyko Plans to Press the Point at Geneva Today

RECALLS LOSSES IN WAR

Herter Replies That Others Suffered Too—Discussion of Basic Issues Delayed

By DREW MIDDLETON
Special to The New York Times.

GENEVA, May 12—The Soviet Union proposed and the Western powers rejected today full participation of Poland and Czechoslovakia in the foreign ministers' conference.

Discussion of Andrei A. Gromyko's plea for participation of the two Soviet satellites occupied all of today's session of the conference at the Palais des Nations.

The Soviet Foreign Minister indicated at the close of the session that he intended to reopen the question tomorrow. The United States, Britain and France made no objection to this at the meeting.

An authoritative United States source said, however, that Secretary of State Christian A. Herter, tomorrow's chairman, would propose that the session begin with the opening statements of the Big Four foreign ministers.

Plan on Germany to Follow

After these speeches, which are traditional at such meetings, the conference could proceed Thursday to presentation of the Western package of proposals on Germany. The future of that country is the subject of the conference.

The Western proposals cover German reunification, the integrity of West Berlin and European security. They answer Soviet demands for liquidation of the West's authority in West Berlin and conclusion of a peace treaty by the Big Four powers with the two Germanys.

Some authoritative sources said they thought the West might agree to allow the Soviet Union to present its proposals first.

The meetings are closed, but all the delegations report on the proceedings at news conferences afterward.

The Soviet intention to push the issue of Polish and Czechoslovak participation was stressed by the introduction of Valerian A. Zorin, Deputy Foreign Minister, as the briefing officer at tonight's Soviet press confer-

Continued on Page 16, Column 1

BRITON IS HOPEFUL ON ATOM TEST BAN

Macmillan Envisions Pact Within a Few Months

By THOMAS P. RONAN
Special to The New York Times.

LONDON, May 12 — Prime Minister Harold Macmillan said today he thought some compromise agreement for stopping nuclear tests would be worked out in the next few months.

He told the House of Commons he thought the compromise would be "along the lines" of the proposal he made to Premier Nikita S. Khrushchev during his recent visit to Moscow.

This was that both sides agree to limit to a specified number the visits that international inspection teams could make each year to the sites of suspected nuclear explosions.

This suggestion was intended to meet the Soviet suspicion that visits would be used for espionage and the Soviet insistence on the right to veto inspections and findings.

Mr. Macmillan noted that Mr. Khrushchev had accepted his proposal and said that President Eisenhower was now prepared to consider it. Early in March the President said that a study of the "new ideas" put forward by Mr. Macmillan in Moscow did not "reassure that they are completely practical."

Mr. Macmillan said recent communications among the President, Mr. Khrushchev and him had "marked an encouraging approach to a common point of view."

"All parties to the Geneva

Continued on Page 18, Column 1

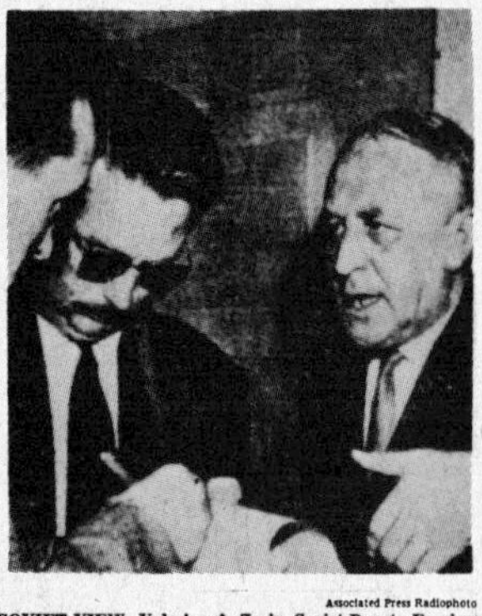

Associated Press Radiophoto

SOVIET VIEW: Valerian A. Zorin, Soviet Deputy Foreign Minister, with newsmen at foreign ministers' conference.

West Vows Berlin Defense 10 Years After the Airlift

Special to The New York Times.

BERLIN, May 12—On the tenth anniversary of the end of the Soviet blockade of Berlin, Western military and political leaders reaffirmed today the West's determination to defend the freedom of the city.

On May 12, 1949, the Soviet Union threw open the barriers on the road, rail and canal access routes to Berlin after eleven months of blockade.

Today tens of thousands of Berliners, in a festive mood, attended ceremonies. They lined the streets under blue skies to cheer Allied leaders and the heroes of the airlift, who had been invited by the city government to attend the celebrations.

Gen. Lucius D. Clay, former United States Military Governor in Germany, warned the Soviet Union at a mass rally in the Deutschlandhalle sports arena that the West was ready to defend the freedom of the city with all available means, including the "horrors of modern war."

No New Airlift Seen

"If there should be further trouble in Berlin, I am convinced that a new airlift would not be the answer," General Clay said.

General Clay shared an enthusiastic ovation with Earl Attlee and Robert Schuman, British and French Government leaders at the time of the blockade.

West Berlin's Mayor, Willy Brandt, thanked the Allies for helping to "wipe off the shame brought upon the German name." He assured the West that the people of Berlin were ready "to brave new hardships and sacrifices if need be."

The mass rally was the climax of the day's events, which began with a wreath-laying ceremony at the Airlift Memorial in front of the city's Tempelhof Airport. The monument honors forty-one British and thirty-one American airmen and five German workers who lost their lives in the operation.

SOVIET EXCHANGE WITH HARVARD SET

Leningrad Professors Will Change Places With U. S. Counterparts in Fall

By HARRY SCHWARTZ

A tentative agreement for exchange of professors has been reached between Harvard University and Leningrad State University.

This was confirmed yesterday by Harvard University. An official of Harvard noted that it was hoped to have the arrangement in operation by September, the beginning of the next academic year. Though the ultimate program is hoped to be extensive, he said, it will probably start with two or three professors.

A similar program is also being negotiated with Moscow State University by Columbia University, and, if successful, may begin in February.

A Columbia delegation headed by Prof. Schuyler Wallace, director of the School of International Relations, visited Moscow University last month. A Moscow University group is expected here next week to complete the negotiations.

Research to Be Stressed

The Harvard-Leningrad exchange will focus mainly upon research work. The exchange professors may give some lectures, but teaching activity will be subordinated to research.

A Harvard delegation visited Leningrad earlier this year to initiate the negotiations and the tentative agreement was reached when a Leningrad delegation visited Harvard last month. The Harvard group was headed by Prof. Merle Fainsod and the Leningrad group by the rector of Leningrad University, Academician Aleksandr D. Aleksandrov, a mathematician.

An informant at Columbia University indicated that more emphasis might be placed on teaching in a Columbia-Moscow exchange than was envisaged in the Harvard-Leningrad agreement. This would be particularly true if the outstanding scholars in physics and oceanography at Moscow University could be brought to Columbia.

Social Science at Issue

A Government official said yesterday that the universities faced a problem with respect to social scientists who might be exchanged. From the Soviet point of view, the teachings of an American economist or historian are regarded as "anti-scientific bourgeois perversions," while the Marxist views of Soviet social scientists are regarded generally here as "Communist propaganda."

The exchanges now being negotiated were originally envisaged in an over-all Soviet-American cultural exchange agreement concluded last year.

The Soviet-American cultural exchange agreement provided specifically for exchange of professors between Harvard and Leningrad and also between Columbia and Moscow.

BRITAIN TO BUILD SPACE SATELLITE WITH AID OF U. S.

Macmillan Tells Commons of Plan—American Rocket May Launch Pay-Load

By WALTER H. WAGGONER
Special to The New York Times.

LONDON, May 12—Britain announced today plans for a space research program that would begin with the development of an earth satellite that might be launched with a United States rocket.

Prime Minister Harold Macmillan told the House of Commons that "substantial but modest sums" would be spent on the design of the satellite's instruments and on studies of the possibility of eventually adopting one of Britain's military rockets as a launching vehicle.

The expenditure, he said, would be "more in hundreds of thousands of pounds than in millions." At the same time, the Prime Minister continued, co-operation with the United States will be sought. He said this would be discussed with a "team of experts" soon to go to Washington.

1,000-Pound Satellite

H. S. W. Massey, Professor of Physics at University College, London, will lead the British scientists.

In addition to seeking details about the design, character and behavior of the United States earth satellites, it was said, he will discuss the American offer, made to the international Committee for Space Research (COSPAR), to launch another country's satellite.

It was disclosed at a news conference after Mr. Macmillan's announcement in Parliament that British scientists envisaged the possibility of developing and launching an instrument-carrying satellite weighing as much as 1,000 pounds, and with an orbiting altitude of "a few hundred miles."

W. H. Stephens, director of the Royal Aircraft Establishment, said the purpose was not to put up a satellite heavier than any of the others but to produce an instrument with a maximum capacity for scientific research.

New Explorations Stressed

The 1,000 pounds, he said, is "just a round number." He added that it might prove more valuable to send a smaller satellite farther into space. The United States indicated in its offer to the international space research group that it had a 150-pound satellite in mind.

Lord Hailsham, Lord President of the Council, whose office is responsible for scientific efforts of this kind, emphasized that Britain's space research program was motivated neither by military nor commercial considerations.

"This is pure science," he said.

He added that it was not to be a moon probe, that it was not a space-travel project, and

Continued on Page 12, Column 1

HOSPITAL SESSION REACHES IMPASSE OVER GRIEVANCES

Management Seeks to Avoid 'Back-Door' Recognition —No New Talks Set

By HOMER BIGART

Negotiations for ending the hospital strike reached an impasse last night on the issue of workers' grievances.

A conference at City Hall broke up shortly after 8 P. M. Mayor Wagner's attempt to find a peace formula was evidently stalemated, for no date was set for a future meeting between union leaders and hospital representatives.

Leaving the Mayor's office, representatives of the hospitals issued a statement attacking the union for an "illegal strike."

The Mayor said that both sides had told him that they would be available for future discussions.

The managements of the six struck hospitals rejected a union proposal that a worker with a grievance select another employe to represent him before an impartial arbitrator.

Hospitals Cite 'Results'

The hospitals told Mayor Wagner that this arrangement would enable the union to channel all grievances through shop stewards and would result in "back-door union recognition."

The hospitals refuse to recognize Local 1199 of the Retail Drug Employes Union, which Friday began a strike of nurses' aides, orderlies, porters, elevator operators, kitchen help and other housekeeping employes at six voluntary institutions.

But the hospitals said yesterday that they were now ready to accept impartial arbitration of labor disputes. They specified that the arbitrator be appointed by some highly placed non-elective official.

Mayor Wagner conferred with the city's Labor Commissioner, Harold Felix, yesterday before resuming talks with the contending sides separately.

Sides Make Statements

Emerging from the Mayor's office shortly before 7 P. M. Morris Iushewitz, secretary of the New York City Central Labor Council, said:

"We have reached a complete stalemate."

After the session ended the Mayor said he would continue his mediation efforts. But the angry statement signed by a committee of presidents of voluntary hospitals showed that little, if any, progress had been made in settling the issue of arbitration of grievances.

The statement also accused the union of "putting union recognition ahead of improvement programs for the employes."

The hospitals had earlier proposed a ten-point program that would provide a minimum wage of $1 an hour, a forty-hour work week and fringe benefits.

During the City Hall talks, hospital representatives said they were also prepared to un-

Continued on Page 28, Column 3

31 KILLED AS PLANE FALLS IN STORM NEAR BALTIMORE; TWO DIE IN LINE'S 2D CRASH

The New York Times — May 13, 1959

TWIN ACCIDENTS: Capital Airlines plane disintegrated in flight near Baltimore (1), and second Capital airliner ran off a runway and crashed at Charleston, W. Va. (2).

NEW YORK FLIGHT

Witness Reports Fiery Debris—2d Craft Skids in Landing

By United Press International.

BALTIMORE, May 12 — A Capital Airlines plane disintegrated in the air during a thunderstorm north of here today. Twenty-seven passengers and the crew of four were killed.

The Viscount turboprop craft was flying from New York to Atlanta.

It was the second disaster to hit Capital, the nation's fifth biggest domestic carrier, in less than an hour.

Earlier a Capital Constellation slid down a mountainside while landing at Charleston, W. Va. Two persons were killed and six sent to hospitals of the more than forty persons aboard. The plane skidded as it landed on a wet runway.

Investigators Go to Scene

The Civil Aeronautics Board sent investigators to the scene of the Baltimore crash. They were led by Oscar Bakke, director of the board's Safety Bureau. With him was the assistant director, Leon Tanguay, and two other top accident investigators from the Washington headquarters.

Reports from witnesses said that the plane appeared to explode in the air.

The wreckage of the British-built plane, powered by four jet engines with conventional propellers, was scattered over a mile-and-a-half long area of open fields near Chase, Md., a village close to the Glenn L. Martin Airport north of Baltimore. A few pieces fell in a swampy area.

The C. A. B. said the plane apparently was flying through "high turbulence" just before the crash. This referred to extreme up-and-down air drafts.

There also was heavy lightning and rain at the time. The plane was flying at 14,000 feet.

Capital said that the pilot of the plane, Capt. W. C. Paddock, 52 years old of Grosse Pointe, Mich., had been flying with the airline for nearly twenty-nine years and never had an accident.

The co-pilot, M. J. Flahaven of Dearborn, Mich., had been

Continued on Page 32, Column 3

Democrats Upset In Camden in Blow To State Chairman

By GEORGE CABLE WRIGHT

The powerful Democratic organization of Mayor George E. Brunner lost control of the Camden city government yesterday for the first time in twenty-four years.

A coalition of Republicans and independent Democrats captured four of the five City Commission posts at stake in the balloting. The only Brunner man to be returned to office was Frank A. Abbott, Director of Public Works.

Mr. Brunner is the Democratic state chairman of New Jersey. The stunning defeat in his own bailiwick may lead to his replacement in that post.

In addition to its local significance, yesterday's loss was a blow to Mr. Brunner's state-wide political prestige.

After serving six consecutive four-year terms, he had not sought re-election. But he named and strongly supported the organization ticket.

'Save Our City' Slate Wins

A move to replace Mr. Brunner as state chairman was begun last year by a number of top party leaders. But it was blocked by Gov. Robert B. Meyner, long a close friend of the Mayor.

The four victorious Commission candidates who opposed the Brunner ticket were two independent Democrats, Alfred R. Pierce and William Shepp, and two Republicans, Frank C. Italiano and Edward C. Garrity, an incumbent. They ran on the "Save Our City" ticket.

They had repeatedly charged during the campaign that Camden was a dying city and accused the Brunner officials of a "do-nothing attitude." They had pointed to a drop in the city's population and a lack of urban-renewal projects.

Among the Brunner men de-

Continued on Page 30, Column 4

HOUSE UNIT VOTES HIGH-COURT CURB

Approves, 17-15, a Measure That Protects State Laws From U. S. Pre-emption

By ANTHONY LEWIS
Special to The New York Times.

WASHINGTON, May 12—The House Judiciary Committee approved today a states' rights bill that the Justice Department has attacked as "the most hazardous" measure before Congress.

The vote was 17 to 15. Nine of the committee's eleven Republicans joined eight Democrats—one from a border state and seven from the South—to form the narrow majority.

The bill, H. R. 3, is sponsored by Representative Howard W. Smith, Democrat of Virginia. He has proposed similar bills, with the same number, for the last several years.

Aimed at High Court

Last year the bill passed the House on a roll-call vote of 241 to 155. It was killed in the Senate, 41 to 40.

The principal section of the measure is designed to prevent Supreme Court decisions holding that Congress has pre-empted a field of legislation. The section reads as follows:

"No act of Congress shall be construed as indicating an intent on the part of Congress to occupy the field in which such act operates to the exclusion of all state laws on the same subject matter, unless such act contains an express provision to that effect, or unless there is a direct and positive conflict between such act and a state law so that the two cannot be reconciled or consistently stand together."

Measure Is Retroactive

The Administration has consistently opposed H. R. 3 on the ground that it might upset established relations of state-Federal law in such areas as labor and railroads. The bill is retroactive, apparently affecting all past statutes.

The label of "hazardous" was applied in recent testimony by Lawrence E. Walsh, the Deputy Attorney General. He said the bill could "lead to relitigation of all the countless cases that have been decided in this field."

Mr. Walsh argued against the bill before the House committee this morning. The vote to report it out followed immediately afterward.

Republicans voting in favor were William M. McCulloch and John E. Henderson of Ohio, William E. Miller of upstate New York, John H. Ray of Staten Island, Richard H. Poff of Virginia, William C. Cramer of Florida, Arch A. Moore Jr. of West Virginia, H. Allen Smith of California and George Meader of Michigan.

Democrats in favor were Frank Chelf of Kentucky, Edwin E. Willis of Louisiana, E. L.

Continued on Page 31, Column 1

PARKING TEST SET BY TRANSIT BOARD

Contract Is Let on 2 Sites—75c Fee to Buy 2 Tokens

By RALPH KATZ

The Transit Authority approved contracts yesterday for the private operation of parking fields on its unused properties adjacent to outlying subway stations in Brooklyn and the Bronx.

Autoists will pay 75 cents a day at the field. That charge will include 45 cents for parking and 30 cents for two tokens for subway trips from the site and back to it. The twin objectives are to tap a new source of revenue and to stimulate subway riding.

The program will be put on a six-month trial period on parts of the Canarsie subway yard in Brooklyn and the Westchester Avenue subway yard in the Bronx. A parking concern will begin operating in Brooklyn about June 1 and will start in the Bronx a month later.

The Canarsie yard, which will accommodate 340 autos, adjoins the Rockaway Park terminal of the BMT Canarsie line. At the Westchester Avenue yard, which adjoins the Westchester Square station of the Pelham Bay line, facilities will be made available for 400 cars about July 1. Eventually, the Bronx field will accommodate 1,500 cars.

Meanwhile, the Transit Authority is surveying ten other sites over the entire periphery of the rapid transit system in

Continued on Page 36, Column 4

2,500-Year-Old Altars Found Near Rome

Believed to Be Part of Lost Sanctuary of Lavinium

By PAUL HOFMANN
Special to The New York Times

PRATICA DI MARE, Italy, May 12—The long-lost sanctuary of Lavinium, linked with the mythical origins of Rome, is believed to have been rediscovered here.

A row of archaic altars dug up near this village and Air Force base eighteen miles south of Rome appears to have been the nucleus of a religious center where Romans 2,500 years ago worshipped their ancestral gods.

Lavinia, wife of Aeneas, is supposed to have given her name to the place. Vergil, in his Aeneid, sings of the landing on the near-by coast by Aeneas, the son of Anchises and the goddess Aphrodite, at the end of his wanderings after the fall of Troy.

In this part of Latium, according to Vergil, Aeneas won Lavinia, a native princess, for his queen. Their remote descendants were Romulus and Remus, legendary founders of Rome.

The old city of Lavinium, according to classical sources, was revered by the Romans for its Aenean traditions. The settlement, an early ally of Rome, reportedly had a temple of Venus, the Latin name for Aphrodite, and a cult of the penates, or household gods, supposed to have been introduced by Aeneas.

Ancient writings and inscriptions contain evidence that every year the newly elected magistrates of republican Rome used to go to Lavinium to venerate the penates of the com-

Continued on Page 6, Column 3

Radiophoto of The New York Times

Ancient altars lie in a row at the excavation site near Pratica di Mare, eighteen miles south of Rome. Wooden structure was built to protect altars from the weather.

NEWS INDEX

News Summary and Index, Page 39

"All the News That's Fit to Print"

The New York Times.

LATE CITY EDITION

U.S. Weather Bureau Report (Page 42) forecast: Mostly fair and warmer today; fair tonight and tomorrow. Temp. range: 75—56; yesterday: 64.3—55.5. Temp.-Hum. Index: near 70; yesterday: 64.

VOL. CVIII..No. 37,037. NEW YORK, SATURDAY, JUNE 20, 1959. 10 cents beyond 50-mile zone from New York City except on Long Island. Higher in air delivery cities. FIVE CENTS

PRESIDENT SCORES STRAUSS' DEFEAT AS LOSS TO NATION

'Sad Episode' Cost People an Able Public Servant, He Says in Statement

REPLACEMENT STUDIED

Commerce Chief's Rejection Shocks the White House—Nixon Blames Johnson

By FELIX BELAIR Jr.

Special to The New York Times.

WASHINGTON, June 19—President Eisenhower assailed today the Senate's refusal to confirm Lewis L. Strauss to be Secretary of Commerce. He called it a "sad episode" that had cost the American people a servant of "proven character, ability and integrity."

The President was unaware, until he reached his office this morning, of the dramatic Senate vote of 49 to 46 shortly after midnight that rejected his appointment of Mr. Strauss.

Informed of the rebuff, he summoned Mr. Strauss to the White House. After a twenty-minute conference the President called reporters into his office and read this handwritten statement:

"Last night the Senate refused to confirm the nomination as Secretary of Commerce of Lewis Strauss—a man who in war and in peace has served his nation loyally, honorably and effectively, under four different Presidents.

Reads Statement Grimly

"I am truly losing a valuable associate in the business of government. More than this—if the nation is to be denied the right to have as public servants in responsible positions men of his proven character, ability and integrity, then indeed it is the American people who are the losers through this sad episode."

President Eisenhower made no attempt to hide his chagrin over the rejection of his nomination. The smile with which he had greeted newsmen who had assembled in his office vanished as he grimly began reading the statement in the clipped phrases of a military commander.

The President's reaction to the Senate's decision contrasted markedly with that of Mr. Strauss.

Talking with newsmen as he left the White House, Mr. Strauss told of his plan to return

Continued on Page 8, Column 4

Eisenhower Unhappy, Strauss Calm on Rejection

President Eisenhower reads a statement expressing regret on the Senate's rejection of Lewis L. Strauss' nomination.

Associated Press Wirephotos

Mr. Strauss displays no visible bitterness at breakfast in Washington following the Senate action in night session.

WORDING OF PACT FOR 7 HOSPITALS REOPENS DISPUTE

Labor Spokesman Protests but After Meeting Says He Still Favors Plan

By HOMER BIGART

Angry bickering over the drafting of the agreement to end the hospital strike here threatened to wreck Mayor Wagner's peace plan last night.

However, after a four-hour meeting that was occasionally interrupted by angry shouting, Harry A. Van Arsdale Jr., president of the City Central Labor Council, said he was still recommending acceptance of the plan by the striking workers.

The tentative agreement, which the Mayor had hailed early yesterday as a formula that dissolved all outstanding issues, was barely twelve hours old when it came under fire.

Mr. Van Arsdale took strong exception to the written version of the agreement.

Felix Calls Meeting

To save the peace, the city's Labor Commissioner, Harold A. Felix, called an emergency meeting of hospital and labor officials. In an attempt to avoid publicity, they met at 30 Broad Street in the office of William H. Davis, chairman of the special mediation panel that had been appointed by the Mayor to settle the strike.

Commissioner Felix conceded that a dispute had arisen over the "language" of certain areas of the settlement, but denied that a major rift had developed.

Meanwhile, picketing continued at the seven struck hospitals. Union officials said that there would be no respite until Monday afternoon, when the 4,000 striking nonprofessional workers will vote on the peace terms. This meeting will be held at 2 P. M. in the Diplomat Hotel.

Mayor Wagner had asked both sides to keep the terms of the agreement secret until Monday.

12-Man Board Provided

It was learned, however, that the settlement makes provision for a wage-review board consisting of six hospital trustees named by the Greater New York Hospital Association and six impartial public figures to be chosen by the chief judge of the Court of Appeals.

There is provision for a worker to pick another to represent him in a grievance case. But union recognition in the normal sense is absent, and hospital officials were congratulating themselves yesterday on the absence of provisions for a shop steward system and across-the-table collective bargaining. They have insisted that union activity on the premises is incompatible with the efficient operation of a hospital.

While it falls short of a normal labor-management contract, the "memorandum of agreement," when reached, was hailed by union leaders. Mr. Van Arsdale then said that he

Continued on Page 43, Column 2

GENEVA TALKS RECESSING TILL JULY 13 IN DEADLOCK; SOVIET IS FIRM ON BERLIN

Khrushchev Urges Big 4 Keep Trying for Solution

Premier's Talk Is Conciliatory in Tone but He Warns of Limit on Price He Will Pay for Summit Parley

By HARRISON E. SALISBURY

Special to The New York Times.

MOSCOW, June 19—Premier Nikita S. Khrushchev proposed today that another effort to reach a formula on the German question be made at Geneva, but

Excerpts from Khrushchev's address on Page 2.

he warned that there was a limit to the price the Soviet Union would pay for a summit meeting.

Mr. Khrushchev made an address that was generally conciliatory in tone in a ceremony in the Kremlin honoring leaders of the East Germany Government who were ending a state visit to the Soviet Union. Once more he said he was ready to go a meeting of the heads of government of East and West as many times as necessary to achieve a solution of difficult world problems.

The Premier emphasized that the Soviet Union was not willing to sign or would not even consider signing an agreement that would make permanent the occupation of Germany, that would preserve for some indefinite time the occupation status of Berlin or that would postpone to the limitless future the signing of a peace treaty for Germany.

In discussing the situation at Geneva, where the Big Four foreign ministers have reached an impasse, Mr. Khrushchev re-examined the Soviet position. He suggested that a temporary arrangement be arrived at in Geneva looking toward a German solution.

He emphasized that the Soviet Union had not and would not confront the West with an

Continued on Page 2, Column 8

FINAL PARLEY SET

Ministers Will Attempt to Write Joint Report Today on Sessions

West's statement and the two Berlin plans, Page 2.

By SYDNEY GRUSON

Special to The New York Times.

GENEVA, June 19—The Big Four foreign ministers agreed today to recess their conference on the German and Berlin problems to July 13. Geneva will again be the meeting place.

The Western powers suggested the recess in the second of two restricted sessions with Andrei A. Gromyko after the Soviet Foreign Minister had renewed his proposal for an interim Berlin settlement with a deadline.

This was Mr. Gromyko's answer to the West's final offer of concessions in return for a guarantee of unrestricted access to West Berlin until Germany's reunification. The Soviet minister kept the West waiting forty-eight hours for his answer.

Khrushchev Talk a Factor

It was made after Nikita S. Khrushchev's speech in Moscow today, in which he substantially maintained the Soviet position toward West Berlin. The Soviet Premier's address, rather than what was happening here, generated the day's excitement.

Excerpts from it were rushed to the Western ministers in their first meeting with Mr. Gromyko at the Russian villa. If it was the cue for Mr. Gromyko it was also a definite enough sign to the West that there was no point in trying to keep the discussions going here for the moment. All that was left, they agreed, was how to wind up here after six weeks of negotiations.

Somewhat to their surprise, the Western ministers got no argument from Mr. Gromyko when they suggested the recess. They proposed July 15. Mr. Gromyko countered with July 13 and the Western powers accepted this date.

Saturday Session Set

Then all four agreed that there should be a brief plenary session tomorrow morning to put the recess agreement on the formal record of the conference. The ministers' deputies will meet beforehand to see if a joint communiqué can be worked out.

Today's two sessions were brief. The first lasted thirty-four minutes. It was almost entirely taken up by Mr. Gromyko's answer and his complaint that the West misunderstood the Soviet intentions about time limits.

The second session, convened after the Western ministers had conferred for two hours, lasted less than an hour. A joint Western statement was presented to Mr. Gromyko and agreement was reached on the recess.

Longer Deadline Offered

The only new thing the West found in Mr. Gromyko's answer this morning was an offer to extend the Soviet deadline from one year to eighteen months.

Though the Soviet Foreign Minister again denied that this was meant as an ultimatum, the Western powers told him that the proposal was as unacceptable now as when originally offered June 9 with the one-year time limit.

The joint statement by Secretary of State Christian A. Herter, Selwyn Lloyd, British Foreign Secretary, and Maurice Couve de Murville, French Foreign Minister, said the renewed offer reserved for the Soviet Union "freedom of unilateral action" against Berlin at the

Continued on Page 2, Column 1

Congress Urged to Study Moses' Housing Actions

By CHARLES GRUTZNER

Robert Moses designated the dummy-held Soundview bungalow tract in the Bronx as a slum clearance site after its owners had failed to obtain city approval of tax abatement for a private housing cooperative.

This came to light yesterday as Representative John V. Lindsay, Republican of New York, asked for a Congressional investigation of this city's Committee on Slum Clearance, of which Mr. Moses is chairman.

Representative Lindsay noted that a Senate-House conference on Thursday struck from the housing bill a provision that he had sponsored. It would have required full disclosure of the identity of sponsors of slum clearance projects.

This action he called "a tragedy" in the light of recent developments.

"The New York City disclosures double the need for a public investigation by Congress," he declared.

Chairman Urged to Quit

Mr. Moses, denying that he had previous knowledge of the ownership of the Soundview tract, charged that published reports as to its ownership were "entirely misleading."

A demand for the resignation of Mr. Moses and a "complete reorganization" of the slum clearance set-up was made by Harris L. Present, chairman of the Council on Housing Relocation Practices.

There were strong indications at City Hall that the Soundview redevelopment, toward which Mr. Moses wants the Federal Government to contribute $2,000,000 and the city to give $1,000,000, would not be approved by the Board of Estimate.

Deputy Mayor Paul T. O'Keefe

Continued on Page 22, Column 1

BANK DEAL LINKED TO SLUM PROJECT

Ungar Offered a $700,000 'Good Faith' Deposit to Shanahan Institution

By WAYNE PHILLIPS

The prospective sponsor of a slum clearance project offered as evidence of "good faith" to deposit $700,000 in a bank headed by Thomas J. Shanahan, it was disclosed yesterday. Mr. Shanahan is vice chairman of the Mayor's Slum Clearance Committee.

The offer was made by Sidney J. Ungar at a time when Mr. Shanahan was investigating the qualifications of competing sponsors for the Riverside-Amsterdam project.

Mr. Ungar was subsequently designated as sponsor of the project on the recommendation of Mr. Shanahan. He is now fighting to retain that designation in the face of revelations of his tenement holdings.

Cleared in Violations

Mr. Ungar was acquitted the day before yesterday in Special Sessions Court of ninety violations of the Multiple Dwelling Law in an old law tenement he owns at 10 West 104th Street.

That building is one of a long list of tenements and other real estate that he owns and manages, including the building at 299 Broadway, which houses the New York City Housing Authority.

Mr. Shanahan, an experienced fund raiser for the Democratic party, is the president of the Federation Bank and Trust

Continued on Page 22, Column 2

U.S. COURT ORDERS TUGMEN REHIRED

Harbor Stoppage Due to End by Midnight as Railroads Say They Will Comply

By JACQUES NEVARD

Ten railroads serving the Port of New York were directed yesterday to reinstate 125 tugboat oilers by midnight tonight. The dismissal of the oilers last Monday set off a tie-up of railroad marine operations here.

The order is expected to end the stoppage by the midnight deadline. It was handed down by Judge Frederick vanPelt Bryan in Federal District Court in Foley Square.

The discharged oilers have been picketing the tugboats since they were laid off. The carriers had said they were no longer needed. Other members of the crews have not crossed their picket lines.

James J. Duffy, chairman of the Marine Labor Committee of the New York Harbor Railroads, said the carriers would comply with the restoration order. But he added that railroad attorneys were considering the possibility of an appeal.

Michael J. Quill, whose Transport Workers Union represents the majority of the oilers, hailed Judge Bryan's order as "a tremendous victory."

He declared in a statement issued after the ruling:

"This decision is an enormously significant step toward the establishment of genuine collective bargaining on every American railroad.

"It is a stern legal warning to all railroad management that they cannot use the courts as

Continued on Page 42, Column 3

Frondizi Struggles To Stave Off a Coup By Argentine Army

By JUAN de ONIS

Special to The New York Times.

BUENOS AIRES, June 19—President Arturo Frondizi clung to the military ministers of his Cabinet today for armed support against a conspiracy to overthrow his Government.

Dr. Frondizi, 51 years old, received a pledge from his three military ministers that they would stand firm. The army's top generals declared after a meeting tonight that they would stand behind the War Secretary, Gen. Hector Solanas Pacheco, and the Constitution.

Army, navy and air force units throughout the country were confined to barracks. Top commanders of the three services held separate meetings in the heavily guarded ministries.

Half a dozen retired officers were under arrest. Orders were out for the capture of a group of prominent military leaders of the revolutionary government that succeeded the dictatorship of Juan D. Perón.

The Presidential press office announced that Dr. Frondizi would preside at all events scheduled for tomorrow, Flag Day, including a military parade.

This was the most serious crisis of Señor Frondizi's turbu-

Continued on Page 6, Column 5

ERHARD CHARGES ADENAUER INSULT

He Says He Cannot Continue Work Unless Criticism by the Chancellor Ceases

By FLORA LEWIS

Special to The New York Times.

BONN, Germany, June 19—The dispute between Dr. Ludwig Erhard, Minister of the Economy, and Chancellor Konrad Adenauer broke out again today. Dr. Erhard declared: "The fate of the party is at stake."

Dr. Erhard said that not only he but also the Christian Democratic Union's Parliamentary delegation had been insulted in an interview that Dr. Adenauer gave to The New York Times. The interview was published Thursday.

Dr. Erhard charged that there was a "method" in Dr. Adenauer's attitude toward him and said: "My reputation is to be systematically lowered." He added that "I cannot continue my work" unless the insults ceased.

Dr. Adenauer had said in the interview that Dr. Erhard lacked the political experience, especially in foreign policy, that was essential for the Chancellorship.

The dispute between the two men erupted June 4 when Dr. Adenauer reversed his decision to run for the Presidency. Dr. Erhard had been generally favored to succeed him as Chancellor.

Although Dr. Adenauer's statements about Dr. Erhard in the interview were milder than

Continued on Page 3, Column 4

HOUSE APPROVES DEBT LIMIT RISE

295 Billion Ceiling Passed by Vote of 255 to 117

By JOHN D. MORRIS

Special to The New York Times.

WASHINGTON, June 19—The House of Representatives approved today a $7,000,000,000 increase in the national debt limit, as requested by President Eisenhower.

A bill fixing the new ceiling at $295,000,000,000 until June 30 of next year was passed on a roll-call vote of 255 to 117. The ballot produced an unexpectedly large protest vote, largely by members who grasped the opportunity to make a gesture against the Government's spending more money than it takes in.

The measure now goes to the Senate. Prompt action there is expected.

The higher ceiling would replace the present temporary limit of $288,000,000,000, which expires at the end of this month. Without new legislation in the meantime, the debt would then be subject to the present permanent ceiling of $283,000,000,000.

The bill would also raise the permanent limit to $285,000,000,000. President Eisenhower had asked for an increase to $288,000,000,000.

The device of a temporary rise, effective only until the end of a fiscal year on June 30, was first adopted in 1954 at the insistence of Senator Harry F. Byrd, Democrat of Virginia. The permanent limit then was $275,000,000,000, where it had been set in 1946.

Since 1954, Congress has ex-

Continued on Page 10, Column 1

Price Rises in May Put Index at Peak

By JOSEPH A. LOFTUS

Special to The New York Times.

WASHINGTON, June 19—The United States Consumers' Price Index set a record in May, the Government reported today.

The index, issued by the Department of Labor's Bureau of Labor Statistics, rose 0.1 per cent in May to 124. The index base of 100 represents the 1947-1949 price average.

All major groups of goods and services went up between mid-April and mid-May.

H. E. Riley, price chief of the bureau, said there was nothing startling or portentous about the rise. For many months the index has been hovering between 123.7 and 123.9. An April-May rise was foreseen for seasonal reasons. Further small rises are in prospect in the next few

Continued on Page 9, Column 1

Emperor's Race Course of Third Century A. D. Is Excavated in Rome

Brick-walled rooms found under grandstand of the arena

Radiophotos of The New York Times

Mosaic discovered in remains of a palace of St. Helena

By PAUL HOFMANN

Special to The New York Times.

ROME, June 19 — Impressive remains of an imperial private circus, or arena, built in the third century A. D. have come to light in excavations on the southeastern outskirts of Rome. Emperor Heliogabalus, the youthful monarch whose short reign from A. D. 218 to 222 marked an extravagant period in the decline of Rome, is believed to have watched horse and chariot races on the site. Government archaeologists, announcing the discovery today, said that what had been unearthed so far indicated that the arena was one of the largest that existed here in ancient times. Prof. Giulio Iacopi, Superintendent of Antiquities in Rome, expressed the opinion that the newly found race course was surpassed in size only by the Circus Maximus, which is said to have accommodated

Continued on Page 4, Column 4

Louisiana Is Ruled By Acting Governor

By The Associated Press.

BATON ROUGE, La., June 19 — Lieut. Gov. Lether Frazar took over as Acting Governor of Louisiana today.

Mr. Frazar, a 54-year-old former college president, moved cautiously to take over the reins after Gov. Earl K. Long had been dragged to a state mental hospital.

As Mr. Frazar acted for the second time in three weeks to guide Louisiana during a political crisis, he showed he was aware that his assumption of power apparently set a precedent for Louisiana.

"Never before has a man taken over as Governor when the Governor was in the state," said Mr. Frazar. "That's what baffles me."

But while he acted on the authority of an opinion by the state's attorney general, the

Continued on Page 11, Column 4

NEWS INDEX

"All the News That's Fit to Print"

The New York Times.

LATE CITY EDITION
U. S. Weather Bureau Report (Page 71) forecasts: Fair and pleasant today and tonight. Partly cloudy tomorrow.
Temp. range: 80—68; yesterday: 81.4—72.9.
Temp.-Hum. Index: low 70's; yesterday: 75.

NEWS SUMMARY AND INDEX, PAGE 71

SECTION ONE

VOL. CVIII..No. 37,073. NEW YORK, SUNDAY, JULY 26, 1959. 35c outside New York City, its suburban area and Long Island. Higher in air delivery cities. TWENTY-FIVE CENTS

BIG FACTORY CITIES LOSING TOP PLACE AS U. S. JOBS RISE

Small Towns Gain as Work Increase Totals a Million in the Last Decade

NEW YORK IS OFF 6.4%

City Club Proposes a $1.50 Hourly Wage Floor Here to Raise Low Level

By A. H. RASKIN

Most of the giant manufacturing cities in the East and Midwest have been losing jobs in the last decade, despite an over-all national gain in factory employment of more than a million.

New York has been hit by this downward trend, but other big centers such as Detroit, Providence and the Albany-Schenectady-Troy industrial area have been even more adversely affected.

These conclusions emerged yesterday from a study of Federal statistics made by Leonard C. Yaseen, an expert in plant location. The study was prompted by a report in The New York Times last Sunday that showed that this city ranked next to last among twenty major manufacturing communities in factory-wage averages.

Wage Level Low

That report, prepared by Nicholas M. Kisburg, research director of Local 210 of the International Brotherhood of Teamsters, disclosed that the New York factory average of $79.22 a week was $25.45 below that of Detroit, the top city in the list. A companion table showed that New York stood ninetieth in the full catalogue of 123 local areas for which factory earnings are reported monthly by the Federal Bureau of Labor Statistics.

The wage analysis brought an announcement by I. D. Robbins, president of the City Club of New York, that his organization was considering a public demand to establish a legal minimum wage of $1.50 an hour in the five boroughs. This would be 50 cents above the existing Federal wage floor.

Sweatshop Harm Seen

The club said that if an industry could not pay its workers at least $1.50 an hour its continued operation "probably does our city more harm than good." The civic group asserted that the city was "subsidizing its sweatshop industries" through its agencies for relief, public housing, health, hospitals and sanitation.

In his survey of the shift in manufacturing employment, Mr. Yaseen emphasized that comparisons of wage rates in big cities were relatively meaningless because the trend was toward building new factories in small towns rather than in metropolitan centers.

He said New York's real competition as a plant site was not with cities like Chicago, Philadelphia or Detroit, but with small communities, where labor costs, taxes, utility rates, union

Continued on Page 35, Column 3

Associated Press Radiophoto

HERTER IN WEST BERLIN: The Secretary of State, right foreground, waves to crowd at ceremony at which thoroughfare was renamed to honor John Foster Dulles.

U. S. DENIES GAINS IN GENEVA JUSTIFY SUMMIT MEETING

Opposes British View That Rift Has Been Bridged—Herter Visits Berlin

By SYDNEY GRUSON

Special to The New York Times.

GENEVA, July 25—The United States was authoritatively represented tonight as unalterably opposed to a summit conference on the basis of what now seem to be the possible results of the foreign ministers' conference here.

This represents a sharp difference from the British position as it is being explained by spokesmen for the British delegation.

But, strangely, this position is not being taken by Selwyn Lloyd, the British Foreign Minister, in the regular meetings he holds with his Western colleagues — Secretary of State Christian A. Herter, Maurice Couve de Murville of France and Dr. Heinrich von Brentano of West Germany. Mr. Herter, incidentally, went to West Berlin and back today.

Minor Differences Noted

The United States delegation concedes that there are differences of approach and of tone in the way Mr. Lloyd acts and talks to the Russians. But it is stated categorically that no difference in substance has been brought out in the Western ministers' strategy meetings.

The main difference in substance between what British spokesmen are saying and the way Mr. Lloyd is understood by his Western colleagues is this:

The British are prepared to go to the summit with a narrowing of differences on the items to be contained in an interim Berlin agreement. This agreement, from the British point of view, could contain a cut-off date for later negotiations on West Berlin without a firm guarantee of the Allies' position there if the negotiations fail.

Chances Believed Slim

In other words, the British, according to their spokesmen, believe that the differences between the West and the East over West Berlin have already been sufficiently narrowed to justify agreement now on a summit meeting.

The American view, which can be stated on high authority, is that this is not the case and that no cut-off date is acceptable unless accompanied by ironclad guarantees for the period beyond the negotiations.

As of tonight, the United States delegation believes there is a slim chance indeed of getting an interim Berlin settlement that would justify a summit meeting.

But the delegation, authoritative sources reported, is more

Continued on Page 4, Column 2

Associated Press Radiophoto

MAN OF THE HOUR: Vice President Richard M. Nixon acknowledges the applause of the crowd as he arrives at the Soviet exposition of agriculture and industry in Moscow.

NIXON WILL SPEND 4 DAYS IN POLAND; PLAN IS SURPRISE

Soviet Refusal to Permit Him to Depart Via East Siberia Alters His Itinerary

POLITICAL ASPECT SEEN

His Trip Will Coincide With Rockefeller's Attendance at Governors' Parley

By OSGOOD CARUTHERS

Special to The New York Times.

MOSCOW, July 25 — Vice President Richard M. Nixon, in a surprise announcement today, said that he and his wife and their party would pay a four-day visit to Poland after leaving the Soviet Union.

The official reason given was that the Soviet Government had rejected the Vice President's request to be permitted to travel home from here via eastern Siberia and across to Alaska.

The move has important foreign and domestic political implications. Furthermore, the visit is of special interest at this time in view of the fury that has been aroused in the Soviet bloc over the proclamation of Captive Nations Week in the United States.

The proposed visit, beginning Aug. 2, was said to have been under discussion between Washington and Warsaw for some time. A spokesman said final arrangements had been under way for approximately a week.

Invitation From Zawadski

The spokesman said the Vice President's party was going to Poland at the invitation of President Aleksander Zawadski.

"The Vice President's visit will provide the occasion for an exchange of views between the American statesman and leading political personalities of the Polish People's Republic," the official announcement said. "It was possible to schedule the visit because the Soviet Union could not schedule the Vice President's departure through eastern Siberia."

This was the Administration's diplomatic way of saying that more than a month ago the Soviet Union had flatly turned down Mr. Nixon's request to be permitted to visit several eastern Siberian cities and then to go on to Vladivostok, long closed to Western visitors, and across the Kamchatka Peninsula and the forty-mile-wide Bering Strait to Alaska.

Siberian Cities Dropped

Because of the refusal to allow this northeastern passage to Alaska, the youngest state in the Union, the Vice President dropped several other Siberian cities from his itinerary. This gave him the extra time to make the visit to Poland, it was explained.

Observers familiar with the American political scene feel that more than mere coincidence is involved in the choice of dates for Mr. Nixon's visit to Poland. The dates coincide with the scheduled visit of Governor Rockefeller of New York to

Continued on Page 2, Column 7

TEAMSTERS PLAN '60 POLITICAL UNIT

Hoffa Pushes Drive to Join in Congress Campaigns—Set to Assess Members

Special to The New York Times.

WASHINGTON, July 25—James R. Hoffa, preparing for what he has called "the day of reckoning at the polls," is polishing up a plan for a department of political action in his International Brotherhood of Teamsters.

The teamster president is expected to present the proposal to the union's general executive board, which he controls, at its September meeting.

A Hoffa spokesman at teamster headquarters here said the plan was to have a national organization functioning in time for the 1960 elections. The aim would be to shape the membership of Congress more to the liking of Hoffa and the union.

The teamsters' new political department, like the Committee on Political Education of the American Federation of Labor and Congress of Industrial Organizations, would work for the election or defeat of Senate and House candidates.

Incumbents seeking re-election would be supported or opposed on the basis of "right" or "wrong" voting records as determined by Hoffa and his associates.

The activities would be financed by "voluntary" check-offs, possibly of 50 cents a month, of the dues from the union's reported membership of 1,600,000, the spokesman said.

Thus members would be asked to authorize the use of a

Continued on Page 43, Column 4

Fiancee Now Says Wedding Tensions Caused Her Flight

Special to The New York Times.

NEWARK July 25—Jacqueline Gay Hart flew home with her father and fiance tonight after admitting that she had run away to Chicago because of tension over her forthcoming marriage. She said she had "sort of exploded."

As she stepped from the plane here shortly before 9 o'clock, Miss Hart was still visibly distraught over the experience, which began Tuesday night when she saw her fiancé, Stanley Noyes Gaines, off on a flight to Pittsburgh.

A thousand persons were at Newark Airport tonight as Miss Hart stepped out of the plane after being questioned for fifteen minutes by Police Director Joseph F. Weldon of Newark.

The blonde, 21-year-old fiancée had admitted to agents of the Federal Bureau of Investigation in Chicago earlier today that her original story of having been abducted was false. Her later account, which both the F. B. I. and Mr. Weldon said they believed, was this:

After seeing Mr. Gaines off Tuesday night, she boarded a bus at the airport for New York and spent the night at the New Yorker Hotel, where she

Continued on Page 41, Column 3

RUSSIANS SWARM THROUGH U.S. FAIR

Throngs Jam Every Exhibit and Strive for Information as Public Gets First Look

By MAX FRANKEL

Special to The New York Times.

MOSCOW, July 25—Tens of thousands of Russians got their first look at the American National Exhibition here today.

They swarmed through the show in Sokolniki Park, having entered with jealously guarded and often mysteriously obtained tickets.

Hundreds found other ways to enter the well-guarded site. Most of them ignored pleas to leave and make room for the oncoming waves.

Judging from the furious note-taking throughout the park, the pressure of crowds against every exhibit and the competitive collections of intended—and some unintended—souvenirs, the visitors learned something about the United States.

And they taught exhibitors a thing or two about this most unusual audience for a United States propaganda effort. The exhibition is the first American effort of its kind here since the Communists won power in 1917.

"Why aren't you showing us your industry, your technology?" asked an elderly woman physician and dozens of other visitors.

"You want to see tractors, then go and see tractors, but leave me alone!" a stout woman shouted to her husband as she headed for the displays of shoes

Continued on Page 7, Column 1

Muscovites Heckle Nixon; He Preaches Free Speech

By HARRISON E. SALISBURY

Special to The New York Times.

MOSCOW, July 25—Vice President Richard M. Nixon praised the virtues of free speech to several hecklers in Moscow today and then went off to spend the night as Premier Nikita S. Khrushchev's guest in the country.

It was another day full of occurrences unusual in the Soviet Union. Mr. Nixon spent most of his time moving through large, friendly crowds of Soviet citizens. He took on several hecklers for impromptu discussions of free speech and the free exchange of ideas.

Tonight Mr. Nixon and Mr. Khrushchev exchanged warm remarks at a private dinner at Spaso House, residence of the United States Ambassador, Llewellyn E. Thompson Jr.

Dr. Eisenhower Among Guests

Dinner ended at 9:30 and half an hour later Mr. Nixon, his wife, Mr. Thompson and Dr. Milton S. Eisenhower, the President's brother, departed for the Khrushchev country house about twenty miles from Moscow.

Never before has Mr. Khrushchev had a leading Western statesman as an overnight guest.

Tomorrow, in a quiet rural setting, the Premier and the Vice President will sit down for hard and serious discussions on world problems.

At tonight's encounter at Spaso House, each man offered the warmest of toasts to the other and his country. Mr. Nixon had especially kind words for the warmth with which the Soviet people had received him and for their dedication to the

Continued on Page 3, Column 1

A POLITICAL GAIN FOR NIXON IS SEEN

Capital Views Soviet Events as Aiding His '60 Hopes—Some Fear Loss by U. S.

By JACK RAYMOND

Special to The New York Times.

WASHINGTON, July 25—There was agreement in Washington today that Vice President Richard M. Nixon had thus far in his visit to the Soviet Union immeasurably advanced his Presidential prospects for next year.

There were some persons who questioned, however, whether the Vice President had advanced the United States' foreign policy, particularly with respect to the image of America abroad.

One side, including some State Department officials, maintains that it pays for the United States to be firm and speak firmly. This side saw merit in the fact that one of the United States' leaders had held the outspoken Soviet Premier, Nikita S. Khrushchev, to at least a draw in their verbal duels.

The other side, including Senator Hubert H. Humphrey, Democrat of Minnesota, himself a Presidential aspirant, thought otherwise. This side held that verbal duels lead nowhere if they are clearly intended for propaganda effects.

The suggestion was made that peoples committed to neither the Communist nor the Western democratic cause might tend to equate the merits of these causes with the merits of the debaters in Moscow.

Officials and experts here be-

Continued on Page 4, Column 2

Debate Goes on TV Over Soviet Protest

By RICHARD F. SHEPARD

The unusual exchange that took place Friday in Moscow between Vice President Richard M. Nixon and Premier Nikita S. Khrushchev was shown dramatically last night over network television.

The nation-wide telecasts of the debate were offered despite a Soviet insistence, which had Mr. Nixon's agreement, that they be delayed until there could be simultaneous showings in the Soviet Union and the United States.

The sixteen-minute tape recording of the lively discussion was shown at 11 P. M. by the American Broadcasting Company, the Columbia Broadcasting System and the National Broadcasting Company after a day of frantic conferences and a telephone call to Moscow. The tape had originally been scheduled for afternoon showings.

The delay was occasioned by a request from the United States

Continued on Page 2, Column 4

Experts Hail Sculpture Discovery in Greece

Bust found in Piraeus

Two Bronze Statues and Marble Work Are Highly Rated

By A. C. SEDGWICK

Special to The New York Times.

ATHENS, July 20—Laborers pulling up pavement to repair sewers in a busy section of the Athens seaport, Piraeus, have discovered three outstanding ancient works of sculpture.

Archaeologists describe the two life-size bronze statues and a marble column surmounted by a man's head as some of the most beautiful art treasures ever brought to light.

Prof. Ioannis Papadimitriou, the Greek Director of Antiquities, said one of the statues, that of a young man, ranked with the Charioteer of Delphi, one of the world's greatest statues. The three works are of different periods and it is surmised that they belonged to a collector.

The statues were discovered July 18 by Nikos Ordonaris, who was operating a pneumatic drill. Officials of the Ministry of Education were notified and archaeologists rushed to the scene.

The police have been assigned to keep crowds from the excavations where it is hoped additional works of art might be found. The statues are now in the Piraeus Archaeological Museum, where they will be cleaned and treated.

If the statues are kept in the Piraeus museum, as the Piraeus people are demanding, the hitherto inconspicuous repository of

Continued on Page 22, Column 1

Statue of a young man may be an Apollo

Bronze figure, slightly larger than life

Castro Foe Caught As Plane Is Downed

By TAD SZULC

Special to The New York Times.

HAVANA, July 25—A man identified as a top leader of a Cuban counter-revolutionary organization operating from the United States was captured at dawn today in his flaming aircraft.

The plane had been shot down by the police outside Havana.

The four-seat Cessna 120 plane was riddled with bullets and set afire when one shot hit the gasoline tank as it prepared to land at 5 A. M. on the Via Blanca, near Guanabo Beach about thirty miles from Havana.

The plane was presumed to have flown from Florida.

One of the two occupants escaped from the wreckage. The other, badly burned and shot several times through the body, was identified by the National Revolutionary Police as Rafael del Pino.

Señor del Pino was described

Continued on Page 27, Column 1

Sports News

BASEBALL

The Yankees defeated the Tigers, 9—8, yesterday at Detroit on Yogi Berra's two-run homer in the ninth inning. Harry Simpson's pinch single in the seventeenth enabled the White Sox to gain a 3-2 triumph over the Baltimore Orioles at Chicago. The victory maintained the White Sox' American League lead of a half-game. The Indians routed the Senators, 8—1, at Cleveland.

HORSE RACING

Sword Dancer, the 3-5 favorite, took the $113,750 Monmouth Handicap by two lengths. Endine scored in the $155,000 Delaware Handicap for the second straight year. Waltz set a track record of 1:54 4-5 for the mile and three-sixteenth in winning the $82,100 Dwyer Stakes at Jamaica. Dunce won the $140,425 Arlington Classic.

TENNIS

Alex Olmedo was upset by Ian Vermaak of South Africa in the semi-final round of the Pennsylvania championships. The scores were 6—2, 6—4, 6—2. Australia clinched its American Zone semi-final Davis Cup series with Canada.

Details in Section 5.

Today's Sections

Index to Subjects

"All the News That's Fit to Print"

The New York Times.

LATE CITY EDITION

U. S. Weather Bureau Report (Page 40) forecasts: Mostly fair, less humid today; fair, cool tonight. Mostly fair tomorrow. Temp. range: 82—70; yesterday: 84.9—75.8.

VOL. CVIII . No. 37,113.

NEW YORK, FRIDAY, SEPTEMBER 4, 1959.

10 cents beyond 50-mile zone from New York City except on Long Island. Higher in air delivery cities

FIVE CENTS

DE GAULLE PLANS TO OFFER ALGERIA ELECTED REGIME

Right of Self-Determination Implied, but Program Is Vague on Ties With Paris

BACKING OF U. S. SOUGHT

Rebel Accord Not Required—Policy Called Blow to French Integrationists

By DANA ADAMS SCHMIDT
Special to The New York Times.

WASHINGTON, Sept. 3 — General Charles de Gaulle's plan for ending the Algerian war calls for creating an Algerian-elected assembly and an Algerian executive.

The French President completed the plan on his trip to Algeria last week and was prepared to discuss it with President Eisenhower yesterday and today.

United States officials who received a report on the plan from Paris assumed that President de Gaulle had in fact outlined it to President Eisenhower. But this part of the talks remained confidential.

The plan is not to be made public officially until the United Nations General Assembly opens Sept. 15. Meanwhile, it is President de Gaulle's aim to gain President Eisenhower's understanding and support.

Parley on Status Envisaged

The French hope is that when the plan is made public it will be backed by France's major allies, even if a majority of the Assembly, based on the African-Asian bloc, rejects it.

General de Gaulle, according to the report received here, would be willing to negotiate the future of Algeria with an executive drawn from the elected legislature. This was the meaning of his recent emphasis on "universal suffrage" as a key to the Algerian problem.

The relationship of the Algerian assembly and executive to institutions in France was not fully worked out in the report of the de Gaulle plan. But it implied that the Algerian people were entitled to self-determination, and that ultimately this could go as far as independence.

Paris Aide Now Rules

At present the main powers of government in Algeria are in the hands of Paul Delouvier, Delegate General, who is appointed by Paris.

In elections held under close supervision of the army last November, Algeria elected seventy-one Deputies, including forty-eight Moslems, and thirty-two Senators, including twenty-two Moslems, to the French Parliament.

General de Gaulle was described as exasperated by what he recognized as a hopeless war, sapping the strength of France and prejudicing her role as a great power. He was said to view his plan as the way out of an impasse.

In contrast to some previous French plans, this one does not insist on a cease-fire as prerequisite to elections. Nor does it call for talks with leaders of the National Liberation Front, which the French believe to be suffering from serious internal dissension between moderates and extremists.

Last October General de

Continued on Page 2, Column 5

Argentina Fights Defiance in Army

By The Associated Press.

BUENOS AIRES, Argentina, Friday Sept. 4—President Arturo Frondizi early today announced that troops were marching on a military school in the heart of Buenos Aires, where the ousted commander in chief of the army announced that he was resuming his command.

Gen. Carlos Toranzo Montero, who was dismissed by Secretary of War Elbio C. Anaya, set up his headquarters in the Army Mechanical School adjoining an arsenal.

He demanded that Secretary Anaya resign.

Economics Minister Alvaro Alsogaray told newsmen at [illegible] "the situation is con[illegible]."

In a [illegible] two hours earlier Señor [illegible] appealed to

Continued on Page 6, Column 2

Finder Says Fossil Links Ape and Man

The New York Times — Sept. 4, 1959

Site of discovery (cross)

Special to The New York Times.

NAIROBI, Kenya, Sept. 3—Dr. Louis S. B. Leakey, a leading British anthropologist, reported today that a recently discovered skull was the link between man and the South African ape man.

He said he and his wife made the discovery July 17 in the Olduvai Gorge, Tanganyika, after an exploration that began there twenty-

Continued on Page 4, Column 2

EISENHOWER GETS ACCORD IN FRANCE

He and de Gaulle Announce 'Complete Agreement' on East-West Relations

Communiqués and remarks by Eisenhower, Page 2.

By ROBERT C. DOTY
Special to The New York Times.

PARIS, Sept. 3—President Eisenhower and President Charles de Gaulle expressed tonight their "complete agreement" on questions of East-West relations and a full and friendly exploration of French-United States problems.

A joint communiqué issued at 11 P. M. at the end of the second day of President Eisenhower's visit to France proclaimed the two leaders' accord on the question of Berlin and on the necessity for making an eventual summit conference with the Soviet Union conditional on the emergence of "some possibility of definite accomplishment."

Two other points of agreement were listed as the desirability of resuming negotiations for "general and controlled disarmament" and on the problem of assistance to underdeveloped areas.

The communiqué and the comments of spokesmen for both Presidents indicated also that they had reached a better understanding of each other's views, without formal agreement, on the problems arising from France's struggle with the Moslem rebellion in Algeria, on General de Gaulle's aspirations for an enhanced role in global strategic planning and on "means of assuring more effective functioning" of the North Atlantic Treaty alliance.

The communiqué was issued

Continued on Page 2, Column 1

1C 'GAS' TAX RISE PASSED BY HOUSE IN A 243-162 VOTE

Roads Bill Goes to Senate—Increase in Interest on Savings Bonds Pushed

By JOHN D. MORRIS
Special to The New York Times.

WASHINGTON, Sept. 3 — The House of Representatives approved a 1-cent increase in the Federal gasoline tax today by a vote of 243 to 162.

The bill to maintain the interstate highway program on a pay-as-you-build basis was passed as the House began to speed action on all legislation standing in the way of adjournment of Congress.

Meanwhile, a bill to permit higher interest rates on savings bonds was rushed to the floor for probable passage tomorrow and a substitute for a $1,216,000,000 civil-works bill vetoed by President Eisenhower was prepared for action tomorrow by the House Appropriations Committee.

Rights Bill May Die

In another development, Congressional sources indicated that chances for Senate passage of a civil rights bill in this session were dead. The Senate is expected to confine itself to extending the life of the Civil Rights Commission.

Passage of the highway bill was a victory for President Eisenhower, although the measure fell somewhat short of his recommendations.

Democratic leaders, who had steadfastly resisted any gasoline-tax rise for most of the session, reluctantly gave their support to the compromise bill and worked for its passage.

Even so, the measure won only a slim majority of the Democrats voting. It was moved along to the Senate only by the help of heavy Republican support.

The Democratic division was 138 for the bill and 127 against it. Republicans divided 105 for the bill and 35 against it.

Tax Now 3 Cents

President Eisenhower's proposal was for a 1½-cent rise in the gasoline tax, now 3 cents a gallon, effective for five years.

The compromise, acceptable to the Administration as a stopgap, was devised by Representative John W. Byrnes of Wisconsin, chairman of the House Republican Policy Committee. It is designed to permit continued construction of the 41,000-mile interstate system of limited-access roads at a rate close to present schedules for at least two years.

The 1-cent tax increase, which also applies to Diesel and other fuels for highway travel, would go into effect on enactment of the bill and expire June 30, 1961. It would produce about $1,000,000,000 for the depleted Highway Trust Fund, created in 1956 to finance the Federal share of road-building programs.

Over the succeeding three

Continued on Page 8, Column 6

Action Against Youth Crime Is Topic of City and State Meetings

At session called by Mayor Wagner at City Hall were, from upper left: Dr. Alfred J. Marrow, head of Commission on Intergroup Relations; Police Commissioner Stephen P. Kennedy; City Council President Abe Stark; the Mayor; Deputy Mayor Paul T. O'Keefe and Abraham D. Beame, Budget Director. Mayor disavowed "coddling."

The New York Times

Governor Rockefeller meeting with other state officials. From left are Attorney General Louis J. Lefkowitz; Assembly Speaker Joseph F. Carlino, Republican of Long Beach; the Senate Majority Leader, Walter J. Mahoney, Republican of Buffalo, and the Governor, in whose office at 22 West Fifty-fifth Street the meeting was conducted.

Senate Approves Labor Reform Bill; House Votes Today

Text of Title VII of labor bill is printed on Page 42.

By JOSEPH A. LOFTUS
Special to The New York Times.

WASHINGTON, Sept. 3—The Senate approved tonight the final draft of what is to be the Labor Reform Act of 1959.

The vote was 95 to 2.

The two Senators opposed were Wayne L. Morse, Democrat of Oregon, and William Langer, Republican of North Dakota.

The House of Representatives reorganized its schedule to permit a vote on final passage tomorrow.

There was no doubt that the House would approve and that President Eisenhower would sign the first general labor control bill since 1947.

Except for a speech of more than four and one-half hours against the measure by Senator Morse, the Senate heard mostly praise of the bill before it voted.

Approval of the reform measure means that in a year or less

Continued on Page 42, Column 1

8 GOVERNORS BID U.S. ACT ON STEEL

Democrats Urge President to Call Parley on Strike—Impact on States Cited

By A. H. RASKIN

Eight Democratic Governors notified President Eisenhower last night that the steel strike was inflicting "critical" damage on their states. In a joint telegram, they asked for an opportunity to meet with the President "at the earliest possible moment."

Their plea for direct White House action to help end the costly tie-up was made public by Gov. David L. Lawrence of Pennsylvania. His state alone has 217,000 workers idle as a result of the fifty-two-day-old shutdown.

The Governors' pressure to budge the President from his hands-off attitude came as James P. Mitchell, Secretary of Labor, accused steel labor and management of failure to exhibit "goodwill and compromise" in their efforts to arrive at a settlement.

Mr. Mitchell declared in a recorded radio interview that both sides had been "derelict in their responsibility to the public, to the [union] members and to the community at large for their failure to negotiate continuously."

His remarks were broadcast over the Columbia Broadcasting System network a few minutes after bargaining teams representing the steel com-

Continued on Page 22, Column 2

Youth Crime Curb, Wider Mental Aid Is Urged in Jersey

Text of summary of report is printed on Page 8.

By GEORGE CABLE WRIGHT
Special to The New York Times.

TRENTON, Sept. 3—An extensive program to improve and expand New Jersey's mental health, correctional and welfare services and to reduce juvenile delinquency was recommended in a report to Gov. Robert B. Meyner today.

The recommendations were made by a commission of prominent citizens, who have just completed a nineteen-month survey of the state's welfare activities—the first since 1918.

The expanded program would be achieved through a reorganization of the Department of Institutions and Agencies.

In its report the commission called on the state to accept responsibility for the promotion and development of intensive mental health services at all governmental levels. It suggested the development of a web of services including clinics in all counties and proposed that the state increase greatly its subsidy of county and local mental health services.

The report warned of extreme shortages of trained personnel in mental health, correction and welfare institutions and agencies throughout the state. That condition, it said, was particularly acute among the top echelon of the State Mental Health Division.

The commission urged the state to erect an institution for

Continued on Page 8, Column 2

2 GANG SUSPECTS ARE DENIED BAIL

Youths Held in Playground Slayings—Court Calls for Firmer Action on Crime

By MILTON BRACKER

Two boys suspected of wielding the weapons in two playground slayings here early Sunday were held without bail on homicide charges yesterday.

The magistrate sitting in the case demanded "more drastic action" in the handling of juvenile delinquency.

During the day, as renewed complaints against "coddling" of young offenders were heard in various parts of the city, the police seized another youth as the thirteenth member of the playground invaders.

The police also made five arrests in the non-fatal stabbing of a teen-ager in Brooklyn Wednesday. Two other youths held as material witnesses in the West Forty-sixth Street playground case were placed under $50,000 bail each.

Malbin Asks Action

In the same case Salvador Agron, and Antonio Hernandez appeared before Magistrate David L. Malbin in Adolescent Court on homicide charges in the deaths of Anthony Krzesinski and Robert Young, both 16. Four other suspects were arraigned earlier this week on homicide charges and held without bail.

Agron, 16 years old, has admitted, according to the police, that he wore a strange, Dracula-like cape to the playground and that he "cut" someone. Hernandez, 17, supposedly had wielded a pointed umbrella.

Magistrate Malbin declared it was getting "very monotonous when you see these young punks coming before us." It is "high time," he said, for more drastic action.

"The rights of the people are being neglected," the magistrate added. "It's high time we all got together and did something quickly."

Agron—his first name has been incorrectly recorded by the police as the Italian Salvatore instead of the Spanish Salvador

Continued on Page 7, Column 2

Associated Press Radiophoto

VISITS FORMER COMMAND: President Eisenhower speaking yesterday at Supreme Headquarters Allied Powers in Europe, outside Paris. At right is Gen. Lauris Norstad, Supreme Allied Commander in Europe. General Eisenhower held post after World War II.

Indians Report Chinese Inroads; Laos Town Awaits Red Attack

Incursions Unconfirmed

By ROBERT TRUMBULL
Special to The New York Times.

NEW DELHI, India, Sept. 3—Widespread Chinese Communist troop incursions are continuing along India's northern frontiers and into the states of Bhutan and Sikkim, according to unconfirmed reports today.

Sources in Kalimpong, Indian trade center near the Sikkim border, said Indian troops were being posted on the approaches to two Himalayan passes, Nathu La and Jelap La. These strategic passes furnish the easiest routes through the Himalayas from Tibet to Sikkim and India.

There were rumors in Calcutta that many Sikkimese were fleeing south in fear of a Chinese advance.

The Press Trust of India, a leading news agency, quoted

Continued on Page 5, Column 5

Samneua Is Threatened

By GREG MacGREGOR
Special to The New York Times.

SAMNEUA, Laos, Sept. 3—Communist troops threatening this town have increased in strength to approximately 4,500 in the last few days, the commander of the royal forces in northern Laos said today.

Earlier this week the enemy strength was estimated to be about 3,000.

North Vietnamese troops and supplies have been crossing the river Song Ma almost continually since the heavy enemy offensive began Sunday morning, said the commander, Brig. Gen. Amkha Soukhavong.

The Red forces have seized all canoes in the river valley and have been using them with small outboard motors for convoys, he added. The husky 39-

Continued on Page 5, Column 2

NEWS INDEX

News Summary and Index, Page 23

ATTACK ON GANGS IS ORDERED HERE BY CITY AND STATE

Rockefeller and Mayor Hold Separate Talks on Rise in Juvenile Violence

SPECIAL CAMPS FAVORED

$2,500,000 for More Police Is Sought Now—Wagner Says 'Coddling' Is Out

By PETER KIHSS

Mayor Wagner and Governor Rockefeller held separate planning conferences with top city and state officials yesterday on ways to counter the rise in juvenile delinquency.

The Mayor's conference resulted in orders to divert $2,500,000 from other municipal programs to bring the police force immediately up to its full quota of 24,508. As of yesterday's roster, this would add 1,089 men. Police Commissioner Stephen P. Kennedy said he hoped to have the new men on the street by Jan. 1.

Both the Mayor and Governor said they favored a long-discussed—and long-stalled—program of special youth camps to counter juvenile crime. The state now has two work camps for young offenders at North Pharsalia and Watkins Glen.

Extra Police Patrols

Mayor Wagner announced the following moves:

¶Extra police patrols as soon as possible "to preserve law and order in the city and to rid the streets of the hoodlums."

¶A call on Governor Rockefeller to provide state camps for youths who are involved in minor difficulties and more state correctional institutions for "tougher youngsters."

¶Immediate increases in lighting in city parks "so the police and any others can be aware of who is in the park."

¶Reviews by the three criminal courts under the Mayor's jurisdiction of criticisms that they may have been too lenient.

¶"No coddling" for hoodlums.

¶Conferences next week with district attorneys and talks in the near future with public and private groups.

¶An appeal to parents—not just governmental agencies—to take responsibility for their children.

4 Murders in a Week

The city and state conferences took place against a background of juvenile crime in which there were four murders here by youths within a week.

Both the Mayor and the Governor opposed suggestions for a curfew on teen-agers here. The Governor said it would be "virtually impossible to enforce, and a law on the books that is not enforced is sometimes worse than no law."

Commissioner Kennedy told reporters that he hoped to get the new policemen on the streets by Jan. 1, but he emphasized that he wanted them fully trained.

There are now 3,539 candidates for appointments to the police force who have passed physical and written tests, according to Deputy Chief Inspector Robert R. J. Gallati, commanding the Police Academy.

However, Commissioner Kennedy and Chief of Detectives James B. Leggett said that only

Continued on Page 7, Column 1

City Code of Ethics Signed by Wagner

By CHARLES G. BENNETT

The city's new Code of Ethics for its 225,000 employes became law yesterday with Mayor Wagner's signature. The code is designed to hold all city officials and employes to rigid standards of conduct.

Other measures signed yesterday by the Mayor will:

¶Bring into being about next Jan. 1, under the jurisdiction of the Traffic Department, a civilian force to enforce regulations at parking meters. One hundred women are expected to make up the force.

¶Permit the New York Telephone Company to install about 2,000 public telephones in streets, near parks and in other public places. These new facilities, depending on the number of multiple booths installed, are expected to yield $800,000 to $1,600,000 a year to the city.

Three bills are involved in

Continued on Page 10, Column [illegible]

"All the News That's Fit to Print"

NEWS SUMMARY AND INDEX, PAGE 95

The New York Times.

LATE CITY EDITION

U. S. Weather Bureau Report (Page 95) forecasts: Mostly cloudy today and tonight. Considerable cloudiness tomorrow. Temp. range: 39—22; yesterday: 35.9—22.1.

SECTION ONE

VOL. CIX. No. 37,241.

NEW YORK, SUNDAY, JANUARY 10, 1960.

35c outside New York City, its suburban area and Long Island. Higher in air delivery cities.

TWENTY-FIVE CENTS

SOVIET BLOC JOINS WEST IN ACCORD ON SPACE STUDIES

Russians, Czechs and Poles Accept COSPAR Plan to Aid in Basic Research

YEAR'S DISPUTE IS ENDED

New Bureau Set Up in World Science Body to Equalize Members' Voting Power

By JOHN HILLABY

Special to The New York Times.

NICE, France, Jan. 9—Scientists from Iron Curtain countries—the Soviet Union, Poland and Czechoslovakia — have agreed to work with Western nations on common problems of fundamental research in space.

This news was announced tonight by Prof. H. C. Van Der Houlst of the Netherlands. He is the new president of the Committee on Space Research, an organization known as COSPAR, now in session here.

The committee was set up in October, 1958, to continue the cooperation in space ventures that marked the International Geophysical Year. Its parent body, the International Council of Scientific Unions, had sponsored the I.G.Y. as the supreme non-governmental body in the scientific world.

Inner Cabinet Formed

After a year of seemingly endless arguments about representation, the executive of COSPAR has achieved a working agreement. It did this by creating an inner cabinet or bureau in which the neutrality of the president, Professor Van Der Houlst, will be matched, it is hoped, by the voting parity of six other bureau members.

The six members are:

Academician Anotoli A. Blagonravov of the Academy of Sciences of the Soviet Union, a vice president of COSPAR; Dr. R. W. Porter, representing the United States National Academy of Scientists, a vice president of COSPAR; Dr. Emil Bucara, representing the Czechoslovak Academy of Sciences; Prof. H. S. W. Massey, representing the British Royal Society; Prof. Maurice Roy of France, representing the International Union of Theoretical and Applied Mechanics; Dr. W. Zonn, representing the Polish Academy of Sciences.

American Sums Up

Dr. Porter of the United States summed up the situation by repeating a remark he made when the new charter of the Committee on Space Research was hopefully drafted a few weeks ago. He said:

"Technicalities and restrictions seem hardly appropriate or necessary in an organization of working scientists concerned only with the encouragement of fundamental research."

In the future, the committee will be composed of representatives designated by international scientific unions, of

Continued on Page 3, Column 5

Nasser Starts Construction Of Aswan Dam on the Nile

He Counts on Big Project to Win a Better Life for the Egyptians

By JAY WALZ

Special to The New York Times.

ASWAN, United Arab Republic, Jan. 9—President Gamal Abdel Nasser set off a ten-ton dynamite explosion today to start construction of the long-planned Aswan High Dam on the Nile.

Mousa Arafa, Minister of Public Works, presided at the ceremonies marking the start of the power and conservation project.

The High Dam, which became an international issue soon after its conception, is being started with a $93,000,000 loan from the Soviet Union for building the first stage of the project.

Ignati T. Novikov, Soviet Minister of Electric Power Station Construction, shared honors in the formalities today. However, President Nasser's honor guest was King Mohamed V of Morocco, in Egypt for a ten-day state visit. Coming here from

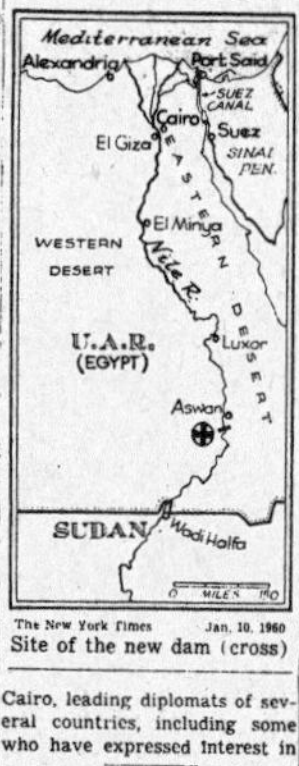

The New York Times Jan. 10, 1960

Site of the new dam (cross)

Cairo, leading diplomats of several countries, including some who have expressed interest in

Continued on Page 8, Column 2

U.S. Seeks Talk With Cuba On Land-Seizure Payments

By E. W. KENWORTHY

Special to The New York Times.

WASHINGTON, Jan. 9—Ambassador Philip W. Bonsal, who is returning to his post in Havana tomorrow, will immediately try to take up with the Cuban Government problems arising out of Cuba's Agrarian Reform Law.

The Government of Premier Fidel Castro has made no concession to the United States' demand that, under international law, United States citizens whose land has been expropriated should receive "prompt, adequate and effective" payment.

The two governments have exchanged several notes on the subject since the law was promulgated last spring. Ambassador Bonsal also sought without success to initiate discussions on the issue several times before he returned home for the Christmas holidays.

Cubans Avoid Meetings

According to officials here, the Cuban Government is apparently willing to let the matter drift. On several occasions Mr. Bonsal has been unable to get appointments with major officials.

The issue between the two governments does not involve Cuba's right to expropriate land held by United States citizens. In a note last June 15, the Cuban Government conceded that the United States Government had always been "consistent and unequivocal" in its support of rural land reform in countries where it was long overdue.

What does concern the United States Government, as it first stated in a note last June

Continued on Page 33, Column 1

BRITISH AID ASKED IN FREEING AFRICA

Nkrumah Asks Macmillan to Help Campaign by Ghana —Says 'Time Is Short'

By HOMER BIGART

Special to The New York Times.

ACCRA, Ghana, Jan. 9 — Prime Minister Kwame Nkrumah urged Britain tonight to assist Ghana in the "liberation" of the remaining colonial territories in Africa.

Speaking at a state dinner in honor of Prime Minister Macmillan, he warned: "The time is short."

He also made a direct request for financial aid, especially in connection with the Volta River power project, an essential part of Ghana's second five-year development plan. Mr. Nkrumah said:

"We will leave no stone unturned to find the funds we need."

This was considered a hint that if help was not forthcoming from Britain, Ghana might turn to the Soviet Union.

Cites Interest in Project

Mr. Macmillan said Britain would follow the progress of the Volta River project "with sympathetic interest."

He told Mr. Nkrumah that there was a strong demand for capital from all over the world and that "the supply is nothing like adequate to the demand."

He said capital would flow to projects that were economically sound and "to those countries which set out to attract investments by creating confidence in their political efficiency and their economic stability."

He said the British "buy a lot of your cocoa and bananas and we could buy a lot of Volta aluminium."

Discussing Ghana's "preoccupation" with the liberation of

Continued on Page 13, Column 1

DEMOCRATS TO ASK $1.25 MINIMUM PAY IN STATE INDUSTRY

Bill to Be Part of Program to Improve Conditions of Labor and Lift Benefits

By STANLEY LEVEY

The State Democratic Committee said yesterday that one of the key points in its 1960 legislative program would be the introduction of a measure to set a state minimum wage of $1.25 an hour.

In his annual message to the Legislature Governor Rockefeller proposed a state minimum wage of $1 an hour.

The Democratic objective is part of a plan for increased labor benefits and improved working conditions. It was announced by Michael H. Prendergast, Democratic State Chairman, and the party's legislative leaders, State Senator Joseph Zaretzki and Assemblyman Anthony J. Travia.

In addition, the three Democrats said they would "strongly urge that Congress be memorialized to enact comparable Federal legislation for a national minimum wage beginning at $1.25 an hour and gradually rising to $1.50 an hour."

Mayor on Record

Mayor Wagner already has announced plans to mobilize the city's political influence in support of a national and state minimum of $1.25. The City Council will hold hearings on a statutory wage floor.

At present there is a Federal minimum wage of $1, which applies to most branches of interstate commerce. There is no such state-wide minimum for workers in intra-state industries. Rather, the Industrial Commissioner sets base rates on an industry-by-industry basis. They are now at or below $1.

The three Democratic leaders also said that "sweeping and far-reaching" amendments were needed in the state's Unemployment Insurance, Workmen's Compensation and Disability Benefits laws "to bring them into line with present conditions."

Changes in Compensation

They proposed changes in the Workmen's Compensation law including an automatic adjustment plan that would set maximum benefits at two-thirds of the average weekly earnings of an injured workmen up to a maximum of $60. They called for the elimination of the present one-week waiting period.

Governor Rockefeller recommended an increase from $45 to $50 in maximum weekly unemployment insurance, sickness, disability and workmen's compensation benefits.

The Democratic program also advocated changes in the Unemployment Insurance law "to effectively off-set the Eisen-

Continued on Page 45, Column 2

STEEL PACT CUTS FACTORS TENDING TO ADD INFLATION

Percentage Rise Is Smallest Since War—Living Cost Escalator Controlled

By JOSEPH A. LOFTUS

Special to The New York Times.

WASHINGTON, Jan. 9 — In more than one way, the new steel labor agreement contains less built-in inflation than its predecessors.

The total package's percentage increase is smaller than any in steel since the war. And the steam has been taken out of the cost-of-living escalator, which many view as a generator of inflation.

The steel workers may get as much as 6 cents in cost-of-living adjustments while the thirty-month contract is in force, compared with 17 cents in the old three-year contract.

On the other hand they may get nothing, no matter how high the cost of living goes. This is the effect of the new, two-way escalation.

The United Steelworkers of America was set on making its insurance coverage noncontributory. It also wanted to preserve the principle of cost-of-living escalation. Management in the beginning held exactly the opposite view.

Novel Idea a Bridge

They slowly moved closer together, but it was a novel, if not unprecedented, idea that bridged the gap. Management insisted that if the employes were entitled to protection against unforeseen rises in retail prices, the companies were entitled to similar protection against probable rises in insurance, particularly medical and hospital insurance.

So they hooked the two together. If insurance costs, being paid by the companies, go up, the added costs can be taken out of cost-of-living rises that the steelworkers would otherwise get.

Actuaries to Check

The insurance costs will be checked by actuaries for each side. If they disagree they may pick a third man to make binding decisions.

If insurance costs do not increase and nothing is taken out of the cost-of-living escalator, the cost-of-living benefits still are held down by a 6-cent ceiling for the thirty months.

On Dec. 1, 1960, the employes may get a cost-of-living adjustment of no more than 3 cents. On Oct. 1, 1961, they may get an additional sum, provided the total for both periods is no more than 6.

Put another way, they may be entitled to 1 cent in the first period and 5 cents additional in the second period, depending on the Consumer Price Index movement, and on how much the insurance escalator reduces it.

Viewed from one angle, the

Continued on Page 70, Column 4

Associated Press Wirephoto

CAMPAIGN PORTRAIT: This new photo of Vice President and Mrs. Nixon was made available in Washington by Robert G. Klein, press secretary to Mr. Nixon, who said the Vice President was a candidate for the Presidency.

Heald Bids City Overhaul Administration of Schools

By GENE CURRIVAN

Dr. Henry T. Heald, president of the Ford Foundation, called yesterday for a "drastic overhaul" of the administrative structure of the city's school system. The former Chancellor of New York University made a sweeping indictment of the system and the Board of Education.

Dr. Heald charged that despite the services of many capable teachers and administrators, there could be no improvement unless "the millstones of administrative inefficiency, political manipulation and official timidity" were removed.

He spoke at the annual luncheon conference of the United Parents Associations at the Waldorf-Astoria Hotel. An overflow audience of more than 3,000 heard him.

Theobald Defends Board

Dr. John J. Theobald, Superintendent of Schools, who spoke before Dr. Heald, defended the board, the administration and the teachers and gave a detailed report of progress.

By November, he said, the board will have completed or have under contract every building project for which money is available.

Mayor Wagner also defended the school system. His speech was read for him by Deputy Mayor Paul T. O'Keefe, because the Mayor, not present, was ill. Outlining progress made by the system, the Mayor cited early identification of exceptional children, educational television, language laboratories, integra-

Continued on Page 35, Column 1

POLITICAL UNREST BREWS IN HARLEM

Powell Group Demands Rise in Negro Representation in City Government

By PETER KIHSS

The political caldron is boiling in Harlem with economic and social complaint. It could spill over with bitter effects on the Democratic party and the city at large.

Representative Adam Clayton Powell Jr., a magnetic orator, and J. Raymond Jones, a skillful behind-the-headlines operator, in effect make up a new Democratic duumvirate over the area.

They are demanding greater Negro patronage and representation in city government. Tomorrow, the group will get its first important patronage at the state level when David B. Jones is sworn in as assistant counsel to the Democratic leader of the State Senate.

Accuses Wagner

Yesterday, at a conference in Harlem, Mr. Powell charged that the Negro was discriminated against in the city government, in the courts and in employment. He accused Mayor Wagner of failing to enforce city laws against discrimination on work done by contractors for the city.

Meanwhile, Mr. Powell has touched off a storm over numbers gambling, which has an illicit play of $2,000,000 to $4,000,000 a month. Many call it Harlem's major industry.

Looming is a likely wrangle over the Manhattan Borough Presidency, now held by Hulan E. Jack. Mr. Jack is under grand jury investigation on his assertion that a $5,500 remodeling job on his apartment was paid for by a real estate operator only as a loan.

Central Harlem cast 130,000

Continued on Page 58, Column 1

NIXON IS PLACED IN RACE BY AIDES; CAMPAIGN LIMITED

He Lets Name Be Entered in New Hampshire, Ohio and Oregon Primaries

BUT WON'T VISIT STATES

A 'Willing' but Not 'Formal' Consent Given to Backers on His 47th Birthday

By W. H. LAWRENCE

Special to The New York Times.

WASHINGTON, Jan. 9—Vice President Nixon became a "willing" but not a "formal" candidate for the Republican Presidential nomination today.

Mr. Nixon's declaration of candidacy took this somewhat unusual form when his office announced that the Vice President had agreed to the entry of his name in Presidential primaries in New Hampshire, Ohio and Oregon.

Mr. Nixon's name was entered today in New Hampshire's primary March 8 when Gov. Wesley Powell laid the signed petitions on the desk of Secretary of State Harry E. Jackson.

Herbert G. Klein, Mr. Nixon's press secretary, told reporters that the Vice President had "answered willingly" when he was asked to allow his name to be entered in the three states.

No Formal Announcement

In response to questions of whether Mr. Nixon planned any formal announcement of his candidacy later, Mr. Klein said:

"This will be as formal an announcement as there will be."

When pressed, Mr. Klein said:

"I see no necessity to make a formal announcement."

The announcement came as the Vice President quietly celebrated his forty-seventh birthday at home with his family.

Mr. Klein said that the Vice President, in giving consent for the entry of his name, had made it quite plain that he would not go into the states to make any campaign speeches.

Mr. Klein said:

"The Vice President has no plans to be in any of these primary states—note even once—as a campaigning candidate."

Presidential Trips Noted

In addition to the usual pressure of business in Washington, Mr. Klein said, the Vice President also took into account the fact that President Eisenhower would be away from Washington for ten days in February and March on a South American goodwill tour and would be going to the East-West summit conference May 16.

Mr. Nixon, Mr. Klein said, makes a point of being in Washington when the President is away.

Mr. Klein said that Gov. Mark O. Hatfield, Republican of Oregon, had called Mr. Nixon and asked permission to enter his name in the primary in that

Continued on Page 44, Column 3

3 MILLION TO GET STATE TAX REFUND

But an Equal Number Ows More Than Was Deducted

By LAYHMOND ROBINSON

Special to The New York Times.

ALBANY, Jan. 9 — About half of New York's wage and salary earners will receive refunds on the state income tax deducted from their pay last year. The others probably will have to make further payments.

The Department of Taxation and Finance said yesterday the refunds were expected to amount to about $50,000,000.

The department expects that 6,800,000 persons will file returns on their 1959 personal income tax by the April 15 deadline.

About 6,000,000 of these are wage and salary earners subject to the new income tax withholding system. The others are mainly self-employed persons who file declarations of estimated income tax and pay in quarterly installments.

Included in the latter group, however, are some wage-earners subject to withholding who

Continued on Page 48, Column 1

U. S. Moves to Curb Drinking on Planes

Special to The New York Times.

WASHINGTON, Jan. 9—The Federal Aviation Agency acted today to reduce drunkenness on airliners. Passengers may still take their own bottles abroad commercial airliners, but the stewardess is supposed to do the pouring.

If the passenger insists upon drinking without the assistance of the aircraft aides, he or she need not be physically restrained, according to a new regulation.

But the "do it yourself" imbiber can be fined up to $1,000, through Federal Aviation Agency enforcement procedures that provide for such penalties.

The new rule will take effect March 10. Airlines are expected

Continued on Page 45, Column 1

Wilkes Is Upheld on 1840 Antarctica Find

American's Sighting Supported—Once Was Ridiculed

By WALTER SULLIVAN

An American whose claim to the discovery of Antarctica as a continent evoked ridicule abroad and a court-martial at home has received vindication from Australian explorers.

He was Lieut. Charles Wilkes of the United States Navy, who led what is often described as the first national exploring expedition sent forth by the United States. In 1840 it sailed about 1,800 miles along what Wilkes interpreted to be the coast of a great continent centered near the South Pole.

The new support relates to the portion of Wilkes' exploration that probably has been the most controversial. It also gives greater credibility to the contention that a United States expedition was the first to sight that side of Antarctica.

The coastline in question is south of eastern Australia. Even on the most recent maps by the United States it shows largely as a dotted line. However, two Australians have drafted a detailed chart based on their own exploration of the last two years and photographs taken by seaplanes from the 1947 expedition of the United States Navy.

They have found a striking similarity between the shape of this coast as it has emerged

Charles Wilkes

Sketch by Wilkes was basis for engraving of the Vincennes

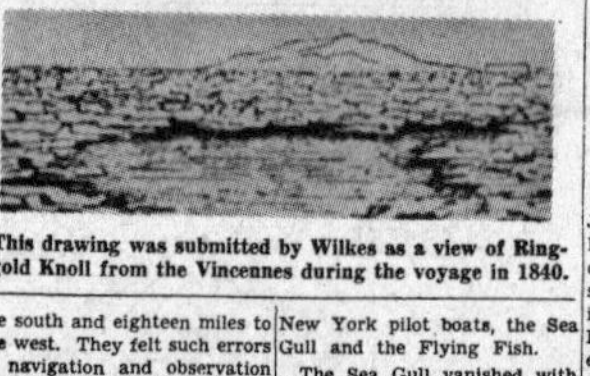

This drawing was submitted by Wilkes as a view of Ringgold Knoll from the Vincennes during the voyage in 1840.

and that sketched by Wilkes in 1840. Hence they believe that "the whole question of the reliability of Wilkes' observations along this sector might well be reviewed."

The study was carried out by B. P. Lambert and Phillip G. Law. Mr. Law has directed all of Australia's operations in Antarctica during the last seven years in behalf of the Australian Department of External Affairs. They presented the results at a recent international symposium on Antarctica held in Buenos Aires.

To achieve a fit between the Wilkes map and their own they shifted his features 116 miles to the south and eighteen miles to the west. They felt such errors in navigation and observation were understandable because of the instruments of that day and Antarctic conditions.

The Wilkes expedition was probably the largest to invade Antarctic waters during the days of sailing ships and was also one of the most unfortunate. It comprised two sloops-of-war — the Vincennes and Peacock—the gun-brig Porpoise, the supply ship Relief and two New York pilot boats, the Sea Gull and the Flying Fish.

The Sea Gull vanished with all hands in a storm. Of the 585 men engaged for the expedition at home and en route, 127 deserted and twenty-three died or were killed by native islanders during stops on the voyage. Wilkes gave a chart of his discoveries to the British explorer, James Clark Ross, who later reported having sailed right

Continued on Page 24, Column 1

Jimmie Davis Wins Louisiana Run-Off

By CLAUDE SITTON

Special to The New York Times.

NEW ORLEANS, Sunday, Jan. 10—Former Gov. Jimmie H. Davis won a sweeping victory over Mayor deLesseps S. Morrison of New Orleans yesterday in a run-off election for the Democratic nomination for Governor of Louisiana.

The nomination of Mr. Davis, ordinarily equivalent to election in traditionally Democratic Louisiana, was attributed partly to his stronger stand on racial segregation in the final campaign period.

Mr. Davis had trailed Mayor Morrison by 65,000 votes in the first primary Dec. 5.

Unofficial returns from 2,081

Continued on Page 47, Column 1

Today's Sections

*Included in all copies in the New York metropolitan area and adjacent territory.

Index to Subjects

"All the News That's Fit to Print"

NEWS SUMMARY AND INDEX, PAGE 95

The New York Times.

LATE CITY EDITION

U. S. Weather Bureau Report (Page 95) forecasts: Variable cloudiness, breezy today; mostly fair tonight and tomorrow. Temp. range: 46—34; yesterday: 53.8—40.7.

SECTION ONE

VOL. CIX—No. 37,269. NEW YORK, SUNDAY, FEBRUARY 7, 1960. TWENTY-FIVE CENTS

35c outside New York City, its suburban area and Long Island. Higher in air delivery cities.

HOME-LOAN FRAUD ON L. I. IS CHARGED; F.B.I. ARRESTS 23

Multimillion Racket Is Laid to Contracting Concerns and Their Salesmen

HOMEOWNERS INVOLVED

Amounts in Excess of Cash Needed for Work Were Split, Officials Say

By McCANDLISH PHILLIPS

The Federal Government moved yesterday against what it described as a "multimillion-dollar" loan racket operated by contracting concerns on Long Island.

Federal Bureau of Investigation agents arrested Nathan Harold Schikler, 45 years old, president of the Kem Home Improvement Corporation of 9 East Merrick Road, Freeport, and nineteen of his employes. They also arrested three Brooklyn real estate agents.

Federal authorities said that investigations of other concerns were being conducted. Further arrests are expected.

The men were charged with having provided false information in order to obtain loans for homeowners from three banks. The banks were backed by the Federal Housing Administration.

Failed to Do Work

In many cases the amounts borrowed were far in excess of the cost of the work actually done and in some cases no work was done at all, the F. B. I. said.

At least 400 homeowners, possibly many more, from Brooklyn to Montauk Point, L. I., were reported to have participated in the scheme in order to obtain cash for pressing expenses, such as funeral or wedding costs.

The three real estate agents were charged with having "verified" the fraudulent information that was given to the banks and the F. H. A. The agents sometimes posed as owners of mortgages and told the banks that payments were up to date, the F. B. I. said.

Part Deducted

Francis Rhinow, assistant United States attorney for the Eastern District of New York, said other companies had been involved in operations running into millions "at least." He would not say how many other companies were under suspicion.

According to the F. B. I., portions of the excess loans were passed on to the homeowners in cash but the company deducted a handsome amount for itself, which it split with its salesmen.

Despite the alleged deductions, the homeowners were obliged to pay back the whole amount of the loan, plus interest, to the banks in three, five or seven years, authorities said.

The following was said to be typical of the operation:

A homeowner needing $3,000

Continued on Page 40, Column 1

The New York Times

DENOUNCE TRUJILLO REGIME: Demonstrators exhibit an effigy of the dictator of the Dominican Republic, top center, near U. N., after picketing the Dominican Consulate.

U.S. Doubts O.A.S. Power To Halt Trujillo's Arrests

Special to The New York Times.

WASHINGTON, Feb. 6—State Department officials expressed the view today that the Organization of American States could condemn the mass arrests reported to be taking place in the Dominican Republic but would be helpless to stop them.

Last night the Venezuelan Ambassador here, Dr. Marcos Falcon-Briceno, requested a meeting of the Council of the Organization of American States to look into charges that mass arrests had been made by the regime of Generalissimo Rafael Leonidas Trujillo Molina.

The request was made to the council's chairman, Vicente Sanchez Gavito of Mexico.

This evening Señor Sanchez Gavito summoned the twenty-one-member council to an extraordinary meeting at 4 P. M. Monday to discuss the Dominican question.

U. S. Stand Uncertain

At the State Department, officials said they did not know what position the United States would take during the council discussions. They said it would be necessary to wait until Venezuela had made her charges and recommendations.

[More than 200 Dominican exiles demonstrated Saturday in front of the Dominican Consulate here and the United Nations. The exiles were protesting against the "persecution" of the Roman Catholic Church and the jailing of citizens in the Dominican Republic.]

It was the opinion of experts on Latin America that the coun-

Continued on Page 34, Column 1

SHAKE-UP IS SEEN IN ALGERIA REGIME

3 French Ministers Arrive to Survey Area in Wake of Anti-de Gaulle Rising

By HENRY TANNER

Special to The New York Times.

ALGIERS, Feb. 6—Three key Ministers in the French Government arrived here today amid reports that they had instructions from President de Gaulle to pave the way for a far-reaching reorganization of the army, civil administration and judiciary in Algeria.

They are Pierre Messmer, new Minister of the Armed Forces; Pierre Chatenet, Interior Minister, and Edmond Michelet, Minister of Justice.

It has been officially acknowledged that almost all locally recruited policemen were in collusion with the European insurgents who rose Jan. 24 against President de Gaulle's policy of self-determination for Algeria. The Government plans to replace a large number of local policemen with men from Continental France.

Poor Judgment Charged

Col. Yves Godard, director of the Sûreté Nationale for Algeria, was relieved of his duties immediately after the collapse of the insurrection last Monday. He was dismissed, officials now say, not for any personal involvement but because it was felt he had showed poor judgment in surrounding himself with men who were drawn to the insurgents.

M. Messmer is reported to have begun an investigation of the role a number of officers played during the insurrection. Some forty are said to be in line for transfer, premature retirement or court-martial.

In addition, it is believed that the Government has tentative

Continued on Page 4, Column 3

ARMS MOVE BY U.S. HINTED IN PARLEY

Herter and Security Chiefs Follow Up President's Talk on Stand Toward East

By JACK RAYMOND

Special to The New York Times.

WASHINGTON, Feb. 6 A new United States move on disarmament appeared to be developing today. Leading officials met in Secretary of State Christian A. Herter's office to discuss Western policies on nuclear tests and disarmament.

These policies have been under intensive study and possible modification in the light of Premier Khrushchev's persistent proposals for total disarmament and his recent public concession that not all nuclear weapons tests can be detected.

The State Department did not announce any details of today's meeting, although one official confirmed that it dealt with disarmament. This already had been indicated by the identification of the participants.

One was Frederick W. Eaton, New York attorney, who will head the United States delegation to the East-West disarmament conference in Geneva March 15. Another was Philip J. Farley, Mr. Herter's special assistant for disarmament and atomic energy.

With the Secretary of State presiding, others at the meeting included Allen W. Dulles, director of the Central Intelligence Agency; John F. Floberg, atomic energy commissioner;

Continued on Page 3, Column 2

MITCHELL EXPECTS MAJOR JOB SHIFTS TO MARK DECADE

More Workers Under 25 and Over 45 Likely—Curb on Discrimination Expected

By JOSEPH A. LOFTUS

Special to The New York Times.

WASHINGTON, Feb. 6—Startling changes in the labor force in the next ten years were forecast today by Secretary of Labor James P. Mitchell.

While the population climbs from 180,000,000 to 208,000,000, or 15 per cent, the number of workers will increase by 13,500,000, or 20 per cent, the Secretary predicted.

If all the manpower that becomes available is used well and wisely, he said, the United States can raise its standard of living 25 per cent in the 1960-1970 decade.

A Labor Department study, titled "Manpower: Challenge of the 1960's," carries special implications for employers and for children born after World War II.

'Major Overhaul' Likely

The changes in the labor force that are coming, said Secretary Mitchell, "will require a major overhaul in the employment policies of many businesses."

"Employers who do not abandon policies against hiring workers because of their age, or sex, or race, religion or nationality, or because they may be handicapped in some way, may have real trouble finding enough workers in the decade ahead."

The Labor Department also predicted that the proportion of older workers would rise. Two of every five employes will be over 45 years old. By 1970, one of every three will be a woman.

Workers under 25 years old, the study said, will account for nearly half of the labor force during the Nineteen Sixties, even though they will stay in school longer.

Fewer in 35-44 Group

There will be a comparatively small increase among workers 25 to 34 years old, it was forecast, but there will be fewer workers aged 35 to 44. Many of those who will be in the 35-to-44 group were born during the depression of the Nineteen Thirties, when birth rates were low.

The expected decline in this age group, Mr. Mitchell said, "will place a heavy burden on personnel management and will force changes in the traditional practices in recruitment, selection and training."

The department also expects that employment will continue to grow faster in the service industries than in the production industries. The employment

Continued on Page 51, Column 4

'Great Debate' in Capital: Is U. S. Misusing Wealth?

One Side Believes Too Many Resources Are Used for Private Consumption Rather Than for Public Services

By EDWIN L. DALE Jr.

Special to The New York Times.

WASHINGTON, Feb. 6—A new "great debate" is raging here.

At the luncheon table, over coffee and brandy after dinner, and to some extent in Congress, it is involving politicians, civil servants, intellectuals and many plain persons.

The debate has been inspired by a single idea: that the basic trouble with American society is that we devote too much of our resources to increasing an already affluent volume of private consumption, and too little to public services of all kinds.

The idea has been emerging gradually for about a year. Its two proponents who appear to have been most widely quoted are Walter Lippmann, the columnist, and John Kenneth Galbraith, the Harvard University economist. Others have also backed it in their writings.

In any case, the idea seems to have had a large impact here. In its most graphic terms, it is stated like this:

"There is something wrong with a country that has bigger and better tailfins at the same time that it has a second-best defense posture, a worsening slum problem, dirty rivers and streams, inadequate health services and wretched under-financing of education."

Some, including Mr. Lippmann, go so far as to contend that the "sense of national purpose" of Americans is being undermined by this condition.

The conclusion of those who support the basic idea is that the nation should spend far more on public purposes, and raise mores taxes as needed to finance the higher expeditures. Their key point is that a higher share of total national income should be spent by Government

Continued on Page 42, Column 1

Huge Atom Service Center Is Under Study for Jersey

By GEORGE CABLE WRIGHT

Special to The New York Times.

WASHINGTON, Feb. 6—The Atomic Energy Commission is studying a New Jersey proposal to establish the first atomic park of its type in this country. Installations would include a multi-million-dollar plant for processing "high level" radioactive waste; facilities for the docking, refueling and servicing of atomic-powered ships, and a combined hospital and research center to treat persons adversely affected through exposure to radiation.

The construction of an atomic reactor is also being considered.

Officials of the commission expressed considerable interest today. The plans will be outlined to the top echelon of the A. E. C. by state officials at a meeting Thursday in the agency's offices here.

Delaware Bay Site Chosen

The park would be on the shores of Delaware Bay in Cape May, Cumberland or Salem Counties and would cover at least 200 acres.

The proposed park has the backing of Gov. Robert B. Meyner's administration, as well as local officials in the three counties. Several major concerns in the state have indicated a strong interest in developing the facilities.

The state, for its part, would make much if not all of the required land available to the builders and extend additional assistance to keep the cost of

Continued on Page 16, Column 3

19 DEMOCRATS ASK CAUCUS IN SENATE

Liberals Seek Party Parley on Interest Rate Rise—'Teamwork' Stressed

By C. P. TRUSSELL

Special to The New York Times.

WASHINGTON, Feb. 6—Senate Democratic liberals are keeping the pressure on Senator Lyndon B. Johnson of Texas, the majority leader, to call more conferences for party discussion of major issues.

Nineteen liberals signed a formal request today for a meeting on the report of the Joint Congressional Economic Committee.

The nineteen found much encouragement in the passage earlier this week of the Federal aid to education bill following such a conference.

Gore Stresses Teamwork

"The sentiment for teamwork is growing," Senator Albert Gore of Tennessee said. He is a leader of the drive for a stronger liberal voice in Senate Democratic party councils.

Senator Gore confirmed that the formal request for another conference had been made. He said the liberals wanted to present their views on interest rates.

"The conference of Democratic Senators on the Federal aid to education bill," Mr. Gore said, "paid off in Democratic unity in the passage of the first strong Federal aid to education bill in eleven years."

Only eleven of the sixty-five Democrats voted against passage.

Mr. Gore said, "This is but an example of what can result from group consideration and formulation of party policy on

Continued on Page 48, Column 3

HOUSE UNIT URGES TV-RADIO DECEIT BE MADE A CRIME

Proposes Laws to Penalize Sponsor and Ad Agency as Well as Station

FEDERAL AGENCIES HIT

Interim Report Calls F.C.C. and F.T.C. Passive in Use of Existing Powers

Recommendations from report are printed on Page 62.

By WILLIAM M. BLAIR

Special to The New York Times.

WASHINGTON, Feb. 6 — House investigators called on Congress today to provide criminal penalties for deceitful radio and television programs and for unfair business practices on the airwaves.

The penalties would cover sponsors and advertising agencies as well as the broadcasters.

The investigators also proposed a powerful economic weapon in the form of short-term suspensions of Federal broadcast licenses if stations and networks failed to heed Government warnings that their programs did not serve the public interest.

Revocation Shunned

Revocations and the refusal to renew licenses, as now provided in law, were so "drastic," they said, that they seldom had been invoked.

The recommendations were offered in an interim report by the House Special Subcommittee on Legislative Oversight which has been investigating TV and radio.

Representative John B. Bennett, Republican of Michigan, a member of the subcommittee, anticipated the panel's report by announcing yesterday that he was introducing legislation that would impose a fine of up to $5,000 or two years in prison or both on persons who used the airwaves to deceive the public.

Drafts Legislation

He also drafted a bill to provide for suspension of licenses for short periods rather than the seldom-used revocation.

Following up the disclosure of rigged TV quiz shows and other deceptive practices in a series of hearings, the subcommittee proposed nine stiff legislative remedies to embrace not only radio and TV stations and networks, but also sponsors and advertising agencies.

The subcommittee assailed the Federal Communications and Federal Trade Commissions for failing to clean up spurious broadcast situations despite "adequate authority." It said the agencies had adopted a "passive" role.

It criticized individual stations, networks, sponsors, and

Continued on Page 62, Column 1

HOUSING PLAN BIDS U. S. REDUCE ROLE

Overhaul of Federal Groups to Wipe Out Slums Urged

By The Associated Press.

WASHINGTON, Feb. 6—Some striking new proposals to subsidize low-income housing and wipe out slums were advanced today in a Government-sponsored study.

The report was prepared at the request of Norman P. Mason, Housing Administrator, by Dr. Ernest H. Fisher, Columbia University housing economist. Dr. Fisher recommended a sweeping overhaul of Federal housing agencies.

His recommendations would reduce Federal control over local housing authorities. These federally aided agencies could become landlords, mortgage lenders and home-improvement contractors in cases where private builders could not afford to take the jobs.

The plan would consolidate the Housing and Home Finance Agency and its five related but independent branches into a single agency that would make all its grants and annual subsidies to each city in a single contract.

Mr. Mason did not endorse the recommendations but made

Continued on Page 40, Column 3

Nu's Faction Leads In Burmese Election

By TILLMAN DURDIN

Special to The New York Times.

RANGOON, Burma, Sunday, Feb. 7—Former Premier Nu's faction of the Anti-Fascist People's Freedom League established a clear lead early today in yesterday's general elections.

By 10 A. M. his candidates were victors in twenty-eight of the thirty-two constituencies tallied. Backers of former Premier Ba Swe, himself apparently defeated, won in the four others.

Though there still were 196 constituencies to be heard from, the victories were so decisive that observers were predicting a majority in the next Parliament for U Nu's group, the so-called Clean faction.

Nation-wide reports indicated

Continued on Page 15, Column 1

Satellite Gives New Data on Radiation Belts

Outer Van Allen Arc Moves, Inner One Is Stable, U. S. Finds

By WALTER SULLIVAN

Explorer VII, the only vehicle still sending scientific data from space, has shown that the rim of the Van Allen radiation belts closest to the earth lies directly across the northern United States.

It seems to be constantly weaving back and forth as much as 500 miles in latitude. Its intensity may vary ten-fold within a few hours. Sometimes sharp spikes of the belt, only a few miles thick, reach toward the earth.

This dynamic picture of the belt has been obtained through daily monitoring of the satellite's signals by the laboratory of Dr. James A. Van Allen at the State University of Iowa in Iowa City. The laboratory has been transcribing the signals directly onto paper, so that the radiation intensity in space can be read immediately.

Thus, as often as seven times a day, Dr. Van Allen can, in effect, look into the sky and see the radiation belt that bears his name. When conditions are good, more than an hour of data is collected daily.

The satellite, launched Oct. 13, carries two Geiger counters. One, the size of a cocktail glass, is coated with a thin layer of lead to keep out the weakest radiation particles. The other, no larger than the eraser on a pencil, is shielded only by the satellite skin.

The orbit lies roughly between 340 and 670 miles above the earth and between Lats. 51 degrees, N. and S. This means that it only skirts the bottom of the inner radiation belt, which lies over the magnetic equator. However, the outer belt, whose heart lies more than 9,000 miles above the Equator, curves in toward the earth, so that its northern and southern rims lie well below the altitude of the satellite.

Signals from the satellite are picked up with a device that seems hardly more elaborate than an ordinary television antenna, mounted atop the university's physics building. The recording equipment in the basement was designed to turn on automatically when the satel-

Continued on Page 20, Column 5

The New York Times — Feb. 7, 1960

Points at which satellites have pierced radiation shells. Observations show that the Outer Van Allen Belt's rim moves north and south several hundred miles at a time. Shells generated by Argus explosions of atomic bombs in space in 1958 were stationary for weeks.

Soviet Eases Visits By U. S. Motorists

By HARRISON E. SALISBURY

For the first time American motorists will be permitted to go it alone in the Soviet Union next summer, traveling on approved routes without guides or Soviet supervision.

The relaxation in auto travel was announced in word sent to Gabriel Reiner of Cosmos Tours, New York travel agency, by Intourist, the official Soviet travel organization.

The elimination of the requirement that each motorist be accompanied by a Soviet guide is one of a series of relaxations in Russian travel rules. New motor routes are being opened. Limitations are being relaxed, and more areas will be open to tourists.

Indicative of the general de-

Continued on Page 2, Column 3

Today's Sections

Index to Subjects

"All the News That's Fit to Print"

The New York Times

LATE CITY EDITION

Weather: Fair, very cold today and tonight. Chance of snow tomorrow. Temp. range: today 24-14; Sunday 33-26. Full U.S. report on Page 30.

VOL. CIX..No. 37,270. | NEW YORK, MONDAY, FEBRUARY 8, 1960. | FIVE CENTS

BLUE CROSS TO ASK FOR A 30-35% RISE IN NEW YORK RATE

Hospital Insurance Group Says It Would Broaden Its Benefits to Members

REQUEST TO STATE DUE

Increase to Go Into Effect This Summer if Approved —Infant Care to Change

The Blue Cross announced yesterday that it would seek to raise its rates 30 to 35 per cent this year so it could broaden hospital insurance benefits for its 7,220,000 subscribers in the metropolitan area.

Announcement of the move came from the Associated Hospital Service of New York, which administers the program in the area.

It said it planned to submit a request for the increase to the state Department of Insurance within "the next month or six weeks," asking that the rise take effect between July and September.

If granted, the basic rate for family contracts under group coverage would rise from $6.60 to $8.58 a month, according to the association. The rate for individuals would go from $2.61 to $3.39 a month.

For persons who pay directly to Blue Cross instead of through their employers, the new rates would be $10.10 for family plans and $4.39 for individual coverage.

Further Requests Hinted

"These should take us at least to the end of 1961," a spokesman said, indicating that further rises might be asked at that time.

With the increases asked for 1960 would go these added services:

¶Infants would be covered from birth. They are not eligible for benefits under present programs before ninety days.

¶Persons with "mental and nervous" disorders would be allowed thirty days of care in general hospitals, other than public ones. Blue Cross now only pays for shock treatment and neurosurgery.

¶The allowance for maternity cases, now $80, would be increased, although the figure has not been set.

¶A rise in the $10-a-day allowance given to subscribers who stay in a private room in a hospital is being considered.

Continued on Page 32, Column 6

Loss of 60,000 Jobs Seen For City Area in 20 Years

But Regional Study Finds New Business Will Ease Impact on Economy

By STANLEY LEVEY

In the next twenty years the metropolitan area will lose 60,000 to 80,000 jobs to more competitive sections of the country, a Harvard study indicates.

Nevertheless, the economic impact of this loss will be cushioned by countervailing forces that will attract new and fast-growing industries to take the places of the ones that will have left.

The jobs that will disappear are in parts of the garment, textile, footwear, electronics and other industries that have a limited need for skilled labor and in which labor costs are a high percentage of total costs. These industries the study calls wage-oriented.

These are some of the major conclusions reached in "Wages in the Metropolis," by Martin Segal, a Dartmouth College economist. The book, published today, is the fourth of nine volumes setting forth the findings in the New York Metropolitan Region Study.

C. McKim Norton, executive vice president of the Regional Plan Association, said the Segal

Conway

C. McKim Norton

book "buttresses the study's previous findings that slices of some industries sensitive to the tug of lower wage rates will depart from the region."

The study was made for the Regional Plan Association by the Harvard Graduate School of Public Administration. It took three years and was financed by grants from the Ford Foundation and the Rockefeller

Continued on Page 58, Column 2

SENATE UNIT MAPS BATTLE FOR BILL TO AID NEGRO VOTE

Committee to Seek Workable Civil Rights Plan Based on Referee Proposals

By ANTHONY LEWIS

Special to The New York Times.

WASHINGTON, Feb. 7—The hard work of drafting a civil rights bill that meets both the legal and the political necessities will begin in the Senate Rules Committee this week.

The problem is to please both Republicans and Northern Democrats and also to produce a workable bill. Both parties now seem agreed that the objective is legislation that will take a major step toward extending the voting of Negroes in the South.

The Attorney General, William P. Rogers, told the Rules Committee bluntly last Friday that workable legislation would have to be based on his proposal for voting referees to be named by the Federal courts. It is probably true also that no bill straying too far from his proposal would get solid Republican support.

On the other hand, Mr. Rogers did leave the way open for some accommodation of views. That was the import of a little-noticed aspect of his tertimony.

Snag in Plan Feared

Some civil rights organizations, and some interested Democrats at Capitol Hill, had feared that Mr. Rogers' plan envisaged Negroes' going through a formal hearing before the referees to qualify as voters. The fear was that few Negroes would be willing to undertake that burden.

For that reason some of these observers preferred the Civil Rights Commission's proposal for registrars who would register Negroes in a simple administrative process. At the same time, these observers recognized the deficiencies found by Mr. Rogers in the registrar plan, notably the fact that it would be limited to Federal elections.

Mr. Rogers, in his testimony on Friday, corrected the impression that his referees would have to hold formal, judicial hearings. He indicated that a Negro would appear alone before the referee and do no more to qualify than a white man would to register.

The Attorney General suggested that any objections by state officials could be voiced not before the referee, but would be submitted later, when he reported to Federal court. The state could file exceptions to his report.

No Objection to Change

The significance of this testimony is that the drafters on the Senate Rules Committee could write Mr. Rogers' view of procedures before the referee into the bill. His draft does not detail the referees' procedure, but he has indicated he would have no objection to the change.

There is some feeling that the Democrats at the Capitol will want to put their own imprint on the civil rights bill that passes. This aim might be satisfied by working with the general approach of Mr. Rogers but making changes such as that one.

Mr. Rogers said he was "not concerned about labels." If a legally sound bill is enacted, he said, he does not care whose name is attached to it.

The Senate is scheduled to begin its civil rights debate a week from tomorrow. There

Continued on Page 14, Column 6

Mikoyan Tells Cubans of Soviet Deterrent Power

Associated Press Wirephoto

First Deputy Premier Anastas I. Mikoyan, center, of the Soviet Union, at the Palace of Workers yesterday in Havana. At right is Maj. Ernesto (Che) Guevara, president of the National Bank of Cuba. Jesus Soto of the Cuban Confederation of Labor is at the left.

Special to The New York Times.

HAVANA, Feb. 7—Anastas I. Mikoyan, a Soviet First Deputy Premier, told the Cuban people today that the Soviet Union's power had put it in a position to demand world peace. "Those who threaten war now know that we have sent a rocket to the moon," he said, "and that we can send it with the same precision to any part of the world. But we threaten no one." Mr. Mikoyan made the statement through an interpreter in a surprise appearance at a meeting of several thousand textile workers. His speech was broadcast over a nation-wide television and

Continued on Page 13, Column 7

U.S.-BRITISH PLAN FOR NUCLEAR BAN TO BE GIVEN SOON

It Is Limited to Tests That Can Be Checked, Excluding Small Subsurface Ones

'THRESHOLD' IS FAVORED

President Said to Seek Way to Meet de Gaulle Stand on Data on Weapons

By E. W. KENWORTHY

Special to The New York Times.

WASHINGTON, Feb. 7 — The United States and Britain will present to the Soviet Union soon, possibly this week, their new plan for a treaty to ban tests of nuclear weapons.

After fifteen months of negotiating in Geneva, the two Western nuclear powers are convinced that the Soviet Union will not agree to an inspection system sufficiently thorough to warrant Western acceptance of a comprehensive ban.

Moreover, the Soviet Union has not accepted the validity or the relevancy of United States scientific data showing that small underground blasts cannot be positively identified by present seismic equipment.

Therefore, according to informed sources here, the United States and Britain will propose a ban on tests that can be monitored. This will include atmosphere, high-altitude and underwater tests, plus—and this is the crucial aspect of the proposal, elements of which have been discussed publicly before—underground explosions above an agreed "threshold."

Shift in U. S. Stand Seen

Meanwhile, President Eisenhower and his top military and diplomatic aides have been discussing means of meeting President de Gaulle's charge that the United States discriminates against France in the realm of nuclear weapons. At his news conference last Wednesday President Eisenhower said he favored changing legislation so that the United States could supply nuclear weapons and information to reliable allies.

On the test ban issue, the proposed threshold, it was learned, will be a seismographic reading and not a fixed rating of explosions. However, the reading will be approximately that resulting from a twenty-kiloton explosion. (A kiloton blast is of a strength equivalent to that of 1,000 tons of TNT.)

According to present plans,

Continued on Page 3, Column 2

NELSON INQUIRER CONCEDES ERROR

Counsel Admits Bypassing Closed Questioning of an Innocent S. I. Witness

By CLAYTON KNOWLES

Whitney North Seymour Jr., chief counsel to the Nelson Commission, acknowledged yesterday that he had put a key witness on the stand at a public hearing without first getting his story in executive session.

The usual investigative practice is to develop the facts in executive, or closed, session and then to present them in public. This is done to guard the rights of witnesses.

"I made a decision, and it came out wrong," Mr. Seymour declared.

The counsel's statement was made as the commission came under attack on a charge of failing to protect the civil rights of individuals testifying in the commission's current investigation into New York City affairs.

The charge was made yesterday by a Democratic Assemblyman on a television program and by the moderator of the program.

The accusation was that Rocco Parisi, executive assistant to Borough President Albert V. Maniscalco of Richmond, had been "seriously damaged by innuendo" when called Jan. 28 to testify about a bank deposit of $2,708.30 he made on Nov. 14, 1958.

The deposit was made the same day that Marvin Klein, a builder who had constructed a

Continued on Page 24, Column 3

Cut in Income Tax For Rail Commuter Sought in Congress

Special to The New York Times.

WASHINGTON, Feb. 7 — Representative Herbert Zelenko of New York today proposed a plan for "freezing commuting expenses forever" by shifting the burden of railroad commuter fare increases to the Federal Government.

Railroad commuters would be allowed to subtract the cost of fare increases after Jan. 1, 1960, from their income tax bills.

Mr. Zelenko, a Manhattan Democrat, said he would introduce a bill to this effect tomorrow. It would be an amendment to the Internal Revenue Code of 1954.

Procedure Outlined

It would allow the commuter, he said, "at the end of each year, when filing his income tax return, to annex his commutation stub with a simple form provided by the Secretary of the Treasury, showing any additional commuter fare that he paid over the rate of Jan. 1, 1960."

Then, "the commuter taxpayer will receive a credit against his income tax of that year or a refund of the amount of increased payments for commutation."

Mr. Zelenko said the bill would "eliminate the necessity for abandoning any more commuter railroads."

The plan would, in effect, be a Federal subsidy to commuter railroads, since increases in fares would be balanced by a reduction in Federal revenue from the income tax. In an ad-

Continued on Page 32, Column 1

POWER AUTHORITY ASKS ATOMIC ROLE

Moses Report Takes Issue With Rockefeller Boards Backing Private Utilities

By WARREN WEAVER Jr.

Special to The New York Times.

ALBANY, Feb. 7—The State Power Authority warned the Rockefeller Administration today against giving private utilities a monopoly on development of atomic energy in the state.

In its annual report to the Governor and the Legislature, the agency maintained that there was "no good reason" it should be barred from the atomic power field if circumstances warranted public participation.

The authority's strong bid for an atomic role appeared to reflect the views as well as some of the sharp language of its chairman, Robert Moses.

"The authority does not seek to be the exclusive agency in the state in the atomic field," the report said, "but rather to be in a position to contribute its share."

Companies' 'Insistence' Cited

The report continued:

"To put it simply, we hold that the state should not at this time and at the insistence of the largest private utility companies commit itself to the proposition that the future development of atomic energy must be exclusively the domain of the private utilities.

"This authority, we believe, has had successful experience. It has talent and facilities, which may well contribute something of value."

The concern expressed by the power authority over exclusive private atomic power development was based on two recent Rockefeller studies.

The first was prepared by the Governor's Committee on Power Resources, headed by John E. Burton, a vice-president of Cornell University. It did not recognize any right of the power

Continued on Page 2, Column 5

Argentina Hunting Foreign Submarine In an Atlantic Inlet

By United Press International.

BUENOS AIRES, Feb. 7—The Government announced tonight that a search was under way for a foreign submarine in the Golfo Nuevo, a small Atlantic inlet on Argentina's southern coast.

The announcement, issued by the Navy Secretary, Rear Admiral Gaston C. Clement, was the closest the Government has yet come to confirming repeated reports that Argentine ships had trapped an undersea craft and were attempting to flush it from a hiding place on the gulf floor.

The Golfo Nuevo, 650 miles southwest of Buenos Aires, is ten miles wide at its mouth, which would mean it could be easily sealed off from access to the open Atlantic.

Newspapers Report an Attack

Newspapers for the last few days have printed reports that a submarine was spotted on the surface of the gulf and was attacked by a patrol craft and damaged.

According to the reports, the submarine then crash-dived, trailing an oil slick, and now lies about ninety feet down on the gulf floor, where it can be spotted on the radar scopes of waiting surface vessels.

The Navy flatly denied that any such attack had been made; but it did say that a foreign underwater craft had been detected by radar in the Golfo Nuevo late last week. The Navy refused any direct comment on whether the submarine had

Continued on Page 2, Column 3

BUDGET DELAYING U. S. ATOM ROCKET

A.E.C.'s Request Is Reduced 25 Per Cent—Slowing of Project by Year Seen

By JOHN W. FINNEY

Special to The New York Times.

WASHINGTON, Feb. 7—Development of a nuclear-powered space rocket would be delayed at least a year by budget cuts imposed by the Administration.

This estimate has been given to the Joint Congressional Committee on Atomic Energy. The committee, which has a successful record of championing such developmental projects as the nuclear submarine and the hydrogen bomb, is becoming increasingly concerned over what it feels is the lack of sufficient budgetary and administrative support for the nuclear rocket program.

In the opinion of many committee members, including Senator Clinton P. Anderson, Democrat of New Mexico and committee chairman, the nuclear rocket offers the best opportunity for the United States to vault ahead of the Soviet Union in the race to place ever bigger payloads further into space.

Pressure is arising from the committee, therefore, to accelerate development of the nuclear rocket program, known as Project Rover.

Of a total of $55,000,000 sought by the Atomic Energy Commission in appropriations and authorizations for the proj-

Continued on Page 4, Column 5

LEGISLATURE SETS BUDGET HEARINGS

2 Meetings Due This Week —Few Changes Expected

Special to The New York Times.

ALBANY, Feb. 7—The Legislature will begin its sixth week of the 1960 session tomorrow, having generated an unusual amount of early activity on measures of little consequence, but with relatively small progress on major bills.

This week the fiscal committees of the Senate and Assembly will hold their annual budget hearings. This year there will be two—one on local assistance spending on Wednesday and the other on state purposes and capital construction on Friday.

The present schedule calls for the committees to report Governor Rockefeller's fiscal plan out for floor action the week of Feb. 22. The expectation is that there will be only relatively minor changes.

$40,000,000 Is Cut

In 1959, having warmed to their job during four years of hacking away at the Democratic budgets of former Gov. W. Averell Harriman, the Republican fiscal committees sliced about $40,000,000 from Mr. Rockefeller's first budget.

This was, to some extent, a party gesture to mollify economy-minded Republicans who were balking at the Governor's tax increase program. This year there is no such tax program, and the Rockefeller budget probably will emerge from committee scrutiny virtually unscathed.

The Wednesday hearing is expected to be the livelier of the two, with Mayor Wagner filing

Continued on Page 22, Column 3

Fragments of 2 Biblical Scrolls Found in Cave in Israeli Desert

Parchment Documents, With Verses of Exodus, Thought to Date From 2d Century

By LAWRENCE FELLOWS

Special to The New York Times.

JERUSALEM (Israeli Sector), Feb. 7—Two fragments of ancient Biblical scrolls with sixteen verses from the Book of Exodus have been discovered by Israeli archaeologists in the dust of a Judaean Desert cave near the Dead Sea.

The fragments, which measure about one by three inches, are yet to be unrolled. They are of parchment and are in good condition except for broken edges on one of them.

Even in their present condition it can be seen that the fragments bear verses and are from a phylactery used in Jewish ritual. One fragment contains the first to the tenth verses of the thirteenth chapter of Exodus. The other contains the eleventh to sixteenth verses.

From coins and various artifacts found with the scroll fragments, it has been determined that they belonged to followers of Bar-Kochba who took refuge in the caves with the collapse

The New York Times Feb. 8, 1960

Site of cave (cross)

of their revolt against the Romans in A. D. 135.

There are eleven rows of script on each of the fragments, written by an accomplished scribe in the same style of Hebrew lettering as was used in the so-called Dead Sea scrolls. These have been found in caves to the north in Jordanian territory.

The discovery was made by an archaeological team led by Dr. Yohanan Aharoni, a lecturer

Continued on Page 9, Column 3

Kramer Defies American Legion Over Hiring of Movie Writers

By MURRAY SCHUMACH

Special to The New York Times.

HOLLYWOOD, Calif., Feb. 7—Stanley Kramer, one of the leading independent producer-directors in the motion-picture industry, defied the American Legion today and said he would hire any writer he pleased, regardless of the writer's "past affiliations or suspected affiliations."

Mr. Kramer termed "un-American" the Legion's attempt to dictate the employment policies of the movie business. He said that while the Legion's "intent is understandable, its methods are reprehensible, to say the least."

"The American Legion," continued Mr. Kramer, "is weighing a procedure in which, literally, the end justifies the means. This is as totally un-American as anything I can imagine."

This strong disagreement with the recent statement by Martin B. McKneally, the National Commander of the Legion, was extraordinary in Hollywood, where the Legion is greatly feared.

Mr. McKneally announced last week that the Legion was opening a "war of information" to combat "a renewed invasion of American filmdom by Soviet-indoctrinated artists."

The National Commander referred specifically to Mr. Kramer for having hired Nedrick Young to write "Inherit the Wind" for the movies. Mr. Young, who makes no secret that he writes under the name of Nathan E.

Continued on Page 35, Column 4

Kurchatov, Soviet Physicist, Dies; Led A-Bomb and H-Bomb Work

His Research for Institute of Atomic Energy Changed Balance of World Power

By The Associated Press.

MOSCOW, Feb. 7—Dr. Igor V. Kurchatov, Soviet physicist who helped to develop the Soviet Union's atomic bomb, died today at the age of 57. The cause of death was given as "paralysis of the heart."

He was a member of the Presidium of the Soviet Academy of Sciences and director of its Institute of Atomic Energy.

His body will lie in state in Trade Union Hall and he will be buried Tuesday in Red Square near the Kremlin wall. These are honors reserved for the most prominent Soviet citizens.

Directed Massive Effort

Igor Vasilevich Kurchatov was the chief scientific organizer and director of the massive Soviet effort that changed the world balance of power by producing the Soviet atomic bomb in 1949 and the Soviet hydrogen bomb in 1953, each feat being accomplished long before the West had thought it would be possible.

Associated Press

Dr. Igor V. Kurchatov

Before he began his work on nuclear weapons during World War II, Dr. Kurchatov had been in the Nineteen Thirties one of the world's pioneer explorers of the atomic nucleus and its properties. In recent years he had been general director of Soviet efforts to harness the power of the hydrogen bomb for peaceful

Continued on Page 4, Column 2

ALGIERS RIGHTISTS FEAR PUNISHMENT

Still Are Defiant in Blaming de Gaulle for Troubles

By HENRY TANNER

Special to The New York Times.

ALGIERS, Feb. 7—The prevailing feelings among Europeans here a week after the collapse of the extremist insurrection are hatred for President de Gaulle and fear of punishment.

The young extremists, and some not so young, are openly boasting that they "will do better next time."

They blame President de Gaulle for all their troubles, from the failure of the insurrection to the conviction, now almost general among them, that the cause of "French Algeria" will not win.

Their bitterness was increased during the last three days by police and administrative measures taken by the Government to prevent a recurrence of the insurrection.

These measures continued today. Brig. Gen. Henri Mirambeau, commander in southwestern Algeria, was recalled to Paris, according to a reliable private report. He was the first general reported to have been

Continued on Page 8, Column 2

NEWS INDEX

"All the News That's Fit to Print"

The New York Times

LATE CITY EDITION
U. S. Weather Bureau Report (Page 95) forecasts: Humid, showers today; mild, chance of showers tonight and tomorrow. Temp. range: 76—68; yesterday: 72.3—67.6. Temp.-Hum. Index: near 74; yesterday: 72.

NEWS SUMMARY AND INDEX, PAGE 95

SECTION ONE

VOL. CIX. No. 37,388. © 1960, by The New York Times Company. Times Square New York 36, N. Y. NEW YORK, SUNDAY, JUNE 5, 1960. 25c outside New York City, its suburban area and Long Island. 50c in 11 Western states, Canada; higher in air delivery cities. TWENTY-FIVE CENTS

NEW TITLE I PLAN OUTLINED FOR CITY BY HOUSING BOARD

Program Alters Practices of Moses' Former Slum Clearance Committee

COMPETITIVE BIDS DUE

'Orderly Rebuilding' Vowed, With Public to Be Kept Informed of Decisions

Text of report to the Mayor is printed on Page 78.

By JOHN SIBLEY

The city's new Housing and Redevelopment Board made public yesterday its plan for "a more orderly rebuilding of the city" under Title I of the Federally aided slum-clearance program.

It said that in the future there would be more competition to sponsor renewal projects, that the public would be kept informed of housing decisions and that projects undertaken would conform to an over-all plan.

The new plan would drastically alter procedures followed by Robert Moses' former Slum Clearance Committee, particularly in the selection of private builders.

Under Title I a city may acquire a substandard area by condemnation or negotiated purchase and resell it at a lower price to a private builder. The Federal Government makes up two-thirds of the city's loss; the city bears the other third. The private builder, or sponsor, then finances the new building.

Mayor Concurs

J. Clarence Davies Jr., chairman of the new board, presented the plan last Wednesday to Mayor Wagner, who released it with the statement: "I concur in the fullest in the approaches set forth and the principles adopted."

At a press briefing, Mr. Davies refused to criticize Mr. Moses or the practices of the defunct committee. But his plan reverses many of the old procedures.

Under Mr. Moses, for instance, there was no competitive bidding after the Slum Clearance Committee had selected a "tentative" sponsor for a project. Mr. Davies' report states:

"We shall exert every effort to interest a large number of sponsors and select the best qualified from among this group. All proposed projects will be advertised in newspapers."

After the selection of a sponsor, there must be a public auction at which other qualified builders may bid for the land involved. However, there will be a "matched bidding" procedure in which the designated sponsor, who by this time will have spent considerable funds for preliminary plans and sur-

Continued on Page 78, Column 3

Democrats to Curb Fights On Loyalty at Convention

Hope to Bar Southern Rebels by Testing 'Good Faith' of Individual and Thus Limit Disputes Over Delegations

By GLADWIN HILL
Special to The New York Times.

LOS ANGELES, June 4—A new strategy will be tried to bar "rebel" Southern delegations from the Democratic National Convention and to minimize the customary floor fighting over credentials.

This was disclosed by authoritative party sources this week as officials pressed ahead with arrangements for the convention, opening here July 11.

There have been movements in a half-dozen Southern states to send delegations instructed to refuse to support distasteful party planks and nominees, particularly on such touchy issues as civil rights.

States conspicuous in such sentiment have included South Carolina, Georgia, Alabama, Mississippi, Louisiana and Arkansas. Northern Democratic leaders habitually demand the delegates' "loyalty" to convention decisions.

Disputes over the validity of certain delegations' "credentials" have caused protracted squabbles during conventions in both the Democratic and Republican parties in recent years. Usually, the argument centers on the circumstances in which the challenged delegations were selected.

This often entails complex and inconclusive examinations of state and county conventions of the party.

Key Northern Democrats propose to reduce the strife, and save convention time, this year by avoiding exhaustive review of the way delegations were chosen. Instead, they will simply challenge the "good faith" of individual delegates.

Thus, one source said, if a delegate could be shown to be a militant segregationist, he

Continued on Page 48, Column 1

U.S. NOTE ACCUSES CASTRO OF WAGING A SLANDER DRIVE

Says Premier and Dorticos Are Sowing 'Animosity'—Cuba Rejects Protest

Text of the United States note will be found on Page 3.

By E. W. KENWORTHY
Special to The New York Times.

WASHINGTON, June 4—The Eisenhower Administration accused Cuba's Premier and President today of having carried on a "campaign of slander" against the United States.

In a note delivered early this afternoon in Havana, the State Department took vigorous exception to statements made by Premier Fidel Castro and President Osvaldo Dorticos Torrado.

These statements, the State Department said, were evidence that the Cuban Government, despite its protestations of friendship and understanding, actually "seeks to sow distrust and animosity" against the United States.

Clarification Sought

In view of this "official campaign of slander," the State Department said, the United States desires to "set the record straight" on its efforts to maintain traditionally friendly relations, "and to make clear to everyone the nature of the response which has been received from the Government of Cuba."

[The Cuban Foreign Ministry "categorically rejected" the protests in the United States note, but said the matters mentioned would be answered in "due course."]

The State Department has been considering sending a sharp note of protest to Cuba for some time, officials said. The decision to do so was taken this week as a result of the attacks on the United States by President Dorticos during a trip to several Latin-American countries.

Complaints Are Specific

The note, delivered by Daniel M. Braddock, counsel at the United States Embassy, listed nine specific complaints. Heading the list was a statement made by President Dorticós in Montevideo, Uruguay, that Cuba had reimbursed American owners for property

"To our knowledge," the note said, "not a single American property owner has been reimbursed for the lands taken from him."

The note reiterated earlier expressions of United States support for "sound policies of agrarian reform." But it charged the Cuban Government with having expropriated property—"frequently without receipt"—and with having physically expelled some American owners from their lands.

The United States Government, the note said, "cannot but protest in the strongest

Continued on Page 3, Column 1

Associated Press Wirephoto

CLASS REUNION: President Eisenhower greets members of the Class of 1915 at West Point. With him, from the left: General of the Army Omar N. Bradley, John Martin, manager of the Bear Mountain Inn, scene of the class party, and Gen. Fred Boye (ret.).

EISENHOWER SAYS KHRUSHCHEV'S IRE AIDS WEST'S UNITY

Asserts Tirades Are Serving to Forge the Strongest Bonds He Has Known

HE DENIES CRISIS EXISTS

President Declares That No Nation Dares Attack U.S. —Joins Class Reunion

Text of Eisenhower's address appears on Page 20.

By WAYNE PHILLIPS
Special to The New York Times.

BEAR MOUNTAIN, N. Y., June 4—President Eisenhower declared tonight that the "ill-tempered expressions" of Premier Khrushchev had united the West more than he had ever known it to be united before.

"We have stanch allies," the President said, speaking extemporaneously. "And as a matter of fact, many of the excesses—particularly the ill-tempered expressions—of Mr. Khrushchev have really brought the West closer together than I have known it, ever since I have been occupying my present office."

The President's remarks were a reply to recent personal attacks by Mr. Khrushchev. Yesterday the Premier said President Eisenhower was too dangerous to lead the United States and ridiculed his executive ability.

The President made the comment in a brief talk to 1,200 Republicans at a testimonial dinner at the Bear Mountain Inn for Representative Katharine St. George.

At 45th Class Meeting

He came to this area to attend the forty-fifth reunion of his class at the United States Military Academy at near-by West Point.

The President made his key point in recalling his West Point days. He said:

"You know at that moment, when the first European war had started, we were still cadets and the world seemed reasonably quiet—indeed, almost leisurely, in its approach to every question, public or private. We had no sense of urgency or tension.

"Now tonight, we meet at a time of bewilderment. I don't like this term, or the using of the term that we are living always in crisis. We are not. There is no nation in this world that dares at this moment to attack the United States and they know it.

"But we wonder what is the outcome of every decent, proper gesture we make to those that live in the other camp. They live in a closed society, secrecy of intent—which we try to penetrate—and in my opinion properly * * *."

The audience applauded en-

Continued on Page 20, Column 4

84 Party Contests Will Go To City's Voters Tuesday

By LEO EGAN

Eighty-four contests for nominations to public office or major positions in the Democratic or Republican parties will be up for decision in New York City in Tuesday's primary election. Elsewhere in the state, seventeen nominations for major public office are at stake.

In five Congressional districts there are contests for delegates and alternates to the Democratic convention.

There are no contests outside the city for seats at the Republican convention.

In the election districts within the city where contests are to be resolved, the polls will be open from 3 P. M. to 10 P. M. Elsewhere the voting hours are noon to 9 P. M. Polling places will be open only to resolve contests. Districts where there are no contests will not have any primaries.

42 for Nominations

Of the major primary contests within the city, forty-two are for nominations to public office, twenty-nine for party district leaderships in Brooklyn and Queens, and thirteen for delegates and alternates to the two national conventions.

Seven of the contests for nominations are in the Republican primary, thirty-five in the Democratic and one, begun by a petition for a write-in vote, in the Liberal.

The contests that have aroused the most attention are being fought on Manhattan's West Side.

They involve the Congressional nomination in the Twentieth District, the State Senate nomination in the Twenty-fifth Senate District, which covers substantially the same area, and

Continued on Page 31, Column 3

RAILROADS GIVEN TAX CUT BY STATE

6 Cities to Lose 12 Million a Year by '62—Aid Is Promised Localities

Special to The New York Times

ALBANY, June 4—The state acted today to cut the taxes railroads pay to six cities including New York. The cuts will reach a level of about $12,000,000 a year in 1962 after starting at $4,000,000 in the fiscal year beginning July 1.

The reductions were ordered under Governor Rockefeller's plan to aid commuter railroads. The state will reimburse the cities about one-half of the tax loss they will suffer.

The order reduced assessments on transportation property owned by railroads. Other property, such as hotels, is not affected. The order was issued by the State Board of Equalization and Assessment under a law passed last year to give railroads tax relief to compensate for low earnings. The exact amounts of the reduction are tentative.

Localities will receive state aid amounting to one-half of the reduction in their tax revenue from railroad property. Where such property is a substantial part of the local assessment roll, state aid will be increased so that no locality will lose more than about 2 per cent of its total taxable assessed valuation in any one year through railroad property exemptions.

In New York City, the reduction in assessments amounts to $64,050,259, or 16 per cent. The

Continued on Page 43, Column 1

REDS' GUNS SHELL QUEMOY HEAVILY

A 500-Round Attack Breaks Peiping Pledge Not to Fire on Even-Numbered Days

By United Press International.

TAIPEI, Taiwan, June 4—Communist China broke today its pledge to bombard Nationalist territory only on odd-numbered days and fired 500 shells at the Quemoy offshore islands in the heaviest barrage this year.

The shelling by coast artillery guns lent strength to a growing Nationalist belief that the Communists may order a new attack on the Quemoy and Matsu offshore island groups to coincide with President Eisenhower's twenty-five-hour visit to Taiwan June 18-19.

He will arrive here from the Philippines aboard the United States Navy heavy cruiser St. Paul. He will come ashore by helicopter.

79 Rounds on Day Before

A Nationalist Defense Ministry communiqué did not mention casualties or damage to the Quemoy complex just off the mainland port of Amoy. It said the barrage lasted thirty minutes.

By contrast, four batteries of Red shore guns fired only seventy-nine rounds at Quemoy and its cluster of smaller islands yesterday—an odd-numbered day.

Early last year, the Communists abruptly ordered a cease-fire on even-numbered days of the month for "humanitarian" reasons. Until today they had abided by it.

The nationalists said today's

Continued on Page 28, Column 1

Herter Cites U.S. 'Disgust' At Soviet Premier's Gibes

By JACK RAYMOND
Special to The New York Times.

WASHINGTON, June 4—Secretary of State Christian A. Herter expressed his "disgust" today at the conduct of Premier Khrushchev in personally attacking President Eisenhower. The Secretary of State accused the Soviet leader of attempting to degrade the standards of international relations. He said Mr. Khrushchev's outbursts "reflect credit neither on himself nor his Government."

Mr. Herter declared that it was "understandable" that the Soviet Premier should seek to divest himself of responsibility for the summit failure, but that this did not excuse the "personal attempts at vilification."

Backed by White House

President Eisenhower, who as a matter of policy says he never indulges in personalities, even on the domestic political scene, was nevertheless indirectly linked to Mr. Herter's comment.

The State Department's spokesman, David Waters, said he "assumed" that Mr. Herter's statement had been cleared with the White House.

The sharp, clearly angry retort was the United States Government's first formal reaction to the scorn and personal abuse that Premier Khrushchev has heaped on the President since the U-2 spy plane affair and the summit collapse.

[The father of Francis Gary Powers, the U-2 pilot downed and imprisoned by the Russians, decided to postpone his scheduled trip to the Soviet Union to see his son.]

For more than two weeks officials here have remained silent, more in wonder than in consternation, at the Soviet

Continued on Page 19, Column 3

KHRUSHCHEV SEEN IN KREMLIN CRISIS

Outburst Against President Is Linked to a Struggle for Power in Soviet

By HARRISON E. SALISBURY

A deepening leadership crisis in the Kremlin lies behind Premier Khrushchev's latest outburst, in the opinion of Soviet affairs experts. The evidence, including diplomatic reports from Moscow, indicates that Mr. Khrushchev is engaged in a tough struggle for power. The final results may not be apparent for weeks or months.

A central role in the tug of war, it was said, is being played by Mikhail A. Suslov, the old Stalin ideologist who has managed to extend his sphere of influence to the point where he is apparently able on occasion to command a majority in the ruling Presidium of the Communist party's Central Committee.

Question Is Parried

It was believed that Mr. Suslov's views have also commanded a majority within the Central Committee, at least on some occasions in the current crisis.

Mr. Khrushchev's public statements, it was said, reflect the harder Suslov line. They also were said to represent an effort by the Premier to strengthen himself against charges that he was "soft" on capitalism and permitted President Eisenhower to take him into camp.

Mr. Khrushchev was asked at his news conference Friday to amplify a remark he made in Paris that internal politics had played a role in the Soviet re-

Continued on Page 24, Column 1

Sports News

BASEBALL

The Yankees lost to the Red Sox, 8—2, at the Stadium yesterday. Roger Maris hit his thirteenth homer and Tony Kubek his fourth for the Yankees' runs. At San Francisco, Jack Sanford of the Giants defeated the St. Louis Cardinals, 2—0, with three-hit pitching. The Detroit Tigers' three-run tenth inning beat the Indians, 7—4, at Cleveland. The Chicago White Sox downed the Athletics at Kansas City, 4—2.

HORSE RACING

Royal Native carried the colors of William B. MacDonald Jr. to a length-and-a-half victory in the $56,900 Top Flight Handicap for fillies and mares before 39,239 racegoers at Belmont Park. Quill was second and Bug Brush third. Bill Hartack rode the favored Royal Native, who paid $4.90 for $2 and ran the mile and a sixteenth in 1 minute 43 seconds under top weight of 126 pounds. Mystic II took the $24,950 Brandywine Turf Handicap at Delaware Park.

TRACK AND FIELD

Al Oerter, the 1956 Olympic champion, won the discus throw at 190 feet 2½ inches in the New York Athletic Club spring games at Travers Island. Tom Carroll of Yale took the 800-yard run.

Details in Section 5

Rockefeller Urges Food Bank for War

By DONALD JANSON
Special to The New York Times

BISMARCK, N. D., June 4—Governor Rockefeller called today for converting much of the nation's farm surplus into a food reserve "to feed our people in the post-attack period in the event of a nuclear attack on this country."

He said the "blow-up" of the summit conference and the revival of East-West tensions made such "greater preparedness" necessary.

In an attack, he asserted, up to a year's supply of food will be needed, "strategically located all over the country." He said this would take nearly half the nation's huge oversupply of wheat.

"It would turn a present liability into a great national as-

Continued on Page 44, Column 1

Ancient Greek Tablet May Rewrite History

The New York Times June 5, 1960

Tablet telling of Greek-Persian conflict was found at Troezen (cross). Routes of Persian forces are indicated. Fleet was at first in two parts, one shown by light line.

By SANKA KNOX

A small and somewhat battered slab of marble discovered in Greece about a year ago may lay a new foundation for rewriting the history of two of the most famous battles of ancient times — Thermopylae and Salamis.

The slab, which is inscribed with a copy of a decree passed in Athens shortly before the historic battles between the Greeks and invading Persians in 480 B. C., was found in Troezen, a village south of Athens in the Peloponnesus.

Prof. Michael H. Jameson, who found the slab, called it the Athenian equivalent to the United States' Declaration of Independence or the Gettysburg Address.

The closest comparison Dr. Jameson could make was to the fragments remaining of the epigrams that were set up after the great Greek victory over

Continued on Page 70, Column 4

The marble tablet contains decree ordering the evacuation of Athens, and a plan for manning Greek ships to meet the Persians in the battles of Artemisium and Salamis.

'Magic' of Freedom Enchants Congolese

By HOMER BIGART
Special to The New York Times

LEOPOLDVILLE, Belgian Congo, June 4—"Does it come wrapped in paper and do we go to the bank and get it?" Lulua tribesmen asked an American missionary in Kasai Province.

They were asking about independence, a kind of magic box that will be given to them June 30. As the hour of freedom from Belgian rule nears, "In-de-pen-dence" is being chanted by Congolese all over this immense land, even by pygmies in the great equatorial forest.

Independence is an abstraction not easily grasped by the Congolese and they are seeking concrete interpretations. All seem to agree that it means an easier life.

To the forest pygmy independence means a little more salt, a little more beer. To ment-

Continued on Page 14, Column 1

Today's Sections

*Included in all copies in the New York metropolitan area and adjacent territory.

Index to Subjects

"All the News That's Fit to Print"

NEWS SUMMARY AND INDEX, PAGE 95

The New York Times.

LATE CITY EDITION

U. S. Weather Bureau Report (Page 95) forecasts: Chance of showers late today and tonight. Partly cloudy tomorrow. Temp. range: 79—60; yesterday: 83.3—56.3. Temp.-Hum. Index: low 70's; yesterday: 72.

SECTION ONE

VOL. CIX. No. 37,395.

NEW YORK, SUNDAY, JUNE 12, 1960.

35c outside New York City, its suburban area and Long Island. 50c in 17 Western states. Canada; higher in air delivery cities.

TWENTY-FIVE CENTS

NIXON URGES G.O.P. TO DEBATE ISSUES, THEN CLOSE RANKS

Tells National Committee 'We'll Lose if Divided' After the Convention

GOVERNOR IS NOT NAMED

States' Leaders Hear Plans Are Geared to Belief That Kennedy Will Be Foe

By WILLIAM M. BLAIR
Special to The New York Times.

WASHINGTON, June 11—Vice President Nixon called on Republicans today to discuss their differences over Administration policies and national issues before their Presidential nominating convention.

But after honest and candid debate, they should fall in solidly behind the party's nominee and platform, he told the Republican National Committee.

Mr. Nixon did not mention Governor Rockefeller in a breakfast talk on the last day of the committee's three-day meeting, saying only that Republicans who were discussing issues today "will discuss them and disagree on them without being disagreeable."

"We know that we have the fight of our lives on our hands," he said. "But we will win if we're united. We'll lose if we are divided."

Meets State Leaders

The standing ovation he received backed up the resolution adopted yesterday by the committee that gave Mr. Nixon equal billing with President Eisenhower on the development of Administration policies and programs.

With this backing, he proceeded to discuss his ideas on policies and programs and campaign plans in three closed meetings with state party leaders. The one-hour sessions were question-and-answer periods.

Committee members said after the first meeting, with mostly Northeastern state leaders, that Governor Rockefeller and his demand that Mr. Nixon clear his stand on major issues before the convention had not been mentioned.

Butler's Appraisal

While the national committee members strongly supported Mr. Nixon, the Democratic National Chairman, Paul M. Butler, characterized the reaction of Republican leaders to Governor Rockefeller as "go away, Nelson, you bother me."

The Republican meeting, he said, showed that the "Republicans would revert to slogans and epithets instead of joining in a great debate with the Democrats."

From the Republican meetings came reports that Mr. Nixon was planning his campaign on the assumption that Senator John F. Kennedy of Massachusetts would be his Democratic opponent. He did not, however, rule out the possibility that Senator Lyndon B.

Continued on Page 48, Column 1

Associated Press Radiophoto

HONORED AT TROOPING THE COLOR: Queen Elizabeth leaving Buckingham Palace yesterday to attend the ceremony. It was the official birthday of the British monarch.

EISENHOWER ASKS HOUSE TO REJECT FOREIGN-AID CUTS

Calls on Leaders to Restore Funds Trimmed by Panel —Sees Free World Peril

By E. W. KENWORTHY
Special to The New York Times

WASHINGTON, June 11 — President Eisenhower urged leaders of the House of Representatives today to use all their influence against heavy reductions in foreign-aid funds.

On the eve of his departure for the Far East, the President sent a telegram to House leaders in which he said that cuts voted by a House Appropriations subcommittee this week would "jeopardize our own security and the defense of the free world."

The President had asked for a total foreign-aid appropriation of $4,175,000,000. Congress had authorized a spending limit of $4,086,300,000.

The House Appropriations subcommittee recommended $3,384,500,000—about $800,000,000 below the original request. The subcommittee is headed by Representative Otto E. Passman, Democrat of Louisiana, a long-time foe of foreign aid.

Will Meet Tomorrow

The full Appropriations Committee will meet Monday to review the recommendations of the subcommittee.

Pointing out that he would be in the Far East when the full committee acts, the President said to the House leaders:

"For our own security, and for the common defense of the free world, I most earnestly request your cooperation in restoring these cuts."

The President directed his plea specifically at a $400,000,000 cut from military assistance and a $75,000,000 cut from defense support. The latter program provides economic aid to nations with which the United States is militarily allied.

Indus Project Defended

The President said nothing about other cuts and restrictions voted by the subcommittee. Many State Department officials, however, were equally, or even more, disturbed by the subcommittee's prohibition against the use of any funds for the Indus River project.

The Indus River development project is essential to the water-sharing agreement between India and Pakistan. It is central to Western plans for eventually getting India and Pakistan on the road to self-sustaining growth.

The total cost of the Indus project is estimated at about $1,000,000,000. However, the amount of American money that would be spent out of next year's funds for initial work would be modest.

The Administration had

Continued on Page 15, Column 1

United Press International Radiophoto

AT DEMONSTRATION IN TOKYO: Some of the sign-carrying marchers outside the U. S. Embassy yesterday.

U.S. Presses Kishi to Curb Threats Against President

By ROBERT TRUMBULL
Special to The New York Times.

TOKYO, Sunday, June 12—Ambassador Douglas MacArthur 2d warned Premier Nobusuke Kishi today of the "strong and adverse reaction" throughout the United States to Left-wing mob action in Japan against President Eisenhower's scheduled visit here June 19 to 22.

In a long meeting with Mr. MacArthur during this morning, Premier Kishi reassured the Ambassador that the "overwhelming majority of Japanese people" strongly disapproved of the Leftist demonstrations against General Eisenhower in recent weeks, and specially the display of anger against James C. Hagerty, the White House press secretary, and the Ambassador.

Mr. MacArthur, acting officially, was understood to have put considerable pressure on the Premier to keep Leftist demonstrations under control and assure the full safety of President Eisenhower during his stay in Japan.

Demonstrators Menacing

The meeting between Mr. MacArthur and Premier Kishi was at Mr. Kishi's request. A statement by the United States Embassy afterward said the Premier was acting on a strong feeling of regret on the part of most Japanese about Friday's outbreaks of anti-Americanism.

The assurances given by Mr. Kishi followed a raging continuance yesterday of the demonstrations.

The police reported that at least 100,000 Japanese milled through Tokyo's streets. Some carried placards voicing threats of violence and harm to President Eisenhower.

Mr. Hagerty, leaving late in the evening for Anchorage, Alaska, to meet President Eisenhower there, was a witness to these hostile demonstrations.

Mr. MacArthur told Premier Kishi at their conference that the attack on Mr. Hagerty, Thomas E. Stephens, the White House appointments secretary, and himself by the Leftist

Continued on Page 3, Column 5

PRESIDENT LEAVES FOR ORIENT TODAY; PLANS UNCERTAIN

Hagerty to Meet Eisenhower Party at Anchorage to Set Details of Itinerary

SHIFTS ON TOKYO LIKELY

But Visit to Japan Is Still Scheduled—Long Motor Trips May Be Curtailed

By WILLIAM J. JORDEN
Special to The New York Times.

WASHINGTON, June 11 Detailed plans for President Eisenhower's three-day visit to Japan were withheld today as he prepared to leave for the Far East on what probably will be his last major overseas trip as President.

The decision to delay releasing the schedule on Japan was made in Tokyo by James C. Hagerty, White House press secretary, after his experience there yesterday with Leftist demonstrators.

Stone-throwing demonstrators imprisoned Mr. Hagerty, Ambassador Douglas MacArthur 2d and Thomas E. Stephens, White House appointments secretary, in their automobile for an hour and twenty minutes at the Haneda International Airport. The three were rescued in a United States Marine Corps helicopter.

To Meet in Anchorage

Mr. Hagerty, who had gone to Japan to arrange for President Eisenhower's visit there on June 19, has left Tokyo to meet the President's party tomorrow in Anchorage, Alaska. It was believed that a final determination of the Tokyo schedule would be made only after Mr. Hagerty had talked with the President. The delay indicated that some revisions were likely in the schedule of the trip.

Despite threats of violence, the President was determined to go ahead with his visit to Japan as the guest of the Japanese Government. Only a suggestion from the Japanese Government could now produce a cancellation of that phase of the Far Eastern trip, it was believed.

7-Hour Flight to Alaska

President Eisenhower's jet will depart from Andrews Air Force Base, outside Washington, at 9 A. M. tomorrow. The flight to Anchorage will take 7 hours 15 minutes, but with time-zone changes, the arrival will be at 10:15 A. M. Alaskan time (4:15 P. M. New York time).

It was considered likely here that several planned public appearances by the President in Japan, including a news conference and an address to the Diet (Parliament), would be canceled. Security men were believed anxious to eliminate as much as possible any long motor trips and movements along exposed routes or through confined quarters.

Officials here were encour-

Continued on Page 8, Column 2

CROWDING EASED IN CITY'S PRISONS

But Mrs. Kross Says Level Is Still Dangerous—Asks for Extensive Reforms

By RUSSELL PORTER

Overcrowding in the city's prisons has been reduced substantially in the six years since Mrs. Anna M. Kross became Commissioner of Correction, but it is still dangerously high.

Mrs. Kross, a former city magistrate, long an advocate of prison reform, is seeking public support to eliminate overcrowding.

Since 1954 new facilities have been built and old ones remodeled or devoted to new uses. So far this year the prisons have held an average of 42 per cent more inmates than their official capacity. In 1954, however, they held an average of 58 per cent more than capacity.

The daily average number of inmates in 1954 was 6,677, compared with a normal rated capacity of 4,200. This year, the capacity is 6,325, but the daily average grew from 7,700 in January to 9,522 in May. The estimated daily average for 1960 is 9,000, on which the 42 per cent estimate is based.

Highest Was 9,834

The highest daily count in the history of the city's prisons was 9,834 on May 16—more than 50 per cent over capacity.

The upsurge in crime since World War II has led to a rapid increase in the number of persons sent to prison. The total number remanded rose from 42,539 in 1945 to 111,091 in 1959—an increase of 161 per cent.

Male prisoners are sent to detention prisons in the various boroughs except Staten Island to await trial. Those convicted and sentenced to city prisons go to the Rikers Island correctional institution or the Hart Island workhouse. The Women's House of Detention on Greenwich Avenue is both a detention and a sentence prison.

Mrs. Kross said the city's

Continued on Page 85, Column 1

Birthday Pageantry For Queen Enlivens A Gray London Day

By WALTER H. WAGGONER
Special to The New York Times.

LONDON, June 11—London's weather today was the kind that optimists say gives the girls of Britain their enviable pink-and-white complexions: mild, moist, an occasional spray of drizzle in the air.

Queen Elizabeth II, straight-backed in her sidesaddle on her chestnut mount, never looked more like a proper Queen, said those viewing their monarch in the Horse Guards Parade marking her official birthday.

She rode just ahead of Prince Philip in the traditional Trooping the Color ceremony. He had returned barely two and a half hours earlier from New York, where he had opened the British Exhibition.

The day had started out threatening rain and there was talk of postponing the pageantry. But the weather relented enough a half hour before the Queen arrived to permit the guardsmen to shed their blue-gray capes.

Traditional Observance

First the troops "keeping the ground" and then the units taking their positions for the parade burst out of their cloaks and blossomed into lines of scarlet tunics, giving the first real touch of color to the day.

The actual birthday of the 34-year-old Queen is April 26, but traditionally a day in June is set aside for official observances.

This morning, as the parade ground crackled with martial music, the barked orders of the Guards officers, the tramp of boots and the rattle of cavalry, the bells of Westminster Abbey pealed out their greetings, too, and a twenty-one-gun salute thundered in from Hyde Park, a mile away.

The Queen wore the scarlet tunic of the Grenadier Guards with the regimental badge and white plume in her black tricorner hat. The Duke of Edinburgh wore his uniform of a colonel in the Welsh Guards.

The color trooped was that of

Continued on Page 16, Column 6

SLUM DRIVE HERE REPORTED EBBING

Morningside Heights Group Finds Weakening of Attack on Problem Buildings

By EDITH EVANS ASBURY

The city is weakening its announced assault on slum buildings, according to a report issued by Morningside Heights, Inc.

The organization, formed by educational, religious and medical institutions in the vicinity of Columbia University, has been watching the operations of the courts and city departments in connection with housing since December, 1958.

Two recent developments of the city's handling of the slum problem were praised in the report. But it found that "there has been a progressive weakening of the attack, with a concomitant lessening of impact."

Recent vigorous prosecution of housing cases by Judah Gribetz, an assistant corporation counsel, and increased referral of cases to the Rent Commission for further action were cited as major steps forward since the organization's last report.

That report, issued last December, recommended referrals to the Rent Commission and said that the lack of a "prosecution attitude" was a major

Continued on Page 44, Column 3

2 LUXURY HOTELS SEIZED IN HAVANA

American-Run Nacional and Hilton Taken Over—Foe of Castro Captured

By R. HART PHILLIPS
Special to The New York Times.

HAVANA, June 11 — The Cuban Government seized the American-operated Habana Hilton and Nacional hotels today on the ground that the managers of these luxury hotels had failed to produce enough tourist business.

In his seizure order, the Minister of Labor, Augusto R. Martinez Sanchez, charged that the American operators had failed to bring in enough tourists "through their ample connections in the United States." He said this had produced a series of labor difficulties making it necessary to take over the hotels.

The Tropicana night club was also taken over by the Government. In addition, the St. John Hotel and the Rosita de Horneda Hotel were seized.

In another development, officials reported the capture of Capt. Manuel Beaton, a former aide of Premier Fidel Castro, who had turned against the regime and had been hunted.

The Cuban army said Captain Beaton was seized in the Sierra Maestra in Oriente Province. Captain Beaton had been in hiding in the mountains where the Castro revolution developed in 1957-58. The Army said he was alone when seized. He was armed with a revolver, the

Continued on Page 41, Column 1

Martha's Vineyard Beats Move To End Strike Tying Up Ferries

Meeting of Islanders Opposes Plan for Settlement—Tax Rise Feared by Many

By STANLEY LEVEY
Special to The New York Times.

EDGARTOWN, Mass., June 11—Martha's Vineyard, which normally lives on summer residents and tourists, is living on hope today.

Since April 15 a strike of ferryboat crews and officers has made it inconvenient—but not impossible—for visitors to get here from the mainland.

Now, with the start of college and high school vacations, islanders are hoping that the strike will be ended and that large numbers of sun-seeking, money-bearing summer people will share their time and wealth with them.

Last night Al Brickman, a successful Vineyard Haven merchant, and a few associates called a public meeting at the Tisbury High School. Their objective was to explain the terms of a tentative agreement between the union and the Steamship Authority, and to bring pressure on the authority to accept them.

Mr. Brickman and his associates thought a formula for settlement had been reached on Thursday when negotiators for the authority worked out a settlement with Local 59 of the International Brotherhood of Teamsters, representing the licensed personnel. But that

The New York Times June 12, 1960

Ferry route (heavy line)

same night the authority repudiated the arrangement.

At Mr. Brickman's meeting, attended by 300 persons, the opposition seized control. Led by Edward Vincent, an Edgartown Selectman and druggist, and Lee Calter, a hotel owner, this group won approval of a motion of its own backing the authority in its no-increase stand and in its ultimatum to the strikers to come back to work by Wednesday or lose their jobs.

This reflects sentiments here, which is not for peace at any price. Everybody wants the state-operated ferries, which also go to neighboring Nantucket, to run again, but almost nobody is saying: "Let's settle this and get down to business and worry about the cost later."

Instead, they are saying: "Don't give in," or "Principle

Continued on Page 46, Column 3

Pilots' Wildcat Strike Grounds 104 Eastern Air Lines Flights

By EDWARD HUDSON

A walkout of Eastern Air Lines pilots yesterday grounded 104 flights out of major cities in the East, Midwest and South. The line operates approximately 400 flights daily.

The pilots' action apparently was in protest against a new regulation issued by the Federal Aviation Agency requiring third pilots on jetliners to relinquish a forward seat when a Federal agency inspector makes a ride to check pilot efficiency.

A spokesman for the pilots' association in Chicago said the stoppages were an unauthorized "spontaneous rebellion." Eastern said the action was an unlawful strike.

The walkout began at Eastern's headquarters base in Miami at midnight Friday. Its effects spread to other cities. Pilots failed to show up for flights, reporting in sick or unable to get to work, according to an Eastern spokesman.

The airline reported last night it had canceled all flights out of Miami and some flights scheduled to depart from Detroit, Chicago, Boston, Minneapolis-St. Paul, St. Louis, Jacksonville, Fla., and New York.

At La Guardia and New York International Airports, twenty of 135 flights were canceled as of last night. Thirteen of forty-five flights were canceled at Newark Airport.

In Miami, approximately 2,000 Eastern Air Lines passengers were stranded yesterday afternoon. National Airlines, a competitor on the Miami-New York run, added extra sections in an effort to accommodate them. Forty-five immobilized Eastern planes created a parking jam

Continued on Page 45, Column 4

Ice Valley Found in Antarctic; Believed to Be 1,300 Miles Long

By WALTER SULLIVAN

Soviet polar scientists believe that a tremendous depression cleaves the central land mass of Antarctica. It may extend under the South Pole.

The Russians have named it the International Geophysical Year Valley in acknowledgment of the role played by Americans, Britons and Australians in progressively bringing it to light.

Where the valley empties into the Indian Ocean it is filled by what appears to be the world's largest glacier. This mountain-flanked river of ice has been charted by the Australians for more than 200 miles. If the valley, or the down-faulting of which it is a part, extends to the South Pole it would be more than 1,300 miles long.

The ice river has been named the Lambert Glacier by Australia. Some of the mountains along it were photographed by seaplanes of the United States Navy in 1947.

The view that the feature extends far inland is based primarily on soundings of the ice sheet by a Soviet tractor party traveling to the Pole of Inaccessibility.

On the way, the group passed over 10,000-foot mountains buried under 3,300 feet of ice. However, as the Russians neared the Pole of Inaccessibility — the point farthest from the sea—the ice sloped down slightly and the land beneath it dropped radically.

A similar drop was observed at the South Pole by Sir Vivian Fuchs and his men on their trans-Antarctic journey in 1957-58. Twenty-five miles on either side of the pole the ice-buried land was 7,000 to

Continued on Page 50, Column 3

Sports News

HORSE RACING

Celtic Ash, an English-bred colt, won the $150,900 Belmont Stakes by five and a half lengths yesterday. Venetian Way was second, Disperse third and the favored Tompion fourth in the ninety-second running of Belmont Park's classic race for 3-year-olds. Joseph E. O'Connell, the owner, netted $96,785 from Celtic Ash's triumph. Willie Hartack rode the victor, who paid $18.80 for $2.

BASEBALL

The Baltimore Orioles took the American League lead by beating the Kansas City Athletics, 6 to 5, in a ten-inning night game. The Yankees scored their fifth straight victory by topping the Cleveland Indians, 6 to 4, in the afternoon. The Indians now are second and the Yankees remain third. In the National League, the St. Louis Cardinals subdued the first-place Pittsburgh Pirates, 7 to 6. The Milwaukee Braves won from the second-place San Francisco Giants, 9 to 5.

TENNIS

Britain regained the Wightman Cup by defeating the United States women, 4—3, at Wimbledon, England.

Details In Section 5.

Today's Sections

Index to Subjects

"All the News That's Fit to Print"

The New York Times.

LATE CITY EDITION
U. S. Weather Bureau Report (Page 44) forecasts: Mostly fair today and tonight. Partly cloudy and warm tomorrow.
Temp. range: 82—64; yesterday: 80.5—61.8.
Temp.-Hum. Index: near 72; yesterday: 74.

VOL. CIX. No. 37,435. NEW YORK, FRIDAY, JULY 22, 1960. FIVE CENTS
10 cents beyond 50-mile zone from New York City except on Long Island. Higher in air delivery cities.

U. N. COUNCIL VOTE ASKS BELGIUM TO PULL OUT OF CONGO SPEEDILY; SOVIET REPLIES TO U.S. WARNING

United Press International Radiophoto

GHANAIAN TROOPS IN THE CONGO: Soldiers get into formation at Leopoldville's airport. The Soviet plane that carried them is in the foreground, before U. S. craft.

MOVE UNANIMOUS

Asian-African Proposal Adopted As Russian Defers Own Plan

Ceylon-Tunisia resolution and excerpts from debate, Page 4.

By THOMAS J. HAMILTON
Special to The New York Times.

UNITED NATIONS, N. Y., Friday, July 22—The Security Council, by unanimous vote, adopted early today a resolution requesting Belgium to proceed "speedily" with the evacuation of her troops from the Congo.

Vasily V. Kuznetsov, a Soviet First Deputy Foreign Minister, did not "press for a vote" on his resolution calling for withdrawal within three days.

The Soviet Union and Poland then joined the other nine members of the Security Council in adopting the milder resolution introduced yesterday by the two Asian-African members, Ceylon and Tunisia.

Second Round Ends

Britain, France and Nationalist China, which abstained on July 14 when the Security Council adopted a resolution recommending the withdrawal of the Belgian forces, supported the new request.

The vote was taken at 12:05 A. M., and the Security Council adjourned at 12:52 A. M. thus ending the second round of its considerat[illegible] that has [illegible] state of A[illegible] independence [illegible] June 30.

The Security Council will meet again this afternoon to take up the Soviet complaint against the United States over the RB-47 plane incident.

The unanimous vote, which is rare in Security Council proceedings, won the thanks of Secretary General Dag Hammarskjold.

Hammarskjold Going to Congo

He said that it would strengthen his efforts to build-up the United Nations Force now in the Congo as authorized by the resolution of July 14. Mr. Hammarskjold plans to leave for Leopoldville tomorrow.

Mr. Kuznetsov took the floor just before midnight to inform Henry Cabot Lodge of the United States that the American was "vastly mistaken" if he thought that his statement early yesterday regarding Soviet troops in the Congo would "frighten" the Soviet Union.

Mr. Lodge, after mentioning reports that the Soviet Union intended to send troops to the Congo, told the Security Council in its Wednesday night-Thursday morning session that, "with other United Nations members, we will do whatever may be necessary to prevent the intrusion of any military forces not requested by the United Nations."

Mr. Kuznetsov commented that "taking into account the

Continued on Page 3, Column 1

NIXON IS COURTING ROCKEFELLER IN BID TO WIN NEW YORK

Concessions on the Platform Look to November and 45 Electoral Votes

SPLIT IN STATE FEARED

Lodge Viewed as Favorite for 2d Spot—Governor Still Firm in Refusal

By LEO EGAN
Special to The New York Times.

CHICAGO, July 21—Vice President Nixon's supporters engaged today in a major effort to conciliate Governor Rockefeller through platform concessions.

Their purpose was to improve Republican chances of carrying New York State, with its rich prize of forty-five electoral votes, in the November elections.

Mr. Nixon, according to his supporters' calculations, is assured of the nomination for President at the Republican National Convention, which opens here Monday. Their concern is not with the nomination but with the election.

Governor Won't Yield

In line with the Nixon strategy of winning Governor Rockefeller over, Senator Thruston B. Morton suggested in a news conference that the eventual platform might be so much to Mr. Rockefeller's liking that he might change his mind about accepting second place on a Nixon ticket.

Robert L. McManus, the Governor's press secretary, countered immediately with a declaration that Mr. Rockefeller definitely would not consider second place.

Although ready to consider Governor Rockefeller for the Vice-Presidential nomination, Nixon supporters appeared to favor Henry Cabot Lodge, United States Ambassador to the United Nations.

President Eisenhower is known to have a high opinion of Mr. Lodge's handling of his United Nations assignment.

Others Considered

Other second-place possibilities receiving serious consideration from Mr. Nixon's supporters are Secretary of the Interior Fred A. Seaton of Nebraska and Senator Morton of Kentucky, national chairman.

Gov. William G. Stratton of Illinois warned today that the Republicans might be in trouble unless they picked a Midwesterner for second place. Unless Mr. Nixon favors some other Midwesterner, he said, he will place the name of Senator Everett McKinley Dirksen in nomination for the Vice-Presidency.

Herbert G. Klein, Mr. Nixon's press secretary, reported that the Vice President expected, if elected, to give his Vice President an even more important role in his Administration than Mr. Nixon had had under President Eisenhower.

"He would want a team-mate who can work closely with him and to whom he could give major domestic and foreign assignments," Mr. Klein said.

The Vice-Presidential choice, he continued, should be in general philosophic agreement with the President, although it is not

Continued on Page 8, Column 2

Rockefeller's Plans Keyed to Platform

By WARREN WEAVER Jr.
Special to The New York Times.

CHICAGO, July 21—Governor Rockefeller will wait until he sees the party platform next week before deciding whether to challenge Vice President Nixon.

This was the picture given today by one of the Governor's political advisers of the strategy he plans to follow when he returns to Chicago Saturday morning for the Republican National Convention. The convention opens Monday.

If the platform reflects enough of the positions he has been taking to satisfy him, Mr. Rockefeller will not authorize his nomination, on the theory that he does not intend to participate in a pure "popularity contest" with Mr. Nixon.

But if Mr. Rockefeller finds the platform substantially short

Continued on Page 9, Column 3

Chrysler President Lost Job Over $450,000 Side Profit

Newberg Agrees to Turn Over His Gains From Suppliers' Deals

By JOSEPH C. INGRAHAM

A difference of opinion on profits that William C. Newberg made from suppliers of parts to the Chrysler Corporation was the compelling reason for his sudden resignation as president of the automotive concern.

The disclosure was made yesterday by directors of Chrysler. They announced after a special secret meeting that a "settlement" agreement had been reached under which Mr. Newberg would turn over profits in excess of $450,000 to Chrysler.

Mr. Newberg, who started with Chrysler as a test mechanic in 1933 and became president last April 28, resigned on June 30 after sixty-four days as chief operating officer. Through his lawyers he emphatically denied any wrongdoing.

In Lansing, the Michigan Attorney General's office said that it had had no part in the investigation made by Chrysler into Mr. Newberg's interests.

"From the meager facts that

The New York Times
William C. Newberg

Continued on Page 45, Column 1

FIRM RIGHTS PLANK OFFERED BY NIXON

Negroes Hail 'Strong' Stand Given to Platform Panel—South Asks Moderation

By WILLIAM M. BLAIR
Special to The New York Times.

CHICAGO, July 21—Vice President Nixon delivered to the Republican National Convention's Platform Committee today what was described as a strong civil rights plank.

Word of Mr. Nixon's action heartened Negro leaders, who were told the plank represented a victory for them. They have pleaded with Republicans to match the strongest civil rights stand ever taken by the Democratic party or to face the loss of Negroes' votes.

The Vice President's proposed plank was brought to Chicago from Washington by Lawrence E. Walsh, deputy attorney general. It was understood that he would confer with Charles H. Percy, Chicago business executive and chairman of the Platform Committee, and that the proposal would be laid before the full committee in executive session tomorrow.

It was drafted by Mr. Nixon, Attorney General William P. Rogers, and Mr. Walsh. The statement for inclusion in the Republican platform was said to be "strong and temperate."

It will recommend actions be-

Continued on Page 8, Column 3

Kennedy Campaign To Open in Hawaii, With Alaska Next

By JOSEPH A. LOFTUS
Special to The New York Times.

HYANNIS PORT, Mass., July 21—Senator John F. Kennedy will formally begin his campaign for President in the two new states, Hawaii and Alaska, about Sept. 1.

This departure from tradition—not only the scenes but also the pre-Labor Day dates—will symbolize his campaign theme, the New Frontier, which he enunciated in his speech accepting the Democratic nomination.

"These two states represent the continuing prospects for growth and vitality in America," the Massachusetts Senator said in a statement at his summer home here. "They are in a sense symbols of the New Frontier."

Democratic nominees for President in recent years have formally opened their campaigns on Labor Day in Cadillac Square, Detroit. Senator Kennedy will speak there this year, on Labor Day, which is Sept. 5, but that speech will be preceded by appearances in Hawaii and Alaska, in that order. The dates for these speeches have not been announced.

"The spirit of adventure which drove men to Hawaii and Alaska must be awakened again in the American people if we are to maintain our position

Continued on Page 9, Column 5

EISENHOWER SEEKS AN EARLY MEETING OF U. N. ARMS BODY

Instructs Lodge to Request It as Soon as Possible in View of Geneva Break-Up

By FELIX BELAIR Jr.
Special to The New York Times.

NEWPORT, R. I., July 21—President Eisenhower moved today for an early meeting of the United Nations Disarmament Commission.

He instructed Henry Cabot Lodge, the United States delegate, to request the earliest possible convening of the commission "so that we and other members of the international community can continue to search for ways and means to achieve the universal desire to reduce the risk of war by controlled steps of disarmament."

The United States move to bring the disarmament issue before the United Nations will be made formally tomorrow by Mr. Lodge in a letter to Secretary General Dag Hammarskjold.

Course Held Imperative

In a statement from the summer White House here President Eisenhower made it clear that his course was imperative in view of the abrupt break-up of the ten-nation talks in Geneva by the Soviet Union last month, when the five Soviet-bloc nations attending walked out of the East-West disarmament conference.

In making available the President's statement, James C. Hagerty, White House press secretary, said in that instructing Mr. Lodge to seek an "early" meeting of the United Nations agency President Eisenhower had in mind "a matter of weeks—not months."

The text of the President's statement read:

"I have been greatly concerned that everything possible be done to make progress on the question of disarmament.

"The abrupt break-up of the ten-nation talks in Geneva by the Soviet Union last month makes it desirable to take further steps so that the vital issue of disarmament can be considered promptly once again. Our efforts to get the Soviet Union to return to the conference table through normal diplomatic channels have not met with success.

"The need for disarmament in the present world situation is too important to set aside at the present time when deliberate efforts are being made to increase tensions.

"The United Nations under the Charter has primary responsibility in this field. I

Continued on Page 2, Column 5

Oldest American Art Is Found

30,000-Year Fossil Revises Dating of Man's Arrival

By SANKA KNOX

Man was in the Western Hemisphere about 30,000 years ago and left the earliest art known in the Americas to document his existence here, two scientists reported yesterday.

The evidence of man's presence—a bit of elephant bone engraved with pictures of beasts—constitutes what was described as a major breakthrough in American archaeological chronology.

The discovery, made last year in Mexico by Dr. Juan Armenta Comacho, appears to push back by 20,000 years the earliest date hitherto found for man in this hemisphere.

Dr. Armenta, who is director of the Department of Anthropology at the University of Puebla in Mexico, said that he had dug his trophy out of desert soil and gravel at Balsequillo, about ten miles southeast of Puebla and sixty miles southeast of Mexico City.

The bit of bone, 6 by 4½ inches in size, is a pelvic fragment of a mastodon or a mammoth. It contains still-crisp impressions of a primitive horse, a camel and a type of mastodon that was thought to have died out 100,000 years ago.

Dr. Armenta's finding that the bone was 30,000 years old has been corroborated by Dr. H. Marie Wormington, curator of archaeology at the Denver Museum of Natural History.

Dr. Wormington, reached by

Continued on Page 20, Column 6

The 30,000-year-old mastodon pelvic bone with animal pictures inscribed on it was found near Puebla, Mexico. The bone fragment measures six by four and a half inches.

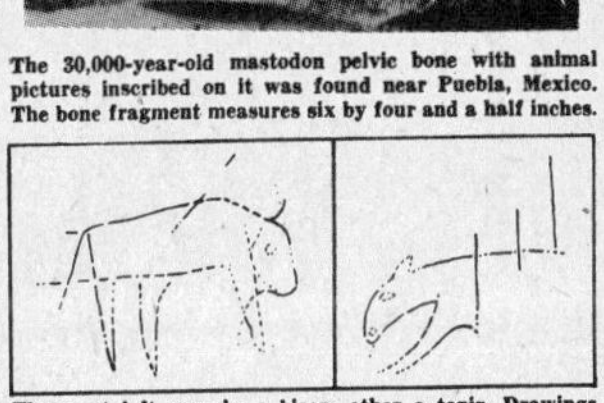

Figure at left may be a bison, other a tapir. Drawings were reproduced from bone by Fernando Ramirez Osorio.

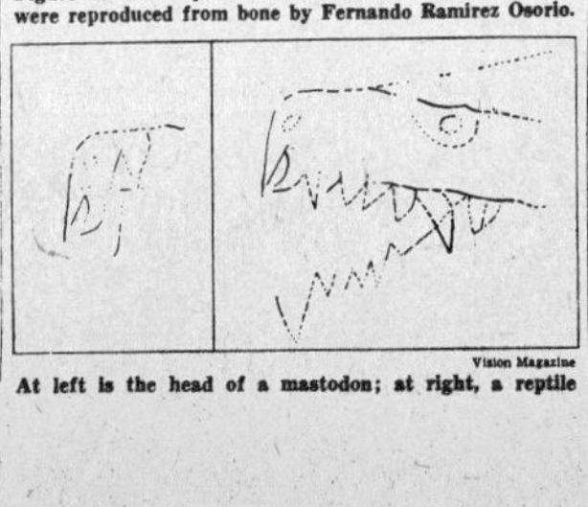

Vision Magazine

At left is the head of a mastodon; at right, a reptile

LUMUMBA COMING TO CONSULT IN U.N.

Decision to Fly Here Eases Tension—Soviet Planes Join Congo Airlift

By HENRY TANNER
Special to The New York Times.

LEOPOLDVILLE, the Congo, July 21—Premier Patrice Lumumba informed the Congo Senate today that he planned to fly to New York to state his case in the United Nations Security Council.

[After the Security Council vote there was speculation in United Nations circles whether Mr. Lumumba would carry through his plan to come here.]

Congolese officials said the Premier would leave tomorrow morning aboard a Ghana Airways plane. They said he would stop in Accra for consultations with President Kwame Nkrumah before flying on to New York.

The Lumumba statement brought some easing of the tension caused by the Congo's threats to invite Soviet troops to expel Belgian forces.

Hunger Threat Rising

However, the food and health crisis grew worse. Congolese women and children searched rubbish dumps for food as United Nation officials rushed to distribute supplies flown in by airlift. A breakdown of water filtration equipment threatened a spread of disease.

Observers now feel that a Congolese appeal for Soviet military intervention has been headed off, at least for the next week.

They doubt that the Government will take drastic action during the Premier's trip or during the subsequent visit to Leopoldville by Secretary General Dag Hammarskjold.

Mr. Hammarskjold was due Next Monday but it is assumed

Continued on Page 3, Column 1

U.S. Grants Poland $130,000,000 More

Special to The New York Times.

WASHINGTON, July 21—The United States agreed today to sell Poland $130,000,000 worth of surplus farm products.

The new agreement raises to $426,300,000 the value of agricultural products covered in agreements between Washington and Warsaw in the last four years. It followed by less than a week another agreement under which Poland pledged to pay $40,000,000 over a twenty-year period to compensate United States citizens whose property was seized in Poland after World War II.

The claims settlement, long in dispute between the two countries, paved the way for the new farm products sale under Public Law 480. It was apparent that without the agreement in the claims dispute, the United States would not have

Continued on Page 6, Column 5

Herter Sees Russian Bluff In Threat to Send Troops

By WILLIAM J. JORDEN
Special to The New York Times.

WASHINGTON, July 21—Secretary of State Christian A. Herter said today that he doubted the Soviet Union would carry out its threat to send combat troops to the Congo. The Secretary read a statement in which he said he found it "hard to believe" that Moscow was ready to "set itself against the United Nations" by a separate action.

Asked if he meant that the Russians were bluffing, the Secretary said at a news conference that that was "a fair implication." [Question 21, Page 2.]

Transcript of Herter's news conference is on Page 2.

Mr. Herter sharply denied a Soviet allegation that United States combat troops had been sent to the Congo. Mr. Herter said the United States personnel there were engaged in air-traffic control, aircraft maintenance and communications work.

U. N. Approval Noted

He said that the men assigned to help with the Congo airlift were in Leopoldville with the approval of the United Nations and that they would stay only as long as they were required by the United Nations.

He called the Soviet demand for their immediate withdrawal a "deliberate, unilateral attempt to obstruct the United Nations efforts in the Congo."

The description of the Soviet move was contained in a statement delivered orally this afternoon to a representative of the Soviet Embassy here by Richard H. Davis, Deputy Assistant Secretary of State for European Affairs. Mr. Herter read the statement at his news conference.

In his statement on the Congo, the Secretary called Premier Khrushchev's threat "recklessly irresponsible" whether the Russian intended to carry it out or not.

Spur to Tensions Seen

Mr. Herter said Moscow's threat, repeated last night at the United Nations by the Soviet delegate, "can only be designed to increase tensions in the area and make more likely the continuation of hostilities and disorder."

The Secretary fully supported the warning of Henry Cabot Lodge, the United States delegate to the United Nations, that Washington would oppose Soviet intervention in the Congo. He said the United States, in cooperation with other members of the United Nations, would "take such action as we thought was required" should Moscow send troops without

Continued on Page 2, Column 1

TRUJILLO SNUBBED IN U.S. SUGAR MOVE

Extra Quota for 12 Nations Omits Dominicans—Cuba Aided in World Market

By TOM WICKER
Special to The New York Times.

WASHINGTON, July 21—The Agriculture Department authorized today the purchase of 617,385 tons of sugar from thirteen countries or foreign possessions to replace amounts cut from Cuba's quota.

[In London, the International Sugar Council increased export quotas to enable Cuba to sell to other countries the sugar the United States has refused to buy. In Washington, Secretary of State Herter said the United States planned no military action against Cuba.]

The action included an unexpected snub to Cuba's chief Caribbean rival, the Dominican Republic of Generalissimo Rafael Leonidas Trujillo Molina, and a windfall for five other Latin-American countries, including Brazil.

A purchase authorization for the Dominican Republic had been expected but was not issued "at this time." The nation has a regular quota for sales in the United States market.

An Agriculture Department spokesman gave no reason for the failure to authorize a Dominican purchase. But he left the way open for the autnor-

Continued on Page 7, Column 1

Soviet Patrol Halted U.S. Ship In International Waters July 7

Vessel Stopped in Pacific

By EDWARD A. MORROW

An American freighter was stopped by an armed Soviet patrol vessel in international waters of the Pacific July 7 and asked to identify herself, it was disclosed yesterday.

Admiralty lawyers said the action constituted a violation of international maritime law. Navy intelligence sources said yesterday that they had been informed of the Soviet action.

It followed by a week the Soviet downing of an American RB-47 reconnaissance plane off the Soviet coast on the Barents Sea. The Russians said the plane had flown over Soviet territorial waters. The United States denied this.

The ship incident, according to Capt. David Baer, assistant vice president of Maritime

Continued on Page 6, Column 2

View on 'Buzzing' Disputed

WASHINGTON, July 21—The United States told the Soviet Union today that it would continue to check on Soviet ships in international waters, particularly those approaching the American coasts.

Washington denied a Soviet allegation that identification flights near Soviet vessels constituted a danger to the safety of such ships. It denounced Russia's warning that she would "take other measures to insure the safety of Soviet vessels in open seas" as a "reckless threat of aggressive action against United States aircraft."

The United States stated its views in a note delivered today to the Soviet Foreign Ministry. It was an answer to a Soviet protest July 13 against "buzz-

Continued on Page 5, Column 3

"All the News That's Fit to Print"

The New York Times.

LATE CITY EDITION
U. S. Weather Bureau Report (Page 58) forecasts: Fair and pleasant today, tonight and tomorrow. Temp. range: 77—62; yesterday: 77.1—62.5. Temp.-Hum. Index: low 70's; yesterday: 71.

VOL. CIX. No. 37,469. | © 1960, by The New York Times Company. Times Square, New York 36, N. Y. | NEW YORK, THURSDAY, AUGUST 25, 1960. | 10 cents beyond 50-mile zone from New York City except on Long Island. Higher in air delivery cities. | FIVE CENTS

PRESIDENT TAUNTS KENNEDY ON SPLIT IN PARTY'S RANKS

Says He Can't Understand Why Senator Wants More Democrats in Congress

HEAVY MAJORITIES CITED

Foreign Policy, Farm Plans and 'Fiscal Responsibility' Called the Chief Issues

Transcript of news conference and summary, Page 22.

By FELIX BELAIR Jr.
Special to The New York Times.

WASHINGTON, Aug. 24—President Eisenhower attacked the Democrats today, using the ammunition of their Presidential candidate to show why the Republicans should win the White House and Congress in the November elections.

At his news conference, the President said he could not understand why Senator John F. Kennedy wanted more Democrats in Congress, when they already had a 2-to-1 majority in both houses and "can do anything they want to if they get together." [Question 1, Page 22.]

The President had been asked to comment on a statement by Senator Kennedy after the Senate defeat yesterday of his version of the medical aid bill. The Senator said that "If we are going to have effective legislation, we are going to have to have an Administration that will provide leadership and a Congress that will act."

Sees Program Lagging

After remarking on the Democrats' inability to pass their own legislative program despite their majorities, the President said he could not see what they would do with even greater numbers.

As for leadership, he said that while the Democrats complained about his request for enactment of his twenty-one-point program in the current short session, the same measures had been pending since January.

The President also told of Vice President Nixon's role in the Administration, saying that Mr. Nixon took part in policy discussions but took no part in making decisions. He said the President alone made the decisions. [Questions 13 and 20.]

At his third straight weekly news conference since returning to Washington from his Newport, R. I., vacation, the President also made these points on political campaign issues, tactics and candidates:

¶In his estimate the chief issues of the campaign would center on his Administration's conduct of foreign policy, the farm problem and his ideas of "fiscal responsibility," which must be followed to prevent

Continued on Page 22, Column 2

Live-Virus Polio Vaccine Approved for Use in U. S.

Public Health Group Ends Dispute by Selection of Sabin Compounds

By BESS FURMAN
Special to The New York Times.

WASHINGTON, Aug. 24—Live-virus poliomyelitis vaccine was approved today as suitable for use in the United States.

The announcement, ending a long controversy, was made by Dr. Leroy E. Burney, Surgeon General of the Public Health Service.

Simultaneously, he laid down exacting rules under which the live-virus vaccine would be licensed for commercial use in this country. His timetable calls for this to take place next spring. He predicted large supplies by the fall of 1961. He said the winter months were best for live polio vaccinations.

The live-virus vaccine, given by mouth, has already been used to immunize millions of persons in the Soviet Union, South America and other parts of the world. It is a virus so weakened as not to cause the disease, but still alive enough to produce antibodies.

In manufacture of the Salk vaccine, used in this country since 1955, the virus is heat-killed to a point where it will not cause disease, but still will produce antibodies. It is given by injection.

Dr. Burney predicted today that the live vaccine would not replace the Salk variety, but that each would complement

Continued on Page 59, Column 3

United Press International Telephoto
Dr. Leroy E. Burney as he told of action on vaccine.

CONGO TROOPS FLY TO KASAI TO STOP SECESSION EFFORT

Lumumba Acts to Crush Bid to Create a New State in Area of Tribal Conflict

By HENRY TANNER
Special to The New York Times.

LEOPOLDVILLE, the Congo, Aug. 24 — Premier Patrice Lumumba sent Congo Army units today to Luluabourg, capital of Kasai Province, in his first serious effort to check a secessionist movement there.

The movement follows nearly two months of bitter fighting by two hostile tribes, the Lulua and the Baluba. It is led by Albert Kalonji, a Baluba chief and political opponent of Premier Lumumba.

Mr. Kalonji has declared the independence of a part of Kasai Province that he calls Mining State and has turned to President Moise Tshombe of the secessionist Katanga Province for support.

Three Companies Sent

Three companies of Congo Army troops — 200 men — left Ndjili Airport at Leopoldville this morning in five planes. This was the first major troop movement by the Congo Army since independence June 30. It was the mutiny of the army early in July that led to United Nations intervention in the Congo.

The Congo Government requisitioned the planes from Air Congo, a subsidiary of the Belgian airline Sabena. The United Nations had refused to make its planes available for the troop movement. Some of the planes bore United Nations markings because they had been chartered earlier by the world organization.

While the official reason given for sending the troops to Luluabourg was to end the tribal fighting that is reported to have cost several hundred lives, officials made it clear that the real reason was to strike at Mr. Kalonji.

New State a Baluba Area

Mr. Kalonji claims the territory to the east, south and west of Luluabourg. His is an all-Baluba state. There have been reports of large-scale population movements, with the Balubas moving south and the Lulua crowding into the Luluabourg area.

Mr. Kalonji formerly was allied with Mr. Lumumba in the Congolese National Movement. Differences before independence caused them to split and each thereafter headed separate factions of the party.

Meanwhile, the United Nations sent Col. Henry Byrne of Ireland to Albertville, in Katanga, to investigate reports that Mali soldiers had mutinied and had killed two Congolese.

Heavy fighting was reported in the Albertville area yesterday but reports conflicted about whether the Mali forces had

Continued on Page 2, Column 4

SENATE RESTORES HOUSE CUT IN AID; VOTES 3.9 BILLION

Bill Now Goes to Conferees —Kennedy Rebuffed Anew on $1.25 Minimum Pay

By TOM WICKER
Special to The New York Times.

WASHINGTON, Aug. 24—The Senate passed a $3,989,054,000 foreign-aid appropriation today, restoring virtually all the cuts made earlier in the House of Representatives.

The vote was 67 to 26, with most of the opposition coming from Southern Democrats. Fifteen of them joined four other Democrats and seven Republicans in opposition to the appropriation. Voting for it were forty-one Democrats and twenty-six Republicans.

Included in the bill was a $100,000,000 item requested by President Eisenhower for use in the Congo and other African emergencies. The appropriation measure now goes to a Senate-House conference for final shaping.

The bill included authority for the President to cut off aid funds for any country giving arms or economic aid to Cuba or weapons to the Dominican Republic.

Democrats Discouraged

The action on foreign aid was one of the few definite accomplishments in a Congressional day of rumor, confusion and growing discouragement on the part of the Democrats.

Their entire legislative program for the post-convention session appeared endangered, and sentiment for a quick adjournment was growing.

There was particularly bitter news in the House for the Democratic Presidential candidate, Senator John F. Kennedy of Massachusetts. There, the Rules Committee joined Republicans and Southern Democrats in opposition to the Kennedy program.

The committee delayed approval of a Senate-House conference on the Kennedy-sponsored minimum-wage bill.

Smith Gives Views

Reports trickling out of its closed meeting indicated that the Democratic chairman, Representative Howard W. Smith of Virginia, had said that the minimum-wage bill would be cleared for conference only at the expense of two other Democratic measures—a school construction bill and another to relax picketing restrictions on building trades unions.

Potential House conferees on the minimum-wage bill made it clear, moreover, that they would fight hard for their version. It would provide an increase from $1 an hour to $1.15, instead of the $1.25 in the Senate bill, and the number of new workers it would cover is much lower.

Representative Graham A. Barden of North Carolina, the Southern Democrat who heads

Continued on Page 23, Column 1

Castro Affirms Red Ties; Challenges Americas Unit

United Press International Telephoto
Premier Fidel Castro speaking early yesterday in Havana

By R. HART PHILLIPS
Special to The New York Times.

HAVANA, Aug. 24—Premier Fidel Castro defied the Organization of American States today and declared that "we are friends of the Soviet Union and of the Chinese People's Republic."

The revolutionary leader spoke as the foreign ministers of the American nations began consideration of the threat of Soviet intervention in the Western Hemisphere through increasingly close relations with the Castro regime.

"With the O. A. S. or without the O. A. S., we will win the fight," the Premier asserted. "With the O. A. S. or without the O. A. S. we will triumph. With the O. A. S. or without

Continued on Page 12, Column 4

Senate Adopts Ban on Aid To Nations Assisting Cuba

By E. W. KENWORTHY
Special to The New York Times.

WASHINGTON, Aug. 24—The Senate voted todav to cut off foreign-aid funds to any nation supplying arms or economic assistance to Cuba. The action came on an amendment to the mutual security appropriations bill offered by Senator Styles Bridges, Republican of New Hampshire.

The amendment declared that United States aid would be denied any country that the President determined "directly or indirectly is selling arms, munitions or implements of war, to the Castro regime in Cuba, or directly or indirectly is giving or loaning military or economic aid to that regime."

Following this action, the Senate approved an amendment by Senator Wayne Morse, Democrat of Oregon, that would apply the same penalty to any nation that, in the President's judgment, was selling arms or giving military aid to any Latin-American country "being subjected to economic or diplomatic sanctions by the Organization of American States."

Action by Voice Vote

Last Saturday the foreign ministers of the American republics voted such sanctions against the Dominican Republic because of its acts of "aggression and intervention" against Venezuela.

Both of the Senate amendments today were approved by voice vote.

At his news conference today President Eisenhower said he did not want to admit that the situation in Cuba was "irretrievable."

Cuba, he said, "has been one of our finest friends." The United States conducted the war that set her free, he said, and "we have tried to keep our hands out of their internal political affairs."

The President said that he would like to see the Organization of American States use its collective "moral and political influence in straightening out

Continued on Page 13, Column 1

DOMINICAN ISSUES STIR CAPITAL RIFT

Some Southern Democrats Defend Trujillo — Dillon Asks Sugar Quota Curb

By WILLIAM J. JORDEN
Special to The New York Times.

WASHINGTON, Aug. 24—A sharp dispute has broken out between the Eisenhower Administration and a number of Southern Democrats in Congress over United States policy toward the Dominican Republic.

Under Secretary of State Douglas Dillon took the Administration's case before the House Agriculture Committee today. He sought support for President Eisenhower's appeal to Congress to cancel the extra sugar quota allotted to the Dominican Republic after the Cuban quota was cut in July.

Mr. Dillon described Generalissimo Rafael Leonidas Trujillo Molina, the Dominican ruler, as a tyrant, a torturer and a murderer.

In the Senate, almost as Mr. Dillon was testifying before the House group, Senator Allen J. Ellender, Democrat of Louisiana, praised General Trujillo as the administrator of a strong democracy.

"I wish there were a Trujillo in every country of South and Central America tonight," Mr. Ellender said.

"To reduce the sugar quota of a country (Cuba) with a Leftist dictator only to grant a substantial portion of that quota to a dictator whose ac-

Continued on Page 16, Column 3

O. A. S. ABANDONS HOPE FOR ACCORD IN U. S.-CUBA FIGHT

Foreign Ministers Move to Counter the Communists' Threat in Hemisphere

HERTER STAND BACKED

Secretary Scores Castro Links With Red Bloc—Urges Parley to Act

Text of Herter's address to O. A. S. is on Page 12.

By TAD SZULC
Special to The New York Times.

SAN JOSE, Costa Rica, Aug. 24—Shocked by Premier Fidel Castro's defiance of the Organization of American States, Latin-American foreign ministers abandoned hope today for a political compromise with the Cuban regime.

The ministers moved instead toward action to counter the threat of Communist intervention in the Western Hemisphere.

The delegates shifted closer to the position of Secretary of State Christian A. Herter, who said today that the Castro regime was leading Cuba "in the Communist direction."

Mr. Herter told the conference of foreign ministers the Hemisphere was faced by "the urgent challenge" of "Sino-Soviet imperialism." H asked the conference to take "the necessary positive decisions to meet the threat."

Others Support Stand

Speeches today by Argentine, Chilean, Guatemalan, Salvadoran and several other ministers following Mr. Herter showed the determination of the Latin-American group to condemn strongly the Communists' infiltration in the Hemisphere. The effort now will be to apply special measures against it.

Dr. Castro, in a speech in Havana, defied the O. A. S. He declared that Cubans were "friends of the Soviet Union and of the Chinese People's Republic."

"The leaders of the Soviet Union and Communist China have made abundantly clear their determination to exploit the situation in Cuba as a means of intervening in inter-American afairs," Mr. Herter declared.

"Their purpose is to break solidarity, sow distrust and fear among the people of the American Hemisphere, and thereby prepare the way for political control of the New World."

The possibility of a Cuban walkout was discounted by diplomats who talked with Foreign Minister Raul Roa of Cuba. Dr. Roa is now believed planning to restate in a speech Dr. Castro's attack on the inter-American system. Until the last minute,

Continued on Page 12, Column 7

NIXON GIVES ARMS BUDGET PRIORITY

Tells V. F. W. Nation Must Hold Its Lead, Even if Taxes Must Go Up

Excerpts from Nixon speech are printed on Page 23.

By DAMON STETSON
Special to The New York Times.

DETROIT, Aug. 24 — Vice President Nixon asserted today that the security of the United States must have the highest priority even if an increase in taxes should be necessary.

He spoke before 10,000 persons at the national convention here of the Veterans of Foreign Wars. The Republican nominee for President emphasized that the United States, if it is to give leadership to the world and guarantee peace, must have military strength that is second to that of no other country.

While he saw no necessity at present for raising taxes, Mr. Nixon made it clear that he would favor higher levies and greater defense spending if that should be required to assure the nation's safety.

U-2 Flight Cited

Although his address was billed as nonpolitical, the Vice President delivered an indirect thrust on an old theme at his Democratic opponent, Senator John F. Kennedy.

Senator Kennedy, who called off an earlier appearance at the V. F. W. convention this week, is now scheduled to address the delegates on Friday.

Mr. Nixon's oblique reference to his opponent was made in connection with the aftermath of the disastrous U-2 flight made over the Soviet Union on May 1.

The Vice President, apparently referring to Mr. Kennedy, noted that some people had suggested that President Eisenhower might have apologized for the U-2 incident and have

Continued on Page 23, Column 4

KENNEDY ATTACKS NIXON 'WEAKNESS'

In Alexandria, He Assails Foreign Policy Leadership —Avoids Rights Issue

Excerpts from Kennedy speech will be found on Page 20.

Special to The New York Times.

ALEXANDRIA, Va., Aug. 24—Senator John F. Kennedy attacked Vice President Nixon's experience and foreign policy leadership tonight as those of "weakness, retreat and defeat."

Moving into the South for the first time since he was nominated at Los Angeles, the Democratic Presidential candidate sidestepped any mention of the controversial civil rights issue that has split his party here.

[In Washington, Mr. Kennedy's office announced that James W. Wine, a lay Protestant leader, had been enlisted to help combat the problems the Senator, as a Roman Catholic, was encountering in the campaign.]

He brought with him his Vice-Presidential running mate, Senator Lyndon B. Johnson of Texas, who also made no mention of the civil rights issue in a brief talk.

15,000 Cheer Speech

The foreign policy speech made by Senator Kennedy was the harshest attack he has yet unleashed against his Republican rival. But his barbs brought applause and cheers from a crowd of more than 15,000 packed into the flood-lighted George Washington High School Stadium.

The Kennedy-Johnson ticket won the endorsement of most of Virginia's ruling Democratic powers, but the most important leader of them all—Senator Harry F. Byrd—was noticeably absent. Pledges of support came, however, from Gov. J. Lindsay Almond Jr. and Senator Byrd's junior colleague,

Continued on Page 20, Column 5

FOLEY SQ. CENTER TO RISE 41 STORIES

Design for Federal Offices Includes Customs Court

The Federal Government announced details yesterday for the $70,000,000 center it will build west of Foley Square. The center will consist of two buildings, one forty-one stories tall, connected in an L-shape to provide a large plaza with a pool.

According to the announcement by the General Services Administration, the construction arm of the Federal Government, the final plans and specifications are scheduled to be completed next spring.

A spokesman for the agency described the design as "two contrasting components" — a Customs Court Building and an office building for eighteen agencies of the Executive Branch of the Government.

The office building will be the forty-one-story one. The court building will be eight stories.

Columns of limestone and black granite will be set around the base of the building, which will be set back from the street. The walls above the plaza will have limestone and metal panels. The buildings will contain 1,800,000 square feet of floor space.

Almost two years ago the

Continued on Page 25, Column 2

A Kennedy and a Rockefeller Seek Puerto Rican Votes Here

Democrat Tours Harlem

By PETER KIHSS

The politicking and the handshaking season on "las veredas de Nueva York"—the sidewalks of New York, specifically Spanish Harlem—started last night when Robert F. Kennedy popped his head out of an open-top radio bus.

He also rode and walked and consumed a pastelillo—a meat pie—in a two-and-a-quarter-hour bid for support for his brother, Senator John F. Kennedy of Massachusetts, as Democratic Presidential nominee among the city's Puerto Ricans.

He tried a few Spanish phrases—"muy bueno" (very good)—for some Puerto Rican coffee, and "hasta la vista" (see you later) when he left one group or another. But he candidly told reporters it had been

Continued on Page 19, Column 1

Post for Governor's Son

By LAYHMOND ROBINSON

Governor Rockefeller's Spanish-speaking eldest son was chosen yesterday to get out the Puerto Rican and Negro votes in the state for the Nixon-Lodge ticket.

The Governor's 28-year-old son, Rodman C. Rockefeller, has been active politically in Puerto Rican and Negro districts since his father's campaign in 1958.

He was selected by state Republicans to coordinate the campaign activities among the two minority groups in what Republican leaders called "the most intensive drive in the party's history" for such votes in a Presidential campaign.

Republican leaders, who were encouraged by defections among Negro and Puerto Rican Democrats to the Republican column

Continued on Page 18, Column 4

Atom Submarine Opens Route Under Ice of Northwest Passage

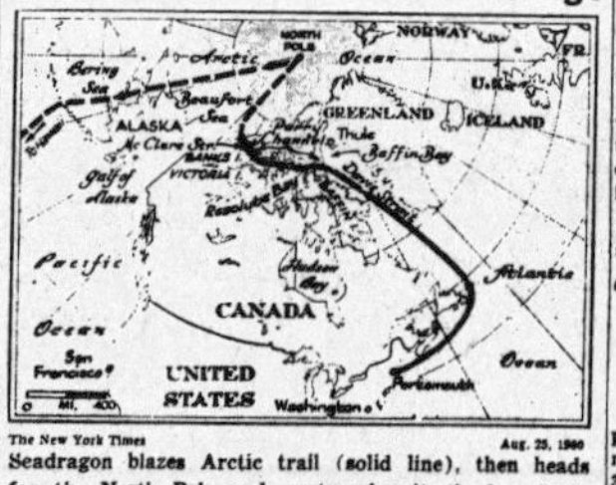

The New York Times Aug. 25, 1960
Seadragon blazes Arctic trail (solid line), then heads for the North Pole and westward exit (broken line).

By PETER BRAESTRUP
Special to The New York Times.

WASHINGTON, Aug. 24—A United States nuclear submarine has made the first underwater transit of the Northwest Passage through the ice-laden waters of the upper Arctic, the Navy said today.

The U. S. S. Seadragon, with Comdr. George P. Steele 2d of Washington serving as captain, made the 850-mile east-west passage in six days. She emerged from the waters of McClure Strait on Sunday.

Tonight, the Seadragon was reported in the Beaufort Sea, heading for the North Pole.

The submarine, by using the Parry Channel route, was said to have opened a more direct passage through the Canadian archipelago from the Atlantic to the Pacific Oceans. Previous explorers used longer, more tortuous "southern" routes.

The Seadragon sailed from Portsmouth, N. H., on Aug. 1, and went up the Greenland-Labrador "slot" through Davis Strait and Baffin Bay. In Baffin Bay, she dived deeper under ice than any submarine had before. She went under one iceberg that was 1,400 feet long and extended 300 feet down into the sea.

In addition to blazing a pos-

Continued on Page 5, Column 2

'Sick' Policeman Made $40,811 On Days Off in Last Five Years

The Police Department reported last night that a patrolman who had been on sick leave 366 days in the last five years had earned $40,811 during that time for outside work.

The patrolman, who had worked as a metallurgist and welding engineer for a Long Island engineering concern, was suspended from the force. Policemen are prohibited from holding outside jobs.

Officials said the patrolman, Salvatore J. Messina, 36 years old, of 148 East Drive, North Massapequa, L. I., had averaged about $6,000 a year in salary from the Police Department for a forty-four-hour week, bringing his total earnings in the last five years to about $70,000.

Among the reasons cited by Patrolman Messina for his absences were virus infections, colds, hay fever, bronchial ailments, other respiratory ailments, peptic ulcers and "effects of a back injury sustained in service."

Deputy Commissioner Walter Arm said, "We don't know how many were legitimate and how many were not."

However, he said it had been established by checking with the engineering concern's rec-

Continued on Page 17, Column 1

NEWS INDEX

BROWNE IS NAMED PURCHASING CHIEF

Deputy Administrator to Be Successor to Spagna

By PAUL CROWELL

Mayor Wagner announced yesterday that he would appoint Deputy City Administrator Roger J. Browne as Commissioner of Purchase. Mr. Browne will succeed Joseph V. Spagna who resigned under fire last Thursday.

The appointment will be made formally as soon as the Board of Estimate and the City Council grant Mr. Browne exemption from the Lyons Residence Law.

That law requires an appointee to city office to have been a resident of the city for at least three years prior to his appointment. Mr. Browne lives at 3 Catereret Place, Garden City, in Nassau County.

The Board of Estimate is expected to approve the exemption unanimously at its meeting today. Approval by the City Council is expected at a meeting Tuesday.

Mr. Browne's annual salary as Commissioner of Purchase will be $20,000, the same amount he receives as deputy city administrator. When he was appointed a deputy city administrator in February, 1959, exemption from the Lyons Law

Continued on Page 32, Column 7

"All the News That's Fit to Print."

The New York Times.

LATE CITY EDITION

U. S. Weather Bureau Report (Page 44) forecasts: Cloudy, some rain today and tonight. Clearing, colder tomorrow. Temp. range: 60—54; yesterday: 65—46.

VOL. CX..No. 37,653.

NEW YORK, SATURDAY, FEBRUARY 25, 1961.

10 cents beyond 50-mile zone from New York City except on Long Island. Higher in air delivery cities.

FIVE CENTS

KENNEDY SUBMITS 2 PLANS TO CURB OUTFLOW OF GOLD

Seeks $100 Limit on Goods Travelers Can Bring Into Country Duty-Free

ACTS ON FOREIGN BANKS

President Also Offers Bills to Aid Medical Training and Improve Facilities

By United Press International.

WASHINGTON, Feb. 24—President Kennedy asked Congress today to help relieve the overseas drain on United States gold and dollars by cutting from $500 to $100 the amount of duty-free goods that American travelers can bring from abroad.

He also submitted a companion bill to exempt from United States taxes the interest received by foreign banks from United States Government securities they hold on a noncommercial basis. The measure was designed to encourage the banks to buy United States securities rather than gold.

At the same time, the President sent Congress two bills to carry out plans in his health program for increasing training opportunities for physicians and dentists and to provide more and better medical facilities.

Scholarships and Grants

The measures would provide Federal scholarships for medical and dental students and would authorize construction grants for teaching and research facilities.

They would also authorize Federal grants for construction of nursing homes and to expand and improve community facilities and services for the care of the aged and others.

The legislation was sent to Congress as the President acted on several fronts. He met with Agriculture Secretary Orville L. Freeman, Theodore C. Sorensen, White House counsel, and Myer Feldman, deputy counsel, on a special farm message he will deliver next month.

The President also chose Anthony J. Drexel Biddle Jr. as Ambassador to Spain.

Mr. Kennedy first advanced his proposals on the gold-dollar problem in a special message Feb. 6. Since then he has taken steps to erase the deficit in the balance of payments. Treasury officials reported that his programs had trimmed the gold outflow.

Buying American Cars

For example, the Administration recently appealed to service men overseas to trim their annual purchases of foreign goods by an average of $100 each.

The Defense Department said today that the service men had cooperated by buying American compact cars instead of foreign models. The armed services helped out by bringing service men and United States auto manufacturers together to arrange a special order.

Under the bill sent to Congress today, the cut in the allowance for duty-free goods would remain in effect for four years. The President said this would meet the immediate situation and provide time for a reappraisal of the balance-of-payments situation. The balance of payments is the measure of payments into and out of the country.

Rockefeller Tuition Plan Gets Support of Regents

Revised Proposal on Aid for College Students Is Backed Unanimously—Passage by Legislature Urged

By LAYHMOND ROBINSON

Special to The New York Times.

ALBANY, Feb. 24—The State Board of Regents gave its unqualified endorsement today to Governor Rockefeller's revised plan for tuition aid to college and university students.

The thirteen-member board, which has general supervision over all education in the state, unanimously endorsed the bill submitted by the Governor to the Legislature on Monday.

The board had previously announced support of the idea of tuition grants but today was the first time it had publicly commented on the specific measure submitted by Mr. Rockefeller.

The Governor in his original proposal outlined in a special message to the legislators, recommended that the state give $200 a year to every undergraduate resident attending college in the state, regardless of his family's financial standing or his academic record.

The new bill scales the award from $100 to $300 a year, depending on the income of the student and his parents. Graduate students would get up to $800 a year toward tuition.

The proposal was changed after it came under considerable criticism from civic groups.

Another major change in the scholar-incentive plan involves the amount of tuition a student must pay to qualify for an award. Under the original proposal, no one who paid less than $500 a year would be eligible.

The new plan would cover all

Continued on Page 24, Column 2

MENZIES CONFERS WITH PRESIDENT; LAOS KING BACKED

Australian, on White House Visit, Also Joins Pledge on U.N. Congo Effort

By WILLIAM J. JORDEN

Special to The New York Times.

WASHINGTON, Feb. 24 — President Kennedy and Prime Minister Robert Gordon Menzies of Australia joined today in public support for King Savang Vathana's peace plan for Laos.

They also "deplored" efforts by the Soviet Union to "twist the tragic events in the Congo into an attack upon the United Nations itself."

Answering Moscow's bitter attacks on Secretary General Dag Hammarskjold, the two leaders pledged joint support of the United Nations official's efforts to bring peace to the Congo.

The President and the Australian Prime Minister conferred for more than two hours at the White House. Their meeting included a luncheon at which Mr. Menzies was the President's guest.

Soviet Policy Reviewed

The White House talk covered a broad range of foreign-policy issues, including an exchange of views on current Soviet policy and on Communist China. But the continuing strife in Laos and the threat to the Southeast Asian country's independence and stability were believed to have occupied the most important place in their conversation.

The United States and Australia are members of the Southeast Asia Treaty Organization. If the crisis in Laos continues, the SEATO Council might have to consider new steps in support of the Government there when the eight-power group meets in Bangkok, Thailand, next month.

In a joint communiqué, the American and Australian statesmen repeated their countries' "strong faith" in the eight-nation defense alliance and in a defense agreement joining Australia, New Zealand and the United States.

Intervention Is Opposed

The Laotian peace plan supported by the President and the Prime Minister was made public earlier this week by King Savang Vathana. He announced Laos' intention to follow a neutral course and opposed any unauthorized foreign interference in Laotian affairs.

The King called on neighboring Burma, Cambodia and Malaya to organize a commission to help restore peace to Laos and to end all foreign intervention.

President Kennedy and Prime Minister Menzies said they hoped the King's efforts would "bear fruit."

However, Mr. Menzies said in a talk with newsmen that the future of the King's proposal was uncertain because definite

Continued on Page 3, Column 3

Associated Press Wirephoto

AUSTRALIAN IS GUEST: Prime Minister Robert Gordon Menzies with President Kennedy yesterday at the White House. They discussed the proposed neutralization of Laos.

U. S. ASKS SOVIET TO DISCUSS PACT FOR AIRLINE LINK

Original Talks, Set to Start Last July, Were Deferred After U-2 Incident

ACCEPTANCE EXPECTED

Release of RB-47 Airmen Held Factor in Decision to Seek Agreement

Special to The New York Times.

WASHINGTON, Feb. 24—The United States has asked the Soviet Union whether it is prepared to make arrangements for reciprocal commercial airline service between the two countries.

The decision to make this move was reached in recent White House conferences on United States-Soviet relations. It was assumed in official circles that Moscow would agree to Washington's suggestion to renew talks on an air agreement.

The talks, if they materialize, may be the first government-to-government negotiations between the Soviet authorities and the Kennedy Administration. But one official said the Government regarded the matter as "a small item in a larger, much larger, picture."

Pledged to Seek Pact

Both the Soviet Union and the United States have formally agreed to try to work out a commercial air pact. A pledge to do so was contained in both the 1958 and 1959 cultural exchange agreements between the two powers.

Preliminary negotiations on technical problems began several years ago between Pan American Airways, which has been authorized to operate any future United States - Soviet service, and Aeroflot, the official Soviet airline.

Any agreement, however, must be based on a formal understanding covering over-all conditions for reciprocal flights, limitations, routing and the like.

Agreed to Open Talks

When an improvement in United States-Soviet relations seemed imminent as a result of meetings between President Eisenhower and Premier Khrushchev in late 1959, the two leaders agreed to open the air agreement talks. They were to have begun last July.

The U-2 incident, the collapse of the summit meeting in Paris in May and the shooting down of a United States Air Force RB-47 plane over the Barents Sea by Soviet fighters July 1 changed the atmosphere.

As a result, the United States Government sent a message to the Soviet authorities suggesting that the talks should take place "in an atmosphere conducive to the achievement of agreement" and proposing that the negotiation be postponed

Continued on Page 2, Column 2

NEW HAVEN SEEKS A $1,500,000 LOAN

Asks I.C.C. for Authority to Issue Note in New Plea for Funds to Keep Running

Special to The New York Times.

WASHINGTON, Feb. 24—The New Haven Railroad informed the Interstate Commerce Commission today that it would need $1,500,000 more to keep the railroad operating.

The amount is the remainder of a $5,000,000 loan guarantee the New Haven sought from the I. C. C. earlier this month.

The commission issued a guarantee on Feb. 14 for the repayments of $3,500,000 and interest at 5 per cent. The remainder was deferred because the New Haven was uncertain whether it could issue a promissory note.

In today's petition, the New Haven asked for authority to issue the $1,500,000 note and said that it would subsequently ask the I. C. C. to guarantee repayment of a loan to be made with the note.

The New Haven used the funds advanced earlier this month to meet payroll and other expenses. The $1,500,000 would be used, it said, to take care of all obligations falling due by March 31.

It anticipated that by that time benefits proposed by state officials in its area would begin to materialize.

On Feb. 21, officials of New York, Connecticut, Massachusetts, Rhode Island, New York City and Westchester County approved a four-year, $54,800,000 emergency-relief program for the New Haven. They will seek the necessary legislation by March 21.

The New Haven told the

Continued on Page 24, Column 2

Auto Makers to Put Seat Belt Fasteners In the 1962 Models

By BERNARD STENGREN

All major American automobile makers will install seat belt hardware as standard equipment on 1962 models, but not the belts themselves.

Announcements of the moves were made almost simultaneously yesterday by Ford, General Motors, Chrysler, American Motors and Studebaker Packard.

Action by the industry came at the close of a two-day visit to Detroit by a group of New York State officials, most of them members of the Legislature.

The group was headed by State Senator Edward J. Speno, Republican of Nassau, long an advocate of mandatory installation of seat belts in automobiles as a safety measure.

Smaller Firms May Act

There was no announcement as yet from the smaller auto manufacturers—including Checker Motors, Willys and International Harvester. However, there was no reason to believe that they would not follow what is now virtually an industry policy.

For a number of years, the makers have resisted installation of seat belts, citing the expense and the apathetic reaction to the devices by the car-buying public.

Several years ago, Ford began promoting their use, but the number of customers interested never went above 7 per cent.

The installation of hardware is a compromise. Reinforcing plates will be attached to floor pans of the cars, and there will be universal brackets to which standard belts can be attached.

If the customer wishes to attach the belts, he can do so easily by paying only for the

Continued on Page 11, Column 3

U.S. HOLDS CUBANS NEED FREE CHOICE

Suggests There Can Be No Settlement Until Castro Allows Political Liberty

By FELIX BELAIR Jr.

Special to The New York Times.

WASHINGTON, Feb. 24—The United States suggested today that there could be no settlement of differences between it and Cuba until the Castro Government permitted freedom of political choice.

In setting forth the Government's position, a State Department spokesman said the United States had only sympathy for the announced aims of the Cuban revolution to improve living conditions. But it is more concerned with the "capture" of that movement by anti-democratic influences, he declared.

[Meanwhile, Cuba realigned her economic ministries by decree, placing Maj. Ernesto Guevara in charge of all industry and the nation's four-year industrialization plan.]

Castro's Fall Foreseen

The policy statement for the State Department by its press officer, Lincoln White, followed a prediction by Senator Kenneth B. Keating, Republican of New York, that "Castro will not last out the year" if the United States pursues the right policies.

In a Senate speech the New York Senator called for a total embargo on exports to Cuba by the Organization of American States, an invitation to Canada to join in O. A. S. deliberations, creation of a Cuban government in exile and convening of a "Cuban forum" to unite anti-Castro factions here and abroad.

In explanation of the Government's view, the State Department spokesman said:

"Our view is that the best way for the Castro regime to demonstrate that it is interested in the independence of the Cuban nation and the welfare of its people is to establish freedom with full guarantees so that the Cuban people may freely choose their own destiny.

"And we are confident that when the Cuban people are given the freedom of choice,

Continued on Page 2, Column 5

Coexistence to Be Dogma In New Soviet Constitution

By United Press International.

MOSCOW, Feb. 24—The Soviet Union published today a preview of a radical new constitution that will make the doctrine of peaceful coexistence a new "scientific principle" of Marxist theory.

The preview, contained in an editorial in Kommunist, official party publication, said the new constitution also would eliminate the last vestiges of private property in Russia.

Kommunist said the constitution would be a historic reflection of the fact that the next stage in the Soviet Union would bring about "a transition of collective, cooperative property into an all-national united Communist property."

This will lead "to elimination of class differences and the establishment of a classless Communist society," the editorial said.

The new fundamental principles of the constitution will be included in a draft program to be submitted at the twenty-second party congress, Kommunist said. The congress is set for Oct. 17.

The new constitution will replace the set of principles adopted in 1919, when the party was in power but Russia was still torn by civil war.

Commission to Report

As previewed by Kommunist, the constitution will give a greater voice to the people in the management of industry, transform the cooperative farms into public property and provide greater intra-party democracy.

A commission on constitutional revision, under the chairmanship of Premier Khrushchev, has been at work on the new principles for several years. It is scheduled to give its report to the congress in October.

According to Kommunist, these historic developments will be reflected in the constitution:

¶That the Soviet Union no longer is under "capitalist encirclement" and is no longer the sole Communist country.

¶That the balance of world power has shifted from the capitalist camp to the Socialist.

¶That the Soviet Union is entering a "second and higher phase."

¶That the Soviet Union has been transformed from a back-

Continued on Page 2, Column 1

U. S. SEEKS ACTION ON CONGO DEATHS

Discusses Step to Condemn Killings—U. N. Considers Plea to World Court

By LINDESAY PARROTT

Special to The New York Times.

UNITED NATIONS, N. Y., Feb. 24—The United States is studying the possibility of new action by the Security Council to condemn political assassinations in the Congo.

Adlai E. Stevenson, the United States representative, held an hour's conversation today with Secretary General Dag Hammarskjold.

He was understood to have made inquiries about the progress being made in implementing the resolution the Council adopted early Tuesday calling for the use of force, as a last resort, to prevent civil war in the Congo.

Issue of U. N. Authority

Secretary General Hammarskjold and his advisory committee on the Congo, meanwhile, were understood to have discussed the possibility of referring an investigation of political killings in the Congo to the International Court of Justice.

The United Nations can ask for advisory opinions from the court. The court, if asked, could decide the authority of the world organization to carry on its own investigation of the killing of former Premier Patrice Lumumba and others as the Security Council resolution suggested.

Congolese authorities have stated, however, that any investigation carried on except by local governmental authorities would violate the provision of the United Nations Charter that prohibits interference in the internal affairs of any member state.

Zorin in Complaint

It was understood that Mr. Hammarskjold had been urged to seek an advisory opinion from the court. So far as was known, however, the matter was scheduled for further discussion.

Valerian A. Zorin, head of the Soviet delegation, complained yesterday that no information was being furnished about the progress of the advisory committee talks. Mr. Zorin asserted particularly that Council members were denied details about steps being taken under the resolution to withdraw Belgian military and tech-

Continued on Page 3, Column 3

ARMY CHIEF NOTES PEIPING'S BUILD-UP

Stahr Warns on Wider Use of Soviet-Made Weapons

By JACK RAYMOND

Special to The New York Times.

WASHINGTON, Feb. 24—Secretary of the Army Elvis J. Stahr Jr. warned today of the growing number of Soviet weapons available to Communist China.

Gen. George B. Decker, Chief of Staff of the Army, cited the increasing long-range-missile capabilities of the Soviet Union and its program of weapons modernization.

General Decker declared that Moscow had not made "large cuts" in military manpower, as it once announced.

The Army leaders stressed Communist improvements in military power, with both nuclear and non-nuclear weapons, in testimony urging modernization of the United States Army.

They testified at a closed "military posture" hearing of the House Armed Services Committee. Their opening statements were released afterward by Representative Carl Vinson, Democrat of Georgia and chairman of the committee.

Secretary Stahr's stress on Red China's military power, in contrast with past focusing on

Continued on Page 4, Column 6

Trial for Pay TV Is Set for Hartford

By The Associated Press.

WASHINGTON, Feb. 24—The country's first over-the-air pay television will start in Hartford, Conn., as soon as sufficient subscribers have been signed up. That is expected in about six months.

The Federal Communications Commission issued final authorization today for a three-year trial of the pay system after ten years of controversy over whether it should be allowed.

Opponents contended that pay TV, once it got started, would gradually black out free television as it is known today by taking over the best programs.

Supporters of the subscription service denied this. They said they would offer programs not normally available to free television and would present

Continued on Page 45, Column 4

New Yorkers Bask in the Sun as Mercury Hits 65°

The New York Times

The mild weather inspired students at Barnard College to take a comfortable sunning

New Yorkers, who have suffered through the hardest winter in years, basked yesterday in sun and warmth. At 3:15 P. M. the temperature rose to 65 degrees, matching the record for the date set in 1930. The spring-like weather caused walkers to doff their coats and slow their pace. College students at Columbia and Barnard and other campuses took their lunches—and conversations—to outside steps. In the suburbs, crocuses and daffodils were spotted nosing out of the warm, soggy ground. Mothers found it difficult to keep sweaters on their excited youngsters, who insisted that "it's practically sum-

Continued on Page 44, Column 2

Bones of Earliest Human, a Child, Reported Dug Up in Tanganyika

By DAVID HALBERSTAM

Special to The New York Times.

WASHINGTON, Feb. 24—A British scientist said here today that he had discovered the bones of the oldest member of the human race known to science.

The relics are considerably more than 600,000 years old, according to Dr. Louis S. B. Leakey, an anthropologist, who discovered them in recent excavations in the Olduvai Gorge of Tanganyika, East Africa.

Dr. Leakey made the announcement at a news conference here today. He said the relics were of an 11-year-old child. He said lesser fragments of another human were also found in the gorge.

He said a more definite date of the child's existence would come later after a more detailed look at the specimens.

Dr. Leakey said these bones, however, were much older than his previous find, the 600,000-year-old "Nutcracker Man," Zinjanthropus Boisei.

The Nutcracker Man — so called because of its huge bone-crushing molars—was considered by most paleontologists to be a contemporary of a host of little man-apes from South Africa called the Australopithecines.

These early hominids, or true tool-making men, have up until now been regarded as inhabitants of the lowest branch of the human evolution tree that leads to the common ancestor of ape and man.

The relics in the latest discovery include the skull, parts of the hands and a foot, the greater part of the jaw and a col-

Continued on Page 11, Column 1

NEWS INDEX

"All the News That's Fit to Print"

The New York Times.

LATE CITY EDITION

U.S. Weather Bureau Report (Page 81) forecasts: Increasing cloudiness today; chance of rain tonight and tomorrow. Temp. range: 54—40; yesterday: 52—43.

VOL. CX..No. 37,699. © 1961 by The New York Times Company. Times Square, New York 36, N. Y. NEW YORK, WEDNESDAY, APRIL 12, 1961. 10 cents beyond 50-mile zone from New York City except on Long Island. Higher in air delivery cities. FIVE CENTS

SOVIET ORBITS MAN AND RECOVERS HIM; SPACE PIONEER REPORTS: 'I FEEL WELL'; SENT MESSAGES WHILE CIRCLING EARTH

HEAD OF RESERVE URGES PRICE CUTS TO RELIEVE SLUMP

Martin Asserts Reductions Would Mean More Jobs and Demand for Goods

By RICHARD E. MOONEY

Special to The New York Times.

WASHINGTON, April 11—The chairman of the Federal Reserve Board made a strong appeal today for price reductions as a means of solving the nation's economic problems.

"Throughout our country, we must not only increase our productivity but also pass some of the gains on to the consumer in the form of lower prices, rather than having all of it go exclusively to labor in higher wages or to management in higher profits," he said.

The chairman, William McC. Martin Jr., said that price cuts could stimulate buying demand that would "provide more jobs for those who are now unemployed, keep the economy moving to higher levels, and [provide] still greater job opportunities in the future."

Some Gains Reported

The Labor Department reported, meanwhile, a modest increase in the factory work week and factory pay for March.

Mr. Martin spoke at the annual meeting of the Association of Reserve City Bankers at Boca Raton, Fla. Copies of his talk were made available here.

It was not the first time that a voice from Washington had been raised in favor of price cuts. It is a point that gets lost, however, in the debates most often heard here, over what the Government should or should not do. In the form presented, it is simply an exhortation. Neither Mr. Martin nor the Kennedy Administration advocates price or wage controls.

Addressing himself to the domestic economy, Mr. Martin said that "at the moment we have pressing need to reduce unemployment and to promote economic growth at the maximum sustainable speed." The way to meet the need, he said, is "a judicious blend" of specific actions, monetary and fiscal policies, and wage-price policies.

Answers Critics of Policy

In such a setting, he said, interest rates need not rise so high nor fall so low as they have in past business cycles.

Mr. Martin used his speech to answer critics who have said that recent Federal Reserve strategy cannot work and has already failed. Seven weeks ago the reserve system abandoned its established policy of buying and selling only the shortest-term securities—Treasury bills—when it sought to impose its influence on credit conditions

Continued on Page 25, Column 5

Realtor Is Indicted In Expense Padding

By EDWARD RANZAL

The president of Pease & Elliman, Inc., a leading real estate concern here, was indicted yesterday on charges of income tax evasion through fraudulent claims for entertainment and travel expenses.

The indictment against the executive, Robert Neaderland, by a Federal grand jury was said to be the first of its kind in the Southern District of New York. It was expected to break ground for future prosecutions for overstatement of business expenses.

Mr. Neaderland, 53 years old, lives at 160 Central Park South. His company is one of the leading developers of apartments on the East Side. He is charged with attempting to evade $27,550 in income taxes in 1954 and 1955, according to

Continued on Page 30, Column 3

Wide College Aid Is Adopted by State

By WARREN WEAVER Jr.

Special to The New York Times.

ALBANY, April 11—A higher-education program that will make $12,300,000 in new financial assistance available to college and university students in New York State this year was approved by Governor Rockefeller today.

He said the program gave assurance that "no young man or woman with the ability and desire for a higher education need be deprived of that opportunity for lack of funds."

The seven higher education measures that were signed included a bill that gave New York City permission to establish a city university to consist of the four municipal colleges and the community colleges in the five boroughs.

One of the bills provides

Continued on Page 48, Column 3

COUNCIL APPROVES OWN CHARTER BILL

Rebuffs Mayor by Spurning State Law Under Which He Named Commission

By CHARLES G. BENNETT

The City Council passed its own bill yesterday calling for the appointment of a commission to draft a new City Charter. The vote was 21 to 3.

Council officers immediately prepared to send the measure directly to Mayor Wagner for his signature or veto. This would be based on a contention by the Council's high command that since the bill merely calls for the appointment of a commission, it does not require Board of Estimate action.

The Council's stand constituted a challenge to the new state law under which Mayor Wagner already has appointed an eleven-member commission to revise the Charter.

Majority Leader Joseph T. Sharkey, who is also Democratic leader of Kings County, repeated his charge that Governor Rockefeller and Mayor Wagner had been "playing together" on Charter revision. Mayor Wagner supported the state bill.

Mr. Sharkey also said he "hoped and expected" that there

Continued on Page 26, Column 3

Population Center Moves West; Census Puts It at Centralia, Ill.

The New York Times April 12, 1961

United States center of population, which was near Portsmouth, Ohio, a hundred years ago, has continued moving west and by 1960 was just northwest of Centralia, Ill.

By The Associated Press.

WASHINGTON, April 11—The population center of the United States has moved again.

Secretary of Commerce Luther H. Hodges announced today that the new center, based on the 1960 census, was near Centralia, Ill., fifty-seven miles west of its 1950 location.

In general, the population center is the point through which a straight line can be drawn in any direction dividing the country's population in half. As many people would live on one side of the line as on the other.

Mr. Hodges had another def-

Continued on Page 27, Column 3

ISRAEL DEFENDS TRIBUNAL'S RIGHT TO TRY EICHMANN

Ex-Nazi Is More Confident as Jerusalem Hearing Enters Its 2d Day

By HOMER BIGART

Special to The New York Times.

JERUSALEM (Israeli Sector), Wednesday, April 12—The Attorney General of Israel, Gideon Hausner, resumed this morning his defense of the right of his country to try Adolf Eichmann for the murder of millions of Jews.

The defendant, as he entered his bulletproof glass cage on the second day of his trial seemed more confident. For the first time, he looked out at the audience. Then he sat down and engaged in an animated conversation with his German lawyer, Dr. Robert Servatius through a microphone in the glass cage. Eichmann smiled at his lawyer and seemed at ease.

On the first day of the trial, Eichmann, stonily impassive, heard his lawyer challenge the court's right to try the former Nazi leader on charges of delivering millions of Jews to Nazi annihilation camps.

The debate over Israel's right to try Eichmann was expected to continue through today's session. The court will not meet tomorrow, Holocaust Day, a day of mourning in Israel for the victims of Nazi terror.

Indictment Is Read

For seventy minutes Eichmann remained standing while the presiding judge, Justice Moshe Landau of the Israeli Supreme Court, read in Hebrew a fifteen-count indictment charging him with crimes against the Jewish people and crimes against humanity. The indictment was translated into German for Eichmann's benefit.

Rigidly erect, his head tilted back and his thin lips tightly compressed, the one-time chief of the Gestapo's Jewish Affairs Section betrayed no emotion during the opening day of trial.

His thin, hawklike visage with its large, sharply pointed nose was fixed intently on the proceedings. Not once did Eichmann turn to gaze on the throng of newsmen, foreign observers and Israeli citizens in the 750 seats in the Beit Haam (House of the People), the converted

Continued on Page 16, Column 1

Former Nazi Hears Indictment Read as Trial Begins in Jerusalem

Adolf Eichmann, charged with crimes against the Jewish people and against humanity, standing in special booth in Beit Haam courtroom yesterday. Justices at bench are, from left, Benyamin Halevi, Moshe Landau, Yitzhak Raveh.

Associated Press Radiophotos

Eichmann peers intently at tribunal during proceedings

U. S. IS DISTURBED BY DELAY ON LAOS

Soviet Lag on Cease-Fire and Increase in Supplies Regarded as Ominous

By WILLIAM J. JORDEN

Special to The New York Times.

WASHINGTON, April 11—Officials said today the United States Government was disturbed by Moscow's delay in accepting a Western plan for an immediate cease-fire in Laos.

A spokesman for the State Department said that continued delay would be regarded here as "a matter of very serious concern."

Adding to the worries of Administration leaders were intelligence reports of a general increase in the flow of Soviet-bloc military supplies to the Pathet Lao movement in recent days. This was regarded as an ominous sign of Soviet intentions in Laos.

Rusk Voices Hope

High officials continued to be hopeful, however, that Moscow would soon give a favorable answer to the cease-fire plan advanced by the British several weeks ago.

That hope was voiced on Capitol Hill today by Secretary of State Dean Rusk. The Secretary told Senators that he expected a Soviet answer "within a very few days."

The presumption here is that continued fighting in Laos contains the seeds of a possibly enlarged conflict and that the Soviet bloc does not want to

Continued on Page 12, Column 4

Centennial of War Rocked by Dispute

By The Associated Press.

CHARLESTON, S. C., April 11—New Jersey accused the National Civil War Centennial Commission of "pathetic mismanagement" tonight and asked that President Kennedy remove Maj. Gen. Ulysses S. Grant 3d as chairman.

Joseph Dempsey, vice chairman of the Jersey Centennial Commission, made the charge at a news conference after General Grant had turned down the state's request for time to rebut a dinner speaker who had criticized its civil rights practices.

General Grant and Donald Flamm, Jersey chairman, engaged in an unscheduled standing debate at the crowded dinner at the Charleston Naval Base. General Grant, to loud appiause, insisted that New

Continued on Page 36, Column 3

BRITISH CONSIDER TRADE UNITY STEP

Kennedy Hopes London Will Enter Common Market

By JAMES RESTON

Special to The New York Times.

WASHINGTON, April 11—President Kennedy now has the impression that the British Government is seriously thinking about joining the European Economic Community, or Common Market.

This impression is based on the fact that during the President's conversations with Prime Minister Macmillan here last week the British leader asked what the United States Government would think if Britain decided to reverse her policy and join the Western European nations now working toward economic and political integration.

Administration to Cooperate

President Kennedy's reply was that the United States would regard this as a major advance toward the unity of the West.

The President did not in any way imply that the United States was thinking of joining the Common Market itself, but he did stress his Government's determination to cooperate fully with its allies in the Organization for Economic Cooperation and Development.

On a recent trip to London it is known that George Ball, United States Under Secretary of State for Economic Affairs, urged upon Viscount Hailsham, the British Lord President of the Council, that Britain give the most serious consideration

Continued on Page 2, Column 3

ADENAUER IN U. S. TO SEE KENNEDY

Arrives for First Talks With President—Stresses Unity

Special to The New York Times.

WASHINGTON, April 11—Chancellor Adenauer of West Germany arrived here tonight for his first meetings with President Kennedy.

He alighted at Andrews Air Force Base from the Lufthansa jet airliner that brought him without stop from Bonn.

In an arrival statement the 85-year-old Chancellor said the German people had already developed "great confidence" in the new President of the United States. He said he was looking forward to establishing personal contact with Mr. Kennedy.

Dr. Adenauer pledged that his country's considerable energy and ability would be devoted to the cause of peace and freedom. He said that his Government realized that its share of responsibility for the future of the world grew "in proportion with our efficiency and capacity."

"Our times are filled with threats and dangers," the Chancellor said, "but I feel sure that the free people of the world will overcome those dangers if they are united and resolute."

The West German leader and his party, including his daughter, Frau Libeth Werhahn, were

Continued on Page 4, Column 5

NEWS INDEX

FRANCE DECLARES ANTI-U.N. 'STRIKE'

De Gaulle Bars Any Role in Armed Ventures—Warns Algerians on Partition

By HENRY GINIGER

Special to The New York Times.

PARIS, April 11—France proclaimed today a virtual strike against the United Nations.

In one of the harshest indictments he has ever made against the organization, President de Gaulle said France "did not wish to participate either by her men or her money in any present or possible enterprise of this organization—or of this disorganization."

The President, in response to a question, confirmed his country's refusal to contribute to the costs of the United Nations force in the Congo. A Foreign Ministry spokesman said that in this context the President's statement referred to present or future military enterprises, although the word "military" did not occur in the text of the news conference.

On another issue, President de Gaulle offered a mixture of incentives for Algerian rebel cooperation with France. He warned anew that a "rupture" might result in the partitioning of Algeria to protect those Algerians who wished to remain under French control.

The President called for reform of the United Nations as well as of the Atlantic Alliance. He made it clear that the future of the alliance would be a major

Continued on Page 3, Column 5

187-MILE HEIGHT

Yuri Gagarin, a Major, Makes the Flight in 5-Ton Vehicle

Text of the Tass statement is printed on Page 22.

By United Press International.

MOSCOW, Wednesday, April 12—The Soviet Union announced today it had won the race to put a man into space. The official press agency, Tass, said a man had orbited the earth in a spaceship and had been brought back alive and safe.

A brief announcement said the first reported space man had landed in what was described as the "prescribed area" of the Soviet Union after a historic flight.

A Moscow radio announcer broke into a program and said in emotional tones:

"Russia has successfully launched a man into space. His name is Yuri Gagarin. He was launched in a sputnik named Vostok, which means "East."

Reports on Landing

Tass said that, on landing, Major Gagarin said: "Please report to the party and Government, and personally to Nikita Sergyevich Khrushchev, that the landing was normal. I feel well, have no injuries or bruises."

He landed at 10:55 A. M. Moscow time [2:55 A. M. New York time].

Earlier, the major reported: "Flight is proceeding normally, I feel well."

After orbiting the earth the major applied a braking device, and the vehicle space landed in the Soviet Union, Tass said.

Major Gagarin, 27 years old, is an industrial technician, and married. He was reported to have received pre-flight training similar to that of the astronauts who will man the United States first space ships.

Soared to 187 Miles

The announcer said the Sputnik reached a minimum altitude of 175 kilometers (109½ miles) and a maximum altitude of 302 kilometers (187¾ miles).

He said the weight of the Sputnik was 10,395 pounds, or slightly over five tons.

The announcement of the launching came at 2 A. M. New York time.

It said everything functioned normally during the flight.

Constant radio contact was maintained between earth and the sputnik, the Moscow radio said.

The announcer said the duration of each revolution around the earth was 89.1 minutes.

The title of the announcement was "The First Human Flight into the Cosmos."

The radio, which was quoting a Tass press agency statement on the launching, said that Maj.

Continued on Page 22, Column 1

White House Confirms Firing; Feat Hailed by U. S. Scientists

By JOHN W. FINNEY

Special to The New York Times.

WASHINGTON, Wednesday, April 12—Pierre Salinger, White House press secretary, announced early today that "American tracking stations have confirmed the fact that the Soviet Union has launched a satellite today."

"We are keeping in close touch with the situation but have no additional comment at this time," he said.

The Soviet success in sending the first man into space left United States officials in a resigned mood of congratulations.

The United States has no chance of equaling the Soviet feat until perhaps late this year.

The Soviet announcement did not take them by surprise, since there had been advance information from United States tracking stations that a satellite had been launched.

James E. Webb, head of the National Aeronautics and Space Administration, described the feat as "a significant accomplishment" that "demonstrates great technical capacity."

"I hope that they can find it possible to make the benefits of this event available to the rest of the world," he said.

Dr. Hugh L. Dryden, deputy administrator of the space agency, commented, "This is something we have been expecting for some time."

"It is only the beginning of man's continued effort of manned exploration of space," he said, "and I think we should continue as rapidly as we can with our own program."

In appraising the achieve-

Continued on Page 24, Column 1

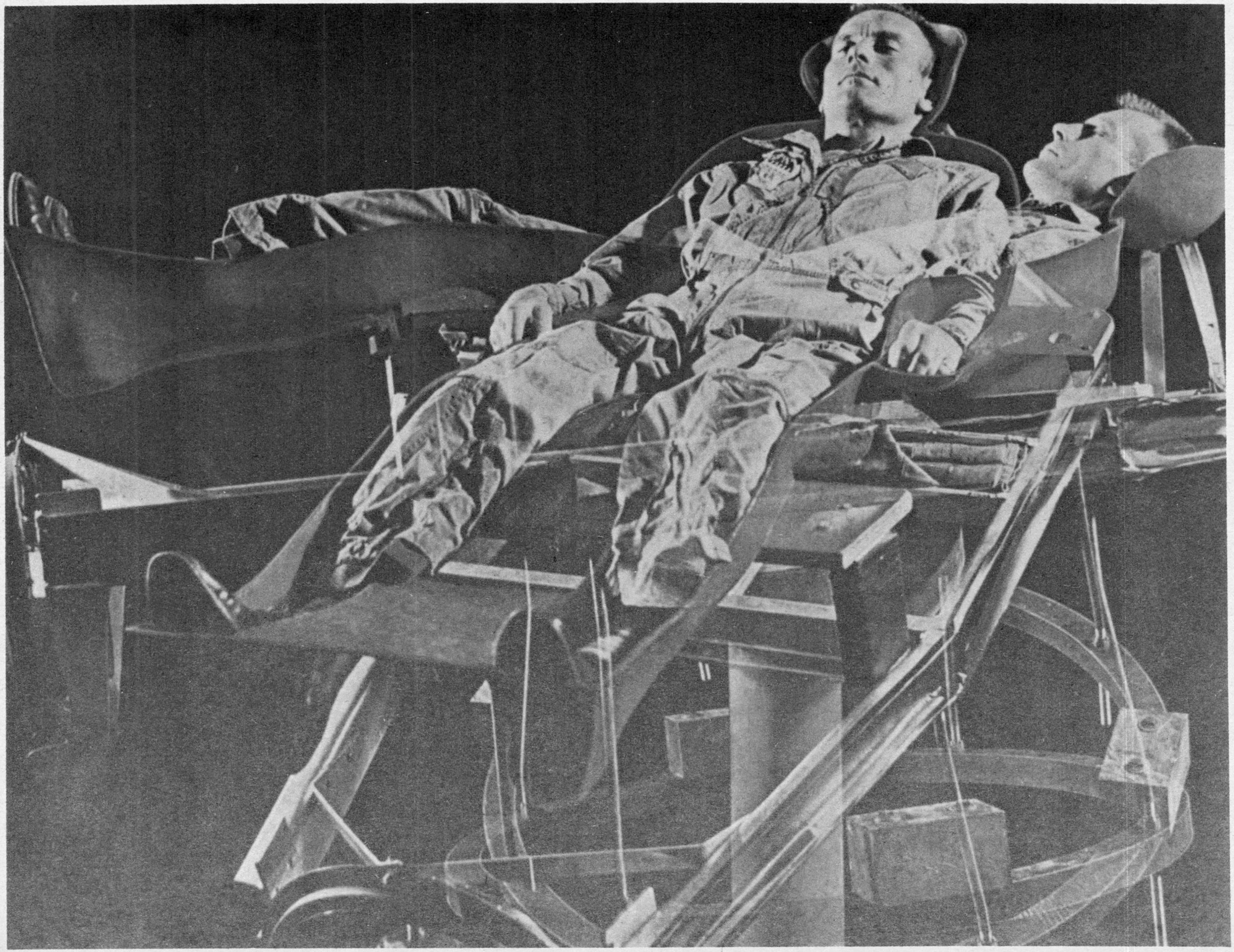

The training of an astronaut for Project Mercury.

"All the News That's Fit to Print"

The New York Times.

LATE CITY EDITION
U. S. Weather Bureau Report (Page 62) forecast: Cloudy, warm, chance of rain late today or tonight and tomorrow. Temp. range: 61–48; yesterday: 70–47.

VOL. CX..No. 37,723.

NEW YORK, SATURDAY, MAY 6, 1961.

10 cents beyond 50-mile zone from New York City except on Long Island. Higher in air delivery cities.

FIVE CENTS

U. S. HURLS MAN 115 MILES INTO SPACE; SHEPARD WORKS CONTROLS IN CAPSULE, REPORTS BY RADIO IN 15-MINUTE FLIGHT

LAUNCHING: Rocket lifts the capsule

RETURN: Astronaut rides in one of helicopters carrying his Mercury capsule to the Lake Champlain

Associated Press Wirephotos

SAFE ABOARD: On the Lake Champlain's deck, Comdr. Alan B. Shepard Jr. views capsule he occupied

ASTRONAUT: Commander Shepard removes space suit.

JOHNSON TO MEET LEADERS IN ASIA ON U.S. TROOP USE

President Says Decision on South Vietnam Action Will Await Report

TALKS SET IN CAPITALS

Ngo Dinh Diem Is Expected to Seek American Units to Deter Red Attack

Transcript of news conference and summary, Page 14.

By WILLIAM J. JORDEN
Special to The New York Times.

WASHINGTON, May 5—President Kennedy said today that the assignment of United States armed forces to South Vietnam would be one of several important matters Vice President Lyndon B. Johnson would discuss on his coming trip to Asia. [Opening statement and Question 4, Page 14.]

The President confirmed that the possibility of sending United States troops to Southeast Asia was under study. He indicated that the final decision would depend on the results of Mr. Johnson's talks in Saigon with President Ngo Dinh Diem and others.

Mr. Kennedy said at a news conference that a special task force in the Government was working on problems related to helping South Vietnam maintain its independence. The question has been considered by the National Security Council as well, he said.

Vital Assignment

Mr. Johnson is expected to leave next Tuesday for the Far East. He also will meet with top Government officials in Bangkok, Thailand; Manila, and other capitals.

The President today described the Johnson mission as "an extremely important assignment."

It is widely assumed here that President Ngo will ask for the assignment of at least a token force of United States troops and regard it as a guarantee of United States' involvement should his country be attacked in force by the Communist North.

Mr. Kennedy did not touch on the matter today, but it is known that the Government is also considering the possibility of sending a similar token force to Thailand. The latter is allied to the United States in the

Continued on Page 3, Column 4

Talks Open in Laos On Truce Details; Meeting 'Friendly'

By JACQUES NEVARD
Special to The New York Times.

HIN HEUP, Laos, May 5—Military representatives of the pro-Western Laotian Government and the pro-Communist Pathet Lao rebels held a preliminary conference here today on machinery for continuing the cease-fire that became effective Wednesday.

The conference lasted one hour and five minutes and was described as "friendly."

According to a Laotian Army spokesman, Col. Oudom Sananikone, the meeting did not take up any political questions.

There appeared to be few tangible results of the talks, but Colonel Oudom Sananikone stressed that the meeting was a preliminary one.

He said that the first Pathet Lao request was that the next meeting take place at Namone, thirty-five miles north of here

Continued on Page 3, Column 2

2 BILLION AID PLAN FOR BRAZIL IS NEAR

U. S. Presses World-Wide Program of New Loans and Debt Deferments

By TAD SZULC
Special to The New York Times.

WASHINGTON, May 5—An international financial rescue package worth more than $2,000,000,000 is being prepared for Brazil. Negotiations, already well advanced, involve the United States, six Western European countries, Japan and the International Monetary Fund.

The agreements, which may be announced late next week, call for new loans totaling nearly $630,000,000. About $340,000,000 of this is to be provided by the United States. The remainder will take the form of a postponement in the repayment of much of Brazil's huge foreign debt.

This international financial operation, the largest ever involving a Latin-American country and one of the largest anywhere in postwar years, is designed to provide President Janio Quadros with extra time and resources to reorganize his economy.

Broad Effort in View

The United States is playing a key role in putting together the Brazilian package. It will also supply separate smaller loans to bolster the economies of Venezuela and Bolivia. Venezuela, which is facing serious budget difficulties, expects to receive soon an initial loan of $50,000,000.

Besides these emergency measures to assist the economics of individual Latin-American republics, the United States moved today to call a special inter-American conference to blueprint long-range economic and social development programs.

President Kennedy announced at his news conference that the United States' delegation to the Council of the Organization of American States had been in-

Continued on Page 17, Column 1

NIXON ASKS DRIVE TO OFFSET SOVIET

Bids Kennedy Rally America to a Fresh Foreign Policy

Excerpts from Nixon speech are printed on Page 2.

By AUSTIN C. WEHRWEIN
Special to The New York Times.

CHICAGO, May 5—Former Vice President Richard M. Nixon urged President Kennedy today to rally the American people for a new start in American foreign policy.

Mr. Nixon called for a "searching reappraisal of the free world's ability, particularly America's ability, to deal with the kind of aggression in which Communists are now engaging."

He further revealed that he had given President Kennedy the "assurance that I will support him to the hilt in backing positive action he may decide is necessary to resist Communist aggression."

[President Kennedy, meanwhile, sent his nuclear test-ban negotiator back to Geneva with an implied warning that the United States might not continue the talks much longer without some prospect of a safeguarded treaty.]

To meet such threats, the former Vice President said that the United States should be prepared to act alone if swift action were needed while machinery for collective action was being set up.

The lesson of Cuba and Laos, he said, is this:

"We must never talk bigger than we are prepared to act.

"When our words are strong and our actions are timid, we

Continued on Page 2, Column 3

Kennedy Plans Aid To Retrain Jobless And Spur Recovery

By PETER BRAESTRUP
Special to The New York Times.

WASHINGTON, May 5—The Kennedy Administration expects to ask Congress for at least $75,000,000 to provide retraining for the long-term unemployed. Other new anti-recession measures also are being considered.

The key question that President Kennedy has yet to decide is whether to break the Administration's self-imposed limit on Federal spending in an effort to stimulate the economy and spur employment.

The $75,000,000 program for retraining workers who have been laid off by technological change and by the decay of their own industries will not materially affect the budget. Nor will the President's orders to the Pentagon to channel more defense contracts to small

Continued on Page 19, Column 2

Elizabeth Visits Pope in Vatican

Associated Press Wirephoto

Pope John XXIII in private audience with Queen Elizabeth

By ARNALDO CORTESI
Special to The New York Times.

ROME, May 5—Pope John XXIII received Queen Elizabeth II and Prince Philip in a private audience today with traditional pomp and ceremony. The meeting was marked by extreme cordiality. Addressing the Queen in French, the Pope said that relations between Britain and

Continued on Page 19, Column 4

MAYOR IS UPHELD ON CHARTER LAW

But Court Reverses Ban on Action by Council, Opening Way to Rival Proposals

By RONALD MAIORANA

Mayor Wagner's right to appoint a Charter Revision Commission was upheld by Justice Irving Saypol yesterday in State Supreme Court.

However, Justice Saypol ruled invalid part of the law under which the Mayor had acted. This part excluded the City Council from Charter-revision activity.

Lawyers said the ruling appeared to make possible the enactment of the City Council's own plan for a Charter Revision Commission. Thus, it is conceivable, they said, that two competing Charters—one drawn by the Mayor's commission and the other by a commission created by the Council—could be submitted to the voters Nov. 7.

In a twenty-two-page decision that caused confusion at City Hall Justice Saypol ruled that the section of the state law that had the effect of bypassing the City Council was invalid because it was an improper delegation of legislative power. He said: "The newly enacted au-

Continued on Page 32, Column 1

Shepard Had Periscope: 'What a Beautiful View'

By JOHN W. FINNEY
Special to The New York Times.

CAPE CANAVERAL, Fla., May 5—"All systems go * * * Everything A-O.K. * * * Mission very smooth * * * What a beautiful view! * * * Coming in for a landing."

These were the reports of Comdr. Alan B. Shepard Jr. as he rode the capsule Freedom 7 115 miles up into space today in the United States' first step toward manned exploration of space. His "A-O.K," is a rocket engineer term meaning double O.K. or perfect.

In a calm, methodical way he reported back by radio on every detail of his fifteen-minute flight, even during the moments of greatest stress as his capsule accelerated from the launching pad and then quickly decelerated upon re-entering the earth's atmosphere.

And there were moments of excitement in his voice, such as when he viewed much of the Eastern Coast of the United States through a periscope from 115 miles up in space.

"What a beautiful view!" he exclaimed into a microphone inside his visored space helmet and then, according to instructions, he returned to scientific observations to report that the cloud cover was three- to four-tenths and was obscuring much of the coast up through Cape Hatteras.

Three-to-four-teenths cloud cover is a description used by

Continued on Page 10, Column 1

PRESIDENT TO ASK INCOME TAX CUTS

Drop Next Year Is Planned, Dillon Tells House Unit

By JOHN D. MORRIS
Special to The New York Times.

WASHINGTON, May 5—The Kennedy Administration plans to lay before Congress next year a tax reform program that will include reduction of individual income taxes.

Secretary of the Treasury Douglas Dillon told the House Ways and Means Committee of the plan today but gave no details. He made it clear, however, that taxpayers with high incomes would probably be among the chief beneficiaries of a proposed reduction in rates.

"I think those in high brackets deserve relief," he said.

Mr. Dillon was questioned for nearly three hours, mainly by Republican committee members, as he completed three days of testimony on tax-revision legislation being sought now by the Administration.

The pending proposals include $1,700,000,000 a year in special tax credits for business enterprises to encourage modernization and expansion of plant and equipment. Tax laws on foreign income, business expense accounts and stock dividends

Continued on Page 22, Column 3

14 Dead, 57 Hurt by Tornado; 2 Towns in Oklahoma Hard Hit

By The Associated Press

POTEAU, Okla., May 5—A vicious tornado tore through two tiny eastern Oklahoma communities near here tonight, killing at least fourteen persons and injuring fifty-seven.

Ten were reported dead at Howe and four at Reichert. The death toll could go higher as rescue workers dug into the debris.

There was a report that a light plane—trying to avoid the massive storm cloud—crashed after a wing tore off. The highway patrol said that a woman who lived in the area reported she saw the plane go down west of Heavener near Summerfield

It was a grim anniversary for this rolling, wooded area some 200 miles southeast of Oklahoma City. Just one year ago twelve were killed when a twister destroyed most of the downtown area of Wilburton.

Tornadoes had plagued Oklahoma for two days, but until tonight there had been only one fatality from the scores of funnels sighted.

Two of the dead were babies. One father died with his 3-month-old son and a mother with her 14-month-old boy.

Tiny farms are scattered throughout the twister-pounded

Continued on Page 62, Column 6

NATION TO WIDEN ITS SPACE EFFORTS

Kennedy Wants More Funds —He Telephones Shepard to Offer Congratulations

Texts of Kennedy statement and call to Shepard, Page 11

By DAVID HALBERSTAM
Special to The New York Times.

WASHINGTON, May 5—An even greater effort in the exploration of space was promised today by President Kennedy.

On the day of this country's first manned space flight, he told a news conference he would make an additional request for appropriations for its space program this year.

"We are going to make a substantially larger effort in space," he declared. [Question 1, Page 14.]

Earlier in the day the President telephoned his personal congratulations to Comdr Alan B. Shepard Jr., the nation's first space traveler, in a call from the White House to the aircraft carrier Lake Champlain.

The President also congratulated the commander's wife and his six fellow-astronauts.

Commander Shepard will visit Washington Monday. There will be a ceremony at noon on

Continued on Page 11, Column 7

IN FINE CONDITION

Astronaut Drops Into the Sea Four Miles From Carrier

Excerpts from radioed reports by Shepard, Page 8

By RICHARD WITKIN
Special to The New York Times.

CAPE CANAVERAL, Fla., May 5—A slim, cool Navy test pilot was rocketed 115 miles into space today.

Thirty-seven-year-old Comdr. Alan B. Shepard Jr. thus became the first American space explorer.

Commander Shepard landed safely 302 miles out at sea fifteen minutes after the launching. He was quickly lifted aboard a Marine Corps helicopter.

"Boy, what a ride!" he said, as he was flown to the aircraft carrier Lake Champlain four miles away.

Extensive physical examinations were begun immediately.

Tonight doctors reported Commander Shepard in "excellent" condition, suffering no ill effects.

Major U. S. Step

The near-perfect flight represented the United States' first major step in the race to explore space with manned space craft.

True, it was only a modest leap compared with the once-around-the-earth orbital flight of Maj. Yuri A. Gagarin of the Soviet Union.

The Russian's speed of more than 17,000 miles an hour was almost four times Commander Shepard's 4,500. The distance the Russian traveled was almost 100 times as great.

But Commander Shepard maneuvered his craft in space—something the Russians have not claimed for Major Gagarin.

All in all, the Shepard flight was welcomed almost rapturous-

Continued on Page 8, Column 1

Nation Exults Over Space Feat; City Plans to Honor Astronaut

By ROBERT CONLEY

The successful flight of America's first astronaut, Comdr. Alan B. Shepard Jr., roused the country yesterday to one of its highest peaks of exultation since the end of World War II.

The achievement brought relief from the strain of hearing about the Soviet Union's success in orbiting a man, feelings of new hope for the future from Maine to Hawaii and dancing in the streets at New York's Columbus Circle.

"Wonderful," "Tremendous," "The greatest thing that ever happened," thousands of persons said as the reaction took hold across the country.

Knots of people crowded sidewalks to watch television screens in store windows. Others jumped up to cheer, pounded friends on the back, ran into neighbors' houses or fell silent.

"He made it," a woman gasped in Chicago, then broke into tears. "He made it."

New York City laid plans for the "most fabulous" ticker tape welcome ever given—one that a city official said would be "even bigger than the one for Charles Lindbergh."

In Washington, Congressmen moved to bestow the nation's

Continued on Page 11, Column 5

NEWS INDEX

Alan Shepard approaching his spacecraft, the *Freedom 7*.

Freedom 7

NASA

Alan Shepard, and his capsule, being retrieved.

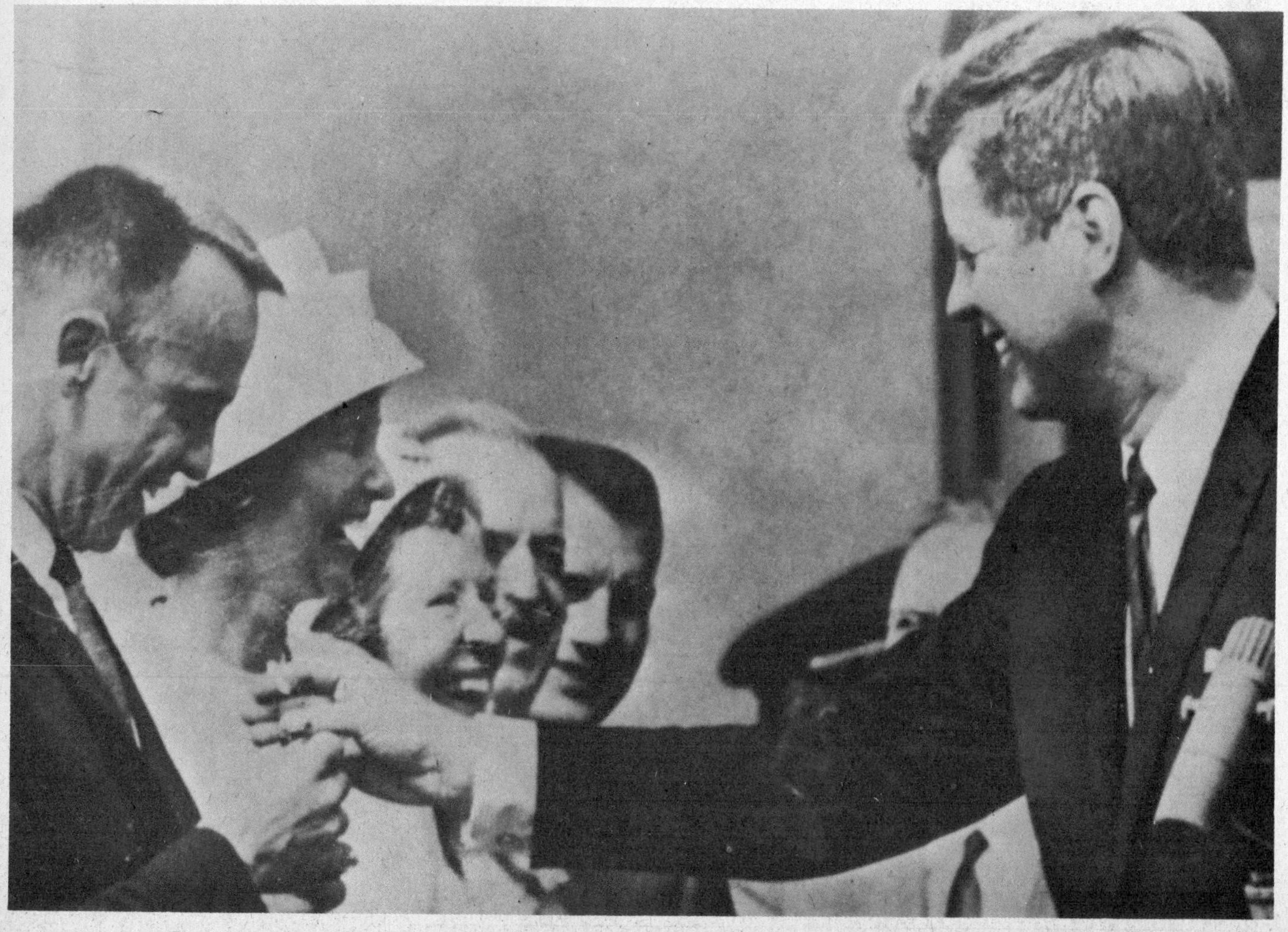

President Kennedy extending the nation's thanks and admiration to Shepard and his wife.

"All the News That's Fit to Print"

The New York Times.

LATE CITY EDITION

U. S. Weather Bureau Report (Page 44) forecasts: Mostly fair, hot, humid, chance of showers late today, part of tomorrow.

Temp. range: 94—75; yesterday: 93—72. Temp.-Hum. Index: low 80's; yesterday: 82.

VOL. CX. No. 37,800. NEW YORK, SATURDAY, JULY 22, 1961. 10 cents beyond 50-mile zone from New York City except on Long Island. Higher in air delivery cities. FIVE CENTS

FRENCH OCCUPY BIZERTE; TUNIS ASKS FOREIGN HELP; CEASE-FIRE URGED IN U. N.

FIGHTING IS HEAVY

Casualty Toll High—Tunisians Seize Oil Pipeline Terminal

By Reuters

BIZERTE, Tunisia, Saturday, July 22—The commander of the French naval base here declared last night that French forces had captured the city of Bizerte.

The announcement, by Admiral Maurice Amman, came after French troops had battered their way into the heart of the city, three miles northeast of the naval base. The Tunisians suffered heavy casualties.

Although the French claimed victory, a Tunisian Government spokesman said early today the fighting was continuing. He said the Tunisian garrison in Bizerte "holds a great part of the town."

As the French forces moved to occupy Bizerte, President Habib Bourguiba said in Tunis he had instructed all Tunisian Embassies to accept foreign volunteers to fight against the French in Tunisia.

[Mr. Bourguiba appealed to "all brother nations to come take part in the battle of Bizerte," it was reported.]

The Tunisian President also said the Government had seized the French coastal oil installation at La Skhira, in eastern Tunisia. La Skhira is the terminal port for the oil pipeline from the Edjele wells in the Sahara.

150 Reported Dead

By THOMAS F. BRADY

Special to The New York Times.

BIZERTE, July 21—The French attacked this city today with troops, tanks and planes.

But after day-long fighting, the Governor's residence was still holding out against the French assault. Heavy firing and explosions could be heard from the central sector and the Arab quarter of Bizerte.

Tunisian sources said military and civilian Tunisian casualties totaled at least 150 today.

About 110 Tunisians were reported killed in the fighting in

Continued on Page 3, Column 3

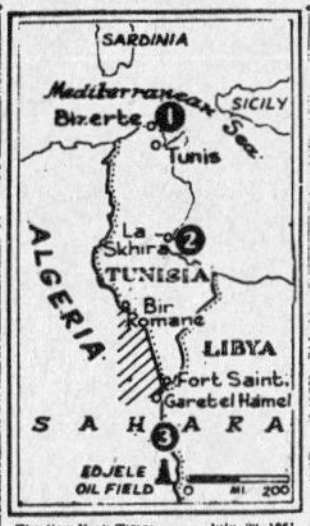

The New York Times July 22, 1961

THE TUNISIAN BATTLE: The French claimed Bizerte (1). Tunisians seized La Skhira oil works (2). There was fighting near Saharan Edjele field (3).

U. S. DRAFTS PLEA

Resolution Will Seek Troop Withdrawal on Both Sides

Excerpts from U. N. debate appear on Page 2.

By SAM POPE BREWER

Special to The New York Times.

UNITED NATIONS, N. Y., July 21—Tunisia and France put their conflicting accounts of the Bizerte crisis before the Security Council today.

Armand Bérard of France renewed a French offer to accept an immediate cease-fire, to be followed by negotiations when conditions had returned to normal. This was made at the close of the session as he spoke in rebuttal of some of the charges made.

Mongi Slim of Tunisia said a cease-fire would be possible only on the basis of a French agreement to leave Tunisia. All the day's speakers agreed on the need for a cease-fire, though they differed in their views on responsibility for the situation.

Seven Nations Speak

Seven nations spoke in today's session, which was summoned hastily in response to a cablegram yesterday from the Tunisian Government charging French aggression. In order, they were Tunisia, France, the United States, the United Arab Republic, Turkey, the Soviet Union and Liberia.

All speakers urged a cease-fire in the growing conflict, but Mr. Slim said it was unacceptable without the withdrawal of French troops.

The United States called for an immediate cease-fire and for the return of all troops to their previous positions as a prelude to negotiations for a permanent settlement. Charles W. Yost, Deputy United States representative, presented this as an appeal to France and Tunisia.

U. S. Works on Accord

The United States delegation was working on a draft resolution incorporating those steps.

Dr. Leopoldo Benites, of Ecuador, this month's President of the Security Council, adjourned the meeting at 8:08 P. M. It will resume at 10 A. M. tomorrow.

During the meeting a message from the Tunisian Government was circulated to the eleven members of the Council. It reported a "very dangerous worsening of the situation." The message, addressed to Secretary General Dag Hammarskjold, was signed by Dr. Sadok Mokkadem, Tunisian Secretary for Foreign Affairs.

The message referring to conditions as of last night, said

Continued on Page 2, Column 3

U.S. WILL SPONSOR AIRLIFT OF CUBANS

Will Pay Havana-to-Miami Passage for 20,000 if Castro Allows Exit

By The Associated Press.

WASHINGTON, July 21—The United States Government announced tonight that it would sponsor a free airlift for more than 20,000 Cubans seeking to come to the United States.

The State Department said that, starting tomorrow, Pan American World Airways would sharply increase its flights to Havana to bring in the waiting Cubans at the rate of 1,000 a day.

The United States Government expects to pay about $350,000 out of its emergency foreign aid fund to finance the mass airlift. The White House has approved the action.

The State Department said the step was being taken because the Cubans had been unable to pay American dollars for the flight to Miami. Instead, they have had only Cuban pesos—unusable to pay their fares on such flights.

Obstacles Possible

Lincoln White, the State Department's press officer, who made the announcement, said no assurance had been received from Premier Fidel Castro as to whether he would let the Cubans out. The United States has not told Dr. Castro about the plan, Mr. White added.

This raised questions about obstacles the airlift might encounter.

The approximately 20,000 Cubans eligible for the flights are those who have visas or waivers issued by the United States Government. Most are relatives

Continued on Page 7, Column 2

RUSK TELLS ALLIES OF U. S. PLANNING FOR BERLIN CRISIS

Confers With Three Powers' Diplomats on Measures to Increase Readiness

By E. W. KENWORTHY

Special to The New York Times.

WASHINGTON, July 21—Secretary of State Dean Rusk conferred today with British, French and West German diplomats on measures to increase the West's readiness to meet a Berlin crisis.

Attending the late afternoon meeting were Viscount Hood, British Minister; Claude Lebel, French Minister Counselor, and Dr. Wilhelm Grewe, West German Ambassador. The British Ambassador, Sir Harold Caccia, and the French Ambassador, Hervé Alphand, were out of town.

At his news conference Wednesday President Kennedy said the National Security Council would conclude on Wednesday afternoon its review of actions to be taken to strengthen the military position of the United States and these decisions would be communicated to its allies this week.

Coordination Is Outlined

Officials said that in addition to disclosing the projected United States moves, Secretary Rusk had suggested in general terms the coordinated actions that the Administration hoped its principal allies would take.

The meeting lasted forty-five minutes. Afterward Dr. Grewe said Mr. Rusk had presented "the Administration's ideas." There was not much discussion, Dr. Grewe said, because "it was the type of meeting where you don't have a great exchange."

He said he was certain West Germany would "step up its defense efforts" if the Council of the North Atlantic Treaty Organization decided this should be done.

West Germany's assigned goal in the alliance is twelve divisions. It now has seven divisions, six of them at full strength. The United States would like West Germany to speed the completion of the seventh and form three more as quickly as possible.

Kennedy Stressed Tension

At his news conference President Kennedy had stressed that the Western alliance was probably facing a period of mounting tensions in relations with the Soviet Union extending beyond the Berlin question, and that it was therefore necessary to consider "what we can in common do."

Tomorrow Secretary of Defense Robert S. McNamara and Gen. Lyman L. Lemnitzer, Chairman of the Joint Chiefs of Staff, will fly to Paris to brief representatives of the Atlantic alliance on United States plans.

They will be accompanied by Paul H. Nitze, Assistant Secretary of Defense for International Security Affairs, and Thomas K. Finletter, United States delegate to NATO headquarters.

Tuesday evening President Kennedy will address the nation

Continued on Page 6, Column 4

U. S. AGAIN FIRES MAN INTO SPACE; CAPSULE LOST AFTER SEA LANDING, BUT ASTRONAUT SWIMS TO SAFETY

Associated Press Wirephoto

Helicopter at right tries vainly to lift space capsule, Liberty Bell 7, from the Atlantic after space flight

Associated Press Wirephoto From N. A. S. A.

Capt. Virgil I. Grissom, behind capsule, waves after trip

United Press International Telephoto From N. A. S. A.

Captain Grissom, aboard carrier, talks with the President

Unplanned Swim Leaves Grissom a 'Little Uneasy'

By JOHN W. FINNEY

Special to The New York Times.

CAPE CANAVERAL, Fla., July 21—Within a half-hour, Capt. Virgil I. Grissom, the second United States astronaut, floated in two elements. For five minutes of his sixteen-minute ride into space he was in the weightless condition of space flight. Then for two to four minutes he floated in his silvery space suit in the Atlantic Ocean.

The first experience, he said, was thrilling. The unexpected dunking left him "a little uneasy," he reported after having been landed by helicopter on the aircraft carrier Randolph. His first words after landing were:

"Give me something to blow my nose. My head is full of sea water."

Why Captain Grissom was forced to end his 118-mile-high trip into space with a swim for his life was a critical question being asked by space agency officials. And for the moment there was no certain answer.

One moment the astronaut was waving to the rescue helicopter overhead through the "picture window" of his capsule, bobbing upright in gentle seas. The next moment the escape hatch had blown from the side of the Liberty Bell 7 capsule, letting water pour into it and forcing the astronaut to swim away from his craft, which was sinking rapidly in 2,800 fathoms—more than three miles—of water.

For more than two minutes, the astronaut, who was described by Comdr. Alan. B. Shepard Jr. as more of a "floater" than a swimmer, was forced to tread water. Around him spread the

Continued on Page 8, Column 3

HATCH BLOWN OFF

Mishap Not Explained—Grissom Reported in Good Condition

Text of Grissom conversation with base, Page 9.

By RICHARD WITKIN

Special to The New York Times.

CAPE CANAVERAL, Fla., July 21—Virgil I. Grissom became the nation's second space explorer today.

The Air Force captain rocketed aboard a Mercury capsule on an arching flight that took him 118 miles into the sky and 303 miles out into the Atlantic.

But the flight was denied complete success. A mishap forced the 35-year-old astronaut to take an unplanned swim and resulted in the sinking of the $2,000,000 capsule with precious films aboard.

From the take-off at 8:20 A. M., Eastern daylight time, until the capsule landed in the ocean sixteen minutes later, the mission appeared as successful as the nearly perfect journey of the nation's first space traveler, Navy Comdr. Alan B. Shepard Jr., on May 5.

Capsule Ships Water

Minutes later, for reasons unknown, explosive bolts blew out the side hatch of the bobbing capsule before a Marine helicopter overhead could hook on and lift the capsule upright.

This hooking-on procedure was provided so that water would not pour into the open hatch when the seventy explosive bolts blew off the cover.

Captain Grissom said he had not pulled the plunger that controls the bolts. The cover blew off before the helicopter had had a chance to lift the capsule to its upright position.

Water rolled into the capsule immediately, and the captain floated out. Two to four minutes later he was hauled to safety by a second helicopter. He had swallowed more sea water than he would have liked. He was somewhat shaky. But he was essentially in excellent condition.

Some observers interpreted the following radio exchange between the capsule and the helicopter as indicating that Captain Grissom had, in fact,

Continued on Page 8, Column 1

SOVIET SAYS NAVY HAS ATOMIC EDGE

Warns U.S. It Has More and Faster Submarines of Missile-Firing Type

By SEYMOUR TOPPING

Special to The New York Times.

MOSCOW, July 21—The Soviet Government newspaper Izvestia declared today that the Soviet Union had a larger and faster fleet of rocket-launching nuclear submarines than the United States.

In the midst of the growing controversy over Berlin, Izvestia asserted that the Soviet Navy boasted "atomic submarines armed with the mightiest rockets of various types."

It was not said, however, whether the Soviet submarines were capable—like the United States Polaris submarines—of launching missiles under water.

The references to nuclear submarines were made in a political commentary written by Observer, a signature reserved for authoritative pronouncements.

Robert Kennedy Scored

It attacked Robert F. Kennedy, the United States Attorney General, for a speech made July 15 at the launching of the Polaris submarine John Marshall at Newport News.

In that speech, the Attorney General, President Kennedy's brother, warned Mr. Khrushchev that the United States could "be pushed too far." He cautioned against "underestimating the American people."

Izvestia denounced the Attorney General as one of a group of United States leaders who had created "military hysteria" over Berlin and had threatened the Soviet Union.

Izvestia contended that Soviet nuclear submarines operated "not at a lesser but at a greater speed than United States submarines and were not fewer in

Continued on Page 7, Column 2

BROOKLYN YOUTH SLAIN OVER DIME

Congresswoman Tours Area After Stomp Killing

An 18-year-old Brooklyn youth was stomped to death in an argument over a dime last night.

Less than three hours after the slaying, Representative Edith Green, Democrat of Oregon, began a scheduled tour of Brooklyn, including the neighborhood where the murder occurred, to study juvenile delinquency conditions.

The victim, Judge Sanders of 939 Lafayette Avenue, was playing handball with his brother Matthew, 17, in a playground at Greene and Stuyvesant Avenues in the Bedford-Stuyvesant section.

According to the police, the brothers heard a cousin involved in a noisy dispute with three other youths at the far end of the playground. The argument was over borrowing 10 cents, the police said.

When the Sanders brothers went to investigate, the older one was attacked by the trio. He was punched and kicked,

Continued on Page 12, Column 2

6,406 APARTMENTS SLATED FOR CITY

Estimate Board to Weigh 9 Middle-Income Projects

By PAUL CROWELL

Proposals for the construction $115,100,000 worth of middle-income housing will go before the Board of Estimate next Thursday.

J. Clarence Davies Jr., chairman of the New York City Housing and Redevelopment Board, said yesterday that the proposals, for 6,406 residential apartments in nine projects, constituted the "biggest single program of middle-income housing ever advanced at once in the city, the state or the nation."

Mr. Davies said the nine projects, all by private builders, would be completed within the next five years. He said 2,043 of the apartments would be available within the year, and the rest would be completed in two to five years.

The Board of Estimate has been asked to review the projects and give them final approval. The plans provide for tax abatement and mortgage loans by the city for the benefit of the builders. The state's

Continued on Page 22, Column 4

ARGENTINA TO GET $204,500,000 AID

U. S. and World Bank Will Grant Development Loans

By TAD SZULC

Special to The New York Times.

WASHINGTON, July 21—Argentina will be granted $204,500,000 in loans for industrial development by the United States and the International Bank for Reconstruction and Development.

It was authoritatively stated today that agreements in principle on the loans had been negotiated here by United States and World Bank officials and an Argentine mission headed by Ambassador Adalbert Krieger Vasena.

Washington also agreed to send a trade mission to Argentina to help her expand her exports to the United States. In addition, Washington will send specialists to Argentina to determine whether the United States ban on the entry of Argentine meat because of foot-and-mouth disease can be lifted for cooked meats.

Surplus Issue Solved

Argentina believes the resumption of substantial exports to the United States can go far to help with her balance-of-payments problems and her financial requirements for imports of industrial equipment.

The negotiators also worked out a solution of the long-standing problem of Argentina's concern that United States loans and donations of surplus commodities, particularly wheat, were threatening her sales abroad.

They agreed to arrange for consultations every six months to determine whether the dis-

Continued on Page 3, Column 1

Strikers Stone Vans at Aqueduct, but Races Go On

Associated Press

Strikers attempt to prevent a horse van from entering the Aqueduct race track in Queens

By STANLEY LEVEY

More than 1,200 stablehands went on strike yesterday at the Aqueduct race track for union recognition and economic gains. Vans carrying horses to the track were stoned and six pickets were arrested on charges of disorderly conduct. However, the violence failed to halt the day's nine-race program. The walkout involved grooms, exercise boys and hot walkers—men who walk horses to cool them off after races and workouts. The New York Racing Association said that today's nine-race card would be held. Taking no chances, however, the association set up an emergency program of

Continued on Page 16, Column 2

NEWS INDEX

News Summary and Index, Page 23

Astronaut Grissom prepares to enter his spacecraft, the *Liberty Bell 7*.

The mighty *Atlas* booster that propelled the *Liberty Bell 7* into space.

"All the News That's Fit to Print"

The New York Times

LATE CITY EDITION
U. S. Weather Bureau Report (Page 90) forecast:
Increasing cloudiness today.
Snow, rain tonight. Rain tomorrow.
Temp. range: 38—26; yesterday: 51—31.

VOL. CXI . No. 38,014. NEW YORK, WEDNESDAY, FEBRUARY 21, 1962. 10 cents beyond 50-mile zone from New York City except on Long Island. Higher in air delivery cities. FIVE CENTS

GLENN ORBITS EARTH 3 TIMES SAFELY; PICKED UP IN CAPSULE BY DESTROYER; PRESIDENT WILL GREET HIM IN FLORIDA

N.A.S.A. via Associated Press Wirephoto
READY: Lieut. Col. John H. Glenn Jr. walks to the van to take him to the launching site at Cape Canaveral, Fla.

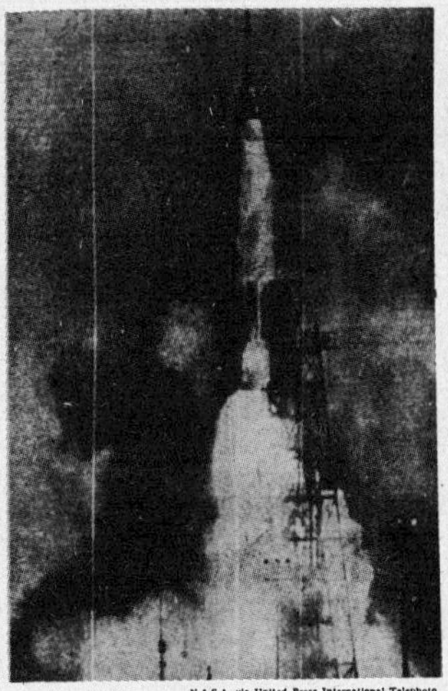

N.A.S.A. via United Press International Telephoto
LIFT-OFF: The Atlas rocket booster bearing the Project Mercury spacecraft roars aloft with 360,000-pound thrust.

N.A.S.A. via Associated Press Wirephoto
RECOVERY: Crewmen of destroyer Noa secure capsule carrying astronaut before lifting it out of the Atlantic.

81,000-MILE TRIP

Flight Aides Feared for the Capsule as It Began Its Re-Entry

Transcript of conversations with Glenn, Pages 25 and 26.

By RICHARD WITKIN
Special to The New York Times.

CAPE CANAVERAL, Fla., Feb. 20—John H. Glenn Jr. orbited three times around the earth today and landed safely to become the first American to make such a flight.

The 40-year-old Marine Corps lieutenant colonel traveled about 81,000 miles in 4 hours 56 minutes before splashing into the Atlantic at 2:43 P. M. Eastern Standard Time.

He had been launched from here at 9:47 A. M.

The astronaut's safe return was no less a relief than a thrill to the Project Mercury team, because there had been real concern that the Friendship 7 capsule might disintegrate as it rammed back into the atmosphere.

There had also been a serious question whether Colonel Glenn could complete three orbits as planned. But despite persistent control problems, he managed to complete the entire flight plan.

Lands in Bahamas Area

The astronaut's landing place was near Grand Turk Island in the Bahamas, about 700 miles southeast of here.

Still in his capsule, he was plucked from the water at 3:01 P. M. with a boom and block and tackle by the destroyer Noa. The capsule was deposited on deck at 3:04.

Colonel Glenn's first words as he stepped out onto the Noa's deck were: "It was hot in there."

He quickly obtained a glass of iced tea.

He was in fine condition except for two skinned knuckles hurt in the process of blowing out the side hatch of the capsule.

The colonel was transferred by helicopter to the carrier Randolph, whose recovery helicopters had raced the Noa for the honor of making the pick-up. After a meal and extensive "de-briefing" aboard the carrier, he was flown to Grand Turk by submarine patrol plane for two days of rest and interviews on technical, medical and other aspects of his flight.

The Noa, nearest ship to the

Continued on Page 20, Column 1

CARLINO CLEARED IN SHELTER CASE BY ETHICS PANEL

Lane Scored in Unanimous Report, Which He Calls 'Cynical and Callous'

Text of concluding sections of report is on Page 50.

By WARREN WEAVER Jr.
Special to The New York Times.

ALBANY, Feb. 20—The Assembly Committee on Ethics and Guidance exonerated Speaker Joseph F. Carlino today of charges of conflict of interest made by Assemblyman Mark Lane.

In a unanimous report submitted to the Legislature, the bipartisan committee said:

¶Mr. Carlino did not "betray the public trust" by serving as a director of a company manufacturing home fall-out shelters while helping to pass school-shelter legislation last November.

¶He did not draft or support the shelter legislation "in any improper manner" for the benefit of the company, Lancer Industries, Inc.

¶The Speaker was not influenced in his official actions in behalf of the bill by the fact that he was a member of the board of directors of Lancer.

¶He did not receive any special benefit from the passage of the legislation.

Charges Unsubstantiated

"The committee concludes with respect to each and every accusation contained in the charges filed," the report said, "that Assemblyman Lane and those who testified in their support failed to submit credible evidence to substantiate them."

In submitting the report, the Ethics Committee requested that the full 150-member lower house vote "with respect to the conclusions reached herein" in the light of the fact that "the charges were directed against its [the Assembly's] highest ranking official."

Assemblyman Donald A. Campbell, Republican of Amsterdam, who is chairman of the committee, said he would move in the Assembly tomorrow for acceptance of the report. Mr. Carlino is expected to be absent during the debate and vote.

Assemblyman Lane, a Democrat of Manhattan, had charged that the Speaker was guilty of

Continued on Page 50, Column 1

ROCKEFELLER BARS KOREA WAR BONUS

Voices Opposition in Face of Legislators' Backing

By LAYHMOND ROBINSON
Special to The New York Times.

ALBANY, Feb. 20—Governor Rockefeller expressed strong opposition tonight to a state bonus for veterans of the Korean war.

Mr. Rockefeller told the New York State Department of the American Legion that he could not "as a responsible leader of government" support the demand for a bonus. The veterans' group had been campaigning for a $100,000,000 bonus for the 482,000 Korean war veterans or their next-of-kin in the state.

The Governor said his stand was backed "unanimously" by the "Republican leadership of the state." This was a reference to the leaders of the Republican-controlled Legislature.

He said that demands for funds for education, mental health, narcotics control and other state services were too great to permit a diversion of money for a veterans' bonus.

Mr. Rockefeller thus took a position in direct opposition to that of most of the Republican and Democratic members of the Legislature, who have been pushing for the bonus. The issue

Continued on Page 51, Column 1

Jersey Bus Strike Settled; Service Is Due Tomorrow

By PETER KIHSS

An agreement to end the New Jersey bus strike was reached last night. The agreement, subject to ratification by the striking employes, was announced by Gov. Richard J. Hughes. The pact will be submitted to the union members at their garages starting at 7 A. M. today.

Union and management men expressed hope that buses could begin operating tomorrow at 4:30 A. M.

The strike against Public Service Coordinated Transport started at 12:01 A. M. Monday and halted 2,511 buses providing 1,000,000 rides a day. The company's 200 routes serve all of New Jersey's twenty-one counties except Warren and Hunterdon and go into New York City and Philadelphia. The Newark subway system was also shut.

Carlin Gets Credit

Governor Hughes credited Mayor Leo P. Carlin of Newark with having "sparkplugged" the successful negotiations. Mayor Carlin flew back from a Miami Beach vacation yesterday and arranged the talks with both sides and with Daniel F. Fitzpatrick, a Federal mediator, and the Governor and himself. The meeting started in Newark at 8:30 P. M., and the agreement was announced at 11:28 P. M.

Earlier, David L. Yunich, president of Bamberger's New Jersey, had asserted that the strike was having a "devastating * * * almost catastrophic" effect on retail business in Newark and elsewhere in the state. A Camden department store reported sales had fallen nearly 50 per cent on Monday, although not that far yesterday.

Despite the drop in shopping, most commuters managed to get to work by alternate means and with a minimum of confusion.

The agreement reached last night provides for a wage increase of 10 cents an hour retroactive to Feb. 1 and extending to next Feb. 1; 4 cents more an hour from then until Aug. 1, 1963, and another 4 cents an hour from then until

Continued on Page 39, Column 3

ROSENTHAL WINS QUEENS ELECTION

But Democrat-Liberal Has Margin of Only 193 Votes —Machines Guarded

By CLAYTON KNOWLES

Benjamin S. Rosenthal, a Democrat-Liberal backed by President Kennedy, squeaked through to victory last night in a special Congressional election in Queens' Sixth District.

By the slim margin of 193 votes, Mr. Rosenthal, a lanky 38-year-old Elmhurst lawyer, edged past Thomas F. Galvin of Flushing, the Republican candidate, to win a three-way race. Emil Levin of Flushing, a Democrat running as an independent, finished far behind.

The unofficial final tally, delayed as the early vote was hastily rechecked for errors, was: Rosenthal, 16,032; Galvin, 15,839, and Levin, 4,216.

Republicans immediately challenged the result and, while Mr. Galvin did not immediately ask for a recount, he sent a telegram demanding that the voting machines be impounded. All voting machines, normally just

Continued on Page 48, Column 3

McNamara Reports Gains by Vietnamese

By JACK RAYMOND
Special to The New York Times.

WASHINGTON, Feb. 20—Secretary of Defense Robert S. McNamara returned to the capital today and reported improvement in the South Vietnamese effort against Communist insurgents.

He had presided at a meeting of United States military and civilian officials yesterday at the headquarters in Hawaii of Admiral Harry S. Felt, commander of United States forces in the Pacific. The meeting was the third in a series of monthly talks on the hostilities in South Vietnam.

A spokesman for Mr. McNamara said that the forces of South Vietnam, supported by the United States, "are hitting

Continued on Page 8, Column 5

NEWS INDEX

KENNEDY PRAISES 'WONDERFUL JOB'

Tells Glenn Nation Is 'Really Proud of You'—Welcome at White House Planned

By TOM WICKER
Special to The New York Times

WASHINGTON, Feb. 20—President Kennedy phoned Lieut. Col. John H. Glenn Jr. today immediately after the astronaut's successful orbital flight and arranged to meet him at Cape Canaveral Friday morning.

The President also set in motion plans for bringing Colonel Glenn to Washington on Monday or Tuesday, for receptions at the White House and the Capitol and a parade down Pennsylvania Avenue

A television set in his office and an open telephone line to Cape Canaveral had kept Mr. Kennedy informed of Colonel Glenn's progress all through the day.

The astronaut's three orbits around the earth, Mr. Kennedy said in a statement, have embarked the United States on a "new ocean"—that of space.

"I believe the United States must sail on it and be in a position second to none," the President said within minutes of Colonel Glenn's safe emergence from his Mercury capsule.

Colonel Glenn, he said, is the "kind of American of whom we are most proud." Mr. Kennedy also praised "all those who participated" in making the astronaut's flight successful.

Then, at 4:10 P. M., Mr. Ken-

Continued on Page 23, Column 7

Leaders of Algeria Back Peace Terms

By THOMAS F. BRADY
Special to The New York Times

TUNIS, Feb. 20—The Algerian nationalist Provisional Government met today and gave full approval to peace accords negotiated with the French by four members of the rebel regime.

One Algerian said afterward: "All twelve members of the Government are in unanimous agreement." This was a reference to five ministers who are prisoners in France, the four negotiators and three ministers who remained in Tunis during the secret talks last week on the French-Swiss border.

The negotiators were Belkacem Krim, M'Hammed Yazid, Saad Dahlab and Lakhdar Ben Tobbal. They met here today

Continued on Page 11, Column 1

The President's Statement

Special to The New York Times.

WASHINGTON, Feb. 20—Following is the text of President Kennedy's statement on Colonel Glenn's flight:

I know that I express the great happiness and thanksgiving of all of us that Colonel Glenn has completed his trip, and I know that this is particularly felt by Mrs. Glenn and his two children.

A few days ago Colonel Glenn came to the White House and visited me, and he is—as are the other astronauts—the kind of American of whom we are most proud.

Some years ago, as a Marine pilot, he raced the sun across this country—and lost. And today he won.

I also want to say a word for all those who participated with Colonel Glenn in Canaveral. They faced many disappointments and delays—the burdens upon them were great—but they kept their heads and they made a judgment, and I think their judgment has been vindicated.

We have a long way to go in this space race. We started late. But this is the new ocean, and I believe the United States must sail on it and be in a position second to none.

Some months ago I said that I hoped every American would serve his country. Today Colonel Glenn served his, and we all express our thanks to him.

ADENAUER WANTS PARLEY ON BERLIN

Suggests Foreign Ministers of Big Four Meet 'Soon'

By SYDNEY GRUSON
Special to The New York Times.

BONN, Germany, Feb. 20—Chancellor Adenauer suggested today that a Big Four foreign ministers' conference on Berlin should be convened "soon." He was speaking to the Parliamentary group of the Christian Democratic Union.

He said that it might be "expedient" to "take a pause" in the Berlin talks now going on between Andrei A. Gromyko, the Soviet Foreign Minister, and Llewellyn E. Thompson Jr., the United States Ambassador to Moscow.

Ambassador Thompson should not continue "negotiating" endlessly, Dr. Adenauer added. There have been four meetings in the last seven weeks between Mr. Gromyko and Mr. Thompson without any advance toward a Berlin settlement.

[A warning by Izvestia, the Soviet Government newspaper, that Moscow was ready to push through a separate peace treaty with East Germany if the United States did not alter its position in the talks raised the possibility of a renewal of the Soviet deadline on a peace pact.]

Dr. Adenauer's advocacy of a new conference of the United States, British, French and Soviet foreign ministers reflected his unhappiness with the course of the Gromyko-Thompson talks.

He is known to believe that Mr. Thompson has made what

Continued on Page 4, Column 2

URBAN PLAN VOTE PUT OFF IN SENATE

Administration Rebuffed on Forcing Issue to Floor

By RUSSELL BAKER
Special to The New York Times.

WASHINGTON, Feb. 20—President Kennedy affronted the Senate's dignity today and got a political rebuff for it.

In a surprising repudiation of the Administration's voting form sheets, the elders turned on the White House and rejected a leadership move to get a quick floor test of the President's urban affairs proposal. The vote was 58 to 42.

Thus, the White House lost its chance to get a favorable Senate vote on the plan before the House could vote to kill it. The Democrats also lost their chance to get the Senate's Republicans clearly on record for or against the plan to create a Cabinet-level Department of Urban Affairs and Housing.

Today's test came on the dusty parliamentary question whether the Senate should take the plan away from the Government Operations Committee and bring it to an immediate floor vote. This is known as "discharging" the committee. It is an extraordinary procedure that is rarely used because it is repugnant to Senate traditions.

Today it became the instrument of the President's defeat.

The move to discharge the Government Operations Committee was undertaken with misgivings yesterday by Mike Mansfield of Montana, Senate Democratic leader. The reason was a sudden threat by the

Continued on Page 16, Column 4

COL. GLENN FLOWN TO ISLE FOR CHECK

He Feels Tired but Elated —Goes to Grand Turk for Report and Examination

By JOHN W. FINNEY
Special to The New York Times

GRAND TURK ISLAND, Feb. 20—An elated but tired John H. Glenn Jr. returned to earth tonight and reported that he "couldn't feel better."

The 40-year-old astronaut also reported that he had felt no sickness or discomfort during his five-hour, three-orbit flight around the earth, even during the extended period of weightlessness.

Colonel Glenn landed at this small British possession at 9:11 P. M. in a Navy S-2-F submarine patrol plane. He was clad in light blue coveralls. He had co-piloted the plane from the carrier Randolph, where he spent several hours after being retrieved from the Atlantic ocean.

Around his ears were the marks of the earphones that he had worn while piloting a plane that traveled at about one-hundredth the speed of his Friendship 7 space capsule And on his face was an excited enthusiastic smile.

Asked how he felt, the red-headed marine replied: "Fine, wonderful, I couldn't feel better."

And he was also hungry. His first comment on stepping into the small hospital arranged for him was: "First I want something to eat—I am hungry." A steak dinner was promptly or-

Continued on Page 22, Column 2

Moscow, Unmoved, Gives News of Orbit

By THEODORE SHABAD
Special to The New York Times.

MOSCOW, Feb. 20—The Russians voiced congratulations tonight on hearing of Lieut. Col. John H. Glenn Jr.'s orbital space flight.

But they showed no enthusiasm on the successful launching and landing of the spacecraft Friendship 7.

These reactions were reported from Moscow University by United States exchange students who had been listening with Russians to radio reports of Colonel Glenn's progress.

"They congratulated us in friendly fashion but were oddly reserved," an American said.

Soviet radio and television were unusually prompt in reporting the flight. The first bul-

Continued on Page 22, Column 5

NEW YORK PAUSES TO 'WATCH' GLENN

Millions Rivet Attention on Astronaut in Flight

By NAN ROBERTSON

The thoughts of millions of New Yorkers were riveted for hours yesterday on one man alone in space.

Minute by minute, they followed the orbital flight of Lieut. Col. John H. Glenn Jr. three times around the earth, waiting in agonizing suspense for his safe return. The life of New York almost stood still during the dramatic countdown.

From then on until Colonel Glenn scrambled "hale and hearty" out of his capsule on the destroyer Noa, people carried on absent-mindedly and in spurts. Millions of working hours were lost during the day, but no one could have begrudged this. Employers and the employed alike were drawn irresistibly to radio and television sets.

The most spectacular display of interest occurred in Grand Central Terminal, where throngs of up to 9,000 persons massed before a huge television screen. The police described it as the largest static crowd in the station's history. The terminal manager said those who

Continued on Page 22, Column 6

Astronaut John Glenn enters his spacecraft, the *Friendship 7.*

A navy helicopter lifts Glenn off the deck of the *Noa* to the carrier *Randolph* after the successful landing of *Friendship 7.*

"All the News That's Fit to Print"

The New York Times.

LATE CITY EDITION
U. S. Weather Bureau Report (Page 50) forecasts: Partly cloudy today, tonight and tomorrow.
Temp. range: 71—59; yestrday: 79—55.
Temp.-Hum. Index: high 60's; yesterday: 70.

VOL. CXII..No. 38,495. NEW YORK, MONDAY, JUNE 17, 1963. TEN CENTS

SOVIET ORBITS WOMAN ASTRONAUT NEAR BYKOVSKY FOR DUAL FLIGHT; THEY TALK BY RADIO, ARE PUT ON TV

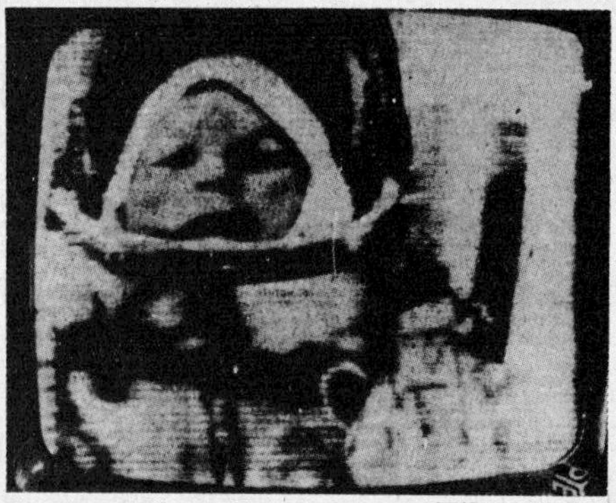

United Press International Radiophoto

IT'S A WOMAN'S UNIVERSE: Lieut. Valentina V. Tereshkova, the first woman in space, as she appeared on TV in Moscow yesterday while orbiting earth in Vostok VI.

PREMIER IS JOYFUL

Phones Spacewoman —She Tells World She Feels Fine

By SEYMOUR TOPPING
Special to The New York Times

MOSCOW, Monday, June 17—Junior Lieut. Valentina V. Tereshkova, the first woman to journey into space, was circling the earth this morning.

She chatted happily by radio telephone with Lieut. Col. Valery F. Bykovsky, who traveled in a nearby orbit.

Lieutenant Tereshkova, 26 years old, a heavy-set parachutist, was launched yesterday at 12:30 P.M. Moscow time (5:30 A.M. Sunday, New York time) aboard the Soviet spaceship Vostok VI.

Premier Khrushchev talked to her by radiotelephone as she orbited.

"Now you see what women are capable of," he said.

Television viewers in Eastern Europe saw the woman astronaut laughing after she reported by radio that she was feeling fine. A communiqué said she had withstood well the transition into weightlessness.

Saw Colonel Launched

Forty-five and a half hours earlier, Lieutenant Tereshkova had watched Colonel Bykovsky launched into space aboard the Vostok V from the Baikonour space center in the Central Asian Republic of Kazakhstan.

Now she was looping around the earth with him in a "group flight" that presumably would test new rendezvous techniques in space.

In the first group flight, by Maj. Andrian G. Nikolayev and Lieut. Col. Pavel R. Popovich last August, the Vostok III and the Vostok IV came within about four miles of each other.

Major Nikolayev circled the earth 64 times in 94 hours 22 minutes. Colonel Popovich orbited 48 times in 70 hours 57 minutes.

Purpose of Flights

The group flights are designed eventually to permit a direct link-up in space of two ships. This would be the first step toward the creation of a staging platform in space for longer voyages to the moon and the planets.

Soon after entering into orbit, the Soviet press agency Tass reported, the spaceship of the woman astronaut passed "in the direct vicinity" of Colonel Bykovsky's. The two astronauts established radio communication and then sent a joint message to Premier Khrushchev.

They reported, "We are at a close distance from each other. All systems in the ships are working excellently. Feeling well."

'Seagull' and 'Hawk'

Lieutenant Tereshkova was operating under the radio call signal "Seagull" and Colonel Bykovsky was designated "Hawk."

The woman astronaut was orbiting the earth every 88.3 minutes at a speed of 18,000 miles an hour. She was traveling in an orbit that was 181 kilometers (about 112 miles) from the earth at the closest point and 231 kilometers (about 141 miles) at the farthest.

Colonel Bykovsky was orbiting every 88.06 minutes and his minimum and maximum distances from the earth were 168.4 kilometers (about 104 miles) and 208.3 kilometers (about 129 miles).

The initial communiqué on the launching of Lieutenant Tereshkova stated:

"The flight is being made to continue the study of the effect of various space-flight fac-

Continued on Page 8, Column 1

PEKING SHARPENS MOSCOW ATTACK, PERILING PARLEY

Letter Assails Coexistence Policy and Insists Upon 'Revolutionary Struggle'

LISTS DISPUTED ISSUES

Ideological Meeting in July Believed Endangered by Uncompromising Stand

Special to The New York Times

HONG KONG, June 16 — A long letter from the Chinese Communists to the Central Committee of the Soviet Communist party appears to have made fruitless the ideological conference between the Chinese and the Russians scheduled to begin July 4 in Moscow.

The letter, sent by the Central Committee of the Chinese party, was made public in full by Hsinhua, the official Chinese press agency.

Dated last Friday, the letter outlined uncompromisingly the Chinese stand on all major points at issue in the ideological dispute. It listed 25 questions Peking wanted discussed at the meeting next month.

The Chinese said their general line was "one of resolute revolutionary struggle by the people of all countries, and of carrying the proletarian world revolution forward to the end." This, they said, would most effectively combat "imperialism" and defend "world peace."

Some Questions Listed

The 25 questions Peking wanted discussed included the following:

¶Defense, as an urgent task, of the revolutionary principles in the Moscow declarations of 1957 and 1960. The 1957 statement by Communist-bloc countries called for unity of all forces opposing "capitalism" and "imperialism." The 1960 declaration warned of the "strengthening of West German militarism" and the "revival of militarist forces in Japan."

¶The general line of the international Communist movement, which should not be reduced one-sidedly to "peaceful coexistence," "peaceful competition" and "peaceful transition."

¶Discussion of the questions of transition from capitalism to Socialism, war and peace, and nuclear weapons.

¶Question concerning the "combating of the cult of the individual" and the opposing of revisionism as the main danger in the international Communist movement.

World Communism's Status

The letter said the questions were crucial and required attention and solution. It was a reply to a Soviet letter of March 30 discussing the forthcoming meeting in Moscow.

The Chinese also asked for discussion of "criticism of Stalin." They proposed discussion of "matters of principle regarding the International Communist movement which were raised at the 20th and 22d congresses of the Soviet Communist party."

The letter expressed hope that the July talks would "yield positive results," but reiteration of China's "hard line" indicated positive results could come only from a retreat by the Soviet party.

The Chinese letter condemned

Continued on Page 5, Column 3

Ben-Gurion Steps Down; Israeli Cabinet Surprised

Premier Cites 'Personal Needs'—Eshkol Seen as Likely Successor

Special to The New York Times

TEL AVIV, June 16—David Ben-Gurion resigned unexpectedly today as the Premier and Defense Minister of Israel and gave up his seat in the Knesset (Parliament).

He announced his resignation at the close of the weekly meeting of his Cabinet. When the surprised ministers pressed him to give reasons for his decision, he said:

"They are personal needs. I propose to keep them to myself."

The 76-year-old leader, who has dominated the 15-year-history of Israel said that no specific national event or state problem had motivated his decision.

Finance Minister Levi Eshkol, 67, is expected to succeed Mr. Ben-Gurion as Premier. A Premier's resignation automatically dissolves the Government and Mr. Eshkol, if he is chosen, will have to form a new one.

Mr. Ben-Gurion apologized for any inconvenience he might cause and suggested that the same four Socialist and

Continued on Page 4, Column 2

Associated Press

David Ben-Gurion

2 SENATORS URGE KENNEDY TO STAY HIS TRIP ABROAD

Goldwater and Scott, Both Republicans, Assert He Is Needed at Home

Special to The New York Times

WASHINGTON, June 16—Two Republican Senators said today that President Kennedy should put off his European trip and stay at home to deal with domestic problems, especially civil rights.

The suggestion came from Senators Barry Goldwater of Arizona and Hugh Scott of Pennsylvania, who are ordinarily at opposite ends of the Republican spectrum. Senator Goldwater is a conservative, Senator Scott a G.O.P. liberal.

The President is scheduled to leave in two weeks for visits to Germany, Ireland, England and Italy. Some newspaper commentators have suggested that the trip is ill-timed in view of the racial crisis here and government uncertainty in Germany, Britain and Italy.

Senator Goldwater called the trip "a very grave mistake." Senator Scott said: "I'd rather see him go to Birmingham than to Berlin just now."

Not Even to Camp David

"What with Cuba still a burning issue," Senator Goldwater said, "with problems here at home—economic and racial—he has no business being out of the White House even to go to Camp David."

Senator Goldwater, who has made clear that he prefers voluntary desegregation efforts to new legislation, said the President should travel at home to use "his great moral persuasive ability with the businessmen of this country where segregation is practised."

The two G.O.P. senators were on a radio-television interview program with their Democratic colleague from Pennsylvania, Joseph S. Clark. The program is broadcast in Pennsylvania.

Senator Clark, while not strongly supporting the President's trip, said "a good case can be made for his going." He said it would be useful, among other things, to have the President in Italy just after the election of a new Pope.

Cites European Side

McGeorge Bundy, the President's special assistant for national security affairs, defended the European trip on a Columbia Broadcasting System show, "Washington Report."

Abandoning the long-planned tour now, he said, would have "quite serious consequences with respect to American clarity of purpose, American decision, the President's own real commitment to and interest in Europe."

The Republican comments

Continued on Page 13, Column 2

TORIES EXPECTED TO WIN IN DEBATE

But Macmillan Resignation Over the Profumo Case Is Predicted in Summer

By SYDNEY GRUSON
Special to The New York Times

LONDON, June 16—Unless the Opposition springs some new shocking surprise, Prime Minister Macmillan is expected to be upheld with a comfortable margin in tomorrow's House of Commons debate on the Profumo scandal.

With rare unanimity, British political commentators believe that it will be a Pyrrhic victory.

Many of them believe that if a formal deal has not been made, then an understanding exists within the Conservative party that Mr. Macmillan will give way to another leader this summer, when the heavy winds from the scandal have spent themselves.

Some Still Favor Resignation

Only among Mr. Macmillan's harshest party enemies and critics is there still a desire to see him overthrown, as the influential weekly periodical, The Economist, put it, "by a 21-year-old trollop," Christine Keeler.

It was the public disclosure 10 days ago that Miss Keeler had conducted simultaneous love affairs with John Profumo, Britain's former Secretary of State for War, and Capt. Yevgeni E. Ivanov, who was the Soviet deputy naval attaché here until last December, that led to the crisis facing Mr. Macmillan and his Government.

[The Soviet press agency Tass denied Sunday that Captain Ivanov was implicated in security matters in the Profumo scandal, United Press International reported in a dispatch from Moscow.]

The Opposition Labor party has charged that Mr. Macmillan was either negligent or naive in not recognizing the seriousness of the situation.

The Conservative back-bench members of Commons are

Continued on Page 3, Column 1

High Court Ruling On School Prayer Is Expected Today

By ANTHONY LEWIS
Special to The New York Times

WASHINGTON, June 16—The Supreme Court is expected to close its current term tomorrow with decisions on a number of significant cases.

Religion in schools is the issue that has captured the most public attention. The Court has before it two cases that followed its decision last year holding unconstitutional the required recitation of the Regents prayer in New York public schools.

The new cases, from Maryland and Pennsylvania, were argued before the Court in February. They are challenges to the practice of reading the Lord's Prayer and selected verses from the Bible at the start of each school day.

Shift in Reaction Seen

Bible reading is required in the public schools of 11 states and permitted in 13 others.

The initial public reaction to the prayer decision a year ago was highly critical. However, opinion has evidently shifted to a significant extent. Even the justices' mail on the issue was become more favorable.

Last month the United Presbyterian Church took a stand against devotional use of the Bible and other religious practices in public schools. Two weeks ago the general board of the National Council of Churches came out against Bible recitations.

In the two pending cases the

Continued on Page 14, Column 2

MILITANCY GROWS IN JACKSON DRIVE

More Aggressive Factions Seeking Leading Roles in Negro Demonstrations

By CLAUDE SITTON
Special to The New York Times

JACKSON, Miss., June 16—Some of the nation's most militant civil rights advocates took steps today, following a riot here, to take over leading roles in this city's racial controversy.

This development, coupled with the flat refusal of white segregationist officials to compromise, indicated that the explosive crisis might be approaching an early showdown.

The Kennedy Adminstration fears this may lead to serious violence. Its concern was demonstrated by a conference this afternoon between Justice Department officials and representatives of some of the more aggressive Negro factions here.

John Doar, Assistant Attorney General in the Civil Rights Division, and Thelton Henderson, a division attorney, met with the Negro group in the Masonic Lodge in Lynch Street.

Officials of the Student Non-Violent Coordinating Committee, in an emergency meeting in Atlanta, decided to throw their support behind continuing mass

Continued on Page 12, Column 3

Talks With Negroes Halted by Leaders In Cambridge, Md.

By The Associated Press

CAMBRIDGE, Md., June 16—White leaders here abruptly ended late today negotiations toward a settlement of racial problems that have placed this Eastern Shore community under modified martial law. They asked Gov. J. Millard Tawes to keep National Guard troops in Cambridge indefinitely.

Their statement came after Mayor Calvin W. Mowbray had met with the City Council, the Dorchester County Commissioners and the county delegation to the Maryland Legislature.

In a telegram to Governor Tawes, the group said that "in view of the breach of faith and the threats of the Negro representatives you invited to meet with you and with us last Friday, further negotiations with these people are impossible."

"We are of the strong opinion that the National Guard should be continued on duty here," the telegram added.

Would Bring in 'Thousands'

Philip Savage, an executive secretary of the National Association for the Advancement of Colored People, had said yesterday that if the racial problems in Cambridge were not resolved by next Friday, "thousands of people will be mobilized in Cambridge."

"I can bring 10,000 people into this city if necessary," he said.

Governor Tawes had met with white and Negro leaders of Cambridge Friday night, shortly after he had ordered the National Guard into the town.

He said after the meeting that he felt the groundwork had been laid for fruitful negotiations on the local level.

The Governor was not immediately available for comment today.

Mrs. Gloria Richardson, chairman of the Cambridge Nonviolent Action Committee, said she would have no statement until

Continued on Page 13, Column 3

MUSCOVITES GLOW OVER SPACE FEAT

Sunday Strollers Smile With Pride as Loudspeakers Blare Word of Flight

By HENRY TANNER
Special to The New York Times

MOSCOW, June 16 — There was pride and joy in the faces of Muscovites today when they received the news that the first woman to be sent into space was a Russian.

Their pleasure was of the quiet sort, relaxed and confident, almost blasé. There were no parades or noisy demonstrations, either organized or spontaneous.

The sidewalks in the center of the city were crowded with Sunday strollers when the loudspeakers on the many squares boomed out the announcement "A woman went into space."

The strollers smiled happily at each other. Some stopped so that they could hear the loudspeakers better. Others continued to walk as they listened, nodded and smiled.

Event Expected

All of them had expected the event.

A young man called out: "Listen to that."

"Now it has actually happened," a woman said.

Another, a little older, said: "I am too old myself, but my children probably will go to the moon." The thought made her smile.

Later, on Red Square, a few compact groups of young people drifted back and forth across the wide expanse, where the cobblestones were gleaming in a fine, drizzling rain.

There the television camera of an American network attracted a crowd of the curious. And the big American cars of reporters were scrutinized knowingly by engine-conscious youngsters. A young man approached a reporter and want-

Continued on Page 8, Column 2

Troops and Tanks Quell Buddhist Riots in Saigon

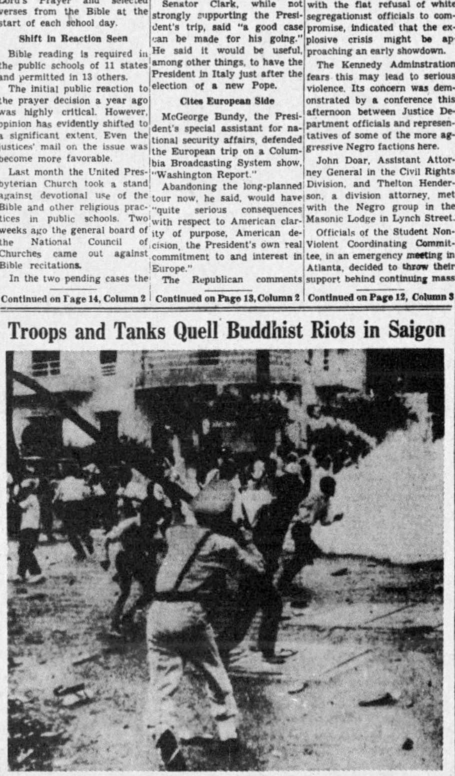

Associated Press Radiophoto

Amid exploding tear gas, branch-wielding policeman chases rioters in a littered street

By The Associated Press

SAIGON, Vietnam, June 16—Security forces restored order in Saigon with tanks and barbed wire tonight, following rioting by Buddhists in the most violent anti-Government outburst in South Vietnam in years. Government forces put down the demonstration with tear gas, clubs and shots fired in the air. The rioting apparently shattered an hours-old accord between leaders of the nation's Buddhist majority and President Ngo Dinh Diem's Government, which is dominated by Roman Catholics. The United States had put pressure on the Saigon regime to meet the Buddhists'

Continued on Page 4, Column 4

Youth Crimes Worry Suburbs; Vandalism and Thefts on Rise

By CLARENCE DEAN

What is wrong with suburban New York teen-agers?

A series of reports in the last few weeks involving thefts, drinking, sex, vandalism and gang fights has revived the question of why youngsters from so-called good homes appear to be seriously misbehaving.

There are those who maintain that the reports are exaggerated, that today's teen-agers are no worse than those of previous years, and that most youngsters in the suburbs are leading orderly and constructive lives.

But the indications are disquieting. For example:

On May 16, the Council of Darien School Parents in Fairfield County, Conn., issued a report saying that teen-age behavior in that commuter town had reached a "point of alarm." The report referred to drinking, stealing, shoplifting, vandalism and sexual misbehavior.

On May 20, the Parent-Teacher Association in Chappaqua, a commuter town in Westchester County, said it had found evidence of "a considerable—even shocking—amount of shoplifting by young people." The association said the activity had become "some sort of game."

On May 23, Long Island state parkway police dispersed with some difficulty about 800 youths who had driven to the parking field at Jones Beach for what the police said had become a beer-drinking brawl.

On May 26, the police arrested 22 youths congregated in a beach area near Smithtown, L. I. The police said the boys were prepared for a "rumble" with a

Continued on Page 11, Column 1

U.S. Role in Arts Called Narrow In Heckscher Report to Kennedy

By TOM WICKER
Special to The New York Times

WASHINGTON, June 16 — An 80-page report sweepingly critical of the Government's attitude toward the arts was made public today by the White House.

The critique was submitted by August Heckscher, President Kennedy's special consultant on the arts. It listed steps by which Washington might foster high cultural standards. Replying to Mr. Heckscher, the President wrote:

"Your report opens up what I am confident will be a new and fruitful relationship between government and the arts."

Mr. Heckscher's report was accompanied by his resignation from the part-time post, not as a protest but because he had served more than twice as long as the six months to which he had agreed.

The resignation evoked a response from Mr. Kennedy headed "Dear Augie." The letter said, "The best tribute to the success of your work is the decision to establish this function on a full-time and, I hope, permanent basis."

Mr. Heckscher was appointed in March, 1962, as the first cultural coordinator between the President and governmental and private agencies. A successor to Mr. Heckscher, who is director of the Twentieth Century Fund, is expected to be named soon.

Mr. Heckscher couched his report in terms of how the Government should stimulate artistic achievement, make the

Continued on Page 22, Column 1

NEWS INDEX

"All the News That's Fit to Print"

The New York Times.

LATE CITY EDITION
U. S. Weather Bureau Report (Page 70) forecasts: Cloudy and foggy, then partly cloudy today; cloudy tonight and tomorrow. Temp. range: 42—38; yesterday: 40—35.

VOL. CXIV..No. 39,136. NEW YORK, FRIDAY, MARCH 19, 1965. TEN CENTS

RUSSIAN FLOATS IN SPACE FOR 10 MINUTES; LEAVES ORBITING CRAFT WITH A LIFELINE; MOSCOW SAYS MOON TRIP IS 'TARGET NOW'

Tass via Associated Press Cablephoto

LEAVING SPACESHIP: Lieut. Col. Aleksei A. Leonov emerges from Voskhod 2 to become first man to float freely in space. Photos were made from videotape broadcast.

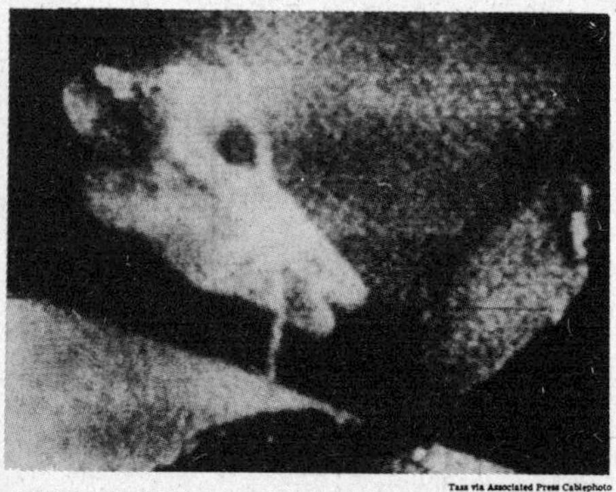

Tass via Associated Press Cablephoto

ALONE IN SPACE: Colonel Leonov outside the ship traveling at nearly five miles a second. He is attached by a lifeline. The projection at right carries movie equipment.

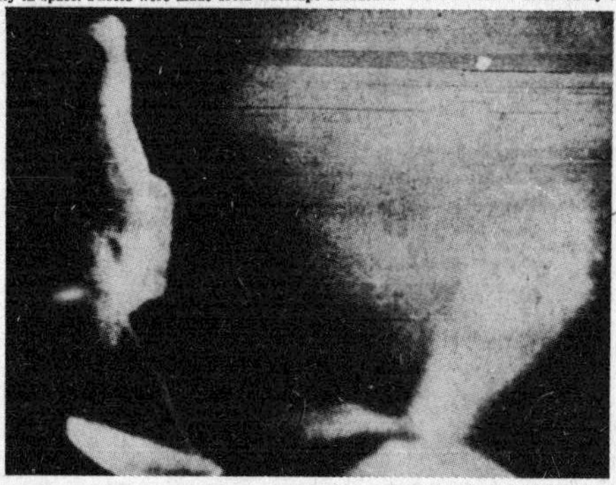

Tass via United Press International Cablephoto

WEIGHTLESS: Colonel Leonov turning behind his craft. Balance between forces of his orbital motion and the pull of gravity produces the condition of weightlessness.

Tass via Associated Press Cablephoto

BEFORE THE FLIGHT: Colonel Leonov in space suit before launching. He spent 10 minutes outside the craft.

JOHNSON OFFERS TO CALL UP GUARD IF WALLACE WON'T

Rejects Governor's Bid for U.S. 'Civilian Forces' to Protect Rights March

Excerpts from address by Gov. Wallace are on Page 20.

By CABELL PHILLIPS
Special to The New York Times

WASHINGTON, March 18 — President Johnson offered tonight to mobilize the Alabama National Guard to protect the Selma-to-Montgomery marchers next week.

In rejecting a request by Gov. George C. Wallace for "federal civilian forces" to police the demonstration, the President pointed out that the Governor could mobilize the Guard if he felt such protection was needed.

He then said that if the Governor did not do so, and conditions warranted, he would call up the Guard himself.

[In Montgomery, Governor Wallace told a joint session of the Alabama Legislature of his request to President Johnson. After he spoke, the Legislature adopted a resolution calling the protest march "asinine and ridiculous." Page 20.]

Delays Ranch Trip

The President's statement was made to a hastily summoned news conference in his White House office at 10:15 o'clock tonight. He had delayed his departure for a weekend at his ranch in Texas because of the developments in the Alabama situation.

The President first read reporters a telegram he had received from Governor Wallace at 8:48 tonight.

The Governor said that in order to maintain maximum security for the march which had been authorized by a Federal Court the state would need the services of more than 6,000 men, 489 vehicles, 15 buses and necessary supporting units.

The President's statement said:

"The questions raised by the Selma-Montgomery march were submitted to the court in Montgomery, Ala.

Cites Court's Ruling

"That court, with an Alabama judge sitting, after hearing all of the evidence, including evidence as to the problems of protecting marchers, determined that a march should be permitted and that the marchers should be protected.

"The Federal Government does not have civilian personnel approaching the figure suggested by Governor Wallace. However, Governor Wallace has at his disposal over 10,000 trained members of the Alabama National Guard which he could call into service.

"If he is unable or unwilling to call up the Guard, and to maintain law and order in Ala-

Continued on Page 20, Column 7

FOWLER IS NAMED DILLON SUCCESSOR

President Nominates Former Under Secretary to Head Treasury Department

By CHARLES MOHR
Special to The New York Times

WASHINGTON, March 18 — President Johnson announced today that he had nominated Henry H. Fowler to succeed Douglas Dillon as Secretary of the Treasury.

Mr. Dillon, who has wanted to leave the Government for some time, is expected to resign soon. Mr. Fowler, 56 years old, a corporate lawyer, is a former Under Secretary of the Treasury. He returned to the practice of law in April of 1964.

Mr. Johnson left tonight for a long weekend at his ranch in Texas. His press secretary, George E. Reedy, said Mr. Johnson would hold a news conference at the ranch at noon Saturday, Eastern standard time.

Shortly before the President's departure, reporters were summoned into his Oval Office, where they found Mr. Fowler, a short, dapper man with carefully groomed white hair.

Different Choice Rumored

Only about an hour earlier, press associations had carried a report asserting that the House Ways and Means Committee had been told by its chairman, Wilbur D. Mills, that the President planned to name David Kennedy, president of the Continental Bank of Chicago, to the Treasury post.

That report may have had some bearing on the unexpected timing of Mr. Fowler's nomination. Mr. Mills, Democrat of Arkansas, denied having made the remark about Mr. Kennedy.

It was known that for several weeks Mr. Johnson had attempted to persuade Donald C. Cook, a New York utility executive, to take the Treasury job.

Mr. Cook, a close personal and political friend of the Pres-

Continued on Page 17, Column 2

2D MAN FLIES SHIP

TV in Soviet Shows Astronaut Turning Slow Somersault

Text of Soviet announcement is printed on Page 14.

By HENRY TANNER
Special to The New York Times

MOSCOW, Friday, March 19 — A Soviet Air Force officer, who yesterday became the first man to leave an orbiting spacecraft and float in space, was still circling the earth early today in the capsule with a fellow astronaut.

Lieut. Col. Aleksei A. Leonov, 30 years old, left the two-man Voskhod 2 as it passed over the Soviet Union while completing its first orbit and beginning its second. He stayed outside the cabin for 10 minutes, according to Tass, official Soviet press agency.

The spaceship, piloted by Col. Pavel I. Belyayev, 39, was launched at 10 A.M. Moscow time yesterday, 2 A.M. Eastern standard time. The launching site, not announced at first, was later said to be the cosmodrome Baekonur in Kazakhstan. All previous Soviet manned space shots have originated there.

[Vasily Seleznev, a leading Soviet space official, said on Moscow television Thursday that "the target before us now is the moon, and we hope to reach it in no distant future," The Associated Press reported.]

New Shot Rumored

There was widespread speculation that a second spaceship might be launched sometime today in an attempt to effect for the first time a link-up of two crafts in space.

As Colonel Leonov traveled through space tethered to his ship at a speed of nearly five miles a second, he was shielded by a specially equipped space suit. This protected him from the intense heat of the sun.

Specialists said that even the slightest penetration of his suit by the sun's rays would have caused instant death.

If the five-yard rope lifeline that connected him with the ship had broken, he could have been lost, orbiting the earth as a human satellite. His body would have burned up on reentry after a week or perhaps months of orbiting.

No Steering Devices

His space suit was not equipped with any devices by which he could have steered his way back to the spacecraft.

Voskhod 2 was orbiting every 90.9 minutes. The apogee, or highest point, of its orbit was approximately 309 miles, higher than any previous manned space flight. Its perigee, or low point, was given as approximately 108 miles.

American space experts said they thought the launching was performed by the same vehicle used in earlier Soviet space flights, developing a thrust of about 900,000 pounds. The fact

Continued on Page 14, Column 1

Court Denies Police Need To Tell Suspect of Rights

By SIDNEY E. ZION

The New York Court of Appeals has ruled that the police do not have to advise a suspect of his right to remain silent and his right to have a lawyer before taking his confession. Legal observers consider the decision of great importance because the courts had appeared to be moving in the direction of requiring the police to inform suspects of their constitutional rights before questioning them.

In fact, the California Supreme Court reversed a conviction in January because the defendant had not been told of his right to have a lawyer and his right to remain silent before confessing.

Thus the two largest states in the country are in direct conflict on what lawyers agree to be one of the most important criminal-law questions of the day.

In the New York case, People v. Gunner, the defendant

Continued on Page 26, Column 1

ALLEN IS UPHELD IN MALVERNE CASE

Court Rules He Has Right to Order Shifts of Pupils

By R. W. APPLE Jr.
Special to The New York Times

ALBANY, March 18 — The Court of Appeals affirmed today the right of the Commissioner of Education to order the reorganization of school districts to promote integration.

By a 5-to-2 vote, the court upheld the order of the Commissioner of Education, James E. Allen Jr., that the elementary schools of Malverne, L. I., be brought into better racial balance. The Malverne situation has been considered an integration test case.

The court's decision was narrowly based. It dealt only with the Commissioner's authority—not with the nature of his order or with his goals.

"Disagreement with the sociological, psychological and educational assumptions relied upon by the Commissioner cannot be evaluated by this court," the decision said. "Such arguments can only be heard in the Legislature, which has endowed the Commissioner with all but absolute power, or by the board of regents, who are elected by the Legislature and make policy."

The Appellate Division of the State Supreme Court, whose decision the Court of Appeals affirmed, had endorsed "the judgment of the Commissioner that correction of racial imbalance is an educational aid to a minority group in attaining the skills and level of education

Continued on Page 21, Column 5

CITY AGAIN FACES WATER SHORTAGE

D'Angelo Says Reserves Are Far Below Normal—Light Snowfall Upstate Cited

By CHARLES G. BENNETT

New York City is facing a possible "serious situation" in its water supply this year, and a summer conservation program will probably be necessary.

Armand D'Angelo, Commissioner of Water Supply, Gas and Electricity, said yesterday that he was concerned that the city's reservoirs were only at 38.1 per cent of their capacity yesterday, a level far below normal for this time of year.

A prime factor in determining whether the city will be short of water this year will be the rainfall between now and June. Mr. D'Angelo said he was heartened that the supply had risen from an all-time low percentage of 24.8 last Feb. 5, but he said the rise was not so great as it should be for this time of year.

Total Capacity Rises

Although the Feb. 5 supply was a record low on a percentage basis, the reserves have been lower because total capacity has increased over the years.

For instance, the 33 per cent of capacity low point reached during the water shortage of 1949-50 represented far less water in storage than the 24.8 per cent of last Feb. 5 because the total capacity of the reservoirs in 1950 was 253 billion gallons, compared with 476.5 billion gallons now.

In mid-February, predictions of heavy snows in the watershed areas had led water authorities to expect that spring runoffs to the reservoirs would raise water levels to normal measurements—near capacity—by June 1, when the summer depletion period usually begins.

On Feb. 18 a spokesman for Mr. D'Angelo accordingly said:

Continued on Page 23, Column 1

Cypriotes Said to Install Soviet-Supplied Missiles

By MAX FRANKEL
Special to The New York Times

WASHINGTON, March 18—The Johnson Administration has acquired apparently convincing evidence that Soviet-made antiaircraft missiles are about to be installed on Cyprus by the Cypriote Government.

Some reports suggest that some of the missiles are already in place.

United States officials, fearing a major crisis, are said to be applying strong pressure upon Greece in a last-minute effort to halt the emplacements.

Although Athens is pledged to give military and diplomatic support to the Greek Cypriote majority on the island, there is some doubt about the extent of its influence over the Government of President Makarios.

Greek-Turkish Clash Feared

Turkey, which has been supporting the Turkish Cypriote minority, has threatened to attack the missile sites from the air.

Some sources feared that preventive raids would be made within the next few days, reviving the danger of war between Greece and Turkey, both members of the North Atlantic Treaty Organization.

The Administration refused today to say anything about its evidence, except to note "press reports" of missile shipments.

A guarded State Department comment betrayed some concern, however. It said that "now more than ever" the parties involved in the Cyprus dispute ought to handle their problem

Continued on Page 4, Column 4

INDONESIAN REDS HARRY AMERICANS

Cut Power for Residences—Try to Seize Oil Plants

By NEIL SHEEHAN
Special to The New York Times

JAKARTA, Indonesia, March 18 — Communist labor unions cut off gas and electricity at a United States Embassy apartment building and the home of the American naval attaché here today and attempted to seize control of United States-owned oil installations in southern Sumatra.

The Jakarta offices of the Indonesian-American Friendship Society, an activity of the embassy, and of The Associated Press were also deprived of electricity.

Antara, the Government press agency, announced that Communist oil workers had actually taken control of the Standard Vacuum Oil Company's refinery at Sungei Gerong near the Sumatran port of Palembang.

However, a company spokesman here said that "the plant was not taken over and operations are normal."

Informed sources said the Communist workers had demonstrated at the refinery and demanded that the American manager hand it over to them.

When he refused, the workers hung posters on the walls of the refinery buildings declaring the installation the property of the Indonesian Government and returned to work. The posters were later removed by the Indonesian police.

A similar demonstration and

Continued on Page 2, Column 5

Senate Defeats Southern Move To Delay Bill on Voting, 67-13

By E. W. KENWORTHY
Special to The New York Times

WASHINGTON, March 18—The bipartisan voting-rights bill started on its legislative journey through both houses of Congress today amid displays of overwhelming support that seemed to augur relatively quick enactment.

In the Senate, Southerners began efforts to delay the bill as soon as it was introduced jointly by the Democratic leader, Mike Mansfield of Montana, and the Republican leader, Everett McKinley Dirksen of Illinois, with 56 co-sponsors from both parties. Later, more Senators joined, bringing the total sponsorship to 66.

The Southerners were overwhelmed on a roll-call vote, 67 to 13.

In the House, where the bill was introduced yesterday, Attorney General Nicholas deB. Katzenbach was the first witness before the Constitutional Subcommittee of the Judiciary Committee.

When the Attorney General completed his explanation of the bill and defense of its constitutionality, Representative William M. McCulloch of Ohio, the ranking Republican on the committee, said that Mr. Katzenbach had made "one of the best statements I have heard in my 17 years in the House."

The Southern challenge came on a motion by Mr. Mansfield to send the bill to the Senate

Continued on Page 21, Column 1

L.I.R.R. 'Slowdown' Delays Thousands

By PETER MILLONES

Thousands of commuters on the Long Island Rail Road were delayed up to several hours last night when engineers refused to move trains until headlights were inspected.

The railroad called the engineers' action a "wildcat slowdown." At its height the slowdown became a full stop as virtually all trains were halted on the line from Manhattan to Montauk.

But shortly after midnight, as the theater crowd strolled into Pennsylvania Station, trains were reported running normally again. There were no indications that service would be affected this morning for the line's 200,000 commuters.

The engineers began calling

Continued on Page 18, Column 6

Kennedy Will Join Mt. Kennedy Climb

By WARREN WEAVER Jr.
Special to The New York Times

WASHINGTON, March 18—Senator Robert F. Kennedy is flying to the Yukon this weekend to join in an attempt to scale for the first time a 13,900-foot peak named after President Kennedy.

The Senator, although an outdoor enthusiast and experienced hiker, has never climbed a mountain. The five other members of the expedition are all experts; one of them is James W. Whittaker, the first American to climb Mount Everest.

The goal of the expedition, Mount Kennedy, is in the St. Elias Mountains, 25 miles north of the Yukon-British Columbia line and just east of the Alas-

Continued on Page 24, Column 1

NEWS INDEX

"All the News That's Fit to Print"

The New York Times

LATE CITY EDITION
U. S. Weather Bureau Report (Page 69) forecasts:
Sunny and cool today, tomorrow.
Fair and cool tonight.
Temp. range: 66—52; yesterday: 70—52.

VOL. CXIV. No. 39,213. | NEW YORK, FRIDAY, JUNE 4, 1965. | TEN CENTS

AMERICAN FLOATS IN SPACE FOR 20 MINUTES AS HE AND PARTNER START 4 DAYS IN ORBIT; FUEL SHORTAGE BARS BOOSTER RENDEZVOUS

ASSEMBLY PASSES A TOTAL REVISION OF THE PENAL LAW

Homosexual Acts Remain as Crimes Under Amendment —Adultery Issue Open

By JOHN SIBLEY
Special to The New York Times

ALBANY, June 3—The Assembly voted approval today of a complete revision of the Penal Law, which lawyers agree has become a bewildering morass since its last major overhaul in 1881.

After intricate parliamentary maneuvering, however, the Assembly left uncertain the outcome of the most controversial issues in today's debate: whether adultery and homosexuality should be treated as matters of law or of morality.

As put forward by a special commission that worked four years to redraft the law, neither adultery nor homosexual acts between consenting adults would be treated as crimes.

From both sides of the aisle today there were applause and lavish praise for the commission chairman, Republican Assemblyman Richard J. Bartlett of Glens Falls. Though there was criticism of specific provisions of the proposed new law, virtually every speaker credited the Bartlett Commission with a brilliant job of tightening and clarifying the penal law as well as bringing it into conformity with current judicial and social thinking.

Churchmen's Fears Cited

From the beginning, there was no doubt that the commission's version would be overwhelmingly approved. After its adoption, the House turned to two bills that would retain adultery and homosexuality in the criminal law.

These measures were introduced by Assemblyman Julius Volker, an Erie County Republican who is a member of the Bartlett Commission. Mr. Volker said his bills were "inspired by the entreaties of churchmen who fear we would be appearing to give passive approval to deviant sexual practices."

The Volker amendment to retain homosexual acts as crimes was passed by a vote of 115 to 16.

Then the Assembly voted, 73

Continued on Page 20, Column 5

SENATORS TIGHTEN STATE ETHICS CODE

But Reject Assembly's Plan for Stricter Control

By RONALD SULLIVAN
Special to The New York Times

ALBANY, June 3 — The Senate voted overwhelmingly late today to strengthen the legislative code of ethics after engaging in the longest and one of the most vigorous debates of the session.

The bill, which was passed 47 to 9, made these changes in and additions to the existing ethics code:

¶Legislators who are lawyers are prohibited from representing clients in actions against the state in the Court of Claims for a fee.

¶Former legislators are forbidden to become lobbyists until they have been out of office at least two years.

¶Former state commissioners and their deputies are barred from appearing before their former agencies on a contingency-fee basis for two years after their resignations.

¶Legislators are required not only to disclose their direct or indirect financial interests in state-regulated companies, but also to identify the companies involved.

Approval of the bill followed the rejection by a close vote of a highly controversial amendment that would have restricted legislators' appearances before state agencies for a fee. This

Continued on Page 20, Column 2

President Asks Quarters And Dimes Without Silver

Half Dollar Content Would Be Reduced —Shortage of Silver Underlies Request for Greater Use of Nickel and Copper

By EDWIN L. DALE Jr.
Special to The New York Times

WASHINGTON, June 3—President Johnson asked Congress today to approve the first major change in United States coinage since 1792.

The change would eliminate silver from dimes and quarters and sharply reduce it in half dollars. The penny and the nickel, neither of which contains silver, would be unchanged.

The sole reason for the change is a growing world shortage of silver.

The first of the new coins, almost certainly dimes, are expected to go into circulation early next year. Quarters would be next.

If Congress approves, as expected, the new dime and quarter would become the world's first "sandwich" coins, with a cupro-nickel exterior and a copper interior. They would be of the same size and design as at present, but they would weigh slightly less than the present coins. Their surface would look and feel like that of the present nickel, and their edges would reveal their copper interior.

The text of Johnson's message will be found on Page 18.

Suited to Coin Devices

Of major importance, the new coins would work in the nation's 12 million coin-operated devices, ranging from vending machines to pay telephones. Modification of the machines to adapt to alternate choices for coinage would have cost at least $100 million and would have put machines out of action for many months.

The new half dollar would also be a sandwich coin, but its appearance would be almost the same as at present. Its outside would be a silver-copper alloy with a high silver content and its inside an alloy with a low silver content, making an overall silver content of 40 per cent, compared with 90 per cent at present.

The half dollar has a low priority in production plans. There is already an acute shortage of the half dollar, but it is far less essential to commerce than are dimes and quarters. The new half dollars, when they eventually appear, will continue to bear the likeness of President Kennedy. The new

Continued on Page 18, Column 7

RATE OF JOBLESS LOWEST SINCE '57

Unemployment in May Down to 4.6 Per Cent—Total at Work Rose 1.3 Million

By JOHN D. POMFRET
Special to The New York Times

WASHINGTON, June 3 — President Johnson announced today that the nation's unemployment rate fell in May to 4.6 per cent, the lowest level since October, 1957, when the rate was 4.5 per cent.

The President reported that unemployment fell between April and May by 220,000, to 3.3 million. The decline, he said, was about triple the seasonal drop expected.

Employment rose by 1.3 million, to 72.4 million, in May. The gain was about 200,000 more than the seasonal expectation.

The drop in unemployment and the rise in employment combined to reduce the jobless rate from the 4.9 per cent level of April.

51st Month of Growth

The President announced the figures at a White House meeting of businessmen active in his program for promoting summer jobs for teen-agers. He made the announcement about an hour and a half before the regular announcement of the figures by the Bureau of Labor Statistics.

The President said that May was the 51st month of the longest peacetime economic expansion in the nation's history.

Since the start of the expansion in February, 1961, he said, unemployment declined by 1.4 million and the unemployment rate dropped from 6.9 to 4.6 per cent. Every worker group showed a marked improvement during the 51-month period except teen-agers, he said.

The President announced that the number of long-term unemployed—those out of work for 15 or more weeks—dropped

Continued on Page 22, Column 2

Johnson Asks Peace In Plea to Russians

By ROBERT B. SEMPLE Jr.
Special to The New York Times

CHICAGO, June 3—President Johnson issued an unusually strong and direct appeal to the people of the Soviet Union tonight to seek new initiatives for world peace.

"There is no American interest," the President declared, "in conflict with the Soviet people anywhere."

He made the appeal in a speech at a Jefferson-Jackson Day dinner sponsored by the Cook County Democratic organization. At the same time he announced that he had ordered the withdrawal of all the remaining United States marines in the Dominican Republic.

The $100-a-plate dinner, attended by approximately 5,000 people, was held in McCormick

Continued on Page 3, Column 5

SOVIET BOMBERS SEEN NEAR HANOI

Russian-Built IL-28 Jets Observed, Pentagon Says

By JACK RAYMOND
Special to The New York Times

WASHINGTON, June 3 — The Defense Department announced today that a "small number" of Soviet jet bombers of an old type had been sighted near Hanoi, the capital of North Vietnam.

The announcement follows reports that six or eight Ilyushin-28 twin-jet bombers had been seen in North Vietnam, but that there was no indication whether they were being flown by Soviet pilots.

The Pentagon's confirmation was made in a brief sentence: "A small number of IL-28 type aircraft have been observed on the ground in the Hanoi area."

A Pentagon source declared that estimates of the number of such planes might change from day to day, presumably as a result of aerial reconnaissance.

The same source also emphasized that the IL-28 warplanes were of comparatively old design and not highly regarded as a military threat, although their range made them capable of use against South Vietnam.

The IL-28 was first tested in 1947. It was used by North Korean and Chinese Communist pilots in the Korean war.

The planes have a range of 1,500 miles. With extra tanks

Continued on Page 3, Column 4

NASA via United Press International Telephoto

TWO MEN FOR SPACE: Maj. James A. McDivitt, commander of the Gemini 4 flight, precedes Maj. Edward H. White 2d to elevator that will take them to top of erector holding capsule. They carry portable air-conditioners.

VIETCONG AMBUSH BATTALION TWICE

Most of 300 Believed Lost in Attacks Near Pleiku— U. S. Marines Balk Foe

By JACK LANGGUTH
Special to The New York Times

SAIGON, South Vietnam, June 3 Two ambushes by the Vietcong 50 miles southeast of Pleiku wiped out another South Vietnamese Army battalion today. The setback raised Government losses in ambushes to 1,000 men during the last week.

[United States marines defending the Danang Air Base repulsed a sharp Vietcong attack early Friday against key bridges near the base, Reuters reported. Page 3.]

Final casualty reports from the two ambush sites in Phoubon have not yet been received. But all but about 80 of the 300-man battalion were said to be dead or missing.

The senior American adviser to the battalion, slightly wounded by enemy fire, called for a helicopter to lift him and two American enlisted men out of the trap.

A United States military spokesman noted that the American officer had been "charged with the safety of his men." When their lives were threatened, he said, "of course it was proper for him to call for evacuation."

Smaller Attacks Made

Smaller Vietcong ambushes in Kontum and Darlac Provinces cost the Government at least 50 more men.

A high-ranking United States officer in Pleiku described the situation as "very serious" and said the American advisers in the II Army Corps had requested more troops.

"The VC are coming out of the bloody hills," the officer said. "We're barely holding our own."

The force of the Vietcong units has caused so[illegible] in the American mission to question official intelligence estimates of Communist strength.

United States military intelligence now lists 64,200 "main force" or full-time professional enemy soldiers, plus 80,000 to 100,000 part-time guerrillas.

Of the "main force" troops, 46,600 men are considered to be field soldiers and 17,600 to be officials in province and district commands and control officials.

These figures represent an increase in the main force's

Continued on Page 3, Column 2

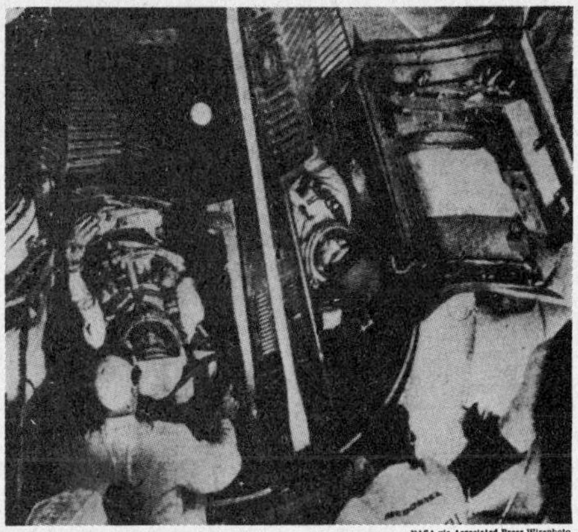

NASA via Associated Press Wirephoto

IN PLACE FOR FLIGHT: Major McDivitt, left, and Major White wait in their seats for technicians to make final adjustments. Exit in space was made through door, right.

Banter in Space: A Textual Account

Excerpts from the conversations of Maj. James A. McDivitt, Maj. Edward H. White 2d, Maj. Virgil I. Grissom, mission control communicator, and ground control crews as gathered by The Associated Press, United Press International and The New York Times:

MAJOR McDIVITT—I am turning around to watch the second stage booster. The second stage looks pretty. It is tumbling about 400 to 500 feet away.

GUAYMAS STATION (in Mexico)—Guaymas, Gemini 4.

MAJOR McDIVITT—Roger, Guaymas. We still have the booster. We're out quite a ways from it now. It's taken a little more fuel than we'd anticipated. We appear right now to be about holding our own with it. Of course we should start to close with it, but it's out farther than we'd hoped to let it get right now.

GUAYMAS STATION — Roger, I copy.

MAJOR McDIVITT—Guaymas, this is Gemini 4. We're going to have to get resolution right away on whether we really make a major effort to close the thing or to save the fuel.

GUAYMAS STATION—I think we should save the fuel.

MAJOR McDIVITT — I guess we've probably expended about 100 feet per second.

GUAYMAS STATION — You've expended 100 feet per second?

MAJOR McDIVITT — I don't think it is worth it.

HOUSTON TO GUAYMAS —You might tell him as far as we're concerned, we want to save the fuel. We're concerned about the lifeline more than we are catching that booster.

GUAYMAS STATION — Gemini 4, Flight advises they'd like to save the fuel. You'll be advised over the Cape.

MAJOR McDIVITT — I just can't wait until I get to the Cape. I guess we're just going to have to watch it go away.

GUAYMAS STATION — Forget it.

HOUSTON—Okay, I guess we'll scrub it.

MAJOR McDIVITT (as the spacecraft neared the East African Coast and as Major White began preparing his equipment to leave the capsule)—It is a bit crowded in here, Gus.

MAJOR GRISSOM — You bet . . . Hey, Jim, you don't have to go upside down unless you want to. Whatever is best for you.

MAJOR McDIVITT—We're running late on the flight plan. . . . We'll wait until next pass around. I don't think we want to try it [floating in space] this time.

GROUND CONTROL—Roger. Gemini 4, we're happy with that.

MAJOR McDIVITT—We just couldn't try that.

GROUND CONTROL—We understand.

MAJOR McDIVITT (an hour and a half later)—It's go.

GROUND CONTROL — We're ready for him to go out whenever he is.

HAWAII STATION — We think he said, "I'm getting out."

MAJOR McDIVITT (to Major White, who is now out of the capsule)—Tell us what you think.

MAJOR WHITE—The maneuvering unit is good. The only problem I have is that I haven't got enough fuel. I've exhausted the fuel now and I was able to maneuver myself down to the bottom of the spacecraft and I was right up on top of the adapter, Jim, and came back into view. The only thing I am . . . over my head and I'm looking right down and it looks like we're coming up on the coast of California. And I'm going in slow rotation to the right. There is absolutely no disorientation association.

MAJOR McDIVITT—One

Continued on Page 14, Column 6

JOKES IN THE VOID

Talk of 2 Astronauts Is Heard by Millions on Radio and TV

By WALTER SULLIVAN
Special to The New York Times

CAPE KENNEDY, Friday, June 4—For 20 minutes yesterday afternoon Maj. Edward H. White 2d of the Air Force was a human satellite of the earth as he floated across North America from the Pacific to the Atlantic.

Tethered to the Gemini 4 spacecraft, he chatted good-humoredly and snapped pictures as he darted about in raw space with the aid of a gas-firing jet gun. Asked how he was doing by Maj. James A. McDivitt of the Air Force, the spaceship commander, Major White replied to his partner in the capsule:

"I'm doing great. This is fun."

When he was told to re-enter the capsule, Major White laughed and said: "I'm not coming in." But later, after more banter, he followed through on orders to return.

Both in 'Great Shape'

At 3 A.M., Eastern daylight time, the spaceship was in its 11th orbit and the astronauts reported that they were in "real great shape." They spent the night taking turns napping and checking radiation levels both in the spacecraft and on its outside surface. The space control center at Houston cut off voice contact with them for more than an hour at a time in order not to disturb them.

Major White's floating venture came after earlier difficulties had forced cancellation of the plan for two close approaches by the spacecraft to the final stage of the rocket that had placed the capsule in orbit.

Attempts to draw near to the rocket during the first orbit had expended roughly half the fuel allocated to such maneuvering. It appeared that the reason for this high fuel consumption would not be known until after analysis of the flight records following the four-day mission.

The mastery of rendezvous techniques is the central goal of the Gemini program, since such operations are essential for landing men on the moon and bringing them home again.

62 Orbits Scheduled

If the two-man vehicle flies its 62 scheduled orbits it should come down about 10 A.M. Monday.

Unlike the Soviet cosmonaut, Lieut. Col. Aleksei A. Leonov, who ventured outside his spaceship in March, Major White apparently suffered no disorientation. During his period in space he pushed himself to various sides of the Gemini craft with his jet gun.

The vehicle's radio circuit was open so that his colleagues on earth could hear the talk between him and Major McDivitt.

Major McDivitt, operating a camera from inside the vehicle, called to his free-floating companion outside:

"Get out in front where I can see you again!"

Major White explained that he could see the California coast. Then he came close enough to brush the ship commander's window.

"You smeared up my windshield, you dirty dog!" called Major McDivitt. His voice traveled by wire to the helmet of his floating companion over the 25-foot tether and also to earth by radio.

The launching from Cape Kennedy had been delayed an hour and a quarter by an electrical failure in the "overspeed regulator" of the erector. The erector is a 130-ton tower,

Continued on Page 14, Column 1

NEWS INDEX

News Summary

"All the News That's Fit to Print"

The New York Times.

LATE CITY EDITION

U. S. Weather Bureau Report (Page 78) forecast: Fair today and tonight. Partly cloudy and milder tomorrow.

Temp. range: 48—30; yesterday: 49—28.

VOL. CXV . No. 39,499.

NEW YORK, THURSDAY, MARCH 17, 1966.

TEN CENTS

GEMINI 8 CREW IS FORCED DOWN IN PACIFIC AFTER SUCCESSFUL LINKUP WITH SATELLITE; SPACEMEN PICKED UP AFTER 3 HOURS IN SEA

JOINT PANEL FINDS EVIDENCE OF NEED FOR NEW TAX RISE

Democratic Majority Urges That Congress Begin Now to Work Out Details

By EILEEN SHANAHAN
Special to The New York Times

WASHINGTON, March 16—Democratic members of the Joint Economic Committee of Congress said unanimously today that there was "increasing evidence daily" that a general tax increase would be needed this year to restrain inflation.

They urged Congress to work out the details of such a tax increase now, so that it could be put into effect quickly later by passage of a simple joint resolution of Congress and the signature of the President.

The Republican members of the committee also said that a tax increase would probably be needed this year, but they argued that it could be avoided if the Administration cut spending and if the Federal Reserve tightened further the availability of credit.

The members of the two parties also came surprisingly close to agreement on another point.

Business Spending Cited

The Democrats recommended outright that the special 7 per cent tax credit given to business on its expenditures for equipment be temporarily suspended, to discourage further rapid rises in such business spending. The Republicans said that suspension of the investment credit, a move that is opposed by most businessmen, should definitely be considered, along with increases in individual and corporate taxes.

The members of the committee expressed these views in the panel's annual report on the January economic report of the President. The committee reviews each year's economic report through hearings, then reports its findings and recommendations to the rest of Congress.

The joint committee itself has no legislative powers, but it has considerable influence as the expert Congressional committee on economic policy issues.

Kennedy Plan Recalled

The committee majority's proposal that Congress begin work now on tax legislation represented a victory for the viewpoint, increasingly held in the Administration and among economists, that procedures are needed whereby tax rates can be changed quickly, up or down, in response to changing conditions in the economy.

Congress rejected, without even the formality of hearings, a proposal by President Kennedy in 1962 that the President be given limited authority to change tax rates to restrain either a boom or a slump.

The joint committee's approach today was a middle-ground one. It would not give any discretionary authority to the President, but it would pro-

Continued on Page 22, Column 1

Watts Is Tense but Quiet; Need for Guard Doubted

Swift Action Is Pledged

By GLADWIN HILL
Special to The New York Times

LOS ANGELES, March 16—A tense and unhappy calm reigned in the Watts area today—bolstered by heavily augmented patrols of shotgun-carrying policemen.

But public officials said they would not be surprised if more disorders developed in the strife-torn center of racial discontent.

However, from Gov. Edmund G. Brown on down, authorities believed that any resumption of yesterday's trouble would be small-scale and quickly contained, rather than burgeoning into anything like last August's six-day rampage of outlawry in the impoverished southwestern Negro district. The Governor said he did not think it would be necessary to call in the National Guard.

In the riot district early today, 212 city policemen were on duty, compared with a normal force of 24. By 9 o'clock tonight, however, the police had removed barricades that had been set up, and patrols appeared to be reduced. During the day 200 dep-

Continued on Page 26, Column 1

Negroes Are Troubled

By THOMAS A. JOHNSON
Special to The New York Times

LOS ANGELES, March 16—"These kids hate white people—they hate them very strongly."

The speaker, a Negro, owns a combination shoeshine parlor and stationery store along riot-torn 103d Street in the Watts district. And he said he had long observed the youths who started a resurgence of violence yesterday in the Los Angeles Negro community.

"This goes for the younger ones and the older ones—they hate white policemen, white delivery men, white teachers and you name it," he added.

The man said that before an attempt was made to end such rioting, "you've got to do something about that hatred."

In a restaurant on Compton Avenue close by, the owner, a Negro, poured containers of strong coffee for Negroes and a few Mexican truckers. The Negroes talked about the riot and the Mexicans talked about the coffee.

"It makes no sense at all to fight when you have no way

Continued on Page 26, Column 5

ANTI-KY PROTEST BY SAIGON MONK DRAWS THOUSANDS

Civilian Regime Demanded —G.I. Paratroop Battalion Said to Kill 142 of Foe

By CHARLES MOHR
Special to The New York Times

SAIGON, March 16 Thousands of South Vietnamese crowded Saigon's Buddhist headquarters compound tonight to listen to a yellow-robed monk demand that military government be ended.

The rally appeared to be a tentative first step by the Unified Buddhist Church to cause the collapse of the Government of Premier Nguyen Cao Ky.

In military action northeast of the capital, Vietcong troops surrounded a United States paratroop battalion. At least 142 guerrillas were said to have died in several hours of fighting. [Page 3.]

Thi Is Sent North

Early today, Air Vice Marshal Ky and his fellow generals sent Lieut. Gen. Nguyen Chanh Thi, whom they had purged from the ruling junta, to the northern area of South Vietnam to try to quiet political unrest and protest that had disrupted that area since Thursday, when General Thi was stripped of power.

Tonight the protest spread to Saigon when a crowd almost filled the several acres at Buddhist headquarters.

In the glare of American television-camera lights, the dirt grounds seemed covered with a sea of earnest faces of lower-middle-class Vietnamese, mostly impassive.

Police Remain Aloof

At least 10,000 people seemed to have assembled although there had been no public or formal announcement of the meeting. The meeting was not violent, and the police did not try to interfere.

Buddhist spokesmen have met with Marshal Ky several times in recent days to demand concessions as a price for calling off their protests, usually reliable sources said.

These demands were not disclosed, but they may have included a request that pro-Buddhist politicians dominate the Democracy-Building Council, an organization that is to recommend a new constitution under which Marshal Ky has promised an election in 1967.

A qualified source suggested that the Buddhists wanted some officials dropped from the Gov-

Continued on Page 5, Column 1

NASA via Associated Press Wirephoto

NEWEST MEN IN SPACE: Maj. David R. Scott, foreground, and Neil A. Armstrong in Gemini 8 capsule before lift-off. Picture has been turned; men actually faced upward.

FLIGHT UNSTABLE

Tumbling Forced Use of Thruster Fuel in Re-entry System

By JOHN NOBLE WILFORD
Special to The New York Times

CAPE KENNEDY, Fla., Thursday, March 17—The Gemini 8 astronauts suddenly lost maneuverability of their craft last night after making the first docking in space.

They were ordered to make an emergency landing in the Western Pacific and splashed down southeast of Okinawa at 10:23 P.M. Eastern standard time.

The astronauts were picked up by the United States Navy destroyer Leonard F. Mason at 1:30 A.M. today after more than [illegible] hours in the choppy waters. They were described as being in good condition and were being taken to Okinawa.

The men climbed aboard the destroyer by way of a rope ladder. The spacecraft was hauled on deck at 1:38 A.M. by a winch. The destroyer is expected to reach Okinawa this evening.

The astronauts' trouble began when a thruster rocket on the spacecraft apparently got stuck in open position and set the linked-up vehicles spinning crazily.

When the trouble occurred during the fifth revolution of the Gemini 8 mission, the astronauts quickly undocked and pulled away from the target Agena. They were able to maintain a stable flight by using a set of rockets normally reserved for re-entry.

The astronauts, Neil A. Armstrong and Major David R. Scott of the Air Force, fired their descent rockets at 9:45 P. M. for the fiery plunge through the earth's atmosphere into the waters of the second recovery area in the Pacific.

Daylight in Area

It was still daylight in the recovery area, one of the reasons for its choice. Such zones are used only for unscheduled splashdowns. The weather was partly cloudy, with visibility of 10 miles.

An Air Force C-54 transport plane spotted the bobbing capsule and parachuted frogmen who attached a flotation collar to the craft.

At 11:30 P.M. the astronauts opened both hatches and were standing up. Their rescuers reported that both of them "looked good."

The trouble developed after what had been a flawless start for a three-day flight.

Even the abrupt ending to the flight could not dim the accomplishment of rendezvous and docking.

The first hint of trouble came about half an hour after the Gemini 8 had achieved the first docking of two space vehicles.

A tracking ship in the Western Pacific relayed to the Manned Spacecraft Center's control room in Houston a message from Mr. Armstrong, the command pilot.

He reported that he had been forced to unlock from the

Continued on Page 20, Column 1

POLICE TO REVIEW MINORITY HIRING

2 Negro Officers to Check Rejected Applicants — Martin Resigns Post

By EMANUEL PERLMUTTER

Police Commissioner Howard R. Leary announced yesterday that he had designated two of his top Negro aides to pass on the character qualifications of Negroes and Puerto Ricans who have been rejected for appointment as policemen.

The reviews are intended, the Commissioner said, to prevent any rejections because of discrimination.

In another development, Deputy Police Commissioner Joseph G. Martin, who was in charge of community relations, resigned his post last night at the request of Commissioner Leary.

Mr. Martin made his resignation known in a telephone call to reporters at Police Headquarters shortly before 8 o'clock. He said that Mr. Leary had "asked me for my resignation in his office" on Tuesday but had added that "there need be no haste on your part in

Continued on Page 46, Column 5

White House Bill To Seek Protection Of Rights Workers

By JOHN HERBERS
Special to The New York Times

WASHINGTON, March 16—The Administration will ask Congress to make it a Federal crime to intimidate or to harm persons engaged in the desegregation of public facilities.

The proposed law, which would not be as broad as some other bills now before Congress, would provide a graduated scale of penalties according to the severity of the crime.

The Administration will also seek to eliminate racial discrimination on juries through two courses of action.

First, Federal juries would be selected only from lists of registered voters or from other representative lists of adult residents that are approved by the appropriate judicial conference.

Second, it would be made illegal to bar persons from state and local jury panels because of race, sex or national origin. In states where there was evidence of violation, the Attorney General could seek relief in a Federal court.

The court could then establish nondiscriminatory standards or appoint a master to

Continued on Page 25, Column 4

SUKARNO ASSERTS HE'S STILL LEADER

Statement, Read on Radio by Deputy Premier, Blurs Picture of Army Role

By SETH S. KING
Special to The New York Times

KUALA LUMPUR, Malaysia, March 16—President Sukarno declared tonight that he was still in full control of Indonesia and had not delegated his authority to anyone.

The President's announcement, read over the radio, added to the confusion in the rapidly changing political picture from Jakarta.

The statement was read by the Third Deputy Premier, Chairul Saleh, who had been reported under "army protection."

Mr. Saleh said there had been considerable misunderstanding since President Sukarno delegated security powers Saturday to Lieutenant General Suharto, the Army Chief of Staff.

Immediately after that General Suharto announced the banning of the Communist party and promised demonstrating students that their demands would be met if they were "constructive and reasonable."

One of the demands was the removal of Dr. Subandrio, First Deputy Premier and Foreign Minister, and other leftists from

Continued on Page 9, Column 1

President Reaffirms Goal Of Moon Landing in 60's

By EVERT CLARK
Special to The New York Times

WASHINGTON, March 16—President Johnson watched the launching of the Gemini 8 spacecraft today and then said that the United States still intended "to land the first man on the surface of the moon in the decade of the sixties."

Mr. Johnson thus reaffirmed a goal set by President Kennedy when he approved the Apollo lunar landing program in 1961.

Because of budget cuts, space officials have recently expressed concern over the chances of meeting the deadline. They have also said that the Soviet Union's chances of landing a man on the moon in this decade appeared better than they did a year ago.

Both Mr. Johnson and Vice President Humphrey seemed today to be telling the National Aeronautics and Space Administration to get on with the lunar landing job regardless of the difficulties. Mr. Humphrey, in a speech to a National Rocket Club dinner, said that the space program "cannot be exempt" from tight budgetary discipline.

Hails Astronauts' Courage

Later tonight, Mr. Johnson voiced relief that the Gemini 8 astronauts, Neil A. Armstrong and Maj. David R. Scott, had landed safely after their flight was cut short.

"All of us are greatly relieved," the President said. "They—and those who are joining in their recovery—have shown remarkable courage and poise under stress."

Although voicing disappointment that the mission could not continue, Mr. Johnson said that Gemini 8, in accomplishing the first docking with another craft in space, had made "a major step on the course we have set."

"The information they have acquired will help us to per-

Continued on Page 21, Column 1

CALM SHATTERED AT SPACE CENTER

Report of Trouble on Gemini Ends a Relaxed Mood— Panic on Craft Denied

By MARTIN WALDRON
Special to The New York Times

HOUSTON, Thursday, March 17—The flight of Gemini 8 changed from a calm and routine space mission into a life or death drama in just a matter of moments last night.

About 7 P.M., Eastern standard time, while Neil A. Armstrong and Maj. David R. Scott apparently were making an uneventful check of their instruments during a docking maneuver, the crowds began to drift away from the Manned Spacecraft Center, where space flights are controlled.

The docking itself had been the high point of the day. It was the first time it had been tried in space by the United States.

Mood Changes

But everyone was confident that it could be done, and when Paul Haney, director of public affairs for the spacecraft center, announced that the docking had been successful, an exodus from the center began.

The only thing left on the schedule for the astronauts during the remainder of their first day in space was a check of the equipment. Then they were to retire for the night, to rest for the next day's scheduled maneuvers outside the spaceship by Major Scott.

When Mr. Armstrong, the first American civilian to fly in space, reported by radio back to Houston that there was serious trouble aboard the spaceship, the mood changed in the twinkling of an eye. Until this announcement, Gemini 8 had been classed as by far the calmest of America's manned spaceflights.

But when the announcement came a number of civilian engineers, on their way to a bar to

Continued on Page 20, Column 5

Dubinsky Retires as President of I.L.G.W.U.

By DAMON STETSON

David Dubinsky, a spry, peppery 74 years old, jolted his colleagues and the garment industry yesterday by resigning as president of the International Ladies Garment Workers Union.

He dabbed his eyes with a handkerchief as his letter of resignation was read in the Biarritz Room of the Americana, where the union's general executive board has been meeting this week.

His letter explained that major union problems had been resolved and that he now felt he could turn to personal considerations. Mr. Dubinsky's retirement is effective April 12.

The occasion came when he invited a few old friends to join him at the hotel.

At 3:10 P. M. he turned from a discussion of the need for raising $300,000 for the fall Congressional campaign to a matter that he said was important to him and to the union.

While he was reviewing his career in the union, Mrs. Dubinsky, wearing a green hat and a dark coat, quietly entered the room and took a seat beside her husband at the green felt-cov-

Continued on Page 29, Column 4

The New York Times (by Ernest Sisto)

David Dubinsky wipes away tear as Luigi Antonini, vice president, presides at Americana

Hughes's Tax Bill Voted by Assembly

By RONALD SULLIVAN
Special to The New York Times

TRENTON, March 16—After six hours of desultory debate, the Assembly gave Gov. Richard J. Hughes the narrowest of victories tonight when it approved a state income tax and an $870-million budget.

The vote on the budget was 32 to 28 and the one on the tax was 31 to 29. The Democratic Governor thus won an initial victory in getting the Legislature to enact a broad base tax to advance the largest spending program in the state's history, much of it for education.

The budget and the tax bills were immediately sent to the Senate tonight and a vote is

Continued on Page 29, Column 3

Pupils Given Right To Wear Yarmulkes

By LEONARD BUDER

Dr. Bernard E. Donovan, the Superintendent of Schools, disregarded the advice of his legal experts and said yesterday afternoon that Jewish pupils would be permitted to wear yarmulkes, or skullcaps, in school.

Earlier in the day it was disclosed that the school system's legal department had advised that wearing yarmulkes "comes under the constitutional prohibition against the use of public schools for religious purposes."

The issue arose after a Manhattan high school student was told by his principal that he could not wear a yarmulke in school. The principal had acted

Continued on Page 33, Column 2

Soviet Space Dogs Returned to Earth

By PETER GROSE
Special to The New York Times

MOSCOW, March 16 — The Soviet Union brought its two space dogs safely back to earth today after 22 days in orbit and frequent transits through the hazardous radiation belt ringing the earth.

The satellite Comos 110, with the two dogs on board, landed "in the prescribed area," Tass, the official press agency, reported. Presumably this referred to a parachute landing in the Soviet space experimental field in Central Asia.

"The animals are in good condition after landing," Tass said.

The two dogs flew higher than any human astronaut and

Continued on Page 21, Column 3

NEWS INDEX

"All the News That's Fit to Print"

The New York Times

LATE CITY EDITION
U.S. Weather Bureau Report (Page 54) forecasts: Partly cloudy and cold today; fair, cold tonight. Fair, warmer tomorrow. Temp. Range: 39—32; yesterday: 44—37.

VOL. CXVI. No. 39,816. NEW YORK, SATURDAY, JANUARY 28, 1967. 10 CENTS

3 APOLLO ASTRONAUTS DIE IN FIRE; GRISSOM, WHITE, CHAFFEE CAUGHT IN CAPSULE DURING A TEST ON PAD

United Press International

BEFORE AN EARLIER TEST: Lieut. Col. Virgil I. Grissom, left, Air Force Lieut. Col. Edward H. White 2d, center, and Navy Lieut. Comdr. Roger B. Chaffee in front of the launching pad. Photograph was released Tuesday.

NASA, via Associated Press Wirephoto

HOURS BEFORE THE TRAGEDY: Colonel Grissom walking to the Apollo spacecraft ahead of Commander Chaffee, yesterday, some 5½ hours before the fire broke out. The capsule was atop a Saturn 1-B rocket, 218 feet above pad.

TRAGEDY AT CAPE

Rescuers Are Blocked by Dense Smoke—Cause Is Studied

Excerpts from news parley on accident, Page 10.

By The Associated Press

CAPE KENNEDY, Fla., Jan. 27—The three-man crew of astronauts for the Apollo 1 mission were killed tonight in a flash fire aboard the huge spacecraft designed to take man to the moon.

Those killed in the blaze on a launching pad were:

VIRGIL I. GRISSOM, 40 years old, Air Force lieutenant colonel, one of the seven original Mercury astronauts.

EDWARD H. WHITE 2d, 36, a lieutenant colonel in the Air Force, the first American to "walk" in space.

ROGER B. CHAFFEE, 31, a Navy lieutenant commander, who had been awaiting his first space flight.

The astronauts were the first American spacemen to be killed on the job and, ironically, died while on the ground. The bodies were removed hours later and a space agency spokesman said death was "instantaneous."

Three other astronauts died in airplane crashes, in the line of duty, but today's tragedy involved the first "on premises" deaths in the American space program—the first time anyone was killed while in space hardware.

Simulation Under Way

The fire broke out at 6:31 P.M. while the three men were taking part in a full-scale simulation of the scheduled Feb. 21 launching that was to take them into the heavens for 14 days of orbiting the earth.

They were trapped behind closed hatches, according to the National Aeronautics and Space Administration.

[Officials said an electrical spark must have ignited the pure oxygen inside the cabin, United Press International reported.]

Paul Haney, spokesman for America's astronauts, said he understood there had been a fire in the cockpit. He said monitors had heard no word from the astronauts during the fire.

Mr. Haney said 26 members of the launching pad crew were treated for smoke inhalation. He said 24 were released and two were hospitalized in good condition.

Space agency officials were alerted by someone on the ground that the fire had broken out, Mr. Haney reported. He said emergency crews tried to reach the astronauts but were blocked by the dense smoke that rolled out of the cockpit.

Officials at Cape Kennedy said that the three astronauts were seated abreast in the rocket in the exercise, just as they would be in actual

Continued on Page 10, Column 1

Fire on Spacecraft Captured on Film

By MARTIN WALDRON
Special to The New York Times

HOUSTON, Jan. 27—The flash fire that killed three astronauts in a spacecraft at Cape Kennedy tonight was filmed, an official of the National Aeronautics and Space Administration said today.

However, the film and recordings made of the astronauts' voices, which were being monitored at Cape Kennedy and at Houston during the test, were sealed immediately after the accident.

Paul P. Haney, director of public affairs for the Manned Spacecraft Center here, said the film and the recordings would be turned over to a board of inquiry that has been given the task of finding out exactly what happened.

The board of inquiry, which will include top officials of the space program, will be appointed tomorrow, Mr. Haney said.

Space officials from Houston

Continued on Page 10, Column 5

500,000 IN THE CITY GO WITHOUT HEAT IN HOUSING STRIKE

Elderly Are the Hardest Hit in Public Developments Affected by Dispute

6,000 EMPLOYES ARE OUT

'Real Progress' Is Reported by Union as Negotiations With Officials Resume

By DAMON STETSON

Nearly all of the 500,000 residents in public housing developments here were left without heat or hot water yesterday by a strike of 6,000 employes of the City Housing Authority.

Elderly persons, mothers and small children huddled around gas stoves in their kitchens in an effort to keep warm. School children and workers returning home through the drenching rain and wind found their apartments cold and cheerless.

A housewife at Riis Houses on East 10th Street summed up her feelings with the comment, "Got no heat, no hot water—they don't get my rent."

The temperature during the day remained close to 40 degrees but dropped to the mid-30's last night.

Governor Rockefeller, taking note of the plight of the thousands of dwellers in public housing in the city, ordered all state armories in the city opened last night to accommodate residents without heat.

'Cold and Damp'

"We've got no hot water or nothing," said Mrs. Ruth Bradley, an elderly tenant in Red Hook Houses in Brooklyn. "It's cold and damp in here anyway, but now it's really cold, and it hurts my arthritis."

The strike by members of Local 237 of the International Brotherhood of Teamsters began officially at 11 P.M. Thursday, but most tenants didn't feel its impact until they got up yesterday morning and found they had no hot water and that their apartments were becoming increasingly chilly.

A spokesman for the authority said that the fuel tanks had been filled to capacity and that the strikers had been requested to set boilers on automatic controls. But Barry Feinstein, vice president of Local 237, said that the union had instructed its members to avoid a possibly dangerous situation that might result from untended boilers and to shut them down.

The authority said that the automatic controls were equipped with safety devices and could have operated for several days without attention. But an official conceded that in 90 per cent of the authority's 147 developments, the boilers had been shut down and that tenants were without heat or hot water.

Negotiations aimed at ending the strike were resumed yesterday afternoon by Mr. Feinstein and his committee and by Walter E. Washington, the chairman, and other officials of the authority. The talks were continuing early this morning.

A union spokesman said that

Continued on Page 24, Column 4

Chicago Is Crippled By a 23-Inch Snow; Police Kill Looter

By DONALD JANSON
Special to The New York Times

CHICAGO, Jan. 27—A city accustomed to snowstorms succumbed to one today.

Chicago is not easy to fell. The nation's third largest city takes in stride weather that makes winter hurt.

But this time wind and snow combined with paralyzing fury in a two-day onslaught that brought Chicago to its knees. It was the worst storm in history here, dumping more than 23 inches of snow on the city and 26 inches on its southern suburbs.

[The Chicago police shot and killed a 10-year-old girl who they said was helping loot a store in the snow-filled streets of the West Side Friday, according to The Associated Press. The storm thundered toward the East during the day and snow warnings were posted as far east as Maine, Vermont and New York.]

Chicagoans trooped to work yesterday, ignoring the heavy

Continued on Page 16, Column 1

LINDSAY ORDERS O'DWYER OUSTED

But Procaccino Says Board Counsel Will Stay On in Transit Subsidy Suit

By SETH S. KING

Mayor Lindsay dismissed Paul O'Dwyer yesterday as a special corporation counsel.

He acted after Mr. O'Dwyer had summoned the Mayor and the Transit Authority to court to explain why they refused to use $84.3-million to subsidize the transit system.

Controller Mario A. Procaccino immediately declared that Mr. O'Dwyer would go right on representing the Board of Estimate in the case.

The board is trying to force the Republican Mayor to use the $84.3-million for a transit subsidy as the Democratic-controlled City Council had directed.

Mr. Procaccino said the dismissal of Mr. O'Dwyer was "an incredible step" in a politically inspired move to thwart the board, which the Democrats also control.

"The Mayor really wants to use $84-million of the taxpayers' money for other purposes," the controller declared. "That money was specifically appropriated to keep the subway fare where it is and not to help the Mayor balance his budget."

The latest phase in the battle over the proposed transit subsidy began Thursday when the board overruled the Mayor and directed Mr. O'Dwyer to go into court for a ruling on whether the city had the right to subsidize the transit system.

Last November, at the insistence of the board, Mr. O'Dwyer, a brother of former Mayor William O'Dwyer and a former Democratic City Councilman, had been appointed by Corporation Counsel J. Lee Rankin to pursue the question

Continued on Page 25, Column 6

NATION'S BANKS SET 5¾% RATE; REBUKING CHASE

Prime Borrowing Cost Falls From 6% but Not to Level of 5½%, Kept by Leader

By H. ERICH HEINEMANN

Business borrowing costs dropped yesterday as banks across the country reduced their prime interest rate to 5¾ per cent from 6 per cent.

The reduction contrasted with the drop to 5½ per cent announced on Thursday by the Chase Manhattan Bank. The question immediately arose whether Chase would adjust its rate to conform to the new industry standard. Late yesterday, a spokesman for Chase said the bank had "no present intention" of doing so.

Meanwhile, it was learned yesterday that there had been discussions between the Chase Bank and the Johnson Administration prior to the bank's announcement of the reduction to 5½ per cent.

Well-informed sources in Washington said last night that the Government "was not taken by surprise" by Chase's action.

Prime Rate Defined

A spokesman for Chase confirmed last night that "as a matter of courtesy" both the Federal Reserve Bank of New York and the Treasury Department had been notified of the decision to lower the rate shortly before the bank's public announcement.

The prime rate, or minimum business-lending rate, according to one major New York bank, "applies to short-term loans to substantial depositors with the highest credit ratings."

[The Bank of Canada announced a reduction in its lending rate to 5 per cent from 5¼ per cent, effective Monday. The rate had remained unchanged since last March 14 when it was raised to 5¼ per cent from 5 per cent.]

A Conspicuous Exception

The general reduction in the prime rate by banks in the United States was the first since Aug. 23, 1960, when it dropped to 4½ per cent from 5 per cent. The new reduction is only the fifth decline since the custom of a prime rate was established in the nineteen-thirties.

The rate reduction was interpreted by bankers and economists as further evidence of the trend toward lower interest rates that started last fall. In time, they said, credit should become more plentiful and its cost should continue to decline—not only for business but for consumers as well, particularly on home mortgages.

The move to 5¾ per cent was led by the First National City Bank of New York. The bank announced its decision about 11 A.M. By the end of the day practically every other large bank in the country had joined in the decision to post a 5¾ per cent rate.

Chase, of course, stayed at 5½ per cent.

Other bankers, though, voiced the opinion that sooner or later

Continued on Page 32, Column 1

Einstein Relativity Theory Challenged

By WALTER SULLIVAN

A leading physicist reported yesterday an observation that, if true and correctly interpreted, would invalidate Albert Einstein's theory of relativity.

Dr. Robert H. Dicke, professor of physics at Princeton University, told a conference on astrophysics here that his observations of the sun last summer showed that its shape was flattened at the poles.

The effect of this flattening, or oblateness, is sufficient, he said, to explain a significant portion of the orbital behavior of Mercury, the planet closest to the sun, without recourse to relativity. It was the precise conformity of Mercury's orbit to Dr. Einstein's predictions that was the chief pillar of his theory.

If Dr. Dicke is correct, this pillar has been undermined.

However, he struck a cautious note in his report to the astrophysical conference. "It wouldn't surprise me," he said, "if general relativity is just plain wrong."

General relativity deals with gravity and its manifestations

Continued on Page 12, Column 4

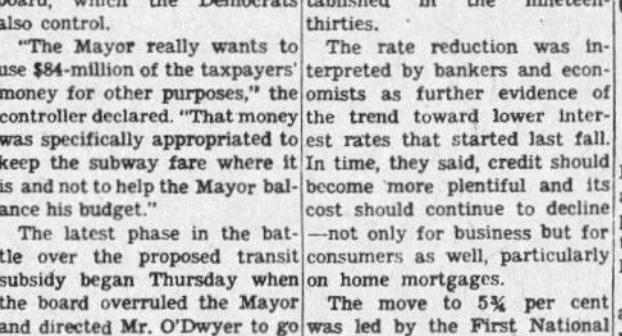

The New York Times (Daniel Brownstein) Jan. 28, 1967

Instrument used by Dr. Robert H. Dicke to determine the sun's shape was based on notched spinning wheel, as shown in upper schematic diagram. As the wheel spun, light of sun passing through notches varied with sun's shape. Light variations during each spin were detected by photocell.

TOWAWAY POLICY IS EASED FOR U.N.

City to Extend Parking Area for Diplomats and Chase Other Motorists Out

The city joined with United Nations officials yesterday in an effort to meet the complaints of diplomats about the towaway crackdown on cars illegally parked in midtown.

The program worked out at a private meeting seeks to reduce the towing away of diplomatic vehicles by the police and provides for various cooperative measures. Specific measures include plans to supply the diplomats with more on-street parking spaces and to chase "squatters" out of parking areas already reserved for the diplomats.

The move to provide more space for diplomats' cars followed similar action regarding handicapped drivers and physicians. On Thursday, the city said that it would designate as many as 700 new special parking places for invalids. A study was also ordered to provide similar spaces for physicians.

The city, however, reserved the right to tow away illegally parked diplomatic vehicles that create a hazard.

Henry A. Barnes, city Traffic Commissioner, said that the city hoped to supply 100 or more reserved on-street parking places—designated by blue traffic signs—for the diplomats. That would raise their midtown total to about 700.

Diplomats have not been carried away by Mayor Lindsay's "no exceptions" towaway program against illegal midtown parking—but a number of their cars have been.

Since the tough policy went into effect Monday—and up to 11:30 P.M. yesterday—998 vehicles have been towed to the "pound" on Pier 74 at the Hudson River and 34th Street. This number includes 22 diplomatic or foreign consular cars.

About a dozen foreign delegations have been affected. Although the diplomats are exempt from the $40 fee—$25 for towing and the $15 fine—they

Continued on Page 28, Column 1

62 Nations Sign Treaty To Curb Arms in Space

By MAX FRANKEL
Special to The New York Times

WASHINGTON, Jan. 27—President Johnson presided today over a White House ceremony at which the United States, the Soviet Union and 60 other countries signed a treaty to limit military activities in outer space.

Mr. Johnson hailed it as an "inspiring moment in the history of the human race" and described the treaty as a "first, firm step toward keeping outer space free forever from the implements of war."

The ceremony took place before the accident at Cape Kennedy, Fla., in which three American astronauts lost their lives.

Treaty-signing ceremonies were held earlier today in Moscow and London, but the pact will not take effect until it is ratified by the United States, the Soviet Union, Britain and two other countries.

For most nations, that is a mere formality, but in the United States, the Senate must give its consent by a two-thirds vote.

Eventual ratification here is expected, because the treaty does not prohibit any present or planned American military activities in space.

It prohibits the placing of nuclear weapons or other weapons of mass destruction in orbit, on the moon or on other celestial bodies. It also bars all military installations and maneuvers from the moon and other planets.

It does not, however, prohibit the orbiting of military spacecraft without large weapons or the use of unmanned satellites for military purposes, such as reconnaissance.

Some opposition here may focus on the difficulties of inspecting Soviet satellites for the presence of nuclear weapons. But American officials expressed confidence that the treaty posed no threat to national security.

They predicted that the Joint

Continued on Page 6, Column 2

ARMY OPPOSITION TO MAO REPORTED

Troops in 2 Regions Said to Resist Orders to Help in Ousting Party Officials

By CHARLES MOHR
Special to The New York Times

HONG KONG, Jan. 27—Disunity and confusion in the Chinese Army seemed apparent to some political analysts here today in the wake of an order to the army to stamp out resistance to Mao Tse-tung's political purge.

There was no immediate confirmation of Peking wall posters reporting that troops in the far western autonomous region of Sinkiang and in Inner Mongolia were opposing orders by Mr. Mao, who is Chairman of the Chinese Communist party, to help oust entrenched party officials.

[Reacting to clashes in Moscow in which Chinese students were hurt, Peking declared that the Soviet Union's leaders were "swine" in the same category as the last Czar, Hitler and the Ku Klux Klan. Page 2.]

The analysts here noted that the troop commander in the Sinkiang military region, Wang En-mao, was concurrently the head of the Communist party's Provincial Committee there. He could hardly be expected to use his troops to oust himself and his comrades from office, the analysts said.

A similar situation prevailed in Inner Mongolia, where Ulanfu, a Mongol, was both military commander and head of the party committee. Whether he is in

Continued on Page 2, Column 4

APOLLO PROGRAM DEALT HARD BLOW

The Slim Margin for Failure Believed Jeopardizing a Moon Landing by '70

By EVERT CLARK
Special to The New York Times

WASHINGTON, Jan. 27—Tonight's accident at Cape Kennedy is expected to deal a serious blow to the Apollo program, which has struggled hard to stay on schedule in the face of annual budget cuts.

Space officials have warned for several years that their margin of operation was thin, that continual economy by the Administration and Congress had left no room for failures if the moon was to be reached by 1970.

Since they first raised this cry, the mishaps have gradually accumulated.

Although it will be some time before the full impact of the accident can be assessed, it means more than the loss of a carefully selected, highly competent crew.

It probably means the loss of a spacecraft and possibly parts of the launching rocket. It also may mean damage to the launching pad that could delay a flight using the backup crew. A backup crew flew the Gemini 9 after the original Gemini 9 pilots were killed in a plane crash.

Last March, President Johnson reaffirmed the goal laid down by President Kennedy when he announced the Apollo program in May of 1961. The United States, Mr. Johnson said, still intends "to land the first man on the surface of the moon" by 1970.

Mr. Johnson's words were interpreted at the time as an answer—and a bit of a reprimand—to the National Aeronautics and Space Administration, which had been complaining to Congress about budget cuts made within the Administration.

On the same day, Vice President Humphrey reminded the space leaders that their program "cannot be exempt" from tight budgetary discipline.

Following the ceremony at

Continued on Page 2, Column 4

Continued on Page 10, Column 2

NEWS INDEX

"All the News That's Fit to Print"

The New York Times

LATE CITY EDITION

Weather: Clearing by afternoon; fair and cool tonight, tomorrow. Temp. range: today 40-35; Tues. 36-30. Full U. S. report on Page 93.

VOL. CXVII..No. 40,226 NEW YORK, WEDNESDAY, MARCH 13, 1968 10 CENTS

M'CARTHY GETS ABOUT 40%, JOHNSON AND NIXON ON TOP IN NEW HAMPSHIRE VOTING

RUSK TELLS PANEL 'WE WILL CONSULT' ON ANY TROOP RISE

He Avoids Pledge to Confer in Advance, but Johnson Is Said to Be Ready To

FULBRIGHT IS CRITICAL

Says Secretary Is Unclear —Vietnam Policy Attacked Again as Hearing Ends

Excerpts from the hearing are on Pages 14 and 15.

By JOHN W. FINNEY
Special to The New York Times

WASHINGTON, March 12—Secretary of State Dean Rusk assured the Senate Foreign Relations Committee today that the Administration would consult with Congress about sending additional troops to Vietnam.

But Mr. Rusk refused to promise that the Administration would consult more closely with Congress than in the past, nor would he commit the Administration to consultations before a decision on additional troops was made.

However, there was some information in Washington tonight that the President would consult Congressional leaders before deciding the troop question. [James Reston's column, editorial page.]

Mr. Rusk, as he concluded more than 10 hours of nationally televised testimony, told the committee: "If more troops are needed, we will, as we have done in the past, consult with appropriate members of Congress."

'He Never Did Answer Us'

This promise, however, fell short of meeting the demands of some committee members, in particular Senator J. W. Fulbright, the chairman.

The Arkansas Democrat wearily observed to reporters after Mr. Rusk had completed his testimony: "He never did answer us on whether there would be consultation before a decision is made. He did not say positively he would and he did not say positively he wouldn't."

The two days of hearings—the first public confrontation between Mr. Rusk and the committee on Vietnam policy in two years—did not lead to any changes of position.

If anything, they caused a hardening of positions as Mr. Rusk reiterated his often-stated arguments and many of the

Continued on Page 15, Column 1

Associated Press

MARINES HONORED: President Johnson congratulating Lieut. John J. McGinty 3d, left, and Maj. Robert J. Modrzejewski in ceremonies at the White House yesterday. Both men won the Medal of Honor for valor during Operation Hastings in Vietnam in July, 1966.

22 in House Ask Congress To Oppose Troop Increase

Bipartisan Group Acts

By HEDRICK SMITH
Special to The New York Times

WASHINGTON, March 12—New resistance to further increases in the number of American troops in Vietnam broke into the open today in debate in the House of Representatives.

A bipartisan group of 22 Representatives, led by William S. Moorehead, Democrat of Pennsylvania, submitted a sense-of-Congress resolution directly opposing the dispatch of any more troops to South Vietnam.

A second resolution, sponsored by 17 House members, sought to put Congress on record as opposing any further increases "without the explicit consent of the Congress" and until President Johnson has presented a "clear justification" to Congress and the American people.

Most Backers Democrats

The original sponsor of this resolution was Edward P. Boland, Democrat of Massachusetts, a senior member of the Appropriations Committee who generally backs Administration policy but has been moving away on Vietnam.

Most of the backers of the two resolutions are House liberals. The preponderance are Democrats.

High Pentagon officials, meanwhile, were urging an initial mobilization of 30,000 infantry reserves to permit the deployment of at least one more combat division to Vietnam in the next several months.

House debate on the troop issue was set off when Paul Findley, Republican of Illinois, announced that a resolution he submitted last Sept. 25, calling for a Congressional reappraisal of American policy in Southeast Asia, now has 120 cosponsors, or more than one-fourth of the 433-man member-

Continued on Page 18, Column 3

Greater Tax Rise Seen

By EILEEN SHANAHAN
Special to The New York Times

WASHINGTON, March 12—Administration officials said today that it would cost something more than $20,000 a man — or $4-billion for 200,000 men — to increase the number of American troops in Vietnam.

Any sizable increase in military force levels in Vietnam, which they emphasized had not yet been decided on, would require the Administration to propose a larger tax increase, reductions in nondefense spending, or both, they said.

Both the troop cost estimate and the warning of possible additional fiscal restraints were given by Administration officials who were testifying before the Senate Finance Committee.

Ostensibly they were testifying on legislation to continue present excise taxes on automobiles and telephone service beyond their scheduled April 1 date for reduction.

The committee went far afield in its questioning, however, and among other things, discussed the possibility of attaching the pending 10 per cent tax surcharge to the excise tax bill.

Two Democratic members of

Continued on Page 19, Column 1

PRESIDENT URGES PATIENCE ON WAR

In Presenting 2 Medals of Honor, He Asserts 'Steady' Nation 'Shall Never Fail'

By MAX FRANKEL
Special to The New York Times

WASHINGTON, March 12—President Johnson took note of the debate over Vietnam here today by imploring Americans not to yield to despair and cautioning the enemy not to misjudge their resolve.

"I think if we are steady, if we are patient, if we do not become the willing victims of our own despair, if we do not abandon what we know is right when it comes under mounting challenge—we shall never fail," the President said.

"Responsibility never comes easy. Neither does freedom come free."

North Vietnam is now openly intervening in South Vietnam, Mr. Johnson said, and there should no longer be any illusions "that this was only a civil war."

"And let no one ever suffer any illusions," he continued, "about the will and about the faith of free men, the American fighting man, the family of citizens who stand by him here and who stand by him out

Continued on Page 15, Column 7

GOVERNOR SIGNS $300-MILLION CUT IN MEDICAID FUND

Says He Saw No Alternative but to Accept Leaders' Plan—Calls Own Better

By SYDNEY H. SCHANBERG
Special to The New York Times

ALBANY, March 12—Governor Rockefeller today signed into law bills that will cut the state's Medicaid program by about $300-million a year—about $100-million more than the Governor had asked for.

The Governor issued no formal comment as he approved the two Republican-sponsored bills, reportedly with personal regret, less than 24 hours after they had been given final passage in the Assembly

Earlier in the day, at an impromptu meeting with newsmen, Mr. Rockefeller said when asked whether he would sign or veto the legislation:

"I don't see frankly that I've got much alternative."

He paused and added: "I proposed what I thought was an effective way to deal with a very difficult problem. They [the legislators] considered, deliberated, and came back with a different plan."

Mayor Scores Cuts

In New York, Mayor Lindsay criticized the Medicaid reductions signed into law by Governor Rockefeller as a "disastrous step backward." The Mayor said that the Governor's action would reduce medical benefits for about 1.6 million New Yorkers and would mean a loss of about $80-million in state aid to municipal and voluntary hospitals.

The legislation—with most of the provisions to go into effect on April 1—will chop about one million persons from the 3.5 million now enrolled in the Medicaid program. About 5.7 million persons were eligible under the present plan, but only 3.5 million signed up.

In addition most of those who will be left on the Medicaid rolls will suffer some cut in the government contribution toward their health-care expenses.

Specifically the bills, which were conceived by Republican leaders in both houses and also drew support from many upstate Democrats, would reduce the cost of Medicaid principally by lowering the net income eligibility level. The level for a family of four, for example, would be reduced from the present $6,000 a year to $5,300.

The Governor's plan would have lowered the income level

Continued on Page 36, Column 3

Friends Say Rockefeller Has Decided to Make Bid

By R. W. APPLE Jr.
Special to The New York Times

ALBANY, March 12—Governor Rockefeller has decided to campaign for the Republican Presidential nomination, according to close friends, but has still not decided upon tactics.

The Governor has told intimates this week that he will choose within the next 10 days one of three courses of action—whichever he believes will best keep alive his chances for the nomination. He has emphasized that his hesitation grows out of a strategic problem, not out of reluctance to seek the nomination or lack of confidence in his ability to make a strong race.

These are the options open to Governor Rockefeller:

1. Wage a full-scale campaign for the Oregon primary election on May 28 in the hope of stopping the drive of former Vice President Richard M. Nixon toward the nomination and dramatically demonstrating his own grass roots popularity.
2. Allow his name to remain in the campaign there, leaving the field work to the draft-Rockefeller committee in that state. He is to meet with leaders of the committee either here or in Manhattan next weekend.
3. File an affidavit of withdrawal from the Oregon primary, in which the Governor's name has been entered by the Oregon Secretary of State. Under the election regulations such an affidavit

Continued on Page 32, Column 1

Effects of Primary

Rockefeller Gets Push Toward Oregon—Kennedy More Than Ever in Dilemma

By TOM WICKER
Special to The New York Times

News Analysis

CONCORD, N. H., March 12—An excellent showing in the New Hampshire Republican primary today by former Vice President Richard M. Nixon probably had the effect of pushing Governor Rockefeller of New York toward entry into the Oregon primary. Another excellent vote-getting performance, by Senator Eugene J. McCarthy of Minnesota in this state's Democratic primary, left Senator Robert F. Kennedy of New York more than ever on the horns of a political dilemma.

Mr. Nixon smashed, by about 80 per cent to 10 per cent, a write-in campaign waged on behalf of, but without the official blessing of, Governor Rockefeller.

Mr. McCarthy took about 40 per cent of the votes from President Johnson, who was a write-in candidate backed by most New Hampshire Democratic party officials.

Mr. Rockefeller disavowed the write-in effort as unauthorized. But the fact remains that fairly conclusive returns showed him winning only about half of the 19,504 votes he got in a full-scale campaign here in 1964.

The Governor's total tonight was also far less than the 15,000 votes the write-in campaign's principal sponsors said they had hoped for.

Behind Nixon of '64

More importantly, the Rockefeller write-in lagged far behind the 15,587 write-in votes cast here in 1964 for Richard M. Nixon. The Nixon write-in of that year was unauthorized, as was the campaign waged for Mr. Rockefeller this year.

Thus, the total for Mr. Rockefeller today, even though he made no effort to increase it, contributed little if any to the "draft" he has said he is awaiting.

Without the development of something resembling such a draft, most political observers believe the New York Governor will be forced into the Oregon primary, where he can do battle openly with Mr. Nixon and possibly Gov. Ronald Reagan of California.

Mr. Rockefeller has until March 22 to decide whether to enter the Oregon primary. He has already made plans to confer with Oregon Republican leaders this week.

As for Senator Kennedy, neither as a write-in possibility for President nor in an unofficial write-in contest between him and Vice President Hum-

Continued on Page 33, Column 2

ROCKEFELLER LAGS

Senator Exceeds Top Primary Predictions on Peace Campaign

By WARREN WEAVER Jr.
Special to The New York Times

CONCORD, N. H., March 12—President Johnson turned back a strong challenge by Senator Eugene J. McCarthy in the first 1968 Democratic primary tonight, but not before the Minnesotan had won about 40 per cent of the vote.

In the parallel Republican contest, Richard M. Nixon routed a write-in effort by supporters of Governor Rockefeller of New York, holding his only current Presidential competitor to about 10 per cent of the vote.

Although the President, a write-in candidate, was headed for certain victory in the popularity contest with nearly 90 per cent of the vote in, incomplete returns indicated that Mr. McCarthy had won about 20 of New Hampshire's 24 delegates to the Democratic National Convention.

This happened because the total Johnson vote was divided among 45 candidates for the 24 delegate openings, while the McCarthy forces had prudently limited their slate to 24, each of whom got the full benefit of the Senator's strength.

Democratic Vote

With 87 per cent of the Democratic vote cast, President Johnson held 50 per cent, or 22,272 votes, to 41 per cent, or 18,032, for Senator McCarthy, whose name was on the ballot.

Rockefeller backers had set a goal of 15,000 for their candidate. With 80 per cent of the Republican returns in, however, he had 11 per cent, or 8,610, which would give him only a little over 10,000 of the expected 102,000 total. Mr. Nixon polled about 80 per cent of the vote, or 63,325.

Despite a heavy snow that began in the late afternoon, the turnover in both party primaries was larger than expected. The projected Republican vote of 102,000 was 15,000 to 20,000 higher than many party leaders had expected, particularly after the with-

Continued on Page 33, Column 1

BIG BOMBS BLAST FOE AT KHESANH

2,000-Pounders Are Used—Saigon Claims 194 of Foe

By GENE ROBERTS
Special to The New York Times

SAIGON, South Vietnam, March 12 — United States aircraft have swarmed over Khesanh repeatedly during the last 24 hours to pound enemy positions with bombs weighing up to a ton.

One of the heaviest bombardments so far around Khesanh, it touched off speculation that the allies wanted to preclude any possibility of an enemy attack there tomorrow.

[South Vietnamese forces reported Wednesday that they had killed 194 North Vietnamese in heavy fighting near the Cua Viet supply base south of the demilitarized zone, United Press International said.]

Tomorrow will be the 14th anniversary of the start of the successful campaign against the French at Dienbienphu, an installation that frequently has been compared with Khesanh, where a force of 6,000 marines is encamped.

As the air assaults raged on, Navy jets from the carrier Enterprise blasted an enemy bunker complex near the encampment with 2,000-pound

Continued on Page 15, Column 3

Poles Oust Fathers Of Demonstrators

By JONATHAN RANDAL
Special to The New York Times

WARSAW, March 12 — In rapid retribution for the Warsaw street riots, the Polish Government dismissed three high government officials tonight. Meanwhile a campaign accusing pro-Zionist Poles and other Jews of having organized the disturbances became more widespread.

The officials were apparently dismissed because their children had been identified in the press as ringleaders of the demonstrations, which protested Communist party controls over cultural affairs.

The dismissals were disclosed following a day of calm, troubled only by minor incidents involving teen-agers whom the Polish press agency P.A.P. de-

Continued on Page 4, Column 4

A Vertebrate Fossil Is Found in Antarctic

By WALTER SULLIVAN

A fossil fragment of a large amphibian that lived in subtropical forests near the South Pole more than 200 million years ago has been found in Antarctica.

This is the first indication that land vertebrates once inhabited that region. It had previously been thought that Antarctica, isolated by hundreds of miles of stormy seas, had never been reached by such animals.

The discovery supports the view that the continent was once linked to other land masses.

This is because animals of this type are thought to have been unable to travel in salt water. Yet closely related species are known to have lived contemporaneously in South Africa, Australia and even as far away as Spitsbergen, near the North Pole.

Dr. Edwin H. Colbert, curator of vertebrate paleontology at the American Museum of Natural History, at 81st Street and Central Park West, termed the discovery one of the most important fossil finds of the century.

It was he who identified the specimen, a fragment of jaw bone only 2½ inches long. He described the animal as resembling a giant salamander about four feet long.

The specimen, he said, should make "very happy" those who believed the continents were once joined and then drifted apart. The ancient animal belonged to the labyrinthodonts, a major group of extinct amphibians. They are of special interest because they may have been ancestral to all modern land vertebrates, including man.

The Antarctic discovery was made last December by a geology team from the Institute of Polar Studies at Ohio University. The team worked from last

Continued on Page 26, Column 4

The American Museum of Natural History

Remains, twice natural size, of jaw of the subtropical amphibian found near South Pole

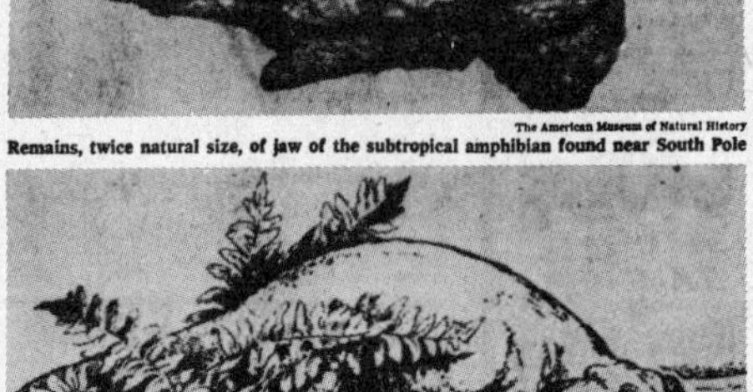

Lois Darling, from "Evolution of the Vertebrates"

An artist's restoration of a labyrinthodont, which lived more than 200 million years ago

Airliner Is Hijacked And Flown to Cuba

By MARTIN WALDRON
Special to The New York Times

MIAMI, March 12 — Two Spanish-speaking gunmen today hijacked a National Airlines DC-8 over south Florida and forced the plane's crew to fly to Havana where the gunmen disembarked with a weeping hostage.

Sarah E. West of Miami, a stewardess, said that the hostage cried "I am killed, I am killed" as he left the plane.

The airliner, on a flight from San Francisco to Miami, had 51 passengers and a crew of seven on board. Cuban authorities released the plane at about 7:30 P.M., after holding it for seven hours, and the plane returned to Miami with its crew and passengers, excepting the two gunmen and

Continued on Page 13, Column 1

NIXON FORECASTS VICTORY IN FALL

Says 'People Don't Want 4 More Years of Johnson'

By ROBERT B. SEMPLE Jr.

A jubilant Richard M. Nixon told 300 supporters last night that his apparently overwhelming victory in New Hampshire meant that "we are going to win in August, and that America is going to get a new leadership in November."

Mr. Nixon, who appeared at 8:45 o'clock in a second-floor room of his new headquarters at 450 Park Avenue, termed the election "the first referendum on Lyndon B. Johnson."

He said that the vote meant "the people of the nation don't want four more years of Johnson in the White House."

The candidate, flanked by Mrs. Nixon and their daughter Tricia, told newsmen that Governor Rockefeller's apparently poor showing in the primary

Continued on Page 33, Column 5

NEWS INDEX

TODAY IS CHRISTMAS DAY! REMEMBER THE NEEDIEST!

"All the News That's Fit to Print"

The New York Times

LATE CITY EDITION

Weather: Mostly sunny, cold today; fair, warmer tonight and tomorrow. Temp. range: today 30-20; Tuesday 34-24. Full U.S. report on Page 62.

VOL. CXVIII—No. 40,513 © 1968 The New York Times Company. NEW YORK, WEDNESDAY, DECEMBER 25, 1968 10 CENTS

3 MEN FLY AROUND THE MOON ONLY 70 MILES FROM SURFACE; FIRE ROCKET, HEAD FOR EARTH

PUEBLO CREWMEN GREETED ON COAST; CAPTORS ASSAILED

Relatives Weep and Scream —Captain Asserts North Koreans Are Inhuman

By BERNARD GWERTZMAN
Special to The New York Times

SAN DIEGO, Dec. 24 — The crew of the intelligence ship Pueblo returned to the United States today in time for Christmas with many of their families.

Led by Comdr. Lloyd M. Bucher, the 82 survivors arrived at the Miramar Naval Air Station outside this city and were met immediately by emotional, sometimes hysterical, greetings and embraces of wives, mothers, fathers and children.

The one man who did not return alive, Duane D. Hodges, was carried from one of the C-141 transports in a flag-draped coffin while the air station band played the Navy hymn.

Commander Bucher, apparently overwrought with emotion, spoke in a low voice as he told the more than 250 relatives, the 300 newsmen and the national television audience about the 11 months his crew spent in North Korean captivity.

Calls Captors Inhuman

He described North Korea as a land "completely devoid of humanity, completely devoted to enslavement of men's minds."

[In Washington, the Navy named Vice Adm. Harold S. Bowen to head a court of inquiry into the Pueblo incident.]

Commander Bucher said that, during the months in North Korea, "the thought that preyed on my mind was the embarrassment to my country because of the loss of one of its fine ships."

At a news conference held in the base theater at Navy Hospital here, Rear Adm. Edwin Rosenberg, the representative of the Commander in Chief, Pacific Fleet, in charge of the Pueblo's repatriation, repeated his past praise

Continued on Page 2, Column 1

Pope Paul Says Mass In a Huge Steel Mill

By ROBERT C. DOTY
Special to The New York Times

TARANTO, Italy, Wednesday, Dec. 25—Pope Paul VI celebrated Christmas midnight mass here for 15,000 workers and members of their families in a huge, echoing rolling mill.

The Pontiff chose the vast Italsider steel plant at this developing industrial center in the heel of the Italian boot as the place to express "the fraternal and radiant presence of Christ among workers throughout the world."

Even while the Pope said mass at an altar consisting of a four-ton slab of steel supported on two broad sections of steel pipe, work continued elsewhere throughout the 2,000-acre plant, the largest in Europe.

Blast furnaces poured plumes of flame into a rainy

Continued on Page 34, Column 1

VIOLATIONS MAR TRUCE IN VIETNAM

80 Incidents Are Reported —22 Enemy Soldiers and an American Killed

By B. DRUMMOND AYRES Jr.
Special to The New York Times

SAIGON, South Vietnam, Wednesday, Dec. 25—The allies and the Vietcong put separate cease-fires into effect yesterday to mark Christmas, but not all the guns fell silent.

At 9 o'clock this morning, the American military command said there had been at least 80 "incidents" involving military contact since the allied cease-fire, scheduled to run 24 hours, went into effect at 6 P.M. yesterday.

The enemy cease-fire began at 1 A.M. yesterday and was scheduled to run for 72 hours. Allied military spokesmen said there were at least eight incidents involving military contact during the first hours of that stand-down.

In about 30 of the incidents, casualties were suffered by one or both sides. The allied spokesmen said that over-all South Vietnamese losses had been light. United States losses were broken down as one soldier killed and 38 wounded.

At least 22 enemy soldiers died.

It was not known whether North Vietnamese troops in South Vietnam were complying with the Vietcong cease-fire order. During previous holiday

Continued on Page 5, Column 3

Col. Frank Borman

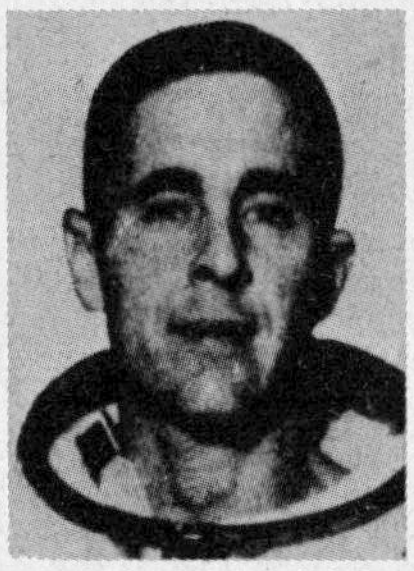

Maj. William A. Anders

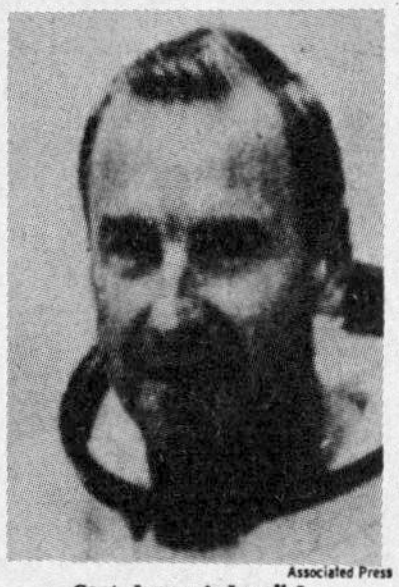

Capt. James A. Lovell Jr.

Associated Press

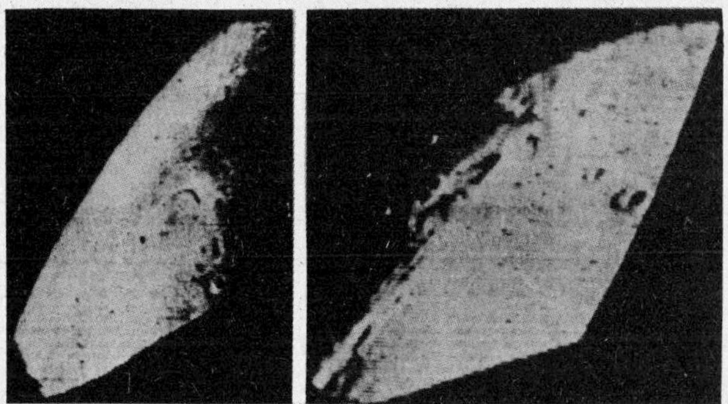

Associated Press

Moon pictures taken through the window of the Apollo 8 spacecraft that were telecast to earth last night. In picture at left of Sea of Crises area, the larger crater is 30 to 40 miles wide. The picture at right was last transmitted.

Astronauts Examine 'Vast, Lonely' Place; Read From Genesis

By JOHN NOBLE WILFORD
Special to The New York Times

HOUSTON, Wednesday, Dec. 25—The three astronauts of Apollo 8 yesterday became the first men to orbit the moon. Early today, after flying 10 times around that desolate realm of dream and scientific mystery, they started their return to earth.

They fired the spacecraft's main rocket engine at 1:10 A.M. to kick them out of lunar orbit

Excerpts from messages to and from Apollo, Page 36.

and to carry them toward a splashdown in the Pacific Ocean on Friday.

Through the static of 231,000 miles, as Apollo 8 swung around from behind the moon and started for earth, one of the astronauts dispelled any doubts, saying, "Please be informed there is a Santa Claus."

57-Hour Return Trip

It would be a 57-hour return trip from the most far-reaching voyage of the space age thus far—or of any other previous age. The astronauts had seen, as no other men had, the ancient lunar craters, plains and rugged mountains from as close as 70 miles.

At 4:59 A.M. yesterday, about 20 hours before the return trip, Col. Frank Borman of the Air Force, Capt. James A. Lovell Jr. of the Navy and Maj. William A. Anders of the Air Force, swept into an orbit of the moon by firing the spacecraft's main rocket. This occurred after they flew around the leading edge of the moon and were directly behind the earth's only natural satellite.

"We got it! We've got it!" exclaimed a mission commentator of the National Aeronautics and Space Administration as the spacecraft emerged from behind the moon 24 minutes later, and was clearly flying a safe and smooth orbit.

Businesslike Report

The calm and laconic Apollo explorers, however, were all business. Captain Lovell's first message to earth was simply:

"Go ahead, Houston. Apollo 8. Burn complete. Our orbit is 169.1 by 60.5—169.1 by 60.5."

The astronauts flew twice around the moon in the egg-shaped orbit, then dropped to a circular orbit nearly 70 miles above the ancient craters, plains and rugged mountains of the lunar surface.

As they beamed their first live television from orbit on Christmas Eve morning, they described the surface of the moon as a colorless gray, "like dirty beach sand with lots of footprints on it" and said it "looks like plaster of Paris."

At about 9:30 P.M. the astronauts began their second and last television show from lunar orbit. It ran some 30 minutes and showed the bright moon, in a pitch black sky, outside the spacecraft window.

Earth Like on 'Oasis'

Colonel Borman described the moon as a "vast, lonely and forbidding sight." adding that it was "not a very inviting place to live or work."

Captain Lovell saw the earth as a "grand oasis in the big vastness of space."

Major Anders was most impressed by "the lunar sunrise and sunsets."

As the telecast neared its end, Colonel Borman said "Apollo 8 has a message for you." With that, Major Anders began reading the opening verses from the Book of Genesis about creation of the earth.

"In the beginning," Major Anders read, "God created the heaven and the earth.

"And the earth was without form and voice; and darkness was upon the face of the deep . . ."

Captain Lovell then took up with the verse beginning, "And God called the light day, and the darkness He called night."

Colonel Borman closed the reading with the verse that read:

"And God called the dry land Earth; and the gathering together of the water called He Seas: and God saw that it was good."

Sends Holiday Greetings

After that Colonel Borman signed off, saying:

"Good-by, good night. Merry Christmas. God bless all of you, all of you on the good earth."

Glynn S. Lunney, one of the flight directors here, told reporters earlier, "we have a completely 'go' spacecraft."

George M. Low, the spacecraft manager at the Manned Spacecraft Center, said he was "altogether happy" with the mission — the most ambitious and daring thus far in the nation's $24-billion Apollo project to land men on the moon next year.

Although the mission's object was not primarily scientific, Dr. John Dietrich of the space center's geology and geochemistry branch, said that the television pictures and astro-

Continued on Page 36, Column 1

At Least 22 Survive Pennsylvania Crash Of Plane With 45

Special to The New York Times

BRADFORD, Pa., Wednesday, Dec. 25—An Allegheny Airlines jetprop plane with 45 persons aboard crashed last night in rugged terrain during a heavy snowstorm while attempting to land at Bradford Regional Airport 15 miles south of here.

There were at least 22 survivors.

The twin-engine plane was Allegheny Flight 736, bound from Detroit to Washington. It had stopped in Erie, Pa., and had been scheduled to stop in Bradford and Harrisburg, Pa.

The wreck, about three miles southeast of the airport, was reported shortly before 9 P.M. by Allegheny Flight 734 out of Cleveland, which said it saw a fire.

It took rescue teams an hour to reach the scene on snowmobiles in freezing temperatures. Several inches of snow had fallen during the day in the heavily wooded area and

Continued on Page 62, Column 1

Christmas Day

Today is Christmas Day. Following is a list of services that are affected:

Public and Parochial Schools—Closed.

Post Office—Closed except for special delivery.

Stores—Most retail and department stores closed.

Banks—Closed.

Stock Exchanges—Closed.

Sanitation—No regular refuse collection.

Parking — Sunday parking regulations in force, permitting parking in alternate-side parking zones and at most parking meters.

Libraries—Closed except for the Main Reading Room of the Library at Fifth Avenue and 42d Street, which will be open from 1 to 10 P.M.

FUEL DELIVERIES FALL SHORT HERE

City's Health Chief Warns of Danger to Sick—Flu Vaccine and Blood Low

By ARNOLD H. LUBASCH

A shortage of heat, vaccine and blood plagued the city yesterday as the Hong Kong flu epidemic continued, and the Health Commissioner warned that many sick people might die unless emergency fuel deliveries were made.

Mayor Lindsay, who said most drivers had stopped fuel deliveries for the holiday, joined Health Commissioner Edward O'Rourke in appealing for fuel deliveries today even though it was Christmas.

With the temperature dropping into the low twenties last night, hundreds of homes, apartment houses and commercial buildings remained without fuel, although oil companies sought to catch up on deliveries delayed by last week's strike.

The city's supply of flu vaccine ran out yesterday as efforts were made to arrange for further shipments before Jan. 2, when 40,000 more doses are scheduled to arrive.

A critical shortage of blood was reported by the Greater

Continued on Page 21, Column 1

Orbit Shows Lunar Interior Is 'Lumpy'

By WALTER SULLIVAN
Special to The New York Times

HOUSTON, Dec. 24—For the first time human beings took a close look today at the earth's nearest celestial neighbor, viewing it from many angles to seek out clues to the events that formed its awesomely rugged terrain.

Until now man has always been forced to look at the moon from a single direction at a great distance, although in the last few years spacecraft have provided glimpses of the far side and close-up views of the earth-facing side.

Today the three Apollo astronauts sailed serenely over the giant craters, looking down their throats, marveling at their crumbling walls and countless strange features that have long puzzled astronomers.

They reported seeing many freshly formed craters, indicating that the cataclysmic events that have pocked the moon and sprinkled it with rubble are continuing. Some of the craters, the astronauts said, looked as though a giant pick had been hacking at a concrete surface, producing fine dust as well as other debris.

Slight Wobbles Observed in Spacecraft's Course

They became the first men to witness a lunar sunrise and found it a strange and unexpected experience. According to Capt. James A. Lovell Jr., about two minutes before sunrise a fine white haze appeared over the horizon where the sun was about to appear.

"It takes the fan shape," he said, "unlike the sunrise on earth, where the atmosphere affects it."

Meanwhile, analysis of the orbital flight by radio antennas on earth showed that, from time to time, the spacecraft wobbled slightly in its path. This confirmed earlier indications that the interior of the moon is "lumpy."

Some scientists, notably Dr. Harold C. Urey of the University of California, San Diego, a Nobel laureate, have suggested that the moon is like a giant raisin cake with lumps of dense iron embedded in material that is far less dense. Such a body could have been formed from a cloud of dust and smaller objects, including chunks of iron, during the formation of the solar system.

If the moon were uniformly dense and perfectly spherical, the gravitational field surrounding it would be perfectly symmetrical. It was this field that held the Apollo spacecraft in orbit. The fact that the spacecraft's road was slightly bumpy, so to speak, revealed an uneven distribution of mass within the moon. In particular, this was noted as the astronauts sailed over Copernicus, one of the largest and most spectacular craters on the moon. It was in darkness but was dimly illuminated by ghostly earthshine—sunlight reflected by the earth.

The lumpiness of the moon

Continued on Page 38, Column 1

A Reflection: Riders on Earth Together, Brothers in Eternal Cold

By ARCHIBALD MacLEISH

MEN'S conception of themselves and of each other has always depended on their notion of the earth. When the earth was the World—all the world there was—and the stars were lights in Dante's heaven, and the ground beneath men's feet roofed Hell, they saw themselves as creatures at the center of the universe, the sole, particular concern of God—and from that high place they ruled and killed and conquered as they pleased.

And when, centuries later, the earth was no longer the World but a small, wet, spinning planet in the solar system of a minor star off at the edge of an inconsiderable galaxy in the immeasurable distances of space — when Dante's heaven had disappeared and there was no Hell (at least no Hell beneath the feet) — men began to see themselves, not as God-directed actors at the center of a noble drama, but as helpless victims of a senseless farce where all the rest were helpless victims also, and millions could be killed in world-wide wars or in blasted cities or in concentration camps without a thought or reason but the reason—if we call it one—of force.

Now, in the last few hours, the notion may have changed again. For the first time in all of time men have *seen* the earth: seen it not as continents or oceans from the little distance of a hundred miles or two or three, but seen it from the depths of space; seen it whole and round and beautiful and small as even Dante—that "first imagination of Christendom" —had never dreamed of seeing it; as the Twentieth Century philosophers of absurdity and despair were incapable of guessing that it might be seen. And seeing it so, one question came to the minds of those who looked at it.

"Is it inhabited?" they said to each other and laughed—and then they did not laugh. What came to their minds a hundred thousand miles and more into space—"half way to the moon" they put it—what came to their minds was the life on that little, lonely, floating planet: that tiny raft in the enormous, empty night. "Is it inhabited?"

THE medieval notion of the earth put man at the center of everything. The nuclear notion of the earth put him nowhere — beyond the range of reason even—lost in absurdity and war. This latest notion may have other consequences. Formed as it was in the minds of heroic voyagers who were also men, it may remake our image of mankind. No longer that preposterous figure at the center, no longer that degraded and degrading victim off at the margins of reality and blind with blood, man may at last become himself.

To see the earth as it truly is, small and blue and beautiful in that eternal silence where it floats, is to see ourselves as riders on the earth together, brothers on that bright loveliness in the eternal cold—brothers who know now they are truly brothers.

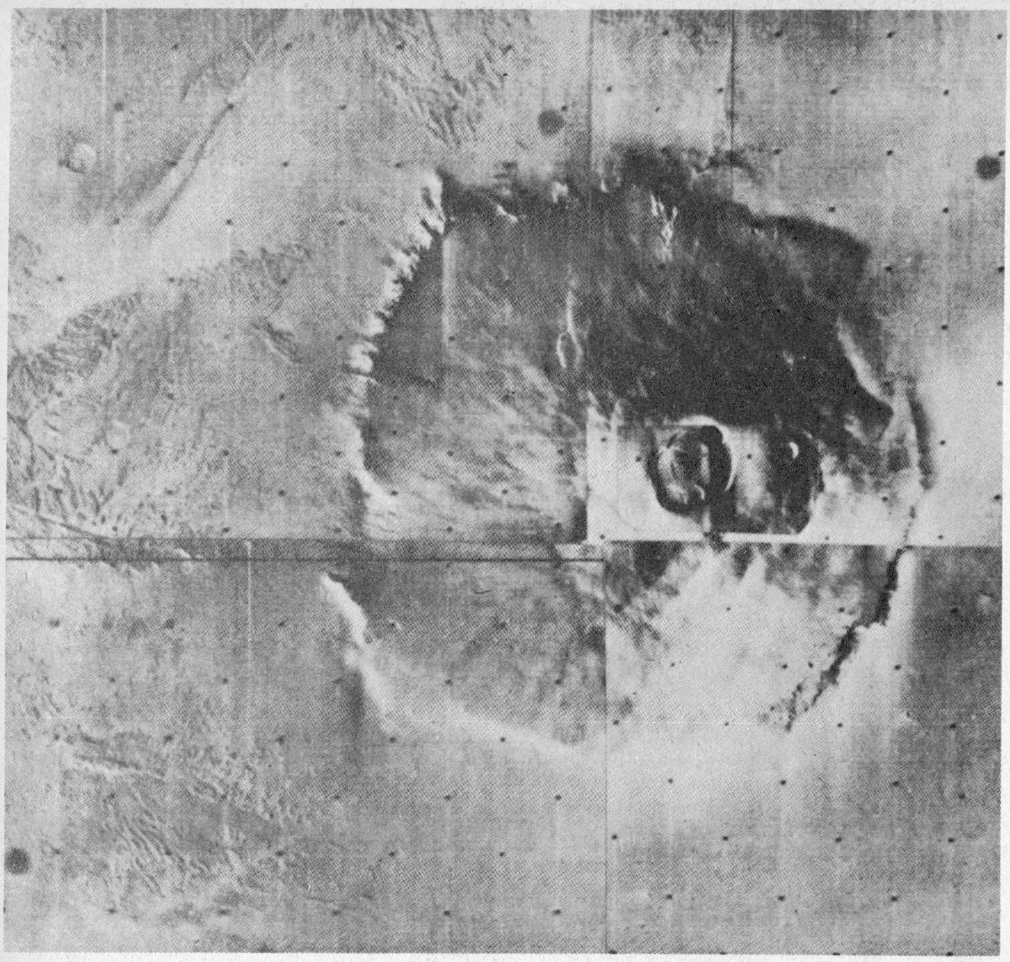

NASA

The towering volcanic mountain is Nix Olympica, approximately 310 miles across at its base. It is more than twice as broad as the most massive volcanic pile on Earth. A large number of possible volcanic features have been identified on Mars, indicating that the planet may have or may have had a molten core.

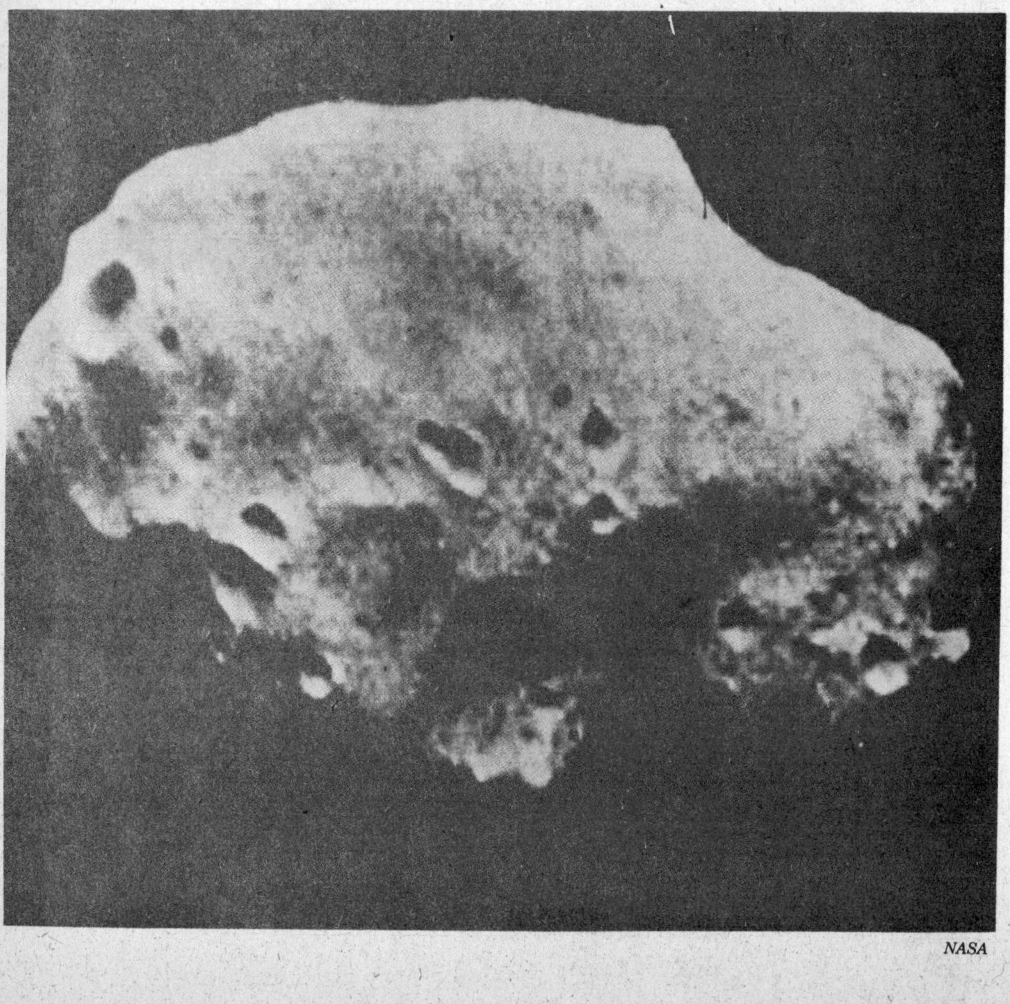

NASA

The first close-up photo of Phobos, the larger of the two Martian moons. Phobos and Deimos appear only as points of light in the most powerful telescopes on Earth.

"All the News That's Fit to Print"

The New York Times

LATE CITY EDITION

Weather: Rain ending by noon today. Fair and mild tonight and tomorrow. Temp. range: today 59-45. Monday 49-42. Full U.S. report on Page 93.

VOL. CXVIII ... No. 40,603 NEW YORK, TUESDAY, MARCH 25, 1969 — 10 CENTS

MAYOR THREATENS HOSPITAL CLOSINGS IN PLEA FOR FUNDS

More State Aid Is Necessary to Prevent Curtailment of Service, He Says

UNION WARNS OF ACTION

Asserts Selective Shutdown Could Spark a Walkout at All Institutions

By CHARLES G. BENNETT

Mayor Lindsay told the State Legislature yesterday that he would have to close some municipal hospitals or reduce their services drastically if the city did not receive more state aid.

The suggestion that selected hospitals might be shut down quickly brought a warning from a labor leader that his union would shut down all 20 municipal hospitals if any were closed by the city.

The Mayor issued his statement after meeting with top hospital officials, who gave him alternative proposals for meeting prospective fund cuts. One suggestion given the Mayor at the City Hall meeting was to close certain hospitals.

A second suggestion was to reduce services for nonacute, ambulatory patients, and outpatient and rehabilitative services. The Mayor said this would reduce hospital services to "only rudimentary care."

Patients Turned Away

The third alternative, the Mayor said, would be to return to state care all psychiatric and tubercular patients. Legally, he said, the responsibility for such care belongs with the state.

In asking for more money, Mr. Lindsay said that all three alternatives were unacceptable.

The hospitals' troubles over lack of funds was dramatized at Harlem Hospital, which has been turning away dozens of patients. The hospital's medical board has voted to close the institution because of lack of funds to hire sufficient personnel.

Yesterday, in addition to the Mayor's City Hall conference with top officials, there were the following developments:

¶Victor Gotbaum, executive director of District Council 37 of the American Federation of State, County and Municipal Employes, said at a crowded meeting of union members at Harlem Hospital that all 20 municipal hospitals would be closed if there was a selective shutdown of any hospital.

¶Legislators of both parties

Continued on Page 34, Column 5

High Court Hints Easing Of Disclosure of Bugging

Grants Hoffa and Clay New Hearings —Indicates Files in Intelligence Cases May Not Have to Be Opened

By FRED P. GRAHAM
Special to The New York Times

WASHINGTON, March 24—The Supreme Court indicated today that the Justice Department might yet be spared the necessity of disclosing the transcripts of conversations overheard in foreign intelligence eavesdropping.

In two brief, unsigned opinions and a tart concurring opinion by Justice Potter Stewart, the Court told the Justice Department that its top officials had become unduly concerned that a Court decision on March 10 would force the Government to disclose intelligence secrets.

The Court sent back for consideration in the lower courts appeals brought by Cassius Clay, former heavyweight boxing champion who prefers to be known as Muhammad Ali, and James R. Hoffa, president of the International Brotherhood of Teamsters, and a dozen other cases in which questions of Government eavesdropping had been raised.

However, no convictions were reversed by the Supreme Court, and today's decisions made it appear that defendants' rights to see Government eavesdrop transcripts were to be more restricted than the ruling on March 10 had seemed to say.

In that decision the Court ruled, in an opinion by Justice Byron R. White, that any crim-

Continued on Page 26, Column 1

NIXON SEEKS BIDS FOR RIGHT TO BUILD LOW-COST HOUSING

Romney Hopes to Pool Needs of Mass Market and Spur Contract Competition

By WARREN WEAVER Jr.
Special to The New York Times

WASHINGTON, March 24—The Nixon Administration is at work on a new housing program that will attempt to spur competition between giant corporations for the right to build hundreds of thousands of low-cost units all over the country.

George Romney, the Secretary of Housing and Urban Development, told reporters today that the key to the new experiment would be encouragement of mass production techniques in an industry where both the laws and the customs have tended to produce buildings one at a time in the past.

Mr. Romney indicated that by pooling the separate housing needs of the major states and cities into a single "mass market," the nation could make profitable use of the assembly line system, originated in his former industry, automobiles, in his former city, Detroit.

Sees Three-Year Wait

Mr. Romney estimated that his plan could produce from 250,000 to 350,000 low-cost housing units a year, but he said that the first of them would probably not become available for about three years.

"You don't design an automobile in a few months; it takes a couple of years," the former president of American Motors declared.

The Housing Secretary has talked informally with Governors of a number of large states and some leaders of the construction trades unions. He said he had been encouraged by their favorable reaction.

Mr. Romney said that the proposal would not involve any Federal spending beyond that already planned for the mortgage interest subsidy program voted by Congress last year. Enough money should be available even if the Vietnam war continues, he added.

A Bidding Procedure

As the Nixon Cabinet officer described his plan over breakfast with reporters, it calls first for Federal authorities to take an informal inventory of housing needs, asking each major state and city how many units it needs and then adding all the figures up.

"If we bring together sufficient volume of demand," Mr. Romney said, "then we can go to the national corporations and say: 'What can you produce for this market?'"

The corporations would be

Continued on Page 28, Column 1

United Press International

AFTER TALKS: President Nixon with Prime Minister Pierre Elliott Trudeau of Canada in Washington yesterday. Mr. Nixon holds coins given men by Canadian Club of Washington.

U.S. PROPOSES BIG 4 OPEN FULL TALKS ON MIDEAST AT U.N.

Yost Is Said to Urge Raising the Bilateral Exchanges to Parley of Chief Delegates

INITIAL ACCORDS CITED

Hope Voiced for a Meeting by Next Week—American Envoy Informs Thant

By JUAN de ONIS
Special to The New York Times

UNITED NATIONS, N. Y., March 24—The United States proposed today to the Soviet Union, Britain and France that talks on the Middle East here be raised from bilateral exchanges to a Big Four meeting.

Diplomatic sources said the proposal was made by Charles W. Yost, the chief United States representative, in separate meetings with the chief delegates of the three other major powers, Yakov A. Malik of the Soviet Union, Armand Bérard of France and Lord Caradon of Britain.

Mr. Yost is reported to have said the United States felt that bilateral talks here and elsewhere between the major powers had established enough points of agreement and had sufficiently clarified areas of difference to make four-sided talks meaningful.

Hope for Early Meeting

The sources did not specify the points on which Mr. Yost indicated that agreement had developed. But it seemed likely that the agreements were more on matters of what the Big Four should discuss and how the talks would be held rather than on any four-power initiative that might be taken toward Israel and the Arab countries.

United States officials hoped that a favorable response to the proposal might make possible a meeting of the Big Four permanent representatives here by next week.

The United States' views on a four-power meeting were communicated to Secretary General Thant by Mr. Yost after he had met with the three ambassadors.

The move, after weeks of bilateral contacts, represented a step forward by the United States in line with President Nixon's decision to undertake a more active approach to the complex Middle Eastern problem.

Eban Opposes Proposal

This type of approach is not welcomed by Israel, whose Foreign Minister, Abba Eban, tried last week to dissuade officials in Washington from moving ahead with a Big-Four effort to break the Middle East stalemate.

Israel has insisted that the Arab leaders must have no illusion that outside forces can bring a settlement to the Middle East. She maintains that the only road to peace is through direct Israeli-Arab negotiations.

United States diplomats have privately informed the heads of various delegations here that this Israeli position is not shared by the Government in Washington. They have been saying the Nixon Administration feels that the major powers can help the rival Middle Eastern states reach agreement by taking an active part in negotiations.

One point on which the Big Four apparently are in agreement is that these negotiations must be conducted through Dr. Gunnar V. Jarring, the Swedish diplomat who is serving as the United Nations' special envoy to the Middle East. The major powers want to strengthen and broaden Dr. Jarring's role as conciliator.

Dr. Jarring's mandate grows out of the Security Council

Continued on Page 20, Column 5

Assembly Votes to Cut Aid In Cases of Campus Crime

By JOHN KIFNER
Special to The New York Times

ALBANY, March 24—The Assembly gave final passage tonight to a bill denying state aid to students convicted of a crime "on the premises of any college." The vote was 86 to 60, with the Democrats voting heavily against it.

After more than three and a half hours of acrimonious debate on student demonstrations the lower house also passed two other Republican bills.

One would require university governing bodies to draw up regulations specifying "precise penalties" for various forms of campus disorders or lose their state financial aid. The bill, sponsored by Charles D. Henderson, Republican of Steuben County and some 50 other Assemblymen, passed 116-30.

A companion measure drawn up by a committee named by Speaker Perry B. Duryea would make disrupting, disturbing or preventing classes on or within 500 feet of college or university property a Class A misdemeanor —aggravated disorderly conduct. It passed 92 to 49.

Another Bill Sidetracked

Another bill, which would have made a second conviction for this crime within six months a felony, was laid aside for further debate after an overwhelming show of hands against it.

In another development, Governor Rockefeller introduced legislation that would remove jurisdiction for most cases involving moving traffic violations from the New York City Criminal courts and give it to the State Department of Motor Vehicles.

"By relieving the criminal courts of most traffic cases," the Governor said, the city courts would be able to "provide prompter handling of serious criminal matters in a more judicious atmosphere."

The Assembly began a general debate over campus demonstrations shortly before 5:30, then voted separately on four bills, with many of the legis-

Continued on Page 43, Column 1

SCHOOL REFORMS FACING SETBACK

Decentralization Bill Is in Trouble as Vote Nears in Senate at Albany

By SYDNEY H. SCHANBERG
Special to The New York Times

ALBANY, March 24—The Senate's Republican majority leader, Earl W. Brydges, said today that he might bring the volatile school decentralization issue to a vote this week. This immediately stirred fears among pro-decentralization legislators that the move would kill the broad plan submitted by the State Board of Regents and result in passage of a much weaker bill.

One such bill was introduced today by Senator John J. Marchi—Mayor Lindsay's chief opponent in the Republican mayoral primary. The Marchi bill would replace New York City's present unsalaried 13-man Board of Education with a three-man paid board and would leave it almost entirely up to the new board to decide how far it might want to go with decentralizing the city's schools. Under the bill, which was immediately reported out of committee to the Senate floor, the board could do virtually nothing, if it so chose.

Senator Brydges, a Niagara Falls Republican, said he "might" take up the more comprehensive Regents bill on Thursday, but when asked about its chances, he shook his head and said: "I don't know how it's going to go."

Proponents of decentraliza-

Continued on Page 43, Column 5

TRUDEAU CONFERS WITH PRESIDENT

ABM, Student Unrest and Race Problems Covered in White House Talks

By JAMES F. CLARITY
Special to The New York Times

WASHINGTON, March 24—President Nixon and Prime Minister Pierre Elliott Trudeau of Canada met privately for 90 minutes today and discussed issues ranging from the President's controversial proposal for an antiballistic missile system to student unrest and racial problems.

The 49-year-old Prime Minister, a forelock of his thinning hair giving him a casual appearance, was the first head of a foreign government to meet with President Nixon on an official state visit to the White House.

The President and the Prime Minister, after listening to their national anthems played by a military band in the drizzle outside the north portico of the White House, went inside and exchanged formal pleasantries on a stage in the West Ballroom.

After their private talk in Mr. Nixon's office the two joined key members of their staffs and talked for 45 minutes longer.

The press secretaries of both Mr. Nixon and Mr. Trudeau, in a briefing after the talks, stressed the amicability of the meeting and parried questions on what the two chiefs of

Continued on Page 11, Column 1

Fruitless Meetings of Eban And Hussein Are Reported

By HEDRICK SMITH
Special to The New York Times

WASHINGTON, March 24—King Hussein of Jordan and Foreign Minister Abba Eban of Israel have held at least two secret meetings in recent months to try to arrange elements of a Middle East settlement, according to reliable sources, but their efforts were unsuccessful.

These neutral sources disclosed that King Hussein was dissatisfied with the terms that Israel had offered and had broken off the meetings for the sake of Arab solidarity.

He is understood to have insisted from the outset that any tentative understandings would have to be made known through Dr. Gunnar V. Jarring of Sweden, the United Nations representative for the Middle East, to insure that other Arab governments would be properly informed. But this never became necessary.

Risks for Hussein

Direct contacts with Israeli officials are a matter of extreme sensitivity for Arab leaders and are considered especially risky for King Hussein. His grandfather, King Abdullah, was assassinated on July 20, 1951, after similar contacts with Israeli leaders, including a meeting with the present Premier, Mrs. Golda Meir.

The assassination is commonly ascribed by historians to popular resentment against King Abdullah's peace efforts, and has acted as a deterrent to face-to-face talks between Arab and Israeli leaders since the war of June, 1967.

For this reason both Israeli and Jordanian officials have repeatedly denied any reports of direct contacts and can be expected to do so again. However, reliable though sketchy accounts have become available here through neutral sources.

According to these accounts, King Hussein and Mr. Eban met in London one or more times last fall, most probably in late September, and again in January. The King was in London

Continued on Page 20, Column 1

GROUND FIGHTING HEAVY IN VIETNAM

Battles Reported in All Four Tactical Zones—Enemy Shells 35 Targets

By B. DRUMMOND AYRES Jr.
Special to The New York Times

SAIGON, South Vietnam, March 24—Moderate to heavy fighting took place in each of South Vietnam's four tactical zones in the last 24 hours, allied military spokesmen reported this afternoon.

They said the battles had resulted in at least 265 enemy deaths and at least seven allied soldiers killed. The fighting reflected the continuing effort by enemy forces to maintain their general offensive, now in its second month.

Concurrent with the battles were 35 rocket and mortar attacks against allied military units and South Vietnamese populated areas. That number was about average for recent weeks but the heavy ground fighting reported was not average. During the offensive, there have been few days when significant battles took place in all four tactical zones.

In an effort to take the initiative away from the enemy, United States marines have begun another major operation in the far northwestern part of South Vietnam. They are maneuvering in a mountainous area next to the Laotian border, about 30 miles south of the demilitarized zone, which runs along the border with North Vietnam.

The area long has been

Continued on Page 5, Column 3

12 GET SUBPOENAS IN ANASTASIA CASE

'New Information' Is Found in 1957 Gangland Killing

By ROBERT M. SMITH

A dozen witnesses to the barbershop murder 11 years ago of Umberto (Albert) Anastasia were subpoenaed yesterday by Manhattan District Attorney Frank S. Hogan.

Anastasia, a master killer for Murder, Inc.—a gangster troop that plagued the city from 1931 to 1940—was riddled with bullets as he sat for a haircut in the barbershop of the Park Sheraton Hotel at Seventh Avenue and 55th Street. Two gunmen had come up behind him and fired 10 shots. Five of them hit Anastasia, who came out of the chair, crashed into the mirror he had been facing, and died on the floor.

A spokesman for Mr. Hogan would not comment on whether detectives had found two men suspected of having carried out the killing.

The spokesman for the District Attorney said that the investigation of the murder of The Executioner has been continuing since the event, on Oct. 25, 1957. He declined to say

Continued on Page 34, Column 1

Eisenhower's Condition Worse; 'Continuous Oxygen' Required

By The Associated Press

WASHINGTON, March 24—Former President Dwight D. Eisenhower has grown weaker and lost ground in his struggle for life.

The 78-year-old General of the Army was conscious but "requiring continuous oxygen and other supportive measures," according to bulletins issued by Walter Reed Army Hospital.

General Eisenhower's wife and brother, Milton, were at his bedside after a weekend that thrust the former President into what the commanding general at Walter Reed called a "crisis." General Eisenhower had suffered congestive heart failure the previous weekend.

In the 9 P.M. bulletin, doctors said there were no significant changes from his condition earlier in the day when he was said to have "grown progressively weaker."

However, the doctors did not make clear whether General Eisenhower's condition had worsened since that midafternoon report.

Doctors said at the beginning of their mid-evening bulletin:

"There is little to add to the 6 P.M. bulletin pertaining to General Eisenhower's condition. No significant changes in the cardiac status and vital signs have developed. The General had a light supper and is resting comfortably."

The term "vital signs" refers to such things as heart rate, blood pressure and breathing rate.

The doctors said that General Eisenhower was being given "oxygen, d[illegible] to strengthen

Continued on Page 31, Column 1

'Proof' of Water on Mars Found, Supporting Idea Life Can Exist

By WALTER SULLIVAN

Astronomers at the McDonald Observatory in Texas said yesterday they had obtained the first "absolutely conclusive proof" that water exists in the atmosphere of Mars.

Although the water content appears to be very low, the observations seem to undermine the arguments of those who say that the air of Mars is so dry that life could not exist there.

Furthermore, the astronomers said, the observations are consistent with the long-postulated migration of water vapor from the martian pole emerging from winter to the pole about to enter winter. This movement was proposed to account for the "wave of darkening" that some have taken as evidence of vegetation.

This darkening of the Martian landscape, as seen through telescopes on earth, begins in spring around the fringes of the polar cap that is melting. The darkening moves toward the Martian equator at about 28 miles a day, as though spring began in the Arctic and moved south.

It has been proposed that melting of polar frost adds enough water vapor to the air to enable plants to flourish, although non-living processes could also account for this color change.

Associated Press

Dr. Harlan J. Smith

The observations were described yesterday in telephone interviews by Dr. Harlan J. Smith, head of the McDonald Observatory, operated by the University of Texas, and by Dr. Ronald Schorn of the Jet Propulsion Laboratory, operated by the California Institute of Technology in Pasadena. Another member of the observing team

Continued on Page 24, Column 3

Doctor Says Sirhan, Hypnotized, Relived Crime in 'Blind Rage'

By DOUGLAS ROBINSON
Special to The New York Times

LOS ANGELES, March 24—The fatal shooting of Senator Robert F. Kennedy was vividly recounted in court today as a psychiatrist who hypnotized Sirhan B. Sirhan in his jail cell told how the defendant had re-enacted the killing.

Under hypnosis, the psychiatrist said, Sirhan jumped from his bed, pulled an imaginary gun from his belt and "fired convulsively over and over again while shouting, 'You son of a bitch!'"

The psychiatrist, Dr. Bernard L. Diamond of the University of California at Berkeley, the key defense witness, described the scene in the jail cell as a "startling experience . . . dramatic and real."

Dr. Diamond, asked by Emile Zola Berman, one of the defense attorneys, what Sirhan's state of mind was at the exact time of the shooting, replied:

"In my opinion, on the basis of hypnotic experiences with Sirhan, the defendant at the precise moment of firing the gun was in a highly abnormal psychotic state of mind."

"He acted in a blind rage," the psychiatrist continued. The shooting, he said, was a "reflex action, an outgrowth not only of chronic psychosis but a very abnormal state that began when he became confused and vague by all the lights and mirrors" outside the pantry where the shooting occurred.

After re-enacting the shooting, Dr. Diamond testified, "Sirhan started to choke as he relived the attempts of those around the Senator to get the

Continued on Page 29, Column 1

NEWS INDEX

IN TODAY'S ISSUE: ANNUAL BUSINESS AND FINANCIAL REVIEW OF ASIA

"All the News That's Fit to Print"

The New York Times

LATE CITY EDITION

Weather: Mostly cloudy today; chance of rain tonight, tomorrow. Temp. range: today 42-26; Thurs. 37-22. Full U.S. report on page 93.

VOL. CXVIII . . No. 40,536

NEW YORK, FRIDAY, JANUARY 17, 1969

10 CENTS

JOHNSON OFFERS PLANS TO CHECK INFLATION IN 1969

ASKS 'COOLING OFF'

But Economic Report Still Sees a 'Highly Prosperous Year'

Text of President's message appears on Pages 14 and 15.

By EDWIN L. DALE Jr.

Special to The New York Times

WASHINGTON, Jan. 16—President Johnson laid out before Congress today an economic strategy for 1969 involving both less boom and less inflation than last year — a strategy known to be endorsed in all its essentials by the incoming Nixon Administration.

Its main elements are a small surplus in the budget and a monetary policy by the Federal Reserve Board allowing money and credit to expand, but at a much lower rate than in the inflationary 1966-68 period.

Mr. Johnson, in his annual Economic Report to Congress, cautioned that restraint on expansion of the economy should not be pushed to the point of bringing on a recession. He said that his strategy involved a "cooling off of the economy and a waning of inflationary forces," but that it still foresaw "a highly prosperous year."

Nixon Team Agrees

His Council of Economic Advisers, in their companion and lengthier report, forecast that "the unemployment rate should remain below 4 per cent" of the labor force this year despite the slowdown. Inflation, according to the forecast, should drop from a rate of more than 4 per cent to "a little more than 3 per cent."

To some extent in public comments, and privately even more, the economic team of President-elect Richard M. Nixon has made plain its view that this basic policy is the right one.

Mr Nixon has reserved the right to change a key element of it—extension of the 10 per cent income tax surcharge—but only if this can be done and still preserve a budget surplus, thanks perhaps to a sharper tapering off of the war in Viet-

Continued on Page 15, Column 1

3.8% Air Fare Rise Is Backed by C.A.B.

Special to The New York Times

WASHINGTON, Jan. 16—The Civil Aeronautics Board announced today that it had tentatively decided to allow the nation's domestic airlines to raise passenger fares an average of 3.8 per cent.

The increase is still subject to final confirmation by the board after it receives public comment.

Under the new rates, effective March 1, first-class air fares would rise by $3 to $10 and certain coach fares by $1 to $2.

The board's decision would increase revenues of the country's 11 trunk airlines by almost $200-million this year, according to airline economists.

Six airlines had sought a larger fare increase. Complaining of falling profits

Continued on Page 93, Column 1

GORE PERILS VOTE ON DAVID KENNEDY

Threatens to Fight Approval as Treasury Secretary if He Retains Bank Stock

By JOHN W. FINNEY

Special to The New York Times

WASHINGTON, Jan. 16—Senator Albert Gore raised potential obstacles today to immediate confirmation of the Nixon Cabinet by objecting that David M. Kennedy would have a conflict of interest as Secretary of the Treasury.

In a move that caught his colleagues by surprise, the Tennessee Democrat threatened to oppose the nomination of Mr. Kennedy to the Treasury post until the Chicago banker agreed to relinquish his stock in the Continental Illinois National Bank and Trust Company. Mr. Kennedy is the former chairman of the bank, one of the nation's largest commercial banks.

In an apparent reversal of position before the Senate Committee on Interior and Insular Affairs, Gov. Walter J. Hickel, the Secretary of the Interior-designate, gave what was considered a firm promise to continue a Federal freeze on the disposition of federally owned Alaska land until Congress settles the issue. The dispute had threatened to block his confirmation.

The Secretary-designate has proposed placing his substantial holdings of Continental Illinois stock in a trust, to be administered by the bank, but Sena-

Continued on Page 16, Column 2

CITY PANEL FINDS 'APPALLING' SIGNS OF RACIAL BIGOTRY

Study Says School Dispute Exposed Intense Feelings Against Whites and Blacks

Excerpts from report to Mayor will be found on Page 19.

By HENRY RAYMONT

A panel appointed by Mayor Lindsay to study bigotry in the city has concluded that "an appalling amount of racial prejudice—black and white—surfaced in and about the school controversy."

In a report made public last night, the nine-member panel said that propaganda and threats used by black extremists during last year's school decentralization dispute contained "a dangerous component of anti-Semitism."

It also condemned manifestations of antiblack bigotry, which it found to be expressed "in more sophisticated and subtle fashion," but "equally evil, corrosive, damaging and deplorable."

Unless adequate measures are taken immediately by the city administration to improve interracial relations, the panel warned, "the school controversy may be only the first" of a number of similar confrontations.

No One Is Named

The 11-page report was prepared by the Special Committee on Racial and Religious Prejudice, headed by Bernard Botein, who retired on Dec. 31 as Presiding Justice of the Appellate Division of the State Supreme Court in Manhattan and the Bronx.

The panel was appointed by Mayor Lindsay on Nov. 9 to determine whether any of the parties in the school dispute were responsible for any of the hate literature that has appeared.

Citing "limitations of time and authority," the panel declined to name any individuals or groups connected with the charges and countercharges of anti-Semitism and racism that has marked the school crisis.

Instead, it recommended that a long-range inquiry into the whole range of racial, religious and ethnic conflicts be entrusted to a permanent conference of representatives from the city's private religious, human relations and civil-rights agencies.

The panel carefully avoided taking sides in the school

Continued on Page 19, Column 6

Paintings Defaced At Metropolitan; One a Rembrandt

By MARTIN ARNOLD

Ten paintings, including a Rembrandt, were defaced at the Metropolitan Museum of Art yesterday, in an apparent protest against the museum's "Harlem on My Mind" exhibition.

Damage to the paintings was slight, but Thomas P. F. Hoving, the museum's director, said in a voice shaking with anger that "the intention of this example of poisonous vandalism is the most grave in the history of this institution."

Protesters against the exhibition, which uses photo murals, slides and recordings, have contended that it shows a white man's view of Harlem. About 35 of them, mostly Negroes, picketed a preview showing and a black-tie cocktail and dinner party at the museum last night.

The vandal or vandals were not caught, and when the

Continued on Page 28, Column 1

REPORT BY JAN. 31, U.S. DIRECTS H.R.A.

City Says Most Irregularities in the Antipoverty Agency Have Been Corrected

This report on the Human Resources Administration was prepared by Richard Reeves, Barnard L. Collier, Richard Phalon and Richard Severo of The New York Times.

The Federal Office of Economic Opportunity has instructed the city's Human Resources Administration to report before Jan. 31 on what action has been taken to correct a long list of alleged irregularities in neighborhood antipoverty agencies.

The irregularities, which H.R.A. officials said yesterday had been "mostly" corrected, ranged from the fact that some local agencies used unnumbered checks to the hiring of consultants who have been paid $1,000 but apparently had no duties.

Those problems were discovered by teams of investigators from the O.E.O., one of the Federal agencies that finances local poverty programs. The investigators visited local agencies last June and reported findings then and last December.

The local organizations —

Continued on Page 20, Column 1

LINDSAY DEFENDS H.R.A. FUND SETUP AS 'PRETTY GOOD'

Denies Laxness and Lauds Ginsberg—An Accountant and O.E.O. Disagree

By MARTIN TOLCHIN

Mayor Lindsay defended the city's antipoverty agency yesterday against charges of fiscal irresponsibility and said that the Human Resources Administration and its subsidiary departments "all have checks and balances and auditing and self-policing systems that are pretty good—that are pretty careful."

"H.R.A. — particularly now, of course, under Dr. Ginsberg —has got some very careful internal auditing and check-and-balance and investigative machinery," Mr. Lindsay told a news conference at City Hall.

Last night, Mitchell Sviridoff, the city's first Human Resources Administrator, said that he would meet today with the Commissioner of Investigations, Robert Ruskin, to discuss "certain individuals and certain situations" in the H.R.A.

W. M. O'Reilly, president of the accounting concern that made a Federal audit of the H.R.A. on Dec. 13, said yesterday of officials of the city's antipoverty agency:

"They do not adequately understand what is meant by fiscal responsibility."

'Tough Administrator'

The Mayor's praise was for Mitchell I. Ginsberg, the Human Resources Administrator, whom he described as "an excellent administrator" and "a very tight-reined, a very tough administrator."

He said Mr. Ginsberg had staffed H.R.A. with "some excellent administrators and fiscal people, and that process has not ended either."

The H.R.A. was set up by Mayor Lindsay 29 months ago as the superagency responsible for the city's $122-million-a-year antipoverty program.

Mr. Lindsay said that "there have been some administrative weaknesses in it [H.R.A.] before Dr. Ginsberg took over."

"Since Dr. Ginsberg has taken over," the Mayor went on, "he's reorganized it and continues to reorganize it, in order to make sure that it's fiscally tight and yet at the same time, according to the command of Congress, the poor are served."

Mr. Lindsay criticized The New York Times, although not by name, for an article yester-

Continued on Page 20, Column 6

EXPANDED VIETNAM TALKS BEGIN IN PARIS TOMORROW; ROUND TABLE AGREED UPON

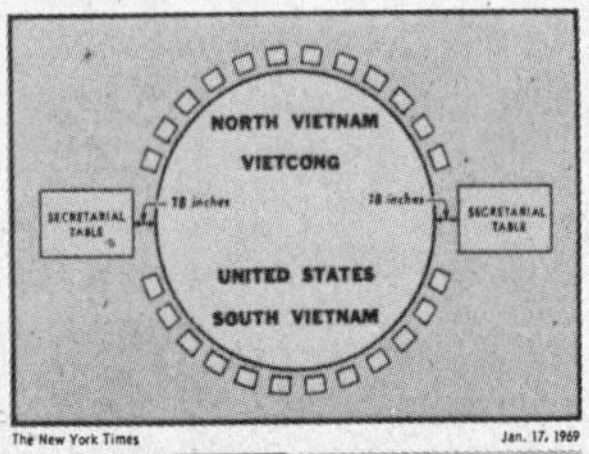

The New York Times Jan. 17, 1969

United Press International

W. Averell Harriman, left, head of U.S. delegation, and Nguyen Thanh Le, Hanoi spokesman, meet newsmen.

DEADLOCK ENDED

Washington and Hanoi Concur on Seating After 10 Weeks

By PAUL HOFMANN

Special to The New York Times

PARIS, Jan. 16—An agreement was announced here today for the opening of the expanded talks on the Vietnam war. The first session is to be held Saturday at 10:30 A.M. (4:30 A.M., New York time).

The accord broke a 10-week deadlock on procedural matters that had blocked negotiations on substantive issues by the participants in the conflict.

Under the terms of the agreement, representatives of the United States, South Vietnam, North Vietnam and the National Liberation Front, or Vietcong, will sit at a circular table without nameplates, flags or markings.

Two rectangular tables, measuring about 3 feet by 4½ feet, will be placed 18 inches from the circular table at opposite sides.

Shape of Table an Issue

The seating arrangements were the main stumbling block to the expanded talks.

The Saigon regime and Washington contended that the round-table proposal would give the Front the same status as South Vietnam and insisted on some device to indicate the existence of only two sides. This would buttress their contention that the Vietcong guerrillas were only agents of North Vietnam.

Today's agreement provided a seating formula elastic enough for the allies to speak of two sides and for the enemy to speak of a four-sided affair. This ambiguity permits all participants to claim victory in the protocol dispute.

Saturday's meeting will take up—and possibly dispose of—the question of procedures to be followed in substantive four-way negotiations on the war.

W. Averell Harriman, the departing head of the United States delegation, and other American officials here said they hoped that the procedural

Continued on Page 2, Column 1

2 Astronauts Board A 2d Russian Craft After Space 'Walk'

By THEODORE SHABAD

Special to The New York Times

MOSCOW, Friday, Jan. 17—Two Soviet manned spacecraft of the Soyuz series docked in orbit around the earth yesterday and remained joined for more than four hours while two astronauts transferred from one vehicle to the other, taking an hour-long "walk" through space.

The link-up between Soyuz 4, with one man aboard, and Soyuz 5, carrying a three-man crew, produced what was described in an official announcement as the "world's first experimental space station" with a total of four compartments providing a shirtsleeve environment.

Soyuz 4, with three astronauts aboard, landed safely today, the Moscow Radio reported.

"The three cosmonauts feel

Continued on Page 12, Column 2

NIXON INTERVENED FOR PARIS ACCORD

He Joined Johnson in Urging Saigon to Accept Plan for Procedural Compromise

Texts of Johnson and Hanoi statements, Page 2.

By HEDRICK SMITH

Special to The New York Times

WASHINGTON, Jan. 16—The incoming Nixon Administration intervened directly with the South Vietnamese Government to urge a procedural compromise in the talks on Vietnam, paving the way for early discussion of substantive issues in Paris.

Through both Ambassador Ellsworth Bunker in Saigon and Secretary of State-designate William P. Rogers in Washington, President-elect Richard M. Nixon informed the Saigon regime last weekend that he joined President Johnson in backing the compromise formula on physical arrangements and appealed for Saigon's support.

In separate statements today, Mr. Johnson and Mr. Nixon acclaimed the breakthrough. Each said that he was pleased by the progress—Mr. Johnson at having pushed the talks into a new phase before he left office and Mr. Nixon at having avoided continued haggling over pro-

Continued on Page 2, Column 7

SENATE DEFEATS FILIBUSTER CURB

Reverses Humphrey, 53-45, on Ruling Aiding Liberals

By WARREN WEAVER Jr.

Special to The New York Times

WASHINGTON, Jan. 16—The latest attempt to curb Senate debate failed today when two Democrats and four Republicans deserted the antifilibuster cause on the second of two critical test votes.

Opponents of the filibuster were able to muster a bare majority, 51 to 47, on a motion to cut off debate, relying on a two-day-old ruling by Vice President Humphrey that he would not require a two-thirds majority for this purpose.

But then the Humphrey ruling itself was challenged, and a coalition of Southern Democrats and conservative Republicans voted the Vice President down, 53 to 45.

For all practical purposes,

Continued on Page 18, Column 7

NEWS INDEX

Galamison to Head Teacher Pact Talks

By LEONARD BUDER

The Rev. Milton A. Galamison, an outspoken critic of the teachers' union, has been appointed chairman of the Board of Education committee that will oversee the forthcoming contract negotiations with the union.

The appointment was made by John M. Doar, president of the city board, who said he regarded Mr. Galamison as "the best man" for that post. Mr. Doar said that the Negro minister, who is the board's vice president, "is independent, will be fair and will meet his responsibility."

Albert Shanker, the president of the United Federation of Teachers, declined yesterday to comment on the selection of Mr. Galamison to head the board's collective bargaining

Continued on Page 19, Column 2

An Enzyme Is Synthesized for First Time

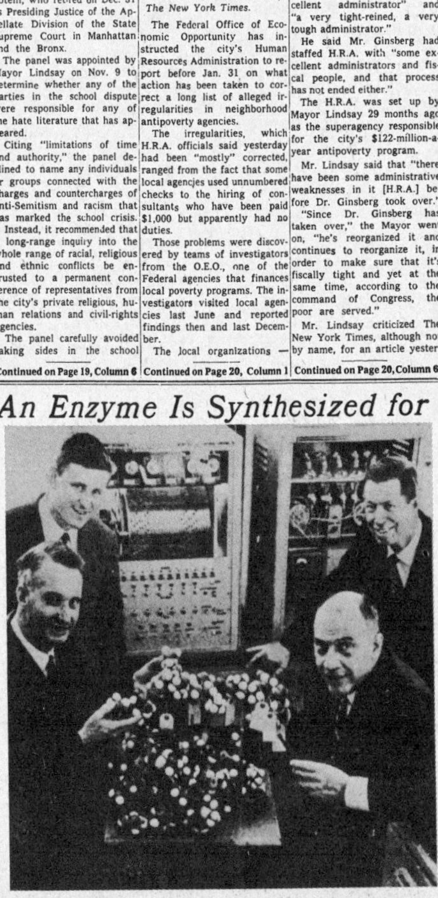

Members of the two research teams that synthesized ribonuclease flank a model of the enzyme. In front are Dr. Ralph F. Hirschmann, left, and Dr. Robert G. Denkewalter of Merck Sharp & Dohme. Behind them are Dr. Bernd Gutte, left, and Dr. R. Bruce Merrifield of Rockefeller University. Apparatus used by Rockefeller team in synthesis is at rear.

By WALTER SULLIVAN

For the first time an enzyme—one of the complex "master chemicals" of life—has been synthesized.

The feat, achieved virtually simultaneously by two laboratories using basically different methods, is expected to open new fields of research into the most intimate chemical processes of life.

"This is probably the beginning of a new generation of therapeutic agents," said Dr. Robert G. Denkewalter, vice president for exploratory research at the Merck Sharp & Dohme Research Laboratories, as the achievements were announced yesterday.

The enzyme ribonuclease has been synthesized not only by the Merck Laboratories, in Rahway, N. J., but also by the Rockefeller University, York Avenue and 66th Street, where yesterday's joint announcement was made.

Ribonuclease, which performs vital functions in almost all cells, has long been a target of research and analysis because of its comparatively simple structure.

Although the Merck researchers spoke of a new generation of drugs, neither they nor the scientists at Rockefeller University expected any immediate applications in medicine. Rather, they said, the door has been

Continued on Page 27, Column 1

Head of Swarthmore Dies During Protest

By United Press International

SWARTHMORE, Pa., Jan. 16—Dr. Courtney C. Smith, president of Swarthmore College, was stricken fatally with a heart attack today while waiting to meet with a faculty committee studying demands by black students who had occupied the admissions office for more than a week. He was 52 years old.

Five hours later, the two dozen black students in the office abandoned their demonstration and left the building. A spokesman said they were acting out of respect for Dr. Smith, but would press their demands later.

Dr. Smith, American Secretary of Rhodes Scholarships since 1953, was pronounced dead in his office at the 104-year-old, Quaker oriented school by Dr. Morris Bowie, a

Continued on Page 44, Column 1

INQUIRY UPHOLDS WARREN REPORT

Finds Autopsy Photos Show 2 Shots Killed President

Discussion and summary of report are on Page 17.

By FRED P. GRAHAM

Special to The New York Times

WASHINGTON, Jan. 16—A panel of four medical experts appointed by Attorney General Ramsey Clark to examine the secret autopsy photographs of President Kennedy's body has confirmed the Warren Commission's conclusion that the President was killed by two shots from behind.

The year-old report was released tonight by the Justice Department.

The department will use the report in court here tomorrow in an attempt to block Jim Garrison, New Orleans District Attorney, from subpoenaing the photographs from the National Archives.

Mr. Garrison has charged that the autopsy material would bolster his upcoming assassination conspiracy trial against a New Orleans businessman by show-

Continued on Page 17, Column 1

The News Summary and Index appears on Page 2.

"All the News That's Fit to Print"

The New York Times

LATE CITY EDITION

Weather: Cloudy today; chance of rain tonight. Fair, mild tomorrow. Temp. range: today 65-54; Monday 69-45. Full U.S. report on Page 92.

VOL. CXVIII.. No. 40,624 | © 1969 The New York Times Company. | NEW YORK, TUESDAY, APRIL 15, 1969 | 10 CENTS

CHINA'S REDS VOTE CHARTER MAKING LIN HEIR TO MAO

Party Congress Approves New Policy Program—Discloses No Details

TO PICK LEADERS TODAY

Full Central Committee Is to Be Elected, Replacing Purged Ruling Group

Text of Chinese communiqué is printed on Page 14.

By CHARLES MOHR

Special to The New York Times

HONG KONG, April 14—The ninth congress of the Chinese Communist party unanimously adopted today a new party charter that stipulates that Defense Minister Lin Piao will eventually succeed Mao Tse-tung as China's leader.

A communiqué made public today by the official press agency Hsinhua said the congress also unanimously adopted a political report by Mr. Lin that will probably become a blueprint for policy in foreign, economic and domestic political fields. But it gave no details of the report.

The communiqué added that the party congress would begin tomorrow to elect a new Central Committee. During the Cultural Revolution initiated by Mr. Mao three years ago, about two-thirds of the members of the old Central Committee were dismissed as "power-holders taking the capitalist road."

Unusual Occasion

A congress is described by Chinese Communists as the highest governing organ of their party, and such convocations are both rare and important. The ninth congress is only the second held since the Communists won control of China in 1949. The last congress was elected in 1956 and last met in 1958.

The 1,512 delegates to the present, or ninth, congress met in Peking 14 days ago on April 1. Until tonight there had been no further news on their deliberations, but today's communiqué indicated that the congress would soon adjourn.

The first two items on the congress agenda, as announced April 1, were the adoption of Mr. Lin's political report and a new party constitution. These tasks have been completed.

Politburo to Be Selected

Tonight's communiqué said the congress would begin electing a new Central Committee "starting from April 15." It was unclear how long this process would take.

The Central Committee will then meet to select a new Politburo, which, in turn, will elect a standing committee. This will be the supreme ruling party body in China.

The new Central Committee would technically be empowered also to elect a new chairman of the committee, but most analysts in Hong Kong assume that Mr. Mao will be re-elected

Continued on Page 14, Column 3

Dubcek Said to Go To Moscow for Talk On Shifts in Prague

By ALVIN SHUSTER

Special to The New York Times

PRAGUE, April 14—Alexander Dubcek, the Communist party chief, was reported today to be going to Moscow for talks on changes expected this week in the Czechoslovak leadership.

There was no official announcement of the trip, with some sources saying that he left today and others reporting that he will go tomorrow. They agreed that he would return to Prague in time for what is looming as a crucial Central Committee meeting on Thursday.

The leadership is expected to yield to Moscow's demands that some progressives be removed from the ruling Presidium. Among those who appear certain of demotion, sources said, is Josef Smrkovsky, deputy chairman of the National Assembly.

The expectation today among progressive forces is that Mr. Smrkovsky, and some others, would be eased

Continued on Page 7, Column 1

YUGOSLAVS PURGE ARMY GENERALS

Officers With Close Links to Moscow Replaced—Strategy Is Revised

By DAVID BINDER

Special to The New York Times

BELGRADE, Yugoslavia, April 14 — Informed sources said today that top generals of the Yugoslav Army had been quietly purged on orders of President Tito, and Yugoslavia's defense strategy had been altered as a result of the Soviet-led invasion of Czechoslovakia last August.

The purged officers, including the former deputy supreme commander, Gen. Ivan Gosnjak, and the chief of the general staff, Gen. Rade Hamovic, were accused of having made inadequate defense preparations and of having a faulty strategic concept.

The sources said at least nine general staff officers, mostly Serbs, had been pensioned off. Some of the names are known to foreign military attachés, but there has been no public discussion of the vast changes that the Yugoslav armed forces have undergone.

A Yugoslav source said that in the days immediately after the invasion of Czechoslovakia, when Yugoslavia underwent mobilization, "shocking" dis-

Continued on Page 8, Column 1

NIXON TELLS O.A.S. LATINS' PROBLEMS GET TOP PRIORITY

Says Alliance for Progress Has Not Accomplished Enough for Hemisphere

By BENJAMIN WELLES

Special to The New York Times

WASHINGTON, April 14 — President Nixon promised today that the problems of the Western Hemisphere would have the "highest priority" in his Administration.

In his first major address on Latin-American relations, Mr. Nixon declared that his Administration would review existing policies with "open eyes, open ears, open mind, open heart."

He chose the 21st anniversary of the founding of the Organization of American States to downgrade the accomplishments of the Alliance for Progress, the development program founded and named in 1961 by President Kennedy and continued by President Johnson. It has invested $1-billion yearly in Latin-American development.

Calls It 'Great Concept'

Speaking in the Pan American Union building before representatives of 22 O.A.S. member states, Mr. Nixon said the alliance was a "great concept."

During his latest visit to Latin America, in 1967, he said, he saw many areas where the alliance had done "much good." However, he added, the overall growth rate of the hemisphere was "not enough" and the results to date of the Alliance for Progress were "disconcerting."

"The per capita growth rate in Latin America since the founding of the Alliance for Progress has been less than that in non-Communist Asia or in Communist East Europe," he said, intimating that new policies, programs and appointments were being planned.

Rate Less than 2%

White House sources were not immediately able to identify the statistics Mr. Nixon had used for his comparisons. However, economists said that the growth rate in Latin America in recent years had been less than 2 per cent—compared with 2 to 4 per cent in non-Communist Asia. Figures for East Europe were unavailable.

The main reason for lagging growth in Latin America is, they said, the 3 per cent annual growth in population, which has been virtually nullifying growth in national output, which averages 5 per cent a year.

Mr. Nixon said that unless

Continued on Page 10, Column 3

The New York Times (by Don Hogan Charles)

OCCUPATION AT COLUMBIA: The scene yesterday on the steps of Hamilton Hall as one of the black students who occupied the Columbia College admissions office in the building talked to the news media and the student community.

Harvard Students Vote New Demands And Extend Strike

By E. W. KENWORTHY

Special to The New York Times

CAMBRIDGE, Mass., April 14—Nearly 6,000 Harvard students voted narrowly at a rally today to continue a student strike three more days. The strike was begun last week to protest use of the police against radical students who had seized a building.

The students said that within the next three days the university administration must inform the students of its response to a list of demands approved today. At the end of that time, the students are to decide what further action they might take.

The strike, which was approved last Thursday at a rally following the police action, was to last three days, ending today.

There are some 15,000 students at Harvard University—6,000 undergraduate men and girls (at Radcliffe, the girls' college that is part of the university) and 9,000 in the graduate and professional schools.

On Friday, the first day of the strike, The Crimson, the student newspaper, estimated that only about one-quarter of the students attended classes. The strike appeared to be about equally effective today. The

Continued on Page 30, Column 2

20 NEGROES STAGE A COLUMBIA SIT-IN

Occupy Admissions Office to Back Demand for Voice in Recruiting Blacks

By SYLVAN FOX

A group of 20 black students occupied a Columbia University office yesterday to back their demands for a greater voice in the recruitment and admission of Negroes to the institution. They were still there at 3 o'clock this morning.

The black students, who took over an office in Hamilton Hall, accused the university of having been "systematically racist and oppressive in its relations with black people" and demanded that black students be given the power to nominate an admission board and an admission staff that would recruit, admit and help finance Negro students.

The university rejected the demands, asserting that Columbia already has a consulting board on black and Puerto Rican admissions and will admit about twice the number of black freshmen this year as last.

Dean Carl F. Hovde headed a university delegation that met with the black students in

Continued on Page 33, Column 1

Council Democrats Plan 10-15% Rent Rise Limit

By DAVID K. SHIPLER

Democratic leaders in the City Council yesterday stiffened the rent guidelines proposed by Mayor Lindsay. Their plan would limit increases to 10 per cent on two-year leases for apartments not under rent control and 15 per cent on leases of three years.

This was a reduction from Mr. Lindsay's formula of 15 and 20 per cent, which the real-estate industry accepted last month.

Since the Democrats control the Council by an overwhelming margin, the new guidelines appear almost certain to be the final ones.

The Council leaders made no other changes in the Mayor's plan for the voluntary regulation of rents in about 425,000 of the city's uncontrolled apartments, except to postpone by six months the date at which the guidelines would be revised on the basis of an operating cost index.

Flexibility in 1970

On the new date—July 1, 1970—the figures of 10 and 15 per cent could be raised or lowered, depending on the index of operating cost increases, still to be formulated by the Mayor's Rent Guidelines Board.

After leaders of the real estate industry had met for three hours with the Council's Special Committee on Rents to discuss the plan, Rexford E. Tompkins, the industry's spokesman, said he was "stunned."

"I just don't know where we'll go with it," he said of the new guidelines. "I think there's going to be general outrage."

Mr. Tompkins predicted that owners would not be able to give wage increases when union contracts for elevator operators, doormen and maintenance men came up for renewal. "Every building is going to be struck," he said.

The new plan was contained in a bill sponsored by the Council leadership, including

Continued on Page 36, Column 5

ROSE SEES 'TREND' TO BACK LINDSAY

Some Liberals Assert Party May Renominate Mayor Without a Primary

By SIDNEY E. ZION

Alex Rose, chief tactician of the Liberal party, said yesterday that an "indicated trend" in favor of the renomination of Mayor Lindsay had "crystallized" within the party.

When asked in an interview if this meant that the Mayor was likely to be nominated at the party's convention tomorrow without having to run in a primary, Mr. Rose said: "That is an open question. I don't know how big the Lindsay majority is and I don't know how many people prefer the Mayor but would also favor a primary."

Despite this qualification, Mr. Rose's report on the situation, which he said was culled from county and district leaders, was considered significant.

Nomination Thought Crucial

Mr. Lindsay and his managers have made no secret of the fact that they consider the Liberal nomination crucial to the Mayor's hopes for reelection. In 1965 the Mayor ran on both the Liberal and Republican lines and many politicians believe that the Liberal vote gave him his margin of victory over Abraham D. Beame, the Democratic candidate.

It was generally believed that the Mayor would again receive the Liberal nomination this year, but the entry of former Mayor Robert F. Wagner into the race last week put this in doubt. Mr. Wagner had been endorsed twice for Mayor by the Liberals and has had excellent relationships with party leaders.

Mr. Rose acknowledged yesterday his "long and good friendship" with Mr. Wagner. He said, however, that the former Mayor had not called him or other party leaders to ask that his name be placed in nomination.

The fact that Mr. Rose chose to go on record with his report of a "crystallization" of

Continued on Page 36, Column 3

PRESIDENT OFFERS 10-POINT PROGRAM IN DOMESTIC AREA

In Message to Congress, He Proposes Tax Reform and Rise in Social Security

DETAILS EXPECTED SOON

Transit Plan, Aid to States, Crime Curb and Equal Job Opportunity Also Cited

The text of Nixon's message appears on Page 28.

By ROBERT B. SEMPLE Jr.

Special to The New York Times

WASHINGTON, April 14—In what amounted to an informal State of the Union Message, President Nixon hinted for the first time today at the details and dimensions of his forthcoming domestic program.

After long weeks of silence on his domestic objectives, the President sent Congress a five-page statement describing, in general terms, 10 recommendations that will begin to flow from the White House to Capitol Hill later this week.

The recommendations appeared to have been chosen carefully so as not to cost the Treasury a great deal of money in the fiscal year beginning July 1. Mr. Nixon himself described the proposals as only a "beginning" and said they would not "carry large price tags for the coming fiscal year."

Other Proposals Coming

Among the major items promised were programs for Federal-state revenue sharing, partial tax reform, an increase in Social Security and development of airways, airports and mass transit systems.

The President also said that he would submit still broader proposals to attack some of the country's basic social ills: hunger and malnutrition, a faltering welfare system and urban decay.

Officials explained that these programs were not in final form—unlike the list of 10—and, even if submitted this year, would probably not have a sizable budgetary impact in the 1970 fiscal year.

Timing the message to coincide with the return of Congress to Capitol Hill after a 10-day Easter recess, Mr. Nixon sought — for the first time—to explain why he had delayed submission of his legislative ideas.

Getting System 'in Order'

He asserted, first of all, that during his first 12 weeks in office he had been preoccupied with the problems of foreign policy, particularly the search for peace in Southeast Asia.

"Peace," he said, "has been the first priority."

Second, he suggested that he had been deterred from rushing quickly into new legislation by "the ruinous rise of inflationary pressures," which dictated a smaller budget.

Third, he said he had discovered that the Federal appa-

Continued on Page 28, Column 1

Chemical Defender of Body Is Deciphered

Scientists Unravel Gamma Globulin's Full Complexity

By WALTER SULLIVAN

The complete structure of one of the chemical soldiers that defend the body against disease has been deciphered for the first time.

The step is considered by scientists working in the field as a milestone along the road toward learning how the body makes the antibodies that fight disease, how that process can be improved upon, and how it can be suppressed to facilitate organ transplants.

The substance involved—a protein antibody known as gamma globulin—was deciphered by Dr. Gerald M. Edelman and his colleagues at Rockefeller University, York Avenue and 66th Street. He reported his results yesterday in Atlantic City to a meeting of the Federation of American Scientists for Experimental Biology.

The development was made possible, in part by the tragedy of a Californian who fell ill of an incurable form of cancer and whose diseased body furnished the material suitable for analysis.

It also came about as the culmination of a long succession of steps along the road to decipherment of an antibody—steps taken at various institutions here and abroad.

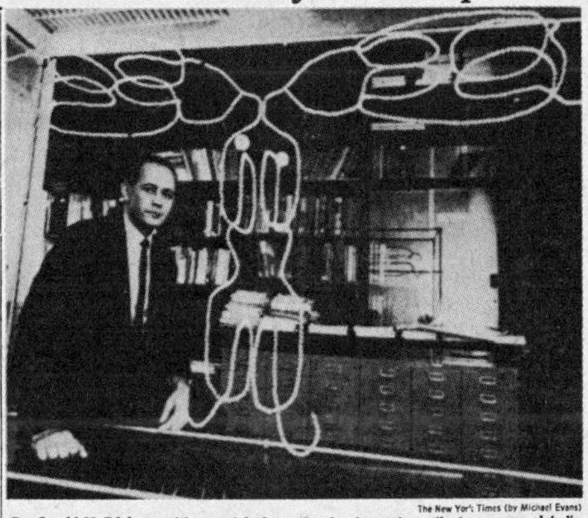

The New York Times (by Michael Evans)

Dr. Gerald M. Edelman with a model of a molecule of protein antibody, gamma globulin, at Rockefeller University. The model is made of plastic poppit beads and ping-pong balls.

Gamma globulin is formed of 19,996 atoms, grouped in 1,320 amino-acid building blocks. Never before has a molecule approaching this complexity been deciphered. The largest heretofore was subtilisin, formed of 274 amino acid units.

The gamma globulins and other immunoglobulins are synthesized by the body when a foreign substance invades it. When one suffers from a disease such as polio or smallpox, the body manufactures such "antibodies" and, if one survives the disease, he retains these defenses and therefore is immune against a recurrence. Vaccination stimulates the production of suitable antibodies—or injects them—without causing illness.

Like all proteins, the gamma globulins are formed from long chains of amino acids hooked together like freight cars. Although thousands of such build-

Continued on Page 32, Column 1

2 Policemen Slain By Chicago Sniper

By United Press International

CHICAGO, April 14—A former marine, named as the bomber of a department store because "I wanted to show them how awful war is," killed two policemen and injured four others with gunfire and grenades before he surrendered in his apartment tonight. A civilian was also injured

Deputy Police Superintendent James Rochford pleaded for an hour before Frank Kulak, a 40-year-old disabled Marine veteran of World War II and the Korean war, agreed to give himself up.

Kulak was unhurt in the five-hour siege, in which hundreds of bullets were fired at his third-floor apartment in a dingy,

Continued on Page 17, Column 2

13 Protesters Guilty In Chicago Disorder

By DONALD JANSON

Special to The New York Times

CHICAGO, April 14—Five New York delegates to the Democratic convention and eight others lost the first round today of the longest disorderly conduct trial in Chicago's history.

Judge Arthur L. Dunne of the Cook County Circuit Court, who had heard the case without a jury, found the 13 guilty of disobeying a police order not to cross an imaginary line the police had drawn last Aug. 29 at Michigan Avenue and 18th Street.

He fined Peter Weiss and the Rev. Richard J. Neuhaus $400 each as leaders of the protest march and Murray Kempton, the columnist, $250. Mr. Weiss

Continued on Page 17, Column 1

NEWS INDEX

Antiwar G.I. Editor Ousted From Army

By BEN A. FRANKLIN

Special to The New York Times

WASHINGTON, April 14 — The Army took today its first formal disciplinary action against a soldier-editor of one of the antiwar antimilitary underground G.I. newspapers that have been appearing at a growing number of military bases in recent months.

Maj. Gen. John C. F. Tillson 3d, the commanding general of Fort Gordon, a basic training base near Augusta, Ga., disclosed that he had ordered the undesirable discharge, effective today, of Pfc. Dennis Davis, identified by Army spokesmen as editor of a clandestine newspaper, The Last Harass. Pub-

Continued on Page 11, Column 1

"All the News That's Fit to Print"

The New York Times

LATE CITY EDITION

Weather: Chance of showers today; clear, cool tonight. Fair tomorrow. Temp. range: today 68-55; Thurs. 75-49. Full U.S. report on Page 92.

VOL. CXVIII... No. 40,662 NEW YORK, FRIDAY, MAY 23, 1969 — 10 CENTS

ASTRONAUTS DIP WITHIN 9.4 MILES OF MOON; SCOUT LANDING SITE, REJOIN MOTHER CRAFT

NIXON INFLUENCED BY FORTAS AFFAIR IN COURT CHOICES

President Says His Friends Were, and Will Be, Ruled Out of Consideration

Excerpts from Nixon's news conference are on Page 27.

By ROBERT B. SEMPLE Jr.
Special to The New York Times

WASHINGTON, May 22—President Nixon said today that the resignation of Abe Fortas from the Supreme Court had helped determine his choice of a new Chief Justice and would influence equally his selection of Mr. Fortas's successor.

The President said the Court required a quick infusion of men whose nominations raised no questions of close political or personal ties to the White House. He asserted that several eminently qualified men had not been chosen for the Chief Justiceship for precisely that reason, and he indicated that he would not appoint a close personal or political friend to the Fortas vacancy.

Mr. Nixon disclosed that four men, who had been seriously considered for the post, had turned it down. They were Attorney General John N. Mitchell, former Attorney General Herbert Brownell, former New York Gov. Thomas E. Dewey and Associate Justice Potter Stewart.

Former Classmate Rejected

A fifth candidate, Charles S. Rhyne, former president of the American Bar Association, who was one of Mr. Nixon's classmates at Duke University Law School, was rejected because he and the President agreed that their personal relationship was so close that charges of "cronyism" might be raised.

Mr. Nixon's views emerged during an unusual 45-minute news conference in his Oval Office this morning—the first exchange of its kind between the President and reporters.

It was different from his televised news conferences in both style and substance. Sitting at his desk and speaking in a low voice, he addressed himself to issues with greater freedom and in greater depth than usual.

He said that the content of his

Continued on Page 26, Column 4

Living Cost Up 0.7% Here; National Increase Is 0.6%

Sales Tax a Factor

By PETER MILLONES

The cost of living in the New York City area rose again in April, and the increase was greater than in other major cities and the country as a whole.

The Labor Department reported that consumer prices here rose 0.7 per cent last month, which means that since January, prices in the area have risen 2.6 per cent and since last April 6.5 per cent.

"We have continued the dubious distinction of being ahead of the national average," said Herbert Bienstock, regional director of the department's Bureau of Labor Statistics.

He said the March-to-April increase could be attributed to the rise in the state sales tax, and higher prices for food, housing, recreation and health services.

Virtually the only things that did not cost more in April than in March were women's clothing, dairy products and public transportation.

The April increase elsewhere was 0.5 per cent in Detroit, 0.5 per cent in Philadelphia, 0.2 per cent in Chicago and 0.2 per cent in Los Angeles.

Continued on Page 16, Column 1

Services Pace U.S. Rise

By EDWIN L. DALE Jr.
Special to The New York Times

WASHINGTON, May 22—Consumer prices rose six-tenths of 1 per cent in April, confirming a faster rate of inflation this year than last, the Labor Department reported today.

The April increase was less than in March. But for the last three months taken together, prices have been rising at an annual rate of 7.6 per cent, or more than in any full year since 1951. There was one three-month period in mid-1956 when prices rose as rapidly, but the rise later slowed.

The Nixon Administration has taken the position that this faster pace of inflation was not unexpected and that it will moderate following an anticipated slowing of the economy later this year. Consumer prices are a "lagging" economic indicator, meaning they follow developments in production, employment and the like.

Once again, increases in the many-sided category of services—ranging from mortgage interest rates to medical care—dominated the April rise in the index. Service prices were

Continued on Page 16, Column 1

G.O.P. Aware in Campaign Of Fortas's Tie to Wolfson

By WARREN WEAVER Jr.
Special to The New York Times

WASHINGTON, May 22—Prominent Republican leaders, including close associates of Richard M. Nixon, were aware at least eight months ago of a potentially explosive relationship between Abe Fortas, then a Supreme Court Justice, and Louis E. Wolfson, then awaiting sentence on perjury and conspiracy convictions.

They did not regard their information as detailed or conclusive enough either to inject it into the controversy over Mr. Fortas's nomination as Chief Justice or to make it an issue in the Presidential campaign, then just getting under way.

A Warning to Javits

The Republican information on the Fortas-Wolfson association did form the basis, however, for a warning passed to Senator Jacob K. Javits, Republican of New York, then seeking re-election to a third term. It was suggested that Mr. Javits avoid any close identification with Mr. Fortas in the campaign.

There is no evidence that these Republican politicians had any knowledge of the $20,000 fee Justice Fortas had received from the Wolfson family foundation for prospective services and returned after 11 months. This transaction led to

Continued on Page 28, Column 1

WARREN SEEKING A CODE OF ETHICS

Judges Will Meet Tomorrow on Proposed Regulations for the Federal Bench

By FRED P. GRAHAM
Special to The New York Times

WASHINGTON, May 22—Chief Justice Earl Warren has called a meeting for Saturday of a committee of top Federal judges to begin drafting a code of ethics and financial reporting rules for all Federal judges.

Mr. Warren hopes to have the new regulations formally adopted by the policy-making arm of the Federal judiciary, the Judicial Conference of the United States, before he retires next month.

If so, they will become the first formal standards of conduct ever to be adopted by the Federal judiciary.

The move marks the first concrete sign that Chief Justice Warren and the Federal judiciary feel an obligation to set their house in order in the wake of the recent Fortas controversy, even before the new Chief Justice takes office.

It sets the stage for a possible conflict with Congress over who should police the courts and what the standards of conduct for Federal judges should be.

The broad outlines of the proposed rules are already under study. The proposals, if adopted, would require annual reporting of income in extensive detail, but the reports would be kept secret within the judicial branch.

The rules would also pro-

Continued on Page 25, Column 1

BLUE CROSS ASKS A 49.5% RATE RISE FOR MOST IN PLAN

State Approval Is Sought to Meet High Hospital Costs —4.8 Million Affected

By MURRAY ILLSON

The Blue Cross asked the State Department of Insurance yesterday to approve a rise of 49.5 per cent in its hospitalization insurance rates.

If the department approves, the increase would affect 4.8 million community-rated subscribers, or 60 per cent of the total enrollment of the Associated Hospital Service of New York, as the insurance plan is formally known.

The organization announced that Blue Shield Medical Insurance rates would not change, nor would the increase apply to the remaining 3.2 million Blue Cross subscribers who are either members of experience-rated groups or subscribers over the age of 65, who supplement their Medicare coverage through the Associated Hospital Service Senior Care program.

Community-rated subscribers are individuals or members of groups who are charged the same rate, regardless of sex, physical condition or age, up to 65, when Medicare takes over. Experience-rated subscribers are rated on the basis of the over-all claim and cost experience of the particular group in which they are enrolled, and the rate is adjusted annually.

Contract Costs Soaring

A typical Blue Cross group family contract, providing 21 days of fully covered hospitalization and 180 more at half cost, now costs $135.84 a year. The comparable service 10 years ago cost $64.08.

Subscribers would be affected by the rate increase in New York City and 12 counties: Columbia, Delaware, Dutchess Greene, Nassau, Orange, Putnam, Rockland, Suffolk, Sullivan, Ulster and Westchester.

Three weeks ago, when the insurance plan disclosed that it was planning to apply for a rate increase, a Blue Cross vice president said it would be "logical to assume" that the increase being sought would be at least as large as the last one, in 1964. That increase averaged 32.92 per cent.

Yesterday's application for a 49.5 per cent rise was made necessary, the announcement said, "to meet hospital costs which have accelerated an unprecedented/83.5 per cent since the last A.H.S. rate adjustment five years ago in 1964, or from $47.38 per day in 1964 to $86.92 in 1969."

The insurance plan said it was also seeking a change of benefits "designed to encourage the use of outpatient facilities and to discourage the

Continued on Page 37, Column 2

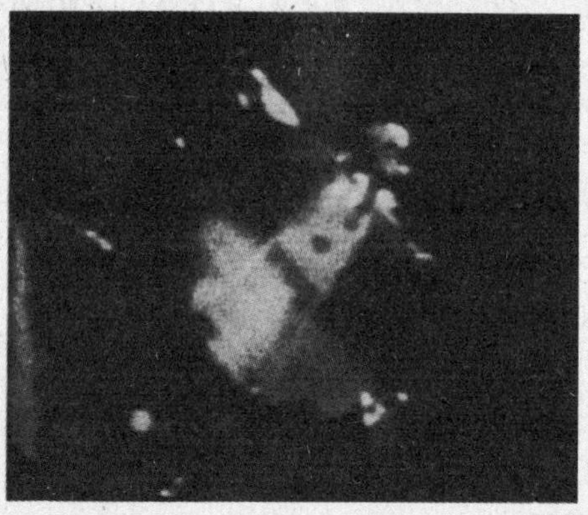

C.B.S. News

SNOOPY DESCENDING: Lunar module of Apollo 10 beginning its successful approach to moon after separation from command ship. View was televised from spacecraft yesterday.

U.S. BATTLE LOSSES STIR NIXON AIDES

Controversy Developing as High Civilian Officials Ask Discretion by Military

By HEDRICK SMITH
Special to The New York Times

WASHINGTON, May 22—A controversy is developing in the Nixon Administration over how to maintain battlefield pressure on the enemy without arousing a political reaction in the United States over high American casualty rates.

Some civilian officials feel that American battlefield commanders are operating with insufficient regard for the impact of the casualty figures on public opinion.

Privately, these high officials express impatience with the Saigon command for undertaking a costly operation such as the assault on Apbia Mountain, in which nearly 50 Americans were killed and 270 wounded. The capture of the mountain Tuesday followed a week of over-all fighting in which 430 Americans were killed — the second highest total in a year.

Sharpened Orders Asked

The concern over such figures has prompted the desire of some officials to have President Nixon sharpen his orders to battlefield commanders to have them use greater discretion.

Mr. Nixon has adopted President Lyndon B. Johnson's strategy of maintaining maximum battlefield pressure on the enemy. But he has ruled out a military solution to the war, insisting that every military move is designed to bolster the allied negotiating position in Paris.

The view of some senior

Continued on Page 2, Column 4

As They Neared the Moon

Special to The New York Times

HOUSTON, May 22—Following is a transcript of comments by Col. Thomas P. Stafford and Comdr. Eugene A. Cernan as they drew closer to the moon in their lunar vehicle, Snoopy:

Hello, Houston, this is Snoopy.

We is going. We is down among them, Charlie.

We're right there. We're right over it.

I just wish we could stay.

I'm telling you, we are low, we're close, babe!

Oh, Charlie, we just saw an earthrise and it's just got to be magnificent.

You can tell Jack [Dr. Harrison H. Shmitt, a geologist-astronaut] that there are enough boulders around here to fill up Galveston Bay, too.

We'll be picking up our landing radar test and taking pictures here and it is a fantastic sight. They do have different shades of browns and grays here. It's like the vulcan . . . vulcanism. There is also a pure white near the edge and the bottom is black and we see some large boulders that are black to blackish gray.

It looks like this landing radar is doing real good.

Straight up ahead you can see the Gulf from the highlands over to the Maria area. It's a beautiful sight. Just like crossing over to a black and gray sea.

Also, it looks like we're getting so close all you have to do is put your tail wheel down and we're there.

We're just coming up on Boot Hill, which is easily distinguishable. Wash Basin is just off to my right. Sidewinder Rille is coming up on my left. O.K., I've got Diamondback Rille. It's very easy to see. These rilles look like they might be a couple of hundred feet deep, very smooth, like wet clay, flat and smooth at the bottom. The edges are definitely rounded.

I've got Smokey on my left coming in. It looks like out in New Mexico or Arizona or some place.

We have been down among them, babe.

Magnificent, Charlie. It's just unbelievable, isn't it?

A transcript of conversations between the crewmen of Apollo 10 and ground controllers appears on Page 22.

LODGE SEES BASIS FOR NEGOTIATION

But Finds Enemy's Stand on Nixon Plan Obscure

By DREW MIDDLETON
Special to The New York Times

PARIS, May 22—Ambassador Henry Cabot Lodge said today at the Vietnam peace talks that there was common ground for discussion and negotiation in President Nixon's eight-point peace program and the plan put forward by the National Liberation Front, or Vietcong.

He cited the issues of reunification, restoration of a truly demilitarized zone between North Vietnam and South Vietnam and respect for the provisional military demarcation line and prisoners of war.

However, Nguyen Thanh Le, spokesman for the North Vietnamese delegation, referring to Mr. Lodge's "pretense" at finding similarities between the two sets of proposals said: "These respective positions are as different as day and night."

As Mr. Lodge left today's session, the 18th of the current negotiations, he said he found the position of North Vietnam and the National Liberation Front on President Nixon's

Continued on Page 4, Column 4

SOVIET DISSIDENTS IN PROTEST TO U.N.

Text Given to Newsmen Says Rights Are 'Repressed'

By BERNARD GWERTZMAN
Special to The New York Times

MOSCOW, May 22 — More than 50 Soviet dissidents, alarmed at the growing number of arrests of their fellows, have drawn up a petition to the United Nations Commission on Human Rights, calling for an investigation of "the repression of basic civil rights in the Soviet Union."

The petition was drafted two days ago and it was not known whether the text had actually been sent out of the Soviet Union. The dissidents made it available to Western correspondents apparently in the hope of reaching the United Nations through Western newspapers.

The petition said the "recent arrests have compelled us to think that Soviet punitive organs have decided finally to bar the activity of people protesting against arbitrariness in our country."

Coincident with the petition, it was also learned today that Ilya Burmistrovich, a 31-year-

Continued on Page 6, Column 1

TEST FOR MODULE

Stafford and Cernan, in 2 Descents, Find 'Smooth' Surface

By JOHN NOBLE WILFORD
Special to The New York Times

HOUSTON, Friday, May 23—Two American astronauts, riding a frail, bug-shaped spacecraft, swooped down within 9.4 land miles of the moon yesterday to demonstrate successfully all the steps of a lunar landing except the actual touchdown.

After three main rocket firings and two dips toward the moon, the two men returned to the orbiting command ship and, by early morning, re-entered it and settled down for the final four days of the Apollo 10 mission.

It was the closest man had ever come to another celestial body.

The feat gave engineers and officials of the Apollo project new confidence that their machines and techniques were up to the task of placing men on the moon this summer.

Get a Close-up View

And it allowed Col. Thomas P. Stafford of the Air Force and Comdr. Eugene A. Cernan of the Navy to get a close-up view of the intended site for the landing. This is an area in the moon's Sea of Tranquility that they described as "very smooth, like wet clay, like a dry river bed in New Mexico or Arizona."

After the second descent, Colonel Stafford and Commander Cernan rode the lunar module back to a rendezvous with the command ship at 10:54 P.M., Eastern daylight time, yesterday.

The two ships rejoined at 11:11 P.M. Shortly after midnight, the command ship jettisoned the unmanned lunar module. The astronauts planned to continued orbiting the moon until early tomorrow morning, when they are to rocket toward the earth and a splashdown in the Pacific Ocean on Monday. The flight began last Sunday.

Difficulties Overcome

A number of difficulties that threatened the mission were overcome during the day.

The astronauts in the lunar module were shaken just before the second descent when the upper stage carrying them went into wild gyrations as it separated from the lower stage. A switch left in a wrong position was blamed for the gyrations.

Three difficulties arose early, before the two craft were separated for the lunar module's descents. They involved inability to vent oxygen from the tunnel connecting the two craft, a slippage of the mechanism linking them and trouble with the command ship's radar unit.

"Snoopy [the lunar module] and Charlie Brown [the com-

Continued on Page 22, Column 1

Televised Take-Off From Moon Planned

By WALTER SULLIVAN
Special to The New York Times

HOUSTON, May 22—Preparations are being made to enable people on earth to watch, by television, the blast-off of a lunar module from the moon.

While it had been hoped that this could be done on the first manned moon landing, the Apollo 11 mission in July, the establishment of an unmanned television station on the moon to record this historic ascent has been deferred.

Whether it will be done on the second landing, that of Apollo 12, will depend on how difficult the Apollo 11 astronauts find working conditions on the lunar surface.

Planners of the Apollo 11 mission are disappointed in the postponement because a view

Continued on Page 22, Column 4

BIG BOARD DEFIED BY MEMBER FIRM

Donaldson, Lufkin Planning Public Share Offering

By TERRY ROBARDS

The New York Stock Exchange was confronted yesterday with a major uprising in its membership, when a leading member firm disclosed its intention to sell shares in itself to the public in defiance of an exchange rule.

Donaldson, Lufkin & Jenrette, Inc., perhaps Wall Street's most aggressive and best known institutional brokerage house, said it had filed a registration statement with the Securities and Exchange Commission covering the public offering of 800,000 of its shares for about $30 a share.

The action was expected to bring to a head the long-simmering controversy over public ownership of brokerage firms, as well as institutional membership on the stock exchange. The brokerage firm indicated that it had acted in a direct effort to confront the exchange's hierarchy with what many officials of the securities industry consider to be a highly significant issue.

"For nearly 200 years the New York Stock Exchange has

Continued on Page 70, Column 1

Goodell Would Back Lindsay as Liberal

By THOMAS F. BRADY

Senator Charles E. Goodell declared yesterday that he would support Mayor Lindsay for re-election next fall even if State Senator John J. Marchi won the Republican nomination for Mayor.

Mr. Marchi retorted later in the day: "I hope Senator Goodell will reconsider his decision to ignore the wishes of the Republican electorate. He would be reading himself out of the party by failure to do so."

Mr. Goodell, a liberal Republican, made his position known at a news conference at the Overseas Press Club that he had called to urge President Nixon to defer construction of the Safeguard antiballistic missile.

Mayor Lindsay has already won the mayoral nomination of

Continued on Page 33, Column 4

N.E.A. Facing Early Removal Of Federal Tax-Exempt Status

By EILEEN SHANAHAN
Special to The New York Times

WASHINGTON, May 22 — The National Education Association is expecting to hear officially at any moment that the Internal Revenue Service has revoked its tax-exempt status, an official of the organization said today.

It would be the second major national organization whose tax-exempt status had been removed in recent weeks. There were indications that these actions might be only the forerunners of a number of others.

The new Commissioner of Internal Revenue, Randolph W. Thrower, has ordered his staff to place "a strict construction" on the requirements of the tax law that organizations be operated "exclusively" for religious, educational and other tax-exempt purposes if they are to retain their exemption.

Mr. Thrower said in an interview that he was particularly concerned about "the ideological organizations that are far from the traditional patterns of religion or education."

He would not spell out what he meant by "ideological organizations."

The other group that has recently lost its exempt status is Americans United for Separation of Church and State, which received its notice of revocation in April but made it public only this week.

The National Education Association, which claims more than one million members, considers itself a professional organization of elementary and second-

Continued on Page 14, Column 4

NEWS INDEX

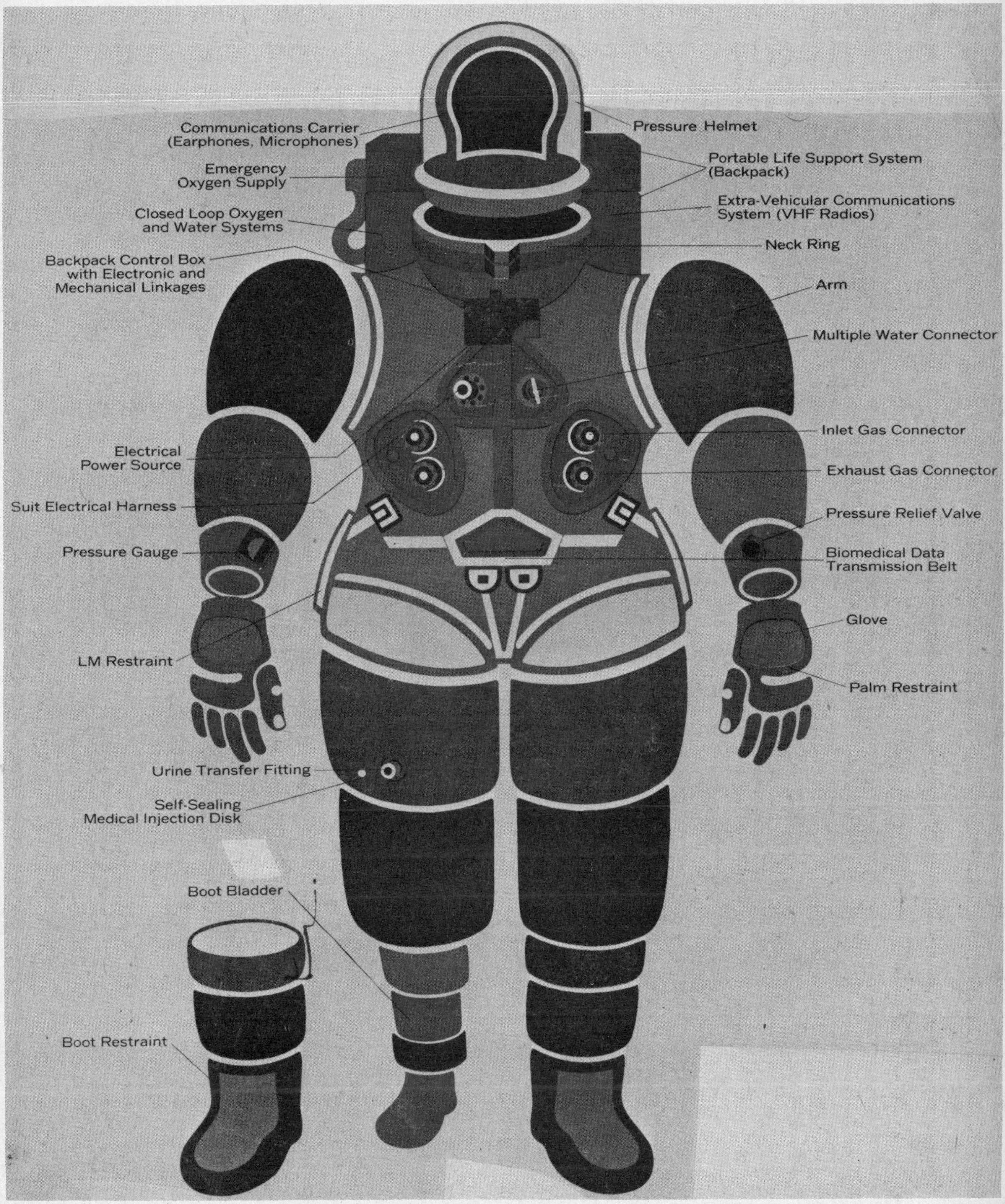
Communications Carrier
(Earphones, Microphones)
Pressure Helmet
Emergency
Oxygen Supply
Portable Life Support System
(Backpack)
Closed Loop Oxygen
and Water Systems
Extra-Vehicular Communications
System (VHF Radios)
Neck Ring
Backpack Control Box
with Electronic and
Mechanical Linkages
Arm
Multiple Water Connector
Inlet Gas Connector
Electrical
Power Source
Exhaust Gas Connector
Suit Electrical Harness
Pressure Relief Valve
Pressure Gauge
Biomedical Data
Transmission Belt
Glove
LM Restraint
Palm Restraint
Urine Transfer Fitting
Self-Sealing
Medical Injection Disk
Boot Bladder
Boot Restraint

What the well-dressed moon man will wear

"All the News That's Fit to Print"

The New York Times

LATE CITY EDITION

Weather: Sunny, hot today; fair tonight. Sunny, hot tomorrow. Temp. range: today 98-76; Wed. 93-74. Temp.-Hum. Index yesterday 84. Complete U.S. report on Page 75.

VOL. CXVIII . . No. 40,717 © 1969 The New York Times Company. NEW YORK, THURSDAY, JULY 17, 1969 10 CENTS

ASTRONAUTS SPEEDING TOWARD THE MOON; FIRST DAY OF APOLLO FLIGHT IS FLAWLESS; NIXON ASKS FOR NATIONAL HOLIDAY MONDAY

DEMOCRATIC GROUP ENDORSES LINDSAY AT UNRULY SESSION

Demonstrators Protesting Ouster of Gerena Hurl Chairs at Delegates

By RICHARD REEVES

The New Democratic Coalition overwhelmingly endorsed Mayor Lindsay for re-election last night after an unruly meeting that ended in a chair-throwing brawl.

Violence ended the noisy session at midnight as a small group of Puerto Ricans, protesting the dismissal of a Puerto Rican city official, began throwing metal chairs and pedestal ashtrays into the crowd of delegates. At the same time in another part of the Hotel Diplomat's ballroom, small clouds of what was apparently tear gas choked screaming men and women.

Fist fights began as young delegates charged into the Puerto Rican group while coughing and crying people ran for the crowded ballroom exits.

One delegate—Jeremiah Elias, 33-year-old campaign chairman of the Village Independent Democrats—was taken to an ambulance with blood streaming from a cut above his left eye by policemen who ran into the room after five minutes of sporadic violence.

Chanting Stops Debate

The brawl—accompanied by a man screaming "Is there a doctor in the house?" over and over into a microphone—climaxed a meeting at which shouting speakers routinely tried to be heard above the noise of roaming delegates to the convention of the city's largest liberal Democratic organization.

Earlier in the meeting, debate had been stopped by the chanting group of Puerto Ricans, by other gas explosions and by brief scuffles including a delegate's attack on a New York Post photographer.

Ironically, little of the debate touched on the qualifications of Mr. Lindsay, a liberal Republican seeking re-election as the candidate of the Liberal party and a proposed independent party, or of his opponents, Controller Mario A. Procaccino, the Democratic nominee, and State Senator John J. Marchi, the candidate of both the Republican and Conservative parties.

There was no official count of the coalition vote last night, but when the endorsement resolution was finally called just

Continued on Page 61, Column 2

Mayor Drops Plans For Express Roads Across 2 Boroughs

By MAURICE CARROLL

The Lower Manhattan Expressway and the Cross-Brooklyn Expressway are dead "for all time," Mayor Lindsay said yesterday.

Confronted with determined community opposition, much of it from the liberal Democrats whose support he has been seeking since he lost the Republican primary last month, the Mayor abandoned plans for the two highly controversial projects.

Alternative routes will be laid out, he said, only when "the community leaders can work out something that is supported by the community."

The Brooklyn road between the Verrazano-Narrows Bridge and the Nassau Expressway would have been the base for the "linear city" that Mr. Lindsay had hailed as "a dramatic new concept for community development."

For the first time," he said, when disclosing plans for the

Continued on Page 51, Column 3

WHITE HOUSE BARS PRICE CONTROLS

Curbs on Wages Also Ruled Out — Democrats Refuse Surcharge Action Now

By EDWIN L. DALE Jr.
Special to The New York Times

WASHINGTON, July 16—The White House, whose spokesman's previous words had left a residue of doubt, finally ruled out wage and price controls today.

Controls had never been under consideration, but it was not until today that Ronald L. Ziegler, the White House press secretary, after instructions from President Nixon and other high officials, said:

"The Administration has ruled out wage and price controls as a way of dealing with inflation under conditions that are now foreseeable. Looking into the future, with the knowledge and experience that this Administration has, and projecting the various alternatives that could be used in the foreseeable future, wage and price controls would not be considered."

Mr. Ziegler emphasized that "the President is not for controls" and has "consistently taken this position." He repeated that the Administration's strategy for cooling the economy "does not include wage and price controls."

Focus on Surcharge

Meanwhile, the attention of the Administration continued to be focused on the real policy question — trying to get the income tax surcharge through the Senate before Congress takes a vacation in mid-August. Despite some expressions of confidence, the news, from the Administration's point of view, was not encouraging.

On the Senate floor, Senator Everett McKinley Dirksen of Illinois, the minority leader, got a firm "no" from his Democratic counterparts when he asked that the surcharge be considered quickly, and certainly before the Congressional recess.

Senators Mike Mansfield of Montana and Edward M. Kennedy of Massachusetts repeated their standing position — that the Democrats would insist on

Continued on Page 62, Column 1

U.S. Is Stressing Cut in Casualties

By MAX FRANKEL
Special to The New York Times

WASHINGTON, July 16 — In planning for a further withdrawal of troops from Vietnam, the Nixon Administration is urging field commanders to redouble efforts to hold down American battle casualties.

A lower casualty rate is viewed here as at least as important as the recall of troops in the effort to appease public opinion in the United States and thus to stiffen the bargaining posture toward North Vietnam. An adjustment of tactics to hold down losses is held to be useful also as "a reply" to the enemy's current but unexplained disengagement from battle.

If Hanoi is trying to signal an interest in mutual but un-

Continued on Page 4, Column 4

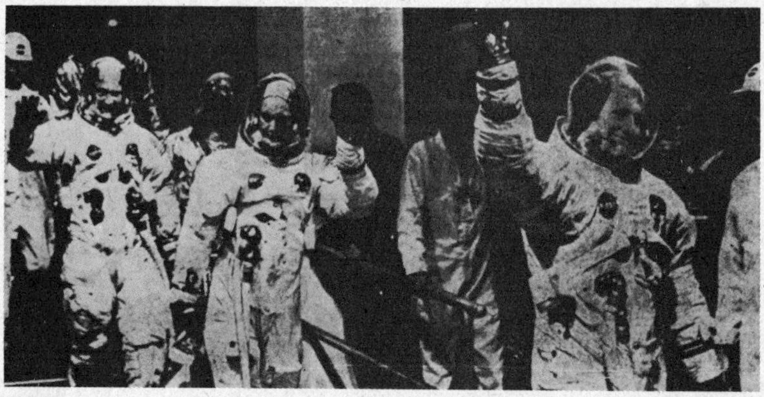

Associated Press

ON WAY TO PAD 39-A: Neil A. Armstrong, at right, Lieut. Col. Michael Collins, center, and Col. Edwin E. Aldrin Jr. as they left their quarters

United Press International

ON THE WAY TO MOON: Saturn 5 rocket carrying the astronauts lifts off at Cape Kennedy. Crowds line banks of lagoon about three miles from site.

CRAFT ON TARGET

World Watches Start of Man's Attempt to Achieve Landing

Excerpts from conversations will be found on Page 20.

By JOHN NOBLE WILFORD
Special to The New York Times

CAPE KENNEDY, Fla., Thursday, July 17—Three American astronauts commissioned to fulfill an age-old dream and a national goal of the decade were streaking across the black sea of space today in man's first attempt to walk on another world — the moon.

All the critical first steps of the epic Apollo 11 flight were made without flaw. The spaceship's course for the moon, an average distance of 238,857 miles from earth, was so accurate that a planned corrective maneuver was canceled as unnecessary.

The men of Apollo 11 — Neil A. Armstrong, a civilian, and Col. Edwin E. Aldrin Jr. and Lieut. Col. Michael Collins of the Air Force — rose from the launching pad here yesterday on a tail of flame from the mammoth Saturn 5 rocket.

The thunderous blastoff at 9:32 A.M., Eastern daylight time, sent a tremor through the ground and staccato shock waves beating at an estimated total of one million people who stood under the hot Florida sun to see the start of the most daring voyage thus far in the age of spacefaring.

First Color TV Show

Millions around the world watched over television relayed by satellites. The first color pictures were transmitted at about 8 P.M., showing the receding earth.

The crew went to sleep an hour later, two hours earlier than scheduled. The extra time became available because the corrective maneuver was skipped.

President Nixon, who watched the launching on television at the White House, was moved to proclaim next Monday — the day Mr. Armstrong and Colonel Aldrin are scheduled to set foot on the lunar crust — a National Day of Participation.

Mr. Armstrong, the shy, intense, 38-year-old commander with a boyish grin, and the 39-year-old Colonel Aldrin, a supremely self-confident pilot and specialist in theoretical astronautics, plan to place the first human footprints and the American flag on the moon early Monday, sometime after 2:21 A.M., following their landing there on Sunday.

The third member of the crew, the 38-year-old Colonel Collins, is to remain in the command ship orbiting about

Continued on Page 20, Column 1

FIGHTING ABATING IN LATIN CONFLICT

Honduras and El Salvador Seem to Lack Equipment

By H. J. MAIDENBERG
Special to The New York Times

GUATEMALA, July 16—The two-day-old war between El Salvador and Honduras appeared today to be abating, largely because of the lack of war materiel, according to neutral diplomatic sources here.

[In Washington, the Council of the Organization of American States received word that both countries had accepted its cease-fire call, though diplomatic arguments broke out over El Salvador's "conditions" for acceptance. The Salvadoran Government made no commitment to withdraw its troops to the frontier.]

Thus far, the conflict has created tens of thousands of refugees, has left an unknown number of people dead in both Central American lands, has undermined the budding Central American Common Market and has raised the specter of future economic and social conflict in the region.

A peace mission of the Organization of American States,

Continued on Page 3, Column 1

Across the Nation Launching Brings Mood of Reflection

By LACEY FOSBURGH

At 9:32 A.M. Eastern daylight time yesterday, when exhaust and flames filled the air at Cape Kennedy and the rocket carrying three men to the moon lifted off the ground, dawn was just reaching the western shores of the United States.

As new light moved along the California beaches and touched the hills, people rose and switched on their television sets. In open-air markets in San Francisco, others already at work by 6:32 A.M. stood in silence amid the flounder and mackerel or asters and roses and listened: "Five, four, three . . ."

Far away in the flat lowlands south of San Diego, Albert J. Gilman, assistant chief of the patrol that polices the border between California and Mexico at Tijuana, sat alone at a television set in his darkened living room.

"I just couldn't believe I was actually watching history in the making" he said, "but I was there. I was part of it. I saw it happen."

Several miles away drivers waiting to go through customs listened to the countdown in

Continued on Page 22, Column 2

AGNEW PROPOSES A MARS LANDING

Manned Mission by End of Century Suggested as Goal

By RICHARD WITKIN
Special to The New York Times

CAPE KENNEDY, Fla., July 16 — Vice President Agnew, here for the Apollo 11 launching, disclosed today that he had been urging that the nation set a new goal of landing men on Mars by the end of the century.

Mr. Agnew said he was a minority voice on a panel that President Nixon assigned last February, to recommend by Sept. 1 what the nation should do in space to follow up the Apollo moon-landing project.

"I don't think," he quickly added, "that the President is the kind of man just to count noses."

The Vice President made his disclosure in interviews here an hour or more before watching the launching of the Apollo 11 on the first manned lunar landing mission.

"It is my individual feeling," the Vice President said, "that we should articulate a simple, ambitious, optimistic goal of a

Continued on Page 22, Column 6

Nixon Calls for a Holiday So All Can Share in 'Glory'

Proclamation Is Issued

By WALTER RUGABER
Special to The New York Times

WASHINGTON, July 16 — President Nixon proposed today that Americans receive a day off from work next Monday to mark the "moment of transcendent drama" when man first sets foot on the moon.

In a proclamation signed hours after he had watched television broadcasts of the Apollo 11 lift-off, the President declared a National Day of Participation for the lunar exploration set for early Monday morning.

Text of Nixon proclamation is printed on Page 22

While he did not have the authority to establish a legal national holiday, his National Day of Participation may amount to the same thing for most private as well as public employes.

All Federal offices will be closed under Mr. Nixon's proclamation except those engaged in essential services, and the President urged Governors, Mayors, heads of school systems and other officials to fol-

Continued on Page 22, Column 2

Public Offices to Shut Here

By SYLVAN FOX

City and state offices will be closed Monday to permit their staffs to join other New Yorkers in commemorating the landing of the Apollo II astronauts on the moon.

In separate statements, Governor Rockefeller and Mayor Lindsay declared that though public buildings would be closed essential services would be maintained.

Their announcements were made shortly after President Nixon issued a call to the nation to observe Monday as a National Day of Participation.

He urged Governors, Mayors, schools and private employers to halt their operations "so that as many of our citizens as possible will be able to share in the significant events of the day."

Governor Rockefeller said: "New York State will follow President Nixon's suggestion that Monday, July 21, be observed as a National Day of Participation. State offices will be closed, but essential services will be maintained."

A spokesman for the Governor said there were "no plans to make this a public, legal

Continued on Page 22, Column 5

Today's 4-Part Issue

This morning's issue of The New York Times is divided into four parts. The second part is a 20-page supplement on "Man and the Moon."

Editorials and Letters to the Editor appear on Page 26 and Obituaries on Page 27. Financial news is in the third part, Sports news in the fourth part. Transportation news and Weather Reports will be found on Page 75.

Following is the News Index for today's issue:

News Summary and Index, Page 40

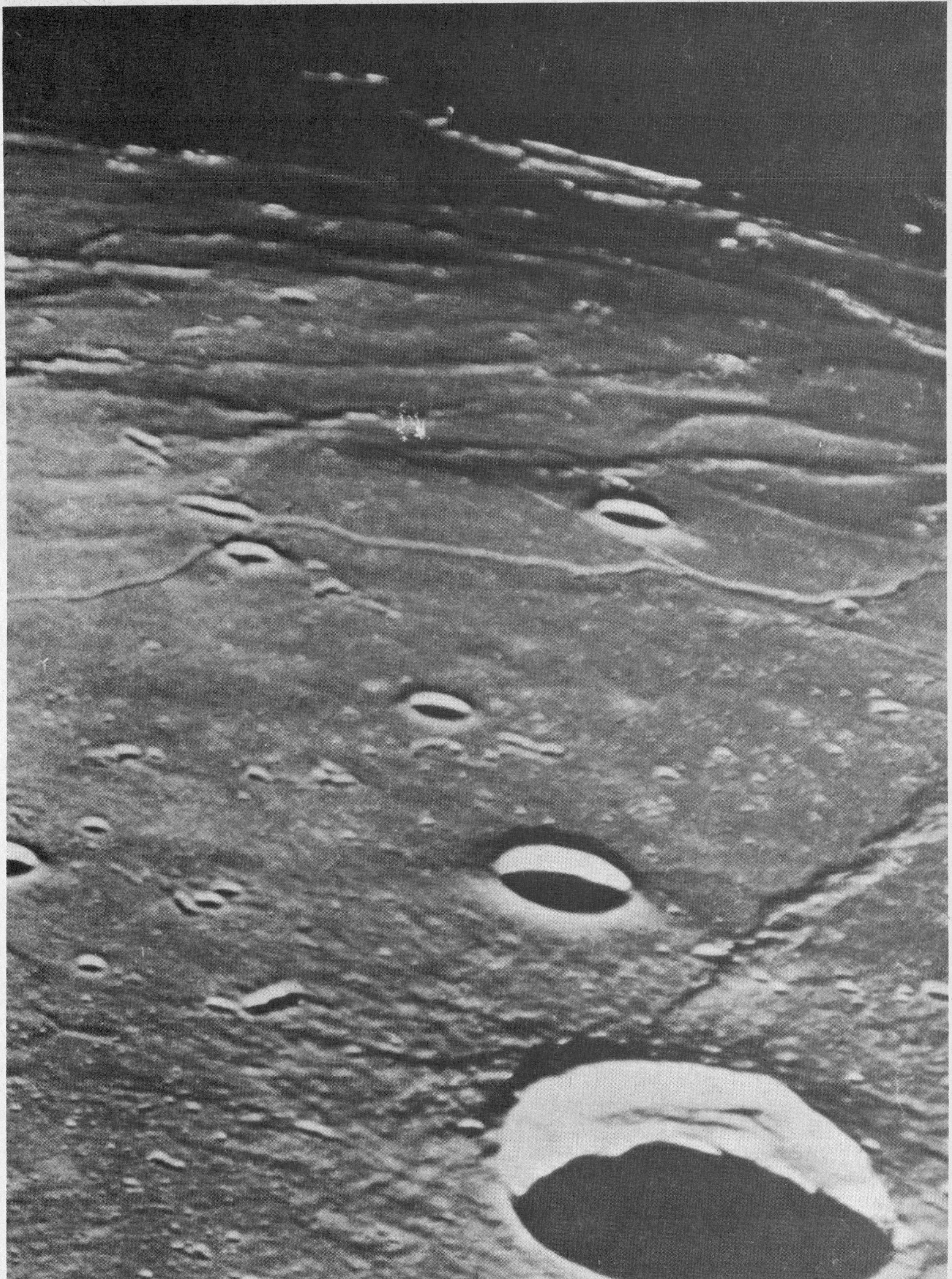

The moon landing approach.

"All the News That's Fit to Print"

The New York Times

LATE CITY EDITION

Weather: Cloudy, showers likely and seasonable through tomorrow. Temp. range: today 79-69; Saturday 82-72. Temp.-Hum. Index yesterday 74. Complete U.S. report on Page 59.

SECTION ONE

VOL. CXVIII . No. 40,720

NEW YORK, SUNDAY, JULY 20, 1969

60¢ beyond 50-mile zone from New York City, except Long Island. 75¢ beyond 200-mile radius. Higher in air delivery cities.

50 CENTS

ASTRONAUTS SWING INTO MOON ORBIT IN PREPARATION FOR TODAY'S LANDING

Woman Passenger Killed, Kennedy Escapes in Crash

Senator Tells the Police He Wandered About in Shock After Car Ran Off Bridge Near Martha's Vineyard

Special to The New York Times

EDGARTOWN, Mass., July 19—A 28-year-old woman passenger drowned today when a car driven by Senator Edward M. Kennedy plunged 10 feet off a bridge into a pond on Chappaquiddick Island near this community on Martha's Vineyard.

Senator Kennedy was at first believed to have escaped injury, but tonight a family physician, Dr. Robert D. Watt, said in Hyannis Port, Mass., that the Senator had "a slight concussion in the back of the head." He said the Senator had been given a sedative.

The woman was Mary Jo Kopechne of Berkeley Heights, N. J., a former secretary to the Massachusetts Democrat's brother, the late Senator Robert F. Kennedy.

The police here said that Edward Kennedy had told them he wandered around in apparent shock after the accident and did not report it to them for about eight hours.

"I remember walking around for a period of time and then going back to my hotel room," Senator Kennedy was quoted by the police as saying. "When I fully realized what had happened this morning, I immediately contacted the police."

In a telephone interview tonight, Police Chief Dominick J. Arena said there was "apparently no criminal negligence involved in the accident itself."

But the Edgartown police said late tonight that a formal charge of leaving the scene of an accident, a misdemeanor, would be filed against Senator Kennedy Monday morning in the Dukes County Courthouse in Edgartown.

The incident was another in a series of violent events that have hounded the Kennedy family ever since it came to prominence in American political life.

Senator Kennedy had come to Martha's Vineyard to join

Continued on Page 50, Column 1

Drug Producer Concedes Investigating Senate Aide

By WALTER RUGABER

Special to The New York Times

WASHINGTON, July 19 — A major pharmaceutical company acknowledged today that it had ordered an investigation into the personal affairs of a Senate aide who helped draft legislation that would affect the drug industry.

Gilbert S. McInerny, vice president and general counsel of the American Home Products Corporation of New York, confirmed in a telephone interview that the corporation had ordered the investigation.

It involved Jay Constantine, a staff member of the Senate Finance Committee, who has worked on legislation involving financial assistance for drug purchases made under the Government's Medicare and Medicaid programs.

The measure, sponsored by Senator Russell B. Long, Democrat of Louisiana, who is chairman of the Finance Committee, would promote the sale of low-cost drugs under their generic names at the expense of higher-priced drugs, sold under trade names, that are chemically equivalent or inferior.

Pharmaceutical manufacturers, who have a substantial interest in the prescribing of drugs by their trade names, are strongly opposed to regulations that would favor prescribing a drug by its generic, or common name, for which the price is frequently lower.

Mr. McInerny said that the

Continued on Page 42, Column 4

CITIES AND STATES AGREE WITH U.S. ON FUND SHARING

Informal Compromise Gives Each Entity a Portion of Federal Revenues

By EDWIN L. DALE JR.

Special to The New York Times

WASHINGTON, July 19—The Nixon Administration and representatives of state and local governments have reached an informal compromise agreement on perhaps the most difficult of several issues involved in the forthcoming Administration proposal for revenue-sharing with the states.

The issue is how much money will go to the states and how much to the cities and other local governments. The compromise, which goes by the name of "Mandatory Pass-through," has been tentatively accepted in principle by all sides, though exact formulas remain to be worked out.

Numerous other questions are still under intensive study by an Administration study group, headed by Murray L. Weidenbaum, Assistant Secretary of the Treasury for Economic Policy. A Presidential message on this major issue—potentially the most important reform in American Government in a generation—is likely later this year, though action by Congress is not expected by anyone until next year.

Formula Being Developed

The compromise on the issue of the city vs. the state was reached at a White House meeting early this month, attended by the key governors, mayors and county officials involved in the revenue-sharing question. There were three possibilities.

First, have all the money go to the states, with distribution to the localities at the discretion of the governor and legislature. This was unacceptable to the cities.

Second, create "two pots," with designated amounts to go to the states and the rest to the localities. This was rejected

Continued on Page 44, Column 1

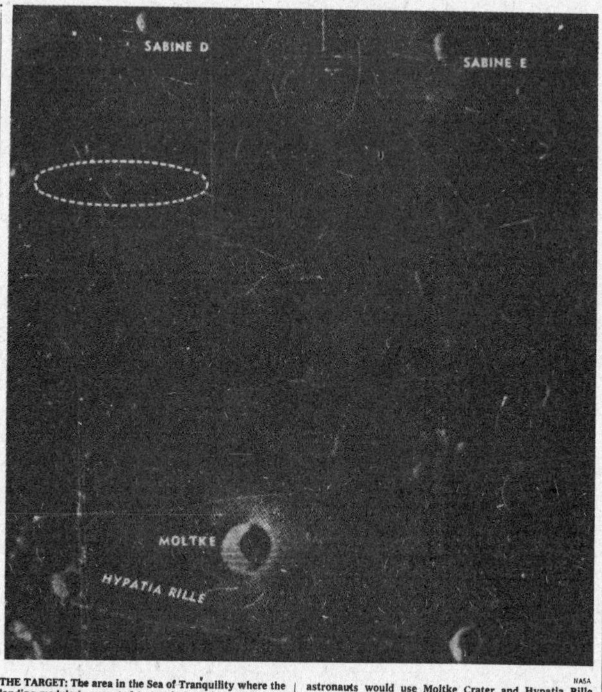

NASA

THE TARGET: The area in the Sea of Tranquility where the landing module is expected to touch down is in the upper left quadrant of this photo, shown by the dotted line. The craft's approach would be from right to left and the astronauts would use Moltke Crater and Hypatia Rille (nicknamed "U.S. 1") as their visual landmarks. The photo—which was taken during the Apollo 10 mission—shows an area of approximately 45 by 45 statute miles.

CREWMEN EAGER

NASA Aides See No Obstacles in the Way of Touchdown

Excerpts from conversations will be found on Page 38.

By JOHN NOBLE WILFORD

Special to The New York Times

HOUSTON, Sunday, July 20—The Apollo 11 astronauts were orbiting the moon early today and eagerly awaiting the mission's most critical and dramatic moment—the landing on a desolate lunar plain.

Neil A. Armstrong, a civilian, and Col. Edwin E. Aldrin Jr. and Lieut. Col. Michael Collins of the Air Force rode their spacecraft into lunar orbit yesterday.

Mr. Armstrong and Colonel Aldrin are scheduled to steer the landing craft to a lunar touchdown at 4:15 P.M. Eastern daylight time today.

Mr. Armstrong, the 38-year-old commander, will open the hatch and plant the first human footprints on the moon at about 2:17 A.M. tomorrow or sooner, if he feels like it.

Colonel Collins will remain in the moon-orbiting command ship while the two other men detach the lunar module and descend to the landing on the moon's Sea of Tranquility.

A Broad, Dry Plain

That is a broad, dry plain that appears from the earth as a dark spot on the right side of the moon—one of the facial features of the legendary man in the moon.

The exact landing spot is in the southwestern part of Tranquility, near the lunar equator and 118 miles southwest of the crater Maskelyne. It will be shortly after dawn—moon time—when the spindly-legged lunar module is to set down.

Flight controllers here said that all systems on the moonship continued to function normally, and that no technical problems stood in the way of the landing.

After the linked command ship and lunar module swept into moon orbit yesterday, Mr. Armstrong radioed across the quarter-million miles of space: "It was like perfect."

The commander reported that the spacecraft's main rocket, a 20,500-pound-thrust engine, had fired for the planned 6 minutes 2 seconds. This slowed the vehicle down so that it could be captured by lunar gravity.

The firing came at 1:22 P.M. after Apollo 11 had swung around the leading edge of the moon and disappeared behind

Continued on Page 38, Column 1

15 NAMED TO STUDY PENTAGON REFORM

Defense Business Concerns Represented on Panel That Will Suggest Changes

By JOHN HERBERS

Special to The New York Times

WASHINGTON, July 19—The membership of a blue-ribbon panel that will make a 12-month study and recommend reforms in the operation of the Department of Defense was announced today by Secretary Melvin R. Laird and Gilbert W. Fitzhugh, chairman of the panel.

Companies that do business with the Pentagon were heavily represented on the group.

Establishment of the panel was announced on June 30. President Nixon announced that Mr. Fitzhugh, chairman of the board and chief executive officer of the Metropolitan Life Insurance Company of New York, would head the study of the department's management, research, procurement and decision-making machinery.

Areas of Inquiry

Formation of the study panel comes at a time when the Pentagon has been under increasing criticism from Congress and other sources for allegedly prodigious waste. In the June 30 announcement, Mr. Laird said the review would be "the most comprehensive" since reorganization studies were made by the Hoover Commission in 1947 and 1953.

Mr. Laird cited some areas of inquiry on which the panel will focus its study and eventual recommendations:

¶Organization and management of the Defense Department and affiliated agencies, the decision-making process and command and control function and facilities.

¶Defense research and development efforts, including the Pentagon's relations with the scientific and industrial community.

¶Defense procurement poli-

Continued on Page 56, Column 1

14 Largest Private Banks Are Nationalized by India

By SYDNEY H. SCHANBERG

Special to The New York Times

NEW DELHI, July 19—The Indian Government, in a bold and unexpected stroke by Prime Minister Indira Gandhi, nationalized the country's 14 largest private banks tonight.

The move does not affect foreign banks with branches in India.

The ordinance empowering an immediate Government takeover of the 14 Indian commercial banks—which control about 75 to 80 per cent of the nation's private banking deposits and are largely dominated by India's most powerful industrial families—was signed by the Acting President, V. V. Giri, shortly after the Cabinet came to a unanimous decision on the measure at an early evening meeting called by Mrs. Gandhi.

Part of India's banking industry is already nationalized in the form of the State Bank. With the ordinance tonight nearly 90 per cent of the country's total bank assets become Government-controlled. The rest are held by small private banks and the foreign banks.

The sudden, aggressive move by Mrs. Gandhi was a clear personal victory for her over the governing Congress party's bosses, with whom she has been openly struggling for control of the party and the Government.

But her fight with them did not appear over tonight, nor did the potential Government crisis that the fight has precipitated.

The Prime Minister, who an-

Continued on Page 8, Column 1

80-Year-Old Myrtle Avenue El To Run for Last Time in October

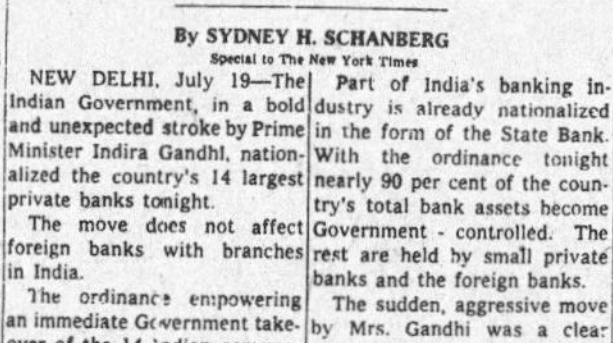

The New York Times July 20, 1969

Myrtle Avenue El between (1) and (2) slated to be razed

By JOSEPH LELYVELD

Brooklyn's 80-year-old Myrtle Avenue Elevated, the only rapid transit line in North America that still uses wooden cars, will be shut down in October and then demolished, the Transit Authority announced yesterday.

The El runs from Jay Street in downtown Brooklyn to Broadway in Williamsburg, passing through a 35-block stretch of the Fort Greene and Bedford-Stuyvesant sections, both inhabited mainly by Negroes and Puerto Ricans. Eight stations, among the last wooden stations in the transit system, will disappear with the closing.

Dr. William J. Ronan, the Transit Authority's chairman, promised increased bus service to the affected neighborhoods and spoke encouragingly of the opening of "a 35-block stretch of Myrtle Avenue to light and air" by the demolition of the elevated structure.

The Myrtle Avenue Line, an extension of the old El, will

Continued on Page 58, Column 2

LUNA 15 IS SHIFTED TO A HIGHER ORBIT

Soviet Says Correction Put Craft 59 Miles From the Moon Instead of 34.5

By BERNARD GWERTZMAN

Special to The New York Times

MOSCOW, July 19—The Soviet Union announced tonight that the orbit of its unmanned lunar spacecraft, Luna 15, had been changed. No reason was given for instituting the new, higher orbit.

Tass, the Soviet press agency, said that the craft was now orbiting the moon at a minimum distance of 59 miles from the surface. It had been as close as 34.5 miles for the last two days.

In the first official report on Luna 15 since it went into orbit on Thursday, Tass said that a correction maneuver was carried out at 4:08 P.M. Moscow time today (9:08 A.M. New York time). This gave Luna 15 an orbit ranging between 59 miles and 136 miles from the surface. The orbit had ranged between 34.5 miles and 126.5 miles.

No Landing Hinted

The report came only minutes before the press agency disclosed that Apollo 11 had gone into moon orbit as part of its plan to land two American astronauts on the moon tomorrow.

There was nothing in the Tass report to indicate whether Luna 15 planned to land on the moon, as some observers here have predicted. According to that theory, the unmanned craft would then attempt to gather some moon rock and to return to earth, supporting the Soviet position that unmanned craft were at least equal in scientific value to manned ones.

The general tenor of recent Soviet commentaries, however, has suggested that Luna 15 will

Continued on Page 38, Column 7

Associated Press

John Fairfax at Hollywood Beach, Fla., waves from boat he rowed from Canary Islands

Briton Is First to Row Atlantic Alone

By MARTIN WALDRON

Special to The New York Times

HOLLYWOOD, Fla., July 19—A 32-year-old London adventurer, John Fairfax, landed his 22-foot-long rowboat in the surf here this afternoon. He had rowed across the Atlantic Ocean, the only person to do it alone.

He called his feat "symbolic," in that he was landing his boat, the Britannia, near the spot where America's three astronauts had been launched on their flight to the moon three days ago.

Mr. Fairfax, cheerful but tired, hopped out of his orange-colored craft at 1:48 P.M., as his girl friend, Sylvia Marrett, was trying to climb aboard.

The surf, stirred by offshore thunderstorms, was preventing Mr. Fairfax from making the last 30 feet to the beach, and Miss Marrett was

Continued on Page 44, Column 4

Today's Sections

Index to Subjects

"All the News That's Fit to Print"

The New York Times

LATE CITY EDITION

Weather: Rain, warm today; clear tonight. Sunny, pleasant tomorrow. Temp. range: today 80-66; Sunday 71-66. Temp.-Hum. Index yesterday 69. Complete U.S. report on P. 50.

VOL. CXVIII . No. 40,721

NEW YORK, MONDAY, JULY 21, 1969

10 CENTS

MEN WALK ON MOON

ASTRONAUTS LAND ON PLAIN; COLLECT ROCKS, PLANT FLAG

Voice From Moon: 'Eagle Has Landed'

EAGLE (the lunar module): Houston, Tranquility Base here. The Eagle has landed.

HOUSTON: Roger, Tranquility, we copy you on the ground. You've got a bunch of guys about to turn blue. We're breathing again. Thanks a lot.

TRANQUILITY BASE: Thank you.

HOUSTON: You're looking good here.

TRANQUILITY BASE: A very smooth touchdown

HOUSTON: Eagle, you are stay for T1. [The first step in the lunar operation.] Over.

TRANQUILITY BASE: Roger. Stay for T1.

HOUSTON: Roger and we see you venting the ox.

TRANQUILITY BASE: Roger.

COLUMBIA (the command and service module). How do you read me?

HOUSTON: Columbia, he has landed Tranquility Base. Eagle is at Tranquility. I read you five by. Over.

COLUMBIA: Yes, I heard the whole thing.

HOUSTON: Well, it's a good show.

COLUMBIA: Fantastic.

TRANQUILITY BASE: I'll second that.

APOLLO CONTROL: The next major stay-no stay will be for the T2 event. That is at 21 minutes 26 seconds after initiation of power descent.

COLUMBIA: Up telemetry command reset to re-acquire on high gain.

HOUSTON: Copy. Out.

APOLLO CONTROL: We have an unofficial time for that touchdown of 102 hours, 45 minutes, 42 seconds and we will update that.

HOUSTON: Eagle, you loaded R2 wrong. We want 10254.

TRANQUILITY BASE: Roger. Do you want the horizontal 55 15.2?

HOUSTON: That's affirmative.

APOLLO CONTROL: We're now less than four minutes from our next stay-no stay. it will be for one complete revolution of the command module.

One of the first things that Armstrong and Aldrin will do after getting their next stay-no stay will be to remove their helmets and gloves.

HOUSTON: Eagle, you are stay for T2. Over.

Continued on Page 4, Col. 1

VOYAGE TO THE MOON

By Archibald MacLeish

Presence among us,

wanderer in our skies,

dazzle of silver in our leaves and on our waters silver,

O
silver evasion in our farthest thought—
"the visiting moon" . . . "the glimpses of the moon" . . .

and we have touched you!

From the first of time,
before the first of time, before the
first men tasted time, we thought of you.
You were a wonder to us, unattainable,
a longing past the reach of longing,
a light beyond our light, our lives—perhaps
a meaning to us . . .

Now
our hands have touched you in your depth of night.

Three days and three nights we journeyed,
steered by farthest stars, climbed outward,
crossed the invisible tide-rip where the floating dust
falls one way or the other in the void between,
followed that other down, encountered
cold, faced death—unfathomable emptiness . . .

Then, the fourth day evening, we descended,
made fast, set foot at dawn upon your beaches,
sifted between our fingers your cold sand.

We stand here in the dusk, the cold, the silence . . .

and here, as at the first of time, we lift our heads.
Over us, more beautiful than the moon, a
moon, a wonder to us, unattainable,
a longing past the reach of longing,
a light beyond our light, our lives—perhaps
a meaning to us . . .

O, a meaning!

over us on these silent beaches the bright
earth,
presence among us

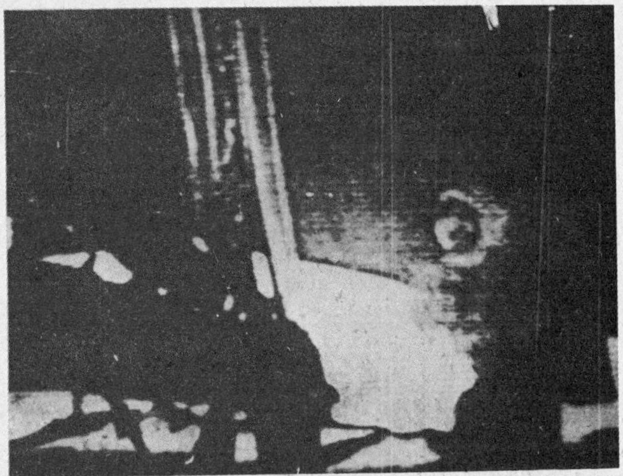

Neil A. Armstrong moves away from the leg of the landing craft after taking the first step on the surface of the moon

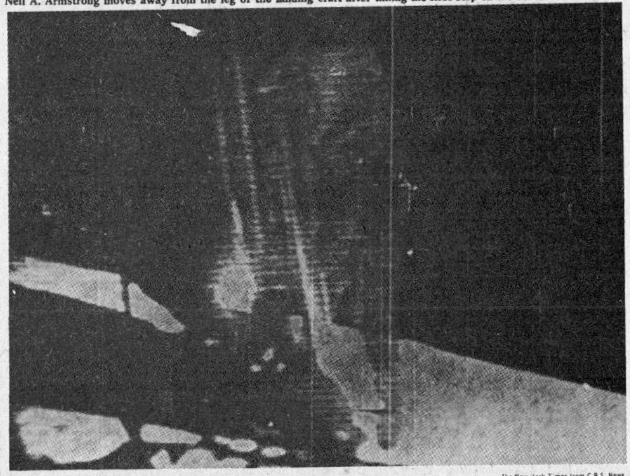

The New York Times from C.B.S. News

Col. Edwin E. Aldrin Jr. climbing down the ladder. The television camera was attached to a side of the lunar module.

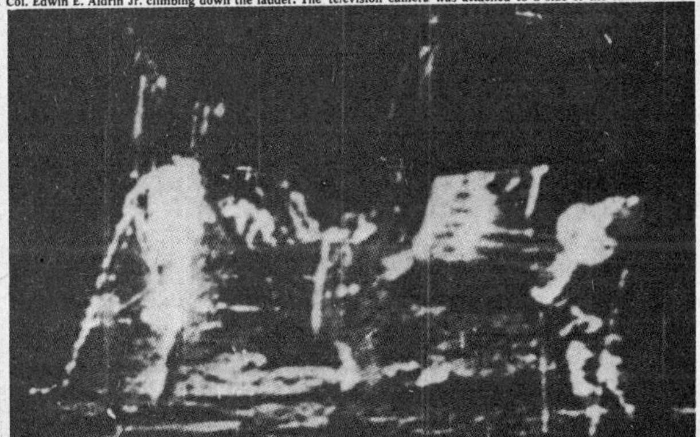

Associated Press

Mr. Armstrong, right, and Colonel Aldrin raise the U.S. flag. A metal rod at right angles to the mast keeps flag unfurled.

A Powdery Surface Is Closely Explored

By JOHN NOBLE WILFORD

Special to The New York Times

HOUSTON, Monday, July 21—Men have landed and walked on the moon.

Two Americans, astronauts of Apollo 11, steered their fragile four-legged lunar module safely and smoothly to the historic landing yesterday at 4:17:40 P.M., Eastern daylight time.

Neil A. Armstrong, the 38-year-old civilian commander, radioed to earth and the mission control room here:

"Houston, Tranquility Base here. The Eagle has landed."

The first men to reach the moon—Mr. Armstrong and his co-pilot, Col. Edwin E. Aldrin Jr. of the Air Force—brought their ship to rest on a level, rock-strewn plain near the southwestern shore of the arid Sea of Tranquility.

About six and a half hours later, Mr. Armstrong opened the landing craft's hatch, stepped slowly down the ladder and declared as he planted the first human footprint on the lunar crust:

"That's one small step for man, one giant leap for mankind."

His first step on the moon came at 10:56:20 P.M., as a television camera outside the craft transmitted his every move to an awed and excited audience of hundreds of millions of people on earth.

Tentative Steps Test Soil

Mr. Armstrong's initial steps were tentative tests of the lunar soil's firmness and of his ability to move about easily in his bulky white spacesuit and backpacks and under the influence of lunar gravity, which is one-sixth that of the earth.

"The surface is fine and powdery," the astronaut reported. "I can pick it up loosely with my toe. It does adhere in fine layers like powdered charcoal to the sole and sides of my boots. I only go in a small fraction of an inch, maybe an eighth of an inch. But I can see the footprints of my boots in the treads in the fine sandy particles.

After 19 minutes of Mr. Armstrong's testing, Colonel Aldrin joined him outside the craft.

The two men got busy setting up another television camera out from the lunar module, planting an American flag into the ground, scooping up soil and rock samples, deploying scientific experiments and hopping and loping about in a demonstration of their lunar agility.

They found walking and working on the moon less taxing than had been forecast. Mr. Armstrong once reported he was "very comfortable."

And people back on earth found the black-and-white television pictures of the bug-shaped lunar module and the men tramping about it so sharp and clear as to seem unreal, more like a toy and toy-like figures than human beings on the most daring and far-reaching expedition thus far undertaken.

Nixon Telephones Congratulations

During one break in the astronauts' work, President Nixon congratulated them from the White House in what, he said, "certainly has to be the most historic telephone call ever made."

"Because of what you have done," the President told the astronauts, "the heavens have become a part of man's world. And as you talk to us from the Sea of Tranquility it requires us to redouble our efforts to bring peace and tranquility to earth.

"For one priceless moment in the whole history of man all the people on this earth are truly one—one in their pride in what you have done and one in our prayers that you will return safely to earth."

Mr. Armstrong replied:

"Thank you Mr. President. It's a great honor and privilege for us to be here representing not only the United States but men of peace of all nations, men with interests and a curiosity and men with a vision for the future."

Mr. Armstrong and Colonel Aldrin returned to their landing craft and closed the hatch at 1:12 A.M., 2 hours 21 minutes after opening the hatch on the moon. While the third member of the crew, Lieut. Col. Michael Collins of the Air Force, kept his orbital vigil overhead in the command ship, the two moon explorers settled down to sleep.

Outside their vehicle the astronauts had found a bleak

Continued on Pages 2, Col. 1

Today's 4-Part Issue of The Times

This morning's issue of The New York Times is divided into four parts. The first part is devoted to news of Apollo 11. and includes Editorials and letters to the Editor (Page 16). Poems on the landing on the moon appear on Page 17.

General news begins on the first page of the second part. The News Summary and Index is on the first page of the third part, which includes sports news, obituaries (Page 51) and transportation news and weather reports (Pages 50 and 52).

Financial and business news begins on the first page of the fourth part.

Following is the News Index for today's issue:

Aldrin descending the steps of the lunar module ladder to the moon's surface.

Man's first footprints on the moon.

The passive seismic experiments package was left to record moon quakes.

Armstrong and the landing craft are reflected in the visor of Aldrin's helmet, as he walks on the moon.

REACTIONS TO MAN'S LANDING ON THE MOON

United Press International

Charles Lindbergh

I feel the development of space should continue. It is of tremendous importance. Undoubtedly things will evolve from it what we don't now foresee, as has always been the case with exploration in the past.

There is, though, a question of how rapidly this should go forward in relation to costs. But I cannot comment on that without making a far more detailed study than I have.

Along with this development of space, which is really a flowering of civilization toward the stars, you might say, we must protect the surface of the earth. That's even more important. Our environment on the surface is where man lives.

If we do that, I think there's almost no limit to the development of space that can be carried on—provided, of course, we protect our human roots in the surface of the earth. We cannot cut off those roots. If we do, none of the flowering, none of the developments we carry on, are going to be of importance.

I think this can be done. I feel sure it can be done; but it must be done in a balanced way.

Dalai Lama

The moon, which is a favorite of the poets and portrayed by the Buddhists as representing the esthetic qualities of peace, serenity and beauty, is now being conquered by man's ever expanding knowledge of science and technology. What was a mere conceptional imagination is today a concrete reality.

The American landing on the moon symbolizes the very acme of scientific achievement. It is indeed a phenomenal feat of far-reaching consequences for the world of science. We Buddhists have always held that firm conviction that there exists life and civilization on other planets in the many systems of the universe, and some of them are so highly developed that they are superior to our own. The perfection of scientific knowledge has enabled man to launch unmanned space-ships toward other planets.

A beginning has been made in space travel. We can now visualize earth people journeying to far-away planets, and opening up communications and relation with beings out in space. Man's limited knowledge will acquire a new dimension of infinite scope, development and dynamism. In this, the high degree of civilization developed in other planetary bodies will be of colossal help.

According to our ancient Buddhist texts, a thousand million solar systems make up a galaxy. . . . A thousand million of such galaxies form a supergalaxy. . . . A thousand million supergalaxies is collectively known as supergalaxy Number One. Again, a thousand million supergalaxy Number Ones form a Supergalaxy Number Two. A thousand million supergalaxy Number Twos make up a supergalaxy Number Three, and of these, it is stated in the texts that there are a countless number in the universe.

The moon landing will, no doubt, be an epoch-making event—a phenomena of awe, unrestrained excitement and sensation. But, the most wondrous event would be if man could relinquish all the stains and defilements of the untamed mind and progress toward achieving the real mental peace and satisfaction when he reaches the moon.

Yes: 'Highest Priority . . .'

R. Buckminster Fuller

Architect and Inventor

Pablo Picasso

It means nothing to me. I have no opinion about it, and I don't care.

No: 'A Symbolic Act of War . . .'

Lewis Mumford

Historian and Urbanologist

Vladimir Nabokov

Poet and Novelist

Treading the soil of the moon, palpating its pebbles, tasting the panic and splendor of the event, feeling in the pit of one's stomach the separation from terra . . . these form the most romantic sensation an explorer has ever known . . . . this is the only thing I can say about the matter . . . . The utilitarian results do not interest me.

Glenn Seaborg

Chairman, Atomic Energy Commission

Even as a scientist who has spent a good deal of his life involved in large-scale technological projects, I find the moon landing an amazing scientific and engineering feat. It personally reinforces my feeling about the great power and potential of science and technology and my belief that through cooperation and concerted efforts man is capable of solving almost any problem, of meeting almost any challenge. I hope the moon landing will have such an uplifting effect on people all over the world and help unite us toward meeting some of our goals here on earth.

Jacques Lipchitz

Sculptor

For me, of course, it is not only an American achievement but a human achievement. Extraordinary. It's something spiritual.

I'm an optimist. I think that humanity will be different after this. I'm happy to live in these times and to witness them. For me it is like humanity stepping out of the womb of nature.

In our art, especially the cubists, we have been announcing this time when men will mature and start a new life. For me it is only beginning.

For me it is something overwhelming. I'm tempted to accord to this event tremendous results. I can't foresee what kind of results, but it will be a kind of mutation of humanity.

Arthur Koestler

Novelist and Journalist

Coincident with cosmic euphoria, the world is in the grip of a cosmic anxiety. Both derive from the same source: the awareness of unprecedented power operating in an unprecedented spiritual vacuum. Prometheus is reaching out for the stars with an empty grin on his face.

Patriarch Athenagoras

Leader of Greek Orthodox Church

The journey of man from the earth to the moon gives to history of mankind a new dimension, a cosmic dimension.

With man's landing on the moon an altogether new era of history is opening, or rather a new kind, the history of the universe, a history of the whole of creation. Therefore it is not a question of an important historical event in the value of evolution in the earthly conception and perspective of history, it is a question of the moving of history to positions and perspectives of such results, which cannot, at this moment be foreseen, results on the subsequent chronicle of the earth as well as the history of other worlds, which only now is beginning for man on this earth.

Philosophically the first reaction that comes with the presence of man on the moon is that man is organically tied not only with one planet but with the whole universe.

Now that man has achieved a cosmic biome we do not know which cosmotheories nor biotheories, to which new ideas, new penetrations and a new scale of values, unimagined at present, this new biome will lead man. The very fact that man is freed from his geocentricism and has become an interplanetary traveler is a great revolution in the world of ideas.

The landing of man on the moon especially opens a new epoch to theology and impels us to a new penetration into theology of the whole creation.

This marvelous enterprise of man as a start of his communication with other regions of the universe means at the same time the beginning of a new epoch in the fields of culture and science and in general in the articulation of the life of tomorrow of the human race on this planet.

Perhaps we are on the eve of the vision of a new wisdom, of a new understanding, of the revelation of God to his creations.

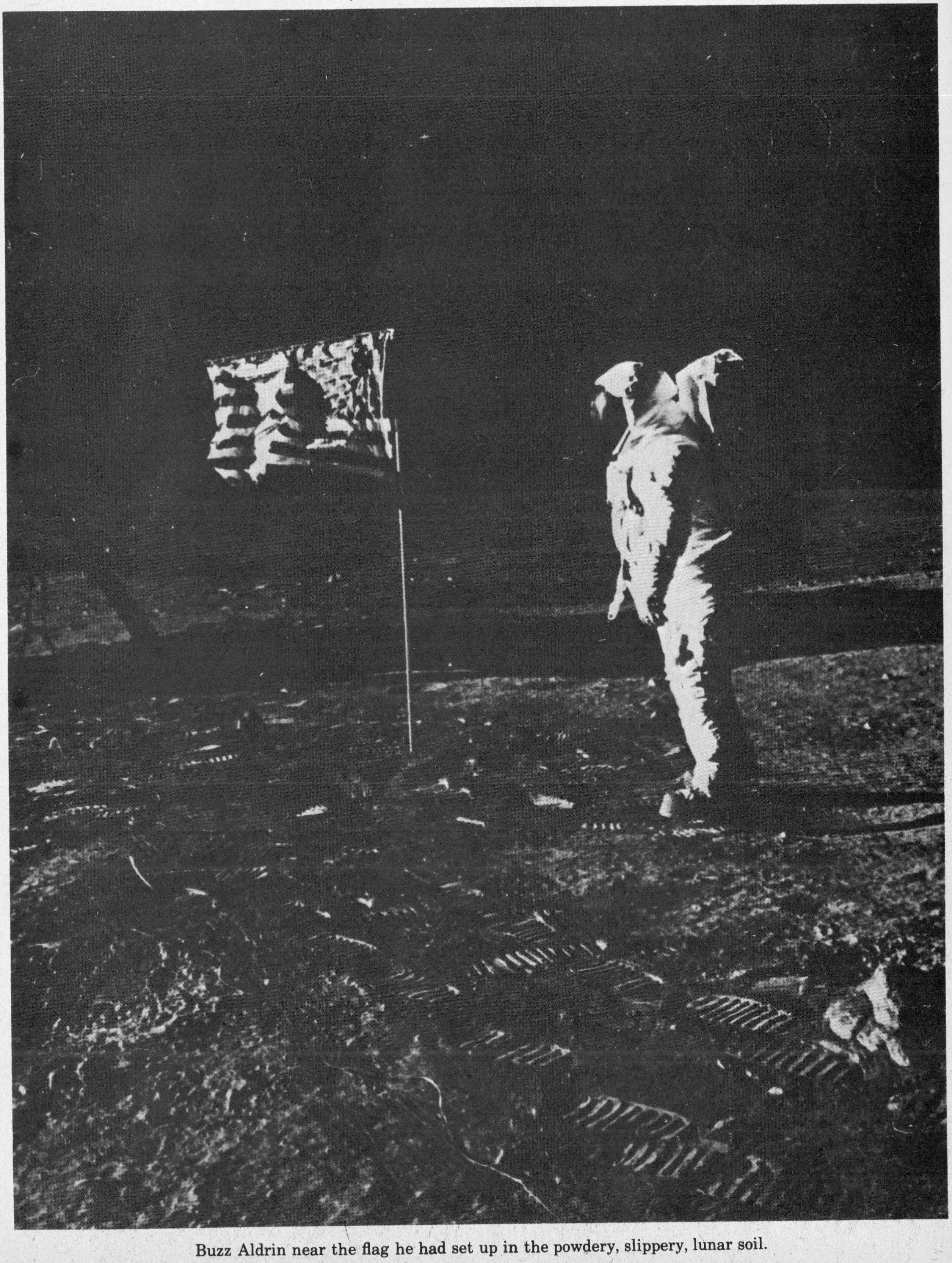

Buzz Aldrin near the flag he had set up in the powdery, slippery, lunar soil.

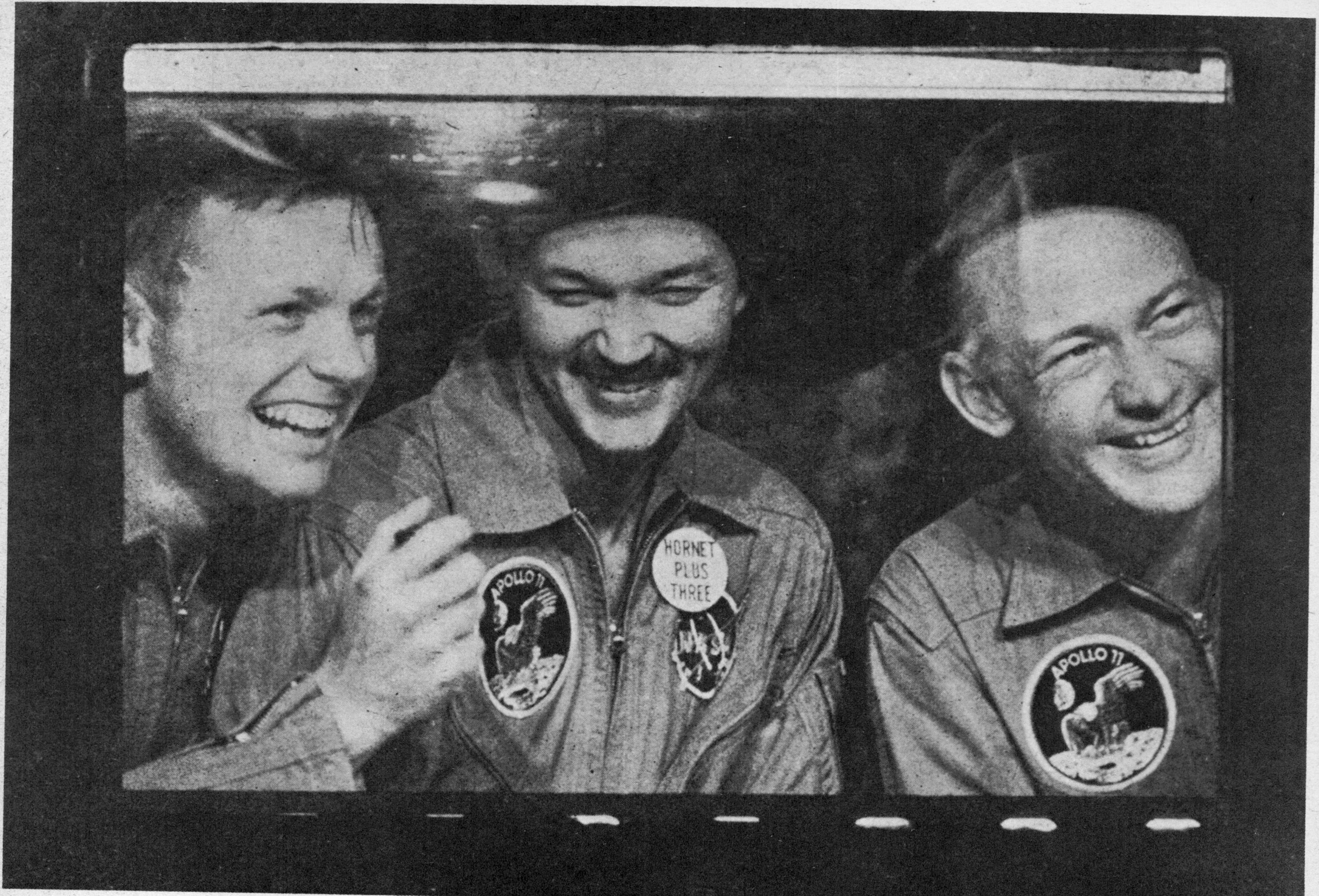

Isolated in a special van to prevent the spread of "moon germs" Armstrong, Collins and Aldrin greet an ecstatic public.

"All the News
That's Fit to Print"

The New York Times

LATE CITY EDITION

Weather: Partly cloudy, chance of rain today. Fair and warm tomorrow. Temp. range; today 77-62; Thurs. 73-63. Temp.-Hum. Index yesterday 70. Complete U.S. report on Page 93.

VOL. CXVIII ... No. 40,725

NEW YORK, FRIDAY, JULY 25, 1969

10 CENTS

ASTRONAUTS BACK FROM MOON; BEGIN 18 DAYS IN QUARANTINE

United Press International

ARRIVE ON RECOVERY SHIP: Back from the moon and enclosed in isolation garments, the Apollo 11 astronauts leave copter that picked them from the Pacific. Dr. Donald Stullken of NASA directs them to quarantine trailer.

Associated Press

TALK WITH PRESIDENT: Neil A. Armstrong, left, Lieut. Col. Michael Collins, with new mustache, and Col. Edwin E. Aldrin Jr., in quarantine, talk with Mr. Nixon. Button means Hornet complement is "plus three" astronauts.

NEW SUEZ BATTLE RAGES FOR 8 HOURS

Both Israel and Egypt Say Other Side Lost 7 Jets—Fighting Worst Since '67

By JAMES FERON

Special to The New York Times

JERUSALEM, July 24 — Israeli and Egyptian forces battled for eight hours with aircraft and artillery along the Suez Canal today. The fighting was the heaviest since the six-day war of June, 1967.

Israeli officials said that their air and ground forces had shot down seven Egyptian fighter planes—six MIG's and a Sukhoi — and had damaged two others.

[In Cairo, the military command said that the Egyptians had downed seven Israeli planes. Cairo denied that it had lost six MIG's but said that a Sukhoi-7 had been lost.]

The Israelis said their planes had also damaged or destroyed four Soviet-made rocket installations, a radar station, antiaircraft and artillery positions and military posts.

Israeli losses were reported to be one soldier killed and five wounded by Egyptian aircraft and three soldiers wounded by artillery fire. All Israeli planes were reported to have returned safely.

The battle—the third in a week—came a day after President Gamal Abdel Nasser told the Egyptian people on the 17th anniversary of the revolution that brought him to power that a "stage of liberation" was beginning in the fight against Israel.

Foreign Minister Abba Eban,

Continued on Page 3, Column 2

Senate's Democrats Adopt Plan to Force Tax Reform

By EILEEN SHANAHAN

Special to The New York Times

WASHINGTON, July 24 — Senate Democrats agreed today on a new legislative strategy in an effort to force a vote on tax reform before considering the Administration's bill extending the 10 per cent tax surcharge.

The strategy for forcing action on tax reform was worked out by members of the Senate Democratic Policy Committee and Democratic members of the Senate Finance Committee. They agreed that they would support extension of the 10 per cent surtax only through the end of November.

At the other end of the Capitol, the House Ways and Means committee neared the end of its work on what has turned into a multibillion-dollar tax reform bill.

It tentatively agreed to eliminate much of the preferential tax treatment accorded the real estate industry and tentatively adopted another proposal that would make it impossible for a person to escape all Federal income tax by combining large deductions with large amounts of tax-free incomes.

The real estate provisions were specifically tailored to preserve most of the present tax incentives for the construction of apartment houses while eliminating or reducing the incentives for commercial and industrial construction.

The new strategy of the Senate Democrats would give the Finance Committee time to work on a major reform bill, which its Democratic members have promised to complete by Oct. 31.

Thus, there would be a full month for Senate debate on the reform package, and for voting on its various elements, before the surtax again expired.

And the vote on extension of

Continued on Page 14, Column 1

KENNEDY TO ENTER COURT PLEA TODAY

He Will Answer Charge of Leaving Scene of Crash in Which Woman Died

Special to The New York Times

EDGARTOWN, Mass., July 24 —Senator Edward M. Kennedy decided today to appear in Dukes County Court tomorrow morning to answer charges that he left the scene of an accident last Saturday in which a 28-year-old Washington secretary, Mary Jo Kopechne, was killed.

The announcement was made tonight by one of Senator Kennedy's three attorneys, Robert Clark Jr. of Brockton, Mass.

A probable-cause hearing had been set for Monday to determine whether the complaint would be issued.

Having waived the right to a hearing, Mr. Kennedy will appear in court, where under state law a complaint could be issued.

Plea to Be Asked

Acting for the court, the clerk will then ask Mr. Kennedy whether he pleads guilty or not guilty. If he pleads not guilty, he may ask for a continuance to prepare his defense. The judge has the right to set the time limit, usually a week or two weeks at the convenience of himself and both sides.

But Mr. Kennedy may also assert that he is ready to stand trial immediately. If the prosecution is ready, the trial will begin with the police presenting their case.

The judge, if he finds Mr. Kennedy guilty, may impose sentence—two months to two

Continued on Page 44, Column 1

ALARM PRECEDED LANDING ON MOON

Overworked Computer Sent Signal, Raising Prospect of Aborting Mission

By RICHARD WITKIN

Apollo officials were seriously worried during the final minutes of the moon landing approach that an overworked computer aboard the lunar module Eagle might compel it to abort the attempt and rocket back into orbit.

This was disclosed yesterday by Christopher C. Kraft Jr., director of flight operations at the National Aeronautics and Space Administration's Manned Spacecraft Center in Houston.

"The computer was right on the ragged edge," Mr. Kraft related. "It was sending alarms that it was working right up to 100 per cent capacity."

Asked if the men in the Mission Control room in Houston were worried that the landing approach would have to be broken off, he said: "You're damn right we were."

Mr. Kraft said that the difficulty arose about eight minutes before Eagle landed and

Continued on Page 30, Column 4

Prayers and Champagne Hail Return of Apollo 11

By LAWRENCE VAN GELDER

With pealing bells, popping champagne corks, cheers, prayers and firecrackers, a jubilant nation celebrated the safe return yesterday af the Apollo 11 astronauts.

Throughout midtown Manhattan and elsewhere across the country, exuberant crowds pressed around store window television sets at midday for a glimpse of the mid-Pacific splashdown of the spacecraft carrying the first men to walk on the moon.

In homes and offices millions suspended activities once again to listen to and watch the final historic adventure that had gripped and held the attention of the world for eight days.

From the lips of the spectators flowed adjectives of awe.

"It's fantastic," said Mrs. Matthew Falco of New York, as she stood with her son near a model of the lunar module at the Time-Life Building in Manhattan.

"I think it's fabulous, just fabulous," said 17-year-old Kathy Hyde, a student, in San Francisco.

"Wonderful," exclaimed Paul Jacobs, a student at Columbia University.

In Birmingham, Ala., where city employes gathered for prayers of thanksgiving for the return of Neil A. Armstrong, Col. Edwin E. Aldrin Jr. and Lieut Col. Michael Collins, Mayor George Seibels asked that church bells, automobile horns and whistles be sounded to convey "the ecstasy that I know abounds within us all."

Firecrackers hurled from high buildings exploded in the air over San Francisco, and from the Presidio came the thumping of a 50-gun salute.

In New York, cheers erupted on the floors of the New York and American Stock Exchanges and on tape that normally carries the latest fluctuations in prices flashed a new message across the Big Board: "Astronauts Armstrong, Aldrin and Collins, so proudly we hail you."

Some individuals remained indifferent and contemptuous of the space exploit. In lower Manhattan, Pat Jones, a Government worker, termed the Apollo 11 mission "totally unrelated to problems in the United States," adding, "It doesn't do anything to help the poor."

But on Fifth Avenue, church bells rang, and in St. Patrick's

Continued on Page 31, Column 2

NIXON SEES CREW

Splashdown in Pacific Is 11 Miles From Carrier Hornet

The text of remarks by Nixon and astronauts, Page 29.

By JAMES T. WOOTEN

Special to The New York Times

ABOARD U.S.S. HORNET, in the Pacific, July 24—The historic mission of Apollo 11 ended today when America's lunar explorers landed safely in the Pacific Ocean, 11 miles from the carrier Hornet, the prime recovery ship.

Neil A. Armstrong, Col. Edwin E. Aldrin Jr. and Lieut. Col. Michael Collins completed their journey from the earth to the moon and back at 12:50 P.M. Eastern daylight time when their charred and peeling spacecraft splashed into the warm, rolling waters 250 miles south of Johnston Island and 950 miles southwest of Hawaii.

By 2 P.M., the astronauts were in a quarantine trailer and had been pronounced in good condition by a physician. And by 2:55 P.M., they were in animated conversation — through glass — with President Nixon.

Spacecraft on Hornet

In another hour, the spacecraft in which Colonel Collins had circled the moon alone, while Mr. Armstrong and Colonel Aldrin were taking man's first steps on the moon Sunday, was hauled aboard the carrier.

"This is the greatest week in the history of the world since the Creation," the President said to the smiling astronauts. They were crowded behind a small window of the Mobile Quarantine Facility, the small, narrow trailer in which they will live until they arrive at the Lunar Receiving Laboratory in Houston early Sunday. Their 18-day quarantine period —21 days from lunar blast-off —will end Aug. 11.

"As I travel into Asia and Europe," Mr. Nixon said, "I'm going to find that as a result of what you've done, the world is closer together. We can reach for the stars as you have."

The President is on an

Continued on Page 28, Column 1

McCarthy Rejects Any Bid for Senate

By WARREN WEAVER Jr.

Special to The New York Times

WASHINGTON, July 24—Senator Eugene J. McCarthy said today that he would not seek re-election to the Senate from Minnesota next year on any ticket or run for the Senate from any other state.

The Senator's statement appeared to leave the way open for him to run for President on an independent ticket in 1972. He said six months ago that he would not seek the Democratic nomination in 1972.

The move also cleared the way for Hubert H. Humphrey, the defeated 1968 Presidential candidate, to return to elective politics by running for the

Continued on Page 26, Column 3

10 NATIONS REACH 'PAPER GOLD' PACT

Compromise Opens Way for a Monetary Reserve Unit

By CLYDE H. FARNSWORTH

Special to The New York Times

PARIS, July 24 — The 10 richest nations reached a monetary compromise today, virtually assuring implementation by September of the first internationally managed reserve unit to share with gold and the dollar the job of lubricating world trade.

After more than five years of intricate and at times hotly contentious negotiations, the last major obstacles have been cleared with a consensus reached by the Group of Ten industrial powers on the amount for distribution of the new Special Drawing Rights, or "paper gold."

The Group of Ten is composed of Belgium, Britain, Canada, France, West Germany, Italy, Japan, Sweden, the Netherlands and the United States. Also, Switzerland is a partial participant.

The officials at today's meeting at the Paris Chateau de la Muette declined to reveal the precise figures. They explained that ministers had yet to approve.

"No, I don't think there will be any changes," said Paul A. Volcker, Under Secretary of the Treasury for International

Continued on Page 79, Column 4

HANOI AIDE SAYS U.S. INVADED LAOS

Troops in Cambodia, Too, Thuy Charges in Paris

By DREW MIDDLETON

Special to The New York Times

PARIS, July 24—North Vietnam charged today that the United States had invaded Laos with 12,000 troops and had started a separate war against that kingdom.

"We demand that the United States cease its aggression, withdraw its troops from Laos and cease the bombing of that country," Xuan Thuy, head of the North Vietnamese delegation, said at the 27th plenary session of the Vietnam peace talks.

Mr. Thuy and his delegation's spokesman, Nguyen Thanh Le, also accused the United States of sending troops into Cambodia.

Some diplomats suspected that the forceful introduction of Laos and Cambodia into talks previously concerned only with South Vietnam signaled a North Vietnamese desire to have the future for these countries included in discussions at the present conference.

Other diplomats thought that the charges against the United States were preparation for further North Vietnamese military activity to "protect" Laos against the alleged American invasion.

Henry Cabot Lodge, the chief

Continued on Page 6, Column 4

Board Vetoes Route Of 2d Ave. Subway

By WILL LISSNER

The Board of Estimate last night rejected a Metropolitan Transportation Authority route for a 3.6-mile stretch of the proposed Second Avenue subway that would have bypassed Manhattan's Lower East Side bulge. The vote was 18 to 4.

The board indicated at the end of a seven-hour meeting, after hearing three hours of public testimony, that the only route it would approve was a compromise plan. It would bend the line into the Lower East Side slums along Avenue A.

Borough President Percy E. Sutton, an advocate of a four-track subway that would run along Avenue C, said he had

Continued on Page 40, Column 1

United Press International

MISSION CONTROLLERS CHEER: Men at space center in Houston arose from their consoles and waved flags when the astronauts' helicopter touched deck of the Hornet.

NEWS INDEX

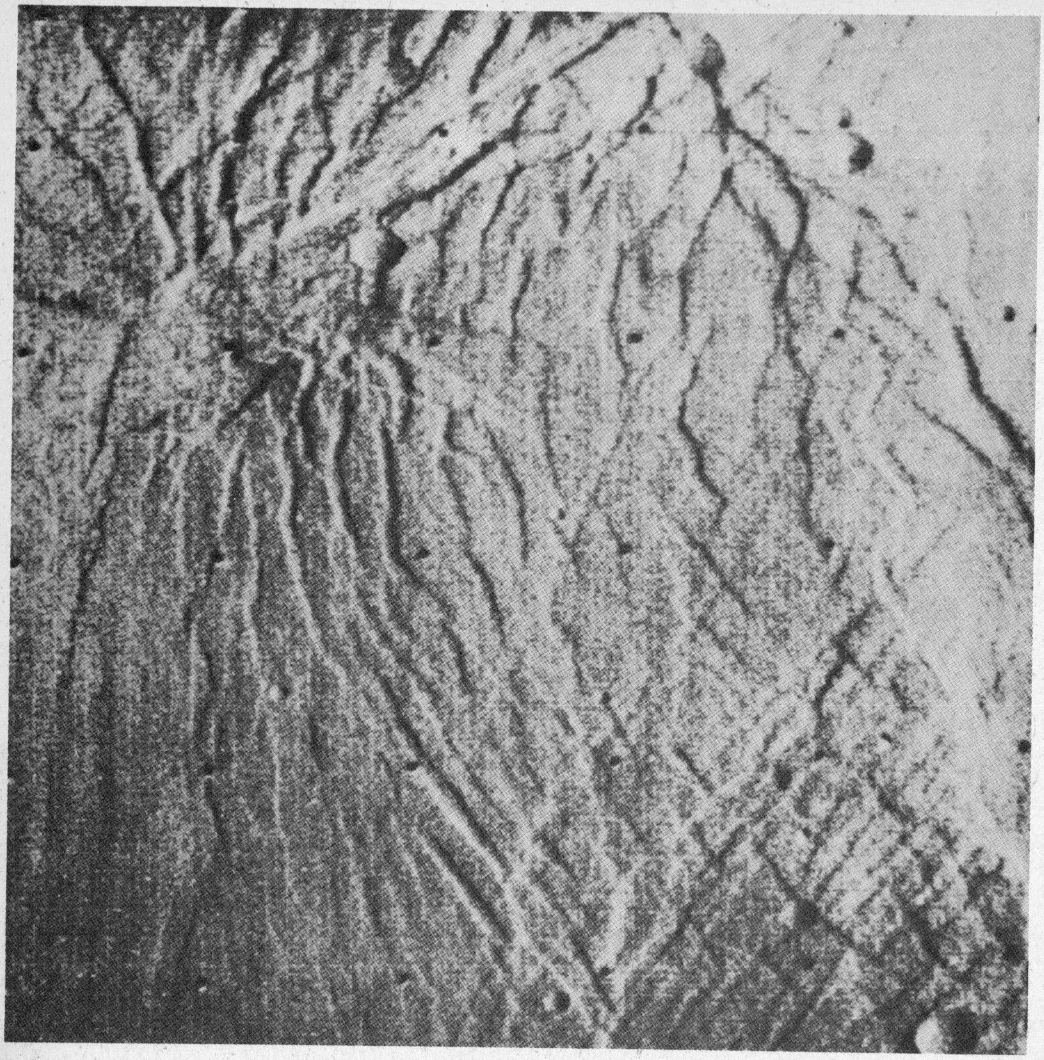

The plateau called Phoenicis Lacus, which stands about 3½ miles above the mean elevation of Mars.

NASA

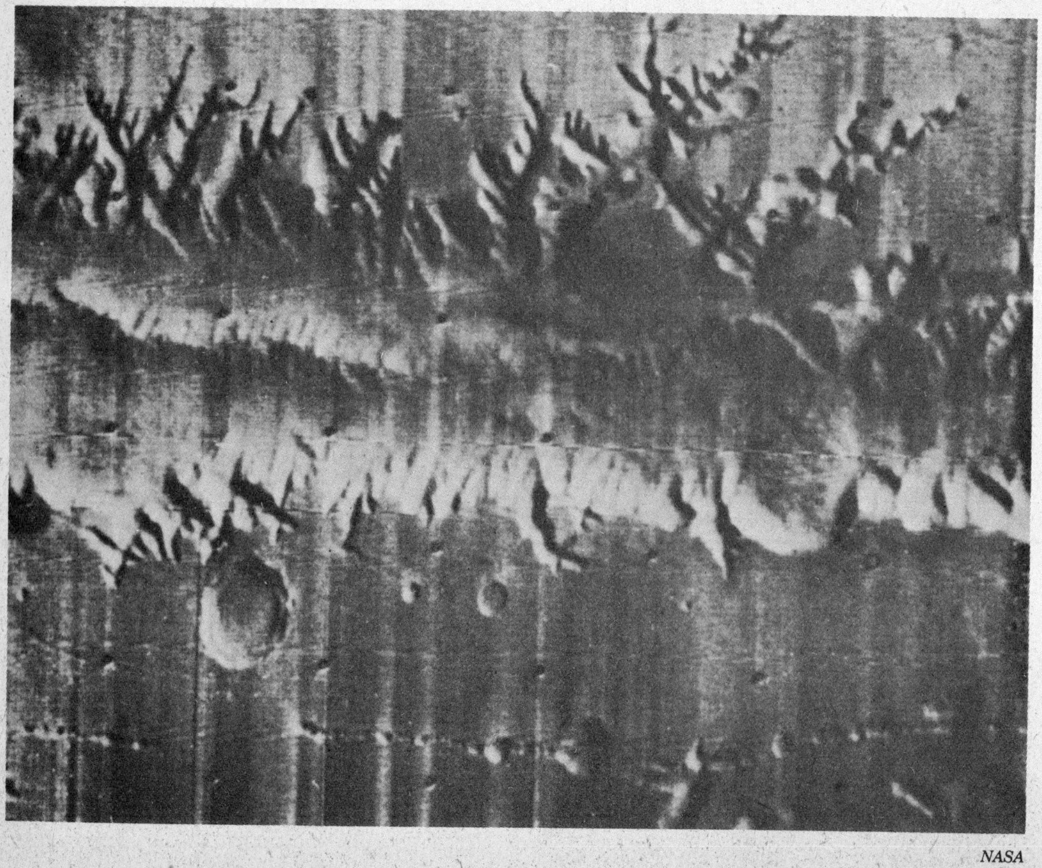

A vast chasm with an area of 235 x 300 miles, stretches across Mars. Recent findings from the Mariner missions have shown that gases that could support life, exist on Mars.

NASA

"All the News That's Fit to Print"

The New York Times

LATE CITY EDITION

Weather: Partly sunny, hot today; fair tonight. Fair, warm tomorrow. Temp. range: today 92-72; Thurs. 89-70. Temp.-Hum. Index yesterday 79. Complete U.S. report on Page 66.

VOL. CXVIII . . No. 40,739 | NEW YORK, FRIDAY, AUGUST 8, 1969 | 10 CENTS

NIXON SAID TO PLAN NEW LINKS IN EAST DESPITE RUSSIANS

He Is Reported to Have Told Kiesinger U.S. Will Move Despite Brezhnev View

BERLIN ALSO DISCUSSED

Proposals for Talks Between East and West Germany Could Test Moscow

By RICHARD HALLORAN

Special to The New York Times

WASHINGTON, Aug. 7—President Nixon was reported to have told Chancellor Kurt Georg Kiesinger of West Germany today that Soviet opposition would not inhibit the United States from dealing directly with the Communist nations of Eastern Europe.

According to informed West German sources, the President made the assertion during a private meeting here in a discussion of Mr. Nixon's visit to Rumania last weekend.

Mr. Nixon and Mr. Kiesinger were also reported to have discussed proposals to Moscow by the Western allies that East and West Germany hold direct discussions on Berlin. The two men were said to have agreed that the proposal could test the Soviet Union's professed desire to ease tensions in Europe.

Brezhnev Doctrine Scorned

In discussing Eastern Europe, Mr. Nixon is said to have told Mr. Kiesinger that the United States did not recognize the Brezhnev doctrine.

That doctrine, enunciated by Leonid I. Brezhnev, General Secretary of the Soviet Communist party, to justify the Russian-led military intervention in Czechoslovakia last summer, holds that the Soviet Union has the right to intervene to protect Eastern European nations from what it considers subversive outside influences.

There were echoes of the doctrine today in Bucharest, when a Soviet delegate to the Rumanian party congress, Konstantin F. Katushev, denounced "perfidious" bridge-building in Eastern Europe, a clear allusion to United States policy. Mr. Katushev, a Soviet party secretary, emphasized Communist cohesion.

State Department officials

Continued on Page 4, Column 4

Associated Press

GREET BONN LEADER: President and Mrs. Nixon welcome Chancellor Kurt Georg Kiesinger to White House dinner. At the rear is Emil Mosbacher, the Chief of Protocol.

Russian, in Rumania, Hints Displeasure at Nixon Visit

By TAD SZULC

Special to The New York Times

BUCHAREST, Aug. 7—A Soviet representative told Rumania's Communist party today that the "perfidious tactic" of bridge-building was "undermining the cohesion of socialist countries" in Eastern Europe. The statement was understood here as a clear criticism of President Nixon's visit to Rumania last weekend.

The statement was made by Konstantin F. Katushev, the chief Soviet delegate to the 10th Congress of the Rumanian Communist party.

Later Mr. Katushev walked out of the hall when a message of greeting from the Chinese Communist party was being read.

The Chinese party sent no delegates to Bucharest and its message consisted mainly of salutations to the Rumanians. It did, however, wish the Rumanian party success in "the defense of national independence in socialism," a remark that could be construed as an allusion to the Soviet pressures on Rumania.

At the moment the announcement was made that the Chinese message would be read, Mr. Katushev, a stocky

Continued on Page 3, Column 1

VIETCONG IMPLY COALITION MOVE

Aide in Paris Reports Talks Have Begun on Forming Regime in Vietnam

By HENRY GINIGER

Special to The New York Times

PARIS, Aug. 7 — The provisional revolutionary government formed by the Vietcong indicated today that it had begun discussions with other groups inside and outside South Vietnam to form a coalition regime.

The indication came after another day of fruitless discussion here among the parties to the Vietnam conflict.

Duong Dinh Thao, the spokesman for the provisional government's delegation, was asked during a news briefing whether there had been contacts with exile groups in Paris.

His answer was that "in South Vietnam as in other places we have begun such consultations to discuss together the questions of re-establishing peace and ending the war of American aggression." He said the goals were peace, independence and neutrality.

No Progress at Talks

Both sides in the peace talks agreed there had been no progress in the 29th plenary session. If anything there was a further hardening of positions.

Appealing for consideration of allied peace proposals, Henry Cabot Lodge, the chief United States delegate, declared in somewhat blunter fashion than in the past that "we remain ready for serious negotiation."

"Until your side shows a similar readiness," he said to the Communist delegates, "we can expect no progress. We have done all that we can do by ourselves to bring a negotiated peace to Vietnam. Now it is time for you to respond."

In answer Mrs. Nguyen Thi Binh, Foreign Minister of the revolutionary government, declared that the plan her delegation had put forward was the only correct one, and Communist spokesmen said the allied peace plan had been categorically rejected because it was absurd.

The essential features of the Communist plan are the unilateral withdrawal of United

Continued on Page 10, Column 3

CON ED PLANNING TO SEEK 15% RISE

Rate Plea Due Before Fall—Inquiry Opens Today

By GENE SMITH

The Consolidated Edison Company is planning to apply for an increase of about 15 per cent in electric rates sometime before Sept. 1.

The company, which has three million customers in the metropolitan area, is expected to argue in its petition to the State Public Service Commission that it needs the higher rates to offset increased costs of labor, fuels, bank credit and taxes.

Just when Con Edison will file its request may depend on the outcome of public hearings that begin before the P.S.C. at 10 A.M. today at 139 Church Street.

A Substantial Increase

The hearings will investigate the utility's reduced power reserves and its request last Monday and on July 18 that customers limit their electric consumption to avert a possible blackout.

The 15 per cent rate increase that Con Edison is expected to ask for is substantially above its last rate increase of 4 per cent on the average. The latter went into effect on Nov. 25, 1966.

The 4 per cent increase—it was considerably higher for some groups of customers—touched off a public controversy when the P.S.C. approved it and then announced it would hold public hearings. After

Continued on Page 20, Column 2

U.S. TO DROP CASE AGAINST DR. SPOCK

Ferber Appeal Also Barred—Time Sought on Others

By ROBERT M. SMITH

Special to The New York Times

WASHINGTON, Aug. 7—The Justice Department said today that it did not intend to ask the Supreme Court to reverse the acquittal of Dr. Benjamin Spock and Michael Ferber on charges of conspiring to counsel evasion of the draft.

But Erwin N. Griswold, the Solicitor General, filed an application with the Supreme Court for an extension of the time the department had to appeal the cases of two other defendants in the conspiracy case, the Rev. William Sloane Coffin Jr. and Mitchell Goodman. The current deadline for an appeal in the cases is next Monday.

On July 11, the United States Court of Appeals for the First Circuit reversed the convictions of all four men. They had been found guilty of conspiracy in 1968. However, the Appeals Court in Boston ordered the cases of Mr. Coffin and Mr. Goodman returned to the Federal District Court for another trial because of an "error" in the original trial.

In the application, Mr. Griswold sought an extension through Sept. 9 of the time the Justice Department had to appeal in the cases of Mr. Coffin, who is chaplain of Yale University, and Mr. Goodman, who is a teacher from New York City.

He gave these reasons for the

Continued on Page 5, Column 1

PAN AM IS STRUCK IN SPITE OF TALKS

Ground Personnel Walk Out as Mediators Postpone Deadline Hour by Hour

Ground personnel of Pan American World Airways began walking off their jobs in at least five cities early today, despite continuing negotiations between the company and the teamsters union in Washington.

A union spokesman said at 3 A.M. that about 1,000 employes had left their posts "without authorization" at Pan Am facilities in New York, Miami, Honolulu, San Francisco and Los Angeles.

The wildcat walkouts began about 2 A.M. just as the negotiators in Washington were announcing the third in a series of strike-deadline extensions. The deadline, originally set for midnight, was extended at the behest of Labor Secretary George P. Shultz.

Clerks Leave Desks

"We have people walking off the job all over the country," the union spokesman, Nicholas Giraffa, said here. "With this hour-to-hour negotiating, we just can't control the membership. We're sending out representatives to get them back to work, but we're having a hell of a time controlling it."

At 2:30 A.M., reservation clerks at the Pan Am Building in Manhattan and at Kennedy International Airport began leaving their desks.

At 3:25 A.M., negotiations were still in session, but there was no word on progress.

The union, representing 8,000

Continued on Page 66, Column 4

L.I.R.R. TO BE BEST IN U.S. IN 2 MONTHS, ROCKEFELLER SAYS

He Tells Riders Line Has Solved 2 Major Problems—Nickerson Skeptical

By BILL KOVACH

Special to The New York Times

GARDEN CITY, L. I., Aug. 7—Governor Rockefeller promised Long Island Railroad commuters today that within two months the line would provide the best service in the country.

Speaking to 300 people at a breakfast meeting of the Long Island Association of Commerce and Industry in the Garden City Hotel, the Governor said his promise of a brighter day for commuters was not a prediction "but an announcement."

"Within the next two months," the Governor repeated, "the Long Island Rail Road service is going to be the finest in the country."

Mr. Rockefeller flew to Nassau by helicopter at the request of local Republicans, who fear commuters' anger will be translated into Democratic votes in the November elections. With him was Dr. William J. Ronan, chairman of the Metropolitan Transportation Authority, which runs the embattled railroad.

Problems Held Solved

The Governor said he based his promise on his belief "that we have the major problems plaguing the railroad solved."

These, he said, were twofold:

1. The new passenger cars purchased by the railroad had come through defective and were not serviceable as quickly as had been hoped.
2. The maintenance of older cars had been much delayed and too many older cars were tied up in repair yards.

Now, the Governor said, the problems with new equipment have been worked out and "we expect to start receiving six or seven serviceable new cars each week" toward the goal of 620 new passenger cars of modern design.

And, he continued, a recent agreement with unions will allow quicker, more efficient maintenance and service of the other railroad equipment.

Political Aspect Minimized

The Governor tended to play down the political implications of his trip to the suburbs, but he conceded that his own chances for re-election could be affected by the operation of the commuter line.

At noon, following the breakfast, Mr. Rockefeller held a private meeting with Nassau Republican leaders in the Hempstead Town Hall. After that meeting, State Senator Edward A. Speno announced plans to have the transportation authority appoint an advisory group of 15 commuters from Nassau and Suffolk.

Nassau County Executive

Continued on Page 39, Column 1

The New York Times (by Robert Walker)

PROMISES BETTER DAYS FOR L.I.R.R.: Governor Rockefeller addressing breakfast meeting of Long Island Association of Commerce and Industry in Garden City, L.I., yesterday.

SENATE, 47 TO 46, ASKS FOR REVIEW OF WEAPON COSTS

Pentagon's Critics Win Vote on Audit—New Attempt to Limit ABM Is Defeated

By WARREN WEAVER Jr.

Special to The New York Times

WASHINGTON, Aug. 7—The Senate voted today to make major Pentagon contracts for weapons subject to the independent scrutiny of the General Accounting Office, the auditing arm of Congress.

The action was taken by a one-vote margin over the strenuous opposition of the chairman of the Senate Armed Services Committee, John C. Stennis, Democrat of Mississippi. He made fruitless parliamentary moves to block and then to reverse the vote of 47 to 46.

Approval of the amendment to the $20-billion authorization bill on military procurement represented the first floor victory for the bipartisan critics of unquestioned military spending who yesterday lost their fight to block the Safeguard missile defense system. The amendment was sponsored by Senator Richard S. Schweiker, Republican of Pennsylvania.

Aided by Economizers

In the vote today, the anti-Pentagon coalition was materially aided by several Senators who were principally voting their desire for economy, such as Harry F. Byrd, Democrat of Virginia, and John J. Williams, Republican of Delaware.

To amount to more than a symbolic assertion of Congressional control over the Pentagon, the Schweiker amendment will have to be approved also by the House, but there the Armed Services Committee, which would oppose such an amendment, is now generally more influential with the membership. As a result, the prospects for passage there are not regarded as promising.

Presented as Compromise

Earlier today, the Senate defeated, 70 to 27, a proposal by Senator Thomas J. McIntyre, Democrat of New Hampshire, to prohibit the Administration from installing weapons in its first two test stations in the Safeguard system but to permit the sites to be otherwise equipped.

Senator McIntyre contended that this plan would be a compromise between President Nixon's request that missiles be installed at the bases in Montana and North Dakota and the Safeguard critics' campaign to restrict the program to research and development for a year.

However, most opponents of Safeguard in the Senate did not regard the McIntyre plan as basically different from what Mr. Nixon had proposed, and they voted against it.

The scene during the debate

Continued on Page 12, Column 5

HOUSE APPROVES TAX RELIEF BILL BY VOTE OF 394-30

California Churches Face Business Tax

Special to The New York Times

SACRAMENTO, Calif., Aug. 7—A bill to collect state corporation taxes from churches and religious organizations on income derived from non-church-related businesses won final approval today from the California Legislature.

A similar provision was included in the tax reform measure passed today in Washington by the House of Representatives.

State Assemblymen voted, 70 to 3, to eliminate the present exemption for churches on the 7 per cent state tax levied on net business incomes. Last month the California Senate approved the bill.

Gov. Ronald Reagan at that time declined to give his views on the bill.

Today, however, aides to State Senator Anthony C. Beilenson, who sponsored the bill, were confident that the Governor would sign it.

Mr. Reagan not only gave

Continued on Page 17, Column 1

SENATE MUST ACT

Its Finance Committee Will Open Hearings Early Next Month

By EILEEN SHANAHAN

Special to The New York Times

WASHINGTON, Aug. 7—A tax reform and relief bill that may involve the most extensive rewriting of the tax laws since adoption of the Federal income tax in 1913 was passed by the House of Representatives today.

The vote was 394 to 30. Most of the opponents were representatives of oil-producing areas who disagreed with provisions reducing — though not eliminating — the tax preferences currently accorded the oil industry.

The bill now goes to the Senate, where the Finance Committee will begin hearings within a few days after the end of the Congressional summer recess, Sept. 3.

The Finance Committee was tentatively planning four weeks of hearings and another four weeks of closed-door meetings at which its version of the bill would be written.

Oct. 31 Commitment

The Democratic members of the Finance Committee, including the chairman, Russell B. Long of Louisiana, are committed to report a bill to the Senate by Oct. 31.

Today's debate and vote in the House came as something of an anticlimax after the months of study and dispute about the bill, beginning with hearings last February in the Ways and Means Committee.

Representative Sam M. Gibbons of Florida, one of the Democratic members of Ways and Means, appeared to speak for most House members when he said the bill would "get votes like motherhood."

Mr. Gibbons was referring mainly to the tax relief provisions, which would take effect gradually from now through 1972.

$9-Billion in Relief

In all, the bill provides for $9.2-billion in tax relief by 1972—not counting the tax reductions that would take place on Jan. 1, 1970, and June 30, 1970, as the 10 per cent tax surcharge is dropped, first to 5 per cent and then to zero.

Elimination of the surcharge by next June would bring another $9-billion, approximately, in tax reductions to individuals and corporations.

The tax reforms contained in the bill would raise a total of $5.2-billion in new revenue by 1972 and somewhat more than that figure, because of some lengthy phasing in of reforms, in subsequent years.

For 1970, a year in which the Government believes that some restraint on the economy

Continued on Page 18, Column 1

FOOD-DRUG BOARD FOUND TOO LIMITED

Panel Terms It Ill-Equipped to Protect the Consumer From Faulty Products

By HAROLD M. SCHMECK Jr.

Special to The New York Times

WASHINGTON, Aug. 7—A study panel of the Food and Drug Administration has concluded that the agency is not equipped to protect the American consumer from bad food, bad drugs, bad cosmetics or faulty products.

"The American public's principal consumer protection is provided by the Food and Drug Administration, and we are currently not equipped to cope with the challenge," says the introduction of a 58-page document transmitted by the study group July 14 to Dr. Herbert L. Ley Jr., commissioner of the Food and Drug Administration.

Panel Set Up in May

The document has not been made public officially, but it is labeled "Final Draft."

Dr. Ley set up the panel May 1, assigning to it the task of defining the consumer protection objectives of the agency, identifying shortcomings and suggesting changes.

"The study group believes there is a fairly common view held by consumers that 'they' (the consumer isn't really sure who) are taking care of all potential hazards associated with the products he ingests or uses," the report says.

"This misconception should

Continued on Page 17, Column 1

2 Gases Associated With Life Found on Mars Near Polar Cap

By WALTER SULLIVAN

Special to The New York Times

PASADENA, Calif., Aug. 7—Two gases intimately associated with the origin and existence of life—methane and ammonia—have been detected in the Martian atmosphere.

In announcing this finding from the Mariner 7 flight past Mars early Tuesday, Dr. George C. Pimentel, professor of chemistry at the University of California at Berkeley, said that the discovery did not necessarily mean there is life on Mars.

However, he speculated that it might exist in areas close to the south polar region of that planet, fed by moisture from the polar ice cap. From infrared spectral observations, he believes the south polar area is capped by clouds of dry ice, but that the surface snows, at least around the outer parts of the polar cap, are of water ice.

Clouds of dry ice, which is frozen carbon dioxide, could protect living organisms from devastating ultraviolet rays of sunlight that otherwise impinge on the surface of Mars.

Dr. Pimentel's speculation was based on his finding that the methane and ammonia were detectable only over the south pole region, implying that the sources of the two gases are localized there.

His findings produced a general gasp among scientists and newsmen assembled to hear reports on the preliminary findings of Mariner 7. No one disputed his identification of me-

Continued on Page 13, Column 2

NEWS INDEX

"All the News That's Fit to Print"

The New York Times

LATE CITY EDITION

Weather: Fair, very cold today and tonight. Chance of snow tomorrow. Temp. range: today 24-14; Sunday 33-26. Full U.S. report on Page 30.

VOL. CXVIII... No. 40,777 — © 1969 The New York Times Company. — NEW YORK, MONDAY, SEPTEMBER 15, 1969 — 10 CENTS

LINDSAY BACKERS SEEK 2D TOP LINE ON NOV. 4 BALLOT

Challenge Petitions Filed by Two Socialist Parties to Force Them Off Machines

DATE OF FILING A FACTOR

Five Groups Vying for Three Spots—Mayor's Foes Have Two Top Places Each

By WILLIAM E. FARRELL

Supporters of Mayor Lindsay, with the blessing of his campaign strategists, are attempting to knock the Socialist Labor party and the Socialist Workers party off the Nov. 4 ballot to assure that the Mayor's Independent party will appear in a top-row column of the voting machines.

The attempt has taken the form of challenges to the petitions filed with the Board of Elections by the two Socialist parties, which have virtually no chance of winning a citywide office.

The Mayor's name already appears once on the top row as the Liberal party candidate; his Independent party backers are hoping to have it appear a second time as well. The other parties with top-row placement are the Republican, Democratic, Conservative and Nonpartisan parties.

7,500 Signatures Needed

Earlier this month, the Socialist Workers party submitted 13,390 signatures to the Board of Elections. The Socialist Labor party filed 10,389 signatures in support of its slate.

Seventy-five hundred valid signatures are required to put a citywide candidate on the ballot. Alexander Bassett, a senior administrator of the elections board, said yesterday that the Lindsay supporters were challenging the validity of about 80 per cent of the signatures obtained by both Socialist parties.

In other political developments yesterday, State Senator John J. Marchi, the Republican-Conservative candidate, said he would be more than willing to debate the Mayor on television if someone else paid for the time.

And City Controller Mario A.

Continued on Page 50, Column 7

The New York Times

REPORTS ON FINANCES: Frederick O'R. Hayes, city's Budget Director, responding to questions yesterday.

CITY SEES SAVING IN WELFARE COSTS

Expects $3-Million to Cover Police Overtime — Crime Rate Down 2.7% in July

By PETER KIHSS

A slowdown in the increase in relief rolls here—even more than in city budget plans last spring — is currently counted on to supply the $3-million for extra police overtime in the next four months.

Frederick O'R. Hayes, the city's Budget Director, said in an interview yesterday that welfare rolls had risen by only 5,000 people in July and that the average monthly increase for the preceding three months had been 7,000.

His budget last April was based on a monthly increase of 7,500—far below the average of 16,000 a month last year and the peak of 23,575 in July, 1968.

Mayor Lindsay has ordered overtime work in both the Sanitation and Police Departments. As many as 1,400 sanitation men are working every Sunday this month, and 500 extra policemen are shortly to begin patrolling each night during high-crime hours.

The police yesterday reported a 2.7 per cent decline in reported crimes here, and a spokesman for the Mayor attributed it in part to the introduction of extra police

Continued on Page 38, Column 4

Northwest Passage Opened

Tanker Near End of Trip Fulfilling a 500-Year Dream

By WILLIAM D. SMITH

Special to The New York Times

ABOARD THE S.S. MANHATTAN, Sept. 14—The S.S. Manhattan churned through the Arctic ice this evening to become the first commercial ship to negotiate the Northwest Passage to Alaska.

The 1,005-foot vessel sailed through the Prince of Wales Strait to the Amundsen Gulf in the Beaufort Sea to raise the prospect of a commercial route that merchant voyagers have dreamed of for 500 years.

The Manhattan still has a week's sailing ahead before she reaches Alaska's shore. But she left behind the most awesome ice at around 1 P.M. Eastern daylight time and was sailing tonight in open water as crew members celebrated their passage with a champagne supper.

800 Miles of Frozen Sea

The big ship has waged a constant battle with ice since she entered Lancaster Sound, the entrance to the Northwest Passage, early on the evening of Sept. 5.

Since then, she has smashed, broken and ground her way through 800 miles of frozen sea with an élan never before seen in the Arctic.

"The Manhattan has put on the most awesome display of icebreaking capability I have ever seen," said Capt. Thomas Pullen, the Canadian Government representative aboard and a man widely acknowledged to be the most experienced ice pilot in the world.

The tanker left Chester, Pa., on Aug. 24 with a 54-man crew and 72 scientists, Canadian and American Government representatives, oil company officials and newsmen. Her destination is Point Barrow on Alaska's oil-rich northern coast.

Purpose of Expedition

The purpose of the expedition is to test the feasibility of using the Northwest Passage as a new and relatively inexpensive route between the recently discovered oil fields of Alaska's North Slope and the oil hungry markets of Europe and the eastern United States.

A successful voyage could lead to development of huge Arctic deposits of iron, sulphur, copper, nickel, lead, silver and other minerals; reshaping of world trade patterns that would allow shorter routes through the Northwest Passage, and the biggest shipbuilding boom since World War II.

The voyage has been a grueling one for the ship's officers and men, who have been under 24-hour-a-day pressure for much of the trip.

They work to a constant accompaniment of clunking and rasping as ice floes scrape along the ship's sides. They work in what is, for many of them, a strange, alien and dangerous world punctuated by 100-foot icebergs and floes 10 feet thick that extend for mile after mile as far as the eye can see.

Rough Ride Through Ice

Yet, contrary to what might be expected, it is not a colorless world, for at this time of the year a bright sun shining from a brilliantly clear sky highlights the subtle blues and greens of the ancient ice.

There is little motion in the specially constructed bow of the Manhattan as it crunches through the ice. Amidships, however, the ship sways like a train riding a roadbed badly in need of improvement. The bulkheads rattle and a passenger feels as if he is flying a small plane through rough weather.

Although the Manhattan has made a mark in history, no one will know until next spring whether her voyage was truly a success.

At that time, all the data gathered from the expedition will have been analyzed and a decision will be made by the

Continued on Page 34, Column 1

Israelis Press Jet Raids on U.A.R. Coast

By JAMES FERON

Special to The New York Times

JERUSALEM, Sept. 14 — Egyptian coastal positions along the Gulf of Suez came under Israeli aerial attack again today, the fourth such assault in five days.

An Israeli Army spokesman said that the raid had lasted 50 minutes, ending at 4 P.M. The earlier attacks occurred in the morning. He said that all Israeli planes had returned safely.

Today's action, like the preceding attacks, was directed against "military objectives" in the 50-mile stretch of the Egyptian-held coast on the western side of the gulf that was attacked last Tuesday by an Israeli armored column.

A spokesman said that two sites struck today were at Ras Ghareb and Ras Zafarana. Both are within the area said to have been devastated by the amphibious force.

[In Cairo, the official Middle East News Agency reported that the Israeli planes were forced to flee eastward after they had attempted to raid Egyptian coastal positions, according to The Associated Press.]

Israeli defense chiefs have stated with unusual bluntness that the raids are intended to demonstrate Egyptian vulnerability outside the immediate area of the Suez Canal.

They have suggested that the commando raids, land attacks and aerial assaults will continue, and perhaps increase in intensity, as long as the United Arab Republic maintains its bombardments along the canal.

Meanwhile, reports of heightened activity on the Israeli-Jordanian border raised the possibility of an Israeli air strike to neutralize the shelling of Israeli settlements.

An army spokesman said that the Gesher settlement, south of the Sea of Galilee, had come under bombardment this morning. Settlers in the area reported another attack tonight. About 50 shells were reported to have been fired.

According to sources in the area, the shells were from heavy artillery pieces or 120-mm. mortars, in either case not part of the guerrilla arsenal. This would mean that Jordanian or Iraqi Army units were taking part in the attacks. The

Continued on Page 15, Column 5

The New York Times — Sept. 15, 1969

Israelis struck again into Egypt at Ras Zafarana (1) and also at Ras Ghareb (2).

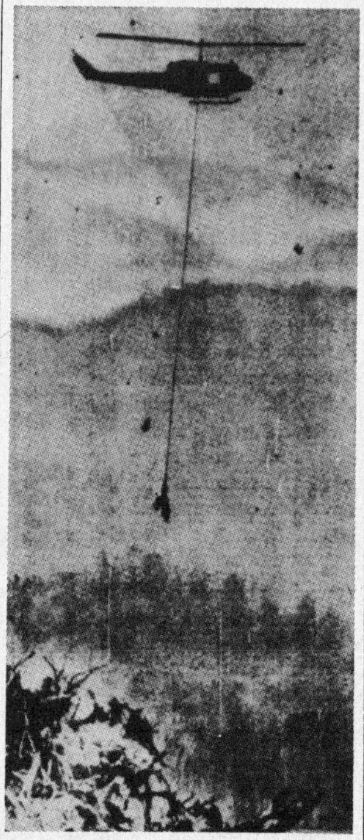

United Press International

RESCUE: Two wounded reconnaissance soldiers being raised by sling to helicopter over Ashau Valley Saturday.

GEN. ABRAMS PAYS THIEU EARLY VISIT UPON HIS RETURN

U.S. Commander Is Thought to Be Relaying Nixon's Views on Withdrawals

THEY TALK 70 MINUTES

25 Rocket Attacks Reported Overnight Against Allied Installations and Towns

By The Associated Press

SAIGON, South Vietnam, Monday, Sept. 15—Gen. Creighton W. Abrams returned to South Vietnam yesterday and went immediately to see President Nguyen Van Thieu, presumably to relay President Nixon's latest thinking on the war and on United States troop withdrawals.

General Abrams, the United States commander in Vietnam, appeared at President Thieu's residence less than two hours after his return from a conference Friday in Washington with Mr. Nixon and key advisers to the President.

The meeting with Mr. Thieu lasted 70 minutes. General Abrams was accompanied by Samuel D. Berger, the Deputy United States Ambassador. Officials would not comment on what was discussed.

[In Washington, there was no announcement on what was decided Friday when President Nixon met with his principal advisers on the war. Over the weekend, there were reports that the Administration was considering major reforms in the draft and would soon announce the withdrawal of 35,000 more troops from Vietnam.]

Unusual Conference Hour

A South Vietnamese official, noting that Mr. Thieu does not ordinarily hold conferences on Sundays or at such early hours—it was 8:10 A.M.—said: "There must be something from Washington—otherwise they wouldn't have met so early."

In a report on the war, the United States command reported enemy shellings and ground fighting decreased generally across the country early today.

Three enemy rockets wounded two Vietnamese civilians in Hue—one of 12 overnight shellings.

In sporadic ground fighting, elements of the United States First Cavalry Division (Airmobile) reported they had killed seven of the enemy with the aid of artillery and air strikes about 75 miles northeast of Saigon. Three Americans were killed and five were wounded.

The command reported 25 rocket and mortar attacks Saturday night against towns and allied bases.

"Ten of these attacks were against United States units or installations," a communiqué said. "Fourteen of the 25 attacks caused casualties or

Continued on Page 10, Column 1

Rise in Infiltration in Delta Said to Follow U.S. Pullout

By TERENCE SMITH

Special to The New York Times

CANTHO, South Vietnam, Sept. 14—United States military authorities here report that North Vietnam has sharply intensified the infiltration of regular army units into the Mekong Delta in the four weeks since the last American troops left the region as part of President Nixon's withdrawal plan.

At least four and possibly seven battalions of predominantly North Vietnamese regulars have crossed the border from Cambodia and slipped into the heart of the delta—the rich, rice-growing southern part of Vietnam—according to the United States military authorities.

Three to four more battalions—1,800 to 2,400 men—have been spotted maneuvering on the Cambodian side of the frontier opposite Chaudoc Province. Intelligence analysts believe one battalion slipped across last Thursday under cover of the series of attacks that followed the 72-hour cease-fire proclaimed by the Vietcong in memory of Ho Chi Minh, President of North Vietnam.

The infiltration of regular units was first spotted last May, but it has intensified sharply in the four weeks since the American units left as part of the initial withdrawal of 25,000 United States troops.

South Vietnamese Army troops have replaced the Americans in Dinhtuong and Kienhoa Provinces, and some officers suspect that the South Vietnamese may well be the target of the North Vietnamese regulars.

"I frankly don't know what they are up to," said Maj. Gen. Roderick Wetherill, senior American military adviser in the delta, in an interview at his headquarters in this town 80 miles southwest of Saigon. He continued:

"But it is possible that they are planning some sort of mini-Tet offensive in the area that was previously protected by the United States Ninth Division. It is one of the things they could do to cause a major political splash in the United States. If they sustained an at-

Continued on Page 11, Column 1

Church 'Reparations' Demanded for Fundamentalists

The Rev. Carl McIntire, accompanied by aides, reading his Christian Manifesto outside Riverside Church yesterday.

Wearing a frock coat and clutching a well-thumbed Bible, the Rev. Carl McIntire, the radio preacher, read his "Christian Manifesto" on the steps of Riverside Church yesterday, demanding $3-billion in "reparations" to fundamentalists.

The demands for payments from churches affiliated with the National Council of Churches, which Mr. McIntire has long opposed, are equal in amount to those requested as "reparations" in a "Black Manifesto" by James Forman from the country's churches and synagogues as compensation for the oppression of Negroes under slavery.

The "reparations" asked for by Mr. McIntire would be used, according to his "manifesto," to restore the idea that everything in the Bible is literally true to its 19th-century ascendance in American religious life. The "manifesto," which Mr. McIntire attached to a panel above the church door when he was finished reading, charges that the liberal "social gospel," which preaches secular activism, has robbed fundamentalism of the institutions it built.

Mr. McIntire was turned away earlier from the chancel of the church at 120th Street and Riverside Drive when he tried to read the 13-page document to the congregation of 1,200 that was filing in for the 11 A.M. service.

"The 'Black Manifesto' is the voice of hell," said Mr. McIntire, who had been refused per-

Continued on Page 51, Column 3

The New York Times (by Michael Evans)

Mr. McIntire, who was turned away from the pulpit, being helped to affix his manifesto over front door of the church.

Greek Opposition Seeks a Joint Front

By ALVIN SHUSTER

Special to The New York Times

ATHENS—In the privacy of their homes, in the shadows of hotel bars and in bustling downtown cafes, opponents of the Greek military regime gather to exchange anxieties, rumors and thoughts for the future.

Not since the army seized power on April 21, 1967, has there been so much talk among the "outs" of the need to settle their differences to avoid the political chaos of pre-coup days.

And the ousted politicians are busy writing a scenario for the future as if the curtain were about to fall on the show now running. In reality, however, it seems the former colonels in power are capable of remaining stage center for some time.

"It all reminds me of that story about how everyone is deciding what to do with the bearskin even though nobody has a plan for killing the bear," said one man here.

Martial law has become a part of life. The Government's informers have been well placed in the universities and in the armed forces.

Moreover, many see the army itself as Greece's "new class," jealous of the prerequisites acquired with power and seemingly unwilling to let them go. Thus, some opponents who a few months ago were hopeful that change would come from within the junta see this possibility fading as the pay of officers goes up along with their new homes, built with special low-cost loans.

This new status of the military is a key topic in Athens. An automobile dealer reports that in some months 8 of 10 new cars are sold to officers. Some jewelers report that more officers' wives have become their customers. One analysis of budget figures shows that salaries of officers have risen by at least 22 per cent since the coup.

Greeks, who have not lost their sense of humor under the authoritarian regime, reflect the new image of the military in their jokes.

A variation of an old story now going the rounds is about the woman on the bus who turns to the man standing beside her and asks:

"Are you an officer?"

"No," he replies.

"Do you have any relatives who are officers?"

"No," he replies.

"Then get your foot off my toe," she says.

All this is not to suggest there are no divergent ele-

Continued on Page 2, Column 4

NEWS INDEX

"All the News That's Fit to Print"

The New York Times

LATE CITY EDITION

Weather: Partly sunny, cool today. Cloudy, cool tonight and tomorrow. Temp. range: today 65-52. Friday 68-51. Full U.S. report on Page 58.

VOL. CXIX..No. 40,782

NEW YORK, SATURDAY, SEPTEMBER 20, 1969

10 CENTS

NIXON CUTS DRAFT CALLS BY 50,000 FOR THIS YEAR; PLEDGES BASIC REFORMS

GROMYKO REBUFFS U.S. BID FOR CURB ON MIDEAST ARMS

Russian, at U.N., Reiterates Demand That Israel Quit Occupied Territories

IS ADAMANT ON VIETNAM

Ignores Nixon's Appeal for Assistance in Bringing the War to an End

Excerpts from Gromyko text will be found on Page 10.

By HENRY TANNER

Special to The New York Times

UNITED NATIONS, N. Y., Sept. 19—Foreign Minister Andrei A. Gromyko, addressing the General Assembly today, rebuffed President Nixon's suggestion of a big-power arms embargo in the Middle East and ignored the President's appeal to United Nations members for diplomatic assistance in ending the Vietnam war.

Both the suggestion and the appeal were presented in Mr. Nixon's speech to the Assembly yesterday.

The Soviet Foreign Minister's address, though considered tough and unyielding by American observers, nevertheless contained an endorsement in principle of the American Administration's concept of "negotiation rather than confrontation."

Eban Another Key Speaker

Abba Eban, Foreign Minister of Israel, was another key speaker in the Assembly's general debate today.

He reiterated Israel's bid for negotiation in the Middle East in dramatic terms.

"The idea of passing from war to peace without negotiation is far less realistic than that of flying to the moon," he said. "The fact is that the moon has been attained by mortal man whereas peace without negotiation has never in all history been achieved at all."

He chided Arab Governments for, as he put it, having "encouraged and indulged" terrorist activity in Israeli-held territory and declared that Israel's "resolve never to change the cease-fire lines except by permanent peace and in favor of agreed boundaries" had become "more passionate than ever" as a result of these attacks.

Mr. Gromyko said that his Government favored "negotiation and a serious-minded attitude and genuine efforts to settle the international issues" facing the Soviet Union, the

Continued on Page 10, Column 6

A New U.S. Delegate Hears Soviet Statement at U.N.

Andrei A. Gromyko, the Soviet Foreign Minister, addressing the General Assembly.

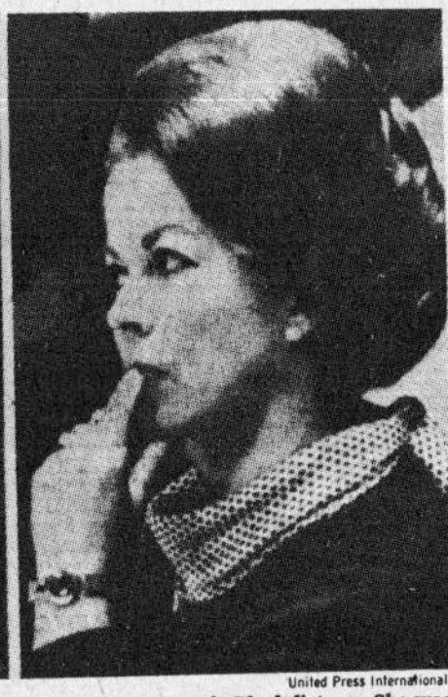

United Press International

Mrs. Shirley Temple Black listens. She was sworn in as a U.S. representative Tuesday.

Thant Says Time to Save Peace of World Runs Out

By SAM POPE BREWER

Special to The New York Times

UNITED NATIONS, N. Y., Sept. 19—Secretary General Thant told the United Nations today that he felt that "time is running out" for efforts to save world peace. He suggested that the decade of the 1970's be dedicated as the "disarmament decade," in which extra efforts should be made to bring the arms race under control and end it.

Progress in disarmament so far has been "indeed, very limited," he said, and he appealed to the United States and the

Excerpts from Thant report are printed on Page 11.

Soviet Union "to begin immediately their bilateral talks to limit and reduce offensive and defensive strategic nuclear weapons."

Mr. Thant's introduction to his annual report, made public today and containing these thoughts, was marked by a sustained tone of gloom.

'Deterioration' Continues

Its first sentence said: "The deterioration of the international situation, which I noted in the introduction to the annual report last year, has continued."

The concluding remarks began with the statement: "I can report very little progress in the world at large toward the goals of the United Nations Charter—to maintain international peace and security, develop friendly relations among nations and achieve international cooperation."

In between, Mr. Thant touched on space and the seabed, the Middle East and Cyprus, economic and social development, human rights and decolonization, among other topics.

There was heavy emphasis, however, on threats to world peace and the need for disarmament.

On the Middle East, he said

Continued on Page 11, Column 1

SOVIET SAID TO CUT DEMANDS ON BONN

Notes Reported Retreating on Berlin and Pact Issue—U.S. Sees Scant Change

By DAVID BINDER

Special to The New York Times

BONN, Sept. 19 — A high Western source disclosed today that the Soviet Union had retreated from its maximum demands on West Germany and West Berlin in notes to Bonn and the three Western allied powers last Saturday.

The notes, replying to Western proposals, concerned improvement of the situation in and around Berlin, isolated 110 miles within Communist East Germany, and agreements to renounce the use of force in relations between Bonn and Moscow.

The unanimous assumption among official analysts here is that the Soviet interest in easing tensions in the region has been prompted by fear of heightened antagonism with Communist China.

Listing details of the notes, the source said the Soviet statement to the United States, Britain and France—the three pow-

Continued on Page 6, Column 1

CANADA TO HALVE FORCES IN EUROPE

Ottawa to Withdraw 4,800 in NATO — 6 Squadrons to Be Reduced to 3

By EDWARD COWAN

Special to The New York Times

OTTAWA, Sept. 19—Canada announced today that she would reduce her military forces in Europe from 9,800 men to 5,000 men and would equip them only with non-nuclear weapons.

The six Canadian squadrons of CF-104 Starfighters in Europe will be reduced to three. From January, 1972, the planes will carry only conventional weapons and will be confined to ground support and reconnaissance roles. A squadron has 15 to 20 aircraft.

The present 5,800-man motorized brigade will be cut to 2,800 men and revamped as a light airmobile force. Canada's Honest John rockets, ground-to-ground missiles capable of carrying nuclear warheads, will be removed from Europe next year.

Saving of $70-Million

Leo Cadieux, Minister of National Defense, estimated that the cuts would save Canada $70-million a year, or half of the present cost of the European force. The reductions would be part of a scaling down of over-all strength of the unified armed services from 98,000 to 82,000 men.

Robert Stanfield, the leader of the Opposition, said that a force of 5,000 men meant that "Canada will be making a token kind of contribution" to NATO. He speculated that the Government might subsequently withdraw the remaining troops after finding out that a 5,000-man force was "relatively ineffective."

Mr. Stanfield, who heads the Progressive Conservative party, called the new level of

Continued on Page 4, Column 4

SENATORS SURVEY DEPTH OF U.S. ROLE IN LAOS STRUGGLE

Symington Group Already at Work—No Combat Units There, Official Insists

By JOHN W. FINNEY

Special to The New York Times

WASHINGTON, Sept. 19—Senator Stuart Symington announced today that the Senate Foreign Relations subcommittee on foreign commitments was already investigating the extent of United States military involvement in Laos.

In informing the Senate, the Missouri Democrat, who heads the subcommittee and is also a member of the Armed Services Committee, said, "We have been at war in Laos for years, and it is time the American people knew more of the facts."

A State Department spokesman, Carl Bartch, declined to comment on Mr. Symington's statement except to reassert that the United States had no "combat troops" in Laos.

That does not exclude the possibility that American planes based in Thailand flew combat missions in support of Royal Laotian troops in their recent successful counteroffensive against North Vietnamese and Communist - supported Pathet Lao troops in Laos.

Preliminary Answer Found

Senate sources indicated that a preliminary inquiry by the Symington subcommittee has confirmed that American planes were flying such missions in addition to the long-acknowledged bombing of North Vietnamese supply routes running through Laos into South Vietnam.

Some State Department officials told Senate sources that the planes were attacking North Vietnamese units assisting the Pathet Lao forces. Under questioning, however, the officials were said to have acknowledged that the presence of North Vietnamese units was not always known for certain prior to the attacks.

The subcommittee investigation was under way but not announced before Senator John Sherman Cooper, Republican of Kentucky, called yesterday for an inquiry by the Senate Foreign Relations and Armed Services Committees to determine whether American troops had already been committed to combat in Laos.

In July two subcommittee staff members—Walter Pincus, chief consultant, and Roland Paul, counsel—spent six days there gathering information on United States programs and personnel.

As a result of the inquiry, a committee member said, "I think we probably know more about what is going on in Laos than the White House."

The next step by the Symington subcommittee will be to hold closed-door hearings beginning Oct. 14. The Senator said that representatives of

Continued on Page 8, Column 1

President Is Disappointed At Slow Pace of Congress

By MARJORIE HUNTER

Special to The New York Times

WASHINGTON, Sept. 19—President Nixon expressed disappointment today over the slow pace on his legislative proposals.

He particularly urged Congress to speed up action on draft law changes, postal reform and a series of anticrime bills.

Democratic leaders promptly renewed their charge, made earlier this week, that the Nixon Administration was responsible for whatever foot dragging existed.

The President's views on lack of Congressional action on many of his proposals were disclosed by the House minority leader, Representative Gerald R. Ford of Michigan, after a conference at the White House.

As he left the White House meeting, Mr. Ford was asked whether he attributed the slow Congressional pace solely to Democratic opposition.

He replied that he did not think the blame should be placed on the Democrats in general, but he added that "there are elements in the Democratic party, in the liberal spectrum, who haven't given as much cooperation as we think they should."

Partisan bickering over who was responsible for the largely unproductive legislative record broke out Tuesday when Republican sources broadly hinted that Mr. Nixon was about to pin a "do-nothing" label on the Democratic controlled Congress.

On Wednesday, House Democrats struck back, accusing the

Continued on Page 14, Column 3

CONGRESS WARNED

Executive Order to Be Issued If Law Is Not Changed in '69

By WILLIAM BEECHER

Special to The New York Times

WASHINGTON, Sept. 19 — President Nixon announced today a 50,000-man cut in planned draft calls for the balance of the year and said that if Congress did not soon vote a draft reform bill he would issue an executive order to effect basic changes himself.

The already announced draft call for 29,000 young men for October will be spaced out over the final three months of the year, it was explained, with calls of 10,000 each in October and November, and 9,000 in December.

Mr. Nixon pointed out that the Administration had programed draft calls of 32,000 for November and 18,000 for December. These, he said, will be "canceled."

Defense Secretary Melvin R. Laird added that a projected call of 35,000 in January would be reviewed in December. The implication was that this, too, might be reduced.

Manpower Needs Stressed

President Nixon, who briefly described the moves at a news conference, and Mr. Laird, who discussed them at some length, stressed falling military manpower needs and a desire to minimize inequities in the 1967 draft law as their motivating rationale.

But other Administration officials conceded that an additional factor in the timing of and emphasis given to the action was the hope that it would lessen anti-war sentiment on college campuses.

A cooling of the campus protests would be expected to improve the bargaining position of the Nixon Administration in trying to achieve a negotiated settlement of the Vietnam war in Paris, these officials said.

In discussing the draft slashes, both Mr. Nixon and Mr. Laird cited the withdrawal of 60,000 men from Vietnam and the reduction of over-all military forces by at least 150,000 as reducing needs.

Mr. Laird said that further

Continued on Page 13, Column 1

Antihijacking Law Enacted by Havana; U.S. Is Not Affected

Special to The New York Times

MIAMI, Sept. 19—The Cuban Government announced today that it had enacted a law under which persons who hijacked airplanes or boats to Cuba could be extradited to their country of origin.

But a Havana communiqué said that the law, signed by President Osvaldo Dorticós Torrado, Premier Fidel Castro and Foreign Minister Raúl Roa, would be applied "only on the basis of equality and strict reciprocity."

A State Department spokesman in Washington, commenting on the Cuban action, said the 1904 extradition treaty between the United States and Cuba "technically remains in effect but as a practical matter is difficult to apply in the absence of direct diplomatic or consular relations."

The new Cuban law, which apparently went into effect today, gives Havana the right to determine whether a hijacker is a common transgressor or a political refugee.

"The Cuban state, in the exercise of its sovereignty, reserves its prerogative of granting the right to asylum when it deems it justified to those persons, who, for political reasons, arrive in our country having found themselves in the necessity of using this extreme means to elude a real danger of death or grave repression," the announcement said. Under the

Continued on Page 58, Column 2

WELFARE CHARGE REBUTTED BY CITY

Officials Deny Deliberately Discouraging Applicants by Tightening of Rules

City officials denied "flatly" yesterday that they had deliberately discouraged the acceptance of new welfare applicants by strictly enforcing procedures that had previously been loosely interpreted.

Mitchell I. Ginsberg, the city's Human Resources Administrator, was asked if the city had tightened these procedures.

"Certainly not," he said. "We would never do that." He used the word "flatly" to characterize his denial.

Several welfare caseworkers and supervisors who had picketed City Hall on Thursday said that they had been ordered to subject welfare applicants to much closer scrutiny, and to enforce some procedures that were "on the books but never enforced."

The procedures involved obtaining statements by relatives of applicants attesting that they

Continued on Page 17, Column 1

Stone Age Indian Tribe Found; Colombians Use Strange Tongue

By WALTER SULLIVAN

The search for a missing fur trader and his guide in the Amazonian jungles of Colombia has brought to light a tribe that seems to be living in the Stone Age and communicates in a tongue unlike any other known language.

The discovery was followed by a bitter clash in which six of the tribesmen were killed. Six others, apparently a family, were taken hostage, but finally released.

Further contact with the tribe and determination of its way of life, in the view of Dr. Robert L. Carneiro of the American Museum of Natural History, is unlikely in the near future. The episode has left the Indians hostile and penetration of the region hazardous, he said.

Dr. Carneiro is curator of South American Ethnology at the museum.

However, he said the missing trader's sister, Cecilia Gil, a Colombian working at the Swiss Bank Corporation in the Wall Street district, still hoped to arouse public support for a new search.

According to Dr. Caneiro, Miss Gil's brother, Julian, left La Pedrera last December with two guides to obtain furs by trading with jungle tribesmen. They were seeking pelts of such animals as jaguar, deer and monkey.

After days of difficult going, including passage across swamps neck-deep in water, they came upon a village of 200 inhabitants living in a single "maloca" — a huge, conical hut 80 feet in diameter.

Apparently hopeful of persuading the natives to hunt for him, Mr. Gil sent one guide back and kept the other with him. The returning guide was told that, if Mr. Gil had not returned within two months a search should be started.

This was done in March by Mr. Gil's brother, Efrain, who was accompanied by a detachment of marines from the Colombian Navy. They found the village and gardens of peach palms and bananas.

Stumps of trees and other vegetation appeared to have been cut with crude tools. Stone ax heads were later found at the site.

Some of the marines went in pursuit of tribesmen seen in the vicinity while Mr. Gil en-

Continued on Page 18, Column 1

Mets' Magic Number Is 7*

The Mets lost a doubleheader to Pittsburgh, 8-2 and 8-0, last night and their National League Eastern Division lead was cut to four games as the Cubs beat St. Louis, 2-1, then lost, 7-2. (Details on Page 34.)

*Any combination of Met victories and Chicago defeats totaling seven will clinch the Eastern Division title for the Mets.

United Press International

ACCUSED OFFICERS EXERCISE IN VIETNAM: Four of six Army Special Forces officers who face courts-martial in the alleged killing of a Vietnamese near the place at Longbinh where they are being held. From left: Capt. Leland J. Brumley, Maj. David E. Crew, Col. Robert B. Rheault and Capt. Budge E. Williams. Two others of lower rank, arrested with the six last July 21, have been paroled, with charges in the slaying of the supposedly duplicitous intelligence agent in abeyance. Three captains will be tried in one group and their seniors at a later time, if ever.

Alitalia Plans $299 Tourist Fare For New York-Rome Round Trip

By ALFRED FRIENDLY Jr.

Special to The New York Times

ROME, Sept. 19 — Alitalia, Italy's state-controlled international airline, announced today that it was planning to break an international rate agreement by offering a $299 round-trip fare for tourist-class passengers between Rome and New York—the lowest ever.

Informed sources said Alitalia was annoyed that the United States Civil Aeronautics Board had approved a new type of discount fare only through next March 31 rather than indefinitely.

The present individual passenger fare is $409. Alitalia said it hoped the new fare would go into effect Nov. 1. The move is viewed by observers here as an effort to force a reduction in trans-Atlantic fares.

[In the United States, the plan was viewed as a tactic to bring pressure to continue lower group fares beyond the March 31 cutoff set by the Civil Aeronautics Board. Transport and Government officials doubted that any trans-Atlantic fare war would develop.]

The Alitalia move will bring about an emergency meeting of the Traffic Conference of the International Air Transport Association, an Alitalia spokesman said. The association agreement, which Alitalia denounced today, governs the air fares charged by member companies.

Alitalia is owned by the Institute for Industrial Reconstruction, the majority of whose shares are held by the Government. The Italian Ministry of Transport will have to approve the new fares, but observers here say such approval is almost automatic.

Italy and the United States have had no formal air traffic treaty since Italy denounced an accord in May, 1966. This treaty would have expired in May, 1967, and has not been renewed because Italy refuses to grant American airlines greater landing rights here and the United States refuses to approve Italy's plan for a Rome-New York-West Coast or Mexico route.

An Alitalia official explained that the airline had decided to reduce individual fares because bulk fare agreements for groups as small as 20 people were not having the desired

Continued on Page 58, Column 6

NEWS INDEX

NASA

Apollo 12 Rollout from the Vehicle Assembly Building at Kennedy Space Center

NASA

Apollo 12 crew: Charles Conrad, Spacecraft Commander; Richard Gordon, Command Module Pilot; Alan Bean, Lunar Module Pilot.

NASA

Apollo 12 launch, Kennedy Space Center, Florida

"All the News That's Fit to Print"

The New York Times

LATE CITY EDITION

Weather: Cloudy, possible showers this afternoon through tomorrow. Temp. range: today 57-51; Tuesday 58-45. Full U.S. report on Page 93.

VOL. CXIX—No. 40,842 NEW YORK, WEDNESDAY, NOVEMBER 19, 1969 10 CENTS

2 ASTRONAUTS LAND ON MOON, 'RIGHT DOWN' ON THE TARGET

PRESIDENT URGES AID TO INDUSTRIES HURT BY IMPORTS

Offers Legislation and Says He Favors Continuation of 'Policy of Freer Trade'

Excerpts from Nixon message appear on Page 38.

By EDWIN L. DALE Jr.
Special to The New York Times

WASHINGTON, Nov. 18 — President Nixon sent to Congress today his long-awaited trade legislation, including new proposals for relief of industries and workers damaged by imports.

The main thrust of the legislation, which the President said was "modest in scope but significant in its impact," was in the direction of freer trade.

Noting that the nation had followed for 35 years "a policy of freer world trade," Mr. Nixon said: "This Administration has reviewed that policy and we find that its continuation is in our national interest."

Parts of the proposed legislation were requested more than a year ago by President Johnson but languished in Congress. Parts were new, but had been suggested in studies made under the former Administration.

New Presidential Power

These were the main points:

¶Modest new Presidential tariff-cutting authority, but with no intention of conducting major new international negotiations for lower tariffs.

¶Repeal of a special device for protection of part of the chemical industry, known as "American selling price," in return for which foreign countries have agreed to cut their chemical tariffs.

¶A major change in the currently dormant "escape clause" provision of present law that will make it easier for industries that can show injury from imports to gain relief through temporary import restrictions. These restrictions will chiefly be higher tariffs.

¶A similar change in the little-used "adjustment assistance" provision, under which groups of workers or individual companies showing injury from imports can obtain financial and other aid.

¶A change in the law that would widen the President's powers to retaliate against nations that erect "unfair" barriers against American exports, agricultural or industrial, or that unfairly subsidize their exports to compete against the United States "in third-country markets."

In New York, delegates to the National Foreign Trade Conference said they wel-

Continued on Page 38, Column 1

Joseph P. Kennedy Dead; Forged a Political Dynasty

Family Tragedies Marred Success in Business and Government

Special to The New York Times

HYANNIS PORT, Mass., Nov. 18 — Joseph P. Kennedy, the patriarch of a political dynasty beset by tragedy, died peacefully today at his summer home at the age of 81.

A family spokesman said that death came at 11:05 A.M. in a second-floor bedroom overlooking Nantucket Sound. Mr. Kennedy had been unconscious since last Saturday when he suffered another in a series of heart attacks.

At his bedside were his wife of 55 years, Mrs. Rose Kennedy, and the last of his four sons, Senator Edward M. Kennedy of Massachusetts.

Also in the room were the widows of two other sons, Mrs. Aristotle Onassis, who was married to President John F. Kennedy, and Mrs. Ethel Kennedy, who was married to Senator Robert F. Kennedy of New York.

President Kennedy was assassinated in 1963 and Robert Kennedy in 1968.

Others present were Mrs. Eunice Kennedy Shriver and her husband, R. Sargent Shriver, Ambassador to France;

Associated Press
Joseph P. Kennedy

Mrs. Joan Kennedy, wife of Edward Kennedy; Mrs. Jean Kennedy Smith, and her husband, Stephen Smith, and Mrs. Patricia Kennedy Lawford.

Mr. Kennedy had been in ill health since 1961 when he suffered a stroke in Palm Beach, Fla. His constant companion since then, Ann Gargan, a niece, was also at the bedside.

President Nixon led the nation in expressing sorrow. In

Continued on Page 51, Column 1

U.S. INVESTIGATING SOME ORGANIZERS OF WAR PROTEST

Kleindienst Sees Possible Antiriot Law Violations—Blount Scores Marches

Special to The New York Times

WASHINGTON, Nov. 18 — Deputy Attorney General Richard G. Kleindienst said today that the Justice Department was investigating some leaders of last week's antiwar demonstration here for possible violations of the Federal antiriot law.

He said that "some members" of the steering committee of the New Mobilization Committee to End the War in Vietnam were among the subjects of the investigation, which could lead to felony indictments under the 1968 antiriot law. The committee sponsored last week's demonstrations.

Earlier, at a White House news conference, another high Nixon Administration official, Postmaster General Winton M. Blount, contended that antiwar demonstrations were prolonging the war and leading to more American casualties. Mr. Blount made his comments after briefing the President on his recent trip to South Vietnam, South Korea and Japan.

Declines to Give Names

Mr. Kleindienst declined to give names of any persons who were being investigated, but during a long news conference in his office he repeatedly associated incidents of violence with David T. Dellinger, who is already being tried under the same antiriot law in Chicago for other alleged activities.

The antiriot law is a section of the Civil Rights Act of 1968. It makes it a Federal crime for persons to cross state lines for the purpose of fomenting riots.

The most violent outburst of last weekend occurred when militants demonstrated at the Justice Department against the Chicago trial.

During his news conference Mr. Kleindienst repeatedly criticized the "New Mobe" leaders and praised those who led the antiwar moratorium of Oct. 15. He said that the New Mobe committee had given assurances throughout the negotiations for parade permits that they would

Continued on Page 33, Column 3

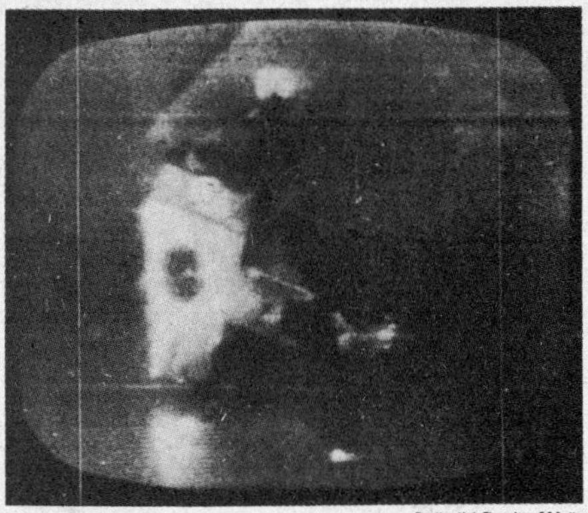

The New York Times from C.B.S. News

SEPARATION OF INTREPID FROM COMMAND SHIP: View of the lunar module, carrying Comdrs. Charles Conrad Jr. and Alan L. Bean, through window of Yankee Clipper.

2 WALKS PLANNED

32-Hour Stay Is Goal in Man's 2d Visit to Lunar Surface

By JOHN NOBLE WILFORD
Special to The New York Times

HOUSTON, Wednesday, Nov. 19—Man returned to the moon early today with the landing of two Apollo 12 astronauts on the rolling plain known as the Ocean of Storms.

Like Columbus returning to the New World he surveyed only briefly the first time, the two astronauts steered their landing ship Intrepid to a landing at 1:54 A.M., Eastern standard time, to conduct a more careful, 32-hour exploration of the lifeless lunar world first reached last July by Apollo 11 astronauts.

The second party of lunar explorers, Comdrs. Charles Conrad Jr. and Alan L. Bean of the Navy, plan to stay on the moon 10 hours longer than their Apollo 11 predecessors and to take two walking excursions on the surface, instead of one. Each moon walk is scheduled to last at least three and a half hours.

Landing Almost Exact

The astronauts bubbled with excitement as they brought the spacecraft down almost exactly on the aiming point, 1,120 feet west of the crater where the Surveyor 3 spacecraft, which they want to inspect, has been standing since 1967.

One of the mission's primary objectives was to demonstrate that men not only could reach the moon, but could also land at the precise point of their choosing. The test of pinpoint navigation is considered necessary for future Apollo flights to more rugged regions of the moon.

"There it is!" shouted Commander Conrad as the spacecraft approached the surface. "There it is! Son of a gun, right down the middle of the road!"

"Outstanding, Pete," the 37-year-old Commander Bean said to the 39-year-old Commander Conrad as the spacecraft touched the surface, stirring up a cloud of dust.

Conrad to Leave Craft

Commander Conrad was scheduled to step down the ladder of the Intrepid at about 6 A.M. today. With all their activities telecast in color to earth, he and Commander Bean are to plant the United States flag and deploy scientific instruments.

The two astronauts planned to take their second excursion after midnight tomorrow. At that time, they hope to walk over to the Surveyor 3.

While Commanders Conrad and Bean are on the moon, the third member of the crew,

Continued on Page 41, Column 3

ROGERS IS GLOOMY ON VIETNAM PEACE

He Discerns 'No Immediate Prospects' Despite Many Contacts With Hanoi

By TAD SZULC
Special to The New York Times

WASHINGTON, Nov. 18—Secretary of State William P. Rogers said today that the United States saw "no immediate prospects" for successful peace negotiations with North Vietnam despite Washington's continuing diplomatic efforts.

After testifying at a closed session of the Senate Foreign Relations Committee, Mr. Rogers said that the United States had had "numerous diplomatic contacts" with North Vietnam, after as well as before the death of President Ho Chi Minh Sept. 3.

"But I think it would be wrong to suggest that they have indicated any success," the Secretary said.

State Department officials asserted later that Mr. Rogers had referred to contacts through third parties and "definitely" not to any new direct secret communications with Hanoi or to a new round of confidential

Continued on Page 14, Column 5

U.S. Paid 39-Million To the Philippines For a Vietnam Unit

By ROBERT B. SEMPLE Jr.
Special to The New York Times

WASHINGTON, Nov. 18 — Nixon Administration officials have conceded to Congress that the United States spent nearly $39-million to finance, equip, and send a small Filipino construction battalion of 2,200 men to South Vietnam in 1966.

Testimony made public today by a Senate Foreign Relations subcommittee disclosed that the money, spent over a three-year period, was four times the amount spent by the Philippine Government to support the battalion, and paid individual soldiers allowances that in effect doubled their pay.

The arrangement was interpreted by Senator J. W. Ful-

Continued on Page 6, Column 4

ROCKEFELLER ASKS CITY PLAN LIAISON

Proposes Joint Committee to Coordinate Efforts on Development Here

By PETER KIHSS

Governor Rockefeller proposed to Mayor Lindsay yesterday that an "informal joint working committee" be set up by the state and the city to coordinate efforts at "carrying out various phases" of the city's new Master Plan.

In a letter to the Mayor, the Governor said he had read the plan "with great interest." He observed that "state programs are increasingly being used by the city to help meet its needs for housing, mass transportation, hospitals, parks, a cleaner environment and the promotion of growing job opportunities."

In the first formal state move on the Master Plan, Governor Rockefeller pledged the Mayor "my fullest support, particularly in your desire to create conditions for rebuilding the core areas of the city and generally for improving the quality of life for all the city's citizens."

The Governor's offer was

Continued on Page 42, Column 1

Words From Moon

Following are conversations between controllers in Houston, Comdrs. Charles (Pete) Conrad Jr. and Alan L. Bean in the lunar module, Intrepid, and Comdr. Richard F. Gordon Jr. in the command module, Yankee Clipper, as transcribed by The New York Times. All of the times given are Eastern standard.

INTREPID: We're loaded to go. . . . I see my crater. . . . That's it. There's LPD [landing point designate].

HOUSTON: Roger, copy, Pete.

INTREPID: There it is! There it is! Son of a gun, right down the middle of the road! Outstanding. 42 degrees, Pete.

Hey, it's targeted right to the center of the crater. I can't believe it

We're passing 3,500. Coming down at about 99 feet a second. You're looking good. About 15 per cent fuel. I'll reset my watch.

I'm going for a landing . . . The boys on the ground do O.K. 1,800 feet 39 degrees. You got 94 seconds to LPD time.

330 feet coming down at 4. Got loads of gas. 300 feet coming down at 5. Oh, look at that crater, right where it's supposed to be! Is it beautiful!

Bean (1:54 A.M.)—42 feet. Coming down at three. Coming down at two. O.K. Start the clock. 42 feet coming down at three, 40 coming down at two. Looking good. 31, 30 feet, coming down at . . . Pete. You've got plenty of gas, plenty of gas, Pete. Stay in there. 18 feet, coming down. He's got it made. Come on in there. 24 feet. Contact lights.

HOUSTON — Roger, copy contact.

INTREPID—Drop.

INTREPID—Command override off. Yes. Main shutoff valve. Yes. Outstanding, man. Beautiful.

INTREPID—Holy . . . . It's beautiful out here.

YANKEE CLIPPER—Hello, Intrepid. Hello, Intrepid.

INTREPID—How are you?

YANKEE CLIPPER — Intrepid, congratulations.

INTREPID—You guys did outstanding piloting, because that thing was right down the middle. Beautiful.

HOUSTON—Glad to hear that, Pete.

APOLLO CONTROL: The third and fourth humans to land on another planetary body, two rather exuberant humans, have completed lunar touchdown at Site 7. Apparently rather close.

HOUSTON: Intrepid, Houston. You can close your fuel vent now and . . .

INTREPID: Roger. Fuel vent closed.

Following are earlier conversations:

YANKEE CLIPPER (11:08 P.M.)—Yankee Clipper here.

HOUSTON—Yankee Clip-

Continued on Page 41, Column 6

Britons Upset by Slaughtering Of Old Horses in Palace Guard

By ANTHONY LEWIS
Special to The New York Times

LONDON, Nov. 18—Animal-loving Britons learned to their horror today that the horses used by the Queen's household troops are sold to slaughterhouses in their old age.

The news, disclosed in banner headlines in The Daily Mirror, set off a day of protest and high-level conferences at the Ministry of Defense. By tonight it appeared that the practice might soon end.

The Royal Society for the Prevention of Cruelty to Animals offered to place the horses in suitable homes. Tonight the army said it would consider the proposal.

But a military spokesman still held to a line that had aroused agitated protest: that the Queen's horses, accustomed to life in London stables, and to the pace of the city, would not adapt to a quiet life in the country.

"It is much more humane to put them down," the spokesman said. "They would just fade away if they were put out to grass."

The horses involved are the ones so familiar to tourists, the ceremonial animals of the Household Cavalry and the Royal Horse Artillery. They are used for the Changing of the Guard and for parades.

Of course, Queen Elizabeth II has horses that she rides at her country places, as well as race horses. They are not involved in the horsemeat controversy. Indeed, a Buckingham Palace spokesman said the whole thing was a matter

Continued on Page 5, Column 3

60 Chanting Militants Break Up Luncheon of 1,500 on Master Plan

The New York Times (by Patrick A. Burns)

Damu Hassan Shabaka, a Community Coalition leader, interrupting yesterday's meeting of the Regional Plan Association at the New York Hilton Hotel. To his left is Morris D. Crawford Jr., board chairman of the Bowery Savings Bank, who adjourned the meeting. At the lectern, Albert D. Merck, association board member, talks to newsman.

A luncheon program at which 1,500 people were to discuss the city's new Master Plan and honor outgoing Gov. Richard J. Hughes of New Jersey was suddenly adjourned yesterday because of disruptions by 60 persons, mainly black militants. The group, with repeated cries of "Damn the masters' plan," had earlier interrupted five out of six morning panel sessions at the 40th annual conference held by the Regional Plan Association at the New York Hilton Hotel.

Governor Hughes told newsmen that he would have summoned the police if such a disruption had been attempted in New Jersey. He said that "free exchange of thought can't exist in the face of anarchy" and that "the time has been reached when government should suppress this anarchy." One of the features of the plan released by the City Planning Commission Saturday is more community involvement in developing city policies. Donald H. Elliott, chairman of the commission, said later that "this was a very small group that came for a purpose of getting some pub-

Continued on Page 43, Column 5

Haynsworth Picks Up Support; Vote on Nominee Is Due Friday

By WARREN WEAVER Jr.
Special to The New York Times

WASHINGTON, Nov. 18—The Supreme Court nomination of Clement F. Haynsworth Jr. continued to gain support today from the ranks of previously uncommitted Senators, but his confirmation remained in doubt.

Senator Ralph T. Smith, Republican of Illinois, who had said only six weeks ago that he could not support Judge Haynsworth and then shifted to an undecided position, called a news conference to announce that he had decided to vote for confirmation.

Senator Smith is serving by appointment in the seat left vacant by the death of Everett McKinley Dirksen. He said that he had made his decision "to support our President and to reflect the views of the people of Illinois," where he must run next fall.

Senator J. Caleb Boggs, Republican of Delaware, was reported to be drafting a speech for delivery tomorrow in which he will endorse Judge Haynsworth's nomination. He has been listed as undecided from the beginning. Senator Smith

Continued on Page 38, Column 5

NEWS INDEX

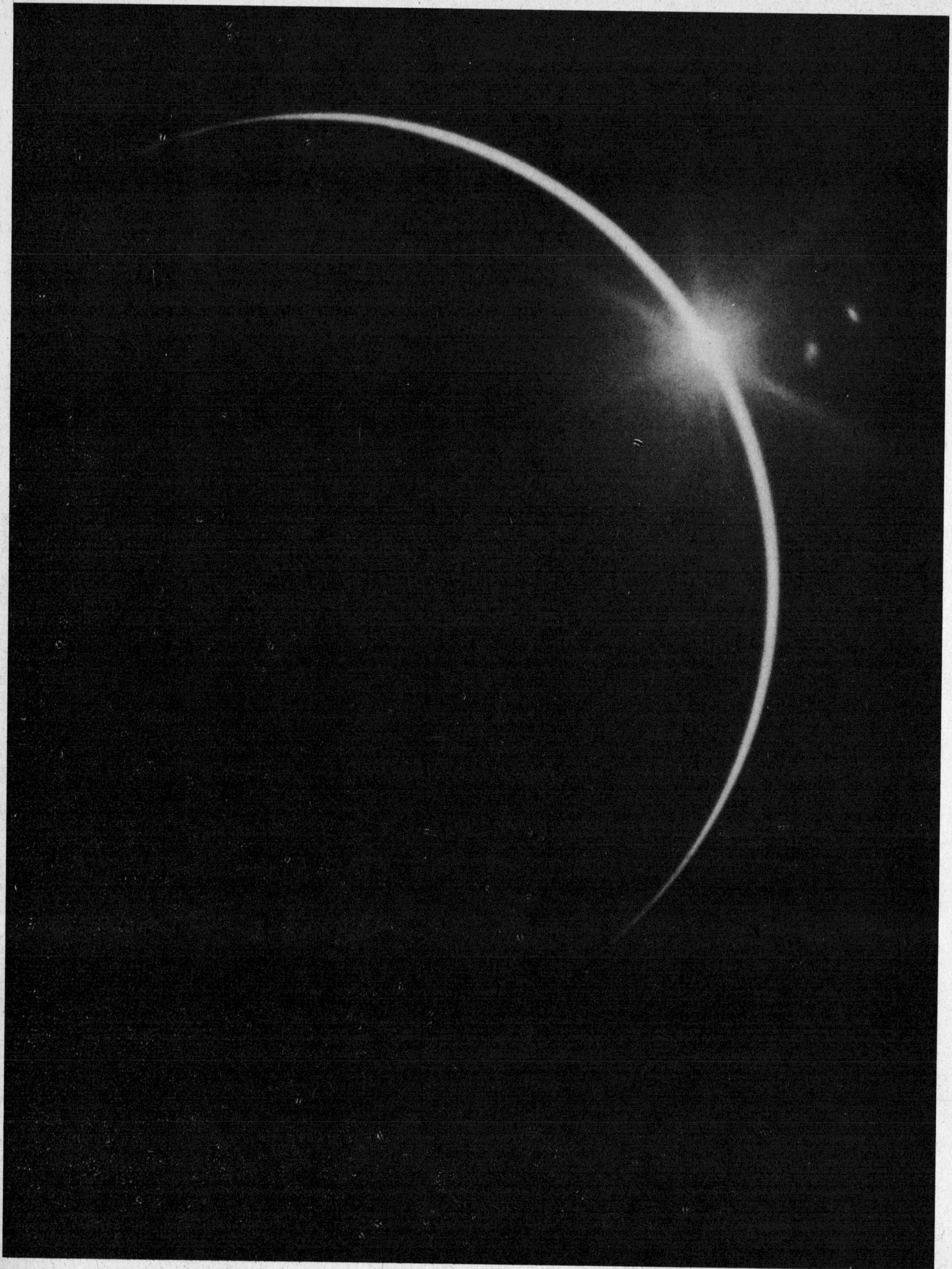

NASA

The earth eclipses the sun in a phenomenon never seen before, photographed by the Apollo 12 crew.

"All the News That's Fit to Print"

The New York Times

LATE CITY EDITION

Weather: Sunny, not as cold today; fair tonight. Fair, mild tomorrow. Temp. range: Today 45-25. Friday 37-27. Full U.S. report on page 74.

VOL. CXIX....No. 40,859 NEW YORK, SATURDAY, DECEMBER 6, 1969 — 10 CENTS

NATO 'RECEPTIVE' TO SECURITY TALKS WITH SOVIET BLOC

But Ministers Declare Parley Depends on a Favorable Attitude on Issues

BERLIN IS EMPHASIZED

An Accord Between East and West Germany Is Urged—Troop Cuts Envisaged

Text of NATO declaration on European security, Page 14.

By DREW MIDDLETON
Special to The New York Times

BRUSSELS, Dec. 5 — The North Atlantic alliance declared today that it was "receptive" to the Warsaw Pact's expression of willingness to hold talks, but emphasized that a conference would depend on a favorable attitude by the East bloc toward concrete issues in Europe.

A declaration issued at the end of a three-day meeting of the 15 member nations' foreign, defense and finance ministers cited free access to West Berlin, a working agreement between East Germany and West Germany and interest in mutual and balanced reductions of forces in Europe as areas where a positive position by the East would encourage the West to move toward larger negotiations.

Answer to East Bloc

The declaration was the North Atlantic Treaty Organization's first detailed answer to the Warsaw Pact's proposal for a European security conference, first made in Budapest in March and repeated, in milder tones, in Prague in October.

The communiqué of the Warsaw Pact meeting in Moscow yesterday did not specifically mention the security conference, but it dealt extensively with the German problem, which NATO regards as one of the keys to easing tension.

The NATO declaration was accompanied by a communiqué describing the routine work of the alliance. In it, the ministers instructed the North Atlantic Council, the alliance's executive body, to watch the development of Soviet naval strength in the Mediterranean "with the greatest attention."

Regarded as Hesitant Step

Aside from the reference to receptivity, the ministers' declaration was regarded as a hesitant step, hedged with conditions, toward any meeting with the Soviet-bloc powers. In essence, it reflects the broad lines of the Nixon Administration's policy on a European détente and United States officials understandably were satisfied with it.

Others were not so happy. One foreign minister, who did not wish to be identified, said he thought that the declaration missed the main point. This, he said, is that "the important thing is to have a conference."

But the policy of the United States, as so often in the past,

Continued on Page 14, Column 6

Premier Meir Joins Welcome of Released Israelis

Associated Press

Premier Golda Meir with Salah Muallem on his return from Syria with Prof. Shlomo Samueloff, not shown here. Men, passengers on jet, were held when it was hijacked by Arabs.

Declaration by Soviet Bloc Called Conciliatory in Bonn

By DAVID BINDER
Special to The New York Times

BONN, Dec. 5—West German officials examining the communiqué issued by Soviet-bloc leaders in Moscow yesterday have concluded that it represents "the most conciliatory stance toward the Federal Republic in recent years" and "the best that one could expect at this time."

Late last night the chief Government spokesman, Conrad Ahlers, said Bonn expected, as a result of the communiqué issued by the seven Warsaw Pact countries after a two-day meeting, that replies to West Germany's November proposals for talks with the Soviet Union and Poland would "soon" be forthcoming from Warsaw and Moscow.

[Walter Ulbricht, the East German Premier, said on his return to East Berlin Friday that he was "very satisfied" with the results of the Moscow conference.]

Key Passage Cited

The key passage of the Moscow communiqué in the view of Bonn analysts, one official said, was:

"The socialist countries taking part in the meeting come out for the expansion and development of relations between all states on the principles of equality, noninterference in internal affairs, respect of sovereignty, territorial integrity and inviolability of frontiers. They are fully resolved to develop relations with other European states wishing to cooperate on the basis of these principles."

This was described here by German officials and East European observers alike as a "green light" for bilateral contacts between the European

Continued on Page 14, Column 3

MANILA ASKING U.S. FOR $100-MILLION

Official Says Marcos Wants Early Payment on Bases to Stave Off Bankruptcy

By PHILIP SHABECOFF
Special to The New York Times

MANILA, Dec. 5 — The Philippine Government, threatened with bankruptcy, decided today to ask the United States to advance $100-million on its 1970 payments for military bases here to stave off the emergency, according to a high-ranking Government source.

The source, who asked not to be identified, said that this decision was reached at a meeting this morning between President Ferdinand E. Marcos and his principal economic advisers.

The President was reported to have instructed his Finance Secretary, Eduardo Z. Romualdez, to approach President Nixon directly with the request for the $100-million advance, which represents about half of the annual United States expenditure on military facilities here.

Mr. Romualdez is in the United States in an effort to raise a large monetary stabilization loan from a consortium of American banks. The loan is needed to relieve what is described here as a desperate shortage of foreign exchange.

According to the official, the Philippine Government has virtually no reserves of convertible currencies even to meet its current operating expenses, much less its international indebtedness. But within the next two months it must repay about $180-million in short-term debt to foreign lenders. But, as sev-

Continued on Page 8, Column 1

2 ISRAELIS FREED BY SYRIA IN TRADE

Hijacked Civilians Released in Exchange for 13 Arabs, Including 2 MIG Pilots

By JAMES FERON
Special to The New York Times

LYDDA, Israel, Dec. 5—Two Israeli civilians held as hostages by Syria since the hijacking of a Trans World Airline jetliner to Damascus on Aug. 29 were released today in exchange for 13 Syrians held in Israel.

The Israelis, Prof. Shlomo Samueloff of Hebrew University and Salah Muallem, a travel agent, returned here this evening to what amounted to a national embrace.

Three Cabinet ministers and Premier Golda Meir, who kissed the unshaven Israelis, were among the hundreds at the Lydda airport, near Tel Aviv, to welcome them home.

They left Damascus on the Boeing 707 that had been hijacked to the Syrian capital by two Arab guerrillas. Damaged in an explosion on the ground, the plane was restored to flying condition two weeks ago.

The Syrians who were involved in the exchange— a deal that Israeli officials had originally said they would never accept — included two pilots who landed their MIG-17's in Israel more than a year ago. Their arrival was said to have been a result of a navigational error.

They were turned over this afternoon to the Red Cross at El Queitra, a now abandoned city in the Israeli-occupied Golan heights of Syria. The re-

Continued on Page 5, Column 3

BURGER NAMES 10 TO OVERSEE ETHICS OF FEDERAL BENCH

3 to Review Financial Data and 7 to Give Advice on Nonjudicial Activities

By JAMES M. NAUGHTON
Special to The New York Times

WASHINGTON, Dec. 5 — Chief Justice Warren E. Burger appointed 10 Federal judges today to oversee financial and out-of-court activities of all Federal judges except members of the Supreme Court.

Three of the judges will review quarterly statements in which their fellow judges will report any receipts of more than $100 for off-bench activities. Such reports were ordered last month by the Judicial Conference of the United States, the 25-member administrative arm of the court system.

On Off-Bench Activities

A separate panel of seven judges will be available, according to Justice Burger's announcement, to advise on various off-bench activities of the judges, such as teaching, lecturing and writing assignments or service on charitable or educational boards.

The Chief Justice said that both committees would serve about a year, until the American Bar Association completes its study of the canons of judicial ethics and the Judicial Conference completes a study of any revision in the canons.

Justice Burger's statement said that any revisions adopted by the Bar Association could be adopted by the judges' group "either in toto or with the special provisions applicable to Federal judges alone."

The Judicial Conference has no authority over Supreme Court members. A spokesman for the Court said that its members would not be subject to the two review committees appointed by Justice Burger.

Controversy Over 2

A controversy over financial and other out-of-court activities of Federal judges arose in recent months from inquiries into the backgrounds of two men nominated to Supreme Court posts.

Former Justice Abe Fortas resigned from the Court last May, after inquiries into his relationship with Louis E. Wolfson, the financier, who is serving a one-year prison sentence for selling unregistered securities. Justice Fortas had been nominated by President Johnson to become Chief Justice, but the nomination was withdrawn amid debate over Justice Fortas's qualifications.

Two weeks ago the Senate rejected President Nixon's nomination of a Federal Ap-

Continued on Page 25, Column 3

Panel on Songmy Questions Calley

United Press International

First Lieut. William L. Calley Jr. arriving at the Pentagon

By E. W. KENWORTHY
Special to The New York Times

WASHINGTON, Dec. 5— First Lieut. William L. Calley Jr., the platoon commander charged with premeditated murder of 109 noncombatants at Songmy, South Vietnam, on March 16, 1968, was questioned for four hours today by a special Army board of inquiry. The eight-member board, headed by Lieut. Gen. William R. Peers, has been directed by Secretary of the Army Stanley R. Resor to determine whether an earlier investigation of the alleged civilian massacre was inadequate and whether there was a cover-up of the alleged incident.

Continued on Page 2, Column 4

SENATE APPROVES $6.5-BILLION RISE IN AGED BENEFITS

Increase in Social Security Added to the Tax Reform Bill on Vote of 48 to 41

VETO THREAT IS DEFIED

Finance Panel's Decision to Place Limit on the Life of Foundations Is Upset

By EILEEN SHANAHAN
Special to The New York Times

WASHINGTON, Dec. 5—The Senate voted a $6.5-billion annual increase in Social Security benefits today as an amendment to the tax reform bill. The vote was 48 to 41.

The action, plus some others the Senate has taken in the last few days, led a number of Republican Senators to protest that the reform bill had been turned into a "Christmas tree bill," with presents on it for everyone.

Senator John J. Williams of Delaware, the ranking Republican on the Finance Committee, declared, "We are doing our Christmas shopping on a credit card. When the American people get the bill, they'll be laboring for years to pay it."

He asserted that amendments to the committee's bill in the last few days totaled $9.9-billion in financial benefits to individuals and businesses, either through reduced Federal income taxes or increased Federal payments.

'Passed by 100 Santas'

These benefits have been "passed around by 100 Santas," he said, referring to the full membership of the Senate, "and they didn't even put on their suits."

In addition to voting the large Social Security increase, the Senate took the following actions on the tax bill today:

¶It reversed a decision of its Finance Committee that would have forced tax-exempt foundations to distribute all their assets and cease operations after 40 years of life, or 40 years from now in the case of existing foundations.

¶It approved a plan to provide tax credits of up to $325 annually per student for the cost of education beyond high school. The amount of the credit would be reduced for families with incomes of $15,000 a year or more and would not be granted at all to families with incomes above $31,250.

¶Authorized the creation of a Presidential commission to study the effects that the tax

Continued on Page 26, Column 4

Packard Foresees Further Troop Cuts Despite Infiltration

By WILLIAM BEECHER
Special to The New York Times

WASHINGTON, Dec. 5 — David Packard, Deputy Secretary of Defense, voiced concern today about what he described as a substantial increase recently in enemy infiltration in South Vietnam. But, he declared, American withdrawals "are going to continue."

Mr. Packard declined to specify numbers involved in the surge in infiltration, but informed officials said that more than 30,000 soldiers were believed to be moving toward the war zone from North Vietnam. Some new units have entered South Vietnam in recent weeks, Mr. Packard declared.

New Offensive Feared

He said that apprehension among military commanders that the enemy might be preparing for another offensive at Tet, the Lunar New Year, was one factor being assessed by Administration officials in trying to decide the size of the next troop reduction and the timing of the announcement. Mr. Packard was speaking at a Pentagon news conference.

On the basis of what he saw and heard during a six-day inspection visit last month, he said: "I am convinced progress in Vietnamization is moving ahead so we can continue our withdrawals."

Asked whether prospects of a major enemy offensive about the time of the Tet holiday on Feb. 6, 7 and 8 might delay the next United States troop withdrawal, Mr. Packard said: "It would depend upon the extent of the Tet offensive and

Continued on Page 4, Column 1

RISING CITY COSTS IMPERIL BUDGET

Increase in Interest Charges Could Result in Deficit Financing, Hayes Says

By RICHARD PHALON

Unexpected increases in operating costs are making it "nip and tuck" whether the city will get through this fiscal year without deficit financing, Budget Director Frederick O'R. Hayes said yesterday.

Rising interest costs are one of the big bugaboos, Mr. Hayes said in an interview. Charges on the temporary borrowing of the city against anticipated revenues, including taxes, are running about $20-million higher than budget projections.

The problem, the Budget Director said, is not so much a higher level of borrowing as the rapid rate at which interest costs have continued to rise.

Police Item a Factor

The $20-million is a small fraction of the $6.6-billion budgeted for the fiscal year that began in July, but it is only one of several unexpected cost items to have materialized since the spending projections were cast.

Among those items, Mr. Hayes said, is $1.1-million in Sanitation Department overtime Mayor Lindsay ordered during his campaign for re-election and a $7-million package of more men and overtime connected with establishing the Fire Department equivalent of a "fourth platoon," mounted in the peak alarm period of 2:30 P.M. to 1 A.M.

Police overtime on the fourth

Continued on Page 30, Column 4

Nixon Induced to Change Signals On No. 1 College Football Team

By ROBERT B. SEMPLE Jr.
Special to The New York Times

WASHINGTON, Dec. 5 — After a couple of near-fumbles and a forced punt from his own end zone, the nation's No. 1 football fan emerged from a brief White House scrimmage today with his southwestern strategy more or less intact.

The scrimmage started earlier this week when it was announced that President Nixon would fly tomorrow to the Texas-Arkansas game in Fayetteville, Ark., and then present the winner with a plaque inscribed to the "No. 1 college football team in college football's 100th year."

Nobody objected except several million residents of Pennsylvania, who bombarded local newspapers and, it is said, the White House with claims that undefeated Penn State was entitled to equal recognition.

In last week's wire-service football polls on which the mythical national championship is based, Texas, Arkansas and Penn State were ranked one, two, three respectively, by The Associated Press, while United Press International placed Penn State second, ahead of Arkansas.

The scrimmage ended abruptly today when Ronald L. Ziegler, the White House press secretary and a former college fullback himself, huddled with his coach in the Oval Room and emerged to tell newsmen that Penn State would be given a plaque too—honoring the Nittany Lions for the longest current undefeated winning streak in college football. Penn State has won 21 games in a row

Continued on Page 51, Column 2

Fossil Called Proof of Continent Link

A Lystrosaurus, Triassic creature of the type whose fossil remains were found by officials of National Science Board. Picture is from Edwin H. Colbert's "The Age of Reptiles."

By WALTER SULLIVAN

The discovery in mountains near the South Pole of the fossil remains of a reptilian counterpart of the hippopotamus that lived, as well, in Africa has established "beyond further question" the former joining of all the southern continents, according to a leading authority on the subject.

The key discovery was made Thursday and reported in a message to the National Science Foundation in Washington by Dr. Laurence M. Gould, scientific leader of Adm. Richard E. Byrd's first expedition to Antarctica in 1928.

Dr. Gould and a fellow geologist, Dr. Grover Murray, president of Texas Technological University, visited the site ofter the discovery, and Dr. Gould said they both considered the find "not only the most important fossil ever found in Antarctica but one of the truly great fossil finds of all time."

Dr Gould and Dr. Murray are members of the National Science Board, which oversees the National Science Foundation.

The fossil was found in the first bed of reptilian and amphibian fossils discovered on the Antarctica continent.

The deposit, apparently an old stream bed, was found a few weeks ago in the Alexandra Range, flanking the Beardmore Glacier on the west. The Beardmore was the route British explorers used in their first attempts to reach the South Pole.

Two years ago, a single fossil fragment was found some 100 miles away in mountains east of the glacier. It was identified as being from a large, salamander-like amphibian that also lived on nearby continents. This was the first fossil hint of a former link between Antarctica

Continued on Page 24, Column 5

Scientists Find Rising Evidence Linking Virus to Some Cancers

By HAROLD M. SCHMECK Jr.
Special to The New York Times

WASHINGTON, Dec. 5 — American scientists are finding increasingly strong evidence linking a virus with certain types of human cancer.

Experts at the National Cancer Institute have published a series of reports during the last year revealing, in total, at least five different but related lines of circumstantial evidence showing that there is a virus associated closely with human sarcomas—cancers that may arise from such tissues as bone, fat and connective tissue.

The question whether viruses are among the causes of human cancer is one of the key unresolved issues of cancer research.

It is widely believed that the chances of preventing some kinds of cancer may improve if a specific virus can be discovered as their cause. Improved understanding of the cancer process and, perhaps, more effective treatment in some cases would also result.

An early clue in the sarcoma research was the discovery that patients with osteosarcoma, a bone cancer, had antibodies in their blood serum against

Continued on Page 23, Column 2

MARIJUANA LAW TERMED 'ABSURD'

2 District Attorneys Here Call Penalties Too Harsh

By DOUGLAS ROBINSON

The District Attorneys of Queens and the Bronx recommended yesterday that the legal penalties for the use or sale of marijuana be drastically reduced to "a more realistic" level.

Although the two men, Thomas J. Mackell of Queens and Burton B. Roberts of the Bronx, differed on the specifics of any new penalties, they agreed that the present sanctions were "absurd and ridiculous."

Mr. Mackell and Mr. Roberts were among several witnesses to appear before a hearing of the State Assembly Democratic Advisory Committee on Crime and Safety in the Streets. The hearing was conducted in the State Office Building, 270 Broadway.

In his presentation, Mr. Mackell said he was opposed to the legalization of marijuana because of the "inescapable conclusion that marijuana can be for many, potentially harmful."

He also cited an estimate by Dr. Stanley Yolles, director of

Continued on Page 35, Column 1

NEWS INDEX

"All the News That's Fit to Print"

The New York Times

LATE CITY EDITION

Weather: Sunny and mild today; turning cloudy tonight, tomorrow. Temp. range: today 43-26; Sunday 36-29. Full U.S. report on Page 57.

VOL. CXIX .... No. 40,882 © 1969 The New York Times Company. NEW YORK, MONDAY, DECEMBER 29, 1969 10 CENTS

CAMP NEAR SAIGON ATTACKED BY FOE; 7 U.S. SOLDIERS DIE

Enemy Approaches During the Night to Open a Heavy Barrage for 10 Minutes

5 G.I.'S ARE WOUNDED

American Death Toll Is the Highest for Single Action Since November Battle

Special to The New York Times

SAIGON, South Vietnam, Dec. 28—Seven American soldiers were killed today by an explosive charge thrown by enemy troops who had crept up to the perimeter of the Americans' field camp in darkness and opened a 10-minute barrage of fire, the United States command reported.

Five other United States soldiers were reported wounded in the attack on the night defensive position of a unit of the 25th Infantry Division near Laikhe, about 25 miles northwest of Saigon.

United States headquarters said the attacking force withdrew, leaving behind three dead, after Air Force jets and a helicopter gunship pounded the enemy positions.

It was the highest American death toll in a single action since 15 soldiers were killed in a three-day battle near Conthien, below the demilitarized zone, in November, a United States spokesman said.

Camp in Grassy Area

According to the United States command and accounts from the field, about 70 soldiers from the 25th Division were camped for the night in an open, grassy area near the Saigon River.

The enemy soldiers, presumably North Vietnamese, slipped unobserved through elephant grass up to the barbed-wire perimeter, studded with Claymore mines, and fired at close range with grenades, rockets, mortars and small arms. The explosion that killed the seven Americans was apparently a grenade or similar explosive charge, a military spokesman said. The five Americans wounded were reportedly hit by small-arms fire.

The Americans returned fire with artillery, small arms and mortars and called in air support.

The attack did not appear to

Continued on Page 12, Column 1

Associated Press

MEDICAL EVACUATION: U.S. helicopter crewman and South Vietnamese soldier lift South Vietnamese marine, wounded in battle in U Minh forest, into helicopter.

Foreign Aid, Under Fire, Faces Further Cutbacks

By FELIX BELAIR Jr.

Special to The New York Times

WASHINGTON, Dec. 28 — Whatever Congress decides to appropriate for foreign aid in the next session, the consensus of development experts in and out of Government is that while the 22-year-old program may survive it will never look the same.

The days of $2.5-billion spending on nation-to-nation economic aid programs by the Agency for International Development or any successor agency are gone forever, say supporters of the program in the Senate and House of Representatives. The same can be said for the relatively lower amounts that have been provided for military assistance grants.

One main force for drastic alteration of foreign aid programs is the prevailing attitude of the Senate.

That attitude was reflected in the report of its Foreign Relations Committee on the aid authorization bill. The report said that "the focus of the committee this year was not on the size or make-up of an aid bill but on whether there should be an aid bill at all."

At another point the report added:

"When all is considered, it is remarkable that the committee has recommended a foreign aid bill at all this year. The fact that it did so is recognition by a majority of committee members that the program is in the national interest and should be continued until a better alternative is found."

Since 1966, Presidential requests for economic and military aid funds have been cut about $1-billion a year. For economic development overseas the amount dropped from $1.89-billion in fiscal 1968 to $1.38-billion the following year.

This year, for the first time since the foreign aid program began, Congress adjourned without agreeing to an aid

Continued on Page 6, Column 3

FRANCE SUMMONS ISRAELI DIPLOMAT IN GUNBOAT AFFAIR

Strain in Relations Likely—Ships Believed Refueling at Rendezvous Off Italy

By HENRY GINIGER

Special to The New York Times

PARIS, Dec. 28—The Israeli chargé d'affaires was summoned to the French Foreign Ministry today amid signs of an impending diplomatic crisis over the mysterious departure of five gunboats from Cherbourg on Thursday.

The French Government proceeded with an inquiry into the departure of the gunboats, which had been built for Israel but placed under an embargo. Relations have already been strained by what the Israelis view as French sympathy for the Arab cause.

The boats left Cherbourg after having been supposedly sold to a Norwegian company for oil-drilling operations, but today they were reported to be in the Mediterranean Sea seemingly headed for Israel.

[Italian port officials indicated that the gunboats were apparently being met in the Mediterranean Sea by Israeli vessels that would refuel them and escort them to Israel.]

Diplomats Are Silent

This afternoon Foreign Minister Maurice Schumann of France conferred with the acting head of the Israeli Embassy, Eyten Ronn, but both the French and the Israelis maintained silence on the tenor of the discussion. The Ambassador, Walter Eytan, is absent from Paris for the New Year holiday.

At the Foreign Ministry, officials indicated that if the inquiry should establish proof that Israel was behind the operation, diplomatic relations would be placed under severe strain. The general assumption

Continued on Page 2, Column 3

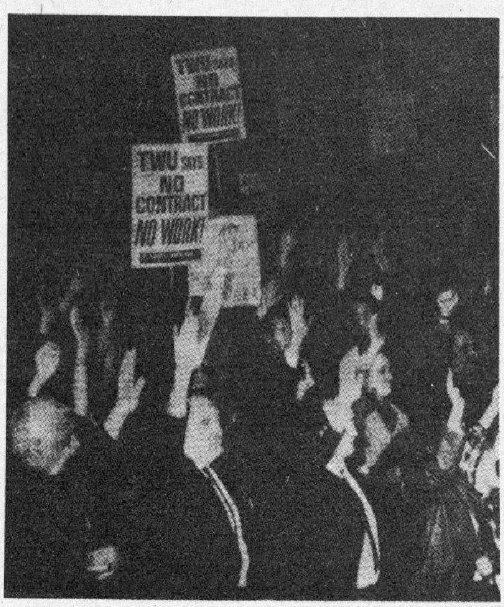

Associated Press

STRIKE VOTE: Union transit workers authorizing strike if contract is not signed by Jan. 1

TRANSIT MEN VOTE TO STRIKE IF PACT IS NOT ACCEPTABLE

Stoppage at 5 A.M. Jan. 1 Is Authorized—Union Says It Has Had No Offer

MAYOR HOLDS A PARLEY

'Countdown' Has Begun, He Says—T.W.U. Threatens to Ignore Taylor Law

By EMANUEL PERLMUTTER

Union transit workers voted unanimously yesterday to strike the city's subways and buses on New Year's Day if they did not have an acceptable contract by then.

Matthew Guinan, international president of the Transport Workers Union, told a wildly cheering overflow crowd of 5,000 at Manhattan Center: "If we do not get a contract we can recommend to the membership, not a bus or subway will roll in this city come 5 A.M., Jan. 1."

This expected strike authorization came as union officers reported that they had not received any offer thus far from the Transit Authority on a new contract for 35,000 workers.

The present two-year contract expires New Year's Eve at midnight and the employes are seeking a 30 per cent wage increase, a four-day work week and other improved benefits.

Present wage rates range from $7,000 to $9,000 a year.

Mayor at Hotel

As a result of the strike vote, Mayor Lindsay met at the Americana Hotel last night with the three mediators in the dispute, Theodore W. Kheel, Vincent D. McDonnell, and Joseph E. O'Grady.

Emerging from the meeting shortly after 11 P.M., the Mayor said:

"I have just met with the three mediators for the past hour. On the basis of our discussions, I have decided to ask both parties in the dispute to meet with me and the mediators at 1 P. M. tomorrow in private session at the Americana Hotel."

Asked whether he planned to be continuously, and personally, involved in the negotiations between now and the deadline, he replied:

"That will depend on the results of the 1 P.M. meeting."

He declined to assess the

Continued on Page 57, Column 1

Budget Benefiting Areas That Supported Lindsay

By MARTIN TOLCHIN

The city's proposed construction program for the coming year apparently follows a time-honored political tradition in often rewarding neighborhoods that voted for the victor—Mayor Lindsay—while removing projects from those that voted against him last month.

Some city officials say that these changes in the 1970-1971 draft capital budget are not political payoffs but rather a reflection of political calculations made during the election campaign. Some neighborhoods were then written off as hopelessly anti-Lindsay, while others were promised major capital improvements and improved services in the hope of winning votes.

The widespread practice is often used by mayors, governors and even Presidents, who view budgets not merely as a tool of government, but also as a technique through which to gain and consolidate political power.

Defenders of the practice view it as part of the bartering of the democratic process, in which a President might use the promise of a Federal power project in the same way that a mayor might use a promised school—to win popularity, and enlist the support of local political leaders for programs that transcend their own districts.

Critics of the practice say that it sets up a priority system based more on the needs of politicians than on the needs of the people.

In New York City, schools, parks, playgrounds and other

Continued on Page 22, Column 1

CITY RESHAPING ITS GOVERNMENT

Program Includes Ending Estimate Board's Role in Budget Process

By MAURICE CARROLL

A major reshaping of the city government is being fashioned by the Lindsay administration and the City Council.

Proponents believe that the rearrangement could provide significant changes in the way the government deals directly with the people.

Private discussions are being held by aides of the Mayor and of the City Council leadership, but none of those involved will talk about the plan. Pieced together through a series of conversations with those who know what is being put together, however, the package appears to embrace:

¶Abolition of the Board of Estimate's role in fashioning of the city budget.

¶Creation of a number of neighborhood service centers, recalling Mr. Lindsay's plan,

Continued on Page 22, Column 5

Parties Mount Drive to Control Senate

By R. W. APPLE Jr.

Special to The New York Times

WASHINGTON, Dec. 28—Quietly, with little national publicity, politicians in Washington and around the country are assembling tickets for the Congressional elections 10 months from now.

By the time Senators and Representatives return in January for the opening of the second session of the 91st Congress, most of the battle lines will have been drawn, particularly for the 35 Senate contests—even if many of the candidates insist on posing as noncandidates for a few weeks longer.

The Republicans are planning a big effort to take control of the Senate for the first time since 1955. President Nixon and Vice President Agnew will travel into key states, according to the Republican National Committee, and it is hoped that a $1,000-a-plate dinner in Washington on March 11 will raise $2-million.

Of the 35 seats at stake, 10 are held by Republicans and 25 by Democrats, which gives the Republicans a tactical advantage. To take control, the Republicans must register a net gain of seven seats, which would make the line-up 50 to 50.

Mr. Agnew would then be able to cast the decisive vote for his party.

Officials of both parties believe that it is possible the Republicans will achieve their goal but will need a number of breaks to do so. This represents a less optimistic view for the Republicans and a less pessimistic view for the Democrats than was commonly held three months ago.

The course of the war in Vietnam and the state of the economy will have a considerable effect on the voting.

So will the fact that many of the Senators seeking re-election next year were elected on the unusually strong Democratic tide of 1958 or in the

Continued on Page 20, Column 1

Temple of Aphrodite Found in Turkey

By SANKA KNOX

The temple of the Aphrodite of Cnidus, the long-lost and most celebrated image of the Greek goddess in antiquity, has been discovered among ruins that may also be the burial place of the statue itself.

The larger-than-life-size marble statue, sculptured by Praxiteles in the fourth century B.C., stood on a height at Cnidus at the southwest tip of a peninsula in Turkey that juts into the Aegean Sea.

The statue, the first nude Aphrodite by a Greek artist, disappeared many centuries ago, but how and when is not known. She was copied many times and copies were made of the copies. There are 52 such examples in existence.

The rediscovered temple, one of the most glamorous archeological finds in years, was partly excavated last summer by Iris C. Love, director of an expedition to Cnidus.

Miss Love, an assistant professor at Long Island University, announced her findings at the annual meeting in San Francisco of the Archaeological Institute of America. The meeting opened Saturday and will conclude tomorrow.

In an interview here before her departure for the West Coast, Miss Love described Aphrodite's temple as Doric and circular, an uncommon form in Greek temple architecture.

Machinery not available at

Continued on Page 25, Column 1

Miss Iris C. Love, director of the expedition to Turkey, next to a marble statue of a priestess of Aphrodite.

Scientist Asserts Violent Noise May Harm Babies Before Birth

By SANDRA BLAKESLEE

Special to The New York Times

BOSTON, Dec. 28 — Violent noise, such as sonic booms, may have permanently damaging effects on unborn babies, a scientist warned today.

The warning, presented to a noise pollution panel at the annual meeting of the American Association for the Advancement of Science, was issued by Dr. Lester W. Sontag, director of the Fels Research Institute in Yellow Springs, Ohio. The paper by Dr. Sontag, who could not be present today, was read by a colleague.

Too much noise in the everyday environment—noise pollution—has been shown to cause health problems in adults. Loss of hearing, increased mental stress and heart disease have been linked to the assault of excess noise in daily living.

The human fetus, according to Dr. Sontag, is equally vulnerable to the noxious effects of too much noise. Forty years ago many people believed that the human fetus was protected from unpleasant conditions in the outside world in the comfort of the mother's womb, but recent experiments have shown that the fetus is not so isolated after all, Dr. Sontag said. The fetus seems to react to harmful environmental conditions just as the mother does, he said.

Supersonic transport jets may therefore pose a threat to the health of unborn infants in that the planes will be one more noxious addition to the total assault of an increasingly noisy environment. It is estimated that one such jet, crossing the United States, would cut a

Continued on Page 25, Column 1

NEWS INDEX

Graham to Rock Fans: 'Tune In to God'

By United Press International

HOLLYWOOD, Fla., Dec. 28—The Rev. Billy Graham told a youthful audience at the Miami rock festival today to get high on God instead of drugs.

But, even as the evangelist spoke, youths passed out stickers calling for the legalization of marijuana.

Wearing a bright gold jacket, dark trousers and a yellow shirt, Mr. Graham appeared beaming and cheerful at the grounds at 11 A.M. and began talking with a bearded man about God.

"Do me a favor and say a prayer to thank God for good friends and good weed," said Donn Kelsey, 33 years old, to Mr. Graham. He said he gets "high" every night.

"You can also get high on Jesus," replied Mr. Graham. "Let us pray for peace," he said.

The evangelist received polite applause as he ascended a 20-foot-high stage and praised the "terrific music" that preceded him in the early morning hours.

He said today's music was a music of protest that was telling the older generation, "We reject your materialism and we want something of the soul."

He told the audience, "Tune in to God today and let Him give you faith. Turn on to His power."

Few of the estimated 2,500 youths in attendance appeared to be listening closely to Mr. Graham, and several passed out material calling for marijuana legalization.

Mr. Graham said at a news conference that he felt a "tremendous response" had been shown to his words.

He said that it was his first appearance at a rock festival but that he planned to attend more because "this is where the young people are I want to reach."

"I love these kids, I really

Continued on Page 38, Column 1

Associated Press

The Rev. Billy Graham listening to a young man at the rock festival in Hollywood, Fla.

"All the News That's Fit to Print"

The New York Times

LATE CITY EDITION

Weather: Cloudy today. Cloudy and cool tonight. Fair, mild tomorrow. Temp. range: today 52-43; Monday 61-42. Full U.S. report on Page 93.

VOL. CXIX..No. 40,988 NEW YORK, TUESDAY, APRIL 14, 1970 10 CENTS

POWER FAILURE IMPERILS ASTRONAUTS; APOLLO WILL HEAD BACK TO THE EARTH

LINDSAY PROPOSES REALTY TAX RISE AND HIGHER FEES

Explains in TV Talk How He Seeks to Close Budget Gap of $630-Million

By MARTIN TOLCHIN

Mayor Lindsay proposed an unspecified increase in real property taxes and city fees last night in a televised "Message to the People" on the fiscal plight of the city.

The proposals were the latest in a series offered by the Mayor to close what he called a gap between income and expenses in the next city budget. The gap was previously estimated at $750-million to $1-billion, but was placed at $630-million by the Mayor yesterday. Most of the Mayor's tax proposals require approval by the State Legislature.

In Albany, legislative sources indicated that the Governor and Legislature were "seriously considering a plan to help meet the city's plea for additional funds with a fiscal package that would include keying percapita aid to a proportion of state income-tax revenues. Per capita aid is that part of the state that is not allocated for specific purposes such as education.

Seeks to Meet Governor

Whatever formula is arrived at, however, it could not affect the state's budget for the present fiscal year, which began April 1. On the other hand, it is possible that a measure passed by this session of the Legislature could become effective during the last quarter of the city's fiscal year, which begins July 1.

The Mayor emphasized in his telecast the "humiliating" aspects of "begging" and "pleading" for funds from the legislative leaders, whom he will meet today in Albany. The Mayor also has requested a meeting with Governor Rockefeller, but such a meeting was not yet scheduled by early last evening.

The four-minute taped speech, which the Mayor read from a prompting device, contained no criticism of Governor Rockefeller or the legislative leaders, but rather assailed "the

Continued on Page 42, Column 3

Legislature Votes That Credit Cards Must Be Requested

By FRANCIS X. CLINES

Special to The New York Times

ALBANY, April 13—The State Senate voted final legislative approval today of a bill that would prohibit the mailing of credit cards to the public unless they were requested specifically in writing.

The measure, which was passed unanimously, was sent to Governor Rockefeller after numerous legislators complained of present conditions in which cards were sent out blindly and frequently misused.

A second credit-card measure was approved by 29 to 20 votes, with the Republican majority having to round

Continued on Page 42, Column 3

NEW CRIME CODE GAINS IN ALBANY

Senate Votes Bill to Revise Penal Law Administration —Assembly Due to Act

By WILLIAM E. FARRELL

Special to The New York Times

ALBANY, April 13 — An extensive revision of the state's Code of Criminal Procedure, containing hundreds of changes in nearly every facet of the criminal justice process, passed the Senate by a vote of 40 to 13 today and was sent to the Assembly.

The measure is expected to be acted on by the Assembly tomorrow, with its chances for passage considered good.

The highly technical, 482-page bill—which the Senate passed after relatively brief debate, considering that its scope covers legal procedures from arrest to post-conviction appeals—is the first major revamping of the state's penal-and the elimination of imprecise, language, some of it dating back to Victorian times.

The product of over four years of drafting by a state commission and many hearings held throughout the state, the controversial bill was originally introduced in the Legislature last year.

However, it drew the fire of

Continued on Page 42, Column 5

BREZHNEV URGES FRESH SOLUTIONS TO ECONOMIC ILLS

On TV, He Strikes Out at Low Productivity of Labor and Poor Management

Excerpts from Brezhnev talk will be found on Page 14.

By BERNARD GWERTZMAN

Special to The New York Times

MOSCOW, April 13—Leonid I. Brezhnev, the Communist party leader, told the Soviet people today that "new methods and new solutions" were needed to solve the country's economic problems.

In a nationally televised speech, Mr. Brezhnev said he was speaking candidly about the problems because the party's Central Committee and Politburo had decided that the people should know about the country's "undoubted successes and about the problems that stand before us."

Striking out at lagging labor productivity, poor economic management and shortages of consumer goods, Mr. Brezhnev attributed the shortcomings partly to "objective reasons," such as unforeseen foreign policy problems requiring unexpected expenditures.

Allusion to China Issue

He was presumably alluding to the Soviet Union's difficulties with China and to the invasion of Czechoslovakia in August, 1968.

He said the economic problems also derived from "subjective reasons," such as poor administration and a lack of work discipline.

In his unusual television address, Mr. Brezhnev essentially repeated what he said in December to a closed meeting of the party's Central Committee. That speech was not published and was discussed only in party cells, although its substance was the subject of an editorial in Pravda, the party newspaper, on Jan. 13.

Since then there have been suggestions in some quarters, especially among intellectuals, that the Soviet cause would be better served by frank, public discussion of the nation's economic ills.

The December speech set off

Continued on Page 14, Column 6

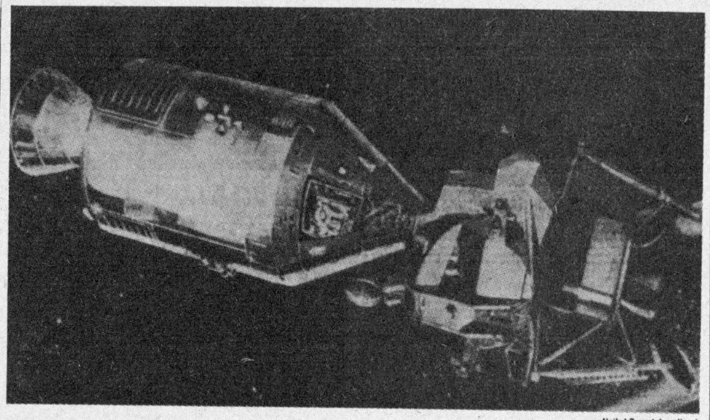

United Press International

THE SPACECRAFT: The Apollo 13 command and service modules, left, attached to lunar module in flight in this artist's conception. Service propulsion rocket is at far left and descent engine of lunar module is at the right. A serious leak of oxygen in the command ship forced the astronauts to use the lunar module for return to earth.

NO MOON LANDING

Men Leave Main Craft for 'Lifeboat' After an Oxygen Leak

Excerpts from conversations with spacecraft, Page 32.

By JOHN NOBLE WILFORD

Special to The New York Times

HOUSTON, Tuesday, April 14—The Apollo 13 astronauts, their lives threatened by a serious oxygen leak, were forced to evacuate their command ship late last night and use their intended moon-landing craft as a "lifeboat" for a fast return to the earth.

In cool and cryptic words, they were instructed by mission control here to use the attached lunar module's rocket to power them back to an emergency splashdown in the Pacific Ocean at about noon on Friday.

There will be great risks and little margin for error or delay.

At a news conference here officials were asked if there was enough oxygen to get the astronauts back to earth safely.

A space agency official answered, "Yes."

"I'm glad to hear it," the questioner said.

The lunar landing module has a supply of 48 pounds of oxygen.

Christopher C. Kraft, deputy director of the Manned Spacecraft Center, said:

"I think their chances are excellent at the moment, assuming their lunar module operates all right."

Emergency Simulated

Houston officials were asked if "this abort situation or altered trajectory had ever been run on simulators, in just this way?"

"On yes, many times," the officials said. "We've run all kinds of abort situations. The Lunar module is designed to carry out the maneuver. We are looking even at the possibilities of dropping the service module, but that particular type of maneuver has not been tested in flight and we'd have to make ourselves certain that we could control the spacecraft under that kind of inertia condition."

The plan is for the three men to keep the hatch open between the lunar module and the command module. One of the astronauts will remain in the command module part of the time to monitor its systems, and it will be necessary to keep the hatch open in order to draw on the lunar module's oxygen supply.

Because of the space limitations in lunar module, it is expected that two of the astronauts will crawl through to the command module to stretch out when it is time to go to sleep. A third astronaut will always remain awake in the lunar

Continued on Page 32, Column 6

INQUIRY BY HOUSE ON DOUGLAS URGED

Rep. Ford Says Justice May Be Impeached—He Plans Speech to List Charges

By WARREN WEAVER Jr.

Special to The New York Times

WASHINGTON, April 13—A bipartisan group of Representatives will press for a House investigation of Justice William O. Douglas's fitness to continue serving on the Supreme Court.

Representative Gerald R. Ford, the Republican floor leader and principal spokesman for the Douglas critics, said today in announcing the plan that he would describe "many charges and allegations" against the Justice in a speech in the House on Wednesday. He declined to provide further details.

Later this week, a resolution creating a House committee to investigate Justice Douglas and report in 90 days will be introduced with bipartisan sponsorship. Such an inquiry, Mr. Ford said, might serve as a preliminary to an impeachment motion in the House.

The House move came in the wake of the Senate's rejection last week of Judge G. Harrold Carswell, the second consecutive Supreme Court nominee of President Nixon to be denied confirmation.

In a television interview, Vice President Agnew said that Judge Carswell and Judge Clement F. Haynsworth Jr. "have been denied seats on the bench for statements that are much less reprehensible than those made, in my opinion, by Justice Douglas."

Last November, when the Senate was considering the Haynsworth nomination, Mr.

Continued on Page 27, Column 1

Drive Against Vietnamese At High Pitch in Cambodia

By HENRY KAMM

Special to The New York Times

PNOMPENH, Cambodia, April 13—An officially inspired campaign of hatred against Vietnamese has reached fever pitch throughout Cambodia. It has resulted in detentions, in disappearances and, in at least one known case, in mass killings that witnesses attributed to Cambodian soldiers.

In the course of the last week or 10 days the campaign against Vietnamese residents has seriously diminished the open sympathy with which many diplomats and other foreigners initially viewed the leadership that overthrew Prince Norodom Sihanouk on March 18.

None of the leading figures of the new regime have said a word, in their flood of statements and communiqués, that might inhibit those who take the official propaganda campaign as a declaration of an open season on Vietnamese.

A standard line of argument appears to have developed among Government officials and private citizens in response to those who intercede on behalf of the frightened Vietnamese.

The Cambodians insist that foreigners simply do not understand the depth of Vietnamese Communist penetration among Vietnamese in Cambodia. They also stress the traditional enmity between the Cambodian and Vietnamese peoples and say that outsiders fail to see the issue in its historical context.

It is often asserted that the Vietnamese have been equally cruel to Cambodians and would do the same in the Cambodians' position.

Vietnamese residents of Cambodia are estimated to number 400,000 in a population of seven million. How many remain at liberty is impossible to tell. In the border provinces, where North Vietnamese and Vietcong forces moved supplies and men and found sanctuary while Prince Sihanouk was in power—his successors have been trying to get rid of them—most of the Vietnamese are believed to be under detention.

The biggest concentration is in the capital, where they live in well-defined sections, particularly along the banks of the Mekong, Bassac and Tonle Sap rivers. Reliable informants reported today that in some sections one member of each family was seized yesterday, apparently as a hostage.

Many Vietnamese, including those who have acquired Cambodian citizenship at consider-

Continued on Page 12, Column 1

MILLS ADVOCATES 2 IMPORT QUOTAS

His Bill Would Limit Textiles and Shoes From Overseas to Their 1967-68 Level

By EDWIN L. DALE Jr.

Special to The New York Times

WASHINGTON, April 13—Chairman Wilbur D. Mills of the House Ways and Means Committee introduced today an omnibus trade bill that would sharply limit imports of textiles and shoes under a new quota system.

Identical bills are expected to be introduced by numerous other members of the House. The bill drafted by Mr. Mills, Democrat of Arkansas, was clearly intended as the vehicle for trade legislation this year, although it could be amended. Hearings are expected to begin early next month.

The new quota system for textiles and shoes would roll back imports in 1970 to the average of 1967-68, with imports limited by country of origin and by category. This major provision of the bill was clearly included because of the impasse in the negotiations between Japan and the United States for a voluntary limitation of textile imports.

The import problems of the shoe and textile industries have dominated Congressional concern. The industries are widely dispersed geographically, and imports have been rising steeply.

The Mills bill includes a provision permitting the President to negotiate international agreements with exporting countries that would permit a somewhat higher level of imports than the 1967-68 average. If no such agreements are ne-

Continued on Page 65, Column 3

U.S. Says Soviet Nuclear Sub Apparently Sank in the Atlantic

By PETER GROSE

Special to The New York Times

WASHINGTON, April 13—The Pentagon reported signs today that a Soviet nuclear submarine had sunk in rough waters of the Atlantic. The site was between 400 and 600 miles northwest of Spain.

United States Navy patrol planes observed the submarine on the surface, apparently in distress, through Friday and Saturday, a Defense Department spokesman said. Two Soviet surface ships—one a freighter, the other an electronic intelligence-gathering vessel—were seen trying to take the submarine in tow.

By yesterday morning naval patrol planes found only two oil slicks on the surface where the submarine had been. The two surface vessels were still patrolling the area, apparently searching, the Pentagon reported.

The spokesman said there was no information about the fate of the crew members of the submarine, some of whom had been sighted on the deck on Saturday, trying to establish the tow-line.

Navy sources at the Pentagon said that the submarine was of the "N," or "November," class, which carries a complement of 88. This is a nuclear-powered attack submarine, not carrying nuclear missiles itself but designed to seek out and attack other submarines.

Jerry Friedheim, the Defense Department spokesman, said that no American vessels of any kind had been in the area. Thus, officials said, the possibility of American aid for the disabled vessel was "only academic, since we didn't have anything anywhere nearby."

Officials said that there were no communications during the incident between the Russians and the Americans, either on the scene or elsewhere. "We did not intercept any distress messages," a Pentagon spokesman said. Officials declined to say whether any other radio communications from the submarine or the accompanying merchant ships had been monitored.

The Pentagon statements appeared to rule out the possi-

Continued on Page 15, Column 3

The New York Times (by Neal Boenzi)

MUSEUM FOUNTAIN OPENS ON BIRTHDAY: The new oval pool area in front of the Metropolitan's Fifth Avenue facade. The 100 jets of water were started by Mayor Lindsay yesterday as part of the institution's centennial celebration. Article is on Page 52.

Air Traffic Protest Appears Near End

By ROBERT LINDSEY

The 20-day-old sick-call slowdown of Federal air traffic controllers appeared to be collapsing last night.

Scores of controllers, facing increasing back-to-work pressure from Federal district courts, returned to their jobs in Federal Aviation Administration airport towers and radar rooms across the country yesterday.

A major break in the dispute was an injunction issued in Brooklyn yesterday afternoon by Federal Judge Orin G. Judd. He told more than 250 New York area air traffic controllers to go back to work "forthwith" or prove to a panel of doctors that they had bona fide illnesses.

Although there was not a significant number of men back

Continued on Page 93, Column 1

NEWS INDEX

Conservation Groups Win Stay Of Start on Alaska Pipeline Road

By E. W. KENWORTHY

Special to The New York Times

WASHINGTON, April 13—A Federal District Court judge enjoined Secretary of the Interior Walter J. Hickel today from issuing a right-of-way permit for a road to parallel the projected Alaska oil pipeline, until complaints of three conservation groups could be tried on their merits.

The effect of the judge's action will be to postpone, probably for a year, the beginning of the road construction. The Trans Alaska Pipeline Systems had assembled $42-million worth of special road machinery in the expectation of obtaining permits so that construction could begin this month.

Lawyers for the three groups—Wilderness Society, Friends of the Earth, and Environmental Defense Fund, Inc. — had asked Judge George L. Hart Jr. to keep Secretary Hickel from issuing right-of-way permits for both the pipeline and the road.

The 48-inch pipeline, which would run 800 miles from Prudhoe Bay on the North Slope to Valdez, would take a 100-foot-wide right-of-way. A 200-foot-wide right-of-way is sought for a 390-mile road from the Yukon River to Prudhoe Bay.

The conservation groups complained that the pipeline permit would violate the 1920 Mineral Leasing Act, which limited right-of-way grants to 25 feet on each side of a pipeline. In this case, they said, the right-of-way could be only 50 feet plus the four feet for the width of the pipe.

They also argued that Secre-

Continued on Page 19, Column 1

"All the News That's Fit to Print"

The New York Times

LATE CITY EDITION

Weather: Sunny and pleasant today; fair, cooler tonight and tomorrow. Temp. range: today 70-48; Friday 61-48. Full U.S. report on Page 58.

VOL. CXIX... No. 40,992 | NEW YORK, SATURDAY, APRIL 18, 1970 | 10 CENTS

ASTRONAUTS LAND GENTLY ON TARGET, UNHARMED BY THEIR FOUR-DAY ORDEAL

NASA, via Associated Press

SAFELY BACK: Fred W. Haise Jr., left, Capt. James A. Lovell Jr., center, John L. Swigert Jr. aboard the Iwo Jima

HINT BY RUSSIANS ON GENEVA PARLEY STIRS U.S. INTEREST

White House Would Explore Possibility of Conference on Indochina Issue

By RICHARD HALLORAN

Special to The New York Times

WASHINGTON, April 17—The White House said today that the United States was interested in exploring with the Soviet Union the possibility of convening an international conference to resolve the conflicts in Indochina.

That was the first expression of the Nixon Administration's desire to draw out the Russians on a Soviet hint that Hanoi had become more receptive to negotiations on Indochina.

It came in response to a comment made in New York yesterday by Yakov A. Malik, the Soviet delegate to the United Nations. Mr. Malik told newsmen: "It appears to be that only a new Geneva conference could bring about a new solution and relax tension on the Indochina peninsula."

Earlier Proposal Rejected

Mr. Malik had been asked about the French proposal made on April 1 for international negotiations on Indochina. If a Geneva conference was the point of that proposal, he said, "then it was deserving of attention."

The White House press secretary, Ronald L. Ziegler, commenting today on the Russians' view, said: "We are interested in exploring what they have in mind." The State Department spokesman, Robert J. McCloskey, used identical words at another news briefing.

If the Soviet delegate's comment was an indication of a change in attitude on negotiations over Indochina, it was the first such indication since Premier Aleksei N. Kosygin rejected President Nixon's letter of March 6 asking for consultations to restore peace to Laos.

It is considered certain here that Soviet diplomats do not

Continued on Page 4, Column 4

Apartment Strike Called 'Certainty'

By DAVID K. SHIPLER

Landlords and apartment house employes broke off negotiations yesterday after the owners rejected a union proposal that would have postponed a strike in 5,000 buildings for 30 days.

No further meetings were scheduled before the expiration of the contract at midnight next Monday.

"A strike appears to be a dead certainty," said Vincent D. McDonnell, chairman of the State Mediation Board.

A walkout would affect 25,000 members of Local 32B of the Building Service Employes Union — doormen, handymen, porters and oth-

Continued on Page 26, Column 5

ANTICRIME PLAN GAINS IN ALBANY

Senate Passes Bill to Set Up State Task Force Under a Deputy Attorney General

By WILLIAM E. FARRELL

Special to The New York Times

ALBANY, April 17—The Senate today passed a bill to establish a statewide task force on organized crime, to be headed by a deputy attorney general, with powers to hold hearings, prosecute cases and grant immunity.

The bill, which passed without debate, empowers the task force to investigate and prosecute such activities of organized crime as gambling, drug trafficking, hijacking, labor racketeering, loansharking, extortion and bribery.

Both houses of the Legislature held lengthy meetings today, plowing through heavy calendars as part of the grueling end-of-the-session push to meet a hoped-for adjournment deadline late Sunday night or early Monday.

With important measures still embedded in choked calendars, there were these major developments today:

¶The $400-million tax and

Continued on Page 16, Column 7

NASA TO REVIEW SPACE ACCIDENT

Special Board to Be Set Up —Paine Hails Return as 'Triumph of Teamwork'

By HAROLD M. SCHMECK Jr.

Special to The New York Times

HOUSTON, April 17—The National Aeronautics and Space Administration began today an official investigation of the accident that forced the Apollo 13 crew to abandon their scheduled moon landing and return to earth.

Dr. Thomas O. Paine, administrator of the space agency, announced here that a special review board was being set up "to investigate the circumstances and causes of the accident aboard the spacecraft Odyssey and the subsequent flight and ground actions taken to recover."

Expressing his gratitude and thankfulness for the safe return of the three astronauts—Capt. James A. Lovell Jr. of the Navy and Fred W. Haise Jr. and John L. Swigert Jr., both civilians—Dr. Paine said the moment of the splashdown in the Pacific was one in which the whole space program could take great pride.

He said Apollo 13 must be counted as a failure because it did not accomplish its prime objective, landing on the moon.

Continued on Page 13, Column 1

NASA, via United Press International

SCENE OF RECOVERY: Capsule hit the water within five miles of aircraft carrier and 800 yards of aiming point.

WORLD REJOICES AT SAFE RETURN

For a Few Minutes, People Forget Their Differences and Cheer Astronauts

By MARTIN ARNOLD

For a few minutes yesterday, all over the world, people of every color and station and political belief seemed as one in their joy over the successful splashdown of Apollo 13.

In many American communities, church bells pealed the safe return of the three astronauts. Churches and synagogues offered prayers of thanksgiving.

Millions watched the splashdown on television here and abroad, from Japan to England. The European Broadcasting Union said in Geneva that it might well be the biggest television audience of all time

In English pubs there were cheers and drinks all around.

Thousands in Lima, Peru, got permission to take early lunch breaks from their work to watch the final moments of the drama.

In New York City, thousands

Continued on Page 12, Column 1

Sea Recovery Swift After Perfect Entry

Aquarius Praised for Vital Role

By JOHN NOBLE WILFORD

Special to The New York Times

HOUSTON, April 17— "Farewell, Aquarius, and we thank you."

That was the tribute today from Mission Control to the tumbling and foresaken lunar module, code-named Aquarius, that had saved the lives of the Apollo 13 astronauts.

Within an hour and a half of their splashdown, Capt. James A. Lovell Jr. of the Navy, Fred W. Haise Jr. and John L. Swigert Jr. crawled back into their command ship and triggered explosive bolts to jettison the lunar module.

The frail craft was built to hold two men for the landing on the moon. But since Monday night's oxygen tank explosion, disabling Apollo 13's primary electrical and life-support systems, the craft had been the three astronauts "lifeboat" for a hasty retreat from 205,000 miles out in space.

Intricate Maneuvers

When the lunar module was cast off at 11:43 A. M. Eastern standard time, it ended some five hours of intricate maneuvering by Apollo 13 to get ready for re-entry into the earth's atmosphere.

The critical maneuvers, improvised by Mission Control and executed by the astronauts, involved rocket firing to sharpen their course toward the entry corridor, jettisoning the service module, where all the trouble began, and then separating the lunar module.

If either module had remained attached, its fuels would probably have exploded during entry, dooming the astronauts.

Courage and Skill

After it was all over, Dr. Thomas O. Paine, head of the National Aeronautics and Space Administration, hailed the astronauts' courage and skill as being "in the great spirit of exploration and bravery."

Dr. George M. Low, NASA's deputy administrator, said that never before had a space mission "demanded as much from the men flying the machines as this one has."

Cantain Lovell, the 42-year-old commander, was making his fourth trip into space and second to the vicinity of the moon. Both Mr. Haise, 36, and Mr. Swigert, 38, were civilian astronauts on their first space

Continued on Page 12, Column 7

Tired Men Found in Good Health

Special to The New York Times

ABOARD U.S.S. IWO JIMA, at Sea, April 17 — The three Apollo 13 astronauts splashed down gently today in the Pacific, ending a four-day fight for survival.

They rode the command module Odyssey to a pinpoint landing at 1:07:44 P.M., Eastern standard time, within five miles of this recovery carrier, 800 yards from their aiming point and 610 miles southeast of American Samoa.

Weary but unharmed after their abortive and perilous moon-landing mission, Capt. James A. Lovell Jr., Fred W. Haise Jr., and John L. Swigert Jr. dropped into a gentle sea for a routine recovery.

When the Odyssey descended from a partly cloudy sky, its orange and white parachutes billowing in the sun, there were cheers from sailors on the flight deck of the Iwo Jima.

The final moments of the space voyage seemed anticlimactic after the hours of harrowing tension that followed a mysterious explosion on the spaceship Monday night.

Crippled in Space

The explosion knocked out the command module's electricity and oxygen systems, crippling Apollo 13 when it was moonbound, 205,000 miles from the earth, and forcing the crew to abandon a plan to land on the lunar mountains.

Despite the long desperate hours when they fought to keep the battered craft going, the astronauts were smiling and walking steadily when they reached the deck of the Iwo Jima.

Avoiding the microphones—they were under orders not to talk to the press until they returned to Houston Sunday—the weary astronauts were led to isolation in the sick bay.

Quick Examinations

A doctor who examined the spacemen only minutes after their return to earth reported that Mr. Haise was suffering from a mild urinary tract infection and had a low-grade fever of 100.6.

Dr. Keith Baird of the space agency, said however, that the astronauts were "all in good health."

"They were considerably more tired than the other crews I have been associated with," said Dr. Baird. "Except for being tired, I think they are all in good health."

Dr. Baird said Mr. Haise had probably acquired his infection because there was a shortage of drinking water in the spacecraft, since the men had to con-

Continued on Page 12, Column 1

Killing of 100 Vietnamese By Cambodians Reported

By HENRY KAMM

Special to The New York Times

TAKEO, Cambodia, April 17—About 100 Vietnamese civilians, including perhaps 30 children, were shot to death by Cambodian soldiers last night in a grade school where they were under detention, survivors said today at the scene of the slayings.

"Take us away or we will all die tonight," an old man pleaded with this correspondent.

The smell of death hung over the school building, where about 150 Vietnamese residents of this provincial capital 50 miles south of Pnompenh were herded together under detention four days ago.

Three bodies—of a man, a boy and a woman—lay under fiber mats at the edge of the pavilion. Four men who would not live until morning lay unattended, eyes vacant, flies crawling on their wounds.

Three groups of men, totaling 40 or 50, sat or lay in terror and pain, awaiting the worst. At least half were wounded and all wore bloodstained clothing.

The small building offered little space for 150 men to live and die, and the dead touched those who survived.

Takeo, like the rest of the region on the frontier with Vietnam, is threatened by Vietcong and North Vietnamese invaders. Throughout the region, Vietnamese residents are being arrested. The purpose, according to the authorities, is to weed out those who help the Vietcong and to save the others from the hostile Cambodian population.

Women and children, who had been gathered up with the men earlier, are being released, but teen-age boys are not considered children by all jailers. Many died here last night.

The survivors said they had given no provocation and did not know what had caused the slayings. The tenor of remarks by soldiers on guard here indicated that they were a reprisal for a Vietcong attack Wednesday night.

Two days ago there were about 150 men under detention according to visitors who were here before and after the killings. Their accounts supported the testimony of the survivors that 100 were killed last night.

Today hundreds of bullet holes scarred the walls, roof and latticework of the build-

Continued on Page 3, Column 1

NEWS INDEX

Jordan Asks Recall Of U.S. Ambassador

By DANA ADAMS SCHMIDT

Special to The New York Times

AMMAN, Jordan, April 17—King Hussein asked today for the recall of the United States Ambassador, Harrison M. Symmes. The request was in protest against the decision of Joseph J. Sisco, the Assistant Secretary of State for Near Eastern and South Asian Affairs, not to go to Jordan on his current visit to the area.

[In Washington, the State Department said that it would comply with the Jordanian request, but would not retaliate by asking the Jordanian Ambassador to leave.]

Mr. Sisco, who is in Israel, having completed a visit to the United Arab Republic, is expected to go to Beirut, Lebanon, tomorrow. The purpose of his

Continued on Page 7, Column 1

United Press International

THE LONG WAIT IS OVER: New Yorkers viewing splashdown on TV at Grand Central Terminal burst into applause

Nixon to Give Medal To Crew in Hawaii

By ROBERT B. SEMPLE Jr.

Special to The New York Times

WASHINGTON, April 17 — President Nixon dropped all other duties today to follow the Apollo 13 astronauts during their final moments of descent. He applauded when they splashed down and lit up a triumphant cigar when they boarded the aircraft carrier Iwo Jima.

He also announced that he would fly to Houston tomorrow to pick up the families of the astronauts and take them to Hawaii, where he will award the Medal of Freedom to the three men.

While in Houston, the President will present the medal, the nation's highest civilian award, to the Apollo 13 ground crew as well. The award will be

Continued on Page 12, Column 7

"All the News That's Fit to Print"

The New York Times

LATE CITY EDITION

Weather: Partly cloudy today; fair tonight. Mostly fair tomorrow. Temp. range: today 56-40; Monday 50-40. Full U.S. report on Page 86.

VOL. CXIX ... No. 40,995 | NEW YORK, TUESDAY, APRIL 21, 1970 | 10 CENTS

NIXON TO PULL OUT 150,000 FROM VIETNAM IN A YEAR; SAYS HANOI BLOCKS PEACE

APPEALS TO FOE

Average Withdrawals of 12,000 a Month Would Continue

The text of Nixon's speech is printed on Page 16.

By ROBERT B. SEMPLE Jr.

Special to The New York Times

SAN CLEMENTE, Calif., April 20—President Nixon pledged tonight to withdraw 150,000 more troops from Vietnam over the next year and once again appealed to the North Vietnamese to undertake serious negotiations.

In a 15-minute address televised from the Western White House, Mr. Nixon set forth a withdrawal plan that seemed designed to reassure his domestic critics that he intended to proceed with his withdrawal strategy yet leave himself and his military commanders wide latitude to determine the pace of disengagement.

On the diplomatic front Mr. Nixon reported no progress. He fixed the blame entirely on the intransigence of the enemy and its insistence on the removal of the Saigon Government of President Nguyen Van Thieu as a precondition to meaningful talks.

"It is Hanoi and Hanoi alone," the President declared, "that stands today blocking the path to a just peace for all the peoples of Southeast Asia."

Commitment to Nation

Mr. Nixon gave a commitment that between now and next April the authorized force in Vietnam—the present ceiling is 434,000—would be reduced by 150,000, to a new ceiling of 284,000.

To his military advisers he gave implicit assurances that the rate of withdrawal could be adjusted to the level of enemy activity and other battlefield factors in South Vietnam.

Since Mr. Nixon announced the first round of withdrawals last June, American troops have been leaving Vietnam at a rate of about 12,000 men a month. The average monthly reductions under the plan announced tonight would remain roughly the same.

But officials here conceded that, while they hoped to undertake "significant" withdrawals in the early stages of the plan, it was entirely possible that more men would be withdrawn near the end of the timetable, especially if battlefield conditions took a sudden turn for the worse. And the President himself said:

"The timing and pace of these new withdrawals within the over-all schedule will be determined by our best judgment of the current military and diplomatic situation."

On balance, however, officials here portrayed the an-

Continued on Page 16, Column 1

Cambodians Battle Reds 15 Miles From Pnompenh

By HENRY KAMM

Special to The New York Times

SAANG, Cambodia, April 20—The war between Cambodia and Vietnamese Communist forces reached within 15 miles of Pnompenh today with a battle for this district capital of a few thousand people. The marketplace marked the front line.

Northward from the market to the Cambodian lines lie about 600 yards of no man's land on both sides of Route 21, from the Bassac River on the left to about 500 yards into the fields on the right. Beyond that line, Government control ends and the command post of the 24th Light Infantry Battalion stands in danger of being outflanked and overrun.

Saang fell to the enemy yesterday afternoon, when outnumbered Government forces were ordered to withdraw. Reinforcements were later moved up and established at the northern edge of the town.

Their mission is a counterattack to recapture the town, but its success is in doubt.

Pnompenh is serenely oblivious to the nearness of war. It is about a half hour's drive from the languor of the swimming pool of the Royal Hotel, where the élite gather for apéritifs around noon, to the farm on Route 21 where Col. Dien Del has installed the command post of the 24th Infantry.

The drive seems longer than the distance because the old French-built road follows the bends and curves of the Bassac for 20 miles. Apéritifs and

Continued on Page 12, Column 1

LAIRD AGAIN NOTES A SOVIET THREAT

Says, in Talk Here, Missile Gains May Compel Major 'Offsetting Actions'

By PETER KIHSS

Secretary of Defense Melvin R. Laird warned yesterday that the United States might have to take "major offsetting actions" if a Soviet build-up of strategic nuclear weapons continued. The United States, he said, has waited until "we are literally at the edge of prudent risk."

The Secretary said that an explanation of the Soviet program would be sought at the conference table during the current talks in Vienna between the United States and the Soviet Union on limitation of strategic arms.

In the last five years, the Soviet Union "has virtually quadrupled the total megatonnage in its strategic offensive force," while the United States has "reduced its megatonnage by more than 40 per cent," Mr. Laird declared in a speech at the annual luncheon of The Associated Press at the Waldorf-Astoria Hotel.

Secretary Laird also said

Continued on Page 2, Column 6

Vietcong Turn Down France's Proposal On Indochina Talks

By JOHN L. HESS

Special to The New York Times

PARIS, April 20—The Vietcong today turned down the French proposal for a new international conference on Indochina.

Mrs. Nguyen Thi Binh, Foreign Minister of the Vietcong's so-called provisional revolutionary government in South Vietnam, said the proposal "could not contribute to solving the problems" of Vietnam, Laos and Cambodia at present.

The French Foreign Minister, Maurice Schumann, suggested the conference on April 1. Last Thursday, the Soviet delegate to the United Nations, Yakov A. Malik, was quoted as having said he favored the convening of such a conference, but Saturday night, in a radio interview, he described the idea as "unrealistic at the present time."

[President Nixon, in his address to the nation, said he had "noted with interest" the statement Thursday by Mr. Malik.]

Mrs. Binh's comments came at a news conference called to denounce what she called the genocide being practiced upon

Continued on Page 11, Column 3

CARSWELL RESIGNS AS JUDGE TO SEEK U.S. SENATE SEAT

Will Oppose Rep. Cramer of Florida in G.O.P. Race for Post Holland Is Leaving

Special to The New York Times

MIAMI, April 20—G. Harrold Carswell announced today that he had resigned from the United States Court of Appeals for the Fifth Circuit to run for the United States Senate.

Mr. Carswell's nomination to the Supreme Court was rejected by the Senate on April 8 by a vote of 51 to 45.

The surprise announcement was made at a news conference by Lieut. Gov. Ray C. Osborne of Florida, who said he was withdrawing from the Senate race in favor of Judge Carswell.

Mr. Osborne said last September that he would be a Republican candidate for the Senate seat being vacated by Spessard L. Holland, a Democrat, who plans to retire.

Top Republicans Present

Mr. Carswell attended today's news conference along with his wife, Virginia; Gov. Claude R. Kirk Jr.; Florida's junior United States Senator, Edward J. Gurney, and other top Republicans.

In his announcement statement, Mr. Carswell said: "The Republican party today offers Floridians the best channel of providing the conservative government in which our citizens believe. For 17 years I have served as prosecutor and in the judicial branches of our government. Now the same sense of service and duty to principle leads me to the Senate race."

Mr. Carswell and his party left the conference quickly and declined to elaborate on the announcement.

Effect Is Pondered

Observers here wondered about the effect of Mr. Carswell's announcement on the Senate candidacy of United States Representative William C. Cramer, Republican, whose campaign plans have had the backing of President Nixon.

The Democrats do not have an announced candidate for the post, but former Gov. Farris Bryant has been strongly mentioned as a possibility.

President Nixon nominated Mr. Carswell to the Supreme Court on Jan. 19, two months after the Senate rejected an earlier nominee from the South, Judge Clement F. Haynsworth Jr. of Greenville, S. C.

Civil rights and labor groups opposed the Carswell nomination after learning of a speech he had made during the 1948 campaign for the Georgia Legislature. He said then: "Segre-

Continued on Page 28, Column 3

United Press International

VISITS LENINGRAD: Henry Ford 2d touring the city on Sunday in a Soviet-made Chaika. St. Isaac's Cathedral is at left, Astoria Hotel at right. The Admiralty is visible at rear.

FORD SAYS SOVIET ASKS AID ON PLANT

In Moscow, He Announces Bid for Technical Help in Building Truck Complex

By JAMES F. CLARITY

Special to The New York Times

MOSCOW, April 20—Henry Ford 2d said today that the Soviet Union had asked the Ford Motor Company to help build a large truck manufacturing complex.

Mr. Ford, chairman of the company, said it would consider the proposal. He declined, at a news conference in the United States Embassy, to say whether his company would accept the proposal to help in building the complex, but he said the company was interested in doing business with the Soviet Union.

He said Soviet officials had also asked Ford to help design the new trucks, to be produced at a plant to be constructed on the Kama River, 550 miles east of Moscow.

The Soviet press, in announcing plans for the project in February, said the plant would be at the Kama River town of Naberezhnye Chelny, 130 miles east of Kazan. It is planned to turn out 150,000 eight-ton trucks by 1974.

The principal questions the company had to resolve, Mr. Ford said, were whether such an arrangement would be prof-

Continued on Page 5, Column 1

BALLOT BILL STIRS FUROR AS SESSION CLOSES IN ALBANY

Victorious Measure Would Put Incumbents on Top Line in City Primary

REFORMERS IN PROTEST

Lindsay-Rockefeller Pact on Aid Voted, Along With a $1.85 Minimum Wage

By PAUL L. MONTGOMERY

Special to The New York Times

ALBANY, April 20—Republicans and regular Democrats combined forces near the end of the exhausted legislative session today to push through a bill that Reformers charged was aimed at the defeat of Democratic insurgents in this year's primary in New York City.

In what G. Oliver Koppell, a Reform Democrat from the Bronx, called "the single most shameless piece of legislation I have ever seen," the Assembly passed a Senate bill that would place incumbents at the top of ballots in the June 23 primary. Previously positions had been determined by lot.

It is a standard rule of politics, particularly in primaries, that the first place on the ballot is the most desirable. In the heated debate on the measure, Assembly Minority Leader Stanley Steingut of Brooklyn sought to defend it as routine.

"This is strictly a bill so that the general public can identify the candidates," he said.

A Hectic Wind-Up

The Republican-dominated session of the legislature, which began on Jan. 7, ended tonight.

The Assembly, which continued its Sunday session until 1 A.M. today, resumed at 7:35 A.M. and ended its hectic deliberations at 5 P.M. The Senate, which had met until 6 o'clock this morning, resumed at 10 A.M. and adjourned at 6:56 P.M.

By the time of adjournment, a number of Assemblymen and Senators had left Albany to observe the Jewish Passover, which began at sundown.

Some of the final measures that cleared the Legislature were ones the legislators had not seen until minutes before they were asked to vote. Through the day the plaintive voices of legislators rose in the two chambers to inquire what matter was under consideration.

The dominant concern of the

Continued on Page 34, Column 1

Ribicoff Urges Expansion Of Welfare Reform Plan

By WARREN WEAVER Jr.

Special to The New York Times

WASHINGTON, April 20—A Democratic version of the Administration welfare reform bill that passed the House last week is taking shape in the Senate. Senator Abraham A. Ribicoff proposed today a series of amendments to the House measure. They appeared likely to form the outline for a considerably broader, more expensive bill headed for Senate approval sometime this summer.

The Connecticut Democrat is an influential member of the Senate Finance Committee, which will begin discussing the House welfare bill this week and open public hearings on it and a number of alternative proposals on April 28.

Senator Ribicoff called for the same level of guaranteed income as President Nixon for the first year of the program's operation—$1,600 a year for a family of four. But his legislation would increase this figure to $1,800 in 1972-73 and $2,000 the following year.

'Glaring Weakness'

He said the Administration bill would set up a "meager level" of benefits, and he called this "the most glaring weakness in the President's welfare program."

Mr. Ribicoff also proposed extending the minimum income guarantee to unmarried people and childless couples. Under the House bill, the guarantee would apply only to families consisting of at least one parent and one child.

The Senator proposed full Federal assumption, over a three-year period, of the cost of the three adult welfare categories: aid to the aged, the blind and the disabled. Under the House bill, the minimum guaranteed monthly benefit would be increased to $110 from $68, but the Federal share would be 90 per cent of the first $65 and 25 per cent of the rest.

As a result of these changes,

Continued on Page 29, Column 1

SUBVERSIVES UNIT LOSES MAIN ROLE

Supreme Court Lets Stand a Ban on Rulings by U.S. Agency on Communists

By FRED P. GRAHAM

Special to The New York Times

WASHINGTON, April 20—The Subversive Activities Control Board was left with virtually no function to perform today after the Supreme Court refused to review a lower court ruling that barred the board from declaring individuals to be members of the Communist party.

Today's action could be the fatal blow to the 20-year-old board, which has been prevented by a string of adverse court decisions from carrying out from its inception its role of registering and exposing Communists.

In the latest lower court decision, the United States Court of Appeals for the District of Columbia declared unconstitutional a 1968 law that authorized the board to publish the names of persons found to be members of the Communist party.

Solicitor General Erwin N. Griswold told the Supreme Court in the Government's appeal that the ruling, if allowed to stand, would cause "the frustration of the Subversive Activities Control Board's reason for existence."

The Court refused, without comment, to hear the appeal. In other actions today, the Court did the following:

¶Agreed to decide if a South-

Continued on Page 30, Column 3

SHANKER WARNS OF A SHUTDOWN

Says Classroom Aides May Strike Next Month

By LEONARD BUDER

Albert Shanker, president of the United Federation of teachers, warned yesterday that there could be a citywide school shutdown next month if the Board of Education did not make a "meaningful" contract offer to the system's paraprofessionals.

Mr. Shanker, who led the teachers' strikes here in 1967 and 1968, said he would urge representatives of the paraprofessionals to authorize a strike at a meeting tomorrow. He added that if they did go on strike, the city's teachers would be asked to respect their picket lines and not report to their classes.

The city system employs about 10,000 paraprofessionals, whose duties range from working with individual pupils or small groups of children to taking attendance and relieving teachers of routine duties. The paraprofessionals, the majority of whom are black or Puerto Rican, hold such job titles as teacher aide, educational assistant or educational associate,

Continued on Page 39, Column 1

Strike in City Apartment Houses Averted by 30-Day Interim Pact

By DAVID K. SHIPLER

A strike by 25,000 apartment-house workers, set for midnight last night, was averted yesterday when landlords and union leaders agreed on a 30-day interim contract that provides for a wage increase of $13 a week.

"This is only what you call a down payment," said Thomas B. Shortman, president of Local 32B of the Building Service Employes Union. He stressed that the union's demand for a $35-a-week raise still held.

The final contract will be negotiated by May 20, according to a joint statement by the union and the Realty Advisory Board, which represents landlords in the talks. Any increase above the $13 will then be paid retroactively, the statement said.

Mayor Lindsay, who had brought the two parties back to the bargaining table after negotiations were broken off last week, announced the interim settlement at a City Hall news conference.

It was the Mayor's pledge to propose modifications in rent control by May 20 that provided

Continued on Page 39, Column 1

NEWS INDEX

Scientists Find Ancient South Pole in the Sahara

By SANDRA BLAKESLEE

A team of earth scientists, dressed in summer shorts and sun hats, searched for the South Pole recently and found it—in the middle of the Sahara.

Dr. Rhodes W. Fairbridge, professor of geology at Columbia University and a member of the team, announced the finding yesterday at a meeting of the American Geophysical Union in Washington.

The expedition, which took scientists from 11 nations to the southeastern corner of Algeria, confirmed what has long been suspected, that the South Pole of 450 million years ago has been slowly edging its way northward, by a sliding action of the earth's crust, to the point where it has arrived today, exposed beneath the desert sun. Inch by inch, the ancient South Pole has traveled a distance of 5,500 miles.

"There is no question about it," Dr. Fairbridge said in an interview. "The territory that was the earth's south polar region in the Upper Ordovician period is now the Central Sahara." The Ordovician geologic period occurred in the Paleozoic era about 500 million years ago. The Taconic mountains in northeastern North America were formed during this period.

The phenomenon of sliding land masses is called the con-

Continued on Page 24, Column 4

The force of melting ice etched this sandstone in the Sahara, according to scientists who found it and said it showed how the South Pole of 450 million years ago moved north.

Yale Strike Urged To Back Panthers

Special to The New York Times

NEW HAVEN, April 20—The Yale College Student Senate, the undergraduate student government of Yale University, urged students tonight to stage a campus strike Wednesday in support of the Black Panthers who are facing trial here.

The student senate approved, 33 to 26, a motion calling on the students to vote for a strike at a mass meeting scheduled for tomorrow night.

Black students at Yale have been demanding a strike since two Panther leaders were jailed for contempt of court last week here. The two, David Hilliard and Emory Douglas, were spectators at pre-trial hearings for Bobby Seale and 13 other Panthers accused of murder, kid-

Continued on Page 26, Column 4

"All the News That's Fit to Print"

The New York Times

LATE CITY EDITION

Weather: Rain ending later today; clear tonight. Partly sunny tomorrow. Temp. range: today 59-56; Saturday 80-62. Full U.S. report on Page 95.

SECTION ONE

VOL. CXIX—No. 41,007 · NEW YORK, SUNDAY, MAY 3, 1970 · 60c beyond 50-mile zone from New York City, except Long Island. 75c beyond 200-mile radius. Higher in air delivery cities. · 50 CENTS

128 U.S. PLANES CARRY OUT ATTACK IN NORTH VIETNAM; SUPPLY LINES ARE TARGETS

NEW HAVEN RALLY ENDS A DAY EARLY; ATTENDANCE DOWN

Protesters Call for a Strike by the Nation's Students Against War in Asia

ADJOURNMENT IS ABRUPT

A Small Group of Radicals Provokes Police Into 2d Tear-Gas Attack

By HOMER BIGART
Special to The New York Times

NEW HAVEN, May 2—Massive demonstrations in support of the Black Panthers ended today with a call for a nationwide student strike, but a small group of white radicals stayed behind and tonight provoked the police into the second tear-gas attack of the generally peaceful protest weekend.

Pelted with bottles, the police, who were aided by a Black Panther sound truck, urged the radicals to leave the New Haven Green, where they had gathered. Backed up by National Guardsmen with fixed bayonets, they gradually forced the bulk of the crowd of 200 into Phelps Gate on the Old Yale campus.

But some youths refused to be dislodged from the green, eluding the police and Yale student marshals, and throwing some rocks and bottles at the police and guardsmen.

Spirits Seemed to Flag

The rally had been adjourned abruptly before tonight's disturbance. It was to have continued tomorrow with a rock music festival, but youthful spirits seemed to be flagging. Attendance today was less than half of the 12,000 to 15,000 who thronged the green on Friday.

The thousands who had gathered here to protest the impending trial of Bobby Seale, the Panther national chairman, and eight other Panthers on murder and kidnapping charges, cheered the proposal for the student strike, which was called

Continued on Page 40, Column 1

The New York Times (by Barton Silverman)

NEW HAVEN GREEN during peaceful rally yesterday in support of Black Panther defendants. Massive demonstrations ended with call for nationwide student strike.

40 of 63 on New York Jet Safe in Caribbean Ditching

A DC-9 jet on a flight from New York to the Caribbean was ditched off St. Croix yesterday with 63 persons aboard. The Coast Guard reported 40 persons rescued last night, seven dead and at least 16 others missing.

The plane was nearly out of fuel when it hit the water about 30 miles east of St. Croix at 3:48 P.M. New York time. The jet left Kennedy International Airport at 11 A.M. and was due at St. Martin, which lies about 150 miles southeast of San Juan, P. R., at 4 P.M.

Flight 980 of the Dutch Antillean Airlines (ALM) ran into a heavy tropical storm. The pilot tried repeatedly to land but was unable to do so. With his fuel gauge almost at zero, he ditched into turbulent waters east of St. Croix.

Most of the passengers were from the New York area, a spokesman for the airline based in Curacao said here last night. There were 55 passengers, 2 infants and 6 crew members on board. The names of those on the flight were withheld pending a determination of the number of fatalities and notification of next of kin.

The Coast Guard reported that seven of those rescued had been injured, at least two seriously. The impact of the ditching shattered the aircraft.

Coast Guard and Navy helicopters dropped life rafts to passengers bobbing in the water, then picked up the survivors.

The helicopters were guided to the rescue site by a Pan American Airways plane, whose pilot reported the ditching by radio, then circled the scene until help came.

Pan American flight 454 from Guadeloupe to San Juan, piloted by Capt. William Prash of Miami, heard the DC-9 report it was low on fuel and about to ditch.

At San Juan, the Federal

Continued on Page 9, Column 1

JOHNSON ACCUSES SOME OF '63 STAFF

On TV, He Asserts Kennedy Holdovers 'Undermined' Him Early in Term

By WARREN WEAVER Jr.
Special to The New York Times

WASHINGTON, May 2—Former President Lyndon B. Johnson has accused some holdover officials of undermining his Administration in the weeks and months after the assassination of President Kennedy.

In a television interview that ranged over the death of President Kennedy and the early disappointments of his own Presidency, Mr. Johnson said that some of the men he inherited from his predecessor in 1963 "did not share either the desire or the hopes that I had for the country and for the Government."

"They, in effect, undermined the Administration and bored from within to create problems for us and leaked information that was slanted, and things of that nature," he continued.

"A good many of them re-

Continued on Page 79, Column 1

LOCAL BOARDS DUE FOR MORE POWER IN SCHOOL AFFAIRS

City Is Taking Steps to Give Community Units Voice in Contract Talks

By LEONARD BUDER

The Board of Education is taking steps to give the city's locally elected community school boards a voice in collective bargaining matters, including the current negotiations with the teacher-aides, and in other school issues.

At the same time, the central board is also planning to grant certain powers to the new local boards to enable them to prepare for a full assumption of duties on July 1, when the city system shifts to a decentralized operation.

The city board's plans, which have been discussed in executive sessions and informally approved, envision the following actions:

¶Establishing a council, composed of one representative from each of the city's 31 community school boards, that would serve in a consultative capacity to the central board and the Chancellor — the post that is to replace Superintendent of Schools — in collective bargaining matters. This would be in line with a provision of the decentralization law.

¶Establishing another council or committee, also composed of 31 local board representatives, that would advise the central board on matters of broad educational policy that would affect the community districts. Although the functions of this council have not yet been defined, a purpose would be to assure close liaison and effective communication between the central and local boards.

¶Granting the new local boards authority to organize, elect officers and formulate their bylaws and to select and even hire district superintendents in advance of July 1. If a new local board hires a superintendent other than the incumbent, this could mean that some districts will have two superintendents for a short period—the outgoing administrator and the incoming official.

¶Operating a training program for the new local board members, as provided by the

Continued on Page 63, Column 1

The New York Times · May 3, 1970

Sites of U.S. raid were given by Hanoi as two provinces (diagonal shading) north of the DMZ. Defense Secretary Melvin R. Laird identified principal enemy sanctuaries (dark shading) across the Cambodian border. Arrows show the two allied ground offensives in Cambodia.

HANOI CAUTIONED

Laird Declares an End to Foe's Sanctuary in Cambodia

By WILLIAM BEECHER
Special to The New York Times

WASHINGTON, May 2—The United States has carried out a heavy bombing raid against supply dumps and other targets north of the demilitarized zone in North Vietnam, well-placed Administration sources said today.

The raid was said to be different in both scope and character from any conducted since November, 1968, when the United States announced the end of most bombing of North Vietnam. Since then, the Government has acknowledged only occasional incidents of "suppressive fire" by small numbers of planes against antiaircraft installations threatening American reconnaissance craft.

The latest raid — conducted yesterday or today—was said to have been carried out by 128 fighter-bombers striking at targets not authorized for attack over the last 18 months. Sources said the supply lines were near the entrance to passes leading into Laos.

Nixon Approval Reported

President Nixon was said to have authorized at least one such raid after his television address Thursday night announcing the attack by American ground troops against enemy installations in Cambodia.

Information about the air raid was obtained here today after a Hanoi radio broadcast charged that more than 100 American planes struck "yesterday and today" in Quangbinh and Nghean Provinces in North Vietnam, killing or wounding "many civilians, including 20 children." It also said two American planes had been shot down.

Official spokesmen here openly acknowledged that there had been a raid in that region, but described it as a reinforced mission of "protective reaction" against antiaircraft guns to protect unarmed reconnaissance aircraft. They refused to discuss the number of planes involved and said they knew nothing about casualties.

Policy Change Denied

The indications here were that the Administration intended to make no special announcement of the raid and hoped it would not attract unusual notice.

Officials did not deny the more detailed information supplied by other reliable sources, but they contended that there was no change in the policy on bombing North Vietnam.

Elsewhere in the Administration, however, the raid was portrayed as a significant departure from past practice, although the sources refused to

Continued on Page 2, Column 5

Allied Search in Cambodia Yields Few Signs of Foe

By TERENCE SMITH
Special to The New York Times

SAIGON, South Vietnam, Sunday, May 3—United States and South Vietnamese soldiers have begun a painstaking search of the Fishhook area of Cambodia amid increasing indications that many enemy troops fled in advance of the allied forces' arrival.

The task force discovered several recently evacuated enemy base areas—but no significant numbers of troops—as the allies began to close a giant ring around the suspected location of the Communist military headquarters for operations in South Vietnam.

Enemy resistance to the allied sweep remained light and scattered. This morning, the United States command reported that eight American soldiers had been killed and 32 wounded—a low number for an operation of such size. A total of about 10,000 South Vietnamese and United States soldiers, including 5,000 American infantrymen, are participating.

Enemy losses were listed as 476 killed, of which 161 were said to be victims of tactical air strikes and assaults by helicopter gunships. In addition, 118 persons were detained, but some of these appeared to be Cambodian civilians.

Some Enemy Bases Found

In an effort to find the enemy, the reconnaissance area of the operation was extended 20 miles deeper into Cambodia yesterday, according to reliable military sources. Teams of low-flying helicopters crisscrossed the area north and west of the Fishhook section throughout the day, searching for signs of enemy troop concentrations.

There was no immediate indication whether the United States command would extend the operation still farther into Cambodia if the task force failed to find significant enemy forces in the Fishhook area.

The battalion-size enemy

Continued on Page 2, Column 3

Conservative Beats Yarborough In Democratic Primary in Texas

By MARTIN WALDRON
Special to The New York Times

HOUSTON, Sunday, May 3—A millionaire businessman from Houston, using President Nixon's "Southern strategy" in a Democratic primary, yesterday defeated Senator Ralph W. Yarborough, the Texas maverick liberal who was bidding for a third term in the Senate.

Lloyd M. Bentsen Jr., a former Representative from the Rio Grande Valley who quit Congress in 1955 to enter business in Houston, charged in a whirlwind campaign from one end of the state to the other that Senator Yarborough had betrayed 10 million Texans with his liberal positions.

Unofficial returns early today from 250 of the state's 254 counties gave these figures:

Bentsen	768,937
Yarborough	678,629

One of Mr. Bentsen's major issues in the campaign against Senator Yarborough, who had long been at odds with the conservatives who have dominated the Democratic party since World War II, was that Senator Yarborough had voted against President Nixon's latest two appointees to the Supreme Court.

Mr. Bentsen also accused the Senator of dividing Texas by speaking out against the Vietnam war and by supporting antiwar demonstrators.

In attempting to overcome the effects of Mr. Bentsen's well financed campaign, which cost an estimated total of $750,000 or more, the Senator had tried to weld together once more the coalition of liberals plus Negroes and Mexican-Americans. But the coalition failed as many voters failed to go to the polls.

Mr. Bentsen claimed victory on the basis of unofficial re-

Continued on Page 44, Column 4

Today's Sections

Index to Subjects

15-to-1 Shot Wins Derby

Dust Commander, a 15-1 shot, won the 96th running of the Kentucky Derby at Churchill Downs yesterday by five lengths. With 17 horses running, the race was worth a record $170,300 and the winner earned $127,800. He paid $32.60 for $2 to win. My Dad George finished second and High Echelon was third. Details in Section 5.

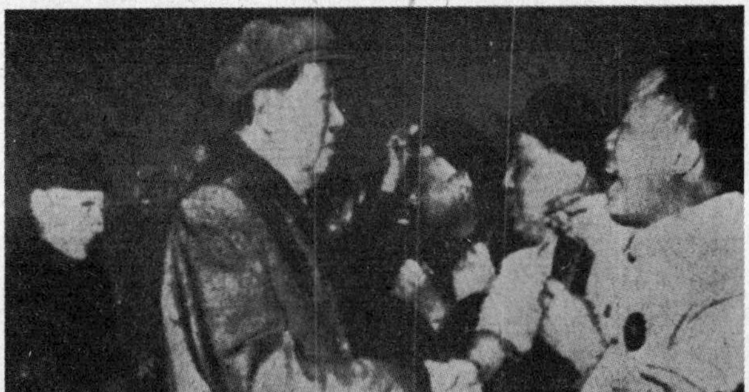

Associated Press

Chairman Mao Tse-tung with Lin Piao, left, at May Day rites in Peking Friday, according to Communist China

Peril to Chinese-Soviet Talks Is Seen in Diatribes

By HARRISON E. SALISBURY

Soviet-Chinese border talks in Peking—and possibly even formal Soviet-Chinese relations—have been imperiled, in the opinion of diplomatic specialists, by new and violent propaganda exchanges.

The Chinese attack on Moscow was in the form of a joint editorial by Peking's three major publications. It attacked Leonid I. Brezhnev, the Soviet party chief, as a "new Hitler" and charged that the Soviet Union had become a "Nazi-type" state, pursuing a racist policy similar to Hitler's "master-race theory" and was planning to conduct a blitzkrieg against China.

The Russians have replied with a special broadcast beamed to China in Mandarin, containing a vituperative attack on Chairman Mao Tse-Tung, charging him with personal responsibility in the death of his first wife, Yang Kai-hui, who was shot by the Chinese Nationalists in 1930, and also, indirectly, for the allegedly mysterious death of his eldest son, Mao An-ying, during the Korean war.

The text of the 6,500 word Chinese declaration, issued April 22 to mark the 100th anniversary of Lenin's birth, is now available in the United States. Like all major pronouncements, it is being given worldwide distribution by the Chinese. The Soviet broadcast was made three days after the editorial was published.

The broadcast accuses Chairman Mao, the Chinese party leader, of "cruelty, selfishness and lust for high position." It charges that he was unfaithful to his second wife, Ho Tze-chen, and that he abandoned his first wife "to her fate."

Diplomatic assessors believed that a blow, conceivably fatal, had been dealt the Soviet-Chinese talks in Peking by the exchanges. They noted that Deputy Foreign Minister Vasily V. Kuznetsov, head of the Soviet delegation, had left Peking for Moscow and doubted that he would return.

The Soviet and Chinese embassies, whose personnel have been sharply reduced, are headed at present by relatively low-ranking diplomats. Recently, Moscow named Vladimir I.

Continued on Page 16, Column 6

Greek Warriors' Bones Found At Site of Battle of Marathon

Special to The New York Times

MARATHON, Greece, May 2—The burial place of Greek warriors who fell in the epoch-making Battle of Marathon, defending Athenian civilization from Persian conquest in 490 B. C., has been discovered by Greek archeologists on this ancient battlefield.

The announcement of the discovery was made on the site today by Prof. Spyridon Marinatos, inspector general of Greek antiquities, as he stood on the edge of the mass grave containing the skeletons of some young soldiers slain in the battle between East and West 2,460 years ago.

The professor told a throng of newsmen that the grave had been identified "beyond any reasonable doubt" as the tomb of the Plataeans, who had volunteered to help the Athenian Army under the leadership of Miltiades fight the Persian invaders, though heavily outnumbered by the enemy.

The mass grave lay under a carefully built stone tumulus, or burial mound, 10 feet high and 50 feet in diameter, its edge marked by hewn stones, on a plain 26 miles northeast of Athens.

Only part of the burial trench has been excavated so far, revealing five perfectly preserved skeletons. According to experts they belong to young soldiers

Continued on Page 14, Column 2

"All the News
That's Fit to Print"

The New York Times

LATE CITY EDITION

Weather: Partly sunny today; clear tonight. Mostly sunny tomorrow. Temp. range: today 70-55; Tuesday 76-56. Full U.S. report on Page 93

VOL. CXIX..No. 41,031 | NEW YORK, WEDNESDAY, MAY 27, 1970 | 10 CENTS

LAIRD SAID TO ASK IF ASIA PULLOUT CAN BE ADVANCED

Query to Abrams Reported to Be Based on Gains Made in Cambodian Operation

REPLY TO DISSENT SEEN

White House Denies It Plans to End Action in Cambodia Before June 30 Deadline

By WILLIAM BEECHER
Special to The New York Times

WASHINGTON, May 26—Secretary of Defense Melvin R. Laird is said to have asked American commanders in Vietnam whether, in light of recent operations against suspected enemy base areas in Cambodia, the United States can withdraw more troops from Vietnam by May 1, 1971 than the 150,000 announced by President Nixon last month.

The reply is expected later this week, according to high-ranking Pentagon sources, who said there were at least three factors behind the request to accelerate the withdrawals, as follows:

¶The capture or destruction of thousands of tons of weapons and ammunition and rice and medicine in the suspected sanctuaries, which, it is estimated, should take North Vietnam 6 to 12 months to replace.

¶A demonstration of combat effectiveness by a large number of previously unimpressive South Vietnamese military units.

¶A desire to cool dissent in Congress and on the campus by demonstrating that the much-criticized assaults across the Cambodian border should speed the American disengagement from Vietnam.

Report Is Questioned

At the White House, the Presidential press secretary, Ronald L. Ziegler, described as inaccurate a report published in The New York Times today to the effect that the Administration's plans contemplated the completion of the withdrawal of American troops from Cambodia ahead of the June 30 deadline set by Mr. Nixon.

Mr. Ziegler said that the operation would be completed by June 30.

"We have no intention of sending any personnel back in," he added. "We've announced our schedule, we are on schedule and everything is proceeding well."

The request for recommendations is said to have been made

Continued on Page 17, Column 1

Nixon Greets Suharto and Briefs Him on Cambodia

United Press International

President Suharto with President Nixon yesterday on the Indonesian leader's arrival

By TAD SZULC
Special to The New York Times

WASHINGTON, May 26—President Nixon welcomed President Suharto of Indonesia to the White House today and told him during a 90-minute conference that the joint United States-South Vietnamese operation in Cambodia was a success.

The two men held the first of two meetings scheduled during President Suharto's three-day stay in Washington. He is on a week-long state visit to the United States. At his arrival at the White House President Suharto said that "my visit comes at a time when the need for sincere and realistic efforts in the interest of peace and stability in the world, and in Southeast Asia in particular, has become ever more pressing." Speaking in Indonesian during the

Continued on Page 6, Column 4

BEIRUT CONSIDERS ASKING TROOP AID FROM ARAB LANDS

Cabinet to Decide Today on Calling In Forces From Morocco and Tunisia

By DANA ADAMS SCHMIDT
Special to The New York Times

BEIRUT, Lebanon, May 26—Premier Rashid Karami said tonight in the National Assembly that the Lebanese Government was considering calling in troops from Morocco and Tunisia or other Arab countries to help defend Lebanon against Israel.

He said that the Cabinet would make a decision on such a move tomorrow and would submit its plan to the Assembly on Thursday.

The Premier's statement was made after a report had reached the Assembly that Israel was planning continuous patrols on both sides of the Israeli-Lebanese border. A statement to that effect was reported to have been made today to newsmen by Maj. Gen. Mordechai Gur, chief of the Israeli Northern Command, during a guided tour of the Israeli side of the border.

Parliament in Turmoil

The news threw the parliament into turmoil. A remark attributed to General Gur that Israel intended to carry out the police duties against Arab guerrillas that the Lebanese Army was unwilling to perform was characterized as arrogant. So was another in which the general was quoted as having said that he hoped that under Israeli protection Lebanese refugees would return to the border area.

Military observers here said that if Lebanon did invite any Arab troops in, it was likely that she would ask for some or all of the 6,000 Iraqi soldiers now in Syria rather than invite troops from North Africa.

The observers pointed out that it would take months to bring in Moroccan or Tunisian forces, while the Iraqis could reach Lebanon in hours. It was also pointed out, however, that Morocco and Tunisia, along with Lebanon, are considered moderate Arab countries.

If the Beirut Government decides that it needs immediate Arab troop reinforcements, the military observers added, it will be under pressure from Lebanese leftists to accept Syrian troops. But, they said, the Lebanese Government is sure to resist such proposals because of its historic fear of absorption by its larger Arab neighbors.

The proposal to bring in Moroccan and Tunisian troops

Continued on Page 4, Column 3

22-Nation Group Suggests U.S. Pay-Price Guidelines

O.E.C.D. Study Asserts Selective Steps Could Help to Achieve Stability and Fuller Employment for Nation

By CLYDE H. FARNSWORTH
Special to The New York Times

PARIS, May 26—An economic body representing 22 nations has cautiously suggested that the United States resolve its growing difficulties in combining high employment with price stability by installing formal wage and price guidelines.

The Organization for Economic Cooperation and Development thrust itself into the policy debate in the United States with a recommendation made in a 46-page review of the American economy.

The O.E.C.D. Secretariat prepares studies of all the member countries such as the United States once a year. These reports are put together with the cooperation of the economic authorities of the countries concerned.

While discreetly worded, the advice was clear. "Even with the easier demand conditions now envisaged, progress toward price stability and an early return to fuller employment might be enhanced if certain selective measures could be applied in support of continued use of traditional demand management policies," the report said.

It cited among these "selective measures" the exercise of influence by the Government on wages and prices—what has come to be known as an incomes policy.

The advice of the international body, in which the United States shares membership with Canada, Japan and 19 Western European countries, was all the

Continued on Page 59, Column 1

NIXON AIDES SAY ECONOMIC MOVES ARE SUCCEEDING

Four Officials Stand Firm on Inflation Policies—Shultz Sees Wall St. 'Neurosis'

PANEL ASKS WAGE RULES

House Unit Seeks to Revive Voluntary Guideposts on Prices and Pay Rises

By EDWIN L. DALE Jr.
Special to The New York Times

WASHINGTON, May 26 — The Nixon Administration, under a barrage of criticism from politicians and financiers, stood firmly by its economic policies today.

Four high officials in four cities commented on the situation, and the theme was the same. Probably the most unequivocal statement came from Harold C. Passer, Assistant Secretary of Commerce for Economic Affairs, who said:

"The economic situation is in control, our policies are working, and we are going to continue these policies."

Secretary of Labor George P. Shultz called the decline in the stock market "a kind of neurosis."

A similar calm reaction to events came from Paul W McCracken, chairman of the

Stocks Tumble Again

The stock market took another tumble yesterday after a brief rally failed to generate momentum. The Dow-Jones industrial average fell 10.20 points to 631.16, the lowest closing since Nov. 19, 1962. Details on Page 57.

Council of Economic Advisers, and Charls E. Walker, Under Secretary of the Treasury.

In Congress today there were these developments:

¶The House Ways and Means Committee approved the Administration's request for an increase of $18-billion in the legal ceiling on the national debt. The committee staff said that the Administration's revenue figures were probably too optimistic and that the budget deficit for the new fiscal year would be more than $4-billion, compared with $1.3-billion projected in the latest revision of the budget.

¶A subcommittee of the House Government Operations Committee approved a bill that would revive the long dormant voluntary wage-price "guideposts." Under the proposal the President's Council of Economic Advisers would establish rules for noninflationary wage increases and permissible price increases and the President would try to persuade business and labor to adhere to the rules. The Administration opposes the bill.

The Administration opposition was made clear by Mr. McCracken in a brief news conference in Los Angeles. He

Continued on Page 20, Column 3

Rogers Backs NATO Move Toward East-Bloc Accord

By DREW MIDDLETON
Special to The New York Times

ROME, May 26—Secretary of State William P. Rogers endorsed today proposals by European allies of the United States for a mutual and balanced reduction of the forces of the Atlantic alliance and the Warsaw pact in central Europe.

Speaking to the other foreign ministers of the 15-nation North Atlantic Treaty Organization here, Mr. Rogers, according to United States sources, called for a declaration to the Soviet Union and the other Warsaw pact states expressing NATO's desire for progress toward a détente.

American sources said his speech marked a definite change in United States policy toward support, in general if not in detail, of a drive toward negotiations with the Soviet bloc. It was noted, however, that although the Secretary's statement went beyond past Nixon Administration positions, it did not go as far as the call of the British Foreign Secretary, Michael Stewart, for the creation by the alliance of a Standing Commission for East-West Affairs in Europe.

Mr. Rogers, American sources said, made no reference to the British proposal or to the call by the Italian Premier, Mariano Rumor, in a speech opening the conference, for rapid and thorough preparation for "forthright conversations between NATO and Warsaw Pact countries with participation open to European neutral and nonaligned countries."

In Mr. Rogers's speech, other diplomats noted, the emphasis

Continued on Page 7, Column 1

SENATE SUPPORTS NIXON ON PULLOUT

Votes on Preamble of Move to Curb Cambodian War as Long Debate Opens

By JOHN W. FINNEY
Special to The New York Times

WASHINGTON, May 26—In the first vote in a prolonged Cambodia debate, the Senate made clear today that it endorsed President Nixon's troop withdrawal plans, although it remained divided on curbing any future military involvement in Cambodia.

The somewhat inconclusive vote came on a revised preamble that was offered for an amendment to a foreign military sales bill. The amendment was sponsored by Senators John Sherman Cooper, Republican of Kentucky, and Frank Church, Democrat of Idaho. The vote was 82-11.

The amendment would provide that the President could spend no funds to "retain" United States forces in Cambodia or to provide military advisers, mercenaries or combat air support to the Cambodian

Continued on Page 14, Column 1

TENANTS ASSAIL RENT PROPOSALS

Some Speakers at Council Hearing Score Capitalism —Candidates Testify

By DAVID K. SHIPLER

Numerous tenants and their organizers threatened rent strikes yesterday if the City Council approved Mayor Lindsay's proposal to relax the city's 27-year-old rent-control law.

Charging that landlords would just put rent increases into their pockets, not into their buildings, about 200 persons—including a parade of candidates for political office—appeared for an all-day hearing at City Hall before the City Council's Housing Committee.

Many criticized the Mayor for inconsistency in advocating rent rises while calling several days ago for Federal wage and price controls.

Others, calling property owners "slumlords," "vultures" and "millionaires," urged complete government take-over of the city's housing.

"We believe it's about time

Continued on Page 44, Column 2

Nixon Meets Heads Of 2 City Unions; Hails War Support

By ROBERT B. SEMPLE Jr.
Special to The New York Times

WASHINGTON, May 26 — President Nixon told leaders of the building trades and longshoremen's unions of New York today that he had found their public demonstrations of support for his Vietnam policy reassuring and "very meaningful."

They, in turn, pledged that their rallies—one of which was marked by violence two weeks ago — would continue, and handed him a statement urging "national support for our fighting men."

There was some difference of opinion over the genesis of the meeting, which lasted for 47 minutes.

Rare Unanimity

Peter J. Brennan, president of the Building and Construction Trades Council of Greater New York and New York State, told newsmen last night that Mr. Nixon had invited the group to the White House during a telephone call last Thursday. The Presidential press secretary, Ronald L. Ziegler, said the initiative had come from the unions.

In any event, there was rare unanimity in the Oval Office today, as the President, who has not been reading or hearing many kind words about his

Continued on Page 18, Column 4

SENATE UNIT BACKS POSTAL REFORMS

Commission Plan and Pay Rise Are Approved but Not Increase in Rates

By United Press International

WASHINGTON, May 26 —The Senate Post Office Committee today approved proposed reforms removing Congress and politics from the postal system and giving post office employes an 8 per cent pay rise.

But the committee, following the example of its House counterpart, left out an increase in postal rates sought by the Administration to finance the $496-million pay increase.

It approved reforms that would let an independent commission set new postal rates as early as next year, with Congress having no voice in the decision or veto power over it.

The Senate bill would make the Postmaster General a non-Cabinet professional hired by nine postal governors. An independent commission of five members would set postal rates, tailoring them to pay 90 per cent of the post office's budget.

Congress would appropriate the other 10 per cent as a "public service" subsidy to maintain rural delivery and other postal operations that

Continued on Page 20, Column 3

SAIGON TO RENEW TIES TO CAMBODIA

Vague Pact Is Also Reached on Troop Withdrawal

Special to The New York Times

SAIGON, South Vietnam, Wednesday, May 27 — The Governments of South Vietnam and Cambodia agreed here today that South Vietnamese troops would be pulled out of Cambodia "as soon as their mission is completed."

The vague agreement, along with an agreement to restore diplomatic relation at the ambassadorial rank, was contained in a joint communiqué prepared by the Foreign Ministers of the two countries at the conclusion of their talks here this morning.

There was no indication in the communiqué when the South Vietnamese troops would conclude their operations in Cambodia or whether South Vietnamese troops would continue to operate after the scheduled withdrawal of United States forces by June 30.

The delegations, headed by Foreign Minister Yem Sambaur of Cambodia and the South Vietnamese Foreign Minister, Tran Van Lam, also agreed to respect for the moment the present boundaries of the two countries, thus bypassing serious discussion over disputed land.

That question was raised

Continued on Page 16, Column 4

Rain Cuts Brooklyn BMT Power, Trapping 5,000 Up to 2½ Hours

By LINDA CHARLTON

About 5,000 subway passengers, some of whom had been trapped for more than two hours, had to be evacuated from powerless trains last night after a heavy downpour caused flooding that resulted in a short circuit on the Fourth Avenue BMT line in Brooklyn.

A total of 17 persons were reported to have been taken to five Brooklyn hospitals for treatment of minor injuries, and others needed emergency oxygen at the scene.

The flow of water that covered all tracks and the third rail began about 6:25 P.M. By 6:30 the power was shut off in both directions along the Fourth Avenue line between DeKalb Avenue and 95th Street, with no service to Coney Island on either Sea Beach or West End line trackage and limited service on the Brighton line.

The Transit Authority said that full service was restored by 11:20 P.M.

An authority spokesman was asked if service would be affected this morning. "Not unless it rains," he said.

The passengers, according to Sgt. Bertram Bergrin of the Bergen Street station, were evacuated with the assistance of about 80 policemen from several precincts and firemen , were called to extinguish insulation fires that followed

Continued on Page 93, Column 6

NEWS INDEX

Moon Rock Believed as Old as Solar System

United Press International

Lunar rock, 1½ inches long, weighs three ounces and apparently dates back to formation of solar system. Slab in foreground was sliced from rock, which resembles earth's granite, for analysis. Numbers refer to Apollo 12, and the rock, the 13th taken from sample box.

By JOHN NOBLE WILFORD

A highly radioactive rock from the moon's Ocean of Storms was reported yesterday to be 4.6 billion years old, making it the oldest lunar material yet discovered and the first lunar rock found that apparently dates back to the formation of the solar system.

Scientists called the observation one of the most exciting and significant findings to be reached in their analysis of the rocks and soil brought back from the moon last year by the Apollo 11 and 12 astronauts.

The discovery was particularly encouraging to scientists who have predicted the moon harbors, in relatively undisturbed condition, materials bearing evidence of the earliest history of the solar system. All the other rocks from two Apollo flights ranged in age from 3.3 billion to 3.7 billion years.

The 4.6 billion-year-old rock was described in an announcement made simultaneously by the Manned Spacecraft Center in Houston and by Dr. Gerald J. Wasserburg of the California Institute of Technology in Pasadena.

Dr. Wasserburg, who performed the dating analysis, made his report in Leningrad at the 13th meeting of the Committee on Space Research (COSPAR) of the International Council of Scientific Unions.

"It now appears we have on the surface of the moon—and in our laboratories — materials which date back to the formation of the solar system," the space center announcement said.

The rock, which was brought back by the Apollo 12 astronauts, was about the size of a small lemon, weighing three ounces and measuring one and a half inches long, an inch wide and three-quarters of an inch thick. Its black and white and gray interior resembled granite found on the earth.

Besides having a great age, the rock was found to have a "unique chemistry" and the highest concentration of radioactive elements yet observed in samples from the moon.

Analysts at Houston said the rock had 20 times more uranium, thorium and potassium than any other rocks from either the Apollo 12 landing site on the Ocean of Storms or the Apollo 11 site on the Sea of Tranquility.

When the radioactivity count

Continued on Page 22, Column 2

Times to Cost 15c; News Accepts Pact

The New York Times announced yesterday that the newsstand price of the daily newspaper would be raised to 15 cents on Monday and that advertising rates would be increased later as a result of a wage settlement with union printers.

At the same time The Daily News reported that it had reached a tentative contract agreement with the printers' union that would provide a wage increase of 41.69 per cent over three years, the same terms agreed to by The Times on Sunday.

Arthur Ochs Sulzberger, president and publisher of The Times, issued the following statement yesterday:

"I am announcing today an increase in the newsstand prices and advertising rates of The New York Times. The newsstand price of the daily New York Times will be raised to

Continued on Page 44, Column 5

"All the News That's Fit to Print"

The New York Times

LATE CITY EDITION

Weather: Sunny, cold today; fair tonight. Chance of rain tomorrow. Temp. range: today 39-28; Saturday 35-23. Full U.S. report on Page 71.

SECTION ONE

VOL. CXX....No. 41,252

NEW YORK, SUNDAY, JANUARY 3, 1971

75¢ beyond 30-mile zone from New York City, except Long Island. Higher in air delivery cities.

50 CENTS

George Davis

BEAUTY DEFENDED: Adirondacks scene. Proposed agency would guide development of the park's six million acres.

NEW POLICY URGED FOR ADIRONDACKS

Report to Rockefeller Calls for Separate State Unit to Guide Development

By BAYARD WEBSTER

Governor Rockefeller yesterday released a two-year study of the Adirondacks that calls for creation of an independent agency with power to regulate the use and development of all land, public and private, in the six-million-acre Adirondack State Park.

The report, prepared for the Governor by the Temporary Study Commission on the Future of the Adirondacks, recommends the formation of a new body called the Adirondack Park Agency, which would set policy for the park, an area slightly larger than the state of Vermont.

Housing Growing in Park

No estimate was given of the cost of carrying out the report's proposals, but one of them calls for a $120-million bond issue to acquire so-called scenic easements, purchase land and construct facilities.

In releasing the study, Governor Rockefeller said that he would study it and, at the appropriate time, submit his recommendations on it to the Legislature.

The new proposed Adirondack Park Agency, which would be bipartisan, would work in conjunction with the State Department of Environmental Conservation to help to slacken the swelling tide of housing developments in the park. It would

Continued on Page 60, Column 1

Graduate Faculties Improve, Poll Finds

By ROBERT M. SMITH

Special to The New York Times

WASHINGTON, Jan. 2—The quality of the faculty in many graduate programs at major universities improved substantially between 1964 and 1969, according to a poll of American college professors. But the professors still hold in highest regard those schools—such as Harvard University and the University of California at Berkeley—that they thought were best six years ago.

At the same time, the professors, in a survey by the American Council on Education, rated 30 per cent of the graduate programs surveyed as marginal or inadequate. In 1964, they gave 28 per cent of the programs the equivalent of those ratings.

One change that has taken place in the attitudes of the professors concerns Columbia University. The survey found that Columbia has slipped noticeably in rank since 1964 in a series of opinion ratings designed to judge the quality of its graduate faculty.

Reaction From Columbia

In addition, the professors often gave the New York school lower ratings for the "effectiveness" of its doctoral programs than for the quality of its faculty. They felt that Columbia as an institution was not as attractive a place to pursue the Ph.D. in many fields as the high caliber of its faculty might imply.

Officials at Columbia, noting the decline in the ratings, said that the quality of the graduate faculty had greatly improved since the early part of 1969, when the survey was completed. They attributed much of the decline to campus unrest.

The council's report, "A Rating of Graduate Programs," is based on questionnaires mailed to faculty members in various fields of study at 130 schools.

The professors were asked their opinion of the graduate programs at universities that offer doctorates in their fields. The fields ranged from art history to zoology.

The ratings reflect the way an average of perhaps 100 teachers in each discipline regarded graduate programs at their own school and others.

A 115-page statistical report summarizing the responses of the professors shows that the graduate faculties at the following schools appear most often in the top five positions

Continued on Page 54, Column 4

Sadat Says He Is Ready For War if the Truce Ends

By RAYMOND H. ANDERSON

Special to The New York Times

CAIRO, Jan. 2—President Anwar el-Sadat declared today that the armed forces of the United Arab Republic were ready for an "all-out battle" against Israel after the Suez Canal cease-fire expires on Feb. 5.

Proclaiming that "it is more honorable to die fighting than to live in surrender," the Egyptian leader reiterated that he would not agree to an extension of the cease-fire unless there was serious progress toward a political settlement involving a timetable for an Israeli withdrawal from Arab lands occupied in the 1967 war.

Mr. Sadat cautioned that Israel might launch a pre-emptive strike before the expiration of the cease-fire and said that the armed forces were alert and ready.

The President spoke to journalists, writers and some prominent intellectuals in Abdin Palace in the first address of a nationwide campaign keyed to the approaching expiration of the cease-fire.

Mr. Sadat will speak at a mass rally in the Nile Delta town of Tanta on Monday and in other towns in Egypt in coming weeks.

In his speech today he said that Israel, with United States support, was adhering to a hard position toward a settlement with the Arabs.

Earlier this week, Mr. Sadat said Israel's decision to resume contact with Dr. Gunnar V. Jarring, the United Nations representative in the Middle East conflict, was a maneuver to obtain an extension of the cease-fire. Israel decided on Monday to resume indirect peace talks, suspended four months when Egypt allegedly violated the cease-fire by moving missie emplacements into the Suez truce zone.

Mr. Sadat reiterated today that he would not stand idle and permit the Suez cease-fire line to become a permanent border.

The President also repeated

Continued on Page 6, Column 1

CITY WILL SUE U.S. ON WELFARE COSTS

Move Seeks to Have Albany and Washington Pay All

By ROBERT D. McFADDEN

Mayor Lindsay directed the city's Corporation Counsel yesterday to sue the Federal and state governments to strike down laws that mandate welfare costs to the city, a sum totaling more than $600-million in the current fiscal year.

The suit also would seek to force the Federal and state governments to finance all welfare and Medicaid programs in New York City.

Under existing laws, the Federal Government sets broad guidelines governing welfare payments and the state sets specific regulations. The city's position is mainly clerical, except that it pays nearly a third of the welfare costs, while the Federal and state governments share the remainder.

The planned suit announced yesterday in a statement at City Hall would thus raise complicated, fundamental issues over the fiscal relationships of

Continued on Page 58, Column 3

FIREMEN CREATING 'GRAVE' SITUATION, MAYOR TELLS CITY

Lindsay Says Officers Join Job Action—Cites Concern for Safety of the People

By EMANUEL PERLMUTTER

Mayor Lindsay said yesterday that the refusal of firemen to perform any duties except fire fighting had created a "very grave" situation because they were now being joined by their superior officers.

"With a breakdown of discipline and command in the field, we are approaching a situation where I am concerned about the safety of the people of this city," the Mayor said at a news conference in City Hall.

He said that superior officers in the department had joined in the firemen's work stoppage by failing to order the men to perform nonemergency duties.

"The firemen's job action is now complete," he said somberly. "It is serious and has grown very grave because they've been joined by their commanders and there is a danger of further escalation."

Maye Accuses City

At about the same time the Mayor was speaking, Michael J. Maye, head of the Uniformed Firefighters' Association, said that "the city is pushing the fire fighters to the wall, and we have just about reached the point of no return."

"I don't want a strike" Mr. Maye said, "and I will do everything in my power to prevent one." But he warned that the firemen might take some unspecified "stronger" action than they had if the city failed to make some "meaningful gestures" in the negotiations.

In a contract dispute with the city, the 11,300 members of the Uniformed Firefighters Association have refused to inspect buildings and fire hydrants, maintain equipment, engage in fire drills and perform firehouse duties.

Mayor Sees Officials

They are protesting their failure to get from the city a new contract that they consider satisfactory. The old contract expired Dec. 31.

The Mayor made his comments about the firemen's job action at City Hall after conferring there for about an hour with members of the Office of Collective Bargaining and with Fire Commissioner Robert O. Lowery and Fire Chief John T. O'Hagan.

The members of the bargaining agency had met previously for two hours at their office, 255 Broadway, where they heard a report from Eric J. Schmertz, the chief mediator in the firemen's dispute, and from others on that mediation

Continued on Page 56, Column 1

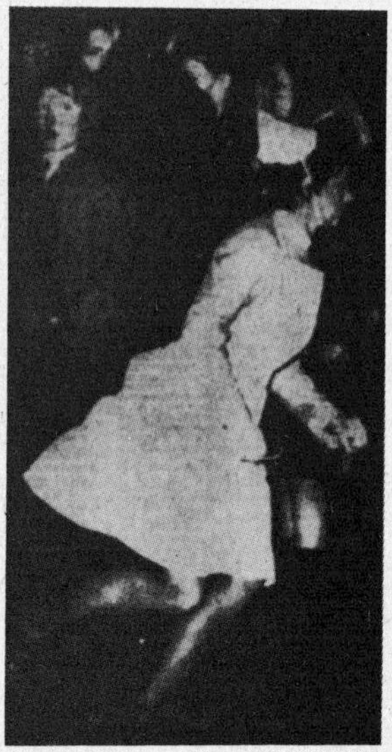

United Press International

EMERGENCY CALL: A nurse rushes into Ibrox Stadium in Glasgow, Scotland, to aid those injured in mishap.

66 Killed as Barrier Falls At Glasgow Soccer Match

Special to The New York Times

GLASGOW, Scotland, Jan. 2—Sixty-six persons were killed today when a crowd barrier collapsed at the Ibrox soccer stadium here.

The tragedy was the worst in the history of British soccer. It came as 80,000 spectators rushed for the exits after the traditional New Year game between the Glasgow Rangers and the Glasgow Celtics.

A police sergeant said there was "a mad rush of people toward exits" at the end of the game. "Then somebody fell," he said. "Somebody fell on top of him. And it snowballed until a crush barrier collapsed."

The officer broke down as he described his search for survivors among "a mound of dead."

More than a hundred other persons were injured, three of them critically. Many more were treated at the stadium according to first-aid attendants.

According to a police spokesman, Ranger supporters leaving the northeast stands heard the roar of the crowd and tried to turn back when the tying goal in the 1-1 draw was scored. Both goals came late in the game. In the confusion a barrier in a sloping exit collapsed and spectators were piled on top of each other.

The New York Times Jan. 3, 1971

One of those injured, John Dawson of Tillicoultry in Clackmannanshire, said: "I am lucky to be alive. When the barrier gave way I was carried along a passageway for 20 yards with three people on top of me and at least three underneath."

Robert Black of Glasgow said there was "terrific pressure in the crowd" when the first goal was scored.

"While I was on the stairway on my way out" he said, "there was so much pressure from behind me that I was tossed down on top of others. Some chaps were on the ground and I was tossed over them."

The Mayor of Glasgow, Sir Donald Liddle, who was present at the game and knelt on

Continued on Page 14, Column 3

CONGRESS CLOSES AS SENATE VOTES SST COMPROMISE

Funding Is Extended Three Months—A Final Decision Is Due in Next Session

LONG DEADLOCK BROKEN

Speaker Eulogized in House—Nixon Vetoes a Pay Rise for Blue-Collar Workers

By JOHN W. FINNEY

Special to The New York Times

WASHINGTON, Jan. 2—The marathon 91st Congress, which met in nearly continuous session for two years, finally adjourned today after one last burst of Senate oratory and then a compromise on the supersonic transport issue.

The compromise broke a deadlock that had kept the session going longer that any other since 1950. The Constitution required adjournment by noon tomorrow.

In essence, the compromise put the SST controversy over to the new Congress, which convenes Jan. 21.

After two hours of oratory, the Senate by a voice vote passed a resolution, approved by the House Thursday, extending the funding for the Department of Transportation, including the supersonic plane project, for three months. The new Congress will have to decide whether to continue the Federal financing of the project beyond March 30.

McCormack Retires

The Senate, after adding a few hours to more than 1,400 hours of debate this session, adjourned at 2:29 P.M. The House spent the afternoon eulogizing the departing Speaker, John W. McCormack, who at the age of 79 is retiring from public life, and then adjourned at 3:11.

President Nixon meanwhile threw down one last rebuke to the Democratic-controlled Congress by vetoing a bill that would have increased the pay of some 800,000 Government blue-collar workers by 4 per cent. The veto came too late for any attempt to override it.

Before Congress adjourned, its leaders received word that the President planned to deliver his State of the Union Message Jan. 22, the day after the new Congress convenes

Just as the McCormack departure marked the changing of the guard in the House, so the climactic SST debate marked the culmination of a challenge by a new generation in the Senate to the power wielded by the House and Senate Appropriations Commit-

Continued on Page 33, Column 1

Today's Sections

Index to Subjects

Israelis Find a Crucifixion Skeleton

By PETER GROSE

Special to The New York Times

JERUSALEM, Jan. 2 — A team of Israeli scholars has announced the discovery in the outskirts of Jerusalem of the skeleton of a man crucified about 2,000 years ago.

The skeleton, its heel bones pierced by a large iron nail, was found more than two years ago in one of several cave tombs in northeastern Jerusalem.

It has long been known from literary sources that crucifixion was a common method of punishment and execution—involving thousands of people — in the ancient world. But the recent discovery is regarded as the first authenticated physical evidence of a crucifixion in Biblical times.

Academic circles in Jerusalem have been eagerly awaiting the publication of definitive reports on the discovery. At the same time, many scholars have privately expressed nervousness over the danger of provoking unwarranted attempts to relate the discovery to the Gospel story of Jesus.

"An initial anthropological approach to the first material evidence of a crucifixion does not exclude a certain emotional concern," wrote Dr. Nicu Haas, senior lecturer in anatomy of the Hebrew University-Hadassah Medical Center, who directed the detailed examination of the bones and other remains.

"We must remember that the act of crucifixion was performed on many thousands of Jews and Gentiles, before and after Jesus of Nazareth. This form of punishment was a customary one in Phoenician and, later, Roman law."

Avraham Biran, director of the Government Department of Antiquities and Museums, said it was "far-fetched and plain silly" to suppose that these were the bones of Jesus, whatever coincidences of timing and circumstances might appear.

"I am sure we have found

Continued on Page 2, Column 3

Associated Press

LAST DAY AS HOUSE SPEAKER: John W. McCormack, Massachusetts Democrat, before the final session of the 91st Congress. Behind him is Representative Hale Boggs, Democrat of Louisiana. Article appears on Page 32.

"All the News
That's Fit to Print"

The New York Times

LATE CITY EDITION

Weather: Sunny, quite cold today; clear, cold tonight. Fair tomorrow. Temp. range: today 22-5; Tuesday 16-4. Full U.S. report on Page 70.

VOL. CXX ... No. 41,269

NEW YORK, WEDNESDAY, JANUARY 20, 1971

15 CENTS

PATROLMEN END SIX-DAY STRIKE, HEEDING UNION DELEGATES' VOTE; PAY AND PENALTIES UNRESOLVED

The New York Times/Jack Manning

BACK TO DUTY: Patrolmen in civilian clothes reporting at station house on 51st Street east of Lexington Avenue

U.S. IS NOW FLYING COPTER MISSIONS FOR LAOS TROOPS

Gunships Attacking Enemy Soldiers and Supplies on the Ho Chi Minh Trail

NEW STEP-UP IN AIR WAR

White House Says Its Policy Barring Use of Ground Forces Is Unchanged

By The Associated Press

SAIGON, South Vietnam, Jan. 19—A further enlargement of the United States air role in Indochina was reported here today as official sources said American helicopter gunships were flying combat missions in Laos in direct support of Laotian ground troops.

The informants said Army, Air Force and Marine helicopter gunships had been supporting the Laotian troops for some time and had been attacking enemy troops and supplies along the Ho Chi Minh Trail through southeastern Laos.

Disclosure of this helicopter activity in Laos followed reports yesterday that United States helicopter gunships were attacking enemy forces in Cambodia in support of an allied drive to reopen a major Cambodian supply route.

[The White House acknowledged a recent step-up in American air operations in Cambodia, but insisted that Administration policy had not changed fom the guidelines laid down by President Nixon last summer forbidding the use of combat troops or advisers to ail Cambodian forces. In Pnompenh, the Cambodian high command reported that all but 10 miles of the highway to the sea had been cleared by allied troops. Pages 3 and 5.]

The informants here said the United States was conducting one of the biggest aerial campaigns of the war in Laos, using B-52 bombers, tactical fighter-bombers, gunships and reconnaissance aircraft with special secret equipment.

The aim, they said, is to slow the flow of North Vietnamese troops and war matériel into Laos, Cambodia and South Vietnam and to prevent the enemy forces from establishing sanctuaries in the three countries.

The United States command said 13 helicopters had been

Continued on Page 3, Column 2

Lithuanian in Soviet Doomed as Hijacker

By BERNARD GWERTZMAN

Special to The New York Times

MOSCOW, Jan. 19 — A Lithuanian was reported today to have been sentenced to death and his pregnant wife to three years in a prison camp for an attempt last November to hijack a plane from the Soviet Union to Sweden.

According to usually reliable sources, a court in Vilna, the Lithuanian capital, imposed the sentences last Thursday after a 10-day trial. The couple have until Thursday to file an appeal with the Lithuanian Supreme Court.

The trial has not yet been reported in newspapers available in Moscow, including the major Lithuanian dailies. No official confirmation could be obtained after the reports had been relayed to Western newsmen through sources fa-

Continued on Page 12, Column 4

EGYPT CRITICIZES ISRAELI POSITION

She Is Said to Find Foe's Proposals on Pullout and Palestinians Inadequate

By HENRY TANNER

Special to The New York Times

UNITED NATIONS, N. Y., Jan. 19—The United Arab Republic was reliably reported today to regard the present Israeli position in the indirect peace talks as inadequate on at least two issues.

One point was understood to be the absence of a commitment by Israel to withdraw her troops from all occupied Arab territories rather than from territories "lying beyond the positions agreed in the peace treaty," as suggested by Israel.

The other point was believed to be the absence from the Israeli suggestions of any reference to the future rights of the Palestinians.

[President Nikolai V. Podgorny of the Soviet Union flew to Moscow after a six-day visit to Egypt amid strong indications that he and the Egyptian leaders had agreed on political and diplomatic pressure as the means of achieving an Israeli withdrawal.]

The Egyptian position was made known last Friday in a memorandum submitted to Dr. Gunnar V. Jarring, the United Nations intermediary, by Dr. Mohammed H. el-Zayyat, the

Continued on Page 11, Column 1

DEMOCRATS NAME ALBERT AND BOGGS TO TOP HOUSE JOBS

Liberals Defeated, 140-88, in Attempt to Elect Udall as Majority Leader

By MARJORIE HUNTER

Special to The New York Times

WASHINGTON, Jan. 19 — Ignoring liberal demands for change, House Democrats chose Carl Albert of Oklahoma as Speaker today and Hale Boggs of Louisiana as majority leader.

Both men were part of the Democratic leadership team under former Speaker John W. McCormack of Massachusetts in the Congress that ended earlier this month.

Liberal - minded reformers were glum as they emerged from the party caucus in the House chamber. While the selection of Mr. Albert had been a foregone conclusion, they had hoped to inject new vitality into the leadership by electing Morris K. Udall of Arizona as majority leader.

However, Mr. Boggs won easily on a second ballot, polling 140 votes to 88 for Mr. Udall and 17 for B. F. Sisk of California.

2 Drop Out of Race

Earlier, James G. O'Hara of Michigan and Wayne L. Hays of Ohio dropped out after trailing the five-man field on the first ballot. On that ballot, Mr. Boggs had 95 votes; Mr. Udall, 69; Mr. Sisk, 31; Mr. Hays, 28, and Mr. O'Hara, 25.

Mr. Hays promptly threw his support to Mr. Boggs, but Mr. O'Hara, contrary to expectations, did not endorse publicly his fellow liberal, Mr. Udall.

The selection of Mr. Albert as Speaker came after only token opposition from John Conyers of Michigan, a Negro. The vote was 220 to 20.

Mr. Conyers entered the race only after Mr. Albert refused to commit himself to strip members of the Mississippi delegation of their seniority. Mr. Conyers had protested that the five Mississippi Representatives had run as members of a state Democratic party that practiced racial segregation and had been refused recognition at the 1968 Democratic National Convention.

The Democrats then rejected, 111 to 55, the move to strip the Mississippians of their seniority, which would have ousted one committee chairman and two subcommittee chairmen.

Mr. Albert is 62 years old and

Continued on Page 14, Column 4

Color-Blind Regime Vowed by Governor Of South Carolina

Special to The New York Times

COLUMBIA, S. C., Jan. 19—Gov. John C. West of South Carolina pledged today in his inaugural address to eliminate "any vestige of discrimination" from state government.

In a public commitment to racial justice that was novel for a Deep South Governor, Mr. West said, "We pledge to minority groups no special status other than full-fledged responsibility in a government that is totally color-blind."

Last Tuesday in Atlanta, Jimmy Carter made a similar statement when he was sworn in as Governor of Georgia.

"I say to you quite frankly that the time for racial discrimination is over," Mr. Carter, a Democrat, said in his inaugural address. "No poor, rural, weak or black person should ever have to bear the additional burden of being deprived of the opportunity of an education, a job or simple justice."

Governor West's speech was punctuated by applause eight times by a crowd of 6,000 persons, who huddled in a chilling

Continued on Page 17, Column 5

PRESIDENT BLOCKS CANAL IN FLORIDA

Halts Project to Bar Harm to Wildlife—Move Hailed by Conservationists

By ROBERT B. SEMPLE Jr.

Special to The New York Times

WASHINGTON, Jan. 19—President Nixon today ordered a halt to further construction of the Cross-Florida Barge Canal "to prevent potentially serious environmental damage."

Conservationists promptly praised the action, which was unusual in that $50-million in Federal funds had already been spent to build nearly one-third of the proposed 107-mile-long canal. The over-all cost of the complete project would have been $180-million.

The canal had been attacked by conservationists as a threat to the environment. Its defenders included many prominent Florida politicians, some of whom lamented the President's action today.

Floridian Upset

Representative Robert L. F. Sikes, Florida Democrat, who is dean of the state's Congressional delegation, said he was "distressed" that Mr. Nixon had acted "summarily." He accused the President of "poor judgment."

In a statement issued this afternoon, Mr. Nixon said he had made his decision on the recommendation of his Council on Environmental Quality. He said the council had told him that "the project could endanger the unique wildlife of the area and destroy this region of unusual and unique natural beauty."

"The step I have taken today," Mr. Nixon said, "will prevent a past mistake from causing permanent damage. But more important, we must assure that in the future we take not only full but also

Continued on Page 54, Column 2

Furious Dissidents Charge 'Sellout' as P.B.A. Votes

Kiernan Is Attacked

By EMANUEL PERLMUTTER

Angry policemen who disagreed with their delegates' decision that they return to work stormed out of the ballroom of the New Yorker Hotel yesterday with such fury that the top of the door frame was torn out. It sounded like a rifle shot.

Shouting, "Strike! Strike!" and "Sellout!," the policemen pushed past newsmen and cameramen with such violence that one television camera was hurled to the floor.

When Edward J. Kiernan, the president of the Patrolmen's Benevolent Association, emerged perspiring and red-faced from the steaming ballroom, he was virtually engulfed by policemen cursing him.

"You sold us out, you fat bum," shouted a grim-faced dis-

Continued on Page 18, Column 2

Frustration Evident

By MURRAY SCHUMACH

The frustration, humiliation and anger that have been building for years among the city's policemen—the basic reasons for their walkout—still smoldered yesterday as they returned to work.

The belief that the court decision in a parity-pay dispute that touched off their wildcat strike was, to them, just a final injustice was expressed over and over again in interviews with policemen, with Council President Sanford D. Garelik, formerly chief inspector, and with former Mayor Robert F. Wagner.

"Everyone took his anger out on this parity issue," said Patrolman Robert Demurjian, who is delegate to the Patrolmen's Benevolent Association from the 14th Precinct. "Parity was an

Continued on Page 18, Column 3

How the City Escaped What Might Have Been

By RICHARD REEVES

City officials, psychologists and a lot of ordinary citizens agreed yesterday that cold weather and the shrewd use of a small force of available police personnel were major factors in saving New York from the spectacular breakdowns in law and order that have hit other cities during police strikes.

There was also a little suspicion that the city might have survived without the crime waves, traffic jams and rioting that hit Montreal 15 months ago and Boston 51 years ago because New Yorkers might just be a special kind of people.

"It was a period of relative calm," said Deputy Mayor Richard R. Aurelio of the wildcat strike by patrolmen, "and the cold obviously had something to do with that.

"So did the superior officers — they really held the town together and a lot of planning went into that. But when all is said and done, the people of the city were unbelievable. I know it sounds corny, but they rise to any occasion."

"New Yorkers are very special cats—they really are different," said Dr. Morton Bard, a professor of psychology at City University who is a former policeman and has worked on several recent police study projects.

"Life in New York requires a special kind of discipline, an

Continued on Page 18, Column 3

PARITY TRIAL IS ON

Services That Acted in Sympathy Return to Work, Too

By LAWRENCE VAN GELDER

The city's patrolmen ended a six-day wildcat strike yesterday after their union delegates, at a tumultuous meeting, voted overwhelmingly to return to work.

Despite vociferous opposition from angry dissidents, delegates of the Patrolmen's Benevolent Association voted 229 to 112 at the New Yorker Hotel to end the walkout, which involved at least 85 per cent of the city's 27,400 patrolmen.

By late afternoon thousands of policemen in all five boroughs had resumed their customary duties, restoring an air of normality to the chill street scene and furnishing an apprehensive populace with a renewal of security.

"I guess everyone's relieved," said a policeman in Brooklyn. "But there wasn't any problem really—everyone was on good behavior."

In the aftermath of the strike, bitterness lingered and some issues remained unresolved. Many who had favored continuation of the strike returned to work reluctantly.

Unfinished Business

Still pending was the resolution of such issues as punishment of the strikers, wage parity and retroactive pay and the injunction sought by the city last Friday as the strike spread.

As the walkout concluded there were these developments:

¶State Supreme Court Justice Irving H. Saypol deferred immediate consideration of the city's request for an injunction and began late yesterday to hear the wage-parity case that precipitated the rebellion.

¶Police Commissioner Patrick V. Murphy ordered the immediate suspension of any member of the force who failed to perform assigned duties, effective at 4 P.M. Shortly thereafter, headquarters reported that no one had been suspended in the 4 P.M. shift.

¶The move to end the walkout was joined by other municipal policemen. Transit and Housing Authority patrolmen,

Continued on Page 19, Column 1

J.D.L. Calls a Halt To Its Harassment Of Soviet Diplomats

By JUAN M. VASQUEZ

Rabbi Meir D. Kahane, leader of the Jewish Defense League, announced yesterday an "indefinite moratorium" in the organization's campaign of harassing Soviet diplomats and members of their families.

The campaign, to protest the treatment of Jews in the Soviet Union, has consisted mainly of trailing members of the Soviet United Nations Mission around the city and directing epithets and obscenities at them.

The activity, together with picketing and demonstrating near the mission on East 67th Street, has been criticized in Government circles, both here and in the Soviet Union, and has exacerbated tensions between the two countries.

The rabbi said that picketing and demonstrating would con-

Continued on Page 12, Column 4

Bone Markings Indicate Ice Age Notation System

By WALTER SULLIVAN

Analysis of markings on fragments of ancient bone, antler and stone has revealed what appears to be a system of notation used throughout most of Europe beginning some 34,000 years ago during the last ice age.

The discovery, according to a number of archeologists and anthropologists, demands radical changes in current beliefs as to the mental capabilities of prehistoric man.

The system of notation seems to anticipate the development of a calendar, the use of abstract symbols and the concept of number. It is thus being hailed as a landmark in the evolution of human cognition.

The nature of the ancient inscriptions has been explored by Alexander Marshack, a research associate at the Peabody Museum of Archeology and Ethnology at Harvard University.

In 1964 Mr. Marshack, then a science writer and amateur archeologist, made the controversial proposal that peculiar scratches, notches and other marks on relics of the ice age might be more than mere decorations. Since then he has toured the museums of Europe and used techniques typical of

Continued on Page 16, Column 1

Copyright, Alexander Marshack

Markings carved in bone 30,000 years ago are thought to be notations on phases of moon. Sequence, starting at A and ending at B, seems to encompass two lunar cycles.

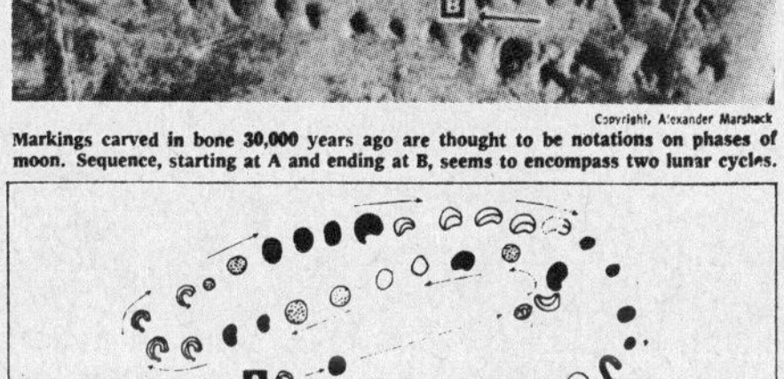

Schematic symbols above highlight nature of markings, with arrows showing progression corresponding to that in top photo. Symbols are arranged below under indicators of lunar cycle: the new moon (black), flanked by crescent moons, and full moon (white), flanked by quarter moons. Symbols are thus said to record lunar phases.

Foreign Policy: The Economic Problem

Following is the third in a series of articles exploring the Nixon Administration's style in foreign policy:

By TAD SZULC

Special to The New York Times

WASHINGTON, Jan. 19—Despite deteriorating economic relations between the United States and the two other great trading powers — the European Common Market and Japan — the Nixon Administration has been unable in the last two years to develop a comprehensive foreign economic policy.

That state of affairs, privately described by high Administration officials as a long period of drift marked by policy contradictions and failures, has been causing concern in Washington, in foreign capitals and in the American business, labor and farm communities.

The foreign view has been that only the exercise of United States leadership can arrest a growing trend toward world economic conflict.

It was in recognition of the need for coordinating divergent domestic and overseas interests at a time of deepening crisis in the international trade, monetary and investment fields that President Nixon today established a Cabinet-level Council on International Economic Policy.

Mr. Nixon, the chairman of the new body, named Peter G. Peterson of Chicago, chairman of the board of Bell & Howell Company, to be executive director. [Details on Page 9.]

The council's task is to pull together military and economic aid, international trade and monetary, financial, investment and commodities matters into a cohesive body of policy, taking into account the requirements of foreign policy.

Until the establishment of the council, recommended by an advisory committee on Government organization, the authority and capacity to manage all the international economic questions have been scattered through the Government. Foreign economic policy was the victim of interagency battles that the White House often had to resolve on an improvised basis.

The establishment of the new machinery was not a simple, bureaucratic move but a

Continued on Page 8, Column 4

NEWS INDEX

Apollo 15 crew: from left to right, David R. Scott, commander; Alfred M. Worden, command module pilot, James B. Irwin, lunar module pilot.

NASA

Irwin stands by the lunar rover on the Moon. Mount Hadley is in the background.

"All the News That's Fit to Print"

The New York Times

LATE CITY EDITION

Weather: Rain today; showers likely tonight. Partly cloudy tomorrow. Temp. range: today 44-26; Thursday 27-20. Full U.S. report on Page 62.

VOL. CXX .. No. 41,285 NEW YORK, FRIDAY, FEBRUARY 5, 1971 — 15 CENTS

2 ASTRONAUTS LAND ON MOON; PREPARE TO EXPLORE SURFACE

TROOPS OF ALLIES MASS NEAR LAOS; CROSSING DENIED

Saigon Refuses to Comment About 'Future Operations' in Northwest Corner

By ALVIN SHUSTER
Special to The New York Times

SAIGON, South Vietnam, Feb. 4 — Thousands of American and South Vietnamese troops, supported by armored columns and planes, were moving near the Laotian border today in the northwestern corner of South Vietnam.

Official South Vietnamese spokesmen said none of their forces had crossed into Laos to strike at the North Vietnamese supply and infiltration trails and bases there. But they refused to comment on what they called "future operations."

American officers on the scene, in Quangtri Province, said they still expected the South Vietnamese troops to move directly against what is known as the Ho Chi Minh Trail in Laos.

Approval by Thieu

Informed sources here said that President Nixon had received advance approval from President Nguyen Van Thieu of South Vietnam to make the decision on whether to send the South Vietnamese troops into Laos after the American troops cleared the way. United States ground combat forces are barred by law from entering Laos.

There was no word here on whether the South Vietnamese forces would in fact carry out what informed sources said was the original plan—to drive into Laos, destroy the vast stockpiles of enemy supplies believed hidden in thick jungle and then withdraw.

Some military sources said they had begun to suspect that President Nixon was having second thoughts about risking a political furor at home over "a widening of the war."

9,000 American Troops

This reportedly was discussed at a 20-minute meeting last night between President Thieu and Ambassador Samuel D. Berger, the senior American official at the embassy in the absence of Ambassador Ellsworth Bunker, who is in Washington for consultations with Mr. Nixon.

The sweep in the northwest, officially announced by the United States command early today after a six-day news blackout here, involves 9,000 Americans and 20,000 South Vietnamese soldiers.

At the same time, 20,000 other South Vietnamese soldiers were reportedly engaged in two new operations in Cambodia in one of the biggest campaigns there since the attacks against enemy supply bases by

Continued on Page 10, Column 1

United Press International

BORDER BUILDUP: American Army vehicles in South Vietnam close to the Laotian line

U.S. Officials Say Invasion Of Laos Is Still Possible

By TERENCE SMITH
Special to The New York Times

WASHINGTON, Feb. 4 — Officials continued today to hold open the possibility of a South Vietnamese strike against the Ho Chi Minh Trail in southern Laos.

They cautioned against published reports that the 20,000 South Vietnamese troops along the Laotian frontier had been ordered by the White House not to cross the border.

Reliable sources indicated that no such final decision had been made. They said there would be little military purpose in mounting a large operation merely to establish control over the uninhabited and strategically insignificant northwestern corner of South Vietnam.

The White House press secretary, Ronald L. Ziegler, declined to say whether the South Vietnamese units might enter Laos, but he told reporters, "You have to keep in mind that this is the first stage of the operations in Miltary Region I."

Military Region I is the designation for the five northernmost provinces of South Vietnam, all of which border the southern Laotian panhandle.

Mr. Ziegler said the enemy had been concentrating supplies and troops throughout the panhandle and that these posed a threat to the security of Military Region I. But asked about the plans of the South Vietnamese troops, he said. "I am not going to project what the future movements would or would not be."

Asked what the American role might be in such an operation, Mr. Ziegler said that, as a matter of general policy, American air power would be used to support South Vietnamese forces "when they take action to prohibit the re-establishment of enemy sanctuaries." No United States ground forces would be used, he said.

Although the six-day news embargo on the campaign was lifted early today, spokesmen still refused to address themselves to the central questions raised by the operation:

¶Has President Nixon decided to authorize a South Vietnamese strike into Laos, or does the decision remain to be made?

¶What factors are being con-

Continued on Page 10, Column 4

6 MAYORS ATTACK THE STATE BUDGET

Warn of 'Hidden' Tax Rise for Localities and Stress Increased Realty Levies

By FRANK LYNN
Special to The New York Times

ALBANY, Feb. 4—The Mayors of the state's six largest cities, including Mayor Lindsay of New York, warned today that Governor Rockefeller's proposed $8.45-billion budget included "hidden tax increases for almost every local government."

Declaring that the budget does not meet their needs, the Big Six Mayors said the "Legislature must recognize that increased local taxation is the inevitable consequence of a state budget that does not adequately help local government."

The Mayors declared that if the state did not increase its aid, they would be forced to increase real-estate taxes, which they described as the "most regressive and economically debilitating tax of them all."

Their reference to the Legislature was viewed by some lawmakers here as a hint that they might be held responsible

Continued on Page 15, Column C

PRESIDENT REBUTS RISING CRITICISM OF REVENUE PLAN

Defends Proposal in Plea to Congress to Act on Aid to States and Cities

Excerpts from Nixon message are printed on Page 40.

By ROBERT B. SEMPLE Jr.
Special to The New York Times

WASHINGTON, Feb. 4—President Nixon formally asked Congress today to turn over to state and local governments $5-billion in unrestricted Federal funds. He also sought to rebut criticisms of the plan that have been gathering momentum on Capitol Hill.

In a 4,000-word message to Congress, Mr. Nixon outlined his proposal for what he calls "general revenue sharing"—a complex plan under which $5-billion would be given to states and cities with virtually no strings attached.

General revenue sharing is the most controversial aspect of the over-all $16-billion program, outlined in Mr. Nixon's State of the Union Message, that is designed to give local governments greater flexibility in the use of Federal tax revenues.

Further Messages Due

The $11-billion "special revenue-sharing" plan is to be financed in large part by dismantling some 100 existing Federal programs with narrow purposes. Details of this plan will be provided in a series of six messages over the next two months. States and cities would have considerable flexiblity in spending the $11-billion for six broad purposes.

The $5-billion plan to which the President addressed himself today, however, carries virtually no restrictions.

It is this aspect of the proposal that has caused much of the early criticism on Capitol Hill, particularly among those who contend that the level of government that collects the tax revenue should remain accountable for how it is spent.

Mr. Nixon said he was well aware of the widespread conviction that "when one level of government spends money that is raised at another level it will spend that money less responsibly." He also noted the related fear that "when those who appropriate tax revenues are no longer the same people who levy taxes, they will no

Continued on Page 40, Column 2

Capt. Alan B. Shepard Jr.

NASA

Comdr. Edgar D. Mitchell

Rolls-Royce Is Bankrupt; Blames Lockheed Project

By JOHN M. LEE
Special to The New York Times

LONDON, Feb. 4—Rolls-Royce, Ltd., Britain's quality symbol for fine automobiles and sophisticated jet engines, declared bankruptcy today. The public reacted with consternation and politicians called it "a major national tragedy."

The company put the blame for its collapse on the huge losses incurred in developing the engine for the Lockheed Aircraft Corporation's new Tristar airbus. Rolls said it could not proceed with the engine under the present fixed-price contract.

The Conservative Government quickly announced it would acquire and maintain those Rolls engine operations it considered vital for national defense, joint military programs with other countries and air forces and civil airlines around the world.

Possibility of Lawsuit

But the Government left open the question of the ill-fated Rolls aircraft engine, known as the RB-211, and said it would explore its future with the Rolls receiver. At the same time, the Government recognized the damage to Britain's commercial reputation and the possibility of a huge lawsuit by Lockheed.

[In Washington it was said that Rolls-Royce's action could threaten to unravel the Administration's plan to rescue Lockheed from possible bankruptcy. Lockheed declared it would see if it could buy an American-built engine for the Tristar. Details and other related stories on Page 41.]

Frederick Corfield, Minister of Aviation Supply, speaking to a stunned House of Commons, said, "Because of the very grave consequences which must follow the decision of the Rolls-Royce board, the Government is also undertaking urgent discussions with the Lockheed

Continued on Page 47, Column 1

INSURERS RAISING STATE AUTO RATES

Increase Likely to Be 15% for Normal Policies and 25% for Assigned Risk

By ROBERT J. COLE

Automobile insurance rates will go up sharply throughout New York State in the next few months. Many car owners have already received bills for higher premiums.

The largest increases—20 to 25 per cent—are expected to be paid by the 700,000 New Yorkers who are in the assigned-risk pool because their driver records or other factors make them unacceptable to the carriers for normal policies.

Rates for an additional 5.5 million people who buy coverage in the normal market are expected to go up by an average of 15 per cent.

State Aide Comments

Alexander E. Fox, deputy superintendent for the State Insurance Department, said he expected the industry to request rate increases in the assigned-risk pool "sometime next week," although he declined to speculate on how large an increase the industry would seek. He said these rates would go up at the latest by March.

Under a law that went into effect in January, 1970, insurance companies may raise normal market rates without the approval of the state; assigned-risk rates, however, remain

Continued on Page 62, Column 5

RIGHT ON TARGET

'A Beautiful Day in the Land of Frau Mauro,' Shepard Reports

By JOHN NOBLE WILFORD
Special to The New York Times

HOUSTON, Friday, Feb. 5 — Two astronauts of Apollo 14—the fifth and sixth human beings ever—landed on the moon early this morning.

Capt. Alan B. Shepard Jr. and Comdr. Edgar D. Mitchell of the Navy steered the four-legged landing craft named Antares to a smooth touchdown at 4:18 A.M., Eastern standard time, on the moon's highlands.

Their landing, the third made by American astronauts, came after a four-day, 250,000-mile voyage across the void of space. It came a year and a half after man's first landing, Apollo 11's pioneering visit to the Sea of Tranquility.

The four other men on the moon were Neil A. Armstrong, the first to set foot on the lunar surface — on July 20, 1969 — and Col. Edwin E. Aldrin Jr. of the Air Force, from Apollo 11, and Comdr. Charles Conrad Jr. and Comdr. Alan L. Bean of the Navy, from Apollo 12.

In a Level Valley

The Apollo 14 astronauts brought their 16-ton landing craft down on a fairly level valley in the Fra Mauro highlands, a cratered and rock-strewn area where the astronauts should be able to find rocks as old as the solar system itself. They plan a 33½-hour visit.

While Maj. Stuart A. Roosa of the Air Force was scheduled to pilot the command module Kitty Hawk in a watchful orbit overhead, Captain Shepard and Commander Mitchell would take two long excursions outside their landing craft to set up a nuclear-powered scientific station and get rock samples.

The descent engine on the lunar module fired at 4:05 A. M., at which time Captain Shepard declared:

"It's a beautiful day in the land of Fra Mauro."

And just before Antares touched down on the moon, Commander Mitchell exclaimed:

"There it is. Right on target. Beautiful. Right out the window. Just like you said it would be."

Comments From Moon

When the craft set down—two minutes behind schedule—the first words were those of Captain Shepherd, who said: "We're on the surface. We made a good landing."

After Mission Control acknowledged the success, the astronaut added:

"That was a beautiful one. We landed on the slope. But other than that, we're in great shape—right on the landing site."

The first of their moon walks, which would last up to five hours each, was to begin around 9 A.M. today. Captain Shepard would take the first steps down the ladder, followed a few minutes later by Commander Mitchell.

All their activities should be seen on earth through a color television transmission from Antares. The second moon walk, scheduled for early tomorrow morning, also was scheduled to be televised.

Captain Shepard and Commander Mitchell were cleared shortly before midnight to be-

Continued on Page 26, Column 7

Memories of the '68 Siege Linger at Foggy Khesanh

By The Associated Press

KHESANH, South Vietnam, Feb. 4—The ghosts of past battles mingle with the fog over this fortress in the mountains of the northwest corner of South Vietnam.

The drizzle is cold and constant, and the hills from which North Vietnamese artillery and mortars once pounded this plateau are shrouded in the thick gray mists.

Abandoned by United States Marines in July, 1968, and visited only occasionally since, Khesanh was transformed this week into a combat base for allied forces massing near the Laotian border.

This time the Americans were Army forces—infantrymen, artillerymen, engineers, helicopter crewmen. Many of them were still in high school when the Marines endured the 77-day siege of Khesanh and the Air Force flew through terrible bombardments to supply them.

Few if any among the ar-

Continued on Page 11, Column 3

Associated Press

American soldiers taking a breather Sunday at Khesanh as copters came in for landing

Laird Gives Rebuff To Moscow on Arms

By WILLIAM BEECHER
Special to The New York Times

WASHINGTON, Feb. 4—Secretary of Defense Melvin R. Laird declared today that the forum for discussing possible reductions in American fighter-bombers deployed within range of the Soviet Union was not the Strategic Arms Limitation Talks but a future conference that should seek mutual reductions of tactical forces in eastern and western Europe.

The proposed talks would involve several countries whereas the strategic-arms talks are between the United States and the Soviet Union.

Mr. Laird's comment came the day after an article in

Continued on Page 2, Column 1

Tuna Stocks Now Called Safe; Mercury Taint Not Widespread

By RICHARD D. LYONS
Special to The New York Times

WASHINGTON, Feb. 4 — The Food and Drug Administration announced today that all stocks of mercury-tainted tuna had been removed from the market and that the contamination problem was not so bad as had been believed.

Commenting on the finish of a seven-week testing program, Dr. Charles C. Edwards Jr., commissioner of the agency, said, "Final statistics showed the problem of mercury in tuna to be less serious than had been feared."

Dr. Edwards said in December that, based on initial samplings, as much as 23 per cent of the tuna stocks might have to be withdrawn.

But the final test results indicated that 3.6 per cent of the 166 million pounds of domestic and imported fish had exceeded the Federal mercury guideline, one-half part of mercury per million parts of fish.

About six million pounds of tuna have been withheld from sale or removed from stores, which led the agency to conclude that "stocks of the fish presently marketed in the United States are within the guideline."

However, the agency said its swordfish testing program, now half completed, had found that 87 per cent of the samples

Continued on Page 7, Column 1

NEWS INDEX

"All the News That's Fit to Print"

The New York Times.

LATE CITY EDITION

U. S. Weather Bureau Reports (Page 54) forecasts: Mostly fair and seasonably cool today, tonight and tomorrow. Temp. range: 60—50. Yesterday: 67.5—54.0.

VOL. CXX.. No. 41,462

NEW YORK, SUNDAY, AUGUST 1, 1971

BQLI 50 CENTS

ASTRONAUTS EXPLORE MOON 6½ HOURS, DRIVE ELECTRIC CAR ON ROUGH TERRAIN

Col. David R. Scott steps from ladder onto moon surface

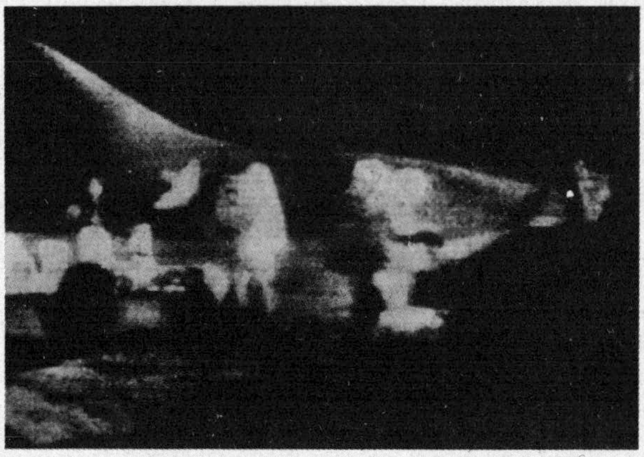

While Lieut. Col. James B. Irwin removes equipment from the LM, right, Colonel Scott carries TV antenna to the Rover

The New York Times/C.B.S. News

Scott removes tool from rack. More photos on Page 48.

U.N. TO SEND TEAM TO EAST PAKISTAN

U.S. Wins Acceptance by Thant and Yahya on Plan for 153-Man Relief Unit

By BENJAMIN WELLES

Special to The New York Times

WASHINGTON, July 31—The United States, working behind the scenes, has won the agreement of both Pakistan and the United Nations to station an international group of 153 civilian relief and rehabilitation experts in East Pakistan under United Nations sponsorship, officials said today.

Moreover, they said, the United States has notified U Thant, Secretary General of the United Nations, that it will contribute $1-million at once as an initial payment to help the group organize and fly necessary equipment to Dacca.

Among the United Nations staff will be 73 monitors, who will be stationed at four area offices in Dacca, Chittagong, Rajshahi and Khulna and at 69 other locations. Each monitor will be linked by radio with a United Nations headquarters in Dacca, qualified informants said.

"The presence of 73 U.N. monitors, each reporting on conditions in his area, may cool

Continued on Page 2, Column 3

Steel Union Votes to Defer Strike Deadline 24 Hours

By PHILIP SHABECOFF

Special to The New York Times

WASHINGTON, July 31—The United Steelworkers of America voted tonight to extend contract negotiations for 24 hours, moving back a deadline for a strike against the nation's steel industry to midnight tomorrow.

The union took the step after a tentative agreement on basic wages was reached with the company negotiators, according to sources close to the bargaining.

The two sides still had not resolved differences on peripheral economic issues, such as incentive pay, which will form a part of the total wage package, and on procedural matters.

About 600 presidents of steel union locals, standing by at the Shoreham Hotel to accept or reject contract proposals, voted to extend the strike deadline, at the suggestion of I. W. Abel, president of the union.

Mr. Abel said at a news conference after the vote that the result was not unanimous but that the great majority had approved the strike postponement.

Appeal by Hodgson

He disclosed that he met earlier in the day with Secretary of Labor James D. Hodgson and J Curtis Counts, director of the Federal Mediation and Conciliation Service. Mr. Hodgson had asked the union to extend negotiations by 48 hours, but Mr. Abel turned him down.

The union president said he had agreed to the one-day postponement because he believed that the remaining differences could be resolved in the meantime.

The tentative agreement on basic wages was reportedly along the lines of contracts negotiated earlier this year by the union for workers in the can, aluminum and copper industries. Those agreements called for wage increases ranging from 95 cents to $1.05 an hour over three years.

The negotiations continued through the night; steel industry management has made no public comment on their progress.

The White House press secretary, Ronald L. Ziegler, said earlier in the day that President Nixon was keeping in close touch with the efforts to head off a steel strike and with developments in the current strike against 10 railroads. The President was said to be in contact with both Mr. Hodgson and Mr. Counts.

Rail Talks Continue

Negotiators of the striking United Transportation Union and the railroads also bargained through the night, to try to resolve a dispute over work rules.

Government sources said that, although differences between the two sides remained, an agreement could be forthcoming soon.

They added, however, that if no real settlement was reached in the next few days, Congress could be expected to act, either on a bill introduced yesterday by Senator Jacob K.

Continued on Page 20, Column 1

I.T.T. WILL GIVE UP LARGE HOLDINGS

Agrees to Divest Itself of Some Recent Purchases to End Hartford Suit

Special to The New York Times

WASHINGTON, July 31—The International Telephone and Telegraph Corporation has agreed to divest itself of several of the largest corporations that it has acquired over the last few years, the Justice Department announced today.

I.T.T. accepted the settlement in return for the ending of a suit filed by the department over its acquisition of the Hartford Fire Insurance Company. The merger of the two companies, with combined assets of more than $7-billion, would have made the new company the largest in United States corporate history. The merger was opposed by the Justice Department on grounds that it would contribute to a "substantial lessening of competition."

The agreement announced today, which must still be approved by the courts, would require I.T.T. to divest itself within two years of its holdings in the Canteen Corporation, a food and vending service company, and the Fire Protection Division of the Grin-

Continued on Page 19, Column 1

Two Tourists View the Moon

Following are conversations between Capcom, the capsule communicator in Houston, and the Apollo crew, as transcribed by The New York Times:

DAVID SCOTT (9:30 A.M. E.D.T.)—As I stand out here in the wonders of the unknown at Hadley, I try to realize there's a fundamental truth to our nature. Man must explore. And this is exploration at its greatest.

Well, I see why we're in a

Col. David R. Scott

tilt. There's so much hummocky ground around here; we're on a slope of probably about 10 degrees and the left rear foot pad is probably about two feet lower than the right rear foot pad. And the left foot's a little low too. But the LM looks like it's in good shape. The Rover's in good shape.

Rather interesting sight, Houston. I can look straight up and see our good earth back there.

JAMES IRWIN (9:34 A.M.) O.K., Dave, I'm going to come on out.

SCOTT—A rather interesting thing, Jim, to see the momentum you generate.

It's easy to get going but you get all that momentum going there, why it takes a bit to stop.

IRWIN—I'm closing the hatch. Oh, it's dirty.

I'm going to move out and get the contingency sample. Oh boy, it's beautiful out here. It reminds me of Sun Valley.

No wonder we slip, Dave, boy, that's really soft dirt there around the front foot pads.

SCOTT (9:52 A.M.) [Removing and unfolding Rover] —Just pull real easy right there. Go easy now. You look pretty sporty there, Jim. Let's see. The engines are unlocked, is that right?

Hold on a minute, I'm not sure the telescoping rods are disconnected. Let's pick it up and move it back and turn it around. Your way. I think maybe if we lift the front end up, can't we?

CAPCOM—Dave and Jim, pull the Rover as far out as you can away from the LM and then pull on the front end if you could.

By that we mean lift up on the front.

IRWIN—We copy, Joe. [Grunts and groans.]

SCOTT—If you want to hold it there I'll get up front of it and try and lift it up. It's off. Let's turn it around, now, Jim.

IRWIN—Give a holler when you're ready to drive Dave, and I'll come out and take some pictures.

SCOTT—Safety belt's on. You sit up a lot higher than in one G. Brake's on, reverse is down. Circuit breakers on. O.K. I get readings [Drives a little distance away].

Still no forward steering. Any suggesttions.

CAPCOM—Cycle over the forward steering circuit-breaker, please.

SCOTT—O.K. No forward steering, Joe.

CAPCOM—Press on.

SCOTT—Jim, I'm going to

Lieut. Col. James B. Irwin

bring her around here and let's get on with it. We're going to have a great time with all these hills and mounds. Jim, as soon as you get that dust brush out I want to brush off so we don't get the Rover too dirty. As I look back behind us it almost looks like we landed in — another, oh, 10 meters aft and we'd have been landed in Surveyor Crater.

IRWIN (11:23 A.M.) [on Rover trip]—Could this be Rhysling right here? It probably is, this large depression off to our left. Well, I can see

Continued on Page 49, Column 6

A FIVE-MILE TRIP

Canyon Rim Is Passed —Two Are Awed by 'Unearthly' Scene

By JOHN NOBLE WILFORD

Special to The New York Times

HOUSTON, July 31 — For hours of "exploration at its greatest," two American astronauts drove across the desolate surface of the moon today in man's first motorized excursion among the ancient lunar rocks, craters and rolling hills.

The Apollo 15 astronauts rode a four-wheel, battery-run vehicle, Rover 1, along the rim of a mile-wide canyon and to the edge of a deep crater in search of rocks from the moon's primeval crust. They covered some five miles and spent about six and a half hours outside their landing craft, Falcon.

From the crater's slope, Col. David R. Scott and Lieut. Col. James B. Irwin of the Air Force transmitted spectacular color television pictures of the lunar vistas, the canyon depths of Hadley Rille, the undulating plain of the Marsh of Decay and the rounded peaks of the Apennine Mountains in the distance.

'This Is Unreal'

An excited Colonel Scott exclaimed: "This is unreal, the most beautiful thing I've ever seen."

When Mission Control described the televised panorama as "absolutely unearthly," Colonel Scott replied:

"Don't tell me this isn't worth doing."

Time and again, the two explorers used the words "fantastic" and "breathtaking" and "spectacular"—or simply "man, oh, man!"—as they rode along at an average speed of five miles an hour. Except for a balky front-wheel steering apparatus, the 10-foot-long roving vehicle did its job well.

Detailed Description

And so did the astronauts, according to geologists monitoring the excursion here at the Manned Spacecraft Center. They said that the astronauts' technical description of the rocks and formations they saw were "first class in an absolute sense"—in other words, far more detailed and informative than the work of any previous crew.

Scientists were particularly impressed by the discovery of such a thick layer of dust in the landing area, the lack of any extensive boulder fields and the generally soft and "weathered" appearance of the hills and crater slopes. Apparently the area has been smoothed out by millions of

Continued on Page 49, Column 1

Today's Sections

Index to Subjects

News and features of special interest in Brooklyn, Queens and Long Island, Pages 59 to 70.

Once-Popular Convertible Is a Victim of Progress

By JERRY M. FLINT

Special to The New York Times

DETROIT, July 31 — No more will that girl driver cross the golden prairie, with her hair blowing wildly in the wind. No more will the young lovers lean back in the car and take in the stars.

The convertibles are finished.

A few are still being turned out, but the end is in sight. There seems to be no room in the modern world for that special car that every boy once wanted. Twentieth-century reality keeps butting in.

"I got behind a sand and gravel truck on the freeway. Nearly blasted me out of the car and took my skin off," said Kenneth Spencer, who designs tomorrow's cars at the Ford Motor Company.

The auto manufacturers of Detroit say the convertible died of cultural shock—it could not adapt. "I supported them like crazy around here," said Joe Sturm, marketing manager at the Chrysler Corporation. "But you run and run after some things, and you just run out of breath." Chrysler has just built its last convertible.

The car makers have a long list of reasons for the death of the convertible.

In the age of air-conditioning, real air has lost its value.

In the age of the freeway, speeds of 70 miles an hour turn a breeze into a hurricane, and the soot and fumes of the big ditch don't help. "When I came out here from the East I had a convertible," recalled Frank Wiley, who works for Chrysler. "You could drive up through the hills and down through the valleys, top down and you felt like you owned the world," he said. "But you can't look at much at 70 miles an hour."

In the age of imitation, the hardtop and the vinyl covered roof stole the sharp look of the convertible—even the word "hardtop" derives from the expression "hardtop convertible."

In the age of Nader and consumerism, the dangers of the convertible in a rollover became an issue and the rattles and leaks that were part of the convertible became unacceptable.

In the age of bored workers and efficiency - minded managers, the convertible became the great nuisance on the assembly line.

In the age of untrained mechanics, service became a headache and repairmen have been known to throw their tools in anger, trying to replace a top.

In the age of crime, protection of the soft top was im-

Continued on Page 51, Column 1

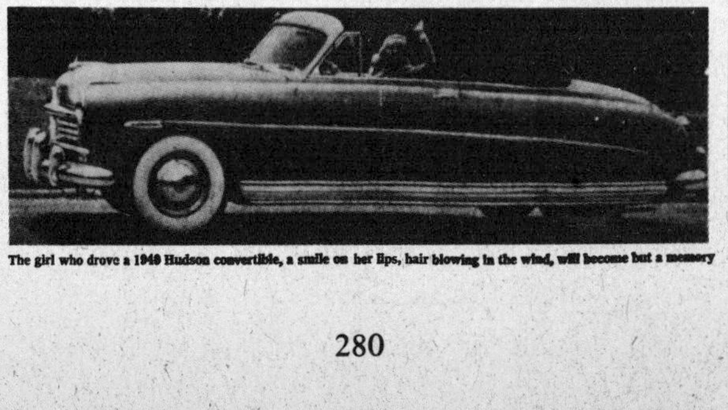

The girl who drove a 1949 Hudson convertible, a smile on her lips, hair blowing in the wind, will become but a memory

Fire Inquiry Scores Transit Authority

By FRANK J. PRIAL

A special panel inquiring into the IRT subway fire two weeks ago reported to Mayor Lindsay yesterday that the subway trainmaster's office had hung up the telephone three times when the fire dispatcher tried to call in requests to have the power cut off so firemen could fight the fire.

A preliminary report on the fire on the Lexington Avenue line, prepared by a panel appointed by Mayor Lindsay, was highly critical of the Transit Authority, charging that the delay in complying with the request for a power cutoff was "inexcusable and cannot be

Continued on Page 46, Column 5

Policeman Kills 2 Pursuing a Robber

By MAURICE CARROLL

Two brothers who ran a Spanish grocery in uptown Manhattan were shot to death in the street early yesterday by an off-duty policeman as they were chasing a third man who had allegedly held up their bodega.

The alleged holdup man was wounded by a bullet fired into his head by one of the brothers.

The policeman, who was in civilian clothes, said later that he had ordered the brothers to "freeze" and that they had turned on him, apparently failing to comprehend that he was a policeman.

One of them shot at him, he

Continued on Page 36, Column 1

NASA

Irwin salutes the American flag raised on the Moon. *Falcon* is in center, lunar roving vehicle at right.

"All the News That's Fit to Print"

The New York Times

LATE CITY EDITION

Weather: Cloudy, humid, showers likely today, tonight, tomorrow. Temp. range: today 74-84; Monday 73-85. Temp.-Hum. Index yesterday 78. Full U.S. report on Page 58.

VOL. CXX ... No. 41,464 NEW YORK, TUESDAY, AUGUST 3, 1971 — 15 CENTS

ASTRONAUTS LEAVE MOON AND DOCK SAFELY; ASCENT OF THE MODULE TELEVISED TO EARTH

U.S. Backs U.N. Seat for Peking, Opposes Ousting Taiwan

OLD POLICY ENDED

Rogers Says He Does Not Know if 2 States Would Sit Together

Transcript of Rogers news briefing is on Page 2.

By TAD SZULC
Special to The New York Times

WASHINGTON, Aug. 2—The United States officially announced its support today for the seating of mainland China in the United Nations this fall but declared its continued opposition to the expulsion of the Taiwan-based Chinese Nationalist Government.

The announcement by Secretary of State William P. Rogers ended 20 years of determined and often bitter United States resistance to the presence of a Peking delegation in the United Nations.

But Mr. Rogers answered with the word "no" when he was asked whether he had received any indication "from either China that they would be prepared to sit with one another in the United Nations."

Looking to Future

In a formal statement at a State Department news briefing, Secretary Rogers said President Nixon had been "forging policies directed to the future while taking fully into account the legacies of the past."

The statement came 18 days after Mr. Nixon's announcement that he would visit mainland China before May, 1972. Mr. Rogers's statement noted that "in Asia and elsewhere in the world we are seeking to accommodate our role to the realities of the world today."

Mr. Rogers said that the decision "is fully in accord with President Nixon's desire to normalize relations with the People's Republic of China in the interests of world peace and in accord with our conviction that the continued representation in the United Nations of the Republic of China will contribute to peace and stability in the world."

U.S. Policy Is Defined

The Secretary said that in Washington's view the opposing contentions by the Communists and the Nationalists to be "the sole government of China and representative of all the people of China" would not necessarily be prejudiced by their simultaneous representation in an international organization. He said that "participation of both in the United Nations need not require that result."

"The United States," he added, "accordingly will support action at the General Assembly this fall calling for seating the People's Republic of China. At the same time the United States will oppose any action to expel the Republic of China or other-

Continued on Page 2, Column 1

The New York Times/Mike Lien

ANNOUNCES CHINA POLICY: Secretary of State William P. Rogers at news conference

Senate Backs Lockheed, 49-48

By EILEEN SHANAHAN
Special to The New York Times

WASHINGTON, Aug. 2—The Senate, by a one-vote margin, gave final Congressional approval today to legislation aimed at saving the Lockheed Aircraft Corporation from bankruptcy.

The bill, passed by the Senate by a vote of 49 to 48, was identical to the one passed by the House on Friday night by a three-vote margin, 192 to 189.

The measure thus goes directly to President Nixon, who hailed the Senate action today as one that was "in the best interests of all the people."

The legislation would permit the Government to guarantee up to $250-million in bank loans to any corporation whose failure would "seriously and adversely" affect the national economy or that of any region. Throughout the long debate on the issue, Administration spokesmen made clear their expectation that the entire $250-million would be used to shore up Lockheed.

Any other corporation that wanted similar help from the Government would have to go to Congress for specific approval of an additional loan-guarantee authority.

Mechanically, guarantees of the loans to Lockheed will have to be authorized first by a three-man board that is created under the legislation. The members of the board are the Secretary of the Treasury, the chairman of the Federal Reserve Board and the chairman of the Securities and Exchange Commission.

The Senate roll-call on the bill was dramatic and the outcome was in doubt until almost the last minute.

The tally stood at 48 to 48 at the end of the normal call, first of the full list of Senators and then of all those present in the chamber who had not voted on the first round. Vice President Agnew was in the presiding officer's chair, ready to cast the tie-breaking vote if needed. But then Senator Marlow W. Cook, Republican of Kentucky, entered the chamber and asked for recognition. When he voted "aye," it was all over.

Senate Democrats split 31 to 22 against the Lockheed loan guarantee and Senate Republicans split 27 to 17 in favor. The Republican showing was not a very strong one for a bill urgently sought by a Republican Administration.

There was no consistent ideological pattern to the voting, however. Liberals and conservatives from both parties voted on both sides.

All of the announced and presumed candidates for the 1972 Democratic Presidential nomination voted against the

Continued on Page 39, Column 1

Soviet Bloc Holds Parley; China Seen as Key Topic

By BERNARD GWERTZMAN
Special to The New York Times

MOSCOW, Aug. 2—The top leaders of all the Soviet-bloc countries except Rumania held a one-day meeting today and issued a communiqué denouncing deviations from Moscow's line and expressing "grave alarm" over the anti-Communist campaign in the Sudan.

Diplomatic sources here believed that the meeting, attended by Leonid I. Brezhnev, the Soviet Communist party leader, was called at Soviet initiative to discuss primarily the latest developments in China's relations with the United States, and to agree on a joint position.

It was believed that the Rumanian President, Nicolae Ceausescu, who recently visited China, boycotted the session since alone of Russia's allies in the Warsaw Pact organization, Rumania strongly supports the moves to improve Chinese-American relations. The gathering was held somewhere in the Crimea, the southern area of European Russia adjacent to the Black Sea.

It was the first time Rumania has been absent from one of the Warsaw Pact's top-level meetings since 1968 when Mr. Ceausescu refused to join in the anti-Czechoslovak actions being planned by the rest of the bloc to end the liberal regime of Alexander Dubcek.

The communiqué itself did not

Continued on Page 5, Column 1

C.I.A. Says It Maintains Army in Laos

By JOHN W. FINNEY
Special to The New York Times

WASHINGTON, Aug. 2—The Nixon Administration acknowledged today, through a Senate subcommittee staff report, that the Central Intelligence Agency was maintaining a 30,000-man "irregular" force now fighting throughout most of Laos.

Many news articles in recent years have described C.I.A. sponsorship of an irregular army in Laos. However, the subcommittee report represented the first time that the agency publicly and officially confirmed its military activities in Laos. The report indicated that the use of the irregular units in Laos was more widespread than had been indicated in the news accounts.

The force has become "the main cutting edge" of the Royal Laotian Army, according to the report, and has been supplemented by Thai "volunteers" recruited and paid by the C.I.A.

The agency's involvement in a secret war in Laos was finally confirmed officially in a staff report prepared for the Senate Foreign Relations subcommittee on foreign commitments by James G. Lowenstein and Richard M. Moose, two former Foreign Service officers who made an inspection trip to Laos in April. A version of their report, once classified top secret, was made public today after clearance by the C.I.A. as well as the State and Defense Departments.

Publication of the detailed 23-page report marks the formal acknowledgment of the secret war that the United States has been conducting in Laos ever since the breakdown of the 1962 Geneva accords, which were supposed to re-establish the neutrality of that country.

In making public the report, Senator Stuart Symington of Missouri, the subcommittee chairman, said: "It is an encouraging sign that the executive branch has finally agreed that much of what the United States Government has been doing in Laos may now be made public. The veil of secrecy which has long kept this secret war in Laos officially hidden from the American people has

Continued on Page 8, Column 1

STEEL PRICE RISE OF 8% ANNOUNCED BY 5 BIG CONCERNS

U.S. Steel Initiates Action —White House Warns of a Bad Effect on Industry

By ROBERT WALKER

Most of the nation's major steel producers announced yesterday that they would raise prices by an average of about 8 per cent on nearly all types of steel products.

The announcements came less than 24 hours after the industry reached a labor agreement calling for wage increases of about 31 per cent over the next three years.

The price changes, which will take effect on a staggered schedule between Aug. 5 and Dec. 1, will be the second round this year and will bring cumulative increases in 1971 to about 15 per cent.

White House Critical

Chicago's Inland Steel Corporation, the country's seventh largest steel concern, which was believed to be the only large producer that might conceivably decline to go along, did not immediately match the action of its competitors.

A White House spokesman said it was "questionable whether the price increase is in the industry's long-run interests."

He added. "Price increases of this magnitude at this time are bound to have an adverse effect on the tonnage of steel produced in the United States and on jobs in the steel industry."

But it was considered highly probable that the new increases would prevail. They were initiated yesterday morning by the United States Steel Corporation, the leading steel company, and were followed, after the White House reaction had been made public, by four other companies in the so-called Big Eight.

Impact on Consumer

In the long run, the higher steel quotations will affect the prices of such items as food and beverage cans, automobiles, appliances and tools.

However, industry analysts did not expect the changes, by themselves, to have an immediate or severe impact on the consumer for these reasons:

¶Prices will not rise for tin-

Continued on Page 12, Column 2

RAIL STRIKE ENDS WITH 42% PAY RISE

42-Month Contract Provides for Change in Work Rules and Binding Arbitration

By PHILIP SHABECOFF
Special to The New York Times

WASHINGTON, Aug. 2 — A damaging rail strike ended today with the signing of a contract that could usher in a new era of labor-management relations for the nation's long-troubled railroad industry.

Negotiators for the United Transportation Union and the railroads reached agreement this morning after almost continuous bargaining over the last three days.

The union withdrew its picket lines, some of which had been up for 18 days, at 12:01 P.M. in each time zone.

Rail officials said that the first passenger trains started to move soon after the pickets had been withdrawn and that the freight trains would begin rolling by midnight. The whole rail system, they said, will be operational by the weekend, although it will take some time until rail service is completely normal again.

The new contract establishes some of the work rule changes that the railroads have sought for many years—rules they insist are needed to make their operations economically viable.

The union also agreed for the first time to submit to binding arbitration involving what had heretofore been jealously guarded prerogatives.

In return, the railroads granted a 42 per cent wage increase over a 42-month period

Continued on Page 56, Column 6

State Panel Named To Study Finances And Service of City

By MARTIN TOLCHIN

All 10 city superagencies and the city's over-all fiscal policies will be examined at public hearings by a new state commission whose full membership was announced yesterday.

Stuart N. Scott, the commission chairman, whose appointment was previously announced, described the scope of the commission's work in his first interview.

"My first impression is of the enormity of the job, and the difficulty of getting a handle on it," he said in his 45th-floor office at the law firm of Dewey, Ballantine, Bushby, Palmer & Wood.

"Obviously high on the list are the city's fiscal problems," Mr. Scott continued. "The general problem is whether the citizens are getting the services from the city government that they ought to get, at a price they can afford."

He said that the panel was planning a total of 20 areas of investigation.

The other unpaid members of

Continued on Page 33, Column 4

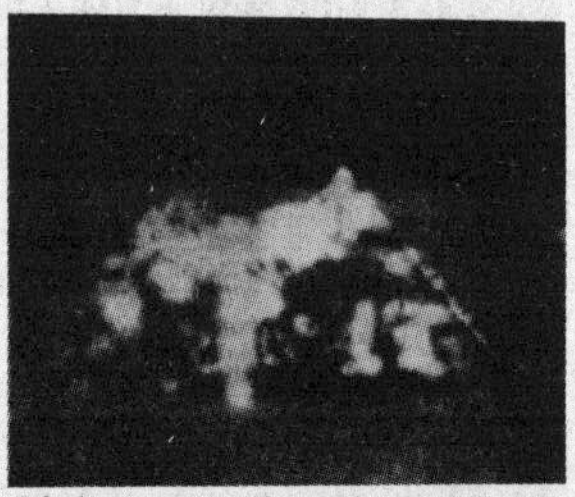

Only the descent stage of the LM remains on the moon. Sequence, beginning at bottom of page, shows lift-off.

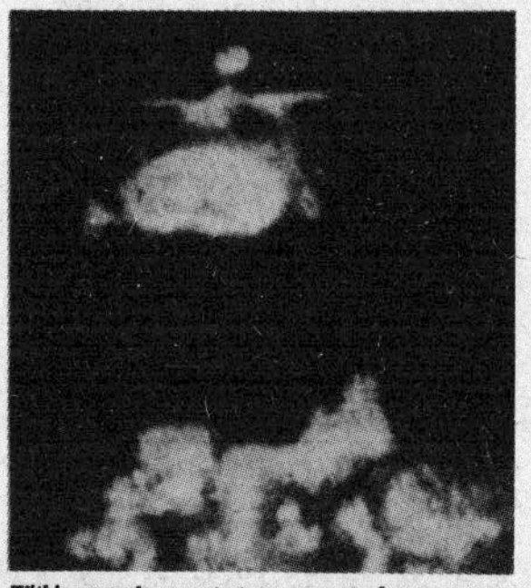

Within seconds, ascent stage was out of camera range

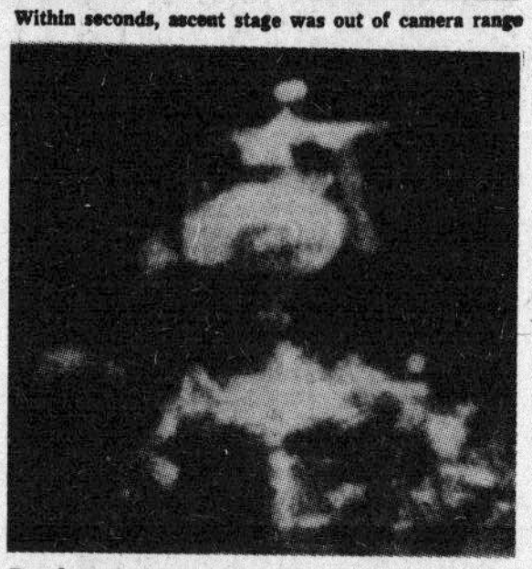

Free from the lower section, Falcon's ascent stage rose

Debris flew in all directions as the ascent engine fired

The New York Times/C.B.S. News

A television camera, still mounted on the lunar vehicle Rover, watched Falcon as the time for lift-off neared.

175-POUND CARGO

Jettisoning of Lunar Module Is Delayed for Two Hours

By JOHN NOBLE WILFORD
Special to The New York Times

HOUSTON, Aug. 2—The two moon-exploring astronauts of Apollo 15 blasted off the lunar surface today in the first televised launching from another world, then rejoined their orbiting command ship two hours later.

Col. David R. Scott and Lieut. Col. James B. Irwin of the Air Force thus ended in a spectacular instant, at 1:11 P.M., Eastern daylight time, nearly three days of man's most extensive and fruitful explorations of the earth's mysterious and desolate satellite planet.

After a link-up with the command ship in lunar orbit, the astronauts overcame what was thought to be a possible oxygen leak in a spacecraft hatch that delayed by two hours the discarding of their spent lunar landing craft. The hatches were rechecked, resealed and then found to be secure for the rest of the mission.

In a Storm of Debris

For the lift-off from the moon, which was watched by millions of television viewers around the world, the lunar module's upper half shot up from its four-legged base, scattering a storm of debris, mostly insulating foil, and a film of lunar dust.

There was no fiery color to the rocket exhaust because there is no air on the moon. The getaway was quick, unlike the launchings from earth, because of the weak lunar gravity and the absence of friction from any atmosphere.

From the lunar module, at the time of lift-off, came the recorded strains of "Off We Go Into the Wild Blue Yonder."

The television camera that gave the earth a picture of the blast-off was left on the moon, mounted on the front of the astronauts' lunar Rover. It was apparently not damaged by the exhaust of the lift-off.

Last Ride on Rover

Before they left the moon, the two astronauts took one last ride on Rover 1, their four-wheel lunar runabout, bouncing west over an undulating plain to look down into a mile-wide canyon called Hadley Rille. What they saw took many scientists by surprise—and could alter theories on how the moon's large basins were formed.

Colonel Scott reported seeing "well-defined" horizontal layers on the west wall of the canyon. This indicated to scientists here at the Manned Spacecraft Center that the moon's basins, called seas, had probably been formed by many lava flows over a long period of time, not by a single event.

Dr. Joseph P. Allen 4th, the scientist-astronaut who acted as capsule communicator, said at a news conference that the layers that Colonel Scott saw and photographed were like "leaves of the history book of that part of the moon."

The scientists were also eagerly awaiting the return of some 175 pounds of rocks and soil that the two astronauts gathered during their three

Continued on Page 14, Column 5

NEWS INDEX

"All the News
That's Fit to Print"

The New York Times

LATE CITY EDITION
Weather: Rain likely today; ending tonight. Fair and cool tomorrow. Temp. range: today 33-45; Saturday 26-39. Full U.S. report on Page 9[illegible].

News of special interest to readers in New Jersey will be found on pages 71 to 90.

VOL. CXXI . . . No. 41,658 © 1972 The New York Times Company NEW YORK, SUNDAY, FEBRUARY 13, 1972 75¢ beyond 50-mile zone from New York City, except Long Island. Higher in air delivery cities. NJ 50 CENTS

18 CITY HOSPITALS SEEK $820-MILLION FOR NEXT BUDGET

Municipal Corporation Asks $130.5-Million Increase Over Present Figure

DIFFICULTIES CONCEDED

English Asserts Organization Tried to Achieve Too Much Too Quickly Since 1970

By JOHN SIBLEY

The City Health and Hospitals Corporation asked yesterday for $820,311,000 for the next fiscal year while acknowledging that it had tried to achieve too much too quickly when it took over the 18 public hospitals in 1970.

"It will take at least a decade to overcome the problems of half a century," said Dr. Joseph T. English, the corporation's president, in a report that also cited current difficulties of the hospital system.

The budget, which is $130.5-million more than the corporation got for the fiscal year ended June 30, will be formally submitted to the Budget Bureau in about three weeks. Granting the request for funds would require an increase of $103-million in tax levy funds from the city, with $26.5-million more expected in receipts from patients and other sources.

State Fund Urged

Dr. English said the state should also provide funds for the hospitals, but did not make a specific dollar request.

"If sufficient funds are not made available," Dr. English warned in a 134-page Report to the People, "it is clear that the City of New York must begin now to plan which facilities and services it will ask the corporation not to provide in fiscal year 1973."

The report contains no mention of specific cuts that would have to be made if the "mandatory budget" is not provided. Nor would Dr. English discuss this when asked, clearly preferring to place the onus on City Hall.

Seven New Facilities

In addition to inflation and mandatory wage increases, the proposed budget includes $40.6-million to operate seven new facilities that are scheduled to open during the fiscal year. These are Gouverneur Hospital, the Sea View Public Health Center Infirmary on Staten Island, a building for psychiatric patients at Metropolitan Hospital, the Morrisania and Mott Haven Neighborhood Family Care Centers in the Bronx, the North Central Bronx Hospital and the new Bellevue Hospital.

Dr. English pointed to progress in a number of areas, but said the corporation got off to a stumbling start because it tried too rapidly to get rid of inefficiencies that had been

Continued on Page 59, Column 2

Portions of Irving's Book Like Hughes Aide's Story

The New York Times/Michael Evans
While court deliberated, Clifford Irving, Edith and son Barnaby strolled to an Automat for lunch.

By WALLACE TURNER
Special to The New York Times

SAN FRANCISCO, Feb. 12—Comparisons made today show that large sections of Clifford Irving's work about Howard R. Hughes are almost exactly like material presented in a manuscript based on the recollections of Noah Dietrich, who once worked for Mr. Hughes.

Details gathered by The New York Times representatives who have seen portions of the book were compared with portions of the forthcoming Dietrich book—"Howard, the Amazing Mr. Hughes."

A comparison of passages in manuscripts, Page 56.

The comparison was made by telephone conversation with Bob Thomas, who writes from Hollywood for The Associated Press and is the co-author with Mr. Dietrich.

Additionally, Mr. Thomas is familiar with the text of the first version of the Dietrich book, which was written by James Phelan, an investigative reporter. Mr. Thomas also has Mr. Phelan's research papers.

Life magazine announced yesterday that it had canceled its plans to publish excerpts from the "autobiography" that had been presented as the product of interviews between Mr. Hughes and Clifford Irving.

McGraw-Hill, Inc., which had purchased the Irving work for $750,000, said that information from Mr. Phelan had caused it to change its mind about the authenticity of the work.

In New York, an appellate court gave permission to Time magazine to publish excerpts over the weekend from the Irving book to prove its contention that the work is a "hoax."

The magazine won an appeal hours after a State Supreme Court justice had enjoined it from publishing any parts of the manuscript.

The appellate ruling, by Justice Theodore R. Kupferman, held that the manuscript was a commercial property, that any restraint would interfere with freedom of speech and that only a relatively small amount of words—up to 1,000—was involved.

Mr. Dietrich, interviewed by

Continued on Page 56, Column 3

The New York Times/Denis Cameron
VIETNAMESE OUTPOST: At Benhet, in central highlands, children watch a military truck move on road flanked by barbed wire. Outpost, near borders with Laos and Cambodia, would be a likely target in event of an enemy offensive.

Bhutto Wants a Defense Pact With U.S.

By C. L. SULZBERGER
Special to The New York Times

RAWALPINDI, Pakistan, Feb. 8—President Zulfikar Ali Bhutto has indicated that Pakistan would like to open "a genuine dialogue" with the United States with a view to reviving and strengthening the bilateral defense agreement that existed

Excerpts from the interview appear on Page 16.

between the two countries until it was more or less discontinued by Washington in 1967. To accomplish this aim there would have to be "a meeting of minds—and also some redrafting," he said.

This apparent request for new military pact was made during a two-hour interview today with President Bhutto. The interview took place in English—a language the President speaks eloquently, holding university degrees from both England and the United States. It

Zulfikar Ali Bhutto

was held in his residence here, near the new capital of Islamabad.

Mr. Bhutto emphasized his feelings of friendship for both China and the United States and said that if it were not embarrassing to the Nixon Administration during an election year, he would be ready "to start talks tomorrow" on obtaining American arms to replace the equipment lost by Pakistan during her war with India last December.

He predicted that Mr. Nixon's visit to Peking — Mr. Bhutto just returned from there—would be "fruitful and productive" although its results would not appear to be "sensational."

Mr. Bhutto strongly praised United States actions during

Continued on Page 16, Column 1

U.S. AIR ATTACKS IN SOUTH VIETNAM HEAVIEST SINCE '70

Bombings Along the Borders to Foil Any Tet Offensive Enter the Fifth Day

BASE AREAS ARE TARGET

Strikes Expected to Go On Until Nixon Leaves on His Trip to China Thursday

By CRAIG R. WHITNEY
Special to The New York Times

SAIGON, South Vietnam, Sunday, Feb. 13—An intense United States bombing campaign against Communist base areas along the Laotian-South Vietnamese border entered its fifth day today as the United Statees command reported the heaviest American air raids in South Vietnam in two years.

A military spokesman in Saigon said today that 13 missions of three planes each bombed suspected enemy positions in Kontum and Pleiku provinces between noon yesterday and 6 A.M. today.

An American military source said privately that the bombing campaign had been ordered at the beginning of the week to blunt a possible Communist offensive, and that it would continue at least until President Nixon left for China on Thursday.

American officials have forecast large-scale attacks during or after the celebrations of Tet, the Lunar New Year, which begin tomorrow evening and Tuesday.

Enemy attacks flared briefly earlier last week with a rocket barrage on Danang and a series of shellings and ground assaults in Binhdinh Province on the central coast, but have diminished over the last few days.

172 Tactical Air Strikes

In the 24-hour period that ended at 6 A.M. yesterday, the United States command said, Air Force and Navy fighter-bombers flew 172 tactical air strikes, all but two of them against enemy base areas bordering the two northern military regions, from the border zone west of Kontum to the demilitarized zone at the North Vietnamese border. The number was the highest since Sept. 24, 1970, the command said.

And according to one military source, "that's just the tip of the iceberg." The source said that at least that number of strikes were flown against enemy supply depots and bunkers across the borders.

United States Air Force B-52's flew 12 missions in the 24 hours ended at noon yesterday, the command said, the most flown in South Vietnam since Jan. 29, 1970. A mission normally has three planes, each dropping up to 36 tons of bombs.

The missions were concentrated against what American

Continued on Page 5, Column 1

The New York Times/Feb. 13, 1972
U.S. jets struck bases on border (heavy line).

U.S. Move to Defer Peace Talks Is Seen As Implicit Warning

By HENRY GINIGER
Special to The New York Times

PARIS, Feb. 12—The indefinite postponement of the Paris peace talks by the United States in protest against a three-day antiwar assembly in Versailles is understood to constitute a warning to North Vietnam that Washington is losing interest in the weekly meetings.

In the official American view, the sessions have been used for propaganda rather than for negotiation and as such they are more important to Hanoi than they are to Washington.

This reasoning is thought to lie behind the complaint raised by the United States over the Versailles gathering. Today, at the meeting, 800 delegates from 75 countries discussed in working commissions plans for stepping up an international campaign to force the United States to accept the peace terms laid down by the Vietnamese Communists.

There had been considerable speculation here over why the United States had chosen to direct attention to the meeting, first by protesting to France, then by refusing to set a date for the next session of the

Continued on Page 6, Column 1

National Commission to Propose Legal Private Use of Marijuana

By FRED P. GRAHAM
Special to The New York Times

WASHINGTON, Feb. 12 — The National Commission on Marijuana and Drug Abuse has unanimously decided to recommend that all criminal penalties for the private use and possession of marijuana be eliminated.

No state has yet gone this far, and the recommendation of the conservatively oriented 13-member commission, which includes nine members appointed by President Nixon, could generate a dramatic shift in the public's attitudes toward the legal status of the drug.

The recommendation comes at a time when marijuana use has become widespread among young people, and yet most political figures have maintained the law-and-order response that criminal penalties should not be abolished.

The report of the commission, which will be presented to Congress and Mr. Nixon March 22, is scheduled to go to the Government's printers Wednesday.

Although a few minor points

Continued on Page 61, Column 4

EASING OF QUOTA ON MEATS HINTED

Rumsfeld Says Move Would Seek to Stem Price Rises by Increase in Imports

By PHILIP SHABECOFF
Special to The New York Times

WASHINGTON, Feb. 12—The Nixon Administration may ease quota restrictions to allow more imported meat to enter the country as a means of slowing the rising spiral of retail meat prices, Donald Rumsfeld, director of the Cost of Living Council, disclosed today.

At a news conference to present the quarterly report of President Nixon's economic stabilization program, Mr. Rumsfeld said that the Administration was worried about rising food prices and that the council was considering doing something about them. The news conference was held yesterday under an embargo that withheld disclosure of the information until today.

Raw agricultural prices, which had been exempted by the council from price controls, rose by 13 per cent in January as against the level in January, 1971. The rise has been reflected in some higher retail food prices, particularly meats.

Talks in Progress

Mr. Rumsfeld declined to discuss the possibility of placing agricultural products under controls. The only "likely possibility" he referred to was an easing of the quota restricting the entry of meat—largely beef and mutton—into the country.

Negotiations between the United States and principal meat-exporting countries, including Australia and New Zealand, are now in progress.

Continued on Page 25, Column 1

A.C.L.U. Is Under Attack For New Activist Stands

By MARTIN ARNOLD

The American Civil Liberties Union, which for nearly 52 years has been defending the rights of others to speak out freely on any issue, now finds, as it undergoes dramatic change, critics attacking its own right to take stands on such issues as the war in Vietnam.

From its beginnings, the union has been involved in controversy. It has been called communistic and socialistic, atheistic and un-American.

But now, for the first time, even some who consider then selves civil libertarians are joining the attack. The charge is that the union is changing its basic character—from simply a defender of constitutional rights to an activist organization committed to a broad range of political and social change.

This charge has grown out of the positions the A.C.L.U. has taken on the Vietnam war, the Berrigan case, the Spock trial, draft resistance, school decentralization and the appointment of William H. Rehnquist to the Supreme Court.

What it is often doing in such cases is expanding the definition of civil liberties to include some illegal acts as a matter of conscience—although the union has steadfastly refused to adopt the position that civil disobedience is a civil liberty that must be defended.

The union, in answering its critics, insists that its change has not been one of basic character, that it still only marches to its traditional drummer—defense of the Constitution and its amendments. The change, then, it says, is one of structure and ability, change made inevitable by its increasing size and affluence.

And its positions on such volatile questions as the war are rooted not in politics, the union says, but in constitutional precepts of free speech and due process. Is the war, for instance, a constitutional war,

Continued on Page 51, Column 1

United Press International
IN MEMORY OF ABRAHAM LINCOLN: On behalf of President Nixon, Representative Robert McClory of Illinois places wreath before the statue at Lincoln Memorial. Ceremony marked birthday, 163 years ago, of 16th President of U.S. Article on Page 48.

TO OUR READERS

The New York Times now offers additional Sunday edition coverage of New Jersey. The supplementary report, consisting of news and features of special interest to readers in the state, appears in the main news section of all copies distributed in New Jersey and Richmond, Rockland and Orange Counties.

New Evidence on Jesus' Life Reported

By PETER GROSE
Special to The New York Times

JERUSALEM, Feb. 12 — Two Israeli scholars believe they have unraveled an elusive mystery of early Christianity—an apparently forged description of Jesus attributed to the Jewish-Roman historian Flavius Josephus.

On the basis of a 10th-century Arabic manuscript by an obscure bishop of the Eastern Church, the scholars think they have strengthened the independent historical evidence for the existence and activities of Jesus of Nazareth.

Shlomo Pines, professor of philosophy at Hebrew University, has reported the discovery of a long-overlooked version of a passage about Jesus attributed to Josephus. He concludes that it is far closer to what the first-century historian may have written than the highly suspect text handed down through the centuries.

Another Hebrew University scholar, David Flusser, professor of comparative religion, carries his colleague's research a step further to

Flavius Josephus

suggest the identity of the man who may have contrived the false text and how he did it.

For more than a century scholars have tried — and failed — to confirm the life and works of Jesus through a non-Christian source — a text that would not have been colored by the militant faith of the early believers. (The earliest Christian sources, the Gospels, are believed to have been written at least a quarter of a century after the Crucifixion.)

The works of Josephus, who lived from A.D. 37 to about 100, were the obvious

Continued on Page 24, Column 1

Index to Subjects

Today's Sections

"All the News That's Fit to Print"

The New York Times

LATE CITY EDITION

Weather: Fair, very cold today and tonight. Chance of snow tomorrow. Temp. range: today 24-14; Sunday 33-26. Full U.S. report on Page 30.

VOL. CXX . . No. 41,467 | NEW YORK, FRIDAY, AUGUST 6, 1971 | 15 CENTS

A SINGLE MARKET FOR STOCK TRADES URGED BY MARTIN

Former Head of Exchange and of Federal Reserve Ends 5-Month Study

MAJOR CHANGES ASKED

Report, Made on Request of Industry, Proposes Antitrust Immunity

Excerpts from Martin report are printed on Page 47.

By TERRY ROBARDS

A sweeping reorganization of the nation's securities industry was recommended yesterday by William McChesney Martin Jr., the former chairman of the Federal Reserve Board.

In a report to the New York Stock Exchange, Mr. Martin called for the integration of that exchange, the American Stock Exchange and all the regional stock exchanges into a single, nationwide, central auction market.

Such a market, he said, would provide centralized reporting of the price and volume of all transactions, so that investors would always be able to judge whether they were getting the best possible prices.

Mr. Martin said new legislation would be required to implement such a system. In the meantime, he said, the New York Stock Exchange should undergo a major restructuring, entailing fundamental changes in its management.

First Comprehensive Study

The Martin report is the first comprehensive analysis to come out of the financial crisis that gripped Wall Street last year. It was presented to the New York Stock Exchange's board of governors, which announced immediately that it would undertake a "detailed study" of the findings and proposals.

The report took five months to complete. It was done, without compensation to Mr. Martin, at the request of Bernard J. Lasker, immediate past chairman of the exchange, with the full approval of its governing board.

While its recommendations are not binding, the report is expected to carry considerable weight in any restructuring of the securities industry that comes about.

Mr. Martin, 64 years old, was the Federal Reserve chairman for 19 years before retiring early last year. He became the

Continued on Page 47, Column 4

U.S. Stand Irritates Peking But Nixon Is Still Welcome

Chinese Counting on Private Talks and Presidential Visit—Blame Japanese and Chiang for Two-China Policy

By JAMES RESTON

Special to The New York Times

PEKING, Friday, Aug. 6—China is taking a hard line against the Nixon Administration for trying to have both the Peking Government and the Chinese Nationalists in the United Nations, but this has not changed its decision to welcome President Nixon here some time before next May.

It can be said on the highest authority that officials here are not only irritated by Secretary of State William P. Rogers's announcement that Washington will vote for the seating of Peking in the United Nations and oppose the expulsion of Taipei, but furious because they think this formula was reached as a result of pressure from both Japan and Chiang Kai-shek, the Chinese Nationalist leader. The Government here is still counting on private negotiations and President Nixon's visit to straighten things out.

Peking has four ways of making its official views known here. In order of importance, they are Government or Communist party official statements, pronouncements in the official press by "Commentator," a signature usually denoting a member of the Central Committee of the Communist party, editorials in the official newspaper, Jenmin Jih Pao, and articles in the official press agency, Hsinhua. The sharp attack on Mr. Rogers's "two China" statement came in the form of a Hsinhua commentary.

The Government here hesitated for a day before its attack on Mr. Rogers's statement. Finally, they characterized the "two China" formula as "absurd," a "preposterous" proposition that proved that the Nixon Administration was "lying" in its determination to support the "Chiang Kai-shek gang" and demonstrate that it was "the enemy of the Chinese people."

There was also a suggestion in the official comment that Peking was not only disappointed but felt that it had

Continued on Page 10, Column 3

CANDIDACY OF KY BARRED BY COURT

Judges Say He Did Not Comply With New Law—Minh May Withdraw

By IVER PETERSON

Special to The New York Times

SAIGON, South Vietnam, Aug. 5—Vice President Nguyen Cao Ky today lost a major round in his fight to get on the ballot for the presidential election Oct. 3. The South Vietnamese Supreme Court rejected his application for candidacy on the ground that it did not comply with the rules established in a stiff electoral law sponsored by Mr. Ky's chief rival, President Nguyen Van Thieu.

The court's rejection of Mr. Ky's candidacy prompted a statement from the third presidential aspirant, Gen. Duong Van Minh. The general said that he was considering withdrawing from the race because Mr. Ky's disqualification proved that President Thieu's Government was using "dishonest tricks" to assure Mr. Thieu's re-election.

In the past General Minh has repeatedly threatened to quit the race if the Vice President

Continued on Page 4, Column 3

Sadat Said to Warn Soviet He'll Resist Reds in Middle East

By JOHN L. HESS

Special to The New York Times

CAIRO, Aug. 5 — President Anwar el-Sadat has told the Soviet Union unequivocally that Egypt will continue to resist Communism in the Arab world, it was reliably reported today. The Kremlin appears to have bowed to his position and to have decided that its strategic interest in the Middle East outweighs the fate of Arab Communists.

At a closed session on July 24 of the Arab Socialist Union, Egypt's only political group, Mr. Sadat recounted a confrontation with the Soviet Union. The speech has not been published but an allusion to it appeared yesterday in Al Akhbar, a popular newspaper.

Mr. Sadat delivered his speech two days after the reversal of the leftist coup d'état in the Sudan.

The paper likened President Sadat's stand to that of his predecessor, Gamal Abdel Nasser, in the late nineteen-fifties. When Premier Nikita S. Khrushchev remonstrated with President Nasser over the repression of Communists in Egypt and over his hostility

Continued on Page 2, Column 6

WHOLESALE INDEX OF PRICES IN JULY CLIMBED SHARPLY

Rise of 0.7%, Biggest Since 1965, Held Back by Drop in the Food Category

By EDWIN L. DALE Jr.

Special to The New York Times

WASHINGTON, Aug. 5—The rise in industrial wholesale prices quickened in July though there was a welcome decline in food prices, the Labor Department reported today.

The closely watched index of industrial wholesale prices, after adjustment for normal seasonal changes, rose seven-tenths of one per cent in July. This was the largest increase for a single month since the current prolonged period of inflation began in late 1965. Before seasonal adjustment the increase was five-tenths of one per cent, the largest this year.

The last time industrial prices rose as much, on a seasonally adjusted basis, was in 1956. The rise in these prices, after easing in late 1970 and early 1971, had averaged four-tenths of a per cent a month in the April-June period, raising new doubts about the progress being made against inflation. The July report, even though one month is never decisive, heightened those doubts.

Over-All Index Up

The portion of the wholesale price index covering farm products, processed foods and feeds declined by one per cent after seasonal adjustment and three-tenths of one per cent before adjustment. This downward movement held back the rise in the wholesale price index as a whole.

The over-all index rose two-tenths of one per cent, seasonally adjusted, the smallest since March. Before adjustment, the rise was three-tenths of one per cent.

At the White House, Ronald L. Ziegler, the President's press secretary, took some comfort in the fact that the rise in the over-all index was the smallest in five months. He conceded that the wholesale price index, like other indicators, contained "some good news, some bad."

He said the Administration "is not losing confidence in the course of action we are taking," though he added that the feeling was not "euphoric" and that "we recognize the problems we face." Mr. Ziegler spoke after a Cabinet meeting at which the state of the economy was a topic.

In Congress, Senator William Proxmire, Democrat of Wisconsin, Chairman of the Joint Economic Committee, called the re-

Continued on Page 45, Column 4

Astronaut Works in Space as His Daughters Watch

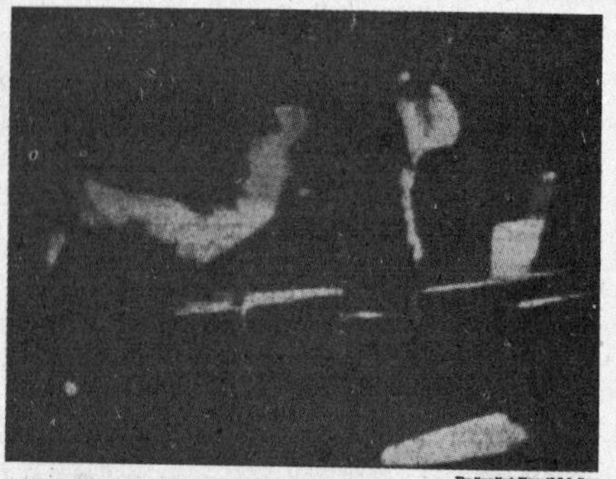

The New York Times/C.B.S. News

Maj. Alfred M. Worden, leg outstretched, retrieving film exposed while he flew Endeavour

Associated Press

As Major Worden moved between cameras and cockpit. Merrill, left, and Alison watched

ASTRONAUT TAKES A WALK IN SPACE TO PICK UP FILMS

Worden's Excursion Outside Cabin Is the First at a Vast Distance From the Earth

SHIP 196,000 MILES OUT

Aides in Houston Surprised at the Speed With Which the Task Is Completed

Excerpts from Apollo reports will be found on Page 12.

By JOHN NOBLE WILFORD

Special to The New York Times

HOUSTON, Aug. 5 — An Apollo 15 astronaut, Maj. Alfred M. Worden of the Air Force, stepped into the black vacuum 196,000 miles from the earth today to become the first man ever to take a floating excursion outside his craft in interplanetary space.

Gripping handrails on the exterior of the spaceship, his legs often drifting high over his head, Major Worden made three trips to the rear section of the craft, the Endeavour, to retrieve film magazines and inspect scientific instruments.

The astronaut spent 16 minutes outside the Endeavour, working all the time, accomplishing his tasks with a speed and ease that surprised Mission Control at the Manned Spacecraft Center here. Only once did the astronaut seem to take note of his environment and the distant scenery.

"You Look Fantastic"

When he looked back and saw one of the two other astronauts standing waist-high in the ship's open hatch, Major Worden said:

"You look absolutely fantastic against that moon back there. That is really a most unbelievable, remarkable thing."

At the time Major Worden began his excursion at 11:40 A.M., Eastern daylight time, Apollo 15 was about 50,000 miles from the moon, coasting toward the earth at a speed of 2,300 miles an hour. If he could see earth at the time, he never commented on it.

Apollo 15 rocketed out of lunar orbit yesterday, after completing man's fourth landing on the moon, and is scheduled to splash down in the Pacific Ocean north of Hawaii Saturday afternoon.

Scott at the Controls

Tomorrow, as they gather speed from the ever stronger pull of earth's gravity, Major Worden, Col. David R. Scott and Lieut. Col. James B. Irwin are scheduled to hold a space-to-ground news conference. For about 30 minutes, starting at 3:54 P.M., they are to answer questions submitted by newsmen here.

While Major Worden was working outside today, Colonel Scott, the Apollo commander, handled the spaceship's controls and Colonel Irwin stood in the open hatch, unreeling a 24-foot tether that attached Major Worden to a ring inside the

Continued on Page 12, Column 2

WALLACE ASSERTS HE'LL RUN IN '72

Barring 'Meaningful Change' in Major Party, He Says He Is in Race 'to Win'

By JAMES T. WOOTEN

Special to The New York Times

MONTGOMERY, Ala., Aug. 5—George C. Wallace says he has decided to run again for the Presidency in 1972.

"The only thing that would keep me out is a meaningful change of direction in the Nixon Administration or the Democratic party," he said here yesterday in an interview, adding: "I have no realistic hopes that such miracles will come to pass."

"I will be running to win," he said. "Some people think I just like to run just to run—but I'll be a serious candidate in 1972 because I believe that a victory for me is quite possible."

In a wide-ranging conversation, the third-party champion of state's rights and segregation confirmed what many of his friends and foes have believed for some time — that he has never really ceased an active pursuit of the Presidency since he captured 10 million votes in the election three years ago.

It was, however, his first outright affirmation that he

Continued on Page 35, Column 6

'72 Draft Lottery Assigns No. 1 to Those Born Dec. 4

Special to The New York Times

WASHINGTON, Aug. 5—The Selective Service System, in a lottery drawing that lasted just over two hours, determined today the order in which about two million young men born in 1952 will be subject to the draft next year.

An hour and 48 minutes after the lottery began, the audience of 100 or so in the Commerce Department Auditorium learned that young men born on Dec. 4, 1952, had been assigned the number 1.

Draft priorities for 1952 appear on Page 32.

A few minutes later, those born on Nov. 1 were paired with No. 366, which, unless draft calls rise far beyond expected levels, means certain immunity from conscription.

The Defense Department's announced draft quota for next year is 100,000 men. Thus, the lottery ceiling could be well below No. 125, according to one Selective Service official. It will depend upon the size of the available manpower pool made up of men born in 1952 who do not hold deferments.

In 1970, when the draft call was 165,000 men, no one holding a lottery number higher than 195 was drafted. This year the call dropped to 140,000, and the highest lottery number reached thus far has been 125. Selective Service officials indicated today that they might have to increase this ceiling to

Continued on Page 32, Column 1

HEALTH COST RISE OF 50% PREDICTED

Federal Study Puts Total at a 'Staggering' $105-Billion in the Fiscal Year 1974

By RICHARD D. LYONS

Special to The New York Times

WASHINGTON, Aug. 5—A major Federal study of the nation's health care costs, made public today, forecasts that medical expenses will rise 50 per cent in the first half of this decade to more than $100-billion.

The increase was termed "staggering" by the five aides who conducted the study. They are statistical experts of the Social Security Administration and its parent body, the Department of Health, Education and Welfare.

The primary aim of the study was to provide Congress with cost estimates of the 12 proposals for national health insurance that have been introduced in the Senate and the House.

Conclusions Listed

The major conclusions of the study are the following:

¶Health expenses will rise from $67-billion to $105-billion between the fiscal years 1970 and 1974, the first year that a national health insurance program may go into operation.

¶The rise in that share of the gross national product that is devoted to health will be as great as the rise in defense spending at the start of the Vietnam war.

¶The average American family may expect to pay additional out-of-pocket medical expenses of $200 a year by 1974

Continued on Page 13, Column 1

Touches of Sidewalk Splendor Planned for Midtown

By MURRAY SCHUMACH

Several of the nation's largest corporations will build promenades, plazas, pools, fountains and underground pedestrian walks to beautify Rockefeller Center and show their faith in the future of the city.

The program is part of a $300-million office building complex rising from 47th to 50th Street, along the west side of the Avenue of the Americas, as part of the expansion of Rockefeller Center. It is due to be completed in 1973.

"We have covenants and faith in the city and want to put our money where our mouth is," Alton G. Marshall, president of Rockefeller Center, Inc., said yesterday at a press conference, where details of the $3.5-million beautification program were announced.

Others who joined him in expressing strong optimism in the city's future were top executives of Time-Life, the Standard Oil Company (New Jersey), McGraw-Hill and Celanese, all of which are part of the skyscraper complex.

The comments predicting a healthy future for the city came at a time when a number of businesses, some big, have either left the city or declared

Continued on Page 28, Column 3

Sketch of proposed buildings on Avenue of the Americas. From left at 47th Street: Celanese, McGraw-Hill and Standard Oil (N.J.). Time-Life, right, is on 50th Street.

Beautification program in the building complex includes promenade behind McGraw-Hill

Giant Incinerator Plan Dropped; City Cites Costs and Pollution

By DAVID BIRD

Plans were officially abandoned by the Lindsay administration yesterday for a giant incinerator that, in 1967, was called the answer to the city's growing garbage crisis.

The city had spent $8-million in planning the facility.

The plant, scheduled to be built at the old Brooklyn Navy Yard, would have been the largest in the world with a capacity of 6,000 tons a day. But in announcing its demise yesterday, Jerome Kretchmer, the city's Environmental Protection Administrator, said it would have been "too expensive and too great a concentrated source of air pollution."

Mr. Kretchmer said that the latest estimate of the incinerator's cost was $200-million.

Although the plant has been canceled, the city has not found an acceptable alternative way of handling the garbage—or solid waste—problem, which has grown steadily.

Sanitation officials estimate that the solid waste generated in the city is increasing at 4 to 6 per cent every year and now stands at about 25,000 tons a day.

Mr. Kretchmer said at a crowded news conference in his Municipal Building office that the next step was to determine where to put the garbage once present dumping sites had been filled up.

Mr. Kretchmer said that "we are actively exploring new techniques for solid waste disposal" but that right now there

Continued on Page 29, Column 2

G.M. to Raise Price Of 1972 Cars $176

By JERRY M. FLINT

Special to The New York Times

DETROIT, Aug. 5 — The General Motors Corporation said today that it would raise 1972 car prices by an average of $176, or 3.9 per cent.

The move assures a large price increase on next fall's cars. The Ford Motor Company and the Chrysler Corporation have said that they plan price increases of around 5 per cent, or about $200 a car.

General Motors, with half the car market, sets the price pattern in the industry; its move apparently insures a price increase of close to $200 a car for the 1972 model year.

A General Motors spokesman said today that the increases took into consideration "to the extent possible" an 8 per cent

Continued on Page 49, Column 2

NEWS INDEX

NASA

The Falcon lifts off from the Moon. This picture marked the first time that a lunar lift-off was seen on Earth.

NASA

The *Endeavor* (Apollo 15 command/service module) in lunar orbit.

NASA

The Moon as seen from the Endeavor in its lunar orbit.

"All the News That's Fit to Print"

The New York Times

LATE CITY EDITION
Weather: Partly cloudy today; fair tonight. Showers likely tomorrow. Temp. range: today 43-64; Saturday 42-52. Full U.S. report on Page 111.

News of special interest to readers in New Jersey will be found on pages 75 to 110.

VOL. CXXI No. 41,728 © 1972 The New York Times Company NEW YORK, SUNDAY, APRIL 23, 1972 75¢ beyond 50-mile zone from New York City, except Long Island. Higher in air delivery cities. NJ 50 CENTS

ASTRONAUTS DRIVE UP MOUNTAIN, COLLECT ROCKS IN 6-MILE TRIP; PLAN TO LIFT OFF MOON TONIGHT

The New York Times/Michael Evans

ANTIWAR MARCH: Protesters heading down Seventh Avenue at Times Square

8 Primaries in 2 Weeks Aim at Blue-Collar Voter

By R. W. APPLE Jr.
Special to The New York Times

PITTSBURGH, April 22—The most intensive period of Presidential primary activity in American political history will take place during the next two weeks.

But the eight primary elections scheduled for states in the South, East and Middle West, as well as the District of Columbia, are unlikely to decide the struggle for the Democratic Presidential nomination. That struggle seems certain to extend through the June primaries in the nation's largest states—California and New York, and probably to the convention floor in Miami Beach.

What may well be decided by May 6 are two critical questions: Will Senator Edmund S. Muskie of Maine or Senator Hubert H. Humphrey of Minnesot.. survive for the next round? Will Gov. George C. Wallace of Alabama, who has encountered nothing but success so far, be slowed a bit?

The answers are by no means clear. The fight will be waged in precincts of every description—from Shaker Heights, Ohio, to the sleepy rural quarters of Eufala, Ala. — but most of all it will be waged among the people who form the backbone of the Democratic party, the blue-collar working people.

They live in Cleveland, Philadelphia, Gary, Memphis and Boston, but also in smaller places like Jeannette, a dingy mill town about 25 miles east of Pittsburgh. And in Jeannette, they seem unsure. They seem that way everywhere.

"I like Humphrey," a glass factory worker said yesterday. "He's against guys who don't pay any taxes, and he's for us. I kind of like Muskie. He's a Polack like me. But that Wallace—ain't he something? He sure kicks hell out of those smart guys down in Washington."

That man, and hundreds of thousands of others like him, will be the main target of Mr. Muskie, Mr. Humphrey, Mr. Wallace and Senator George McGovern of South Dakota, who must also court the blue-collar vote, in the two weeks ahead.

More and more, the Democrats' campaign is taking on a populist coloration, as all the candidates seek to identify themselves with the issues that Mr. Wallace brought to the fore: tax reform, the remoteness of government, urban disorder and decay, and an overwhelming sense of frustration.

Pennsylvania and Massachusetts are to vote Tuesday. A week later, on May 2, there will be four primaries: Ohio, Indiana, the District of Columbia and Alabama. Then come

Continued on Page 39, Column 1

Coming Primaries

Massachusetts and Pennsylvania	Tuesday
Alabama, District of Columbia, Indiana, Ohio	May 2
Tennessee	May 4
North Carolina	May 6

WAR FOES MARCH IN THE RAIN HERE

Turn Out by the Thousands —Weather Curbs Other Rallies Across Nation

By MARTIN ARNOLD

There was driving rain and biting cold, but still many thousands of people marched and rallied peacefully for hours on the city's streets yesterday to protest the war in Vietnam.

They had come from Massachusetts and Vermont and from as far west as Ohio to take part. They jammed the Penn Central and Long Island Rail Road lines and filled the early morning buses and the Hudson tubes from New Jersey to get here. Many of them were high school students.

The marchers' estimates of the crowd ranged from 30,000 to 100,000, but most news people put the figure at 35,000.

Across the nation, bad weather cut the crowds considerably in such places as Washington, where peace demonstrations had been scheduled. But 30,000 people attended a rally in Golden Gate Park in San Francisco, where many paid a quarter to throw darts at pictures of President Nixon and J. Edgar Hoover, the director of the Federal Bureau of Investigation.

In Los Angeles, only about

Continued on Page 54, Column 1

ENEMY LAUNCHES ASSAULT ON ANLOC FROM FOUR SIDES

Big Infantry Attack Comes After Heavy Shelling— 2d City in Area Hit

By MALCOLM W. BROWNE
Special to The New York Times

SAIGON, South Vietnam, Sunday, April 23 — After pounding the besieged provincial capital of Anloc with artillery for three hours this morning, North Vietnamese forces began a major infantry attack from four sides, in what appeared to be the beginning of the terminal battle for the town.

Military sources spoke gloomily of the tremendous strength the enemy was reportedly using in the attack. The position of the 8,000 defenders seemed grim.

The new attack on Anloc came after a day in which enemy forces seemed to be on the offensive from one end of South Vietnam to the other, striking at positions from the Mekong Delta in the south to the northernmost provinces.

All last night the rumble of heavy bombs, presumably dropped by B-52's near Anloc, could be heard in Saigon, and the northern sky flickered red from the detonations.

2-Week Siege

Anloc has been under siege since April 8, when Locninh, another plantation town further north on Route 13, fell to the Communists.

In the same general region, what appeared to be a coordinated attack was launched this morning on Dautieng, a town 85 miles northwest of Saigon.

Large enemy forces have been moving into Tayninh Povince and nearby Binhlong Province for some time. Anloc is the capital of Binhlong Province.

The two Sunday attacks clearly were intended to secure the northwestern approaches to Saigon for the North Vietnamese.

To buttress the defenses of the capital of Saigon itself from

Continued on Page 20, Column 3

NASA via Associated Press

LUNAR CURIOSITY: Large boulder draws attention of Lieut. Col. Charles M. Duke Jr., left, and Capt. John W. Young. Astronauts found it during walk up Stone Mountain.

3D WALK IS TODAY

Some Samples Found Are Crystalline Type in the Original State

By JOHN NOBLE WILFORD
Special to The New York Times

HOUSTON, Sunday, April 23 —The astronauts of Apollo 16 roamed the slopes of a mountain on the moon yesterday, chatting happily, turning over rocks and eagerly collecting samples as they set a record for the longest lunar trek.

Over a period of 7 hours and 23 minutes, the two seemingly inexhaustible explorers gathered a few crystalline rocks that scientists hope will contain clues to the early history of the rugged Descartes landing site.

Capt. John W. Young of the Navy and Lieut. Col. Charles M. Duke Jr. of the Air Force covered about six miles by foot and by lunar rover on the second of three scheduled excursions outside their landing craft, Orion. They ranged about three miles south of Orion to the rock-strewn slopes of Stone Mountain.

Their record EVA, for extravehicular activity, ran from 11:33 A.M., Eastern standard time, to 6:56 P.M.—12 minutes longer than their trek Friday and 11 minutes longer than a journey by Apollo 15 astronauts last August.

Captain Young and Colonel Duke retired at 11:18 P.M. yesterday for a scheduled eight-hour rest period.

Today, they plan to take their final excursion, a five-hour trip north of Orion to a large crater with light-colored rocky debris extending outward in distinctive ray patterns.

Last Excursion Curtailed

The third EVA is scheduled to start at 10:57 A.M. Its planned duration was curtailed by two hours because of Apollo 16's delay in landing on the moon Thursday night.

After the final moon walk, the two astronauts are scheduled to lift off the lunar surface at 8:22 P.M. today and rejoin Lieut. Comdr. Thomas K. Mattingly 2d of the Navy. Commander Mattingly has been steering the command ship, Casper, in lunar orbit. The two ships are supposed to link up at 10:17 P.M.

Apollo 16's return voyage to earth is now scheduled to begin at 9:15 P.M. tomorrow—nearly a day earlier than originally planned. This change was dictated by the flight controllers' concern over the faulty second-

Continued on Page 52, Column 1

Astronauts' Final Day on Moon

10:57 A.M.—Third moon walk begins.
3:52 P.M.—Astronauts return to lunar module.
8:22 P.M.—Lift-off for return to earth.
10:17 P.M.—Lunar module docks with command module.

9:16 P.M. tomorrow—Engine firing for return to earth.
2:42 P.M. Thursday—Splashdown.

SOVIET PREPARES BIG NEW MISSILE

U.S. Aides Say Tests Could Be Held Before Nixon's Journey to Moscow

By WILLIAM BEECHER
Special to The New York Times

WASHINGTON, April 22— The Soviet Union is preparing to test-fire a new intercontinental ballistic missile that is significantly larger than any now in operation, American analysts said today.

The analysts said that the missile has a diameter of about 12 feet, about a third larger than that of the SS-9, the biggest Soviet missile that has been deployed.

Although American officials in several branches of Government agree that the new missile could be test-fired in a matter of days, some doubt that the Russians will test it before President Nixon's visit to Moscow on May 22.

A Mystery Solved

The recent appearance of the new missile at the test complex at Tyuratam, north of the Aral Sea, apparently resolves some of the mystery surrounding the more than 90 large new missile silos of two different sizes on which construction began in late 1970.

After the new silos had been discovered, weapons specialists in and out of Government speculated that they were designed for one of three purposes: to give added protection to existing missiles, to house modified versions of the two basic So-

Continued on Page 5, Column 1

Jersey's Relief Rolls Rose 2½ Times From '66 to '71

By EDWARD C. BURKS

New Jersey's welfare rolls increased by more than two and a half times over the five-year period ended in 1971, a rate of growth matching that of New York City.

A New York Times analysis of the latest official state figures shows that the number of New Jersey residents receiving welfare assistance increased from 174,298 in October, 1966, to 461,623 in October, 1971.

The rapid climb occurred in urbanized areas, large and small. But the biggest additions to the rolls were in such "old cities" as Newark, Paterson, Camden, Atlantic City, Jersey City and Union City, where the poor have migrated into decaying residential areas.

Newark, for example, accounts for 83 per cent of all the welfare recipients in Essex County, although it has only about 40 per cent of the county's population.

Of the 461,623 welfare clients in the state last October, 367,-477—or 8 out of 10—were receiving payments under the Aid for Dependent Children category. The clients in this category are generally mothers and their children in fatherless households.

In a survey of 750 such mothers who applied for assistance in one month in Essex County, 49 per cent were found to be "single girls with out-of-wedlock children," according to Philip K. Lazaro, director of the county welfare board.

Two-thirds of the mothers had been born and raised in New Jersey. Only 37 of the 750 had lived in the state fewer than five years.

In addition to the 461,623 welfare clients, the state by last October had 45,000 people eligible for Medicaid and 13,056 refugees from Cuba enrolled under a special Federal relief program.

Excluding the Cubans and the 45,000 people eligible for Medicaid, the money paid out to welfare recipients in October, 1971, was $34.6-million, nearly four times the $8.9-million total of five years earlier. The state and municipalities paid out $19.1-million of the $34.6-million; the remainder was paid by the Federal Government.

Essex, New Jersey's most populous county, was at the top of the list, accounting for

Continued on Page 53, Column 1

U.S. Farm Agency Reported to Foster Abuse of Migrants

By PHILIP SHABECOFF
Special to The New York Times

WASHINGTON, April 22—An extensive study by the Labor Department, obtained here today, indicates that the department's Rural Manpower Service has failed to curb widespread exploitation of migrant farm workers.

The study, started 10 months ago after complaints by migrant worker groups, also reports that the rural program is helping in many cases to institutionalize abuses against farm workers, such as racial discrimination, neglect of minimum-wage and child-labor laws, and substandard housing, health and sanitary facilities.

The study also reports extensive evidence that the Labor Department service often represents growers' rather than workers' interests. However, the study does not directly address itself to the worker groups' recommendation that the serv-

Continued on Page 29, Column 1

Bing Says Farewell to the Met

By ISRAEL SHENKER

Twenty-two years after he grasped the silken threads of power over the Metropolitan Opera, Sir Rudolf Bing yesterday said farewell to the premier opera company of the world.

In the silence of a damp and dismal morning, in the full-throated matinee glory of the final opera, and in the extraordinary evening gala that brought down the curtain on his reign as general manager, Sir Rudolf was the star triumphant.

A heavenly chorus of great singers—stars he had brought to the opera during his 22 years there—turned up to sing him fond adieu. It was the kind of homage that only the Met can pay.

The 70-year-old autocrat of Lincoln Center, who was born in Vienna, knighted in Britain and blooded at the Met, began his great day in the most pedestrian way—walking his dog, Pip, in Central Park.

For the occasion, Pip wore a green wool sweater and Sir Rudolf a gray coat and bowler. Then the two returned to their apartment in the Essex House, where Lady Bing had prepared the breakfast Sir Rudolf has eaten daily for a good 30 years: porridge, tea and toast.

At his office, the bill of fare was something else again—stacks of letters and telegrams

Continued on Page 65, Column 1

The New York Times/Edward Hausner

Sir Rudolf Bing with his dog, Pip, in Central Park before attending a gala evening in his honor at the opera house.

Ideal of Unity Stirs Appalachian Poor

By GEORGE VECSEY
Special to The New York Times

CHARLESTON, W. Va., April 22—In other parts of the country, the pop wall posters feature Dennis Hopper on his Easy Rider motorcycle or Che Guevara staring moodily into the future. But here in a storefront office in Appalachia, the pop poster features Mother Jones, a prim old lady who looks like everybody's grandmother.

"Pray for the dead and fight like hell for the living," implored Mother Jones in an epic coal field battle in the early nineteen-hundreds. Now her words and her image are being used to help a new generation of Appalachians struggle toward a common movement or experience.

Something is stirring in Appalachia, according to many people from the core of the coal region. Numbers of mountain people are coming down from their isolated hollows to forge bonds with former Appalachian Volunteers or VISTA workers who stayed behind and put down roots. But while some of the impetus undoubtedly comes from such outsiders, everyone agrees that this loose, amorphous "movement" depends on people who were born and raised in the hills and who intend to remain in the hills.

There is no single organization that speaks for Appalachia, and no single group of goals. Indeed, the splinter groups often seem at odds with one another or ignorant of one another. There are the widows of union miners, for example, who refuse to have anything to do with the widows of nonunion miners. And there are ecology groups that contend with the welfare groups that contend with the miners' groups—all in a region long notorious for lack of corporate compassion and grassroots cohesion.

But lately many of the groups have been broadening, sending out signals over the rocky ridges and around the narrow valleys, trying to beat the physical and spiritual isolation that has kept the mountaineer in his place—up in the head of the hollow—for over a hundred years.

"I can remember a few years ago when you couldn't get people to call you on the phone," says one long-time Appalachian adviser. "Now I get phone calls from people all over the area. We're losing our shyness."

Many Appalachian people have been brought together

Continued on Page 47, Column 1

Today's Sections

Index to Subjects

"All the News
That's Fit to Print"

The New York Times

LATE CITY EDITION

Weather: Sunny and pleasant today; fair, pleasant tonight, tomorrow. Temp. range: today 64-78; Friday 73-83. Temp.-Hum. Index yesterday 75. Full U.S. report on Page 52.

VOL. CXXI ... No. 41,832 • © 1972 The New York Times Company NEW YORK, SATURDAY, AUGUST 5, 1972 15 CENTS

MAJOR-WAR PLANS ARE BEING REVISED BY WHITE HOUSE

Decision Made to Develop but Not Deploy Bigger, More Accurate Arms

KISSINGER HEADS STUDY

More Options for President Sought—Move Is Made Quietly to Curb Debate

By WILLIAM BEECHER
Special to The New York Times

WASHINGTON, Aug. 4 — The Nixon Administration is quietly moving to shift the emphasis of American strategic planning in case of a major war and to develop bigger, more accurate warheads and other weapons to carry out such plans.

The purpose underlying such a shift, senior Administration officials say, is to give the President greater flexibility in answering any kind of nuclear attack on the United States, or even the threat of such an attack.

The present war plans provide a handful of alternatives. But all are on so massive a scale, officials say, that on Russian radar screens the approaching missiles and bombers would probably appear headed for Soviet cities, whether they were or not.

Campaign Issue Seen

Thus the search, on Mr. Nixon's part, is for a series of limited retaliatory options that planners say would be aimed both at deterring war and at avoiding a cataclysm.

To do this the Administration's planners have begun to move toward more advanced weapons that could destroy "hard targets" in the Soviet Union, such as nuclear weapons storage bunkers and missile silos. Such weapons, while not banned by the recent strategic arms limitation accords, are expected to touch off a debate in the Presidential campaign over whether the Administration is setting the stage for another upward spiral in the arms race.

The move toward this new policy has taken several forms. Without public announcement, the President recently named Henry A. Kissinger, his national security adviser, to head a top-level interdepartmental group to come up with additional nuclear war options, officials disclose.

Mr. Nixon also has sanctioned the development of weapons improvements, some designed to make selective retaliatory strikes more precise and effective, others designed

Continued on Page 9, Column 1

U.S. Tells of a 2d Pipeline From China to Fuel Hanoi

Pentagon Aides Expect It to Increase Supply to Meet Daily Need

By BENJAMIN WELLES
Special to The New York Times

WASHINGTON, Aug. 4 — Senior Defense Department officials said today that North Vietnam had virtually completed a second new fuel pipeline from China to Kep, a town 30 miles northeast of Hanoi.

When it is completed later this month, the new line, which parallels one completed in July, is expected to increase North Vietnam's fuel supplies from China to 1,000 tons daily. That figure would approximate the current operating needs of the North.

While the new pipelines in the constantly bombed North would be of some help in sustaining the enemy offensive, the defense officials said that they doubted that Hanoi would be able to mount another offensive of similar scope. They pointed to North Vietnam's estimated losses—65,000 to 70,000 soldiers killed since the offensive began in April.

Moreover, they assert, the American "interdiction," as the Pentagon calls it, of North Vietnamese ports with mines has been 100 per cent effective in cutting off all water-borne supplies except those brought in by sampans or junks.

The New York Times/Aug. 5, 1972

Second pipeline (1) is being completed to augment line that was finished last month (2).

The new pipeline, the officials said, is nearly identical with the one started in June and completed in July, about two months after the announcement by President Nixon on May 8 that North Vietnam's territorial waters would be mined.

The first line, which starts

Continued on Page 4, Column 3

FOOD PRICES RISE BUT JOBLESS RATE IS STEADY IN JULY

Farm Products in Sharpest Jump in Last 18 Months—Unemployment at 5.5%

By EDWIN L. DALE Jr.
Special to The New York Times

WASHINGTON, Aug. 4—The nation's unemployment remained in July at the reduced June level, but another jump in farm and food prices caused a significant increase in the Wholesale Price Index, the Labor Department reported today.

At 5.5 per cent of the labor force, the unemployment rate in July tended to confirm the improvement recorded in June. Prior to the most recent two months, unemployment had hovered near 6 per cent since late 1970.

Although the over-all Wholesale Price Index rose steeply, the closely watched index of industrial commodities showed improvement. The rise of two-tenths of one per cent was the smallest since Phase Two wage and price controls began last November.

For the index as a whole, dominated by rising agricultural prices, the increase was eight-tenths of one per cent, or seven-tenths after adjustment for normal seasonal changes in some prices. The index for farm and food prices rose 2.2 per cent, or 1.8 per cent after seasonal adjustment. The two-tenths rise for industrial products was the same both before and after adjustment.

Recorded Early in Month

Entirely because of the burst of farm and food prices, the Wholesale Price Index has risen slightly more rapidly in the eight months of Phase Two than in the eight months preceding the price and wage freeze last August. The index for July was 119.7, with 1967 prices taken as 100.

The wholesale price rise for food products signals a further increase in the Consumer Price Index for this category. However, Ezra Solomon, a member of President Nixon's Council of Economic Advisers, found one hopeful sign today. He said, "We now know that live cattle prices peaked during the first week in July and that they have since fallen by about 6½ per cent."

The steep July wholesale increase—recorded early in the month—was not limited to livestock, however. There were also large increases in prices of poultry, eggs, fruits and vegetables, and green coffee.

For farm products as a whole the increase was 3.2 per cent, the largest for a single month in a year and a half. Farm

Continued on Page 22, Column 4

Associated Press

Senator Edmund S. Muskie leaving his residence in Bethesda, Md., on his way to Maine, to consider accepting the Democratic Vice-Presidential nomination.

M'GOVERN OFFERS MUSKIE 2D PLACE IN 2-HOUR PARLEY

Maine Senator Flies Home to Confer With His Wife on 'Reasons to Do It'

'APPEALING CHALLENGE'

Staff Is Urging Nominee to Keep Shriver Available in Event of Refusal

By JAMES M. NAUGHTON
Special to The New York Times

WASHINGTON, Aug. 4 — Senator George McGovern has offered the Democratic nomination for Vice President to Senator Edmund S. Muskie of Maine, and Mr. Muskie said tonight he was "looking for reasons to do it."

Senator Muskie confirmed that the Presidential nominee asked him to join the Democratic ticket when they met for two hours last night at Mr. Muskie's house in nearby Maryland.

But he added, in a telephone conversation tonight from his summer cottage in Maine, that he was wrestling with the decision, weighing both the anxieties of his wife, Jane, and "practical questions" about his role on a McGovern ticket.

Challenge Is 'Appealing'

"I have to decide," Mr. Muskie said, "whether I thought my accepting such a nomination would make a difference not only to George McGovern and to the party, but to the country. The challenge, of course, is always appealing."

He said that he hoped to be able to give a reply to Senator McGovern tomorrow morning, but that "my wife and I are still discussing it."

Key members of the McGovern campaign staff, including Frank Mankiewicz, the political director, and Henry A. Kimelman, the finance chairman, renewed their efforts in the meantime to persuade Senator McGovern to turn to a Kennedy in-law, Sargent Shriver, if Mr. Muskie should say no.

Mr. Mankiewicz reportedly telephoned Mr. Shriver, a former Ambassador to France and director of the Peace Corps, at the Kennedy family compound in Hyannis Port, Mass., to encourage him to remain available.

4th Senator Asked

Senator Muskie was the fourth of Senator McGovern's colleagues who had been asked since Monday night to consider joining the ticket after Senator Thomas F. Eagleton of Missouri had reluctantly yielded to Mr. McGovern's request that he resign the nomination.

In a meeting yesterday with reporters, Mr. McGovern said that he had asked Senators Edward M. Kennedy of Massachusetts, Abraham A. Ribicoff of Connecticut and Hubert H. Humphrey of Minnesota to reconsider their rejections of the Vice-Presidential spot at the Democratic National Convention last month. All three told him they had not changed their minds.

Mr. McGovern's turn last

Continued on Page 12, Column 4

ANTIPOVERTY UNIT BUYS A COMPANY

Purchase of Harlem Concern Reflects Immediate Aim 'to Generate Profits'

By C. GERALD FRASER

As part of its economic development plan, a Harlem antipoverty agency has purchased the Shultz Company, Inc., a Harlem-based manufacturer of wood, metal and plastic interiors for supermarkets, for $1-million.

The Commonwealth Holding Company, a profit-making corporation owned by the Harlem Commonwealth Council, said yesterday that it would use the annual profits from the manufacturing company to attack social problems. But it said the immediate aim of the purchase was to make money.

"The responsibility of a local development group," said James H. Dowdy, president of both the holding company and the council, "is to generate profits."

"It has no responsibility to cure any of the social ills," he added.

"It's cold, up and down business," Mr. Dowdy explained.

He said, for instance, that the white management team at the Shultz company, at 44 West

Continued on Page 10, Column 2

Fischer Wins Again; 6½-3½ Lead Dims Hopes for Spassky

By HAROLD C. SCHONBERG
Special to The New York Times

REYKJAVIK, Iceland, Aug. 4 —Bobby Fischer won today's adjourned game from Boris Spassky, pulling far ahead in the world championship chess match.

The Russian resigned on the 56th move, making the score 6½ to 3½ in favor of the American challenger.

Fischer now needs only six more points to win the title. Spassky needs 8½ to retain it.

The game, the 10th in the match, was resumed at 2 P.M. instead of the usual 5 P.M. starting time so that Fischer could observe his Sabbath, which starts at sundown Friday.

Nobody here gives the champion much of a chance. "There is very little hope for Spassky," Svetozar Gligoric, Yugoslavian grandmaster, said after the game. "Spassky's chess is inferior to Fischer's. After the second game it has been a disaster for him."

Spassky won the first game, on July 11, on a blunder by Fischer, and won the second on a forfeit when Fischer failed to show up. But in the eight games after that he has been able to get only 1½ points, all on draws.

"Fischer has been ahead in

Continued on Page 22, Column 1

JUDGE SHIFT HERE TO EASE BACKLOG

11 Justices Will Transfer to Felony Trials Under New Case Processing Plan

By MICHAEL KNIGHT

Eleven State Supreme Court justices here will be transferred from civil cases to felony cases next month in a move expected to make significant inroads into the city's growing backlog of felony trials.

Governor Rockefeller and Chief Judge Stanley H. Fuld of the Court of Appeals announced yesterday that the 11 judges would bring to 72 the number sitting in Manhattan, Brooklyn, Queens and the Bronx.

The increase will be the first step in implementing the Emergency Felony Case Processing Program approved by the Legislature this year in response to the growing outcry from judges, district attorneys and prisoners that it takes too long to try persons accused of murder, rape, armed robbery and other felonies.

Focus on Brooklyn

In addition, five mobile probation teams will be set up to provide the presentencing reports that are required before a judge may sentence a prisoner.

The lack of these reports has been a major complaint, especially in Brooklyn, where, according to a spokesman for the Judicial Conference of the State of New York, 1,564 defendants are being held, awaiting presentencing reports.

The mobile units will concentrate first in Brooklyn, the spokesman said, and then in the other boroughs as they are needed.

The vacancies in the Supreme Court's civil parts will be filled by shifting New York City Civil and Criminal Court judges and by increasing the use of "individual calendar" parts, said the spokesman, Michael McEneney.

The "individual calendar" al-

Continued on Page 17, Column 1

Bremer Guilty in Shooting Of Wallace, Gets 63 Years

By HOMER BIGART
Special to The New York Times

UPPER MARLBORO, Md., Aug. 4—Arthur H. Bremer was found guilty and sentenced to 63 years in prison today for the shooting of Gov. George C. Wallace of Alabama and three other persons at a political rally in Laurel, Md., May 15.

The jury of six men and six women took only 90 minutes to find that Bremer was sane when he fired the bullets that paralyzed Governor Wallace and forced him to end his campaign for the Democratic Presidential nomination.

The defense had raised the question of Bremer's sanity, and that was the main issue of this speedy five-day state trial.

Bremer, a 21-year-old busboy and odd-job worker from Milwaukee who had stalked President Nixon before making Mr. Wallace his prime target, heard without emotion the jury's verdict and—30 minutes later—the sentence imposed by Judge Ralph W. Powers.

His father, William Bremer, a truck driver who lost an eye at the age of 9, was standing against the wall in the rear of the courtroom. He had been coldly ignored by his son, but he flushed with anger over the verdict.

"The boy was sick," he said, and he added bitterly, "Probably if he was a black, or some Communist agitator, he'd be free."

When the jury was dismissed, Judge Powers asked Arthur Bremer if he had anything to say. Standing beside his attorney, Benjamin Lipsitz, Bremer said in a firm, clear voice:

"Well, Mr. Marshall [State's Attorney Arthur A. Marshall] tells me he'd like society to

Continued on Page 54, Column 2

Leslie Bacon Freed In Capitol Bombing

By United Press International

WASHINGTON, Aug. 4—The Justice Department announced tonight that it had dropped a perjury indictment against Leslie Ann Bacon in connection with the bombing of the United States Capitol March 1, 1971.

The department said it had sought the dismissal of the indictment and obtained a Federal District Court's permission to do so "because the decision was made not to answer defendant's motions of disclosure of electronic surveillance" regarding the case.

The department would not say what the nature of the surveillance was or what persons were involved. The Fed-

Continued on Page 53, Column 2

China Hails Discovery of 2,100-Year-Old Han Tomb

By JOHN BURNS
The Globe and Mail, Toronto

PEKING, Aug. 4—The discovery of a western Han Dynasty tomb dating back more than 2,100 years is being hailed in China as one of the most important archeological finds in decades.

The unearthing of the tomb near the southern city of Changsha was announced this week by the Communist party newspaper Jenmin Jih Pao in an account illustrated with a set of striking photographs.

Although the tomb belonged to the wife of a relatively insignificant nobleman who held sway over the region of Changsha, its discovery is important because of the extraordinary state of preservation in which it was found.

Greatest among the treasures that were found within is the corpse itself, described by the Chinese newspaper as being "fairly well preserved." That description is borne out by an accompanying photograph, which showed the corpse lying in the coffin, face up, its features clearly distinguishable as those of a woman.

Associated Press

The coffin that was found in the tomb unearthed at Changsha, in southern China

Chinese tombs have never before yielded a recognizable corpse that was even remotely as old as the one found in Changsha. The corpse appears to have benefited from the unusually determined effort that was made to seal it from the decaying effects of air.

The paper did not disclose how the discovery was made, or when, other than saying that it was "recently found." But sources in Peking disclosed later that workers digging evacuation tunnels came upon it earlier this year.

According to these sources, the discovery so seized the imagination of the Chinese leaders that they sent one of their own number, the octogenarian poet and historian Kuo Mo-jo, to inspect the site. It is also reported that the leaders ordered work on the tomb to be given the highest priority among a number of competing archeological finds.

The leaders' interest in the tomb may have been height-

Continued on Page 2, Column 5

NEWS INDEX

City's Patrol Force Smallest Since 1968

By ERIC PACE

Donald F. Cawley, the chief of the Police Department's patrol force, disclosed yesterday that the number of uniformed patrolmen in his command had fallen to 15,740—the lowest level in about four years.

Chief Cawley said the shrinkage in the force—which is generally considered the backbone of the city's law enforcement efforts—was due largely to attrition under City Hall's present policy of not engaging new municipal employes.

But he said it had also coincided with an increase in police efficiency due to many innovations — such as "vertical patrols" in skyscrapers—made under Police Commissioner Patrick V. Murphy.

"The encouraging part of the picture is that while we have a reduced number of men assigned to patrol, we have had significant reversals in crime [statistics] and our arrest activity is up," the chief said in a headquarters interview a year after taking his post.

Chief Cawley's title of chief of the Patrol Services Bureau puts him at the top of the vast pyramid of uniformed police commands, whose foundation has always been the thousands of individual patrolmen that the public encounters in the city's 74 precincts.

He said the number of policemen with the rank of patrolman —the department's lowest grade—in the Patrol Services Bureau had declined by about 1,300 between July 1, 1971 and July 15, 1972, when the 15,740 figure, the most recent head count, was reported.

Knowledgeable officials at Police Headquarters said this figure was the lowest since about 1968. A year-by-year breakdown was not available late yesterday, but the figure for 1967 was 13,921, and for 1962 it was 13,700.

The attrition is expected to continue at the rate of 10 per cent a year—which would mean the loss of 1,500 patrolmen within a total police force of 30,107, as compared to a total of 31,286 a year ago.

Other, lesser factors contributed to the drop, Chief Cawley said, in addition to the freeze on hiring, which is an economy move. For one thing, a few hundred patrolmen have been promoted to sergeant, a supervisory rank.

This upgrading — having more sergeants and fewer patrolmen — gives each sergeant fewer men to supervise, which is considered a good thing by theoreticians of police administration. Ideally, they say, this

Continued on Page 11, Column 3

"All the News That's Fit to Print"

The New York Times

LATE CITY EDITION

Weather: Sunny, cool today; cold tonight. Chance of rain tomorrow. Temp. range: today 29-42; Wed. 37-52. Full U.S. report on Page 94.

VOL. CXXII..No. 41,963 — © 1972 The New York Times Company — NEW YORK, THURSDAY, DECEMBER 14, 1972 — 15 CENTS

ASTRONAUTS END WALKS ON MOON AFTER UNVEILING PLAQUE TO PEACE AND DEDICATING A ROCK TO YOUTH

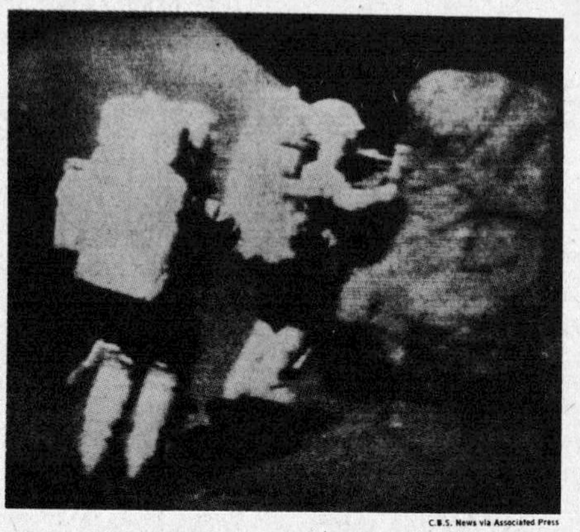

C.B.S. News via Associated Press

Capt. Eugene A. Cernan chips away at a lunar rock as Dr. Harrison H. Schmitt watches

LIFT-OFF TONIGHT

Last Exploration Fails to Uncover Volcanic Traces at Crater

By JOHN NOBLE WILFORD

Special to The New York Times

HOUSTON, Thursday, Dec. 14—The Apollo 17 astronauts completed man's last lunar trek for years to come with a ceremony last night dedicating a moon rock to the youth of the world, "the promise of the future."

It was one of the many rock samples Capt. Eugene A. Cernan of the Navy and Dr. Harrison H. Schmitt, a geologist, gathered on their third and final excursion outside the landing craft, the Challenger.

Their journey took them among striking boulders at the foot of a mountain and to another crater that scientists had thought might be volcanic. They were disappointed, however, when they discovered none of the orange and red soils similar to those found on the previous excursion at an apparent volcanic vent.

Plaque to Remain

The two astronauts later unveiled a plaque that they attached to one of the legs of the landing craft. The lower half of the craft will remain on the moon. In words reminiscent of the plaque left by the first men to walk on the moon, the Apollo 17 plaque read:

Here man completed his first Explorations of the moon December 1972, A.D.
May the spirit of peace in which we came
Be reflected in the lives of all mankind.

It was signed by President Nixon and the three men of Apollo 17, Captain Cernan, Comdr. Ronald E. Evans of the Navy and Dr. Schmitt.

Apollo 17, the sixth manned landing on the moon, is the last scheduled mission of the $25-billion project. No American astronauts are expected to return to the moon in this decade, probably not for many years beyond that.

The two members of the crew who explored the moon, Captain Cernan and Dr. Schmitt, held the 10-minute ceremony shortly before midnight as they were preparing to re-enter the landing craft following their final excursion out on the surface.

Hatch Is Closed

They closed the hatch for the last time at 12:38 A.M., Eastern standard time, today.

The Challenger is scheduled to rocket off the cratered surface at 5:56 P.M. today to rejoin the command ship, America, in lunar orbit. Commander Evans is piloting the command ship.

After circling the moon for nearly two days, the three astronauts are to blast out of lunar orbit at 6:32 P.M. Saturday to begin the three-day return trip to a splashdown in the Pacific Ocean on Tuesday afternoon.

In dedicating a rock from the Taurus-Littrow landing site, Captain Cernan stood near the landing craft and stated:

"I think probably one of the most significant things we can think about when we think about Apollo is that it has opened for us—for us, being the world—a challenge for the future. The door is now cracked, but the promise of the future lies in the young people all over the world, learning to live and learning to work together. "In order to remind all the

Continued on Page 52, Column 3

KISSINGER LEAVES FOR U.S. AS ROUND OF TALKS CLOSES

Discussions in Paris Fail to Solve Issue of Political Control of Vietnam

AIDES ARE STAYING ON

President Will Confer With Chief Negotiator Today on Apparent Impasse

By FLORA LEWIS

Special to The New York Times

PARIS, Dec. 13—Henry A. Kissinger flew home tonight, ending an arduous round of Vietnam cease-fire talks without having solved the central problem—political control of South Vietnam.

In a brief departure statement before leaving by special plane at 9 P.M., Mr. Kissinger said: "I am returning to Washington and will exchange messages with special adviser Le Duc Tho as to whether a further meeting is necessary."

"In the meantime, Ambassador Sullivan and two members of my staff are staying here and will be meeting under the direction of Ambassador Porter with experts of the other side."

Thanks to France

Mr. Kissinger thanked the French Government for "the privileges and cooperation they have extended to me."

The technical experts staying on—including William H. Sullivan, Deputy Assistant Secretary of State for East Asian Affairs, and William J. Porter, the American representative at the formal Vietnam peace conference here—will continue bargaining sessions over details of a draft cease-fire text and related protocols about such things as an international control commission for Vietnam.

[In Washington, the White House said President Nixon would see Mr. Kissinger "first thing" Thursday morning. Officials foresaw critical decisions facing the President in view of the apparent impasse. Page 14.]

In Paris, authoritative sources said there had been some progress on details, clarifying language and assuring a simultaneous cease-fire in Laos, though not in Cambodia. But the central issue — political power in South Vietnam — remained unsettled. All efforts to bridge the disagreement with ambiguous language have reportedly failed.

Saigon Visit Planned

On the central issue of the war, the negotiations thus were deadlocked. The agreement between Mr. Kissinger and Mr. Tho to maintain their communications and the possibility of further meetings indicated that the talks had not broken down. But they had not made progress on any but peripheral issues either.

Last October, in a phrase that most of the world took literally, Mr. Kissinger said that "peace is at hand" and that an agreement could be completed in one more negotiating round lasting "not more than three or four days." That round began on Nov. 20 and continued, except for a nine-

Continued on Page 14, Column 5

U.S. Wins Move in U.N. To Reduce Contribution

General Assembly, 81 to 27, Approves Cut to 25% of Organization's Budget —Soviet Opposition Is Bitter

By ROBERT ALDEN

Special to The New York Times

UNITED NATIONS, N. Y., Dec. 13—The United States tonight won its uphill fight to reduce its contribution to the United Nations budget.

The General Assembly adopted its Finance Committee's recommendation that the United States' contribution be reduced from 31.5 per cent to 25 per cent of the world organization's budget "as soon as practicable."

The vote was 81 to 27 with 22 abstentions. A two-thirds vote, or a minimum of 72, was required for adoption.

The margin of victory was unexpectedly large in view of what had been a determined and bitter effort by the Soviet bloc, led by the Soviet Union itself, to bar the proposed reduction.

Assessments to the budget have, since the United Nations' founding, been based on a member's ability to pay—although, even in the earliest years the majority view was that the United Nations should not be overly dependent on any single member nation.

Thus a ceiling was established on what a member nation should pay and that ceiling has been reduced over the years until it now stands "in principle" at 30 per cent of the regular United Nations budget.

This year the United States mounted a determined effort to reduce its contribution to 25 per cent.

The timing of the effort was linked to the expected admission of the two Germanys at

Continued on Page 17, Column 1

'72 Growth Rate Lowest In 10 Years, Kosygin Says

By THEODORE SHABAD

Special to The New York Times

MOSCOW, Dec. 13—Premier Aleksei N. Kosygin, in his second major pronouncement on the economy this fall, has disclosed that the Soviet Union's rate of growth in 1972 was the lowest in the last 10 years.

The disclosure, in the form of a national-income statistic, reflects for the first time the over-all impact of this year's serious grain-crop failure on the Soviet economy. The bad crop forced Soviet leaders to buy large quantities of grain abroad to insure adequate food supplies and save the nation's livestock herds.

Figures given by the Premier in a published review of the economy show that national income increased by only 4 per cent in 1972, compared with the 6 per cent planned. It was the lowest annual growth rate since the catastrophic crop year of 1963.

1973 Plan Revised Upward

Mr. Kosygin said that the economic plan for next year, to be announced Monday, had been revised upward to make up for the decline in the growth rate in 1972.

"The planned rates of growth of national income have been raised compared with the preceding two years," Mr. Kosygin said in the economic report, published in the current issue of Kommunist, an authoritative Communist party journal.

National income, a key index of economic performance in

Continued on Page 12, Column 3

POMPIDOU FAVORS U.S.-EUROPE TALKS

Asks Discussions at 'Highest Level' on Economic and Political Relationship

By JAMES RESTON

Special to The New York Times

PARIS, Dec. 13—President Pompidou is now in favor of consultations "at the highest level" to clarify United States-European monetary, trade and political relations in the coming year.

In an interview at the Elysée Palace, the French President said that world politics would be entering a new and difficult phase in 1973, but that the main thing was to get a better political understanding—he emphasized "political"—of the objectives of the United States, the expanded Common Market and Japan.

Sees a New Situation

Questions of money and trade, he said, tend to divide nations, but, important and urgent as these questions are, they are secondary to the larger political and philosophical questions that require more discussion in the future than in the last few years.

His main point seemed to be that as 1973 approaches, all the major nations find themselves in a new situation, as they did at the end of World War II.

With the reorganization of Europe, the reconciliation of old feuds between Western Europe and the Soviet Union, the entrance of Britain into the Common Market, the spec-

Continued on Page 3, Column 1

STATE REGISTERS WELFARE DECLINE, ITS FIRST IN YEARS

Rural Areas Show Big Drop in Rolls, Cutting Average 2,151 Persons a Month

By PETER KIHSS

A sharp drop in welfare rolls upstate, notably in rural areas, has led to a statewide decline in relief rolls averaging 2,151 persons a month in the July-August-September quarter compared with the previous quarter. This was the first such decline in many years.

The upstate decline, attributed to administrative tightening of eligibility and improved economic conditions, averaged 7,491 persons a month. In this period, New York City, where Mayor Lindsay set a zero-growth target for welfare rolls for the budget year started last July 1, showed a monthly rise averaging 5,340 persons.

Upstate Urban Areas Down

Rural counties showed the strongest declines, with the welfare rolls in these areas down 4,900 persons from an April-May-June monthly average of 140,600. Eight upstate urban counties, involving such areas as Buffalo, Rochester and Syracuse, went down 2,200, from 217,900 to 215,700.

The other declines were in the metropolitan area's suburbs—Nassau, Suffolk, Westchester and Rockland—down 400 from 180,300. The New York City rise in the state reports was from 1,267,628 to 1,272,968.

Both the city and upstate areas are expected to show declines in still-to-be-completed October figures, which will reflect people being dropped as ineligible because of the 20 per cent increases in Social Security benefits.

Available data for every year from 1966 to 1971 had shown a statewide increase in relief recipients from the April-June to July-September quarters. This year's reports, still in preliminary form, were described as showing mainly decreases in the home-relief category, which includes the working poor who get supplements to low wages.

Jobs Being Pushed

At the same time, Board of Education officials here said yesterday that adults in the aid-to-dependent-children family category were being "pushed" into any kind of jobs, and reported sharp slashes in adult education programs for such recipients had taken place Dec. 1.

The State Labor Department said the so-called Talmadge Amendment to the Work Incentive program (WIN) put into effect by Congress July 1 had compelled "more emphasis on

Continued on Page 53, Column 2

CITY TO BROADEN TAX ON EMPLOYES

Future Municipal Workers Living in Suburbs Would Pay Full Resident Rate

By FRANCIS X. CLINES

A bill requiring all future New York City employes who reside in the suburbs to pay the full city resident income tax was passed unanimously yesterday by the City Council.

The measure, which the Mayor's office said would be signed into law, would require future job applicants from outside the city to agree to pay the full resident tax—which is four to eight times the nonresident levy—as a condition of employment.

"It's a matter of protecting the suburban workers from themselves," said Councilman Mario Merola, a Bronx Democrat who sponsored the measure. "If the city goes down, they go down."

Lindsay Calls It 'Fair'

Mayor Lindsay hailed the bill as a "fair taxation" measure. "It should encourage civil servants to live in and know first-hand the communities that they are sworn to serve," he said in a statement.

Municipal union leaders have found difficulty with this reasoning and have opposed the bill as discriminatory because suburbanites working for the city would pay full taxes for services they use only partially.

As of next January, job applicants would have to agree to the full tax, which would go into effect in 1974.

No present employe would be affected by the bill.

A court challenge to the bill is considered likely, since the

Continued on Page 41, Column 3

United to Cut Fares June 1 Under New Charter Rules

By ROBERT LINDSEY

In the first domestic application of a radical new charter-fare concept, United Air Lines announced yesterday plans to slash fares up to 65 per cent on several major routes, effective June 1. However, travelers must buy their tickets 90 days in advance to qualify for the bargains.

Under the plan, a New York-to-Los Angeles round trip ticket would cost $129 as against the present $336. And the price of a New York-to-Honolulu round-trip would be $229, as against the present $468.

Meanwhile, five months of turbulent negotiations by 40 airlines over new trans-Atlantic fares collapsed yesterday in Geneva. Spokesmen for the negotiators said that the deadlock meant that each airline would be able to set its own fare on flights between North America and Europe after Feb. 1, and the outlook was that at least some lines were prepared for a price war.

The two developments yesterday were closely related, although they occurred more than 3,000 miles apart. United's plan will initiate a new category of airline ticket, promulgated Sept. 27 by the Civil Aeronautics Board, that for the first time will allow any traveler to fly on low-cost nonscheduled charter flights.

Heretofore, only members for six months of clubs, unions, student groups and other so-called "affinity" organizations could get together to take advantage of the wholesale-buying advantages inherent in charter flights. Under the new C.A.B. rule, it will not be necessary to belong to an organization.

In Geneva, officials of the International Air Transport Association, the organization of 107 airlines that sets fares for scheduled flights on most international routes, said that it was largely because of the aeronautics board's action that the airlines had been unable to reach agreement on new fares.

Under the rules of the air transport association, airlines will be able to set their own rates on trans-Atlantic routes beginning Feb. 1 unless they can break their impasse. In the past, the airlines frequently came close to a breakdown in agreements to charge identical rates but in virtually all cases reached agreement in the end.

However, an official at the

Continued on Page 94, Column 5

Drug Agency Acts to Restrict Use of Diet Pills and Vitamins

By RICHARD D. LYONS

Special to The New York Times

WASHINGTON, Dec. 13—The Food and Drug Administration announced moves today to restrict unnecessary and potentially harmful use of diet pills and vitamins.

The probable result of today's actions, if they take effect next year, will be a further drop in the number of amphetamine prescriptions written by doctors for weight reduction and a cut in the amounts of vitamins A and D in self-treatment remedies. The market for these two types of pills is $500-million a year.

The action against diet pills was made public in testimony before a Senate subcommittee by Dr. Henry E. Simmons, director of the F.D.A.'s Bureau of Drugs.

A series of diet pill studies made for the Federal agency between 1969 and 1971 and involving 10,000 Americans found, Dr. Simmons said, that the drugs were almost worthless.

"There is nothing of outstanding value except diet" in controlling weight, he said.

Dr. Simmons said that a series of actions already taken by the Federal agency to tighten the prescribing of amphetamines for reducing diets had resulted in a drop from 2 million prescriptions a month at the start of 1970 to 673,000 a month now.

But weight-reducing drugs, most of which contain amphetamines, are still being prescribed

Continued on Page 18, Column 1

2 Soviet Aides Visit a Dissident In Hotel Here and Lift Passport

By MICHAEL T. KAUFMAN

Valery N. Chalidze, a leader of Soviet dissidents who has been lecturing in this country on the Soviet human rights movement, was visited in his East Side hotel yesterday by two Soviet officials who confiscated his passport and told him that he had been deprived of his citizenship.

Dr. Chalidze, a 34-year-old physicist, is one of a small group of intellectuals who have spoken out openly against political repression in the Soviet Union. Since Thanksgiving Day, he has been in the United States lecturing on the dissident movement at law schools here and in Washington.

Yesterday about 11 A.M., Dr. Chalidze said, he was awakened by a phone call saying that two Soviet officials were waiting for him in the lobby of his hotel, the Volney, at 23 East 74th Street.

The slight, dark-haired scientist, said that when he went downstairs, one of the Russians, Yuri Galishnikov, a consular secretary from Washington, asked him for his passport "to check my identity." Dr. Chalidze said that he gave the document to the man, who then passed it to his associate, who did not identify himself.

"It ended up in the other man's pocket," said Dr. Chalidze.

Dr. Chalidze continued that

The New York Times

Dr. Valery N. Chalidze at his hotel here yesterday.

the officials then told him he had been stripped of his citizenship by a decree passed Tuesday by the Presidium of the Supreme Soviet, the nation's nominal legislature.

The grounds for the decree, Mr. Galishnikov reportedly told Dr. Chalidze, were "acts discrediting a Soviet citizen."

In his statement Dr. Chalidze, a Georgian, denied any such acts. "In the United States I have been occupied with conversations with jurists and with lectures on human rights in the U.S.S.R. and, in particular,

Continued on Page 11, Column 1

Truman's Condition Is Termed Weaker

Special to The New York Times

KANSAS CITY, Mo., Dec. 13—Former President Harry S. Truman, hospitalized for lung congestion and an irregular heartbeat, was reported tonight to be weaker and less responsive than he was yesterday.

Officials at Research Hospital and Medical Center, where the 88-year-old Mr. Truman was admitted eight days ago, continued to list his condition as "serious" rather than "critical," but added:

"He is semiconscious but is not as responsive as last night. He remains relatively unchanged except he is weaker."

The hospital's definition of "serious" is as follows: "Acutely ill with recovery uncertain. Vital signs may be unstable

Continued on Page 25, Column 1

Keogh, Former Aide to Nixon, Is Chosen as Head of U.S.I.A.

By LINDA CHARLTON

Special to The New York Times

WASHINGTON, Dec. 13 — President Nixon announced today the nomination of James Keogh, a former White House speech-writer who has criticized news coverage of Mr. Nixon, to head the United States Information Agency.

The President's intention of nominating Mr. Keogh to succeed Frank J. Shakespeare Jr., who is returning to private life, was one of three high-level appointments announced by the White House press secretary, Ronald L. Ziegler.

Mr. Ziegler said that the President would nominate Joseph T. Sneed, dean of the Duke University Law School in Durham, N. C., as Deputy Attorney General.

Mr. Nixon also designated to head the National Park Service Ronald H. Walker, who was once an assistant to former Secretary of the Interior Walter J. Hickel and since June, 1969, has been in charge of organizing the President's travels. Mr. Nixon met with Mr. Walker this afternoon.

The nominations of Mr. Keogh and Mr. Sneed require Senate approval, but the appointment of Mr. Walker does not.

Mr. Ziegler also noted that Mr. Nixon met this afternoon with Treasury Secretary George P. Shultz, his chief economic spokesman.

Associated Press

James Keogh

At the Justice Department, Mr. Sneed will replace Ralph E. Erickson, whose departure for a "high judicial post" was previously announced. Mr. Ziegler said that Mr. Sneed was "widely respected in the legal profession" and that the President was confident he would play an important role in the law enforcement drive that the President feels has "highest importance among the responsibilities that he owes the American people."

Mr. Sneed, who is 52 years old, taught in the law schools of Cornell and Stanford Universities and the University of

Continued on Page 21, Column 1

NEWS INDEX

"All the News That's Fit to Print."

The New York Times.

LATE CITY EDITION
POSTSCRIPT
WEATHER—Possibly showers today; tomorrow fair and warmer.
Temperatures Yesterday—Max., 55; Min., 44.

VOL. CXXIII . . No. 42,410 — © 1974 The New York Times Company — NEW YORK, WEDNESDAY, MARCH 6, 1974 — 30c beyond 50-mile radius of New York City, except Long Island. Higher in air delivery cities. — 15 CENTS

BRITISH PROPOSING 35% FOR MINERS, TWICE HEATH'S BID

Wilson, Anxious to Resolve Coal Strike, Is Expected to Accept Board's Plan

NEW CABINET IS NAMED

Michael Foot, the Leader of Party's Left Wing, Is Employment Secretary

By ALVIN SHUSTER
Special to The New York Times

LONDON, March 5 — The board studying the pay of Britain's striking coal miners has proposed raises of about 35 per cent, more than double what Edward Heath had offered before resigning as Prime Minister.

The disclosure, by informed sources who have seen the report, came as Mr. Heath's successor, Harold Wilson, leader of the Labor party, named his new Cabinet, balanced between left-wing and moderate leaders, and moved to end the crippling three-week-old strike.

It was the miners' rejection of a 16.5 per cent offer that led to their strike—against the Government, which owns Britain's mines — and brought Mr. Heath's order for an election to strengthen his hand.

Acceptance Is Expected

But his party lost, and today it appeared that the higher raise would be accepted by Prime Minister Wilson. He is clearly anxious to settle quickly to provide the image of achievement for his one-day-old Labor party Government, even though militant leaders of other unions will find their appetites whetted. Negotiations must follow between the National Union of Mine Workers and the National Coal Board, which runs the industry.

"I hope we can be in a position by tomorrow night to finalize a wage agreement," said Joseph Gormley, the union's president.

The Major Surprise

The recommendations of the board, set up by the Conservative party Government of Mr. Heath, were discussed today by union officials and Michael Foot, a favorite of the trade unions, who was named as Secretary for Employment.

The selection of Mr. Foot, 60-year-old leader of the left wing in the party, was the major surprise in the Cabinet choices. He is to deal not only with the mine strike but also with attempts to keep wage demands of other restive unions

Continued on Page 7, Column 1

Selassie Pledges to Seek Democratic Government

Plan for a Constitutional Convention Follows Ethiopian Unrest

By CHARLES MOHR
Special to The New York Times

ADDIS ABABA, Ethiopia, March 5—Emperor Haile Selassie, confronted by continued unrest and increasing demands for sweeping change, announced tonight that he had agreed to a constitutional convention to create a new system of elected democratic government.

The step was generally regarded as one that would lead to the end of absolute monarchy in the eastern African country, where an army mutiny last week forced the dismissal of the Emperor's Cabinet.

It was not certain, however, that the move toward a constitutional convention would guarantee peace. Many elements in the country are demanding quick and radical change now that the military mutiny has relaxed the hard grip of authority.

Labor leaders said a general strike called for Thursday would probably begin on schedule. The workers are demanding more rights and benefits.

In a radio and television address tonight, the 81-year-old Emperor, who uses the royal first person plural in his speeches, said, "We are instituting constitutional reform for the lasting benefit of the country."

Camera Press
Emperor Haile Selassie

He said the constitutional reforms would be meant to bring such changes as making the Premier "responsible to Parliament." He said the reforms would also be aimed at "defining and clarifying the institutional relationships between different branches of the imperial Ethiopian Government" and "guaranteeing further the civil rights of our people."

The Emperor announced that

Continued on Page 11, Column 1

Hope Is Seen for Easing Of Oil Curb at Arab Talks

By JUAN de ONIS
Special to The New York Times

KUWAIT, March 5—The meeting of Arab oil ministers to be held in Libya Sunday holds out strong prospects for a relaxation of Arab oil restrictions, including the embargo against the United States, according to Arab diplomatic sources.

But there were indications of continuing doubts in some Arab governments about a complete abandonment of the "oil weapon" until more progress is made on Israeli withdrawal from occupied Arab territories.

The key to what is decided in Libya on the embargo and Arab oil-production cutbacks is expected to be the position taken by Syria, which is in the first stage of negotiating a troop-separation agreement with Israel on the Golan Heights.

[In Washington, Secretary of State Kissinger conferred with President Nixon while authoritative sources forecast an end to the oil embargo and a drop in oil prices.]

There are still doubts over what the Syrian position will be when the oil ministers meet in Tripoli. If the Syrians are not in favor of an immediate end to the embargo or production cutbacks, the result could be a decision for a partial lifting of

Continued on Page 20, Column 2

U.S. SAYS ALLIES FAIL TO CONSULT

Complains That Trade Bloc Gave No Advance Notice on Offer of Aid to Arabs

By DAVID BINDER
Special to The New York Times

WASHINGTON, March 5 — The State Department complained today that the nine-nation European Economic Community had failed to consult the United States in advance of its offer of long-term economic and technical cooperation to the Arab countries yesterday.

The department spokesman, George S. Vest, said at an afternoon press briefing: "The United States was not consulted on that particular activity. It was informed about it after it became public."

The community announced its proposal to 20 Arab countries in Brussels at about the same time that Mr. Kissinger arrived in the Belgian capital yesterday to brief representatives of the North Atlantic Treaty Organization on his latest diplomatic efforts in the Middle East.

According to West German

Continued on Page 4, Column 1

Stock Prices Soar

The stock market climbed 19.24 points yesterday, registering its biggest advance in two months in heavy trading spurred by hopes of an early end to the Arab oil embargo. Page 47.

HOUSE MANEUVER ON TRANSIT BILL PERILS 35C FARE

Brinegar Opposition Stalls Measure—Ronan Predicts Subway Charge of 60c

By MARTIN TOLCHIN
Special to The New York Times

WASHINGTON, March 5—Transportation Secretary Claude S. Brinegar said today that he was "flatly opposed" to a House-Senate conference bill on urban mass transit and had urged President Nixon to veto the legislation, which appeared all but doomed today in a parliamentary quagmire in the House.

If the legislation is killed, the 35-cent fare in New York City will go to 60 cents, "no question about it," Dr. William J. Ronan, chairman of the Metropolitan Transportation Authority, said on being informed of the day's events.

Mayor Beame of New York was equally gloomy. "At this critical time—when we must turn to mass transportation as the savior in our energy crisis—failure on the part of the Congress or the National Administration to come to our aid will have disastrous results," he said. Under an arrangement with the state, the 35-cent fare will stay in effect until May 1.

The setback for the legislation stunned the bill's sponsors as well as New York politicians and transportation officials. President Nixon, who had initially opposed the legislation, finally accepted the concept of mass-transit operating subsidies in meetings with Mayor Beame, Governor Wilson and former Gov. Nelson A. Rockefeller.

White House View Given

Governor Wilson questioned whether today's actions truly reflected Mr. Nixon's views. Some legislators felt that Mr. Brinegar's statement reflected the position of the powerful Office of Management and Budget and not the White House. However, a high White House aide said the action did reflect the President's thinking.

Representative Dave Martin of Nebraska, the ranking Republican on the Rules Committee, supported this contention on the bill when he told the members of the committee that "I've had word from the White House that if it comes to the President's desk, he's going to veto it."

A more common view among metropolitan-area legislators was that President Nixon had never viewed the cities as part of his constituency. "He sees the cities as the anti-Nixon coalition," said Representative Edward I. Koch, Manhattan Democrat. "There's no question that the major voices raised on impeachment come from urban areas, and it may be that he's trying to punish them. He may just be so angry that he's flailing the cities."

Mr. Brinegar said that the legislation, which would provide New York City with $150-million, "is heavily weighted to a handful of big cities with

Continued on Page 44, Column 1

Associated Press
Thomas A. Luken, Democrat, being congratulated at campaign headquarters in Cincinnati after winning seat from Ohio's First Congressional District. At right is wife, Shirley.

G.O.P. Loses House Seat In Ohio, Leads on Coast

By R. W. APPLE Jr.
Special to The New York Times

CINCINNATI, March 5—Thomas A. Luken, a 48-year-old Democrat, eked out a narrow victory tonight in a special election in Ohio's First Congressional District—an election in which Watergate played a role.

It was the third straight formerly Republican district captured by the Democrats this year, and Mr. Luken's defeat of Willis D. Gradison Jr., the Republican nominee, appeared likely to create severe apprehension among Republican incumbents who must campaign for re-election this November.

[In California, State Senator Robert J. Lagomarsino, a Republican, led seven Democrats in the race for the 13th Congressional District seat. With nearly two-thirds of the vote counted, Mr. Lagomarsino had 30,846 votes to 27,234 for all the Democrats. If he maintained a clear majority, Mr. Lagomarsino would be elected without a runoff.]

The outcome here could also increase the pressure on President Nixon to resign from members of his own party.

With all 478 precincts reporting, the unofficial tally was as follows:

Luken	55,171
Gradison	51,057

A Democratic official had described the district, which had gone Democratic only three times in this century, as "damned tough turf for us." The previous incumbent, Representative William J. Keating, who resigned to become president of The Cincinnati Enquirer, won in the Nixon landslide of 1972 with 70.3 per cent of the vote.

It was not immediately clear how large a part Watergate

Continued on Page 16, Column 4

Mitchell Is Linked To Vesco by Sears

By MARTIN ARNOLD

The Government started yesterday to get to the core of its case against John N. Mitchell and Maurice H. Stans, with the first testimony linking former Attorney General Mitchell to Robert L. Vesco, the financier who is now a fugitive.

This was done through Harry L. Sears, the former Republican majority leader of the New Jersey Senate, who told of introducing Mr. Vesco to Mr. Mitchell and of inducing Mr. Mitchell to intervene in a Federal investigation of Mr. Vesco's financial dealings.

He also told how Mr. Mitchell helped get Mr. Vesco out of a Swiss jail where he was being held while the Swiss

Continued on Page 22, Column 5

A DOUBLE DEFENSE OF NIXON DRAFTED

Lawyers Planning Rebuttal to Implications by Grand Jury on Hush Money

By JOHN HERBERS
Special to The New York Times

WASHINGTON, March 5 — White House lawyers are preparing a two-pronged defense against the implication in last Friday's grand jury indictments that President Nixon may not have opposed hush money payments to the Watergate defendants.

The grand jury did not say directly that Mr. Nixon had approved such payments. But one of its charges against H. R. Haldeman, the former White House chief of staff, was that he lied when he testified under oath that the President said in a meeting last March 21 that "it would be wrong" to raise $1-million to insure the silence of the seven original Watergate burglars.

First, according to sources close to the White House, the lawyers are ready to argue that the President did use a phrase in the course of a conversation to the effect that "It would be wrong." However, they said that although he used it in the context of a proposal to award executive clemency to the defendants he was also conveying his belief that

Continued on Page 22, Column 5

RODINO PANEL BIDS LAWYERS OBTAIN GRAND JURY DATA

Impeachment Inquiry Also Seeking to Learn if White House Will Give Evidence

IMPLICIT THREAT IS SEEN

House Group May Use Its Subpoena Powers Against Courts and President

By JAMES M. NAUGHTON
Special to The New York Times

WASHINGTON, March 5—The House Judiciary Committee directed its lawyers today to obtain a sealed grand jury report on President Nixon's possible role in the Watergate cover-up and to determine by Thursday if the White House would supply evidence for use in an impeachment inquiry.

Implicit in both decisions by the committee was a threat to use if necessary the panel's broad subpoena powers against both the White House and the courts to obtain evidence for the investigation of the President's conduct in office.

The committee chairman, Representative Peter W. Rodino Jr., Democrat of New Jersey, scheduled meetings Thursday and Friday to "take further action" if the committee's quest for information was not successful.

Meanwhile, it was learned that the special Watergate prosecutor, according to a letter he sent to the chief judge of United States District Court here, would seek at least a dozen more major indictments. [Details on Page 22.]

Two Developments Cited

The committee's actions, at a closed two-hour briefing this morning, were intended to bring to a climax tomorrow two developments that could determine the duration of the impeachment inquiry.

The committee authorized its two senior impeachment lawyers, John M. Doar and Albert E. Jenner Jr., to take part in a hearing tomorrow before Chief Judge John J. Sirica of the United States District Court on what is to be done with the grand jury's sealed report and a briefcase said to contain evidence supporting the jurors' conclusions about Mr. Nixon's role in an alleged conspiracy to obstruct the Watergate investigation.

The House panel specifically instructed the lawyers to tell Judge Sirica that the committee was entitled under the Constitution to any material bear-

Continued on Page 23, Column 1

DAYAN WILL JOIN CABINET IN ISRAEL

Mrs. Meir to Finish Setting Up New Coalition Today

Special to The New York Times

TEL AVIV, March 5—Premier Golda Meir announced today that she would complete the formation of a new coalition tomorrow and that it would include Moshe Dayan as Defense Minister.

A statement from her office, issued after a special Cabinet meeting in Jerusalem, said that the Minister of Communications, Shimon Peres, had also agreed to serve in the new coalition.

This reversal of both their decisions to withdraw from the Government was made known in a statement from her office after an extraordinary Cabinet meeting attended by the chief of staff, Lieut. Gen. David Elazar, and the director of military intelligence, Maj. Gen. Eliahu Zeira. It was also announced

Continued on Page 3, Column 3

NEWS INDEX

Sol Hurok, the Impresario, Dies at 85

Jack Mitchell
Sol Hurok in his office before a portrait of Pavlova

By ALDEN WHITMAN

Sol Hurok, one of the world's foremost impresarios, died yesterday afternoon of a massive heart attack at the age of 85.

He had had lunch with Andrés Segovia, the guitarist and close friend who was among the many distinguished artists whose appearances here he had sponsored, and then was on his way to a meeting with David Rockefeller, president of the Chase Manhattan Bank, at his 17th-floor office at 1 Chase Manhattan Plaza.

But he was driven instead to 1 New York Plaza, several blocks away in the financial section, where Chase Manhattan also maintains offices. Mr. Hurok went to the 17th floor, where he collapsed. He was taken to Beekman Downtown Hospital, where he was pronounced dead.

The marquee headline "S. Hurok Presents" had been customarily followed by the name of a famous musical artist, bal-

Continued on Page 40, Column 1

World's Oldest Song Reported Deciphered

Near-East Origin

By LACEY FOSBURGH
Special to The New York Times

BERKELEY, Calif., March 5—The soft sounds of what is now believed to be the oldest song in the world were played here today at the University of California.

"This has revolutionized the whole concept of the origin of Western music," Richard L. Crocker, professor of music history at Berkeley, said today.

The discovery proves that Western music is about 1,400 years older than previously known and dates back to the ancient Near-Eastern civilization of at least the second millenium B.C.

Scholars have always believed that Western music originated in Greece, but this indicates it came from the Near East.

"We always knew there was music in the earlier Assyro-Babylonian civilization, but until this, we did not know," Professor Crocker said, "that it had the same heptatonic diatonic scale that is characteristic of contemporary Western music and Greek music of the first millenium B.C."

The song, which sounds to contemporary Western ears like a lullaby, a hymn or a gentle folk song, was last heard, scholars said, about

Continued on Page 18, Column 1

The New York Times/Teresa Zabala
Richard L. Crocker playing reproduction of a lyre

Out of Prehistory

By HAROLD C. SCHONBERG

The startling discovery of the Hurrian cuneiform tablet containing a cult love song pushes back the frontier of notated music well over a thousand years.

An Appraisal

Up to now, the oldest piece of music in notated form has been a fragment of Greek papyrus containing a song in the "Orestes" of Euripides. That dates from the fourth century B.C. The new discovery is put at about 1800 B.C.

Listening to this music (heard in a two-minute excerpt on the telephone) puts a listener back into musical prehistory. The sound of the lyre, constructed by Prof. Robert R. Brown from 4,600-year-old instructions, has the primitive quality associated with crude plucked instruments. The music, proceding in double notes and short rhythmic phrases, usually in semitonal up-and-down shifts, sounds equally primitive as far as its actual texture goes.

But there is one surprise. Professor Brown, Prof. Anne D. Kilmer, who worked on the text, and Prof. Richard L. Crocker of the music department of the University of California in Berkeley, are confident that the piece of

Continued on Page 18, Column 3

Skylab with a missing solar wing as seen by the departing astronauts.

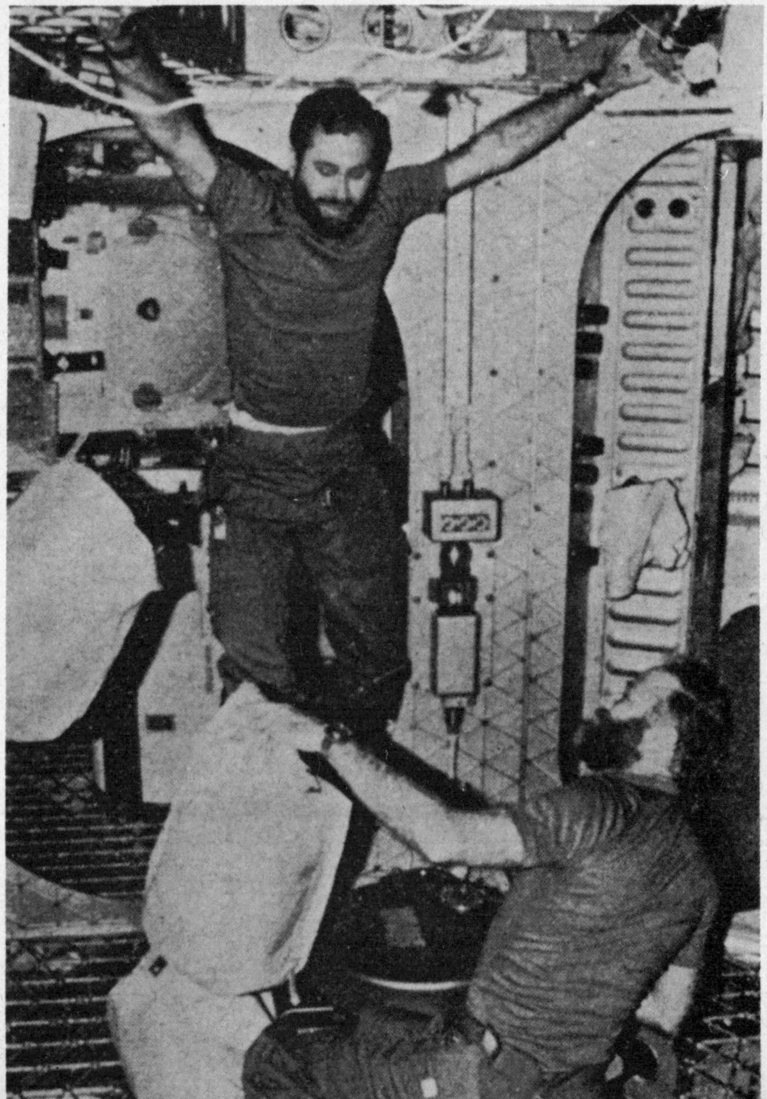

Astronauts Pogue and Carr disposing of garbage aboard *Skylab*.

"All the News That's Fit to Print"

The New York Times

LATE CITY EDITION

Weather: Chance of flurries today; very cold tonight. Cloudy tomorrow. Temp. range: today 19-23; Friday 20-25. Additional details on Page 58.

VOL. CXXIII ... No. 42,385 | NEW YORK, SATURDAY, FEBRUARY 9, 1974 | 15 CENTS

Court Blocks Ervin Panel On Request for 5 Tapes

Gesell Decides Pretrial Publicity Could Prejudice Rights of Defendants—Nixon Argument Is Also Rejected

By DAVID E. ROSENBAUM
Special to The New York Times

WASHINGTON, Feb. 8—Judge Gerhard A. Gesell of the United States District Court dismissed today a suit by the Senate Watergate committee to obtain five White House tapes on the ground that the "blazing atmosphere" of the committee's hearings might prejudice rights of potential defendants, including President Nixon.

It was not clear whether the committee would appeal the ruling. Senator Sam J. Ervin Jr. of North Carolina, the committee's chairman, and Samuel Dash, the chief counsel, declined to make immediate comment. Senator Howard H. Baker Jr. of Tennessee, the ranking Republican on the panel, said that he did not favor an appeal.

Excerpts from Gesell's order are printed on Page 60.

Judge Gesell, a Democrat who has the reputation of being one of the most liberal judges on the Federal bench here, rejected Mr. Nixon's contention that 'the public interest is best served by a blanket, unreviewable claim of confidentiality over all Presidential communications."

For example, Congressional demands for similar evidence during impeachment proceedings "would present wholly different considerations," the judge declared.

But the factor of "critical importance" in this particular set of circumstances, Judge Gesell said, is "the need to safeguard pending criminal prosecutions from the possibly prejudicial effect of pretrial publicity."

"That the President himself may be under suspicion does not alter this fact, for he no

Continued on Page 60, Column 2

BYRNE ANNOUNCES MANDATORY PLAN OF 'GAS' RATIONING

Statewide Effort, 2d in U.S., Uses Car-Plate System—Program Starts Monday

By RONALD SULLIVAN
Special to The New York Times

TRENTON, Feb. 8—Governor Byrne announced a mandatory statewide gasoline-rationing program for New Jersey today, imposing a system based on alternate-day purchasing that will begin Monday.

New Jersey thus joins Hawaii as the only states with statewide mandatory rationing.

Under the plan, which is identical with the voluntary system announced in New York yesterday by Governor Wilson, automobiles in New Jersey with odd-numbered plates will be resricted to purchases on odd-numbered days, and cars with even-numbered plates will be restricted to even-numbered days.

'Tank Topping' Countered

In responding to a gasoline shortage that he called the worst in the country, Governor Byrne said the rationing program would also require service stations to refuse gasoline to motorists whose automobiles had at least a half-tankful of fuel to discourage the "tank topping" that has resulted in long lines throughout the state.

Also, no service station in New Jersey, with the exception of those on the New Jersey Turnpike and on the Garden State Parkway, will be permitted to restrict any motorist to less than five gallons of fuel at a time.

In New York, reaction to that state's voluntary rationing plan, which is to go into effect Monday at 12:01 A.M., was mixed. Upstate station operators endorsed it, but in the New York City area, the response was generally negative.

Commitment From Simon

In Connecticut, the first major rationing plan in the New York region went into its second day in Bridgeport and appeared to be a success. Officials said the plan drastically reduced and in some cases eliminated lines of motorists at the pumps. In Hartford, Gov. Thomas J. Meskill said he would ask the General Assembly for broad powers to deal with the crisis.

Mr. Byrne, who spoke at a news conference at the studios of the New Jersey Public Broadcasting Authority, also said he had received a commitment from William E. Simon, director of the Federal Energy Office, for an additional emergency gasoline allocation for New Jersey this month. But he said he did not know how much the allocation would amount to.

New Jersey is to receive 204 million gallons of gasoline this month, 8C per cent of what it used in February, 1972.

"Neither the implementation of controls nor the emergency

Continued on Page 15, Column 1

United Press International

A snow plow at work on a driveway at the White House yesterday. Conditions in the Washington area were so bad that President Nixon, headed for Bethesda, Md., for a medical checkup, had to turn back.

WORST SNOWFALL OF WINTER TIES UP MOST ROADS HERE

Afflicts Much of East Coast—First Emergency Since '69 Declared by City

3 KILLED IN ACCIDENTS

Medical Check-Up Canceled by Nixon as He Is Caught in Traffic in Capital

By ROBERT D. McFADDEN

The heaviest snowstorm of the winter so far blustered over the metropolitan area yesterday, causing huge traffic jams and hundreds of minor vehicular accidents and prompting the city to declare its first snow emergency in five years.

The storm, which had been expected to pass south of the city, instead struck in the early afternoon and left snow accumulations of nearly six inches by late evening. The overnight total here was expected to be between six and seven inches.

Snow and a glaze of ice forced the closing of the West Side Highway and the eastern half of the Long Island Expressway, and turned nearly all highways in the region into treacherous skidways. Three persons were killed in accidents on suburban roads.

Motorists Stranded

As motorists tried to inch their way home last night, major routes to Long Island became clogged with abandoned cars that made the highways impassible and forced hundreds of drivers onto Queens side streets, where they sought in vain for hotel rooms, gas... and a way to get home.

The police used bullhorns to force motorists off the Clearview Expressway and the Cross Island Parkway because of stalled cars, many of them out of gas, and on Northern Boulevard, one driver reported that it had taken him three hours to travel six blocks.

Though the police used two busses to pick up dozens of motorists stranded on the highways, they seemed at a loss to cope with the constant stream of drivers who appeared at stationhouses seeking a place to spend the night.

"All we can do," one officer said at the 111th precinct in Bayside, "is to make them welcome here."

Nixon Trip Thwarted

The snow was part of a storm extending up from Virginia, with New York City and Long Island on its northern edge. Elsewhere on the Eastern Seaboard, the storm closed schools and slowed travel.

In Washington, President Nixon set out from the White House by car in the morning for his annual physical checkup at the Bethesda Naval Medical Center in suburban Maryland. But driving snow and heavy traffic prompted him to

Continued on Page 12, Column 4

Wobbly Skylab Astronauts End 84-Day Orbital Flight

By VICTOR K. McELHENY
Special to The New York Times

HOUSTON, Feb. 8—Wobbly-legged but cheerful, the Skylab 3 astronauts returned this morning from 84 days in orbit around the earth, man's longest space flight. Except for a link-up between United States and Soviet spacecraft planned for next year, the Skylab mission that ended today was the last scheduled flight by American astronauts until a two-stage shuttle rocket now being developed begins operations in 1979 or later.

President Nixon, in a message radioed to the recovery carrier U.S.S. New Orleans, 176 miles southwest of San Diego, praised the three Skylab missions flown since last May as "one of the most scientifically productive endeavors in the history of human exploration."

Meanwhile, engineers in the Mission Control Center 20 miles southeast of here ran a series of tests of the now-abandoned Skylab workshop in orbit, which is to be made completely "dormant" by midafternoon tomorrow, deprived of power, air-conditioning and life-sustaining atmosphere.

Aboard the carrier, the Skylab 3 crew, Lieut. Col. Gerald P. Carr, of the Marines, Dr. Edward G. Gibson, a civilian scientist, and Lieut. Col. William R. Pogue of the Air Force, experienced a rapidly diminishing dizziness and were soon pronounced by flight surgeons to be at least as fit as the astronauts who flew 59 days aboard the Skylab orbiting workshop from last July 28 to Sept. 25.

Overcoming the partial failure of a gyroscope system for

Continued on Page 23, Column 1

EGYPTIANS DECIDE ON 3 MAJOR STEPS

Some Demobilization Due—Censorship Is Eased—Sadat Cabinet Stays

By HENRY TANNER
Special to The New York Times

CAIRO, Feb. 8—President Anwar el-Sadat has shelved plans to revise his Cabinet and will continue as his own Premier until "every inch" of Israeli-occupied Egyptian territory has been recovered, the authoritative newspaper Al Ahram said today.

At the same time, the newspaper reported, all but military censorship of the Government-owned Egyptian press will be lifted, beginning tomorrow, and preparations for partial demobilization of the Egyptian Army are being started, through a Presidential letter to all soldiers asking them to state their wishes for their futures.

This was the first hint to be given here that a part of the army might be demobilized as a result of the initial disengagement on the Suez Canal front. The strength of the Egyptian forces has never been disclosed here, but reports from abroad

Continued on Page 8, Column 3

RATIONING SYSTEM WORKS IN OREGON

Voluntary Gasoline Buying Based on License Plates Has Eliminated Panic

By EARL CALDWELL
Special to The New York Times

PORTLAND, Ore., Feb. 8—A gasoline rationing plan similar to the one requested in New York and mandated in New Jersey has been in effect here in Oregon for three weeks, and from all indications it has worked extremely well.

"It doesn't alleviate the shortage," Ted Birrer, director of the Western Conference of Petroleum Retailers, said, but he added: "It has accomplished what we hoped it would. It has leveled out the chaotic situation we experienced here in December and January."

In the weeks since rationing went into effect here the impact has been noticeable and in some instances even dramatic.

The program works because, in the view of motorists interviewed on the dwindling gas-station lines, they are no longer as worried that they will not be able to get gasoline and, therefore, they visit the stations less frequently. The knowledge that half the motorists in the state are not supposed to go to a gas station on any given day has eliminated most of the panic buying, they say.

And this slowdown in the daily assault on the gas station has, in effect, left stations with more gas, so that they can stay open longer. This, in turn, has engendered further confidence among motorists.

There seemed to be, too, a wide willingness to cooperate in the plan, simply because there was a plan.

Under the Oregon plan, also

Continued on Page 14, Column 5

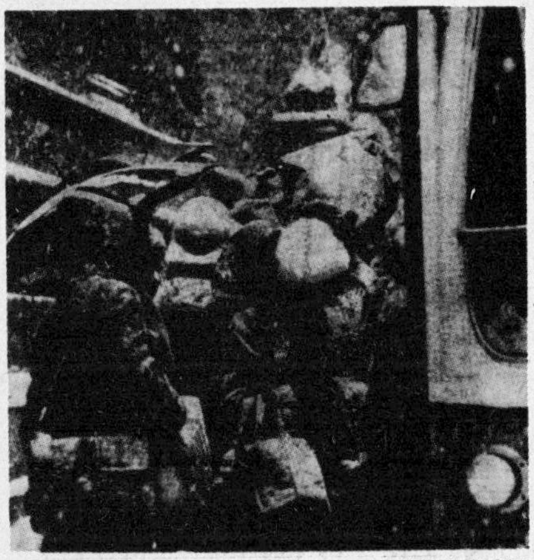

The New York Times/Joyce Dookeen

In the New York area, too, the storm made travel conditions very bad, and people who could get early starts for home did so. Here, passengers board a Madison Avenue bus.

Most Truckers Still Idle; Confusion on Pact Is Wide

By PHILIP SHABECOFF
Special to The New York Times

WASHINGTON, Feb. 8—Most of the striking independent truckers apparently remained off the nation's highways today despite optimistic statements by Administration officials that over-the-road freight traffic would be back to normal soon.

Reports from around the country indicated considerable confusion among the truckers on what to do in following a tentative agreement yesterday between some of their representatives and the Government.

The reports indicated that a trickle of the independent owner-operators had gone back to work. It also appeared that the level of violence that had characterized the work stoppage had tapered off sharply.

But a majority of the truckers apparently kept their rigs at home or parked at truck stops.

Some areas reported that shortages, particularly of foodstuffs, continued to worsen. Unemployment caused by the strike was down slightly.

The strike has had a much sharper impact on meat supplies for the Northeast than for the rest of the country and the situation could get much worse next week, the president of the American Meat Institute said in Chicago.

Richard Lyng, who heads the national trade organization for the meat packing and processing industry, said customers in the Northeast had been espe-

Continued on Page 14, Column 5

SHULTZ OPPOSED TO OIL REPRISALS

Angry Treasury Chief Tells Congress 'Cooperation' Is Aim in Arab Dispute

By United Press International

WASHINGTON, Feb. 8—An angry Treasury Secretary George P. Shultz denounced today suggestions that the United States retaliate against the Arab oil embargo by controlling American exports and cutting foreign aid.

The retaliatory actions, which Representative Barber B. Conable Jr., Republican of New York, said had been suggested by several of his Congressional friends, would be contrary to the United States position of "not confrontation but cooperation," Mr. Shultz testified before the Joint House-Senate Economic Committee.

Senator Jacob Javits, Republican of New York, charged that the Arab oil-producing countries were getting so rich they might try to buy such giants of United States business as Sears, Roebuck and Company and, he noted, they were making bilateral oil-supply deals with consuming countries such as France.

Did the Administration have any contingency plans "if this thing really gets nasty and threatens to bring the world down," Senator Javits asked?

Mr. Shultz replied: "I think it's important that we not only

Continued on Page 39, Column 3

British Miners Reject Appeal; To Strike Now Despite Election

By ALVIN SHUSTER
Special to The New York Times

LONDON, Feb. 8—Leaders of Britain's coal miners decided today to go ahead with their national strike Sunday, rejecting an appeal by Prime Minister Heath to postpone it until after the election later this month.

Refusal to delay the strike means that the election campaign here will take place amid industrial strife and continued emergency measures, including the three-day work week ordered by the Government for most of British industry.

Violence between the police and pickets is considered possible, although the union's leaders today urged the miners to remain peaceful and announced steps to limit picketing.

Meanwhile, Parliament was dissolved at 12:57 P.M. after traditional formalities during which members of the House of Commons were summoned to the House of Lords. There was one last pre-election fight in the Commons, focusing on the expenses of British delegates to the European Parliament.

Mr. Heath, who yesterday called the election for Feb. 28, expressed regret that "we are now prevented from holding an election in an atmosphere of industrial peace." But other members of his Conservative party felt that the strike should help Mr. Heath's bid for re-election by underscoring his appeal to the British to vote against disruptive militants.

Mr. Heath, whose struggle with the miners over their

Continued on Page 6, Column 4

Business Activity Set a Record Pace For State in 1973

By DAVID A. ANDELMAN
Special to The New York Times

ALBANY, Feb. 8—The state's index of business activity—a key indicator of the health of New York's economy—reached a record high in 1973 despite the energy crisis, the state's Department of Commerce reported today.

The index reported record highs for five of its key components, according to the State Commerce Commissioner, Neal L. Moylan. In addition, he said, unemployment was substantially below 1972 figures and personal income climbed to record levels in 1973.

The business index—a measure of the physical output of goods and services in the private sector—averaged 112, compared with 100 in the base year of 1967, and was five points above the previous record of 107, first set in 1969 and re-established in 1973.

The largest gain was in construction, showing an increase of 12 points in its index over

Continued on Page 18, Column 1

NEWS INDEX

United Press International

Dr. Edward G. Gibson of Skylab 3 greets NASA team at opening door of module aboard the New Orleans

"All the News That's Fit to Print"

The New York Times.

Copyright, 1953, by The New York Times Company.

VOL. CXXIII ... No. 42,434 · © 1974 The New York Times Company · NEW YORK, SATURDAY, MARCH 30, 1974 · 35c beyond 50-mile radius of New York City except Long Island. Higher in air delivery cities. · 15 CENTS

5:00 A.M. EXTRA

Fair today, tonight and tomorrow, little change in temperature.
Temperature Range Today—Max., 78; Min., 62
Temperatures Yesterday—Max., 78; Min., 66
Full U. S. Weather Bureau Report, Page 54

WHITE HOUSE YIELDS DATA SUBPOENAED BY JAWORSKI IN POLITICAL-GIFT INQUIRY

U.S. JURY INDICTS 8 IN CAMPUS DEATHS AT KENT STATE U.

One Present and 7 Former Members of Guard Charged in May 4, 1970, Killings

NO CONSPIRACY FOUND

20-Man Panel Does Not Cite Any Officers or Officials of Government for Roles

By AGIS SALPUKAS
Special to The New York Times

CLEVELAND, March 29—A Federal grand jury today indicted one present member and seven former members of the National Guard of Ohio on charges of violating the civil rights of four Kent State University students who were shot to death and nine others who were wounded.

But the grand jury of 20 men and women found no conspiracy among the guardsmen to shoot the students, a theory that had been raised in previous investigations.

It also did not cite any Guard officers or Government officials who have been criticized in several private investigations as having helped create an atmosphere on the campus that contributed to the shootings.

Assistant Attorney General J. Stanley Pottinger, who is in charge of the Civil Rights Division of the Justice Department, said that the grand jury would not be discharged and could be reconvened to hear further evidence.

Resolution of Evidence

When he was asked if the indictments today meant the resolution of the evidence that has been presented so far, Mr. Pottinger said, "Yes."

The grand jury, which was convened last Dec. 18, met for 39 days, heard from 173 witnesses, looked at 250 exhibits and produced a transcript of 6,800 pages.

Those indicted today were charged with willfully assaulting and intimidating demonstrators on the Kent State campus who were protesting against the United States invasion of Cambodia. The indicted men were charged with firing guns in the direction of the protesters and violating their constitutional rights on May 4, 1970.

Penalty upon conviction is one year imprisonment and a $1,000 fine. When death results from the action the penalty may be any number of years up to life in prison.

The men indicted today were five members of G Troop and three members of A Company — two of the three units total-

Continued on Page 64, Column 3

SOLZHENITSYNS ARE REUNITED: Aleksandr I. Solzhenitsyn with his wife and children in Zurich after they joined him there yesterday. Mr. Solzhenitsyn was deported from Soviet Union six weeks ago. Details, Page 8. — Associated Press

Burning of Coal by Con Ed Banned After Tomorrow

By DAVID BIRD

The Consolidated Edison Company will not be allowed to burn coal after tomorrow, the city's Environmental Protection Administration said yesterday.

The administration turned down a request from the utility for an extension of the variance it received last December to burn coal because there was a danger of running out of the cleaner oil during the fuel shortage.

With increasing supplies of oil becoming available in recent weeks, Con Edison based its new request on economy. It said that burning coal would save $100-million a year and mean a cut of 4 to 7 per cent in the average bill for its 2.9 million customers in New York City and Westchester County.

The Environmental Protection Administration said the Con Edison estimates were exaggerated because they did not take into account that oil prices were now dropping and coal prices rising. The administration said a more realistic estimate of savings would be 2 per cent of the average bill, or 40 cents a month.

"This is a very small investment which I believe New Yorkers are more than willing to make to preserve clean air in our city," said Robert A. Low, the Environmental Protection Administrator.

Although both city and state variances would have been needed for the utility to burn coal, a denial by either one blocks the practice. The state, however, is reportedly about to make a response almost identical to the city's.

No Federal action is now required. If the variance had been granted, it might have run into difficulty with the Federal Environmental Protection Agency on the ground that the burning of coal would add an intolerable burden to the city's already over-polluted air at a time when cleaner oil was available.

The Federal agency reluctantly allowed the burning of coal last December when it appeared there would not be enough oil. But it has made it clear that it sees no need

Continued on Page 43, Column 4

Shubert Executives Are Sued by State

By MURRAY SCHUMACH

Two of the three top executives of the Shubert theatrical and real-estate empire and some members of the family were accused yesterday by Attorney General Louis J. Lefkowitz of obtaining millions of dollars from the Shubert estate with claims that were "grossly excessive, unjustified and unreasonable."

Specifically named were Gerald Schoenfeld and Bernard B. Jacobs, two of the three men who dominate the coast-to-coast Shubert operations; Lawrence Shubert Lawrence, who was deposed as president about two years ago, and Mrs. Kerttu Helena Shubert, widow of the

Continued on Page 15, Column 1

SOVIET HOPEFUL ON ARMS ACCORD

Brushing Aside 'Pessimism' in West, It Says Pact Can Be Arranged by June

By HEDRICK SMITH
Special to The New York Times

MOSCOW, March 29 — The Soviet Union today brushed aside "pessimistic" Western press appraisal of Secretary of State Kissinger's mission to Moscow and asserted that a new accord on strategic-arms limitation "can be worked out by the time of" President Nixon's visit here in late June.

This Soviet assessment contrasted sharply with the version given American reporters traveling home with Mr. Kissinger after his talks here this week with Leonid I. Brezhnev, the Soviet Communist party leader.

[In Washington, the Administration sought to counter what the State Department called "an unusual amount of gloom" in the press over the results of Mr. Kissinger's talks in Moscow. It said that it would be useful for Mr. Nixon to make the trip in June even though Mr. Kissinger did not achieve the breakthrough on arms limitation he had sought.]

Another Visit Held Possible

Meanwhile, American officials here said the Soviet Foreign Minister, Andrei A. Gromyko, would probably go to Washington to carry on the dialogue on such key issues as arms control on about April 9, when he attends the United Nations General Assembly.

They also held out some prospect that Mr. Kissinger might come back to Moscow in May for another attempt at a breakthrough on the arms accord, despite the failure to achieve major progress during

Continued on Page 11, Column 3

Gross Is Convicted Of All 5 Charges In Campaign Fraud

By JOSEPH F. SULLIVAN
Special to The New York Times

NEWARK, March 29 — Nelson G. Gross, the former state Republican chairman, was convicted today on five tax fraud and perjury counts that stemmed from his activities as chairman of the 1969 gubernatorial campaign of William T. Cahill.

Mr. Gross sat impassively as the jury of seven men and five women repeated the word "guilty" 60 times as they were polled on each of the five counts by Judge Lawrence A. Whipple in Federal District Court.

The 42-year-old political leader faces jail terms up to 23 years and fines totaling $32,000.

Mr. Gross was convicted of advising William H. Preis, president of the Triple S Blue Stamp Company, to disguise a $5,000 contribution to the Cahill campaign as a tax-deductible business expense and then advising Mr. Preis to lie about the scheme to a grand jury last year.

The defendant was accompanied in court today by his wife, Mrs. Noel Gross; his father, Albert Gross, and a brother. Mrs. Gross is president of the State Federation of Republican Women's Clubs.

The verdict was announced

Continued on Page 35, Column 4

Transit Talks Intensify

Negotiations aimed at heading off a transit strike threatened for Monday intensified, but crucial wage issues have not been resolved. Page 29.

Cook Concedes More Lies Relating to Vesco Inquiry

By MARTIN ARNOLD

George Bradford Cook, one of the Government's chief witnesses, admitted yesterday at the Mitchell-Stans trial that he had lied under oath on three occasions to the grand jury that investigated this case and twice to Congressional committees.

He did it, he said, to protect Maurice H. Stans and also to protect the reputation of the Securities and Exchange Commission, which he headed at the time.

Under cross-examination, Mr. Cook was accused by defense attorneys of having also lied in the White House to Gen. Alexander M. Haig Jr., President Nixon's chief of staff, and to Leonard Garment, the President's special counsel.

For Mr. Cook it was a day in which he underwent withering cross-examination. He heard himself depicted over and over again as a liar, and was forced to admit that this was so. And he listened to not so veiled hints that he was an ambitious young man who had subtly tried to blackmail Mr. Stans into helping him further his career in government.

On Thursday, Mr. Cook's second day on the witness stand, he testified under direct examination by the Government that he lied only twice to the grand jury before changing his mind and deciding to tell the truth. He also told of many meetings and conversations with Mr. Stans about the S.E.C.'s investigation of Robert L. Vesco, a financier, who was also indicted in this case, but who has fled the country.

Mr. Cook's testimony Thursday was the first hard testimony of the trial to really tie Mr. Stans in with the alleged crimes in this case. Mr. Stans, former Secretary of Commerce, and John N. Mitchell, former Attorney General, are accused of perjury, obstruction of justice and conspiracy for allegedly attempting to impede an

Continued on Page 14, Column 2

FIGHT IS AVERTED

But Talks Continue on Impeachment Panel's Plea for Documents

By JOHN HERBERS
Special to The New York Times

WASHINGTON, March 29—The White House agreed today to surrender all the materials subpoenaed March 15 by the special Watergate prosecutor, Leon Jaworski.

President Nixon, in deciding not to fight the subpoena, made an important concession in his efforts to limit, on the ground of executive privilege, the number of documents and tape recordings he turns over to the investigations of alleged wrongdoing in his Administration.

Still pending was the dispute between Mr. Nixon and the House Judiciary Committee, which asked for additional tapes and documents for its impeachment inquiry. However, lawyers for the two sides were negotiating on the committee's request, and there were some indications that a compromise might soon be reached.

New Subpoenas Expected

The materials covered by the Jaworski subpoena pertained to documents concerning political contributions, one of the areas still under grand jury investigation. Mr. Jaworski is expected to issue further subpoenas for materials in the milk price controversy and the International Telephone and Telegraph Corporation antitrust case.

There was also the possibility that he would subpoena additional material to be used in the prosecution of defendants indicted in the cover-up of the Watergate burglary.

Ronald L. Ziegler, the White House press secretary, informally disclosed the breakthrough in the constitutional struggle as if it were a routine decision that had never been in doubt.

Yielding of Materials

He wandered into the White House press room this morning and, in the course of chatting with a small group of reporters, said that James D. St. Clair, the President's chief attorney for Watergate matters, had told him "all of the materials requested" by Mr. Jaworski would be turned over later in the day. Today was the deadline for surrendering the material.

A spokesman for Mr. Jaworski said that the materials were delivered to the prosecutor's office in a brown paper package at 5:15 P.M.

Mr. Jaworski had issued the subpoena only after he was

Continued on Page 13, Column 1

Women Make Strides: On Bases and Into Mory's

Jersey Court Acts

By JOSEPH B. TREASTER
Special to The New York Times

TRENTON, March 29—The State Superior Court ruled today that girls must be permitted to play Little League baseball along with boys in New Jersey.

In a decision that is expected to have a national impact, a panel of three Appellate Division judges voted 2 to 1 that the Little League was a public accommodation that under state law could not discriminate against players on the basis of sex.

Officials of the National Organization for Women who originally challenged the Little League's boys-only rules have said they hope the New Jersey case will serve as a model for ending sex-discrimination by the baseball organization throughout the country.

Earlier this week, a mother in West Haven, Conn., filed a complaint with the Connecticut

Continued on Page 25, Column 1

Yale's Bar Gives In

By MICHAEL KNIGHT
Special to The New York Times

NEW HAVEN, March 29—Mory's, the legendary dark-paneled restaurant here celebrated in song by generations of male Yale University students and faculty members, today gave up its three-year fight to exclude women.

In a carefully negotiated agreement marking the end of one of the best-known and most-dogged fights to preserve a masculine enclave, advocates of women's rights who had succeeded in getting the restaurant-club's liquor license revoked agreed to call off renewed legal action in return for a promise by the restaurant to admit women to "full-fledged membership."

The agreement paves the way for the speedy approval of a new liquor license for the former stronghold of male exclusiveness as early as next week and the admission of

Continued on Page 25, Column 2

Nixon Said to Reject Amending His Taxes

By The Associated Press

WASHINGTON, March 29—President Nixon's tax lawyers have rejected any suggestion that he voluntarily amend his returns and pay additional taxes, and have asked to argue their case before an investigating Congressional committee, sources close to the inquiry said today.

The sources said the Joint Committee on Internal Revenue Taxation would receive within a week a staff report concluding that President Nixon owes substantially more than the $78,651 he paid on income totaling more than $1-million in the years 1969 through 1972.

The suggestion that Mr. Nixon voluntarily file new returns for the years in question was made publicly by Representative Wilbur D. Mills, Democrat of Arkansas, vice chairman of the Joint committee and chairman of the House Ways and Means Committee.

The White House has not responded publicly, but there have been strong indications to

Continued on Page 14, Column 1

Mercury Found to Have Magnetic Field

By WALTER SULLIVAN
Special to The New York Times

PASADENA, Calif., March 29—Mariner 10 zoomed in today for the first close-up look at the planet Mercury and sent back television pictures showing an intensely crater-marked surface gouged, torn and blasted by space debris and 4.6 billion years of proximity to the sun.

The surface, criss-crossed here and there by strange-looking valleys of unknown origin, bears many resemblances to those of the moon and Mars. Yet it differs in ways that should ultimately be indicative of Mercury's separate history.

Probably the biggest surprise has been in indications that Mercury has a magnetic field with a strength about 1 per cent that of the earth's. Even so weak a field was unexpected, since it is stronger than any magnetism observed near Venus, Mars or the moon.

The earth's magnetism is believed caused by a dynamo effect from the churning of molten material within the core of a spinning planet. The spin rate of Mercury is so slow that little or no field was expected.

Another surprise has been the presence of a tenuous but appreciable atmosphere formed of helium, neon and argon, with some hydrogen present.

There is apparently no oxy-

Continued on Page 43, Column 1

Jet Propulsion Laboratory, via Associated Press

Mariner 10 photo of Mercury at distance of 21,700 miles

Britain No Longer Foreign Tax Haven

By TERRY ROBARDS
Special to The New York Times

LONDON, March 29 — Turmoil erupted in the foreign business community here today in response to Britain's demise as an international tax haven following the presentation of the labor Government budget.

The Government has closed a tax loophole that enabled thousands of foreign businessmen and others working here for foreign companies to avoid or substantially reduce their personal income-tax bills. The impact of the move could be substantial because one of the chief attractions of working in

Continued on Page 36, Column 1

NEWS INDEX

Unexpected Snow Snarls Traffic Here

The New York Times/Gene Maggio

Motorists separating their cars after a tangle on snowy Palisades Interstate Parkway

By JUDITH CUMMINGS

Spring suffered an unexpected setback yesterday with the arrival of several inches of snow, to the chagrin of thousands of city and suburban motorists who were caught with their guard down and their snow tires off.

Highway traffic was slowed throughout the metropolitan region and in a few cases brought to a standstill as automobiles floundered on slippery roads. Although no official snow emergency was declared, traffic authorities from just north of Poughkeepsie to southern New Jersey were advising drivers to stay off the roads.

A number of major employers in the city sent their workers home early, as the accumulation had reached nearly three inches by 4 P.M. By 7 P.M., the snowfall began to slacken somewhat, the National Weather Service said, after 3.2 inches had fallen in the city. With temperatures rising slowly in the evening, the forecast was for rain and possible freezing rain into the morning.

Traffic on the Hudson River crossings was described as light to moderate by the Port Authority, with the exception of the Holland Tunnel, which saw heavy traffic and some delays.

Movement on the Triborough Bridge, however, was slowed to a crawl during the afternoon rush—a condition that later became what the police described as a "massive traffic jam." The delays were laid to the difficulty of maneuvering tow trucks through the congestion to remove stranded vehicles from the lanes.

The National Weather Service, which had predicted "cloudy skies but no precipitation" in its forecast for yesterday, said it had been caught short because "the big intense storm systems" that normally bring snow had not developed.

Why the snow came despite

Continued on Page 35, Column 6

"All the News That's Fit to Print"

The New York Times

LATE CITY EDITION

Weather: Chance of rain today and tonight. Seasonable tomorrow. Temp. range: today 68-78; Saturday 67-76. Temp.-Hum. Index yesterday 73. Full U.S. report on Page 63.

SECTION ONE

VOL. CXXII .. No. 42,211 NEW YORK, SUNDAY, AUGUST 19, 1973 — 75¢ beyond 30-mile zone from New York City, except Long Island. Higher in air delivery cities. — 50 CENTS

CITY PATROL CARS 50% UNDERMANNED DURING EVERY DAY

800 Fewer Police Officers Available Here for Foot or Motor Duty in Year

5 BOROUGHS AFFECTED

But Manhattan's Reduction of Personnel Is Termed Greatest by Survey

By PRANAY GUPTE

Nearly half of the available patrol cars in the city are unmanned every day. And, say high police officials, that fact can be viewed two ways:

There's "a temporary excess of cars," or

There's "a manpower shortage."

A study by The New York Times of manning in the city's 71 precincts showed that the number of uniformed officers available for foot and radio motor patrol had decreased by nearly 1,000 over the last year. In July, 1972, there were 15,409 police officers; in July, 1973, the figure was 14,608.

The study showed that while all the boroughs lost manpower, the largest decrease was in Manhattan, from 4,911 police officers last year to 4,682 this year.

Situation Aggravated

The situation is aggravated by the assignment of policemen to courts, hospitals, consulates and, especially during the summer months, to beaches and parks.

High police officials readily acknowledged the decrease in manpower.

Hugo J. Masini, the Police Department's chief of operations, said, "From February, 1970, to October, 1972, we suffered a loss of 3,116 police officers and 320 civilians due to the job freeze.

"This shortage has been felt in every command of the city. Obviously, any manpower shortage is most immediately felt and most visible at the precinct level."

As for the unused patrol cars, Chief Masini said, "At the moment, we have a temporary excess of cars." One car is allocated to each of the city's 808 radio patrol sectors.

P.B.A. Opposed Plan

This "excess" according to Mr. Masini, was caused by the over-all police manpower shortage and the purchase, several years ago of about 200 additional patrol cars when the department intended to implement a one-man, one-car concept. Opposition by the Patrolmen's Benevolent Association thwarted that plan.

However Mr. Masini disclosed last week that he would offer proposals to Police Commissioner Donald F. Cawley "within four or five weeks" for instituting the one-man car concept on a limited basis.

"There are sectors of the city where it appears to me

Continued on Page 50, Column 3

U.S. Shortages Peril World Food Aid Plan

Supplies for 80 Million Needy Overseas Will Have to Be Cut Back or Abandoned

By KATHLEEN TELTSCH
Special to The New York Times

UNITED NATIONS, N. Y., Aug. 18—In Colombia's poorest rural areas, a school-lunch program faces shutdown. Elderly patients in a hospital in Haiti will have to go without an extra daily hot meal. And in India, the promising development of a new food fo. babies is threatened.

These operations and hundreds more will be abandoned or drastically cut back in coming weeks because private United States relief agencies will no longer have the commodities to continue helping 80 million to 100 million needy people in 100 countries around the world.

The agencies have been informed in the last week by Washington officials that the Department of Agriculture will not be able to purchase commodities for the Food for Peace program during August and possibly not in September.

Moreover, the agencies were told the commodity situation was so unsettled that it was uncertain when they could again expect to get supplies of wheat, flour, vegetable oil and other foodstuffs on which they have based their free distribution of relief overseas for almost 20 years.

Calamitous Effect Seen

The effect will be calamitous, according to administrators of the voluntary agencies, as they are called.

"I have not seen a situation like this in my 28 years in overseas assistance," said Fred W. Devine of CARE — the Cooperative for American Relief Everywhere. "It's going to be disastrous."

CARE and Catholic Relief Services operate the two most extensive programs supplying supplementary foods to the

Continued on Page 21, Column 1

Beef Price Freeze Upheld By Federal Appeals Court

By The Associated Press

WASHINGTON, Aug. 18 — A Federal appellate court upheld the beef price freeze today, rejecting contentions of the meat industry that the Cost of Living Council was arbitrary and capricious and had exceeded its authority.

A three-judge special panel of the United States Court of Appeals said that it was clear the Pacific Coast Meat Jobbers Association, Inc., and the National Association of Meat Purveyers, Inc., "had not made the showing necessary to entitle them to a preliminary injunction."

The decision upheld a ruling on Aug. 6 by United States District Court Judge Robert F. Peckham in San Francisco.

"For several reasons," the appeals court said, "it was entirely reasonable for the C.L.C. to decide to keep the ceiling on beef longer than on other meats."

The council continued strict price ceilings on beef until Sept. 12 while lifting them on the rest of the meat industry.

"There was evidence to show that beef prices were rising faster than other meat prices, and that live poultry, sheep and swine were being destroyed, while beef was only being withheld from the market," the court said.

President's Power Cited

It rejected contentions that the Cost of Living Council had acted illegally, "since the President and those to whom he delegates this power are specifically given by the Economic Stabilization Act the power to institute price controls."

"While there was testimony in the record to show that plaintiffs are experiencing losses from the beef price freeze, it is not clear that the harm will be irreparable," the court said.

It added that the freeze would end Sept. 12, and individual merchants "may avail themselves of the C.L.C. exemption procedures where un-

Continued on Page 23, Column 1

Expected Yield From OTB In City Cut by $20-Million

By EMANUEL PERLMUTTER

The city and state will get $20-million less than expected from offtrack betting on horses in the city for the fiscal year that ended June 30, according to an audit released yesterday by State Controller Arthur Levitt.

Mr. Levitt said the indications were that about $41.6-million would be available as net revenues for distribution by the city's Offtrack Betting Corporation.

The OTB had originally estimated that it would be able to turn over more than $62-million for the fiscal year. The city receives 80 per cent and the state 20 per cent of the net revenues under the law that established the OTB as a public corporation.

Television Blamed

The offtrack betting agency revised its estimates last February because "during the first seven and one-half months of the 1972-73 fiscal year, net revenues available for distribution were well below the amounts budgeted," Mr. Levitt said.

"While OTB did not meet its profitability estimates for the initial budget for the 1972-73 year, we were told that this was primarily due to the inability to televise races during the first half of the year," he said.

"With the commencement of television of races (early this year), OTB betting volume improved. OTB expected that the full year results would match the revised budget estimate."

Originally, the OTB has expected that betting for the fiscal year would exceed $700-million. It revised this figure to $568-million in February. It had expected to turn over $23.9-million to the city and

Continued on Page 35, Column 1

WRITER DECLARES SHE WAS G.O.P. SPY IN M'GOVERN CAMP

Says Chotiner, Nixon Friend, Paid Her $1,000 a Week to Travel as Reporter

A freelance writer says she was recruited by one of President Nixon's closest political advisers and received $1,000 a week to travel with the press corps accompanying Senator George McGovern during the 1972 Presidential campaign. She says she made daily reports on the Democratic candidate's personal and political activities.

The writer, Mrs. Lucianne Cummings Goldberg, said in an interview in today's editions of The Washington Star-News that she was recruited and paid directly by Murray M. Chotiner, a long-time associate of President Nixon.

During the eight weeks of "hard, gruesome 24-hour days" she spent with the McGovern campaign, Mrs. Goldberg said in a later interview last night, she reported to Mr. Chotiner or his secretary once or twice a day over a special telephone line in his Washington law office. She said she used the code name "Chapman's friend."

Paid by Check

Mrs. Goldberg said that Mr. Chotiner paid her directly by personal check and that she had no connection with the Committee for the Re-election of the President. She said she did not know what use Mr. Chotiner made of the information she gave him, which she said "was never anything more than The Washington Post had the next day."

"I don't think I was a very good spy," Mrs. Goldberg said. She added that she had once been told that "someone at the White House" had complained: "Why doesn't she just get an earlier edition?"

Asked why Mr. Chotiner continued to pay her $1,000 a week if her information was not useful, she said: "I was doing the job he had asked me to do. There was no reason to yank me off."

Spoke With Chotiner

Mrs. Goldberg said that she had spoken yesterday by telephone to Mr. Chotiner in Newport Beach, Calif., and told him that she had told her story to The Star-News. She said Mr. Chotiner had not seemed concerned and told her to tell "the whole truth."

The operator at the Newporter Hotel, where Mrs. Goldberg said Mr. Chotiner was staying, said last night that there was no one registered there by that name. Other efforts to reach him for comment were also unsuccessful.

Mrs. Goldberg said that "the implication was very strong" that President Nixon knew and approved of her activities, but that Mr. Chotiner had never told her explicitly that the President was involved in her aspect of the campaign. Mr. Chotiner is "a very shrewd man

Continued on Page 44, Column 4

44% in Poll Find Nixon's TV Address Not Convincing and 27% Are Persuaded

By JOHN HERBERS
Special to The New York Times

WASHINGTON, Aug. 18 — About 44 per cent of the people who watched President Nixon's Watergate address on television Wednesday night found the speech "not at all" convincing, while 27 per cent concluded it was "completely" or "quite a lot" convincing, according to a Gallup Poll commissioned by The New York Times.

Other highlights of the poll showed that half of those who watched the address did not believe the President's statement that he had no involvement in the planning or cover-up of the Watergate burglary, that 56 per cent believed he should turn over tape recordings of his meetings with aides to the Senate Watergate committee and the courts, and that 58 per cent disagreed with the President's statement that civil rights and antiwar protests helped create the atmosphere that led to the Watergate crimes.

The survey was conducted by telephone Thursday night from a national sample of 810 adults. On a sample of that size, according to polling experts, the margin of error can be as much as 4 percentage points either way.

Public opinion is considered particularly important in the current phase of the Watergate scandals because President Nixon's address, a defense of his conduct in the matter, was designed to go over the heads of Congress and his critics and appeal directly to the people.

Sampling by Congress

Further, opinion sampling by members of Congress, who are now in recess, may determine how hard Congressional committees push investigations into various aspects of Watergate and other government corruption.

The poll showed that 77 per cent of those questioned saw the Nixon address on television, an unusually high figure that indicated a strong interest in the subject.

Following are the major questions and the responses, based on replies of those who watched the speech:

¶"Did President Nixon's speech increase your confidence in the Nixon administration, or not?" 27 per cent, yes; 66 per cent, no; 7 per cent, no opinion.

¶"Did you believe President Nixon when he said he had no involvement in the planning or cover-up of Watergate, or not?" 38 per cent, yes; 50 per cent, no; 12 per cent, no opinion.

¶"President Nixon said he has not turned over the tapes of his conversations with former aides because people in the future would be reluctant to talk freely with the President. Do you think this a valid reason for not turning over the tapes?" 41 per cent, yes; 51 per cent, no; 8 per cent, no opinion.

¶"Do you think he should turn over the tapes?" 56 per cent, yes; 36 per cent, no; 8 per cent, no opinion.

¶"President Nixon said that the civil rights and antiwar protests helped create the atmosphere that led to the Watergate situation. Do you agree or disagree?" 28 per cent, agree; 58 per cent disagree; 12 per

Continued on Page 41, Column 5

U.S. TO SELL SPAIN 8 BRITISH PLANES

Move Involving Jets Made for Marine Corps Angers Opposition in London

By ALVIN SHUSTER
Special to The New York Times

LONDON, Aug. 18 — The United States has decided to sell eight British-made jet fighters to Spain, touching off a political controversy here.

The Spanish Government, which has been unable to buy arms from Britain for years, will purchase eight British Harrier vertical take-off jets, worth about $30-million, under the existing defense agreement with the United States. The warplanes are made for the United States Marine Corps by the Hawker Siddeley factories in Britain.

The eight warplanes, given the American designation AV-8, would be delivered to Spain between November, 1975, and January, 1976, a Defense Department spokesman said in Washington. Training for pilots and ground crews will be provided by the United States as part of the deal. The spokesman noted that purchasing arms from one nation and then selling them to another "is not done as often as the more direct arrangement."

Harold Wilson, the leader of the Labor party Opposition, promptly denounced what he called a "back-door sale," and noted the long-standing policy here against selling weapons to "Fascist Spain." He accused the Conservative Government of "employing the United States as an arms trafficker."

"Spain is a blatantly fascist

Continued on Page 22, Column 4

Reputed Donor Disclaims Aiding Agnew '66 Drive

By MARTIN WALDRON
Special to The New York Times

BALTIMORE, Aug. 18—The retired controller of a consulting engineering concern under investigation in Maryland denied today that he contributed to Vice President Agnew's 1966 campaign for Governor despite an official contributions report showing that he gave $2,500.

Frank R. Taylor, 76 years old, said, "I wouldn't give those people the sweat off my brow."

An employe of the J. E. Greiner Co. for 23 years, Mr. Taylor retired Dec. 31, 1965, and lives in McLean, Va.

Another retired Greiner company official, Harry M. Brown, now dead, was also listed as having given $2,500. At the time of the reported contribution, he had been retired for 10 years and was living in St. Augustine, Fla., but the official report gave his address as 1106 North Charles Street, Baltimore.

The names of the two men were turned up by The New York Times in a check of contributors shown by Mr. Agnew's official reports to have given him $1,000 or more for campaign purposes.

The 1966 report is the second Agnew campaign document to show up with apparently false information.

31 Donations Listed

A report filed May 19, 1972, with the General Accounting Office in Washington on a "Salute to Ted Agnew Dinner" listed 31 donations totaling $49,900 that sponsors of the dinner later admitted were bogus. The money came from the re-election funds of President Nixon and was attributed to individuals so as to make the testimonial dinner appear to be a success.

Mr. Agnew's 1966 records were subpoenaed Aug. 10 by United States Attorney George Beall, the Federal prosecutor

Continued on Page 43, Column 4

Air Force Chief Resigns As Key Minister in Chile

By MARVINE HOWE
Special to The New York Times

SANTIAGO, Chile, Aug. 18—The truckers' strike that has poisoned the life of this country went into its 24th day today with new violence and the resignation of the military officer who had been brought into the Cabinet last week as Minister of Public Works and Transport.

President Salvador Allende Gossens, in announcing the resignation from the Cabinet of Gen. César Ruiz Danyau, commander of the air force, said that the general, in his letter of resignation, had contended that he had not had the means to solve the transport strike.

Dr. Allende declared that the general had been given "the broadest freedom" to act and had been free to seek his assistants at all levels.

Under Secretary Replaced

In what was obviously a gesture of appeasement to the truckers, the Government announced the removal of the Under Secretary of Transport, Jaime Faivovich, who was considered the main obstacle to a settlement.

After an emergency Cabinet session at noon, the Government announced that General Ruiz had been replaced as Minister of Public Works by Brig. Humberto Magliochetti Barahona, the former operations chief of the air force.

Gen. Gustavo Leigh Guzmán, former head of the Air Force Academy, was named the new commander in chief of the air force.

Another military man, Gen. Hermán Brady, director of the War Academy, was named General Commissioner of Highway Associations, replacing Mr. Faivovich.

Appearing weary and troubled, President Allende swore in the new Public Works Minister and air force commander this afternoon.

He pledged that his Government would seek "a rational, just and democratic solution" to the country's problems and warned, "Those who break the law will be relentlessly punished."

Some fifty wives of air force officers marched on the Presidential Palace tonight protesting against the removal of General Ruiz as commander in chief.

"General Ruiz resigned as

Continued on Page 3, Column 1

U.S. RENTAL DEALS AID NIXON BACKERS IN BALTIMORE AREA

Democrats Who Shifted to Him in 1972 Are Found to Get Millions in Leases

3 MAJOR PARTNERSHIPS

73.6 Per Cent of Rent Paid by G.S.A. Since 1969 Is Going to One Group

By DENNY WALSH
Special to The New York Times

WASHINGTON, Aug. 18—Nearly three-fourths of the rent paid by the Federal Government for space leased in the Baltimore area during the Nixon Administration goes to a small group of businesses associated with prominent Democrats who switched their support to President Nixon in the 1972 campaign.

An examination of records at the General Services Administration, the Government's acquisition and housekeeping agency, shows that, of the $4,744,000 paid out every year in rent under leases awarded by the G.S.A. in the Baltimore area since January, 1969, 73.6 per cent of it goes to this group.

$18-Million Extension

Even if renewal options attached to certain of the leasing contracts are not exercised, the leases awarded to this group during the Nixon Administration will yield from $50-million to $60-million in rental income before they expire.

Since July, 1969, the group, operating through three partnerships, has successfully negotiated three leases with the G.S.A. worth $3,491,000 in yearly rental.

In addition to these new leases, one of which was negotiated while the potential lessors were raising money for the Nixon campaign and donating to it themselves, the agency three months ago extended one of the group's contracts from the era of President Johnson, making it worth $18-million more.

Justice Department Acted

The Justice Department looked into the matter, but nothing came of its investigation.

There has been no indication that the questions involved are connected in any way with investigations, in which Vice President Agnew has been told he is a target, of alleged kickbacks by construction industry figures in Maryland.

Much the same set of partners were able to secure three lucrative leases from the agency during the last two years of the Administration of the late Lyndon B. Johnson whom they supported financially in his successful 1964 campaign for the Presidency. They are all strong supporters of Maryland's Democratic Governor, Marvin Mandel.

Last year, however, while the Governor acted as co-chairman of the Maryland campaign for Senator George McGovern, the Federal lease-holders were key figures in the state's Democrats for Nixon organization.

In most of the Federal deals

Continued on Page 42, Column 4

U.S. Reviewing a Customs Regulation That Could Cost Two Airlines Millions

By NICHOLAS GAGE

The Treasury Department is planning to soften a Customs Service regulation that, if left unchanged, might cost Pan American World Airways and Trans World Airlines millions of dollars in duties and penalties, according to Federal Government sources.

They said that two Customs Service civil cases, alleging that Pan Am and T.W.A. had frequently violated the regulation, had been stalled for months in Washington.

At the same time the Treasury Department, of which Customs is a part, has been moving quietly to revise the regulation, which deals with repairs made abroad on American planes, to provide a basis for a settlement of the cases favorable to the airlines, according to the sources.

While the cases would still be valid despite any revision of the regulation, because the violations occurred before the revision, the sources said, the fact of the revision would weaken the justification for demanding strong penalties for the violations.

The regulation calls for the levying of a duty on repairs made abroad on American ships and planes. The duty, which amounts to 50 per cent of the cost of the repairs, is intended to protect American labor from having to compete with cheaper labor abroad.

Shultz Orders Review

J. B. Clawson, deputy assistant secretary of the Treasury, acknowledged that the regulation was under review but denied that the reason was to affect the cases against the airlines.

The review was ordered by Treasury Secretary George P. Shultz after receiving a complaint from the airline industry last April, he said. The complaint came in the form of a letter from Paul Ignatius, head of the Air Transport Association and former Secretary of the Navy.

"Obviously, pending cases against the airlines are the reason they are complaining," Mr. Clawson said. "But we're looking at the regulation because it was drafted a long time ago and deserves re-evaluation." The regulation was drafted in 1948, he said.

Vernon Acree, the Commissioner of Customs, said the main reason action on the cases against Pan Am and T.W.A. had not been taken was that investigations of other airlines were continuing and Customs wanted to wait and move at once on all cases involving the regulation.

He acknowledged that the usual practice in law enforcement was to proceed on each case as it was developed but said in this instance it made

Continued on Page 49, Column 1

A Cave in Greece Yields Clues To Prehistoric Travels by Sea

By MARIO S. MODIANO
Special to The New York Times

KOILADA, Greece, Aug. 18—American archeologists in Greece have dug up evidence of the world's earliest seafaring, dating from about 7500-7000 B.C.—at least a thousand years before sea travel was known to have been practiced.

Proof of this was said to have been found at Franchthi, a cave near here used as a home by humans almost without interruption from at least 20,000 B.C. to 3000 B.C. Experts regard the cave, in southern Greece, as the most important prehistoric site in Europe and the Middle East.

Dr. Thomas W. Jacobsen, of Indiana University, spent six years exploring the site. "The cave," he said, "produced evidence of continuous human occupation and activity from the upper Paleolithic through the Mesolithic and the Neolithic. In this sense it is unique. There is no such sequence anywhere else in the Old World."

Archeologists had explored many Stone Age sites in Greece; some revealed human occupation in the remote Paleolithic period, before 9000 B.C., while others showed evi-

Continued on Page 16, Column 1

Eban Rejects Prodding

Foreign Minister Abba Eban, declaring Israel's Middle East policy a success, in an interview scoffed at State Department suggestions that Israel produce fresh ideas to break the stalemate. Page 9.

Today's Sections

Index to Subjects

The New York Times

LATE CITY EDITION

Weather: Showers, then part sunny today; clear tonight, tomorrow. Temp. range: today 51-65. Sunday 53-72. Additional details on Page 62.

VOL.CXXIII...No.42,478

NEW YORK, MONDAY, MAY 13, 1974

20c beyond 50-mile radius of New York City, except Long Island. Higher in air delivery cities.

15 CENTS

LEVITT CONFIRMS CON EDISON NEEDS 'IMMEDIATE' HELP

Reports a 'Grave Financial Condition' as Utility Chief Presses for State Aid

LEGISLATIVE MOVE SEEN

Luce Indicates That Without $500-Million Assistance, Rates Would Go Up

By DAVID A. ANDELMAN

State Controller Arthur Levitt said yesterday that he had "verified the need for immediate relief" for Consolidated Edison, and the utility's board chairman said that without state aid, an extra 25 per cent electric rate increase or other "extraordinary measures" would be needed.

The Controller's statement, including his view that Con Edison was in "grave financial condition," was the first independent confirmation, demanded repeatedly by skeptics in Albany, of the utility's repeated claims that without state aid it was in danger of bankruptcy.

The statement, together with comments Saturday by Mayor Beame of his concern over the continued viability of the utility, were aimed at breaking the legislative logjam on Con Edison as the State Legislature moves into what is expected to be the final week of the 1974 session.

Rate Increase Pending

In an interview yesterday, Charles F. Luce, Con Edison's board chairman, said that his estimate of an extra 25 per cent increase was based on the company's immediate need for $500-million—about 25 per cent of its annual revenues of $2-billion.

And this 25 per cent increase would be over and above a 29 per cent increase now pending before the Public Service Commission, of which 12 percentage points were granted on an interim basis last February.

Beyond that, Mr. Luce said, the utility would, if unsuccessful in Albany, seek other aid, including a Congressional loan or loan guarantee, as was authorized for the ailing Lockheed Aircraft Corporation two years ago.

"I think we could make a case for that," Mr. Luce said.

Last month Governor Wilson proposed that the Legislature give the Power Authority of the State of New York the authority to take over two Con Edison plants now under construction—a nuclear unit at Indian Point and an oil-fired unit at

Continued on Page 36, Column 3

Nixon Seems Determined To Resist Calls to Resign

Family and Aides Deny Rumors and Say That Impeachment Is the Only Way He Will Be Forced to Yield Office

By JOHN HERBERS
Special to The New York Times

WASHINGTON, May 12 — There were a number of indications today that President Nixon, whatever he may decide in the future about relinquishing his office, is now acting like a man who has made up his mind: to let the constitutional impeachment process in Congress run its course.

The President returned to the White House this morning after an Oklahoma speaking engagement in which he reiterated, in response to new rounds of rumors that he would resign, his determination not to quit.

Meanwhile, J. Fred Buzhardt Jr., the White House counsel, said in a television broadcast today that the publication of some of Mr. Nixon's privately spoken, reportedly ethnic references was part of a "concerted campaign to poison the public mind against the President by any means, fair or foul." [Details on Page 18.]

More convincing than Mr. Nixon's avowal of his intention to stay in office, however, were some other indications that seemed to confirm a rather well-established policy, at least for the time being, as Mr. Nixon's Administration was buffeted by a serious erosion of conservatives within his own party.

Even though Mr. Nixon has retreated many times from adamant positions, his staff and his family have maintained a solid front of insistence that Mr. Nixon has not been deterred by the avalanche of criticism of his conduct in office.

His aides have pointed out that the rumors of resignation have circulated largely in Congress, many members of which would welcome a resignation to relieve them of going through the painful process of impeachment. The rumors have received little credence within the White House, where Mr. Nixon's mood and intentions are better known.

Mrs. David Eisenhower, who is the President's younger daughter, Julie, said in a news conference yesterday that Mr. Nixon told his family Friday night that he would not resign as long as there is one friendly Senator who supports him in his fight against impeachment.

So far, the President has retained the support of the one

Continued on Page 18, Column 7

Franklin National Moves To Assure Its Liquidity

By ROBERT E. BEDINGFIELD

The Franklin National Bank, one of New York's major commercial banks, received a pledge of financial support from the Federal Reserve System yesterday and announced a series of proposed actions of its own to bolster its financial position.

Both developments are designed to assure the bank's liquidity. The Federal Reserve's pledge of advances to the bank "as needed" and the bank's own moves were decided upon after a series of unusual all-day Sunday meetings here and in Washington.

The two moves followed a statement issued on Friday afternoon by Harold V. Gleason, chairman and chief executive officer of both the bank and of its parent, the Franklin New York Corporation, a one-bank holding company, calling for a passing of the regular quarterly dividends that normally would be paid on Aug. 1 out of the current quarter's earnings.

The bank's own program, which will be submitted to both its directors and those of the holding company at meetings scheduled at 9 A.M. today in Manhattan, calls for the raising of $50-million of new capital.

At the meetings, directors also will be asked to approve several major management changes "and certain other programs to improve the bank's performance," according to a three-page statement issued in Mr. Gleason's name about 8 o'clock last night.

Mr. Gleason's statement of last night disclosed that the bank since March 31 has sustained losses of $14-million and a possible additional $25-million in its foreign-currency trading. This has resulted, the statement said, because of an employe in the bank's foreign currency exchange department "operating beyond his authority and without the bank's knowledge."

The "appropriate authorities" as well as the bank's insurance company have been notified, and the bank, according to Mr. Gleason's statement, believes

Continued on Page 48, Column 6

President Hafez al-Assad of Syria and aides inspecting the battlefront during a visit to Golan Heights Friday night

Associated Press and United Press International

Secretary of State Kissinger, Abba Eban of Israel right, and Kenneth B. Keating, U.S. envoy, at Jerusalem meeting

KISSINGER MEETS SYRIAN PRESIDENT AND NOTES GAINS

Secretary Returns to Israel After Talks in Damascus —Accord Eludes Him

MEETS WITH MRS. MEIR

Israeli Cabinet Will Discuss Situation Today — U.S. Hopes for Compromises

By BERNARD GWERTZMAN
Special to The New York Times

JERUSALEM, May 12—Secretary of State Kissinger said in Damascus today that he and Syrian leaders had gone from the general to "a detailed and complete examination" of all issues in a Syrian-Israeli agreement on troop separation but that an accord still eluded them.

Speaking to newsmen before shuttling back to Israel for renewed talks tonight with senior Israeli officials here, Mr. Kissinger said "some progress" was again achieved in his third trip to the Syrian capital on this Middle East journey. There were other favorable signs, but newsmen were told that Mr. Kissinger remained uncertain that he could soon bridge the gap separating Syria and Israel.

Mr. Kissinger and his top aides met with Premier Golda Meir and other Israeli officials for more than two hours at her office tonight.

Foreign Minister Abba Eban told newsmen, "We discussed ways some of the differences may be reconciled." He added that the Israeli Cabinet would meet tomorrow to consider the situation.

New Meeting Set

A meeting between the Israeli negotiators and Mr. Kissinger's team was set for tomorrow afternoon after the Cabinet meeting. American officials said that Mr. Kissinger hoped that Israel would make the additional compromises needed to help him bring about a disengagement accord when he returns to Damascus on Tuesday.

Mr. Kissinger told newsmen outside the Premier's office that the talks tonight were "very detailed" but he declined to predict whether an agreement was possible.

After almost daily conversations with Israeli and Syrian officials, Mr. Kissinger knows by now what compromises would be necessary to resolve the disengagement negotiations, American officials said. Although he has narrowed the differences between Syria

Continued on Page 8, Column 4

U.S. Energy Goals Are Still Far Off As Supplies Rise

By EDWARD COWAN
Special to The New York Times

WASHINGTON, May 12—Six months after President Nixon penciled "Project Independence" into his Nov. 7 energy speech, several hundred people in a dozen Federal agencies are involved in the most ambitious exercise in peacetime economic forecasting, planning and policy making in the history of the United States—trying to develop a working definition.

As now conceived, the effort—centered in the Federal Energy Administration—will be a continuing exercise, refined from year to year in light of changing conditions.

At the moment, then, Project Independence is little more than an idea. Even Mr. Nixon's more limited; initial use of the phrase—"the potential to meet our own energy needs without depending on any foreign sources"—lacked clear content.

What then, does "Project Independence" mean?

Without exception, the Pres-

Continued on Page 49, Column 3

RACE ISSUE MUTED IN NEWARK VOTE

5-Way Campaign, Headed by Gibson and Imperiale, Closing on Calm Note

By MICHAEL T. KAUFMAN

In contrast to the racially polarized campaign for Mayor of Newark four years ago, the contest among the five contenders in tomorrow's election wound down yesterday in a mood of low-key amity.

"Happy Birthday," said Anthony Imperiale to Mayor Kenneth A. Gibson as the two chief opponents in the race met, along with three other candidates, on a television panel.

"With victory on Tuesday," responded Mayor Gibson, teasing the State Senator, who has been his chief critic.

The issues in the nonpartisan election, this time around, are general and broad: the crime rate, the tax structure and, most of all, the personalities of the two major antagonists. Four years ago, when national attention focused on

Continued on Page 35, Column 3

Foreign Appeals for Food Raise Price Specter Here

By EDWIN L. DALE Jr.
Special to The New York Times

WASHINGTON, May 12—The United States Government is slowly approaching an agonizing decision on whether to give away more food to nations approaching starvation at the risk of starting a new surge of food prices at home.

Secretary of Agriculture Earl L. Butz recognizes that there are problems involved in increasing aid, but does not believe they are imminent because of the enormous American harvest in prospect for this year.

Dr. Butz said in an interview that the larger crops would permit some increase in food aid in the coming 12 months, above what had been planned, without any important impact on domestic prices. Other officials are less confident, particularly in the light of the possibility of large requests for food from India.

In the background is Secretary of State Kissinger, who favors more food aid, for foreign-policy as well as humanitarian purposes. No immediate decisions are expected.

"There's no doubt that the situation poses a grave potential dilemma," said Gary L. Seevers, the member of the President's Council of Economic Advisers who deals with agricultural matters, and who emphasized the crucial importance of food prices to the general level of consumer prices this year and next.

Mr. Seevers supports Dr. Butz's view that some additional aid will be possible above what had been planned, but adds, "It all depends on the magnitude."

There have been some estimates that India alone may need to import five million tons or more of food grain, mainly

Continued on Page 10, Column 1

Proposal for Human Colonies in Space Is Hailed by Scientists as Feasible Now

By WALTER SULLIVAN

A conference of physicists, astronauts and space flight technologists discussed last week the likelihood that it is now possible and, in fact, desirable to establish self-sufficient human colonies in space.

The conferees had been invited to Princeton University by Dr. Gerard K. O'Neill, professor of physics there, to discuss his proposals for such an effort, and they expressed varying degrees of enthusiasm for the scheme. It was even suggested that a century from now most of humanity will be living in space.

The initial goal would be construction of a "small" colony of about 2,000 people at a site, along the orbital path of the moon, known as the L5 libration point.

From the studies of the 18th century French mathematician Joseph Louis Lagrange it became evident that there are five points in space where the gravitation fields of the earth and moon balance one another. An object at one of these points would tend to remain there rather than falling toward the earth or moon.

The two most stable such points are known as L4, which lies ahead of the moon on the latter's orbital path, and L5, which lies behind it, each being separated from the moon by a distance equal to that from the earth to the moon.

The New York Times/May 13, 1974

L5 is one of five points in space where the gravitation fields of the earth and the moon balance each other and where a space station could remain.

The initial station would be built, using the space shuttle and space tug systems now under development, and its cost would be comparable to that of the Apollo moon-landing program.

It would take advantage of abundant building materials available on the moon and one of two novel cargo-launching systems to export such material from the moon.

Dr. O'Neill is internationally known, not as a designer of space systems but for his role in setting in motion what has become one of the most productive areas of physics research—that in which beams of high energy particles are fired head on at one another.

He pointed out that "virtually unlimited" resources exist in space and that sunlight provides a continuous source of free energy with no nighttime interruption. Furthermore, in the asteroid belt are great chunks of almost pure nickel-iron that can be fabricated into steel with minimal processing. (Samples of this material lie in museums as nickel-iron meteorites.)

His initial colony would require the transport of 10,000 tons of material from the earth and fabrication of a cylinder 200 meters in diameter and 100 meters long (the meter being

Continued on Page 23, Column 4

Prosecutor Guarded

Federal investigators believe someone last week drugged Assistant United States Attorney Peter R. Schlam, the chief prosecutor at the extortion-conspiracy trial of a Long Island Congressman, and the prosecutor has been placed in protective custody by United States marshals at an undisclosed location. Page 62.

Associated Press

BOSTON CELTICS WIN CHAMPIONSHIP: The Celtics defeated the Bucks, 102-87, at Milwaukee yesterday, to win the National Basketball Association title for the first time since 1969. Above, Don Nelson of the Celtics scoring against Cornell Warner as Dave Cowens (18) and Kareem Abdul-Jabbar watched. Details, Page 41.

Airlines and Agents Aim To Foil Youth Fare Ban

By ROBERT LINDSEY

If you are more than 15 years old—and less than 24—there's $50 waiting for you in Amsterdam after June 1, but you have to answer a few questions.

Or, if you are under 24 and are willing to throw away a valid airline ticket between Toronto and New York, you can save up to $350 on the price of a ticket from New York to Europe this summer.

Despite the nominal demise of the trans-Atlantic youth fares, these stratagems have cropped up recently on the threshold of the annual summer tourist rush to Europe—which promises to be more of a trickle than a flood this year.

The start of the summer season is still a month away, but already the trans-Atlantic airlines are feuding, as they do about every year at this time.

Pan American World Airways has called "illegal" a plan by KLM, the Dutch-flag airline, and the Netherlands National Tourist Office, to pay young people $50 for answering questionnaires in Amsterdam. Pan Am officials say the plan is nothing more than a subterfuge to circumvent a United States Government decision to end international youth fares—and an illegal rebate scheme.

The Dutch plan may launch what some people in the airline industry already are calling the "questionnaire war," recalling the "sandwich war" of more than a decade ago, when trans-Atlantic airlines vied with one another to offer the fanciest sandwiches.

Under the plan, young people who fly directly to Amsterdam via KLM after June 1 from New York or Chicago and stay in the Dutch city at least two nights, will be paid $50 after they complete a questionnaire.

What will the survey cover? "Your preferences, tastes, ambitions, peeves, pleasures and desires," a straight-faced advertisement for the plan says.

"Extraordinary," a Civil Aeronautics Board investigator said last week when told about the plan, adding that it would be investigated for possible violation of Federal law.

Meanwhile, Pan American said it hoped to block imple-

Continued on Page 62, Column 5

NEWS INDEX

"All the News That's Fit to Print"

The New York Times

LATE CITY EDITION

Weather: Partly cloudy today; fair and pleasant tonight and tomorrow. Temp. range: today 60-75; Monday 67-78. Temp.-Hum. Index yesterday 78. Additional details on Page 78.

VOL. CXXIII...No. 42,514

NEW YORK, TUESDAY, JUNE 18, 1974

20¢ beyond 50-mile radius of New York City, except Long Island. Higher in air delivery cities.

15 CENTS

Kalmbach Given Jail Term Of 6-18 Months by Sirica

Nixon's Former Lawyer Is Also Fined $10,000 for Illegal Fund-Raising on Behalf of White House

By ANTHONY RIPLEY
Special to The New York Times

WASHINGTON, June 17—Herbert W. Kalmbach, President Nixon's former personal lawyer, was sentenced today to six to 18 months in prison and fined $10,000 for illegal fund-raising activities on behalf of the White House.

The sentence was imposed by Judge John J. Sirica in United States District Court on the second anniversary of the break-in at the Democratic National Committee headquarters in the Watergate Office Building.

Mr. Kalmbach, a low-key figure who usually remained in the background while raising millions for Mr. Nixon's re-election campaign and other political activities, told the judge before the sentencing:

"Your honor, I'd like to let you know how deeply embarrassed I am and how much I regret standing here before you this afternoon."

He pleaded guilty Feb. 25 to a two-count criminal information drawn by the Watergate special prosecutor, Leon Jaworski, and had promised to cooperate with the Watergate investigation.

His sentence followed the general pattern of light penalties imposed on Watergate figures who have negotiated pleas and agreed to cooperate.

Judge Sirica said he had recommended that Mr. Kalmbach, who is 52 years old, be placed in a minimum security prison such as the Federal Prison Farm at Allenwood, Pa. He gave Mr. Kalmbach two weeks to clear up his personal affairs before beginning his sentence.

Mr. Kalmbach had pleaded guilty to a charge of operating an illegal campaign com-

Continued on Page 24, Column 1

The New York Times
Herbert W. Kalmbach after he was sentenced.

OIL NATIONS RAISE COMPANIES' COST FOR ROYALTIES 2%

Saudi Arabia Blocks Attempt to Raise Prices of Crude Several Dollars a Barrel

By JUAN de ONIS
Special to The New York Times

QUITO, Ecuador, June 17—A majority of the world's large oil-exporting countries announced today an increase of 2 per cent in royalties levied on Western oil companies after Saudi Arabia, the biggest exporter, had blocked an attempt to raise oil prices several dollars a barrel.

The Organization of Petroleum Exporting Countries decided at a ministerial meeting here to continue the posted price of oil at present record levels for another three months, from July 1.

The effect of maintaining the posted price (on which oil-exporting countries calculate their tax-take) and imposing the new royalty levy is to squeeze profits of the oil companies unless they can pass the added cost on to consumers.

Outlook on Pricing

If the new levy is passed along in full, as has been the oil companies' practice with tax increases in the past, the increase in crude oil prices could be about 10 to 15 cents a barrel, or less than 2 per cent of prevailing prices.

Saudi Arabia said she is not going to apply the royalty increase for the time being. The increase, which applies to oil exported by the companies, was adopted partly as an effort to reduce their profits. Approximately 30 million barrels of oil a day are exported from the nations that are members of OPEC.

The leaders of the drive for increased government income from oil exports were Kuwait, Iran, Venezuela, Indonesia, Libya and Algeria. They insist that the new levy is necessary to offset inflationary price increases in major industrial goods and foods that oil-producing nations must import.

Producers' View

"Until the industrial countries do something about the inflation in their price, the oil producers must protect the real value of a barrel of oil by increasing the government take," said Jamshid Amouzegar, Iran's chief delegate.

Iran was also a leader in the sudden increase in the posted price last December, which raised the export price of oil from Iran, Saudi Arabia, Kuwait and other Middle East sources from $3.65 a barrel in September, before the Middle East war and Arab production cutbacks, to more than $7 a barrel.

The oil companies must pay 60 per cent of the posted price in taxes and royalties, which have been 12.5 per cent of the

Continued on Page 51, Column 2

United Press International
Flames and smoke issuing from Westminster Hall in London yesterday after a bomb explosion. The police said a phone call from man using a code word of the Provisional wing of the Irish Republican Army warned of the blast.

NIXON PROMISES LONG-TERM HELP FOR THE ISRAELIS

Pledges Arms and Economic Aid—Bids New Cabinet Take Risks for Peace

NUCLEAR PACT PLANNED

Joint Statement Says U.S. Will Negotiate Accord on Atomic Cooperation

By TERENCE SMITH
Special to The New York Times

JERUSALEM, June 17—President Nixon today concluded a 26-hour visit here in which he assured Israel of long-term military and economic assistance and urged the new Government to demonstrate its statesmanship by taking risks for peace.

This dual theme dominated Mr. Nixon's tightly scheduled visit, which included two working sessions with Israeli leaders, a state banquet and a somber ceremony this morning at Yad Vashem, the memorial to the six million Jews killed during World War II.

U.S. to Supply Nuclear Fuel

Like the United States-Egyptian agreement announced last week, the communiqué issued here today included an announcement that the two Governments would soon negotiate an agreement on cooperation in the field of "nuclear energy, technology and the supply of [nuclear] fuel from the United States under agreed safeguards."

As an immediate step, the communiqué said, "Israel and the United States will in the current month reach provisional agreement on the further sale of nuclear fuel to Israel."

This provision represents less of a breakthrough in Israeli-American relations than it did in the American-Egyptian agreement. The United States already sells nuclear fuel to Israel for use in Nahal Soreq, an American-financed nuclear research station on the Mediter ranean coast. Israel has a second nuclear reactor at Dimona, southwest of the Dead Sea.

Crowds Line the Route

On the way to the Yad Vashem memorial, Mr. Nixon twice halted his motorcade to greet the enthusiastic crowds of Israelis who lined his route. At one point he clambered up a dusty bank to grasp the hands of some excited schoolchildren who were waving to him.

The President and his huge entourage of officials, security men and accompanying newsmen left this afternoon for Amman, Jordan, the last Middle Eastern stop on his tour. Secretary of State Kissinger took off an hour earlier on a separate plane for a meeting of the foreign ministers of the

Continued on Page 14, Column 5

4 More Regents Tests Off As Gold Tells of 3 Thefts

By LEONARD BUDER

State education authorities canceled four more Regents examinations yesterday, making a total of nine called off, as Brooklyn District Attorney Eugene Gold said that he now believed that test booklets or answer sheets had been stolen from three schools in the borough and widely distributed.

The latest statewide tests to be canceled were the revised chemistry and physics examinations and the comprehensive social studies and third-year Hebrew tests. Last Friday the State Education Department canceled four tests outright and on Sunday it called off another.

The department also last week scrapped its original chemistry and physics tests, which were supposed to have been given tomorrow and had said it would give revised examinations in these subjects on Thursday.

But late yesterday, after obtaining information from District Attorney Gold that the original tests were being sold to students, the department dropped the new tests as well. A department aide said that the new tests had contained some questions from the original examinations.

The other canceled examinations were those in English, ninth-grade mathematics, 10th-grade mathematics (geometry), and 11th-grade mathematics and biology. A total of 650,000 students throughout the state had been earlier expected to take 21 different Regents tests this week including those now canceled.

The developments caused

Continued on Page 28, Column 1

White May Get Seat Rezoned for a Black

By FRANK LYNN

A Brooklyn congressional district that had been reapportioned under a Justice Department order so that a black could be elected will instead very likely have a white Representative.

City Councilman Samuel D. Wright, the black Democrat who had been expected to run for Congress in the new 14th Congressional district, said yesterday that he would not run because he could not win the district even though figures of the Joint Legislative Committee on Reapportionment show that blacks constitute 45 per cent of the population and

Continued on Page 29 Column 3

CATTLEMEN TO GET SUPERMARKET AID

Bid to Cut Meat Prices and Promote Sales Promised at White House Meeting

By WILLIAM ROBBINS
Special to The New York Times

WASHINGTON, June 17—An effort to reduce meat prices and promote sales was promised today by supermarket spokesmen during a White House meeting of Government and food-industry officials on the plight of the nation's troubled cattle producers.

An agreement by the retailers' representatives to send telegrams calling for the action was announced by Kenneth Rush, President Nixon's economic counselor, after the two-hour session, which was attended by producers and meat packers as well as the food-chain executives.

"Your serious consideration" of Government and producer requests for "an emergency maximum promotion effort to move currently excessive supplies of beef and pork into consumption," was urged by Clarence G. Adamy, president of the National Association of Food Chains, in telegrams sent immediately after the White House discussion.

Mr. Adamy said the telegrams were being sent to all members of his association as well as to other retail groups.

"Our people have always responded to such appeals," Mr. Adamy said in a telephone interview. "I have every reason to expect almost universal response."

Sales promotions were given an immediate sendoff by Secretary of Agriculture Earl L. Butz at a news briefing following

Continued on Page 51, Column 2

Bomb in London Damages Oldest Hall of Parliament

By ALVIN SHUSTER
Special to The New York Times

LONDON, June 17—A bomb exploded today in the most historic part of the Houses of Parliament, damaging Westminster Hall, the 900-year-old chamber that has seen much of British history. Eleven people were injured, none seriously.

The police said that the bombing was the work of the Provisional wing of the Irish Republican Army. A man with an Irish accent telephoned the Press Association, the local news agency, giving six minutes warning of the explosion and using a code word of the I.R.A. to identify a genuine alert.

For several hours after the blast at 8:28 A.M. smoke shrouded Big Ben as firemen fought the fire fed by an ignited gas main. The hall's annex, which housed a canteen and some offices, was wrecked.

The great hall itself, the oldest remaining part of the original Royal Palace of Westminster, appeared only slightly damaged. The famous ceiling of curved arches of oak and carved hammer beams remained intact.

Windows along both sides of the hall were blown out, along with panels of glass over the northern entrance. The stained glass window at the southern end—the area tourists pass when they enter Parliament for tickets to the galleries—was undamaged.

There was also no damage to the House of Commons or the House of Lords, both of which are some distance from the hall. But the smell of smoke lingered in the corri-

Continued on Page 3, Column 1

ATOMIC EXPLOSION SET OFF BY CHINA

U.S. Reports Relatively Big Test in Air, but Schlesinger Shows Little Concern

Special to The New York Times

WASHINGTON, June 17—China conducted a relatively large nuclear test early today, the United States Atomic Energy Commission announced.

The commission said the explosion took place in the atmosphere at about 2 A.M. Eastern Daylight Time, at the test range in northwestern China. The blast was in the "intermediate range" between 200 kilotons and one megaton, according to the announcement. A kiloton is the equivalent of 100 tons of TNT and a megaton is equal to one million tons of TNT.

At a Pentagon news conference, Secretary of Defense James R. Schlesinger expressed no particular concern over the Chinese test. He said the test "simply reflects the slow-paced Chinese program," which he described as deliberate but "moderately successful."

Since October, 1964, China has conducted 16 nuclear tests—15 in the atmosphere and one underground. The tests have ranged from about 20 kilotons—the size of the bomb detonated over Hiroshima in 1945—to five in the one-megaton to three-megaton range.

Presumably today's Chinese test was of a thermonuclear device for later incorporation in a warhead for the intermediate-range and intercontinental ballistic missiles China is known to be developing.

The announcement here of

Continued on Page 6, Column 4

Court Says States Can Bar Job Benefits in Pregnancy

By WARREN WEAVER Jr.
Special to The New York Times

WASHINGTON, June 17—The Supreme Court ruled 6 to 3 today that states can deny disability benefits to women incapacitated by normal pregnancy without committing unconstitutional discrimination.

The decision was a serious setback for advocates of equal rights for women, who have won limited victories in the courts recently on issues that have included mandatory pregnancy leaves for public school teachers and allowances for the husbands of servicewomen.

Justice Potter Stewart wrote for the majority that under the California law in question "there is no risk from which men are protected and women are not" and "likewise there is no risk from which women are protected and men are not."

In his dissent, however, Justice William J. Brennan Jr. noted that the program protects men when they are incapacitated by prostate trouble or circumcision, which affect only members of their sex, and hemophilia and gout, which are largely confined to males.

In a number of states, disability benefits are paid under an insurance system to workers who are incapacitated by sickness. The programs are similar to those in which on-the-job accidents are covered by workmen's compensation. Under the California law before the high court, the program was entirely supported by a 1 per cent tax on employe wages.

In the majority opinion, Jus-

Continued on Page 25, Column 1

2,200-Year-Old Ship Found Off Cyprus to Be Shown

By STEVEN V. ROBERTS
Special to The New York Times

KYRENIA, Cyprus—About 2,200 years ago a merchant ship set off on a journey through the eastern Mediterranean, stopping at such islands as Samos, Kos and Rhodes, trading in oil and wine, millstones and almonds.

Less than two miles outside this port on the north coast of Cyprus, the ship sank in 100 feet of water, probably while trying to ride out a storm.

A bit off schedule, the old ship has finally made it to Kyrenia. Salvaged from the sea floor by a team of archeologists, she is the oldest vessel ever recovered from underwater, according to Michael L. Katsev, the director of the excavation.

After seven years of work, this "time capsule," as Mr. Katsev calls it, is going on public display soon, with air-conditioning to preserve the wood. The setting will be the former barracks room of a crusaders' castle that has guarded the entrance to this lovely harbor since A.D. 1200.

The worm-eaten, weather-

Continued on Page 4, Column 3

John Veltri
Diver with underwater breathing apparatus aiding preparation of a 2,200-year-old ship for raising off Kyrenia, Cyprus. At left are storage jars. Ship will be displayed soon.

Blacks Return to South In a Reverse Migration

By B. DRUMMOND AYRES Jr.
Special to The New York Times

ATLANTA, June 17—Driven out by racism and lack of economic opportunity, Southern blacks have been migrating North in huge numbers for more than a century, riding the Illinois Central, the Greyhound and the old family Ford toward the promise of Chicago's South Side and New York's Harlem.

But now, with the promise unfulfilled in many cases, significant numbers of blacks are returning to the South, coming "back down home" to a region that seems, at last, to offer as many economic opportunities and as much brotherhood as any other section of the United States.

"I didn't see any reason to stay up there in that madhouse when all I found was just as much discrimination and poverty, and even more crime, than there is down here," said Freddie Lee Reese, a 32-year-old native of Montgomery, Ala., who recently returned to his home town to work as a building supervisor after several years of disenchantment in Chicago.

Significant numbers of Northern-born blacks have gone South these days, too—many

Continued on Page 49, Column 4

NEWS INDEX

Associated Press
President and Mrs. Nixon at Yad Vashem, memorial to Jews killed during World War II, in Jerusalem. Mr. Nixon wears hat, following Jewish law. At right is chief cantor.

"All the News That's Fit to Print"

The New York Times

LATE CITY EDITION

Weather: Sunny and hot today; fair tonight. Not so warm tomorrow. Temp. range: today 70-93; Saturday 65-88. Highest Temp.-Hum. Index yesterday: 77. Details on Page 47.

SECTION ONE

VOL. CXXIII . . No. 42,540 — NEW YORK, SUNDAY, JULY 14, 1974 — 60 CENTS

90c beyond 50-mile zone from New York City, except Long Island. Higher in air delivery cities.

The New York Times/Micha Bar-Am

Under the gaze of curious Lebanese children, an Israeli works on barbed-wire section of a fence at Avivim. Israel, in an attempt to curtail terrorist attacks, is constructing the fence and a protected strip along her border with Lebanon.

Israel Builds New Border Fence

By TERENCE SMITH

Special to The New York Times

MALKIYA, Israel, July 13—The dense coils of concertina wire are studded with tiny razor blades and rooted to the ground by iron stakes. The 12-foot-high hurricane fence is alive with electric warning devices and topped with strands of barbed wire.

Both are being strung across the 50-mile length of Israel's northern frontier as part of a major new defensive system designed to seal the Lebanese border against infiltration by Arab guerrillas.

[Israel's conditional offer to negotiate with Palestinian guerrilla organizations received big headlines in Arab newspapers in Beirut, but Palestinian leaders withheld official comment and were privately skeptical of the offer. Page 17.]

Work on the elaborate new fence began two months ago and is expected to take several more weeks to complete. Similar obstacles are already in place along the Syrian and Jordanian borders.

The objective, according to Israeli military sources, is to make it as difficult and dangerous as possible for small guerrilla units to cross from their bases in southern Lebanon. Four such squads have made it in the last three months and 51 Israelis have died in the ensuing attacks on civilian settlements.

"We realize it's impossible to seal the border completely," an Israeli major who commands the frontier force near this border kibbutz told a visitor. "But this fence will at least slow a terrorist down," he said. "If the system works properly, we'll be able to kill him before he manages to cut his way through."

The decision to go ahead with the construction of the fence was made shortly after the guerrilla attack on Qiryat Shemona on April 11, in which 18 Israelis were killed. The three guerrillas who carried out that assault simply climbed over the six-foot chain-link fence at the bor-

Continued on Page 17, Column 1

Inflation Replaces Energy As Nation's Main Concern

48% in a Gallup Poll Cite Rising Costs as No. 1 Problem—Consumers Assert Prices 'Trap' and 'Depress' Them

By MICHAEL C. JENSEN

Inflation, overshadowed earlier this year by the energy crisis, has leaped back into prominence as the nation's No. 1 concern, according to the latest Gallup Poll and a series of interviews across the country.

"I didn't leave Ireland to be poor here too," said Eileen Dugan, a 27-year-old dental assistant from New York's upper East Side who earns about $9,000 a year.

"If I were to get married soon, I'd think long and hard about having a child. I don't want to give my child a third-rate home and education, and end up living a depressing life myself. It's just not worth it."

The results of the Gallup Poll indicate that Miss Dugan is not alone in considering inflation an overriding concern.

Forty-eight per cent of those polled by Gallup named the high cost of living as the nation's paramount problem, far exceeding the next highest category, 15 per cent who were more concerned with "lack of trust in Government," and the 11 per cent who named "corruption in Government" and "Watergate."

"You feel trapped," said Richard Spohn of Los Angeles, a Harvard-trained lawyer who heads Ralph Nader's California Citizen Action Group. Mr. Spohn questioned how he could survive "on a Nader salary of $100 a week."

Citing soaring interest rates for home mortgages, he said his plans to buy a house had been dampened. He said, "You buy one and end up paying three times the price [in mortgage interest], and the way things are going it's going to cost four times the price."

The Gallup Poll revealed that concern over inflation cut across both age and income barriers, and was widespread throughout the nation.

High income Americans seemed to take a more benign attitude toward inflation. A total of 41 per cent of the Gallup Poll's business and professional respondents named the cost of living as the nation's major problem. In less affluent groups, the totals ranged from 47 per cent to 54 per cent.

Robert Kholos, one of the individuals interviewed, said his $20,000-a-year salary was ade-

Continued on Page 28, Column 4

City and 2 Unions Agree

City labor negotiators have reached tentative understandings with representatives of the fire and sanitation unions on basic wage increases in a two-year contract. Page 36.

2 Convicts in Court Siege Permit Inmates' Transfer

7 Hostages Still Held

By JOHN W. FINNEY

Special to The New York Times

WASHINGTON, July 13—Two armed convicts holding seven hostages in the cell block of a Federal Court building permitted the release today of 14 other prisoners as they continued negotiations with Justice Department officials.

The released prisoners, who were transfered to other jails, had been in the basement cell block when the two convicts seized control on Thursday afternoon.

George K. McKinney, the United States marshal for the District of Columbia, called the move a "helpful sign" that "the situation can be worked out peacefully."

Justice Department officials cautioned, however, that the situation was "still potentially dangerous." The two convicts

Continued on Page 34, Column 3

Baltimore Jail Stormed

By The Associated Press

BALTIMORE, July 13—City jail inmates took three hostages tonight while striking guards picketed outside, but the police stormed into the building and returned the inmates to their cells.

No shots were fired and no serious injuries were reported.

The police said the hostages were members of the supervisory staff who had replaced striking jail guards. About 75 inmates were in the large open room where the hostages were held for about an hour, but the police said they did not know how many of them had participated in the revolt.

Nonstriking policemen using dogs and nightsticks put down the disturbance at the City Jail in downtown Baltimore.

"We hit the door and we did

Continued on Page 35, Column 1

The New York Times/George Tames

Senator Sam J. Ervin Jr. collecting his papers after news session on final report. At right is Samuel Dash, the Senate Watergate committee's chief counsel.

ERVIN PANEL ASKS SWEEPING REFORM OF ELECTION LAWS

Watergate Committee Final Report Recommends 35 Legislative Changes

17-MONTH INQUIRY ENDS

Document Avoids Assessing the Possible Involvement of Nixon and Aides

By JOHN M. CREWDSON

Special to The New York Times

WASHINGTON, July 13—The Senate Watergate committee, in its last official action, released today a final report that included proposals for a sweeping overhaul of campaign and other statutes that, it predicted, would go far toward precluding another Watergate.

The 2,217-page report, concluding a 17-month investigation that first focused attention on the scandals surrounding the Nixon Administration, was drawn almost entirely from testimony and documents previously made public. It provided no new revelations and carefully refrained from assigning guilt or innocence in particular areas to President Nixon or his aides.

Excerpts from final report are printed on Page 30.

Noting that its mandate had been limited to the recommendation o legislative reforms to prevent the recurrence of such abuses, the seven-member panel set forth a total of 35 proposals for legislative change.

'Lessons of Watergate'

"Surely one of the most penetrating lessons of Watergate," the report declared, "is that campaign practices must be effectively supervised and enforcement of the criminal laws vigorously pursued against all offenders—even those of high estate—if our free institutions are to survive."

The committee proposed, among other innovations, the creation of an independent public attorney, in effect a permanent version of the special Watergate prosecutor, who

Continued on Page 31, Column 1

Nixon Reaffirms Support Of Kissinger on Wiretaps

By BERNARD GWERTZMAN

Special to The New York Times

WASHINGTON, July 13—President Nixon has come to the support of Secretary of State Kissinger with a letter to the Senate Foreign Relations Committee reaffirming his responsibility for the wiretapping of 17 officials and newsmen between 1969 and 1971.

Senator J. W. Fulbright, chairman of the committee, which has begun an investigation of Mr. Kissinger's role in the wiretapping, confirmed today that he received the one-and-a-quarter-page letter last night.

He declined to make it public before the rest of the committee had seen it, but he said the letter was a clear and "positive statement" by Mr. Nixon justifying the wiretapping program on the ground of national security and stating that he had ordered that the project be instituted to get to the source of news leaks at the time.

The willingness of Mr. Nixon to come to Mr. Kissinger's support has tended to scotch some of the speculation that was current in Washington after the Secretary's recent threat to resign after accusations that he had misled the committee about his role in the wiretapping.

Some political observers believed that a rift was developing between Mr. Kissinger and the White House over the apparent reluctance of Mr. Nixon or Gen. Alexander M. Haig Jr., the Presidential chief of staff who was formerly Mr. Kissinger's deputy on the National Security Council staff, to speak out more strongly on the Secretary of State's behalf.

The President's letter apparently repeated in essence what Mr. Nixon has already said in taking responsibility for the wiretapping program.

In a statement issued on May 22, 1973, Mr. Nixon, noting that there had been leaks of

Continued on Page 31, Column 2

Federal Aides Discount Sludge Threat

By DAVID A. ANDELMAN

Two Federal agencies said yesterday that the sludge reported to be creeping toward the beaches of Long Island was no threat to swimmers and might even be of natural origins.

But the associate administrator of the National Oceanic and Atmospheric Administration, one of the two Federal agencies that held a joint meeting here Friday on the sludge problem, conceded that within two years it would be necessary to find new disposal areas for sewage sludge farther offshore because of the increasing volumes of the material being dumped.

David H. Wallace, the administrator in charge of marine resources, was careful to draw a distinction between sewage sludge that may contain disease-carrying bacteria and dangerous concentrations of heavy metals, and sludge of natural origin that he said might build up in sedimentary deposits on the ocean floor consisting of natural marine waste of dead plants and animal life.

"The health hazard [along the South Shore beaches of Long Island] was about as low as you could expect anywhere," Mr. Wallace said yesterday when reached in Washington. "There is no evidence at all that this is deteriorating the water quality of the area in which people swim."

The meeting Friday that included officials of the oceanic and atmospheric administration and the United States Environmental Protection Agency, was called to determine whether the situation involving sludge had developed in the offshore area of Long Island to a point that warranted changing substantially the timetable for finding new sitees for dumping sludge in deeper waters.

Last year, Federal officials said that such new sites would be needed in 1978 or later. Yesterday, however, Mr. Wallace

Continued on Page 40, Column 3

Ford Doubts House Will Impeach Nixon

Special to The New York Times

SAN CLEMENTE, Calif., July 13—Vice President Ford, emerging from a meeting with President Nixon at the President's estate here, indicated today that he expected the House Judiciary Committee to recommend impeachment proceedings against Mr. Nixon.

However, he said that the Judiciary Committee did not reflect the attitude of the House of Representatives as a whole and asserted that he expected the full House to reject the impeachment bill.

Mr. Ford said that some members of the Judiciary Committee had begun the proceedings with the preconceived idea that the President was guilty and would therefore push through a recommendation for impeachment.

But "the preponderance of evidence" indicates that the President is innocent of any criminal wrongdoing in relation to the cover-up of the Watergate break-in, he declared.

Mr. Ford, who was Republican leader of the House before succeeding Spiro T. Agnew as Vice President, said that he thought the chairman of the Judiciary Committee, Peter W. Rodino Jr., was being fair in his conduct of the proceedings, and that some members of the committee were fair.

But he said that other members had prepared bills of impeachment even before the hearings started. He seemed to be intimating that a majority of the committee members had prejudged the President and would possibly not treat Mr. Nixon fairly.

Yesterday, Gerald L. Warren, the White House deputy press secretary, told newsmen that the President believed the

Continued on Page 31, Column 5

The New York Times/Theodore L. Sullivan

View of a fissured area in the Thingvellir rift zone, northeast of Reykjavik, Iceland. Lasers and other distance-measuring devices have shown an apparent widening of one or two inches across this zone over past few years.

Continental Drift Is Traced to an Iceland Volcano

By WALTER SULLIVAN

Intensive international efforts to determine what is slowly pushing the land masses of Europe and America farther apart have shown that, in a broad sense, a large part of the North Atlantic is one vast volcanic structure centered on Iceland.

This emerged at a conference of specialists from both sides of the Atlantic held at the University of Iceland in Reykjavik during the week of July 1 to 7.

Such evidence has been seized upon by those earth scientists who believe a great plume, or upwelling, of hot, relatively plastic rock from a depth of 1,000 miles or more is rising beneath Iceland, making that the most volcanic region on earth and pushing apart the eastern and western halves of the ocean.

However, other explanations were offered at the meeting. It was proposed, for example, that the hot, swollen nature of the North Atlantic floor arises from the slowness of spreading from its centerline.

Perhaps the most striking discovery reported at the meeting was the manner in which, chemically speaking, the second highest volcano in Iceland serves as the focal point of eruptions that extend at least 1,000 miles down the Mid-Atlantic Ridge.

Dr. G. E. Sigvaldason of the Nordic Volcanological Institute in Reykjavik described the analysis of 513 samples of lava collected from all over Iceland. These showed that, in a strikingly uniform manner, those specimens of a potash-rich variety showed less and less po-

Continued on Page 26, Column 1

Gary Player Victor In British Open Golf

Gary Player of South Africa won the British Open golf championship at Lytham St. Annes, England, by shooting a final-round 70 yesterday. He finished with a 72-hole total of 282, four strokes better than Peter Oosterhuis of Britain, the runner-up, and five better than Jack Nicklaus of the United States.

Player earned $13,200 in winning the event for the third time; he also triumphed in 1959 and 1968. He entered the final round with a three-stroke lead over Oosterhuis, shot birdies on the first two holes and took command with an eagle on the sixth.

Details in Section 5

Associated Press

Mr. Ford and Mr. Nixon meeting in San Clemente, Calif.

Today's Sections

Index to Subjects

"All the News That's Fit to Print."

The New York Times.

THE WEATHER
Thundershowers today, cooler at night; tomorrow fair.
Temperatures yesterday—Max., 79; min., 67.
For weather report see Page 25.

VOL.CXXIV...No.42,644 | NEW YORK, SATURDAY, OCTOBER 26, 1974 | 20 CENTS
rice higher in air delivery cities.

ARAB ENVOYS BACK PALESTINIANS' BID TO GET WEST BANK

Stand of Foreign Ministers at Rabat Is Subject to Change by Leaders

ISSUE DOMINATES TALKS

Representatives of 19 Lands Also Affirm Concept of a Separate Nation

By HENRY TANNER
Special to The New York Times

RABAT, Morocco, Oct. 25—The foreign ministers of 19 Arab countries voted today to support the Palestine Liberation Organization's claim to control over all territories on the West Bank of the Jordan River that might be evacuated by Israel.

The vote, however, was on a recommendation to the Arab heads of state and government who will open their meeting here tomorrow, and the stand taken today could undergo changes when the leaders meet. The issue has dominated the four days of preliminary talks by the foreign ministers that ended today and it is certain to dominate the meeting of the Arab leaders.

A 'Rejection Front'

The foreign ministers, in their recommendation, also reaffirmed the right of the Palestinians to set up a "national authority in the liberated area" —in other words, to create a state of their own. The results of the vote were announced by Jordanian and Palestinian delegates at rival news conferences.

The Palestinian issue and the question of war or peace are intimately linked. Jordanians and others have been arguing that acceptance of the Palestinian demands by the other Arabs would amount to blocking all chances of peace because Israel will not deal with the Palestinians.

But significantly, the Palestinian delegation joined the majority in rejecting an amendment, proposed by Iraq, that would have barred the new Palestinian entity from entering into Arab-Israeli talks for a negotiated Middle East settlement. Iraq and Libya form the "rejection front" that is opposed to any peace talks involving Israel.

U. S. Is Implicated

A leading member of the Palestinian delegation strongly stated the willingness of the over-all guerrilla organization to join the quest for a negotiated settlement. "With the kind of support we got here and a strong resolution in the United Nations Assembly next month, we can go to the Geneva conference or any other place where a Mideast settlement is discussed," the delegate told a reporter.

The United States was implicated openly for the first time today in the controversy between Jordan and the Palestinians.

The spokesman for the Jor-

Continued on Page 3, Column 1

Associated Press
President Ford and two of the civil rights leaders with whom he met yesterday at the White House: Vernon E. Jordan Jr., center, of the National Urban League, and the Rev. Jesse L. Jackson of Operation PUSH.

Fossils in Ethiopia Said to Show Man As Million Years Older Than Believed

By Reuters

ADDIS ABABA, Ethiopia, Oct. 25—Anthropologists said today that they had found fossilized human remains three million to four million years old that, they predicted, would revolutionize thinking on the origins of man.

Members of a joint American-French-Ethiopian expedition held a news conference to show parts of jawbones discovered this month in the central region of Ethiopia, near the Awash River.

Preliminary dating indicates the fossils may be as much as 1.5 million years older than those discovered by the American anthropologist Richard Leakey on the shores of Lake Rudolf, in Kenya. These were said to be the oldest relics of humans.

The latest finds consist of a complete upper jaw with all the teeth in place, half of an upper jaw and half of a lower jaw, both with teeth.

The expedition was led by Dr. Karl Johanson, an anthropologist from Case Western Reserve University and the Cleveland Museum of Natural History, and Dr. Maurice Taieb of the French Scientific Research Center.

A statement by the expedition said: "These specimens clearly exhibit traits which must be considered as indicative of the genus homo. Taken together they represent the most complete remains of this genus from anywhere in the world at a very ancient time. All previous theories of the origin of the lineage which lead to modern man must now be totally revised. We must throw out many existing theories and consider the possibility that man's origins go back to well over four million years."

The statement recalled that discoveries from Lake Rudolf and from Olduvai Gorge, in Tanzania—where Mr. Leakey's father, the late Dr. Louis S. B. Leakey, the archeologist, made historic fossil finds—had taken man's earliest remains back to over two million years. Two years ago Richard Leakey presented a manlike skull from Lake Rudolf that he said was 2.6 million years old.

The New York Times/Oct. 26, 1974
Fossils were found near an Ethiopian river (1). Earlier finds were at a lake in Kenya (2) and a Tanzanian gorge (3).

The finds in Ethiopia are "perhaps the most provocative human fossils ever discovered on the African Continent," the statement said, adding, "It is certain that anthropologists from all over the world will meet these discoveries with extreme controversy and amazement."

It said the location of the finds suggested the "revolutionary postulate" that human origins lay outside Africa—Richard Leakey maintains that Africa was the cradle of humankind—but it conceded that this idea would be greeted with extreme skepticism.

Wealth of Recent Finds

If further study confirms that the fossils found in Ethiopia are indeed what their discoverers have asserted, they should prove to be of considerable significance in understanding how man evolved.

In recent years scientists

Continued on Page 12, Column 6

BLACKS TELL FORD HE WEAKENS LAW

But the President Reassures Leaders Who Criticize His View on Busing

By JOHN HERBERS
Special to The New York Times

WASHINGTON, Oct. 25—A group of black civil rights leaders told President Ford in blunt language today that his recent public statement on the Boston school violence had the effect of encouraging whites to violate the law.

Mr. Ford replied that he understood their concern and promised there would be full enforcement of the civil rights law that makes it a Federal crime to interfere with court-ordered school desegregation.

The exchange of views, as reported by the black leaders and an aide to the President, occurred at a meeting in the Oval Office that "senior statesmen" of the civil rights movement had requested with Mr. Ford to impress their views on him.

Gratified at Meeting

Although Mr Ford made no further promises to them, the leaders expressed gratification that for the first time since 1968 they were able to meet on a regular basis with the President. They said Mr. Ford had assured them that more such meetings would be held. Mr. Ford and black members of Congress have also met since he took office on Aug. 9.

The statement at issue was one Mr. Ford made at a news conference on Oct. 9 in which he said, "I deplore the violence that I have read about and seen on television." But he added: "The court decision in that case, in my judgment, was not the best solution to quality educa-

Continued on Page 17, Column 2

Air Force Fires ICBM Successfully From Plane

Launching of Minuteman Is Regarded as Step Toward Developing Missile With Mobility on Land and in Air

By JOHN W. FINNEY
Special to The New York Times

WASHINGTON, Oct. 25—The Air Force, in a step toward development of a strategic missile with mobility in the air and on land, has successfully test-fired for the first time an intercontinental ballistic missile dropped from an airplane, the Defense Department announced today.

A Minuteman 1 missile, normally launched from an underground silo, was fired yesterday after being dropped from a C5A transport flying at 20,000 feet over the Pacific Ocean off the Southern California coast.

A New Concept

The 78,000-pound missile, mounted on a carriage, was pulled by drogue parachutes out of the rear door of the huge transport. Held upright by parachutes, it fell to 8,000 feet before its engines were ignited. The engines burned for 10 seconds, carrying the missile to 20,000 feet, before they were turned off, letting it fall into the ocean.

A Pentagon spokesman said the test was successful. With its carriage, the missile weighed 86,000 pounds, the largest object ever dropped from an airplane. One purpose of the test was to study the stability of a plane when it drops such a heavy object.

The test was part of a potentially revolutionary concept being pursued by the Air Force—the development of a mobile intercontinental ballistic missile that could be launched from an airplane, from truck or railroad cars on the ground, or from underground silos.

In part, the concept springs from at least a theoretical concern that the present generation of fixed land-based missiles in their underground silos may become vulnerable to the larger missiles with multiple warheads, known as MIRV's, being developed by the Soviet Union.

The Navy already has a force of mobile missiles that are invulnerable from attack in the Poseidon missiles, which are mounted on nuclear submarines.

The concept of a land-air mobile missile, however, is being pushed, partly for political reasons, in an attempt to get the Soviet Union to agree on a halt to development of mobile intercontinental missiles.

Funds May Be Sought

A Pentagon spokesman said it was coincidental that the test firing came on the day Secretary of State Kissinger arrived in Moscow to resume discussions with Soviet leaders on future limitations on strategic arms. He pointed out that the test pro-

Continued on Page 8, Column 1

JURY HEARS SIRICA SAY DEFENSE DID 'GOOD JOB' ON DEAN

Says He Thinks Lawyers Succeeded in Portraying Role of the Witness

MOVE DRAWS OBJECTION

Judge Appears to Regret the Remark, Saying That He Expressed No Opinion

By LESLEY OELSNER
Special to The New York Times

WASHINGTON, Oct. 25 — Judge John J. Sirica caused something of a furor today on the 19th day of the Watergate cover-up trial with a remark about John W. Dean 3d, the prosecution's chief witness.

In the presence of the jury, Judge Sirica asked a defense lawyer if he was trying with his questions to make Mr. Dean appear to be a liar.

Without waiting for a reply, the judge then remarked that he thought all the defense lawyers had done a "pretty good job."

The judge appeared to regret his remark as soon as he made it, and seemed to amend his comments as he went on, limiting them to the fact that the defense lawyers had brought out to the jury Mr. Dean's admitted participation in the Watergate case.

Thus, Judge Sirica's entire statement was as follows: "I think you have done a pretty good job, all of you—that he has admitted his participation in this alleged cover-up case."

'Expressed No Opinion'

Later, after lawyers for the prosecution put an objection on the record and asked the judge to make a statement to the jury that would erase any possible damage, Judge Sirica told the jurors that they were the "sole judges" of the case.

He told them that though judges in the Federal courts were permitted to comment to the jurors on the evidence, it was not his practice to comment.

"Thus I have expressed no opinion regarding this witness or his testimony, and I will express no opinion," he said.

But the court record of a bench conference held after Judge Sirica made his remark shows that the prosecution lawyers, led by James F. Neal, had wanted the judge to make a somewhat stronger statement to the jury.

According to the court

Continued on Page 17, Column 4

Kissinger Discusses Arms With Brezhnev Five Hours

By BERNARD GWERTZMAN
Special to The New York Times

MOSCOW, Oct. 25 — Secretary of State Kissinger and Leonid I. Brezhnev, the Soviet Communist party leader, met for more than five hours today and talked almost exclusively about putting further curbs on each side's arsenal of offensive strategic weapons.

A brief communiqué issued at the close of tonight's session said that the two men regarded the exchange of views as "useful" and would continue discussions tomorrow, Mr. Kissinger's final day in the Soviet capital. He will leave for New Delhi early Sunday on the second leg of his three-week trip to more than a dozen countries.

Officials from both sides declined to go into details on today's discussions, which lasted two hours 45 minutes in the morning and two and one-half hours tonight. They limited themselves to saying that Mr. Kissinger, Mr. Brezhnev and their aides "gave detailed consideration to matters related to possible further measures on the further limitation of strategic arms."

An American spokesman added that the atmosphere had been "very friendly and very cordial," in keeping with the tone set in yesterday's first day of talks, which were devoted primarily to issues other than limiting strategic arms.

The noncommittal nature of the joint statement shed little light on whether Mr. Kissinger had made much progress with the "fairly concrete ideas" that reporters were told he had brought with him from Washington on how to accelerate the talks on limiting strategic arms.

Mr. Kissinger hopes to get the Russians to accept certain concepts that could be announced by the time President Ford and Mr. Brezhnev hold their first meeting, widely believed here to be all but set for next month somewhere in the Far East.

These ideas are more

Continued on Page 11, Column 3

Miss Furtseva Dies

Yekaterina A. Furtseva, the only woman in Soviet history to become a member of the ruling inner circle of the Communist party, died in Moscow yesterday of a heart attack. Miss Furtseva was Minister of Culture from 1960 to her death. Page 34.

World Fish Supply Too Depleted to Fill Needs of the Hungry

By HAROLD M. SCHMECK Jr.
Special to The New York Times

WASHINGTON, Oct. 25—New England haddock has been a staple of American fish markets since Colonial days. Today the fish are so scarce that stocks are endangered and commercial fishermen are forbidden to seek them anywhere off the East Coast.

There used to be a large-scale sardine fishery off California. Today California sardines are commercially extinct. There are a few left, but so few that it is not worth putting to sea after them.

This is another in a series of articles on the world food situation.

Herring have virtually disappeared from the North Sea and the Atlantic coast of Europe. Fishermen learned all their migration points and systematically fished them out.

Such is the reality behind the popular conception of the teeming seas as a source of limitless food for the world's hungry humans.

In various ways mankind is already putting unprecedented strain on the resources of the seas and showing these resources to be finite. The impetus has come from expanding population, the world's increasing need for food and, in the case of some nations, from affluence.

The lure of large-scale sun-

Continued on Page 24, Column 3

Unemployment Up Here Despite Decline in State

By MICHAEL STERN

Unemployment worsened sharply in the city in September while it was easing in the suburbs and in the state as a whole, the State Department of Labor reported yesterday.

The jobless rate for the city rose from 7 per cent in August to 7.4 per cent last month, and the number of people out of work increased by 7,000 to 231,200.

In contrast, the rate fell from 4.9 per cent to 4.5 per cent in Nassau County, from 6.2 per cent to 5.6 per cent in Suffolk County, from 4.5 per cent to 4.2 per cent in Westchester County, from 5.2 per cent to 4.8 per cent in Rockland County and from 6.3 per cent to 6.1 per cent in the state as a whole.

Economists with the department said the continuation of the high rate of unemployment here was another indication of the relative weakness of the city's economy. While all the suburban counties had rates below the 5.8 per cent national unemployment rate for September, the city's figure was 1.6 per cent higher.

The acuteness of the job situation here has been apparent since April, when the state agency revised its method of computing unemployment to make it conform with the method used by the Federal Department of Labor, and found that city unemployment rates were significantly higher than national rates.

Still another indicator of the relative weakness of the local economy is the September total for employment.

The number of people working in the city fell by 54,300 to 2,903,300, compared with 2,957,800 in September, 1973. The September-to-September fall in the summer jobs is more than triple the average rate of monthly declines all through 1973.

Commenting on the new figures, Herbert Bienstock, head of the New York office of the Federal Bureau of Labor Statistics, said the worsening of the city's rate probably reflected the return to the job market of recent college graduates who were unable to get work in June.

"The city is the center, you might call it 'the big apple,' of the professional job market for the state and the region," he said, "and the inability of young people to find a place in this market shows that there are worms at the core of the

Continued on Page 43, Column 6

REGENTS TO ALLOW APPEALS ON BUSING

Parents Can Contest Orders if Lower-Quality Education or Pupil Danger Is Seen

By IVER PETERSON
Special to The New York Times

ALBANY, Oct. 25—The State Board of Regents issued a statement on integration policy today that, for the first time, gives parents a procedure for challenging an integration busing order if they believe the bus ride would endanger their children's health and safety or lower the quality of their education.

Manifestly sensitive to the expected charges that the new statement represents a dilution of the Regents' past support for busing, the board devoted four pages to quotations from past position papers favoring integration as the ideal for a multiracial society. Not until the fifth and last page are the new restrictions on busing spelled out.

The long-awaited statement, hammered out in unusually lengthy meetings over the last three days, was attacked by Dr. Kenneth B. Clark, the board's only black member. Dr. Clark said the document "panders to the primitive fears and racial prejudices of the majority of the American people."

Although Chancellor Joseph W. McGovern maintained that

Continued on Page 64, Column 2

G.M. Profit Slumps By 94% in Quarter

The announcement of gloomy figures from the auto industry continued yesterday as the General Motors Corporation, the No. 1 auto maker, reported that its earnings for the third quarter plummeted 94 per cent from the same period of 1973. Its earnings for the first nine months of the year were the lowest in 16 years.

The net for the quarter was the second lowest since World War II. The corporation lost $77.1 million in the 1970 third quarter due to a two-month strike by the United Automobile Workers union.

The report came a day after the corporation announced the indefinite layoff of 6,000 more workers and as the Ford Motor Company and the Chrysler Corporation also announced layoffs and cutbacks caused by the severe sales slump in which the industry finds itself.

Details, Page 41. An article on layoffs at G.M.'s plant in North Tarrytown, N. Y., appears on Page 33.

NEWS INDEX

Associated Press
CALDER'S 'FLAMINGO' DEDICATED IN CHICAGO: Release of many balloons marked ceremony yesterday in the plaza of the Federal Center. Alexander Calder, sculptor of the steel work, attended. Works by Marc Chagall and Picasso are on sites nearby.

"All the News That's Fit to Print"

The New York Times

LATE CITY EDITION

Weather: Partly sunny today; mild tonight. Fair and warm tomorrow. Temp. range: today 68-85; Friday 73-89. Highest Temp.-Hum. Index yesterday: 80. Details on Page 44.

VOL. CXXIV ... No. 42,666 NEW YORK, SUNDAY, NOVEMBER 17, 1974

$1.00 beyond 50-mile zone from New York City, except Long Island. Higher in air delivery cities.

60 CENTS

Ford Flies to Tokyo Today

United Press International

On the Ginza, welcome signs and U.S. flags suspended from lampposts hailed the visit of President Ford.

Associated Press

Elsewhere in Tokyo, a group opposing the visit staged a demonstration. About 350 marched. Page 12.

DEMOCRATIC PLAN FAVORS CONTROLS IF ALL ELSE FAILS

Party's National Committee Gives Proposal—Decries Ford Economic Policies

By PHILIP SHABECOFF

Special to The New York Times

WASHINGTON, Nov. 16—The Democratic National Committee proposed today a tentative economic program that would open the door for Congressional action on mandatory wage and price controls and fuel conservation as an alternative to the policies of the Ford Administration.

The program, prefaced by a stinging attack on President Ford's leadership, was prepared by the Democratic Advisory Council of Elected Officials, an arm of the National Committee.

Democratic officials within the committee and in Congress cautioned that the program was not their party's final answer to Mr. Ford. The proposals set forth by the council are general and in some cases ambiguous.

Step Toward Unity

But these officials emphasized that the program represented an important step by the party to reach unity on economic policy before the heavily Democratic 94th Congress convenes in January.

Many of the most influential economic policymakers in the House and Senate are members of the Council. So, too, are powerful state and city executives, including Mayor Beame of New York City.

The program was informally cleared with the Democratic leadership of both Houses, according to one member of the council. Perhaps more important, it was worked out in consultation with the American Federation of Labor and Congress of Industrial Organizations, he said.

A recent attack on the Democrats in Congress by George Meany, president of the federation, indicated a potential conflict between the party and organized labor over economic policy. The committee's proposed program is an indication that that conflict can be avoided, the council official said.

G.O.P. Failure Discerned

On the key issue of wage and price controls, the Democrats' paper asserts, "The Republican Administration's failure to apply them equitably in 1971-73 makes it difficult to recommend them now."

However, it adds that "extraordinary increases" in food and fuel costs may be starting another price-wage spiral.

"If so, and if the anti-inflationary steps outlined above are not sufficient to control this spiral, then we would support an across-the-board system of economic controls, including prices, wages, executive compensation, profits and rents," it said. "We would also support creation of whatever governmental monitoring systems are necessary to insure the equitable application of these controls. We do not propose recreation of a system that discriminates against salaried and hourly workers."

The last sentence probably

Continued on Page 37, Column 1

United Press International

President Anwar el-Sadat of Egypt conferring in Cairo yesterday with his top advisers. They are, from left, Lieut. Gen. Mohammed Abdel Ghany el-Gamasy, Army Chief of Staff; Field Marshal Ahmed Ismail, War Minister; Mamdouh Salem, Interior Minister; Ismail Fahmy, Foreign Minister. Mideast tensions were the topic.

Tension in Mideast Stirs Wide Concern; Israel Explains Alert, Citing Syrian Move

Warnings and Uncertainty Are Voiced in the Area and by U.S. and U.N.

Military activity in the Middle East precipitated warnings and expressions of concern yesterday in Tel Aviv, the Arab capitals, Washington and the United Nations.

While tension and talk of war increased during the day, worry about the consequences of recent events was mixed with uncertainty about their meaning. Israel and her Arab neighbors all denied any hostile intent on their own parts, saying that they were merely reacting to the intentions of the other side.

Charge by Syrian

In Damascus, Abdel Halim Khaddam, the Syrian Foreign Minister, said that Israel, which has partly mobilized her reserve forces, was planning an attack against his country. He said Syrian forces were ready and would retaliate "firmly and strongly against any Israeli aggression."

Informed sources said the Syrian armed forces had been placed on a "higher state" of alert.

Newspapers close to the Palestinian guerrillas said in Beirut that an Israeli attack was imminent in southern Lebanon, where the guerrillas have bases.

In Cairo, the Egyptian Foreign Minister, Ismail Fahmy, canceled all previously made appointments for the day and held urgent meetings with the Soviet and American Ambassadors to tell them of his Government's concern.

Meetings in Washington

In Washington, Administration officials held urgent diplomatic consultations with representatives of the nations concerned in an effort to dampen tensions, but officials continued to emphasize that they did not believe an outbreak of fighting in the Middle East was imminent or likely.

The United States was reported to have received assurances from both Israel and Syria that neither intended to go to war—assurances that Administration officials tended to take at face value.

Secretary General Waldheim of the United Nations said he was concerned about develop-

Continued on Page 4, Column 1

Tel Aviv Sees Acts as a Precaution

Special to The New York Times

TEL AVIV, Nov. 16—Defense Minister Shimon Peres tonight described a partial mobilization of Israel's reserves and Israeli movements in the Golan Heights as a response to "unexplained movements" by Syrian forces. He did not amplify.

Statements by Mr. Peres on television and in a meeting with Israeli military correspondents were the first official confirmation by the Israeli Government of a partial mobilization yesterday of the Israeli reserve forces. For 48 hours previously, military censorship here prevented the developments from being officially made public.

The only related news that could clear censorship had references to foreign sources, such as statements by Secretary of State Kissinger that reports of imminent warfare were exaggerated.

[An Arab girl was killed, scores of people were injured and 50 were arrested as riots swept through the West Bank of the Jordan, The Associated Press reported.]

Mr. Peres said nothing tonight about the scale of the call-up. However, the disruption to civilian life was nothing like that on Yom Kippur last year, when Israeli forces were attacked by Egypt and Syria.

The Defense Minister said that the Israelis were viewing these military developments

Continued on Page 5, Column 1

FORD SETS A QUOTA ON CANADIAN BEEF

He Says Retaliatory Move Is Aimed at 'Unjustifiable' Curbs on U.S. Exports

By The Associated Press

WASHINGTON, Nov. 16—President Ford imposed a quota system today on the shipment of beef and pork from Canada, charging that the neighboring nation had erected "unjustifiable import restrictions" against United States products.

The action was in retaliation for quotas set by Canada last August limiting imports of United States-produced cattle and meat.

A White House spokesman said that Mr. Ford's goal in signing the proclamation was "to bring about an end to the Canadian quotas.'

Move Held 'Necessary'

The action came as sources reported that Mr. Ford was also considering lifting all restrictions on domestic sugar production and shifting to a new quota system on United States purchases of foreign sugar.

The President contended that the Canadian meat restrictions "violate the commitments of Canada made to the United States . . . oppress the commerce of the United States and prevent the expansion of trade on a mutually advantageous basis."

He said he deemed it "necessary and appropriate" to impose restrictions on Canadian products "in order to obtain

Continued on Page 56, Column 1

FOOD CONFERENCE, IN LAST DAY, FORMS NEW U.N. AGENCY

130-Nation Parley Approves Organization to Supervise Anti-Hunger Programs

A COMPROMISE ACCORD

Talks in Rome Also Set Up Agricultural-Aid Projects for Poorer Countries

By WILLIAM ROBBINS

Special to The New York Times

ROME, Nov. 16—A new United Nations agency to supervise programs to give the world, and particularly the less-developed nations, more and better food, was approved by the World Food Conference here today.

The new organization, to be called the World Food Council, will have a secretariat in Rome, associated with the Food and Agriculture Organization, but will report to the United Nations in New York.

Though it requires endorsement of the parent organizations, that action is expected to be a formality, considering the worldwide representation at the conference here.

A Key Accomplishment

The new structure represents a key accomplishment of the conference, whose plans it is to help carry out. It was the result of an intricate compromise between underdeveloped and developed nations that was reached in the final session of this 11-day meeting of 130 nations.

Edwin M. Martin, deputy chairman of the American delegation, said that the United States was pleased with the results of the conference.

"This conference was not called to get food to people tomorrow but to lay out a plan of action to prevent the crisis that we have now from recurring," Mr. Martin said.

His apparent allusion was to President Ford's refusal to commit the United States to a million-ton increase in emergency food aid. However, Mr. Martin acknowledged publicly what others have said privately, that "we will probably be giving that much" in additional food aid, but added, "It would not be useful to announce a figure."

As the delegates gathered here Nov. 5, many hoped that pledges of immediate aid for some 460 million people imperiled by hunger would be

Continued on Page 15, Column 1

Carey Plans to Overhaul Mental-Health Operations

By MURRAY SCHUMACH

Governor-elect Hugh L. Carey has decided that dismissal of top officials of the State Department of Mental Hygiene will be only the first step in a sweeping overhaul of a system that has come under heavy attack from voluntary agencies, local officials, community leaders and legislators.

According to those in the field close to Mr. Carey, the Governor-elect intends to reorganize the state's mental-health operations to end the indiscriminate release of mental patients who get little or no aftercare; to build close cooperation between the state and community agencies working with mental patients, and to greatly increase the emphasis on preventive mental-health treatment.

"What I want," Mr. Carey recently told one of his closest advisers, "is a system that will make good mental-health treatment available to every New Yorker as a right, not a privilege."

Although he has not yet decided on details of reorganization, the Governor-elect has planned the outline of top priority changes. According to those to whom he has confided his decisions, they include the following points:

¶No mental patient will be released from a state institution until a place in the community has first been chosen and approved as appropriate for his aftercare. This could lengthen the stays of some patients in state institutions.

¶Far more power, from the

Continued on Page 68, Column 4

New and Surprising Type Of Atomic Particle Found

By WALTER SULLIVAN

Experiments conducted independently on the East and West Coasts have disclosed a new type of atomic particle.

Its properties are so unexpected that there are differing views as to how it might fit into current theories on the elementary nature of matter.

The experiments were done at the Stanford Linear Accelerator in Palo Alto, Calif., by a team under Dr. Burton Richter and at the Brookhaven National Laboratory in Upton, L.I., by a group under Dr. Samuel C. C. Ting of the Massachusetts Institute of Technology.

In a statement yesterday, the two men said:

"The suddenness of the discovery coupled with the totally unexpected properties of the particle are what make it so exciting. It is not like the particles we know and must have some new kinds of structure.

"The theorists are working frantically to fit it into the framework of our present knowledge of the elementary particle. We experimenters hope to keep them busy for some time to come."

Some scientists believe that the new particle will prove to be the long-sought manifestation of the so-called weak force—one of the four basic forces in nature. The others are gravity, electromagnetism and the strong force that binds together the atomic nucleus.

It is also suspected that the particle may be related to a recently developed theory equating two of those forces — electromagnetism and the weak force— as manifestations of the same phenomenon. However, the properties of the newly discovered particle are not those predicted for either

Continued on Page 29, Column 1

The South Africans and Apartheid Today

This is the first of a series of articles on the racial situation in South Africa.

By CHARLES MOHR

Special to The New York Times

JOHANNESBURG, South Africa, Nov. 16 — South Africa is making a sudden effort to improve her tarnished image in the world — but she seems unlikely to make major changes in the fundamental policies that gave her a harsh reputation in racial relations.

In recent weeks the National party Government of Prime Minister John Vorster has undertaken once again to achieve dialogue and improved relations with some of its closest neighbors in black Africa. Embattled at the United Nations in New York, it has also attempted to parry attacks on its apartheid policies by hinting that it would try to move away from discrimination based on color in day-to-day relations.

Speculation and Optimism

At home Mr. Vorster told domestic critics this month to give the country a "six months' chance," adding, "If South Africa is given that chance, they will be amazed at where the country stands in 6 to 12 months' time."

Enigmatic though the words were, his pronouncements and those of other leaders of the National party brought a flurry of speculation and of optimism that the white-supremacy policies — apartheid, or separate development of the races —

Continued on Page 38, Column 1

United Press International

During last year's South African games in Pretoria, black athletes were allowed to swim in the pool of a hotel where only whites had been permitted. But this change in apartheid lasted only as long as the games.

Flanigan Is Dropped

President Ford withdrew the controversial nomination of Peter M. Flanigan to be Ambassador to Spain yesterday. Page 13.

Colleges Fighting Law Opening Files to Students

By EDWARD B. FISKE

Colleges around the country are adopting strategies ranging from the destruction of documents to Congressional lobbying to avoid what they describe as "unintended" and "unethical" consequences of a new Federal law giving parents and students the right to examine school files.

A major objection to the law, which becomes effective Tuesday, is that it seems to require institutions to make available letters of recommendation and other documents that were solicited under a pledge of confidentiality.

The colleges received some hope of a reprieve Friday when Senator Claiborne Pell, Democrat of Rhode Island, chairman of the Senate Education Subcommittee, announced that he was ready to seek legislation postponing enactment of the law pending hearings on the controversial sections.

Supporters of the new legislation, while acknowledging that some of its language needs clarification, remain vigorously opposed to any delay. They see such delay as a disguised means of undermining the law and postponing the enactment of long overdue civil rights.

"A great number of parents and students will be awfully upset if it is delayed," said a spokesman for Senator James L. Buckley, Conservative-Republican of New York, who was the author of the legislation.

At issue is the so-called "Buckley amendment" to the Elementary and Secondary School Act that was signed by President Ford on Aug. 20 in one of his first official actions as President.

The section, entitled the Family Educational Rights and Privacy Act, prohibits Federal funds to any educational institution that "has a policy of denying, or which effectively prevents, the parents of students . . . the right to inspect and review any and all official records, files, and data directly related to their children."

The law requires an institution to hold hearings if a parent, or a student over the age of 18 years, wishes to challenge the content of the student's records. It also restricts the release of file documents to third parties without the consent of the parent or student.

The bill, which was not the subject of formal hearings, was introduced by Senator

Continued on Page 66, Column 3

Today's Sections

Index to Subjects

"All the News That's Fit to Print."

The New York Times.

LATE CITY EDITION
Mostly cloudy, moderate temperature today. Tomorrow mostly cloudy, temperature unchanged.
Temperatures Yesterday—Max., 93; Min., 75

VOL. CXXIV...No. 42,781 © 1975 The New York Times Company NEW YORK, WEDNESDAY, MARCH 12, 1975 Price higher in air delivery cities. 20 CENTS

GULF OIL ACCUSED BY S.E.C. OF HIDING $10-MILLION FUND

Money Was Allegedly Used to Make Illegal Political Gifts From 1960 to 1974

AN EX-AIDE ALSO NAMED

Company Agrees, as Suit Is Filed, to an Order to Bar It From Similar Action

By EILEEN SHANAHAN
Special to The New York Times

WASHINGTON, March 11 — The Securities and Exchange Commission charged the Gulf Oil Corporation today with falsifying its reports to hide the existence of a $10-million secret fund that was used to make illegal political contributions between 1960 and 1974.

The $10-million secret fund is by far the largest corporate political fund that has been alleged to exist by any law-enforcement agency since disclosures of illegal corporate campaign contributions began in 1973, as an outgrowth of the Nixon Administration scandals.

The S.E.C. simultaneously announced the filing of its suit against Gulf, in United States District court here, and the company's agreement to an order against it that will bar it from taking similar illegal actions

Additional Steps

The company will also be required to take some additional steps to determine just how the illegal fund was set up and by whom and to correct its false reports.

The S.E.C.'s complaint also named as a defendant the former head of Gulf's Washington office, Claude C. Wild Jr., who was also a vice president of the company. Mr. Wild has not agreed to a settlement of the charge against him.

In a case brought by the Watergate special prosecutor's office, he pleaded guilty in November, 1973, to contributing illegally $100,000 in corporate funds to the 1972 Nixon re-election campaign. He was fined $1,000.

The S.E.C.'s complaint did not say to whom the illegal campaign contributions had been given. The complaint merely said that "in excess of $10-million in corporate funds" had been channeled to Bahamas Exploration Company, Ltd., a wholly owned Gulf subsidiary,

Continued on Page 9, Column 1

Gas Hunt Plan Is Off

A projected deal for the three metropolitan gas utilities to invest in a hunt for new gas supplies in the Gulf of Mexico was suddenly withdrawn yesterday. Page 43.

The New York Times/Paul Hosefros

Assembly Majority Leader Albert H. Blumenthal, standing at left, and Minority Leader Perry B. Duryea, right, at what was to have been a joint session of the Legislature yesterday in Albany. However, members of the Senate refused to attend, and the election of three new members of State Board of Regents was postponed several hours.

DEMOCRATS NAME THREE AS REGENTS

G.O.P. Senators Boycott Vote and Assembly Republicans Denounce 'Rump' Session

By MAURICE CARROLL
Special to The New York Times

ALBANY, March 11—Three Regents were chosen tonight by a tired and grumbling Legislature at a session boycotted by Republican Senators and denounced as a "rump" meeting by Assembly Republicans.

With the Republicans refusing to take part, the Democrats made the only nominations and then proceeded to elect Jorge L. Battista, deputy borough president of the Bronx, for the Manhattan-Bronx district; Mary Alice Kendall, a member of the West Irondequoit school board, for the Rochester-area district, and Louis E. Yavner, a Manhattan lawyer, for an at-large seat.

Court Action Foreseen

Democrats cast the only votes for those nominated to the 15-member board, which sets educational policy for the state. Earlier in the day, the Republicans had supported a slate consisting of Dr. Rhoda L. Lorand, a Manhattan psychologist, for the Manhattan-Bronx district; Janet W. Richardson of Painted Post, for the Rochester area, and Dr. Gaetano L. Vincitoria, a St. John's University professor, for the at-large assignment.

The Republican leader of the Assembly, Perry B. Duryea of Montauk, L.I., said that unnamed citizens had assured him that they would go to court to upset the election. A majority of the Senate was not there in the Assembly chamber, he said, "and we cannot—we cannot—participate in a sham."

The squabble was precipi-

Continued on Page 26, Column 1

Egypt Wants New Accord To Include Pledges of '74

By HENRY TANNER
Special to The New York Times

ASWAN, Egypt, March 11—Egypt has suggested that a new disengagement agreement with Israel in Sinai contain some of the language used in the first such agreement, in January last year, Egyptian officials indicated here today.

In that agreement, Egypt and Israel formally pledged scrupulous observance of their cease-fire. They promised to "refrain from all military and paramilitary action" from the moment of the signing of the document.

While putting no time limit on their promise not to take military action, they stated that the document was not a final peace agreement but a first step toward a durable peace in keeping with resolutions of the United Nations Security Council and within the framework of the Geneva peace conference.

The Egyptians have also suggested that a new disengagement agreement include naval units in the Mediterranean and the Red Sea so as to give both sides protection against being outflanked at sea, the officials indicated.

These points were believed to be at the core of the proposals or ideas submitted to Secretary of State Kissinger by President Anwar el-Sadat here Saturday. But officials here today declined to discuss details of the meeting.

The Egyptians appear to be taking the position that the phrasing of last year's document was so clear and definitive that it should meet Israel's demand for guarantees against the eruption of a new war. They seem to think that the absence of a time limit combined with the suggestion of progress toward peace under the resolutions of the United Nations should enable the negotiators to get around the block that has appeared as a result of public statements on both sides.

The Israelis have been asking for a no-war pledge of several years. The Egyptians have been saying that any such assurances must be linked with progress toward peace.

Egyptian officials here frequently point out that the

Continued on Page 4, Column 3

Common Market Gives Easier Terms to Britain

By ALVIN SHUSTER
Special to The New York Times

DUBLIN, March 11 — The heads of government of the Common Market countries reached agreement tonight on easier terms for Britain in the nine-nation community.

After two days of bargaining in Dublin Castle, Prime Minister Harold Wilson completed his bid for "fundamental renegotiation" of Britain's terms of entry in the European Economic Community. The bargaining involved substantial difficulty for the heads of government who gathered here to try to head off a British withdrawal and the disintegration of the Market.

With concessions on lower budget payments to the Market, Mr. Wilson was now ready to return to London to call a special Cabinet meeting to decide on his Government's recommendations to the British electorate. It will vote in June in a referendum on remaining inside the community.

A Protest Vote Possible

A majority of the Cabinet and Mr. Wilson are now expected to urge the people to vote "yes" on remaining in the community. But there is no certainty that the British will go along with the recommendation, given the widespread unease in the country over British membership and a vocal opposition to it.

Recent polls showed that the vote may well be close. The latest estimated that less than half of the British people were in favor of belonging to the Market.

Moreover, there is the prospect that British voters would use the referendum as a vote of protest against high prices and other economic ills rather than to demonstrate their true feelings on Europe. This is a fear that haunts British offi-

Continued on Page 8, Column 1

FIGHTING PICKS UP IN SOUTH VIETNAM

Battle Over Ban Me Thuot Remains Undecided—Attacks Widespread

By JAMES M. MARKHAM
Special to The New York Times

SAIGON, South Vietnam, Wednesday, March 12—As fighting picked up sharply across South Vietnam, the battle for Ban Me Thuot in the Central Highlands remained undecided this morning after the Government brought in three battalions of rangers from the north of the city, military sources said.

The arrival of the 1,200 rangers was believed to have almost doubled the size of the defending garrison of regular troops and militiamen.

One informant in touch with the beseiged city said that last night was "quieter" than the night before, though street fighting persisted.

New Thrust Is Seen

This morning a South Vietnamese military source said that a new thrust against the city appeared to be developing from the northwest, with some North Vietnamese tanks and troops clashing with some Government defenders on the outskirts of Ban Me Thuot.

Government and North Vietnamese artillery units were said to have exchanged fire yesterday while frightened civilians hid in their houses. According to one account, a Government spotter plane with a loudspeaker hovered over the city warning residents not to venture outside lest they be mistaken for invaders.

The Saigon command said that North Vietnamese troops, who twice reportedly penetrated the heart of the city Monday supported by tanks,

Continued on Page 12, Column 3

Lon Nol Shuffles Cabinet And Ousts Chief of Forces

He Asks Premier to Form a New Government—Little Change Seen

By DAVID A. ANDELMAN
Special to The New York Times

Associated Press

Premier Long Boret

The New York Times

Gen. Sosthene Fernandez

PHNOM PENH, Cambodia, March 11—President Lon Nol removed the commander of Cambodia's armed forces today and asked the Premier to form a new Cabinet.

The changes were announced by the President in a radio broadcast tonight after days of Cabinet-level meetings and political maneuvering. Cabinet changes were not immediately disclosed by Premier Long Boret, but no major surprises were expected.

Military Situation Grim

The President's announcements were seen as gestures toward the Cambodian insurgents and toward leaders of the United States Congress who have called for replacement of Marshal Lon Nol and his entire Government. But the moves may also be partly attributable to a power struggle within the army and the Government.

However, the formation of the new Cabinet and the installation of the new armed forces commander is likely to produce little real change either in the Government or in the immediate military picture, which continued to show no improvement today on any front.

In his brief radio address, Marshal Lon Nol gave no clue to the composition of the new Government except that he and Premier Long Boret would remain. But he did announce that the military commander, Gen. Sosthene Fernandez, had been removed and Lieut. Gen. Saksut Sakhan had been named chief of staff. General Sosthene Fernandez's position as commander has been eliminated.

The governmental changes seem unlikely to have any major impact on either the Cambodian insurgents or the United States Congress.

The insurgents have named seven "criminals" who they say must be "hanged" before any

Continued on Page 12, Column 1

Lisbon Says It Foiled Coup After Attack on Loyal Unit

By The Associated Press

LISBON, March 11—Two air force training planes attacked an artillery barracks today in what officials said was an attempted coup against Portugal's left-wing military Government.

Loyal officers said reactionary elements were behind the uprising and that the Government was in complete control of the situation.

[One soldier was reported to have been killed and many wounded, some seriously, according to reports from Reuters news agency. A military spokesman said on Portuguese television that the soldier had died during fighting at an artillery barracks on the outskirts of Lisbon. Planes bombed and strafed the barracks and paratroopers tried to storm them. Another soldier interviewed on television said that at least 10 of his comrades had been injured in the attack.]

Brig. Gen. Otelo de Carvalho, chief of security forces, hinted that he believed the United States was involved. He told Portuguese reporters that the United States Ambassador, Frank C. Carlucci "had better leave after what happened today." He added that he could not guarantee Mr. Carlucci's safety.

Mr. Carlucci issued a statement that said: "I have full confidence that Gen. Otelo de Carvalho and the Government of Portugal are capable and have the intention of insuring my security." [In Washington, the State Department denied any involvement.]

[The leader of the revolution in Portugal last April, Gen. António de Spínola, arrived in Spain with his wife and 18 officers who fled with him, The Times of London reported. They were detained by authorities there, and the Spanish Foreign Ministry denied any involvement in the events in Lisbon.]

Military units took up posi-

Continued on Page 2, Column 4

SENATE UNIT BACKS COMPROMISE PLAN ON CAMBODIAN AID

Surprise 4-3 Vote Favors Administration Proposal for $125-Million Arms

JAVITS SHIFT IS THE KEY

House Panel Splits, 3-3, on Alternative Offering Help in Limited Installments

By JOHN W. FINNEY
Special to The New York Times

WASHINGTON, March 11—A Senate Foreign Relations subcommittee, in a surprise vote of 4 to 3, approved a Ford Administration compromise today to provide $125-million in additional military aid to Cambodia.

A House Foreign Affairs subcommittee, meanwhile, split by 3 to 3 on a proposal to provide $45-million a month in emergency military aid to the Lon Nol Government. Each installment would be dependent upon a Presidential certification that good-faith efforts were being made to achieve a negotiated settlement.

The original Administration request had been for $222-million in supplemental aid to see Cambodia through the dry-season warfare.

The Senate subcommittee's action—and to a lesser extent that of the House subcommittee—gave at least a temporary reprieve to the Administration in its uphill struggle to win Congressional approval.

According to the Administration, without the additional assistance, largely in ammunition, the Government would fall to the Communist-led insurgent forces within a matter of weeks.

Humphrey Was Confident

Though the Administration was winning some support at the subcommittee level, Democratic and Republican leaders still felt it to be extremely doubtful that the House of Representatives, and the Senate, but with less doubt, would approve any additional military aid.

The Senate subcommittee action came after its chairman, Senator Hubert H. Humphrey, Democrat of Minnesota, had gone into the closed-door meeting confident that even the compromise would be defeated.

The swing vote, according to subcommittee members, was provided by Senator Jacob K. Javits, Republican of New York. He had been wavering, and the White House was lobbying with him intensively.

Senator Javits said after the two-hour meeting that he had decided to vote for the aid because he believed "that is the more likely course to bring about an orderly transition of government."

Basically, he explained, he

Continued on Page 12, Column 3

Fossil of Giant Winged Reptile Is Found

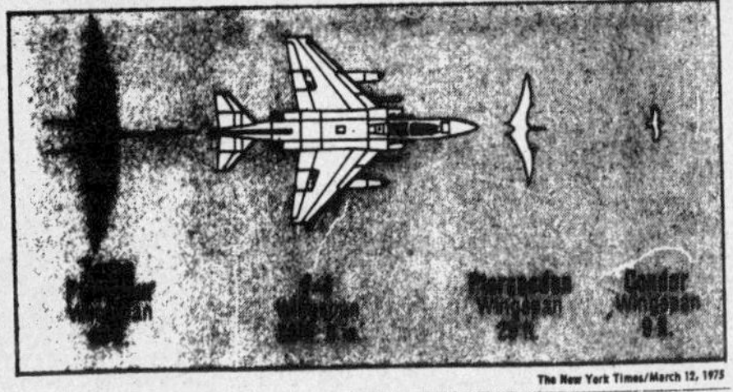

The New York Times/March 12, 1975

By BOYCE RENSBERGER

The largest known creature ever to have flown, an extinct winged reptile with an estimated wingspan of 51 feet—the length of an IRT subway car—has been discovered by fossil hunters in Texas.

The animal, which lived something more than 60 million years ago, had twice the wingspan of the biggest previously known pterodactyl, or winged reptile, and nearly six times the wingspan of the condor, the largest flying bird now alive.

The estimated size of the creature is derived from calculations based on the sizes of many fragmentary and some complete bones found in excavations during the last three years in Big Bend National Park in Brewster County, Texas.

Announcement of the discovery, in the March 14 issue of Science, is expected to rekindle a half-century-old debate among paleontologists over whether flying reptiles flapped their featherless, leathery wings like birds or merely climbed up onto high perches and leaped into the air currents to soar like gliders.

One scientist familiar with the discovery said that the great size of the newly found creature might make it seem improbable to some experts that it was able to rise into the air under wing power alone. He noted, however, that because no one had any reliable estimate of how much winged reptiles weighed, it was virtually impossible to calculate their aerodynamic properties.

The fossils were found by Douglas A. Lawson, a graduate student at the University of California at Berkeley, who began searching in the Big Bend

Continued on Page 11, Column 2

NEWS INDEX

United Press International

Soldiers and civilians in a trench in front of a Lisbon artillery barracks that was attacked by two training planes

"All the News That's Fit to Print"

The New York Times

LATE CITY EDITION

Weather: Sunny, warm today; fair tonight. Partly cloudy tomorrow. Temp. range: today 68-85; Sunday 63-83. Highest Temp.-Hum. Index yesterday: 75. Details on Page 57.

VOL. CXXIV . . No. 42,908 — © 1975 The New York Times Company — NEW YORK, THURSDAY, JULY 17, 1975 — Price higher in air delivery cities. — 20 CENTS

KISSINGER ASSAILS WARNING BY CAIRO ON U.N.'S MANDATE

Says Threat Not to Renew Term of Force in Sinai Disrupts Peace Effort

MOTIVATION UNCERTAIN

Rabin Feels Egyptian Move Could Undermine Accord on Separation of Troops

By BERNARD GWERTZMAN
Special to The New York Times

WASHINGTON, July 16—Secretary of State Kissinger said today that Egypt's threat not to renew the mandate of the United Nations peace-keeping force in Sinai was "extremely unfortunate" and complicated American efforts to bring about a new Egyptian-Israeli agreement.

Speaking at a news conference in Milwaukee before flying back to Washington from a Middle West visit, Mr. Kissinger seemed exasperated by the Egyptian move, which he said had come as a surprise to the United States.

Top officials were consulting here all day on the significance of the ambiguously worded letter from Foreign Minister Ismail Fahmy yesterday to Secretary General Waldheim.

Mandate Expires July 24

The letter seemed to leave open a possibility of keeping the approximately 4,000-member United Nations force in place beyond the July 24 expiration only if an accord was reached before then or if the United Nations Security Council adopted a resolution—certain to be rejected by Israel—demanding an Israeli withdrawal from all Arab territories occupied since the war of 1967.

[In Jerusalem Premier Yitzhak Rabin warned that Egypt's threatened refusal to renew the United Nations mandate could jeopardize negotiations on a new Sinai accord and undermine the existing disengagement agreement. Page 4.]

Secretary of State Kissinger and his aides were worried that Cairo's letter on the mandate issue could make it more difficult for Premier Rabin to obtain wide support for the concessions required for an accord on Sinai.

It was particularly troublesome, one official said, because the letter was made public at a time when the Kissinger me-

Continued on Page 9, Column 1

United Press International

NEW SAUDI KING VISITS EGYPT: King Khalid being welcomed to Cairo yesterday by President Anwar el-Sadat on his first trip abroad as a monarch. Page 8.

Lisbon Dissolves Coalition After 2d Key Party Quits

By HENRY GINIGER
Special to The New York Times

LISBON, Thursday, July 17—Portugal's military rulers dissolved the coalition Government today, hours after the withdrawal of the second of the nation's two moderate parties.

The armed forces ended the coalition after the desertion of the centrist Popular Democratic party, which followed by less than a week the withdrawal of the Socialist party from the coalition.

The armed forces leaders are now expected to form a military Cabinet with civilian technicians. This was the alternative to governing alone, with the Communist party as their ally. Military men had already occupied most of the posts in the outgoing Government.

The dissolution was not surprising. The withdrawal of the Popular Democrats signified a widening of the breach between the armed forces and the exponents of parliamentary democracy.

Two Popular Democratic ministers will be leaving the Government. They are Joaquim Magalhaes Mota, who was Minister Without Portfolio, and Jorge Sa Borges, who headed the Social Affairs Ministry.

Mr. Sa Borges had hesitated about joining the Socialists in opposition to the military because he feared such a move could foster civil war. But after a 2½-hour meeting with President Francisco da Costa Gomes

Continued on Page 3, Column 5

Navy's Estimates on F-18 Found $1.6-Billion Short

By JOHN W. FINNEY
Special to The New York Times

WASHINGTON, July 16—The Defense Department has concluded that the Navy, which was under instructions to come up with a "low-cost fighter," has understated by at least $1.6-billion the long-term cost of its program to build a new carrier plane.

The finding, contained in a secret "issue paper" made available by Navy sources, introduces a new complication in the Navy's announced plans to buy the F-18 as its "low-cost fighter" for modernizing carrier squadrons in the nineteen-eighties.

One alternative would be to raise the projected Navy budget over the next five years to accommodate the increased costs of the F-18 program. But this solution would be difficult for the Navy, which already finds itself $2-billion short on the projected costs of its shipbuilding program over the next five years.

Another alternative—and one raised by the Defense Department—would be to scrap the F-18 program and have the Navy go back to industry to design a lower-cost fighter that would fit within the Navy's original budget. This alternative might not be too unacceptable to the admirals, who were never enthusiastic in the first place about building the F-18.

Under pressure from both the Defense Department and Congress, the Navy in May announced that it had selected the F-18 as its lightweight, low-cost fighter for the future rather than the F-16 chosen by the Air Force.

The twin-engine F-18 is a version of the plane unsuccessfully entered by the Northrop Corporation in the Air Force competition for a lightweight fighter. Northrop then teamed up with the McDonnell Douglas Corporation, which will build the carrier version of the F-18, to win the Navy competition.

The Navy at that time estimated that each F-18 would

Continued on Page 21, Column 2

Associated Press

RARE FIND IN CHINA: A figure of a warrior, one of about 6,000 life-sized pottery figures of warriors and horses found near Sian, in northwest China. The statues are believed to memorialize Chin Shih-huang, founding emperor of Chin dynasty, 221-207 B.C., and were said to constitute one of the rarest finds anywhere in the world.

NEWS INDEX

PAY PLAN CHANGED FOR POLICE RAISES

Beame Says Funds Will Come From City Expense Budget Rather Than Borrowings

By FRED FERRETTI

In reversal of one of the city's traditional bookkeeping "gimmicks," Mayor Beame announced yesterday that the long-delayed raises for 23,000 policemen would be paid with $31-million from last year's expense budget rather than with borrowings from the current capital budget.

"Under the law, we could have charged these to judgments and claims [in the capital budget]," Mr. Beame said, "but I didn't want to do that. I want to avoid borrowing wherever possible."

Controller Harrison J. Goldin, who on Tuesday said that based on Budget Bureau procedures the salary increase would come from current capital-budget funds set aside for such salary adjustments, said yesterday that he was "delighted the method's being changed." He said Mr. Beame had called him early in the morning to tell him "they've changed direction and so we'll follow it."

Taxes are Discussed

In another fiscal turnaround yesterday, the Mayor indicated through a spokesman that he had "no intention of twisting arms" to persuade an increasingly reluctant City Council to support $32-million worth of nuisance taxes that he proposed early this week as a way of restoring the jobs of 2,100 laid-off workers.

Paying normal operating costs, such as salaries and salary increases, with money from the capital budget has been one of the city's budgetary procedures that has been severely criticized by the financial and investment communities.

The state legislation creating the Municipal Assistance Corporation has as one of its provisons the gradual withdrawal of all expense-budget items from the capital budget which is primarily concerned with capital construction and main-

Continued on Page 15, Column 1

BEAME WEIGHING A CITY PAY FREEZE TO AID BOND SALE

M.A.C. Said to Be Facing Difficulty in Placing Its Next $1-Billion Issue

By STEVEN R. WEISMAN

Mayor Beame, under pressure from members of the Board of Estimate, told them yesterday that he would consider imposing a freeze on municipal wage increases as a step toward restoring the confidence of investors who had refused to lend the city any more money.

Word that Mr. Beame had agreed to a possible freeze came last night after reports that the Municipal Assistance Corporation, which was set up to raise the $3-billion the city needed this summer, was heading toward failure to sell its own bonds.

The Mayor's agreement followed a series of unusual developments during the day that saw what one City Hall source said was an open revolt by the Board of Estimate members, who charged that both Mr. Beame and Controller Harrison J. Goldin had not been keeping the others abreast of the city's deteriorating fiscal position.

Sharp Exchange

A prolonged breakfast meeting with the Mayor at Gracie Mansion, according to an official, produced a heated exchange after which the Board of Estimate met in an unusual session—without Mr. Beame—in the office of Council President Paul O'Dwyer.

A spokesman for Mr. Beame, reached at Gracie Mansion last night, declined to comment on the idea of a wage freeze except to say that "the subject did come up" at a second meeting between the Mayor and Board of Estimate members toward evening.

"The Mayor says he would prefer to reserve comment on that question until he meets with Big Mac," said the spokesman, Sidney J. Frigand, referring to a meeting scheduled for today with the directors of the Municipal Assistance Corporation.

The idea of a wage freeze—which would mean rolling back a 6 per cent increase that city employes were due to get on July 1—raised several questions that various officials could not answer.

Some Doubts

It was not clear whether Mr. Beame had the authority to impose a freeze without authorization from the Legislature. Nor was it clear how much money could be gained from it, nor whether such a freeze would cover retroactive increases won in court recently by the Patrolmen's Benevolent Association.

The deliberations took place yesterday as it became known

Continued on Page 16, Column 1

Vote on Sex Bias

The House, by one vote, forbade the Department of Health, Education and Welfare to spend money to enforce the sex integration of physical-education classes. The action could weaken sex-discrimination regulations going into effect Monday. Page 30.

Moscow Is Buying Wheat From Two U.S. Concerns

Cook Industries Sells 73 Million Bushels and Cargill 44 Million—Current Value of Deals Would Be $470-Million

By WILLIAM ROBBINS
Special to The New York Times

WASHINGTON, July 16—The Soviet Union has agreed to buy 3.2 million metric tons of wheat, or about 117 million bushels, from two major United States corporations.

The sales were by Cook Industries of Memphis and Cargill, Inc., of Minneapolis. Cook will supply 2 million metric tons, or 73 million bushels, and Cargill 1.2 million tons, or 44 million bushels.

The value of the American sales was not immediately available, but the deals would be worth about $470-million on the basis of current prices of wheat for future delivery and a normal extra charge for delivery to Gulf of Mexico ports. The Russian contracts call for future delivery.

The Cook Industries sale was first announced by the Department of Agriculture, which did not identify the company.

But Edward W. Cook, chairman of Cook Industries, confirmed his company's sale by telephone from the Memphis airport shortly after landing on the last leg of his return flight from Moscow, where he had negotiated the sale.

In a brief statement, he said that the sale allows "for shipment from origins other than the United States."

"While most will probably be shipped from the United States, it is also highly probable that some will be shipped from other grain-producing countries," he said.

Saying that "this transaction was conducted with the full knowledge of the United States Department of Agriculture and the Administration," Mr. Cook continued: "It was personally reported to the U.S.D.A. and the Senate Permanent Investigations subcommittee promptly upon our return to the United States today."

A spokesman for Cargill confirmed tonight its sale of wheat, which was done through a subsidiary, Tradex of Geneva, and said that some of the wheat would be shipped in the summer of 1976. Roy Wallace, the company's director of public relations, said that he could not give more information at this

Continued on Page 39, Column 6

Exxon's Italian Payments Tied to Specific Benefits

By ROBERT M. SMITH
Special to The New York Times

WASHINGTON, July 16—The Exxon Corporation's Italian affiliate made payments, approved by higher Exxon officials, to Italian political parties in order to get specific legislative benefits from the Italian Government.

The payments, tied by amount to particular corporate objectives, such as the interest-free use of excise taxes collected in Italy, were disclosed in a 1972 report by auditors within Exxon. The report was discussed today at a hearing of the Senate Foreign Relations subcommittee on multinational corporations.

The payments to the political parties were camouflaged—for example, by the issuance of vouchers for goods that were never bought. In reviewing the system of disguised payments, the Exxon auditors at one point suggested that if the payments were to continue they could assist by developing "special procedures"—presumably more sophisticated than the use of dummy vouchers.

According to the Exxon audit, one of the reasons for camouflaging the payments was to permit the company to deduct them from its Italian income taxes.

The practice, according to Senator Frank Church, the Idaho Democrat who heads the subcommittee, permits "only one conclusion—the company was practicing a fraud on the Italian Government."

Senator Church also pointed out that the payments to the parties "not only relate to questions that were before the Italian Government, but they track [in time] with the issues

Continued on Page 47, Column 2

Associated Press

Archie L. Monroe of Exxon Corporation testifying.

Canada to Reduce Gas Sent to U.S.

By ROBERT TRUMBULL
Special to The New York Times

OTTAWA, July 16—Exports of Canadian natural gas to the United States will be reduced because of an impending shortage, the Minister for Energy, Mines and Resources, Donald S. Macdonald, announced today.

Mr. Macdonald, commenting in the House of Commons on a report by the National Energy Board recommending restraints on the consumption and export of natural gas, said that the cutbacks would be taken in consultation with Washington to insure that American consumers dependent on Canadian supplies would be protected as far as possible in the new export schedule.

Canadian users of natural gas will also be restricted in expansion of their present con-

Continued on Page 47, Column 2

APOLLO AND SOYUZ SHIFT THEIR ORBITS FOR LINK-UP TODAY

Soviet Astronauts Put Craft on a Circular Course 140 Miles Above Earth

12:15 P.M. RENDEZVOUS

Americans Fire Rockets as They Maneuver to Bring 2 Spaceships Closer

By JOHN NOBLE WILFORD
Special to The New York Times

HOUSTON, July 16—Apollo and Soyuz, two spaceships on separate courses but with one common goal, maneuvered smoothly into new orbits today in preparation for tomorrow's first international rendezvous in space.

The Soviet astronauts, Col. Aleksei A. Leonov and Valery N. Kubasov, fired the Soyuz propulsion system to settle into an almost circular orbit some 140 miles above the earth. The firing came at 3:43 P.M., Moscow time (8:43 A.M., Eastern daylight time).

This put the Soyuz into its prearranged position where it is to orbit passively while the American astronauts steer the Apollo higher and closer, homing in for the planned link-up between the two ships at 12:15 P.M., Eastern daylight time, tomorrow.

Apollo Rockets Fired

A brief firing of the Apollo's small maneuvering rockets at 4:18 P.M. altered slightly the plane and altitude of its orbit, which is now ranging from a low of 108 miles to a high of 143 miles.

The American astronauts—Brig. Gen. Thomas P. Stafford of the Air Force, Vance D. Brand and Donald K. Slayton—plan a series of similar rocket maneuvers tomorrow morning that should bring the two spaceships within direct radio contact over the Pacific Ocean and within sight of each other over Chile.

The docking is to take place about 140 miles over Germany, and will be televised. A short while later, General Stafford and Colonel Leonov are to meet, shake hands and begin two days of joint activities in the linked spacecraft.

No Big Problems Reported

Soviet and American space officials reported that no problems had arisen thus far that would interfere with the rendezvous and docking. The spacecraft were launched yesterday, first the Soyuz from the Baikonur Cosmodrome in Soviet Central Asia and then the Apollo from the Kennedy Space Center in Florida.

At a news conference here, Frank Littleton, the American flight director in charge of maintaining liaison with the Soviet mission control, said:

"We have a good situation going here. Things are going smoothly on both sides."

M. P. Frank, the chief flight director for Apollo, reported that "everything seems to be going well" and that the American astronauts were "working efficiently and in good spirits."

Two mechanical problems, one Soviet and one American, turned out to be minor.

A Soyuz television camera,

Continued on Page 12, Column 8

The New York Times/Joe Traver

AT CAPACITY: The Ashokan Reservoir near Kingston, N.Y. Though city's reservoirs are full, the city is using more water than is safe. Page 26.

THE NEW YORK TIMES

The members of the Apollo-Soyuz crew. U.S. team: Donald Slayton, Thomas Stafford, Vance Brand. Soviet team: Valeriy Kubasov, Aleksei Leonov.

"All the News That's Fit to Print"

The New York Times

LATE CITY EDITION

Weather: Partly cloudy, warm and humid today, tonight and tomorrow. Temperature range: today 73-88; Thursday 73-83. Details on Page 60.

VOL. CXXIV . . No. 42,909 | NEW YORK, FRIDAY, JULY 18, 1975 | Price higher in air delivery cities. | 20 CENTS

U.S. AND SOVIET ASTRONAUTS UNITE SHIPS AND THEN JOIN IN HISTORIC HANDSHAKES

City Will Dismiss 1,434 In Sanitation Force Today

Beame Says Union Fund Is Running Out—Tells M.A.C. He'll Do 'Whatever Is Necessary' to Open Bond Market

By RONALD SMOTHERS

Mayor Beame said late yesterday that 1,434 sanitationmen would be dismissed this afternoon, and that 750 others would have to be laid off at the end of the month because the unusual $1.6-million fund pledged by their union to pay their wages was running out.

John J. DeLury, president of the Uniformed Sanitationmen's Association, urged all union members who still had jobs to report to work as scheduled, and not repeat the wildcat walkout of two weeks ago.

He noted that the union was in State Supreme Court pressing its challenge of any layoffs of garbagemen. "Let the courts decide it," he said.

The layoff announcement was the most concrete development of a day in which municipal officials and outside fiscal experts struggled with the city's seemingly endless financial crisis. Among the other actions yesterday were the following:

¶Officials of the Municipal Assistance Corporation suggested to Mayor Beame that, in addition to a proposed wage freeze, he might have to consider pay cuts for city workers, increased transit fares, and tuition at the City University to restore investor confidence in the corporation's bonds. The Mayor pledged to do "whatever is necessary" to regain access to money-lending markets. [Page 10.]

¶Leaders of municipal unions angrily denounced the proposal to freeze or roll back the 6 per cent raise that went into effect July 1, saying it would be illegal contract-breaking. And lawyers for the politically divided Legislature differed on whether the city or state would have the authority to suspend the raises. [Page 7.]

¶The Mayor said he would announce today the dismissal of more than 30 appointees in "high-level positions," drawing salaries ranging from $18,000 to $33,000 a year. He did not give the names of those to be dismissed, but said the action might save the city $750,000 a year.

The announcement of the layoff of sanitationmen signaled the loss of a gamble taken by the sanitation union on July 3.

Sanitationmen had gone on a two-day wildcat strike to protest the scheduled dismissal

Continued on Page 3, Column 1

Estimate Board Assuming Sharper Role With Mayor

By STEVEN R. WEISMAN

A week ago Mayor Beame was assuring his fellow political leaders that the city's "crisis" had lifted, at least for a while. But within the last 48 hours he has found himself in something approaching a state of siege, faced with demands for drastic steps to bring the city, for the second time in a month back from the brink of possible default.

For the first time in the history of his mayoralty, Mr. Beame was dealing with a Board of Estimate—long-accustomed to docility—acting independently, taking the initiative and to even criticizing the Mayor to his face. Some members of the board questioned, in private, whether Mr. Beame had been sufficiently aware recently of the seriousness of the city's weakening fiscal position.

The focus of the new moves by the Board of Estimate yesterday and the day before was the suggestion—long discussed at City Hall, but never really taken seriously—of freezing municipal wages as a step to impress investors who are refusing to lend money either to the city or to the Municipal Assistance Corporation.

The idea of the freeze emerged Wednesday morning at a sometimes heated breakfast meeting between the Board of Estimate and Mr. Beame. It was later discussed at an informal session held

Continued on Page 8, Column 3

ISRAEL GIVES U.S. NEW PROPOSALS FOR SINAI ACCORD

Plan, to Be Relayed to Cairo, Said to Include an Offer to Pull Back in Passes

Special to The New York Times

WASHINGTON, July 17 — Ambassador Simcha Dinitz of Israel today gave Secretary of State Kissinger the latest Israeli proposals for breaking the deadlocked talks with Egypt on a new Sinai agreement. Americans and Israelis said later that "progress" had been made toward an accord.

The 90-minute session was reported to have covered all major geographic and political points of an accord.

Despite an Egyptian threat not to renew the mandate of the United Nations peace-keeping force in Sinai, a cause of concern here and in Israel, the American mediation efforts still appear to be on the course that seemed charted last week when the first signs of definite progress emerged.

If the Egyptians refuse to allow the United Nations force to be extended, however, the current negotiations are expected to collapse. At this time, this is not anticipated.

Talks Depend on Mandate

Senior officials in Israel said today that the future of the negotiations hinged on whether a way could be found to extend the mandate, which expires next Thursday. An Israeli policy-maker said that the negotiations were "still on track" but frozen.

The official Egyptian view appears to be that Cairo has instilled a sense of urgency into the search for a settlement, but has closed no door that had previously been opened. [Page 3.]

Mr. Dinitz and Mr. Kissinger will meet again tomorrow morning for further clarification of the Israeli position. The new Israeli ideas will then be given to Hermann F. Eilts, Ambassador to Cairo, for relay to Egypt over the weekend.

It is hoped by Americans and Israelis that the latest ideas will be sufficient to persuade the Egyptians to accept a new mandate for the United Nations force, and thereby forestall a bitter debate next week in the United Nations Security Council.

Mr. Dinitz, who brought the

Continued on Page 3, Column 5

Inside the Soyuz spacecraft, astronauts listen to message from President Ford. From left: Valery N. Kubasov, Col. Aleksei A. Leonov, Brig. Gen. Thomas P. Stafford and Donald K. Slayton. Vance D. Brand remained in the Apollo craft.

'GLAD TO SEE YOU'

Crewmen Eat Lunch—Brezhnev and Ford Praise Link-Up

By JOHN NOBLE WILFORD

Special to The New York Times

HOUSTON, July 17—Astronauts of the United States and the Soviet Union united spaceships today and then joined hands in the first international meeting away from earth, a symbolic gesture of the two nations' expressed desire to cooperate in the exploration of space.

The American Apollo made physical contact with the Soviet Soyuz at 12:09 P.M., Eastern daylight time, about 140 miles over the Atlantic Ocean, 620 miles west of Portugal. Then, three and a half minutes later, the two ships achieved a firm link-up.

"We have capture," Brig. Gen. Thomas P. Stafford of the Air Force, the Apollo commander, radioed in Russian to the Soyuz commander, Col. Aleksei A. Leonov.

'Well Done, Tom'

"Well done, Tom, it was a good show," Colonel Leonov responded in English. The two crews, when speaking to each other, use the listener's language.

The Soviet and American crews met face to face more than three hours and two orbits of earth later. The linked spaceships were passing over Amsterdam at the moment.

Peering through the opened hatches into the Apollo's connecting module, Colonel Leonov welcomed General Stafford with the English words, "Glad to see you."

General Stafford, replying in Russian, said:

"A, zdravstvuite, ochen rad vas videt" ("Ah, hello, very glad to see you.")

Commanders Shake Hands

The two astronauts then shook hands through the hatches, an event that would have been all but unthinkable a few years ago when the two nations were rivals in space, as in most other affairs.

General Stafford and Donald K. Slayton crawled into the Soyuz where they presented a gift of flags to the Soviet astronauts, listened to messages from the leaders of their two countries and ate lunch together.

The 16-ton Apollo and 7½-ton Soyuz are scheduled to remain docked for two days, until Saturday morning. During that time, the astronauts will exchange gifts, share meals and conduct some scientific experiments.

The other member of the Soyuz crew is Valery N. Kubasov. The third member of the Apollo crew is Vance D. Brand, who remained in the Apollo during the first crew transfer.

Back on earth, in Moscow and Washington and at the Johnson Space Center here, officials of both nations offered

Continued on Page 12, Column 1

LEVELING IS FOUND IN NATION'S OUTPUT

G.N.P.'s Total in 2d Quarter Seen as Further Evidence of a Waning Recession

By EDWIN L. DALE Jr.

Special to The New York Times

WASHINGTON, July 17—The nation's total output of goods and services was essentially flat in the second quarter, providing further evidence that the recession has hit bottom, the Commerce Department reported today.

Preliminary figures showed that the gross national product, the broadest measure of the total economy, declined at an annual rate of three-tenths of 1 per cent in the April-June quarter, after adjusting for higher prices. This nominal drop in the "real" G.N.P. is within the range of statistical error and means basically that the total output went neither up nor down. The G.N.P. plummeted at a rate of 11.4 per cent in the first quarter and had declined in every quarter since the end of 1973.

There would have been a rise in the second quarter but for a

Continued on Page 41, Column 1

Destruction of LSD Data Laid to C.I.A. Aide in '73

By NICHOLAS M. HORROCK

Special to The New York Times

WASHINGTON, July 17 — The staff of the Rockefeller commission concluded that the chief of the Central Intelligence Agency's testing of LSD destroyed the drug program's records in 1973 to hide the details of possibly illegal actions, commission sources said today.

These sources said that the chief of the program, Dr. Sidney Gottlieb, a 57-year-old biochemist, was personally involved in a fatal experiment in November, 1953, in which the commission has said a researcher was surreptitiously given LSD, a potent mind-altering drug. The researcher, Frank R. Olson, jumped to his death from a New York City hotel room less than two weeks later after reportedly showing symptoms of anxiety.

The Rockefeller commission staff, on the basis of its investigation, concluded that 20 years after Mr. Olson's death, and 10 years after the LSD experiments were purportedly halted, Dr. Gottlieb ordered the destruction of all the records of the program, including a total of 152 separate files, commission sources said.

The record destruction came shortly after other records had been destroyed by Richard Helms, then director of Central Intelligence, these sources said.

Dr. Gottlieb retired from the agency a few months after Mr. Helms left in January, 1973, they said.

The Rockefeller commission previously reported the destruction of records on the LSD experiments, but did not mention Dr. Gottlieb by name. It also reported a program through the Federal Bureau of Drug Abuse Control in which the C.I.A. had arranged to test LSD on "unsuspecting volunteers" in two programs, one in the West and the other along the East Coast.

Staff sources on the Rockefeller commission said this program was also commanded by Dr. Gottlieb.

For a short time after he resigned from the C.I.A., Dr.

Continued on Page 6, Column 1

LSD Report Disputed

Robert V. Lashbrook, a former employe of the Central Intelligence Agency, said he believed Frank R. Olson, a scientist who committed suicide in 1953, had knowingly participated in an experiment with LSD. The statement appeared to contradict the Rockefeller commission's finding that Mr. Olson had been given the drug surreptitiously. Page 6.

A.T.&T. DISCLOSES SAUDI FINANCING

$100-Million, Six-Year Note, Bearing Rate of 8.40%, Is Placed With OPEC Nation

By REGINALD STUART

The American Telephone and Telegraph Company has placed a $100-million note issue with the Government of Saudi Arabia, the giant telecommunications company said yesterday.

The six-year note, bearing a 8.40 per cent interest rate, is the first such financing of its type by A.T.&T., which has traditionally restricted its borrowings to domestic financial markets.

"The private placement relieves some of the demand on the domestic capital market and should make it easier to raise the remainder of the year's financing by Bell operating companies," said a brief A.T.&T. statement that quoted Charles L. Brown, the company's executive vice president and chief financial officer.

Although Mr. Brown's statement made no reference beyond his assertion that the Saudi deal would ease the domestic capital-market situation, A. T. & T. itself has had some problems in the money market. The most recent example was its inability to raise more than $160-million through the exercise of 31.3 million stock-purchase warrants in May. Had they all been exercised, A. T. & T. would have realized about $1.6-billion.

Negotiations for the loan were underway since April, the company said, with the interest rate set on April 29. A.T.&T.

Continued on Page 41, Column 1

United Press International

ROYAL COUPLE ATTACKED IN OKINAWA: Crown Prince Akihito of Japan and Princess Michiko, left, leap back as a fire bomb hurled by a radical explodes before them. The couple were laying flowers at a monument to the war dead, near Naha, when the incident took place. Both escaped unhurt. Two men were arrested. Page 4.

City's Biggest Scofflaw: U.S., at $6-Million a Year

By MAX H. SEIGEL

The Parking Violations Bureau here has disclosed that the biggest scofflaw in the city is the Federal Government, which is running up unpaid bills estimated at $6-million a year.

The problem, according to bureau officials, is that there is very little the city has been able to do about it.

A confidential memorandum being circulated among executives of the city's Transportation Administration the parent agency of the bureau, also says that indirectly the Federal Government, as host to the United Nations, will be responsible for more than $14.5-million in unpaid parking tickets issued to cars with diplomatic and consular license plates.

Explaining the Federal Government's direct responsibility, bureau officals said cars assigned to many of the 77 Federal agencies in the city get 5,000 summonses a month, which, with penalties for nonpayment, add up to $2.7-million a year.

In addition, the officials disclosed, more than 10,000 undercover cars that operate in the city on any given day get 6,000 summonses a month, which add up to $3.3-million a year.

As one official put it, "the F.B.I., the C.I.A., Customs, Treasury, the Drug Enforcement Administration and other agencies have cars registered to fictitious names and addresses. We don't know whether it's an undercover vehicle unless it's towed away. We find out when someone comes to pick it up."

A few months ago, when the city police towed away a half-dozen Federal cars illegally parked, those who came

Continued on Page 29, Column 5

NEWS INDEX

City Proposes to Grant Builders Option of Hiring Own Inspectors

By ROBERT E. TOMASSON

The city's Department of Buildings, with 45 of its 270 inspectors and 15 other employes charged with graft, is planning to seek authorization to give builders the option to hire their own inspectors.

Building Commissioner Jeremiah T. Walsh said that within a month a special board would submit to the City Council amendments to the building code to permit the change in the procedures for new construction.

"We've taken a careful look at the question of whether we're closing the door on one system of graft and just opening another," Mr. Walsh said in an interview. "I don't think we are."

The official said that while he did not want to characterize one group as being more prone than another group to accepting bribes, "it's been said that a $500 or $1,000 bribe to an inspector making $11,000 a year seems like a mighty big hunk of cash."

"I just don't think that's going to be the case with a state-licensed architect or engineer, even though he's hired by the builder," Mr. Walsh said.

"It would have to be a very big bribe for that professional man to jeopardize his career," he added.

Last January, a law giving builders the option to hire their

Continued on Page 29, Column 4

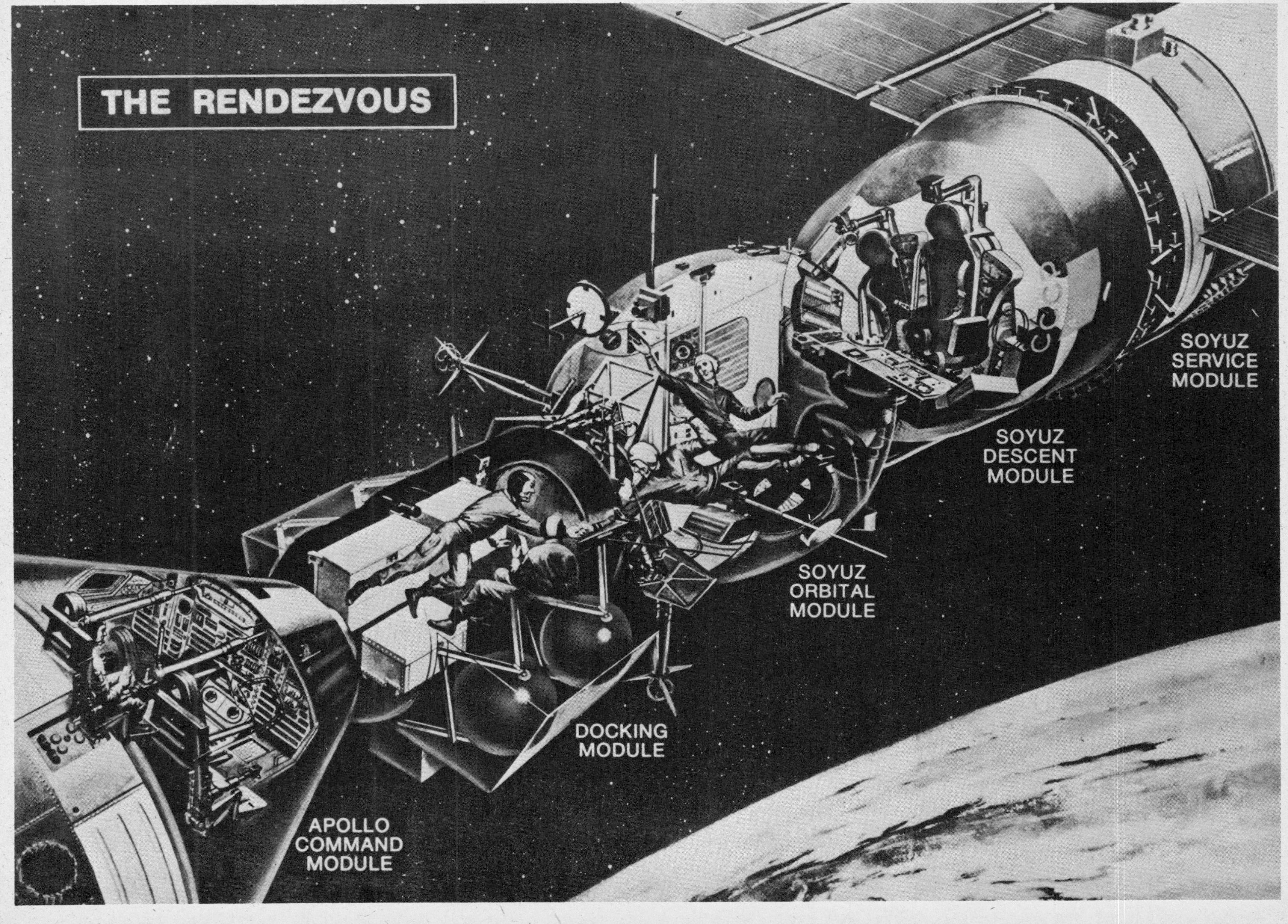
THE RENDEZVOUS
SOYUZ SERVICE MODULE
SOYUZ DESCENT MODULE
SOYUZ ORBITAL MODULE
DOCKING MODULE
APOLLO COMMAND MODULE

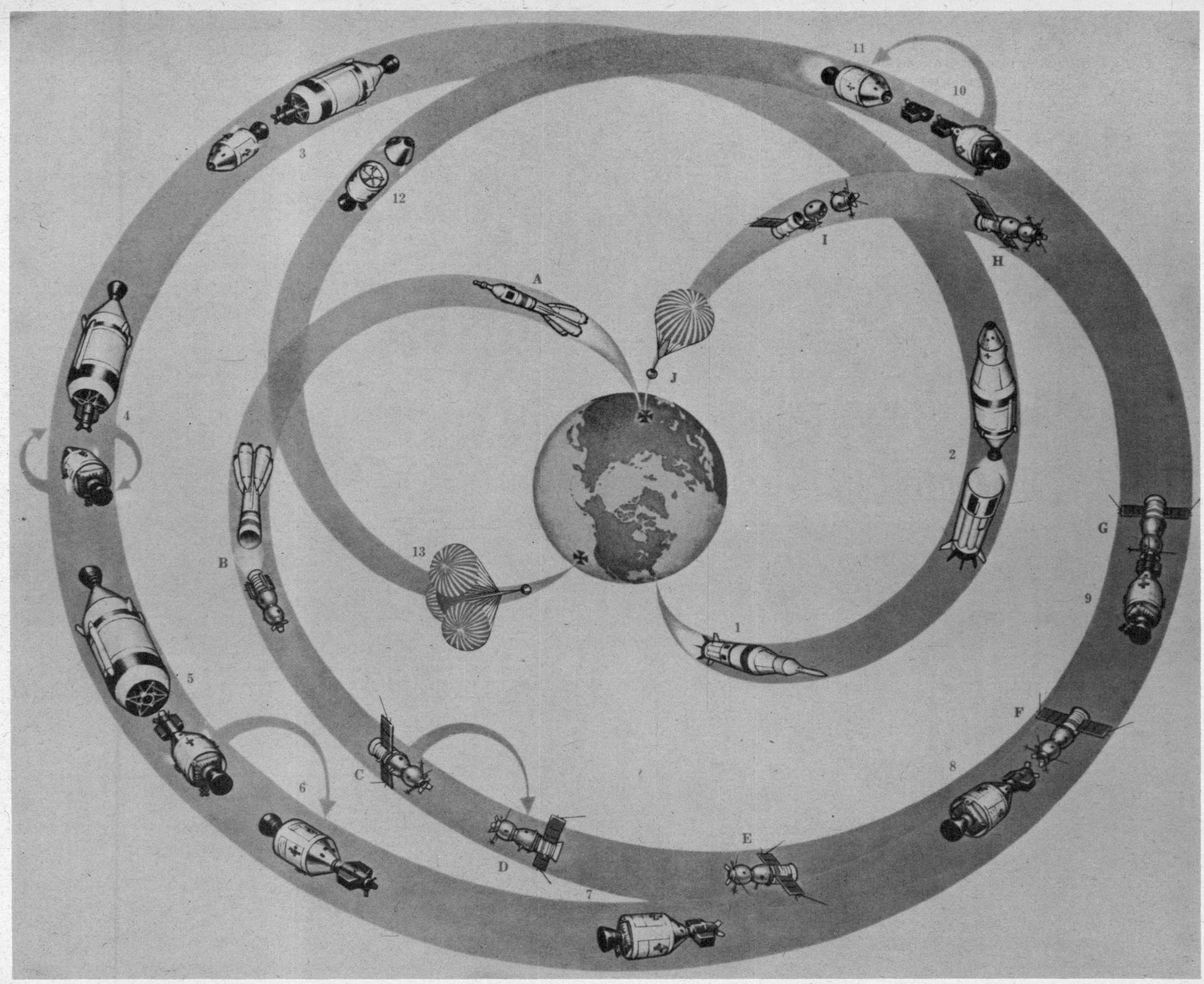

NASA

1 **Soyuz launch.**
Soyuz rockets from the Baikonur launch complex near the Aral Sea in Kazakhstan, U.S.S.R.

2 **Apollo launch.**
About 7½ hours later, Apollo is launched from the John F. Kennedy Space Center on the Atlantic coast of Florida, U.S.A.

3 **Apollo-Soyuz rendezvous.**
Rendezvous occurs about 50 hours after Soyuz launch. The spacecraft dock about an hour later.

4 **Historic meeting in space.**
Astronaut and cosmonaut greet each other with handshake. Two astronauts are in Docking Module. The other is in Apollo Command Module. Both cosmonauts are in the Orbital Module of Soyuz. Descent Module is behind Orbital Module.

5 **Apollo-Soyuz Mission Profile.**

Soyuz

- A Launch
- B Soyuz—launch vehicle separation.
- C Solar panels, that generate electricity from sunlight, unfold.
- D Soyuz turnaround.
- E Soyuz continues to final orbit.
- F(8) Rendezvous.
- G(9) Joint activities.
- H Deorbit.
- I Separation of Orbital, Descent, and Instrument Modules.
- J Descent and landing of Descent Module in Kazakhstan, U.S.S.R.

Apollo

- 1 Launch.
- 2 Separation of Saturn 1B first stage.
- 3 Second-stage separation.
- 4 Apollo turnaround.
- 5 Apollo extracts Docking Module from second stage.
- 6 Apollo turnaround to face in direction of flight.
- 7 Apollo orbit circularization and rendezvous maneuvers.
- 8(F) Rendezvous.
- 9(G) Joint activities.
- 10 Apollo jettisons Docking Module.
- 11 Turnaround and rocket firing for deorbit.
- 12 Service Module jettison.
- 13 Descent and landing of Command Module in Pacific near Hawaii.

"All the News
That's Fit to Print"

The New York Times

LATE CITY EDITION

Weather: Sunny and pleasant today; fair and mild tonight, tomorrow. Temperature range: today 60-78; Friday 67-85. Details on Page 54.

VOL. CXXIV... No. 42,882 — NEW YORK, SATURDAY, JUNE 21, 1975 — Price higher in air delivery cities. — 20 CENTS

Jersey Is Told Budget Gap Will Halt State Operations

Attorney General Warns the Constitution Bars Spending of Any Funds July 1 Unless the Deficit Is Eliminated

By RONALD SULLIVAN
Special to The New York Times

TRENTON, June 20—State Attorney General William F. Hyland warned today that "state government as we know it in New Jersey will stop July 1 unless the Legislature approves a balanced state budget."

At a news conference following an emergency cabinet meeting in Governor Byrne's State House office, Mr. Hyland declared that the State Constitution prevented the administration from spending any funds beginning July 1 unless a $412-million deficit in its $2.8-billion budget was eliminated by then.

The Attorney General's warning followed a similar pronouncement by the Governor, who warned a group of South Jersey officials in Camden this morning that $50-million in state aid to municipalities would most likely end in 10 days unless the Legislature appropriated enough new revenue to eliminate the $412-million deficit.

The Governor is already prepared to cut $257-million from the state's $807-million school-aid program if the budget is not balanced by July 1, the beginning of the new fiscal year.

However, Webster B. Todd, the Republican state chairman, ridiculed the sense of urgency being conveyed by the Governor, particularly since the Democrats in the Legislature took today off to cruise New York Harbor at the invitation of the Port Authority of New York and New Jersey.

He said, "I think it's sickening for the Democrats to tell everyone they are holding a Sunday legislative session to create a sense of urgency while at the same time they are taking a champagne-and-caviar cruise up the Hudson."

The Assembly is scheduled to meet Sunday in a highly unusual session to approve the budget, without any revenue to eliminate its deficit, as the Senate did on Monday. And while there was talk of a compromise package of sales, business and

Continued on Page 14, Column 3

CITY'S PROSPECT FOR ADDING TAXES GAINS IN ALBANY

Compromise With G. O. P. by Carey on Aid for Schools Is Expected to Help

By LINDA GREENHOUSE
Special to The New York Times

ALBANY, June 20—Prospects for additional taxing authority for New York City rose today.

Governor Carey, under growing pressure from his own party to assist in the city's fiscal crisis by compromising with Republicans or a major aid-to-education bill, is expected to propose early next week a statewide increase of about $140-million in aid to schools.

The increase, which is in the range that Republican Senate sources indicated today would be acceptable as a key to giving New York City more taxing authority, will require an appropriation of $35-million in the current state fiscal year.

This is $10-million more than the Governor has insisted for weeks is available in his "fiscal plan."

The Governor is expected to take some pains to explain that the extra $10-million comes from a rate of spending under the current $2.8-billion education formula that is lower than expected, and that it was not artificially found in response to the demands of the Senate Republican majority.

The Final Step

But several of the few people here who are aware of the proposal conceded privately today that the added money did indeed represent an effort by Mr. Carey, after weeks of carefully cultivated noninvolvement with the city fiscal crisis, to put in place the final pieces necessary to resolve the two remaining crucial issues of the legislative session.

For days now the Republicans, led by the Senate majority leader, Warren M. Anderson, have demanded passage of a statewide school-aid package in return for approving new city taxes beyond the level of $150-million.

Originally, the demand was for the Democratic-controlled Assembly to pass and the Governor to sign a specific bill, a $197-million package co-sponsored by Senator Anderson that passed the Senate last month.

This position had softened recently to the point where

Continued on Page 14, Column 2

The New York Times/Tyrone Dukes

Commissioner Michael J. Codd at Police Headquarters. He told officers about operations—such as drives against prostitution, drugs and auto crime—that would be curtailed because of budgetary layoffs of 5,834 members of the department.

CONSUMER PRICES ROSE 0.4% IN MAY AND 9.5% IN YEAR

Figures Indicate Continued Easing in Inflation Despite Increase in Cost of Beef

'REAL EARNINGS' HIGHER

Spendable Income Up 4.4%, a Record, Making Up About All of 12-Month Loss

By EDWIN L. DALE Jr.
Special to The New York Times

WASHINGTON, June 20—Inflation as measured by consumer prices continued to moderate in May, the Labor Department reported today.

Despite a big rise in beef prices and also higher prices for gasoline, the Consumer Price Index last month climbed by only four-tenths of 1 per cent, both before and after adjustment for normal seasonal changes in some prices. It thus reached 159.3 per cent of the 1967 average of 100.

Except for last March—when food prices were falling—this was the smallest rise in the index since July, 1973. The rise from March to April was six-tenths of 1 per cent. For the last three months the index has risen at an annual rate of 5 per cent, a major improvement as against the peak rate of 13.6 per cent reached in the three months ended last October.

Decline in Demand

The slowing of inflation has coincided with a sharp decline in demand and production in the economy and a corresponding rise in unemployment.

In the New York-northeastern New Jersey area the prices of the goods and services bought by consumers rose 0.4 per cent last month, responding to an increase in the prices of meat, women's apparel and medical care costs, according to the United States Bureau of Labor Statistics. [Page 54.]

Nationally, prices were up 9.5 per cent from May a year ago.

While this is a big rise in prices, last month was the first since the beginning of 1974 when inflation, measured as the rise from the same month a year earlier, was not in the "double-digit" category, meaning 10 per cent or more.

Wages rose nearly as much as prices last month, and in addition, paychecks began to reflect the $8.7-billion 1975 tax reduction for individuals voted by Congress. The result was that "real spendable earnings" rose by a record 4.4 per cent, making up nearly all the ground lost over the last year.

Rebates Not Counted

The "real spendable earnings" gain of 4.4 per cent reflected only the reductions in withholding taxes resulting from the 1975 tax cut, not the rebates on 1974 taxes, the distribution of which began last month.

Ron Nessen, the White House press secretary, said President Ford was gratified by the moderation of inflation, but "thinks Congress must act in a responsible way to avoid rekindling" inflationary pressure by adding to Federal spending.

The sharp increase in beef prices—essentially a delayed reaction from last year's poor corn crop—was accompanied by higher prices for pork and poultry. This rise in the meat category was enough to pull up the food portion of the index by five-tenths of 1 per cent, seasonally adjusted, even though many food prices declined. These included sugar, cereal and bakery products (reflecting at last the large decline in wheat prices), dairy products and processed fruits and vegetables.

To economists, the best news in the index came in

Continued on Page 54, Column 1

Giancana, Gangster, Slain; Tied to C.I.A. Castro Plot

By SETH S. KING
Special to The New York Times

CHICAGO, June 20—Sam Giancana, a Chicago crime syndicate leader reported to have been a key participant in a Central Intelligence Agency plot to assassinate Premier Fidel Castro of Cuba in 1961, was shot to death last night in his suburban Oak Park nome.

Shortly after 11 P.M. the Chicago gangster's 81-year-old caretaker found his body on the floor of a small basement kitchen. The police said that Mr. Giancana had been shot seven times in the head and neck with a .22-caliber pistol.

There were no signs of struggle. Oak Park detectives assumed that the killer had entered the basement through an outside stairway and that Mr. Giancana knew him.

An empty wallet lay near the body, but the police also found $1,400 in a money clip in Mr. Giancana's trousers and have discounted robbery as a motive for the killing.

Vincent Inserra, head of the Federal Bureau of Investigation's Organized Crime Squad in Chicago, called the slaying "a professional hit." He speculated that friction between the slain gangster and other Chicago crime leaders was the reason for the murder.

Neighbors reported that they saw two men in dark suits standing on the street outside the Giancana home shortly after 9 P.M.

Later today, James Scannell, Deputy Chief of Police in Oak Park, said that the two had been identified as "law enforcement officials." But he declined to identify them further or to explain why they were there.

The Oak Park police said they now believed that two or three other persons had been in Mr. Giancana's home, but that they had left before 10:30 P.M. when the caretaker re-

Continued on Page 12, Column 1

U.S. Says Russians Now Have Deployed 60 MIRV Missiles

By JOHN W. FINNEY
Special to The New York Times

WASHINGTON, June 20—Secretary of Defense James R. Schlesinger said today that the Soviet Union in the last six months had deployed 60 intercontinental ballistic missiles armed with multiple independently targetable warheads.

Mr. Schlesinger, who said last Jan. 15 that the Soviet Union had begun deploying two new intercontinental missiles presumably armed with multiple warheads, told a Pentagon news conference today that he did not regard the deployment of the 60 missiles as particularly surprising or alarming.

Mr. Schlesinger provided the review of recent Soviet missile developments in a summary of a secret briefing he gave a group of defense ministers of the North Atlantic Treaty Organization earlier this month.

The Secretary also said that the Soviet Union was dismantling some of its older intercontinental missiles as it built up its number of submarine-launched ballistic missiles beyond 740. He said the

Continued on Page 8, Column 3

INQUIRY REVEALS I.R.S. MASTER LIST

House Unit Releases Names of Groups and Persons Kept Under Scrutiny

By EILEEN SHANAHAN
Special to The New York Times

WASHINGTON, June 20—The Mayor of Los Angeles, a member of Congress, a former Ambassador to Britain, a former Attorney General, the American Legion and the American Civil Liberties Union are listed in what appears to be part of a master index of persons and organizations that were under scrutiny by the Internal Revenue Service.

The list was made public today at a hearing by a House Government Operations subcommittee that is looking into improper enforcement activities on the part of Internal Revenue.

I.R.S. officials said that they could not vouch for the authenticity of the document, but they conceded that it appeared to be a genuine copy of a part of the index to a master list of 466,442 names that was kept in an Internal Revenue computer at the Detroit I.R.S. data center.

The master list is part of a computerized data collection and storage system known as the tax agency's Intelligence Gathering and Retrieval System, created in 1973. The operation of the system was suspended earlier this year after disclosures that the files contained much information not related to tax-law enforcement.

Donald C. Alexander, the Commissioner of Internal Revenue, who testified today before the subcommittee, said repeatedly, as he has previously, that he believed it was wrong for Internal Revenue to collect information unrelated to the enforcement of the tax laws.

The system was supposed to

Continued on Page 54, Column 2

Dr. Ray Quits State Dept.; Critical of Kissinger Policy

By BERNARD GWERTZMAN
Special to The New York Times

WASHINGTON, June 20—Dr. Dixy Lee Ray resigned today as the State Department's top science official, charging Secretary of State Kissinger and other high aides with deliberately not consulting her office on key policy matters.

It was the first time in Mr. Kissinger's 21-month tenure as Secretary that a senior official had quit and made complaints public.

But the 60-year-old former chairman of the Atomic Energy Commission has been well known in Washington for speaking her mind, and today, after sending her letter of resignation to Mr. Kissinger, Dr. Ray was no less outspoken in a conversation in her seventh floor suite.

Dr. Ray's irritation seemed directed primarily at being excluded from important policy matters dealing with scientific subjects such as research and development of new energy sources, something she said had been taken over by the department's Office for Economic and Business Affairs with Mr. Kissinger's approval.

Not in 'Inner Circle'

It was also evident from conversations with her and her aides that Dr. Ray believed that Mr. Kissinger had not delegated to her bureau the responsibility it was due by Congressional mandate. Mr. Kissinger has often been criticized for keeping policy decisions confined to a dozen or so top aides.

It is readily acknowledged even by Mr. Kissinger's closest associates that Dr. Ray, while highly regarded professionally, was not a member of the Secretary's "inner circle."

Mr. Kissinger, through a spokesman, said only that he was "sorry" that Dr. Ray was resigning and that he had forwarded the letter of resignation to President Ford, who formally must accept it since he appointed her.

Thomas O. Enders, the Assistant Secretary for Economic and Business Affairs, declined to comment publicly on Dr. Ray's resignation.

Dr. Ray joined the State Department five months ago as the first Assistant Secretary for Oceans and International Environmental and Scientific Affairs. The new bureau was set up by Congress to give added prestige and importance to these matters within the department.

In her letter to Mr. Kissinger,

Continued on Page 20, Column 5

United Press International

Dr. Dixy Lee Ray

Coast City Hails 1937 Soviet Polar Flight

By ANDREW H. MALCOLM
Special to The New York Times

VANCOUVER, Wash., June 20—It took almost four decades, but this little city of 40,000 people put on its best rain gear today to hail a group of aging Russian aviators and dedicate what is believed to be the first monument in the United States honoring an achievement of Soviet citizens.

The occasion was the 38th anniversary of the unplanned landing here of three Russian fliers completing the world's first nonstop airplane flight from Europe to North America over the North Pole, a journey of 5,288 miles.

Two of the fliers—Georgi F. Baidukov, now 69 years old, who was the co-pilot, and Aleksandr V. Belyakov, 78, who was the navigator—attended today's ceremonies. Also attending was Igor V. Chkalov, the 47-year-old son of the late Valery P. Chkalov, the chief pilot.

The achievement, despite hazardous weather and severe navigational difficulties, never received the fame in the United States that Charles Lindbergh did after his trans-Atlantic flight to Paris in 1927. In fact, over the years most non-Russians who had ever heard of the Russians' polar flight probably forgot about it.

But now Vancouver, which also happens to be celebrating its 150th anniversay, is trying to rekindle memories of that accidental landing here through memorial plaques, memorial coins and memorial speeches. The city even named a new

Continued on Page 54, Column 4

Associated Press

Top: Mayor Jim Gallagher of Vancouver, Wash., is kissed by Aleksandr Belyakov at dedication of monument commemorating the 1937 flight on which Mr. Belyakov was navigator. Bust depicts Valery Chkalov, pilot. Center: plane, Stalinist Route. The crew, from left: Mr. Belyakov, Mr. Chkalov and Georgi Baidukov after landing in Vancouver.

State Correction Panel Urged to Resign

By SELWYN RAAB

Declaring that the State Commission of Correction failed to investigate abuses in New York's prison system properly, state investigators yesterday called for the resignations of the remaining four members of the watchdog agency.

In a report, the State Commission of Investigation essentially substantiated charges that officials of the beleaguered prison agency had ignored irregularities and possible crimes by jail authorities.

The S.C.I. said it had found that the correction group had adopted a general policy of a "no action" commission that "was not supposed to rock the boat and not make waves."

Denying the charges, Albert Berkowitz, chairman of the correction agency, said most of his panel's shortcomings had been caused by budget and staff limitations. He said he would not resign unless asked to do so by Governor Carey.

A bill expected to be approved by the Legislature in this session would bring about a major reorganization of the correction commission. It would replace seven part-time commissioners with three full-time commissioners responsible for supervising prison investigations and reviewing grievances.

The investigation commission said that the current correction commissioners had failed to "fulfill their statutory obligations," declaring:

"They have attempted to explain away this failure by claiming their role was only as a citizens' board—despite statutory language to the contrary. It would appear to this commission that such a misconception of their role arose for reasons of convenience rather than conviction.

"Furthermore, using their own standard of acting as a citizens' board, the incumbent commissioners even failed to satisfy the lesser demands of this more modest role."

In the aftermath of the 1971 riot at the Attica state prison, which resulted in the death of 43 persons, the correction commission was severed from the Department of Correction and reorganized as an independent, ombudsman type of agency in January of 1973. The commission was given vast powers by the Legislature to remedy prison complaints, including the closing of substandard institutions.

Last April 10 The New York

Continued on Page 55, Column 4

NEWS INDEX

"All the News That's Fit to Print"

The New York Times

LATE CITY EDITION

Weather: Sunny, warm today; cool tonight. Sunny and warm tomorrow. Temperature range: today 58-82; Wednesday 56-78. Details, Page 78.

VOL. CXXV . . No. 43,006 | © 1975 The New York Times Company | NEW YORK, THURSDAY, OCTOBER 23, 1975 | 25 cents beyond 50-mile zone from New York City, except Long Island. Higher in air delivery cities. | 20 CENTS

Reds Win First Series in 35 Years

By JOSEPH DURSO

Special to The New York Times

BOSTON, Oct. 22—In the final inning of the final game, the Cincinnati Reds finally subdued the rambunctious Boston Red Sox, 4-3, tonight and won the 72d World Series in seven games.

There were two outs in the ninth, the 67th inning played by the teams over a 12-day span, when Joe Morgan singled to center field off the 50th pitcher used in the Series. The hit dropped about 10 feet in front of Fred Lynn while Ken Griffey scored the run that snapped a 3-3 tie. Half an inning later, the big bad "mean machine" of Cincinnati had captured the Reds' first championship in 35 years.

It was the end of a Series filled with new heroes, new geography and even new rivals, and the first ever played between Boston and Cincinnati since the American and National Leagues began grappling for baseball's first prize in 1903. It also was the third time in six years that the Reds had tried to win the Series, and, when they finally did it, they squeaked past an underdog

Continued on Page 51, Column 8

Associated Press

Joe Morgan of the Reds lining a single to center in the ninth to drive in the winning run. Jim Burton was pitching. Behind the plate are Carlton Fisk and Art Frantz, umpire.

CONSUMER PRICES UP 0.5%, HALF RATE OF EARLY SUMMER

September Index 7.8% Over Year Ago—Subway Fare a Factor in Rise Here

By EDWIN L. DALE Jr.

Special to The New York Times

WASHINGTON, Oct. 22—Consumer prices rose five-tenths of 1 per cent in September, more than in August but only half the worrisome inflation rate of early summer, the Labor Department reported today.

Food prices essentially stabilized last month, but increases in many other items, including New York City transit fares, pushed up the index.

The 15-cent increase in bus and subway fares pushed the Consumer Price Index for the New York-Northeastern New Jersey area up by 1.1 per cent in September, the largest monthly increase this year. [Page 29.]

'Basic' Rate of 6%

Several Government officials said the September increase was in line with the present "underlying" or "basic" inflation rate of about 6 per cent. August was below this level, and June and July above it.

The Consumer Price Index for September was 7.8 per cent above September, 1974, the lowest inflation rate for a 12-month period in two years. The last time this measure showed a lower rate of inflation was in September, 1973.

Thus the deepest recession in the economy since the Depression of the nineteen-thirties has had the effect of significantly moderating the "double-digit" inflation of 1974 but has far from eliminated it.

Drop in 'Real' Earnings

For the three months ended in September the index rose at an annual rate of 7.3 per cent.

The rise in prices last month, together with a decline in the average work week, meant another drop in "real" earnings of the average production or nonsupervisory worker last month. The decline was six-tenths of 1 per cent.

The tax reduction of last spring, however, more than offset the decline in real wages so that real spendable earnings, or take-home pay, improved by 1 per cent as against a year ago.

The index stood at 163.6 in September. This means that the same goods and services that cost $100 in 1967 now cost $163.60.

Lower prices for fresh fruits

Continued on Page 29, Column 1

Carey Suspends Lottery Over Duplicate Numbers

Governor Halts Games Pending Inquiry Into Sales of Faulty Tickets Caused by 'Computer Complications'

By ROBERT McG. THOMAS Jr.

Governor Carey ordered the immediate suspension of the state's lotteries yesterday after it was learned that a programing error had caused hundreds of duplicate tickets to be printed for the special $1.4-million jackpot drawing on Oct. 31.

Although lottery officials said hat a computer check indicated that there were no programing errors and no duplicate tickets printed for the regular weekly Double-Up lottery, the Governor's order applied to the Double-Up drawing as well.

There was no indication how many Double-Up tickets might have been sold for today's canceled drawing. But lottery officials said that about 1.8 million of the four million tickets that went on sale Oct. 8 for the Oct. 31 drawing known as the Super Colossus, had been sold before yesterday's suspension order.

There was no indication how long the suspension would last, but the Governor's office said that those who had purchased tickets for the canceled drawings "will be protected." This will be done by a mechanism to be devised, presumably through direct refunds or an exchange for new tickets.

In explaining the suspension, Governor Carey seemed to go beyond the immediate problem of duplicate tickets and to touch on other problems that have plagued the lottery recently.

"The chance odds of the game are substantial enough, and the public should not be subject to inexcusable, unreasonable, incredible lengthening of those odds due to mechanical or human deficiencies," he said.

This was an apparent allusion to recent criticism of the former $250,000 Colossus lottery, which held its last regular

Continued on Page 28, Column 4

AID PLAN FOR CITY, BALKED IN SENATE, GAINS IN THE HOUSE

2 Southern Senators Prevent Committee Session on Bill Pressed by Proxmire

REPRESENTATIVES MOVE

11-2 Vote Agrees to Support Legislation to Help Avoid a Default by New York

By MARTIN TOLCHIN

Special to The New York Times

WASHINGTON, Oct. 22—Congressional action to enable New York City to avert a default suffered a parliamentary setback in the Senate today, but gained support in the House.

In the Senate, Southern opponents prevented the Committee on Banking, Housing and Urban Affairs from meeting to draft legislation while the Senate was in session, touching off a brief but acrimonious debate.

In the House, the Democratic Steering and Policy Committee voted in a closed session to support legislation to avert a default although no specific legislation was endorsed. The vote was 11 to 2, with two members abstaining.

Situation Serious

"It was an overwhelming vote to go ahead," said Representative John J. McFall of California, the Democratic whip. "We felt that the situation is so serious to the country that we have to go ahead."

President Ford, meanwhile, was said to be "irritated" by published accounts of his willingness to sign legislation easing the city's fiscal plight. The White House press secretary, Ron Nessen, again refused, as he had done for several days, to respond directly when asked if the President would veto any such legislation. [Page 31.]

On Capitol Hill, visiting Republican and Democratic leaders of the New York State Legislature expressed vigorous opposition to any increase in state taxes as part of a Congressional package to ease the financial crisis. [Page 33.]

A Reason for Speed

It was understood that the Steering and Policy Committee was eager to get the bill on the House floor so that, at the very least, if the bill failed and New York defaulted, the Democrats could blame President Ford and the Republicans for any ensuing chaos.

However, Representative Thomas P. O'Neill Jr., the House majority leader, said that "at this point in time, I don't read the votes in the House for New York City. If there were a vote today, I would have to say that New York would not prevail."

On the other hand, Representative Phillip Burton of California, chairman of the Democratic caucus, said that he had found "a reluctant facing up to the facts" that had translated into "improved sup-

Continued on Page 31, Column 4

PACT WITH MADRID TO GO TO CONGRESS

State Department, in Shift, Will Submit New 5-Year Agreement for Approval

By BERNARD GWERTZMAN

Special to The New York Times

WASHINGTON, Oct. 22—The State Department will break with precedent and submit for Congressional approval the military, political, economic and cultural agreement with Spain that is close to completion, high Administration officials said today.

Previous accords with Spain, dating from 1953 and renewed periodically, have been regarded by successive administrations as "executive agreements" requiring no Congressional action.

A wide-ranging debate on United States relations with Spain is expected on Capitol Hill.

The decision to seek a formal vote in Congress on the five-year pact, which includes provisions for the continued use by American air and naval forces of Spanish bases, was made before Generalissimo Francisco Franco's latest ill-

Continued on Page 4, Column 4

Franco Said to Gain

Generalissimo Francisco Franco was reported to be recovering from an acute heart ailment, but the question of his remaining in power was unresolved. Page 33.

Peking Atmosphere Chilly As Kissinger Ends Talks

By LESLIE H. GELB

Special to The New York Times

PEKING, Thursday, Oct. 23—Secretary of State Kissinger's four-day visit to China ended last night as it began, with disagreement over Washington's policy of détente with Moscow, but with relations between the United States and China intact.

Mr. Kissinger and Foreign Minister Chiao Kuan-hua exchanged dinner toasts in a somewhat chilly atmosphere.

In the toasts, both men used words that rank near the bottom of the Chinese diplomatic vocabulary: Mr. Chiao referred to the "friendly atmosphere" of the talk between Mr. Mao and Mr. Kissinger, but characterized the other conversations as "frank" and "useful." Similar words were used in the communiqué issued when Mr. Kissinger visited here last November.

Visit For Ford Is Set

Mr. Kissinger, who looked somber, said he was satisfied with the exchanges and indicated that he was alert to danger from Moscow but would nevertheless continue his policy of détente.

Diplomats said a date had been set for President Ford to visit China in the coming weeks, but would not say when. Arranging this visit was the express purpose of the Kissinger trip.

According to American diplomats, the Chinese persisted in the theme that the United States had been appeasing the Soviet Union and was thus risking another world war. Mr. Kissinger was said to have responded that détente was not viewed as a substitute for a strong defense and that détente served as a lever to restrain Soviet expansion.

On Western Europe and Soviet-American talks to limit strategic arms, the Chinese were said to have criticized American policy without offering alternatives. Mr. Kissinger did not ask for alternatives, and the Chinese indicated that their role was simply to alert and not

Continued on Page 9, Column 1

Helms Says Search Of Mail Was Illegal

By LINDA CHARLTON

Special to The New York Times

WASHINGTON, Oct. 22—Richard Helms, Director of Central Intelligence from 1966 to 1973, testified today that he knew then that the agency's mail-opening program was illegal. But he said he assumed that Allen W. Dulles, the intelligence agency's director who started the operation in 1953, had "made his legal peace with it."

Mr. Helms, the only witness this afternoon before the Senate Select Committee on Intelligence, also conceded that a 1970 report to President Nixon that he and others had signed, and that stated that the mail-

Continued on Page 12, Column 3

ELECTION AGENCY SET BACK IN HOUSE

Hays Leads in Defeating Rule to Require Filing of Fund Data With Commission

By WARREN WEAVER Jr.

Special to The New York Times

WASHINGTON, Oct. 22—The House of Representatives killed today a regulation proposed by the Federal Election Commission that would have required members of Congress to file their campaign financial reports with the new agency.

Representative Wayne L. Hays, Democrat of Ohio, who led the fight against the regulation, said that the 257-to-148 vote was a "warning" to the commission "not to be capricious and not to rewrite the law."

This was the second successive loss by the commission in its first two attempts to win Congressional approval for its regulations. Two weeks ago the Senate rejected, 48 to 47, a rule that made members of Congress politically accountable for their office funds.

Supporters of the filing regulation, outnumbered in debate as well as votes, argued that the 1974 campaign finance law clearly required the initial filing of contribution and spending reports with the commission, rather than the Senate secretary and House clerk.

Thomas B. Curtis, chairman of the commission, said he was "disappointed" by the action because the agency believed

Continued on Page 27, Column 1

Football League Folds

The World Football League, beset by financial problems since its inception a year ago, announced it would cease operations immediately. Page 51.

State Phone Rate Increase Of 12 Per Cent Approved

By PETER KIHSS

The New York Telephone Company was authorized yesterday to increase its rates by $297,989,000 annually, or about 12 per cent over current intrastate revenues, in a decision by the State Public Service Commission. The major effect will be on businesses, whose costs may rise 15 to 25 per cent.

The commission rejected a controversial proposal by the company, endorsed by a commission examiner last August, that would have introduced timing of single-message local calls in New York City, Nassau and Suffolk Counties, lower Westchester County and the Buffalo metropolitan area.

The commission said the increased cost would be 34 cents a month on the basic charge for residential customers with only one telephone; this is now $7 in New York City before taxes, and it allows 50 calls. A similar business customer's basic charge, now $11.25 before taxes, will go up $1.04.

The average residential monthly bill in the city before taxes has been $19.79. This could increase more than 34 cents, because the commission approved a reduction in the initial period for multimessage-unit areas from five minutes to three minutes and also cut the initial period for long-distance calls to points within the state from three minutes to two minutes.

Less than half the gross increase of $297,989,000 will go to the company; the rest will be taken by Federal, state and local taxes, whose sum was

Continued on Page 34, Column 1

Parks Agency Plight Epitomizes the City's

By LEE DEMBART

Present and former officials and employes of the Parks Department and outside experts who have studied the agency agree that a complete management overhaul is not just the major way to save money during the city's fiscal crisis, but may also be the only way to keep the city's parks functioning at all.

They paint a picture of archaic work rules, ineptitude, shortsightedness and a "baroque bureaucracy" that combine to keep out new ideas and stymie old ones.

In a sense, they say, the department is a microcosm of the worst of city government: an entrenched Civil Service, a middle management loyal to the workers but not always to management objectives, and a rotating top management, heavy with patronage appointees, that barely has time to implement any plans it may come up with.

Lack of Imagination Seen

Some experts say that what the department needs most is the hardest commodity to come by—imagination. But others say that no amount of thinking or planning or experimenting will prove a match for "The System."

There have been any number of proposals put forward to improve the efficiency and services of the Parks Department, but few have been acted on. To make matters worse, many of the money-saving ideas would cost money to start, though they would save money

This is the 11th in a series on new proposals being discussed or implemented to help the city save money and improve or tighten services as a result of the fiscal crisis.

in the end, and the city is in no position to increase spending now.

In fact, the Parks Department, which officially is part of the soon-to-be-disbanded

Continued on Page 30, Column 2

Soviet Spacecraft Lands on Venus and Sends Back Photo of Rocks

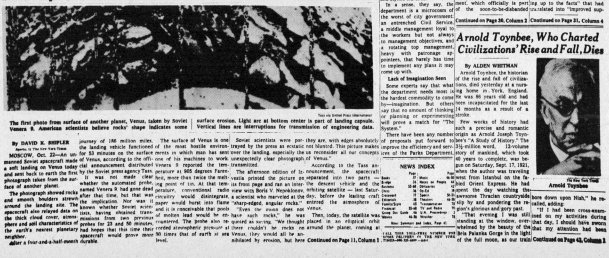

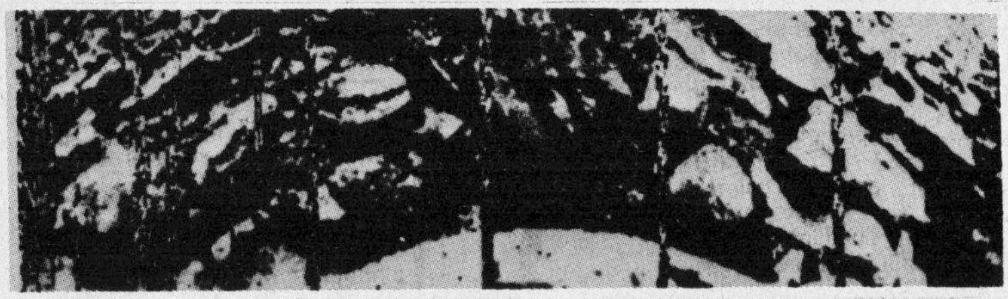

Tass via United Press International

The first photo from surface of another planet, Venus, taken by Soviet Venera 9. American scientists believe rocks' shape indicates some surface erosion. Light arc at bottom center is part of landing capsule. Vertical lines are interruptions for transmission of engineering data.

By DAVID K. SHIPLER

Special to The New York Times

MOSCOW, Oct. 22—An unmanned Soviet spacecraft made a soft landing on Venus today and sent back to earth the first photograph taken from the surface of another planet.

The photograph showed rocks and smooth boulders strewn around the landing site. The spacecraft also relayed data on the thick cloud cover, atmosphere and soil characteristics of the earth's nearest planetary neighbor.

After a four-and-a-half-month journey of 186 million miles, the landing vehicle functioned for 53 minutes on the surface of Venus, according to the official announcement distributed by the Soviet press agency Tass.

It was not made clear whether the automated probe, named Venera 9, had gone dead after that time, but that was the implication. Nor was it known whether Soviet scientists, having obtained transmissions from two previous probes for 23 and 50 minutes, had hopes that this time their spacecraft would prove more durable.

The surface of Venus is one of the most hostile environments in which man has sent one of his machines to work. Venera 9 reported the temperature at 905 degrees Farenheit, more than twice the melting point of tin. At that temperature, conventional radio circuitry would disintegrate, paper would burst into flame and it is conceivable that pools of molten lead would be encountered. The probe also recorded atmospheric pressure at 90 times that of earth at sea level.

Soviet scientists were portrayed by the press as ecstatic over the landing, especially the unexpectedly clear photograph transmitted.

The afternoon edition of Izvestia printed the picture on its front page and ran an interview with Boris V. Nepoklonov, a scientist who marveled at the "sharp-edged, angular rocks."

"Even the moon does not have such rocks," he was quoted as saying. "We thought there couldn't be rocks on Venus, they would all be annihilated by erosion, but here they are, with edges absolutely not blunted. This picture makes us reconsider all our concepts of Venus."

According to the Tass announcement, the spacecraft separated into two parts — the descent vehicle and the orbiting satellite — last Saturday, before the leading craft entered the atmosphere of Venus.

Then, today, the satellite was placed in an elliptical orbit around the planet, coming at

Continued on Page 11, Column 1

NEWS INDEX

Arnold Toynbee, Who Charted Civilizations' Rise and Fall, Dies

By ALDEN WHITMAN

The New York Times

Arnold Toynbee

Arnold Toynbee, the historian of the rise and fall of civilizations, died yesterday at a nursing home in York, England. He was 86 years old and had been incapacitated for the last 14 months as a result of a stroke.

Few works of history had such a precise and romantic origin as Arnold Joseph Toynbee's "A Study of History." The 3½-million word, 12-volume story of mankind, which took 40 years to complete, was begun on Saturday, Sept. 17, 1921, when the author was traveling west from Istanbul on the fabled Orient Express. He had spent the day watching the awesome Thracian countryside slip by and pondering the region's glorious and gory past.

"That evening I was still standing at the window, overwhelmed by the beauty of the Bela Palanka Gorge in the light of the full moon, as our train bore down upon Nish," he recalled, adding:

"If I had been cross-examined on my activities during that day, I should have sworn that my attention had been

Continued on Page 42, Column 2

"All the News That's Fit to Print"

The New York Times

LATE JERSEY EDITION
New Jersey news, Pag 37.
North: Sunny cold today; clear not as cold tonight. Temp. range 30-48. South: Sunny, cool today; partly cloudy, cold tonight. Temp. range 32-52. Details on Page 66.

VOL. CXXV.... No. 43,014 © 1975 The New York Times Company NEW YORK, FRIDAY, OCTOBER 31, 1975 25 cents beyond 50-mile zone from New York City, except Long Island. Higher in air delivery cities. 20 CENTS

Prince Assumes Powers With Franco Near Death

Juan Carlos Named Chief of State to Fill Leadership Vacuum but He Will Not Become King Until General Dies

By HENRY GINIGER

Special to The New York Times

MADRID, Friday, Oct. 31—With Generalissimo Francisco Franco apparently near death, Prince Juan Carlos de Borbón assumed the powers of Chief of State last night in a move that virtually marked the end of 36 years of the general's rule.

The Government decision to fill the power vacuum came after 11 days of waiting as General Franco continued to fight off heart failure and as the conflict over the territory of Spanish Sahara built to a crisis.

The Prince will preside over a Cabinet meeting today in his palace of Zarzuela outside Madrid, to signal the start of his rule and a new era in Spain. He will not be crowned King, however, until General Franco dies. Theoretically, the Prince is assuming power for the time of the general's illness, but nobody in Spain expects any other outcome than the 82-year-old leader's death soon.

A 3-Man Regency

When he dies, a three-man Council of the Regency, headed by the ultraconservative Speaker of Parliament, Alejandro Rodríguez de Valcárcel, will take over power for the time necessary to assemble the Council of the Realm and Parliament for the swearing in of Juan Carlos as King.

The dramatic news that the only ruler most of the Spanish people have ever known was out of power came shortly after 9 P.M., and all radio and television programs were interrupted to broadcast it. The Prince was reported to be in the Zarzuela Palace with his wife, Princess Sophia, at the time. But the decision was believed to have been made final yesterday morning during an hour-long conference between Premier Carlos Arias Navarro and the Prince.

For 11 days the Premier had carried the main burden of decision-making, hurrying to and from the Pardo Palace, where the general lay dying, to conferences with Moroccan officials who had come here to press their nation's claims to the Sahara. A second round of talks ended yesterday with an agreement reported near, but an Algerian delegation was still trying to block it by insisting that the Saharan population be given the right of self-determination.

Sahara Conflict Feared

King Hassan II of Morocco is preparing to lead several hundred thousand of his subjects in a peaceful march into the Sahara, and the possibility of armed conflict has grown daily. A liberation group in the Sahara called Polisario is operating with Algerian support and has vowed to oppose the march and the Moroccan push southward to an area rich in phosphates and other minerals.

The need for a chief of state able to approve treaties and deploy troops as commander of the armed forces became urgent. There were also more routine matters that had piled up awaiting final approval. But for the

Continued on Page 11, Column 5

The New York Times

Prince Juan Carlos de Borbón

At the Helm in Spain

Juan Carlos

Special to The New York Times

MADRID, Oct. 30—Prince Juan Carlos de Borbón, who assumed power "temporarily" in Spain today, comes to his task with a stronger sense of duty than enthusiasm. He is more at ease at the helm of his racing yacht than at a Cabinet meeting and much more expert in sports than in politics.

Man in the News

The 37-year-old Prince exudes physical vigor and health. His tall frame is kept in shape by daily workouts and by horseback riding, yachting, hunting and golf when he can get around to it.

But he was carefully reared and trained to be a king and he has gone through a daily routine of audiences and receptions with grace and charm. What has been lacking has been active and frequent experience in national problems, for he was constantly kept at arms' length and confined to largely ceremonial duties.

People who have talked to him, however, report an awareness of the problems and a desire to get Spain off on a new footing. He has traveled abroad, speaks excellent French and English and has been exposed to the difficulties Spain has had in getting along in the Western world. He is also understood to be aware that much remains to be done before he wins complete acceptance at home.

Aside from the fact that, after 44 years without a king, the country is not especially monarchist, Juan Carlos is facing outright hostility from a broad range of groups who think that the political protégé and the designated successor of Generalissimo Francisco Franco is more or less committed to the system founded after the Civil War.

One of the crosses Juan Carlos has to bear is his father, Don Juan, Count of Barcelona, who considers himself titular head of the royal house and has never formally abandoned his rights to the throne. Don Juan is reserved about his son's capacity to apply and enforce a democratic course for Spain and is expected to wait a while before recogniz-

Continued on Page 11, Column 2

PRESIDENT ASKING $4.7-BILLION IN AID, MOST FOR MIDEAST

Hard Scrutiny by Congress Seen in Light of Ford's Refusal to Help City

By BERNARD GWERTZMAN

Special to The New York Times

WASHINGTON, Oct. 30—President Ford asked Congress today to approve foreign aid of nearly $5-billion for the current fiscal year, an unusually large amount that includes $3.4-billion for Israel and the Arab countries.

The long-awaited $4.7-billion military and support-assistance request would supplement about $1.3-billion in economic and humanitarian aid that is already close to approval by Congress.

In addition, the Administration is asking for aid to international organizations and will allocate about $1.5-billion in food assistance, bringing the over-all foreign-aid program ending next June 30 to approximately $8-billion.

Challenge Is Expected

This large sum is sure to face close scrutiny on Capitol Hill, particularly in light of Mr. Ford's refusal to help New York City. Administration officials and Congressional aides predicted today that the aid bill submitted by Mr. Ford today would run into opposition even though Israel is the single largest beneficiary.

Of the $4.7-billion requested today, 70 per cent was designated for the Middle East, in part as fulfillment of Administration promises to Israel and Egypt during negotiations that led to the recent Sinai agreement.

"I believe the hope for a lasting solution to the Arab-Israeli dispute is stronger today than at any time in the previous quarter century," Mr. Ford said in his message to Congress, made public by the White House today. "A new era also is opening in our relations with Arabs and Israelis. This security assistance program will give substance to those new relationships and help preserve the momentum toward peace."

Three Main Categories

The $4.7-billion was broken down into three categories—$424.5-million in outright military grants for material and training; $2.4-billion in military credits; $1.9-billion in security support assistance, a form of economic aid.

The high points of the request include:

¶A request of $2.24-billion for Israel, of which $1.5-billion would be in military credits and $740-million in economic aid. But $500-million of the military credits would not have to be repaid. Israel had originally sought about $3.3-billion, but

Continued on Page 5, Column 1

SENATE UNIT, 8 TO 5, BACKS LOAN GUARANTEE FOR CITY DESPITE THREATENED VETO

Shanker Doesn't Oppose Aid From Pension Funds

By FRED FERRETTI

Albert Shanker, president of the United Federation of Teachers, who reluctantly and at the last minute consented to the release of teachers' pension fund money that prevented the city's default two weeks ago, said yesterday that he was "not opposed in principle" to a plan that would use city pension funds to guarantee loans and prevent future default.

However, Mr. Shanker said, "It has to be done with a view to the integrity of the funds."

Under the plan, drafted by Herbert Elish, executive director of the Municipal Assistance Corporation, and Jack Bigel, a pension consultant to city unions, the $8.5-billion in assets of the five city retirement systems would be used to guarantee $4-billion in loans. The loans would be used to buy M.A.C. bonds, which would in turn retire the city's short-term debt and ease its recurring cash flow crises.

There was cautious optimism about the plan yesterday as a result of Mr. Shanker's statement, coupled with a similar response from Michael Maye, president of the Uniformed Firefighters Association that "we'll do whatever we can if it's possible," and the earlier tacit approval of the plan by Victor Gotbaum, executive director of District Council 37 of the Municipal Employes Union, one of the architects of the plan.

Even skepticism about the plan's workability and opposition to it from among some banking sources failed to dampen the efforts of its proponents, for the feeling persists among the city's elected officials and among union officials that the plan is preferable as an alternative to the bankruptcy reorganization proposed on Wednesday by President Ford.

Felix G. Rohatyn, chairman of M.A.C., and Governor Carey

Continued on Page 13, Column 1

VOTE HELD FUTILE

But Proxmire Says He Has Seen President Reverse His Stand

By MARTIN TOLCHIN

Special to The New York Times

WASHINGTON, Oct. 30—The Senate Banking Committee approved 8 to 5 today legislation that would provide a $4-billion loan guarantee to prevent default by New York City. It rejected the argument that such action was "futile" because of a threatened filibuster and veto.

"I've seen the President turn around before," said Senator William Proxmire, committee chairman and a Wisconsin Democrat, in pressing for committee approval. "President Nixon turned around on a dime on the subject of price control."

And Senator Harrison A. Williams Jr., New Jersey Democrat, said of Mr. Ford, "There's nothing absolute in his thinking."

"The President promised a veto on mass-transit operating assistance and then worked with us to get a bill out of the House," he added.

Package Planned

In the House of Representatives, meanwhile, Speaker Carl Albert of Oklahoma said that the Democratic leadership was "100 per cent committed to get a guarantee-type of bill." The leadership agreed this afternoon to make President Ford's bankruptcy proposal part of the loan-guarantee legislation, with which it would then be inextricably linked.

The unexpectedly wide margin in the Senate Banking Committee was provided by Senator Bob Packwood of Oregon, the only Republican to vote in favor of the measure.

"I don't think the President and the committee are that far apart," he said.

The other Republicans insisted, however, that the legislation was doomed.

'Exercise in Futility'

"There ain't gonna be no loan-guarantee legislation," said Senator John G. Tower of Texas, ranking Republican on the committee. "It's not going to pass in the first place. The fact of the matter is that New York City is going into default, and there's nothing that we can do to prevent that."

Senator Edward W. Brooke, Massachusetts Republican, who had also opposed the loan-guarantee legislation from the start, added that "the President's speech had made it clear that this is an exercise in futility."

"There is literally no possibility of overriding a Presidential veto," he said.

Senator Brooke failed to

Continued on Page 12, Column 4

City a '76 Issue for Ford; Democrats Doubt Its Value

By R. W. APPLE Jr.

Special to The New York Times

WASHINGTON, Oct. 30—President Ford and his advisers have found what they consider a central and potentially highly productive theme for his 1976 campaign: New York City must pay for its sins, and the rest of the country must learn from New York's errors or be doomed to repeat them.

Having vowed yesterday to veto any Congressional measure designed to help the city to stave off default, Mr. Ford made New York's problems the centerpiece in his political rhetoric in a speech today in San Francisco in which he derided city officials for seeking Federal assistance. [Page 12.]

Democrats do not contest the Republicans' conviction that the President's position reflects the attitude of the electorate as of today. But they are not persuaded that the issue will be drawn next November as it is now, and many of them doubt that Mr. Ford will benefit from New York's troubles.

White House officials are reluctant to admit that the President's hard line grows out of anything more than his deeply ingrained small-town Middle Westerner's belief in fiscal prudence and self-reliance.

But officials at the Ford campaign committee privately acknowledged today that one element in the President's stance was the conviction, as one of them put it, that "what he's saying now will play well on Election Day." They believe, furthermore, that it will help to

Continued on Page 12, Column 1

CAREY MOBILIZING RESPONSE TO FORD

He Calls for City-Unity Rally to Rebut President's Stand —Cheered by Union Aides

By FRANCIS X. CLINES

Angry and combative, Governor Carey yesterday announced that he would soon schedule a citywide demonstration—Operation Alive and Kicking—as a reply to President Ford, a plea for Federal help, and a boost for the city's image and industry.

Later, it became known that the Governor regarded Times Square as an appropriate site for such a rally and had suggested to business leaders Nov. 16 as a tentative date.

Obviously still seething at President Ford's rejection of special help for the city to avoid default, Mr. Carey characterized the Presidential message as "a kick in the groin" to the city.

During the day, the Governor addressed the State A.F.L.-C.I.O. in Kiamesha Lake, N.Y., where he brought 1,500 state

Continued on Page 13, Column 3

In Moroccan March, Sand Stifles Fervor

By HENRY KAMM

Special to The New York Times

TARFAYA, Morocco, Oct. 29—South of Agadir, the joy goes out of the Moroccan march to annex Spanish Sahara, and the sandstorms take over.

By the time the truck convoys carrying thousands upon thousands of volunteers, who by then may have been on the road for 1,000 miles, reach the one-track road that begins at Tantan, where the Sahara meets the Atlantic, what started as a joyride has turned into misery.

For those last 100 miles to the final staging area here, 40 miles from the border, the endless convoys are often stopped to wait out the cruel winds that blind the eyes and choke the lungs with the sands of the desert. They blow turbans loose and make the ends stand out like windsocks in a gale.

The men—there are only occasional truckloads of women in the caravans—cower against the sides of the open trucks and huddle against each other. The cheers with which they greet passing traffic or waving villagers in greener parts of the country turn sour on this final stretch, and the marchers' waves perfunctory.

Halfway between here and Tantan a truck overturned yesterday, and its passengers, apparently uninjured, crouched pathetically in its upended bed or lay face down in the desert to present a minimal target to the winds. Accidents are not rare, but help arrives quickly.

The logistics of this unprecedented movement, which is to put 350,000 people from every province of Morocco into marching order here within the next 10 days, are a miracle of planning and organization. They attest to the thoroughness of the preparations for this innovative attempt at peaceful annexation.

Planning and organization were particularly striking today, when three busloads of foreign journalists were brought to the staging camps on an officially sponsored visit. The enthusiasm that greeted them was as care-

Continued on Page 4, Column 5

Troubled Oil Men Blaming Government for Problems

By JAMES P. STERBA

Special to The New York Times

HOUSTON, Oct. 30—From their luncheon tables at the Houston Petroleum Club atop the Exxon Building, oil and energy executives look with wrinkled brows these days over booming Houston, the self-proclaimed "energy capital of the world."

They are not happy men.

Two years after the Arab oil embargo, they are not—as most had hoped—leading their companies and the nation into massive new energy development projects, for the benefit of both. Instead, they are leading an industry that has never, they assert, been more uncertain and troubled.

In the aftermath of the embargo, while the country continues to debate its energy course, the captains of the energy industry contend they remain handcuffed by the lack of a national energy policy, hamstrung by Federal controls, hounded by environmentalists, picked at by politicians, misunderstood by the press, and distrusted by almost everybody else.

Their efforts to find and produce offshore oil, to mine Western coal, and to build nuclear power plants continue to be delayed, insuring a larger and longer dependence on imported oil to meet the nation's growing energy needs.

These three alternatives to imports are technologically feasible and economical, they say. But even if governmental and environmental obstacles were cleared immediately, energy from these sources could not be generated fast enough—

Continued on Page 43, Column 1

This is the third of five articles examining the energy situation two years after the Arab oil embargo.

Agnew Denies Guilt

Former Vice President Spiro T. Agnew, in an interview in Crofton, Md., again denied that he had been guilty of anything except the single count of income-tax evasion to which he had pleaded no contest. Page 42.

Man Traced 3.75 Million Years By Fossils Found in Tanzania

By BOYCE RENSBERGER

Special to The New York Times

WASHINGTON, Oct. 30—Fossil evidence that true man had evolved and lived in East Africa by almost 3.75 million years ago, nearly a million years earlier than had been previously established, has been found in Tanzania by Dr. Mary Leakey.

Dr. Leakey, widow of Louis Leakey, the archeologist, said at a news conference here today that she had found the jaws and teeth of at least 11 creatures that appear to belong to the genus homo, the scientific classification that includes modern man, homo sapiens.

Although pre-human creatures, some perhaps transitional between ape and man, have been found in older fossil deposits, Dr. Leakey's new discoveries are said to be the oldest reliably dated examples of true man. Most experts consider that some of modern man's ancestors, though less advanced than homo sapiens, should be regarded as true man.

The fossils were found in a region called Laetolil, a remote, semi-arid place 25 miles south of Olduvai Gorge, where the Leakeys have made many spectacular fossil discoveries over the last two decades.

Laetolil, a local tribal name for the area, was first explored by Louis and Mary Leakey in 1935, but they found nothing other than the remains of extinct animals. Last December, however, Dr. Leakey returned to the area and found spe-

Continued on Page 43, Column 1

NEWS INDEX

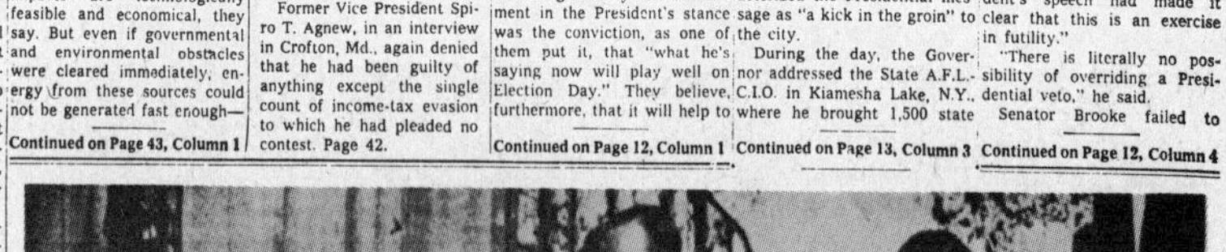

The New York Times/Tyrone Dukes

Governor Carey, seated, at the meeting at which he announced plans for a demonstration. Standing, from left, are Mayor Beame, Kenneth S. Axelson, Deputy Mayor for Financial Affairs, and David Rockefeller, chairman of Chase Manhattan Bank. Mr. Carey sharply criticized the President.

"All the News That's Fit to Print"

The New York Times

LATE CITY EDITION

Weather: Humid, thundershowers likely today through tomorrow. Temperature range: today 67-80; Sunday 66-84. Details on page 58.

VOL. CXXV .... No. 43,248 NEW YORK, MONDAY, JUNE 21, 1976 25 cents beyond 50-mile zone from New York City, except Long Island. Higher in air delivery cities. 20 CENTS

2,800-Year-Old Fortress Is Discovered in Sinai

By TERENCE SMITH

Special to The New York Times

KUNTILLET AJRUD, Israeli-Occupied Sinai — On this lonely, isolated hill overlooking a vast and empty desert plain, an Israeli archeological team has discovered an ancient Judean fortress containing a rare collection of Hebrew and Phoenician inscriptions dating to about 800 B.C.

The inscriptions were discovered on pottery and the plaster walls of a remarkable 2,800-year-old fortress apparently built by King Jehoshophat of Judea to protect the Solomonic route to the port of Elath and the rich Red Sea trade lanes to the biblical Ophir.

The inscriptions are considered doubly significant because several refer to "Jehovah," the traditional name of God that the ancient Jews wrote rarely because it was so extremely sacred. It is the largest collection of eighth century B.C. inscriptions ever found at a single site.

The site itself had been discovered in the 19th century by a Briton who drew erroneous conclusions from what he found.

Clues From Inscriptions

Some of the inscriptions are still being deciphered at Tel Aviv University and the Israel Museum in Jerusalem. But Zeev Meshel, the archeologist who headed the dig, has reached some tentative conclusions. The more provocative include the following:

¶The fortress is the southernmost and westernmost Judean site ever discovered. It stands at a crossroads between the ancient Gaza-Elath route and a track leading to the southern Sinai region. To Mr. Meshel, this suggests that effective control of the Judean kingdom of the period extended much farther south and west than had previously been believed.

¶Mr. Meshel believes that the Judean kings probably passed this way as they headed for Elath, which, according to the Bible, King Solomon developed as a major port for the Red Sea trade. The existence of this fortress raises the possibility that others like it may lie undiscovered on the Gaza-Elath route.

¶The Phoenician inscriptions on the walls are evidence that some Phoenicians passed this way, again probably going to Elath, then known as Etzion Geber. In the Book of Kings, the Bible records that Solomon made a pact with the Phoenician King Hiram of Tyre to provide Lebanon cedars to build Solomon's Red Sea fleet.

The Phoenician inscriptions found here tend to support the speculation that the ships were actually assembled in what is now Lebanon, were sailed down the Mediterranean to a point near Gaza, broken down there into sections and then hauled across the desert by the shortest route to Elath, which passes Kuntillet Ajrud.

"The theory makes sense," Mr. Meshel said at the site. "We can't prove it by what we have found here, but there was no wood in Elath to build the ships, and it is a fact that later in history the Crusaders hauled ships in sections across the desert in order to surprise their enemies in the Gulf of Elath."

The inscriptions at the site are unusually poetic and religious, leading Mr. Meshel to conclude that the fortress had some sacred tradition associated with it. He stops short of calling it a temple because of its design, but the rich ornamentation, the extensive plastering over the stone-and-mud walls, altars and benches suggest strongly that there was something special about the place.

"It could have been built to commemorate the religious tradition associated with the Sinai," Mr. Meshel said during a break in the digging. "Even in those days, the Jews knew the biblical stories of the wanderings of the children of Israel in the desert, the accounts of Moses receiving the Commandments on Mount Sinai. Those things had happened 400 or 500 years earlier. Perhaps the Judean kings wanted to commemorate that tradition."

Quality of Ancient Life

One inscription, carved on the rim of a stone bowl, has a more topical reference. It reads, in ancient Hebrew: "May Obadyo, son of Adnah, be blessed by God." Mr. Meshel believes this may refer to the Obadyo—or Obadiah — mentioned in Chronicles as the commander of King Jehoshaphat's army at the time.

In addition to the inscriptions, the archeologists discovered beautiful drawings. One shows a cow nursing a calf, another depicts a young girl seated on a bench with her legs crossed, playing a harp, still another portrays the Egyptian god Bes, a popular figure of fertility and protection.

The site is on top of an isolated hill halfway between Gaza and Elath. It rises only about 120 feet above the surrounding plain but affords an unbroken view for at least 20 miles in every direction.

At the foot of the hill a green clump of desert scrub surrounds the 10 wells of Ajrud. The wells, which still work and are used by the Bedouins today, date to antiquity. Mr. Meshel assumes that it was these wells, which provide the only water for miles around, that originally drew travelers to the site 2,800 years ago.

The New York Times/Micha Bar-Am

Israeli archeologists and volunteers dig through ruins of ancient Judean fortress on a hill between Gaza and Elath

"All the News That's Fit to Print"

The New York Times

LATE CITY EDITION

Weather: Chance of rain late today, tonight. Partly sunny tomorrow. Temperature range: today 72-86; Tuesday 66-90. Details on page 65.

VOL. CXXV .... No. 43,278 NEW YORK, WEDNESDAY, JULY 21, 1976

25 cents beyond 50-mile zone from New York City, except Long Island. Higher in air delivery cities.

20 CENTS

VIKING ROBOT SETS DOWN SAFELY ON MARS AND SENDS BACK PICTURES OF ROCKY PLAIN

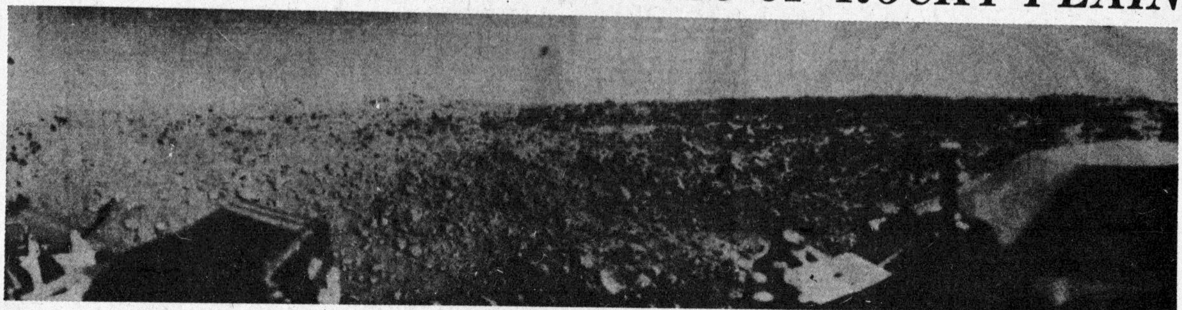

A composite photo showing a 300-degree panorama of the surface of Mars, made by a camera on the Viking 1 landing craft just after touchdown on the planet yesterday morning. Parts of the craft are visible in foreground.

Associated Press

Foot pad of the Viking 1 resting on Mars. Center of this picture is five feet from camera and the rock at center is approximately four inches across.

Associated Press

3¼-HOUR DESCENT

Scientists Are Jubilant as News Is Flashed, Taking 19 Minutes

By JOHN NOBLE WILFORD

Special to The New York Times

PASADENA, Calif., July 20—An explorer from Earth, the robot craft Viking 1, made the first successful landing on Mars today and transmitted spectacular photographs of a rocky, wind-scoured desert plain, the site for the first direct search for life on another world.

The squat, three-legged Viking landing craft came to rest, upright and intact, on the Chryse Plain of Mars at 7:53 A.M. Eastern daylight time after a voyage of 11 months and nearly half a billion miles. The final and most suspenseful step, the craft's descent to the surface from its mother ship in Mars orbit, took 3 hours 13 minutes.

Then, Touchdown

Responding to automatic computer commands, the lander's rockets fired, its parachute unfurled, protective shielding broke away, more rockets were fired—and then, touchdown. It was 19 minutes, because of the great distance between Mars and Earth, now more than 212 million miles, before confirmation of the safe landing reached the control rooms here at the Jet Propulsion Laboratory.

"Touchdown!" announced Richard Bender, one of the flight controllers. "We have touchdown. We have several indications of touchdown."

It was an emotional moment for the scientists and engineers of the $1 billion Viking project, many of whom had spent eight years preparing for this day.

Applause and Amazement

There was applause in the control room and throughout the laboratory. There were broad smiles and moist eyes. There were soft expressions of numbed amazement at what they had wrought.

With the Viking landing begins the first surface exploration of Mars (two Soviet landings failed to produce usable data). The planet has fascinated man for centuries and been the object of legend and endless scientific speculation.

In eight days, if all continues to go according to plan, a mechanical arm on the lander is to reach out and scoop up soil samples for chemical and biological analysis by onboard instruments. This will mark the beginning of the mission's search for signs of possible life on Mars.

Though Mars is no longer seriously thought of as an

Continued on Page 12, Column 1

Ford Gains 10 Delegates And Needs Only 18 More

By JAMES M. NAUGHTON

Special to The New York Times

WASHINGTON, July 20—President Ford gained substantial delegate strength today to pull within 18 votes of the total needed to gain a first-ballot nomination at the Republican National Convention.

Amid conflicting claims from the rival Republican camps, The New York Times determined from the best available information and a canvass of the delegates involved that Mr. Ford had a net gain of 10 delegates while Ronald Reagan had a net increase of one.

The new tally by The Times listed 1,112 delegates for Mr. Ford—18 short of the 1,130 needed for nomination — and 1,064 for Mr. Reagan, with 83 still uncommitted. Thirteen of the 83 said they were leaning to Mr. Ford and three to Mr. Reagan.

James A. Baker, a deputy chairman of the President Ford Committee, claimed the conversion of several delegates and proposed to certify the President's strength by making public the identities of all Ford delegates once they constitute a convention majority.

The proposal to list the delegates by name and address was the latest move in a war of nerves between supporters of the President and of Mr. Reagan.

Mr. Baker dismissed as "blowing smoke" the largely unsubstantiated claim yesterday by John P. Sears, the Reagan campaign manager, to 1,140 delegates for the former Californian governor—10 more than needed for nomination.

Mr. Sears retaliated later to-

Continued on Page 22, Column 1

U.S. AGENCY FINDS DRUG TESTING LAX

Says F.D.A., Makers and Others Expose the Public to Needless Risks

By RICHARD HALLORAN

Special to The New York Times

WASHINGTON, July 20—Congressional investigators have issued a blistering indictment of the Food and Drug Administration, pharmaceutical makers, doctors and research scientists, charging them with exposing humans to unnecessary risks in testing new drugs.

The General Accounting Office also reported that the testing procedures could result in F.D.A. approval of a new drug for public use based on "inaccurate and unreliable data."

The Congressional investigating unit disclosed instances of "alarming adverse reactions" to new drugs that went unreported and the death of eight soldiers in an Army test of a drug intended to prevent malaria.

Despite continued controversy over many aspects of the regulation of prescription drugs in recent years, the general ac-

Continued on Page 8, Column 1

South African Black Is Reported Killed In Renewed Rioting

By JOHN F. BURNS

Special to The New York Times

JOHANNESBURG, July 20—At least one black man was reported killed tonight when police reinforcements were rushed to the coal-mining center of Witbank, 75 miles east of here, which was in the grip of the most serious rioting since the widespread anti-Government upheavals last month.

Reports from the scene said that about 3,000 black youths had poured out of black townships and attacked people and buildings in areas occupied by Indians and people of mixed descent, who are called colored here.

Few details were available, and it was unclear how the reported death had occurred. However, the riot policemen, armed with automatic rifles, were acting under standing Government orders to suppress fresh outbreaks of violence with all necessary force.

The possibility of a chain reaction was raised by a police report of at least one outbreak elsewhere. At midnight, rioters were said to have set fire to several buildings in Khutsong, a black township near Carletonville, a mining town southwest of Johannesburg.

The death would be the first since the end of the rioting

Continued on Page 4, Column 7

GOLD PLUNGES 12% IN WEEK TO $107.75

Slump Hurts South Africa —Heavy Soviet Selling Is Seen as Part of Cause

By PETER T. KILBORN

Special to The New York Times

LONDON, July 20 — The turmoil that has been swirling through many nations' currencies has now swept into gold, long a major component, along with the dollar, of the world's monetary reserves.

In only five business days, the price of gold has tumbled nearly 12 percent, from $122 an ounce last Wednesday to $107.75 at its close today in London. Today alone it fell nearly $6.

The drop has been so abrupt, gold experts here said, that South Africa, the world's leading producer of gold, now faces political as well as economical consequences unless the price recovers quickly.

"If you take the gold out of South Africa," said Richard Lockwood, a mining expert for a brokerage firm in London, "you've got one of the worst economies in the world."

Experts also expected difficulties for the Soviet Union, another major producer. Ironically, they said, the Russians helped bring on the decline in

Continued on Page 47, Column 5

Flight Offers Clue to Air of Mars

By WALTER SULLIVAN

Special to The New York Times

PASADENA, Calif., July 20—The first definitive analysis of the Martian atmosphere has provided long-sought clues to the planet's history, including the possibility that enough water is hidden beneath its surface to cover the planet one mile deep.

The chief surprise has been Viking's discovery that argon, an inert gas, constitutes far less of the Martian atmosphere than scientists previously believed. Whereas estimates of the argon level on Mars had been as high as 30 percent, data from Viking indicate that it is only about 3 percent, compared with about 1 percent in the Earth's atmosphere.

This and other detailed determinations should help explain why the air of Mars has so little nitrogen and should bear on such questions as the history of the Earth's known atmosphere, including the proposal that the atmosphere of both Earth and Mars were formed in eruptions very early in each planet's history.

Such an early formation of the atmosphere would mean, as well, the early appearance of oceans or smaller water bodies suitable for the evolution of life.

When the Soviet Union's Mars 6 plunged into the Mars atmosphere in its unsuccessful landing attempt in 1974 it was thought that perplexing features of its data transmissions could be explained if 30 percent of the Martian air consisted of argon. The possibility of so large a percentage also offered an explanation for observations made near one of the Martian poles a few days ago by the Viking mother ship that cast loose the lander today.

Level Is About 3 Percent

Today's measurement, which is considered definitive, put the argon level at about 3 percent.

The lower abundance of argon is good news for those experimenters hoping to learn the composition of Mars's surface materials. Their instrument aboard the lander will determine such compositions with a gas chromatograph mass spectrometer that could have been rendered useless by an atmosphere rich in argon.

The project's scientists believe that today's measurements will help clarify whether, as some of them believe, there is still enough water hidden beneath the surface of Mars to cover that planet to a depth of one mile.

The abundance of argon in the air of Mars today is a critical index of the atmosphere's history. If volcanic eruptions and other processes generated the same atmospheric constituents as those produced by such activity on Earth the present abundance of argon could, it was argued, have been as high as reported by the Russians.

The reasoning is that since argon is chemically inert and too heavy to diffuse away from either the earth or Mars, all of it orginally in both atmospheres should still be there. On Earth it constitutes only 1 percent of the air, which is 78 percent nitrogen.

If, however, the original at-

Continued on Page 12, Column 4

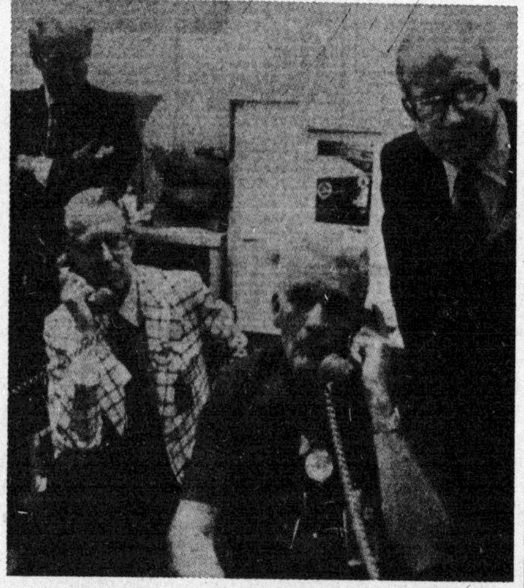

Dr. James Fletcher, left, and James S. Martin, on phones, being congratulated by President Ford as other officials watched a television set for first Mars photographs.

United Press International

Rao Indictments Obtained By Nadjari Are Reinstated

By MAX H. SEIGEL

The Appellate Division in Brooklyn yesterday reinstated perjury indictments obtained by Maurice H. Nadjari against Judge Paul P. Rao Sr. of United States Customs Court; his son, Paul Jr., and another lawyer, Salvatore Nigrone.

The indictments had been dismissed last Dec. 2 by the late Justice John M. Murtagh of State Supreme Court on the ground that undercover agents had made statements to the grand jury that "were highly prejudicial to the defendants." Justice Murtagh also had questioned whether the evidence before the grand jury was legally sufficient to establish the offense charged.

Several weeks after the dismissal of the indictments, which involved a manufactured "robbery" case, Governor Carey cited the Rao reversal—and others that had occurred less than a month earlier—in announcing his intention to dismiss Mr. Nadjari as the special state prosecutor looking into the criminal-justice system in New York City.

In its 4-to-1 decision reinstating the indictments, the Appellate Division majority said that it acted "on the law" without going into the actual merits of the case.

The majority found that Justice Murtagh had said improperly that he was dismissing the indictments "in the interests of justice" while he had actually ordered the dismissal

Continued on Page 67, Column 1

Long Offers 2d Vote In Tax-Aid Dispute

By EILEEN SHANAHAN

Special to The New York Times

WASHINGTON, July 20—Russell B. Long, chairman of the Senate Finance Committee, promised today to give the panel a new opportunity to vote for or against each of 73 provisions of the pending tax bill, most of which benefit just one company or industry.

Senator Long made the commitment after an unusually heated session of the committee during which Senator Edward M. Kennedy was, in effect, called a demagogue by one Republican member and accused of not knowing what he was talking about by another.

Mr. Kennedy, Democrat of Massachusetts, has emerged as a leading foe of the kind of narrow-interest tax legislation

Continued on Page 42, Column 4

Attica Is Termed as Bad As Before 1971 Rebellion

By FRED FERRETTI

Special to The New York Times

ATTICA, N.Y., July 20 — The chief of a State Commission of Correction team sent into the Attica prison last week following the most recent outbreak of violence there described conditions within the facility today as "just as bad, perhaps worse" than in September 1971, just before an inmate rebellion that resulted in the deaths of 43 persons.

"What we have is a combat situation," said Scott Christianson, director of the Correction Commission's State Prison Unit, following five days of investigation and interrogation of inmates and guards. "The environment is so physical, so potentially dangerous, the power of both the inmates and the guards is so awesome, that it can go off at any time. Both sides have the power of death in their hands."

The superintendent of the prison, Harold J. Smith, conceded in an interview that an inmate rebellion could happen again. "Yes, it could," he said, "I'd be a damn fool to say otherwise."

The Correction Commission has reported formally to Governor Carey that a set of parallels exists between the situation here today and what it was in Attica just before Sept. 9, 1971, when the prisoners revolted. The prison was subsequently recaptured by state troopers who stormed it.

The new report urged the

Continued on Page 65, Column 1

NEWS INDEX